W9-ASE-709

DIRECTORY OF
Archives and Manuscript Repositories
IN THE UNITED STATES

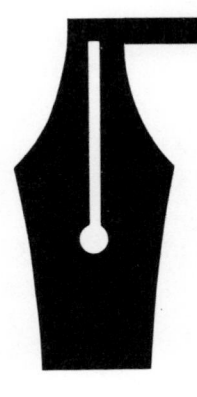

DIRECTORY OF
Archives and Manuscript Repositories

IN THE UNITED STATES

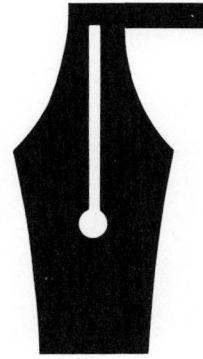

SECOND EDITION

National Historical
Publications and
Records Commission

Phoenix • New York
ORYX PRESS
1988

The rare Arabian Oryx is believed to have inspired the myth of the unicorn. This desert antelope became virtually extinct in the early 1960s. At that time several groups of international conservationists arranged to have 9 animals sent to the Phoenix Zoo to be the nucleus of a captive breeding herd. Today the Oryx population is over 400, and herds have been returned to reserves in Israel, Jordan, and Oman.

Copyright © 1988 by
The Oryx Press
2214 North Central at Encanto
Phoenix, Arizona 85004-1483
No claim of copyright for material created by U.S. Government.

Published simultaneously in Canada

Printed and Bound in the United States of America

∞ The paper used in this publication meets the minimum requirements of American National Standard for Information Science—Permanence of Paper for Printed Library Materials, ANSI Z39.48, 1984.

Library of Congress Cataloging-in-Publication Data

Directory of archives and manuscript repositories in the United
    States.—2nd ed.
      p. cm.
    Includes index.
    ISBN 0-89774-475-6
      1. Archives—United States—Directories. I. United States.
National Historical Publications and Records Commission.
CD3020.D49 1988   87-30157
016.091′025′73—dc 19   CIP

CONTENTS

Foreword   vii
Preface   ix
Introduction   xi
Key to Short Title Citations   xiii
Alabama   1
Alaska   6
American Samoa   9
Arizona   10
Arkansas   16
California   20
Colorado   64
Connecticut   72
Delaware   89
District of Columbia   92
Florida   118
Georgia   126
Guam   134
Hawaii   135
Idaho   138
Illinois   141
Indiana   168
Iowa   186
Kansas   196
Kentucky   206
Louisiana   224
Maine   231
Mariana Islands   239
Maryland   240
Massachusetts   252
Michigan   291
Minnesota   312

Mississippi   329
Missouri   334
Montana   346
Nebraska   349
Nevada   355
New Hampshire   357
New Jersey   363
New Mexico   381
New York   387
North Carolina   478
North Dakota   490
Ohio   492
Oklahoma   516
Oregon   522
Pennsylvania   532
Puerto Rico   571
Rhode Island   572
South Carolina   577
South Dakota   583
Tennessee   588
Texas   597
Utah   618
Vermont   621
Virgin Islands   627
Virginia   628
Washington   642
West Virginia   680
Wisconsin   683
Wyoming   699
Repository Index   703
Subject Index   759

FOREWORD

Publication of the second edition of the *Directory of Archives and Manuscript Repositories in the United States* is one of several ways that the National Historical Publications and Records Commission seeks to assist researchers interested in historical topics. Through its records and publications grant programs, the Commission supports improved preservation and access to original source materials relating to American history. Besides the first edition of the *Directory*, published in 1978, the Commission staff has produced several books about historical research materials, including *A Guide to Archives and Manuscripts in the United States* (1961), edited by Philip M. Hamer. The Commission's *Historical Documentary Editions* (1986) cites titles and publishers of documentary book and microform publication series that have been supported by the publications grant program.

The *Directory* was produced under the general direction and supervision of the Commission's Acting Executive Director, Richard A. Jacobs, and the Director of the Records Program, George L. Vogt. It is hoped that it will prove beneficial to both casual and scholarly researchers.

Frank G. Burke
Acting Chairman
National Historical Publications
and Records Commission

PREFACE

The National Historical Publications and Records Commission was established as the National Historical Publications Commission by an act of Congress in 1934. The Commission was authorized in 1964 to provide grants from federal and private sources for historical documentary publication projects. The Commission's name was changed to its present form in 1974 and it began a program of providing grants for archives and records projects. By law the Commission consists of 17 members, including the Archivist of the United States, who serves as chair. The Commission is an independent statutory body affiliated with the National Archives and Records Administration

This second edition of the *Directory of Archives and Manuscript Repositories in the United States* is a revision of the 1978 edition and includes descriptions of approximately 1,400 repositories not described in the earlier volume, as well as updated entries for previously listed institutions. The *Directory* has been produced entirely with electronic data processing techniques, from initial entry of data to composition of copy for printing.

The Commission wishes to thank the thousands of archivists, manuscript curators, librarians, museum personnel, and volunteers who completed repository information questionnaires, as well as the many individuals who contributed information on repository locations and bibliographic citations. These contributions helped to make this a truly national directory.

Richard A. Noble served as the supervisory editor for this edition. Other Commission staff members who contributed substantially to the work are Mary A. Giunta, Susan R. F. Goff, Theresa L. Mack, Patricia R. Mallard, Cynthia M. Masszonia, Nancy A. Sahli, Richard N. Sheldon, and George L. Vogt. Several other NHPRC staff members helped conduct the 1986 telephone survey of repositories.

In addition, a number of student interns and other volunteers offered assistance throughout the project. National Archives staff members who deserve special thanks are Shelby G. Bale, Ross J. Cameron, John A. Constance, Katherine V. Coram, Matthew C. Dinkel, John H. Hedges, James L. Jones, Dennis R. Means, Ann L. Mohan, Mary C. Ryan, Richard B. Smith, and Timothy G. Walch. Assistance was also provided by the Computer Center of the Division of Computer Research and Technology, National Institutes of Health.

Also contributing key advice were staff members at three institutions that conducted statewide records surveys funded by the Commission: the Kentucky Department for Libraries and Archives, the New York Historical Resources Center at the Olin Library of Cornell University, and the Archives and Records Management Division of the Washington Secretary of State. Barbara A. Teague, archivist at the Kentucky Department for Libraries and Archives, and David W. Hastings, archivist at the Washington State Archives and Records Management Division, were particularly helpful regarding the computer aspects of the project. The Commission also is grateful for the assistance of Dimity S. Berkner, Susan Slesinger, and the rest of the staff of The Oryx Press.

The Commission hopes that the *Directory* will have an impact beyond that of providing researchers with information about where to locate source materials. The descriptions of repositories' acquisitions policies, for example, should enable archivists and curators of historical materials to devise future acquisitions policies in a more informed manner; moreover, donors should be in a better position to determine which institutions are most appropriate to receive certain materials. In sum, this book reflects the Commission's broader goal of contributing to a general understanding of American history.

Richard A. Jacobs
Acting Executive Director
National Historical Publications
and Records Commission

INTRODUCTION

How the Second Edition Was Prepared

This volume updates the first edition of the *Directory of Archives and Manuscript Repositories in the United States*, which was published in 1978. That volume included full listings for approximately 2,675 repositories and abbreviated listings for approximately 575 repositories. In 1980 the Commission staff sent questionnaires to all fully listed repositories requesting additions and corrections to their entries. Information also was solicited from some 10,000 repositories not included in the first edition.

From the completed questionnaires, from additional information solicited by telephone, and from comprehensive field surveys conducted by Commission-supported projects in Kentucky, New York State, and Washington State, the *Directory* staff prepared approximately 1,400 new entries and revised the majority of first-edition entries. A number of repositories in the first edition were deleted from the second edition because they either had become defunct or had deaccessioned their manuscripts and archives.

Because of federal budget cuts, the *Directory* project experienced heavy reductions in staff during the fall and winter of 1981–82. The staff reductions compounded problems inherent in the SPINDEX computer programs used for processing data, such as the lack of an interactive mode for correcting and updating files.

Because of these problems, the remaining staff in 1982 reordered priorities and simplified the ambitious plans for the *Directory*. The greatest emphasis was placed on the preparation of basic, accurate data for as many repositories as possible. To this end, the staff recanvassed all responding institutions by mail in the spring of 1983 to confirm addresses, telephone numbers, and hours of operation. The responses received before September 1, 1983, were incorporated into the second edition. In early 1986, repository telephone numbers were updated again. The staff called as many numbers as was practical and checked the remainder against current institutional directories, such as the American Association for State and Local History's *Directory of Historical Agencies in North America* (1986).

As a result of the emphasis on supplying basic data, the staff exercised broad discretion over repositories' suggestions for revision of acquisitions policy statements and descriptions of holdings. Minor revisions were ignored; major additions were placed in new paragraphs, which could be added without disturbing the previous information.

The staff also decided to limit changes in the bibliographic citations. The editors corrected major errors and added new citations for guides describing one repository's entire holdings. The editors, however, did not routinely add or change citations for multi-repository guides, which generally list many institutions in a particular state or region or with holdings on a particular topic. The staff deviated from this rule in one major way—by creating short citations to important multi-repository guides. A key to these citations follows this introduction.

How to Use the Directory: Main Text

The *Directory* is arranged alphabetically by state or equivalent political unit and thereunder by city and institutional name within the city. Preceding each state's entries is a description of its program for local government records prepared by the Commission staff and verified by appropriate state officials. Each institutional entry begins with a unique access code, corresponding to the state, city, and institution. For example, in the access code CA421-40, CA stands for California; 421, Los Angeles; and 40, The Arnold Schoenberg Institute Archives.

For each institution, information in the following categories may be included: name of institution, street address, mailing address, and telephone number; days and hours of service; user fees; general restrictions on access to the institution (i.e., membership requirements, minimum ages, or advance arrangements); availability of copying facilities for users; acquisitions policy; volume of total holdings of historical source materials expressed in standard abbreviations, such as l.f. (linear feet), c.f. (cubic feet), and vols. (volumes); inclusive dates of holdings; a brief description of the institution's documentary or records holdings; and bibliographic references to selected guides and printed finding aids published since 1958 that cite the repository. For telephone numbers, the phrase "no telephone" may signify that the repository has no telephone, that the repository does not wish its telephone number to be listed, or that the *Directory* staff has been unable to ascertain the number.

Bibliographic references may be listed either in full or abbreviated form. A list of the latter is provided in the "Key to Short Title Citations," which immediately follows this introduction. Instances of abbreviated references include Hinding; Meckler and McMullin; Winroth; and New York State county guides. Readers should be aware that use of the references is not consistent; many guides are listed variously either as full or short citations. For example, Alan M. Meckler and Ruth McMullin, comps., *Oral History Collections* (Bowker, 1975) may appear in full, or simply as Meckler and McMullin in the short form.

Historical source materials found in the *Directory* include paper documents, architectural drawings, photographs, sound recordings, machine-readable records, motion pictures, and microforms. Materials relating to all countries, eras, and topics are included, although emphasis is on U.S. history.

This volume contains full entries for approximately 4,225 repositories in all states, the District of Columbia, Puerto Rico, and the U.S. Virgin Islands. (Eliminated from the second edition are entries for the Canal Zone, now part of the Republic of Panama.) An additional 335 institutions are included with abbreviated entries containing minimal identifying information. These institutions, which are listed in two standard guides, did not return the repository informational questionnaire for the *Directory* by the September 30, 1981, deadline. The two standard guides are *A Guide to Archives and Manuscripts in the United States* (1961), edited by Philip M. Hamer, and the *National Union Catalog of Manuscript Collections (NUCMC)*, published by the Library of Congress (1962–).

The style manual prepared for internal use by the staff combines features of the *United States Government Printing Office Style Manual* (1973) and *A Manual of Style*, 12th ed. rev. (University of Chicago Press, 1975). The user should bear in mind, however, that the volume was prepared working from forms submitted by approximately 4,225 repositories, making uniformity of entries difficult to achieve. Although the staff has made its best effort to attain consistency throughout the volume, the information in the *Directory* can only be as accurate as that submitted on the repository questionnaires or contained in the bibliographic sources consulted by the staff. *Readers are urged to contact repositories before visiting to ascertain whether addresses or hours have changed since they last were reported.*

How to Use the Directory: Indexes

Following the text entries are a repository index and a subject index. The indexes use repository access codes instead of page numbers. The repository index cites each institution and subordinate division included in the *Directory*. In some cases, this index includes the previous names of repositories, conforming to their listings in the Hamer *Guide* or *NUCMC*.

The subject index cites personal names, subjects, and geographical terms derived from the narrative descriptions of holdings and bibliographic references. Acquisitions policy statements are not indexed. Subject terms usually have been adapted from the language of the entries themselves.

Geographical locations are indexed only if they fall outside the state in which the repository is located or if they are areas of national significance or interest. Standard post office abbreviations for state names are used for indexing cities, as in OSHKOSH WI, but not for states, as in WISCONSIN. The term UNITED STATES has been avoided as a main entry, except when it is part of a corporate or institutional name. Federal and other government agencies may be listed (a) in strict alphabetical order, such as BUREAU OF INDIAN AFFAIRS, (b) under the most significant word relating to their activity, such as INDIAN AFFAIRS, BUREAU OF, and/or (c) under a broader rubric, such as GOVERNMENT AGENCIES.

The subject index omits certain broad categories, such as churches and schools, which appear in many repository listings, particularly those of local historical societies. More specific references, such as those to particular denominations or educational institutions and their records, have been included. The forms of source materials, such as diaries, account books, and oral history recordings, generally are not used as index entries. Key exceptions are photographs and motion pictures, which are indexed if a repository holds them in substantial quantity.

Users should keep in mind that many index terms refer to the abbreviated bibliographic references listed in the "Key to Short Title Citations." Moreover, although the subject index includes numerous cross-references, users should consult the broadest range of subject terms possible, since similar subjects may be entered in more than one form.

Because of certain computer system requirements for filing, terms followed by a space precede terms followed by a punctuation mark. Similarly, spaces and punctuation marks always precede letters. Thus BOOK TRADE precedes BOOK-OF-THE-MONTH CLUB, which precedes BOOKS. Since the computer system permits a maximum of 99 characters per index term or subheading, certain longer terms have been abbreviated.

KEY TO SHORT TITLE CITATIONS

Subject or National Guides:

SHORT TITLE	FULL TITLE

Allard, Crawley, and Edmison: Dean C. Allard, Martha L. Crawley, and Mary W. Edmison, *U.S. Naval History Sources in the United States* (Department of the Navy, Naval History Division, 1979).

Armstrong: Robert D. Armstrong, *Territorial Nevada: A Guide to the Records* (Nevada Historical Society, 1978).

Bean and Vane: Lowell John Bean and Sylvia Brakke Vane, *California Indians: Primary Resources, A Guide to Manuscripts, Artifacts, Documents, Serials, Music and Illustrations* (Ballena Press, 1977).

Beers-Confederate: Henry Putney Beers, *Guide to the Archives of the Government of the Confederate States of America* (National Archives, 1968).

Beers-Southwest: Henry Putney Beers, *Spanish & Mexican Records of the American Southwest: A Bibliographical Guide to Archive and Manuscript Sources* (University of Arizona Press, 1979).

Bhatt: Purnima Mehta Bhatt, *Scholars' Guide to Washington, D.C., for African Studies* (Smithsonian Institution Press, 1980).

Davis: Richard C. Davis, *A Guide to North American Forest History: Archives and Manuscripts in the United States and Canada* (Clio Books, 1977).

Dillon: Kenneth J. Dillon, *Scholars' Guide to Washington, D.C., for Central and East European Studies* (Smithsonian Institution Press, 1980).

Duignan: Peter Duignan, *Handbook of American Resources for African Studies* (Hoover Institution, 1967).

Gehring: Charles Gehring, ed., *A Guide to Dutch Manuscripts Relating to New Netherland in United States Repositories* (New York State Library, 1978).

Grant: Steven A. Grant, *Scholars' Guide to Washington, D.C., for Russian and Soviet Studies* (Smithsonian Institution Press, 1977).

Grow: Michael Grow, *Scholars' Guide to Washington, D.C., for Latin American and Caribbean Studies* (Smithsonian Institution Press, 1979).

Hamer: Philip M. Hamer, ed., *A Guide to Archives and Manuscripts in the United States* (Yale University Press, 1961).

Hinding: Andrea Hinding, ed., *Women's History Sources: A Guide to Archives and Manuscript Collections in the United States* (R. R. Bowker, 1979).

Hines: Donald M. Hines, *An Index of Archived Resources for a Folklife and Cultural History of the Inland Pacific Northwest Frontier* (University Microfilms International, 1976).

Hounshell: David A. Hounshell, comp., *Manuscripts in U.S. Depositories Relating to the History of Electrical Science and Technology* (Smithsonian Institution, n.d.).

Ingram: Kenneth E. Ingram, *Manuscripts Relating to Commonwealth Caribbean Countries in United States and Canadian Repositories* (Caribbean Universities Press, 1975).

Kim: Hong N. Kim, *Scholars' Guide to Washington, D.C., for East Asian Studies* (Smithsonian Institution Press, 1979).

Krichmar: Albert Krichmar, *The Women's Rights Movement in the United States, 1848–1970: A Bibliography and Sourcebook* (Scarecrow Press, 1972).

Larson: David R. Larson, ed., *Guide to Manuscripts Collections and Institutional Records in Ohio* (Society of Ohio Archivists, 1974).

Leventhal and Mooney-I: Herbert Leventhal and James E. Mooney, eds., "A Bibliography of Loyalist Source Material in the United States: Part I," American Antiquarian Society, *Proceedings* 85 (April 1975).

Leventhal and Mooney-II: Herbert Leventhal and James E. Mooney, eds., "A Bibliography of Loyalist Source Material in the United States: Part II," American Antiquarian Society, *Proceedings* 85 (October 1975).

Leventhal and Mooney-III: Herbert Leventhal and James E. Mooney, eds., "A Bibliography of Loyalist Source Material in the United States: Part III," American Antiquarian Society, *Proceedings* 86 (October 1976).

Martin: Thomas J. Martin, comp., *North American Collections of Islamic Manuscripts* (G. K. Hall, 1977).

Meckler and McMullin:	Alan M. Meckler and Ruth McMullin, comps., *Oral History Collections* (R. R. Bowker, 1975).
Mehr:	Linda Harris Mehr, comp. and ed., *Motion Pictures, Television and Radio: A Union Catalogue of Manuscript and Special Collections in the Western United States* (G. K. Hall, 1977).
Novotny:	Ann Novotny, ed., *Picture Sources* (Special Libraries Association, 1975).
NUCMC:	*National Union Catalog of Manuscript Collections* (Library of Congress, 1959–).
Parkinson:	George Parkinson, *Guide to Coal Mining Collections in the United States* (West Virginia University Library, 1978).
Paszek:	Lawrence J. Paszek, comp., *United States Air Force History: A Guide to Documentary Sources* (Office of Air Force History, 1973).
Robbins:	J. Albert Robbins, ed., *American Literary Manuscripts: A Checklist of Holdings in Academic, Historical and Public Libraries, Museums, and Authors' Homes in the United States* (University of Georgia Press, 1977).
Rowan:	Bonnie G. Rowan, *Scholar's Guide to Washington, D.C., Film and Video Collections* (Smithsonian Institution Press, 1980).
Schatz:	Walter Schatz, ed., *Directory of Afro-American Resources* (R. R. Bowker, 1970).
Spalek:	John M. Spalek, *Guide to the Archival Materials of the German-Speaking Emigration to the United States after 1933* (University Press of Virginia, 1978).
Svoboda and Dunning:	Joseph G. Svoboda and David G. Dunning, comps., *Preliminary Guide to Ethnic Resource Materials in Great Plains Repositories* (University of Nebraska at Lincoln, 1978).
Swanson and Gibb:	Duane P. Swanson and Hugh R. Gibb, *The Historical Records of the Components of Conrail: A Survey and Inventory* (Eleutherian Mills Historical Library, 1978).
Whistler:	Nancy Whistler, *Colorado Oral History Guide* (Denver Public Library, 1980).
White:	Bruce M. White, comp., *The Fur Trade in Minnesota: An Introductory Guide to Manuscript Sources* (Minnesota Historical Society, 1977).
Wilson and Zabrosky:	Robert E. Wilson and Frank A. Zabrosky, comps., *Resources on the Ethnic and Immigrant in the Pittsburgh Area* (Pittsburgh Council on Higher Education, 1979).
Winroth:	Elizabeth Winroth, *Union Guide to Photograph Collections in the Pacific Northwest* (Oregon Historical Society, 1978).
Zobrist:	Benedict Zobrist, "Resources of the Presidential Libraries for the History of the Second World War," in *World War II: An Account of its Documents* edited by James E. O'Neill and Robert W. Krauskopf, National Archives Conferences, vol. 8 (Howard University Press, 1976).

Geographical Guides:

SHORT TITLE	FULL TITLE
Allegany County Guide:	*Guide to Historical Resources in Allegany County, New York, Repositories* (Cornell University, Olin Library, New York Historical Resources Center, 1980).
Broome County Guide:	*Guide to Historical Resources in Broome County, New York, Repositories* (Cornell University, Olin Library, New York Historical Resources Center, 1980).
Cayuga County Guide:	*Guide to Historical Resources in Cayuga County, New York, Repositories* (Cornell University, Olin Library, New York Historical Resources Center, 1980).
Chemung County Guide:	*Guide to Historical Resources in Chemung County, New York, Repositories* (Cornell University, Olin Library, New York Historical Resources Center, 1980).
Chenango County Guide:	*Guide to Historical Resources in Chenango County, New York, Repositories* (Cornell University, Olin Library, New York Historical Resources Center, 1980).
Cortland County Guide:	*Guide to Historical Resources in Cortland County, New York, Repositories* (Cornell University, Olin Library, New York Historical Resources Center, 1981).
Delaware County Guide:	*Guide to Historical Resources in Delaware County, New York, Repositories* (Cornell University, Olin Library, New York Historical Resources Center, 1980).
Livingston County Guide:	*Guide to Historical Resources in Livingston County, New York, Repositories* (Cornell University, Olin Library, New York Historical Resources Center, 1981).
Schuyler County Guide:	*Guide to Historical Resources in Schuyler County, New York, Repositories* (Cornell University, Olin Library, New York Historical Resources Center, 1981).
Seneca County Guide:	*Guide to Historical Resources in Seneca County, New York, Repositories* (Cornell University, Olin Library, New York Historical Resources Center, 1980).
Steuben County Guide:	*Guide to Historical Resources in Steuben County, New York, Repositories* (Cornell University, Olin Library, New York Historical Resources Center, 1981).

Tioga County
Guide:
Guide to Historical Resources in Tioga County, New York, Repositories (Cornell University, Olin Library, New York Historical Resources Center, 1981).

Tompkins County
Guide:
Guide to Historical Resources in Tompkins County, New York, Repositories (Cornell University, Olin Library, New York Historical Resources Center, 1981).

Wayne County
Guide:
Guide to Historical Resources in Wayne County, New York, Repositories (Cornell University, Olin Library, New York Historical Resources Center, 1981).

Wyoming County
Guide:
Guide to Historical Resources in Wyoming County, New York, Repositories (Cornell University, Olin Library, New York Historical Resources Center, 1981).

Yates County
Guide:
Guide to Historical Resources in Yates County, New York, Repositories (Cornell University, Olin Library, New York Historical Resources Center, 1980).

Washington
Repository Guide:
Historical Records of Washington State: Records and Papers Held at Repositories (Washington State Historical Records Advisory Board, 1981).

DIRECTORY OF
Archives and Manuscript Repositories
IN THE UNITED STATES

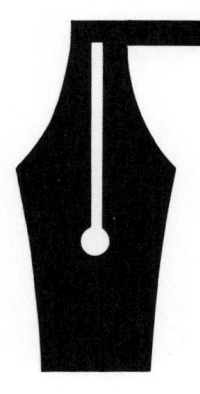

ALABAMA

Since 1955, when the State and County Records Commissions were created, the Archives and History Department has administered a statewide program for preserving local public records. In 1971 a division of the Archives was created that has had the responsibility for preparing retention schedules for state and county records. The *Code of Alabama* contains a section pertaining to the disposition of certain municipal records.

The Archives is the repository for permanent official records of the State of Alabama.

The Archives has begun an inventory of county records and some permanent records have been transferred to the Department.

The Archives and History Department has a small in-house microfilming unit and has begun the microfilming of county records.

AUBURN UNIVERSITY

AL80-40
Auburn University
Archives
Ralph B. Draughon Library
Auburn University AL 36849

(205) 826-4465

OPEN: M-F 8-5; closed weekends and holidays
ACCESS: qualified researchers
COPYING FACILITIES: yes
MATERIALS SOLICITED: University-related records, papers, and manuscript collections relating to history of Alabama, particularly material relating to agriculture, architecture, pharmacy, journalism, engineering, politics, and the Alabama Republican Party. Will also accept genealogical material.

HOLDINGS:
   Total volume: 2,945 l.f.
   Inclusive dates: 1798 -
   Description: 500 manuscript collections dating from 1798 concerning regional history, primarily Alabama material. Includes personal and family papers, organizational records, church records, genealogical collections, architectural records, and political papers. University records include videotapes, films, photographs, oral history tapes, as well as personal and professional papers of University personnel and offices on campus dating from 1856.

SEE: Hamer; NUCMC, 1959-61.

SEE: Allard, Crawley, and Edmison; Meckler and McMullin; Davis; Hinding.

SEE ALSO: *Map Collections in the United States and Canada, A Directory* (Special Libraries Assn., 1970); Alan M. Meckler and Ruth McMullin, comps., *Oral History Collections* (Bowker, 1975); Deborah W. Austin and Allen W. Jones, 'Georgia Manuscripts in the Auburn University Archives,' *Georgia Archive* (Winter 1974).

BIRMINGHAM

AL120-100
Birmingham Public Library
Department of Archives and Manuscripts
2115 7th Avenue, North
Birmingham AL

MAILING ADDRESS:
2020 Park Place
Birmingham AL 35203

(205) 595-5821

OPEN: M-Sa 9-6; closed Sundays and holidays
COPYING FACILITIES: yes
MATERIALS SOLICITED: Manuscripts, archives and non-current records, visual documents, audible documents of research or archival value, microforms and other copies of manuscripts, and scrapbooks. Will also accept non-current machine-readable records of research or archival value.

HOLDINGS:
   Total volume: 6,500 l.f.
   Inclusive dates: 1790 -
   Description: Archives, manuscripts, visual and audio documents, microforms, and scrapbooks relating to the history of Birmingham, Jefferson County, and north central Alabama. Subjects include urban real estate development, iron, steel, and coal industries, textile manufacture, civil rights, education, family history, local government, and civic and social organizations. Concentration beyond the north central Alabama area occurs in the J. Hubert Scruggs postal history collection, documenting Alabama and Confederate postal history.

SEE: Hamer.

SEE: Schatz; Parkinson.

AL120-104
Birmingham Public Library
Southern Women's Archives
2115 7th Avenue, North
Birmingham AL

MAILING ADDRESS:
2020 Park Place
Birmingham AL 35203

(205) 595-5821

OPEN: M-Sa 9-6; closed Sundays and holidays
COPYING FACILITIES: yes
MATERIALS SOLICITED: Manuscripts, diaries, journals, audio recordings, photographs, and organization records relating to Alabama women.

HOLDINGS:
   Total volume: 250 l.f.
   Inclusive dates: 1840 -
   Description: Alabama women's materials, primarily 20th century, consisting of correspondence, diaries, manuscripts, minutes, photographs, scrapbooks, and oral histories. Also included are biographical summaries and photographs of Distinguished Service Award recipients.

AL120-110
Birmingham-Southern College
Charles Andrew Rush Learning Center
Special Collections
Birmingham AL 35254

(205) 328-5250, Ext. 202

OPEN: M-F 8-noon; closed weekends and holidays
COPYING FACILITIES: yes
MATERIALS SOLICITED: Materials relating to the history of Birmingham-Southern College and its predecessors, Southern University and Birmingham College, and to the Methodist church in Alabama, particularly records of churches within the North Alabama Conference. Will also accept personal records of persons connected with Birmingham-Southern College or the Methodist church.

HOLDINGS:
   Total volume: not specified
   Inclusive dates: 19th Century -
   Description: Records of Southern University, Birmingham College, and Birmingham-Southern College and church records of membership, marriages, baptisms, and funerals.

AL120-200
Episcopal Diocese of Alabama
Diocesan Headquarters
521 North 20th Street
Birmingham AL 35203

(205) 328-8374

OPEN: M-Th 9-4, F 9-noon by
  appointment; closed weekends
COPYING FACILITIES: yes
MATERIALS SOLICITED: Materials relating
  to the Diocese of Alabama.

HOLDINGS:
  Total volume: 90 l.f.; 30 file drawers
  Inclusive dates: 1830 -
  Description: Parish histories, registers
  of defunct parishes, early registers of
  some active parishes, diocesan records
  such as newsletters and annual journals,
  letters and papers of bishops, photographs
  of churches and church members, and
  other materials relating to the Diocese of
  Alabama.

AL120-720
Samford University
Harwell G. Davis Library
800 Lakeshore Drive
Birmingham AL 35229

(205) 870-2749

OPEN: M-F 8-4:30; closed weekends and
  holidays
COPYING FACILITIES: yes
MATERIALS SOLICITED: Alabama history
  and people, the Baptist church in Alabama, and Irish materials. Will also accept genealogical source material.

HOLDINGS:
  Total volume: 213,000 items
  Inclusive dates: 1800 -
  Description: Chiefly 19th and 20th
  century materials relating to the southeastern U.S., Alabama history, the Baptist
  church in Alabama, genealogy, and Ireland.

AL120-810
The University of Alabama in
  Birmingham
Lister Hill Library of the Health
  Sciences
Alabama Museum of the Health
  Sciences
1700 University Blvd.
Birmingham AL

MAILING ADDRESS:
University Station
Birmingham AL 35294

(205) 934-4475

OPEN: M-F 8-5; closed weekends and
  holidays
COPYING FACILITIES: yes
MATERIALS SOLICITED: Materials of or
  relating to persons, organizations and
  institutions affiliated with all aspects of
  health care in Alabama.

HOLDINGS:
  Total volume: 10,000 items
  Inclusive dates: 19th century -
  Description: A collection of papers,
  documents, photographs, and tape recordings reflecting the history of health care
  in Alabama, including medicine, nursing,
  dentistry, optometry, individual practi-
  tioners, schools, hospitals, clinics, and organizations.

AL120-815
The University of Alabama in
  Birmingham
Lister Hill Library of the Health
  Sciences
Reynolds Historical Library
1700 University Blvd.
Birmingham AL

MAILING ADDRESS:
University Station
Birmingham AL 35294

(205) 934-4475

OPEN: M-F 8-5; closed weekends and
  holidays
COPYING FACILITIES: yes
MATERIALS SOLICITED: Records, correspondence, or manuscripts dealing with
  the history of science, medicine, or
  dentistry.

HOLDINGS:
  Total volume: 75 items
  Inclusive dates: 1450 -
  Description: A collection of correspondence of Osler, Pasteur, and Nightingale,
  and single items of other significant figures in scientific, medical, and dental history.

GUIDES: *Rare Books and Collections of
  the Reynolds Historical Library: A Bibliography* (Univ. of Alabama Press,
  1968).

SEE: Hinding.

CULLMAN

AL130-333
Herman J. Heidrich Library and St.
  Bernard Abbey
Cullman AL 35055

(205) 734-3730, 8292

OPEN: by appointment
COPYING FACILITIES: no
MATERIALS SOLICITED: Will accept ma-
  terial relating to the school.

HOLDINGS:
  Total volume: not specified
  Inclusive dates: not specified
  Description: Collection consists of correspondence, diaries, manuscripts, sermons and addresses, minutes, photographs, records, scrapbooks, and wills of
  persons in any way connected with the
  monastery, school, or parish of St. Bernard.

FORT RUCKER

AL380-800
United States Army Aviation Museum
Building 6007
Fort Rucker AL 36362

no telephone

OPEN: M-F 10-5, Sa, Su 1-5; closed
  Christmas
COPYING FACILITIES: no
MATERIALS SOLICITED: Visual documents and manuscripts concerning
  Army aviation from 1942 to the
  present. Will also accept audible documents of research value, such as oral
  history tapes and transcripts, or sound
  recordings concerning Army aviation
  from 1942 to the present.

HOLDINGS:
  Total volume: 500 items
  Inclusive dates: 1942 -
  Description: Materials relating to Army
  aviation, including major theaters of op-
  erations in World War II, the Korean
  War, and the Vietnam War.

SEE: Hinding.

HUNTSVILLE

AL440-560
National Speleological Society
Archives
Cave Avenue
Huntsville AL 35810

(205) 852-1300

OPEN: by appointment
COPYING FACILITIES: no
MATERIALS SOLICITED: Correspondence
  between committees within the Society,
  committee reports, and other Society
  materials. Will also accept other materials concerning caves or caving.

HOLDINGS:
  Total volume: 25 l.f.
  Inclusive dates: 1938 -
  Description: Records of the National
  Speleological Society's activities and history, including correspondence, committee reports, membership lists, proceedings
  of meetings, and information on conventions. There are also materials on grottos
  and regions, science and research, and
  other subjects related to caving.

SEE ALSO: an index available from the
  Society.

AL440-800
The University of Alabama at
  Huntsville
The Library
Archives and Special Collections
Huntsville AL

MAILING ADDRESS:
P.O. Box 1247
Huntsville AL 35807

(205) 895-6540

OPEN: M-F 8-5; closed weekends and
  holidays
COPYING FACILITIES: yes

MATERIALS SOLICITED: University records and related historical materials. Will also accept materials of historical interest concerning northern Alabama.

HOLDINGS:
Total volume: 320 l.f.
Inclusive dates: 1947 -
Description: Congressional papers of Robert E. Jones, including correspondence and office files; the University archives; and some manuscripts and papers of space scientist Willy Ley.

MARION

AL540-400

Judson College
Bowling Library
Marion AL 36756

(205) 683-6161, Ext. 175

OPEN: Su 2-10, M-Th 8-10, F 9-4; closed Saturdays, College holidays and July-Aug.
USER FEES: $5 annually
ACCESS: appointment requested
COPYING FACILITIES: yes
MATERIALS SOLICITED: Will accept records relating to the history of Judson College or the town of Marion.

HOLDINGS:
Total volume: not specified
Inclusive dates: 1840 -
Description: Records pertaining to Judson College and Marion, including letters by alumnae concerning celebration of the College's 75th anniversary, 1913.

SEE: Hinding.

MAXWELL AFB

AL560-720

Albert F. Simpson Historical Research Center
Building 1405
Maxwell Air Force Base AL

MAILING ADDRESS:
AFSHRC/HOA
Maxwell AFB AL 36112

(205) 293-5958, 5962

OPEN: M-F 8-5; closed weekends and holidays
COPYING FACILITIES: yes
MATERIALS SOLICITED: Material dealing with the history of the Army Air Forces/U.S. Air Force, especially personal papers of retired general officers and other key personnel in aviation.

HOLDINGS:
Total volume: 18,000 c.f.
Inclusive dates: 1907 -
Description: The major portion of the collection consists of unit histories of various Air Force organizations prepared since 1942. Also included are reference materials on the early period of military aviation; course materials of the Air Corps Tactical School of the 1920's and 1930's; working papers of major staff offices of Headquarters, Army Air Forces, during World War II; histories and related documents of various joint and combined commands; miscellaneous documents or collections of various organizations including the U.S. Army, the British Air Ministry, and the German Air Force; and a large collection of material relating to USAF activities in the war in Southeast Asia.

Other special collections include historical monographs and studies; oral history tapes and transcripts; End of Tour Reports; USAF individual aircraft record cards; the German Air Force Document Collection (also known as the Karlsruhe Document Collection), 265 binders of German military directives, situation reports, war diaries, maps, etc., concerning the German Air Force 1914-45; a unique bound German collection of aircraft data with photographs and some drawings of aircraft from countries of the world 1909-45 (by country and aircraft manufacturing company) taken from the Central Aviation Library, Berlin, at the end of World War II (63 volumes); and personal papers of many retired general officers and other Air Force personnel.

SEE: Hamer; NUCMC, 1968, 77.

SEE: Paszek; Hinding.

SEE ALSO: Gloria L. Atkinson, 'The Archives of the USAF Historical Division,' *Special Libraries* 59 (July-Aug. 1968); and the following publications of the Center: Gloria L. Atkinson, *Personal Files in the U.S. Air Force Historical Collections* (1975); *U.S. Air Force Oral History Catalog* (1977); *Research Guide to the Project CHECO Reports 1964-1976* (1977); Gloria L. Atkinson, *German Air Force Monograph Project* (1972).

MOBILE

AL580-510

Mobile Public Library
Special Collections Division
704 Government Street
Mobile AL 36602

(205) 438-7094, 7093

OPEN: M-Sa 9-5; closed Sundays and holidays
COPYING FACILITIES: yes
MATERIALS SOLICITED: Mobile, Alabama, and Gulf coast history.

HOLDINGS:
Total volume: 100,000 items
Inclusive dates: 1539 -
Description: Manuscripts relating to the history of the Mobile Bay area and the Gulf coast. Included are papers relating to colonial Mobile and Pensacola, FL, concerned with the building of the submarine *Hunley,* and microfilm on the colonial enterprises of the French and Spanish, 1539-1763.

SEE: NUCMC, 1959-61, 70, 78.

SEE: Schatz; Allard, Crawley, and Edmison.

SEE ALSO: Ruth Warren and Herndon Smith, *River Echoes* (Mobile Public Library, 1972).

AL580-530

Museum of the City of Mobile
355 Government Street
Mobile AL 36609

(205) 438-7569

OPEN: Tu-F 10-5; closed Mondays, weekends and holidays
ACCESS: by appointment only
COPYING FACILITIES: yes
MATERIALS SOLICITED: Materials pertaining to the history of Mobile and the surrounding area. Will also accept materials relating to the history of the Gulf coast in such areas as government, the military, law, commerce, music, transportation, and suffrage.

HOLDINGS:
Total volume: 144 l.f.
Inclusive dates: 1702 -
Description: Collections include personal papers of prominent Mobile residents and their families; Civil War papers of such figures as Raphael Semmes, David G. Farragut, and Edward Richard Sprigg Canby; public records of the City and County of Mobile; legal documents; commercial papers; records of volunteer fire companies of Mobile; materials relating to suffrage and slavery in Mobile; extensive collection of personal papers of Mary McNeil Fenollosa dealing with her life in Japan and Mobile.

Remaining papers of Roderick D. MacKenzie including glass negatives he made in India as studies for his series of monotypes and etchings and progress photographs of the murals in the Alabama Capitol; Chester Root papers dealing with papers of the commanding officer of Fort Bowyer during the 1819 Spanish Florida crisis; papers of George Walton the Signer, and his wife Dorothy; Maria Leyette Sheip (Marie Stanley) papers; and the extensive Dr. Thomas M. McMillan collection of several thousand Confederate documents.

GUIDES: A processed guide is available from the Museum.

SEE: Hinding.

AL580-650

The Protestant Episcopal Church in the Diocese of the Central Gulf Coast, Inc.
Office of the Bishop
3809 Old Shell Road
Mobile AL

MAILING ADDRESS:
P.O. Box 8547
Mobile AL 36608

(205) 344-3360

OPEN: M-F 8-8; closed weekends and holidays
ACCESS: appointment required
COPYING FACILITIES: yes
MATERIALS SOLICITED: Bishops' correspondence and diaries, financial records, parochial reports, visual records of inactive congregations, minutes of the standing and finance committees, and issues of the diocesan journal and newspaper. Will also accept photographs of diocesan history and ar-

chitectural drawings of church buildings.

HOLDINGS:
Total volume: 50 l.f.
Inclusive dates: 1900 -
Description: Records of the Protestant Episcopal Diocese of the Central Gulf Coast, established in 1971 with jurisdiction over northern Florida and southern Alabama. Included are bishops' correspondence, standing committee and finance committee minutes, and diocesan journals and newspapers. Also held are records of inactive congregations, including correspondence and parish, confirmation, baptism, marriage, and death records.

AL580-800
University of South Alabama
Library
Special Collections Department
Mobile AL 36688

(205) 460-7025

OPEN: M-F 8-5; closed weekends, holidays and between quarters
ACCESS: faculty, graduate students, and serious scholars
COPYING FACILITIES: yes
MATERIALS SOLICITED: Gulf coast history, old and unique material. Will also accept unique graphic materials.

HOLDINGS:
Total volume: 72 l.f.; several filing cabinets
Inclusive dates: 1890's - 1950's
Description: Manuscript collection of letters and other pieces of NAACP material related to early civil rights movement in this Gulf coast area.

MONTEVALLO

AL600-800
University of Montevallo
Carmichael Library
Archives
Montevallo AL 35115

(205) 665-2521

OPEN: M 8-10, Tu-F 8-5; closed weekends, Thanksgiving, Christmas, spring holidays, and between school terms
COPYING FACILITIES: yes
MATERIALS SOLICITED: Materials relating to University of Montevallo and Shelby County, AL, history. Will also accept mining and related industrial material of central Alabama.

HOLDINGS:
Total volume: 75 l.f.; 9 file cabinets
Inclusive dates: 1890 -
Description: Materials relating chiefly to University of Montevallo, including presidential correspondence and files, photographs, 1896- , maps, and mining documents of 19th century Shelby County, AL.

MONTGOMERY

AL620-20
Alabama Department of Archives and
History
624 Washington Avenue
Montgomery AL 36130

(205) 261-4361

OPEN: M-Sa 8-5; closed July 4th, Thanksgiving, Christmas, and New Year's
COPYING FACILITIES: yes
MATERIALS SOLICITED: Materials relating to Alabama and Alabamians, state and county archives, machine-readable records and audible documents of archival value.

HOLDINGS:
Total volume: 22,000 c.f.
Inclusive dates: 1700 -
Description: Official archives of the Territory and State of Alabama; county records; private manuscript collections beginning with the 18th century; military records and soldiers' correspondence from all wars in which Alabamians have participated; and compilations of correspondence and other material of genealogical interest. The private manuscript collections consist of papers of Alabamians.

SEE: Hamer; NUCMC, 1959-61.

SEE: Davis; Duignan; Schatz; Novotny; Allard, Crawley, and Edmison; Hinding; Robbins; Beers - Confederate.

AL620-60
Alabama State University
Levi Watkins Learning Center
University Library and Learning
Resources Center
University Archives and Special
Collections
915 South Jackson
Montgomery AL 36195-0301

(205) 293-4112, 4106

OPEN: M-Th 8-9, F 8-5; closed weekends and holidays
COPYING FACILITIES: yes
MATERIALS SOLICITED: Materials of historical value to the University. Will also accept personal manuscripts and music scores.

HOLDINGS:
Total volume: 40 l.f.
Inclusive dates: 1921 -
Description: Records relating to the history of the University, including correspondence, budget appropriation reports, diaries, photographs and papers of individual faculty members.

SEE: Hinding; Schatz.

AL620-320
Huntingdon College
Houghton Memorial Library
1500 East Fairview Avenue
Montgomery AL 36106

(205) 265-0511

OPEN: Su 2-10, M-Th 8-10, F 8-5, Sa 9-5; closed holidays
COPYING FACILITIES: yes
MATERIALS SOLICITED: Materials regarding Huntingdon College and the (South) Alabama-West Florida Conference of the United Methodist church.

HOLDINGS:
Total volume: 126 l.f.
Inclusive dates: 1808 -
Description: The college archives consisting of correspondence, records, photographs, publications, and mementoes pertaining to Huntingdon College, its students, faculty, administration and alumni. Also, as the official repository of the Alabama-West Florida Conference of the United Methodist Church and its antecedent conferences and its constituent institution Huntingdon College, includes geneaological data on 2,500 ministers; historical data on individual churches; official records of boards, committees and agencies.

NORMAL

AL640-40
Alabama A & M University
J. F. Drake Memorial Learning
Resources Center
Normal AL 35762

(205) 859-7455, 7309

OPEN: M-F 8-5; closed weekends and holidays
COPYING FACILITIES: yes
MATERIALS SOLICITED: Materials on the history of Alabama A & M. Will also accept materials on the history of black Americans in the State of Alabama.

HOLDINGS:
Total volume: 312 c.f.; 481 boxes
Inclusive dates: 1875 -
Description: Materials that relate to Alabama A & M, including papers, letters, photographs, blueprints, books, catalogues, yearbooks, and other documents dealing with or emphasizing the institution's development.

SEE: Schatz.

TALLADEGA

AL760-760
Talladega College
Talladega College Historical
Collections
Talladega AL 35160

(205) 362-0206, Ext. 283

OPEN: M-F 8:30-5; closed weekends and academic holidays

ACCESS: serious researchers; non-Talladega undergraduates need letter of introduction from supervising faculty

COPYING FACILITIES: yes

MATERIALS SOLICITED: Generally any material dealing with black America or Talladega alumni; in particular, papers dealing with the black church, African missions, especially southern Africa, civil rights, and education.

HOLDINGS:
Total volume: 126 l.f.
Inclusive dates: 1867 - 1977
Description: The archives of the College preserves a documentary record of the history of the College, 1867- . The collection is strongest in material dealing with the black church, African missions, especially southern Africa, civil rights, and historical developments in education for blacks.

GUIDES: Leon P. Spencer, A Guide to the Archives of Talladega College (1972); Leon P. Spencer, A Guide to the Collections (1972).

SEE: NUCMC, 1961, 71-72, 74.

SEE: Schatz; Hinding.

TROY

AL780-760
Troy State University
Library
Troy AL 36081

(205) 566-3000, Ext. 256

OPEN: M-F 8-5; closed weekends and holidays
COPYING FACILITIES: yes
MATERIALS SOLICITED: University archives, and other materials regarding local and regional history.

HOLDINGS:
Total volume: 42 l.f.
Inclusive dates: 1809 -
Description: Records of the University; journals of 19th century Alabamians; transcripts of oral history tapes; and the

Paul V. Yoder collection of 700 original scores and recordings of band music.

SEE: NUCMC, 1978.

TUSKEGEE INSTITUTE

AL820-765
Tuskegee Institute
Hollis Burke Frisell Library
Tuskegee Institute AL 36088

no telephone

SEE: Hamer.

Questionnaire not returned.

UNIVERSITY

AL840-280
Geological Survey of Alabama
Library
Walter Bryan Jones Hall
University AL

MAILING ADDRESS:
P.O. Drawer O
University AL 35486

(205) 349-2852, Ext. 215

OPEN: M-F 8-5; closed weekends and holidays
COPYING FACILITIES: yes
MATERIALS SOLICITED: Will accept information pertaining to early Alabama geology.

HOLDINGS:
Total volume: 50,000 pages
Inclusive dates: 1873 - 1937
Description: A collection of manuscripts, field notes, and letters relating to the geology, geography, flora, and economic activity of Alabama. Included are papers of Eugene Allen Smith and of his associates, chiefly Henry McCalley, Charles Mohr, and H. H. Smith.

AL840-820
University of Alabama
Library
Special Collections
University AL

MAILING ADDRESS:
Drawer 'S'
University AL 35486

(205) 348-5512

OPEN: M-F 8-5; closed weekends and holidays
COPYING FACILITIES: yes
MATERIALS SOLICITED: Industries, urban collections, Congressional and Senatorial collections, Confederate (diaries, letters, etc.), and genealogical materials concerned with Alabama families. Will also accept visual and audio materials relating to ethnic, folk, minority, and women's culture in the Deep South and the United States.

HOLDINGS:
Total volume: 5,500 l.f.
Inclusive dates: 1797 -
Description: Manuscript collection related chiefly to Alabama and the South. Includes collections relating to prominent Alabama political leaders (State and National), educators, businessmen, scientists, clergy, plantation owners, industries, small businesses, associations, Civil War items, and Alabama women.

Collections covering interdisciplinary field research in 19th and 20th century sociocultural history of ethnic, folk, minority and women's groups in the United States, focusing on field work and media documentation in Alabama and the Deep South. The emphasis is on audio and visual materials, principally sound recordings, photographs, and video tapes of oral history and folklore interviews.

SEE: Hamer; NUCMC, 1959-62, 68, 80.

SEE: Schatz; Duignan; Davis; Hinding.

ALASKA

There is no statewide program for preserving local government records in Alaska. Political subdivisions normally retain custody of their records.

ANCHORAGE

AK50-25
Alaska Pictorial Service
99515 Lakeside Drive
Anchorage AK

MAILING ADDRESS:
Box 190144
Anchorage AK 99519-0144

(907) 344-1370

OPEN: by appointment
USER FEES: variable, depending upon usage
COPYING FACILITIES: no
MATERIALS SOLICITED: Photographs relating to Alaska.

HOLDINGS:
 Total volume: 150,000 items
 Inclusive dates: 1915 -
 Description: Photographs of virtually all subject material pertaining to Alaska.

SEE ALSO: Ann Novotny, ed., *Picture Sources 3* (Special Libraries Assn., 1975).

AK50-66
Anchorage Historical and Fine Arts Museum
Museum Archives
121 West Seventh Avenue
Anchorage AK 99501

(907) 264-4326, 4327

OPEN: Monday by appointment, Tu-F 9-5; closed weekends and holidays
COPYING FACILITIES: yes
MATERIALS SOLICITED: Historical Alaska, with emphasis on Anchorage, Matanuska Valley, including Alaska Railroad.

HOLDINGS:
 Total volume: 20,000 photographs; 200 maps; additional materials
 Inclusive dates: 1870 -
 Description: Photographs dealing with Alaska's history and development with emphasis on South Central Alaska, Valdez, and the Alaska Railroad. Also includes slides of Alaskan art and native artifacts, diaries, and the museum archives. Included are photos and other holdings of the Cook Inlet Historical Society.

SEE: Novotny; Hinding.

AK50-800
University of Alaska, Anchorage
Library System
Archives and Manuscripts Department
3211 Providence Drive
Anchorage AK 99508

(907) 786-1849

OPEN: M-F 8-5; closed holidays and spring recess
COPYING FACILITIES: yes
MATERIALS SOLICITED: Papers and records of individuals, families, businesses, and organizations which document the political, social, cultural, and economic development of Alaska, primarily south central Alaska and Anchorage, in addition to records of the University of Alaska, Anchorage. Will also accept materials concerning the Arctic region and the Pacific Northwest.

HOLDINGS:
 Total volume: 800 c.f.; 500 oral history tapes; 1,300 microfilm reels; 15,000 photographs
 Inclusive dates: 1850 -
 Description: Materials of or pertaining to Alaskan political, social, and cultural action groups; 19th and 20th century individuals and families; and native American leaders and organizations. Included are personal papers, organization records, photographs, oral histories, and recordings.

CORDOVA

AK250-110
Cordova Historical Society, Inc.
1st Street
Cordova AK

MAILING ADDRESS:
P.O. Box 391
Cordova AK 99574

(907) 424-7443

OPEN: M, Tu, Th, F 1-9, Sa, Su 1-5; closed Wednesdays and holidays
USER FEES: $20 per hour for supervision of outside researchers
ACCESS: prior approval required
COPYING FACILITIES: yes
MATERIALS SOLICITED: Materials that relate to Cordova's past, including its history as a fishing village, and materials on the railroad era.

HOLDINGS:
 Total volume: 500 photographs; 75 maps; additional materials
 Inclusive dates: early 20th century -
 Description: Manuscript maps of the Copper River, the Northwest Railroad, and Cordova; charts; technical drawings and aerial photographs; correspondence of State and local officials; and other materials relating to the history of Cordova and its environs.

ELMENDORF

AK320-40
Alaskan Air Command
Office of History
Elmendorf Air Force Base AK 99506-5001

(907) 552-5217, 4763

OPEN: M-F 8-4; closed weekends and holidays
COPYING FACILITIES: yes
MATERIALS SOLICITED: Air Force activities in Alaska, 1920 - .

HOLDINGS:
 Total volume: 250 c.f.; 200 microfilm reels; 2,000 items
 Inclusive dates: 1920 -
 Description: Annual histories of the Alaskan Air Command, World War II unit histories, studies, plans, oral history interviews, photographs, and other documents relating to Air Force activities and operations in Alaska.

SEE: Paszek.

FAIRBANKS

AK350-120
Catholic Diocese of Fairbanks
Diocesan Archives
1316 Peger Road
Fairbanks AK 99709

(907) 456-6753

OPEN: M-F 9-5; closed weekends, holidays and some church holy days
USER FEES: yes
ACCESS: limited to specific requests
COPYING FACILITIES: no
MATERIALS SOLICITED: Religious history in the State of Alaska, especially the northern part. Will also accept diaries and journals.

HOLDINGS:
 Total volume: 8 file drawers
 Inclusive dates: 1947 -
 Description: Correspondence between diocesan administrators and local pastors and materials dealing with relationships

between the Church and Federal, State and local government agencies on subjects such as socio-economic and educational problems of the area.

AK350-800
University of Alaska
E. E. Rasmuson Library
Rare Books, Archives and
Manuscripts
Fairbanks AK 99701

(907) 474-7481

OPEN: M-F 9-5; closed weekends and holidays
COPYING FACILITIES: yes
MATERIALS SOLICITED: Material related to the history and development of Alaska and the work of its people, political representatives, businesses, organizations, etc. Will also accept some polar exploration materials.

HOLDINGS:
> *Total volume:* 4,922 c.f.
> *Inclusive dates:* 1800 -
> *Description:* Approximately 1,500 c.f. of official records of the University, as well as approximately 3,350 c.f. of manuscripts, 88,000 photographic prints and negatives, 1,650 audio and video recordings, 982 reels of microfilm, 490 reels of movie film, and other materials relating primarily to Alaska. The bulk of the collection falls after 1868, although some microfilm collections and individual pieces date from the early 19th century. The manuscript collections are particularly strong in documenting Alaska's political development.

SEE: Hamer; NUCMC, 1965, 68, 73.

SEE: Hounshell; Novotny; Davis.

SEE ALSO: G. Q. Flynn, 'The New Deal and Local Archives: The Pacific Northwest,' *American Archivist* 33 (Jan. 1970).

Indexes and registers to individual collections are available at the Library.

AK350-815
Alaska Native Language Center
University of Alaska
Fairbanks AK

MAILING ADDRESS:
P.O. Box 111
Fairbanks AK 99775-0120

(907) 474-7874

OPEN: M-F 9-5; closed weekends and holidays
COPYING FACILITIES: yes
MATERIALS SOLICITED: Materials in or on Alaskan native languages and similar languages outside of Alaska. Will also accept materials in or on other American Indian languages, or on bilingual education or linguistics.

HOLDINGS:
> *Total volume:* 2,600 items
> *Inclusive dates:* 1700's -
> *Description:* Originals or copies of a large proportion of all unpublished writings in and about Alaskan native languages, including vocabularies, dictionaries, grammars, field notes and notes

and lists of all kinds, as well as historical, sociolinguistic, and educational materials and documents concerning bilingual education in Alaska.

GUIDES: Michael Krauss and Mary Jane McGary, *Alaska Native Languages, A Bibliographic Catalogue, Part One: Indian Languages* (Alaska Native Language Center, 1980).

HAINES

AK400-720
Chilkat Valley Historical Society
The Sheldon Museum and Cultural Center
25 Main Street
Haines AK

MAILING ADDRESS:
Box 623
Haines AK 99827

(907) 766-2207

OPEN: summer, daily 1-4; winter, M, W 1-4 and by appointment; closed Christmas, New Year's and Easter
USER FEES: one dollar per adult; children under 18 free if accompanied by parent or teacher
COPYING FACILITIES: yes
MATERIALS SOLICITED: Local history and Indian material. Will also accept correspondence and other materials dealing with pioneers even previous to their arrival in Alaska.

HOLDINGS:
> *Total volume:* 36 l.f.
> *Inclusive dates:* 1881 -
> *Description:* Correspondence collected for autographs; a journal and manuscript deeds from about 1900; photographs (1897-); 5,600 feet of home movies; a few maps, charts and blueprints; account books of the Porcupine Mining Co. (1897-1916); and logs of two harbor boats (1910-30).

SEE: Hinding.

HOMER

AK450-320
Homer Society of Natural History, Inc.
Pratt Museum
3779 Bartlett Street
Homer AK 99603

(907) 235-8635

OPEN: Oct. - May, Tu-Sa 10-5; June - Sept., daily 10-5; closed Jan. and holidays
COPYING FACILITIES: no
MATERIALS SOLICITED: Will accept historical photographs or documents concerning the Kenai Peninsula, particularly the lower Cook Inlet and Kachemak Bay area.

HOLDINGS:
> *Total volume:* 2 c.f.
> *Inclusive dates:* 1890 - 1974
> *Description:* Historical photographs of Homer and its residents; correspondence, invoices, and certificates of recognition

concerning the Museum and local residents; and papers from the *S.S. Cordova.*

JUNEAU

AK500-20
Alaska Division of State Libraries and Museums
Alaska Historical Library
333 Willoughby Avenue
Juneau AK

MAILING ADDRESS:
Pouch C
Juneau AK 99811

(907) 465-2925

OPEN: M-F 8-5; closed weekends and holidays
COPYING FACILITIES: yes
MATERIALS SOLICITED: Materials relating to Alaska and Arctic regions, with selective coverage of Siberia, the Yukon Territory, the Northwest Territories and British Columbia. Will also accept other selected materials concerning Siberia, the Yukon and the Northwest Territories, British Columbia, and the northwest coast of the United States.

HOLDINGS:
> *Total volume:* 335 l.f.
> *Inclusive dates:* 1847 -
> *Description:* A collection of manuscripts and archival records relating to Alaska and the Yukon Territory, primarily from the 1900's. Included are a few diaries, Russian Orthodox church records, business records, city records of Sitka and Nome, Federal and Territorial records and records of a few community associations. The collection includes photograph files of several government agencies concerning road construction, communications and tourism, as well as a historical photograph file relating to communities, native peoples, and other topics.

SEE: Hamer; NUCMC, 1965, 70, 75.

SEE: Parkinson; Bean and Vane; Robbins; Hinding; Novotny; Meckler and McMullin.

SEE ALSO: Alaska Division of State Libraries and Museums, *Pathfinder for Historical Research: A Selective Key to the Alaska Historical Library Resources* (1976).

AK500-40
Alaska State Archives
141 Willoughby Avenue
Juneau AK

MAILING ADDRESS:
Pouch C-0207
Juneau AK 99811

(907) 465-2275

OPEN: M-F 8-4:30; closed weekends and holidays
COPYING FACILITIES: yes
MATERIALS SOLICITED: Alaska public records.

HOLDINGS:
Total volume: 1,500 c.f.
Inclusive dates: 1884 -
Description: Public records of the State and Territorial governments of Alaska.

SEE: Hamer (as Office of the Secretary of Alaska).

NOME

AK700-120
Carrie McLain Memorial Museum
Front Street
Nome AK

MAILING ADDRESS:
P.O. Box 53
Nome AK 99762

(907) 443-2566

OPEN: M-F 10-6; closed weekends and holidays
COPYING FACILITIES: yes
MATERIALS SOLICITED: Materials pertaining to the history of early Nome during the Gold Rush and Eskimo art and history.

HOLDINGS:
Total volume: 50 documents; 6,000 photographs
Inclusive dates: 1877 -
Description: Chiefly documents, correspondence, personal recollections and photographs pertaining to Eskimos and life in Nome during the years of the great Gold Rush. The photograph collection includes pictures of Nome and the immediate vicinity, residents and Eskimo portraits.

PETERSBURG

AK750-120
Clausen Memorial Museum
301 Fram Street
Petersburg AK

MAILING ADDRESS:
Box 708
Petersburg AK 99833

(907) 772-3598

OPEN: summer, daily 1-4; winter, by appointment only
COPYING FACILITIES: no
MATERIALS SOLICITED: Materials relating to the Petersburg area, and local subjects such as pioneer families, the fishing industry, and fox farming.

HOLDINGS:
Total volume: 10 l.f.
Inclusive dates: early 1900's -
Description: A collection of manuscripts, journals, ledgers, legal documents and correspondence relating to Petersburg and southeastern Alaska. Included are photographs of old Petersburg, many related to the fishing industry.

VALDEZ

AK900-840
Valdez Historical Society
Royal Center on Egan Drive
Valdez AK

MAILING ADDRESS:
P.O. Box 6
Valdez AK 99686

(907) 835-4367

OPEN: M-F 1:30-5, Sa, Su by appointment
COPYING FACILITIES: yes
MATERIALS SOLICITED: Materials pertaining to Alaska, especially Valdez, Prince William Sound, and the Copper River Basin.

HOLDINGS:
Total volume: 100 l.f.
Inclusive dates: 1890 -
Description: Materials relating to the Valdez area, including Recording District records, slides and films, philately and religion.

AMERICAN SAMOA

There is no program for the preservation of local government records of American Samoa. Local public agencies normally retain custody of their permanently valuable records.

ARIZONA

Since 1937 the Arizona Department of Library, Archives and Public Records has administered a statewide program for preserving state and local public records. Although many permanently valuable local public records remain in the custody of local officials, more than 1,500 cubic feet of county records, about 40 percent of which date from the Territorial period (1864-1912), have been transferred to the State Archives in Phoenix. The Archives also houses additional county records preserved on some 900 reels of microfilm.

CAMP VERDE

AZ75-240
Fort Verde State Historic Park
Lane Street
Camp Verde AZ

MAILING ADDRESS:
P.O. Box 397
Camp Verde AZ 86322

(602) 567-3275

OPEN: daily 8-5:30; closed Christmas
USER FEES: fifty cents per person, age 18 and older
COPYING FACILITIES: no
MATERIALS SOLICITED: Records, letters, ledgers, and maps of the 1865-90 period pertaining to Arizona military history.

HOLDINGS:
>*Total volume:* 8 items
>*Inclusive dates:* 1865 - 1940
>*Description:* Diaries, ledgers, and account books, dating mostly from 1865-91, relating to Arizona.

CASA GRANDE

AZ100-120
Casa Grande Valley Historical Society
110 West Florence Blvd.
Casa Grande AZ 85222

(602) 836-2223

OPEN: M-F 9-12, pm by appointment; closed weekends and holidays
COPYING FACILITIES: yes
MATERIALS SOLICITED: Materials pertaing to local history. Will also accept materials relating to people in the area, including early Indians.

HOLDINGS:
>*Total volume:* 24 l.f.; 16 file drawers
>*Inclusive dates:* late 1700's -
>*Description:* Materials relating to the history of the Casa Grande area and its people, including prehistoric and contemporary Indian tribes.

COOLIDGE

AZ175-120
Casa Grande Ruins National Monument
Coolidge AZ

MAILING ADDRESS:
P.O. Box 518
Coolidge AZ 85228

(602) 723-3172

OPEN: daily 7-6
ACCESS: advance arrangements preferred
COPYING FACILITIES: no
MATERIALS SOLICITED: Will accept information relating to the history and archaeology of Casa Grande Ruins and other Hohokam sites in the area.

HOLDINGS:
>*Total volume:* not specified
>*Inclusive dates:* 1880's -
>*Description:* Correspondence, logbooks, public documents, and unpublished manuscripts pertaining to the administration and archaeology of Casa Grande Ruins National Monument. Maps, drawings, and photographs documenting excavations and repairs of the site and construction of park facilities; and records and photographs relating to the establishment of Hohokam-Pima National Monument.

DRAGOON

AZ225-40
The Amerind Foundation, Inc.
Dragoon AZ

MAILING ADDRESS:
P.O. Box 248
Dragoon AZ 85609

(602) 586-3003

OPEN: M-F 8-5; closed weekends and holidays
ACCESS: scholars by appointment
COPYING FACILITIES: yes
MATERIALS SOLICITED: Will accept anthropological or historical materials.

HOLDINGS:
>*Total volume:* 40 l.f.
>*Inclusive dates:* 1450 - 1821
>*Description:* 352 microfilm reels of records of the colonial period of New Spain in northern Mexico, known as Nueva Vizcaya, 1631-1821. Field notes, maps, slides, and photographs of prehistoric sites excavated by Amerind in southeastern Arizona and Chihuahua, in northern Mexico.

SEE ALSO: Charles C. Di Peso, Renato Rosaldo, and Robert R. Anderson, *Index to El Archivo de Hidalgo del Parral, 1631-1821* (Arizona Silhouettes, 1961).

FLAGSTAFF

AZ250-480
Lowell Observatory
Archives
Mars Hill Road 1400 W.
Flagstaff AZ 86001

(602) 774-3358

OPEN: by appointment only; closed weekends and holidays
ACCESS: appointment required
COPYING FACILITIES: yes

HOLDINGS:
>*Total volume:* 35,000 items
>*Inclusive dates:* 1894 -
>*Description:* Scientific correspondence and manuscripts of publications of Observatory staff, observing logbooks, business records, and other materials pertaining to the Lowell Observatory and its study of the stars and solar system.

SEE ALSO: *Source Materials for the Recent History of Astronomy and Astrophysics: A Checklist of Manuscript Collections in the United States* (American Institute of Physics, 1971).

AZ250-520
Museum of Northern Arizona
Harold S. Colton Memorial Library
Museum Archives and Manuscripts Collection
Flagstaff AZ

MAILING ADDRESS:
Route 4, Box 720
Flagstaff AZ 86001

(602) 774-5211

OPEN: M-F 9-5; closed weekends
COPYING FACILITIES: yes
MATERIALS SOLICITED: Materials on northern Arizona and the Colorado plateau, including manuscripts on natural and environmental sciences, art,

archaeology, ethnology, and history of northern Arizona.

HOLDINGS:
> *Total volume:* 321 l.f.
> *Inclusive dates:* 1875 -
> *Description:* Correspondence, diaries, journals, field notes, maps, photographs, sound recordings, and tapes concerning Hopi, Navajo, Havasupai, Walapai and Maricopa Indians of Arizona; archaeology of the Flagstaff area; northern Arizona geographic exploration, geology, paleontology, early mining claims, plants, birds, animals, and history and biography of early scientists, pioneers, and artists; and history of the Museum of Northern Arizona.

SEE: NUCMC, 1973.

AZ250-575
Northern Arizona University
Library
Special Collections Division
Flagstaff AZ

MAILING ADDRESS:
C.U. Box 6022
Flagstaff AZ 86001

(602) 523-2171

OPEN: M-F 8-5; closed holidays and some school vacations
COPYING FACILITIES: yes
MATERIALS SOLICITED: Archival materials relating to Arizona, with a special emphasis on northern Arizona. Will also accept materials relating to southwestern U.S.

HOLDINGS:
> *Total volume:* 1,720 l.f.; 12,000 photographs
> *Inclusive dates:* 1870 -
> *Description:* A collection of archival material reflecting the history of northern Arizona, including letters, diaries, pioneer reminiscences, company and business records, photographs, and oral history recordings. Included are materials relating to lumbering and mercantile activities in the Flagstaff area, the Lowell Observatory, Mormon colonization in northern Arizona, the Northern Arizona Pioneers' Historical Society, and the Emery Kolb Photographic Collection.

SEE: NUCMC, 1981.

SEE: Davis; Hinding.

SEE ALSO: Sarah Pederson, *Emery Kolb: A Guide to the Kolb Collection in the Northern Arizona University Libraries* (Northern Arizona University Press, 1980).

Unpublished guides to specific collections available at the Library.

AZ250-690
Riordan State Historic Park
Riordan Ranch Street
Flagstaff AZ

MAILING ADDRESS:
P.O. Box 217
Flagstaff AZ 86002

(602) 779-4395

OPEN: by appointment only

COPYING FACILITIES: no
MATERIALS SOLICITED: Materials concerning Flagstaff and the Riordan family.

HOLDINGS:
> *Total volume:* not specified
> *Inclusive dates:* 1880's -
> *Description:* Political, social, business, and domestic materials relating to the pioneer Riordan families of Flagstaff. Included are accounting and business records, correspondence, diaries, maps, and photographs.

FLORENCE

AZ275-520
McFarland State Historical Park
Main and Ruggles Streets
Florence AZ

MAILING ADDRESS:
P.O. Box 109
Florence AZ 85232

(602) 868-5216

OPEN: by appointment only, Su, M, Th-Sa 8-5; closed Tuesdays, Wednesdays and Christmas
USER FEES: fifty cents for persons 18 years and older
ACCESS: appointment required
COPYING FACILITIES: no
MATERIALS SOLICITED: Photographs and written materials relating to the lifestyle and development of Territorial Pinal County, AZ, and medical information relating to the local hospital, 1865-1938. Will also accept personal histories, diaries, anecdotes, and interviews of early residents of Pinal County.

HOLDINGS:
> *Total volume:* 200 items
> *Inclusive dates:* 1875 - 1938
> *Description:* Photographs of Territorial Pinal County, AZ, and of E. W. McFarland, former Governor, U.S. Senator, and Supreme Court Justice.

GRAND CANYON

AZ350-290
Grand Canyon National Park
Study Collection
Grand Canyon AZ

MAILING ADDRESS:
P.O. Box 129
Grand Canyon AZ 86023

(602) 638-7769, 7768

OPEN: M-F 8-5; closed weekends and holidays
COPYING FACILITIES: no
MATERIALS SOLICITED: Natural and human history of Grand Canyon and Grand Canyon National Park.

HOLDINGS:
> *Total volume:* 10,000 items
> *Inclusive dates:* 1860 -
> *Description:* Photographs, letters, ledgers, journals, mining claims, master plans, oral history tapes, and files relating to the early settlement of the Grand

Canyon's South Rim, exploration of the Colorado River in the Canyon, the development of mining and tourism, and the management of the Park.

SEE: NUCMC, 1968.

SEE: Davis.

HEREFORD

AZ375-120
Coronado National Memorial
Hereford AZ

MAILING ADDRESS:
Box 126, RR 1
Hereford AZ 85615

(602) 366-5515

OPEN: daily 8-5
COPYING FACILITIES: no
MATERIALS SOLICITED: Materials relating to the Coronado expedition and related events and peoples. Will also accept materials related to the Spanish Empire, its cultural contributions, and the history of Spanish-Mexican movement into the United States and northwestern Mexico until the present day.

HOLDINGS:
> *Total volume:* 8 l.f.
> *Inclusive dates:* 1896 -
> *Description:* Collection of materials documenting the formation and development of Coronado National Memorial.

MESA

AZ435-520
Mesa Museum
53 North Macdonald
Mesa AZ 85201

(602) 834-2230

OPEN: Tu-Sa 10-4; closed Sundays, Mondays, and holidays
ACCESS: appointment requested
COPYING FACILITIES: yes

HOLDINGS:
> *Total volume:* not specified
> *Inclusive dates:* 19th century -
> *Description:* The John Hale collection of materials relating to 19th and 20th century cattle ranching and Maricopa County brand registrations; Frank Midvale field notes, maps, and illustrations of petroglyphs in Arizona and of the prehistoric Hohokam canal system; and oral history recordings of pioneers and settlers of the Mesa region.

MOCCASIN

AZ450-640
Pipe Spring National Monument
Monument Library
Moccasin AZ 86022

(602) 643-7105

OPEN: daily 8-4:30; closed Thanksgiving, Christmas, and New Year's
COPYING FACILITIES: no

MATERIALS SOLICITED: Manuscripts on early pioneer life in southern Utah and northern Arizona.

HOLDINGS:
Total volume: 1.5 file drawers
Inclusive dates: 1850 -
Description: A general collection of Mormon and Western history with a few diaries, journals, and reminiscences.

NOGALES

AZ475-640
Pimeria Alta Historical Society
  Museum
Library and Archives
223 Grand Avenue
Nogales AZ

MAILING ADDRESS:
P.O. Box 228
Nogales AZ 85628

(602) 287-5402

OPEN: M-F 10-5, Sa 10-1, Su 1-4; closed Christmas and New Year's
ACCESS: advance appointment required
COPYING FACILITIES: no
MATERIALS SOLICITED: Materials relating to the development of northern Sonora, Mexico and southern Arizona, 1783- .

HOLDINGS:
Total volume: 20 Hollinger boxes
Inclusive dates: 1783 -
Description: Logbooks of Durango Mine, Sonora, Mexico; documents from businesses in Santa Cruz County, late 19th and early 20th centuries; records of the City of Nogales; archives of ranching and mining interests, 19th and 20th centuries; oral history collection pertaining to ranchers, businesses, descendants of Geronimo and other materials.

PAGE

AZ500-400
The John Wesley Powell Memorial
  Museum
6 Lake Powell Blvd.
Page AZ

MAILING ADDRESS:
P.O. Box 547
Page AZ 86040

(602) 645-2741

OPEN: M-F 9-6; closed weekends and holidays
ACCESS: must present proper credentials
COPYING FACILITIES: no
MATERIALS SOLICITED: Materials on John Wesley Powell and films of the Colorado River and its tributaries prior to the Glen Canyon Dam.

HOLDINGS:
Total volume: 12 file drawers
Inclusive dates: 1869 - 1957
Description: Written and photographic material relating to John Wesley Powell and his explorations of the Colorado Plateau areas of Utah and Arizona, Colorado, and the Green River; diaries of other explorers following Powell.

PHOENIX

AZ550-040
Arizona Department of Library,
  Archives and Public Records
Archives Division
1700 West Washington
Phoenix AZ 85007

(602) 255-4159

OPEN: M-F 8-5; closed weekends and holidays
COPYING FACILITIES: yes
MATERIALS SOLICITED: Official territorial and non-current statehood records of State, county, and municipal governments and agencies; institution records; papers of State legislators and officials; papers of individuals closely associated with the State's history; records of State and local organizations and State chapters of National organizations; and school records, especially teachers' registers, 1930- . Will also accept manuscripts, maps, and pictures of historical value.

HOLDINGS:
Total volume: 4,500 c.f.; 7,723 microfilm reels
Inclusive dates: 1863 -
Description: Records of the territorial period, including materials relating to military and Indian affairs and relations with Mexico, New Mexico, and the borderlands; journals and bills of legislatures; and records of the territorial prison at Yuma, 1876-1907. Records of the statehood period include those of the Office of the Governor, State departments and agencies, the Supreme Court, and lower courts of record; selected records of the Office of the Secretary of State; and official records of the fourteen Arizona counties.
  Personal papers include those of George W. P. Hunt, State Governor from 1912 to 1932, concerning State politics, prison reform, capital punishment, labor rights, women's suffrage, and securing of the Colorado River compact; and those of George Hebard Maxwell, 1897-1949, concerning flood control, reclamation, and the National Recovery Administration in Arizona and the Southwest.

GUIDES: Steven P. Brown, comp. and ed., *An Introductory Guide to the Arizona State Archives* (1981).

SEE: Hamer.

SEE: Novotny; Krichmar; Hinding; Beers-Southwest.

AZ550-45
Arizona Historical Society
Phoenix Chapter
1242 North Central Avenue
Phoenix AZ 85004

(602) 255-4470

OPEN: Tu-Sa 10-4; closed Sundays, Mondays, and holidays
COPYING FACILITIES: yes
MATERIALS SOLICITED: Materials relating to Phoenix and the Salt River Valley. Will also accept materials on Arizona in general.

HOLDINGS:
Total volume: 300 l.f.
Inclusive dates: 1860's - 1960's
Description: A collection of papers of individuals, records of organizations, unpublished memoirs and histories, diaries, and audio-visual materials dealing with the development of Phoenix and the Salt River Valley.

AZ550-640
Phoenix Public Library
Arizona Room
12 East McDowell Road
Phoenix AZ 85004

(602) 262-6537

OPEN: M, Tu 10-9, W-Sa 10-5; closed Sundays and holidays
COPYING FACILITIES: yes
MATERIALS SOLICITED: Will accept collections concerning Arizona or Phoenix.

HOLDINGS:
Total volume: 12 file drawers
Inclusive dates: 1890 - 1930
Description: The newspaper 'morgue,' or personal reference file, of Colonel James Harvey McClintock. About 75 percent of the file is clippings, and the other 25 percent correspondence relating to the newspaper and other projects of McClintock.

PIMA

AZ600-200
Eastern Arizona Museum and
  Historical Society of Graham
  County
4 North Main Street
Pima AZ

MAILING ADDRESS:
Box 274
Pima AZ 85543

no telephone

OPEN: M-F 8-4; closed weekends and holidays
COPYING FACILITIES: yes
MATERIALS SOLICITED: Materials concerning the Pima area, including records, individual histories, diaries, journals, genealogical data, and photographs of people, events, and buildings. Will also accept scrapbooks and death and funeral records.

HOLDINGS:
Total volume: 5 c.f.
Inclusive dates: 18th Century -
Description: Local history materials, including a record book of canal company transactions, records of the Sons and Daughters of Pima Pioneers, town council meeting records of the 1930's, and manuscripts of the centennial book published in 1979 relating to the history of Pima.

PRESCOTT

AZ625-630
Prescott Historical Society
Sharlot Hall Museum
415 West Gurley
Prescott AZ 86301

(602) 445-3122

OPEN: Tu-F 9-4:30; closed Mondays,
    weekends and holidays
COPYING FACILITIES: yes
MATERIALS SOLICITED: Materials per-
    taining to mining; Arizona politics; pio-
    neer oral histories; ranching; and Pres-
    cott businesses, services, and clubs.
    Will also accept any material which re-
    lates to the history of Prescott and its
    surrounding area, northern Arizona,
    Arizona, or the Southwest in general.

HOLDINGS:
    Total volume: 3,500 c.f.
    Inclusive dates: 1864 -
    Description: Photographs, manuscripts,
    diaries, oral histories, political papers,
    and pioneer biographies relating to the
    Prescott area, northern Arizona, Arizona
    and the Southwest.

SEE: Hamer; NUCMC, 1966.

SEE: Hinding.

SPRINGERVILLE

AZ700-40
Apache - Sitgreaves National Forest
Springerville AZ

MAILING ADDRESS:
P.O. Box 640
Springerville AZ 85938

(602) 333-4301

OPEN: weekdays by appointment; closed
    weekends and holidays
COPYING FACILITIES: yes
MATERIALS SOLICITED: Will accept ma-
    terials relating to the Apache-Sitgreaves
    National Forest.

HOLDINGS:
    Total volume: 9 c.f.
    Inclusive dates: 1906 -
    Description: Manuscripts relating to
    the history of the Apache - Sitgreaves
    National Forest, focusing on the growth
    in management and use of the Forest's
    resources, such as timber, range lands,
    soil, water, and recreational facilities. In-
    cluded are correspondence, diaries,
    logbooks, account books, business
    records, maps, charts, and aerial photo-
    graphs.

TEMPE

AZ750-10
Arizona Historical Foundation
Hayden Library
Arizona State University
Tempe AZ 85287

(602) 966-8331, 965-3283

OPEN: M-F 8-5; closed weekends and
    holidays
ACCESS: academic and scholarly
    researchers
COPYING FACILITIES: yes
MATERIALS SOLICITED: Papers of Ari-
    zona historical and political figures.
    Will also accept materials relating to
    Arizona and northern Mexico, Sonora
    in particular.

HOLDINGS:
    Total volume: 2,378 l.f.
    Inclusive dates: 1862 -
    Description: About 60 collections in-
    cluding records and papers of individuals,
    families, and firms with focus on Arizona
    politics, mining, mercantile and cattle in-
    dustries, especially Goldwater mercantile
    enterprises and papers of U.S. Senator
    Barry Goldwater; photograph collection
    of 14,000 stills, prints, postcards, 35 mm
    slides, and negatives on related subjects;
    and the Dr. Benjamin Sacks' collection of
    Arizona reference cards; maps of territo-
    rial Arizona; and photocopies and micro-
    film of Arizona materials from other de-
    positories.

SEE ALSO: Preliminary inventories and
    guides available at the institution.

AZ750-32
Arizona State University
Department of Music
Southwest Tape Archive
Tempe AZ 85287

(602) 965-7568

OPEN: M-F 8-5; closed weekends and
    holidays
COPYING FACILITIES: yes
MATERIALS SOLICITED: Manuscripts per-
    taining to ethnomusicology, linguists,
    and anthropology, and music scores in
    manuscript related to
    ethnomusicological topics.

HOLDINGS:
    Total volume: 6 c.f.; 400 hours of
    recordings
    Inclusive dates: 1890 -
    Description: Tape recordings and re-
    lated manuscript documentation pertain-
    ing to ethnomusicology, with an emphasis
    on the southwestern United States and
    northwestern Mexico. Also included is
    material on Black American culture,
    Anglo-American folk culture in the
    Southwest, and Hispanic-American, Viet-
    namese, African, and Latin American
    music.

AZ750-45
Arizona State University
Library
Tempe AZ 85281

(602) 965-3417

OPEN: M-F 8-5; closed weekends and
    holidays
ACCESS: right to control access reserved
COPYING FACILITIES: yes
MATERIALS SOLICITED: University
    records. Will also accept Arizona politi-
    cal papers, materials relating to Ari-
    zona history, and literary manuscripts.

HOLDINGS:
    Total volume: 5,000 l.f.
    Inclusive dates: 1500 -
    Description: Materials relating to the
    history of the University, Arizona, and
    surrounding States. The papers of several
    Arizona politicians, holding both State
    and National office, are deposited here.
    These materials are complemented by pa-
    pers and records of other individuals, or-
    ganizations, and businesses. The library
    also houses a literary manuscript collec-
    tion, the Paolo Soleri Archive, and the
    Arizona State University Archives.

SEE: NUCMC, 1970, 72, 77.

SEE: Davis; Meckler and McMullin;
    Novotny; Robbins; Hinding; Mehr;
    Beers - Confederate.

SEE ALSO: Charles C. Colley, 'The Papers
    of Carl T. Hayden: Arizona's Silent
    Senator of Record,' *Journal of the West*
    14 (Oct. 1975); Charles C. Colley, 'The
    Papers of Senator Carl T. Hayden of
    Arizona: The Monumental Record of a
    Distinguished Career,' *Manuscripts*
    (Fall 1976); *Man-Environment Systems*
    5 (1975, p. 277).

AZ750-760
Tempe Historical Society
Tempe Historical Museum
3500 South Rural Road
Tempe AZ 85282

(602) 966-7253

OPEN: Tu-Sa 9-5; closed Sundays,
    Mondays, and holidays
COPYING FACILITIES: no
MATERIALS SOLICITED: Materials relating
    to the history of Tempe, including its
    economic, educational, political, social,
    and religious history.

HOLDINGS:
    Total volume: 65 boxes
    Inclusive dates: 1849 - 1978
    Description: Materials relating to
    Tempe, including Charles Trumbull
    Hayden and the political career of Sena-
    tor Carl T. Hayden. The holdings also
    include biographies and oral history re-
    cordings of early settlers, early photo-
    graphs of Tempe, maps, and ephemera.

TOMBSTONE

AZ760-760

Tombstone Courthouse State
   Historical Park
3rd and Toughnut Streets
Tombstone AZ

MAILING ADDRESS:
P.O. Box 216
Tombstone AZ 85638

(602) 457-3311

OPEN: daily 8-5:30; closed Christmas
USER FEES: fifty cents per individual,
   age 17 and under admitted free
ACCESS: appointment requested
COPYING FACILITIES: yes
MATERIALS SOLICITED: Will accept
   manuscripts and visual documents relating to Tombstone during the time it
   was Cochise County seat (1882-1929).

HOLDINGS:
   Total volume: 20 c.f.
   Inclusive dates: 1879 - 1929
   Description: Primarily records of
Tombstone from the early 1880's to the
late 1920's. Some records relating to oth-
er areas of Cochise County during the
same period.

TUBAC

AZ775-790

Tubac Presidio State Historic Park
Broadway and River Road
Tubac AZ

MAILING ADDRESS:
P.O. Box 1296
Tubac AZ 85646

(602) 398-2252

OPEN: daily 8-5:30; closed Christmas
ACCESS: appointment requested
COPYING FACILITIES: no
MATERIALS SOLICITED: Spanish materials relating to southern Arizona and
   northwestern Mexico. Will also accept
   materials relating to Arizona prior to
   1900.

HOLDINGS:
   Total volume: 2 l.f.
   Inclusive dates: 1600 - 1940
   Description: Maps and other materials
relating to the period of Spanish occupa-
tion of Arizona, as well as materials relat-
ing to the history of Tubac and southern
Arizona.

TUCSON

AZ800-30

Arizona Historical Society
Manuscripts Division
949 E. 2nd Street
Tucson AZ 85719

(602) 628-5774

OPEN: M-F 10-4, Sa 10-1; closed
   Sundays and holidays
COPYING FACILITIES: yes

MATERIALS SOLICITED: Social, economic
   and political history of Arizona, the
   Southwest and Mexico-Sonora.
HOLDINGS:
   Total volume: 2,300 c.f.; 1,000
manuscript collections; 12,000
biographical files
   Inclusive dates: 1750's -
   Description: 7,000 collections and biographical files and 250,000 photographs
relating chiefly to Arizona, the Southwest
and Mexico.

GUIDES: Charles C. Colley, *Documents of
   Southwestern History* (1972).

SEE: Hamer; NUCMC, 1959-62 (as Arizona Pioneers' Historical Society), 75.

SEE: Duignan; Schatz; Davis; Hounshell;
   Novotny; Bean and Vane; Robbins;
   Hinding; Mehr.

SEE ALSO: Paul and Greta Ezell, *The
   Aguiar Collection in the Arizona Pio-
   neers' Historical Society* (San Diego
   State College Press, 1964).

AZ800-790

University of Arizona
Arizona State Museum
Documentary Relations of the
   Southwest
Tucson AZ 85721

(602) 621-6278

OPEN: M-F 8-5; closed weekends and
   holidays
ACCESS: qualified researchers only
COPYING FACILITIES: yes
MATERIALS SOLICITED: Materials relating
   to the American Southwest and
   northwestern Mexico in the Spanish colonial and mission periods, 1520-1820.

HOLDINGS:
   Total volume: 620 reels microfilm
   Inclusive dates: 1550 - 1810
   Description: Microfilms of foreign
archival holdings pertaining to the greater
American Southwest with stress on Jesuit
missionary activities in northern Mexico,
with the largest concentration in 17th and
18th century materials. Contains considerable material on the ethnohistory of the
region.

SEE ALSO: A partial guide is available at
   the institution.

AZ800-800

University of Arizona
Arizona State Museum
Library
Tucson AZ

MAILING ADDRESS:
Building 30
Tucson AZ 85721

(602) 621-4695

OPEN: Tu-Th 8-4, F 8-2; closed other
   days and holidays
ACCESS: qualified researchers with
   approved research project
COPYING FACILITIES: yes
MATERIALS SOLICITED: Anthropological
   archives, including ethnological field
   diaries and reports, archaeological excavation logs, linguistic data, and pro-

fessional correspondence of anthropologists, especially materials relating to the
Southwest and northwestern Mexico.
Will also accept general materials in
anthropology, history and linguistics.

HOLDINGS:
   Total volume: 450 c.f.
   Inclusive dates: 1920 -
   Description: Archaeological archives of
the greater Southwest. Included are archaeological excavation logs, field diaries,
site survey inventories, ethnological field
diaries, linguistic field materials, oral history and linguistic tapes, manuscripts relating to Indians and other ethnic groups,
professional anthropological correspondence, and other unpublished manuscripts.

SEE: Bean and Vane; Hinding; Novotny;
   Meckler and McMullin.

AZ800-803

University of Arizona
Arizona State Museum
Photographic Collections
Tucson AZ 85721

(602) 621-2445

OPEN: M-F 8-5; closed weekends and
   holidays
COPYING FACILITIES: yes
MATERIALS SOLICITED: Ethnographic
   and archaeological film material on the
   historic and prehistoric peoples of the
   Greater Southwest and northwestern
   Mexico. Will also accept such materials
   on North American Indians and peoples of Mexico and Central and South
   America.

HOLDINGS:
   Total volume: 150,000 items
   Inclusive dates: late 19th century -
   Description: A collection of photographs depicting prehistoric and historic
archaeology and ethnology of the Indians
of the southwestern United States and
northwestern Mexico. Also documented
are museum artifacts and displays, Arizona history, the ecology and environment of Arizona and the greater Southwest, and the prehistory of North America, Mexico, Central and South America,
Europe, and Africa.

SEE: Novotny.

AZ800-820

University of Arizona
Library
Center for Creative Photography
843 East University Blvd.
Tucson AZ 85719

(602) 621-7968

OPEN: M-F 9-5, Su noon-5; closed
   Saturdays and holidays
ACCESS: advance arrangements
   requirement
COPYING FACILITIES: yes
MATERIALS SOLICITED: Photographic ar-
   chives and manuscript collections relat-
   ing to the history of photography.

HOLDINGS:
Total volume: not specified
Inclusive dates: 1840 -
Description: Photographs, manuscripts, and other materials of 20th century photographers, including Ansel Adams, Wynn Bullock, Harry Callahan, Aaron Siskind, Frederick Somers, and W. Gene Smith. Also included are examples of 19th century photographic processes, such as daguerreotypes, albumen prints, and calotypes.

AZ800-830

University of Arizona
Library
Special Collections
Tucson AZ 85721

(602) 621-6424

OPEN: M-F 9-5, Sa 12-4; closed Sundays and holidays
COPYING FACILITIES: yes
MATERIALS SOLICITED: Materials relating to Arizona and other southwestern States and literary materials of Arizona authors or relating to the Southwest. Will also accept photographs and technical drawings.

HOLDINGS:
Total volume: 940 l.f.
Inclusive dates: 1592 -
Description: 500 collections relating chiefly to Arizona and the Southwest including manuscripts from the Spanish missionary period, and diaries, reminiscences and correspondence of pioneers, business records, mining records, papers of outstanding Arizonans and records of the Hubbell trading post at Ganado. Also literary manuscripts of writers on Arizona, the Southwest and other topics.

SEE: Hamer; NUCMC, 1959-65, 68-69, 72, 74, 78, 80.

SEE: Bean and Vane; Duignan; Novotny; Schatz.

SEE ALSO: Morris Rieger, 'Africa-Related Papers of Persons and Organizations in the United States,' *African Studies Bulletin* 8 (Dec. 1965); Todd Mills, 'Western Manuscripts in the University of Arizona Library,' *Arizona and the West* 22 (Spring 1980); Henry Putney Beers, *Spanish & Mexican Records of the American Southwest: A Bibliographic Guide to Archive and Manuscript Sources* (Univ. of Arizona Press, 1979).

WILLCOX

AZ850-120

Chiricahua National Monument
Dos Cabezas Star Route
Willcox AZ

MAILING ADDRESS:
P.O. Box 6500
Willcox AZ 85643

(602) 824-3560

OPEN: daily 8-5; closed Christmas and New Year's
COPYING FACILITIES: no
MATERIALS SOLICITED: Items relating to historical and scientific knowledge of the Monument.

HOLDINGS:
Total volume: 5 l.f.
Inclusive dates: early 1900's -
Description: Maps, blueprints, architectural drawings, aerial photographs, photographs, and oral history tapes relating to Chiricahua National Monument, Fort Bowie National Historic Site, and the surrounding area.

WINDOW ROCK

AZ900-560

Navajo Tribal Museum
Native American Research Collection
Highway 264
Window Rock AZ

MAILING ADDRESS:
P.O. Box 308
Window Rock AZ 86515

(602) 871-6673

OPEN: M-F 8-5; closed weekends and holidays
COPYING FACILITIES: yes
MATERIALS SOLICITED: Materials regarding Navajo history, culture, and archaeology. Will also accept materials relating to other North American Indian tribes.

HOLDINGS:
Total volume: 90 l.f.
Inclusive dates: 1600's -
Description: Materials relating to Navajo history and culture. Included are copies of manuscripts from various sources; oral history tapes; microfilms of archival documents; maps; photographs; archaeological site reports and photographs; material relating to Navajo scouts; genealogical records; pension records; birth and death certificates of Navajos born prior to 1868; hospital records; and typescripts of 19th century newspaper articles on the Navajo.

YUMA

AZ950-40

Arizona Historical Society
Yuma County Historical Society Collections
240 Madison Avenue
Yuma AZ 85364

(602) 783-8020

OPEN: Tu-Sa 9-4; closed Sundays, Mondays and holidays
COPYING FACILITIES: no
MATERIALS SOLICITED: Materials pertaining to the history of the lower Colorado River region.

HOLDINGS:
Total volume: 20 l.f.; 4 file cabinets
Inclusive dates: 1850 - 1960
Description: Maps, diaries, business records, manuscripts, oral history tapes, and photographs related to people and places of significance in the lower Colorado River region, with emphasis on Yuma.

AZ950-950

Yuma Territorial Prison State Historic Park
Penitentiary Avenue and Prison Hill
Yuma AZ

MAILING ADDRESS:
P.O. Box 792
Yuma AZ 85364

(602) 783-4771

OPEN: daily 10-5; closed Christmas and Tuesdays and Wednesdays July 1-Sept. 30
COPYING FACILITIES: no
MATERIALS SOLICITED: Material related to the history of the Arizona Territorial Prison at Yuma between 1876 and 1909, including photographs of the prison and immediate vicinity, or persons associated with the Prison. Will also accept material before or after the prison operating dates if related to Arizona Territorial law and/or law enforcement with respect to the prison.

HOLDINGS:
Total volume: 30 vols.; 100 photographs
Inclusive dates: 1876 - 1909
Description: A compilation of materials which outline the history of the Arizona Territorial Prison at Yuma. Included are four volumes of newspaper articles, personal accounts, correspondence, and official superintendents' reports. There are about 100 photographs of the penitentiary and persons associated with it.

SEE: Hinding.

ARKANSAS

Since 1976 the Arkansas History Commission has administered a statewide program for preserving local public records. Permanently valuable local public records normally remain in the custody of local officials, but the State Archives in Little Rock makes available to researchers microfilm copies of county vital, probate, and land records, county court administrative records, circuit and chancery court records, selected tax books, and some municipal records, filmed by the Church of Jesus Christ of Latter-day Saints. The typical cutoff date for microfilming is 1900. Inventories are available at the State Archives for those county records which have been microfilmed.

ARKADELPHIA

AR60-120

Clark County Library
609 Caddo Street
Arkadelphia AR 71923

(501) 246-2271

OPEN: Tu-F 8:30-5, Sa 9-4; closed
  Sundays, Mondays and holidays
COPYING FACILITIES: yes
MATERIALS SOLICITED: Material relating to Clark County. Will also accept material pertaining to the southern U.S.

HOLDINGS:
  Total volume: 80 l.f.
  Inclusive dates: 1770 -
  Description: A collection of materials relating to Arkansas. Included are diaries, scrapbooks, maps, film strips, and materials relating to the history of early settlers, forts, colonization, and the Civil War.

AR60-600

Ouachita Baptist University
Riley Library
Clark County Historical Association
  Archives
Arkadelphia AR 71923

(501) 246-4531, Ext. 120

OPEN: by appointment only; closed
  University holidays
ACCESS: advance arrangements advisable
COPYING FACILITIES: yes
MATERIALS SOLICITED: Materials relating to Arkadelphia, Clark County, and Arkansas.

HOLDINGS:
  Total volume: 1,809 items
  Inclusive dates: 1801 - 1977
  Description: Materials relating to Clark County and Arkadelphia, including biographies of early settlers, personal correspondence, photographs, diaries, scrapbooks, a collection of plays relating to the history of Clark County, and oral history recordings.

BRAVETTE

AR200-322

Benton County Historical Society
3rd and Charollett Streets
Bravette AR 72736

(501) 524-3217

OPEN: by appointment only
COPYING FACILITIES: no
MATERIALS SOLICITED: Materials pertaining to Benton County. Will also accept other materials.

HOLDINGS:
  Total volume: 12 boxes; 70
photographs
  Inclusive dates: 1850 -
  Description: Photographs and manuscripts, including correspondence, relating to the Benton County area and its history.

SEE: NUCMC, 1959-61.

CONWAY

AR240-320

Hendrix College
Olin C. Bailey Library
Washington and Front Streets
Conway AR 72032

(501) 450-1303

OPEN: M-Th 8-midnight, F 8-5, Sa 1-5,
  Su 2-midnight; closed weekends and
  evenings June - mid-Sept., and holidays
COPYING FACILITIES: yes
MATERIALS SOLICITED: Will accept manuscripts, archives, visual documents, and audible documents regarding the Methodist church in Arkansas.

HOLDINGS:
  Total volume: 50 l.f.
  Inclusive dates: 1843 - 1950's
  Description: Records of the Methodist Episcopal Church, South and the Methodist Protestant church in Arkansas. Included are minutes of annual conferences (local and district), personal diaries, and unpublished church histories (local congregations).

SEE: Hamer.

AR240-810

University of Central Arkansas
Torreyson Library
Arkansas Room
Conway AR 72032

(501) 329-2931, Ext. 449

OPEN: M-Th 8-11, F 8-5, Sa 8:30-4, Su
  1-10; closed holidays
COPYING FACILITIES: yes
MATERIALS SOLICITED: Materials by and
  about Arkansas natives.

HOLDINGS:
  Total volume: 27 vols.
  Inclusive dates: 1969 -
  Description: Typescripts of the tapes of the oral history project at the University of Central Arkansas.

SEE: Meckler and McMullin; Hinding.

DOLPH

AR270-360

Izard County Historical Society
Dolph AR

MAILING ADDRESS:
P.O. Box 84
Dolph AR 72528

(501) 297-3751

OPEN: by appointment only
COPYING FACILITIES: no
MATERIALS SOLICITED: Materials concerning Izard County and/or pioneers in the Ozark area. Will also accept pictures, diaries, and other materials related to the Ozarks.

HOLDINGS:
  Total volume: 20 c.f.
  Inclusive dates: 1810 -
  Description: A collection of manuscripts relating to the Ozark area, including genealogies, autobiographies, and diaries.

FAYETTEVILLE

AR330-830

University of Arkansas
Libraries
Special Collections
Fayetteville AR 72701

(501) 575-5577

OPEN: M-F 8-5, Sa 9-1; closed Sundays,
  holidays, and Saturdays between
  semesters

COPYING FACILITIES: yes
MATERIALS SOLICITED: Materials related to Arkansas history. Will also accept other historical and literary collections which are of significant research potential in support of the University's graduate program.

HOLDINGS:
Total volume: 2,785 c.f.
Inclusive dates: 1763 -
Description: Principally historical manuscripts collections consisting of private papers of political leaders and other prominent persons closely associated with Arkansas and of the archives of nongovernmental Arkansas institutions. There are also a few historical collections which are not Arkansas related; a few collections which include the literary manuscripts, as well as the correspondence, of poets, novelists, and other writers, some of whom are Arkansas related; and a collection of Arkansas and Ozark mountain folklore materials.

SEE: Hamer; NUCMC, 1959-62, 70, 72, 74-77, 79.

SEE: Davis; Parkinson; Hines; Hinding; Robbins.

SEE ALSO: Walter Schatz, ed., *Directory of Afro-American Resources* (Bowker, 1970); David A. Hounshell, comp., *Manuscripts in U.S. Depositories Relating to the History of Electrical Science and Technology* (Smithsonian Institution, n.d.); Samuel A. Sizer, *A Guide to Selected Manuscript Collections in the University of Arkansas Library* (Univ. of Arkansas Library, 1976).

AR330-880
Washington County Historical Society
30 South College
Fayetteville AR 72701

(501) 521-2970

OPEN: irregular hours
COPYING FACILITIES: yes
MATERIALS SOLICITED: Materials pertaining to Washington County, its events, inhabitants, and records. Will also accept other materials.

HOLDINGS:
Total volume: 1,000 items
Inclusive dates: 1826 -
Description: Materials relating to Washington County, AR, including church and business records, some military records, and some genealogical material.

SEE: Hamer; NUCMC, 1966.

GILLETT

AR360-40
Arkansas Post County Museum
Gillett AR

MAILING ADDRESS:
P.O. Box 32
Gillett AR 72055

(501) 548-2634

OPEN: Tu-Sa 9-4, Su 1-4:30; closed Mondays and holidays

COPYING FACILITIES: no
MATERIALS SOLICITED: Materials relating to Arkansas County and Arkansas. Will also accept material pertaining to early U.S. history.

HOLDINGS:
Total volume: 400 items
Inclusive dates: 1786 - 1966
Description: Deeds, letters, bills of sale for slaves, contracts made at Arkansas Post (1805-19), homestead grants, an 1810 account book of Scull & Co., court proceedings, wills, and a Civil War diary.
Also includes early maps, an 1837 census of the Arkansas Territory; genealogical information, 1786-1875.

HOT SPRINGS

AR390-280
Garland County Historical Society
914 Summer Street
Hot Springs AR 71913

(501) 623-5875

OPEN: by appointment
COPYING FACILITIES: no
MATERIALS SOLICITED: History of Hot Springs and Garland County.

HOLDINGS:
Total volume: 4 file cabinets
Inclusive dates: 1800 -
Description: Materials relating to the history of Hot Springs and Garland County.

AR390-760
Tri-Lakes Regional Library
200 Woodbine
Hot Springs AR 71901

(501) 623-4161

OPEN: Tu, Th 11-8, W, F, Sa 9:30-5:30; closed Sundays, Mondays, and holidays
COPYING FACILITIES: no
MATERIALS SOLICITED: Historical records, including photographs and oral histories, of Garland, Montgomery and Clark counties, AR. Will also accept materials on Arkansas.

HOLDINGS:
Total volume: 350 items
Inclusive dates: 1900 -
Description: Oral history recordings concerning bath houses in Hot Springs and the administration of Leo P. McLaughlin, mayor of Hot Springs from 1926-47, as well as photographs and slides of the area.

JONESBORO

AR480-130
Crowley Ridge Regional Library
315 West Oak
Jonesboro AR 72401

(501) 935-5133

OPEN: M-W 9-9, Th-Sa 9-5:30; closed Sundays and holidays
COPYING FACILITIES: yes

MATERIALS SOLICITED: Materials relating to Arkansas. Will also accept materials pertinent to the ancestry of residents of northeastern Arkansas, southeastern Missouri, and western Tennessee.

HOLDINGS:
Total volume: 500 l.f.
Inclusive dates: 1790 -
Description: Materials relating to Arkansas and the Jonesboro area, including family and area histories, censuses, cemetery records, and other materials used in genealogical research.

AR480-320
Holy Angels Convent
Off Highway 141 North
Jonesboro AR

MAILING ADDRESS:
P.O. Drawer 130
Jonesboro AR 72403

(501) 935-5810

OPEN: by appointment only; closed Sundays and major holidays
COPYING FACILITIES: yes

HOLDINGS:
Total volume: 25 file boxes
Inclusive dates: 1887 -
Description: Record of the Olivetan Benedictine Sisters of Jonesboro, including papers of the foundress and major superiors, rules and constitutions, chronicles of early years, financial records, scrapbooks, and records of institutions and of deceased sisters.

SEE: Hinding.

LITTLE ROCK

AR510-13
Arkansas Department of Natural and Cultural History
Arkansas Territorial Restoration
3rd and Scott
Little Rock AR 72201

(501) 371-2348

OPEN: M-Sa 9-5, Su 1-5; closed holidays
ACCESS: advance arrangements required
COPYING FACILITIES: no
MATERIALS SOLICITED: Arkansas history, 1800-1850's. Will accept other materials relevant to the restoration sites.

HOLDINGS:
Total volume: 900 items
Inclusive dates: early 19th century -
Description: Collections include documents pertaining to Arkansas Territory and early statehood.

SEE: Hinding.

AR510-25
Arkansas History Commission
One Capitol Mall
Little Rock AR 72201

(501) 371-2141

OPEN: M-Sa 8-4:30; closed Sundays and holidays
COPYING FACILITIES: yes

MATERIALS SOLICITED: All materials related to Arkansas history, genealogy, folklore, and culture.

HOLDINGS:
> *Total volume:* 700 c.f.
> *Inclusive dates:* 1764 -
> *Description:* State governmental records; private manuscript collections relating to the history of Arkansas and its people; county and municipal records; papers of business, industry, and agriculture; records of religious, social, and ethnic institutions and organizations; and cartographic and pictorial materials.

SEE: Hamer; NUCMC, 1968.

SEE: Schatz; Beers - Confederate; Novotny; Hinding.

AR510-30

Arkansas Library Commission
506 1/2 Center Street
Little Rock AR 72201

no telephone
SEE: Hamer.

Questionnaire not returned.

AR510-145

Diocese of Little Rock
Archives
2415 North Tyler Street
Little Rock AR

MAILING ADDRESS:
P.O. Box 7239
Little Rock AR 72217

(501) 664-0340

OPEN: by appointment only; closed church holidays
USER FEES: variable
ACCESS: serious researchers; appointment suggested
COPYING FACILITIES: yes
MATERIALS SOLICITED: Materials relating to the Roman Catholic Church in Arkansas, including its growth, clergy, members, institutions, and organizations.

HOLDINGS:
> *Total volume:* 250 c.f.
> *Inclusive dates:* late 18th Century -
> *Description:* Materials relating to the Roman Catholic Church in Arkansas, including correspondence of bishops and priests, parish reports, parish celebration booklets, parish histories, records of diocesan institutions, early sacramental records, diocesan financial records, photographs, and diocesan celebration and history materials.

AR510-520

Missionary Baptist Seminary
Glover Library
Missionary Baptist Archives
5220 Stage Coach Road
Little Rock AR 72204

(501) 455-4588, 4589

OPEN: Tu-F 8-1; closed other days and holidays
ACCESS: appointment requested
COPYING FACILITIES: no

MATERIALS SOLICITED: Baptist historical materials, U. S. and foreign; material relating to the American Baptist Association and the "Landmark" Movement; James Robinson Graves; and "Missionary Baptists" and Benjamin Marcus Bogard. Will also accept other materials relating to Baptists.

HOLDINGS:
> *Total volume:* 5 c.f.
> *Inclusive dates:* 1800's -
> *Description:* Church records for Arkansas and association minutes of Arkansas and other States.

AR510-680

Quapaw Quarter Association
1315 South Scott
Little Rock AR

MAILING ADDRESS:
P.O. Box 1104
Little Rock AR 72203

(501) 371-0075

OPEN: M-F 9-5; closed weekends and holidays
COPYING FACILITIES: yes
MATERIALS SOLICITED: Materials on historic preservation of buildings and neighborhoods, with emphasis on late 19th and early 20th century Little Rock.

HOLDINGS:
> *Total volume:* 10 l.f.; 5 file drawers
> *Inclusive dates:* 1821 -
> *Description:* Survey records, 1977; historic records; photographs; slides; and maps of structures in the Quapaw Quarter area of Little Rock.

AR510-810

University of Arkansas at Little Rock
Library
Archives and Special Collections
33rd and University
Little Rock AR 72204

(501) 371-1071

OPEN: M-F 8-5; closed weekends, holidays, and Christmas vacation
COPYING FACILITIES: yes
MATERIALS SOLICITED: Materials relating to the history and cultural development of Arkansas.

HOLDINGS:
> *Total volume:* 300 l.f.
> *Inclusive dates:* 1810 -
> *Description:* Materials relating to the political, economic, social, and literary history of Arkansas, including major collections on the Arkansas Knights of Labor, the Populist Party, the Arkansas Republican Party, poet John Gould Fletcher, Jr., U.S. Congressman David D. Terry, Jr., and the 1957 Little Rock crisis period.

AR510-825

University of Arkansas for Medical Sciences
Library
History of Medicine/Archives Division
4301 West Markham
Little Rock AR

MAILING ADDRESS:
4301 West Markham/Slot 586
Little Rock AR 72205

(501) 661-5980

OPEN: M-F 8-4:30; closed weekends and University holidays
ACCESS: University alumni and students, scholars, and others with permission
COPYING FACILITIES: yes
MATERIALS SOLICITED: Materials concerning the University of Arkansas for Medical Sciences and the history of medicine, with emphasis on Arkansas.

HOLDINGS:
> *Total volume:* 123 l.f.
> *Inclusive dates:* 1844 -
> *Description:* Records of the University of Arkansas for Medical Sciences and materials relating to the history of medicine, particularly in Arkansas. The holdings include publications, minutes, office files, theses, dissertations, photographs, and personal papers.

MONTICELLO

AR600-160

Drew County Historical Museum
Southeast Research and Archives Center
404 South Main Street
Monticello AR 71655

(501) 367-7446

OPEN: M-F 9-5, Sa, Su 2-5
COPYING FACILITIES: no
MATERIALS SOLICITED: Materials relating to the history of Drew County. Will also accept materials pertaining to Arkansas in general.

HOLDINGS:
> *Total volume:* 300 items
> *Inclusive dates:* 1860 -
> *Description:* Manuscripts and photographs documenting the history of Drew County, as well as Arkansas. Included are daybooks, account books, letters, genealogical research materials, and oral history tapes.

STATE UNIVERSITY

AR890-20

Arkansas State University
Dean B. Ellis Library
Arkansas Room
P.O. Box 2040
State University AR 72467

(501) 972-3077

OPEN: M-F 8-4:30, or by appointment; closed weekends and holidays
COPYING FACILITIES: yes

MATERIALS SOLICITED: Material relating to Arkansas, including government records and records of private organizations.

HOLDINGS:

Total volume: 315 l.f.; 109 items
Inclusive dates: 1874 -
Description: Letters from Judge J. C. Parker to Clerks of the Court of the U.S. District Court for the Western District of Arkansas (1874-1904); papers of Francis Cherry, governor of Arkansas (1953-55); papers of E. C. 'Took' Gathings, U.S. Representative; and papers and other materials relating to children's author Lois Lenski.

SEE: Robbins.

AR890-30
Arkansas State University
Museum Library
State University AR

MAILING ADDRESS:
P.O. Box 490
State University AR 72467

(501) 972-2074

OPEN: First Su 2-5, M-F 9-4; closed Saturdays, holidays, and holiday weekends
ACCESS: advance arrangements required
COPYING FACILITIES: yes
MATERIALS SOLICITED: Materials on northeastern Arkansas history and development.

HOLDINGS:

Total volume: 37 l.f.
Inclusive dates: 1840 - 1950
Description: Courthouse records for Sharp County, AR; Arkansas postal ledgers; Kansas and Arkansas teaching contracts; Civil War correspondence; New England family papers; land grants, maps, photographs, and scrapbooks.

SEE: Robbins.

WASHINGTON

AR950-600
Old Washington Historic State Park
Washington AR

MAILING ADDRESS:
P.O. Box 98
Washington AR 71862

(501) 983-2684

OPEN: M, W-Sa 8-4, Su 1-5; closed Tuesdays and holidays
COPYING FACILITIES: yes
MATERIALS SOLICITED: Materials relating to the history of the southwestern United States.

HOLDINGS:

Total volume: 25 boxes
Inclusive dates: 1800 - 1880
Description: Documents and letters relating to old Washington and to the history of the southwestern United States.

CALIFORNIA

California has no statewide program for the management and preservation of local government records of permanent value. Commonly, counties and municipalities maintain custody of the records, but few provide adequate archival care; and appraisal is highly imprecise. Some records of six counties, largely court records dating from 1850, and records of numerous school districts are housed at the State Archives in Sacramento.

Although it has no comprehensive statutory responsibility for local government records, the State Archives provides technical resource materials to cities and counties through its Information Center for Archives and Records Management and, in 1981, published *Identification of the Historical Records of County Government in California*, a manual widely distributed to county officials and historical agencies to assist them in problems of records appraisal.

ANGWIN

CA32-640
Pacific Union College
Nelson Memorial Library
Angwin CA 94508

(707) 965-6241

OPEN: Su 9-10, M-Th 7:30-10, F 7:30-1; shorter hours June 12 - Sept. 25; closed Saturdays and holidays
COPYING FACILITIES: yes

HOLDINGS:
Total volume: 11 boxes
Inclusive dates: not specified
Description: Records of Japanese war crime trials held after World War II, collected by an interpreter during the trials.

SEE: Hamer.

ARCADIA

CA40-60
Arcadia Public Library
20 West Duarte Road
Arcadia CA 91006

(213) 446-7111

OPEN: M-Th 9:30-9, F, Sa 9:30-5:30; closed Sundays and holidays
COPYING FACILITIES: yes

MATERIALS SOLICITED: Materials relating to Arcadia history, including Rancho Santa Anita, E. J. 'Lucky' Baldwin and his descendants, the World War I U.S. Army Balloon School at Ross Field, the Santa Anita Assembly Center for Japanese-Americans in World War II, and the Army Ordnance Training Center, Camp Santa Anita, during World War II. Will also accept materials relating to the history of the Santa Anita Race Track.

HOLDINGS:
Total volume: 1,000 items
Inclusive dates: early 1900's -
Description: Photographs relating to the history of Arcadia, covering such subjects as E. J. 'Lucky' Baldwin and his daughter Anita, Rancho Santa Anita, the U.S. Army Balloon School at Ross Field during World War I, and the Santa Anita Assembly Center for Japanese-Americans during World War II. There are also a few blueprints, manuscript maps, and oral history tapes, as well as documents relating to the Library's founding and operation.

CA40-480
Los Angeles State and County Arboretum
Historical Section
301 North Baldwin Avenue
Arcadia CA 91006

(818) 446-8251

OPEN: M-F 8-4:30; closed weekends and holidays
ACCESS: advance appointment required
COPYING FACILITIES: no
MATERIALS SOLICITED: Photographs of the Los Angeles Basin, especially the San Gabriel Valley (1875-1950), and postcards of the Los Angeles area (1900-50).

HOLDINGS:
Total volume: 1,010 items
Inclusive dates: 1875 - 1950
Description: Photographs emphasizing the development of the Baldwin Ranch holdings in the San Gabriel Valley; a postcard collection concentrating on views of Los Angeles (1900-15); and oral history tapes and transcripts of interviews with local residents relating to the Baldwin Ranch era (1875-1936).

ATASCADERO

CA48-40
Atascadero Historical Society Museum
6500 Palma Avenue
Atascadero CA

MAILING ADDRESS:
P.O. Box 1047
Atascadero CA 93423

(805) 466-0506

OPEN: M-F 1-4, or by appointment; closed weekends and holidays
COPYING FACILITIES: yes
MATERIALS SOLICITED: Materials relating to Atascadero history.

HOLDINGS:
Total volume: not specified
Inclusive dates: 1790 -
Description: Materials relating to the founding of Atascadero and Palos Verdes Estates, and University City, MO, by E. G. Lewis. Included is information on the Lewis family and others related to early Atascadero, as well as photographs, records of real estate transactions, blueprints, and journals of several early residents.

BANNING

CA66-80
Banning Public Library
21 West Nicolet Street
Banning CA 92220

(714) 849-3192

OPEN: M, Th 9-8, Tu, W, F 9-6, Sa 9-1; closed Sundays and holidays
COPYING FACILITIES: yes
MATERIALS SOLICITED: Materials relating to the early history of California and Riverside and San Bernardino counties.

HOLDINGS:
Total volume: not specified
Inclusive dates: early 1800's -
Description: Materials relating to the history of the West, southern California, Riverside County, CA, and the Banning area. Included are biographies and photographs of early settlers of Banning and the San Gorgonio Pass, and other materials documenting local Mexican and Indian history.

CA66-520

Malki Museum, Inc.
11-795 Fields Road
Morongo Indian Reservation
Banning CA 92220

(714) 849-7289

OPEN: Tu-Su 10-5; closed Mondays
COPYING FACILITIES: no
MATERIALS SOLICITED: Materials related
to the Indian tribes of southern California. Will also accept materials related
to the Indians of North America.

HOLDINGS:
   Total volume: not specified
   Inclusive dates: not specified
   Description: Materials, including
manuscripts, photographs, and oral history tapes, relating to the Indian tribes of
southern California. There are considerable field notes by various anthropologists, including John Peabody Harrington.

SEE: Bean and Vane.

BELMONT

CA78-740

Sisters of Notre Dame de Namur
California Province
Archives
College of Notre Dame
1500 Ralston Avenue
Belmont CA 94002

(415) 592-2939, 593-1681

OPEN: M-F 9-3, or by appointment
COPYING FACILITIES: yes
MATERIALS SOLICITED: Records of the
convents and schools of the Sisters of
Notre Dame, California Province. Will
also accept materials relating to the
educational work of the Sisters of
Notre Dame in Oregon (1844-51) and
in California (1851-1960).

HOLDINGS:
   Total volume: 362 l.f.
   Inclusive dates: 1843 - 1960
   Description: Records relating to the
Sisters of Notre Dame de Namur, California Province (including Oregon, Washington, and Hawaii). Types of materials
include letters, diaries of sisters and students, annuals, journals, accounts, photographs, and minutes.

SEE: Hinding.

BERKELEY

CA86-50

Armstrong College
Library
2222 Harold Way
Berkeley CA 94704

(415) 848-2500, Ext. 22

OPEN: M-Th 8-7, F 8-4; closed weekends
and holidays
COPYING FACILITIES: yes
MATERIALS SOLICITED: Material relating
to the history of Armstrong College.

HOLDINGS:
   Total volume: 7 l.f.
   Inclusive dates: 1918 -
   Description: 45 M.B.A. theses, a collection of photographs, and a few pieces of
correspondence.

CA86-120

Citizens for Farm Labor
Berkeley CA

MAILING ADDRESS:
P.O. Box 1173
Berkeley CA 94701

no telephone

OPEN: by appointment only
COPYING FACILITIES: no

HOLDINGS:
   Total volume: 25 c.f.
   Inclusive dates: 1953 - 1973
   Description: Materials from the National Agricultural Workers Union, Agricultural Workers Association, Agricultural Workers Organizing Committee,
and United Farm Workers Organizing
Committee, documenting efforts to organize farm laborers in California. Included are correspondence, photographs,
diaries, and tape recordings of mass
meetings and interviews with organizing
leaders and laborers.

CA86-280

Graduate Theological Union
Library
c/o Graduate Theological Union
   Library
2400 Ridge Road
Berkeley CA 94709

(415) 841-8222

OPEN: by appointment only
SEE: NUCMC, 1979.

Questionnaire not returned.

CA86-385

Judah L. Magnes Memorial Museum
Goldstein Library
2911 Russell Street
Berkeley CA 94705

(415) 849-2710

OPEN: Su-F 10-4; closed Saturdays, legal
holidays, and Jewish holidays
COPYING FACILITIES: yes
MATERIALS SOLICITED: Materials on the
Jews of India, Morocco and Egypt.

HOLDINGS:
   Total volume: 75 l.f.
   Inclusive dates: 1401 -
   Description: The Belkin papers, concerning the Jewish World Relief Organization's mission for Russia and the
Ukraine, 1920-21; 47 items on the
Karaite community of Cairo, Egypt; correspondence of Max Liliethal concerning
his mission to Russia, 1839-45; and materials concerning the Holocaust.

SEE: NUCMC, 1978, 80.

CA86-400

Judah L. Magnes Memorial Museum
Western Jewish History Center
2911 Russell Street
Berkeley CA 94705

(415) 849-2710

OPEN: M-F 10-3; closed weekends,
holidays and Jewish holy days
COPYING FACILITIES: yes
MATERIALS SOLICITED: Western American Jewish history, David Lubin and
Judah L. Magnes. Will also accept materials relating to non-Western American Jewish communities and institutions and some Latin American material.

HOLDINGS:
   Total volume: 485 c.f.; 70 microfilm
reels; 3,135 items
   Inclusive dates: 1849 -
   Description: Manuscripts, photographs,
clippings, oral histories, diaries, scrapbooks, genealogies, biographies, and
archival records of Jewish institutions of
eleven western States designed to illustrate the cultural, philanthropic, business,
and other contributions of Jewish people
and institutions to the American West.
Most of the information is on California,
Oregon, Arizona, and Washington, and
dates from 1849, except for some background information on individuals who
came west later in their lives, including
some early European records.
   Includes materials pertaining to western Canada and Mexico, Alaska and Hawaii, documenting the business, cultural,
intellectual, philanthropic and social contributions of Jewish people and their institutions to the American West.

SEE: NUCMC, 1978, 80.

SEE: Hinding.

SEE ALSO: Joan Hoff Wilson and Lynn B.
Donovan, 'Women's History: A Listing
of West Coast Archival and Manuscript
Sources, Part II,' *California Historical
Quarterly* 55 (Summer 1976); Alan M.
Meckler and Ruth McMullin, comps.,
Oral History Collections (Bowker,
1975); Celeste L. MacLeod, 'The Western Jewish History Center,' *American
Jewish Historical Quarterly* 63 (1968);
and the following publications of the
Center by Sara G. Cogan: *Pioneer Jews
of the California Mother Lode, 1849-80*
(1968), *The Jews of San Francisco and
the Greater Bay Area, 1849-1919*
(1973), *The Jews of Los Angeles,
1849-1945.*

Suzanne Nemiroff, comp., *Western Jewish
History Center of the Judah L. Magnes
Memorial Museum: Catalog of Manuscripts Collections* (1977).

CA86-520

Meiklejohn Civil Liberties Institute
1715 Francisco Street
Berkeley CA 94703

(415) 848-0599

OPEN: M-F 9-5; closed weekends and
holidays
COPYING FACILITIES: yes

MATERIALS SOLICITED: Materials related to civil liberties, civil rights, and due process, particularly sex discrimination, grand and petit juries, affirmative action, police misconduct, and prisoners' rights.

HOLDINGS:
>   Total volume: 80 l.f.; 8,000 files
>   Inclusive dates: 1936 -
>   Description: Papers relating to civil liberties and civil rights, including records, correspondence, legal files, and scrapbooks pertaining to voter registration drives in the South during the 1960's and the legal fight to dissolve the House Committee on Un-American Activities; records of the National Lawyers Guild, 1936-76; and extensive holdings of briefs and other legal documents from cases in all aspects of civil liberties.

SEE: Schatz; Bean and Vane; Hinding.

SEE ALSO: Finding aids to individual collections are available at the institution.

CA86-630

Pacific School of Religion
Archives
1798 Scenic Avenue
Berkeley CA 94709

(415) 848-0528, Ext. 249

OPEN: M-F 8:30-5; closed weekends
ACCESS: by prior arrangement
COPYING FACILITIES: yes
MATERIALS SOLICITED: Church records, primarily from California, of the United Church of Christ (Congregational), the Christian church (Disciples of Christ), and the Methodist church. Will also accept related materials.

HOLDINGS:
>   Total volume: 45 l.f.
>   Inclusive dates: 1850 -
>   Description: Records relating primarily to Congregational, Methodist, and Christian church congregations and ministers in California, with papers and records from other areas. Included are some papers of the Spanish and Mexican periods in California; records of missionary work among the Chinese and Japanese in California; and manuscript materials of the Women's Board of Missions for the Pacific, the Northern California Conference of the United Church of Christ, and the California-Nevada Conference of the United Methodist church.

SEE: Hamer; NUCMC, 1959-62, 70.

SEE: Beers - Southwest; Schatz; Duignan; Bean and Vane.

CA86-780

University of California, Berkeley
The Bancroft Library
Manuscripts Division
Berkeley CA 94720

(415) 642-6481

OPEN: M-F 9-5, Sa 1-5; closed Sundays
COPYING FACILITIES: yes
MATERIALS SOLICITED: Materials relating to the history of western North America and to the humanities.

HOLDINGS:
>   Total volume: 37,000,000 items
>   Inclusive dates: 16th century -
>   Description: Manuscripts focusing on the history of California, other Western States, and Mexico, as well as other collections of papers of persons prominent in literature, politics, journalism, law, science, and other professions; records of organizations and business firms; and individual items, such as diaries and journals.

GUIDES: Dale L. Morgan and George P. Hammond, eds., A Guide to the Manuscript Collections of the Bancroft Library, Vol. 1, Pacific and Western Manuscripts (Univ. of California Press, 1963); George P. Hammond, ed., A Guide to the Manuscript Collections of the Bancroft Library, Vol. 2, Mexican and Central American Manuscripts (Univ. of California Press, 1972). Other volumes to be published.

SEE: Hamer; NUCMC, 1963-67, 70-71, 75.

SEE: Robbins; Hinding; Martin; Ingram; Spalek; Allard, Crawley, and Edmison; Bean and Vane; Parkinson; Beers - Southwest.

SEE ALSO: Joan Hoff Wilson and Lynn B. Donovan, 'Women's History: A Listing of West Coast Archival and Manuscript Sources, Part II,' California Historical Quarterly 55 (Summer 1976); Ann Novotny, ed., Picture Sources 3 (Special Libraries Assn., 1975); Albert Krichmar, The Women's Rights Movement in the United States, 1848-1970: A Bibliography and Sourcebook (Scarecrow Press, 1972); David A. Hounshell, comp., Manuscripts in U.S. Depositories Relating to the History of Electrical Science and Technology (Smithsonian Institution, n.d.); Robert H. Becker, 'Library Resources: The Bancroft Library--Then and Now,' California Historical Quarterly 52 (Fall 1973).

Peter Duignan, Handbook of American Resources for African Studies (Hoover Institution, 1967); Dale L. Morgan, 'Western Travels and Travelers in the Bancroft Library,' in John Francis McDermott, ed., Travelers on the Western Frontier (Univ. of Illinois Press, 1970); Andrea Hinding and Rosemary Richardson, comps., Archival and Manuscript Resources for the Study of Women's History: A Beginning (Univ. of Minnesota Libraries, Social Welfare History Archives Center, 1972); Source Materials for the Recent History of Astronomy and Astrophysics: A Checklist of Manuscript Collections in the United States (American Institute of Physics, 1971).

CA86-790

University of California, Berkeley
The Bancroft Library
The Mark Twain Project
480 General Library
Berkeley CA 94704

MAILING ADDRESS:
480 Main Library
University of California
Berkeley CA 94720

(415) 642-6480

OPEN: M-F 9-5; closed weekends and holidays
COPYING FACILITIES: yes
MATERIALS SOLICITED: Materials relating to the life and work of Samuel Langhorne Clemens.

HOLDINGS:
>   Total volume: 160 l.f.
>   Inclusive dates: 1800 -
>   Description: Materials relating to the life and work of Samuel Langhorne Clemens. Included are 45 of his notebooks and journals; 3,000 letters by Clemens and members of his family; over 10,000 letters to Clemens; and about 600 literary manuscripts. There are also contemporary documents and clippings, photographs, scrapbooks, and other items.

SEE: Hamer; NUCMC, 1965, 71.

CA86-810

University of California, Berkeley
The Bancroft Library
Regional Oral History Office
486 The Bancroft Library
Berkeley CA 94720

(415) 642-7395

OPEN: M-F 8-5; closed weekends and holidays
COPYING FACILITIES: yes
MATERIALS SOLICITED: Will accept tapes on all aspects of western history.

HOLDINGS:
>   Total volume: 468 oral history memoirs
>   Inclusive dates: 1880 -
>   Description: Oral history tapes and transcripts, and related papers and pictorial material relating to the history of California and the West. Major topics include agriculture, water resources, and land use in northern California; art, photography, and writing in the San Francisco Bay area; Russian immigrants to California; conservation and State and National parks; fine printing in the San Francisco Bay area; forest service and forest policy; the Earl Warren era in California (1926-53); the tenures of governors Goodwin Knight and Pat Brown (1953-66); the California wine industry; the social history of northern California; the California Jewish community; the history of the University of California at Berkeley; woman suffragists; California women political leaders; and biography.

GUIDES: Suzanne B. Riess and Willa K. Baum, eds., Catalogue of the Regional Oral History Office, 1954-1979 (1980).

SEE: NUCMC, 1970.

SEE: Krichmar.

SEE ALSO: Alan M. Meckler and Ruth McMullin, comps., *Oral History Collections* (Bowker, 1975); Willa K. Baum, 'Oral History: A Revived Tradition at the Bancroft Library,' *Pacific Northwest Quarterly* 58 (April 1967); 'History on Tape: The Regional Oral History Office at the Bancroft Library,' *California Historical Quarterly* 54 (Spring 1975).

CA86-815

University of California, Berkeley
The Bancroft Library
University Archives
281 Library
Berkeley CA 94720

(415) 642-2933

OPEN: M-F 9-5; closed weekends and holidays
COPYING FACILITIES: yes
MATERIALS SOLICITED: Manuscripts, photographs, tape recordings, and memorabilia relating to the University of California.

HOLDINGS:
   Total volume: 9,000,000 items
   Inclusive dates: 1855 -
   Description: Records of the University of California from its inception in 1868, and documentation generated by its predecessor, the College of California. Included are office files, Academic Senate records, student and alumni publications, photographs, memorabilia, and printed materials. Also held are records of the systemwide administration of the University and of the Berkeley campus, as well as materials concerning other campuses in the University of California system.

CA86-820

University of California, Berkeley
Department of Architecture
313A Wurster Hall
Berkeley CA 94720

(415) 642-5124

OPEN: variable hours
ACCESS: advance arrangements advised
COPYING FACILITIES: yes
MATERIALS SOLICITED: Material related to architecture and landscape architecture in California.

HOLDINGS:
   Total volume: 1,500,000 items
   Inclusive dates: 1885 -
   Description: Consists of 30,000 architectural drawings for California, as well as landscape architectural drawings for California, the eastern United States, and England. Also included are 1,000,000 blueprints for the San Francisco Bay area and the William W. Wurster collection of architectural drawings, photographs, and papers. Collections of private papers of California architects include those of Bernard Maybeck, Charles Sumner Green, Julia Morgan, John Galen Howard, Willis Polk, and the landscape architects Beatrix Farrand and Gertrude Jekyll.

SEE: Hinding.

CA86-850

University of California, Berkeley
Forestry Library
The Metcalf-Fritz Photograph
   Collection
260 Mulford Hall
Berkeley CA 94720

(415) 642-2936

OPEN: M-Th 9-9, F 9-5, Sa, Su 1-5; summer, M-F 9-5; closed holidays, and weekends in summer
COPYING FACILITIES: yes
MATERIALS SOLICITED: Photographs which show forestry activities in California, particularly those associated with the University's Department of Forestry and Conservation.

HOLDINGS:
   Total volume: 36 l.f.
   Inclusive dates: 1910 -
   Description: Over 8,000 photographs (many with matching negatives) illustrating logging equipment, logging operations, reforestation, lumber mills, specimens of tree species, and activities of the University of California's School of Forestry. Most of the photographs were taken in California. About 20 percent concern forestry in other parts of the United States (particularly Oregon and Washington), and there are some pictures of logging in Europe during World War I.

SEE: Davis.

CA86-882

University of California, Berkeley
Lawrence Berkeley Laboratory
Archives and Records
1 Cyclotron Road
Building 69-107
Berkeley CA 94720

(415) 486-5525

OPEN: M-F 8-4; closed weekends and holidays
COPYING FACILITIES: yes
MATERIALS SOLICITED: Official administrative and research records of Lawrence Berkeley Laboratory, including papers of noteworthy scientists; business records of the Manhattan Engineering District; and records reflecting interdisciplinary group research, particularly in physics, nuclear science, and medical physics.

HOLDINGS:
   Total volume: 15,000 c.f.
   Inclusive dates: 1941 -
   Description: Records of Lawrence Berkeley Laboratory, including Director's Office documents, business records, division and department files, and individual scientist files. Included are correspondence, photographs, official files, magnetic tapes, film containing raw data, and drawings. The records relate to basic research at the Laboratory and reflect the relationship of science to government and to the University.

CA86-890

University of California, Berkeley
Music Library
240 Morrison Hall
Berkeley CA 94720

(415) 642-2623

OPEN: M-Th 9-9, F, Sa 9-5, Su 1-5; summer and semester breaks, M-F 9-5; closed holidays
ACCESS: an appointment is advised
COPYING FACILITIES: yes
MATERIALS SOLICITED: Manuscripts of so-called Western art music and music treatises dating from the Middle Ages to the present which have demonstrable research value for musicologists.

HOLDINGS:
   Total volume: 250 l.f.
   Inclusive dates: 11th century -
   Description: More than 2,000 volumes of musical scores and treatises (11th century - 19th century); 250 music manuscripts by 20th century composers such as Ernst Bloch, Sigmund Romberg, Darius Milhaud, Luigi Dallapiccola, and local composers of the San Francisco Bay area; musicological papers of Manfred Bukofzer and Alfred Einstein; and the correspondence, diaries, and musical compositions of Alfred Hertz, conductor of the San Francisco Symphony Orchestra. There is also a sound archive of 22,000 78 rpm discs.

SEE: Spalek.

SEE ALSO: Vincent Duckles and Minnie Elmer, *Thematic Catalog of a Manuscript Collection of Eighteenth-Century Italian Instrumental Music in the University of California, Berkeley, Music Library* (Univ. of California Press, 1963).

CA86-895

University of California, Berkeley
Office for History of Science and
   Technology
Archive for History of Quantum
   Physics
470 Stephens Hall
Berkeley CA 94720

(415) 642-4581

OPEN: M-F 9-5; closed weekends and holidays
COPYING FACILITIES: yes

HOLDINGS:
   Total volume: 317 microfilms
   Inclusive dates: 1898 - 1933
   Description: A microfilm collection of primary source materials for the study of the history of quantum physics, including letters, manuscripts, notebooks, and personal commentaries of major physicists.

SEE ALSO: Thomas S. Kuhn, John L. Heilbron, Paul Forman, and Lini Allen, *Sources for the History of Quantum Physics: An Inventory and Report* (1967).

A duplicate of the collection is held by the American Philosophical Society, Library, in Philadelphia, PA.

CA86-910
University of California, Berkeley
University Herbarium
Department of Botany
Berkeley CA 94720

(415) 642-2465

OPEN: M-F 8-5; closed weekends and
  holidays
COPYING FACILITIES: yes
MATERIALS SOLICITED: Field books relating to botanical specimens deposited
  here and maps necessary to identify
  collecting localities.

HOLDINGS:
  Total volume: 100 l.f.
  Inclusive dates: 1870's -
  Description: Field books kept by collectors, correspondence relating to transactions involving the University Herbarium
  and its collections, and photographs related to persons and events connected
  with the Herbarium's history.

CA86-920
University of California, Berkeley
Water Resources Center
Archives
410 O'Brien Hall
Berkeley CA 94720

(415) 642-2666

OPEN: M-F 8-5; closed weekends and
  academic holidays
COPYING FACILITIES: yes
MATERIALS SOLICITED: Materials relating
  to water resources.

HOLDINGS:
  Total volume: 100,000 items
  Inclusive dates: 1890 -
  Description: Materials relating to water
  resources, including technical and scientific reports, proceedings from conferences
  and symposia, photographs, maps and
  other illustrative material, as well as the
  papers of persons prominent in water engineering, law, management, and related
  fields.

GUIDES: *Dictionary Catalog of the Water
  Resources Center Archives* (G. K. Hall,
  1970), and supplements.

SEE: NUCMC, 1971.

SEE: Davis; Hounshell.

SEE ALSO: the following publications of
  the Center Archives: Lois Judd, comp.,
  *Bibliography of the Reports and Pub-
  lications of James Dix Schuyler* (1961);
  Lois Judd and Clare Bullitt, comps.,
  *Water Resources Reports by Walter Le-
  roy Huber: An Annotated Listing*
  (1962); Gerald J. Giefer and Anelle
  McCarty Kloski, comps., *Water Re-
  sources Reports and Papers in the J. B.
  Lippincott Collection* (1970); Michael
  Poniatowski, comp., *Ocean and Water
  Resources Engineering Reports, College
  of Engineering, University of California,
  Berkeley* (1973).

BEVERLY HILLS

CA90-30
Academy of Motion Picture Arts &
  Sciences
Margaret Herrick Library
8949 Wilshire Blvd.
Beverly Hills CA 90211

(213) 278-4313

OPEN: M, Tu, Th, F 9-5; closed
  Wednesdays, weekends, and holidays
COPYING FACILITIES: yes
MATERIALS SOLICITED: Documents and
  photographs relating to motion pic-
  tures.

HOLDINGS:
  Total volume: 3,500 l.f.
  Inclusive dates: 1894 -
  Description: Photograph collection con-
  sists of four million motion picture stills,
  and includes the stillbooks of Metro-
  Goldwyn-Mayer, Paramount Pictures,
  RKO Pictures, and Cecil B. DeMille.
  Manuscript collection consists of personal
  papers, business records, scrapbooks and
  scripts, and includes the produced script
  files of Paramount Pictures; scrapbooks
  of Jean Hersholt, Robert Z. Leonard,
  Irene, Hedda Hopper and Louella Par-
  sons; and personal papers of Mack
  Sennett, William N. Selig, Jules White,
  Jesse L. Lasky, George Cukor, George
  Stevens, and others.

SEE: NUCMC, 1980.

SEE: Spalek; Mehr.

BISHOP

CA94-360
Inyo National Forest
873 North Main Street
Bishop CA 93514

(619) 873-5841

OPEN: M-F 8-5; closed weekends and
  holidays
ACCESS: advance arrangements required
COPYING FACILITIES: yes
MATERIALS SOLICITED: Manuscripts,
  photographs, and other documents pertaining to the prehistory and history of
  the general area, which included western Nevada and central eastern California.

HOLDINGS:
  Total volume: 20 l.f.
  Inclusive dates: 1830 -
  Description: A collection of reports,
  documents, letters, photographs, oral history tapes, and historic maps relating to
  prehistoric and historic period occupation, settlement, land use, and development of central eastern California and
  adjacent portions of western Nevada.

CA94-480
Laws Railroad Museum and
  Historical Site
Silver Canyon Road
Bishop CA

MAILING ADDRESS:
P.O. Box 363
Bishop CA 93514

(714) 873-5950

OPEN: March 1 - Nov. 15, daily 10-4;
  rest of year, Sa, Su 10-4; closed
  Thanksgiving, Christmas, and New
  Year's
ACCESS: advance arrangements advised
COPYING FACILITIES: no
MATERIALS SOLICITED: Will accept ma-
  terials pertinent to the history of the
  Owens Valley, CA.

HOLDINGS:
  Total volume: not specified
  Inclusive dates: late 19th century -
  Description: Photographs and pioneer
  family histories of the Owens Valley, CA.

BUENA PARK

CA110-600
Order of Servants of Mary
Western Province
Somerset Archives
5210 Somerset Street
Buena Park CA 90621

(714) 523-5810

OPEN: by appointment weekday
  mornings
COPYING FACILITIES: yes
MATERIALS SOLICITED: Material related
  to members and religious communities
  of the Western Province of Servites.

HOLDINGS:
  Total volume: 4 file cabinets
  Inclusive dates: 1924 -
  Description: Community records and
  personal papers of members of the Order
  of Servants of Mary who founded individual religious communities throughout the western part of the United States,
  particularly in the Denver area, Belen,
  NM, Portland, OR, and California. Also
  included are provincial files from the
  founding of the Western Province in
  1967, microfiche and original copies of
  all earlier Western Province material, and
  personnel and student records from
  seminaries of the order located in Riverside, San Francisco, and Anaheim, CA.

BURBANK

CA114-880
Walt Disney Productions
Walt Disney Archives
500 South Buena Vista Street
Burbank CA 91521

(213) 840-5424

OPEN: by appointment only
COPYING FACILITIES: yes

MATERIALS SOLICITED: Materials related to Walt Disney, Walt Disney Productions, Disneyland, and Walt Disney World.

HOLDINGS:
>*Total volume:* not specified
>*Inclusive dates:* 1920 -
>*Description:* The history of Walt Disney and the organization he founded, in business records, creative records, and examples of products. General categories are animated cartoons, motion pictures, television, theme amusement parks, and other forms of family entertainment.

SEE: Novotny; Mehr.

CAMARILLO

CA118-720
St. John's Seminary
Edward Laurence Doheny Memorial Library
The Estelle Doheny Collection
5012 East Seminary Road
Camarillo CA 93010

(805) 482-0637, 4115

OPEN: M, W, F 9-1; closed other days
ACCESS: appointment required
MATERIALS SOLICITED: Will accept manuscripts related to present holdings.

HOLDINGS:
>*Total volume:* 2,500 items
>*Inclusive dates:* 9th century - 20th century
>*Description:* Manuscripts and autograph material, including autographs of signers of the Constitution and the Declaration of Independence, authors, politicians, and royalty.

SEE: Hamer; NUCMC, 1959-62, 70.

SEE: Beers - Southwest; Schatz; Bean and Vane; Robbins; Hinding.

CARMEL

CA122-320
Harrison Memorial Public Library
Ocean and Lincoln Avenues
Carmel CA

MAILING ADDRESS:
P.O. Box 800
Carmel CA 93921

(408) 624-4629

OPEN: M-Th 9-9, F, Sa 9-6; closed Sundays and holidays
COPYING FACILITIES: yes
MATERIALS SOLICITED: Local history of Carmel-By-The-Sea and its environs.

HOLDINGS:
>*Total volume:* 90 c.f.
>*Inclusive dates:* 1900 -
>*Description:* A collection of visual materials relating to the history of Carmel-By-The-Sea, including photographs, memoirs and scrapbooks.

SEE: Robbins.

CHATSWORTH

CA132-120
Chatsworth Historical Society
Historical Collection
10385 Shadow Oak Drive
Chatsworth CA

MAILING ADDRESS:
P.O. Box 413
Chatsworth CA 91311

no telephone

OPEN: by appointment
COPYING FACILITIES: no
MATERIALS SOLICITED: Materials pertaining to Chatsworth's history, as well as to that of the San Fernando Valley and California in general.

HOLDINGS:
>*Total volume:* 260 items
>*Inclusive dates:* 1885 -
>*Description:* Slides, photographs, and some documents pertaining to Chatsworth's history, as well as that of the San Fernando Valley and California in general. Included are some photographs of farm machinery and equipment used in the Valley, and of early pioneers, and oral history tapes of early Valley residents.

CA132-160
Dataproducts Corporation
9657 Mason Avenue
Chatsworth CA

MAILING ADDRESS:
6200 Canoga Avenue, MS 2034
Woodland Hills CA 91365

(213) 888-4162, 709-1637

OPEN: M-F 8-5; closed weekends and holidays
ACCESS: by written request to Records Administrator and Historian
COPYING FACILITIES: yes
MATERIALS SOLICITED: Materials relating to the development of Dataproducts Corporation, its operating divisions, and subsidiaries, and products, and the activities of its founders in such companies as Engineering Research Associates, Univac, Telemeter Magnetics, and Ampex Computer Products. Will also accept materials relating to Dataproducts predecessor companies and subsidiaries.

HOLDINGS:
>*Total volume:* 150 l.f.
>*Inclusive dates:* 1961 -
>*Description:* Historical records of Dataproducts Corporation, including financial statements, business plans, correspondence of the founders, board of directors minutes, monthly activity reports, annual and quarterly reports, product design and development records, advertisements, and photographs. Also included are 67 recorded oral history interviews with corporate founders, managers, and long term employees, including Erwin Tomash, Dr. George Brown, Irving L. Wieselman, and other computer industry pioneers and specialists in the peripheral products field, as well as Dr. Walter F. Bauer, Werner Frank, and

Frank Wagner, early software and data processing specialists and founders of Informatics, Inc.

CHICO

CA136-40
Association for Northern California Records and Research
Chico CA

MAILING ADDRESS:
P.O. Box 3024
Chico CA 95927

(916) 895-5710

OPEN: by appointment only
COPYING FACILITIES: no

HOLDINGS:
>*Total volume:* not specified
>*Inclusive dates:* not specified
>*Description:* Primarily inactive public records of the assessor, auditor, clerk, recorder, sheriff, treasurer and tax collector of Butte County, CA.

SEE ALSO: *Public Records of Butte County, California, in the Northeastern California Collection, Learning Activities Resource Center, California State University, Chico* (Assn. for Northern California Records and Research, 1976).

CA136-90
California Department of Parks and Recreation
Bidwell Mansion State Historic Park.
525 Esplanade Avenue
Chico CA 95926

(916) 895-6144

OPEN: M-F 10-5; closed weekends and holidays
USER FEES: fifty cents
COPYING FACILITIES: no
MATERIALS SOLICITED: Materials pertaining to the Bidwell family.

HOLDINGS:
>*Total volume:* 12 l.f.
>*Inclusive dates:* 1850's - 1918
>*Description:* Correspondence of John and Annie Bidwell; Bidwell family diaries, account books, and photographs; maps; charts; and architectural drawings.

SEE: Bean and Vane.

CA136-120
California State University, Chico
Library
Special Collections Department
1st & Hazel Street
Chico CA 95929

(916) 895-5710

OPEN: M-Th 8-10, F 8-5; Summer, M-F 7-4:15; closed weekends and Christmas week
COPYING FACILITIES: yes
MATERIALS SOLICITED: Public records of cities, counties, and special government districts, business records, family records, and photographs, all pertaining to the northeastern California counties of Butte, Colusa, Glenn, Lassen,

Modoc, Plumas, Shasta, Siskiyou, Sutter, Tehama, Trinity, and Yuba. Will also accept other materials pertaining to the history of these counties.

HOLDINGS:
> *Total volume:* 750 l.f.
> *Inclusive dates:* 1850s - 1955
> *Description:* Non-official manuscript records and photographs pertaining to several northeastern California counties. Included are 20,000 photographs, maps, scrapbooks, oral histories, engineering drawings, music scores, folklore items, and genealogical sources.

SEE: Davis; Hinding.

SEE ALSO: Finding aids to individual collections are available from the institution.

CLAREMONT

CA143-80
Blaisdell Institute for Advanced Study in World Cultures and Religions
143 East 10th Street
Claremont CA 91711

(714) 621-8194

OPEN: M-F 9-3; closed weekends and holidays
COPYING FACILITIES: yes

HOLDINGS:
> *Total volume:* 3.5 l.f.
> *Inclusive dates:* 1943 -
> *Description:* Typescripts of Blaisdell Institute *Journal* articles, 1966- , on world cultures and religions, and the implications of the sciences for human beings; the 4-volume 'Story of a Life' by James A. Blaisdell; 7 reports of research on Oriental topics, by Mokusen Miyuki; and oral history transcripts relating to the history of the Blaisdell family and the Blaisdell Institute.

CA143-240
The Francis Bacon Foundation, Inc.
The Francis Bacon Library
655 North Dartmouth Avenue
Claremont CA 91711

(714) 624-6305

OPEN: M-F 9-4:30; closed weekends and holidays
ACCESS: by prior arrangement
COPYING FACILITIES: yes
MATERIALS SOLICITED: 16th and 17th century English material. Will also accept material from poets, writers, painters of the 'Arensberg Circle.'

HOLDINGS:
> *Total volume:* 18 l.f.; 25 vols.
> *Inclusive dates:* 1561 - 1961
> *Description:* The Arensberg Archives (Walter Conrad Arensberg) consists of six collections covering family correspondence, legal documents, correspondence with American literary figures, French poets and painters, and anti-Shakespeareans. Other holdings include letters of Francis Bacon and his family, Privy Council documents, heraldic documents and other manuscript material of the 17th century.

SEE: NUCMC, 1978.

SEE: Robbins.

SEE ALSO: Copies of calendars available at a fee from the institution.

CA143-280
Galleries of the Claremont Colleges
Claremont University Center
Collections (Photography)
Humanities Building
Scripps College
10th Street and Columbia Avenue
Claremont CA 91711

(714) 621-8000, Ext. 3397, 2241

OPEN: M-F 8-5; closed weekends and holidays
ACCESS: by appointment only
COPYING FACILITIES: yes
MATERIALS SOLICITED: Will accept photography of Native Americans.

HOLDINGS:
> *Total volume:* 300 items
> *Inclusive dates:* 1880 - 1930
> *Description:* Photographs relating to ethnic art collections of the Claremont University Center. Subjects covered include Indians of the Coachella Valley of southern California, especially baskets and basketmakers; the Panama-California International Exposition of 1916; and missionary photographs of Angola.

SEE: Bean and Vane.

CA143-470
Libraries of the Claremont Colleges
Honnold Library
Special Collections Department
Ninth and Dartmouth Streets
Claremont CA 91711

(714) 621-8000, Ext. 3977

OPEN: M-F 9-noon, 2-5; closed weekends and holidays
ACCESS: academic institution identification required; by prior arrangement
COPYING FACILITIES: yes
MATERIALS SOLICITED: Materials relating to southern California water resources development, as well as the Claremont Colleges.

HOLDINGS:
> *Total volume:* 500 l.f.
> *Inclusive dates:* 1450 -
> *Description:* Manuscripts, scrapbooks, maps, and photographs, mostly related to California history, particularly Southern California, Claremont town and Colleges, water resources development, agriculture, institutions, transportation, and literature. The Archives contain correspondence, official documents, photographs, oral histories and literary and other manuscripts pertaining to all aspects of the development and activities of the Claremont Colleges.
> Other holdings include papers of H. Jerry Voorhis and Jose Maria Maytorena, and collections on Oxford University, the Italian Renaissance, music, and a wide variety of English and American literary and historical figures.

SEE: Hamer; NUCMC, 1963-64, 76.

SEE: Meckler and McMullin; Hines; Bean and Vane; Robbins; Mehr.

SEE ALSO: Andrea Hinding and Rosemary Richardson, comps., *Archival and Manuscript Resources for the Study of Women's History: A Beginning* (Univ. of Minnesota Libraries, Social Welfare History Archives Center, 1972); Alan M. Meckler and Ruth McMullin, comps., *Oral History Collections* (Bowker, 1975); Joan Hoff Wilson and Lynn B. Donovan, 'Women's History: A Listing of West Coast Archival and Manuscript Sources, Part I,' *California Historical Quarterly* 55 (Spring 1976); Catherine K. Firman, ed., *The William W. Clary Oxford Collection, Supplement* (Honnold Library of the Claremont Colleges, 1965).

CA143-480
Libraries of the Claremont Colleges
Norman F. Sprague Memorial Library
Harvey Mudd College
Claremont CA 91711

(714) 621-8000 Ext. 3921

OPEN: M-F 8-5; closed weekends and holidays
ACCESS: by prior arrangement
COPYING FACILITIES: yes
MATERIALS SOLICITED: Materials in the field of aviation history, especially vintage aircraft, lighter-than-air vehicles and ballooning, and World Wars I and II. Will also accept materials dealing with the early history of mining and metallurgy.

HOLDINGS:
> *Total volume:* 3,000 items
> *Inclusive dates:* 1900 -
> *Description:* 300 letters between Herbert Hoover and booksellers in Europe and the United States, 1900-14, concerning rare books on mining and metallurgy; and the Carruthers Aviation History Collection, containing photographs, reminiscences of aviators, and letters, 1920-50.

CA143-490
Libraries of the Claremont Colleges
Pomona College
Geology Library
6th and College Avenue
Claremont CA 91711

(714) 621-8000, Ext. 2952

OPEN: M-F 8-5; closed weekends and holidays
COPYING FACILITIES: yes

HOLDINGS:
> *Total volume:* 50 items
> *Inclusive dates:* 1920's - 1940's
> *Description:* Manuscript maps (geologic) of limited areas within southern California, mostly derived from student master's or senior theses.

CA143-690

Rancho Santa Ana Botanic Garden
1500 North College Avenue
Claremont CA 91711

(714) 626-3922

OPEN: M-F 8-5; closed weekends and
holidays
COPYING FACILITIES: no
MATERIALS SOLICITED: Will accept materials pertaining to botany or horticulture, especially materials on California's native flora.

HOLDINGS:
Total volume: 2 boxes; 30 books
Inclusive dates: 1880 -
Description: Manuscripts, correspon-
dence, and field books of Philip Munz;
field books of Marcus Jones.

CA143-720

The School of Theology at Claremont
1325 North College Avenue
Claremont CA 91711

(714) 626-3521, Ext. 263

OPEN: M-F 8:30-5; closed weekends and
holidays
ACCESS: advance appointment is
advisable
COPYING FACILITIES: yes
MATERIALS SOLICITED: Materials on the
following ecclesiastical bodies in southern California and Arizona: United
Methodist church, Protestant Episcopal
church, Christian church-Disciples of
Christ. Will also accept materials relating to the history of Christianity in
southern California.

HOLDINGS:
Total volume: 200 l.f.
Inclusive dates: 1875 -
Description: Papers of church officials,
scholars associated with the church, and
official church records for the United
Methodist church, the Protestant Episco-
pal church, and the Christian church-
Disciples of Christ in southern California
and Arizona.
Also held are documentary films of
Robert Flaherty.

SEE: NUCMC, 1962.

SEE: Mehr.

COLUMBIA

CA159-120

Columbia College
Library
Sawmill Flat Road
Columbia CA

MAILING ADDRESS:
P.O. Box 1849
Columbia CA 95310

(209) 533-5100

OPEN: M-Th 8-9, F 8-4:30; closed
weekends and holidays
COPYING FACILITIES: yes
MATERIALS SOLICITED: Materials relating
to the history of the Mother Lode, local
history, and Columbia Junior College,
as well as microform copies of archives

of community groups and churches.
Will also accept materials relating to
Miwok Indian culture.

HOLDINGS:
Total volume: 1,000 items
Inclusive dates: 1850 -
Description: A collection of materials
relating to the Mother Lode region of
California, including photographs of miners and mining areas, and oral history
tapes of local residents. There are also
tapes of Miwok Indian legends,
microform copies of community group
and local church records, and engineering
drawings for the Columbia Junior College
campus.

GUIDES: Roy Tennant, comp., *Mother
Lode Bibliography* (1980).

SEE: Bean and Vane.

SEE ALSO: Guides to parts of the collection available from the institution.

CORONADO

CA168-120

Coronado Historical Association, Inc.
718 Orange Avenue
Coronado CA

MAILING ADDRESS:
P.O. Box 393
Coronado CA 92118

(619) 435-5892, 4483

OPEN: Wednesdays 10-12, or by
appointment
COPYING FACILITIES: no
MATERIALS SOLICITED: Materials pertaining to local history of Coronado
and San Diego County, CA.

HOLDINGS:
Total volume: 3,000 items
Inclusive dates: 1886 -
Description: Materials pertaining to the
history of Coronado and San Diego
County, CA, including early city and
school records, photographs of local resi-
dents and scenes, films, slides, and maps.

CRESCENT CITY

CA180-160

Del Norte County Historical Society
Main Museum
577 H Street
Crescent City CA 95531

(707) 464-3922

OPEN: June-Sept., M-F noon-5; by
appointment otherwise
COPYING FACILITIES: no
MATERIALS SOLICITED: Business records,
military diaries, weather bureau reports
and other materials relating to Del
Norte County, CA.

HOLDINGS:
Total volume: 140 vols.
Inclusive dates: 1855 - 1970
Description: Early Del Norte County
lumber company ledgers, general mer-
chandise business ledgers, printing company records, Crescent City weather bureau reports, 1917-45, post office records,

and Del Norte County school, census,
club, burial, and church records.

SEE: Bean and Vane.

DAVIS

CA206-790

University of California, Davis
Library
Department of Special Collections
Davis CA 95616

(916) 752-1621

OPEN: Su-F 8-5; closed Saturdays and
holidays
COPYING FACILITIES: yes
MATERIALS SOLICITED: Agricultural technology; American literature; apiculture;
University of California at Davis archives; California history; English literature and history; the French Revolution; the performing arts; and viticulture and enology.

HOLDINGS:
Total volume: 493,000 items
Inclusive dates: 17th century -
Description: Materials relating to agricultural machinery, pomology, horticulture, viticulture, enology, apiculture, and
meteorology; American, English, and German literature; the French Revolution;
and California history. There are also oral
history interviews with American Indians,
as well as the University archives.

GUIDES: A guide is available from the
Library.

SEE: NUCMC, 1970.

SEE: Spalek; Bean and Vane; Hinding;
Robbins; Mehr.

SEE ALSO: Don Kunitz, 'The Higgins Library: A Source for the Study of Agricultural History,' *Agricultural History*
49 (Jan. 1975); *Map Collections in the
United States and Canada, A Directory*
(Special Libraries Assn., 1970); Alan
M. Meckler and Ruth McMullin,
comps., *Oral History Collections*
(Bowker, 1975); Ann Novotny, ed., *Picture Sources 3* (Special Libraries Assn.,
1975); Richard C. Davis, *North American Forest History: A Guide to Archives
and Manuscripts in the United States
and Canada* (Clio Books, 1977).

CA206-940

Yolo County Library
Davis Branch
315 East 14th Street
Davis CA 95616

(916) 756-2332

OPEN: M 12-9, Tu, W 9-9, Th-F 9-6, Sa
9-5:30; closed Sundays and holidays
COPYING FACILITIES: yes
MATERIALS SOLICITED: Will accept photographic materials dealing with the
history of Davis.

HOLDINGS:
Total volume: 3 c.f.
Inclusive dates: 1850 - 1968
Description: Manuscript and research
notes for Jean Leach Larkey's *Davisville,*
published in 1968. The collection also

contains many photographs of Davis and its residents.

DEATH VALLEY

CA210-160
Death Valley National Monument
Death Valley CA 92328

(619) 786-2331, Ext. 27

OPEN: M-F 8-5; closed weekends and holidays
COPYING FACILITIES: yes
MATERIALS SOLICITED: Material regarding early pioneers and travelers in the Death Valley region, as well as other material relating specifically to Death Valley's natural and human history.

HOLDINGS:
> Total volume: 15 l.f.
> Inclusive dates: 1870 -
> Description: A collection of diaries, letters, manuscripts, newspaper clippings, and other matter about pioneers, early travelers, and employees in the Death Valley region, as well as a historic and current photograph file of Death Valley.

DOMINGUEZ HILLS

CA222-120
California State University
Educational Resources Center
1000 East Victoria Street
Dominguez Hills CA 90247

no telephone

SEE: NUCMC, 1975.

Questionnaire not returned.

DOWNEY

CA226-170
Downey Historical Society
12540 Rives Avenue
Downey CA

MAILING ADDRESS:
P.O. Box 554
Downey CA 90241

(213) 927-5255, 869-7367

OPEN: Tu, W 9-2 and by appointment
COPYING FACILITIES: yes
MATERIALS SOLICITED: Manuscript histories of local organizations and institutions; deeds and maps; account books and other financial records of local businesses, churches, schools, and government agencies; genealogical data on pioneers of the area; photographs; and any source material on John G. Downey. Will also accept personal correspondence, bills of sale, diaries, and architectural drawings of local historical significance.

HOLDINGS:
> Total volume: 14 l.f.
> Inclusive dates: 1884 -
> Description: Materials relating to the history of Downey and the Los Nietos Valley, including account books of early

school districts, insurance company registers, photographs, manuscript histories of local organizations, reminiscences of pioneers, genealogical materials, stock certificate books of the Los Nietos and Ranchito Walnut Growers Association, and miscellaneous deeds, bills of sale, and personal correspondence.

SEE: Hinding.

ENCINO

CA246-480
Los Encinos State Historic Park
Archives and
Encino Historical Society
Library
16756 Moorpark Street
Encino CA 91436

(818) 784-4849

OPEN: Sa-Tu 8-5, W-F 10-5; closed holidays
COPYING FACILITIES: no
MATERIALS SOLICITED: Historical material directly related to Los Encinos State Historic Park. Will also accept historical material related to Encino in general, as well as the San Fernando Valley, Los Angeles, and the State of California.

HOLDINGS:
> Total volume: 20 l.f.
> Inclusive dates: 1700's - 1900's
> Description: Manuscripts, photographs, deeds, and genealogical material directly related to Encino, the San Fernando Valley, Los Angeles, and California.

ESCONDIDO

CA248-200
Escondido Historical Society
321 N. Broadway
Escondido CA

MAILING ADDRESS:
P.O. Box 263
Escondido CA 92025

(714) 743-8207

OPEN: Tu-Su 1-4; closed Mondays and holidays
COPYING FACILITIES: yes
MATERIALS SOLICITED: Materials relating to the early history of Escondido, especially the Battle of San Pasqual.

HOLDINGS:
> Total volume: not specified
> Inclusive dates: 1840 -
> Description: Materials documenting the history of Escondido, including oral history recordings, a diary, scrapbooks, family histories, and a photograph collection, 1888 -

EUREKA

CA250-120
Clarke Memorial Museum
240 E Street
Eureka CA 95501

(707) 443-1947

OPEN: Tu-Sa 9-5; closed Sundays, Mondays, holidays, and last Saturday in March to second Tuesday in May
COPYING FACILITIES: no
MATERIALS SOLICITED: Photographs of Humboldt County, CA, and manuscripts from early pioneers of the county.

HOLDINGS:
> Total volume: not specified
> Inclusive dates: 1851 - 1910
> Description: Humboldt County manuscripts and business journals from the late 1800's, and photographs depicting local maritime history, Indian tribes, homesteads, railroads, streetcars, logging, storefronts, and portraits.

FALL RIVER MILLS

CA258-240
Fort Crook Historical Society
Fort Crook Museum
Fort Crook Avenue
Fall River Mills CA

MAILING ADDRESS:
P.O. Box 397
Fall River Mills CA 96028

(916) 336-5110

OPEN: May-Nov. 1, daily 1-5; closed rest of year
COPYING FACILITIES: yes
MATERIALS SOLICITED: Historical materials pertaining to the Fort Crook area and Intermountain Valley, including business records, genealogical data, unpublished manuscripts, music scores and records of local institutions and organizations.

HOLDINGS:
> Total volume: not specified
> Inclusive dates: 1863 -
> Description: Manuscripts, records, visual documents, scrapbooks, and genealogical data pertaining to towns, businesses, pioneers, and Indians of the Intermountain Valley.

FREMONT

CA270-520
Mission San Jose
Archives
43148 Mission Blvd.
Fremont CA

MAILING ADDRESS:
P.O. Box 3276, Mission San Jose Station
Fremont CA 94539

(415) 656-2364

OPEN: by appointment only

HOLDINGS:
Total volume: 35 vols.
Inclusive dates: 1837 -
Description: Register of deaths of Mission San Jose, 1837-59, and parish records of baptisms, marriages, confirmations, first communions, and deaths, 1859 - .

Original death registers, 1797 - 1837, and original baptism and marriage records, 1797 - 1859, have been transferred to the Roman Catholic Archdiocese of San Francisco, in San Francisco, CA. Mission San Jose holds copies of these materials.

FRESNO

CA274-40
Academy of California Church History and Monterey-Fresno Diocesan Chancery
Fresno CA

MAILING ADDRESS:
P.O. Box 1668
Fresno CA 93717

no telephone

SEE: Hamer; NUCMC, 1966.

Questionnaire not returned.

CA274-120
California State University, Fresno
Henry Madden Library
Department of Special Collections
Fresno CA 93740

(209) 294-2595

OPEN: M-F 10-5; closed weekends
COPYING FACILITIES: yes
MATERIALS SOLICITED: Materials pertaining to the San Joaquin Valley; viticulture and enology; international fairs and expositions, 1851-1940; the Credit Foncier of Sinaloa Company; William Saroyan; the Sierra Nevada mountains; and Yosemite National Park. Will also accept significant materials complete enough for master's thesis research.

HOLDINGS:
Total volume: 77 l.f.; 1,232 photographs
Inclusive dates: 1850 -
Description: The University archives; manuscript collections and photographs relating to the Credit Foncier of Sinaloa Company and its colony at Topolobampo, Mexico; promotional materials relating to an attempt to exploit a mineral area of Peru, 1881; selected papers of Luis Murillo regarding economic promotion of the west coast of Mexico, and Gerardo Murillo's (Dr. Atl) articles against Venustiano Carranza; records of two local businesses, 1899-1971; correspondence and a diary relating to the cattle industry in the San Joaquin Valley; an 1840 Seminole War diary and two Civil War diaries; and a collection of photographs, 1910-15, of the lumber industry in Madera County, CA.

GUIDES: A guide is available from the institution.

SEE: Hamer (as Fresno State College); NUCMC, 1965-66, 74.

SEE ALSO: *Map Collections in the United States and Canada, A Directory* (Special Libraries Assn., 1970); Richard C. Davis, *North American Forest History: A Guide to Archives and Manuscripts in the United States and Canada* (Clio Books, 1977).

CA274-130
Center for Mennonite Brethren Studies
Hiebert Library
1717 S. Chestnut
Fresno CA

MAILING ADDRESS:
4824 E. Butler
Fresno CA 93727-5097

(209) 251-7194, Ext. 1055

OPEN: Tu-F 8-5, or by appointment; closed other days and holidays.
COPYING FACILITIES: yes
MATERIALS SOLICITED: Materials dealing with the origins, history, and current activities of the Mennonite Brethren denomination. Will also accept Anabaptist materials, materials of other Mennonite denominations, and materials related to the Mennonite heritage.

HOLDINGS:
Total volume: 155 l.f.
Inclusive dates: 1860 -
Description: Records of the Mennonite Brethren denomination in the United States, Canada and South America, including its mission work around the world. There are also personal papers of missionaries and leaders of the denomination, and items dealing with the migration of early settlers in the United States.

SEE ALSO: A. J. Klassen, ed., *The Seminary Story, Twenty Years of Education and Ministry, 1955-1975* (Pacific Printing Press, 1975).

CA274-240
Fresno County Free Library
Local History Collection
2420 Mariposa Street
Fresno CA 93721

(209) 488-3191

OPEN: M, Tu 9-9, W, F 9-6, Th noon-9, Sa 1-5; closed Sundays and holidays
ACCESS: adults only
COPYING FACILITIES: yes
MATERIALS SOLICITED: Materials related to the city of Fresno, Fresno County and the central San Joaquin Valley; production items for plays of William Saroyan; pioneer reminiscences.

HOLDINGS:
Total volume: 12,000 items
Inclusive dates: 1885 -
Description: A collection of materials reflecting the history of the city of Fresno, Fresno County and the central San Joaquin Valley. Included are ordinances and resolutions of the city of Fresno.

SEE: NUCMC, 1977.

SEE: Meckler and McMullin.

CA274-250
Fresno County Historical Society
7160 West Kearney Blvd.
Fresno CA 93706

no telephone

OPEN: by appointment only
COPYING FACILITIES: no
MATERIALS SOLICITED: Materials related to Fresno County.

HOLDINGS:
Total volume: 500 l.f.
Inclusive dates: 1850's -
Description: The collection covers primarily Fresno County. Municipal and county records are irregular, but cover 1850-1970 and include road and sewer records, criminal court records, and material relating to irrigation projects. There are over 10,000 photographs of people of the area, a collection of old commercial discs concerning Chinatown, and 20 major and 75 minor manuscript collections dealing with Fresno County, including diaries, personal papers, and business papers.

SEE: Davis; Hinding.

CA274-720
Sierra National Forest
Information Office
1130 O Street
Fresno CA 93721

(209) 487-5143

OPEN: by appointment only; closed weekends and holidays
COPYING FACILITIES: yes
MATERIALS SOLICITED: Materials relating to the history and development of the Sierra Forest Reserve or Sierra National Forest.

HOLDINGS:
Total volume: 18 l.f.
Inclusive dates: 1900 -
Description: Manuscripts, diaries, maps and photographs dealing with the history of the Sierra Forest Reserve (Sierra National Forest).

FULLERTON

CA278-120
California State University, Fullerton
Geography Department
Map Library
Fullerton CA 92634

(714) 773-3161

OPEN: M-F 9-3; closed weekends and holidays; July - Aug., by appointment only
COPYING FACILITIES: no

HOLDINGS:
Total volume: 1 file cabinet
Inclusive dates: 1952 - 1970
Description: Aerial photographs of Orange County, CA, for 1952-53 and 1970.

CA278-130
California State University, Fullerton
Library
University Archives and Special
   Collections
800 North State College Blvd.
Fullerton CA

MAILING ADDRESS:
P.O. Box 4150
Fullerton CA 92634

(714) 773-3444, 2633

OPEN: M, Tu 1-7, W-F 9-noon; closed
   weekends and holidays
COPYING FACILITIES: yes
MATERIALS SOLICITED: Science fiction
   manuscripts, local history materials
   stressing citrus and water, and other
   materials relating to the collections.

HOLDINGS:
   Total volume: 800 l.f.
   Inclusive dates: 1920 -
   Description: The University archives;
   manuscripts of science fiction authors; local history materials, including citrus
   business records, oral history tapes, and
   manuscripts; Walkup Theatre Collection
   materials; Donal Michalsky music manuscripts; kinescopes and outtakes of the
   television series *Adventure Tomorrow*;
   materials concerning angling; records of
   the California Speech and Hearing Association; collections of the Orange County
   Historical Society, including Haven Seed
   Company business records; Fay
   MacFadden botany correspondence, emphasizing bryophytes; World War II propaganda films; regional records of the
   United States Volleyball Association; and
   oral history recordings of the University's
   history department.

SEE: NUCMC, 1975.

SEE: Meckler and McMullin; Mehr.

CA278-240
Fullerton College
William T. Boyce Library
321 East Chapman Avenue
Fullerton CA 92634

(714) 871-8000, Ext. 244

OPEN: M-Th 7:30-10, F 7:30-4, Sa
   8:30-12:30; closed Sundays, holidays,
   Aug., and during semester breaks
COPYING FACILITIES: yes
MATERIALS SOLICITED: Material pertaining to the history of the College and
   the Fullerton community.

HOLDINGS:
   Total volume: 140 l.f.
   Inclusive dates: 1900 -
   Description: Archives of Fullerton Col-
   lege, and papers, photographs, and oral
   history tapes and transcripts dealing with
   the history of the College and the
   Fullerton area.

GARDEN GROVE

CA282-280
Garden Grove Historical Society
Stanley House Museum
12174 Euclid Avenue
Garden Grove CA 92640

(714) 530-8871

OPEN: Su 1-4:30, or by prior
   arrangement; closed holidays
COPYING FACILITIES: no
MATERIALS SOLICITED: Materials relating
   to Garden Grove and the surrounding
   area, including Orange County. Will also
   accept materials related to southern California, California, the western United
   States, or the United States as a whole.

HOLDINGS:
   Total volume: 20 l.f.
   Inclusive dates: 1876 -
   Description: Ledgers of an early settler
   in Garden Grove, 1876-1900; photographs of Garden Grove and the surrounding area; a few early maps and related documents; and 12 oral history
   tapes of long-time residents of the area.

CA282-480
W. Everett Miller Library of Vehicles
12172 Sheridan Lane
Garden Grove CA 92640

no telephone

OPEN: by appointment only
ACCESS: records closed to general public;
   research will be performed at $20 per
   hour
COPYING FACILITIES: yes
MATERIALS SOLICITED: Any material relating to design, construction, selling,
   and servicing of vehicles for use on the
   common roads and biographical material of persons involved in these processes. Will also accept material relating to phrenology, physiognomy, and
   certain religious studies.

HOLDINGS:
   Total volume: 3 file drawers
   Inclusive dates: 1890's -
   Description: Letters and photographs
   about America's first gasoline automobile
   from its builder, J. Frank Duryea. Notes
   on the carriage industry by George J.
   Mercer. Letters, photographs, engineering
   drawings, etc., of carriages, automobiles,
   trucks and other vehicles.

GLEN ELLEN

CA288-400
Jack London State Historic Park
2400 London Ranch Road
Glen Ellen CA 95442

(707) 938-5216

OPEN: daily 10-5; closed Thanksgiving,
   Christmas, and New Year's
USER FEES: $2 per vehicle
ACCESS: advance arrangements required
COPYING FACILITIES: no
MATERIALS SOLICITED: Will accept ma-
   terials relating to Jack London.

HOLDINGS:
   Total volume: 2 file cabinets
   Inclusive dates: 1898 - 1930
   Description: Papers of Jack London,
   including notebooks, manuscripts, and
   blueprints of his home.

SEE: Robbins.

GLENDALE

CA290-240
Forest Lawn Memorial Parks
Forest Lawn Museum
1712 South Glendale Avenue
Glendale CA 91205

(213) 254-3131

OPEN: daily 10-6
ACCESS: advance notification requested
COPYING FACILITIES: no

HOLDINGS:
   Total volume: 60 items
   Inclusive dates: 19th century -
   Description: Copies of letters and other
   manuscripts by Americans and Europeans prominent in literature, politics, the
   military, and other fields.

SEE: Robbins.

CA290-280
Glendale Public Libraries
Special Collections
222 East Harvard Street
Glendale CA 91205

(213) 956-2020

OPEN: M-F 10-5; closed weekends and
   holidays
COPYING FACILITIES: yes
MATERIALS SOLICITED: Materials related
   to local history and to cats and cat
   genealogy. Will also accept materials
   related to California history.

HOLDINGS:
   Total volume: 3,500 items
   Inclusive dates: 1900 -
   Description: A collection of stud books
   for domestic cats dating from 1904 and
   materials relating to anatomy and pathology of cats. There are also local history
   materials, including oral history tapes.

CA290-720
Sons of the Revolution Library
600 South Central Avenue
Glendale CA 91204

(213) 240-1775, 246-1775

OPEN: Th-Sa 10-4, W noon-8, Tu by
   appointment; closed Sundays,
   Mondays, holidays, and October
USER FEES: $1 donation per visit or $10
   donation per year
COPYING FACILITIES: yes
MATERIALS SOLICITED: Manuscripts per-
   taining to the period of the American
   Revolution, as well as family geneal-
   ogies.

HOLDINGS:
Total volume: 5,000 vols.
Inclusive dates: late 19th century -
Description: Family genealogies for the period since 1620, primarily for the United States.

HAYWARD

CA314-120

California State University, Hayward
Library
Special Collections
Hayward CA 94542

(415) 881-3676

OPEN: M-Th 1-4; closed other days and holidays
COPYING FACILITIES: yes
MATERIALS SOLICITED: Local history manuscripts.

HOLDINGS:
Total volume: 3,000 leaves
Inclusive dates: 1830 - 1920
Description: Materials relating to the Jensen family, chiefly in German. Included are letters and journals of the families of Jens Christian Jensen and Erich Rickert Jensen, natives of Fohr, North Frisian Islands, Germany, who settled in the Hayward - Castro Valley area in the 1860's.

SEE: Hinding.

CA314-320

Hayward Area Historical Society
22701 Main Street
Hayward CA

MAILING ADDRESS:
Box 555
Hayward CA 94543

(415) 581-0223

OPEN: M-F 12-4; closed weekends and holidays
COPYING FACILITIES: yes
MATERIALS SOLICITED: Materials relating to Hayward and the surrounding area.

HOLDINGS:
Total volume: 80 vols.
Inclusive dates: 1876 -
Description: Materials pertaining to the history and life of the Hayward area, including Eden Township, Alameda County, and California in general, their organizations, population, and government. Scrapbooks and local government records, including Hayward's tax records, 1876-1950, form a large part of the collection.

SEE: Hinding.

HOLLYWOOD

CA318-320

Homosexual Information Center
Library
6758 Hollywood Blvd., 208
Hollywood CA 90028

(213) 464-8431

OPEN: M-F noon-5, Sa by appointment; closed Sundays
COPYING FACILITIES: yes
MATERIALS SOLICITED: Homosexual movement records, correspondence and papers of movement leaders, audio-visual materials, and unpublished manuscripts. Will also accept microfilm versions of otherwise unavailable materials.

HOLDINGS:
Total volume: not specified
Inclusive dates: 1948 -
Description: A collection of homosexual movement materials from the United States and some European countries, consisting of organization records such as minutes, financial accounts, correspondence and papers of movement and organization leaders, audio broadcasts, tapes of discussions and business meetings of early groups, scholarly research papers, school term papers, and unpublished manuscripts.

CA318-640

Pacific Pioneer Broadcasters
1500 North Vine
Hollywood CA

MAILING ADDRESS:
P.O. Box 4866
North Hollywood CA 91607

(213) 462-9606/461-2121

OPEN: by appointment only
COPYING FACILITIES: no
MATERIALS SOLICITED: Materials pertaining to the history of radio and television broadcasting, including photographs, recordings, scripts, and publications.

HOLDINGS:
Total volume: 300 l.f.; 270 vols.; 3,000 items
Inclusive dates: early 1920's - 1950's
Description: Radio scripts, tape recordings of original radio broadcasts, music scores from radio programs, television scripts, and oral history recordings and photographs of radio personalities.

SEE: Mehr.

CA318-700

Science Fiction Museum
2495 Glendower Avenue
Hollywood CA 90027

(213) MOON FAN (666-6326)

OPEN: M-Sa 10-5; closed Sundays, Thanksgiving, Christmas, and New Year's
USER FEES: $50 per hour for unassisted research; $150 per hour for curator-assisted research
ACCESS: advance arrangements required

COPYING FACILITIES: yes
MATERIALS SOLICITED: Still photographs, clippings, scripts, and other materials relating to science fiction and fantasy films, domestic and foreign, before 1930. Will also accept other materials pertaining to the fantasy genre.

HOLDINGS:
Total volume: 300,000 items
Inclusive dates: 1800's -
Description: Photographs, newspaper and magazine clippings, tape recordings, scripts, and other materials concerning science fiction and fantasy films, television and radio programs, and plays.

SEE: Mehr.

JOLON

CA352-520

Mission San Antonio
Jolon CA

MAILING ADDRESS:
P.O. Box 803
Jolon CA 93928

(408) 385-4478

OPEN: M-Sa 9-4:30, Su 11-5
COPYING FACILITIES: no
MATERIALS SOLICITED: Maps, drawings and records related to Indian history and early California, including Spanish and Mexican land grants. Will also accept materials relating to mission history, agriculture and architecture.

HOLDINGS:
Total volume: 5 file drawers
Inclusive dates: 1769 -
Description: Photographs, documents and copies of documents pertaining directly or indirectly to the missions of California and particularly to the Mission San Antonio.

SEE: Beers - Southwest

KING CITY

CA360-720

San Antonio Valley Historical Association
Public Library
King City CA

MAILING ADDRESS:
P.O. Box 184
Lockwood CA 93932

(408) 385-3587

OPEN: M, W-F 2-9, Tu 10-4; closed weekends and holidays
COPYING FACILITIES: yes
MATERIALS SOLICITED: Materials pertaining to the history of southern Monterey County.

HOLDINGS:
Total volume: 19 oral histories; 9 items
Inclusive dates: 1860 -
Description: Oral history tapes relating to local history and local residents, 8 family histories, and a paper on the history of the Soil Conservation Service in southern Monterey County.

LA JOLLA

CA368-120

Copley Press, Inc.
James S. Copley Library
1134 Kline Street
La Jolla CA

MAILING ADDRESS:
P.O. Box 1530
La Jolla CA 92038

(619) 454-0411

OPEN: by appointment only; closed
holidays
ACCESS: by prior arrangement
COPYING FACILITIES: yes
MATERIALS SOLICITED: Materials relating
to the American Revolution, Mark
Twain, John C. Fremont, Robinson
Jeffers, and western United States his-
tory, particularly California and San
Diego items. Will also accept Ameri-
cana in general.

HOLDINGS:
Total volume: 190 items
Inclusive dates: 1770 -
Description: 150 letters on the American Revolution, and 30 letters of a historical nature from other periods of
American history. There are also Daniel
Chamier's accounts, 1774-77, giving the
cost of the American Revolution to England, and John Lansing's narrative of the
proceedings of the Convention of 1787.

CA368-800

University of California, San Diego
Library
La Jolla CA

MAILING ADDRESS:
Box 109
La Jolla CA 92037

(619) 452-3339

SEE: NUCMC, 1966, 72.

Questionnaire not returned.

CA368-820

University of California, San Diego
Scripps Institution of Oceanography
Historical Archives Section
8602 La Jolla Shores Drive
La Jolla CA

MAILING ADDRESS:
Code C-075-C
University of California, San Diego
La Jolla CA 92093

(619) 452-3274

OPEN: M-F 9-3 or by appointment;
closed weekends and holidays
COPYING FACILITIES: yes
MATERIALS SOLICITED: Manuscript materials relating to the history of American oceanography, specifically at the
Scripps Institution; biographical material on former and present staff members; photographs; and tape recordings.
Will also accept some general material
on the history of oceanography and
early San Diego people who founded
the institution.

HOLDINGS:
Total volume: 800 l.f.
Inclusive dates: 1880 -
Description: A correspondence and
manuscript collection on the establishment and development of the Scripps Institution of Oceanography. Included are
correspondence of the directors and of
some staff members, in part material formerly classified for military security. Also
included are photographs, daily ship logs,
annual or biennial reports of the Institution, a few diaries and unpublished autobiographical accounts, newspaper and
magazine clippings, original manuscripts
of textbooks, films, and tape recordings.
The largest single collection is the personal and professional files of Carl L.
Hubbs. Other materials include papers of
William Emerson Ritter, Thomas
Wayland Vaughan, and correspondence
of the Scripps family.

SEE ALSO: Guides to the Ritter, Scripps
family, and Vaughan materials are
available through the Archives Section.

LA PUENTE

CA376-480

La Puente Valley Historical Society,
Inc.
Heritage Room
La Puente City Hall
15900 East Main
La Puente CA

MAILING ADDRESS:
P.O. Box 522
La Puente CA 91744

(818) 336-7644, 2382, 3384

OPEN: Su and W 1-4, Tu 2-4; closed
other days and holidays
COPYING FACILITIES: no
MATERIALS SOLICITED: Historical materials relating to the Rowland Workman
land grant area.

HOLDINGS:
Total volume: 2 file cabinets
Inclusive dates: 1841 -
Description: Materials related to the
Rowland Workman land grant area.

LAFAYETTE

CA382-480

Lafayette Historical Society
Lafayette Library
Lafayette CA

MAILING ADDRESS:
P.O. Box 133
Lafayette CA 94549

no telephone

OPEN: M 12-9, Tu 10-6, W 12-9, Th
10-9, F 10-6, Sa 10-6; closed Sundays
and holidays
COPYING FACILITIES: yes
MATERIALS SOLICITED: Local history of
Lafayette and the surrounding area, including materials pertaining to early
pioneers, schools, associations, and city
government.

HOLDINGS:
Total volume: 16 l.f.
Inclusive dates: 1846 -
Description: Over 900 photographs of
early pioneers, oral history tapes and
transcripts, maps and city records, diaries, and letters.

LAGUNA NIGUEL

CA386-560

National Archives and Records
Administration
Federal Archives and Records Center
Archives Branch
24000 Avila Road
Laguna Niguel CA 92677

(714) 831-4220

OPEN: M-F 8-4:30; closed weekends and
holidays
ACCESS: Records are open, subject to
Federal agency restrictions and
restrictions based upon current
legislation relevant to confidentiality
and security classification. See General
Information Leaflet No. 2, 'Regulations
for the Public Use of Records in the
National Archives.'
COPYING FACILITIES: yes
MATERIALS SOLICITED: The Federal Ar-
chives and Records Center is responsi-
ble for non-current records of agencies
of the Federal government in Arizona,
Clark County, NV, and the southern
California counties of Imperial, Inyo,
Kern, Los Angeles, Orange, Riverside,
San Bernardino, San Diego, San Luis
Obispo, Santa Barbara, and Ventura.
Will also accept other materials subject
to the appropriate guidelines of the Na-
tional Archives and Records Service.

HOLDINGS:
Total volume: 8,858 c.f.
Inclusive dates: 1851 - 1965
Description: Federal records, including
records of Government agencies within
the geographic area of interest of this
Federal Archives and Records Center.
More significant materials include the
records of the Territorial and District
Courts, Bureau of Customs, Bureau of
Land Management, and Bureau of Indian
Affairs.
Also, records of the U.S. Army Corps
of Engineers, National Aeronautics and
Space Administration, and the United
States Coast Guard.

SEE: Schatz; Davis; Allard, Crawley, and
Edmison; Bean and Vane; Hinding;
Beers - Southwest.

SEE ALSO: Walter Schatz, ed., Directory of
Afro-American Resources (Bowker,
1970); Norman E. Tutorow, 'Library
Resources: Potpourri of Graphic Ma-
terials in the Los Angeles Federal
Records Center,' California Historical
Quarterly 52 (Winter 1973); Joan Hoff
Wilson and Lynn B. Donovan,
'Women's History: A Listing of West
Coast Archival and Manuscript
Sources, Part I,' California Historical
Quarterly 55 (Spring 1976). Prelimi-
nary inventories and other descriptive
pamphlets are available for some of the
record groups.

LAKEPORT

CA390-480
Lake County Historical Society
Lake County Museum
175 3rd Street
Lakeport CA

MAILING ADDRESS:
P.O. Box 1011
Lakeport CA 95453

(707) 279-4466

OPEN: M-F 1-4, Sa 11-4; closed Sundays
and holidays
ACCESS: special arrangements required
to view photographs
COPYING FACILITIES: no
MATERIALS SOLICITED: Lake County history, written and oral, including genealogical data on County residents.

HOLDINGS:
Total volume: 2,200 photographs;
8,200 pages
Inclusive dates: 1860's -
Description: Materials reflecting Lake
County history, including photographs,
recollections of Pomo Indians and materials on their culture, recollections of
early white settlers, genealogical data, and
a few oral history recordings.

SEE: Bean and Vane.

LODI

CA402-720
San Joaquin County Historical
Museum
San Joaquin County Archives
11793 North Micke Grove Road
Lodi CA

MAILING ADDRESS:
P.O. Box 21
Lodi CA 95241

(209) 368-9154, 463-4119

OPEN: M-F 8-5; closed weekends and
holidays
ACCESS: by prior arrangement only
COPYING FACILITIES: yes
MATERIALS SOLICITED: Manuscript materials relating to San Joaquin County
and the adjacent area, and photographs
and other visual documents relating to
County agriculture, businesses, homes,
and communities.

HOLDINGS:
Total volume: 3,000 items
Inclusive dates: 1850 -
Description: A collection covering the
growth and development of San Joaquin
County. Included are reports, maps, and
papers related to the reclamation and
production of the Sacramento - San
Joaquin River delta.

SEE: Bean and Vane.

LOMA LINDA

CA406-480
Loma Linda University
Library
Loma Linda CA 92354

(714) 796-7311

OPEN: M-Th 9-9, F 9-2; closed weekends
and holidays
ACCESS: prior application and approval
COPYING FACILITIES: yes
MATERIALS SOLICITED: Materials relating
to Adventist history and to Loma Linda University. Will also accept rare or
19th century materials.

HOLDINGS:
Total volume: 350 l.f.
Inclusive dates: 1814 -
Description: Manuscript collection of
Adventist and Loma Linda University
history dating from 1814 and pertaining
to the activities of the University and of
the Seventh-day Adventist church, mainly
in the United States.

SEE: Hamer; NUCMC, 1959-61 (as College of Medical Evangelists).

LOMPOC

CA410-120
La Purisima Mission State Historical
Park
Lompoc CA

MAILING ADDRESS:
R.F.D. Box 102
Lompoc CA 93436

(805) 733-3713

OPEN: by appointment
COPYING FACILITIES: no
MATERIALS SOLICITED: Documentation
of restoration of southern California
missions, specifically material pertaining to the 1933-41 NPS/CCC restoration of La Purisima Mission. Will also
accept material relating to the history
of La Purisima Mission.

HOLDINGS:
Total volume: 10 c.f.
Inclusive dates: 1933 -
Description: Documentation covering
restoration and preservation of La
Purisima Mission from 1933. Included
are correspondence, architectural
drawings, manuscripts and photographs.
In addition there is archaeological material and documentation dealing with the
early history of La Purisima Mission,
1813-1933.

SEE: Bean and Vane; Hinding.

LONG BEACH

CA414-150
California State University, Long
Beach
Library
Special Collections
1250 Bellflower Blvd.
Long Beach CA 90840

(213) 498-4087

OPEN: M-F 8-5, by appointment only;
closed weekends
COPYING FACILITIES: yes
MATERIALS SOLICITED: Materials that
document the history of California
State University, Long Beach, and the
Long Beach area. Oral histories concerning social and cultural developments in southern California,
1920-present, as seen from the vantage
point of the Japanese-American and
Mexican-American experience, the social history of women, and the contribution of the German emigre community.

HOLDINGS:
Total volume: 900 l.f.
Inclusive dates: 1920 -
Description: Archives of the University, including correspondence, photographs, microforms and oral histories. Political papers of Congressmen Richard
Hanna and Mark Hannaford, and State
Assemblyman Vincent Thomas. Musical
tapes and scores of Wesley Kuhnle relating to research in historic tuning of early
keyboard instruments. Oral histories concerning University and community history, cultural development and the minority experience in southern California.
Non-current files of the State Coastal
Commission, Long Beach office.

SEE: Hinding; Mehr.

CA414-320
Historical Society of Long Beach
116, Long Beach Senior Center
1150 East 4th Street
Long Beach CA 90802

MAILING ADDRESS:
P.O. Box 1869
Long Beach CA 90801

(213) 435-7511

OPEN: W, Th 10-3, F, Sa by
appointment; closed other days
COPYING FACILITIES: no
MATERIALS SOLICITED: Material pertinent to the area.

HOLDINGS:
Total volume: 5,000 photographs; 20
oral histories
Inclusive dates: 1880's -
Description: The collection consists of
about 5,000 photographs, including some
20,000 negatives. There are also 20 reels
of oral history tapes and scrapbook and
pamphlet files.

SEE: Mehr.

SEE ALSO: A computerized survey of historical resources in southern California
is under way at Placentia Public Library.

CA414-470
Long Beach Public Library
California Petroleum Industry
  Collection
101 Pacific Avenue
Long Beach CA 90802-4482

(213) 437-2949

OPEN: Su 1-5, M-Th 10-9, F, Sa 10-5:30;
  closed holidays
ACCESS: by prior arrangement
COPYING FACILITIES: yes
MATERIALS SOLICITED: Materials relating
  to the history of the California petroleum industry, 1859-1959.

HOLDINGS:
    Total volume: 1,000 items
    Inclusive dates: 1859 - 1959
    Description: Materials, including pho-
  tographs and diagrams, relating to the
  history of the California petroleum industry.

CA414-480
Long Beach Public Library
Long Beach Collection
101 Pacific Avenue
Long Beach CA 90802-4482

(213) 437-2949

OPEN: Su 1:30-5, M 10-8, Tu-Sa 10-5:30
COPYING FACILITIES: yes
MATERIALS SOLICITED: Materials of, by,
  or about Long Beach and local activities.

HOLDINGS:
    Total volume: 50 l.f.
    Inclusive dates: 1890 -
    Description: Material on local history,
  including about 8,500 photographs,
  10,000 negatives, scrapbooks, a diary,
  other manuscripts, and some oral history
  tapes and transcripts.

SEE: Meckler and McMullin; Novotny;
  Hinding.

CA414-490
Long Beach Public Library
Marilyn Horne Archives
101 Pacific Avenue
Long Beach CA 90802-4482

(213) 437-2949

OPEN: M-Th 10-9, F, Sa 10-5:30, Su
  1:30-5; closed holidays
COPYING FACILITIES: yes
MATERIALS SOLICITED: Classical and
  popular music, television interviews
  and programs, correspondence, diaries,
  music scores, and sound and film recordings of or related to Marilyn
  Horne. Will also accept microforms of
  archival materials relating to Ms.
  Horne if originals are not available.

HOLDINGS:
    Total volume: 7 l.f.
    Inclusive dates: 1950 -
    Description: A collection of biographi-
  cal materials on the life and music of
  Marilyn Horne. The collection includes
  correspondence, television scripts, seminar tapes, tape recordings of performances, professional and amateur photographs, and oral history recordings.

CA414-500
Long Beach Public Library
Rancho Los Cerritos
Historical Collection
4600 Virginia Road
Long Beach CA 90807

(213) 424-9423

OPEN: W-Su 1-5; closed Mondays,
  Tuesdays, Thanksgiving, Christmas,
  and New Year's
COPYING FACILITIES: no
MATERIALS SOLICITED: Materials relating
  to southern California history, local
  history, the Rancho period of California history, Jonathan Temple, Manuel
  Nieto, the Cota family, Lewellyn Bixby,
  Jotham Bixby, and Sarah Bixby Smith.
  Will also accept materials relating to
  western American regional history,
  California history, Spanish-Colonial architecture and furnishings, and Victorian (American) furniture and antiques.

HOLDINGS:
    Total volume: 6 l.f.
    Inclusive dates: 1830 -
    Description: A collection of manu-
  scripts relating to Rancho Los Cerritos
  history. The collection includes correspondence, diaries, journals, account
  books and business records, genealogical
  source data, maps and charts, architectural drawings and renderings, photographs, oral history tapes and transcripts,
  focusing on the Temple, Bixby, Flint, and
  Hathaway families.

SEE: Bean and Vane.

LOS ALTOS HILLS

CA418-200
Foothill Electronics Museum
De Forest Memorial Library
Foothill College
12345 El Monte Road
Los Altos Hills CA 94022

(415) 948-8590, Ext. 381

OPEN: Su 1-4:30, Th,F 9-4:30; closed
  holidays
USER FEES: one dollar, adults;
  twenty-five cents, children
ACCESS: by prior consent
COPYING FACILITIES: yes
MATERIALS SOLICITED: Materials on surveillance and early California Bay area
  electronics. Will also accept material
  on early wireless and television.

HOLDINGS:
    Total volume: 3,300 c.f.
    Inclusive dates: 1873 - 1975
    Description: The Lee De Forest collec-
  tion consists of 128,444 items, including
  handwritten and typed papers, transcripts, correspondence, diaries, journals,
  notebooks detailing scientific work and
  inventions, documents relating to patents
  and other legal matters, awards, and
  scrapbooks. Other collections deal with
  early wireless, radio, television, California
  Bay area electronics, and surveillance.

SEE: NUCMC, 1974, 79.

SEE: Mehr.

SEE ALSO: Earl G. Goddard, ed., *Guide to
  Foothill Electronics Museum: Miracles
  in Trust* (Perham Foundation, 1974).

LOS ANGELES

CA421-015
American Film Institute
Louis B. Mayer Library
2021 North Western Avenue
Los Angeles CA 90027

(213) 856-7660

OPEN: M-F 10:30-5:30; closed weekends
  and holidays
ACCESS: graduate students, scholars,
  writers and members of the
  entertainment industry
COPYING FACILITIES: yes
MATERIALS SOLICITED: Motion pictures
  and television, primarily from an
  entertainment/theatrical approach, including documentaries and video art,
  but not educational or industrial topics.

HOLDINGS:
    Total volume: 2,800 items
    Inclusive dates: 1910 -
    Description: 17 special collections,
  2,000 motion picture scripts, 800 television scripts, transcripts, approximately
  400 seminar transcripts, and a collection
  of motion picture stills and personal photographs.

SEE: NUCMC, 1974.

SEE: Meckler and McMullin; Novotny;
  Hinding; Mehr.

SEE ALSO: Joan Hoff Wilson and Lynn B.
  Donovan, 'Women's History: A Listing
  of West Coast Archival and Manuscript
  Sources, Part I,' *California Historical
  Quarterly* 55 (Spring 1976).

CA421-20
American Historical Association
Pacific Coast Branch
University of Southern California
Los Angeles CA 90089-0034

(213) 743-2368

SEE: NUCMC, 1959-61.

Questionnaire not returned.

CA421-30
Archdiocese of Los Angeles
Chancery Archives
1531 West Ninth Street
Los Angeles CA 90015

(213) 251-3200

OPEN: by appointment
ACCESS: professional scholars
COPYING FACILITIES: yes
MATERIALS SOLICITED: Western Americana documentation, with special emphasis on the development of the Roman Catholic church in that area. Will
  also accept other material on the
  Catholic church in America.

HOLDINGS:
    Total volume: 150,000 items
    Inclusive dates: 1769 -
    Description: A collection of manuscripts, documents, and assorted memorabilia pertaining to the Catholic history of California and the Pacific West.

SEE: Beers - Southwest.

SEE ALSO: 'The Los Angeles Chancery Archives,' *The Americas* 21 (April 1965); 'The Chancery Archives of the Archdiocese of Los Angeles: An Historical Perspective,' *Records of the American Catholic Historical Society* 82 (Sept. 1971); 'Printed Guides to Archival Centers for American Catholic History,' *American Archivist* 32 (Oct. 1969); 'California's Catholic Heritage,' *American Ecclesiastical Review* 113 (July 1965); 'Chancery Archives,' *American Archivist* 28 (April 1965); *A Select Guide to California Catholic History* (1966).

CA421-40
The Arnold Schoenberg Institute
Archives
University of Southern California
University Park MC-1101
Los Angeles CA 90089-1101

(213) 743-5393

OPEN: M-F 9-5; closed weekends and holidays
ACCESS: by appointment only
COPYING FACILITIES: yes
MATERIALS SOLICITED: Materials concerning composer Arnold Schoenberg.

HOLDINGS:
    Total volume: 6,000 pages; 24 reels; 3 l.f.; 1,500 photographs
    Inclusive dates: 1880's - 1951
    Description: Papers of Arnold Schoenberg, including most of his original music manuscripts and sketchbooks of compositions, manuscripts of his literary and theoretical works, and microfilm copies of music manuscripts and correspondence held by other repositories, as well as related photographs, tape recordings, and films.

SEE: NUCMC, 1978.

SEE: Spalek.

SEE ALSO: Jan Maegaard, *Studien zur Entwicklung des Dodekaphonen Satzes bei Arnold Schoenberg* 1 (Wilhelm Hansen, 1972); Josef Rufer, *The Works of Arnold Schoenberg* (Faber and Faber, 1962); Arnold Schoenberg Institute *Journal* (before 1977, *Bulletin*), 1975 to date.

CA421-100
Blue Cross of California
Frances B. Linke Library
21555 Oxnard Street
Woodland Hills CA 91367

(213) 666-3473

OPEN: M-F 7:30-4:30; closed weekends
ACCESS: librarians only
COPYING FACILITIES: yes
MATERIALS SOLICITED: Health care and related legislation; medical and health care economics.

HOLDINGS:
    Total volume: 160 l.f.
    Inclusive dates: 1964 -
    Description: Archival material relating to Blue Cross, Blue Cross of Southern California, and health care.

CA421-115
California Historical Society
Southern California Branch
6300 Wilshire Blvd.
Los Angeles CA 90048

(213) 651-5655

OPEN: M-Th 9-5; closed other days and holidays
COPYING FACILITIES: yes
MATERIALS SOLICITED: Photographs relating to the history of the greater southern California area.

HOLDINGS:
    Total volume: 15,000 items
    Inclusive dates: 1860 -
    Description: Photographs and related materials, 1890-1940, of Los Angeles commercial photographer C. C. Pierce, and photographs, 1900, of George Wharton James, depicting Indian groups and activities of the Southwest. The collection focuses on activities and people of the greater southern California area, especially Los Angeles.

CA421-180
Church of Jesus Christ of Latter-day Saints
Genealogical Society
Southern California Area Genealogical Library
10741 Santa Monica Blvd.
Los Angeles CA 90025

(213) 474-9990

OPEN: M, F 9-5, Tu-Th 9-9, Sa 9-3; closed Sundays, holidays, and last two weeks of December.
COPYING FACILITIES: yes
MATERIALS SOLICITED: Family histories, local histories, vital record compilations, and church, court, military, immigration, and other materials of genealogical significance.

HOLDINGS:
    Total volume: 18,000 microfilm reels
    Inclusive dates: 18th century -
    Description: Family histories and other genealogical material.

SEE ALSO: a brochure available from the Library.

The Library also holds copies of materials from the Church of Jesus Christ of Latter-day Saints Genealogical Society in Salt Lake City, UT.

CA421-218
El Pueblo de Los Angeles State Historic Park
History and Public Affairs
845 North Alameda Street
Los Angeles CA 90012

(213) 628-1274

OPEN: by appointment only

COPYING FACILITIES: yes
MATERIALS SOLICITED: Photographs of the Los Angeles area. Will also accept other materials relating to the history of Los Angeles since its founding in 1781.

HOLDINGS:
    Total volume: 5 file cabinets; 25 c.f.
    Inclusive dates: 1833 -
    Description: Materials relating to the history of Los Angeles and its environs, including maps, photographs, architectural drawings, records of organizations and institutions, ephemera, and scrapbooks.

CA421-250
Hebrew Union College
Skirball Museum
3077 University Mall
Los Angeles CA 90007

(213) 749-3424

OPEN: Su 10-5, Tu-F 11-4; closed Mondays, Saturdays, and holidays
ACCESS: appointment required
COPYING FACILITIES: yes
MATERIALS SOLICITED: Medieval illuminated Bibles, ritual texts, marriage contracts, Esther scrolls, Haggadoth (Passover liturgy), and documentary photographs relating to Judaica and Jewish history.

HOLDINGS:
    Total volume: 300 items
    Inclusive dates: 16th century - 20th century
    Description: Illuminated Hebrew marriage contracts, chiefly from 18th century Italy; 50 Esther scrolls, chiefly from 18th-20th century Italy, Germany, and Eastern Europe; and photographs covering such subjects as synagogue architecture, famous Jewish people, ceremonial art, and early 20th century Palestine.

SEE: Novotny.

CA421-322
Los Angeles (Inner City) Cultural Center
Libraries
Langston Hughes Memorial Library
1308 South New Hampshire Avenue
Los Angeles CA 90006

(213) 387-1161

OPEN: M-F 10-5, Sa 10-4; closed Sundays and holidays
ACCESS: students and serious researchers
COPYING FACILITIES: no
MATERIALS SOLICITED: Materials relating to the arts, particulary minority arts, including scripts and plays. Will also accept related music and documents.

HOLDINGS:
    Total volume: not specified
    Inclusive dates: 1900 -
    Description: Unpublished plays and music scores by black, Asian American, Native American, and other minority artists, conference reports on psychology and education, early 1900's- , and a file of the Center's periodical publication *Neworld,* 1974- .

CA421-330

Los Angeles City Clerk's Office
Los Angeles City Archives
Piper Technical Center, Room 320
555 Ramirez Street
Los Angeles CA 90012

(213) 485-3512, 5705

OPEN: M-F 7:30-5; closed weekends and holidays
ACCESS: identification required
COPYING FACILITIES: yes

HOLDINGS:
Total volume: 500 vols.
Inclusive dates: 1827 - 1900
Description: Collections and files relating to Los Angeles history and government, including city maps, council minutes, ordinances, tax records, annexation records, and census reports.

Post-1900 records of a similar nature, in part ongoing, are also available at the Office.

CA421-340

Los Angeles City College
Earth Science Department
855 North Vermont Avenue
Los Angeles CA 90029

(213) 669-4228

OPEN: M-F 8-2; closed weekends and holidays
ACCESS: faculty or other responsible individuals
COPYING FACILITIES: yes

HOLDINGS:
Total volume: 1,000 slides
Inclusive dates: 1929 - 1945
Description: A collection of 4x5 glass slides, most dealing with geological subjects. Some are copies of textbook illustrations, but many are of southern California during the period indicated.

CA421-360

Los Angeles City Recreation and Parks Department
Hollywood Museum Collection
200 North Spring Street
Los Angeles CA 90012

(213) 485-5515

OPEN: by appointment only
ACCESS: collections in storage as of August 1980
COPYING FACILITIES: no
MATERIALS SOLICITED: Will accept motion picture scripts and photographs.

HOLDINGS:
Total volume: 51,000 items
Inclusive dates: 1920 -
Description: 40,000 still photographs, 10,000 transcription discs, 600 oral history tapes and 100 personal collections of memorabilia, all relating to motion pictures and their history.

SEE: Meckler and McMullin; Mehr.

CA421-385

Barlow Society for the History of Medicine
634 South Westlake Avenue
Los Angeles CA 90057

(213) 483-4555

SEE: NUCMC, 1959-61.

Questionnaire not returned.

CA421-390

Los Angeles County Museum of Natural History
History Division Historic Records Center
900 Exposition Blvd.
Los Angeles CA 90007

(213) 744-3301

OPEN: Tu-F 1-4; closed other days and holidays
COPYING FACILITIES: yes
MATERIALS SOLICITED: Manuscript and iconographic materials relating to southern California and the Los Angeles area, 1600-1940. Will also accept materials relating to the American Southwest and the Pacific area, 1600-1900, with emphasis on Baja California, Arizona, New Mexico, and northwestern Mexico.

HOLDINGS:
Total volume: 950 l.f.
Inclusive dates: 1650 - 1950
Description: Materials relating chiefly to Los Angeles and southern California. There are WPA notes for southern California county histories; maps; 100,000 photographic prints and negatives; and collections on early aviation, the early motion picture industry, and the socio-economic development of southern California.

SEE: Hamer; NUCMC, 1959-61.

SEE: Bean and Vane; Beers - Southwest; Hinding; Novotny; Schatz.

CA421-400

Los Angeles Public Library
Central Library
630 West Fifth Street
Los Angeles CA 90071

(213) 626-7555

OPEN: M-Th 10-9, F, Sa 10-5:30; closed Sundays and holidays
COPYING FACILITIES: yes
MATERIALS SOLICITED: Materials relating to California, especially Los Angeles.

HOLDINGS:
Total volume: 16,000 items
Inclusive dates: 1800 -
Description: Materials relating primarily to Los Angeles and southern California, including the *Mercury* Case, concerning contraband trade on the California coast; literary manuscripts and letters of Theodore Dreiser; autobiographical sketches of prominent citizens; a photograph collection of the area, 1850 to present; the Performing Arts Photograph Collection, which is nationwide in scope;

and some aerial photographs and manuscript maps.

SEE: Hamer; NUCMC, 1962, 70.

SEE: Bean and Vane; Mehr.

CA421-470

Mount Saint Mary's College
Charles Willard Coe Memorial Library
Archives
12001 Chalon Road
Los Angeles CA 90049

(213) 476-2237, Ext. 233

OPEN: Su 2-10, M-Th 8-10, F 8-4:30, Sa 10-6; closed holidays
COPYING FACILITIES: yes
MATERIALS SOLICITED: Archives of Mount Saint Mary's College.

HOLDINGS:
Total volume: not specified
Inclusive dates: 1925 -
Description: Papers and photographs relating to Mount Saint Mary's College.

SEE: Mehr.

CA421-510

Occidental College
Library
Special Collections Department
1600 Campus Road
Los Angeles CA 90041

(213) 259-2640, 2852

OPEN: M-F 1-5; closed holidays and during late August and late December
ACCESS: scholarly researchers with advance arrangements
COPYING FACILITIES: yes
MATERIALS SOLICITED: Materials relating to Lincoln and the Civil War, the West, California history, history of the College, romantic literature, modern American literature, and William Jennings Bryan.

HOLDINGS:
Total volume: not specified
Inclusive dates: 1810 -
Description: Manuscript collections focusing on William Jennings Bryan, Robinson Jeffers, William Mellors Henry, Charles F. Lummis, mystery and detective fiction (correspondence and book manuscripts), conditions in Mexico between 1917 and 1919, and American railroads from the 1840's to the late 1950's.

SEE: Hamer.

SEE: Robbins; Mehr.

SEE ALSO: Indexes, checklists, and other finding aids are available at the institution.

CA421-520

ONE, Incorporated
Baker Memorial Library
2256 Venice Blvd.
Los Angeles CA 90006

(213) 735-5252

OPEN: M-F 9-5; closed weekends and holidays
COPYING FACILITIES: no
MATERIALS SOLICITED: Materials relating to male and female homosexuality, transsexualism, and transvestism, primarily in the United States, but also in foreign countries.

HOLDINGS:
Total volume: not specified
Inclusive dates: 1950 -
Description: Materials relating to homosexuality, including material on personal lives and social movements for homosexual rights.

SEE ALSO: Vern L. Bullough, W. Dorr Legg, Barrett Elcano, and James L. Keppner, comps., *Comprehensive Bibliography of Homosexuality* (Garland, 1976).

CA421-565

Sisters of Social Service
Archives
1120 Westchester Place
Los Angeles CA 90019

(213) 731-2117

OPEN: by appointment only
COPYING FACILITIES: yes
MATERIALS SOLICITED: Materials relating to the history of the Sisters of Social Service, social change in Hungary and the United States in the early 20th century, and social change in the Catholic church and in religious life. Will also accept materials on the history of social work in Hungary and the United States.

HOLDINGS:
Total volume: 100 l.f.
Inclusive dates: 1908 -
Description: Non-current records of the administration and membership of the Sisters of Social Service in Los Angeles since 1926, as well as manuscripts, letters, photographs, and work reports relating to the community's U.S. activities and its founding and activities in Hungary.

SEE: Hinding.

CA421-610

Southwest Museum
Library
234 Museum Drive
Los Angeles CA 90065

MAILING ADDRESS:
P.O. Box 128
Highland Park Station
Los Angeles CA 90024

(213) 221-2163

OPEN: Tu-F 1-4:45; closed weekends and Mondays
COPYING FACILITIES: no
MATERIALS SOLICITED: American anthropologists, American Indians of the Southwest and also Northwest Coast, and Charles F. Lummis and friends. Will also accept Arizona, New Mexico, and California history and Mexican and South American archaeology and anthropology.

HOLDINGS:
Total volume: 300 c.f.; 90,000 items
Inclusive dates: 1800 -
Description: Correspondence, diaries, and manuscripts of Charles Fletcher Lummis; correspondence and anthropological and archaeological papers of Frank Hamilton Cushing, Frederick Webb Hodge, and George Bird Grinnell; other historical, anthropological, and literary papers and archaeological field reports pertaining to Arizona, New Mexico, and southern California, mainly 1880-1930; photographs of American Indians, especially the Pueblos and other Southwest tribes; and South American archaeology.

SEE: Hamer; NUCMC, 1962.

SEE: Novotny; Bean and Vane; Robbins; Hinding; Beers-Southwest.

CA421-620

Theatre and Film Arts
691 South Irolo Street
Los Angeles CA

MAILING ADDRESS:
P.O. Box 98, Ambassador Station
Los Angeles CA 90070

no telephone

OPEN: by appointment
COPYING FACILITIES: yes
MATERIALS SOLICITED: Materials pertaining to theater, music, burlesque, and vaudeville.

HOLDINGS:
Total volume: 300 items
Inclusive dates: 1803 -
Description: Letters, scores, manuscripts, correspondence, and annotated volumes related to the history of music and the theater.

SEE: Novotny.

CA421-660

University of California, Los Angeles
Biomedical Library
History & Special Collections Division
12-077 Center for the Health Sciences
University of California, Los Angeles
Los Angeles CA 90024

(213) 825-6940

OPEN: M-F 8-5; closed weekends and holidays
COPYING FACILITIES: yes

HOLDINGS:
Total volume: 30 l.f.
Inclusive dates: 19th century -
Description: Manuscripts, documents, and photographs relating to the development of medical institutions in Los Angeles, Florence Nightingale, the history of the neurosciences in North America and Europe, and the history of medicine.

SEE: Hinding.

CA421-665

University of California, Los Angeles
Bureau of Governmental Research
Library
Los Angeles CA 90024

no telephone

SEE: NUCMC, 1962.

Questionnaire not returned.

CA421-710

University of California, Los Angeles
Law Library
405 Hillgard Avenue
Los Angeles CA 90024

(213) 825-3960, 7826

OPEN: late Aug. - late May, M-F 8-midnight, Sa 9-6, Su 1-midnight; variable summer hours; closed holidays
COPYING FACILITIES: yes

HOLDINGS:
Total volume: 3 boxes
Inclusive dates: 1949 - 1953
Description: Manuscripts, typescripts of published works, speeches, class notes and lectures, class assignments and examinations, correspondence, and other papers of Roscoe Pound, primarily concerning law and legal education.

SEE: Bean and Vane.

CA421-750

University of California, Los Angeles
Music Library
Schoenberg Hall
Los Angeles CA 90024

(213) 825-4881, 4882

OPEN: Su 1-9, M-Th 8-10, F 8-5, Sa 9-5; closed holidays and University intersessions
COPYING FACILITIES: yes
MATERIALS SOLICITED: Music manuscripts and documents of contemporary composers, especially those in the Los Angeles area, UCLA faculty composers, and Austrian emigre composers; music manuscripts and documents of American film and television composers; and manuscripts and documents relating to music development in Los Angeles. Will also accept manuscripts generally relating to Western art music, documents relating to the development of popular American music, and microforms of manuscripts, especially medieval and Renaissance music, in foreign libraries.

HOLDINGS:
Total volume: 500 l.f.
Inclusive dates: 1400 -
Description: Manuscripts and documents relating to Ernst Toch, Eric Zeisl, film and television music, popular American music, women composers, and contemporary composers from the University and Los Angeles communities.

SEE: Spalek; Hinding; Mehr.

SEE ALSO: Don L. Hixon, ed., *A Directory of Special Music Collections in Southern California Libraries and in the Libraries of the University of California and the California State Universities and Colleges* (Music Library Assn., Southern California Chapter, Music Library Survey Committee, 1976); *Repertoire internationale des sources musicales* (International Inventory of Musical Sources); *Series B: Music Manuscripts* (Barenreiter, 1960-).

CA421-760

University of California, Los Angeles
Theater Arts Department
NATAS-UCLA Television Library
1438 Melnitz Hall
University of California
Los Angeles CA 90024

(213) 825-4480

OPEN: M-F 9-5:30; closed weekends and holidays
COPYING FACILITIES: no
MATERIALS SOLICITED: All formats of television programs (both public and commercial) from the inception of the medium to the present, including public service spots and commercials. Will also accept supportive material such as scripts, production notes, budgets, memorabilia, etc.

HOLDINGS:
    Total volume: 10,000 programs
    Inclusive dates: 1948 -
    Description: Kinescopes, films and tapes of all formats of U.S. television broadcasting. The collection is particularly strong in dramatic and comedy variety shows from 1948 to the present. Documentaries and public affairs programs are also well represented. Sample holdings include: Hallmark Hall of Fame series (163 shows from 1951 to 1972), Jack Benny programs (243 shows from 1951 to 1967), three Alcoa-sponsored anthology series (222 shows from 1956 to 1963), and a large collection of materials from John F. Kennedy's 1958 senatorial and 1960 presidential campaigns.

SEE: Hinding.

SEE ALSO: an annual title catalog available from the Library at a nominal cost, and other finding aids for use at the institution.

CA421-763

University of California, Los Angeles
Theater Arts Department
The UCLA Film Archives
Melnitz, Room 1438
Los Angeles CA 90024

(213) 206-8013

OPEN: by appointment only, M-F 9-5; closed weekends, holidays, and University holidays
COPYING FACILITIES: no
MATERIALS SOLICITED: Prints and pre-print material of motion pictures from all countries and time periods.

HOLDINGS:
    Total volume: 12,000 films
    Inclusive dates: 1912 -
    Description: Motion pictures in both print and pre-print form, especially sound films produced by such companies as 20th Century Fox, Paramount Studios, Warner Brothers, and Republic Pictures. There is also pre-print material on American animation and a growing collection of foreign films.

GUIDES: *UCLA Film Archive Catalogue* (1975).

SEE: Hinding.

CA421-766

University of California, Los Angeles
Theater Arts Department
The UCLA Radio Archives
Melnitz, Room 1438
Los Angeles CA 90024

(213) 206-8013

OPEN: M-F 9-5:30; closed weekends and holidays
COPYING FACILITIES: no
MATERIALS SOLICITED: Original broadcast transcriptions, master tapes, and wire recordings of radio broadcasts dating from radio's inception to the present.

HOLDINGS:
    Total volume: 10,050 items
    Inclusive dates: 1932 -
    Description: Disc and tape recordings, including radio materials deposited by Hallmark Cards and the Carnation Company and 50 collections related to such radio performers as Jack Benny, 1932-55, Bing Crosby, 1946-54, and Ed Wynn, 1933-36.

SEE: Hinding.

CA421-770

University of California, Los Angeles
University Research Library
Department of Special Collections
405 Hilgard Avenue
Los Angeles CA 90024

(213) 825-4879

OPEN: M-Sa 9-5; closed Sundays and holidays
COPYING FACILITIES: yes
MATERIALS SOLICITED: Materials relating to the humanities, fine arts, and social sciences. Will also accept other materials.

HOLDINGS:
    Total volume: 2,000,000 items
    Inclusive dates: 13th century -
    Description: Manuscripts, documents, maps, pamphlets, photographs, ephemera, microfilm, tape recordings, and phonograph records, specializing in the humanities, fine arts, and social sciences. Included are collections relating to English 19th century fiction, early children's books, California, the West, popular literature, and 20th century authors; historical manuscripts for mainly English and American history, especially local history, Asian-American studies, and the entertainment world; materials for the history

of science, technology and photography; and the University's archives.

SEE: Hamer; NUCMC, 1959-64, 70-71, 73, 76.

SEE: Davis; Paszek; Allard, Crawley, and Edmison; Parkinson; Robbins; Hinding; Mehr.

SEE ALSO: James V. Mink, *The Papers of General William Starke Rosecrans and the Rosecrans Family: A Guide to Collection 663* (Univ. of California Library, 1961); Walter Schatz, ed., *Directory of Afro-American Resources* (Bowker, 1970); Peter Duignan, *Handbook of American Resources for African Studies* (Hoover Institution, 1967); Joan Hoff Wilson and Lynn B. Donovan, 'Women's History: A Listing of West Coast Archival and Manuscript Sources, Part II,' *California Historical Quarterly* 55 (Summer 1976).

CA421-774

University of California, Los Angeles
William Andrews Clark Memorial
Library
2520 Cimarron Street
Los Angeles CA 90018

(213) 731-8529

OPEN: M-F 9-4:45; closed weekends and holidays
COPYING FACILITIES: yes
MATERIALS SOLICITED: English manuscripts, 1640-1750; Oscar Wilde and the 1890's; Eric Gill. Will also accept materials related to Montana history.

HOLDINGS:
    Total volume: 14,000 items
    Inclusive dates: 1600 -
    Description: Major collections of manuscripts cover English literature, music, economics, history, and theology (1640-1750); Oscar Wilde and the 1890's (1800-1945); Eric Gill diaries, journals, workbooks, and letters (1890-1945); Montana history (1839-1930); business records of Alexander Warfield, Albert G. Boone, and Warfield & Boone, traders, Indian Territory (1851-61); and California printers (1925-75). There are also small collections of manuscripts relating to Spanish discoveries and administration in Alta California (1750-1800); letters of musicians and composers (1789-1926); and documents and letters of rulers and statesmen (1800-1900).

GUIDES: *Dictionary Catalog of the William Andrews Clark Memorial Library* (G. K. Hall, 1974).

SEE: Hamer; NUCMC, 1972.

SEE: Robbins.

SEE ALSO: Richard C. Davis, *North American Forest History: A Guide to Archives and Manuscripts in the United States and Canada* (Clio Books, 1977).

CA421-825
University of Southern California
Library
University Archives
University Park
Los Angeles CA 90007

(213) 743-5174

OPEN: appointment preferred M-F 10-6; closed weekends and holidays
ACCESS: the University community, alumni, and researchers with specific projects
COPYING FACILITIES: yes
MATERIALS SOLICITED: Materials relating to the history of the University of Southern California. Will also accept materials concerning the history of Los Angeles as it bears upon the University.

HOLDINGS:
Total volume: 250 l.f.
Inclusive dates: 1870's -
Description: Inactive University records, campus publications, faculty monographs, ephemera, visual and audible documents, published studies on the University, and memorabilia relating to the history of the University of Southern California.

CA421-830
University of Southern California
Library
Special Collections Department
University Park
Los Angeles CA 90007

(213) 743-6058

OPEN: M-F 8:30-5, Sa 9-5; closed Sundays, and Saturdays when classes not in session
COPYING FACILITIES: yes
MATERIALS SOLICITED: Performing arts history and production, American literary manuscripts, and California history and government. Will also accept other collections of scholarly value.

HOLDINGS:
Total volume: 4,850 l.f.
Inclusive dates: 1826 -
Description: Over 156 collections cover the fields of performing arts history and production. There are also 19 collections of American literary manuscripts from 1850 to the present and 54 collections covering miscellaneous subjects. 14 collections comprise the Library of Aeronautical History.

SEE: Hamer; NUCMC, 1963-64, 70.

SEE: Allard, Crawley, and Edmison; Hinding; Mehr; Robbins; Spalek.

SEE ALSO: Christopher D. Wheaton and Richard B. Jewell, *Primary Cinema Resources: An Index to Screenplays, Interviews, and Special Collections at the University of Southern California* (G. K. Hall, 1975); Alan M. Meckler and Ruth McMullin, comps., *Oral History Collections* (Bowker, 1975); Joan Hoff Wilson and Lynn B. Donovan, 'Women's History: A Listing of West Coast Archival and Manuscript Sources, Part II,' *California Historical Quarterly* 55 (Summer 1976).

MADERA

CA432-520
Madera County Museum
210 West Yosemite
Madera CA

MAILING ADDRESS:
P.O. Box 478
Madera CA 93639

(209) 673-0291

OPEN: Sa, Su 1-4:30, or by appointment
COPYING FACILITIES: no
MATERIALS SOLICITED: Historical materials related to Madera County.

HOLDINGS:
Total volume: 3,000 items
Inclusive dates: 1874 -
Description: Materials pertaining to the geography and political history of Madera County, the genealogy of its residents, lumbering, mining, and agriculture, as well as to the local Indian population. Included are maps and photographs.

MALIBU

CA436-640
Pepperdine University
Payson Library
Malibu CA 90265

(213) 456-4243

OPEN: M-F 8-5; closed weekends
COPYING FACILITIES: yes
MATERIALS SOLICITED: Archives of Church of Christ, the Disciples church, and Pepperdine University, as well as movie shooting scripts and materials relating to California history; children's literature manuscripts; and 19th century French history manuscripts. Will also accept materials on missions or other church topics, as well as manuscripts of contemporary California authors.

HOLDINGS:
Total volume: 40 l.f.
Inclusive dates: 1800 -
Description: Shooting scripts for movies and television shows written by Ivan Goff, several unpublished manuscripts, Civil War correspondence, picture postcards, a manuscript book from the late 1700's, and archival materials relating to Pepperdine University and the Church of Christ.

MARYSVILLE

CA452-400
John Packard Library of Yuba County
303 Second Street
Marysville CA 95901

no telephone

SEE: Hamer (as Marysville City Library).

Questionnaire not returned.

MENDOCINO

CA454-520
Mendocino Historical Research, Inc.
45007 Albion
Mendocino CA

MAILING ADDRESS:
P.O. Box 922
Mendocino CA 95460

(707) 937-5791

OPEN: daily 1-4 or by appointment; closed holidays
COPYING FACILITIES: yes
MATERIALS SOLICITED: Photographs and other materials on the history of lumbering and logging of redwoods on the Mendocino coast, materials concerning shipping and loading ships, 1852-1930's, genealogical records of coast residents, photographs, maps, deeds, and letters.

HOLDINGS:
Total volume: 12 l.f.
Inclusive dates: 1852 - 1930's
Description: Materials documenting the history of the Mendocino area, including genealogical files, letters, family biographies, deeds, maps, histories of early settlers from New England and Prince Edward Island, and photographs of the redwood lumber industry, towns, and ships.

SEE: Hinding.

MENLO PARK

CA456-530
Menlo Park Public Library
Local History Collection and
Menlo Park Historical Association
History Room
Civic Center
Menlo Park CA 94025

(415) 858-3460

OPEN: Su 2-5, M-W 10-9, Th, F 10-6, Sa 10-5; closed holidays
ACCESS: Local History Collection - see reference librarian; History Room - by prior appointment.
COPYING FACILITIES: yes
MATERIALS SOLICITED: Anything pertaining to the history of Menlo Park or surrounding areas, such as Atherton and Portola Valley.

HOLDINGS:
Total volume: 6 file drawers; 24 l.f.; 24 boxes
Inclusive dates: 1840's -
Description: Clippings from the *Menlo Park Recorder*, 1970- , photographs of early Menlo, 12 oral history tapes and transcripts, maps and documents relating to the development of and early land ownership in southern San Mateo County, materials relating to Camp Fremont, a World War I military training camp, and other materials relating to Menlo Park history.
Collections from local school and government sources; World War I posters.

CA456-730
Sport Balloon Society of the United
   States of America
Sonnichsen Collection
Menlo Oaks Balloon Field
Menlo Park CA

MAILING ADDRESS:
P.O. Box 2247
Menlo Park CA 94025

(415) 326-7679

OPEN: by appointment
USER FEES: variable
ACCESS: aeronauts engaged in scholarly
   research
COPYING FACILITIES: no
MATERIALS SOLICITED: Aerostations in
   the United States, 1700's- . Will also
   accept worldwide balloon and airship
   data.

HOLDINGS:
   Total volume: 60 l.f.
   Inclusive dates: 1870 -
   Description: Correspondence; logbooks
of aerostats and aeronauts; data and results of balloon competitions sanctioned
by the Society; records of all Whiskey
Hill, Atherton and Menlo Oaks Ballooning and Sporting Society rally events,
1965 to date; manuscripts; and data on
the Model Balloon League.

MILL VALLEY

CA460-520
Mill Valley Historical Society
375 Throckmorton Avenue
Mill Valley CA 94941

(415) 388-2190

OPEN: M 2-4, 7-9, Tu, Th 10-4, 7-9, W,
   Sa 10-4, F 2-4; closed Sundays and
   holidays
COPYING FACILITIES: yes
MATERIALS SOLICITED: Materials relating
   to Mill Valley.

HOLDINGS:
   Total volume: not specified
   Inclusive dates: 1850 -
   Description: Photographs, oral histor-
ies, and newspaper clippings relating to
Mill Valley.

MODESTO

CA476-520
McHenry Museum of Art and History
1402 I Street
Modesto CA 95354

(209) 577-5366

OPEN: Tu-F 7-4; closed other days,
   Christmas and New Year's
COPYING FACILITIES: yes
MATERIALS SOLICITED: Materials per-
   taining to Stanislaus County.

HOLDINGS:
   Total volume: several thousand items
   Inclusive dates: 1840's -
   Description: Photographs, court files,
diaries, maps, and deeds relating to the
history of Stanislaus County; oral histor-

ies, photographs, and genealogical files of
local pioneers; and records of community
organizations.

MONTEREY

CA480-120
Colton Hall Museum
Pacific Street
Monterey CA 93940

(408) 646-3851, 375-9944

OPEN: Tu-Su 10-5; closed Mondays and
   holidays
COPYING FACILITIES: yes
MATERIALS SOLICITED: Material concerned with California's Constitutional
   Convention of 1849, Colton Hall
   School, and local history. Will also accept State and local history material,
   early school books and materials, and
   photographs and drawings.

HOLDINGS:
   Total volume: 100 l.f.
   Inclusive dates: 1840 -
   Description: Materials pertaining to
California's Constitutional Convention of
1849; Colton Hall School photographs,
papers, and other memorabilia; and local
historical materials.

CA480-500
Monterey History and Art Association
Allen Knight Maritime Museum
550 Calle Principal
Monterey CA

MAILING ADDRESS:
P.O. Box 805
Monterey CA 93940

(408) 375-2553

OPEN: Tu-F 10-4, Sa, Su 2-4; closed
   Mondays and holidays; Sept. 15 - June
   15, afternoons only
COPYING FACILITIES: yes
MATERIALS SOLICITED: Will accept maritime materials, with emphasis on subjects related to Monterey Bay.

HOLDINGS:
   Total volume: 32 l.f.
   Inclusive dates: 1839 -
   Description: 61 ships' logs; towage
records, 1908-22, mostly from the San
Francisco Bay area; 157 photograph al-
bums of 19th and 20th century ships and
captains; and a diary, 1851, kept by Israel
Whitney Lyon on the ship *Flying Cloud*
from New York to San Francisco.

CA480-510
Monterey History and Art Association
Mayo Hayes O'Donnell Library
155 Van Buren Street
Monterey CA

MAILING ADDRESS:
P.O. Box 805
Monterey CA 93940

(408) 372-2608

OPEN: W, F, Sa, Su afternoons; closed
   other days and holidays
COPYING FACILITIES: yes

MATERIALS SOLICITED: Materials relating
   to California history, particularly that
   of the Monterey Peninsula.

HOLDINGS:
   Total volume: 20 l.f.
   Inclusive dates: 1850 -
   Description: A collection relating to the
Monterey Peninsula. Included are approximately 4,000 photographs of people
and places; correspondence, personal and
institutional; account books; business and
financial records; records of government
agencies; maps and charts; architectural
drawings; aerial photographs; genealogical
source data; three literary manuscripts;
and oral history tapes.

SEE: Bean and Vane.

CA480-530
Monterey Public Library
625 Pacific Street
Monterey CA 93940

(408) 646-3930

OPEN: Su 1-5, M-Th 9-9, F 9-6, Sa 9-5
ACCESS: serious researchers only;
   identification and registration required
COPYING FACILITIES: yes
MATERIALS SOLICITED: Any items relat-
   ing to California or Monterey (city and
   County) history.

HOLDINGS:
   Total volume: not specified
   Inclusive dates: 17th century -
   Description: Several 17th century English manuscripts; Monterey's jail register,
1850-72; business records of Monterey
firms of the late 19th century; book
manuscripts, letters, and journals; 1,500
historical photographs, mostly of Monterey; and drawings and photographs by
architect William O. Raiguel.

SEE: Robbins.

CA480-720
Stevenson House State Historical
   Monument
530 Houston Street
Monterey CA 93940

no telephone

SEE: NUCMC, 1962.

   Questionnaire not returned.

CA480-800
U.S. Army Museum, Presidio of
   Monterey
Building 113
Monterey CA 93940

(408) 242-8414

OPEN: Th-M 9-4; closed Tuesdays,
   Wednesdays, and holidays
ACCESS: advance arrangements required
COPYING FACILITIES: no
MATERIALS SOLICITED: Presidio of Mon-
   terey, 1902- , its predecessor institution
   Fort Mervine, 1846-1902, and associ-
   ated units and individuals. Will also
   accept materials pertaining to the U.S.
   Army and the history of Monterey.

HOLDINGS:
Total volume: 200 items; 10 file drawers
Inclusive dates: 1847 - 1920
Description: Photographs, maps, correspondence, and papers of individuals relating to Monterey, Fort Mervine, and the Presidio of Monterey.

MORAGA

CA488-520
Moraga Historical Society
Archive
St. Mary's College Library
Moraga CA 94575

no telephone

OPEN: Su 1-4, M-F 9-5, Sa 1-5; closed holidays, and weekends during summer
COPYING FACILITIES: yes
MATERIALS SOLICITED: All material related to residents of the area granted to Joaquin Moraga and Juan Bernal in 1841, called Rancho Laguna de los Palos Colorados, or more widely called today 'Lamorinda,' which includes the cities of Lafayette, Moraga, Orinda, and the town of Canyon. Will also accept materials related to the Moraga family in California.

HOLDINGS:
Total volume: 37 l.f.
Inclusive dates: 1835 -
Description: Manuscripts or copies thereof, newspaper clippings and photographs of residents of Rancho Laguna de los Palos Colorados area, Contra Costa County, CA. Included are trial transcripts, deeds, vital records (church), letters, ledgers, minutes, rosters, etc.

SEE: Meckler and McMullin.

CA488-720
St. Mary's College of California
Moraga CA 94575

(415) 376-4411, Ext. 233

OPEN: M-F 10-noon; other times by appointment
COPYING FACILITIES: yes
MATERIALS SOLICITED: Materials related to St. Mary's College, 1863- . Will also accept materials related to Catholic higher education in 19th century California.

HOLDINGS:
Total volume: 93 l.f.
Inclusive dates: 1863 -
Description: Materials concerning St. Mary's College and extracurricular activities sponsored by its students and administration, at the College's three locations, San Francisco, 1863-89, Oakland, 1889-1928, and Moraga, 1928- . Included are letters, manuscript histories, account books, scrapbooks, architectural and engineering drawings, aerial photographs, motion pictures, and history recordings.

MOUNTAIN VIEW

CA496-520
Mountain View Pioneer and Historical Association
Pioneer Room
Mountain View Public Library
585 Franklin Street
Mountain View CA

MAILING ADDRESS:
P.O. Box 252
Mountain View CA 94041

(415) 968-6595

OPEN: M 10-5, W 10-8; closed other days and holidays
COPYING FACILITIES: yes
MATERIALS SOLICITED: Materials relating to the history of Mountain View.

HOLDINGS:
Total volume: not specified
Inclusive dates: 1860 -
Description: Materials relating to the Mountain View area, including records of organizations and churches, papers of individuals, family histories, unpublished papers, student papers, clippings, correspondence, ephemera, photographs, and oral history tapes.

NAPA

CA500-560
Napa County Historical Society
1219 1st Street
Napa CA 94558

(707) 224-1739

OPEN: Tu, Th noon-4, M, W, F, Sa by appointment; closed Sundays and holidays
COPYING FACILITIES: yes
MATERIALS SOLICITED: Manuscripts, archives, and non-current records of community clubs and groups, architectural drawings, and photographs, all pertaining to Napa County and especially to the cities of Napa, St. Helena, and Calistoga.

HOLDINGS:
Total volume: 450 l.f.
Inclusive dates: 1850 -
Description: Manuscripts and photographs of Napa County pioneers, businesses, churches, schools, and government agencies.
Artifacts and relics of early pioneers and native Americans of Napa County and California.

NATIONAL CITY

CA504-560
National City Public Library
Archives Room
200 East 12th Street
National City CA 92050

(619) 474-8211

OPEN: M, Tu 1-9, W, Th 10-8, F 10-6; closed weekends and holidays
COPYING FACILITIES: yes

MATERIALS SOLICITED: Materials relating to National City. Will also accept materials relating to the South Bay area of San Diego County, CA.

HOLDINGS:
Total volume: 110 l.f.
Inclusive dates: 1834 -
Description: Account books, business and financial records, correspondence, diaries, records of local organizations and government agencies, manuscript maps, charts, architectural drawings, aerial photographs, photographs, oral history tapes, sound recordings of local events, scrapbooks, and biographies of pioneer residents, all primarily concerned with National City.

SEE: Bean and Vane.

NEVADA CITY

CA508-560
Nevada County Historical Society
Searls Historical Library
214 Church Street
Nevada City CA 95959

MAILING ADDRESS:
P.O. Box 1300
Nevada City CA 95959

(916) 265-5910

OPEN: M-Sa 1-4; closed Sundays and holidays
COPYING FACILITIES: yes
MATERIALS SOLICITED: Nevada County history.

HOLDINGS:
Total volume: 150 l.f.
Inclusive dates: 1848 - 1942
Description: Manuscripts relating to Nevada County. Included are deeds, mining claims, statistics, legal documents, tapes, diaries, letters, maps, charts, pictures, negatives, and genealogical information on Nevada County pioneers.

SEE: Hinding.

NORTHRIDGE

CA524-140
California State University, Northridge
Map Library
18111 Nordhoff Street
Northridge CA 91330

(213) 885-3465

OPEN: M-F 8-5; closed weekends and holidays
COPYING FACILITIES: no
MATERIALS SOLICITED: All subjects for which map coverage is available.

HOLDINGS:
Total volume: 65,000 items
Inclusive dates: 20th century
Description: A collection of aerial photographs covering areas of California and the eastern United States.

CA524-160
California State University,
  Northridge
Urban Archives Project
18111 Nordhoff Street
Northridge CA 91330

(818) 885-2487

OPEN: M-F 9-4:30; closed weekends and
  holidays
COPYING FACILITIES: yes
MATERIALS SOLICITED: Records of
voluntary associations in Los Angeles
County, CA, including labor unions,
ethnic organizations, social service
agencies, chambers of commerce, civic
associations, and social action groups.
Will also accept papers of individuals
closely associated with these organizations and papers of prominent public
citizens in the San Fernando Valley.

HOLDINGS:
  Total volume: 550 c.f.
  Inclusive dates: 1900 -
  Description: Primarily records of
  voluntary organizations in Los Angeles
  County, CA, and also personal papers
  and records of statewide organizations
  after 1930. Included are records of the
  Los Angeles County Federation of Labor,
  Industrial Association of San Fernando
  Valley, League of Women Voters of
  Greater Los Angeles, and California Fed-
  eration of Teachers.

OAKLAND

CA540-520
Mills College
Library
5000 MacArthur Blvd.
Oakland CA 94613

(415) 430-3302

OPEN: M-F 10-5; school vacations, M-F
  1-5; closed weekends and holidays
COPYING FACILITIES: yes

HOLDINGS:
  Total volume: 9,505 items
  Inclusive dates: 1730 -
  Description: Materials relating chiefly
  to English, American, and California
  writers and literature, and Albert M.
  Bender, San Francisco art patron. There
  are also a few collections of family papers, as well as the College archives,
  which contain files of the College presidents.

GUIDES: *A Brief Description of the Manuscript Collections of the Mills College
  Library* 1 (1975).

SEE: Hamer; NUCMC, 1959-62, 71,
  74-75, 77, 80.

SEE: Spalek; Robbins; Hinding.

SEE ALSO: Joan Hoff Wilson and Lynn B.
  Donovan, 'Women's History: A Listing
  of West Coast Archival and Manuscript
  Sources, Part I,' *California Historical
  Quarterly* 55 (Spring 1976).

CA540-590
Oakland Museum
History Department
1000 Oak Street
Oakland CA 94607

(415) 273-3842

OPEN: M-F by appointment only; closed
  weekends and holidays
COPYING FACILITIES: yes
MATERIALS SOLICITED: Materials per-
taining to the San Francisco Bay area,
California, and the western United
States, with emphasis on photographs.
Will also accept materials concerning
the United States in general.

HOLDINGS:
  Total volume: 110 c.f.
  Inclusive dates: 1700's -
  Description: Maps, government documents, business records, diaries, correspondence and photographs relating to
  ethnographic, agricultural, social, political
  and industrial aspects of California and
  western United States history.

SEE: Novotny; Schatz.

CA540-610
Oakland Public Library
Oakland History Room
125 14th Street
Oakland CA 94612

(415) 834-7446

OPEN: Tu, Th noon-8:30,W, F 10-5:30;
  closed weekends, Mondays, and
  holidays
COPYING FACILITIES: yes
MATERIALS SOLICITED: Materials covering the history of Oakland and its environs, including ephemera and photographs.

HOLDINGS:
  Total volume: not specified
  Inclusive dates: 1852 -
  Description: Newspaper clippings, photographs, letters, and other materials covering California and East Bay history,
  with emphasis on Oakland and its environs. Included is the Jack London collection of clippings, letters, periodical articles, and other materials.

SEE: Hamer; NUCMC, 1959-61.

SEE: Robbins; Hinding; Novotny.

PACIFIC GROVE

CA566-640
Pacific Grove Public Library
550 Central Avenue
Pacific Grove CA 93950

(408) 373-0603

OPEN: M-Th 10-9, F-Sa 10-5; closed
  Sundays and holidays
COPYING FACILITIES: yes
MATERIALS SOLICITED: Materials on the
history of Pacific Grove, including pho-
tographs.

HOLDINGS:
  Total volume: 3 vols.; 1 box
  Inclusive dates: 1878 -
  Description: Three typed, bound volumes of the journals of Hayes Perkins,
  world traveler and Pacific Grove resident,
  and minutes and other records of a local
  women's study group and book review
  group, the Muricata Club, which flourished from 1911 to 1974.

SEE: Hinding.

PALOS VERDES PENINSULA

CA574-640
Palos Verdes Library District
650 Deep Valley Drive
Palos Verdes Peninsula CA 90274

no telephone

SEE: Hamer.

Questionnaire not returned.

PASADENA

CA578-130
California Institute of Technology
Archives
1201 East California Blvd.
Pasadena CA 91125

(818) 356-6433, 6405

OPEN: M-F by appointment; closed
  weekends
ACCESS: scholars, students, and writers,
  by appointment
COPYING FACILITIES: yes
MATERIALS SOLICITED: History of 20th
century science and technology, particularly as related to the California Institute of Technology. Will also accept
papers of non-Caltech scientists, if they
complement existing collections; materials relating to the history of the California Institute of Technology; sound
recordings; and photographs of scientists, equipment, and the campus.

HOLDINGS:
  Total volume: 500,000 items
  Inclusive dates: 1830's -
  Description: Over 60 collections relating to the history of the Institute and to
  20th century science and technology. Included are records of divisions, administrative officers, and faculty committees;
  papers of individual Caltech scientists;
  sound recordings; and over 5,000 photographs of scientists. Subjects documented include 19th century American
  scientists; 19th century social conditions
  in Russia; 20th century Italian mathematics; American political, social, and intellectual history; the development of the
  physical sciences, aeronautics, molecular
  biology, and seismology; and social and
  political conditions in Europe before
  World War II.

GUIDES: *A Brief Guide to the California
  Institute of Technology Archives* (1977).

SEE: Hamer; NUCMC, 1959-61, 69, 71.

SEE: Paszek; Spalek.

SEE ALSO: Ann Novotny, ed., *Picture Sources 3* (Special Libraries Assn., 1975); Joan Nelson Warnow, *A Selection of Manuscript Collections at American Repositories* (American Institute of Physics, 1969); Albert Gunns and Judith R. Goodstein, *Guide to the Robert Andrews Millikan Collection at the California Institute of Technology* (American Institute of Physics, 1975). Guides to other individual collections are available at the institution.

CA578-560

National Aeronautics and Space
  Administration
Jet Propulsion Laboratory
of the California Institute of
  Technology
4800 Oak Grove Drive
Pasadena CA 91109

(818) 354-4200, 4321

OPEN: M-F 7:30-4:30; closed weekends and holidays
ACCESS: by prior arrangement
COPYING FACILITIES: yes
MATERIALS SOLICITED: Materials on aeronautics, astronautics and related subjects.

HOLDINGS:
  Total volume: 5,000 items
  Inclusive dates: 1936 -
  Description: A collection of materials on aeronautics and astronautics, especially these concerned with NASA and its predecessor agency, the National Advisory Committee for Aeronautics. Material on such subjects as foreign and military aeronautics and astronautics, science, technology, public policy, military missiles, unmanned deep space exploration, and the operation of the Laboratory itself is also held.

CA578-630

Norton Simon Museum of Art at
  Pasadena
The Blue Four Galka Scheyer Archive
411 West Colorado Blvd.
Pasadena CA 91105

(213) 681-2484, (818) 449-6840

OPEN: by appointment only
COPYING FACILITIES: yes
MATERIALS SOLICITED: Will accept documents concerning Paul Klee, Alexis Jawlensky, Lyonel Feininger, and Wassily Kandinsky (the Blue Four) and Galka Scheyer.

HOLDINGS:
  Total volume: 800 items
  Inclusive dates: 1924 - 1945
  Description: Photocopies of correspondence between Galka Scheyer and the artists of the Blue Four-Paul Klee, Alexis Jawlensky, Lyonel Feininger, and Wassily Kandinsky.

SEE: Hamer; NUCMC, 1965 (as Pasadena Art Museum).

CA578-640

Pasadena Historical Society
Pasadena Historical Museum Library
470 West Walnut
Pasadena CA 91103

(818) 577-1660

OPEN: Tu, Th 1-4; closed other days, holidays, and August
COPYING FACILITIES: yes
MATERIALS SOLICITED: Pasadena history. Redevelopment plans and maps, school board integration records, personal histories, photographs.

HOLDINGS:
  Total volume: 167 l.f.
  Inclusive dates: 1880 -
  Description: Materials relating to the history of Pasadena, including family histories, diaries, and scrapbooks, mostly dating from before 1920.
    Some older records concern the adjacent communities of Altadena, San Marino, South Pasadena, and Sierra Madre. Included are a large photograph collection, local business records, Pasadena Land Company and tract maps, scrapbooks, Thaddeus Lowe family records, and records of the Mt. Lowe Incline Railway and resort.

SEE: Bean and Vane; Hinding.

CA578-675

Pasadena Urban Conservation
  Department
Room 111
100 N. Garfield
Pasadena CA 91109

(818) 405-4228

OPEN: by appointment only
ACCESS: advance arrangements required
COPYING FACILITIES: yes
MATERIALS SOLICITED: Records and photographs relating to architecture, landscape design, parks, urban design, planning, and history of Pasadena and its environs. Will also accept other materials relating to these subjects.

HOLDINGS:
  Total volume: 400 l.f.
  Inclusive dates: 1886 -
  Description: Materials concerning buildings and land use in Pasadena, including city assessment records, 1886-1970, city building permits, 1902- , park department records, 1923-34, materials relating to architects and landscape architects, photographs of buildings, aerial photographs, maps, and historical materials.

PERRIS

CA582-600

Orange Empire Railway Museum
2201 South A Street
Perris CA

MAILING ADDRESS:
P.O. Box 548
Perris CA 92370

(714) 657-2605

OPEN: Sa, Su 11:30-3; closed weekdays and holidays
ACCESS: by two weeks advance notice
COPYING FACILITIES: yes
MATERIALS SOLICITED: Diaries, manuscripts, company records and photographs related to railroad and street railway activity, primarily in southern California.

HOLDINGS:
  Total volume: 60 l.f.
  Inclusive dates: 1875 -
  Description: Over 4,000 pieces, with emphasis on company records of the San Diego Electric Railway and California Southern Railroad, with lesser quantities from the Los Angeles street railway operations, 1920-63. The collections focus on the development and operation of selected public transportation firms in southern California in the 1885-1963 period.

PLEASANT HILL

CA594-120

Contra Costa County Library
Central Library at Pleasant Hill
1750 Oak Park Blvd.
Pleasant Hill CA 94523

(415) 944-3434

OPEN: M-Th 10-9, F, Sa 10-6; closed Sundays and holidays
COPYING FACILITIES: yes
MATERIALS SOLICITED: Papers of local notables.

HOLDINGS:
  Total volume: 10 l.f.
  Inclusive dates: 1847 - 1966
  Description: Papers, 1847-85, of Thomas A. Brown, a judge who lived in Pleasant Hill, consisting of letters, journals, and account books of business transactions of Brown and his relative, Elam Brown. There are also papers of Representative John F. Baldwin, 1954-66, consisting of letters and materials relating to constituents and legislative activity.

POMONA

CA601-120

California State Polytechnic
  University, Pomona
Library
3801 West Temple Avenue
Pomona CA 91768

(714) 598-4671

OPEN: M-F 8-5; closed weekends and holidays
COPYING FACILITIES: yes

HOLDINGS:
  Total volume: 16 l.f.
  Inclusive dates: 1925 - 1928
  Description: Kellogg Arabian Horse Ranch (Pomona) correspondence files, pamphlets, maps, newspaper clippings, photographs and business records. Most of the material is concerned with the construction, operation, and horse purchases of the Ranch.

CA601-640
Pomona Public Library
Special Collections Department
625 South Garey
Pomona CA

MAILING ADDRESS:
P.O. Box 2271
Pomona CA 91769

(714) 620-2026

OPEN: M, Tu 10-9, W, Th 10-6, F 10-5,
Sa noon-5; closed Sundays and
holidays
COPYING FACILITIES: yes
MATERIALS SOLICITED: Materials relating
to all areas of the collections.

HOLDINGS:
Total volume: not specified
Inclusive dates: 1850's -
Description: Records of the California
citrus industry, Pomona Valley water
companies and businesses, and Pomona
organizations; diaries of James C. Truman, Mabel White, and Mary White; correspondence of the Pomona Centennial-
U.S. Bicentennial Committee; local oral
histories; Pomona Valley land and tax
records; and 92,125 photographs of Pomona Valley, southern California, and
the Southwest.

SEE: Robbins; Krichmar; Meckler and
McMullin.

PORT HUENEME

CA605-510
CEC-Seabee Museum
Code 2232
Naval Construction Battalion Center
Port Hueneme CA 93043

(805) 982-5163

OPEN: M-F 7:30-4; closed weekends and
holidays
COPYING FACILITIES: yes
MATERIALS SOLICITED: Permanent, historical records of the Naval Facilities Engineering Command, the Naval Construction Force (Seabees) and the Navy's Civil
Engineer Corps. Will also accept records
which pertain to the aforementioned military organizations, but which are not a
part of their official holdings.

HOLDINGS:
Total volume: 12,000 c.f.
Inclusive dates: 1940 -
Description: Official historical records
of the Naval Facilities Engineering Command, the Naval Construction Force
(Seabees), and the Navy's Civil Engineer
Corps. The Naval Facilities Engineering
Command (formerly the Bureau of Yards
and Docks) records deal with the acquisition, construction, and maintenance of
the Naval shore establishment both in the
United States and abroad. Naval Construction Force records document the
operational accomplishments of this combat construction arm of the Navy from
its inception to the present. Civil Engineer Corps records relate to the evolving role of the civil engineer in the U.S.
Navy.

CA605-530
Naval School, Civil Engineer Corps
  Officers
Moreell Library
Moreell Collection
Port Hueneme CA 93041

(805) 982-3241

OPEN: M-F 7:30-4; closed weekends
ACCESS: authorization required from
commanding officer of the Naval
School or of the Naval Construction
Battalion Center
COPYING FACILITIES: yes

HOLDINGS:
Total volume: 30 l.f.
Inclusive dates: 1917 - 1978
Description: Correspondence, tape recordings, reports and other documents
pertinent to the official and personal activities of Admiral Ben Moreell, organizer
of the Navy Seabees.

SEE: NUCMC, 1972.

SEE: Allard, Crawley, and Edmison.

QUINCY

CA613-640
Plumas County Museum
500 Jackson Street
Quincy CA

MAILING ADDRESS:
P.O. Box 776
Quincy CA 95971

(916) 283-1750

OPEN: M-F 8:30-5, Sa 11-4; closed
Sundays and holidays
COPYING FACILITIES: no
MATERIALS SOLICITED: Material pertain-
ing to Plumas County history.

HOLDINGS:
Total volume: 500 items
Inclusive dates: 1852 -
Description: Diaries, records and
manuscripts from early pioneers.

SEE: Bean and Vane.

RAMONA

CA616-690
Ramona Pioneer Historical Society
  and Museum
729 Main Street
Ramona CA

MAILING ADDRESS:
P.O. Box 625
Ramona CA 92065

(619) 789-1062

OPEN: W-Sa 1-4 or by appointment
COPYING FACILITIES: yes
MATERIALS SOLICITED: Early pioneers
and Indians of southern California,
particularly of Ramona and the former
post offices at Ballena, Witch Creek,
and Santa Ysabel, CA. Will also accept
manuscripts, news clippings, and pictures of the Juian, Warner's, and
Ranchita areas.

HOLDINGS:
Total volume: 795 items
Inclusive dates: 1890's -
Description: Photographs of Ramona,
1890's-1920's, oral history recordings of
local residents, and manuscript biographies of early residents.

RED BLUFF

CA620-760
Tehama County Library
Californiana Section
909 Jefferson Street
Red Bluff CA 96080

(916) 527-0604

OPEN: M-Th 10-9, F, Sa 10-4; closed
Saturdays June - Aug., Sundays, and
holidays
COPYING FACILITIES: yes
MATERIALS SOLICITED: Local history for
Tehama County and northern Califor-
nia. Will also accept Calfornia history
materials.

HOLDINGS:
Total volume: 400 l.f.
Inclusive dates: 1856 -
Description: 2,000 photographs of
Tehama County, including logging scenes,
1900-10, and the eruption of Mount
Lassen, 1914-16; papers of U.S. Senator
Clair Engle, 1959-64, Don Smith, farm
advisor for Tehama County, 1940's-1972,
Leo McCoy, 1930, and John D. Sweeney;
and oral history recordings and tran-
scripts of Tehama County residents.

REDDING

CA624-710
Shasta College
Museum and Research Center
1065 North Old Oregon Trail
Redding CA 96001

MAILING ADDRESS:
P.O. Box 6006
Redding CA 96099

(916) 241-3523

OPEN: by appointment only
COPYING FACILITIES: yes
MATERIALS SOLICITED: Materials pertaining to the history of Shasta,
Tehama, and Trinity counties. Will
also accept materials relating to the
western United States in general.

HOLDINGS:
Total volume: 35 l.f.
Inclusive dates: 1850 -
Description: A general local history collection relating chiefly to northern California. Included are correspondence, business records, photographs, oral history
tapes, engineering drawings, and aerial
photographs, which document gold and
copper mining, logging, farming, development of towns, the eruption of Mt.
Lassen, and the lives of residents. There
are also Shasta County coroner's records,
1851-1939, and Caltrans (State highway
department) photographic negatives,
1933-68, for much of northern California.

SEE: Bean and Vane.

CA624-730
Shasta Historical Society
1911 Rio Drive
Redding CA

MAILING ADDRESS:
P.O. Box 277
Redding CA 96099

(916) 225-4155

OPEN: by appointment only
ACCESS: appointment required
COPYING FACILITIES: yes
MATERIALS SOLICITED: Documents, diaries, maps, and photographs relating to Shasta County and northern California. Will accept West Coast history materials.

HOLDINGS:
  Total volume: 10,000 items
  Inclusive dates: 1834 -
  Description: Photographs, correspondence, cemetery records, and family records relating to local history.

CA624-740
Shasta-Trinity National Forest
2400 Washington Avenue
Redding CA 96001

(916) 246-5066, 5222

OPEN: M-F 8-4:45; closed weekends and holidays
COPYING FACILITIES: no

HOLDINGS:
  Total volume: 3 c.f.
  Inclusive dates: 1940 - 1950
  Description: Forest Service pictures, largely restricted to the old Shasta Forest. Many pictures are of former employees, some of landscape and daily activities.

REDLANDS

CA628-40
A. K. Smiley Public Library
Special Collections and
Lincoln Memorial Shrine
125 West Vine Street
Redlands CA

MAILING ADDRESS:
P.O. Box 751
Redlands CA 92373

(714) 793-2201

OPEN: Tu-Sa 9-5; closed Sundays, Mondays and holidays
COPYING FACILITIES: yes
MATERIALS SOLICITED: Materials related to local history, southern California, the Civil War and Abraham Lincoln. Will also accept materials on southern California Indians.

HOLDINGS:
  Total volume: 2,500 l.f.
  Inclusive dates: 1840 -
  Description: The California and Local History Collection contains manuscripts, pamphlets, ephemeral material, photographs, maps, and oral history material relating chiefly to southern California.

The Civil War Collection is based upon Lincoln's life and the Civil War period itself, and includes manuscripts, pamphlets and photographs.

SEE: Bean and Vane; Robbins.

SEE ALSO: *A Selective Bibliography of Books, Pamphlets, Letters, Documents and Other Materials in the Lincoln Memorial Shrine* (1975); *A Selective Bibliography of Books, Pamphlets, Letters, Documents and Other Materials in the Heritage Collection of the A. K. Smiley Library* (1975).

CA628-720
San Bernardino County Museum
2024 Orange Tree Lane
Redlands CA 92373

(714) 793-6345

OPEN: Su 1-5, Tu-Sa 9-5; closed Mondays and holidays
COPYING FACILITIES: yes
MATERIALS SOLICITED: Will accept any materials relating to the history of San Bernardino County or its residents.

HOLDINGS:
  Total volume: 6,065 items
  Inclusive dates: 1858 -
  Description: Diaries, correspondence, and 6,000 photographs dealing primarily with the history of San Bernardino County, especially its mid-19th century settlers from Salt Lake City, UT.

SEE: Hinding.

REDWOOD CITY

CA636-690
Redwood City Public Library
881 Jefferson Avenue
Redwood City CA 94063

(415) 369-3738

OPEN: M-Th 10-9, F, Sa 10-5; closed Sundays and holidays
ACCESS: serious researchers
COPYING FACILITIES: yes
MATERIALS SOLICITED: Materials relating to the history of Redwood City. Will also accept materials relating to San Mateo County.

HOLDINGS:
  Total volume: 240 l.f.
  Inclusive dates: 1850 -
  Description: Materials concerning Redwood City, as well as other San Mateo County communities, including photographs, maps, 16 oral history tapes of pioneer residents, deeds, and other historical memorabilia. The collection also contains 187 notebooks of the former City Historian, including 62 on Redwood City, 20 on other communities in San Mateo County, 43 on San Francisco, and 62 on other counties and western States.

SEE: Hinding.

SEE ALSO: Indexes to some of the local history notebooks are available at the institution.

RIALTO

CA640-640
Rialto Historical Society
201-05 North Riverside Avenue
Rialto CA

MAILING ADDRESS:
P.O. Box 413
Rialto CA 92376

(714) 875-1750

OPEN: Th, Sa 2-4; closed other days
COPYING FACILITIES: no
MATERIALS SOLICITED: Maps, diaries, photographs, institutional records, audio tapes, and other items pertaining to Rialto and its residents.

HOLDINGS:
  Total volume: 6 c.f.
  Inclusive dates: 1853 -
  Description: Records of the Semi-Tropic Land & Water Company, the Mutual Land & Water Company, and other local water companies; minutes of the Rialto Cemetery Association; a historic church registry, including information about the First Christian Church, built in 1907; and photographs of early scenes in Rialto.

RICHMOND

CA644-690
Richmond Public Library
Richmond Collection
Civic Center Plaza
Richmond CA 94804

(415) 233-2348

OPEN: Su 2-5, M-W 9-9, Th-Sa 9-6; closed holidays
COPYING FACILITIES: yes
MATERIALS SOLICITED: Materials relating to Richmond and western Contra Costa County, including archives and visual and audible documents.

HOLDINGS:
  Total volume: 12 c.f.
  Inclusive dates: 1905 -
  Description: Materials relating to the history of Richmond and western Contra Costa County. Included are reminiscences of pioneers, documents on the history of the Richmond Art Center, 1936- , photographs, oral history interviews, and films on local history.

SEE: NUCMC, 1977.

SEE: Schatz; Meckler and McMullin.

RIO VISTA JUNCTION

CA650-322
Bay Area Electric Railroad Association
Western Railway Museum
5848 State Highway 12
Rio Vista Junction CA 94585

(415) 534-0071

OPEN: weekends and holidays except Christmas

COPYING FACILITIES: no
MATERIALS SOLICITED: Photographs, negatives, timetables, correspondence files, maps, and valuation reports. Will also accept other railroad materials.

HOLDINGS:
> *Total volume:* 900 sq.f.
> *Inclusive dates:* not specified
> *Description:* Railroad photographs, negatives, timetables, maps, financial reports, valuation reports, correspondence files, surveys, and vouchers.

RIVERSIDE

CA652-795
University of California, Riverside
California Museum of Photography
University of California
Riverside CA 93921

(714) 787-4787

OPEN: M-W, F, Sa 10-5, Th 10-7; closed Sundays and holidays
ACCESS: appointment required
COPYING FACILITIES: yes
MATERIALS SOLICITED: Prints, stereoviews, and other materials relating to the history of photography.

HOLDINGS:
> *Total volume:* 457,000 items
> *Inclusive dates:* 1840's -
> *Description:* Photographic prints, daguerreotypes, calotypes, and glass plate negatives covering the worldwide history of photography.

SEE: Novotny.

CA652-800
University of California, Riverside
Library
Special Collections
Riverside CA

MAILING ADDRESS:
Box 5900
Riverside CA 92517

(714) 787-3233

OPEN: M-F 9-5; closed weekends and holidays

SEE: NUCMC, 1970, 75.

Questionnaire not returned.

SACRAMENTO

CA676-110
California Office of the Secretary of State
California State Archives
1020 O Street
Sacramento CA 95814

(916) 445-4293

OPEN: M-F 7:45-5; closed weekends and holidays
COPYING FACILITIES: yes
MATERIALS SOLICITED: Records of the agencies of the California State government and of the public schools of California. Will also accept records of California county governments.

HOLDINGS:
> *Total volume:* 45,000 c.f.
> *Inclusive dates:* 1784 -
> *Description:* Manuscript records of the branches and divisions of the California State government (1849-), documenting State government policies and programs and containing information on the people, places, organizations, ideas, and activities with which those programs have dealt. Also copies of Spanish-Mexican land grant records (1784-1846), case files of county courts of several counties, and a collection of public school records from many school districts throughout the State.

SEE: Davis; Bean and Vane; Schatz; Novtny; Hinding; Armstrong; Beers - Southwest.

SEE ALSO: Joan Hoff Wilson and Lynn B. Donovan, 'Women's History: A Listing of West Coast Archival and Manuscript Sources, Part I,' *California Historical Quarterly* 55 (Spring 1976); and the following publications of the California State Archives: *The California State Archives* (1972); and *Genealogical Research in the California State Archives* (1976). Inventories to specific groups of records available from the institution.

CA676-130
California State Library
California Section
Library and Courts Building
9th and Capitol Mall
Sacramento CA

MAILING ADDRESS:
P.O. Box 2037
Sacramento CA 95809

(916) 445-4027

OPEN: M-F 8-5; closed weekends and holidays
COPYING FACILITIES: yes
MATERIALS SOLICITED: California history and materials relating to cultural, social, political, and economic aspects of California life. Will also accept material focusing on other States if it is significant and related to California.

HOLDINGS:
> *Total volume:* 1,000 l.f.
> *Inclusive dates:* 1769 -
> *Description:* A collection of manuscripts, photographs, and other materials, relating chiefly to California, especially in the pioneer period, and also containing material on Nevada. Included are diaries, reminiscences of pioneers, business records, and letters. Subjects covered include gold and silver mining, commercial and banking business, overland travel, sea voyages, transportation, and social and cultural life.

SEE: Hamer; NUCMC, 1959-62, 74, 76, 80.

SEE: Bean and Vane; Hinding; Robbins; Mehr; Beers - Southwest.

SEE ALSO: Ann Novotny, ed., *Picture Sources 3* (Special Libraries Assn., 1975); *Map Collections in the United States and Canada, A Directory* (Special Libraries Assn., 1970); Joan Hoff Wilson and Lynn B. Donovan, 'Women's History: A Listing of West Coast Archival and Manuscript Sources, Part I,' *California Historical Quarterly* 55 (Spring 1976); *Directory of Archival and Manuscript Repositories in California* (Society of California Archivists, 1975); Richard C. Davis, *North American Forest History: A Guide to Archives and Manuscripts in the United States and Canada* (Clio Books, 1977).

CA676-140
California State University, Sacramento
Library
University Archives
2000 Jed Smith Drive
Sacramento CA 95819

(916) 278-6926

OPEN: M-F 10-3 or by appointment
COPYING FACILITIES: yes
MATERIALS SOLICITED: Materials relating to California State University, Sacramento.

HOLDINGS:
> *Total volume:* 2,356 l.f.
> *Inclusive dates:* 1947 -
> *Description:* Materials relating to California State University, Sacramento, the legislative activities and career of Congressman John E. Moss, the Sacramento Peace Center, the Sacramento Citizens Committee on Local Governmental Reorganization, and Charles M. Goethe.

SEE: Hinding.

CA676-170
Diocese of Northern California
1318 27th Street
Sacramento CA

MAILING ADDRESS:
Box 161268
Sacramento CA 95816

(916) 442-6918

OPEN: by appointment only
ACCESS: by arrangement with diocesan Historiographer or Secretary
COPYING FACILITIES: yes
MATERIALS SOLICITED: Information from parishes of the Episcopal Diocese of Northern California.

HOLDINGS:
> *Total volume:* 5 file cases
> *Inclusive dates:* 1848 -
> *Description:* Historical documents having to do with the Episcopal church in the northern third of California, including records of meetings of conventions, legal documents, photographs, journals, and notebooks.

CA676-740
Sacramento History Center
Sacramento Museum and History
  Division
1930 J Street
Sacramento CA 95814

(916) 447-2958

OPEN: M-F 8-5; closed weekends and
  holidays
COPYING FACILITIES: yes
MATERIALS SOLICITED: Sacramento Valley related subjects, including manuscripts, photographs, film, and public
  records. Will also accept materials concerning California, especially the
  capital and political issues.

HOLDINGS:
  Total volume: 2,350 l.f.; 1,000,000
  items; 3,750,000 feet of film
    Inclusive dates: 1850 -
    Description: A repository for non-
  current public records from the City and
  County of Sacramento. Included are
  records from such County departments as
  the Clerk, Recorder, Assessor, Auditor,
  Treasurer, and Board of Supervisors. City
  records come from the City Clerk, Assessor, Treasurer, and City Council. The
  Museum also houses complete television
  film archives, including day logs, of local
  NBC affiliate station KCRA-TV, since its
  establishment in 1955. One million photographs relating to Sacramento, 1855- ,
  cover such topics as land reclamation,
  railroads, commercial growth and industry, residential scenes, agriculture, Sacramento River traffic, and individual and
  group portraits.

CA676-750
Sacramento Pioneer Association
1930 J Street
Sacramento CA 95814

(916) 447-2958

OPEN: M-F 8-5; closed weekends and
  holidays
COPYING FACILITIES: no

HOLDINGS:
  Total volume: 100 l.f.
    Inclusive dates: 1854 -
    Description: Letters, diaries, records
  and archives relating to the history of the
  Association and its members.

GUIDES: Cheryl Anne Lundstrom, *Report
  to the Sacramento Pioneer Association
  Regarding the Organization and Inventory of Their Archives* (1976).

CA676-770
Sutter's Fort State Historical
  Monument
2701 L Street
Sacramento CA 95816

(916) 445-4422

SEE: Hamer; NUCMC, 1965.

Questionnaire not returned.

SAINT HELENA

CA680-720
The Silverado Museum
1490 Library Lane
St. Helena CA

MAILING ADDRESS:
P.O. Box 409
St. Helena CA 94574

(707) 963-3757

OPEN: Tu-Su 12-4; closed Mondays and
  holidays
ACCESS: qualified researchers
COPYING FACILITIES: yes
MATERIALS SOLICITED: Materials relating
  to the life and works of Robert Louis
  Stevenson and his immediate circle.

HOLDINGS:
  Total volume: 10 l.f.
    Inclusive dates: 1850 -
    Description: The collection traces Ste-
  venson's entire career, through Scotland,
  England, France, New York, California,
  Hawaii, and Samoa. It includes items on
  family members and a large collection of
  letters, diaries, and manuscripts of his
  stepdaughter Isobel Field.

SEE: NUCMC, 1971.

SEE: Hinding; Robbins.

SALINAS

CA688-720
Salinas Public Library
John Steinbeck Collection
110 West San Luis
Salinas CA 93901

(408) 758-7311

OPEN: M-Th 10-9, F-Sa 10-6; closed
  Sundays and holidays
COPYING FACILITIES: yes
MATERIALS SOLICITED: Materials related
  to John Steinbeck.

HOLDINGS:
  Total volume: 2.5 l.f.
    Inclusive dates: 1902 -
    Description: A collection of correspon-
  dence, photographs, and oral history
  tapes concerning John Steinbeck, Salinas
  author and Nobel Prize winner.

SEE: Robbins.

SEE ALSO: John Gross and Lee Richard
  Hayman, *John Steinbeck: a guide to the
  collection of the Salinas Public Library*
  No. 31979.

SAN ANDREAS

CA692-130
Calaveras County Museum and
  Archives
30 North Main Street
San Andreas CA

MAILING ADDRESS:
Government Center
San Andreas CA 95249

(209) 754-4203

OPEN: M-F 8:30-5, Sa by appointment;
  closed Sundays and holidays
USER FEES: $5
COPYING FACILITIES: yes
MATERIALS SOLICITED: Materials pertaining to the history of Calaveras
  County, including diaries, genealogical
  information, correspondence, business
  and financial records, maps, photographs and oral histories.

HOLDINGS:
  Total volume: 407 l.f.
    Inclusive dates: 1850 -
    Description: Calaveras County public
  records. Non-public materials include hotel and business records, mining records,
  diaries, photographs, aerial photographs,
  insurance maps, architectural and engineering drawings, scrapbooks, and oral
  history tapes.

SAN ANSELMO

CA696-720
San Francisco Theological Seminary
Library
San Anselmo CA 94960

no telephone

SEE: Hamer; NUCMC, 1959-61.

Questionnaire not returned.

SAN BERNARDINO

CA700-720
San Bernardino County Library
741 South Lugo Street, Suite E
San Bernardino CA

MAILING ADDRESS:
104 West Fourth Street
San Bernardino CA 92415

(714) 383-1734

OPEN: by appointment Tu, F 9-4; closed
  other days
COPYING FACILITIES: yes
MATERIALS SOLICITED: Materials relating
  to the history of San Bernardino County
  and California.

HOLDINGS:
  Total volume: 18 l.f.
    Inclusive dates: 1855 -
    Description: Materials relating primar-
  ily to the history of San Bernardino
  County. Included are an unpublished
  Federal Writers' Project history of the
  County; 19th century letters; a ferryman's
  diary, 1855-58; County school histories

and a student register for the Sturges Academy of San Bernardino, 1883-88.

Photostats of early land grants; unpublished histories of local communities; maps; business records of the Italian Vineyard Company and other area firms; photographs; and oral history tapes.

SEE: Hamer; NUCMC, 1968.

SEE: Davis; Bean and Vane.

CA700-760
San Bernardino Public Library
401 North Arrowhead
San Bernardino CA 92401

(714) 383-5277

OPEN: M-Th 9-9, F, Sa 9-6, Su 1-5; closed holidays
COPYING FACILITIES: yes
MATERIALS SOLICITED: San Bernardino city and county history. Will also accept southern California history.

HOLDINGS:
Total volume: 30 l.f.
Inclusive dates: 1860's -
Description: Materials pertaining to the city and county of San Bernardino, including city records and 500 photographs dating as early as the 1860's.

SEE: Bean and Vane.

SAN BRUNO

CA704-560
National Archives and Records Administration
Federal Archives and Records Center
Archives Branch
1000 Commodore Drive
San Bruno CA 94066

(415) 876-9009, 9018

OPEN: M-F 7:45-4:15; closed weekends and holidays
ACCESS: Records are open, subject to Federal agency restrictions and restrictions based upon current legislation relevant to confidentiality and security classification. See General Information Leaflet No. 2, 'Regulations for the Public Use of Records in the National Archives.'
COPYING FACILITIES: yes
MATERIALS SOLICITED: Records of Federal agencies in northern California, Nevada (except Clark County), Hawaii, and American possessions in the Pacific Ocean area.

HOLDINGS:
Total volume: 9,800 c.f.
Inclusive dates: 1850 - 1960
Description: Records of Federal agencies in northern California, Nevada, Hawaii, and the Pacific Ocean area. Of particular interest are the records of the Government of American Samoa, the Federal courts, and the Bureau of Customs.

SEE: Hamer (listed under South San Francisco).

SEE: Allard, Crawley, and Edmison; Bean and Vane; Hinding; Beers - Southwest; Armstrong.

SEE ALSO: Joan Hoff Wilson and Lynn B. Donovan, 'Women's History: A Listing of West Coast Archival and Manuscript Sources, Part I,' *California Historical Quarterly* 55 (Spring 1976); Richard C. Davis, *North American Forest History: A Guide to Archives and Manuscripts in the United States and Canada* (Clio Books, 1977).

SAN DIEGO

CA712-120
Citizens United for Racial Equality
San Diego CA 92182

(619) 265-5715

OPEN: by appointment only
COPYING FACILITIES: no

HOLDINGS:
Total volume: 8 file drawers
Inclusive dates: 1968 -
Description: Correspondence, minutes, financial records, etc., relating to the activities of the organization, primarily in the areas of school desegregation, housing and equal employment opportunities.

Records transferred to San Diego University, San Diego Historical Research Center, San Diego CA 92182.

CA712-570
Naval Training Center
Historical Museum
San Diego CA 92133

(619) 225-4011

OPEN: M-F 8-4; closed weekends and holidays
COPYING FACILITIES: yes

HOLDINGS:
Total volume: 1 item
Inclusive dates: 1877
Description: The 'forwarding book' of Captain Edward Simpson during the cruise of the *U.S.S. Omaha* along the western coast of the Americas. Enclosures include position reports and watercolor drawings of ports visited.

CA712-630
Photophile
2311 Kettner Blvd.
San Diego CA 92101

(619) 234-4431

OPEN: M-F by appointment only; closed weekends and holidays
ACCESS: Educational, editorial, or commercial use only.
COPYING FACILITIES: no
MATERIALS SOLICITED: Color transparencies of contemporary subject matter.

HOLDINGS:
Total volume: 200,000 items
Inclusive dates: 1960 -
Description: Color transparencies of national and international subjects relating to travel, people, industry, nature, and recreation.

SEE ALSO: Ann Novotny, ed., *Picture Sources 3* (Special Libraries Assn., 1975).

CA712-700
San Diego County Law Library
1105 Front Street
San Diego CA 92101

(619) 236-2307

OPEN: M-Th 8-8, F 8-5, Sa, Su noon-4; closed holidays
COPYING FACILITIES: yes
MATERIALS SOLICITED: Legal history materials relating to San Diego County and California. Will also accept other Anglo-American legal history materials.

HOLDINGS:
Total volume: 30 l.f.
Inclusive dates: 1850 - 1964
Description: Memorabilia of early San Diego lawyers and judges; materials relating to local courts, the bar association, and the legal secretaries' association; original court records for 13 trials and probates, 1850-1910; scrapbooks of early San Diego lawyers, including letters and photographs; local court judgment books, 1853-84; photographs of 152 lawyers and judges of San Diego; photographs and pictures of local legal buildings; and a 4-volume diary, 1885-1917.

SEE: Novotny.

CA712-708
San Diego Historical Society
Research Archives
1649 El Prado
San Diego CA

MAILING ADDRESS:
P.O. Box 81825
San Diego CA 92138

(619) 232-6203

OPEN: Tu-F 10-4, Sa noon-4; closed Sundays, Mondays, and holidays
USER FEES: no charge to members; research card or fee for nonmembers
ACCESS: adults only
COPYING FACILITIES: yes
MATERIALS SOLICITED: Material relating to the history of San Diego County. Will also accept material on California, the southwestern United States, and Baja California, when they involve events or individuals relating to the history of San Diego.

HOLDINGS:
Total volume: 750 c.f.; 700 l.f.
Inclusive dates: 1767 -
Description: Materials relating chiefly to San Diego County, such as manuscripts, including correspondence, diaries, journals, account books, and business, financial, and government records; archival records of institutions and organizations; maps; architectural drawings, blueprints, and photographs; oral history tapes and transcripts; and microfilm copies of unpublished theses and manuscript material not available locally.

The archival collection contains records of the City of San Diego, the County of San Diego, and the various courts of San Diego. The photo collection contains over 150,000 images.

SEE: Hamer (as Junipero Serra Museum); NUCMC, 1962, 71-72.

SEE: Mehr; Beers - Southwest; Bean and Vane; Hinding.

SEE ALSO: Ann Novotny, ed., *Picture Sources 3* (Special Libraries Assn., 1975); Joan Hoff Wilson and Lynn B. Donovan, 'Women's History: A Listing of West Coast Archival and Manuscript Sources, Part I,' *California Historical Quarterly* 55 (Spring 1976).

CA712-713
San Diego Museum of Man
Photo Archives and Archaeological Archives
1350 El Prado
San Diego CA 92101

(619) 239-2001

OPEN: M-F 8:30-2:30; closed weekends and holidays
ACCESS: advance arrrangements required
COPYING FACILITIES: yes
MATERIALS SOLICITED: Ethnographic photographic materials, oral histories, recordings, and manuscripts relating to the Eskimo and North and South American Indian cultures, particularly those of the West, as well as archaeological site data and photographs from the American Southwest and the Channel Islands. Will also accept ethnographic materials relating to other native cultures.

HOLDINGS:
Total volume: 30,000 items; additional materials
Inclusive dates: 1840's -
Description: Ethnographic historical photographs of western American Indian, Eskimo, and Mexican and South American Indian cultures. Included are glass positives of Eskimos by F. H. Nowell, stereo cards of the aftermath of the Boxer Rebellion, and a journal and photograph album of San Diego County Indians by Constance Goddard Dubois. Also held are records of 4,200 archaeological sites in the Southwest and Channel Islands, many relating to work of Malcolm J. Rogers.

SEE: Bean and Vane.

CA712-720
San Diego Public Library
California Room
820 E Street
San Diego CA 92101

(619) 236-5834

OPEN: M-Th 10-9, F 9:30-5:30, Sa 9-5:30; closed Sundays and holidays
COPYING FACILITIES: yes
MATERIALS SOLICITED: San Diego city records; personal and business papers of San Diego city and County pioneers and persons of prominence; and papers of civic and cultural groups. Will also accept materials pertaining to music and the theater.

HOLDINGS:
Total volume: 210 c.f.; 250 l.f.
Inclusive dates: 1775 -
Description: A collection of manuscripts, financial and other records, and papers of civic leaders relating chiefly to San Diego city and County. Included are

diaries, letters, personal documents, photographs, and architectural drawings.

SEE: Hamer; NUCMC, 1959-61, 70.

SEE: Mehr; Bean and Vane; Hinding.

SEE ALSO: *Map Collections in the United States and Canada, A Directory* (Special Libraries Assn., 1970); Ann Novotny, ed., *Picture Sources 3* (Special Libraries Assn., 1975); Walter Schatz, ed., *Directory of Afro-American Resources* (Bowker, 1970); Joan Hoff Wilson and Lynn B. Donovan, 'Women's History: A Listing of West Coast Archival and Manuscript Sources, Part I,' *California Historical Quarterly* 55 (Spring 1976).

CA712-726
San Diego Society of Natural History
Natural History Museum
Library
San Diego CA

MAILING ADDRESS:
P.O. Box 1390
San Diego CA 92112

(619) 232-3821

OPEN: M-F 8-4:30; closed weekends and holidays
COPYING FACILITIES: yes
MATERIALS SOLICITED: Natural history, paleontology, and geology of the Southwest and Mexico. Will also accept natural history, paleontology, geology, marine invertebrate studies, herpetology, entomology, and botany throughout the world.

HOLDINGS:
Total volume: 60,000 vols.
Inclusive dates: 19th century -
Description: Natural history and other materials concerning the Southwest and Baja California, including field notes and diaries of curators who worked at the Natural History Museum, as well as papers, letters, manuscripts, and scrapbooks relating to the development of the Museum.

SEE: Hamer; NUCMC, 1968.

CA712-743
San Diego State University
Library
Map Collection
San Diego CA 92182-0511

(619) 265-5650

OPEN: M-F 8-4:30; closed weekends and holidays
COPYING FACILITIES: no
HOLDINGS:
Total volume: 227 items
Inclusive dates: 1939 - 1967
Description: 167 aerial photographs, mainly of San Diego County, 1939-55; 14 index mosaics of San Diego County, 1953; and 46 incomplete index mosaics of counties in California, Arizona, Colorado, North Dakota, Oregon, Texas, Utah, and Washington, produced during the 1950's.

CA712-750
San Diego State University
Library
Center for Regional History
San Diego CA 92182

(619) 265-5751

OPEN: M-F 9-4:30; closed weekends and holidays
COPYING FACILITIES: yes
MATERIALS SOLICITED: Materials relating to San Diego, including business, labor, cultural, religious, social service agency, personal, and military records.

HOLDINGS:
Total volume: 900 l.f.
Inclusive dates: 1887 -
Description: A manuscript and photograph collection relating primarily to the urban development of San Diego in the 20th century. Included are records of organizations and businesses, papers of individuals, and unpublished diaries and journals documenting migration and demographic history, the growth of organized labor, economic development, cultural dynamics, social evolution, the experiences of religious groups, Mexican-American border interactions, and the influence and activities of the military.
Includes records of Citizens United for Racial Equality, listed separately in 1978 *Directory*.

GUIDES: Stephen A. Colston, comp., *A Guide to the Collection of the San Diego History Research Center* (San Diego State Univ. Library, 1978).

CA712-810
University of San Diego
James S. Copley Library
Alcala Park
San Diego CA 92110

(714) 291-6480, Ext. 4315

OPEN: M-F 9-4; closed weekends and holidays
ACCESS: upon written request
COPYING FACILITIES: yes

HOLDINGS:
Total volume: 175 items
Inclusive dates: 1920 - 1970
Description: A collection of material relating to Emmett Culligan and the establishment and operation of the Culligan Water Company. Includes printed and manuscript copies of books and papers, speeches, items of a personal nature and documents.

SEE: Bean and Vane; Robbins.

SAN FRANCISCO

CA720-10
African-American Historical and Cultural Society, San Francisco
Building C-165
Fort Mason Center
San Francisco CA 94123

(415) 441-0640

OPEN: Tu-Sa 10-6; closed Sundays, Mondays, and holidays

COPYING FACILITIES: yes
MATERIALS SOLICITED: Materials pertaining to African-Americans and people of African descent in the West. Will also accept other materials on African-American history and culture.

HOLDINGS:
Total volume: 20 c.f.
Inclusive dates: 1858 - 1978
Description: Materials pertaining to African-American history in California and the western United States, including records of the NAACP Educational Committee, 1958-68, papers of the Cape Verde Club, photographs of blacks in the West, civil rights photographs, 1950-70, and 24 oral history interviews.

CA720-104

Bank of America NT&SA
Bank of America Archives 3218
315 Montgomery Street
San Francisco CA

MAILING ADDRESS:
P.O. Box 37000
San Francisco CA 94012

(415) 622-4997

OPEN: M-F 8:30-4:30; closed weekends and holidays
ACCESS: restricted to properly accredited researchers; some records restricted
COPYING FACILITIES: yes
MATERIALS SOLICITED: All subject areas relating to the Bank, with particular emphasis on the Bank's management and major policy decisions.

HOLDINGS:
Total volume: 1,910 l.f.
Inclusive dates: 1862 -
Description: 1,200 volumes of minute books, stock journals, cancelled stock certificates, ledgers, bylaws and articles of incorporation of banks acquired by Bank of America; 19 l.f. of photographs taken at ceremonies, events, and occasions related to bank activities.
Approximately 670 l.f. of evaluated records consisting of correspondence files of executives of the Bank and heads of selected administrative departments, documenting the founding, growth, and development of the Bank and its overall management at the policy-making level.

SEE ALSO: California Historical Society, *Inventory of Historical Collections in San Francisco*; O. G. Wilson, 'Bank of America's Archival Program,' *American Archivist* 29 (Jan. 1966). Copies of various inventories available at the institution.

CA720-148

California Academy of Sciences
Library
Golden Gate Park
San Francisco CA 94118

no telephone

SEE: Hamer.

Questionnaire not returned.

CA720-161

California Department of Conservation
Division of Mines and Geology
Library
Room 2022
Ferry Building
San Francisco CA 94111

no telephone

OPEN: M-F 8-5; closed weekends and holidays
COPYING FACILITIES: yes
MATERIALS SOLICITED: Mining, geology, and natural hazards in California.

HOLDINGS:
Total volume: 50 l.f.
Inclusive dates: 1850 -
Description: Open file reports of geologists concerning geology, geophysics, and geologic hazards in California.

CA720-180

California Historical Society
Library
2099 Pacific Avenue
San Francisco CA

MAILING ADDRESS:
2090 Jackson Street
San Francisco CA 94109

(415) 567-1848

OPEN: W-Sa 10-4; closed other days and holidays
USER FEES: one dollar for non-members, fifty cents for students
COPYING FACILITIES: yes
MATERIALS SOLICITED: Materials relating to women, labor history, artists, literary figures, city and state politics and development, San Francisco businesses, neighborhood associations, and civic, cultural, and social organizations. Will also accept papers relating to individuals and materials focusing on California history with emphasis on San Francisco.

HOLDINGS:
Total volume: 4,000 collections
Inclusive dates: 1767 -
Description: Manuscripts relating to the history of California, including diaries, letters, account books, maps, sketches, and records of politicians, businesspersons, literary figures, and philanthropists. Organization records include those of the League of Women Voters, the San Francisco Young Men's Christian Association, and the San Francisco Chamber of Commerce. There are also materials relating to the Mexican War of 1846-47, the 1849 gold rush and mining, and the history of western printing and publishing.

SEE: Hamer; NUCMC, 1971, 75.

SEE: Schatz; Krichmar; Novotny; Bean and Vane; Allard, Crawley, and Edmison; Hinding; Robbins; Armstrong; Beers - Southwest.

SEE ALSO: Bernice M. Nece, 'The Kirsten Flagstad Memorial Collection,' *American Archivist* 30 (July 1967); Richard C. Davis, *North American Forest History: A Guide to Archives and Manuscripts in the United States and Canada* (Clio Books, 1977); and the following articles by Lynn B. Donovan in the *California Historical Quarterly*: 'Library Resources: CHS Collections on the History of Women in California,' 52 (Spring 1973); with Linda Chiswick, 'Day-by-Day Records: Diaries from the CHS Library,' 54 and 56 (Winter 1975 and Spring 1977); and, with Joan Hoff Wilson, 'Women's History: A Listing of West Coast Archival and Manuscript Sources, Part I,' 55 (Spring 1976).

CA720-203

California State Library
Sutro Branch
480 Winston Drive
San Francisco CA 94132

(415) 731-4477

SEE: Hamer; NUCMC, 1959-62.

Questionnaire not returned.

CA720-220

Chinese Historical Society of America
17 Adler Place
San Francisco CA 94133

(415) 391-1188

OPEN: Tu-Sa 1-5; closed Sundays, Mondays, and holidays
COPYING FACILITIES: no
MATERIALS SOLICITED: Materials pertaining to the Chinese in America.

HOLDINGS:
Total volume: not specified
Inclusive dates: late 19th century -
Description: Materials relating to the Chinese in America, including oral history tapes, newspaper clippings, photographs and manuscripts. Special areas of interest include records of the Chinatown Factfinding Committee, Ah Louis family letters, the Chinese Constitutionalist Party archives, and photographs of early 20th century Chinese in America.

CA720-307

Forest Service
Recreation Management Staff
Cultural Resource Management
Research and Archives Center
630 Sansome Street
San Francisco CA 94111

no telephone

OPEN: M-F 8-4; closed weekends and holidays
COPYING FACILITIES: yes
MATERIALS SOLICITED: Manuscripts, visual and audible documents, and non-current machine-readable records pertaining to the history of California Indians, and Euro-American, Chinese and other cultural and ethnic groups within National Forests in California, 1800 to the present.

HOLDINGS:

Total volume: 1,700 items

Inclusive dates: 1800 -

Description: Manuscripts, records and oral history material concerned primarily with the early history of 17 National Forests in California, particularly with the history of railroad and other types of logging, and mining, grazing, forestry, recreation, and subsistence uses.

CA720-316

The Foundation for San Francisco's Architectural Heritage
2007 Franklin Street
San Francisco CA 94109

(415) 441-3000

OPEN: by appointment only; closed weekends and holidays
ACCESS: advance arrangements required
COPYING FACILITIES: yes
MATERIALS SOLICITED: Materials pertaining to historic buildings in San Francisco.

HOLDINGS:

Total volume: 3 file cabinets

Inclusive dates: 1972 -

Description: Research files and photographs pertaining to a survey and evaluation of historic architecture in downtown San Francisco, as well as materials pertaining to the architectural history of San Francisco in general, including recordings of lectures on San Francisco Bay region architecture.

CA720-356

International Longshoremen's and Warehousemen's Union
Anne Rand Research Library
1188 Franklin Street
San Francisco CA 94109

(415) 775-0533

OPEN: M-F 9-5; closed weekends and holidays
ACCESS: advance approval required
COPYING FACILITIES: yes
MATERIALS SOLICITED: Materials that pertain to operations and activities of the ILWU.

HOLDINGS:

Total volume: 280 l.f.; 350 file drawers

Inclusive dates: 1934 -

Description: The ILWU Archives include major collective bargaining agreements; complete records of major negotiations, with research exhibits; arbitration awards and hearings; records of International Executive Board meetings; correspondence; some materials from locals; 'ILWU History' file organized by subject; and materials from deportation trials of Harry R. Bridges. Three additional collections record ILWU participation in maritime committees: the Maritime Federation of the Pacific archives, the Committee for Maritime Unity archives, and the Pacific Coast Maritime Industry Board archives.

SEE ALSO: Paul Lewinson and Morris Rieger, 'Labor Union Records in the United States,' *American Archivist* 25 (Jan. 1962).

CA720-365

Japanese American Citizens League
National Headquarters
1765 Sutter Street
San Francisco CA 94115

(415) 921-5225

OPEN: M-F 9-5; closed weekends and holidays
ACCESS: members, scholars, and students; advance arrangements required
COPYING FACILITIES: yes
MATERIALS SOLICITED: Materials pertaining to Japanese-American history.

HOLDINGS:

Total volume: not specified

Inclusive dates: 1929 -

Description: Non-current records of the national organization of the Japanese American Citizens League; photographs and films relating to Japanese-American immigration, the anti-Japanese movement from 1900 to 1946, World War II evacuation and relocation, 1942-46, and postwar resettlement and progress.

CA720-405

Lutheran Church-Missouri Synod
California-Nevada-Hawaii District
465 Woolsey Street
San Francisco CA 94134

(415) 468-2336

OPEN: by appointment only
COPYING FACILITIES: yes
MATERIALS SOLICITED: Materials pertinent to the history of the California and Nevada District of the Lutheran Church-Missouri Synod.

HOLDINGS:

Total volume: 40 l.f.

Inclusive dates: 1860 -

Description: Documents pertaining to the history of the California-Nevada-Hawaii District of the Lutheran Church-Missouri Synod.

CA720-485

National Maritime Museum
J. Porter Shaw Library
Foot of Polk Street
San Francisco CA 94109

(415) 556-3002

OPEN: winter M-F 10-5, summer M-F 10-6
MATERIALS SOLICITED: West Coast and Pacific Basin maritime history. Will also accept materials related to 19th and early 20th century sail and steam shipping and shipbuilding in the continental U.S.

HOLDINGS:

Total volume: 12,000 vols.; 400 logbooks; 700 ship plans

Inclusive dates: 1849 - 1940

Description: World-wide maritime history, including shoreside technology, focusing on commercial sail and steam shipping and shipbuilding on the Pacific Coast of the United States and in the Pacific Basin. Subjects include shipbuilding, whaling, biography, vessel histories, shipboard life, and local history.

The collection includes more than 100,000 historical photographs of West Coast maritime activity from 1848 to 1940, over 200 oral history tapes, 650 charts and maps, 2,085 groupings of ephemera, and more than 75 feet of archives.

SEE: Novotny.

CA720-546

Pacific Telephone and Telegraph Company
Library
140 New Montgomery Street
San Francisco CA 94105

no telephone

SEE: Hamer.

Questionnaire not returned.

CA720-548

Poetry Center
American Poetry Archives
1600 Holloway
San Francisco CA 94132

(415) 469-1056, 2227

OPEN: M-W 10-5, Th 9-noon; closed other days and holidays
ACCESS: advance arrangements required
COPYING FACILITIES: no
MATERIALS SOLICITED: Audio and video recordings of poetry readings, talks, and lectures by poets and fiction writers.

HOLDINGS:

Total volume: 1,860 items

Inclusive dates: 1954 -

Description: Audio and video collections of modern and contemporary poetry, primarily in English.

CA720-550

Presidio Army Museum
Corner of Lincoln and Funston
San Francisco CA 94129-5502

(415) 561-3319

OPEN: Tu-Su 10-4; closed Mondays and holidays
ACCESS: by appointment only
COPYING FACILITIES: no
MATERIALS SOLICITED: Materials relating to the military history of California. Will also accept materials relating to United States military history.

HOLDINGS:

Total volume: 4 file cabinets; 5,010 items

Inclusive dates: 1776 -

Description: A collection of correspondence, records, diaries, logbooks, photographs, and oral history tapes relating to the history of the Presidio of San Francisco, as well as the history of San Francisco and California in general, with emphasis on military history.

CA720-579
Roman Catholic Archdiocese of San
  Francisco
Chancery Archives
445 Church Street
San Francisco CA 94114

MAILING ADDRESS:
P.O. Box 1799
Colma CA 94014

(415) 994-5211

OPEN: M, W 9-4; closed weekends,
  holidays, and holy days
ACCESS: a written request, addressed to
  the Chancellor's Office, is required
COPYING FACILITIES: yes
MATERIALS SOLICITED: All manuscript
  and photographic materials relating to
  the Archdiocese including its religious
  orders and its bishops and priests. Will
  also accept similar materials pertaining
  to the Roman Catholic church in the
  western United States.

HOLDINGS:
    Total volume: 375 vols.; 118 boxes
    Inclusive dates: 1770 - 1950
    Description: Personal papers of
  laypersons and missionaries of upper and
  Baja California, as well as records of baptisms, deaths, and marriages, and papers
  regarding the Pious Fund, all pre-dating
  1840. Records since 1840 relate to such
  topics as episcopal visitations, parish
  boundaries, and council meetings.

SEE: Beers - Southwest.

SEE ALSO: Francis J. Weber, 'The San
  Francisco Chancery Archives,' The
  Americas 20 (Jan. 1964).

CA720-623
San Francisco Conservatory of Music
Library
1201 Ortega Street
San Francisco CA 94122

(415) 564-8086

OPEN: M-Th 9-9, F 9-5, Sa 9-3; closed
  Sundays and holidays; shorter hours
  during school vacations
COPYING FACILITIES: yes
MATERIALS SOLICITED: Manuscripts of
  living American composers.

HOLDINGS:
    Total volume: not specified
    Inclusive dates: 1907 -
    Description: A small collection which
  includes correspondence of Ada Clement,
  Lillian Hodghead, Harold Bauer and
  Ernst Bloch. There are also lecture notes
  of Bloch and Josef Lhevinne, some photographs, and a few manuscripts and
  sketches.

CA720-675
San Francisco Public Library
San Francisco Room
Civic Center
San Francisco CA 94102

(415) 558-3949, 3191

OPEN: M, F, Sa 10-6, Tu-Th 10-9, Su
  1-5; closed holidays
COPYING FACILITIES: yes

MATERIALS SOLICITED: San Francisco
  and California history, with emphasis
  on municipal government documents
  and papers of mayors. Will also accept
  materials pertaining to local businesses,
  associations, and community groups.

HOLDINGS:
    Total volume: 1,900 boxes
    Inclusive dates: 1845 -
    Description: Manuscripts, maps, pho-
  tographs, aerial photographs, building
  plans, ethnic collections, city and county
  records dating from 1849 to 1906, and
  business and shipping papers, from the
  San Francisco area, and papers relating to
  the Indian occupation of Alcatraz Island.

SEE: NUCMC, 1959-62.

SEE: Bean and Vane; Hinding; Robbins.

SEE ALSO: Andrea Hinding and Rosemary
  Richardson, comps., Archival and
  Manuscript Resources for the Study of
  Women's History: A Beginning (Univ.
  of Minnesota Libraries, Social Welfare
  History Archives, 1972); Joan Hoff
  Wilson and Lynn B. Donovan,
  'Women's History: A Listing of West
  Coast Archival and Manuscript
  Sources, Part I,' California Historical
  Quarterly 55 (Spring 1976); Walter
  Schatz, ed., Directory of Afro-American
  Resources (Bowker, 1970); Ann
  Novotny, ed., Picture Sources 3 (Special
  Libraries Assn., 1975).

CA720-739
Sisters of the Presentation of the
  Blessed Virgin Mary
Presentation Archives
2340 Turk Blvd.
San Francisco CA 94118

(415) 751-0406

OPEN: by appointment only
COPYING FACILITIES: yes
MATERIALS SOLICITED: Materials relating
  to the Sisters of the Presentation of the
  Blessed Virgin Mary.

HOLDINGS:
    Total volume: 38 boxes; 5 file
  cabinets; 50 vols.
    Inclusive dates: 1854 -
    Description: Records of the education-
  al, pastoral, and social ministries of the
  Sisters of the Presentation in Washington,
  California, New Mexico, Mexico, and
  Guatemala. Included are annals, account
  books, financial records, genealogical
  source data, unpublished memoirs and
  histories, photographs, and audio-visual
  materials.

CA720-746
Society of California Pioneers
Library
456 McAllister Street
San Francisco CA 94102

(415) 861-5278

OPEN: M-F 1-4; closed weekends,
  holidays, and July
COPYING FACILITIES: yes
MATERIALS SOLICITED: Early California
  history, particularly the pre-1869 period, with emphasis on San Francisco.

Will also accept California history up
to 1918.

HOLDINGS:
    Total volume: not specified
    Inclusive dates: 1837 - 1918
    Description: Photographs of early Cali-
  fornia and San Francisco; manuscript collections including many pioneer diaries,
  letters, and ranch and business records;
  scrapbooks; materials on California mining operations; and records of Society
  members including autobiographies, ora-
  tions, and obituaries.

SEE: Hamer; NUCMC, 1959-61, 75.

SEE: Novotny; Beers-Southwest.

CA720-798
Strybing Arboretum Society
Helen Crocker Russell Library
9th Avenue at Lincoln Way
San Francisco CA 94122

(415) 661-1514

OPEN: daily 10-4; closed holidays
COPYING FACILITIES: yes
MATERIALS SOLICITED: History of Gold-
  en Gate Park, San Francisco. Will also
  accept early California horticultural
  manuscripts.

HOLDINGS:
    Total volume: 6 l.f.
    Inclusive dates: 1870 - 1910
    Description: The William Hammond
  Hall archives includes letters and business
  and financial records for the years
  1870-80. The G. T. Lane archives consists of correspondence and lecture manuscripts on economic botany in India.

SEE: Novotny.

CA720-886
University of California, San
  Francisco
The Library
Oriental Medicine Division
513 Parnassus Avenue
San Francisco CA 94143

(415) 666-2334

OPEN: M-F 8:30-4:30; closed weekends
  and University holidays
ACCESS: qualified users
COPYING FACILITIES: yes
MATERIALS SOLICITED: Materials related
  to Chinese, Japanese, or Korean medicine, and also to the influence and development of Western medicine in
  those countries.

HOLDINGS:
    Total volume: 674 vols.
    Inclusive dates: 1500 - 1867
    Description: Materials of Japanese ori-
  gin, written in Japanese or Chinese, relating chiefly to Chinese or Japanese medicine, especially methods of diagnosis,
  treatments, prescriptions for human be-
  ings and for horses, medical schools, and
  education. Included are unpublished
  books, oral instructions, notes, letters,
  Buddhist sutras, anatomical and technical
  drawings, acupuncture and moxibustion
  charts, and drawings of medicinal herbs
  and materia medica.
      Also includes materials of Chinese ori-
  gin.

CA720-890

University of California, San
Francisco
The Library
Special Collections: Archives
257 Medical Sciences Building
San Francisco CA 94143

(415) 666-2334

OPEN: M-F 8:30-5; closed weekends and
holidays
ACCESS: prior arrangement requested;
identification required
COPYING FACILITIES: yes
MATERIALS SOLICITED: Materials of historical significance related specifically
to the development of the University
of California's San Francisco campus
and its personnel. Will also accept photographs, manuscripts, memorabilia,
and biographical information relating
to the University of California at San
Francisco and its personnel.

HOLDINGS:
Total volume: 1,034 l.f.
Inclusive dates: 1864 -
Description: Records of the University
of California at San Francisco. Included
are faculty minutes, financial records,
matriculation records for the schools of
medicine, dentistry and pharmacy; papers
and correspondence of faculty and alumni; photographs of the campus and campus personnel; oral history tapes; and motion pictures.

SEE: Hamer (as University of California
Medical Center Library).

SEE: Hinding.

SEE ALSO: Joan Hoff Wilson and Lynn B.
Donovan, 'Women's History: A Listing
of West Coast Archival and Manuscript
Sources, Part II,' California Historical
Quarterly 55 Summer 1976).

CA720-894

University of California, San
Francisco
The Library
Special Collections: History
257 Medical Sciences Building
San Francisco CA 94143

(415) 666-2334

OPEN: M-F 8-5; closed weekends and
University holidays
ACCESS: University of California
students, faculty, and employees, and
San Francisco Bay area health
professionals; certain other categories
of users upon approval of the Librarian
COPYING FACILITIES: yes
MATERIALS SOLICITED: Manuscripts
dealing with California health sciences,
diaries of physicians and nurses, William Osler, anesthesia, and homeopathy. Will also accept manuscripts and
letters of general interest in the history
of the health sciences.

HOLDINGS:
Total volume: 1,200 items
Inclusive dates: 15th century -
Description: A manuscript collection
relating chiefly to California and San
Francisco area health science individuals
and groups in the medical, dental, pharmaceutical, nursing and homeopathic
fields. Included are lecture notebooks of
medical students, chiefly from the 19th
century; pharmacy prescription files and
formularies; oral histories relating to dentistry; papers and minutes of San Francisco area health science groups; manuscript medical articles; and correspondence relating to anesthesia and William
Osler.
There are also more than 1,000 letters
of noted physicians and scientists from
the first half of the 20th century, and
miscellaneous Arabic, Latin, and Mexican
manuscripts.

SEE: Hamer (as University of California
Medical Center Library).

SEE ALSO: Alan M. Meckler and Ruth
McMullin, comps., Oral History Collections (Bowker, 1975); 'Oral History
Project in San Francisco,' Bulletin of
the History of Dentistry 23 (Dec.
1975).

CA720-910

University of San Francisco
Richard A. Gleeson Library
Special Collections Department
San Francisco CA 94117

(415) 666-6686

OPEN: M-W, F 9-5; Th 1-9:30; closed
weekends and holidays
COPYING FACILITIES: yes
MATERIALS SOLICITED: Charles Carroll
of Carrollton, Eric Gill, Robert Graves,
Richard Le Gallienne, and California.
Will also accept other materials per-
tinent to the collections.

HOLDINGS:
Total volume: 950 items; 15 boxes
Inclusive dates: 1679 -
Description: Literary manuscripts and
letters of Eric Gill, Robert Graves, and
Richard Le Gallienne; historical manuscripts relating to Charles Carroll of
Carrollton, U.S. women's suffrage, San
Francisco mayors Adolph Sutro and Roger D. Lapham, and the Spanish colonization of Mexico and Baja California,
1679-1846. Also held are the archives of
the University of San Francisco, 1855- ,
and materials concerning the American
period of Roman Catholicism in California, 1846- .

SEE: Hamer; NUCMC, 1968.

SEE: Bean and Vane.

CA720-955

Utah International Inc.
Archives
550 California Street
San Francisco CA 94104

(415) 981-1515

OPEN: by appointment only
ACCESS: qualified researchers;
appointment required

COPYING FACILITIES: yes
MATERIALS SOLICITED: Materials relating
to the history of the corporation.

HOLDINGS:
Total volume: 120 l.f.
Inclusive dates: 1900 -
Description: Photographs, correspondence, memorandums, ledgers, internal
reports, and other materials documenting
the corporation's development from a
construction firm to a multinational mining firm. Included are photographs of the
company's railroad, dam, and industrial
construction projects, primarily in the
western United States, 1920-60.

CA720-960

Wells Fargo Bank
Archives, History Room, Research
Library
475 Sansome Street
San Francisco CA 9411 1

(415) 396-4157, 3209

OPEN: M-F 10-3; closed weekends and
holidays
ACCESS: by prior arrangement; history
room is open to public
COPYING FACILITIES: no
MATERIALS SOLICITED: Records and oth-
er materials generated by Wells Fargo
Bank and its subsidiaries and affiliates.
Will also accept other materials per-
taining to the Bank.

HOLDINGS:
Total volume: 2,500 l.f.
Inclusive dates: 1852 -
Description: Records of Wells Fargo
Bank and contributing organizations, covering banking and financial history in the
western United States. The collection includes records of predecessor banks, financial journals, executive correspondence, photographs, tapes, film, and
records of express operations,
1850's-1950's.
Also materials of general interest in
Western history, such as banking, express-
ing, mining, and stagecoaches.

CA720-980

Wine Institute
165 Post Street
San Francisco CA 94108

(415) 986-0878

OPEN: M-F 9-5; closed weekends and
holidays
ACCESS: by appointment, qualified
individuals only
COPYING FACILITIES: no

HOLDINGS:
Total volume: 5,000 items
Inclusive dates: mid-1800's -
Description: Photographs and clippings
relating to the California wine industry.

SEE ALSO: Ann Novotny, ed., Picture
Sources 3 (Special Libraries Assn.,
1975).

The clipping file has been microfilmed and deposited in the library of
the University of California at Davis.

SAN GABRIEL

CA724-730
San Gabriel Mission Church
Archives
537 West Mission Drive
San Gabriel CA 91776

(818) 282-5191

OPEN: daily 9-4; closed Thanksgiving, Christmas, Easter, and Mondays, Sept.-May
COPYING FACILITIES: yes
MATERIALS SOLICITED: Current records of baptisms, marriages, deaths, and confirmations.

HOLDINGS:
Total volume: 50 vols.
Inclusive dates: 1771 -
Description: Baptismal, confirmation, marriage and death records, dating from the 1770's; an index of neophytes, 1825; and one volume of biannual reports, 1773-1832.

SEE: Bean and Vane; Hinding; Beers - Southwest.

SAN JOSE

CA728-730
San Jose Historical Museum
635 Phelan Avenue
San Jose CA 95112

(408) 287-2290

OPEN: M-F 8:30-4:30; closed weekends and holidays
ACCESS: by prior arrangement
COPYING FACILITIES: yes
MATERIALS SOLICITED: Materials relating to the history of the Santa Clara Valley.

HOLDINGS:
Total volume: 1,300 l.f.
Inclusive dates: 1792 -
Description: A collection relating to the social, economic, and political history of the Santa Clara Valley. Included are records of early Spanish settlers, 1792-1859, materials relating to American settlers, accounts and records of businesses and local government, maps, and a photograph collection relating to Valley life and institutions.

SEE: Beers - Southwest

CA728-850
Sourisseau Academy for California State and Local History
Room 315, Library
San Jose State University
San Jose CA

MAILING ADDRESS:
History Department
San Jose State University
San Jose CA 95192

(415) 324-0161

OPEN: by appointment only, at (408) 227-2657
COPYING FACILITIES: yes

MATERIALS SOLICITED: Materials pertaining to California State and local history.

HOLDINGS:
Total volume: 11 c.f.
Inclusive dates: 1850 -
Description: Photographs of Santa Clara County, the New Almaden Mine, Big Basin State Park, and Yosemite; diaries of artist and conservationist Andrew P. Hill; and materials relating to braceros in California.

SAN LEANDRO

CA740-710
San Leandro Community Library Center
300 Estudillo Avenue
San Leandro CA 94577

(415) 577-3480

OPEN: M-Th 9-9, F 9-6, Sa 9-5; closed Sundays and holidays
COPYING FACILITIES: yes
MATERIALS SOLICITED: Local history materials dealing with the city of San Leandro and the surrounding area.

HOLDINGS:
Total volume: 2,540 items
Inclusive dates: 1860 - 1960
Description: Historical photographs and documents relating to San Leandro, including street scenes, buildings and houses, local events, citizens, and membership photographs of societies and organizations.

SEE: Hinding.

SEE ALSO: Ann Novotny, ed., *Picture Sources 3* (Special Libraries Assn., 1975).

SAN LUIS OBISPO

CA744-120
California Polytechnic State University
Library
Special Collections Department - Archives
San Luis Obispo CA 93407

(805) 546-2305

OPEN: M-F 9-4; closed weekends and holidays
ACCESS: written and in person requests subject to screening by the Section
COPYING FACILITIES: yes
MATERIALS SOLICITED: San Luis Obispo County and California Central Coast area history; history of printing, graphic design, and their related fields; architecture, landscape architecture, and environmental design; history and development of California Polytechnic State University, San Luis Obispo. Also accepts materials relating to agriculture, engineering, and thoroughbred horse breeding and training.

HOLDINGS:
Total volume: 675 l.f.
Inclusive dates: 1850 -
Description: Materials relating to the history and development of San Luis Obispo County and the California Central Coast region, including manuscripts, inactive public documents, photographs, maps, and oral histories.
Architectural drawings, correspondence, records, photographs, and memorabilia relating to the life and work of California architect Julia Morgan, along with the development of the Hearst-San Simeon State Monument. Materials comprising the archives of California Polytechnic State University, San Luis Obispo.

SAN MARINO

CA756-320
The Huntington Library
1151 Oxford Road
San Marino CA 91108

(213) 792-6141

OPEN: M-Sa 8:30-5; closed Sundays and holidays
COPYING FACILITIES: yes
MATERIALS SOLICITED: British and American history and literature, 11th century to 1837 (British history), to 1900 (American history), to present (California history). Will also accept materials on printing history.

HOLDINGS:
Total volume: 5,000,000 items
Inclusive dates: 10th century -
Description: British and American history and literature; American history from the beginnings through today relating to Spanish explorations, the colonial-revolutionary period, the Civil War, westward movement, and California.

SEE: Hamer; NUCMC, 1959-62, 68, 71, 77, 81.

SEE: Allard, Crawley, and Edmison; Armstrong; Bean and Vane; Beers - Southwest; Gehring; Ingram; Martin; Mehr; Novotny; Parkinson; Robbins.

SEE ALSO: Morris Rieger, 'Africa-Related Papers of Persons and Organizations in the United States,' *African Studies Bulletin* 8 (Dec. 1965); Nathan Reingold, 'The Anatomy of a Collection: The Rhees Papers,' *American Archivist* 27 (April 1964); Walter Schatz, ed., *Directory of Afro-American Resources* (Bowker, 1970);

Andrea Hinding and Rosemary Richardson, comps., *Archival and Manuscript Resources for the Study of Women's History: A Beginning* (Univ. of Minnesota Libraries, Social Welfare History Archives Center, 1972); Huntington Library, *Bulletin, Quarterly,* and *Annual Report*; Hubert C. Schultz, Norma B. Cuthbert, and Haydee Noya, *Ten Centuries of Manuscripts in the Huntington Library* (Huntington Library, 1962); J. E. Patterson, comp., 'Checklist of Prescott Manuscripts,' *Hispanic American Historical Review* 39 (Feb. 1959); Peter Duignan, *Handbook of American Resources for African Studies* (Hoover Institution, 1967);

David A. Hounshell, comp., *Manuscripts in U.S. Depositories Relating to the History of Electrical Science and Technology* (Smithsonian Institution, n.d.); William P. Cumming, *British Maps of Colonial America* (Univ. of Chicago Press, 1974); American Institute of Physics, Neils Bohr Library, *Source Materials for the Recent History of Astronomy and Astrophysics: A Checklist of Manuscript Collections in the United States* (American Institute of Physics, 1971); Albert Krichmar, *The Women's Rights Movement in the United States, 1848-1970: A Bibliography and Sourcebook* (Scarecrow Press, 1972); Joan Hoff Wilson and Lynn B. Donovan, 'Women's History: A Listing of West Coast Archival and Manuscript Sources, Part I,' *California Historical Quarterly* 55 (Spring 1976);

Richard C. Davis, *North American Forest History: A Guide to Archives and Manuscripts in the United States and Canada* (Clio Books, 1977).

SAN MATEO

CA760-710
San Mateo County Historical
Association and Museum
1700 West Hillsdale Blvd.
San Mateo CA 94402

(415) 574-6441

OPEN: W-F 10-4:30, Sa, Su noon-4; closed Mondays, Tuesdays, and holidays
COPYING FACILITIES: yes
MATERIALS SOLICITED: Materials relating to the history and development of San Mateo County.

HOLDINGS:
    Total volume: 89 l.f.; 50 c.f.; 17 map drawers
    Inclusive dates: 1805 -
    Description: Materials relating to the history and development of San Mateo County, including maps, photographs, manuscripts, government records, documents, business records, journals, logbooks, architectural drawings, transcriptions, oral histories, and school and organization records.
    Also account books, correspondence, diaries, aerial photographs, and scrapbooks.

SEE: Hamer; NUCMC, 1959-61.

SEE: Bean and Vane; Robbins.

SEE ALSO: Joan Hoff Wilson and Lynn B. Donovan, 'Women's History: A Listing of West Coast Archival and Manuscript Sources, Part I,' *California Historical Quarterly* 55 (Spring 1976); Richard C. Davis, *North American Forest History: A Guide to Archives and Manuscripts in the United States and Canada* (Clio Books, 1977).

SAN PEDRO

CA762-40
American Cetacean Society
745 Paseo del Mar
San Pedro CA

MAILING ADDRESS:
P.O. Box 2639
San Pedro CA 90731

(213) 548-6279

OPEN: M-F 9-5; closed weekends and holidays
ACCESS: advance arrangements required
COPYING FACILITIES: yes
MATERIALS SOLICITED: Materials pertaining to whales, whaling, and other marine mammals. Will also accept environmental ocean reports.

HOLDINGS:
    Total volume: 500 items
    Inclusive dates: 1969 -
    Description: Account books, programs, newsletters, and journals of the American Cetacean Society, as well as position papers on whaling, whale watch reports, and recordings of meetings and speakers.

SAN RAFAEL

CA764-160
Dominican College
Library
San Rafael CA 94901

no telephone

SEE: Hamer.

Questionnaire not returned.

CA764-165
Dominican Convent of San Rafael
1520 Grand Avenue
San Rafael CA 94901

(415) 454-9221, Ext. 27

OPEN: M-F 9-11:30 or by appointment; closed weekends
COPYING FACILITIES: no
MATERIALS SOLICITED: Will accept materials relating to early education in California and Nevada, early days in Monterey and Benicia, and the foundation and development of the Dominican Order (priests and sisters) in California.

HOLDINGS:
    Total volume: 80 l.f.; 22 vols.
    Inclusive dates: 1850 - 1980
    Description: Manuscripts relating chiefly to the development of educational work by the Dominican Sisters of San Rafael. Included are letters concerning the first school in Monterey and pioneer conditions, reminiscences of pioneer sisters, ledgers, educational materials, and accounts of schools in the San Francisco Bay area and the San Joaquin Valley, pioneering in Nevada, and the founding of the first hospital in Reno.

SEE: Hinding.

CA764-510
Marin County Free Library
California History Collection
Civic Center Administration Building
San Rafael CA 94903

(415) 499-7419

OPEN: M-F 10-3; closed weekends and holidays
ACCESS: students, professors, and bona fide researchers; advance arrangements requested
COPYING FACILITIES: no
MATERIALS SOLICITED: Materials relating to California and to Marin County history and biography. Will also accept materials relating to authors of Marin County and California.

HOLDINGS:
    Total volume: 10 cases; 24 file cabinets
    Inclusive dates: mid-1800's -
    Description: Materials relating primarily to Marin County, including records of government agencies, associations, and community groups, diaries, logbooks, genealogical materials, literary manuscripts, photographs, oral history recordings and transcripts, and scrapbooks concerning artists, authors, the Marin County civic center building, and other subjects.

SANTA ANA

CA770-40
American Aviation Historical Society
2333 Otis Street
Santa Ana CA

MAILING ADDRESS:
P.O. Box 99
Garden Grove CA 92642

(714) 549-4818

OPEN: by appointment
ACCESS: members of the Society only; special permission required for outside users
COPYING FACILITIES: no
MATERIALS SOLICITED: Photographs of military and civilian aircraft. Will also accept biographical data on persons associated with aviation.

HOLDINGS:
    Total volume: 10,000 items
    Inclusive dates: 1900 -
    Description: Photographic negatives of aircraft.

GUIDES: A catalog is available at cost from the repository.

SEE: Meckler and McMullin.

CA770-120
The Bowers Museum
2002 North Main Street
Santa Ana CA 92706

(714) 972-1900

OPEN: by appointment only
ACCESS: professional scholars by advance appointment
COPYING FACILITIES: no

MATERIALS SOLICITED: Orange County and Santa Ana history, including businesses, citriculture and other agriculture, photographs, and pre-history of the Pacific coastline.

HOLDINGS:
Total volume: 20 l.f.
Inclusive dates: 1870 -
Description: A collection of manuscripts relating chiefly to Santa Ana, Orange County, and California. Included are diaries, land titles, water surveys, early Santa Ana municipal records, financial records of two citriculture packing houses, archives of churches and community groups, and late 19th-early 20th century photographs.

SEE: Hamer.

SEE: Hinding; Bean and Vane.

SEE ALSO: Henry Putney Beers, *Spanish & Mexican Records of the American Southwest: A Bibliographical Guide to Archive and Manuscript Sources* (Univ. of Arizona Press, 1979).

SANTA BARBARA

CA774-710
Santa Barbara Historical Society
Library
136 East De la Guerra Street
Santa Barbara CA

MAILING ADDRESS:
P.O. Box 578
Santa Barbara CA 93102

(805) 966-1601

OPEN: Tu-F 1-5; closed other days and holidays
COPYING FACILITIES: yes
MATERIALS SOLICITED: Materials relating to Santa Barbara city and county.

HOLDINGS:
Total volume: 40 file drawers; 100 l.f.
Inclusive dates: 1800 -
Description: Manuscripts, photographs, maps, ledgers, account books, diaries, logbooks, genealogical records, tapes and films relating to Santa Barbara city and county.

CA774-720
The Santa Barbara Mission
Archive-Library
Old Mission
Santa Barbara CA 93105

no telephone

OPEN: M-Sa 9-4; closed Sundays, Mondays, and holidays
ACCESS: by appointment
COPYING FACILITIES: no
MATERIALS SOLICITED: Materials relating to the history of the Santa Barbara Mission and Franciscan activity in California, and genealogical data and vital records concerning Hispanic America and early California.

HOLDINGS:
Total volume: 100,000 pages
Inclusive dates: 1769 - 1885
Description: Records relating to the history of the Mission and its college, as well as to California, Spain, Mexico, and Latin America. Most documents are in Spanish and other foreign languages.

SEE: Hamer; NUCMC, 1975.

SEE: Bean and Vane; Beers - Southwest.

CA774-800
University of California, Santa Barbara
Library
Department of Special Collections
Santa Barbara CA 93106

(805) 961-3420

OPEN: M-Th 8-10, F 8-5, Sa 11-5, Su noon-3; during intersessions, M-F 8-5
COPYING FACILITIES: yes
MATERIALS SOLICITED: Civil War, Reconstruction, slavery, westward movement, California and local history, birth control, and fine printing history. Will also accept materials related to all teaching areas of the University.

HOLDINGS:
Total volume: 208,177 items
Inclusive dates: 1780 -
Description: Over 120 small and large collections of manuscripts, chiefly materials on community development, conservation, the Civil War, natural history, birth control, avant garde writing and opera.

GUIDES: *A Checklist of Manuscripts* (1970).

SEE: Hamer (as Santa Barbara College Library, University of California, Goleta); NUCMC, 1968-69.

SEE: Davis; Mehr; Schatz; Meckler and McMullin; Spalek; Hinding; Robbins.

SEE ALSO: *William Wyles Collection: University of California at Santa Barbara* (1970).

SANTA CLARA

CA778-710
Santa Clara County Historical and Genealogical Society
City Library
2635 Homestead Road
Santa Clara CA 95051

(408) 998-5596

OPEN: M-F 9-9, Sa 9-6, Su 1-5; closed holidays
COPYING FACILITIES: yes
MATERIALS SOLICITED: Genealogies, oral histories, records of old-timers, and other historical information on Santa Clara County.

HOLDINGS:
Total volume: not specified
Inclusive dates: mid-1800's -
Description: Several local family histories and files on pioneer native Californians.

CA778-780
University of Santa Clara
Archives
Michel Orradre Library
Santa Clara CA 95053

(408) 554-4117

OPEN: by appointment
COPYING FACILITIES: yes
MATERIALS SOLICITED: Materials relating to the history of the Mission Santa Clara and the University of Santa Clara. Will also accept materials relating to the history of the Santa Clara Valley area.

HOLDINGS:
Total volume: 500 c.f.
Inclusive dates: 1777 -
Description: Records of Mission Santa Clara, 1777-1851. Also materials relating to the history of the University of Santa Clara.
Included are the papers of prominent alumni and faculty; the photographic collection of Alaskan explorer Bernard Hubbard; the seismographic and meteorological records of the campus's Ricard Observatory; the papers of the university's first president, John Nobili; photos and other materials of aviation pioneer John J. Montgomery; and the papers of Bernard J. Reid, early teacher and Civil War participant.
The Archives also preserves a collection of miscellaneous materials relating to the history of the Santa Clara Valley.

SEE ALSO: Beryl Hoskin, *A History of the Santa Clara Mission Library* (Biobooks, 1961); Francis J. Weber, 'Sources for a Catholic History of California: A Biblio-Archival Survey,' *Southern California Quarterly* 57 (Fall 1975).

CA778-800
University of Santa Clara
Michel Orradre Library
Santa Clara CA 95053

(408) 554-4415

OPEN: M-F 8-midnight, Sa 9-5, Su 1-midnight; closed holidays
ACCESS: qualified researchers, by appointment
COPYING FACILITIES: yes
MATERIALS SOLICITED: Materials relating to Mexican-Americans and migrant farm workers.

HOLDINGS:
Total volume: 62 l.f.
Inclusive dates: 1910 -
Description: Papers and play manuscripts of Clay Meredith Greene; papers and literary manuscripts of Mexican-American writer Jose Villarreal; papers of government official James Carr; scripts from the *Daniel Boone* television series; and scores by motion picture music composer Lionel Newman.

SEE: NUCMC, 1965, 77.

SEE: Beers - Southwest; Mehr.

SEE ALSO: A guide to the Greene collection is available at the library.

SANTA CRUZ

CA782-240

Forest History Society
109 Coral Street
Santa Cruz CA 95060

(408) 426-3770

OPEN: M-F 8-5; closed weekends
ACCESS: advance arrangements requested
COPYING FACILITIES: yes
MATERIALS SOLICITED: Records and papers of national conservation, forestry, and forest industry organizations, and of individuals of national importance in the forest and conservation field. Will also accept records of individuals or organizations of regional importance.

HOLDINGS:
   Total volume: 523 l.f.
   Inclusive dates: 1875 -
   Description: Records of national conservation, forestry, and forest industry organizations including the American Forestry Association, Natural Resources Council of America, Society of American Foresters, National Forest Products Association, and American Forest Institute; records and papers of individuals and regional organizations involved in conservation, forestry, and the forest industries; and photographs, oral histories, field diaries, correspondence, and scrapbooks of foresters, loggers, conservationists, and forest industry leaders.

SEE: Hamer; NUCMC, 1968, 76.

SEE: Davis; Meckler and McMullin.

CA782-720

Santa Cruz County Historical Museum
118 Cooper Street
Santa Cruz CA 95060

(408) 425-2540

OPEN: M-Sa noon-5; closed Sundays and holidays
COPYING FACILITIES: yes
MATERIALS SOLICITED: Materials regarding the history of Santa Cruz County or California.

HOLDINGS:
   Total volume: not specified
   Inclusive dates: 1850's -
   Description: Journals, diaries, manuscript maps, photographs, and other materials concerning the history, geography, water resources, architecture, families, and businesses of Santa Cruz County.

CA782-730

Santa Cruz Historical Society, Inc.
Santa Cruz CA

MAILING ADDRESS:
P.O. Box 246
Santa Cruz CA 95061

(408) 427-3240

OPEN: by appointment
ACCESS: members of the Society, and others with written permission of the Society's president
COPYING FACILITIES: no

MATERIALS SOLICITED: Materials relating to regional and local history, especially documents and papers from the Spanish and Mexican colonial periods, and early photographs and daguerreotypes of Santa Cruz and the Monterey Bay area. Will also accept pre-1920's advertising material, maps, and materials relating to railroads.

HOLDINGS:
   Total volume: 450 items
   Inclusive dates: 1844 -
   Description: Materials relating primarily to Santa Cruz history. Included are letters from the gold rush era, a history of the town band, photographs of the area, 1870-1900, and tape recordings by local historians.

CA782-800

University of California, Santa Cruz Library
Santa Cruz CA 95064

(408) 429-2547, 2364, 2076

OPEN: by appointment
COPYING FACILITIES: yes
MATERIALS SOLICITED: Materials relating to Santa Cruz local history, including maps of contiguous counties; the history of Lick Observatory; the economic, agricultural, ethnic, labor, and social history of the California central coastal region; and the institutional history of the University of California. Will also accept materials relating to the history of astronomy, and maps, especially of Canada, Micronesia, Melanesia, and Polynesia.

HOLDINGS:
   Total volume: 73 l.f.; 40,000 items
   Inclusive dates: 1797 -
   Description: Photographs and manuscripts relating to the history of Santa Cruz, including diaries, legal and business records, materials from the pre-statehood period, and oral history interviews on the history of Santa Cruz County, the University, and Lick Observatory. There are also maps and aerial photographs of the County; letters, diaries, and other papers, 1874-1944, relating to astronomy and to Lick Observatory; T. J. Jaggar's journal and other papers on the history and customs of the Fiji Islands, 1838-42; letters of Thomas Carlyle, relating to his publications and other business dealings; and diaries, papers, and correspondence relating to research in the South Pacific, 1947-70, and the South Pacific Commission.

SEE: NUCMC, 1959-62.

SEE: Mehr; Hinding; Bean and Vane.

SEE ALSO: *Source Materials for the Recent History of Astronomy and Astrophysics: A Checklist of Manuscript Collections in the United States* (American Institute of Physics, 1971); *Map Collections in the United States and Canada, A Directory* (Special Libraries Assn., 1970); Ann Novotny, ed., *Picture Sources 3* (Special Libraries Assn., 1975); Joan Hoff Wilson and Lynn B. Donovan, 'Women's History: A Listing of West Coast Archival and Manuscript Sources, Part II,' *California Historical Quarterly* 55 (Summer 1976); Alan M.

Meckler and Ruth McMullin, comps., *Oral History Collections* (Bowker, 1975); Richard C. Davis, *North American Forest History: A Guide to Archives and Manuscripts in the United States and Canada* (Clio Books, 1977).

SANTA MONICA

CA790-720

Santa Monica Public Library
California Special Collection
1343 Sixth Street
Santa Monica CA 90401

(213) 451-8859

OPEN: M-Th 10-9, F, Sa 10-5:30; closed Sundays and holidays
COPYING FACILITIES: yes
MATERIALS SOLICITED: Photographs of the Santa Monica Bay region of western Los Angeles County.

HOLDINGS:
   Total volume: 749 photographs
   Inclusive dates: 1870 -
   Description: A collection of photographs, including panoramas, of the Santa Monica Bay region of western Los Angeles County, including Venice, Santa Monica, Santa Monica Canyon, Pacific Palisades and Topanga Canyon. The bulk of the collection was taken between 1875 and 1940.

SANTA ROSA

CA798-720

Society of Wireless Pioneers, Inc.
Santa Rosa CA

MAILING ADDRESS:
P.O. Box 530
Santa Rosa CA 95402

(707) 542-0898

OPEN: by appointment
COPYING FACILITIES: yes
MATERIALS SOLICITED: Materials relating to wireless telegraphy, maritime history, 1900 to date, and lighthouses. Will also accept materials on the history of ships, shipping, and navigational aids, especially in the field of electronics, such as radar and sonar.

HOLDINGS:
   Total volume: 3,000 pages; 1,000 items
   Inclusive dates: 1850 -
   Description: Materials relating to the development of wireless telegraphy, as well as to ships, shipping, and maritime disasters.

SAUSALITO

CA810-700
Sausalito Historical Society
Museum
420 Litho Street
Sausalito CA

MAILING ADDRESS:
P.O. Box 352
Sausalito CA 94966

(415) 332-1005

OPEN: M, W, Sa 10-4 or by
appointment; closed other days and
holidays
COPYING FACILITIES: yes
MATERIALS SOLICITED: Southern Marin
County, CA, Rancho Sausalito, the fer-
ryboat and railroad era, yachting, local
architecture, local artists, and William
A. Richardson. Will also accept
Victoriana.

HOLDINGS:
Total volume: 15 file drawers
Inclusive dates: 1870 -
Description: Local photographs,
railroad maps from 1875, scrapbooks and
other documentation of Sausalito artists
in the 1950's, a personal names index,
and tax records, applications to join the
fire department, and other records of the
City of Sausalito.

SHASTA

CA814-120
California Department of Parks and
Recreation
Shasta State Historic Park
Shasta CA

MAILING ADDRESS:
P.O. Box 2430
Shasta CA 96087

(916) 243-8194

OPEN: daily 10-5; closed Thanksgiving,
Christmas, and New Year's
COPYING FACILITIES: yes
MATERIALS SOLICITED: Materials pertaining to the northern California gold
rush, particularly in the town of Shasta
and Shasta County, 1846-1900, as well
as records of pre-1900 general stores.

HOLDINGS:
Total volume: 40 l.f.
Inclusive dates: 1848 - 1940
Description: Materials pertaining to the
California gold rush, particularly in the
town of Shasta and Shasta County;
records of the Litsch General Store,
1855-1961; and scrapbooks and files of
Mae Helene Bacon Boggs concerning
California art and artists.

SEE: Hinding.

SIMI VALLEY

CA830-720
Simi Valley Historical Society
R. P. Strathearn Historical Park
137 Strathearn Place
Simi Valley CA

MAILING ADDRESS:
P.O. Box 351
Simi Valley CA 93062

(805) 526-6453, 0879

OPEN: by appointment Su 1-4, M, Tu,
Th, F 9:30-2; closed Wednesdays,
Saturdays, and holidays
ACCESS: with prior arrangements only
COPYING FACILITIES: no
MATERIALS SOLICITED: Materials relating
to the Simi Valley area. Will also ac-
cept materials relating to the history of
southern California.

HOLDINGS:
Total volume: 500 items
Inclusive dates: 1874 - 1960
Description: Letters of a local ranching
family, letters of a local oologist, and
some local business letters.

SEE: NUCMC, 1978.

SONOMA

CA838-720
Sonoma Valley Historical Society
Depot Park Museum
270 First Street West
Sonoma CA

MAILING ADDRESS:
P.O. Box 861
Sonoma CA 95476

(707) 938-9765

OPEN: W-Su 1-4:30; closed Mondays,
Tuesdays, Thanksgiving, Christmas,
and New Year's
ACCESS: advance arrangements with
Museum Director required
COPYING FACILITIES: no
MATERIALS SOLICITED: Materials per-
taining to Sonoma Valley.

HOLDINGS:
Total volume: 500 items
Inclusive dates: 1850 - 1950
Description: Materials relating to peo-
ple, businesses, activities, and structures
in the Sonoma Valley.

SONORA

CA842-760
Tuolumne County Historical Society
158 West Bradford Avenue
Sonora CA

MAILING ADDRESS:
P.O. Box 695
Sonora CA 95370

(209) 532-1317

OPEN: M-F 9-4:30 by appointment only;
closed weekends except in summer
10-3:30

COPYING FACILITIES: no
MATERIALS SOLICITED: Materials relating
to the history of Tuolumne County and
its relationship to the culture and economy of California. Will also accept
records of Tuolumne County government and Stanislaus National Forest.

HOLDINGS:
Total volume: 4,050 items
Inclusive dates: 1850's -
Description: Photographs and oral his-
tory interviews relating to Tuolumne
County history.

SOUTH LAKE TAHOE

CA846-480
Lake Tahoe Historical Society
980 Star Lake Avenue
South Lake Tahoe CA

MAILING ADDRESS:
P.O. Box 404
South Lake Tahoe CA 95705

(916) 544-2312

OPEN: Memorial Day - Labor Day, daily
10-2; closed rest of year
ACCESS: noncommercial purposes only,
except by special arrangement
COPYING FACILITIES: no
MATERIALS SOLICITED: Material relating
to the Lake Tahoe Basin, such as historical photographs and pioneers' memoirs.

HOLDINGS:
Total volume: 6 c.f.
Inclusive dates: 1875 -
Description: Photographs and manuscripts, including correspondence, diaries,
an autobiography, oral history tapes; one
motion picture film pertaining to the history of the South Shore of Lake Tahoe
and its inhabitants.

SOUTH PASADENA

CA850-720
South Pasadena Public Library
1115 El Centro Street
South Pasadena CA 91030

(213) 799-9108

OPEN: M-W 10-8, Th 10-6, Sa 10-5;
closed other days and holidays.
COPYING FACILITIES: yes
MATERIALS SOLICITED: Materials relating
to the history of the South Pasadena
area.

HOLDINGS:
Total volume: 102 l.f.
Inclusive dates: 1889 -
Description: Minutes of the Oneonta
Club and the South Pasadena Library
Board, photographs of Cawston's Ostrich
Farm, a Cultural Heritage Commission
slide show and script, and some oral his-
tory tapes.

STANFORD

CA858-320

Hoover Institution on War,
 Revolution and Peace
Archives
Stanford University
Stanford CA 94305

(415) 497-3563

OPEN: M-F 8:15-4:45; closed weekends
 and holidays
COPYING FACILITIES: yes
MATERIALS SOLICITED: 20th century political, social, and economic history for
 most geographical areas of the world.
 Emphasis on military history, diplomacy, politics and government, political
 ideologies, economics, journalism, international relief, and intellectual history.

HOLDINGS:
> Total volume: 18,000 l.f.
> Inclusive dates: 1880 -
> Description: Over 3,800 collections
> covering the field of 20th century politi-
> cal, social, and economic history for most
> geographical areas, including North
> America, eastern Europe and Russia
> (Soviet Union), western Europe, East and
> Southeast Asia, the Middle East, Africa,
> and Latin America. Included are records
> of organizations, papers of individuals,
> unpublished memoirs and histories, col-
> lections of ephemera, and audio-visual
> materials.
>
> These materials document internation-
> al relations, major political ideologies,
> war relief, world migrations, revolution-
> ary upheavals, military and diplomatic
> history, intellectual history, and activities
> of governments, international bodies, and
> resistance movements throughout the
> 20th century.

GUIDES: Charles G. Palm and Dale Reed,
 Guide to the Hoover Institution Archives
 (1980).

SEE: Hamer; NUCMC, 1968-69, 71-72,
 75, 77.

SEE: Paszek; Schatz; Allard, Crawley, and
 Edmison; Spalek; Hinding; Robbins.

SEE ALSO: *The Library Catalogs of the
 Hoover Institution on War, Revolution
 and Peace: Catalog of the Western Language Collections* (G. K. Hall, 1969);
 *Archival and Manuscript Materials at
 the Hoover Institution on War, Revolution and Peace, A Checklist of Major
 Collections* (1975); Gerhard L.
 Weinberg, *Supplement to Guide to Captured German Documents* (1959);

Agnes F. Peterson, *Western Europe, A Sur-
 vey of Holdings at the Hoover Institution
 on War, Revolution and Peace* (1970);
 Peter Duignan, George Rentz, Karen
 Fung, and Michel Nabti, *African and
 Middle East Collections, A Survey of
 Holdings at the Hoover Institution on
 War, Revolution and Peace* (1971);
 Kenneth M. Glazier and James R. Hob-
 son, *International and English-language
 Collections, A Survey of Holdings at the
 Hoover Institution on War, Revolution
 and Peace* (1971);

John T. Ma, *East Asia, A Survey of Holdings
 at the Hoover Institution on War, Revolu-
 tion and Peace* (1971); Joseph W.
 Bingaman, *Latin America, A Survey of
 Holdings at the Hoover Institution on
 War, Revolution and Peace* (1972);

Joan Hoff Wilson and Lynn B. Donovan,
 'Women's History: A Listing of West
 Coast Archival and Manuscript Sources,
 Part I,' *California Historical Quarterly* 55
 (Spring 1976).

Richard C. Davis, *North American Forest
 History: A Guide to Archives and Manu-
 scripts in the United States and Canada*
 (Clio Books, 1977).

CA858-790

Stanford University
Libraries
Archive of Recorded Sound
The Knoll
Stanford CA 94305

(415) 497-9312

OPEN: M-F 8-5, by appointment only;
 closed weekends and holidays
COPYING FACILITIES: yes
MATERIALS SOLICITED: Sound recordings
 of drama, literature, poetry, Stanford
 University subjects, and events of political, social, or historical significance,
 as well as related textual materials.
 Will also accept folk and ethnic recordings relating to Stanford University
 academic programs.

HOLDINGS:
> Total volume: not specified
> Inclusive dates: 1930's -
> Description: Sound recordings, includ-
> ing those of student protests and political
> events at Stanford University,
> 1960's-70's, poetry readings at the Uni-
> versity, oral history interviews concerning
> civil rights in the South, and radio broad-
> casts, 1930's-40's.

SEE: Meckler and McMullin.

CA858-810

Stanford University
Libraries
Department of Special Collections
Manuscripts Division
Stanford CA 94305

(415) 497-4054

OPEN: M-F 8-5, Sa 9-5; closed Sundays
 and holidays
ACCESS: by prior arrangement for
 Saturday use
COPYING FACILITIES: yes
MATERIALS SOLICITED: 19th and 20th
 century British and American literature;
 U.S. history, particularly Civil War, western, and California; California farm labor
 and related minority histories; 18th century European social history; transportation; politics and government with emphasis on California.

HOLDINGS:
> Total volume: 2,918 l.f.
> Inclusive dates: 12th century -
> Description: Collections relating to
> most disciplines dating from the 12th
> century to the present, with an emphasis
> on the 19th and 20th centuries. Especially

strong are collections relating to 19th and
20th century British and American literature; U.S. history, particularly history of
the Civil War, the West, and California;
18th century European social history;
California farm labor and related minority histories; transportation; and politics
and government, especially in California.

SEE: Hamer; NUCMC, 1959-61, 63-65,
 67, 69, 71-72, 74.

SEE: Krichmar; Duignan; Hounshell; Schatz;
 Davis; Allard, Crawley, and Edmison;
 Bean and Vane; Robbins; Novotny;
 Hinding; Mehr; Beers - Southwest.

SEE ALSO: *Cataloged Manuscripts: Department of Special Collections, Manuscript
 Division, Stanford University Library*
 (1973).

Joan Hoff Wilson and Lynn B. Donovan,
 'Women's History: A Listing of West
 Coast Archival and Manuscript Sources,
 Part I,' *California Historical Quarterly* 55
 (Spring 1976).

CA858-820

Stanford University
Libraries
University Archives
Stanford CA 94305

(415) 497-2952

OPEN: M-F 8-5; closed weekends,
 holidays, and vacations
COPYING FACILITIES: yes
MATERIALS SOLICITED: Stanford University history, including personal papers of
 Stanford founders, faculty members, and
 trustees, as well as administrative records.

HOLDINGS:
> Total volume: 5,000 l.f.
> Inclusive dates: 1845 -
> Description: Manuscript collections,
> record groups, printed materials, photo-
> graphs, maps, prints and ephemera relat-
> ing to the history of Stanford University.
> Included are personal papers of Stanford
> University's founders, presidents, trustees,
> and faculty members.

SEE: Hamer (as Stanford Collection);
 NUCMC, 1967, 70, 72, 74, 76-77.

SEE: Bean and Vane; Spalek; Hinding.

SEE ALSO: *List of Holdings, Stanford University Archives* (1973); Ann Novotny,
 ed., *Picture Sources 3* (Special Libraries
 Assn., 1975); David A. Hounshell,
 comp., *Manuscripts in U.S. Depositories
 Relating to the History of Electrical Science and Technology* (Smithsonian Institution, n.d.); Andrea Hinding and
 Rosemary Richardson, comps., *Archival
 and Manuscript Resources for the Study
 of Women's History: A Beginning*
 (Univ. of Minnesota Libraries, Social
 Welfare History Archives Center,
 1972); Joan Hoff Wilson and Lynn B.
 Donovan, 'Women's History: A Listing
 of West Coast Archival and Manuscript
 Sources, Part I,' *California Historical
 Quarterly* 55 (Spring 1976).

Roxanne-Louise Nilan, comp., *Guide to the
 Manuscript and Archival Collections of the
 Stanford University Archives* (1979).

CA858-895
Stanford University
School of Medicine
Lane Medical Library
Stanford CA 94305

(415) 497-6831

OPEN: M-F 8-5; variable summer and
holiday hours; closed weekends
COPYING FACILITIES: yes
MATERIALS SOLICITED: Materials related
to the Stanford University School of
Medicine. Will also accept any materials related to the field of medicine.

HOLDINGS:
Total volume: 720 l.f.
Inclusive dates: 1732 -
Description: Manuscripts relating chiefly to the Cooper Medical College and to
the physicians involved in the early history of the College; the Seidel collection
of Oriental manuscripts relating to medical and other scientific subjects;
catalogued photographs; and records and
papers of several medical institutions and
individuals.

SEE: Hamer; NUCMC, 1959-61, 63-64.

SEE: Martin; Hinding.

STOCKTON

CA862-630
Pioneer Museum and Haggin
Galleries
Petzinger Memorial Library
1201 North Pershing Avenue
Stockton CA 95203

(209) 462-4116

OPEN: Tu, Th, Sa 1:30-4:30, by
appointment; closed other days and
holidays
ACCESS: appointment one week in
advance
COPYING FACILITIES: yes
MATERIALS SOLICITED: California and
San Joaquin County history. Will also
accept art and art history and general
history items relating to the Museum's
collection of California history and
19th and 20th century French and
American art.

HOLDINGS:
Total volume: 150 l.f.; 8,000
photographs
Inclusive dates: 1849 - 1950
Description: Materials relating to
Stockton, San Joaquin County and California. Included are a large photograph
collection, business records of local manufacturers, materials relating to local biography and agricultural technology, editorial cartoons, and drawings of early
Stockton.

SEE: Hamer; NUCMC, 1970.

SEE ALSO: Ann Novotny, ed., Picture
Sources 3 (Special Libraries Assn.,
1975).

CA862-730
Stockton-San Joaquin County Public
Library
California Room
605 North El Dorado
Stockton CA 95202

(209) 944-8415

OPEN: M, W, Th 10-9, Tu, F 10-6, Sa
10-5; closed Sundays and holidays
COPYING FACILITIES: yes
MATERIALS SOLICITED: Materials relating
to Stockton, San Joaquin County, the
gold mining region of California, and
the State in general.

HOLDINGS:
Total volume: 1,000 items
Inclusive dates: 1850 -
Description: Original writings of Stockton and San Joaquin County pioneers
pertaining to library development, the
theater, and government; early public
documents; and logbooks relating to Library activities.

SEE: Hinding.

CA862-810
University of the Pacific
Pacific Center for Western Historical
Studies
Stockton CA 95211

(209) 946-2169

OPEN: M-F 9-5; closed weekends and
holidays
ACCESS: serious scholars
COPYING FACILITIES: yes
MATERIALS SOLICITED: Materials relating
to the American Trans-Mississippi
West, especially the Far West. Will also
accept materials relating to Pacific Basin history, including Latin America.

HOLDINGS:
Total volume: 1,100 l.f.
Inclusive dates: 1550 -
Description: Over 150 major collections and about 300 minor collections
covering primarily California and Oregon, 1850-1950. Subjects covered include ethnic minorities, Spanish-
American history, the Pacific Northwest,
the fur trade, modern Latin America,
crime and criminals, business history, the
Civil War, environment, mining, transportation, Western literature, education,
theater, church history, politics, medicine,
historiography, art history, agriculture,
Stockton and Bay Area history, and
women.

SEE: Hamer; NUCMC, 1972.

SEE: Hines; Bean and Vane; Robbins;
Hinding.

SEE ALSO: Joan Hoff Wilson and Lynn B.
Donovan, 'Women's History: A Listing
of West Coast Archival and Manuscript
Sources, Part II,' California Historical
Quarterly 55 (Summer 1976).

Richard C. Davis, North American Forest
History: A Guide to Archives and Manu-
scripts in the United States and Canada
(Clio Books, 1977).

SUNNYVALE

CA870-710
Sunnyvale Historical Society and
Museum Association
Sunnyvale Historical Museum
Sunnyvale Avenue and California
Street
Sunnyvale CA

MAILING ADDRESS:
P.O. Box 61301
Sunnyvale CA 94088

(408) 749-0220

OPEN: M, Tu, Th-Sa 12-3:30, Su 1-4;
closed Wednesdays and holidays
COPYING FACILITIES: no
MATERIALS SOLICITED: Materials relating
to the Martin Murphy, Jr., family and
to Ida Trubschenck, as well as to
Sunnyvale and California in general.

HOLDINGS:
Total volume: 5 c.f.
Inclusive dates: 1902 - 1960
Description: Photographs, oral history
interviews, and other materials relating to
the Martin Murphy, Jr., family and the
history of Sunnyvale, as well as maps,
aerial photographs, insurance records,
and records of the city clerk.

SEE: Hinding.

THREE RIVERS

CA882-720
Sequoia National Park
Division of Interpretation
Three Rivers CA 93271

(209) 565-3341

OPEN: M-F 8-4:30; closed weekends and
holidays
COPYING FACILITIES: yes
MATERIALS SOLICITED: Will accept materials if need is evident.

HOLDINGS:
Total volume: 6 boxes
Inclusive dates: 1884 -
Description: Logs, manuscripts, theses,
photographs and diaries relating to the
cultural and administrative histories of
the Sequoia and the Kings Canyon Na-
tional Parks, including the records of the
Kaweah Co-operative Commonwealth
Company.

SEE: Hamer; NUCMC, 1962.

SEE ALSO: Richard C. Davis, North
American Forest History: A Guide to
Archives and Manuscripts in the United
States and Canada (Clio Books, 1977).

TOPANGA

CA886-240

Feminist History Research Project
19988 Observation Drive
Topanga CA

MAILING ADDRESS:
P.O. Box 1156
Topanga CA 90290

(213) 455-1028

OPEN: by appointment
COPYING FACILITIES: no
MATERIALS SOLICITED: Oral history materials relating to women's lives in the 20th century, values and daily life patterns, women in the labor movement, women's work patterns, and birth control practices. Will also accept other oral history materials on women.

HOLDINGS:
Total volume: 500 hours of tapes
Inclusive dates: not specified
Description: Oral history interviews with women born prior to 1910 about their lives and activities in the home, in social movements, and at work outside the home, with emphasis on the 'unknown' woman.

GUIDES: A list of holdings is available from the institution.

SEE: Hinding.

TURLOCK

CA906-120

California State College, Stanislaus
Library
800 Monte Vista Avenue
Turlock CA 95380

no telephone
SEE: NUCMC, 1968.

Questionnaire not returned.

VALLEJO

CA922-840

Vallejo Naval and Historic Museum
Research and Accessions Division
734 Marin Street
Vallejo CA 94590

(707) 643-0077

OPEN: Tu-Sa 10-5; closed other days and holidays
MATERIALS SOLICITED: Materials relating to the history of the northern San Francisco Bay area and to the history of the U.S. Navy in the West.

HOLDINGS:
Total volume: not specified
Inclusive dates: 1800 -
Description: Materials relating to the cultural history of the northern San Francisco Bay area, with particular emphasis on the history of the 'North Bay Counties,' and to the history of the U.S. Navy in the West, especially the Mare Island Naval Shipyard. Documented is the influ-

ence of the Bay, area rivers, inland waterways, and other geographic features on the historical development of the region. Included are records of organizations, governments, and individuals, as well as unpublished memoirs and histories, photographs, and other audio-visual materials.

SEE: Allard, Crawley, and Edmison.

VENTURA

CA934-720

San Buenaventura Mission
Historical Museum
225 East Main Street
Ventura CA

MAILING ADDRESS:
211 East Main Street
Ventura CA 93001

(805) 648-4496

OPEN: M-Sa 10-5, Su 10-4; closed Christmas and Easter
COPYING FACILITIES: no
MATERIALS SOLICITED: Any materials related to the Mission's history.

HOLDINGS:
Total volume: 146 vols.
Inclusive dates: 1782 -
Description: A complete set of register books.

SEE: Bean and Vane; Beers - Southwest.

CA934-835

Ventura County Historical Museum
Historical Library
100 East Main Street
Ventura CA 93001

(805) 653-0323

OPEN: Tu-F 10-5; closed other days and holidays
COPYING FACILITIES: yes
MATERIALS SOLICITED: Materials pertaining to the history of Ventura County, southern California, and California in general. Will also accept other research materials.

HOLDINGS:
Total volume: 120 l.f.
Inclusive dates: 1836 -
Description: Materials pertaining chiefly to the history of Ventura County and its people, including records of businesses, churches, clubs, and local government, as well as personal papers.

SEE: Hamer (as Ventura County Free Library); NUCMC, 1965 (as Ventura County and City Free Library).

VISALIA

CA942-940

Tulare County Free Library
Historical Research Collection
200 West Oak Street
Visalia CA 93277

(209) 733-8440

OPEN: Tu 12-9; closed other days and holidays
COPYING FACILITIES: yes
MATERIALS SOLICITED: History of Tulare County. Will also accept local genealogies, photographs, and maps of the San Joaquin Valley.

HOLDINGS:
Total volume: 60 l.f.
Inclusive dates: 1852 -
Description: Correspondence of George W. Stewart relating to the establishment and later enlargement of Sequoia National Park; official agreements and other legal papers of Park-related land purchases kept by Stewart when he was associated with the U.S. Land Office; and miscellaneous letters, bulletins, announcements and other papers related to the Park. There are also materials relating to the California National Guard and the Council of Defense, United War Work Campaign during World War I; photographs; maps; records of Tulare County government agencies; records of local institutions and organizations; account books; title abstracts; and diaries of Forrest Hopping.

SEE: NUCMC, 1974.

WALNUT CREEK

CA954-720

Shadelands Ranch Historical Museum
2660 Ygnacio Valley Road
Walnut Creek CA

MAILING ADDRESS:
Box 4562
Walnut Creek CA 94596

(415) 935-7871

OPEN: by appointment only; closed holidays
COPYING FACILITIES: no
MATERIALS SOLICITED: Local history.

HOLDINGS:
Total volume: not specified
Inclusive dates: 1850 -
Description: Materials relating to the history of the Walnut Creek area since 1849 and to the life of Joseph Reddeford Walker, American trapper and guide.

WATSONVILLE

CA958-640

Pajaro Valley Historical Association
William H. Volck Museum
261 East Beach Street
Watsonville CA 95076

(408) 722-0305

OPEN: Tu-Th 9-3 or by appointment;
closed other days and holidays
COPYING FACILITIES: no
MATERIALS SOLICITED: History of the
Pajaro Valley.

HOLDINGS:
Total volume: 90 l.f.
Inclusive dates: 1865 -
Description: Letters and literary manuscripts; genealogical source materials; account books, business and financial records; non-current records of schools, city and county government agencies, and community groups and associations; architectural drawings and aerial photographs; oral history tapes and transcripts; and a photograph collection. All materials relate to the history and growth of the Pajaro Valley, with emphasis on Watsonville.

WHITTIER

CA966-860

Whittier College
Department of Geology
Fairchild Aerial Photography
Collection at Whittier College
13615 Earlham Drive
Whittier CA 90608

(213) 693-0771, Ext. 363

OPEN: by appointment only; closed
weekends and holidays
COPYING FACILITIES: yes
MATERIALS SOLICITED: Will accept historic flight records for California and surrounding states.

HOLDINGS:
Total volume: 130,000 negatives;
300,000 prints
Inclusive dates: 1927 - 1965
Description: A collection of vertical aerial photographs originating from Fairchild Aerial Surveys, including negatives, prints, and photomosaics at scales from 500 ft. to 6,000 ft. per inch. Coverage is concentrated in southern California and scattered in the rest of California and adjoining States. The exposures preserve a record of land-surface configuration prior to urbanization, of rates of change in natural features, and of changing patterns in land use and urban development.

GUIDES: *Flight Inventory, Fairchild Aerial Photograph Collection at Whittier College* (1974).

SEE ALSO: *Flight Index Maps, Fairchild Aerial Photograph Collection at Whittier College* (Whittier College, n.d.).

CA966-880

Whittier College
Wardman Library
Whittier CA 90608

(213) 693-0771, Ext. 247

OPEN: M-Th 8-10:30, F 8-5, Sa 1-5, Su
1-10:30; closed holidays and weekends
between sessions
COPYING FACILITIES: yes
MATERIALS SOLICITED: Materials relating to the Society of Friends, Richard M. Nixon, John Greenleaf Whittier, and Jessamyn West.

HOLDINGS:
Total volume: 30 l.f.
Inclusive dates: 1750 - 1969
Description: A collection of Quaker journals, meeting house records and other manuscripts, 1750-1900. There are also a small number of documents relating to Richard M. Nixon, 50 holograph letters of John Greenleaf Whittier, and 67 portfolios of manuscripts of Jessamyn West.

SEE: NUCMC, 1971.

SEE: Meckler and McMullin; Robbins.

WILLOWS

CA978-520

Mendocino National Forest
420 East Laurel Street
Willows CA 95988

(916) 934-3316

OPEN: M-F 8-4:30; closed weekends and
holidays
ACCESS: serious researchers; advance
arrangements required
COPYING FACILITIES: yes
MATERIALS SOLICITED: Materials relating to the geographic area of the Mendocino National Forest.

HOLDINGS:
Total volume: 4 file cabinets
Inclusive dates: 1907 -
Description: Records of the area encompassed by the Mendocino National Forest, including correspondence, photographs, oral history recordings and transcripts, and maps.

WILMINGTON

CA982-480

Los Angeles Harbor College
Library
1111 Figueroa Place
Wilmington CA 90744

(213) 518-1000

OPEN: M-Th 8-9, F 8-4, by appointment
only; closed weekends and holidays
ACCESS: by prior arrangement
COPYING FACILITIES: yes
MATERIALS SOLICITED: Materials relating to the history, development, and culture of the San Pedro-Wilmington, Lomita, Palos Verdes Peninsula, and Carson areas of the Los Angeles Harbor region, including development of the Harbor and maritime history.

HOLDINGS:
Total volume: 1,500 items
Inclusive dates: 1850 -
Description: Photographs, oral history tapes, and documents relating to the history and development of the Los Angeles Harbor area, including material about early residents.

YOSEMITE NATIONAL PARK

CA994-940

Yosemite National Park
Research Library and Records Center
Yosemite National Park CA

MAILING ADDRESS:
P.O. Box 577
Yosemite National Park CA 95389

(209) 372-4461, Ext. 261

OPEN: M-F 8-5; closed weekends and
holidays
ACCESS: by prior arrangement
COPYING FACILITIES: yes
MATERIALS SOLICITED: Materials relating to the history of Yosemite National Park and the surrounding region.

HOLDINGS:
Total volume: 100 l.f.
Inclusive dates: 1851 -
Description: A collection of manuscripts, correspondence, and other papers documenting the human history of the Yosemite region, with particular emphasis on the Yosemite Commissioners, the Army administration, the National Park Service, and business concessions within the Park.

SEE: Hamer.

SEE ALSO: Richard C. Davis, *North American Forest History: A Guide to Archives and Manuscripts in the United States and Canada* (Clio Books, 1977).

YREKA

CA998-440

Klamath National Forest
1312 Fairland Road
Yreka CA 96097

(916) 842-6131

OPEN: M-F 8-4:30; closed weekends and
holidays
COPYING FACILITIES: no
MATERIALS SOLICITED: Materials relating to the history of Siskiyou County, CA, northern California, forestry, and the Forest Service.

HOLDINGS:
Total volume: 30 l.f.; 300 vols.; 75
items
Inclusive dates: 1850 -
Description: Photographs, 75 oral history recordings, documents, aerial photographs, and typescript histories relating to the history of Siskiyou County, CA, Klamath National Forest, and northern California.

CA998-720
Siskiyou County Museum
910 South Main Street
Yreka CA 96097

(916) 842-3836

OPEN: Tu-Sa 9-5; closed Sundays, Mondays, and holidays
COPYING FACILITIES: yes

MATERIALS SOLICITED: History of Siskiyou County and northern California.

HOLDINGS:
Total volume: 4 l.f.
Inclusive dates: 1850 -
Description: A collection of documents relating generally to northern California and specifically to the history of Siskiyou County. Materials focus on the period 1880-1920, and relate to the development of the County's mining, agricultural, and logging industries.

SEE: Winroth.

COLORADO

The Division of State Archives and Public Records is responsible for the preservation of local public records in Colorado. Although local governments normally retain custody of their permanent records, the Archives has acquired some of these records in original or on microfilm: marriage records, incorporation papers of cities and towns, and early Denver record books.

ARVADA

CO36-40
Arvada Center for the Arts and
  Humanities
Museum
6901 Wadsworth Blvd.
Arvada CO 80003

(303) 431-3080

OPEN: by appointment only, M-F 9-5;
  closed weekends and holidays
ACCESS: advance arrangements required
COPYING FACILITIES: yes
MATERIALS SOLICITED: Photographs which document traditional and contemporary crafts and the Arvada region.

HOLDINGS:
  Total volume: 1,500 items
  Inclusive dates: 1875 - 1933
  Description: Glass negatives and slides from the studio of W.J. Collins of Rapid City, SD, depicting mining, lumbering, and cattle ranching in the Black Hills region, studio portraits of Black Hills residents, and scenes of Rapid City, Deadwood, Hot Springs, and other South Dakota towns.

ASPEN

CO54-40
Aspen Historical Society
624 West Bleeker
Aspen CO

MAILING ADDRESS:
P.O. Box 1323
Aspen CO 81611

(303) 925-3721

OPEN: M, W 9-5 and by appointment
USER FEES: $2 adults, $.50 children
ACCESS: by prior arrangement
COPYING FACILITIES: yes
MATERIALS SOLICITED: Mining information; old photographs; items 1880-1945 pertaining to skiing; biographies.

HOLDINGS:
  Total volume: 5 file cabinets
  Inclusive dates: 1879 -
  Description: Photographs, private journals, business papers, schools records, county records, and historical surveys related to the Aspen area and Pitkin County. Interest areas stressed include mining of the silver period, the Music Festival, the Aspen Institute of Humanistic Studies, and Aspen's skiing industry.

SEE: Whistler.

BAYFIELD

CO90-280
The Gem Village Museum
Bayfield CO

MAILING ADDRESS:
Route 1
Bayfield CO 81122

(303) 884-2811

OPEN: by appointment only
COPYING FACILITIES: no
MATERIALS SOLICITED: Regional geology and archaeology.

HOLDINGS:
  Total volume: 2 boxes
  Inclusive dates: 1948 - 1959
  Description: Field notes, cards, and photographs pertaining to the Pine River drainage area, 1948-50, and to the pithouse site on the San Juan River, 1956-59.

BOULDER

CO108-85
Boulder Public Library
Carnegie Branch Library
1125 Pine Street
Boulder CO

MAILING ADDRESS:
P.O. Drawer H
Boulder CO 80306

(303) 441-3110, 3100

OPEN: Tu-Th 1-9, F, Sa 9-1 or by appointment; closed Mondays, Sundays and holidays
COPYING FACILITIES: yes
MATERIALS SOLICITED: Materials relating to social, cultural, economic, and political developments in the city of Boulder and Boulder County, CO. Will also accept oral history tapes about Colorado.

HOLDINGS:
  Total volume: 9,200 items
  Inclusive dates: 1890's -
  Description: Manuscripts, records, photographs, and other materials relating to the history of Boulder and Boulder County, CO. Included are records of the Boulder Chamber of Commerce, documents on the history of Allenspark, CO, records of county cemeteries, architectural, engineering, and technical drawings of Boulder, records of the Boulder County Historic Site Inventory, and oral history recordings and transcripts concerning mining and women in Colorado.

SEE: Whistler.

CO108-560
National Oceanic and Atmospheric
  Administration
National Geophysical Data Center
325 Broadway
Boulder CO

MAILING ADDRESS:
E-GC
Boulder CO 80303

(303) 497-6215

OPEN: M-F 8-5; closed weekends and holidays
COPYING FACILITIES: yes
MATERIALS SOLICITED: Observational data on earthquakes, tsunami, volcanos, geothermal and heat flow, marine geology and geophysics, coastal bathymetry, solar phenomena, interplanetary phenomena, the magnetosphere, the ionosphere, cosmic rays (galactic and solar), aurora, and airglow; as well as marine seismic profiles; geomagnetic field measurements; and historical records on earthquakes and their effects. Will also accept other data associated with the fields of solid earth geophysics and solar-terrestrial physics.

HOLDINGS:
  Total volume: 20,200 c.f.
  Inclusive dates: 19th century -
  Description: Data on all aspects of seismology, marine geology and geophysics, geomagnetism, solar activity, interplanetary phenomena, the ionosphere, cosmic rays, auroras and airglow. About one quarter of the data is stored on magnetic tape. A historical file about U.S. earthquakes includes data from as early as 1638, although information before 1900 is spotty.

SEE ALSO: Ann Novotny, ed., *Picture Sources 3* (Special Libraries Assn., 1975). Catalogs of some of the holdings are available upon request.

CO108-740
University of Colorado
Institute of Behavioral Science
Boulder CO

MAILING ADDRESS:
Campus Box 481
Boulder CO 80306

(303) 492-8147

OPEN: by appointment only
USER FEES: $20 per hour for viewing video tapes
ACCESS: serious researchers; advance arrangements required
COPYING FACILITIES: yes
MATERIALS SOLICITED: Videotaped oral histories concerning coal mining in the West and historical photographs concerning coal mining and other forms of energy development in the West.

HOLDINGS:
Total volume: 12,000 items; 550 hours of recordings
Inclusive dates: 1890's -
Description: Audio and video recordings of interviews with coal miners and 12,000 historical photographs, relating to coal mining in the West.

SEE: Parkinson.

CO108-810
University of Colorado
Libraries
Western Historical Collections
Boulder Campus
Boulder CO

MAILING ADDRESS:
Campus Box 184
Boulder CO 80302

(303) 492-7242

OPEN: M-F 8-5; closed weekends and holidays
COPYING FACILITIES: yes
MATERIALS SOLICITED: Materials pertaining to the development of Colorado and the Rocky Mountain region, including political, economic, social, and intellectual history. Will also accept significant historical manuscripts of National interest.

HOLDINGS:
Total volume: 6,000,000 items
Inclusive dates: 1810 -
Description: Holdings principally about the settlement and development of Colorado and the Rocky Mountain region since 1860. Included are manuscript collections on politics, mining, labor, and higher education, as well as other western and local subjects.

GUIDES: Ellen Arguimbau, comp., and John A. Brennan, ed., *A Guide to Manuscript Collections* (1977).

SEE: Hamer; NUCMC, 1959-62, 65-66, 68, 70, 76-77.

SEE: Hinding; Hines; Parkinson; Svoboda and Dunning; Whistler.

SEE ALSO: John A. Brennan, 'University of Colorado's Western History Collections,' *Great Plains Journal* 2 (Spring 1972); Albert Krichmar, *The Women's Rights Movement in the United States, 1848-1970: A Bibliography and Sourcebook* (Scarecrow Press, 1972); Lawrence J. Paszek, comp., *United States Air Force History: A Guide to Documentary Sources* (Office of Air Force History, 1973); Richard C. Davis, *North American Forest History: A Guide to Archives and Manuscripts in the United States and Canada* (Clio Books, 1977). Published guides to many of the collections are available.

CASCADE

CO150-840
Ute Pass Historical Society
Ute Pass Library Building, Research Room
8010 Severy
Cascade CO

MAILING ADDRESS:
P.O. Box 2
Cascade CO 80809

(303) 684-2201

OPEN: W 10-5; other days by appointment only
COPYING FACILITIES: no
MATERIALS SOLICITED: Material relating to the history of the Ute Pass area from Manitou to Divide, CO, including Pikes Peak, Colorado Midland Railway, and areas on the Ute Trail west of Divide.

HOLDINGS:
Total volume: 2 4-drawer file cabinets
Inclusive dates: 1870's -
Description: Letters, scrapbooks, legal papers, oral histories, and 2,500 photographs relating to the development of the Ute Pass area.

COLORADO SPRINGS

CO180-120
Colorado College
Library
Special Collections
Colorado Springs CO 80903

(303) 473-2233, Ext. 668

OPEN: M-Th 9-5, F 9-4; closed weekends and holidays
COPYING FACILITIES: yes
MATERIALS SOLICITED: History of Colorado College and Colorado Springs. Will also accept materials relating to southwestern history, and literary manuscripts and letters.

HOLDINGS:
Total volume: 100 l.f.
Inclusive dates: 1812 -
Description: Manuscripts pertaining primarily to the history of Colorado College, Colorado Springs, and the American West. In addition, there are collections of letters of British poets, early U.S. history manuscripts, 18th and 19th century British literary letters, southwestern U.S. oral

history tapes, and folklore and folk music materials.

SEE: Hamer; NUCMC 1967, 76, 80.

SEE: Robbins; Hinding; Svoboda and Dunning.

CO180-640
Pikes Peak Regional Library District
Local History Collection
20 North Cascade
Colorado Springs CO

MAILING ADDRESS:
P.O. Box 1579
Colorado Springs CO 80901

(303) 473-2080

OPEN: M-Th 10-9, F, Sa 10-6; closed Sundays and holidays
COPYING FACILITIES: yes
MATERIALS SOLICITED: Materials pertaining to the history and development of the Pikes Peak region and Colorado. Will also accept material on Indians, railroading, homesteading, western exploration and expansion, health resorts and tourism, mining and cattle industries, and military installations in the region.

HOLDINGS:
Total volume: 10,000 items
Inclusive dates: 1859 -
Description: City directories and newspapers of the region; 75,000 photographic prints and negatives of the region, including works of W. H. Jackson, Horace S. Poley, Laura Gilpin, and Myron Wood; blueprints and architectural drawings; manuscript diaries, correspondence, business records, and club records; oral history interviews; pamphlets, maps, government documents; audio-visual programs; monographs and secondary writings.

SEE: Meckler and McMullin; Hinding; Robbins.

CO180-650
Pioneers' Museum
Library and Archives
215 South Tejon Street
Colorado Springs CO 80903

(303) 578-6786

OPEN: Tu-Sa 10-4; closed Mondays, weekends and holidays
COPYING FACILITIES: yes
MATERIALS SOLICITED: Material relating to Colorado Springs, the Pikes Peak region, and Colorado, including memorabilia.

HOLDINGS:
Total volume: 30 vols.; 2,000 items
Inclusive dates: 1858 -
Description: A collection of manuscripts relating chiefly to Colorado. Included are diaries, reminiscences of pioneers, Pikes Peak region photographs, genealogies, letters, documents, account books, business records, hotel registers, literary manuscripts and maps.

SEE: Hamer; NUCMC, 1959-61.

SEE: Svoboda and Dunning.

CO180-750

United States Air Force Academy
Library
Special Collections Branch
USAF Academy
Colorado Springs CO 80840

(303) 472-1818

OPEN: M-F 7:15-4:30; closed weekends
and holidays
ACCESS: by written request to the
Director of Academy Libraries
COPYING FACILITIES: yes
MATERIALS SOLICITED: Papers of military and aviation leaders, and selec-
tions from papers relative to the history of the Air Force Academy. Will
also accept materials related to the history of aeronautics.

HOLDINGS:
Total volume: 1,800 l.f.
Inclusive dates: 1907 -
Description: Manuscript collections
pertaining to the origin and development
of civil and military aeronautics in the
United States. Included are the U.S. Air
Force Academy archives, 1942 to the
present, containing official correspondence, memoranda, staff studies, reports,
minutes of meetings, and related records.
Other significant collections relate to air
warfare in World Wars I and II and the
Korean and Vietnam wars, and consist of
correspondence, memoranda, diaries,
photographs, oral history tapes and transcripts, and related materials.

SEE: NUCMC, 1979.

SEE: Meckler and McMullin; Paszek.

SEE ALSO: *Map Collections in the United
States and Canada, A Directory*
(Special Libraries Assn., 1970).

DENVER

CO252-30

The American Humane Association
Roberta Wright Reeves Memorial
Library
9725 East Hampden Avenue
Denver CO

MAILING ADDRESS:
P.O. Box 1266
Denver CO 80201

(303) 695-0811

OPEN: M-F 9-5; closed weekends and
holidays
ACCESS: by appointment only to
qualified researchers
COPYING FACILITIES: yes
MATERIALS SOLICITED: Manuscript, document, and record material relating to
animal welfare and child protection.
Will also accept agency and society materials.

HOLDINGS:
Total volume: 50,000 items
Inclusive dates: 1850 -
Description: Records, reports, and photographs pertaining to all phases of the
animal welfare and child protection
movements, chiefly in the United States,

but including international materials as
well.

SEE: Novotny.

CO252-42

Auraria Higher Education Center
Library
University Archives and Special
Collections
11th at Lawrence Street
Denver CO 80204

(303) 866-3401

OPEN: M-Th 8-5, F noon-5; closed
weekends and holidays
COPYING FACILITIES: yes
MATERIALS SOLICITED: Records and materials relating to the University and
Colleges, their faculty and alumni,
criminal justice, environmental design,
public and urban affairs, and the site
of Auraria.

HOLDINGS:
Total volume: 450 l.f.
Inclusive dates: 1860 -
Description: University records relating
to the three institutions coordinated by
the Auraria Higher Education Center,
which are the University of Colorado at
Denver, Metropolitan State College, and
the Community College of Denver. Included are governing board and administrative unit records, student publications, and faculty papers.
Special collections include the papers
of literary critic and author Donald Sutherland, the papers of the Colorado Wom-
en's Conference, the Kirschner Science
Fiction Collection, landscape architecture
lantern slides, and materials relating to
the Auraria site selection and historic
Ninth Street.

SEE: Meckler and McMullin.

CO252-70

Colorado Department of
Administration
Division of State Archives and Public
Records
1313 Sherman Street
Denver CO 80203

(303) 866-2055

OPEN: M-F 8-4:45; closed weekends and
holidays
COPYING FACILITIES: yes
MATERIALS SOLICITED: Records of Colorado State and local public agencies.

HOLDINGS:
Total volume: 53,000 c.f.; 180,000
reels of microfilm
Inclusive dates: 1859 -
Description: Records of Colorado State
and local government agencies, including
the official papers of governors.

SEE: Hamer.

SEE: Hinding; Beers - Southwest; Svoboda
and Dunning.

SEE ALSO: Ann Novotny, ed., *Picture
Sources 3* (Special Libraries Assn.,
1975); Richard C. Davis, *North American Forest History: A Guide to Archives
and Manuscripts in the United States
and Canada* (Clio Books, 1977).

CO252-80

Colorado Department of Natural
Resources
Division of Mines
1313 Sherman Street
Room 719
Denver CO 80203

(303) 839-3401

OPEN: M-F 7-5; closed weekends and
holidays
COPYING FACILITIES: yes

HOLDINGS:
Total volume: 15 file cabinets
Inclusive dates: early 1800's -
Description: Materials about mining in
Colorado, including information and annual operator's reports for all metal,
nonmetal, and coal mines; maps of all
coal mines; claim and general mining
maps; and historical information concerning mines and mining areas.

SEE: Parkinson.

CO252-90

Colorado Department of Natural
Resources
Division of Parks and Outdoor
Recreation
Information and Education Section
1313 Sherman
Room 618
Denver CO 80226

(303) 866-3437

OPEN: M-F 8-5; closed weekends and
holidays
COPYING FACILITIES: yes
MATERIALS SOLICITED: Material dealing
with Colorado local history, especially
Division of Parks and Outdoor
Recreation property, and with the development of natural resource management in Colorado.

HOLDINGS:
Total volume: 18 items
Inclusive dates: 1979 -
Description: Oral history interviews
and documents concerning the cultural
history of property administered by the
Division, as well as interviews with people active in developing natural resource
management in Colorado.

CO252-100

Colorado Historical Society
Stephen H. Hart Library
1300 Broadway
Denver CO 80203

(303) 866-2305

OPEN: Tu-Sa 9-5; closed Sundays,
Mondays, and holidays
COPYING FACILITIES: yes
MATERIALS SOLICITED: Materials relative
to or illustrative of the past, present,
and current history of Colorado.

HOLDINGS:
Total volume: 7,000,000 pieces
Inclusive dates: 1800 -
Description: Manuscripts and archives,
photographs, maps, newsfilm, oral history
tapes, and television newsfilm relating to

the history of Colorado dating principally from 1858 to the present.

GUIDES: *A Guide to the Research Collections of the State Historical Society of Colorado.*

SEE: Hamer; NUCMC, 1968-69, 71, 74-76.

SEE: Meckler and McMullin; Schatz, Novotny, Davis; Krichmar; Hines; Parkinson; Allard, Crawley, and Edmison; Hinding; Robbins; Mehr; Svoboda and Dunning; Whistler; Beers-Southwest.

CO252-120

The Colorado Mountain Club
2530 West Alameda Avenue
Denver CO 80219

(303) 922-8315

OPEN: M-F 9-2 and M, Tu, Th 7-9; closed weekends and holidays
COPYING FACILITIES: yes
MATERIALS SOLICITED: Reports on outdoor trips in the Rocky Mountains and other areas.

HOLDINGS:
Total volume: 8 l.f.
Inclusive dates: 1930's -
Description: Trip reports on mountaineering in Colorado and elsewhere in the Rocky Mountain region of the United States, including many reports by leaders of the Club's outings.

SEE: NUCMC, 1975.

CO252-152

Denver Museum of Natural History
Archives Department
Montview and Colorado Blvd.
Denver CO 80205

(303) 575-3610

OPEN: by appointment only
ACCESS: appointment requested
COPYING FACILITIES: yes
MATERIALS SOLICITED: Materials documenting the history of the Denver Museum of Natural History, its employees, Board members, and associated individuals, as well as materials relating to its collections.

HOLDINGS:
Total volume: 450 l.f.
Inclusive dates: late 1800's -
Description: Archives of the Museum, including field notes documenting international expeditions and work in the United States; manuscripts concerning anthropology and natural history; still photographs, movie film, and video tapes documenting Museum activities and field work; and audio recordings of Museum programs and oral histories.

CO252-159

Denver Public Library
Collection Development
1357 Broadway
Denver CO 80203

(303) 571-2038, 2000

OPEN: by appointment only; closed holidays

COPYING FACILITIES: no
MATERIALS SOLICITED: Eugene Field, works in verse and prose, letters, pictures. Will also accept letters addressed to Field or concerning him.

HOLDINGS:
Total volume: 400 items
Inclusive dates: 1850 - 1930
Description: 281 manuscript items by Eugene Field, plus additional items concerning him, including letters to his wife, children, and other persons.

CO252-163

Denver Public Library
Conservation Library
1357 Broadway
Denver CO 80203

(303) 571-2009, 2000

OPEN: M-W 10-9, F, Sa 10-5:30; closed Sundays, Thursdays and holidays
ACCESS: by prior arrangement
COPYING FACILITIES: yes
MATERIALS SOLICITED: All areas of conservation, including natural history, energy, fish, floods, parks, population, and wildlife biology.

HOLDINGS:
Total volume: 600 c.f.; 35,000 photographs and slides; 178 oral histories
Inclusive dates: 1900 -
Description: Papers of individuals, records of organizations and government agencies, and other materials covering the history of the environmental movement, primarily in the United States, but also in Latin America and other parts of the world. Federal lands, wildlife, forestry, water, and grazing are among the areas of strength.

SEE ALSO: Alan M. Meckler and Ruth McMullin, comps., *Oral History Collections* (Bowker, 1975); Richard C. Davis, *North American Forest History: A Guide to Archives and Manuscripts in the United States and Canada* (Clio Books, 1977). A descriptive brochure is available from the repository.

CO252-172

Denver Public Library
Genealogy Division
1357 Broadway
Denver CO 80203

(303) 571-2190, 2000

OPEN: M-W 10-9, F, Sa 10-5:30; closed Sundays, Thursdays and holidays
COPYING FACILITIES: yes
MATERIALS SOLICITED: Family histories.

HOLDINGS:
Total volume: 20 drawers
Inclusive dates: 1930 -
Description: Collection emphasizes the states east of the Mississippi. Notebook file of Colorado pioneers; genealogical clippings and manuscripts, charts and maps. Obituary index for Denver area 1940-present; notebook file of non-local obituaries.

CO252-181

Denver Public Library
Western History Department
1357 Broadway
Denver CO 80203

(303) 571-2009, 2000

OPEN: M-Th 10-9, F-Sa 10-5:30; closed Sundays and holidays
COPYING FACILITIES: yes
MATERIALS SOLICITED: Trans-Mississippi West. Strong emphasis on Denver, Colorado and Rocky Mountain region. All subject areas included.

HOLDINGS:
Total volume: 1,425 l.f.; 300 oral histories; 280,000 photographs
Inclusive dates: 19th century -
Description: Materials reflecting all phases of the development of States west of the Mississippi River, with emphasis on those in the Rocky Mountain region. Materials cover the earliest explorations, Spanish land grants, and the gold rush era to the present day, and include manuscripts, microfilm, oral histories and photographs.

SEE: Hamer; NUCMC 1969, 74, 79.

SEE: Hounshell; Parkinson; Hinding; Whistler.

SEE ALSO: Ann Novotny, ed., *Picture Sources 3* (Special Libraries Assn., 1975). Alan M. Meckler and Ruth McMullin, comps., *Oral History Collections* (Bowker, 1975).

Richard C. Davis, *North American Forest History: A Guide to Archives and Manuscripts in the United States and Canada* (Clio Books, 1977).

CO252-360

The Iliff School of Theology
Ira J. Taylor Library
2201 South University Blvd.
Denver CO 80210

(303) 744-1287, Ext. 164

OPEN: M-F 8-4:30; closed weekends and holidays
ACCESS: An interview with the Conference Archivist, the Librarian of The Iliff School of Theology, or their representatives is required.
COPYING FACILITIES: yes
MATERIALS SOLICITED: Records and papers generated by the Iliff School of Theology and persons connected with it; records and papers generated by the Rocky Mountain United Methodist Conference and persons connected with it. Will also accept material of archival value related to the Methodist church and religion in the Rocky Mountain area, particularly in Colorado.

HOLDINGS:
Total volume: 300 l.f.
Inclusive dates: 1863 -
Description: A joint archives of The Iliff School of Theology and the Rocky Mountain United Methodist Conference. Most of the material is at present unprocessed, so the extent of the collection is not known. It does include records of some of the Methodist, Evangelical United Brethren, and United Methodist

churches in Colorado, some of the records of The Iliff School of Theology, and correspondence and other personal papers of several prominent figures in Colorado Methodism.

SEE: Hamer (as Colorado Methodist Historical Society).

CO252-550

National Archives and Records
    Administration
Archives Branch
Building 48, Denver Federal Center
Denver CO 80225

(303) 776-0817

OPEN: M-F 7:30-4; closed weekends and holidays
ACCESS: Records are open, subject to Federal agency restrictions and restrictions based upon current legislation relevant to confidentiality and security classification. See General Information Leaflet No. 2, 'Regulations for the Public Use of Records in the National Archives.'
COPYING FACILITIES: yes
MATERIALS SOLICITED: Records of Federal agencies located in GSA Region 8. Until 1972 it covered the States of Arizona, Colorado, New Mexico, Utah, and Wyoming. Since 1972 the region consists of Colorado, Montana, North and South Dakota, Utah, and Wyoming. Will also accept other materials when approval is granted by the Records Disposition Division and approved by officials of the Office of the National Archives.

HOLDINGS:
   Total volume: 10,731 c.f.
   Inclusive dates: 1847 - 1965
   Description: Included are records, 1847-1965, created by Federal agencies primarily located in the Rocky Mountain area. There are records of the Bureau of Indian Affairs, U.S. District Courts, Bureau of Land Management, U.S. Forest Service, Bureau of Reclamation, Denver Mint, War Assets Administration, and Civilian Conservation Corps. The records concern the activities of each special agency and take the form of case files, correspondence, and reports.
    There are also 30,000 still pictures of the Bureau of Reclamation, ca. 1905-1965.

SEE: Hamer.

SEE: Paszek; Hinding; Beers - Southwest.

SEE ALSO: *Research Opportunities* (Denver Federal Records Center, 1967); Frances L. Swadesh, 'Analysis of Records of the Southern Ute Agency, 1877 through 1952, National Archives RG 75, in the Federal Records Center, Denver, Colorado,' in Omer C. Stewart, *Ethnohistorical Bibliography of the Ute Indians of Colorado* (Univ. of Colorado Press, 1971). Preliminary inventories for some record groups available at the repository.

Richard C. Davis, *North American Forest History: A Guide to Archives and Manuscripts in the United States and Canada* (Clio Books, 1977).

CO252-680

Regis College
Library
West 50th Avenue and Lowell Blvd.
Denver CO 80221

no telephone

SEE: Hamer.

Questionnaire not returned.

CO252-780

United Bank of Denver, N.A.
Archives Center
1740 Broadway
Denver CO

MAILING ADDRESS:
P.O. Box 5247
Denver CO 80217

(303) 861-8811

OPEN: M-F 8-5; closed weekends and holidays
ACCESS: by written request
COPYING FACILITIES: yes
MATERIALS SOLICITED: Materials relating to United Bank of Denver and its predecessor banks, the United States National Bank (in Denver), the Denver National Bank, the National Bank of Commerce, the Daniels Bank, and the Hamilton National Bank.

HOLDINGS:
   Total volume: 250 items; 25 l.f.
   Inclusive dates: 1884 -
   Description: Materials documenting United Bank of Denver and its predecessors, including ledgers, scrapbooks, photographs, and oral history interviews.

CO252-820

University of Denver
Penrose Library
2150 East Evans Avenue
Denver CO 80208

(303) 871-2212

OPEN: M-F 8-5; closed weekends and holidays
ACCESS: prior communication or an interview with the Archivist
COPYING FACILITIES: yes
MATERIALS SOLICITED: Records, papers and publications generated by the University of Denver and persons associated with it and materials from organizations or individuals noted for their historic or community involvement. Will also accept Western Americana, early State and Territory records, documents, and correspondence pertaining to historic activities in the Rocky Mountain region.

HOLDINGS:
   Total volume: not specified
   Inclusive dates: 1862 -
   Description: Records and manuscripts, photographs, maps, and oral history tapes relating to the history of the University of Denver (Colorado Seminary) since 1862 and documents pertaining to the development of Colorado Territory and State, including railroads in Colorado and the Rocky Mountain area.

SEE: NUCMC, 1976-77.

SEE: Robbins.

DURANGO

CO270-240

Fort Lewis College
Library
Center of Southwest Studies
College Heights
Durango CO 81301

(303) 247-7456, 7713

OPEN: M-F 8-5; closed weekends and holidays
ACCESS: Librarian or Director of Center must give permission for the use of the material
COPYING FACILITIES: yes
MATERIALS SOLICITED: Material about the Southwest: Colorado, New Mexico, Arizona, Utah, western Texas, Nevada, southern California.

HOLDINGS:
   Total volume: not specified
   Inclusive dates: 1850 -
   Description: A collection of microfilm and original materials on the southwestern United States and Mexico. Included are documents relating to the Ute Indians, mining, water surveys, military activities, Spanish exploration and colonization, the Rio Grande Southern Railroad, the Western Colorado Power Company, and various businesses in the Durango area.

GUIDES: *Center of Southwest Studies: Opportunities for Research* (n.d.).

ENGLEWOOD

CO306-200

Englewood Public Library
3400 South Elati Street
Englewood CO 80110

(303) 761-4376

OPEN: M-Th 9-9, F-Sa 9-5:30; closed Sundays and holidays
COPYING FACILITIES: yes
MATERIALS SOLICITED: Englewood history. Will also accept materials relating to nearby areas.

HOLDINGS:
   Total volume: 20 l.f.
   Inclusive dates: 1870 -
   Description: Englewood city documents, mostly recent, including minutes of boards and commissions and City Council agenda items; photographs and slides; manuscripts; and 37 oral history interviews on Englewood history.

SEE: Whistler.

FORT COLLINS

CO378-110
Colorado State University
Germans from Russia in Colorado
Study Project
Fort Collins CO 80523

(303) 491-1844, 5911

OPEN: by appointment only
COPYING FACILITIES: yes
MATERIALS SOLICITED: Materials of or relating to Germans from Russia (also known, incorrectly, as 'Volga' Germans). Will also accept materials pertaining to German-Americans and to the Soviet Union's minority policies and activities.

HOLDINGS:
    Total volume: 350 items
    Inclusive dates: 1850 -
    Description: A collection of theses, dissertations, articles, oral history tapes and transcripts, family documents and manuscripts, and other items relating to Germans from Russia who settled in Colorado.

SEE: Whistler.

SEE ALSO: Germans from Russia in Colorado Study Project *Newsletter* (July and Dec. 1976).

CO378-120
Colorado State University
Libraries
Special Collections
University Archives
Fort Collins CO 80523

(303) 491-1844, 5911

OPEN: M, W, F 8-12, Tu, Th 1-5; closed weekends and holidays
COPYING FACILITIES: yes
MATERIALS SOLICITED: Materials pertaining to the history of Colorado State University. Will also accept materials related to the areas of study and research at Colorado State University.

HOLDINGS:
    Total volume: 2,000 l.f.
    Inclusive dates: 1872 -
    Description: Records of Colorado State University and papers of its faculty members, papers of William E. Morgan, correspondence of Elwood Mead, the Peace Corps and Peace Research collections, and records of the Colorado Forestry Association.

SEE: Hamer; NUCMC, 1965, 69, 80.

SEE: Hinding; Robbins; Davis.

CO378-250
Fort Collins Museum
200 Mathews Street
Fort Collins CO

MAILING ADDRESS:
Avery House
328 West Mountain Avenue
Fort Collins CO 80521

(303) 221-6738

OPEN: by appointment only; closed Mondays and major holidays
ACCESS: by prior appointment
COPYING FACILITIES: yes
MATERIALS SOLICITED: Historic materials relating to the development of Fort Collins, Larimer County, and northern Colorado.

HOLDINGS:
    Total volume: not specified
    Inclusive dates: 1862 -
    Description: A collection pertaining to pioneer movement and settlement in Fort Collins and Larimer County, including letters, diaries, journals, sheet music, records of early organizations, and scrapbooks.

CO378-260
Fort Collins Public Library
Local History
201 Peterson Street
Fort Collins CO 80524

(303) 221-6740

OPEN: M-F 1:30-5:30; closed weekends and holidays
COPYING FACILITIES: yes
MATERIALS SOLICITED: Photographs and written materials of Larimer County, CO.

HOLDINGS:
    Total volume: 58,515 items
    Inclusive dates: 1866 -
    Description: Materials relating to Colorado, with emphasis on Larimer County, CO, including oral history recordings and transcripts, 58,000 photographs, and manuscripts relating to Colorado State University and Fort Collins.

SEE: Whistler.

GEORGETOWN

CO414-280
Georgetown Society, Inc.
Georgetown CO

MAILING ADDRESS:
P.O. Box 667
Georgetown CO 80444

(303) 569-2840

OPEN: M-F 8-5; closed weekends and holidays
ACCESS: appointment required
COPYING FACILITIES: yes
MATERIALS SOLICITED: Local history of Georgetown and the surrounding area. Will also accept materials on early local inhabitants before or after their residence in Georgetown.

HOLDINGS:
    Total volume: 100 l.f.
    Inclusive dates: 1860's -
    Description: The collection includes photographs and slides of Georgetown buildings, people, and events since the 1960's. Most of the manuscripts consist of business records of William A. Hamill, from the 1880's to the early 1900's, and subsequent business records, continuing through 1920, of mining companies formerly owned by Hamill.

GOLDEN

CO458-80
Buffalo Bill Memorial Museum
Golden CO

MAILING ADDRESS:
Box 950, Route 5
Golden CO 80401

(303) 526-0744

OPEN: daily 9-5 May 1-Oct. 1, daily 9-4 other months; closed Mondays (winter) and holidays
ACCESS: appointment required
COPYING FACILITIES: yes
MATERIALS SOLICITED: Materials concerning William F. Cody, Johnny Baker, and the Buffalo Bill Wild West Show and persons involved with it.

HOLDINGS:
    Total volume: 4,500 items
    Inclusive dates: 1850 -
    Description: A collection of approximately 2,500 letters, receipts, account books, travel schedules, and vouchers pertaining to the life of William F. Cody and his Wild West Show, as well as 2,000 related photographs and negatives.

SEE ALSO: Ann Novotny, ed., *Picture Sources 3* (Special Libraries Assn., 1975).

CO458-110
Colorado Railroad Historical
    Foundation, Inc.
Colorado Railroad Museum
17155 West 44th Avenue
Golden CO

MAILING ADDRESS:
P.O. Box 10
Golden CO 80402

(303) 279-4591

OPEN: daily 9-5; closed holidays
COPYING FACILITIES: yes
MATERIALS SOLICITED: Materials regarding the railroads of Colorado and the West.

HOLDINGS:
    Total volume: 30 tons
    Inclusive dates: 1840's -
    Description: Office and operating files of various Colorado and regional railroads, including photographs, maps, and blueprints, along with correspondence, timetables, and other related material.

CO458-130
Colorado School of Mines
Arthur Lakes Library
Golden CO 80401

(303) 273-3694, 3665

OPEN: M-F 8-5; closed weekends and holidays
ACCESS: advance arrangements requested
COPYING FACILITIES: yes
MATERIALS SOLICITED: History of the Colorado School of Mines, careers of its graduates, the mineral industries, and mining in the Rocky Mountains.

Will also accept materials concerning the mineral industries worldwide.

HOLDINGS:
Total volume: not specified
Inclusive dates: not specified
Description: Materials concerning the history of the Colorado School of Mines, careers of its graduates, and the mineral industries primarily in Colorado, but also worldwide.

SEE: Hamer; NUCMC, 1968.

GRAND JUNCTION

CO476-520
Mesa County Public Library
530 Grand Avenue
Grand Junction CO 81501

(303) 243-4442

OPEN: M-W 10-9, Th-Sa 10-5; closed Sundays and holidays
COPYING FACILITIES: yes
MATERIALS SOLICITED: Materials relating to the history of Mesa County and the western slope of Colorado. Will also accept materials relating to Colorado history.

HOLDINGS:
Total volume: 25 l.f.
Inclusive dates: 1880 -
Description: Manuscripts, newspaper clippings, biographical information on settlers, oral history interviews, reminiscences of early setters, and an obituary file, relating to Mesa County history.

SEE: Whistler.

CO476-540
Museum of Western Colorado
Archives
4th and Ute
Grand Junction CO 81501

(303) 242-0971

OPEN: Su 2-5, Tu-Sa 10-5; closed Mondays and holidays
COPYING FACILITIES: yes
MATERIALS SOLICITED: Oral history tapes, especially pertaining to the Glade Park and Plateau Valley areas; historical material on Mesa County, Ute Indians in western Colorado, and development of western Colorado oil shale; and photographs of Mesa County pioneers and early towns. Will also accept documents, business records, unpublished manuscripts, genealogical data, etc., pertaining to the settling of the Western Slope of Colorado and its more recent history.

HOLDINGS:
Total volume: 3,000 items
Inclusive dates: 1880 -
Description: A collection of manuscripts, photographs, and oral history tapes (as yet untranscribed), relating chiefly to western Colorado. Included are diaries, letters, histories written by pioneers, and papers on transportation, oil shale, the Ute Indians, exploration, and businesses.

GREELEY

CO498-40
American Historical Society of Germans from Russia
Archives and Historical Library
Greeley Public Library
Greeley CO 80631

(303) 353-4955, 6123

OPEN: M-Th 9-9, F, Sa 9-6; closed Sundays and holidays
COPYING FACILITIES: yes
MATERIALS SOLICITED: Anything relating to the history of Germans from Russia, including genealogical data.

HOLDINGS:
Total volume: 1,056 volumes
Inclusive dates: 1763 -
Description: Materials relating to the history of Germans from Russia.

CO498-270
City of Greeley Museums
919 7th Street
Greeley CO 80631

(303) 353-6123, Ext. 391

OPEN: Tu-Sa 9-5; closed Sundays, Mondays, and holidays
COPYING FACILITIES: yes
MATERIALS SOLICITED: Materials pertaining to the history of Greeley and Weld County. Will also accept historical materials on Colorado and the surrounding region.

HOLDINGS:
Total volume: 40 l.f.
Inclusive dates: 1869 -
Description: Maps, diaries, letters, scrapbooks, ledgers, Union Colony records and minute books, records of other local businesses, and a large photograph collection, 1870 to date.

LEADVILLE

CO640-480
Lake County Public Library
Colorado Mountain History Collection
1115 Harrison Avenue
Leadville CO 80461

(303) 486-0569

OPEN: M-Th 11-8, F, Sa 1-5; closed Sundays and holidays
COPYING FACILITIES: yes
MATERIALS SOLICITED: Materials regarding the town of Leadville and Lake County. Will also accept materials regarding the surrounding areas.

HOLDINGS:
Total volume: 10 c.f.
Inclusive dates: 1880 -
Description: Miscellaneous letters, mining maps from 1880's. Also account books and guest registers from the Vendome (Tabor Grand) Hotel, 1892-1970; as well as a catalogued photograph collection of the Leadville area.

LONGMONT

CO676-480
Longmont Pioneer Museum
Archives
375 Kimbark Street
Longmont CO 80501

(303) 776-6050, Ext. 374

OPEN: by appointment only
COPYING FACILITIES: yes
MATERIALS SOLICITED: Family histories, Seth Terry diaries and information, and Charles Boynton photographs relating to the history of Longmont and Boulder County, CO. Will also accept other photographs and records concerning Longmont and the St. Vrain Valley.

HOLDINGS:
Total volume: 1 file cabinet; 12 l.f.
Inclusive dates: 1859 - mid-1940's
Description: Family histories of pioneers in the Longmont area, 1859-1929, the Charles Boynton photograph collection, and records, diaries, and photographs relating to the history of Longmont and the St. Vrain Valley.

LOVELAND

CO685-480
Loveland Public Library
205 East 6th
Loveland CO 80537

(303) 667-4040

OPEN: Tu-Th 10-9, F, Sa 10-5; closed Sundays, Mondays and holidays
COPYING FACILITIES: yes
MATERIALS SOLICITED: Oral history tapes of the Loveland area.

HOLDINGS:
Total volume: 70 items
Inclusive dates: 1972 -
Description: Materials relating to the history of the Loveland area, including oral history interviews and biographies of settlers.

SEE: Whistler.

NEW CASTLE

CO730-280
Garfield County Public Library
New Castle CO

MAILING ADDRESS:
P.O. Box 320
New Castle CO 81647

(303) 984-2346

OPEN: M-Th 9-8, F, Sa 9-5; closed Sundays and holidays
COPYING FACILITIES: yes
MATERIALS SOLICITED: Photographs and oral history tapes and transcripts pertaining to the history of Garfield County and Colorado. Will also accept records of local institutions and organizations.

HOLDINGS:
Total volume: 3 l.f.
Inclusive dates: 1908 -
Description: A collection of old and rare photographs of local interest and oral history recordings pertinent to local and Colorado State history.

PUEBLO

CO768-640
Pueblo Library District
Western Research Room
100 East Abriendo Avenue
Pueblo CO 81004

(303) 544-1940

OPEN: Tu noon-4, 7-9, Th noon-4:30, F 9-6; other times by appointment
COPYING FACILITIES: yes
MATERIALS SOLICITED: Materials on Pueblo, southeastern Colorado, and Colorado, with emphasis on ethnicity.
HOLDINGS:
Total volume: 16,515 items; 24 l.f.; 61 boxes
Inclusive dates: 1870's -
Description: Materials relating to the history of Pueblo and southeastern Colorado, including homestead records; pho-tographs; maps; oral history interviews relating to ethnicity, water rights, and women; oral histories, photographs, and school records relating to country schools in Colorado; records of Woodcroft Hospital, the Gobatti Manufacturing Company, and the Columbian Federation, an Italian-American fraternal organization; and data sheets and photographs documenting local buildings.

SEE: Parkinson; Whistler.

STEAMBOAT SPRINGS

CO856-80
Bud Werner Memorial Library
The Routt County Collection
Steamboat Springs CO

MAILING ADDRESS:
P.O. Box 774568
Steamboat Springs CO 80477

(303) 879-0240

OPEN: M-Th 10-8, F, Sa 10-5; closed Sundays and holidays
COPYING FACILITIES: yes
MATERIALS SOLICITED: Materials relating to Routt County, particularly its ranching, mining, and skiing history.

HOLDINGS:
Total volume: 6 file drawers
Inclusive dates: 1877 -
Description: Manuscripts, studies, dissertations, diaries, clippings, oral history recordings, maps and photographs relating to the history of Routt County.

SEE: Whistler.

TRINIDAD

CO910-120
Carnegie Public Library
Trinidad CO 81082

no telephone

SEE: Hamer.

Questionnaire not returned.

CONNECTICUT

Since 1903 the Connecticut State Library has been authorized to accept and preserve local government records of permanent value. Most town and city records are locally held, but the State Library in Hartford has accessioned town meeting records, tax lists, voters' lists, justice of the peace papers, and other similar records, dating from 1700 to the present. The Library also has microfilm copies of vital, land, and probate records of localities, 1635 to 1850, which were filmed by the Church of Jesus Christ of Latter-day Saints. Guides to some record groups of local public records are available at the Library.

ANSONIA

CT4-160
Derby Historical Society
Gen. David Humphreys House
37 Elm Street
Ansonia CT

MAILING ADDRESS:
P.O. Box 331
Derby CT 06418

(203) 735-1908, 3016

OPEN: M-F 9-4:30; closed weekends and holidays
COPYING FACILITIES: yes
MATERIALS SOLICITED: Materials relating to the lower Naugatuck Valley (Ansonia, Derby, Seymour, Shelton, and Oxford).

HOLDINGS:
  Total volume: 100 c.f.
  Inclusive dates: 1650 -
  Description: Materials relating to regional history and particularly to Commodore Isaac Hull, General David Humphreys, and the Rev. Dr. Richard Mansfield.

BRIDGEPORT

CT36-80
Bridgeport Public Library
Historical Collections
925 Broad Street
Bridgeport CT 06604

(203) 576-7417

OPEN: M-W, F, Sa 9-5; closed Thursdays, Sundays, holidays and Saturdays in summer

ACCESS: serious researchers at discretion of Library
COPYING FACILITIES: yes
MATERIALS SOLICITED: Materials on Bridgeport and regional activities in greater Bridgeport area, pertaining to government, business, labor, ethnic groups, community organizations, health, welfare and religion. Circus materials, especially those pertaining to P. T. Barnum and associates.

HOLDINGS:
  Total volume: 750 l.f.
  Inclusive dates: 1700 -
  Description: Over 200 collections pertaining to Bridgeport and Fairfield County. Included are personal papers, organizational records, city archives and audio-visual materials. Personal papers and organizational records concern business activities (shipping, railroading, local manufacturing, retail business), architecture, cultural and scientific activities, education, military affairs (Revolutionary War, War of 1812, Civil War, World War II), health, welfare and community organizations. City archives are represented by records of several major departments, recent mayors and the Common Council. A collection of circus material is centered primarily around Phineas T. Barnum and his associates.
  Also included are oral history materials and military materials concerning World War 1, the Korean War and the Vietnam War.

SEE: Hamer; NUCMC, 1966.

SEE: Hinding; Robbins.

SEE ALSO: Ann Novotny, ed., *Picture Sources 3* (Special Libraries Assn., 1975); *Map Collections in the United States and Canada, A Directory* (Special Libraries Assn., 1970); Nelle Neafie, *A P. T. Barnum Bibliography Selected by Nelle Neafie* (Bridgeport Public Library, 1965).

BRISTOL

CT48-40
American Clock and Watch Museum, Inc.
Edward Ingraham Library
100 Maple Street
Bristol CT 06010

(203) 583-6070

OPEN: April - Oct., daily 11-5; closed Nov. - March
ACCESS: appointment required
COPYING FACILITIES: yes
MATERIALS SOLICITED: Records relating to horology.

HOLDINGS:
  Total volume: 60 c.f.
  Inclusive dates: late 18th century -
  Description: Historical and technical information on handcrafting and manufacturing of clocks and watches, with emphasis on U.S. production. Included are photographs, manuscripts, accounting records of clock makers, diaries of clock makers, and director's minutes of clock manufacturing companies.

CT48-80
Bristol Public Library
5 High Street
Bristol CT 06010

no telephone

SEE: Hamer.

Questionnaire not returned.

COLEBROOK

CT102-120
Colebrook Historical Society, Inc.
Colebrook CT

MAILING ADDRESS:
Curator
Box 85
Colebrook CT 06021

(203) 379-3130

OPEN: Memorial Day - Columbus Day, Sa, Su, and holidays 2-4, or by appointment; closed rest of year
ACCESS: prior arrangements required
COPYING FACILITIES: no
MATERIALS SOLICITED: Materials pertaining to the history of Colebrook and its inhabitants.

HOLDINGS:
  Total volume: 500 items
  Inclusive dates: 1800 -
  Description: Correspondence, local histories, diaries, logbooks, account books, and genealogical source data pertaining to people and places of Colebrook, as well as photographs, lists of voters and school students, and school reports.

COLLINSVILLE

CT108-120
The Canton Historical Society
Canton Historical Museum
Library
11 Front Street
Collinsville CT 06022

(203) 693-2793

OPEN: Tu-Th 12-4, Su 2-5; closed
Mondays, Fridays, Saturdays and Dec.
1-April 1
USER FEES: one dollar for non-members,
25 cents for students and senior
citizens
COPYING FACILITIES: no
MATERIALS SOLICITED: Historical documents pertaining to the history of Canton, 1806 to the present. Will also accept historical documents pertaining to
surrounding area and documents of
general interest pertaining to the Victorian period.

HOLDINGS:
Total volume: 75 items
Inclusive dates: 1850 - 1910
Description: A collection pertaining to
the history of Canton and the surrounding area. Included are materials relating
to the Collins Company, old deeds, photographs, and memorabilia from local
families.
Collection contains oral history tapes
and manuscripts.

CORNWALL

CT120-120
Cornwall Historical Society
Pine Street
Cornwall CT

MAILING ADDRESS:
P.O. Box 115
Cornwall CT 06796

no telephone

OPEN: Su 12-5, Sa 10-5, and by
appointment; closed Nov. 1 - May 1
ACCESS: by prior arrangement
COPYING FACILITIES: yes
MATERIALS SOLICITED: Will accept materials relating to the history of Cornwall.

HOLDINGS:
Total volume: 300 c.f.
Inclusive dates: 1740 -
Description: Papers connected with the
history of Cornwall and its residents, including the town archives, early genealogical and vital records, school records,
and materials concerning officers in the
Revolutionary War and Civil War.

SEE: Hamer (as Cornwall Free Library).

SEE: Hinding.

DANBURY

CT144-150
Danbury Scott-Fenton Museum and
Historical Society
43 Main Street
Danbury CT 06810

(203) 743-5200

OPEN: Tu-F 10-5, Sa, Su 2-5; closed
Mondays and holidays
COPYING FACILITIES: yes
MATERIALS SOLICITED: Maps of the
Danbury area; account books, diaries,
photographs, and manuscripts relating
to Danbury history and people; Charles
E. Ives materials; and genealogical
data.

HOLDINGS:
Total volume: 10 l.f.; 2 file cabinets
Inclusive dates: 1740 -
Description: Danbury history materials;
Charles E. Ives biographical materials,
clippings, and photographs; documents,
patents, diaries, scrapbooks, ledgers,
clippings, and photographs relating to the
hatting industry; a mid-19th century farm
diary; and Civil War diaries.

CT144-880
Western Connecticut State College
Ruth A. Haas Library
Archives
181 White Street
Danbury CT 06810

(203) 797-4118, 4052, 4343

OPEN: M-Th 8-11, F 8-4:30, Sa 9-4, Su
1-9; closed holidays
COPYING FACILITIES: yes
MATERIALS SOLICITED: Historical materials, with emphasis on Danbury and
Fairfield County, CT, adjoining areas
of New York State, and New England
in general, as well as Western Connecticut State College archives.

HOLDINGS:
Total volume: 125 l.f.; 170 c.f.
Inclusive dates: 1764 - 1963
Description: Records from Danbury
City Hall, including tax lists, voting
records, vital statistics, city utility
records, correspondence of selectmen, city
court records, minutes of school board
meetings, welfare applications and histories, WPA records, military enrollment
records, and a collection of early maps.
There are also Civil War letters, local
diaries covering the period 1852-92, and
documents pertaining to social life and
student government at the College since
its establishment in 1904.

GUIDES: Doris Ann Rourke, 'Guide to
Archival Materials in the Ruth A. Haas
Library, Western Connecticut State
College,' (1977) is available from the
Library.

EAST HADDAM

CT174-200
East Haddam Historical Society
Rathbun Free Memorial Library
Main Street, Route 149
East Haddam CT 06423

(203) 873-8210

OPEN: Tu, W, F 10-5, Th 10-8; closed
weekends, Mondays and holidays
COPYING FACILITIES: yes
MATERIALS SOLICITED: Historical materials pertaining to East Haddam.

HOLDINGS:
Total volume: 96 sq.f.
Inclusive dates: 1704 -
Description: Scrapbooks, vital statistics,
account books, diaries, documents, and
land, probate, and cemetery records.

EAST HARTFORD

CT186-800
United Technologies Corporation
Archives
400 Main Street
MS124-22I
East Hartford CT 06114

MAILING ADDRESS:
400 Main Street (Airport Office
Annex)
East Hartford CT 06108

(203) 565-5401

OPEN: by appointment only
ACCESS: serious researchers; prior
approval and appointment required
COPYING FACILITIES: yes
MATERIALS SOLICITED: Materials relating
to the history, product, and technology
of United Technologies Corporation
and its divisions. Will also accept related materials pertaining to customers,
including airlines, the U. S. Army,
Navy, and Air Force, continental and
international customers, and owners
and operators of United Technologies
Corporation products.

HOLDINGS:
Total volume: 1,300 c.f.
Inclusive dates: 1908 -
Description: Technical, business, legal,
and general records pertaining primarily
to corporation aviation activities, including the Pratt & Whitney Aircraft, Sikorsky Aircraft, and Hamilton Standard
companies. Included are correspondence,
technical reports, photographs, engineering drawings, company publications, oral
history recordings and transcripts, audio-
visual records, manuscripts, microforms,
motion pictures, and scrapbooks.

EAST HAVEN

CT198-80

Branford Electric Railway Association, Inc.
Branford Trolley Museum
Kuhn Memorial Library
17 River Street
East Haven CT 06512

(203) 467-6927

OPEN: by appointment only
COPYING FACILITIES: no
MATERIALS SOLICITED: Materials related to the technological, social, and economic history of electric railway transportation, including streetcars, interurbans, and rapid transit. Will also accept materials dealing with related modes of public transportation, including cable cars, buses, and railroads.

HOLDINGS:
Total volume: not specified
Inclusive dates: 1880's -
Description: Photographs, blueprints, maps, and business records related to the technology and history of the electric railway industry and its role in American life.

FAIRFIELD

CT234-230

Fairfield Historical Society
636 Old Post Road
Fairfield CT 06430

(203) 259-1598

OPEN: M-F 9:30-4:30, Su 1-5 by appointment; closed Saturdays and holidays
COPYING FACILITIES: yes
MATERIALS SOLICITED: Materials relating to the town of Fairfield.

HOLDINGS:
Total volume: 200 l.f.; 5,000 photographs
Inclusive dates: early 18th century -
Description: Family papers, church records, school records, account books of merchants and craftspeople, tax lists, organization records, photographs, and newspaper clippings relating to the history of Fairfield County in particular and Connecticut and New England in general. Topics covered include genealogy, geography, agriculture, industry, biography, and domestic and fine arts, with strongest holdings for the 19th century.

SEE: Hamer; NUCMC, 1977.

CT234-250

Fairfield Public Library
1080 Old Post Road
Fairfield CT 06430

(203) 255-8250

OPEN: M-F 9-8:30, Sa 9-5; closed Sundays and holidays
COPYING FACILITIES: yes
MATERIALS SOLICITED: Will accept material on Hungarian-Americans in Fairfield.

HOLDINGS:
Total volume: 20 items
Inclusive dates: 1973 -
Description: Oral history of Fairfield, covering transportation at the turn of the century and the development of the local Hungarian-American community.

SEE: NUCMC, 1975.

CT234-260

Fairfield University
Nyselius Library
University Archives
North Benson Road
Fairfield CT 06430

(203) 254-4000, Ext. 2179

OPEN: M-F 8:30-4:30; closed weekends and holidays
ACCESS: by application to University Reference Librarian
COPYING FACILITIES: yes
MATERIALS SOLICITED: Fairfield University and Fairfield College Preparatory School archival materials.

HOLDINGS:
Total volume: 80 l.f.
Inclusive dates: 1940 -
Description: Miscellaneous records and publications of or pertaining to Fairfield University and Fairfield College Preparatory School; some sound and video tapes of University forums and programs; master's theses of Fairfield University School of Corporate and Political Communication; and some related photographs and news clippings.

FARMINGTON

CT247-240

Farmington Village Green and Library Association
Farmington Museum
37 High Street
Farmington CT 06032

(203) 677-9222

OPEN: by appointment only
COPYING FACILITIES: no
MATERIALS SOLICITED: Materials relating to life in Farmington.

HOLDINGS:
Total volume: 200 items
Inclusive dates: 1750 -
Description: Chiefly 18th and 19th century materials pertaining to Farmington, including account books, sermons and church records, a journal, photographs, and genealogical source data.

SEE: Hamer.

The Museum is also known as the Stanley-Whitman House.

CT247-640

Miss Porter's School
Archives
Farmington CT 06032

no telephone

SEE: NUCMC, 1979.

Questionnaire not returned.

GLASTONBURY

CT254-320

Historical Society of Glastonbury
1944 Main Street
Glastonbury CT

MAILING ADDRESS:
P.O. Box 46
Glastonbury CT 06033

(203) 633-6890

OPEN: M 10-1, or by appointment; closed holidays
COPYING FACILITIES: no
MATERIALS SOLICITED: Materials relating to Glastonbury history, including photographs and research relating to old houses.

HOLDINGS:
Total volume: 45 l.f.; 22 file drawers
Inclusive dates: 1750 -
Description: Chiefly 18th and 19th century materials relating to Glastonbury, including account books, business accounts, diaries, letters, sermons, genealogical data, research relating to 18th and 19th century houses, school records, photographs, and tax lists.

SEE: Hamer.

GOSHEN

CT261-280

Goshen Historical Society
Old Middle Road
R.D. 1
Goshen CT 06756

(203) 491-2665

OPEN: by appointment only
COPYING FACILITIES: no
MATERIALS SOLICITED: Materials relating to Goshen.

HOLDINGS:
Total volume: 100 vols; 1 file cabinet
Inclusive dates: late 18th century -
Description: Correspondence, deeds, account books, diaries, journals, genealogical source data, records, and scrapbooks relating to Goshen.

GRANBY

CT268-720
Salmon Brook Historical Society
Reference and Educational Center
208 Salmon Brook Street
Granby CT 06035

(203) 653-3965

OPEN: Su 2-4, and by appointment
COPYING FACILITIES: no
MATERIALS SOLICITED: Local and area history. Will also accept State and regional history.

HOLDINGS:
  Total volume: 20 c.f.
  Inclusive dates: 1786 -
  Description: Correspondence, business and organization records, photographs, maps, genealogical records, and a few diaries, covering the history of Granby and its environs, including such topics as Newgate Prison, the Farmington Canal, the Connecticut Home Guard, turnpikes, whaling voyages, and the Civil War.

GREENWICH

CT275-280
Greenwich Library
Oral History Collection
101 West Putnam Avenue
Greenwich CT 06830

(203) 622-7900

OPEN: M-F, Sa 9-5, Su 9-9; closed Sundays May 1-Oct. 1 and holidays
COPYING FACILITIES: yes

HOLDINGS:
  Total volume: 825 items
  Inclusive dates: 1972 -
  Description: A collection of oral history tapes and transcripts dealing with the town of Greenwich, 1890-1970.

SEE: Hinding.

CT275-800
U.S. Tobacco Museum
96 West Putnam Avenue
Greenwich CT

MAILING ADDRESS:
100 West Putnam Avenue
Greenwich CT 06830

(203) 869-5531

OPEN: Tu-Sa 9-4:30; closed Mondays and holidays
ACCESS: appointment required
COPYING FACILITIES: yes
MATERIALS SOLICITED: Materials relating to tobacco, including records of tobacco brands; agricultural records; photographs of tobacco fields, processing, harvesting, and early tobacco shops; and information on tobacco wars and monopoly, and early tobacco companies, trademarks, and labels. Will also accept photographic negatives related to tobacco.

HOLDINGS:
  Total volume: 506 vols.; 2 file cabinets
  Inclusive dates: 17th century -
  Description: Tobacco brand records, 1895- , records of early package designs, ephemera, papers of individuals, records of companies, photographs, slides, and other materials concerning the tobacco industry.

GROTON

CT282-720
Submarine Force Library and Museum
Naval Submarine Base
Groton CT

MAILING ADDRESS:
Box 16
Naval Submarine Base New London
Groton CT 06349

(203) 449-3174

OPEN: M-F 10-4 by appointment; closed weekends and holidays
ACCESS: Not open to general public. Researchers admitted during normal weekday hours by appointment only; contact director ten days in advance of visit.
COPYING FACILITIES: yes
MATERIALS SOLICITED: Materials relating to active or retired naval personnel and civilians involved with submarines. Will also accept materials relating to submarines.

HOLDINGS:
  Total volume: 1,500 items; 50,000 photographs; motion pictures
  Inclusive dates: late 19th century -
  Description: A collection of materials relating to the history and development of submarines throughout the world, but particularly those of the U.S. Navy. Personal paper collections include those of submarine operators, designers and builders, especially John Philip Holland.
  The collection includes the papers of Simon Lake and individual histories on each U.S. Navy submarine.

SEE: Novotny; Allard, Crawley, and Edmison.

GUILFORD

CT288-280
Guilford Keeping Society, Inc.
171 Boston Street
Guilford CT

MAILING ADDRESS:
Box 363
Guilford CT 06437

(203) 453-3176

OPEN: Tu-Su 11-4 June through Labor Day; by appointment Sept. through May
COPYING FACILITIES: no
MATERIALS SOLICITED: Materials relating to the town of Guilford.

HOLDINGS:
  Total volume: 10,500 items
  Inclusive dates: 1750 -
  Description: A collection of photographs, diaries, deeds, store records, town records, and other materials relating to the town of Guilford.

Town documents on indefinite loan to the Guilford Free Library.

HARTFORD

CT316-40
Antiquarian and Landmarks Society, Inc., of Connecticut
394 Main Street
Hartford CT 06103

no telephone

SEE: NUCMC, 1978.

Questionnaire not returned.

CT316-105
United Church of Christ
Connecticut Conference
125 Sherman Street
Hartford CT 06105

(203) 233-5564

OPEN: M-F 9-4; closed weekends and holidays
COPYING FACILITIES: yes
MATERIALS SOLICITED: Association, missionary society, conference, and other records of the Congregational Christian church and the United Church of Christ in Connecticut.

HOLDINGS:
  Total volume: 100 l.f.
  Inclusive dates: 1708 -
  Description: Association, missionary society, conference, and other records of the Congregational Christian church and the United Church of Christ in Connecticut. Few records of individual churches are held.

SEE: Hamer.

SEE: Hinding.

SEE ALSO: Jack T. Ericson, ed., *Missionary Society of Connecticut Papers, 1759-1948, A Guide to the Microform Edition* (Microfilming Corp. of America, 1976).

CT316-110
The Connecticut Historical Society
1 Elizabeth Street
Hartford CT 06105

(203) 236-5621

OPEN: M-Sa 9-5; closed Sundays, holidays and Saturdays between Memorial and Labor Days
COPYING FACILITIES: yes
MATERIALS SOLICITED: Papers of individuals and records of organizations from Connecticut. Will also accept Connecticut family papers.

HOLDINGS:
> *Total volume:* 1,194 l.f.
> *Inclusive dates:* 1600 -
> *Description:* A collection of manuscripts relating chiefly to Connecticut. Included are diaries, reminiscences, papers of individuals, records of organizations, and collections of ephemera.

SEE: Hamer; NUCMC, 1959-67, 69, 71, 73.

SEE: Allard, Crawley, and Edmison; Robbins; Ingram; Leventhal and Mooney - I.

SEE ALSO: Walter Schatz, ed., *Directory of Afro-American Resources* (Bowker, 1970); Ann Novotny, ed., *Picture Sources 3* (Special Libraries Assn., 1975); *Map Collections in the United States and Canada, A Directory* (Special Libraries Assn., 1970); David A. Hounshell, comp., *Manuscripts in U.S. Depositories Relating to the History of Electrical Science and Technology* (Smithsonian Institution, n.d.).

CT316-120

Connecticut State Library
Archives, History and Genealogy Unit
231 Capitol Avenue
Hartford CT 06115

(203) 566-3690

OPEN: M-F 8:30-5; closed weekends and holidays
COPYING FACILITIES: yes
MATERIALS SOLICITED: State and local government records. Will also accept manuscripts and archives of Connecticut agencies, institutions, businesses and individuals.

HOLDINGS:
> *Total volume:* 18,000 c.f.
> *Inclusive dates:* 1635 -
> *Description:* Holdings consist of two main categories: noncurrent official records held by the Library as the State's archival agency, and other papers relating chiefly to Connecticut and New England. In the first category are included colonial and State legislative and court records, local tax, land and probate records, official files of Connecticut governors, and administrative records of various State agencies. Manuscript collections include the papers of prominent Connecticut individuals, family papers, church and society records, business records, and genealogical material.

GUIDES: Robert Claus, comp., *Guide to Archives in the Connecticut State Library* (1978).

SEE: Hamer; NUCMC, 1959-65, 69, 71, 75, 78.

SEE: Allard, Crawley, and Edmison; Hinding; Robbins; Ingram; Leventhal and Mooney - I; Gehring.

SEE ALSO: Walter Schatz, ed., *Directory of Afro-American Resources* (Bowker, 1970); Silvie Turner, 'The Connecticut Archives,' *Connecticut Historical Society Bulletin* 33 (July 1968); Ann Novotny, ed., *Picture Sources 3* (Special Libraries Assn., 1975); Albert

Krichmar, *The Women's Rights Movement in the United States, 1848-1970: A Bibliography and Sourcebook* (Scarecrow Press, 1972). Checklists on specific types of records available from the Library.

Checklists on specific types of records are available from the library.

CT316-210

Episcopal Diocese of Connecticut
Archives
1335 Asylum Avenue
Hartford CT 06105

(203) 233-4481

OPEN: by appointment only
COPYING FACILITIES: yes
MATERIALS SOLICITED: Materials concerning the Episcopal church in Connecticut and New England, including tapes, recordings, pictures, music scores, slides, and maps.

HOLDINGS:
> *Total volume:* not specified
> *Inclusive dates:* 1704 -
> *Description:* Manuscripts and other materials concerning the history of the Episcopal church (Church of England) in Connecticut and New England on the diocesan and parish levels. Included are the papers of persons and organizations prominent in its history, especially of its bishops.

SEE: Hamer.

SEE: Hinding.

CT316-310

Hartford Medical Society
Library
230 Scarborough Street
Hartford CT 06105

(203) 236-5613

OPEN: M-F 9-5; closed weekends and holidays
COPYING FACILITIES: yes

HOLDINGS:
> *Total volume:* 200 items
> *Inclusive dates:* 1600's - 1942
> *Description:* Manuscripts relating to the history of medicine and the medical profession in the United States, especially Hartford. Included are materials relating to Gershom Bulkeley and correspondence of Sir William Osler.

SEE: Hamer; NUCMC, 1960.

CT316-320

Hartford Public Library
Hartford Collection
500 Main Street
Hartford CT 06103

(203) 525-9121

OPEN: M, W 9-9, Tu, Th-Sa 9-5; closed Sundays and holidays
COPYING FACILITIES: yes
MATERIALS SOLICITED: Materials pertaining to the history of the Hartford area.

HOLDINGS:
> *Total volume:* 3,000 items
> *Inclusive dates:* 18th century -
> *Description:* Materials relating to Hartford, including manuscript letters, record books, music scores, business records, archives, photographs, tapes, and motion pictures.

SEE: Robbins.

SEE ALSO: Ann Novotny, ed., *Picture Sources 3* (Special Libraries Assn., 1975).

CT316-330

Hartford Seminary Foundation
Case Memorial Library
Archives
77 Sherman Street
Hartford CT 06105

(203) 232-4451, Ext. 305, 307

OPEN: M-F 9-4:30 by appointment; closed weekends and holidays
COPYING FACILITIES: yes
MATERIALS SOLICITED: Materials concerning Protestant foreign missions, religion, Christian churches, and Christian-Muslim relations, as well as official records and correspondence of the Foundation. Will also accept missionary papers, and papers of theologians, educators, and historians.

HOLDINGS:
> *Total volume:* 1,350 l.f.
> *Inclusive dates:* 10th century -
> *Description:* Manuscript collections of about 1,000,000 pieces, consisting of sermons of prominent New England ministers since 1705; diaries, journals, correspondence, and other papers of 18th-20th century theologians, missionaries, historians, and educators; papers relating to the French and Indian War and Civil War; materials relating to the Hartford Seminary Foundation and its predecessors, 1833- , including the official records of the institution; and Arabic, Turkish, Armenian, Hebrew, Syriac, Ethiopian, Coptic, and Persian manuscripts, 10th-20th centuries.

GUIDES: Nafi Donat, *Archival Material in the Case Memorial Library* (1976), and *The Archives of the Case Memorial Library* (1975).

SEE: Hamer; NUCMC, 1959-61, 66, 77.

SEE: Hinding; Martin; Robbins.

SEE ALSO: Nafi Donat, 'Archival Material in the Metal Cases, Glass Cases, and in the Annex to the Archives of the Case Memorial Library,' (Hartford Seminary Foundation, 1974); Avedis K. Sanjian, *A Catalogue of Medieval Armenian Manuscripts in the United States* (Univ. of California Press, 1976); Robert O. Collins and Peter Duignan, *Americans in Africa* (Hoover Institution, 1963).

CT316-360
Institute of Social Ethics
National Gay Liberation Archives
One Gold Street
22-BC
Hartford CT

MAILING ADDRESS:
Central Station, P.O. Box 3417
Hartford CT 06103

(203) 547-1281

OPEN: by appointment
COPYING FACILITIES: no
MATERIALS SOLICITED: Materials relating to the gay liberation movement.

HOLDINGS:
Total volume: 80 l.f.
Inclusive dates: 1950 -
Description: Materials relating to the gay liberation movement in the United States, Canada, and Europe, including some materials on the general subject of homosexuality.

CT316-520
Mark Twain Memorial
351 Farmington Avenue
Hartford CT 06105

(203) 247-0998

OPEN: M-F 9-5; closed weekends and holidays
COPYING FACILITIES: yes
MATERIALS SOLICITED: Materials, chiefly American, pertaining to Mark Twain, his family, and his contemporaries, as well as to decorative arts, architecture, and photography of the period from 1840 to 1910.

HOLDINGS:
Total volume: 7,500 items
Inclusive dates: 1840 - 1910
Description: Letters, manuscripts, and documents of or pertaining to Mark Twain and his family, in addition to letters of his contemporaries, and architectural drawings and photographs of the Victorian era.

SEE: NUCMC, 1966.

SEE: Robbins.

SEE ALSO: Ann Novotny, ed., *Picture Sources 3* (Special Libraries Assn., 1975).

CT316-560
The Nook Farm Research Library
The Stowe-Day Memorial Library
77 Forest Street
Hartford CT 06105

(203) 522-9258

OPEN: M-F 9-5; closed weekends and holidays
COPYING FACILITIES: yes
MATERIALS SOLICITED: 19th century Americana with particular emphasis on architecture, landscape architecture, the decorative arts, woman suffrage and black history. Will also accept materials related to the family of the Reverend Lyman Beecher and Hartford's Nook Farm residents.

HOLDINGS:
Total volume: 95,000 items
Inclusive dates: 1770 - 1910
Description: Thirty collections focusing on 19th century America relating chiefly to the career and children of the Reverend Lyman Beecher. Also included are materials relating to the woman suffrage associates of Isabella Beecher Hooker; theatrical history and William H. Gillette; literary manuscripts of Charles Dudley Warner and Samuel L. Clemens; Thomas Wentworth Higginson and abolitionism; industrial firms; Lydia Huntley Sigourney; and Katharine Seymour Day. There are also 19th century architectural drawings, wallpaper samples, and regional photographs.

SEE: NUCMC, 1969.

SEE: Robbins; Hinding.

SEE ALSO: Walter Schatz, ed., *Directory of Afro-American Resources* (Bowker, 1970); *The Manuscripts of Harriet Beecher Stowe* (Stowe-Day Foundation, 1976); *The Stowe, Beecher, Hooker, Seymour, Day Foundation Bulletin* (1958-61). Descriptive brochure available from Library.

CT316-750
Travelers Insurance Companies
Corporate Library
One Tower Square
Hartford CT 06115

(203) 277-0270

OPEN: by appointment only; closed weekends and holidays
ACCESS: appointment required
COPYING FACILITIES: yes
MATERIALS SOLICITED: Will accept materials on the history of The Travelers Insurance Companies.

HOLDINGS:
Total volume: 5 file cabinets; 20 l.f.
Inclusive dates: 1863 -
Description: Materials covering the history of the Travelers Insurance Companies, including company business and financial records, advertisements, publications, architectural drawings, and photographs of company buildings and Hartford.

CT316-763
Trinity College
Library
Archives
300 Summit Street
Hartford CT

MAILING ADDRESS:
Trinity College Library
300 Summit Street
Hartford CT 06106

(203) 527-3151, Ext. 493

OPEN: M-F 8:30-4:30; closed weekends and holidays
ACCESS: appointment required
COPYING FACILITIES: yes
MATERIALS SOLICITED: Manuscripts, student publications, College records, and photographs relating to the history of Trinity College, fomerly Washington College, and its students, faculty, administration, trustees, and alumni.

HOLDINGS:
Total volume: 350 l.f.
Inclusive dates: 1800 -
Description: Manuscripts, student publications, College records, and photographs relating to the history of Trinity College and its students, faculty, administration, trustees, and alumni. Included are 450 architectural drawings by William Burges and Francis H. Kimball documenting the design and construction of College buildings, 1872-78, and the papers of the William E. Curtis family of Watertown, CT, 1800-95.

SEE: Hinding.

CT316-770
Trinity College
Watkinson Library
300 Summit Street
Hartford CT 06106

(203) 527-3151, Ext. 307

OPEN: M - F 8:30-4:30; closed holidays and weekends
ACCESS: by appointment
COPYING FACILITIES: yes
MATERIALS SOLICITED: General literary and historical materials, particularly 19th century Americana.

HOLDINGS:
Total volume: 250 manuscript boxes
Inclusive dates: 1700 -
Description: Historical, literary, and music manuscripts, including papers of 19th century Connecticut figures like musician and composer Nathan H. Allen, educator Henry Barnard, historian, philologist, and bibliographer James Hammond Trumbull, and essayist, novelist, and newspaper editor Charles Dudley Warner. There are also 18th and 19th century American copybooks and choir parts, Connecticut family papers, Revolutionary and Civil War material, and E. A. Robinson and Robert Frost collections.

SEE: Hamer; NUCMC, 1959-62, 71.

SEE: Schatz; Martin; Allard, Crawley, and Edmison; Robbins; Hinding; Leventhal and Mooney, I.

SEE ALSO: *Edwin Arlington Robinson: A Bio-Bibliography* (Trinity College, 1969); *The Robert Frost Collection in the Watkinson Library* (Trinity College, 1974).

CT316-880
Wadsworth Atheneum
600 Main Street
Hartford CT 06103

(203) 278-2670, Ext. 341, 342

OPEN: Tu-Sa 11-3, Su 1-5; closed Mondays and holidays
ACCESS: by prior arrangement
COPYING FACILITIES: yes
MATERIALS SOLICITED: Will accept materials on art, artists, and local cultural history.

HOLDINGS:
Total volume: 500 manuscripts; 7,500 photographs
Inclusive dates: late 18th century -
Description: Collections relating chiefly to the history of New England, but also including a number of papers of National importance. There are a few papers of Samuel Colt and John Trumbull, letters of Jeremiah Wadsworth and his family, small quantities of papers of other distinguished persons, a collection of autograph letters of U.S. Presidents and others prominent in American history, a collection of artists' autographs, and a large photograph collection pertaining to fine art.

SEE: Hamer.

SEE: Novotny; Martin.

HARWINTON

CT323-320
T.A. Hungerford Memorial Library
Burlington Road
Harwinton CT 06791

(203) 485-1555

OPEN: M, W 2-8:30, Tu 9:30-5, Th, F 2-5, Sa 9:30-1; closed Sundays and holidays
COPYING FACILITIES: yes
MATERIALS SOLICITED: Any items relevant to the history of the town of Harwinton. Will also accept any materials relative to New England or Connecticut history, particularly that of northwestern Connecticut.

HOLDINGS:
Total volume: not specified
Inclusive dates: 1730's -
Description: A collection of items related chiefly to the history of Harwinton, including Civil War photographs and memorabilia, some diaries and letters, several collections of personal records dating from the 1700's, and a variety of other manuscripts and photographs.

KENSINGTON

CT351-640
Peck Memorial Library
Kensington CT 06037

no telephone
SEE: Hamer; NUCMC, 1973.

Questionnaire not returned.

LITCHFIELD

CT393-480
The Litchfield Historical Society, Inc.
Ingraham Memorial Research Library
On-the-Green
Litchfield CT

MAILING ADDRESS:
P.O. Box 385
Litchfield CT 06759

(203) 567-5862

OPEN: Tu-Sa 11-4:30; closed Sundays, Mondays, and holidays
COPYING FACILITIES: yes
MATERIALS SOLICITED: Litchfield and general area history.

HOLDINGS:
Total volume: 292 l.f.
Inclusive dates: 1700 -
Description: Manuscripts, account books, and bound volumes relating to Litchfield (borough, town and county) and its inhabitants. Business, social, civic, and personal records are included.

SEE: Hamer; NUCMC, 1971-72, 74.

SEE: Allard, Crawley, and Edmison; Robbins; Leventhal and Mooney - I.

MADISON

CT400-520
Madison Historical Society
853 Boston Post Road
Madison CT

MAILING ADDRESS:
P.O. Box 17
Madison CT 06443

(203) 245-4567

OPEN: May-Oct., W, Sa 1-4; other times by appointment; closed Nov.-April
ACCESS: by prior arrangement
COPYING FACILITIES: no
MATERIALS SOLICITED: Manuscript and graphic material pertaining to the town and people of Madison. Will also accept materials pertaining to the Battle of the Merrimac and the Monitor during the Civil War.

HOLDINGS:
Total volume: 14 l.f.
Inclusive dates: 19th century -
Description: Account books, aerial photographs, a few diaries, a small collection of photographs pertaining to Madison, a vertical file of newspaper clippings and local history essays, and additional materials concerning the history of Madison and other Connecticut towns.

MIDDLETOWN

CT428-520
Middlesex County Historical Society
151 Main Street
Middletown CT 06457

no telephone
SEE: Hamer.

Questionnaire not returned.

CT428-865
Wesleyan University
Archives
Olin Library, Church Street
Middletown CT 06457

(203) 347-9411, Ext. 2456

OPEN: M-F 9-5; closed weekends and University holidays
ACCESS: appointments should be made for vacation and summer use

COPYING FACILITIES: yes
MATERIALS SOLICITED: University history and directly related material.

HOLDINGS:
Total volume: 700 l.f.
Inclusive dates: 19th century -
Description: Primarily the University archives, dating from its founding in 1831. Other holdings relate to Wilbur Olin Atwater and agricultural chemistry; 18th and 19th century English and American Methodists; Gorham Munson and social credit; Henry Bacon, including architectural drawings; Elia Kazan; and the production of the *Omnibus* television series.

SEE: Hamer; NUCMC, 1959-61.

SEE: Spalek; Robbins; Hinding.

MILFORD

CT435-520
Milford Historical Society, Inc.
34 High Street
Milford CT

MAILING ADDRESS:
P.O. Box 337
Milford CT 06460

(203) 874-2664

OPEN: June - Sept., Su 2-5; closed rest of year
COPYING FACILITIES: no
MATERIALS SOLICITED: Materials pertaining to Milford, its famous residents, and local industry.

HOLDINGS:
Total volume: not specified
Inclusive dates: 1639 -
Description: Three documents signed by President Martin Van Buren and H. S. Gill regarding land tracts for services in the War of 1812, a genealogy of the P. T. Barnum family, as well as other genealogies, historic sketches, notebooks, account books, architectural drawings, diaries, letters, photographs, deeds, discharge papers, and public school and town reports.

MYSTIC

CT463-520
Mystic Seaport Museum, Inc.
G. W. Blunt White Library
Mystic CT 06355

(203) 572-0711, Ext. 261

OPEN: M-F 9-5, Sa 9-5 by appointment; closed Sundays and holidays
COPYING FACILITIES: yes
MATERIALS SOLICITED: American maritime history up to 1900, including logs and journals, shipping records, shipmaster's papers, marine law, maritime art and literature, social and economic records of maritime communities, maritime arts and crafts, related maritime industries such as shipbuilding, sailmaking, ropemaking, and coopering, seamen's life and welfare, and other materials.

HOLDINGS:
Total volume: 500 l.f.
Inclusive dates: 1780 - 1920
Description: Business records of ships, shipowners, shipmasters, shipping agents, and other maritime related trades and topics, concentrated primarily along the Northeast coast from Maine to New York. Included are ships' logs and journals, ledgers, diaries, account books, cash books, shipping articles, charter parties, protests, marine insurance policies, ships' plans, and general correspondence.

SEE: Hamer; NUCMC, 1959-66, 68, 80 (as Marine Historical Association).

SEE: Allard, Crawley, and Edmison; Hinding; Robbins; Novotny; Duignan; Schatz.

NEW BRITAIN

CT477-130
Central Connecticut State University
Elihu Burritt Library
New Britain CT 06062

(203) 827-7524

OPEN: M-F 8-4; closed weekends and holidays
COPYING FACILITIES: yes
MATERIALS SOLICITED: Materials pertaining to Elihu Burritt and Central Connecticut State University. Will also accept manuscripts and letters of Walter Hart Blumenthal.

HOLDINGS:
Total volume: 35 l.f.
Inclusive dates: 1754 -
Description: Records of the First Church in New Britain, including handwritten records, sermons, and reports, covering the period 1754-1931; Central Connecticut State University archives 1849 to the present; the Elihu Burritt collection of manuscripts and letters by and about 'The Learned Blacksmith.'

Also business records of the Middletown and Berlin Turnpike company; the Charles Lanman collection of manuscripts related to his 'Dictionary of the United States Congress'; and 2 photographs and 3 engravings by Mathew Brady.

SEE: NUCMC, 1974.

CT477-570
New Britain Public Library
Local History Room
20 High Street
New Britain CT 06050

(203) 224-3155, Ext. 43

OPEN: M, Tu, Th 9-9, W, F, Sa 9-5; closed Sundays, holidays, and Saturdays in summer
ACCESS: advance arrangements with Curator required
COPYING FACILITIES: yes
MATERIALS SOLICITED: Materials pertaining to New Britain and its history, people, industries, institutions, associations, and government. Will also accept materials concerning neighboring towns and Connecticut.

HOLDINGS:
Total volume: not specified
Inclusive dates: 1750 -
Description: Elihu Burritt materials, consisting of 21 vols. of his journals, 1841-59, correspondence, notes for published works, and manuscripts for unpublished works. There are also materials relating to the history of New Britain and its people, industries, institutions, and associations, consisting of manuscript maps; photographs; research papers; records of local associations such as the New Britain Tract Society, 1852-81, Woman's Christian Temperance Union, and Civil War Veterans.

Unpublished memoirs of local historian Alfred Andrews; two Civil War recollections; account books; manuscripts for published works by authors other than Burritt; and manuscript material relating to the New Britain Institute, 1853- .

SEE: NUCMC, 1962.

SEE: Robbins.

NEW CANAAN

CT484-550
New Canaan Historical Society
13 Oenoke Ridge
New Canaan CT 06840

(203) 966-1776

OPEN: Tu-Sa 9:30-4:30; closed Sundays and Mondays
COPYING FACILITIES: yes
MATERIALS SOLICITED: Local material, including diaries, business and personal papers and records, family records, land records, and photographs. Will also accept material dealing with Fairfield County.

HOLDINGS:
Total volume: not specified
Inclusive dates: 1710 -
Description: Materials concerning the Noyes family and Hoyt Nursery; papers, letters, diaries, and other materials of the Silliman, Seeley and Jones, and Pennoyer families; records of New Canann Congregational Church and St. Mark's Episcopal Church; an index for the local Methodist church; New Canaan town records, including assessor's books, 1854-1960; and local cemetery records.

SEE: NUCMC, 1970.

CT484-570
New Canaan Library
151 Main Street
New Canaan CT 06840

no telephone

SEE: NUCMC, 1959-61.

Questionnaire not returned.

NEW HAVEN

CT505-120
Connecticut Agricultural Experiment Station
123 Huntington Street
New Haven CT

MAILING ADDRESS:
P.O. Box 1106
New Haven CT 06504

(203) 789-7265

OPEN: M-F 8:30-4:30; closed weekends and holidays
COPYING FACILITIES: yes
MATERIALS SOLICITED: Station records. Will also accept other materials related to agriculture.

HOLDINGS:
Total volume: 90 microfilm reels; 50 vols.
Inclusive dates: 1875 -
Description: Records of the Connecticut Agricultural Experiment Station, including 11 volumes of typed correspondence of Samuel W. Johnson, microfilm copies of correspondence of the genetics department, notebooks of Donald F. Jones, correspondence of Thomas B. Osborne, and materials on the discovery of vitamins and the need for amino acids.

CT505-560
New Haven Colony Historical Society Library
114 Whitney Avenue
New Haven CT 06510

(203) 562-4183

OPEN: Tu-F 10-5; closed weekends, Mondays, and holidays
COPYING FACILITIES: yes
MATERIALS SOLICITED: History and genealogy of New Haven.

HOLDINGS:
Total volume: 1,200 l.f.
Inclusive dates: 1638 -
Description: Corporate records of business, insurance and railroad companies, such as the Farmington Canal Co. and the New Haven Water Co.; a maritime collection of logs and diaries; school and church records and papers of civic organizations and clubs; family genealogies; New Haven city/county documents; and personal papers of New Haven individuals and families.

SEE: Hamer; NUCMC, 1976-77, 80.

SEE: Allard, Crawley, and Edmison; Hinding; Robbins.

CT505-890

Yale University
Libraries
Beinecke Rare Book and Manuscript
  Library
121 Wall Street
New Haven CT

MAILING ADDRESS:
Box 1603A Yale Station
New Haven CT 06520

(203) 436-8438, 0833

OPEN: M-F 8:30-5; closed weekends and
  holidays
COPYING FACILITIES: yes
MATERIALS SOLICITED: Primarily Western civilization material in all areas except music, law, and the history of
  medicine. Will also accept any literary
  manuscripts of value.

HOLDINGS:
  Total volume: 1,000,000 items
  Inclusive dates: 14th century -
  Description: British and continental
  manuscripts, 1450-1600, many illuminat-
  ed; English literature and history, 1450 to
  the present, especially James Barrie,
  James Boswell, Joseph Conrad, George
  Meredith, and Robert Louis Stevenson;
  American literature, especially James
  Fenimore Cooper, Eugene O'Neill, Ezra
  Pound, Gertrude Stein, Walt Whitman,
  and William Carlos Williams; American
  black writers, especially Langston Hughes,
  James Weldon Johnson, and Richard
  Wright; western Americana; French, German, and Russian literature of the 19th
  and 20th centuries; Near Eastern history
  and literature, especially Arabic; alchemy;
  and Oriental literary manuscripts of ancient texts, 14th to 19th centuries.

GUIDES: *The Beinecke Rare Book and
  Manuscript Library: A Guide to its Collections* (1974).

SEE: Hamer (as Yale University Library:
  Rare Book Room, Western Americana
  Collection, Yale Collection of Ameri-
  can Literature, and Yale Collection of
  German Literature); NUCMC, 1968,
  72, 74, 76-77, 80.

SEE: Paszek; Martin; Spalek; Robbins.

SEE ALSO: Ann Novotny, ed., *Picture
  Sources 3* (Special Libraries Assn.,
  1975); George L. McKay, ed., *A Steven-
  son Library: Catalogue of a Collection
  of Writings by and about Robert Louis
  Stevenson formed by Edwin J. Beinecke,*
  6 vols. (Yale Univ., 1951-64);
  Archibald Hanna, 'An American West
  Treasure Hunt in Connecticut: The
  Frederick W. Beinecke Collection, Yale
  University,' *American West* 9 (Sept.
  1972).

Archibald Hanna, 'Manuscript Resources in
  the Yale University Library for the Study
  of Western Travel,' in John Francis
  McDermott, ed., *Travelers on the Western
  Frontier* (Univ. of Illinois Press, 1970);
  Jeanne M. Goddard and Charles Kritzler,
  comps., and Archibald Hanna, ed., *A
  Catalogue of the Frederick and Carrie S.
  Beinecke Collection of Western Ameri-
  cana* (Yale Univ. Press, 1965); Walter

Schatz, ed., *Directory of Afro-American
  Resources* (Bowker, 1970); Richard C.
  Davis, *North American Forest History: A
  Guide to Archives and Manuscripts in the
  United States and Canada* (Clio Books,
  1977).

CT505-900

Yale University
Libraries
Divinity School Library
409 Prospect Street
New Haven CT 06510

(203) 436-8440

OPEN: M-F 8:30-5; closed weekends and
  holidays
COPYING FACILITIES: yes
MATERIALS SOLICITED: Materials pertaining to missions, church and society,
  and American clergy and scholars, especially those associated with the Yale
  Divinity School.

HOLDINGS:
  Total volume: 1,400 l.f.
  Inclusive dates: 1692 -
  Description: Papers of American Protestant missionaries in China and elsewhere, 1834-1950; papers of New England clergymen and of prominent Yale
  faculty members; records documenting
  religious work among college and university students including the archives of the
  YMCA Student Division, 1886-1967,
  World Student Christian Federation,
  1895-1938, and Student Volunteer Movement for Foreign Missions, 1883-1960.
  Records related to Congregational
  church history including archives of the
  Council for Christian Social Action.

SEE: Hamer; NUCMC, 1976-77, 80.

SEE: Hinding.

CT505-905

Yale University
Libraries
Forestry and Environmental Studies
  Library
22 Sage Hall
205 Prospect Street
New Haven CT 06520

(203) 436-0577

SEE: Hamer (as Yale University, School of
  Forestry, Library).

Questionnaire not returned.

CT505-910

Yale University
Libraries
John Herrick Jackson Music Library
98 Wall Street
New Haven CT 06520

(203) 436-8240

OPEN: M-F 8:30-5; closed weekends and
  holidays
COPYING FACILITIES: yes
MATERIALS SOLICITED: Manuscript music and related material (letters, diaries,
  etc.) from all stylistic eras.

HOLDINGS:
  Total volume: 475 l.f.
  Inclusive dates: 1400 -
  Description: Individual music manu-
  scripts of all historical periods since 1400,
  as well as the papers and complete music
  manuscripts of composers such as Charles
  E. Ives, Carl Ruggles, Horatio Parker,
  Leo Ornstein, Richard Donovan, and
  Quincy Porter.
  Also included are music manuscripts
  of Virgil Thomson.

SEE: Hamer (as Yale University, Library
  of the School of Music); NUCMC,
  1974, 76, 78.

SEE: Meckler and McMullin; Spalek;
  Hinding.

CT505-930

Yale University
Libraries
Medical Library
Historical Library
333 Cedar Street
New Haven CT 06510

(203) 785-4354

OPEN: M-F 8:45-4:45; closed weekends
  and Christmas
COPYING FACILITIES: yes
MATERIALS SOLICITED: Yale Medical
  School and Yale New Haven Medical
  Center material. Will also accept ma-
  terials in the history of medicine.

HOLDINGS:
  Total volume: not specified
  Inclusive dates: 13th century -
  Description: Materials relating to medicine and medical history. Included are
  collections of letters, medical reports, and
  other papers of physicians prominent in
  the development of medical science in
  both the United States and abroad. There
  are also the archives of the Yale Medical
  School and the Yale New Haven Medical
  Center.

SEE: Hamer.

SEE: Martin.

In 1978 most of the manuscript col-
lection was transferred to the Yale
University Library, Department of
Manuscripts and Archives.

CT505-945

Yale University
Libraries
Sterling Memorial Library
Franklin Collection
Room 230, Sterling Memorial Library
120 High Street
New Haven CT

MAILING ADDRESS:
Box 1603A Yale Station
New Haven CT 06520

(203) 436-8646

OPEN: M-F 9-5; closed weekends and
  University holidays
COPYING FACILITIES: yes
MATERIALS SOLICITED: Will accept any
  materials of or relating to Benjamin
  Franklin or the Marquis de Lafayette.

HOLDINGS:

> *Total volume:* 1,400 items
> *Inclusive dates:* 1699 -
> *Description:* Letters and manuscripts by and pertaining to Benjamin Franklin, his family, and his literary, political, and scientific interests; other contemporary manuscripts; and manuscripts of modern research based on the collection. The Stuart Jackson collection of 400 letters of or pertaining to the Marquis de Lafayette is also housed in the Franklin Collection.

SEE: Hamer.

CT505-960

Yale University
Libraries
Sterling Memorial Library
Manuscripts and Archives
120 High Street
New Haven CT

MAILING ADDRESS:

Box 1603A Yale Station
New Haven CT 06520

(203) 436-0907, 0908

OPEN: M-F 8:30-4:45; closed weekends and holidays
COPYING FACILITIES: yes
MATERIALS SOLICITED: Materials pertaining to 20th century legal, political and public affairs, and contemporary medical care and health policy. Will also accept materials relating to the history of Yale or which supplement and complement current areas of strength.

HOLDINGS:

> *Total volume:* 25,000 l.f.
> *Inclusive dates:* pre-1400 -
> *Description:* A general collection of historical manuscripts and Yale University archives consisting primarily of non-literary American papers dating from the 18th century to the present, with strong holdings in the following areas: U.S. history, politics, and government; special collections relating to Africa, Russia, and Latin America from the 17th to 19th centuries, and China, Japan, Germany and Europe in the 20th century; Connecticut and New Haven history; family history; women; Indians of North America; religion and missionary movements; medical care, health policy and social medicine; forestry; education; business; history of science; history of legal theory and practice; journalism; drama; fine arts; architecture; aviation; railroads; western U.S. history; reform movements; military and maritime history; economics; anthropology; sociology; and philosophy.

SEE: Hamer (as Yale University Library: Historical Manuscripts Collection and Yale University Archives, and Yale Law School Library); NUCMC, 1959-66, 68-69, 71-72, 74, 76-77.

SEE: Parkinson; Spalek; Allard, Crawley, and Edmison; Novotny; Hines; Bean and Vane; Ingram; Leventhal and Mooney - I; Beers - Southwest; White.

SEE ALSO: Peter Duignan, *Handbook of American Resources for African Studies* (Hoover Institution, 1967); Gerald Friedberg, 'Sources for the Study of Socialism in America, 1901-1919,' *Labor History* 6 (Spring 1965); Walter Schatz, ed., *Directory of Afro-American Resources* (Bowker, 1970); *Source Materials for the Recent History of Astronomy and Astrophysics: A Checklist of Manuscript Collections in the United States* (American Institute of Physics, 1971); Andrea Hinding and Rosemary Richardson, comps., *Archival and Manuscript Resources for the Study of Women's History: A Beginning* (Univ. of Minnesota Libraries, Social Welfare History Archives Center, 1972).

David A. Hounshell, comp., *Manuscripts in U.S. Depositories Relating to the History of Electrical Science and Technology* (Smithsonian Institution, n.d.); J. E. Patterson, 'Checklist of Prescott Manuscripts,' *Hispanic American Historical Review* 39 (Feb. 1959); Lawrence J. Paszek, comp., *United States Air Force History: A Guide to Documentary Sources* (Office of Air Force History, 1973); Richard C. Davis, *North American Forest History: A Guide to Archives and Manuscripts in the United States and Canada* (Clio Books, 1977).

CT505-970

Yale University
Libraries
Sterling Memorial Library
Map Collection
120 High Street
New Haven CT

MAILING ADDRESS:

Box 1603A Yale Station
New Haven CT 06520

(203) 436-8638

OPEN: M-F 10-5; closed weekends and holidays
COPYING FACILITIES: yes
MATERIALS SOLICITED: Manuscript maps of all areas and periods.

HOLDINGS:

> *Total volume:* 500 items
> *Inclusive dates:* 2500 B.C. -
> *Description:* Manuscript maps, primarily topographic, covering all parts of the world, with emphasis on American and English material.

SEE ALSO: *Map Collections in the United States and Canada, A Directory* (Special Libraries Assn., 1970).

CT505-975

Yale University
Libraries
Sterling Memorial Library
Vertical Files Collection
120 High Street
New Haven CT

MAILING ADDRESS:

Box 1603A Yale Station
New Haven CT 06520

(203) 436-8336

OPEN: M-F 8:30-5 by appointment only; closed weekends and holidays
ACCESS: members of the Yale community, and others with permission
COPYING FACILITIES: yes

MATERIALS SOLICITED: Will accept any non-duplicate material within the scope of the Crawford Theatre Collection.

HOLDINGS:

> *Total volume:* 1,500 photographs; 52 l.f.
> *Inclusive dates:* 1838 -
> *Description:* The Crawford Theatre Collection of journals, scrapbooks, production materials, and photographs on individual performers and productions, with emphasis on English and American theater, mid-19th century to the present; and the Technology and Society Collection, containing 46 linear feet of research materials and other papers from the Yale Technology Project's studies on automation and its effects on personnel in 12 companies, 1946-62.

CT505-976

Yale University
Libraries
Sterling Memorial Library
Yale Collection of Historical Sound Recordings
High Street
New Haven CT

MAILING ADDRESS:

Box 1603A, Yale Station
New Haven CT 06520

(203) 436-1822

OPEN: M-F 1-5; closed weekends, holidays, and Christmas week
ACCESS: advance arrangements required
COPYING FACILITIES: no
MATERIALS SOLICITED: Concert music (classical, American musical theater, and jazz) recordings and recordings of spoken material (literary, dramatic, and documentary, especially in politics), with emphasis upon representation of important performers. Will also accept early recordings of popular songs and folk music.

HOLDINGS:

> *Total volume:* 100,000 items
> *Inclusive dates:* 1888 -
> *Description:* Recordings which document performance practice in the fields of Western concert music, jazz, theater, poetry, American musical theater, literature, history, and politics. Special subject areas of concentration are 19th century styles of singing, piano recordings, recordings of the music of Johann Sebastian Bach, and the music of Cole Porter. The collection includes both commercial and non-commercial recordings.

SEE ALSO: Karol Berger, 'The Yale Collection of Historical Sound Recordings,' *The Journal of the Association for Recorded Sound Collection* 6.

CT505-977

Yale University
Libraries
Yale Editions of the Private Papers of
    James Boswell
Beinecke Rare Book and Manuscript
    Library
121 Wall Street
New Haven CT 06520

(203) 436-2207

OPEN: M-F 8:30-5, Sa 8:30-12:15; closed
    Sundays and holidays
ACCESS: serious scholars only, upon
    approval of written form
COPYING FACILITIES: yes
MATERIALS SOLICITED: Will accept
    manuscripts pertaining to James Bos-
    well.

HOLDINGS:
    Total volume: 29 c.f.
    Inclusive dates: 1500 - 1864
    Description: The collection is about
    equally divided between Boswell family
    papers, dating from the 16th century and
    earlier, and Boswell's personal papers.
    Among the latter are several thousand
    letters between Boswell and such people
    as Burke, Chatham, Garrick, Goldsmith,
    Malone, Reynolds, Rousseau, Voltaire,
    and Wilkes; Boswell's journal, 1761-94;
    other manuscripts by him, including *Life
    of Johnson, The Journal of a Tour to the
    Hebrides,* and *An Account of Corsica;* his
    personal accounts; legal papers from his
    law practice; and accounts, deeds,
    workbooks, and letters relating to his
    management of his estate of Auchinleck,
    1782-95. The collection as a whole pro-
    vides information on Boswell's life, his
    artistic skills, and the creative process;
    18th century literary, political, and social
    history; 17th century political history; and
    17th and 18th century Scottish agricul-
    tural history.

SEE ALSO: unpublished finding aids avail-
    able at the repository.

CT505-980

Yale University
Peabody Museum of Natural History
170 Whitney Avenue
New Haven CT 06520

(203) 436-0850

OPEN: M-F 8:30-5; closed weekends and
    holidays
ACCESS: permission of Curator in charge
    of material to be viewed
COPYING FACILITIES: yes

HOLDINGS:
    Total volume: 500 l.f.
    Inclusive dates: 1820 -
    Description: Materials related to collec-
    tions of the several divisions of the Mu-
    seum: anthropology, zoology, paleontol-
    ogy, botany, scientific instruments, and
    other fields. Correspondence, manu-
    scripts, catalogs, field notes, maps, pho-
    tographs, drawings, and business records
    are included.

NEW LONDON

CT512-120

Connecticut College
Library
Department of Special Collections
Mohegan Avenue
New London CT 06320

(203) 447-7622

OPEN: by appointment only
ACCESS: appointment required
COPYING FACILITIES: yes
MATERIALS SOLICITED: New London
    area history. Will also accept materials
    which relate to the history of the Col-
    lege and of Connecticut, or which
    would strengthen existing collections.

HOLDINGS:
    Total volume: 75 boxes; 96 l.f.
    Inclusive dates: 1800 -
    Description: Materials on American
    women, consisting of papers and letters
    relating to Alice Hamilton, Margaret
    Fuller, Belle Moskowitz, Frances Perkins,
    Lydia Sigourney, Prudence Crandall
    Philleo, and Lillian Wald. There is also a
    collection of 18th and 19th century let-
    ters, including a letter from George
    Washington to Major General Nathanael
    Greene; letters of the Gallup family of
    Groton relating to meteorological obser-
    vations and the publication of the *New
    England Almanac and Farmer's Friend;*
    papers relating to the construction of the
    Groton Monument in 1829-30 and its
    modification in 1882-83; the abstract of a
    journal of a Mediterranean cruise of the
    frigate *United States* in the 1830's; and
    numerous miscellaneous letters and docu-
    ments relating to inhabitants of the New
    London area.
    A small collection of literary manu-
    scripts includes letters of Eugene O'Neill,
    Robert, Elinor, and Lesley Frost, and Al-
    ice B. Toklas, and typescripts of the nov-
    els of Cecilia Holland. The Connecticut
    College archives contains extensive files
    of correspondence of former presidents
    and faculty members; several hundred
    photographs of buildings and people;
    tapes of poetry readings, addresses, and
    recitals; typescript copies of master's the-
    ses and honors papers; and photographs
    of the American Dance Festival,
    1950's-60's.

SEE: Hamer; NUCMC, 1971.

SEE: Robbins.

SEE ALSO: Walter Schatz, ed., *Directory of
    Afro-American Resources* (Bowker,
    1970).

CT512-550

New London County Historical
    Society
Shaw Mansion
11 Blinman Street
New London CT 06320

(203) 443-1209

OPEN: Tu-Sa 1-4; closed Sundays,
    Mondays and holidays
USER FEES: adults one dollar; children
    50 cents
ACCESS: serious researchers only

COPYING FACILITIES: no
MATERIALS SOLICITED: Materials on
    New London County, preferably 16th
    to 19th century. Will also accept pho-
    tographs.

HOLDINGS:
    Total volume: 32 l.f.
    Inclusive dates: 1644 - 1900
    Description: Manuscripts relating chief-
    ly to New London County, including pa-
    pers of Nathaniel Shaw, Jr., dealing with
    his naval service during the Revolution-
    ary War, as well as his shipping business;
    papers of a New London whaling firm;
    whaling logs; business account books; led-
    gers; day books; school records; diaries;
    rate books; society records; genealogical
    and historical workbooks; family collec-
    tions of letters, bills, and deeds; ship
    manifests; insurance papers; maps; charts;
    and photographs.

SEE: Hamer; NUCMC, 1965.

SEE: Allard, Crawley, and Edmison.

CT512-800

United States Coast Guard Academy
Library
New London CT 06371

(203) 444-8510

OPEN: by appointment only
ACCESS: by prior arrangement
COPYING FACILITIES: yes
MATERIALS SOLICITED: Material related
    to the Coast Guard and predecessor
    services.

HOLDINGS:
    Total volume: 2,500 items
    Inclusive dates: 1790 -
    Description: Letters and documents re-
    lated to lighthouses, revenue cutters, and
    the Coast Guard, including a few
    Alexander Hamilton manuscripts.

SEE: Hamer; NUCMC, 1959-61.

SEE: Allard, Crawley, and Edmison.

NEW MILFORD

CT519-560

New Milford Historical Society
6 Aspetuck Avenue
New Milford CT

MAILING ADDRESS:
P.O. Box 566
New Milford CT 06776

(203) 354-3069

OPEN: M-Sa 1-4 or by appointment;
    closed Sundays and Nov. - April
COPYING FACILITIES: no
MATERIALS SOLICITED: Diaries, letters,
    memoirs and other papers of local resi-
    dents. Will also accept other docu-
    ments, such as deeds, wills and con-
    tracts, pertaining to New Milford.

HOLDINGS:
    Total volume: 550 items
    Inclusive dates: 1713 - 1900
    Description: Deeds, wills, correspon-
    dence, Revolutionary War papers, and
    Civil War records relating to New Mil-

ford. There are also sermons of Daniel Boardman, Nathaniel Taylor, and others.

SEE: Hinding.

NEWTOWN

CT533-120
Cyrenius H. Booth Library
25 Main Street
Newtown CT 06470

(203) 426-4533

OPEN: daily, irregular hours; closed holidays
COPYING FACILITIES: yes

HOLDINGS:
Total volume: 25 items
Inclusive dates: 1733 - 1863
Description: A collection of papers and maps pertaining to Newtown history. Included are proclamations, registers, ledgers, deeds, summons, tax lists, election papers, and photographs.

SEE: Hamer.

NORWALK

CT582-80
Burndy Corporation
Library
Richards Avenue
Norwalk CT 06852

no telephone

SEE: NUCMC, 1965.

Questionnaire not returned.

CT582-550
Norwalk Historical Commission
Norwalk Historical Reference Library
141 East Avenue
Norwalk CT 06851

(203) 866-0202

OPEN: Su-Th 1-5, mornings by appointment; closed Fridays, Saturdays and holidays
COPYING FACILITIES: yes
MATERIALS SOLICITED: Materials pertaining to the history of Norwalk, especially its industrial and maritime history. Will also accept pre-1800 materials pertaining to neighboring towns.

HOLDINGS:
Total volume: 15 l.f.
Inclusive dates: 1650 -
Description: Records of local industries, merchants, families, and churches, relating to the history of Norwalk and including ledgers, account books of farmers, correspondence, and biographical information.

OLD LYME

CT596-480
Lyme Historical Society
Archives
96 Lyme Street
Old Lyme CT 06371

(203) 434-5542, 5844

OPEN: M-F 9-5 by appointment only; closed weekends and holidays
COPYING FACILITIES: yes
MATERIALS SOLICITED: Materials on Lyme and Old Lyme and the members of the Old Lyme Art Colony.

HOLDINGS:
Total volume: 100 l.f.
Inclusive dates: 1704 -
Description: Family papers, business accounts, town records, correspondence, diaries, account books, and photographs relating to the present-day towns of Lyme and Old Lyme. There are also papers and correspondence relating to the Old Lyme Art Colony, 1899-1936.

GUIDES: An unpublished guide is available at cost from the institution.

SEE: NUCMC, 1978.

OLD MYSTIC

CT603-360
The Indian and Colonial Research Center
Main Street
Old Mystic CT 06372

(203) 536-9771

OPEN: Tu, Th, Sa 2-4; closed other days and holidays
COPYING FACILITIES: no
MATERIALS SOLICITED: Early colonial history, 1600-1780, and early Indian history.

HOLDINGS:
Total volume: 4,000 items; 9 file drawers
Inclusive dates: 1700's -
Description: Materials concerning Connecticut, New England, and New York history, including early Indian and colonial history. Included are manuscripts, maps, glass negatives, city and town records, court records, and wills, in addition to notebooks of Eva L. Butler on genealogy, Indians, anthropology, and other subjects.

ROCKY HILL

CT673-690
Rocky Hill Historical Society, Inc.
The Academy Hall Museum-Library
785 Old Main Street
Rocky Hill CT

MAILING ADDRESS:
P.O. Box 185
Rocky Hill CT 06067

(203) 563-8710

OPEN: by appointment only

COPYING FACILITIES: no
MATERIALS SOLICITED: Documents relating to Rocky Hill's history.

HOLDINGS:
Total volume: 10 c.f.
Inclusive dates: early 19th century - mid-20th century
Description: Materials documenting the history of Rocky Hill, including letters, medical records, tax records, account books, church association record books, a record book of a meadow farming land association, school record books, photographs, and taped interviews with old residents.

SEE: Hinding.

SALISBURY

CT687-710
Salisbury Association
Salisbury CT 06068

no telephone

SEE: NUCMC, 1971.

Questionnaire not returned.

CT687-730
Scoville Memorial Library
Salisbury CT 06068

no telephone

SEE: NUCMC, 1971.

Questionnaire not returned.

SIMSBURY

CT718-720
Simsbury Historical Society, Inc.
Massacoh Plantation
800 Hopmeadow Street
Simsbury CT

MAILING ADDRESS:
P.O. Box 2
Simsbury CT 06070

(203) 658-2500

OPEN: by appointment only
ACCESS: serious researchers only
COPYING FACILITIES: no
MATERIALS SOLICITED: Simsbury area and Farmington Valley.

HOLDINGS:
Total volume: 60 l.f.
Inclusive dates: 1800's -
Description: Family records, correspondence, genealogies, and Simsbury town records.

SOMERS

CT723-720
Somers Historical Society
574 Main Street
Somers CT

MAILING ADDRESS:
Box 302
Somers CT 06071

(203) 749-7273

OPEN: by appointment
COPYING FACILITIES: no
MATERIALS SOLICITED: History of Somers and its inhabitants, as well as Connecticut and New England history, 1700-1900.

HOLDINGS:
Total volume: 1 c.f.
Inclusive dates: 1725 -
Description: Early deeds and sermons; correspondence, 1850-1930; photographs; music scores; church records of Somers; and some oral history interviews on early schools, industries, and houses of Somers.

SOUTHPORT

CT751-640
Pequot Library
720 Pequot Avenue
Southport CT 06490

(203) 255-0779, 259-0346

OPEN: M, W 9-8:30, Tu, Th, F 9-5:30, Sa 9-5, Su 2-6; closed holidays
ACCESS: at librarian's discretion
COPYING FACILITIES: yes

HOLDINGS:
Total volume: 3,300 items; 700 vols.
Inclusive dates: 1740 - 1880
Description: A collection of 18th and 19th century manuscripts relating to the Fairfield area. Included are ledgers, account books and logs of local trading sloops and brigs; personal papers and diaries; and a collection of miscellaneous correspondence of signers of the Declaration of Independence and other notable Americans.

SEE: Hamer.

SEE ALSO: *Monroe, Wakeman, and Holman Collections* (Yale Univ. Library, 1960).

Part of the collection is on deposit at The Beinecke Rare Book and Manuscript Library, Yale University, New Haven, CT.

STAMFORD

CT765-710
Stamford Genealogical Society Library
Ferguson Library
96 Broad Street
Stamford CT

MAILING ADDRESS:
P.O. Box 249
Stamford CT 06904

no telephone

OPEN: M-F 9-9, Sa 9-5:30; closed Sundays and holidays
COPYING FACILITIES: yes
MATERIALS SOLICITED: Local history and genealogy, primarily for Stamford, Connecticut, and New England.

HOLDINGS:
Total volume: 3 file drawers
Inclusive dates: 19th century -
Description: Genealogical and other local history materials, including some 19th century letters.

SEE ALSO: unpublished guides available at the repository.

STONINGTON

CT772-720
Stonington Historical Society Library
Whitehall Mansion
Whitehall Avenue
Stonington CT

MAILING ADDRESS:
P.O. Box 103
Stonington CT 06378

(203) 536-2428

OPEN: Th 2-4 or by appointment
COPYING FACILITIES: no
MATERIALS SOLICITED: Stonington's history, including records of early families, of whaling, sealing, and ocean shipping voyages, and of land warfare. Will also accept similar materials regarding adjacent areas, such as Waverly, RI, and New London, Mystic, and Groton, Ct.

HOLDINGS:
Total volume: 700 items
Inclusive dates: 1672 - 1902
Description: Letters, diaries, records, and accounts pertaining to the history of Stonington and the families of the first settlers, Miner, Stanton, Trumbull, Palmer, Williams, and Chesebrough. Other materials related to Stonington include ships' logs and other records of whaling, sealing, exploration, and merchant shipping, including the China trade.

SEE: NUCMC, 1962.

SEE: Ingram.

SEE ALSO: Walter Schatz, ed., *Directory of Afro-American Resources* (Bowker, 1970).

STORRS

CT779-520
Mansfield Historical Society, Inc.
954 Storrs Road
Storrs CT

MAILING ADDRESS:
P.O. Box 145
Storrs CT 06268

(203) 429-6575

OPEN: May-June, Th, Su 1-4; closed other times
COPYING FACILITIES: no
MATERIALS SOLICITED: Manuscripts, visual documents, audible documents, and scrapbooks. Will also accept microforms.

HOLDINGS:
Total volume: 22 l.f.
Inclusive dates: 1724 -
Description: Business, social, industry, and church records relating to Mansfield and genealogies and correspondence of local families.

SEE: NUCMC, 1974.

CT779-785
University of Connecticut Libraries
Historical Manuscripts and Archives
Room 227, Wilbur Cross Library
Route 195 (Storrs Road)
Storrs CT

MAILING ADDRESS:
Box U-205
Storrs CT 06268

(203) 486-2893, 4777

OPEN: M-W 1-4:30 or by appointment; closed weekends and holidays; by appointment only during summer and intersessions
COPYING FACILITIES: yes
MATERIALS SOLICITED: Connecticut history since 1850, with emphasis on labor and urban affairs, immigration and ethnicity, politics and public affairs, and business and industry, as well as non-current records of the University and materials relating to the University's history.

HOLDINGS:
Total volume: 4,400 l.f.
Inclusive dates: 1790 -
Description: Manuscripts and related materials pertaining to the University of Connecticut and the history of Connecticut, with strong holdings of railroad and business records. Also included are records of individuals and organizations in the fields of politics, immigration and ethnicity, public affairs, labor, and urban affairs.

SEE: Schatz; Robbins.

SEE ALSO: Duane P. Swanson and Hugh R. Gibb, *The Historical Records of the Components of Conrail: A Survey and Inventory* (Eleutherian Mills Historical Library, 1978).

CT779-790
University of Connecticut
Libraries
Music Library
Storrs CT

MAILING ADDRESS:
U-Box 12
Storrs CT 06268

(203) 486-2502

SEE: NUCMC, 1976.

Questionnaire not returned.

CT779-800
University of Connecticut
Center for Oral History
Wood Hall 206
Storrs CT

MAILING ADDRESS:
Box U-103
Storrs CT 06268

(203) 486-3722, 4951, 5245, 3251

OPEN: by appointment
ACCESS: permission of the director of
the Center for Oral History required
COPYING FACILITIES: yes
MATERIALS SOLICITED: Papers and tapes
of prominent participants in recent history, particularly in government, education, labor, and business.

HOLDINGS:
Total volume: 25 vols.; 264
interviews
Inclusive dates: 1969 -
Description: Transcriptions of taped interviews with persons who have played
important roles in recent Connecticut history.

SEE ALSO: Alan M. Meckler and Ruth
McMullin, comps., *Oral History Collections* (Bowker, 1975).

CT779-812
University of Connecticut
Roper Public Opinion Research
Center
Storrs CT

MAILING ADDRESS:
Box U-164
Storrs CT 06268

no telephone

SEE: Hamer.

Questionnaire not returned. This
institution was formerly located in
Williamstown, MA.

STRATFORD

CT786-720
The Stratford Historical Society
967 Academy Hill
Stratford CT

MAILING ADDRESS:
Box 382
Stratford CT 06497

(203) 378-0630

OPEN: by appointment only
COPYING FACILITIES: no
MATERIALS SOLICITED: Will accept materials relating to the history of Stratford.

HOLDINGS:
Total volume: 45 c.f.
Inclusive dates: 1674 -
Description: Genealogies, correspondence, reminiscences of residents, account
books and logbooks, diaries, notebooks,
probate papers, deeds, some early school
records and tax lists, photographs, and a
few oral history tapes, chiefly relating to
the history of Stratford and its environs.

SEE ALSO: Walter Schatz, ed., *Directory of
Afro-American Resources* (Bowker,
1970).

SUFFIELD

CT793-440
Kent Memorial Library
Historical Room
50 North Main Street
Suffield CT 06078

(203) 668-2325

OPEN: Tu-Th 10-8:30, F 10-6, Sa 10-5;
closed Sundays, Mondays and holidays
COPYING FACILITIES: yes
MATERIALS SOLICITED: Materials pertinent to Suffield.

HOLDINGS:
Total volume: not specified
Inclusive dates: 1635 -
Description: A collection of items relating to the history of Suffield and Connecticut, including town and church archives, papers of individuals and organizations, photographs and maps, data on
early buildings in Suffield, and genealogical and biographical information.

SEE: Hamer.

TERRYVILLE

CT797-480
Lock Museum of America, Inc.
130 Main Street
Terryville CT

MAILING ADDRESS:
P.O. Box 104
Terryville CT 06786

(203) 589-6359

OPEN: Tu-Su 1:30-4:30 or by
appointment; closed Mondays and
holidays

COPYING FACILITIES: yes
MATERIALS SOLICITED: Materials concerning the development and manufacture of locks in the United States.

HOLDINGS:
Total volume: 12 l.f.
Inclusive dates: 1910 - 1930
Description: The financial and sales
records of the Eagle Lock Company in
Terryville.

TORRINGTON

CT821-760
Torrington Historical Society, Inc.
192 Main Street
Torrington CT

MAILING ADDRESS:
61 Main Street
Torrington CT 06790

(203) 482-8260

OPEN: M-F 8-4; closed weekends and
holidays
COPYING FACILITIES: no
MATERIALS SOLICITED: Torrington and
Litchfield County history and genealogy. Will also accept Connecticut history materials.

HOLDINGS:
Total volume: 27 items
Inclusive dates: 1740 -
Description: Account books of
individuals, businesses, and manufacturers of Torrington and the surrounding
area.

Also has local histories, maps, pictures,
newspapers, genealogies and slides.

WALLINGFORD

CT849-880
Wallingford Historical Society, Inc.
180 South Main Street
Wallingford CT 06492

MAILING ADDRESS:
P.O. Box 73
Wallingford CT 06492

(203) 265-0313

OPEN: Su 2-5; closed during winter
months, except for tours and special
appointments
COPYING FACILITIES: no
MATERIALS SOLICITED: Material relating
to Wallingford, Cheshire and Meriden.
Will also accept material relating to
former residents of these areas.

HOLDINGS:
Total volume: 150 l.f.
Inclusive dates: 1670 -
Description: Manuscripts of Wallingford's history, including diaries, scrapbooks, legal papers, maps, and photographs.

SEE: Hamer.

WASHINGTON

CT863-280
Gunn Memorial Library, Inc.
Historical Museum
Wykeham Road
Washington CT 06793

(203) 868-7756

OPEN: Tu, Th 2-5, Sa 1-4; closed other
  days and holidays
COPYING FACILITIES: yes
MATERIALS SOLICITED: History of Washington, as well as of New Preston, CT.

HOLDINGS:
  Total volume: 19 l.f.
  Inclusive dates: 1740 -
  Description: 347 glass plate negatives
  by Joseph West of houses and scenes in
  Washington; many photographs of
  houses, people, and other local subjects;
  newspaper clippings about the town; correspondence of several families, including
  a holograph history of one family; and
  the logbook of a local inn, 1924-65.

WATERBURY

CT870-520
Mattatuck Historical Society
Mattatuck Museum
119 West Main Street
Waterbury CT 06702

(203) 753-0381

OPEN: by appointment only
ACCESS: appointment required
COPYING FACILITIES: yes
MATERIALS SOLICITED: Material related
  to the social history of greater Water-
  bury and Connecticut artists.

HOLDINGS:
  Total volume: 158 boxes; 180 items
  Inclusive dates: 1674 -
  Description: Materials relating to the
  social history of the greater Waterbury
  area, including business records of Plume
  & Atwood Company, Waterbury Button
  Company, Great Brook Reservoir Association, and railroads; personal papers, including those of local families; collections
  concerning professions and organizations;
  records of the city of Waterbury; and
  other materials.

CT870-730
Silas Bronson Library
267 Grand Street
Waterbury CT 06702

(203) 574-8200

OPEN: M, W 9-9, Tu, Th-Sa 9-5:30;
  closed Sundays, holidays, and
  Saturdays in summer
COPYING FACILITIES: yes

HOLDINGS:
  Total volume: 6 file cabinets; 1 item
  Inclusive dates: not specified
  Description: A microfilm of the manu-
  script *Census of the City and Town of
  Waterbury, Connecticut, 1876,* by Sturges
  M. Judd, and materials concerning ser-
  vicemen, manufacturing, civil defense,

and other aspects of Waterbury's role in
World War II.

SEE: Hamer.

WATERTOWN

CT884-870
Watertown Historical Society
22 DeForest Street
Watertown CT 06795

(203) 274-1634

OPEN: W 2-4 and by appointment
COPYING FACILITIES: no
MATERIALS SOLICITED: Will accept materials relating to Watertown history
  and genealogy.

HOLDINGS:
  Total volume: 36 items
  Inclusive dates: 1780 -
  Description: A small collection of diaries, maps, deeds, scrapbooks, business
  account books, and other items relating
  chiefly to Watertown.

CT884-890
Watertown Library
470 Main Street
Watertown CT 06714

no telephone

SEE: Hamer.

Questionnaire not returned.

WEST HARTFORD

CT891-400
Jewish Historical Society of Greater
  Hartford
335 Bloomfield Avenue
West Hartford CT 06117

(203) 236-4571, Ext. 35

OPEN: M, Th 10-2 and by appointment;
  closed other days and holidays
COPYING FACILITIES: yes
MATERIALS SOLICITED: Materials relating
  to the history and growth of the Jewish
  community in the greater Hartford
  area.

HOLDINGS:
  Total volume: 4 file cabinets; 20 c.f.
  Inclusive dates: mid-1800's -
  Description: Records, manuscripts, pictures, slides, films, tape recordings, and
  related materials concerning the history
  of the Jews in the Hartford area.

CT891-550
The Noah Webster Foundation and
  Historical Society of West Hartford,
  Inc.
227 South Main Street
West Hartford CT 06107

(203) 521-5362

OPEN: M-F 9-5; closed weekends and
  holidays

ACCESS: a letter explaining the use the
  researcher would make of the collection
  is requested
COPYING FACILITIES: yes
MATERIALS SOLICITED: Documents and
  illustrative material concerning Noah
  Webster and his times, as well as the
  history of the town of West Hartford.

HOLDINGS:
  Total volume: 2 file cabinets
  Inclusive dates: 1730 - 1900
  Description: Correspondence by and
  relating to Noah Webster; material relating to the town of West Hartford, including photographs, diaries, documents and
  ledgers.
    Also included are Butler family papers,
  the Shelden family collection including
  materials on local voluntary associations,
  and West Hartford tax lists.

CT891-820
University of Hartford
Hartt College of Music
Library
West Hartford CT 06117

no telephone

SEE: NUCMC, 1978.

Questionnaire not returned.

WEST WILLINGTON

CT905-880
Willington Historical Society
Jared Sparks Road
West Willington CT

MAILING ADDRESS:
c/o Robertson
Mirtl Road
West Willington CT 06279

(203) 429-3451

OPEN: by appointment only
COPYING FACILITIES: no
MATERIALS SOLICITED: Letters, photographs, diaries, and memorabilia concerning the history of Willington.

HOLDINGS:
  Total volume: not specified
  Inclusive dates: 1759 - 1850's
  Description: Photographs, research papers on early industries, Congregational
  church records, indenture papers, historical speeches delivered during centennial
  and bicentennial celebrations, genealogical records of the earliest settlers, letters,
  and scrapbooks, primarily concerning the
  history of Willington.

WESTON

CT919-880
The Weston Historical Society, Inc.
Weston CT

MAILING ADDRESS:
P.O. Box 1092
Weston CT 06883

no telephone

OPEN: by appointment only

COPYING FACILITIES: no
MATERIALS SOLICITED: The history of Weston and its inhabitants.

HOLDINGS:
Total volume: 20 items
Inclusive dates: 1832 -
Description: Oral history tapes, photographs of Weston schools and students, diaries, and a record book.

WESTPORT

CT926-480

The Lifwynn Foundation, Inc.
30 Turkey Hill Road South
Westport CT 06880

(203) 227-4139

OPEN: M-F 9-5; closed weekends and holidays
COPYING FACILITIES: yes

HOLDINGS:
Total volume: 35 l.f.
Inclusive dates: 1920 - 1950
Description: Papers of Trigant Burrow, phylobiologist and psychiatrist, concerning the establishment and early history of the American Psychoanalytic Association, as well as Burrow's introduction of group analysis and the development of his phylobiological research. The collection contains manuscripts of published and unpublished works, laboratory notes, references to and reviews of Burrow's writings, and correspondence with leading figures in science, education, literature, psychoanalysis, and other fields.

SEE: NUCMC, 1977.

WETHERSFIELD

CT933-870

Webb Deane Stevens Museum
211 Main Street
Wethersfield CT 06109

no telephone

SEE: NUCMC, 1959-61 (as Webb House).

Questionnaire not returned.

CT933-890

Wethersfield Historical Society
Old Academy Museum Library
150 Main Street
Wethersfield CT 06109

(203) 529-7656

OPEN: M-F 10-4, Sa June-Oct. 10-4 or by appointment; closed Sundays and holidays
ACCESS: must be over 14 years old
COPYING FACILITIES: yes
MATERIALS SOLICITED: Local history and genealogical materials. Will also accept materials related to State history.

HOLDINGS:
Total volume: 50 l.f.; three file cabinets
Inclusive dates: 1670 -
Description: Materials relating chiefly to Wethersfield history and genealogy. Included are photographs, letters, diaries, account books and miscellaneous papers.

SEE: Hamer; NUCMC, 1966.

WILTON

CT947-880

Wilton Historical Society
Wilton Heritage Museum
249 Danbury Road
Wilton CT 06897

(203) 762-7257

OPEN: Tu-F 10-4; closed Mondays, weekends and holidays
COPYING FACILITIES: no
MATERIALS SOLICITED: Private papers pertinent to Wilton and its inhabitants. Will also accept land records and other materials pertaining to Wilton's town government and cultural organizations.

HOLDINGS:
Total volume: 12 l.f.
Inclusive dates: 1650 -
Description: Diaries, letters, deeds, journals, and store account books relating primarily to Wilton, but including some references to surrounding towns.

SEE: NUCMC, 1959-62 (listed under Cannondale, CT).

WINDSOR

CT961-210

Emhart Industries, Inc.
Hartford Division Library
123 Day Hill Road
Windsor CT

MAILING ADDRESS:
P.O. Box 2809
Hartford CT 06101

(203) 688-8551, Ext. 320

OPEN: M-F 8-4:30; closed weekends and holidays
ACCESS: serious researchers; special arrangements required
COPYING FACILITIES: yes
MATERIALS SOLICITED: Materials regarding glass technology and packaging.

HOLDINGS:
Total volume: 100 l.f.
Inclusive dates: 1912 -
Description: 2,000 photographs of glassmaking equipment and glass factories, Emhart Industries records, and technological information, all covering the history of the glass container industry.

SEE ALSO: Ann Novotny, ed., *Picture Sources 3* (Special Libraries Assn., 1975).

CT961-880

Windsor Historical Society
96 Palisado Avenue
Windsor CT 06095

(203) 688-3813

OPEN: Tu-Sa 10-4; closed Sundays, Mondays, July 4, Thanksgiving, and Dec. 1 - April 1
USER FEES: one dollar
ACCESS: an appointment is necessary
COPYING FACILITIES: yes
MATERIALS SOLICITED: Material about Windsor history and Windsor genealogy. Will also accept Connecticut material and United States history.

HOLDINGS:
Total volume: 1,000 items
Inclusive dates: 1610 - 1900's
Description: A collection focusing primarily on the history of Windsor. Holdings include manuscript music books of the late 18th to mid-19th centuries, collections of recipes, manuscript books on penmanship, and account books of local businesses in the 18th and 19th centuries. There are also genealogical materials relating to over 100 families and historical materials relating to local churches.

WINDSOR LOCKS

CT963-120

Connecticut Aeronautical Historical Association, Inc.
New England Air Museum
Bradley International Airport
Windsor Locks CT 06096

(203) 623-3305

OPEN: daily 10-7; closed Christmas and Thanksgiving
COPYING FACILITIES: no
MATERIALS SOLICITED: Personal memorabilia and business records pertaining to aviation, as well as aviation history manuscripts and visual and audible documents dealing with New England. Will also accept aviation history materials not dealing with New England.

HOLDINGS:
Total volume: 200 c.f.
Inclusive dates: not specified
Description: Photographs, motion pictures, and oral history tapes and transcripts relating to aviation history; corporate records of the Burnelli Aircraft Company; and personal scrapbooks and other memorabilia of local aviation personalities.

WOODBURY

CT982-280

Glebe House
Woodbury CT 06798

no telephone

SEE: Hamer; NUCMC, 1965.

Questionnaire not returned.

CT982-600
Old Woodbury Historical Society
Hollow Road
Woodbury CT

MAILING ADDRESS:
Town Office Building
P.O. Box 705
Woodbury CT 06798

no telephone

OPEN: July - Aug., Su 2-4, and by
   appointment
ACCESS: advance arrangements required
COPYING FACILITIES: no

HOLDINGS:
   Total volume: not specified
   Inclusive dates: late 18th century -
   Description: Account books, business
records, photographs, maps, scrapbooks,
and genealogical records relating to local
history.

DELAWARE

The Division of Historical and Cultural Affairs of Delaware has recently been administering a statewide program for preserving local public records. Many permanently valuable local public records remain in the custody of local officials, but the Hall of Records in Dover holds a significant body of county and municipal records dating from the 18th century. The Hall of Records also makes available to researchers microfilm copies of vital, probate, land, and other county and municipal records filmed by the Division and by the Church of Jesus Christ of Latter-day Saints.

DELAWARE CITY

DE60-240
Fort Delaware Museum
Fort Delaware State Park
Pea Patch Island
Delaware City DE

MAILING ADDRESS:
P.O. Box 1251
Wilmington DE 19899

(302) 834-7941

OPEN: May - Sept., Sa, Su by
  appointment only
ACCESS: prior arrangements required
COPYING FACILITIES: no
MATERIALS SOLICITED: Materials pertaining to Fort Delaware, 1813-1942. Will also accept Civil War documents having Delaware State significance.

HOLDINGS:
  Total volume: 200 items
  Inclusive dates: 1822 - 1942
  Description: A collection of 50 letters by Confederate prisoners at Fort Delaware, some letters of Union guards stationed there, and other documents, all of Civil War vintage; some letters and documents of 1822-27; and about 50 photographs of the Fort and prisoners, 1863-65.

DOVER

DE90-140
Delaware Division of Historical and
  Cultural Affairs
Bureau of Archives and Records
Hall of Records
Dover DE 19901

(302) 736-5318

OPEN: Tu-F 8:30-4:15, Sa 8-3:45; closed
  Sundays, Mondays and holidays
COPYING FACILITIES: yes
MATERIALS SOLICITED: Public records of the State of Delaware and its counties and municipalities. Will also accept other Delaware material.

HOLDINGS:
  Total volume: 75,000 c.f.
  Inclusive dates: 1638 -
  Description: Public records of the State of Delaware, including county records continuous from about 1680, and State records of varying content and completeness. There are also numerous collections of private papers, mainly concerned with Delaware history.

SEE: Hamer; NUCMC, 1959-61, 63-64, 70, 73 (as Delaware Public Archives Commission).

SEE: Davis; Ingram; Leventhal and Mooney - I; Novotny; Paszek; Schatz.

SEE ALSO: Leon deValinger, Jr., comp., *Calendar of Sussex County, Delaware, Probate Records, 1680-1800* (Delaware Public Archives Commission, 1964); Leon deValinger, Jr., and Virginia E. Shaw, *A Calendar of Ridgeley Family Letters, 1742-1899, in the Delaware State Archives,* vol. 3 (Delaware Public Archives Commission, 1961); Joanne Mattern and Harold B. Hancock, comps., *A Preliminary Inventory of the Older Records in the Delaware Archives,* State of Delaware Archives Inventory, no. 1 (Delaware Division of Historical and Cultural Affairs, 1978).

GREENVILLE

DE270-200
Hagley Museum and Library
Wilmington DE

MAILING ADDRESS:
P.O. Box 3630
Wilmington DE 19807

(302) 658-2400

OPEN: M-F 8:30-4:30, second Saturday of month 9-4:30; closed other Saturdays, Sundays, and holidays

ACCESS: all researchers must file a Library identification form and be interviewed
COPYING FACILITIES: yes
MATERIALS SOLICITED: Business and industrial history of the mid-Atlantic area (Delaware, Pennsylvania, New Jersey, and Maryland). Will also accept any materials pertaining to Delaware and the du Pont family.

HOLDINGS:
  Total volume: 12,000,000 items
  Inclusive dates: 1588 -
  Description: Business and industrial records, particularly those relating to production and manufacturing, including major bodies concerning the iron and steel industry in Pennsylvania and the explosives and chemical industries in Delaware and Pennsylvania. Records relating to coal, transportation, railroads, shipbuilding, oil and petroleum, leather, paper, machinery, textiles, canning, merchandising, and shipping, chiefly in the 19th and 20th centuries, are also held. The collection also contains personal papers of the du Pont family, John J. Raskob, and others.

GUIDES: John Beverley Riggs, *A Guide to the Manuscripts in the Eleutherian Mills Historical Library: Accessions Through the Year 1965* (1970).

SEE: Hamer (as Eleutherian Mills-Hagley Foundation, Wilmington, DE, and Longwood Library, Kennett Square, PA); NUCMC, 1959-61, 71-73.

SEE: Parkinson; Allard, Crawley, and Edmison; Hines; Hinding; Robbins; Swanson and Gibb.

SEE ALSO: Ann Novotny, ed., *Picture Sources 3* (Special Libraries Assn., 1975); Walter Heacock, 'Business Archives and Museum Development,' *American Archivist* 29 (Jan. 1966); Alan M. Meckler and Ruth McMullin, comps., *Oral History Collections* (Bowker, 1975); David A. Hounshell, comp., *Manuscripts in U.S. Depositories Relating to the History of Electrical Science and Technology* (Smithsonian Institution, n.d.); Lawrence J. Paszek, comp., *United States Air Force History: A Guide to Documentary Sources* (Office of Air Force History, 1973); Richard C. Davis, *North American Forest History: A Guide to Archives and Manuscripts in the United States and Canada* (Clio Books, 1977).

NEWARK

DE540-780

University of Delaware
Archives
78 East Delaware Avenue
Newark DE 19711

(302) 451-8006

OPEN: M-F 8:30-5; closed weekends and
   holidays
ACCESS: 50-year restriction on
   unpublished University materials and
   records, unless access is necessitated
   under provisions of the Freedom of
   Information Act of the State of
   Delaware
COPYING FACILITIES: yes
MATERIALS SOLICITED: University
   records. Will also accept personal papers of faculty and alumni, but only if
   refused by the Library's Special Collections Department.

HOLDINGS:
   Total volume: 2,500 l.f.
   Inclusive dates: 1769 -
   Description: 5,400 volumes, 7,500 photographic negatives and prints, and 1,500
   cubic feet of paper records, consisting of
   the archives of the University of Delaware and its predecessor institution, the
   Academy of Newark. Included are
   records of the board of trustees; the University president, vice-president, treasurer, and secretary; deans, directors, and
   department chairpersons; and committees
   and commissions; as well as theses and
   dissertations.

SEE: Hamer (as University of Delaware,
   Library); NUCMC, 1970.

DE540-790

University of Delaware
Libraries
Department of Special Collections
South College Avenue
Newark DE 19711

(302) 451-2229, 2965

OPEN: M-F 10-5; closed weekends and
   holidays
ACCESS: users must conform to
   Regulations Concerning the Use of
   Manuscripts, a printed guide available
   at the Library
COPYING FACILITIES: no
MATERIALS SOLICITED: American political and historical manuscripts and 20th
   century literary manuscripts. Will also
   accept manuscript maps and charts, architectural and engineering drawings,
   photographs, other visual documents,
   and records of institutions and organizations in Delaware.

HOLDINGS:
   Total volume: 550 l.f.
   Inclusive dates: 1580 -
   Description: Over 400 collections of
   business, diplomatic, educational, historical, legal, literary, political, and technological records. They are primarily centered on 19th and 20th century America,
   but Africa, the Far East, Latin America,
   the Pacific, and western Europe also are
   represented. Included are diaries, memoirs, ships' logs, papers of individuals,

company records, archives of 20th century literary magazines, records of organizations, archives of government bodies,
collections of ephemera, original sketches
and drawings, and maps.

SEE: Hamer (as University of Delaware,
   Library); NUCMC, 1959-62, 68, 71,
   77-78, 80.

SEE: Parkinson; Hines; Robbins.

SEE ALSO: Peter Duignan, *Handbook of*
   American Resources for African Studies
   (Hoover Institution, 1967); Richard C.
   Davis, *North American Forest History:*
   A Guide to Archives and Manuscripts in
   the United States and Canada (Clio
   Books, 1977).

WILMINGTON

DE810-150

Delaware Art Museum
Library
2301 Kentmere Parkway
Wilmington DE 19806

(302) 571-9590

OPEN: M-F 10-4:30; closed weekends
   and holidays
ACCESS: appointment required
COPYING FACILITIES: yes
MATERIALS SOLICITED: Materials related
   to the English Pre-Raphaelites and to
   American artists, especially Howard
   Pyle and his pupils and John Sloan and
   'The Eight'.

HOLDINGS:
   Total volume: 60 file drawers
   Inclusive dates: mid-19th century -
   Description: Archives of the Wilming-
   ton Society of the Fine Arts, 1912- ;
   items relating to the Samuel and Mary R.
   Bancroft collection of Pre-Raphaelite
   paintings, including correspondence of
   Samuel Bancroft, Jr., some Dante Gabriel
   Rossetti letters, and 45 manuscripts of
   Rossetti sonnets; archives and logbooks
   of artists Albert Lindsay, Jerome Myers,
   Everett Shinn, Frank E. Schoonover, and
   Gayle Hoskins; and photographs of artist
   Howard Pyle and his pupils Gayle Hos-
   kins, Stanley Arthurs, Frank E.
   Schoonover, Jessie Willcox Smith,
   Elizabeth Shippen Green Elliott, and Vio-
   let Oakley.

SEE: Hamer (as Wilmington Society of the
   Fine Arts).

DE810-170

Diocese of Delaware
Vault of the Cathedral Church of St.
   John
10 Concord Avenue
Wilmington DE

MAILING ADDRESS:
Diocesan Registrar
2020 Tatnall Street
Wilmington DE 19802

(302) 656-5441

OPEN: by appointment only
ACCESS: arrangements made by letter to
   Diocesan Registrar
COPYING FACILITIES: yes

MATERIALS SOLICITED: Parish histories
   and records; records of diocesan institutions; journals of diocesan conventions; records of annual meetings of the
   Episcopal Church Women; and diocesan and parish periodicals. Will also
   accept press clippings relating to the
   Episcopal Diocese of Delaware and its
   bishops, clergy, lay leaders, and parish
   anniversary celebrations, as well as
   photographs of churches, bishops, clergy, church groups, and other subjects.

HOLDINGS:
   Total volume: 170 sq. ft.
   Inclusive dates: 1792 -
   Description: A complete set of diocesan convention journals dating since
   1792; manuscript sermons, journals, and
   diaries of Delaware bishops; microfilm
   copies of parish registers; and annual reports of the Episcopal Church Women.

DE810-330

The Historical Society of Delaware
Library
505 Market Street Mall
Wilmington DE 19801

(302) 655-7161

OPEN: M 1-9, Tu-F 9-5; closed weekends
   and holidays
COPYING FACILITIES: yes
MATERIALS SOLICITED: Materials relating
   to the history of Delaware and its citizens, from 1683 to the present. Will
   also accept most materials relating to
   adjoining States.

HOLDINGS:
   Total volume: 1,100 vols.; 950 l.f.
   Inclusive dates: 1683 -
   Description: Diaries, letters, journals,
   photographs, maps, and other papers relating to business, religion, politics, government, the military, abolitionism, temperance, and suffrage in Delaware and
   adjoining Pennsylvania and Maryland
   counties.

SEE: Hamer; NUCMC, 1968, 70-71.

SEE: Allard, Crawley, and Edmison;
   Gehring; Hinding; Ingram; Leventhal
   and Mooney - I.

SEE ALSO: H. Clay Reed, 'Manuscript
   Books in The Historical Society of
   Delaware,' *Delaware History* 11 (1964);
   Ann Novotny, ed., *Picture Sources 3*
   (Special Libraries Assn., 1975); Walter
   Schatz, ed., *Directory of Afro-American*
   Resources (Bowker, 1970); Richard C.
   Davis, *North American Forest History:*
   A Guide to Archives and Manuscripts in
   the United States and Canada (Clio
   Books, 1977).

DE810-690

Rockwood Museum
Research Archives
610 Shipley Road
Wilmington DE 19809

(302) 571-7776

OPEN: Tu-F 11-4; closed Mondays,
   weekends and holidays
COPYING FACILITIES: no

MATERIALS SOLICITED: Will accept manuscripts, archives, visual documents, and scrapbooks pertaining to Wilmington and Quaker history, particularly the Shipley, Bringhurst, and Hargraves families.

HOLDINGS:
Total volume: 87 l.f.
Inclusive dates: 1700 - 1940
Description: Records of the Shipley, Bringhurst, and Hargraves families, Quaker and Wilmington history, and Anglo-American trade, including account books, business and financial records, correspondence, diaries, genealogical source data, maps, architectural and technical drawings, aerial photographs, motion pictures, and scrapbooks.

WINTERTHUR

DE900-320

The Henry Francis du Pont
Winterthur Museum, Inc.
The Joseph Downs Manuscript and
Microfilm Collection
Winterthur DE 19735

(302) 656-8591

OPEN: M-F 8:30-4:30 and the first Saturday of each month March through Dec.; closed weekends and holidays
ACCESS: access granted to all responsible researchers upon presentation of reliable identification, the completion of a researcher's registration form and a brief interview
COPYING FACILITIES: yes
MATERIALS SOLICITED: The arts of the United States and Great Britain, 1630-1914.

HOLDINGS:
Total volume: 7,000 lots of manuscript materials; 3,150 reels of microfilm; 4,858 microfiche
Inclusive dates: 1630 -
Description: Manuscripts pertaining to the decorative arts, with emphasis on American craftspeople from the 17th through the 19th centuries. The manuscripts are comprised of household inventories, wills, court records, estate records, bills, account books, diaries, designs and drawings for objects and buildings, merchant and business letterbooks, import and export records, personal and business letters, surveys and records of fire insurance companies, and other items.
Among the special collections are the Edward Deming Andrews Memorial Shaker Collection; the Thelma S. Mendson Card Collection; the Maxine Waldron Collection and Children's Books and Paper Toys; the Waldron Phoenix Belknap Collection and photographs for Ledlie I. Laughlin's book *Pewter in America;* and R. W. Symonds' research notes on English furniture and craftspeople.
Also included are the research notes, diaries, letters and manuscripts of Irving W. Lyon; the research notes, photographs pertaining to articles by Irving Phillips Lyon on New England Colonial furniture; the Joseph Downs Collection of research papers and notes; the papers and research materials of Charles F. Montgomery; and the records of William G. Pahlmann, interior designer, New York, 1930-1977.
Microfilm holdings emphasize probate court records, out-of-print books, and prints from original papers in collections in museums, libraries and historical societies. Also on deposit are family papers, account books, letters, photographs, scrapbooks of memorabilia (on microfilm) relating to the Corbit-Sharpe House and the Wilson-Warner House, both in Odessa, Delaware, or to the surrounding area.

SEE: Hamer.

SEE: Allard, Crawley, and Edmison.

SEE ALSO: Ann Novotny, ed., *Picture Sources 3* (Special Libraries Assn., 1975).

DE900-330

The Henry Francis du Pont
Winterthur Museum, Inc.
Winterthur Archives
Winterthur DE 19735

(302) 656-8591

OPEN: M-F 8:30-4:30 and first Saturday of each month, March - Dec.; closed Sundays and holidays
ACCESS: responsible researchers upon presentation of identification and completion of brief interview and registration procedures; appointment advised
COPYING FACILITIES: yes
MATERIALS SOLICITED: Items pertaining to Henry Francis du Pont, Winterthur Farms, Winterthur Gardens, Chestertown House Corporation, and Winterthur Museum. Will also accept papers of Henry du Pont, and Henry Algernon du Pont, and records of the Col. Henry A. du Pont Company.

HOLDINGS:
Total volume: 1,300 l.f.
Inclusive dates: 1800 -
Description: Materials relating to: the military, political, and business activities of Henry Algernon du Pont; the horticultural, agricultural, and antique collecting activities of Henry Francis du Pont; the farming, cattle breeding, arboretum and property maintenance operations of the Winterthur Farms; and the acquisitions and installation of the collections of the Winterthur Museum, including the Museum properties in Odessa.

SEE: Ingram.

SEE ALSO: Barbara Hearn, comp., *Summary Guide* (1975). Another guide to family and corporate records, 1846-1951, is available from the institution.

DISTRICT OF COLUMBIA

Since 1985 the Office of Public Records, District of Columbia Archives, in Washington, DC, has had legal responsibility for maintaining the permanently valuable records of the District of Columbia government and its predecessors. The Archives has not accessioned any records, pending completion of an archival facility. Currently, some 1,408 cubic feet of fiscal, engineering, police, and other District of Columbia government records are preserved at the National Archives in Washington, DC. Most of these are described in its 1976 publication, *Preliminary Inventory of the Records of the Government of the District of Columbia* (P.I. 186). The National Archives also houses some 1,130 cubic feet of related records of Federal authorities with jurisdiction over the District of Columbia.

DC1-40

ACTION (The Agency For Volunteer Service)
Photo Library
Room 200, 806 Connecticut Avenue, N.W.
Washington DC 20525

MAILING ADDRESS:
Room P305, 806 Connecticut Avenue, N.W.
Washington DC 20525

(202) 254-7523

OPEN: M-F 9-5; closed weekends and holidays
ACCESS: appointment requested
COPYING FACILITIES: yes

HOLDINGS:
Total volume: 10,000 items
Inclusive dates: 1960 -
Description: Photographs of ACTION volunteers and their work for the following agencies: Peace Corps, Volunteers in Service to America (VISTA), Foster Grandparent Program, Retired Senior Volunteer Program (RSVP), Service Corps of Retired Executives (SCORE), and Active Corps of Executives (ACE).

SEE: Novotny.

SEE ALSO: Michael Grow, *Scholars' Guide to Washington, D.C., for Latin American and Caribbean Studies* (Smithsonian Institution Press, 1979); Shirley L. Green, comp., *Pictorial Resources in the Washington, D.C., Area* (Library of Congress, 1976).

DC1-160

African Methodist Episcopal Church
Financial Department
2311 M Street, N.W.
Washington DC 20037

(202) 337-3930

OPEN: M-F 8:30-5; closed weekends and holidays
COPYING FACILITIES: yes
MATERIALS SOLICITED: Financial records of the institutions of higher education supported by the African Methodist Episcopal church.

HOLDINGS:
Total volume: 100 vols.; additional materials
Inclusive dates: 1856 -
Description: Financial records, including annual budgets, of the following educational institutions supported by the African Methodist Episcopal church: Daniel Payne College, Birmingham, AL; Shorter Junior College, North Little Rock, AR; Edward Waters College, Jacksonville, FL; Morris Brown College, Atlanta, GA; Turner Theological Seminary, Atlanta, GA; Kittrell Job Corps Center, Kittrell, NC; Payne Theological Seminary, Wilberforce, OH; Wilberforce University, Wilberforce, OH; Allen University, Columbia, SC; and Paul Quinn College, Waco, TX.

DC1-180

Agency for International Development (AID)
Bureau for External Affairs
401 23rd Street, N.W.
Washington DC 20523

(202) 647-4330

OPEN: Su-F 9-5; closed Saturdays and holidays
ACCESS: advance arrangements required
COPYING FACILITIES: no
MATERIALS SOLICITED: Photographs of AID projects in the third world.

HOLDINGS:
Total volume: 30,000 items
Inclusive dates: 1966 -
Description: Black and white photographs and color slides of foreign aid projects involving agriculture, public health, family planning, education, and disaster relief in Africa, Asia, and Latin America.

SEE: Novotny; Grow; Bhatt.

DC1-200

Air Force
Office of Air Force History

MAILING ADDRESS:
HQ USAF/CHOR
Building 5681
Bolling AFB
Washington DC 20332-6098

(202) 767-5088

OPEN: M-F 9-4; closed weekends and holidays
ACCESS: The general public is limited to access to unclassified documents only. Access to classified materials is based on a 'need-to-know' and granted only by the Office of Information (SAF/OIPM), Department of the Air Force, Washington, DC 20330.
COPYING FACILITIES: no
MATERIALS SOLICITED: Military aviation history.

HOLDINGS:
Total volume: 178 c.f. microfilm; 728 c.f. documents
Inclusive dates: 1915 -
Description: Unclassified and classified documents and microfilm, covering all aspects of the history of the Air Force, as well as other aspects of military aviation history.

SEE ALSO: Lawrence J. Paszek, *United States Air Force History: A Guide to Documentary Sources* (Office of Air Force History, 1973); and the following publications of the Albert F. Simpson Historical Research Center: Hugh N. Ahmann, *U.S. Air Force Oral History Catalog of Selected Interviews* (1975); Eleanor E. Peets, *USAF History of Women in the Armed Forces: A Selected Bibliography* (1976); Gloria L. Atkinson, *German Air Force Monograph Project* (1972); and *Selected Historical Studies* (1974).

DC1-280

Amalgamated Transit Union
5025 Wisconsin Avenue, N.W.
Washington DC 20016

(202) 537-1645

OPEN: M-F 8-4; closed weekends and holidays
COPYING FACILITIES: no

HOLDINGS:
Total volume: 48 file drawers
Inclusive dates: 1900 -
Description: Copies of all labor contracts of the Amalgamated Transit Union's local organizations since 1900, as well as financial statements of some local unions.

DC1-295

American Alliance for Health,
  Physical Education and Recreation
Archives
1201 16th Street, N.W.
Washington DC 20036

(703) 476-3423

OPEN: M-F, by appointment only; closed
  weekends and holidays
COPYING FACILITIES: yes
MATERIALS SOLICITED: Records of the
  seven associations of the Alliance.

HOLDINGS:
  Total volume: 100 l.f.
  Inclusive dates: 1886 -
  Description: Correspondence, minutes,
  annual reports, conference records, and
  other records, dating chiefly since 1945,
  relating to the Alliance and the seven
  associations which comprise it. Also included are papers of Alliance presidents
  and incomplete records of its national
  conventions dating from the early 1900's.

DC1-300

American Association for the
  Advancement of Science
1333 H Street, N.W.
Washington DC 20005

(202) 467-4428

OPEN: M-F 9-5; closed weekends and
  holidays
ACCESS: appointment required
COPYING FACILITIES: yes
MATERIALS SOLICITED: Will accept Asso-
  ciation records.

HOLDINGS:
  Total volume: 2,000 l.f.
  Inclusive dates: 1846 -
  Description: Records of the American
  Association for the Advancement of Sci-
  ence, including its council and board, ex-
  ecutive office, *Science* magazine, and of-
  fices, committees, and annual meetings.
  Also held are 2 vols. of manuscript min-
  utes, 1846-80.

DC1-340

American Association of University
  Women
Archives
2401 Virginia Avenue, N.W.
Washington DC 20037

(202) 785-7763, 7708

OPEN: by appointment only
USER FEES: none unless extended use of
  Archivist's time for research purposes
  or aid is required
ACCESS: open to members of Association
  and professionals, academicians,
  historians, and doctoral candidates
COPYING FACILITIES: yes
MATERIALS SOLICITED: Material created
  by the Association, its divisions,
  branches, and members, and related to
  its work. Will also accept manuscript
  material relating to prominent Association members and officers and activities in which they engaged.

HOLDINGS:
  Total volume: 175 l.f.; 322 boxes
  Inclusive dates: 1881 -
  Description: Material relating to the
  Association and its predecessor and affiliated organizations. Included are records
  of the Association of Collegiate Alumnae,
  including studies on health, housing, and
  professions for women; the Southern Association of College Women; the Western
  Association of Collegiate Alumnae; the
  International Federation of University
  Women, including refugee dossiers; the
  Association's Status of Women Committee, with materials covering suffrage,
  equal pay, women in public office and
  the armed forces, and minimum wages;
  the Education Committee, dealing with
  elementary, secondary, and higher education; and the White House Conferences
  on Children and Youth.

DC1-400

American Federation of Labor and
  Congress of Industrial
  Organizations
Library
815 16th Street, N.W.
Washington DC 20006

(202) 637-5297

OPEN: M-F 9-4:30; closed weekends and
  holidays
COPYING FACILITIES: yes
MATERIALS SOLICITED: Photographs concerning the AFL-CIO, as well as selected records of the organization.

HOLDINGS:
  Total volume: 239 boxes; 20 vols.; 5
  l.f.; additional materials
  Inclusive dates: 1881 -
  Description: Records and other materials relating to the American Federation of
  Labor (AFL) and Congress of Industrial
  Organizations (CIO), both before and
  after their merger. Much of the material
  is on microfilm. Included are executive
  council minutes of the AFL, 1893-1924;
  convention proceedings of the AFL, the
  CIO, and the AFL-CIO; and correspondence, reports, and copies of agreements
  exchanged between the AFL headquarters
  and its local unions, 1898-1953, concerning contract negotiations, strikes, and settlements.
  Papers of Samuel Gompers include letters dealing with a variety of political,
  social, and economic issues, as well as his
  notes from the Paris Peace Conference of
  1918 and from meetings of the advisory
  committee of the Council of National
  Defense. William Green's papers,
  1915-52, pertain mostly to the period
  since 1934, with emphasis on AFL and
  CIO relations and labor problems of
  World War II. There are also 5 linear feet
  of photographs of Gompers, Green, international union presidents, conventions,
  meetings, and other subjects.

SEE: Novotny.

DC1-460

American Forestry Association
1319 18th Street, N.W.
Washington DC 20036

(202) 467-5810

OPEN: M-F 9-4:30; closed weekends and
  holidays
COPYING FACILITIES: yes
MATERIALS SOLICITED: Photographs related to forestry and trees.

HOLDINGS:
  Total volume: 4,000 items
  Inclusive dates: 1900 -
  Description: An uncatalogued collec-
  tion of photographs relating to trees and
  forestry.

DC1-480

American Institute of Architects
Library
1735 New York Avenue, N.W.
Washington DC 20006

(202) 626-7493

OPEN: M-F 8:30-5; closed weekends and
  holidays
ACCESS: appointment required for use of
  architectural drawings
COPYING FACILITIES: no
MATERIALS SOLICITED: Will accept
  records and papers of or pertaining to
  the American Institute of Architects.

HOLDINGS:
  Total volume: not specified
  Inclusive dates: late 18th century -
  Description: Corporate records of the
  American Institute of Architects, including minutes, annual reports, and some
  photographs; several thousand architectural drawings of Richard Morris Hunt
  and the firm Hunt and Hunt; 5,500 19th
  century photographs of American and
  European architecture and art, primarily
  the works of Richard Morris Hunt; and
  drawings of architects Ammi B. Young
  and William Thornton, including
  Thornton's design for the U.S. Capitol.

SEE ALSO: Hong N. Kim, *Scholars' Guide
  to Washington, D.C., for East Asian
  Studies* (Smithsonian Institution Press,
  1979); Shirley L. Green, comp., *Pictorial Resources in the Washington, D.C.,
  Area* (Library of Congress, 1976).

DC1-500

American Iron and Steel Institute
Photo Library
1000 16th Street, N.W.
Washington DC 20036

(202) 452-7100

OPEN: M-F 9-5; closed weekends and
  holidays
COPYING FACILITIES: yes
MATERIALS SOLICITED: Photographs and
  other visual items relating to steel companies. Will also accept other materials
  relating to steel manufacturing.

HOLDINGS:
  Total volume: 5,000 items
  Inclusive dates: 1860's -
  Description: Historical and current
  photographs of the iron and steel indus-
  try, covering transportation, mining of

coal, limestone, and iron ore, and manu-facturing facilities and processes. There are also charts and drawings of recent steel making processes.

SEE: Novotny.

DC1-560
American National Red Cross
Archives
18th and D Streets, N.W.
Washington DC 20006

(202) 639-3480

OPEN: M-F 8:30-4:45; closed weekends and holidays
ACCESS: subject to review by library personnel
COPYING FACILITIES: yes
MATERIALS SOLICITED: Records of the American National Red Cross. Will also accept special papers relating to the American Red Cross.

HOLDINGS:
    Total volume: 1,894 l.f.
    Inclusive dates: 1947 -
    Description: Noncurrent records of the Red Cross. Included are official Ameri-can Red Cross Board minutes, correspon-dence, reports on war and disaster relief and other activities of the Red Cross, records of international conventions and conferences, and records pertaining to the Red Cross societies of other countries.

SEE: Hamer; NUCMC, 1959-61.

SEE: Novotny; Hinding; Allard, Crawley, and Edmison; Kim; Grant; Grow.

DC1-580
American Petroleum Institute
Public Relations
Photographic and Film Services
Room 701, 2101 L Street, N.W.
Washington DC 20037

(202) 682-8042

OPEN: M-F 9-5; closed weekends and holidays
COPYING FACILITIES: no
MATERIALS SOLICITED: Materials from member companies of the American Petroleum Institute. Will also accept materials having to do with supplemen-tal energy sources.

HOLDINGS:
    Total volume: 20,000 photographs; 100 films; 6,000 slides
    Inclusive dates: 1860 -
    Description: Films dealing with the technology of the petroleum industry, in-cluding obsolete technology, as well as more recent developments in exploration, production, and fire protection. There are also slides and photographs of refining, production, exploration, offshore drilling, and other aspects of the petroleum in-dustry since the 1850's. Included are pho-tographs predating 1940, depicting early gasoline stations and Pennsylvania and Texas oil fields.

SEE: Novotny.

SEE ALSO: *Movies About Oil* (American Petroleum Institute, 1978).

An inventory of slides and photographs is available at the repository.

DC1-600
American Pharmaceutical Association
  Foundation
2215 Constitution Avenue, N.W.
Washington DC 20037

(202) 429-7523

OPEN: M-F 8:30-5; closed weekends and holidays
ACCESS: by appointment only
COPYING FACILITIES: yes
MATERIALS SOLICITED: Current records of pharmacy schools, pharmacy related associations and boards of pharmacy, as well as of the American Pharmaceu-tical Association.

HOLDINGS:
    Total volume: 230 l.f.
    Inclusive dates: 1852 -
    Description: Records of the American Pharmaceutical Association, related and affiliated organizations, schools of phar-macy and boards of pharmacy, including bylaws, annual meeting abstracts and pro-ceedings, speeches, manuscripts, news re-leases and clippings, photographs, corre-spondence, manuscript minutes and mis-cellaneous papers, and other related ma-terial.

SEE ALSO: 'Structure of the Archives of the American Pharmaceutical Associ-ation,' *Pharmacy in History* 7 (1962); Ann Novotny, ed., *Picture Sources 3* (Special Libraries Assn., 1975).

DC1-640
American Psychiatric Association
  Archives
Library and Archives
1400 K Street N.W.
Washington DC 20005

(202) 682-6080

OPEN: by appointment only
ACCESS: student researchers required to present letter of introduction from professor
COPYING FACILITIES: yes
MATERIALS SOLICITED: Records of the American Psychiatric Association, per-sonal papers of its members, oral his-tories of psychiatrists, and photographs and memorabilia relating to the history of the Association and its members. Will also accept papers, photographs, and memorabilia relative to the history of psychiatry.

HOLDINGS:
    Total volume: 700 l.f.
    Inclusive dates: 1846 -
    Description: Official records of the American Psychiatric Association since the early 1940's, in addition to some membership records, correspondence of secretaries, and letters of founders from the mid-1800's to 1940. There are also photographs of psychiatrists, mental hos-pitals and psychiatric meetings; tapes and transcripts of oral history interviews with more than 50 prominent psychiatrists; record copies of all APA publications; microfilms of records; private papers of persons important in the history of psy-

chiatry; and memorabilia relating to psy-chiatry.

SEE: NUCMC, 1977.

SEE: Meckler and McMullin; Spalek; Hinding.

DC1-680
American Trucking Associations, Inc.
Room 503, 1616 P Street, N.W.
Washington DC 20036

(202) 797-5291

OPEN: M-F 8:30-4:30; closed weekends and holidays
COPYING FACILITIES: no
MATERIALS SOLICITED: Photographs re-lated to the trucking industry.

HOLDINGS:
    Total volume: 7,000 items
    Inclusive dates: late 1800's -
    Description: Black and white photo-graphs and color slides of a variety of trucks, such as automobile transporters, cement mixers, circus trucks, coal haulers, farm vehicles, and dump trucks. Other subjects covered include accidents, bridges, mass transit vehicles, highways, lumber operations, maintenance, truck stops, pollution, railroads, ships, highway signs, cities, and computers.

SEE: Novotny.

SEE ALSO: A catalog of photographs and slides is available at the repository.

DC1-700
American University
Battelle Memorial Library
University Archives
Nebraska and Massachusetts Avenues, N.W.
Washington DC 20016

(202) 785-8400, Ext. 273, 216

OPEN: M-W, F 9-4:30; closed Thursdays, weekends, and holidays
COPYING FACILITIES: yes
MATERIALS SOLICITED: Materials per-taining to the development and opera-tion of the University.

HOLDINGS:
    Total volume: 421 l.f.
    Inclusive dates: 1889 -
    Description: Records pertaining to the founding of American University, includ-ing correspondence and plans, as well as records of University departments, re-flecting their growth and relationship to the University community as a whole.

SEE: NUCMC, 1977.

DC1-705
American University
Music Library
Washington DC 20016

no telephone
SEE: NUCMC, 1977.

    Questionnaire not returned.

DC1-740

Archdiocese of Washington
Chancery Office
5001 Eastern Avenue
Washington DC

MAILING ADDRESS:
P.O. Box 29260
Washington DC 20017

(301) 853-3800

OPEN: by appointment only
ACCESS: All searching for materials is performed by the Archdiocese's Archivist.
COPYING FACILITIES: yes
MATERIALS SOLICITED: Records of events in the Archdiocese's parishes.

HOLDINGS:
  Total volume: 60 l.f.
  Inclusive dates: 1939 -
  Description: Records of the Archdiocese's parishes, relating to the establishment of each parish, priests who served in them, personnel appointments made by the Archbishop, and anniversaries and other special events. Also included are papers of the Archbishops and records of communications between the Archdiocese and the Vatican.

DC1-760

Armed Forces Institute of Pathology
Armed Forces Medical Museum
Otis Historical Archives
Alaska Avenue and 14th Street, N.W.
Washington DC 20306

(202) 576-2334, 2341, 2348

OPEN: M-F 8-4; closed weekends and holidays
ACCESS: visitor's pass available at information desk of Institute upon registration
COPYING FACILITIES: yes
MATERIALS SOLICITED: Military and civilian medical manuscripts; military and civilian memorabilia relating to the history of medicine.

HOLDINGS:
  Total volume: 200 l.f.
  Inclusive dates: 1649 -
  Description: Collections of manuscripts, personal correspondence, letterbooks, photographs and scrapbooks relating to the history of medicine, to military medicine, to the history of the Medical Museum and to developments in the science of pathology. Focuses on early history of Army Medical Museum; pioneer efforts in photomicroscopy; and photographs of medical and surgical cases resulting from Civil War injuries. Also included are collected papers and correspondence of former curators and directors of the Institute; correspondence, manuscripts, case studies, and research papers of notable pathologists and handwritten sections of old Museum accessions catalogues.

SEE: Novotny; Hinding.

DC1-775

Armenian Assembly of America
Oral History Project
Suite 101
1420 N Street, N.W.
Washington DC 20005

(202) 393-3434

OPEN: M-F 9-5; closed weekends and holidays
ACCESS: serious researchers; advance arrangements required
COPYING FACILITIES: yes
MATERIALS SOLICITED: Taped oral history interviews with survivor-immigrants of the Armenian genocide from 1915 to 1923. Will also accept related photographs, films, and other documentation.

HOLDINGS:
  Total volume: 400 items
  Inclusive dates: 1976 -
  Description: Taped interviews with survivors of the Armenian genocide from 1915 to 1923 who emigrated to the United States, including descriptions of early village life, the massacres and deportations, and resettlement in the United States. About half the interviews have been translated and transcribed.

DC1-805

Army Corps of Engineers
Office of the Chief of Engineers
Library
Room 3E066, 1000 Independence Avenue, S.W.
Washington DC 20314

(202) 272-0457

OPEN: M-F 8-4; closed weekends and holidays
COPYING FACILITIES: yes
MATERIALS SOLICITED: Contemporary materials related to the Corps of Engineers.

HOLDINGS:
  Total volume: not specified
  Inclusive dates: 1775 -
  Description: Annual reports of the Office of the Chief of Engineers, from 1775 to the present; state reports, association reports, board reports, and Federal government records concerning roads, canals, and other improvements in the United States, with emphasis on the 1820-70 period; reports submitted by the Corps of Engineers to the Congressional public works committee concerning river and harbor improvements; reports on Corps explorations and surveys since 1830; and reports, background materials, and memoranda concerning studies made in 1947, 1960, and 1970 concerning a second canal route across Central America, as an alternate to the Panama Canal.

DC1-810

Army Corps of Engineers
Office of the Chief of Engineers
Public Affairs Office
Audio Visual Division
20 Massachusetts Avenue, N.W.
Washington DC 20314

MAILING ADDRESS:
HQDA (DAEN-PAV)
20 Massachusetts Avenue, N.W.
Washington DC 20314

(202) 272-0017

OPEN: by appointment only; closed weekends and Federal holidays
COPYING FACILITIES: yes
MATERIALS SOLICITED: Photographs from Corps field offices showing current projects.

HOLDINGS:
  Total volume: 45 vols.
  Inclusive dates: 19th century -
  Description: Historical photographs, including those of Revolutionary War sketches, 19th century railroad construction, early exploration of the Rocky Mountains, gold mining in the 1850's, the Mexican-American War, U.S. generals, World War II engineering, construction of the Pentagon and Capitol, and other construction in the District of Columbia. Contemporary photographs document ship navigation, flood control, hydroelectric power construction projects, and other fields of Corps activity.

SEE: Novotny.

DC1-860

Association for Childhood Education International
Archives
3615 Wisconsin Avenue, N.W.
Washington DC 20016

(202) 942-2443

OPEN: M-F 8:30-4:30; closed weekends and holidays
ACCESS: advance arrangements required
COPYING FACILITIES: yes
MATERIALS SOLICITED: Will accept papers of persons in the field of early childhood education.

HOLDINGS:
  Total volume: 108 l.f.
  Inclusive dates: 1820's -
  Description: Materials pertaining to early childhood education and child development, chiefly records of the Association for Childhood Education International (ACEI) and its predecessor organizations, the International Kindergarten Union and the National Council of Primary Education, as well as papers of Friedrich Froebel, Winifred E. Bain, Susan E. Blow, Patty Smith Hill, Eugenia Hunter, Mary Leeper, Agnes Snyder, and others involved in children's education. There are also research materials, oral history interviews, and photographs of ACEI members, kindergartens, and related subjects.

GUIDES: Elizabeth Neterer, 'Archival and Historical Collections at ACEI Center,' (n.p., 1976).

SEE: Hinding.

DC1-890

Association of American Medical
   Colleges
Archives
One Dupont Circle, N.W.
Washington DC 20036

(202) 828-0551

OPEN: by appointment only
ACCESS: bona fide scholars and
   researchers upon approval
COPYING FACILITIES: yes
MATERIALS SOLICITED: Materials related
   to the history of the Association of
   American Medical Colleges.

HOLDINGS:
   Total volume: 150 l.f.
   Inclusive dates: 1876 -
   Description: Collection consists of
   2,000 items relating to administrative and
   program records of the Association of
   American Medical Colleges, including
   founding and evolution, and data on U.S.
   and Canadian medical schools and teaching hospitals.

GUIDES: Mary H. Littlemeyer, *AAMC Ar-*
chives Preliminary Inventory, 1876-1973
(Assn. of American Medical Colleges,
1974).

SEE ALSO: Finding aids to collections are
   available at the institution.

DC1-920

Association of American Railroads
Office of Information and Public
   Affairs
1920 L Street, N.W.
Washington DC 20036

(202) 835-9387

OPEN: M-F 8:30-5; closed weekends and
   holidays
ACCESS: qualified researchers only
COPYING FACILITIES: yes
MATERIALS SOLICITED: Photographs
   from railroad companies.

HOLDINGS:
   Total volume: 13,000 items
   Inclusive dates: 19th century -
   Description: 11,000 black and white
   photographs showing the history of
   railroads in the United States. Construction of tracks, dormitory cars for workers,
   equipment, early locomotives and trains,
   Chinese laborers, and the building of the
   transcontinental railroad are among the
   topics covered. There are also 2,000 color
   slides depicting recent developments in
   railroading.

SEE: Novotny.

DC2-200

B'nai B'rith Museum
Archival Collection
1640 Rhode Island Avenue, N.W.
Washington DC 20036

(202) 857-6583

OPEN: Su-F 10-5; closed Saturdays, and
   legal and Jewish holidays
ACCESS: qualified researchers only

COPYING FACILITIES: yes
MATERIALS SOLICITED: Materials related
   to Jewish history.

HOLDINGS:
   Total volume: 8,000 vols.
   Inclusive dates: late 16th century -
   Description: Papers relating to the history of the Jewish people in the United
   States, and their role in immigration, assimilation, development of social service
   societies, politics, agricultural movements,
   human and civil rights causes, and urban
   development. There is also a collection of
   Hebrew illuminated manuscripts, including scrolls of Esther.

DC2-600

Broadcast Pioneers Library
730 24th Streeet, N.W.

(202) 223-0088

OPEN: M-F 9-5, by appointment only;
   closed weekends and holidays
COPYING FACILITIES: yes
MATERIALS SOLICITED: Oral history interviews with early radio and television
   broadcasters.

HOLDINGS:
   Total volume: not specified
   Inclusive dates: early 20th century -
   Description: Materials documenting the
   history of radio and television broadcasting, including personal papers and scrapbooks; 4,500 photographs; and 1,235
   audio tapes containing speeches, interviews, and more than 300 oral history
   interviews.

SEE: NUCMC, 1978.

SEE: Meckler and McMullin; Novotny;
   Hinding.

DC2-850

Business and Professional Women's
   Foundation
Library
2012 Massachusetts Avenue, N.W.
Washington DC 20036

(202) 293-1200

OPEN: M-F 9-5; closed weekends and
   holidays
COPYING FACILITIES: yes

HOLDINGS:
   Total volume: 10 l.f.; 250 items
   Inclusive dates: 1955 -
   Description: Correspondence, budget-
   ary data, minutes, and other records of
   the Business and Professional Women's
   Foundation, documenting such activities
   as providing loans and sponsoring research, scholarships, and seminars. Also
   included are photographs, scrapbooks,
   and 250 sound recordings of oral history
   interviews with members of the National
   Federation of Business and Professional
   Women's Clubs and speeches by notable
   women.

SEE: Meckler and McMullin; Hinding.

DC3-210

The Catholic University of America
Department of Archives, Manuscripts,
   and Museum Collections
Washington DC 20064

(202) 635-5065

OPEN: M-F 9-1; closed weekends,
   holidays, and holy days
ACCESS: subject to the Archivist's
   approval
COPYING FACILITIES: yes
MATERIALS SOLICITED: Labor history,
   Catholic organization materials, social
   welfare history, Catholic historical materials, personal papers of Catholic
   church hierarchy, and University archives.

HOLDINGS:
   Total volume: 6,100 l.f.
   Inclusive dates: 1607 -
   Description: Labor history materials,
   including papers of prominent leaders of
   the Knights of Labor, Congress of Industrial Organizations, American Federation
   of Labor, and United Mine Workers;
   records of Catholic social welfare organizations in the United States; papers of
   outstanding Catholic scholars in anthropology, history, theology, philosophy, economics, and other fields; Catholic church
   history materials and papers of Catholic
   clergy; and the archives of The Catholic
   University of America. Historical topics
   covered include domestic expansion, international relations, labor unionization,
   war relief, Catholic Indian missions, and
   frontier settlement.

SEE: Hamer; NUCMC, 1959-62, 66.

SEE: Parkinson; Allard, Crawley, and
   Edmison; Hinding; Kim; Grow.

SEE ALSO: George A. Hruneni, Jr., 'A
   Touch of Western Americana in the
   Archives of The Catholic University of
   America,' *Manuscripts* 27 (Spring
   1975), reprinted in *American Indian*
   Quarterly: A Journal of History and Lit-
   erature (Winter 1976); George A.
   Hruneni, Jr., 'Bicentennial Potpourri in
   The Catholic University of America
   Archives,' *Manuscripts* 28 (Winter
   1976); Francis J. Weber, 'The Catholic
   University of America Archives,'
   Records of the American Catholic His-
   torical Society of Philadelphia 77
   (March 1966); Walter Schatz, ed., *Di-*
   rectory of Afro-American Resources
   (Bowker, 1970); Andrea Hinding and
   Rosemary Richardson, comps., *Archival*
   and Manuscript Resources for the Study
   of Women's History: A Beginning
   (Univ. of Minnesota Libraries, Social
   Welfare History Archives Center,
   1972).

DC3-226

The Catholic University of America
The Oliveira Lima Library
Washington DC 20064

(202) 635-5059

OPEN: M-F 9-5; closed weekends and
   holidays
COPYING FACILITIES: yes

MATERIALS SOLICITED: Personal papers of the Library's founder, Manoel de Oliveira Lima, and manuscripts and public documents from Portugal, other Lusophone (Portuguese-speaking) countries, and former areas of Portuguese influence, especially for the period of the Old Empire (prior to 1825).

HOLDINGS:
Total volume: 121,831 items
Inclusive dates: 16th century - 1940
Description: Oliveira Lima family papers, 1867-1940; Sousa Correia papers, 1852-1900; Portuguese materials concerning the Peace of Utrecht, 1713; manuscripts of unpublished treatises on the Portuguese in India and Africa in the 17th century; diplomatic correspondence from the Portuguese ambassador to the Vatican, 18th century; private correspondence of Diogo de Mendonca Corte-Real, Portuguese Minister of State, 18th century; and photographs of the art and architecture of Brazil and Portugal.

GUIDES: *Catalog of the Oliveira Lima Library, The Catholic University of America,* 2 vols. (G. K. Hall, 1970).

SEE: Grow.

DC3-320
Center of Military History
Pulaski Building
20 Massachusetts Avenue, N.W.
Washington DC 20314-0200

(202) 272-0317

OPEN: M-F 8-4; closed weekends and holidays
ACCESS: non-citizens of the United States must obtain permission from the Assistance Chief of Staff for Intelligence, Department of the Army, through their military attache in Washington, D.C.; clearance is required for viewing classified documents; requests should be sent to the Department of the Army, Office of the Adjutant General, Washington, DC 20314
COPYING FACILITIES: no

HOLDINGS:
Total volume: 900 l.f.
Inclusive dates: 20th century
Description: Materials documenting the history of the United States Army, including 500 linear feet of research materials and papers concerning the history of the Army since 1776; 5,000 unpublished histories of the Department of Defense and its predecessor agencies since 1940; and 300 linear feet of documents and histories of the Office of the Surgeon General.

DC3-550
Columbia Historical Society
Library
1307 New Hampshire Avenue, N.W.
Washington DC 20036

(202) 785-2068

OPEN: by appointment only
COPYING FACILITIES: yes
MATERIALS SOLICITED: Land records, papers of businesspersons and local government officials, and other materials

concerning the development of the non-Federal sector of Washington, DC.

HOLDINGS:
Total volume: 60 l.f.
Inclusive dates: 1698 - 1969
Description: Materials documenting the history of Washington, DC, with emphasis on the non-Federal sector. Among the textual documents are private papers, records of local government agencies, business and organization records, a few Presidential letters, records of predecessor companies of the Capital Transit Company, bound copies of the 1880 Federal census for the District of Columbia, and unpublished histories.

Also held are 12,000 photographs of street scenes, buildings, and other local subjects, and recordings of oral history interviews, many transcribed, with District of Columbia residents.

SEE: Hamer; NUCMC, 1973.

SEE: Novotny.

DC3-750
Corcoran Gallery of Art
Archives
Curatorial Library
17th Street and New York Avenue, N.W.
Washington DC 20006

(202) 638-3211

OPEN: M-F 10-4:30 by appointment only; closed weekends and holidays
ACCESS: by appointment only
COPYING FACILITIES: yes
MATERIALS SOLICITED: Materials relating to American art, including graphics, painting and sculpture. Will also accept materials relating specifically to the permanent collections of the institution.

HOLDINGS:
Total volume: 15 file drawers
Inclusive dates: 18th century -
Description: Manuscript material about American artists, especially during the 1880's to 1940's. Included are correspondence of artists, dealers, and collectors; records of the Corcoran Gallery; records of the Washington Gallery of Modern Art, absorbed by the Corcoran Gallery in 1969; and early 19th century correspondence on microfilm.

SEE: Novotny.

DC3-760
Corcoran Gallery of Art
Permanent Collection
17th Street and New York Avenue, N.W.
Washington DC 20006

(202) 638-3211

OPEN: Tu-Su 11-5; closed Mondays and holidays
ACCESS: by appointment only
COPYING FACILITIES: yes
MATERIALS SOLICITED: Contemporary photographic art.

HOLDINGS:
Total volume: 250 items
Inclusive dates: 1920's -
Description: Photographs by Ansel Adams, Manuel Bravo, Lewis Hine, August Sander, William Christenberry, William Eggleston, and Walker Evans, as well as 100 photographs by Thos Taylor. There is also a collection of photographs relating to Washington, DC, or taken by Washington, DC, photographers, including the work of John Gossage and Jan Groover.

SEE: Novotny.

DC3-800
The Cosmetic, Toiletry & Fragrance Association
1110 Vermont Avenue, N.W.
Washington DC 20005

(202) 331-1770

OPEN: M-F 9-5; closed weekends and holidays
ACCESS: advance arrangements required
COPYING FACILITIES: yes

HOLDINGS:
Total volume: 10 l.f.
Inclusive dates: 1913 -
Description: Records relating to the history of the cosmetics, toiletries, and fragrance industry, including proceedings of the Manufacturers Perfumers Association, 1913-20, audio-visual materials, unpublished scientific data, and other materials.

DC4-260
Department of Agriculture
Office of Governmental Affairs
Photographic Division
Room 4407, South Building, USDA
12th Street and Independence Avenue, S.W.
Washington DC 20250

(202) 447-6633

OPEN: M-F 8:30-5; closed weekends and holidays
COPYING FACILITIES: yes
MATERIALS SOLICITED: Photographs related to agriculture.

HOLDINGS:
Total volume: 100,000 items
Inclusive dates: 1940's -
Description: Black and white photographs and color transparencies concerning U.S. agriculture and such related topics as conservation, forestry, wildlife, natural resources, pollution, irrigation, and farmers' cooperatives and other farm-related organizations.

SEE: Novotny.

SEE ALSO: Shirley L. Green, comp., *Pictorial Resources in the Washington, D.C., Area* (Library of Congress, 1976).

A guide to the black and white photograph collection is available.

DC4-322

Department of Energy
History Division
Room 7E-054, Forrestal Building
1000 Independence Avenue, S.W.
Washington DC 20585

(202) 252-5235

OPEN: M-F 8:30-5; closed weekends and
holidays
COPYING FACILITIES: no
MATERIALS SOLICITED: Historically valuable records of offices of the Department of Energy or its predecessor agencies in the Washington DC area. Will
also accept personal papers documenting the history of energy development
and use in the United States, and
energy-related photographic material.

HOLDINGS:
    Total volume: 3,000 c.f.; 67,000
    photographs
    Inclusive dates: 1945 -
    Description: Records of the Depart-
    ment of Energy, 1977- , and its predeces-
    sor agencies. Included are records of the
    Atomic Energy Commission, 2,000 c.f.,
    the Energy Research and Development
    Administration, 225 c.f., the Federal En-
    ergy Administration, 260 c.f., and the De-
    partment of the Interior, 200 c.f., and
    black and white photographs and color
    slides of the programs of the United
    States Department of Energy.

DC4-450

Department of Housing and Urban
    Development
Printing and Visual Arts Division
Room B116
451 7th Street, S.W.
Washington DC 20410

(202) 755-7310

OPEN: by appointment only M-F 9-5;
closed weekends and Federal holidays
COPYING FACILITIES: no
MATERIALS SOLICITED: Photographs
dealing with housing projects, slums,
college housing, community centers, urban demolition and renewal projects,
and other subjects concerning American housing and urban development,
with emphasis on programs of the U.S.
Department of Housing and Urban Development. Will also accept related col-
or slides.

HOLDINGS:
    Total volume: 180,000 negatives
    Inclusive dates: late 1950's -
    Description: Photography related to
    projects sponsored by the U.S. Depart-
    ment of Housing and Urban Develop-
    ment, including housing projects, urban
    renewal, parks, public works, and public
    buildings. There are also photographs of
    people, especially children and the elder-
    ly, HUD-sponsored tours under such pro-
    grams as Model Cities and Operation
    Breakthrough, some HUD conferences,
    Secretaries of HUD, and riot destruction
    and renewal, as well as artists' renderings
    of renewal projects and aerial photo-
    graphs of rural and urban scenes. The
    collection is chiefly comprised of black
    and white photographs, with some color
    prints and slides.

SEE ALSO: Ann Novotny, ed., *Picture
    Sources 3* (Special Libraries Assn.,
    1975).

DC4-940

Dumbarton Oaks Research Library
and Dumbarton Oaks Garden Library
1703 32nd Street, N.W.
Washington DC 20007

(202) 342-3280

OPEN: by appointment only
ACCESS: serious researchers
COPYING FACILITIES: yes

HOLDINGS:
    Total volume: several hundred items
    Inclusive dates: mid-1800's -
    Description: Correspondence of literary
    figures and holograph music scores.

SEE: Hamer.

SEE: Robbins.

DC5-600

Environmental Protection Agency
Project DOCUMERICA (A-107)
401 M Street, S.W.
Washington DC 20460

(202) 382-5923

OPEN: M-F 9:30-3:30; closed weekends
and holidays
COPYING FACILITIES: yes

HOLDINGS:
    Total volume: 16,000 items
    Inclusive dates: 1972 -
    Description: A collection of 35mm col-
    or slides documenting positive and nega-
    tive aspects of U.S. environmental con-
    ditions from 1972 to 1976, covering both
    natural and human-made environments.

DC5-800

Episcopal Diocese of Washington
    Archives
Washington Cathedral Library
Mount Saint Alban
Washington DC 20016

(202) 537-6586

OPEN: by appointment only
ACCESS: special arrangements with
    Diocesan Historiographer required
COPYING FACILITIES: no
MATERIALS SOLICITED: Will accept his-
torical materials related to the Epis-
copal Diocese of Washington.

HOLDINGS:
    Total volume: 90 c.f.
    Inclusive dates: 1848 -
    Description: Records of the Episcopal
    Diocese of Washington, including records
    of the office of the bishop, with strongest
    holdings for the period 1895-1945; bish-
    ops' papers, chiefly of Henry Yates
    Satterlee, Alfred Harding, and James Ed-
    ward Freeman; 12 linear feet of account
    books, vestry minutes, and birth, death,
    marriage, and confirmation records of de-
    funct churches in the District of Colum-
    bia, 1838-1935; and photographs of Di-
    ocesan personnel and activities.

SEE: Hamer; NUCMC, 1966 (as Washing-
    ton Cathedral Library).

DC6-500

Fish and Wildlife Service
Office of Audio Visual
18th and C Streets, N.W.
Washington DC 20240

(202) 343-8770

OPEN: M-F 7:45-4:15; closed weekends
and holidays
COPYING FACILITIES: yes
MATERIALS SOLICITED: Photographs of
wildlife on National Wildlife Refuges
and of endangered species of plants
and animals in the United States.

HOLDINGS:
    Total volume: 15,000 items
    Inclusive dates: 1880 -
    Description: Black and white photo-
    graphs and color slides of endangered
    plant and animal species in the United
    States and of wildlife on National
    Wildlife Refuges.

SEE: Novotny.

DC6-600

Folger Shakespeare Library
201 East Capitol Street
Washington DC 20003

(202) 544-4600

OPEN: M-Sa 8:45-4:45; closed Sundays
and holidays
ACCESS: restricted to serious students
with appropriate qualifications needing
to use the Folger's special resources
COPYING FACILITIES: yes
MATERIALS SOLICITED: Manuscripts
which would complement or supplement the present collections.

HOLDINGS:
    Total volume: 50,000 items
    Inclusive dates: 1300 -
    Description: Primarily English manu-
    scripts, including collections of family pa-
    pers, letters, diaries, account books, Par-
    liamentary reports, commonplace books,
    literary manuscripts, and plays. Signifi-
    cant holdings include materials relating to
    English actors and theater managers Da-
    vid Garrick and Charles Kean, New York
    theater manager Augustin Daly, and
    American theater critic William Winter.
    There are also records of the Drury Lane
    Theatre, transcripts of documents of var-
    ious Italian states, the personal papers of
    Henry Clay Folger and Emily Jordan
    Folger, records of the founding and build-
    ing of the Library, architectural drawings,
    and blueprints.

GUIDES: *Catalog of Manuscripts of the
    Folger Shakespeare Library* (G. K.
    Hall, 1971).

SEE: Hamer; NUCMC, 1963-65.

SEE: Dillon; Novotny; Robbins; Ingram.

SEE ALSO: A. Harbage, *Annals of English
    Drama, 975-1700*, revised by S.
    Schoenbaum (1964), and supplements
    (1966, 1970); 'Nineteenth-Century
    Holdings at the Folger,' *The Victorian
    Newsletter* 22 (Fall 1962); 'French His-
    tory Holdings in the Folger Library,'

French Historical Studies 9 (Spring 1976); 'Theatrical Holdings of the Folger Shakespeare Library,' in E. Perry, ed., *Performing Arts Resources* (1974); *The Widening Circle* (Folger Shakespeare Library, 1976).

DC6-650
Ford's Theatre National Historic Site
Lincoln Library
511 10th Street, N.W.
Washington DC 20004

(202) 426-6924

OPEN: daily 9-5 preferably by appointment; closed Christmas
ACCESS: appointment required; serious scholars only
COPYING FACILITIES: yes
MATERIALS SOLICITED: Materials concerning the Lincoln assassination.

HOLDINGS:
   Total volume: 500 items
   Inclusive dates: 1865 -
   Description: John Wilkes Booth's diary; papers of Joseph Messmer concerning the trial of the accused Lincoln assassination conspirators; a few letters of Mary Lincoln and of the doctors who treated President Lincoln after his shooting; 10 glass negatives of Lincoln and his home in Springfield, IL; several hundred cartes-de-visite showing Lincoln and his contemporaries, including Civil War generals and Cabinet members; and several hundred photographs relating to the assassination and subsequent trials.

SEE: Hamer.

DC6-800
Franciscan Monastery
Library
1400 Quincy Street, N.E.
Washington DC 20017

(202) 526-6800

OPEN: M-Sa by appointment only; closed Sundays, Christmas, and Easter
COPYING FACILITIES: yes
MATERIALS SOLICITED: Manuscripts relating to the Franciscan order or the history of the Holy Land.

HOLDINGS:
   Total volume: 2 vols.; 28 items
   Inclusive dates: 13th century - 18th century
   Description: A collection primarily composed of medieval and Renaissance manuscripts, but also containing two documents of the Latin Patriarch of Jerusalem, 1776-77, granting permission to captains of two ships to fly the flag of the Holy Land in the waters of the Levant.

SEE: Hamer.

DC7-100
Gallaudet College
The Edward Miner Gallaudet
  Memorial Library
Archives
7th and Florida Avenues, N.E.
Kendall Green
Washington DC 20002

(202) 651-5582

OPEN: M-F 8-5; closed weekends and holidays
COPYING FACILITIES: yes
MATERIALS SOLICITED: Materials relating to faculty of Gallaudet College, alumni, academic and administrative departments of the College, State and foreign schools for the deaf, and State and foreign organizations for the deaf.

HOLDINGS:
   Total volume: 1,350 l.f.
   Inclusive dates: 1818 -
   Description: A collection of records relating to The Columbia Institution for the Deaf, Gallaudet College, Model Secondary School for the Deaf, other State schools and foreign schools for the deaf, and deaf organizations. The collection includes correspondence, diaries, scrapbooks, blueprints, photographs, account books, and financial records; academic, administrative, and departmental records; and student organization records.

SEE: Hinding.

DC7-300
General Federation of Women's Clubs
Archives
1743 N Street, N.W.
Washington DC 20036

(202) 347-3168

OPEN: M-F 8:30-4:30; closed weekends and holidays
ACCESS: advance arrangements required
COPYING FACILITIES: yes

HOLDINGS:
   Total volume: 100 l.f.; 16 file drawers
   Inclusive dates: 1890 -
   Description: Records of the General Federation of Women's Clubs, including transcripts, programs, and other records of annual conventions, as well as annual reports, resolutions, materials about Federation programs in art and education, a complete set of the periodical *General Federation Clubwomen*, 1890- ; correspondence; and photographs.

SEE: Hinding.

DC7-510
George Washington University
Dimock Gallery
Lower Lisner Auditorium
730 21st Street, N.W.
Washington DC 20006

(202) 676-7091

OPEN: M-F 10-5; closed weekends and holidays
ACCESS: advance appointment required
COPYING FACILITIES: yes
MATERIALS SOLICITED: Materials related to Washington, DC.

HOLDINGS:
   Total volume: 245 items
   Inclusive dates: 16th century - 20th century
   Description: A collection of 130 manuscripts, photographs, and newspaper clippings relating to Ulysses S. Grant, III, and his family; 80 photographs of Washington, DC, mostly of the 19th century; and 35 miscellaneous items, including a 16th century Latin manuscript and reproductions of George Washington letters.

DC7-540
George Washington University
Library
Special Collections Division
2130 H Street, N.W.
Washington DC 20052

(202) 676-7497

OPEN: M-F 9-5 and by appointment; closed weekends and holidays
ACCESS: researchers must register to use materials and must present adequate identification
COPYING FACILITIES: yes
MATERIALS SOLICITED: Material relating to American labor, the China Salt Gabelle (1930-52), U.S. journalism, 19th century political cartoons, U.S. politics, urban planning, and Washington, DC; and George Washington University archival documents. Will also accept collections which offer significant research potential and which support the University's curriculum.

HOLDINGS:
   Total volume: 90 l.f.
   Inclusive dates: 1810 - 1968
   Description: Fourteen collections comprising personal papers of people prominent in labor, international relations, journalism, politics, urban planning, and higher education in 19th and 20th century America. Collections include correspondence, diaries, manuscripts, records, oral history transcripts, and photographs.

SEE: Hamer; NUCMC, 1971.

SEE: Grant; Dillon; Meckler and McMullin; Robbins.

DC7-650
Georgetown University
Library
Special Collections Division
37th and O Streets, N.W.
Washington DC 20057

(202) 625-3230, 4160

OPEN: M-F 9-5; closed weekends and holidays
COPYING FACILITIES: yes
MATERIALS SOLICITED: Materials relating to diplomatic history, political science, American history, and Roman Catholic (especially Jesuit) history. Will also accept materials relating to English and American literature, languages and linguistics, and other collections strong enough to be self-sustaining.

HOLDINGS:
> *Total volume:* 4,400 l.f.
> *Inclusive dates:* 1450 -
> *Description:* More than 130 collections covering a wide range of subjects, including U.S. Catholic (Jesuit) history, diplomatic history, American history, North American Indian linguistics, English and American literature, lexicography, U.S. political science, the Panama Canal, astronomy, and the history of Georgetown University.
>
> Also included are the archives, 1867-1974, of Woodstock College of Woodstock, MD, and the archives of the Maryland Province of the Society of Jesus, including papers of Province officials and of other Jesuits, records of Jesuit estates in southern Maryland, and materials relating to Mexico, 1816-48, and to the Missouri Province of the Society during the 1830's.

SEE: Hamer (as Georgetown University Archives); NUCMC, 1959-61, 67, 72-73, 79.

SEE: Dillon; Grow; Kim; Rowan; Bhatt; Meckler and McMullin; Hines; Robbins; Martin; Allard, Crawley, and Edmison; Hinding.

SEE ALSO: Richard C. Davis, *North American Forest History: A Guide to Archives and Manuscripts in the United States and Canada* (Clio Books, 1977); unpublished preliminary inventories available at the repository.

DC7-660

Georgetown University
Medical Center
John Vinton Dahlgren Memorial Library
The Alexis Carrel Collection
3900 Reservoir Road, N.W.
Washington DC 20007

(202) 625-2495

OPEN: M-F 9-5; closed weekends and holidays
ACCESS: by appointment; usually restricted to those in the health science professions and others engaged in research on the work of Alexis Carrel
COPYING FACILITIES: yes

HOLDINGS:
> *Total volume:* 35,000 items
> *Inclusive dates:* 1901 - 1941
> *Description:* A collection of papers and manuscripts of Nobel Prize winner Alexis Carrel, consisting of laboratory notes, journals, slides, and tapes. There are also materials relating to Carrel's work in the transplantation of organs, as well as data on the suturing of blood vessels and tissue cultivation.

DC8-500

Holy Name College
Library
Franciscan House of Studies
14th and Shepherd Streets, N.W.
Washington DC 20017

no telephone

SEE: Hamer.

Questionnaire not returned.

DC8-850

Howard University
Moorland-Spingarn Research Center
Manuscript Division
500 Howard Place, N.W.
Washington DC 20059

(202) 636-7480

OPEN: M-F 9-5 preferably by appointment; closed weekends and holidays
COPYING FACILITIES: yes
MATERIALS SOLICITED: Materials related to the history and culture of people of African descent.

HOLDINGS:
> *Total volume:* 6,000 l.f.; 850 oral histories; several thousand photographs
> *Inclusive dates:* late 18th century -
> *Description:* Over 400 collections of personal papers, organization archives, and other materials, mostly from the mid- 19th century to the present, covering black history and culture, primarily in the United States.

SEE: Hamer; NUCMC, 1962.

SEE: Robbins; Hinding; Grow; Bhatt.

SEE ALSO: Peter Duignan, *Handbook of American Resources for African Studies* (Hoover Institution, 1967); Walter Schatz, ed., *Directory of Afro-American Resources* (Bowker, 1970): see also under Civil Rights Documentation Project; Vincent J. Browne and Norma O. Leonard, eds., *Bibliography of Holdings of the Civil Rights Documentation Project* (Howard Univ., Civil Rights Documentation Project, 1974); Alan M. Meckler and Ruth McMullin, comps., *Oral History Collections* (Bowker, 1975): as Civil Rights Documentation Project; Albert Krichmar, *The Women's Rights Movement in the United States, 1848-1970: A Bibliography and Sourcebook* (Scarecrow Press, 1972); *Dictionary Catalog of the Jesse E. Moorland Collection of Negro Life and History* (G. K. Hall, 1970), *First Supplement* (1976).

DC9-450

International Bank for Reconstruction and Development (World Bank)
Photo Library
Room N-260, 801 19th Street, N.W.
Washington DC

MAILING ADDRESS:
1818 H Street, N.W.
Washington DC 20433

(202) 477-2345

OPEN: M-F 9-5:30; closed weekends and holidays
COPYING FACILITIES: yes
MATERIALS SOLICITED: Photographs of appropriate projects related to the World Bank in developing countries.

HOLDINGS:
> *Total volume:* 30,000 items
> *Inclusive dates:* 20th century -
> *Description:* Black and white photographs and color slides covering projects affiliated with the World Bank in 70 developing nations. Such subjects as trans-portation, industry, agriculture, flood control, fishing, rural development, social services, education, tourism, birth control, and making of handicrafts are depicted.

SEE: Novotny.

DC9-580

U.S. Information Agency
Associate Directorate for Programs
Agency Library
Agency Archives
1425 K Street, N.W.
Room 740
Washington DC 20547

(202) 485-7700

OPEN: M-F 8:30-4; closed weekends and Federal holidays
ACCESS: serious researchers, with permission of the Office of Congressional and Public Liaison (CPL), 1750 Pennsylvania Avenue, N.W., Washington DC 20547.
COPYING FACILITIES: yes
MATERIALS SOLICITED: Will accept materials pertaining to the history of the U.S. government's international information, educational, and cultural exchange programs.

HOLDINGS:
> *Total volume:* 470 l.f.
> *Inclusive dates:* 1938 -
> *Description:* Records of the U. S. Information Agency and its predecessor agencies, the Office of War Information and the International Information Administration, including the Voice of America, and records of the Bureau of Educational and Cultural Affairs of the Department of State. Also held are 66 tapes of oral history interviews with persons employed by or associated with the Bureau of Educational and Cultural Affairs.

DC10-500

Jewish Historical Society of Greater Washington
Lilian and Albert Small Jewish Museum
701 3rd Street, N.W.
Washington DC 20001

(202) 789-0900 or (301) 881-0100

OPEN: by appointment only
COPYING FACILITIES: no
MATERIALS SOLICITED: Materials concerning Jewish history, particularly of the Washington, DC, area.

HOLDINGS:
> *Total volume:* not specified
> *Inclusive dates:* 19th century -
> *Description:* Correspondence, records of synagogues and of organizations, photographs, scrapbooks, notes, news clippings, and other materials relating to the Jewish community of Washington, DC, and its organizations and individuals.

SEE ALSO: Sylvan M. Dubow, 'The Jewish Historical Society of Greater Washington: Its Archival Program,' *American Archivist* 30 (Oct. 1967).

DC12-100
Library of Congress
African and Middle Eastern Division
Hebraic Section
Room 1006
John Adams Building
2nd Street and Independence Avenue,
S.E.
Washington DC 20540

(202) 287-5422

OPEN: M-F 8:30-5, Sa 8:30-12:30; closed
Sundays and holidays
COPYING FACILITIES: yes

HOLDINGS:
Total volume: 400 items
Inclusive dates: Medieval period -
20th century
Description: A miscellaneous collection
of Hebrew manuscripts.

SEE: Hamer (as Orientalia Division).

DC12-105
Library of Congress
African and Middle Eastern Division
Near East Section
Room 1005
John Adams Building
2nd Street and Independence Avenue,
S.E.
Washington DC 20540

(202) 287-5421

OPEN: M-F 8:30-5, Sa 8:30-12:30; closed
Sundays and holidays
COPYING FACILITIES: yes

HOLDINGS:
Total volume: 1,400 items
Inclusive dates: 17th century - 19th
century
Description: Material relating to
Islamic and Arabic cultures, consisting of
manuscripts dealing primarily with
Islamic religion, history, and science.

SEE: Hamer (as Orientalia Division).

SEE: Martin.

DC12-150
Library of Congress
Asian Division
Room 1016
John Adams Building
2nd Street and Independence Avenue,
S.E.
Washington DC 20540

(202) 287-5420

OPEN: M-F 8:30-5, Sa 8:30-12:30; closed
Sundays and holidays
COPYING FACILITIES: yes

HOLDINGS:
Total volume: 1,200 items
Inclusive dates: not specified
Description: Japanese handwritten
texts contained in Tokugawa feudal government records; other pre-Meiji transcripts of commentary and ritual of Shinto and Buddhism, history, geography, essays, and arts; Tibetan manuscripts,
mainly of religious texts; South Asian
handwritten texts or copies of texts; and a

holographic letter of M. K. Gandhi. Languages represented are Sanskrit, Pali
(Sinhalese, Thai, Burmese, and Khmer
versions), Tamil, Telugu, Oriya, Malay,
and Bugis.

SEE: Hamer (as Orientalia Division).

DC12-190
Library of Congress
Geography and Map Division
James Madison Memorial Building,
Room B01
101 Independence Avenue, S.E.
Washington DC 20540

(202) 287-MAPS

OPEN: M-F 8:30-5, Sa 8:30-12:30; closed
Sundays and holidays
COPYING FACILITIES: yes
MATERIALS SOLICITED: Cartographic ma-
terials covering all periods, subjects,
and geographical areas.

HOLDINGS:
Total volume: 3,600,000 maps;
44,000 atlases
Inclusive dates: 1800 -
Description: Manuscript maps, charts,
and atlases, and other cartographic materials, chiefly of the early period of
American history, with strong holdings
for the exploration and colonial periods
and for the Revolutionary War. Also included are early maps of China, Korea
and Japan, and photoreproductions of
manuscript maps housed in other repositories in Europe and the United States.

GUIDES: The Geography and Map Division: A Guide to Its Collections and
Services (1975).

SEE: Hamer.

SEE ALSO: The Library of Congress Quarterly Journal (until 1964 Quarterly
Journal of Current Acquisitions), 1943
to date. Finding aids published by the
Geography and Map Division are cited
in its 'List of Publications' (May 1976).

DC12-200
Library of Congress
Hispanic Division
Thomas Jefferson Building
10 First Street, S.E.
Washington DC 20540

(202) 287-5400

OPEN: M-F 8:30-5; closed weekends and
holidays
COPYING FACILITIES: yes
MATERIALS SOLICITED: Recorded poetry
and prose from Hispanic cultures.

HOLDINGS:
Total volume: 400 tapes
Inclusive dates: 1942 -
Description: Audio tapes of writers
from Spain, Portugal, Latin America, and
the Caribbean reading their poetry and
prose in such languages as Spanish, Portuguese, Catalan, French, Quechua,
Nahuatl, and Zapotec. There are also recorded interviews and commentaries of
Hispanic literary figures, as well as
textual materials.

GUIDES: Francisco Aguilera, comp., and
Georgette M. Dorn, ed., The Archive of
Hispanic Literature on Tape: A Descrip-
tive Guide (1974).

SEE ALSO: Georgette M. Dorn, 'The Ar-
chive of Hispanic Literature on Tape,'
Federal Linguist 7 (1976); Michael
Grow, Scholars' Guide to Washington,
D.C., for Latin American and Carib-
bean Studies (Smithsonian Institution
Press, 1979); the Library of Congress
Quarterly Journal (until 1964 Quarterly
Journal of Current Acquisitions), 1943
to date.

DC12-300
Library of Congress
Manuscript Division
James Madison Memorial Building
First Street and Independence
Avenue, S.E.
Washington DC 20540

(202) 287-5387

OPEN: M-Sa 8:30-5; closed Sundays and
holidays
ACCESS: readers engaged in serious
research; college and university
undergraduates are not admitted as
researchers, except for those engaged in
senior theses or equivalent research
projects, with letters of introduction
from faculty advisors
COPYING FACILITIES: yes
MATERIALS SOLICITED: All areas of
American history and culture. Will also
accept photographic copies of collections located elsewhere but within the
scope of solicitation.

HOLDINGS:
Total volume: 38,000,000 items
Inclusive dates: 17th century -
Description: Personal papers and organization records mainly from the colonial period of American history to the
present time, in the subject areas of politics, literature, science, religion, military
and naval history, and Afro-American
history and culture. Included are microfilm copies of more than 2,000,000
manuscripts in foreign archives and libraries relating to U.S. history.

SEE: Hamer; NUCMC, 1959-74, 76.

SEE: Bean and Vane; Spalek; Hinding;
Hines; Allard, Crawley, and Edmison;
Parkinson; Robbins; Ingram; White;
Kim; Bhatt; Grow; Gehring; Leventhal
and Mooney - II; Armstrong.

SEE ALSO: Walter Schatz, ed., Directory of
Afro-American Resources (Bowker,
1970); Peter Duignan, Handbook of
American Resources for African Studies
(Hoover Institution, 1967); Robert O.
Collins and Peter Duignan, Americans
in Africa (Hoover Institution, 1963);
Morris Rieger, 'Africa-Related Papers
of Persons and Organizations in the
United States,' Africa Studies Bulletin 8
(Dec. 1965); Albert Krichmar, The
Women's Rights Movement in the Unit-
ed States, 1848-1970: A Bibliography
and Sourcebook (Scarecrow Press,

1972); Andrea Hinding and Rosemary Richardson, comps., *Archival and Manuscript Resources for the Study of Women's History: A Beginning* (Univ. of Minnesota Libraries, Social Welfare History Archives Center, 1972).

David A. Hounshell, comp., *Manuscripts in U.S. Depositories Relating to the History of Electrical Science and Technology* (Smithsonian Institution, n.d.); Joan Nelson Warnow, *A Selection of Manuscripts Collections at American Repositories* (American Institute of Physics, 1969); *Source Materials for the Recent History of Astronomy and Astrophysics: A Checklist of Manuscript Collections in the United States* (American Institute of Physics, 1971); Dean C. Allard and Betty Bern, comps., *U.S. Naval History Sources in the Washington Area and Suggested Research Topics* (Naval History Division, 1970); Lawrence J. Paszek, comp., *United States Air Force History: A Guide to Documentary Sources* (Office of Air Force History, 1973).

Gerald Friedberg, 'Sources for the Study of Socialism in America, 1901-1919,' *Labor History* 6 (Spring 1965); Richard C. Davis, *North American Forest History: A Guide to Archives and Manuscripts in the United States and Canada* (Clio Books, 1977); Jerome S. Handler, *A Guide to Source Materials for Study of Barbados History, 1627-1834* (Southern Illinois Univ. Press, 1971); Paul T. Heffron, 'Manuscript Sources in the Library of Congress for a Study of Labor History,' *Labor History* 10 (Fall 1969).

Roy R. Thomas, *Women in American History, 1896-1920: Their Manuscripts in the Library of Congress* (Bowie State College, 1972); James E. O'Neill, 'Copies of French Manuscripts for American History in the Library of Congress,' *Journal of American History* 51 (March 1965); the Library of Congress *Annual Reports,* 1897 to date, and *Quarterly Journal* (until 1964 *Quarterly Journal of Current Acquisitions*), 1943 to date; and calendars, indexes and registers listed in *Library of Congress Publications in Print.*

DC12-400
Library of Congress
Microform Reading Room Section
Thomas Jefferson Building
First Street, S.E.
Washington DC 20540

(202) 287-5471

OPEN: M-F 8:30-9:30, Sa 8:30-5, Su 1-5; shorter hours on certain holidays; closed other holidays
COPYING FACILITIES: yes

HOLDINGS:
  Total volume: 30,000 microfilm reels and microfiche cards
  Inclusive dates: 6th century -
  Description: Microform reproductions of manuscripts and archives chiefly located in European and other foreign repositories. Materials copied include early records (mainly pre-1900) of U.S. State governments; archives of the Japanese Ministry of Foreign Affairs, 1868-1945; 12th through 14th century notarial chartularies in Genoa, Italy; literary ma-

terials microfilmed by the Modern Language Association; and manuscripts in St. Catherine's Monastery on Mount Sinai and in the libraries of the Greek and Armenian Patriarchates in Jerusalem.

SEE: Bhatt.

SEE ALSO: the Library of Congress *Quarterly Journal* (until 1964 *Quarterly Journal of Current Acquisitions*), 1943 to date.

DC12-450
Library of Congress
Motion Picture, Broadcasting and Recorded Sound Division
James Madison Memorial Building, Room 338
First Street and Independence Avenue, S.E.
Washington DC 20540

(202) 287-5840

OPEN: M-F 8:30-5 by appointment; closed weekends and holidays
ACCESS: serious researchers, with advance appointment
COPYING FACILITIES: yes
MATERIALS SOLICITED: Film, television programs, radio programs and sound recordings relating to history and cultural heritage.

HOLDINGS:
  Total volume: 250,000 reels; 1,000,000 sound recordings
  Inclusive dates: films since 1890's; recordings since 1880's
  Description: Holdings derived primarily from copyright deposits, but also from gifts, exchanges, occasional purchases; important World War II materials via Alien Property Custodian. Important film collections include American Film Institute Collection, Paper Print Collection, and Theodore Roosevelt Collection.
  Important recorded sound collections include National Broadcasting Company Radio Collection, American Forces Radio and Television Service Collection, OWI Collection, Berliner Collection, Joel Berger Collection, House of Representatives Debates, and collections of individual music artists.

SEE: Kim; Dillon; Bhatt; Rowan.

SEE ALSO: Kemp Niver, *Motion Pictures from the Library of Congress Paper Print Collection, 1894-1912* (Univ. of California Press, 1967); the Library of Congress *Quarterly Journal* (until 1964 *Quarterly Journal of Current Acquisitions*), 1943 to date; a brochure describing the collection available on request from the Motion Picture Section.

DC12-510
Library of Congress
Music Division
Reference Section
James Madison Memorial Building, Room 113
First Street and Independence Avenue, S.E.
Washington DC 20540

(202) 287-5504

OPEN: daily 8:30-5; closed holidays
COPYING FACILITIES: yes
MATERIALS SOLICITED: Music manuscripts, letters and other manuscripts of significant importance to the history of music. Will also accept materials which strengthen existing holdings.

HOLDINGS:
  Total volume: 237,663 items
  Inclusive dates: 12th century -
  Description: 35,463 music manuscripts and 202,200 letters of or relating to composers and other musicians of all nationalities. Greatest strengths are in American music and in the period since the 18th century.
  The Division has particularly strong holdings in American music, Mendelssohn, Brahms, Rachmaninoff and the Second Vienna School.

GUIDES: *The Music Division: A Guide to Its Collections and Services* (1972).

SEE: Hamer; NUCMC, 1959-61, 67-70, 72-74, 76, 81.

SEE ALSO: the Library of Congress *Quarterly Journal* (until 1964 *Quarterly Journal of Current Acquisitions*), 1943 to date. Finding aids to parts of the collection have been published by the Music Division.

DC12-600
Library of Congress
Prints and Photographs Division
James Madison Memorial Building, Room 339
First Street and Independence Avenue, S.E.
Washington DC 20540

(202) 287-6394

OPEN: M-F 8:30-5; closed weekends and holidays
COPYING FACILITIES: yes
MATERIALS SOLICITED: Photographs and architectural materials.

HOLDINGS:
  Total volume: 8,500,000 photographs; additional materials
  Inclusive dates: late 18th century -
  Description: Photographs, architectural drawings, and other visual items, covering all geographic and subject areas, with emphasis on American history.

SEE: Hamer; NUCMC, 1978.

SEE: Bhatt; Dillon; Grow.

SEE ALSO: Ann Novotny, ed., *Picture Sources 3* (Special Libraries Assn., 1975); Dean C. Allard and Betty Bern, comps., *U.S. Naval History Sources in the Washington Area and Suggested Research Topics* (Naval History Division, 1970); Lawrence J. Paszek, comp., *United States Air Force History: A Guide to Documentary Sources* (Office of Air Force History, 1973); and the following publications of the Library of Congress: *Quarterly Journal* (until 1964 *Quarterly Journal of Current Acquisitions*), 1943 to date; *Viewpoints* (1975); and Hirst D. Milhollen and Donald H.

Mugridge, *Civil War Photographs, 1861-1865: A Catalog of Copy Negatives Made from Originals Selected from the Mathew B. Brady Collection in the Prints and Photographs Division of the Library of Congress* (1961).

DC12-650
Library of Congress
Rare Book and Special Collections
Division
Thomas Jefferson Building, Rm. 256
Washington DC 20540

(202) 287-5434

OPEN: M-F 8:30-5; closed weekends and holidays
COPYING FACILITIES: yes
MATERIALS SOLICITED: Will accept manuscript materials closely related to printing history or forming part of a collection of chiefly printed materials.

HOLDINGS:
Total volume: 500,000 items
Inclusive dates: 13th century -
Description: Manuscripts and photographs which complement the Library's rare book collections. Included are medieval and Renaissance manuscripts, literary manuscripts, autograph documents of notable Americans and Europeans, and U.S. copyright records, 1870-97.

GUIDES: *The Rare Book Division: A Guide to Its Collections and Services* (1965).

SEE: Hamer; NUCMC, 1959-62, 65, 72.

SEE: Bhatt; Grow.

SEE ALSO: the Library of Congress *Quarterly Journal* (until 1964 *Quarterly Journal of Current Acquisitions*), 1943 to date.

Some manuscripts held by the Rare Book and Special Collections Division are housed at the Alverthorpe Gallery in Jenkintown, PA.

DC12-900
Lutheran Church-Missouri Synod
Southeastern District
5121 Colorado Avenue, N.W.
Washington DC

MAILING ADDRESS:
P.O. Box 8608
Washington DC 20011

(202) 293-3031

OPEN: M-F 8:30-4, or by appointment; closed holidays
ACCESS: with approval of Archivist
COPYING FACILITIES: yes
MATERIALS SOLICITED: Written and oral materials dealing with the history of Lutherans on the East coast and especially in the Southeastern District: North Carolina, South Carolina, Virginia, the District of Columbia, Maryland, and Delaware. Will also accept related machine-readable and microform records.

HOLDINGS:
Total volume: 10 file drawers
Inclusive dates: 1935 -
Description: Materials of or relating to the Southeastern District of the Lutheran Church-Missouri Synod, consisting of manuscripts, congregation histories, presidential papers, and official District records.

DC13-210
Department of the Navy
Headquarters, U.S. Marine Corps
History and Museums Division
Building 58, Marine Corps Historical
Center
Washington Navy Yard
Washington DC

MAILING ADDRESS:
Commandant of the Marine Corps
(Code HD)
Headquarters, U.S. Marine Corps
Washington DC 20380

(202) 433-3914

OPEN: M-F 8-4:30; closed weekends and holidays
ACCESS: The general public has access to unclassified material. Access to classified material is based on a 'need-to-know' and appropriate security clearance, and is granted only by the Director of the Marine Corps History and Museums Division.
COPYING FACILITIES: yes
MATERIALS SOLICITED: Personal papers of distinguished Marines, and oral history tapes, photographs, motion pictures, and official records relating to the U.S. Marine Corps. Will also accept any other materials relating to Marine Corps history.

HOLDINGS:
Total volume: 4,500 c.f.
Inclusive dates: 1775 -
Description: Classified and unclassified documents, military music, personal papers, oral history tapes and transcripts, and still and moving pictures, covering all aspects of Marine Corps history.

SEE: Hamer (as Historical Branch, Headquarters, U.S. Marine Corps); NUCMC, 1970, 77.

SEE: Allard, Crawley, and Edmison; Hinding; Grow; Grant; Kim.

SEE ALSO: Alan M. Meckler and Ruth McMullin, comps., *Oral History Collections* (Bowker, 1975); Dean C. Allard and Betty Bern, comps., *U.S. Naval History Sources in the Washington Area and Suggested Research Subjects* (Naval History Division, 1970); Lawrence J. Paszek, comp., *United States Air Force History: A Guide to Documentary Sources* (Office of Air Force History, 1973); and the following publications of the History and Museums Division: Charles Anthony Wood, comp., *Marine Corps Personal Papers Collection Catalog* (1974); Benis M. Frank, comp., *Marine Corps Oral History Collection Catalog* (1975); and 9 pamphlets comprising the *Marine Corps History and Museums Division Manuscript Register Series*.

Still and motion picture holdings have been transferred to the Defense Audio-Visual Agency in Washington, DC.

DC13-300
Martin Luther King, Jr., Memorial
Library
Washingtoniana Division
901 G Street, N.W.
Washington DC 20001

(202) 727-1213

OPEN: M-Th 9-9, F, Sa 9-5:30; closed Sundays and holidays
COPYING FACILITIES: yes
MATERIALS SOLICITED: Materials concerning the District of Columbia's local government and private citizens, and the Federal government as it relates to the District of Columbia.

HOLDINGS:
Total volume: 1,016,000 items; 51 l.f.; 18 file drawers; 2 boxes
Inclusive dates: 1811 -
Description: Materials of or relating to residents, businesses, institutions, and local government agencies of Washington, DC. Included are miscellaneous deeds, letters, and other manuscripts; scrapbooks; papers of Theodore Noyes, editor of the Washington *Star*; records of the District of Columbia Office of Emergency Preparedness relating to protest demonstrations, 1968-72; records of the Martin Luther King, Jr., Memorial Library and the District of Columbia public library system; 1,000,000 newspaper clippings, primarily since 1930; 15,000 photographs; 1,000 glass slides; and 4 file cabinets of photographs from the Washington *Daily News*.

GUIDES: *Inventory of the Archival Records of the Washingtoniana Division* (1979).

DC14-100
National Academy of Sciences
2101 Constitution Avenue, N.W.
Washington DC 20418

(202) 334-2125

OPEN: M-F 9-4; closed weekends and holidays
ACCESS: All holdings considered privileged until 50 years old. Exceptions are made on a case-by-case basis for qualified scholars.
COPYING FACILITIES: yes

HOLDINGS:
Total volume: 1,800 c.f.
Inclusive dates: 1863 -
Description: Administrative records of the National Academy of Sciences, and of the organizations established under its corporate charter: the National Research Council, the National Academy of Engineering, and the Institute of Medicine. Of particular interest are correspondence concerning the Academy and the Research Council from the files of Edwin Bidwell Wilson; the records of the Science Advisory Board (1933-35); and the records of the Chairman of the Board of Directors of the Canal Zone Biological Station (1940-46).

SEE: Hinding.

DC14-120

National Aeronautics and Space
  Administration
Audio-Visual Branch
400 Maryland Avenue, S.W.
Washington DC 20546

(202) 453-8375

OPEN: M-F 8-4:30; closed weekends and
  holidays
COPYING FACILITIES: no
MATERIALS SOLICITED: Materials related
  to National Aeronautics and Space Administration (NASA) flights and operations.

HOLDINGS:
  Total volume: 100,000 items
  Inclusive dates: 1958 -
  Description: Photographs of NASA
  manned flights, including all steps from
  construction through launch, as well as
  satellite photographs of the earth, other
  planets, and stars.

SEE: Novotny; Allard, Crawley, and
  Edmison.

DC14-140

National Aeronautics and Space
  Administration
Headquarters History Office
Room 706, 7th and D Streets, S.W.
Washington DC

MAILING ADDRESS:
Code LH - 14, NASA
Washington DC 20546

(202) 453-2999

OPEN: M-F 8-4:30; closed weekends and
  holidays
COPYING FACILITIES: yes
MATERIALS SOLICITED: Aeronautics and
  astronautics. Will also accept related
  subject material.

HOLDINGS:
  Total volume: 900 c.f.
  Inclusive dates: 20th century -
  Description: Materials on aeronautics
  and astronautics, with greatest emphasis
  on recent American civilian activities, especially those connected with NASA or
  its predecessor agency, the National Advisory Committee for Aeronautics. Material
  in related fields, such as foreign and military aeronautics and astronautics, science,
  technology, and public policy, is also
  held.

SEE: Novotny; Meckler and McMullin;
  Allard, Crawley, and Edmison.

SEE ALSO: *Astronautics and Aeronautics,* a
  yearly chronology prepared by the History Office using material in the archives (1961-).

DC14-180

National Arboretum
24th and R Streets, N.E.
Washington DC 20002

(202) 475-4815

OPEN: M-F 8-4:30; closed weekends and
  Christmas
ACCESS: with permission only
COPYING FACILITIES: no
MATERIALS SOLICITED: Materials per-
  taining to botany, horticulture, plant
  exploration, bonsai, and landscape ar-
  chitecture.

HOLDINGS:
  Total volume: 12 l.f.; 5 boxes
  Inclusive dates: 1907 -
  Description: Notes and other papers of
  Arie F. den Boer, concerning crab apples;
  copies of letters and other documents relating to the Potomac Park Japanese
  flowering cherry trees; and early photographs of U.S. Department of Agriculture
  plant exploration trips, mainly to China
  and Russia.

SEE ALSO: Ann Novotny, ed., *Picture
  Sources 3* (Special Libraries Assn.,
  1975).

DC14-250

National Archives and Records
  Administration
Office of the National Archives
8th Street and Pennsylvania Avenue,
  N.W.
Washington DC 20408

(202) 523-3218

OPEN: M-F 8:45-5:15; closed weekends
  and holidays; reading rooms open
  evenings and Saturdays
ACCESS: Restrictions on access are
  described in General Information
  Leaflet No. 2, 'Regulations for the
  Public Use of Records in the National
  Archives.'
COPYING FACILITIES: yes
MATERIALS SOLICITED: Will accept all
  records created by agencies of the United States Government that have been
  determined by the Archivist of the
  United States to have sufficient historical or other value to warrant their con-
  tinued preservation by the United
  States Government.

HOLDINGS:
  Total volume: 1,332,149 items
  Inclusive dates: 1774 -
  Description: Records created or collected by headquarters offices of agencies of
  the legislative, executive, and judicial
  branches of the United States Government since its establishment, including
  the records of the Continental and Confederation Congresses. The records comprise more than 400 record groups, each
  of which generally consists of the records
  of a single agency, or major part of an
  agency, and predecessor units, if any.
  Records of field offices of U.S. agencies,
  including the U.S. District Courts, are
  found in regional archives branches in
  eleven different cities.

GUIDES: *Guide to the National Archives of
  the United States* (GPO, 1974).

SEE: Hamer; NUCMC, 1965, 74, 76.

SEE: Allard, Crawley, and Edmison; Arm-
  strong; Bean and Vane; Beers - South-
  west; Bhatt; Dillon; Grant; Grow;
  Hinding; Hounshell; Ingram; Kim;
  Leventhal and Mooney - II; Parkinson;
  Rowan; Spalek; White.

SEE ALSO: Walter Schatz, ed., *Directory of
  Afro-American Resources* (Bowker,
  1970); Dean C. Allard and Betty Bern,
  comps., *U.S. Naval History Sources in
  the Washington Area and Suggested Research Subjects* (Naval History Division, 1970); Lawrence J. Paszek, comp.,
  *United States Air Force History: A
  Guide to Documentary Sources* (Office
  of Air Force History, 1973); Richard C.
  Davis, *North American Forest History:
  A Guide to Archives and Manuscripts in
  the United States and Canada* (Clio
  Books, 1977); Ann Novotny, ed., *Picture Sources 3* (Special Libraries Assn.,
  1975); Harold T. Pinkett, 'Recent Federal Archives as Sources for Negro History,' *Negro History Bulletin* 30 (Dec.
  1967); Meyer H. Fishbein, 'Business
  History Resources in the National Archives,' *Business History Review* 38
  (Summer 1964).

Carmelita S. Ryan, 'The Written Record
  and the American Indian: The Archives
  of the United States,' *Western Historical
  Quarterly* 6 (April 1975); Meyer H. Fishbein, 'Labor History Resources in the National Archives,' *Labor History* 8 (Fall
  1967); James R. Browning and Bess
  Glenn, 'The Supreme Court Collection at
  the National Archives,' *American Journal
  of Legal History* 4 (July 1960); Joseph B.
  Howerton, 'The Resources of the National Archives for North-Central States Ethnic Research,' *Illinois Libraries* 57
  (March 1975); Harold B. Hancock,
  'Materials for Company History in the
  National Archives,' *American Archivist* 29
  (Jan. 1966). General Information Leaflet
  No. 3, 'Select List of Publications of the
  National Archives and Records Service,'
  describes finding aids available from the
  institution.

DC14-350

National Business League
4324 Georgia Avenue, N.W.
Washington DC 20011

(202) 829-5900

OPEN: by appointment only; closed
  holidays
COPYING FACILITIES: no
MATERIALS SOLICITED: Materials related
  to the National Business League. Will
  also accept materials related to small
  businesses and minority businesses.

HOLDINGS:
  Total volume: 14 l.f.
  Inclusive dates: 1900 -
  Description: Records of the National
  Business League and its predecessor organization, the National Negro Business
  League. Holdings include the articles of
  incorporation, the early bylaws and constitution, annual convention proceedings
  since 1900, with some gaps between 1924
  and 1956, minutes of national board of
  directors' meetings, newspaper clippings
  on the League's activities, 1920-44, correspondence of Booker T. Washington,

founder of the League, photographs and sound recordings, a 1928 survey of black-operated businesses in 33 cities, and a similar survey compiled in the 1940's.

DC14-370

National Capital Planning Commission
1325 G Street, N.W.
Washington DC 20576

(202) 724-0194

OPEN: M-F 8-4:30; closed weekends and holidays
ACCESS: by appointment only
COPYING FACILITIES: yes
MATERIALS SOLICITED: Maps of proposed developments in the National Capital Region. Will also accept aerial photographs.

HOLDINGS:
Total volume: 566 c.f.
Inclusive dates: 1793 -
Description: Large-scale maps submitted to the Commission by Federal agencies showing proposed development plans in the National Capital Region, consisting of Washington, DC; Arlington, Fairfax, Loudoun, and Prince William counties, VA; Alexandria, VA; and Montgomery, Prince Georges, and Charles counties, MD. Included are maps showing master plans, land use, site development, and transportation plans. There are also sample plans prepared by the Commission, as well as aerial photographs of the Washington, DC, area.

SEE ALSO: list of map subjects available at the repository.

DC14-380

National Catholic News Service
1312 Massachusetts Avenue, N.W.
Washington DC 20005

(202) 659-6720

OPEN: by appointment only
USER FEES: variable
ACCESS: appointment required
COPYING FACILITIES: no
MATERIALS SOLICITED: Photographs related to contemporary Roman Catholic affairs.

HOLDINGS:
Total volume: 50,000 items
Inclusive dates: 1920's -
Description: Black and white news photographs, mostly pertaining to the Roman Catholic church, particularly the Vatican, Catholic organizations, church activities, and prominent Catholics, both clerical and lay.

SEE: Novotny.

DC14-410

National Defense University
Library
Room 12, Building 61
Fort McNair
4th and P Streets, S.W.
Washington DC 20319

(202) 475-1905

OPEN: M-F 8-4:15; closed weekends and holidays
ACCESS: bona fide researchers only; advance appointment required
COPYING FACILITIES: yes

HOLDINGS:
Total volume: 33 l.f.; 3,000 items
Inclusive dates: 1860's -
Description: Personal papers of General Maxwell Taylor, 1943-77, including correspondence, copies of official documents, and research materials for his book *Swords and Plowshares.* There are also 3,000 photographic negatives of Fort McNair, the National Defense University, and Arsenal Point, where the University is located, including some photographs of the hanging of Mary E. Surratt on Arsenal Point.

SEE: Paszek.

DC14-420

National Federation of Business and Professional Women's Clubs, Inc.
Archives Department
2012 Massachusetts Avenue, N.W.
Washington DC 20036

(202) 293-1100

OPEN: M-F 9-5; closed weekends and holidays
COPYING FACILITIES: yes

HOLDINGS:
Total volume: 348 c.f.
Inclusive dates: 1919 -
Description: Records of the National Federation of Business and Professional Women's Clubs, including correspondence, budgets, incomplete membership records, financial records, minutes of board of directors meetings, records and proceedings of national conventions of the Federation since 1919, photographs of women and of national conventions, records of National Businesswomen's Week, materials on the International Federation of Business and Professional Women's Clubs, and records relating to the founding of the World Center for Women's Archives.

SEE: Hinding.

DC14-450

National Gallery of Art
Library
Washington DC 20565

(202) 842-6614

OPEN: Tu-F 10-5; closed Mondays, weekends, and holidays
ACCESS: qualified researchers only
COPYING FACILITIES: yes
MATERIALS SOLICITED: Correspondence and related papers of artists. Will also accept materials of research value.

HOLDINGS:
Total volume: 500 items
Inclusive dates: Renaissance period -
Description: Correspondence of Mary Cassatt; 300 letters, chiefly of artists whose works are in the National Gallery of Art's collections, including some by Bernhard Berenson and Frederic Remington; and other manuscripts by and about artists represented in the collections.

DC14-460

National Gallery of Art
Photographic Archives
Washington DC 20565

(202) 842-6026

OPEN: M-F 10-5, by appointment only; closed weekends and holidays
COPYING FACILITIES: no
MATERIALS SOLICITED: Photographs of works of art.

HOLDINGS:
Total volume: 800,000 items
Inclusive dates: 19th century -
Description: Black and white photographs of paintings, sculpture, architecture, and other works of art, with emphasis on Western art.

DC14-470

National Genealogical Society
1921 Sunderland Place, N.W.
Washington DC 20036

(202) 785-2123

OPEN: M, W, F, Sa 11-4; closed other days, holidays, and 1st and 3rd Saturdays of winter months
USER FEES: $1 per day or $10 per year
COPYING FACILITIES: yes
MATERIALS SOLICITED: Materials pertaining to genealogy and local history. Will also accept biographical materials.

HOLDINGS:
Total volume: 100 l.f.
Inclusive dates: not specified
Description: 40 collections of genealogical source data, including correspondence, diaries, photographs, newspaper clippings, and Bible records.

DC14-490

National Grange
Memorial Library
1616 H Street, N.W.
Washington DC 20006

(202) 628-3507

OPEN: M-F 9-5; closed weekends and holidays
ACCESS: appointment required
COPYING FACILITIES: no

HOLDINGS:
Total volume: 30 boxes
Inclusive dates: 1874 -
Description: Journal of Proceedings of the National Grange, 1874 to date; National Grange correspondence with Congress; copies of Grange testimony before Congress during the 1960's and 1970's; and some photographs pertaining to the organization.

SEE ALSO: Helen T. Finneran, 'Records of the National Grange in its Washington Office,' *American Archivist* 27 (Jan. 1964).

DC14-500
National Guard Association of the
United States
1 Massachusetts Avenue, N.W.
Washington DC 20001

(202) 789-0031

OPEN: M-F 8-4; closed weekends and
holidays
ACCESS: serious writers or students of
military history
COPYING FACILITIES: yes
MATERIALS SOLICITED: Photographs of
National Guard activities. Will also accept written material describing National Guard activities.

HOLDINGS:
Total volume: 20 l.f.
Inclusive dates: 1949 -
Description: A collection of photographs of National Guard activities including equipment, training, riots, and disaster relief. Also included are photographs of individuals who hold or have
held positions of importance in the National Guard or who have contributed to
the effectiveness of the Guard.

DC14-520
National Organization for Women
1401 New York Avenue, N.W., Suite
800
Washington DC 20005

(202) 347-2279

OPEN: M-F 9-5; closed weekends and
holidays
COPYING FACILITIES: no
MATERIALS SOLICITED: Records of the
National Organization for Women.
Will also accept personal papers of for-
mer officers of the Organization.

HOLDINGS:
Total volume: not specified
Inclusive dates: 1968 -
Description: Archives and other non-
current records of the National Organiza-
tion for Women.

Other records of the Organization
are held by the Schlesinger Library,
Radcliffe College, Cambridge, MA.

DC14-530
National Park Service
Division of Cultural Resources
Management
1100 L Street N.W.
Washington DC 20240

MAILING ADDRESS:
Assistant Director, Cultural
Resources-560
National Park Service
Department of Interior
Washington DC 20240

(202) 343-2723, 2532, 4747

OPEN: M-F 7:45-4:15; closed weekends
and holidays
COPYING FACILITIES: yes
MATERIALS SOLICITED: Will accept studies, reports, and scholarly dissertations
dealing with National Park Service
areas.

HOLDINGS:
Total volume: 6,500 items
Inclusive dates: 1920's -
Description: Studies, guides, and reports by Park Service personnel dealing
with approximately 300 National Park
areas, including historical reports, architectural data, structure reports, archaeological survey and excavation reports,
remote sensing studies, special studies for
proposed areas, planning guides, and other miscellaneous information.

DC14-540
National Park Service
Photo Library
Room 8068, 19th and E Streets, N.W.
Washington DC 20240

(202) 343-7394

OPEN: M-F 7:45-4:15; closed weekends
and holidays
COPYING FACILITIES: yes
MATERIALS SOLICITED: Materials related
to the National Parks and related areas.

HOLDINGS:
Total volume: 1,075,000 items
Inclusive dates: 1860's -
Description: A collection of 1,075,000
photographs, both black and white and
color, of National Parks, arranged geo-
graphically by park. Most depict natural
scenery from 1930 to the present; other
subjects include wildlife, plant life, outdoor recreation, city parks, historic buildings, monuments, and archaeology.
Textual records include park proposals
and geological, energy, and other studies
of parks.

SEE: Novotny.

DC14-552
National Press Club
Archives
National Press Building
Washington DC 20045

(202) 662-7500

OPEN: M-F 9-5, Sa, Su by appointment;
closed holidays
ACCESS: advance arrangements required
COPYING FACILITIES: yes
MATERIALS SOLICITED: Materials concerning the history of journalism, the
Washington correspondent, journalists,
cartoonists, and photographers. Will
also accept award-winning entries in
journalism competitions.

HOLDINGS:
Total volume: 120 l.f.
Inclusive dates: 1908 -
Description: The records of the National Press Club, including correspondence, minutes, legal and financial
records, biographical information on journalists, photographs, cartoons, tapes and
transcripts of speeches, materials on the
construction of the National Press Building, scrapbooks, unpublished
reminiscences, and ephemera.

DC14-580
National Shrine of the Immaculate
Conception
4th Street and Michigan Avenue, N.E.
Washington DC 20017

(202) 526-8300

OPEN: by appointment only
ACCESS: Researchers must obtain
permission of the Director of the
Shrine in advance of visit, and must
present identification at the door.
COPYING FACILITIES: yes
MATERIALS SOLICITED: Personal papers
and photographs relating to the Shrine
or to people affiliated with it.

HOLDINGS:
Total volume: 125 boxes; 4 file
cabinets
Inclusive dates: 1920 -
Description: Materials relating to the
National Shrine of the Immaculate Conception, including newsletters, correspondence, memoranda, proclamations, financial records, and other official records of
the Shrine; papers of clergy and others
associated with the Shrine; photographs,
including those of the Shrine's construction; engineering and technical drawings;
motion pictures; and oral history interviews.

DC14-590
National Society of the Daughters of
the American Revolution
Americana Collection in the Archives
Room
1776 D Street, N.W.
Washington DC 20006

(202) 628-1776, Ext. 256

OPEN: M-F 9-4; closed weekends and
holidays
USER FEES: one dollar
ACCESS: advance arrangements required
COPYING FACILITIES: yes
MATERIALS SOLICITED: Materials related
to American history prior to 1830.

HOLDINGS:
Total volume: 5,000 documents
Inclusive dates: 17th century - 1830
Description: Microfilmed documents
related to U.S. history before 1830, with
emphasis on the Revolutionary War period. Included are deeds, wills, family letters, church records, marriage records,
diaries, 14 documents signed by George
Washington, letters and papers of all delegates to the Constitutional Convention of
1787, papers of signers of the Declaration
of Independence, and papers relating to
the American Revolution signed by European political figures and French military officers. There is also a collection of
photographs of U.S. Presidents and their
wives.

SEE: Hamer; NUCMC, 1966.

SEE: Allard, Crawley, and Edmison.

DC14-600

National Society of the Daughters of
the American Revolution
Genealogical Library
1776 D Street, N.W.
Washington DC 20006

(202) 628-1776, Ext. 226

OPEN: M-F 9-4; closed weekends and
holidays
COPYING FACILITIES: yes
MATERIALS SOLICITED: Genealogical materials, especially those useful in tracing
lineage to participants in the Revolutionary War.

HOLDINGS:
   Total volume: 1,591 vols.; 200 file
drawers; additional materials
   Inclusive dates: 18th century -
   Description: Genealogical materials
from a variety of sources, relating to all
areas of the United States, with emphasis
on the East. Included are church, cemetery, town, Bible, and other records, in
bound volumes, compiled by the genealogical records committee for each state
and the District of Columbia. There are
especially strong collections for New
York, 584 volumes, and Maryland, 34
volumes. Additional materials include
334 volumes of typewritten abstracts of
Revolutionary War pension applications,
including 101 volumes for New Hampshire; Tennessee and West Virginia county government records compiled by the
Work Projects Administration; and miscellaneous genealogical records of Alabama counties.

SEE: Hamer; NUCMC, 1966.

DC14-640

National Trust for Historic
Preservation
Audiovisual Collections
1785 Massachusetts Avenue, N.W.
Washington DC 20036

(202) 673-4038

OPEN: M-F 9-5; closed weekends and
holidays
USER FEES: charged for use of films by
non-members
COPYING FACILITIES: yes
MATERIALS SOLICITED: Slides and photographs dealing with historic preservation and the built environment.

HOLDINGS:
   Total volume: 27 films; 25,000 slides;
16 drawers of photographs
   Inclusive dates: 20th century -
   Description: Photographs, slides, and
films documenting historic preservation
and covering such topics as adaptive use,
transportation, restoration, destruction,
building crafts, maritime preservation, architectural styles, building types, street
furniture, landscaping and gardens, and
commercial archaeology.

SEE: Novotny.

SEE ALSO: *Films: Historic Preservation
and Related Subjects* (National Trust
for Historic Preservation, 1976).

DC14-650

National Trust for Historic
Preservation
Library
1785 Massachusetts Avenue N.W.
Washington DC 20036

MAILING ADDRESS:
740 Jackson Place, N.W.
Washington DC 20006

(202) 673-4000

OPEN: M-F 9-5 members only by
appointment; closed weekends and
holidays
COPYING FACILITIES: yes

HOLDINGS:
   Total volume: 60 microfilm rolls; 250
l.f.
   Inclusive dates: 1949 -
   Description: Records of the National
Trust for Historic Preservation, including
correspondence of the Trust and its
member organizations, as well as miscellaneous records, 1949- , relating to
such topics as property acquisitions and
preservation legislation. There are also
records of the Williamsburg Seminar for
Historical Administrators, 1965- .

DC14-715

Naval Aviation History Office
Building 159E, Room 584
Washington Navy Yard
Washington DC 20374

(202) 433-4355

OPEN: M-F 8-4:30; closed weekends and
holidays
COPYING FACILITIES: yes
MATERIALS SOLICITED: Official documents relating to U.S. Navy and Marine Corps aviation. Will also accept
private papers, including correspondence and photographs.

HOLDINGS:
   Total volume: 1,000 c.f.
   Inclusive dates: 1911 -
   Description: Collections pertaining to
the history of U.S. Navy and Marine
Corps aviation and space exploration. Included are yearly squadron histories, reports of major battles, and photographs
of aircraft.

SEE: Allard, Crawley, and Edmison.

DC14-720

Naval Historical Center
Naval History Division
Curator Branch
Photographic Section
Building 108
Washington Navy Yard
Washington DC 21374

(202) 433-2765

OPEN: M-F 9-4 preferably by
appointment; closed weekends and
holidays
ACCESS: appointment suggested
COPYING FACILITIES: yes
MATERIALS SOLICITED: Materials of naval and maritime interest.

HOLDINGS:
   Total volume: 100,000 items
   Inclusive dates: 19th century -
   Description: Black and white photographs, color photographs, color transparencies, and drawings relating to U.S. naval history, primarily for the period before 1920, covering such subjects as ships,
personnel, flags, ceremonies, and naval
warfare.

SEE: Novotny.

SEE ALSO: Michael Grow, *Scholars' Guide
to Washington, D.C., for Latin American and Caribbean Studies*
(Smithsonian Institution Press, 1979).

DC14-725

Naval Historical Center
Naval History Division
Navy Department Library
Building 44
Washington Navy Yard
Washington DC 20374

(202) 433-4131

OPEN: M-F 9-4; closed weekends and
holidays
COPYING FACILITIES: yes
MATERIALS SOLICITED: History, science,
biography, and exploration, relating to
the U.S. Navy. Will also accept materials concerning military history and science, and international relations.

HOLDINGS:
   Total volume: 3,000 items
   Inclusive dates: 1690 -
   Description: Letters and other papers,
mostly of U.S. naval officers, but also of
government officials, including Presidents; Congressional documents, reports,
hearings, and legislation concerning the
U.S. Navy; reports of the Secretary of the
Navy and of special boards and panels;
graduate theses on naval history; and 350
volumes of manuscript administrative
histories of World War II naval offices
and commands.

SEE: Allard, Crawley, and Edmison;
Paszek.

DC14-730

Naval History Division
Operational Archives
Building 57, Washington Naval Yard
Washington DC 20374

(202) 433-3170

OPEN: M-F 7:30-4:30; closed weekends
and holidays
COPYING FACILITIES: yes
MATERIALS SOLICITED: Records relating
to recent U.S. naval operations, strategy, and policy; histories of naval commands and activities; and office files of
senior naval officers.

HOLDINGS:
   Total volume: 9,500 c.f.
   Inclusive dates: late 18th century -
   Description: U.S. Navy records since
1939, including records of the Office of
the Chief of Naval Operations, records of
Fleet commands, manuscript histories of
naval activities, officer biographies, and
files of some senior flag officers. Materials relating to the British, German, and

Japanese navies in World War II are also held, in addition to a small collection of pre-1939 U.S. materials, including biographical data on 19th century naval officers.

GUIDES: 'Declassified Records in the Operational Archives' is available upon request.

SEE: Hamer; NUCMC, 1972, 74, 77, 81.

SEE: Paszek; Hinding; Allard, Crawley, and Edmison; Dillon; Grow; Kim.

SEE ALSO: *Partial Checklist: World War II Histories and Historical Reports in the U.S. Naval History Division* (Naval History Division, 1977); William C. Heimdahl and Edward J. Maroida, comps., *Guide to United States Naval Administrative Histories of World War II* (1976).

DC14-740
Naval Historical Foundation
Building 210, Washington Navy Yard
Washington DC 20374

(202) 433-2005

OPEN: M-F 8-4; closed weekends and holidays
ACCESS: appointment required
COPYING FACILITIES: yes
MATERIALS SOLICITED: Personal papers and manuscripts pertaining to the history and traditions of the United States Navy and maritime affairs.

HOLDINGS:
   Total volume: 75 l.f.; 500 items
   Inclusive dates: mid-18th century -
   Description: Personal naval papers, manuscripts, diaries and journals relating to naval and maritime history.

SEE: Allard, Crawley, and Edmison.

DC14-750
Naval Observatory
Library
34th Street and Massachusetts
   Avenue, N.W.
Washington DC 20390

(202) 653-1499

OPEN: M-F, by appointment only; closed weekends and holidays
COPYING FACILITIES: yes

HOLDINGS:
   Total volume: 10 l.f.
   Inclusive dates: 1860's - 1960's
   Description: Several journals containing results of telescope observations, notebooks listing purchases and functions of various telescopic instruments, notebooks and copies of letters of William Harkness, an astronomer at the Observatory in the late 19th century, and research worksheets relating to astronomy and telescopic observations.

SEE: Allard, Crawley, and Edmison.

DC14-770
Naval Imaging Command
Film Depository Division
Building 168, Naval Station,
   Anacostia
Washington DC

MAILING ADDRESS:
Chief of Information, Department of
   the Navy (0I220)
Room 2D340, Pentagon
Washington DC 20350

(202) 433-2156, 2116

OPEN: M-F 7:15-3:45; closed weekends and holidays
ACCESS: Outside researchers must secure permission from the Naval Public Affairs Office to use the depository.
COPYING FACILITIES: yes
MATERIALS SOLICITED: Films of the U.S. Navy and related subjects.

HOLDINGS:
   Total volume: 60,000,000 feet of film
   Inclusive dates: 1941 -
   Description: Stock film pertaining to the U.S. Navy and related subjects, including ships, planes, personnel, operational exercises, animal life such as sharks and seals, the Vietnam War, and meteorology. The collection is indexed.

SEE: Kim; Paszek; Rowan.

DC14-780
Naval Imaging Command
Still Picture Depository
Naval Station, Anacostia
Washington DC 20374

(202) 433-2168

OPEN: M-F 7:15-3:45; closed weekends and holidays
USER FEES: possible fee for lengthy search for requested materials
COPYING FACILITIES: yes
MATERIALS SOLICITED: Photographs of U.S. Navy subjects.

HOLDINGS:
   Total volume: 500,000 items
   Inclusive dates: 1958 -
   Description: Color and black and white photographs relating to the U.S. Navy and its aircraft, ships, personnel, and bases.

SEE: Novotny; Paszek.

SEE ALSO: Hong N. Kim, *Scholars' Guide to Washington, D.C., for East Asian Studies* (Smithsonian Institution Press, 1979); Michael Grow, *Scholars' Guide to Washington, D.C., for Latin American and Caribbean Studies* (Smithsonian Institution Press, 1979); Steven A. Grant, *Scholars' Guide to Washington, D.C., for Russian/Soviet Studies* (Smithsonian Institution Press, 1977).

DC14-850
New National Theatre Corporation
National Theatre
Library
1321 E Street, N.W.
Washington DC 20004

(202) 628-6161

OPEN: Tu-Sa noon-9; closed Sundays and Mondays
COPYING FACILITIES: yes
MATERIALS SOLICITED: Information relating to the National Theatre of Washington and to other theaters. Will also accept other performing arts information.

HOLDINGS:
   Total volume: 5 l.f.; 20 file drawers
   Inclusive dates: 1835 -
   Description: Materials relating to the National Theatre and to other historic theaters of Washington, DC. Included are correspondence, logbooks, journals, account books, business records, music scores, sound recordings, and photographs.

DC14-870
The Newspaper Guild
1125 15th Street, N.W.
Washington DC 20005

(202) 296-2990

OPEN: M-F, by appointment only; closed weekends and holidays
COPYING FACILITIES: yes

HOLDINGS:
   Total volume: not specified
   Inclusive dates: 1933 -
   Description: Letters, convention proceedings, public statements, and other records of The Newspaper Guild, as well as photographs of Guild employees, strikes, picket lines, and other subjects.

Most of the archives of The Guild have been transferred to Wayne State University, Archives of Labor History and Urban Affairs, Detroit, MI. Permission to use these archives must be obtained from The Newspaper Guild.

DC15-50
Order of Preachers
Province of St. Joseph
Archives
Dominican House of Studies
487 Michigan Avenue, N.E.
Washington DC 20017

(202) 529-5300

OPEN: by appointment
COPYING FACILITIES: no
MATERIALS SOLICITED: Materials relating to the Dominican Order in the United States.

HOLDINGS:
   Total volume: 2,016 c.f.
   Inclusive dates: 1800 -
   Description: Records of the Dominican Order in the United States, concentrating on the eastern half of the country after 1939. There are records and other documents of the Order's institutions and

members, including letters, diaries, memoirs, unpublished manuscripts, financial records, maps, charts, architectural plans, photographs of persons, places and events, aerial photographs, oral histories, microfilms and hand copies from Roman archives. There are also papers of foreign missions in China, Kenya, Peru, Chile, and Pakistan. Much of the material pertains to the growth of the Roman Catholic church in the Ohio and Mississippi valleys, especially Ohio and Kentucky.

SEE: Hamer (as Dominican College).

DC15-500
Organization of American States
Records Management Center
19th Street and Constitution Avenue, N.W.
Washington DC

MAILING ADDRESS:
17th Street and Constitution Avenue, N.W.
Washington DC 20006

(202) 789-3849, 3973

OPEN: M-F 9:30-5; closed weekends and holidays
ACCESS: qualified scholars only; advance arrangements required
COPYING FACILITIES: yes

HOLDINGS:
    Total volume: 900 c.f.
    Inclusive dates: 1889 -
    Description: Records of the Organization of American States (OAS) and its agencies and activities, including General Assemblies; Meetings of Consultation of Ministers of Foreign Affairs; meetings of the Inter-American Economic and Social Council, the Inter-American Council for Education, Science and Culture and its committees, and the Inter-American Juridical Committee; general and special conferences; and conferences sponsored by OAS specialized agencies.
    Other holdings include record copies of the proceedings of the Council of the OAS; reports of the Secretary General; multilateral and bilateral treaties, conventions, and agreements signed by OAS member countries, with accompanying instruments of ratification or denunciation; 26,000 photographs of Latin American subjects; and tape recordings of speeches by representatives of OAS member countries.

SEE: Hamer (as Pan American Union).

SEE: Novotny; Grow.

DC16-300
The Phillips Collection
1600 21st Street, N.W.
Washington DC 20009

(202) 387-2151

OPEN: Tu-F 10-5; closed weekends, Mondays and holidays
ACCESS: serious students of the arts and scholars; appointments must be made in advance by writing or by phone
COPYING FACILITIES: yes
MATERIALS SOLICITED: Photographs of articles of modern art.

HOLDINGS:
    Total volume: 1,000 photographs; other items
    Inclusive dates: 1825 -
    Description: Material relating to modern art and some of its 19th century sources, chiefly photographs and supporting documentation on works of art in the Collection.

SEE ALSO: Ann Novotny, ed., Picture Sources 3 (Special Libraries Assn., 1975).

DC16-680
Public Broadcasting Service
Program Data and Analysis
475 L'Enfant Plaza West, S.W.
Washington DC 20024

(202) 488-5227

OPEN: M-F 9-5; closed weekends and holidays
ACCESS: advance arrangements required
COPYING FACILITIES: no
MATERIALS SOLICITED: Nationally distributed public television programs on film or video tape, textual records of the programs' contents and distribution, and production and promotion photographs and slides.

HOLDINGS:
    Total volume: 34,400 items; 50 file cabinets
    Inclusive dates: 1953 -
    Description: Films and video recordings of nationally distributed public television programs and of programs from the Educational Television Stations Program Service, later titled the Public Television Library. Included are 100 classic theatrical films, performance programs in music and drama, in-depth news programs, Congressional hearings, science documentaries, and interviews and profiles of figures in the arts, politics, and science.

SEE: Rowan.

DC19-40
St. Albans School for Boys
Ellison Library
St. Albans Archives
Massachusetts and Wisconsin Avenues, N.W.
Washington DC 20016

(202) 537-6409

OPEN: M-Th 8-5, F 8-3; closed weekends, holidays, last 2 weeks of March and December, and June 1-Sept. 15
COPYING FACILITIES: yes

HOLDINGS:
    Total volume: 275 l.f.
    Inclusive dates: 1904 -
    Description: Records of St. Albans School for Boys, including records of the headmaster, registrar, bursar, and the Cathedral Chapter of the National Cathedral Foundation; as well as records of affiliated organizations; materials concerning School activities and development; photographs; and manuscripts.

GUIDES: 'Inventory of the Records of St. Albans School,' (n.p., 1970).

SEE ALSO: Sherrod East, 'St. Albans Archives,' American Archivist 34 (Oct. 1971).

DC19-130
Scottish Rite of Freemasonry
Supreme Council
Archives
1733 Sixteenth Street, N.W.
Washington DC 20009

(202) 232-3579

OPEN: M-F 8-4; closed weekends and holidays
COPYING FACILITIES: yes
MATERIALS SOLICITED: Materials concerning Freemasonry in the United States.

HOLDINGS:
    Total volume: 2,500,000 items
    Inclusive dates: 1801 -
    Description: Materials relating to the Scottish Rite of Freemasonry and its founding. Included are correspondence between subordinate bodies and the Supreme Council; correspondence of Grand Commanders, 1801- ; the Albert Pike collection of his letters, translations from Sanskrit and ancient Hebrew, and other papers; and the Maurice H. Thatcher collection of papers relating to his Congressional career and the construction of the Panama Canal.

SEE: Hamer; NUCMC, 1959-61.

DC19-160
Senate
Historical Office
S413, U.S. Capitol
Washington DC 20510

(202) 224-6900

OPEN: M-F 9-5; closed weekends and holidays
ACCESS: appointment required
COPYING FACILITIES: yes
MATERIALS SOLICITED: Photographs of U.S. Senators.

HOLDINGS:
    Total volume: 30,000 items
    Inclusive dates: 19th century -
    Description: Photographs of U.S. Senators, with especially strong holdings for those who have held office since 1950.

DC19-220
Seventh-day Adventists
General Conference
Archives
6840 Eastern Avenue, N.W.
Washington DC 20012

(202) 722-6000

OPEN: M-Th 8:30 - 5:30, F 8:30 - 12; closed weekends and holidays
ACCESS: by letter of recommendation from college or university, or from an Adventist church administrator
COPYING FACILITIES: yes
MATERIALS SOLICITED: Organization and administrative records of the General Conference of Seventh-day Adventists. Will also accept personal papers of leading Adventist ministers and educators.

HOLDINGS:
> *Total volume:* 4,000 l.f.
> *Inclusive dates:* 1863 -
> *Description:* Records of over 100 administrative or distinct functional units of the world headquarters of the Seventh-day Adventist church, including the presidential office; secretariat; treasury; administrative and legal entities; general departments; bureaus, associations, and services; General Conference institutions; Seventh-day Adventist professional organizations; and world divisions. Much of the material involves the mission outreach of the church in the United States and abroad.

SEE: Hinding.

DC19-250
Shipbuilders Council of America
1110 Vermont Avenue, N.W.
Washington DC 20005

(202) 775-9060

OPEN: M-F 9-5; closed weekends and holidays
COPYING FACILITIES: no
MATERIALS SOLICITED: Materials relating to the historical relevance of U.S. shipyards to national security and economic growth.

HOLDINGS:
> *Total volume:* 750 items
> *Inclusive dates:* 1920 -
> *Description:* Records of the Council, including minutes of board of directors, minutes of committee meetings, and mailings to members.

DC19-310
Smithsonian Institution
Archives
900 Jefferson Drive, S.W.
Washington DC

MAILING ADDRESS:
Room 2135, Arts and Industries Building
Washington DC 20560

(202) 357-1420

OPEN: M-F 9-5; closed weekends and holidays
COPYING FACILITIES: yes
MATERIALS SOLICITED: Official records of the Smithsonian Institution, and of Washington, DC, scientific societies.

HOLDINGS:
> *Total volume:* 7,500 c.f.
> *Inclusive dates:* 1820 -
> *Description:* The holdings consist chiefly of official records of the Smithsonian Institution and also include manuscripts, private papers, and collections relating to Smithsonian staff members and other scientists. The collection is particularly rich in the history of 19th century American science and includes the private papers of Smithsonian Secretaries Joseph Henry, Spencer F. Baird, and Samuel P. Langley, as well as the papers of their 20th century successors, Charles D. Walcott, Charles G. Abbot, and Alexander Wetmore.

GUIDES: *Guide to the Smithsonian Archives* (Smithsoniaan Institution Press, 1978).

SEE: Hamer; NUCMC, 1971-72, 74, 76, 78, 80.

SEE: Spalek; Allard, Crawley, and Edmison; Hinding; Kim; Grant; Grow; Dillon.

SEE ALSO: 'Preliminary Guide to the Smithsonian Institution Archives,' *Archives and Special Collections of the Smithsonian Institution,* no. 1 (Smithsonian Institution Press, 1971); David A. Hounshell, comp., *Manuscripts in U.S. Depositories Relating to the History of Electrical Science and Technology* (Smithsonian Institution, n.d.); Richard C. Davis, *North American Forest History: A Guide to Archives and Manuscripts in the United States and Canada* (Clio Books, 1977).

DC19-320
Smithsonian Institution
Archives of American Art
Room 331, National Portrait Gallery Building
Eighth and F Streets, N.W.
Washington DC 20506

(202) 357-2781

OPEN: M-F 10-5; closed weekends and holidays
ACCESS: scholars above the undergraduate level
COPYING FACILITIES: yes
MATERIALS SOLICITED: History of American visual arts.

HOLDINGS:
> *Total volume:* 3,700 l.f.; 3,775 rolls of microfilm
> *Inclusive dates:* 18th century -
> *Description:* About 3,000 collections relating to American visual arts, chiefly painting and sculpture, including the personal papers of artists, craftspeople, collectors, dealers, art historians, critics, and records of art museums, galleries, schools, art societies, and relevant government agencies. In addition, the Archives has more than 2,000 oral history interviews with artists and others in the art world.

GUIDES: Garnett McCoy, *Archives of American Art: A Directory of Resources* (Bowker, 1972); Arthur J. Breton, Nancy Zembala, and Anne P. Nicastro, *Archives of American Art: A Checklist of the Collection* (Smithsonian Institution, 1977).

SEE: NUCMC, 1967, 69, 71-72, 74.

SEE: Schatz; Meckler and McMullin; Spalek; Allard, Crawley, and Edison; Dillon; Grant.

SEE ALSO: *Archives of American Art Journal,* 1961 - .

Card Catalogue of the Manuscript Collections of the Archives of American Art 10 vols. (Scholarly Resoources, 1981).

The Archives maintains offices in New York City, Boston, Detroit, Los Angeles, and San Francisco. Copies of the microfilm collections are available at all of the offices.

DC19-327
Smithsonian Institution
Freer Gallery of Art
Department of Near Eastern Art
12th Street and Jefferson Drive, S.W.
Washington DC 20560

(202) 357-2091

OPEN: M-F 10-5 by appointment; closed weekends and Christmas
ACCESS: appointment preferred
COPYING FACILITIES: yes
MATERIALS SOLICITED: Manuscripts, slides, photographs and microfilms on Near Eastern cultures.

HOLDINGS:
> *Total volume:* 90,000 items; 4 file drawers
> *Inclusive dates:* 3rd century -
> *Description:* 600 Christian, Islamic, Buddhist and Hindu bound manuscripts and single folios, including religious works in Greek, Syriac, Coptic, and Armenian, and secular and religious works in Arabic, Persian, Turkish, and Hindi. Also included are 1,600 items of the Herzfeld collection of drawings, photographs, journals, and notebooks of expeditions to the Near East, 1903-36; 87,000 similar items in the Smith collection on Persia, 1930-60; and the Agaoglu collection of four drawers of notes and photographs concerning Islamic metalwork, 1930-50.

SEE: Hamer.

SEE: Kim; Grant; Martin; Spalek.

SEE ALSO: Ann Novotny, ed., *Picture Sources 3* (Special Libraries Assn., 1975); S. Der Nersessian, *Armenian Manuscripts in the Freer Gallery of Art,* Oriental Studies, no. 6 (Smithsonian Institution, 1963).

DC19-330
Smithsonian Institution
Freer Gallery of Art
Library
12th and Jefferson Drive, S.W.
Washington DC 20560

(202) 357-2091

OPEN: M-F 10-4:30; closed weekends and Christmas
ACCESS: written request to Librarian preferred
COPYING FACILITIES: yes

HOLDINGS:
> *Total volume:* 15,000 items
> *Inclusive dates:* 1886 - 1919
> *Description:* 30 volumes of carbon copy letters from Charles L. Freer and 29 diaries of Freer, in addition to correspondence of Abbott H. Thayer, Thomas W. Dewing, James Abbott McNeill Whistler, Dwight W. Tryon, and numerous friends and business acquaintances of Freer.

DC19-340
Smithsonian Institution
Hirshhorn Museum and Sculpture
    Garden
8th Street and Independence Avenue,
    S.W.
Washington DC 20560

(202) 357-3222

OPEN: M-F 10-5; closed weekends and
    holidays
ACCESS: students and scholars with prior
    written permission
COPYING FACILITIES: yes
MATERIALS SOLICITED: Archival material
    relating to the Museum's permanent
    collection of painting and sculpture.

HOLDINGS:
    Total volume: 3,311 items
    Inclusive dates: 1870 -
    Description: Correspondence of artists,
    art galleries, and museums relating to the
    permanent collection of painting and
    sculpture of the Hirshhorn Museum and
    Sculpture Garden. Included are materials
    on Elmer MacRae, the Armory Show,
    Thomas Eakins, Samuel Murray, and
    Louis Eilshemius.

SEE: Novotny.

DC19-440
Smithsonian Institution
Museum of African Art and
Frederick Douglass Institute
    Archives
316-18 A Street, N.E.
Washington DC 20002

(202) 287-3490

OPEN: M-F 10-5; closed weekends,
    Thanksgiving, and Christmas
ACCESS: appointment required
COPYING FACILITIES: no
MATERIALS SOLICITED: Historical and
    current   materials,   including
    ethnographic data, pertaining to Afri-
    can art and to Afro-Americans, espe-
    cially Frederick Douglass. Will also ac-
    cept materials on cubism, post-
    impressionism, and the effects of Af-
    rican art upon European art, as well as
    educational materials pertaining to the
    arts and museum education.

HOLDINGS:
    Total volume: 100 c.f.; 30 items
    Inclusive dates: 1699 -
    Description: Financial, attendance, and
    other records of the Museum of African
    Art, Institute for Cross-Cultural Studies,
    and Frederick Douglass Institute, dating
    from 1960, in addition to 30 manuscript
    maps of Africa, mostly 18th century.

SEE: Bhatt.

DC19-450
Smithsonian Institution
Museum of African Art and
Frederick Douglass Institute
Eliot Elisofon Archives
316-318 A Street, N.W.
Washington DC 20002

(202) 287-3490

OPEN: by appointment only; closed
    Christmas
ACCESS: appointment requested
COPYING FACILITIES: yes
MATERIALS SOLICITED: Visual materials
    relating to African or Afro-American
    art and culture. Will also accept ma-
    terials from other cultures that have
    been influenced by African culture.

HOLDINGS:
    Total volume: 80,000 items
    Inclusive dates: 1949 -
    Description: Primarily color slides and
    black and white photographs of African
    and Afro-American art and culture. Much
    of the collection is composed of still pho-
    tographs and film outtakes by photo-
    graphic journalist Eliot Elisofon.

SEE ALSO: Purnima Mehta Bhatt, *Schol-
    ars' Guide to Washington, D.C. for Af-
    rican Studies* (Smithsonian Institution
    Press, 1980).

DC19-500
Smithsonian Institution
National Air and Space Museum
    Library
7th Street and Independence Avenue,
    S.W.
Washington DC 20560

(202) 357-3133, 3134, 3135

OPEN: M-F 10-4; closed weekends and
    holidays
ACCESS: serious research scholars
COPYING FACILITIES: yes
MATERIALS SOLICITED: Aeronautics, avi-
    ation, astronautics, and space science,
    as well as biographical information on
    air and space personalities. Will also
    accept material relating to earth and
    planetary sciences, astronomy, and as-
    trophysics.

HOLDINGS:
    Total volume: 1,100,000 items;
    additional materials
    Inclusive dates: 1783 -
    Description: 600,000 photographs and
    drawings covering all aspects of the his-
    tory of aeronautics and astronautics, in-
    cluding rocketry, ballooning, airships, his-
    torical events, notable aviators, and as-
    tronauts. There are also manuscript col-
    lections of aviation historians and
    500,000 technical reports on aeronautics,
    astronautics, earth and planetary sciences,
    and astronomy.

SEE: Allard, Crawley, and Edmison; Kim;
    Grant; Dillon.

SEE ALSO: Catherine D. Scott, 'National
    Air and Space Museum Library,' in
    Madeline Miele, Roberta Moore, and
    Sarah Prakken, eds., *The Bowker An-
    nual of Library and Book Trade In-
    formation, 1976* (Bowker, 1976); Alan
    M. Meckler and Ruth McMullin,
    comps.,   *Oral   History   Collections*
    (Bowker, 1975); Ann Novotny, ed., *Pic-
    ture Sources 3* (Special Libraries Assn.,
    1975); Dean C. Allard and Betty Bern,
    comps., *U.S. Naval History Sources in
    the Washington Area and Suggested Re-
    search Subjects* (Naval History Divi-
    sion, 1970); Lawrence J. Paszek, comp.,
    *United States Air Force History: A
    Guide to Documentary Sources* (Office
    of Air Force History, 1973).

DC19-520
Smithsonian Institution
National Anthropological Archives
10th Street and Constitution Avenue,
    N.W.
Washington DC 20560

(202) 357-1986

OPEN: M-F 9-5; closed weekends and
    holidays
COPYING FACILITIES: yes
MATERIALS SOLICITED: History and an-
    thropology of native Americans, history
    of anthropology, and non-current
    records of anthropological organiza-
    tions. Will also accept material con-
    cerning disciplines closely related to an-
    thropology.

HOLDINGS:
    Total volume: 4,000 c.f.
    Inclusive dates: 1840 -
    Description: Private papers of anthro-
    pologists and American ethnologists, and
    records of the Smithsonian Department
    of Anthropology, River Basin Surveys, In-
    stitute for Social Anthropology, and sev-
    eral private anthropological and native
    American organizations. Also included
    are photographs, cartographic materials,
    and sound recordings. The collections are
    strongly related to North American In-
    dians and Eskimos.

SEE: Hamer (as Bureau of American
    Ethnology Archives).

SEE: Grow; Kim; Bean and Vane;
    Hinding.

SEE ALSO: *Catalog to Manuscripts at the
    National Anthropological Archives* (G.
    K. Hall, 1975); Ann Novotny, ed., *Pic-
    ture Sources 3* (Special Libraries Assn.,
    1975). Two pamphlet guides, 'Selected
    Portraits of Prominent North American
    Indians' (1973) and 'Selected Photo-
    graphs Illustrating North American In-
    dian Life' (1974), published by the
    Smithsonian Press, are also available.

DC19-536
Smithsonian Institution
National Museum of American Art
    Archives
8th and G Streets, N.W.
Washington DC 20560

(202) 357-1381, 1771, 2593

OPEN: M-F 10-5:15; closed weekends
    and holidays
ACCESS: advance arrangements required
COPYING FACILITIES: yes
MATERIALS SOLICITED: Archives and
    non-current records of the Museum
    and its staff and related manuscripts,
    visual documents, and audible docu-
    ments.

HOLDINGS:
    Total volume: 379 c.f.
    Inclusive dates: 1906 -
    Description: Records of the National
    Museum of American Art (formerly the
    National Collection of Fine Arts) and its
    staff including official and personal cor-
    respondence; account books; financial
    records; administrative material; literary
    manuscripts; unpublished memoirs; dia-
    ries; journals; personal papers; logbooks;

scrapbooks; exhibition research material including biographical and bibliographical information; architectural and technical drawings; audio materials; and photographs.

SEE: Hinding; Novotny.

DC19-539

Smithsonian Institution
National Museum of American Art
Slide and Photograph Archive
8th and G Streets, N.W.
Washington DC 20560

(202) 357-1626, 1348, 2283

OPEN: by appointment only M-F 9-5; closed weekends and Federal holidays
COPYING FACILITIES: yes
MATERIALS SOLICITED: American art.

HOLDINGS:
  Total volume: 160,000 items
  Inclusive dates: 1897 -
  Description: Photographs documenting art, primarily American. Included are 127,000 negatives of the New York photographic firm of Peter A. Juley and Son, depicting art works and artists since 1897 and including many works now lost, destroyed, or altered in appearance.

DC19-542

Smithsonian Institution
National Museum of American History
Archives Center
12th and Constitution Avenue, N.W.
Washington DC 20560

(202) 357-3270

OPEN: M-F 10-4:30; closed weekends and holidays
ACCESS: advance arrangements encouraged
COPYING FACILITIES: yes
MATERIALS SOLICITED: Personal papers; business and other organization records; historical photograph collections; and audio and video recordings especially in areas relating to the Museum's artifact collections and to American history. Of special interest is the history of science and technology, selected aspects of the history of American society, records of and advertising ephemera.

HOLDINGS:
  Total volume: 5,000 l.f.
  Inclusive dates: 1700 -
  Description: Manuscript collections transferred from other divisions of the National Museum of American History. Strengths are in the history of electricity, electronic communications, pharmacy, and other areas of science and technology. Also held is the Collection of Business Americana, including business advertising, related ephemera, and greeting cards; several large collections of historical photographs; and descriptive information on collections held by the Museum's other divisions and units.

GUIDES: *Guide to Manuscript Collections in the National Museum of History and Technology* (Smithsonian Institution Press, 1978).

DC19-545

Smithsonian Institution
National Museum of American History
Department of Social and Cultural History
Division of Ceramics and Glass
AHB 4613
12th Street and Constitution Avenue N.W.
Washington DC 20560

(202) 357-1786

OPEN: M-F 9-5:15; closed weekends and holidays
ACCESS: prior appointment required
COPYING FACILITIES: yes
MATERIALS SOLICITED: Materials relating to ceramics and glass.

HOLDINGS:
  Total volume: 13 c.f.
  Inclusive dates: 1920's -
  Description: Photographic images of ceramics and glassware and of ceramics manufacturing equipment, and formulas for the production of stained glass used in the Washington Cathedral.

GUIDES: *Guide to Manuscript Collections in the National Museum of History and Technology* (Smithsonian Institution Press, 1978).

DC19-550

Smithsonian Institution
National Museum of American History
Department of Social and Cultural History
Division of Community Life
AHB 4101
12th Street and Constitution Avenue, N.W.
Washington DC 20560

(202) 357-2385

OPEN: M-F 9-5:15; closed weekends and holidays
ACCESS: prior appointment required
COPYING FACILITIES: yes
MATERIALS SOLICITED: Materials relating to popular culture and sports.

HOLDINGS:
  Total volume: 38 c.f.; 103 vols.
  Inclusive dates: 1778 -
  Description: Photographs, manuscripts, legal documents, scrapbooks, and other materials concerning U.S. community and urban life and popular culture, including education, immigration, entertainment, the labor movement, ethnic groups, and blacks. Included are 103 volumes of clippings concerning boxer Joe Louis, compiled by his manager Julian Black.

GUIDES: *Guide to Manuscript Collections in the National Museum of History and Technology* (Smithsonian Institution Press, 1978).

DC19-555

Smithsonian Institution
National Museum of American History
Department of Social and Cultural History
Division of Costumes
AHB 4202
12th Street and Constitution Avenue, N.W.
Washington DC 20560

(202) 357-3185

OPEN: M-F 9-5:15; closed weekends and holidays
ACCESS: prior appointment required
COPYING FACILITIES: yes
MATERIALS SOLICITED: Materials relating to costumes and textiles.

HOLDINGS:
  Total volume: 23 c.f.
  Inclusive dates: 1888 -
  Description: Business records of U.S. textile and clothing manufacturers; papers of Dorothy Shaver, fashion and design industry executive; information files concerning fashion designers; and photographs of garments.

GUIDES: *Guide to Manuscript Collections in the National Museum of History and Technology* (Smithsonian Institution Press, 1978).

SEE: NUCMC, 1980.

DC19-560

Smithsonian Institution
National Museum of American History
Department of Social and Cultural History
Division of Domestic Life
AHB 4117
12th Street and Constitution Avenue, N.W.
Washington DC 20560

(202) 357-2308

OPEN: M-F 9-5:15; closed weekends and holidays
ACCESS: prior appointment required
COPYING FACILITIES: yes
MATERIALS SOLICITED: Materials relating to furnishings and other aspects of domestic life.

HOLDINGS:
  Total volume: 50 c.f.
  Inclusive dates: 1749 -
  Description: Materials relating to crafts, amusements, furniture, architecture, and other aspects of American culture. Included are photographs, family papers, materials concerning pottery makers, records of amusement park carousel manufacturers, papers on New England gravestone carving, architectural materials such as records of a Gothic Revival style house in Connecticut, a scrapbook concerning cigar store figures, and papers of William Ramsay, who helped found Alexandria, VA.

GUIDES: *Guide to Manuscript Collections in the National Museum of History and Technology* (Smithsonian Institution Press, 1978).

SEE: NUCMC, 1980.

All manuscripts and archives have been transferred to the National Museum of American History, Archives Center **(DC19-542).**

DC19-565
Smithsonian Institution
National Museum of American History
Department of Social and Cultural History
Division of Graphic Arts
AHB 5703
12th Street and Constitution Avenue, N.W.
Washington DC 20560

(202) 357-2877

OPEN: M-F 9-5:15; closed weekends and holidays
ACCESS: prior appointment required
COPYING FACILITIES: yes
MATERIALS SOLICITED: Materials relating to graphic arts.

HOLDINGS:
Total volume: 14 c.f.
Inclusive dates: 1906 -
Description: Photographs, correspondence, notes, and business records concerning fine arts, type and typography, engraving, printing, and other aspects of graphic arts.

GUIDES: *Guide to Manuscript Collections in the National Museum of History and Technology* (Smithsonian Institution Press, 1978).

SEE: NUCMC, 1980.

DC19-570
Smithsonian Institution
National Museum of American History
Department of Social and Cultural History
Division of Musical Instruments
AHB 4123
12th Street and Constitution Avenue, N.W.
Washington DC 20560

(202) 357-1707

OPEN: by appointment only; closed weekends and Christmas
ACCESS: prior appointment required
COPYING FACILITIES: yes
MATERIALS SOLICITED: Materials concerning musical instruments.

HOLDINGS:
Total volume: 79 c.f.
Inclusive dates: 20th century -
Description: Photographs of musical instruments and of works of art containing musical instruments; photographs and manuscripts relating to organs and organ design; 100 tape recordings of musical performances at the Museum; an oral history interview with organist E. Power

Biggs; and tape recordings and other materials concerning traditional music in Vermont, Virginia, North Carolina, and Mexico.

GUIDES: *Guide to Manuscript Collections in the National Museum of History and Technology* (Smithsonian Institution Press, 1978).

DC19-576
Smithsonian Institution
National Museum of American History
Department of Social and Cultural History
Division of Political History
AHB 4109
12th Street and Constitution Avenue, N.W.
Washington DC 20560

(202) 357-2008

OPEN: M-F 9-5:15; closed weekends and holidays
ACCESS: prior appointment required
COPYING FACILITIES: yes
MATERIALS SOLICITED: Political history materials.

HOLDINGS:
Total volume: 75 c.f.; 3 vols.
Inclusive dates: 1764 -
Description: Largely a collection of photographs pertaining to U.S. politics, as well as papers of persons active in public life, including small collections of John Adams and John Hancock family papers.

GUIDES: *Guide to Manuscript Collections in the National Museum of History and Technology* (Smithsonian Institution Press, 1978).

SEE: Allard, Crawley, and Edmison; Hinding.

DC19-581
Smithsonian Institution
National Museum of American History
Department of Social and Cultural History
Division of Textiles
AHB 4131
12th Street and Constitution Avenue, N.W.
Washington DC 20560

(202) 357-1889

OPEN: M-F 9-5:15; closed weekends and holidays
ACCESS: prior appointment required
COPYING FACILITIES: yes
MATERIALS SOLICITED: Materials relating to textiles.

HOLDINGS:
Total volume: 47 c.f.
Inclusive dates: 19th century -
Description: Weavers' account books, specifications and drawings issued by the U.S. Patent Office for sewing machines and other textile machinery, and photographs of garments, rugs, linen, embroidery sewing machines, quilts, and other textiles and textile machinery.

GUIDES: *Guide to Manuscript Collections in the National Museum of History and Technology* (Smithsonian Institution Press, 1978).

DC19-586
Smithsonian Institution
National Museum of American History
Department of History of Science and Technology
Division of Electricity and Modern Physics
AHB 5025
12th Street and Constitution Avenue, N.W.
Washington DC 20560

(202) 357-1840

OPEN: M-F 9-5:15; closed weekends and holidays
ACCESS: prior appointment required
COPYING FACILITIES: yes
MATERIALS SOLICITED: Materials documenting the history and technology of electricity, nuclear energy, and modern physics.

HOLDINGS:
Total volume: 437 c.f.
Inclusive dates: 1840 -
Description: Materials concerning the technology and theory of electricity and modern physics. Included are biographical files on figures prominent in the field of electricity; blueprints, photographs, and papers concerning a variety of inventions; patents and other documents on the development of the transformer; records of telegraph companies; records of a scientific instrument manufacturing company; and papers of Elisha Gray, William Joseph Hammer, Elihu Thomson, Russell Harrison Varian, and others.

GUIDES: *Guide to Manuscript Collections in the National Museum of History and Technology* (Smithsonian Institution Press, 1978).

SEE: Hounshell.

DC19-591
Smithsonian Institution
National Museum of American History
Department of History of Science and Technology
Division of Extractive Industries
AHB 5032
12th Street and Constitution Avenue, N.W.
Washington DC 20560

(202) 357-2095, 2813, 2323

OPEN: M-F 9-5:15; closed weekends and holidays
ACCESS: prior appointment required
COPYING FACILITIES: yes
MATERIALS SOLICITED: Materials concerning extractive industries.

HOLDINGS:
Total volume: 165 c.f.
Inclusive dates: 1820 -
Description: Business records, personal papers, organization records, photographs, patents, and blueprints, pertaining

to mining, agriculture, food processing, and the fishing industry, primarily in the United States. Included are records of coal and iron mining companies, coal mining machinery manufacturers, railroads, railroad and canal construction companies, and textile mills; photographs of cattle from around the world; and records of the Association of Living Historical Farms and Agricultural Museums.

GUIDES: *Guide to Manuscript Collections in the National Museum of History and Technology* (Smithsonian Institution, 1978).

DC19-596

Smithsonian Institution
National Museum of American History
Department of History of Science and Technology
Division of Mathematics
AHB 5002
12th Street and Constitution Avenue, N.W.
Washington DC 20560

(202) 357-2392

OPEN: M-F 9-5:15; closed weekends and holidays
ACCESS: prior appointment required
COPYING FACILITIES: yes
MATERIALS SOLICITED: Materials concerning mathematics and computers.

HOLDINGS:
Total volume: 108 c.f.
Inclusive dates: 20th century -
Description: Materials documenting the history of mathematics, computers, other calculating devices, and psychology. Included are oral histories concerning computers and other mathematical devices, records generated by computer societies and user groups, photographs, drawings, flow charts, blueprints, notebooks, and correspondence.

GUIDES: *Guide to Manuscript Collections in the National Museum of History and Technology* (Smithsonian Institution Press, 1978).

DC19-601

Smithsonian Institution
National Museum of American History
Department of History of Science and Technology
Division of Mechanical and Civil Engineering
AHB 5020
12th Street and Constitution Avenue, N.W.
Washington DC 20560

(202) 357-2058

OPEN: M-F 9-5:15; closed weekends and holidays
ACCESS: prior appointment required
COPYING FACILITIES: yes
MATERIALS SOLICITED: Materials concerning mechanical and civil engineering, and related business and technological history.

HOLDINGS:
Total volume: 1,500 c.f.
Inclusive dates: 1823 -
Description: Personal papers of and biographical information about U.S. mechanical, civil, chemical, petroleum, electrical, mining, aeronautical, and automotive engineers; and business records, photographs, drawings, blueprints, and other records documenting a wide variety of engineering, construction, and manufacturing activities in the United States. Companies represented include tunnel, dam, bridge, and railroad construction firms; diesel engine and automobile manufacturers; ironworks; paper manufacturers; shipbuilders; foundries; and breweries. Of particular importance are 400 cubic feet of records of the Baldwin Southwark Corporation, 1868-1945, concerning the manufacturing of engines, boilers, and other machinery, and 24 cubic feet of glass negatives of machine tools, presses, engines, and other machinery manufactured by Ohio companies.

GUIDES: *Guide to Manuscript Collections in the National Museum of History and Technology* (Smithsonian Institution Press, 1978).

SEE: NUCMC, 1980.

DC19-606

Smithsonian Institution
National Museum of American History
Department of History of Science and Technology
Division of Mechanisms
AHB 5015
12th Street and Constitution Avenue, N.W.
Washington DC 20560

(202) 357-3188

OPEN: M-F 9-5:15; closed weekends and holidays
ACCESS: prior appointment required
COPYING FACILITIES: yes
MATERIALS SOLICITED: Materials concerning clocks, watches, and small mechanical devices.

HOLDINGS:
Total volume: 37 c.f.
Inclusive dates: 1822 -
Description: Photographs and manuscripts pertaining to clocks, watches, and other types of light machinery. Also included are business records, drawings of tools used in making timepieces, papers of inventor Charles Sumner Tainter, and War Production Board records concerning regulation and production of clocks and watches during World War II.

GUIDES: *Guide to Manuscript Collections in the National Museum of History and Technology* (Smithsonian Institution Press, 1978).

SEE: NUCMC, 1980.

SEE: Hinding.

DC19-611

Smithsonian Institution
National Museum of American History
Department of History of Science and Technology
Division of Medical Sciences
AHB 5000
12th Street and Constitution Avenue, N.W.
Washington DC 20560

(202) 357-2145

OPEN: by appointment only
ACCESS: prior appointment required
COPYING FACILITIES: yes
MATERIALS SOLICITED: Materials concerning medicine.

HOLDINGS:
Total volume: 68 c.f.; 402 items
Inclusive dates: 1740 -
Description: Photographs of medical equipment, pharmaceutical manufacturing, hospitals, and physicians; medical account books; papers of the medical and chirurgical faculty of the University of Maryland; and papers of dentists, physicians, and others in the field of medicine, including William Thomas Green Morton and Samuel Guthrie.

GUIDES: *Guide to Manuscript Collections in the National Museum of History and Technology* (Smithsonian Institution Press, 1978).

SEE: NUCMC, 1980.

DC19-616

Smithsonian Institution
National Museum of American History
Department of History of Science and Technology
Division of Military History
AHB 4013
12th Street and Constitution Avenue, N.W.
Washington DC 20560

(202) 357-1883

OPEN: M-F 9-5:15; closed weekends and holidays
ACCESS: prior appointment required
COPYING FACILITIES: yes
MATERIALS SOLICITED: Military history materials.

HOLDINGS:
Total volume: 109 c.f.
Inclusive dates: 19th century -
Description: Photographs, personal papers, muster rolls, biographical information, and other materials concerning military personnel, ordnance makers and inspectors, weapons, forts, flags, and other aspects of military history.

GUIDES: *Guide to Manuscript Collections in the National Museum of History and Technology* (Smithsonian Institution Press, 1978).

SEE: NUCMC, 1980.

DC19-621

Smithsonian Institution
National Museum of American History
Department of History of Science and Technology
Division of Armed Forces History
AHB 4020
12th Street and Constitution Avenue, N.W.
Washington DC 20560

(202) 357-2249

OPEN: M-F 9-5:15; closed weekends and holidays
ACCESS: prior appointment required
COPYING FACILITIES: yes
MATERIALS SOLICITED: Naval history materials.

HOLDINGS:
Total volume: 299 c.f.
Inclusive dates: 1813 -
Description: U.S. Navy, Marine Corps, and Coast Guard historical materials. Included are papers of engineers, naval officers, seamen, inventors, and manufacturers, and a purser's journal documenting Matthew C. Perry's 1852-54 mission to Japan. Photographs, biographical files, ship drawings and plans, lighthouse and buoy drawings, and a collection concerning the Smithsonian Institution's efforts to salvage and restore the U.S.S. *Tecumseh*, a Civil War ironclad, also are included.

GUIDES: *Guide to Manuscript Collections in the National Museum of History and Technology* (Smithsonian Institution Press, 1978).

SEE: NUCMC, 1980.

SEE: Allard, Crawley, and Edmison.

DC19-626

Smithsonian Institution
National Museum of American History
Department of History of Science and Technology
Division of Photographic History
AHB 5713
12th Street and Constitution Avenue, N.W.
Washington DC 20560

(202) 357-2059

OPEN: Wednesdays 10-4
ACCESS: prior appointment required
COPYING FACILITIES: yes
MATERIALS SOLICITED: Materials concerning the history of photography.

HOLDINGS:
Total volume: 51 c.f.
Inclusive dates: 1881 -
Description: Patent specifications and drawings of inventions of photographic and optical equipment; and press releases, biographical information, and correspondence dealing with photographic and optical equipment, photographic art, and photographers.

GUIDES: *Guide to Manuscript Collections in the National Museum of History and Technology* (Smithsonian Institution Press, 1978).

SEE: NUCMC, 1980.

SEE: Novotny.

SEE ALSO: Shirley L. Green, comp., *Pictorial Resources in the Washington, D.C., Area* (Library of Congress, 1976).

DC19-631

Smithsonian Institution
National Museum of American History
Department of History of Science and Technology
Division of Physical Sciences
AHB 5123
12th Street and Constitution Avenue, N.W.
Washington DC 20560

(202) 357-2482, 2089

OPEN: M-F 9-5:15; closed weekends and holidays
ACCESS: prior appointment required
COPYING FACILITIES: yes
MATERIALS SOLICITED: Materials concerning the physical sciences.

HOLDINGS:
Total volume: 85 c.f.; 9 items
Inclusive dates: 1797 -
Description: Personal papers of the John William Draper family, Andrew Ellicott, and other scientists, inventors, and surveyors; records of scientific instrument and equipment manufacturers; photographs of scientists and equipment; patents and illustrations of instruments used in chemistry and other sciences; and figures and notes comparing barometers in branch offices of the National Weather Service with standard instruments.

GUIDES: *Guide to Manuscript Collections in the National Museum of History and Technology* (Smithsonian Institution Press, 1978).

SEE: NUCMC, 1980.

DC19-636

Smithsonian Institution
National Museum of American History
Department of History of Science and Technology
Division of Transportation
AHB 5010
12th Street and Constitution Avenue, N.W.
Washington DC 20560

(202) 357-2025

OPEN: M-F 9-5:15; closed weekends and holidays
ACCESS: prior appointment required
COPYING FACILITIES: yes
MATERIALS SOLICITED: Transportation materials.

HOLDINGS:
Total volume: 591 c.f.
Inclusive dates: 1831 -
Description: Photographs of sailing ships, other marine craft, fire fighting equipment, non-rail land transportation, streetcars, streetcar construction, shipyards, and railroad cars, including 13,000 negatives of Pullman cars. Other materials include drawings and charts concerning marine transportation, plans of lighthouses, business records of locomotive manufacturers, papers of marine architects and a railroad president, an Army Corps of Engineers study of inland waterways, 1956, and WPA Historic American Merchant Marine Survey records.

GUIDES: *Guide to Manuscript Collections in the National Museum of History and Technology* (Smithsonian Institution Press, 1978).

SEE: NUCMC, 1980.

SEE: Allard, Crawley, and Edmison.

DC19-641

Smithsonian Institution
National Museum of American History
Dibner Library
12th Street and Constitution Avenue, N.W.
Washington DC 20560

(202) 357-1568

OPEN: by appointment only
COPYING FACILITIES: yes

HOLDINGS:
Total volume: 16 c.f.; 200 vols. and boxes
Inclusive dates: 13th century -
Description: Materials concerning the history of science and technology since the Renaissance, covering electricity, magnetism, astronomy, chemistry, and early physics. Among the holdings are papers, photographs, and portraits of notable scientists, including Isaac Newton, John Dalton, Max Planck, Albert Einstein, and Benjamin Silliman; scientific manuscripts of Newton, and manuscript copies of works by Aristotle, Johannes de Sacrobosco, Boethius, and Renaissance authors; and speeches given by prominent scientists, including Guglielmo Marconi's Nobel Prize acceptance address.

GUIDES: *Guide to Manuscript Collections in the National Museum of History and Technology* (Smithsonian Institution Press, 1978).

SEE: Spalek.

DC19-646

Smithsonian Institution
National Museum of American History
National Numismatics Collections
AHB 4000
12th Street and Constitution Avenue, N.W.
Washington DC 20560

(202) 357-1798

OPEN: M-F 9-5:15; closed weekends and holidays
ACCESS: prior appointment required
COPYING FACILITIES: yes
MATERIALS SOLICITED: Materials concerning numismatics.

HOLDINGS:
Total volume: 20 c.f.
Inclusive dates: 1930 -
Description: Papers of Herbert H. Bratter, consultant to the Departments of Commerce and Treasury, concerning monetary policy, international monetary conferences, inflation, and related financial issues. There are also clippings about numismatic history and photographs of coins.

GUIDES: *Guide to Manuscript Collections in the National Museum of History and Technology* (Smithsonian Institution Press, 1978).

DC19-651
Smithsonian Institution
National Museum of American History
National Philatelic Collections
AHB 4004
12th Street and Constitution Avenue, N.W.
Washington DC 20560

(202) 357-1796

OPEN: M-F 9-5:15; closed weekends and holidays
ACCESS: prior appointment required
COPYING FACILITIES: yes
MATERIALS SOLICITED: Postal history materials.

HOLDINGS:
Total volume: 367 c.f.
Inclusive dates: 1863 -
Description: Records of the U.S. Postal Service; and its predecessor, the U.S. Post Office Department, 1894- ; Railway Mail Service records, 1922-66, documenting railway post offices in the United States; Internal Revenue Service records, 1863-1925, concerning commodity tax stamps; 19th century records of local U.S. post offices; and photographs and other documents concerning stamps and postal history.

GUIDES: *Guide to Manuscript Collections in the National Museum of History and Technology* (Smithsonian Institution Press, 1978).

SEE: NUCMC, 1980.

DC19-700
Society of the Cincinnati
2118 Massachusetts Avenue, N.W.
Washington DC 20008

(202) 785-0540

OPEN: M-F 10-4 by appointment only; closed weekends and holidays
ACCESS: by prior appointment
COPYING FACILITIES: yes
MATERIALS SOLICITED: Materials concerning the Society of the Cincinnati and the Revolutionary War and its participants. Will also accept papers of Society members and materials concerning Anderson House and its contents.

HOLDINGS:
Total volume: 60 l.f.
Inclusive dates: 1720 -
Description: Primarily the archives of the General Society of the Cincinnati, founded in 1783, but also including records of State chapters. Additional holdings include papers of the Larz Anderson family, mostly concerning the Society's headquarters building, and private papers, muster rolls, orderly books and other manuscripts pertaining to the Revolutionary War and other aspects of U.S. history.

SEE: Allard, Crawley, and Edmison.

SEE ALSO: John D. Kilbourne, 'French Manuscripts in the Archives of the Society of the Cincinnati,' *Manuscripts* 27 (Winter 1975).

DC19-750
Society of Woman Geographers
1619 New Hampshire Avenue, N.W.
Washington DC 20009

(202) 265-2669

OPEN: Tu, F 9:30-2:30; closed other days
ACCESS: by appointment
COPYING FACILITIES: no
MATERIALS SOLICITED: Material by and about members of the Society.

HOLDINGS:
Total volume: 17 l.f.
Inclusive dates: 1925 -
Description: Correspondence, biographical and professional activities data, photographs, oral history tapes and other materials relating to members. Also contained are business and financial records of the Society, an organization of women engaged in geographical work and its allied disciplines.

SEE: Hinding.

DC19-800
Soil Conservation Service
Information Division
Audio-Visual Branch
14th Street and Independence Avenue, S.W.
Washington DC

MAILING ADDRESS:
P.O. Box 2890
Washington DC 20250

no telephone

OPEN: M-F 8-4:30; closed weekends and holidays
ACCESS: qualified researchers
COPYING FACILITIES: yes
MATERIALS SOLICITED: Black and white photographs concerning soil conservation.

HOLDINGS:
Total volume: 75,000 items
Inclusive dates: 1934 -
Description: Black and white photographs, arranged alphabetically, documenting agricultural problems, particularly soil erosion. Subjects covered include environmental programs, irrigation, dams, reservoirs, flood control, bank erosion and stabilization, poor farming practices, pollution, and urban and rural erosion problems.

SEE: Novotny.

DC19-900
Supreme Court of the United States
Curator's Office
Washington DC 20543

(202) 479-3298

OPEN: M-F 9-4:30; closed weekends and holidays
COPYING FACILITIES: yes
MATERIALS SOLICITED: Papers and other materials concerning Supreme Court Justices, past and present, with emphasis on their service on the Court.

HOLDINGS:
Total volume: 1,200 items
Inclusive dates: 1782 -
Description: 200 items of personal correspondence, representing most members of the Supreme Court since 1789; 1,000 individual and group photographs of Supreme Court Justices, including a photograph of each one's official portrait; and 20 audio tapes and films of interviews with Justices.

DC20-600
Trinity College
Archives
Washington DC 20017

(202) 939-5000

OPEN: M-F 10-5; closed weekends and College holidays
ACCESS: appointment preferred
COPYING FACILITIES: yes

HOLDINGS:
Total volume: 500 c.f.
Inclusive dates: 1897 -
Description: Non-current records of Trinity College, including complete minutes of the board of trustees since 1897; minutes of advisory and auxiliary board, student government, and faculty meetings; notebooks and scrapbooks from the dean of students' office; and photographs of students, faculty members, and campus buildings.

SEE: Hinding; Robbins.

DC21-510
University of the District of Columbia
Learning Resources Division
Archives and Special Collections
425 2nd Street, N.W.
Washington DC 20001

(202) 727-2200 through -2211

OPEN: M-F 9-5; closed weekends and holidays
COPYING FACILITIES: yes
MATERIALS SOLICITED: Materials related to the history of the University of the District of Columbia and its predecessors.

HOLDINGS:
Total volume: 102 l.f. and 60 file drawers
Inclusive dates: 1851 -
Description: Official documents, correspondence and reports relating to the history and activities of the University of the District of Columbia since its founding.

DC22-500

Alexander Graham Bell Association for the Deaf
Library
3417 Volta Place
Washington DC 20007

(202) 337-5220

OPEN: M-F 9-4:30; closed weekends and holidays
ACCESS: appointment suggested
COPYING FACILITIES: yes
MATERIALS SOLICITED: Alexander Graham Bell family materials. Will also accept early materials related to the education of the deaf.

HOLDINGS:
Total volume: 75 l.f.
Inclusive dates: 1870 - 1925
Description: Materials concerning work on behalf of the deaf, chiefly comprised of papers of Alexander Graham Bell. Included are 350 letters from Bell, 150 from his father, Alexander Melville Bell, 150 from Helen Keller, and others from Annie Sullivan, John Hitz, and Gardiner Greene Hubbard. There are also 20 boxes of business correspondence addressed to Bell, 1880-1922; 40 laboratory notebooks of Bell; his unpublished manuscripts; and 500 photographs of Bell, Helen Keller, conventions attended by Bell, and schools for the deaf.

SEE: Hamer.

DC23-70

Walter Reed Army Medical Center
Libraries
Medical Library Building 2
Room 2G
Walter Reed Army Medical Center
Washington DC 20307

(202) 576-1238

OPEN: M-Th 8-8, F 8-5, Sa 9-5, Su 1-5; closed holidays
ACCESS: special arrangements required
COPYING FACILITIES: yes

HOLDINGS:
Total volume: 3 vols.
Inclusive dates: not specified
Description: A manuscript history of the Walter Reed Center, entitled, 'Borden's Dream.'

DC23-100

Washington Cathedral
Central Files
Mount Saint Alban
Washington DC 20016

(202) 537-6247

OPEN: M-F by appointment only; closed weekends and holidays
ACCESS: serious researchers only; permission for use must be requested in writing from Provost of the Cathedral
COPYING FACILITIES: yes
MATERIALS SOLICITED: Records of the Washington Cathedral.

HOLDINGS:
Total volume: 200 file drawers
Inclusive dates: 1890's -
Description: Records of the Washington Cathedral, including sermons, magazine articles, financial records, minutes of chapter meetings, records of the committee to establish the Cathedral, a copy of the act of Congress establishing the Cathedral in 1893, and records of its construction.

DC23-250

Washington Hospital Center
Medical Library
110 Irving Street, N.W.
Washington DC 20010

(202) 541-6221

OPEN: M-F 8:30-5; closed weekends and holidays
ACCESS: approved researchers
COPYING FACILITIES: yes
MATERIALS SOLICITED: Materials concerning the Washington Hospital Center and its three predecessor hospitals.

HOLDINGS:
Total volume: 95 l.f.
Inclusive dates: 1870 -
Description: Official records, correspondence, photographs, diaries, personnel materials, and 33 oral history interviews with physicians, administrators, and others, concerning the Washington Hospital Center and its predecessor hospitals: Central Dispensary and Emergency Hospital, Garfield Memorial Hospital, and the Episcopal Eye, Ear and Throat Hospital.

SEE: Meckler and McMullin.

DC23-500

Wesley Theological Seminary
Library
4400 Massachusetts Avenue, N.W.
Washington DC 20016

(202) 363-0922

OPEN: M-F 8:30-10, Sa 9-1, Su 6-9; shorter hours during summer
COPYING FACILITIES: yes

HOLDINGS:
Total volume: 200 items; 75 vols.
Inclusive dates: 1760 - 1940
Description: Materials related chiefly to Methodism, especially the former Methodist Protestant church. Included are sermons of Nicholas Snethen; letters of John Wesley, 1760-90; letters of Francis Asbury, 1790-1805; and conference journals of the Methodist Protestant and Methodist Episcopal churches.

SEE: Hamer.

DC23-700

Whitefriars Hall
Library
1600 Webster Street, N.W.
Washington DC 20017

(202) 526-1221

OPEN: M-F 9-5; closed weekends and holidays
ACCESS: appointment required
COPYING FACILITIES: yes
MATERIALS SOLICITED: Materials related to the history of the Carmelite Order.

HOLDINGS:
Total volume: 70 microfilm reels
Inclusive dates: 13th century - 17th century
Description: Microfilm copies of European manuscripts relating to the Carmelite Order or written by members of the Order. Most of the manuscripts are in Latin, and the remainder in French and German.

DC23-800

William Alanson White Psychiatric Foundation
Archives
1610 New Hampshire Avenue, N.W.
Washington DC 20009

(202) 667-3008

OPEN: by appointment only
ACCESS: appointment required
COPYING FACILITIES: yes

HOLDINGS:
Total volume: 2,000 discs; several dozen manuscripts
Inclusive dates: 1927 - 1948
Description: Unpublished manuscripts and original recordings of lectures of psychiatrist Harry Stack Sullivan.

FLORIDA

Since 1968 the Division of Archives, History and Records Management of Florida's Department of State has administered a statewide program for preserving local public records. County and municipal officials are responsible by statute for maintaining disposition schedules of records in their offices. The State Archives in Tallahassee maintains a central file of all approved disposition authorizations.

Permanently valuable records may be retained at the local level or transferred to the State Archives, which also has some 3,000 reels of microfilm of vital, probate, land, and other county records filmed by the Church of Jesus Christ of Latter-day Saints. The Florida State Archives also provides a security microfilm storage service for local governmental agencies.

BOCA RATON

FL40-250
Florida Atlantic University
Library
Boca Raton FL 33431

(305) 393-3762

OPEN: M-Th 8-midnight, F 8-6, Sa 9-5, Su 1-midnight; closed holidays
COPYING FACILITIES: no
MATERIALS SOLICITED: Materials by and about Theodore Pratt. Will also accept history of Palm Beach County, FL.

HOLDINGS:
Total volume: 20 l.f.
Inclusive dates: 1901 -
Description: Work papers and records of author Theodore Pratt, including manuscripts of his books. Also held are his notes, outlines, research material, galley proofs, records of submissions, correspondence, and records of royalties.

SEE: NUCMC, 1969.

BRADENTON

FL60-720
South Florida Museum and Bishop Planetarium
201 10th Street, West
Bradenton FL 33505

(813) 746-4132

OPEN: Tu-F 10-5, Sa, Su 1-5; closed Mondays, Thanksgiving, Christmas, and New Year's
COPYING FACILITIES: no

HOLDINGS:
Total volume: not specified
Inclusive dates: 1772 -
Description: A ledger, a log book of the yacht 'Ripple', used in Manatee County, FL, in the 1920's-30's, and photographs of construction of the Panama Canal, troops in Cuba and the Philippines during the Spanish-American War, France during World War I, Seminole Indians in 1900, and Melanesia in the 1930's.

CORAL GABLES

FL80-120
City of Coral Gables Historical Archives
Coral Gables Police Station
Room B-2
2801 Salzedo Street
Coral Gables FL

MAILING ADDRESS:
P.O. Drawer 141549
Coral Gables FL 33114

(305) 442-6443

OPEN: M-F 8-5; closed weekends and holidays
ACCESS: advance arrangements with historian or other staff required
COPYING FACILITIES: yes
MATERIALS SOLICITED: Materials relating to Coral Gables history, including photographs, written histories, or oral histories. Will also accept materials relating to Dade County, FL.

HOLDINGS:
Total volume: 400 sq.f.
Inclusive dates: early 20th century -
Description: Materials relating to the City of Coral Gables, including photographs dating from its earliest development, architectural records, plans, oral histories or early pioneers, and written histories.

FL80-160
Dermatology Foundation of Miami
Tape Studio and Library
480 Casuarina Concourse
Coral Gables FL 33143

(305) 667-3224

OPEN: M-Th 9-1; closed other days and holidays
ACCESS: prior arrangements required
COPYING FACILITIES: yes
MATERIALS SOLICITED: Oral history interviews with dermatologists. Will also accept other taped material relating to the goals of the project.

HOLDINGS:
Total volume: 118 items
Inclusive dates: 1962 -
Description: Taped interviews with senior and leading dermatologists throughout the world. There are also video recordings of interviews and of lectures and symposiums.

SEE: Meckler and McMullin.

FL80-820
University of Miami
Richter Library
Archives Division
Coral Gables FL 33124

(305) 284-3247

OPEN: M-F 9-4; closed weekends and holidays
COPYING FACILITIES: yes
MATERIALS SOLICITED: Materials on the history of the University. Will also accept materials relating to local history, personal and corporate papers, and photographs.

HOLDINGS:
Total volume: 362 l.f.
Inclusive dates: 1926 -
Description: Materials relating to the University, including records and correspondence of the founders and first presidents, non-current faculty personnel records, a photograph collection, tape recordings of campus events, and films of basketball games. There are also 55 literary manuscripts, chiefly relating to Florida.

DAYTONA BEACH

FL120-330
Halifax Historical Society, Inc.
224 1/2 South Beach Street
Daytona Beach FL

MAILING ADDRESS:
P.O. Box 5051
Daytona Beach FL 32018

(904) 252-6659

OPEN: M-F 1-4, Su 2-5; closed Saturdays
and holidays
COPYING FACILITIES: no
MATERIALS SOLICITED: Historical materials pertaining to Daytona Beach and eastern Florida. Will also accept U.S. history materials.

HOLDINGS:
> *Total volume:* 12 file drawers; 2,500 photographs
> *Inclusive dates:* 1870 -
> *Description:* Manuscripts and photographs relating chiefly to eastern Volusia County, FL. Included are hotel registers, court records, and diaries and reminiscences of early pioneers.

DELAND

FL140-240
Florida Baptist Historical Society
DeLand FL

MAILING ADDRESS:
Stetson University, Box 1353
DeLand FL 32720

(904) 734-4121, Ext. 545

OPEN: M-F 8-4; closed weekends,
Christmas, Easter, July 4, and term
breaks
ACCESS: approval of library staff or
curator required
COPYING FACILITIES: yes
MATERIALS SOLICITED: Baptist historical
materials.

HOLDINGS:
> *Total volume:* 2 file cabinets; 50 l.f.
> *Inclusive dates:* 1800 -
> *Description:* Diaries of early Baptist leaders, biographies, early church records, manuscripts on Baptist history, and microfilms of Baptist historical materials in other libraries.

GUIDES: Harry Garwood, *The Florida
Baptist Historical Collection Index*
(1960).

FL140-710
Stetson University
Archives
DeLand FL

MAILING ADDRESS:
Box 1418
DeLand FL 32720

(904) 734-4121

OPEN: M-F 9-noon; closed weekends and
holidays
COPYING FACILITIES: yes

MATERIALS SOLICITED: Materials relating
to Stetson University. Will also accept
materials relating to DeLand and
Volusia County.

HOLDINGS:
> *Total volume:* 150 l.f.; 5 file cabinets
> *Inclusive dates:* 1883 -
> *Description:* A collection of correspondence relating chiefly to Stetson University. There are also personal letters from early DeLand settlers; photographs of the campus, faculty, students and athletic teams; and biographies of all presidents and former and present faculty members.

FORT LAUDERDALE

FL160-240
Fort Lauderdale Historical Society,
Inc.
219 S.W. 2nd Avenue
Fort Lauderdale FL 33301

MAILING ADDRESS:
P.O. Box 14043
Fort Lauderdale FL 33302

(305) 463-4431

OPEN: M-F 9:30-4:30; closed weekends
and holidays
ACCESS: advance arrangements required
COPYING FACILITIES: yes
MATERIALS SOLICITED: Local history.

HOLDINGS:
> *Total volume:* 220 l.f.; 165,000 photo negatives
> *Inclusive dates:* early 19th century -
> *Description:* Data files on Fort Lauderdale history, including biographical information on local families, photo negatives and map collections and oral history collection of more than 150 tapes.

SEE ALSO: a subject guide to the collection available from the institution.

FORT MYERS

FL180-210
Edison Winter Home and Museum
2350 McGregor Blvd.
Fort Meyers FL 33901

(813) 334-3614

OPEN: M-Sa 9-4, Su noon-4; closed
Christmas
ACCESS: by appointment only
COPYING FACILITIES: no
MATERIALS SOLICITED: Thomas A. Edison materials.

HOLDINGS:
> *Total volume:* 250 items
> *Inclusive dates:* 1847 - 1931
> *Description:* A collection of correspondence, journals, logbooks, and manuscripts relating to Thomas A. Edison. Included are letters to and from Edison, experiment logbooks, inter-office correspondence, business records, photographs, technical drawings, and original phonograph recordings.

GAINESVILLE

FL220-280
Gainesville Public Library
Reference Department
222 East University Avenue
Gainesville FL 32601

(904) 374-2091

OPEN: M-Th 9-9, F 9-5, Sa 9-5, Su 1-5;
closed holidays and weekends when
followed by a Monday holiday
COPYING FACILITIES: yes
MATERIALS SOLICITED: Local history
materials.

HOLDINGS:
> *Total volume:* 250 items
> *Inclusive dates:* 1900 -
> *Description:* Historical photographs of Gainesville and Alachua County, FL, with accompanying captions.

FL220-792
University of Florida
Florida State Museum
Gainesville FL 32611

(904) 392-1721

OPEN: Su 1-5, M-Sa 9-5, holidays 1-5;
closed Christmas
ACCESS: appointment required
COPYING FACILITIES: yes
MATERIALS SOLICITED: Audible documents and other materials dealing with the natural and social history of the Caribbean and Southeast.

HOLDINGS:
> *Total volume:* 350 sq.f.
> *Inclusive dates:* 1895 -
> *Description:* Archives of the Museum, 1895- , Florida oral history interviews, field notes pertaining to the natural history and ethnography of Florida and the circum-Caribbean region, and a bioacoustical archive of animal recordings.

FL220-795
University of Florida
Libraries
P. K. Yonge Library of Florida
History
441 Library West
Gainesville FL 32611

(904) 392-0319

OPEN: M-F 8-5; closed weekends and
holidays
COPYING FACILITIES: yes
MATERIALS SOLICITED: Correspondence, manuscripts, and maps relating to Florida history, and microfilm of government documents from the British and Spanish colonial periods. Will also accept historical photographs and postcards.

HOLDINGS:
> *Total volume:* not specified
> *Inclusive dates:* 1513 -
> *Description:* Materials relating to the colonial, territorial, and statehood periods of Florida history, including correspondence of politicians and other prominent persons, diaries, journals, manuscript maps, business records, and photographs.

Also preserved are microfilm copies of colonial Spanish Florida documents from the Archivo General de Indias in Seville and other Spanish archives, as well as British colonial materials from the Public Record Office.

GUIDES: *Dictionary Catalog of the P. K. Yonge Library of Florida History*, (G. K. Hall, 1977).

SEE: Hamer.

SEE: Hinding; Davis; Allard, Edmison, and Crawley; Beers-Confederate.

SEE ALSO: Published guides to collections of Spanish colonial documents are available from the institution.

FL220-800

University of Florida
Libraries
Rare Books and Manuscripts
  Department
531 Library West
Gainesville FL 32611

(904) 392-0321

OPEN: M-F 8-5; closed weekends and holidays
COPYING FACILITIES: yes
MATERIALS SOLICITED: Materials by or pertaining to women literary figures in particular and literary writers in general. Will also accept materials dealing with the Caribbean area.

HOLDINGS:
   Total volume: 550 l.f.
   Inclusive dates: late 17th century -
   Description: Historical manuscripts dealing with Haiti's war of independence, 1801-03, and related earlier documents; notary papers from Jeremie, Haiti; papers of M. K. Rawlings, Zora Neale Hurston, Lillian Smith, Edith Pope, John D. McDonald, Alden Hatch and Margaret Dreier Robins.

SEE: Hamer; NUCMC, 1959-64, 69, 74, 78.

SEE: Meckler and McMullin; Robbins; Ingram; Leventhal and Mooney - III.

SEE ALSO: Laura V. Monti, comp., *A Calendar of Rochambeau Papers at the University of Florida Libraries* (Univ. of Florida Libraries, 1972); Andrea Hinding and Rosemary Richardson, comps., *Archival and Manuscript Resources for the Study of Women's History: A Beginning* (Univ. of Minnesota Libraries, Social Welfare History Archives Center, 1972); Thomas H. English, *Roads to Research: Distinguished Library Collections of the Southeast* (Univ. of Georgia Press, 1968).

FL220-805

University of Florida
Libraries
University Archives
450 Library East
Gainesville FL 32611

(904) 392-6547

OPEN: M-F 9-1; closed weekends and holidays
COPYING FACILITIES: yes

MATERIALS SOLICITED: Material relating to the University of Florida, including non-current records of the institution and organizations, photographs, and scrapbooks.

HOLDINGS:
   Total volume: 950 l.f.; 388 c.f.; 11 file cabinets
   Inclusive dates: 1886 -
   Description: Correspondence relating chiefly to the University of Florida, letters of the University's builders, campus photographs, and biographies of University presidents and faculty members.

SEE: Hamer.

JACKSONVILLE

FL280-380

Jacksonville Historical Society
Jacksonville University
University Blvd.
Jacksonville FL 32211

(904) 744-3950, Ext. 3278

SEE: Hamer.

Questionnaire not returned.

FL280-390

Jacksonville Public Library
Delius Collection
122 North Ocean Street
Jacksonville FL 32202

(904) 633-2426

OPEN: M-F 9-9, Sa 9-6; closed Sundays and holidays
COPYING FACILITIES: yes
MATERIALS SOLICITED: Deliana, especially materials relating to Frederick Delius in Florida.

HOLDINGS:
   Total volume: 4 l.f.
   Inclusive dates: 1896 -
   Description: A collection of Frederick Delius music scores, including his first published composition. There are also copies of 15 letters; manuscript accounts of the rediscovery of Delius' home at Solano Grove; copies of all Delius materials relating to Florida in the Delius Trust, London; monographs; clippings; photographs; and performance programs.

FL280-400

Jacksonville Public Library
Florida Collection
122 North Ocean Street
Jacksonville FL 32202

(904) 633-3305

OPEN: M-F 9-5:30; closed weekends and holidays
COPYING FACILITIES: yes
MATERIALS SOLICITED: Floridiana, especially Jacksonville-related material.

HOLDINGS:
   Total volume: 205 boxes; 5,054 items; 100 reels microfilm; 2 drawers photographs; 325 maps
   Inclusive dates: 1591 -
   Description: A collection of materials on Florida with particular emphasis on northeastern Florida and Jacksonville.

SEE: Leventhal and Mooney - III.

FL280-420

Jacksonville University
Carl S. Swisher Library
2800 University Blvd., North
Jacksonville FL 32211

(904) 744-3950

OPEN: M-F 8:30-4; closed weekends and holidays
ACCESS: visitor's pass required
COPYING FACILITIES: yes
MATERIALS SOLICITED: Material relating to Florida and Frederick Delius. Will also accept other materials relating to the University's liberal arts curriculum.

HOLDINGS:
   Total volume: not specified
   Inclusive dates: 1895 -
   Description: The manuscript score of *Koanga*, and letters of Frederick Delius; materials relating to Florida; and the University archives, including University reports, presidents' papers, and trustee reports.

MELBOURNE

FL420-240

Florida Institute of Technology
Library
Melbourne FL

MAILING ADDRESS:
P.O. Box 1150
Melbourne FL 32901

(305) 723-3701

OPEN: M-Th 8-11, F 8-5, Sa noon-8, Su 2-10; closed holidays; variable summer hours
COPYING FACILITIES: yes
MATERIALS SOLICITED: Space program manuscripts relating to Cape Kennedy. Will also accept original manuscripts of well-known authors.

HOLDINGS:
   Total volume: 100 l.f.
   Inclusive dates: 20th century
   Description: The collection consists of the Institute's archives, the personal papers of General John B. Medaris, and some materials relating to Cape Kennedy.

MIAMI

FL440-150
Dade County Public Schools
Social Studies Office
Black Archives and Oral History
    Collection
Historical Museum of Southern
    Florida
3280 South Miami Avenue
Miami FL

MAILING ADDRESS:
1444 Biscayne Blvd.
Miami FL 33132

(305) 375-1492

OPEN: M-F by appointment; closed
    weekends and holidays
COPYING FACILITIES: yes
MATERIALS SOLICITED: Materials con-
    cerning the black community in south-
    ern Florida, including photographs,
    manuscripts, oral history recordings
    and transcripts, non-current records of
    local organizations such as churches,
    schools, businesses, and community
    groups, and public records which re-
    flect racial discrimination.

HOLDINGS:
    Total volume: 250 items
    Inclusive dates: 1835 - 1964
    Description: Photographs, manuscripts
    and oral history recordings tracing the
    experience of early black settlers in Dade
    County, and copies of local ordinances
    and resolutions relating to racial discrimi-
    nation.

FL440-320
Historical Association of Southern
    Florida
Charlton W. Tebeau Library of
    Florida History
101 West Flagler Street
Miami FL 33130

(305) 854-3289

OPEN: by appointment only; closed
    holidays
COPYING FACILITIES: yes
MATERIALS SOLICITED: Materials relating
    to the development and/or history of
    southern Florida, including archaeologi-
    cal topics.

HOLDINGS:
    Total volume: 160 l.f.; 45,000
    photographs
    Inclusive dates: 1743 -
    Description: Collections relating to
    southern Florida, with emphasis on Dade
    County. Included are the papers of
    individuals, some diaries and
    unpublished materials, literary manu-
    scripts, and records of organizations.
    Audio-visual materials include oral his-
    tory tapes and transcripts, and photo-
    graphs and negatives, including some of
    Cuba and the Bahamas.

SEE: Hamer.

FL440-530
Miami-Dade Public Library
Florida Collection
1 Biscayne Blvd.
Miami FL 33132

(305) 579-5001

OPEN: M-Sa 9-6; closed Sundays and
    holidays
COPYING FACILITIES: yes
MATERIALS SOLICITED: Florida and local
    history.

HOLDINGS:
    Total volume: 17,662 items
    Inclusive dates: late 19th and 20th
    century
    Description: The collection is com-
    prised chiefly of 17,500 photographic neg-
    atives of the Miami area, 1895-1950's. It
    also contains 98 manuscripts by Florida
    authors and oral history interviews with
    22 Florida pioneers.

SEE: Hamer; NUCMC, 1965.

SEE: Robbins.

ORLANDO

FL560-40
American Lawn Bowls Association
420 North Hughey Street
Orlando FL

MAILING ADDRESS:
P.O. Box 6141-C
Orlando FL 32803

no telephone

OPEN: by appointment only
COPYING FACILITIES: no
MATERIALS SOLICITED: Records of lawn
    bowls tournaments throughout the
    United States. Will also accept pho-
    tographs, minutes of meetings, and oth-
    er items pertaining to organizations af-
    filiated with the American Lawn Bowls
    Association.

HOLDINGS:
    Total volume: 28 l.f.
    Inclusive dates: 1915 -
    Description: Tournament records, min-
    utes of meetings, financial reports, histori-
    cal sketches of clubs, promotional re-
    leases, and photographs, relating to the
    sport of lawn bowls in the United States.

FL560-590
Orange County Historical
    Commission
812 East Rollins Street
Loch Haven Park
Orlando FL 32803

(305) 898-8320

OPEN: Tu, W 10-4 by appointment only;
    closed Mondays and holidays
ACCESS: serious researchers, high school
    age or older
COPYING FACILITIES: no
MATERIALS SOLICITED: Documents and
    photographs relating to central Florida.

HOLDINGS:
    Total volume: 3,000 photographs;
    500 items
    Inclusive dates: 1859 - 1940
    Description: Photographs of Orange
    County, chiefly 1879-1910. Documents
    include the county's oldest deed (1859),
    business account books, hotel guest regis-
    ters, and the civil records of Orlando and
    Orange County.

PALM BEACH

FL580-320
The Henry Morrison Flagler Museum
Whitehall Way
Palm Beach FL

MAILING ADDRESS:
P.O. Box 969
Palm Beach FL 33480

(305) 655-2833

OPEN: Tu-Sa 10-5, Su noon-5; closed
    Mondays, Christmas and New Year's
    Day
ACCESS: by appointment only
COPYING FACILITIES: yes
MATERIALS SOLICITED: Area history,
    concentrating on H. M. Flagler, the
    Flagler System, Florida east coast de-
    velopment, the Flagler family, and
    Palm Beach County.

HOLDINGS:
    Total volume: 550 boxes
    Inclusive dates: 1880 - 1920
    Description: Records of the building of
    the railroad from Jacksonville to Key
    West; records of Florida land companies,
    hotels, farms, etc., of the Flagler System;
    letter books of H. M. Flagler; family let-
    ters; photographs; and plans and drawings
    of railroads and buildings.

PENSACOLA

FL600-640
Pensacola Historical Museum
405 South Adams Street
Pensacola FL 32501

(904) 433-1559

OPEN: M-Sa 9-4:30; closed Sundays and
    holidays
COPYING FACILITIES: yes
MATERIALS SOLICITED: Pensacola,
    Escambia County, and northwestern
    Florida history.

HOLDINGS:
    Total volume: 90 boxes; 6 l.f.; 3,600
    genealogical sheets; 35,000 photographs;
    10 hours of tapes
    Inclusive dates: 1500 -
    Description: Manuscripts relating to
    the history of Pensacola, Escambia Coun-
    ty and northwest Florida. Included are
    diaries, letters, photographs and negatives
    of local persons and events, and genea-
    logical records.

SEE: Novotny; Hinding.

SEE ALSO: Richard C. Davis, *North
    American Forest History: A Guide to
    Archives and Manuscripts in the United
    States and Canada* (Clio Books, 1977).

FL600-800
The University of West Florida
John C. Pace Library
Pensacola FL 32514

(904) 474-2492

OPEN: M-F 8-4:30, Sa 8-noon; closed
Sundays, holidays and Saturdays during
Intersession
COPYING FACILITIES: yes
MATERIALS SOLICITED: Materials relating
to western Florida history, Florida
counties west of the Apalachicola Riv-
er, and Pensacola and its environs.
Will also accept materials relating to
the southern and Gulf coasts.

HOLDINGS:
Total volume: 650,000 items
Inclusive dates: 1700 -
Description: Manuscripts, family papers, business records, and other materials, with emphasis on the period
1821-1940, relating primarily to the history, life, and culture of Pensacola, and
the 10 western counties in the Florida
panhandle.

GUIDES: The First One Hundred: A Catalog of Manuscripts and Special Collections (Univ. of West Florida, Library,
1972).

SEE: NUCMC, 1969, 76.

SEE: Allard, Crawley, and Edmison;
Hinding.

SEE ALSO: Ann Novotny, ed., Picture
Sources 3 (Special Libraries Assn.,
1975); Alan M. Meckler and Ruth
McMullin, comps., Oral History Collections (Bowker, 1975); Marion Viccars,
'The First One Hundred,' Manuscripts
25 (Winter 1973). Inventories of individual collections available at the repository.

Richard C. Davis, North American Forest
History: A Guide to Archives and Manu-
scripts in the United States and Canada
(Clio Books, 1977).

FL600-880
West Florida Regional Library
Local History Collection
200 West Gregory Street
Pensacola FL 32501

(904) 438-5479

OPEN: M-Th 8-8, F, Sa 8-5; closed
Sundays and holidays
COPYING FACILITIES: yes

HOLDINGS:
Total volume: 30 items
Inclusive dates: early 1890's - 1960's
Description: Maps and photographs of
Pensacola.

St. Augustine

FL660-120
Castillo de San Marcos National
  Monument and
Fort Matanzas National Monument
1 Castillo Drive
St. Augustine FL 32084

(904) 829-6506

OPEN: M-F 8:15-5; closed weekends and
holidays
ACCESS: appointment required
COPYING FACILITIES: no
MATERIALS SOLICITED: Materials related
to the construction, repair, and operation of Castillo de San Marcos,
1672-1900, under Spanish, British, and
American control, and of Fort
Matanzas, 1742-1821, under Spanish
and British control, as well as items
concerning the political, social, and
economic history of Florida in the
same period. Will also accept materials
documenting the art of war, military
architecture and engineering, artillery
practice and operations, and individual
and unit drills and maneuvers from
1518 to 1821.

HOLDINGS:
Total volume: 178 microfilm reels
Inclusive dates: 1518 - 1833
Description: Microfilmed Spanish and
British records regarding Florida's colonial history, with emphasis on the construction and repair of Castillo de San
Marcos and Fort Matanzas, and military,
administrative, ecclesiastical, financial,
and personal matters in the area known
by the British as 'East Florida.'

SEE: Hamer.

SEE: Leventhal and Mooney - III.

SEE ALSO: Luis R. Arana, et al., Castillo
de San Marcos and Fort Matanzas National Monuments Historical Research
Management Plan (National Park Service, Office of Archaeology and Historic Preservation, 1967).

FL660-510
Marineland, Inc.
St. Augustine FL

MAILING ADDRESS:
Box 122, Route 1
St. Augustine FL 32084

(904) 471-1111

OPEN: daily 8-5
COPYING FACILITIES: yes
MATERIALS SOLICITED: Manuscripts, archives, visual documents, and recordings pertaining to all aspects of marine
life and phenomena.

HOLDINGS:
Total volume: not specified
Inclusive dates: 1938 -
Description: Daily weather data,
records of ocean conditions and unusual
marine phenomena, marine-related research manuscripts, business and other
records of Marineland, and photographs
and films of Marineland.

SEE ALSO: Ann Novotny, ed., Picture
Sources 3 (Special Libraries Assn.,
1975).

FL660-720
St. Augustine Historical Society
271 Charlotte Street
St. Augustine FL 32084

(904) 824-2872

OPEN: M-F 9-5; closed weekends and
holidays
ACCESS: advance notice requested
COPYING FACILITIES: yes
MATERIALS SOLICITED: Materials related
to Florida history, 1512-1763, east
Florida, 1763-1821, and St. Augustine
and northeast Florida, 1821- . Will also
accept materials related to Florida history, 1763- .

HOLDINGS:
Total volume: 25 l.f.; 20 items
Inclusive dates: 1740 -
Description: Deeds, business records,
family papers, city records, and oral his-
tory tapes.

SEE: Hamer.

SEE: Leventhal and Mooney - III.

St. Leo

FL680-720
St. Leo Abbey
Library
St. Leo FL 33574

(904) 588-8290

SEE: Hamer.

Questionnaire not returned.

St. Petersburg

FL720-720
St. Petersburg Historical Society
Waterfront Museum
335 Second Avenue, N.E.
St. Petersburg FL 33701

(813) 894-1052

OPEN: M-Sa 11-5, Su 1-5; closed
holidays
COPYING FACILITIES: no

HOLDINGS:
Total volume: 10 boxes
Inclusive dates: 1922 -
Description: Materials relating to the
history of St. Petersburg and its inhabitants, including some genealogical data,
as well as materials covering other varied
topics.

SEE: Hamer.

SEE: Hinding.

SANFORD

FL740-720
Sanford Memorial Library
520 East First Street
Sanford FL 32771

(305) 322-2182

SEE: Hamer; NUCMC, 1962.

Questionnaire not returned.

SEFFNER

FL750-200
Eleventh Bombardment Group (H)
   Association, Inc.
Historical Archives
P.O. Box 637
Seffner FL 33584

(813) 681-3544

OPEN: by appointment
COPYING FACILITIES: no
MATERIALS SOLICITED: Materials relating
   to the operation of U.S. Army Air
   Force bombardment units in the South
   Pacific from January 1940 to Decem-
   ber 1945. Will also accept materials re-
   lating to the combat air war in the
   Pacific, 1940-45.

HOLDINGS:
   Total volume: 28 l.f.; 2 trunks; 10
boxes
   Inclusive dates: 1940 -
   Description: Photographs, official reports, personal histories, logbooks, journals, microfilms of official reports and
records, mission reports, clippings, films,
and other materials relating to the Eleventh Bombardment Group (H) and its
combat activities in the Pacific during
World War II.

TALLAHASSEE

FL800-200
Florida A & M University
Black Archives, Research Center, and
   Museum
Tallahassee FL

MAILING ADDRESS:
FAMU Box 809
Tallahassee FL 32307

(904) 599-3020, 3021

OPEN: M-F 8-5; closed weekends
ACCESS: appointment required
COPYING FACILITIES: yes
MATERIALS SOLICITED: Records and pa-
   pers relating to Afro-Americans and
   their institutions in Florida and the
   United States, as well as relating to
   Africans. Will also accept materials on
   persons and organizations which influ-
   enced Afro-American history.

HOLDINGS:
   Total volume: 300 c.f.
   Inclusive dates: 1850's -
   Description: Correspondence of black
college presidents, records of black or-
ganizations primarily in Florida, records

of Florida A & M University, photographs of prominent blacks who visited
the University since the 1890's, and oral
history recordings of blacks over 65 years
old.

SEE: Schatz.

FL800-235
Florida Department of Natural
   Resources
Division of Resource Management
Bureau of State Lands
Elliot Building
401 South Monroe Street
Tallahassee FL

MAILING ADDRESS:
Crown Building
202 Blount Street
Tallahassee FL 32304

(904) 488-9380

OPEN: M-F 8-5; closed weekends and
   holidays
COPYING FACILITIES: yes

HOLDINGS:
   Total volume: 835 vols.; 222 c.f.
   Inclusive dates: 1775 -
   Description: Records, surveys, plats,
maps, field notes, patents and other ma-
terial relating to the title and description
of the public domain in Florida. Included
are the records transferred in 1907 from
the Office of the U.S. Surveyor-General
of Florida; records of the U.S. Land Of-
fice in Gainesville; records of the Florida
Department of Natural Resources; and
'Briefed Translations of Spanish Land
Grants in Florida,' prepared by the Work
Projects   Administration   Historical
Records Survey.

FL800-245
Florida Division of Archives, History
   and Records Management
Florida State Archives
R. A. Gray Building
South Bronough Street
Tallahassee FL

MAILING ADDRESS:
Department of State, The Capitol
Tallahassee FL 32304

(904) 487-2073

OPEN: M-F 8-5; closed weekends and
   holidays
COPYING FACILITIES: yes
MATERIALS SOLICITED: Florida State and
   territorial government records. Will
   also accept records of local governments, and private manuscripts which
   reflect upon State government activity.

HOLDINGS:
   Total volume: 16,000 c.f.
   Inclusive dates: 1821 -
   Description: Public records of Florida
territorial and State government offices
and agencies, including Governor, Secretary of State, Commissioner of Education, State Board of Pensions, Board of
Commissioners of State Institutions, Supreme Court, and various legislative committees. Also included are microfilms of
deed, marriage, and probate records of
most Florida counties, and a small num-

ber of manuscript collections relative to
government activities.

GUIDES: *Catalog of the Florida State Archives: Catalog Number 1* (1975).

SEE: Hamer (as Florida State Library).

SEE: Allard, Crawley, and Edmison;
   Hinding.

SEE ALSO: Richard C. Davis, *North
   American Forest History: A Guide to
   Archives and Manuscripts in the United
   States and Canada* (Clio Books, 1977);
   individual finding aids for most collec-
   tions available on request.

FL800-262
Florida State University
Robert Manning Strozier Library
Special Collections
Tallahassee FL 32306

(904) 644-3271

OPEN: M-Th 9-10, F 9-5, Su 2-6; closed
   Saturdays and holidays
COPYING FACILITIES: yes
MATERIALS SOLICITED: Historical, political, and family papers and business
   records of the area. Will also accept
   records of specialized organizations in
   subject fields studied at Florida State
   University.

HOLDINGS:
   Total volume: 315,800 items
   Inclusive dates: 1516 -
   Description: Historical papers and
records of the area, including those of
local businesses, individuals, families, and
officeholders, as well as papers of such
organizations as the Blue Ridge Institute
for Southern Community Service Executives.

SEE: Hamer; NUCMC, 1969-71.

SEE: Robbins; Hinding.

SEE ALSO: Walter Schatz, ed., *Directory of
   Afro-American   Resources* (Bowker,
   1970); Richard C. Davis, *North American Forest History: A Guide to Archives
   and Manuscripts in the United States
   and Canada* (Clio Books, 1977); annual
   description of collections in April issue
   of *Florida Historical Quarterly*, 1908- .

FL800-266
Florida State University
State Photographic Archives
Room 66, Strozier Library
Tallahassee FL 32306

(904) 487-2073

OPEN: M-F 9-1; closed weekends and
   holidays
COPYING FACILITIES: yes
MATERIALS SOLICITED: Photographs of
   Florida. Will also accept photographs
   of subjects related to Florida.

HOLDINGS:
   Total volume: 78,144 items
   Inclusive dates: 1849 -
   Description: Mounted and identified
photographs of Florida or Florida related
people and places.

SEE: Novotny; Hinding.

FL800-575
Forest Service
National Forests in Florida
2586 Seagate Drive, Suite 200
Tallahassee FL

MAILING ADDRESS:
P.O. Box 13549
Tallahassee FL 32308

(904) 681-7265

OPEN: M-F 7:30-5; closed weekends and
holidays
COPYING FACILITIES: yes
MATERIALS SOLICITED: Documents, diaries, correspondence, photographs and
other materials relating to National
Forests in Florida prior to as well as
after establishment. Will also accept
materials relating to settlers, explorers,
settlements, life styles, and events in
the areas of Florida's National Forests.

HOLDINGS:
   Total volume: 20 c.f.; 300 items
   Inclusive dates: 1850 -
   Description: Diaries, land transactions,
agency correspondence, and aerial pho-
tographs relating to National Forests in
Florida. Much of the material consists of
copies from private collections.

TAMPA

FL820-240
Florida Historical Society
Library
University of South Florida Library
Tampa FL 33620

(813) 974-2731

OPEN: M-Th 8-9, F 8-5, Su 1-5; closed
Saturdays and during University
Library vacations; limited hours
between academic quarters
COPYING FACILITIES: yes
MATERIALS SOLICITED: Significant
manuscripts relating to the history of
Florida. Will also accept significant
non-historical Florida material, such as
literary manuscripts of Florida authors.

HOLDINGS:
   Total volume: 60 l.f.
   Inclusive dates: 1492 -
   Description: Collections and individual
items relating to the history of Florida.
Included are personal papers of several
Florida governors, family and business
papers, and journals. Coverage is most
extensive in the territorial period of Florida's history. Also held are the archives of
the Florida Historical Society, including
correspondence relating to topics in Florida history.

SEE: Hamer.

SEE: Hinding.

FL820-480
Lutheran Church in America
Florida Synod
3838 West Cypress Street
Tampa FL 33607

(813) 876-7660

OPEN: M-F 8-4; closed weekends and
holidays
ACCESS: members of Lutheran Church
in America congregations; others with
permission
COPYING FACILITIES: no

HOLDINGS:
   Total volume: 1,100 c.f.
   Inclusive dates: 1938 -
   Description: Documents pertinent to
the development and operations of the
Lutheran Church in America's judicatory
unit for Florida. Correspondence, histories, reports, and other significant documents of all Lutheran Church in America
congregations in Florida are included.

FL820-780
University of South Florida
Library
Special Collections Department
Tampa FL 33620

(813) 974-2731

OPEN: M-Th 8-9, F 8-5, Su 1-5; closed
Saturdays and during University
Library vacations; limited hours
between academic quarters
COPYING FACILITIES: yes
MATERIALS SOLICITED: Material relating
to Florida, 19th century American literature, and American juvenile literature in the 19th and early 20th centuries. Will also accept material relating
to southern history, private presses,
American textbooks (pre-1865), and
subjects suitable to support the programs of the University of South Florida.

HOLDINGS:
   Total volume: 1,050 l.f.
   Inclusive dates: 1700 -
   Description: Florida-related manuscript
collections, including the papers of Flo-
ridians prominent in political, social and
artistic life. The collections include
ephemera, memorabilia and audio-visual
material. There are also several collections of non-Florida manuscripts in areas
such as economics, American literature,
history of the South, and drama, as well
as the University of South Florida Archives, consisting of materials relating to
the history and operation of that institution.

SEE: Hinding.

FL820-810
University of Tampa
Merl Kelce Library
401 West Kennedy Blvd.
Tampa FL 33606

(813) 253-8861, Ext. 385

OPEN: M-Th 8-midnight, F 8-5, Su
1-midnight preferably by appointment;
closed holidays and Christmas vacation
COPYING FACILITIES: yes

MATERIALS SOLICITED: Materials regarding the history of Florida military personnel.

HOLDINGS:
   Total volume: 17 file cases
   Inclusive dates: 1800 -
   Description: Correspondence, committee reports, and other papers of William
C. Cramer, U.S. Representative from
Florida; correspondence, diaries, photographs, and memorabilia relating to activities of U.S. military personnel from
1800 through the Vietnam War; and correspondence, photographs, memorabilia,
research materials, and author's drafts of
Stanley P. Kimmel relating to his book,
The Mad Booths of Maryland, with emphasis on John Wilkes Booth and the
assassination of Abraham Lincoln.

TAVARES

FL840-480
Lake County Historical Society
315 North New Hampshire Avenue
Tavares FL 32778

no telephone

OPEN: Su, W 1-4; open holidays
COPYING FACILITIES: no
MATERIALS SOLICITED: Local history.

HOLDINGS:
   Total volume: 100 photographs; 100
tapes
   Inclusive dates: 1870 -
   Description: Photographs and oral his-
tory tapes relating to the history of
Tavares and Lake County.

VALPARAISO

FL860-320
Historical Society of Okaloosa and
   Walton Counties, Inc.
Museum
115 Westview Avenue
Valparaiso FL

MAILING ADDRESS:
P.O. Box 488
Valparaiso FL 32580

(904) 678-2615

OPEN: Tu-Sa 11-4, closed Sundays,
Mondays, holidays and Dec. 22-Jan. 2
COPYING FACILITIES: no
MATERIALS SOLICITED: History of
Okaloosa and Walton counties, particularly early settlers, area industries, local
institutions, and organizations. Will
also accept material relating to the
growth and development of
northwestern Florida.

HOLDINGS:
   Total volume: 3 file cabinets; 37
boxes
   Inclusive dates: 1851 -
   Description: A collection of letters,
business records and other documents relating to the early Scottish settlers of Walton County, a Ft. Walton Beach pioneer
family (1830-50), the L and N Railroad,
and the cities of Ft. Walton Beach and
Valparaiso in the 1920's; records of an

early hotel in Ft. Walton Beach; and over 50 tapes and transcriptions of reminiscences of members of pioneer families.

WHITE SPRINGS

FL940-240
Florida Folklife Program
Florida Folklife Archive
White Springs FL

MAILING ADDRESS:
P.O. Box 265
White Springs FL 32096

(904) 397-2192, 2193

OPEN: M-F 8:30-5; closed weekends and holidays
COPYING FACILITIES: yes
MATERIALS SOLICITED: Information on folk ways, crafts, and lore, local histories, and oral interviews.

HOLDINGS:
Total volume: 16 c.f.; 500 hours of sound recordings
Inclusive dates: 1950 -
Description: Materials relating chiefly to Florida folklore, including transcribed oral history interviews with craftsmen,

folk artists, and others, materials on ethnic groups such as Czechs, Greeks, Cubans, and Seminole Indians, and tape recordings of the Florida Folk Festival, 1954- .

WINTER PARK

FL960-680
Rollins College
Archives
Mills Memorial Library
Winter Park FL 32789

(305) 646-2000, Ext. 2421

OPEN: M-F 9-5; closed weekends and holidays
COPYING FACILITIES: yes
MATERIALS SOLICITED: Rollins College records.

HOLDINGS:
Total volume: 860 l.f.; 68 file drawers
Inclusive dates: 1884 -
Description: Non-current records of Rollins College and a small collection of photographs and information about people and places connected with the College.

SEE: NUCMC, 1977.

FL960-690
Rollins College
Mills Memorial Library
Winter Park FL 32789

(305) 646-2521

OPEN: M-Th 8-11, F 8-10, Sa 9-5, Su 2-11; closed holidays
COPYING FACILITIES: yes
MATERIALS SOLICITED: Florida history and culture.

HOLDINGS:
Total volume: 100 l.f.; 2,260 items
Inclusive dates: 17th century -
Description: Two 17th century breviaries, various literary manuscripts and papers of botanical and horticultural interest, papers of journalist and Rollins College president Hamilton Holt, and the Floridiana collection of more than 600 photographs, chiefly of Winter Park scenes.

SEE: Hamer; NUCMC, 1962, 65.

SEE: Robbins.

SEE ALSO: Peter E. Robinson, ed., *Register: Hamilton Holt Papers* (Rollins College, Mills Memorial Library, 1964). Listings are available for many of the collections.

GEORGIA

In 1957 the Department of Archives and History of the Georgia Secretary of State's Office initiated a statewide program for preserving local government records of lasting significance. These records normally are retained by their creating agencies, but some 4,000 cubic feet of original probate, marriage, and other county records have been acquired by the Department of Archives in Atlanta. Researchers at the Archives also are provided with some 19,000 reels of microfilm of vital, land, probate, and other county records, mostly dated before 1900, filmed by the Department and the Church of Jesus Christ of Latter-day Saints.

ATHENS

GA75-790
University of Georgia
Libraries
Richard B. Russell Memorial Library
Athens GA 30602

(404) 542-5788

OPEN: M-F 8-5; closed weekends and holidays
ACCESS: prospective researchers must apply in advance; application forms available from the above address
COPYING FACILITIES: no
MATERIALS SOLICITED: Any material relating to Senator Richard B. Russell, including papers of former staff, family, and friends, and papers of other members of the Georgia Congressional delegation.

HOLDINGS:
    Total volume: 2,537 l.f.
    Inclusive dates: 1905 -
    Description: Approximately 1,700 linear feet of manuscripts covering all areas of the career of Richard B. Russell from the time he was Speaker of the Georgia House of Representatives until the time of his death in 1971, when he was President Pro Tempore of the U.S. Senate. Additionally, there are 148 oral history interviews, and photographs, motion pictures, and sound recordings. The Library also contains smaller collections of papers of other members of the Georgia Congressional delegation and papers relating to Russell.

SEE: NUCMC, 1979.

GA75-800
University of Georgia
Libraries
Science Library
Map Collection
Ag Drive
Athens GA 30602

(404) 542-4535

OPEN: M-Th 8-10, F 8-6, Sa 1-6, Su 1-10; closed holidays; variable hours during school vacations
COPYING FACILITIES: yes
MATERIALS SOLICITED: Aerial photography of Georgia and all post-1900 mapping of Georgia. Will also accept other maps or aerial imagery material of the Southeast and Georgia.

HOLDINGS:
    Total volume: 170,000 items
    Inclusive dates: 1938 -
    Description: A collection of aerial photographs of Georgia arranged by counties. Most Georgia counties are covered at 5- to 10-year intervals from 1938 to 1968. Photo indexes are available for the coverage. Most of the photography was produced for either the Agricultural Stabilization and Conservation Service or the Soil Conservation Service.

GUIDES: John Sutherland, *Aerial Photographic Coverage of Georgia; Map Collection, Science Library, University of Georgia Libraries* (1977).

SEE ALSO: *Map Collections in the United States and Canada, A Directory* (Special Libraries Assn., 1970).

GA75-810
University of Georgia
Libraries
Special Collections
Manuscript Department
Athens GA 30602

(404) 542-2972

OPEN: M-F 8-5; closed weekends and holidays
COPYING FACILITIES: yes
MATERIALS SOLICITED: Materials pertaining to Georgia; the southeastern States; selected contemporary literature, music, costume and theater; and blacks.

HOLDINGS:
    Total volume: 1,511,000 items
    Inclusive dates: 1450 -
    Description: Over 1,000 collections covering 18th-20th century America, with particular emphasis on Georgia and the southeastern States. Included are records of organizations, papers of individuals, unpublished memoirs and diaries, legal records, typescripts of books, and audiovisual materials, documenting such subjects as military and political history, business, education, literature, theater, and music.

SEE: Hamer; NUCMC, 1959-64, 72, 79.

SEE: Spalek; Allard, Crawley, and Edmison; Robbins; Hinding; Leventhal and Mooney - III; Beers - Confederate.

SEE ALSO: *Map Collections in the United States and Canada, A Directory* (Special Libraries Assn., 1970); Walter Schatz, ed., *Directory of Afro-American Resources* (Bowker, 1970); Ann Novotny, ed., *Picture Sources 3* (Special Libraries Assn., 1975); David A. Hounshell, comp., *Manuscripts in U.S. Depositories Relating to the History of Electrical Science and Technology* (Smithsonian Institution, n.d.); Albert Krichmar, *The Women's Rights Movement in the United States, 1848-1970: A Bibliography and Sourcebook* (Scarecrow Press, 1972).

ATLANTA

GA90-30
Atlanta Historical Society, Inc.
Archives
3101 Andrews Drive, N.W.
Atlanta GA 30305

(404) 261-1837

OPEN: M-F 9-4:45; closed weekends and holidays
COPYING FACILITIES: yes
MATERIALS SOLICITED: Materials relating to the Atlanta metropolitan area, and records of the city of Atlanta and Fulton County, GA. Will also accept materials on horticulture in the South.

HOLDINGS:
    Total volume: 3,103 c.f.
    Inclusive dates: 1837 -
    Description: Materials relating chiefly to Atlanta, including over 800 collections of papers of individuals, organizations and businesses; architectural drawings; maps and plat diagrams; subject and personality files; formal unpublished manuscripts; official records of the city of Atlanta and of Fulton County; and a visual arts collection including over 30,000 photographs.

GUIDES: *A Guide to the Manuscript Collections of the Atlanta Historical Society* (1976).

SEE: Hamer; NUCMC, 1979.

SEE ALSO: Richard T. Eltzroth, 'The Atlanta Historical Society: Its Archival and Library Holdings,' *Georgia Archive* 1 (Fall 1972); Ann Novotny, ed., *Picture Sources 3* (Special Libraries Assn., 1975); *Map Collections in the United States and Canada, A Directory* (Special Libraries Assn., 1970); Albert Krichmar, *The Women's Rights Movement in the United States, 1848-1970: A Bibliography and Sourcebook* (Scarecrow Press, 1972); David B. Gracy, II, 'Data in the Raw: A Guide to Atlanta's Archives,' *Georgia Archive* 3 (Summer 1975).

GA90-60

Atlanta University Center
Arnett Library
273 Chestnut Street, S.W.
Atlanta GA 30314

SEE: Hamer.

Questionnaire not returned.

GA90-130

The Coca-Cola Company
Archives
310 North Avenue, N.W.
Atlanta GA

MAILING ADDRESS:
P.O. Drawer 1734
Atlanta GA 30301

(404) 898-3491, 3492

OPEN: M-F 9-5; closed weekends and holidays
ACCESS: advance arrangements required except for company personnel
COPYING FACILITIES: yes
MATERIALS SOLICITED: Materials relating to the history of The Coca-Cola Company and the Coca-Cola bottling industry. Will also accept materials relating to the soft drink industry and major figures in The Coca-Cola Company's history.

HOLDINGS:
> *Total volume:* 2,500 l.f.
> *Inclusive dates:* 1886 -
> *Description:* Records relating to the history of the product Coca-Cola and to the activities of the corporation. Holdings include department and administrative files, minutes, reports, correspondence, internal publications, news releases, publicity, photography, annual reports, print advertising, radio and television commercials, audio-visual and print training material, promotional material, oral histories, and ephemera.

GA90-190

Emory University
Pitts Theology Library
Atlanta GA 30322

(404) 727-4166

OPEN: M-F 8-5; closed weekends and holidays
COPYING FACILITIES: yes
MATERIALS SOLICITED: Materials relating to Methodism in the South; papers of southern Methodist ministers and faculty members of Candler School of Theology, Emory University; and records of academic societies in the field of religion. Will also accept Methodist materials from areas other than the South.

HOLDINGS:
> *Total volume:* 21 l.f.
> *Inclusive dates:* 1831 -
> *Description:* The collection includes manuscript volumes of the minutes of the annual meetings of the North Georgia Conference of the Methodist church (1831-1921), and records of committees, boards and societies of the North Georgia Conference, as well as the records of individual district conferences and organizations. Also included are manuscript sermons and sermon outlines of Linus Parker and Joseph Staunton Key, the papers of Candler School of Theology faculty members, and the minutes and records of the American Academy of Religion, Southeastern Section (1949-75).

SEE: Hinding.

GA90-200

Emory University
Robert W. Woodruff Library
Special Collections Department
Atlanta GA 30322

(404) 727-6887

OPEN: M-Sa 9-6; closed Sundays and holidays
COPYING FACILITIES: yes
MATERIALS SOLICITED: Southern Americana, particularly materials relating to Georgia and materials relating to Emory University. Will also accept materials relating to existing collections or other materials appropriate for inclusion.

HOLDINGS:
> *Total volume:* 3,500 l.f.
> *Inclusive dates:* 1700 -
> *Description:* Materials concentrating geographically on the South, particularly Georgia, and emphasizing the Civil War, literary figures (primarily late 19th century), journalists, Methodism, politics and civil rights. Included are papers of individuals and organizations, collections of memorabilia, and the Emory University Archives.
>
> Additional collections emphasize the Communist Party of the United States of America and Anglo-Irish literary materials.

SEE: Hamer; NUCMC, 1959-62, 65, 68-69, 71-72, 75, 77.

SEE: Hinding; Robbins; Martin.

SEE ALSO: Peter Duignan, *Handbook of American Resources for African Studies* (Hoover Institution, 1967); Walter Schatz, ed., *Directory of Afro-American Resources* (Bowker, 1970).

David B. Gracy, 'Data in the Raw: A Guide to Atlanta's Archives,' *Georgia Archive,* Vol. III, No. 2 (Summer 1975).

Richard C. Davis, *North American Forest History: A Guide to Archives and Manuscripts in the United States and Canada* (Clio Books, 1977).

GA90-210

Emory University
School of Dentistry
Sheppard W. Foster Library
1462 Clifton Road, N.E.
Atlanta GA 30322

(404) 727-6695

OPEN: M-F 9-5; closed weekends and holidays
ACCESS: an appointment is desirable
COPYING FACILITIES: no

HOLDINGS:
> *Total volume:* 5 vols.
> *Inclusive dates:* 1869 - 1925
> *Description:* Minutes of the Georgia State Dental Society, 1869-79, and of the Atlanta Dental College faculty, 1893-95; papers of the National Association of Dental Faculties, 1894-1901; and building specifications, including one drawing, for Atlanta Southern Dental College, 1925.

SEE: Hamer.

GA90-230

The First National Bank of Atlanta
Corporate Secretary's Department
2 Peachtree Street, N.W.
Atlanta GA

MAILING ADDRESS:
P.O. Box 4148
Atlanta GA 30302

(404) 894-4586

OPEN: M-F 9-4; closed weekends and holidays
COPYING FACILITIES: yes

HOLDINGS:
> *Total volume:* 4 boxes
> *Inclusive dates:* 1865 -
> *Description:* Various non-confidential records pertaining to the Atlanta National Bank, as well as other banks with which it has merged.

GA90-260

Georgia Department of Archives and History
330 Capitol Avenue, S.E.
Atlanta GA 30334

(404) 656-2350

SEE: Hamer.

Questionnaire not returned.

GA90-265

Georgia Department of Natural Resources
Parks, Recreation and Historic Sites Division
Historic Preservation Section
Room 701
270 Washington Street, S.W.
Atlanta GA 30334

(404) 656-2840

OPEN: M-F 8-4:30; closed weekends and holidays
ACCESS: an appointment is recommended
COPYING FACILITIES: yes

MATERIALS SOLICITED: Material relating to State-owned historic sites.

HOLDINGS:
Total volume: 30 boxes
Inclusive dates: 1790's -
Description: A collection of manuscripts relating chiefly to Georgia historic sites that are or were owned by the State, especially those acquired under the Georgia Historical Commission, 1951-73. Some of the material relates to the individuals who owned the sites prior to State control.

GUIDES: *Inventory and Key to Catalogue System of Manuscripts, Documents, Microfilm, Pictures and Maps in the Possession of the Georgia Historical Commission* (1976), available from the Historic Preservation Section.

GA90-270
Georgia Department of State
Surveyor General Department
330 Capitol Avenue, S.E.
Atlanta GA 30334

(404) 656-2367

OPEN: M-F 8-4:30; closed weekends and holidays
COPYING FACILITIES: yes
MATERIALS SOLICITED: Copies of all dissertations and theses based on records of the Department; maps of the Southeast. Will also accept historical and geographical works on the Southeast.

HOLDINGS:
Total volume: 1,507,000 items
Inclusive dates: 1599 -
Description: Maps and associated documents relating to land surveying; geography; forest ecology; botany; geology; history, including land use, land development, migrations, frontier defenses, early roads and trails; Creek and Cherokee Indians, including land reservations, removal from Georgia, mounds, and agricultural improvements; Georgia boundary surveys; municipal annexations; and original grants and surveys of land from about 1756 to 1909.

GA90-280
Georgia Institute of Technology
Library
Atlanta GA 30332

(404) 894-4586

OPEN: M-F 8-5; closed weekends and holidays
COPYING FACILITIES: yes
MATERIALS SOLICITED: Archives and non-current records of the Georgia Institute of Technology.

HOLDINGS:
Total volume: 730 l.f.
Inclusive dates: 1885 -
Description: The archives of the Georgia Institute of Technology, including correspondence, business ledgers, registrar's records, tapes and recordings, photographs, and clippings, a large part of which is on microfilm. Also, there is a large collection of maps and aerial photographs, concentrating on Georgia and the southeastern United States.

SEE ALSO: *Map Collections in the United States and Canada, A Directory* (Special Libraries Assn., 1970).

GA90-300
Georgia State University
Southern Labor Archives
Urban Life Center 1028
Atlanta GA 30303

MAILING ADDRESS:
Box 1027
University Plaza
Atlanta GA 30303

(404) 658-2476, 2477

OPEN: M-F 8:30-5:30; closed weekends, holidays and Christmas vacations
ACCESS: qualified researchers
COPYING FACILITIES: yes
MATERIALS SOLICITED: Organized labor, particularly in the South, and related organizations and activities (e.g., civil rights).

HOLDINGS:
Total volume: 2,800 c.f.
Inclusive dates: 1871 -
Description: Manuscript collections from labor organizations and members, chiefly concerning the South. Files (correspondence, printed proceedings, contracts, financial and legal documents) discussing organizing activity and internal functioning of unions focus on the rise, development and politics of organized labor in the South. Included are records from local, city, State, regional and international organizations. Holdings are especially strong in the Deep South during the period since 1930, and for the following unions: Woodworkers, Machinists, Service Employees, United Textile Workers, and Typographers.

SEE: NUCMC, 1973, 77, 80.

SEE: Hinding.

SEE ALSO: David B. Gracy, 'Data in the Raw: A Guide to Atlanta's Archives,' *Georgia Archive,* Vol. III, No. 2 (Summer 1975). A list of holdings describing collections processed and major collections received is published each year by the Archives.

Richard C. Davis, *North American Forest History: A Guide to Archives and Manuscripts in the United States and Canada* (Clio Books, 1977).

GA90-360
Interdenominational Theological
  Center
Archives and Special Collections
671 Beckwith Street, S.W.
Atlanta GA 30314

(404) 522-8980

OPEN: M-F 8:30-5; closed weekends and holidays
COPYING FACILITIES: yes
MATERIALS SOLICITED: Materials pertaining to the black religious experience. Will also accept materials relating to black history in general.

HOLDINGS:
Total volume: not specified
Inclusive dates: 1883 -
Description: Manuscripts and other archival records emphasizing the black religious experience. Included are institutional records of the Interdenominational Theological Center and its 7 constituent seminaries; papers and records of black churches, religious leaders, institutions, and organizations; records of the Freedmen's Aid Society of the Methodist Episcopal church; and records of National and local organizations related to blacks and civil rights. Most of the materials focus on the South, but include coverage of the rest of the United States, as well as Africa.

SEE ALSO: Walter Schatz, ed., *Directory of Afro-American Resources* (Bowker, 1970); David B. Gracy, II, 'Data in the Raw: A Guide to Atlanta's Archives,' *Georgia Archive* 3 (Summer 1975).

GA90-490
Martin Luther King, Jr., Center for
  Social Change
King Library and Archives
449 Auburn Avenue, N.E.
Atlanta GA 30312

(404) 524-1956

OPEN: by appointment only
ACCESS: advance arrangements advised
COPYING FACILITIES: yes
MATERIALS SOLICITED: Manuscripts, organization records, photographs, audio and video tapes, and other materials relating to the American civil rights movement, 1950's-60's.

HOLDINGS:
Total volume: 575 l.f.
Inclusive dates: 1940's -
Description: Personal papers, organization records, and tape recordings relating to the civil rights movement in the United States. Included are papers of Dr. Martin Luther King, Jr., and records of the Martin Luther King, Jr., Center for Social Change, Southern Christian Leadership Conference, Student Nonviolent Coordinating Committee, Congress of Racial Equality, Delta Ministry, Mississippi Freedom Democratic Committee, Episcopal Society for Cultural and Racial Unity, and National Lawyers Guild.

SEE: Schatz; Meckler and McMullin.

GA90-600
Oglethorpe University
Library
4484 Peachtree Road, N.E.
Atlanta GA 30319

(404) 261-1441

OPEN: by appointment
COPYING FACILITIES: yes

HOLDINGS:
Total volume: 1 file cabinet; 21 boxes
Inclusive dates: 1835 -
Description: Materials relating to Oglethorpe University, including minutes of the board of trustees, 1835-71; the 'Founder's Book,' 1916; a gift ledger; records of the 'Crypt of Civilization' at Oglethorpe; papers and drawings of the

original Oglethorpe buildings, 1913-30; and related photographs.

SEE: Robbins.

GA90-700

Southern Education Foundation, Inc.
811 Cypress Street, N.E.
Atlanta GA 30308

(404) 523-0001

OPEN: M-F 9-4:30; closed weekends and holidays
ACCESS: qualified researchers only
COPYING FACILITIES: yes
MATERIALS SOLICITED: The Foundation's own records, dealing with black education and philanthropy. Will also accept materials dealing with any aspect of education or philanthropy in the South.

HOLDINGS:
Total volume: 10 file drawers; 20 l.f.
Inclusive dates: 1876 - 1937
Description: A collection of correspondence, minutes of meetings, and related files of three private foundations: the Peabody Fund, the Slater Fund, and the Jeanes Fund. Materials relate both to education in the South, especially black education, and to the history of philanthropy. The early files include correspondence with Booker T. Washington.

SEE ALSO: Walter Schatz, ed., *Directory of Afro-American Resources* (Bowker, 1970).

AUGUSTA

GA105-690

Richmond County Historical Society
Reese Library
Augusta College
2500 Walton Way
Augusta GA 30910

(404) 737-1745

OPEN: Su 2-10:30, M-Th 7:45-10:30, F 7:45-5, Sa 9:30-5
ACCESS: Society members or students, faculty, and alumni of Augusta College; others by special arrangement with curator or assistant curator
COPYING FACILITIES: yes
MATERIALS SOLICITED: Local and State history and genealogy.

HOLDINGS:
Total volume: 3 file cabinets
Inclusive dates: 1700 -
Description: Personal and family papers, records of churches, schools, and organizations, oral history tapes and transcripts, and other materials relating to the history of Augusta, Richmond County, and the surrounding area, including South Carolina.

GA105-720

St. Paul's Church
605 Reynolds Street
Augusta GA 30902

(404) 724-2485

OPEN: daily 9-5
COPYING FACILITIES: no

HOLDINGS:
Total volume: 4,000 items
Inclusive dates: 1755 -
Description: Church records, including minutes of vestry meetings; letters from church officers; church registers; marriage, baptism, and communicant records. 18th century material relates to a time when the church, through parish representatives, served as administrator of local government.

CALHOUN

GA180-280

Gordon County Historical Society, Inc.
S. Wall Street
Calhoun GA

MAILING ADDRESS:
P.O. Box 342
Calhoun GA 30701

(404) 629-1515

OPEN: Tu, Th, F 10-4 or by appointment; closed weekends and holidays
COPYING FACILITIES: yes

HOLDINGS:
Total volume: 8 l.f.
Inclusive dates: 1830 -
Description: Materials pertaining to Gordon County and northwestern Georgia, including the history of local participation in America's wars, church histories (mostly Baptist), and family histories.

CARROLLTON

GA210-880

West Georgia College
Library
Special Collections
Carrollton GA 30117

(404) 834-1370

OPEN: M-Th 7:30-10, F 7:30-5, Sa 10-5, Su 3-10; closed holidays and Christmas vacation
COPYING FACILITIES: yes
MATERIALS SOLICITED: History and records of West Georgia College and its predecessor, Fourth District A & M School; history of Carroll and surrounding counties; and manuscripts of local authors. Will also accept rare monographs and other manuscript material on Georgia.

HOLDINGS:
Total volume: 9,094 items
Inclusive dates: 1860 -
Description: Records of the Fourth District Agricultural and Mechanical School (1907-33) and of West Georgia

College (1933-), including annual reports, yearbooks, minutes of the faculty, bulletins, and special projects, as well as documentation of the 'College in the Country' concept of continuing education.

GA210-900

West Georgia Regional Library
Special Collections
710 Rome Street
Carrollton GA

MAILING ADDRESS:
P.O. Box 160
Carrollton GA 30117

(404) 836-1325

OPEN: M-F 9-5; closed weekends and holidays
ACCESS: advance arrangements required
COPYING FACILITIES: yes
MATERIALS SOLICITED: Materials relating to Carroll County history and genealogy. Will also accept materials relating to other counties in the region, including Heard, Douglas, Haralson, and Paulding counties.

HOLDINGS:
Total volume: 53 items
Inclusive dates: 1900 -
Description: Materials relating chiefly to Carroll County settlers, including photographs and scrapbooks.

COLUMBUS

GA245-110

Columbus College
Archives
Simon Schwob Memorial Library
Columbus GA 31993

(404) 568-2247

OPEN: M, Th, F 1:30-5:30, Tu, W 1:30-10:30, Sa 1-6, between quarters M-F 1:30-5:15; closed Sundays and holidays
COPYING FACILITIES: yes
MATERIALS SOLICITED: Materials relating to the history of Columbus and the surrounding Chattahoochee valley area. Will also accept other materials.

HOLDINGS:
Total volume: 500 l.f.
Inclusive dates: 1820's - 1970's
Description: Materials focusing on the history of Columbus, Fort Benning, GA, and Phenix City, AL, with some materials pertaining to surrounding counties. Included are records of orphanages, a free kindergarten and settlement house association, family welfare bureau, radio station, and Columbus College, in addition to papers of businessmen, politicians, a slave dealer, newspaper women, and inventor.

EAST POINT

GA405-560
National Archives and Records
  Administration
Federal Archives and Records Center
Archives Branch
1557 St. Joseph Avenue
East Point GA 30344

(404) 763-7477

OPEN: M-F 8-5; closed weekends and
  holidays
ACCESS: Records are open, subject to
  Federal agency restrictions and
  restrictions based upon current
  legislation relevant to confidentiality
  and security classification. See General
  Information Leaflet No. 2, 'Regulations
  for the Public Use of Records in the
  National Archives.'
COPYING FACILITIES: yes
MATERIALS SOLICITED: Federal govern-
  ment records of historic value from the
  States of Alabama, Georgia, Florida,
  Kentucky, Mississippi, North Carolina,
  South Carolina, and Tennessee. Will
  also accept donated material of historic
  value relating to Federal activity.

HOLDINGS:
  Total volume: 33,542 c.f.
  Inclusive dates: 1716 -
  Description: Federal records produced
  in the eight southeastern States within the
  geographic area of interest of this Federal
  Archives and Records Center. Included
  are records of the Federal Courts and
  other Federal agencies.

SEE: Davis; Paszek; Allard, Crawley, and
  Edmison; Leventhal and Mooney - III;
  Beers - Confederate.

SEE ALSO: David B. Gracy, 'Data in the
  Raw: A Guide to Atlanta's Archives,'
  Georgia Archive, Vol. III, No. 2
  (Summer 1975); Walter Schatz, ed., *Di-
  rectory of Afro-American Resources*
  (Bowker, 1970). A pamphlet, *Research
  Opportunities* (1977), is available upon
  request. Preliminary inventories are
  also available at the institution for
  some record groups.

LA GRANGE

GA660-480
La Grange College
William and Evelyn Banks Library
La Grange GA 30240

(404) 882-2911, Ext. 34

OPEN: M-Th 8-10, F 8-5, Sa 1-5, Su
  1-10; closed holidays
USER FEES: permission granted under
  direct observation of a staff member
COPYING FACILITIES: yes
MATERIALS SOLICITED: Materials pertaining to the history of La Grange
  College, to Georgia authors, particularly those who graduated from the College, and to the Marquis de Lafayette.

HOLDINGS:
  Total volume: 1,500 vols.; 40 items
  Inclusive dates: 17th and 18th
century
  Description: A collection of manuscripts by and about Georgia authors and
  the Marquis de Lafayette.

MACON

GA735-520
Mercer University
Stetson Memorial Library
Georgia Baptist Historical Collection
1330 Edgewood Avenue
Macon GA 31207

(912) 744-2960

OPEN: M-F 9-5; closed weekends and
  holidays
COPYING FACILITIES: yes
MATERIALS SOLICITED: Georgia Baptist
  history and materials on Mercer University. Will also accept local history
  materials.

HOLDINGS:
  Total volume: 30 c.f.
  Inclusive dates: 1794 -
  Description: Correspondence of educa-
  tor W. H. Kilpatrick, a journal of U.S.
  Senator A. O. Bacon, Georgia Baptist
  church records, 1794 to date, and records
  of Mercer University.

SEE: NUCMC, 1965.

GA735-540
Middle Georgia Historical Society,
  Inc.
Archives and Special Collections
Washington Memorial Library
1180 Washington Avenue
Macon GA 31201

(912) 743-3851

OPEN: M-F 9-5; closed weekends, Easter,
  Jefferson Davis Day, and Christmas
COPYING FACILITIES: yes
MATERIALS SOLICITED: Materials relating
  to the history of Bibb, Jones, Monroe,
  Twiggs, Houston, Crawford, and Peach
  counties, GA, including documents,
  manuscripts, photographs, and social,
  economic, religious, and political materials. Will also accept materials relating to other sections of Georgia.

HOLDINGS:
  Total volume: 150 c.f.
  Inclusive dates: 1825 -
  Description: Materials documenting the
  history of Macon and Bibb County, GA,
  including literary manuscripts of Harry
  Stillwell Edwards, Sidney Lanier, and
  other middle Georgia authors; records of
  Christ Episcopal Church; records of the
  Macon volunteers, the first local militia
  group; papers of W. A. Huff, mayor of
  Macon; the Douglass Theatre collection
  of cinema and burlesque papers, financial
  records, and materials concerning black
  vaudeville; records of the Republican
  Party of Bibb County; and Macon photographs.

MARIETTA

GA765-440
Kennesaw Mountain National
  Battlefield Park
Marietta GA

MAILING ADDRESS:
P.O. Box 1167
Marietta GA 30061

(404) 427-4686

OPEN: daily 9-5; closed Christmas and
  New Year's
COPYING FACILITIES: yes
MATERIALS SOLICITED: Items relating to
  the Civil War, especially the Atlanta
  Campaign of 1864. Will also accept
  any item of National historical interest.

HOLDINGS:
  Total volume: not specified
  Inclusive dates: 1850 - 1900
  Description: Materials relating chiefly
  to the Civil War, including wartime let-
  ters of the Faw family of Georgia, a diary
  of Sgt.-Major Lyman S. Widney, letters of
  Col. Columbus Sykes, and papers of Lt.
  Col. James W. Langley.

MILLEDGEVILLE

GA780-270
Georgia College
Library
Flannery O'Connor Collection
231 West Hancock Street
Milledgeville GA 31061

(912) 453-4047

OPEN: M-F 9-4; closed weekends,
  holidays, and Christmas vacation
ACCESS: graduate students and other
  scholars by prearrangement; letters not
  available for research
COPYING FACILITIES: no
MATERIALS SOLICITED: Correspondence
  of Flannery O'Connor.

HOLDINGS:
  Total volume: 4,300 pages; other
materials
  Inclusive dates: 1941 -
  Description: A collection of 135 manuscripts, and letters of the Georgia writer,
  Flannery O'Connor. Also included are 4
  audio recordings, 5 motion pictures, critical writings, clippings, photographs and
  memorabilia.

SEE: Robbins; Hinding.

SEE ALSO: Gerald Becham, 'The Flannery
  O'Connor Collection,' *The Flannery
  O'Connor Bulletin* 1 (1972).

GA780-290
Georgia College
Library
Special Collections
231 West Hancock Street
Milledgeville GA 31061

(912) 453-4047

OPEN: M-F 8-5; closed weekends,
  holidays, and Christmas vacation
COPYING FACILITIES: yes

MATERIALS SOLICITED: Georgia history and local history.

HOLDINGS:
Total volume: 47 l.f.; 1,500 items
Inclusive dates: 1791 -
Description: Archives of the College, 1887 to date, and 1,500 other items, relating chiefly to Georgia. Included are 446 pages of manuscripts, plus ledgers, account books, plantation records, indentures, land grants, and diaries.

SEE: Hamer.

GA780-310
Georgia College
Museum and Archives of Georgia Education
131 South Clark Street
Milledgeville GA

MAILING ADDRESS:
P.O. Box 702
Milledgeville GA 31061

(912) 453-4391

OPEN: M-F noon-5; closed weekends and College vacations
ACCESS: advance arrangements required
COPYING FACILITIES: yes
MATERIALS SOLICITED: Oral documents and other materials relating to the development of education in Georgia.

HOLDINGS:
Total volume: not specified
Inclusive dates: 19th century -
Description: Materials relating to the development of education in Georia, including oral history interviews with black educators.

SEE: Hinding.

MT. BERRY

GA810-80
The Berry Schools
Archives
Memorial Library
Mt. Berry GA 30149

(404) 232-5374

OPEN: M-Th 8-midnight, F 8-5, Sa 9-5, Su 2-midnight; variable hours during College vacations
ACCESS: advance arrangements perferred
COPYING FACILITIES: yes
MATERIALS SOLICITED: Materials relating to The Berry Schools and their founder Martha Berry.

HOLDINGS:
Total volume: 651 l.f.; 3,000 items
Inclusive dates: 1902 - 1942
Description: Records of The Berry Schools, including holographs, financial records, correspondence, architectural drawings, board minutes, photographs, scrapbooks, and promotional materials. Included are correspondence of the schools' founder Martha Berry with political, social, economic, intellectual, and religious leaders, as well as photographs of The Berry Schools, prominent persons associated with them, and life in the rural South in the early 20th century.

OXFORD

GA825-200
Emory University
Oxford College
Library
Oxford GA 30267

(404) 786-7051, Ext. 281

OPEN: M-Th 8-11, F 8-5, Sa 2-5, Su 2-11; closed holidays; shorter summer hours
COPYING FACILITIES: yes
MATERIALS SOLICITED: Materials concerning Emory University and local history. Will also accept materials concerning the Methodist church and Georgia authors.

HOLDINGS:
Total volume: not specified
Inclusive dates: 1958 -
Description: Church histories of Newton County, GA, genealogical materials, Emory University materials, Methodist church minutes, local history recordings, and a Georgia authors clipping file.

RABUN GAP

GA840-240
The Foxfire Fund, Inc.
Rabun Gap GA 30568

(404) 746-5318

OPEN: by appointment only
COPYING FACILITIES: no
MATERIALS SOLICITED: Will accept old photographs, journals, and other materials relating to the northern Georgia/western North Carolina section of the southern Appalachians.

HOLDINGS:
Total volume: 35 l.f. of tapes; 30,000 items
Inclusive dates: 1966 -
Description: Audio tape interviews with elderly natives of the southern Appalachians, primarily northern Georgia and western North Carolina, relating to cultural traditions. There are also 30,000 black and white negatives relating to the same topic.

SEE: Meckler and McMullin.

RINCON

GA860-280
The Georgia Salzburger Society Museum
Rincon GA

MAILING ADDRESS:
Box 477, Route 1
Rincon GA 31326

(912) 754-6333

OPEN: W, Sa, Su 3-5; closed other days
COPYING FACILITIES: no
MATERIALS SOLICITED: Materials relating to the early Salzburger settlers and their descendants. Will also accept materials relating to the silk industry in the colony of Georgia.

HOLDINGS:
Total volume: not specified
Inclusive dates: 1754 -
Description: Records of the Jerusalem Lutheran Church, 1754 to date (in German before 1823), and genealogical data concerning descendants of the original Salzburger settlers in Ebenezer, GA.

ROME

GA870-730
Shorter College
Memorabilia Room
Rome GA 30161

(404) 291-2121

OPEN: by appointment only
COPYING FACILITIES: yes
MATERIALS SOLICITED: Materials related to Shorter College students, alumni, faculty, and trustees.

HOLDINGS:
Total volume: 16 c.f.
Inclusive dates: 1840's -
Description: Photographs, slides, motion pictures, sound recordings, and manuscripts related to Shorter College, 1873 to date. Also included is a travel account from the 1840's.

ST. SIMONS ISLAND

GA885-120
Coastal Georgia Historical Society
Museum of Coastal History
610 Beachview Drive
St. Simons Island GA

MAILING ADDRESS:
P.O. Box 1151
St. Simons Island GA 31522

(912) 638-4666

OPEN: M-F 8:30-5:30 by appointment only; closed weekends and holidays
ACCESS: advance arrangements required
COPYING FACILITIES: no
MATERIALS SOLICITED: Materials pertaining to the social, economic, political, religious, technological, sociological, and anthropological history of coastal Georgia, including the interpretation of historical archaeology.

HOLDINGS:
Total volume: 16 l.f.
Inclusive dates: 1788 -
Description: Materials relating to coastal Georgia, including early prominent families of St. Simons Island, construction of the first lighthouse in 1810, the Brunswick-Altamaha Canal in the 1830's - 1900's, lumber milling in the 1870's and 1880's, naval stores production in the 1870's - 1900's, shipbuilding in World Wars I and II, and the resort era since 1900. Also held are taped interviews and talks, slides, and photographs.

SEE: Hinding.

GA885-240
Fort Frederica National Monument
Park Library
St. Simons Island GA

MAILING ADDRESS:
Route 4, Box 286-C
St. Simons Island, GA 31522

(912) 683-3639

OPEN: by appointment only
COPYING FACILITIES: no
MATERIALS SOLICITED: Materials relating to 18th century English history, the history of the town and fort of Frederica, 1736-50, American southern history, 1700-50, and settlers and inhabitants of Frederica. Will also accept materials relating to the history of Frederica since 1750.

HOLDINGS:
Total volume: 100 l.f.
Inclusive dates: 1854 -
Description: Materials relating to the political, economic, social, and military history of Fort Frederica from 1736 to 1750 and the town of Frederica through the present day.

GA885-520
Methodist Museum
St. Simons Island GA

MAILING ADDRESS:
Box 407
Epworth-by-the-Sea
St. Simons Island GA 31522

(912) 638-4050

OPEN: M 1-4, Tu-F 9-4, Sa 9-noon; closed Sundays, Thanksgiving, Christmas, and New Year's
COPYING FACILITIES: yes
MATERIALS SOLICITED: Materials relating to the history of the Methodist church, John and Charles Wesley, and Coastal Georgia, specifically St. Simons Island.

HOLDINGS:
Total volume: 3,760 items
Inclusive dates: 1744 -
Description: Diaries and manuscripts of Methodist ministers, records of the South Georgia Methodist Conference, scrapbooks concerning missionaries and women's work for the Methodist church, biographical information concerning clergy and lay people active in the church, financial records of the Dodge Meigs lumber mill, 1878, and visual materials concerning the history of coastal Georgia.

SEE: Hinding.

SAVANNAH

GA895-120
Chatham-Effingham-Liberty Regional Library
Reference Department
Georgia History Collection
2002 Bull Street
Savannah GA 31499

(912) 234-5127

OPEN: Su 3-6, M-Th 9-9, F, Sa 9-6; closed holidays
COPYING FACILITIES: yes
MATERIALS SOLICITED: Local and State government documents, local history papers, and genealogies of Georgia. Will also accept works by Georgia authors and genealogies from other States.

HOLDINGS:
Total volume: 18 l.f.; 600 items
Inclusive dates: 1920 -
Description: Texts of speeches, photographs, and other materials compiled about Savannah by Mayor Thomas Gamble in the 1930's.

GA895-160
Diocese of Savannah
Chancery Archives and Diocesan Archives
302 East Liberty Street
Savannah GA

MAILING ADDRESS:
P.O. Box 8789
Savannah GA 31402

(912) 238-2320

OPEN: M-F 10-5; closed weekends, holidays and some holy days
COPYING FACILITIES: yes
MATERIALS SOLICITED: Diocesan church records, 1796-1898, and histories of individual parishes, especially the very old ones. Will also accept Diocese-related newspaper clippings, scrapbooks, photographs, and personal letters, as well as biographies of bishops.

HOLDINGS:
Total volume: 120 l.f.
Inclusive dates: 1796 -
Description: Manuscripts relating to the Diocese of Savannah, including journals, personal and official letters, scrapbooks, typescripts, papers on the growth of the Catholic church during the Spanish and French colonization of Georgia, Civil War diaries, and stories of the Indian tribes of Georgia and of the experiences of early missionaries.

GA895-280
Georgia Historical Society
501 Whitaker Street
Savannah GA 31401

(912) 944-2128

OPEN: M-F 10-6, Sa 9:30-1; closed Sundays and holidays
COPYING FACILITIES: yes
MATERIALS SOLICITED: Materials regarding Georgia and the southeastern United States.

HOLDINGS:
Total volume: 1,500 collections
Inclusive dates: 1740 -
Description: Manuscripts relating chiefly to Georgia and Savannah, including diaries and other papers of families, plantation and business records, minutes and other records of organizations, and official and semi-official records of the colony and State of Georgia.

SEE: Hamer; NUCMC, 1979.

SEE: Allard, Crawley, and Edmison; Beers - Confederate; Hinding; Hines; Ingram; Leventhal and Mooney - III; Novotny; Robbins; Schatz.

GA895-290
Girl Scouts of the U.S.A.
Juliette Gordon Low Girl Scout National Center
142 Bull Street
Savannah GA 31401

(912) 233-4501

OPEN: M-F 10-4; closed weekends and holidays
COPYING FACILITIES: yes
MATERIALS SOLICITED: Will accept materials related to Juliette Gordon Low, founder of the Girl Scouts of the U.S.A.; documentation of the architectural history of her birthplace, the Wayne-Gordon House in Savannah; and documentation of the founding and early years of the Girl Scouts in Savannah, 1912-15.

HOLDINGS:
Total volume: 3 file drawers
Inclusive dates: 1818 - 1927
Description: Manuscripts relating to Juliette Gordon Low, the history of the Wayne-Gordon House, and the Gordon family.

SEE: Hinding.

STATESBORO

GA915-280
Georgia Southern College
Library
Statesboro GA

MAILING ADDRESS:
Landrum Box 8074
Statesboro GA 30460

(912) 681-5417

OPEN: M-F 8-5; closed weekends and holidays
COPYING FACILITIES: yes
MATERIALS SOLICITED: Papers of Georgia Southern College faculty, College publications and office files; public papers and publications relevant to the history of the College and to the history of Georgia, the city of Statesboro and Bulloch County. Will also accept notable manuscripts and personal papers.

HOLDINGS:
Total volume: 175 c.f.
Inclusive dates: 1812 -
Description: Primarily papers concerning Georgia Southern College. Included are photographs, faculty publications, theses, bulletins and other College publications, and material relating to the 1969 inauguration of President John O. Eidson. Other holdings relate to the city of Statesboro and the State of Georgia, Margaret Mitchell, the Civil War, and the War of 1812.

SEE: Hinding.

TIFTON

GA940-280

Georgia Agrirama Development
  Authority
State Museum of Agriculture
U.S. I-75 at 8th Street Exit
Tifton GA

MAILING ADDRESS:
P.O. Box Q
Tifton GA 31794

(912) 386-3344

OPEN: Winter, M-Sa 9-5, Su noon-5,
  summer, daily 9-6; closed holidays
ACCESS: appointment required
COPYING FACILITIES: yes
MATERIALS SOLICITED: Materials relating
to the history of agriculture in Georgia,
especially rural development in southern Georgia, 1870-1900.

HOLDINGS:
  Total volume: 110 items
  Inclusive dates: 1820 -
  Description: Materials chiefly relating
to southern Georgia from 1870 to 1900,
including account books of local turpentine commissaries, general stores, and
professionals, church records, family papers, oral history interviews, and research
reports on the material history of the
area.

VALDOSTA

GA950-480

Lowndes County Historical Society
305 West Central Avenue
Valdosta GA

MAILING ADDRESS:
P.O. Box 434
Valdosta GA 31601

(912) 247-4780

OPEN: Su 2-5; closed other days
COPYING FACILITIES: no
MATERIALS SOLICITED: Materials per-
taining to the city of Valdosta and
Lowndes County.

HOLDINGS:
  Total volume: not specified
  Inclusive dates: 1860 -
  Description: Letters, 400 photographs,
biographical sketches, organization and
county government records, and genea-
logical materials pertaining to Lowndes
County and its residents.

GA950-720

South Georgia Regional Library
300 Woodrow Wilson Drive
Valdosta GA 31601

(912) 333-5285

OPEN: M-Th 10-9, F, Sa 10-5:30, Su
2:30-5:30; closed holidays
COPYING FACILITIES: yes

HOLDINGS:
  Total volume: 10 items
  Inclusive dates: 19th century -
  Description: Manuscript histories of
four Georgia localities: Valdosta,
Kinderlou, Lowndes County, and Echols
County; a pictorial history of Valdosta;
and a woman's memoirs, giving first im-
pressions of Valdosta in 1863.

SEE: Hinding.

YOUNG HARRIS

GA990-940

Young Harris College
Duckworth Libraries
Young Harris GA

MAILING ADDRESS:
P.O. Box 38
Young Harris GA 30582

(404) 379-3526

OPEN: M-Th 8-10:30, F 8-5, Su 1-10:30;
closed Saturdays, holidays, and
quarterly intersessions
ACCESS: advance arrangements required
COPYING FACILITIES: yes
MATERIALS SOLICITED: Materials relating
to Young Harris College, north Georgia, southern Appalachia, and Byron
Herbert Reece.

HOLDINGS:
  Total volume: 26 l.f.
  Inclusive dates: 1891 -
  Description: Materials relating to the
history of Young Harris College and
manuscripts and correspondence of poet
Byron H. Reece.

GUAM

The Nieves M. Flores Memorial Library has been designated the official Archives of the Government of Guam records. A records survey is being conducted to determine locations and types of records, to appraise records for permanent preservation, and to analyze storage conditions and costs.

HAWAII

Hawaii has no statewide program for preserving the records of its political subdivisions. Because the State government administers typically local functions, all vital, land, probate, court, tax, education and welfare records are generated by State agencies. Such records of permanent value are housed at the State Archives in Honolulu, or are on microfilm in the agencies. Police, fire, sewage, zoning, and other records of the four counties (municipalities) normally remain in the custody of local authorities.

HILO

HI250-480

Lyman House Memorial Museum
276 Haili Street
Hilo HI 96720

(808) 935-5021

OPEN: M-Sa 10-4; closed Sundays and holidays
COPYING FACILITIES: no
MATERIALS SOLICITED: Hawaii materials.

HOLDINGS:
 Total volume: 90 c.f.; 6,000 photographs
 Inclusive dates: 1800 -
 Description: Correspondence, diaries, business records, genealogical source data, public documents, church and school records, manuscript maps, and photographs pertaining to Hawaii, its history, and its ethnic groups.

HONOLULU

HI350-73

Bernice P. Bishop Museum
Library and Sound Archives
1525 Bernice Street
Honolulu HI

MAILING ADDRESS:
P.O. Box 19000A
Honolulu HI 96819

(808) 847-3511

OPEN: W 8-4 and by appointment
COPYING FACILITIES: yes
MATERIALS SOLICITED: Hawaii and Pacific history, anthropology, and natural history. Sound documentation of music, folklore, and history. Will also accept photographs of informants, and sheet music with accompanying English translations.

HOLDINGS:
 Total volume: 294 l.f.; 24 file drawers; 40 map case drawers; and 3,500 recordings
 Inclusive dates: 1750 -
 Description: Historical materials acquired from Hawaiian royal family collections, including correspondence, memorabilia, genealogies, diaries, musical scores, public documents, and collections relating to chant, legend, and lore. Museum staff collections include Museum-generated records of expeditions and research in the Pacific area, 1898 to date, including materials in the fields of natural history, anthropology, material culture, and linguistics of the Pacific islands and Hawaii. There are also maps, drawings, plans, and other visual documents.
 Oral documentation of the music, cultural practices, beliefs, and history of Hawaii, with some coverage of Polynesia, Micronesia, Melanesia, and Asia. Recording media include cylinders; acetate, aluminum, and vinyl discs; and wire, magnetic tape, and cassette recordings.

GUIDES: *Dictionary Catalog of the Library of Bernice P. Bishop Museum, Honolulu* (G. K. Hall, 1964-69).

SEE: Novotny; Robbins; Allard, Crawley, and Edmison.

SEE ALSO: A. L. Kaeppler, 'Acculturation in Hawaiian Dance,' *Yearbook of the International Folk Music Council* 4 (1972); A. L. Kaeppler, 'Music in Hawaii in the Nineteenth Century,' *Die Musikkulturen Asiens, Afrikas and Ozeaniens im 19. Jahrhundert* (Bosse, 1973); E. Williamson, 'Hawaiian Chants . . .,' *Ethnomusicology* 18 (1974); K. P. Emory, M. K. Pukui, and E. Williamson, *Directions in Pacific Traditional Literature* (Bishop Museum Press, 1976); W. Kikuchi and C. Stauder, *Archaeology on Kauai*, vol. 5 (Kauai Community College, 1976).

HI350-80

Bernice P. Bishop Museum
Pacific Scientific Information Center
1525 Bernice Street
Honolulu HI

MAILING ADDRESS:
P.O. Box 19000A
Honolulu HI 96819

(808) 847-3511

OPEN: by appointment only
COPYING FACILITIES: yes
MATERIALS SOLICITED: Materials on the oceanic Pacific area and closely related areas to the west, focusing on geography in its broad sense, including man, plants, animals and their environment.

HOLDINGS:
 Total volume: 50 c.f.; 70,000 aerial photographs; maps and drawings
 Inclusive dates: 1890 -
 Description: Biogeographical and descriptive notes regarding Pacific islands, chiefly Polynesia and Micronesia. There are also aerial photographs of Pacific islands.

HI350-150

Daughters of Hawaii
Queen Emma Summer Palace
2913 Pali Highway
Honolulu HI 96817

(808) 595-6291

OPEN: M-F 9-4, Sa 9-noon; closed Sundays and holidays
ACCESS: by approval of board of directors of Daughters of Hawaii
COPYING FACILITIES: no
MATERIALS SOLICITED: History and culture of Hawaii from beginnings through the Hawaiian monarchy. Will also accept materials pertaining to the history of the Daughters of Hawaii.

HOLDINGS:
 Total volume: not specified
 Inclusive dates: 1903 -
 Description: Records pertaining to the history of Hulihee Palace in Kailua-Kona, and the Queen Emma Summer Palace in Honolulu, the two historic houses maintained and operated as museums by the Daughters of Hawaii. There are also records of the Daughters of Hawaii (1903-).

HI350-295

Hawaii Chinese History Center
Room 410, 111 North King Street
Honolulu HI 96817

(808) 521-5948

OPEN: M, W, F 10-1; closed other days and holidays
COPYING FACILITIES: no
MATERIALS SOLICITED: Materials relating to the Chinese in Hawaii, including genealogies, records of organizations, memoirs, records of Chinese historical sites, old documents, and photographs. Will also accept records relating to the Chinese in America and throughout the world, and Chinese historical or cultural materials of background value to the history of the Chinese in Hawaii.

HOLDINGS:
 Total volume: 12 l.f.
 Inclusive dates: 1788 -
 Description: A collection relating chiefly to the Chinese in Hawaii. Included are genealogies, records of organizations, oral

history recordings of old Chinese, maps, photographs, and rare documents.

HI350-300
Hawaii Department of Accounting and General Services
Archives Division
Iolani Palace Grounds
Honolulu HI 96813

(808) 548-2355

OPEN: M-F 7:45-4:30; closed weekends and holidays
COPYING FACILITIES: yes
MATERIALS SOLICITED: Hawaiian government records, covering its various forms, including kingdom, provisional government, republic, Territory, and State, as well as private papers of government officials and members of Hawaii's royal family. Will also accept manuscripts concerning Hawaiian history that do not conflict with collection specialties of other local repositories.

HOLDINGS:
Total volume: 8,000 c.f.
Inclusive dates: 1790 -
Description: Archives of the governments of Hawaii, and 425 collections of private papers, primarily of members of Hawaii's royal family and government officials, including Delegates to Congress for the Territory of Hawaii.

GUIDES: 'The Archives of Hawaii' (1966), a mimeographed description of the collection, is available on request.

SEE: Hamer (as Public Archives); NUCMC, 1970.

SEE: Allard, Crawley, and Edmison; Hinding.

SEE ALSO: Agnes Conrad, 'Indexes to Records in the State of Hawaii Archives,' *Hawaii Library Association Journal* 28 (Dec. 1971); Ann Novotny, ed., *Picture Sources 3* (Special Libraries Assn., 1975); *Map Collections in the United States and Canada, A Directory* (Special Libraries Assn., 1970); Richard C. Davis, *North American Forest History: A Guide to Archives and Manuscripts in the United States and Canada* (Clio Books, 1977).

HI350-311
Hawaii State Library
Hawaii and Pacific Section, Hawaii Documents Center
478 South King Street
Honolulu HI 96813

(808) 548-2346

OPEN: M, W, F, Sa 9-5, Tu, Th 9-8; closed weekends
ACCESS: identification required
COPYING FACILITIES: yes
MATERIALS SOLICITED: Manuscripts and other materials concerning Hawaii and the Pacific.

HOLDINGS:
Total volume: 1 l.f.
Inclusive dates: 1841 - 1960
Description: Letters, papers, and other materials relating to Admiral Richard Thomas and the Sandwich Islands; the

journal of William Miller, British consul of Honolulu in 1844, describing Hawaii and its people; reminiscences of Henry L. Sheldon about his experiences in Honolulu, 1846-53; and papers of Nils Paul Larsen, 1890-1960.

HI350-315
Hawaiian Historical Society
Library
560 Kawaiahao Street
Honolulu HI 96813

(808) 537-6271

OPEN: M-F 10-4; closed weekends and holidays
ACCESS: advance notice recommended
COPYING FACILITIES: no
MATERIALS SOLICITED: Personal papers and photographs relating to the history of Hawaii. Will also accept archives of community organizations and business records.

HOLDINGS:
Total volume: 57 l.f.
Inclusive dates: 1817 -
Description: Letters, journals, diaries, research notes, and papers relating to the history of Hawaii, including those of Joel Turrill, Gorham Gilman, William DeWitt Alexander, Sereno Bishop, and John Stokes. Also held are photographs of Hawaii by Ray Jerome Baker, Theodore Kelsey, Robin Kay, and others.

SEE: NUCMC, 1959-61.

HI350-320
Hawaiian Mission Children's Society
Library
553 South King Street
Honolulu HI 96813

(808) 531-0481

OPEN: M-F 10-4; Saturdays by appointment; closed Sundays and holidays
COPYING FACILITIES: no
MATERIALS SOLICITED: Writings of the Protestant missionaries to Hawaii during 19th century, their first-generation descendants, and later generations' writings if pertinent to Hawaii or missionary endeavors, including Micronesia. Will also accept writings of non-missionary people in Hawaii, if relating to missionary personnel, work, etc.; church records, photographs, drawings, and early travellers' descriptions of Hawaii, especially material showing the relation of missions and missionaries to the community.

HOLDINGS:
Total volume: 230 l.f.
Inclusive dates: 1818 - 1945
Description: Reports, journals, and correspondence of the Protestant missionaries to Hawaii who arrived 1820-48; correspondence with the American Board of Commissioners for Foreign Missions in Boston; and statistics on schools, churches, population and migrations.

SEE: Hamer; NUCMC, 1966, 76.

SEE: Hinding.

HI350-340
Honolulu Municipal Reference & Records Center
City Hall Annex
558 South King Street
Honolulu HI 96813

(808) 523-4577

OPEN: M-F 7:45-4:30; closed weekends and holidays
COPYING FACILITIES: yes
MATERIALS SOLICITED: Records and historical materials pertinent to the history of the municipal government of Honolulu.

HOLDINGS:
Total volume: 400 c.f.
Inclusive dates: 1887 -
Description: The bulk of the holdings consists of Honolulu city legislative records since 1905. Other materials include photographs of public works projects since the 1920's, bound ledgers, journals, financial records, and a series of engineering maps dated 1887.

SEE ALSO: Jean T. Kadooka-Mardfin, 'Archival Responsibilities of the Special Librarian,' *Special Libraries* 67 (Dec. 1976).

HI350-720
St. Louis-Chaminade Education Center
Marianist Archives
3140 Waialae Avenue
Honolulu HI 96816

no telephone

OPEN: by appointment only
COPYING FACILITIES: yes
MATERIALS SOLICITED: Materials relating to Catholic church history in the Hawaiian islands, especially photographs, manuscripts, and oral histories.

HOLDINGS:
Total volume: 72 c.f.
Inclusive dates: 1881 - 1970
Description: A collection concentrating on the history of St. Louis College, the second oldest private school in the Hawaiian islands. Included are 170 volumes of non-current student and financial records; 813 glass negatives of the campus, College activities, and cities and churches of Hawaii; 2 volumes of photograph prints; oral histories; and miscellaneous manuscripts, journals, and minutes.

For access to this material please write: Brother Lawrence Scrivani, P.O. Box AC, Cupertino CA 95015.

HI350-770
United States Army Museum, Hawaii
Battery Randolph
Kalia and Saratoga Roads
Fort DeRussey
Honolulu HI

MAILING ADDRESS:
Director
US Army Museum, Hawaii
DPT, USASCH
Fort Shafter HI 96858

(808) 543-2639

OPEN: Tu-Su 10-4:30; closed Mondays
  and holidays
ACCESS: University of Hawaii staff and
  graduate students, and other
  researchers by prior appointment
COPYING FACILITIES: no
MATERIALS SOLICITED: U.S. military history, primarily in East Asia and the
  Pacific Ocean.

HOLDINGS:
  Total volume: 15 l.f.
  Inclusive dates: 1898 - 1946
  Description: Materials chiefly documenting the activities of the U.S. Army
  in East Asia and the Pacific Ocean islands, including photographs of the Korean and Vietnam wars; unpublished unit
  histories, some dating from the 1920's;
  land records; official military records; and
  private papers.

HI350-790
University of Hawaii at Manoa
Department of History
Pacific Regional Oral History
  Program
2530 Dole Street
Honolulu HI 96822

(808) 948-7708, 8486

OPEN: by appointment only
ACCESS: appointment recommended
COPYING FACILITIES: yes
MATERIALS SOLICITED: Oral histories
  concerning plantation life in Hawaii,
  including labor organization, work experiences, and ethnic culture. Will also
  accept related photographs.

HOLDINGS:
  Total volume: 120 oral histories
  Inclusive dates: 1970 -
  Description: Recorded interviews and
  transcripts, mostly relating to labor on
  Hawaiian sugar and pineapple planta-
  tions.

SEE ALSO: Alan M. Meckler and Ruth
  McMullin, comps., *Oral History Collections* (Bowker, 1975).

HI350-808
University of Hawaii at Manoa
Library
Archives and Manuscripts
2425 Campus Road
Honolulu HI 96822

(808) 948-8264, 8473

OPEN: M-F 8-5; closed weekends and
  holidays
COPYING FACILITIES: yes
MATERIALS SOLICITED: Material by or
  about the University of Hawaii, its faculty, staff, and students. Will also accept materials relating to Hawaii during World War II (part of the Hawaii
  War Records Depository); faculty, staff
  and student personal papers; records of
  campus organizations; and faculty, staff
  and student publications, if done while
  at the University.

HOLDINGS:
  Total volume: 1,575 l.f.
  Inclusive dates: 1824 -
  Description: Manuscript material, photographs, maps, charts, drawings, and
  other items on the University of Hawaii,
  and on Hawaii during World War II; and
  materials related to sugar planters, scientists, educators, government officials,
  travellers and authors who visited or
  worked in Hawaii.

SEE: Hamer (as both University of Hawaii, Library and Hawaii War Records
  Depository); NUCMC, 1962, 66, 78.

SEE: Hinding; Allard, Crawley, and
  Edmison; Robbins.

The repository holds materials previously reported separately as the University of Hawaii at Manoa, Library,
Hawaiian Collection (HI350-810 in
first edition).

LAHAINA

HI400-480
Lahaina Restoration Foundation
Front and Dickenson Streets
Lahaina HI

MAILING ADDRESS:
P.O. Box 338
Lahaina HI 96767

(808) 661-3262

OPEN: M-F 10-4; closed weekends and
  holidays
COPYING FACILITIES: yes

HOLDINGS:
  Total volume: not specified
  Inclusive dates: 1820 - 1860
  Description: Copies of letters, shipping
  notices, court records, and other papers
  dealing with buildings, personalities,

whalers, sites, natural events, and other
aspects of the history of Lahaina, early
capital of the Hawaiian Kingdom.

The repository's holdings consist
mainly of copies of manuscripts
housed at the Hawaiian Mission Children's Society in Honolulu, HI.

LAIE

HI450-75
Brigham Young University-Hawaii
  Campus
Archives and Manuscripts
55-220 Kulanui Street
Laie HI 96762

(808) 293-3869

OPEN: M-F 8-5; closed weekends and
  holidays
ACCESS: advance arrangements required
COPYING FACILITIES: yes
MATERIALS SOLICITED: Materials relating
  to the impact of Mormonism in the
  Pacific and records of the Laie and
  Kahuku plantations. Will also accept
  pictures and other items relating to
  Polynesia.

HOLDINGS:
  Total volume: 360 l.f.
  Inclusive dates: 1850 -
  Description: Archival material relating
  to Brigham Young University-Hawaii
  Campus and photographs, oral histories,
  and news clippings covering local history
  and history of the Pacific Ocean area.

HI450-80
Brigham Young University - Hawaii
  Campus
Oral History Program
55-220 Kulanui Street
Laie HI 96762

(808) 293-3834

OPEN: by appointment only
COPYING FACILITIES: yes
MATERIALS SOLICITED: History of the
  Mormon church in the Pacific. Will
  also accept Pacific materials in general.

HOLDINGS:
  Total volume: 156 items
  Inclusive dates: 1971 -
  Description: Oral history interviews
  conducted in New Zealand, Tonga, Samoa, and the United States about the
  Maori Agricultural College, a Mormon
  school in New Zealand which operated
  from 1913 to 1931.

SEE: Meckler and McMullin.

IDAHO

Since about 1970 the Idaho State Historical Society has administered a statewide program for preserving local public records. The majority of Idaho's permanently valuable local public records remain in the custody of local officials, but most of the permanently valuable records for a third of the counties and the city of Boise are located at the Idaho State Historical Society in Boise.

BOISE

ID80-90
Boise State University
Library
Special Collections Department
1910 University Drive
Boise ID 83725

(208) 385-1736

OPEN: M-F 8-5; closed weekends and holidays
COPYING FACILITIES: yes
MATERIALS SOLICITED: Materials relating to Boise State University, Boise city, southwestern Idaho, and western poets.

HOLDINGS:
> *Total volume:* 754 c.f.
> *Inclusive dates:* 1875 -
> *Description:* Manuscripts and institution records documenting the growth of Boise State University, Boise city, and southwestern Idaho. There are collections dealing with local politics, teaching, education, Idaho history, and literary endeavors, primarily poetry. Included are oral history interviews, photographs, and records of organizations, individuals, and University faculty, including correspondence, minutes, scrapbooks, diaries, and financial records.

SEE: Hinding; Winroth.

ID80-365
Idaho State Historical Society
Division of Manuscripts and
Idaho State Archives
610 North Julia Davis Drive
Boise ID 83702

(208) 334-3356

OPEN: M-F 8-5; closed weekends and holidays
COPYING FACILITIES: yes
MATERIALS SOLICITED: Records of State agencies, cities, counties, and special districts; manuscripts, documents, files; and business, law office, bank, commercial, labor organization, church,

and personal records relating to Idaho and the Pacific Northwest. Will also accept other files and materials from Idaho sources worthy of preservation.

HOLDINGS:
> *Total volume:* 19,400 l.f.
> *Inclusive dates:* 1860 -
> *Description:* Over 900 collections, including 94 agencies in the Archives and 410 larger manuscript collections, relating primarily to Idaho and its history. Files of attorneys, defunct banks, labor organizations, lumber companies, ranches, merchants, church councils, mining companies, and newspapers comprise most of the non-government materials.

SEE: Hamer; NUCMC, 1959-62, 69, 71.

SEE: Davis; Novotny; Winroth; Hines; Hinding; Meckler and McMullin.

SEE ALSO: Merle M. Wells, 'The Idaho State Archives,' *Intermountain Archivist* (June 1976); G. Q. Flynn, 'The New Deal and Local Archives: The Pacific Northwest,' *American Archivist* 33 (Jan. 1970).

ID80-375
Idaho State Historical Society
Idaho Oral History Center
210 North Main Street
Boise ID

MAILING ADDRESS:
610 North Julia Davis Drive
Boise ID 83702

(208) 334-3863

OPEN: M-F 8-5; closed weekends and holidays
ACCESS: advance arrangements required
COPYING FACILITIES: no
MATERIALS SOLICITED: Oral history tapes and transcripts. Will also accept related photographs and research materials.

HOLDINGS:
> *Total volume:* 360 reels; 4 file cabinets
> *Inclusive dates:* 1958 -
> *Description:* Tape recordings and transcripts of oral history interviews, largely descriptions of early pioneer life in Idaho but also including interviews on historic sites and buildings.

CALDWELL

ID160-130
The College of Idaho
Regional Studies Center, Folklore
 Archives
Caldwell ID 83605

(208) 459-5214

OPEN: M-F 9-4; closed weekends and holidays
COPYING FACILITIES: yes
MATERIALS SOLICITED: Folklore and oral history of the Snake River region (Wyoming, Idaho, Utah, Oregon, and Washington).

HOLDINGS:
> *Total volume:* 150 items
> *Inclusive dates:* 1960 -
> *Description:* Oral history tapes, copies of student projects, and over 100 photographs of buildings, fences, and other scenes of the region.

SEE: Meckler and McMullin.

COEUR D'ALENE

ID240-520
Museum of North Idaho, Inc.
North Idaho College
Coeur d'Alene ID

MAILING ADDRESS:
P.O. Box 812
115 Northwest Blvd.
Coeur d'Alene ID 83814

(208) 664-3448

OPEN: Tu-Sa 11-5; closed Sundays, Mondays, holidays and Nov.-March
ACCESS: by prior arrangement
COPYING FACILITIES: yes
MATERIALS SOLICITED: Materials relating to northern Idaho.

HOLDINGS:
> *Total volume:* 3,000 items
> *Inclusive dates:* 1875 -
> *Description:* Photographs pertaining to Coeur d'Alene region of northern Idaho. Some records on early schools and a small collection of early newspapers.

SEE: Davis; Winroth; Hines.

ID240-560
North Idaho College
Library
1000 West Garden Avenue
Coeur d'Alene ID 83814

(208) 769-3355

OPEN: M-Th 8-10, F 8-4:30, Sa 10-4;
closed Sundays, holidays and school
vacations
COPYING FACILITIES: no
MATERIALS SOLICITED: Local oral history.

HOLDINGS:
Total volume: 225 oral history tapes
Inclusive dates: 1972 -
Description: Oral history interviews of
Coeur d'Alene residents relating to the
history of Coeur d'Alene, Kootenai County, and the State of Idaho.

SEE: Meckler and McMullin.

LAVA HOT SPRINGS

ID400-720
South Bannock County Historical
Center
Lava Hot Springs Museum
8 Main Street
Lava Hot Springs ID

MAILING ADDRESS:
P.O. Box 387
Lava Hot Springs ID 83246

(208) 776-5254

OPEN: daily 10-5
ACCESS: advance arrangements required
COPYING FACILITIES: yes
MATERIALS SOLICITED: Histories of settlers, manuscripts of authors, and other
materials relating to the history of
southeastern Bannock County. Will
also accept local contemporary photographs and manuscripts.

HOLDINGS:
Total volume: 2,500 items; 1 vol.
Inclusive dates: 1900 -
Description: Local history photographs
of early trappers, Indians, the city of
Lava Hot Springs, family portraits, buildings, and the local hot mineral water resort. Also held are recordings and transcripts from a local history project, city
records, cemetery and chamber of commerce records, family histories, and diaries.

MOSCOW

ID480-40
Appaloosa Horse Club, Inc.
Museum
Pullman Highway
Moscow ID

MAILING ADDRESS:
P.O. Box 8403
Moscow ID 83843

(208) 882-5578

OPEN: M-F 9-5; closed weekends and
holidays

COPYING FACILITIES: yes
MATERIALS SOLICITED: Materials concerning Appaloosa horses, the Nez
Perce Indians, the Nez Perce War, and
the Palouse country.

HOLDINGS:
Total volume: 28 items
Inclusive dates: 19th century -
Description: Photographs and letters
relating to the Columbia Plateau area,
Appaloosa horses, Nez Perce Indians,
cowboys, and mountain men.

ID480-480
Latah County Historical Society, Inc.
110 South Adams Street
Moscow ID 83843

(208) 882-1004

OPEN: W-Sa 1-4; closed other days and
holidays
COPYING FACILITIES: no
MATERIALS SOLICITED: Materials relating
to the settlement of Latah County,
1860 to date, with particular emphasis
on mining, farming, lumbering, and
other aspects of the County's economic
development. Will also accept materials
relating to Nez Perce Indians and to
the economic, social, cultural, and political development of northern Idaho
and eastern Washington.

HOLDINGS:
Total volume: 50 l.f.
Inclusive dates: 20th century
Description: Materials pertaining to all
aspects of the settlement and development of Latah County, including letters,
business records, genealogical materials,
photographs, manuscripts, and recordings
and transcripts of interviews with over
200 County pioneers.

SEE: Winroth; Hines.

SEE ALSO: Sam Schrager, ed., Guide to the
Latah County, Idaho, Oral History Collection (Latah County Museum Society,
1977); Alan M. Meckler and Ruth
McMullin, comps., Oral History Collections (Bowker, 1975).

ID480-770
University of Idaho
Archive of Pacific Northwest
Archaeology
Moscow ID 83843

(208) 885-6123

OPEN: M-F 8-5; closed weekends and
holidays
COPYING FACILITIES: yes
MATERIALS SOLICITED: Archaeology
(prehistory, historical archaeology, rock
art, archaeologists) of the Pacific
Northwest and osteometric and other
physical anthropological materials. Will
also accept ethnographic and linguistic
manuscript material.

HOLDINGS:
Total volume: 3,400 items
Inclusive dates: 1805 -
Description: A collection of manuscripts on the archaeology of the Pacific
Northwest, including British Columbia,
Idaho, Oregon, Washington, and parts of
Alaska, Alberta, California, and Montana.
Includes manuscript copies of site reports

and surveys, field notebooks, correspondence of regional archaeologists, maps,
drawings, photographs, film clips, English
translations of published works, taped interviews of regional archaeologists, and
osteometric data sheets.

SEE: Winroth.

ID480-810
University of Idaho
Library
Special Collections and Archives
Moscow ID 83843

(208) 885-7951

OPEN: M-F 8-5; closed weekends and
holidays
COPYING FACILITIES: yes
MATERIALS SOLICITED: University archives, as well as materials pertaining
to mining, lumbering, business, and
people in Idaho.

HOLDINGS:
Total volume: 966 l.f.; other materials
Inclusive dates: 1880 -
Description: The archives and noncurrent records of the University of Idaho, and 84 groups of papers relating to
various businesses and individuals in Idaho, especially mining.

SEE: Hamer; NUCMC, 1959-61, 66, 70.

SEE: Hinding; Hines; Robbins; Mehr; Davis.

SEE ALSO: Ann Novotny, ed., Picture
Sources 3 (Special Libraries Assn.,
1975); Alan M. Meckler and Ruth
McMullin, comps., Oral History Collections (Bowker, 1975); A Descriptive Inventory of the Papers of George Frederick Jewett (Univ. of Idaho Publications, No. 5, 1969).

MURPHY

ID520-600
Owyhee County Historical Museum
Murphy ID

MAILING ADDRESS:
Box 67
Murphy ID 83650

(208) 495-2319

OPEN: W-F 10-4; closed other days and
holidays
COPYING FACILITIES: no
MATERIALS SOLICITED: Materials relating
to the history of Owyhee County.

HOLDINGS:
Total volume: not specified
Inclusive dates: 1863 -
Description: Materials relating to
Owyhee County, including photographs,
oral histories, reminiscences of pioneers,
and materials concerning early mining activity.

SEE: Winroth.

NAMPA

ID560-560
Northwest Nazarene College
Archives
Nampa ID 83651

(208) 467-8605

OPEN: by appointment only
COPYING FACILITIES: yes
MATERIALS SOLICITED: Materials relating
to the history of the College.

HOLDINGS:
  Total volume: 247 document cases;
  14 filing cases
  Inclusive dates: 1898 -
  Description: Papers pertaining to the
  College, including the correspondence of
  its presidents; financial records; student
  codes; taped speeches; architectural
  drawings and aerial photographs; and
  other related manuscripts and photographs.

SEE ALSO: an index to major holdings
available from the institution.

OROFINO

ID600-130
Clearwater National Forest
12730 Highway 12
Orofino ID 83544

(208) 476-4541

OPEN: M-F 8-4:30; closed weekends and
holidays
COPYING FACILITIES: no
MATERIALS SOLICITED: Materials regarding prehistoric and historic human activity within and adjacent to
Clearwater National Forest.

HOLDINGS:
  Total volume: 6 items
  Inclusive dates: 1910 -
  Description: Photographs, films, reports
and narratives regarding prehistoric and
historic human activity within and adjacent to Clearwater National Forest, including information about the history of
the National Forest, forest fires, logging,
and technical information about the Forest.

POCATELLO

ID640-345
Idaho State University
Archives
Pocatello ID

MAILING ADDRESS:
P.O. Box 8089
Pocatello ID 83209

(208) 236-3661, 3677, 2954

OPEN: by appointment only; closed
holidays
ACCESS: advance arrangements required
COPYING FACILITIES: yes
MATERIALS SOLICITED: Materials dealing
with Idaho history and records of Idaho State University. Will also accept
historical materials on states bordering
Idaho.

HOLDINGS:
  Total volume: 332 l.f.
  Inclusive dates: 1880's -
  Description: Historical manuscripts,
  scrapbooks, correspondence, and other
  materials relating to Idaho history, including papers of Senator Fred T. Dubois
  and local historian Dr. Minnie F. Howard and records of the Lemhi Indian
  agency.

SEE: Hamer; NUCMC, 1959-62, 70 (as
Idaho State University Museum, Archives Division).

ID640-360
Idaho State University
Idaho Museum of Natural History
Pocatello ID

MAILING ADDRESS:
Campus Box 8096
Pocatello ID 83209

(208) 236-3168

OPEN: M-F 8:30-4:30; closed weekends
and holidays
COPYING FACILITIES: yes

HOLDINGS:
  Total volume: 150 items
  Inclusive dates: 1930 -
  Description: Manuscripts pertaining to
archaeology, anthropology, and the early
history of the region.

REXBURG

ID680-690
Ricks College
David O. McKay Learning Resources
  Center
Archives and Special Collections
Rexburg ID 83440

(208) 356-2376, 2377, 2356

OPEN: M-F 9-3; closed weekends and
holidays
COPYING FACILITIES: yes
MATERIALS SOLICITED: Materials relating
to the history of Ricks College, Mormon history, and eastern Idaho.

HOLDINGS:
  Total volume: 500 c.f.
  Inclusive dates: 1888 -
  Description: Manuscripts, photographs,
  and oral history interviews concerning
  Ricks College and the settlement of the
  Church of Jesus Christ of Latter-day
  Saints in the Upper Snake River Valley,
  as well as oral history and photographs of
  the Teton Dam flood of 1976.

SEE: Meckler and McMullin; Hinding.

SANDPOINT

ID880-80
Bonner County Historical Society
Bonner County Museum
Lakeside Park
Ontario and South Ella Streets
Sandpoint ID

MAILING ADDRESS:
P.O. Box 1063
Sandpoint ID 83864

(208) 263-2344

OPEN: M 10-4; Tu-F 8:30-4:30; closed
weekends and holidays
COPYING FACILITIES: yes
MATERIALS SOLICITED: Materials pertaining to Bonner County history, especially logging and railroads.

HOLDINGS:
  Total volume: 30 l.f.
  Inclusive dates: 1809 -
  Description: Materials relating to the
  history of Bonner County, including the
  papers of individuals and businesses, particularly in the fields of logging and
  railroading, as well as 2,000 photographs.
  There are also copies of mid-19th century
  surveying materials (maps and sketches)
  by James Alden.

SEE: Winroth; Hines.

ILLINOIS

Under the Illinois Regional Archival Depository system, established in 1976 in conformance with the Illinois Local Records Act of 1961, the State is divided into six sections, for which the State universities in Carbondale, Charleston, DeKalb, Macomb, Normal, and Springfield serve as repositories of permanently valuable local public records. These depositories have accessioned some 5,300 cubic feet of such material. The State Archives in Springfield has acquired some 1,600 reels of microfilm of pre-1900 vital, land, probate, and other county records filmed by the Church of Jesus Christ of Latter-day Saints.

Chicago and Cook County are excluded from the Illinois Regional Archival Depository system.

ARGONNE

IL35-40

Argonne National Laboratory
Technical Information Services
    Department
Building 203, 9700 South Cass
    Avenue
Argonne IL 60439

(312) 972-5618, 2000

OPEN: by appointment only
ACCESS: Files are in storage with varying degrees of accessibility, and are available to researchers by appointment, subject to time limitations of Laboratory staff.
COPYING FACILITIES: no

HOLDINGS:
    Total volume: not specified
    Inclusive dates: 1942 -
    Description: Documents and records concerned with the history and operation of the Metallurgical Laboratory (1942-46), U.S. Atomic Energy Commission, and the Argonne National Laboratory.

AURORA

IL45-30

Aurora College
Library
347 South Gladstone
Aurora IL 60507

(312) 892-6431, Ext. 61, 62

OPEN: Su 1-9, M-Th 8-10, F 8-5, Sa 10-4; closed holidays and Aug.
ACCESS: appointment required with Jenks Curator, College Archivist, or Library Director
COPYING FACILITIES: yes
MATERIALS SOLICITED: Manuscripts, archival records, Christian education materials, photographs, oral history tapes, and scrapbooks related to the Millerite movement and the Advent Christian church and missions.

HOLDINGS:
    Total volume: 89 l.f.
    Inclusive dates: 1814 -
    Description: The Jenks collection, including materials of William Miller, the Millerite movement, Advent Christian church, Seventh-Day Adventists, and Life and Advent Union. The collection also relates to missionary activities of the Advent Christian church among black freedmen and Western pioneers and foreign missionary work in India, the Congo, China, and Japan.

SEE: Hamer.

SEE: Hinding.

IL45-45

Aurora Historical Museum
Cedar and Oak Streets
Aurora IL

MAILING ADDRESS:
P.O. Box 905
Aurora IL 60507

(312) 897-9029

OPEN: W, Su 2-4:30; closed other days
USER FEES: $3 annual membership encouraged
COPYING FACILITIES: yes
MATERIALS SOLICITED: Will accept Aurora area material.

HOLDINGS:
    Total volume: 50 l.f.; 5 file cabinets
    Inclusive dates: 1770 -
    Description: Documents, photographs, and other materials covering the history of the Aurora area.

IL45-640

Paramount North Island Centre
Archives
23 East Galena Blvd.
Aurora IL

MAILING ADDRESS:
11 East Galena Blvd.
Aurora IL 60506

(312) 896-7676

OPEN: by appointment only
ACCESS: appointment required with Director of Theatre Operation
COPYING FACILITIES: yes
MATERIALS SOLICITED: Documents pertaining to the theater in Illinois since 1930, restoration and preservation of theaters and movie palaces, the Paramount Theater chain and Bablan and Katz theaters, and the use of stencils in renovation.

HOLDINGS:
    Total volume: 37 c.f.
    Inclusive dates: 1977 -
    Description: Records of performances at the Paramount Theater, including programs, photographs, press releases, and newspaper clippings, and records of the Paramount Arts Centre renovation, including soil testing results, blueprints, and schedules.

BARRINGTON

IL55-80

Barrington Area Historical Society
    Museum
218 West Main Street
Barrington IL 60010

(312) 381-1730

OPEN: M-F by appointment; closed weekends and Federal holidays
COPYING FACILITIES: yes
MATERIALS SOLICITED: Materials pertaining to the history and development of the Barrington area.

HOLDINGS:
    Total volume: 24 l.f.; 1 fireproof file
    Inclusive dates: 1840 -
    Description: Manuscripts, including genealogical source data, logbooks, account books, business records, and literary manuscripts; archives of schools, businesses, government agencies, churches, and community groups; photographs and maps; oral history tapes and transcripts.

IL55-120
Carmelite Order
The Province of the Most Pure Heart
    of Mary
Archive
Carmelite Provincial House
45 East Dundee Road
Barrington IL 60010

(312) 381-6790, 6791

OPEN: by appointment only
ACCESS: qualified historians and
    researchers
COPYING FACILITIES: yes
MATERIALS SOLICITED: Personal papers
    of Carmelites in the U.S.; materials
    concerning the Carmelites in the U.S.
    from the Sacred Propaganda Fide Ar-
    chives, Rome; and records from Car-
    melite missions in Peru and Chile. Will
    also accept any records pertaining to
    Carmelite activities and apostolates in
    the U.S. and Canada.

HOLDINGS:
    Total volume: 300 l.f.
    Inclusive dates: 1864 -
    Description: Records of the Carmelite
    Province of the Most Pure Heart of
    Mary, in the U.S. and Canada, and mis-
    sions in Palestine, Chile, and Peru. In-
    cluded are acts and correspondence from
    Rome; Provincial acts, statutes, necrol-
    ogies, and letters; and registers of the
    Province, its apostolates and activities.
    There are also records and correspon-
    dence of the priors provincial from 1864;
    personnel records; documents and histori-
    cal material of each foundation, extant
    and suppressed; chronicles of the Prov-
    ince and friaries; diaries; collections of
    papers of Carmelites; financial records of
    the Province, friaries, and parishes; maps;
    technical drawings; photographs; and mo-
    tion pictures.

BELVIDERE

IL74-360
Ida Public Library
320 North State Street
Belvidere IL 61008

(815) 544-3838

OPEN: M-F 12-9, Sa 10-6; closed
    Sundays and holidays
COPYING FACILITIES: yes

HOLDINGS:
    Total volume: 45 items
    Inclusive dates: 1885 -
    Description: Personal reminiscences, a
    set of letters from Civil War days, an
    informal history of Belvidere, and inven-
    tories of local flora, architecture, cemetery
    inscriptions, and other aspects of Boone
    County history. Also included are
    blueprints from the 1913 library building,
    as well as the records, accession books,
    and Board of Trustee minutes from the
    Library, dating from 1885.

BERWYN

IL84-120
Czechoslovak Society of America
    Fraternal Life
Archives
2701 South Harlem Avenue
Berwyn IL

MAILING ADDRESS:
CSA Plaza
Berwyn IL 60402

(312) 795-5800

OPEN: M-F 9-4:30; closed weekends and
    holidays
COPYING FACILITIES: yes
MATERIALS SOLICITED: Minute and
    record books of lodges, and materials
    relating to early Czech, Moravian, or
    Slovak immigration to the United
    States.

HOLDINGS:
    Total volume: 1,103 l.f.; 1,388 items
    Inclusive dates: 1854 -
    Description: Records of the Czechoslo-
    vak Society of America, including minute
    books, financial and insurance records,
    death claims, and correspondence con-
    cerning such subjects as lodges, scholar-
    ships, real estate, mortgages, sick benefits,
    and election of lodge officers.

IL84-600
Order of Servants of Mary
Eastern Province
Provincial Archives
3401 South Home Avenue
Berwyn IL 60402

(312) 484-0063

OPEN: by appointment only
ACCESS: Each request is judged
    individually, consideration being given
    to the qualifications of the researchers,
    the purpose of the research, and the
    sensitivity of certain records, especially
    personnel records.
COPYING FACILITIES: no
MATERIALS SOLICITED: Material relating
    to the life and activities of the mem-
    bers of the Eastern Province of
    Servites. Will also accept other materi-
    als related in some way to the Eastern
    Province of Servites.

HOLDINGS:
    Total volume: 230 l.f.
    Inclusive dates: 1870 -
    Description: Financial and administra-
    tive records of the Province and provin-
    cial administration of the Eastern Prov-
    ince of Servites (1967-75); its predecessor,
    the Our Lady of Sorrows Province
    (1870-1967); records of the Novena of
    Our Sorrowful Mother (1937-75); person-
    al papers of some deceased members of
    the Servite Order; and local archives of
    houses of the Province which have been
    closed. Some records also refer to the
    foundations made in Ireland and the Re-
    public of South Africa.

BLOOMINGTON

IL94-360
Illinois Wesleyan University
Sheean Library
Bloomington IL 61701

(309) 556-3172

OPEN: M-F 8-5; summer, M-F 8-4;
    closed weekends and holidays
ACCESS: at the discretion of the Library
COPYING FACILITIES: yes
MATERIALS SOLICITED: Materials relating
    to Leslie C. Arends and to Illinois Wes-
    leyan University.

HOLDINGS:
    Total volume: 50 c.f.
    Inclusive dates: 1850 -
    Description: Papers of Leslie C.
    Arends; archives of Illinois Wesleyan
    University, including faculty minutes,
    trustee minutes, correspondence, reports,
    records of the non-resident degree pro-
    gram(1874-1910), and theses; and records
    of Chaddock College and Hedding Col-
    lege.

SEE: NUCMC, 1959-61, 78.

SEE: Hinding.

IL94-510
McLean County Historical Society
Archives
201 East Grove Street
Bloomington IL 61701

(309) 827-0428

OPEN: M-F 9-5; closed weekends and
    holidays
COPYING FACILITIES: yes
MATERIALS SOLICITED: Material pertain-
    ing to McLean County, including cor-
    respondence, diaries, academic manu-
    scripts and records of railroads, farms,
    social clubs, political movements, and
    religious groups.

HOLDINGS:
    Total volume: 100 l.f.
    Inclusive dates: 1820 -
    Description: Manuscripts, diaries,
    photos, correspondence, maps; business,
    church, and social records relating to
    McLean County. In particular, records,
    letters, and diaries relating to the 33rd
    and 94th Illinois Volunteer Regiments
    (Civil War). William Wantling collection
    of correspondence and manuscripts
    (contemporary poetry); McLean County
    Home Bureau papers (rural home eco-
    nomics); and Milo Custer papers
    (Kickapoo Indians and genealogy).

SEE: Hamer.

SEE: Hinding.

IL94-800

United Methodist Church
Central Illinois Conference
Commission on Archives and History
Conference Historical Society
1211 North Park Street
Bloomington IL 61701

(309) 828-5092

OPEN: M-F 8-4:30; closed weekends and holidays
COPYING FACILITIES: yes
MATERIALS SOLICITED: Materials relating to the United Methodist church in central Illinois and the United States.

HOLDINGS:
Total volume: 760 c.f.
Inclusive dates: 1780 -
Description: Local church records, especially of closed churches; correspondence, diaries, etc., of ministers and church officials; unpublished histories and reports; conference officials' records; and ledgers, reports, and early records of church-sponsored organizations, such as colleges, hospitals, and benevolent homes.

SEE: Hamer.

SEE ALSO: Robert H. Williams, *A Partial Inventory of Primary Source Documents and Unpublished Materials, Illinois Conference Historical Society* (1960).

CAIRO

IL109-130
Cairo Public Library
1609 Washington Avenue
Cairo IL 62914

(618) 734-1840

OPEN: M-F 9-7, Sa 9-5; closed Sundays and holidays
COPYING FACILITIES: yes
MATERIALS SOLICITED: Local family genealogies, materials concerning burials in Pulaski County, IL, Cairo photographs, and Civil War memoirs, particularly for Cairo. Will also accept other Cairo materials.

HOLDINGS:
Total volume: 100 vols.
Inclusive dates: 1858 -
Description: Civil War materials pertaining to the Sisters of the Holy Cross at the Mound City, IL, hospital, two Civil War diaries, steamboat photographs and information compiled by Captain William H. Tippet, and Alexander County, IL, cemetery records.

SEE: Hamer; NUCMC, 1966.

CANTON

IL119-240
Fulton County Historical and
 Genealogical Society
Parlin-Ingersoll Library
205 West Chestnut Street
Canton IL

MAILING ADDRESS:
45 North Park Drive
Canton IL 61520

(309) 647-0771, 0328

OPEN: M-F 9-6, Sa 9-4, Su 1-4; closed holidays
COPYING FACILITIES: yes
MATERIALS SOLICITED: Historical and genealogical materials related to Fulton County and its inhabitants.

HOLDINGS:
Total volume: 10 l.f.
Inclusive dates: 1833 -
Description: Materials chiefly pertaining to the settlement and development of Fulton County and Illinois, and to the history of settlers before they migrated to Illinois. Much of the collection consists of family histories and Daughters of the American Revolution genealogical materials.

CARBONDALE

IL124-725
Southern Illinois University at
 Carbondale
Morris Library
Special Collections
Carbondale IL 62901

(618) 453-2543

OPEN: M-F 9-5, Sa 9-noon; closed Sundays, state and University holidays
COPYING FACILITIES: yes
MATERIALS SOLICITED: Materials of or pertaining to 20th century American, British, and Irish authors, especially expatriates; American philosophers; southern Illinois history; and theater, particularly political theater and that of the Irish renaissance.

HOLDINGS:
Total volume: 6,000 c.f.
Inclusive dates: 1860 -
Description: Most of the collection is divided between personal papers and other manuscripts (215 collections) and University Archives (including 65 series of administrative records, university publications, faculty publications, dissertations, theses, and research papers). Serves as one of six Illinois Regional Archives Depositories containing local government records. Also included are photographs, films, and sound recordings.

SEE: Hamer; NUCMC, 1959-61, 69-71, 74, 77.

SEE: Parkinson; Spalek; Robbins; Hinding.

SEE ALSO: Ralph McCoy, 'Manuscript Collections in Morris Library,' *ICarbS* 1 (Spring-Summer 1974); John W. Presley, *The Robert Graves Manuscripts and Letters at Southern Illinois University: An Inventory* (Whitston, 1976); Stanley B. Kimball, comp., *Sources of Mormon History in Illinois, 1839-48; An Annotated Catalog of the Microfilm Collection at Southern Illinois University* (Southern Illinois Univ. Library, 1966); Alan M. Meckler and Ruth McMullin, comps., *Oral History Collections* (Bowker, 1975); David A. Hounshell, *Manuscripts in U.S. Depositories Relating to the History of Electrical Science and Technology* (Smithsonian Institution, n.d.).

Albert Krichmar, *The Women's Rights Movement in the United States, 1848-1970: A Bibliography and Sourcebook* (Scarecrow Press, 1972); Walter Schatz, ed., *Directory of Afro-American Resources* (Bowker, 1970); 'Midwest Research Institutions Directory,' *Illinois Libraries* 53 (Jan. 1971); Richard C. Davis, *North American Forest History: A Guide to Archives and Manuscripts in the United States and Canada* (Clio Books, 1977).

CARTHAGE

IL139-320
Hancock County Historical Society
Courthouse, 3rd Floor
Carthage IL

MAILING ADDRESS:
Box 68
Carthage IL 62321

no telephone

OPEN: M-Th 9-3 by appointment; closed Fridays and weekends
ACCESS: serious researchers
COPYING FACILITIES: yes
MATERIALS SOLICITED: Genealogical materials relating to local families. Will also accept early photographs of Hancock County.

HOLDINGS:
Total volume: not specified
Inclusive dates: 1829 -
Description: Scrapbooks, genealogical materials, records of organizations and schools, doctor's account books, and oral history recordings, all relating to Hancock County.

CHAMPAIGN

IL140-322
Illinois Department of Energy and
 Natural Resources
Illinois State Geological Survey
 Division
Natural Resources Building
615 East Peabody Drive
Champaign IL 61820

(217) 344-1481

OPEN: M-F 8-5; closed weekends and holidays
COPYING FACILITIES: yes
MATERIALS SOLICITED: Correspondence, drill hole logs, geologic and mine notes, unpublished manuscripts, Geological Survey archives, manuscript maps, charts, photographs, and unpublished translations.

HOLDINGS:
Total volume: 1,000 c.f.
Inclusive dates: 1905 -
Description: Materials relating mainly to geology and mineral resources of the State of Illinois. Included are correspondence files of National committees, field notes, mine notes, manuscript work maps, photographs, logs and related records from over 220,000 mineral test drillings, and other materials.

CHARLESTON

IL154-130

Coles County Historical Society
County Clerk
Court House
Charleston IL

MAILING ADDRESS:
P.O. Box 255
Charleston IL 61920

(217) 345-2057

OPEN: M-F 8-4; closed weekends and
   holidays
COPYING FACILITIES: yes
MATERIALS SOLICITED: Burials in Coles
   County from 1832 to present.

HOLDINGS:
   Total volume: 40,000 items
   Inclusive dates: 1832 -
   Description: A card file on all burials
   within what is now known as Coles
   County. Each card lists name of person
   buried, location, birth date, date of death,
   and other pertinent data.

CHICAGO

IL169-52

American Bar Foundation
Program on Oral History
1155 East 60th Street
Chicago IL 60637

(312) 988-6500

OPEN: M-F 9-5; closed weekends
COPYING FACILITIES: yes

HOLDINGS:
   Total volume: 100 hours of taped
interviews
   Inclusive dates: 1935 -
   Description: Taped interviews relating
   to the history of the organized bar in the
   United States, with special emphasis on
   the history of the American Bar Foundation, American Bar Association, and the
   American Bar Endowment. Covers not
   only institutional history but also important issues that the legal profession has
   faced since about 1936 to the present
   time.

IL169-78

American Dental Association
Bureau of Library Services
211 East Chicago Avenue
Chicago IL 60611

(312) 440-2653, 2500

OPEN: M-F 8:30-5; closed weekends and
   holidays
COPYING FACILITIES: yes
MATERIALS SOLICITED: Materials concerned with the history of the American Dental Association. Will also accept historical materials concerned with
   dentistry.

HOLDINGS:
   Total volume: 250 l.f.
   Inclusive dates: 1869 -
   Description: Records of the American
   Dental Association and its predecessor
   organizations, including correspondence,
   publications, and biographical informa-
   tion on persons important to dentistry.

SEE: Novotny.

IL169-127

The Arnold H. Crane Library of
   Photography
134 North LaSalle Street
Chicago 60602

no telephone

OPEN: by appointment only
USER FEES: research fee for assistance by
   library staff
ACCESS: all research performed by
   library staff
COPYING FACILITIES: yes
MATERIALS SOLICITED: Materials relating
   to photography and modern art, with
   emphasis on Dada and Surrealism.

HOLDINGS:
   Total volume: 12,000 items
   Inclusive dates: 1800 -
   Description: Photographs of historical
   or aesthetic value.

SEE: Novotny.

IL169-130

Art Institute of Chicago
Ryerson and Burnham Libraries
Michigan Avenue at Adams Street
Chicago IL 60603

(312) 443-3666

OPEN: M-Sa 10:30-4:30; closed Sundays,
   holidays, and Saturdays in summer
ACCESS: members of the Art Institute,
   students of the School of the Art
   Institute, visiting curators
COPYING FACILITIES: yes
MATERIALS SOLICITED: Manuscripts, letters, architectural records and
   drawings, and photographs pertaining
   to the visual fine arts and to architecture.

HOLDINGS:
   Total volume: 68 vols.; 853 items;
   10,000 architectural drawings; 18,460
photographs
   Inclusive dates: 19th century - 20th
century
   Description: The Ryerson Library has
   minutes of the Society for the Advancement of Truth in Art, and artists' business letters from the Art Institute of Chicago, including several letters of Georgia
   O'Keeffe, Mary Cassatt, and John Singer
   Sargent. The Architecture Archive in the
   Burnham Library has Daniel H.
   Burnham material, including diaries, office letters, and personal letters; Louis
   Henri Sullivan material, including his
   manuscript for 'System of Ornament'
   (with 20 drawings), and correspondence
   with Charles H. Whitaker and John Van
   Allen; Frank Lloyd Wright correspondence concerning a bank in Dwight, IL; a
   business letter book, a scrapbook, and
   two small sketchbooks of Howard Van
   Doren Shaw; Edward H. Bennett papers;

and materials concerning the World's Columbian Exposition of 1893, including
photographs, Burnham's final report as
Director of Work, and a letter book of
McKim, Mead, and White.

There is also a major collection of
architectural drawings and blueprints
from the offices of Burnham and Root;
D. H. Burnham and Company; Adler and
Sullivan; Louis H. Sullivan; Tallmadge
and Watson; and other Chicago architects. Also held are 39 microfilm reels
containing architectural drawings of early
buildings in the Chicago area and documents concerning them, and 18,460
mounted photographs of architecture. Illuminated medieval and Renaissance
manuscripts are housed in the Institute's
Department of Prints and Drawings.

SEE: Hamer; NUCMC, 1966-67.

SEE: Novotny; Hinding.

SEE ALSO: John Zukowsky, 'Burnham's
   Gift to Chicago: The Burnham Library
   of Architecture,' *Illinois Libraries* 63
   (April 1981).

IL169-169

Balzekas Museum of Lithuanian
   Culture
6500 South Pulaski
Chicago IL 60629

(312) 847-2441

OPEN: daily 1-4:30; closed Christmas
   and New Year's
USER FEES: one dollar
COPYING FACILITIES: no
MATERIALS SOLICITED: Materials relating
   to eastern Europe, Lithuanian artists,
   and Lithuanian history and humanities
   in the 19th and 20th centuries. Will
   also accept material on American
   Presidents.

HOLDINGS:
   Total volume: 25 l.f.
   Inclusive dates: 1930's -
   Description: Individuals' papers,
   unpublished memoirs and histories, and
   records of various Lithuanian institutions.

IL169-247

Center for Research Libraries
6050 South Kenwood Avenue
Chicago IL 60637

(312) 955-4545

OPEN: M-F 9-5; closed weekends and
   holidays
USER FEES: $8 per request for
   nonmember libraries
ACCESS: serious researchers may use
   materials on the premises; loans made
   only to libraries
COPYING FACILITIES: yes
MATERIALS SOLICITED: Materials geared
   to needs of member libraries. Will also
   accept other materials.

HOLDINGS:
   Total volume: 60 l.f.; undetermined
amount of microform
   Inclusive dates: 16th century -
   Description: Two collections of original
   records; one audio tape collection; holdings in microform of government archives (principally British, German and
   Japanese); archives of businesses, soci-

eties, and individuals; and unpublished foreign doctoral dissertations.

GUIDES: *Center for Research Libraries: Handbook* (1976).

SEE: Hamer (as Midwest Inter-Library Center).

SEE: Duignan.

SEE ALSO: Finding aids and microform guides are available at the institution.

IL169-286

Chicago Academy of Sciences
2001 North Clark Street
Chicago IL 60614

(312) 549-0606

OPEN: daily 10-5; closed Christmas
ACCESS: by appointment only
COPYING FACILITIES: yes
MATERIALS SOLICITED: Materials relating to natural history. Will also accept Chicago Academy of Sciences manuscript minutes, biographical files, financial records, publications, and other material relating to the Academy's activities and history.

HOLDINGS:
> *Total volume:* 25,000 items; 5 file drawers; other materials
> *Inclusive dates:* 1857 -
> *Description:* Material relating to natural history; manuscripts, minutes, biographical files, and copies of correspondence of early Academy directors with the Smithsonian Institition; and records of the Academy and its activities.

IL169-325

Chicago Historical Society
Clark Street at North Avenue
Chicago IL 60614

(312) 642-4600

OPEN: Tu-Sa 9:30-4:30; closed Sundays, Mondays, and holidays; July - Aug., M-F 9:30-4:30
COPYING FACILITIES: yes
MATERIALS SOLICITED: Records of Chicago organizations, personal papers of Chicagoans, and other materials concerning Chicago. Will also accept significant items (but generally not collections) which are likely to be used in the Society's exhibits program and which concern Illinois, the Old Northwest, the Civil War, and Abraham Lincoln.

HOLDINGS:
> *Total volume:* 7,200 l.f., excluding the Chicago Architectural Archive
> *Inclusive dates:* 1635 -
> *Description:* Manuscripts chiefly relating to social, political, business, and working conditions in Chicago, as well as cultural, religious, educational and other activities from the city's earliest days to the present. Plus a new Chicago Architectural Archive containing papers and records of Chicago architects and architectural firms.
>
> There are also significant holdings on life in Illinois from earliest settlement through the Civil War years, along with smaller but important lots of papers concerning the Civil War and the American Revolution, and individual pieces and

small lots of papers of Americans in various regions of the country during the 18th and 19th centuries.

SEE: Hamer; NUCMC, 1959-64, 66, 69, 71, 75.

SEE: Krichmar; Duignan; Paszek; Davis; Parkinson; Allard, Crawley, and Edmison; Hines; Ingram; Robbins; Hinding.

SEE ALSO: *Libraries and Information Centers in the Chicago Metropolitan Area* (Illinois Regional Library Council, 1976); Archie Motley, 'Chicago Historical Society,' *Illinois Libraries* 57 (March 1975); William L. Burton, *Descriptive Bibliography of Civil War Manuscripts in Illinois* (Northwestern Univ. Press, 1966); Walter Schatz, ed., *Directory of Afro-American Resources* (Bowker, 1970); Ann Novotny, ed., *Picture Sources 3* (Special Libraries Assn., 1975); David A. Hounshell, comp., *Manuscripts in U.S. Depositories Relating to the History of Electrical Science and Technology* (Smithsonian Institution, n.d.); Andrea Hinding and Rosemary Richardson, comps., *Archival and Manuscript Resources for the Study of Women's History: A Beginning* (Univ. of Minnesota Libraries, Social Welfare History Archives Center, 1972).

Articles and reports describing the Society's holdings appear frequently in *Chicago History: The Magazine of the Chicago Historical Society.*

IL169-396

The Chicago Public Library
Conrad Sulzer Regional Library
4455 North Lincoln Avenue
Chicago IL 60625

(312) 728-8652

OPEN: by appointment only, M-Th 9-9 F, Sa 9-5; closed Sundays and holidays
COPYING FACILITIES: yes
MATERIALS SOLICITED: Materials relating to the Ravenswood-Lakeview area of Chicago. Will also accept other materials relating to the history of Chicago.

HOLDINGS:
> *Total volume:* 175 l.f.
> *Inclusive dates:* pre-Civil War -
> *Description:* Diaries, correspondence, maps, photographs, and newspaper clippings relating to the history of the Ravenswood-Lakeview area of Chicago.

SEE: Hinding.

IL169-403

The Chicago Public Library
Pullman Branch
11001 South Indiana Avenue
Chicago IL 60628

no telephone

SEE: NUCMC, 1972.

Questionnaire not returned.

IL169-416

The Chicago Public Library
Special Collections Division
78 East Washington Street
Chicago IL 60602

(312) 269-2926

OPEN: M-F 10-4, Sa by appointment; closed Sundays and holidays
ACCESS: identification must be presented; appointments preferred for extensive research
COPYING FACILITIES: yes
MATERIALS SOLICITED: Material on the World's Columbian Exposition of 1893; material from the Goodman Theatre files and family of Kenneth Sawyer Goodman; and historical documents relating to the history of libraries in Chicago. Will also accept Civil War diaries, correspondence, rosters; typescripts and annotated galley proofs of works by Chicago authors; and Carl Sandburg correspondence.

HOLDINGS:
> *Total volume:* 2,000 items; 170 c.f.; 10,000 c.f. of archival material
> *Inclusive dates:* 1570 -
> *Description:* Autograph specimens of prominent 16th-20th century literary, historical, and art figures; materials relating to John S. Wright, James W. Ellsworth, Ralph G. Newman, Nathan Leopold, Otto Eisenschiml, the World's Columbian Exposition, the Goodman Theatre of the Art Institute of Chicago, and Carl Sandburg; manuscripts and photographs concerning the Civil War and the Grand Army of the Republic; graphic material including cartoons of John T. McCutcheon.
>
> The Chicago Public Library Archives includes blueprints, financial records, correspondence, Director's files, photographs, scrapbooks, and publications.

SEE: Hamer; NUCMC, 1959-61.

SEE: Schatz; Robbins.

SEE ALSO: *Treasures of the Chiary(1978); Susan Prendergast Schoelwer, 'The Chicago Public Library Special Collections Division,' Illinois Libraries 63 (April 1981); Dictionary Catalog of the Vivian G. Harsh Collection of Afro-American History and Literature* (G.K. Hall, 1978).

IL169-468

Chicago State University
Douglas Library
95th Street and King Drive
Chicago IL 60628

(312) 995-2235

OPEN: M-F 8-8:30, Sa 8-4; closed Sundays and holidays
COPYING FACILITIES: yes
MATERIALS SOLICITED: History of Chicago State University.

HOLDINGS:
> *Total volume:* 8 file cabinets
> *Inclusive dates:* 1869 -
> *Description:* A collection of information related to Chicago State University, including the University archives and the Paul and Emily Douglas Collection.

IL169-507

Chicago Theological Seminary
Hammond Library
5757 South University Avenue
Chicago IL 60637

(312) 752-5757

OPEN: M-F 9-5; closed weekends and
   holidays
COPYING FACILITIES: yes
MATERIALS SOLICITED: Church records
   on midwest Congregationalism; personal papers of theological faculty members; Congregational church merger papers.

HOLDINGS:
   Total volume: 500 vols.; 200 l.f.
   Inclusive dates: 1840 - 1965
   Description: Records of individual
   midwest Congregational churches. Included are reports of synods of Evangelical
   and Reformed churches, especially in the
   midwest; reports of the American Board
   of Commissioners for Foreign Missions;
   and yearbooks of the Congregational
   church in the U.S., England and Wales.
   There are also papers of individuals,
   unpublished diaries and histories of Congregational ministers, and the records of
   the Chicago Community Renewal Society.

SEE: Hamer; NUCMC, 1960.

IL169-565

Congregation of Our Lady of the
   Cenacle
Central Archives
513 Fullerton Parkway
Chicago IL 60614

(312) 528-6300

OPEN: by appointment only; closed
   Sundays and holidays
ACCESS: appointment required
COPYING FACILITIES: no
MATERIALS SOLICITED: History of the
   Congregation in the United States,
   New Zealand, the Philippines, Peru,
   and Canada; religious life in the United
   States; and the contemporary religious
   ministry.

HOLDINGS:
   Total volume: 9 file cabinets; 20 file
   cabinet drawers
   Inclusive dates: 1820 -
   Description: Records of the Congregation of the Cenacle in three American
   provinces and its origins in France, including correspondence, documents, journals, chapter papers, biographical information relating to Sisters, minutes, scrapbooks, photographs, motion pictures, and
   other audiovisual materials.

IL169-580

Cook County Hospital
Libraries and Archives
Nurses Residence
1900 West Polk Street
Chicago IL 60612

(312) 633-7538

OPEN: M-F 9-5; closed weekends and
   holidays
COPYING FACILITIES: yes

MATERIALS SOLICITED: Materials relating
   to Cook County Hospital, Cook County School of Nursing, and the Health
   and Hospitals Governing Commission
   of Cook County.

HOLDINGS:
   Total volume: 600 c.f.
   Inclusive dates: 1872 -
   Description: Administrative records for
   Cook County Hospital, Cook County
   School of Nursing, and the Health and
   Hospitals Governing Commission of
   Cook County. Also included are a photo-
   graph collection, Florence Nightingale let-
   ters, engineering drawings, Cook County
   Hospital Warden's Register of Patients,
   and items from the Illinois Training
   School for Nurses.

SEE: Hinding.

SEE ALSO: Terrence S. Norwood, 'The
   Cook County Hospital Archives,' *Illinois Libraries* 63 (April 1981).

IL169-599

DePaul University
Libraries
Lincoln Park Campus Library
Department of Special Collections
2323 North Seminary Avenue
Chicago IL 60614

(312) 341-8088

OPEN: M-F 8:30-4:30, evenings and
   weekends by appointment; closed
   holidays
COPYING FACILITIES: yes
MATERIALS SOLICITED: Will accept
   manuscripts.

HOLDINGS:
   Total volume: 86 items
   Inclusive dates: 13th century - 1925
   Description: Facsimiles of 9 letters of
   Napoleon and his associates; 10 illumi-
   nated manuscripts; various autograph let-
   ters.

SEE: Hamer.

IL169-651

Episcopal Diocese of Chicago
Archives and Historical Collections
65 East Huron Street
Chicago IL 60611

(312) 787-6410

OPEN: M-F 9-4:30; closed weekends and
   holidays
COPYING FACILITIES: yes
MATERIALS SOLICITED: American church
   history, especially relating to the Episcopal church nationally or regionally;
   Illinois church history; Chicago church
   history. Will also accept materials relating to civil rights, race relations, urban
   problems, population shifts, ethnic
   groups, American Indians, church-state
   relations, inter-church relations, abor-
   tion, penal reform, women's liberation,
   gay liberation, drugs, drug problems, al-
   coholism, and pornography.

HOLDINGS:
   Total volume: 1,000 vols.; 230.5 l.f.
   Inclusive dates: 1835 -
   Description: Records of the parishes,
   chapels, missions, schools, charitable institutions, organizations and guilds of the
   Episcopal church in Illinois, especially in
   the Diocese of Chicago. Included are diocesan Journals of Convention, annual
   reports, and statistics. There is also correspondence of the former bishops of the
   diocese; biographical items concerning
   bishops, priests, deacons, deaconesses,
   members of religious orders, and laity;
   and items concerned with the formation
   of the Reformed Episcopal church.

SEE: NUCMC, 1976 (as Protestant Episcopal Church, Diocese of Chicago, Archives and Historical Collections).

IL169-677

Evangelical Covenant Church of
   America
Covenant Archives/Historical Library
5125 North Spaulding Avenue
Chicago IL 60625

(312) 583-2700, Ext. 5267

OPEN: M-F 8-noon by appointment;
   closed weekends and holidays
ACCESS: prior arrangements required
COPYING FACILITIES: yes
MATERIALS SOLICITED: Official records
   of the denominational institutions, regional conferences, local churches and
   mission stations; diaries, journals,
   logbooks of missionaries, pastors, and
   church members; oral history tapes;
   translations of early documents; photographs related to churches at home or
   in mission areas. Will also accept motion pictures; old audio records of music; tapes of sermons; books related to
   the history of the denomination or its
   people.

HOLDINGS:
   Total volume: 700 microfilm reels;
   194 file drawers; 108 letter boxes
   Inclusive dates: 1868 -
   Description: Records of the Evangelical
   Covenant Church of America and its prehistory, from 1868, including parent organizations, regional conferences, local
   churches, biographical information on
   pastors and lay leaders. Records of institutions, both denominational and conference, are also included. Likewise
   records, logbooks, and correspondence
   from missions in Alaska, China-Taiwan,
   Colombia, Ecuador, Japan, Mexico, Thailand, and Zaire.

SEE: Hamer; NUCMC, 1966-67.

SEE: Hinding.

SEE ALSO: Sigurd F. Westberg, 'The Archives of the Evangelical Covenant
   Church of America,' *Illinois Libraries*
   63 (April 1981).

IL169-703
Farm and Industrial Equipment
   Institute
Suite 680
410 North Michigan Avenue
Chicago IL 60611

(312) 321-1470

OPEN: by appointment only, M-F
   8:30-4:30; closed weekends and
   holidays
COPYING FACILITIES: yes

HOLDINGS:
   Total volume: 30 l.f.
   Inclusive dates: 1893 -
   Description: Archives of the Farm and
   Industrial Equipment Institute, including
   periodicals and minutes of meetings.

IL169-729
Field Museum of Natural History
Library
Roosevelt Road at Lake Shore Drive
Chicago IL 60605

(312) 922-9410, Ext. 282

OPEN: M-F 8:30-4:30; closed weekends
   and holidays
ACCESS: advance arrangements required
COPYING FACILITIES: yes
MATERIALS SOLICITED: Materials relating
   to the founding, development, and or-
   ganization of the Field Museum of
   Natural History.

HOLDINGS:
   Total volume: 182 c.f.
   Inclusive dates: 1893 -
   Description: Archival materials relating
   to the Museum's building, growth, and
   activities since its founding.

SEE: Hamer; NUCMC, 1966 (as Chicago
   Natural History Museum).

SEE: Hinding; Novotny; Bean and Vane;
   Spalek.

IL169-753
First National Bank of Chicago
Library
One First National Plaza
Chicago IL 60670

no telephone

SEE: Hamer.

Questionnaire not returned.

IL169-826
Hedrich-Blessing Ltd.
11 West Illinois Street
Chicago IL 60610

(312) 321-1151

OPEN: M-F 9-5; closed weekends and
   holidays
COPYING FACILITIES: no

HOLDINGS:
   Total volume: 1,500,000 items
   Inclusive dates: 1930 -
   Description: Photographs relating primarily to midwestern architecture, including interior and exterior views of industries and residences.

SEE: Novotny.

IL170-39
The John Crerar Library
35 West 33rd Street
Chicago IL 60616

no telephone

SEE: Hamer.

Questionnaire not returned.

IL170-53
Lithuanian American Council, Inc.
2606 West 63rd Street
Chicago IL 60629

(312) 778-6900

OPEN: M-F 9-2 by appointment only;
   closed weekends and holidays
ACCESS: advance arrangements required
COPYING FACILITIES: yes
MATERIALS SOLICITED: Documents con-
   cerning the Lithuanian American
   Council and the freedom of Lithuania.

HOLDINGS:
   Total volume: not specified
   Inclusive dates: 1940 -
   Description: Minutes of meetings and
   other records of the Lithuanian American
   Council; correspondence with Lithuanian
   diplomatic representatives, consulates, the
   Supreme Committee for the Liberation of
   Lithuania, the Lithuanian community in
   America, and the United States govern-
   ment; statements of Lithuanian refugees;
   records of the Kersten Committee; and a
   list of Lithuanians persecuted by the So-
   viet Union.

IL170-61
Lithuanian Photo Library, Inc.
2345 West 56th Street
Chicago IL 60636

(312) 737-8400

OPEN: by appointment only
COPYING FACILITIES: yes
MATERIALS SOLICITED: Visual materials
   relating to Lithuanian immigration to
   the United States and Lithuanian ethnic activities, particularly in the United
   States.

HOLDINGS:
   Total volume: 20,035 items
   Inclusive dates: not specified
   Description: Photographs, films, and
   video tapes about the Lithuanian com-
   munity in the United States and abroad.

IL170-78
Loyola University of Chicago
Archives
E. M. Cudahy Memorial Library
6525 North Sheridan Road
Chicago IL 60626

OPEN: M-F 9-5; closed weekends and
   holidays
COPYING FACILITIES: yes
MATERIALS SOLICITED: Materials relating
   to the Catholic church in Chicago and
   Loyola University of Chicago. Will also
   accept materials relating to the Catholic church in the United States.

HOLDINGS:
   Total volume: 30 l.f.
   Inclusive dates: 1890 -
   Description: Loyola University records,
   including its parent institution, St. Igna-
   tius College; Catholic Church Extension
   Society Papers, 1905-1962; Dorr E. Felt
   Pamphlet Collection; Chicago Inter-
   Student Catholic Action Papers; Alliance
   of Catholic Laity Papers; William T.
   Kane, S.J., Photo Collection.

SEE: NUCMC, 1971.

SEE: Hinding; Spalek.

IL170-91
Lutheran Church in America
Archives
Lutheran School of Theology
1100 East 55th Street
Chicago IL 60615

(312) 667-3500, 653-0766

OPEN: M-F 8:30-4:30; closed weekends
   and holidays
COPYING FACILITIES: yes
MATERIALS SOLICITED: Will accept materials related to the Lutheran Church
   in America and its predecessor bodies.

HOLDINGS:
   Total volume: 3,000 l.f.
   Inclusive dates: 1820 -
   Description: Archives of the Lutheran
   Church in America and its predecessors:
   United Lutheran Church in America
   (mostly German), Augustana Lutheran
   church (Swedish), American Evangelical
   Lutheran church (Danish), and Finnish
   (Suomi) Evangelical Lutheran church.
   The documents broadly relate to church
   administration in the United States and
   Canada, and include information on in-
   dividual congregations, parish education,
   worship and church music, and missionary activities abroad. The institution is
   also the depository for records of the Illinois and Iowa synods of the Lutheran
   Church in America.

GUIDES: Joel W. Lundeen, comp., *Pre-
   serving Yesterday for Tomorrow: A
   Guide to the Archives of the Lutheran
   Church in America* (1977).

SEE: Hinding.

IL170-182
McCormick Theological Seminary
McGaw Library
800 West Belden Avenue
Chicago IL 60614

no telephone

SEE: Hamer.

Questionnaire not returned.

IL170-195
Meadville Theological School of
   Lombard College
5701 South Woodlawn Avenue
Chicago IL 60637

(312) 753-3196, 3195

OPEN: M-F 9-5; closed weekends and
   holidays
COPYING FACILITIES: yes

MATERIALS SOLICITED: Material relating to the Unitarian Universalist denominations and ministry.

HOLDINGS:
> *Total volume:* 250 l.f.
> *Inclusive dates:* not specified
> *Description:* Sermon manuscripts and correspondence of William Ellery Channing; correspondence, papers, sermons, and scrapbooks of Jenkin Lloyd Jones; papers and correspondence of A. Powell Davies; and materials of Unitarian and Universalist churches and ministers throughout America but especially in the Midwest.

SEE: Hamer; NUCMC, 1966.

IL170-234
Moody Bible Institute
Library
Historical Collection
820 North LaSalle Street
Chicago IL 60610

(312) 329-4140

OPEN: M-F 8-10:45, Sa 8-8; closed Sundays and holidays
COPYING FACILITIES: yes
MATERIALS SOLICITED: Correspondence of Dwight L. Moody and presidents of the Moody Bible Institute, and documents and photographs relating to the history of the Institute.

HOLDINGS:
> *Total volume:* 66 l.f.
> *Inclusive dates:* 1854 -
> *Description:* A manuscript collection of 1,000 pieces, comprised mainly of letters of Dwight L. Moody, R. A. Torrey, and James M. Gray. There are also 200 biographical files concerning persons affiliated with the Institute, an extensive photograph collection, and documents relating to the founding of the Institute.

SEE: Hamer.

SEE: Hinding.

SEE ALSO: 'Midwest Research Institutions Directory,' *Illinois Libraries* 53 (Jan. 1971).

IL170-250
Mundelein College
Learning Resource Center
6339 North Sheridan Road
Chicago IL 60660

(312) 262-8100

OPEN: Su-Th 9-10, F, Sa 9-11; closed holidays
COPYING FACILITIES: yes

HOLDINGS:
> *Total volume:* 75 items
> *Inclusive dates:* late 15th century -
> *Description:* A small collection of autograph letters and other documents of signers of the Declaration of Independence and of various other persons, including Isabella I, Queen of Castile.

SEE: Hamer.

SEE: Hinding.

IL170-273
Museum of Science and Industry
Library
57th Street and Lake Shore Drive
Chicago IL 60637

(312) 684-1414, Ext. 428, 429

OPEN: daily by appointment only; closed Christmas
ACCESS: prior arrangements required
COPYING FACILITIES: yes

HOLDINGS:
> *Total volume:* 40 c.f.; 3,000 items
> *Inclusive dates:* 1850 - 1950
> *Description:* Locomotive drawings; documentary materials on the Chicago Century of Progress Exposition (1933-34) and the Chicago Railroad Fair (1950), consisting of architectural blueprints, correspondence, and other material; records of the Huegely Mill of Nashville, IL (1850-75), including ledgers, orders, and correspondence reflecting wheat prices and methods of production; and glass slides relating to the history of the Museum of Science and Industry, other science museums, international expositions and various scientific and technical fields (1926-37).

SEE: Hamer.

IL170-280
National Archives and Records
   Administration
Federal Archives and Records Center
Archives Branch
7358 South Pulaski Road
Chicago IL 60629

(312) 581-7816

OPEN: M-F 8-4:15 by appointment only; closed weekends and holidays
ACCESS: Records are open, subject to Federal agency restrictions and restrictions based upon current legislation relevant to confidentiality and security classification. See General Information Leaflet No. 2, 'Regulations for the Public Use of Records in the National Archives.'
COPYING FACILITIES: yes
MATERIALS SOLICITED: Federal records within the geographic area of interest of this Federal Archives and Records Center. Will also accept non-Federal records related to Federal holdings, subject to the appropriate guidelines of the National Archives and Records Service.

HOLDINGS:
> *Total volume:* 37,540 c.f.
> *Inclusive dates:* 1803 -
> *Description:* Records of field offices of Federal agencies in Illinois, Indiana, Michigan, Minnesota (except U.S. Court records), Ohio, and Wisconsin. Included are records of the U.S. Circuit and District Courts, the Bureau of Indian Affairs (primarily Wisconsin), U.S. Attorneys and Marshals, and the U.S. Immigration and Naturalization Service.

SEE: Hamer.

SEE: Davis; Allard, Crawley, and Edmison; Hinding.

SEE ALSO: Bruce C. Harding, 'Sources for Ethnic Studies in the Region 5 Archives Branch,' and 'Regional Archives Branch - Chicago,' *Illinois Libraries* 57 (March 1975). Microfilm lists, preliminary inventories, and other finding aids available at the institution.

IL170-283
National Board of Young Men's
   Christian Associations of the
   United States
101 North Wacker Drive
Chicago IL 60606

(312) 977-0031

OPEN: M-F 9-4; closed weekends and holidays
COPYING FACILITIES: yes
MATERIALS SOLICITED: Papers of retired YMCA directors and foreign service secretaries; records of local YMCAs; and materials pertaining to YMCA relief work in World Wars I and II. Will also accept records of young men's societies which preceded the YMCA and materials on the history of physical education and World War I relief work.

HOLDINGS:
> *Total volume:* 2,500 l.f.
> *Inclusive dates:* 1844 -
> *Description:* Records of the YMCA, including archives of the National Board of YMCAs and its predecessor, the International Committee of YMCAs; minutes and reports of the World Alliance of YMCAs; records of local YMCAs in the United States and abroad; a large collection of photographs covering National and foreign YMCA activities; unpublished manuscripts and personal papers of staff members and others associated with the organization; and some recordings of interviews with former YMCA directors.

SEE: Schatz.

IL170-312
National Insurance Association
2400 South Michigan Avenue
Chicago IL 60616

(312) 842-5125

OPEN: M-F 9:30-4:30; closed weekends and holidays
ACCESS: students and business or social researchers
COPYING FACILITIES: no
MATERIALS SOLICITED: Will accept correspondence and other records of minority life insurance firms and predecessors, such as burial societies.

HOLDINGS:
> *Total volume:* 9 c.f.
> *Inclusive dates:* 1921 -
> *Description:* Correspondence, minutes, and convention proceedings of the National Negro Insurance Association, 1921-54, and the National Insurance Association, 1954- .

SEE: Schatz.

IL170-351
The Newberry Library
60 West Walton Street
Chicago IL 60610

(312) 943-9090

OPEN: Tu-Th 9-9:40, F-Sa 9-5:40; closed
 Sundays, Mondays, and holidays
ACCESS: undergraduates required to
 show letter from an advisor
COPYING FACILITIES: yes
MATERIALS SOLICITED: Personal papers
 of Midwestern figures, particularly
 Chicagoans, and club papers and company archives, for the fields of social
 history, politics, literature, journalism,
 music, and fine printing, in addition to
 materials documenting the history of
 The Newberry Library. Will also accept
 other manuscript materials which en-
 hance the Library's collections.

HOLDINGS:
 Total volume: 4,110 l.f.; 2,950 sq. f.
 Inclusive dates: late Middle Ages -
 Description: Personal papers, club and
 company archives, and other modern
 manuscripts, primarily of the Midwest
 and emphasizing history, literature, music, and printing. Included are archives of
 the Illinois Central Railroad, the Chicago,
 Burlington and Quincy Railroad, and the
 Pullman Company.
 Also held are Philippine, Hispanic,
 and Portuguese historical documents; materials documenting the westward movement in America; manuscript maps and
 atlases; pre-1500 books of hours, treatises,
 and manuscript fragments; post-1500 European and American manuscripts; and
 Oriental manuscripts, including those in
 Arabic, Hebrew, Persian, Pali, and Sanskrit.

SEE: Hamer; NUCMC, 1959-62, 65-67,
 69-70, 73, 80.

SEE: Novotny; Davis; Parkinson; Bean
 and Vane; Martin; Robbins; Hinding;
 Ingram.

IL170-403
North Park College
Library
5125 North Spaulding Avenue
Chicago IL 60625

(312) 583-2700, Ext. 340

OPEN: M-Th 7:45-11, F 7:45-10, Sa 10-5,
 Su 1-11; closed holidays and Christmas
 week

SEE: Hamer.

Questionnaire not returned.

IL170-416
Northwestern Memorial Hospital
Archives
516 West 36th Street
Chicago IL

MAILING ADDRESS:
303 East Superior Street
Chicago IL 60611

(312) 908-3090, 4671

OPEN: M-F 9-5; closed weekends and
 holidays

ACCESS: advance arrangements required
COPYING FACILITIES: yes
MATERIALS SOLICITED: Materials related
 to Northwestern Memorial Hospital
 and its predecessor institutions.

HOLDINGS:
 Total volume: 3,800 c.f.
 Inclusive dates: 1849 -
 Description: Records of Northwestern
 Memorial Hospital and its numerous pre-
 decessor institutions.

SEE: Hinding.

IL170-429
Northwestern University
Dental School
Library
311 East Chicago Avenue
Chicago IL 60611

(312) 908-8332

OPEN: M-Th 8-10, F 8-6, Sa 9-5; closed
 Sundays and holidays
COPYING FACILITIES: yes
MATERIALS SOLICITED: Materials relating
 to dental research, dental education
 and Northwestern University Dental
 School.

HOLDINGS:
 Total volume: 30 l.f.; 3 file drawers
 Inclusive dates: 1867 -
 Description: A collection of manuscripts relating to dentistry, dental research, and allied subjects. Included are
 letters, research reports and other papers
 of Greene Yardeman Black, Charles W.
 Freeman and George W. Teuscher. There
 is also a single letter from John Greenwood to George Washington about his
 dental charges. The collection includes 14
 linear feet of Northwestern University
 Dental School archives.

SEE: Hamer; NUCMC, 1964.

SEE: Novotny.

IL170-442
Northwestern University
Law Library
Chicago IL 60611

(312) 908-8451

SEE: NUCMC, 1962.

Questionnaire not returned.

IL170-455
Northwestern University
Medical School
Library
303 East Chicago Avenue
Chicago IL 60611

(312) 908-8136

SEE: Hamer; NUCMC, 1965.

Questionnaire not returned.

IL170-475
Our Lady of Sorrows Basilica
Archives
3121 West Jackson Blvd.
Chicago IL 60612

(312) 638-5800

OPEN: by appointment only
ACCESS: Each request is judged
 individually, consideration being given
 to the qualifications of the researcher,
 the purpose of the research, and the
 sensitivity of certain types of records.
COPYING FACILITIES: no
MATERIALS SOLICITED: Records of Our
 Lady of Sorrows Basilica. Will also accept other materials related in some
 way to the Basilica.

HOLDINGS:
 Total volume: 450 vols.; 36 l.f.
 Inclusive dates: 1874 -
 Description: Administrative and financial records of Our Lady of Sorrows Parish and its related parish organizations
 and the monastery of Servite priests and
 brothers.

SEE ALSO: inventories of some materials
 available at the institution.

IL170-520
Polish Museum of America
Library
984 Milwaukee Avenue
Chicago IL 60622

(312) 384-3352

SEE: Hamer.

Questionnaire not returned.

IL170-637
Roosevelt University
Archives
430 South Michigan Avenue
Chicago IL 60605

(312) 341-3643

OPEN: M-Th 9-9, F 9-6:30, Sa, Su 12-5;
 closed holidays
COPYING FACILITIES: yes

HOLDINGS:
 Total volume: 80 l.f.; 200 vols.
 Inclusive dates: 1886 -
 Description: Primarily Roosevelt University records. There are also the Labor
 Oral History Project, currently encompassing 24 volumes and 48 interviews; 85
 holograph letters and other documents,
 chiefly 19th century, by German composers and writers; and the Chicago Auditorium Association Papers, including early
 records, minutes, and correspondence.

SEE: Hamer; NUCMC, 1966, 77.

SEE: Meckler and McMullin; Parkinson;
 Spalek; Hinding.

IL170-650
Roosevelt University
Oral History Project
430 South Michigan Avenue
Chicago IL 60605

(312) 341-3643

OPEN: M-Th 9-8, F 9-6, Sa, Su noon-6;
closed holidays
COPYING FACILITIES: yes
MATERIALS SOLICITED: Labor history;
women in the labor movement; and
immigration history. Will also accept
materials relating to family history and
Afro-American history.

HOLDINGS:
Total volume: 63 items
Inclusive dates: 1890 -
Description: Transcripts of interviews
with people who have been involved in
the labor movement in the Chicago area.
A small number of interviews are with
people who have immigrated to Chicago
or who are involved in the labor movement in other areas.

SEE: Meckler and McMullin; Hinding.

IL170-780
Spertus College of Judaica
Asher Library
Chicago Jewish Archives
618 South Michigan Avenue
Chicago IL 60605

(312) 922-9012

OPEN: M-Th 9-5, F 9-3; closed
weekends, holidays, and Jewish
holidays
ACCESS: serious researchers
COPYING FACILITIES: yes
MATERIALS SOLICITED: All material doc-
umenting the history of the Chicago
Jewish community.

HOLDINGS:
Total volume: 120 l.f.
Inclusive dates: 1880's -
Description: A collection tracing the
growth of the Chicago Jewish community, including records of synagogues and
of philanthropic, cultural, social service,
and religious organizations, and papers of
individuals who contributed to the development of the community.

SEE: Hinding.

IL170-832
Trans Union Corporation
111 West Jackson Blvd.
Chicago IL 60604

(312) 645-6000

OPEN: by appointment only
ACCESS: company employees only,
except by special arrangement with a
company officer
COPYING FACILITIES: yes

HOLDINGS:
Total volume: 17,800 c.f.
Inclusive dates: not specified
Description: Trans Union Corporation
records.

IL170-884
The University of Chicago
Library
Department of Special Collections
1100 East 57th Street
Chicago IL 60637

(312) 962-8704

OPEN: M-F 9-5, Sa 9-1; closed Sundays
and holidays
ACCESS: non-University-affiliated
readers must obtain visitor's pass at
Library
COPYING FACILITIES: yes
MATERIALS SOLICITED: 20th-century
American and European social and intellectual history; the history of the social sciences; modern physics and its
social consequences and implications;
the history of the University of Chicago and related institutions and their
members.

HOLDINGS:
Total volume: 10,000 c.f.
Inclusive dates: 13th century -
Description: Over 700 collections spanning the social and cultural history of
England, 13th-20th centuries; Ireland,
17th-19th centuries; continental Europe,
18th-20th centuries; and Southeast Asia,
20th century; as well as those covering
U.S. literary, social, political, and religious history. Important American topics
include the Civil War era; Kentucky and
settlement of the Ohio Valley; Chicago
and regional history; 20th century literature and literary criticism; social ame-
lioration and reform; philanthropy; socialism; religious history; and the history of
American sociology and social research.
There are also collections dealing with
medieval and classical philology and the
history of science, especially atomic science and physics and their social implications.

GUIDES: A Preliminary Guide to the
Manuscripts and Archives in The University of Chicago Library (1973).

SEE: Hamer; NUCMC, 1963-64, 66,
68-69, 71.

SEE: Davis; Parkinson; Bean and Vane;
Ingram; Allard, Crawley, and Edmison;
Spalek; Robbins; Martin.

SEE ALSO: Mary Janzen Wilson, Guide to
the James Franck Papers (Univ. of Chicago Library, 1976); Robert C.
Emmett, Guide to the Albert Mayer Papers on India (Committee on Southern
Asian Studies and Southern Asia Reference Center, 1977); Andrea Hinding
and Rosemary Richardson, comps.,
Archival and Manuscript Resources for
the Study of Women's History: A Beginning (Univ. of Minnesota Libraries, Social Welfare History Archives Center,
1972); Walter Schatz, ed., Directory of
Afro-American Resources (Bowker,
1970); Peter Duignan, Handbook of
American Resources for African Studies
(Hoover Institution, 1967); Source Materials for the Recent History of Astronomy and Astrophysics: A Checklist of
Manuscript Collections in the United
States (American Institute of Physics,
1971).

Albert Krichmar, The Women's Rights
Movement in the United States,
1848-1970: A Bibliography and
Sourcebook (Scarecrow Press, 1972); Joan
Nelson Warnow, A Selection of Manu-
script Collections at American Repositories
(American Institute of Physics, 1969);
Thomas S. Kuhn, John L. Heilbron, Paul
Forman, and Lini Allen, Sources for His-
tory of Quantum Physics: An Inventory
and Report (American Philosophical Soci-
ety, 1967); Gerald Friedberg, 'Sources for
the Study of Socialism in America,
1901-1919,' Labor History 6 (Spring
1965); William S. Coker and Jack D. L.
Holmes, 'Sources for the History of the
Spanish Borderlands,' Florida Historical
Quarterly 49 (April 1971); Lawrence J.
Paszek, comp., United States Air Force
History: A Guide to Documentary Sources
(Office of Air Force History, 1973).

Finding aids for individual collections are
available at the institution.

IL170-891
University of Chicago
National Opinion Research Center
Library and Data Archives
6030 South Ellis Avenue
Chicago IL 60637

(312) 753-1200

OPEN: M-F 8:30-5; closed weekends and
holidays
COPYING FACILITIES: yes
MATERIALS SOLICITED: Sample survey
data collected by National Opinion Research Center. Will also accept sample
survey data collected by other organizations.

HOLDINGS:
Total volume: 500 studies
Inclusive dates: 1941 -
Description: Sample survey data on
punched cards and magnetic tapes collected by the National Opinion Research
Center on a variety of subjects and from
a wide range of populations. Supporting
documentation and related materials are
also available.

GUIDES: John W. Allswang and Patrick
Bova, NORC Social Research, 1941-64:
An Inventory of Studies and Publica-
tions in Social Research (NORC, 1964);
Bibliography of Publications, 1941 - .

SEE: Schatz; Hinding.

IL170-897
The University of Chicago
The Oriental Institute Museum
The Archaeological Archives
1155 East 58th Street
Chicago IL 60637

(312) 962-9520

OPEN: M-F 9-4 by appointment only;
closed weekends and holidays
ACCESS: advance arrangements
recommended
COPYING FACILITIES: yes
MATERIALS SOLICITED: Photographic
and field record materials concerning
Oriental Institute excavations and artifacts of the ancient Near East. Will
also accept photographs and papers of
other travellers or scholars relating to

the ancient or modern Near East, as well as records of artifacts and excavations from other institutions.

HOLDINGS:
Total volume: 2,500 sq.f.; 300 l.f.
Inclusive dates: 1860's -
Description: Photographic and field records collections pertaining to archaeological and philological research conducted in the ancient Near East by Oriental Institute scholars, including prints, negatives, slides, maps, drawings, field registers, diaries, manuscripts, artifact card catalogues, and personal papers.

SEE: Novotny; Hinding; Martin; Spalek.

IL170-910
University of Illinois at Chicago Circle
The Library
Manuscript Department
801 South Morgan
Chicago IL

MAILING ADDRESS:
Box 8198
Chicago IL 60680

(312) 996-2742

OPEN: M-F 8:30-4:45; closed weekends and holidays
COPYING FACILITIES: yes
MATERIALS SOLICITED: Manuscripts, archives, and visual and audible material pertaining to the social, political, economic, and cultural history of the Chicago metropolitan area, 1860- .

HOLDINGS:
Total volume: 6,805 l.f.
Inclusive dates: 1860 -
Description: Manuscript and archival collections relating chiefly to the history of the Chicago metropolitan region and Chicago's leadership role in Progressive Era reforms. Holdings include organization records, personal papers, subject collections, and photographs.
Subject strengths include the settlement movement, social welfare and reform, child welfare, philanthropy, ethnic and racial population groups, housing, political activism, community organization, economics, business, and civic and cultural life. Two specialized holdings are the Jane Addams Memorial Collection and the Midwest Women's Historical Collection.

GUIDES: *Guide to the Manuscript Collections* (n.d.).

SEE: NUCMC, 1968-72, 75-77.

SEE: Spalek; Parkinson; Hinding; Davis; Robbins; Schatz.

IL170-936
University of Illinois at the Medical Center
Library of the Health Sciences
Archives and Special Collections
1750 W. Polk
Chicago IL

MAILING ADDRESS:
P.O. Box 7509
Chicago IL 60680

(312) 966-8977

OPEN: M-F 8:30-5; closed weekends and holidays
COPYING FACILITIES: yes
MATERIALS SOLICITED: Materials relating to the history of Chicago's West Side Medical Center, particularly the official records and manuscripts of the University, its faculty, staff, and students. Will also accept materials relating to the history of medicine and the health sciences in Chicago.

HOLDINGS:
Total volume: 250 c.f.
Inclusive dates: 1871 -
Description: Archives of the Medical Center campus of the University of Illinois, including manuscripts, photographs, and University publications.

SEE: Hamer; NUCMC, 1975, 78.

DANVILLE

IL186-170
Danville Public Library
307 North Vermilion Street
Danville IL 61832

(217) 446-7420

OPEN: M-Th 9-9, F, Sa 9-5:30; closed Sundays and holidays
COPYING FACILITIES: yes
MATERIALS SOLICITED: Local history and genealogy manuscript materials of Vermilion County, IL, and its environs, and records of local government agencies, organizations, schools, and families.

HOLDINGS:
Total volume: 26 c.f.
Inclusive dates: 1826 - 1900
Description: Genealogical source materials, photographs, and records of county government and local groups.

DECATUR

IL192-510
Macon County Historical Society
Macon County Museum Complex
State and Local History Room
5580 North Fork Road
Decatur IL

MAILING ADDRESS:
P.O. Box 146
Decatur IL 62525

(217) 422-4919

OPEN: by appointment only; closed holidays

COPYING FACILITIES: yes
MATERIALS SOLICITED: Materials relating to Macon County or Abraham Lincoln. Will also accept rural school materials.

HOLDINGS:
Total volume: 5 c.f.
Inclusive dates: 1850 -
Description: Materials concerned with Macon County, including audio-visual materials; account books; business records of Morehouse and Wells hardgoods store, Michls Cigar Store, and Walrus Manufacturing Company, all of Decatur; and early 20th century research by a Decatur woman on care of lingerie and feminine hygiene.

DEKALB

IL202-550
Northern Illinois University
Regional History Center
268 Swen Parson Hall
DeKalb IL 60115

(815) 753-1779

OPEN: M-F 8-5; closed weekends, holidays, and when University is closed
COPYING FACILITIES: yes
MATERIALS SOLICITED: Official records of the University and faculty papers; public records from 18 counties of northern Illinois (except Cook); private manuscripts and records from 20 counties of northern Illinois (except Cook).

HOLDINGS:
Total volume: 3,400 l.f.; 180,000 photographs
Inclusive dates: 1834 -
Description: The Regional History Center has three sets of historical records. First, the University Archives serves as the repository for all official records of the university dating from 1895. Second, the local government records collection is part of the Illinois Regional Archives Depository System established by the Illinois State Archives and contains county, township, and municipal records (1830-1970) from 18 counties of northern Illinois (except Cook).
The Center's third major collection contains private manuscripts and records from 20 counties of northern Illinois (except Cook). Areas of emphasis in this collection include: agriculture, ethnic and religious history, local and regional politics, business history, urban expansion, and transportation.

SEE: NUCMC, 1971, 78.

SEE: Hinding; Robbins.

DES PLAINES

IL207-160
Des Plaines Historical Society
Museum
789 Pearson Street
Des Plaines IL

MAILING ADDRESS:
Box 225
Des Plaines IL 60016

(312) 391-5399

OPEN: Tu-Th 2-4; closed other days
COPYING FACILITIES: yes
MATERIALS SOLICITED: Local history and
biographies of the Des Plaines River
valley, including Cook County and
Chicago, IL. Will also accept Illinois
materials.

HOLDINGS:
Total volume: not specified
Inclusive dates: 1860 -
Description: Reminiscences, photographs, scrapbooks, and other materials
documenting the Des Plaines River valley.

SEE: Hinding.

DOWNERS GROVE

IL212-280
George Williams College
Library
555 31st Street
Downers Grove IL 60515

(312) 964-3100, Ext. 218

OPEN: M-F 8-5, variable hours during
summer and between sessions; closed
weekends
COPYING FACILITIES: yes
MATERIALS SOLICITED: Records of
George Williams College. Will also accept personal papers of faculty members of the College.

HOLDINGS:
Total volume: 150 l.f.
Inclusive dates: 1854 -
Description: Records of George Williams College and the personal and business papers of Robert Weidensall, including Civil War correspondence, 42 vols. of
diaries, and materials relating to the
Young Men's Christian Association.

SEE: Hamer; NUCMC, 1971.

EAST PEORIA

IL231-240
Fondulac District Library
Local History Collection
235 Everett Street
East Peoria IL 61611

(309) 699-3917

OPEN: M-F 9-6, Su 2-6; closed holidays
COPYING FACILITIES: yes
MATERIALS SOLICITED: East Peoria his-
tory.

HOLDINGS:
Total volume: 150 items
Inclusive dates: 1873 -
Description: A collection of photographs, correspondence, and other manuscripts relating to East Peoria. Included is
a file on volunteer efforts of East Peoria
women during World War I and an
1886-88 grocery store ledger.

EDWARDSVILLE

IL236-520
Madison County Historical Society
715 North Main Street
Edwardsville IL 62025

(618) 656-7562

OPEN: W-F 9-4, Su 1-4; closed other
days and holidays
COPYING FACILITIES: yes
MATERIALS SOLICITED: Manuscripts, archives, and visual material pertaining
to Madison County.

HOLDINGS:
Total volume: 44 l.f.
Inclusive dates: 1818 - 1950
Description: Materials relating to
Madison County history, consisting of
County government documents, including
a ledger of a land office for military
bounty lands in Illinois Territory; research materials of the Land of Goshen
Historical Society concerning pioneers,
settlements, and institutions; record
books of businesses, organizations, and
individuals; and miscellaneous materials,
such as letters, land grants, post office
records, and genealogies.

SEE: Hamer; NUCMC, 1971.

IL236-730
Southern Illinois University
Elijah P. Lovejoy Library
Map Section
Edwardsville IL 62025

(618) 692-2422

OPEN: M-F 7:30-10, Sa 9-5, Su 2-7;
closed holidays
COPYING FACILITIES: yes
MATERIALS SOLICITED: Original rare
maps. Will also accept copies of historic maps.

HOLDINGS:
Total volume: 300 items
Inclusive dates: 1819 - 1910
Description: Manuscript maps.

IL236-760
Southern Illinois University
Elijah P. Lovejoy Library
Research Collections
Edwardsville IL 62026

(618) 692-2665

OPEN: M-F 9-4:30; closed weekends and
holidays

SEE: NUCMC, 1972.

Questionnaire not returned.

ELGIN

IL241-120
Church of the Brethren
General Board

Brethren Historical Library and
Archives
1451 Dundee Avenue
Elgin IL 60120

(312) 742-5100, Ext. 294

OPEN: M-F 9-4; closed weekends and
holidays
ACCESS: advance appointment requested
COPYING FACILITIES: yes
MATERIALS SOLICITED: Materials relating
to the cultural, socio-economic, theological, genealogical, and institutional
history of the Church of the Brethren.
Will also accept materials relating to
Brethren groups which trace their origins to Schwarzenau, Germany, in
1708.

HOLDINGS:
Total volume: 2,000 c.f.
Inclusive dates: 1731 -
Description: Records of national agencies of the Church of the Brethren, including correspondence, photograph collections, and audio-visual items, related
to the church's activities in the United
States, India, China, Nigeria, Ecuador,
and other nations; records of regional and
local Brethren organizations; and manuscript collections, diaries, and journals by
and biographical information about people active in the church.

ELK GROVE VILLAGE

IL245-322
Congregation of Alexian Brothers
Provincial Archives
600 Alexian Way
Elk Grove Village IL 60007

(312) 640-7550

OPEN: M-F 7:30-4; closed weekends and
holidays
ACCESS: researchers must have verified
reasons for seeking access to repository
COPYING FACILITIES: yes
MATERIALS SOLICITED: Materials relating
to the institutions of the Alexian Brothers.

HOLDINGS:
Total volume: 702 l.f.
Inclusive dates: 1866 -
Description: Materials relating to hos-
pitals, nursing homes, and Roman Catho-
lic church history in areas served by the
Alexian Brothers: Oshkosh, WI, Gresham,
WI, Chicago, IL, Elk Grove Village, IL,
St. Louis, MO, Elizabeth, NJ, San Jose,
CA, Signal Mountain, TN, and Boys
Town, NE; materials relating to the
Brothers' schools of nursing for men in
Chicago and St. Louis; and data relating
to ethnic groups' roles in immigration
and church-oriented development.

SEE: Hinding.

ELMHURST

IL246-190

Elmhurst College
A. C. Buehler Library
190 Prospect
Elmhurst IL 60126

(312) 279-4100, Ext. 229

OPEN: M-Th 8-11, F 8-9, Sa 9-5, Su 2-11; closed holidays
ACCESS: advance arrangements required
COPYING FACILITIES: yes
MATERIALS SOLICITED: Materials pertaining to the city of Elmhurst, particularly its Germanic antecedents, the United Church of Christ, and the College's relationship to the city. Will also accept materials relating to Reinhold Niebuhr.

HOLDINGS:
 Total volume: 75 l.f.
 Inclusive dates: 1871 -
 Description: The College archives, documenting the German heritage of Elmhurst and covering community attitudes during World War I. Materials include correspondence of board members, the former president, and faculty members.

IL246-200

Elmhurst Historical Museum
120 East Park Avenue
Elmhurst IL 60126

MAILING ADDRESS:
P.O. Box 84
Elmhurst IL 60126

(312) 833-1457

OPEN: Tu, Th 1-5, Sa 10-5; closed other days and holidays
COPYING FACILITIES: yes
MATERIALS SOLICITED: Materials relating to the history and present population of Elmhurst.

HOLDINGS:
 Total volume: 160 l.f.
 Inclusive dates: 1850 -
 Description: Materials relating to the history of Elmhurst, including public records of the city; school records; Elmhurst College records; personal papers and family records and collections; organizational records; maps and surveys; tapes of radio broadcasts; records of commemorative observances; scrapbooks and albums; photographs, negatives, and slides; vital statistics, cemetery records, and other genealogical data; greeting card and sheet music collections.

SEE: NUCMC, 1978.

SEE: Meckler and McMullin; Hinding.

ELSAH

IL251-630

Principia College
Archives
Elsah IL 62028

(618) 374-2131, Ext. 311

OPEN: M-F 9-4; closed weekends and holidays
ACCESS: persons affiliated with Principia College, and others by special arrangement
COPYING FACILITIES: yes
MATERIALS SOLICITED: Materials pertaining to the history of Principia College. Will also accept materials on alumni accomplishments of special significance.

HOLDINGS:
 Total volume: 600 l.f.
 Inclusive dates: 1897 -
 Description: Materials pertaining to the history of Principia College, including non-current records, as well as some local history materials of special interest.

SEE: Hinding.

EUREKA

IL256-200

Eureka College
Melick Library
Eureka IL 61530

(309) 467-3721, Ext. 219

OPEN: M-Th 8-10, F 8-4:30, Su 2-10; closed Saturdays and holidays
ACCESS: users must be accompanied by a librarian
COPYING FACILITIES: yes
MATERIALS SOLICITED: Materials relating to Eureka College history and education and the Disciples of Christ church. Will also accept materials relating to the city of Eureka and Woodford County history.

HOLDINGS:
 Total volume: 12 l.f.; 5 file cabinets
 Inclusive dates: 1860 -
 Description: Manuscripts, photographs and microfilm, relating mainly to Eureka College.

EVANSTON

IL261-200

Evanston Historical Society
225 Greenwood Street
Evanston IL 60201

(312) 475-3410

OPEN: M, Tu, Th-Sa 1-5; closed Wednesdays, Sundays, and holidays
COPYING FACILITIES: yes
MATERIALS SOLICITED: Any material relating to Evanston, in particular its architecture and history. Will also accept material relating to Gen. Charles Gates Dawes, Vice President (1924-1929).

HOLDINGS:
 Total volume: 27 files cabinets; 300 l.f.
 Inclusive dates: 1840 -
 Description: Large collection of Evanston material; since 1907 the official repository of the records of the city of Evanston and its predecessors. Nearly complete newspaper files, 1872-present, large biographical collection, extensive photographic collection; records and archives of Evanston churches, clubs, and businesses, etc.; collection relating to Charles G. Dawes; local maps, 1850-present.

SEE: Hamer.

SEE: Hinding.

IL261-280

Garrett-Evangelical Theological Seminary
Library
2121 Sheridan Road
Evanston IL 60201

(312) 866-3910

OPEN: M-F 9-4:30; closed weekends and holidays
COPYING FACILITIES: yes
MATERIALS SOLICITED: Papers of former faculty and church leaders. Will also accept significant materials of religious interest, especially those relating to the Methodist Episcopal church, the Methodist church, and the United Methodist church.

HOLDINGS:
 Total volume: 250 l.f.
 Inclusive dates: 1860 -
 Description: Correspondence, lecture notes and other papers of the faculty of the Garrett Biblical Institute; sermons, correspondence and journals of early Methodist preachers in the Midwest; papers of Methodist bishops; and research materials on Mormons and polygamous marriage.

SEE: Hamer (as Garrett Biblical Institute in Evanston, IL, and as Evangelical Theological Seminary in Naperville, IL); NUCMC, 1966, 69.

SEE: Hinding.

IL261-545

National Woman's Christian Temperance Union
Frances E. Willard Memorial Library
1730 Chicago Avenue
Evanston IL 60201

(312) 864-1396, 1397, 1322

OPEN: M-F 9-4:30, Sa by appointment only; closed Sundays and holidays
COPYING FACILITIES: yes
MATERIALS SOLICITED: Materials concerning alcohol, narcotics, and tobacco, and documentation of the Prohibition and temperance movements. Will also accept materials pertaining to the family, home protection, and social and moral concerns.

HOLDINGS:
Total volume: 4,500 items
Inclusive dates: 1874 -
Description: Materials from the United States and many other countries, regarding intemperance and related social problems; manuscripts of U.S. and foreign temperance leaders, most notably Frances E. Willard; annual minutes of the National Woman's Christian Temperance Union and other temperance organizations in most of the fifty States; and other temperance organization materials.

SEE: Hamer; NUCMC, 1965.

SEE: Krichmar; Hinding.

IL261-565

Northwestern University
Library
Map Collection
1935 Sheridan Road
Evanston IL 60201

(312) 491-7603

OPEN: M-F 8:30-5; closed weekends and holidays
COPYING FACILITIES: yes
MATERIALS SOLICITED: Will accept aerial photographs.

HOLDINGS:
Total volume: 1,540 aerial photographs; 23 negatives
Inclusive dates: 1934 - 1950's
Description: Aerial photographs and negatives given to the Map Collection by the Department of Geography, reflecting areas in which field work was being done.

IL261-566

Northwestern University
Library
Melville J. Herskovits Library of
  African Studies
1935 Sheridan Road
Evanston IL 60201

(312) 491-7684, 7685

OPEN: M-F 8:30-5; closed weekends and holidays
COPYING FACILITIES: yes
MATERIALS SOLICITED: Records of U.S. associations concerned with Africa; archival materials bearing on U.S. relations with African countries; primary research materials of Africanist scholars; and original documents relating to African history, society, and politics.

HOLDINGS:
Total volume: 1,200 c.f.
Inclusive dates: 1799 -
Description: Manuscripts and other materials relating to Africa, including the Melville J. Herskovits papers; the Gwendolen M. Carter/Thomas G. Karis collection on African nationalist organizations in South Africa; the papers of Umar Falke and other collections from northern Nigeria; the papers of A. Abdurahman and Z. Gool.
   The papers of Vernon A. Anderson, Dennis Brutus, Lavinia Scott, Alex Hepple, Leo Kuper, Vernon McKay, Eva L.R. Meyerowitz, the African Studies Association (noncurrent), the Program of African Studies at Northwestern University (noncurrent), the American Committee to Keep Biafra Alive, the Black Sash organization, the Economic Survey of Liberia, and the Claude Barnett Clipping Collection.
   In addition, the library holds microfilm copies of the archives of the Church Missionary Society, the Danish archives concerning West Africa, the Dutch archives concerning West Africa, a select series of the National Archives of Zambia, the archives of the Presbyterian Church in the U.S.A., Board of Foreign Missions, the archives of the Propaganda Fide bearing on Africa, and the archives of the Treasury and Colonial Offices, Great Britain.

SEE: Duignan; Schatz.

SEE ALSO: *Catalog of the Melville J. Herskovits Library of African Studies* (G. K. Hall, 1972).

IL261-568

Northwestern University
Library
Music Library
1935 Sheridan Road
Evanston IL 60201

(312) 491-3434

OPEN: M-F 9-5, Sa 10-noon; closed Sundays and holidays
COPYING FACILITIES: yes
MATERIALS SOLICITED: Music manuscripts, including letters, with an emphasis on the 20th century. Will also accept anything relating to music.

HOLDINGS:
Total volume: 10,000 items
Inclusive dates: 1750 -
Description: A collection of music manuscripts, letters, and memorabilia with an emphasis on the 20th century.

SEE: Hinding.

IL261-570

Northwestern University
Library
Special Collections
1937 Sheridan Road
Evanston IL 60201

(312) 491-3635

OPEN: M-F 8:30-5, Sa 8:30-noon; closed Sundays, holidays and Saturdays during intersessions
COPYING FACILITIES: yes
MATERIALS SOLICITED: Literary and little magazines and theater history. Will also accept social history, especially 1960-79, student uprisings, and literary and political history.

HOLDINGS:
Total volume: 520 l.f.
Inclusive dates: 1750's - 1970's
Description: Manuscripts of Anais Nin's novels, papers of Vice President Charles G. Dawes, archives of The Dublin Gate Theatre, papers of Jan Herman and his little magazine *San Francisco Earthquake*, papers of the little magazine *The Outsider*, archives of the American Economic Association and the *American Economic Review*, archives of the Berkeley Folk Festival, and other materials.

SEE: Hamer; NUCMC, 1959-61.

SEE: Hinding; Martin; Robbins.

IL261-585

Northwestern University
Library
University Archives
Room 110 Deering
Northwestern University Library
Evanston IL 60201

(312) 491-3354, 3136

OPEN: M-F 8:30-5; closed weekends and holidays
ACCESS: A number of collections are closed. In some instances, access to restricted collections may be granted by written permission from the donor, the creating office, or the University Archivist.
COPYING FACILITIES: yes
MATERIALS SOLICITED: Official records of the University and documentation pertaining to the activities and functions of all components of the University community. Will also accept documentation relating to the University's academic strengths and interests, the city of Evanston, and the entire Chicago 'North Shore' area.

HOLDINGS:
Total volume: 3,500 l.f.
Inclusive dates: 1850 -
Description: Official records of Northwestern University and other records which document the origins, development, and internal functions of the University and its role in society. Included are the minutes of the Board of Trustees and other administrative bodies; financial records; catalogues and bulletins; the papers of University presidents and distinguished members of the faculty; runs of various administrative, faculty, and student publications; records of student and alumni organizations; a photograph collection; audio and video tapes; sound recordings; microfilm; architectural drawings; and biographical files.

SEE: Hinding.

SEE ALSO: Patrick M. Quinn, 'Profile in Purple: The Northwestern University Archives,' *Illinois Libraries* 57 (March 1975).

FREEPORT

IL296-720

Stephenson County Historical
  Museum
1440 South Carroll Avenue
Freeport IL 61032

(815) 232-8419

OPEN: F-Su 1:30-5, other times by appointment only; closed holidays
COPYING FACILITIES: no
MATERIALS SOLICITED: Local historical items.

HOLDINGS:
Total volume: not specified
Inclusive dates: 1830 -
Description: Papers of Jane Addams, including 30 letters, 1860's-1930's, relating to childhood, college, travel to Europe, and Hull-House, as well as other school and family documents; and 10 Civil War letters, including those of Ulysses S. Grant, William Tecumseh Sherman, Stephen Hurlbut, and Admiral David Porter.

GALENA

IL301-280
Galena Historical Museum
211 South Bench Street
Galena IL 61036

(815) 777-9129

OPEN: M-F 8:30-5; closed weekends and holidays
ACCESS: advance arrangements required
COPYING FACILITIES: no
MATERIALS SOLICITED: Materials associated with the history of Galena, Jo Daviess County, IL, and the upper lead mining region. Will also accept oral history tapes.

HOLDINGS:
Total volume: not specified
Inclusive dates: 19th century -
Description: Account books, business, financial, and court records, correspondence, diaries, journals, scrapbooks, and genealogical source data, pertaining to Galena, Jo Daviess County, IL, the upper lead mining region, Ulysses S. Grant, and the Civil War.

GALESBURG

IL305-280
Galesburg Public Library
Special Collections
40 East Simmons Street
Galesburg IL 61401

(309) 343-6118

OPEN: M-Th 9-9, F, Sa 9-5; closed Sundays and holidays
ACCESS: identification required
COPYING FACILITIES: yes
MATERIALS SOLICITED: Local history materials including items on broader subjects that relate to the Galesburg area; materials pertaining to the history of Illinois, especially its early pioneers. Will also accept first edition material relating to Carl Sandburg and Abraham Lincoln and their connection with the Galesburg area.

HOLDINGS:
Total volume: 2,000 items
Inclusive dates: 1830 -
Description: A collection consisting chiefly of photographs and slides, with some manuscripts, dealing mainly with local history.

IL305-430
Knox College
Seymour Library
College Archives
Galesburg IL 61401

(309) 343-0112, Ext. 392

OPEN: M-F 1-5; closed Thanksgiving, Christmas, New Year's, and June - Aug.
COPYING FACILITIES: yes
MATERIALS SOLICITED: Records of Knox College and papers of its faculty and alumni, as well as materials concerning the settlement of Illinois and the upper Mississippi Valley, Galesburg and Knox County history, and literature.

HOLDINGS:
Total volume: 2,500 l.f.
Inclusive dates: 1800 -
Description: Manuscript collections relating chiefly to Knox College and Illinois history, especially 1820-90. Included are letters of literary, political, and scientific leaders, since 1800; papers of Knox College alumni and faculty; and the archives of Knox College, since 1835, Lombard College, 1851-1931, and the city of Galesburg, 1835-75. Photographs, tapes, slides, and motion pictures are also available.

SEE: Hamer; NUCMC, 1966, 73-74, 77-78, 80.

SEE: Meckler and McMullin; Robbins; Hinding.

GLENVIEW

IL325-270
Glenview Area Historical Society
1121 Waukegan Road
Glenview IL 60025

(312) 724-2235

OPEN: by appointment only
COPYING FACILITIES: no
MATERIALS SOLICITED: Materials pertinent to Glenview history.

HOLDINGS:
Total volume: 15 l.f.
Inclusive dates: 1830 -
Description: A collection of biographies, letters, records of early businesses, photographs, and other materials pertaining to the history of the Glenview area.

IL325-290
Glenview Public Library
1930 Glenview Road
Glenview IL 60025

(312) 729-7500

OPEN: M-F 9-9, Sa 9-5, Su 2-5; closed holidays
COPYING FACILITIES: yes
MATERIALS SOLICITED: Material on the history and growth of the Glenview area; articles from periodicals, photographs, maps, family histories, business histories, manuscripts, diaries.

HOLDINGS:
Total volume: 3 file drawers
Inclusive dates: 1940 -
Description: Pamphlets, photographs, clippings, letters, microfilm, on the history and growth of the Glenview area including the Kennicott Grove (National Historical Landmark).

GRANITE CITY

IL340-280
Granite City Public Library
2001 Delmar Avenue
Granite City IL 62040

(618) 452-6238

OPEN: M-Th 9-9, F, Sa 9-5; variable summer hours; closed Sundays and holidays
ACCESS: identification required
COPYING FACILITIES: yes
MATERIALS SOLICITED: Materials relating to Granite City and Madison County, IL.

HOLDINGS:
Total volume: not specified
Inclusive dates: 20th century
Description: Materials relating chiefly to Granite City and Madison County, IL, including biographies of early settlers, photographs, and a one-volume city history prepared by the Work Projects Administration.

GREENVILLE

IL354-80
Bond County Historical Society, Inc.
Historical Society Museum
414 W. Main Street
Greenville IL

MAILING ADDRESS:
RR2 Box 44
Greenville IL 62246

(618) 664-0819

OPEN: 1st Sunday May-Oct. 2-5
COPYING FACILITIES: yes
MATERIALS SOLICITED: History of Bond County, 1818-1918, or related subjects.

HOLDINGS:
Total volume: not specified
Inclusive dates: 1824 -
Description: Materials include a local history film, covering 1933 to 1940; 100 slides of historic buildings of Bond County; a file of statements by old local settlers, 1900; diaries and account books; a minute book of Almira College, 1850; a surveyor's map, 1824; a list of county voters, 1817; microfilm copies of the local paper, 1858 to 1979; copies of Bond County census 1820-1900; some genealogical data, including cemetery records.

HIGHLAND PARK

IL374-310
Highland Park Historical Society
326 Central Avenue
Highland Park IL

MAILING ADDRESS:
P.O. Box 56
Highland Park IL 60035

(312) 432-7090

OPEN: Su 2-4, Tu-F 1-5, Sa by appointment; closed Mondays, Christmas, New Year's, and July 4
COPYING FACILITIES: no
MATERIALS SOLICITED: Materials related to the history of Highland Park and Lake County, IL.

HOLDINGS:
  Total volume: 60 l.f.; 12 file drawers; 3,000 slides
    Inclusive dates: mid-19th century -
    Description: Old and new slides of Highland Park and vicinity; some genealogical material relating to early families; papers of H.P. Building Company, 1867-72; Ravinia Festival archives; early Illinois and local maps; many local photographs.

SEE: Hinding.

HINSDALE

IL384-320
Hinsdale Public Library
20 East Maple Street
Hinsdale IL 60521

(312) 986-1976

OPEN: M-Th 9-9, F, Sa 9-6, Su 1-5; closed holidays and Sundays June-August
ACCESS: access to collection supervised by "Friends of the Library" and librarian
COPYING FACILITIES: yes
MATERIALS SOLICITED: Any local history materials.

HOLDINGS:
  Total volume: 8 file drawers
    Inclusive dates: 1873 -
    Description: Local biographical and genealogical materials, property abstracts and maps, various reminiscences of early residents, a 1943 religious survey, Hinsdale centennial records, and a collection of Hinsdale photographs, 1873- , including historical and current photographs of many houses.

SEE: Hinding.

JACKSONVILLE

IL394-360
Illinois College
Schewe Library
Jacksonville IL 62650

(217) 245-7126, Ext. 227

OPEN: M-F 8-5, Sa 10-5, Su 2-5; June - Aug., M-F 8-4; closed Thanksgiving week, two weeks at Christmas, and weekends in summer
ACCESS: Head Librarian must be present
COPYING FACILITIES: yes
MATERIALS SOLICITED: History of Illinois College.

HOLDINGS:
  Total volume: 10 l.f.
    Inclusive dates: 1829 -
    Description: Materials concerning Illinois College and its presidents, faculty, and students.

SEE: Hamer; NUCMC, 1968.

SEE: Robbins.

IL394-400
Jacksonville Public Library
201 West College Avenue
Jacksonville IL 62650

no telephone

SEE: Hamer (as Morgan County Historical Society).

Questionnaire not returned.

IL394-500
MacMurray College
Henry Pfeiffer Library
Jacksonville IL 62650

(217) 245-6151, Ext. 285

OPEN: M-Th 7:45-10:30, F 7:45-5, Sa 12-4, Su 2-10:30; closed holidays and school vacations; variable summer hours
COPYING FACILITIES: yes
MATERIALS SOLICITED: Historical materials relating to MacMurray College. Will also accept materials relating to the College curriculum or local history materials.

HOLDINGS:
  Total volume: 600 items
    Inclusive dates: 1851 - 1942
    Description: Papers related to the history of MacMurray College and of the Methodist church in the area; personal journals and diaries; and papers of former presidents of the College, particularly Joseph R. Harker.

SEE: Hamer; NUCMC, 1966, 73.

SEE: Schatz; Hinding; Robbins.

JOLIET

IL404-410
Joliet Public Library
150 North Ottawa Street
Joliet IL 60431

(815) 740-2667

OPEN: M-F 9-9, Sa 9-4; closed Sundays and holidays
COPYING FACILITIES: yes
MATERIALS SOLICITED: Will accept local history items.

HOLDINGS:
  Total volume: 3 items
    Inclusive dates: 1882 - 1978
    Description: A register of pioneers compiled by the Will County Pioneers Association; 'Factors Which Make Joliet a Good Convention City,' by the Joliet Association of Commerce, 1927; and 'War? Or Good? It's Our Choice,' a collection of poems by Josiah S. Watson.

KANKAKEE

IL409-440
Kankakee County Historical Society Library
Kankakee County Collection
Eighth and Water Streets
Kankakee IL 60901

(815) 932-5279

OPEN: M, Th 9-3:30; closed other days
COPYING FACILITIES: yes
MATERIALS SOLICITED: Kankakee County historical events.

HOLDINGS:
  Total volume: 20 c.f.; 7 file cabinets
    Inclusive dates: 1853 -
    Description: Materials concerning the history of Kankakee County, including correspondence, account books, financial records, genealogical source data, manuscripts, photographs, films, oral history recordings, and biological information.

KENILWORTH

IL414-440
Kenilworth Historical Society
415 Kenilworth Avenue
Kenilworth IL 60043

(312) 251-2565

OPEN: M 1-3, or by appointment
COPYING FACILITIES: no
MATERIALS SOLICITED: Kenilworth local government, schools, churches, and civic organizations, and the historical and architectural background of homes in the community.

HOLDINGS:
  Total volume: 3 file drawers; 85 items
    Inclusive dates: 1875 -
    Description: Photographs of Kenilworth people and scenes, a small collection of local diaries and letters, and photographs and historical data about the first 60 homes built in Kenilworth, one of

the first completely planned communities in the United States.

KEWANEE

IL417-440
Kewanee Historical Society, Inc.
211 North Chestnut Street
Kewanee IL 61443

(309) 894-9701

OPEN: W-Sa 1-4, Su 1-4 in summer; closed Mondays and Tuesdays
COPYING FACILITIES: no
MATERIALS SOLICITED: Materials concerning the history of Kewanee, 1854-, and Wetherfield, IL, 1836-1924, including factories, schools, business, sports, churches, streetcars, prominent citizens, city government, and genealogy.

HOLDINGS:
Total volume: 833 items
Inclusive dates: 1911 -
Description: Scrapbooks of photographs and other materials about Kewanee history, photographs of cornhusking, and slides of local businesses and homes.

LA GRANGE

IL424-480
La Grange Area Historical Society
First Congregational Church
6th Avenue
La Grange IL

MAILING ADDRESS:
53 South La Grange Road
La Grange IL 60525

(312) 482-4248

OPEN: by appointment only
ACCESS: advance arrangements with curator required
COPYING FACILITIES: no
MATERIALS SOLICITED: La Grange records of historical significance.

HOLDINGS:
Total volume: not specified
Inclusive dates: 1894 -
Description: Materials pertaining to the La Grange area, including bills, account books, log books, village documents, architectural drawings, aerial photographs, photographs, scrapbooks, and records of school districts, community groups, and churches.

LACON

IL429-520
Marshall County Historical Society
406 Fifth Street
Lacon IL

MAILING ADDRESS:
506 North High Street
Lacon IL 61540

(309) 246-2349

OPEN: M-F by appointment; closed weekends
COPYING FACILITIES: yes
MATERIALS SOLICITED: Materials concerning Marshall County history, including railroads, steamboating, pioneers, and family history.

HOLDINGS:
Total volume: not specified
Inclusive dates: 1829 -
Description: Photographs of Marshall County courthouse, steamboats on the Illinois River, and navigational locks at Henry, IL; excerpts of secretary's minutes of the Crow Meadow Horse Thief Association, 1846; materials relating to Dr. Robert Beal, physician and local campaign manager for Abraham Lincoln; materials concerning Jeriah Bonham, newspaperman, writer, and local promoter of Lincoln's candidacy; and newspaper clippings.

LAKE FOREST

IL434-490
Lake Forest College
Donnelley Library
College Archives
Lake Forest IL 60045

(312) 234-3100, Ext. 405

OPEN: M-F 8:30-5; closed weekends and holidays
ACCESS: qualified undergraduates, graduate students, faculty members, and other researchers, by application only
COPYING FACILITIES: yes
MATERIALS SOLICITED: Lake Forest College history and archival records, and related community materials. Will also accept materials pertaining to the history of Lake Forest, Lake County, and Chicago.

HOLDINGS:
Total volume: 158 l.f.
Inclusive dates: 1856 -
Description: Primarily archival records of Lake Forest College, including administrative papers of its presidents, as well as other materials concerning the history of the College and of individuals and institutions associated with it. Materials on the early history of Chicago, the city of Lake Forest, and Lake County also are held.

SEE: NUCMC, 1978.

SEE ALSO: finding aids to individual collections and record groups available at the repository.

LEBANON

IL444-720
McKendree College
Holman Library
Lebanon IL 62254

(618) 537-4481, Ext. 142

OPEN: by appointment
COPYING FACILITIES: yes
MATERIALS SOLICITED: All materials relating to McKendree College and to the Southern Illinois Conference of the United Methodist church and its antecedents.

HOLDINGS:
Total volume: not specified
Inclusive dates: not specified
Description: Financial records, trustees' records and minutes, materials used to write the College's centennial history in 1928, programs, photographs, memorabilia, and manuscripts of literary society writings. The Library also serves as a repository for the archives of the Southern Illinois Conference of the United Methodist church.

SEE: Hinding.

LIBERTYVILLE

IL449-480
Libertyville-Mundelein Historical Society
413 North Milwaukee Avenue
Libertyville IL 60048

(312) 362-3130

OPEN: by appointment only
COPYING FACILITIES: yes
MATERIALS SOLICITED: Historical and genealogical materials relating to Lake County.

HOLDINGS:
Total volume: 100 l.f.; 16 file drawers; and other items
Inclusive dates: early 1800's -
Description: Materials relating to Lake County. Included are records of local businesses, schools, churches, and other organizations; a collection of early maps; and some genealogical material, oral history tapes, and photographs.

SEE: NUCMC, 1970.
SEE: Hinding.

LINCOLN

IL454-470
Lincoln College
Library
700 North Ottawa
Lincoln IL 62656

no telephone
SEE: Hamer.

Questionnaire not returned.

LISLE

IL459-360

Illinois Benedictine College
Theodore Lownik Library
5700 College Road
Lisle IL 60532

(312) 960-1500, Ext. 850

OPEN: by appointment only; closed
  holidays
ACCESS: advance arrangements required
COPYING FACILITIES: yes
MATERIALS SOLICITED: Sherlock Holmes
  and Arthur Conan Doyle materials and
  the College archives. Will also accept
  Abraham Lincoln materials.

HOLDINGS:
  Total volume: not specified
  Inclusive dates: not specified
  Description: The College archives, relating to St. Procopius Abbey, St. Procopius College, and Illinois Benedictine College; 20,000 photographs and other materials concerning Abraham Lincoln; photographs and other materials concerning
  Arthur Conan Doyle's character Sherlock
  Holmes; and manuscripts, letters from
  immigrants, and genealogical materials,
  relating to Czech-speaking persons in
  northern Illinois and Nebraska.

IL459-520

The Morton Arboretum
Sterling Morton Library
Lisle IL 60532

(312) 968-0074

OPEN: Tu-F 9-5, Sa 10-4; closed
  Sundays, Mondays, and holidays
ACCESS: serious researchers; advance
  arrangements preferred
COPYING FACILITIES: yes
MATERIALS SOLICITED: Landscape plans,
  letters, photographs, clippings, and oth-
  er materials of Jens Jensen and Ossian
  Cole Simonds.

HOLDINGS:
  Total volume: 43 file drawers; 30 l.f.
  Inclusive dates: 1900 -
  Description: The Jens Jensen collection
  of correspondence, photographs,
  clippings, and plans for residential, park,
  and other landscape work; the May
  Theilgaard Watts collection of book
  manuscripts, ecological notebooks, correspondence, and related materials of the
  author of *Reading the Landscape of
  America* and *Reading the Landscape of
  Europe*; and the Morton Arboretum archives, including correspondence between
  Joy Morton and Sterling Morton.

SEE: Novotny; Hinding.

LOCKPORT

IL464-880

Will County Historical Society
803 South State Street
Lockport IL 60441

(815) 838-5080

OPEN: daily 1-4:30; closed Thanksgiving
  week, Christmas week through Jan. 3,
  and all other holidays
USER FEES: $2 search fee
COPYING FACILITIES: no

HOLDINGS:
  Total volume: 100,000 items
  Inclusive dates: 1830 - 1935
  Description: Property records, a sur-
  name file, and cemetery records, all per-
  taining to Will County, in addition to
  Illinois and Michigan Canal records.

LOMBARD

IL469-480

Lombard Historical Society
Museum
23 West Maple Street
Lombard IL 60148

(312) 629-1885

OPEN: Su, W 1-4, and by appointment;
  closed holidays
COPYING FACILITIES: no
MATERIALS SOLICITED: Materials relating
  to the history of Lombard and its inhabitants.

HOLDINGS:
  Total volume: 7 file drawers
  Inclusive dates: 1840's -
  Description: A miscellaneous collection
  of manuscripts, records, maps, photographs, and other materials relating to the
  history of the village of Lombard. Taped
  interviews with village residents, village
  board minutes from 1869, and copies of
  York Township (Dupage County) board
  minutes, 1850-51, are included.

SEE: Hinding.

MACOMB

IL489-890

Western Illinois University
Library
Archives and Special Collections
  Department
Macomb IL 61455

(309) 298-1845, Ext. 272

OPEN: M-F 8-5; closed weekends and
  holidays
COPYING FACILITIES: yes
MATERIALS SOLICITED: Records of Western Illinois University and of other institutions of west central Illinois; materials about members of Congress and
  other prominent figures of the region;
  materials by regional authors; and documents related to the Icarian movement.

HOLDINGS:
  Total volume: 750 c.f.
  Inclusive dates: 1825 -
  Description: Congressional papers of
  Representative Thomas Railsback, including materials related to Watergate,
  juvenile delinquency, and gun control; a
  Burl Ives collection, related to his Johnny
  Horizon program; Edgar Lee Masters correspondence; and a collection of manuscripts by Western Illinois University faculty. A collection on west central Illinois
  includes diaries, correspondence, and
  audio-visual materials, 1880 to the
  present.

SEE: Hinding.

SEE ALSO: 'Midwest Research Institutions
  Directory,' *Illinois Libraries* 53 (Jan.
  1971).

METAMORA

IL542-360

Illinois Prairie District Public Library
208 East Partridge Street
Metamora IL 61548

(309) 367-4594

OPEN: M, Tu, F 11-5, W 7-9, Sa 9-noon;
  closed Sundays, Thursdays, and
  holidays
COPYING FACILITIES: yes
MATERIALS SOLICITED: Materials related
  to Woodford County, IL, Metamora,
  Abraham Lincoln in Illinois, and agricultural history.

HOLDINGS:
  Total volume: 15 vols.
  Inclusive dates: late 1800's -
  Description: Minutes of the Town
  Board of Metamora.

MOLINE

IL548-150

Deere & Company
Corporate Archives
John Deere Road
Moline IL 61265

(309) 752-4733

OPEN: M-F 8-4; closed weekends and
  holidays
ACCESS: persons within the firm and
  scholars upon request and approval
COPYING FACILITIES: yes
MATERIALS SOLICITED: Non-current account books, business records, financial
  records, correspondence, photographs,
  and publications which document the
  workings of the firm. Will also accept
  geographical and historical material of
  the Quad-City and Ogle County, IL,
  areas and material relating to the development of the agricultural implement industry in the United States.

HOLDINGS:
  Total volume: 2,000 c.f.
  Inclusive dates: 1837 -
  Description: Financial records, correspondence, minutes, reports, house organs, news releases, product information,
  policy statements, and pictorial material
  relating to the worldwide operations of

Deere & Company or any of its acquisitions. Personal papers of John Deere and his descendants and items relating to the development of the agricultural implement industry in the United States and the history of the Quad-City area are also held.

MONMOUTH

IL553-520
Monmouth College
Hewes Library
Monmouth IL 61462

(309) 457-2190

OPEN: M-Th 8-midnight, F 8-10, Sa 9-5, Su 1-midnight; closed holidays and shorter hours between terms
COPYING FACILITIES: yes
MATERIALS SOLICITED: Materials relating to Monmouth College.

HOLDINGS:
Total volume: 160 l.f.
Inclusive dates: 1853 -
Description: A collection of materials dealing with Monmouth College, including minutes of societies, clippings, programs, yearbooks and photographs.

MORRISON

IL567-520
Morrison Historical Society
129 1/2 East Main Street
Morrison IL

MAILING ADDRESS:
100 East Main Street
Morrison IL 61270

no telephone

OPEN: M, Tu, W, F 9-5, Th 9-noon; closed weekends and holidays
COPYING FACILITIES: no
MATERIALS SOLICITED: Morrison area materials, primarily relating to Whiteside County, IL. Will also accept other historical items.

HOLDINGS:
Total volume: not specified
Inclusive dates: 1860's -
Description: Household Science Club records, 1904-65, Progressive Reading Circle records, 1897-1968, Knights of Pythias records, 1899-1913, and photographs of people, cities, farms, and other subjects.

IL567-600
Odell Public Library
202 East Lincolnway
Morrison IL 61270

(815) 772-4089

OPEN: M-W, F 2-8:30, Th 2-5:30, Sa 10:30-5; closed Sundays and holidays
COPYING FACILITIES: yes
MATERIALS SOLICITED: Whiteside County History.

HOLDINGS:
Total volume: not specified
Inclusive dates: 1865 -
Description: Materials concerning Whiteside County, including cemetery records, county supervisor's reports, letters of early settlers, a World War I scrapbook, the guest register from the Worthington House in Morrison, Morrison Congregational church records, and genealogical materials.

MOUNT CARROLL

IL585-720
Shimer College
Library
Mount Carroll IL 61053

no telephone

SEE: Hamer.

Questionnaire not returned.

MOUNT VERNON

IL599-520
Mount Vernon Public Library
101 South 7th Street
Mount Vernon IL 62864

(618) 242-6322

OPEN: M-F 10-8, Sa 11-5; closed Sundays and holidays
COPYING FACILITIES: yes
MATERIALS SOLICITED: History of southern Illinois, especially Mount Vernon and Jefferson County, IL, including photographs and genealogical materials.

HOLDINGS:
Total volume: 300 l.f.; 4 file drawers
Inclusive dates: 1800 -
Description: Jefferson County histories, family histories, immigrant passenger lists, birth and death records, cemetery records, photographs and news clippings of early Mount Vernon, city records, and oral history materials.

NAPERVILLE

IL609-120
Naperville Heritage Society
Naper Settlement
Caroline Martin-Mitchell Museum
201 West Porter Avenue
Naperville IL 60540

(312) 420-6010

OPEN: W, Sa, Su 1:30-4:30 and by appointment; closed holidays
COPYING FACILITIES: no
MATERIALS SOLICITED: Information about the George Martin and Edward Grant Mitchell families. Will also accept manuscripts or documents dealing with Naperville history and oral history tapes dealing with Naperville pioneers.

HOLDINGS:
Total volume: 4,500 items
Inclusive dates: 1500 -
Description: Business ledgers, 1860's-90, Presidential autographs, Civil War correspondence and diaries, diaries of early local residents, George Martin correspondence from Scotland, assorted Martin-Mitchell correspondence, indentures, photographs, oral histories, a child's manuscript about early pioneer experiences, records of community groups, maps, family histories, and miscellaneous documents of Victorian Naperville.

SEE: Hinding.

NORMAL

IL624-370
Illinois State University
Milner Library
Map Room
Normal IL 61761

(309) 438-3486

OPEN: M-F 8:30-5; closed weekends and holidays
COPYING FACILITIES: yes
MATERIALS SOLICITED: Maps and aerial photographs. Will also accept manuscript maps, charts, and genealogical source data.

HOLDINGS:
Total volume: 40,500 aerial photos; 227,355 maps
Inclusive dates: 20th century
Description: Aerial photographs from throughout the United States, furnished by the Agricultural Stabilization and Conservation Service. The largest group is from Pennsylvania.

IL624-380
Illinois State University
Milner Library
Special Collections/University Archives
Normal IL 61761

(309) 438-7450

OPEN: by appointment only
COPYING FACILITIES: yes
MATERIALS SOLICITED: University archives, records of local literary clubs, papers of regional families, circus materials, and central Illinois county records. Will also accept any materials of regional interest.

HOLDINGS:
Total volume: 1,720 l.f.
Inclusive dates: 1738 -
Description: Archives and non-current records of Illinois State University; public records of central Illinois counties; records of Bloomington-Normal literary clubs; correspondence and diaries of McLean County families; correspondence and literary manuscripts of American and English authors; correspondence of circus performers, entrepreneurs and impresarios; account books, business records and financial records of the Barnum and Bailey and Ringling Brothers circuses and also of the Dobritch International Circus;

and photographs and slides of circus performers and circuses.

SEE: Hamer; NUCMC, 1970, 72.

SEE: Hinding; Robbins.

SEE ALSO: *Guide to the University Archives* (Illinois State Univ., Milner Library, 1976); Robert Sokan, *A Descriptive and Bibliographical Catalog of the Circus and Related Arts Collection at Illinois State University* (The Scarlet Ibis Press, 1976); 'Midwest Research Institutions Directory,' *Illinois Libraries* 53 (Jan. 1971).

NORTH CHICAGO

IL629-40
Abbott Laboratories
Archives
Routes 43 and 137
Abbott Park IL 60064

(312) 937-2362

OPEN: M-F 9-4; closed weekends and holidays
ACCESS: appointment required
COPYING FACILITIES: yes
MATERIALS SOLICITED: Materials relating to the history of Abbott Laboratories.

HOLDINGS:
  Total volume: 2 vertical files
  Inclusive dates: 1888 -
  Description: A collection documenting the activities of Abbott Laboratories from its founding in 1888, including some materials relating to Dr. Wallace Calvin Abbott from earlier dates.

OAK BROOK

IL644-80
Bethany Theological Seminary and Northern Baptist Theological Seminary
Library
Special Collections and Archives
Butterfield and Meyers Roads
Oak Brook IL 60521

(312) 620-2214

OPEN: by appointment only
COPYING FACILITIES: yes
MATERIALS SOLICITED: Faculty papers and other records and papers pertaining to Bethany Theological Seminary and Northern Baptist Theological Seminary.

HOLDINGS:
  Total volume: 110 l.f.
  Inclusive dates: 1905 -
  Description: Administrative records and faculty papers of Bethany Theological Seminary, formerly Bethany Biblical Seminary in Chicago, Baptist Association records, Danish and Norwegian Baptist Seminary material, and faculty papers of Northern Baptist Theological Seminary.

SEE: Hamer; NUCMC, 1966 (as Northern Baptist Theological Seminary).

OAK PARK

IL649-600
Oak Park Public Library
Local History and Local Authors Collections
834 Lake Street
Oak Park IL 60301

(312) 383-8200

OPEN: M-F 9-9, Sa 9-5, Su 1-5; closed holidays and Sundays June - Aug.
ACCESS: identification required
COPYING FACILITIES: yes
MATERIALS SOLICITED: Materials by or about Frank Lloyd Wright and other Prairie School architects, and by or about Ernest Hemingway; Oak Park history material. Will also accept works by or about Oak Park authors.

HOLDINGS:
  Total volume: 1,200 items
  Inclusive dates: 1855 - 1960
  Description: A collection of Frank Lloyd Wright materials including photographs of Wright buildings, negatives and prints of Wright's work from files of Grant Manson; colored slides of Wright buildings in Oak Park and River Forest; and two original pencil drawings from Wright's studio. Hemingway materials include letters, photographs and tape recordings, while the local history collection includes photographs of Oak Park.

SEE: Robbins.

SEE ALSO: *Frank Lloyd Wright - Prairie School of Architecture: A Selection of Materials in the Oak Park Public Library* (Oak Park Public Library, 1974); *Ernest Hemingway Collection* (Oak Park Public Library, 1974).

ORION

IL674-880
Western Township Public Library
1111 4th Street
Orion IL

MAILING ADDRESS:
P.O. Box 70
Orion IL 61273

(309) 526-8375

OPEN: M 1-8, Tu, Th 6-8, W 9-8, F 1-5, Sa 9-1; closed Sundays and holidays
COPYING FACILITIES: yes
MATERIALS SOLICITED: Materials pertaining to the history of Western Township and Orion. Will also accept materials relating to the history of Henry County, IL, or towns near Orion.

HOLDINGS:
  Total volume: 100 l.f.
  Inclusive dates: 1838 -
  Description: Records of early Western Township, property deeds, assessor books, LaGrange and Deanington lyceum records, library records, biographies and family histories, a Civil War petition, various photographs and drawings, and other materials relating to the history of Orion and its environs.

PALOS PARK

IL693-640
Palos Park Historical Society
Community Center Foundation
127 and Southwest Highway
Palos Park IL 60464

no telephone

OPEN: by appointment only
COPYING FACILITIES: yes
MATERIALS SOLICITED: Materials pertaining to local residents, churches, libraries, and village and county offices. Will also accept tax records, proceedings of senior citizen groups, public documents, and related photographs.

HOLDINGS:
  Total volume: 8 file drawers
  Inclusive dates: early 19th century -
  Description: Materials pertaining to the history of Palos Park and its environs, including church records, land records, scrapbooks, and other papers.

PARK FOREST SOUTH

IL703-300
Governors State University
Library
Park Forest South IL 60466

(312) 534-5000

OPEN: by appointment only; closed Sundays and holidays
ACCESS: identification, statement of purpose, and references required
COPYING FACILITIES: yes
MATERIALS SOLICITED: Records of the University's academic and support units, and brochures, directories, and other publications of the University, dating from its initial planning stages. Will also accept publications of the Board of Governors of Illinois State Colleges and Universities; writings and tape recordings of University personnel; and items of local interest bearing on the University.

HOLDINGS:
  Total volume: 50 l.f.; 33 c.f.
  Inclusive dates: 1969 -
  Description: Records of Governors State University (excluding office correspondence and fiscal records), covering the planning of the University, the development of its administration, academic departments, and physical layout, and its daily operations since 1971.

PARK RIDGE

IL708-40
American Society of Anesthesiologists
Wood Library-Museum of Anesthesiology
515 Busse Highway
Park Ridge IL 60068

(312) 825-5586

OPEN: M-F 9-4:45; closed weekends and holidays
COPYING FACILITIES: yes

HOLDINGS:
Total volume: 53 l.f.; 50 tapes
Inclusive dates: 1905 -
Description: Records of the American Society of Anesthesiologists and its predecessors, the Long Island Society of Anesthetists, the New York Society of Anesthetists, and the American Society of Anesthetists. Included are audio and video recordings about persons active in anesthesiology; audio tapes of highlights of annual meetings of the American Society of Anesthesiologists; and biographical files about prominent pioneers in anesthesiology.

SEE: Meckler and McMullin.

PEKIN

IL718-200
Everett McKinley Dirksen
Congressional Leadership Research Center
Broadway and Fourth Street
Pekin IL 61554

(309) 347-7113

OPEN: by appointment only
ACCESS: identification required; advance arrangements preferred
COPYING FACILITIES: yes
MATERIALS SOLICITED: Materials pertinent to party leadership positions in the U.S. Senate and House of Representatives.

HOLDINGS:
Total volume: 2,000 l.f.
Inclusive dates: 1900 -
Description: Manuscripts, audio-visual items, and memorabilia relating chiefly to the political and Congressional career of Everett McKinley Dirksen. Included are legislative files, working papers, personal papers, correspondence from constituents, and political materials.

PEORIA

IL723-80
Bradley University
Cullom-Davis Library
Virginius H. Chase Special Collections Center
Peoria IL 61625

(309) 671-5945

OPEN: M-F 9-4:30 and by appointment; closed weekends, Christmas-New Year's, Memorial Day and July
COPYING FACILITIES: yes
MATERIALS SOLICITED: Materials pertaining to the history of Bradley University, the Peoria area, and central Illinois, especially materials relating to Jubilee College and Bishop Philander Chase.

HOLDINGS:
Total volume: 150 l.f.
Inclusive dates: 1824 -
Description: A general collection of photographs, letters, and other materials concerning Peoria area history; manuscripts pertaining to Bishop Philander Chase and Jubilee College; miscellaneous

Bradley University administrative papers and publicity materials; archives of Sigma Phi fraternity, 1911-49.

The repository holds materials reported by the Peoria Historical Society, Inc., **(IL723-630)** in the first edition.

IL723-650
Peoria Public Library
107 N.E. Monroe Street
Peoria IL 61602

(309) 672-8845

OPEN: M-Th 9-9, F, Sa 9-6; closed Sundays, Saturdays during summer, and holidays

SEE: Hamer.

Questionnaire not returned.

PRINCETON

IL762-80
Bureau County Historical Society
109 Park Avenue West
Princeton IL 61356

(815) 875-2184

OPEN: Th, Sa, Su 1-5; closed other days, Thanksgiving, Christmas, and New Year's
ACCESS: appointment recommended
COPYING FACILITIES: no

HOLDINGS:
Total volume: 6 bookcases; 2 file cabinets
Inclusive dates: 1828 -
Description: Historical materials relating to Bureau County, focusing on schools, churches, the historical society, and families, particularly the Bryants and the Lovejoys. There are also data and letters regarding local participants in the Civil War and later wars, photograph collections, genealogies, maps, and scrapbooks.

SEE: Robbins.

QUINCY

IL767-320
Historical Society of Quincy and Adams County
425 South 12th Street
Quincy IL 62301

(217) 222-1835

OPEN: by appointment only
COPYING FACILITIES: no
MATERIALS SOLICITED: Materials of local interest only: Quincy and Adams County, IL.

HOLDINGS:
Total volume: not specified
Inclusive dates: 1840 -
Description: Local history and genealogy, including manuscripts of early pioneers and of Civil War soldiers and officers; other materials about the Civil

War; Abraham Lincoln materials; and industrial histories.

SEE: Hamer; NUCMC, 1962.

SEE: Hinding.

IL767-680
Quincy College
Library
1800 College Avenue
Quincy IL 62301

(217) 228-5345, 222-8020

OPEN: M-Th 7:50-10, F 7:50-8, Sa 11-5, Su 1-10; closed Thanksgiving, Christmas, and New Year's
COPYING FACILITIES: yes
MATERIALS SOLICITED: Materials pertaining to the history of Quincy College. Will also accept materials relating to Quincy and Adams County.

HOLDINGS:
Total volume: 960 c.f.
Inclusive dates: 1866 -
Description: Materials relating chiefly to Quincy College. Included are correspondence, account books, and business records.

RED BUD

IL770-40
Adorers of the Blood of Christ
Province of Ruma
Red Bud IL

MAILING ADDRESS:
Box 115, R.R. 1
Red Bud IL 62278

(618) 282-3848, Ext. 47

OPEN: by appointment only
COPYING FACILITIES: yes
MATERIALS SOLICITED: Materials pertaining to the history of immigrants to Illinois from Baden, Germany, 1870-73; to changes in the lives of Catholic sisters resulting from Vatican Council II, 1962-65; and to the early history of member groups in Italy and Germany. Will also accept archival materials related to the congregation of the Adorers of the Blood of Christ or groups of German immigrants to Clinton and Hamilton counties, IL.

HOLDINGS:
Total volume: 25 c.f.; additional materials
Inclusive dates: 1870 -
Description: Letters, house annals, biographical materials, photographs, and taped interviews dealing with Ruma Province of the Adorers of the Blood of Christ. Much of the collection concerns the immigration of members of the congregation from Germany to Illinois, and German-American social history, as exemplified by this community.

SEE: Hinding.

RIVER FOREST

IL772-120
Concordia College
Archives
7400 Augusta
River Forest IL 60305

(312) 771-8300, Ext. 448, 359

OPEN: by appointment only
COPYING FACILITIES: yes
MATERIALS SOLICITED: Materials relating
to history of the College.

HOLDINGS:
  Total volume: 96 l.f.
  Inclusive dates: 1864 -
  Description: Correspondence, financial
  records, photographs, and materials relat-
  ing to the history of the College.

ROCK ISLAND

IL801-20
Augustana College
Library
Special Collections
7th Avenue and 35th Street
Rock Island IL 61201

(309) 794-7317

OPEN: M-F 8-4:30; closed weekends and
  holidays
COPYING FACILITIES: yes
MATERIALS SOLICITED: Materials relating
  to the history of Swedish immigrants in
  the United States and the history of the
  Upper Mississippi Valley. Will also accept Augustana College records, including publications, letters and papers of
  the College presidents, records of organizations, and registrar's records.

HOLDINGS:
  Total volume: 450 l.f.
  Inclusive dates: 1850 - 1935
  Description: Materials relating to
  Swedish immigrants in the United States,
  including papers of early Swedish-
  American clergy. Other holdings relate to
  Indians in and around Rock Island and
  Moline, with emphasis on the Sauk and
  Fox tribes.
    Hauberg collection, including early set-
  tlement in Upper Mississippi Valley;
  business records of Rock Island Sash and
  Door Works; depository for archives of
  National Association of Geology Teach-
  ers; limited number of historical maps.

SEE: Hamer; NUCMC, 1959-61, 70, 72,
80.

SEE: Hinding.

Holdings on Swedish immigration
to the United States, primarily
Swedish-language materials, have been
transferred to the Swenson Swedish
Immigration Research Center in the
Augustana College Library.

ROCKFORD

IL806-695
Rockford College
Howard Colman Library
Archives
5050 East State Street
Rockford IL 61101-2393

(815) 226-4037

OPEN: by appointment only
ACCESS: prior notice of researcher's visit
  and area of archival interest is
  requested
COPYING FACILITIES: yes
MATERIALS SOLICITED: Any materials
  dealing with the history of Rockford
  College or people associated with Rockford College.

HOLDINGS:
  Total volume: 530 l.f.
  Inclusive dates: 1845 -
  Description: Presidential correspondence, trustees' minutes, scrapbooks, pictures, financial records, etc., relating to
  the history of Rockford Female Seminary, later Rockford College. Included are
  materials relating to Jane Addams and
  Julia Lathrop, her assistant at Hull House
  in Chicago; The Molly and John Grimes
  Collection, dealing with history events in
  northern Illinois between 1949 and 1961;
  and the working files of art and music
  critic Clarence Bulliet.

SEE: Hinding.

SEE ALSO: *Rockford College Archives
Handbook* (1976) is available from the
institution.

IL806-705
Rockford Museum - Midway Village
6799 Guilford Road
Rockford IL 61107

(815) 397-9112

OPEN: Th-Su 1-4; closed other days and
  holidays
USER FEES: one dollar
ACCESS: advance arrangements required
COPYING FACILITIES: yes
MATERIALS SOLICITED: Items dealing
  with Rockford, Winnebago County, IL
  and northern Illinois.

HOLDINGS:
  Total volume: not specified
  Inclusive dates: 1850's -
  Description: Photographs of the
  'Double Eagle II' Atlantic balloon flight
  in 1978, photographs and financial
  records of industries, and oral histories.

IL806-710
Rockford Public Library
Local History and Genealogy Division
215 North Wyman Street
Rockford IL 61101

(815) 965-6731

OPEN: M-W, F 9-6, Th noon-9, Sa 1-5;
  closed Sundays and holidays
COPYING FACILITIES: yes

HOLDINGS:
  Total volume: 13 l.f.
  Inclusive dates: 1840 - 1940
  Description: Records of early churches
  and organizations, business correspondence of an early industrial family, correspondence concerning information-
  gathering about people in the Pecatonica
  area, family materials gathered in the
  1940's concerning social changes in the
  Argyle settlement, scrapbooks concerning
  Camp Grant during World War II, and
  oral history recordings.

SEE: Novotny; Hinding.

ROCKTON

IL811-690
Rockton Township Historical Society
Rockton IL

MAILING ADDRESS:
Box 2
Rockton IL 61072

no telephone

OPEN: June-Sept., Su 1-4; other times by
  appointment
USER FEES: fifty cents
COPYING FACILITIES: no
MATERIALS SOLICITED: Materials concerning Stephen Mack, his family, and
  the early history of the Rockton area.

HOLDINGS:
  Total volume: not specified
  Inclusive dates: 1800 - 1900
  Description: Documents of or relating
  to Indians and early settlers of Rockton,
  including the Stephen Mack family.

IL811-760
Talcott Free Library
101-03 East Main Street
Rockton IL 61072

(815) 624-7511

OPEN: M 12-9, Tu, Th 9-9, W, F 9-5:30,
  Sa 9-1; closed Sundays and holidays
COPYING FACILITIES: yes
MATERIALS SOLICITED: Will accept oral
  history recordings and family geneal-
  ogies.

HOLDINGS:
  Total volume: 2 l.f.
  Inclusive dates: early 18th century -
  Description: Genealogies and family
  histories, as well as other local history
  documents.

ST. CHARLES

IL826-730
St. Charles Public Library District
One South Sixth Avenue
St. Charles IL 60174

(312) 584-0076

OPEN: M-F 9-9, Sa 9-5, Su 1-5; closed
  holidays and Sundays June-Aug.
COPYING FACILITIES: yes
MATERIALS SOLICITED: Materials relating
  to St. Charles and Kane County, IL.

HOLDINGS:
Total volume: not specified
Inclusive dates: 19th century -
Description: Materials relating to St. Charles and Kane County, IL, including biographies, photographs, reminiscences, interviews, historic accounts, and diaries.

SCHAUMBURG

IL841-520

Motorola, Inc.
Archives
1303 East Algonquin Road
Schaumburg IL 60196

(312) 576-5305

OPEN: by appointment only
ACCESS: advance request required
COPYING FACILITIES: no
MATERIALS SOLICITED: Materials concerning certain types of Motorola equipment and products.

HOLDINGS:
Total volume: 10 file cabinets
Inclusive dates: 1928 -
Description: Photographs, tapes, and papers documenting the history of Motorola, its contributions to technology, and its areas of specialization, particularly in communications and navigation.

SHELBYVILLE

IL851-720

Shelby County Historical and Genealogical Library
303 North Morgan
Shelbyville IL

MAILING ADDRESS:
P.O. Box 287
Shelbyville IL 62565

no telephone

OPEN: by appointment only
COPYING FACILITIES: yes
MATERIALS SOLICITED: Materials dealing with Shelby County and the State of Illinois.

HOLDINGS:
Total volume: 17 l.f.
Inclusive dates: 1850 -
Description: Material pertaining to Shelby County, including oral history tapes, historical and genealogical records, and tax records, 1854-1900.

SEE: Hinding.

SOUTH HOLLAND

IL856-730

South Suburban Genealogical and Historical Society
Roosevelt Community Center
320 East 161st Place
South Holland IL

MAILING ADDRESS:
P.O. Box 96
South Holland IL 60473

(312) 333-9474

OPEN: Tu, W 1-9, F 10-4, second Saturday of month 11:30-1:30; closed other days and holidays
COPYING FACILITIES: yes
MATERIALS SOLICITED: Genealogical source data, land records, naturalization records, and other manuscripts of local historical and genealogical interest.

HOLDINGS:
Total volume: 3 file cabinets
Inclusive dates: 1835 -
Description: Photocopies of abstracts of land purchases in southern Cook County, 1835- , naturalization records from the City Court of Calumet City, IL and information on American families with Bishop, Eddy, and Cone surnames.

SPRINGFIELD

IL866-200

Episcopal Diocese of Springfield
821 South 2nd Street
Springfield IL 62704

(217) 525-1876

OPEN: M-Sa 9-4; closed Sundays and holidays
COPYING FACILITIES: no
MATERIALS SOLICITED: Local church records; correspondence of bishops of Springfield; and pictures of church buildings. Will also accept materials related to records of the Episcopal church in Illinois.

HOLDINGS:
Total volume: 75 Hollinger boxes
Inclusive dates: 1835 -
Description: Records of existing and defunct parishes and missions within the Diocese; records of diocesan commissions and departments; personal files of the bishops of Springfield; and other material relating to the Episcopal church within the Diocese and nationally.
Collection also contains journals of synods: Illinois, 1835-1872; Springfield, 1877-present; general convention journals, 1823-present; Episcopal church annual, 1845-present.

IL866-320

Hospital Sisters of Third Order of St. Francis
St. Francis Convent
Sangamon Avenue
Springfield IL

MAILING ADDRESS:
P.O. Box 42
Springfield IL 62705

(217) 522-3386

OPEN: M-F 8-3, weekends by appointment; closed holidays and holy days
ACCESS: open to serious researchers
COPYING FACILITIES: no
MATERIALS SOLICITED: Materials relating to the Order's hospitals and school of nursing and to the religious community style of living. Will also accept materials pertaining to hospital equipment and early maps of the Springfield area.

HOLDINGS:
Total volume: 20 file cabinets; 260 boxes
Inclusive dates: 1844 -
Description: Manuscripts pertaining to the early history of the Hospital Sisters of the Third Order of St. Francis in Germany and to its founding in America in 1875; records of the Order for the countries of Germany, Poland, China, Japan, Taiwan, and the states of Illinois, Wisconsin, Missouri, Louisiana, and Arizona.
Also, correspondence, account books, financial records, photographs, newspaper clippings, slides, tapes, books, films; miscellaneous information regarding the Catholic church, clergy, state organizations, and personnel.

IL866-355

Illinois Office of the Secretary of State
Archives Division
Archives Building
Springfield IL 62756

(217) 782-4682

OPEN: M-F 8-4:30, Sa 8:30-12; closed Sundays and holidays
COPYING FACILITIES: yes
MATERIALS SOLICITED: Records of official Illinois State and local government agencies of permanent legal, administrative or research value.

HOLDINGS:
Total volume: 75,000 c.f.
Inclusive dates: 1780 -
Description: Records from all branches of Illinois territorial and State governments, such as gubernatorial correspondence; journals, committee reports, and laws of the General Assembly; and 5,000 cubic feet of Illinois Supreme Court case files, 1820-1936. Also included are records of land grants to early French, British, and American settlers in Illinois and all records of initial Federal and State land sales in Illinois; as well as materials concerning the planning, financing, and construction of the Illinois and Michigan Canal; the organization and development of State financial institutions; the establishment and administration of State mental, penal, and educational in-

stitutions; and the planning and construction of State buildings and public works.

There are also materials from all six State constitutional conventions; territorial and State population censuses, 1818-65; schedules for Illinois of U.S. censuses of agriculture, manufacturing, mortality, and social statistics, 1850-80, and population, 1880; military records of Illinois residents' participation in the Black Hawk, Mexican, Civil, Spanish-American, and Korean Wars, and World Wars I and II; and reports filed with the Secretary of State and the Auditor of Public Accounts by banks, savings and loan associations, and profit and non-profit corporations. The Archives Division also holds all unpublished material and research data gathered by the Illinois Historical Records Survey of the Work Projects Administration.

GUIDES: *Descriptive Inventory of the Archives of the State of Illinois* (1978).

SEE: Hamer.

SEE ALSO: Mary Lynn McCree, 'Illinois State Archives: Guide to Records Holdings,' *Illinois Libraries* 46 (May 1964); 'Preliminary Report of the Land Records,' *Illinois Libraries* 41 (April 1959); Earnest E. East, 'Records of Illinois Soldiers at War,' *Illinois Libraries* 41 (April 1959); Emma M. Scheffler, 'Maps in the Illinois State Archives,' *Illinois Libraries* 44 (June 1962); Walter Schatz, ed., *Directory of Afro-American Resources* (Bowker, 1970); Wayne C. Temple, 'Government Records as Historical Sources,' *Illinois Libraries* 52 (Feb. 1970); Richard C. Davis, *North American Forest History: A Guide to Archives and Manuscripts in the United States and Canada* (Clio Books, 1977).

IL866-365

Illinois State Historical Library
Old State Capitol Building
Springfield IL 62706

(217) 782-4836

OPEN: M-F 8:30-5; closed weekends and holidays
COPYING FACILITIES: yes
MATERIALS SOLICITED: Materials relating to Illinois, the Midwest, and Abraham Lincoln. Will also accept other materials.

HOLDINGS:
Total volume: 7,860 l.f. of manuscripts; 120,000 photographs; 3,275 tapes; 55,000 reels of microfilm; 700 films and videotapes
Inclusive dates: 1274 -
Description: The Library has an estimated four million manuscript items, consisting of 200 large collections and over 2,000 smaller ones. The collections relate to all phases of State history, with most of the items dating from 1818, the year of Statehood. Outstanding are holdings relating to Abraham Lincoln and his contemporaries; papers of political leaders, including U.S. Senators and Representatives, governors, legislators, and other State officials; and military collections pertaining to the Black Hawk War and the Civil War. Records of education, reli-

gious, business, labor, and social groups are also held.

SEE: Hamer; NUCMC, 1963-66, 72, 77.

SEE: Davis; Paszek; Allard, Crawley, and Edmison; Parkinson; Robbins; Hinding.

SEE ALSO: Thomas E. Felt, 'The Stephen A. Douglas Letters in the State Historical Library,' *Journal of the Illinois State Historical Society* 56 (Winter 1963); Robert L. Brubaker, 'The State Historical Library's Collection,' *Illinois History* 18 (March 1965); Bernard Wax, 'The Illinois State Historical Library Oral History Project,' *Illinois Libraries* 45 (Feb. 1963); Walter Schatz, ed., *Directory of Afro-American Resources* (Bowker, 1970); Alan M. Meckler and Ruth McMullin, *Oral History Collections* (Bowker, 1975); 'Microfilm Collections of Periodicals, Manuscripts and Miscellany in the Illinois State Historical Library,' *Illinois Libraries* 47 (March 1965); Ann Novotny, ed., *Picture Sources 3* (Special Libraries Assn., 1975).

William L. Burton, *Descriptive Bibliography of Civil War Manuscripts in Illinois* (Northwestern Univ. Press, 1966); 'Illinois Manuscript and Archival Collections - A Checklist of Published Guides,' *Journal of the Illinois State Historical Society* 66 (Winter 1973); 'Recent Manuscript Acquisitions,' *Journal of the Illinois State Historical Society*, 1958 - ; and the following publications of the Library: *Manuscripts Acquired During 1964-1965* (1967); and, by Robert L. Brubaker, *The David Davis Family Papers, 1816-1943: A Descriptive Inventory* (1965); *The King Family Papers, 1798-1927: A Descriptive Inventory* (1963); *Manuscripts Acquired During 1963: A Descriptive Inventory* (1964).

IL866-480

Lincoln Library
Sangamon Valley Collection
326 South 7th Street
Springfield IL 62701

(217) 753-4910

OPEN: M-Th 9-9, F 9-6, Sa 9-5; closed Sundays and holidays
COPYING FACILITIES: yes
MATERIALS SOLICITED: Materials relating to Springfield and central Illinois history and genealogy, Vachel Lindsay, Brand Whitlock, Illinois State Fair, central Illinois businesses, citizens, and organizations.

HOLDINGS:
Total volume: 20 l.f.
Inclusive dates: 1830 -
Description: Materials relating to the social, political, cultural, architectural, geographic and genealogical make-up of central Illinois. Includes photographs, obituary and other special indexes, ephemera, family histories, Illinois State Fair materials, selected business and organization records, journals, diaries, architectural drawings, broadsides, and Springfield city documents.

Also items relating to area authors, including Vachel Lindsay and Brand Whitlock.

SEE: Robbins.

IL866-715

Sangamon State University
Library
University Archives and Special Collections
Brookens Library
Springfield IL 62708

(217) 786-6520

OPEN: M-Th 9-7, F 9-5; closed weekends and holidays
COPYING FACILITIES: yes
MATERIALS SOLICITED: Records of Sangamon State University and related materials, including personal papers of faculty, staff, and students; papers and records of Illinois community colleges; local history materials; and county records of central Illinois.

HOLDINGS:
Total volume: 500 c.f.
Inclusive dates: 1820 -
Description: Sangamon State University records, including personal papers of faculty members relating to their business and academic careers. Additional materials include collections documenting the growth of the community college system in Illinois, and records of 14 central Illinois counties, concerning land sales, taxation, circuit court cases, and the history of the region in general.

SEE: NUCMC, 1976, 80.

SEE: Parkinson.

IL866-720

Sangamon State University
Oral History Office
Springfield IL 62708

(217) 786-6521

OPEN: M-F 9-4; closed weekends and holidays
COPYING FACILITIES: yes
MATERIALS SOLICITED: 20th century American history, especially Illinois. Will also accept photographs, documents, and manuscripts relating to the oral history memoirs.

HOLDINGS:
Total volume: 450 oral histories
Inclusive dates: 1880 -
Description: A collection of 450 oral histories relating to modern American history, but focusing principally on Illinois political and social history. Subject areas covered include State and central Illinois politics, agriculture, coal mining, labor relations, business enterprise, ethnic groups, student activism, blacks, women, education, and mental health practices.

SEE: NUCMC, 1976.

SEE: Meckler and McMullin.

SEE ALSO: Subject descriptions and inventories are available at the institution.

IL866-840

Vachel Lindsay Association
603 South Fifth Street
Springfield IL

MAILING ADDRESS:
1529 Noble Avenue
Springfield IL 62704

(217) 528-9254

OPEN: Tu, Th June-Aug. 9-4; otherwise
  by appointment only
USER FEES: one dollar
ACCESS: endorsed applicants
COPYING FACILITIES: no

HOLDINGS:
  Total volume: 300 items
  Inclusive dates: 1875 -
  Description: Copies and originals of
  Vachel Lindsay's poems, literary manu-
  scripts, correspondence and other papers,
  as well as related photographs and schol-
  arly dissertations. Also have original
  Lindsay artwork.

SEE: Robbins.

SULLIVAN

IL886-520

Moultrie County Historical and
  Genealogical Society
117 East Harrison Street
Sullivan IL

MAILING ADDRESS:
P.O. Box M M
Sullivan IL 61951

(217) 728-4085

OPEN: M, Sa 1-5; closed other days and
  holidays
COPYING FACILITIES: no
MATERIALS SOLICITED: Materials pertaining to the history of Moultrie
  County or adjacent counties, and data
  on pioneer families of the county. Will
  also accept family histories or genealogical reference material.

HOLDINGS:
  Total volume: 200 l.f.
  Inclusive dates: 1840's -
  Description: Materials pertaining to
  Moultrie County of historical and genealogical importance. Included are correspondence, account books, business
  records, diaries, journals, and genealogical
  source material; biographical data on county
  inhabitants; archives and noncurrent
  records of churches, schools, and civic
  associations; county and township
  records; photographs and scrapbooks;
  obituary files, cemetery books, and sexton's books.

URBANA

IL916-40

American Library Association
Archives
Room 19, Library
University of Illinois
1408 West Gregory Drive
Urbana IL 61801

(217) 333-0798

OPEN: M-F 8-5; closed weekends and
  holidays
COPYING FACILITIES: yes
MATERIALS SOLICITED: Records of the
  American Library Association and its
  constituent units and affiliated bodies;
  papers of officers and members relating
  to the Association's activities; and photographs of libraries and librarians.

HOLDINGS:
  Total volume: 846 c.f.
  Inclusive dates: 1850 -
  Description: 320 record series relating
  to the organizational development of the
  American Library Association, concepts
  of librarianship and library service, library education, library buildings, library
  extension and international assistance
  programs, technical and institutional services, and library war service and the
  wartime contributions of librarians.

GUIDES: Maynard J. Brichford, ed., *Guide
  to the American Library Association Archives* (American Library Assn., 1979).

SEE: NUCMC, 1971 (in Chicago, IL).

IL916-795

University of Illinois
Illinois Historical Survey
Library
Library 346
1408 W. Gregory Drive
Urbana IL 61801

(217) 333-1777

OPEN: M-F 9-5, Sa 9-12; closed
  University holidays and interterms
COPYING FACILITIES: yes
MATERIALS SOLICITED: Materials relating
  to the history of the Illinois Country,
  the Old Northwest, the Upper Mississippi Valley; colonial policy in the
  Great Lakes area; history and settlement of Illinois; and Illinois farming,
  businesses, organizations, professions,
  politicians, and citizens. Will also accept materials concerning the development of the Midwest in the 19th century and communitarianism in the
  United States.

HOLDINGS:
  Total volume: 500 l.f.
  Inclusive dates: 1547 -
  Description: Manuscript and archival
  materials relating to the history of Illinois, the Midwest, the Old Northwest,
  the Upper Mississippi Valley, and colonial policy in the Great Lakes area; Illinois farming, business, organizations,
  professions, politicians, and citizens; and
  communitarianism in the United States.

GUIDES: Maynard J. Brichford, Robert
  M. Sutton, and Dennis F. Walle,
  *Manuscripts Guide to Collections at the
  University of Illinois at Urbana-
  Champaign* (Univ. of Illinois Press,
  1976).

SEE: Hamer; NUCMC, 1959-62, 69,
  71-72, 74, 76-77.

SEE: Robbins.

SEE ALSO: Robert M. Sutton, 'The Illinois
  Historical Survey: A Half-Century of
  Selective Acquisitions,' *Illinois Librar-
  ies* 50 (Feb. 1970).

Richard C. Davis, *North American Forest
  History: A Guide to Archives and Manu-
  scripts in the United States and Canada*
  (Clio Books, 1977).

IL916-810

University of Illinois
University Archives
Room 19, Library
1408 West Gregory Drive
Urbana IL 61801

(217) 333-0798

OPEN: M-F 8-5; closed weekends and
  holidays
COPYING FACILITIES: yes
MATERIALS SOLICITED: Materials relating
  to higher education, student life and
  organizations, academic disciplines and
  organizations, accountancy, agriculture,
  architecture, educational organizations,
  engineering, English language education, international athletic competition,
  international development programs, library science, quality control, Russian
  area studies, and vocational education.

HOLDINGS:
  Total volume: 9,598 c.f.
  Inclusive dates: 1776 -
  Description: Archives of the University, including 804 series of office records,
  656 series of personal papers, and 1,939
  series of University publications, largely
  for the post-1893 period. The Archives
  also administers holdings of business archives.

GUIDES: Maynard J. Brichford, Robert
  M. Sutton, and Dennis F. Walle, *Manuscripts Guide to Collections at the University of Illinois at Urbana-Champaign*
  (1976); Maynard Brichford, *Guide to
  the University of Illinois Archives*
  (1980).

SEE: Hamer; NUCMC, 1965, 67, 69,
  71-72, 75, 77.

SEE: Hounshell; Davis; Paszek; Meckler
  and McMullin; Novotny; Parkinson;
  Spalek; Allard, Crawley, and Edmison;
  Hinding; Schatz; Robbins.

SEE ALSO: Annual reports of the archives
  list new accessions.

IL916-820
University of Illinois
University Libraries
Music Library
Music Building
1114 West Nevada Street
Urbana IL 61801

(217) 333-1173

OPEN: M-Th 8-10, F 8-5, Sa 9-5, Su
2-10; M-F 8-5 when classes are not in
session; closed holidays
COPYING FACILITIES: yes

HOLDINGS:
    Total volume: 1,200 microfilm reels;
    4,000 reels recorded tape; 150
    phonograph records; 100 c.f.
    miscellaneous archival materials
      Inclusive dates: pre-1800's -
      Description: Microfilms of medieval
    and Renaissance polyphonic music manu-
    scripts for the period 1450-1530, largely
    from Western European repositories. Re-
    cordings of University of Illinois School
    of Music concerts and recitals,
    1945-present. Archival materials pertain-
    ing to miscellaneous individuals and in-
    stitutions, including Rafael Joseffy, Harry
    Partch, Maud Powell, Joseph Szigeti, and
    Chicago radio station WGN.

SEE: Spalek.

SEE ALSO: Charles Hamm, ed., *Census-*
Catalogue of Manuscript Sources of
Polyphonic Music 1400-1550 (American
Institute of Musicology, 1977 -).

IL916-840
Urbana Free Library
Archives
201 South Race Street
Urbana IL 61801

(217) 367-4025

OPEN: M-Sa 9:30-4:30; closed Sundays,
holidays, and third Monday in March
COPYING FACILITIES: yes
MATERIALS SOLICITED: History and genealogy of Champaign County, IL.

HOLDINGS:
    Total volume: 70 l.f.; 80 drawers
    Inclusive dates: 1833 -
    Description: Collections relating to the
    history and genealogy of Champaign
    County, IL, including correspondence,
    ledgers, photographs, slides, oral history
    tapes, maps, and records of churches,
    families, organizations, and local govern-
    ments.

VANDALIA

IL921-840
Vandalia Historical Society
307 N. 6th Street
Vandalia IL 62471

(618) 283-0024

OPEN: by appointment only
USER FEES: $5
COPYING FACILITIES: no

HOLDINGS:
    Total volume: 6 c.f.
    Inclusive dates: 1819 -
    Description: Illinois manuscripts, in-
    cluding lectures, letters, reminiscences of
    persons living in the early 20th century, a
    description of Vandalia in 1819, letters of
    author James Hall, papers relating to
    Abraham Lincoln, such as 'Vandalia in
    Lincoln Literature,' radio and bicenten-
    nial talks, literary manuscripts, photo-
    graphs, and correspondence between au-
    thors who have written about early Il-
    linois history.

SEE: Hinding.

WALTONVILLE

IL936-640
The Prairie Historians
Cole and Elm Streets
Waltonville IL

MAILING ADDRESS:
P.O. Box 301
Waltonville IL 62894

no telephone

OPEN: by appointment or on special
occasions announced locally
COPYING FACILITIES: no
MATERIALS SOLICITED: Materials relating
to local history, including records of
Justice of the Peace courts, school districts, and townships; family records;
and business records over 50 years old.

HOLDINGS:
    Total volume: 12 c.f.
    Inclusive dates: 1822 - 1949
    Description: A collection of materials
    relating to the history of Waltonville and
    the surrounding area. Included are
    records of schools, churches, railroads,
    businesses, highways, and local families.

WATSEKA

IL946-360
Iroquois County Genealogy Society
Genealogy Library
Old Courthouse Museum
103 West Cherry Street
Watseka IL 60970

(815) 432-2215

OPEN: M-F 1-5; closed weekends and
holidays
COPYING FACILITIES: yes
MATERIALS SOLICITED: All materials relating to the history of Iroquois County. Will also accept genealogical materials relating to persons who migrated to
the County or who have lived there at
any time.

HOLDINGS:
    Total volume: 1,000 c.f.
    Inclusive dates: 1850 -
    Description: Primarily court records,
    including birth, death, marriage, tax,
    land, and naturalization records; family
    Bibles; cemetery data; and school records.
    Of particular interest is a group of his-
tories of each school in the County, written in 1918.

SEE: Hinding.

WAUCONDA

IL951-480
Lake County Forest Preserve
  Headquarters
Lake County Museum
Lakewood Forest Preserve
Wauconda IL 60084

(312) 526-7878

OPEN: M-F 8:30-4:30; closed weekends
and holidays
ACCESS: advance arrangements required
COPYING FACILITIES: no
MATERIALS SOLICITED: Will accept ma-
terials pertinent to Lake County.

HOLDINGS:
    Total volume: 390 c.f.
    Inclusive dates: 1830 - 1970's
    Description: Manuscripts, visual mate-
    rials, and oral tape recordings pertaining
    to early Lake County history.

SEE: Hinding.

WAUKEGAN

IL956-870
Waukegan Historical Society
Library
1917 North Sheridan Road
Waukegan IL 60085

(312) 336-1859

OPEN: W, F 10-2, Sa 11-1, or by
appointment; closed holidays
COPYING FACILITIES: yes
MATERIALS SOLICITED: Materials per-
taining to Waukegan and Little Fort,
including materials about Dr. Norman
Roberts, Jane Addams, Mrs. Joseph T
Bowen, John C. Haines, Hull House
summer camp, and Abraham Lincoln.
Will also accept materials pertaining to
Lake County, IL, or western Lake
Michigan.

HOLDINGS:
    Total volume: 1 file cabinet; 10 boxes
    Inclusive dates: 1830 -
    Description: Materials relating to the
    area, including correspondence, diaries,
    genealogies, personal papers of Dr. Nor-
    man Roberts, photographs, slides, oral
    history tapes, and records of organiza-
    tions and businesses.

SEE: Hinding.

WHEATON

IL976-850
Wheaton College
Archives
Wheaton IL 60187

MAILING ADDRESS:
Box 607
Wheaton IL 60187

(312) 260-5157

OPEN: M-F 8:30-4:30, Sa 8-12; closed
Sundays and holidays
COPYING FACILITIES: yes
MATERIALS SOLICITED: Records dealing
with interdenominational or nonde-
nominational Protestant evangelism
and missions from the 1700's to the
present, both archives and private papers. Will also accept microfilm of non-
American missionary and/or evangelism materials, and records of U.S.
Protestant evangelical institutions and
leaders.

HOLDINGS:
Total volume: 190 c.f.
Inclusive dates: 1917 -
Description: The Center's collection includes materials dealing with nondeno-
minational Protestant evangelism and missions in the United States as well as data
on evangelical congresses, conferences,
and institutions. The records deal with
political, economic, and social events, as
well as religious.
Types of records include correspondence, reports, business records, photographs, films, audio tapes, videotapes,
maps, posters, slides, and scrapbooks.

SEE: NUCMC, 1981.

IL976-890
Wheaton College
Buswell Memorial Library
Archives and Special Collections
Irving at Franklin
Wheaton IL 60187

(312) 260-5705

OPEN: M-F 1-5; closed weekends and
holidays
COPYING FACILITIES: yes
MATERIALS SOLICITED: Materials relating
to the history of Wheaton College and
persons connected with the college.

HOLDINGS:
Total volume: 400 l.f.
Inclusive dates: 1831 -
Description: Records pertaining to
Wheaton College; papers of college presi-
dents including Jonathan Blanchard,
Charles Blanchard, V. Raymond Edman,
and Hudson T. Armerding; materials re-
lating to the history of evangelicalism;

papers of college faculty members; papers
of author Madeleine L'Engle.
Literary society minutes; glass plate
negatives of the local area; and alumni
papers including Arthur Christy, Kenneth
Taylor, and Theodore B. Wallin.

SEE: Hamer; NUCMC, 1968.

SEE: Schatz.

IL976-900
Wheaton College
Buswell Memorial Library
Marion E. Wade Collection
Irving at Franklin
Wheaton IL 60187

(312) 260-5908

OPEN: M-F 1-5; closed weekends and
holidays
COPYING FACILITIES: yes
MATERIALS SOLICITED: Materials relating
to the authors listed below.

HOLDINGS:
Total volume: 25 c.f.
Inclusive dates: 1880's -
Description: Letters and manuscripts of
authors Owen Barfield, G. K. Chesterton,
C. S. Lewis, George MacDonald, Dorothy
L. Sayers, J. R. R. Tolkien, and Charles
Williams; and additional material con-
cerning their lives and works.

WILMETTE

IL981-560
National Spiritual Assembly of the
Baha'is in the United States
National Baha'i Archives
Baha'i House of Worship
Linden and Sheridan
Wilmette IL

MAILING ADDRESS:
Baha'i National Center
Wilmette IL 60091

(312) 869-9039

OPEN: M-F by appointment only; closed
weekends and holidays
ACCESS: advance permission required

COPYING FACILITIES: yes
MATERIALS SOLICITED: Materials relating
to the history of the Baha'i faith in the
United States. Will also accept Baha'i
materials of other countries.

HOLDINGS:
Total volume: 1,400 l.f.
Inclusive dates: 1897 -
Description: Collections relating to the
history of the Baha'i faith, primarily for
North America but also covering Central
and South America, Europe, Asia, Africa,
and Australasia. Included are the records
of the National Spiritual Assembly of the
Baha'is of the United States, papers of
individuals, photographs, unpublished
memoirs, and local histories.

ZION

IL996-980
Zion Historical Society, Inc.
Shiloh House
Rev. Anton Darms Library
1300 Shiloh Blvd.
Zion IL

MAILING ADDRESS:
P.O. Box 333
Zion IL 60099

(312) 746-2427

OPEN: June - Aug. by appointment only
ACCESS: open by appointment by mail
only, or some summer weekend hours
COPYING FACILITIES: no
MATERIALS SOLICITED: Material relating
to Zion history and the founder of the
city of Zion, Dr. John Alexander
Dowie.

HOLDINGS:
Total volume: 80 l.f.; 4 file drawers
Inclusive dates: 1850 -
Description: Miscellaneous materials
pertaining to the life of John Alexander
Dowie (Zion's founder) and Zion's early
history including: many books and pho-
tographs; some films and oral histories;
Dowie and period artifacts; and papers of
Dowie, Alexander Ford Wilson, and An-
ton Darms.

SEE: Hinding.

INDIANA

Since 1939 county records commissions have maintained authority over the disposition of local public records in Indiana. Under this program some 4,118 cubic feet of permanently valuable items have been transferred to the Archives Division of the Indiana Commission on Public Records in Indianapolis. Most other records of political subdivisions remain in the custody of local officials.

There are also more than 600 microfilm reels of vital, land, probate, and other local government documents, held by the Archives Division, Indiana Commission on Public Records and the Genealogy Division of the State Library.

AKRON

IN5-40
Akron Carnegie Public Library
Akron IN 46910

(219) 893-4113

OPEN: M-Sa 9-6; closed Sundays and holidays
COPYING FACILITIES: yes
MATERIALS SOLICITED: Manuscripts, archives of local institutions and organizations, visual documents, and audible documents.

HOLDINGS:
  Total volume: 9 c.f.
  Inclusive dates: 1850 -
  Description: Local history and genealogy materials, including Akron Methodist Church records, records of discontinued churches, photographs, lodge records, oral history recordings, motion pictures, and slides.

ANDERSON

IN22-50
Anderson College
School of Theology
Library
Anderson IN 46011

(317) 649-9071, Ext. 2077

OPEN: M-F 7:30-11:30, Sa 8:30-12:30, Su 1-5; closed holidays
COPYING FACILITIES: yes
MATERIALS SOLICITED: Materials by Church of God authors or about the Church of God. Will also accept ma-

terials from members of groups which split from the church.

HOLDINGS:
  Total volume: 48 drawers; 109 boxes; 70 l.f.
  Inclusive dates: 1880 -
  Description: Materials regarding Warner Press, formerly the Gospel Trumpet, publishing institution for the Church of God, in Anderson, IN; records of Anderson College and other Church of God colleges; papers of minister David Sidney Warner; written and recorded sermons; oral histories; and materials concerning the history of the Woman's Missionary Society.

SEE: NUCMC, 1959-61.

SEE: Hinding.

IN22-510
Madison County Historical Society, Inc.
Anderson Public Library Annex
8th and Jackson Streets
Anderson IN

MAILING ADDRESS:
P.O. Box 523
30 West 11th Street
Anderson IN 46015

(317) 644-2578

OPEN: by appointment only
COPYING FACILITIES: yes
MATERIALS SOLICITED: Madison County government. Will also accept business archives and hospital archives.

HOLDINGS:
  Total volume: 800 c.f.
  Inclusive dates: 1823 -
  Description: Manuscripts and government records of the 14 townships, 13 towns, 3 cities, 35 taxing units, and 5 school districts in Madison County. Records of certain defunct towns and villages and the old county school and township school systems are also included.

AUBURN

IN33-40
Auburn Automotive Heritage, Inc.
Auburn-Cord-Duesenberg Museum
1600 South Wayne Street
Auburn IN

MAILING ADDRESS:
P.O. Box 271
Auburn IN 46706

(219) 925-1444

OPEN: M-F 10-5; closed weekends, Thanksgiving, Christmas, and New Year's
ACCESS: Museum members or serious historians and automobile owners
COPYING FACILITIES: yes
MATERIALS SOLICITED: Records of automobile companies of Auburn.

HOLDINGS:
  Total volume: 120 c.f.
  Inclusive dates: 1835 -
  Description: Collections documenting automobile models manufactured in Auburn, including the Auburn, Kiblinger, Imp, Eckhart, DeSoto, Cord, McIntyre, and Zimmerman, as well as the Dusenberg, manufactured in Indianapolis, IN. Included are photographs, drawings, blueprints, information on Indiana automotive pioneers, business records of automobile companies, and materials concerning Auburn and De Kalb County, IN.

BEDFORD

IN55-80
Bedford Public Library
Indiana Room
Old Lawrence Collection
1323 K Street
Bedford IN 47421

(812) 275-4471

OPEN: M-Th 10-9, F, Sa 10-5; closed Sundays
COPYING FACILITIES: yes
MATERIALS SOLICITED: Materials of historical significance relating to Lawrence County, IN, and Indiana. Will also accept historical materials of national and international significance, oral histories, and microforms and copies of manuscripts with restricted availability.

HOLDINGS:
  Total volume: 4 c.f.
  Inclusive dates: 1839 - 1974
  Description: Records of civic organizations in Bedford and Lawrence County, IN, photographs of the library and Bedford, minutes of library trustee meetings, unpublished manuscripts relating to the history of Bedford, Lawrence County, and the library, photographs of national and international personalities, and stereoscopes of geography and peoples of the world.

BLOOMINGTON

IN66-340

Indiana University
Folklore Institute
Folklore Archives
510 North Fess Avenue
Bloomington IN 47401

(812) 335-1027

OPEN: M-F 9-4; closed weekends and
holidays
COPYING FACILITIES: yes
MATERIALS SOLICITED: Folklore and oral
history.

HOLDINGS:
Total volume: not specified
Inclusive dates: 1947 -
Description: Over 30,000 field collections, in typewritten or manuscript form,
collected primarily in Indiana, Michigan,
Ohio, and Kentucky, providing information on folklore genres and folklore data.
In addition to these collections, the Archives also has a large slide and tape
collection and copies of dissertations and
theses completed in the Folklore Institute.

SEE ALSO: James S. Rikoon, ed., *Guide to
the Indiana University Folklore Archives*
(1979).

A summary description of holdings is available from the Archives.

IN66-350

Institute for Sex Research
Indiana University
Morrison 416
Bloomington IN 47405

(812) 335-7686

OPEN: M-F 9-5; closed weekends and
holidays
USER FEES: $30 for out-of-state visitors
ACCESS: qualified scholars with
demonstrable research needs
COPYING FACILITIES: yes
MATERIALS SOLICITED: Materials relating
to sexual behavior and attitudes.

HOLDINGS:
Total volume: 85 l.f.; 7 file cabinets
Inclusive dates: 1855 -
Description: A collection of 50,000
photographs ranging from art photography to pornography, 1855- ; a film collection including scientific documentary
films, commercial pornography, and experimental avant-garde works; biographical materials; diaries; love letters; records
of sexual activity; and personal essays.
There is also a small collection of phonograph records and tapes, unpublished
literary manuscripts, and folklore material.

IN66-380

Indiana University
Libraries
Lilly Library
Manuscripts Department
7th and Jordan
Bloomington IN 47401

(812) 335-2452

OPEN: M-F 9-5, Sa 9-noon; closed
Sundays and holidays
COPYING FACILITIES: yes
MATERIALS SOLICITED: Materials relating
to modern British, French, German,
and American literature; Indiana history and letters; and publishing and
book selling records. Will also accept
materials relevant to general library
holdings and University curriculum.

HOLDINGS:
Total volume: 3,224,877 items
Inclusive dates: 5th century -
Description: Over 770 collections covering a wide variety of subjects and most
geographical regions of the world. Particular emphasis has been placed on 19th
and 20th century British and American
literature, Latin American history and
culture before independence, Indiana history and letters, and U.S. history and
politics. Included are diaries, scrapbooks,
correspondence, art materials, records of
publishing firms, and photographs.

SEE: Hamer; NUCMC, 1978.

SEE: Parkinson; Ingram; Spalek; Martin;
Allard, Crawley, and Edmison; Robbins; Hinding.

SEE ALSO: J. E. Patterson, comp.,
'Checklist of Prescott Manuscripts,'
Hispanic American Historical Review
39 (Feb. 1959); C. R. Boxer,
'Preliminary Report on a Collection of
Documents Looted at Manila in
1762-64, and Now in the Lilly Library,
Indiana University,' *Southeast Asian
Archives* 2 (July 1969); Rebecca Camp-
bell Mirza, *A Guide to Selected Latin
American Manuscripts in the Lilly Li-
brary of Indiana University* (Indiana
Univ., 1974); Elfrieda Lang,
*Manuscritos Latinoamericanos en la
Biblioteca Lilly* (Indiana Univ., 1970);
C. R. Boxer, *Catalogue of Philippine
Manuscripts in the Lilly Library*
(Indiana Univ., Asian Studies Research
Institute, 1968); occasional articles in
The Indiana University Bookman.

Richard C. Davis, *North American Forest
History: A Guide to Archives and Manu-
scripts in the United States and Canada*
(Clio Books, 1977).

IN66-385

Indiana University
Museum
601 East 8th Street
Bloomington IN 47405

(812) 335-5445

OPEN: Tu-F 9-4:30, Sa, Su 1-4:30: closed
Mondays and holidays
COPYING FACILITIES: yes
MATERIALS SOLICITED: Photographs of
American Indians and of Indiana history subjects. Will also accept
ethnographic photographs from
throughout the world and photographs
depicting the history of the Midwest.

HOLDINGS:
Total volume: 10,000 items
Inclusive dates: 1900 -
Description: 8,000 negatives of the
Rodman Wannamaker collections of
American Indian photographs taken by
Joseph Dixon from 1908 to 1926, and

2,000 photographs covering Indiana and
Midwest history.

SEE: Bean and Vane.

IN66-390

Indiana University
Oral History Research Project
512 North Fess Avenue
Bloomington IN 47401

(812) 335-2856

OPEN: M-F 8-5; closed weekends and
holidays
COPYING FACILITIES: yes
MATERIALS SOLICITED: Oral history recordings concerning any aspect of Indiana's history, with emphasis on the
period since 1945.

HOLDINGS:
Total volume: 852 sound tapes, 14
video tapes, 24,000 pp. of transcripts
Inclusive dates: 1968 -
Description: Oral history interviews, including transcripts, concentrating on
20th-century Indiana. Major areas covered include community histories, state
politics, industry in Indiana. Among subjects not related specifically to Indiana
are histories of the American Negro
Press, environmental groups, and the theater, as well as biographies of several
public figures and interviews dealing with
U.S.-British relations during World War
II.

GUIDES: *Guide to Indiana University Oral
History Research Project and Related
Studies* (1977).

SEE: Hinding.

IN66-395

Indiana University
School of Music
Library
Sycamore Hall
Bloomington IN 47401

(812) 335-8541

OPEN: M-Th 8-10:30, F, Sa 8-5, Su
12-10:30; closed holidays
ACCESS: must have some form of
identification
COPYING FACILITIES: yes
MATERIALS SOLICITED: Music manuscripts from 15th-18th and 20th centuries; student compositions; black music; Latin American music; and sound
recordings and tapes of Latin American
music. Will also accept correspondence,
diaries, journals, and other documents
of composers, musicologists, and performers; and any literary works relating
to music.

HOLDINGS:
Total volume: 3,000 items
Inclusive dates: 900 -
Description: 20th century manuscripts;
black and Latin American music manuscripts; tapes of Latin American music;
correspondence, journals, and historical
writings of Bruno Nettl; and original and
photocopied manuscripts from 15th-19th
centuries.

SEE: Spalek.

IN66-520

Monroe County Public Library
Indiana Room
303 East Kirkwood Avenue
Bloomington IN 47401

(812) 339-2271

OPEN: M-Th 9-9, F, Sa 9-5, Su 1-5;
closed holidays
COPYING FACILITIES: yes
MATERIALS SOLICITED: Genealogies of
local families and Bloomington and
Monroe County history.

HOLDINGS:
Total volume: not specified
Inclusive dates: 1818 -
Description: Early 20th century school
census books for Monroe County townships; papers of John Stapleton, Monroe
County surveyor; local family histories;
minutes of the Monroe County Historical
Society; a card file of Bloomington residents in World War II; photographs; video tapes of southern Indiana craftspeople;
60 oral history recordings and transcripts;
and microfilms of local history documents and scrapbooks.

SEE: NUCMC, 1977.

BRISTOL

IN77-200

Elkhart County Historical Society
Rush Memorial Center
Bristol IN

MAILING ADDRESS:
P.O. Box 434
Bristol IN 46507

(219) 848-4322

OPEN: Sa 1-4, Su 1-5; closed other days,
holidays, and Dec. 1 - Feb. 28
COPYING FACILITIES: no
MATERIALS SOLICITED: Manuscripts and
visual materials relating to the history
of Elkhart County.

HOLDINGS:
Total volume: 200 l.f.; 16 file drawers
Inclusive dates: 1830 -
Description: Elkhart County history
materials, including county and township
government records relating to local government administration, public buildings,
prisons, poor relief, public works, schools,
railroads, and corporations. Also held are
photographs and genealogical material, as
well as diaries, business records, and organization records bearing on social life,
temperance, the local economy, the Civil
War, and early residents.

BROWNSTOWN

IN92-80

Brownstown Public Library
200 West Walnut Street
Brownstown IN 47220

(812) 358-2853

OPEN: M, W, F 1-9, Sa 9-5; closed other
days and holidays
COPYING FACILITIES: yes

MATERIALS SOLICITED: Material relating
to Brownstown and Jackson County,
IN.

HOLDINGS:
Total volume: not specified
Inclusive dates: 1816 -
Description: Materials relating chiefly
to Jackson County, IN, including
reminiscences and letters of pioneers,
cemetery records, histories and photographs of Brownstown and other towns in
Jackson County, the 'Story of the Reno
Gang' by John Reno, films of the sesquicentennial celebration of the Brownstown
area and of the first watermelon festival
in 1967, and records of the county superintendent of schools, 1913-65.

COLUMBUS

IN121-80

Bartholomew County Historical
Society
524 Third Street
Columbus IN 47201

(812) 372-3541

OPEN: M-F 9-5, Sa 1-4; closed Sundays
and holidays
COPYING FACILITIES: yes
MATERIALS SOLICITED: Materials relating
to the history of Bartholomew County.

HOLDINGS:
Total volume: 2,000 items
Inclusive dates: 1820 -
Description: A collection of manuscripts relating to Bartholomew County.
Included are County records,
reminiscences of pioneers, letters, and papers on various aspects of County life,
business, and industry.

CONNERSVILLE

IN132-310

Historic Automotive Data Collection
Route Five
Connersville IN 47331

(317) 825-9259

OPEN: Sa 9-5; closed other days
COPYING FACILITIES: no
MATERIALS SOLICITED: Materials pertaining to the American automotive industry.

HOLDINGS:
Total volume: 3,500 items
Inclusive dates: 1891 -
Description: Materials pertaining to the
American automotive industry, with spe-
cial emphasis on Connersville and Indi-
ana.

COVINGTON

IN143-120

Covington Public Library
Fountain County Historical Society
Collection
622 Fifth Street
Covington IN

MAILING ADDRESS:
Box 148
Kingman IN 47952

(317) 793-2572

OPEN: summer, M-Sa 1-5; winter, M-F
5-9, Sa 1-5; closed Sundays and
holidays
COPYING FACILITIES: no
MATERIALS SOLICITED: Historical material related to Fountain County.

HOLDINGS:
Total volume: 6 file drawers
Inclusive dates: 1850's -
Description: Typescript histories of lo-
cal families, churches, and agriculture,
diaries, letters, and photographs of the
Wabash and Erie Canal and of the Attica,
IN, sesquicenntennial celebration.

CRAWFORDSVILLE

IN154-880

Wabash College
Lilly Library
Crawfordsville IN 47933

(317) 364-4330

OPEN: M-F 9-4:30; closed weekends and
holidays
ACCESS: advance arrangements requested
COPYING FACILITIES: yes
MATERIALS SOLICITED: History of Wabash College including official records
and personal papers of administrators,
faculty, students, and alumni.

HOLDINGS:
Total volume: 200 l.f.; 5 file cabinets
Inclusive dates: 1832 -
Description: The history of Wabash
College, including records and personal
papers of college offices, organizations,
clubs, presidents, administrators, faculty,
and students. Included are materials of
founder and professor Edmund Otis Hovey, letters and diaries of Wabash participants in the Civil War, and files of president Joseph Farrand Tuttle, including
materials on late 19th century college
education in America.

There is also a collection of 19th century history of Montgomery County, IN,
and the Upper Wabash Valley, including
letters and ledgers of early settlers, community leaders such as Isaac Compton
Elston and Henry Smith Lane, and
churches and voluntary organizations
such as the National Horse Theft Detective Association.

SEE: Hamer; NUCMC, 1959-61.

SEE: Hinding; Robbins.

EAST CHICAGO

IN187-40

Association of Romanian Catholics of America, Inc.
Archives Section
4309 Olcott Avenue
East Chicago IN 46312

(219) 398-3760

OPEN: by appointment only
ACCESS: authorized representatives of Romanian Catholic parishes in U.S., recognized responsible civic or ethnic organization representatives, and serious researchers
COPYING FACILITIES: no
MATERIALS SOLICITED: Material relating to Romanian Catholic parishes, individuals, communities of Romanian Catholics non-organized as parishes, and Romanian ethnic-cultural activities. Will also accept anything relating to these areas or relating to the history, traditions, and customs of Romanians in any part of the world.

HOLDINGS:
    Total volume: 2 file cabinets; 20 l.f.
    Inclusive dates: 1700 -
    Description: Materials relating to activities of the Association, 1948 to date, as well as other materials dealing with the ethnic, cultural, historical, and religious background of Romanians both in the United States and Romania.

IN187-200

East Chicago Historical Society
East Chicago Public Library
2401 East Columbus Drive
East Chicago IN 46312

(219) 397-2453

OPEN: F 1-5; closed other days
COPYING FACILITIES: yes
MATERIALS SOLICITED: Materials relating to East Chicago city government and the history of industries, organizations, and institutions; memoirs and pictures. Will also accept northern Indiana history materials.

HOLDINGS:
    Total volume: 30 c.f.
    Inclusive dates: 1850 -
    Description: Materials relating to the government, industries, organizations, institutions, and individuals of East Chicago and the surrounding area.

EVANSVILLE

IN209-140

Daughters of Charity of St. Vincent de Paul
Mater Dei Provincialate
Archives
9400 New Harmony Road
Evansville IN 47712

(812) 963-3341

OPEN: M-F 9-5; closed weekends and holidays
COPYING FACILITIES: yes
MATERIALS SOLICITED: Materials pertaining to the history of missions in the East Central Province of the Daughters of Charity and to related areas of U.S. history.

HOLDINGS:
    Total volume: not specified
    Inclusive dates: 1600 -
    Description: Correspondence; diaries; journals; logbooks; account books; archives and non-current records of institutions and organizations such as churches, schools, hospitals, social agencies, government agencies, businesses, and community groups; photographs; tapes; and dissertations; all pertaining to the Daughters of Charity of St. Vincent de Paul. Other collections cover areas of U.S. history which relate to the Daughters of Charity missionary activities.

SEE: Hinding.

IN209-200

Evansville Museum of Arts and Science, Inc.
Archives Office
411 S.E. Riverside Drive
Evansville IN 47713

(812) 425-2406

OPEN: Tu-F 10-5; closed other days and holidays
COPYING FACILITIES: yes
MATERIALS SOLICITED: Chiefly Vanderburgh County history, plus surrounding areas of Indiana, Kentucky and Illinois; also artists' biographies, photographs, and other materials. Will also accept some National history items, chiefly wars, politics, and the famous people associated with them.

HOLDINGS:
    Total volume: not specified
    Inclusive dates: 1770 -
    Description: Manuscript materials, chiefly from the 19th century, focusing on Evansville and Vanderburgh County. Included are personal letters from early settlers and some letters of notable Americans; papers of James L. Orr; records of an Illinois Sons of Temperance group (1862); records of local businesses, churches and schools; items relating to the Ohio River; artists' biographies, chiefly contemporary; and papers of the Evansville, Suburban and Newburgh Railway Company (1888-1948), including records, maps, photographs, building plans, and glass negatives.

SEE: Hamer; NUCMC, 1966.

SEE ALSO: 'Midwest Research Institutions Directory,' *Illinois Libraries* 53 (Jan. 1971).

IN209-360

Indiana State University at Evansville
Special Collections and University Archives
8600 University Blvd.
Evansville IN 47712

(812) 464-1896

OPEN: M-F 8-4:30; closed weekends and holidays
COPYING FACILITIES: yes
MATERIALS SOLICITED: Local history material, especially business records, materials relating to the Jewish and black communities, and personal and family papers. Will also accept local regional papers.

HOLDINGS:
    Total volume: not specified
    Inclusive dates: 1780 -
    Description: Materials relating to Vanderburgh, Warrick, Posey, and Gibson counties, including personal and family papers, literary manuscripts, business records, records of community organizations, and Evansville city records. Audiovisual holdings include photograph collections, glass slides used in teaching social studies, and an oral history collection of interviews with local individuals. There are also the University Archives, containing official files, as well as personal papers of faculty and staff.

GUIDES: Josephine M. Elliott, *Preliminary Guide to the Special Collections of Indiana State University* (1975).

SEE: NUCMC, 1978.

SEE: Hinding.

IN209-800

University of Evansville
Clifford Memorial Library
Archives
1800 Lincoln Avenue
Evansville IN 47714

(812) 479-2488

OPEN: M-F 8-5; closed weekends and holidays
COPYING FACILITIES: yes
MATERIALS SOLICITED: Materials relating to Moores Hill College, 1854-1919; Evansville College, 1919-67; and the University of Evansville, 1967- ; and their students, alumni, faculty, and trustees. Will also accept photographs and other materials relating to Evansville and Moores Hill, IN.

HOLDINGS:
    Total volume: 105 l.f.; 8 file cabinets
    Inclusive dates: 1853 -
    Description: Records of the University of Evansville and its predecessors, Moores Hill College and Evansville College, including programs, photographs, financial records, recordings of events, correspondence, reports of officers, minutes of the board of trustees and faculty and University senate, accreditation applications and documents, student records of Moores Hills College, and personnel files of faculty, trustees, and alumni.

SEE: Hinding.

IN209-880

The Willard Library of Evansville
Regional and Family History Center
21 First Avenue
Evansville IN 47710

(812) 425-4309

OPEN: Tu-Sa 9-5:30, Su 1:30-5; closed Mondays and holidays
COPYING FACILITIES: yes

MATERIALS SOLICITED: Manuscript materials, pictorial records, and genealogical records bearing on individuals, companies, institutions, and events of Evansville and neighboring communities. Will also accept materials relevant to the history of the tri-State region, comprised of southwestern Indiana and adjacent areas of Illinois and Kentucky.

HOLDINGS:
Total volume: 100 l.f.
Inclusive dates: 1800 -
Description: Manuscript and documentary materials relating to the history of Evansville and Vanderburgh County, IN, and adjacent areas of Indiana, Illinois, and Kentucky. Important holdings include records of Willard Library and its predecessors; materials of the Southwest Indiana Historical Society and the Vanderburgh Historical and Biographical Society; papers of author Annie Fellows Johnston, social reformer Albion Fellows Bacon, and businessman and civic leader Norman A. Shane, Sr.; scripts of radio newscasts; records of the Evansville Station of the U.S. Weather Service; and miscellaneous personal papers and city, township, and county records.

SEE: Hinding.

SEE ALSO: Walter Schatz, ed., *Directory of Afro-American Resources* (Bowker, 1970).

FORT WAYNE

IN231-40
Allen County-Fort Wayne Historical Society
302 East Berry Street
Fort Wayne IN 46802

(219) 426-2882

OPEN: M-F 11-5; closed weekends and holidays
COPYING FACILITIES: yes
MATERIALS SOLICITED: 20th century social, economic and political history in Allen County and environs, with emphasis on business records, personal papers, and photographs of ethnic and minority groups, as well as architectural records.

HOLDINGS:
Total volume: 1,275 l.f.
Inclusive dates: 1809 -
Description: Manuscripts concerning northeastern Indiana, including papers of entrepreneurs Samuel Hanna and Allen Hamilton, mayors Ivan Lebamoff and Harold Zeis, Democratic politician Henry Branning, and Congressman George Gillie; business records of the Bowser Pump Company (gasoline pump manufacturer), the Nickel Plate Railroad, and the National Appliance Retail Dealers Association; government records; and renderings of public buildings in the Midwest by architects John Wing, S. F. Mahurin, Brentwood J. Tolan, and Straus and Associates.

IN231-130
Concordia Theological Seminary Archives
6600 North Clinton
Fort Wayne IN 46825

(219) 482-9611, Ext. 244

OPEN: M-F 8-5; weekends by appointment; closed holidays
COPYING FACILITIES: yes
MATERIALS SOLICITED: History of the Seminary, including papers and records of professors and students; history of the Lutheran Church-Missouri Synod as it relates to the Seminary from 1846.

HOLDINGS:
Total volume: 110 l.f.; 15 file drawers; 100 items
Inclusive dates: 1846 -
Description: Business and academic records, publications, writings of the faculty, and student records of Concordia Theological Seminary from its founding in 1846, including material pertinent to the history of the Missouri Synod. The collection also contains composite photographs of graduating classes, photographs and architectural plans of the campus and a few related slides and motion pictures.

IN231-240
Fort Wayne Public Library
Indiana Collection
900 Webster Street
Fort Wayne IN 46802

(219) 424-7241

OPEN: M-F 9-9, Sa 9-6; closed Sundays and holidays
COPYING FACILITIES: yes

HOLDINGS:
Total volume: not specified
Inclusive dates: 20th century
Description: The Cocks Collection relating to the history of the motion picture industry, containing 10,000 stills, autographed pictures of movie stars, promotional material, sample film contracts, booking records, and profit and loss records.

SEE ALSO: Ann Novotny, ed., *Picture Sources 3* (Special Libraries Assn., 1975).

IN231-370
Indiana Jewish Historical Society
203 West Wayne Street
Fort Wayne IN 46802

(219) 422-3862

OPEN: M-F 9-3; closed weekends and legal and Jewish holidays
COPYING FACILITIES: yes
MATERIALS SOLICITED: Materials documenting the history of Jewish life in Indiana.

HOLDINGS:
Total volume: 4,000 items
Inclusive dates: 1764 -
Description: Materials concerning Jewish life and culture in Indiana, including records of congregations and organizations, family histories, information on Indiana Jews who served in the U.S. armed forces, materials about Jewish cemeteries, and oral histories.

SEE: Hinding.

IN231-470
Lincoln National Life Foundation
1300 South Clinton Street
Fort Wayne IN

MAILING ADDRESS:
P.O. Box 1110
Fort Wayne IN 46801

(219) 427-3864, 3916

OPEN: Nov. - May, M-Th 8-4:30, F 8-12:30; May - Nov., M-F 8-4:30, Sa 10-4:30; closed other days and holidays
COPYING FACILITIES: yes
MATERIALS SOLICITED: Photographs, letters of Abraham Lincoln and his biographers, and other materials relating to Lincoln, his political associates, Civil War politics, and Indiana in the mid-19th century. Will also accept Presidential autographs, and items relating to Henry Clay and to other prominent political, cultural, and literary figures of Lincoln's day.

HOLDINGS:
Total volume: not specified
Inclusive dates: 1780's -
Description: Manuscript materials by, about, or associated with Abraham Lincoln, including over 100 Lincoln letters and autographs; the Richard W. Thompson papers; papers by Lincoln's cabinet members and family; and letters by Lincoln's contemporaries and biographers. Large collections of Kentucky courthouse records, some dating from the late 1700's, and of genealogical data concerning the Hanks family, also are included.

SEE: Robbins; Hinding.

SEE ALSO: Walter Schatz, ed., *Directory of Afro-American Resources* (Bowker, 1970).

IN231-490
The Lutheran Church-Missouri Synod
Indiana District Archives
1145 South Barr Street
Fort Wayne IN 46802-3180

(219) 423-1511

OPEN: by appointment only
COPYING FACILITIES: yes
MATERIALS SOLICITED: Indiana District records and records of congregations which are members of the District. Will also accept general records of the Synod and collections pertaining to individuals connected with the Synod or District.

HOLDINGS:
Total volume: 400 l.f.
Inclusive dates: 1847 -
Description: Records of the former Central District of the Lutheran Church-Missouri Synod (Indiana, Ohio, Kentucky, West Virginia) and of the Indiana District of the same church body. The Central District was divided in 1963 into the Indiana and Ohio Districts. The Indiana District now embraces all of Indiana and the northern part of Kentucky.

Most of the records date from 1928 and later, and consist of minutes, reports, and correspondence of various officials and boards.

FRANKFORT

IN237-240
Frankfort Community Public Library
208 West Clinton Street
Frankfort IN 46041

(317) 654-8746

OPEN: M-Th 9-8, F, Sa 9-5; closed Sundays and holidays
COPYING FACILITIES: yes
MATERIALS SOLICITED: Frankfort and Clinton County, IN, genealogical materials.

HOLDINGS:
   Total volume: 9 items; 7 vols.
   Inclusive dates: 1879 -
   Description: Local history materials, including a history of the First Christian Church of Frankfort, scrapbook of deaths in the Mulberry area, 1929- , Heavilon family notebooks, high school diaries of Claude G. Bowers, scrapbook of Clinton County and Indiana, 1895 census of Warren Township, and materials concerning the Kent family, deaths of servicemen in World War II, and pioneers.

FRANKLIN

IN242-230
Franklin College
Library
Special Collections
Franklin IN 46131

(317) 736-8441, Ext. 262, 257

OPEN: M-F 8-5; evenings and weekends by appointment only; closed holidays and Dec. 25 - Jan. 1
COPYING FACILITIES: yes
MATERIALS SOLICITED: Materials concerning the Baptist church in Indiana. Will also accept materials concerning Indiana authors and Indiana history in general.

HOLDINGS:
   Total volume: 906 l.f.
   Inclusive dates: 1799 -
   Description: 239 collections documenting Indiana history, including records of Baptist churches and associations, papers of Baptist clergy, papers and other materials relating to authors and public officials, and Franklin College materials.

SEE: Hamer; NUCMC, 1966, 69, 75.

SEE: Hinding.

SEE ALSO: Robert Y. Coward and Hester H. Coward, eds., *Catalog of the David Demaree Banta Indiana Collection* (Franklin College, 1965); 'Midwest Research Institutions Directory,' *Illinois Libraries* 53 (Jan. 1971).

IN242-250
Franklin-Johnson County Public Library
Madison at Home Avenue
Franklin IN 46131

(317) 738-2833

OPEN: M-Th 9:30-8, F, Sa 9:30-6; closed Sundays and holidays
COPYING FACILITIES: yes
MATERIALS SOLICITED: Materials pertaining to Johnson County and its inhabitants.

HOLDINGS:
   Total volume: 43 vols.; 95 items
   Inclusive dates: 1813 - 1913
   Description: Legal and business records, burial records, and a Civil War diary, all pertaining to Johnson County residents. Concerns represented include a tile company, threshing machine operators, a leather shop, and a horse thief and felony detective firm.

GARY

IN253-360
Indiana University Northwest
Calumet Regional Archives
3400 Broadway
Gary IN 46408

(219) 980-6661

OPEN: M-F 9-5; closed weekends and holidays
ACCESS: must contact one of the co-directors, Ronald D. Cohen or James B. Lane
COPYING FACILITIES: yes
MATERIALS SOLICITED: Any manuscript or archival materials dealing with the history of the Calumet region (Lake and Porter counties, IN).

HOLDINGS:
   Total volume: 36 file cabinets
   Inclusive dates: mid-1800's -
   Description: Materials relating to the history of the Calumet region (Lake and Porter counties, IN). Included are personal papers; photographs; church, labor union, settlement house, and other institutional records; and local publications. Materials focus on the history of urban institutions, organizations, government agencies, and ethnic groups.

GOSHEN

IN264-40
Archives of the Mennonite Church
1700 South Main Street
Goshen IN 46526

(219) 533-3161, Ext. 477

OPEN: M-F 8-5; closed weekends and holidays
COPYING FACILITIES: yes
MATERIALS SOLICITED: Mennonite church and Amish Mennonite history. Will also accept historical materials concerning other Mennonites and related groups.

HOLDINGS:
   Total volume: 2,301 l.f.
   Inclusive dates: early 19th century -
   Description: Materials relating chiefly to the Mennonite church in the United States and Canada and its mission and relief activities throughout the world. Included are papers of officers, committees, and institutions of the Mennonite General Board, Board of Missions, Board of Education, and Board of Publication; some records of Mennonite district conferences and local congregations; records of the Mennonite Central Committee in Akron, PA; records of other Mennonite organizations; papers of individual Mennonite and Amish Mennonite leaders; and microfilms, slides, photographs, and recordings.

SEE: Hamer; NUCMC, 1979.

SEE: Hinding.

SEE ALSO: 'Midwest Research Institutions Directory,' *Illinois Libraries* 53 (Jan. 1971).

GREENCASTLE

IN275-150
DePauw University
Archives of DePauw University and Indiana United Methodism
Roy O. West Library
Greencastle IN 46135

(317) 658-4500

OPEN: M-F 8-5; closed weekends, holidays and school vacations
COPYING FACILITIES: yes
MATERIALS SOLICITED: Official records of DePauw University and the United Methodist church in Indiana, and personal papers of people prominent in these institutions. Will also accept personal papers of alumni of DePauw University in art, education, business, government, and science.

HOLDINGS:
   Total volume: 1,500 c.f.
   Inclusive dates: 1806 -
   Description: Ledgers, minute books, personal papers, and official records of DePauw University (1836-), including tapes, microfilm, photographs, and maps. Indiana United Methodism materials include church record books, personal papers of prominent church members, reports, photographs, and historical material for individual local churches.

SEE: Hamer; NUCMC, 1959-61, 68, 70.

SEE: Hinding; Robbins.

SEE ALSO: Eleanore Cammack, comp., *Indiana Methodism: A Bibliography of Printed and Archival Holdings in the Archives of DePauw University and Indiana Methodism* (DePauw Univ., 1964); David J. Olson, comp., *Select Bibliographic Guide to the Archives of DePauw University and Indiana Methodism* (DePauw Univ., 1972);

Richard C. Davis, *North American Forest History: A Guide to Archives and Manuscripts in the United States and Canada* (Clio Books, 1977).

IN275-170
DePauw University
Roy O. West Library
Greencastle IN 46135

(317) 658-4512

OPEN: M-Th 8-5, F 8-4; shorter summer hours; closed weekends, holidays, and University vacations
COPYING FACILITIES: yes
MATERIALS SOLICITED: Will accept materials from faculty, alumni, and trustees.

HOLDINGS:
Total volume: 50 items
Inclusive dates: 1920 - 1960
Description: Literary correspondence of Leon Edel, William James, Fred Lewislattes, Bliss Perry, William Lyon Phelps, Mackenzie King, MacKinlay Kantor, Richard Halliburton, Edwin Markham, Sara Teasdale Filsinger, Vachel Lindsay, Sherwood Anderson, Hamlin Garland, Elinor Frost, Mabel Leigh Hunt, Hugh Walpole, Harriet Monroe, Max Ehrmann, and George Ade.

SEE: Robbins.

IN275-640
Putnam County Historical Society
Roy O. West Library
DePauw University
Greencastle IN 46135

(317) 658-4501

OPEN: M-F 8-5; closed weekends, holidays and school vacations
COPYING FACILITIES: yes
MATERIALS SOLICITED: Materials relating to Putnam County history and genealogy.

HOLDINGS:
Total volume: 50 c.f.
Inclusive dates: 1823 -
Description: Official records of the County (court records); diaries, correspondence and other personal papers; family histories; local business records; unpublished accounts of local persons, institutions and events; slides, tape recordings and microfilm; and records of social clubs.

SEE: Hinding.

GREENFIELD

IN286-280
Greenfield Public Library
700 N. Broadway
Greenfield IN 46140

(317) 462-5141

OPEN: M-F 10-8, Sa 10-6; closed Sundays and holidays
COPYING FACILITIES: yes
MATERIALS SOLICITED: Genealogical materials pertaining to Hancock County, IN, as well as histories of local organizations and institutions.

HOLDINGS:
Total volume: 2 vols.; 2 microfilm reels
Inclusive dates: 1836 - 1920
Description: Birth, marriage, and death records of Hancock County.

GREENWOOD

IN297-600
OMS International
Greenwood IN

MAILING ADDRESS:
Box A
Greenwood IN 46142

(317) 881-6751

OPEN: M-Sa 8-5; closed Sundays, holidays, and first week in July
COPYING FACILITIES: yes
MATERIALS SOLICITED: Manuscripts, archives, and visual and audible records.

HOLDINGS:
Total volume: 30 l.f.; 2 file cabinets
Inclusive dates: 1880 -
Description: Materials relating to founders and missionaries of the OMS, formerly the Oriental Missionary Society. Included are unpublished manuscripts on missionaries, primarily in East Asia, India, and South America; items concerning other Christian notables, especially of the early 20th century; and the OMS magazine, 1902- . Materials cover such subjects as the Tokyo earthquake of 1923, war years, and imprisonments in China during World War II.

SEE: Duignan.

HAMMOND

IN308-330
Hammond Public Library
Calumet Room Collection
564 State Street
Hammond IN 46320

(219) 931-5100

OPEN: M-F 9-9, Sa 9-5; closed Sundays and holidays
COPYING FACILITIES: yes
MATERIALS SOLICITED: Materials pertaining to the Calumet region.

HOLDINGS:
Total volume: 1,500 items; 20 file drawers
Inclusive dates: 1850 -
Description: Materials pertaining to history of Hammond and the Calumet region of Indiana and Illinois, including unpublished manuscripts, letters, family papers and other genealogical data, photographs of local people, places and events, plat books, maps, and oral history tapes.

IN308-640
Purdue University Calumet Library
Archives and Special Collections
2233 171st Street
Hammond IN 46323-2094

(219) 844-0520, Ext. 530, 434

OPEN: M-W 9-noon or by appointment; closed weekends and holidays
COPYING FACILITIES: yes
MATERIALS SOLICITED: Materials relating to northwestern Indiana and the Calumet area and records of Purdue University Calumet, its faculty, and its alumni.

HOLDINGS:
Total volume: 124 l.f.
Inclusive dates: 19th century -
Description: Records of Purdue University Calumet, as well as papers of individuals, records of organizations, and audio-visual materials relating to the history of northwestern Indiana and the Calumet area.

HANOVER

IN319-330
Hanover College
The Duggan Library
Hanover IN

MAILING ADDRESS:
Box 287
Hanover IN 47243

(812) 866-2151, Ext. 338

OPEN: by appointment only
COPYING FACILITIES: yes
MATERIALS SOLICITED: Hanover College records and related materials, as well as local history. Will also accept materials relating to the Synod of Indiana of the United Presbyterian Church in the United States of America.

HOLDINGS:
Total volume: 280 c.f.
Inclusive dates: 1810 -
Description: Correspondence (1813-1900) of John Finley Crowe and his family and heirs relating to the origin and history of Hanover College; minutes and other records of the faculty and board of trustees of Hanover College (1834-1927) and of the literary societies of Hanover College (1836-1914); and records of the Synod of Indiana of the United Presbyterian Church in the United States of America.

HOBART

IN341-320
Hobart Historical Society, Inc.
Pleak Memorial Library
706 East 4th Street
Hobart IN

MAILING ADDRESS:
P.O. Box 24
Hobart IN 46342

OPEN: Sa 10-3, other days by appointment

COPYING FACILITIES: no
MATERIALS SOLICITED: Materials relating to Hobart and Lake County history and Hobart genealogy.

HOLDINGS:
Total volume: 30 file drawers
Inclusive dates: 1850 -
Description: Manuscripts, journals, business records, genealogical material, and other primary sources relating to Hobart and Lake County history, including records of clubs, civic groups, and some churches.

SEE: Hinding.

HUNTINGTON

IN352-320
Huntington College
Loew-Alumni Library
Huntington College Archives
Huntington IN 46750

(219) 356-6000, Ext. 161

OPEN: M-F 11:15-12:15; closed weekends and holidays
ACCESS: by appointment only
COPYING FACILITIES: yes
MATERIALS SOLICITED: Records of Huntington College, the women's auxiliary, and other United Brethren in Christ colleges, as well as correspondence of Huntington College alumni and officials. Will also accept material relating to Huntington, IN.

HOLDINGS:
Total volume: 100 items
Inclusive dates: 1897 -
Description: Material relating to Huntington College, including minutes of literary societies and the women's auxiliary, treasurer's account books, club records, and records of college classes. Also included are trustees' minutes and treasurer's records from Huntington's predecessor, Hartsville College.

SEE: Hinding.

IN352-800
United Brethren in Christ
Archives
United Brethren Building
302 Lake Street
Huntington IN 46750

(219) 356-2312

OPEN: M, W, F 9-4 or by appointment; closed weekends and holidays
ACCESS: appointment advisable
COPYING FACILITIES: yes
MATERIALS SOLICITED: United Brethren in Christ records of general and annual conferences, departments, boards, and correspondence of church officials.

HOLDINGS:
Total volume: 180 l.f.
Inclusive dates: 1830 -
Description: Journals of general church and annual conferences; church records; letters from missionaries; and biographical files on church bishops, including correspondence.

SEE: Hinding.

INDIANAPOLIS

IN363-40
American Legion National
  Headquarters
Library
700 North Pennsylvania Street
Indianapolis IN

MAILING ADDRESS:
P.O. Box 1055
Indianapolis IN 46206

(317) 635-8411

OPEN: M-F 8-4:30; closed weekends and holidays
COPYING FACILITIES: yes
MATERIALS SOLICITED: Correspondence dealing with the establishment of the American Legion, including papers and memorabilia of its founders, as well as materials concerning its programs and activities. Will also accept war diaries; unit histories of World Wars I and II and of the Korean and Vietnam wars; and State, district, county, and post histories of the American Legion.

HOLDINGS:
Total volume: 7,400 vols.; 1,140 file drawers
Inclusive dates: 1919 -
Description: Archives of the American Legion headquarters, including minutes, proceedings, and reports of National conventions, National executive committee meetings, and special and standing committee meetings. There are also biographical sketches, letters, diaries, military and naval service records, speeches, scrapbooks, photographs, and oral histories of American Legion National commanders and other Legion officers and members who have held National or State office. Some records of State and local organizations of the Legion also are housed at the repository.

SEE: Hamer.

SEE ALSO: Susan A. Cady, ed., *Directory of Library Resources in Central Indiana* (Central Indiana Area Library Services Authority, 1975).

IN363-50
The Catholic Center
Archives
1400 N. Meridian Street
Indianapolis IN

MAILING ADDRESS:
P.O. Box 1410
Indianapolis IN 46206

(317) 236-1400

OPEN: by appointment only
COPYING FACILITIES: yes
MATERIALS SOLICITED: Material related to the history of the Catholic church in Indiana.

HOLDINGS:
Total volume: 200 boxes
Inclusive dates: 1834 -
Description: Parish annual reports; diaries, letters, reports, and records of bishops and priests; biographies of priests connected with the dioceses of Vincennes and Indianapolis; unpublished disserta-

tions; and photographs of priests, churches, and religious ceremonies.

IN363-90
Butler University
The Irwin Library
4600 Sunset Avenue
Indianapolis IN 46208

(317) 283-9227

OPEN: M-Th 8-11, F 8-5, Sa 9-5, Su 2-10; closed July 4, Thanksgiving, and Christmas; variable hours between semesters
COPYING FACILITIES: yes
MATERIALS SOLICITED: History of Butler University.

HOLDINGS:
Total volume: 129 l.f.
Inclusive dates: 1857 -
Description: Archives and non-current records of Butler University.

SEE: Robbins.

SEE ALSO: a printed brochure available from the repository describing part of the holdings.

IN363-110
The Children's Museum
3000 North Meridian
Indianapolis IN 46208

(317) 924-5431

OPEN: closed weekends and holidays
ACCESS: serious researchers; appointment required
COPYING FACILITIES: yes
MATERIALS SOLICITED: Records relating to the history of the Children's Museum, as well as the history of neighborhoods and businesses of Indianapolis.

HOLDINGS:
Total volume: 500 l.f.
Inclusive dates: 1821 -
Description: Materials relating to the founding, development, and history of The Children's Museum, and historical materials, particularly photographs, concerning Indianapolis citizens, neighborhoods, and businesses.

IN363-125
Christian Theological Seminary
Manuscript Collection
1000 West 42nd Street
Indianapolis IN 46208

(317) 924-1331, Ext. 114

OPEN: M-F 8-5; closed weekends, holidays and week between Christmas and New Year's
ACCESS: archives users must obtain written permission from originating office
COPYING FACILITIES: yes
MATERIALS SOLICITED: Materials relating to the Christian church (Disciples of Christ). Will also accept religious and other materials.

HOLDINGS:
>*Total volume:* 189 l.f.
>*Inclusive dates:* 1816 -
>*Description:* Material relating to the Christian church in the U.S. and Great Britain, including sermons and correspondence.

SEE: NUCMC, 1970.

SEE: Hinding.

IN363-342

Indiana Commission on Public Records
Archives Division
Room 117, Indiana State Library Building
140 N. Senate Avenue
Indianapolis IN 46204-2215

(317) 232-3660, 3737

OPEN: M-F 8-4:30; closed weekends and holidays
COPYING FACILITIES: yes
MATERIALS SOLICITED: Records of Indiana State government and its political subdivisions having permanent legal, administrative, or research value.

HOLDINGS:
>*Total volume:* 27,000 c.f.
>*Inclusive dates:* 1785 -
>*Description:* Records of Indiana State government, including constitutional offices and education, natural resources, corrections, institutional services, public health, taxation and finance, internal improvements, civil rights, law, charities and welfare, business, and transportation agencies.
>
>Major series include Territorial case files of the General Court of the Indiana Territory; Indiana Supreme and Appellate Court case files; laws enacted and bills of the General Assembly; original land sales to Indiana settlers by the Federal government; military records of Indiana citizens who fought in the Mexican War, Blackhawk War, Civil War, Spanish-American War, World Wars I and II, and the Korean Conflict; articles of incorporation and annual reports of corporations doing business in Indiana; and records of the Board of State Charities.
>
>Other major series are blueprints of public and private buildings; official files of Indiana governors, auditors of State, attorneys general, superintendents of public instruction, and adjutants general; public utility annual reports; State election returns; records of the State Bank; records of the Wabash and Erie Canal and the Michigan Road; agricultural, manufacturing, and social statistics census schedules, 1850-80; and minutes of meetings of State boards and commissions.

GUIDES: Guide is being created as records are processed and finding aids created. Individual entries are in the *Indiana History Bulletin* published by the Indiana Historical Bureau. Publication of entries began in August, 1980. Eventually entries will be combined and edited in a guide to the entire holdings.

SEE: Hamer (as Indiana State Library, Archives Division).

IN363-350

Indiana Historical Society
Library
315 West Ohio Street
Indianapolis IN 46202

(317) 232-1879

OPEN: M-F 8:15-5, Sa 8:15-4; closed Sundays, holidays, and Saturdays June-August
COPYING FACILITIES: yes
MATERIALS SOLICITED: Materials relating to the Northwest Territory, Indiana Territory, Indiana, and travel in these areas, primarily in the 18th and 19th centuries, but also including the 20th century.

HOLDINGS:
>*Total volume:* 1,800 l.f.
>*Inclusive dates:* 1699 -
>*Description:* Manuscripts relating to the Northwest Territory, Indiana Territory, and Indiana, including correspondence, diaries, journals, account books, and business records.

SEE: Hamer; NUCMC, 1959-62, 71, 75, 80.

SEE: Parkinson; Hines; Allard, Crawley, and Edmison; Robbins; Hinding.

SEE ALSO: 'Midwest Research Institutions Directory,' *Illinois Libraries* 53 (Jan. 1971); Walter Schatz, ed., *Directory of Afro-American Resources* (Bowker, 1970); Ann Novotny, ed., *Picture Sources 3* (Special Libraries Assn., 1975).

Richard C. Davis, *North American Forest History: A Guide to Archives and Manuscripts in the United States and Canada* (Clio Books, 1977).

IN363-360

Indiana State Library
Indiana Division
140 North Senate Avenue
Indianapolis IN 46204

(317) 232-3675

OPEN: M-F 8:15-5; closed weekends and holidays
ACCESS: identification required
COPYING FACILITIES: yes
MATERIALS SOLICITED: All categories of non-government materials pertaining to Indiana and its people, with the exception of architectural, engineering and technical drawings, church records, and genealogical data. Will also accept the latter types of materials.

HOLDINGS:
>*Total volume:* 3,450,000 items
>*Inclusive dates:* 1713 -
>*Description:* A collection of personal papers and other private materials relating to Indiana, including diaries, correspondence, account books, business and financial records, non-current records of State and local institutions and organizations, a few manuscript maps and charts, photographs, oral history tapes and transcripts, and a few videotapes. Subjects represented are pioneer settlements and trade with Indians, the War of 1812, the Mexican War, the Civil War, politics, social life, and economic conditions.

SEE: Hamer; NUCMC, 1969.

SEE: Hinding; Robbins; Parkinson.

SEE ALSO: Edwin T. Layton, Jr., ed., *A Regional Union Catalog of Manuscripts Relating to the History of Science and Technology Located in Indiana, Michigan, and Ohio* (Case Western Reserve Univ., 1971); David A. Hounshell, comp., *Manuscripts in U.S. Depositories Relating to the History of Electrical Science and Technology* (Smithsonian Institution, n.d.); Walter Schatz, ed., *Directory of Afro-American Resources* (Bowker, 1970); Ann Novotny, ed., *Picture Sources 3* (Special Libraries Assn., 1975).

Alan M. Meckler and Ruth McMullin, comps., *Oral History Collections* (Bowker, 1975); Albert Krichmar, *The Women's Rights Movement in the United States, 1848-1970: A Bibliography and Sourcebook* (Scarecrow Press, 1972); Gerald Friedberg, 'Sources for the Study of Socialism in America, 1901-1919,' *Labor History* 6 (Spring 1965); 'Midwest Research Institutions Directory,' *Illinois Libraries* 53 (Jan. 1971); Richard C. Davis, *North American Forest History: A Guide to Archives and Manuscripts in the United States and Canada* (Clio Books, 1977). Some partial lists of holdings are also available.

IN363-385

Indiana University-Purdue University at Indianapolis
Archives
420 Blake Street
Indianapolis IN 46202

(317) 264-8278, Ext. 2

OPEN: M-F 8-5; closed weekends and holidays
COPYING FACILITIES: yes
MATERIALS SOLICITED: Records and papers relating to the history of Indiana University-Purdue University at Indianapolis, its fourteen schools and divisions, and its predecessor private schools.

HOLDINGS:
>*Total volume:* 916 l.f.
>*Inclusive dates:* 1866 -
>*Description:* Records and other materials documenting the history of Indiana University-Purdue University at Indianapolis, its fourteen schools and divisions, and its predecessor private schools, including Normal College of the American Gymnastic Union, 1866-1941, and the John Herron School of Art, 1902-67.

IN363-400

Indianapolis-Marion County Public Library
40 East St. Clair Street
Indianapolis IN

MAILING ADDRESS:
P.O. Box 211
Indianapolis IN 46206

(317) 269-1774

OPEN: M-F 9-5; closed weekends and holidays

COPYING FACILITIES: yes
MATERIALS SOLICITED: Indianapolis authors.

HOLDINGS:
Total volume: not specified
Inclusive dates: 1890 -
Description: The May Wright Sewall collection of autographed letters relating to literature, art, politics, the women's suffrage movement, and the stage; the typed manuscript of *Kate Fennigate*, by Booth Tarkington, and his manuscript of 'Hardest Wife to Be,' which was included in *Fennigate*.
Typed manuscripts of Felix Salten's *Good Comrades* and of Harry Emerson Wilder's *Anthony Wayne*, and the James Whitcomb Riley collection, including correspondence, manuscripts, photographs, business records, galley proofs, and other materials.

SEE: NUCMC, 1959-62, 69.

SEE: Hinding; Robbins.

IN363-480
Lutheran Church in America
Indiana-Kentucky Synod
3733 North Meridian Street
Indianapolis IN 46208

(317) 926-1554

OPEN: M-F 8:30-5; closed weekends and church and National holidays
ACCESS: clearance from Synod staff required
COPYING FACILITIES: no
MATERIALS SOLICITED: Congregational and synodical records. Will also accept papers of clerical and lay leaders.

HOLDINGS:
Total volume: 50 l.f.
Inclusive dates: 1840 -
Description: Records and other materials covering the history of the Indiana-Kentucky Synod of the Lutheran Church in America, its predecessor bodies, and its constituent parishes.

SEE ALSO: mimeographed outline of holdings available from the repository.

IN363-660
President Benjamin Harrison
Memorial Home
1230 North Delaware Street
Indianapolis IN 46202

(317) 631-1898

OPEN: M-Sa 9-5, Su 12:30-5; closed Thanksgiving, Christmas, and New Year's
COPYING FACILITIES: yes
MATERIALS SOLICITED: Archival materials relating to Benjamin Harrison and his family, including political Americana, 1880-1892.

HOLDINGS:
Total volume: 3 c.f.; 1 file cabinet
Inclusive dates: 1854 - 1945
Description: Harrison family letters and photographs.

SEE: Hinding.

KOKOMO

IN407-320
Howard County Historical Museum
1200 West Sycamore Street
Kokomo IN 46901

(317) 452-4314

OPEN: Su 2-4, M, W, F 1-4; closed other days, holidays, and Jan.
ACCESS: advance arrangements required
COPYING FACILITIES: no
MATERIALS SOLICITED: Items relating to Howard County.

HOLDINGS:
Total volume: not specified
Inclusive dates: 1840 -
Description: Materials relating to Howard County, including diaries, photographs, early county records, maps, and genealogical material.

SEE: NUCMC, 1959-61.

LAFAYETTE

IN440-160
Diocese of Lafayette in Indiana
Chancery Archives
610 Lingle Avenue
Lafayette IN

MAILING ADDRESS:
P.O. Box 260
Lafayette IN 47902

(317) 742-0275

OPEN: M-F 9-4; closed weekends, holy days, and holidays
ACCESS: appointment required
COPYING FACILITIES: yes
MATERIALS SOLICITED: Items of Diocesan institutions, parishes, and personnel.

HOLDINGS:
Total volume: 7 l.f.
Inclusive dates: 1838 - 1958
Description: Papers regarding the Roman Catholic Diocese of Lafayette, including minutes of its 1958 synod and data from its 1964 census; official papers and correspondence of John George Bennett, 1945-57; records of the St. Joseph Orphanage, 1876-1937; a family tree and correspondence of John Francis Noll; and a Loganport missionary register, 1838-55.
Official letters of John Joseph Carberry, 1957-65, and Raymond Joseph Gallagher, 1965-80; biographies of deceased diocesan priests; microfilm of diocesan newspaper, 1945-80; working papers of first diocesan assembly, 1968, and priests' senate, 1969-79.

IN440-760
Tippecanoe County Historical
Association
909 South Street
Lafayette IN 47901

(317) 742-8411

OPEN: Tu-Sa 1-5; closed Sundays, Mondays, holidays, and Jan.
COPYING FACILITIES: yes

MATERIALS SOLICITED: Items pertaining to Tippecanoe County. Will also accept other materials.

HOLDINGS:
Total volume: not specified
Inclusive dates: 1826 -
Description: Materials relating primarily to Tippecanoe County, including genealogical items, photographs, maps, early County records. Also included are personal papers, diaries, records of businesses and community groups, oral history tapes and transcripts.

SEE: Hamer.

SEE: Hinding.

MARION

IN506-870
The Wesleyan Church
Archives and Historical Library
Highway 37 and 50th Street
Marion IN

MAILING ADDRESS:
P.O. Box 2000
Marion IN 46952

(317) 674-3301, Ext. 162

OPEN: M-F 8-4:30; closed weekends and holidays
COPYING FACILITIES: yes
MATERIALS SOLICITED: Local church and conference records of the Wesleyan church, records of its members, and general headquarters records.

HOLDINGS:
Total volume: 400 l.f.
Inclusive dates: 1843 -
Description: Correspondence, minute books, and other records of the Wesleyan church headquarters, as well as many items relating to its predecessor bodies and to its affiliated churches, institutions, and conferences.

MICHIGAN CITY

IN517-520
Michigan City Historical Society, Inc.
Old Lighthouse Museum
Michigan City IN

MAILING ADDRESS:
P.O. Box 512
Michigan City IN 46360

(219) 872-6133

OPEN: closed Mondays and holidays
COPYING FACILITIES: yes
MATERIALS SOLICITED: Local genealogical materials and lighthouse records.

HOLDINGS:
Total volume: 20 l.f.
Inclusive dates: 1832 -
Description: Materials pertaining to the history of shipping and lighthouse service in Michigan City, La Porte County, IN, and the Lake Michigan area.

MT. VERNON

IN533-640
Posey County Historical Society
Mt. Vernon IN

MAILING ADDRESS:
P.O. Box 171
Mt. Vernon IN 47620

no telephone

OPEN: by appointment only
COPYING FACILITIES: no
MATERIALS SOLICITED: Materials relating
to Posey County.

HOLDINGS:
Total volume: not specified
Inclusive dates: not specified
Description: Oral history interviews
with citizens of the county, a handwritten
daybook and log of a justice of the peace,
and scrapbooks of turn-of-the-century
postcards, Valentines and advertisements.

MUNCIE

IN539-80
Ball State University
Bracken Library
Althea L. Stoeckel Delaware County
  Archives & Local History
  Collection
Muncie IN 47306

(317) 285-5078

OPEN: M-F 8-5 and W 7:30-9:30 p.m.;
closed weekends and holidays
COPYING FACILITIES: yes
MATERIALS SOLICITED: Manuscripts,
county and municipal government
records, maps, photographs and oral
histories relating to the history of industry, labor, education, minorities, religious groups, and political, social, and
fraternal organizations in Delaware
County and the surrounding area.

HOLDINGS:
Total volume: 1,525 l.f.
Inclusive dates: 1827 -
Description: Public records of Delaware County, including deed and mortgage records, tax duplicates, assessment
lists, marriage records, and circuit and
superior court documents. The collection
also contains more than 500 historical
maps, with emphasis on Delaware County; oral history interviews; photographs of
Muncie; papers and diaries of local leaders; records of local businesses, churches,
women's groups, professional and fraternal organizations.

IN539-83
Ball State University
Bracken Library
Center for Middletown Studies
Muncie IN 47306

(317) 285-8037

OPEN: M-Sa 8-5, Wednesday evenings
7:30-9:30; closed weekends and
holidays
COPYING FACILITIES: yes

MATERIALS SOLICITED: Items pertaining
to Muncie's past and data compiled
from Middletown (Muncie) studies.

HOLDINGS:
Total volume: 50 l.f.
Inclusive dates: 1829 -
Description: Photograph negatives of
the 1920's depicting the early automotive
industry in Muncie, Ku Klux Klan activities, business and factory interiors,
storefronts, and other local scenes. Also
included are papers of a local railroad
detective, an investigation of 19th century criminal charges in Middletown, and
other manuscript collections.

IN539-86
Ball State University
Bracken Library
Music Archives
Muncie IN 47306

(317) 285-5078

OPEN: M-F 8-5; closed weekends and
holidays
COPYING FACILITIES: yes

HOLDINGS:
Total volume: 20 l.f.
Inclusive dates: 1920's -
Description: Archives of the International Horn Society, including tape recordings of annual workshops and memorabilia of Max Pottag, John Graas, and
Alfred Brain; and the Cecil Leeson
archival saxophone collection, including
music manuscripts, correspondence,
scrapbooks of Leeson's career, and files of
Dr. Hewitt A. Waggener, researcher in
the early history of the saxophone.

IN539-90
Ball State University
Bracken Library
Special Collections
Muncie IN 47306

(317) 285-5078

OPEN: M-F 8-5; closed weekends and
holidays
COPYING FACILITIES: yes
MATERIALS SOLICITED: Letters and
manuscripts of John Steinbeck and
contemporary poets. Will also accept
any material of Sir Norman Angell.

HOLDINGS:
Total volume: 140 l.f.; 8 file drawers
Inclusive dates: 1833 -
Description: Literary manuscripts and
correspondence of literary figures, primar-
ily those of Sir Norman Angell and of
John Steinbeck. One letter by Herbert
Hoover, and three Ku Klux Klan warning
notes, 1870, are also included.

SEE: Hinding; Robbins.

IN539-100
Ball State University
College of Architecture and Planning
Archive of Drawings and Documents
Muncie IN 47306

(317) 285-8441, 1922

OPEN: variable hours; closed school
holidays and vacations

ACCESS: advance arrangements advised
COPYING FACILITIES: yes
MATERIALS SOLICITED: Plans, drawings,
photographs, and other documents regarding historic sites and structures in
Indiana and careers of Indiana architects, landscape architects, planners, engineers, and builders. Will also accept
documents regarding historic sites and
structures in neighboring states.

HOLDINGS:
Total volume: 12,000 items
Inclusive dates: 1725 -
Description: Documents concerning the
history of architecture, landscape archi-
tecture, planning, and engineering in In-
diana. Major collections include drawings
by Allen & Kelly, S. G. Bartel, R. Bishop,
R. F. Daggett, Sr. and Jr., R. P. Daggett,
C. W. Gerrard, C. Kibele, S. Nolan,
Pierre & Wright, L. W. Scholl, and R. K.
Zimmerly. Photographs and Historic
American Buildings Survey drawings in-
clude works by these and other practi-
tioners.

IN539-545
Muncie Public Library
301 East Jackson Street
Muncie IN 47305

(317) 747-8200

OPEN: M-F 9-9, Sa 9-6; closed Sundays
and holidays
COPYING FACILITIES: yes
MATERIALS SOLICITED: Local materials.

HOLDINGS:
Total volume: 3 l.f.
Inclusive dates: 1964 -
Description: Transcripts of local radio
station editorials.

NASHVILLE

IN550-80
Brown County Historical Society, Inc.
Archives, Oral History, Genealogy
State Road 135 North
Nashville IN

MAILING ADDRESS:
Archives and Oral History
P.O. Box 668
Nashville IN 47448

Genealogy
Box 261 R.R. 6
Columbus IN 47201

(812) 988-6311, 4297

OPEN: by appointment only
COPYING FACILITIES: yes
MATERIALS SOLICITED: Oral history interviews with knowledgeable County
residents and general County history
materials, particularly those relating to
Indians and to participation in U.S.
wars.

HOLDINGS:
Total volume: 130 l.f.
Inclusive dates: 1818 -
Description: Varied collections relating
to the County's history, including church
history materials, genealogical research
notes, letters, and aerial photographs.

NEW ALBANY

IN561-560
New Albany-Floyd County Public
    Library
Indiana History Room
180 West Spring Street
New Albany IN 47150

(812) 944-8464

OPEN: M-Th 9-8:30 F, Sa 9-5:30; closed
    Sundays and holidays
COPYING FACILITIES: yes
MATERIALS SOLICITED: Manuscripts and
    visual documents relating to Floyd
    County and New Albany. Will also ac-
    cept materials relating to surrounding
    Indiana counties, especially Clark and
    Harrison counties.

HOLDINGS:
    Total volume: 20 l.f.
    Inclusive dates: 19th century -
    Description: Manuscripts relating chief-
    ly to Floyd County, including account
    books, business records, correspondence,
    club minute books and programs, as well
    as oral history interviews relating to New
    Albany history and a photograph collec-
    tion including over 500 steamboat pic-
    tures.

NEW CASTLE

IN572-320
Henry County Historical Museum
606 S. 14th Street
New Castle IN 47362

(317) 529-4028

OPEN: M-Sa 1-4:30; closed Sundays and
    holidays
COPYING FACILITIES: no
MATERIALS SOLICITED: Materials of his-
    torical significance pertaining to Henry
    County.

HOLDINGS:
    Total volume: 4 file cabinets
    Inclusive dates: 1816 -
    Description: Considerable genealogical
    material on Henry County families, as
    well as papers of the local Society of
    Friends and those of County officials and
    local celebrities, such as Omar Bundy,
    Arthur Osborn, and Thomas B. Redding.

SEE: Hamer.

NEW HARMONY

IN583-560
New Harmony Workingmen's
    Institute
Tavern and West Streets
New Harmony IN

MAILING ADDRESS:
Box 368
New Harmony IN 47631

(812) 682-4806

OPEN: Tu-F 10-5, Sa 10-4; closed
    Sundays, Mondays, and holidays

ACCESS: researchers required to apply
    for permission in advance
COPYING FACILITIES: yes
MATERIALS SOLICITED: Manuscript ma-
    terials relating to New Harmony and
    Posey County, IN, or to people who
    were involved in the area.

HOLDINGS:
    Total volume: 720 l.f.
    Inclusive dates: 1805 - 1949
    Description: Papers relating mainly to
    the New Harmony Community of
    Equality and to the town of New Har-
    mony. Included are records of organiza-
    tions; correspondence; diaries and travel
    accounts from Europe, 1805-13, the West
    Indies, and the United States, 1816-17;
    and papers of individuals relating to the
    educational, political and social ideas of
    the early 19th century.

SEE: Hamer; NUCMC, 1959-61.

SEE: Hinding; Robbins.

SEE ALSO: 'Midwest Research Institutions
    Directory,' *Illinois Libraries* 53 (Jan.
    1971); Edwin T. Layton, Jr., ed., *A Re-
    gional Union Catalog of Manuscripts
    Relating to the History of Science and
    Technology Located in Indiana, Michi-
    gan, and Ohio* (Case Western Reserve
    Univ., 1971).

NOBLESVILLE

IN594-120
Conner Prairie Pioneer Settlement
Conner Prairie Research Library
13400 Allisonville Road
Noblesville IN 46060

(317) 773-3633, Ext. 46

OPEN: M-F 10-5; closed weekends and
    holidays
ACCESS: researchers with proper
    credentials and permission of
    Historian; appointment required
COPYING FACILITIES: yes
MATERIALS SOLICITED: Manuscripts re-
    lating to the Midwest, central Indiana,
    Hamilton County, and the Conner fam-
    ily in the 19th century. History, social
    life, folklore and folklife, commerce,
    music, and agriculture are among
    topics of interest.

HOLDINGS:
    Total volume: 9 l.f.
    Inclusive dates: 1808 - 1963
    Description: A collection of manu-
    scripts relating to central Indiana and two
    of its early settlers, John and William
    Conner, including Conner family papers
    and genealogical data, as well as ledgers,
    correspondence, photographs, maps,
    reminiscences, and other materials.

IN594-560
Noblesville Public Library
16 South 10th Street
Noblesville IN 46060

(317) 773-1384

OPEN: M-Th 9:30-8:30, F, Sa 9:30-5:30;
    closed Sundays and holidays
COPYING FACILITIES: yes

MATERIALS SOLICITED: Materials related
    to Hamilton County, IN, including
    Noblesville, Fishers, Clarksville,
    Durbin, Clare, Strawtown, Aroma, and
    Omega, IN.

HOLDINGS:
    Total volume: 78 l.f.; 300 microfilm
    reels
    Inclusive dates: 1832 -
    Description: Collections concerning the
    history of Hamilton County, IN, and its
    families, including indexes to county
    records and to death notices from 1837
    to 1920, records of cemetery inscriptions,
    family histories, and the Roberts collec-
    tion of early photographs of Noblesville
    and Hamilton County.

NOTRE DAME

IN627-640
Priests of Holy Cross
Indiana Province
Province Archives Center
Douglas Road
Notre Dame IN

MAILING ADDRESS:
P.O. Box 568
Notre Dame IN 46556

no telephone

OPEN: M-F 9-4; closed weekends and
    holidays
ACCESS: advance arrangements required
COPYING FACILITIES: yes
MATERIALS SOLICITED: Materials related
    to the Congregation of Holy Cross.
    Will also accept other materials.

HOLDINGS:
    Total volume: 300 l.f.
    Inclusive dates: 1841 -
    Description: Manuscripts, archives, vi-
    sual and audible documents, and micro-
    films of manuscripts, relating chiefly to
    the Congregation of Holy Cross in the
    United States. Materials relating to the
    Indiana Province include provincial ad-
    ministration papers, provincial chapter
    papers, chronicles, account books, ledgers,
    manuscripts of members of the province,
    photographs, oral history recordings, and
    microfilms.

IN627-720
Saint Mary's College
Archives
Regina Hall
Notre Dame IN 46556

no telephone

OPEN: M-F 8:45-4:30; closed weekends
    and holidays
COPYING FACILITIES: yes

HOLDINGS:
    Total volume: 205 document cases; 7
    boxes
    Inclusive dates: 1844 -
    Description: Papers of Sister M.
    Madeleva Wolff, including manuscripts
    relating to higher education, theology,
    and literature. Also included are research
    papers from the Graduate School of Sa-
    cred Theology, 1943-69, and ledgers, jour-
    nals, notebooks, minutes, scrapbooks,

photographs, and religious society, organization, and corporation papers.

SEE: Hinding.

IN627-760
Theatre Historical Society
Province Archives Center
Douglas Road
Notre Dame IN

MAILING ADDRESS:
P.O. Box 101
Notre Dame IN 46556

(219) 239-5000

OPEN: M-F 9-3; closed weekends and holidays
ACCESS: prior arrangements required
COPYING FACILITIES: yes
MATERIALS SOLICITED: Materials relating to theaters and their history, particularly architectural.

HOLDINGS:
    Total volume: 40 l.f.
    Inclusive dates: 1890 -
    Description: Photographs of theaters and movie houses, covering interiors, exteriors, and theaters under construction; the Loew's collection of photographs of theaters previously owned or operated by the Loew's chain; and photographs of non-dramatic stage productions ('presentations').

IN627-780
University of Notre Dame
Archives
Notre Dame IN

MAILING ADDRESS:
607 Memorial Library
Notre Dame IN 46556

(219) 239-6447

OPEN: M-F 8-5; closed weekends and holidays
COPYING FACILITIES: yes
MATERIALS SOLICITED: Materials related to the University of Notre Dame and American Catholicism. Will also accept other materials of scholarly interest to researchers.

HOLDINGS:
    Total volume: 5,000 l.f.
    Inclusive dates: 1576 -
    Description: Manuscript and archival materials, visual and audible documents, and microfilms of manuscript material in Europe and Canada, principally from the 19th and 20th centuries, relating chiefly to the Catholic church in the U.S. and to the University of Notre Dame. Materials relating to the University include office files, account books and ledgers, personal manuscript collections of members of the faculty, photographs, oral history tapes, microfilms and related materials. Papers relating to the Catholic church in the U.S. are divided into four categories - diocesan, clerical, lay and organizational - and are composed of the same types of materials.

SEE: Hamer; NUCMC, 1967-69, 75, 77.

SEE: Spalek; Parkinson; Allard, Crawley, and Edmison; Hinding; Hines; Robbins.

SEE ALSO: Thomas T. McAvoy, 'Catholic Archives and Manuscript Collections,' *American Archivist* 24 (Oct. 1961); Wendy Clauson Schlereth, 'The Christian Family Movement,' *American Catholic Studies Newsletter* 2 (Nov. 1976).

Published guides to microfilmed collections are available from the institution.

IN627-800
University of Notre Dame
Libraries
Department of Rare Books and
  Special Collections
Notre Dame IN 46556

(219) 239-6489

OPEN: M-F 8-5; closed weekends and holidays
COPYING FACILITIES: yes
MATERIALS SOLICITED: British and American authors, including Catholic authors; Dante; international sports and games and other materials of scholarly interest.

HOLDINGS:
    Total volume: 50,000 items
    Inclusive dates: 1450 -
    Description: Philosophical, theological, liturgical and literary codex manuscripts; documents and letters of popes, cardinals, bishops and other historical figures; modern letters and literary manuscripts of British and American authors, including Catholic authors in general; photographs of Catholic authors; single-leaf manuscripts relating to Europe and America; and motion pictures, photographs, tape recordings, and microforms relating to international sports and games.

SEE: Robbins.

IN627-810
University of Notre Dame
The Medieval Institute
715 Memorial Library
Notre Dame IN 46556

(219) 239-6603

OPEN: M-F 8-5; evenings and Saturdays by appointment; closed weekends and holidays
ACCESS: scholars engaged in serious research; visiting scholars should make prior written arrangements
COPYING FACILITIES: yes

HOLDINGS:
    Total volume: 24,000 microfilm reels; 22,000 photographs
    Inclusive dates: 7th century - 18th century
    Description: A collection of microfilm copies of medieval and Renaissance manuscripts located in European libraries, including the complete manuscript holdings of the Ambrosiana Library in Milan and the Cathedral Chapter Library in Monza. Virtually all historical disciplines are represented, but the collection is particularly strong in the history of universities, the history of science, medieval liturgies, and Italian humanism.

SEE: Martin.

SEE ALSO: Antonio Ceruti, *Inventario dei Manoscritti della Biblioteca Ambrosiana* (Etimar, 1973); O. Lofgren and R. Traini, *Catalogue of the Arabic Manuscripts in the Bibliotheca Ambrosiana* (Neri Pozza, 1975); A. Luzzatto and L. Mortara Ottolenghi, *Hebraica Ambrosiana* (Il Polifilo, 1972); Renata Cipriani, *Codici Miniati dell'Ambrosiana* (Neri Pozza, 1968); Astrik L. Gabriel, *A Summary Catalogue of Microfilms of 1000 Scientific Manuscripts in the Ambrosiana* (The Medieval Institute, 1968); Carl T. Berkhout, *Ambrosiana Manuscripts: Catalogues* (The Medieval Institute, 1976).

PERU

IN649-520
Miami County Historical Society
Miami County Historical Museum
Junction of U.S. Route 24 and
  Business U.S. Route 31
Peru IN 46970

(317) 472-1570

OPEN: M-F 9-4; closed other days and holidays
COPYING FACILITIES: yes
MATERIALS SOLICITED: Material pertaining to the history of Miami County. Will also accept material pertaining to Indiana history.

HOLDINGS:
    Total volume: not specified
    Inclusive dates: 1830 -
    Description: Materials reflecting the history of Miami County and Peru, including correspondence of political figures and government officials; diaries of Civil War soldiers and others; school rosters, probation report books, and enrollment records; 30 volumes of oral history interviews with elderly County residents; and photographs of persons, places, and events.

IN649-650
Miami County Historical Society
Puterbaugh Museum
11 North Huntington Street
Peru IN 46970

(317) 472-1570

OPEN: M-Sa 9-4; closed Sundays, holidays, winter months
COPYING FACILITIES: yes
MATERIALS SOLICITED: Materials pertaining to the history of Miami County. Will also accept Indiana history materials.

HOLDINGS:
    Total volume: not specified
    Inclusive dates: 1830 -
    Description: Papers and photographs relating to the early history of Miami County, including many relating to the Miami and other American Indians; correspondence and diaries, including those of Civil War soldiers; account books and other financial records of early residents; and several papers relating to Henry Conradt and his family.

PLAINFIELD

IN660-620

Plainfield Friends Meeting
Western Yearly Meeting of Friends
105 South East Street
Plainfield IN 46168

(317) 839-6490

OPEN: M-F 9-4; closed weekends
ACCESS: prior arrangement only
COPYING FACILITIES: yes
MATERIALS SOLICITED: History of the Society of Friends in the State of Indiana, including original documents from the earliest Quaker settlers.

HOLDINGS:
  Total volume: 500 items
  Inclusive dates: 1823 -
  Description: Records of the Western Yearly Meeting of the Society of Friends, including materials relating to its founding, as well as proceedings of its 72 constituent local meetings.

IN660-640

Plainfield Public Library
Guilford Township Historical Collection
1120 Stafford Road
Plainfield IN 46168

(317) 839-6602

OPEN: Tu-Th 12-5; also last Saturday of each month 9-5; closed Sundays and holidays
ACCESS: prior arrangements recommended
COPYING FACILITIES: yes
MATERIALS SOLICITED: Any materials relating to Guilford Township, Hendricks and surrounding counties, and Indiana in general.

HOLDINGS:
  Total volume: 75 l.f.
  Inclusive dates: 1820 -
  Description: Correspondence, deeds, diaries, logbooks, account books, and genealogical data, pertaining to the history of Hendricks County, IN, and the surrounding area. There is also a collection of County tax records and local school and court records.

SEE: Hinding.

PLYMOUTH

IN671-520

Marshall County Historical Society Museum
317 West Monroe Street
Plymouth IN 46563

(219) 936-2306

OPEN: M-F 9-5, Su 1-5; closed Saturdays and holidays
COPYING FACILITIES: yes
MATERIALS SOLICITED: Materials relating to Marshall County, including genealogy.

HOLDINGS:
  Total volume: 100 l.f.
  Inclusive dates: 1834 -
  Description: Diaries, account books, genealogical source data, maps, photographs, and oral history tapes pertaining to Marshall County.

REMINGTON

IN687-690

Remington-Carpenter Township Public Library
Ohio Street
Remington IN

MAILING ADDRESS:
P.O. Box 65
Remington IN 47977

(219) 261-2543

OPEN: M-W, F 10-5, Sa 10-noon; closed Sundays, Thursdays and holidays
ACCESS: advance arrangments required
COPYING FACILITIES: yes
MATERIALS SOLICITED: Materials relating to the history of Remington and Jasper County, IN. Will also accept materials relating to Indiana history.

HOLDINGS:
  Total volume: 15 l.f.
  Inclusive dates: 1898 -
  Description: Photographs and newspaper clippings of Remington and the surrounding area.

RENSSELAER

IN693-710

Saint Joseph's College
Archives
Rensselaer IN 47978

(219) 866-7111

OPEN: by appointment
COPYING FACILITIES: yes
MATERIALS SOLICITED: Materials pertaining to the history of Saint Joseph's College.

HOLDINGS:
  Total volume: 150 c.f.
  Inclusive dates: 1889 -
  Description: Account books of school organizations, music scores in manuscript, photographs, motion pictures, tapes and transcripts of people and events, all related closely to the College.

RICHMOND

IN704-200

Earlham College
Lilly Library
Richmond IN 47374

(317) 962-6561

OPEN: M-F 8-11, Sa 8-5, Su 1-11; summer, M-F 8-5; irregular hours during College vacations
COPYING FACILITIES: yes
MATERIALS SOLICITED: Material pertaining to the Society of Friends.

HOLDINGS:
  Total volume: 500 l.f.
  Inclusive dates: 18th century -
  Description: Manuscript materials relating chiefly to the Society of Friends, including scattered minutes of some monthly meetings, records of Young Friends activities, and records, including photographs, relating to the work of the Associated Executive Committee of Friends on Indian Affairs. There are also personal paper collections of individual Quakers and materials relating to the history of Earlham College.

SEE: Hamer; NUCMC, 1959-64, 75.

SEE: Schatz; Parkinson; Robbins; Hinding.

IN704-240

Friends United Meeting
Wider Ministries Commission Archives
101 Quaker Hill Drive
Richmond IN 47374

(317) 962-7573

OPEN: M-F 8-5; closed weekends and holidays
ACCESS: advance arrangements requested; identification required
COPYING FACILITIES: yes
MATERIALS SOLICITED: Materials relating to Friends World Mission activities.

HOLDINGS:
  Total volume: 53 l.f.
  Inclusive dates: 1890 - 1975
  Description: Reports, photographs, and microfilmed correspondence relating to overseas mission work in Cuba, Kenya, Jamaica, Mexico, and Palestine.

IN704-360

Indiana Yearly Meeting of Friends
Custodian of Records
First Friends Meeting
15th and East Main Streets
Richmond IN 47374

no telephone

OPEN: by appointment only
COPYING FACILITIES: no

HOLDINGS:
  Total volume: 600 vols.
  Inclusive dates: early 1800's - 1970
  Description: Membership lists, birth and death records, marriage records, and minutes of early monthly meetings of Friends who were members of the Indiana Yearly Meeting of Friends.

IN704-520

Morrisson-Reeves Library
80 North 6th Street
Richmond IN 47374

(317) 966-8291

OPEN: M-Th 9-9, F, Sa 9-5:30; July-Aug., M-Sa 9-5:30; closed Sundays and holidays
COPYING FACILITIES: yes
MATERIALS SOLICITED: Will accept manuscript or archival materials relating to local organizations, prominent families or individuals, and Richmond and Wayne County, IN, history.

HOLDINGS:
Total volume: not specified
Inclusive dates: late 19th century -
Description: Materials relating to local organizations, including special interest clubs, chapters of the American Association of University Women and the Daughters of the American Revolution, and the Richmond Sisterhood, an affiliate of the National Federation of Temple Sisterhoods. Also included are manuscripts of books by Esther Kellner.

IN704-880

Julia Meek Gaar Wayne County
Historical Museum
1150 North A Street
Richmond IN 47374

(317) 962-5756

OPEN: Tu-F 12-4, Sa, Su 1-5; closed Mondays, holidays, and mid-Dec. - mid-Feb.
ACCESS: prior appointment required
COPYING FACILITIES: no
MATERIALS SOLICITED: Genealogical and historical material concerning Wayne County.

HOLDINGS:
Total volume: 80 c.f.
Inclusive dates: 1800 -
Description: Genealogies, diaries, justice of the peace records, school records, letters, and land patents, pertaining to the history of Wayne County.

ROCHESTER

IN726-240

Fulton County Historical Society
7th and Pontiac
Rochester IN 46975

(219) 223-4436

OPEN: M-F 9-5; closed weekends and holidays
COPYING FACILITIES: no
MATERIALS SOLICITED: Written records and photographs pertaining to families and businesses of Fulton County.

HOLDINGS:
Total volume: 200 c.f.
Inclusive dates: 1800 -
Description: Diaries; correspondence; unpublished genealogical manuscripts; records of businesses, churches, and community groups; materials concerning one-room schools; photographs; oral history tapes; motion pictures of Elmo Lincoln, the first movie Tarzan; and other materials relating chiefly to Fulton County history.

SEE: Hinding.

SAINT MEINRAD

IN759-710

Saint Meinrad Archabbey
Library
St. Meinrad IN 47577

(812) 357-6756, 6611

OPEN: by appointment only

SEE: Hamer; NUCMC, 1962.

Questionnaire not returned.

SALEM

IN770-880

Washington County Historical Society
307 East Market Street
Salem IN 47167

(812) 883-6495

OPEN: Su, Tu-Sa 1-5; closed Mondays and holidays
COPYING FACILITIES: yes
MATERIALS SOLICITED: Family history; local history or history of other counties and States; and court records.

HOLDINGS:
Total volume: 5,000 items
Inclusive dates: 1700 -
Description: Genealogies, war records, school records, diaries, scrapbooks, marriage records, obituaries, death records, censuses, church records, county histories, and account books.

SEE: NUCMC, 1959-61.

SHELBYVILLE

IN781-360

Inlow Foundation
Library
103 West Washington Street
Shelbyville IN 46176

no telephone

SEE: Hamer; NUCMC, 1966.

Questionnaire not returned.

SOUTH BEND

IN792-160

Discovery Hall Museum
Research Library
120 South St. Joseph Street
South Bend IN 46601

(219) 284-9714

OPEN: M-F 9-5; closed weekends and holidays
COPYING FACILITIES: yes
MATERIALS SOLICITED: Materials relating to the history of business, industry, and technology in St. Joseph County, Indiana, including business records, trade catalogs, photographs, and personal papers.

HOLDINGS:
Total volume: 3,000 l.f.
Inclusive dates: 1850 -
Description: Business records from St. Joseph County, primarily South Bend and Mishawaka, including sales records, photographs, advertising material, and correspondence. Industries represented include Studebaker Brothers Manufacturing Company (wagons and automobiles), Birdsell Manufacturing Company (clover hullers and wagons), N. P. Bowsher Manufacturing Company (feed grinding mills), and Oliver Chilled Plow Company.

SEE ALSO: An inventory of the Studebaker archives is available from the institution.

IN792-560

Northern Indiana Historical Society
112 South Lafayette Blvd.
South Bend IN 46601

(219) 284-9664

OPEN: M-F 9-5; closed weekends and holidays
ACCESS: advance notice preferable
COPYING FACILITIES: no
MATERIALS SOLICITED: Materials pertaining to St. Joseph County, IN, and its environs.

HOLDINGS:
Total volume: 200 l.f.
Inclusive dates: 1803 -
Description: Materials concerning St. Joseph County, IN, and its environs, including papers of early traders, materials concerning business and government, early maps and drawings, photographs, and oral history recordings.

SEE: Hamer; NUCMC, 1965.

SEE: Hinding.

SEE ALSO: 'Midwest Research Institutions Directory,' *Illinois Libraries* 53 (Jan. 1971); Alan M. Meckler and Ruth McMullin, comps., *Oral History Collections* (Bowker, 1975).

IN792-720

South Bend Public Library
Local History Department
122 West Wayne Street
South Bend IN 46601

(219) 282-4625

OPEN: M-Th 9-9, F, Sa 9-6; closed Sundays and holidays
COPYING FACILITIES: yes
MATERIALS SOLICITED: Any historical materials covering St. Joseph County, IN, and pre-1830 materials concerning northern Indiana and southern Michigan.

HOLDINGS:
Total volume: 115 c.f.
Inclusive dates: 1850 -
Description: Local history materials, consisting of personal papers, logbooks, radio scripts of the Library's story hour, scrapbooks of the TB (Tuberculosis) Society, County history scrapbooks, newspaper clipping files, and genealogical materials.

SEE ALSO: Walter Schatz, ed., *Directory of Afro-American Resources* (Bowker, 1970).

SPEEDWAY

IN803-360

The Indianapolis Motor Speedway
Hall of Fame Museum
4790 West 16th Street
Speedway IN 46224

(317) 241-2501

OPEN: daily 9-5; closed Christmas
USER FEES: adults, one dollar; children under 16, free
ACCESS: by appointment only
COPYING FACILITIES: no
MATERIALS SOLICITED: Records of the Contest Board of the American Automobile Association; manuscript material dealing with the history of the motor car. Will also accept racing memorabilia, and manuscript material related to the history of transportation.

HOLDINGS:
Total volume: 5 file cabinets
Inclusive dates: 1909 - 1956
Description: Records of the Contest Board of the American Automobile Association.

TERRE HAUTE

IN825-200

Eugene V. Debs Museum and Library
451 North 8th Street
Terre Haute IN

MAILING ADDRESS:
P.O. Box 843
Terre Haute IN 47808

(812) 232-2163

OPEN: Su-Th, Sa 2-5; closed Fridays and holidays
ACCESS: bona fide scholars, researchers, and college students
COPYING FACILITIES: no
MATERIALS SOLICITED: Materials pertaining to the life of Eugene V. Debs, including letters, photographs, and memorabilia. Will also accept materials relating to Norman Thomas and the Socialist Party.

HOLDINGS:
Total volume: 32 vols.; 300 items
Inclusive dates: 1834 - 1968
Description: 20 bound volumes of convention proceedings of the Brotherhood of Locomotive Firemen, 1873-1968; scrapbooks of materials relating to Debs, including 3 scrapbooks of his wife which contain many intimate notes and poems; and 300 photographs of Debs in public and private life.

SEE: Parkinson; Robbins; Hinding.

IN825-350

Indiana State University
Cunningham Memorial Library
Department of Rare Books and
Special Collections
Terre Haute IN 47809

(812) 237-2610, 2580

OPEN: M-F 8-4:30; closed weekends and holidays
ACCESS: interview with Head of Department of Rare Books and Special Collections required
COPYING FACILITIES: yes
MATERIALS SOLICITED: Papers in lexicography; materials relating to Indiana history; Eugene V. Debs items.

HOLDINGS:
Total volume: 160 l.f.
Inclusive dates: 1850 -
Description: University archives; Indiana Federal Writers' Project materials and photographs; Eugene V. Debs and Theodore Debs correspondence, memorabilia and photographs; Mitford McLeod Mathews correspondence; Jesse Stuart items; miscellaneous correspondence.

SEE: NUCMC, 1978.

SEE: Robbins.

SEE ALSO: Thomas Krasean, 'Guide to the Indiana Sesquicentennial Manuscript Project Index' (n.p., 1968).

IN825-830

Vigo County Historical Society, Inc.
John G. Biel Library
1411 South 6th Street
Terre Haute IN 47802

(812) 235-9717

OPEN: Su-F 1-4; closed Saturdays and holidays
ACCESS: by appointment only
COPYING FACILITIES: yes
MATERIALS SOLICITED: Material related to local history.

HOLDINGS:
Total volume: 19 file drawers; 16 l.f.
Inclusive dates: 1800 -
Description: Correspondence and papers dealing with local history, including Terre Haute, Vigo County, and the Wabash Valley.

SEE: NUCMC, 1971.

SEE: Robbins.

IN825-850

Vigo County Public Library
Special Collections
One Library Square
Terre Haute IN 47807

(812) 232-1113

OPEN: Su 1-5, M-Th 9-9, F 9-6, Sa 9-5; closed Sundays June - Sept., and holidays
ACCESS: prior appointment required
COPYING FACILITIES: yes
MATERIALS SOLICITED: Materials pertaining to local history and genealogy; archival materials of local individuals and organizations.

HOLDINGS:
Total volume: 12,610 items
Inclusive dates: 1400 -
Description: Aside from several late medieval manuscripts, the collection is chiefly comprised of 18th and 19th century Americana, including early travel descriptions and maps; Indiana history materials, such as oral history tapes, journals, and letters; and a genealogy collection of census and church records, diaries, charts, and scrapbooks. There is also a scrapbook containing letters by Lord Byron and other materials associated with Byron.

SEE: Hinding.

SEE ALSO: Alan M. Meckler and Ruth McMullin, comps., *Oral History Collections* (Bowker, 1975).

VALPARAISO

IN858-835

Valparaiso University
Archives
Valparaiso IN 46383

(219) 464-5482

OPEN: M-F 8:30-12; closed weekends and holidays
ACCESS: qualified researchers only
COPYING FACILITIES: yes
MATERIALS SOLICITED: Official records of Valparaiso University and personal papers of administrators, faculty, and alumni.

HOLDINGS:
Total volume: 180 c.f.
Inclusive dates: 1859 -
Description: Materials concerning the administrative history, student life, and faculty research of Valparaiso University.

IN858-850

Valparaiso University
Henry F. Moellering Memorial
Library
Valparaiso IN 46383

(219) 464-5366

OPEN: M, Tu, Th, F 10-noon; closed other days and holidays
ACCESS: qualified researchers only
COPYING FACILITIES: yes
MATERIALS SOLICITED: All material concerning Valparaiso University.

HOLDINGS:
Total volume: 102 l.f.
Inclusive dates: 1859 -
Description: Official records of the University, correspondence of presidents, some manuscripts of faculty articles, and a collection of 3,000 photographs of the campus, students, and similar subjects.

VINCENNES

IN902-80
The Brute Library
205 Church Street
Vincennes IN 47591

(812) 882-7016

OPEN: M-Sa 10-5, Su 1-5; closed Oct.
1-April 1
USER FEES: $5 for research
COPYING FACILITIES: yes
MATERIALS SOLICITED: Materials relating
to history, government, religion, education, and art.

HOLDINGS:
Total volume: 3 file drawers
Inclusive dates: 1749 -
Description: Materials relating to the
early history of the old Northwest Territory and Christianity in this area during
the 18th century, and other documents
relating to religion, medicine, geography,
and Indian lore.

SEE: Hamer (as Old Cathedral Library).

IN902-840
Vincennes University
Byron R. Lewis Historical Collections
Library
1001 North 1st Street
Vincennes IN 47591

(812) 885-4330

OPEN: M-F 8:30-4:30, also Su-Th 7-10
during fall and spring semesters; closed
Saturdays
COPYING FACILITIES: yes
MATERIALS SOLICITED: Indiana local,
county, and State manuscripts; oral history and other materials relating to the
British, French, Northwest Territory,
and Indiana Territory periods; and
Vincennes University archives. Will
also accept materials relating to genealogy, Indiana authors, and the military.

HOLDINGS:
Total volume: 360 boxes; 30 file
drawers; 55 items
Inclusive dates: 1760 -
Description: A regional history collection dealing with the development of
French and British influence in the Wabash Valley and the development of Indiana Territory and State and Vincennes.
Included are personal papers of government and private individuals.

SEE: NUCMC, 1976.

SEE: Parkinson; Hinding; Robbins.

WABASH

IN913-880
Wabash Carnegie Public Library
188 West Hill Street
Wabash IN 46992

(219) 563-2972

OPEN: M-Th 9-8, F, Sa 9-6; June - Aug.,
M-Sa 9-6; closed Sundays and holidays
COPYING FACILITIES: yes

MATERIALS SOLICITED: Local oral history, including material relating to
Mark C. Honeywell and Honeywell
business operations, and Ku Klux Klan
activities. Will also accept typed manuscripts of local history reminiscences.

HOLDINGS:
Total volume: 120 tapes
Inclusive dates: 1970 -
Description: Oral history tapes, many
transcribed and indexed, relating to local
history, and emphasizing Mark C.
Honeywell; Honeywell, Inc.; the Ku Klux
Klan; and Spanish-American War
reminiscences.

SEE ALSO: Alan M. Meckler and Ruth
McMullin, comps., *Oral History Collections* (Bowker, 1975); partial index in
Indiana Magazine of History 68 (Dec.
1972).

A partial index appears in *Indiana Magazine* 68 (Dec. 1972).

IN913-900
Wabash County Historical Museum
Memorial Hall
Wabash IN 46992

no telephone

OPEN: M, Tu, Th, F 9-4, W 9-noon;
closed weekends and holidays
COPYING FACILITIES: no
MATERIALS SOLICITED: Materials relating
to Wabash County and Indiana history.

HOLDINGS:
Total volume: not specified
Inclusive dates: 1830's -
Description: Manuscripts, archives, visual documents, and scrapbooks relating
chiefly to Wabash County. Included are
biographies of early settlers, Civil War
records, Wabash-Erie Canal records, and
reminiscences of pioneers.

WAKARUSA

IN917-880
Wakarusa Public Library
124 North Elkhart Street
Wakarusa IN 46573

(219) 862-2465

OPEN: M, Tu 9-5:30, Th, F 9-8, Sa 9-4;
closed Wednesdays and Sundays
COPYING FACILITIES: yes
MATERIALS SOLICITED: Town histories,
genealogies, and cemetery indexes. Will
also accept local photographs and diaries.

HOLDINGS:
Total volume: 30 l.f.; 6 c.f.
Inclusive dates: 1908 -
Description: Local history materials, including histories of organizations and
clubs, church histories, school board
records, teacher contracts, trustee and assessor books, and ledger and account
books of early merchants and doctors.

WEST LAFAYETTE

IN935-640
Purdue University
Krannert Graduate School of
Management
Krannert Library
West Lafayette IN 47907

no telephone

SEE: NUCMC, 1978.

Questionnaire not returned.

IN935-650
Purdue University
Libraries
Special Collections
West Lafayette IN 47907

(317) 494-2904

OPEN: M-F 8-5; closed weekends and
holidays
COPYING FACILITIES: yes
MATERIALS SOLICITED: Manuscript materials pertaining to Purdue University
and its students, alumni, benefactors,
faculty, and staff.

HOLDINGS:
Total volume: 3,218 l.f.; 75 c.f.; 24
file cabinets
Inclusive dates: 1834 -
Description: Materials of or pertaining
to Purdue University in West Lafayette,
including student theses, papers of faculty
members, administrators and alumni,
and the Purdue oral history collection.
Included are papers of George Ade, John
T. McCutcheon, Bruce Rogers, Charles
Major, Frank B. and Lillian M. Gilbreth,
Richard Owen, John Purdue, Earl L.
Butz, Benjamin F. Meissner, and Amelia
Earhart.
There are also records of the Midwest
Program on Airborne Television Instruc-
tion and a collection relating to New Har-
mony, IN.

SEE: Hamer; NUCMC, 1959-62, 73 (listed
under Lafayette, IN).

SEE: Hinding; Robbins.

SEE ALSO: Ann Novotny, ed., *Picture
Sources 3* (Special Libraries Assn.,
1975); Alan M. Meckler and Ruth
McMullin, comps., *Oral History Collec-
tions* (Bowker, 1975); Edwin T. Layton,
Jr., ed., *A Regional Union Catalog of
Manuscripts Relating to the History of
Science and Technology Located in In-
diana, Michigan, and Ohio* (Case West-
ern Reserve Univ., 1971); Richard C.
Davis, *North American Forest History:
A Guide to Archives and Manuscripts in
the United States and Canada* (Clio
Books, 1977).

WINONA LAKE

IN990-240

Free Methodist Church of North
   America
Marston Memorial Historical Center
   of the Free Methodist Church
901 College
Winona Lake IN 46590

(219) 267-7656, 7161

OPEN: M-F 9-4; closed weekends and
   holidays
COPYING FACILITIES: yes
MATERIALS SOLICITED: Materials specifically relating to the history of Methodism or Free Methodism, including
   missions, colleges, and conferences.

HOLDINGS:
   Total volume: 4 file cabinets
   Inclusive dates: 1850 -
   Description: Letters, diaries, journals,
   sermon manuscripts, and documents
   from the beginning of the Free Methodist
   church in 1860, including many items
   related to mission work overseas. Also, a
   collection of photographs, and cassette recordings made from old phonograph
   records.

IN990-280

Grace Theological Seminary
Library
200 Seminary Drive
Winona Lake IN 46590

(219) 372-5177

OPEN: M-F 8-10, Sa 9-10, Su 2-5; closed
   holidays

ACCESS: advance arrangements required
COPYING FACILITIES: yes
MATERIALS SOLICITED: Will accept docu-
   ments relating to the life and career of
   William A. 'Billy' Sunday.

HOLDINGS:
   Total volume: 28 c.f.
   Inclusive dates: 1882 - 1974
   Description: Correspondence, sermon
   notes, campaign memorabilia, photo-
   graphs and miscellaneous documents of
   Billy Sunday and his wife. The collection
   documents Sunday's career as an evangel-
   ist and as a player for the Chicago White
   Stockings baseball team.

SEE: NUCMC, 1981.

IOWA

Most of Iowa's permanently valuable local public records remain in the custody of local officials.

The Newspaper/Census Library of the Iowa State Historical Department in Des Moines makes available to researchers several thousand reels of microfilm of selected county records, filmed by the Genealogical Society of Utah. When this microfilming project is completed it will include records of all counties.

The State Historical Department has published retention and disposition schedules for both county and municipal records. The State Archives in Des Moines provides records management, historical records appraisal, and conservation and preservation advice to local political subdivisions in Iowa. The State Historical Society in Iowa City has some county records which are available for research to the public and provides records management, historical records appraisal, and conservation/preservation advice to governmental agencies and individuals.

AMANA

IA22-40
Amana Heritage Society
Amana IA 52203

(319) 622-3567

OPEN: by appointment only
COPYING FACILITIES: no
MATERIALS SOLICITED: Materials concerning Amana history.

HOLDINGS:
> *Total volume:* 770 items
> *Inclusive dates:* 1600's -
> *Description:* Diaries, photographs, letters, deeds, other records, and oral history tapes concerned with the immigration, travel, and settlement of the Amana people. The majority of written documents are in old German script.

SEE: Hinding.

AMES

IA33-350
Iowa Department of Transportation
Library
800 Lincoln Way
Ames IA 50010

(515) 239-1200

OPEN: M-F 7:30-5; closed weekends and holidays
COPYING FACILITIES: yes
MATERIALS SOLICITED: Historical materials related to transportation in Iowa.

HOLDINGS:
> *Total volume:* 3 file cabinets
> *Inclusive dates:* 1900 - 1980
> *Description:* Correspondence and other materials concerning the registry and upkeep of historic roads and trails in Iowa, and a collection of some 1,000 photographs depicting road-building in the State, 1900-40.
> Materials relating to the history of the former Iowa State Highway Commission and the present Iowa Department of Transportation, 1900-present. Also publications relating to aeronautics, river, and railroad history in Iowa.

IA33-364
Iowa State University
Library
American Archives of the Factual
  Film
Ames IA 50011

(515) 294-6672

OPEN: M-F 8-5; closed weekends
COPYING FACILITIES: yes
MATERIALS SOLICITED: Education, business, science, technology, medicine, and other non-entertainment films and related textual materials. Will also accept papers of film producers, files of film units within businesses, records of film organizations, oral history interviews, still photographs, filmstrips, and slides.

HOLDINGS:
> *Total volume:* 2,540 items; 140 l.f.
> *Inclusive dates:* 1911 -
> *Description:* Factual films, including documentaries, in-house training films, and educational films, in addition to related textual materials.

IA33-370
Iowa State University
Library
Department of Special Collections
Ames IA 50011

(515) 294-6672

OPEN: M-F 8-5; closed weekends and holidays
COPYING FACILITIES: yes
MATERIALS SOLICITED: University archives, including papers of faculty, staff and alumni and records of administrative units of the University; manuscript collections in agriculture, science and technology, factual films, business, banking and finance, conservation, veterinary medicine, rural sociology and labor relations.

HOLDINGS:
> *Total volume:* 1,640 l.f.
> *Inclusive dates:* 1850 -
> *Description:* Materials relating chiefly to Iowa State University, Iowa, and the Midwest. Topics covered include agriculture, business, science, technology, finance and banking.

GUIDES: *Guide to the Manuscript Collections in the ISU Library* (1978).

SEE: Hamer; NUCMC, 1965, 71-72, 75, 78.

SEE: Schatz; Meckler and McMullin; Davis; Krichmar; Parkinson; Hinding; Robbins.

BETTENDORF

IA43-80
Bettendorf Public Library
2950 18th Street
Bettendorf IA 52722

(319) 332-7427

OPEN: M-Th 9-9, F, Sa 9-5; closed Sundays and holidays
COPYING FACILITIES: yes

HOLDINGS:
> *Total volume:* 5 items
> *Inclusive dates:* early 1900's - 1970's
> *Description:* Oral history tapes concerning Bettendorf and scrapbooks entitled *Fifty Years in the Onion Business*, by Russell Rice, containing newspaper clippings and photographs of Pleasant Valley, Bettendorf, and Davenport, IA, articles on raising onions, and a typescript of Rice's experiences.

SEE: Meckler and McMullin.

BOONE

IA58-540
Mamie Doud Eisenhower Birthplace
Museum and Library
709 Carroll Street
Boone IA

MAILING ADDRESS:
P.O. Box 55
Boone IA 50036

(515) 432-1896

OPEN: April 1 - Dec. 31, Tu-Su 1-5; by
appointment rest of year; closed
Mondays, Thanksgiving, Christmas,
and New Year's
USER FEES: one dollar
COPYING FACILITIES: yes
MATERIALS SOLICITED: Materials per-
taining to Mamie Doud and Dwight D.
Eisenhower and their families. Will
also accept related materials on Boone
County, IA, history.

HOLDINGS:
Total volume: 10 c.f.; 3 file cabinets
Inclusive dates: 19th century -
Description: Correspondence, genealogical materials, tape recordings, photographs, and scrapbooks of Mamie Doud
and Dwight D. Eisenhower and the
Doud, Carlson, and Eisenhower families;
business records of the Carlson family
milling business in Boone; records of the
Mamie Doud Eisenhower Birthplace
Foundation; and photographs, blueprints,
and landscape plans of the Birthplace restoration project.

BURLINGTON

IA66-80
Burlington Public Library
501 N. 4th Street
Burlington IA 52601

(319) 753-1649

OPEN: M-Th 9-9, F-Sa 9-5; closed
Sundays and holidays
COPYING FACILITIES: yes
MATERIALS SOLICITED: Diaries, journals,
correspondence, photographs and maps
relating to settlement and development
of the Territory of Iowa, particularly
southeastern Iowa.

HOLDINGS:
Total volume: 50 l.f.; 8 file drawers
Inclusive dates: 1830 - 1920
Description: Letters, diaries, and photographs of individuals and families in
southeastern Iowa in the 19th century
and photographs of Burlington and southeastern Iowa in the late 19th and early
20th centuries.

SEE: Hamer.

SEE: Hinding.

BURR OAK

IA74-480
Laura Ingalls Wilder Park & Museum,
Inc.
Burr Oak IA 52101

no telephone

OPEN: daily 9-5:30; closed Oct. 15 - May
1
USER FEES: $1.25
ACCESS: advance arrangements required
COPYING FACILITIES: no
MATERIALS SOLICITED: Materials con-
cerning Laura Ingalls Wilder and her
childhood home in Burr Oak.

HOLDINGS:
Total volume: not specified
Inclusive dates: 1973 -
Description: Correspondence of persons across the United States and
Canada, account books, financial records,
photographs, and biographical information relating to Laura Ingalls Wilder's
years at her childhood home in Burr Oak.

CEDAR FALLS

IA88-120
Cedar Falls Historical Society
303 Clay Street
Cedar Falls IA 50613

(319) 277-8817

OPEN: W-Su 2-4; closed other days and
holidays
COPYING FACILITIES: no
MATERIALS SOLICITED: Items pertinent
to the history of Cedar Falls, the adjacent county and Iowa. Will also accept
other materials for museum display.

HOLDINGS:
Total volume: 400 items; 4 file
cabinets
Inclusive dates: 1833 -
Description: Material relating to the
history of Cedar Falls and the surrounding area, including diaries, letters, and
other materials. There are also photographs documenting the fifty oldest
homes in the area.

IA88-800
University of Northern Iowa
Library
Special Collections
Cedar Falls IA 50613

(319) 273-6307

OPEN: M-F 8-4
COPYING FACILITIES: yes
MATERIALS SOLICITED: Materials relating
to all facets of University of Northern
Iowa history and to education and edu-
cational organizations, particularly in
Iowa and in rural areas. Will also ac-
cept local history materials.

HOLDINGS:
Total volume: 1,200 l.f.
Inclusive dates: 1840 -
Description: Personal papers, official
records, and other materials relating pri-
marily to the history of the University of
Northern Iowa (formerly Iowa State
Teachers College) and to Iowa education
in general.

GUIDES: 'Classification Schedule of the
University of Northern Iowa Archives'
is available.

SEE: NUCMC, 1969.

CEDAR RAPIDS

IA99-40
Ancient Free and Accepted Masons
Grand Lodge of Iowa
Iowa Masonic Library
813 First Avenue, S.E.
Cedar Rapids IA

MAILING ADDRESS:
Box 279
Cedar Rapids IA 52406

(319) 365-1438

OPEN: M-F 8-5; closed weekends and
holidays
ACCESS: permission of Library office
COPYING FACILITIES: yes
MATERIALS SOLICITED: Will accept ma-
terials at discretion of Librarian.

HOLDINGS:
Total volume: 32 l.f.; 50 items
Inclusive dates: 1838 -
Description: Diaries (1838-1900) of T.
S. Parvin, discussing social conditions,
politics, Masonic and personal affairs; letters on scientific and literary topics; and
materials relating to early radiology ex-
periments and activities and publications
of radiological societies.

SEE: Hamer.

SEE: Hinding.

CHEROKEE

IA122-120
Cherokee County Historical Society
Spurgeons Building
Main Street
Cherokee IA

MAILING ADDRESS:
P.O. Box 247
Cleghorn IA 51014

no telephone

OPEN: M-Th 8-5, F-Sa 8-12; closed
Sundays and holidays
ACCESS: bona fide researchers
COPYING FACILITIES: yes
MATERIALS SOLICITED: Cherokee County
historical materials, including diaries,
journals, records, letters, authenticated
pictures, and photocopies.

HOLDINGS:
Total volume: 500 items
Inclusive dates: 1856 -
Description: Material relating to Cherokee County, including County tax
records; journals and diaries; indexes to
County births, deaths, burials, and marriages; township records; and genealogical
material on pioneer families.

IA122-720
Sanford Museum and Planetarium
117 East Willow Street
Cherokee IA 51012

(712) 225-3922

OPEN: M-F 9-5, Sa, Su 2-5; closed
  holidays
ACCESS: appointment required at least
  one week prior to visit
COPYING FACILITIES: no
MATERIALS SOLICITED: Materials related
  to archaeological and ethnographical
  subjects and to local history.

HOLDINGS:
  Total volume: 10 l.f.
  Inclusive dates: 1857 - 1920
  Description: Collections of journals,
  documents, photographs and correspondence of early settlers of the area,
  unpublished reminiscences of the area,
  accounts of archaeological excavations
  (including maps and plans of local sites),
  and assorted memorabilia.

SEE: Hinding.

CLERMONT

IA133-520
Montauk
Highway 18 E.
Clermont IA

MAILING ADDRESS:
P.O. Box 372
Clermont IA 52135

(319) 423-7173

OPEN: M-F 8-5; closed weekends and
  holidays
ACCESS: appointment required
COPYING FACILITIES: no
MATERIALS SOLICITED: Papers concern-
  ing William Larrabee.

HOLDINGS:
  Total volume: 19 l.f.
  Inclusive dates: 1860 - 1910
  Description: A collection of letters,
  journals, deeds, and account books of
  Iowa Governor William Larrabee, as well
  as photographs and memorabilia of the
  Larrabee family.

COUNCIL BLUFFS

IA177-240
Free Public Library
200 Pearl Street
Council Bluffs IA 51501

(712) 323-7553

OPEN: M-Th 9-9, F 9-6, Sa 9-5, Su
  1-4:30; closed Sundays mid-May -
  mid-Sept. and holidays
COPYING FACILITIES: yes
MATERIALS SOLICITED: Materials relating
  to the Council Bluffs area.

HOLDINGS:
  Total volume: 50 l.f.; 715 items; 14
  file drawers
  Inclusive dates: 1850 -
  Description: Correspondence received
  by Amelia Bloomer, Grenville Mellen
  Dodge's correspondence and autobiography, Mormon history and railroad history
  materials, photographs, and other materials.

SEE: Hamer; NUCMC, 1965.

SEE: Hinding; Krichmar.

IA177-320
Historic General Dodge House
605 Third Street
Council Bluffs IA 51501

(712) 322-2406

OPEN: Tu-Sa 10-5, Su 1-5; closed
  Thanksgiving, Christmas, and January
ACCESS: advance arrangements required
COPYING FACILITIES: yes
MATERIALS SOLICITED: Materials relating
  to Major-General Grenville M. Dodge,
  his family and associates, and his home
  in Council Bluffs. Will also accept materials relating to the Civil War,
  railroad building and operation in the
  nineteenth century, Republican party
  politics and development of western
  Iowa.

HOLDINGS:
  Total volume: 1,100 items
  Inclusive dates: 1845 - 1920
  Description: Journals, manuscripts and
  other materials relating chiefly to the life
  and career of General Dodge, his family
  and his business, military, and political
  associates, including 400 photographs and
  600 Keystone stereo views.

IA177-340
Historical Society of Pottawattamie
  County
232 Bennett Avenue
Council Bluffs IA 51501

(712) 322-7491

OPEN: by appointment only
COPYING FACILITIES: no

HOLDINGS:
  Total volume: 200 l.f.
  Inclusive dates: 1870 -
  Description: Original court records, in-
  cluding certificates of birth and death, of
  Pottawattamie County.

DAVENPORT

IA188-160
Davenport Public Library
321 Main Street
Davenport IA 52801

(319) 326-7832

OPEN: M-Th 9-9, F, Sa 9-5:30, also Su
  1-5 Oct. - April; closed holidays and
  Sundays, May - Sept.

SEE: Hamer.

Questionnaire not returned.

IA188-360
Iowa-Illinois Gas & Electric Company
206 East 2nd Street
Davenport IA 52808

(319) 326-7127

OPEN: M-F 8-5; closed weekends and
  holidays
ACCESS: authorization required
COPYING FACILITIES: yes
MATERIALS SOLICITED: Account books,
  business records, and financial records
  of predecessor companies.

HOLDINGS:
  Total volume: 25 l.f.
  Inclusive dates: 1900 - 1942
  Description: Materials on the predecessor companies of Iowa-Illinois Gas &
  Electric Company as well as local gas,
  electric, and transportation utilities. Includes corporate records, financial and
  operating data.

IA188-520
Marycrest College
Cone Library
Archives
1607 West 12th Street
Davenport IA 52804

(319) 326-9254

OPEN: M-F by appointment only; closed
  weekends
COPYING FACILITIES: yes
MATERIALS SOLICITED: Official records
  of the College. Will also accept materials of a local nature.

HOLDINGS:
  Total volume: 50 l.f.; 20 file drawers
  Inclusive dates: 1939 -
  Description: A collection relating to the
  history of Marycrest College. Included are
  materials relating to the woman
  foundress and first president; materials
  prepared for all official accrediting agencies; faculty studies and institutional data;
  minutes of faculty and committee meetings; news releases; college publications;
  and photographs of student activities and
  the physical plant.

SEE: Hinding.

IA188-650
Putnam Museum
1717 West 12th Street
Davenport IA 52804

(319) 324-1933

OPEN: Tu-F 9-5 by appointment only;
  closed other days and holidays
ACCESS: by appointment only;
  researchers in specific topics relating to
  the Museum's holdings
COPYING FACILITIES: yes
MATERIALS SOLICITED: Materials relating
  to local and regional history.

HOLDINGS:
  Total volume: 2,000 l.f.
  Inclusive dates: 1800 -
  Description: Collections of correspondence and business records, photographs
  and other research materials concerning
  the Iowa-Illinois region. Included are materials relating to steamboats, railroads,
  early settlement, the Civil War, growth of

the area, and letters and documents of famous people.

SEE: NUCMC, 1970, 72, 75 (as Davenport Museum).

SEE ALSO: Carol Hunt, 'Manuscript Collections: The Putnam Museum in Davenport,' *Annals of Iowa* 44 (Summer 1978).

IA188-777

Sisters of the Humility of Mary
820 W. Central Park Avenue
Davenport IA 52804

(319) 323-9466

OPEN: by appointment only
COPYING FACILITIES: yes

HOLDINGS:
> *Total volume:* 15,000 items
> *Inclusive dates:* 1750 -
> *Description:* Letters of Dan A. Shields, youngest son of General James Shields; a letter of Mother Mary of the Angels Maujean concerning the death of General Shields at the home of the Sisters of Humility; papers of real estate speculator Mary Quinn Tally; family documents, letters, and slides relating to Abbe J. J. Begel, founder of the Sisters of Humility of Mary in France in 1854; and letters of Bishop J. J. Hogan, first bishop of the diocese of St. Joseph, MO.

SEE: Hinding.

DECORAH

IA211-480

Luther College
Library
Decorah IA 52101

(319) 387-1163

OPEN: M-F 9-noon, or by appointment; closed holidays and one week at Christmas
COPYING FACILITIES: yes
MATERIALS SOLICITED: 19th century Norwegian-American immigrant manuscripts; manuscripts relating to the Synod of the Norwegian Evangelical Lutheran Church of America; archival materials of Luther College; and Winneshiek County, IA, history materials. Will also accept Norwegian-American ethnic materials, and manuscripts of persons from outside Winneshiek County having a connection with Luther College or the County.

HOLDINGS:
> *Total volume:* 342,000 items
> *Inclusive dates:* 1835 -
> *Description:* Materials relating chiefly to Norwegian-Americans, the Norwegian Lutheran church, Luther College, and the history of Winneshiek County, IA. Included are records of the Synod for the Norwegian Lutheran Church of America, 1853-1917; papers of its presidents and several of its pastors and district officials; records of Luther College and Luther Seminary and papers of some of its presidents and faculty members; records of Fort Atkinson, IA, built to protect the Winnebago Indian tribe; papers relating to the Civil War and World War I; and

records of local lumber companies and a local publishing firm.

SEE: Hamer; NUCMC, 1959-62.

SEE: Hinding.

SEE ALSO: An unpublished list of collections is available from the institution.

DES MOINES

IA233-160

Drake University
Cowles Library
Special Collections
28th Street and University Avenue
Des Moines IA 50311

(515) 271-2862

OPEN: M-F 8-5; closed weekends and holidays
COPYING FACILITIES: yes
MATERIALS SOLICITED: Literary manuscripts and other papers of Iowa authors associated with the University, including Philip Duffield Stong, Susan Glaspell, MacKinlay Kantor, and Thomas Duncan. Will also accept records, faculty papers, and other materials relating to the University, as well as Iowa and Des Moines historical materials.

HOLDINGS:
> *Total volume:* 26 drawers; 6,800 items
> *Inclusive dates:* 1881 -
> *Description:* Archives and other materials relating to the history of Drake University, and 1,200 pieces of correspondence of novelist Philip Duffield Stong, mostly to and from his mother.

SEE: NUCMC, 1966 (as Drake University, Divinity School Library).

SEE: Robbins.

IA233-280

Grand View College
Library
Archives Collection
1351 Grandview Avenue
Des Moines IA 50316

(515) 263-2877

OPEN: M-F 8-9, Sa 1-4, Su 5-9; M-F 8-3 during summer; closed holidays
ACCESS: by arrangement with the Librarian or Archivist
COPYING FACILITIES: yes
MATERIALS SOLICITED: Danish-American materials.

HOLDINGS:
> *Total volume:* 50 l.f.
> *Inclusive dates:* 1870 -
> *Description:* Materials pertaining to Danish-American immigrants, the Danish Evangelical Lutheran church, and Grand View College. Most materials are in the Danish language.

IA233-360

Iowa State Historical Department
Division of Historical Museum and Archives
E. 7th and Court Avenue
Des Moines IA 50319

(515) 281-3007, 5113

OPEN: M-F 8-4; closed weekends and holidays
COPYING FACILITIES: yes
MATERIALS SOLICITED: Historically valuable executive, legislative, and judicial records of the State of Iowa from territorial times to present. Will also accept materials of local political subdivisions of Iowa, as well as church and business records under special circumstances.

HOLDINGS:
> *Total volume:* 12,000 c.f.
> *Inclusive dates:* 1838 -
> *Description:* Official records of the State of Iowa, dating from territorial times to the present, including the official papers of all Iowa governors, all Legislative Acts, and the records of the Supreme Court of Iowa.

SEE: Hamer; NUCMC, 1962-64, 77-78.

SEE: Duignan; Schatz; Krichmar; Davis; Parkinson; Hinding; Robbins.

IA233-450

Iowa State Medical Library
East 12th Street and Grand Avenue
Des Moines IA 50319

no telephone

SEE: Hamer; NUCMC, 1959-61.

Questionnaire not returned.

IA233-640

Public Library of Des Moines
Franklin Avenue Library
5000 Franklin Avenue
Des Moines IA 50310

(515) 283-4271

OPEN: M-F 9-9, Sa 9-5, Su 2-5; closed holidays, and Sundays in summer
COPYING FACILITIES: yes
MATERIALS SOLICITED: Local oral history interviews.

HOLDINGS:
> *Total volume:* 58 cassettes
> *Inclusive dates:* 1972 -
> *Description:* Oral history recordings, completely transcribed, containing recollections of Des Moines residents about the early history of Des Moines, Polk County, and central Iowa.

SEE ALSO: Alan M. Meckler and Ruth McMullin, comps., *Oral History Collections* (Bowker, 1975).

DUBUQUE

IA244-30

The American Lutheran Church
Archives
Wartburg Theological Seminary
Dubuque IA 52001

(319) 589-0320

OPEN: M-F 8-5; closed weekends and
holidays
COPYING FACILITIES: yes
MATERIALS SOLICITED: Materials related
to the American Lutheran church and
its antecedent German-American and
Danish-American bodies.

HOLDINGS:
Total volume: 2,300 l.f.
Inclusive dates: 1812 -
Description: The archives of the
American Lutheran church and its antecedent bodies of German-American and
Danish-American background, including
the papers of many prominent
individuals associated with these
churches. The Archives also includes materials concerning missionary activities in
Ethiopia, India, and New Guinea, and
about 90 sets of theological lecture notes
from German universities, 1830-80.

SEE: Hamer; NUCMC, 1967, 69, 71, 75.

SEE: Hinding.

SEE ALSO: typewritten guides available
from the institution.

Another archival repository for the
American Lutheran church is located
at Luther Theological Seminary, St.
Paul, MN (MN763-50).

IA244-120

Catholic Chancery Office
1104 Bluff Street
Dubuque IA 52001

no telephone
SEE: Hamer.

Questionnaire not returned.

IA244-160

Dubuque County Historic Society
2nd Street Harbor
Dubuque IA

MAILING ADDRESS:
P.O. Box 305
Dubuque IA 52001

(319) 557-9545

OPEN: M-F 10-5 by appointment; closed
weekends and holidays
COPYING FACILITIES: no
MATERIALS SOLICITED: Materials pertaining to the history of the upper Mississippi River, Dubuque County and
steamboating.

HOLDINGS:
Total volume: 50 l.f.
Inclusive dates: 1830 -
Description: Historical records of Du-
buque County, including business and
school records, public documents, genea-

logical data, correspondence, diaries, photographs and oral history tapes.

IA244-480

Loras College
Wahlert Memorial Library
1450 Alta Vista Street
Dubuque IA 52001

(319) 588-7164

OPEN: M-Th 8-11:30, F 8-8, Sa 10-7, Su
noon-11:30; closed holidays
COPYING FACILITIES: yes
MATERIALS SOLICITED: Political and historical papers.

HOLDINGS:
Total volume: 75 l.f.
Inclusive dates: 12th century - 20th
century
Description: Political papers and other
correspondence of Maurice Connolly,
1877-1921 (150 items); Italian documents
of the 15th-19th centuries, chiefly related
to the Roman Catholic church, and various medieval codices (1,500 items); and
City Council records of Dubuque,
1842-1941, including notices, ordinances,
petitions, reports, resolutions, and other
papers (28 drawers).
Also correspondence of John T.
Corbett concerning national lobbying efforts of the Brotherhood of Locomotive
Engineers, 1933-1951 (2 l.f.).

SEE: Hamer; NUCMC, 1968.

SEE ALSO: a printed catalog of the codices
available from the repository.

GRINNELL

IA377-280

Grinnell College
Burling Library
Grinnell IA 50112

(515) 236-2531

OPEN: M 9-5, Tu 9-noon, W-F 9-5;
closed weekends and holidays
COPYING FACILITIES: yes
MATERIALS SOLICITED: Faculty and
alumni manuscripts, especially related
to Grinnell College history; and local
history, including maps, manuscripts,
and papers of historical interest about
the town of Grinnell and Poweshiek
County.

HOLDINGS:
Total volume: 70 l.f.
Inclusive dates: 1846 -
Description: Materials relating primarily to Grinnell College, its faculty and
alumni. Other holdings document Congregational educational and religious activities in Iowa, and the life of James Norman Hall.

SEE: Hamer; NUCMC, 1971.

SEE: Paszek; Hinding; Robbins.

INDIANOLA

IA455-720

Simpson College
Dunn Library
Indianola IA 50125

(515) 961-6251, Ext. 663

OPEN: by appointment only
COPYING FACILITIES: yes
MATERIALS SOLICITED: Records and other materials relating to the life of Simpson College.

HOLDINGS:
Total volume: 143 boxes; 5 vols.
Inclusive dates: 1860 -
Description: Archives of Simpson College, in addition to minutes of the Methodist Episcopal church, dating from the
mid-19th century; memorabilia and photographs of George Washington Carver;
and papers of newspaper editor Don Berry.

SEE ALSO: Walter Schatz, ed., Directory of
Afro-American Resources (Bowker,
1970).

IOWA CITY

IA466-40

American College Testing Program
Library
2201 North Dodge Street
Iowa City IA

MAILING ADDRESS:
P.O. Box 168
Iowa City IA 52240

(319) 337-1165

OPEN: M-F 8:30-4:30; closed weekends
and holidays
ACCESS: program officials and qualified
researchers, with permission
COPYING FACILITIES: yes
MATERIALS SOLICITED: Internal documents and other items relating directly
to the Program.

HOLDINGS:
Total volume: 8 file drawers
Inclusive dates: 1959 -
Description: A collection of internal
documents, correspondence, news releases, and related materials, dealing with
the American College Testing Program
since its establishment in 1959.

SEE ALSO: unpublished guide to the collections available at the institution.

IA466-360

Iowa State Historical Department
State Historical Society Division
Manuscript Collection
402 Iowa Avenue
Iowa City IA 52240

(319) 338-5471

OPEN: M-F 8-4:30; closed weekends and
holidays
COPYING FACILITIES: yes
MATERIALS SOLICITED: Materials relating
to political, social, religious, ethnic,
and economic life and culture in Iowa;

papers of Iowans and records of Iowa organizations, schools, and businesses. Will also accept materials relating to the Midwest, and the Missouri and Mississippi rivers.

HOLDINGS:
  Total volume: 2,800 l.f.
  Inclusive dates: 1830's -
  Description: Personal papers and records of businesses, organizations, and churches documenting all aspects of Iowa history. Included are political papers of late 19th and early 20th century U.S. Representatives, records of millwork companies, materials relating to the Civil War, and many single letters, documents, diaries, account books, and research papers. There is also a photograph collection including glass and paper images, 1853 to the present.

GUIDES: Katherine Harris, comp., *Guide to Manuscripts* (1973).

SEE: Hamer; NUCMC, 1976, 79.

SEE: Hinding; Robbins; Allard, Crawley, and Edmison; Parkinson.

SEE ALSO: Boyd Keith Swigger, comp., *A Guide to Resources for the Study of the Recent History of the United States in the Libraries of the University of Iowa, the State Historical Society of Iowa, and in the Herbert Hoover Presidential Library* (Univ. of Iowa, 1977); Richard C. Davis, *North American Forest History: A Guide to Archives and Manuscripts in the United States and Canada* (Clio Books, 1977).

Published inventories available from the institution.

Listing in NUCMC 1962-64 includes holdings of the Department's division in Des Moines.

IA466-800
University of Iowa
Libraries
Special Collections Department
Iowa City IA 52242

(319) 353-4854

OPEN: M-F 9-5; closed weekends and holidays
COPYING FACILITIES: yes
MATERIALS SOLICITED: Historical and literary manuscripts relating to Iowa and the Midwest and archival records of the University of Iowa.

HOLDINGS:
  Total volume: 7,500 l.f.
  Inclusive dates: 1800 -
  Description: 10,000 individually cataloged letters or manuscript items of English and American authors or historical figures, principally of the 19th and 20th centuries. In addition there are 400 collections of papers and records relating to Iowa and midwestern history, more than 600 manuscripts by Iowa authors, and 3,700 l.f. of records relating to the history of the University of Iowa.
  The University Archives includes an extensive collection of photographs and oral history transcripts. The Map Room has a large collection of aerial photographs of Iowa.

SEE: Hamer; NUCMC, 1959-65, 69, 71-72, 74-77, 79.

SEE: Hinding; Hounshell; Martin; Meckler and McMullin; Novotny; Parkinson; Robbins; Schatz; Spalek.

SEE ALSO: Richard C. Davis, *North American Forest History: A Guide to Archives and Manuscripts in the United States and Canada* (Clio Books, 1977); Frank Paluka, 'American Literary Manuscripts in the University of Iowa Libraries: A Checklist,' *Resources for American Literary Study* 3 (Spring 1973); Frank Paluka, 'English Literary Manuscripts in the University of Iowa Libraries,' *The Library Scene* 1 (Summer 1972); O. M. Brack, Jr., and D. H. Stefanson, *A Catalogue of the Leigh Hunt Manuscripts in the University of Iowa Libraries* (Friends of the Univ. of Iowa Libraries, 1973).

Frederick P. W. McDowell and E. Sharon Graves, *The Angus Wilson Manuscripts in the University of Iowa Libraries* (Friends of the Univ. of Iowa Libraries, 1969); *Books at Iowa,* 1964- , semi-annual journal of the Friends of the University of Iowa Libraries; Boyd Keith Swigger, comp., *A Guide to Resources for the Study of the Recent History of the United States in the Libraries of the University of Iowa, the State Historical Society of Iowa, and in the Herbert Hoover Presidential Library* (Univ. of Iowa, 1977).

KALONA

IA499-520
Mennonite Historical Society of Iowa
Mennonite Archives
Kalona IA

MAILING ADDRESS:
Box 576
Kalona IA 52247

(319) 656-3271

OPEN: M-F 1-5; closed weekends and Oct. 15-April 15 except by appointment
ACCESS: appointment required
COPYING FACILITIES: no
MATERIALS SOLICITED: Materials concerning Mennonite and Amish church history, genealogy records, local history, diaries and scrapbooks.

HOLDINGS:
  Total volume: 40 boxes; 75 items; 3 file cabinets
  Inclusive dates: 1700 -
  Description: Materials pertaining to Amish and Mennonite history, including marriage records, obituaries, deeds, legal transactions, day school registers, photographs and conference records for Iowa and Nebraska.

SEE: Hinding.

KEOKUK

IA511-450
Keokuk Public Library
210 North 5th Street
Keokuk IA 52632

(319) 524-1483

OPEN: M-Th 10-9, F, Sa 10-6; closed Sundays and holidays
COPYING FACILITIES: yes
MATERIALS SOLICITED: Materials concerning Keokuk, Lee County, IA, Van Buren County, IA, Hancock County, IL, and Clark County, MO, including such subjects as history, biography, genealogy, authors, upper Mississippi River history, boats and boating, the Half-Breed Tract, and Mark Twain. Will also accept materials relating to the later life of former Keokuk residents.

HOLDINGS:
  Total volume: 78 l.f.; 8 file drawers
  Inclusive dates: 1850 -
  Description: Minutes, membership lists, and other records of early Keokuk clubs and organizations, including the Keokuk Rifles militia; journals of doctors during the Civil War and late 1800's; photograph albums depicting building of Keokuk lock and dam, 1913; scrapbooks including photographs, invoices, programs, sale bills, and handbills; and the Davis papers on microfilm.

SEE: Hamer.

LAMONI

IA533-280
Graceland College
Frederick Madison Smith Library
Restoration History Manuscript
  Collection
Lamoni IA 50140

(515) 784-5362

OPEN: M-F 10-2, some evenings; closed other days and school holidays
ACCESS: qualified scholars or students in any undergraduate or graduate institution
COPYING FACILITIES: yes
MATERIALS SOLICITED: Documents, manuscripts, photographs, and archival materials relating to the founding, maintenance, and outreach of the Latter-day Saints church, the Reorganized Church of Jesus Christ of Latter Day Saints or any of the 375 dispersed groups. Will also accept materials dealing with the town of Lamoni, Graceland College, or the political, social, or religious climate of the United States as it relates directly to the foundation of Mormonism.

HOLDINGS:
  Total volume: 210 l.f.
  Inclusive dates: 1828 -
  Description: 'Scripture' manuscripts, diaries, letters, account books, genealogical materials, manuscripts, music scores, photographs, oral history tapes, microfilm and translations of manuscripts relating to the origin, growth, and expansion of

the Latter-day Saints movement until 1844 and the diverse movements emerging after the assassination of Joseph Smith. Included are materials relating to the history of the organization; various church institutions; towns (Lamoni, IA, Kirtland, OH, Far West, MO, Salt Lake City, UT) directly related to the growth of the church; Graceland College; the Independence Sanitarium; and missionary activities throughout the world.

LE MARS

IA544-880
Westmar College
Charles A. Mock Library
Le Mars IA 51031

(712) 546-7081, Ext. 217

OPEN: M-Th 8-10:30, F 8-5, Sa 1-5, Su 2-10:30; closed holidays
COPYING FACILITIES: yes
MATERIALS SOLICITED: Current materials relating to Westmar College, and historical materials concerning Westmar College; its predecessor Western Union College; York College, which merged with Westmar College; and the predecessors of York College, which were Kansas City University, Campbell College, Lane University, Leander Clark College, Gould College, Avalon College, Gibbon Collegiate Institute, and Le Mars Normal School.

HOLDINGS:
Total volume: 60 l.f.
Inclusive dates: 1857 -
Description: Administrative records and other materials concerning Westmar College, Western Union College, and York College.

LOGAN

IA600-322
Harrison County Historical Village
109 E. 6th Street
Logan IA 51546

(712) 644-2006, 2519

OPEN: Su 1-6, Mondays by appointment, Tu-Sa 10-5
COPYING FACILITIES: no
MATERIALS SOLICITED: Local history and genealogy.

HOLDINGS:
Total volume: 80 vols.
Inclusive dates: 1861 - 1928
Description: Collection of local historical materials, including school and township records, scrapbooks, family genealogical charts, a soldier's history of the Civil War and the minute book of the Farmers' Wives Society, 1884-97.

MCGREGOR

IA622-200
Effigy Mounds National Monument
McGregor IA

MAILING ADDRESS:
Box K
McGregor IA 52157

(319) 873-2356

OPEN: daily 8-5
ACCESS: general visitors must be accompanied by staff member; microfilm copies will be used except in special circumstances
COPYING FACILITIES: no
MATERIALS SOLICITED: Archaeological field notes from northeastern Iowa.

HOLDINGS:
Total volume: 3 file drawers
Inclusive dates: 1900 - 1960
Description: Manuscripts of Ellison Orr covering his archaeological survey work and excavation in northeastern Iowa during the early 1900's, and National Park Service research papers, mostly from the 1950's and 1960's.

SEE: Hamer; NUCMC, 1966.

MISSOURI VALLEY

IA661-160
DeSoto National Wildlife Refuge
P.O. Box 114, Route 1
Missouri Valley IA 51555

(712) 642-2772

OPEN: M-F 8-5; closed weekends and holidays
COPYING FACILITIES: yes
MATERIALS SOLICITED: Materials related to the steamer *Bertrand* on the Missouri River; and maps, diaries, and accounts of mid-19th century travelers describing flora and fauna of Iowa and Nebraska bordering the Missouri River. Will also accept materials on the natural environment of the central plains in Iowa and Nebraska before 1800.

HOLDINGS:
Total volume: 120 l.f.
Inclusive dates: 1800 -
Description: Slides and documentation relating to the excavation of the steamboat *Bertrand* in 1969-70, as well as reports on the condition and treatment of all artifacts retrieved from the wreckage. Also included are 19th century maps of the Missouri River and other records documenting the activities of the *Bertrand*.

MOUNT PLEASANT

IA688-360
Iowa Wesleyan College
J. Raymond Chadwick Library
Archives
Broad Street
Mt. Pleasant IA 52641

(319) 385-8021, Ext. 130, 131

OPEN: M-F mornings; closed weekends and holidays
ACCESS: appointment requested
COPYING FACILITIES: yes
MATERIALS SOLICITED: Records of Iowa Wesleyan College, German Methodist College, and the United Methodist church and its predecessors. Will also accept materials concerning Iowa, Henry County, IA, and Mt. Pleasant.

HOLDINGS:
Total volume: 1,014 l.f.; 20 4-drawer file cabinets
Inclusive dates: 1839 -
Description: Minutes, journals, record books, and biographical materials on pastors, all relating to the United Methodist church of Iowa, including the Evangelical Association, United Brethren church, Evangelical United Brethren, Methodist Episcopal church, and Methodist Protestant church.

Also held are records of Iowa Wesleyan College, materials relating to the German Methodist College, the Zwingli F. Meyer collection relating to German Methodism in Iowa, Missouri, and surrounding areas, materials on German Methodism in Germany, and correspondence and papers of John Edward Newsom and Emma Day Newsom, 1876-1922.

SEE: Hinding; Schatz.

IA688-520
Midwest Old Settlers and Threshers Association
Museum of Repertoire America
Mount Pleasant IA

MAILING ADDRESS:
R.R. 1
Mount Pleasant IA 52641

(319) 385-8937

OPEN: by appointment only; closed holidays
USER FEES: donations
COPYING FACILITIES: no
MATERIALS SOLICITED: Materials relating to American theater, specifically touring repertoire companies (tent and opera house), Chautauqua, showboats, and minstrel shows. Also related theater memorabilia.

HOLDINGS: *Total volume:* 100 tapes; 1,000 scripts; 2,000 photographs; 50 scrapbooks; 100 account books
Inclusive dates: 1840 -
Description: Play manuscripts and adaptations, photographs of performers, music scores and other materials relating to repertoire companies.

MOUNT VERNON

IA699-120
Cornell College
Russell D. Cole Library
Mt. Vernon IA 52314

(319) 895-8811

OPEN: M, Th 10-3 by appointment
ACCESS: permission of Library Director
  required
COPYING FACILITIES: yes
MATERIALS SOLICITED: Materials relating
  to the history of Cornell College.

HOLDINGS:
  Total volume: 11.5 l.f.
  Inclusive dates: 1858 -
  Description: Cornell College holdings,
  1858- , including presidential and faculty
  correspondence, trustee and faculty diaries, literary society and religious group
  minute books, faculty music compositions, films, video tapes, and oral history
  tapes. There are also records of the First
  Methodist Church in Mt. Vernon,
  1911-26, including board minutes and
  records, quarterly conference records,
  mission society membership lists and
  minutes, trustee minutes, and building
  committee records.

SEE: Hinding.

ORANGE CITY

IA755-560
Northwestern College
Ramaker Library
Dutch Heritage Collection
101 7th Street, S.W.
Orange City IA 51041

(712) 737-4821

OPEN: by appointment only
COPYING FACILITIES: yes
MATERIALS SOLICITED: Material relating
  to the history of Northwestern Classical
  Academy, Northwestern College and
  the Reformed Church in America, particularly the midwestern and far western areas and the Particular Synod of
  the West. Will also accept materials relating to the history of northwestern
  Iowa, particularly Sioux County, missionaries of the Reformed Church in
  America, histories of families with
  Dutch ancestry, and graduates of
  Northwestern College.

HOLDINGS:
  Total volume: 40 l.f.
  Inclusive dates: 1870 -
  Description: Manuscripts relating to
  Northwestern Classical Academy;
  Northwestern Junior College and Academy; Northwestern College; and the Reformed Church in America, especially the
  midwestern and far western classes. There
  are also family histories and town histories.

GUIDES: *A Guide to the Archives of the
  Ramaker Library* (n.d.).

SEE: NUCMC, 1974.

SEE: Hinding.

SEE ALSO: *The Manuscript and Archival
  Holdings of the Dutch Heritage Collec-
  tion, Ramaker Library* (Northwestern
  College, n.d.).

OSAGE

IA766-520
Mitchell County Historical Society
Museum
200 North Sixth Street
Osage IA

MAILING ADDRESS:
R.R. 4
Osage IA 50461

(515) 732-4118

OPEN: weekends and holidays 2-5 from
  Memorial Day through Labor Day;
  closed weekdays and rest of year
COPYING FACILITIES: yes
MATERIALS SOLICITED: Will accept diaries, scrapbooks, and other materials
  pertaining to the lives of early Iowa
  pioneers.

HOLDINGS:
  Total volume: 100 sq.f.
  Inclusive dates: 1858 -
  Description: The collection includes rural school registers dating from 1870,
  manuscript histories of the County (1883,
  1911, 1917, 1973), scrapbooks and genealogical items related to Mitchell County
  residents, and original centennial histories
  of the churches and towns in the County.

PELLA

IA811-110
Central College
Learning Resource Center
Department of Archives
Pella IA 50219

(515) 628-5219, 4151 Ext. 219

OPEN: M-F 11-3; closed weekends and
  holidays
COPYING FACILITIES: yes
MATERIALS SOLICITED: Materials pertaining to local history, the Dutch in
  America, and family history. Will also
  accept Central College archival material.

HOLDINGS:
  Total volume: 2,000 items
  Inclusive dates: 1825 -
  Description: Papers of H. P. Scholte,
  minister in the Netherlands and founder
  of Pella, containing 860 letters and documents concerning church matters in the
  Netherlands from 1825 to 1846. Collections documenting Pella history include
  family and personal letters, financial
  records of colonists, abstracts of land titles, court records, business records, plats,
  church membership records, financial
  records of Central College, and a small
  collection of oral history recordings.

GUIDES: 'A Guide to the Archives of
  Central College,' (1978).

SEE: Hamer; NUCMC, 1966.

PRIMGHAR

IA822-600
O'Brien County Historical Society
541 15th Street
Primghar IA

MAILING ADDRESS:
Box 385
Primghar IA 51245

(712) 324-2068

OPEN: summer, second and fourth
  Sunday of each month 2-5, or by
  appointment with Secretary
COPYING FACILITIES: yes
MATERIALS SOLICITED: Any written document or oral history which relates to
  the history of O'Brien County and the
  surrounding area.

HOLDINGS:
  Total volume: 10 items
  Inclusive dates: 1920's -
  Description: Church histories, school
  records, and family histories relating to
  O'Brien County and northwestern Iowa.

ROCKWELL CITY

IA833-120
Calhoun County Historical Society
8th and South Streets
Rockwell City IA

MAILING ADDRESS:
c/o Judy Webb
RR 2
Rockwell City IA 50579

(712) 297-8307

OPEN: Sundays 2-5 May to Sept.; closed
  other days, and Oct. 15 - April 15
  except by appointment
COPYING FACILITIES: no
MATERIALS SOLICITED: Histories of
  towns, schools, churches, and patriotic
  and civic organizations in the county.
  Will also accept early photographs.

HOLDINGS:
  Total volume: 8 l.f.; 1.5 file cabinets;
  342 items
  Inclusive dates: 1876 -
  Description: Calhoun County history
  materials, including manuscripts, family
  histories, aerial and plat maps, scrapbooks, and music manuscripts by George
  A. Craft.

SEE: Hinding.

SCOTCH GROVE

IA840-400
Jones County Iowa Historical Society
Rural Route 1
Scotch Grove IA

MAILING ADDRESS:
P.O. Box 124
Monticello IA 52310

(319) 465-3564

OPEN: May - Sept., Su 1-5; by
  appointment other times

COPYING FACILITIES: yes
MATERIALS SOLICITED: Materials documenting Jones County and its environs.

HOLDINGS:
Total volume: 24 sq.f.
Inclusive dates: 1839 - 1940
Description: Letters, diaries, legal documents, pioneer reminiscences, and audio tapes pertaining to Jones County history.

SIOUX CENTER

IA855-150
Dordt College
Archives and Dutch Memorial
    Collection
498 4th Avenue, N.E.
Sioux Center IA 51250

(712) 722-3771, Ext. 6042

OPEN: M-F 9-4:30; closed Sundays and holidays
COPYING FACILITIES: yes
MATERIALS SOLICITED: Archival materials of Dordt College and materials on the life, culture, and institutions of Dutch settlers of the Midwest. Will also accept Dutch-American materials from a wider geographical area.

HOLDINGS:
Total volume: 2,000 items
Inclusive dates: 19th century -
Description: Materials preserving the historical record of Dutch settlers in Iowa, Minnesota, North and South Dakota, and parts of Canada. Included are records of schools and Christian Reformed churches, some letters and diaries, and a few oral history tapes.

SIOUX CITY

IA866-160
Diocese of Sioux City
1821 Jackson Street
Sioux City IA

MAILING ADDRESS:
P.O. Box 3379
Sioux City IA 51102

(712) 255-7933

OPEN: M-F 9-5; closed weekends and holy days
ACCESS: specific approval needed in every case
COPYING FACILITIES: yes

HOLDINGS:
Total volume: not specified
Inclusive dates: 1918 -
Description: Complete baptismal, confirmation, marriage, and financial records for all Roman Catholic parishes in the 24 northwestern counties of Iowa.

IA866-730
Sioux City Public Museum
2901 Jackson Street
Sioux City IA 51104

(712) 279-6174

OPEN: M-F 9-5; closed weekends and holidays
COPYING FACILITIES: yes
MATERIALS SOLICITED: Written materials, photographs, and oral histories of historical or scientific importance relating to Sioux City and the surrounding tri-state region. Will also accept State or regional historical accounts pertaining to Iowa, Nebraska, or South Dakota, Civil War history, and Upper Missouri River history.

HOLDINGS:
Total volume: 500 l.f.
Inclusive dates: 19th century -
Description: Collections pertaining primarily to the history of Sioux City and northwestern Iowa, with substantial documentation of Sioux City from the 1850's to 1890's. Included are oral history interviews concerning Sioux City and personal papers of Iowa Governor William L. Harding.

SEE: Hamer.

SEE: Hinding.

WATERLOO

IA922-280
Grout Museum of History and
    Science
503 South Street
Waterloo IA 50701

(319) 234-6357

OPEN: Tu-F 9-1 by appointment only and 1-4:30, Sa 1-4; closed Sundays, Mondays, and holidays
COPYING FACILITIES: yes
MATERIALS SOLICITED: Old photographs, reminiscences, diaries pertaining to local area. Will also accept articles of a scientific nature pertaining to local area.

HOLDINGS:
Total volume: 7,000 items
Inclusive dates: 1853 - early 20th century
Description: Collections relate to the history of Black Hawk County and surrounding area. Archives include Civil War correspondence, diaries, photographs, Black Hawk County courthouse records, unpublished memoirs by local historian, rural school registers and ledgers, hotel ledgers, and non-current records of social organizations and businesses.

WAVERLY

IA944-880
Wartburg College
Engelbrecht Library
College Archives
Waverly IA 50677

(319) 352-8200

OPEN: Su 1-11:30, M-Th 7:30-11:30, F 7:30-6, Sa 9-5; closed holidays
COPYING FACILITIES: yes
MATERIALS SOLICITED: Materials pertaining to the history of Wartburg College, including its organization, administration, faculty, students, and buildings.

HOLDINGS:
Total volume: 7 files; 72 l.f.
Inclusive dates: 1870's -
Description: Records of Wartburg College, including board, faculty, and building committee minutes, news releases, and alumni and student affairs material, and a large photograph collection. Also included are records of colleges which merged to form Wartburg College.

WEBSTER CITY

IA955-440
Kendall Young Library
1201 Willson Avenue
Webster City IA 50595

(515) 832-2565

OPEN: M-Th 9-9, F 9-6, Sa 9-5; closed Sundays and holidays
COPYING FACILITIES: yes
MATERIALS SOLICITED: Historical material relating to Hamilton County, IA.

HOLDINGS:
Total volume: 32 c.f.
Inclusive dates: 1857 -
Description: A local historical collection relating to Webster City and Hamilton County, including personal papers; reminiscences of pioneers; scrapbooks on businesses, churches, schools, the Library, authors and artists, and women's organizations; 1,000 slides and photographs of historical sites and events; and an information file about early residents. Also included is a collection of autographs of political, military, literary and other figures, as well as a manuscript of *Happy Land* by MacKinlay Kantor and a manuscript history of Hamilton County.

SEE: Hamer; NUCMC, 1978.

SEE: Hinding; Robbins.

SEE ALSO: *Kendall Young and the Kendall Young Library* (Kendell Young Library, 1976).

WEST BRANCH

IA966-320
Herbert Hoover Library
West Branch IA

MAILING ADDRESS:
P.O. Box 488
West Branch IA 52358

(319) 643-5301

OPEN: M-F 9-5; closed weekends and
holidays
ACCESS: serious researchers; adequate
identification and satisfactory
completion of forms required
COPYING FACILITIES: yes
MATERIALS SOLICITED: Material relating
directly to Herbert Hoover or to the
period of his public career, 1914-64.

HOLDINGS:
Total volume: 3,061 l.f.
Inclusive dates: 1861 -
Description: Papers of Herbert Hoover
constitute about two-thirds of the holdings. They are supplemented by an oral
history collection, a large still photograph
and motion picture collection, and 70
other collections covering a wide range of
political, social, and economic topics, primarily for the period 1920-64.

GUIDES: *Historical Materials in the Herbert Hoover Presidential Library* (1977).

SEE: NUCMC, 1967, 69-70, 72, 74, 79.

SEE: Allard, Crawley, and Edmison;
Hinding; Parkinson.

SEE ALSO: *Guide to the National Archives
of the United States* (GPO, 1974); Boyd
Keith Swigger, comp., *A Guide to Re-
sources for the Study of the Recent His-
tory of the United States in the Librar-
ies of the University of Iowa, the State
Historical Society of Iowa, and in the
Herbert Hoover Presidential Library*
(Univ. of Iowa, 1977); Ann Novotny,
ed., *Picture Sources 3* (Special Libraries
Assn., 1975); Lawrence J. Paszek,
comp., *United States Air Force History:
A Guide to Documentary Sources*
(Office of Air Force History, 1973);
Richard C. Davis, *North American For-
est History: A Guide to Archives and
Manuscripts in the United States and
Canada* (Clio Books, 1977).

WEST UNION

IA972-240
Fayette County Helpers Club and
Historical Society
100 North Walnut
West Union IA 52175

(319) 422-9213

OPEN: M-F 8-5, weekends by
appointment only; closed holidays
COPYING FACILITIES: yes
MATERIALS SOLICITED: Materials pertinent to the people of Fayette County.

HOLDINGS:
Total volume: not specified
Inclusive dates: 1849 -
Description: Fayette County cemetery
records, school records, war records, fam-
ily files, and scrapbooks.

KANSAS

Since 1961 the Archives Department of the Kansas State Historical Society has administered a statewide program for preserving official county records. The Archives Department advises county governments and local historical societies on the preservation of county archives through microfilming and the various phases of collection processing. Currently, the department is preparing records retention schedules which will ensure the preservation of records with enduring value.

County officials must offer records to the Archives Department before seeking authority from the district court for their disposition. Local governments usually retain custody of their records of lasting significance; consequently, the state archives has not acquired many permanently valuable local records.

ABILENE

KS10-150
Dickinson County Historical Society
412 South Campbell
Abilene KS

MAILING ADDRESS:
P.O. Box 506
Abilene KS 67410

(913) 263-2681

OPEN: by appointment only; closed holidays
COPYING FACILITIES: yes
MATERIALS SOLICITED: Materials of historical interest pertaining to Dickinson County.

HOLDINGS:
  Total volume: 150 c.f.
  Inclusive dates: 1861 -
  Description: Materials pertaining to the social, political, and economic history of Dickinson County, primarily consisting of public, business, church, cemetery, organization, and school records, personal papers, obituaries, and photographs.

SEE: Hinding.

KS10-170
Dwight D. Eisenhower Library
Abilene KS 67410

(913) 263-4751

OPEN: M-F 9-4:45, Saturdays by appointment; closed Sundays and holidays
ACCESS: all researchers must complete a research application
COPYING FACILITIES: yes
MATERIALS SOLICITED: United States diplomatic and military history, 1935-69; and United States political, economic, and social history, 1953-69.

HOLDINGS:
  Total volume: 19,250,000 pages; other items
  Inclusive dates: 1900 - 1980
  Description: Approximately 332 manuscript collections, 473 oral history transcripts and tapes, 1,000 hours disc and tape audio recordings, 180,000 still photographs, and 600,000 feet of motion picture film pertaining to 20th century United States diplomatic, military, political, economic, and social history. Major areas of emphasis are World War II, the origins and early history of the Cold War, and the Dwight D. Eisenhower Presidency, 1953-61.

GUIDES: *Historical Materials in the Dwight D. Eisenhower Library* (1977).

SEE: NUCMC, 1971, 73, 76.

SEE: Hinding; Parkinson; Allard, Edmison, and Crawley; Paszek; Svoboda and Dunning.

SEE ALSO: Alan M. Meckler and Ruth McMullin, comps., *Oral History Collections* (Bowker, 1975); David A. Hounshell, comp., *Manuscripts in U.S. Depositories Relating to the History of Electrical Science and Technology* (Smithsonian Institution, n.d.); Ann Novotny, ed., *Picture Sources 3* (Special Libraries Assn., 1975); Richard C. Davis, *North American Forest History: A Guide to Archives and Manuscripts in the United States and Canada* (Clio Books, 1977).

KS10-520
Museum of Independent Telephony
412 South Campbell
Abilene KS 67410

MAILING ADDRESS:
P.O. Box 625
Abilene KS 67410

(913) 263-2681

OPEN: M-F 10-4:30; closed weekends, Thanksgiving, and Christmas

USER FEES: $20 for lengthy research by Curator
ACCESS: advance arrangements requested
COPYING FACILITIES: yes
MATERIALS SOLICITED: Historical materials concerning independent telephony. Will also accept materials from related independent fields.

HOLDINGS:
  Total volume: not specified
  Inclusive dates: 1890's -
  Description: Materials concerning telephony, including manuscripts dealing with independent telephone systems in the United States, histories of exchanges and people, oral histories, and photographs.

ARKANSAS CITY

KS52-120
Cherokee Strip Landrush Museum
Arkansas City KS

MAILING ADDRESS:
Box 230
Arkansas City KS 67005

(316) 442-6750

OPEN: Tu-Sa 10-5, Su 1-5; closed Mondays, weekdays Nov. - April, and holidays
ACCESS: advance notice of research intent required
COPYING FACILITIES: no
MATERIALS SOLICITED: Materials pertaining to the history of the Cherokee Strip, Kansas, Oklahoma, and the western United States.

HOLDINGS:
  Total volume: 5,000 photographs; additional materials
  Inclusive dates: 1880 - 1930
  Description: Photographs centering around the Cherokee Strip Run of 1893 and its participants. There are also some journals and diaries related to the same subject.

ATCHISON

KS80-40
Atchison Public Library
401 Kansas Avenue
Atchison KS 66002

(913) 367-1902

OPEN: M-Th 9-9, F, Sa 9-5, Su 2-4; closed holidays
COPYING FACILITIES: yes

MATERIALS SOLICITED: Materials relating to the history of Atchison County and Kansas in general, including genealogical materials.

HOLDINGS:
 Total volume: 3 vols.
 Inclusive dates: 1840 - 1920
 Description: Three scrapbooks containing photographs and other materials relating to the history of Atchison, its residents, and its buildings.

KS80-720
St. Benedict's Abbey
Archives
Atchison KS 66002

(913) 367-5340

OPEN: by appointment only

SEE: Hamer; NUCMC, 1965.

Questionnaire not returned.

ATWOOD

KS94-690
Rawlins County Historical Museum
308 State Street
Atwood KS

MAILING ADDRESS:
203 S. 6th Street
Atwood KS 67730

(913) 626-9423

OPEN: by appointment only
COPYING FACILITIES: no
MATERIALS SOLICITED: Manuscripts, scrapbooks, and visual and audible documents relating to Rawlins County.

HOLDINGS:
 Total volume: 20 l.f.
 Inclusive dates: 1875 -
 Description: Obituary newspaper clippings, family histories, and photographs, pertaining to Rawlins County history.

SEE: Svoboda and Dunning.

BALDWIN CITY

KS108-70
Baker University
Archives and Historical Library
Special Collections
Collins Library
606 8th Street
Baldwin City KS 66006

(913) 594-6451, Ext. 380

OPEN: M-W, F 9-noon, or by appointment; closed Thursdays, weekends, and University vacations
COPYING FACILITIES: yes
MATERIALS SOLICITED: History of early Kansas, Kansas Methodism, and Baker University, including materials of alumni and missionaries.

HOLDINGS:
 Total volume: 100 l.f.
 Inclusive dates: 1854 -
 Description: Correspondence, diaries, and journals, primarily ministerial, pertaining to early settlement in Kansas; conference and local records of the Methodist Episcopal church; records of the Methodist Protestant and Evangelical United Brethren churches; photographs; and records of the University, including presidential correspondence, faculty minutes, and letters of alumni and missionaries.

SEE: Hinding.

BONNER SPRINGS

KS136-880
Wyandotte County Museum
Harry M. Trowbridge Research
 Library
631 North 126 Street
Bonner Springs KS 66012

(913) 721-1078

OPEN: March - Dec., Tu-Sa 10-5, Su 1-5; Jan. - Feb., F-Su 1-5; closed Mondays, Thanksgiving and Christmas
COPYING FACILITIES: yes
MATERIALS SOLICITED: Materials relating to Wyandotte County and Kansas.

HOLDINGS:
 Total volume: 55 l.f.
 Inclusive dates: 19th century -
 Description: Materials relating to the history of settlement and the people of Wyandotte County, including manuscripts, photographs, diaries, correspondence, maps, county and city records, and organization records.

SEE: Hinding.

CHANUTE

KS164-520
Martin and Osa Johnson Safari
 Museum, Inc.
16 South Grant
Chanute KS 66720

(316) 431-2730

OPEN: by appointment only; closed holidays
ACCESS: restrictions, if any, are determined by the Board of Directors of the Museum; individual cases must be discussed
COPYING FACILITIES: yes
MATERIALS SOLICITED: African and South Pacific and Borneo exploration materials, particularly those related to Martin and Osa Johnson. Will also accept exploration documents, 1840 - present; vaudeville material (Midwest circuit) ca. 1911-1917; Jack London materials, 1906-1916; materials relating to the people, flora, and fauna of Africa, South Pacific, and Borneo.

HOLDINGS:
 Total volume: 500 l.f.
 Inclusive dates: 1884 - 1953
 Description: A collection related chiefly to the exploration and photographic work of Martin and Osa Johnson in the South Pacific islands, 1908 and 1916-20; eastern and central Africa, 1921-34; and North Borneo, 1919 and 1935. Included are photographs, unpublished manuscripts, articles, fragmentary diaries, letters and other correspondence.

SEE: Hinding.

COLBY

KS192-760
Thomas County Historical Society
1525 West 4th Street
Colby KS 67701

(913) 462-6972

OPEN: Tu-F 9-5, Sa, Su 1-5; closed Mondays and holidays
COPYING FACILITIES: yes
MATERIALS SOLICITED: Diaries, letters, and other original records, books, and pamphlets written by or about people of Thomas County; photographs and maps of the county.

HOLDINGS:
 Total volume: 675 l.f.
 Inclusive dates: 1880 -
 Description: Pioneer reminiscences, family histories, business records, church and cemetery records, school records, and a large collection of photographs, relating primarily to the history of Thomas County.

CONCORDIA

KS213-120
Cloud County Historical Museum
7th and Broadway
Concordia KS

MAILING ADDRESS:
P.O. Box 635
Concordia KS 66901

(913) 243-2866

OPEN: daily 1-5; closed Christmas and Easter
ACCESS: advance permission required
COPYING FACILITIES: no
MATERIALS SOLICITED: Material relating to Cloud County.

HOLDINGS:
 Total volume: 40 l.f.
 Inclusive dates: 1793 -
 Description: Letters, including one each of Martha Washington and Abraham Lincoln; early Cloud County histories; early photographs; church records; card catalog of births, deaths, marriages from 1870-1919; dental appointment calendars; school records; scrapbooks.

KS213-560
Nazareth Convent and Academy
Nazareth Motherhouse Archives
13th Street and Washington Street
Concordia KS 66901

(913) 243-2113

OPEN: M-F 9-5; closed weekends and
holidays
ACCESS: advance appointment required
COPYING FACILITIES: yes
MATERIALS SOLICITED: Official documents and personal papers relating to
the Sisters of St. Joseph congregation
in Concordia and its activities in the
fields of education, health care, and
charity. Will also accept materials pertaining to Roman Catholic church history and to the work of the Federation
of the Sisters of St. Joseph in the United States and Canada.

HOLDINGS:
Total volume: 132 l.f.
Inclusive dates: 1883 -
Description: Administrative records,
letters, photographs, memorabilia, and
oral histories tracing the history of the
Sisters of St. Joseph congregation in
Concordia, including information on its
members and the people they serve in the
United States and Brazil.

SEE: Hinding.

DIGHTON

KS241-480
Lane County Historical Society
Museum
333 North Main
Dighton KS

MAILING ADDRESS:
P.O. Box 821
Dighton KS 67839

(316) 397-5652

OPEN: Tu-Su 1-5; closed Mondays and
holidays
COPYING FACILITIES: no
MATERIALS SOLICITED: Materials pertaining to Lane County and Kansas
history. Will also accept fiction by
Kansans or about Kansas and pioneer
life.

HOLDINGS:
Total volume: 6 bookcases
Inclusive dates: 1873 -
Description: Materials relating to the
history of Lane County, including maps,
photographs, personal and business correspondence, business account books, papers, memoirs, minutes of clubs and organizations, school materials, and land
records.

DODGE CITY

KS255-720
St. Mary of the Plains College
Archives
Dodge City KS 67801

(316) 225-4171

OPEN: M-Th 9-4, F 9-noon, or by
appointment; closed weekends and
holidays
COPYING FACILITIES: yes
MATERIALS SOLICITED: Archives and
non-current records of St. Mary of the
Plains College and its predecessor institutions. Will also accept personal papers and oral histories pertaining to the
institution.

HOLDINGS:
Total volume: 150 l.f.
Inclusive dates: 1884 -
Description: Records and other histori-
cal materials concerning St. Mary of the
Plains College and the institutions which
preceded it.

EL DORADO

KS269-80
Butler County Historical Society
Museum
383 E. Central Street
El Dorado KS

MAILING ADDRESS:
P.O. Box 696
El Dorado KS 67042

(316) 321-9333

OPEN: Tu-F 1-5; closed weekends,
Mondays, and holidays
COPYING FACILITIES: no
MATERIALS SOLICITED: Oral history
, tapes and transcripts covering local his-
tory.

HOLDINGS:
Total volume: 1,700 items
Inclusive dates: mid-1800's -
Description: Historical materials concerning Butler County, including 100 oral
history recordings, 100 diaries, letters,
and other manuscripts, and 1,500 photographs and tintypes.

EMPORIA

KS283-200
Emporia State University
William Allen White Library
Special Collections Division
1200 Commercial Street
Emporia KS 66801

(316) 343-1200, Ext. 5205

OPEN: M-F 8-5; closed weekends and
holidays; hours vary during school
vacations
ACCESS: advance arrangements
recommended
COPYING FACILITIES: yes
MATERIALS SOLICITED: Will accept any
materials of or relating to William Allen White, Emporia Kansas State College and its Library (including non-
current records), May Massee and authors and illustrators who worked with
her, Lois Lenski, Elizabeth Yates, Mary
White, and the William Allen White
Children's Book Award and its recipients.

HOLDINGS:
Total volume: 70 l.f.; 8,000 items
Inclusive dates: 1857 -
Description: 3,770 papers and photographs of William Allen White and his
family; 36 l.f. of non-current records of
Emporia Kansas State College; 8.5 l.f. of
records of White Library, 1931-52; 3,957
items, including papers and audio-visual
records, regarding May Massee and the
authors and illustrators with whom she
worked; 218 manuscripts and photographs related to Lois Lenski's regional
books; 27 manuscripts and photographs
of Elizabeth Yates, the first recipient of
the William Allen White Children's Book
Award; 24 l.f. of papers regarding that
award, since 1953; and 50 papers and
photographs of Mary White.

SEE: NUCMC, 1978.

SEE: Robbins.

SEE ALSO: *A Bibliography of William
White Prepared by Kansas State Teach-
ers College from the William Allen
White Collection* (Teachers College
Press, 1969); Elizabeth (Gray) Vining
and Annis Duff, *The May Massee Col-
lection: Creative Publishing for Children*
(Kansas State Teachers College, 1972).

GARDEN CITY

KS335-240
Finney County Historical Society
Finnup Park
Garden City KS

MAILING ADDRESS:
P.O. Box 59
Garden City KS 67846

(316) 275-6664

OPEN: daily 1-5; closed holidays
COPYING FACILITIES: yes
MATERIALS SOLICITED: Records, manu-
scripts, and photographs relating to
Finney County.

HOLDINGS:
Total volume: not specified
Inclusive dates: 1870 -
Description: Materials relating primarily to Finney County, including records
of organizations and individuals, county
court and township records, and photographs of southwestern Kansas.

SEE: Hinding.

HAYS

KS377-200

Ellis County Historical Society
Museum
100 W. 7th Street
Hays KS 67601

MAILING ADDRESS:
Box 9
Hays KS 67601

(913) 628-2624

OPEN: by appointment only
ACCESS: appointment with Archivist-Historian required
COPYING FACILITIES: yes
MATERIALS SOLICITED: Manuscripts, photographs, and oral history tapes pertaining to the history of Ellis County.

HOLDINGS:
Total volume: 52 l.f.
Inclusive dates: 1867 -
Description: Materials relating to all phases of Ellis County history, including papers of the short-lived town of Hays City, 1868; civil and criminal justice of the peace dockets of Big Creek Township, 1872-85; some papers of Katheryn O'Loughlin McCarthy, first U.S. Congresswoman from Kansas; records of Munjor Town and Grazing Co., 1876-1911; and about 3,000 photographs.

KS377-250

Fort Hays State University
Forsyth Library
Archives Collection
Hays KS 67601

(913) 628-4433

OPEN: M-Th 8-10:30, Sa 9-5, Su 2-10 during school sessions; otherwise M-F 1-5; closed holidays
COPYING FACILITIES: yes
MATERIALS SOLICITED: Non-current records and other materials pertaining to the history of Fort Hays State University, history of western Kansas. All materials relating to ethnic groups in western Kansas, especially the Germans from Russia. Will also accept genealogical materials and family histories pertaining to western Kansas; county histories of western Kansas.

HOLDINGS:
Total volume: 48 file drawers; 300 tapes; 350 hours of recordings
Inclusive dates: 1860 -
Description: Documents relating to the history of Fort Hays Kansas State College; 350 hours of oral history interviews covering the history of the College and western Kansas; and 300 audio tape recordings concerning Kansas folklore.

SEE: Hinding; Svoboda and Dunning.

SEE ALSO: Alan M. Meckler and Ruth McMullin, comps., *Oral History Collections* (Bowker, 1975).

HILL CITY

KS385-280

Graham County Historical Society
414 North West
Hill City KS

MAILING ADDRESS:
406 South East
Hill City KS 67642

no telephone

OPEN: Su 2-4 or by appointment
COPYING FACILITIES: yes
MATERIALS SOLICITED: Manuscripts, photographs, and other materials concerning the history of Graham County.

HOLDINGS:
Total volume: not specified
Inclusive dates: 1879 -
Description: Manuscripts concerning family history, documents pertaining to Graham County history, photographs, tax receipts and other county courthouse records, oral histories, cemetery records, and records of Hill City, townships, and school districts.

JOHNSON

KS461-720

Stanton County Historical Society
Stanton County Library
Johnson KS

MAILING ADDRESS:
c/o Roger Jones
Route 2
Johnson KS 67855

(316) 495-3191

OPEN: M-F 9-6, Sa 9-2; closed Sundays and holidays
COPYING FACILITIES: yes
MATERIALS SOLICITED: Correspondence of early settlers in Stanton County. Will also accept any materials relative to the early history of the County.

HOLDINGS:
Total volume: 101 items
Inclusive dates: 1887 -
Description: A collection of early photographs of Stanton County people and scenes, and a notebook containing daily weather observations for 1894-95.

KANSAS CITY

KS475-440

Kansas City Public Library
625 Minnesota Avenue
Kansas City KS 66101

no telephone

SEE: Hamer.

Questionnaire not returned.

KS475-800

University of Kansas
Medical Center
College of Health Sciences and Hospital
Clendening History of Medicine Library
Rainbow Blvd. at 39th Street
Kansas City KS 66103

(913) 588-7040

OPEN: M-F 8-4:30; closed weekends and holidays
COPYING FACILITIES: yes
MATERIALS SOLICITED: Materials of medical interest. Will also accept other materials by persons in the medical field.

HOLDINGS:
Total volume: 18,000 volumes
Inclusive dates: 1400 -
Description: 100 series of diverse materials pertaining to the history of medicine, including medical reports, texts, notes, memoirs, manuscripts of books and articles, and related papers, as well as other materials by medical persons.

SEE: Hamer; NUCMC, 1959-61, 80.

SEE: Martin; Robbins.

SEE ALSO: Ann Novotny, ed., *Picture Sources 3* (Special Libraries Assn., 1975).

LARNED

KS513-250

Fort Larned National Historic Site
Route 3
Larned KS 67550

(316) 285-3571, 6911

OPEN: daily 8:30-5 by appointment only; closed holidays and Dec. 1
ACCESS: prior arrangements required
COPYING FACILITIES: no
MATERIALS SOLICITED: Materials pertaining to Fort Larned from 1859-1959; U.S. military documents and items, 1859-78. Will also accept Civil War era items and Santa Fe Trail materials.

HOLDINGS:
Total volume: 351 items
Inclusive dates: 1860 -
Description: Collection of military documents, letters and photographs pertaining to the U.S. Army and Fort Larned; items of Lt. C. H. Hoyt, Company H, 5th Regiment U.S. Vols.; diary of Chaplain David White; diary of Lt. Col. Koert S. Van Voorhees, 137th New York Vol. Infantry, 1864; photographs of Fort Larned, Civil War soldiers, and the Larned area.

KS513-720
Santa Fe Trail Center
Research Library
U.S. Highway 56
Larned KS

MAILING ADDRESS:
Route 3
Larned KS 67550

(316) 285-2054

OPEN: M-F 9-5; closed weekends,
Christmas, and first week in November
COPYING FACILITIES: yes
MATERIALS SOLICITED: Historic items
pertaining to the Santa Fe Trail area
from the prehistoric Indian culture to
the present. Will also accept records
pertaining to Pawnee County.

HOLDINGS:
Total volume: 1,000 c.f.; 1,700
photographs; 2,300 glass lantern slides
Inclusive dates: 1800 -
Description: A collection of manuscripts, letters and public documents relating chiefly to commerce on the Santa
Fe Trail. Included are some
reminiscences of settlers and papers on
the Civil War and the Indian wars relating mainly to Ft. Larned, KS. There are
also Pawnee County records, including
school records, dating from the 1870's.

LAWRENCE

KS527-160
Douglas County Historical Society
Elizabeth M. Watkins Community
  Museum
Library
1047 Massachusetts Street
Lawrence KS 66044

(913) 841-4109

OPEN: Tu-Sa 10-4, Su 1:30-4; closed
Mondays
COPYING FACILITIES: yes
MATERIALS SOLICITED: Correspondence,
records, and photographs relating to
the history of Douglas County.

HOLDINGS:
Total volume: 16 l.f.
Inclusive dates: 1854 -
Description: Materials concerning
Douglas County, including letters, diaries,
and journals of early settlers, records of
rural schools, business records, oral history tapes and transcripts, and photographs of residents, buildings, and scenes.

KS527-790
University of Kansas
Libraries
Kenneth Spencer Research Library
Department of Special Collections:
  Manuscripts Section
Lawrence KS 66045

(913) 864-4334

OPEN: M-F 8-6, Sa 9-1; closed Saturdays
except spring and fall semesters; closed
Sundays and holidays
ACCESS: advance arrangements
recommended

COPYING FACILITIES: yes
MATERIALS SOLICITED: Historical material from Britain and Europe,
1000-1900; authors' archives; theatrical
archives; medieval texts; commonplace
books; scientists' archives, especially
natural historians; maps, sea-charts;
early technology; 18th-century agriculture.

HOLDINGS:
Total volume: 1,016 l.f.
Inclusive dates: 1000 -
Description: A general collection with
strengths in Italian politics, history, law,
economics, daily life; Roman Catholic
church governance and diplomacy; British family papers; Portuguese political
correspondence, 1800-50; English legal
documents; medieval texts.
  Correspondence of English and Irish
literary-political figures (Rossetti, Yeats,
Porter, Tennyson, Moore, O'Shaughnessy,
Shields); papers of natural historians
Francis Harper, Ralph Ellis, T. J.
Fitzpatrick; neurologists C. Judson Herrick and George Ellett Coghill.

GUIDES: Alexandra Mason, *A Guide to
the Collections* (1972).

SEE: Hamer; NUCMC, 1967, 77, 80.

SEE: Spalek; Ingram; Robbins; Martin.

SEE ALSO: Walter Schatz, ed., *Directory of
Afro-American Resources* (Bowker,
1970); Thomas R. Smith and Bradford
L. Thomas, *Maps of the 16th to 19th
Centuries in the University of Kansas
Libraries: An Analytical Carto-
bibliography* (Univ. of Kansas Libraries, 1963); additional articles and descriptions of collections published three
times a year in *Books and Libraries at
the University of Kansas.*

Additional descriptions of collections appear
in *Books and Libraries at the University
of Kansas.*

KS527-795
University of Kansas
Libraries
Kenneth Spencer Research Library
Kansas Collection
Lawrence KS 66045

(913) 864-4274

OPEN: M-F 8-5, Sa 9-1; closed Sundays,
holidays, and Saturdays during
university vacations
COPYING FACILITIES: yes
MATERIALS SOLICITED: Kansas history,
economics, literature and culture. Will
also accept materials relating to surrounding States and western America.

HOLDINGS:
Total volume: 4,000 l.f.; 200,000
photographs; 135 oral histories; 486
architectural drawings
Inclusive dates: 1830 -
Description: Manuscript and photographic material relating to the economic,
political, and social history of Kansas,
including diaries, letters, account books,
and records of individuals, churches,
businesses, and other organizations, as
well as gubernatorial and senatorial papers. A collection of U.S. left- and right-
wing contemporary political movements
is also maintained.

SEE: Hamer; NUCMC, 1962, 65, 67.

SEE: Novotny; Schatz; Davis; Robbins.

SEE ALSO: Steve Jansen and Tom Brown,
'Preliminary Guide to Manuscript Materials in the Kansas Collection, Spencer Research Library, University of
Kansas' (n.p., 1979).

KS527-805
University of Kansas
Libraries
Kenneth Spencer Research Library
University Archives
Lawrence KS 66045

(913) 864-4188

OPEN: M-F 8-5; closed weekends and
holidays
COPYING FACILITIES: yes
MATERIALS SOLICITED: Materials relating
to the University of Kansas.

HOLDINGS:
Total volume: 9,000 c.f.
Inclusive dates: 1866 -
Description: Official records of the
University, supplemented by personal papers of faculty members and alumni and
materials from other sources. Included
are papers, documents, photographs,
sound recordings, and motion pictures.

GUIDES: Patricia Michaelis, *University of
Kansas Archives: A Guide* (1975).

SEE ALSO: Albert Krichmar, *The Women's
Rights Movement in the United States,
1848-1970: A Bibliography and
Sourcebook* (Scarecrow Press, 1972).

LEAVENWORTH

KS541-470
Leavenworth County Historical
  Society
334 5th Avenue
Leavenworth KS 66048

(913) 682-7759

OPEN: Tu-Su 1-4:30; closed Mondays
and third week Dec. - third week Feb.
USER FEES: one dollar
COPYING FACILITIES: no
MATERIALS SOLICITED: Materials pertaining to the Victorian period. Will
also accept any materials pertaining to
the history of Leavenworth.

HOLDINGS:
Total volume: 4 file cabinets
Inclusive dates: 1854 -
Description: Materials pertaining to the
families, industries and community af-
fairs of early Leavenworth.

KS541-490
Leavenworth Public Library
5th and Walnut Streets
Leavenworth KS 66048

(913) 682-5151, Ext. 200, 201

OPEN: M-F 8:30-9, Sa 9-5; closed
Sundays and holidays
COPYING FACILITIES: yes

MATERIALS SOLICITED: Materials relating to the history of Leavenworth and the surrounding area.

HOLDINGS:
Total volume: 20 items
Inclusive dates: 1859 -
Description: Photograph albums and scrapbooks relating to the early history of Leavenworth and its environs; records of county cemeteries; oral histories of Leavenworth County; county maps; and photographs of the town of Leavenworth.

KS541-720
Saint Mary College
DePaul Library
Special Collections Department
Leavenworth KS 66048

(913) 682-5151, Ext. 263

OPEN: by appointment only
COPYING FACILITIES: yes
MATERIALS SOLICITED: Will accept materials related to Abraham Lincoln, the Holy Scriptures, Kansas and Leavenworth history, Shakespeare, and the theater as related to Shakespeare.

HOLDINGS:
Total volume: not specified
Inclusive dates: 11th century -
Description: Letters, legal and business documents, and other American papers, including many focusing on the periods of the Revolutionary and Civil wars; a collection of Biblical codices and vellum leaves; and the archives of the College.

SEE: Schatz (listed under Xavier, KS); Robbins.

SEE ALSO: Duplicated guides are available for several collections.

LINDSBORG

KS555-80
Bethany College
Wallerstedt Learning Center
Lindsborg KS 67456

(913) 227-3311

OPEN: M-Th 7:30-10:30, F 7:30-5, Sa 11-4, Su 2:30-10:30; summer hours may vary; closed holidays and school vacations
ACCESS: scholars with references
COPYING FACILITIES: yes
HOLDINGS:
Total volume: 60 l.f.
Inclusive dates: 1881 - 1904
Description: Correspondence of Carl Aaron Swensson, founder and former president of Bethany College.

LYNDON

KS569-600
Osage County Historical Society
Osage County Museum
631 Topeka Avenue
Lyndon KS

MAILING ADDRESS:
P.O. Box 361
Lyndon KS 66451

(913) 828-3477, 4844

OPEN: M-F 8-4; closed weekends and holidays
COPYING FACILITIES: no
MATERIALS SOLICITED: Photographs, manuscripts, journals, records, and other materials relating to the history of Osage County and Kansas in general.

HOLDINGS:
Total volume: 2.5 l.f.
Inclusive dates: 1869 -
Description: Maps, manuscripts, photographs, and other materials pertaining to the Santa Fe Trail, the 110 Crossing, other old trails, post offices, jails, schools and classes, and other aspects of the history of Osage County and its environs.

LYONS

KS579-690
Coronado-Quivera Historical Museum
105 W. Lynn
Lyons KS 67554

(316) 257-3941

OPEN: Tu-Sa 10-5, Su 1-5; closed Mondays, Thanksgiving, Christmas, and New Year's
COPYING FACILITIES: yes
MATERIALS SOLICITED: Materials concerning Francisco Vasquez Coronado's visit to the area in 1541 and Father Juan Padilla, photographs of county history, and materials concerning the county's oil and salt industries.

HOLDINGS:
Total volume: 2,000 items
Inclusive dates: 1880's -
Description: Family genealogies and photographs of settlements, towns, schools, churches, clubs, families, and events relating to Rice County history.

MCPHERSON

KS593-510
McPherson College
Miller Library
Brethren Collection
1600 E. Euclid
McPherson KS 67460

(316) 241-0731, Ext. 212

OPEN: M-Th 7:30-10, F 7:30-5, Sa 1-5, Su 2-10, except June M-F 8-5; closed July-Aug. except by appointment
COPYING FACILITIES: yes
MATERIALS SOLICITED: Materials by and about the Church of the Brethren, its people, and McPherson College. Will

also accept materials about McPherson city and county and Kansas.

HOLDINGS:
Total volume: not specified
Inclusive dates: not specified
Description: Church records and correspondence of defunct congregations of the Church of the Brethren, materials relating to regional and district church bodies, the McPherson College archives, and early McPherson city government records.

SEE: Hinding.

MANHATTAN

KS607-450
Kansas State University
Library
Special Collections and University Archives
Manhattan KS 66506

(913) 532-6516

OPEN: M-F 8-5; closed weekends and holidays
COPYING FACILITIES: yes
MATERIALS SOLICITED: Materials documenting the history of Kansas State University, and papers of prominent Kansans.

HOLDINGS:
Total volume: 100 l.f.
Inclusive dates: mid-18th century -
Description: Manuscripts, oral history tapes and transcripts, and other materials relating to the history of Kansas State University and prominent Kansans. Particularly notable are letters and other papers relating to General Steven J. Casement and his son Daniel D., which include a colonial Virginia land patent signed by Patrick Henry.

GUIDES: Evan W. Williams, *Special Collections and the University Archives at the Kansas State University Library* (1979).

SEE: NUCMC, 1959-61, 70.

SEE: Meckler and McMullin; Hinding.

KS607-690
Riley County Historical Museum
2309 Claflin Road
Manhattan KS 66502

(913) 537-2210

OPEN: Tu-Sa 8:30-5; closed Sundays, Mondays and holidays
COPYING FACILITIES: no
MATERIALS SOLICITED: Writings or other records by or about individuals and organizations of Riley County. Will also accept similar materials from adjacent counties.

HOLDINGS:
Total volume: 80 l.f.
Inclusive dates: 1855 -
Description: A local history collection, containing all original Riley County marriage records; scrapbooks of the Riley County Historical Society; papers of the Manhattan city clerk's office, Chamber of Commerce, and cemetery sexton; genea-

logical materials; school records; photographs; and other items about churches and towns in Riley County.

SEE: Hinding; Svoboda and Dunning.

MINNEAPOLIS

KS635-600
Ottawa County Historical Museum
Minneapolis KS 67467

no telephone

OPEN: Tu-Su 1-5; closed Mondays, Thanksgiving, Christmas, and New Year's
COPYING FACILITIES: no
MATERIALS SOLICITED: Materials relating to Ottawa County or the State of Kansas. Will also accept materials relating to other subject areas.

HOLDINGS:
Total volume: 4,179 items
Inclusive dates: 19th century -
Description: Materials relating chiefly to Ottawa County. Included are documents relating to local churches, schools, businesses, and institutions from pioneer times to the present. There is also a photograph collection that emphasizes life in the pioneer period, as well as materials relating to 'Rock City,' a group of sandstone concretions near Minneapolis.

SEE: NUCMC, 1962.

NORTH NEWTON

KS676-520
Mennonite Library and Archives
Bethel College
E. 27th Street
North Newton KS

MAILING ADDRESS:
P.O. Box B
North Newton KS 67117

(316) 283-2500, Ext. 213

OPEN: M-F 8-5; closed weekends and holidays
ACCESS: access to official archives restricted by creating agency; prior arrangements should be made with the Archivist
COPYING FACILITIES: yes
MATERIALS SOLICITED: General Conference Mennonite church files, material relating to conscientious objectors, genealogy, relief, disaster work, and Mennonite and College-related oral history. Will also accept materials on peace, nonresistance and other related Mennonite subjects; and sound recordings, microfilm, manuscripts, photographs, slides, and personal archival collections of Mennonite leaders.

HOLDINGS:
Total volume: 955 l.f.
Inclusive dates: 1665 -
Description: Archival and manuscript materials relating to the General Conference Mennonite church, and especially to the German-Russian Mennonites who migrated to America and settled west of the Mississippi. There are also records of

Bethel College and related Mennonite institutions, microfilm and manuscript church and parish record books, taped interviews with World War I and II conscientious objectors, and other tapes of interviews, addresses, and dramatic and commemorative events.

SEE: Hamer (as Bethel College Historical Library); NUCMC, 1959-62, 73-74, 80.

SEE: Meckler and McMullin; Hinding; Svoboda and Dunning.

SEE ALSO: *Voices Against War: A Guide to the Schowalter Oral History Collection on World War I Conscientious Objection* (Bethel College, n.d.).

OBERLIN

KS690-160
Decatur County Historical Society, Inc.
Last Indian Raid in Kansas Museum
258 South Penn Avenue
Oberlin KS 67749

(913) 475-2712

OPEN: Tu-Sa 10-5 except 10-7 June-Aug., Su 1:30-5; closed Mondays, holidays, and Dec. 1-April 1
COPYING FACILITIES: yes
MATERIALS SOLICITED: Materials relating to the history of Decatur County, early pioneers, and the last Indian raid in Kansas history.

HOLDINGS:
Total volume: not specified
Inclusive dates: 1874 - 1880
Description: Historical materials relating to the last Indian raid in Kansas in 1878, including biographies of early settlers involved in the raid and oral history interviews.

OTTAWA

KS718-600
Ottawa University
Myers Library
Ottawa KS 66067

(913) 242-5200, Ext. 270

OPEN: M-Th 7:45-10:30, F 7:45-5, Sa 9:30-5, Su 3-10:30; closed Thanksgiving, Christmas, and New Year's week
COPYING FACILITIES: yes
MATERIALS SOLICITED: Materials relating to Ottawa University, the Ottawa Indians, and Kansas Baptists. Will also accept materials relating to local history and American Baptist history.

HOLDINGS:
Total volume: 40 l.f.; 12 file drawers
Inclusive dates: 1864 -
Description: Documents, letters, treaties, transcripts, meeting minutes, contracts, scrapbooks, and photographs related to Ottawa University, the Ottawa Indians and Kansas Baptists.

PITTSBURG

KS746-120
Crawford County Historical Society
305-307 East Madison
Pittsburg KS 66762

no telephone

OPEN: by appointment
COPYING FACILITIES: no
MATERIALS SOLICITED: Local history relating to Crawford County and adjacent areas, including letters, manuscripts, and photographs.

HOLDINGS:
Total volume: 1 file cabinet
Inclusive dates: 1900 -
Description: Materials on the history of Crawford County, including oral history tapes of recollections of local history by older townspeople.

KS746-640
Pittsburg State University
Library
Pittsburg KS 66762

(316) 231-7000

OPEN: M-F 8-4:30, weekends and evenings by appointment only; closed holidays
ACCESS: advance arrangements preferred
COPYING FACILITIES: yes
MATERIALS SOLICITED: Historical and literary materials pertaining to southeast Kansas, Pittsburg State University, its faculty and its alumni. Will also accept photographs, manuscripts, and other materials dealing with socialism, populism, and spiritualism.

HOLDINGS:
Total volume: 120 l.f.
Inclusive dates: 19th century -
Description: Materials relating to southeast Kansas history and literature, including business records and correspondence of E. Haldeman-Julius, J. A. Wayland, Eva Jessye, D. J. Saia, Joseph Skubitz, Phil and Ida Hayman Callery, Percy Daniel, and University faculty in several disciplines; archives of Pittsburg State University; the Irene P. Ertman science fiction collection; and the Ted Watts sports art collection.

SEE: Schatz; Robbins; Hinding.

PLEASANTON

KS760-480
Linn County Historical Society
Linn County Archives
Linn County Museum
Dr. Dunlap Park
Pleasanton KS

MAILING ADDRESS:
P.O. Box 137
Pleasanton KS 66075

(913) 352-8739

OPEN: winter, Sa, Su 1-5; summer, daily 1-5
COPYING FACILITIES: yes

MATERIALS SOLICITED: Materials pertaining to the history of Linn County and its residents.

HOLDINGS:
Total volume: 40 l.f.; 1,000 photographs; 3 file cabinets
Inclusive dates: 1850 -
Description: Records of Potosi Township, 1870-1960; photographs of Linn County scenes and residents; and a notebook of the records of the local Old Settlers organization.

RUSSELL

KS774-690
Russell County Historical Society, Inc.
Fossil Station Museum
331 Kansas Street
Russell KS 67665

(913) 483-3637

OPEN: May 31 - Sept. 1, M-F 10-5, Sa, Su 1-5; rest of year by appointment only
COPYING FACILITIES: no
MATERIALS SOLICITED: Photographs or genealogy pertaining to Russell County.

HOLDINGS:
Total volume: 55 drawers
Inclusive dates: 1872 - 1938
Description: Russell County family history file, 1872-1938, compiled by the Work Projects Administration and covering marriages, births, and deaths; and courthouse records, 1872-1927, including road tax rolls, abstract records, township officer records, and warrant records.

ST. PAUL

KS819-720
St. Francis Monastery
Papers
St. Francis Rectory
St. Paul KS 66771

no telephone

SEE: Hamer.

Questionnaire not returned.

SALINA

KS833-440
Kansas Wesleyan University
Memorial Library
Wesleyan Archives
100 East Claflin
Salina KS 67401

(913) 827-5541, Ext. 298

OPEN: M-Th 8-10, F 8-5, Sa 1-5, Su 2-10, initial appointment only M-F 8-5; summer hours vary; closed holidays
COPYING FACILITIES: yes
MATERIALS SOLICITED: Kansas Wesleyan University records, papers of faculty members, and records of student organizations. Will also accept other materials related to University history.

HOLDINGS:
Total volume: 185 l.f.
Inclusive dates: 1886 -
Description: Historical and non-current records of Kansas Wesleyan University, including account books, business and financial records and correspondence, and personal papers of faculty.

SEE: Hinding.

SHAWNEE MISSION

KS850-720
The Smoky Hill Railway Museum and Historical Society, Inc.
The Kansas City Railroad Museum
Shawnee Mission KS

MAILING ADDRESS:
P.O. Box 124
Shawnee Mission KS 66201

(816) 761-4494

OPEN: Sa, Su 1-5; closed other days
ACCESS: advance arrangements required
COPYING FACILITIES: no
MATERIALS SOLICITED: Materials relating to railroading in the Midwest.

HOLDINGS:
Total volume: 10 c.f.
Inclusive dates: 1900 -
Description: Railroad records including depot information, time tables, rules, train orders, maps, diagrams of engines and cars, pictures, and descriptions of rebuilding steam engines.

TOPEKA

KS878-200
Episcopal Diocese of Kansas
Diocesan Office
830 S.W. Polk
Topeka KS 66612

(913) 235-9255

OPEN: M-F 8:30-4:30; closed weekends and holidays
ACCESS: appointment required
COPYING FACILITIES: yes

HOLDINGS:
Total volume: 175 l.f.
Inclusive dates: 1837 -
Description: Materials relating to the Episcopal church in Kansas, including bishops' papers, organization records, parish registers, and other papers.

SEE: NUCMC, 1969.

SEE: Hinding.

KS878-430
Kansas State Historical Society
120 West Tenth Street
Topeka KS 66612

(913) 296-3251

OPEN: M-F 8-5; closed weekends and holidays
ACCESS: identification and registration required
COPYING FACILITIES: yes

MATERIALS SOLICITED: Manuscripts, photographs, and maps relating to the past and present history of Kansas and Kansans, including papers of individuals, businesses, churches, associations, and other organizations. Records of state, county, and municipal government agencies. Will also accept items pertaining to the western U.S. and westward expansion.

HOLDINGS:
Total volume: 12,500 c.f.; 140,000 photographs; 8,600 maps; 4,900 rolls of microfilm
Inclusive dates: 1800 -
Description: Papers relating to individuals, businesses, churches, organizations, and events in Kansas and the Midwest; westward migration and territorial expansion; and the Civil War. Included in the holdings of the Manuscript Department are correspondence and payroll records of the Atchison, Topeka and Santa Fe Railway and its predecessors.

Papers of Frederick Funston, Lucy B. Johnston, Alf M. Landon, Isaac McCoy, the New England Emigrant Aid Company, Theodore Schellenberg, Eugene F. Ware, and the St. Louis Superintendency of the Office of Indian Affairs; photographs of Kansas, the central plains, and the western U.S.; manuscript maps of Kansas and the West; and microfilm copies of records and papers of individuals, churches and businesses in private hands.

The Department of Archives holds records of the Supreme Court, Board of Agriculture, Office of the Governor, Insurance Department, Secretary of State, and other State agencies, as well as original State and territorial censuses and enumerations, territorial records, and some county and municipal records. The society's library also holds a small collection of manuscript materials, primarily genealogical in nature.

SEE: Hamer; NUCMC, 1959-62, 65, 77.

SEE: Novotny; Krichmar; Paszek; Parkinson; Allard, Crawley, and Edmison; Robbins; Hinding; Svoboda and Dunning.

SEE ALSO: Walter Schatz, ed., *Directory of Afro-American Resources* (Bowker, 1970); Richard C. Davis, *North American Forest History: A Guide to Archives and Manuscripts in the United States and Canada* (Clio Books, 1977); Eugene Donald Decker, *A Selected, Annotated Bibliography of Sources in the Kansas State Historical Society Pertaining to Kansas in the Civil War* (Kansas State Teachers College, 1961); guides to microfilmed collections available from the Society.

KS878-520
The Menninger Foundation
Division of Museums and Archives
5800 W. 6th Street
Topeka KS

MAILING ADDRESS:
Box 829
Topeka KS 66601

(913) 273-7500

OPEN: M-F 8:30-5 by appointment only; closed weekends and holidays
COPYING FACILITIES: yes
MATERIALS SOLICITED: Materials relating to American psychiatry. Will also accept materials in such related fields as psychology, social work, and occupational therapy.

HOLDINGS:
Total volume: 1,100 l.f.
Inclusive dates: late 19th century -
Description: Materials focusing on the history of the Menninger Foundation and the Menninger family. There are also materials relating to figures in the field of mental health, such as Clifford Beers, Emil Oberholzer, Ugo Cerletti, and Dorothea Dix; records of such organizations as the Group for the Advancement of Psychiatry; 1,500 audio tapes of lectures by such people as Anna Freud, Aldous Huxley, Karl Menninger, W. C. Menninger, Margaret Mead, Konrad Lorenz, and Gregory Zilboorg; and a photograph collection.

SEE: Hinding.

KS878-880
Washburn University of Topeka
Mabee Library
Congregational Collection and
    Washburn Archives
1700 College
Topeka KS 66621

(913) 295-6479

OPEN: M-Th 8-11, F 8-5, Sa 10-4, Su 2-11; irregular hours when University is not in session; closed holidays
COPYING FACILITIES: yes
MATERIALS SOLICITED: Records of church membership or financial transactions; minutes of church meetings; family records; correspondence; other manuscripts dealing with history of local churches in Kansas and Oklahoma as well as State church organizations, all of the United Church of Christ. Will also accept journals reporting early Kansas church history and sermons and speeches by church leaders in the United Church of Christ.

HOLDINGS:
Total volume: 2,000 items; 5 file cabinets
Inclusive dates: 1850 -
Description: A collection of local and State church records and miscellaneous manuscripts relating to the early history of midwestern churches and missions, gathered for the Kansas-Oklahoma Conference, United Church of Christ.
Included are miscellaneous materials pertaining to the founding, history, and continuous operation of Washburn University. A special collection relates to graphic designer Bradbury Thompson and the publication of the Washburn Bible.

SEE: Hinding.

ULYSSES

KS892-280
Grant County Historical Society
Grant County Museum
300 East Oklahoma
Ulysses KS

MAILING ADDRESS:
P.O. Box 906
Ulysses KS 67880

(316) 356-3009

OPEN: Tu-Su 1-5; closed Mondays, Thanksgiving, and Christmas Eve through New Year's
COPYING FACILITIES: yes
MATERIALS SOLICITED: Diaries, letters, genealogies, and photographs pertaining to Grant County.

HOLDINGS:
Total volume: 12 l.f.; 2 file drawers
Inclusive dates: 1887 -
Description: Materials relating chiefly to Grant County, including an 1887 census, biographies of early settlers, tax rolls, 1888 - 1900, pioneer reminiscences, cemetery records, photographs, and diaries.

WELLINGTON

KS934-120
Chisholm Trail Museum
502 North Washington Avenue
Wellington KS 67152

(316) 326-3820, 2174

OPEN: summer, Sa, Su, Tu-Th 2-4; winter, Sa, Su 2-4; closed other times except by prior arrangement
COPYING FACILITIES: no
MATERIALS SOLICITED: Materials peculiar to Sumner County, KS. Will also accept genealogical materials.

HOLDINGS:
Total volume: 5,000 items
Inclusive dates: 1839 -
Description: Diaries, logbooks, letters, wedding announcements, school, church, and public records, photographs, and other materials relating to the history of Sumner County and its inhabitants.

WICHITA

KS948-240
Friends University
Library
Quaker Collection
2100 University Avenue
Wichita KS 67213

(316) 261-5800, Ext. 720

OPEN: M-Th 8-10, F 8-4, Su 5-10; closed Saturdays, holidays, and some days during school vacations
COPYING FACILITIES: yes
MATERIALS SOLICITED: Quaker records, and personal diaries, letters, and accounts of Quakers, especially of the Great Plains area; unpublished manuscripts of Quaker historical import; and

Quaker genealogical materials including family Bibles. Will also accept Garfield University material, and early photographs of Kansas Quaker activities and personnel and of Friends University.

HOLDINGS:
Total volume: 100 l.f.
Inclusive dates: late 1700's -
Description: Records of the Kansas Yearly Meeting of Friends, both evangelical and conservative, and records of monthly meetings; collections of manuscripts, diaries, and reminiscences of pioneers; papers concerning missions and Quaker work among American Indians; unpublished poetry of Quaker Kansans (including Henry Coffin Fellows, Asa Dillon, and Juliet Reeve); and research about the Quakers and Daniel Defoe and other English writers.

KS948-870
Wichita Historical Museum
204 South Main
Wichita KS 67202

(316) 265-9314

OPEN: Tu-Su 1-5; closed Mondays and holidays
ACCESS: prior arrangements necessary
COPYING FACILITIES: yes
MATERIALS SOLICITED: Manuscripts and documents relating to the settlement and development of the city of Wichita and the immediate area.

HOLDINGS:
Total volume: 15 file drawers
Inclusive dates: 1865 -
Description: Photographs, diaries, and other documents relating to the history of Wichita.

SEE: Hinding.

KS948-880
Wichita Public Library
Reference Department
223 South Main Street
Wichita KS 67202

(316) 262-0611

OPEN: M-Th 8:30-9, F, Sa 8:30-5:30, Su 1-5; closed Christmas, New Year's, and Memorial Day
COPYING FACILITIES: yes

HOLDINGS:
Total volume: 1,800 items
Inclusive dates: 18th century -
Description: Literary manuscripts by Charles B. Driscoll and Paul I. Wellman, and a ship's log, a diary of a Spanish corsair, and some other papers in Driscoll's piracy collection.

SEE: Hamer (as Wichita City Library).

SEE: Hinding.

KS948-890
Wichita State University
Library
Special Collections
1845 Fairmount
Wichita KS 67208

(316) 689-3590

OPEN: M-F 8-5; closed weekends and holidays
COPYING FACILITIES: yes
MATERIALS SOLICITED: Congressional papers, materials regarding local and regional history, aviation history, 19th-century anti-slavery materials, and 20th-century radical organizations' materials.

HOLDINGS:
Total volume: 588 l.f.
Inclusive dates: 1760 -
Description: Over 60 manuscript collections on a wide variety of subjects, including several collections of Congressional papers, letters and papers of William Lloyd Garrison, literary manuscripts, papers of prominent Wichitans, and some aircraft drawings.

SEE: Schatz; Allard, Crawley, and Edmison; Robbins; Hinding.

WINFIELD

KS962-120
Cowley County Historical Society
Museum and Library
1011 Mansfield
Winfield KS

MAILING ADDRESS:
1714 East 11th
Winfield KS 67156

(316) 221-9736, 4141

OPEN: Sa, Su 2-5; closed other days
COPYING FACILITIES: no
MATERIALS SOLICITED: Northern Cowley County events and people. Will also accept selected items concerning Kansas.

HOLDINGS:
Total volume: not specified
Inclusive dates: 1870 -
Description: Materials relating to the history of northern Cowley County, especially Winfield, including photographs, diaries, family histories, letters, business records, newspaper accounts, and oral history interviews relating to families.

KS962-730
Southwestern College
Memorial Library
100 N. College Street
Winfield KS 67156

(316) 221-4150, Ext. 225

OPEN: Su 5-9:30, M-Th 8-9:30, F 8-4, Sa 9-1; closed holidays; summer hours M-F 9-4
COPYING FACILITIES: yes

HOLDINGS:
Total volume: not specified
Inclusive dates: 1890 -
Description: Materials pertaining to the history of Southwestern College, including about 150 photographs and some oral history tapes.

KS962-800
United Methodist Church
Kansas West Conference
Commission on Archives and History
Southwestern College
Winfield KS 67156

(316) 221-4150

OPEN: by appointment only
COPYING FACILITIES: yes
MATERIALS SOLICITED: Anything relating to the Methodist church and Evangelical United Brethren church in Kansas, specifically within the present Kansas West Conference. Will also accept materials in Methodist and Kansas church history and general Evangelical United Brethren church history.

HOLDINGS:
Total volume: 57 c.f.
Inclusive dates: 1856 -
Description: Material relating to local United Methodist churches in Kansas; correspondence and autobiographical information on United Methodist ministers in Kansas; files of the Board of Missions, Central Kansas Conference; manuscripts and memorabilia of Roy L. Smith; and the Southwestern College archives.

SEE: Hamer (as Historical Society of the Central Kansas Conference); NUCMC, 1968.

SEE: Hinding; Svoboda and Dunning.

KENTUCKY

Since 1967, the Public Records Division, Kentucky Department for Libraries and Archives, Frankfort, has directed a statewide program for preserving local public records. Although local government officials are responsible for maintaining their permanently valuable records, the Division has physical custody of approximately 50,000 cubic feet of records and 15,000 reels of microfilm from all of Kentucky's 120 counties, with a heavy concentration on 19th- and 20th-century materials.

Filming was done by the Church of Jesus Christ of Latter-day Saints and the Division's micrographics laboratory. Indexes are available to this film.

Local government record series include judicial, real estate, fiduciary, tax and administrative records. Among other repositories in the state, the Kentucky Historical Society in Frankfort has 3,600 reels of microfilm of local public records and the Department of Special Collections, King Library, University of Kentucky, houses 7,775 reels of similar material. Finding aids to these microfilmed records are available at the institutions.

ASHLAND

KY2A-80
Boyd County Historical Society
Ashland Public Library
1740 Central Avenue
Ashland KY 41101

(606) 329-0090

OPEN: M, Tu, Th, F 9-9, W, Sa 9-6; closed Sundays
COPYING FACILITIES: yes
MATERIALS SOLICITED: Materials concerning the history of Ashland, Boyd County, surrounding counties of eastern Kentucky, local corporate history, river traffic on the Ohio and Big Sandy rivers, genealogy, and family history.

HOLDINGS:
Total volume: 20 c.f.
Inclusive dates: 1850 - 1975
Description: Manuscripts and photographs documenting the development of Ashland and its iron, steel, coal, and lumber industries, river traffic on the Big Sandy and Ohio rivers, local floods, and

the history of eastern and northeastern Kentucky.

BARBOURVILLE

KY24-800
Union College
Abigail E. Weeks Memorial Library
Barbourville KY 40906

(606) 546-4151, Ext. 243

OPEN: M-Th 8-10, F 8-5, Sa 8-4, Su 6-10
ACCESS: with Librarian's permission
COPYING FACILITIES: yes
MATERIALS SOLICITED: Material dealing with Union College, Barbourville, Abraham Lincoln, and the Civil War.

HOLDINGS:
Total volume: 6 c.f.
Inclusive dates: 1860's - 1979
Description: Material dealing with Abraham Lincoln and Union College.

BEATTYVILLE

KY3S-480
Lee County Public Library
Beattyville KY

MAILING ADDRESS:
P.O. Box V
Beattyville KY 41311

(606) 464-8014

OPEN: M-F 9-5, Sa 11-5; closed Sundays
COPYING FACILITIES: yes
MATERIALS SOLICITED: Materials dealing with the history of Lee County and surrounding counties.

HOLDINGS:
Total volume: 0.4 c.f.
Inclusive dates: 1885 -
Description: Holdings dealing largely with genealogy, family history, county and regional history, and the history of church groups and associations.

BEDFORD

KY42-800
Trimble County Library
Main and Church Streets
Bedford KY

MAILING ADDRESS:
Box 212
Bedford KY 40006

(502) 255-7362

OPEN: M-F 9:30-5, Sa noon-5; closed Sundays
COPYING FACILITIES: yes
MATERIALS SOLICITED: Materials concerning Bedford and Trimble County.

HOLDINGS:
Total volume: 17 items
Inclusive dates: 1900 -
Description: Trimble County materials, including oral history recordings, scrapbooks on obituaries and the 1937 flood, and a manuscript of family history, containing land deeds, bills, receipts, photographs, correspondence, local histories, and maps.

BENTON

KY5M-520
Marshall County Public Library
1003 Poplar Street
Benton KY 42025

(502) 527-9969

OPEN: M 9-8, Tu-Sa 9-5; closed Sundays
COPYING FACILITIES: yes
MATERIALS SOLICITED: Materials dealing with the history of the Marshall County area.

HOLDINGS:
Total volume: 0.6 c.f.; 4 vols.; 23 items
Inclusive dates: 1861 -
Description: Genealogical source data and other materials of local interest, including histories of the Library and a copy of a Civil War diary by a Marshall County native who served in the Confederate army.

BEREA

KY80-70
Berea College
Appalachian Museum
Berea KY

MAILING ADDRESS:
C.P.O. Box 2298
Berea KY 40404

(606) 986-9341, Ext. 520

OPEN: M-F 10-5; closed weekends and holidays
COPYING FACILITIES: no
MATERIALS SOLICITED: Materials relating to the culture and history of the southern Appalachian mountain region.

HOLDINGS:
Total volume: not specified
Inclusive dates: 1750 - 1930
Description: Photographs, correspondence, commercial records, ledgers, diaries, oral history tapes, relating to the lifestyle of the people of the southern Appalachian region.

KY80-90

Berea College
Library
Special Collections
Berea KY 40404

(606) 986-9341, Ext. 289, 290

OPEN: M-F 9:30-4:30; closed weekends and College vacations
COPYING FACILITIES: yes
MATERIALS SOLICITED: History and culture of the Appalachian region; history of Berea College and the Berea community. Will also accept small collections of general historical interest, such as Civil War letters.

HOLDINGS:
Total volume: 600 l.f.
Inclusive dates: 1840 -
Description: Materials relating to the antislavery movement in the United States and the founding of Berea College, the history of the College and its interracial and Appalachian commitments, and the history and culture of the Appalachian region.

SEE: Hamer.

SEE: Robbins; Hinding.

SEE ALSO: Walter Schatz, ed., *Directory of Afro-American Resources* (Bowker, 1970).

Guides to several collections have been published by the College.

BOONEVILLE

KY9U-600

Owsley County Public Library
Booneville KY

MAILING ADDRESS:
P.O. Box 176
Booneville KY 41314

(606) 593-5700

OPEN: M-Sa 9-5; closed Sundays
COPYING FACILITIES: yes
MATERIALS SOLICITED: Materials on local and family history and genealogy.

HOLDINGS:
Total volume: 1.5 c.f.
Inclusive dates: not specified
Description: County cemetery records.

BOWLING GREEN

KY94-845

Western Kentucky University
Archives
Helm-Cravens Library
Bowling Green KY 42101

(502) 745-4793

OPEN: M-F 8-4; closed weekends and holidays
COPYING FACILITIES: no
MATERIALS SOLICITED: Pictures and other materials pertaining to the University or its antecedents.

HOLDINGS:
Total volume: 1,000 l.f.
Inclusive dates: 1884 -
Description: Materials relating to the University and its predecessor institutions, including correspondence of presidents, financial records, yearbooks, college newspapers, minutes of college and department organizations, faculty senate proceedings, scrapbooks, photographs, slides, bulletins, catalogs, maps, building plans, architectural blueprints, and manuscripts and correspondence of faculty and others affiliated with the University.

KY96-850

Western Kentucky University
Folk-lore, Folk-life and Oral History Archives
Helm-Cravens Library
Bowling Green KY 42101

(502) 745-3951

OPEN: M-F 8-4:30; closed weekends and holidays
COPYING FACILITIES: yes
MATERIALS SOLICITED: Folklore and oral history of Kentucky. Will also accept folklore and oral history of surrounding geographic areas, and any other folk or music materials relevant to the collection.

HOLDINGS:
Total volume: 2,100 tapes; 150 l.f.
Inclusive dates: 1950 -
Description: Tapes of local performers of traditional songs and music, a large collection of folk songs, oral history recordings and transcriptions, and manuscripts of field collection projects performed by students and faculty. The collections cover folklore, country music, and traditional music, mainly in Kentucky and the surrounding region.

SEE ALSO: 'Research Guide to Western Kentucky University Folk-lore and Folk-life Archive,' *Academic Services Library Bulletin* 8 (Western Kentucky Univ., 1974); Alan M. Meckler and Ruth McMullin, comps., *Oral History Collections* (Bowker, 1975).

KY96-870

Western Kentucky University
Kentucky Library
Bowling Green KY 42101

(502) 745-2592

OPEN: M, W, Th, F 8-4:30, Tu 8-9, Sa 9-4:30; closed Sundays and holidays
COPYING FACILITIES: yes
MATERIALS SOLICITED: Family papers and other manuscripts dealing chiefly with south central Kentucky, with emphasis on the Civil War, Mammoth Cave, and Shakers of South Union, KY.

HOLDINGS:
Total volume: 702 l.f.
Inclusive dates: 1715 -
Description: Chiefly 19th and 20th century materials, relating mainly to Bowling Green, Warren County, and south central Kentucky. Included are papers of politicians, authors, editors, lawyers, and clergy; papers of many Kentucky families and much genealogical material; personal papers pertaining to the Civil War, the Spanish-American War, and World Wars I and II; business and church records; papers of the South Union Society of Believers in South Union, KY (1800-1916); a land grant collection; legal records of Warren, Logan, and Nelson counties; and the Ellis Collection of about 3,500 photographs of steamboats and associated subjects on the Ohio and Mississippi rivers.

SEE: Hamer; NUCMC, 1970-72, 74, 76-77, 80.

SEE: Davis; Hinding; Novotny; Parkinson; Paszek; Robbins; Schatz.

BRANDENBERG

KY98-520

Meade County Public Library
Library Place
Brandenburg KY 40108

(502) 422-2094

OPEN: M 8:30-5, Tu, W 8:30-4:30, Th 8:30-4:30, 7-9, F 9-5, Sa 10-4; closed Sundays
COPYING FACILITIES: yes
MATERIALS SOLICITED: Genealogical data on Meade County and surrounding areas.

HOLDINGS:
Total volume: 4 c.f.
Inclusive dates: 1974 -
Description: Meade County genealogical files, family charts, clippings, microfilmed county court records of marriages since 1824, and an index to the marriage records.

CAMPBELLSVILLE

KY126-120
Campbellsville College
Library
Campbellsville KY 42718

(502) 465-8158

OPEN: M-Th 8-10, F 8-5, Sa 9-5; closed
   Sundays and holidays
COPYING FACILITIES: yes
MATERIALS SOLICITED: Materials relating
   to Kentucky authors, the State of Kentucky, education in the United States,
   and the history of Campbellsville College.

HOLDINGS:
   Total volume: 100 items
   Inclusive dates: 1790 -
   Description: A growing genealogical
   collection on Kentucky; an obituary in-
   dex (1953-65) to the Central Kentucky
   News Journal; minutes of the Russell
   Creek Association of Baptists and Taylor
   County Baptist Association; church his-
   tories in the area.

KY126-760
Taylor County Historical Society
Old Clerk's Office
Courthouse Square
Campbellsville KY

MAILING ADDRESS:
P.O. Box 14
Campbellsville KY 42718

no telephone

OPEN: third Tuesday evenings of
   alternate months or by appointment
COPYING FACILITIES: no
MATERIALS SOLICITED: Taylor County
   items.

HOLDINGS:
   Total volume: 9.2 c.f.
   Inclusive dates: 1815 -
   Description: Court records, photographs, personal items, copies of store
   ledgers, Historical Society materials,
   cemetery records, genealogical files, and
   other historical documents of
   Campbellsville and Taylor County.

KY126-770
Taylor County Public Library
205 North Columbia Avenue
Campbellsville KY 42718

(502) 465-2562

OPEN: M-Sa 9-5; closed Sundays
COPYING FACILITIES: yes
MATERIALS SOLICITED: Will accept material relating to the genealogy and history of Taylor County.

HOLDINGS:
   Total volume: 3.5 c.f.
   Inclusive dates: 1900 -
   Description: Genealogical and historical data relating to Taylor County and an
   oral history collection concerning local
   history and related topics.

CARLISLE

KY13U-560
Nicholas County Memorial Library
223 Broadway
Carlisle KY 40311

(606) 289-5595

OPEN: M 11:30-7:30, Tu, F-Sa 9-5;
   closed Wednesdays and Sundays
COPYING FACILITIES: yes
MATERIALS SOLICITED: Will accept materials relating to local history and genealogy.

HOLDINGS:
   Total volume: 0.5 c.f.
   Inclusive dates: 1860 -
   Description: Historical photographs of
   Carlisle and Nicholas County.

CARROLLTON

KY13Y-120
Port William Historical Society
Masterson House
Highway 42
Carrollton KY 41008

(502) 732-4287

OPEN: Monday 11:30-7, Tu-Sa 9:30-5;
   closed Sundays
COPYING FACILITIES: yes
MATERIALS SOLICITED: Will accept ma-
   terials relating to the history of Carroll
   County.

HOLDINGS:
   Total volume: 0.6 c.f.
   Inclusive dates: 1816 - 1979
   Description: Oral history tapes, Historical Society records, papers or records collected by Society members, subject files
   of papers and clippings, and photographs.

CLINTON

KY17S-320
Hickman County Public Library
209 Mayfield Road
Clinton KY 42031

no telephone

OPEN: M 6-8, Tu-Sa 2-5; closed Sundays
COPYING FACILITIES: no
MATERIALS SOLICITED: Will accept ma-
   terials on Hickman County.

HOLDINGS:
   Total volume: 0.2 c.f.; 18 items
   Inclusive dates: 1962 -
   Description: Local history clippings,
   correspondence relating to Hickman
   County's sesquicentennial celebration in
   1971, and an oral history collection describing life in the area in the early 20th
   century.

COVINGTON

KY176-160
Diocese of Covington
Archives
1140 Madison Avenue
Covington KY 41012

(606) 291-4240

OPEN: by appointment only
ACCESS: items made available to
   individual researchers at the discretion
   of the Archivist
COPYING FACILITIES: yes
MATERIALS SOLICITED: Manuscripts and
   photographs pertaining to the history
   of the Catholic church in eastern Kentucky. Will also accept similar materials pertaining to the history of the
   Catholic church in the United States,
   particularly in Kentucky and Cincinnati, OH.

HOLDINGS:
   Total volume: 170 l.f.; 150 vols.
   Inclusive dates: 1827 -
   Description: Materials relating to the
   Diocese, including episcopal correspon-
   dence, personnel records, parish reports,
   and financial ledgers, dating primarily
   from 1853 to date.

KY176-720
Benedictine Sisters of Covington,
   Kentucky
St. Walburg Convent
Community Archives
2500 Amsterdam Road
Covington KY 41016

(606) 331-6333, 6324, 6771

OPEN: by appointment only
COPYING FACILITIES: yes
MATERIALS SOLICITED: Any material applicable to the life, work, and spiritual-
   ity of the Benedictine Sisters of
   Covington, Kentucky, since 1859. Will
   also accept materials relating to parishes, missions, schools, and centers
   staffed by the Benedictine Sisters.

HOLDINGS:
   Total volume: 150 l.f.
   Inclusive dates: 1859 -
   Description: Archives of the Benedictine Sisters of St. Walburg Convent, both
   as individuals and as an institution, including material on their foundations,
   work, activities, and spiritual life.

SEE ALSO: Indices and catalogue available at the institution.

KY188-440
Kenton County Public Library
5th and Scott Streets
Covington KY 41011

(606) 491-7610

OPEN: M-Th 10-8, F 10-6, Sa 10-5;
   closed Sundays and holidays
COPYING FACILITIES: yes
MATERIALS SOLICITED: Materials relating
   to Kenton County, northern Kentucky,
   and Kentucky.

HOLDINGS:
Total volume: not specified
Inclusive dates: 19th century -
Description: Materials relating chiefly to Kenton County and northern Kentucky, including city ordinance and record books of Covington, biographies, photographs, church and cemetery records, oral history interviews, maps, genealogical source data, scrapbooks, and research papers.

CYNTHIANA

KY189-320
Cynthiana Public Library
Cynthiana KY

MAILING ADDRESS:
Box 217
Cynthiana KY 41031

(606) 234-4881

OPEN: M, W, F, 9-5, Tu, Th 9-9, Sa 9-1; closed Sundays
COPYING FACILITIES: yes
MATERIALS SOLICITED: Materials relating to the history of Cynthiana and Harrison County, KY.

HOLDINGS:
Total volume: 3.2 c.f.
Inclusive dates: 1857 -
Description: Genealogical and family history records, histories prepared for the U.S. Bicentennial celebration, papers presented by members of the Inquisitor's Club, scrapbooks, and ledgers.

DANVILLE

KY192-200
Kentucky Medical Association
McDowell House and Apothecary Shop
125 South Second Street
Danville KY 40422

(606) 236-2804

OPEN: M-Sa 10-4, Su 2-4; closed Mondays Nov. - Feb. and holidays
USER FEES: $1.50 admission fee
COPYING FACILITIES: yes
MATERIALS SOLICITED: Any materials relating to physician Ephraim McDowell.

HOLDINGS:
Total volume: 7 items
Inclusive dates: mid-18th century - mid-19th century
Description: 5 letters by or to Dr. Ephraim McDowell and members of his family, discussing both personal and medical matters, and 2 McDowell family Bibles, with genealogical records.

DIXON

KY22W-920
Webster County Public Library
300 East Leiper Street
Dixon KY 42409

(502) 639-9171

OPEN: M-Sa 10-5; closed Sundays and holidays
COPYING FACILITIES: yes
MATERIALS SOLICITED: Will accept materials on Webster County history.

HOLDINGS:
Total volume: 5.7 c.f.; 5 vols.
Inclusive dates: 1892 -
Description: Materials relating to Dixon and Webster County history and people, including photographs of local authors Cale Young and Laban Lacy Rice, histories of the Poole Church of Christ, Onton School, and Webster County, and a report on Webster County folklore compiled by students at Webster County High School.

EMINENCE

KY230-320
Henry County Library and
Henry County Historical Society
Eminence Terrace
Eminence KY 40019

(502) 845-5682

OPEN: M-W, F, Sa 9-5, Th 9-9; closed weekends
COPYING FACILITIES: yes
MATERIALS SOLICITED: Genealogical and other materials relating to Eminence and Henry County.

HOLDINGS:
Total volume: 7.5 l.f.; 30 items
Inclusive dates: 1858 -
Description: Motion pictures and photographs relating to Henry County and Eminence events and residents, business ledger books of Pleasureville, KY, and scrapbooks relating to Henry County, the local Daughters of the American Revolution, and the Homemakers Club. Also held are the Henry County Historical Society's genealogical files relating to county families, institutions, churches, and cemeteries, including family charts, newsclippings, photographs, and correspondence.

KY230-440
Kentuckiana Regional Library
Eminence Terrace
Eminence KY 40019

(502) 845-7059

OPEN: M-F 8-4:30; closed weekends
COPYING FACILITIES: yes
MATERIALS SOLICITED: Materials about the Library and local history.

HOLDINGS:
Total volume: 3 l.f.; 1 vol.
Inclusive dates: 1925 -
Description: Records of the Library, including correspondence, press releases, memoranda, annual reports, and financial statements concerning the development of the library system in Henry County. There are also oral history reminiscences of local residents and a scrapbook of the Bland Ballard Chapter of the Daughters of the American Revolution.

FLORENCE

KY240-80
Boone County Public Library
7425 U.S. Route 42
Florence KY 41042

(606) 371-6222

OPEN: M, W, F, Sa 9-6, Tu, Th 9-4; closed Sundays
COPYING FACILITIES: yes
MATERIALS SOLICITED: Will accept materials relating to the history of Florence and Boone County.

HOLDINGS:
Total volume: 1 c.f.
Inclusive dates: 1876 -
Description: Boone County history materials.

FORT CAMPBELL

KY250-160
Army 101st Airborne Division and Fort Campbell
Don F. Pratt Museum
Wickam Hall
Fort Campbell KY 42223

(502) 798-3215, 4986

OPEN: M-F 12:30-4:30, Sa-Su 1-4:30; closed Christmas Eve, Christmas, New Year's Day
ACCESS: Researcher should notify the Museum at least one day in advance of visit so that materials will be available when he or she arrives.
COPYING FACILITIES: no
MATERIALS SOLICITED: Materials dealing with the history of the 101st Airborne Division, 12th and 14th Armored Divisions, 11th Airborne Division, and Fort Campbell. Will also accept any materials dealing with World War II, the Korean War, and the Vietnam War, with a special emphasis on airborne, airmobile, and air assault operations.

HOLDINGS:
Total volume: 173 l.f.
Inclusive dates: 1942 -
Description: A collection of photographs, slides, and taped interviews dealing primarily with the 101st Airborne Division from World War II to the present. Included are personal papers, documents, and unit histories about the 101st Airborne Division, 11th Airborne Division, and Fort Campbell.

FORT KNOX

KY272-45
Army, Armor School
Library
Building 2369
Fort Knox KY 40121

(502) 624-6231

OPEN: M-F 9-4:30; closed weekends
COPYING FACILITIES: yes

HOLDINGS:
> *Total volume:* 181 c.f.
> *Inclusive dates:* 1942 - 1974
> *Description:* Student papers written at
the Armor School, after action reports
concerning World War II and the Korean
War, and historical documents on microfilm concerning World War II.

KY272-635
Patton Museum of Cavalry and
  Armor
Fayette Avenue near Chaffee Avenue
Fort Knox KY

MAILING ADDRESS:
P.O. Box 208
Fort Knox KY 40121-0208

(502) 624-3812

OPEN: M-F 9-4; weekends and holidays
  10-4:30; May 1 - Sept. 30, open until 6
  p.m.
COPYING FACILITIES: yes
MATERIALS SOLICITED: Items of historical interest relating to armor and
  mechanized cavalry, Fort Knox, and
  General George S. Patton.

HOLDINGS:
> *Total volume:* 80 c.f.
> *Inclusive dates:* 1870's -
> *Description:* Photographs, scrapbooks,
after action reports, manuscripts, maps,
and private military papers of Generals I.
D. White, Harry Johnson, and Harold
Blakely. There are also materials documenting the development of tank warfare, Fort Knox, and the career of General George S. Patton.

FORT MITCHELL

KY280-760
Thomas More College
Archives
Fort Mitchell KY 41017

(606) 341-5800

OPEN: by appointment only
COPYING FACILITIES: yes
MATERIALS SOLICITED: Non-current
  records of Thomas More College and
  other materials pertaining to its history
  and development.

HOLDINGS:
> *Total volume:* 100 l.f.
> *Inclusive dates:* 1931 -
> *Description:* Non-current records of the
presidents and departments of Thomas
More College.

FRANKFORT

KY288-395
Kentucky Arts Council
Berry Hill
Frankfort KY 40601

(502) 564-3757

OPEN: M-F 8-4:30; closed weekends and
  holidays
COPYING FACILITIES: yes

HOLDINGS:
> *Total volume:* 25 c.f.
> *Inclusive dates:* 1966 -
> *Description:* Inactive program file
records, a grant applications logbook, and
videotapes of artists in school.

KY288-425
Kentucky Department of Library and
  Archives
Division of Archives and Records
  Management
Box 537
300 Coffee Tree Road
Frankfort KY 40602

(502) 875-7000

OPEN: M-Sa 8-4:30; closed Sundays and
  holidays
COPYING FACILITIES: yes
MATERIALS SOLICITED: 18th - 20th century public records of the Commonwealth of Kentucky and its subdivisions. Will also accept other public
  records and private records relating to
  State public record holdings.

HOLDINGS:
> *Total volume:* 70,000 c.f.; 15,000
> reels
> *Inclusive dates:* 1784 - 1960
> *Description:* State and local archives of
Kentucky, including material on political,
economic, scientific and social topics.

SEE: Davis; Parkinson; Hinding.

SEE ALSO: Inventories to many collections
have been published by the institution.

KY288-440
Kentucky Historical Society
200 Broadway
Frankfort KY

MAILING ADDRESS:
P.O. Box H
Frankfort KY 40601

(502) 564-3016

OPEN: daily 8-4:30; closed Christmas
  and Easter
COPYING FACILITIES: yes
MATERIALS SOLICITED: Family records,
  political oral history collections and
  other significant manuscripts. Will also
  accept any significant items dealing
  with Kentucky history.

HOLDINGS:
> *Total volume:* 3,000 collections
> *Inclusive dates:* 1700's -
> *Description:* Chiefly pre-20th century
materials relating to Kentucky, including
maps, account books, diaries, church,
military, land and tax records, family cor-

respondence, and papers relating to slavery. There are also the public papers of
Kentucky governors from 1792 to 1923,
consisting of official appointments, election returns, pardons and appeals for pardons, and other materials. Also included
are photographic and oral history collections.

SEE: Hamer; NUCMC, 1966, 72.

SEE: Novotny; Robbins; Hinding.

SEE ALSO: *Kentucky Historical Society Microfilm Catalog* (Kentucky Historical
  Society, 1975).

KY288-460
Kentucky State University
Blazer Library
Frankfort KY 40601

(502) 227-6852

OPEN: M-Th 8-10, F 8-4:30, Sa 9-4, Su
  2-8; closed holidays
COPYING FACILITIES: yes
MATERIALS SOLICITED: Afro-American
  and African history and culture. Also
  material about Kentucky State University and black history in Kentucky.

HOLDINGS:
> *Total volume:* 5,000 items
> *Inclusive dates:* 1880's -
> *Description:* Materials relating to Ken-
tucky State University, including records,
correspondence, and publications. There
are also holdings relating to the history of
black people in Kentucky and to Afro-
American and African history in general.

GEORGETOWN

KY304-280
Georgetown College
Cooke Memorial Library
Special Collections
Georgetown KY 40324

(502) 863-8046

OPEN: M-F 8:30-5; closed weekends and
  holidays
COPYING FACILITIES: yes
MATERIALS SOLICITED: Will accept materials on Kentucky, especially those relating to Georgetown College.

HOLDINGS:
> *Total volume:* 8 l.f.
> *Inclusive dates:* 1850 -
> *Description:* Materials pertaining to the
history of Georgetown College, and the
papers of George M. Spears, including
diaries and letters from several American
authors.

GRAYSON

KY310-440
Kentucky Christian College
Lusby Memorial Library
College and Landsdown
Grayson KY 41143

(606) 474-6613

OPEN: M-F 9-4; closed weekends
COPYING FACILITIES: yes

MATERIALS SOLICITED: Materials related to the College's history and the activities of its staff and graduates.

HOLDINGS:
Total volume: 3 c.f.
Inclusive dates: 1885 - 1978
Description: Photographs documenting the College's history and the activities of its faculty and students, as well as the work of early twentieth century evangelist R. B. Neal and the Gospel Dollar League in the eastern Kentucky mountains. Also held are papers relating to administrative and faculty activities of the College.

GREENSBURG

KY316-280

Green County Public Library
116 South Main Street
Greensburg KY 42743

(502) 932-7081

OPEN: M-Sa 9-5; closed Sundays
COPYING FACILITIES: yes
MATERIALS SOLICITED: Historical and genealogical records relating to Green County and the region.

HOLDINGS:
Total volume: 3 c.f.
Inclusive dates: 1960 -
Description: Local history and genealogy records for Green County and the surrounding area, as well as an oral history collection.

HARRODSBURG

KY352-320

Harrodsburg Historical Society Library
220 South Chiles Street
Harrodsburg KY

MAILING ADDRESS:
P.O. Box 316
Harrodsburg KY 40330

no telephone

OPEN: by appointment only
USER FEES: $2 per hour
COPYING FACILITIES: yes
MATERIALS SOLICITED: Family genealogical records. Will also accept materials relating to the history of Harrodsburg, Mercer County, and Kentucky in general.

HOLDINGS:
Total volume: 6 file drawers; 9 vols.
Inclusive dates: 1774 -
Description: Family files, genealogical records, and other materials relating to local history, and bound volumes of records of a local Shaker community.

SEE: Hinding; Robbins.

HODGENVILLE

KY358-40

Abraham Lincoln Birthplace National Historic Site
Route 1
Hodgenville KY 42748

(502) 358-3874

OPEN: daily 8-5; closed Christmas
COPYING FACILITIES: no
MATERIALS SOLICITED: Materials pertaining to the Lincoln family's association with the Sinking Spring Farm and to the building and development of the National historic site.

HOLDINGS:
Total volume: 3 c.f.; 3 vols; 370 items; 1 microfilm reel
Inclusive dates: 1808 -
Description: Correspondence concerning the Lincoln Farm Association, scrapbooks concerning the association and the historic site, lantern slides and other photographs documenting the history and construction of the historic site, and microfilmed records of the Lincoln farm.

KY358-480

La Rue County Public Library
201 Lincoln Boulevard
Hodgenville KY 42748

(502) 358-3851

OPEN: M-F 9-4:30, Sa 9-noon; closed Sundays
COPYING FACILITIES: no
MATERIALS SOLICITED: Material concerning Abraham Lincoln, Thomas Lincoln and his family, associates of the Lincoln family, the Lincoln Birthplace National Historic Site, and Hodgenville and La Rue County history.

HOLDINGS:
Total volume: 1.25 l.f.; 5 items; 9 vols.
Inclusive dates: 1921 - 1979
Description: A vertical file on Hodgenville and La Rue County, scrapbooks concerning the local area and the Abraham Lincoln Birthplace National Historic Site, oral history recordings, and information derived from county court records pertaining to the Lincoln family and its associations in the area.

HYDEN

KY37S-480

Leslie County Library
Hyden KY

MAILING ADDRESS:
P.O. Box 112
Hyden KY 41749

no telephone

OPEN: M-F 9-5, Sat 9-1; closed Sundays
COPYING FACILITIES: yes
MATERIALS SOLICITED: Materials relating to the history and culture of Leslie County and the surrounding region, as well as genealogical and family history data.

HOLDINGS:
Total volume: 0.4 c.f.
Inclusive dates: 1927 - 1979
Description: Two films, manuscript and oral history materials, and documents, relating to early Presbyterian churches and schools in Leslie County, early medical care in the county, and local and family history.

JACKSON

KY38U-80

Breathitt County Public Library
1024 College Avenue
Jackson KY 41339

(606) 666-5541

OPEN: M-F 8-4:30, Sa 9-3; closed Sundays
COPYING FACILITIES: yes
MATERIALS SOLICITED: Materials on genealogy and local history for the county and its environs.

HOLDINGS:
Total volume: 0.7 c.f.
Inclusive dates: 1774 -
Description: Transcriptions of local cemetery records and family histories.

KY38U-470

Lees Junior College
Library-Oral History Center
601 Jefferson Street
Jackson KY 41339

(606) 666-7521

OPEN: M-Th 8-9, F 8-4, Su 5-9; closed Saturdays and holidays
ACCESS: appointment required
COPYING FACILITIES: yes
MATERIALS SOLICITED: Information relating to the founding and early years of Lees Junior College, and records of early life in the local region.

HOLDINGS:
Total volume: 1,000 cassette tapes; 10 l.f.
Inclusive dates: 1950's -
Description: Oral history interviews with residents of eastern Kentucky, concentrating on local history and culture. A small collection of yearbooks, faculty newsletters, and other records of Lees Junior College also is included.

SEE: Parkinson.

SEE ALSO: *The Appalachian Oral History Project Union Catalog* (Appalachian Oral History Project, 1977).

JAMESTOWN

KY380-720

Russell County Public Library
N. Main Street
Jamestown KY

MAILING ADDRESS:
P.O. Box 246
Jamestown KY 42629

(502) 343-3545

OPEN: M-Sa 8-5; closed Sundays
COPYING FACILITIES: yes
MATERIALS SOLICITED: Material on local
history.

HOLDINGS:
Total volume: not specified
Inclusive dates: 1960 - 1979
Description: An oral history collection,
local history records, library scrapbooks,
and records of the Jamestown Business
and Professional Women's Club.

LA GRANGE

KY41E-160
Duerson - Oldham County Public
Library
106 East Jefferson Street
La Grange KY 40031

(502) 222-1133

OPEN: Tu, W, F, Sa 10-5, M, Th 10-9;
closed Sundays
COPYING FACILITIES: yes
MATERIALS SOLICITED: Local history and
genealogy, especially oral history.

HOLDINGS:
Total volume: 2 l.f.; 3 vols.; 38 items
Inclusive dates: 1802 -
Description: Abstracts of minutes, reports, news clippings, photographs, genealogical files and notes, and oral history on
Oldham County, including its history,
economic development, library, schools,
and families.

LANCASTER

KY41M-280
Garrard County Public Library
101 Lexington Street
Lancaster KY 40444

(606) 792-3424

OPEN: M-F 9-5, Sa 9-3; closed Sundays
COPYING FACILITIES: yes
MATERIALS SOLICITED: Will accept ma-
terials relating to Lancaster and
Garrard County.

HOLDINGS:
Total volume: 3.8 c.f.
Inclusive dates: 1814 -
Description: Files on Garrard County
history, genealogy, cemeteries, and houses
and a ledger of the Lancaster Library
Company, 1814-21.

LAWRENCEBURG

KY410-40
Anderson County Public Library
114 North Main Street
Lawrenceburg KY 40342

(502) 839-6420

OPEN: M-F 8:30-5, Sa 9-5; closed
Sundays
COPYING FACILITIES: yes
MATERIALS SOLICITED: Will accept ma-
terials relating to the history of
Lawrenceburg and Anderson County.

HOLDINGS:
Total volume: 3.3 c.f.
Inclusive dates: 1890 -
Description: Photographs, family gene-
alogies, and clippings relating to the his-
tory of Lawrenceburg and Anderson
County.

LEBANON

KY418-520
Marion County Public Library
201 E. Main
Lebanon KY 40033

(502) 692-4698

OPEN: Tu 9-9, W-F 9-5:30, Sa 9-5;
closed Sundays and Mondays
COPYING FACILITIES: yes
MATERIALS SOLICITED: Materials con-
cerning the history of Lebanon and
Marion County.

HOLDINGS:
Total volume: 5.5 c.f.; 10 vols.
Inclusive dates: 1830 - 1978
Description: Family histories, local history manuscripts, a biography of Edwin
Carlile Litsey, listings from Catholic
cemeteries in the area, copies of a church
register of two Catholic churches in Lebanon, copies of church baptismal records,
oral history recordings, copies of records
concerning Lebanon and Marion County
history, institutions, and organizations,
and photographs, slides, and a transcript
concerning area historic buildings.

LEITCHFIELD

KY430-280
Grayson County Public Library
130 E. Market Street
Leitchfield KY

MAILING ADDRESS:
P.O. Box 512
Leitchfield KY 42754

(502) 259-5455

OPEN: M noon-8, Tu-Sa 9-5; closed
Sundays
COPYING FACILITIES: yes

HOLDINGS:
Total volume: 14 vols.
Inclusive dates: 1976 -
Description: Typescript records of area
cemeteries and family histories of the
Haynes family, the John Whitely family,
and the Joseph Day family.

LEXINGTON

KY464-50
American Saddle Horse Museum
4093 Iron Works Pike
Lexington KY 40511

(606) 259-2746

OPEN: M-Sa 10-4, Su 1-5
COPYING FACILITIES: no
MATERIALS SOLICITED: Materials con-
cerning American saddle horses.

HOLDINGS:
Total volume: 0.5 l.f.
Inclusive dates: 1961 - 1979
Description: Minutes of the Kentucky
Breeders and Exhibitors Association,
1961-63, and the Board of Trustees of the
American Saddle Horse Museum,
1963-79, describing the founding of the
American Saddle Horse Museum at
Spindletop Farm in Lexington, KY.

KY464-440
Keeneland Association
Library
4201 Versailles Road
Lexington KY

MAILING ADDRESS:
P.O. Box 1690
Lexington KY 40510

(606) 254-3412, Ext. 223

OPEN: M-F 9-4; race days, 9-11; closed
weekends and holidays
COPYING FACILITIES: no
MATERIALS SOLICITED: Materials dealing
with thoroughbred horses worldwide,
including breeding, training, racing,
prominent persons in these areas, race
tracks, race meetings, and horse farms.

HOLDINGS:
Total volume: 115 c.f.
Inclusive dates: 1829 - 1972
Description: Photographs dealing with
the breeding, sale, and racing of thoroughbred horses, including horse farms,
race tracks, prominent thoroughbred
horses, and owners, breeders, trainers,
and others active in horse racing and the
thoroughbred horse industry. Other materials include scrapbooks, farm records,
manuscripts, and records.

SEE: Novotny.

KY464-460
Kentucky Rivers Coalition
207 Woodland Drive
Lexington KY

MAILING ADDRESS:
P.O. Box 1306
Lexington KY 40590

no telephone

OPEN: M-F 9-6; closed weekends
ACCESS: advance arrangements advised
COPYING FACILITIES: no

HOLDINGS:
Total volume: 20.5 c.f.
Inclusive dates: 1976 -
Description: Administrative records
and project files documenting the Coalition's educational, research, and citizen
action programs to protect Kentucky rivers and the environment.

KY464-490
Lexington Theological Seminary
Library
631 South Limestone
Lexington KY 40508

(606) 252-0361

OPEN: M-F 8-9; closed weekends and
holidays

COPYING FACILITIES: yes
MATERIALS SOLICITED: Materials relating to the Christian church (Disciples of Christ) in the southeastern United States, congregations in the Lexington area and clergy of the Disciples, as well as records of Disciple missionary activities. Will also accept materials related to hymnody, liturgics, and church unity movements.

HOLDINGS:
  Total volume: 100 file cabinets
  Inclusive dates: 1800 -
  Description: Early records of the Christian church, especially of leaders related to the Seminary; manuscript sermons of leaders; congregational records; records of missionaries to the Belgian Congo, 1900-50; materials concerning work in China, 1880's-1945; minutes; and records.

SEE: Hamer (as College of the Bible).

SEE: Hinding.

KY464-495
Lexington-Fayette County Historic
  Commission
253 Market Street
Lexington KY 40508

(606) 255-8312

OPEN: M-F 8:30-5; closed weekends
COPYING FACILITIES: no

HOLDINGS:
  Total volume: 4.2 c.f.
  Inclusive dates: not specified
  Description: Survey sheets for historic sites in Lexington and Fayette County, prepared by the Historic Commission in conjunction with the Kentucky Heritage Commission and the U.S. Department of the Interior's National Register program.

KY464-760
Transylvania University
Frances Carrick Thomas Library
Special Collections Department
Lexington KY 40508

(606) 233-8227, 8225

OPEN: M-F 8:30-4:30; closed weekends
  and holidays
ACCESS: advance arrangements preferred
COPYING FACILITIES: yes
MATERIALS SOLICITED: Transylvania University materials, Rafinesque manuscripts and materials, 19th century natural science of the eastern seaboard and Ohio River Valley, Kentucky history, and materials relating to existing collections.

HOLDINGS:
  Total volume: 269.5 l.f.
  Inclusive dates: 1780 -
  Description: Manuscripts of local and Transylvania University figures such as Joseph Buchanan, Thomas H. Chivers, Charles Caldwell, Robert Peter, and C. S. Rafinesque; documents of Jefferson Davis representing his incarceration after the Civil War; Henry Clay papers; materials in the J. Winston Coleman collection of Kentucky history; and archives of Transylvania University, including correspondence, memoranda, minutes, financial

and business records, ledger books, and photographs.

SEE: Hamer.

SEE: Martin.

KY464-780
United Methodist Church
Kentucky Conference
Commission on Archives and History
1387 New Circle Road N.E.
Lexington KY

MAILING ADDRESS:
P.O. Box 5107
Lexington KY 40555

(606) 254-7388

OPEN: M-F 8:30-4:30
COPYING FACILITIES: no
MATERIALS SOLICITED: Materials pertaining to the history and development of Methodism. Will also accept materials relating to Christian theology and to the impact of religion on various aspects of human existence.

HOLDINGS:
  Total volume: 5.8 c.f.
  Inclusive dates: 1853 -
  Description: Letters, reports, histories, and other papers relating to the history of the Kentucky Conference of the United Methodist church, as well as to Methodism and Christianity in general, with particular emphasis on their influence on political issues.

KY464-800
University of Kentucky
King Library
Department of Special Collections
Lexington KY 40506

(606) 257-8611

OPEN: M-F 8-4:30, Sa 8-12; closed
  Sundays and holidays
ACCESS: advance permission to use
  Diocese of Lexington materials
COPYING FACILITIES: yes
MATERIALS SOLICITED: Kentucky, Ohio
  Valley, and Appalachian materials.

HOLDINGS:
  Total volume: 10,050 c.f.
  Inclusive dates: 1700 -
  Description: Archives of the University, as well as materials relating to history and literature in Kentucky, the Ohio Valley, and the Appalachian region. Collections include records of social, business, philanthropic, professional, and church organizations; personal and public papers of individuals; diaries and journals; oral history interviews; and photographs.
  There are also 7,775 microfilm reels of records of 113 Kentucky counties, dating from the late 18th to the early 20th century. Also included are the records of the Episcopal Diocese of Lexington.

SEE: Hamer; NUCMC, 1959-65, 72, 75.

SEE: Parkinson; Hinding; Robbins.

SEE ALSO: 'Midwest Research Institutions Directory,' *Illinois Libraries* 53 (Jan. 1971); Walter Schatz, ed., *Directory of Afro-American Resources* (Bowker, 1970); Peter Duignan, *Handbook of American Resources for African Studies* (Hoover Institution, 1970); Albert Krichmar, *The Women's Rights Movement in the United States, 1848-1970: A Bibliography and Sourcebook* (Scarecrow Press, 1972); Alan M. Meckler and Ruth McMullin, comps., *Oral History Collections* (Bowker, 1975).

KY464-880
Waveland State Shrine
Higbee Mill Road
Lexington KY 40503

(606) 272-3611

OPEN: Tu-Sa 9-4, Su 1:30-4:30; closed
  Mondays, Christmas, and New Year's
ACCESS: appointment required
COPYING FACILITIES: yes

HOLDINGS:
  Total volume: 1,000 items
  Inclusive dates: 1794 -
  Description: Business ledgers, manuscript books, scrapbooks, surveyors' notebooks, diaries, family history charts of Kentuckians, bills of sale, receipts, bills, and land grants, all relating to Lexington and Kentucky history. Also included are daguerreotypes, photographs of the Civil War period, World War I photographs, and pictures of Kentucky families.

LIBERTY

KY467-120
Casey County Public Library
Middleburg Street
Liberty KY 42539

(606) 787-9381

OPEN: M, W, F 9-5:30, Tu 11-6, Sa
  9-4:30; Tuesday evenings until 7 in
  summer; closed Thursdays
COPYING FACILITIES: yes
MATERIALS SOLICITED: Local historical
  and genealogical materials.

HOLDINGS:
  Total volume: 1.5 c.f.
  Inclusive dates: 1956 -
  Description: Local history and genealogy materials, including family histories, cemetery records, and oral history tapes.

LONDON

KY48V-480
Laurel County Public Library
116 East Fourth Street
London KY 40741

(606) 864-5759

OPEN: M 8-8, Tu-Sa 8-6; closed Sundays
COPYING FACILITIES: no
MATERIALS SOLICITED: Will accept genealogical materials.

HOLDINGS:
Total volume: 1.5 c.f.
Inclusive dates: 1800 - 1900
Description: Genealogical files and histories of Laurel County and surrounding areas.

KY48V-495
Levi Jackson Wilderness Road State Park
Mountain Life Museum
London KY

MAILING ADDRESS:
Route 7 Box 595
London KY 40741

(606) 878-8000

OPEN: May - Labor Day, daily 9-5; closed rest of year
ACCESS: advance arrangements required
COPYING FACILITIES: no
MATERIALS SOLICITED: Will accept documents dealing with Laurel County, KY and its first residents.

HOLDINGS:
Total volume: 1.5 c.f.
Inclusive dates: 1828 - 1917
Description: Historical documents of London, Laurel County, KY, and their first residents, as well as court records and an 1868 impeachment document.

KY48V-720
Sue Bennett College
Library
100 College Street
London KY 40741

(606) 864-6770

OPEN: M-F 8-4; closed weekends
COPYING FACILITIES: yes
MATERIALS SOLICITED: Will accept materials dealing with Sue and Belle Bennett and the College.

HOLDINGS:
Total volume: 6.5 c.f.
Inclusive dates: 1896 - 1979
Description: Materials dealing with the history of Sue Bennett College, Methodism in Kentucky, and Laurel County, KY.

LOUISVILLE

KY496-70
Bellarmine College
Library
Newburg Road
Louisville KY 40205

(502) 452-8137

OPEN: M-Th 8-10, F 8-5, Sa 9-5, Su 1-10; closed weekends during summer and College vacations, and holidays
COPYING FACILITIES: yes
MATERIALS SOLICITED: Materials relating to the Catholic church and to history in the Archdiocese of Louisville and Kentucky areas, and materials by and about Robert Bellarmine.

HOLDINGS:
Total volume: 50 l.f.; 67 oral history tapes
Inclusive dates: late 19th century -
Description: Materials relating to the history of Bellarmine College and the history of Louisville. Included are oral history tapes collected by the Louisville Historical League and the Catholic Archdiocese of Louisville.

KY496-90
Bellarmine College
Thomas Merton Collection
Newburg Road
Louisville KY 40205

(502) 452-8187

OPEN: Tu-F 9-5; closed Mondays, weekends, and holidays
ACCESS: Restrictions on unpublished material vary according to item and to status of person seeking access.
COPYING FACILITIES: yes; $12 minimum charge
MATERIALS SOLICITED: Material by and about Thomas Merton. Will also accept all materials ancillary to Thomas Merton, monasticism, and related topics.

HOLDINGS:
Total volume: 30,000 items
Inclusive dates: 1915 -
Description: Writings, lectures, correspondence, diaries and journals, manuscripts, drawings, photographs and other memorabilia of Thomas Merton.

SEE: Robbins.

SEE ALSO: Marquita Breit, *Thomas Merton: A Bibliography* (Scarecrow Press, 1974).

KY496-200
Episcopal Diocese of Kentucky
421 South 2nd Street
Louisville KY 40202

(502) 584-7148

OPEN: M-F 8:30-5; closed weekends and holidays
ACCESS: appointment required
COPYING FACILITIES: yes
MATERIALS SOLICITED: Materials pertaining to Kentucky Episcopal parishes. Will also accept materials pertaining to the Episcopal church in Indiana, southern Ohio, and Tennessee.

HOLDINGS:
Total volume: 2 safes
Inclusive dates: 1796 -
Description: Materials related to the Diocese, including records of churches and their activities (1796-), papers of bishops, and records of the Diocese (1829-).

KY496-400
Jefferson County Archives and Records Service
531 Court Place
101 Fiscal Court Building
Louisville KY 40202

(502) 625-5761, 5751

OPEN: M-F 8-4:30; closed weekends and holidays
COPYING FACILITIES: yes
MATERIALS SOLICITED: Materials relating to Jefferson County government, including selected judicial records. Will also accept related visual documents, particularly photographs and architectural, engineering, and technical drawings.

HOLDINGS:
Total volume: 14,000 c.f.
Inclusive dates: 1780 -
Description: Jefferson County government records, including county clerk's records, judicial and fiscal documents, and administrative correspondence, reports, and other records of county executive departments and joint county/city agencies. There are also county judges' papers, 1945 to the present.

SEE ALSO: 'An Inventory of Jefferson County Records,' *The Filson Club History Quarterly* 44 (Oct. 1970).

KY496-498
Louisville Free Public Library
Iroquois Branch Library
601 West Woodlawn
Louisville KY 40215

(502) 367-1236

OPEN: M-W 2-8, Th-Sa 10-5; closed Sundays
COPYING FACILITIES: yes
MATERIALS SOLICITED: Will accept materials concerning the library's construction and area organizations active in the library's development.

HOLDINGS:
Total volume: 1 c.f.
Inclusive dates: 1939 -
Description: Photographs, news clippings, scrapbooks, correspondence, reports, and meeting minutes of the Beechmont Civic Club covering the building of the branch library in south Louisville and its dedication in 1939.

KY496-518
Louisville Free Public Library
Southwest Branch Library
7219 Dixie Highway
Louisville KY 40258

(502) 937-6296

OPEN: M-W 2-8, Th-Sa 10-5; closed Sundays
COPYING FACILITIES: no

HOLDINGS:
Total volume: 4 items
Inclusive dates: 1974 - 1975
Description: Cassette tapes relating to southwestern Jefferson County and Valley Station, KY, including topography, archaeology, education, the history of

Valley Station Christian Church, and re-membrances.

KY496-520
Louisville Free Public Library
Western Branch Library
604 South 10th Street
Louisville KY 40203

(502) 584-5526

OPEN: M-F 8:30-11, Sa 10-1, Su 7-10; shorter hours June - Aug.; closed holidays
COPYING FACILITIES: no
MATERIALS SOLICITED: Materials concerning all aspects of the black experience, including materials pertaining to local black citizens and the Western Branch Library.

HOLDINGS:
Total volume: 5.5 l.f.
Inclusive dates: 1900 -
Description: Papers of Joseph Cotter, including manuscripts of poetry, plays, stories, music, and jokes, as well as clippings, correspondence, memoranda, and photographs; papers concerning Thomas F. Blue, including correspondence, speeches, and photographs documenting Blue's association with the library; and scrapbooks containing clippings, correspondence, photographs, and tape recordings, covering the library's history, activities, employees, and patrons, as well as its near closing in 1980 and community efforts to maintain it in operation.

SEE: Schatz.

KY496-530
Louisville Presbyterian Theological
  Seminary
Library
1044 Alta Vista Road
Louisville KY 40205

(502) 895-3413

OPEN: M-F 8:30-11, Sa 10-1, Su 7-10; shorter hours June-Aug.; closed holidays
COPYING FACILITIES: yes
MATERIALS SOLICITED: Records of Presbyterian churches in Kentucky. Will also accept materials relating to church history, especially Presbyterian church history.

HOLDINGS:
Total volume: 87,500 vols.
Inclusive dates: not specified
Description: Manuscripts relating to the Presbyterian church in Kentucky, including minutes of Kentucky synods and presbyteries and session records of churches.

SEE: Hamer.

SEE: Hinding.

KY496-540
Louisville Zoological Garden and
  Louisville Zoological Society
1100 Trevillian Way
Louisville KY

MAILING ADDRESS:
P.O. Box 37250
Louisville KY 40233

(502) 459-2181

OPEN: Winter, Tu-Su 10-5; summer, daily 10-6
COPYING FACILITIES: yes
MATERIALS SOLICITED: Records pertaining to the administration of the Zoo and its animals.

HOLDINGS:
Total volume: 16 l.f.
Inclusive dates: 1963 -
Description: Minutes, animal records, daily reports, animal donation records, and zoo hospital reports, documenting the history of the Louisville Zoological Garden since its establishment as the Louisville Zoological Commission, as well as the history, health, and maintenance of the Zoo's animals. Also held are minutes of the Louisville Zoological Society, documents concerning its organization and the promotion of exhibits, special events, and other Zoo programs.

KY496-687
Saints Mary and Elizabeth Hospital
4400 Churchman Avenue
Louisville KY 40215

(502) 361-6011

OPEN: M-F 8-4:30; closed weekends
COPYING FACILITIES: yes
MATERIALS SOLICITED: Materials concerning the hospital, including papers of staff and non-current records.

HOLDINGS:
Total volume: 0.75 l.f.
Inclusive dates: 1921 -
Description: Materials primarily concerning the history and development of Saints Mary and Elizabeth Hospital, including a history of its library, photographs of an earlier hospital on 12th and Magnolia Streets, news clippings, memorandums, constitutions, and by-laws describing the hospital's development and expansion, and early materials listing surgical procedures and staff members.

KY496-720
Southern Baptist Theological
  Seminary
Library
2825 Lexington Road
Louisville KY 40206

SEE: Hamer; NUCMC, 1959-61.

Questionnaire not returned.

KY496-725
Southern Baptist Theological
  Seminary
School of Church Music
The American Liszt Society Collection
2825 Lexington Road
Louisville KY 40206

(502) 897-4115

OPEN: not specified
ACCESS: permission required in advance
COPYING FACILITIES: yes
MATERIALS SOLICITED: Materials pertaining to the life, works, and professional career of Franz Liszt.

HOLDINGS:
Total volume: 12 l.f.
Inclusive dates: early 19th century -
Description: Records of the American Liszt Society's annual festivals, since 1967, including a complete series of programs, tape recordings of all festival performances, and copies of papers read at the festivals. In addition, there is a copy of the manuscript of Liszt's Don Sanche.

KY496-730
Spalding College
Archives
851 South Fourth Street
Louisville KY 40203

(502) 585-9911, Ext. 279

OPEN: M-F 9-4:30; closed weekends, Thanksgiving, Christmas, and Easter
COPYING FACILITIES: yes
MATERIALS SOLICITED: Official records from all campus offices; personal papers of faculty and administrative staff; and records of student and faculty organizations. Will also accept letters, journals, notebooks, diaries, scrapbooks, and photographs.

HOLDINGS:
Total volume: 250 c.f.
Inclusive dates: 1920 -
Description: Records of Spalding College, founded in 1920 under the name Nazareth College. Included are official records, personal papers of faculty, students and alumnae, and pictorial materials.

SEE: Hinding.

KY496-765
The Filson Club
Manuscript Department
118 West Breckinridge Street
Louisville KY 40203

(502) 582-3727

OPEN: M-F 9-5; closed weekends and holidays
ACCESS: All users are asked to sign a daily register and must complete a form listing collections used and giving basic personal data.
COPYING FACILITIES: yes
MATERIALS SOLICITED: Kentucky history and literature; materials relating to the Ohio Valley. Will also accept materials relating to colonial Virginia and southern Indiana.

HOLDINGS:
Total volume: 588 l.f.
Inclusive dates: 1609 -
Description: Manuscripts relating chiefly to Kentucky history and literature, with greatest strength in the pioneer, antebellum and Civil War periods. The collection includes personal and family papers, records of organizations and societies, account books, autograph collections, diaries, and genealogical materials.
Also church records, some manuscript maps, architectural drawings, large photographic collection.

SEE: Hamer; NUCMC, 1962, 65-66, 68, 70, 76.

SEE: Robbins; Hinding; Bean and Vane; Parkinson; Novotny.

SEE ALSO: Walter Schatz, ed., *Directory of Afro-American Resources* (Bowker, 1970); Albert Krichmar, *The Women's Rights Movement in the United States, 1848-1970: A Bibliography and Sourcebook* (Scarecrow Press, 1972).

Richard C. Davis, *North American Forest History: A Guide to Archives and Manuscripts in the United States and Canada* (Clio Books, 1977).

KY496-785
University of Louisville
Archives and Records Center
Louisville KY 40292

(502) 588-6674

OPEN: M-F 8-4:30; closed weekends and holidays
COPYING FACILITIES: yes
MATERIALS SOLICITED: Records of the University of Louisville and its predecessor schools; papers of persons associated with the University and manuscripts and other materials related to the social, political, economic, and cultural development of the Louisville area.

HOLDINGS:
Total volume: 7,250 l.f.
Inclusive dates: 1779 -
Description: Institutional records and personal papers relating to the University; personal papers of twentieth century political figures and social activists, cultural leaders, scientists, historians, educators, and other men and women of the Louisville area; and records of regional railroads and other businesses, cultural institutions, settlement houses and other social agencies, schools, colleges, churches and local government bodies.

SEE: NUCMC, 1977, 81.

SEE: Parkinson.

SEE ALSO: 'Midwest Research Institutions Directory,' *Illinois Libraries* 53 (Jan. 1971); 'A Selective Guide to Research Sources in the University of Louisville Archives' (1981).

KY496-795
University of Louisville
Kornhauser Health Sciences Library
502 South Preston Street
Louisville KY 40202

no telephone

SEE: NUCMC, 1970 (as University of Louisville, Medical School Library).

Questionnaire not returned.

KY496-800
University of Louisville
Law Library
Belknap Campus
Louisville KY 40292

(502) 588-6392

OPEN: M-F 8-5; closed weekends and holidays
COPYING FACILITIES: yes
MATERIALS SOLICITED: Papers written by U.S. Supreme Court Justices John Marshall Harlan (1833-1911) and Louis Dembitz Brandeis. Will also accept materials written about Harlan and Brandeis.

HOLDINGS:
Total volume: 148 l.f.
Inclusive dates: 1854 - 1938
Description: 1,500 items relating chiefly to John Marshall Harlan's (1833-1911) activities as an Associate Justice of the U.S. Supreme Court, including correspondence, daybooks, account books, briefs, dockets, legal records, clippings, and other papers; and 250,000 items relating to Louis D. Brandeis, including personal correspondence and other papers, and materials focusing on Brandeis' activities on the Court, World War I, Zionism, government, savings bank life insurance, and the law firm of Nutter, McClennen and Fish.

SEE: Hamer; NUCMC, 1959-61, 68.

SEE: Schatz.

SEE ALSO: William E. Read and William C. Berman, 'Papers of the First Justice Harlan at the University of Louisville,' *American Journal of Legal History* 11 (1967); 'Midwest Research Institutions Directory,' *Illinois Libraries* 53 (Jan. 1971).

KY496-808
University of Louisville
Music Library
Shelby Campus
Louisville KY 40222

no telephone

SEE: NUCMC, 1980.

Questionnaire not returned.

KY496-812
University of Louisville
Oral History Center
University Archives and Records Center
Louisville KY 40292

(502) 588-6674

OPEN: M-F 9-4:30; closed weekends and holidays
COPYING FACILITIES: yes
MATERIALS SOLICITED: Oral histories of local black groups, Kentucky women, Louisville history, etc., designed to supplement the textual holdings of the University's Archives and Records Center.

HOLDINGS:
Total volume: 1,000 individual interviews
Inclusive dates: 1968 -
Description: A collection of taped interviews, relating chiefly to the history of Louisville and Kentucky. Subject strengths include black history, the local Jewish community, the Louisville & Nashville Railroad, Kentucky women, and the desegregation of Louisville schools.

SEE: Meckler and McMullin; Hinding.

KY496-823
University of Louisville
University Library
Photographic Archives
Louisville KY 40292

(502) 588-6752

OPEN: M-W, F 8-4:30, Th 8-8; closed weekends and holidays
COPYING FACILITIES: yes
MATERIALS SOLICITED: Documentary photographs, principally American. Will also accept photography-related letters, manuscripts, and other materials.

HOLDINGS:
Total volume: 750,000 photographs
Inclusive dates: 1840's - 1960's
Description: Photographs relating chiefly to Louisville, the State of Kentucky, and the surrounding area. Also included are negative files from the Standard Oil of New Jersey Company, photographs of Europe in the nineteenth century, theatrical photographs, contemporary photographs, and materials relating to Roy Stryker.

SEE: Novotny.

SEE ALSO: 'Midwest Research Institutions Directory,' *Illinois Libraries* 53 (Jan. 1971); Steven Lewis, James McQuaid, and David Tait, *Photography Source and Resource* (Turnip Press, 1973).

KY496-825
University of Louisville
University Library
Rare Books and Special Collections
Belknap Campus
Louisville KY 40292

(502) 588-6762

OPEN: M-F 9-5; closed weekends and holidays
COPYING FACILITIES: yes
MATERIALS SOLICITED: Literary manuscripts to complement the rare book collections, including those by Edgar Rice Burroughs, Isak Dinesen, H. L. Mencken, and Irish authors. Will also accept materials relating to the history of books and of World War I, and parchment deeds and indentures.

HOLDINGS:
Total volume: 1,500 items
Inclusive dates: 1800 -
Description: A collection of literary manuscripts, personal papers, and memorabilia of American authors from the early 19th century to the present. Materials focusing on Mary Austin Holley, H. L. Mencken, Hortense Flexner King, and Philip L. Barbour are complemented by individual items of most major American authors.

SEE: NUCMC, 1968, 78.

SEE: Hinding; Robbins.

SEE ALSO: 'Midwest Research Institutions Directory,' Illinois Libraries 53 (Jan. 1971).

KY496-850
Ursuline Sisters of the Immaculate Conception of Louisville, Kentucky Archives
3115 Lexington Road
Louisville KY

MAILING ADDRESS:
3105 Lexington Road
Louisville KY 40206

(502) 897-1811

OPEN: M-F 9-3; closed weekends and holidays
ACCESS: appointment recommended; some folders restricted or reserved to permission of General Superior
COPYING FACILITIES: yes
MATERIALS SOLICITED: Materials relating to this Ursuline community, including administrative records and manuscripts of members; material from other Ursuline communities; archives and non-current records of churches and schools staffed by the Ursuline Sisters; and related photographs, oral history tapes and transcripts, slides, and sound recordings. Will also accept manuscript collections from people who have had some special connection with this community.

HOLDINGS:
Total volume: 250 l.f.
Inclusive dates: 1858 -
Description: Records of the Ursuline Sisters of the Immaculate Conception of Louisville, Kentucky, for schools and parishes served in the eastern, midwestern, and southern states and Peru and correspondence with religious organizations in France, Germany and Italy.

Included are records of organizations; manuscripts of individuals; unpublished histories and diaries; taped recordings of meetings, lectures and oral histories; photographs, slides and memorabilia; scrapbooks.

SEE: Hinding.

MADISONVILLE

KY504-310
Historical Society of Hopkins County
107 Union Street
Madisonville KY 42431

(502) 821-3986

OPEN: M-F 1-5; closed weekends and holidays
COPYING FACILITIES: yes
MATERIALS SOLICITED: Materials relating to the history of Hopkins County, its people and industries.

HOLDINGS:
Total volume: 31 c.f.; 72 vols.
Inclusive dates: 1809 -
Description: Materials relating to the history of Hopkins County. Included are items relating to pioneers, and industries, particularly the coal industry, as well as family papers.

KY504-510
Madisonville Community College
Learning Resource Center
University Drive
Madisonville KY 42431

(502) 821-2250, Ext. 151

OPEN: M-F 8-9; summer, M-F 8-6; closed weekends and holidays
COPYING FACILITIES: yes
MATERIALS SOLICITED: Will accept materials relating to Madisonville Community College, Madisonville, and Hopkins County, KY.

HOLDINGS:
Total volume: 1.8 c.f.; 2 vols; 22 items
Inclusive dates: 1836 - 1978
Description: Materials concerning the College's establishment and development, as well as copies of the minutes of the University of Kentucky Board of Trustees and of the records of the Community College Council and the University Senate Rules Committee for 1972 and 1977.

MARION

KY514-120
Crittenden County Historical Society
Bob Wheeler Museum
222 West Carlisle
Marion KY

MAILING ADDRESS:
Box 25
Marion KY 42064

(502) 965-9257

OPEN: M, Th, F 8-4; closed other days
COPYING FACILITIES: no
MATERIALS SOLICITED: Will accept materials on Crittenden County and the Museum.

HOLDINGS:
Total volume: 100 items
Inclusive dates: 1910's - 1960's
Description: Photographs of Crittenden County natives, including ministers, teachers, county school superintendents, physicians, politicians such as U.S. Senator Ollie M. James, as well as photographs of one-room school houses in the county.

KY514-130
Crittenden County Public Library
204 West Carlisle Street
Marion KY 42064

(502) 965-3354

OPEN: M 9-8, Tu, Th-Sa 9-5; closed Wednesdays and Sundays
COPYING FACILITIES: yes
MATERIALS SOLICITED: Will selectively accept materials on Crittenden County and its history.

HOLDINGS:
Total volume: 4 c.f.; 5 vols.; 51 items
Inclusive dates: 1842 - 1978
Description: An oral history collection, a historical file documenting the county, genealogical materials on local families, court records, and a history of county men who served in World War I.

MAYFIELD

KY520-280
Graves County Public Library
6th and College Streets
Mayfield KY 42066

(502) 247-2911

OPEN: Tu 10-9, W-F 10-5, Sa 10-4; closed Sundays and Mondays
COPYING FACILITIES: yes
MATERIALS SOLICITED: Will accept material on Graves County.

HOLDINGS:
Total volume: 5 vols.; 12 items
Inclusive dates: 1920 - 1978
Description: Manuscript histories of the area, a family history, and an oral history collection.

KY520-530
Mid-Continent Baptist Bible College
Route 2
Mayfield KY 42066-9647

(502) 247-8521

OPEN: M-F 9-5; closed weekends
COPYING FACILITIES: yes
MATERIALS SOLICITED: Will accept religious and secular materials on regional history.

HOLDINGS:
 Total volume: 2.8 c.f.; 5 microfilm reels; 3 items
 Inclusive dates: 1825 -
 Description: Records of the College, materials on area religious schools which preceded the College, microfilmed records of churches in Graves County, KY, copies of minute books of local Baptist associations, and clippings on Baptist and other history of the area.

MAYSVILLE

KY526-520
Mason County Museum
215 Sutton Street
Maysville KY 41056

(606) 564-5865

OPEN: Tu-Sa 10-4, Su 2-4; closed Mondays and holidays
USER FEES: one dollar per visit or $10 annual membership fee
ACCESS: serious researchers
COPYING FACILITIES: yes
MATERIALS SOLICITED: Genealogical and historical material relating to the Mason County and surrounding areas.

HOLDINGS:
 Total volume: 50 microfilm reels; 7 boxes
 Inclusive dates: early 1800's -
 Description: Land grants, other documents, photographs, and microfilms of courthouse and census records, pertaining to Mason County history.

McKEE

KY53N-400
Jackson County Public Library
Courthouse Square
McKee KY

MAILING ADDRESS:
P.O. Box 160
McKee KY 40447

(606) 287-8113

OPEN: M, Tu 8:30-5, W-F 8:30-4, Sa 9-1; closed Sundays
COPYING FACILITIES: yes
MATERIALS SOLICITED: Will accept local history materials.

HOLDINGS:
 Total volume: 1 c.f.
 Inclusive dates: 1894 - 1976
 Description: Local history, genealogy, and other materials relating to Jackson County, including an oral history collection.

MELBOURNE

KY532-720
Sisters of Divine Providence of Kentucky
Saint Anne Convent
Melbourne KY 41059

(606) 441-0679

OPEN: by appointment only
COPYING FACILITIES: yes
MATERIALS SOLICITED: Materials pertaining to older members of the order, former students in the order's schools, and the history of the order's missions and houses.

HOLDINGS:
 Total volume: 12 file cabinets
 Inclusive dates: 1889 -
 Description: Manuscripts and other records pertaining to the history of the Sisters of Divine Providence in the United States, as well as materials relating chiefly to the history of the Roman Catholic church in the United States, especially in the Diocese of Covington, and materials on the Sisters of Divine Providence of St. Jean de Bassel, France.

SEE: Hinding.

MIDWAY

KY54G-520
Midway College
Marrs Library
Midway KY 40347

(606) 846-4421, Ext. 216

OPEN: M, W 8-11, Tu, Th 8-10, F 8-5, Sa 11-4, Su 6-10; closed Thanksgiving, Christmas, and College vacations
ACCESS: permission of Head Librarian required
COPYING FACILITIES: yes
MATERIALS SOLICITED: Will accept items relating to the history of the College and Kentucky.

HOLDINGS:
 Total volume: 13 file cabinets
 Inclusive dates: 1847 -
 Description: Materials related to the history of Kentucky Female Orphan School and its successor institution Midway College and to the history of the Christian church (Disciples of Christ). Included are pictures, letters, school catalogs, and other publications.

SEE: Hinding.

MILLERSBURG

KY54Q-520
Millersburg Military Institute
Alumni Office
North Main Street
Millersburg KY 40348

(606) 484-3352

OPEN: M-F 8-4:30; closed weekends
COPYING FACILITIES: yes

MATERIALS SOLICITED: Official Institute records. Will also accept materials relating to the Institute's history, alumni, faculty, and staff.

HOLDINGS:
 Total volume: 2.3 c.f.
 Inclusive,dates: 1884 -
 Description: Millersburg Military Institute stockholder and board of trustee minutes, photographs, alumni correspondence, Institute yearbooks, early Institute catalogs, student newspapers and other publications, and student grade records and catalogs of Millersburg Female College, prior to the acquisition of its campus in 1931 by the Institute.

MONTICELLO

KY55L-920
Wayne County Public Library and Wayne County Historical Society
159 South Main
Monticello KY 42633

(606) 348-8565

OPEN: M, Tu, Th, F 8-4:30, Sa 8-4; closed Wednesdays and Sundays
ACCESS: advance arrangements required
COPYING FACILITIES: yes
MATERIALS SOLICITED: Genealogical and historical materials dealing with the Monticello area and Kentucky.

HOLDINGS:
 Total volume: 22.5 c.f.
 Inclusive dates: 1800 -
 Description: Family histories, an oral history collection, Wayne County genealogical materials and historical documents, and County court records.

MOREHEAD

KY558-520
Morehead State University
Johnson Camden Library
Special Collections
Morehead KY 40351

(606) 783-2829

OPEN: Su 1-10, M-Th 8-10, F 8-6, Sa 9-4:30; closed holidays and school vacations
COPYING FACILITIES: yes
MATERIALS SOLICITED: Materials relating to Morehead State University and its predecessor schools; papers associated with the University; and manuscripts and other materials related to the social, cultural, political, and economic development of the community extending into Kentucky Appalachia east and south of Morehead.

HOLDINGS:
 Total volume: 21 l.f.
 Inclusive dates: 1942 -
 Description: Primarily University archives and presidential papers, as well as correspondence and financial papers of local women's clubs, and letters from Morehead students serving in the military in World War II.

SEE: NUCMC, 1969.

MOUNT STERLING

KY56N-520
Montgomery County Public Library
241 W. Locust Street
Mount Sterling KY 40353

(606) 498-2404

OPEN: M-F 9-5, Sa 9-1; closed Sundays
COPYING FACILITIES: yes
MATERIALS SOLICITED: Materials dealing
with county and local history, genealogy, and family history.

HOLDINGS:
Total volume: 4 c.f.
Inclusive dates: 1859 - 1975
Description: Scrapbooks documenting local organization history, transcriptions of cemetery records, minute books of local societies, church histories, oral histories, and early glass negative studio portraits.

MURRAY

KY564-520
Murray State University
Pogue Special Collections Library
Murray KY 42071

(502) 762-6152

OPEN: M-F 8-4:30, Sa 10-3; closed
Sunday, holidays, and spring vacation
COPYING FACILITIES: yes
MATERIALS SOLICITED: Materials relating to the history, literature, and culture of Tennessee and Kentucky, especially the western sections of those States; materials, including genealogical data, relating to Virginia, North Carolina, South Carolina, Maryland, Georgia, Missouri, and Illinois, especially their influence on the settlement and development of western Kentucky and Tennessee.

HOLDINGS:
Total volume: 750 l.f.
Inclusive dates: 1800 -
Description: Materials relating principally to western Kentucky and western Tennessee. Included are diaries, correspondence, official papers and records of political figures, manuscripts of works by regional writers, scrapbooks, labor union records, records of churches and civic groups, and an oral history tape collection.

SEE: Hinding.

SEE ALSO: 'Midwest Research Institutions Directory,' *Illinois Libraries* 53 (Jan. 1971); Charles F. Hinds, 'Kentucky Records: How to Use Them and Where They Are,' *National Genealogical Society Quarterly* 59 (March 1971).

NAZARETH

KY569-720
Sisters of Charity of Nazareth
Archival Center
Nazareth KY 40048

(502) 348-1500, Ext. 412

OPEN: M-F 9-4, and by appointment;
closed weekends, Christmas, and Easter
COPYING FACILITIES: yes

HOLDINGS:
Total volume: 35 vols.; 15 boxes
Inclusive dates: 1812 -
Description: Materials relating chiefly to Kentucky, as well as other southern States. Included are the papers of Catherine Spalding and John Baptist Mary David, and letters of Stephen Badin, Benedict Joseph Flaget, and Martin John Spalding. Records of Nazareth Academy (1814-1956) are also included.

GUIDES: A mimeographed guide is available from the institution.

SEE: Hamer; NUCMC, 1966, 68.

SEE: Parkinson; Hinding.

NERINX

KY57W-720
Sisters of Loretto
Archives
Loretto Motherhouse
Nerinx KY 40049

(502) 865-5811

OPEN: by appointment only
ACCESS: serious researchers;
appointment required
COPYING FACILITIES: yes
MATERIALS SOLICITED: Will accept materials on the history of the Sisters of Loretto.

HOLDINGS:
Total volume: 23 microfilm reels; 329 l.f.
Inclusive dates: 1794 -
Description: Materials relating to the history of the Sisters of Loretto since their establishment in Kentucky, including administrative, financial, school, religious, and legal records, as well as papers, correspondence, foreign archival material, diaries, journals, memoirs, photographs, and tapes.
The materials document missions in the United States, China, and South America, the life of Father Charles Nerinckx, schools with which the Sisters are associated, lives of early Catholic missionaries and clergy, members of the Society, and the assemblies, general chapters, provincial chapters, Loretto Houses, and administrations of the Sisters of Loretto.

OWENSBORO

KY598-600
Owensboro-Daviess County Public
Library
Kentucky Room
450 Griffith Avenue
Owensboro KY 42301

(502) 684-0211

OPEN: M-F 1-9, Sa 9-6, Su 2-5; closed
holidays
COPYING FACILITIES: yes
MATERIALS SOLICITED: Materials on Owensboro, Daviess County, Muhlenberg County, and the counties of the Green River region (Hancock, Henderson, Union, Webster, Ohio, and McLean counties). Will also accept materials on other Kentucky counties.

HOLDINGS:
Total volume: 50 l.f.
Inclusive dates: 1813 -
Description: Local history manuscripts; photographs; records of the Daviess County Historical Society, Rotary Club, Married Ladies Reading Club, Carnegie Free Public Library and Owensboro-Daviess County Public Library, and Investigators Club; Owensboro city documents; student papers; oral history tapes; letters; and scrapbooks of local women's clubs.

OWENTON

KY600-600
Owen County Public Library and
Owen County Historical Society
N. Main Street
Owenton KY

MAILING ADDRESS:
Box 296
Owenton KY 40359

(502) 484-3450

OPEN: M-Sa 10:30-5; closed Sundays and
holidays
COPYING FACILITIES: yes
MATERIALS SOLICITED: Manuscripts, oral history tapes, and other materials relating to the history of Owen County and its communities.

HOLDINGS:
Total volume: 4.7 c.f.
Inclusive dates: 1846 -
Description: Business records and ledgers of 19th century Owen County stores, minutes of the Owen County Union Agricultural and Mechanical Association, 1859-66, family photograph albums, reference files on local history, genealogy, and cemeteries, and oral history tapes, all relating to the history of Owen County.

OWINGSVILLE

KY602-80
Bath County Library
Main Street
Owingsville KY

MAILING ADDRESS:
Box 136
Owingsville KY 40360

(606) 674-2531

OPEN: M-Sa 10:30-5; closed Sundays
COPYING FACILITIES: yes
MATERIALS SOLICITED: Materials relating
to Bath County history, including genealogy and family history.

HOLDINGS:
Total volume: 0.1 c.f.
Inclusive dates: 1974 - 1978
Description: Local church histories and
oral history tapes concerning county his-
tory.

PADUCAH

KY604-40
Alben W. Barkley Museum
533 Madison Street
Paducah KY

MAILING ADDRESS:
P.O. Box 252
Paducah KY 42001

(502) 444-9356, 554-9690

OPEN: Sa, Su 1-4 and by appointment
USER FEES: 50 cents
COPYING FACILITIES: no
MATERIALS SOLICITED: Will accept ma-
terials relating to Alben W. Barkley,
Linn Boyd, George Rogers, William
Clark, Irvin S. Cobb, the history of
Paducah, the Jackson Purchase region,
and river lore.

HOLDINGS:
Total volume: 15 c.f.; 63 vols.; 1,100
items
Inclusive dates: 1855 - 1979
Description: Photographs, scrapbooks,
and other materials relating to U.S. Vice
President Alben W. Barkley, and the history of Paducah, the Jackson Purchase
region, and Kentucky.

KY604-630
Paducah Community College
Library
Alben Barkley Drive
Paducah KY

MAILING ADDRESS:
P.O. Box 7380
Paducah KY 42002-7380

(502) 442-6131

OPEN: M-Th 8-8:30, F 8-4, Sa 9-noon;
closed Sundays
COPYING FACILITIES: yes

HOLDINGS:
Total volume: 5 items
Inclusive dates: 1976 -
Description: Videotape recordings of
interviews with the president of Paducah
Junior College and the director of its suc-
cessor institution, Paducah Community
College, describing the history of the Col-
lege and its merger with the University of
Kentucky community college system in
1968.

KY604-640
Paducah Public Library
555 Washington Street
Paducah KY 42001

(502) 442-2510

OPEN: M-F 10-8:45, Sa 10-5:45, Su
2-5:45; closed holidays
COPYING FACILITIES: yes
MATERIALS SOLICITED: Materials relating
to history of Paducah, western Kentucky, and Irvin S. Cobb.

HOLDINGS:
Total volume: 66 items; 9.5 l.f.; 3
vols.
Inclusive dates: 1837 - 1977
Description: Oral history interviews
with western Kentucky residents relating
to local history, business, pioneer travels,
and folk crafts, including an interview
with Lela Scopes, whose brother John
was tried in the 'monkey trial.'
Also held are correspondence and
manuscripts of author and humorist Irvin
S. Cobb, including the manuscript of *Exit
Laughing*; local history manuscripts; materials relating to a hotel, general store,
and the library; newspaper clippings
about Vice President Alben W. Barkley;
and newspaper clippings, photographs,
and correspondence relating to Paducah.

KY604-890
William Clark Market House
Museum, Inc.
2nd and Broadway
Paducah KY

MAILING ADDRESS:
P.O. Box 12
Paducah KY 42001

(502) 443-7759

OPEN: Tu-Sa noon-4, Su 1-5; closed
Mondays
USER FEES: 50 cents
COPYING FACILITIES: no
MATERIALS SOLICITED: Will selectively
accept material on Paducah and the
Jackson Purchase area.

HOLDINGS:
Total volume: 2.2 c.f.; 2 vols.
Inclusive dates: 1890 -
Description: Correspondence and
clippings relating to the Museum, a prescription ledger from the turn of the century, clippings about Vice President
Alben W. Barkley, deeds signed by Paducah founder William Clark, an early map,
and land grants signed by Kentucky governors.

PARIS

KY61A-640
Paris-Bourbon County Library
701 High Street
Paris KY 40361

(606) 987-4419

OPEN: M-F 9-5, Sa 9-3; closed Sundays
COPYING FACILITIES: yes
MATERIALS SOLICITED: Will accept documents and papers relating to the historic development of Paris and Bourbon County.

HOLDINGS:
Total volume: 3.3 c.f.
Inclusive dates: 1888 - 1968
Description: Photographs depicting late
19th and early 20th century development
of Paris and Bourbon County, as well as
scrapbooks of clippings compiled by Paris
author Edna Talbott Whitley.

PETERSBURG

KY62G-120
Chapin Memorial Library
Market Street
Petersburg KY 41080

(606) 586-5265

OPEN: Tu 1-3, W 10-noon, Th 6-8;
closed other days
COPYING FACILITIES: no
MATERIALS SOLICITED: Will accept ma-
terials relating to the history of
Petersburg.

HOLDINGS:
Total volume: 0.5 c.f.
Inclusive dates: 1857 - 1949
Description: Diaries of Petersburg resi-
dent Lewis A. Loder relating to the early
Petersburg community and correspon-
dence of the Library's founder E. Y.
Chapin.

PIPPA PASSES

KY630-40
Alice Lloyd College
Appalachian Oral History Project
Pippa Passes KY 41844

(606) 368-2101

OPEN: M-F 8-4:30; closed weekends and
holidays
COPYING FACILITIES: yes
MATERIALS SOLICITED: History and folklore of the central Appalachian region.

HOLDINGS:
Total volume: 2,000 hours of tapes
and 5,000 photographs
Inclusive dates: late 19th century -
Description: Oral history tapes and historical photographs dealing with the life,
history, and folklore of the Appalachian
area.

SEE: Parkinson; Hinding.

SEE ALSO: Alan M. Meckler and Ruth McMullin, comps., *Oral History Collections* (Bowker, 1975); *The Appalachian Oral History Project Union Catalog* (Appalachian Oral History Project, 1977).

PRESTONSBURG

KY6-640

Prestonsburg Community College Library
HC 69, P.O. Box 230
Prestonsburg KY 41653

(606) 886-3863

OPEN: M-Th 8-8, F 8-4:30; closed weekends
COPYING FACILITIES: yes

HOLDINGS:
Total volume: 0.3 c.f.
Inclusive dates: 1962 - 1979
Description: Genealogy and family histories, as well as a scrapbook detailing the community college's construction and early activities.

RICHMOND

KY680-180

Eastern Kentucky University
Archives Division
Richmond KY

MAILING ADDRESS:
University Archives
Room 26, Cammack Building
Richmond KY 40475-0937

(606) 622-2820

OPEN: M-F 8-4:30; closed weekends and holidays
COPYING FACILITIES: yes
MATERIALS SOLICITED: Records that relate to the history and administration of the University and its predecessor institutions; papers of persons or organizations associated with the University; and manuscripts and related materials of individuals and groups outside the University which document cultural, social, political, economic, and historical developments of the region served by the University.

HOLDINGS:
Total volume: 1,100 c.f.; 1,200 oral history tapes; 250 films
Inclusive dates: 1810 -
Description: Official university records; personal papers of university presidents, faculty and alumni; collections of family, business and civic manuscripts from Richmond and Madison County; church records from Madison and surrounding counties; collections of personal papers of Kentucky politicians, including Governor Keen Johnson and William L. Wallace.
Inactive records of academic and professional organizations, including the Ohio Valley Athletic Conference and the Kentucky Academy of Science; and oral history collections on Kentucky county judges, school superintendents, newspaper editors, politicians, and the University's historical development.

SEE ALSO: Inventories of papers of University presidents and faculty members available from the repository.

KY680-190

Eastern Kentucky University
Crabbe Library
Townsend Room
Richmond KY 40475

(606) 622-1792

OPEN: M-F 8-4:30; closed weekends and when University is not in session
COPYING FACILITIES: yes
MATERIALS SOLICITED: Material related to Kentucky.

HOLDINGS:
Total volume: 3,200 items
Inclusive dates: 1900 -
Description: A collection of letters, manuscripts, and papers relating chiefly to the history and literature of Kentucky. Included are letters and papers of Irvin S. Cobb, Willard R. Jillson, John Wilson Townsend, French Tipton and Turley Noland.

SEE: Hamer.

SEE: Hinding; Robbins.

SEE ALSO: Charles F. Hinds, 'Kentucky Records: How to Use Them and Where They are Located,' *National Genealogical Society Quarterly* 59 (March 1971).

ST. CATHARINE

KY710-160

Dominican Sisters of St. Catharine of Siena
Archives
St. Catharine Motherhouse
St. Catharine KY 40061

(606) 336-9303, Ext. 41

OPEN: M-F 10-5 by appointment only; closed holidays, Christmas week, and Holy Week
ACCESS: advance permission required
COPYING FACILITIES: yes
MATERIALS SOLICITED: Materials pertaining to the ministry activities of the Dominican Sisters of St. Catharine of Siena. Will also accept materials made or received by the Dominican Sisters or any institution staffed by them.

HOLDINGS:
Total volume: 185 l.f.; 16 file drawers; blueprint cabinet
Inclusive dates: 1822 -
Description: Manuscripts relating to the history of the Dominican Sisters of St. Catharine of Siena Congregation.

SEE: Hinding.

SHELBYVILLE

KY76Y-760

Shelby County Library
309 8th Street
Shelbyville KY 40065

(502) 633-3803

OPEN: M-Sa 9:30-5:30; closed Sundays
COPYING FACILITIES: yes
MATERIALS SOLICITED: Family histories and other historical materials concerning Shelbyville and Shelby County.

HOLDINGS:
Total volume: 7 l.f.; 1 vol.
Inclusive dates: 1860 -
Description: Genealogical files, cemetery indexes, news clippings, and photographs of homes and buildings, relating to Shelby County history.

SHEPHERDSVILLE

KY760-720

Ridgway Memorial Library
2nd and Walnut Streets
Shepherdsville KY

MAILING ADDRESS:
P.O. Box 146
Shepherdsville KY 40165

(502) 543-7675

OPEN: M 9-6, Tu-Sa 9-5; closed Sundays
COPYING FACILITIES: yes
MATERIALS SOLICITED: Archival material on Bullitt County, KY.

HOLDINGS:
Total volume: 5 l.f.
Inclusive dates: 1965 -
Description: News clippings, family histories, reports, and an oral history collection, concerning Bullitt County, KY, and Shepherdsville, with reference to Bernheim Forest, government, politics, education, the salt works, churches, parks, shrines, clubs, organizations, schools, Camp Crescendo, and Camp Shantituck.

SOMERSET

KY78J-650

Pulaski County Public Library and Pulaski County Historical Society
North Main Street
Somerset KY

MAILING ADDRESS:
Box 36
Somerset KY 42501

(606) 679-1734

OPEN: Tu-Th 9-6, F 9-9, Sa 9-5; closed Sundays and Mondays
COPYING FACILITIES: yes
MATERIALS SOLICITED: Local history materials and genealogical materials dealing with Kentucky and the surrounding States.

HOLDINGS:
Total volume: not specified
Inclusive dates: 1600 -
Description: Family histories, local histories, copies of public records and other genealogical materials, records of the Somerset Chapter of the Daughters of the American Revolution, and county court records, 1806-15.

KY78J-760
Somerset Community College
Harold D. Strunk Learning Resource Center
808 Monticello Road
Somerset KY 42501

(606) 678-8174

OPEN: M-Th 8-7, F 8-5; closed weekends
COPYING FACILITIES: yes
MATERIALS SOLICITED: Will accept materials dealing with the local area.

HOLDINGS:
Total volume: 1 c.f.
Inclusive dates: 1880 - 1960
Description: Photographs and clippings dealing with the destruction and relocation of Old Burnside.

STANFORD

KY79F-320
Harvey Helm Memorial Historical Library and Museum
415 West Main
Stanford KY

MAILING ADDRESS:
301 Third Street
Stanford KY 40484

(606) 365-7513

OPEN: W 1:30-3:30, Sa 1-4, or by appointment
COPYING FACILITIES: yes
MATERIALS SOLICITED: Will accept materials relating to the development of Stanford and Lincoln County, KY.

HOLDINGS:
Total volume: 4.9 c.f.
Inclusive dates: 1819 -
Description: Records and papers relevant to the history of Lincoln County and a file of genealogical materials.

STURGIS

KY800-760
Sturgis Public Library
Seventh Street
Sturgis KY 42459

(502) 333-5547

OPEN: M-F 12:30-5, Sa 10:30-4; closed Sundays and holidays
COPYING FACILITIES: yes
MATERIALS SOLICITED: Will accept material relating to Sturgis and Union County, KY.

HOLDINGS:
Total volume: 6 vols.
Inclusive dates: 1954 - 1967
Description: Scrapbooks dealing with the community and the library.

VERSAILLES

KY834-480
Logan Helm-Woodford County Public Library
115 North Main Street
Versailles KY 40383

(606) 873-5191

OPEN: M, Th-Sa 10-5:30, Tu, W 10-9, Su 2-5
COPYING FACILITIES: yes
MATERIALS SOLICITED: Will accept materials relating to the history of Versailles and Woodford County.

HOLDINGS:
Total volume: 3.3 c.f.
Inclusive dates: 1804 - 1976
Description: Scrapbooks of Woodford County organizations and residents, 19th century ledgers, photographs of historic homes and businesses in Versailles and Midway, KY, and oral history tapes of interviews and reminiscences of Woodford County residents.

WARSAW

KY85G-290
Gallatin County Public Library
West Pearl Street
Warsaw KY 41095

no telephone

OPEN: M-W, F, Sa 9-5, Th 9-8; closed Sundays
COPYING FACILITIES: yes
MATERIALS SOLICITED: Materials relating to the development of Warsaw and Gallatin County.

HOLDINGS:
Total volume: 0.5 c.f.
Inclusive dates: 1957 -
Description: Genealogical research papers, family history papers, manuscript county histories, and oral history tapes.

WHITLEY CITY

KY87S-520
McCreary County Public Library
Whitley City KY

MAILING ADDRESS:
P.O. Box 8
Whitley City KY 42653

(606) 376-8738

OPEN: M 9-7, Tu-F 9-5:30, Sa 9-4; closed Sundays
COPYING FACILITIES: yes
MATERIALS SOLICITED: Oral history and local history materials.

HOLDINGS:
Total volume: not specified
Inclusive dates: 1912 -
Description: An oral history collection and a pictorial history.

WILLIAMSBURG

KY876-120
Cumberland College
Hagan Memorial Library
821 Walnut Street
Williamsburg KY 40769

(606) 549-2200, Ext. 329

OPEN: M-F 7:45-11, Sa noon-11, Su 2:30-11; closed holidays
COPYING FACILITIES: yes
MATERIALS SOLICITED: Materials concerning Baptists, Kentucky Baptists, and southeastern Kentucky history, as well as local photographs, manuscripts, and genealogical materials.

HOLDINGS:
Total volume: 1,000 items
Inclusive dates: 1870 -
Description: Manuscripts, photographs, and genealogical materials concerning southeastern Kentucky.

WILMORE

KY886-30
Asbury College
Morrison-Kenyon Library
North Lexington Avenue
Wilmore KY 40390

(606) 858-3511

OPEN: M-Th 7:30-10:45, F 7:30-9, Sa 9-9; variable summer hours; closed Sundays
COPYING FACILITIES: yes
MATERIALS SOLICITED: Records of Asbury College. Will also accept other materials relating to the College's history.

HOLDINGS:
Total volume: 42.4 c.f.
Inclusive dates: 1923 -
Description: Records of Good News, an evangelical Methodist publisher in Wilmore, papers of Methodist missionary Alex J. Reid, annual reports of the college registrar, other college records and faculty and staff papers, college bulletins and catalogs, alumni newsletters, student yearbooks and publications, and student handbooks, including publications of Bethel Academy, a four-year high school operated by the college, 1927-38.

KY886-50
Asbury Theological Seminary
B. L. Fisher Library
North Lexington Avenue
Wilmore KY 40390

(606) 858-3581, Ext. 246

OPEN: M-F 8-4, Sa 9-4; closed Sundays and holidays
ACCESS: prior arrangements must be made

COPYING FACILITIES: yes

MATERIALS SOLICITED: Materials pertaining to Methodism and the Holiness movement. Will also accept papers of noted preachers in those fields, noted missionaries, and Christian and social service organizations.

HOLDINGS:
Total volume: 334 l.f.
Inclusive dates: 1900 -
Description: Papers of the Christian Holiness Association, the Asa Mahan Society, theologians John Paul and Albert Day and various Christian and social service organizations, and the archives of the Asbury Theological Seminary.

SEE: NUCMC, 1978.

LOUISIANA

In 1968 the State Archives and Records Service of the Louisiana Secretary of State's Office implemented a preservation program for local public records. Permanently valuable parish and municipal records normally remain in the custody of local authorities, but small quantities of these records are housed in Baton Rouge at the State Archives and at the Department of Archives of the Louisiana State University Library. Researchers at the State Archives also have access to some 300 reels of microfilm of land and police records for 12 parishes of the period 1740-1960.

ALEXANDRIA

LA26-480
Louisiana State University at
  Alexandria
James C. Bolton Library
Alexandria LA 71301

(318) 473-6437

OPEN: M-Th 7:30-8, F 7:30-4:30, Sa 8:30-12:30; closed Sundays, holidays, and evenings and Saturdays when University is not in session
COPYING FACILITIES: yes
MATERIALS SOLICITED: Will accept materials documenting the history of Louisiana, especially its central region.

HOLDINGS:
  Total volume: 13 l.f.
  Inclusive dates: 1796 -
  Description: Land deeds, slave sale papers, diaries, ledgers, and letter books, 1796-1857, and 11 l.f. of student term papers on central Louisiana (1969-), including some tapes and snapshots.

BATON ROUGE

LA62-430
Louisiana Division of Historic
  Preservation
666 N. Foster
Baton Rouge LA

MAILING ADDRESS:
P.O. Box 44247
Baton Rouge LA 70804

(504) 922-0358

OPEN: M-F 8-4:30; closed weekends and holidays
COPYING FACILITIES: yes

HOLDINGS:
  Total volume: 30 c.f.
  Inclusive dates: late 18th century -
  Description: Files concerning 271 Louisiana properties built from the late 18th to early 20th centuries and listed in the National Register of Historic Places. Included are historical evaluations, architectural evaluations, photographs, slides, and copies of land deeds and title searches.

LA62-470
Louisiana Secretary of State
Archives and Records Division
1515 Choctaw Drive
Baton Rouge LA

MAILING ADDRESS:
P.O. Box 94125
Baton Rouge LA 70804

(504) 342-5440

OPEN: M-F 8-4:30; closed weekends and holidays
COPYING FACILITIES: yes

HOLDINGS:
  Total volume: 2,000 cubic feet
  Inclusive dates: 1702 -
  Description: State government records and other papers pertaining to the history of Louisiana, including church records, journals and diaries, land records, surveying notes, acts of State, treaties, and executive orders, as well as the records of several parishes and cities.

SEE: Hinding.

SEE ALSO: Calendars of colonial documents and a guide to the St. Landry Parish archives are available from the repository.

LA62-490
Louisiana State Library
Louisiana Division
760 Riverside North
Baton Rouge LA

MAILING ADDRESS:
P.O. Box 131
Baton Rouge LA 70821

(504) 342-4914

OPEN: M-F 8-4:30; closed weekends and holidays
COPYING FACILITIES: yes
MATERIALS SOLICITED: Will accept photographs.

HOLDINGS:
  Total volume: 112 l.f.
  Inclusive dates: 1930 -
  Description: Research and related materials of the WPA Writers' Program, Louisiana, including 28 unpublished interviews with former slaves. There is also a large collection of black and white photographs of Louisiana people and scenes, mostly from the 1930's.

SEE: Hamer; NUCMC, 1959-61.

SEE: Hinding.

SEE ALSO: Ann Novotny, ed., *Picture Sources 3* (Special Libraries Assn., 1975).

LA62-500
Louisiana State University
Hill Memorial Library
Special Collections
Baton Rouge LA 70803-3300

(504) 388-6551

OPEN: M-F 7:30-4, Sa 8-12; closed Sundays and holidays
COPYING FACILITIES: no
MATERIALS SOLICITED: Materials pertaining to Louisiana and the lower Mississippi Valley. Will also accept other materials of interest to the southern United States provided they are of sufficient scholarly value.

HOLDINGS:
  Total volume: 3.5 million items; 250 c.f.
  Inclusive dates: 1650 -
  Description: Over 3,500 collections, pertaining mainly to the history, culture, economy and other aspects of Louisiana and the lower Mississippi River Valley. Materials include papers of individuals and families, records of businesses and organizations, unpublished histories and memoirs, military records, public records, institutional records, photographs, and audio tape recordings. They document, in particular, plantation economy, slavery, the Civil War, southern political history of the 19th and 20th centuries, and southern economic, cultural, religious and intellectual life. Included are archives of Louisiana State University, containing papers of faculty members and campus organizations, historical materials, records and reports of academic departments, and official administrative records.

SEE: Hamer; NUCMC, 1969-72, 75, 78.

SEE: Hinding; Robbins; Allard, Crawley, and Edmison; Beers - Confederate.

SEE ALSO: V. L. Bedsole, 'Collections in the Department of Archives and Manuscripts, Louisiana State University,' *Louisiana History* 1 (Fall 1960); Walter Schatz, ed., *Directory of Afro-American Resources* (Bowker, 1970); Peter Duignan, *Handbook of American Resources for African Studies* (Hoover Institution, 1967); Ann Novotny, ed., *Picture Sources 3* (Special Libraries Assn.,

1975); Albert Krichmar, *The Women's Rights Movement in the United States, 1848-1970: A Bibliography and Sourcebook* (Scarecrow Press, 1972); T. Harry Williams and John Milton Price, 'The Huey P. Long Papers at Louisiana State University,' *Journal of Southern History* 36 (May 1970); Thomas H. English, *Roads to Research* (Univ. of Georgia Press, 1968); Richard C. Davis, *North American Forest History: A Guide to Archives and Manuscripts in the United States and Canada* (Clio Books, 1977).

LA62-710

Southern University
Library
Black Heritage Collection
Baton Rouge LA 70813

(504) 771-2843, 4990

OPEN: M-F 8-5; closed weekends
ACCESS: prior notification preferred
COPYING FACILITIES: yes
MATERIALS SOLICITED: Southern University and blacks in America.

HOLDINGS:
    Total volume: 619 c.f.
    Inclusive dates: 1880 -
    Description: University records, faculty papers, and papers of a University president, dating from 1914.

HAMMOND

LA286-720

Southeastern Louisiana University
Library
Archives Department
Hammond LA

MAILING ADDRESS:
P.O. Drawer 896
University Station
Hammond LA 70402

(504) 549-2234

OPEN: by appointment only
ACCESS: advance arrangements preferable
COPYING FACILITIES: yes
MATERIALS SOLICITED: Materials pertaining to the Florida parishes of Louisiana.

HOLDINGS:
    Total volume: 80 c.f.
    Inclusive dates: late 1800's -
    Description: The papers of U.S. Representative James H. Morrison, in addition to a few diaries and papers of local residents and some photographs.

LAFAYETTE

LA358-160

Diocese of Lafayette
Archives
515 Cathedral Street
Lafayette LA

MAILING ADDRESS:
P.O. Drawer 3387
Lafayette LA 70701

(318) 233-7788

OPEN: M-F 8-4:30; closed weekends, holidays, and holy days
ACCESS: advance arrangements recommended
COPYING FACILITIES: yes
MATERIALS SOLICITED: Materials concerning the secular and religious history of southwestern Louisiana.

HOLDINGS:
    Total volume: 150 l.f.; 300 vols.; 150 reels of film
    Inclusive dates: 1756 -
    Description: Archives of the Roman Catholic Diocese of Lafayette, 1918 to the present, covering the area of 12 civil parishes in southwestern Louisiana. Also included are materials relating to parishes and priests involved in the separation from the Archdiocese of New Orleans.

SEE ALSO: Computerized index to several collections of correspondence.

LA358-165

Diocese of Lake Charles
Archives
515 Cathedral Street
Lafayette LA

MAILING ADDRESS:
P.O. Box 3223
Lake Charles LA 70602

(318) 439-7400

OPEN: M-F 8-4:30; closed weekends, holidays and religious holidays
ACCESS: serious scholars, thesis writers, church historians; advance arrangements preferred
COPYING FACILITIES: yes
MATERIALS SOLICITED: Archival materials concerning the secular and religious history of southwest Louisiana (Imperial Calcasieu).

HOLDINGS:
    Total volume: 20 l.f.
    Inclusive dates: 1850 -
    Description: Archives of the Roman Catholic Diocese of Lake Charles, established in 1980, covering Calcasieu, Cameron, Jefferson Davis, Allen, and Beauregard parishes. Also included are materials on priests and parishes of the area when under the jurisdiction of the Archdiocese of New Orleans and Diocese of Lafayette.

LA358-800

University of Southwestern Louisiana
Dupre Library
Southwestern Archives and Manuscripts Collections
302 E. St. Mary Boulevard
Lafayette LA

MAILING ADDRESS:
U.S.L. Box 4-0199
Lafayette LA 70504

(318) 231-5702

OPEN: M-F 8-5; closed weekends and holidays
COPYING FACILITIES: yes
MATERIALS SOLICITED: Louisiana history and customs, rice industry, petroleum industry (Gulf Coast only), area business records, and family papers. Will also accept sugar industry papers, petroleum industry papers, and parish and municipal records of the Lafayette area.

HOLDINGS:
    Total volume: 1,234 l.f.
    Inclusive dates: 1605 -
    Description: Collections covering the history, social life, and customs of the French-speaking people and other residents of Louisiana, particularly the region of Acadiana. Included are records of industries and business concerns, particularly the rice industry, papers of pioneer families and individuals, photographs, maps, and ledgers. Microfilmed copies of Louisiana colonial records deposited in the archives of Paris, London, and Madrid cover the period from 1605 to 1805.
    Also included are archives of the University of Southwestern Louisiana, particularly presidential papers and faculty and alumni materials.

SEE: NUCMC, 1967, 69, 76.

SEE: Hinding; Schatz.

LAKE CHARLES

LA395-520

McNeese State University
Frazar Memorial Library
Archives and Special Collections
Lake Charles LA 70609

(318) 437-5000

OPEN: M-Th 7:45-10, F 7:45-4:30, Sa 8-6, Su 1-10; closed Thanksgiving, Christmas, and Mardi Gras
COPYING FACILITIES: yes
MATERIALS SOLICITED: Materials relating to McNeese State University, Lake Charles, and southwestern Louisiana.

HOLDINGS:
    Total volume: 18 l.f.
    Inclusive dates: 1865 -
    Description: Materials relating to the history of McNeese State University, records of John McNeese, manuscripts of University faculty, and photographs, maps, correspondence, diaries, and personal papers concerning the early history of the culture, finance, politics, and religion of Lake Charles and southwestern Louisiana.

MANSFIELD

LA465-480

Mansfield State Commemorative Area
LA 175 South
Mansfield LA

MAILING ADDRESS:
Route 2, P.O. Box 459
Mansfield LA 71052

(318) 872-1474

OPEN: W-Su 9-5; closed Mondays,
Tuesdays, Thanksgiving, Christmas,
and New Year's
USER FEES: students 50 cents, adults one
dollar
COPYING FACILITIES: no
MATERIALS SOLICITED: Anything relating
to the Civil War, especially the Red
River campaign.

HOLDINGS:
Total volume: 125 items
Inclusive dates: 1850 - 1865
Description: Correspondence, diaries,
and other material concerning the Civil
War, especially the Red River campaign.
Copies of original diaries about the cam-
paign are also available.

MONROE

LA535-560

Northeast Louisiana University
Sandel Library
Archives and Special Collections
Monroe LA 71201

(318) 342-2011

OPEN: M-F 8-5; closed weekends and
holidays
COPYING FACILITIES: yes
MATERIALS SOLICITED: Materials on
Northeast Louisiana University and the
eleven-parish region of northeastern
Louisiana.

HOLDINGS:
Total volume: 300,000 items
Inclusive dates: 1713 -
Description: Records and publications
of Northeast Louisiana University from
its inception as Ouachita Junior College
in 1931. Also manuscripts, diaries and
papers from and about northeastern Louisiana and its people.

GUIDES: *Catalog of Manuscript Collections* (1979).

SEE ALSO: A published inventory of the
Otto E. Passman collection is available
from the institution.

LA535-600

Ouachita Parish Public Library
Special Collections
1800 Stubbs Avenue
Monroe LA 71201

(318) 387-1950

OPEN: Su 2-5, M, Tu, Th, F 9-6, W
12:30-9, Sa 9-5; closed holidays
COPYING FACILITIES: no

MATERIALS SOLICITED: Manuscripts,
records, and visual documents relating
to local history.

HOLDINGS:
Total volume: 700 items
Inclusive dates: 1860 -
Description: Local history materials, including photographs of northeastern Louisiana, 1900-40, genealogical records, funeral home ledgers, collections of ephemera, and manuscripts of the Work
Projects Administration, Writers' Program, fifth district, Louisiana.

NATCHITOCHES

LA570-540

Northwestern State University of
Louisiana
Watson Library
Archives Division
Natchitoches LA 71497

(318) 357-4585

OPEN: M-F 8-5:30; closed weekends and
state holidays
COPYING FACILITIES: yes
MATERIALS SOLICITED: Local, colonial,
women's, political, and social history,
photographs, family history, literary
manuscripts, and personal collections
of writers. Will also accept maps,
drawings, and historical and literary
materials from areas other than
northwestern Louisiana.

HOLDINGS:
Total volume: 1,100 c.f.
Inclusive dates: 1725 - 1970
Description: Materials dealing with
18th century social and political history
of the area governed by the commandant
of the Natchitoches post; 19th century
family and Civil War correspondence,
diaries, and business and plantation
records; and 20th century literary and
journalistic writings, local genealogies,
notes from oral history interviews with
local Indians, and papers on the botany
of northwestern Louisiana.

SEE: NUCMC, 1968.

SEE: Schatz; Robbins; Davis; Hinding.

NEW ORLEANS

LA600-20

Amistad Research Center
Old U.S. Mint Building
400 Esplanade Avenue
New Orleans LA 70116

(504) 522-0432

OPEN: M-Sa 8:30-5; closed Sundays and
holidays
COPYING FACILITIES: yes
MATERIALS SOLICITED: Materials relating
to the history of America's ethnic minorities and race relations. Will also
accept materials related to the history
of the United Church of Christ.

HOLDINGS:
Total volume: 8,500,000 items
Inclusive dates: 1793 -
Description: Materials relating primarily to black history and race relations in
the United States. Papers of clergy and of
missionaries and teachers and religious
societies, especially those involved in race
relations, are prominent among the collections. There are clusters of collections
relating to arts and letters, women, and
legal matters. Other ethnic groups for
which there are materials are Native
Americans, Chinese Americans, and Hispanic Americans.

GUIDES: 'Holdings of the Amistad Research Center' is available on request.

SEE: NUCMC, 1969, 71-72, 74, 76, 78.

SEE ALSO: Walter Schatz, ed., *Directory of
Afro-American Resources* (Bowker,
1970); Clifton H. Johnson, 'Some
Archival Sources on Negro History in
Tennessee,' *Tennessee Historical Quarterly* 28 (Winter 1969); Ann Novotny,
ed., *Picture Sources 3* (Special Libraries
Assn., 1975); Andrea Hinding and
Rosemary Richardson, comps., *Archival
and Manuscript Resources for the Study
of Women's History: A Beginning*
(Univ. of Minnesota Libraries, Social
Welfare History Archives Center,
1972); and several published guides to
microfilm editions of collections.

Several guides to original or microfilmed
collections have been published, and
typescript registers for all collections are
available.

The Amistad Research Center was
formerly located at Fisk University in
Nashville, TN.

LA600-40

Archdiocese of New Orleans
Archives of the Roman Catholic
Archdiocese of New Orleans
1100 Chartres Street
New Orleans LA 70116

(504) 529-2651

OPEN: M-F 9-5; closed weekends,
religious and legal holidays
USER FEES: general fee of $10 per day or
fraction thereof; fee of $10 per hour for
the time required of the archivist in
locating and retrieving materials
ACCESS: advance arrangements required;
genealogical inquiries must be in
writing and are handled exclusively by
the staff
COPYING FACILITIES: yes
MATERIALS SOLICITED: All records pertaining to the work of the Catholic
church in the New Orleans Archdiocese. Will also accept materials directly
or indirectly associated with former (or
present) bishops, clergy, and religious
men or women, including photographs,
artifacts, biographies, and published or
unpublished works by the diocesan
hierarchy and clergy.

HOLDINGS:
Total volume: 725 l.f.
Inclusive dates: 1739 -
Description: Records of the Archdio-
cese of New Orleans, including some ma-
terials pertaining to suffragan sees. Also

in the collection are proceedings of synods and provincial councils, and documents dealing with the establishment of the diocese and the appointment of bishops. Approximately 15,000 manuscripts date from the 19th century, the majority from Louisiana pastors concerning the material and spiritual status of their parishes. There are also photographs of clergy, churches, schools, and other institutions; records of institutions and religious organizations; and architectural blueprints and specifications.

Parish registers of St. Louis Cathedral, New Orleans: baptisms, marriages, burials for the years 1720-1890.

SEE ALSO: Charles E. Nolan, ed., *A Southern Catholic Heritage: An Inventory of the Catholic Archives of Alabama, Louisiana, and Mississippi, Vol. I, 1704-1813* (Archdiocese of New Orleans, 1976).

LA600-160

Dillard University
Will W. Alexander Library
2601 Gentilly Blvd.
New Orleans LA 70122

(504) 283-8822, Ext. 301

OPEN: Su 1-5, Tu-Th 8-10, F 8-8, Sa 9-4; closed holidays
COPYING FACILITIES: yes
MATERIALS SOLICITED: Will accept materials relating to black Americans.

HOLDINGS:
Total volume: 113 vols.
Inclusive dates: 1784 -
Description: McPherson Freedom Memorial Collection, including abolition society minutes, books, pamphlets, and newspapers; also, materials relating to the Mississippi Mission Conference and the Louisiana Conference.

SEE ALSO: Walter Schatz, ed., *Directory of Afro-American Resources* (Bowker, 1970).

LA600-310

The Historic New Orleans Collection
Archives-Manuscripts Division
533 Royal Street
New Orleans LA 70130

(504) 523-4662

OPEN: Tu-Sa 10-4:30; closed Sundays, Mondays, and holidays
COPYING FACILITIES: yes
MATERIALS SOLICITED: Primary materials to complement the Collection's current holdings in New Orleans, Louisiana, and regional history, chiefly papers and records of local persons and events. Will also accept other materials relating to holdings of other divisions in the museum.

HOLDINGS:
Total volume: 100 l.f.
Inclusive dates: 1642 -
Description: Materials relating to the colonial and territorial periods in Louisiana; the Battle of New Orleans; the Civil War and Reconstruction; slavery and free blacks in Louisiana; and local music, business, families, and individuals. Significant materials deal with Pierre Clem-

ent de Laussat, the Louisiana Relief Committee, Louisianians in the Civil War, and the E. G. W. Butler family.

SEE: NUCMC, 1979.

SEE: Hinding; Novotny.

SEE ALSO: *Guide to Research at the Historic New Orleans Collection* (Historic New Orleans Collection, 1978).

LA600-320

Hotel Dieu Hospital
Library
2021 Perdido Street
New Orleans LA

MAILING ADDRESS:
P.O. Box 61262
New Orleans LA 70161

(504) 588-3470

OPEN: M-F 8-4:30; closed weekends and holidays
COPYING FACILITIES: yes
MATERIALS SOLICITED: Materials of historical significance relating to Hotel Dieu.

HOLDINGS:
Total volume: 50 vols.
Inclusive dates: 1859 -
Description: Historical materials pertaining to Hotel Dieu Hospital, including registers of patients, 1859-1900, photographs, and publications of the institution.

SEE: Hamer.

SEE: Hinding.

LA600-455

Louisiana Army and Air National Guard
Office of the Adjutant General
Military Library
Jackson Barracks
New Orleans LA 70146

(504) 271-6262, Ext. 242

OPEN: M-F 7:30-4 by appointment; closed Saturdays, Sundays, and holidays
ACCESS: advance arrangements requested
COPYING FACILITIES: no
MATERIALS SOLICITED: Materials relating to Louisiana State military history.

HOLDINGS:
Total volume: 20 l.f.; 11 file cabinets; 51 boxes
Inclusive dates: 1860 -
Description: The Commissioner of Louisiana military records collection, including records of Louisiana Confederate soldiers and commands.

SEE: Hamer (as Louisiana Military Department, AGO Military Archives).

SEE: Beers - Confederate.

LA600-465

Louisiana Department of Culture, Recreation, and Tourism
Louisiana State Museum
Louisiana Historical Center
Old U.S. Mint
400 Esplanade Avenue
New Orleans LA

MAILING ADDRESS:
P.O. Box 2458
New Orleans LA 70176

(504) 568-8214

OPEN: M-F 8:30-5; closed weekends and holidays
ACCESS: serious scholars; appointments requested
COPYING FACILITIES: yes
MATERIALS SOLICITED: Materials relating to the social, cultural, and political history of Louisiana. Will also accept other materials on an individual basis.

HOLDINGS:
Total volume: 550 l.f.
Inclusive dates: 18th century - early 20th century
Description: Judicial papers of the French Superior Council and Spanish Cabildo of Louisiana, 1718-1803, containing successions; contracts; birth, death and marriage records; ships' and personal estate inventories; correspondence; decrees; and litigation records, all documenting life in French and Spanish colonial Louisiana. There are also miscellaneous collections of personal papers, correspondence, maps and other materials.

Important collections deal with James Wilkinson, John McDonogh, George Hebard Maxwell, the Louisiana State Board of Agriculture and Immigration, Louisianans in the Civil War and Reconstruction, and the Louisiana Committee on the Panama Canal Exposition.

SEE: Hamer; NUCMC, 1976, 80.

SEE: Hinding; Beers - Confederate.

LA600-490

Louisiana State University
Medical Center
Division of Libraries
1542 Tulane Avenue
New Orleans LA 70112

no telephone

SEE: Hamer.

Questionnaire not returned.

LA600-505

Loyola University of New Orleans
Library, Spanish Documents Project
6363 St. Charles Avenue
New Orleans LA

MAILING ADDRESS:
P.O. Box 198
New Orleans LA 70118

(504) 865-3346

OPEN: M-F 9-4:30; closed weekends and religious and legal holidays
COPYING FACILITIES: no

MATERIALS SOLICITED: Papeles Procedentes de Cuba, Archivo General de Indias, Seville.

HOLDINGS:
Total volume: 272 microfilm rolls
Inclusive dates: 1622 - 1891
Description: Microfilm of the Santo Domingo Papers, housed in the Archivo General de Indias, Seville, Spain, which were compiled under the Spanish colonial administrative body, the Audencia de Santo Domingo, and relate to the Spanish colony of Louisiana. French documents on microfilm include the Archives Nationale's series of correspondence received in France from colonial officials in Louisiana, as well as a series of ships' logs, 1676-1793. Other microfilms include Propaganda Fide records from the archives of the papal Congregatio de Propaganda Fide, relating to the missionary activities on the African continent of the papal Sacra Congregatio de Propaganda Fide.

SEE ALSO: Catalogo de documentos del Archivo General de Indias, seccion V, gobierno, Audiencia de Santo Domingo, sobre la epoca espanola de Luisiana (Direccion General de Archivos y Bibliotecas and Loyola Univ., 1968); Nicola Kowalsky, 'Inventario dell'Archivo storico della S. Congregazione 'de Propaganda Fide,' *Neue Zeitschrift fur Missionswissenschaft/Nouvelle Revue de science missionnaire* 17 (1961). Other catalogs and finding aids available at the institution.

LA600-540

New Orleans Baptist Theological
   Seminary
Library
3939 Gentilly Boulevard
New Orleans LA 70126

(504) 282-4455

OPEN: M-F 7:45-10, Sa 9-3; closed Sundays and holidays
COPYING FACILITIES: yes
MATERIALS SOLICITED: Materials relating to theology, religion, the Bible, church music, religious education, and Baptists.

HOLDINGS:
Total volume: not specified
Inclusive dates: 1854 -
Description: Materials pertaining to the New Orleans Baptist Theological Seminary and individuals connected with that institution, including correspondence, scrapbooks, manuscript sermons, logs, and letters.

LA600-555

New Orleans Public Library
Louisiana Division
219 Loyola Avenue
New Orleans LA 70140

(504) 596-2550

OPEN: Tu-Sa 10-6; closed Sundays, Mondays, and holidays
COPYING FACILITIES: yes

MATERIALS SOLICITED: City of New Orleans municipal records; photographic materials on Louisiana; and Mardi Gras materials. Will also accept other materials, although collections which do not add to already existing strengths are referred to other repositories in the State.

HOLDINGS:
Total volume: 12,000 vols.; 1,000,000 pieces
Inclusive dates: 1769 -
Description: A collection of records relating chiefly to colonial Louisiana and the municipal government of the City of New Orleans. Included are ledgers, letters, maps and plans, photographs, sound and silent films, microfilms, and sound recordings documenting the city. Nongovernmental records in the collection include those of the Women's Anti-Lottery League; the ERA Club (Equal Rights Association); Local Council of Women of New Orleans; and the Girod Asylum.

SEE: Hamer (as Department of Archives, New Orleans Public Library); NUCMC, 1965, 69, 77-78.

SEE: Krichmar; Hinding; Robbins.

SEE ALSO: Collin B. Hamer, Jr., 'Records of the City of Lafayette (1833-52) in the City Archives Department of the New Orleans Public Library,' *Louisiana History* 13 (Fall 1972); Collin B. Hamer, Jr., *Genealogical Materials in the New Orleans Public Library* (New Orleans Public Library, 1975); Collin B. Hamer, Jr., 'Records of the City of Jefferson (1850-70) in the City Archives Department of the New Orleans Public Library,' *Louisiana History* 17 (Winter 1976). Several unpublished guides are available for sections of the collection.

Collin B. Hamer, Jr., *Researchers' Guide to the Resources of the Louisiana Division of the New Orleans Public Library* (New Orleans Public Library, 1978).

LA600-690

Religious Sisters of Mercy
Archives, Louisiana Area
301 N. Jefferson Davis Parkway
New Orleans LA 70119

MAILING ADDRESS:
P.O. Box 19024
New Orleans LA 70179

(504) 486-7361

OPEN: by appointment only
ACCESS: serious scholars
COPYING FACILITIES: yes
MATERIALS SOLICITED: Materials concerning the Sisters of Mercy in New Orleans community branch convents in Florida, Alabama, Mississippi, and Louisiana.

HOLDINGS:
Total volume: 25 l.f.
Inclusive dates: 1869 - 1929
Description: Financial records, chronicles, annals, board and chapter minutes, registers of sisters, lists of deceased sisters, school and asylum roll books, records of institutions administered by sisters, copies of Roman records and records of other Sisters of Mercy

jurisdictions, one letter of Catherine McAuley, letters and business correspondence of Austin Carroll, and international newspaper clippings concerning the Sisters of Mercy.

LA600-710

St. Mary's Dominican College
The John XXIII Library
550 Pine Street
New Orleans LA 70118

no telephone

SEE: Hamer.

Questionnaire not returned.

LA600-755

Tulane University
Howard-Tilton Memorial Library
Special Collections Division
Manuscripts Collection
7001 Freret Street
New Orleans LA 70118

(504) 865-5685, 5686

OPEN: M-F 8:30-5, Sa 9-1; closed Saturdays between semesters, and Sundays and holidays
COPYING FACILITIES: yes
MATERIALS SOLICITED: Historical and political materials pertaining to New Orleans, Louisiana, and the Mississippi Valley, including family papers, business records, church and synagogue records, agricultural records, and materials from charitable and philanthropic organizations. Will also accept literary papers, especially those related to Southern writers.

HOLDINGS:
Total volume: 2,500,000 pieces
Inclusive dates: late 17th century -
Description: Over 2,000 collections mainly relating to New Orleans and Louisiana during the 19th and 20th centuries. Collections include family papers, individual and corporate business records, papers of Louisiana political leaders, Civil War papers (including those of the Louisiana Historical Association), papers of social, civil, charitable and philanthropic organizations, records of the history of medicine, papers of leading women in Louisiana, plantation and slavery materials.

Records of religious organizations, especially those of the Episcopal church in Louisiana and New Orleans synagogues, steamboat materials, and oral history of New Orleans. Literary materials include correspondence, notes and manuscripts of George Washington Cable, William Faulkner, Charles Gayarre, and Lyle Saxon.

SEE: Hamer; NUCMC, 1959-65, 78, 80.

SEE: Schatz; Davis; Hinding; Ingram; Robbins; Martin; Krichmar; Beers - Confederate.

SEE ALSO: Connie G. Griffith, 'Summary of Inventory: Louisiana Historical Association Collection,' *Louisiana History* 9 (1968); Connie G. Griffith, 'Collections in the Manuscripts Sections of Howard-Tilton Memorial Library, Tulane University,' *Louisiana History* 1 (1960); Wilbur E. Meneray, *A Brief Guide to the Manuscripts Section of the Special Collections Division, Tulane University Library* (Tulane Univ. Library, 1977).

Catalogues of several collections have been published by the Tulane University Library.

LA600-760
Tulane University
Latin American Library
New Orleans LA 70118

(504) 865-5681

OPEN: M-F 8-10, Sa 10-4:45; closed Sundays and University holidays
COPYING FACILITIES: yes
MATERIALS SOLICITED: Materials relating to Mexico, Central and South America, and the Caribbean. Will also accept papers or collections of Latin Americanists.

HOLDINGS:
   Total volume: 150 c.f.; 26 file cabinets
   Inclusive dates: 1520 - 1970
   Description: Primarily collections of Mexican manuscripts dealing chiefly with civil and ecclesiastical matters. Included are original and photocopied manuscripts in Amerindian languages and photocopies relating to 16th century Mexico from Spanish and Mexican repositories as well as notes and transcriptions of documents relating to art and architecture in colonial Peru.
   There are papers of 19th century individuals and families including Porter Cornelius Bliss, U.S. diplomat in Mexico; Erwin Paul Dieseldorff, German coffee planter in Guatemala; the Gordoa family, holders of Zacatecas mining and ranching interests; Francisco Morazan, Central American political figure; and Ephraim George Squier, U.S. diplomat and traveler in Latin America; as well as 20th century papers of historian Lewis Hanke. Collections of ethnographic, architectural, and art photographs from Peru, Guatemala, Mexico, and Spain also are held.

SEE: Hamer (as Tulane University, Middle American Research Institute Library).

LA600-761
Tulane University
Howard-Tilton Memorial Library
Special Collections Division
Southeastern Architectural Archive
7001 Freret Street
New Orleans LA 70118

(504) 865-5697

OPEN: M-F 1-5; closed weekends and holidays
COPYING FACILITIES: yes
MATERIALS SOLICITED: Architectural and related materials pertaining to the Southeast, particularly records of architectural offices, including drawings, correspondence, building contract specifications, and photographs.

HOLDINGS:
   Total volume: 1,000,000 items
   Inclusive dates: late 18th century
   Description: Architectural and architecture-related materials pertaining to the Southeast, with emphasis on Louisiana. Included are records of architectural offices, mostly in New Orleans, photographs of historic architecture, and records of the New Orleans Chapter of the American Institute of Architects, Louisiana Landmarks Society, and Tulane School of Architecture.

LA600-764
Tulane University
Howard-Tilton Memorial Library
Special Collections Division
William Ransom Hogan Jazz Archive
7001 Freret Street
New Orleans LA 70118

(504) 865-5688

OPEN: M-F 1-5, Sa 10-noon; closed Sundays and holidays
COPYING FACILITIES: yes
MATERIALS SOLICITED: Business or financial records, correspondence, diaries, journals, logbooks, manuscript public documents, music scores in manuscript, musician's union records, photographs, motion pictures, video tapes, oral history tapes, sound recordings, and scrapbooks, pertaining to jazz.

HOLDINGS:
   Total volume: not specified
   Inclusive dates: early 19th century-
   Description: Primarily jazz materials, with emphasis on early jazz and New Orleans. Also included are materials pertaining to related musical forms.

SEE: Meckler and McMullin; Hinding.

LA600-765
Tulane University
Rudolph Matas Medical Library
New Orleans LA 70112

(504) 588-5155

SEE: Hamer.

Questionnaire not returned.

LA600-775
University of New Orleans
Earl K. Long Library
Archives and Manuscripts/Special Collections Department
New Orleans LA 70148

(504) 286-6543, 7273

OPEN: M-F 8-4:30, Sa 9-1; closed Sundays and University holidays
COPYING FACILITIES: yes
MATERIALS SOLICITED: Materials relating to the urban aspects of contemporary New Orleans, especially records of businesses and labor unions, ethnic groups, and community oriented organizations. Will also accept materials on the history of New Orleans and Louisiana.

HOLDINGS:
   Total volume: 1,800 l.f.
   Inclusive dates: 1821 -
   Description: Over 130 collections relating chiefly to 20th-century New Orleans, but including some material on other parts of the state and nation. Holdings emphasize records of business and labor, and the ethnic and urban aspects of the New Orleans area.
   The archives of the Southern District of the Lutheran Church-Missouri Synod, as well as records of its congregations, pastors, and agencies, are also included, as are the legal archives of the Supreme Court of Louisiana for the period 1813-79, and the records of the Chamber of Commerce of the New Orleans area.

SEE: NUCMC, 1980.

SEE: Hinding; Robbins.

SEE ALSO: unpublished inventory/guides to most of the individual collections available at the repository.

LA600-920
Xavier University of Louisiana
Library
Black Collection
7325 Palmetto Street
New Orleans LA 70125

(504) 486-7411, Ext. 655

OPEN: M-Th 8-10, F 8-5, Sa 9-2, Su 2-10; closed holidays
ACCESS: graduate students and legitimate scholars; written request required at least one day before research visit
COPYING FACILITIES: yes
MATERIALS SOLICITED: Materials relating to slavery in Louisiana, and papers of black families, especially Louisiana residents.

HOLDINGS:
   Total volume: 20 boxes; 2,000 items
   Inclusive dates: 1758 - 1897
   Description: Manuscript collections relating to slaves and free blacks, chiefly in Louisiana and especially in New Orleans. Letters, deeds, wills, mortgages, bonds, licenses, receipts, and municipal records comprise the bulk of the holdings.

SEE: Hamer; NUCMC, 1979.

SEE ALSO: Walter Schatz, ed., *Directory of Afro-American Resources* (Bowker, 1970); Robert O. Collins and Peter Duignan, *Americans in Africa* (Hoover Institution, 1963).

PINEVILLE

LA670-480
Louisiana College
Norton Memorial Library
1140 College Drive
Pineville LA 71359

(318) 487-7201

OPEN: M-Th 7:45-10, F 7:45-5, Sa 10-5:30; closed two weeks at Easter
COPYING FACILITIES: yes

HOLDINGS:
Total volume: 12 l.f.
Inclusive dates: 1920 - 1979
Description: Tapes, records, manuscripts, scrapbooks, and related materials of white composer and whistler Robert Hunter MacGimsey, who composed 'Sweet Little Jesus Boy,' 'Shadrack,' and other black spiritual pieces.

RUSTON

LA780-490
Louisiana Tech University
Prescott Memorial Library
University Archives
Ruston LA 71272

(318) 257-3555, 2217

OPEN: M-F 8-4; closed weekends and holidays
COPYING FACILITIES: yes
MATERIALS SOLICITED: Northern Louisiana materials. Will also accept other materials.

HOLDINGS:
Total volume: 64 l.f.
Inclusive dates: 1800 -
Description: Mainly private and corporate papers relating to northern Louisiana. The University archives also form part of the collection.

SEE: NUCMC, 1981.

SEE ALSO: Richard C. Davis, *North American Forest History: A Guide to Archives and Manuscripts in the United States and Canada* (Clio Books, 1977).

SHREVEPORT

LA885-120
Centenary College of Louisiana
Magale Library
Cline Room
Shreveport LA

MAILING ADDRESS:
P.O. Box 4188, Centenary Station
Shreveport LA 71134-0188

(318) 869-5170

OPEN: by appointment only; closed holidays
USER FEES: hourly rate charged for research requests by mail taking an inordinate amount of staff time
ACCESS: serious researchers; permission of the Archivist required
COPYING FACILITIES: yes
MATERIALS SOLICITED: Northern Louisiana, Shreveport, Arkansas, Louisiana, and Texas history and culture; Centenary College of Louisiana history including papers of faculty and alumni;

Louisiana Conference of the United Methodist church, including papers of ministers and other persons active in the conference. Will also accept materials relating to Louisiana, southern history, or Methodist history in general.

HOLDINGS:
Total volume: 60 boxes; 30 file drawers; 60 vols.
Inclusive dates: 1825 -
Description: Archives of Centenary College of Louisiana, including records of its predecessor institutions; archives of the Louisiana Conference of the United Methodist church, including a few district and individual church records as well as material on the Methodist Episcopal and Methodist Protestant churches in Louisiana; and a collection assembled by the North Louisiana Historical Association focusing on the history and culture of northern Louisiana.

SEE: Hamer; NUCMC, 1965, 78, 80.

SEE: Hinding.

LA885-480
Louisiana State University, Shreveport
Library
Archives Department
8515 Youree Drive
Shreveport LA 71115

(318) 797-5226

OPEN: M-F 8-4:30; closed weekends and holidays
COPYING FACILITIES: yes
MATERIALS SOLICITED: Historical manuscript materials and public and private organizational records relating to or originating in northwest Louisiana, especially materials on the Red River, the oil and gas industry, agriculture, government and politics, and family papers. Will also accept materials on other sections in Louisiana, southwestern Arkansas or northeastern Texas.

HOLDINGS:
Total volume: 1,015 l.f.
Inclusive dates: 1790 -
Description: 75 collections covering 19th and 20th century political, social and economic history of northwestern Louisiana and the Red River. Included are records of business, political, economic and educational organizations; papers of significant individuals; account books and business records of plantations; diaries; journals; logbooks; maps; and oral history tapes, all documenting the social and economic development of the Red River, the Mississippi River, the oil and gas industry in the area, political, educational and legal events and the activities of city and parish governments.

SEE ALSO: a brochure on the Archives available upon request.

LA885-690
R. W. Norton Art Gallery
Reference Library
4747 Creswell Avenue
Shreveport LA 71106

(318) 865-4201

OPEN: W 1-5, Sa 1-5; closed other days and holidays
COPYING FACILITIES: yes
MATERIALS SOLICITED: Materials on artists represented in the Museum's permanent collection; local and State material of historical value.

HOLDINGS:
Total volume: 3 l.f.
Inclusive dates: early 20th century -
Description: Account books, business records, and other records of the Little Theater of Shreveport and the Cotillion Board of Holiday in Dixie; letters of Frederic Remington; photostatic copies of manuscripts relating to Charles M. Russell; 2 bound volumes of personal war telegrams and dispatches, belonging to Jefferson Davis; miscellaneous letters relating to the Civil War and Sam Houston; and a collection of letters written by Presidents of the United States.

THIBODAUX

LA920-560
Nicholls State University
Ellender Memorial Library
Allen J. Ellender Archives
Thibodaux LA

MAILING ADDRESS:
P.O. Box 2028 NSU
Thibodaux LA 70301

(504) 446-8111, Ext. 406

OPEN: M-F 8-4; closed weekends, holidays and University spring break
COPYING FACILITIES: yes
MATERIALS SOLICITED: Manuscripts, visual and audible documents relating to south central Louisiana.

HOLDINGS:
Total volume: 40,000 items
Inclusive dates: 1800 -
Description: The papers of U.S. Senator Allen J. Ellender and other collections relating chiefly to south central Louisiana, including personal correspondence, business correspondence, sugar plantation diaries, business records, accounting records, music scores in manuscript, scrapbooks, photographs and oral history tapes.

SEE: NUCMC, 1971.

MAINE

Since 1973 the Maine State Archives has administered a statewide program for preserving local public records. Most permanently valuable records generated by political subdivisions have remained in the custody of local officials, but a small number of county and municipal records have been transferred to the State Archives in Augusta. The State Archives also makes available to researchers microfilm copies of town vital records, town meeting records, and other local public records which were filmed by the Church of Jesus Christ of Latter-day Saints. In the initial phase of its own microfilm program, the State Archives has been filming all pre-1850 municipal records not previously microfilmed. In 1976 the State Archives published a revised edition of *Public Record Repositories in Maine,* a guide to the availability, location, and microfilm status of local records.

ALFRED

ME12-640
Parsons Memorial Library
Alfred ME 04002

no telephone
SEE: Hamer.

Questionnaire not returned.

AUBURN

ME25-30
Androscoggin Historical Society
2 Turner Street
Auburn ME 04210

no telephone
SEE: Hamer.

Questionnaire not returned.

ME25-50
Auburn Public Library
Court and Spring Streets
Auburn ME 04210

(207) 782-3191

OPEN: Mondays 9-8, Tu-F 9-6, Sa 9-5 except Summer; closed Sundays between Memorial Day and Labor Day

SEE: Hamer.

Questionnaire not returned.

AUGUSTA

ME37-440
Kennebec Historical Society
91 Western Avenue
Augusta ME 04330

no telephone
SEE: Hamer.

Questionnaire not returned.

ME37-525
Maine State Archives
Augusta ME 04333

(207) 289-2451

OPEN: M-F 8:30-4; closed weekends and holidays
COPYING FACILITIES: yes
MATERIALS SOLICITED: Permanently valuable records of public agencies of the State and its political subdivisions.

HOLDINGS:
Total volume: 50,000 c.f.
Inclusive dates: 1635 -
Description: Records of the executive, legislative, and judicial branches of the Maine State government, in addition to records of the State's political subdivisions.

SEE: Hinding; Davis.

SEE ALSO: *Microfilm List: Maine Town and Census Records* (Maine State Archives, 1980).

Brochures describing military, land, local historical, local genealogical, and other records are available on request.

ME37-535
Maine State Library
Cultural Building
State House Station No. 64
Augusta ME 04333

(207) 289-3561

OPEN: M, W, F 9-5, Tu, Th 9-9, Sa 11-5 during school year; closed Sundays and holidays
COPYING FACILITIES: yes
MATERIALS SOLICITED: Will accept manuscripts pertaining to Maine.

HOLDINGS:
Total volume: 27.7 l.f.; 42.8 c.f.; and maps
Inclusive dates: 1636 -
Description: Papers relating chiefly to Maine. Included are numerous family histories and other genealogical materials; a few diaries and journals; collections of miscellaneous documents pertaining to a number of Maine towns; transcripts and other papers concerning the northeastern boundary; returns of the election of 1819 on the Maine constitution; plans of the Maine State House by Charles Bulfinch; various materials on Maine's participation in the Civil War; blueprints and drawings from the Historic American Buildings Survey; and the Edward B. Draper collection of slides and photographs of Maine scenes, with emphasis on lumbering operations.

SEE: Davis; Hinding.

SEE ALSO: Guides and indexes to some individual collections are available at the institution.

ME37-540
Maine State Museum
State House Station No. 83
Augusta ME

MAILING ADDRESS:
State House Station 83
Augusta ME 04333

(207) 289-2301

OPEN: M-F 9-5; closed weekends and holidays
ACCESS: advance arrangements preferred
COPYING FACILITIES: yes
MATERIALS SOLICITED: Papers of individuals and of non-government organizations with strong relevance to Maine history.

HOLDINGS:
Total volume: 350 l.f.
Inclusive dates: 1700 - 1950
Description: Holdings relating to the history of human activity in Maine, with primary emphasis upon economic activity and socio-political organization.

SEE: Hinding.

SEE ALSO: Ann Novotny, ed., *Picture Sources 3* (Special Libraries Assn., 1975); Richard C. Davis, *North American Forest History: A Guide to Archives and Manuscripts in the United States and Canada* (Clio Books, 1977).

BANGOR

ME50-70
Bangor Historical Society
159 Union Street
Bangor ME 04401

(207) 942-5766

OPEN: Tu-F 10-2; closed other days
COPYING FACILITIES: no
MATERIALS SOLICITED: Bangor-related materials; materials relating to lumbering, shipping, the military, mercantile activities, social history, and biography. Will also accept personal papers, institutional records, and ephemera.

HOLDINGS:
  Total volume: 60 c.f.
  Inclusive dates: 1770's -
  Description: Manuscript materials relating to early Bangor and Maine events, including account books, logs, music scores, correspondence, visual documents, local television station film, glass plates and photographs.

ME50-80
Bangor Public Library
145 Harlow Street
Bangor ME 04401

no telephone

SEE: Hamer.

Questionnaire not returned.

BAR HARBOR

ME62-80
Bar Harbor Historical Society, Inc.
34 Mt. Desert Street
Bar Harbor ME 04609

(207) 288-3838

OPEN: June 15 - Sept. 14, M-Sa 1-4; by appointment Sept. 15 - June 14; closed Sundays and holidays
COPYING FACILITIES: no
MATERIALS SOLICITED: Material concerning Bar Harbor's past.

HOLDINGS:
  Total volume: 1,300 items
  Inclusive dates: 1870's -
  Description: A collection of early photographs of Bar Harbor, account books of hotels and businesses, records and correspondence of early organizations, documents concerning the incorporation of the town of Eden (Bar Harbor) in 1796, blueprints of some early summer cottages, maps and motion pictures of the town in 1928 and 1938.

BATH

ME75-520
Maine Maritime Museum
Library/Archives
963 Washington Street
Bath ME 04530

(207) 443-1316

OPEN: M-F 9-5 by appointment only; closed weekends and holidays
ACCESS: appointment required
COPYING FACILITIES: yes
MATERIALS SOLICITED: Maritime history of Bath, Maine, and New England. Will also accept local and regional history pertaining to the Bath area.

HOLDINGS:
  Total volume: 800 boxes; 765 vols.
  Inclusive dates: 1607 -
  Description: Materials relating to maritime history, especially shipbuilding and related industries in Bath during the 19th century. Included are captains', shipbuilders', and ship owners' letters, account books, and logs; papers of Sewall & Co.-built ships; vessel plans; and a collection of photographs of Bath-built vessels.

SEE: Novotny.

BELFAST

ME87-80
Belfast Museum, Inc.
66 Church Street
Belfast ME 04915

(207) 338-1875, 2078

OPEN: June - Sept., Su 1-4, and by appointment
COPYING FACILITIES: no
MATERIALS SOLICITED: Materials pertaining to life in Belfast from 1770 to the present.

HOLDINGS:
  Total volume: not specified
  Inclusive dates: 1770 -
  Description: Various papers, including ledgers, account books, letters, journals, music scores, and photographs related to the history and life of Belfast and its environs.

BETHEL

ME95-80
Bethel Historical Society, Inc.
Moses Mason Museum
15 Broad Street
Bethel ME

MAILING ADDRESS:
P.O. Box 12
Bethel ME 04217

(207) 824-2908

OPEN: M-F 9-5; closed weekends
COPYING FACILITIES: yes
MATERIALS SOLICITED: Materials relating to Maine, Oxford County, and the White Mountains. Will also accept materials relating to the Bethel area.

HOLDINGS:
  Total volume: 100 l.f.
  Inclusive dates: late 18th century -
  Description: Manuscripts, maps, and photographs relating to western Maine.

SEE: Hinding.

BLUE HILL

ME112-80
Blue Hill Public Library
Blue Hill ME 04614

(207) 374-5515

OPEN: M-Sa 10-5, evening hours Thursdays; closed Sundays, holidays, and 3rd week in April
COPYING FACILITIES: no

HOLDINGS:
  Total volume: 5 l.f.
  Inclusive dates: late 1700's -
  Description: Some town records, records of the Library and its predecessors, since 1796, and some business records, including those of a fulling mill and two granite companies of the late 19th century.

SEE: Hamer (as Ladies' Social Library).

SEE: Hinding.

ME112-400
Jonathan Fisher Memorial, Inc.
Blue Hill ME 04614

(207) 374-2780

OPEN: July 1 - Sept. 15, Tu, F, Sa by appointment only; closed other days and rest of year
COPYING FACILITIES: no
MATERIALS SOLICITED: Papers by or about Jonathan Fisher, his family, and his works.

HOLDINGS:
  Total volume: not specified
  Inclusive dates: 1768 - 1847
  Description: Manuscripts dealing with Jonathan Fisher and his work as pastor, his home, and his pursuits.

BRUNSWICK

ME162-100
Bowdoin College
Peary-Macmillan Arctic Museum
Hubbard Hall
Brunswick ME 04011

(207) 725-5416, 5289, 5304

OPEN: Tu-F 10-4, Sa 10-5, Su 2-5; closed Mondays and holidays
ACCESS: advance arrangements required
COPYING FACILITIES: no

HOLDINGS:
  Total volume: not specified
  Inclusive dates: 1862 -
  Description: Personal memorabilia, photographs and glass slides pertaining to the Arctic exploration of Admirals Robert E. Peary and Donald B. MacMillan, held by the Peary-MacMillan Arctic Museum; and the Winslow Homer collection held by the Bowdoin College Museum of Art,

including a daybook, letters, photographs, photograph albums, scrapbooks, postcards, an address book, and a Civil War pass.

ME162-120
Bowdoin College
Library
Special Collections
Brunswick ME 04011

(207) 725-8731, Ext. 5288

OPEN: M-F 8:30-5; closed weekends and holidays
COPYING FACILITIES: yes
MATERIALS SOLICITED: Materials pertaining to Hawthorne, Longfellow, and other Bowdoin-related authors, and other Maine materials.

HOLDINGS:
Total volume: 400,000 items
Inclusive dates: 1790 -
Description: Primarily a collection of personal and family papers relating to the history of Maine, New England, and Bowdoin College. Also included are some literary manuscripts; the archives of the Atlantic & St. Lawrence Railroad, 1844-89; the Robert A. Bartlett papers, consisting of 15,000 manuscripts, photographs, clippings, and other items concerning his career as an Arctic explorer and shipmaster; and the Oliver Otis Howard papers, consisting of approximately 150,000 items, primarily correspondence to and from General Howard for the period 1843-1908, and covering his service as a Civil War general, founder of the Freedmen's Bureau, president of Howard University, and superintendent of the United States Military Academy.

SEE: Hamer; NUCMC, 1971.

SEE: Hines; Robbins; Hinding.

SEE ALSO: *Hawthorne-Longfellow Library: A Catalogue of Endowed Funds & Selected Special Collections,* Bowdoin College Bulletin, no. 338 (March 1973); Walter Schatz, ed., *Directory of Afro-American Resources* (Bowker, 1970).

ME162-640
Pejepscot Historical Society
Archives Room
Curtis Library
Middle and Pleasant Streets
Brunswick ME 04011

(207) 729-6606, 725-5242

OPEN: by appointment
COPYING FACILITIES: yes
MATERIALS SOLICITED: Materials pertaining to the Brunswick, Harpswell, and Topsham area.

HOLDINGS:
Total volume: 60 l.f.
Inclusive dates: 1732 - 1900
Description: Records, letters, ledgers, and other papers relating to Brunswick and surrounding towns since the colonial period.

SEE: Hamer; NUCMC, 1965.

SEE: Davis.

BUCKSPORT

ME175-80
Bucksport Historical Society, Inc.
Main Street
Bucksport ME

MAILING ADDRESS:
P.O. Box 798
Bucksport ME 04416

(207) 469-2591

OPEN: July-Aug. W-F 1-4; other times by appointment
USER FEES: fifty cents
COPYING FACILITIES: no

HOLDINGS:
Total volume: 275 items
Inclusive dates: 1797 -
Description: Local histories of the fire department, shipbuilding, seagoing vessels, and other topics; ships' logs; account books; copies of memorandum books and surveying notes of Jonathan Buck, founder of Bucksport; and 200 photographs of such subjects as shipbuilding, other local industries, and the ship *Roosevelt,* sailed by Robert Peary on his voyage to discover the North Pole.

BURLINGTON

ME187-730
Stewart M. Lord Memorial Historical Museum
Burlington ME 04417

(207) 732-4121

OPEN: summer, Su, W 2-4; closed rest of year
COPYING FACILITIES: no
MATERIALS SOLICITED: Materials pertaining to the history of Burlington and Lowell, ME.

HOLDINGS:
Total volume: not specified
Inclusive dates: early 1800's -
Description: Scrapbooks, organization records, surveyors' records, photographs, some town records, and other materials pertaining to the history of Burlington and Lowell and their environs.

CALAIS

ME200-120
Calais Free Library
Union Street
Calais ME 04619

(207) 454-3223

OPEN: M-Th 12-8, F 12-6, Sa 1-5; closed Sundays and holidays
COPYING FACILITIES: yes
MATERIALS SOLICITED: Local history.

HOLDINGS:
Total volume: 475 items; 60 notebooks
Inclusive dates: 1600 - 1958
Description: A collection of photographs, journals, scrapbooks and diaries relating chiefly to the history of Calais and the surrounding St. Croix Valley,

which includes parts of New Brunswick, Canada. Included are the James Shepherd Pike papers, 440 items, containing letters on the abolition of slavery, and Richard V. Hayden's notebooks, covering lumbering, shipping, surveying, and personal matters in Robbinston, ME, and its environs.

SEE: Hamer; NUCMC, 1969, 75.

SEE ALSO: Richard C. Davis, *North American Forest History: A Guide to Archives and Manuscripts in the United States and Canada* (Clio Books, 1977).

CAMDEN

ME212-120
Camden-Rockport Historical Society
Old Conway Homestead
Cramer Museum
Camden ME

MAILING ADDRESS:
P.O. Box 897
Camden ME 04843

(207) 236-2720

OPEN: by appointment only
USER FEES: admission charged
COPYING FACILITIES: no
MATERIALS SOLICITED: Will accept records, photographs, and other materials pertinent to early life in Camden and Rockport.

HOLDINGS:
Total volume: 1,000 items
Inclusive dates: 1780 - 1920's
Description: Ships' logs and other records, centering around the history of Camden and Rockport and the shipbuilding industry.

SEE: NUCMC, 1959-61.

CASTINE

ME231-120
Castine Scientific Society
Archives Department
Perkins Street
Castine ME 04421

(207) 326-8753

OPEN: by appointment only
ACCESS: serious researchers
COPYING FACILITIES: yes
MATERIALS SOLICITED: Will accept local manuscripts and photographs.

HOLDINGS:
Total volume: 20 c.f.; other items
Inclusive dates: 1760's - 1880's
Description: Material relating to Castine and the surrounding area, including letters, business papers, diaries, ships' logs, ledgers, maps, and photographs.

DEER ISLE

ME275-160
Deer Isle-Stonington Historical
  Society
Deer Isle ME

MAILING ADDRESS:
RFD Box 46
Deer Isle ME 04627

(207) 348-2886

OPEN: July - Labor Day, W, Sa, Su 2-5;
  other months by appointment
COPYING FACILITIES: no
MATERIALS SOLICITED: Maritime and local history materials.

HOLDINGS:
    Total volume: 400 items
    Inclusive dates: 1865 - 1930's
    Description: A collection of photo-
graphs, original papers, Customs House
books and records, as well as genealogical
material, centering around Deer Isle during its most active years as a maritime
center.

SEE: Hinding.

DEXTER

ME287-160
Dexter Historical Society
Dexter ME 04930

no telephone

OPEN: June 15 - Sept. 15, M-Sa 1-5; rest
  of year, by appointment only; closed
  Sundays
COPYING FACILITIES: no
MATERIALS SOLICITED: Manuscripts,
  maps, photographs, and recordings pertaining to the history of Dexter and its
  environs. Will also accept records of
  local institutions and organizations.

HOLDINGS:
    Total volume: 1,000 items
    Inclusive dates: 1820 -
    Description: Materials of local histori-
cal significance, including materials regarding the businesses, recreational activities, homes, and farms of local residents.

DOVER-FOXCROFT

ME300-760
Thompson Free Library
76 E. Main Street
Dover-Foxcroft ME 04426

(207) 564-3350

OPEN: M-Th 1-8, F 10-6, Sa 1-5;
  June-Sept. closes at 5; closed Sundays
  and holidays

SEE: Hamer.

Questionnaire not returned.

ELLSWORTH

ME337-120
The Colonel Black House
Ellsworth ME 04605

no telephone
SEE: Hamer.

Questionnaire not returned.

FARMINGTON

ME350-560
The Nordica Memorial Association,
  Inc.
53 Holley Road, Route 3
Farmington ME 04938

(207) 778-2042

OPEN: June 1 - Labor Day, Tu-Su 10-5;
  by appointment May, Sept., and Oct.;
  closed Mondays and rest of year
COPYING FACILITIES: no
MATERIALS SOLICITED: Any materials
  pertaining to the life and career of opera singer Lillian Nordica.

HOLDINGS:
    Total volume: not specified
    Inclusive dates: mid-18th century -
early 20th century
    Description: 200 letters between
Nordica and her mother and other rela-
tives, 300 photographs related to Nordica
and her career, her personally noted opera scores, and early Cape Cod deeds of
her ancestors' homes.

ME350-800
University of Maine at Farmington
Mantor Library
41 High Street
Farmington ME 04938

(207) 778-3501, Ext. 349

OPEN: M-Th 8-11, F 8-10, Sa 10-5, Su
  1-11; closes after 4:30 and closed
  weekends when college not in session;
  closed holidays
COPYING FACILITIES: yes
MATERIALS SOLICITED: Materials pertaining to local, regional, and state history and to the University of Maine at
  Farmington.

HOLDINGS:
    Total volume: 20 l.f.
    Inclusive dates: 1800 -
    Description: University records, 1863- ,
historical records and photographs of the
Farmington and Franklin County area,
and oral history recordings of life in the
area, including Flagstaff Lake and
Sugarloaf Mountain.

HALLOWELL

ME425-320
Hubbard Free Library
115 2nd Street
Hallowell ME 04347

(207) 622-6582

OPEN: M, W, F, Sa 2-5:30, Tu, Th 2-6;
  closed Sundays
ACCESS: material to be used in library
COPYING FACILITIES: yes
MATERIALS SOLICITED: Hallowell-related
  materials.

HOLDINGS:
    Total volume: 200 items; several file
drawers
    Inclusive dates: not specified
    Description: Photographs, maps, scrap-
books, and ledgers.

SEE: Hamer.

HOULTON

ME437-120
Cary Library
107 Main Street
Houlton ME 04730

(207) 532-3967

OPEN: M-F 9-8, Sa 9-1; closed Sundays
  and holidays; shorter summer hours
COPYING FACILITIES: yes
MATERIALS SOLICITED: Will accept ma-
  terial concerning Houlton, Aroostook
  County, and Maine.

HOLDINGS:
    Total volume: 6 l.f.; 7 vols.; 135
cassettes
    Inclusive dates: 1794 -
    Description: Collections concerned
mainly with Houlton and Aroostook
County history. Included are four early
19th century letterbooks containing old
deeds, notices of land sales, boundary dispute records, lists of Houlton families,
and logging permits; two account books
covering New Salem, MA, 1805-06, and
Houlton Plantation, 1809-33; complete
records of the Houlton Woman's Club
since 1904 and of the Free Bed Association of the Aroostook Hospital since
1921; and a scrapbook of the local
Pamond Grange, 1878-1929. A collection
of 135 oral history cassettes relates to life
in the County since 1890 and includes
conversations with French and Swedish
settlers.

SEE: Hamer; NUCMC, 1965.

SEE: Meckler and McMullin; Hinding.

ISLESFORD

ME453-40
Acadia National Park
Islesford Historical Museum
Islesford ME

MAILING ADDRESS:
P.O. Box 177
Bar Harbor ME 04609

(207) 288-3338

OPEN: June 20 - Labor Day, 10-4 by
appointment only
COPYING FACILITIES: no
MATERIALS SOLICITED: Manuscripts pertaining to social and economic history
of the area, old Acadia, east coastal
Maine and the Canadian Maritime
Provinces; genealogies of early families
in the area. Will also accept genealogical material to complete existing files.

HOLDINGS:
Total volume: 1,500 items
Inclusive dates: 1640 - 1933
Description: Papers, manuscripts, genealogical data, maps, and photographs;
ships' logs, freight slips, pilot slips, and
other papers pertaining to the schooner
trade from Cranberry Isles, 1796-1890,;
real estate and town papers from the
towns of Cranberry Isles and Mount
Desert; and materials relating to the early
history of Acadia National Park.

KENNEBUNK

ME460-80
The Brick Store Museum
117 Main Street
Box 177
Kennebunk ME

MAILING ADDRESS:
P.O. Box 177
Kennebunk ME 04043

(207) 985-4802

OPEN: Library open Tu-Sa 10-4:30;
research by appointment only; closed
Sundays and Mondays
ACCESS: appointment required
COPYING FACILITIES: yes
MATERIALS SOLICITED: History and ge-
nealogy of Kennebunk, York County,
ME, and Maine.

HOLDINGS:
Total volume: not specified
Inclusive dates: late 18th century -
19th century
Description: Town and family records,
shipbuilding and other industry materials,
maps, and photographs, relating to local
and county history.

ME460-440
Kennebunk Free Library
112 Main Street
Kennebunk ME 04043

(207) 985-2173

OPEN: M, W, F 1-9, Tu, Th, Sa 9:30-5;
closed Sundays, holidays, and at noon
on Saturdays July and Aug.

COPYING FACILITIES: yes
MATERIALS SOLICITED: Kennebunk area
history in text or photographs.
HOLDINGS:
Total volume: 5 boxes; 2 file drawers
Inclusive dates: early 1800's -
Description: Diaries of Andrew Walker, 1851-97, covering events in the
Kennebunks, local and national government news, real estate transactions, and
the lives of local residents. Also included
are a manuscript record book, including
correspondence of the Kennebunk Soldiers' Relief Society, 1861-65, as well as
19th century photographs by Kenneth
Joy of the Kennebunk area and its residents.

SEE: Hamer.

SEE: Hinding.

KENNEBUNKPORT

ME462-440
Kennebunkport Historical Society
North Street
Kennebunkport ME

MAILING ADDRESS:
P.O. Box 405
Kennebunkport ME 04046

(207) 967-2751

OPEN: July - Aug., Tu, Th 1-4; June and
Sept., Tu 1-4; and by appointment
ACCESS: during winter months material
available by prior arrangement
COPYING FACILITIES: no
MATERIALS SOLICITED: Custom House
records, District of Kennebunk,
1800-1913, and related papers. Will
also accept most materials relating to
the history of Kennebunkport.

HOLDINGS:
Total volume: not specified
Inclusive dates: 1678 -
Description: Letters, diaries, journals,
logbooks, account books, hand-written
school books, business and finance
records, photographs, oral history tapes
and transcripts, and a photographic copy
of the Kennebunkport Proprietor's Book,
1678-1790. There are records of the Custom House of the District of Kennebunk,
and documents and business records relating to shipping, shipbuilding, sail makers, riggers, and related occupations.

LEWISTON

ME487-90
Bates College
Library
Lewiston ME 04240

no telephone

SEE: Hamer; NUCMC, 1966.

Questionnaire not returned.

LINCOLN

ME500-480
Lincoln Historical Society
47 Fleming Street
Lincoln ME 04457

no telephone

SEE: Hamer.

Questionnaire not returned.

MACHIAS

ME512-80
Burnham Tavern Museum
Main and Free Streets
Machias ME

MAILING ADDRESS:
60 Court Street
Machias ME 04654

(207) 255-4432

OPEN: Mid-June - Labor Day, M-F 1-5;
rest of year by appointment; closed
weekends
COPYING FACILITIES: no
MATERIALS SOLICITED: Materials pertaining to the history of the Machias
area and eastern Maine.

HOLDINGS:
Total volume: 70 vols.
Inclusive dates: 1763 -
Description: Account books and other
papers of early local settlers, daybooks of
the Civil War period, and about 20 vol-
umes of secretary's reports of the Hannah
Weston Chapter of the Daughters of the
American Revolution.

NEW GLOUCESTER

ME575-560
New Gloucester Historical Society
New Gloucester ME

MAILING ADDRESS:
P.O. Box 3
New Gloucester ME 04260

(207) 926-4437

OPEN: by appointment only
COPYING FACILITIES: no
MATERIALS SOLICITED: Any materials re-
lating to the history of New Gloucester.

HOLDINGS:
Total volume: 10 l.f.
Inclusive dates: 1737 -
Description: Proprietors' records,
record books, church records, organiza-
tion records, letters, diaries, and genea-
logical data relating to the history of New
Gloucester.

SEE: NUCMC, 1959-61.

OGUNQUIT

ME625-600
Ogunquit Free Library
Shore Road
Ogunquit ME 03907

no telephone

SEE: Hamer.

Questionnaire not returned.

ORONO

ME650-780
University of Maine at Orono
Department of Anthropology
Northeast Archives of Folklore and
   Oral History
South Stevens Hall
Orono ME 04469

(207) 581-1891

OPEN: M-F 10-5; closed weekends
ACCESS: an appointment is
   recommended
COPYING FACILITIES: yes
MATERIALS SOLICITED: Oral histories
   and materials relating to the folklore
   and folklife of Maine and the Maritime
   Provinces of Canada. Will also accept
   photographs.

HOLDINGS:
   Total volume: 1,100 reels tape; 1,000
   photographs
   Inclusive dates: 1958 -
   Description: Manuscript and tape-
   recorded material relevant to the folklore,
   folklife, and local history of Maine and
   the Maritime Provinces of Canada. The
   Archives is especially strong in materials
   relating to late 19th and early 20th century lumber camps and river-drives.

SEE: Davis; Hinding.

SEE ALSO: Florence Ireland, 'The Northeast Archives of Folklore and Oral History: A Brief Description and Catalog
   of its Holdings 1958-72,' *Northeast
   Folklore* 13 (1972); Alan M. Meckler
   and Ruth McMullin, comps., *Oral History Collections* (Bowker, 1975).

ME650-810
University of Maine at Orono
Raymond H. Fogler Library
Special Collections Department
Orono ME 04469

(207) 581-1686

OPEN: M-F 8-4:30; Sundays 1-5 during
   fall and spring semesters; closed
   Saturdays
ACCESS: identification required
COPYING FACILITIES: yes
MATERIALS SOLICITED: Materials relating
   to Maine and its people. Will also accept materials relating to maritime history.

HOLDINGS:
   Total volume: 900 boxes; 3,000 l.f.
   Inclusive dates: 1700 -
   Description: Archival records, manuscripts, diaries, logbooks, ledgers and account books, genealogies, correspondence,
   family papers, and other materials relating to Maine history, people and institutions. Included are maps, photographs,
   some recordings and audio items.

SEE: Hamer; NUCMC, 1965, 67, 74, 78.

SEE: Davis; Hinding; Robbins; Allard,
   Crawley, and Edmison.

SEE ALSO: *A Guide to the Special Collections, Raymond H. Fogler Library*
   (Univ. of Maine at Orono, 1974).

PATTEN

ME667-480
The Lumberman's Museum, Inc.
Route 159
Shin Pond Road
Patten ME

MAILING ADDRESS:
P.O. Box 300
Patten ME 04765

(207) 528-2650, 2547

OPEN: Memorial Day - Labor Day,
   Tu-Sa 9-4, Su 1-4; Labor Day -
   Columbus Day, Sa, Su 1-4; closed rest
   of year
USER FEES: one dollar
COPYING FACILITIES: no
MATERIALS SOLICITED: Photographs, ac-
   count books, and other materials relat-
   ing to logging.

HOLDINGS:
   Total volume: not specified
   Inclusive dates: 1880's - 1940's
   Description: Materials relating to logging, including account books, business
   records, and financial records of logging
   camps and stores, scrapbooks, 1,000 photographs, correspondence, diaries, and
   journals.

PORTLAND

ME712-280
Greater Portland Landmarks, Inc.
Resource Library
165 State Street
Portland ME 04101

(207) 774-5561

OPEN: M-F 8-5; closed weekends and
   holidays
COPYING FACILITIES: yes
MATERIALS SOLICITED: Technical data
   relating to the preservation of historical
   New England properties.

HOLDINGS:
   Total volume: 2,135 items
   Inclusive dates: 19th century -
   Description: Materials concerning architecture and historic preservation in the
   greater Portland area, including reports,
   photographs, buildings surveys, and Historic American Buildings Survey
   drawings.

ME712-530
Maine Historical Society
485 Congress Street
Portland ME 04101

(207) 774-1822

OPEN: Tu, W, F 9-5, Th 9-8; open
   second Saturday of month; closed
   Sundays, Mondays, and holidays
USER FEES: one dollar per day for
   non-members
COPYING FACILITIES: yes
MATERIALS SOLICITED: Materials covering Maine history and genealogy: personal and family papers, political
   manuscripts, business records, religious
   history and church records, records of
   cultural, fraternal, and patriotic organizations, and local and town histories.
   Will also accept manuscripts pertaining
   to American history, and maps, architectural drawings, and engineering
   drawings.

HOLDINGS:
   Total volume: 1,095 l.f.; 105 map
   drawers
   Inclusive dates: 1492 -
   Description: Personal papers, genealogical materials, organization records, business records, and other non-government
   documents relating primarily to Maine
   history. The collection is especially rich in
   19th century material, but also includes
   much 18th century material.

SEE: Hamer; NUCMC, 1966, 70-71, 76.

SEE: Allard, Crawley, and Edmison; Davis; Hinding; Hounshell; Leventhal and
   Mooney - I.

ME712-790
Union Mutual Life Insurance
   Company
2211 Congress Street
Portland ME

MAILING ADDRESS:
P.O. Box 9548
Portland ME 04122

(207) 780-2347

OPEN: by appointment only
ACCESS: permission for use granted by
   Head of Information Services
COPYING FACILITIES: yes

HOLDINGS:
   Total volume: 100 l.f.
   Inclusive dates: 1848 -
   Description: Ledger books, correspon-
   dence, pictures, policies, and other busi-
   ness and financial records.

ME712-880
Westbrook College
Maine Women Writers Collection
9716 Stevens Avenue
Portland ME 04103

(207) 797-7261

OPEN: Tu-Th 10-4, appointment
   preferred; closed other days and
   holidays
MATERIALS SOLICITED: Materials relating
   to Maine women authors.

HOLDINGS:
Total volume: 52 l.f.
Inclusive dates: 1797 -
Description: Manuscripts, correspondence, and memorabilia of Maine women authors.

SEE: NUCMC, 1969.

SEE: Hinding.

ROCKLAND

ME725-880
William A. Farnsworth Library and Art Museum
19 Elm Street
Rockland ME

MAILING ADDRESS:
P.O. Box 466
Rockland ME 04841

(207) 596-6457

OPEN: by appointment only
ACCESS: with permission of curator
COPYING FACILITIES: yes
MATERIALS SOLICITED: Materials relating to American art and the decorative arts, with emphasis on artists who worked in Maine.

HOLDINGS:
Total volume: 45 l.f.; 5 map drawers
Inclusive dates: 1790 -
Description: Papers, drawings, diaries, etc., of Rev. Jonathan Fisher of Blue Hill; papers and correspondence of wood carver John H. Bellamy of Kittery Point; Louise Nevelson Archives, containing correspondence, memorabilia, working drawings, etc., of this 20th century sculptor; correspondence of George Bellows.

Also, ledgers, correspondence and other personal and business records of the Museum's patron, William A. Farnsworth, prominent businessman, and his family; Historic American Buildings Survey architectural drawings of 1930-40; diaries, journals, ledgers, and drawings of Stephen R. Deane, 19th century American calligrapher.

SACO

ME750-160
Dyer-York Library and Museum
371 Main Street
Saco ME 04072

(207) 283-0754

OPEN: Tu, Th, F 10-5, W 2-8, Sa 9-12; closed other days, holidays, and last two weeks of August
COPYING FACILITIES: yes
MATERIALS SOLICITED: Materials covering York County history and genealogy, personal and family papers, political manuscripts, church records, local and town histories, maps, architectural drawings, records of local cultural and educational organizations.

HOLDINGS:
Total volume: 6,000 items
Inclusive dates: 1681 - 1900
Description: Documents relating to York County, including deeds, indentures, letters, public documents, church records, logbooks, business records, maps, plans, architectural drawings, one diary of the Revolutionary War period, and one Civil War diary.

A collection of sermons, letters, philosophical writings, historical observations and political documents relating to events in the last part of the 18th century and the early 19th century, by George Thatcher of Biddeford, ca. 1860.

SEE: Hamer (as York Institute).

SEE ALSO: Richard C. Davis, *North American Forest History: A Guide to Archives and Manuscripts in the United States and Canada* (Clio Books, 1977).

SEARSPORT

ME762-640
Penobscot Marine Museum
Church Street
Searsport ME 04974

(207) 548-6634

OPEN: by appointment only M-F 8:30-3:30; closed weekends and holidays
ACCESS: appointment required
COPYING FACILITIES: yes
MATERIALS SOLICITED: Maritime history.

HOLDINGS:
Total volume: 300 items; 15 l.f.
Inclusive dates: not specified
Description: Logbooks, journals, account books, and other maritime items, as well as ships' papers, custom records, and builders' records.

SEE: Hamer; NUCMC, 1965.

SEDGWICK

ME775-720
Sedgwick-Brooklin Historical Society
Sedgwick ME 04676

(207) 359-8930

OPEN: Su 2-4; closed other days
COPYING FACILITIES: no
MATERIALS SOLICITED: Pictures and letters about life in Sedgwick or Brooklin before 1970. Will also accept other materials relating to these towns before 1970.

HOLDINGS:
Total volume: 2 c.f.
Inclusive dates: 1805 - 1915
Description: Early maps, local church records, postcards, and photographs.

SOUTH PORTLAND

ME825-730
South Portland Public Library
482 Broadway
South Portland ME 04106

(207) 799-2204

OPEN: M, Tu, Th, F 9-9, W 1-9, Sa 9-5; closed Sundays, holidays, and Saturdays in summer
COPYING FACILITIES: yes
MATERIALS SOLICITED: Manuscripts and materials by and about James Otis Kaler.

HOLDINGS:
Total volume: 7 boxes; 2 notebooks
Inclusive dates: 1890 - 1912
Description: Two unpublished manuscripts of American children's author James Otis Kaler, as well as letters to Kaler, including seven boxes of correspondence from Civil War Medal of Honor winners and two notebooks of typed copies of original letters from children concerning Kaler's book *Toby Tyler*.

SPRINGVALE

ME837-560
Nasson College
Anderson Learning Center-Library
Springvale ME 04083

(207) 324-5340, Ext. 25

OPEN: M-Th 8:30-10, F 8:30-5, Sa 9-5, Su 1-10; closed holidays, and weekends between sessions
COPYING FACILITIES: yes
MATERIALS SOLICITED: Materials relating to the State of Maine, York County, women's studies, Jewish life and literature, and Canada, as well as Nasson College archives.

HOLDINGS:
Total volume: 1,200 items
Inclusive dates: 18th century -
Description: Various materials relating primarily to Maine, and to York County in particular, including information on early exploration and nature studies, as well as non-current records and other materials pertaining to the history of Nasson College.

SEE: Hinding.

WATERVILLE

ME925-130
Colby College
Library
Special Collections
Waterville ME 04901

(207) 873-1131, 3284

OPEN: M-F 8:30-4:30; closed weekends and holidays
COPYING FACILITIES: yes
MATERIALS SOLICITED: American regional authors, especially those with a connection to Maine; Irish authors, 1800 to present; Kennebec River Valley history; and Colby College archives.

HOLDINGS:
   Total volume: 35,000 manuscripts;
170 l.f.
   Inclusive dates: 19th century -
   Description: Literary manuscripts and other papers of 19th and 20th century American authors whose works reflect life in Maine and New England, as well as collections relating to English and Irish writers of the same period. Represented are such individuals as Edwin Arlington Robinson, Sarah Orne Jewett, Thomas Hardy, and George Bernard Shaw. The Colby College archives contains historical files relating to the College, as well as the papers of several alumni prominent in American history.

SEE: Hamer; NUCMC, 1959-61, 76.

SEE: Spalek; Robbins; Hinding.

SEE ALSO: *Colby Library Quarterly,* 1948 -

ME925-870

Waterville Historical Society
Redington Museum
64 Silver Street
Waterville ME 04901

(207) 872-9439

OPEN: Tu-Sa 2-6 May 17-Sept. 23; closed Sundays, Mondays, and from Sept. 23-May 17 except by appointment
COPYING FACILITIES: no
MATERIALS SOLICITED: Manuscripts relating to the Waterville area and its people, especially diaries and account books.

HOLDINGS:
   Total volume: 500 c.f.
   Inclusive dates: 1780 - 1950
   Description: Diaries; account books of merchants, lawyers, physicians, and artisans; early deeds, wills, and mortgages; records of early land proprietors, toll bridge owners, banks, and associations; correspondence; and a photograph collection.

SEE: Hamer; NUCMC, 1970.

SEE: Davis; Hinding.

WILTON

ME937-870

Wilton Free Public Library
(Goodspeed Memorial)
104 Main Street
Wilton ME 04294

(207) 645-4831

OPEN: Tu, W 10:30-5, Th 10:30-5:30; closed other days and holidays
COPYING FACILITIES: no
MATERIALS SOLICITED: Historical materials relating to the town of Wilton and its environs.

HOLDINGS:
   Total volume: 43 vols.; 62 items
   Inclusive dates: 1822 -
   Description: Local tax records, 1822-95, and a collection of about 37 manuscripts and 25 photographs pertaining to town history.

SEE: Hamer (as Goodspeed Memorial Library).

WISCASSET

ME950-480

Lincoln County Cultural and
   Historical Association
Lincoln County Museum
Archives
Federal Street
Wiscasset ME

MAILING ADDRESS:
P.O. Box 61
Wiscasset ME 04578

(207) 882-6817

OPEN: by appointment only
ACCESS: serious researchers only
COPYING FACILITIES: no
MATERIALS SOLICITED: Documents relating to Lincoln County. Will also accept documents relating to mid-coastal Maine.

HOLDINGS:
   Total volume: 3,500 items
   Inclusive dates: 1730 - 1900
   Description: Materials relating to Samuel Goodwin, proprietor of the Kennebec Purchase Company, and his descendants, who settled Pownalborough on Kennebec, now Dresden, ME. Other holdings include town officers' day books and local ships' logs.

SEE: NUCMC, 1975.

YARMOUTH

ME965-520

Merrill Memorial Library
Box 315
Yarmouth ME 04096

(207) 846-4763

OPEN: M 10-5, Tu 2-8, W 10-5, Th 2-8, F, Sa 10-5; closed Sundays and Saturdays in July and Aug.
COPYING FACILITIES: yes
MATERIALS SOLICITED: Will accept materials about the towns of Yarmouth and North Yarmouth, Cumberland County, and the State of Maine with emphasis on genealogy, shipping, ocean commerce, shipbuilding, and fishing.

HOLDINGS:
   Total volume: 34 l.f.
   Inclusive dates: 1640 - 1920's
   Description: Deeds, church records, account books, local histories, diaries, photographs, genealogies relating to early settlements and the shipbuilding industry.

YORK

ME980-600

Old York Historical Society
Lindsay Avenue
York ME

MAILING ADDRESS:
P.O. Box 312
York ME 03909

(207) 363-3872

SEE: Hamer.

Questionnaire not returned.

MARIANA ISLANDS

There is no program for the preservation of local records of the Mariana Islands. Most records of lasting significance are housed at the agency of origin.

MARYLAND

Legislation passed in 1935 empowered the Maryland Hall of Records to administer a records preservation program for local governments. Many permanently valuable local records remain at the agency of origin, but some 35,000 cubic feet of local public records, including all courthouse documents prior to 1788, are located at the Hall of Records in Annapolis.

Also housed there are some 41,000 microfilm reels of land, probate, and other county and municipal records, 17th century to date, which were filmed by the Hall of Records, by local government agencies, and by the Church of Jesus Christ of Latter-day Saints.

In 1963 the Hall of Records published *The County Courthouses and Records of Maryland, Part Two: The Records*, which describes materials housed at the State capital and in county seats. *A Series Summary Guide to the Public Records of Baltimore City* was printed in 1977, and the first volume of a series unit guide to county records on microfilm was published in 1978. The second volume was published in 1981. Indexes to probate, land, and marriage records at the Hall of Records are also available for use there.

ANNAPOLIS

MD57-500

Maryland Department of General
  Services
Maryland Hall of Records
St. John's Street and College Avenue
Annapolis MD

MAILING ADDRESS:
P.O. Box 828
Annapolis MD 21404

(301) 269-3916

OPEN: M-Sa 8:30-4:30; closed Sundays
  and holidays
COPYING FACILITIES: yes
MATERIALS SOLICITED: Maryland State, county and local records of permanent historical value. Will also accept private papers and memorabilia relating to the history of Maryland.

HOLDINGS:
  Total volume: 60,000 c.f.
  Inclusive dates: 1635 -
  Description: Archives of the State and colony of Maryland, including records of State, county, and local government agencies. There are also personal papers, church and business records, maps, and photographs relating to Maryland history.

SEE: Hamer; NUCMC, 1968.

SEE: Parkinson; Allard, Crawley, and Edmison; Levanthal and Mooney - I.

SEE ALSO: Gust Skordas, ed., *The Early Settlers of Maryland: An Index to Names of Immigrants Compiled from Records of Land Patents, 1633-1680, in the Hall of Records, Annapolis, Maryland* (Genealogical Publishing, 1968); Walter Schatz, ed., *Directory of Afro-American Resources* (Bowker, 1970); Morris L. Radoff, 'The Maryland Hall of Records,' *Manuscripts* 20 (Spring 1968); Dean C. Allard and Betty Bern, comps., *U.S. Naval History Sources in the Washington Area and Suggested Research Subjects* (Naval History Division, 1970).

The following publications of the Maryland Hall of Records: Edward C. Papenfuse, Gregory A. Stiverson, and Mary D. Donaldson, *An Inventory to the Maryland State Papers, Volume One: The Revolutionary War Era, 1775-1789* (1977); Patricia M. Vanorny, comp., *A Series Summary Guide to the Public Records of Baltimore City* (1975), originally published in *Maryland Historical Magazine* 70 (Fall 1975); *A Guide to the Microfilm Holdings of the Maryland Hall of Records* (1978); Phebe R. Jacobsen, *Quaker Records in Maryland* (1966); and various calendars and other finding aids to individual collections.

MD57-800

United States Naval Academy
Museum
Annapolis MD 21402

(301) 267-2108

OPEN: M-F 9-4:50 by appointment;
  closed weekends, Thanksgiving,
  Christmas, and New Year's
ACCESS: appointments are recommended
COPYING FACILITIES: yes
MATERIALS SOLICITED: Manuscript material relating to United States naval history with particular interest in items by, to or about naval officers or pertaining to objects in the Museum's historical collections.

HOLDINGS:
  Total volume: 70 l.f.
  Inclusive dates: 1770 -
  Description: Manuscripts relating primarily to American naval history and famous naval officers, documenting naval battles, exploration, diplomatic missions, technological developments, and personal lives. Included are correspondence, diaries, ship journals and public documents. Individuals documented include John Paul Jones, David G. Farragut, Horatio Nelson, and Robert Fulton.

SEE: Hamer; NUCMC, 1959-61.

SEE: Allard, Crawley, and Edmison; Hinding.

SEE ALSO: Dean C. Allard and Betty Bern, comps., *U.S. Naval History Sources in the Washington Area and Suggested Research Subjects* (Naval History Division, 1970). Other finding aids and catalogs are available at the Museum.

MD57-810

United States Naval Academy
Nimitz Library
Special Collections Division
Annapolis MD 21402

(301) 267-2220

OPEN: M-F 7:45-4:30; closed weekends
  and holidays
COPYING FACILITIES: yes
MATERIALS SOLICITED: Manuscripts, ships' logs, journals, letterbooks, photographs, and other materials relating to U.S. Navy ships, stations and personnel. Will also accept other Annapolis and naval materials.

HOLDINGS:
  Total volume: 890 l.f.; 250 vols.;
  11,000 photographs; 44 photograph
  albums
  Inclusive dates: 1759 -
  Description: Ships' logs, journals, letterbooks, and watch-station-quarter bills, 1778-1943, relating chiefly to the U.S. Navy; papers of American naval officers; photographs of American naval and merchant ships, the U.S. Naval Academy, American naval officers, and Naval Academy midshipmen; and the Edward J. Steichen Collection of photographs, including World War II combat prints and general works by 20th century American photographers.

SEE: Allard, Crawley, and Edmison.

SEE ALSO: *The Edward J. Steichen Collection* (Nimitz Library, 1972); Dean C. Allard and Betty Bern, comps., *U.S. Naval History Sources in the Washington Area and Suggested Research Subjects* (Naval History Division, 1970).

MD57-820

United States Naval Institute
Oral History Office
Annapolis MD 21402

(301) 268-6110

OPEN: M-F 8-4:30; closed weekends and
holidays
COPYING FACILITIES: yes
MATERIALS SOLICITED: Oral history interviews of individuals in all branches
of the Naval service.

HOLDINGS:
Total volume: 2,800 hours of tape;
70,000 pages of transcripts
Inclusive dates: 1969 -
Description: Oral history interviews
with individuals representing all branches
of naval service; interviews on particular
subjects such as the Polaris submarine,
naval aviation, the WAVES, Chester
Nimitz, prisoners of war, and the U.S.
Coast Guard.

SEE: NUCMC, 1970.

SEE: Allard, Crawley, and Edmison;
Hinding.

SEE ALSO: Alan M. Meckler and Ruth
McMullin, comps., *Oral History Collections* (Bowker, 1975); Dean C. Allard
and Betty Bern, comps., *U.S. Naval
History Sources in the Washington Area
and Suggested Research Subjects* (Naval
History Division, 1970).

Card index available to researchers.

All interviews are transcribed;
copies are on deposit at the Naval
Historical Center in Washington, DC,
and the Nimitz Library at the U.S.
Naval Academy.

MD57-830

United States Naval Institute
Photographic Library
Annapolis MD 21402

(301) 268-6110

OPEN: M-F 8-4:30; closed weekends and
holidays
COPYING FACILITIES: yes
MATERIALS SOLICITED: Photographs of
ships and aircraft since the Civil War
period, and photographs covering the
Civil War, World Wars I and II, and
the Korean and Vietnam wars.

HOLDINGS:
Total volume: 250,000 items
Inclusive dates: 1860 -
Description: Photographs of U.S.
Navy, Coast Guard, Marine Corps, and
Merchant Marine subjects, including air-
craft, combat, personnel and operations
(chiefly naval), most Navy ships, some
Coast Guard and Merchant Marine ships,
and some foreign vessels.

SEE: Novotny; Allard, Crawley, and
Edmison.

SEE ALSO: A registry of ship photographs
is available.

BALTIMORE

MD76-20

Ancient Free and Accepted Masons of
Maryland
Grand Lodge
Museum
225 North Charles Street
Baltimore MD 21201

(301) 752-1198

OPEN: M-F 9-4:30; closed weekends and
holidays
COPYING FACILITIES: yes
MATERIALS SOLICITED: Will accept ma-
terials related to Masonry and famous
Masons, local and worldwide.

HOLDINGS:
Total volume: 500 items
Inclusive dates: mid-18th century -
Description: Masonic certificates, patents, and other papers, including some
from England, but chiefly from America,
particularly Maryland.

MD76-30

Archdiocese of Baltimore
Archives
320 Cathedral Street
Baltimore MD 21201

(301) 547-5443

OPEN: M-F 9-4:30 by appointment only
COPYING FACILITIES: yes
MATERIALS SOLICITED: Letters and docu-
ments of the archbishops of Baltimore.

HOLDINGS:
Total volume: 335 boxes
Inclusive dates: 1745 - 1961
Description: Letters, documents,
records and diaries of the archbishops of
Baltimore; Propaganda Fide documents
and papal letters; a Henry Latrobe drawing of the Baltimore Cathedral; materials
relating to missionary activity throughout
the United States, especially in New England and the Kentucky-Michigan area;
letters of Gabriel Richard; and letters of
U.S. Presidents, including George Washington, Thomas Jefferson, Theodore Roosevelt, and William Howard Taft.

SEE: Hamer; NUCMC, 1971.

Papers generally are closed until 35
years after the death of the
archbishop.

MD76-60

Baltimore Department of Legislative
Reference
Division of City Archives and
Records Management
Room 201
211 East Pleasant Street
Baltimore MD 21202

(301) 396-4861, 4863

OPEN: M-F 8:30-4:30; closed weekends
and holidays
COPYING FACILITIES: yes

HOLDINGS:
Total volume: 3,000 c.f.
Inclusive dates: 1729 -
Description: Tax records, 1798-present;
ship passenger lists, 1833-66; Mayoral
and City Council records, 1799-present;
Town Commissioners and other early
municipal agencies, 1729-97; records of
numerous municipal agencies including
City Commissioners, Appeal Tax Court,
Civil Service Commission, Law Department, Department of Education, City
Register, and Board of Estimates,
1797-present.
Election records, 1800-present; cartographic records, 1730-present; and
records of special commissions appointed
by the Mayor and City Council, ca.
1835-present.

MD76-70

Baltimore Hebrew College
Joseph Meyerhoff Library
5800 Park Heights Avenue
Baltimore MD 21215

(301) 578-6936

OPEN: by appointment only; closed
Jewish holidays
ACCESS: appointment required
COPYING FACILITIES: yes
MATERIALS SOLICITED: Will accept
manuscripts and synagogue records.

HOLDINGS:
Total volume: 3 file cabinets
Inclusive dates: 1880 - 1960
Description: Correspondence and journals of Dr. Harry Friedenwald; correspondence of Dr. Herman Seidel and
some business records; and correspondence of Prof. Leo J. Kanner relating to
efforts to rescue Jewish physicians from
Nazi Germany.

SEE: Hinding.

MD76-80

The Baltimore Museum of Art
The Cone Collection, Archives
Art Museum Drive
Baltimore MD 21218

(301) 396-7100, 7101

OPEN: by appointment only
COPYING FACILITIES: yes

HOLDINGS:
Total volume: 6 drawers
Inclusive dates: early 20th century
Description: Correspondence and pho-
tographs related to Etta and Claribel
Cone and their collection of paintings,
sculpture, prints, drawings, and artifacts,
which is housed at the Museum. Materi-
als related to Gertrude and Leo Stein in
Paris are also included.

SEE: Hinding.

MD76-100

Carmelite Monastery of Baltimore
Archives
1318 Dulaney Valley Road
Baltimore MD 21204

(301) 823-7415

OPEN: by appointment only
COPYING FACILITIES: no
MATERIALS SOLICITED: Materials concerning the history of the Carmelite community and related aspects of Roman Catholicism and secular life.

HOLDINGS:
  Total volume: not specified
  Inclusive dates: 1642 -
  Description: Manuscripts relating to the community of the Carmelite nuns since its founding in 1790 in Port Tobacco, MD. Included in the collection are correspondence, a diary of the Carmelites' 1790 voyage from Europe to America, sermons, poems, wills, legal records, community annals, profession and death records, and the deed to the community's original property.

SEE: Hinding.

MD76-118

College of Notre Dame of Maryland
Archives
4701 North Charles Street
Baltimore MD 21210

(301) 435-0100

OPEN: by appointment only
COPYING FACILITIES: yes
MATERIALS SOLICITED: Materials relating to early 19th century Baltimore. Would also accept materials concerned with 19th century education and Maryland history.

HOLDINGS:
  Total volume: not specified
  Inclusive dates: 1863 -
  Description: Records relating to the College of Notre Dame of Maryland, Baltimore, higher education, and early architecture.

SEE: NUCMC, 1959-62.

MD76-190

Enoch Pratt Free Library
400 Cathedral Street
Baltimore MD 21201

no telephone

SEE: Hamer; NUCMC, 1959-61.

Questionnaire not returned.

MD76-240

Fort McHenry National Monument
  and Historic Shrine
Library
East Fort Avenue
Baltimore MD 21230

(301) 962-4290

OPEN: by appointment only; closed Christmas and New Year's

ACCESS: clearance to use materials must be made through the Superintendent, Chief of Visitor Services, or Historian
COPYING FACILITIES: yes
MATERIALS SOLICITED: Materials pertaining to the War of 1812, particularly the Battle of Baltimore and the defense of Fort McHenry, and to 'The Star-Spangled Banner.' Will also accept materials covering other periods of Fort McHenry history.

HOLDINGS:
  Total volume: 21,000 items; 1,500 photographs
  Inclusive dates: 1776 -
  Description: Manuscripts relating to the history of Fort McHenry, the War of 1812, the Key and Armistead families, and to Mrs. Reuben Ross Holloway and the movement to establish 'The Star-Spangled Banner' as the National anthem. Photographs relate chiefly to Fort McHenry and the Baltimore area, particularly the World War I Army Hospital No. 2 at Fort McHenry.

SEE: Hamer; NUCMC, 1965.

SEE: Allard, Crawley, and Edmison.

MD76-300

Jewish Historical Society of Maryland, Inc.
Embassy Apartment
3809 Clark's Lane
Baltimore MD 21215

(301) 358-9417

OPEN: M-F 9:30-3, preferably by appointment; closed weekends and Jewish holidays
COPYING FACILITIES: yes
MATERIALS SOLICITED: Material relating to the history of the Jews of Maryland.

HOLDINGS:
  Total volume: 80 c.f.; 75 tapes
  Inclusive dates: 1840 -
  Description: Collections on Maryland Jewish families and personalities, including the papers of Benjamin and Henrietta Szold, Harry Friedenwald, and Herman Seidel, and taped oral history interviews with important members of the Baltimore Jewish community.

MD76-315

The Johns Hopkins Medical
  Institutions
The Alan Mason Chesney Medical
  Archives
35 Turner
720 Rutland Avenue
Baltimore MD 21205

(301) 955-3043

OPEN: by appointment M-Th 9-5, F 9-4:30; closed holidays
COPYING FACILITIES: yes
MATERIALS SOLICITED: Administrative records of The Johns Hopkins Medical Institutions and papers of faculty and staff.

HOLDINGS:
  Total volume: 1,600 l.f.
  Inclusive dates: 1876 -
  Description: The archives of The Johns Hopkins Medical Institutions, including the Hospital, School of Nursing, School of Hygiene and Public Health, The Harriet Lane Home, Colored Orphan's Asylum, Welch Medical Library, and School of Health Services. Included are fiscal files, official correspondence, architectural drawings, photographs, and personal papers of faculty and staff of the Medical Institutions, including John Jacob Abel, William Henry Welch, Howard Kelly, Thomas Cullen, Adolf Meyer, and Horsley Gantt.

GUIDES: Archives and Manuscripts in the Alan Mason Chesney Medical Archives of The Johns Hopkins Medical Institutions (The Johns Hopkins University and The Johns Hopkins Hospital, 1980).

SEE: Hamer; NUCMC, 1965 (as Welch Medical Library).

SEE: Hinding.

MD76-325

The Johns Hopkins University
The Ferdinand Hamburger, Jr.,
  Archives
3400 North Charles Street
Baltimore MD 21218

(301) 338-8323

OPEN: M-F 8:30-5; closed weekends and holidays
ACCESS: advance arrangements required
COPYING FACILITIES: yes
MATERIALS SOLICITED: Records of the non-medical divisions of The Johns Hopkins University; papers of prominent Hopkins faculty and alumni; photographs and ephemera.

HOLDINGS:
  Total volume: 2,000 l.f.
  Inclusive dates: 1867 -
  Description: Official repository for records of five Johns Hopkins University divisions: Arts and Sciences, Engineering, Evening College and Summer Session, School of Advanced International Studies, and Central Administration, including records of the Board of Trustees, the President, Vice Presidents, Provost, Registrar, Academic Council, financial offices, the Library, academic departments, research institutes, student activities, and The Johns Hopkins University Press.
  University publications. Over 5,500 catalogued photographs of Hopkins subjects. Collections of personal and professional papers of Hopkins faculty and students.

MD76-333

The Johns Hopkins University
George Peabody Library
17 E. Mount Vernon Place
Baltimore MD 21202

(301) 659-8197, 8179

OPEN: Su-F 9-5, Sa 9-5 during academic year; closed holidays
COPYING FACILITIES: yes
MATERIALS SOLICITED: Genealogy.

HOLDINGS:
   Total volume: 130 vols.
   Inclusive dates: 1812 - 1870
   Description: Letters, journals, and other papers of U.S. Secretary of the Navy John Pendleton Kennedy.

SEE: Hamer; NUCMC, 1969.

SEE: Novotny; Hinding.

MD76-340

The Johns Hopkins University
John Work Garrett Library
4545 North Charles Street
Baltimore MD 21210

(301) 338-7641

OPEN: M-F 9-5; closed weekends and holidays
COPYING FACILITIES: yes
MATERIALS SOLICITED: Materials pertaining to the history of Baltimore and Maryland, or related to present collections.

HOLDINGS:
   Total volume: 90,000 items
   Inclusive dates: 1776 - 1960
   Description: Seven collections of artistic, literary, and historical materials, including diplomatic materials of John Work Garrett, 1872-1942, and architectural materials, such as letters, plans, and sketches, of Laurence Fowler, which together comprise the bulk of the holdings. Music manuscripts by Sidney Lanier and an autograph collection of literary, artistic, and political figures are also included. Also papers of Francis White, 1914-57, U.S. ambassador.

SEE: Allard, Crawley, and Edmison.

MD76-360

The Johns Hopkins University
Milton S. Eisenhower Library
North Charles and 34th Streets
Baltimore MD 21218

(301) 338-8348, 8372

OPEN: M-F 8:30-5; closed weekends and holidays
COPYING FACILITIES: yes
MATERIALS SOLICITED: Political science interviews. Will also accept materials relating to the history and current activities of The Johns Hopkins University.

HOLDINGS:
   Total volume: 87,000 items
   Inclusive dates: 1450 -
   Description: Primarily correspondence of the 19th and 20th centuries, chiefly of persons associated with The Johns Hopkins University. Letters of Daniel Coit Gilman, first president of the University, form the largest single part of the collection. There are also a few medieval manuscripts, a group of Icelandic manuscripts of the 18th and 19th centuries, the Kurrelmeyer collection of over 1,600 letters of German literary figures, and the Dexter collection of political science interviews.

SEE: Hamer; NUCMC, 1959-64, 74, 76.

SEE: Spalek; Martin; Robbins.

SEE ALSO: Richard K. Smith, comp. and ed., *The Hugh L. Dryden Papers, 1898-1965: A Preliminary Catalogue of the Basic Collection* (The Johns Hopkins Univ., Milton S. Eisenhower Library, 1974); Walter Schatz, ed., *Directory of Afro-American Resources* (Bowker, 1970).

MD76-478

Loyola College
Archives
4501 North Charles Street
Baltimore MD 21210

(301) 323-1010

OPEN: M-F 9:30-4; closed weekends, holidays, and religious holidays
ACCESS: qualified scholars
COPYING FACILITIES: yes
MATERIALS SOLICITED: Loyola College materials. Will also accept Baltimore social, educational, intellectual, and religious history materials.

HOLDINGS:
   Total volume: 19 l.f.; 3 file cabinets
   Inclusive dates: 1850 -
   Description: Records of Loyola College including minutes of meetings, correspondence, office files, reports, recommendations, proposals, policy statements, memorandums, registers, programs, speeches, financial records, ledgers, budgets, property appraisals, athletic records, scrapbooks, plats, maps, building plans, photographs, motion picture film, audio records, audio tapes, and scripts.

MD76-490

Lutheran Church in America
Maryland Synod
7604 York Road
Baltimore MD 21204

(301) 825-9520

OPEN: M-F 9-5; closed weekends and holidays
ACCESS: approval of Synod Secretary or President
COPYING FACILITIES: yes

HOLDINGS:
   Total volume: 3 l.f.
   Inclusive dates: 1820 -
   Description: Proceedings of the annual conventions of the Synod since its organization in 1820, containing lists of congregations, pastors, board of trustee members, and committee members, as well as budgets, summary histories of congregations, and other data.

MD76-515

Maryland Historical Society
Manuscripts Division
201 West Monument Street
Baltimore MD 21201

(301) 685-3750

OPEN: Tu-F 11-4:30, Sa 9-4:30; closed Sundays, Mondays, and holidays
USER FEES: $2.50 per day for non-members
ACCESS: Undergraduates must have a letter of introduction from a faculty member; high school students and below are not allowed access to the

collections; all researchers will be screened by the Division staff.
COPYING FACILITIES: yes
MATERIALS SOLICITED: Materials on Maryland history and people. Will sometimes accept materials relating to the history of the Middle Atlantic region, principally Pennsylvania and Virginia, and usually with specific connection to Maryland.

HOLDINGS:
   Total volume: 2,500,000 items
   Inclusive dates: 1515 -
   Description: Over 2,200 manuscript collections, mainly from the 18th to early 20th centuries, covering the whole spectrum of Maryland history from the Calvert family (Maryland colonial proprietors) of the 16th century to the papers of political and social leaders; businesses; civic, literary and social organizations; published and unpublished literary manuscripts; diaries; accounts; and correspondence. All areas of the State are represented with emphasis on the Baltimore area. Although the vast majority of the manuscript collections are private, there are records of official State, county, and city government organizations, chiefly from the colonial and early National periods.

GUIDES: Avril J. M. Pedley, comp., *The Manuscript Collections of the Maryland Historical Society* (1968).

SEE: Hamer; NUCMC, 1967, 69-71, 73, 75-76, 78, 81.

SEE: Parkinson; Duignan; Robbins; Hinding; Ingram; Allard, Crawley, and Edmison; Davis.

SEE ALSO: Walter Schatz, ed., *Directory of Afro-American Resources* (Bowker, 1970); James M. Merrill, 'The Naval Historian and His Sources,' *American Archivist* 32 (July 1969). Articles describing specific collections, as well as broader descriptions of holdings, appear frequently in the *Maryland Historical Magazine*. Guides to microfilms of individual collections are available at the institution.

Other guides to collections available at institution.

MD76-525

Maryland Historical Society
Oral History Office
201 West Monument Street
Baltimore MD 21201

(301) 685-3750

OPEN: Tu-Sa 9-4:30; closed Sundays, Mondays, and holidays
USER FEES: $2.50 per day for non-members.
ACCESS: advance arrangements necessary
COPYING FACILITIES: yes
MATERIALS SOLICITED: Oral histories covering Maryland history. Will also accept voice recordings of the State's past leaders and taped speeches about Maryland subjects.

HOLDINGS:
  Total volume: 400 interviews; 500 hours of tape
  Inclusive dates: 1971 -
  Description: 325 hours of taped interviews covering Maryland history. Included are 85 interviews concerning civil rights activities, as well as collections focusing on Baltimore craftspeople, the B & O Railroad, artists and writers, business leaders, and highway development.
  Also, Baltimore neighborhood profiles, veterans of Civilian Conservation Corps service and perspectives on the aging.

SEE: Meckler and McMullin; Hinding.

SEE ALSO: Alan M. Meckler and Ruth McMullin, comps., *Oral History Collections* (Bowker, 1975).

MD76-526
Maryland Historical Society
Prints and Photographs Division
201 West Monument Street
Baltimore MD 21201

(301) 685-3750

OPEN: Tu-Sa 9-4:30; closed Sundays, Mondays, and holidays
USER FEES: $2.50 a day for non-members
ACCESS: advance arrangements requested
COPYING FACILITIES: yes
MATERIALS SOLICITED: Graphic materials pertaining to Maryland, including photographs, maps, and ephemera.

HOLDINGS:
  Total volume: 3,000 maps; 200,000 photographs; 90 l.f. ephemera
  Inclusive dates: 1500's -
  Description: Maps, 19th and 20th century photographs, and other visual documents relating to Maryland, with emphasis on the Baltimore area.

SEE: Novotny.

Architectural drawings are now in the Gallery Division.

MD76-527
Medical and Chirurgical Faculty of the State of Maryland
Library
1211 Cathedral Street
Baltimore MD 21201

(301) 539-0872, Ext. 215

OPEN: M-F 9-5; closed weekends and holidays
USER FEES: extensive reference service will be billed at cost
ACCESS: appointment requested
COPYING FACILITIES: yes
MATERIALS SOLICITED: Materials relating to the development of medicine and its related disciplines in Maryland; letters and correspondence to or from Maryland physicians; and diaries, journals and logbooks of Maryland physicians. Will also accept medical school instructors' lecture notes, notebooks of medical students, and manuscripts of medical texts.

HOLDINGS:
  Total volume: not specified
  Inclusive dates: 1700 -
  Description: Financial records, transactions of meetings, committee reports, records of library use, and licensing information about Maryland physicians, of the Medical and Chirurgical faculty of the state of Maryland; lecture notes of instructors at Maryland medical schools; notebooks of medical students; diaries, journals, logbooks, and business and financial records of Maryland physicians; clinical, business, and financial records of hospitals; patients' records; and notebooks of Maryland students attending medical schools in Europe in the early 1800's.

MD76-540
Morgan State University
Soper Library
Hillen Road and Cold Spring Lane
Baltimore MD 21239

no telephone
SEE: NUCMC, 1980.

Questionnaire not returned.

MD76-640
Peabody Institute of The Johns Hopkins University
Conservatory of Music
Library
21 E. Mount Vernon Place
Baltimore MD 21202

(301) 8154, 8157

OPEN: M-F 9-5; closed weekends and holidays
ACCESS: advance arrangements requested
COPYING FACILITIES: yes
MATERIALS SOLICITED: Manuscripts of Peabody composers; correspondence, diaries, journals, logbooks, and concert programs of Peabody faculty and alumni; sound recordings of Peabody performers; non-current records of the Peabody Institute of the City of Baltimore and the Peabody Institute of The Johns Hopkins University (1977-); photographs. Will also accept manuscript scores and personal papers of Baltimore-area and American composers.

HOLDINGS:
  Total volume: 1,000 l.f.
  Inclusive dates: 1850 -
  Description: Records of the Peabody Institute of the City of Baltimore and its component parts: Conservatory of Music, Library, Art Gallery, Lecture Series, Preparatory School. Includes business and financial records, correspondence, diaries, logbooks, scrapbooks, concert programs, photographs, etc.
  Special collections include manuscript music scores of Louis Cheslock, Asger Hamerik, John Itzel, Theodore Hemberger, Howard Thatcher, Gustav Strube, W. Edward Heimendahl, Hugh Newsom; scrapbooks of Enrico Caruso; memorabilia of John Charles Thomas; papers of Louis Lombard; clipping file of Israel Rosen.

MD76-650
The Peale Museum
225 Holliday Street
Baltimore MD 21202

(301) 396-1149, 3523

OPEN: W-F 10-4:30; closed other days and holidays
COPYING FACILITIES: yes
MATERIALS SOLICITED: Visual documents related to the history of Baltimore, including maps; architectural, engineering, and technical drawings; still photographs; scrapbooks containing primary visual documents. Will also accept archives and non-current records of Baltimore institutions and organizations, provided they contain primarily visual documents; audible documents, motion pictures and videotapes related to Baltimore.

HOLDINGS:
  Total volume: 50,000 photographs; 1,300 prints
  Inclusive dates: 1800 -
  Description: Still photographs, architectural and engineering drawings, and maps depicting Baltimore or created by Baltimoreans.

SEE: Novotny.

MD76-720
Society of Friends
Baltimore Yearly Meeting
Homewood Friends Meeting House
3107 North Charles Street
Baltimore MD 21218

no telephone
SEE: Hamer.

Questionnaire not returned.

MD76-748
Sulpician Archives Baltimore
711 Maiden Choice Lane
Baltimore MD 21228

(301) 242-4499

OPEN: by appointment only
COPYING FACILITIES: yes
MATERIALS SOLICITED: History of various Sulpician seminaries in the United States, with emphasis on their personnel and alumni. Will also accept material dealing with U.S. church history.

HOLDINGS:
  Total volume: 600 l.f.
  Inclusive dates: 1790 -
  Description: Records of St. Mary's Seminary and University and other Sulpician Seminaries in Washington DC, San Francisco, Seattle, Honolulu, Detroit, Louisville, Boston, and New York City.

MD76-790
United Methodist Historical Society
Lovely Lane Museum
2200 St. Paul Street
Baltimore MD 21218

(301) 889-4458

OPEN: M, F 10-4; closed other days, Christmas, New Year's, and July 4

COPYING FACILITIES: yes
MATERIALS SOLICITED: United Methodist history, with focus on the Baltimore Conference area.

HOLDINGS:
  Total volume: 12,000 items; 400 vols. of manuscripts; 4,000 printed volumes
  Inclusive dates: 1711 -
  Description: Minutes of Baltimore and Washington United Methodist Conferences, 1800- ; reports and papers of Baltimore Conference committees; records of closed Methodist churches in Baltimore and vicinity; stewards' books of Baltimore, Frederick, Berkeley, Great Falls, Harford, and a few other circuits, 1794-1925; journals of preachers, including Nelson Reed, John Kobler, Henry Slicer, and James Hyatt; 63 letters of Francis Asbury; scrapbooks of Bishop A. W. Leonard; letters of many other bishops; papers of John F. Goucher; Methodist sesquicentennial and bicentennial papers, 1934 and 1966; documents, 1879-1963, relating to Methodist unions of 1939 and 1968; and genealogical lists and indexes.

SEE: Hamer (as Methodist Historical Society of the Baltimore Conference).

SEE: Schatz.

MD76-800
University of Baltimore
Baltimore Region Institutional Studies Center
Charles and Mount Royal Street
Baltimore MD 21201

(301) 625-3238, 3135

OPEN: M-F 9-4:30; closed weekends and holidays
USER FEES: extended research by staff will be charged at cost
ACCESS: access subject to completion of an application and adherence to the regulations stipulated
COPYING FACILITIES: yes
MATERIALS SOLICITED: Records originating in or collected by agencies and associations important to social institutions of the region, including materials relating to city planning; housing; community organization; family planning; citizen business and political participation; social welfare; Model Cities and urban renewal; and church groups. Will also accept related materials complementary to the collections.

HOLDINGS:
  Total volume: 4,500 l.f.; 350 tapes
  Inclusive dates: 1819 -
  Description: Records of public, private and quasi-public agencies and associations functioning in the Baltimore area, including the Maryland Council of Churches, the Baltimore City Planning Department, the Independent Order of Odd Fellows, Planned Parenthood, the Greater Baltimore Committee, the Belvedere Hotel Corporation, and the Maryland Conference for Social Concern.

  Also tapes and transcripts from the Baltimore Neighborhood Heritage Project, among others. Holdings include minutes, correspondence, financial records, program files, survey data, photographs, and other associated non-print material.

SEE: NUCMC, 1977.

SEE: Hinding.

SEE ALSO: Various guides available through the institution.

MD76-810
University of Baltimore
Library
Steamship Historical Society Collection
1420 Maryland Avenue
Baltimore MD 21201

(301) 625-3134

OPEN: M-F 8-4, and by appointment; closed weekends and holidays
COPYING FACILITIES: yes
MATERIALS SOLICITED: Company records, photographs, charts, and other materials dealing with powered vessels of coastal or inland waters or the ocean.

HOLDINGS:
  Total volume: 420 c.f.; 87 l.f.
  Inclusive dates: 1790 -
  Description: A collection documenting the technical development of powered marine transport and related business and social developments. Included are promotional materials, and business records produced by various steamship lines and associations, including the complete records of the Hudson River Day Line.

  There are also approximately 25,000 negatives and 50,000 photographs of vessels and shipping; blueprints and specification drawings of steamships built in the United States; and a collection of maritime maps, charts and harbor plans.

SEE: Allard, Crawley, and Edmison.

MD76-880
The Walters Art Gallery
Department of Manuscripts and Rare Books
600 North Charles Street
Baltimore MD 21201

(301) 547-9000

OPEN: by appointment only M-F; closed weekends and holidays
ACCESS: scholars and advanced graduate students with letter of introduction; advance appointment required
COPYING FACILITIES: yes
MATERIALS SOLICITED: Manuscripts and rare printed books, illustrated.

HOLDINGS:
  Total volume: 800 manuscripts; 1,300 incunabula
  Inclusive dates: 700 A.D. - 19th century
  Description: 794 Western and Near Eastern manuscripts, most of them illuminated, 8th-20th century; 56 letters of Catherine the Great; 230 letters of Henry Walters, also shipping lists, relating to the formation of the manuscript and book collection and to the founding of the School of Art as Applied to Medicine at The Johns Hopkins University; 200 letters from artists pertaining to works of art in the Walters collection.

  Diaries and financial agendas of George A. Lucas, spanning the years 1852-1909, recording purchases made abroad for William and Henry Walters as well as other American collectors.

SEE: Hamer; NUCMC, 1965.

SEE: Martin.

SEE ALSO: Dorothy E. Miner, 'Since De Ricci: Western Illuminated Manuscripts Acquired Since 1934, A Report in Two Parts,' *Journal of the Walters Art Gallery* 29-30 (1966/67) and 31-32 (1968/69); Dorothy E. Miner, 'The Collecting of Islamic Manuscripts in America,' *Acts of the Seventh International Congress of Bibliophiles (1971)* (1974); C. U. Faye and W. H. Bond, *Supplement to the Census of Medieval and Renaissance Manuscripts in the United States and Canada* (Bibliographical Society of America, 1962); Dorothy E. Miner's bibliography, in U. McCracken, L. Randall, and R. Randall, eds., *Gatherings in Honor of Dorothy E. Miner* (1974).

Catalog of Western manuscripts in progress.

BEL AIR

MD114-310
Harford Community College
Learning Resources Center
Library Services Division
401 Thomas Run Road
Bel Air MD 21014

(301) 836-4131, 4146

OPEN: M-Th 9-9, F 9-4:30; closed weekends, major holidays, and evenings between semesters
COPYING FACILITIES: yes
MATERIALS SOLICITED: Maryland materials.

HOLDINGS:
  Total volume: 25 l.f.
  Inclusive dates: 1967 -
  Description: Papers and correspondence of the Maryland Constitutional Convention of 1967, focusing on delegate Charles Willis, and studies and working papers for the Rosenberg Report on Higher Education in Maryland.

MD114-330
Historical Society of Harford County, Inc.
Bel Air MD

MAILING ADDRESS:
324 South Kenmore Avenue
Bel Air MD 21014

(301) 838-7691

OPEN: Archives by appointment only Wednesday 9:30-noon; court records open Wednesday 1-4
ACCESS: collection closed to public; a small staff will perform research on request
COPYING FACILITIES: no
MATERIALS SOLICITED: Materials relating to the history and inhabitants of Harford County. Will also accept materials concerning adjacent counties.

HOLDINGS:
  Total volume: 80 file drawers; 10 plat drawers
  Inclusive dates: 1675 - 1925
  Description: A collection of manuscripts relating to the history of Harford County, including materials on genealogy, social history, economics, industry, transportation, culture, architecture, and religion.

Court records are located at County Service Building, North Philadelphia Blvd., Aberdeen, MD 21001.

BELTSVILLE

MD133-160

Department of Agriculture
National Agricultural Library
Beltsville MD 20705

(301) 344-3876

OPEN: M-F 8-4; closed weekends and holidays

SEE: NUCMC, 1970, 74, 79.

Questionnaire not returned.

BETHESDA

MD152-550

National Library of Medicine
History of Medicine Division
8600 Rockville Pike
Bethesda MD 20894

(301) 496-5963

OPEN: M-F 8:30-4:45; closed weekends
COPYING FACILITIES: yes
MATERIALS SOLICITED: Private or personal papers, oral history tapes and transcripts of individuals who have influenced the evolution of contemporary medicine; papers of health-related organizations and societies; and nonclinical photographs relating to the history of medicine.

HOLDINGS:
  Total volume: 900 collections; 140 oral histories; 70,000 pictures
  Inclusive dates: 15th century -
  Description: Materials relating to the history of medicine and other health professions and related institutions. Manuscripts and oral histories are largely modern American in their focus.

SEE: Hamer; NUCMC, 1966, 69, 71, 76.

SEE: Martin; Allard, Crawley, and Edmison; Novotny; Meckler and McMullin; Paszek; Hinding; Grant.

MD152-560

National Naval Medical Center
Naval Medical School
Edward Rhodes Stitt Library
Bethesda MD 20014

no telephone

SEE: NUCMC, 1970.

Questionnaire not returned.

MD152-720

Sisters of Mercy of the Union
Generalate Archives
10000 Kentsdale Drive
Bethesda MD

MAILING ADDRESS:
P.O. Box 34446
Bethesda MD 20034

(301) 469-9221

OPEN: M-F 9-4; closed weekends and holidays
ACCESS: appointment with Archivist required
COPYING FACILITIES: yes
MATERIALS SOLICITED: Materials significant to the history of the Sisters of Mercy in the United States and non-current records of the Generalate administration.

HOLDINGS:
  Total volume: 450 l.f.
  Inclusive dates: 1830 -
  Description: Archives, manuscripts, and memorabilia tracing the history of the Sisters of Mercy, primarily in the United States but also in Ireland. Included are detailed records of the Sisters of Mercy of the Union beginning in 1929; letters, 1837-41, of Catherine McAuley, founder of the congregation; papers of members of the congregation, including reminiscences of a Crimean War nurse, a diary of a nurse in the Spanish-American War, and a typescript of Civil War experiences; and three early 18th century illuminated manuscripts.

CATONSVILLE

MD209-80

Baltimore County Public Library
Catonsville Branch
1100 Frederick Road
Catonsville MD 21228

no telephone
SEE: NUCMC, 1975.

Questionnaire not returned.

CHESTERTOWN

MD228-870

Washington College
Clifton M. Miller Library
Archives
Chestertown MD 21620

(301) 778-2800, Ext. 241

OPEN: M-Th 8:30-10, F 8:30-4:30, Sa 10-2, Su 1-5, 7-10; in summer and when college not in session M-F 8:30-4:30
ACCESS: serious researchers only; prior arrangements are advised
COPYING FACILITIES: yes
MATERIALS SOLICITED: Materials relating to the College.

HOLDINGS:
  Total volume: 30 file drawers
  Inclusive dates: late 1700's -
  Description: Manuscripts, documents, printed materials, and pictures relating to the history of Washington College.

SEE: Robbins.

CLINTON

MD255-720

The Mary Surratt House
Surratt Society Library
9110 Brandywine Road
Clinton MD

MAILING ADDRESS:
P.O. Box 427
Clinton MD 20735

(301) 868-1121

OPEN: Th, F 11-3, Sa, Su 12-4; closed other days, January, February, and holidays
ACCESS: members only, or by appointment
COPYING FACILITIES: no
MATERIALS SOLICITED: Records relating to the Lincoln assassination, John Wilkes Booth, the Surratt family and the mid-19th century especially in the Washington, D.C. and Maryland area. Will also accept some Civil War materials.

HOLDINGS:
  Total volume: 1 file cabinet
  Inclusive dates: 1930 -
  Description: Unpublished manuscripts and scrapbooks pertaining to Lincoln's assassination or persons involved in it; audiovisual slides and tapes relating to the Surratt story; cassettes relating to the Lincoln assassination; and unpublished pamphlets and photographs relating to the Booth escape route.

COCKEYSVILLE

MD266-80

Baltimore County Historical Society
Agriculture Building
9811 Van Buren Lane
Cockeysville MD 21030

(301) 666-1876

OPEN: Sa 10-3; also open on Sundays of meetings or by appointment
COPYING FACILITIES: yes
MATERIALS SOLICITED: Baltimore County and Maryland history; genealogy; data on agriculture and crafts; local cemetery inscriptions; and information on significant buildings.

HOLDINGS:
  Total volume: 2 rooms
  Inclusive dates: 19th century -
  Description: Papers of Lizette Woodworth Reese; ledgers of the Baltimore County Alms House and farmer-miller Charles Jessop; transcribed inscriptions from Baltimore County cemeteries; unpublished school papers and reports on county history; materials, including photographs, relating to several hundred local

buildings; genealogical materials and family group sheets; and glass negatives, 1900-20, taken by Emma K. Woods of Lutherville, MD.

MD266-800
Unitarian and Universalist
  Genealogical Society
10605 Lakespring Way
Cockeysville MD 21030

(301) 628-2490

OPEN: by mail or appointment only
ACCESS: Society members and interested scholars
COPYING FACILITIES: yes
MATERIALS SOLICITED: Genealogical source data, international in scope, such as anecdotal correspondence, ancestor charts, Bible records, wills, and baptismal, marriage and funeral records, from the 16th century to the present, on Unitarians and Universalists, as well as Deists, Ethicists, Freethinkers, Hicksite Quakers, Humanists, Latitudinarian Anglicans, Pantheists, Reform Jews, and Transcendentalists. Will also accept correspondence revealing the philosophical or religious values and denominational affiliations of persons in the liberal religious tradition.

HOLDINGS:
  Total volume: 19 l.f.
  Inclusive dates: 20th century
  Description: Information files documenting the religious affiliations and beliefs of over 8,000 religious liberals of many nationalities since the 16th century, including genealogical data.

SEE: NUCMC, 1978.

COLLEGE PARK

MD285-200
Entomological Society of America
4603 Calvert Road
College Park MD 20740

(301) 864-1334

OPEN: M-F 8:30-5; closed weekends and holidays
ACCESS: members of the Society or others engaged in recognized entomological research
COPYING FACILITIES: yes
MATERIALS SOLICITED: Historical files of the Society's five geographical branches and papers of individual entomologists, as appropriate.

HOLDINGS:
  Total volume: 50 l.f.
  Inclusive dates: 1954 -
  Description: Historical records of the Society, relating to entomological activities in North America, including records of meetings, minutes, correspondence, research, and other materials.

SEE: Novotny.

MD285-360
International Fortean Organization
  (INFO)
7317 Baltimore Avenue
College Park MD 20740

no telephone

OPEN: by appointment only
COPYING FACILITIES: no
MATERIALS SOLICITED: Materials relating to unidentified flying objects (UFOs), the Loch Ness monster, Bigfoot, archaeological oddities, and other anomalies.

HOLDINGS:
  Total volume: 40 file drawers
  Inclusive dates: early 19th century -
  Description: Research, reports, clippings, photographs, art work, and other materials relating to anomalous and curious phenomena around the world.

SEE ALSO: Subject inventory available at repository.

MD285-805
University of Maryland
McKeldin Library
Archives and Manuscripts
  Department
College Park MD 20742

(301) 454-2318, 3035

OPEN: M-F 8:30-5, Sa 10-5; closed Sundays and holidays
COPYING FACILITIES: yes
MATERIALS SOLICITED: Materials relating to agriculture and the environment, political and social history, and literary collections.

HOLDINGS:
  Total volume: 3,000 c.f.
  Inclusive dates: 1700 -
  Description: Post-Civil War personal papers and manuscripts relating to agriculture, and political and social history, including correspondence, diaries, account books, music scores, photographs, and sound recordings. There are also the University archives, and 20th century American and European literary manuscripts.

SEE: NUCMC, 1973, 75-76, 78, 80.

SEE: Hinding; Robbins; Schatz; Novotny; Kim.

SEE ALSO: Various printed guides available through the institution.

CUMBERLAND

MD304-80
Allegany County Historical Society,
  Inc.
History House
218 Washington Street
Cumberland MD 21502

(301) 777-8678

OPEN: Tu-Su 1:30-4; closed Mondays, holidays, and from November through April
ACCESS: appointment requested Nov. - May

COPYING FACILITIES: no
MATERIALS SOLICITED: Records relating to Allegany County and Maryland history. Will also accept genealogical data.

HOLDINGS:
  Total volume: 875 items
  Inclusive dates: 1820 - 1960
  Description: Photographs, diaries, ledgers and financial records, personal documents including school certificates, and genealogical information relating to the social, economic, and transportation history of Allegany County, including records relating to the Baltimore and Ohio Railroad and the Chesapeake and Ohio Canal.

EASTON

MD323-520
Talbot County Free Library
Maryland Room
100 West Dover Street
Easton MD 21601

(301) 822-1626, 1676

OPEN: M 9-9, Tu-Sa 9-5; closed Sundays and holidays
COPYING FACILITIES: yes
MATERIALS SOLICITED: Will accept account books, business or financial records, genealogical source data, and literary manuscripts.

HOLDINGS:
  Total volume: 5 c.f.; 6 file drawers
  Inclusive dates: 18th century -
  Description: Correspondence, day books, ledgers, photographs and genealogical data relating to Talbot County; papers of James A. Michener, 1976-78, and manuscript of *Chesapeake*; and correspondence of H. L. Mencken.

ELLICOTT CITY

MD361-320
Howard County Historical Society,
  Inc.
Library
P.O. Box 109
8328 Court Avenue
Ellicott City MD 21043

(301) 461-1050, 465-2681

OPEN: Tu 1-4, first and third Sunday of month 1-4; other times by appointment
COPYING FACILITIES: yes
MATERIALS SOLICITED: Materials relating to Howard County and Maryland history and genealogy, including photographs, maps, and papers. Will also accept diaries, letters, and scrapbooks related to the history of Howard County.

HOLDINGS:
  Total volume: not specified
  Inclusive dates: 1730 -
  Description: Plats, deeds, account books, tax and court records, draft records, minutes books of organizations, oral history transcripts, and photographs relating to Howard County and adjacent parts of Maryland.

EMMITSBURG

MD380-160

Daughters of Charity of St. Vincent
de Paul
St. Joseph's Provincial House
333 South Seton Avenue
Emmitsburg MD 21727

(301) 447-3121

OPEN: by appointment only M-F 9-4:45
and weekends 10-4; closed holidays
ACCESS: appointment required
COPYING FACILITIES: yes
MATERIALS SOLICITED: Materials pertinent to the activities of the Daughters
of Charity in Emmitsburg.

HOLDINGS:
Total volume: 288 boxes
Inclusive dates: 1786 -
Description: Manuscripts dealing with
the history of the Sisters of Charity of St.
Joseph in Emmitsburg since 1809, and
papers of the congregation's founder,
Elizabeth Ann Seton, 1786-1820. Addi-
tional materials consist of correspondence
of American Catholic bishops, 1805-42,
Civil War and Spanish-American War
papers, and mission histories.

SEE: Hamer.

SEE: Hinding.

MD380-520

Mount Saint Mary's College
Hugh J. Phillips Library
Emmitsburg MD 21727

(301) 447-6122

OPEN: M-F 9-5; closed weekends and
holidays
ACCESS: serious researchers; prior
arrangements must be made
COPYING FACILITIES: yes
MATERIALS SOLICITED: Catholicism in
Maryland (especially western Maryland); Catholic Traditionalist Movement; early Catholic Americana.

HOLDINGS:
Total volume: 460 l.f.
Inclusive dates: 1805 -
Description: Manuscripts, journals, pictures, papers and artifacts relating to Catholicism, not only in western Maryland
but often following the careers of Mount
St. Mary's faculty and graduates as they
were appointed to different dioceses as
the nation and church expanded. Includes
some local genealogical materials.

SEE ALSO: General inventory available at
institution; extensive cataloging under
way.

FREDERICK

MD399-240

Frederick County Public Libraries
C. Burr Artz Library
110 East Patrick Street
Frederick MD 21701

(301) 694-1628

OPEN: M 1-9, Tu, W, F 9-9, Sa 9-5;
closed Sundays, Thursdays, and
holidays
ACCESS: some materials available only
by prior arrangement
COPYING FACILITIES: yes
MATERIALS SOLICITED: Frederick County
history.

HOLDINGS:
Total volume: 30 items
Inclusive dates: 1768 - 1824
Description: Letters relating mainly to
Maryland, including some from George
Washington and other prominent men to
Thomas Johnson.

SEE: Hamer.

GLEN ARM

MD475-280

Gunpowder Falls State Park
10815 Harford Road
Glen Arm MD 21057

(301) 592-2897

OPEN: M-F 8-4:30; closed weekends and
holidays
ACCESS: special arrangements required
COPYING FACILITIES: no

HOLDINGS:
Total volume: 4 items
Inclusive dates: 1976
Description: Audio tapes covering the
history of Gunpowder Falls State Park,
containing information about historical
sites, Indian settlements, and the creation
of the Park.

GREENBELT

MD513-640

Prince George's County Memorial
Library
Greenbelt Branch Library
Rexford G. Tugwell Room
11 Crescent Road
Greenbelt MD 20770

(301) 345-5800

OPEN: M-Th 9-9, F 9-6, Sa 9-5; closed
Sundays and holidays
COPYING FACILITIES: yes
MATERIALS SOLICITED: Greenbelt towns,
especially Greenbelt, MD; planned
communities and new towns; consumer
cooperatives and the cooperative movement. Will also accept materials relating to urban and regional planning.

HOLDINGS:
Total volume: 3 file drawers
Inclusive dates: 1935 -
Description: Business and financial
records of several town of Greenbelt
agencies and associations, including town
council minutes, Greenbelt Consumer
Services minutes, and Woodway Homes
records; and Farm Security Administration photographs of early Greenbelt
scenes as well as photographs by private
citizens.

HAGERSTOWN

MD532-880

Washington County Historical Society
Simms A. Jamieson Memorial Library
135 W. Washington Street
Hagerstown MD

MAILING ADDRESS:
P.O. Box 1281
Hagerstown MD 21740

(301) 797-8782

OPEN: M 9-4; closed other days and
holidays
COPYING FACILITIES: yes
MATERIALS SOLICITED: Materials relating
to the history and genealogy of the region.

HOLDINGS:
Total volume: not specified
Inclusive dates: 19th century -
Description: Photographs and manuscripts relating to the history of Washington County and the surrounding area.
Included are 2,700 photographs; genealogical materials; a few diaries, daybooks,
ledgers, and letters; a log of the U.S.S.
Constellation in 1885; and a diary from
the Spanish-American War.

HYATTSVILLE

MD551-640

Prince George's County Memorial
Library
Hyattsville Branch Library
Maryland Room
6530 Adelphi Road
Hyattsville MD 20782

(301) 779-9330

OPEN: M-F 9-9, Sa 9-5; closed Sundays
and holidays
ACCESS: by appointment only
COPYING FACILITIES: yes
MATERIALS SOLICITED: Maryland materi-
als. Will also accept other materials.

HOLDINGS:
Total volume: not specified
Inclusive dates: 20th century
Description: Materials relating to the
history of Maryland, Prince George's
County and municipalities within the
County. Included are oral history tapes,
photographs, organization records, maps
and ephemera.

SEE: Rowan.

KENSINGTON

MD575-333

Bakery and Confectionary Workers
   International Union
Public Relations
10401 Connecticut Avenue
Kensington MD 20895

(301) 933-8600

OPEN: M-F 9-5; closed weekends and
   holidays
ACCESS: appointment required
COPYING FACILITIES: yes
MATERIALS SOLICITED: Records of local
   unions affiliated with the Bakery and
   Confectionary Workers International
   Union.

HOLDINGS:
   Total volume: not specified
   Inclusive dates: 1900 -
   Description: Records of the Bakery and
   Confectionary Workers International
   Union, including ledgers, executive board
   minutes, and microfilms of contracts,
   1958; and of correspondence between the
   Union and its local organizations.

LA PLATA

MD580-120

Charles County Community College
Learning Resource Center
Southern Maryland Room
Mitchell Road
Box 910
La Plata MD 20646

(202) 870-3008, Ext. 331; (301)
   934-2251, Ext. 331

OPEN: M-F 1-4:30; other hours by
   appointment; closed weekends, college
   holidays, and Christmas week
ACCESS: advance arrangements suggested
COPYING FACILITIES: yes
MATERIALS SOLICITED: Materials relating
   to the history of southern Maryland,
   including Charles, Calvert, and St.
   Mary's counties and Prince George's
   County before 1865, as well as
   Maryland-related genealogy. Will also
   accept materials relating to Prince
   George's County after 1865 and Mary-
   land history.

HOLDINGS:
   Total volume: 300 c.f.
   Inclusive dates: 1651 -
   Description: Visual and aural materials
   relating to southern Maryland history including manuscripts, oral history tapes,
   slides, photographs, scrapbooks, papers of
   individuals, collections of ephemera, business archives and records of community
   organizations, genealogical data, and papers relating to the historic homes and
   sites in the area.

LEONARDTOWN

MD608-710

St. Mary's County Historical Society
11 Court House Drive
Leonardtown MD

MAILING ADDRESS:
P.O. Box 212
Leonardtown MD 20650

(301) 475-2467

OPEN: Tu-Sa 10-4; closed Sundays,
   Mondays, July 4, Thanksgiving, and
   Dec. 19 through Jan. 1
USER FEES: 50 cents per hour for use of
   microfilm viewer by non-members
COPYING FACILITIES: no
MATERIALS SOLICITED: Genealogical
   data, papers, diaries, and pictures relat-
   ing to St. Mary's County. Will also ac-
   cept County land deeds.

HOLDINGS:
   Total volume: 16 file drawers
   Inclusive dates: 1636 -
   Description: A collection of deeds,
   cemetery records, assessment and land
   records on microfilm, genealogical papers,
   and similar materials referring to St.
   Mary's County.

POTOMAC

MD703-40

Academy of American Franciscan
   History
Library
9901 Carmelita Drive
Potomac MD

MAILING ADDRESS:
P.O. Box 34440
Bethesda MD 20817

(301) 365-1763

OPEN: M-F 9-5; closed weekends and
   holidays
ACCESS: qualified graduate students or
   equivalent
COPYING FACILITIES: yes
MATERIALS SOLICITED: Franciscans in
   Latin America.

HOLDINGS:
   Total volume: 14 vols.; 70 items; 200
   microfilm reels
   Inclusive dates: 1550 - 1900
   Description: Manuscripts concerning
   the missionary and cultural activities of
   the Franciscan friars in Brazil, Latin
   America, New Mexico and California. Included are 50 original letters from missionaries in California and two
   catechisms in Indian languages. Also included are 200 microfilm rolls from the
   Vatican Archives, Archivo General de Indias (Seville), Arquivo Nacional and
   Arquivo Historico Ultramarino (Lisbon),
   and from various public and private archives of South America.

SEE: Beers - Southwest; Grow.

SEE ALSO: Lino Gomez Canedo, *Los
Archivos Historicos de la Historia de
America* (Instituto Panamericano de
Geografia e Historia, 1961); Thomas T.
McAvoy, 'Catholic Archives and Manu-
script Collections,' *American Archivist*
24 (Oct. 1961).

REISTERSTOWN

MD745-690

Baltimore County Public Library
Reisterstown Branch
Cockeys Mill Road
Reisterstown MD 21136

no telephone

SEE: NUCMC, 1976.

Questionnaire not returned.

RIVERDALE

MD755-560

National Oceanic and Atmospheric
   Administration
National Ocean Service
Charting and Geodetic Services
Data Control Section
WSC2, Room 151
N/CG243
6001 Executive Boulevard
Riverdale MD 20840

(301) 443-8408

OPEN: M-F 7-3:30; closed weekends and
   holidays
USER FEES: according to material
   supplied
ACCESS: all inquiries by mail or
   telephone; copies supplied by mail
COPYING FACILITIES: yes
MATERIALS SOLICITED: Hydrographic
   data concerning coastal areas of the fifty States, Puerto Rico, the Virgin Islands, and the Great Lakes.

HOLDINGS:
   Total volume: not specified
   Inclusive dates: 1835 -
   Description: 23,000 survey sheets and
   related material, both hydrographic and
   topographic.

SEE ALSO: Shirley L. Green, comp. *Pictorial Resources in the Washington, D.C.,
Area* (Library of Congress, 1976).

ROCKVILLE

MD760-530

Montgomery County Historical
   Society
103 West Montgomery Avenue
Rockville MD 20850

(301) 762-1492

OPEN: Tu-Sa 12-4, first Sunday of
   month 2-5; closed Mondays and
   holidays
USER FEES: 50 cents
COPYING FACILITIES: yes

MATERIALS SOLICITED: History of Montgomery County. Will also accept materials on the history of Maryland and genealogy of Maryland families.

HOLDINGS:
Total volume: 55 file drawers
Inclusive dates: 1776 -
Description: Materials relating to Maryland and Montgomery County. Included are a photograph collection, genealogical files, copies of early county records, collections of family papers, and oral history tapes.

SEE ALSO: Elizabeth Lawton and Raymond Sweeney, *Maryland History, A Selective Bibliography* (Montgomery County Historical Society, 1975).

ST. MICHAELS

MD770-120
Chesapeake Bay Maritime Museum
Library
St. Michaels MD

MAILING ADDRESS:
P.O. Box 636
St. Michaels MD 21663

(301) 745-2916

OPEN: M-F 9-4; closed weekends
ACCESS: appointment required
COPYING FACILITIES: yes
MATERIALS SOLICITED: Records relating to 19th century Chesapeake Bay boats and the seafood industry. Will also accept records relating to Chesapeake Bay history in general.

HOLDINGS:
Total volume: not specified
Inclusive dates: 19th century
Description: Photographs, logs, receipts, and manuscripts relating to 19th century Chesapeake Bay, especially bay boats and lighthouses and the seafood industry.

SHARPSBURG

MD798-40
Antietam National Battlefield Site
Library
Sharpsburg MD

MAILING ADDRESS:
P.O. Box 158
Sharpsburg MD 21782

(301) 432-5124

OPEN: M-F 8:30-5; closed weekends, Thanksgiving, Christmas and New Year's
ACCESS: Researchers, students, and writers only; all users must register; special permission for use of certain rare materials by written request only.
COPYING FACILITIES: no
MATERIALS SOLICITED: Diaries, letters, and maps of soldiers who fought in the Battle of Antietam and the Civil War. Will also accept materials relating to the history of Washington County; maps, sketches, and photographs relating to the Battle of Antietam; and military documents pertaining to the 1862 Maryland campaign.

HOLDINGS:
Total volume: 70 l.f.
Inclusive dates: 1862 -
Description: Research reports, manuscripts, diaries, letters, pay books, vouchers, receipts, ledgers, and reminiscences relating to the Battle of Antietam and the Civil War.

SILVER SPRING

MD800-322
International Federation of
Professional and Technical
Engineers
818 Roeder Road, Suite 702
Silver Spring MD 20910

(301) 565-9016

OPEN: M-F 9-5; closed weekends and holidays
ACCESS: by appointment and with permission of President of the Federation
COPYING FACILITIES: yes

HOLDINGS:
Total volume: not specified
Inclusive dates: 1918 -
Description: National convention proceedings of the Federation, 1918 to the present, and photographs of Federation officials and other labor leaders.

SOLOMONS

MD836-120
Calvert Marine Museum
Solomons MD

MAILING ADDRESS:
P.O. Box 97
Solomons MD 20688

(301) 326-2042

OPEN: M-F 10-4:30, weekends by appointment only; closed Thanksgiving, Christmas, and New Year's
COPYING FACILITIES: no
MATERIALS SOLICITED: Local maritime history, including ships' logs, maritime business records, photographs of ships, shipbuilding, and the seafood industry, architectural drawings, and oral history tapes. Will also accept genealogical source data.

HOLDINGS:
Total volume: 21 l.f.
Inclusive dates: 1854 -
Description: Maritime collections concentrating on Calvert County, the Patuxent River, and the western Chesapeake Bay, including photographs; records of marine businesses (such as oyster houses); oral history tapes, containing genealogical information; ship blueprints; and ships' logs and account books.

TOWSON

MD950-520
Maryland House and Garden
Pilgrimage
1105A Providence Road
Towson MD 21204

(301) 821-6933

OPEN: M-F 9-1; closed weekends, holidays, Dec. 25 - Jan. 1, and June 15 - Sept. 15
COPYING FACILITIES: no
MATERIALS SOLICITED: Historical and descriptive data and photographs of houses and gardens in the state of Maryland.

HOLDINGS:
Total volume: 5,000 items
Inclusive dates: 1930 -
Description: Photographs of Maryland homes and record copies of *Annual Maryland House and Garden Pilgrimage.*

MD950-760
Towson State University
Archives
Cook Library
8000 York Road
Towson MD 21204

(301) 321-2398

OPEN: M 8-3; closed other days, holidays, and University intersessions
COPYING FACILITIES: yes
MATERIALS SOLICITED: Towson State University records. Will also accept material illustrative of student, alumni, faculty, staff, and adminstrative activities and institutional development.

HOLDINGS:
Total volume: 210 l.f.; 9 file cabinets
Inclusive dates: 1866 -
Description: Records of Towson State University and its predecessor institutions, Maryland State Normal School, The State Teachers College at Towson, and Towson State College. Included are minutes of faculty, department, and committee meetings; financial records; correspondence; student and faculty organization records; student academic records; notebooks and class histories; scrapbooks, photographs, sound recordings, and architectural drawings.

SEE: Hinding; Robbins.

WESTMINSTER

MD978-320
Historical Society of Carroll County
210 East Main Street
Westminster MD 21157

(301) 848-6494

OPEN: Tu-F 9-4; closed Mondays, weekends, and holidays
USER FEES: one dollar per hour for non-members
COPYING FACILITIES: yes
MATERIALS SOLICITED: Materials pertaining to the history of Carroll County. Will also accept materials relating

to the history of Maryland as it pertains to Carroll County.

HOLDINGS:
> *Total volume:* not specified
> *Inclusive dates:* early 19th century -
> *Description:* Correspondence, diaries, journals, account books, genealogical source data, deeds, church records, photographs, maps, oral history tapes, and vertical files, providing information on the development and contemporary life of Carroll County.
> Collection includes photographic materials.

SEE: Hinding.

MD978-880
Western Maryland College
Archives
Westminster MD 21157

(301) 848-7000

OPEN: by appointment only
ACCESS: by arrangement with the College Archivist; access to College archival material varies according to restrictions established by College offices and departments
COPYING FACILITIES: no

MATERIALS SOLICITED: Materials relating to Western Maryland College, including history, diaries, correspondence, working papers, and memorabilia.

HOLDINGS:
> *Total volume:* not specified
> *Inclusive dates:* 1867 -
> *Description:* Materials, including diaries, correspondence, and business records, relating to Western Maryland College. The collection includes photographs, non-current working papers of the College, microform copies of student records, and College journals and publications.

SEE: Hinding.

WHEATON

MD985-560
National Capital Historical Museum
of Transportation, Inc.
National Capital Trolley Museum
1313 Bonifant Road
Northwest Branch Regional Park
Wheaton MD

MAILING ADDRESS:
P.O. Box 4007
Colesville Branch
Silver Spring MD 20904

(301) 384-9797, 589-4676

OPEN: Sa, Su noon-5; closed other days and Dec. 15 - Jan. 1
ACCESS: prior arrangement required by calling Librarian
COPYING FACILITIES: no
MATERIALS SOLICITED: Materials relating to electric traction, especially street railway companies. Will also accept materials relating to railroading.

HOLDINGS:
> *Total volume:* 2 c.f.
> *Inclusive dates:* 1890 -
> *Description:* Primarily materials of the traction companies of Washington, DC.

MASSACHUSETTS

Acting under the authority of legislation enacted in 1889, the Division of Public Records of the Office of the Massachusetts Secretary of State has supervisory responsibilities for the preservation and management of local and county records. Since 1973, the Division has accelerated its supervisory activities by means of a comprehensive field survey program. Towns, cities, and counties traditionally have been responsible for the safekeeping of their records.

ABINGTON

MA5-160
Dyer Memorial Library
Centre Avenue
Abington MA

MAILING ADDRESS:
P.O. Box 2245
Abington MA 02351

(617) 878-8480

OPEN: M, Tu, Th, F 1-5; closed
weekends, Wednesdays, and holidays
COPYING FACILITIES: yes
MATERIALS SOLICITED: Will accept all
materials relating to the history of Abington.

HOLDINGS:
Total volume: not specified
Inclusive dates: 1600's -
Description: Materials relating to Abington, including logbooks, account books, petitions, deeds, maps, photographs, oral history tapes and genealogical materials.

AMESBURY

MA17-40
Amesbury Public Library
149 Main Street
Amesbury MA 01913

(617) 388-0312

OPEN: M-F 10-9, Sa 10-5; closed
Sundays and holidays
COPYING FACILITIES: yes
MATERIALS SOLICITED: Local history material, especially on manufacturing and genealogy. Will also accept other materials relating to local events or personalities.

HOLDINGS:
Total volume: 100 l.f.
Inclusive dates: 1600 -
Description: Historical and biographical materials relating to Amesbury; maps and photographs of local scenes and events; and records of local churches, schools and organizations.

SEE: Hamer.

SEE: Robbins.

MA17-400
John Greenleaf Whittier Home
86 Friend Street
Amesbury MA 01913

(617) 388-1337

OPEN: Tu-Sa 10-4; closed Sundays,
Mondays, Thanksgiving, Christmas,
January and February
USER FEES: adults 50 cents, children 25
cents
ACCESS: by prior arrangement
COPYING FACILITIES: no
MATERIALS SOLICITED: Materials relevant to John Greenleaf Whittier.

HOLDINGS:
Total volume: 80 items
Inclusive dates: 1836 - 1892
Description: Materials relating to John Greenleaf Whittier, including correspondence, manuscript poems, and a diary written by Whittier's sister. Also included are citations and proclamations connected with Whittier's political activities and photographs of his associates in the antislavery movement.

SEE: Robbins.

AMHERST

MA21-40
Amherst College
Robert Frost Library
Archives and Special Collections
Amherst MA 01002

(413) 542-2299

OPEN: M-F 8:30-4:30 (academic year);
M-F 8-4 (summer months); closed
weekends and holidays
ACCESS: serious researchers at college
level or above with adequate personal
identification
COPYING FACILITIES: yes
MATERIALS SOLICITED: Amherst College records; 19th and 20th century literary manuscripts. Will also accept Amherst College faculty and graduates' records and papers, and materials relating to the French and Indian War and William Wordsworth.

HOLDINGS:
Total volume: 10,800 c.f.
Inclusive dates: 1450 -
Description: Materials relating chiefly to New England and to English and American literature. Among the individuals represented are Emily Dickinson, Robert Frost, William Wordsworth, Louise Bogan, and Lord Jeffrey Amherst. The College Archives, in addition to containing the non-current records of the College, also includes personal papers of notable faculty amd alumni, such as Dwight W. Morrow.

SEE: Hamer; NUCMC, 1959-62, 75, 78, 80.

SEE: Hinding; Robbins; Martin.

MA21-400
The Jones Library, Inc.
Special Collections
43 Amity Street
Amherst MA 01002

(413) 256-0246

OPEN: M-Sa 9-5; closed Sundays and
holidays
COPYING FACILITIES: yes
MATERIALS SOLICITED: Amherst history and Amherst authors. Will also accept materials relating to the history of area towns.

HOLDINGS:
Total volume: 203 l.f.
Inclusive dates: 1700 -
Description: Materials relating primarily to the history of Amherst, its inhabitants, area towns, and materials by and about Amherst authors. Included are some personal papers of Emily Dickinson and the personal correspondence of Charles Kellogg Field and family.

SEE: Hamer; NUCMC, 1969, 72.

SEE: Schatz; Robbins.

MA21-770
University of Massachusetts at Amherst
Archives and Manuscripts
Department
University Library
Amherst MA 01003

(413) 545-2780

OPEN: M-F 8:30-5; closed weekends and
holidays
COPYING FACILITIES: yes
MATERIALS SOLICITED: Materials relating to the University of Massachusetts. Will also accept materials relating to western Massachusetts and New England.

HOLDINGS:
>*Total volume:* 3,000 l.f.
>*Inclusive dates:* 1812 -
>*Description:* Historical manuscripts, theses, photographs, tapes, faculty and student papers, and records of the University of Massachusetts. There are also manuscript collections relating principally to Massachusetts in the 20th century, including materials concerning W. E. B. Du Bois, Joseph and Tamara Obresky, Maurice A. Donahue, Robert Francis, John W. Haigis, the Linguistic Atlas of New England, the Valley Peace Center of Amherst, the Hampshire-Franklin County Chapter of the Civil Liberties Union of Massachusetts, the Friends of the Belchertown State School, the New England Intercollegiate Lacrosse League, military government of Europe after World War II, and contemporary Soviet authors. Also papers of Horace Mann Bond and family and Harvey Swados.

SEE: Hamer (as University of Massachusetts Library).

SEE: Hinding; Robbins.

SEE ALSO: unpublished guides to parts of the collection available at the repository.

MA21-800

University of Massachusetts at Amherst
Labor Relations and Research Center
125 Draper Hall
Amherst MA 01003

(413) 545-2884

OPEN: M-F 8:30-4:30; closed weekends and holidays
ACCESS: open to Five-College Consortium students, faculty, staff; others by permission of director
COPYING FACILITIES: yes
MATERIALS SOLICITED: Materials relating to labor unions and industrial relations, especially in Massachusetts; records and correspondence of the Labor Relations and Research Center.

HOLDINGS:
>*Total volume:* 5 drawers; 5 vols.; 1 folder
>*Inclusive dates:* 1900 -
>*Description:* Letters on the AFL-CIO merger in Massachusetts, account books of Fall River textile industry unions, and archives and correspondence of the Labor Relations and Research Center.

SEE: Meckler and McMullin.

ANDOVER

MA25-40

Andover Historical Society
97 Main Street
Andover MA 01810

(617) 475-2236

OPEN: Su 2-4, M-F 9-5 or by appointment; closed Saturdays and holidays
ACCESS: advance arrangements required
COPYING FACILITIES: yes

MATERIALS SOLICITED: Andover documents, with focus on family, business, manufacturing, church, architectural, and school records.

HOLDINGS:
>*Total volume:* 250 l.f.
>*Inclusive dates:* 1694 -
>*Description:* Materials relating to Andover and the surrounding area, especially notable Andover families and Massachusetts settlers. Included are deeds, wills, diaries, letters, and miscellaneous manuscripts.

MA25-520

Memorial Hall Library
Elm Square
Andover MA 01810

(617) 475-6960

OPEN: M-F 9-9, Sa 9-5, Su 2-5; closed holidays
COPYING FACILITIES: yes
MATERIALS SOLICITED: Genealogy, local history.

HOLDINGS:
>*Total volume:* 55 vols.; 12 file drawers; several cartons
>*Inclusive dates:* colonial period -
>*Description:* Notebooks of genealogical data on Andover families, several 19th century maps of the area, papers relating to the Civil War, and miscellaneous photographs and other materials relating to the history of Andover.

SEE: Hamer.

SEE: Hinding.

MA25-650

Phillips Academy
Oliver Wendell Holmes Library
Andover MA 01810

(617) 475-3400, Ext. 188

OPEN: Su 2:30-9:30, M-Th 9-9:30, F 8-6, Sa 9-5; closed Labor Day, Christmas, and New Year's
COPYING FACILITIES: yes
MATERIALS SOLICITED: Materials relating to Phillips Academy.

HOLDINGS:
>*Total volume:* not specified
>*Inclusive dates:* 18th century -
>*Description:* Materials relating chiefly to Phillips Academy and the people associated with it. Included are records of the Academy; letters, genealogical materials, and miscellaneous papers of the Phillips family; and papers of alumni and others connected with the Academy.

SEE: NUCMC, 1969, 80.

SEE: Hinding; Robbins.

ARLINGTON

MA29-40

Arlington Historical Society
Museum
7 Jason Street
Arlington MA 02174

(617) 648-4300

OPEN: M, Th, F 9-4, Tu 9-1; closed Wednesdays, weekends, and holidays
ACCESS: by appointment only
COPYING FACILITIES: no

HOLDINGS:
>*Total volume:* 325 c.f.
>*Inclusive dates:* early 18th century -
>*Description:* Materials relating to the history of Arlington, including correspondence of the early 18th century; a few account books and diaries; church and school records; town warrants; sermons of Samuel Cooke and Thaddeus Fiske, dating from the 18th and 19th centuries; thousands of deeds; and photographs of townspeople and houses.

ASHLAND

MA41-40

Ashland Historical Society
Town Hall
Main Street
Ashland MA

MAILING ADDRESS:
P.O. Box 321
Ashland MA 01721

(617) 881-3075

OPEN: by appointment only
ACCESS: Some material is housed in the Ashland Public Library and is available during the regular library hours, M-Sa 2-9, to members of the Society or to others with the permission of the Curator; some microfilm copies are available without restriction.
COPYING FACILITIES: no
MATERIALS SOLICITED: Ashland history or subjects pertaining to the local area.

HOLDINGS:
>*Total volume:* 28 l.f.; 204 items; 47 vols.
>*Inclusive dates:* 1754 -
>*Description:* Historical materials relating to Ashland, as well as to Hopkinton, Holliston, and Framingham prior to 1846. Included are industrial, school, and organization records, genealogical material relating to local families, and 19th century photographs of local citizens. The bulk of the holdings fall between 1800 and 1945.

ATTLEBORO

MA48-20

Attleboro Area Industrial Museum,
Inc.
42 Union Street
Attleboro MA 02703

(617) 222-0801

OPEN: M-F 9-4; closed weekends and
holidays
COPYING FACILITIES: no
MATERIALS SOLICITED: Attleboro area
material, especially industrial materials.

HOLDINGS:
Total volume: 1 vertical file; 90 sq. f.
Inclusive dates: 1661 -
Description: Materials pertaining to Attleboro history, including manuscripts,
business records, genealogical source data,
photographs, and scrapbooks. Also held
are materials of the Attleboro Historical
Commission, including a journal of the
Revolutionary War period, letters, school
reports, and slides of the town's 1969
275th anniversary celebration.

MA48-40

Attleboro Public Library
Joseph L. Sweet Memorial
74 North Main Street
Attleboro MA 02703

(617) 222-0157

OPEN: M 9-8:30, Tu 9-5:30, W, Th
1-8:30, F, Sa 9-5:30; closed Saturdays
mid-June to mid-Sept.
ACCESS: permission granted through
Librarian's office
COPYING FACILITIES: yes
MATERIALS SOLICITED: 18th and 19th
century manuscript items; papers of
clergyman Peter Thacher and church
organizations. Will also accept documents, manuscripts, photographs, and
other materials pertaining to Attleboro.

HOLDINGS:
Total volume: 40 l.f.
Inclusive dates: 1661 -
Description: Collections focusing on
the Town of Attleborough, later the City
of Attleboro (1914), including the separa-
tion of Attleborough from North
Attleborough in 1887, covering social,
economic, political, religious and military
history, with emphasis on military history
of the years 1814 to 1863. Included are
records of organizations, sermons, journals of individuals, records of military
organizations, papers and letters,
unpublished histories and genealogies, genealogical finding aids, scrapbooks, account books and maps.

SEE: Hamer; NUCMC, 1968.

AUBURN

MA52-50

Auburn Public Library
Auburn MA 01501

no telephone

SEE: Hamer.

Questionnaire not returned.

BARNSTABLE

MA67-720

The Sturgis Library
Stanley W. Smith Collection
3090 Main Street
Barnstable MA

MAILING ADDRESS:
P.O. Box 606
Barnstable MA 02630

(617) 362-6636

OPEN: M, F 2-5, Tu, Th 2-9, W, Sa 9-5;
closed Sundays
COPYING FACILITIES: yes
MATERIALS SOLICITED: Local history,
maritime history, and genealogy.

HOLDINGS:
Total volume: 1,500 items
Inclusive dates: mid-17th century -
late 19th century
Description: Documents about Cape
Cod, including land deeds, financial
records, and maps.

BARRE

MA70-70

Barre Historical Society, Inc.
Common Street
Barre MA 01005

no telephone

OPEN: Tu-F 2-9, Sa 2-5; closed Sundays,
Mondays, holidays, and Saturdays
before holidays
COPYING FACILITIES: no
MATERIALS SOLICITED: Materials relating
to the town of Barre and its people.

HOLDINGS:
Total volume: 30 l.f.
Inclusive dates: 1763 - 1900's
Description: Diaries relating to the gold
rush and building of canals; and records,
documents, and pictures of businesses, industries, schools, churches, families, articles and events of or pertaining to the
town of Barre and its people.

SEE: Hamer (as Barre Town Library);
NUCMC, 1971.

SEE: Davis; Hinding.

BEDFORD

MA77-80

Bedford Historical Society
15 The Great Road
Bedford MA 01730

no telephone

OPEN: by appointment only
COPYING FACILITIES: no
MATERIALS SOLICITED: Materials relating
to the history of Bedford. Will also
accept material on flags, especially the
Bedford Flag, the battles of Lexington
and Concord, and muralist Rufus Porter.

HOLDINGS:
Total volume: 2,400 items
Inclusive dates: 18th century -
Description: A collection relating chiefly to the history of Bedford. Included are
deeds, wills, legal documents, receipts,
school and church records, photographs,
and materials on the Bedford Flag.

MA77-520

The MITRE Corporation
Burlington Road
K-450
Bedford MA 01730

(617) 271-7854

OPEN: by appointment only
ACCESS: for corporate use only
COPYING FACILITIES: yes

HOLDINGS:
Total volume: 1,100 c.f.
Inclusive dates: 1942 -
Description: Photographs, slides, motion picture film, tape recordings, microfilm, microfiche, viewgraphs, annual reports, house organs, press clippings, training brochures, memorabilia, work tasks
documentation, minutes, and correspondence, all relating to The MITRE Corporation.

BELCHERTOWN

MA81-80

The Belchertown Historical
Association
The Stone House
20 Maple Street
Belchertown MA 01007

(413) 323-6573

OPEN: by appointment only; closed
holidays
USER FEES: adults, one dollar
ACCESS: appointment required for
research
COPYING FACILITIES: no
MATERIALS SOLICITED: Materials relating
to Belchertown.

HOLDINGS:
Total volume: not specified
Inclusive dates: 1700's -
Description: Materials relating chiefly
to Belchertown, including deeds, tax
records, genealogical materials, church
records, photographs, and diaries. Other
holdings include items on the French and

Indian and Revolutionary wars, land surveying in western Massachusetts (1740-1810), and missionary activities in China.

SEE: NUCMC, 1962.

BELMONT

MA84-50

Armenian Library and Museum of America
Archives and Manuscripts Department and Oral History Collection
380 Concord Avenue
Belmont MA

MAILING ADDRESS:
P.O. Box 147
Belmont MA 02178

(617) 484-4779

OPEN: by appointment only
COPYING FACILITIES: no
MATERIALS SOLICITED: Oral histories, diaries, letters and photographs of first-generation Armenian-Americans, including survivors of the massacres in Turkey during World War I. Will also accept manuscripts and non-current records of Armenian institutions in America, in the former Armenian republic, in the Soviet Socialist Republic of Armenia, and in Armenian settlements elsewhere.

HOLDINGS:
>*Total volume:* 600 hours of oral histories; additional materials
>*Inclusive dates:* 1890 -
>*Description:* A collection of photographs and Armenian language diaries, manuscripts, and oral histories of survivors of the Turkish massacres of Armenians in 1895 and during World War I. The oral histories relate to Armenian life before 1914, the events of the massacres, and the subsequent emigration to America by the survivors, including the experiences of first-generation Armeniaan-Americans. There is also a small collection of miscellaneous materials pertaining to Armenian culture.

BEVERLY

MA92-70

Beverly Historical Society and Museum
Cabot House
117 Cabot Street
Beverly MA 01915

(617) 922-1186

OPEN: summer, Tu-F 10-4; closed holidays and rest of year
USER FEES: one dollar per day
COPYING FACILITIES: no
MATERIALS SOLICITED: Materials relating to the history of Beverly.

HOLDINGS:
>*Total volume:* 200 l.f.
>*Inclusive dates:* 1650 -
>*Description:* About 20,000 items, including family papers; records of local churches, societies, and other organizations; town and school records; and records of the U.S. Naval office at Beverly, 1784-1800. Other holdings include diaries, logbooks, business records, genealogical source data, maps, and photographs.

SEE: Hamer.

SEE: Hinding; Allard, Crawley, and Edmison.

SEE ALSO: Peter Duignan, *Handbook of American Resources for African Studies* (Hoover Institution, 1967); Walter Schatz, ed., *Directory of Afro-American Resources* (Bowker, 1970); G. Bhagat, 'Materials Relating to Eighteenth and Nineteenth Century Indo-American Trade and Consular Relations in Private Archives in the United States,' *Indian Archives* 17 (Jan. 1967/Dec. 1968).

MA92-90

Beverly Public Library
32 Essex Street
Beverly MA 01915

(617) 922-0310

OPEN: Su 1-5, M-Th 9-9, F 9-6, Sa 9-5; closed holidays
COPYING FACILITIES: yes

HOLDINGS:
>*Total volume:* not specified
>*Inclusive dates:* not specified
>*Description:* Correspondence of Massachusetts author and teacher Lucy Larcom.

SEE: Hamer.

The papers of Asa Gray, listed in NUCMC, 1969, have been transferred to the Beverly Historical Society, in Beverly, MA.

BOLTON

MA104-80

Bolton Historical Society, Inc.
Great Road
Bolton MA 01740

no telephone

OPEN: by appointment only
COPYING FACILITIES: no
MATERIALS SOLICITED: Anything relating to Bolton and its people.

HOLDINGS:
>*Total volume:* 8 l.f.
>*Inclusive dates:* 1790 -
>*Description:* Materials relating to the history and people of Bolton.

BOSTON

MA108-10

Allied Orders of the Grand Army of the Republic
Memorial Shrine to the Grand Army of the Republic
Room 27, State House
Boston MA 02133

no telephone

OPEN: M, W, F 10-3 and by appointment
COPYING FACILITIES: no
MATERIALS SOLICITED: Materials relating to the Civil War and the Grand Army of the Republic.

HOLDINGS:
>*Total volume:* not specified
>*Inclusive dates:* 1800's -
>*Description:* Materials relating primarily to the involvement of Massachusetts citizens in the Civil War and their postwar contributions to society.

MA108-80

Ancient and Honorable Artillery Company of Massachusetts
Faneuil Hall
Boston MA 02109

(617) 227-1638

OPEN: M-F 10-4; closed weekends, holidays, and first two weeks in October
COPYING FACILITIES: no
MATERIALS SOLICITED: History of the Company and individual members.

HOLDINGS:
>*Total volume:* 10 l.f.
>*Inclusive dates:* 1680 -
>*Description:* Manuscripts relating to the history of the Company and biographical notes on members.

MA108-110

Austro-American Association of Boston, Inc.
88 Marlborough Street
Boston MA 02116

no telephone

OPEN: by appointment only
COPYING FACILITIES: no
MATERIALS SOLICITED: Materials on Austria, including personal letters and notes from Austrian Nobel prize winners, Austrian scientists, musicians, and physicians and current Austrian writers, poets, composers, and painters. Will also accept materials on Austrian-Americans and their contributions in the United States.

HOLDINGS:
>*Total volume:* 6 l.f.
>*Inclusive dates:* 1970 -
>*Description:* Program announcements of meetings, correspondence, minutes of board meetings, records of scholarship awards, annual financial reports, and incorporation papers of the Austro-American Association.

MA108-140
Boston Athenaeum
10 1/2 Beacon Street
Boston MA 02108

(617) 227-0270

OPEN: M-F 9-5:30, Sa 9-4; closed
   Sundays, holidays, and Saturdays Oct. -
   May
COPYING FACILITIES: yes
MATERIALS SOLICITED: Will accept let-
   ters and other materials relating to Bos-
   ton history and life.

HOLDINGS:
   Total volume: not specified
   Inclusive dates: 1690 -
   Description: The archives of the Athenaeum and personal papers of its
   founders and librarians, 1790- ; correspondence, diaries, essays, sermons, and
   other papers of merchants, ministers, literary figures, and others, 1690-1960;
   logbooks, orderly books, receipt books,
   notarial records, and court records,
   1670-1930; architectural plans, drawings,
   and sketchbooks of Boston, 1800-1950;
   and institution and organization records
   of Boston, 1850-1950.

SEE: Hamer; NUCMC, 1959-61, 70, 76.

SEE: Allard, Crawley, and Edmison;
   Hinding; Ingram; Leventhal and Mooney - I; Martin; Robbins; Schatz.

MA108-200
Boston Public Library
Copley Square
Boston MA

MAILING ADDRESS:
Box 286
Boston MA 02117

no telephone

SEE: Hamer; NUCMC, 1963-65, 69,
   73-75.

Questionnaire not returned.

MA108-240
Boston University
Mugar Library
Department of Special Collections
771 Commonwealth Avenue
Boston MA 02215

(617) 353-3696

OPEN: M-F 9-5; closed weekends and
   holidays
ACCESS: qualified scholars and
   researchers; identification required
COPYING FACILITIES: yes
MATERIALS SOLICITED: 20th century literature, journalism, public affairs, and
   the arts, especially theater, film, radio,
   television and music; pre-1820 American materials; materials relating to the
   Victorian era, military history, nursing,
   and Robert Frost; and Presidential papers, especially those of Abraham Lincoln and Theodore Roosevelt.

HOLDINGS:
   Total volume: 10,000 l.f.
   Inclusive dates: 1400 -
   Description: Primarily English and
   American manuscripts of the 19th and
   20th centuries. The Twentieth Century
   Archives contains the papers of 832
   individuals prominent in contemporary
   literature, public affairs, journalism, the-
   ater, film, radio, television, and music.
   Other holdings relate to Martin Luther
   King, Jr., John W. McCormack, Ameri-
   can colonial history, the Foxcroft and
   Mayhew families, the history of nursing,
   Florence Nightingale, the Military Historical Society of Massachusetts and the
   First Corps of Cadets (Massachusetts),
   Theodore Roosevelt and other American
   Presidents and government leaders, Robert Frost, Franz Liszt, the Boston Sym-
   phony Orchestra, and Boston University
   (archives).

SEE: Hamer; NUCMC, 1959-61, 63-67,
   69-71, 77 (also, Military Historical Society of Massachusetts, 1966).

SEE: Allard, Crawley, and Edmison;
   Hinding; Ingram; Leventhal and Mooney - I; Paszek; Robbins; Spalek.

SEE ALSO: Walter Schatz, ed., *Directory of
   Afro-American Resources* (Bowker,
   1970); Peter Duignan, *Handbook of
   American Resources for African Studies*
   (Hoover Institution, 1967); Lorenzo J.
   Greene, 'Negro Manuscripts Collections
   in Libraries,' *Negro History Bulletin* 30
   (March 1967); Lois A. Monteiro, ed.,
   *Letters of Florence Nightingale in the
   History of Nursing Archives, Special
   Collections, Boston University Libraries*
   (Boston Univ., Nursing Archives,
   1974); Alan M. Meckler and Ruth
   McMullin, comps., *Oral History Collec-
   tions* (Bowker, 1975). Brochures are
   available describing holdings in the
   Twentieth Century Archives and in the
   History of Nursing Archives.

MA108-320
The Bostonian Society
Library
15 State Street, 3rd Floor
Boston MA

MAILING ADDRESS:
Old State House, 206 Washington
Street
Boston MA 02109

(617) 242-5614

OPEN: M-F 9:30-4:30; closed weekends
   and holidays
COPYING FACILITIES: no
MATERIALS SOLICITED: Will accept
   manuscripts, archives and non-current
   records of Boston institutions and organizations, and manuscript maps and
   architectural drawings that are Boston
   related.

HOLDINGS:
   Total volume: 20 l.f.
   Inclusive dates: 18th century - 20th
   century
   Description: Materials relating to the
   history of Boston.

SEE: Hamer; NUCMC, 1959-61.

SEE: Leventhal and Mooney - I.

MA108-480
Congregational Library
14 Beacon Street
Boston MA 02108

(617) 523-0470

OPEN: M-F 9-4:30; closed weekends and
   holidays
COPYING FACILITIES: yes
MATERIALS SOLICITED: Congregational
   church records and Congregational Association records. Will also accept
   manuscript sermons and correspondence and papers of Congregational
   leaders.

HOLDINGS:
   Total volume: 5,000 items
   Inclusive dates: 1669 -
   Description: Manuscripts relating to
   Congregationalism, including many indi-
   vidual sermons and letters, materials on
   Congregational history and records of
   churches, chiefly in New England.

SEE: Hamer; NUCMC, 1959-64, 68, 76,
   78, 80.

SEE ALSO: Walter Schatz, ed., *Directory of
   Afro-American Resources* (Bowker,
   1970).

MA108-520
Emerson College
Library
150 Beacon Street
Boston MA 02116

(617) 578-8673, 8668

OPEN: M-F 7:45-10, Sa noon-6, Su
   noon-10; closed holidays and week
   after Christmas
COPYING FACILITIES: yes
MATERIALS SOLICITED: Women in the
   performing arts and Emerson College
   history.

HOLDINGS:
   Total volume: 4 videotapes; 6 l.f.; 4
   scrapbooks
   Inclusive dates: 1880 -
   Description: Videotapes of performances by women and interviews with
   women in the fields of stage, film, radio,
   and television. There are also manuscripts of Charles Wesley Emerson and
   early records of Emerson College.

MA108-580
Episcopal Diocese of Massachusetts
Diocesan Library and Archives
1 Joy Street
Boston MA 02108

(617) 742-4720

OPEN: M-F 9-5; closed weekends and
   holidays
COPYING FACILITIES: yes
MATERIALS SOLICITED: Materials relating
   to the history of the Diocese and its
   parishes; sermons by prominent clergy
   within the Diocese; materials related to
   the bishops of the Diocese. Will also
   accept liturgical works relevant to the
   Diocese.

HOLDINGS:

Total volume: 500 vols.; 350 c.f.
Inclusive dates: 1682 -
Description: Materials relating to American history, colonial church history, and Episcopal clergy; official records of the Episcopal Diocese of Massachusetts and its organizations; vital records of closed parishes in the Diocese; parish histories; and papers and memorabilia of the bishops of the Diocese of Massachusetts.

SEE: Hamer (as Massachusetts Diocesan Library); NUCMC, 1978.

SEE: Hinding; Leventhal and Mooney - I; Robbins.

MA108-600

The First Church of Christ, Scientist
Archives and Library of The Mother
  Church
Christian Science Center
Boston MA 02115

(617) 262-2300

OPEN: M-F 8:15-4; closed weekends and holidays
ACCESS: Application must be made in writing and include full details of applicant's personal and/or professional qualifications, specific nature of materials to be consulted, and the intended use of materials. Each application is judged in the light of donor restrictions and basic church policies.
COPYING FACILITIES: yes
MATERIALS SOLICITED: Materials relating to Christian Science, Mary Baker Eddy and her students, and The First Church of Christ, Scientist (The Mother Church) and its branches around the world. Will also accept Bible materials.

HOLDINGS:

Total volume: 5,000 l.f.
Inclusive dates: 1800 -
Description: Manuscripts written by Mary Baker Eddy, primarily letters and articles concerning her Bible study, her discovery of Christian Science as a healing ministry, and her founding of The Mother Church; letters written to Eddy, reminiscences of her, and visual and legal documents; archives and other material relating to the Church, its branch churches and societies, and its members.

SEE: Hinding.

MA108-750

Harvard University
Graduate School of Business
  Administration
Baker Library
Manuscripts and Archives
  Department
Soldiers Field Road
Boston MA 02163

(617) 495-6411

OPEN: M-F 9-5; closed weekends and holidays
COPYING FACILITIES: yes
MATERIALS SOLICITED: New England business records. Will also accept other business records of national signifi-cance, official school records, and faculty papers.

HOLDINGS:

Total volume: 10,000 l.f.
Inclusive dates: 1300 -
Description: Over 1,300 collections, comprising records of business firms and people engaged in business activities, mainly for New England. Foreign trade, shipping, railroads, textiles, and other manufacturing interests are represented; also farming, general storekeeping and many other commercial activities. A collection of account books of a branch of the Medici family constitutes the earliest material.

Also included are the Harvard Business Archives, consisting of official school records, faculty papers, and school ephemera.

GUIDES: Robert W. Lovett and Eleanor C. Bishop, comps., *Manuscripts in Baker Library: A Guide to Sources for Business, Economic, and Social History* (1978).

SEE: Hamer; NUCMC, 1959-68, 70, 72, 74, 76, 78, 80.

SEE: Robbins; Hinding; Allard, Crawley, and Edmison; Parkinson; Spalek; Ingram; Davis; Paszek; Meckler and McMullin; Schatz; Hounshell; Swanson and Gibb.

SEE ALSO: Morris Rieger, 'Africa-Related Papers of Persons and Organizations in the United States,' *African Studies Bulletin* 8 (Dec. 1965); Herman Freudenberger, 'Records of the Bohemian Iron Industry, 1964-1875: The Basis for a Comprehensive Study of Modern Factories,' *Business History Review* 43 (Autumn 1969)

Robert W. Lovett, 'The Heard Collection and Its Story,' *Business History Review* 35 (Winter 1961); Robert Freeman Smith, 'Thomas W. Lamont and United States-Mexican Relations: Some Aspects of the Usefulness of a Private Manuscript Collection,' *Harvard Library Bulletin* 15 (Jan. 1967); G. Bhagat, 'Materials Relating to Eighteenth and Nineteenth Century Indo-American Trade and Consular Relations in Private Archives in the United States,' *Indian Archives* 17 (Jan. 1967/Dec. 1968).

MA108-770

Harvard University
The Francis A. Countway Library of
  Medicine
10 Shattuc Street
Boston MA 02115

(617) 732-2171

OPEN: M-F 9-5; closed weekends and holidays
ACCESS: qualified scholars and researchers
COPYING FACILITIES: yes
MATERIALS SOLICITED: Anything relating to medical history, as well as the Harvard Medical Archives.

HOLDINGS:

Total volume: not specified
Inclusive dates: 11th century -
Description: Materials relating to medical history and medical personalities, with particular strength in New England, Massachusetts, and Boston medicine, including the Harvard Medical Archives, but also relating to the subject in an international perspective.

SEE: Hamer (as Boston Medical Library); NUCMC, 1962.

SEE: Novotny; Martin; Hinding; Robbins.

SEE ALSO: Morris Rieger, 'Africa-Related Papers of Persons and Organizations in the United States,' *African Studies Bulletin* 8 (Dec. 1965).

MA108-900

Institute of Contemporary Art
955 Boylston Street
Boston MA 02115

(617) 266-5152

OPEN: M-F 10-4; closed weekends
ACCESS: advance arrangements required

HOLDINGS:

Total volume: 1,000 sq. f.
Inclusive dates: 1936 -
Description: Business and financial records, correspondence, and scrapbooks relating to the exhibition program, design program, and other activities of the Institute of Contemporary Art since its founding.

MA108-920

Insurance Library Association of
  Boston
156 State Street
Boston MA 02109

(617) 227-2087

OPEN: M-F 8:45-4:30; closed weekends and holidays
USER FEES: $25-$250 for insurance professionals; free to general public
COPYING FACILITIES: yes
MATERIALS SOLICITED: Materials relating to insurance.

HOLDINGS:

Total volume: 3 file drawers
Inclusive dates: 1760's -
Description: Materials from insurance agents, agencies, and companies: insurance policy registers, company ledgers, agents' reports, correspondence, signed agreements, charters and constitutions, court decisions, lectures, and miscellaneous records. The collection also includes photographs, the majority of which are of fires, fire fighters, and fire apparatus, as well as photographs of people in the insurance business.

SEE: Hamer.

MA108-940

Isabella Stewart Gardner Museum
2 Palace Road
Boston MA 02115

(617) 566-1401

OPEN: by appointment
ACCESS: by appointment only to qualified researchers
COPYING FACILITIES: yes
MATERIALS SOLICITED: Correspondence of Isabella Stewart Gardner and papers relating to the collection and Ms. Gardner.

HOLDINGS:
>   *Total volume:*   6,539 items; 10 boxes;
> 75 vols.
>   *Inclusive dates:*   1835 -
>   *Description:* Papers relating to Isabella
> Stewart Gardner and the Museum collec-
> tion. Included are dealers' invoices, busi-
> ness records, correspondence with musi-
> cal performers and their agents, an ar-
> chitect's diary, and the manuscript for
> Ms. Gardner's *A Choice of Books.* Per-
> sonal papers include travel journals, dia-
> ries, photographs, and correspondence,
> much of it relating to people in art, mu-
> sic, literature, and the theater.

SEE: Hamer; NUCMC, 1965.

SEE: Hinding.

SEE ALSO: Paula M. Kozol, ed., *Guide to
the Collection, Isabella Stewart Gardner
Museum* (1976); *Correspondence of Isabella Stewart Gardner at the Gardner
Museum, Boston, Massachusetts* (1976);
and articles on the archives in the Museum's annual reports, 1970 - .

Many materials are available on
microfilm at the Archives of American Art.

MA108-965
John F. Kennedy Library
Columbia Point
Boston MA 02125

(617) 929-4535, 4500

OPEN: M-F 8:30-4:30; closed weekends
and holidays
ACCESS: access according to National
Archives and Records Service
regulations
COPYING FACILITIES: yes
MATERIALS SOLICITED: Materials relating
to modern American politics and government, especially people and events
associated with John F. Kennedy.

HOLDINGS:
>   *Total volume:*   28,000,000 pages
>   *Inclusive dates:*   1925 -
>   *Description:* Collections of official and
> personal papers of people in government
> and politics, chiefly at the national level
> and primarily related to the career of
> John F. Kennedy. Also extensive motion
> picture film, audiotape, and photographs
> on the same subjects.

GUIDES: *Historical Materials in the John
F. Kennedy Library* (1981).

SEE: NUCMC, 1978.

SEE: Meckler and McMullin; Paszek;
Schatz; Novotny; Robbins; Davis;
Allard, Crawley, and Edmison; Zobrist.

MA109-120
Massachusetts Historical Society
1154 Boylston Street
Boston MA 02215

(617) 536-1608

OPEN: M-F 9-4:45; closed weekends and
holidays
COPYING FACILITIES: yes
MATERIALS SOLICITED: Personal and institutional papers pertaining to Massachusetts history.

HOLDINGS:
>   *Total volume:*   30,000 sq.f.
>   *Inclusive dates:*   1450 -
>   *Description:* Materials,   particularly
> from the 17th, 18th, and early 19th cen-
> turies, relating chiefly to Massachusetts
> and New England. Included are family
> and personal papers, such as those of the
> Adams, Quincy, and Saltonstall families,
> materials pertaining to such varied or-
> ganizations as Brook Farm and the Soci-
> ety of the Cincinnati, and other holdings
> relating to ships and shipping, merchan-
> dising, and other businesses.

GUIDES: Massachusetts Historical Society,
*Library Catalog of Manuscripts of the
Massachusetts Historical Society* (G. K.
Hall, 1969).

SEE: Hamer; NUCMC, 1959-62, 65-66,
68-69, 71-72, 74, 77, 79.

SEE: Allard, Crawley, and Edmison;
Gehring; Ingram; Krichmar; Leventhal
and Mooney - I; Novotny; Paszek;
Robbins.

SEE ALSO: Peter Duignan, *Handbook of
American Resources for African Studies*
(Hoover Institution, 1967); Walter
Schatz, ed., *Directory of Afro-American
Resources* (Bowker, 1970); J. E.
Patterson, comp., 'Checklist of Prescott
Manuscripts,' *Hispanic American His-
torical Review* 39 (Feb. 1959); G.
Bhagat, 'Materials Relating to Eigh-
teenth and Nineteenth Century Indo-
American Trade and Consular Rela-
tions in Private Archives in the United
States,' *Indian Archives* 17 (Jan.
1967/Dec. 1968); Jerome S. Handler, *A
Guide to Source Materials for the Study
of Barbados History, 1627-1834*
(Southern Illinois Univ. Press, 1971).

Morris Rieger, 'Africa-Related Papers of
Persons and Organizations in the United
States,' *African Studies Bulletin* 8 (Dec.
1965). Articles describing the collections
can be found in the Massachusetts Historical Society *Miscellany.* Guides to microfilms and other finding aids are available at the Society.

Richard C. Davis, *North American Forest
History: A Guide to Archives and Manu-
scripts in the United States and Canada*
(Clio Books, 1977).

MA109-140
Massachusetts Horticultural Society
Library
300 Massachusetts Avenue
Boston MA 02115

(617) 536-9280

OPEN: M-F 9-4:30; closed weekends and
holidays
COPYING FACILITIES: yes
MATERIALS SOLICITED: Materials relating
to horticulture.

HOLDINGS:
>   *Total volume:*   30 collections
>   *Inclusive dates:*   1830 - 1968
>   *Description:* Materials relating to gar-
> dening, plant culture, flower arrange-
> ment, and other horticultural subjects. Also in-
> cluded are papers, letters, and photo-
> graphs relating to the history of the Soci-
> ety.

GUIDES: *Massachusetts Horticultural Society, Dictionary Catalog of the Library*
(G. K. Hall, 1962-71).

MA109-180
Massachusetts Metropolitan District
Commission
20 Somerset Street
Boston MA 02108

(617) 727-5218

OPEN: M-F 8:30-4; closed weekends and
holidays
ACCESS: appointment required
COPYING FACILITIES: yes
MATERIALS SOLICITED: Materials relating
to the development of parks, water service, and sewers in the Boston area.
Will also accept materials relating to
seacoast fortification.

HOLDINGS:
>   *Total volume:*   1,500 vols.
>   *Inclusive dates:*   1830 -
>   *Description:* Materials relating to the
> history of water, sewer, and park develop-
> ment in the Boston area. Included are
> unpublished reports and proposals to the
> State legislature; records of transactions
> between vendors and park boards;
> records of court cases involving land ac-
> quisition for the Quabbin Reservoir; and
> photographs of projects, including con-
> struction contracts, types of equipment,
> and pictures of actual construction.

MA109-200
Massachusetts New-Church Union
Swedenborg Library
175 Newbury Street, N.
Boston MA 02116

no telephone

SEE: Hamer.

Questionnaire not returned.

MA109-220
Massachusetts Secretary of State
Archives Division
220 Morrisey Boulevard
Columbia Point
Boston MA 02125

(617) 727-2816

OPEN: M-F 9-5; closed weekends and
holidays
COPYING FACILITIES: yes
MATERIALS SOLICITED: Records of all
branches of State government, especially executive and administrative agencies.

HOLDINGS:
>   *Total volume:*   5,000 c.f.
>   *Inclusive dates:*   1620 -
>   *Description:* Public records of the colo-
> ny, province, and Commonwealth of
> Massachusetts, of Plymouth Colony, and
> of Maine, dating prior to 1820. Included
> are a collection of 300 volumes of histori-
> cal records and papers, dating prior to
> 1800, commonly cited as *Mass. Archives;*
> a full set of legislative records, including
> drafts and engrossed copies of all laws
> and bills, 1628- ; Governor's Council
> records; records of the Secretary of State;
> Treasury records; military records, pri-

marily from the Revolutionary War and Civil War; original Federal census schedules, 1850-80; and various small groups from other administrative agencies.

SEE: Hamer.

SEE: Ingram; Robbins; Allard, Crawley, and Edmison; Gehring.

MA109-230

Massachusetts Society of Mayflower Descendants
101 Newbury Street
Boston MA 02116

(617) 266-1624

OPEN: by appointment only
USER FEES: $10 per mail inquiry or $.10 per item reproduction for site visits
ACCESS: Society Historian has access to materials; reproductions available to researchers for a fee
COPYING FACILITIES: yes
MATERIALS SOLICITED: Genealogical materials related to Mayflower descendants.

HOLDINGS:
Total volume: 60 file drawers
Inclusive dates: 1896 -
Description: The 'Bowman File' of genealogical materials about descendants of Mayflower passengers.

MA109-240

Massachusetts State Library
341 State House
Boston MA 02133

(617) 727-2590

OPEN: M-F 9-5; closed weekends and holidays
COPYING FACILITIES: yes
MATERIALS SOLICITED: Massachusetts State documents and State officials' papers.

HOLDINGS:
Total volume: not specified
Inclusive dates: 1602 -
Description: Massachusetts legislative and executive documents, chiefly from the colonial period to the 1930's, and records of quasi-State organizations.

SEE: Hamer; NUCMC, 1967-68.

MA109-360

Museum of Fine Arts
Library
465 Huntington Avenue
Boston MA 02115

(617) 267-9300

OPEN: by appointment only

SEE: Hamer.

Questionnaire not returned.

MA109-380

Museum of Science
Science Park
Boston MA 02114

(617) 723-2500

OPEN: M-F 9-5; closed weekends and holidays
COPYING FACILITIES: yes
MATERIALS SOLICITED: Corporate records of the Museum.

HOLDINGS:
Total volume: 81 l.f.
Inclusive dates: 1820 -
Description: Corporate records and descriptions of the activities of the Boston Society of Natural History, and correspondence, journals, drawings, and other manuscripts by the Society's naturalists or their correspondents, 1820-1900.

SEE: Hamer (as Boston Society of Natural History).

MA109-440

New England Conservatory of Music
Libraries and Audio Department
33 Gainsborough Street
Boston MA 02115

(617) 262-1120

OPEN: Su 9-1, M-Th 8:30-10:30, F 8:30-6; Sa 9-5; Audio Dept., weekdays 9-5; reduced summer hours; closed major holidays
ACCESS: reason for requesting use of rare materials must be indicated
COPYING FACILITIES: yes
MATERIALS SOLICITED: Will accept music manuscripts; musicians' letters; photographs; and recorded materials.

HOLDINGS:
Total volume: 100 l.f.; other items
Inclusive dates: 16th century -
Description: Principally holograph manuscripts of music scores of the late 19th and early 20th centuries, emphasizing the 'Boston School' of composers and works with saxophone. There are also composers' letters, Vaughn Monroe and 'Voice of Firestone' arrangements, and 'Voice of Firestone' kinescopes.
Includes concert tapes.

SEE: Hamer.

MA109-460

New England Historic Genealogical Society
101 Newbury Street
Boston MA 02116

(617) 536-5740

OPEN: M-Sa 9-4:45; closed State and National holidays and Saturdays before holidays
USER FEES: $10 per day for non-members
ACCESS: Restricted to members of the Society; other qualified researchers by special arrangement.
COPYING FACILITIES: yes
MATERIALS SOLICITED: Will consider original and transcribed manuscripts relating to New England local and family history. Documents of special interest include compiled genealogies, genealogical charts and notes, diaries, travel journals, correspondence, indentures, deeds, wills, inventories, muster rolls, Bible records, account books, cemetery inscriptions, tax lists, board of selectmen minutes, voting lists, town treasurer's records, church records, and family photographs.

HOLDINGS:
Total volume: 5,800 l.f.
Inclusive dates: 1630 -
Description: Material relating to the history of New England and the genealogies of its families. Included are family papers, the Massachusetts Direct Tax List of 1798, papers of the Corporation for the Propagation of the Gospel in New England, business papers of Thomas and John Hancock, papers of Trinity Church in the City of Boston, a collection of Civil War letters, and diaries, personal letters, and accounts.

SEE: Hamer; NUCMC, 1976.

SEE: Allard, Crawley, and Edmison; Hinding; Leventhal and Mooney - I; Robbins.

MA109-480

New England Methodist Historical Society
Library
745 Commonwealth Avenue
Boston MA 02215

(617) 353-3034

OPEN: M-F 9-5; closed weekends and holidays
COPYING FACILITIES: yes
MATERIALS SOLICITED: Legal records of churches of the Southern New England Conference of the United Methodist church that have been closed or merged. Will also accept documents dealing with New England Methodism.

HOLDINGS:
Total volume: 50 l.f.
Inclusive dates: 1793 -
Description: Materials dealing with the history of Methodism in New England, primarily older records of churches that have been closed or merged in Massachusetts. Since 1974 other areas of New England have submitted their records for deposit.

SEE: Hamer; NUCMC, 1965.

SEE ALSO: William E. Lind, 'Methodist Archives in the United States,' *The American Archivist* 24 (Oct. 1961).

MA109-530

Northeastern University
Libraries
University Archives
211 Dodge Library
360 Huntington Avenue
Boston MA 02115

(617) 437-2351

OPEN: M-F 8:30-4:30; closed weekends and holidays
COPYING FACILITIES: yes

MATERIALS SOLICITED: Documents relating to the history of the University and especially the Cooperative Plan of Education.

HOLDINGS:
Total volume: 9,828 l.f.
Inclusive dates: 1898 -
Description: Records of University community, including official departmental reports, faculty publications, Ph.D. theses, graphics, multimedia formats, and other materials.

MA109-560
Old South Meeting House
310 Washington Street
Boston MA 02108

(617) 482-6439

OPEN: by appointment only M-F 9:30-5; closed weekends, Thanksgiving, and Christmas

SEE: Hamer.

Questionnaire not returned.

MA109-595
Roman Catholic Archdiocese of
Boston
Archives
2121 Commonwealth Avenue
Boston MA 02135

(617) 254-0100, Ext. 145, 142

OPEN: M-F 9-4:45; closed weekends, holidays, and holy days
ACCESS: a written application is required
COPYING FACILITIES: yes
MATERIALS SOLICITED: Material from the Archdiocese and from the parishes within its jurisdiction. Will also accept significant materials regarding activities, organizations, individuals, and groups relevant to the mission of the Roman Catholic church in the Boston area.

HOLDINGS:
Total volume: 1,500 l.f.
Inclusive dates: 1789 -
Description: Parish records, including baptismal, marriage and confirmation records; diaries of parishes and individuals; official correspondence relating to administration, the establishments of parishes, theological problems, financial problems, and philanthropic activities; and collateral material on such topics as schools, social service agencies, and the effect of Irish immigration on the establishment of parishes.

GUIDES: James M. O'Toole, *Guide to the Collections of the Archives of the Archdiocese of Boston* (Garland Press, 1982).

SEE ALSO: Peter J. Rahill, 'Archives of the Archdiocese of Boston,' *American Archivist* 22 (Oct. 1959).

Various guides to portions of the collections are available at the repository.

MA109-630
Simmons College
Archives
Beatley Library
300 The Fenway
Boston MA 02115

(617) 738-3141

OPEN: M-F 9-4:30, Summer hours vary; closed weekends and holidays; appointments recommended
ACCESS: advance arrangements suggested
COPYING FACILITIES: yes
MATERIALS SOLICITED: History of Simmons College and the Fenway neighborhood of Boston; working women of Boston; papers of Simmons administrators, professors, students, and staff; vocational education for women; and records of Garland Junior College. Will also accept records of social welfare agencies in Boston associated with or once associated with the Simmons School of Social Work; records regarding the development of careers for women, e.g. retailing, public health nursing, librarianship, business administration, and teaching.

HOLDINGS:
Total volume: 920 l.f.
Inclusive dates: 1899 -
Description: Archives of Simmons College, Simmons School of Social Work, and Garland Junior College. Included are records of these institutions, oral history interviews, photographs of the College and Boston taken by students, and many materials relating to the Women's Educational and Industrial Union of Boston.

SEE: NUCMC, 1980.

SEE: Hinding.

SEE ALSO: Unpublished inventories and registers are available for most collections, and a brief description of the entire collection in typescript form is available upon request.

MA109-660
Social Law Library
1200 Court House
Boston MA 02108

(617) 523-0018

OPEN: M-F 9-5; closed weekends and holidays
COPYING FACILITIES: yes
MATERIALS SOLICITED: Legal historical materials.

HOLDINGS:
Total volume: 2,500 manuscripts; 100 vols.; 360,000 file papers
Inclusive dates: 1692 - 1860
Description: Personal and professional letters concerning Lemuel Shaw's family and his legal practice, as well as letters relating to the Massachusetts Supreme Judicial Court, notes on cases, early drafts of opinions, and charges to juries. There are also records of the Suffolk (Boston) Inferior Court of Common Pleas, 1692-1820, including Extended Records Books and file papers, documenting Boston legal and political developments and issues of public interest, and containing materials relating to such people as John

Adams, James Otis, Jr., John Hancock, and Paul Revere.

MA109-680
Society for the Preservation of New
England Antiquities
Library
141 Cambridge Street
Boston MA 02114

(617) 227-3956

OPEN: M-F 9:30-5; closed weekends
ACCESS: advance arrangements requested
COPYING FACILITIES: yes
MATERIALS SOLICITED: Photographic and architectural history of New England; historic properties owned by the Society. Will also accept materials relating to the social and decorative arts history of New England.

HOLDINGS:
Total volume: 1,000,000 items
Inclusive dates: 1840 -
Description: Over 1,000,000 photographic images, in all forms, relating to the architectural, photographic, social, and economic history of New England. Manuscript holdings include account books relating to New England commerce, and documentation relating to the historic properties owned by the Society.
Includes materials relating to architects Luther Briggs, Frank Chouteau Brown, William Place, Julius Pomeroy, Alexander Parris, Asher Benjamin, and Ogden Codman, Jr.; manuscript materials of the Codman family, Coffin family, Harrison Gray Otis, Sara Orne Jewett, and the Rundlet-May Collection.

SEE: Hamer.

SEE: Novotny.

SEE ALSO: Unpublished guides, inventories, and indexes are available at the repository for individual collections of manuscripts, photographs, and architectural drawings.

MA109-720
The South End Historical Society, Inc.
698 Tremont Street
Boston MA 02118

(617) 536-4445

OPEN: by appointment only or for regular monthly meetings
COPYING FACILITIES: no
MATERIALS SOLICITED: Historical papers and photographs of the South End section of Boston. Will also accept miscellaneous historical materials relating to Boston, and materials relating to architecture and the decorative arts, particularly of the Victorian period.

HOLDINGS:
Total volume: not specified
Inclusive dates: 1820 -
Description: Papers, photographs, and other materials relating to Boston's South End. Included is an architectural survey of buildings in the area as well as papers from local organizations.

MA109-750

Unitarian Universalist Association
25 Beacon Street
Boston MA 02108

(617) 742-2100, Ext. 250

OPEN: Mon-Fri 9-5; closed weekends
COPYING FACILITIES: yes
MATERIALS SOLICITED: Manuscripts and papers of Unitarian clergy and laity and records of Unitarian Universalist churches and denominationally related organizations.

HOLDINGS:
   Total volume: 450 c.f.
   Inclusive dates: 1919 -
   Description: Records of the Unitarian Universalist Association and its denominationally related organizations. Included are correspondence of presidents, clergy files, church files, departmental files, audio-visual materials, and biographical materials relating to famous Unitarian Universalists.

MA109-830

University of Massachusetts at Boston Library
Manuscripts and Archival Collections Department
Harbor Campus
Boston MA 02125

(617) 929-7611, 7635

OPEN: M-F 9-4; closed weekends and holidays
COPYING FACILITIES: yes
MATERIALS SOLICITED: Materials relating to the history of Dorchester, 19th century Boston private welfare organizations, and post-1960 community voluntary organizations, especially radical and alternative groups.

HOLDINGS:
   Total volume: 375 c.f.
   Inclusive dates: 1800 -
   Description: Archives of the major 19th and early 20th century private child welfare agencies of Boston, including photographs, material relating to the history of the Dorchester section of Boston and records of post-1960 community organizations, such as the Beacon Hill Free School.

MA109-850

U.S.S. Constitution Museum
Samuel Eliot Morison Library
Boston MA

MAILING ADDRESS:
P.O. Box 1812
Boston MA 02129

(617) 426-1812

OPEN: daily 9-5; closed Thanksgiving, Christmas and New Year's
ACCESS: advance arrangements with Curator or Director
COPYING FACILITIES: yes
MATERIALS SOLICITED: Materials relating to the *U.S.S. Constitution*, 1790's- . Will also accept materials relating to American naval history, 1790- , and British and French naval history, 1790-1850.

HOLDINGS:
   Total volume: 200 l.f.
   Inclusive dates: 1790's -
   Description: Materials relating to the *U.S.S. Constitution*, including logbooks, journals, manuscripts, maps, charts, account books, correspondence, photographs, and microfilm of logs and correspondence between captains and the Secretary of the Navy.

BOYLSTON

MA123-80

Boylston Public Library
695 Main Street
Boylston MA 01505

(617) 869-2371

OPEN: M 2-5, Tu 10:30-8, W 10:30-5, Th 2-8, F 2-7, Sa 10-2; closed Sundays and holidays
COPYING FACILITIES: yes
MATERIALS SOLICITED: Materials pertaining to Boylston and its people.

HOLDINGS:
   Total volume: 6 c.f.
   Inclusive dates: 1750 -
   Description: Manuscripts, maps, and photographs relating to Boylston and the Wachusett Reservoir, records of social clubs, manuscripts of local authors, and genealogical information for local families.

SEE: Hamer.

BREWSTER

MA134-80

Brewster Ladies' Library
1822 Main Street
Brewster MA

MAILING ADDRESS:
P.O. Box LL
Brewster MA 02631

(617) 896-3913

OPEN: W 12-8, Th-Sa 10-4; July-Aug. W-F 10-2 and 7-9, Sa 10-2; closed Su-Tu
COPYING FACILITIES: yes
MATERIALS SOLICITED: Materials relating to Brewster and Cape Cod.

HOLDINGS:
   Total volume: 1 l.f.
   Inclusive dates: 19th century -
   Description: Manuscripts relating to the social history of Brewster and its 18th and 19th century shipmasters, genealogy of Brewster residents, and research and photographs primarily of the late 19th century.

SEE: Hinding.

MA134-560

New England Fire and History Museum
1439 Main Street
Brewster MA 02631

(617) 896-5711

OPEN: Mid-June - Mid-Sept., 10-5 daily; Mid-Sept. - Columbus Day, 10-5 weekends; closed rest of year
USER FEES: $2.25 per day
ACCESS: an appointment is required
COPYING FACILITIES: no
MATERIALS SOLICITED: Material relating to early American fire fighting, fires, and the role played by fire fighters in social and political life; material relating to early blacksmithing, apothecary and medicinal herbs, and insurance company history. Will also accept material relating to Benjamin Franklin.

HOLDINGS:
   Total volume: not specified
   Inclusive dates: 17th century - early 20th century
   Description: Material relating to fire fighting, apothecary herb culture, and blacksmithing.

BRIDGEWATER

MA139-90

Bridgewater Public Library
Historical Room
15 South Street
Bridgewater MA 02324

(617) 697-3331

OPEN: by appointment only M-Th 11-9, F, Sa 11-5; closed Sundays and holidays
ACCESS: advance arrangements required
COPYING FACILITIES: yes
MATERIALS SOLICITED: Materials relating to the history of Bridgewater.

HOLDINGS:
   Total volume: 75 vols.; 4 file drawers
   Inclusive dates: 1848 -
   Description: Materials relating to the history of Bridgewater, a manuscript of Joshua Crane, Scotland Trinity Church records, Ousa Mequin Club records, records of the Bridgewater Public Library, and historical photographs and picture postcards of Bridgewater.

BROOKLINE

MA154-310

Hebrew College
Jacob and Rose Grossman Library
43 Hawes Street
Brookline MA 02146

(617) 232-8710

OPEN: Fall-spring Su 9-3:30, M, Tu 10-9, W, Th 9-9; summer M, Th 8:30-5, Tu, W 8:30-8:15, F 8:30-2; intersessions M-Th 9-5, F 9-1
ACCESS: recognized scholars or by recommendation of recognized scholars in the field
COPYING FACILITIES: yes

MATERIALS SOLICITED: Hebraica and Judaica.

HOLDINGS:
Total volume: 5 c.f.
Inclusive dates: 1548 - 1932
Description: Hebraic, Judeo-Arabic, and Aramaic manuscripts from a variety of locations relating to the Bible, Talmud, liturgy, poetry, history, ethical works, and Chassidic and Kabbalistic works. Included are personal letters and private lectures.

GUIDES: A photocopied list of manuscripts (1976) is available from the Library.

MA154-480
Longyear Historical Society
Mary Baker Eddy Museum
120 Seaver Street
Brookline MA 02146

(617) 277-8943

OPEN: Su 1-5, Tu-Sa 10-5; Nov. 1-March 31, Tu-Sa 10-4, Su 1-4; closed Mondays, holidays, and February
ACCESS: researchers must be approved by Director
COPYING FACILITIES: yes
MATERIALS SOLICITED: Materials relating to Mary Baker Eddy, her students and associates. Will also accept materials relating to John Munro Longyear or Mary Beecher Longyear.

HOLDINGS:
Total volume: 400 c.f.
Inclusive dates: 1800 - 1950
Description: Manuscripts, correspondence, diaries, journals, logbooks, account books, business records, financial records, genealogical source data, and literary manuscripts covering principally the life of Mary Baker Eddy, and the lives of the Baker family and students of Mrs. Eddy and her associates. Most material relates to activities in Massachusetts and New Hampshire.

MA154-640
Public Library of Brookline
361 Washington Street
Brookline MA 02146

(617) 734-0100

OPEN: Su 1-5, M-Th 9:30-9, F 9:30-6, Sa 9:30-5:30; closed holidays
COPYING FACILITIES: yes
MATERIALS SOLICITED: Material pertaining to Brookline and its people. Will also accept other materials on an individual basis.

HOLDINGS:
Total volume: 3,075 items
Inclusive dates: 1630 -
Description: Manuscripts, maps, and photographs relating to Brookline, and including records of social and political clubs, legal documents, manuscripts of local authors, and town notices and department reports. There are also papers of local families, including wills, letters, military documents, diaries and account books; and photographs of the town taken since the 1860's.

SEE: Hamer; NUCMC, 1972 (as Brookline Historical Society).

SEE: Hinding.

SEE ALSO: unpublished guides to parts of the collection available at the Library.

BUZZARDS BAY

MA165-520
Massachusetts Maritime Academy
Captain Charles H. Hurley Library
Nantucket Avenue
Taylor's Point
Buzzards Bay MA

MAILING ADDRESS:
P.O. Box D
Buzzards Bay MA 02532

(617) 759-5761, Ext. 271

OPEN: M-Th 8-11, F 8-5, Su 2-11; closed Saturdays and holidays
COPYING FACILITIES: yes
MATERIALS SOLICITED: Any materials on the Massachusetts Maritime Academy (formerly the Massachusetts Nautical Training School and the Massachusetts Nautical School).

HOLDINGS:
Total volume: 25 l.f.
Inclusive dates: 1874 -
Description: Manuscripts, public documents, videotapes, motion pictures, photographs, and audio tapes relating to the history of the Massachusetts Maritime Academy and its graduates. Materials document training ships, cruises, cadet life, the curriculum, and the careers of graduates.

CAMBRIDGE

MA169-30
American Academy of Arts and Sciences
Norton's Woods
136 Irving Street
Cambridge MA 02138

(617) 492-8800

OPEN: by appointment only
COPYING FACILITIES: no

HOLDINGS:
Total volume: not specified
Inclusive dates: not specified
Description: Materials relating to American scientific and learned societies from the Revolutionary War to the present, materials relating to the Academy's projects, 1940's- , and data on deceased fellows of the Academy, 1940's- .

SEE: Hamer (listed under Boston, MA).

MA169-40
Archives of the First Church in Cambridge, Congregational
11 Garden Street
Cambridge MA 02138

(617) 547-2724

OPEN: by appointment only
COPYING FACILITIES: no

MATERIALS SOLICITED: Records, documents, and manuscripts pertaining to the history of the Church and local government; current records of the Church and affiliated organizations. Will also accept maps, photographs, and other materials relating to Church members.

HOLDINGS:
Total volume: 103 l.f.
Inclusive dates: 1630 -
Description: Materials, including correspondence and sermons, relating chiefly to the First Church in Cambridge, Congregational.

SEE: Hamer.

MA169-50
Cambridge Historical Commission
Cambridge City Hall Annex
57 Inman Street
Cambridge MA 02139

(617) 498-9040

OPEN: M-F 8:30-5; closed weekends and holidays
COPYING FACILITIES: yes
MATERIALS SOLICITED: Photographs, plans, and documents relating to Cambridge architecture; maps of Cambridge; and documents relating to urban development in historical perspective.

HOLDINGS:
Total volume: 125 c.f.
Inclusive dates: 1634 -
Description: Architectural survey materials, including more than 20,000 negatives and photographic prints of Cambridge buildings; maps; and a cross-index of Cambridge architects and builders.

MA169-110
Episcopal Theological School
Library
99 Brattle Street
Cambridge MA 02138

no telephone

SEE: Hamer; NUCMC, 1962, 65.

Questionnaire not returned.

MA169-170
Harvard University
Archives
Pusey Library
Cambridge MA 02138

(617) 495-2461

OPEN: M-F 9-5; closed weekends and holidays
ACCESS: Official records of the University are unavailable for research use for a period of 50 years unless the written permission of the head of the department or office involved has been obtained.
COPYING FACILITIES: yes
MATERIALS SOLICITED: History of Harvard University, its affiliated organizations, and persons connected with it (papers of University graduates are not collected).

HOLDINGS:
> *Total volume:* 40,000 l.f.
> *Inclusive dates:* 1636 -
> *Description:* Official University records, personal papers of members of Harvard faculty, records of student and other organizations, student and faculty notes and course papers relating to the curriculum, and other miscellaneous manuscripts relating to Harvard history. There are 500 collections of faculty papers, as well as correspondence and other papers of Harvard presidents and minutes of governing boards. Other holdings include University doctoral theses and publications by and about the University.

GUIDES: Clark A. Elliott, *A Descriptive Guide to the Harvard University Archives* (Harvard Univ. Library, 1974).

SEE: Hamer; NUCMC, 1965, 69, 71, 76.

SEE: Allard, Crawley, and Edmison; Bean and Vane; Hinding; Ingram; Leventhal and Mooney - I; Paszek; Spalek.

SEE ALSO: Clark A. Elliott, 'Sources for the History of Science in the Harvard University Archives,' *Harvard Library Bulletin* 22 (Jan. 1974); David A. Hounshell, comp., *Manuscripts in U.S. Depositories Relating to the History of Electrical Science and Technology* (Smithsonian Institution, n.d.); Clifford K. Shipton, 'The Harvard University Archives in 1938 and 1969,' *Harvard Library Bulletin* 18 (April 1970); *Source Materials for the Recent History of Astronomy and Astrophysics: A Checklist of Manuscript Collections in the United States* (American Institute of Physics, Neils Bohr Library, 1971).

MA169-190

Harvard University
Arnold Arboretum
The Arborway
Jamaica Plain MA and
22 Divinity Avenue
Cambridge MA

MAILING ADDRESS:
22 Divinity Avenue
Cambridge MA 02138

(617) 495-2366

OPEN: M-F 9-5; closed weekends and holidays
ACCESS: by prior arrangement
COPYING FACILITIES: yes

HOLDINGS:
> *Total volume:* 16 file drawers
> *Inclusive dates:* 1872 - 1927
> *Description:* A collection of letters of Charles Sprague Sargent, Alfred Rehder, and Elmer D. Merrill, relative to Arboretum affairs; miscellaneous records of plant acquisitions; botanical drawings; notebooks of E. H. Wilson's expeditions to China, India, and Japan; and glass negatives and photographs of the Wilson expeditions.

MA169-200

Harvard University
Busch-Reisinger Museum
Gropius Archives and Feininger
  Archives
29 Kirkland Street
Cambridge MA 02138

(617) 495-2338

OPEN: by appointment only; closed Sundays and holidays
ACCESS: advance arrangements required
COPYING FACILITIES: yes
MATERIALS SOLICITED: Materials related to the Bauhaus, Walter Gropius, and Lyonel Feininger.

HOLDINGS:
> *Total volume:* 1,500 c.f.
> *Inclusive dates:* 1900 - 1960
> *Description:* Materials documenting the careers of Walter Gropius and Lyonel Feininger and the Bauhaus school of architecture, including photographs and correspondence.

SEE: Spalek; Novotny.

MA169-210

Harvard University
Carpenter Center for the Visual Arts
Cambridge MA 02138

(617) 495-3251

OPEN: by appointment only; closed weekends, holidays, and June-Oct.
COPYING FACILITIES: no
MATERIALS SOLICITED: Photographs relating to the social history of America.

HOLDINGS:
> *Total volume:* 40,000 items
> *Inclusive dates:* 1840 -
> *Description:* Photographs depicting social conditions and relating to social ethics and reform in America.

SEE ALSO: Ann Novotny, ed., *Picture Sources 3* (Special Libraries Assn., 1975).

MA169-230

Harvard University
Divinity School
Andover-Harvard Theological Library
Manuscript Department
45 Francis Avenue
Cambridge MA 02138

(617) 495-5770

OPEN: M-F 9-5; closed weekends and holidays
COPYING FACILITIES: yes
MATERIALS SOLICITED: Papers of faculty members of Harvard Divinity School, records and papers of individuals related to the American Unitarian Association, the Universalist Church of America, the Unitarian Universalist Service Committee, and the Unitarian Universalist Association.

HOLDINGS:
> *Total volume:* 1,659 l.f.
> *Inclusive dates:* 1504 -
> *Description:* A collection of manuscripts dating chiefly after 1800 relating to the faculty of Harvard Divinity School, the archives of the American Unitarian Association, the Universalist Church of America, and the Unitarian Universalist Service Committee. Included are the papers of ministers and lay persons and records of individual churches and organizations from both denominations. The material is chiefly American.

SEE: Hamer; NUCMC, 1971-72, 74-75, 77, 80.

SEE: Hinding; Spalek.

SEE ALSO: Alan Seaburg, 'Some Unitarian Manuscripts at Andover-Harvard,' *Harvard Library Bulletin* 26 (Jan. 1978).

MA169-270

Harvard University
Farlow Reference Library
20 Divinity Avenue
Cambridge MA 02138

(617) 495-2369

OPEN: M-F 9-5; closed weekends and holidays
COPYING FACILITIES: yes
MATERIALS SOLICITED: Letters and papers of botanists, especially those of cryptogamic botanists. Will also accept photographs of botanists, manuscripts and proof sheets of botanical papers.

HOLDINGS:
> *Total volume:* 4,263 c.f.
> *Inclusive dates:* 1830 -
> *Description:* Manuscripts, letters, photographs and memorabilia of botanists of the 19th and 20th centuries. The holdings include the papers and correspondence of the curators of the Farlow Herbarium, beginning with those of William G. Farlow, as well as those of other botanists interested in cryptogamic botany. There are several unique collections of scientific paintings of fungi.

SEE: Hamer.

SEE: Davis; Hinding.

MA169-300

Harvard University
Fogg Art Museum
Archives Department
32 Quincy Street
Cambridge MA 02138

(617) 495-2384

OPEN: M-F 10-4; closed weekends and holidays
ACCESS: appointment required
COPYING FACILITIES: no

HOLDINGS:
> *Total volume:* 129 file drawers
> *Inclusive dates:* 1895 -
> *Description:* Files of former museum directors Charles H. Moore, Edward W. Forbes, Paul J. Sachs, Arthur Pope, John Coolidge, and (for her directorship only) Agnes Mongan. Records of past Fogg exhibitions; curatorial records for the collection of Western painting and sculpture; papers of Fogg patron Grenville L. Winthrop.

SEE: Hamer.

SEE: Martin.

MA169-305

Harvard University
Graduate School of Design
Frances Loeb Library
Cambridge MA 02138

(617) 495-2574

OPEN: M-F 9-10, Su 2-10; summer schedule varies; closed Saturdays and holidays
ACCESS: advance arrangements advisable
COPYING FACILITIES: no
MATERIALS SOLICITED: Will accept architecture, landscape architecture, and urban design and planning, especially if related to the Graduate School of Design's alumni or of local interest.

HOLDINGS:
    Total volume: 1,000 vols.; 20,000 items
    Inclusive dates: 1700 -
    Description: Materials in architecture, landscape architecture, and urban design and planning, as well as related fields, with the strongest concentration in United States and 20th century materials. Included are manuscripts in the collections relating to Charles Eliot, Charles Mulford Robinson, Le Corbusier, H. H. Richardson, and the archaeological research of Kenneth J. Conant at the abbey in Cluny, France, as well as manuscripts of Frederick Law and John Charles Olmsted.
    There also are archival materials of the Graduate School of Design and an audio-visual collection of slides, photographs, and working drawings.

SEE: Hamer.

MA169-310

Harvard University
Gray Herbarium
22 Divinity Avenue
Cambridge MA 02138

(617) 495-2366

OPEN: M-F 10-5; closed weekends and holidays
ACCESS: by prior arrangement
COPYING FACILITIES: yes

HOLDINGS:
    Total volume: 300 c.f.
    Inclusive dates: 1783 -
    Description: 800 folders of letters of Asa Gray, and 8,000 letters to him, chiefly from distinguished European and American scientists, particularly botanists, as well as letters of other botanists. There are also Gray's journals, manuscripts, and papers related to the Herbarium.

SEE: Hamer; NUCMC, 1975.

SEE: Beers - Southwest; Hinding; Robbins.

MA169-340

Harvard University
Harvard College Library
Fine Arts Library
Fogg Art Museum
32 Quincy Street
Cambridge MA 02138

(617) 495-3374

OPEN: M-F 9-5; closed weekends and holidays
USER FEES: members of Harvard University pay no fees; flexible rules apply to others
COPYING FACILITIES: yes

HOLDINGS:
    Total volume: 118 boxes; 1,000,000 items
    Inclusive dates: mid-19th century -
    Description: Papers and photographs of art historians Prentice Duell, Fiske Kimball, and Clarence Kennedy, and photographs illustrating fine art of all types, including architecture, sculpture, painting, minor arts, and manuscript art.

SEE: NUCMC, 1973.

SEE: Novotny.

MA169-370

Harvard University
Harvard College Library
The Houghton Library
Manuscript Department
Cambridge MA 02138

(617) 495-2440

OPEN: M-F 9-5; closed weekends and holidays
ACCESS: open to all mature scholars
COPYING FACILITIES: yes
MATERIALS SOLICITED: Early and literary manuscripts.

HOLDINGS:
    Total volume: 24,300 l.f.
    Inclusive dates: 3500 B.C. -
    Description: Manuscripts of every period and place, especially those relating to American literature (particularly New England) and history, and English literature.

SEE: Hamer; NUCMC, 1959-61, 65, 67, 70-71, 81.

SEE: Allard, Crawley, and Edmison; Hinding; Ingram; Leventhal and Mooney - I; Martin; Robbins; Spalek.

SEE ALSO: 'Afro-American Studies: A Guide to Resources of the Harvard University Library,' Guides to the Harvard Libraries, No. 10 (Harvard Univ., 1969); R. S. Robin, Annotated Catalogue of the Papers of Charles S. Peirce (Univ. of Massachusetts, 1967); P. Obermueller and H. Steiner, Katalog der Rilke-Sammlung Richard von Mises (1966); The Kilgour Collection of Russian Literature, 1750-1920 (Harvard Univ., 1959); M. Glatzer, Hebrew Manuscripts in the Houghton Library of the Harvard College Library (Harvard Univ., 1975); J. Clemons, 'A Checklist of Syriac Manuscripts in the United States and Canada,' Orientalia Christiana Periodica 23 (1966); G. M. Browne, 'Ostraca Harvardiana,' Harvard Studies in Classical Philology 76 (1972); Walter Schatz, ed., Directory of Afro-American Resources (Bowker, 1970).

J. E. Patterson, comp., 'Checklist of Prescott Manuscripts,' Hispanic American Historical Review 39 (Feb. 1959); Andrea Hinding and Rosemary Richardson, comps., Archival and Manuscript Resources for the Study of Women's History:

A Beginning (Univ. of Minnesota Libraries, Social Welfare History Archives Center, 1972); D. C. Watt, 'U.S. Documentary Resources for the Study of British Foreign Policy, 1919-1959,' International Affairs 38 (Jan. 1962).

MA169-400

Harvard University
Harvard-Yenching Library
2 Divinity Avenue
Cambridge MA 02138

(617) 495-2756

OPEN: M-F 9-5; closed weekends and holidays
USER FEES: annual fees for persons not affiliated with Harvard; faculty and other, $100; students, $50; alumni, $30; optional monthly fees, $10
ACCESS: special permission required for access to materials in the Rare Books Room
COPYING FACILITIES: yes
MATERIALS SOLICITED: Materials relating to East Asia in the humanities and social sciences. Will also accept audio-visual materials.

HOLDINGS:
    Total volume: 9,000 items
    Inclusive dates: 14th century -
    Description: Materials relating to East Asia, including religious (mostly Buddhist) manuscripts; historical manuscripts on political and social developments in the Chinese empire during the 19th century; literary and artistic manuscripts, including holographic versions; and transcribed manuscripts, dating from antiquity to the end of the 19th century.
    Includes archives of the Lingnam University (Canton) Board of Trustees, 1884-1950; personal papers of Hu Hanmin and George and Geraldine Fitch.

SEE: Hamer.

SEE ALSO: A. K'ai-ming Chiu, An Annotated Catalogue of Ming Encyclopedias and Reference Works in the Chinese-Japanese Library of the Harvard-Yenching Institute at Harvard (Harvard-Yenching Institute, 1961).

MA169-440

Harvard University
Law School
Manuscript Division
Langdell Hall
Cambridge MA 02138

(617) 495-4550

OPEN: M-F 9-5; closed weekends and holidays
ACCESS: qualified researchers with specific projects; letter from advisor or instructor required from Ph.D. candidates and undergraduates
COPYING FACILITIES: yes
MATERIALS SOLICITED: Personal and professional papers of members of the American legal profession, such as judges, attorneys and law professors; papers relating to specific court cases; papers created by legal research projects; and semi-archival material of the Harvard Law School with emphasis on persons and projects associated with the Harvard Law School. Will also ac-

cept important legal papers of persons or court cases not connected with the Harvard Law School.

HOLDINGS:
Total volume: 1,480 l.f.
Inclusive dates: 1715 -
Description: Primarily 20th century collections relating to the three branches of the legal profession, specifically the bench, the bar, and the teaching profession. Included are drafts of opinions and administrative files of members of the judiciary; correspondence, activities files, drafts of writings and speeches, and biographical items of judges, law professors, and practicing attorneys; teaching notes; research projects conducted or initiated by the Harvard Law School, particularly in the fields of international law and of crime and delinquency.

There are also Harvard Law School semi-archival material, diaries, journals, and photographs.

SEE: Hamer; NUCMC, 1972, 74-76, 80.

SEE: Hinding; Robbins.

MA169-460
Harvard University
Littauer Center
Manpower and Industrial Relations Library
Cambridge MA 02138

no telephone

SEE: Hamer (as Harvard University, Industrial Relations Library, and Littauer Center of Public Administration, Library).

Questionnaire not returned.

MA169-500
Harvard University
Museum of Comparative Zoology
24 Oxford Street
Cambridge MA 02138

(617) 495-2463

OPEN: M-F 9-5; closed weekends and holidays
COPYING FACILITIES: yes
MATERIALS SOLICITED: Official records and other manuscripts concerning the zoological collections of this museum. Pictures of museum building, staff, and students. Will also accept personal and professional papers of zoologists and geologists associated with this museum. Portraits, all media, of figures in the history of science.

HOLDINGS:
Total volume: 300 l.f.
Inclusive dates: 1810 -
Description: The museum archives' holdings include museum records, 1859-1910, and other manuscripts concerning the growth of American scientific institutions and the history of American zoology and geology, including paleontology and oceanography.

Included are papers of the museum's founder Louis Agassiz, Alexander Agassiz, and ornithologist William Brewster; departmental catalogs and curatorial correspondence; records of museum-sponsored expeditions; papers of staff and

students; some historical collections such as correspondence of Thomas Say; zoological drawings and photographs; portraits of scientists in all media; and ephemera.

SEE: Hamer.

SEE: Hinding.

MA169-530
Harvard University
Peabody Museum
Tozzer Library
Divinity Avenue
Cambridge MA 02138

no telephone

SEE: Hamer.

Questionnaire not returned.

MA169-590
Longfellow National Historic Site
105 Brattle Street
Cambridge MA 02138

(617) 876-4491

OPEN: daily 10-4:30; closed Thanksgiving, Christmas, and New Year's
COPYING FACILITIES: no
MATERIALS SOLICITED: Will accept historic photographs and other documentary materials relating to the architecture, landscaping, and furnishings of the Vassall-Craigie-Longfellow House.

HOLDINGS:
Total volume: 175 l.f.
Inclusive dates: 1685 - 1928
Description: Manuscript collection relating chiefly to the domestic life of Henry Wadsworth Longfellow, his family, friends, and associates, including the Wadsworth, Longfellow, Dana, and Appleton family papers. The collection consists mainly of correspondence, focusing on genealogy, politics, travel, and the personal life of the Longfellows in Cambridge, Boston, Portland, ME, and elsewhere. There is also a photograph collection, particularly of China and Japan, 1871-73.

SEE: Hamer.

SEE: Hinding; Robbins.

MA169-610
Massachusetts Institute of Technology
Museum
Francis Russell Hart Nautical Collections
77 Massachusetts Avenue
Cambridge MA 02139

(617) 253-5942

OPEN: by appointment only
COPYING FACILITIES: yes

HOLDINGS:
Total volume: 30,000 items
Inclusive dates: 1870 -
Description: Materials relating to naval architecture and marine engineering, including technical drawings, blueprints, and photographs of U.S. Naval vessels, private yachts, and other ships. Collec-

tions include ship drawings from the Herreshoff Manufacturing Company, photographs of yachts from 1880 to 1940, the design file of ship designer Gordon Monroe, and photographs of shipyard construction activity.

MA169-625
Massachusetts Institute of Technology
Museum
265 Massachusetts Avenue
Cambridge MA 02139

(617) 253-4444

OPEN: M-F 9-6; closed weekends and holidays
COPYING FACILITIES: yes
MATERIALS SOLICITED: Photographs, tapes, films, disk and video recordings, oral history tapes and transcripts, sound recordings, architectural drawings and renderings relating to the history of M.I.T. and developments in 19th- and 20th-century technology. Will also accept memorabilia relating to the Institute, faculty, students, staff.

HOLDINGS:
Total volume: 12,000 architectural drawings; 5 million photographs; 300 audio-visuals.
Inclusive dates: 1865 -
Description: Materials relating to the history of the Massachusetts Institute of Technology, including photographs, architectural theses, documents, records, correspondence, and memorabilia.

SEE: Hinding.

MA169-650
Massachusetts Institute of Technology
Institute Archives and Special Collections
14N-118
Cambridge MA 02139

(617) 253-5136

OPEN: M-F 9-5; closed weekends and holidays
COPYING FACILITIES: yes
MATERIALS SOLICITED: Official records of the Massachusetts Institute of Technology; collections of papers of individual faculty and research staff members, and of individuals important in the development of 20th century technology and science, with emphasis on areas relevant to M.I.T. teaching and research.

HOLDINGS:
Total volume: 3,000 l.f.
Inclusive dates: early 1800's -
Description: Official records of the Massachusetts Institute of Technology from its founding in 1861 to date, including those of its presidents, administrative offices, schools and departments. Also, collections of professional and personal papers principally of individuals connected with the Institute, with an emphasis on science and technology.

Subject strengths include public works projects, hydraulics, engineering education, cybernetics, computers, scientific research during World War II, science policy, recombinant DNA technology regulations, energy research and policy, and physics.

SEE: Hamer; NUCMC, 1971, 80.

SEE: Hinding.

SEE ALSO: *Source Materials for the Recent History of Astronomy and Astrophysics: A Checklist of Manuscript Collections in the United States* (American Institute of Physics, 1971); Thomas S. Kuhn, John L. Heilbron, Paul Forman, and Lini Allen, *Sources for History of Quantum Physics: An Inventory and Report* (American Philosophical Society, 1967). Inventories and/or finding aids for some collections of papers are available at the Archives.

MA169-800
Modern Greek Studies Association
Box 337 Harvard Square Branch
Cambridge MA 02138

no telephone

OPEN: M-Th 9:30-3:30; closed Fridays, weekends, holidays, and Aug.
ACCESS: appointment required, members only
COPYING FACILITIES: no
MATERIALS SOLICITED: Materials relating to modern Greeks, including diaries, literary manuscripts and photographs.

HOLDINGS:
Total volume: not specified
Inclusive dates: 1930 -
Description: Materials relating to U.S.-Greek relations, including the Marshall Plan, Greek War relief, the Cyprus War of Independence, and the Turkish invasion.

MA169-855
Radcliffe College
Archives
3 James Street
Cambridge MA 02138

(617) 495-8662

OPEN: M-F 9-5; closed weekends and holidays
COPYING FACILITIES: yes
MATERIALS SOLICITED: Records of Radcliffe College offices; alumnae publications, papers and memorabilia; and College history.

HOLDINGS:
Total volume: 2,088 l.f.
Inclusive dates: 1879 -
Description: Non-current records and other materials documenting and relating to the history of Radcliffe College.

SEE: Hinding.

MA169-860
Radcliffe College
The Arthur and Elizabeth Schlesinger Library on the History of Women in America
10 Garden Street
Cambridge MA 02138

(617) 495-8647, 8648

OPEN: M-F 9-5 and limited evening hours during fall and spring semesters; closed weekends and holidays
COPYING FACILITIES: yes
MATERIALS SOLICITED: American women, women's organizations, and family papers.

HOLDINGS:
Total volume: 3,024 l.f.
Inclusive dates: 1790 -
Description: Manuscripts relating primarily to American women in the 19th and 20th centuries, with some emphasis on New England and Massachusetts. Subject areas covered include women's rights, suffrage, and feminism; education; politics and government service; social service and settlements; medicine and health; birth control; labor organizing; prisons; voluntary organizations; and, to a lesser degree, literature, the theater, music, and the visual arts.

GUIDES: *Arthur and Elizabeth Schlesinger Library on the History of Women in America: The Manuscript Inventories and the Catalogs of the Manuscripts, Books and Pictures* (G. K. Hall, 1973).

SEE: Hamer (as Radcliffe Women's Archives); NUCMC, 1959-66, 69-71, 73-74, 77, 79-80.

SEE: Schatz; Meckler and McMullin: Krichmar; Allard, Crawley, and Edmison; Hinding; Robbins; Hines.

SEE ALSO: Reports of the Library have been issued annually, 1953-64, and triennially thereafter.

MA169-885
Radcliffe College
Henry A. Murray Research Center
10 Garden Street
Cambridge MA 02138

(617) 495-8140

OPEN: M-F 9-5; closed weekends and holidays
COPYING FACILITIES: yes
MATERIALS SOLICITED: Social science data, especially longitudinal studies, concerning the changing life experiences of American women, as well as similar data about men for comparative purposes.

HOLDINGS:
Total volume: 50 data sets
Inclusive dates: 20th century
Description: Textual and machine readable data sets gathered for social science studies of American women, including marriage, child rearing, divorce, retirement, and experiences of educated women engaged in professional activities.

MA169-970
Women's Educational Center, Inc.
Women's Movement Archives
46 Pleasant Street
Cambridge MA 02139

(617) 354-8807

OPEN: by appointment only; closed Sundays and holidays
USER FEES: advance arrangements required
COPYING FACILITIES: no

MATERIALS SOLICITED: Materials relating to the contemporary women's liberation movement, particularly groups in the greater Boston area. Will also accept materials relating to the contemporary women's movement and to the history of women in Boston and Massachusetts.

HOLDINGS:
Total volume: 18 l.f.
Inclusive dates: 1966 - 1979
Description: Records of women's movement groups in the Boston area, including correspondence, financial records, records of extant organizations, and records of the Women's Educational Center.

CANTON

MA172-160
Daugavas Vanagi of Boston, Massachusetts, Inc.
Library of Latvian Plays and Theater
67 Randolph Street
Canton MA 02021

no telephone

OPEN: by appointment only
COPYING FACILITIES: no
MATERIALS SOLICITED: Manuscripts of plays by Latvian and Latvian-American authors and other materials concerning Latvian theaters and drama ensembles, both in Latvia and elsewhere.

HOLDINGS:
Total volume: 4 file cabinets
Inclusive dates: 1945 -
Description: Manuscripts of plays by Latvian and Latvian-American authors and photographs of Latvian theater productions and of drama assemblies outside Latvia.

CENTERVILLE

MA180-120
Centerville Historical Society and Museum
513 Main Street
Centerville MA

MAILING ADDRESS:
P.O. Box 491
Centerville MA 02632

(617) 775-0331

OPEN: late June to early Oct., Th-Su 2-4:30; closed other days and rest of year
COPYING FACILITIES: no
MATERIALS SOLICITED: Material on Centerville sea captains of the mid-1800's. Will also accept any historical material pertaining to the village of Centerville and the surrounding area.

HOLDINGS:
Total volume: 250 items
Inclusive dates: 1820 -
Description: Materials relating to the history of Centerville, including business records, ships' logs, photographs, a diary, minutes of the Centerville Public Lyceum (1885-86), and one oral history tape.

CHELMSFORD

MA190-120
Chelmsford Historical Society, Inc.
40 Byam Road
Chelmsford MA 01824

no telephone
SEE: NUCMC, 1970.

Questionnaire not returned.

CHESTERFIELD

MA196-120
Chesterfield Historical Society
Edwards Memorial Museum
North Road
Chesterfield MA 01012

(413) 296-4759

OPEN: by appointment
COPYING FACILITIES: no
MATERIALS SOLICITED: Chesterfield history and genealogy. Will also accept regional history and memoirs.

HOLDINGS:
Total volume: 500 items
Inclusive dates: 1760 - 1860
Description: Deeds, indentures, records of churches and other organizations, store ledgers, lists of voters, manuscript maps, personal diaries and memoirs, town welfare records, and oral history tapes.

CHESTNUT HILL

MA199-90
Boston College
Libraries
Special Collections
Chestnut Hill MA 02167

(617) 552-3282

OPEN: M-F 9-5; closed weekends and holidays
ACCESS: primarily for faculty, graduate students, and other mature scholars
COPYING FACILITIES: yes
MATERIALS SOLICITED: Early Boston; West Indies; Ireland; Catholic church in the U.S.; Jesuit travels and missions in North America; manuscripts and letters of, to or about Maurice Baring, Hilaire Belloc, G. K. Chesterton, James B. Connolly, Eleanor Early, Thomas Merton, Alice and Wilfrid Meynell and their circle, Coventry Patmore, Bruce Rogers, and Francis Thompson. Will also accept literary manuscripts, published or unpublished; papers of retired public figures; local history; items by or about Jesuits outside North America; and anti-Jesuit material.

HOLDINGS:
Total volume: 7,400 items
Inclusive dates: 1621 - 1969
Description: Materials relating to the natural, cultural, and political history of the West Indies, especially Jamaica; the Irish home rule movement; Boston history; and Coventry Patmore, Francis Thompson, Alice and Wilfrid Meynell,

Thomas Merton, and Eleanor Early, including literary manuscripts.

SEE: Hamer; NUCMC, 1959-61.

SEE: Robbins; Ingram.

SEE ALSO: Jerome S. Handler, *A Guide to Source Materials for the Study of Barbados History, 1627-1834* (Southern Illinois Univ. Press, 1971).

MA199-100
Boston College
University Archives
140 Commonwealth Avenue
Chestnut Hill MA 02167

(617) 552-3248

OPEN: M-F 9-5; closed weekends and holidays
ACCESS: authorized members of the University and qualified scholars
COPYING FACILITIES: yes
MATERIALS SOLICITED: Non-current records of Boston College. Will also accept personal papers of University personnel, and visual documents of research and archival value.

HOLDINGS:
Total volume: 1,000 l.f.
Inclusive dates: 1842 -
Description: Non-current files, records, documents and publications pertaining to the activities of Boston College, its officers, administrators, faculty, students and alumni. Also included are personal papers of some faculty and alumni.

CLINTON

MA207-120
Clinton Historical Society
Holder Memorial
210 Church Street
Clinton MA 01510

(617) 368-0084, 365-4877

OPEN: by appointment only
COPYING FACILITIES: no
MATERIALS SOLICITED: Materials concerning textile and carpet manufacturing, 1840-1930. Will also accept materials related to the history of Clinton, including its citizens, politics, and manufacturing.

HOLDINGS:
Total volume: not specified
Inclusive dates: 1700 -
Description: Materials relating to the history of Clinton, including documents of the Bigelow Carpet Company, Lancaster Gingham Mills, and Clinton Wire Cloth Company, as well as Civil War records and diaries.

CONCORD

MA217-130
Concord Free Public Library
129 Main Street
Concord MA 01742

(617) 369-5324, 2309

OPEN: M-Th 9-1, M-Th 1-6 by appointment; Friday and Saturday schedules vary; closed Sundays and holidays
ACCESS: prior letter of inquiry to Library Director encouraged; registration with Reference Department required
COPYING FACILITIES: yes
MATERIALS SOLICITED: Materials relating to Concord history. Will also accept materials relating to Concord authors.

HOLDINGS:
Total volume: 300 l.f.
Inclusive dates: 1635 - 1950
Description: Materials relating to Concord history, including the lives of such residents as Amos Bronson Alcott, Louisa May Alcott, Ephraim Wales Bull, Ralph Waldo Emerson, Franklin Benjamin Sanborn, and Henry David Thoreau. Types of records include deeds, indentures, business records, glass negatives, photographs, microfilmed town records, and letters.

SEE: Hamer; NUCMC, 1966, 75.

SEE: Schatz; Allard, Crawley, and Edmison; Robbins.

MA217-480
Louisa May Alcott Memorial
 Association
Orchard House
399 Lexington Road
Concord MA

MAILING ADDRESS:
P.O. Box 343
Concord MA 01742

(617) 369-4118

OPEN: by appointment
ACCESS: by appointment only; write at least two weeks in advance
COPYING FACILITIES: no
MATERIALS SOLICITED: Will accept manuscripts, photographs, and other materials relating to the Alcott family.

HOLDINGS:
Total volume: 100 items
Inclusive dates: 1799 - 1888
Description: Photographs, letters and other manuscripts relating to the Alcott family, particularly the years spent at Orchard House (1857-77).

MA217-520
Minute Man National Historical Park
174 Liberty Street
Concord MA

MAILING ADDRESS:
P.O. Box 160
Concord MA 01742

(617) 369-6993, 484-6192

OPEN: M-F 8-5; closed weekends,
Christmas, and New Year's
ACCESS: by appointment
COPYING FACILITIES: no

HOLDINGS:
Total volume: 12 file drawers
Inclusive dates: 1860 - 1940
Description: Documents, such as
manuscripts, correspondence, and person-
al records of author Margaret Sidney.

SEE: Robbins.

DALTON

MA227-120
Crane & Company, Inc.
Museum
30 South Street
Dalton MA 01226

(413) 684-2600, Ext. 231

OPEN: June 1 - Sept. 30, M-F 2-5; other
months by appointment; closed
weekends, July 4, and Labor Day
COPYING FACILITIES: no

HOLDINGS:
Total volume: 9 file cabinets
Inclusive dates: 19th century -
Description: Letters, photographs, and
other materials dealing with the history of
Crane & Company, paper manufacturers
since 1801, as well as the Crane family.

DANVERS

MA231-640
Peabody Institute Library
Danvers Archival Center
15 Sylvan Street
Danvers MA 01923

(617) 774-0554

OPEN: M 1-7:30, W, F 1-5, Tu and Th
by appointment; closed other days and
holidays
COPYING FACILITIES: yes
MATERIALS SOLICITED: Materials relating
to witchcraft, particularly in Salem in
1692; materials relating to the history
and development of Salem and
Danvers.

HOLDINGS:
Total volume: 384 l.f.; 509 vols.;
5,300 items
Inclusive dates: 1670 -
Description: Manuscripts, genealogical
material, town records, and court transcripts relating to the Salem and Danvers
communities. Included are materials relating to witchcraft, the Revolutionary
War, the abolitionist movement, and other aspects of American history.

SEE: NUCMC, 1978.

SEE: Hinding.

SEE ALSO: a brochure, 'A Guide to the
Danvers Archival Center,' available
from the institution.

DEDHAM

MA235-150
Dedham Historical Society
612 High Street
Dedham MA

MAILING ADDRESS:
Box 215
Dedham MA 02026

(617) 326-1385

OPEN: W, Th 1-5, Sa 1-4; closed other
days, Saturdays Oct. - May, and
holidays
COPYING FACILITIES: yes
MATERIALS SOLICITED: Dedham history.

HOLDINGS:
Total volume: 140 l.f.
Inclusive dates: 1635 -
Description: Diaries, maps, and papers
relating to Dedham, Nathaniel Ames,
Fisher Ames, Horace Mann, and a turn-
pike corporation.

SEE: Hamer; NUCMC, 1962, 77.

SEE: Leventhal and Mooney - I; Robbins.

DEERFIELD

MA238-520
Memorial Libraries
Henry N. Flynt Library of Historic
Deerfield, Inc., and
Pocumtuck Valley Memorial
Association Library
Memorial Street
Deerfield MA

MAILING ADDRESS:
P.O. Box 53
Deerfield MA 01342

(413) 774-5581, Ext. 125

OPEN: M-F 9-4; closed weekends and
holidays
COPYING FACILITIES: yes
MATERIALS SOLICITED: Family and other
manuscripts of Deerfield area; account
books, diaries, local history and genealogy of western Massachusetts and Connecticut Valley. Will also accept materials on American decorative arts, architecture, craftsmanship, social customs, museum economy, restoration,
and collecting practices.

HOLDINGS:
Total volume: 710 boxes; 184 l.f.
Inclusive dates: 1670 -
Description: Materials relating to the
Deerfield area, including account books,
sermons, diaries, town records, church
records, records of organizations, papers
of more than 225 families, photographs,
microfilms, maps, and sketches and patterns for needlework.

SEE: Hamer.

SEE: Hinding; Leventhal and Mooney - I.

SEE ALSO: a pamphlet, *Research at
Deerfield: An Introduction to the Collection of The Memorial Libraries* (1973)
available on request. Finding aids to
specific parts of the collection available
at repository.

DENNIS

MA242-160
Dennis Historical Society
Josiah Dennis Manse Library
Whig Street and Nobscusset Road
Dennis MA

MAILING ADDRESS:
P.O. Box 607
South Dennis MA 02660

(617) 398-8035, 385-3338

OPEN: by appointment
COPYING FACILITIES: no
MATERIALS SOLICITED: Material pertaining to Cape Cod history and genealogy,
the cranberry and fishing industries,
the sea, and ships. Will also accept old
photographs, maps, letters, diaries,
manuscripts, and scrapbooks.

HOLDINGS:
Total volume: 550 l.f.
Inclusive dates: 1700 -
Description: Materials pertaining to Josiah Dennis, founder of the town;
logbooks, account books, and journals relating to Cape Cod history; Fairbank
family items, including correspondence
and diaries; town of Dennis annual reports, dating from 1850; some Plymouth
Colony records; and records and minutes
of the Dennis Historical Society.

DIGHTON

MA246-160
Dighton Historical Society, Inc.
1217 Williams Street
Dighton MA 02715

(617) 669-5514

OPEN: M 9-11:30; closed other days and
holidays
ACCESS: by appointment only
COPYING FACILITIES: no
MATERIALS SOLICITED: Materials relating
to the history of Dighton and the surrounding area.

HOLDINGS:
Total volume: not specified
Inclusive dates: 1700 -
Description: A varied collection relating to the history of Dighton. Included
are Civil War and World War I correspondence; diaries, journals, logbooks,
account books, genealogical source data,
and maps; charts and file cards on the
town cemeteries; photographs, motion
pictures, slides, and sound recordings of
town events; and town meeting records
from 1864 to date.

SEE: Hinding.

DORCHESTER

MA250-160

Dorchester Historical Society, Inc.
195 Boston Street
Dorchester MA 02125

(617) 436-8367

OPEN: Saturdays and other times by
  appointment
COPYING FACILITIES: no
MATERIALS SOLICITED: Dorchester family papers, genealogies, records, and
  manuscripts.

HOLDINGS:
  Total volume: 50 c.f.
  Inclusive dates: 1635 -
  Description: Materials chiefly relating
  to the history of Dorchester. Included are
  family papers; documents pertaining to
  Shay's Rebellion, the Revolutionary War,
  and the Civil War; diaries and personal
  papers; and photographs.

SEE: Hamer.

SEE: Hinding.

DUXBURY

MA265-160

Duxbury Rural and Historical Society
King Caesar Road
Duxbury MA

MAILING ADDRESS:
P.O. Box 176, Snug Harbor
Duxbury MA 02331

(617) 934-6106

OPEN: June 15 - Sept. 15, Tu-Su 2-5, or
  by appointment
USER FEES: one dollar
ACCESS: serious researchers
COPYING FACILITIES: no
MATERIALS SOLICITED: Material related
  to Duxbury and the Duxbury area.

HOLDINGS:
  Total volume: not specified
  Inclusive dates: 1620 -
  Description: Materials relating to the
  history of Duxbury, with particular em-
  phasis on the Pilgrims and shipbuilding.

EASTHAM

MA278-200

Eastham Historical Society, Inc.
1869 Schoolhouse Museum
Route 6
Eastham MA

MAILING ADDRESS:
Box 8
Eastham MA 02642

(617) 255-4968

OPEN: by appointment only
USER FEES: 50 cents
COPYING FACILITIES: no
MATERIALS SOLICITED: Manuscripts, vi-
  sual documents, and scrapbooks.

HOLDINGS:
  Total volume: 2 file drawers
  Inclusive dates: not specified
  Description: Materials concerning Cape
  Cod history and genealogy, and photo-
  graphs of shipwrecks, buildings and local
  storm damage in 1978.

SEE: Hinding.

EDGARTOWN

MA285-160

Dukes County Historical Society
School and Cooke Streets
Edgartown MA

MAILING ADDRESS:
Box 827
Edgartown MA 02539

(617) 627-4441

OPEN: summer, Tu-Sa 10-4:30; winter,
  Th, F 1-4, Sa 10-4; closed other days
  and holidays
COPYING FACILITIES: yes
MATERIALS SOLICITED: Whaling, geneal-
  ogy, and local history.

HOLDINGS:
  Total volume: 700 l.f.
  Inclusive dates: 1642 -
  Description: Materials relating chiefly
  to the history of Martha's Vineyard, in-
  cluding whaling logs, ships' logs, genea-
  logical material, account books and led-
  gers, oral history tapes, and photographs.
  There are also sermons of Nathaniel
  Hancock, Edgartown Customs House
  records, and footage from a Katherine
  Cornell movie.

SEE: Hinding; Leventhal and Mooney - I.

ESSEX

MA293-200

Essex Historical Society, Inc.
Essex Shipbuilding Museum
Main Street
Essex MA

MAILING ADDRESS:
39 Eastern Avenue
Essex MA 01929

(617) 768-7541

OPEN: Th-Su 1-4; closed Oct. 15-May 31
  except by appointment
COPYING FACILITIES: no
MATERIALS SOLICITED: Essex history,
  particularly shipbuilding.

HOLDINGS:
  Total volume: 3 l.f.
  Inclusive dates: 1634 - 1940
  Description: A collection of manuscripts, photographs, diaries, daybooks,
  journals, genealogical papers, and public
  documents pertaining to the history of
  the town of Essex. The collection focuses
  on the history of schooner building in
  Essex, but also includes military and personal material.

FALL RIVER

MA304-230

Fall River Historical Society
451 Rock Street
Fall River MA 02720

no telephone

SEE: NUCMC, 1959-62, 68.

Questionnaire not returned.

FALMOUTH

MA307-230

Falmouth Historical Society
Palmer Avenue at the Village Green
Falmouth MA

MAILING ADDRESS:
Box 174
Falmouth MA 02541

(617) 548-4857

OPEN: W 9-noon, F 8-4; closed weekends
  and holidays
ACCESS: advance arrangements required
COPYING FACILITIES: no
MATERIALS SOLICITED: Materials relating
  to the town of Falmouth, including
  records of early industry and the development of the town as a resort community, records of early families, and
  items relating to Cape Cod history and
  seafaring. Will also accept maps and
  charts of Cape Cod, and family
  records, such as Bibles, deeds, and wills
  of locally important families.

HOLDINGS:
  Total volume: 1,050 l.f.
  Inclusive dates: 1700 -
  Description: Materials relating to the
  founding and development of Falmouth,
  including records of the founding families, and their deeds and wills; records
  and photographs of early industry; materials on the town's maritime history,
  including whaling ship specifications;
  logbooks and other records of whaling
  voyages; and photographs of ship captains.

SEE ALSO: a list of logbooks available
  from the institution.

FITCHBURG

MA311-240

Fitchburg Historical Society
50 Grove Street
Fitchburg MA

MAILING ADDRESS:
P.O. Box 953
Fitchburg MA 01420

(617) 345-1157

OPEN: W, Th 10-4, Su 2-4 Sept. 15-June
  15; closed other days and holidays
ACCESS: access on application to
  Librarian
COPYING FACILITIES: no
MATERIALS SOLICITED: Will accept ma-
  terials relating to Fitchburg.

HOLDINGS:
Total volume: not specified
Inclusive dates: not specified
Description: Materials relating to Fitchburg and the surrounding area.

FOXBORO

MA319-240
Foxborough Historical Commission
Memorial Hall
Foxboro MA

MAILING ADDRESS:
Town Hall
Foxboro MA 02035

(617) 543-7040, 3866

OPEN: W 7-9; closed other days
COPYING FACILITIES: no
MATERIALS SOLICITED: Items relating to the history of Foxboro. Will also accept other materials.

HOLDINGS:
Total volume: not specified
Inclusive dates: not specified
Description: Materials relating to the history of Foxboro.

FRAMINGHAM

MA323-230
Framingham Public Library
Framingham Room
49 Lexington Street
Framingham MA 01701

(617) 872-4383

OPEN: M, W, F 9-5:30, Tu, Th 1-9; closed weekends and holidays
COPYING FACILITIES: yes
MATERIALS SOLICITED: Materials pertaining to Framingham.

HOLDINGS:
Total volume: 25 items; additional materials
Inclusive dates: not specified
Description: Materials relating to the history of Framingham and its people, including manuscripts, maps, photographs, and town records.
SEE: Hamer (as Edgel Memorial Library, Framingham Center, MA).
SEE: Hinding.

MA323-250
Framingham Historical and Natural History Society
Framingham MA

MAILING ADDRESS:
Box 2032
Framingham MA 01701

no telephone

SEE: Hamer (as Framingham Natural History and Historical Society, Framingham Center, MA).

Questionnaire not returned.

GLENDALE

MA334-120
Chesterwood
Library
Off Route 183
Glendale MA

MAILING ADDRESS:
P.O. Box 827
Stockbridge MA 01262

(413) 298-3579

OPEN: by appointment only; closed holidays and weekends Nov. - April
ACCESS: scholars; advance arrangements required
COPYING FACILITIES: yes
MATERIALS SOLICITED: Materials relating to the American sculptor Daniel Chester French. Will also accept materials relating to beaux arts sculpture, historic preservation in the Berkshire region, and Daniel Chester French's family.

HOLDINGS:
Total volume: 5,000 items
Inclusive dates: 1866 -
Description: Collections relating to the sculptor Daniel Chester French and his father, Henry Flagg French, wife, Mary French, daughter, Margaret French Cresson, and son-in-law, William Penn Cresson. Included are letters, diaries, account books, blueprints, sketchbooks, drawings, photographs, negatives, oral history tapes, scrapbooks, genealogical data, literary manuscripts, architectural drawings, sound recordings, and motion pictures.
SEE: Hinding.

GLOUCESTER

MA338-280
Gloucester Lyceum & Sawyer Free Library
Audio-Visual Department
2 Dale Avenue
Gloucester MA 01930

(617) 283-0376

OPEN: M-F 9-8, Sa 9-5; closed Sundays, holidays, and Saturdays 1 p.m. in summer
COPYING FACILITIES: yes
MATERIALS SOLICITED: Oral histories relating to fishing, art, immigrant groups, and tourism.

HOLDINGS:
Total volume: 9 l.f.
Inclusive dates: 1978 -
Description: Recordings of 103 oral history interviews relating to the area of Cape Ann, MA, including history, fishing, art, immigrant groups, tourism, Charles Olson, Clarence Birdseye, seafaring, shipbuilding, quarries, literature, and music.

MA338-840
Village Hall Association
Annisquam Historical Society
Walnut Street, Annisquam
Gloucester MA

MAILING ADDRESS:
102 Leonard Street
Gloucester MA 01930

(617) 283-1426

OPEN: June 15-Sept. 30, M 2:30-5:30, Th 7:30-9:30, and by appointment
COPYING FACILITIES: no
MATERIALS SOLICITED: Materials relating to the history of Annisquam; related material applicable to Cape Ann, the North Shore, and Massachusetts.

HOLDINGS:
Total volume: 6 file cabinets; 500 items
Inclusive dates: 17th century -
Description: Materials relating to Annisquam, with emphasis on the 18th and 19th centuries, including store ledgers; ship provisioning records; diaries; accounts of the ship trade to South America, Europe, and the Orient; special papers on local history and industries, ships' logs, letters, family scrapbooks, and genealogies.
Other materials relate to Cape Ann and the North Shore. Includes a large collection of glass negatives and photographic prints of Cape Ann subjects from 1880-1930, featuring Martha Hale Harvey.
SEE: Hinding.

GREAT BARRINGTON

MA349-30
Albert Schweitzer Friendship House
Hurlburt Road
Great Barrington MA 01230

no telephone
SEE: NUCMC, 1977.

Questionnaire not returned.

GREENFIELD

MA352-270
Greenfield Community College
Archibald MacLeish Collection
One College Drive
Greenfield MA 01301

(413) 774-3131

OPEN: Su 2-10, M-Th 8-10, F 8-5; closed Saturdays and holidays
ACCESS: appointment required
COPYING FACILITIES: yes
MATERIALS SOLICITED: Materials by and about Archibald MacLeish. Will also accept materials relating to MacLeish's peer poets.

HOLDINGS:
Total volume: 600 items
Inclusive dates: 1890 -
Description: Manuscripts and audio-visual documents relating to Archibald MacLeish. Included are correspondence, literary manuscripts, photographs, videotapes and audiotapes.

GROTON

MA356-120
Congregation of the Holy Union of the Sacred Hearts
Sacred Heart Province
One Main Street
Groton MA 01450

(617) 448-6042

OPEN: by appointment
COPYING FACILITIES: no
MATERIALS SOLICITED: Material pertaining to the origins and growth of the Congregation and the Sacred Heart Province. Will also accept all materials, 1826-1977, which have a bearing on the growth of religious congregations in France, Belgium, South America, especially Argentina, and the United States, especially the Atlantic seaboard States.

HOLDINGS:
Total volume: not specified
Inclusive dates: 1825 -
Description: Materials relating to the history of the Congregation of the Holy Union of the Sacred Hearts, including correspondence of the founder and the early members of the Congregation, circular letters, memoirs, newspaper clippings, photographs, and reports.

SEE: Hinding.

GROVELAND

MA359-480
Langley-Adams Library
Groveland MA 01830

no telephone
SEE: Hamer.

Questionnaire not returned.

HADLEY

MA363-640
Porter Phelps Huntington Foundation, Inc.
Porter Phelps Huntington House Museum
130 River Drive
Hadley MA 01035

(413) 584-4699

OPEN: M-F by appointment only
ACCESS: advance arrangements required
COPYING FACILITIES: no

HOLDINGS:
Total volume: 35,000 items
Inclusive dates: 1669 - 1960
Description: Papers of the Porter-Phelps-Huntington family which resided in the Hadley homestead from 1752 to 1960, including account books, business and financial records, family correspondence, 18th and 19th century diaries of women, journals, logs, genealogical data, and manuscript public accounts.

Also included are manuscript maps, photographs, and a tape of the first curator and founder of the museum collection. Persons represented in the collection include Elizabeth Porter Phelps, Elizabeth Whiting Phelps Huntington, Frederick Dan Huntington, James Otis Sargent Huntington, Dan Huntington, Ruth Huntington Sessions, and James Lincoln Huntington.

The materials are on temporary loan to the Amherst College Library, Amherst, MA 01002.

HARVARD

MA383-240
Fruitlands Museums, Inc.
102 Prospect Hill Road
Harvard MA 01451

(617) 456-3924

OPEN: by appointment only M-F 9-5; closed weekends and holidays
ACCESS: advance arrangements required
COPYING FACILITIES: yes
MATERIALS SOLICITED: Historical manuscripts and journals relating to the Shakers; 19th century American painting, history, and literature; and American Indians.

HOLDINGS:
Total volume: not specified
Inclusive dates: 19th century -
Description: Manuscripts and other materials concerning American Indians, Shakers, and American paintings, history, and literature.

SEE: Hinding.

HAVERHILL

MA394-330
Haverhill Public Library
99 Main Street
Haverhill MA 01830

no telephone
SEE: Hamer; NUCMC, 1966-67 (as Haverhill Historical Society).

Questionnaire not returned.

HINGHAM

MA398-330
Hingham Public Library
Hingham Bicentennial Collection
66 Leavitt Street
Hingham MA 02043

(617) 749-0907

OPEN: M-Th 9-9, F, Sa 9-6; Sundays by appointment; closed holidays, Saturday afternoons in summer
ACCESS: identification required
COPYING FACILITIES: yes
MATERIALS SOLICITED: Materials relating to the history of Hingham.

HOLDINGS:
Total volume: 2,200 items
Inclusive dates: 1632 -
Description: Materials relating to the history of Hingham, including manuscripts, diaries, account books, day books, correspondence, vital records, deeds, wills, indentures, and photographs. Subject areas covered include businesses, institutions, churches, clubs, societies, town papers, military history, and local families. Most of the collection is available on microfilm.

SEE ALSO: 'Hingham Bicentennial Collection Index,' a photocopied inventory of the materials on microfilm, available from the institution.

HOLLISTON

MA407-320
Holliston Historical Society
Holliston MA 01746

no telephone
SEE: Hamer; NUCMC, 1971.

Questionnaire not returned.

HOPEDALE

MA411-80
Bancroft Memorial Library
50 Hopedale Street
Hopedale MA 01747

(617) 473-7692

OPEN: M-W 2-8, Th-F 2-6, Sa 10-2; summer hours M, T, Th 2-6, W, 2-8, F 10-2; closed Sundays and holidays
COPYING FACILITIES: yes
MATERIALS SOLICITED: Materials relating to the Hopedale Community and Adin Ballou.

HOLDINGS:
Total volume: not specified
Inclusive dates: 1848 - 1908
Description: Papers and manuscripts of Adin Ballou and photographs and other materials on the Hopedale Community. There are also ledgers of the Draper family.

SEE: Hamer.

HULL

MA425-520
The Means Library
5 Vautrinot Avenue
Hull MA 02045

no telephone

OPEN: by appointment only
ACCESS: advance request by letter that delineates purpose of research is required.
COPYING FACILITIES: no
MATERIALS SOLICITED: All significant historical material relating to Hull, which includes the resort area of Nantasket Beach: especially pre-1920 manuscripts, photographs, and printed ephemera. Will also accept materials which strengthen existing collections.

HOLDINGS:
Total volume: 12 c.f.
Inclusive dates: 1641 -
Description: Material documenting the history of Hull and Nantasket Beach, including Paragon Park. Postcard, photograph, and printed ephemera collections; ecclesiastical papers; hotels, transportation, and public works and utilities materials; 19th century memorabilia of the Lucihe/James families; manuscripts and scrapbooks pertaining to the operatic career of Mme. Bernice De Pasquali, and the lifesaving activities of Captain Joshua James, the Massachusetts Humane Society, and U.S. Life-Saving Service.

HYDE PARK

MA432-320
Hyde Park Historical Society
30 Ayles Road
Hyde Park MA

MAILING ADDRESS:
Hyde Park Library
Harvard Street
Hyde Park MA 02136

(617) 361-4398

OPEN: M, Th 12-8, Tu, W, F 10-5, Sa 9-5; closed Sundays
ACCESS: by prior arrangement
COPYING FACILITIES: yes

HOLDINGS:
Total volume: 50 l.f.
Inclusive dates: 1850 -
Description: Business records of the Hyde Park Water Company, oral history tapes relating to Hyde Park history, photographs of the town, town records, club records, and maps of the community.

SEE: Hinding.

IPSWICH

MA436-350
Ipswich Historical Society
53 South Main Street
Ipswich MA 01938

no telephone
SEE: Hamer.

Questionnaire not returned.

MA436-360
Ipswich Public Library
25 North Main Street
Ipswich MA 01938

(617) 356-4646

OPEN: M-Th 10-8, F 10-5:30, Sa 9-4; closed Sundays and holidays

SEE: Hamer.

Questionnaire not returned.

MA436-370
Ipswich Town Hall
Ipswich MA 01938

no telephone
SEE: Hamer.

Questionnaire not returned.

LANCASTER

MA448-470
Lancaster Historical Commission
Town Hall
Lancaster MA 01523

(617) 365-2762

OPEN: Tu, W 9-1; closed other days
COPYING FACILITIES: yes
MATERIALS SOLICITED: Letters, diaries, photographs, and other materials pertaining to people or events connected with the town of Lancaster.

HOLDINGS:
Total volume: 3,500 items
Inclusive dates: 1790 - 1938
Description: Manuscripts, 1790-1900, relating to the town of Lancaster, and 3,000 photographs, 1890-1938, of people and events in the town.

SEE: Hinding.

MA448-490
Lancaster Town Library
Main Street
Lancaster MA 01523

(617) 365-2008

OPEN: Tu-F 10-8; Sa 2-5 Sept. - June; closed Sundays, Mondays

SEE: Hamer.

Questionnaire not returned.

LAWRENCE

MA451-360
Immigrant City Archives, Inc.
38 Lawrence Street
Lawrence MA 01840

(617) 686-9230

OPEN: by appointment only
ACCESS: advance arrangements suggested
COPYING FACILITIES: no
MATERIALS SOLICITED: Materials relating to immigrants and to organizations formed by and for immigrants in greater Lawrence. Will also accept materials relating to Lawrence history.

HOLDINGS:
Total volume: 45 l.f.
Inclusive dates: 1850 -
Description: Records of the Lawrence YWCA and International Institute; records of the German School, German Free Bed Society, and other German-American organizations; records of the Lithuanian National Catholic church, Social Camp Association, and cemetery; scrapbooks of organizations; oral history recordings of Lawrence citizens; and photographs of subjects important to immigrant history in Lawrence.

LEXINGTON

MA462-480
Lexington Historical Society, Inc.
36 Hancock Street
Lexington MA

MAILING ADDRESS:
P.O. Box 514
Lexington MA 02173

(617) 861-0928

OPEN: by appointment only
COPYING FACILITIES: no
MATERIALS SOLICITED: Material pertaining to Lexington, particularly of the American Revolutionary period. Will also accept other pertinent Lexington material.

HOLDINGS:
Total volume: 90 c.f.
Inclusive dates: 1690 -
Description: Material relating to Lexington's origin and growth, with emphasis on the town's participation in the American Revolution. Included are proclamations, petitions, correspondence, account books, journals, oral history tapes, maps, photographs, motion pictures, genealogical source data, and church records.

SEE: Hamer; NUCMC, 1980.

SEE: Novotny.

LINCOLN

MA466-480

Lincoln Public Library
Bedford Road
Lincoln MA 01773

(617) 259-8465

OPEN: M, W, Th 9-8:30, Tu, F 9-6, Sa
10-5; closed Sundays and holidays
COPYING FACILITIES: yes
MATERIALS SOLICITED: Materials relating
to the history of Lincoln.

HOLDINGS:
Total volume: 41 l.f.
Inclusive dates: 1735 -
Description: Town records, 1745- ,
records of early churches, family papers
and genealogies, materials relating to the
history of old houses in Lincoln, including slides, and some oral history tapes.

LONGMEADOW

MA474-690

Richard Salter Storrs Library
693 Longmeadow Street
Longmeadow MA 01106

no telephone

SEE: NUCMC, 1962.

Questionnaire not returned.

LOWELL

MA478-730

Society for the Preservation of
Colonial Culture
52 New Spalding Street
Lowell MA 01851

no telephone

OPEN: by appointment only
COPYING FACILITIES: no

HOLDINGS:
Total volume: 3,000 vols.
Inclusive dates: 1767 - 1779
Description: Copies of muster rolls of
the 10th Foot British Army Regiment, as
well as other units of the British Army
which took part in the battles of Lexington and Concord.

MA478-800

University of Lowell
Libraries
Special Collections
1 University Avenue
Lowell MA 01854

(617) 452-5000, Ext. 2388

OPEN: M-F 8:30-5; closed weekends and
holidays
COPYING FACILITIES: yes
MATERIALS SOLICITED: Social, political,
and economic history of Lowell; material relating to the Middlesex Canal.

HOLDINGS:
Total volume: 70 hours oral history
tapes; 210 l.f.; 5,000 photographs; 600
drawings
Inclusive dates: 1780 -
Description: Manuscripts relating to
Lowell, including the records of local
churches, companies, hospitals, and associations; city records; and diaries, journals, literary manuscripts and correspondence. There are also records of the
Middlesex Canal Company; papers of the
Warren Manning family; photographs
taken by the Locks and Canals Company
depicting Lowell architecture; architectural, engineering, and technical drawings relating to waterpower and the textile industry; and oral history interviews relating to the history of Lowell.

SEE: Hinding.

LYNN

MA486-470

Lynn Historical Society, Inc.
Manuscript Collection
125 Green Street
Lynn MA 01902

(617) 592-2465

OPEN: M-F 9-4, Sa 1-4; closed Sundays
and holidays
ACCESS: an appointment is advised
COPYING FACILITIES: yes
MATERIALS SOLICITED: Will accept any-
thing connected with the history of
Lynn.

HOLDINGS:
Total volume: not specified
Inclusive dates: 1629 -
Description: Manuscripts relating to
the history of Lynn. Included are correspondence, diaries, journals, logbooks,
business records, religious records, manuscript schoolbooks, school records, and
records of clubs and charitable organizations. Subject focuses include Quakers,
the shoe industry, the antislavery movement, and the Hutchinson Family Singers. There is also a photograph collection.

SEE: Hinding.

MANCHESTER

MA499-520

Manchester Historical Society
10 Union Street
Manchester MA 01944

(617) 526-7230

OPEN: Tu, W, Th, and F afternoons;
afternoons only in July and Aug., other
times by appointment; closed weekends
and Mondays
COPYING FACILITIES: yes

HOLDINGS:
Total volume: not specified
Inclusive dates: 1835 -
Description: Ledgers, account books,
family and genealogical records, including
wills and deeds, and other materials relating to the history of Manchester and its
inhabitants, including an 1835 manuscript history of the town.

SEE: Hinding.

MARBLEHEAD

MA506-520

Marblehead Historical Society
161 Washington Street
Marblehead MA

MAILING ADDRESS:
P.O. Box 1048
Marblehead MA 01945

(617) 631-1069

OPEN: mid-May to mid-Oct., M-Sa
9:30-4; closed Memorial Day and
Sundays
COPYING FACILITIES: no
MATERIALS SOLICITED: Items relating to
Marblehead history, including photo-
graphs.

HOLDINGS:
Total volume: 30 file drawers
Inclusive dates: 1715 -
Description: Genealogical material on
Marblehead families; material on Marble-
head's involvement in the Revolutionary
War, the War of 1812, and the Civil
War; letters, deeds, bills, and other papers
of Marblehead families; and records of
Marblehead schools and organizations, es-
pecially the Marblehead Academy. Most
materials predate 1900.

SEE: Hamer; NUCMC, 1959-61.

SEE: Hinding; Leventhal and Mooney - I.

MARLBOROUGH

MA513-530

Marlborough Public Library
35 West Main Street
Marlborough MA 01752

(617) 485-0494

OPEN: M-F 9-8:30, Sa 9-5; closed
Sundays and holidays
COPYING FACILITIES: yes
MATERIALS SOLICITED: Materials relating
to the history of Marlborough.

HOLDINGS:
Total volume: 526 items
Inclusive dates: 1670 - late 19th
century
Description: Correspondence, deeds,
account books, and other personal, family, and genealogical papers of the
Brigham, Gates, Jones, Newton, Rice,
Stevens, and Witherbee families of Marlborough; church records of Marlborough,
including letters from Cotton Mather, Increase Mather, and Artemas Ward, and
reports, petitions, bills, receipts, and attendance books of the first parish church.

There are also local military records,
including muster rolls, orders, appointments, inventories, and copies of monthly
reports; and diaries and notebooks of Edward Barnes, Silas Barnes, Cyrus Felton,
Silas Bolman, and Emily Rice.

SEE: Hamer; NUCMC, 1968.

SEE: Robbins; Hinding

MEDFORD

MA528-510
Medford Historical Society
24 Iural Avenue
Medford MA 02155

no telephone

SEE: Hamer.

Questionnaire not returned.

MA528-740
Tufts University
Fletcher School of Law and
    Diplomacy
Edward R. Murrow Center for Public
    Diplomacy
Mugar Hall
Packard Avenue
Medford MA 02155

(617) 628-7010

OPEN: M-F 9-5; closed weekends and
    holidays
ACCESS: qualified scholars and
    researchers at the discretion of the
    Curator
COPYING FACILITIES: yes
MATERIALS SOLICITED: Will accept ma-
    terials relating to Edward R. Murrow.

HOLDINGS:
    Total volume: 400 l.f.
    Inclusive dates: 1839 - 1965
    Description: A manuscript collection
relating to the professional life of Edward
R. Murrow, including correspondence, reports, speeches, interviews, tapes
and films. Also included are some personal correspondence, memorabilia, and
clippings.

SEE: NUCMC, 1976.

MA528-780
Tufts University
Library
Archives and Special Collections
Medford MA 02155

(617) 628-5000

OPEN: M-F 9-5; closed weekends and
    holidays
ACCESS: scholarly researchers
COPYING FACILITIES: yes
MATERIALS SOLICITED: Archival materi-
    als pertaining to the history of Tufts
    University, and letters by P. T.
    Barnum. Will also accept manuscript
    collections relating directly to Tufts
    University, its existing library collec-
    tions and the research interests of
    scholars at Tufts, and single items or
    collections of historic or literary value
    that do not clearly belong in some oth-
    er repository.

HOLDINGS:
    Total volume: 422 l.f.
    Inclusive dates: 1700's -
    Description: Manuscripts, documents,
minutes, logbooks, and correspondence
relating to the history of Tufts University,
1840's to date; papers of Hosea Ballou,
II, Phineas Taylor Barnum, Amos Emerson Dolbear, and John Holmes; ser-

mons of William Bentley; and materials
relating to the Confederacy, as well as
other items of general interest.
    Also, the papers of Henri Goiran.

SEE: Hamer; NUCMC, 1962, 70.

SEE: Leventhal and Mooney - I; Robbins.

SEE ALSO: Gabor Erdelyi, comp., 'John
    Holmes: A Bibliography of Published
    and Unpublished Writings in the Spe-
    cial Collections of the Tufts University
    Library,' *Bulletin of the New York Pub-
    lic Library* 73 (June 1969); Russell E.
    Miller, 'College and University Ar-
    chives: The Experience of One Institu-
    tion,' *College and Research Libraries*
    28 (March 1967); Walter Schatz, ed.,
    Directory of Afro-American Resources
    (Bowker, 1970); *Source Materials for
    the Recent History of Astronomy and
    Astrophysics: A Checklist of Manuscript
    Collections in the United States*
    (American Institute of Physics, 1971).

MA528-800
Universalist Historical Society
Library
Tufts University
Medford MA 02155

no telephone

SEE: Hamer.

Questionnaire not returned.

MENDON

MA538-520
Mendon Historical Society
Mendon Historical Museum
Main Street
Mendon MA

MAILING ADDRESS:
P.O. Box 403
Mendon MA 01756

no telephone

OPEN: by appointment only June-Sept.
COPYING FACILITIES: no
MATERIALS SOLICITED: Manuscripts,
    photographs and other material relating
    to the history of Mendon.

HOLDINGS:
    Total volume: 129 items; 30 vols.
    Inclusive dates: 1800 -
    Description: A collection relating to the
history of the town of Mendon since its
first settlement in 1660. Included are accounts of locations of early homes,
schools, churches, and businesses, photographs, manuscript papers written by
Society members, literary manuscripts, a
film, and other materials.

SEE: Hamer.

METHUEN

MA540-800
United Methodist Church
New Hampshire Conference
Historical Society
First United Methodist Church
Corner of Lowell and Pelham Streets
Methuen MA

MAILING ADDRESS:
54 Lowell Street
Methuen MA 01844

(617) 683-0068

OPEN: by appointment only
COPYING FACILITIES: no
MATERIALS SOLICITED: Materials relating
    to the New Hampshire United Meth-
    odist Conference.

HOLDINGS:
    Total volume: not specified
    Inclusive dates: 18th century -
    Description: Records of the New
Hampshire Conference, including photographs, newspaper clippings, journals, diaries, logbooks, and correspondence.

MIDDLEBORO

MA542-200
Eddy Family Association, Inc.
1 Cedar Street
Middleboro MA

MAILING ADDRESS:
570 Washington Street, Box 354
Duxbury MA 02332

(617) 934-6058

OPEN: July - Aug., Sa, Su 10-6; other
    days June - Sept., by appointment;
    closed rest of year
ACCESS: prior arrangements required
COPYING FACILITIES: no
MATERIALS SOLICITED: Letters, deeds,
    and legal papers, particularly those re-
    lating to the Eddy family and their de-
    scendants. Will also accept other docu-
    ments, diaries, genealogical records,
    and similar materials.

HOLDINGS:
    Total volume: 1 l.f.
    Inclusive dates: 1645 -
    Description: Letters, deeds, and legal
papers, particularly relating to the Eddy
family and their descendants.

MA542-520
Middleborough Historical Association
Jackson Street
Middleboro MA

MAILING ADDRESS:
Box 272
Middleboro MA 02346

no telephone

SEE: NUCMC, 1959-61.

Questionnaire not returned.

MILTON

MA554-530

Robert Bennett Forbes House
Archives
215 Adams Street
Milton MA 02186

(617) 696-1815

OPEN: by appointment only
COPYING FACILITIES: yes
MATERIALS SOLICITED: Written or audible documents, photographs, and maps relating to U.S. trade with China, 1784-1912. Will also accept similar materials relating to European trade with China until 1912 and to U.S. trade with other East Asian countries, as well as copies of documents of U.S.-China trade.

HOLDINGS:
Total volume: 43 l.f.; 3,000 items
Inclusive dates: 1768 - 1930
Description: Materials concerning U.S. trade with China in the late 18th century and the 19th century. Documents include personal and business letters, account books, maps, log books, diaries, and other papers of Americans indirectly or directly involved in the trade. Photographs include records of China and Japan and of American traders, in the 19th century and the first decade of the 20th century.

SEE: Leventhal and Mooney - I.

MOUNT HERMON

MA568-560

Northfield Mount Hermon School
Mount Hermon Libraries
Mount Hermon MA

MAILING ADDRESS:
P.O. Box 200
Mount Hermon MA 01354

(413) 498-5311, Ext. 443

OPEN: M-F 8-10, Sa 11-3, Su 1:30-10; closed holidays and school vacations, including summers
ACCESS: permission of Librarian and/or Archivist required
COPYING FACILITIES: yes
MATERIALS SOLICITED: Will accept materials pertaining to the history of the Northfield Mount Hermon School and its alumni.

HOLDINGS:
Total volume: 150 boxes
Inclusive dates: 1879 -
Description: Material relating to the history of Mount Hermon School, its founder Dwight L. Moody, and Northfield Mount Hermon School.

NANTUCKET

MA572-540

Nantucket Maria Mitchell Association
Science Library
Maria Mitchell Memorabilia
2 Vestal Street
Nantucket MA 02554

(617) 228-9198

OPEN: June - Sept., M-F 10-5, Sa 10-noon; winter hours M-Th 2-5; closed Sundays and holidays
COPYING FACILITIES: no

HOLDINGS:
Total volume: 70 items; 9 l.f.; 9 microfilm reels
Inclusive dates: 1838 - 1880
Description: A collection of correspondence, diaries, lecture notes, meteorological and astronomical observations belonging to Maria Mitchell, America's first woman astronomer. The collection concerns her work in astronomy and her views on life with emphasis on education for women.

SEE: Hinding.

MA572-560

Nantucket Historical Association
Peter Foulger Museum
Library
Broad Street
Nantucket MA

MAILING ADDRESS:
Box 1016
Nantucket MA 02554

(617) 228-1894

OPEN: M-F 10-4; closed weekends and holidays
COPYING FACILITIES: yes
MATERIALS SOLICITED: Whaling, Nantucket, and maritime history.

HOLDINGS:
Total volume: 1,000 l.f.
Inclusive dates: 1650 -
Description: Logbooks, manuscripts, and other materials relating to whaling, Nantucket, and maritime history.

SEE: Hamer.

SEE ALSO: Robert O. Collins and Peter Duignan, *Americans in Africa* (Hoover Institution, 1963).

NATICK

MA576-520

Morse Institute
Library
14 East Central Street
Natick MA 01760

(617) 651-7300

OPEN: M, Tu, Th, Sa 9-6, W, F 9-9; closed Sundays, holidays, and Saturdays during July-Aug.
COPYING FACILITIES: yes
MATERIALS SOLICITED: Materials related to Natick history.

HOLDINGS:
Total volume: 40 l.f.; 15 microfilm reels
Inclusive dates: late 18th century -
Description: Photographs, early maps, vital records of the town on microfilm, papers of individuals, and biographical material.

SEE: Hamer.

NEEDHAM

MA580-550

Needham Free Public Library
Laura G. Willgoose Archives Room
1139 Highland Avenue
Needham MA 02194

(617) 444-0087

OPEN: M-Th 9-9, F, Sa 9-5:30; Su 2-5 Nov.-March; closed weekends Memorial Day-Labor Day, and closed other holidays; archives by appointment only
ACCESS: advance arrangements required
COPYING FACILITIES: yes
MATERIALS SOLICITED: Material pertaining to the history of Needham.

HOLDINGS:
Total volume: 63 l.f.
Inclusive dates: 1711 -
Description: Maps, manuscripts, church records, diaries, town reports, pictures, records of the assessors and selectmen, and other documents pertaining to the history of the town of Needham.

MA580-570

Needham Historical Society, Inc.
53 Glendoon Road
Needham MA 02192

(617) 444-3181

OPEN: Monday evenings 7:30-9; weekends by appointment; closed other times
COPYING FACILITIES: no
MATERIALS SOLICITED: Records and historical materials of the town of Needham. Will also accept historical materials relating to the Needham area.

HOLDINGS:
Total volume: not specified
Inclusive dates: 1711 -
Description: Materials relating to the history of Needham, including town records, maps, photographs, journals, manuscripts, and other materials.

NEW BEDFORD

MA584-550

New Bedford Free Public Library
Melville Whaling Room Collection
613 Pleasant Street
New Bedford MA 02740

(617) 999-6291

OPEN: M-Sa 9-5; closed Sundays and holidays
COPYING FACILITIES: yes

MATERIALS SOLICITED: Materials relating to American whaling, geographical areas affected by whaling, and the history and genealogy of southeastern New England and Long Island. Will also accept material on 19th century shipping, the history of American sea warfare prior to the 20th century, and the *Alabama* claims.

HOLDINGS:
Total volume: 90,000 items
Inclusive dates: 1767 - 1925
Description: Whaling manuscripts relating primarily to the port of New Bedford. Included are logbooks, account books, letter books, and other materials related to the whaling industry; Custom House records, including crew lists, manifests, bonds, oaths, and enrollments; and miscellaneous letters and papers of individuals and ships employed in the whaling industry.

SEE: NUCMC, 1972.

SEE: Schatz; Robbins.

SEE ALSO: Reginald B. Hegarty, comp., *A List of Log Books of Whaling Voyages in the Collection of the Melville Room in the Free Public Library, New Bedford, Massachusetts* (New Bedford Free Public Library, 1963).

MA584-600

Old Dartmouth Historical Society
18 Johnny Cake Hill
New Bedford MA 02740

(617) 997-0046

OPEN: M-F 9-5, Saturdays by appointment; closed Sundays and holidays
COPYING FACILITIES: yes
MATERIALS SOLICITED: History of American whaling and local history. Will also accept European whaling material.

HOLDINGS:
Total volume: 750 l.f.; 10 file drawers; 1,800 microfilm reels; 15,000 photographic negatives; 2,000 photographs
Inclusive dates: 1712 - 1930
Description: Over 1,000 logbooks and journals as well as whaling agents' account books and records; correspondence, diaries, business and financial records pertaining to the history of New Bedford and its surrounding towns. Microfilm holdings reflect acquisition of International Marine Archives, Inc., formerly of Nantucket; copies of logbooks, journals, correspondence, and accounts in U.S. and foreign institutions and in private hands.

SEE: Hamer; NUCMC, 1959-61.

SEE: Duignan; Allard, Crawley, and Edmison.

SEE ALSO: *Checklist of Logbooks in the Collection of the New Bedford Whaling Museum* (Oct. 1980); Morris Rieger, 'Africa-Related Papers of Persons and Organizations in the United States,' *African Studies Bulletin* 8 (Dec. 1965).

The repository currently holds all manuscript and archival materials formerly at the International Marine Ar-

chives, Inc. (MA572-360 in first edition).

NEWTON

MA590-400

The Jackson Homestead
Historical Center and Community Museum
527 Washington Street
Newton MA 02158

(617) 552-7238

OPEN: M-F 8-4; closed weekends and holidays
COPYING FACILITIES: yes
MATERIALS SOLICITED: Materials relating to Newton history, including family papers of Newton residents or former residents, such as wills, deeds, diaries, and journals; business papers; club and organization records; and photographs.

HOLDINGS:
Total volume: 40 l.f.
Inclusive dates: 1700 -
Description: Materials relating to Newton history, including diaries, journals, correspondence, accounts, copybooks, and wills. There are records of Newton churches, clubs, and organizations, and photographs of buildings and people. The bulk of the material is from the second half of the 19th century.

SEE: NUCMC, 1959-61.

SEE: Novotny.

MA590-570

Newton Free Library
414 Centre Street
Newton MA 02158

(617) 552-7152

OPEN: M-Th 9-9, F 9-6, Sa 9-5, Su 1-5; closed holidays and mid-June - mid-Sept.
ACCESS: no public access to uncatalogued material
COPYING FACILITIES: yes
MATERIALS SOLICITED: Materials relating to the city of Newton including archives and non-current records of institutions and organizations, visual documents, such as photographs, videotapes, oral history tapes; sound recordings; and scrapbooks containing the types of materials mentioned above. Will also accept material including diaries, journals, genealogical source data, and literary manuscripts relating to the city of Newton, and her people.

HOLDINGS:
Total volume: 500 vols.
Inclusive dates: 1856 -
Description: Records, reports and scrapbooks from Newton institutions, organizations, and government agencies; a photograph collection, including glass plates, circa 1900; oral history interviews; and four sound recordings and videotapes.

SEE: Hinding.

MA590-720

Swedenborg School of Religion
Library
48 Sargent Street
Newton MA 02158

(617) 244-0504

OPEN: by appointment only
ACCESS: at the discretion of the faculty
COPYING FACILITIES: yes
MATERIALS SOLICITED: Materials relating to Emanuel Swedenborg; materials written by Swedenborgians; records of Swedenborgian churches, groups, and other organizations. Will also accept materials useful in the Swedenborg School of Religion.

HOLDINGS:
Total volume: not specified
Inclusive dates: 1790 -
Description: Sermon manuscripts; minutes, reports, and letters concerning the activities of Swedenborgian church organizations; and photographs, architectural plans, personal letters, genealogies, birth, marriage, and death records, all relating to Swedenborgians.

SEE: Schatz.

NEWTON CENTRE

MA593-40

Andover Newton Theological School
Library
169 Herrick Road
Newton Centre MA 02159

(617) 964-1100, Ext. 251

OPEN: M-F 8:30-4:30; closed weekends and holidays
COPYING FACILITIES: yes
MATERIALS SOLICITED: New England Baptist church records and United Church of Christ and Congregational church materials. Will also accept any manuscript material complementary to scope of the repository.

HOLDINGS:
Total volume: 250 l.f.
Inclusive dates: 1715 -
Description: New England Baptist and Congregational church records and personal papers of clergy. Also included are the archives of Andover Theological Seminary, the Newton Theological Institution, Andover Newton Theological School, the American Baptist churches of Massachusetts, the Society of Brethren, and the Society of Inquiry.

SEE: Hamer; NUCMC, 1959-61.

SEE: Hinding; Robbins.

NORTH AMHERST

MA603-560
New England Quaker Research
Library
Mt. Toby Friends Meetinghouse
Leverett MA

MAILING ADDRESS:
P.O. Box 655
North Amherst MA 01059

(617) 549-1226

OPEN: Su 9:30-1, and by appointment
COPYING FACILITIES: no
MATERIALS SOLICITED: Materials relating
to Quakers. Will also accept materials
pertaining to Quaker concerns, such as
way of life, religion, God, prayer, medi-
tation, pacifism, civil liberties, race relations, feminism, prisons, and poverty.

HOLDINGS:
Total volume: 2 file drawers
Inclusive dates: 1800 -
Description: 19th century letters, and
20th century correspondence by Quakers
who were members of the Mt. Toby
(Middle Connecticut Valley) Monthly
Meeting of Friends.

NORTH ANDOVER

MA606-530
Museum of American Textile History
800 Massachusetts Avenue
North Andover MA 01845

(617) 686-0191

OPEN: Tu-F 9-5; closed Mondays and
weekends
COPYING FACILITIES: yes
MATERIALS SOLICITED: Textile industry
business records such as account books,
correspondence, production records,
engineering reports, architectural
drawings and photographs from mills,
selling agents, consulting firms, machinery manufacturers and industry associations; also correspondence, diaries
and literary or scientific manuscripts
from individuals active in the industry.

HOLDINGS:
Total volume: 1,560 l.f.; 25,000 items
Inclusive dates: 1810 - 1970
Description: Materials on the American
textile industry, especially in New England, and related developments abroad.
Included are business records of textile
manufacturing companies, textile machinery manufacturers, textile trade associations, engineering consultants, and water
power developers; papers of inventors,
weavers, dyers, chemists, and students of
textile technology; architectural, engineering, and technical drawings; and photographs. Subjects covered include textile
technology, mill architecture and power
engineering, textile trading and marketing, tariffs, raw materials, labor, and
workers' housing.
Also held are the collections of the
North Andover Historical Society, relating chiefly to the local history of Andover
and North Andover.

SEE: NUCMC, 1969, 71.

SEE: Hinding.

SEE ALSO: the following publications of
the Museum: *Business Manuscripts in
the Merrimack Valley Textile Museum*
(1969); *Minor Manuscript Holdings*
(1971); *Checklist of Prints, Drawings
and Paintings in the Merrimack Valley
Textile Museum, Part One: Maps,
Plans, and Town Views* (1972) and *Part
Two: Mills and Factories* (1973).

Also, *Part Three: Textile Technology* (1980).

MA606-560
North Andover Historical Society
153 Academy Road
North Andover MA 01845

(617) 686-4035

OPEN: Tu-F 9-5; closed Mondays,
weekends, Christmas, New Year's, and
Easter
COPYING FACILITIES: yes
MATERIALS SOLICITED: Materials relating
to North Andover history, or Andover
before 1855, including photographs,
correspondence, diaries or journals,
maps, account books, architectural information, business, church, or club
records.

HOLDINGS:
Total volume: 60 l.f.
Inclusive dates: 1650 -
Description: Deeds, letters, journals,
documents, photographs, and other material relating to North Andover history
and surrounding area, including records
of local organizations and churches, local
architectural information, and microfilm
of early town records.

MA606-720
Stevens Memorial Library
345 Main Street
North Andover MA

MAILING ADDRESS:
P.O. Box 8
North Andover MA 01845

(617) 682-6260

OPEN: M-Th 9-9, F, Sa 9-5, Su 2-5;
closed holidays, and weekends
July-August
COPYING FACILITIES: yes
MATERIALS SOLICITED: Anne Bradstreet,
the Bradstreet family, the Stevens fam-
ily, and the history and genealogy of
North Andover and Essex County, MA.

HOLDINGS:
Total volume: 80 l.f.; 800 items
Inclusive dates: 1644 -
Description: Manuscript works and a
journal of poet Anne Bradstreet, materials pertaining to the Bradstreet family,
and slides on the poet's English background; a scrapbook on Walter and Louise Stevens Arensberg, genealogical
sources, and other Stevens family materials.
North Andover history materials, including photographs, an aerial view of the
town, oral history, interviews with senior
citizens, genealogical materials on the
Appleton, Bailey, Johnson, and Tucker
families, a tape of graveside services and
readings from poet Richard Hovey, and

letters of Phillips Brooks; and materials
concerning the Stevens Memorial Library, including records, letters, and photographs of construction.

SEE: Hinding.

NORTH DARTMOUTH

MA612-720
Southeastern Massachusetts
University
Library Communication Center
Archives and Special Collections
Old Wesport Road
North Dartmouth MA

MAILING ADDRESS:
Old Westport Road
P.O. Box 6
North Dartmouth MA 02747

(617) 999-8686

OPEN: M-F 8:30-4:00; closed weekends
COPYING FACILITIES: yes
MATERIALS SOLICITED: Records pertain-
ing to the history of the New Bedford
Textile Institute, the Bradford Durfee
Textile Institute, and the Southeastern
Massachusetts Technological
Institute/Southeastern Massachusetts
University, including business records,
minutes of meetings, and information
about administrators, faculty, and
alumni. Will also accept materials relat-
ing to the Bristol County, MA area.

HOLDINGS:
Total volume: not specified
Inclusive dates: 1890 -
Description: Records of New Bedford
Textile Institute, Bradford Durfee Textile
Institute, Southeastern Massachusetts
Technological Institute/Southeastern Mas-
sachusetts University, including corre-
spondence, account books, financial
records, photographs and biographical in-
formation relating to administrators, fac-
ulty, and alumni of the three colleges.

NORTH EASTON

MA615-80
Borderland State Park
Massapoag Avenue
North Easton MA 02356

(617) 238-6566

OPEN: by appointment only
USER FEES: $2 seasonal State Park
parking fee
ACCESS: Prior arrangements must be
made with the Massachusetts
Department of Environmental
Management, Supervisor of
Interpretive Services, 100 Cambridge
Street, Boston, MA 02202.
COPYING FACILITIES: no
MATERIALS SOLICITED: Materials relating
to the Ames and Butler families, including correspondence, account books,
business papers, appointment books,
pocket diaries, household accounts,
bills, financial records, miscellaneous
papers and documents, and photographs.

HOLDINGS:
  Total volume: 22 file drawers; 90 boxes
  Inclusive dates: 1840 - 1969
  Description: Records and papers relating to Blanche Ames Ames, Oakes Ames, and the social, political, military, and scientific activities of the Ames and Butler families, including Civil War general Benjamin F. Butler.

MA615-710
Stonehill College
Arnold B. Tofias Industrial Archives
Donahue Hall
320 Washington Street
North Easton MA 02357

(617) 238-1081, Ext. 396

OPEN: M-F 8:30-4:30 during academic year; closed weekends and holidays
ACCESS: by appointment only
COPYING FACILITIES: yes

HOLDINGS:
  Total volume: 2,000 l.f.
  Inclusive dates: 1774 - 1956
  Description: Records and correspondence of the Ames Shovel Company, including material on the building of the Union Pacific Railroad.

SEE ALSO: a brochure, 'The Arnold B. Tofias Industrial Archives at Stonehill College, Easton, Massachusetts,' available from the institution.

MA615-720
Stonehill College
Cushing-Martin Library
Joseph W. Martin Collection
Washington Street
North Easton MA 02357

(617) 238-1081, Ext. 328

OPEN: M-Th 8-10:30, F 8-5, Sa 10-5, Su 1-10:30; shorter summer hours; closed holidays
COPYING FACILITIES: yes

HOLDINGS:
  Total volume: 14,000 items
  Inclusive dates: 1912 - 1968
  Description: Manuscripts relating chiefly to the political career of Joseph W. Martin, Speaker and Minority Leader, U.S. House of Representatives, 1939-59.

SEE ALSO: unpublished finding aids available at the institution.

MA615-730
Stonehill College
Michael Novak Papers
Donahue Hall
320 Washington Street
North Easton MA 02357

(617) 238-1081, Ext. 396

OPEN: M-F 8:30-4:30 during academic year; closed weekends and holidays
ACCESS: Michael Novak's permission required
COPYING FACILITIES: yes

HOLDINGS:
  Total volume: 110 l.f.
  Inclusive dates: 1955 -
  Description: Materials related to Michael Novak, a philosopher, author, journalist, and professor of philosophy and religious studies. Included are drafts of manuscripts, correspondence, interviews, contracts and political papers.

NORTHAMPTON

MA624-240
Forbes Library
20 West Street
Northampton MA 01060

(413) 584-8399

OPEN: Tu-Sa 9-5, minor holidays 1-5; closed Sundays, Mondays, and major holidays
ACCESS: researchers on doctoral candidate level and above
COPYING FACILITIES: yes
MATERIALS SOLICITED: History of Northampton, Hampshire County, and western Massachusetts. Local authors and notables. Genealogical works and material relating to western Massachusetts. Calvin Coolidge material.

HOLDINGS:
  Total volume: 900 vols.; 25,000 items
  Inclusive dates: 1661 -
  Description: Sylvester Judd manuscript on the Connecticut Valley consisting of 60 manuscript volumes of genealogical, historical, and antiquarian researches, particularly with reference to the towns of Hampshire County, but extending also to the whole state of Massachusetts and that of Connecticut.

SEE: Hamer; NUCMC, 1962, 64, 68.

SEE: Hinding; Leventhal and Mooney - I; Robbins; Schatz.

SEE ALSO: A descriptive brochure on the Calvin Coolidge Memorial Room is available from the Library. Finding aids to the Judd manuscript may be used at the Library.

MA624-560
Northampton Historical Society
46 Bridge Street
Northampton MA 01060

(413) 584-6011

OPEN: M-F 9-5; closed weekends and holidays
ACCESS: college age and above; prefer accredited scholars
COPYING FACILITIES: no
MATERIALS SOLICITED: Materials relating to Northampton history.

HOLDINGS:
  Total volume: not specified
  Inclusive dates: 1659 -
  Description: Materials relating to the history of Northampton, including wills, court records, deeds, correspondence, account books, indenture articles, receipts, Revolutionary War discharge warrants, Civil War documents, travel notebooks, marriage certificates, architectural blueprints, surveyors' drawings, military materials from World War I, and pho-

tographs, including 700 glass plate negatives.

SEE: Hamer.

SEE: Hinding.

MA624-700
Smith College
Archives
Northhampton MA 01063

(413) 584-2700, 2970

OPEN: M-F 9-5; closed weekends and holidays
ACCESS: high school age or above; accredited scholars preferred
COPYING FACILITIES: yes
MATERIALS SOLICITED: Archives of Smith College, including official College records and publications, academic and administrative department files, buildings and grounds records, faculty files, alumnae records and memorabilia, and records of student activities.

HOLDINGS:
  Total volume: 1,400 l.f.
  Inclusive dates: 1871 -
  Description: Materials documenting the history, organization, and development of the College, including records of its founders, presidents, administrators, faculty, academic and administrative departments, student activities, alumnae association, graduate schools, intercollegiate activities, and buildings and grounds.

SEE: Hinding.

MA624-740
Smith College
The Sophia Smith Collection
Northampton MA 01063

(413) 584-2970

OPEN: M-F 9-5; summer M-F 8-4; closed weekends and holidays
ACCESS: high school age or above; prefer accredited scholars
COPYING FACILITIES: yes
MATERIALS SOLICITED: Manuscript sources relating to women, especially in the following subject areas: birth control, civil rights, education, government, humanities, fine arts, industry, the professions, peace, religion, suffrage, women's rights, and women's liberation. Will also accept late 19th- and 20th-century photographs relating to women and their activities.

HOLDINGS:
  Total volume: 2,067 l.f.
  Inclusive dates: 1794 -
  Description: Materials documenting the history, status, and role of women throughout the world, with emphasis on the United States. Included are papers of the Ames, Garrison, and Hale families; personal papers of such women as Margaret H. Sanger, Carrie Chapman Catt, Ellen Gates Starr, Mary Van Kleeck, and Ruth Frances Woodsmall; and other items relating to such subject areas as birth control, women's rights, peace, suffrage, religion, and the arts.

GUIDES: *Manuscript, Subject, and Author Catalogs of the Sophia Smith Collection (Women's History Archive)* (G. K. Hall, 1975).

SEE: Hamer; NUCMC, 1967, 69, 71, 77.

SEE: Meckler and McMullin; Novotny; Schatz; Krichmar; Robbins; Hinding.

SEE ALSO: Published catalogs of the Sophia Smith Collection are available.

MA624-750
Smith College
William Allan Neilson Library
Rare Book Room
Northampton MA 01063

(413) 584-2910

OPEN: M-F 9-5; closed weekends and holidays
COPYING FACILITIES: yes

HOLDINGS:
> *Total volume:* 17,500 items
> *Inclusive dates:* 1325 - 1975
> *Description:* A general collection of letters, historical documents, and literary manuscripts supportive of the printed books collection, principally English and American in orientation.

SEE: Hamer; NUCMC, 1969.

SEE: Hinding; Robbins.

NORTHBOROUGH

MA627-560
Northborough Historical Society, Inc.
52 Main Street
Northborough MA

MAILING ADDRESS:
P.O. Box 661
Northborough MA 01532

no telephone

OPEN: by appointment only; closed holidays and during winter months
COPYING FACILITIES: no
MATERIALS SOLICITED: Items and papers relating to present and past Northborough residents.

HOLDINGS:
> *Total volume:* 300 items
> *Inclusive dates:* 1750's -
> *Description:* Materials relating to Northborough, including diaries of former residents, deeds, genealogical materials, and records of town organizations.

SEE: Hamer; NUCMC, 1968.

SEE: Schatz; Davis.

NORTON

MA636-880
Wheaton College
Library
College Archives
Norton MA 02766

(617) 285-7722, Ext. 513

OPEN: M-F 8:30-4:30, other times by appointment; closed weekends and holidays
COPYING FACILITIES: yes
MATERIALS SOLICITED: Records from College administrative offices, academic departments, and faculty committees; alumnae publications, correspondence, diaries and class letters; and College history.

HOLDINGS:
> *Total volume:* 290 l.f.
> *Inclusive dates:* 1721 -
> *Description:* Archives of Wheaton College, including official college records and publications, administrative department files, records and photographs of student and faculty organizations and activities, student and faculty notes and papers; alumni records, photographs, and other memorabilia; Wheaton family records including correspondence, deeds and financial material; manuscripts, class notes, diaries, and correspondence of Lucy Larcom.
> Other holdings include senior honors theses, and tapes of lectures by Eleanor Roosevelt, Kurt Vonnegut, Jr., Jessamyn West, and others.

SEE: Schatz; Robbins; Hinding.

NORWOOD

MA642-560
Norwood Historical Society
93 Day Street
Norwood MA

MAILING ADDRESS:
135 Day Street
Norwood MA 02062

(617) 762-9197

OPEN: by appointment
USER FEES: nominal
COPYING FACILITIES: no
MATERIALS SOLICITED: Correspondence and photographs. Will also accept records of community groups.

HOLDINGS:
> *Total volume:* 6 l.f.
> *Inclusive dates:* 1890 - 1930
> *Description:* A collection of letters and other materials relating to photography.

OXFORD

MA654-590
Oxford Free Public Library
Oxford Museum
339 Main Street
Oxford MA 01540

(617) 987-2882

OPEN: M 10-1, Tu-F 10-8, Sa 10-4; closed Sundays and holidays, Saturdays during summer
COPYING FACILITIES: yes
MATERIALS SOLICITED: Will accept manuscripts, photographs, materials on Clara Barton, Elliott P. Joslin, the Nipmuck Indians, and Huguenot emigration to Massachusetts, and genealogies. Will also accept Nipmuck Indian artifacts, old postcards of Oxford, maps and pictures.

HOLDINGS:
> *Total volume:* 1,000 vols.
> *Inclusive dates:* 1800 -
> *Description:* Materials relating to Oxford history, including town, school, and business records; materials on Clara Barton and Elliott P. Joslin; genealogical data; and photographs of the town.

PEABODY

MA662-640
Peabody Historical Society
35 Washington Street
Peabody MA 01960

no telephone

SEE: Hamer.

Questionnaire not returned.

PETERSHAM

MA673-640
Petersham Historical Society, Inc.
North Main Street
Petersham MA 01366

(617) 724-3380

OPEN: by appointment only
COPYING FACILITIES: yes
MATERIALS SOLICITED: Local history; genealogy relating to Petersham residents; and material on Shay's Rebellion.

HOLDINGS:
> *Total volume:* 24 files
> *Inclusive dates:* 1738 -
> *Description:* Material relating to the history of Petersham, including church, town, and school records. There is also material on Shay's Rebellion; genealogical data relating to Petersham families; photographs of local houses with supporting documentation on their owners; cemetery records; military records; and business records relating to straw hats, blacksmithing, and mercantile activities.

SEE: Hamer; NUCMC, 1959-61.

SEE: Davis.

PITTSFIELD

MA677-70

Berkshire Athenaeum
Local History and Literature Services
1 Wendell Avenue
Pittsfield MA 01201

(413) 499-9480

OPEN: M-Th 10-9, F, Sa 10-5; closed
   Sundays and holidays
ACCESS: qualified researchers
COPYING FACILITIES: yes
MATERIALS SOLICITED: Herman Mel-
   ville, Berkshire region authors, Shakers,
   Berkshire County in the Revolutionary
   War, industrial history of Berkshire
   County, oral history, and genealogical
   source data. Will also accept non-
   current records of Berkshire County in-
   stitutions and organizations, visual doc-
   uments, and microforms.

HOLDINGS:
   Total volume: 3,240 items
   Inclusive dates: 1761 -
   Description: Materials relating to the
   history and culture of the Berkshire region of Massachusetts. Holdings focus on
   Herman Melville, the Berkshire literary
   tradition, the American Shaker movement, the industrial development of Berkshire County, and the colonial and Revolutionary War period in the Berkshires.
   Included are records of organizations,
   miscellaneous manuscripts, and audio-
   visual materials.

SEE: Hamer.

SEE: Leventhal and Mooney - I; Robbins.

SEE ALSO: Jay Leyda, ed., *The Melville
   Log* (Gordian Press, 1969); Mary L.
   Richmond, comp., *Shaker Literature: A
   Bibliography* (Univ. Press of New Eng-
   land, 1977).

MA677-720

Hancock Shaker Village, Inc.
U.S. Route 20
Pittsfield MA

MAILING ADDRESS:
P.O. Box 898
Pittsfield MA 02360

(413) 447-7284

OPEN: M, W, F 10-4; closed other days
   and holidays
ACCESS: serious researchers only; written
   permission of the Director is required
COPYING FACILITIES: no
MATERIALS SOLICITED: Manuscripts and
   records relating to the Shaker communities at Hancock, MA, Enfield, CT,
   and Tyringham, MA; visual documents
   relating to these communities; and oral
   history interviews with former Shakers.
   Will also accept materials relating to
   other utopian organizations and groups,
   such as the Moravians, the Oneida
   Community, the Swedish community
   at Bishop Hill, Mormons, and Harmo-
   nists, and utopian studies and history.

HOLDINGS:
   Total volume: 500 items
   Inclusive dates: 1780 -
   Description: Manuscripts relating to
   the United Society of Believers (Shakers)
   at Hancock and 11 other eastern United
   States communitarian settlements. Included are letters, diaries, business records
   (primarily from the New Lebanon, NY,
   community), and articles of organization
   and instruction.

SEE: Hinding.

PLYMOUTH

MA685-520

Mayflower Society House
4 Winslow Street
Plymouth MA

MAILING ADDRESS:
P.O. Box 297
Plymouth MA 02360

(617) 746-2590

OPEN: daily 9-4; closed mid-Sept. -
   Memorial Day
USER FEES: nominal admission
ACCESS: morning hours are primarily for
   members only; non-members are
   welcome in the afternoon
COPYING FACILITIES: yes
MATERIALS SOLICITED: Material relating
   to Mayflower descendants, Ralph Waldo Emerson, the Winslow family, and
   early American history.

HOLDINGS:
   Total volume: 6 items
   Inclusive dates: 1599 - 1914
   Description: 17th century American
   documents, pertaining to the Mayflower
   and the various owners of the Edward
   Winslow House. There is also a copy of
   the rough draft of the Declaration of Independence.

MA685-630

The Pilgrim Society
75 Court Street
Plymouth MA 02360

(617) 746-1620

OPEN: by appointment only M-F
   9:30-4:30; closed Christmas and New
   Year's
COPYING FACILITIES: yes
MATERIALS SOLICITED: Materials relating
   to the history of Plymouth and the Pilgrims. Will also accept materials relating to nearby towns.

HOLDINGS:
   Total volume: 6,000 vols.; 9,200
   manuscripts, maps, prints, etc.
   Inclusive dates: 1594 -
   Description: Materials by and about
   the Pilgrims, and materials relating to
   Plymouth and its inhabitants, organiza-
   tions, agencies, and industries.

GUIDES: Charlotte S. Price, *A Guide to
   Manuscripts of the Pilgrim Society*
   (1976), available at cost from the Society.

SEE: NUCMC, 1978.

SEE: Robbins.

SEE ALSO: Lawrence D. Geller, *Between
   Concord and Plymouth: The Transcen-
   dentalists and the Watsons, with the
   Hillside Collection of Manuscripts*
   (Pilgrim Society, 1973).

MA685-640

Plimoth Plantation
Research Department
Warren Avenue
Plymouth MA

MAILING ADDRESS:
Box 1620
Plymouth MA 02360

(617) 746-1622

OPEN: M-F 9-4; closed weekends and
   holidays
ACCESS: by written request
COPYING FACILITIES: yes

HOLDINGS:
   Total volume: 9 files
   Inclusive dates: 1631 - 1686
   Description: Photocopies and type-
   scripts of wills and inventories of Plym-
   outh Colony.

QUINCY

MA697-680

Quincy Historical Society
Library and Museum
8 Adams Street
Quincy MA 02169

(617) 773-1144

OPEN: W 9:30-3:30, Sa 12:30-3:30; also
   by appointment; closed holidays
COPYING FACILITIES: yes
MATERIALS SOLICITED: Materials relating
   to Quincy and the surrounding area.

HOLDINGS:
   Total volume: 6 l.f.; 12 file drawers
   Inclusive dates: 1620 -
   Description: Deeds, maps, unpublished
   literary and historical manuscripts, genealogical data, account books, journals,
   tapes, and other materials relating to the
   history of Quincy and its environs.

READING

MA705-680

Reading Antiquarian Society
103 Washington Street
Reading MA

MAILING ADDRESS:
26 Vine Street
Reading MA 01867

(617) 944-5051

OPEN: Su 2-5 May-Nov.
COPYING FACILITIES: no
MATERIALS SOLICITED: Materials related
   to the history of Reading.

HOLDINGS:
Total volume: 16 l.f.
Inclusive dates: 1706 -
Description: Manuscripts and photographs relating to the history of Reading.

SEE: Hamer; NUCMC, 1959-61.

REHOBOTH

MA708-40

Annawan Historical Society of
Rehoboth
Rehoboth MA

MAILING ADDRESS:
P.O. Box 71
Rehoboth MA 02769

(617) 669-6464

OPEN: by appointment only
COPYING FACILITIES: no
MATERIALS SOLICITED: Historical and genealogical materials relating to Rehoboth. Will also accept other materials.

HOLDINGS:
Total volume: 100 items
Inclusive dates: 1771 - 1940
Description: Records of individuals and organizations in Rehoboth, chiefly dating from the 19th century. Included are annual school reports, copies of Oak Swamp Baptist Church records, Town of Rehoboth financial records, and a record book of Lemuel Morse, 1800-40.

REVERE

MA711-690

Revere Public Library
Revere MA 02151

no telephone

SEE: Hamer.

Questionnaire not returned.

ROYALSTON

MA725-320

Royalston Village Improvement and
Historical Society
Society Building-The Common
Royalston MA

MAILING ADDRESS:
Fernald Road
South Royalston MA 01331

(617) 249-2598, 2081

OPEN: by appointment only
ACCESS: appointment required
COPYING FACILITIES: no
MATERIALS SOLICITED: Logs, ledgers, journals, and diaries of Royalston activities.

HOLDINGS:
Total volume: 8 c.f.
Inclusive dates: mid 1800's -
Description: Financial records of local business, original handwritten sermons of local clergy, a few town records, and some correspondence.

MA725-640

Phinehas S. Newton Library
Main Street
Royalston MA 01368

(617) 249-3572

OPEN: Tu, Th 1-8:30, Sa 9-noon; closed other days and holidays
COPYING FACILITIES: no

HOLDINGS:
Total volume: 3 vols.
Inclusive dates: 1914 - 1916
Description: Addresses and papers of Fred Wilder Cross, representative to the General Court, 1914-16.

SALEM

MA733-210

Essex Institute
James Duncan Phillips Library
132 Essex Street
Salem MA 01970

(617) 744-3390

OPEN: M-F 9-4:30; closed weekends and holidays
USER FEES: free to members of Essex Institute and residents of Salem; all others $1.25.
ACCESS: must be over 18 years of age
COPYING FACILITIES: yes
MATERIALS SOLICITED: Materials relating to early New England shipping and Essex County artists, authors, businesses, clubs, churches, schools, charitable organizations, and residents.

HOLDINGS:
Total volume: 4,000 l.f.
Inclusive dates: 1630 -
Description: Documents relating to the maritime history of Massachusetts, including 1,850 logbooks and sea journals; customs records of Salem, Marblehead, Beverly, Newburyport, Ipswich, and Gloucester; entrances and clearances of Boston and Essex County ports, 1686-1765; and materials relating to trade with China, India, West Africa, the West Indies, and other ports. There are also papers relating to Essex County families; collections of genealogies, sermons, maps, photographs, all of Essex County; and records of county churches, clubs, businesses, charitable organizations, and schools.

SEE: Hamer; NUCMC, 1962, 67, 71, 73, 78, 80.

SEE: Allard, Crawley, and Edmison; Bean and Vane; Hinding; Ingram; Leventhal and Mooney - I; Robbins.

SEE ALSO: Walter Schatz, ed., *Directory of Afro-American Resources* (Bowker, 1970); G. Bhagat, 'Materials Relating to Eighteenth and Nineteenth Century Indo-American Trade and Consular Relations in Private Archives in the United States,' *Indian Archives* 17 (Jan. 1967/Dec. 1968); Robert O. Collins and Peter Duignan, *Americans in Af-*

rica (Hoover Institution, 1963); Ann Novotny, ed., *Picture Sources 3* (Special Libraries Assn., 1975); Jerome Handler, *A Guide to Source Materials for the Study of Barbados History* (Southern Illinois Univ. Press, 1971).

Morris Rieger, 'Africa-Related Papers of Persons and Organizations in the United States,' *African Studies Bulletin* 8 (Dec. 1965); Norman R. Bennett, George E. Brooks, and Alan R. Booth, 'Materials for African History,' *African Studies Bulletin* 5 (Oct. 1962); annual reports of the Institute in the *Essex Institute Historical Collections*. Finding aids for individual collections are available at the Institute.

Richard C. Davis, *North American Forest History: A Guide to Archives and Manuscripts in the United States and Canada* (Clio Books, 1977).

MA733-660

Peabody Museum of Salem
Phillips Library
East India Square
Salem MA 01970

(617) 745-1876

OPEN: M-F 10-4:30; closed weekends and holidays
USER FEES: $1.50 per week
COPYING FACILITIES: yes
MATERIALS SOLICITED: Ethnology of the Pacific islands and maritime history of New England. Will also accept material relating to the natural history of Essex County.

HOLDINGS:
Total volume: 900 l.f.
Inclusive dates: late 1700's -
Description: 2,500 logbooks, journals and account books; 2,000 boxes of papers on Salem shipbuilding and trade with Africa, the Far East and Pacific islands. Other holdings relate to North American Indians.

SEE: Hamer; NUCMC, 1972.

SEE: Allard, Crawley, and Edmison; Ingram; Martin; Hinding.

SEE ALSO: Morris Rieger, 'Africa-Related Papers of Persons and Organizations in the United States,' *African Studies Bulletin* 8 (Dec. 1965); Robert O. Collins and Peter Duignan, *Americans in Africa* (Hoover Institution, 1963); Peter Duignan, *Handbook of American Resources for African Studies* (Hoover Institution, 1967); Walter Schatz, ed., *Directory of Afro-American Resources* (Bowker, 1970); G. Bhagat, 'Materials Relating to Eighteenth and Nineteenth Century Indo-American Trade and Consular Relations in Private Archives in the United States,' *Indian Archives* 17 (Jan. 1967/Dec. 1968); Norman R. Bennett, George E. Brooks, and Alan R. Booth, 'Materials for African History,' *African Studies Bulletin* 5 (Oct. 1962).

Richard C. Davis, *North American Forest History: A Guide to Archives and Manuscripts in the United States and Canada* (Clio Books, 1977).

SANDWICH

MA738-700
Sandwich Archives & Historical
  Center
145 Main Street
Sandwich MA 02563

(617) 888-0340

OPEN: by appointment only; closed
  holidays
COPYING FACILITIES: yes
MATERIALS SOLICITED: Materials relating
  to 17th century New England Quakers;
  the town of Sandwich; Boston & Sandwich Glass Company; Thornton W.
  Burgess; and the Cape Cod branch
  railroad. Will also accept Sandwich genealogy; Cape Cod Canal plans, construction, and operations; materials relating to Joseph Jefferson's career and
  paintings; and early maps of Barnstable
  County, MA.

HOLDINGS:
  Total volume: 200 l.f.
  Inclusive dates: 1651 -
  Description: Records of Sandwich
  town meetings; birth, death, and marriage
  records; proprietors' land, road, and military records; real estate and personal
  property valuations and tax records; selectmen's correspondence; genealogical
  records and correspondence; newspaper
  transcripts; census records; cemetery
  records; maps; church records; and civic
  records.

SEE: Hinding.

MA738-720
The Sandwich Historical Society
Sandwich Glass Museum
129 Main Street
Sandwich MA

MAILING ADDRESS:
P.O. Box 103
Sandwich MA 02563

(617) 888-0251

OPEN: M-F 9:30-4; Nov. 1 - April 1, by
  appointment only; closed weekends and
  holidays
ACCESS: advance arrangements required
COPYING FACILITIES: yes
MATERIALS SOLICITED: Materials relating
  to Sandwich glass, the Boston & Sandwich Glass Company, its founder
  Deming Jarves and its glass workers,
  the Cape Cod Glass Works, and the
  history of Sandwich. Will also accept
  materials relating to the history of
  glassmaking.

HOLDINGS:
  Total volume: 4 file drawers; 3 boxes
  Inclusive dates: 1679 -
  Description: Financial and business
  records of the Boston & Sandwich Glass
  Company, including correspondence of
  Deming Jarves and associates and patents
  for glassmaking. Also included are diaries
  and journals of Sandwich citizens, deeds,
  legal documents, records of Sandwich organizations, and photographs of Sandwich.

SHARON

MA748-440
Kendall Whaling Museum
27 Everett Street
Sharon MA

MAILING ADDRESS:
P.O. Box 297
Sharon MA 02067

(617) 784-5642

OPEN: M-F 1-4; closed weekends and
  holidays
COPYING FACILITIES: yes
MATERIALS SOLICITED: Documents on
  the history of whaling.

HOLDINGS:
  Total volume: 700 vols.
  Inclusive dates: 1760 -
  Description: Manuscripts pertaining to
  the whaling industry, including logbooks,
  journals, diaries, account books, and correspondence.

GUIDES: 'Whaling Logbooks and Journals
  in the Kendall Whaling Museum Collection,' (1977).

SEE: Hinding.

SHIRLEY

MA761-320
Hazen Memorial Library
Lancaster Road
Shirley MA 01464

(617) 425-9645

OPEN: M, Th 1-5, W 1-8, Sa 11-4; closed
  other days and holidays
COPYING FACILITIES: no

HOLDINGS:
  Total volume: 90 l.f.; 1 file cabinet
  Inclusive dates: 18th century -
  Description: Materials relating chiefly
  to the history of Shirley, including biographies of famous townspeople, diaries,
  letters from the Civil War and other
  periods, and histories of local organizations.

MA761-720
Shirley Historical Society
Center Road
Shirley MA

MAILING ADDRESS:
Shirley MA 01464

(617) 425-9460, 6623

OPEN: by appointment only
COPYING FACILITIES: no
MATERIALS SOLICITED: Materials relating
  to the Town of Shirley and its residents. Will also accept Shaker materials
  and MacKaye materials.

HOLDINGS:
  Total volume: 3 file cabinets
  Inclusive dates: 1750 -
  Description: Shirley town reports,
  school committee reports, valuation lists,
  diaries, scrapbooks, letters, photographs
  of town residents, oral history recordings,
  and Shirley Congregational Church

records. Included are diaries, scrapbooks,
letters, and photographs of Steele
MacKaye, Percey MacKaye, Benton
MacKaye and Hazel MacKaye.

SHREWSBURY

MA765-730
Shrewsbury Historical Society
232 Gulf Street
Shrewsbury MA 01545

no telephone

SEE: Hamer.

Questionnaire not returned.

SOMERVILLE

MA772-120
Charles H. Stewart & Co.
8 Clarendon Avenue
Somerville MA

MAILING ADDRESS:
P.O. Box 187
Somerville MA 02144

(617) 625-2407

OPEN: M-Sa 9-5; closed Sundays and
  holidays
COPYING FACILITIES: no
MATERIALS SOLICITED: Materials relating
  to Boston theaters.

HOLDINGS:
  Total volume: 1,000 vols.
  Inclusive dates: 1800 -
  Description: Records relating to the
  history of theaters, particularly in the
  Boston area, including programs, 1850- .

SOUTH HADLEY

MA776-515
Mount Holyoke College
The Skinner Museum
South Hadley MA 01075

(413) 538-2085

OPEN: May - Oct., Su, W 2-5; rest of
  year, by appointment only
ACCESS: advance arrangements required
COPYING FACILITIES: yes

HOLDINGS:
  Total volume: 1,000 items
  Inclusive dates: 1598 - 1940
  Description: Papers of the Museum's
  founder, Joseph Allen Skinner, a
  19th-century New England textile entre-
  preneur, and papers relating to the colonial, early National, and industrial
  periods of western Massachusetts.

MA776-530
Mount Holyoke College
Williston Memorial Library
South Hadley MA 01075

(413) 538-2441, 2225

OPEN: M-Sa 9-5; closed Sundays and
holidays
ACCESS: records less than 50 years old
can be seen only with advance
permission
COPYING FACILITIES: yes
MATERIALS SOLICITED: Information
about Mount Holyoke alumnae, classes,
academic departments, and student organizations; personal memorabilia of
alumnae and faculty, especially collected papers of alumnae. Will also accept
materials relating to all aspects of
Mount Holyoke history, including
alumnae; materials dealing with early
education and educational institutions
for women, and with those early wom-
en's colleges for which Mount Holyoke
served as a model, including Huguenot
(South Africa), the International Institute for Girls (Spain), Lake Erie, Mills,
Western, and Women's Christian College, Madras, India.

HOLDINGS:
Total volume: 2,100 l.f.
Inclusive dates: 1815 -
Description: Materials dealing with all
aspects of Mount Holyoke history, including the lives of individuals connected
with it. Included are holdings relating to
Mary Lyon and the development of education for women; educational institutions founded or staffed by alumnae;
alumnae missionary activities; and photographs of the College campus and student activities.

SEE: Hamer; NUCMC, 1966, 72.

SEE: Hinding.

SEE ALSO: Morris Rieger, 'Africa-Related
Papers of Persons and Organizations in
the United States,' *African Studies Bul-
letin* 8 (Dec. 1965); Walter Schatz, ed.,
Directory of Afro-American Resources
(Bowker, 1970); Peter Duignan, *Hand-
book of American Resources for African
Studies* (Hoover Institution, 1967).
Guides to individual collections are
available at the institution.

SOUTH NATICK

MA785-720
Natural History and Library Society
of South Natick
4 Merrill Road
South Natick MA 01760

no telephone

SEE: Hamer; NUCMC, 1968.

Questionnaire not returned.

SOUTH SUDBURY

MA788-280
Goodnow Public Library
21 Concord Road
Sudbury MA 01776

(617) 443-9112

OPEN: M-W 9-9, Th-Sa 9-5, Su 1-5;
closed Sundays Memorial
Day-Columbus Day, Saturdays
July-Labor Day, and holidays

SEE: Hamer.

Questionnaire not returned.

SOUTHBRIDGE

MA797-400
Jacob Edwards Library
236 Main Street
Southbridge MA 01550

(617) 764-2544

OPEN: M-Th 10-9, F 10-6, Sa 10-4;
closed Sundays and holidays
COPYING FACILITIES: yes
MATERIALS SOLICITED: Materials relating
to Southbridge and to the southern
Worcester County, MA, area, especially
photographs and genealogical materials.

HOLDINGS:
Total volume: 12 l.f.
Inclusive dates: 1790's -
Description: Personal papers, deeds, account books, and ledgers of the Marcy
family, including William Marcy, lawyer
and Secretary of State; maps, deeds, commissions, and photographs pertaining to
the local area.

SEE: Hinding.

SPRINGFIELD

MA804-50
American International College
Oral History Center
170 Wilbraham Road
Springfield MA

MAILING ADDRESS:
1000 State Street
Springfield MA 01109

(413) 737-7000

OPEN: M-Th 8-10, F 8-5, Sa 11-5, Su
3-10; closed holidays, and Sundays
during school recesses and summer
COPYING FACILITIES: yes
MATERIALS SOLICITED: Oral history relating to western Massachusetts and
New England, particularly in the area
of non-elite history. Will also accept
documents supporting the oral history
collection.

HOLDINGS:
Total volume: 600 tapes
Inclusive dates: 1971 -
Description: Tapes and supporting doc-
umentation dealing primarily with west-
ern Massachusetts and the Connecticut
River Valley, including communities in

Connecticut. There is specific emphasis
on non-elite members of the community
and their role in society.

MA804-130
Connecticut Valley Historical
Museum
194 State Street
Springfield MA 01103

(413) 732-3080

OPEN: by appointment only M-F 9-5;
closed weekends and Monday holidays
ACCESS: advance arrangements required
COPYING FACILITIES: no
MATERIALS SOLICITED: Personnel, business, and legal records from the Connecticut River Valley, 1635-1950.

HOLDINGS:
Total volume: 3,500 items
Inclusive dates: 1635 - 1950
Description: Records relating to the
business history of western Massachu-
setts. There are account books,
1651-1702; and the former files of the
Smith College Council of Industrial Stud-
ies, consisting of records of defunct area
business firms, such as Farr Alpaca,
Ames Manufacturing Company, and the
Clement Manufacturing Company.

SEE: Hamer; NUCMC, 1959, 61, 63-64.

SEE ALSO: a pamphlet, *Connecticut Valley
Collection of Business History,* available
upon request.

MA804-710
Springfield College
Babson Library
Dr. Ernest M. Best Archives Room
Springfield MA 01108

(413) 788-3307

OPEN: M-F 8:30-4; closed weekends and
holidays
COPYING FACILITIES: yes
MATERIALS SOLICITED: Materials pertaining to physical education, sports,
physiology, and Springfield College faculty and graduates.

HOLDINGS:
Total volume: 124 l.f.; 20 file
drawers; 16 boxes
Inclusive dates: 1700 -
Description: A collection relating to
Springfield College's philosophy of devel-
oping the student's mind, spirit, and
body. Included are materials relating to
Lawrence L. Doggett, Ernest M. Best, Lu-
ther H. Gulick, and Peter V. Karpovich.

STOCKBRIDGE

MA811-720
Stockbridge Library Association
Historical Room
Main Street
Stockbridge MA 01262

(413) 298-5501

OPEN: Tu-F 9-5, Sa 9-4; closed Sundays,
Mondays and holidays
COPYING FACILITIES: yes

MATERIALS SOLICITED: Family letters, genealogical information, pictures, and oral history tapes of local residents.

HOLDINGS:
Total volume: 4,000 items
Inclusive dates: 1710 -
Description: A manuscript collection relating to the Sergeant, Edwards, Sedgwick, Field, and other local families; Congregational church records; over 100 account books, 1775-1905; journals; records of local institutions; early maps; photographs; Indian records; genealogical source data; oral history tapes; literary manuscripts; and manuscript public documents.

SEE: Hamer.

SEE: Hinding; Leventhal and Mooney - I; Robbins.

STOUGHTON

MA817-720
Stoughton Historical Society, Inc.
6 Park Street
Stoughton MA

MAILING ADDRESS:
P.O. Box 542
Stoughton MA 02072

(617) 344-5456

OPEN: W 2-4, Th 7-9, Su 10-noon, other hours by appointment
ACCESS: appointment required
COPYING FACILITIES: yes
MATERIALS SOLICITED: Papers and genealogical materials relating to the town of Stoughton and Norfolk County.

HOLDINGS:
Total volume: 48 l.f.
Inclusive dates: Civil War -
Description: Photos, diaries, journals and account books relating to Stoughton families; records of Commonwealth of Massachusetts Great and General Court; town reports, street listings, and tax lists of Stoughton; and a small oral history collection.

STURBRIDGE

MA823-610
Old Sturbridge Village
Research Library
Route 20
Sturbridge MA 01566

(617) 347-3362

OPEN: M-F 8:30-5; closed weekends and holidays
COPYING FACILITIES: yes
MATERIALS SOLICITED: Materials relating to all aspects of life and work in rural New England, 1790-1850, with emphasis on early industrial development.

HOLDINGS:
Total volume: 185 l.f.
Inclusive dates: 1790 - 1850
Description: Materials relating to rural life and industry in New England. Included are letters, diaries, and family papers; daybooks and account books of farmers, storekeepers, artisans, clergy, and teachers; town and school records; records of cultural, religious, and charitable organizations; and business records of manufacturers and saw, grist, textile, starch, and paper mills.

SEE: NUCMC, 1976.

SEE: Hinding.

SWANSEA

MA837-720
Swansea Historical Society
Luther Corner
Swansea MA 02777

MAILING ADDRESS:
Box 67
Swansea MA 02777

no telephone

OPEN: by appointment only
COPYING FACILITIES: yes
MATERIALS SOLICITED: Any materials relating to the history of Swansea and its environs.

HOLDINGS:
Total volume: 105 vols.; 1 box; 105 items
Inclusive dates: 17th century -
Description: Materials relating to the history of Swansea and its residents. Included are 17th century deeds and records, including those of town meetings; account books of general stores, farmers, shoemakers, and clock makers; records of shipping, cotton manufacturing, and church societies; logbooks of voyages by Swansea mariners; photographs; 2 manuscript maps; and 5 oral history tapes on the historical houses and sections of the town.

TAUNTON

MA841-600
Old Colony Historical Society
66 Church Green
Taunton MA 02780

(617) 822-1622

OPEN: Tu-Sa 10-4; closed Sundays, Mondays, and holidays
USER FEES: one dollar daily fee for non-members
COPYING FACILITIES: yes

HOLDINGS:
Total volume: 3,500 items
Inclusive dates: 1639 -
Description: A collection of manuscripts consisting of wills, deeds, diaries, journals, account books, business records, genealogical data, music scores, maps, and pictures, mostly pertaining to the Old Colony, but a few of the Bay Colony and Plymouth Colony.

SEE: Hamer; NUCMC, 1959, 61.

SEE: Leventhal and Mooney - I.

TEMPLETON

MA845-560
Narragansett Historical Society
The Common
Templeton MA 01468

no telephone
SEE: Hamer.

Questionnaire not returned.

TOPSFIELD

MA849-750
Topsfield Historical Society
1 Howell Street
Topsfield MA

MAILING ADDRESS:
29 Perkins Row
Topsfield MA 01983

no telephone

OPEN: Tu-Su 1-4:30; closed Mondays and Sept. 15 to June 15
USER FEES: fifty cents
COPYING FACILITIES: no
MATERIALS SOLICITED: Documents or photographs relating to the history of Topsfield.

HOLDINGS:
Total volume: 10 c.f.
Inclusive dates: 1750 -
Description: Materials relating to residents of Topsfield, including account books, diaries, correspondence, sermons, programs, and the papers of George Francis Dow, antiquarian and founder of the Historical Society. There are also records of the Parson Capen House, site of the repository, a National Historic Landmark.

WAKEFIELD

MA865-880
Wakefield Historical Society
Museum
Americal Civic Center
Main Street
Wakefield MA

MAILING ADDRESS:
21 Chestnut Street
Wakefield MA 01880

(617) 245-0010

OPEN: by appointment
COPYING FACILITIES: no

HOLDINGS:
Total volume: 16 file drawers; 600 items
Inclusive dates: early 1700's -
Description: Documents, records, and photographs related to the history of Wakefield and its predecessor towns of South Reading and Reading.

WALTHAM

MA871-40

American Jewish Historical Society
Library
2 Thornton Road
Waltham MA 02154

(617) 891-8110

OPEN: M-F 8:30-5; closed Fridays during
summer and Friday mornings during
winter; closed weekends, holidays and
Jewish holidays
ACCESS: primarily graduate students and
serious scholars
COPYING FACILITIES: yes
MATERIALS SOLICITED: Materials relating
to the American Jewish experience.

HOLDINGS:
> *Total volume:* 4,000,000 items
> *Inclusive dates:* 1572 -
> *Description:* Approximately 600 collec-
> tions pertaining to the history of the Jew-
> ish communities in the Western Hemi-
> sphere, including papers of individuals,
> plus archives of numerous Jewish com-
> munal institutions on both local and Na-
> tional levels.

GUIDES: Two publications of the Society,
*A Preliminary Survey of the Manuscript
Collections Found in the American Jewish Historical Society* (1967) and *Manuscript Collections in the American Jewish Historical Society: Cataloged January 1968-June 1969* (n.d.).

SEE: Hamer (listed under New York City);
NUCMC, 1968-70, 72, 77-78, 80.

SEE: Krichmar; Duignan; Allard, Crawley,
and Edmison; Hinding; Ingram; Robbins.

SEE ALSO: Jerome S. Handler, *A Guide to
Source Materials for the Study of Barbados History, 1627-1834* (Southern Illinois Univ. Press, 1971); Andrea
Hinding and Rosemary Richardson,
comps., *Archival and Manuscript Resources for the Study of Women's History: A Beginning* (Univ. of Minnesota
Libraries, Social Welfare History Archives Center, 1972); Philip P. Mason,
ed., *Directory of Jewish Archival Institutions* (Wayne State Univ., 1975); Walter Schatz, ed., *Directory of Afro-
American Resources* (Bowker, 1970).

An introductory guide to the collections is
available at the institution.

MA871-60

Bentley College
Baker-Vanguard Library
College Archives
Beaver and Forest Streets
Waltham MA 02154

(617) 891-2233

OPEN: M-Th 8-11, F 8-10, Sa 10-5, Su
1-10; M-F 8:30-4:30 during College
vacations; closed holidays
ACCESS: prior arrangements for use of
material should be made
COPYING FACILITIES: yes
MATERIALS SOLICITED: Correspondence
and other materials pertaining to accounting, the Bentley School of Ac-

counting and Finance, and its founder
and first president, Harry Clark Bentley. Will also accept handwritten account books and ledgers.

HOLDINGS:
> *Total volume:* 600 items
> *Inclusive dates:* 19th century -
> *Description:* Correspondence of Harry
> Clark Bentley; several dozen typewritten
> or handwritten notes from him and other
> officers of the School to instructors;
> unpublished manuscript material on the
> teaching of accounting, goodwill, and
> autobiographical information; 19th cen-
> tury manuscript account books; and par-
> tial records of the School and College,
> including printed materials, ephemera,
> student notebooks, and audio-visual ma-
> terials.

MA871-85

Brandeis University
The Dretzin Living Biographies
   Program
Abram L. and Thelma Sachar
   International Center
Waltham MA 02154

(617) 647-2272

OPEN: M-F 9-5; closed weekends and
holidays
COPYING FACILITIES: yes

HOLDINGS:
> *Total volume:* not specified
> *Inclusive dates:* 1967 -
> *Description:* Audio-visual tapes of dis-
> cussions with David Ben-Gurion, Grete
> Bibring, General Carlos Romulo, David
> Seegal, Earl Warren, and Averell Har-
> riman; tape cassette interviews conducted
> by Abram L. Sachar with Harry S Tru-
> man, Edwin Reischauer, Howard Rusk,
> and others; and cassettes of Sachar's pro-
> gram, 'The Course of Our Times.'

SEE: Meckler and McMullin.

MA871-90

Brandeis University
Goldfarb Library
Special Collections
415 South Street
Waltham MA 02254

(617) 647-2513

OPEN: M-F 8:30-4:30; closed weekends,
holidays, and Jewish holidays
COPYING FACILITIES: yes
MATERIALS SOLICITED: Materials relating
to the Spanish Civil War and to the
Sacco-Vanzetti case.

HOLDINGS:
> *Total volume:* 73 l.f.
> *Inclusive dates:* 1718 -
> *Description:* Manuscripts, clippings,
> and photographs dealing with various
> topics, including the Spanish Civil War,
> the cases of Alfred Dreyfus, Leo Frank,
> and Sacco and Vanzetti, socialism, and
> Daniel Webster.

SEE: NUCMC, 1970.

SEE: Novotny; Martin; Spalek; Robbins.

MA871-280

Gore Place Society
52 Gore Street
Waltham MA 02154

(617) 894-2798

OPEN: Tu-Sa 10-5, Su 2-5; closed
Mondays, holidays, and Nov. 15-April
15
ACCESS: serious scholars and researchers
COPYING FACILITIES: no
MATERIALS SOLICITED: Materials relating
to the life of Christopher Gore and
subsequent owners and occupiers of
Gore Place. Will also accept material
relating to the history of Waltham and
Watertown.

HOLDINGS:
> *Total volume:* 300 items
> *Inclusive dates:* 1790 -
> *Description:* Letters from Christopher
> Gore dealing with politics, agriculture,
> and personal affairs; documents relating
> to Gore's term as Governor of Massachu-
> setts; account books and correspondence
> of later owners of Gore Place; photo-
> graphs and maps of Gore Place; and ge-
> nealogical data on the Gore family.

MA871-540

National Archives and Records
   Administration
Federal Archives and Records Center
Archives Branch
380 Trapelo Road
Waltham MA 02154

(617) 647-8100

OPEN: M-F 8-4:30; closed weekends and
holidays
ACCESS: Records are open, subject to
Federal agency restrictions and
restrictions based upon current
legislation relevant to confidentiality
and security classification. See General
Information Leaflet No. 27, 'General
Restrictions on Access to Records in
the National Archives of the United
States.'
COPYING FACILITIES: yes
MATERIALS SOLICITED: Permanently
valuable records of Federal agencies in
Maine, New Hampshire, Vermont,
Massachusetts, Connecticut, and Rhode
Island.

HOLDINGS:
> *Total volume:* 10,591 c.f.
> *Inclusive dates:* 1789 - 1948
> *Description:* Permanently valuable
> records of Federal agencies in New Eng-
> land, especially records of United States
> District and Circuit Courts, the Bureau of
> Customs, the U.S. Coast Guard and the
> Corps of Army Engineers.

SEE: Davis; Allard, Crawley, and
Edmison.

SEE ALSO: *List of Pre-1840 Federal Dis-
trict and Circuit Courts* (National Ar-
chives Special List No. 31, 1972);
James K. Owens, 'Federal Court
Records of New Hampshire,' *Historical
New Hampshire* 25 (Fall 1970).

MA871-860
Waltham Historical Society, Inc.
Lyman House
185 Lyman Street
Waltham MA 02154

no telephone

OPEN: by appointment
COPYING FACILITIES: no
MATERIALS SOLICITED: Photographs, diaries, account books, deeds, indentures, sermons, record books, and other manuscripts on Waltham. Also general material on adjacent towns, such as Watertown, Weston, and Newton. Will also accept glass negatives and photographs.

HOLDINGS:
    Total volume: 1,700 items; 4 file drawers
    Inclusive dates: 1702 -
    Description: Manuscripts, photographs, and glass negatives relating to the history of Waltham and its environs, including both public records and personal papers of its residents.

MA871-870
Waltham Museum, Inc.
7 Viles Court
Waltham MA

MAILING ADDRESS:
15 Noonan Street
Waltham MA 02154

(617) 893-8017, 894-2609

OPEN: Su 1-4:30, other days by appointment; closed holidays
COPYING FACILITIES: no
MATERIALS SOLICITED: Records relating to the history of Waltham.

HOLDINGS:
    Total volume: 8 file drawers
    Inclusive dates: 1813 -
    Description: Records relating to the city of Waltham, Waltham Watch Company, Metz Automobile Company, Boston Manufacturing Company, and other area industries.

MA871-890
Waltham Public Library
Genealogy and Local History Room
735 Main Street
Waltham MA 02154

(617) 893-1750

OPEN: Tu, W, F 9-5, Th 1-5; closed weekends, Mondays, and holidays
ACCESS: serious researchers, with permission of Reference Librarian or Director
COPYING FACILITIES: yes
MATERIALS SOLICITED: Local history, genealogy and biography.

HOLDINGS:
    Total volume: 83 vols.; 559 items
    Inclusive dates: 1703 - 1958
    Description: Materials relating to Waltham residents and organizations, including receipts, sermons, legal documents, and typewritten copies of original manuscripts done during a 1937-38 WPA project.

SEE: Hamer.

WAYLAND

MA883-870
Wayland Free Public Library
5 Concord Road
Wayland MA 01778

(617) 358-2311

OPEN: M-Th 9-9, F 9-5, Sa 10-5, Su 2-5; closed holidays and on summer weekends
COPYING FACILITIES: yes
MATERIALS SOLICITED: Materials relating to Wayland history and people, including records and photographs.

HOLDINGS:
    Total volume: 200 vols.
    Inclusive dates: 1706 -
    Description: Materials relating to the history of Wayland. Included are the constitution of the East Sudbury Social Library (1796); deeds, reports, letters, and other material pertaining to the East Sudbury Ministerial Fund (1789-1843); an account book of a blacksmith; photographs of Wayland and the construction of the Wayland Water Works; records of the Library; town reports; evaluation lists; maps; and other materials.

SEE: Hamer.

WELLESLEY

MA891-80
Babson College
The Horn Library
Special Collections
Babson Park
Wellesley MA 02157

(617) 235-1200, Ext. 570

OPEN: by appointment only
ACCESS: advance arrangements required
COPYING FACILITIES: no

HOLDINGS:
    Total volume: not specified
    Inclusive dates: 17th century -
    Description: Memorabilia and photographs pertaining to Roger W. Babson; documents, manuscripts, and photographs documenting the history of Babson College; and manuscripts of Sir Isaac Newton.

MA891-860
Wellesley College
Archives
Wellesley MA 02181

(617) 235-0320, Ext. 2128

OPEN: M-F 9-5; closed weekends and holidays; closes at 4:30 when the College is not in session
COPYING FACILITIES: yes
MATERIALS SOLICITED: Records of Wellesley College and papers of people or groups associated in some way with the College.

HOLDINGS:
    Total volume: 1,000 l.f.
    Inclusive dates: 1780 -
    Description: Archives of Wellesley College including the personal papers of some Wellesley faculty and alumnae. The collection focuses on the operation of the College and the higher education of women, with most materials dating after 1870.

SEE: Hinding; Meckler and McMullin.

MA891-880
Wellesley College
Library
Special Collections
Wellesley MA 02181

(617) 235-0320, Ext. 2129

OPEN: M-F 10-5; closed weekends and holidays, closes at 4:30 when the college is not in session
ACCESS: written appointment required June - Aug.; appointment desirable during academic terms
COPYING FACILITIES: yes
MATERIALS SOLICITED: Literary manuscripts, especially of poetry in English, literary and historical material by and about women, and history of books and printing. Will also accept juvenile literature, literary and historical material of 20th century Italy, and historical material of the Caribbean.

HOLDINGS:
    Total volume: 6,000 items
    Inclusive dates: 14th century -
    Description: Medieval and Renaissance manuscripts, many illuminated; poetry in English, including manuscripts and letters, especially of Robert and Elizabeth Browning and William Wordsworth; U.S. history, including Nathan Dane's 'Moral and Political Survey...' and a journal of Charles Sumner.
    Included are a collection of American Indian languages, chiefly Micmac; manuscripts by and about women, including Jeannette Marks papers, Madeleine Henrey papers, letters of Alice Stone Blackwell, and two manuscripts of Storm Jameson; correspondence and drawings of John Ruskin; and William Hunter letters concerning 19th century China.

SEE: Hamer; NUCMC, 1962.

SEE: Robbins; Schatz.

WELLFLEET

MA894-880
Wellfleet History Society, Inc.
Main Street
Wellfleet MA

MAILING ADDRESS:
Box 58
Wellfleet MA 02667

no telephone

OPEN: July - Aug., Tu-Sa 2-5; closed other days and rest of year
USER FEES: fifty cents
COPYING FACILITIES: no
MATERIALS SOLICITED: Material related to Wellfleet, such as maritime records, school records, and organization min-

utes. Will also accept material directly related to Cape Cod.

HOLDINGS:
Total volume: 1.5 l.f.
Inclusive dates: 1756 - 1910
Description: Minutes of the Wellfleet Marine Benevolent Society, records of the now defunct Second Congregational Church, an Indian reservation document (1756), a page from H. D. Thoreau's manuscript, *Cape Cod*, some early wills, letters, early school records, and copies of papers related to the division of common lands.

WENHAM

MA897-880
Wenham Historical Association and Museum, Inc.
Timothy Pickering Library
132 Main Street
Wenham MA 01984

(617) 468-2377

OPEN: M-F 9:30-4:30, Su 2-5; closed Saturdays, holidays, and February
COPYING FACILITIES: yes
MATERIALS SOLICITED: Materials pertaining to Wenham history and to farming in Massachusetts.

HOLDINGS:
Total volume: 5 file cabinets; 4 file drawers; 1,500 items
Inclusive dates: mid-17th century -
Description: Papers and records of the Massachusetts Society for Promoting Agriculture, and papers, photographs, and other material on Wenham history.

SEE: Hinding.

WEST BARNSTABLE

MA901-120
Cape Cod Community College
Library-Learning Resource Center
West Barnstable MA 02668

(617) 362-2131, Ext. 245

OPEN: M, W 8-4, Tu, Th, F 10-3; closed weekends and holidays
ACCESS: identification and sign-in required
COPYING FACILITIES: yes
MATERIALS SOLICITED: Cape Cod history. Will also accept other materials of value to the College or community.

HOLDINGS:
Total volume: 1,600 items
Inclusive dates: 17th century -
Description: Manuscripts, photographs, and tapes relating to Cape Cod history. Includes archives of the State Normal School in Hyannis.

WEST BOXFORD

MA903-80
Ingalls Memorial Library Association
Boxford Historic Document Center
Washington Street
West Boxford MA 01885

(617) 592-1460

OPEN: by appointment only
COPYING FACILITIES: yes
MATERIALS SOLICITED: Materials pertaining to Boxford, MA. Will also accept materials about nearby towns.

HOLDINGS:
Total volume: 133 file boxes; 10 map drawers
Inclusive dates: 1685 -
Description: Materials relating to Boxford and nearby towns, including manuscripts, letters, and maps.

WEST BOYLSTON

MA904-80
Beaman Memorial Public Library
West Boylston Collection
8 Newton Street
West Boylston MA 01583

(617) 835-3711

OPEN: M 6-8:30, Tu 2-8:30, W 10-5, Th 1-8:30, F, Sa 2-5; closed Sundays, holidays; closed Mondays and Saturdays, July-Aug.
COPYING FACILITIES: yes
MATERIALS SOLICITED: Materials pertaining to West Boylston history and genealogy.

HOLDINGS:
Total volume: 12 vols.; 112 items
Inclusive dates: 1603 - 1958
Description: Letters, photographs, legal papers, manuscript histories, essays, church and cemetery records, and historical maps of West Boylston, including materials on the period prior to the town's incorporation. Of particular interest in the collection are the records of a local Grand Army of the Republic post.

SEE: Hamer; NUCMC, 1966.

WEST BROOKFIELD

MA910-680
Quabeag Historical Society
Main Street
West Brookfield MA 01585

no telephone
SEE: Hamer.

Questionnaire not returned.

WESTBOROUGH

MA925-880
Westborough Historical Society
7 Parkman Street
Westborough MA 01581

no telephone
SEE: Hamer.

Questionnaire not returned.

WESTFIELD

MA928-730
Westfield State College
Raymond Patterson Alumni Archive
Westfield MA

MAILING ADDRESS:
History Department
Westfield State College
Westfield MA 01085

(413) 568-3311, Ext. 340

OPEN: M-F 9-4; closed weekends and holidays
COPYING FACILITIES: yes
MATERIALS SOLICITED: Materials relating to local history and the history of education. Will also accept New England historical materials.

HOLDINGS:
Total volume: 50 l.f., 60 rolls of film
Inclusive dates: 1839 -
Description: Records of Westfield State College, 1839- , primarily papers of faculty and alumni. Also included are civil court records of Hampden County, 1866-1920, and other materials of local historical interest.

WESTFORD

MA931-400
J. V. Fletcher Library
Historical Collections
50 Main Street
Westford MA

MAILING ADDRESS:
P.O. Box 367
Westford MA 01886

(617) 692-5555

OPEN: M-Th 10-8, F, Sa 10-5; closed Sundays, holidays, and Saturdays July-Aug.
COPYING FACILITIES: yes
MATERIALS SOLICITED: Materials on Dr. Nettie Maria Stevens and Ellen Swallow Richards. Will also accept materials on local history and genealogy.

HOLDINGS:
Total volume: 18 file drawers
Inclusive dates: 1755 -
Description: Papers and drawings of Dr. Nettie Maria Stevens, 1861-1912; Civil War correspondence of the Jubb family, 1861-66; correspondence concerning the New England Freedmen's Aid Society, 1865-66; correspondence of the New England Women's Auxiliary Associ-

ation and the Soldier's Aid Society of Westford, 1861-65; and manuscripts, documents, and photographs of local historical interest, including articles of National import, such as the covenant to boycott British trade during the blockade of Boston harbor, 1774.

SEE: Hamer.

WESTON

MA937-280
Golden Ball Tavern Trust
662 Boston Post Road
Weston MA

MAILING ADDRESS:
Box 223
Weston MA 02193

(617) 894-1751

OPEN: by appointment only
ACCESS: prior arrangements required
COPYING FACILITIES: no
MATERIALS SOLICITED: Materials relating to Isaac Jones and his descendants.

HOLDINGS:
Total volume: 3 file drawers
Inclusive dates: 1700 - 1900
Description: Collections relating to Isaac Jones, Weston innkeeper and shipping agent, his associates, and his descendants. Included are ledgers of local residents (1750-1830); wills, deeds, and other legal documents; and transaction receipts.

WESTWOOD

MA943-880
Westwood Public Library
Baker Historical Collection
668 High Street
Westwood MA 02090

(617) 326-7562

OPEN: M-F 9-9, Sa 10-5, Su 2-5; closed holidays and weekends during July and August
COPYING FACILITIES: yes
MATERIALS SOLICITED: State and local history.

HOLDINGS:
Total volume: 30 vols.; 4 file drawers
Inclusive dates: 1700 -
Description: Photographs and lantern slides of Westwood; slides and a tape recording of a 1972 parade; property deeds and maps dating to the 18th century; account books; journals; records of an early fire company; and letters to Franklin Delano Williams from his wife, 1861-65.

SEE: Hinding.

WEYMOUTH

MA947-880
Weymouth Public Libraries
The Tufts Library
46 Broad Street
Weymouth MA 02188

(617) 337-1402

OPEN: M-F 9-9, Sa 9-5, Su 2-5; closed holidays and weekends July-Aug.
COPYING FACILITIES: yes
MATERIALS SOLICITED: Weymouth history.

HOLDINGS:
Total volume: 5 vols.; 25 items; additional materials
Inclusive dates: not specified
Description: The diary of Dr. Cotton Tufts, 1778-1809, letters of the Fifield family concerning antislavery issues, microfilm of early town and church records, and records of the Reynolds Womens Relief Corps, an auxiliary of the Grand Army of the Republic.

SEE: Hamer.

WILLIAMSTOWN

MA961-870
Williams College
Chapin Library of Rare Books
Stetson Hall
Williamstown MA

MAILING ADDRESS:
Box 426
Williamstown MA 01267

(413) 597-2462

OPEN: M-F 9-5; closed weekends and holidays; shorter hours during vacations
ACCESS: qualified researchers; certain special materials may require additional references from visiting scholars and researchers
COPYING FACILITIES: yes
MATERIALS SOLICITED: Materials relating to American authors and literature, 1900-75.

HOLDINGS:
Total volume: 25 l.f.
Inclusive dates: 1750 - 1950
Description: Principal collections: Presidential letters and manuscripts; Gregory Mason papers; Samuel Gridley and Julia Ward Howe papers; Emily F. and Israel T. Talbot papers; Ted Shawn-Jacob's Pillow Dance Collection; William Cullen Bryant; 20th-century American fine printers and graphic artists.
A general American manuscript file includes significant items of George Ade, Stephen Crane, Ralph Waldo Emerson, William Faulkner, Thomas Wentworth Higginson, Oliver Herford, James Russell Lowell, George Barr McCutcheon, Edgar Lee Masters, Walt Whitman, Aaron Burr, Benjamin Franklin, George Mason, et al.

SEE: Robbins.

SEE ALSO: a brochure describing the collections available from the Chapin Library.

MA961-890
Williams College
Library
Williamstown MA 01267

no telephone
SEE: Hamer.

Questionnaire not returned.

WINCHENDON

MA964-880
Winchendon Historical Society, Inc.
50 Pleasant Street
Winchendon MA 01475

(617) 297-0300

OPEN: Tu 6:30-8:30 July - Aug.; by appointment in winter
COPYING FACILITIES: yes
MATERIALS SOLICITED: Materials pertaining to Winchendon history.

HOLDINGS:
Total volume: 15 vols.; 505 items
Inclusive dates: 1800 -
Description: Materials relating to the history of Winchendon and its residents, including church records, diaries, account books, railroad history materials, slides of historic homes, and materials related to the Civil War and the local chapter of the Grand Army of the Republic.

SEE: Hinding.

WINCHESTER

MA967-880
Winchester Archival Center
15 High Street
Winchester MA 01890

(617) 721-7146

OPEN: W 1-4, Th 7-9, other times by appointment
COPYING FACILITIES: yes
MATERIALS SOLICITED: Any materials pertaining to Winchester, its government, organizations and people. Also records pertaining to areas of Woburn, MA, that are now known as Winchester. Will also accept materials pertaining to neighboring towns or dealing with families who once lived in Winchester.

HOLDINGS:
Total volume: 75 l.f.
Inclusive dates: 1694 -
Description: Photographs, diaries, family papers, biographical information and other unpublished materials on the people, churches, businesses, and organizations of Winchester.

WINTHROP

MA970-890
Winthrop Public Library
2 Metcalf Square
Winthrop MA 02152

(617) 846-1703

OPEN: M, Tu, Th 1-9, W 10-9, F 10-6, Sa 10-5; closed Sundays and holidays
COPYING FACILITIES: yes
MATERIALS SOLICITED: Historical material relating to Winthrop and the area of Boston Harbor Islands.

HOLDINGS:
> Total volume: not specified
> Inclusive dates: not specified
> Description: A diary, letters, and pictures of Mrs. R. Pomeroy from the Civil War period; glass negatives by Harry Whorf of Winthrop in the 1880's; local history scrapbooks and tape recordings; local engineering reports, architectural plans, church records, town reports, and typescript histories; a register of the Old Suffolk Chapter of the Sons of the American Revolution; a history of Winthrop Community Hospital; letters; bills of sale; and deeds.

SEE: Hamer.

WOBURN

MA975-890
Woburn Public Library
45 Pleasant Street
Woburn MA 01802

(617) 933-0148

OPEN: M-Th 8:30-8, F, Sa 8:30-5:30; closed Wednesday afternoons and Saturdays in summer; closed Sundays and holidays

SEE: Hamer; NUCMC, 1966, 71.

Questionnaire not returned.

WOLLASTON

MA978-200
Eastern Nazarene College
Archives
Wollaston MA 02170

(617) 773-6350

OPEN: by appointment
COPYING FACILITIES: yes
MATERIALS SOLICITED: Trustee, administration, faculty and student records of the College. Will also accept materials concerning the Church of the Nazarene in the Eastern Educational Zone.

HOLDINGS:
> Total volume: 105 l.f.
> Inclusive dates: 1900 -
> Description: Archives of Eastern Nazarene College, including trustee records, transcripts of interviews with students and faculty, a photograph collection, presidential correspondence, correspondence of the academic dean, and faculty minutes.

WOODS HOLE

MA981-890
Woods Hole Oceanographic
  Institution
Data Library/Archive
McLean Buildings
Quissett Campus
Woods Hole MA 02543

(617) 548-1400, Ext. 2481, 2471

OPEN: M-F 8-5; closed weekends and holidays
COPYING FACILITIES: yes
MATERIALS SOLICITED: Materials in oceanography, geology, biology, climatology, meteorology, hydrography, bathymetry, geophysics and ocean chemistry. Will also accept underwater photographs, coastal photographs, charts, maps, aerial photographs of coastal regions, New England climatological data, bathymetric surveys, and historical maps and charts of the New England region.

HOLDINGS:
> Total volume: 6,500 sq. f.
> Inclusive dates: 1840 -
> Description: Materials relating to oceanography focusing on scientific observations taken at sea since 1930. Included are cruise, aircraft flight, and submarine dive records; marine charts; hydrographic surveys; scientific notebooks and more than 1,000,000 photographs of the ocean floor.
>
> Special collections include World War II German and Japanese war atlases pertaining to oceanography; New England climatological data from 1896 to present; large U.S. and Canadian map collections.

WORCESTER

MA985-70
American Antiquarian Society
185 Salisbury Street
Worcester MA 01609

(617) 755-5221

OPEN: M-F 9-5; closed weekends and holidays
ACCESS: open to serious scholars, most graduate students, and selected undergraduates engaged in directed, original research
COPYING FACILITIES: yes
MATERIALS SOLICITED: History of the book trade in North America to 1876; Society archives. Will also accept materials pertaining to central Massachusetts, 1620-1880, or materials which complement existing collection strengths (e.g., colonial and early National religion, early diaries and account books).

HOLDINGS:
> Total volume: 1,850 l.f.
> Inclusive dates: 1620 -
> Description: Manuscripts relating to the American book trade to 1876; colonial and early National religion, politics, and military activities; and the growth of central Massachusetts to 1880. There are also holdings of early National diaries and account books, as well as the Soci-

ety's own records, tracing its growth as an institution from 1812 to the present.

GUIDES: Catalogue of the Manuscript Collections of the American Antiquarian Society 4 vols. (G. K. Hall, 1979).

SEE: Hamer; NUCMC, 1962-65, 69, 72, 74-75, 77.

SEE: Allard, Crawley, and Edmison; Bean and Vane; Davis; Hinding; Ingram; Leventhal and Mooney - I; Robbins.

SEE ALSO: Morris Rieger, 'Africa-Related Papers of Persons and Organizations in the United States,' African Studies Bulletin 8 (Dec. 1965); Peter Duignan, Handbook of American Resources for African Studies (Hoover Institution, 1967); Walter Schatz, ed., Directory of Afro-American Resources (Bowker, 1970); Robert O. Collins and Peter Duignan, Americans in Africa (Hoover Institution, 1963); Ann Novotny, ed., Picture Sources 3 (Special Libraries Assn., 1975); and the Proceedings and Newsletter of the Society.

MA985-100
Clark University
Archives
950 Main Street
Worcester MA 01610

(617) 793-7206

OPEN: M-F 9-4:30; closed weekends, holidays and during University winter break
COPYING FACILITIES: yes
MATERIALS SOLICITED: University-related material: institutional records; papers of the founder, presidents, and prominent faculty; student materials; photographs; building plans and drawings; and institutional memorabilia.

HOLDINGS:
> Total volume: 850 l.f.
> Inclusive dates: 1850 -
> Description: Non-current institutional records of permanent value from principal departments and offices, as well as other materials relating to the history of the University, its faculty and its students.

SEE: Hamer (as Clark University Library); NUCMC, 1970, 73.

SEE: Hinding.

SEE ALSO: finding aids to the G. Stanley Hall and Wallace W. Atwood papers available at the repository.

MA985-110
Clark University
Goddard Library
Department of Rare Books and
  Special Collections
950 Main Street
Worcester MA 01610

(617) 793-7572

OPEN: M-F 9-4:30; closed weekends, holidays and during University winter break
COPYING FACILITIES: yes

MATERIALS SOLICITED: Materials relating to Robert Hutchings Goddard; manuscripts of Worcester area authors.

HOLDINGS:
> *Total volume:* 104 l.f.
> *Inclusive dates:* 1778 -
> *Description:* Papers, diaries, patents, and other materials by and relating to Robert Hutchings Goddard and the Goddard family, and early rocketry; and literary manuscripts and other papers of Worcester authors Esther Forbes and Olive Higgins Prouty. There are also a few miscellaneous items, such as nine Revolutionary War era Army orderly books, 1778-83.

SEE: Hamer; NUCMC, 1970.

SEE: Hinding; Robbins.

SEE ALSO: *The Goddard Biblio-Log,* published by the Friends of the Goddard Library.

MA985-120
Clark University
Graduate School of Geography
Guy H. Burnham Map and Aerial
    Photograph Library
950 Main Street
Worcester MA 01610

(617) 793-7322

OPEN: M-F 9-5; closed weekends and holidays
COPYING FACILITIES: yes
MATERIALS SOLICITED: Areas of importance to current geographic studies, such as Africa, international development, economic geography, cultural geography, and physical geography. Will also accept other items of cartographic interest and statistical material on all countries.

HOLDINGS:
> *Total volume:* 13,000 items
> *Inclusive dates:* 1870 -
> *Description:* Slides, aerial photographs, and glass plates relating to various areas of geographic study.

MA985-130
College of the Holy Cross
Archives
1 College Street
Worcester MA 01608

(617) 793-2506

OPEN: M-F 8:30-4; closed weekends and holidays

ACCESS: restricted to professional researchers
COPYING FACILITIES: yes
MATERIALS SOLICITED: Papers of professional alumni and retired politicians. Will also accept data on the history of New England education.

HOLDINGS:
> *Total volume:* 2,150 l.f.
> *Inclusive dates:* 1840 -
> *Description:* Materials relating to the history of Holy Cross College, including holdings relating to the trustees, presidents, deans, treasurers, departments, honor societies, faculty, admissions, the registrar's office, extracurricular activities, sports, alumni, and publications.

SEE: Duignan.

SEE ALSO: An index to the Archives is available at the institution.

MA985-140
College of the Holy Cross
Library
Worcester MA 01610

no telephone

SEE: Hamer; NUCMC, 1959-61.

Questionnaire not returned.

MA985-860
Worcester Historical Museum
39 Salisbury Street
Worcester MA 01609

(617) 753-8278

OPEN: Tu-Sa 10-4; closed Sundays, Mondays, and holidays
ACCESS: arrangements must be made in advance
COPYING FACILITIES: yes
MATERIALS SOLICITED: Material pertaining to Worcester. Will also accept material pertaining to Worcester County.

HOLDINGS:
> *Total volume:* 300 l.f.
> *Inclusive dates:* 1725 -
> *Description:* Manuscript collections pertaining to Worcester and Worcester County. Included are family papers, institutional records, correspondence, deeds, legal agreements, genealogical and biographical notes, typescripts, lectures, and ephemera.

SEE: Hamer.

SEE: Schatz; Meckler and McMullin; Davis; Hinding; Robbins.

MA985-870
Worcester Polytechnic Institute
Archives
George C. Gordon Library
Worcester MA 01609

(617) 793-5413

OPEN: open weekday mornings; closed weekends and holidays
ACCESS: advance appointment with the Special Collections Librarian
COPYING FACILITIES: yes
MATERIALS SOLICITED: Materials relating to Worcester Polytechnic Institute and the Washburn Machine Shops.

HOLDINGS:
> *Total volume:* 700 l.f.
> *Inclusive dates:* 1865 -
> *Description:* A collection relating to the history of engineering education at Worcester Polytechnic Institute. Included are papers of faculty and alumni, president's papers relating to the Institute's philosophy of combining practical training with theoretical education, photographs and other archival holdings.

MA985-890
Worcester Public Library
Salem Square
Worcester MA 01608

(617) 799-1655

OPEN: M-Th 9-8:30, F, Sa 9-5:30, Su 1-5:30; closed holidays, and Sundays in summer
COPYING FACILITIES: yes
MATERIALS SOLICITED: Will accept materials pertaining to the City of Worcester and notable Worcester people.

HOLDINGS:
> *Total volume:* 82 items
> *Inclusive dates:* 1784 - 1806
> *Description:* Letters of the Green family, chiefly by Dr. John Green, II, father of the founder of the Worcester Public Library.

MICHIGAN

Since 1952 the State Archives of Michigan has administered a statewide program for preserving local public records. Many permanently valuable local public records remain in the custody of local officials, but several thousand cubic feet have been transferred either to the State Archives in Lansing or to one of five regional depositories: Western Michigan University, Central Michigan University, Michigan Technological University, Oakland University, and the Detroit Public Library. The first four regional depositories hold mainly county records, while the Burton Historical Collection at the Detroit Public Library holds mainly Detroit city archives.

Researchers at the State Archives have access to microfilm copies of vital, tax, probate, and other local public records filmed by the Church of Jesus Christ of Latter-day Saints. Inventories of records held by a select number of counties and municipalities, including the city of Detroit, also are available for reference at the Archives.

ADRIAN

MI8-20
Adrian College
Shipman Library
Adrian MI 49221

(517) 265-5161

OPEN: M-Th 8-11, F 8-5, Sa 9:30-4:30, Su 2-11; closed Easter and Christmas; shorter summer hours
COPYING FACILITIES: yes
MATERIALS SOLICITED: Historical archives of Adrian College.

HOLDINGS:
Total volume: not specified
Inclusive dates: 1859 -
Description: College-related materials, including trustee minutes, 1859 to date, literary periodicals, a journal and notebook of College founder Asa Mahan, and sound recordings of campus singing groups and of original musical compositions.

SEE: Hamer.

MI8-30
Adrian Public Library
141 East Maumee Street
Adrian MI 49221

(517) 263-2161, Ext. 277

OPEN: M, Tu, Th 10-9, W, F 10-5:30, Sa 9:30-5:30; closed Sundays and holidays
COPYING FACILITIES: yes
MATERIALS SOLICITED: Materials concerning Adrian and Lenawee County. Will also accept some materials on Michigan history.

HOLDINGS:
Total volume: 250 items
Inclusive dates: 1830 -
Description: A collection relating chiefly to businesses and social activities of Adrian and Lenawee County, including account books, a few diaries, records of organizations, and photographs of people.

SEE: Hamer.

MI8-480
Lenawee County Historical Museum
110 East Church
Adrian MI

MAILING ADDRESS:
P.O. Box 511
Adrian MI 49221

(517) 265-6071

OPEN: Tu-Sa 1-5; closed Sundays, Mondays, and holidays
COPYING FACILITIES: no
MATERIALS SOLICITED: Materials concerning Lenawee County.

HOLDINGS:
Total volume: 30 l.f.
Inclusive dates: 1830's -
Description: Lenawee County historical materials, including photographs and business, school board, tax, and government records.

SEE: Hinding.

MI8-720
Siena Heights College
Library
1247 East Siena Heights Drive
Adrian MI 49221

(517) 263-0731, Ext. 242

OPEN: M-Th 8:30-10, F 8:30-4, Sa 1-5, Su 2-10; closed holidays; shorter hours between sessions and during summer
COPYING FACILITIES: yes
MATERIALS SOLICITED: College archives.

HOLDINGS:
Total volume: 2 file cabinets
Inclusive dates: 1919 -
Description: College archival material, chiefly consisting of committee reports, division and department reports, audit reports, and minutes. Also included is a 15th century illuminated manuscript.

SEE: Hamer.

MI8-800
United Methodist Church
Detroit Conference
Archives and History
Shipman Library
Adrian College
Adrian MI 49221

(517) 265-5161

OPEN: M-Th 8-11, F 8-5, Sa 9:30-4:30, Su 2-11; shorter hours during summer; closed holidays
COPYING FACILITIES: yes
MATERIALS SOLICITED: Biographies of ministers and histories of churches.

HOLDINGS:
Total volume: 35 monographs
Inclusive dates: 1950 -
Description: Typewritten monographs dealing with different aspects of Methodist church history.

ALBION

MI12-10
Albion College
Stockwell Memorial Library
Albion MI 49224

no telephone

SEE: NUCMC, 1971 (as United Methodist Church, West Michigan Conference, Commission on Archives and History).

Questionnaire not returned.

ALLEGAN

MI20-50
Allegan Public Library
331 Hubbard Street
Allegan MI 49010

(616) 673-4625

OPEN: M-Th 12-9, F, Sa 9-5:30; closed Sundays and holidays
COPYING FACILITIES: yes

HOLDINGS:
    Total volume: not specified
    Inclusive dates: 1833 -
    Description: Township records and other local materials, including letters to U.S. Representative and Senator Lucius Lyon.

SEE: Hamer.

ALLENDALE

MI28-280
Grand Valley State College
Zumberge Library
Archives
Allendale MI 49401

(616) 895-3513

OPEN: by appointment only
COPYING FACILITIES: yes
MATERIALS SOLICITED: Michigan milling and related materials and Michigan business records.

HOLDINGS:
    Total volume: 180 l.f.
    Inclusive dates: 1870 - 1952
    Description: Journals, ledgers, letter books, correspondence, sales records, shipping records, and payroll and related business and financial records of the Voigt flour milling enterprise and its predecessors, related to Grand Rapids, and the company's distribution area throughout the eastern United States.

ALMA

MI32-40
Alma College
Monteith Library
Archives
614 West Superior
Alma MI 48801

(517) 463-7227

OPEN: by appointment only
ACCESS: access and use by permission of Archivist
COPYING FACILITIES: yes
MATERIALS SOLICITED: Material from administrative and academic offices of the College, current and retired faculty, and College alumni. Will also accept manuscripts of works by Alma College faculty, students and alumni; items dealing in any way with Alma College; or other materials of intrinsic value.

HOLDINGS:
    Total volume: 204 l.f.; 4,680 slides, tapes, films
    Inclusive dates: 1886 - 1965
    Description: Minutes and records of the Board of Trustees and College community government bodies, academic and extra-curricular programs and their development, and a photographic record of late 19th and 20th century campus activities. Also in the collection are correspondence and manuscript sermons of two College presidents and a few manuscripts of works published by alumni and friends of the College.

ALPENA

MI36-400
Jesse Besser Museum
491 Johnson Street
Alpena MI 49707

(517) 356-2202

OPEN: by appointment only M-F 9-4; closed weekends and holidays
ACCESS: appointment required
COPYING FACILITIES: yes
MATERIALS SOLICITED: Records relating to the history of Alpena and northeastern Michigan.

HOLDINGS:
    Total volume: not specified
    Inclusive dates: 1830's - 1960's
    Description: Manuscripts, data, and photographs relating to the history of Alpena and northeastern Michigan, including early industries, lighthouses, fisheries, shipping, and development.

ANN ARBOR

MI40-300
Gerald R. Ford Library
1000 Beal Avenue
Ann Arbor MI 48109

(313) 668-2218

OPEN: M-F 8:45-4:45, Sa 8:30-12:30 by appointment only; closed Sundays and holidays
COPYING FACILITIES: yes
MATERIALS SOLICITED: Materials relating to the Presidential administration of Gerald R. Ford and to his life and public career.

HOLDINGS:
    Total volume: 14,000,000 pages
    Inclusive dates: 1929 -
    Description: Papers of Gerald R. Ford covering his career as Congressman, Vice President, and President, including White House central files and 150 files from White House and Domestic Council staff, 1974-77. Also included are papers of friends and associates, federal records, organization records, and audio-visual materials.

MI40-784
University of Michigan
Bentley Historical Library
Michigan Historical Collections
1150 Beal Avenue
Ann Arbor MI 48109-2113

(313) 764-3482

OPEN: M-F 8:30-5, Sa 9-12:30; closed Sundays and holidays, and Saturdays during summer
COPYING FACILITIES: yes
MATERIALS SOLICITED: Michigan and the University of Michigan. Will also accept other materials if donor has some Michigan connection.

HOLDINGS:
    Total volume: 22,000,000 items
    Inclusive dates: 1704 -
    Description: Over 3,500 collections relating chiefly to the history of Michigan and the University of Michigan. Subject holdings of special note include the temperance and prohibition movement, America's interest in the Philippine Islands, 20th century American government and politics, the Civil War, lumbering, church history, conservation, women's history, black history, pacifism and conscientious objection, journalism, medicine, agriculture, and the life of immigrant groups in Michigan. Included are records of organizations, papers of individuals, and audio-visual materials.
    Also held are the records of the Episcopal Diocese of Western Michigan and its affiliated parishes and organizations, dating 1874- , with emphasis on recent years.

GUIDES: Thomas Powers and William McNitt, *Guide to Manuscripts in the Bentley Historical Library* (1976).

SEE: Hamer; NUCMC, 1963-65, 81.

SEE: Davis; Meckler and McMullin; Novotny; Hounshell; Krichmar; Schatz; Paszek; Robbins; Hinding; Bean and Vane; Spalek; Ingram; Parkinson.

SEE ALSO: The Collections also have issued finding aids to individual collections and bulletins relating to such special areas of study as black history, mass communications, natural resources and conservation, the Philippines, the Detroit Urban League, and pacifism and conscientious objection.

MI40-796
University of Michigan
Engineering-Transportation Library
312 Undergraduate Library Building
Ann Arbor MI 48109

(313) 764-7494

OPEN: M-F 8-5; closed weekends and holidays
ACCESS: appointment required prior to visit
COPYING FACILITIES: yes
MATERIALS SOLICITED: Will accept materials on any phase of transportation history, including technology, travel, planning and construction, and social impact. Formats may comprise correspondence, diaries, maps, photographs, engineering and technical drawings, and business and financial records of transport industries.

HOLDINGS:
    Total volume: 31,000 items
    Inclusive dates: 1625 - 1945
    Description: Transportation history with emphasis on 19th century North America. There are 1,000 pieces of correspondence, 12,000 prints and photographs covering all modes of transportation, 60 minute books and ledgers of the Detroit United Railway Lines, and 18,000 items of the personal and business papers of Charles Ellet, Jr., American civil engineer.

SEE: NUCMC, 1962.

SEE ALSO: Ann Novotny, ed., *Picture Sources 3* (Special Libraries Assn., 1975); Edwin T. Layton, Jr., ed., *A Regional Union Catalog of Manuscripts Relating to the History of Science and Technology Located in Indiana, Michigan, and Ohio* (Case Western Reserve Univ., 1971); Richard C. Davis, *North American Forest History: A Guide to Archives and Manuscripts in the United States and Canada* (Clio Books, 1977).

MI40-800

University of Michigan
History of Art Department
Asian Art Archives
Room 50, Tappan Hall
Ann Arbor MI 48109-1357

(313) 764-5555

OPEN: M-F 8-5; closed weekends, holidays, and Christmas vacation
COPYING FACILITIES: no
MATERIALS SOLICITED: Black and white photographs and color slides of art, particularly painting, sculpture, and architecture, from China, Japan, South Asia, and Southeast Asia. Will also accept related architectural plans.

HOLDINGS:
　　Total volume: 50,000 items
　　Inclusive dates: not specified
　　Description: Photographs of paintings, bronzes, ceramics, and minor arts in the collection of the National Palace Museum in Taiwan; photographs of Far Eastern art, primarily painting, covering all periods of art history, although with limited 20th century coverage; photographs of South Asian architecture, sculpture, and painting, with emphasis on cave architecture and sculpture; photographs of Southeast Asian sculpture, murals, and monuments; and photographs of Islamic art, including monuments, decorative arts, and book illuminations.

MI40-808

University of Michigan
Library
Department of Rare Books and
　　Special Collections
Room 711, Hatcher Graduate Library
Ann Arbor MI 48109-1205

(313) 764-9377

OPEN: M-F 10-5, Sa 10-12; closed Sundays, holidays, and Christmas week
ACCESS: qualified scholars engaged in research
COPYING FACILITIES: yes
MATERIALS SOLICITED: Materials relating to the 19th and 20th century theater, literary and scientific topics, protest movements, and historical papers of more than local interest. Will also accept materials of potential research value, in areas not covered by nearby repositories for local, State, and early American materials.

HOLDINGS:
　　Total volume: 75,000 items; 700 vols.; 250 l.f.
　　Inclusive dates: 17th century -
　　Description: Over 100 collections relating chiefly to literature, the theater, music, science, history, economics, and pro-

test movements in the United States and Europe in the 19th and 20th centuries. Included are personal correspondence and papers, literary manuscripts, promptbooks, music scores, government documents, records of literary and civil rights organizations, photographs, and scrapbooks.

SEE: Hamer; NUCMC, 1959-61, 76, 78.

SEE: Robbins; Martin; Hinding.

SEE ALSO: Walter Schatz, ed., *Directory of Afro-American Resources* (Bowker, 1970); Lorenzo Green, 'Negro Manuscript Collections in Libraries,' *Negro History Bulletin* 30 (March 1967); Ann Novotny, ed., *Picture Sources 3* (Special Libraries Assn., 1975).

MI40-814

University of Michigan
Museum of Anthropology
4009 Museums Building
Ann Arbor MI 48109

(313) 764-0485

OPEN: M-F 8-5; closed weekends and holidays
COPYING FACILITIES: yes
MATERIALS SOLICITED: Materials relating to ethnobotany in North America and the history of archaeological research in Michigan, elsewhere east of the Rocky Mountains, and the Philippine Islands. Will also accept ethnographic and archaeological field notes, photographs, and films.

HOLDINGS:
　　Total volume: 60 l.f.
　　Inclusive dates: late 1800's -
　　Description: Materials relating to the history of ethnobotany in North America, the beginnings of scientific archaeology in Michigan and the National Research Council state surveys, anthropological field work in the Philippines, and the history of the Museum of Anthropology. Included are field notes and correspondence of Melvin R. Gilmore and Carl E. Guthe, photographs by Dean C. Worchester, papers of prominent amateur archaeologists in Michigan and museum curators, and administrative records of the Museum.

SEE: Bean and Vane.

MI40-820

University of Michigan
William L. Clements Library
909 South University Avenue
Ann Arbor MI 48109

(313) 764-2347

OPEN: M-F 9-5; closed weekends and holidays
ACCESS: serious researchers only; letter of introduction required from non-residents of Ann Arbor
COPYING FACILITIES: yes
MATERIALS SOLICITED: Americana, 1500-1865. Will also accept American sheet music in manuscript, prior to 1900.

HOLDINGS:
　　Total volume: 300,000 items
　　Inclusive dates: 1542 - 1950
　　Description: 350 collections, chiefly British and American materials relating to the colonial and Revolutionary War periods, the War of 1812, and other aspects of American history, including the antislavery movement and the Civil War. There are also collections pertaining to Latin American history, including some dating as early as 1542, and papers of bibliophiles.

GUIDES: Arlene P. Shy, ed., *Guide to the Manuscript Collections of the Clements Library* (G. K. Hall, 1978).

SEE: Hamer; NUCMC, 1959-64, 68, 70.

SEE: Allard, Crawley, and Edmison; Hinding; Robbins; Ingram; Beers - Southwest.

SEE ALSO: *History of the William L. Clements Library, 1923-1973* (Univ. of Michigan, 1973); Christian Brun, comp., *Guide to the Manuscript Maps in the William L. Clements Library* (Univ. of Michigan, 1959); Douglas W. Marshall, ed., *Research Catalog of Maps of America to 1860 in the William L. Clements Library* (Univ. of Michigan, 1972); Walter Schatz, ed., *Directory of Afro-American Resources* (Bowker, 1970); Edwin T. Layton, Jr., ed., *A Regional Union Catalog of Manuscripts Relating to the History of Science and Technology Located in Indiana, Michigan, and Ohio* (Case Western Reserve Univ., 1971).

Ann Novotny, ed., *Picture Sources 3* (Special Libraries Assn., 1975); William F. Welke, 'The Papers of the Viscounts Melville,' *American Archivist* 26 (Oct. 1963); Peter Duignan, *Handbook of American Resources for African Studies* (Hoover Institution, 1967); Richard C. Davis, *North American Forest History: A Guide to Archives and Manuscripts in the United States and Canada* (Clio Books, 1977).

MI40-880

Washtenaw Historical Society
2708 Brockman Blvd.
Ann Arbor MI 48104

no telephone

SEE: Hamer.

Questionnaire not returned.

AUGUSTA

MI44-520

McKay Library
105 South Webster Street
Augusta MI 49102

no telephone

SEE: NUCMC, 1977.

Questionnaire not returned.

BATTLE CREEK

MI60-420
Kimball House Historical Society of
Battle Creek
196 Capital Avenue, N.E.
Battle Creek MI 49017

(616) 965-2613

OPEN: Tu, Th 1-4:30 and by
appointment; closed holidays and
entire month of January
COPYING FACILITIES: no
MATERIALS SOLICITED: Materials pertaining to the history of Battle Creek.

HOLDINGS:
  Total volume: not specified
  Inclusive dates: 1850 -
  Description: Photographs, letters, diaries, journals, manuscripts, pioneer papers, and other materials relating to the
  history of Battle Creek and its immediate
  environs.

MI60-440
Kingman Museum of Natural History
175 Limit Street
Battle Creek MI 49017

(616) 965-5117

OPEN: Su 1-5, M-F 10-5; closed
Saturdays and holidays
COPYING FACILITIES: yes

HOLDINGS:
  Total volume: 15,000 slides
  Inclusive dates: 1940's - 1950's
  Description: Slides dealing chiefly with
  the National Parks, wildlife, and Indian
  tribes in the western United States and
  Mexico.

MI60-880
Willard Library
Local History Collection
7 West Van Buren Street
Battle Creek MI 49016

(616) 968-8166

OPEN: M-Th 9-9, F, Sa 9-5; closed
Sundays and holidays
ACCESS: appointment preferred
COPYING FACILITIES: yes
MATERIALS SOLICITED: Battle Creek ma-
terials, 1831- ; Michigan materials,
1837- ; and family histories.

HOLDINGS:
  Total volume: 20,000 items
  Inclusive dates: 1831 -
  Description: Materials relating to
  Michigan history, specializing in the
  Calhoun County and Battle Creek areas.
  Included are manuscripts, photographs,
  glass slides, Michigan and Battle Creek
  government documents, and correspon-
  dence and scrapbooks of Dr. John Har-
  vey Kellogg, who was active in Seventh-
  Day Adventist church activities, such as a
  health-related periodical and the Battle
  Creek sanitarium.

SEE: Hinding.

BAY CITY

MI64-70
Bay County Historical Society
Historical Museum of Bay County
1700 Center Avenue
Bay City MI 48708

(517) 893-5733

OPEN: M-F 10-5; closed weekends and
holidays
COPYING FACILITIES: yes
MATERIALS SOLICITED: Historical mate-
rials concerning Bay County and the
Great Lakes.

HOLDINGS:
  Total volume: not specified
  Inclusive dates: 1830 -
  Description: Manuscripts and photographs regarding the history of Bay County and the Great Lakes, particularly Lake
  Huron. Bay County materials include
  manuscripts relating to Indians, records
  of lumbering companies and other industries, memoirs of the first settlers, Civil
  War letters, and documents pertaining to
  the Bay City *Times.*

SEE: Hamer (as Bay County Historical
Museum).

SEE: Davis.

BELDING

MI68-640
Process Equipment Corporation
500 Reed Street
Belding MI 48809

(616) 794-1230

OPEN: M-F 9-5; closed weekends and
holidays
ACCESS: prior approval, based on nature
of research
COPYING FACILITIES: yes

HOLDINGS:
  Total volume: 20 file drawers
  Inclusive dates: 1945 -
  Description: Ledgers, financial state-
  ments, tax returns, corporate minutes,
  and other Corporation records.

BENTON HARBOR

MI80-80
Benton Harbor Public Library
213 East Wall Street
Benton Harbor MI 49022

(616) 926-6139

OPEN: M-W 9:30-8:30, Th, F 9:30-6, Sa
9:30-5; certain collections by
appointment only; closed Saturdays,
June-Aug.; closed Sundays and holidays
COPYING FACILITIES: yes
MATERIALS SOLICITED: Materials per-
taining to the history of Benton
Harbor-St. Joseph area, Berrien Coun-
ty, House of David, and the Great
Lakes, particularly Lake Michigan.

HOLDINGS:
  Total volume: 200 items
  Inclusive dates: 1856 -
  Description: Materials relating to
  Michigan, Benton Harbor-St. Joseph,
  Berrien County, and surrounding town-
  ships, including early marriage and ceme-
  tery records, family genealogies, Daugh-
  ters of the American Revolution lineage
  books, and early photographs.

SEE: Hamer.

BERRIEN SPRINGS

MI90-30
Andrews University
James White Library
Heritage Room
Berrien Springs MI 49104

(616) 471-3274

OPEN: Su 1-5, M-Th 8-5, F 8-12, Tu and
Th evenings; closed Saturdays and
major holidays
COPYING FACILITIES: yes
MATERIALS SOLICITED: Materials dealing
with the history of the Seventh-Day
Adventist church and the Millerite
movement; personal papers of church
pioneers, missionaries and ministers;
and United States and Michigan history materials.

HOLDINGS:
  Total volume: 605 l.f.
  Inclusive dates: 1844 -
  Description: Research materials on the
  history of the advent movement and the
  Seventh-Day Adventist church. Included
  are the personal papers of John Byington,
  John N. Loughborough, George
  McCready Price, and James L.
  McElhany; and missionary materials, in-
  cluding a collection about Pitcairn Island
  beginning in 1890.

SEE: Hamer (as Seventh-Day Adventist
Theological Seminary Library in Tako-
ma Park, MD); NUCMC, 1970.

BIG RAPIDS

MI100-240
Ferris State College
Library
College Archives
901 South State Street
Big Rapids MI 49307

(616) 796-0461, Ext. 5690

OPEN: M-W, F 8-5, Th 9-5; closed
weekends and holidays
COPYING FACILITIES: yes
MATERIALS SOLICITED: Items relating to
the history of the College, the city of
Big Rapids, and the surrounding area.
Will also accept selected items relating
to Michigan and subjects emphasized
by the College curriculum.

HOLDINGS:
  Total volume: 112 l.f.
  Inclusive dates: 1860 -
  Description: Noncurrent records of
  Ferris State College, 1884 to date, and
  papers of its administrators and faculty

members, including Woodbridge N. Ferris, College founder and U.S. Senator. There are additional materials relating to the history of Big Rapids and the surrounding area.

Papers of Dr. Chauncey J. Howe, O.D., optometrist and secretary of the Michigan Board of Examiners in Optometry, 1909-72.

SEE: Hamer (as Ferris Institute Library); NUCMC, 1968.

SEE: Meckler and McMullins.

SEE ALSO: A register of the Chauncey J. Howe archives of optometry has been published by the Library.

BLOOMFIELD HILLS

MI110-120

Cranbrook Educational Community Archives
380 Lone Pine Road
Bloomfield Hills MI

MAILING ADDRESS:
P.O. Box 801
Bloomfield Hills MI 48013

(313) 645-3154

OPEN: by appointment only
COPYING FACILITIES: yes
MATERIALS SOLICITED: Noncurrent business records of the Cranbrook Institutions and materials relating to the history of Cranbrook.

HOLDINGS:
Total volume: 300 l.f.
Inclusive dates: 1880 -
Description: Records of the Cranbrook Institutions (Cranbrook School, Kingswood School, Brookside School, Cranbrook Academy of Art, Cranbrook Institute of Science, Christ Church Cranbrook, Cranbrook Foundation, and Cranbrook Educational Community), including minutes of the boards, photographs, taped interviews with individuals, as well as papers and correspondence of George G. Booth, founder of Cranbrook.

CADILLAC

MI122-880

Wexford County Historical Society-Museum
127 Beech Street
Cadillac MI

MAILING ADDRESS:
P.O. Box 124
Cadillac MI 49601

no telephone

OPEN: June-Aug., Tu-F 2-5, Sa 12-4; Sept.-May, by appointment only
ACCESS: appointment requested
COPYING FACILITIES: no
MATERIALS SOLICITED: Manuscript, archives, and visual materials relating to Wexford County. Will also accept public documents relating to the County.

HOLDINGS:
Total volume: 64 c.f.
Inclusive dates: 1870 - 1960
Description: Materials relating to Wexford County, including the logging industry, the 'Shay' engine, early schools, and people, as well as photographs of architecture, dress, and other subjects.

CARO

MI126-880

Watrousville-Caro Area Historical Society
770 Norma Drive
Caro MI 48723

(517) 673-4643

OPEN: June - Sept., M-F 2-4; closed weekends
ACCESS: contact secretary if additional access is necessary
COPYING FACILITIES: no
MATERIALS SOLICITED: Family histories, oral history tapes, documents, photographs, correspondence, journals, account books, and business records relating to the history of the Watrousville-Caro area.

HOLDINGS:
Total volume: 25 items
Inclusive dates: 1851 - 1935
Description: Materials relating to the Watrousville-Caro area. Included are records of Juniata Township, oral history tapes, records of a general store, school board records, documents pertaining to school reunions, chattel mortgages, and materials relating to a local Methodist church.

CASPIAN

MI130-360

Iron County Museum
Route 424, Museum Street
Caspian MI

MAILING ADDRESS:
P.O. Box 272
Caspian MI 49915

(906) 265-3942, 2617

OPEN: M-Sa 9-5, Su 1-5; June-Labor Day; other months by appointment only
USER FEES: $.50 children, $1.50 adults
COPYING FACILITIES: no
MATERIALS SOLICITED: Letters and records of local pioneers, organizations, and mining and lumbering companies.

HOLDINGS:
Total volume: 300 l.f.
Inclusive dates: 1700's -
Description: Manuscripts of various individuals and concerns of Iron County, mostly dating from the 1920's. Also included are a mining company's payrolls and voucher books, as well as mining maps, manuscripts and proofs of local history books, about 150 oral history interviews, and 3,000 photographs of local scenes and people.

CHELSEA

MI160-520

McKune Memorial Library
221 South Main
Chelsea MI 48118

(313) 475-8732

OPEN: M 10-5, 7-9, Tu 12-5, W 12-5, 7-9, Th 10-9, F 12-5, Sa 10-3; closed Sundays and holidays
COPYING FACILITIES: yes
MATERIALS SOLICITED: Historical materials dealing with Chelsea Village, surrounding townships, and Washtenaw County. Will also accept items covering Michigan history.

HOLDINGS:
Total volume: not specified
Inclusive dates: 1800 -
Description: Materials relating to Chelsea Village, surrounding townships, and Washtenaw County, including diaries, scrapbooks, accounting records, and a complete cemetery file of the Chelsea area, cross-indexed by family name.

CHESANING

MI164-120

Chesaning Public Library
227 East Broad Street
Chesaning MI 48616

(517) 845-3211

OPEN: M, Tu 9-5, Th 8:30-8:30, F 11-7, Sa 9-1; closed Sundays, Wednesdays, and holidays
COPYING FACILITIES: yes
MATERIALS SOLICITED: Local history materials. Will also accept materials dealing with Michigan history.

HOLDINGS:
Total volume: 7 boxes; 3,085 items
Inclusive dates: mid-19th century -
Description: Over 3,000 family history data sheets of local families, 75 photographs of local scenes and people, 10 oral history tapes, 6 boxes of cemetery records, and 1 box of research materials for Mark Ireland's history of Chesaning (1842-1950), *Place of the Big Rock.*

CLAWSON

MI172-120

Clawson Historical Commission
Clawson Historical Museum
41 Fisher Court
Clawson MI

MAILING ADDRESS:
425 North Main
Clawson MI 48017

(313) 588-9169

OPEN: M-F 1-4:30, Su 1-4; closed Saturdays and holidays
COPYING FACILITIES: yes
MATERIALS SOLICITED: Local history materials, including personal papers, government records, and oral histories.

Will also accept materials pertaining to Michigan history.

HOLDINGS:
> *Total volume:* 4 file drawers
> *Inclusive dates:* 1900 -
> *Description:* Photographs, biographical sketches, recollections, newsclippings, and other materials relating to Clawson and the surrounding area.

COPPER HARBOR

MI200-240
Fort Wilkins State Park
Copper Harbor MI 49918

(906) 289-4215

OPEN: daily M-F; closed weekends and holidays
ACCESS: serious academic researchers
COPYING FACILITIES: no
MATERIALS SOLICITED: Photographs and documents relating to the history of Fort Wilkins, Copper Harbor lighthouse and range lighthouse; and Keweenaw Peninsula settlement, copper mining, commercial fishing and lumbering.

HOLDINGS:
> *Total volume:* 12 l.f.
> *Inclusive dates:* 1843 - 1870
> *Description:* Photographs and documents relating to Fort Wilkins, its military personnel and dependents; Copper Harbor lighthouse, range lighthouse, and personnel; and Keweenaw Peninsula copper mining and shipping industries.

DEARBORN

MI214-140
Dearborn Department of Libraries
Henry Ford Centennial Library
Audio-Visual Division
16301 Michigan Avenue
Dearborn MI 48126

(313) 943-2344

OPEN: M, Tu, Th 9-9, W 1-9, F 9-5; Sa 1-5; Su 1-5 in winter; closed holidays
COPYING FACILITIES: yes

HOLDINGS:
> *Total volume:* 4 reels
> *Inclusive dates:* 1915 - 1950
> *Description:* Nearly 5,000 feet of silent 16mm home movies taken by Henry Ford 1915-1930, depicting the Ford family at home in Fairlane Manor and on vacations throughout the world. The library also has nearly 4,000 documentary and fiction films.

MI214-150
Dearborn Historical Museum
915 Brady Street
Dearborn MI 48124

(313) 565-3000

OPEN: M-F 8:30-5:30; Sa 9-5 May-Nov., 1-5 Nov.-May; closed Sundays and holidays
COPYING FACILITIES: yes

MATERIALS SOLICITED: Dearborn history.

HOLDINGS:
> *Total volume:* 1,000 l.f.
> *Inclusive dates:* 1833 -
> *Description:* A collection of manuscripts, archives, history files, maps, photographs, and oral history tapes and transcripts related to all aspects of Dearborn history. Included is information on buildings and residences, business and industry, churches and organizations, education, events, families and genealogies, government, streets, roads, bridges, and transportation. There is a special emphasis on the Arsenal-Commandant's Quarters and the McFadden-Ross House. The collection also includes extensive materials on Henry Dearborn, the city's namesake.

GUIDES: *A Guide to the Manuscript Collections and an Outline to History, Photograph and Newspaper Files of the Dearborn Historical Commission* (1976).

SEE: Hamer; NUCMC, 1959-62, 77.

SEE: Hinding.

MI214-260
Greenfield Village and Henry Ford Museum
Ford Archives
20900 Oakwood Boulevard
Dearborn MI

MAILING ADDRESS:
P.O. Box 1970
Dearborn MI 48121

(313) 271-1620, Ext. 650

OPEN: M-F 8:30-5; closed weekends and holidays
USER FEES: subject to change and adjustment according to circumstances
ACCESS: by approval of Director of Archives upon written application
COPYING FACILITIES: yes
MATERIALS SOLICITED: Materials related to Henry Ford and family, Ford Motor Company and Ford nonautomotive enterprises.

HOLDINGS:
> *Total volume:* 12,000 l.f.
> *Inclusive dates:* 1903 - 1960
> *Description:* Personal papers and business files of Henry Ford; records from offices of the Ford Motor Company, as well as subsidiary companies and companies owned by Henry Ford. Company records include information on production, public relations, sales and advertising, finance, subsidiaries, legal operations, international operations, organization, and administration. There are also personal papers of individuals associated with Henry Ford or the Company, as well as nearly 400,000 photographs and 400 oral histories.

SEE: Hamer.

SEE: Hounshell; Meckler and McMullin; Davis; Novotny; Parkinson; Paszek.

SEE ALSO: Edwin T. Layton, Jr., ed. *A Regional Union Catalog of Manuscripts Relating to the History of Science and Technology Located in Indiana, Michigan, and Ohio* (Case Western Reserve Univ., 1971).

A booklet, *The Ford Archives* (1974), is available from the institution.

MI214-280
Greenfield Village and Henry Ford Museum
Robert Hudson Tannahill Research Library
20900 Oakwood Boulevard
Dearborn MI

MAILING ADDRESS:
P.O. Box 1970
Dearborn MI 48121

(313) 271-1620, Ext. 540

OPEN: by appointment only M-F 8:30-5; closed weekends
ACCESS: appointment required
COPYING FACILITIES: yes
MATERIALS SOLICITED: Manuscripts, business archives, and related materials relating to American agriculture, power and shop machinery, glass and ceramics, home arts, lighting, communications, furniture, and transportation, for the period from 1650 to 1950. Will also accept other materials documenting American material culture for the same period.

HOLDINGS:
> *Total volume:* 250 l.f.; 4 file cabinets
> *Inclusive dates:* 1549 - 1940
> *Description:* Personal and business papers of Thomas A. Edison, the Detroit Publishing Company archives, materials concerning the Boston & Sandwich Glass Company, and a manuscript collection.

DETROIT

MI230-50
Archdiocese of Detroit
Archives
1234 Washington Boulevard
Detroit MI 48226

(313) 237-5846

OPEN: by appointment only M-F 8:30-4; closed weekends and holidays
COPYING FACILITIES: yes

HOLDINGS:
> *Total volume:* 500 l.f.
> *Inclusive dates:* 1704 -
> *Description:* Records chiefly of the central administration of the Roman Catholic Archdiocese of Detroit, founded in 1833, and its bishops, as well as early records of the Catholic community in the Detroit area prior to 1833 and parish records of historical interest. The records include correspondence, account books, financial and legal records, photographs, and early printed items.

SEE: Hamer.

MI230-148

The Detroit Institute of Arts
Museum Archives and Record Center
5200 Woodward Avenue
Detroit MI 48202

(313) 833-1462, 1728

OPEN: M-F 9:30-5; closed weekends and holidays
COPYING FACILITIES: yes
MATERIALS SOLICITED: Records of the Detroit Institute of Arts and related associations and personal papers of individuals associated with the museum. Will also accept materials relating to the history of American puppetry.

HOLDINGS:
Total volume: 800 c.f.; 390 vols.
Inclusive dates: 1876 -
Description: Records pertaining to the administration, curatorial activities, governance, and history of the museum, including papers of individuals and organizations such as the Alger House Branch Museum records, the Paul McPharlin puppetry in America collection, and the Robert H. Tannahill papers; calendars, catalogs, minutes, administrative data, and publicity materials; architectural drawings and blueprints of the museum buildings; photographs of staff, buildings, exhibitions, events, and Detroit streets; oral histories; minute books; and scrapbooks.

MI230-153

The Detroit Institute of Arts
Registrar's Office
5200 Woodward Avenue
Detroit MI 48202

(313) 833-7933

OPEN: M-F 9-5; closed weekends and holidays
COPYING FACILITIES: yes
MATERIALS SOLICITED: Materials documenting items in the collection.

HOLDINGS:
Total volume: 60 file drawers
Inclusive dates: 1885 -
Description: Records pertaining to the works of art in the collections of the Founders Society and Detroit Institute of Arts (approximately 40,000 objects). Included are slides; photographs; invoices; correspondence with dealers, donors, lenders, borrowers, and scholars; accessions and catalog information; and materials from previous special exhibitions. Manuscript artist letters.
Computerized access through the Detroit Art Registration Information Systems.

MI230-155

The Detroit Institute of Arts
Research Library
5200 Woodward Avenue
Detroit MI 48202

(313) 833-7926

OPEN: M-Sa 9-5; closed Sundays and holidays
ACCESS: graduate students and majors in art history
COPYING FACILITIES: yes

HOLDINGS:
Total volume: 20 vols.; 40,575 items
Inclusive dates: 13th century -
Description: 7 volumes of medieval and Renaissance illuminated manuscripts; 575 items and 13 volumes of the correspondence, travel journals, notes, and other papers of artist Thomas Cole; and 40,000 entry forms, with biographical information, submitted by Michigan artists for annual exhibitions since 1945.
Architectural drawings by Albert Kahn, including designs by Nettleton and Kahn for the James E. Scripps Library and other early works.

SEE: Hamer; NUCMC, 1959-61.

SEE: Martin.

MI230-165

Detroit Public Library
Burton Historical Collection
5201 Woodward Avenue
Detroit MI 48202

(313) 833-1480

OPEN: Tu, Th, F, Sa 9:30-5:30, W 1-9; closed Sundays, Mondays, and holidays
COPYING FACILITIES: yes
MATERIALS SOLICITED: Materials relating to the history of the Old Northwest, Michigan, and Detroit; automotive history; black music and musicians; and fine arts.

HOLDINGS:
Total volume: 10,000 l.f.
Inclusive dates: 1700 -
Description: The Burton Historical Collection at the Library includes over 6,500 l.f. of letters, papers, ledgers, and other documents relating to the history of Detroit, Michigan, and the Old Northwest, including papers of pioneers, officeholders, businesspersons, traders, and organizations, as well as non-current records of the city and county. Other collections include papers and photographs regarding black music and musicians, literature, fine arts, and automotive history.

SEE: Hamer; NUCMC, 1966-73, 76, 79, NUCMC, 1967 (as Detroit Public Library, Automotive History Collection).

SEE: Beers - Southwest; Hinding; Robbins; Parkinson; Spalek; Ingram; Allard, Crawley, and Edmison; Bean and Vane; Hines.

SEE ALSO: *The Automotive History Collection of the Detroit Public Library; A Simplified Guide to its Holdings* (G. K. Hall, 1966); Edwin T. Layton, Jr., ed., *A Regional Union Catalog of Manuscripts Relating to the History of Science and Technology Located in Indiana, Michigan, and Ohio* (Case Western Reserve Univ., 1971); David A. Hounshell, comp., *Manuscripts in U.S. Depositories Relating to the History of Electrical Science and Technology* (Smithsonian Institution, n.d.).

Walter Schatz, ed., *Directory of Afro-American Resources* (Bowker, 1970); Ann Novotny, ed., *Picture Sources 3* (Special Libraries Assn., 1975); David J. Olson, comp., *Bibliography of Sources Relating to Women* (Michigan History Division, Michigan Department of State, 1975); Albert Krichmar, *The Women's Rights Movement in the United States, 1848-1970: A Bibliography and Sourcebook* (Scarecrow Press, 1972).

Richard C. Davis, *North American Forest History: A Guide to Archives and Manuscripts in the United States and Canada* (Clio Books, 1977).

MI230-180

Dossin Great Lakes Museum
Ship Data Registry
100 Strand, Belle Isle
Detroit MI 48207

(313) 267-6440
ACCESS: appointment required
COPYING FACILITIES: no
MATERIALS SOLICITED: Photographs and records pertaining to Great Lakes ships and shipping.

HOLDINGS:
Total volume: 250 l.f.; 25,000 items
Inclusive dates: 1850 -
Description: Materials dealing with Great Lakes and St. Lawrence River navigation, including photographs, official lists of vessels, and data sheets and career information about individual ships. No genealogical materials are included.

SEE: Novotny.

MI230-500

Marygrove College
Library
8425 West McNichols Road
Detroit MI 48221

no telephone
SEE: Hamer.

Questionnaire not returned.

MI230-720

Sacred Heart Seminary
Leo J. Ward Memorial Library
Rare Book Collection and Archives
2701 West Chicago Boulevard
Detroit MI 48206

(313) 868-2700

OPEN: M-F 9-9, Sa, Su 12-5; closed Catholic holy days
COPYING FACILITIES: yes
MATERIALS SOLICITED: Materials on the Catholic church in Michigan, the Archdiocese of Detroit, and Gabriel Richard. Will also accept other materials.

HOLDINGS:
Total volume: 13 l.f.; 28 items
Inclusive dates: 1800 -
Description: Notebooks, diaries, and manuscript textbooks of Gabriel Richard, and the Sacred Heart Seminary archives.

MI230-730

Southeast Michigan Council of
  Governments
8th Floor, Book Building
1249 Washington Boulevard
Detroit MI 48226

(313) 961-4266

OPEN: M-F 8:30-4:30; closed weekends
  and holidays
ACCESS: permission required
COPYING FACILITIES: yes
MATERIALS SOLICITED: Noncurrent
  records, minutes, reports, maps, aerial
  photographs, and noncurrent machine
  readable records of research value, pertaining to southeastern Michigan.

HOLDINGS:
  Total volume: 50 boxes
  Inclusive dates: 1952 - 1969
  Description: Files of three regional
  planning organizations for southeastern
  Michigan, particularly focusing on
  Wayne, Oakland, and Macomb counties
  of the Detroit metropolitan area. Minutes
  of meetings, correspondence, planning
  notes, aerial photography, and data files
  are represented.

MI230-740

The Stroh Brewery Company
100 River Place
Detroit MI 48207

(313) 446-2000

OPEN: M-F by appointment; closed
  weekends and holidays
COPYING FACILITIES: yes
MATERIALS SOLICITED: Visual materials
  pertaining to the Stroh family, its brewery, and the brewing industry of Detroit and Michigan before World War
  II.

HOLDINGS:
  Total volume: not specified
  Inclusive dates: 1880 -
  Description: A collection of photo-
  graphs, advertisements, and records of
  The Stroh Brewery Company, including
  materials on its manufacture of ice cream
  and visual materials on other breweries in
  Michigan.

SEE ALSO: Edwin T. Layton, Jr., ed., *A
  Regional Union Catalog of Manuscripts
  Relating to the History of Science and
  Technology Located in Indiana, Michi-
  gan, and Ohio* (Case Western Reserve
  Univ., 1971).

MI230-780

Ukrainian-American Archives and
  Museum
11756 Charest Street
Detroit MI 48212

(313) 366-9764

OPEN: Sa 3-6, Su 10-2, or by
  appointment
COPYING FACILITIES: yes
MATERIALS SOLICITED: Materials pertaining to American and Ukrainian history.

HOLDINGS:
  Total volume: 863 boxes
  Inclusive dates: not specified
  Description: Materials concerning
  Ukrainian settlement in America and
  Canada, correspondence of organizations
  and individuals, materials concerning
  eastern Europe in World War I and II,
  papers and correspondence pertaining to
  refugees and displaced persons, and ma-
  terials concerning the city of Hamtramck,
  MI.

MI230-800

University of Detroit
Main Library
Rare Book Room and Archives
4001 West McNichols Road
Detroit MI 48221

(313) 927-1071, 1090

OPEN: M-F 8-5; closed weekends,
  holidays, and last two weeks of
  December
ACCESS: must have permission of
  Director and/or reference or archives
  staff
COPYING FACILITIES: yes
MATERIALS SOLICITED: Books, manuscripts, photographs relating to literature, engineering, technology, architecture, fine printing, and the University
  of Detroit.

HOLDINGS:
  Total volume: 285 l.f.; 1,000 vols.;
  10,000 photos
  Inclusive dates: 1565 - 1979
  Description: Theological manuscripts,
  including two antiphonals dated 1581
  and 1688; materials relating to the history
  of early Detroit; and letters of literary
  and historical figures, including some
  from British novelist Marie Corelli to the
  painter Arthur Severn. There are also the
  archives of the University, including letters, photographs, negatives, student papers, publications, clippings, press releases, and other materials.
  Book, short story, film scripts, and
  manuscripts of Elmore Leonard; Ernest
  Larue Jones collection of photographs illustrating history of aeronautics from
  1863-1917.

SEE: Hamer; NUCMC, 1966.

SEE ALSO: Walter Schatz, ed., *Directory of
  Afro-American Resources* (Bowker,
  1970).

MI230-880

Wayne State University
Archives of Labor History and Urban
  Affairs
Walter P. Reuther Library
Detroit MI 48202

(313) 577-4024

OPEN: M-F 9-5; closed weekends,
  holidays, and week after Christmas
ACCESS: available for serious scholarly
  research
COPYING FACILITIES: yes
MATERIALS SOLICITED: American labor
  history and related social and economic
  reform movements. 20th century urban
  America.

HOLDINGS:
  Total volume: 40,000 l.f.; 8,000 tapes;
  250,000 photographs
  Inclusive dates: 1860's -
  Description: The Archives serves as the
  official depository for the American Federation of State, County and Municipal
  Employees, American Federation of
  Teachers, Air Line Pilots Association, Industrial Workers of the World, The
  Newspaper Guild, United Auto Workers,
  United Farm Workers, and state and local labor organizations. Collections include oral history and photographs, as
  well as the personal papers of union leaders and other political and labor activists.

GUIDES: Warner W. Pflug, ed., *A Guide
  to the Archives of Labor History and
  Urban Affairs: Wayne State University*
  (Wayne State Univ. Press, 1974).

SEE: Hamer; NUCMC, 1966, 68, 70-74,
  77, 79.

SEE: Hinding; Parkinson; Davis.

SEE ALSO: Ann Novotny, ed., *Picture
  Sources 3* (Special Libraries Assn.,
  1975); Alan M. Meckler and Ruth
  McMullin, comps., *Oral History Collec-
  tions* (Bowker, 1975); Walter Schatz,
  ed., *Directory of Afro-American Re-
  sources* (Bowker, 1970); David J.
  Olson, comp., *Bibliography of Sources
  Relating to Women* (Michigan History
  Division, Michigan Dept. of State,
  1975); Archives of Labor History and
  Urban Affairs, *Newsletter.*

Philip P. Mason, 'Labor History Archives at
  Wayne State University,' *Labor History* 5
  (Winter 1964); Philip P. Mason, 'Wayne
  State University: The Archives of Labor
  and Urban Affairs,' *Archivaria* 4
  (Summer 1977).

MI230-890

Wayne State University
Department of Anthropology
Museum of Anthropology
6001 Cass (north door)
Detroit MI

MAILING ADDRESS:
137 Manoogian Building
Wayne State University
Detroit MI 48202

(313) 577-2598, 2935

OPEN: by appointment
ACCESS: advance arrangements required
COPYING FACILITIES: no
MATERIALS SOLICITED: Will accept ma-
  terials relating to Michigan archaeology
  and Indians.

HOLDINGS:
  Total volume: 11 c.f.
  Inclusive dates: 1958 -
  Description: Manuscripts relating primarily to Detroit area archaeology, land
  use histories, manufacturing companies,
  and Michigan Indians.

MI230-905
Wayne State University
University Archives
Walter P. Reuther Library
Detroit MI 48202

(313) 577-4024

OPEN: M-Sa 9-5; closed Sundays,
holidays, and other University closings
ACCESS: non-University collections open
under conditions arranged with
individual donor
COPYING FACILITIES: yes
MATERIALS SOLICITED: University
records, photographs, films, and sound
recordings; personal papers of faculty;
and professional and organizational
records, in particular relating to medicine and medical education.

HOLDINGS:
Total volume: 4,075 l.f.; 4,000 tapes;
25,000 photographs
Inclusive dates: 1868 -
Description: Materials, dating primarily
after 1930, documenting the growth and
development of Wayne State University
from its inception as the Detroit Medical
College in 1868. Included are University
files, faculty papers, and non-University
organization records reflecting medical
education and organizations, community
activities, and professional involvement
and research.

SEE: NUCMC, 1973.

SEE: Hinding.

SEE ALSO: David J. Olson, comp., Bibliog-
raphy of Sources Relating to Women
(Michigan History Division, Michigan
Dept. of State, 1975).

DEXTER

MI235-160
Dexter Area Museum, Inc.
3443 Inverness Street
Dexter MI 48130

(313) 426-2519

OPEN: Tu 1-3, second and fourth Sa 1-3,
or by appointment; closed other days
and holidays
COPYING FACILITIES: yes
MATERIALS SOLICITED: Genealogies, letters, diaries, memoirs, reminiscences,
histories, and other papers related to
persons, places, and events of the Dexter area.

HOLDINGS:
Total volume: 7 file drawers; 70
items
Inclusive dates: 1800 -
Description: Photographs, marriage,
death, and cemetery records, school
records, genealogies, and other papers relating to the history of the village of Dexter and the surrounding townships of
Lima, Scio, and Webster. All aspects of
development, including social, architectural, and educational, are represented.

EAST LANSING

MI255-530
Michigan State University
Libraries
Special Collections Division
East Lansing MI 48824

(517) 355-3770

OPEN: M-F 9-5, Sa 9-1; closed Sundays
and holidays
ACCESS: identification must be presented
and will be held while material is in
use
COPYING FACILITIES: yes
MATERIALS SOLICITED: Materials related
to American right- and left-wing activism, social change, etc. Will also accept
manuscript material in any area that is
judged to have potential research value.

HOLDINGS:
Total volume: 1,401 l.f.
Inclusive dates: 15th century -
Description: Africana collections relating to the Congo, German railway construction in Southwest Africa, and the
1895 French Madagascar War; African
travel diaries of Hungarian explorer Samuel Teleki (1845-1916); papers of German
political scientist Adolf Grabowsky, Russian literary critic Alexander Il'in, printing historian Douglas McMurtrie, agricul-
turist Perry G. Holden; and notebooks
and diaries of entomologist Francis Hemming.
Correspondence of journalist Harold
Frederic, materials concerning labor relations at the Safran Printing Co. (Detroit),
account books and photographs from the
Henderson Stock Co. (Midwest tent show
organization), materials relating to American political activity, especially CPUSA,
various Trotskiite groups, and the Students for a Democratic Society.

SEE: Hamer; NUCMC, 1959-62.

SEE: Duignan; Novotny; Parkinson; Robbins.

MI255-545
Michigan State University
University Archives and Historical
Collections
Room EG-13, Library
East Lansing MI 48824

(517) 355-2330

OPEN: M-F 8-5; closed weekends and
holidays
COPYING FACILITIES: yes
MATERIALS SOLICITED: Inactive University records of legal, administrative or
historical value; personal papers of faculty, staff, and alumni of the University; records of student and faculty organizations; manuscript materials relating to University interests such as agriculture, rural life, veterinary medicine, and international development;
and records of individuals and organizations that document Michigan history or the origin of the land grant
philosophy of education.

HOLDINGS:
Total volume: 6,500 c.f.
Inclusive dates: 1470 -
Description: The University Archives
comprises official University records, including those of the central administration, the individual colleges and departments and the Cooperative Extension
Service; University publications; and private papers of individuals and organizations associated with the University. The
Historical Collections consist of biblical
and liturgical texts dating from 1470 to
1927, and 19th and 20th century materials relating primarily to Michigan
individuals, families, businesses, and other organizations; rural life; agriculture; the
Civil War; and the lumbering and automobile industries. There are also microfilm copies of papers of members of Congress and others connected with the land
grant movement.
Pictorial records consist of over 30,000
items, many of them relating to campus
life and activities of Michigan State University. The Oral History Collection contains materials on University history and
a set of interviews relating to lumbering
in Michigan.

GUIDES: Frederick L. Honhart, Suzann
M. Pyzik and Saralee R. Howard, eds.,
A Guide to the Michigan State University Archives and Historical Collections
(1976).

SEE: Hamer; NUCMC, 1959-64, 66,
69-70, 80.

SEE: Duignan; Davis; Hinding.

SEE ALSO: Morris Rieger, 'Africa-Related
Papers of Persons and Organizations in
the United States,' African Studies Bulletin 8 (Dec. 1965).

EMPIRE

MI268-200
Empire Township Historical Museum
Main Street
Empire MI 49630

no telephone

OPEN: June - Labor Day, Tu, Th, Sa, Su
1-4; closed other days
COPYING FACILITIES: no
MATERIALS SOLICITED: Material pertaining to the lumbering industry on the
Lake Michigan shore around the turn
of the century. Will also accept local
history materials.

HOLDINGS:
Total volume: not specified
Inclusive dates: 1890's - 1920
Description: Photographs of early
homes and people of Empire Township
and the surrounding area.

FLINT

MI314-60
Alfred P. Sloan, Jr., Museum
1221 East Kearsley Street
Flint Michigan 48503

(313) 762-1169

OPEN: M-F 8-5; closed weekends and
holidays
COPYING FACILITIES: yes
MATERIALS SOLICITED: Material relating
to Flint and Genesee County, MI, and
records relating to the General Motors
Corporation, especially Buick.

HOLDINGS:
    Total volume: 50 l.f.
    Inclusive dates: 1865 -
    Description: Materials relating to Flint
and Genesee County, MI, especially General Motors Corporation, including
manuscripts, photographs, and local television news footage.

SEE: Hinding.

MI314-250
Flint Public Library
Michigan Room
1026 East Kearsley Street
Flint MI 48502

(313) 232-7111, Ext. 260

OPEN: M-Th 9-9, F, Sa 9-6; closed
Sundays and holidays
ACCESS: special permission required
COPYING FACILITIES: yes

HOLDINGS:
    Total volume: 70 vols.; 40 tapes; 221
aerial photographs
    Inclusive dates: 1880 -
    Description: Local historical materials,
including oral history tapes; photographs
of Flint buildings, churches, officials, etc.;
Flint and Genesee County postcards; library archives; and family and local histories.

SEE: Hamer; NUCMC, 1966.

SEE: Meckler and McMullin.

The materials listed in Hamer and
NUCMC, 1966, have been transferred
to the Sloan Museum, also in Flint.

MI314-265
General Motors Institute
Alumni Foundation's Collection of
    Industrial History
1700 West Third Avenue
Flint MI 48502

(313) 762-9890

OPEN: M-F 8-4:30; closed weekends,
Thanksgiving, Christmas recess, Good
Friday, and summer recess
ACCESS: permission of the Director
COPYING FACILITIES: yes
MATERIALS SOLICITED: Papers of busi-
nessmen, and other materials relating
to the establishment and growth of
American business and industry, espe-
cially transportation. Will also accept
materials relating to products.

HOLDINGS:
    Total volume: 1,300 l.f.
    Inclusive dates: 1635 -
    Description: Manuscripts, correspon-
dence, records, and photographs relating
to the development of American business
and industry, with emphasis on the private transportation industry. Included are
papers of businessmen William C. Durant, Charles Stewart Mott, John Lee
Pratt, and Charles F. Kettering; complete
records of Frigidaire Corporation and the
Industrial Mutual Association of Flint,
Michigan; and records of General Motors
Institute.

MI314-840
The University of Michigan at Flint
Library
Flint MI 48502

(313) 762-3405

OPEN: by appointment only
COPYING FACILITIES: yes
MATERIALS SOLICITED: Materials con-
cerning Flint and Genesee County and
Michigan history, especially industrial
and labor history, as well as genealogy.

HOLDINGS:
    Total volume: 16 l.f.; 150 items
    Inclusive dates: 1895 -
    Description: University records; files of
persons important in campus development; scrapbooks, ledgers, journals, and
pictures of prominent local industrialists;
and tapes and memorabilia relating to the
labor movement, especially the Flint sit-
down strike of 1935.

FRANKENMUTH

MI322-240
Frankenmuth Historical Association
Frankenmuth Historical Museum
613 South Main Street
Frankenmuth MI 48734

(517) 652-9701

OPEN: M-Sa 9-5; closed Sundays,
Thanksgiving, and Christmas
COPYING FACILITIES: yes
MATERIALS SOLICITED: Material relating
to Frankenmuth and to the Franconian
colonies of Saginaw Valley.

HOLDINGS:
    Total volume: 4 c.f.
    Inclusive dates: 1816 - 1977
    Description: Documents, mostly in
German, relating to the founding and development of Frankenmuth as a Lutheran
missionary colony to the Indians, emphasizing the relationship between
Frankenmuth and the founding of the
Lutheran Church-Missouri Synod. Included are diaries, letters, unpublished dissertations, research papers, photographs,
and other materials relating to social
clubs, businesses, and individuals.

GARDEN

MI343-280
Fayette Historic State Park
13700 13.25 Lane
Garden MI 49835

(906) 644-2603

OPEN: June 15 - Labor Day, daily 9-7;
Labor Day - Oct. 15 and May 15 -
June 14, M-F 9-4:30; Oct. 16 - May 14,
by appointment only
USER FEES: motor vehicle permit one
dollar daily, $5 annually
ACCESS: with permission of Park
Manager
COPYING FACILITIES: no
MATERIALS SOLICITED: Correspondence,
journals, logbooks, account books, and
business records pertaining to the Park
and its environs.

HOLDINGS:
    Total volume: 2 file boxes
    Inclusive dates: 1867 - 1894
    Description: Papers of the Jackson Iron
Company pertaining to its charcoal iron
operations.

Some materials have been trans-
ferred to the Michigan Department of
State, Michigan History Division,
State Archives Unit, in Lansing, MI.

GRAND HAVEN

MI350-760
Tri-Cities Historical Society
Museum
1 North Harbor Avenue
Grand Haven MI

MAILING ADDRESS:
Box 234
Grand Haven MI 49417

(616) 842-0700

OPEN: June 1-Labor Day W-Su 2-10;
weekends May 15-30 and Labor
Day-Oct. 15
USER FEES: 50 cents per adult; children
with parents free; senior citizens free;
society members free
COPYING FACILITIES: yes
MATERIALS SOLICITED: Materials pertaining to the history of the Grand Haven area and its inhabitants.

HOLDINGS:
    Total volume: 8 l.f.; 12 boxes
    Inclusive dates: 1836 -
    Description: Letters by early pioneers,
journals, scrapbooks, logbooks, photographs, and court, tax, post office, cemetery and other records, all pertaining to
the history of Grand Haven, Ottawa
County, and their environs.

GRAND RAPIDS

MI355-110

Calvin College and Seminary
Heritage Hall-Library
Colonial Origins Collection
3201 Burton Street, S.E.
Grand Rapids MI 49506

(616) 957-6316

OPEN: M-F 9-4; closed weekends and
holidays
COPYING FACILITIES: yes
MATERIALS SOLICITED: Materials relating
to Dutch settlers and their descendants
in the United States and Canada.

HOLDINGS:
Total volume: 761 l.f.; 580 tapes;
2,132 microfilm reels
Inclusive dates: 1830 -
Description: Minutes and records of
713 Christian Reformed churches in the
Midwest, New Jersey, New York, Colorado, California, Washington, and
Canada; materials concerning defunct
churches and Dutch settlements in the
United States and Canada; inactive seminary and college records; personal papers
of presidents, faculty and alumni of Calvin College and Seminary.
Papers of ministers and missionaries
of the Christian Reformed church; the
Dutch Immigrant Letter Collection, correspondence, documents, travel accounts,
diaries and other records relating the
Dutch immigrants' experiences and cultural adaptation in the United States.

SEE: NUCMC, 1968, 71.

SEE ALSO: Herbert Brinks, ed., *Guide to
the Dutch-American Historical Collections of Western Michigan*
(Dutch-American Historical Commission, 1967).

MI355-160

Diocese of Grand Rapids
Diocesan Archives
650 Burton Street, S.E.
Grand Rapids MI 49507

(616) 243-0491

OPEN: by appointment only
ACCESS: open to serious researchers on
presentation of letter of
recommendation; an appointment is
advised
COPYING FACILITIES: yes
MATERIALS SOLICITED: Material relating
to the Catholic church in western
Michigan. Will also accept Michigan
history materials which relate to Catholic church history.

HOLDINGS:
Total volume: 70 l.f.
Inclusive dates: 1882 -
Description: Official correspondence
and records of the Catholic church in
Michigan, especially western Michigan.

SEE: NUCMC, 1975.

MI355-270

Grand Rapids Public Library
Michigan Room
60 Library Plaza, NE
Grand Rapids MI 49503

(616) 456-3600

OPEN: Tu, W 12-9, Th-Sa 9-5:30; closed
Sundays, Mondays, and holidays
ACCESS: appointment by telephone
advisable
COPYING FACILITIES: yes
MATERIALS SOLICITED: Materials per-
taining to the history of Grand Rapids,
Kent County, and western central
Michigan. Will also accept materials re-
lating to Michigan in general.

HOLDINGS:
Total volume: 125,000 items
Inclusive dates: 1829 -
Description: Personal papers, records
of businesses, organizations, churches,
and governments, and photographs reflecting life in Grand Rapids and western
Michigan. Included are correspondence of
early land speculator John Ball, papers of
archaeologist Wright L. Coffinberry, pioneer collections, League of Women Voters' scrapbooks, Kent County tax rolls
and census records, and military records
from World Wars I and II.

SEE: Hamer; NUCMC, 1959-61.

SEE ALSO: Edwin T. Layton, Jr., ed., *A
Regional Union Catalog of Manuscripts
Relating to the History of Science and
Technology Located in Indiana, Michi-
gan, and Ohio* (Case Western Reserve
Univ., 1971); *Map Collections in the
United States and Canada, A Directory*
(Special Libraries Assn., 1970).

MI355-290

Grand Rapids Public Museum
Pictorial Materials Collection
54 Jefferson, S.E.
Grand Rapids MI 49503

(616) 456-3977

OPEN: by appointment only; closed
weekends and holidays
COPYING FACILITIES: yes
MATERIALS SOLICITED: Pictorial materials of Grand Rapids and vicinity. Will
also accept materials produced by residents of the Grand Rapids area.

HOLDINGS:
Total volume: 50,000 items
Inclusive dates: 1850 -
Description: A collection of photo-
graphs relating primarily to the Grand
Rapids area.

SEE: Hamer.

SEE ALSO: Richard C. Davis, *North
American Forest History: A Guide to
Archives and Manuscripts in the United
States and Canada* (Clio Books, 1977).

GRANDVILLE

MI360-280

Grandville Historical Association and
Museum
3195 Wilson, S.W.
Grandville MI 49418

(616) 531-3030

OPEN: by appointment only
COPYING FACILITIES: yes
MATERIALS SOLICITED: Materials per-
taining to the early history of
Grandville and Jenison, MI.

HOLDINGS:
Total volume: 4 l.f.
Inclusive dates: 1865 -
Description: Records and photographs
pertaining to Grandville's and Jenison's
pioneer families, early landmarks,
schools, churches, early businesses, local
government, fire department, and
railroad, and to the Grand River.

GRAYLING

MI368-320

Hartwick Pines State Park
Interpretive Center and Logging
Camp Museum
Grayling MI

MAILING ADDRESS:
Route 3, Box 3840 M-93
Grayling MI 49738

(517) 348-7068

OPEN: daily 9-4; Nov.-May, by
appointment only
USER FEES: motor vehicle permit $2
daily, $7 annually
COPYING FACILITIES: no

HOLDINGS:
Total volume: 100 items
Inclusive dates: 1860 - 1916
Description: Photographs pertaining to
logging in Michigan, 1860-1900, and to
the life of Edward E. Hartwick.

The Hartwick papers listed in
Hamer and NUCMC, 1966, (under
Hartwick Pines Memorial Hall) have
been transferred to the Michigan De-
partment of State, Michigan History
Division, in Lansing.

HANCOCK

MI390-720

Suomi College
Finnish-American Historical Archives
Hancock MI 49930

(906) 482-5300, Ext. 273

OPEN: by appointment only; closed
holidays and school vacations
COPYING FACILITIES: yes
MATERIALS SOLICITED: Anything by or
about Finnish-Americans and Finnish-
Canadians: works of authors (published
or manuscript), organizations and soci-

eties, the Finnish-American churches, and immigration to America.

HOLDINGS:
> *Total volume:* 80,000 items
> *Inclusive dates:* 1890 -
> *Description:* Manuscripts, published works, photographs, scrapbooks, record books, correspondence, music, and oral history relating to the life and work of Finnish immigrants and Finnish-Americans. Included are materials on church and temperance activities, aid to Finland during the war years, the cooperative movement, and labor organizations; Finnish language newspapers; Immigrants' Library (1890's); records of Suomi College; and a local history collection.

HARTLAND

MI414-120
Cromaine Library
3688 North Hartland Road
Hartland MI 48029

no telephone

SEE: Hamer.

Questionnaire not returned.

HILLSDALE

MI440-320
Hillsdale College
Mossey Learning Resources Center
Hillsdale MI 49242

(517) 437-7341, Ext. 225

OPEN: M-F 8-11, Sa 9-6, Su 1-11; closed Christmas and New Year's
COPYING FACILITIES: yes
MATERIALS SOLICITED: Materials by and about Will Carelton.

HOLDINGS:
> *Total volume:* 1,394 items; 21 l.f.
> *Inclusive dates:* 1865 - 1979
> *Description:* Audio tape recordings of The Manion Forum, a national radio commentary program hosted by Clarence E. Manion, 1954-79, including filmed interviews with General Douglas MacArthur, Barry Goldwater, Eddie Rickenbacker, and other national and international figures. Also held are personal papers, notebooks, correspondence, and diaries of Michigan poet Will Carelton.

SEE: Spalek.

HOLLAND

MI445-310
Herrick Public Library
300 River Avenue
Holland MI 49423

(616) 394-1400

OPEN: Su 2-5, M-F 9-9, Sa 9-6; closed Sundays, June - Sept.; closed Saturdays, 2-6 July and Aug.

USER FEES: $6 annual fee for those residing outside the area serviced by the Lakeland Library Federation
COPYING FACILITIES: yes
MATERIALS SOLICITED: Membership records of area churches organized before 1900, genealogies, and oral history. Will also accept other materials relating to local history and genealogy.

HOLDINGS:
> *Total volume:* 180 l.f.
> *Inclusive dates:* 1840 -
> *Description:* Materials focusing on family history and local history of the Holland area, especially the Dutch background of the inhabitants.

SEE: Hinding.

MI445-320
Hope College
Archives
Holland MI 49423

(616) 392-5111, Ext. 2130

OPEN: M-F 8-noon; closed weekends and holidays; between sessions by appointment only
COPYING FACILITIES: yes
MATERIALS SOLICITED: Photographs, programs, diaries, letters, and other materials connected with the history of Hope College, its alumni, and missionaries of the Reformed Church in America who served in China. Will also accept materials concerning the history of the Dutch in western Michigan.

HOLDINGS:
> *Total volume:* 225 l.f.
> *Inclusive dates:* 1825 -
> *Description:* Papers related to the history of Hope College and its alumni. Included are correspondence and papers of administrators, trustees, and faculty; committee minutes and reports; student society minutes; papers and diaries of students; programs of events; photographs and slides; audio tapes of visiting speakers and of some events; alumni papers; and papers connected with intercollegiate organizations, church support, and the Dutch in western Michigan.
> Includes materials of the Hope College Polar Bear Oral History Project, pertaining to American Expeditionary Forces in Russia, 1918-1919.

GUIDES: Andrew Vander Zee, *Guide to the Archives of Hope College* (1981).

SEE: NUCMC, 1968, 71, 73.

SEE: Hinding.

SEE ALSO: Herbert Brinks, ed., *Guide to the Dutch-American Historical Collections of Western Michigan* (Dutch-American Historical Commission, 1967).

MI445-560
Netherlands Museum
8 East 12th Street
City Hall
Holland MI 49423

(616) 392-9084, 394-1362

OPEN: M-Sa 9-5; Su 11:30-5, summer; closed New Year's, Thanksgiving, and Christmas

COPYING FACILITIES: yes
MATERIALS SOLICITED: Materials relating to the history of Dutch settlements in Michigan and Dutch migration to the Midwest. Will also accept any materials about the Dutch in the United States.

HOLDINGS:
> *Total volume:* 200 l.f.
> *Inclusive dates:* 1846 -
> *Description:* A collection of manuscripts, diaries, letters, and documents relating chiefly to Dutch immigration to the United States, beginning in 1847, and records of the city of Holland.

GUIDES: Elton J. Bruins, *A Guide to the Archives of the Netherlands Museum* (1978).

SEE: Hamer; NUCMC, 1968.

SEE: Hinding.

SEE ALSO: Herbert Brinks, ed., *Guide to the Dutch-American Historical Collections of Western Michigan* (Dutch-American Historical Commission, 1967); Richard C. Davis, *North American Forest History: A Guide to Archives and Manuscripts in the United States and Canada* (Clio Books, 1977).

MI445-880
Western Theological Seminary
85 East 13th Street
Holland MI 49423

(616) 392-8555

OPEN: M-F 8-5; closed weekends and holidays
COPYING FACILITIES: yes
MATERIALS SOLICITED: Records of Western Theological Seminary; papers of its professors and alumni; and materials relating to the history of the Reformed Church in America. Will also accept materials relating to Dutch-American religious institutions and Dutch immigration.

HOLDINGS:
> *Total volume:* 300 l.f.
> *Inclusive dates:* 1770 -
> *Description:* Materials dealing largely with the history of the Seminary, including financial and office records, papers of professors and alumni, sermons and other papers of ministers of the Reformed Church in America, and papers and photographs of missionaries in China, Japan, and India.

GUIDES: Elton J. Bruins, *The Manuscript and Archival Holdings of Beardslee Library, Western Theological Seminary, Holland, Michigan* (1978).

SEE: NUCMC, 1968, 70-71.

SEE: Hinding.

SEE ALSO: Herbert Brinks, ed., *Guide to the Dutch-American Historical Collections of Western Michigan* (Dutch-American Historical Commission, 1967).

HOLLY

MI450-560

Northwest Oakland County Historical
  Society
Patterson House
502 Maple Street
Holly MI

MAILING ADDRESS:
4053 Elliot Road
Holly MI 48442

(313) 634-4673

OPEN: by appointment only
COPYING FACILITIES: yes
MATERIALS SOLICITED: Local history
materials for Groveland, Holly, Rose
and Springfield townships in Oakland
County, as well as research materials
not necessarily concerning Oakland
County.

HOLDINGS:
  Total volume: 2 boxes; 10 recordings
  Inclusive dates: early 19th century -
  Description: Land grants, probate
  records, pioneer journals, diaries, letters,
  oral history tapes, and other materials
  relating to the history of Oakland County
  and its residents.
      Also includes the Michigan Pioneer
  Collection, atlases, and maps relating to
  Oakland County.

SEE: Hinding.

HOUGHTON

MI464-530

Michigan Technological University
  Library
Archives
Houghton MI 49931

(906) 487-2505

OPEN: M-F 1-5; closed weekends and
  holidays
COPYING FACILITIES: yes
MATERIALS SOLICITED: Materials pertaining to the economic, cultural, political, and social life of the people and
institutions of the Copper Country,
Michigan's western upper peninsula,
and the Lake Superior region.

HOLDINGS:
  Total volume: 1,700 c.f.
  Inclusive dates: 1830 -
  Description: Business records, personal
  papers, and photographs relating primarily to copper mining in Michigan, including a special collection about Isle Royale.
  Also included are personal papers of U.S.
  Bureau of Mines director Scott Turner, as
  well as correspondence and reports relating to the activities of the Arctic Coal
  Company on Spitzbergen in the early
  1900's.

SEE ALSO: Robert D. Patterson and David
H. Thomas, 'Michigan Technological
University Library Archives,' *Historical
Society of Michigan Chronicle* 9 (First
Quarter 1973); Richard C. Davis,
*North American Forest History: A
Guide to Archives and Manuscripts in
the United States and Canada* (Clio
Books, 1977).

HUDSON

MI476-320

Hudson Public Library
205 South Market Street
Hudson MI 49247

(517) 448-3801

OPEN: M-W 12-8, F, Sa 9-5; closed
  Sundays, Thursdays, and holidays
SEE: Hamer.

Questionnaire not returned.

ITHACA

MI505-760

Thompson Home Library
Michigan Collection
125 West Center Street
Ithaca MI 48847

(517) 875-4184

OPEN: Sept. 10-May 1, M 9-9, Tu-F 9-5;
  closed weekends and holidays
COPYING FACILITIES: yes
MATERIALS SOLICITED: Genealogical
source data and photographs relating to
Gratiot County, MI. Will also accept
records of local institutions.

HOLDINGS:
  Total volume: 30 vols.; 150
  photographs
  Inclusive dates: 1862 -
  Description: Primarily genealogical materials of Gratiot County and vicinity,
  including cemetery records, civil records,
  biographical albums of surrounding counties, and a typescript list of Civil War
  soldiers buried in the County. Also included are local church records of the
  19th century and records of the Ithaca
  Grange.

SEE: Hamer.

JACKSON

MI510-200

Ella Sharp Museum
3225 Fourth Street
Jackson MI 49203

(517) 787-2320

OPEN: by appointment only M-F 8:30-5;
  closed weekends and holidays
ACCESS: scholarly researchers
COPYING FACILITIES: yes
MATERIALS SOLICITED: Will accept materials reflecting Victorian life or relating to local history.

HOLDINGS:
  Total volume: 40 boxes; 2 file
  cabinets
  Inclusive dates: 1835 -
  Description: Correspondence, diaries,
  account books, photographs and family
  documents related to Victorian life and
  Jackson County history. Most of the collection is connected with the Merriman
  and Sharp families, who operated a suc-
  cessful local farm from the 1850's to the
  1910's.

SEE: Hinding.

MI510-390

Jackson City Public Library
244 West Michigan Avenue
Jackson MI 49201

no telephone
SEE: Hamer.

Questionnaire not returned.

KALAMAZOO

MI518-50

American Institute for Exploration
Main Administrative Office and
  Library
1809 Nichols Road
Kalamazoo MI 49007

no telephone

OPEN: M-Th 3-5, F 10-3; closed
  weekends and holidays
USER FEES: $5 per hour for assistance
  from staff member
ACCESS: restricted to qualified scholars;
  advance appointment required
COPYING FACILITIES: yes
MATERIALS SOLICITED: Field journals,
manuscript maps and charts, and historical documents relating to exploration in general and more specifically to
Aleut-Eskimo culture, prehistoric cultural contacts between Alaska and Asia,
Aleutian-Bering Sea history, land use
and conservation in western Alaska,
history and culture of Hokkaido, Japan, northeast Asia, and North Pole
region. Will also accept contemporary
research on scientific expeditions and
on technological innovations of application to exploration.

HOLDINGS:
  Total volume: 8 file cabinets
  Inclusive dates: 1741 -
  Description: Materials relating to field
  research in Alaska, the Canadian Arctic,
  northern Japan, and Southeast Asia between 1944 and the present. Research
  fields represented include anthropology,
  botany, archaeology, bioecology,
  ethnobotany, linguistics, marine biology,
  geology, medicine, and ethnology. There
  are original Aleut-Eskimo texts and linguistic tapes and diaries; manuscripts and
  field data collected by 19th century expeditions in the Aleutians; copies of
  ships' logs and journals of Russian explorers; and manuscripts and rough field
  data from expeditions in Sumatra and
  Formosa, 1928-35.

SEE: Hinding.

MI518-425
Kalamazoo College
Library
College and Baptist Room
Thompson and Academy Streets
Kalamazoo MI 49007

(616) 383-8482

OPEN: M-F by appointment; closed
weekends and holidays
COPYING FACILITIES: yes
MATERIALS SOLICITED: College records
and materials pertaining to its alumni
or faculty.

HOLDINGS:
Total volume: 150 l.f.; 65 boxes; 24
file drawers
Inclusive dates: 1832 -
Description: Materials relating to the
College, 1832-1933; the Michigan Baptist
State Convention Collection, 1825-1906,
of letters, pastoral reports, record books
of the Convention, and journals and
daybooks of missionaries and circuit rid-
ers in western Michigan; and correspondence, diaries, manuscript magazine articles, and other papers, 1930-63, of Maynard Owen Williams, chief of the foreign
staff of National Geographic Magazine.

SEE: Hamer; NUCMC, 1979.

SEE ALSO: Lawrence H. Conrad, Sr., Maynard Owen Williams, Class of 1910,
Kalamazoo College (Kalamazoo College, 1966).

MI518-445
Kalamazoo Public Library
Reference Division
315 South Rose Street
Kalamazoo MI 49007

(616) 342-9837, Ext. 243

OPEN: M-F 9-9, Sa 9-6; Sundays 1-5
during school years; closed holidays
ACCESS: prior arrangement is necessary
with Local History Librarian for use of
vault materials
COPYING FACILITIES: yes
MATERIALS SOLICITED: Kalamazoo city,
township and County items; personal,
club, and governmental items. Will also
accept materials of a local history nature that relate to Kalamazoo and
southwestern Michigan.

HOLDINGS:
Total volume: 95 l.f.; 34 file drawers
Inclusive dates: 1836 -
Description: Records of local churches;
area school district minutes; Public Library historical materials; papers of local
organizations, such as the Woman's
Christian Temperance Union, the Child
Welfare League, and the Kalamazoo
County Agricultural Society; and letters
dealing with the establishment of a woman's professorship at the University of
Michigan. There are also several hundred
glass negatives (1870-1910) of Kalamazoo
people, buildings, and industries; most
are identified although not all have prints
for examination.

SEE: Hamer; NUCMC, 1966.

SEE: Krichmar

MI518-455
Kalamazoo Public Museum
315 South Rose Street
Kalamazoo MI 49007

(616) 345-7092

OPEN: by appointment only M-F 10-4;
closed weekends and holidays
COPYING FACILITIES: yes
MATERIALS SOLICITED: Manuscripts,
photographs, postcards pertaining to local history, especially before 1925; issues of Kalamazoo Gazette and Kalamazoo Telegraph, 1860-65.

HOLDINGS:
Total volume: 500 c.f.
Inclusive dates: 1800 -
Description: Letters, diaries, and travel
accounts of Kalamazoo area residents in
the late 19th century, describing farm and
city life; local church records, business
ledgers, and sermons, dating from 1830; a
large collection of photographs; personal
collections, including those of Colonel Orlando Moore, who fought in the Civil
War, and Thaddeus Smith, a colleague of
John Philip Sousa; and the Edward J.
Stevens Collection of data concerning
Michigan pioneers, 1815-50.

SEE: Hamer.

MI518-860
Western Michigan University
Adams Center for Ecological Studies
Kalamazoo MI 49001

no telephone

SEE: Hamer.

Questionnaire not returned.

MI518-870
Western Michigan University
Archives and Regional History
Collections
Kalamazoo MI 49008

no telephone

SEE: Hamer (as Western Michigan University, Library); NUCMC, 1968.

Questionnaire not returned.

LAKE LINDEN

MI530-320
Houghton County Historical Museum
Highway M-26
Lake Linden MI 49945

no telephone

SEE: Hamer (as Keweenaw Historical Society, Houghton, MI).

Questionnaire not returned.

LANSING

MI550-505
The Library of Michigan
Information Services Unit
735 East Michigan Avenue
Lansing MI

MAILING ADDRESS:
Box 30007
Lansing MI 48909

(517) 373-1593

OPEN: M-F 1-5; closed weekends and
holidays
COPYING FACILITIES: yes
MATERIALS SOLICITED: Genealogical
source data for the Great Lakes area,
primarily Michigan.

HOLDINGS:
Total volume: 200 l.f.
Inclusive dates: 1800 -
Description: Materials relating to
Michigan history and genealogy, includ-
ing vital, church, and family records.

SEE: Hamer (as Michigan State Library).

SEE: Krichmar; Parkinson; Hinding.

SEE ALSO: Walter Schatz, ed., Directory of
Afro-American Resources (Bowker,
1970); Richard J. Hathaway, ed., Directory of Historical Collections in the
State of Michigan (Michigan Archivists
Assn., 1969); and the following semi-
annual publication of the Department
of Education: Family Trails (1967-).

MI550-530
Michigan Department of State
Michigan History Division
State Archives Unit
3405 North Logan Street
Lansing MI 48918

(517) 373-0512

OPEN: M-F 8-5; closed weekends and
holidays
COPYING FACILITIES: yes
MATERIALS SOLICITED: State and local
public records; private materials that
pertain to the State and its government. Will also accept photographs and
maps.

HOLDINGS:
Total volume: 14,000 c.f.
Inclusive dates: 1810 -
Description: State of Michigan Archives, including records of the Executive
Office, and the offices of the Secretary of
State, Attorney General, Auditor General,
as well as other departments, commissions, and special legislative study committees. There are also local government
records, including county, city, and township materials. Special collections include
the personal papers of individuals prominent in Michigan government, as well as
maps and visual documents.

GUIDES: Valerie Gerrard Browne and Da-
vid Jerome Johnson, A Guide to the
State Archives of Michigan: State
Records (1977).

SEE: Hamer (as Michigan Historical Commission Archives).

SEE: Hinding.

SEE ALSO: Ann Novotny, ed., *Picture Sources 3* (Special Libraries Assn., 1975); *Map Collections in the United States and Canada, A Directory* (Special Libraries Assn., 1970); Walter Schatz, ed., *Directory of Afro-American Resources* (Bowker, 1970); David J. Olson, comp., *Bibliography of Sources Relating to Women* (Michigan History Division, Michigan Dept. of State, 1975); Edwin T. Layton, Jr., ed., *A Regional Union Catalog of Manuscripts Relating to the History of Science and Technology Located in Indiana, Michigan, and Ohio* (Case Western Reserve Univ., 1971). Other printed finding aids are available at the institution.

Richard C. Davis, *North American Forest History: A Guide to Archives and Manuscripts in the United States and Canada* (Clio Books, 1977).

LUDINGTON

MI585-520

Mason County Historical Society
Rose Hawley Museum-Archives
305 East Filer Street
Ludington MI 49431

(616) 843-2001

OPEN: by appointment only
ACCESS: advance arrangements preferred
COPYING FACILITIES: yes
MATERIALS SOLICITED: Ludington city, township, and county items. Will also accept materials that relate to Mason County and western Michigan.

HOLDINGS:
 Total volume: 1,000 vols.; 16 file drawers; 1,500 items
 Inclusive dates: 1800 -
 Description: Business and financial records, correspondence of early settlers, diaries and journals pertaining to the lumbering era, genealogical source data of approximately 500 area families, photographs of the Ludington area and townships, and scrapbooks. Also included are noncurrent records of organizations, such as churches, schools, associations, and community groups, and audio tapes and transcripts.

SEE: NUCMC, 1973, 76, 79.

MACKINAC ISLAND

MI590-520

Mackinac Island State Park
 Commission
Mackinac Island MI

MAILING ADDRESS:
P.O. Box 370
Mackinac Island MI 49747

(906) 847-3328

OPEN: by appointment only M-F; closed weekends and May 15 - Oct. 1
ACCESS: by appointment only
COPYING FACILITIES: yes

MATERIALS SOLICITED: Mackinac Island history and archaeology, including Fort Mackinac; Fort Michilimackinac history and archaeology, and Mackinaw City history. Will also accept items pertaining to 18th and 19th century military activity and French and British culture in North America, and documents or photographs pertaining to the Straits of Mackinac area.

HOLDINGS:
 Total volume: 3,000 photographs; 50 microfilm reels
 Inclusive dates: 1700 -
 Description: Photographs, both originals and copies, of Fort Mackinac, Mackinac Island, and the Straits of Mackinac region; microfilms from the British Museum and photostats of other manuscripts relating to the Fort and Island; and oral history tapes and transcripts of reminiscences of Mackinac Island residents.

Most of the collection is kept in the Commission's Lansing office, which is closed from May 15 to September 30. The staff moves to Mackinac Island during this time to run historic site programs.

MI590-720

Stuart House Museum of Astor Fur
 Post
Market Street
Mackinac Island MI 49757

no telephone

SEE: Hamer.

Questionnaire not returned.

MARQUETTE

MI605-80

Bishop Baraga Association
239 Baraga Avenue
Marquette MI 49855

no telephone

SEE: NUCMC, 1962.

Questionnaire not returned.

MI605-520

Marquette County Historical Society
213 North Front Street
Marquette MI 49855

(906) 226-3571

OPEN: M-F 9-4:30; closed weekends and holidays
USER FEES: one dollar for students, $5 for others
COPYING FACILITIES: yes
MATERIALS SOLICITED: Materials relating to the history of Marquette County, including pertinent materials from the upper peninsula.

HOLDINGS:
 Total volume: 435 l.f.
 Inclusive dates: 1840 -
 Description: Collections pertaining to the history of Marquette County and the upper peninsula. Included are business

records, manuscripts, correspondence, genealogical data, maps, charts, engineering and architectural drawings, photographs, journals, and logbooks.

SEE: Hamer; NUCMC, 1959-61.

SEE: Davis.

MARSHALL

MI609-520

Marshall Historical Society
Museum
Archives
Marshall MI

MAILING ADDRESS:
P.O. Box 68
Marshall MI 49068

(616) 781-8544

OPEN: third week of May - end of Sept., M, W-Su 10-1; closed Tuesdays and holidays; rest of year by appointment only
USER FEES: $10 per hour
COPYING FACILITIES: yes
MATERIALS SOLICITED: Will accept materials pertaining to Marshall from 1834 to 1925.

HOLDINGS:
 Total volume: not specified
 Inclusive dates: 1834 - 1925
 Description: Scrapbooks, correspondence, photographs, and ledgers relating to Marshall.

MAYVILLE

MI615-520

Mayville Historical Museum
22 Turner
Mayville MI

MAILING ADDRESS:
Box 242
Mayville MI 48744

(517) 843-6429

OPEN: F, Sa 9-4, and by appointment
COPYING FACILITIES: no

HOLDINGS:
 Total volume: 15 l.f.
 Inclusive dates: 1870 -
 Description: Materials relating to the village of Mayville and its environs, including official records, private papers, genealogical data, and historical research papers.

MENOMINEE

MI620-520

Menominee County Historical Society
Menominee County Museum
902 2nd Street
Menominee MI

MAILING ADDRESS:
P.O. Box 151
Menominee MI 49858

(906) 863-2679

OPEN: Su 2-5, M-Sa 10-5; open June,
July, and August
ACCESS: advance arrangements required
COPYING FACILITIES: yes
MATERIALS SOLICITED: Menominee
County and city records, church
records, diaries, and other materials re-
lating to the early history of the area.
Will also accept materials relating to
logging, early industry, and military
veterans.

HOLDINGS:
Total volume: 1,500 vols.; other items
Inclusive dates: 1863 -
Description: A collection focusing on
the history of the Menominee area. Included are tax and enrollment lists, probate records, oral history tapes, diaries,
materials relating to local military history
and marine history, and films of logging
activities.

MONROE

MI650-510

Monroe County Historical
    Commission
Archives
126 South Monroe Street
Monroe MI 48161

(313) 243-7137

OPEN: May 1 - Oct. 31, Tu-Su 10-5;
Nov. 1 - April 30, Tu-Su 1-5; closed
Mondays
ACCESS: call in advance for weekends
and holidays
COPYING FACILITIES: yes
MATERIALS SOLICITED: Materials relating
to Monroe County.

HOLDINGS:
Total volume: 300 l.f.
Inclusive dates: 1782 -
Description: Materials relating to Monroe County, including personal papers
and scrapbooks of local families, items
relating to George Armstrong Custer,
school records, Monroe city and County
records, local business records, photographs, and the files of an architectural
survey of the County done in the 1970's.

SEE: NUCMC, 1977.

MI650-530

Monroe County Library System
3700 South Custer Road
Monroe MI 48161

(313) 241-5277

OPEN: M-Th 9-9, F, Sa 9-5; closed
Sundays and holidays
ACCESS: two to four weeks advance
arrangements required
COPYING FACILITIES: yes
MATERIALS SOLICITED: Materials per-
taining to George Armstrong Custer,
the Battle of the Little Big Horn,
American Indians, and Indian wars.
Will also accept materials pertaining to
Monroe and Michigan history, the
American West, and westward expan-
sion.

HOLDINGS:
Total volume: 1,000 vols,; 500 items
Inclusive dates: 19th century -
Description: Manuscripts, photographs,
and correspondence; motion pictures; aerial photographs concerning the career of
George Armstrong Custer; materials by
and about Eduard Dorsch, including poetry, plays, botanical works, and photographs of the Dorsch home; photographs
and oral history recordings concerning
Monroe County history.

SEE: Meckler and McMullin.

MI650-720

Sisters, Servants of the Immaculate
    Heart of Mary
Archives
610 West Elm Street
Monroe MI 48161

(313) 241-3660

OPEN: M-F 10-4; closed weekends,
holidays, and holy days
ACCESS: appointment preferred
COPYING FACILITIES: yes
MATERIALS SOLICITED: Materials pertinent to the Sisters, Servants of the Immaculate Heart of Mary congregation
in Monroe, its members and founder,
Louis Florent Gillet, and related
Catholic church materials. Will also accept selected materials related to the
congregation in Scranton and Philadelphia, PA.

HOLDINGS:
Total volume: 250 l.f.
Inclusive dates: 1845 -
Description: Materials relating primarily to the congregation, including its parochial schools and noneducational institutions in Michigan, other States, and
abroad. Included are annual chronicles of
institutions affiliated with the congregation, annual assignments, records of the
general superiors, and personal records of
congregation members.

SEE: Hinding.

MOUNT PLEASANT

MI665-120

Central Michigan University
Clarke Historical Library
Mt. Pleasant MI 48859

(517) 774-3352

OPEN: M-F 8-5; closed weekends,
holidays, and whenever the University
is officially closed
ACCESS: manuscripts available upon
completion of an application form,
which must be approved by the
Director
COPYING FACILITIES: yes
MATERIALS SOLICITED: Michigan, the
Northwest Territory, and the Great
Lakes area. Will also accept graphic
materials and items which relate to the
Library's geographical area of solicita-
tion.

HOLDINGS:
Total volume: 207,035 items; 2,648
vols.; 1,182 l.f.
Inclusive dates: 1711 -
Description: Collections relating to the
history and culture of Michigan, the
Northwest Territory, and the Great
Lakes area. Included are records and
papers of organizations, businesses,
military and political figures, pioneer
settlers, literary artists, religious
figures, families, and individuals;
unpublished memoirs and histories; and
collections of ephemera and
audio-visual materials.

SEE: Hamer; NUCMC, 1962, 68.

SEE: Hinding; Bean and Vane; Robbins.

SEE ALSO: Walter Schatz, ed., *Directory of
Afro-American Resources* (Bowker,
1970); David J. Olson, comp., *Bibliography of Sources Relating to Women*
(Michigan History Division, Michigan
Dept. of State, 1975); Alan M. Meckler
and Ruth McMullin, comps., *Oral History Collections* (Bowker, 1975); David
A. Hounshell, comp., *Manuscripts in
U.S. Depositories Relating to the History of Electrical Science and Technology* (Smithsonian Institution, n.d.); Edwin T. Layton, Jr., ed., *A Regional
Union Catalog of Manuscripts Relating
to the History of Science and Technology Located in Indiana, Michigan, and
Ohio* (Case Western Reserve Univ.,
1971); William Miles, comp., *Women's
History: A Guide to Unpublished Resources in the Clarke Historical Library*
(Clarke Historical Library, 1976).

William Miles, comp., *Manuscripts on Microfilm* (Clarke Historical Library, 1976);
and the annual report of the Library,
1971 - .

Richard C. Davis, *North American Forest
History: A Guide to Archives and Manu-
scripts in the United States and Canada*
(Clio Books, 1977).

MUNISING

MI670-40

Alger County Historical Society
203 W. Onota Street
Munising MI

MAILING ADDRESS:
Box 201
Munising MI 49862

(906) 387-4186

OPEN: July and Aug. M 10-12, Tuesday
evenings 7-9, W-F noon-4; closed
weekends; other months by
appointment only
USER FEES: $5 per visit, or free with $5
annual membership
ACCESS: appointment required
COPYING FACILITIES: no
MATERIALS SOLICITED: Materials concerning Alger County history, including
photographs, newspaper clippings,
ephemera, and oral history recordings.
Will also accept related manuscripts,
genealogies, and documentation of
community and ethnic groups.

HOLDINGS:
Total volume: 500 items
Inclusive dates: 1896 -
Description: Oral history recordings relating chiefly to early settlers and the history of Alger County, photographs, an obituary file, 1966- , and pioneer reminiscences.

MUSKEGON

MI675-320

Hackley Public Library
316 West Webster Avenue
Muskegon MI 49440

(616) 722-7276

OPEN: M-Th 9-8; F 9-5 (summer only);
Sa 9-5 (fall through spring only)
COPYING FACILITIES: yes
MATERIALS SOLICITED: Will accept local history records.

HOLDINGS:
Total volume: 25 l.f.
Inclusive dates: 1868 -
Description: Materials relating chiefly to Muskegon, consisting mainly of the records of three organizations and photographs of local people and scenes.

SEE: Hamer; NUCMC, 1966.

SEE: Davis; Hinding.

MI675-510

Muskegon County Museum
430 W. Clay
Muskegon MI 49440

(616) 722-0278

OPEN: Tu-F 10-5, Sa 10-3; closed
Sundays, Mondays, and holidays
ACCESS: appointment required
MATERIALS SOLICITED: Materials concerning the history of Muskegon County and surrounding areas.

HOLDINGS:
Total volume: 8 file drawers
Inclusive dates: 19th century -
Description: Local diaries and correspondence from the Civil War and lumbering eras; the Yates collection of photographs and typescript newspaper articles concerning Muskegon through the 1950's; school, county government, and city government documents; and recorded interviews with County residents.

NEW BALTIMORE

MI690-560

New Baltimore Public Library
51150 Washington Avenue
New Baltimore MI 48047

(313) 725-0273

OPEN: M, Tu, Th 12-8:30, W 10-8:30, F
12-5, Sa 10-4; closed Sundays and holidays
COPYING FACILITIES: yes
MATERIALS SOLICITED: Photographs, oral histories, and manuscripts relating to the Hatheway Institute and New Baltimore.

HOLDINGS:
Total volume: 15 albums; 10 oral histories; 12 items
Inclusive dates: 1845 -
Description: Photographs of people and scenes in New Baltimore, including the Hatheway Institute; research papers on local history; diaries, containing information about social life and weather in the early 20th century; account books and ledgers; and oral history interviews with elderly residents of New Baltimore.

NILES

MI700-240

Fort St. Joseph Museum
508 East Main Street
Niles MI 49120

(616) 683-4702

OPEN: Tu-Sa 10-4; closed Sundays, Mondays, and holidays
ACCESS: appointment and references are required
COPYING FACILITIES: no
MATERIALS SOLICITED: Will accept materials related to the history of Niles, Berrien County, and Michigan.

HOLDINGS:
Total volume: not specified
Inclusive dates: 1829 -
Description: Manuscripts, letters, diaries, scrapbooks, photographs, account books, and organization records reflecting the history of the Niles-Berrien County area and its people.

MI700-560

Niles Community Library
620 East Main Street
Niles MI 49120

(616) 683-8545

OPEN: Tu-Th 9-9, F, Sa 9-5:30;
June-Aug. Tu-F 9-7, Sa 9-5:30; closed Sundays, Mondays, holidays, and two middle weeks of August
ACCESS: identification required
COPYING FACILITIES: yes
MATERIALS SOLICITED: Materials pertaining to the history of Niles and Michigan, including unpublished biographies, oral histories, and letters and diaries of former area residents.

HOLDINGS:
Total volume: 279 l.f.; 6 file cabinets
Inclusive dates: 1670 -
Description: Histories of 900 local families; 25 volumes of bound minutes of the Ladies Reading Club, 1880- ; and various theses and other materials pertaining to local and State history.
Materials pertaining to Fort St. Joseph, including translations and abstracts of French language documents; various local government records; account and day books of early businesses.

GUIDES: A guide to the collection is available on request.

SEE: Hinding.

NORTHVILLE

MI705-560

Northville Historical Society
Griswold Avenue
Northville MI

MAILING ADDRESS:
P.O. Box 71
Northville MI 48167

(313) 349-0767, 0408

OPEN: by appointment only; Saturdays
9-noon, and May-Oct. 31 Sundays 1-4
USER FEES: one dollar
COPYING FACILITIES: no
MATERIALS SOLICITED: Materials pertaining to the history of Northville.

HOLDINGS:
Total volume: 2,000 items
Inclusive dates: 1843 -
Description: A collection of papers dealing with the political, economic, and social history of Northville. Included are government records, papers of individuals, collections of ephemera, and photographs.

OLIVET

MI720-600

Olivet College
Libraries
College Archives
Olivet MI 49076

(616) 749-7608

OPEN: M-Th 8-10, F 8-5, Sa 9-5, Su
2-10; closed holidays
COPYING FACILITIES: yes
MATERIALS SOLICITED: Any materials relating to the history of Olivet College and community; materials relating to literary figures associated with Olivet in the 1930's and 1940's, such as Katherine Anne Porter, Ford Maddox Ford, Sherwood Anderson, Padraic and Mary Colum, and Carl Sandburg. Will also accept materials of unusual value or interest.

HOLDINGS:
Total volume: 205 l.f.
Inclusive dates: 1844 -
Description: Records of Olivet College and papers of individuals associated with the College and its community. There are also records, photographs, and correspondence of Ezra Pound, Ford Maddox Ford, Katherine Anne Porter, and Sherwood Anderson, relating primarily to the association of these writers with Olivet College in the 1930's and 1940's.

SEE: Hinding.

ONTONAGON

MI725-600

Ontonagon County Historical Society
Museum
233 River Street
Ontonagon MI

MAILING ADDRESS:
Box 7
Ontonagon MI 49953

(906) 884-2342

OPEN: M-F 9-5, Sa 9-2; closed Sundays
COPYING FACILITIES: no
MATERIALS SOLICITED: Materials pertaining to the history of Ontonagon County and the State of Michigan.

HOLDINGS:
Total volume: not specified
Inclusive dates: 1860 - 1920
Description: Records of the Victoria Mining Company, including correspondence, journals, maps, payroll records, cancelled checks, invoices, and drawings of underground workings and the hydraulic system by which the mine was operated.

OWOSSO

MI735-720

Shiawassee County Historical Society
Mathews Building, Suite 302
Owosso MI

MAILING ADDRESS:
P.O. Box 145
Durand MI 48867

no telephone

OPEN: M-Th 8-4, F 8-12; closed weekends and holidays
ACCESS: advance arrangements required
MATERIALS SOLICITED: Materials relating to the early history of Shiawassee County.

HOLDINGS:
Total volume: 100 c.f.
Inclusive dates: 1837 -
Description: Manuscript letters, diaries, histories, and personal records relating to the early history of Shiawassee County and its pioneers, and a survey of American Indian artifacts found in it.

PLYMOUTH

MI765-640

Plymouth Historical Society
Archives
155 South Main Street
Plymouth MI 48170

(313) 455-8940

OPEN: Th, Sa, Su 1-4; closed other days
USER FEES: one dollar
ACCESS: serious researchers
COPYING FACILITIES: no
MATERIALS SOLICITED: Photographs, diaries, local government records, genealogical materials, oral histories, and other items tracing Plymouth history.

HOLDINGS:
Total volume: 23 boxes; 3 file cabinets
Inclusive dates: 1825 -
Description: Materials pertaining to the history and genealogy of Plymouth and the surrounding area, including materials on the 24th Michigan Infantry during the Civil War. Collections include account books, maps, photographs, scrapbooks, oral histories, genealogical records, and correspondence.

PONTIAC

MI770-600

Oakland County Pioneer and
Historical Society
405 Oakland Avenue
Pontiac MI 48058

(313) 338-6732

OPEN: Tu-F 10-3; closed other days, holidays, and mid-Dec. - Jan. 2
COPYING FACILITIES: no
MATERIALS SOLICITED: Letters, journals, scrapbooks, and other materials relating to Oakland County.

HOLDINGS:
Total volume: 81 l.f.; 40 boxes
Inclusive dates: 1818 -
Description: Materials relating to Oakland County schools, churches, social and political organizations (including records of the Lincoln Republican Club), families, and businesses, including 40 file boxes of lineage records.

MI770-640

Pontiac City Library
60 East Pike Street
Pontiac MI 48058

no telephone

SEE: Hamer.

Questionnaire not returned.

PORT HURON

MI775-520

Port Huron Museum of Arts and
History
1115 Sixth Street
Port Huron MI 48060

(313) 982-0891

OPEN: by appointment only M-F 9-4:30, Sa, Su 1-4:30; closed holidays
ACCESS: appointment requested
COPYING FACILITIES: yes
MATERIALS SOLICITED: Materials pertaining to the history of the Port Huron and St. Clair County area, the life of Thomas Edison, and marine lore of the St. Clair River and Great Lakes.

HOLDINGS:
Total volume: 250 l.f.
Inclusive dates: 1820 -
Description: Materials of local interest, including maps, photographs, ledgers, U.S. customs records, records of the Ladies Library Association and the Museum of Arts and History, township records, correspondence, and other personal manuscript materials pertaining to the Port Huron area, including old Fort Gratiot.

MI775-710

St. Clair County Library
W. L. Jenks Historical Collection
210 McMorran Blvd.
Port Huron MI 48060

(313) 987-7323

OPEN: by appointment only M 5:30-8:30, Tu-Th 9-4:30; closed Fridays, weekends, and holidays
COPYING FACILITIES: yes
MATERIALS SOLICITED: Historical material pertaining to Port Huron, St. Clair County, and Michigan. Will also accept historical material on other Michigan counties and cities and material on Lambton County, Ontario, and Sarnia, Ontario.

HOLDINGS:
Total volume: 726 sq.f.
Inclusive dates: 1818 -
Description: A collection relating chiefly to Port Huron, St. Clair County, and Michigan. Included are correspondence, State maps, photographs, literary manuscripts, and county census records (1830-94).

SEE: Hamer.

Some materials are on loan to the Clarke Historical Library, Central Michigan University, and to the Burton Historical Collection, Detroit Public Library.

ROCHESTER

MI795-600

Oakland University Library
Rochester MI 48063

(313) 370-2471

OPEN: by appointment only M-F 8-5; closed weekends, holidays, and week after Christmas
COPYING FACILITIES: yes
MATERIALS SOLICITED: Will accept records related to Oakland County.

HOLDINGS:
Total volume: 3 l.f.
Inclusive dates: 1902 - 1955
Description: Records relating to the investigation by Frederick Black of the death of John Wilkes Booth; Oakland tax records, 1840-80; and the archives of Oakland University.

ROMEO

MI812-690
Romeo Historical Society
P.O. Box 412
Romeo MI 48065

(313) 752-4111, 6013

OPEN: M, W, F 1-4; other times by
  appointment
USER FEES: one dollar suggested
  donation for nonresidents
COPYING FACILITIES: yes
MATERIALS SOLICITED: Photographs, diaries, records, genealogical materials,
  oral histories, and other items pertaining to Romeo, Bruce, and Washington
  townships.

HOLDINGS:
  Total volume: 300 items
  Inclusive dates: 1800 - 1900
  Description: Photographs of Romeo's
  families and homes. Documents of early
  settlement, diaries, letters, and local literary society and farmers' club minutes.

SAGINAW

MI824-320
Hoyt Public Library
Eddy Historical & Genealogical
  Collection
505 Janes Avenue
Saginaw MI 48605

(517) 755-0904

OPEN: M-Th 9-9, F, Sa 9-5; closed
  Sundays
COPYING FACILITIES: yes
MATERIALS SOLICITED: Photographs, ge-
  nealogies, and other materials pertain-
  ing to Saginaw Valley history and its
  lumbering and automobile industries.
  Will also accept records of Saginaw
  County schools, churches, and social or
  service organizations.

HOLDINGS:
  Total volume: not specified
  Inclusive dates: 19th century -
  Description: Business and personal pa-
  pers of families with lumbering interests
  in the Saginaw Valley, including
  references to lumbering in the Pacific
  Northwest.

SEE: Hamer; NUCMC 1968 (as Saginaw
  Public Libraries).

SEE: Davis; Parkinson.

ST. CLAIR SHORES

MI828-720
St. Clair Shores Public Library
St. Clair Shores Historical
  Commission's Archival Collections
22500 Eleven Mile Road
St. Clair Shores MI 48081

(313) 771-9020

OPEN: M-Th; closed Fridays, weekends,
  and holidays
COPYING FACILITIES: yes

MATERIALS SOLICITED: Archival and
  photographic material on the history of
  St. Clair Shores.

HOLDINGS:
  Total volume: 20 l.f.; 50 items
  Inclusive dates: 1911 -
  Description: Materials relating to the
  village and city of St. Clair Shores and
  Lake Township, including Lake Township clerks' and treasurers' records; village
  and city records; histories of buildings,
  institutions, and families; photographs;
  and oral history interviews.

ST. JOSEPH

MI845-40
The American Society of Agricultural
  Engineers
2950 Niles Road
St. Joseph MI 49085

(616) 429-0300

OPEN: M-F 8-5; closed weekends and
  holidays
ACCESS: appointment required
COPYING FACILITIES: no
MATERIALS SOLICITED: Manuscripts pertaining to the history of agricultural
  machinery and farmstead equipment.

HOLDINGS:
  Total volume: 200 l.f.
  Inclusive dates: 1907 -
  Description: Meeting and business
  records, correspondence, and original
  manuscripts of ASAE publications, including the *Seven Decades That Changed
  America* manuscript, which relates the
  history of the Society, 1907-77.

SAULT STE. MARIE

MI865-80
Bayliss Public Library
Judge Joseph R. Steere Room
541 Library Drive
Sault Ste. Marie MI 49783

(906) 632-9331

OPEN: Tu, Th 9-9, W, F 9-5:30, Sa 9-4;
  closed Sundays and holidays
ACCESS: adults doing historical or
  genealogical research
COPYING FACILITIES: yes
MATERIALS SOLICITED: Materials on the
  eastern Upper Peninsula of Michigan.

HOLDINGS:
  Total volume: 12,350 items; 150 vols.
  Inclusive dates: 1802 - 1940's
  Description: Collections chiefly relating
  to Sault Ste. Marie and Port Mackinac,
  primarily concerned with local businesses
  and social clubs, land purchases, the fur
  trade, relations with the Indians, and
  shipping on the upper Great Lakes. Included are some of the records of the
  American Fur Company from 1834 to
  1848.

SEE: Hamer (as Carnegie Public Library).

SEE: Hinding.

MI865-480
Lake Superior State College
Library
1000 College Drive
Sault Ste. Marie MI 49783

(906) 632-6841, Ext. 402

OPEN: M-Th 8-11, F 8-5, Sa 12-5, Su
  1-11; closed holidays
COPYING FACILITIES: yes
MATERIALS SOLICITED: Materials con-
  cerning the marine history of the Great
  Lakes, especially Lake Superior and the
  Sault locks; the Hiawatha epic of H.
  W. Longfellow and related source ma-
  terial by H. R. Schoolcraft; Indians of
  Michigan and Ontario, Canada; and
  the career of U.S. Senator Philip A.
  Hart.

HOLDINGS:
  Total volume: not specified
  Inclusive dates: 19th century -
  Description: Logbooks, visual documents, and other Michigan history materials, with emphasis on Sault Ste. Marie, the eastern end of the Upper Peninsula, Chippewa and Ojibway Indians, and
  the marine history of the Great Lakes,
  especially Lake Superior and the Sault
  locks.

STURGIS

MI890-720
Sturgis Public Library
130 N. Nottawa Street
Sturgis MI 49091

(616) 651-7907

OPEN: M-Th 9:30-8:30, F, Sa 9:30-5:30;
  closed Sundays and holidays
COPYING FACILITIES: yes
MATERIALS SOLICITED: Materials pertaining to genealogy, Michigan history,
  and local history.

HOLDINGS:
  Total volume: 200 items
  Inclusive dates: 19th century -
  Description: Letters, diaries, family
  trees and other papers of area residents,
  and some local club and association materials, including records of the Daughters
  of the American Revolution, the Grand
  Army of the Republic, and the local historical society.

TECUMSEH

MI910-770
Tecumseh Public Library
Clara Waldron Historical Room
215 North Ottawa
Tecumseh MI 49286

(517) 423-2238

OPEN: F 3-5, Sa 12-4, or by special
  arrangement
COPYING FACILITIES: yes
MATERIALS SOLICITED: Materials pertaining to Tecumseh area history, including economic, political, social, and
  cultural development. Will also accept
  materials pertaining to Lenawee County history, and Michigan history.

HOLDINGS:
Total volume: not specified
Inclusive dates: 1824 -
Description: Business, church, and school records; photographs; records of social and service organizations; and a slide collection pertaining to the history and development of the Tecumseh County area.

THREE RIVERS

MI920-760
Three Rivers Public Library
920 West Michigan Avenue
Three Rivers MI 49093

(616) 273-8666

OPEN: M, W, F 10-7, Tu, Th 11-8, Sa 10-4; closed Sundays and holidays
COPYING FACILITIES: yes
MATERIALS SOLICITED: Materials pertaining to the history of Three Rivers and St. Joseph County. Will also accept Michigan history materials.

HOLDINGS:
Total volume: 20 l.f.; 6 vols.
Inclusive dates: 1890 -
Description: Genealogies, cemetery records, manuscript histories, journals, scrapbooks, and photographs relating to the history of Three Rivers, its environs, and its residents.

SEE: Hamer.

TRAVERSE CITY

MI925-120
Con Foster Museum
Traverse City MI 49684

no telephone
SEE: Hamer.

Questionnaire not returned.

MI925-560
Northwestern Michigan College
Mark Osterlin Library
Traverse City MI 49684

(616) 922-1060

OPEN: M-Th 8-10, F 8-5, Sa 9-4, Su 1-5; summer hours M, Th, F 8:30-4:30, Tu, W 8:30-9:30; closed weekends
COPYING FACILITIES: yes
MATERIALS SOLICITED: Items pertinent to the historical record of northwestern Michigan.

HOLDINGS:
Total volume: 30 microfilm reels
Inclusive dates: 1802 -
Description: Materials pertaining to northwestern Michigan history, including church records, organization records, township records, authors' working papers, ledgers, diaries, a lighthouse log, business records, and post office records.

MI925-640
Pioneer Study Center
11930 West Bayshore
Traverse City MI

MAILING ADDRESS:
Box 1032
Traverse City MI 49684

(616) 946-3151

OPEN: M-F 8:30-3:30; closed other days and holidays
COPYING FACILITIES: yes
MATERIALS SOLICITED: Oral history tapes, documents, photographs, and postcards of log boom days in the history of the Grand Traverse region, 1860-1910; diaries, manuscripts, and genealogy records of the pioneer era of the region, 1860-80. Will also accept other photographs and tapes of contemporary leaders in the community.

HOLDINGS:
Total volume: 3 c.f.; 14 file drawers
Inclusive dates: 1860 - 1965
Description: Materials relating to the Grand Traverse region, encompassing Grand Traverse, Antrim, and Leelanau counties. Emphasis is on the log boom era, 1860-1910. Included are manuscripts, photographs, oral history tapes, and other items.

TRENTON

MI930-760
Trenton Historical Museum
St. Joseph and 3rd Streets
Trenton MI

MAILING ADDRESS:
Trenton City Hall
2800 3rd Street
Trenton MI 48183

(313) 675-2130

OPEN: Sa 2-5 by appointment only; closed holidays and other days
COPYING FACILITIES: yes
MATERIALS SOLICITED: History of the museum property and house. Will also accept materials concerning the downriver and Trenton area.

HOLDINGS:
Total volume: 64 sq.f.
Inclusive dates: 1850 - 1942
Description: Photographs of Trenton people and properties, as well as local deeds.

TROY

MI935-770
Troy Museum
60 West Wattles Road
Troy MI 48098

(313) 524-3570

OPEN: Su 2-4, M-F 9-4; closed Saturdays and holidays
COPYING FACILITIES: no
MATERIALS SOLICITED: Materials relating to Troy, Oakland County, and Michigan. Will also accept items pertaining

to American military history (1860-1950) and architectural development of the Troy area and Oakland County.

HOLDINGS:
Total volume: 2 files; 500 vols.
Inclusive dates: 1820 -
Description: Biographies of past and current Troy residents, tracing westward settlement; township records and maps, including cemetery maps; six oral histories; and diaries, 1812-1930's.

WYANDOTTE

MI982-80
Bacon Memorial Public Library
Local History Collection
45 Vinewood Street
Wyandotte MI 48192

(313) 282-7660

OPEN: M-Th 10-9; Oct.-June, Sa 10-5 and closed Fridays; June-Oct., F 10-5 and closed Saturdays; closed holidays and Sunday
COPYING FACILITIES: yes
MATERIALS SOLICITED: All materials concerning Wyandotte and significant materials concerning downriver Detroit, Wayne County, and Michigan.

HOLDINGS:
Total volume: 22 file drawers
Inclusive dates: 1800 -
Description: Several unpublished manuscripts; over 3,000 photographs of local subjects; records, of community organizations; Wyandotte public records, including the Registration of Electors, 1868-1932; Ford City government records; and oral history interviews with area residents, recorded in the 1950's.
Also includes maps and scrapbooks.

MI982-880
Wyandotte Museums
2610 Biddle Avenue
Wyandotte MI 48192

(313) 246-4520

OPEN: M-F 9-5; closed weekends and holidays
COPYING FACILITIES: yes
MATERIALS SOLICITED: Any materials relating to Wyandotte and its residents and Detroit materials. Also interested in locating records of Michigan Alkali, J. B. Ford Plate Glass Industry, and Eureka Iron Works and items relating to the Wyandotte shipbuilding industry.

HOLDINGS:
Total volume: 25 file drawers
Inclusive dates: 1800 -
Description: Ledgers, scrapbooks, clippings, photographs, tape recordings, and miscellaneous manuscripts relating chiefly to the history of Wyandotte.

YPSILANTI

MI990-180

Eastern Michigan University
Center of Educational Resources
University Archives and Special
  Collections
Ypsilanti MI 48197

(313) 487-3423

OPEN: M-F 9-noon; closed weekends and
  holidays
COPYING FACILITIES: yes
MATERIALS SOLICITED: Materials related
  to Eastern Michigan University.

HOLDINGS:
  Total volume: 1,023 l.f.; 171 file
drawers
  Inclusive dates: 1849 -
  Description: Noncurrent records relating to Eastern Michigan University including University publications, photographs, transcripts of oral history tapes, correspondence, papers of individuals, and collections of ephemera.

MI990-940

Ypsilanti Historical Museum
220 North Huron
Ypsilanti MI 48197

(313) 482-4990

OPEN: by appointment and M-F 9-12;
  closed two weeks at Christmas and
  New Year's

ACCESS: City Historian or Museum
  Archivist must be present
COPYING FACILITIES: yes
MATERIALS SOLICITED: Historical and
  current materials pertaining to Ypsilanti and Washtenaw County.

HOLDINGS:
  Total volume: 6 file drawers
  Inclusive dates: 1820 -
  Description: Letters, deeds, church records, and other materials pertinent to the history of Ypsilanti and Washtenaw County.

MINNESOTA

In 1955 the Minnesota State Archives, now a part of the Division of Archives and Manuscripts of the Minnesota Historical Society, initiated a records preservation program for local governments. Counties, municipalities, townships, and school districts ordinarily maintain custody of archival documents, but small quantities have been acquired by the Historical Society in St. Paul and nine regional research centers operate under its auspices.

ADA

MN14-560
Norman County Historical Society
Museum
1st Street East
Ada MN

MAILING ADDRESS:
404 West 5th Avenue
Ada MN 56510

(218) 784-4911

OPEN: Tu, Th, Sa 2-5; closed other days and holidays
USER FEES: fees for opening outside regular hours
COPYING FACILITIES: no
MATERIALS SOLICITED: Letters, diaries, club records, public records, church records, family histories, and business records pertaining to Norman County. Will also accept legal documents related to the Norman County area.

HOLDINGS:
Total volume: 4,500 items
Inclusive dates: 1871 -
Description: Family histories; rural school and business records dating from 1900; legal documents; discharge papers from the Grand Army of the Republic, World War I, World War II, Korean and Vietnam wars; materials pertaining to the Woman's Christian Temperance Union and other organizations; photographs and slides; and oral history tapes pertaining to the Norman County area.

ALBERT LEA

MN28-240
Freeborn County Historical Society
Museum and Research Library
Freeborn County Fairgrounds
North Bridge
Albert Lea MN

MAILING ADDRESS:
P.O. Box 403
Albert Lea MN 56007

(507) 373-8003

OPEN: 1:30-4:30 (days vary with month)
ACCESS: prior arrangements required
COPYING FACILITIES: yes
MATERIALS SOLICITED: History of Freeborn County and surrounding counties.

HOLDINGS:
Total volume: 200 l.f.
Inclusive dates: 1849 -
Description: A collection of materials on Freeborn County and surrounding counties, including manuscripts, diaries, and genealogies relating to Colonel Albert Miller Lea and other individuals.

ANNANDALE

MN38-520
Minnesota Pioneer Park
Highway 55 W.
Annandale MN 55302

(612) 274-8489

OPEN: daily May-Oct.; other months by appointment
USER FEES: $2
COPYING FACILITIES: yes
MATERIALS SOLICITED: Letters from soldiers and sailors during war time.

HOLDINGS:
Total volume: not specified
Inclusive dates: 1860's - 1900
Description: Litchfield hotel register; records of Corinna and Litchfield; map of Stearns County, 1900; and photographs.

ANOKA

MN42-40
Anoka County Historical/Genealogical
Society
1900 Third Avenue South
Anoka MN 55303

(612) 421-0600

OPEN: Tu-F 12:30-4; closed other days and holidays
COPYING FACILITIES: yes
MATERIALS SOLICITED: Records from churches, schools, local government, and similar institutions. Will also accept items of historic interest to Anoka County.

HOLDINGS:
Total volume: 2,000 sq.f.
Inclusive dates: early 19th century -
Description: Manuscripts relating to early Anoka County, its history, formation, educational system, commerce, settlement, aboriginal peoples, and early settlers and their genealogy.

SEE: Hinding.

AUSTIN

MN49-520
Mower County Historical Society
Austin MN

MAILING ADDRESS:
Box 426
Austin MN 55912

SEE: NUCMC, 1980.

Questionnaire not returned.

BEMIDJI

MN63-70
Bemidji State University
Library
University Archives
Bemidji MN 56601

(218) 755-3349, 2955

OPEN: M-F 8-4:30; closed weekends and holidays
COPYING FACILITIES: yes
MATERIALS SOLICITED: Records and other materials relating to University activities, functions, organizations, and departments, as well as the faculty, staff, and students. Will also accept private and personal records of faculty and staff.

HOLDINGS:
Total volume: 116 boxes; 23 file drawers
Inclusive dates: 1919 -
Description: Records of University faculty, students, and staff, including personal papers.

SEE: Hinding.

MN63-75
Bemidji State University
North Central Minnesota Historical Center
Bemidji MN 56601

SEE: NUCMC, 1977.

Questionnaire not returned.

BRECKENRIDGE

MN126-880
Wilkin County Historical Society
704 Nebraska Avenue
Breckenridge MN

MAILING ADDRESS:
P.O. Box 212
Breckenridge MN 56520

(218) 630-5841

OPEN: Su 1:30-4:30, Tu 11-4 or by appointment; closed other days and holidays
COPYING FACILITIES: yes
MATERIALS SOLICITED: Materials relating to Wilkin County. Will also accept other materials.

HOLDINGS:
Total volume: not specified
Inclusive dates: 1860 -
Description: Local newspapers from 1881; some biographies of early pioneers; Family History Book - Wilkin County, 1977; recreated rooms.

CARLTON

MN185-120
Carlton County Historical Society
Box 245
Carlton MN 55718

(218) 384-3271

OPEN: M, W, F 12-4; closed other days and holidays
COPYING FACILITIES: yes
MATERIALS SOLICITED: Materials on military roads, logging, lumbering, railroads, and the brick industry.

HOLDINGS:
Total volume: 12 file drawers
Inclusive dates: 1700 -
Description: Oral history tape about logging; school records; township clerk's records; county records, including deeds and licenses; and minutes of a local women's organization.

SEE: NUCMC, 1979.

SEE: Hinding.

CASS LAKE

MN198-120
Chippewa National Forest
Cass Lake MN

MAILING ADDRESS:
Route 3, P.O. Box 244
Cass Lake MN 56633

(218) 335-2226

OPEN: M-F 8-4:30; closed weekends and holidays
USER FEES: none, except for extensive search and photographic work
COPYING FACILITIES: yes
MATERIALS SOLICITED: Oral history materials relating to Chippewa National Forest. Will also accept photographs and manuscripts relating to the Forest.

HOLDINGS:
Total volume: 10 l.f.
Inclusive dates: 1915 -
Description: Manuscripts, photographs, and oral history interviews relating to the history of Chippewa National Forest. Included is material relating to early logging as well as recollections of area pioneers.

COLLEGEVILLE

MN226-700
St. John's Abbey
Kritzeck Collection
Collegeville MN 56321

(612) 363-2546

OPEN: by appointment only
ACCESS: prior arrangement required
COPYING FACILITIES: yes

HOLDINGS:
Total volume: several hundred items
Inclusive dates: 1450 -
Description: Holograph letters, including ecclesiastical manuscripts of Doctors of the Church, Saints and Blessed, and Supreme Pontiffs; and secular manuscripts of Holy Roman Emperors, czars of Russia, kings of England, France, and Spain, and Presidents of the United States.

SEE ALSO: An unpublished inventory of the Kritzeck Collection is available at the institution.

MN226-705
St. John's Abbey
Archives
Collegeville MN 56321

(612) 363-2699

OPEN: by appointment only
ACCESS: open to researchers by prior arrangement with Archivist
COPYING FACILITIES: yes
MATERIALS SOLICITED: Any materials relating to the Abbey and the history and spiritual customs of areas and peoples served by the Abbey and its foundations.

HOLDINGS:
Total volume: 1,134 l.f.
Inclusive dates: 1846 -
Description: Records of the Abbey and its subsidiary institutions, St. John's University, Preparatory School, and the Liturgical Press. Institutional and corporate records include legal and ecclesiastical documents, correspondence of officials, minutes, and financial records. Also included is an extensive collection of personal papers, including manuscript histories, letters, diaries, notes, sermons, and other writings; clippings; a large collection of photographs, slides, and motion pictures dating from before 1875; maps; and oral records.

In addition to documenting life, work, and prayer at Collegeville, records document missionary activity of the upper Midwest since 1856. Also documented are activities in Washington State, New York, Saskatchewan, the Dakotas, Oklahoma, Japan, the Philippines, the Bahamas, Puerto Rico, and Mexico. The Collection also includes liturgical and spiritual materials, local histories, and memorabilia.

SEE: Hamer (as St. John's University Library).

MN226-720
St. John's University
Bush Center
Hill Monastic Manuscript Library
Collegeville MN 56321

(612) 363-3514

OPEN: M-F 8-4:30; closed weekends and holidays
COPYING FACILITIES: yes
MATERIALS SOLICITED: Manuscript books from the early Middle Ages to the 17th century.

HOLDINGS:
Total volume: 50,000 items
Inclusive dates: early Middle Ages - 17th century
Description: Microfilmed copies of manuscript books and archival units from libraries and archives in Austria, Spain, Malta, Ethiopia, and elsewhere. Much of the material dates from before 1450, but since many collections are only partially cataloged by the foreign repositories, and since only approximate dates are known for many items, it is difficult to determine what proportion pertains to the pre-1450 period. Languages of documents include Latin, German, Greek, Hebrew, Italian, and Ge'ez. The strength of the collections lies in literary manuscripts, and there is an important Austrian *wappenbucher* collection.

SEE: NUCMC, 1975.

SEE: Martin.

SEE ALSO: Julian G. Plante, 'The Hill Monastic Manuscript Library: Its Origins, Microfilmed Collections, and Activities,' *Res Publica Litterarum: Studies in the Classical Tradition* 2 (1979).

The Library has published several finding aids to portions of its microfilmed collections and irregularly publishes the Hill Monastic Manuscript Library *Progress Reports.*

MN226-725
St. John's University
University Archives
Collegeville MN 56321

(612) 363-2129

OPEN: M-F 2:30-4:30; closed weekends
and holidays
COPYING FACILITIES: yes
MATERIALS SOLICITED: Material relating
to the University, its faculty, staff, students, and alumni.

HOLDINGS:
   Total volume: 615 l.f.
   Inclusive dates: 1856 -
   Description: Administrative, academic
   and financial records and correspondence; publications; photographs; slides
   and motion pictures; oral records; plans;
   maps and graphics; memorabilia; and collections of personal papers relating to
   University life, academics, activities,
   events, programs, staff, faculty, students,
   and alumni. Also included are records of
   the Preparatory School, Seminary, and
   ancillary programs sponsored by the institution such as the Institute for Mental
   Health, Institute for Ecumenical and Cultural Research, Minnesota Public Radio,
   and the Hill Monastic Manuscript Library.

CROOKSTON

MN233-160
Diocese of Crookston
The Chancery Office
1200 Memorial Drive
Crookston MN 56716

(218) 281-4533

OPEN: M-F 9-5; closed weekends,
holidays, and holy days
ACCESS: permission of Chancellor
required
COPYING FACILITIES: yes
MATERIALS SOLICITED: Records of the
Diocese of Crookston and official decrees and correspondence of the Roman Catholic church. Will also accept
personal papers of diocesan personnel.

HOLDINGS:
   Total volume: 600 c.f.
   Inclusive dates: 1875 -
   Description: Sacramental and historical
   records of the parishes comprising the
   Diocese of Crookston in northwestern
   Minnesota.

DULUTH

MN261-40
Army Corps of Engineers
Canal Park Marine Museum
Canal Park
Duluth MN 55802

(218) 727-2497

OPEN: M-F 8-4:30; closed weekends,
Thanksgiving, Christmas, and New
Year's
COPYING FACILITIES: no

MATERIALS SOLICITED: Materials relating
to ships and shipping on the upper
Great Lakes, shipwrecks, upper Lakes
ports, and geology and geography of
Lake Superior basin. Will also accept
any regional history related to the upper Great Lakes.

HOLDINGS:
   Total volume: 50 l.f.
   Inclusive dates: 1865 -
   Description: Historical manuscripts relating to the development of Duluth-
   Superior Harbor and other Lake Superior
   ports, commodities and cargo records,
   and photographs; manuscript data sheets
   on Lakes ships, and photographs and
   slides; vessel log books and operating
   records; clippings and ephemera on similar subjects; and construction drawings
   for selected vessels.

MN261-170
Duluth Public Library
520 West Superior Street
Duluth MN 55802

(218) 723-3802

OPEN: M, Tu 10-8:30, W-F 10-5:30, Sa
10-4; closed Sundays and holidays
COPYING FACILITIES: yes
MATERIALS SOLICITED: Materials relating
to Duluth and the Great Lakes with
emphasis on local history and Indians
of the area.

HOLDINGS:
   Total volume: 750 l.f.
   Inclusive dates: 1850 -
   Description: Manuscripts, clipping files,
   photographs, maps, and local government
   records.

MN261-730
Superior National Forest
515 West 1st Street
Duluth MN

MAILING ADDRESS:
P.O. Box 338
Duluth MN 55801

(218) 720-5324

OPEN: M-F 8-4; closed weekends and
holidays
COPYING FACILITIES: yes
MATERIALS SOLICITED: Materials relating
to the Boundary Waters Canoe Area,
Selke Committee Reports, Superior National Forest, and the general Forest
area.

HOLDINGS:
   Total volume: 40 c.f.
   Inclusive dates: 1909 -
   Description: A collection relating to the
   history of the Superior National Forest,
   including the Boundary Waters Canoe
   Area, Forest personnel, and actions and
   activities pertaining to the Forest.

MN261-810
University of Minnesota at Duluth
Northeast Minnesota Historical
   Center
Room 375, Library
Duluth MN 55812

(218) 726-8526

OPEN: M-F 8-4:30; closed weekends and
holidays
COPYING FACILITIES: yes
MATERIALS SOLICITED: Materials relating
to northeastern Minnesota; the counties
of Carlton, Cook, Lake, and St. Louis;
and Lake Superior; including manuscripts, archives, visual documents, audible documents, microforms, and
scrapbooks. Will also accept public
records.

HOLDINGS:
   Total volume: 2,000 l.f.
   Inclusive dates: 1690 - 1980
   Description: Materials relating to ship-
   ping, mining, fur trade, settlement, and
   early families in Duluth and St. Louis
   County, MN, including the diaries of
   Rev. Edmund F. Ely, an early missionary
   to the Indians, and the papers of the
   Merritt family, discoverers of iron ore on
   the Mesabi Range.
      Also includes the records of the
   Duluth-Superior Transit Company; the
   Great Lakes-St. Lawrence Tidewater As-
   sociation, which paved the way for the St.
   Lawrence Seaway; the records of Duluth
   area conservation, civic, and cultural
   groups; public records; and the papers of
   Julius Barnes, local businessman and
   friend of Herbert Hoover.

SEE: Hinding.

The materials at the Northeast
Minnesota Historical Center were deposited there by the St. Louis County
Historical Society (MN261-710 in the
1978 *Directory*).

MN261-830
University of Minnesota at Duluth
Library and Learning Resources
   Service
University Archives
Room 375, Library
Duluth MN 55812

(218) 726-6157

OPEN: M-F 8-4:30; closed weekends
COPYING FACILITIES: yes
MATERIALS SOLICITED: Noncurrent
records of the University of Minnesota
at Duluth, 1947- , and its predecessor,
Duluth State Teacher's College,
1902-47. Will also accept personal papers of faculty, staff, and alumni.

HOLDINGS:
   Total volume: not specified
   Inclusive dates: 1902 -
   Description: Noncurrent records, pho-
   tographs, printed materials, and other
   materials relating to the history, curricu-
   lum, and physical development of the
   University of Minnesota at Duluth.

EDINA

MN275-200

Edina Historical Society
4801 West 50th Street
Edina MN 55424

(612) 927-8861

OPEN: by appointment only
COPYING FACILITIES: no
MATERIALS SOLICITED: Manuscripts, archival material, and visual and audible documents reflecting local history, elementary education before 1900, the Grange (Patrons of Husbandry), and flour milling.

HOLDINGS:
Total volume: 200 l.f.
Inclusive dates: 1857 -
Description: A collection of manuscripts, photographs, and audible documents pertaining to the history of Edina. Included are reminiscences of pioneers and papers relating to 19th century local history, including the Edina Mills, Cahill School, Minnehaha Grange, and Jonathan Grimes House.

SEE: Hinding.

ELYSIAN

MN300-480

Le Sueur County Historical Society
Corner of Frank and Fourth Streets
Elysian MN

MAILING ADDRESS:
Box 557
Elysian MN 56028

(507) 362-8350, 267-4620

OPEN: June - Aug., W-Su 1:30-5:30; May and Sept., open Sa, Su, by appointment; closed rest of year
ACCESS: appointment advised; access to church records only in company of local Curator
COPYING FACILITIES: no
MATERIALS SOLICITED: Church, school, cemetery, and city vital records. Will also accept lodge, society, and business records and recordings of senior citizens.

HOLDINGS:
Total volume: 20 l.f.; 5 vols.
Inclusive dates: 1831 -
Description: A collection relating to the history of Le Sueur County. Included are a five-volume diary (1831-68), church records, school records, organization records, and tape recordings of senior citizens.

SEE: Hinding.

EXCELSIOR

MN307-200

Excelsior Lake Minnetonka Historical
Society
339 Third Street
Excelsior MN

MAILING ADDRESS:
P.O. Box 305
Excelsior MN 55331

(612) 474-5880

OPEN: W 9-noon; closed other days and holidays
COPYING FACILITIES: yes
MATERIALS SOLICITED: Materials relating to the history of the Lake Minnetonka area.

HOLDINGS:
Total volume: 2,500 items
Inclusive dates: 1852 -
Description: Materials documenting the Lake Minnetonka area, including records of churches, schools, government, civic and social organizations, and businesses; diaries, journals, logbooks, and correspondence of families and individuals; maps and plat books; photographs; oral history tapes and transcripts; and scrapbooks.

MN307-360

InterStudy
Library - Information Center
5715 Christmas Lake Road
Excelsior MN

MAILING ADDRESS:
P.O. Box 458
Excelsior MN 55331

(612) 474-1176

OPEN: M-F 8-4:30; closed weekends and holidays
ACCESS: appointment required
COPYING FACILITIES: yes
MATERIALS SOLICITED: Materials relating to alternative delivery systems in health care, including health maintenance organizations, health policy analysis, health insurance, and medical economics.

HOLDINGS:
Total volume: 200 items
Inclusive dates: 1976 -
Description: Records relating to health policy analysis, health insurance, medical economics, and alternative delivery systems, including health maintenance organizations.

FAIRMONT

MN314-520

Martin County Historical Society
Pioneer Museum
304 E. Blue Earth Avenue
Fairmont MN 56031

(507) 235-5178, 9812

OPEN: Tu-F 1:30-4:30; closed other days and Oct. 1 - May 1
COPYING FACILITIES: yes

MATERIALS SOLICITED: Fairmont and Martin County history.
HOLDINGS:
Total volume: 5 c.f.
Inclusive dates: 1860's -
Description: Materials relating to Martin County, including school, court, and township records; personal papers; reminiscences; oral history tapes; and tapes of town events made by the local radio station.

SEE: Hamer.

Researchers must provide their own tape recorders.

FARIBAULT

MN321-690

Rice County Historical Society
1814 2nd Avenue
Faribault MN 55021

no telephone

OPEN: M-F 8-4:30, Sa, Su 1-4:30; closed holidays
COPYING FACILITIES: no
MATERIALS SOLICITED: Material relating to Rice County history, particularly the milling industry.

HOLDINGS:
Total volume: 22 l.f.
Inclusive dates: 1858 -
Description: Materials pertaining to Rice County, including papers written for Historical Society meetings, letters, diaries, organization and business records, sermons of Bishop Henry B. Whipple, and World War I aerial photographs.

SEE: Hamer.

SEE: Davis.

FERGUS FALLS

MN328-600

Otter Tail County Historical Society
1110 Lincoln Avenue West
Fergus Falls MN 56537

(218) 736-6038

OPEN: Sa, Su 1-4, M-F 11-5; closed holidays
COPYING FACILITIES: yes
MATERIALS SOLICITED: Materials pertaining to the history of Otter Tail County and the surrounding area, including genealogical and biographical materials. Will also accept Minnesota history materials.

HOLDINGS:
Total volume: 82 l.f.; 280 oral histories
Inclusive dates: 1850 -
Description: Materials relating to the history of Otter Tail County and the genealogies and biographies of its people. The collection contains record books of businesses, church and cemetery records, clippings, scrapbooks, photographs, correspondence, oral history recordings, and some diaries.

SEE: Hinding.

GILBERT

MN338-360
Iron Range Historical Society
Division of Historical Service
Research Library and Archives
City Hall
Broadway
Gilbert MN

MAILING ADDRESS:
Box 786
Gilbert MN 55741

(218) 749-3150

OPEN: M-F 8-4; closed weekends and
holidays
COPYING FACILITIES: yes
MATERIALS SOLICITED: Materials relating
to the history of the iron ranges of
Minnesota including photos, manuscripts, records, company histories, and
family histories.

HOLDINGS:
Total volume: 1,000 l.f.
Inclusive dates: 1880 -
Description: Records, including oral
history tapes, photographs, and slides, relating to the mining regions of
northeastern Minnesota, Michigan, and
Wisconsin, and the labor and ethnic history of the region.

GRAND MARAIS

MN356-120
Cook County Historical Society
225 North First Avenue West
Grand Marais MN 55604

(218) 387-1678

OPEN: M, Th 1-5, W 1-9, F 10-5, Sa 1-4;
closed Su, Tu
SEE: Hamer; NUCMC, 1975.

Questionnaire not returned.

GRAND RAPIDS

MN363-360
Itasca County Historical Society
Museum
Old Central School
Grand Rapids MN

MAILING ADDRESS:
P.O. Box 664
Grand Rapids MN 55744

(218) 326-6461

OPEN: M-Sa 10-5; closed Sundays and
holidays
COPYING FACILITIES: no
MATERIALS SOLICITED: Oral and written
history, genealogy, and photographs relating to Itasca County. Will also accept all manuscript materials.

HOLDINGS:
Total volume: 30 l.f.; 2 file cabinets
Inclusive dates: 1819 -
Description: Family, business, government, and organizational records, personal journals, photographs, and oral histories relating to the history and culture of
Itasca County, especially early settlement
and pioneer activities in logging, mining,
and farming.

GRANITE FALLS

MN370-920
Valdres Samband
Sacred Heart MN

MAILING ADDRESS:
Route 2, P.O. Box 14A
Sacred Heart MN 56285

(612) 765-2595

OPEN: by appointment only
COPYING FACILITIES: no
MATERIALS SOLICITED: Materials dealing
with folk in and from the Valdres Valley of Norway, including genealogical,
historical, and cultural information.

HOLDINGS:
Total volume: 1,200 items
Inclusive dates: 1899 -
Description: Records of the Valdres
Samband, the oldest and largest Norse
bygdelag (community association) in
America; genealogies of member families;
photographs; manuscripts; and oral tapes.

HIBBING

MN391-310
Hibbing Historical Society
First Settlers Association
First Settlers Museum
21st and 4th Avenue East
Hibbing MN 55746

(218) 262-3486

OPEN: M-F 9-5, June -Sept., Tu, W 9-4,
Oct. - May; closed weekends and
holidays
ACCESS: appointment required
COPYING FACILITIES: yes
MATERIALS SOLICITED: Records, manu-
scripts, documents, diaries, maps, and
photographs relating to North Hibbing,
St. Louis County, and Minnesota.

HOLDINGS:
Total volume: 2,500 items
Inclusive dates: 1892 -
Description: Records of early women's
clubs, including correspondence, financial
records, membership lists, and minutes;
records, minutes, and scrapbooks relating
to the establishment of the Western chapter of the Northland chapter of the Red
Cross; manuscripts on memories of its
early settlers; photographs; and architectural and engineering drawings relating to
Hibbing.

HOPKINS

MN405-320
Hopkins Historical Society
33 14th Avenue North
Hopkins MN

MAILING ADDRESS:
1010 1st Street South
Hopkins MN 55343

(612) 935-8474

OPEN: Su 2-5, other days by
appointment
COPYING FACILITIES: yes
MATERIALS SOLICITED: Materials concerning the history of the Hopkins
area. Will also accept any documents
having historical value.

HOLDINGS:
Total volume: 4 l.f.; 6,000 items
Inclusive dates: 1850 -
Description: Materials concerning the
history of Hopkins and its vicinity, including records of the Hopkins Women's
Club and its civic activities, 1908-61; documents and photographs, some reflecting
the Bohemian ethnic background of
many of the local residents; and an information file, including genealogical data
regarding local families.

SEE: Hinding.

HUTCHINSON

MN412-520
McLeod County Historical Society
115 South Jefferson Street
Hutchinson MN 55350

SEE: Hamer.

Questionnaire not returned.

INTERNATIONAL FALLS

MN419-440
Koochiching County Historical
Society
214 6th Street
International Falls MN

MAILING ADDRESS:
Box 1147
International Falls MN 56649

(218) 283-4316

OPEN: M-Sa 10-4 Memorial-Labor Days;
by appointment during winter; closed
Sundays and holidays
USER FEES: 50 cents in summer
ACCESS: advance arrangements requested
during winter season
COPYING FACILITIES: no
MATERIALS SOLICITED: Family histories
and other materials pertaining to the
history of Koochiching County and the
surrounding area.

HOLDINGS:
Total volume: 75 l.f.
Inclusive dates: 1890 -
Description: Materials relating to
Koochiching County history, including
account books, business records, corre-

spondence, diaries, genealogical data, literary manuscripts, minute books, scrapbooks, photographs, motion pictures, and oral histories and transcripts. The collection documents clubs, organizations, churches, schools, industry, businesses, government agencies, families, and community history.

SEE: NUCMC, 1959-61.

SEE: Hinding.

LAKE BRONSON

MN433-440
Kittson County Historical Society
Lake Bronson MN

MAILING ADDRESS:
P.O. Box 98
Lake Bronson MN 56734

(218) 754-4100

OPEN: M-F 9-5, Sa, Su 1-5; closed weekends Labor Day to Memorial Day; closed Thanksgiving, Christmas, and New Year's
COPYING FACILITIES: no
MATERIALS SOLICITED: Selective items pertaining to history of county and area.

HOLDINGS:
Total volume: 1.5 l.f.
Inclusive dates: 1894 - 1960
Description: A collection relating to the history of Kittson County. Included are court calendars, ledger books, oral history tapes, and personal papers. Many materials relate to persons of Scandinavian background.

LAKE CITY

MN438-880
Wabasha County Historical Society
204 South Oak Street
Lake City MN 55041

SEE: Hamer.

Questionnaire not returned.

LITCHFIELD

MN459-520
Meeker County Historical Society
308 North Marshall
Litchfield MN 55355

(612) 693-8911

OPEN: M-F 9-5, Sa, Su 1-5 Apr.-Oct.; F, Sa, Su 1-5, M, W 9-5 Oct.-Apr.; closed holidays except Memorial Day, and Tu, Th Oct.-Apr.

SEE: Hamer; NUCMC, 1966.

Questionnaire not returned.

LITTLE FALLS

MN466-520
Morrison County Historical Society
Charles A. Weyerhaeuser Memorial Museum
County Road 52 (Lindbergh Drive)
Little Falls MN

MAILING ADDRESS:
P.O. Box 239
Little Falls MN 56345

(612) 632-4007

OPEN: Tu-Sa 10-5, Su 1-5; closed Sundays, Nov. - April, and Mondays
COPYING FACILITIES: yes
MATERIALS SOLICITED: Manuscript materials relating to the history of Morrison County.

HOLDINGS:
Total volume: not specified
Inclusive dates: 19th century -
Description: Primarily manuscript materials relating to people, places, and events in Morrison County, as well as photographs and oral history recordings.

SEE: Hamer.

LONG LAKE

MN473-880
West Hennepin Pioneers Association
1953 W. Highway 12
Long Lake MN

MAILING ADDRESS:
235 N. Lakeview
Long Lake MN 55356

(612) 473-6557

OPEN: summer, Tu-Su 2-5; rest of year, Su 2-5 and by appointment; closed Mondays
COPYING FACILITIES: yes
MATERIALS SOLICITED: Materials pertaining to the history of Hennepin County and its residents.

HOLDINGS:
Total volume: 100 c.f.
Inclusive dates: 1850 -
Description: Papers, diaries, organization records, photographs, and recordings relating to the history of Hennepin County, particularly the western half.

MADELIA

MN492-880
Watonwan County Historical Society
423 Dill Avenue, S.W.
Madelia MN

MAILING ADDRESS:
P.O. Box 126
Madelia MN 56062

(507) 642-3247

OPEN: M-Th 8:30-4, F 8:30-11:30, Su 1-4 in Summer; W 1-4 and by appointment in winter
COPYING FACILITIES: no

MATERIALS SOLICITED: Materials relating to the history of Watonwan County and its residents.
HOLDINGS:
Total volume: 4 file cabinets
Inclusive dates: 1870 -
Description: Materials pertaining to the Watonwan County area.

MADISON

MN499-480
Lac qui Parle County Historical Society
Historic Center
S. Highway 75
Madison MN

MAILING ADDRESS:
P.O. Box 124
Madison MN 56256

(612) 598-7678

OPEN: W-F 1-5; Su 1-5, April - Sept.; closed other days and holidays
COPYING FACILITIES: no
MATERIALS SOLICITED: Diaries, family histories, business records, and other materials relating to Lac qui Parle County and its early settlers.

HOLDINGS:
Total volume: 20 l.f.
Inclusive dates: 1870 -
Description: Family histories, business and military records, photographs, and oral history recordings of significance to the history of Lac qui Parle County.

MANKATO

MN506-80
Blue Earth County Historical Society
606 South Broad Street
Mankato MN 56001

(507) 345-4154

OPEN: Tu-F 1-5 and by appointment; closed holidays
COPYING FACILITIES: yes
MATERIALS SOLICITED: Manuscript materials, photographs, and oral histories relating to Blue Earth County and its residents.

HOLDINGS:
Total volume: 36 c.f.; 3 file cabinets
Inclusive dates: 1850 -
Description: Account books; business and financial records; correspondence; diaries; genealogical materials; records of schools, local government agencies, businesses, associations, and community organizations; manuscript maps; oral history recordings and transcripts; and photographs, all relating to the history of Blue Earth County and south central Minnesota.

SEE: Hamer.

MN506-530
Mankato State University
Southern Minnesota Historical Center
Mankato MN 56001

SEE: NUCMC, 1977.

Questionnaire not returned.

MARSHALL

MN520-700
Southwest State University
Southwest Minnesota Historical
Center
Marshall MN 56258

(507) 537-7373

OPEN: M 8-4, Tu-F 9-4 by appointment;
closed weekends, holidays, and summer
COPYING FACILITIES: yes
MATERIALS SOLICITED: Ethnic and local
history of southwest Minnesota. Will
also accept materials on farm organizations in Minnesota and genealogical
source materials on the upper Midwest.

HOLDINGS:
Total volume: 600 l.f.
Inclusive dates: 1860 -
Description: Manuscripts relating chiefly to the 19 counties in southwestern
Minnesota. Included are about 200 oral
history interviews, diaries, business
records and correspondence, legislators'
papers, microfilm copies of church
records of closed churches in the area,
and records of farm organizations in the
State.

GUIDES: James E. Fogerty, comp., Pre-
liminary Guide to the Holdings of the
Minnesota Regional Research Centers
(Minnesota Historical Society, 1975).

SEE: NUCMC, 1977.

SEE: Hinding.

MINNEAPOLIS

MN541-16
Abbott-Northwestern Hospital, Corp.
Sister Kenny Institute
800 E. 28th Street
Minneapolis MN 55407

(612) 874-4312

OPEN: M-F 7:30-9; closed weekends and
holidays
ACCESS: appointment required;
restrictions set at that time
COPYING FACILITIES: yes
MATERIALS SOLICITED: Material related
to the work of Sister Kenny or to poliomyelitis. Will also accept archival
material relating to physical therapy
and rehabilitation of physical illnesses,
and papers of employees of the Sister
Kenny Institute up to 1975.

HOLDINGS:
Total volume: 35 boxes
Inclusive dates: 1900 -
Description: Material relating to the ca-
reer of Sister Elizabeth Kenny and the
founding of the Institute named for her.
Annual reports are included, as is ma-

terial relating to the early treatment of
poliomyelitis and the discovery of polio
virus vaccines.

SEE: Hinding.

MN541-64
American Swedish Institute
2600 Park Avenue
Minneapolis MN 55407

(612) 871-4907

OPEN: by appointment; closed Mondays
and holidays
ACCESS: notification of Director or
Curator required
COPYING FACILITIES: yes
MATERIALS SOLICITED: Will accept
manuscripts, records of organizations,
and visual and audible documents re-
lating to Swedish immigration to the
United States.

HOLDINGS:
Total volume: 60 l.f.
Inclusive dates: 1850 -
Description: Collections relating to the
settlement of Swedes in North America,
including family papers, correspondence,
record books of Swedish organizations, a
collection of Bibles with genealogical information, photographs, a few diaries,
and microfilm records of former Swedish
churches in Minnesota.

MN541-80
Augsburg College
George Sverdrup Library
Archives
731 21st Avenue South
Minneapolis MN 55454

(612) 330-1017

OPEN: M-Th 8-11, F 8-5, Sa 10-5, Su
2-11; closed weekends during school
vacation and holidays
ACCESS: permission required
COPYING FACILITIES: yes
MATERIALS SOLICITED: College records
and lectures and papers of College
presidents and faculty. Will also accept
visual documents, oral history recordings, and transcripts, as well as manuscripts of persons associated with the
College.

HOLDINGS:
Total volume: 265 c.f.
Inclusive dates: 1860's -
Description: Archives of Augsburg College and its predecessor, Augsburg College
and Theological Seminary, including business records, biography and reference
files, materials concerning missions and
student organizations, photographs, and
letters, lectures, and papers of College
presidents, founders, and church leaders.

SEE: Hamer.

MN541-216
Episcopal Diocese of Minnesota
309 Clifton Avenue
Minneapolis MN 55403

(612) 871-5311

OPEN: M-F 9-4; closed weekends and
holidays
ACCESS: appointment requested

COPYING FACILITIES: yes
MATERIALS SOLICITED: Records of the
Episcopal Diocese of Minnesota. Will
also accept other materials regarding
the Episcopal church in Minnesota.

HOLDINGS:
Total volume: 250 l.f.
Inclusive dates: 1857 -
Description: Diocesan financial
records, correspondence regarding diocesan property, records of baptisms, marriages, and burials from defunct parishes,
journals of diocesan conventions, and diocesan periodicals.

MN541-320
Hennepin County Historical Society
2303 Third Avenue South
Minneapolis MN 55404

(612) 870-1329

OPEN: Tu-F 9-4:30; closed other days
and holidays
COPYING FACILITIES: yes
MATERIALS SOLICITED: Pre-1900 materials documenting the history of Hennepin County, including agricultural,
church, and women's history. Will also
accept selected post-1900 materials.

HOLDINGS:
Total volume: 200 l.f.
Inclusive dates: 1845 -
Description: Collections covering the
social, economic, and political history of
Hennepin County, including business
records, account books, personal papers,
diaries, records of clubs and organizations, and photographs. There is substantial documentation of early settlers' experiences and 19th century businesses,
particularly the flour milling industry.

SEE: Hamer.

MN541-496
Minneapolis Institute of Arts
2400 3rd Avenue S.
Minneapolis MN 55404

(612) 870-3114

OPEN: Su 12-5, Tu, W, F, Sa 10-5, Th
10-9; closed Mondays and holidays
ACCESS: advance arrangements required
COPYING FACILITIES: yes
MATERIALS SOLICITED: Photographs of
works of art.

HOLDINGS:
Total volume: 175 boxes; 125 file
drawers
Inclusive dates: 1883 -
Description: Records of the Minneapolis Institute of Arts and the Minneapolis
Society of Fine Arts, including correspondence, minutes, exhibitions, documents,
loan forms, memoranda, and photographs. Also, Van Derlip Collection of
photographs of works of art and architecture (8,700 items).

SEE: Novotny; Martin.

MN541-512

Minneapolis Public Library and
Information Center
Art/Music Department and
Athenaeum
300 Nicollet Mall
Minneapolis MN 55401

(612) 372-6520

OPEN: M-F 9-5; closed weekends and
holidays
USER FEES: borrowing fee of $30 for
nonresidents; deposit card available for
$25 ($22 refundable)
ACCESS: special restrictions apply to the
AIMF tape recordings
COPYING FACILITIES: yes
MATERIALS SOLICITED: Will accept mu-
sic manuscripts by local composers.

HOLDINGS:
Total volume: not specified
Inclusive dates: not specified
Description: Examples of 15th century
Gregorian chant and a collection of music manuscripts by local composers, including 80 scores by Willard Patton and
21 scores by Emil Oberhoffer.
Materials by and about J. G. Hinderer,
including paintings, press notices, pamphlets, correspondence, photographs, and
teaching materials. Also, American International Music Fund tape recordings of
338 premiere performances of contemporary works by leading orchestras of the
United States and Canada.

SEE: Hamer.

MN541-592

Minneapolis Public Library and
Information Center
Minneapolis History Collection
300 Nicollet Mall
Minneapolis MN 55401

(612) 372-6648

OPEN: M-F 9-5:30, Sa 9:30-5:30; closed
Saturdays, Memorial Day to Labor
Day, and holidays
ACCESS: users should be at least senior
high school level
COPYING FACILITIES: yes
MATERIALS SOLICITED: Materials relating
to Minneapolis and the surrounding
area, except municipal government information. Will also accept materials
on Minnesota and its cities and counties.

HOLDINGS:
Total volume: not specified
Inclusive dates: 1851 -
Description: Collections relating chiefly
to the history of Minneapolis. Included
are records of the Minnesota Academy of
Science, women's club papers, and photographs from the morgue of the Minneapolis Times and other sources. Other
materials include organization reports,
correspondence, family papers, and scrapbooks on the Minneapolis Aquatennial.

SEE: Hamer; NUCMC, 1959-62.

SEE: Novotny.

MN541-600

Minneapolis Public Library and
Information Center
North Regional Library
Ralph Waldo Emerson Room
1315 Lowry Avenue North
Minneapolis MN 55411

(612) 522-3333, 372-6522

OPEN: by appointment only
ACCESS: written requests for
appointments preferred
COPYING FACILITIES: yes

HOLDINGS:
Total volume: 128 items; 5,000 vols.
Inclusive dates: 19th century -
Description: Letters and manuscripts
by 19th century New England writers,
notably Ralph Waldo Emerson, John
Greenleaf Whittier, Henry Wadsworth
Longfellow, James Russell Lowell, Emily
Dickinson, Oliver Wendell Holmes, and
Henry David Thoreau.

SEE: Robbins.

MN541-777

United Methodist Church
Minnesota Annual Conference
Commission on Archives and History
122 West Franklin Avenue
Minneapolis MN 55404

no telephone

OPEN: M-F by appointment; closed
weekends and holidays
ACCESS: advance arrangements requested
COPYING FACILITIES: yes
MATERIALS SOLICITED: Materials related
to the United Methodist church in
Minnesota.

HOLDINGS:
Total volume: not specified
Inclusive dates: 1850 -
Description: Journals and other materials documenting the history of the church
and its antecedents in Minnesota, including the Church of the United Brethren in
Christ, Evangelical Association, Evangelical church, Evangelical United Brethren
church, Methodist Episcopal church, and
Methodist church. Included are records of
discontinued churches and papers of ministers serving in the Conference.

SEE: Hamer.

SEE: Hinding.

MN541-822

University of Minnesota
Libraries
Ames Library of South Asia
S-10 Wilson Library
309 19th Avenue S.
Minneapolis MN 55445

(612) 373-2890

OPEN: M-F 8-5; closed weekends and
holidays
ACCESS: permission of Librarian must
be obtained
COPYING FACILITIES: yes

MATERIALS SOLICITED: South Asian culture. Will also accept materials relating
to other parts of Asia if they relate to
South Asia in some definite way.
HOLDINGS:
Total volume: 15 l.f.
Inclusive dates: 1646 -
Description: Over 1,500 items dealing
mainly with South Asia as it is presently
defined, including Burma. The collection
consists of letters, diaries, ships' logs, political papers, Persian, Arabic and Urdu
historical writings, letterbooks, and con-
sultations.

SEE: Martin.

Other University of Minnesota repositories are in St. Paul.

MN541-838

University of Minnesota
Libraries
Children's Literature Research
Collections
109 Walter Library
117 Pleasant Street, S.E.
Minneapolis MN 55445

(612) 373-9731

OPEN: M-F 7:45-4:30; closed weekends
and holidays
COPYING FACILITIES: yes
MATERIALS SOLICITED: Manuscripts for
contemporary children's books. Will
also accept related research materials
and correspondence.

HOLDINGS:
Total volume: 200 l.f.
Inclusive dates: 1846 -
Description: The Kerlan Collection of
manuscripts of 1,500 children's books, including award-winning books, books by
Minnesota authors or with a Minnesota
setting, books about the American Indian
(especially Dakota and Ojibway), and
Scandinavian children's books. There is
also the Gag Family Collection of 10
linear feet of manuscripts by Wanda Gag,
1928-46.

SEE: NUCMC, 1981.

SEE: Robbins; Hinding.

SEE ALSO: The Kerlan Collection (Univ. of
Minnesota Libraries, 1974).

MN541-854

University of Minnesota
Libraries
James Ford Bell Library
462 Wilson Library
309 19th Avenue S.
Minneapolis MN 55445

(612) 373-2888

OPEN: M-F 8-5; closed weekends and
holidays
COPYING FACILITIES: yes
MATERIALS SOLICITED: European overseas expansion, 1200-1800.

HOLDINGS:
> *Total volume:* 1,000 items
> *Inclusive dates:* 1200 - 1800
> *Description:* Manuscripts relating to European overseas expansion prior to 1800, including maps and charts, logbooks, records and documents pertaining to overseas trading companies, reports from missionaries in the Orient, and other materials concerning commercial, colonial, and missionary activities of Europeans abroad.

GUIDES: *The James Ford Bell Library Catalog* (G. K. Hall, 1981).

SEE: Hamer; NUCMC, 1963-65.

SEE ALSO: John Parker and Carol Urness, comps., *The James Ford Bell Collection: A List of Additions* (Univ. of Minnesota Press, 1961, 67, 70, 75).

MN541-902
University of Minnesota
Libraries
Social Welfare History Archives
109 Walter Library
117 Pleasant Street, S.E.
Minneapolis MN 55445

(612) 373-4420

OPEN: M-F 8-4:30, Sa by appointment; closed Sundays and holidays
ACCESS: serious researchers on completion of application form
COPYING FACILITIES: yes
MATERIALS SOLICITED: Records and papers of organizations and individuals involved in organized efforts to deal with social problems or prevent their occurrence, whether as planners, providers, or consumers of services. Emphasis is on private sector activities, either at the national level or in the Twin Cities metropolitan area.

HOLDINGS:
> *Total volume:* 3,500 l.f.
> *Inclusive dates:* 1880 -
> *Description:* More than 150 collections relating to social service and social reform, especially after World War I, including records of national welfare associations, Twin Cities social work agencies, and some settlement houses across the country.
> Subjects covered include public welfare, child welfare, child study, urban renewal, community organization, professional social work, social work education, neighborhood centers, social health, recreation, public health, group health and consumer cooperatives, voluntary sterilization, fertility control, assistance to single mothers, adoption, traveler's aid, Junior Leagues, problems of aging, welfare journalism, international social welfare, community music education, and administration and funding of voluntary associations.

GUIDES: David Klassen and William Wallach, comps., *Social Welfare History Archives: Guide to Holdings* (Univ. of Minnesota, 1979)

SEE: NUCMC, 1967, 70.

SEE: Schatz; Krichmar; Hinding; Robbins; Spalek.

SEE ALSO: Steven A. Grant and John Brown, *The Russian Empire and Soviet Union: A Guide to Manuscripts and Archival Materials in the United States* (G. K. Hall, 1981); *Descriptive Inventories of Collections in the Social Welfare History Archives Center* (Greenwood, 1970).

'Social Welfare History Archives: Inventory of Holdings' is issued periodically and is available by request from the institution.

MN541-918
University of Minnesota
Libraries
Special Collections Department
466 Wilson Library
309 19th Avenue S.
Minneapolis MN 55445

(612) 373-2897

SEE: Hamer; NUCMC, 1965, 67.

Questionnaire not returned.

MN541-925
University of Minnesota
Libraries
University Archives
10 Walter Library
117 Pleasant Street, S.E.
Minneapolis MN 55445

(612) 373-2891

OPEN: M-F 8-5; closed weekends and holidays
COPYING FACILITIES: yes
MATERIALS SOLICITED: University records; papers of staff and faculty; and records of student, staff, faculty, or University-related organizations. Will also accept papers of outstanding alumni, or of people or organizations with some University association.

HOLDINGS:
> *Total volume:* 9,150 l.f.; 32,000 photographs; 5,000 tapes and films
> *Inclusive dates:* 1851 -
> *Description:* Materials relating chiefly to the University of Minnesota, its administration, faculty, staff, students and related organizations and activities. The collection comprises official records, professional and personal papers, University of Minnesota theses and doctoral dissertations, maps, blueprints, ephemera, and audio-visual materials.

SEE: Hamer (as University of Minnesota Library); NUCMC, 1965, 67, 69, 76, 78.

SEE: Davis; Hinding; Robbins.

MN541-934
University of Minnesota
Libraries
Map Division
S-76 Wilson Library
309 19th Avenue S.
Minneapolis MN 55445

(612) 373-2825

OPEN: M-F 8-5; closed weekends and holidays
COPYING FACILITIES: yes

MATERIALS SOLICITED: Minnesota aerial photographs of various scales.

HOLDINGS:
> *Total volume:* 136,578 photographs
> *Inclusive dates:* 1937 -
> *Description:* Aerial photography of Minnesota, including large-scale county coverage, small-scale statewide coverage, detailed coverage of Minneapolis, and aerial photography mosaics of portions of the State. There are also many aerial photographs of urban areas in Michigan, Montana, North Dakota, South Dakota, and Wisconsin, as well as mosaics of selected urban areas of the United States.

GUIDES: *Catalog of Aerial Photography in the Map Division, Wilson Library, University of Minnesota* (1977).

MONTEVIDEO

MN555-120
Chippewa County Historical Society
221 North First Street
Montevideo MN 56265

no telephone
SEE: Hamer; NUCMC, 1968.

Questionnaire not returned.

MOORHEAD

MN562-110
Clay County Historical Society
202 1st Avenue N.
Moorhead MN

MAILING ADDRESS:
Box 501
Moorhead MN 56560

(218) 233-4604

OPEN: M-F 9-5; closed weekends and holidays

SEE: Hamer; NUCMC, 1959-62.

Questionnaire not returned.

MN562-520
Moorhead State University
Northwest Minnesota Historical Center
Moorhead MN 56560

(218) 236-2346, 2343, 2922

OPEN: M-F 9-4; closed weekends and holidays
COPYING FACILITIES: yes
MATERIALS SOLICITED: Materials pertaining to the history of northwestern Minnesota, including business and industry, legislative records, education, churches, and community groups.

HOLDINGS:
> *Total volume:* not specified
> *Inclusive dates:* 1860 -
> *Description:* Manuscript collection relating to the history of northwestern Minnesota with emphasis on local government, business development, agribusiness, area legislators, church history, and education; personal journals, maps,

and photographs; and an oral history collection relating to Scandinavian and ethnic history, rural life during the Depression, state legislators, and World War II.

SEE: NUCMC, 1977.

SEE: Hinding.

MORRIS

MN583-890

University of Minnesota at Morris
Morris Campus Archives
Briggs Library
Morris MN 56267

(612) 589-2211, Ext. 6175, 6172

OPEN: M-F 8-5; closed weekends and
holidays
ACCESS: by application indicating
purpose of research
COPYING FACILITIES: yes
MATERIALS SOLICITED: Inactive files of
individuals, offices and organizations
affiliated with the University. Will also
accept other materials related to the
history and operation of the institution.

HOLDINGS:
Total volume: 100 l.f.
Inclusive dates: 1959 -
Description: Records of the chief administrative officer of the campus, mostly
pertaining to finances, the faculty, and
relations with other University departments. Also included are newsclipping
scrapbooks and a file of the campus
newspaper.

MN583-920

University of Minnesota at Morris
West Central Minnesota Historical
    Center
Briggs Library
Morris MN 56267

(612) 589-2211, Ext. 6170

OPEN: M-F 3-5 during academic year;
closed weekends and holidays
COPYING FACILITIES: yes
MATERIALS SOLICITED: Materials pertaining to the history of west central
Minnesota, including the period prior
to European settlement.

HOLDINGS:
Total volume: 610 l.f.; 200 oral
histories
Inclusive dates: 1870 -
Description: Manuscript collections relating to the history of west central Minnesota and containing extensive business
records and political collections, with emphasis on the State legislature. Includes
town, county, and regional public records
and computerized data base of census
data for Stevens County, 1870-1905. Oral
histories emphasizing ethnicity, the Great
Depression, and World War II.

GUIDES: James E. Fogerty, comp., Manuscript Collections of the Minnesota Regional Research Centers (Minnesota
Historical Society, 1980).

SEE: NUCMC, 1977.

SEE: Hinding.

NEW ULM

MN618-80

Brown County Historical Society
2 N. Broadway
New Ulm MN 56073

(507) 354-2016

OPEN: M-Sa 1-5; closed Sundays and
holidays
COPYING FACILITIES: yes
MATERIALS SOLICITED: Genealogical and
historical materials relating to Brown
County and materials dealing with the
Dakota War of 1862 in Minnesota.

HOLDINGS:
Total volume: 30,000 items
Inclusive dates: 1830 -
Description: Primarily a collection of
Brown County and Minnesota Valley historical materials comprising papers of
pioneer families; papers relating to the
Sioux Indians; church, school, business
and local government records; land company records; military records and soldiers' diaries; a collection of autographs
of notable persons; and 525 glass plate
negatives from a New Ulm portrait photograph studio, 1880's-early 1900's.

SEE: Hamer.

NORTHFIELD

MN625-120

Carleton College
Library
Northfield MN 55057

(507) 663-4270

SEE: Hamer.

Questionnaire not returned.

MN625-550

Northfield Public Library
Local History Collection
3rd and Washington Streets
Northfield MN 55057

(507) 645-6606

OPEN: M-Th 1-9, F 1-7, Sa 9-4, Su 2-4;
closed holidays
COPYING FACILITIES: yes
MATERIALS SOLICITED: History of
Northfield and environs, exclusive of
Carleton and St. Olaf Colleges.

HOLDINGS:
Total volume: 5 c.f.
Inclusive dates: 1855 -
Description: Materials relating to
Northfield and the surrounding area from
the time of first settlement in 1855. Included are manuscripts, archives, and visual materials, with significant holdings
relating to local architecture.
Also materials relating to the James-Younger gang bank raid of 1876.

SEE: Hamer.

SEE: Hinding.

MN625-570

Norwegian-American Historical
    Association
St. Olaf College
Northfield MN 55057

(507) 663-3221

OPEN: M, W, F 8-3, T, Th 8-12; closed
weekends and holidays
COPYING FACILITIES: yes
MATERIALS SOLICITED: Materials relating
to Norwegian migration to America
and immigrants' life in America.

HOLDINGS:
Total volume: 900 l.f.
Inclusive dates: 1800 -
Description: Letters, diaries, ledgers,
minutes, reminiscences, speeches, family
histories, photographs, stories, poetry, and
other materials relating to Norwegian immigration to America.

GUIDES: Lloyd Hustvedt, comp. and ed.,
Guide to Manuscripts Collections of the
Norwegian-American Historical Association (1979).

SEE: Hamer; NUCMC, 1968-71.

SEE: Schatz; Davis; Robbins; Hinding.

SEE ALSO: A detailed description and inventory of each collection is available
at the repository.

MN625-710

St. Olaf College
Archives
Rolvaag Memorial Library
Northfield MN 55057

(507) 663-3229

OPEN: M-F 8:30-12:30; closed weekends
and holidays
COPYING FACILITIES: yes
MATERIALS SOLICITED: Faculty and administrative office files. Will also accept personal papers and other material
of faculty, administrators, students, and
alumni.

HOLDINGS:
Total volume: 900 l.f.
Inclusive dates: 1874 -
Description: Materials relating to St.
Olaf College. Included are papers of Lars
W. Boe relating to his presidency of the
College, the National Lutheran Council,
the Lutheran World Federation, and the
Lutheran church in both the United
States and Europe; records of the St. Olaf
Choir and its first director, F. Melius
Christiansen; and papers relating to
WCAL, the campus radio station.
Also photograph collection of O. G.
Felland, 1886-1928, relating to the history
of the College and to Norwegian pioneer
life in Minnesota and Wisconsin; music
manuscripts of F. Melius Christiansen.

SEE: NUCMC, 1973.

SEE: Hinding.

ORTONVILLE

MN632-80

Big Stone County Historical Society
Highways 12 and 75
Ortonville MN 56278

(612) 839-3359

OPEN: by appointment only
ACCESS: restricted to Society members; materials will be copied for outside researchers
COPYING FACILITIES: yes
MATERIALS SOLICITED: Genealogical materials, personal papers of early settlers, and other materials of interest to Big Stone County history.

HOLDINGS:
　　Total volume: 1 file drawer
　　Inclusive dates: 1844 -
　　Description: Correspondence, 1844-46; diaries, 1886-1947; school records, 1882-99; and photographs relating to the history of Big Stone County and its residents.

OWATONNA

MN646-720

Steele County Historical Society
Owatonna MN

MAILING ADDRESS:
P.O. Box 204
Owatonna MN 55060

no telephone

OPEN: by appointment only
USER FEES: $1.50 per person, $2 per family, 50 cents for students
COPYING FACILITIES: no
MATERIALS SOLICITED: Records, journals, and oral histories relating to Steele County. Will also accept letters, documents, and deeds.

HOLDINGS:
　　Total volume: not specified
　　Inclusive dates: 1800's -
　　Description: Records relating to Steele County and its early residents, including oral histories.

PIPESTONE

MN674-630

Pipestone County Historical Society
113 S. Hiawatha
Pipestone MN

MAILING ADDRESS:
Box 175
Pipestone MN 56164

(507) 825-2563

OPEN: M-Sa 10-5 June-Aug., Su 1-5 June-Aug., Tu-Sa 1-5 Sept.-May; closed holidays
COPYING FACILITIES: yes
MATERIALS SOLICITED: Manuscripts, business records, genealogical source data, and personal papers of early settlers.

HOLDINGS:
　　Total volume: 30 l.f.
　　Inclusive dates: 1880 -
　　Description: Materials relating to Pipestone County and the surrounding area, including township records; school records; land sales records of the Close Brothers Company, 1883-1910; genealogical source data; photographs, 1880- ; and public library records.

SEE: Hamer.

MN674-650

Pipestone National Monument
Pipestone MN

MAILING ADDRESS:
P.O. Box 727
Pipestone MN 56164

no telephone

SEE: NUCMC, 1967.

Questionnaire not returned.

ROCHESTER

MN721-520

Mayo Foundation
Archives
200 1st Street, S.W.
Rochester MN 55901

no telephone

SEE: Hamer.

Questionnaire not returned.

MN721-600

Olmsted County Historical Society
Research Center
Salem Road and County Road 122
Rochester MN

MAILING ADDRESS:
Box 6411
Rochester MN 55901

(507) 282-9447

OPEN: Tu-F 9-5, Sa 9-4; closed Sundays, Mondays, and holidays
COPYING FACILITIES: yes
MATERIALS SOLICITED: Olmsted County and city of Rochester manuscripts, archival materials, and visual documents. Will also accept materials pertaining to the history of Minnesota, particularly southeastern.

HOLDINGS:
　　Total volume: 88 l.f.
　　Inclusive dates: 1826 -
　　Description: Diaries, letters, military records, club journals, industrial records, reminiscences, photographs, technical drawings, and research papers, chiefly concerning Rochester and Olmsted County.

SEE: Hamer.

SEE: Hinding.

ROSEAU

MN728-690

Roseau County Museum
108 2nd Avenue, N.E.
Roseau MN 56751

(218) 463-1918

OPEN: Tu-Sa 9-5, closed other days and holidays
COPYING FACILITIES: no
MATERIALS SOLICITED: Will accept items pertaining to the natural or cultural history of the County.

HOLDINGS:
　　Total volume: 9.9 l.f.
　　Inclusive dates: 1889 -
　　Description: Materials relating to Roseau County, including correspondence, ledgers, church records, agricultural society records, bank books, court dockets, school records, scrapbooks, township records, business records, and the papers of Mike Holm.

SEE: Hamer; NUCMC, 1962 (as Roseau County Historical Society).

ROYALTON

MN735-690

Royalton Historical Society
Library and Museum
Center Street
Royalton MN 56373

(612) 584-5900, 5641

OPEN: by appointment only
COPYING FACILITIES: no
MATERIALS SOLICITED: Materials documenting the history of Morrison and Benson counties, MN.

HOLDINGS:
　　Total volume: 650 items
　　Inclusive dates: 1858 -
　　Description: Papers of local settlers and organizations and 500 photographs of Royalton residents, early logging scenes, and high school graduating classes since the early 1900's.

ST. CLOUD

MN742-700

St. Cloud State University
Central Minnesota Historical Center
St. Cloud MN 56301

(612) 255-3254

OPEN: M-F by appointment; closed June-Aug.
COPYING FACILITIES: yes
MATERIALS SOLICITED: Material on the history of central Minnesota.

HOLDINGS:
　　Total volume: 300 l.f.
　　Inclusive dates: 1840 -
　　Description: A collection focusing on the history of central Minnesota. Included are oral history interviews with area legislators, as well as records of organizations, such as the St. Cloud branch of the

American Association of University Women.

GUIDES: James E. Fogerty, comp., *Preliminary Guide to the Holdings of the Minnesota Regional Research Centers* (Minnesota Historical Society, 1975).

SEE: NUCMC, 1977.

SEE: Hinding.

The Central Minnesota Historical Center is no longer a branch of the Minnesota Historical Society.

MN742-720

St. Cloud State University
Learning Resources Services
University Archives and Rare Books
and Manuscripts
Centennial Hall
St. Cloud MN 56301

(612) 255-4753, 2084

OPEN: M-F 8-4; closed weekends and holidays
COPYING FACILITIES: yes
MATERIALS SOLICITED: Personal papers of individuals and records of organizations associated with the University, local history for central Minnesota, and records of professional media organizations.

HOLDINGS:
>*Total volume:* 200 l.f.
>*Inclusive dates:* 1869 -
>*Description:* Collections focusing on the history of Stearns County, including correspondence and records of businesses, government agencies, churches, schools, and social organizations; personal papers; oral history recordings; and photographs.

SEE: Hamer (as St. Cloud State Teachers College); NUCMC, 1966.

SEE: Hinding.

MN742-750

Stearns County Historical Society
235 33rd Avenue S.
St. Cloud MN

MAILING ADDRESS:
P.O. Box 702
St. Cloud MN 56302

(612) 253-8424

OPEN: M-F 9-4; closed weekends and holidays
COPYING FACILITIES: yes
MATERIALS SOLICITED: Manuscripts, archives, visual and audible documents, and scrapbooks dealing with Stearns County. Will also accept machine-readable records and microforms.

HOLDINGS:
>*Total volume:* 205 l.f.
>*Inclusive dates:* 1842 -
>*Description:* Collections focusing on the history of Stearns County, including correspondence and records of businesses, government agencies, churches, schools, and social organizations; personal papers; oral history recordings; and photographs.

SEE: Hamer.

ST. JOSEPH

MN749-120

College of Saint Benedict
Library
St. Joseph MN 56374

(612) 363-5610

OPEN: M-F 8-4; closed weekends and holidays
ACCESS: appointment requested
COPYING FACILITIES: yes
MATERIALS SOLICITED: Records of the College of Saint Benedict.

HOLDINGS:
>*Total volume:* 4 file drawers
>*Inclusive dates:* 1961 -
>*Description:* Records of the College of Saint Benedict since its incorporation as an institution separate from St. Benedict's Convent. The records contain minutes of Board of Trustees meetings, financial reports, accreditation reports, College publications, academic reports, and minutes of organizations and committees of students, faculty, and the administration.

SEE: Hamer.

MN749-720

St. Benedict's Convent
Archives
St. Joseph MN 56374

(612) 363-5157

OPEN: M-F 8-4; closed weekends and holidays
ACCESS: appointment requested
COPYING FACILITIES: yes
MATERIALS SOLICITED: Records of St. Benedict's Convent, a Roman Catholic institution, as well as papers of its members. Will also accept material documenting the schools, hospitals, nursing homes, and missions administered by the order.

HOLDINGS:
>*Total volume:* 260 l.f.
>*Inclusive dates:* 1857 -
>*Description:* Records of St. Benedict's Convent and papers of its members. There are also records of affiliated institutions, including schools and hospitals in Minnesota, North Dakota, and Utah; missions in China, Japan, Puerto Rico, and the Bahamas; parish schools, chiefly in Minnesota, Wisconsin, North Dakota, Montana, and Washington; Indian missions; and orphanages. The collection contains correspondence, financial reports, chronicles, newsletters, theses, family histories, data about members of the order, scrapbooks, photographs, and audible documents.

SEE: Hinding.

ST. PAUL

MN763-50

The American Lutheran Church
Archives
Luther Northwestern Theological
Seminary
2481 Como Avenue W.
St. Paul MN 55108

(612) 641-3205

OPEN: M-F 9-12:15 and by appointment; closed weekends and holidays
COPYING FACILITIES: yes
MATERIALS SOLICITED: Materials regarding the Norwegian Lutheran Church of America and its predecessors and related bodies.

HOLDINGS:
>*Total volume:* 700 l.f.
>*Inclusive dates:* 1837 - 1961
>*Description:* Records of American and antecedent Norwegian Lutheran churches, including minutes and correspondence of National and district offices; pictures, slides, filmstrips, and tapes; papers of prominent individuals associated with these churches, such as Johan A. Aasgaard, T. O. Burntvedt, J. A. O. Stub, and Carl M. Weswig; and missionary research materials regarding work in China, Hong Kong, Taiwan, South Africa, and Madagascar.

SEE: Hamer (as Evangelical Lutheran Church, Archives); NUCMC, 1967, 69, 72.

SEE: Hinding.

SEE ALSO: Typewritten guides are available from the institution.

Another archival repository for The American Lutheran Church is located at Wartburg Theological Seminary in Dubuque, IA.

MN763-80

Baptist General Conference
Archives
Bethel Theological Seminary
3949 Bethel Drive
St. Paul MN 55112

(612) 638-6282

OPEN: by appointment
COPYING FACILITIES: yes
MATERIALS SOLICITED: Materials relating to the Baptist General Conference.

HOLDINGS:
>*Total volume:* 400 l.f.; 800 vols.
>*Inclusive dates:* 1852 -
>*Description:* Records of the Baptist General Conference, formerly the Swedish Baptist General Conference of America. Included are records of missionary activities in various parts of the world, records of Bethel College and Seminary, records and histories of individual churches, papers of clergy, and a collection of oral histories and other recordings.

SEE: Hamer (as Historical Committee of the Baptist General Conference).

SEE: Hinding.

MN763-100
Catholic Historical Society of Saint
    Paul
2260 Summit Avenue
St. Paul MN 55105

(612) 690-4355

OPEN: by appointment only; closed
    holidays
COPYING FACILITIES: yes
MATERIALS SOLICITED: Correspondence
    of archibishops John Ireland, John
    Gregory Murray, and Leo Binz. Will
    also accept other materials related to
    Catholicism in the upper Midwest.

HOLDINGS:
    Total volume: 50 l.f.
    Inclusive dates: 1840 -
    Description: Materials related to the
    early history of Roman Catholicism in
    the upper Midwest, principally Minnesota
    and the Dakotas. The collection includes
    manuscripts, photographs, scrapbooks,
    files on parish history, and papers of pio-
    neer priests and bishops, such as Joseph
    Cretin, John Ireland, Augustin Ravoux,
    and James Reardon.

SEE: Hamer; NUCMC, 1959-61.

MN763-110
College of St. Catherine
Library
Archives
2004 Randolph Avenue
St. Paul MN 55105

(612) 690-6553

OPEN: M-Th 8-3; closed F, Sa, Su and
    holidays
ACCESS: general public with reliable
    recommendation; faculty with
    permission of the Archivist; students
    with supervision
COPYING FACILITIES: yes
MATERIALS SOLICITED: Materials per-
    taining to the College, its faculty, stu-
    dents, and alumnae, as well as its spon-
    soring religious congregation, the Sis-
    ters of St. Joseph, and its relationships
    with civic organizations. Will also ac-
    cept realia, especially that which tends
    to complement areas of the curriculum.

HOLDINGS:
    Total volume: 58 l.f.; 9 file drawers
    Inclusive dates: 19th century -
    Description: A collection of records of
    the College of St. Catherine, scrapbooks,
    and newspaper clippings of student and
    faculty activities. Included are 43 oral his-
    tory tapes of faculty and administrators.
    There are also a number of letters and
    autographs, as well as photographs and a
    few items related to Minnesota Roman
    Catholic church leaders who were closely
    related to the College.

SEE: Hamer; NUCMC, 1980.

SEE: Hinding.

MN763-120
College of St. Thomas
Archives
2115 Summit Avenue
St. Paul MN 55105

(612) 647-5726

OPEN: by appointment only
COPYING FACILITIES: yes
MATERIALS SOLICITED: College history.
    Will also accept neighborhood history.

HOLDINGS:
    Total volume: 342 l.f.
    Inclusive dates: 1885 -
    Description: Archives of the College,
    consisting of photographs, biography files,
    news clippings, College publications, and
    papers of offices, organizations, and de-
    partments of the College.

SEE: NUCMC, 1959-61, 67.

SEE: Robbins.

MN763-310
Hamline University
Bush Memorial Library
Archives
1536 Hewitt
St. Paul MN 55104

(612) 641-2288, 2373

OPEN: M-F 8:30-4; closed weekends and
    holidays
ACCESS: appointment required
COPYING FACILITIES: yes
MATERIALS SOLICITED: Manuscripts,
    records, and publications relating to
    Hamline University and its faculty, ad-
    ministration, and alumni.

HOLDINGS:
    Total volume: 165 l.f.
    Inclusive dates: 1853 -
    Description: Materials related to
    individuals and organizations associated
    with the institutional, academic, and cor-
    porate life of Hamline University.

MN763-400
James Jerome Hill Reference Library
80 West Fourth Street
St. Paul MN 55102

(612) 227-9531

OPEN: M-F 9-5 by appointment; closed
    weekends and holidays
COPYING FACILITIES: yes
MATERIALS SOLICITED: Will accept busi-
    ness and economic materials with em-
    phasis on the 9th Federal Reserve Dis-
    trict and the Washington-Oregon re-
    gion.

HOLDINGS:
    Total volume: 350 items
    Inclusive dates: 1842 -
    Description: A miscellaneous collec-
    tion, including papers relating to merger
    of the Great Northern Railroad and the
    Northern Pacific Railroad and briefs of
    the Great Northern Iron Ore Properties
    Trust case.

SEE: Hamer.

SEE: Davis.

MN763-500
Macalester College
Library
1600 Grand Avenue
St. Paul MN 55105

(612) 696-6346

OPEN: M-F 9-4:30; closed weekends
COPYING FACILITIES: yes
MATERIALS SOLICITED: Materials per-
    taining to Macalester College and its
    faculty, students, and alumni.

HOLDINGS:
    Total volume: 150 boxes; 3 file
    cabinets
    Inclusive dates: 1874 -
    Description: Records of Macalester
    College, including correspondence, news-
    letters, theses, family histories, data on
    faculty members, visual documents, au-
    dible documents, and scrapbooks.

SEE: Hamer; NUCMC, 1966.

SEE: Robbins.

MN763-510
Midwest China Center
Room 308, Gullixon Hall
2481 Como Avenue
St. Paul MN 55108

(612) 641-3238

OPEN: M-F 8-4:30; closed weekends and
    holidays
COPYING FACILITIES: yes
MATERIALS SOLICITED: Materials per-
    taining to China, 1880-1950, including
    taped interviews, records of organiza-
    tions, unpublished manuscripts, jour-
    nals, correspondence, photographs,
    movies, and personal papers.

HOLDINGS:
    Total volume: 50 l.f.; 110 oral
    histories
    Inclusive dates: 1880 - 1952
    Description: Oral history interviews,
    with emended transcripts, of persons who
    lived and worked on mainland China:
    missionaries, church staff, doctors, educa-
    tors, military personnel, businesspersons,
    and their children. The interviewees are
    primarily Americans and Chinese who
    live in or are associated with the Mid-
    west. Complementary archival materials
    include records of organizations,
    unpublished manuscripts, journals, corre-
    spondence, photographs, and personal pa-
    pers, many of which contain information
    on Christian missions in China.

SEE: Hinding.

MN763-530
Minnesota Historical Society
Audio-Visual Library
690 Cedar Street
St. Paul MN 55101

(612) 296-2489

OPEN: M-Sa 8:30-5; closed Sundays and
    holidays
COPYING FACILITIES: yes
MATERIALS SOLICITED: Materials relating
    to Minnesota people, places, and activi-
    ties.

HOLDINGS:
Total volume: 150,000 photographs; 700 oral history tapes; 400 16mm films
Inclusive dates: 1840 -
Description: Materials relating to Minnesota, including black and white photographs and oral history tapes. Subject strengths include lumbering, mining, agriculture, Indians, industry, labor, and commerce. There are special oral history projects on blacks and Mexican-Americans in Minnesota.

SEE: Novotny; Meckler and McMullin; Hinding.

MN763-540
Minnesota Historical Society
Division of Archives and Manuscripts
1500 Mississippi Street
St. Paul MN 55101

(612) 296-6980

OPEN: M-F 8:30-5, Sa 9-1; closed Sundays and holidays
COPYING FACILITIES: yes
MATERIALS SOLICITED: Manuscripts and archives relating to Minnesotans and Minnesota history. Current collecting emphasis on business, labor, transportation industry, politics and government, conservation and environment, women, minority and ethnic groups, and cooperatives. Statutorily responsible for preservation of permanent and historically valuable Minnesota public records (State, county, and local).

HOLDINGS:
Total volume: 60,000 l.f.
Inclusive dates: 1472 -
Description: Territorial, State, local, and Federal records dating from 1849 to the present. Manuscript materials relating primarily to Minnesota and the Northwest in the 19th and 20th centuries.

SEE: Hamer; NUCMC, 1959-67, 69-70, 72, 74, 76.

SEE: Allard, Crawley, and Edmison; Bean and Vane; Davis; Hinding; Hines; Hounshell; Ingram; Krichmar; Parkinson; Paszak; Robbins; Schatz; Spalek.

SEE ALSO: Descriptions of materials also are contained in guides to microfilmed collections, annual reports of the Division and Society, and articles in *Minnesota History*. Many additional collection and subject guides available from the Society.

MN763-573
Minnesota State Agricultural Society
Minnesota State Fair History Museum
Building 273F, Heritage Square
St. Paul MN

MAILING ADDRESS:
Administration Building 332
Minnesota State Fairgrounds
St. Paul MN 55108

(612) 642-2200

OPEN: daily 9-9 for 12 days before Labor Day; by appointment other times
COPYING FACILITIES: no

MATERIALS SOLICITED: Materials relating to the history of the Minnesota State Fair and similar expositions.

HOLDINGS:
Total volume: 80 vols; 2,000 items; additional materials
Inclusive dates: 1885 -
Description: Materials documenting the Minnesota State Fair, including contracts, other records, photographs, and scrapbooks of newspaper clippings.

MN763-580
Minnesota State Law Library
117 University Avenue
St. Paul MN 55155

(612) 296-2775

OPEN: M-F 7:30-5, Sa 8:30-12:30; closed holidays and Saturdays in summer; appointment required for Saturday use
COPYING FACILITIES: yes
MATERIALS SOLICITED: Lower court transcripts of cases decided by the Minnesota Supreme Court.

HOLDINGS:
Total volume: not specified
Inclusive dates: 1800's -
Description: Lower court transcripts of cases decided by Minnesota Supreme Court.

MN763-690
St. Paul Companies
Library
385 Washington Street
St. Paul MN 55102

(612) 221-8226, 7448

OPEN: by appointment only
COPYING FACILITIES: yes

HOLDINGS:
Total volume: 50 c.f.
Inclusive dates: 1849 -
Description: The St. Paul Fire and Marine Insurance Company archives (1853 to date); 3 file drawers of letters (1849-64) of Alexander Wilkin, his family, and his friends; and other papers dealing with early settlement in the St. Paul area.

MN763-710
St. Paul Public Library
Highland Park Branch
Perrie Jones Memorial Room
1974 Ford Parkway
St. Paul MN 55116

(612) 292-6622

OPEN: M, Th 9-9, Tu, W 12:30-9, F, Sa 9-5:30 (winter); M, Th 9-9, Tu, W, F 9-5:30 (summer); closed other days and holidays
COPYING FACILITIES: yes
MATERIALS SOLICITED: Works by St. Paul authors and materials pertaining to St. Paul history.

HOLDINGS:
Total volume: 16 items
Inclusive dates: 1699 -
Description: Reminiscences, letters, and other papers, including two albums of letters by and to Robert Robitschek

and the reminiscences of Rear Admiral George Collier Remey, as well as some letters relating to the Library.

MN763-720
Sisters of St. Joseph of Carondelet
St. Paul Province
1884 Randolph Street
St. Paul MN 55105

(612) 698-0323

OPEN: M-F 9:30-4:30; closed weekends and holidays
COPYING FACILITIES: yes
MATERIALS SOLICITED: Materials relating to the 19th century Catholic church and religious communities in Minnesota. Will also accept materials on Minnesota and North Dakota history.

HOLDINGS:
Total volume: 225 l.f.
Inclusive dates: 1840's -
Description: Materials relating to the work of the Sisters of St. Joseph of Carondelet in Minnesota, North Dakota, and Wisconsin. Included are the records of the first hospital in Minnesota and the records of schools, colleges, and hospitals staffed by the order, as well as a variety of other materials.

SEE: Hinding.

MN763-790
University of Minnesota
Immigration History Research Center
826 Berry Street
St. Paul MN 55114

(612) 373-5581

OPEN: M-F 8-4:30, Sa 9-1; closed Sundays and holidays
COPYING FACILITIES: yes
MATERIALS SOLICITED: American immigration and ethnic history of groups whose origins are in eastern, central, and southern Europe and the Middle East.

HOLDINGS:
Total volume: 2,600 l.f.; 500 photographs; 600 reels of microfilm; 6 oral history tapes
Inclusive dates: 1880 -
Description: Over 225 collections relating to the American ethnic groups whose origins are in eastern, central, and southern Europe and the Middle East. The collections focus on the sub-societies these immigrants established in America, the formation of such groups, their internal structure, and their impact upon major institutions in the country. Included are the records of such ethnic institutions as fraternal societies, churches, and publishing companies. Other materials included are personal papers from ethnic leaders, clergy, journalists, labor leaders, writers, poets, and politicians.

GUIDES: *Guide to Manuscript Holdings, January 1976* (Univ. of Minnesota, Immigration History Research Center, 1976).

SEE: NUCMC, 1972, 75, 78.

SEE: Hinding; Spalek; Parkinson.

SEE ALSO: Rudolph J. Vecoli, 'The Immigration Studies Collection of the University of Minnesota,' *American Archivist* 32 (April 1969); *Spectrum* (newsletter of the Center), 1975 - . Guides to materials on specific ethnic groups are available from the Center.

The IHRC Ethnic Collection Series, Nos. 1-9, published by the Center, describes materials on specific ethnic groups.

Other University of Minnesota repositories are in Minneapolis.

MN763-800

University of Minnesota
Libraries
Manuscripts Division
826 Berry Street
St. Paul MN 55114

(612) 376-7271

OPEN: M-F 8-5; closed weekends and holidays
ACCESS: grades K-12 ordinarily restricted from using repository
COPYING FACILITIES: yes
MATERIALS SOLICITED: Literary manuscripts of Minnesota authors; Minnesota performing arts materials; and architectural records from Minnesota, Iowa, South Dakota, North Dakota, and Wisconsin.

HOLDINGS:
    Total volume: 2,500 c.f.
    Inclusive dates: 16th century -
    Description: Architectural records solicited from architects, engineers, contractors, and others involved in built environments, including drawings, specifications, photographs, and job files; performing arts records solicited from dance, theater, and music organizations and individuals, including correspondence, photographs, promptbooks, publicity material, and financial records; and personal papers of authors and other literary figures from Minnesota, including correspondence, diaries, photographs, manuscripts, and notes for writings.

SEE: NUCMC, 1972-75.

SEE: Robbins.

SEE ALSO: Alan K. Lathrop, 'Architectural Records: A Heritage on Paper,' *Historic Preservation* 25 (Oct.-Dec. 1973); Ann Novotny, ed., *Picture Sources 3* (Special Libraries Assn., 1975); *Northwest Architectural Archives* (Univ. of Minnesota Libraries, 1974).

St. Peter

MN769-280

Gustavus Adolphus College
College and Minnesota Synod of
    Lutheran Church in America
    Archives
St. Peter MN 56082

(507) 931-7572, 8000

OPEN: M-F 8:30-noon; closed weekends and holidays
ACCESS: permission from Archivist required

COPYING FACILITIES: yes
MATERIALS SOLICITED: Records of Gustavus Adolphus College and the Minnesota Synod of the Lutheran Church in America. Will also accept family histories, diaries, manuscripts from professors and alumni, and photographs.

HOLDINGS:
    Total volume: 1,100 l.f.
    Inclusive dates: 1850 -
    Description: Records of Gustavus Adolphus College, Minnesota College, the Minnesota Synod of the Lutheran Church in America, and two of its predecessors, the Minnesota Conference of the Augustana Lutheran church and the English Evangelical Lutheran Synod of the Northwest. Included are correspondence and writings of Conference and College presidents (500,000 items), diaries, family histories, manuscripts, photographs, and microfilms of congregational records of approximately 250 Lutheran congregations.

SEE: Hamer (as Gustavus Adolphus College Library); NUCMC, 1959-61.

SEE: Krichmar.

MN769-560

Nicollet County Historical Society
St. Peter MN

MAILING ADDRESS:
P.O. Box 153
St. Peter MN 56082

no telephone

OPEN: daily 1-4 May-Oct.

SEE: Hamer; NUCMC, 1959-61 (as Nicollet County Historical Museum).

Questionnaire not returned.

Sauk Center

MN790-720

Sinclair Lewis Foundation, Inc.
Sauk Centre MN

MAILING ADDRESS:
P.O. Box 222
Sauk Centre MN 56378

(612) 352-5202

OPEN: Memorial Day - Labor Day, Sundays 10-6, Sept. - May by appointment only
COPYING FACILITIES: no
MATERIALS SOLICITED: Materials relating to Sinclair Lewis.

HOLDINGS:
    Total volume: 36 items
    Inclusive dates: not specified
    Description: Correspondence and other documents relating to Sinclair Lewis.

SEE: Robbins.

Sauk Rapids

MN794-80

Benton County Historical Society
218 1st Street N.
Sauk Rapids MN 56379

(612) 253-9614

OPEN: M-F 8-4:30; closed weekends and holidays
ACCESS: by application one working day prior to intended examination of materials
COPYING FACILITIES: no
MATERIALS SOLICITED: Benton County history.

HOLDINGS:
    Total volume: 6 l.f.
    Inclusive dates: 1890 - 1960
    Description: Personal papers, photographs, oral histories, manuscript public documents, account books, business records, and genealogical data, all relating to Benton County history.

Spring Valley

MN821-720

Spring Valley Community Historical
    Society, Inc.
Washington Avenue and Main Street
Spring Valley MN

MAILING ADDRESS:
c/o Secretary
909 South Broadway
Spring Valley MN 55975

(507) 346-2763

OPEN: Sundays 2-4, June - Oct; closed other times
COPYING FACILITIES: no
MATERIALS SOLICITED: Genealogical materials, histories, and photographs relating specifically to the Spring Valley area. Will also accept records relating to Fillmore County, Minnesota.

HOLDINGS:
    Total volume: 6 l.f.
    Inclusive dates: 1890 -
    Description: Photographs, diaries, journals, scrapbooks, and other records relating to Spring Valley and local families.

Stillwater

MN835-720

Stillwater Public Library
Minnesota Room
223 North 4th Street
Stillwater MN 55082

(612) 439-1692

OPEN: M-Th 10-9, F, Sa 10-5; closed Sundays and holidays
USER FEES: $5 for non-residents of State
COPYING FACILITIES: yes
MATERIALS SOLICITED: Materials relating to Minnesota, specifically the St. Croix River area on the eastern boundary between Wisconsin and Minnesota.

HOLDINGS:
Total volume: 560 vols.; 8 file cabinets; 3 photo files; 1 map case
Inclusive dates: 1802 -
Description: Materials relating to Washington County and the St. Croix River Valley. Included are oral history interviews; photographs, especially of lumbering; and scrapbooks on Civil War veterans and Abraham Lincoln.

MN835-880
Washington County Historical Museum
602 North Main Street
Stillwater MN

MAILING ADDRESS:
P.O. Box 167
Stillwater MN 55082

(612) 436-7032

OPEN: Tu, Th, Sa, Su 2-5 or by appointment Tu-F
USER FEES: one dollar, adults; fifty cents, under age 16
COPYING FACILITIES: no
MATERIALS SOLICITED: Materials pertaining to the history of the St. Croix Valley and Washington County.

HOLDINGS:
Total volume: 18 scrapbooks
Inclusive dates: 1840 - 1950's
Description: Scrapbooks containing letters, clippings, and other papers and photographs relating to the history of Stillwater, Washington County, and Minnesota in general, including materials regarding residents before they arrived in Minnesota.

TWO HARBORS

MN863-480
Lake County Historical Society
Depot Building
Two Harbors MN 55616

(218) 834-4898

OPEN: M-Sa 9-4, Su 1-4; closed in winter
SEE: NUCMC, 1959-61.

Questionnaire not returned.

WABASSO

MN884-880
County Center Historical Society
Wabasso MN

MAILING ADDRESS:
South Street
Wabasso MN 56293

(507) 342-5328

OPEN: M-F by appointment; closed weekends and holidays
COPYING FACILITIES: no
MATERIALS SOLICITED: Materials pertaining to the history of the Wabasso area of southwestern Minnesota and its inhabitants.

HOLDINGS:
Total volume: not specified
Inclusive dates: 1860's -
Description: Manuscripts, diaries, and record books of early settlers of the Wabasso area of southwestern Minnesota.

SEE: Hinding.

WILLMAR

MN961-440
Kandiyohi County Historical Society
610 N.E. Old Highway 71
Willmar MN 56201

(612) 235-1881

OPEN: by appointment only; closed weekends and holidays
COPYING FACILITIES: yes
MATERIALS SOLICITED: Business and personal papers, diaries, family histories, and genealogies pertaining to Kandiyohi County. Will also accept other original manuscripts pertaining to Kandiyohi County.

HOLDINGS:
Total volume: 150 l.f.
Inclusive dates: 1860 -
Description: Materials pertaining to local history in Kandiyohi County. Included are public and private business records, legal records, personal papers, unpublished manuscripts, wills, deeds, petitions and other documents, maps, and 9 oral history tapes.

SEE: Hinding.

WINDOM

MN968-120
Cottonwood County Historical Society
812 Fourth Avenue
Windom MN 56101

(507) 831-1134

OPEN: M-F 9-4; closed holidays and weekends except by appointment
COPYING FACILITIES: no
MATERIALS SOLICITED: Will accept materials relating to Windom and other areas in Minnesota.

HOLDINGS:
Total volume: 200 items
Inclusive dates: 1860 - 1960
Description: Original deeds, manuscript histories, diaries, public documents, logbooks, and memorabilia pertaining to Windom, Cottonwood County, and other parts of Minnesota.

SEE: Hinding.

WINONA

MN975-120
College of St. Teresa
Archives
Winona MN 55987

(507) 454-2930, Ext. 349

OPEN: by appointment only
ACCESS: with permission of College Archivist
COPYING FACILITIES: yes
MATERIALS SOLICITED: Materials relevant to the College of St. Teresa.

HOLDINGS:
Total volume: 135 boxes; 15 file cabinets; additional materials
Inclusive dates: 1894 -
Description: Archival materials of the College of St. Teresa, including correspondence, clippings, publicity materials, financial records and ledgers, and other materials related to the College's administration, faculty, and students.

SEE: Hinding.

MN975-160
Diocese of Winona
55 West Sanborn
Winona MN

MAILING ADDRESS:
P.O. Box 588
Winona MN 55987

(507) 454-4643

OPEN: by appointment only
COPYING FACILITIES: yes
MATERIALS SOLICITED: Correspondence, financial records, genealogical data, photographs, architectural drawings, and other materials pertaining to the Roman Catholic Diocese of Winona. Will also accept records of individual churches.

HOLDINGS:
Total volume: 220 c.f.
Inclusive dates: 1860 -
Description: Diocesan records, including correspondence, biographical data about priests, parish histories, account books and other financial records, photographs, and architectural drawings.

MN975-720
St. Mary's College
Fitzgerald Library
Winona MN 55987

(507) 452-4430, Ext. 1563

OPEN: M-Th 8-5, F 8-4:30, Sa 1-4; closed Sundays and during school recesses
ACCESS: appointment recommended
COPYING FACILITIES: yes
MATERIALS SOLICITED: Papers relating to the College.

HOLDINGS:
Total volume: 300 l.f.
Inclusive dates: 1913 -
Description: Bulletins, reports, official documents, office missives, and related material on the business, academic life, and history of Saint Mary's College.

MN975-730

St. Mary's College
Southeast Minnesota Historical Center
Winona MN 55987

(507) 452-4430, Ext. 1563

OPEN: M-F 9-4; closed weekends and
holidays
ACCESS: prior arrangements should be
made
COPYING FACILITIES: yes
MATERIALS SOLICITED: Items relating to
business and economic activity, social
and cultural life, higher education, family history and genealogy, local church
records, and selected public records.

HOLDINGS:
Total volume: 325 l.f.
Inclusive dates: 1850 -
Description: Manuscripts, photographs,
maps, audio and oral history tapes, microfilm, and some published materials relating to Minnesota history, with particular emphasis on the eight southeastern
counties. Emphasis is upon business, labor, and economic activity; family history

and genealogy; higher education; politics;
and social, cultural, and religious life.
Also included are some public records of
law enforcement agencies, courts, and
town governments.

GUIDES: James E. Fogerty, comp., *Pre-
liminary Guide to the Holdings of the
Minnesota Regional Research Centers*
(Minnesota Historical Society, 1975);
*Catalog of the Southeast Minnesota
Historical Center Collections* (1979).

SEE: NUCMC, 1977.

SEE: Hinding.

MN975-860

Winona County Historical Society,
Inc.
Laird Lucas Memorial Library
160 Johnson Street
Winona MN 55987

(507) 454-2723

OPEN: M-F 10-5; closed weekends and
holidays

COPYING FACILITIES: yes
MATERIALS SOLICITED: Winona County,
Minnesota, and the Mississippi River.
Will also accept materials relating to
Trempealeau, Buffalo, and Pepin coun-
ties in Wisconsin and Huston and
Wabasha counties in Minnesota.

HOLDINGS:
Total volume: 400 l.f.
Inclusive dates: 1830 -
Description: Materials pertaining to
Winona County, the State of Minnesota,
and steamboating on the Mississippi Riv-
er.

SEE: Hinding.

MISSISSIPPI

Mississippi does not have a statewide program for preserving local public records. Permanently valuable local public records normally remain in the custody of local officials. The Mississippi Department of Archives and History in Jackson makes available to researchers more than 6,000 reels of microfilm of vital, probate, land, and other county records dating through the end of the 19th century. The Department of Archives and History also has been systematically microfilming similar county records for the 20th century and regularly adds this microfilm to its collection.

ABERDEEN

MS20-200
Evans Memorial Library
Historical Division
130 S. Long Street
Aberdeen MS 39730

(601) 369-4601

OPEN: M-Sa 9-4:30; closed Sundays and holidays
COPYING FACILITIES: yes

HOLDINGS:
Total volume: 100,000 items
Inclusive dates: early 19th century -
Description: Materials relating chiefly to the South, with many items from the Civil War and World Wars I and II. Included are records of local organizations, account books, county records, papers of lawyers and politicians, materials relating to steamboats, railroads, and early Indian land owners, and local church records dating from 1819. There are also family history charts and other genealogical materials, as well as a collection of 14,000 glass negatives and accompanying photographers' record books.

SEE: Hinding.

SEE ALSO: Typescript finding aids to the manuscript collections are available at the repository.

BAY ST. LOUIS

MS50-560
Naval Oceanographic Office
Technical Publications Group
Bay St. Louis MS

MAILING ADDRESS:
Commanding Officer
Naval Oceanographic Office
Attn: Technical Publications Group
Code 4603
Bay St. Louis NSTL MS 39522-5001

(601) 688-4015

OPEN: M-F 8-4; closed weekends and holidays
ACCESS: written and telephone inquiries only
COPYING FACILITIES: no
MATERIALS SOLICITED: Materials dealing with Naval exploration, hydrography, oceanography, charting, and navigation.

HOLDINGS:
Total volume: 30 file drawers
Inclusive dates: 1735 -
Description: Manuscript and cartographic materials dealing with the U.S. Navy hydrographic and oceanographic development; cartographic work from several foreign hydrographic offices (England, Spain, Germany, Japan); and administrative correspondence of the U.S. Navy Hydrographic Office and the Naval Oceanographic Office.

BILOXI

MS80-40
American Patriot Archives Society, Inc.
815 Caillavet Street
Biloxi MS

MAILING ADDRESS:
P.O. Box 1036
Biloxi MS 39533

no telephone

OPEN: by appointment only
COPYING FACILITIES: yes
MATERIALS SOLICITED: Records of any nonprofit organization.

HOLDINGS:
Total volume: 89 c.f.
Inclusive dates: 1973 -
Description: Letters and other manuscripts relating to the commitment to freedom demonstrated by Americans. Included are letters concerning the American Bicentennial from President Ford, Vice President Rockefeller, and many U.S. Senators and Representatives.

MS80-80
Biloxi Chamber of Commerce
1036 Fred Haise Boulevard
Biloxi MS

MAILING ADDRESS:
P.O. Drawer 1928
Biloxi MS 39533

(601) 374-2717

OPEN: M-F 8:30-5; closed weekends and holidays
ACCESS: advance arrangements required
COPYING FACILITIES: yes

HOLDINGS:
Total volume: 25 boxes
Inclusive dates: 1930's -
Description: Materials primarily concerning Biloxi and Harrison County, MS, including board of director's minutes, committee reports, correspondence with State and Federal officials, and other records of the Biloxi Chamber of Commerce, as well as newspaper clippings, photographs, slides, and motion pictures.

BOONEVILLE

MS140-560
Northeast Regional Library
George E. Allen Library
Church Street
Booneville MS 38829

(601) 728-6553

OPEN: M, Tu, Th 10-8, W, F, Sa 10-6; closed Sundays and holidays
COPYING FACILITIES: yes
MATERIALS SOLICITED: Documents dealing with U.S. Presidents or other prominent politicians. Will also accept genealogical materials.

HOLDINGS:
Total volume: 10,000 items
Inclusive dates: 1935 - 1965
Description: Papers and photographs of U.S. politicians, including Franklin D. Roosevelt, Harry S Truman, Dwight D. Eisenhower, John F. Kennedy, Richard M. Nixon, and J. Edgar Hoover.

CLARKSDALE

MS200-120
Carnegie Public Library
114 Delta Avenue
Clarksdale MS

MAILING ADDRESS:
P.O. Box 280
Clarksdale MS 38614

(601) 624-4461

OPEN: M-Tu 9-8, W-Th 9-6, F-Sa 9-5; closed Sundays and holidays; shorter hours in summer
COPYING FACILITIES: yes
MATERIALS SOLICITED: Clarksdale and Coahoma County pictures, maps, diaries, genealogies, and other archival materials.

HOLDINGS:
Total volume: 2 file drawers
Inclusive dates: early 1900's -
Description: Photographs, pioneer reminiscences, and unpublished histories, relating to Clarksdale and Coahoma County.

CLEVELAND

MS230-160
Delta State University
W. B. Roberts Library
Cleveland MS 38733

(601) 846-4430

OPEN: Su 2-10, M-Th 8-10, F 8-5, Sa 8-12; closed Easter, Christmas, Labor Day, and July 4
COPYING FACILITIES: yes
MATERIALS SOLICITED: Materials pertaining to the Mississippi delta region.

HOLDINGS:
Total volume: 350 c.f.
Inclusive dates: 1807 -
Description: Diaries, pictures, writings, and other papers of Walter Sillers, Sr., Florence Warfield Sillers, and other members of the Sillers family. Additional manuscripts include a diary of Philip H. Sherman, 1873-79; papers of Lucy Nugent Somerville and Judge Lucy S. Howorth; and literary manuscripts. The primary focus of the collections is on Mississippi politics since 1900.
Additional materials include papers of James Hand, Jr., and George Messenger.

SEE: Hinding.

CLINTON

MS260-500
Mississippi College
Library
Clinton MS

MAILING ADDRESS:
Box 127
Clinton MS 39056

(601) 924-6530

OPEN: M-F 8:30-4:30; closed weekends and holidays

COPYING FACILITIES: yes
MATERIALS SOLICITED: Materials and records relating to the Baptist church in Mississippi.

HOLDINGS:
Total volume: 5,000 items
Inclusive dates: 1836 -
Description: The Mississippi Baptist Historical Commission collection, including church records, association minutes, manuscripts, subject and biographical files, slides, photographs, scrapbooks, diaries, and oral history tapes and transcripts, relating to the Mississippi Baptist Convention and affiliated associations and churches.

SEE: Hinding (as Mississippi Baptist Historical Collection).

The Henry Bellamann papers, listed in NUCMC, 1968, have been transferred to the University of Mississippi Library, University, MS.

COLUMBUS

MS300-520
Mississippi University for Women
J. C. Fant Memorial Library
Columbus MS 39701

(601) 329-4750, Ext. 332

OPEN: M, Tu 8:30-5, Th 8:30-12; closed W, F, Sa, Su, holidays, and June-Aug.
COPYING FACILITIES: yes
MATERIALS SOLICITED: Will accept materials relating to prominent Mississippi persons and the University.

HOLDINGS:
Total volume: 27 boxes; 35 items; 1 c.f.
Inclusive dates: 1885 -
Description: Material relating to the history of Columbus, the State of Mississippi, and the University.

SEE: NUCMC, 1980.

SEE: Hinding.

MS300-550
Mississippi University for Women
M.U.W. Archives and Museum
Columbus MS 39701

(601) 329-4750, Ext. 325

OPEN: Aug. - April, M, W 8-4:30, Th 8-noon; closed other times
COPYING FACILITIES: no
MATERIALS SOLICITED: Will accept documents and artifacts relating to the University and prominent Mississippi persons.

HOLDINGS:
Total volume: 595 c.f.
Inclusive dates: 1885 -
Description: The M.U.W. collection, 1885- , relating to the University and the history of Columbus and Mississippi, including correspondence, financial records, diaries and journals, manuscript public documents, institution records, and visual documents such as architectural drawings and photographs. Also held is the Tenn-Tom collection, 1929- , relating to the Tennessee-Tombigbee Waterway Devel-

opment Authority, Corps of Engineers, and other government agencies.

HATTIESBURG

MS490-810
University of Southern Mississippi
William David McCain Library and Archives
Hattiesburg MS

MAILING ADDRESS:
Southern Station
P.O. Box 5148
Hattiesburg MS 39406-5148

(601) 266-4347

OPEN: M-Th 8-9, F 8-5, Sa 1-5, Su 2-6; closed school holidays
ACCESS: restricted to scholarly researchers
COPYING FACILITIES: yes
MATERIALS SOLICITED: Materials used in publication of children's books; records of the University; and materials relating to William M. Colmer and Theodore G. Bilbo. Will also accept materials related to Mississippi, Southern history, the Confederacy, the Civil War, and genealogy.

HOLDINGS:
Total volume: 5,500 l.f.
Inclusive dates: 1820 -
Description: Manuscript collections in two principal divisions: the de Grummond Collection relating to children's literature and several collections relating to Mississippi history, including the papers of State Governor and U.S. Senator Theodore G. Bilbo and U.S. Representative William M. Colmer. The de Grummond materials include correspondence, book manuscripts, and art work by over 800 authors and illustrators. The McCain Library also houses the archives of the University of Southern Mississippi.

SEE: Meckler and McMullin; Hinding.

SEE ALSO: The University of Southern Mississippi Press has published finding aids to two collections at the Library: the William M. Colmer Papers and the Merritt Mauzey Collection.

HOLLY SPRINGS

MS520-520
Marshall County Historical Society, Inc.
Marshall County Historical Museum
220 East College Avenue
Holly Springs MS

MAILING ADDRESS:
P.O. Box 806
Holly Springs MS 38635

(601) 252-4437, 2943

OPEN: by appointment only
ACCESS: appointment requested
COPYING FACILITIES: no
MATERIALS SOLICITED: Manuscripts, records of institutions and organizations, visual documents, and audible

documents pertaining to Marshall County.

HOLDINGS:
Total volume: 24 l.f.
Inclusive dates: 1837 -
Description: Biographies, photographs, reminiscences, correspondence, and diaries relating to Marshall County; family papers of artist Kate Freeman Clark; and correspondence, scrapbooks, and diaries of Senators L.Q.C. Lamar and E.C. Walthall.

SEE: Hinding.

JACKSON

MS550-120

Catholic Diocese of Jackson
237 E. Amite Street
Jackson MS

MAILING ADDRESS:
P.O. Box 2248
Jackson MS 39225-2248

(601) 969-1880

OPEN: by appointment only
COPYING FACILITIES: yes
MATERIALS SOLICITED: Records and papers relating to the Catholic church in Mississippi.

HOLDINGS:
Total volume: 80 file drawers
Inclusive dates: 1800 -
Description: Records of the Catholic church in Mississippi.

MS550-410

Jackson State University
Henry T. Sampson Library
Special Collections
1325 John R. Lynch Street
Jackson MS 39217

(601) 968-2123

OPEN: M-F 9-5; closed weekends and holidays
COPYING FACILITIES: yes
MATERIALS SOLICITED: Literary manuscripts, correspondence, archives and noncurrent records of the University, Margaret Walker Alexander papers, oral history tapes and transcripts, manuscripts of speeches, galleys, papers and correspondence of Jacob L. Reddix, photographs and tapes. Will also accept diaries, music scores in manuscript and sound recordings, and materials relating to prominent Mississippians.

HOLDINGS:
Total volume: 21 l.f.
Inclusive dates: 1877 -
Description: A manuscript collection of records of formerly all black schools seeking accreditation by the Southern Association of Colleges and Schools, 1960-69; papers and correspondence of Margaret Walker Alexander and of Jacob L. Reddix (fifth President of Jackson State University).

A collection of athletic activities of the "Big 8 Conference"; tapes, literary manuscripts, programs, etc., of significant events in the history and development of

Jackson State University; transcripts of the Radcliffe College Black Women Oral History Project; and letters, scrapbooks and photographs.

SEE: NUCMC, 1978.

SEE: Hinding.

SEE ALSO: 'A Guide to Elementary and Secondary School Reports Submitted to the Mississippi Negro Accrediting Commission Located in the H. T. Sampson Library' is available on request.

MS550-460

Millsaps College
Millsaps-Wilson Library
Lehman Engel Collection
Jackson MS 39210

(601) 354-5201, Ext. 245

OPEN: M-F 8:30-12 or by appointment; closed weekends and holidays
ACCESS: only persons over 18 years
COPYING FACILITIES: yes

HOLDINGS:
Total volume: 1,000 items
Inclusive dates: 1940's -
Description: Correspondence, musical scores, and other materials related to the stage, theater, and music donated by Lehman Engel from his personal files and collections.

MS550-500

Mississippi Department of Archives and History
Archives and Library Division
100 South State Street
Jackson MS

MAILING ADDRESS:
P.O. Box 571
Jackson MS 39205

(601) 359-1424

OPEN: M-F 8-5, Sa 8:30-4:30
COPYING FACILITIES: yes
MATERIALS SOLICITED: Mississippi history, especially social, economic, military, and political history. Will also accept other materials relating to Mississippi, including maps and photographs.

HOLDINGS:
Total volume: 8,830 c.f.
Inclusive dates: 1699 -
Description: Official State archives and private manuscripts relating primarily to Mississippi. Included are records of land titles and French, British, and Spanish administration of the region that is now Mississippi; records of the Mississippi Territory; executive, legislative, and judicial records of the State of Mississippi; county records; and papers of individuals, organizations, churches, and businesses.

SEE: Hamer; NUCMC, 1959-62, 69-70.

SEE: Allard, Crawley, and Edmison; Robbins; Hinding; Ingram; Krichmar; Davis.

SEE ALSO: William S. Coker and Jack D. L. Holmes, 'Sources for the History of the Spanish Borderlands,' *Florida Historical Quarterly* 49 (April 1971); Walter Schatz, ed., *Directory of Afro-American Resources* (Bowker, 1970); Ann Novotny, ed., *Picture Sources 3* (Special Libraries Assn., 1975); and the following publications of the Department: Thomas W. Henderson and Ronald E. Tomlin, comps., *Guide to Official Records in the Mississippi Department of Archives and History* (1975); Patti Carr Black and Maxyne Madden Grimes, comps., *Guide to Civil War Source Material in the Department of Archives and History, State of Mississippi* (1962); *Biennial Reports*, to 1969; and *Annual Report*, 1969 - .

MS550-540

Mississippi Methodist Archives
Millsaps-Wilson Library
Millsaps College
Jackson MS 39210

(601) 354-5201, Ext. 277

OPEN: by appointment
USER FEES: fees for special research
COPYING FACILITIES: yes

HOLDINGS:
Total volume: 750 l.f.
Inclusive dates: 19th century -
Description: Church records, personal papers of ministers, and other research materials relating to Methodism in Mississippi and the South.

SEE: Hamer (as Mississippi Conference, Methodist Historical Society); NUCMC, 1962.

LORMAN

MS570-40

Alcorn State University
Library
Reference Department
Lorman MS 39096

(601) 877-6357

OPEN: M, Tu, Th 8-5, W 1-5, F 8-4; closed weekends
COPYING FACILITIES: yes
MATERIALS SOLICITED: Material on the history and development of Alcorn State University and Oakland College.

HOLDINGS:
Total volume: not specified
Inclusive dates: 1830 -
Description: Materials relating to the history and development of Alcorn State University. Included are departmental records and other historical materials relating to the growth of the institution.

MISSISSIPPI STATE

MS610-520
Mississippi State University
Mitchell Memorial Library
Special Collections
Mississippi State MS

MAILING ADDRESS:
P.O. Drawer 5408
Mississippi State MS 39762

(601) 325-3060

OPEN: M-F 8-5, Sa 9-noon; closed
Sundays and holidays
COPYING FACILITIES: yes
MATERIALS SOLICITED: Materials pertaining to Mississippi politics, journalism, social history, and agriculture;
Mississippi State University; and Senator John C. Stennis. Will also accept
other Mississippi historical materials.

HOLDINGS:
Total volume: 2,550 l.f.
Inclusive dates: 1784 -
Description: Collections relating primarily to Mississippi political, social, and
agricultural history. Included are the papers of families, organizations, and
individuals such as Senator John C.
Stennis, as well as the archives of Mississippi State University.

SEE: Hamer; NUCMC, 1966, 69, 72, 79.

SEE: Schatz; Meckler and McMullin;
Krichmar; Davis; Hinding; Beers -
Confederate.

NATCHEZ

MS640-400
Judge George W. Armstrong Library
South Commerce and Washington
Streets
Natchez MS

MAILING ADDRESS:
P.O. Box 1406
Natchez MS 39120

(601) 445-8862

OPEN: M-Th 9-6, F 9-5, Sa 9-1; closed
Sundays and holidays
COPYING FACILITIES: yes
MATERIALS SOLICITED: Will accept ma-
terials relating to Natchez and Adams
County history.

HOLDINGS:
Total volume: 150 items
Inclusive dates: 1800 -
Description: Materials dealing primar-
ily with Natchez, Adams County and
Concordia Parish, and Louisiana local
history from the early 1800's to 1900's.
Included are correspondence, photo-
graphs, city directories, public documents,
newspapers and items relating to the
Natchez Pilgrimage, and houses from its
origin in the 1930's.

MS640-520
Myrtle Bank Galleries
408 North Pearl Street
Natchez MS 39120

(601) 442-4090

OPEN: M-Sa 10-4; Su noon-4
ACCESS: written requests for
photographs will be acknowledged;
information can be obtained by phone
or by visiting the galleries, but requests
for specific photographs will not be
filled based upon telephone
conversations
COPYING FACILITIES: yes

HOLDINGS:
Total volume: 75,000 negatives
Inclusive dates: 1850's - 1950's
Description: Original photographic negatives, including glass plate and celluloid
negatives, by Henry Gurney, Henry Norman, and Earl Norman relating to street
scenes, river scenes and river boats,
houses, people, rural scenes, trains, celebrations and other special occasions, and
portraits of all ages that reveal fashions
and tastes of the Victorian period up
through World War II.

TOUGALOO

MS870-760
Tougaloo College
Coleman Library
Lillian Pierce Benbow Room of
Special Collections
Tougaloo MS 39174

(601) 956-4942, Ext. 272

OPEN: M-F 8-5; closed weekends and
holidays
COPYING FACILITIES: yes
MATERIALS SOLICITED: Oral and written
materials pertaining to civil rights and
the civil rights movement, and papers
of black and white leaders and educators, black families, and the black aged
in Mississippi.

HOLDINGS:
Total volume: 370 l.f.
Inclusive dates: 1900 -
Description: A collection focusing on
black people and civil rights in Mississippi. Included are papers of civil rights
workers; records of organizations such as
the U.S. Commission on Civil Rights and
the Delta Ministry; a large collection of
legal papers, including those of the
NAACP Legal Defense Fund and the
Lawyers Constitutional Defense Committee; research papers on Mound Bayou,
MS, and other State history topics; and
materials concerning *Kudzu,* an underground newspaper in Jackson, MS.

GUIDES: 'Research Collections Available
at L. Zenobia Coleman Library, Lillian
Pierce Benbow Room of Special Collections,' (n.d.).

TUPELO

MS880-560
Natchez Trace Parkway
Library
Rural Route 1
Tupelo MS

MAILING ADDRESS:
Rural Route 1, NT-143
Tupelo MS 38801

(601) 842-1572

OPEN: daily 8-5; closed Christmas
COPYING FACILITIES: no
MATERIALS SOLICITED: Materials relating
to the history of the Natchez Trace
Parkway and of the surrounding regions through which it passes. Will also
accept histories of people, and events
associated with Indians and the Old
Natchez Trace.

HOLDINGS:
Total volume: 12 l.f.
Inclusive dates: 1935 -
Description: Historical documents,
manuscripts, photographs, and maps relating to the historical aspects, people and
events, associated with the Old Trace and
its modern counterpart, the Natchez
Trace Parkway.

UNIVERSITY

MS900-870
University of Mississippi
John Davis Williams Library
Department of Archives and Special
Collections
University MS 38677

(601) 232-7408

OPEN: M-Th 8:30-8, F 8:30-5, Sa
9-noon; closed Sundays and holidays
COPYING FACILITIES: yes
MATERIALS SOLICITED: Materials relating
to Mississippi, including literary manuscripts, political papers, materials on
the Mississippi lumber industry, and
translations and criticism of William
Faulkner, Eudora Welty, Tennessee
Williams, Richard Wright, and other
Mississippi authors. Will also accept
sound recordings, diaries, photographs,
letters, and other papers relating to
Mississippi.

HOLDINGS:
Total volume: 8,200 vols.; 3,500 l.f.
Inclusive dates: early 1800's -
Description: Manuscripts relating to
Mississippi, including materials on the
University of Mississippi, folklore, music,
and the lumber industry. There is particular emphasis on the papers of Mississippi political figures. Also included are
music manuscripts of Charles Ives and
other composers.

SEE: Hamer; NUCMC, 1980.

SEE: Paszek; Krichmar; Davis; Hinding;
Robbins.

VICKSBURG

MS950-830
Vicksburg and Warren County
   Historical Society
Old Court House Museum
Vicksburg MS 39180

SEE: Hamer; NUCMC, 1962.

Questionnaire not returned.

WEST POINT

MS970-520
Mary Holmes College
Library
Oral History Program
West Point MS 39773

(601) 494-6820, Ext. 59

OPEN: M-F 8-5; closed weekends, and
   Thanksgiving, Christmas, and Spring
   vacations

COPYING FACILITIES: yes
MATERIALS SOLICITED: Interviews with
   rural black Mississippians concerning
   all areas of their lives.

HOLDINGS:
   Total volume: 600 tapes
   Inclusive dates: 1969 -
   Description: Oral histories of rural
   black Mississippians relating to their education, sex life, economic status, religion,
   environment, share cropping, and civil
   rights experiences.

MISSOURI

In 1972 the Missouri Records Management and Archives Service assumed responsibility for scheduling local records in that State. The Church of Jesus Christ of Latter-day Saints has microfilmed vital, land, probate, and other records of almost all counties and the city of St. Louis, from the time of formation through a typical cut-off date of 1900. Some 7,100 reels of these documents, as well as finding aids to them, are available to researchers at the State Archives in Jefferson City.

Most original records of counties and municipalities remain in the custody of local agencies.

ARROW ROCK

MO30-80
Arrow Rock State Historical Site
Arrow Rock MO 65320

(816) 837-3300

SEE: Hamer.

Questionnaire not returned.

CANTON

MO120-120
Culver-Stockton College
Library
Canton MO 63435

no telephone

SEE: Hamer.

Questionnaire not returned.

CASSVILLE

MO160-80
Barry County Historical Society
Barry County Court House
Cassville MO 65625

no telephone

OPEN: M-F 9-4, Sa 9-noon; closed
   Sundays and holidays
COPYING FACILITIES: no

HOLDINGS:
   Total volume: 20 items
   Inclusive dates: 1910 - 1920
   Description: Photographs of Barry County scenes, including a railway depot and trains.

CHARLESTON

MO170-520
Mississippi County Historical Society
Museum
Russell Hotel
Charleston MO

MAILING ADDRESS:
500 North Green Street
Charleston MO 63834

(314) 683-4348

OPEN: by appointment
COPYING FACILITIES: no
MATERIALS SOLICITED: Will accept material relating to Mississippi County.

HOLDINGS:
   Total volume: 160 c.f.
   Inclusive dates: 1790 -
   Description: Material relating to the genealogy and history of Mississippi and Charleston counties.

CLAYTON

MO200-720
St. Louis County Department of Parks and Recreation
Grant and Kingston Drive
St. Louis MO 63125

(314) 544-5714

OPEN: Su 1-5, W-Sa 8-5; closed
   Mondays, Tuesdays, and holidays
COPYING FACILITIES: no
MATERIALS SOLICITED: Will accept materials related to the Jefferson Barracks and the units stationed there.

HOLDINGS:
   Total volume: 4 items; 249 photographs
   Inclusive dates: 1864 - 1945
   Description: A roll book, supply log, topographic map, and marriage license from the Jefferson Barracks, as well as photographs of the Barracks, of various military units, and of scenes from the Spanish-American War, the Pancho Villa campaigns, and World War I.

COLUMBIA

MO210-780
University of Missouri at Columbia
Central Administration
University Archives
Room 701, Lewis Hall
Columbia MO 65211

(314) 882-7567

OPEN: M-F 8-5; closed weekends and
   holidays
COPYING FACILITIES: yes
MATERIALS SOLICITED: Official records of the University; papers of faculty, students, and administrators; and records of student and faculty organizations.

HOLDINGS:
   Total volume: 2,344 c.f.
   Inclusive dates: 1839 -
   Description: Records and papers of faculty, students and administrators documenting the history of the University, including manuscripts, photographs, tape recordings, films, official reports, and memorabilia.

SEE: Hinding.

MO210-815
University of Missouri at Columbia
Joint Collection
University of Missouri Western
   Historical Manuscript
   Collection-Columbia and
State Historical Society of Missouri
   Manuscripts
Room 23, Ellis Library
Columbia MO 65211

(314) 882-6028

OPEN: M-F 8-4:45; closed weekends and
   holidays
ACCESS: identification is required
COPYING FACILITIES: yes
MATERIALS SOLICITED: Materials relating to Missouri history, the westward movement, agriculture, lumbering, politics, social welfare, labor, women, and science.

HOLDINGS:
   Total volume: 11,600 l.f.
   Inclusive dates: 1576 -
   Description: Papers of Missouri political, legal, business, and religious leaders; New Deal agricultural leaders; University of Missouri faculty and departments; local unions and state labor organizations; and WPA Historical Records Survey of Missouri; pre- and early statehood records; lumber industry records; church records; antebellum family papers; wom-

en's personal and organizational papers; Missouri River steamboat materials; and archives of professional and other organizations.

SEE: Hamer; NUCMC, 1959-62, 63-64, 68, 70, 74.

SEE: Schatz; Meckler and McMullin; Krichmar; Davis; Hines; Allard, Crawley, and Edmison; Robbins; Hinding; Parkinson; Paszek; Spalek.

SEE ALSO: Lewis E. Atherton, 'Western Historical Manuscripts Collection: A Case Study of a Collecting Program,' *American Archivist* 26 (Jan. 1963); *Source Material for the Recent History of Astronomy and Astrophysics: A Checklist of Manuscript Collections in the United States* (American Institute of Physics, Neils Bohr Library, 1971).

Complete card catalogs to the Joint Collection are located at University branches in Kansas City, Rolla, and St. Louis; interlibrary loan is available.

MO210-840

University of Missouri at Columbia
Museum of Anthropology
Archives
Room 104, Swallow Hall
Columbia MO 65211

(314) 882-3764

OPEN: Tu-F 10-3; closed M, Sa, Su and University holidays
COPYING FACILITIES: no
MATERIALS SOLICITED: Census documents from colonial Latin America, with emphasis on Mexico and Central America. Will also accept manuscript materials pertaining to the Indian and colonial European cultures of North and South America or to linguistic, archaeological, or anthropological studies of world cultures.

HOLDINGS:
Total volume: 100 items
Inclusive dates: 16th century -
Description: Copies of census and other documents in the Archivo General de Centro America and the Archivo General de Indias, relating to Hidalgo and central Mexico, Chiapas, Guatemala, and El Salvador. The collection also contains lists of holdings of other museums in Missouri, a Diegueno (southern California) Indian card file dictionary, and an early 20th century notebook in Alaskan Eskimo.

CONCEPTION

MO220-120

Conception Abbey
Archives
Conception MO 64433

(816) 944-2211

OPEN: by appointment only
ACCESS: consideration given to requests for historical research on an individual basis
COPYING FACILITIES: yes

MATERIALS SOLICITED: Manuscripts, letters, newspaper clippings, photographs, and other materials relating to members of Conception Abbey and to where they have worked.

HOLDINGS:
Total volume: 30 l.f.
Inclusive dates: 1873 -
Description: Records documenting the history of Conception Abbey and its members and their work. Included are records and letters between the Abbey superior and monks stationed in parishes and missions outside the Abbey, primarily in the Midwest and including Standing Rock Indian Reservation at Fort Yates, ND, and St. Joseph's parish in Springfield, MO. Also held are records pertaining to Benedictine monasteries worldwide, files on individual monks, local histories, and records of a college and seminary under the Abbey's jurisdiction.

SEE: Hamer; NUCMC, 1966.

DIAMOND

MO240-280

George Washington Carver National Monument
Diamond MO

MAILING ADDRESS:
Box 38
Diamond MO 64840

(417) 325-4151

OPEN: daily 8:30-5; closed Christmas
ACCESS: advance arrangements recommended
COPYING FACILITIES: no
MATERIALS SOLICITED: Will accept materials pertaining to the life of George Washington Carver.

HOLDINGS:
Total volume: 3,000 items
Inclusive dates: 1860 - 1948
Description: Materials related to the life of George Washington Carver, including original correspondence and oral history tapes with Carver and contemporaries. Included also are copies of letters, deeds, and other records.

SEE: Schatz.

FAYETTE

MO290-120

Central Methodist College
George M. Smiley Memorial Library
Methodist Collection
Fayette MO 65248

(816) 248-3391

OPEN: M-Th 8-10:30, F 8-9:30, Sa 8:30-11:30, Su 2:30-10:30; summer, M-F 8:30-4:30; closed weekends in summer and during school vacations
COPYING FACILITIES: yes
MATERIALS SOLICITED: Material relating to Methodism, particularly in Missouri. Will also accept materials from churches that have merged with the Methodist church.

HOLDINGS:
Total volume: 50 items
Inclusive dates: 1700's -
Description: Material relating to the Methodist church in Missouri and throughout the world. Included are manuscript congregational histories, reports, and photographs.

SEE: Hinding.

GRAHAM

MO350-280

Graham Historical Society, Inc.
Graham MO

MAILING ADDRESS:
P.O. Box 72
Graham MO 64455

(816) 939-2275

OPEN: appointment required
COPYING FACILITIES: no
MATERIALS SOLICITED: Will accept any material relating to the genealogy or history of Hughes Township.

HOLDINGS:
Total volume: 4 file cabinets
Inclusive dates: 1800 -
Description: Birth, marriage, death, and land records of area. Also includes oral history tapes and photographs of elderly residents and slides of local buildings.

SEE: Hinding.

HANNIBAL

MO370-520

Mark Twain Home Board
Mark Twain Museum
208 Hill Street
Hannibal MO 63401

(314) 221-9010

OPEN: open daily except New Year's, Thanksgiving, and Christmas; advance arrangements suggested
COPYING FACILITIES: yes
MATERIALS SOLICITED: Material relating to Samuel Langhorne Clemens' (Mark Twain) life and writings. Will also accept items relating to Hannibal, 1840-55.

HOLDINGS:
Total volume: 300 items
Inclusive dates: 1840 - 1940
Description: Materials relating to the life of Samuel Langhorne Clemens (Mark Twain). Included are correspondence; genealogical data on the Clemens and Lampton families; historical and genealogical data on early Hannibal families; maps of early Hannibal; photographs and motion picture films, including one of Clemens; recordings of men imitating Clemens; and one book manuscript.

SEE: Robbins.

INDEPENDENCE

MO400-320

Harry S. Truman Library
Independence MO 64050

(816) 833-1400

OPEN: M-Sa 8:45-4:45; closed Sundays
and holidays
ACCESS: applicants for research must
complete an application providing
detailed information on their topics
COPYING FACILITIES: yes
MATERIALS SOLICITED: Materials relating
to the history of the administration of
President Harry S. Truman and to his
life and public career.

HOLDINGS:
Total volume: 12,804,000 pages;
73,863 photographs; 2,625 recordings;
292,784 l.f. of motion pictures
Inclusive dates: 1903 -
Description: Papers of Harry S. Truman, including White House files for his
Presidential administration, and nearly
300 other manuscript collections of Truman's associates in various capacities.
Also included are records of commissions
and committees appointed by Truman as
President, as well as organizations associated with his career. There are collections of photographs, motion pictures,
sound recordings, and transcripts of oral
history interviews.

GUIDES: Historical Materials in the Harry
S. Truman Library (1979).

SEE: Hamer; NUCMC, 1965-66, 68,
71-72, 74-76.

SEE: Novotny; Schatz; Meckler and
McMullin; Davis; Hindings; Allard,
Crawley, and Edmison; Bean and Vane;
Parkinson; Paszek.

MO400-400

Jackson County Historical Society
Research Library and Archives
Room 103
Independence Square Courthouse
Independence MO 64050

(816) 252-7454

OPEN: M-Th 10-3; closed other days and
holidays
COPYING FACILITIES: yes
MATERIALS SOLICITED: Materials relating
to the history of Jackson County, particularly 19th century subjects such as
the Santa Fe Trail, the migration of
pioneers to Oregon and California, and
guerilla warfare during the Civil War.

HOLDINGS:
Total volume: 575 l.f.
Inclusive dates: 1825 -
Description: Letters, diaries, and
records of families, businesses, and organizations of Jackson County. Included
are records of literary societies, social organizations, mills, the Jackson County superintendent of schools, and horse and
livestock shows. There is also a collection
of the work of local photographers.

SEE: NUCMC, 1980.

SEE: Hinding.

MO400-690

Reorganized Church of Jesus Christ of
Latter Day Saints
History Commission
Church Archives
The Auditorium
River and Walnut
Independence MO

MAILING ADDRESS:
P.O. Box 1059
Independence MO 64051

(816) 833-1000

OPEN: M-F 8-5, Sa 9-1; closed Sundays
and holidays
COPYING FACILITIES: yes
MATERIALS SOLICITED: Material relating
to the formation and development of
the Latter Day Saint (Mormon) movement, its post-1844 dispersion, and the
subsequent organization and growth of
the Reorganized Church of Jesus Christ
of Latter Day Saints.

HOLDINGS:
Total volume: 300 l.f.
Inclusive dates: 1795 -
Description: Manuscripts and records
relating to the Latter Day Saint
(Mormon) movement, chiefly in the
United States, particularly New York,
Ohio, Missouri, Illinois, and Iowa, and
some papers concerned with activity in
Australia, the British Isles, French Polynesia, and other world mission areas. Included are correspondence, diaries,
letterbooks, photographs, records and reports of local jurisdictions, and official
records originating from Church headquarters.

SEE: Hinding.

JEFFERSON CITY

MO410-40

Adjutant General of Missouri
Records and Archives
1717 Industrial Drive
Jefferson City MO 65101

(314) 751-2321

OPEN: M-F 8-5; closed weekends and
holidays
COPYING FACILITIES: no
MATERIALS SOLICITED: Military records
and other materials relating to Missouri inhabitants who served in the armed
forces of the Confederacy. Will also accept military information pertaining to
Missourians who participated in any
war.

HOLDINGS:
Total volume: 2,000,000 items
Inclusive dates: 1812 -
Description: Military service records of
Missouri citizens, including participants
in all domestic and foreign wars since
1812.

MO410-120

Cole County Historical Society
109 Madison
Jefferson City MO 65101

(314) 635-1850

OPEN: Tu-Sa 1-5; closed Sundays and
Mondays
USER FEES: determined by amount of
staff time needed
ACCESS: appointment requested
COPYING FACILITIES: yes
MATERIALS SOLICITED: Material relating
to Cole County. Will also accept ma-
terials relating to Missouri governors
and other state officials.

HOLDINGS:
Total volume: 3 file drawers; 12
scrapbooks
Inclusive dates: 1869 - 1976
Description: Fire maps, atlases, photographs, cemetery records, diaries, scrapbooks and oral history tapes relating to
the history of Cole County and its residents.

MO410-545

Missouri Office of Secretary of State
Records Management and Archives
Service
1001 Industrial Drive
Jefferson City MO

MAILING ADDRESS:
P.O. Box 778
Jefferson City MO 65102

(314) 751-3280

OPEN: M-F 8-4:30; closed weekends and
holidays
COPYING FACILITIES: yes
MATERIALS SOLICITED: Records of the
State of Missouri. Will also accept other public and private records relating
to public record holdings of the State
of Missouri.

HOLDINGS:
Total volume: 9,500 c.f.
Inclusive dates: 1805 -
Description: Primarily government
records of the State of Missouri. Also
included are some territorial records and
early county records on microfilm, a
small manuscripts collection of local
church records on microfilm, and several
groups of historical photographs.

SEE: Hinding.

KANSAS CITY

MO430-120

Church of the Nazarene
International Headquarters
Archives
6401 The Paseo
Kansas City MO 64131

(816) 333-7000, Ext. 437

OPEN: by appointment only
ACCESS: advance arrangements required
COPYING FACILITIES: yes
MATERIALS SOLICITED: Church of the
Nazarene records at the denomination-
al level and records of precedent or

related religious bodies. Will also accept records of institutions of the Church of the Nazarene, personal materials of prominent Nazarenes, and records of related non-Nazarene bodies, such as camp meeting associations, schools, and missionary bodies.

HOLDINGS:
> *Total volume:* 1,500 c.f.
> *Inclusive dates:* 1884 -
> *Description:* Records of the International Headquarters for the Church of the Nazarene; its governing boards, agencies, assemblies, and their departments and officers; foreign missions; local and regional organizations; and precedent or related religious bodies, including regional holiness associations and churches, principally in the Northeast, West Coast, Tennessee, Texas, North Dakota, and Iowa. Included are photographs, audio recordings, correspondence, statistical charts, minutes, reports, financial records, and personal papers.

MO430-420
Kansas City Museum of History and
    Science
Archives
3218 Gladstone Boulevard
Kansas City MO 64123

(816) 483-8300

OPEN: Tu-F 8-5:30 by appointment;
    closed Sa, Su, M, and holidays
COPYING FACILITIES: yes
MATERIALS SOLICITED: Materials relating to the history of the Kansas City region and materials that document artifacts in the Museum's collections.

HOLDINGS:
> *Total volume:* 200 l.f.
> *Inclusive dates:* 1634 -
> *Description:* Materials covering Kansas City regional history from 1836 to the present, with emphasis on Kansas City, MO, in the 20th century. Included are records of cultural organizations, mayoral papers, papers relating to aviation, motion pictures, and a large collection of photographs from the late 19th and early 20th centuries. There are also a number of European legal documents dating from 1634.

SEE: NUCMC, 1980.

SEE: Hinding.

SEE ALSO: an unpublished guide to the manuscript collections available for use at the Museum.

MO430-540
National Archives and Records
    Administration
Kansas City Federal Archives and
    Records Center
Archives Branch
2312 E. Bannister Road
Kansas City MO 64131

(816) 926-7271

OPEN: M-F 8-4; closed weekends and all
    Federal holidays
COPYING FACILITIES: yes

MATERIALS SOLICITED: Archives of Federal agencies in Missouri, Kansas, Iowa, and Nebraska.

HOLDINGS:
> *Total volume:* 13,000 c.f.
> *Inclusive dates:* 1833 - 1977
> *Description:* Administrative records of Federal agencies operating in the states of Missouri, Kansas, Iowa, Nebraska, North Dakota, South Dakota, and Minnesota. Documentation of the activities of Indian agencies and federal courts is of particular interest, but all types of government records are included.

SEE: Allard, Crawley, and Edmison; Davis; Hinding.

MO430-700
St. Luke's Hospital of Kansas City
Archives
Wornall Road at 44th Street
Kansas City MO

MAILING ADDRESS:
P.O. Box 1647
Kansas City MO 64141

(816) 932-2517, 2000

OPEN: M-F 8-4:30; closed weekends and
    holidays
ACCESS: appointment required
COPYING FACILITIES: yes
MATERIALS SOLICITED: Records and memorabilia relating to the history of St. Luke's Hospital of Kansas City and its medical staff, personnel, and students.

HOLDINGS:
> *Total volume:* 24 l.f.
> *Inclusive dates:* 1882 -
> *Description:* Copies of news clippings about St. Lukes's Hospital of Kansas City, 1882- ; Hospital records, including minutes, publications, departmental pamphlets, annual reports, and statistical information; a photograph collection; and other materials.

MO430-775
University of Missouri at Kansas City
Archives
Room 203, General Library
5100 Rockhill Road
Kansas City MO 64110

(816) 276-1539

OPEN: M-F 8-5; closed weekends and
    holidays
COPYING FACILITIES: yes
MATERIALS SOLICITED: Official records of the University; papers of faculty, students, administrators, and alumni; records of student and faculty organizations; papers and records relating to the Conservatory of Music and the Schools of Dentistry, Law, and Pharmacy prior to their merger with the University; and records of the University of Kansas City, 1929-63.

HOLDINGS:
> *Total volume:* 800 c.f.
> *Inclusive dates:* 1895 -
> *Description:* Official records; professional and personal papers of administrators, faculty, students, and alumni; dissertations and theses; faculty and Univer-

sity publications, tape recordings, photographs, films, manuscripts, and memorabilia, relating to the University of Missouri at Kansas City.

MO430-790
University of Missouri at Kansas City
Conservatory Library
General Library
Kansas City MO 64110

(816) 276-1675

OPEN: M-Th 8-8:30, F 8-5, Sa 10-5;
    closed Sundays and holidays
USER FEES: $15 (Friends of the Library
    membership) for non-University users
COPYING FACILITIES: yes
MATERIALS SOLICITED: American music with particular attention to Kansas City, MO, and midwestern materials.

HOLDINGS:
> *Total volume:* 30 l.f.
> *Inclusive dates:* 1640 -
> *Description:* Materials collected by the Institute for Studies in American Music relating to American music of all types and periods. Other holdings include music manuscripts and related papers of local composers, as well as the papers of area music performers and organizations.

SEE: Hinding.

SEE ALSO: two publications of the Conservatory: *Treasures from the Collection of the Institute for Studies in American Music* (1972) and *Landmarks of American Music History, an Exhibit in Honor of Oscar George Sonneck, 1873-1928* (1973).

MO430-800
University of Missouri at Kansas City
Joint Collection
University of Missouri Western
    Historical Manuscript
    Collection-Kansas City and
State Historical Society of Missouri
    Manuscripts
Room 302, Newcomb Hall
5100 Rockhill Road
Kansas City MO 64110

(816) 276-1543

OPEN: M-F 8-5; closed weekends and
    holidays
COPYING FACILITIES: yes
MATERIALS SOLICITED: Architectural drawings and blueprints of Kansas City architectural firms, primarily commercial and public buildings located in Kansas City.

HOLDINGS:
> *Total volume:* 450 c.f.; 3,500
> blueprints
> *Inclusive dates:* 1858 -
> *Description:* Manuscripts relating to the development of Kansas City and the adjacent area; architectural records, blueprints, and drawings for more than 3,500 Kansas City buildings. Also, papers reflecting the political and economic history of Kansas, including papers of Charles B. Wheeler, Jr., the 1970 Jackson County Charter Commission, the Civic Research Institute, and Lou E. Holland.

Social and cultural history, represented by such collections as the Kansas City Jazz Oral History Collection, the Kansas City Browning Society Records, and the papers of Herbert Perry Wright.

SEE: NUCMC, 1962.

SEE: Novotny.

KIRKSVILLE

MO460-560
Northeast Missouri State University
Pickler Memorial Library
Kirksville MO 63501

(816) 785-4526

OPEN: M-F 8-5; other times by appointment; closed holidays
COPYING FACILITIES: yes

HOLDINGS:
Total volume: 125 l.f.
Inclusive dates: 1867 -
Description: Papers of Glenn Frank and Harry Laughlin; records of the now defunct Central Wesleyan College; and faculty, financial, and administrative records of Northeast Missouri State University.

SEE: NUCMC, 1968.

LAWSON

MO490-880
Watkins Woolen Mill State Historic Site
Route 2
Lawson MO

MAILING ADDRESS:
P.O. Box 270
Lawson MO 64062

(816) 296-3357

OPEN: M-F 8:30-4; closed weekends and holidays
COPYING FACILITIES: no
MATERIALS SOLICITED: Records relating to the textile industry of the Midwest and the operation of Watkins Woolen Mill.

HOLDINGS:
Total volume: 30 l.f.
Inclusive dates: 1812 - 1920
Description: A collection of manuscripts relating primarily to the W. L. Watkins family and their business and personal affairs.

SEE: Hinding.

LEXINGTON

MO520-440
Lexington Library and Historical Association
Lexington Historical Museum
112 South 13th Street
Lexington MO

MAILING ADDRESS:
P.O. Box 121
Lexington MO 64067

(816) 259-6313

OPEN: by appointment only
COPYING FACILITIES: no
MATERIALS SOLICITED: Materials relating to the history of Lexington and Lafayette County, MO.

HOLDINGS:
Total volume: not specified
Inclusive dates: 1825 -
Description: Materials covering the history of the Lexington area, including business records and records of educational and cultural organizations.

SEE: Hamer; NUCMC, 1966.

LIBERTY

MO530-110
Clay County Historical Society
Clay County Archives
Box 99
Liberty MO 64068

no telephone

OPEN: W, Sa 9-3; closed other days and first two Saturdays of month
USER FEES: one dollar daily or $5 membership annually
COPYING FACILITIES: yes
MATERIALS SOLICITED: Clay County probate, marriage, land grant, and family records. Will also accept materials relating to Clay County residents before immigration to Missouri.

HOLDINGS:
Total volume: not specified
Inclusive dates: 1822 -
Description: County probate records, 1822- ; marriage records, 1822-1915; land patent records, 1822-78; and family records.

MO530-120
Clay County Museum Association
Library and Archives
14 North Main
Liberty MO 64068

(816) 781-8062

OPEN: Su 2-5, Tu-Sa 1-4; closed Mondays and Christmas
USER FEES: $2 for nonmembers
COPYING FACILITIES: yes
MATERIALS SOLICITED: Materials relating to the history of Liberty, Clay County, and Missouri.

HOLDINGS:
Total volume: not specified
Inclusive dates: late 1700's -
Description: Materials relating to Liberty and Clay County, including diaries and probate records.

MARYVILLE

MO570-560
Nodaway County Historical Society Museum
422 West 2nd Street
Maryville MO 64468

(816) 582-4955

OPEN: by appointment only
COPYING FACILITIES: no
MATERIALS SOLICITED: Missouri; Nodaway County, MO; and Maryville.

HOLDINGS:
Total volume: 15 l.f.
Inclusive dates: 1846 -
Description: Records relating to northwestern Missouri.

MEMPHIS

MO590-720
Scotland County Historical Society
311 S. Main
Memphis MO 63555

(816) 465-2259, 2404

OPEN: M-F 1-4; closed weekends and holidays
COPYING FACILITIES: yes
MATERIALS SOLICITED: Materials pertaining to the history of Scotland County.

HOLDINGS:
Total volume: 2,000 items
Inclusive dates: 1842 -
Description: Manuscripts pertaining to the founding and history of Scotland County, including diaries, genealogies, and organization records.

MOBERLY

MO607-520
Moberly Historical and Railroad Museum
100 N. Sturgeon Street
Moberly MO 65270

no telephone

OPEN: Su, Sa 1-4; closed other days
ACCESS: appointment required
COPYING FACILITIES: yes
MATERIALS SOLICITED: History of Moberly; history and building of the Wabash Railroad and Norfolk and Western Railroad; General Omar M. Bradley; Randolph County, MO; and Missouri.

HOLDINGS:
Total volume: 800 sq.f.
Inclusive dates: 1873 -
Description: Records relating to the Wabash Railroad, Norfolk and Western Railroad, Omar M. Bradley, the U.S.

Coast Guard frigate *Moberly*, and the early history of Moberly.

NEVADA

MO620-80
Bushwhacker Museum
Archives
231 North Main
Nevada MO 64772

(417) 667-5841

OPEN: by appointment only
COPYING FACILITIES: no
MATERIALS SOLICITED: Local history of Nevada and Vernon County, MO; regional history of western Missouri, including the Civil War period; Osage Indians and early explorers; the border war; bushwhackers; and post-Civil War outlaws.

HOLDINGS:
  Total volume: not specified
  Inclusive dates: 1719 -
  Description: Records relating to regional and local history including John Brown's raid in 1858 and James Addison Reavis, the 'Baron of Arizona.'

PLATTE CITY

MO675-640
Platte County Historical Society, Inc.
Ben Ferrel-Platte County Museum
220 Ferrel Drive
Platte City MO

MAILING ADDRESS:
P.O. Box 103
Platte City MO 64079

(816) 431-5121

OPEN: by appointment only
COPYING FACILITIES: yes
MATERIALS SOLICITED: Platte County history.

HOLDINGS:
  Total volume: 12 file drawers
  Inclusive dates: 1839 -
  Description: Family histories, unpublished articles, oral histories, and photographs relating to Platte County history.

POINT LOOKOUT

MO700-720
The School of the Ozarks
Ralph Foster Museum
Lois Brownell Research Library
Point Lookout MO 65726

(417) 334-6411, Ext. 407

OPEN: Su 1-5, M-Sa 9-5; closed Thanksgiving, Christmas, and New Year's
COPYING FACILITIES: no
MATERIALS SOLICITED: Ozarkiana materials.

HOLDINGS:
  Total volume: 100 l.f.
  Inclusive dates: 1840 -
  Description: Manuscripts and historical photographs pertaining to the Ozarks region. Included are a few diaries, some reminiscences of pioneers and military figures, a collection of autographed letters from famous people all over the world, and a collection of historical photographs of The School of the Ozarks.

SEE: Hinding.

REPUBLIC

MO730-800
Wilson's Creek National Battlefield
Route 2
Republic MO

MAILING ADDRESS:
Postal Drawer C
Republic MO 65738

(417) 732-2662

OPEN: by appointment only
COPYING FACILITIES: no
MATERIALS SOLICITED: Records from the 1852-1870 era relating to the Battle of Wilson's Creek, participants in the battle, partisan activities in southwest Missouri, and the families living on the battlefield at the time of the engagement.

HOLDINGS:
  Total volume: 3 file drawers
  Inclusive dates: 1852 - 1870
  Description: Records relating to the Battle of Wilson's Creek, its participants, local families in the area at the time of the battle, and partisan activities in southwest Missouri.

ROLLA

MO760-530
Missouri Department of Natural Resources
Division of Geology and Land Survey
Buehler Park
Rolla MO

MAILING ADDRESS:
P.O. Box 250
Rolla MO 65401

(314) 364-1752

OPEN: M-F 8-5; closed weekends and holidays
COPYING FACILITIES: yes

HOLDINGS:
  Total volume: not specified
  Inclusive dates: 1850 -
  Description: Field notebooks, correspondence, and miscellaneous documents relating to geology and geography of Missouri.

MO760-760
University of Missouri at Rolla
Archives
G-2 Library
Rolla MO 65401

(314) 341-4815

OPEN: M-F by appointment only; closed weekends and holidays
COPYING FACILITIES: yes
MATERIALS SOLICITED: Official records of the University; papers of faculty, students, and administrators; and records of student and faculty organizations.

HOLDINGS:
  Total volume: 300 c.f.
  Inclusive dates: 1870 -
  Description: Records and papers of faculty, students, and administrators documenting the history of the University, including manuscripts, photographs, tape recordings, films, and official reports.

MO760-780
University of Missouri at Rolla
Department of Geology and
  Geophysics
Rolla MO 65401

(314) 341-4616

OPEN: M-F 8-5; closed weekends and holidays
COPYING FACILITIES: yes

HOLDINGS:
  Total volume: 300 c.f.
  Inclusive dates: 1975 -
  Description: Geologic maps, cross-sections, and diagrams, all originals of materials included in theses written for the Department. There are also originals of some thesis materials prepared prior to 1975.
  Repository for all USGS maps, both geological and geophysical.

MO760-800
University of Missouri at Rolla
Joint Collection
University of Missouri Western
  Historical Manuscript
  Collection-Rolla and
State Historical Society of Missouri
  Manuscripts
Room G-3 Library
Rolla MO 65401

(314) 341-4874

OPEN: M-F 8-5; closed weekends and holidays
COPYING FACILITIES: yes
MATERIALS SOLICITED: Historical manuscripts and materials related to science and technology, including technological applications of scientific advances, especially in mining and engineering, and records of cultural and commercial enterprises in the Ozarks and southern Missouri.

HOLDINGS:
> *Total volume:* 25 c.f.
> *Inclusive dates:* 1825 -
> *Description:* Collections documenting social history and technological advances in southern Missouri, including correspondence, diaries, photographs, business and financial records, unpublished histories and reminiscences, and genealogical data.

ST. CHARLES

MO770-480

The Lindenwood Colleges
Lindenwood College Archives
St. Charles MO 63301

(314) 946-6912

OPEN: by appointment only
COPYING FACILITIES: yes
MATERIALS SOLICITED: Materials documenting the history of the Lindenwood Colleges. Will also accept historical materials concerning St. Charles and St. Louis, MO.

HOLDINGS:
> *Total volume:* 12 l.f.; 8 file cabinets
> *Inclusive dates:* 1800 -
> *Description:* Diaries (1800-50) of Mary Easton and George C. Sibley and pictures, letters, yearbooks, catalogs, and other records of the Lindenwood Colleges.

SEE: Hamer.

The diaries of Mary Easton and George C. Sibley are on permanent loan to the Missouri Historical Society, St. Louis, MO.

MO770-710

St. Charles County Historical Society
Archives and Library
101 South Main Street
St. Charles MO 63301

(314) 723-2939

OPEN: M, W, F 10-3; closed other days and holidays
USER FEES: one dollar
COPYING FACILITIES: yes
MATERIALS SOLICITED: Materials pertaining to the history of St. Charles County and its residents.

HOLDINGS:
> *Total volume:* 12 file cabinets; 6 book shelves
> *Inclusive dates:* 1769 -
> *Description:* Materials pertaining to St. Charles County and the surrounding area. Included are genealogical materials, city and county records, personal papers, records relating to the architectural design of local houses, photographs, and oral history interviews.

SEE: Hinding.

ST. JOSEPH

MO800-730

St. Joseph Museum and Pony Express Stables Museum
11th and Charles
St. Joseph MO 64501

(816) 232-8471

OPEN: M-F 8-5 by appointment; closed weekends and holidays
ACCESS: permission from the staff
COPYING FACILITIES: yes
MATERIALS SOLICITED: Materials on the Pony Express, St. Joseph history, archaeology, and other 19th century history. Will also accept other material after evaluation by staff.

HOLDINGS:
> *Total volume:* 8 l.f.
> *Inclusive dates:* 1840 - 1925
> *Description:* Manuscripts, including the Joseph Robidoux family history and genealogy, the journal of Julius Robidoux, records of the Pony Express, and correspondence of Harry L. George, an Indian artifact collector. There are also archaeological records pertaining to the Indians in the area and a photograph collection relating to St. Joseph history.

ST. LOUIS

MO810-190

Center for Reformation Research
6477 San Bonita Avenue
St. Louis MO 63105

(314) 727-6655

OPEN: M, W, F 9-5, other times by appointment
COPYING FACILITIES: yes
MATERIALS SOLICITED: Materials on the history of late medieval and early modern Europe.

HOLDINGS:
> *Total volume:* 2,070 microfilm reels
> *Inclusive dates:* 1450 - 1650
> *Description:* The political archives of Landgrave Philip of Hesse from the Marburg Staatsarchiv; the Simmler collection from the Zurich Zentralbibliothek; the Thesaurus Baumianus from the Bibliotheque Nationale et Universitaire, Strasbourg; the Celle collection of correspondence from the Niedersachsische Staatsarchiv, Hannover; the archives of Westminster Cathedral; materials from the Herzog August Bibliothek, Wolfenbuttel; and smaller collections from individuals, primarily Lutheran theologians of the 16th century.

SEE: NUCMC, 1969 (as Foundation for Reformation Research).

MO810-200

Concordia Historical Institute
801 DeMun Avenue
St. Louis MO 63105

(314) 721-5934, Ext. 320, 321

OPEN: M-F 8-5; closed weekends, New Year's, July 4, and Christmas
ACCESS: serious researchers upon application
COPYING FACILITIES: yes
MATERIALS SOLICITED: History of Lutheranism in America with special concentration on the history of the Lutheran Church-Missouri Synod. Will also accept materials relating to German-Americans or the Lutheran Reformation.

HOLDINGS:
> *Total volume:* 8,298 l.f.
> *Inclusive dates:* 1520 -
> *Description:* Archives of the Lutheran Church-Missouri Synod, its boards, agencies, and commissions. Also included are the archives of auxiliary organizations, such as the Lutheran Laymen's League, Lutheran Women's Missionary League, some districts of the Missouri Synod, and records of a small number of congregations. These records include minutes, correspondence, reports, financial data, and photographs. Another major portion of the collection contains the personal papers of a number of individuals who were prominent in the Lutheran church in America.

SEE: Hamer; NUCMC, 1959-64, 66, 69, 71-72.

SEE: Hinding; Bean and Vane.

SEE ALSO: Morris Rieger, 'Africa-Related Papers of Persons and Organizations in the United States,' *African Studies Bulletin* 8 (Dec. 1965); August R. Suelflow, *Microfilm Index and Bibliography of the Concordia Historical Institute, The Department of Archives and History, Lutheran Church-Missouri Synod* (Concordia Press, 1966); Robert O. Collins and Peter Duignan, *Americans in Africa* (Hoover Institution, 1963); Walter Schatz, ed., *Directory of Afro-American Resources* (Bowker, 1970); Alan M. Mecker and Ruth McMullin, comps., *Oral History Collections* (Bowker, 1975); Concordia Historical Institute *Quarterly*, 1928- . Inventories of many collections are available at the Institute.

MO810-260

Eugene Field House and Toy Museum
634 South Broadway
St. Louis MO 63102

(314) 421-4689

OPEN: Tu-Sa 10-4, Su 12-5; closed Mondays and holidays
ACCESS: graduate students presenting a letter from their dean; other professionals with appropriate credentials
COPYING FACILITIES: no

HOLDINGS:
  Total volume: 3 boxes
  Inclusive dates: 1850 - 1895
  Description: Manuscripts, correspondence, photographs, royalty records, and other materials pertaining to the life and literary works of Eugene Field.

SEE: Hinding; Robbins.

MO810-270

Evangelical and Reformed Church and United Church of Christ
475 East Lockwood Avenue
St. Louis MO 63119

(314) 961-3627

OPEN: Tu-Th mornings; closed other times
COPYING FACILITIES: yes
MATERIALS SOLICITED: Congregational and church agency records of the Evangelical Synod of North America, including current United Church of Christ ministers, congregations, and agencies. Will also accept any materials pertaining to institutions and persons related to the Evangelical Synod of North America.

HOLDINGS:
  Total volume: 1,500 sq.f.
  Inclusive dates: 1740's -
  Description: Records of ministers, churches, and agencies of the German Reformed church (1740's-), the Evangelical Synod of North America (1840-), the Evangelical and Reformed church (1934-), and the United Church of Christ (1957-). Included are diaries of founders and correspondence of such persons as Richard and Reinhold Niebuhr, the minutes of general and district conferences, and the records of Eden Seminary and of local churches. There are also materials regarding missionary activities in India, Honduras, Japan, and Iraq.

MO810-330

Harris-Stowe State College
Library
Harris Teachers College/Stowe Teachers College Archives
3026 Laclede Avenue
St. Louis MO 63103

(314) 533-3366, Ext. 36

OPEN: M-Th 7:30-8:30, F 7:30-4, Sa 9-4; closed Sundays and holidays
ACCESS: persons not students of the College or teachers in the St. Louis Public Schools should apply to the Coordinator of Library and Media Services
COPYING FACILITIES: yes
MATERIALS SOLICITED: Official publications, documents, records, and memorabilia of the Harris Teachers and Stowe Teachers Colleges and the St. Louis public schools.

HOLDINGS:
  Total volume: 82 l.f.; 6 file cabinets
  Inclusive dates: 1854 -
  Description: Documents, records, memorabilia, and other materials relating to the Harris Teachers and Stowe Teachers Colleges and the St. Louis public schools.

SEE: Hinding.

MO810-390

Jefferson National Expansion Memorial National Historical Site
11 North Fourth Street
St. Louis MO 63102

(314) 425-4465

OPEN: M-F 8:30-4; closed weekends and holidays
COPYING FACILITIES: no
MATERIALS SOLICITED: Will accept materials relating to westward expansion in the area west of the Mississippi River, 1803-90 and materials relating to the history of the city of St. Louis during that same time period.

HOLDINGS:
  Total volume: 253 c.f.
  Inclusive dates: 1750 -
  Description: Records and research materials gathered principally for the purpose of furnishing background information for the Museum of Westward Expansion, covering the time period 1803-90, and including material on explorers, mountain men, trappers and traders, soldiers, Indians, miners, cattlemen, sodbusters, settlers, and the overland experience.

MO810-470

The May Department Stores Company
Corporate Information Center
611 Olive Street
St. Louis MO 63101

(314) 342-6300

OPEN: M-F 8:30-5; closed weekends and holidays
ACCESS: corporate personnel and bonafide researchers with permission of Director
COPYING FACILITIES: yes
MATERIALS SOLICITED: Corporate documents including real estate information, federal filings, stockholder information, minutes, and histories.

HOLDINGS:
  Total volume: 116.67 l.f.
  Inclusive dates: 1790's -
  Description: Documents concerning The May Department Stores Company and its subsidiaries.

MO810-490

Missouri Botanical Garden
Archives
2345 Tower Grove Avenue
St. Louis MO

MAILING ADDRESS:
P.O. Box 299
St. Louis MO 63166

(314) 577-5143

OPEN: M-F 9-5; closed weekends and holidays
ACCESS: by appointment only and upon completion of a background and request form
COPYING FACILITIES: yes

MATERIALS SOLICITED: Materials relating to Henry Shaw and to the fields of horticulture, systematic botany, landscape architecture, plant ecology, and plant geography. Will also accept papers of benefactors and trustees of the Botanical Garden and materials relating to botanical illustration and the history of the Shaw neighborhood.

HOLDINGS:
  Total volume: 550 c.f.
  Inclusive dates: 1450 -
  Description: Photographs, scientific illustrations, blueprints, landscape plans, biographical data, and other papers relating to the history of the Missouri Botanical Garden and properties of its founder, Henry Shaw. Also included are personal and professional papers of botanists, horticulturists, landscape architects, and people in allied fields. Much of the material relates to the scientific exploration of the American West and tropical regions of the world, as well as to local history.

SEE: Hamer; NUCMC, 1971-72.

SEE: Davis; Hinding.

SEE ALSO: The Botanical Garden Archives has published inventories to several collections.

MO810-510

Missouri Historical Society
Archives
Jefferson Memorial Building
Forest Park
St. Louis MO 63112

(314) 361-1424

OPEN: Tu-F 9:30-4:45; closed Sa, Su, M and holidays
USER FEES: $5 per day or $20 per year for nonmembers
COPYING FACILITIES: yes
MATERIALS SOLICITED: Materials pertaining to the history of Missouri and St. Louis: economic, political, social, business, military, aeronautical, literary, blacks, women, native Americans; westward expansion and exploration; early American fur trade; transportation of the Mississippi and Missouri river valleys; Louisiana Purchase Exposition; Lewis and Clark Expedition; American Fur Company; and major local figures.

HOLDINGS:
  Total volume: 2,000,000 items
  Inclusive dates: 1664 -
  Description: Manuscripts emphasizing the post-1750 development of the trans-Mississippi West as it relates to the history of Missouri and St. Louis. The collection covers western exploration, the fur trade, frontier and modern medicine, Missouri politics, military history, women's suffrage, aeronautics, literature, and business. Included are the archives of colonial capitals St. Louis, New Madrid, and St. Charles, containing tax, census, and court records.

SEE: Hamer; NUCMC, 1962-68, 70, 73, 76.

SEE: Schatz; Novotny; Krichmar; Hinding; Robbins; Allard, Crawley, and Edmison; Bean and Vane.

MO810-590

Protestant Episcopal Church
Diocese of Missouri
Diocesan Archives
1210 Locust Street
St. Louis MO 63103

(314) 231-1220

OPEN: M-F 9-5; closed weekends and
holidays
ACCESS: qualified researchers as
determined by interview
COPYING FACILITIES: yes
MATERIALS SOLICITED: Manuscripts,
journals, diaries, and archives of the
Diocese and parish churches.

HOLDINGS:
Total volume: 800 l.f.; 1,120 vols.
Inclusive dates: 1832 -
Description: Papers of bishops of Missouri; official files of letters and personal
histories of clergy serving in the Diocese;
parochial registers of closed and aban-
doned parishes; vestry minute books; financial records; records and registers of
Daniel Sylvester Tuttle, Bishop of Montana, Idaho, and Utah; tapes of interviews relating to Diocesan history and
convention addresses; motion pictures of
summer youth conferences; and archives
of the Metropolitan Church Federation of
Greater St. Louis.

SEE: Hinding.

MO810-600

St. Louis Art Museum
Richardson Memorial Library
Archives Division
Forest Park
St. Louis MO 63110

(314) 721-0067

OPEN: Tu-F 10-4:45; closed Sa, Su, M
and holidays
ACCESS: by prior arrangement with
Librarian or Archivist
COPYING FACILITIES: yes
MATERIALS SOLICITED: Material relating
to the history of the St. Louis School
and Museum, of Fine Arts, the City
Art Museum, and the St. Louis Art
Museum. Will also accept documents
of research value on the development
of the fine arts in the St. Louis area
and the Fine Arts Department of the
1904 St. Louis World's Fair.

HOLDINGS:
Total volume: 900 l.f.
Inclusive dates: 1879 -
Description: Records and correspondence of the St. Louis Art Museum and
its predecessors, the St. Louis School and
Museum of Fine Arts, and the City Art
Museum. Also included are account
books and business and financial records;
records of exhibitions; material relating to
the Fine Arts Department of Louisiana
Purchase Exposition (1904 St. Louis
World's Fair); plans, blueprints, and photographs of the Art Museum building;
and tape recordings of lectures and other
events associated with the Art Museum.

MO810-630

St. Louis Mercantile Library
Association
510 Locust Street
St. Louis MO

MAILING ADDRESS:
P.O. Box 633
St. Louis MO 63188

(314) 621-0670

OPEN: by appointment only

SEE: Hamer; NUCMC, 1966.

Questionnaire not returned.

MO810-650

St. Louis Metropolitan Medical
Society
St. Louis Society for Medical and
Scientific Education
St. Louis Medical Museum
Oak Knoll Park
Clayton MO 63105

(314) 726-2888

OPEN: M-F 8:30-5; closed weekends and
holidays
COPYING FACILITIES: yes
MATERIALS SOLICITED: Materials relating
to history of medicine in St. Louis and
entire state of Missouri and the history
of the St. Louis City and County Medical Societies.

HOLDINGS:
Total volume: 6,000 items
Inclusive dates: 1835 -
Description: Records relating to the
history of medicine in Missouri, especially in St. Louis, including photographs
and records of local medical organizations and medical schools.

MO810-670

St. Louis Post-Dispatch
Reference Department
900 North Tucker Boulevard
St. Louis MO 63101

(314) 622-7536

OPEN: M-F 9-4; closed holidays and
weekends
USER FEES: $25 per hour research fee
ACCESS: appointment by telephone
required
COPYING FACILITIES: no
MATERIALS SOLICITED: Historical pho-
tographs of metropolitan area.

HOLDINGS:
Total volume: 2,000,000 items
Inclusive dates: 1900 -
Description: Photographic collection relating chiefly to the St. Louis area, including buildings, landmarks, streets, trolleys,
costumes, etc.

MO810-690

St. Louis Public Library
Gardner Rare Book Room
1301 Olive Street
St. Louis MO 63103

(314) 241-2288, Ext. 381

OPEN: M 3-7, Tu-Th 12-3, 1st and 3rd F
12-3, 2nd and 4th Sa 12-3; closed 2nd
and 4th F, 1st and 3rd Sa, Sundays
and holidays
COPYING FACILITIES: yes

HOLDINGS:
Total volume: 200 l.f.
Inclusive dates: 15th century -
Description: Archives of the St. Louis
Public Library; typescripts by authors
Fannie Hurst, George Sterling, and Ba-
bette Deutsch; indenture documents from
17th century England; a 15th century
manuscript French romance; a small col-
lection of material relating to Susan
Blow; and a collection of miscellaneous
American and English letters, 1772-1930,
including items by George Washington,
Samuel Colt, Ulysses S. Grant, and Ed-
ward Everett Hale.

SEE: NUCMC, 1959-61.

SEE: Schatz; Robbins.

MO810-700

St. Louis Science Center
Oak Knoll Park
St. Louis MO 63105

(314) 726-2888

OPEN: M-F 9-5; closed weekends and
holidays
ACCESS: by appointment
COPYING FACILITIES: yes

HOLDINGS:
Total volume: 2 l.f.
Inclusive dates: 1856 - 1941
Description: Council meeting minutes
and other minutes of the St. Louis Acad-
emy of Science.

MO810-730

St. Louis University
Pius XII Memorial Library
Vatican Film Library
3655 West Pine Boulevard
St. Louis MO 63108

(314) 658-3090

OPEN: M-F 8-5; closed weekends and
holidays
COPYING FACILITIES: yes
MATERIALS SOLICITED: Microfilms of
Greek and Latin manuscripts of the
Middle Ages and Renaissance. Color
slides of medieval and Renaissance
manuscript illuminations.

HOLDINGS:
Total volume: 26,194 reels
Inclusive dates: 5th century - 19th
century
Description: Microfilms of Latin,
Greek, Hebrew, Arabic, and Ethiopic
manuscripts from the Vatican Library,
with selected manuscripts from other European and British libraries, all representing numerous phases of Mediterranean
and Western European cultural and in-

tellectual history from classical antiquity to the early 19th century.

Includes microfilms of Jesuit documents from various archives in the western hemisphere and Europe (but no baptismal, marriage, or burial records), relating to North and South America and the Philippines.

SEE: Hamer.

SEE: Robbins; Beers - Southwest.

SEE ALSO: issues of the Library's journal, *Manuscripta*; Harry La Plante, 'The Vatican Microfilm Library: A Bibliography,' *The Catholic Library World* 33 (Dec. 1961); and three articles by Lowrie J. Daly: 'Some Examples of Theological Materials Available on Microfilm,' *Library Trends* 9 (Oct. 1960); 'Manuscripts in Microfilm,' *Library Journal* 86 (Sept. 1961); 'Microfilmed Documents about the Southwest at Saint Louis University,' *Manuscripts* 21 (Fall 1969).

Published and unpublished manuscript catalogs are available at the Vatican Film Library.

The manuscripts relating to the Jesuit order, listed in Hamer, are no longer housed at the repository.

MO810-750

Sisters of St. Joseph of Carondelet
St. Louis Province
Archives Department
6400 Minnesota Avenue
St. Louis MO 63111

(314) 481-8800

OPEN: M-F 9-4 with prior appointment; closed weekends and holidays
USER FEES: variable
COPYING FACILITIES: yes
MATERIALS SOLICITED: Materials relating to the history of the order, including correspondence, diaries, journals, logbooks, account books, business records, financial records, photographs, slides, tapes, literary manuscripts, music scores in manuscript, and manuscript documents. Will also accept archives and noncurrent records of institutions, such as churches, schools, and community groups.

HOLDINGS:
Total volume: 160 boxes
Inclusive dates: 1650 -
Description: A collection focusing on the history and activities of the Sisters of St. Joseph of Carondelet. Included are materials from approximately one hundred houses in eleven states, Japan, South America, and Ghana.

SEE: Hinding.

MO810-760

Sisters of St. Mary of the Third Order of St. Francis
1100 Bellevue Avenue
St. Louis MO 63117

(314) 645-8922, Ext. 250

OPEN: by appointment only
COPYING FACILITIES: yes

HOLDINGS:
Total volume: not specified
Inclusive dates: 1872 -
Description: Correspondence, especially from Superiors General and Rome; histories of the congregations; and annual reports of the Order's hospitals.

SEE: Hinding.

MO810-780

University of Missouri at St. Louis
Archives
Thomas Jefferson Library
St. Louis MO 63121

(314) 553-5143

OPEN: M-F 8-5; closed weekends
ACCESS: permission required
COPYING FACILITIES: yes
MATERIALS SOLICITED: Official records of the University; papers of faculty, students, and administrators; and records of student, faculty, and staff organizations. Will also accept materials relating to the establishment of the University.

HOLDINGS:
Total volume: 400 l.f.
Inclusive dates: 1945 -
Description: Records and papers of faculty, students, and administrators documenting the history of the University, including manuscripts, photographs, tape records, official publications and reports, serials, and memorabilia.

SEE: Hinding.

MO810-800

University of Missouri at St. Louis
Joint Collection
University of Missouri Western Historical Manuscript Collection
and
State Historical Society of Missouri Manuscripts
Thomas Jefferson Library
St. Louis MO 63121

(314) 553-5143

OPEN: M, W-F 8-5, Tu 8-9; closed weekends, holidays, and breaks
ACCESS: permission required for use of University Archives material
COPYING FACILITIES: yes
MATERIALS SOLICITED: St. Louis and Missouri history, including immigration, urban development, politics, education, voluntary organizations, businesses, blacks, and women. Will also accept materials in similar areas in American history.

HOLDINGS:
Total volume: 4,000 l.f.
Inclusive dates: 1809 -
Description: Papers of Missouri individuals and records of organizations involved in politics, civil rights, education, religion, feminism, socialism, ecology, consumerism, business, and labor.

SEE: NUCMC, 77-78, 80.

SEE: Hinding.

SEE ALSO: Alan M. Meckler and Ruth McMullin, comps., *Oral History Collections* (Bowker, 1975); Irene E. Cortinovis, 'Documenting an Event with Manuscripts and Oral History: The St. Louis Teachers' Strike, 1973,' *Oral History Review* (1974); Margaret Sullivan, 'Into Community Classrooms: Another Use for Oral History,' *Oral History Review* (1974).

MO810-880

Washington University
Gallery of Art
St. Louis MO 63130

(314) 889-5385, 5490

OPEN: Th afternoons; other times by appointment
COPYING FACILITIES: yes
MATERIALS SOLICITED: Original manuscripts and correspondence relating to the history of the Gallery, its collection and patrons.

HOLDINGS:
Total volume: 2,500 items
Inclusive dates: 1904 - 1969
Description: Letters concerning works of art, written by Jules Breton, Harriet Hosmer, and Tom Wesselman; photographs, slides, negatives of art work in the collection; and annotated bibliography of history of the Gallery.

SEE: Novotny.

MO810-920

Washington University
Libraries
Department of Rare Books and Special Collections
John M. Olin Library
Lindell and Skinker Boulevards
St. Louis MO

MAILING ADDRESS:
Campus Box 1061
St. Louis MO 63130

(314) 889-5413

OPEN: M-F 8:30-5; closed weekends and holidays
ACCESS: open to bona fide researchers
COPYING FACILITIES: yes
MATERIALS SOLICITED: Literary papers of selected American and British contemporary authors and literary groups, and papers of persons significant in the history of 20th century printing, with emphasis on the modern private press and the book arts. Will also accept historical papers relating to the St. Louis area in the 18th and 19th centuries; 19th and 20th century materials documenting Pierre de Ronsard and his literary circle in France; and documents of or relating to 19th century British and American literary and political figures.

HOLDINGS:
Total volume: 52,700 items
Inclusive dates: 1660 -
Description: Manuscript collections, chiefly of the 19th and 20th centuries, documenting literary activity in the United States and Great Britain and centering on the personal papers of authors and the

records of literary organizations and small publishing firms. Included are correspondence, notebooks, poetry worksheets, prose drafts, proof materials, ephemera, and audiotape recordings. Additional materials relate to 20th century book arts and to St. Louis area history.

SEE: Hamer; NUCMC, 1959-62, 68-72, 74, 76-77, 80.

SEE: Schatz; Robbins.

SEE ALSO: William Matheson, 'An Approach to Special Collections,' *American Libraries* (Dec. 1971); *Checklist of Audiotape Recordings in the John M. Olin Library,* Washington University Library Studies No. 14 (Washington Univ., 1975); Walter Schatz, ed., *Directory of Afro-American Resources* (Bowker, 1970).

MO810-940
Washington University
Libraries
University Archives and Research
  Collection
John M. Olin Library
Lindell and Skinker Boulevards
St. Louis MO 63130

(314) 889-5444

OPEN: M-F 8:30-5; closed weekends and holidays
ACCESS: open to bona fide researchers
COPYING FACILITIES: yes
MATERIALS SOLICITED: University records, including archives of student and alumni organizations; personal and professional papers of University trustees, administrators, and faculty members; papers of 20th century political figures; and records of local organizations and businesses. Will also accept related photographs, architectural and engineering drawings, maps, and audiovisual materials.

HOLDINGS:
> *Total volume:* 3,000 c.f.
> *Inclusive dates:* 1853 -
> *Description:* Materials focusing on political, business, and social welfare history in the St. Louis metropolitan area in the 20th century. Included are local government records, records of Washington University and other private institutions, and memoirs, diaries, and other private papers. The collections document community and governmental relations, regional planning, women's suffrage, the history of science, higher education, student protest movements, anti-war and anti-draft campaigns, civil rights activities of the St. Louis black community, and military, engineering, architectural, and transportation history.

SEE: Meckler and McMullin.

SEE ALSO: Missouri Urban Studies Group *Newsletter* 2 (May 1973); *Checklist of Audiotape Recordings in the John M. Olin Library,* Washington University Library Studies, No. 14 (Washington Univ., 1975); Joan Nelson Warnow, *A Selection of Manuscript Collections at*

American Repositories (American Institute of Physics, 1969); Albert Krichmar, *The Women's Rights Movement in the United States, 1848-1970: A Bibliography and Sourcebook* (Scarecrow Press, 1972).

MO810-960
Washington University
School of Medicine
Library
Archives
615 South Taylor Street
St. Louis MO

MAILING ADDRESS:
660 S. Euclid Avenue
St. Louis MO 63110

(314) 534-0643

OPEN: M-F 8:30-5; closed weekends and holidays
ACCESS: restricted to alumni and students of the School; scientists, historians, and other qualified scholars; and interested researchers with permission
COPYING FACILITIES: yes
MATERIALS SOLICITED: Records of the Washington University School of Medicine, personal papers of its alumni and faculty members, and papers of prominent figures in the history of medicine.

HOLDINGS:
> *Total volume:* 1,200 l.f.
> *Inclusive dates:* 1802 -
> *Description:* Materials relating to the history of medicine; and to the history of the Washington University School of Medicine, its faculty members, alumni, and students; and the University Medical Center. Holdings include correspondence, records, photographs, sound recordings, maps, and microfilmed materials.

GUIDES: *Guide to the Archival Collections in the Library of the Washington University School of Medicine* (1974).

SEE: Hamer; NUCMC, 1959-61, 65, 68, 76.

SEE: Hinding.

SEE ALSO: Phoebe A. Cassidy and Robert S. Sokol, comps., *Index to the Wm. Beaumont, M.D. (1785-1853) Manuscript Collection* (Washington Univ. Libraries, Library of the School of Medicine, 1968); Alan M. Meckler and Ruth McMullin, comps., *Oral History Collections* (Bowker, 1975).

SALISBURY

MO830-120
Chariton County Historical Society
115 E. 2nd Street
Salisbury MO 65281

(816) 388-5338

OPEN: May 31-Oct. 31, Sa, Su 2-4; other times by appointment only
COPYING FACILITIES: no

HOLDINGS:
> *Total volume:* not specified
> *Inclusive dates:* late 19th century -
> *Description:* Oral histories of early 20th century citizens; research papers on one-room schools, late 19th and early 20th century; family histories of early settlers; a photograph collection; a catalog of family, church, and city cemeteries in the county; and documents and maps concerning Missouri history, with emphasis on rural prairie life.

STOUTSVILLE

MO870-520
Mark Twain Birthplace State Historic
  Site
Route 1
Stoutsville MO 65283

(314) 565-3449

OPEN: Su 12-5, M-Sa 10-4; closed New Year's, Easter, Thanksgiving, and Christmas.
USER FEES: fifty cents, adults; twenty-five cents, children 6 to 12
COPYING FACILITIES: no
MATERIALS SOLICITED: First editions of Twain's works or original photographs of Twain and family.

HOLDINGS:
> *Total volume:* 110 items
> *Inclusive dates:* 1850 - 1970
> *Description:* The original manuscript of *The Adventures of Tom Sawyer*, the contract for its publication; 30 photographs of Twain, his family, and his associates; steamboat memorabilia; inventions by Twain; and first editions and published critiques.

SEE: NUCMC, 1962.

SEE: Robbins.

UNITY VILLAGE

MO894-800
Unity School of Christianity
Library
Unity Village MO 64065

(816) 524-3550

OPEN: M, Tu, Th 8-5, W 8-noon, F 8-4:30; closed weekends and holidays
COPYING FACILITIES: yes
MATERIALS SOLICITED: Materials relating to New Thought, conduct of life, mental healing, and suggestive therapeutics. Will also accept materials relating to Christian Science.

HOLDINGS:
> *Total volume:* 40,000 items
> *Inclusive dates:* 1866 -
> *Description:* Archives of Unity School of Christianity, which began as a liberal Christian movement in 1889, and the archives of the International New Thought Alliance.

VERSAILLES

MO902-520
Morgan County Historical Society
120 North Monroe Street
Versailles MO 65084

no telephone

OPEN: M-Sa 1-5 June-Sept.; closed
Sundays and holidays
ACCESS: appointment required
COPYING FACILITIES: yes
MATERIALS SOLICITED: Will accept materials pertaining to the history of Morgan County.

HOLDINGS:
Total volume: not specified
Inclusive dates: 1823 -
Description: Local history materials, including 30 hotel registers, chiefly dating after 1900; World War I photographs; a church ledger; post office record books; and teachers' daily registers from the 19th century.

WARRENSBURG

MO920-120
Central Missouri University
Ward Edwards Library
Special Collections
Warrensburg MO 64093

(816) 429-4148, 4154

OPEN: M-F 7:30-10:30, Sa 9-5, Su 2-10:30; closed holidays
COPYING FACILITIES: yes
MATERIALS SOLICITED: Will accept materials that strengthen the University's curriculum.

HOLDINGS:
Total volume: 21 items
Inclusive dates: 1855 - 1950's
Description: Letters between the Buckley and Pelot families of Sweet Springs, MO (1855-65); Civil War period letters of Isaac Adair; and the manuscript of Loula Grace Erdman's novel, *Separate Star.*

MONTANA

Montana does not have a statewide program for preserving local public records. Permanently valuable county and municipal records normally remain in the custody of local officials.

BILLINGS

MT100-200
Eastern Montana College
Library
Special Collections
Billings MT 59101

(406) 657-2262

OPEN: M-F by appointment only; closed weekends and holidays
COPYING FACILITIES: yes
MATERIALS SOLICITED: Materials related to the history of eastern Montana.

HOLDINGS:
> *Total volume:* 15,000 items
> *Inclusive dates:* 1855 -
> *Description:* Correspondence, ledgers, orders, photographs, diaries, maps, and reports of George Armstrong Custer, Edward Settle Godfrey, Francis Marion Gibson, Donald McIntosh, Simon Snyder, and James M. DeWolf, army officers; David F. Barry, photographer; Charles A. DeWar, civil engineer and surveyor; Fred Dustin, archaeologist and historian; Willard E. Fraser, anthropologist and Mayor of Billings; Glen Hallam, labor leader, American Federation of State, County, and Municipal Employees; and Laura Bell Clark Yegen.
> Also included are a ledger of the Billings Bridge Company; correspondence of the Crow Agency, Bureau of Indian Affairs; and records of the U.S. Army 7th Cavalry.

SEE: NUCMC, 1978.

SEE: Hinding.

BOZEMAN

MT130-535
Montana State University
Roland R. Renne Library
Archives
Renne Library
Bozeman MT 59717

(406) 994-4243

OPEN: M-F 1-5; closed weekends and holidays
COPYING FACILITIES: yes

MATERIALS SOLICITED: Records and publications of Montana State University, the Montana Agricultural Experiment Station, and the Montana Extension Service.

HOLDINGS:
> *Total volume:* 4,500 c.f.
> *Inclusive dates:* 1893 -
> *Description:* Archives of Montana State University, including the Montana Agricultural Experiment Station and the Montana Extension Service. Much material relates to the agricultural history of the State. Papers of some faculty members are also included.

SEE: Hinding.

SEE ALSO: Brian Cockhill and Dale L. Johnson, eds., *Guide to Manuscripts in Montana Repositories* (Univ. of Montana Library, 1973).

MT130-540
Montana State University
Library
Special Collections
Bozeman MT 59715

(406) 994-4242

OPEN: M-F 8-5; closed weekends and holidays
COPYING FACILITIES: yes
MATERIALS SOLICITED: Materials relating to Montana local history; agriculture and agricultural business; Yellowstone National Park; and Montana Indian culture. Will also accept materials relating to Abraham Lincoln; children's literature; and literature of the Northwest.

HOLDINGS:
> *Total volume:* 1,390 collections
> *Inclusive dates:* 1865 -
> *Description:* A collection relating to the history of Montana and Yellowstone National Park, including Indians, the fur trade, the livestock industry, agriculture, mining, and the environment.

SEE: NUCMC, 1967, 71, 79.

SEE: Davis; Parkinson; Svoboda and Dunning; Hinding.

SEE ALSO: Alan M. Meckler and Ruth McMullin, comps., *Oral History Collections* (Bowker, 1975); Brian Cockhill and Dale L. Johnson, eds., *Guide to Manuscripts in Montana Repositories* (Univ. of Montana Library, 1973); Terry Abraham, comp., *A Union List of the Papers of Members of Congress from the Pacific Northwest* (Washington State Univ. Library, 1976).

CASCADE

MT180-880
Wedsworth Memorial Library
9 1/2 Front Street North
Cascade MT 59421

(406) 468-2848

OPEN: M 9-noon, 3-9, Tu 9-5, W 2-5, Th, F 3-5; closed weekends and holidays
COPYING FACILITIES: yes
MATERIALS SOLICITED: Photographs, account books, correspondence, diaries, journals, and logbooks. Will also accept all material of a historical nature, including photographs and business histories.

HOLDINGS:
> *Total volume:* not specified
> *Inclusive dates:* 1890's -
> *Description:* Primarily photographs of early Cascade, especially buildings, street scenes, and people.

SEE: Winroth.

CROW AGENCY

MT270-130
Custer Battlefield National Monument
Crow Agency MT

MAILING ADDRESS:
P.O. Box 39
Crow Agency MT 59022

(406) 638-2622

OPEN: M-F 8-4:30; closed weekends, Thanksgiving, Christmas, and New Year's
ACCESS: advance arrangements required
COPYING FACILITIES: yes
MATERIALS SOLICITED: Items of the 7th Cavalry, 1870's; Little Big Horn and Plains Indian items.

HOLDINGS:
> *Total volume:* 7,400 items
> *Inclusive dates:* 1850 - 1930
> *Description:* Over 7,000 museum items associated with the Battle of the Little Big Horn and the persons involved; includes the Elizabeth B. Custer Collection of photographs, clothing, and correspondence associated with her husband's military career; 7th Cavalry documents of the 1870's; and records of organizations, papers of individuals, unpublished memoirs and histories, collections of ephemera, and audio-visual materials.

SEE: Hamer; NUCMC, 1966.

SEE: Winroth.

GREAT FALLS

MT430-320

Historic Landmark Society of
  Montana
501 Ford Building
Great Falls MT

MAILING ADDRESS:
Box 1653
Great Falls MT 59401

no telephone

OPEN: by appointment only
COPYING FACILITIES: no
MATERIALS SOLICITED: Material dealing
  with early history of Montana, especially the region around Virginia City.
  Will accept other material relating to
  Montana, railroads, automatic musical
  instruments, advertising items, and grocery items.

HOLDINGS:
  Total volume: 300 c.f.
  Inclusive dates: 1863 - 1920
  Description: Letters (1863-1900) sent
  to Virginia City and other early Montana
  towns; indexes to these letters; records of
  the Elling Bank, and ledgers and account
  books of the S. R. Buford Company and
  other Virginia City businesses; merchan-
  dise catalogs; and other related advertising, business, and personal letters.

SEE: Winroth.

HELENA

MT530-500

Montana Historical Society
Division of Archives and Manuscripts
225 North Roberts Street
Helena MT 59601

(406) 444-2694

OPEN: M-F 8-5, Sa 10-5; closed Sundays
  and holidays
COPYING FACILITIES: yes
MATERIALS SOLICITED: Materials relating
  to Montana, the Pacific Northwest, and
  the northern Plains, with particular emphasis on political, social, and cultural
  activities of the post-1910 era. Will
  also accept materials outside normal
  areas of acquisition to ensure preservation if a collection appears in danger of
  destruction or damage.

HOLDINGS:
  Total volume: 10,000 c.f.; 70,000
  photographs; 600 maps
  Inclusive dates: 1806 -
  Description: Materials relating to Montana, the northern Rocky Mountain and
  Plains regions, and the Pacific Northwest.
  Included are materials on emigrant travel,
  mining, livestock raising and agriculture,
  banking, politics, freighting, merchandising, Indian relations, the military, the fur
  trade, government, business, and natural
  resources utilization. In addition to
  manuscript collections, the Society also
  houses the State archives.

SEE: Hamer; NUCMC, 1971-72, 79.

SEE: Davis; Robbins; Hinding; Winroth;
  Parkinson; Svoboda and Dunning.

SEE ALSO: Brian Cockhill and Dale L.
  Johnson, eds., *Guide to Manuscripts in
  Montana Repositories* (Univ. of Mon-
  tana Library, 1973); Albert Krichmar,
  *The Women's Rights Movement in the
  United States, 1848-1970: A Bibliography and Sourcebook* (Scarecrow Press,
  1972); Ann Novotny, ed., *Picture
  Sources 3* (Special Libraries Assn.,
  1975); Jeffrey J. Safford, 'The Montana
  Livestock Industry Through Oral History,' *Agricultural History* 49 (Jan.
  1975); Terry Abraham, comp., *A Union
  List of the Papers of Members of Congress from the Pacific Northwest*
  (Washington State Univ. Library,
  1976); descriptions of holdings in *Montana: The Magazine of Western History*, 1951 - .

MT530-690

Roman Catholic Diocese of Helena
515 N. Ewing
Helena MT

MAILING ADDRESS:
P.O. Box 1729
Helena MT 59601

(406) 442-5820

OPEN: M-F 9-4; closed weekends and
  holidays
ACCESS: advance arrangements required
COPYING FACILITIES: yes
MATERIALS SOLICITED: Parish and in-
  stitution records and correspondence.
  Will also accept material relating to the
  Roman Catholic church in the area.

HOLDINGS:
  Total volume: not specified
  Inclusive dates: 1884 -
  Description: Records of the Roman
  Catholic Diocese of Helena, including
  records of parishes and institutions (some
  on microfilm), correspondence of bishops, diaries of priests, and general historical data on Montana relating to the Roman Catholic church.

MISSOULA

MT700-800

University of Montana
Library
Missoula MT 59812

(406) 243-2053

OPEN: M-F 8-5, Sa 12-6, Su-Th 7-9
  when classes in session; M-F 8-5 other
  times of year; closed holidays
COPYING FACILITIES: yes
MATERIALS SOLICITED: Visual and
  manuscript materials relating to Montana's past, including archives of the
  University and of community groups;
  business records; political papers; and
  manuscript materials of Montana authors. Will also accept related oral histories and microforms of privately held
  manuscript collections.

HOLDINGS:
  Total volume: 7,250 l.f.; 20,000
  photographs
  Inclusive dates: 1860 -
  Description: Archives of the University
  of Montana and manuscript collections
  covering the political, business, and social
  history of Montana in the 20th century,
  with emphasis on western Montana.

SEE: Hamer (as Montana State University); NUCMC, 1971, 73, 78.

SEE: Hinding; Robbins; Winroth; Svoboda
  and Dunning.

SEE ALSO: Brian Cockhill and Dale L.
  Johnson, comps., *Guide to Manuscripts
  in Montana Repositories* (Univ. of
  Montana Library, 1973); Alan M.
  Meckler and Ruth McMullin, comps.,
  Oral History Collections (Bowker,
  1975); Terry Abraham, comp., *A Union
  List of the Papers of Members of Congress from the Pacific Northwest*
  (Washington State Univ. Library,
  1976); Richard C. Davis, *North American Forest History: A Guide to Archives
  and Manuscripts in the United States
  and Canada* (Clio Books, 1977).

RICHEY

MT750-690

Richey Historical Society
Richey Museum
Richey MT

MAILING ADDRESS:
Box 218
Richey MT 59259

no telephone

OPEN: daily 2-5 (Su by appointment);
  closed Christmas, New Year's, July 4
COPYING FACILITIES: no
MATERIALS SOLICITED: History of home-
  steaders in the Richey area of Dawson
  County, MT. Will also accept maps,
  charts, account books, and scrapbooks.

HOLDINGS:
  Total volume: 5 l.f.
  Inclusive dates: 1913 - 1975
  Description: Biographies of homestead-
  ers of Dawson and Richland counties,
  MT; photographs; school records; oral
  histories of local residents; and scrap-
  books.

WEST GLACIER

MT870-280

Glacier National Park
The George C. Ruhle Library
West Glacier MT 59936

(406) 888-5441, Ext. 302

OPEN: M-F 8-4:30; closed weekends and
  holidays
ACCESS: serious researchers, Park
  employees, and local residents
COPYING FACILITIES: yes

HOLDINGS:
   Total volume: 12 file drawers
   Inclusive dates: 1880's -
   Description: Materials dealing with the administration, history, and natural history of Glacier National Park, comprised chiefly of reports by superintendents, rangers, and other officials and agencies.

SEE: Hamer.

SEE: Davis; Winroth.

NEBRASKA

In 1969 the State Archives Division of the Nebraska State Historical Society assumed responsibility for the archival preservation of local government records in that State. Local public agencies normally retain custody of such permanently significant records as deeds and probate records, but the Archives Division has accessioned many court, tax, and other records, primarily of counties. Microfilm copies of selected records also are available at the Archives Division in Lincoln. The Division will furnish copies of finding aids to specific series upon request.

ALLIANCE

NE32-40
Alliance Knight Museum
908 Yellowstone
Alliance NE 69301

(308) 762-2384

OPEN: M-Sa 10-5, Su 2-5; closed Nov. 1-Apr. 30
ACCESS: serious researchers
COPYING FACILITIES: yes
MATERIALS SOLICITED: Materials on the Box Butte County area, including information on families, records of businesses and other organizations, and oral histories, particularly concerning Alliance, Hemingford, and early cities of the area. Will also accept maps, charts, drawings, photographs, and scrapbooks.

HOLDINGS:
  Total volume: 10 l.f.
  Inclusive dates: 1885 -
  Description: Photographs; oral histories; and records of local schools, churches, and organizations.

BELVIDERE

NE112-760
Thayer County Historical Museum
Belvidere NE 68315

(402) 768-2147

OPEN: Su, W 2-5; other days by appointment
COPYING FACILITIES: no
MATERIALS SOLICITED: Materials relating to Thayer County and Nebraska.

HOLDINGS:
  Total volume: 300 items
  Inclusive dates: 1865 -
  Description: Materials reflecting the history of Thayer County, including a large photograph collection, a few oral history interviews, and record books of businesses, schools, churches, doctors, veterinarians, women's clubs, and the Woman's Christian Temperance Union.

BLAIR

NE144-160
Dana College
C. A. Dana - LIFE Library
Blair NE 68008

(402) 426-4101, Ext. 119

OPEN: Su 3-10, M-Th 8-11, F 8-5, Sa 9-4; closed College holidays and vacations
COPYING FACILITIES: yes
MATERIALS SOLICITED: Materials pertaining to Danish-Americans, Dana College, and local oral history. Will also accept materials relating to the history of the United Danish Evangelical Lutheran church.

HOLDINGS:
  Total volume: 45 cassette tapes
  Inclusive dates: 1973 -
  Description: A collection of oral history interviews dealing with Dana College, local history, and Danish-American immigration.

SEE: Meckler and McMullin.

CENTRAL CITY

NE224-520
Merrick County Historical Museum
Central City NE

MAILING ADDRESS:
c/o T.C. Reeves
Rte 1, Box 64
Central City NE 68826

(308) 946-3309

OPEN: M, Tu 10-4, daily afternoons until 4
USER FEES: donations accepted
COPYING FACILITIES: no
MATERIALS SOLICITED: Copies of land grants, historical photographs of public buildings and families, and other materials relating to the history of Merrick County.

HOLDINGS:
  Total volume: not specified
  Inclusive dates: 1860's -
  Description: Materials relating to the history of Merrick County. Included are 300 photographs, oral history interviews, and scrapbooks.

SEE: Hamer.

CHADRON

NE240-560
Nebraska National Forest
270 Pine Street
Chadron NE 69337

(308) 432-3367

OPEN: M-F 8-5; closed weekends and holidays
COPYING FACILITIES: yes
MATERIALS SOLICITED: History of Nebraska National Forest and Oglala National Grasslands in Nebraska, and Buffalo Gap and Ft. Pierre National Grasslands in South Dakota. Will also accept materials relating to the history of the Great Plains Shelterbelt Program.

HOLDINGS:
  Total volume: 5 c.f.
  Inclusive dates: 1902 -
  Description: A collection of manuscripts, correspondence, financial records, and photographs relating to the establishment of the Nebraska National Forest and Bessey Nursery, the first Federal tree nursery. Included are some reminiscences of early rangers and nursery workers.

CRAWFORD

NE284-560
Nebraska State Historical Society
Fort Robinson Museum
Crawford NE

MAILING ADDRESS:
P.O. Box 304
Crawford NE 69339

(308) 665-2852

OPEN: M-Sa 8-5, Su 1:30-5; closed weekends, holidays, and Nov. 15-Apr. 1
COPYING FACILITIES: yes
MATERIALS SOLICITED: Fort Robinson; Indian Wars, especially pertaining to the Fort Robinson region; photographs; motion pictures depicting military use of Fort Robinson; and oral histories and manuscripts of former military and civilian personnel. Will also accept

items pertaining to the U.S. Army from the Indian Wars through World War II and historic Indian tribes of the region.

HOLDINGS:
Total volume: not specified
Inclusive dates: 1874 -
Description: Maps, charts, and building plans of Fort Robinson; oral histories of former Fort Robinson military and civilian personnel and World War II prisoners of war held at the Fort Robinson Prison Camp; and photographs and motion pictures of Fort Robinson, the Timber Reserve, 1939, and Sioux Indians.

CRETE

NE288-160
Doane College
Perkins Library
College Archives
Crete NE 68333

(402) 826-2161, Ext. 224, 287

OPEN: Su 2-11, M-Th 8-11, F 8-5, Sa 10-5; June-Aug., M-F 8-5; closed Christmas to New Year's and July 4
ACCESS: nonscholarly researchers need permission
COPYING FACILITIES: yes
MATERIALS SOLICITED: Materials relating to Doane College; its predecessors, Tabor and Gates Colleges; its founder, Thomas Doane; its early church sponsor, the United Church of Christ; and the early history of southeast Nebraska.

HOLDINGS:
Total volume: 5,000 items
Inclusive dates: 1872 -
Description: The collection includes audio tapes of former administrators and alumni, diaries, files, minutes, photographs, and other items, all relating to Doane College or its predecessors, Tabor and Gates Colleges; its founder, Thomas Doane; its early church sponsor, the United Church of Christ (Congregational church); or to the early history of southeastern Nebraska.

NE288-400
J-B Publishing Company
430 Ivy Avenue
Crete NE 68333

no telephone

OPEN: by appointment only
ACCESS: written permission is required
COPYING FACILITIES: yes
MATERIALS SOLICITED: Photographs of post offices, locomotives, rolling stock, railroad stations, railroad bridges, and other railroad-related buildings and structures. Will also accept documents related to these subjects.

HOLDINGS:
Total volume: 6,500 photographs and negatives
Inclusive dates: 1960 -
Description: A collection of photographs of post offices, railroad stations, railroad bridges, and other railroad-related structures in North America and Great Britain.

SEE ALSO: a catalog of railroad station photographs available upon request.

ELKHORN

NE320-520
Mount Michael Benedictine Abbey and High School
Elkhorn NE 68022

(402) 289-2541

OPEN: by appointment only
ACCESS: at the discretion of the Archivist
COPYING FACILITIES: yes

HOLDINGS:
Total volume: 16.5 c.f.
Inclusive dates: 1953 -
Description: Papers, documents, and related items concerning the foundation and history of Mount Michael Abbey and Mount Michael High School.

SEE: NUCMC, 1966.

FORT CALHOUN

NE352-880
Washington County Historical Association
Washington County Historical Museum
14th and Monroe Streets
Ft. Calhoun NE 68023

(402) 468-5740

OPEN: Su, W, F, Sa 1:30-4:30, other times by appointment; closed Nov.-Apr.
COPYING FACILITIES: yes
MATERIALS SOLICITED: Family histories.

HOLDINGS:
Total volume: 900 photographs; 800 items
Inclusive dates: 1856 - 1935
Description: Manuscripts relating to Washington County. Included are diaries, letters of pioneers describing area life, account books, business records, a card file of family names, Fort Atkinson records, cemetery and church records, records of women's organizations, school attendance books, and tax assessor books. There are also tapes of interviews with citizens and of community events.

SEE: Hamer; NUCMC, 1963-64.

FREMONT

NE368-160
Dodge County Historical Society
Louis E. May Museum
Library
1643 Nye Avenue
Fremont NE

MAILING ADDRESS:
Box 766
Fremont NE 68025

(402) 721-4515

OPEN: W-Su 1:30-4:30; closed M, Tu and Jan.-Apr.
COPYING FACILITIES: yes
MATERIALS SOLICITED: History of Fremont, Dodge County, and Nebraska.

HOLDINGS:
Total volume: 1,500 photographs and glass negatives
Inclusive dates: 1880 -
Description: Materials relating to Fremont, Dodge County, and Nebraska history. Included are manuscripts by George McVicker dealing with early settlement in the County; hotel registers; county road ledgers and cash ledgers; diaries; and photographs.

SEE: Hamer (in Hooper, NE).

GERING

NE384-560
North Platte Valley Historical Association, Inc.
North Platte Valley Museum
11th and J Streets
Oregon Trail Park
Gering NE

MAILING ADDRESS:
P.O. Box 495
Gering NE 69341

(308) 436-5411

OPEN: May 1 to August 31, M-Sa 8:30-5, Su and holidays 1-5
COPYING FACILITIES: no
MATERIALS SOLICITED: Any materials pertaining to the history of the North Platte Valley and its residents.

HOLDINGS:
Total volume: 150 c.f.
Inclusive dates: 1887 -
Description: Diaries, letters, club minutes, photographs, and other personal writings pertaining to the settlement and development of the North Platte Valley.

GRAND ISLAND

NE416-320
Hall County Historical Society
1720 N. Kruse Street
Grand Island NE 68801

(308) 382-5392

OPEN: by appointment only

SEE: Hamer.

Questionnaire not returned.

NE416-720
Stuhr Museum of the Prairie Pioneer
Stuhr Research Library
3133 West Highway 34
Grand Island NE 68801

(308) 384-1380

OPEN: M-F 9-5, Sa and Su by appointment; closed Christmas and New Year's
ACCESS: special permission required
COPYING FACILITIES: yes

MATERIALS SOLICITED: Materials pertaining to the history of the Great Plains, Nebraska, Hall County, and Grand Island. Will also accept materials relating to individuals of those areas, as well as organization records.

HOLDINGS:
Total volume: 100 l.f.
Inclusive dates: 1840 - 1910
Description: Diaries of early pioneers, church and school records, photographs, and other materials relating to the history of Grand Island and Nebraska.

SEE: Hinding.

HASTINGS

NE496-40
Adams County Historical Society
Archives
1330 North Burlington Avenue
Hastings NE

MAILING ADDRESS:
Box 102
Hastings NE 68901

(402) 463-5838

OPEN: Sa, Su 12-4:45, M-F 9-4:45; closed holidays
COPYING FACILITIES: yes
MATERIALS SOLICITED: Adams County history.

HOLDINGS:
Total volume: 250 c.f.
Inclusive dates: 1871 -
Description: Materials relating to the Great Plains, Nebraska, south central Nebraska, and its people and activities. Present holdings include photographs, motion pictures, records of county organizations, schools and churches, personal papers, and oral history tapes, in addition to inventories.

SEE: Hinding; Svoboda and Dunning.

NE496-330
Hastings Museum
Highway 281 at 14th Street
Hastings NE 68901

(402) 461-2399

SEE: Hamer.

Questionnaire not returned.

LINCOLN

NE560-50
American Old Time Fiddlers
   Association
Fiddling Archive
6141 Morrill Avenue
Lincoln NE 68507

no telephone

OPEN: by appointment only
COPYING FACILITIES: no
MATERIALS SOLICITED: Materials pertaining to the history of fiddle playing in all countries.

HOLDINGS:
Total volume: 41 file drawers
Inclusive dates: 1843 -
Description: Materials relating to fiddlers and their instruments and tunes in all time periods and countries, including sound tapes, discs, photographs, letters, and music.

SEE: Hinding.

NE560-550
Nebraska State Historical Society
State Archives Division
1500 R Street
Lincoln NE

MAILING ADDRESS:
Box 82554
Lincoln NE 68501

(402) 471-3270

OPEN: M-Sa 8-5; closed Sundays and holidays
ACCESS: researcher registration required
COPYING FACILITIES: yes
MATERIALS SOLICITED: Private and institutional manuscripts relating to Nebraska and the Great Plains, and public records from State and local governments. Will also accept photographs and maps.

HOLDINGS:
Total volume: 24,000 c.f.
Inclusive dates: 1854 -
Description: Materials relating to all aspects of Nebraska history. Included are records of State and local government units, held by the Society as the State's official archives, personal papers, institutional records, and business records.

SEE: Hamer; NUCMC, 1963-65, 67, 71, 76, 78, 81.

SEE: Novotny; Schatz; Meckler and McMullin; Hounshell; Krichmar; Davis; Hinding; Robbins; Allard, Crawley, and Edmison; Paszek.

SEE ALSO: *A Guide to The Manuscript Division of the State Archives* (Nebraska State Historical Society, 1974).

NE560-790
United Church of Christ
Nebraska Conference
History and Archives Room
2055 E Street
Lincoln NE 68510

(402) 477-4131

OPEN: M-F 8:30-5, Sa 8:30-12; closed Sundays and holidays
COPYING FACILITIES: yes
MATERIALS SOLICITED: Conference-related materials, including records of defunct churches, histories of churches, papers of pastors and prominent lay people, and records of Conference agencies.

HOLDINGS:
Total volume: 121,126 items; 20 vols.
Inclusive dates: 1855 -
Description: Records of the Nebraska Conference of the United Church of Christ and its associations and defunct churches, as well as related private papers such as diaries and correspondence.

NE560-810
The United Methodist Church
Nebraska Conference
Historical Center
Nebraska Wesleyan University
52nd and St. Paul Street
Lincoln NE

MAILING ADDRESS:
P.O. Box 4553
Lincoln NE 68504

(402) 465-2175

OPEN: M-F 9-noon; closed weekends and holidays
COPYING FACILITIES: yes
MATERIALS SOLICITED: Archives of the United Methodist church and its predecessor denominations in Nebraska, including records of churches, organizations, pastors, and prominent lay persons. Will also accept records of United Methodism and its predecessor denominations outside of Nebraska.

HOLDINGS:
Total volume: 14,000 items
Inclusive dates: 1856 -
Description: Manuscripts, correspondence, and scrapbooks pertaining to members of the Methodist church in Nebraska and their activities; biography files on clergy and prominent lay persons of the Nebraska Conference of the United Methodist church, and historical research papers. Also included are minutes and other records of various churches, conferences, and church related activities, and a photograph collection.

SEE: Hamer (as Methodist Historical Society).

SEE: Hinding.

NE560-860
University of Nebraska at Lincoln
Library
Special Collections Division
Room 308, Love Library
University of Nebraska
Lincoln NE 68588

(402) 472-2531

OPEN: M-F 7:30-4:30; closed weekends and holidays
COPYING FACILITIES: yes
MATERIALS SOLICITED: Materials relating to Czechs and Slovaks outside Czechoslovakia (ethnic group materials) with the emphasis on Czech-Americans and materials relating to American folklore, World War I, World War II, Great Plains, and Nebraska literary figures.

HOLDINGS:
Total volume: 1,000 c.f.
Inclusive dates: 1600 -
Description: Manuscripts and collections of literary figures and folklorists, notably Mari Sandoz and Benjamin Botkin; materials, including tape recordings and other documentation, of Czechs in the United States, particularly in Nebraska; and railroad freight tariffs, 1890-1945.

SEE: Hamer; NUCMC, 1959-61, 68, 72, 80.

SEE: Robbins; Martin; Hinding; Svoboda and Dunning.

SEE ALSO: Elizabeth S. ten Houten, 'Some Collections of Special Use for Women's History Resources in the U.S.,' *American Association of University Women Journal* (April 1974).

NE560-870

University of Nebraska at Lincoln Library
University Archives
Room 308, Love Library
University of Nebraska
Lincoln NE 68588

(402) 472-2531

OPEN: M-F 7:30-4:30; closed weekends and holidays
COPYING FACILITIES: yes
MATERIALS SOLICITED: Materials relating to the University of Nebraska. Will also accept materials relevant to research conducted in University departments.

HOLDINGS:
   Total volume: 3,000 c.f.
   Inclusive dates: 1869 -
   Description: Historical records of the University of Nebraska, including papers of chancellors, administrative records, records of faculty and student organizations, and personal and professional papers of emeriti and alumni in all academic fields.

SEE: NUCMC, 1970, 76.

SEE: Davis; Hinding.

MINDEN

NE592-440

Kearney County Historical Society
Sixth Street and Nebraska Avenue
Minden NE

MAILING ADDRESS:
129 S. Kearney Avenue
Minden NE 68959

(308) 832-2813

OPEN: Sa, Su 2-5; closed other days
COPYING FACILITIES: no
MATERIALS SOLICITED: Kearney County history.

HOLDINGS:
   Total volume: 2 c.f.
   Inclusive dates: 1870's -
   Description: Materials pertaining to the history of Kearney County and its residents, including family histories and pioneer memoirs and reminiscences.

OMAHA

NE624-130

Creighton University
Alumni Memorial Library
2500 California Street
Omaha NE 68178

(402) 280-2705

OPEN: M-F 9-4; closed weekends and holidays
ACCESS: advance arrangements required
COPYING FACILITIES: yes
MATERIALS SOLICITED: Will accept materials of scholarly interest.

HOLDINGS:
   Total volume: 25 l.f.
   Inclusive dates: 1840 - 1941
   Description: A collection of letters, diaries, and records of residents of Holt County, NE, and of John and Edward Creighton, founders of the University.

SEE: NUCMC, 1975.

SEE: Novotny; Martin; Hinding.

NE624-150

The Danish Brotherhood in America
3717 Harney Street
Omaha NE

MAILING ADDRESS:
P.O. Box 31748
Omaha NE 68131

(402) 341-5049

OPEN: M-F 8-4:30 by appointment; closed weekends and holidays
ACCESS: no public access; research done by office personnel on a time available basis
COPYING FACILITIES: no
MATERIALS SOLICITED: Will accept society records, district society records, and lodge records.

HOLDINGS:
   Total volume: 20 l.f.
   Inclusive dates: 1882 -
   Description: Archives of The Danish Brotherhood in America, including accounting records; minutes; the Brotherhood's monthly publication, 1916- ; membership applications; information on members; and records of lodges.

NE624-240

First Central Congregational Church (United Church of Christ)
Church History Collection
421 South 36th Street
Omaha NE 68131

(402) 345-1533

OPEN: M-F 8:30-4:30; summer, M-F 8:30-noon; closed weekends and holidays
ACCESS: appointment required
COPYING FACILITIES: no
MATERIALS SOLICITED: Historical diaries or journals, correspondence, and photographs relating to the establishment and growth of the Congregational denomination in Omaha.

HOLDINGS:
   Total volume: 2 file cabinets
   Inclusive dates: 1856 -
   Description: Handwritten documents and records, as well as photographs of founders and early sites, pertaining to the First Congregational church and other churches that merged to form the First Central Congregational church (United Church of Christ).

NE624-400

Joslyn Art Museum
2200 Dodge Street
Omaha NE 68102

(402) 342-3300

OPEN: Tu-Sa 10-5, Su 1-5; closed Mondays and holidays
ACCESS: prior arrangements should be made
COPYING FACILITIES: yes

HOLDINGS:
   Total volume: 125 items; 815 photographs
   Inclusive dates: 15th century -
   Description: Primarily materials relating to the history of Nebraska, Iowa, and the Great Plains in the 19th century. Included are letters from members of an Iowa family that emigrated to Oregon Territory and California, a journal describing travel on the Missouri River, a Civil War diary, and photographs of American Indians and of Omaha. There are small collections of medieval and Renaissance manuscripts and Sanskrit and Hindi documents.

SEE: Hamer.

SEE ALSO: Ann Novotny, ed., *Picture Sources 3* (Special Libraries Assn., 1975).

NE624-520

Mutual of Omaha Insurance Company
Mutual of Omaha Plaza
Omaha NE 68175

(402) 342-7600

OPEN: M-F 8-4:30; closed weekends and holidays
ACCESS: closed to general public; staff will provide information on request
COPYING FACILITIES: yes
MATERIALS SOLICITED: Records relating to the company, conservation of animal and material resources, and Indians.

HOLDINGS:
   Total volume: 12 5-drawer cabinets; 75 l.f.
   Inclusive dates: 1909 -
   Description: Records relating to Mutual of Omaha and its Wild Kingdom Show.

NE624-620

Omaha Public Library
215 S. 15th Street
Omaha NE 68102

(402) 444-4800

OPEN: M-F 9-8:30, Sa 9-5:30; closed
Sundays, holidays and Tu, F at 5:30
during July-Aug.

SEE: Hamer; NUCMC, 1962.

Questionnaire not returned.

NE624-800

Union Pacific Historical Museum
1416 Dodge Street
Omaha NE 68179

(402) 271-3530

OPEN: M-F 9-5, Sa 9-1; closed Sundays
and holidays
ACCESS: restricted to serious scholars
COPYING FACILITIES: yes
MATERIALS SOLICITED: Will accept materials pertaining to railroads and the
settlement of the West.

HOLDINGS:
  Total volume: 100,000 items;
  additional materials
  Inclusive dates: 1900 -
  Description: Some materials relating to
  Abraham Lincoln, a miscellaneous collection of Union Pacific Railroad records,
  and over 100,000 photographs and slides
  relating to railroads and various aspects
  of the American West and Midwest.

SEE: Hamer.

SEE: Novotny.

Most of the papers described in
Hamer have been transferred to the
Nebraska State Historical Society in
Lincoln.

NE624-830

University of Nebraska
Medical Center
Library of Medicine
42nd and Dewey Avenue
Omaha NE 68105

(402) 559-7091

OPEN: by appointment only
COPYING FACILITIES: yes
MATERIALS SOLICITED: Materials per-
taining to Nebraska medical history.
Will also accept materials relating to
the history of medicine.

HOLDINGS:
  Total volume: 170 l.f.
  Inclusive dates: 1854 -
  Description: A collection of manuscripts relating to medical education and
  practice in Nebraska. Included are correspondence files, logbooks, financial
  records and photographs, as well as
  noncurrent records of the University of
  Nebraska Medical Center and its predecessor, the Omaha Medical College.

SEE: Hinding.

PILGER

NE712-760

Stanton County Museum
N. Main Street
Pilger NE 68768

no telephone

OPEN: June - Aug., Su 2-4; others times
by appointment
COPYING FACILITIES: no
MATERIALS SOLICITED: Materials relating
to Stanton County, including account
books, business records, public documents, church records, school records,
county government records, and oral
history tapes of pioneer families.

HOLDINGS:
  Total volume: not specified
  Inclusive dates: 1880's -
  Description: Collections relating to the
history of Stanton County.

PLATTSMOUTH

NE720-120

Cass County Historical Society
Museum
666 Main Street
Plattsmouth NE 68048

(402) 296-4770

OPEN: M, Tu, Th, F 9-5, Sa, Su 2-5;
closed Wednesdays and holidays
COPYING FACILITIES: no
MATERIALS SOLICITED: Will accept ma-
terials relating to the history of Cass
County.

HOLDINGS:
  Total volume: 6 l.f.
  Inclusive dates: 1853 -
  Description: Land grant papers, town
histories, pioneer reminiscences, family
histories, photographs, public school
records, tax records, personal and business papers and letters, autograph books,
scrapbooks, and other materials pertaining to the history of Cass County and its
residents.

RED CLOUD

NE736-560

Nebraska State Historical Society
Willa Cather Historical Center
338 North Webster Street
Red Cloud NE 68970

(402) 746-3285

OPEN: M-Sa 8-5, Su 1:30-5; closed
Christmas, New Year's, Thanksgiving
ACCESS: advance arrangements suggested
COPYING FACILITIES: yes
MATERIALS SOLICITED: Will accept ma-
terials relating to Willa Cather's life
and writings. Will also accept materials
relating to Red Cloud and Webster
County, NE.

HOLDINGS:
  Total volume: 4,000 items
  Inclusive dates: 1873 -
  Description: 400 letters, about half by
Willa Cather and the remainder written
to or about her, including about 110 by
Carrie Miner Sherwood. There are also
20 unpublished studies of Willa Cather,
1,600 photographs, and films about Cath-
er. Also included are extensive clippings,
papers, and ephemera relating to Red
Cloud history.

SEE: Hinding; Robbins; Svoboda and
Dunning.

SEWARD

NE800-110

Concordia Teachers College
Archives
800 North Columbia Avenue
Seward NE 68434

(402) 643-3651, Ext. 7257

OPEN: by appointment only
COPYING FACILITIES: yes
MATERIALS SOLICITED: College publications; photographs; materials relating to
student activities, concerts, and recit-
als; faculty publications; materials on
faculty activities; and interviews with
former students. Will also accept materials pertinent to the history of the
College.

HOLDINGS:
  Total volume: 50 l.f.
  Inclusive dates: 1894 -
  Description: Materials pertaining to the
history of Concordia Teachers College,
including College and student publications, materials relating to student and
faculty activities, and tape recorded interviews and papers of former faculty members.

NE800-480

Lutheran Church - Missouri Synod
Nebraska District
Archives
152 South Columbia
Box 407
Seward NE 68434

(402) 643-2961

OPEN: M-F 8-5 by appointment; closed
weekends and holidays
COPYING FACILITIES: yes
MATERIALS SOLICITED: Historical materials relating to Nebraska District congregations, officials, boards, publications, and agencies. Will also accept
records of disbanded congregations.

HOLDINGS:
  Total volume: not specified
  Inclusive dates: 1844 -
  Description: Materials relating to the
Nebraska District, including congregation
files, church records, biographies and lists
of professional church workers, records of
district officials and boards, and district
convention proceedings. There are also

materials pertaining to social agencies, Concordia Teachers College, the Lutheran Laymen's League, the Lutheran Women's Missionary League, and the Walther League.

NEVADA

Since 1977 the Division of Archives has administered a statewide program for scheduling local government records, according to Nevada Revised Statutes 239.125, Sub Section 2. Most permanently valuable county and municipal records have remained in the custody of local officials, but the State Archives does have significant holdings of county records dating from the mid-19th century.

CARSON CITY

NV90-530
Nevada State Library
Division of State, County, and
  Municipal Archives
101 South Fall Street
Capitol Complex
Carson City NV 89710

(702) 885-5210

OPEN: M-F 8-5; closed weekends and holidays
COPYING FACILITIES: yes
MATERIALS SOLICITED: State, county, and city government records. Will also accept materials relating to government representatives, employees, or officials.

HOLDINGS:
  Total volume: 6,900 c.f.
  Inclusive dates: 1851 -
  Description: State, county, and city government archives of Nevada, as well as materials relating to government representatives, officials, and employees. Among the holdings are governors' records; records of State agencies; various military records relating to U.S. military posts in Nevada, as well as Nevada servicemen; State Supreme Court documents; miscellaneous county records; and personal papers, such as the Walter S. Baring and Patrick McCarran collections.

GUIDES: *A Guide to the Collections and Records: State, County and Municipal Archives* (1974).

SEE: Hinding; Armstrong.

SEE ALSO: Frederick C. Gale, 'The Nevada State, County and Municipal Archives,' *Intermountain Archivist* (June 1976).

The Baring and McCarran collections have recently been transferred to the Nevada Historical Society in Reno, NV.

EAST ELY

NV200-920
White Pine County Historical Society
11th and A Avenue
Nevada Northern Depot
East Ely NV

MAILING ADDRESS:
P.O. Box 1117
Ely NV 89301

(702) 235-7504

OPEN: by appointment only
COPYING FACILITIES: no
MATERIALS SOLICITED: Nineteenth century photographs of gold and silver boom camps of Nevada. Will also accept other materials relating to Nevada history.

HOLDINGS:
  Total volume: not specified
  Inclusive dates: 1860 -
  Description: Materials relating to White Pine County, including several hundred photographs, slides on the county's gold and silver boom camps, and card index files for county newspapers.

ELKO

NV270-560
Northeastern Nevada Museum
1515 Idaho Street
Elko NV

MAILING ADDRESS:
P.O. Box 2550
Elko NV 89801

(702) 738-3418

OPEN: M-Sa 9-5, Su 1-5; closed Thanksgiving, Christmas, and New Year's
ACCESS: serious researchers
COPYING FACILITIES: yes
MATERIALS SOLICITED: Material relating to northeastern Nevada. Will also accept materials relating to the West.

HOLDINGS:
  Total volume: 7,162 items
  Inclusive dates: 1840 -
  Description: Materials relating to northeastern Nevada. Included are documents; unpublished manuscripts on northeastern Nevada history; photographs, negatives, and slides, including such subjects as mining camps, railroads, and ranching; oral history tapes of area pioneers; and manuscript maps, charts, and blueprints.

SEE: Hinding.

FALLON

NV450-120
Churchill County Museum and
  Archives
1050 South Maine Street
Fallon NV 89406

(702) 423-3677

OPEN: M-W, Sa 9-4; closed Th, F, Su and holidays
ACCESS: advance arrangements requested
COPYING FACILITIES: yes
MATERIALS SOLICITED: Materials relating to the development of Churchill County and northern Nevada.

HOLDINGS:
  Total volume: 200 c.f.
  Inclusive dates: 1860 -
  Description: Northern and central Nevada material, including business and financial records; correspondence; unpublished oral history transcriptions; uncataloged papers from a variety of mines and mills; records of Harmony Social Club, Veterans of Foreign Wars, and other local organizations; and records of the Newlands Reclamation Project, 1904-20. Also included are public records of Churchill County and documents from the city of Fallon. The photograph archive includes over 1,000 catalogued photographs.

SEE: Armstrong.

LAS VEGAS

NV630-800
University of Nevada at Las Vegas
James Dickinson Library
Special Collections Department
4505 Maryland Parkway
Las Vegas NV 89154

(702) 739-3252

OPEN: M-F 9-4:30; closed weekends and holidays
COPYING FACILITIES: yes
MATERIALS SOLICITED: Materials relating to gambling and Nevada history, and the archives of the University of Nevada at Las Vegas.

HOLDINGS:
  Total volume: 250 l.f.
  Inclusive dates: 19th century -
  Description: Materials relating to gambling and similar activities in both the United States and abroad; materials on Nevada, particularly the southern part of the State, including photographs, oral histories, maps, manuscripts, and motion

pictures; and the archives of the University of Nevada at Las Vegas.

SEE: NUCMC, 1980.

SEE ALSO: Stephen Powell, *A Gambling Bibliography Based on the Collection* (Univ. of Nevada, 1972).

OVERTON

NV870-480

Lost City Museum of Archaeology
721 S. Highway 169
Overton NV

MAILING ADDRESS:
P.O. Box 807
Overton NV 89040

(702) 397-2193

OPEN: daily 8:30-4:30 by appointment; closed holidays
ACCESS: archaeological site information restricted to accredited professionals and students with professional supervision; advance arrangements required
COPYING FACILITIES: yes
MATERIALS SOLICITED: Materials relating to the Overton area, including archaeological site records, diaries, journals, manuscript histories, manuscript maps, aerial photographs, and oral history tapes.

HOLDINGS:
   Total volume: 1 file cabinet
   Inclusive dates: 1924 -
   Description: The collection consists mainly of archaeological site sheets and artifact catalog cards for sites in the southern Nevada area, particularly the Pueblo Grande de Nevada or 'Lost City', which was originally excavated by the Civilian Conservation Corps. Also available are maps, and journals dealing with the excavations, archaeological site maps, and some local family histories.

RENO

NV940-560

Nevada Historical Society
1650 North Virginia Street
Reno NV 89503

(702) 789-0190

OPEN: W-Su 10-5; closed Mondays, Tuesdays, and holidays
COPYING FACILITIES: yes

MATERIALS SOLICITED: Nevada and western Americana, 1840 to the present, relating to mining, lumbering, politics and government, transportation, and other topics. Will also accept other materials at the discretion of the Society.

HOLDINGS:
   Total volume: 2,500 l.f.
   Inclusive dates: 1846 -
   Description: Approximately 3,000 collections, including the papers of political leaders; records of educational, fraternal and business groups, and mining companies; personal papers of prominent citizens; and the records of such organizations as the Nevada Federation of Women's Clubs. Also pioneer diaries, photograph collections, recorded and written reminiscences, some territorial and early statehood archival records, and the complete records of the Episcopal Diocese of Nevada.

GUIDES: L. James Higgins, Jr., *A Guide to the Manuscript Collections at the Nevada Historical Society* (1975).

SEE: Hamer.

SEE: Davis; Hinding.

SEE ALSO: Robert D. Armstrong, *A Preliminary Union Catalog of Nevada Manuscripts* (Univ. of Nevada/Nevada Library Assn., 1967); L. James Higgins, Jr., Eric N. Moody, and Lee Mortensen, *A Preliminary Checklist of the Manuscript Collections at the Nevada Historical Society* (Nevada Historical Society, 1974); Ann Novotny, ed., *Picture Sources 3* (Special Libraries Assn., 1975).

NV940-800

University of Nevada at Reno
Library
Basque Studies Program
Reno NV 89557

(702) 784-4854

OPEN: M-F 8-5; closed weekends and holidays
COPYING FACILITIES: yes
MATERIALS SOLICITED: Basque-related materials from the Old or New World.

HOLDINGS:
   Total volume: 7,000 items
   Inclusive dates: 17th century -
   Description: Basque materials, including records of organizations; family papers; photographs, church records, and copies of original documents from the Spanish and French Basque regions; and

slides and photographs of Basque festivals, sheepherding, and other activities, chiefly in the western United States, 1960- .

NV940-810

University of Nevada at Reno
Library
Special Collections Department
Reno NV 89557

(702) 784-6538

OPEN: M-F 8-5, Sa 1-5; closed Sundays, holidays, and Saturdays in summer
COPYING FACILITIES: yes
MATERIALS SOLICITED: Materials relating to north and central Nevada and contiguous areas lying within the Great Basin.

HOLDINGS:
   Total volume: 2,423 l.f.
   Inclusive dates: 1850 -
   Description: 1,200 collections relating primarily to Nevada history, with emphasis on mining, politics, and water resources. There are materials on Nevada Indians, as well as the archives of the University.

SEE: NUCMC, 1965, 67, 69, 77, 80.

SEE: Davis; Robbins; Hinding; Bean and Vane.

SEE ALSO: Robert D. Armstrong, comp. and ed., *A Preliminary Union Catalog of Nevada Manuscripts* (Univ. of Nevada Library/Nevada Library Assn., 1967); Walter Schatz, ed., *Directory of Afro-American Resources* (Bowker, 1970); Mary Ellen Glass, 'A Historian's Look at the Archives, University of Nevada,' *Intermountain Archivist* (June 1976).

NEW HAMPSHIRE

Since 1977 the retention schedule for New Hampshire's local public records has been the responsibility of a municipal records board, including officers of municipal organizations as well as gubernatorial appointees. Current rules call for microfilming many local records with a copy of the film to be deposited in the New Hampshire Division of Records Management and Archives. The New Hampshire State Library has microfilm copies of records of each town and county to 1900 (if records existed at the time of filming by the Church of Jesus Christ of Latter-day Saints).

The State Library has an individual name index to the microfilmed records dating through 1825. Early original records of many towns, long on deposit at the New Hampshire Historical Society, have now been transferred to the Division of Records Management and Archives.

CENTER SANDWICH

NH108-720
Sandwich Historical Society
Museum
Maple Street
Center Sandwich NH

MAILING ADDRESS:
Box 106
Center Sandwich NH 03227

(603) 284-6269

OPEN: July 4-Sept. 3, M-Sa 11-5; May 28-July 2, Sept. 5-Oct. 1, M-F 2-5; closed rest of year
COPYING FACILITIES: no
MATERIALS SOLICITED: Materials, chiefly in social, political, and ecclesiastical history, of primarily local significance. Will also accept photographs, maps, and ledgers.

HOLDINGS:
   Total volume: not specified
   Inclusive dates: 1769 -
   Description: Materials pertaining to the Sandwich area, including documents relating to the military, churches, schools, and town government, as well as personal letters.

CHARLESTOWN

NH118-600
Old Fort Number 4
Route 11
Charlestown NH

MAILING ADDRESS:
P.O. Box 336
Charlestown NH 03603

(603) 826-5700

OPEN: late June - Labor Day, daily 10-5; closed other times
ACCESS: advance arrangements required
COPYING FACILITIES: no
MATERIALS SOLICITED: Materials relating to Fort Number 4 and Charlestown history prior to 1800, New Hampshire's participation in the French and Indian War, and individuals and families who lived at Fort Number 4. Will also accept materials relating to the history of Charlestown and the surrounding area.

HOLDINGS:
   Total volume: 2 l.f.
   Inclusive dates: 1778 -
   Description: Photographs of Charlestown and journals, manuscripts, and maps relating to the Charlestown area and Fort Number 4.

CONCORD

NH134-530
New Hampshire Department of State
Division of Records Management and Archives
71 South Fruit Street
Concord NH 03301

(603) 271-2236

OPEN: M-F 8-4:30; closed weekends and holidays
COPYING FACILITIES: yes
MATERIALS SOLICITED: Records generated by public service on the State and local levels and by individuals who have created public records on public service. Will also accept privately created records that bear on service or property within the State (e.g., records of land surveyors).

HOLDINGS:
   Total volume: 1,700 vols.; 900 c.f.
   Inclusive dates: 1623 - 1918
   Description: New Hampshire records, including provincial deed and probate records; provincial court records; materials relating to the French and Indian, Revolutionary, and Civil Wars, and World War I; gubernatorial, executive council, legislative, secretary of state, and treasury papers; and boundary dispute records and Masonian land maps.

SEE: Leventhal and Mooney - I.

NH134-540
New Hampshire Historical Society
30 Park Street
Concord NH 03301

(603) 225-3381

OPEN: Sept.-May, M-Sa 9-4:30; June-Aug., M, Tu, Th, F 9-4:30, W 9-8; closed holidays, Sundays Sept.-May, weekends June-Aug.
COPYING FACILITIES: yes
MATERIALS SOLICITED: Manuscripts, archives, and noncurrent records, visual documents, microforms, and scrapbooks pertaining to all aspects of New Hampshire history, with special emphasis on 18th and 19th century materials.

HOLDINGS:
   Total volume: 1,000 l.f.
   Inclusive dates: 1623 -
   Description: Materials relating to the history of New Hampshire, primarily its political leaders and public officials. There are also papers of New Hampshire families, diaries, personal and official papers of State militia members, early town records, 18th and 19th century account books, shipping records, minutes of literary societies and other social organizations, school and church records, corporation records, genealogical miscellany, and 25,000 photographs. Significant collections include papers of President Franklin Pierce and records of the Abbot-Downing Company, manufacturers of the Concord Coach.

SEE: Hamer; NUCMC, 1968-69, 71, 73-74, 76.

SEE: Allard, Crawley, and Edmison; Davis; Duignan; Hinding; Leventhal and Mooney - I; Novotny; Robbins; Schatz.

NH134-560
New Hampshire State Library
20 Park Street
Concord NH 03301

(603) 271-2394

OPEN: M-F 8:30-4:30; closed weekends and holidays

SEE: Hamer; NUCMC, 1966.

Questionnaire not returned.

DOVER

NH194-160

Dover Public Library
73 Locust Street
Dover NH 03820

(603) 742-3513

OPEN: M-F 9-8, Sa 9-5; closed Sundays
and holidays
COPYING FACILITIES: yes
MATERIALS SOLICITED: Materials relating
to the Dover area.

HOLDINGS:
Total volume: 151 vols.
Inclusive dates: 1826 - 1865
Description: The journals of the Reverend Enoch Place, of Strafford and Barrington, primarily detailing his religious duties, such as marriages and funerals.

SEE: Hamer; NUCMC, 1968.

SEE: Schatz; Hinding.

NH194-560

Northam Colonists Historical Society
182 Central Avenue
Dover NH

MAILING ADDRESS:
Route 1, Box 449
Dover NH 03820

(603) 742-4674

OPEN: M-Th 9-8:30, F 9-5:30, Sa 9-5;
closed Sundays
ACCESS: permission of the Society
required
COPYING FACILITIES: no

HOLDINGS:
Total volume: 1 file cabinet
Inclusive dates: 1623 -
Description: Materials relating to the history of Dover, including information on early settlers, addresses given to the Republican State conventions of the 1870's, records of the local fire department in the 1860's and 1870's, maps, and papers presented at Society meetings.

DURHAM

NH206-800

University of New Hampshire
Dimond Library
Special Collections
Durham NH 03824

(603) 862-2714

OPEN: M-F 9-4:30; closed weekends and
holidays
COPYING FACILITIES: yes
MATERIALS SOLICITED: Materials relating
to the history and development of the University, the town of Durham, and adjacent areas; and papers of authors and social and political leaders who were born in or lived in New Hampshire. Will also accept materials of historical and/or research importance for the University.

HOLDINGS:
Total volume: 950 c.f.
Inclusive dates: 1578 -
Description: Manuscripts, archives, and visual and audible documents relating chiefly to New Hampshire after 1732. Included are records of the University and the town of Durham, papers of local families and organizations, and records of various New Hampshire towns, counties, and churches. Papers of individuals include the Congressional files of Norris Cotton and the literary archives of Oscar Maria Graf and Friedrich Grosshut, German exile novelists. American authors represented include Conrad Aiken, Witter Bynner, Robert Frost, and Edwin Arlington Robinson. There are also several collections of literary and music manuscripts of contemporary New Hampshire artists.
Also included are papers of Thomas McIntyre, composers Amy Beach and Robert Manton, and poet Donald Hall.

SEE: Hamer; NUCMC, 1965, 73-74.

SEE: Hinding; Robbins; Spalek; Leventhal
and Mooney - I.

EXETER

NH254-210

Exeter Public Library
Front Street
Exeter NH 03833

(603) 772-3101

SEE: Hamer.

Questionnaire not returned.

NH254-640

Phillips Exeter Academy
Library
Exeter NH 03833

(603) 772-4311, Ext. 326

OPEN: M-F 8-9, Sa 8-4, Su 2-9; shorter
hours during academic vacations
COPYING FACILITIES: yes
MATERIALS SOLICITED: Local and State
history; manuscripts of alumni; and memorabilia and records of the school.

HOLDINGS:
Total volume: not specified
Inclusive dates: 17th century -
Description: Archives of Phillips Exeter Academy; papers of members of the faculty and alumni; deeds, and other manuscripts from colonial New Hampshire; literary manuscripts; and several items relating to 19th century sailing vessels.

SEE: Hamer; NUCMC, 1970.

SEE: Robbins.

FARMINGTON

NH266-280

Goodwin Library
South Main Street
Farmington NH 03835

(603) 755-2944

SEE: Hamer.

Questionnaire not returned.

FRANKLIN

NH312-240

Franklin Public Library
310 Central Street
Franklin NH 03235

(603) 934-2911

OPEN: M 9:30-6, Tu-F 9:30-8, Sa 9:30-4;
closed Sundays and holidays
COPYING FACILITIES: yes
MATERIALS SOLICITED: Materials pertaining to the history of Franklin and its environs.

HOLDINGS:
Total volume: 4 vols.; 50 photographs
Inclusive dates: 1820 - early 20th
century
Description: Historical photographs of Franklin and account books of local businesses of the early 19th century.

HAMPTON

NH368-320

Hampton Historical Society
Meeting House Green Memorial and
Historical Association, Inc.
Tuck Memorial Museum
40 Park Avenue
Hampton NH 03842

(603) 926-3287

OPEN: daily 1-4 July-Aug. only, other
times by appointment
ACCESS: advance arrangements required
COPYING FACILITIES: no
MATERIALS SOLICITED: Material relating
to local Hampton history, including manucripts, documents, letters, deeds, and photographs.

HOLDINGS:
Total volume: 500 vols.
Inclusive dates: 1600 -
Description: Material relating to Hampton history including histories, biographies, albums, and scrapbooks.

HANOVER

NH372-160
Dartmouth College
Library
Hanover NH 03755

(603) 646-2037

OPEN: M-F 8-4:30; closed weekends and holidays

SEE: Hamer; NUCMC, 1963-65, 67, 70-71, 74-76, 78, 81.

Questionnaire not returned.

HENNIKER

NH396-560
New England College
Danforth Library
Henniker NH 03242

(603) 428-2344

OPEN: M-F 9-5 by appointment; closed weekends and holidays
COPYING FACILITIES: yes
MATERIALS SOLICITED: New England College archives. Will also accept manuscripts and audible documents.

HOLDINGS:
Total volume: 100,000 items; 16 l.f.
Inclusive dates: 1923 -
Description: The papers of Styles Bridges, including correspondence, political files, speeches, memorabilia, and audiovisual materials documenting his State and National political career. There are also the New England College archives, consisting of 16 linear feet of publications.

SEE: NUCMC, 1969.

SEE ALSO: James J. Kiepper, *Styles Bridges, A Register of his Papers in the New England College Library* (New England College, 1972).

HOLLIS

NH430-320
Hollis Historical Society
20 Main Street
Hollis NH

MAILING ADDRESS:
P.O. Box 138
Hollis NH 03049

(603) 465-7696

OPEN: M-Sa afternoons by appointment
COPYING FACILITIES: no
MATERIALS SOLICITED: Genealogical source data including diaries and journals relating to the Hollis area.

HOLDINGS:
Total volume: 2,100 items
Inclusive dates: 1760 -
Description: Records, photographs, and manuscripts relating to Hollis and its people.

HOPKINTON

NH444-560
New Hampshire Antiquarian Society
Main Street
Hopkinton NH 03301

(603) 746-4292

OPEN: W 2-4 by appointment

SEE: Hamer; NUCMC, 1966.

Questionnaire not returned.

KEENE

NH468-800
University of New Hampshire
Keene State College
Mason Library
Preston Collection
229 Main Street
Keene NH 03431

(603) 352-1909, Ext. 237

OPEN: M-Th 8-11, F 8-5, Sa 10-5, Su 2-11; hours shortened during class recesses
COPYING FACILITIES: yes
MATERIALS SOLICITED: Materials dealing with New Hampshire history.

HOLDINGS:
Total volume: 4 c.f.
Inclusive dates: 1750 - 1950
Description: Property records of the Masonian Proprietors in New Hampshire and documentation of land speculation in the New Hampshire, Vermont, and Connecticut Valley region under the aegis of Governor Benning Wentworth.

MADISON

NH588-520
Madison Historical Society
Main Street
Madison NH

MAILING ADDRESS:
P.O. Box 9
Madison NH 03849

(603) 367-4687

OPEN: Tuesday afternoons during summer and by appointment
COPYING FACILITIES: no
MATERIALS SOLICITED: Manuscripts and scrapbooks relating to Madison history. Will also accept oral histories relating to Madison.

HOLDINGS:
Total volume: 12 file drawers
Inclusive dates: 1830 -
Description: An extensive collection of veterans' records from the Revolution and the Civil War; death-burial certificates issued before and shortly after 1900; and billings, inventories, and related material from Madison stores before and shortly after 1900. Also included are mortgage transactions and town business records, 1870-1900; scrapbooks, dia-
ries, and letters; along with maps and sketches relating to Madison history.

MANCHESTER

NH600-30
American-Canadian Genealogical Society
172 Belmont Street
Manchester NH

MAILING ADDRESS:
P.O. Box 668
Manchester NH 03105-0668

(603) 622-2883

OPEN: Tu, W noon-4, 6:30-9, Th noon-4, F 9-9; other times by appointment only
ACCESS: membership required after two visits
COPYING FACILITIES: yes
MATERIALS SOLICITED: Materials relating to research of Canadian genealogical ancestries, Americans with Canadian ancestries, and Canadians with French ancestries, in addition to all genealogical and historical source data. Will also accept city, town and church histories, annual reports, vital records and judicial proceedings from areas of French settlement.

HOLDINGS:
Total volume: 1,000 volumes
Inclusive dates: 1608 -
Description: Genealogical resources relating to Americans of Canadian ancestry of all ethnic backgrounds, with a specialty in French Canadian material.

NH600-510
Manchester City Library
New Hampshire Room
405 Pine Street
Manchester NH 03104

(603) 624-6550

OPEN: M-F 9-5:30, Sa 9-5; closed Sundays and holidays
COPYING FACILITIES: yes
MATERIALS SOLICITED: Will accept materials relating to New Hampshire and the Manchester area.

HOLDINGS:
Total volume: 113 l.f.
Inclusive dates: 1748 -
Description: Materials relating to Manchester government agencies, churches, clubs, and citizens, and to New Hampshire. Included are 140 scrapbooks of newspaper clippings, early land grants, orderly books of the New Hampshire Militia, Civil War papers of Dr. W. A. Webster, papers of composer Zo Elliot, speeches of Cyrus Little, and writings of George C. Carter, Fred Lamb, and George Brown. There are also records of the New Hampshire Medical Society and a photograph collection of Manchester and vicinity, including three boxes of photos from the Amoskeag Corporation.

NH600-530
Manchester Historic Association
129 Amherst Street
Manchester NH 03104

(603) 622-7531

OPEN: Tu-F 11-4, Sa 1-4; closed Su, M
  and holidays
USER FEES: $3 minimum charge for
  research done by staff taking more than
  30 minutes
COPYING FACILITIES: yes
MATERIALS SOLICITED: Materials relating
  to Manchester industry, social service
  agencies, cultural agencies, ethnic
  groups, and small business; family albums, letters, and photographs; personal diaries; tape recorded reminiscences;
  architectural photographs and
  renderings; maps; other photographs;
  engineers' plans and schedules; glass
  plate negatives of early 20th century
  industry and local scenes; materials relating to Major General John Stark and
  family; and textile sample books. Will
  also accept materials relating to contiguous small towns.

HOLDINGS:
  Total volume: 1,685 l.f.
  Inclusive dates: 1759 -
  Description: Records of the Amoskeag
  Manufacturing Company textile plant,
  1828-1936; including fabric sample
  books; the Smyrl Textile Designer Collection, 1928-63, relating to the design of
  automobile interior fabrics and tire side
  walls; archives of the local United Fund;
  local photographs; small retail business
  and professional account books; the Walter Dignam Collection of 19th century
  music; and other materials relating primarily to Manchester history.

SEE: Hamer.

NH600-740
Smyth Public Library
Manchester NH

MAILING ADDRESS:
Box 306, R.F.D. 1
Manchester NH 03104

(603) 624-6550

SEE: Hamer.

Questionnaire not returned.

MILFORD

NH660-880
Wadleigh Memorial Library
Nashua Street
Milford NH 03055

(603) 673-3330

SEE: NUCMC, 1959-61.

Questionnaire not returned.

NASHUA

NH672-570
Nashua Public Library
2 Court Street
Nashua NH 03060

(603) 883-4141

OPEN: M-F 8:30-9, Sa 8:30-5:30, Su 1-5
COPYING FACILITIES: yes
MATERIALS SOLICITED: Letters, diaries,
  literary manuscripts, maps, and photographs on Nashua history.

HOLDINGS:
  Total volume: 12 items; 3 file
  drawers
  Inclusive dates: 1746 -
  Description: Several literary manuscripts, a letter book pertaining to General John G. Foster, a large book of
  handwritten sketches pertaining to
  records of Civil War veterans in Nashua,
  and the original charter of Dunstable,
  1746, which later became the city of
  Nashua.

NEW CASTLE

NH680-760
New Castle Archives and Records
  Committee
New Castle NH 03854

(603) 431-6854

OPEN: First Monday each month 9-11,
  other times by appointment
ACCESS: only when accompanied by
  member of Archives Committee
COPYING FACILITIES: no
MATERIALS SOLICITED: Original manuscripts, documents, maps, and pictures
  pertaining to New Castle, especially
  concerning ships, shipping, and the
  fishing industry, as well as genealogical
  information pertaining to the townspeople. Will also accept scrapbooks
  concerning town events.

HOLDINGS:
  Total volume: 45 l.f.; 12 boxes
  Inclusive dates: 1623 -
  Description: Materials relating to the
  town of New Castle, including records of
  town meetings, 1693- ; copies of city
  records concerning New Castle when it
  was part of the city of Portsmouth,
  1652-93; and vital statistics. Also included is the Meloon collection of complete
  copies of wills, deeds, and probate
  records from Rockingham County,
  1637-1900; 14 photostatic copies of maps
  and drawings of Fort William and Mary
  (Fort Constitution) and Portsmouth harbor, 1699-1720; and early maps of the
  area.

NEW HAMPTON

NH688-280
Gordon-Nash Library
New Hampton NH 03256

(603) 744-8061

OPEN: Su-F 10:30-9, Sa 10-2; closed
  holidays
COPYING FACILITIES: yes
MATERIALS SOLICITED: Material relating
  to New Hampton history, including papers, letters, pictures, scrapbooks, and
  ledgers.

HOLDINGS:
  Total volume: 4 l.f.
  Inclusive dates: 1777 - 1940
  Description: Papers, records, and tapes
  relating to New Hampton history and to
  the genealogy of its early families. Included are records of the town churches,
  of the New Hampton School, and of
  town reports.

NEW IPSWICH

NH696-560
New Ipswich Historical Society
Main Street
New Ipswich NH 03071

no telephone

OPEN: Tu, Th 2-4 July-Aug. only, other
  times by appointment
COPYING FACILITIES: no
MATERIALS SOLICITED: Materials pertaining to New Ipswich.

HOLDINGS:
  Total volume: not specified
  Inclusive dates: early 19th century -
  Description: A small collection of New
  Ipswich manuscripts, including 19th cen-
  tury account books, town records, records
  of Appleton Academy, and school re-
  ports.

SEE: Hamer.

NEWMARKET

NH720-560
New Market Historical Society
Stone School Museum
Newmarket NH 03857

(603) 659-3652

OPEN: Memorial Day - Labor Day, Th
  2-4; closed other days
COPYING FACILITIES: no
MATERIALS SOLICITED: Newmarket history, especially French-Canadian and
  Polish ethnic groups. Will also accept
  other local southeastern New Hampshire historical materials and materials
  on New England industries.

HOLDINGS:
  Total volume: 200 items
  Inclusive dates: 1791 -
  Description: Payroll ledgers of a textile
  firm, the Newmarket Manufacturing
  Company; local diaries; a motion picture
  of the Sam Smith Shoe Company; maps;
  photographs; records of local churches

and community groups; and manuscript cemetery indexes.

NOTTINGHAM

NH732-560
Nottingham Historical Society
Blaisdell Public Library
Route 152
Nottingham NH

MAILING ADDRESS:
Star Route, P.O. Box 4
Nottingham NH 03290

(603) 679-8741

OPEN: Sa 2:30-4 June 18-Sept. 17, other times by appointment
COPYING FACILITIES: no
MATERIALS SOLICITED: Town records and family papers from the Nottingham area.

HOLDINGS:
Total volume: not specified
Inclusive dates: 1722 -
Description: 14 microfilm rolls and numerous boxes of Nottingham town records, 1722 to date, including highway tax records, boundary documents, and records of the poorhouse, in addition to some private papers of local residents.

PETERBOROUGH

NH748-630
Peterborough Historical Society
Grove Street
Peterborough NH

MAILING ADDRESS:
P.O. Box 58
Peterborough NH 03458

(603) 924-3235

OPEN: M-W 10-4; closed Christmas week
SEE: Hamer.

Questionnaire not returned.

NH748-650
Peterborough Town Library
Main and Concord Streets
Peterborough NH 03458

(603) 924-6401

OPEN: M, W, F 10-6, Tu, Th 10-8, Sa 9-1; closed Sundays and holidays
USER FEES: 3-month temporary card, $2; nonresidents, $8 per annum
COPYING FACILITIES: yes

HOLDINGS:
Total volume: 42,000 vols.
Inclusive dates: 1800 -
Description: A small collection of manuscripts including material relating to Edward MacDowell, Stephen Foster, Abiel Abbot, and Nathaniel Holmes.

PLYMOUTH

NH772-640
Plymouth State College
Herbert H. Lamson Library
Plymouth NH 03264

(603) 536-1550, Ext. 257

OPEN: M-F 8-5; closed weekends and holidays
COPYING FACILITIES: yes
MATERIALS SOLICITED: Materials on Robert Frost, Plymouth and New Hampshire history, and the College archives.

HOLDINGS:
Total volume: 28 file drawers
Inclusive dates: 1770's -
Description: Letters from Robert Frost to George H. Browne, 1915-20, and related materials; American Revolutionary era documents of a local nature; manuscripts of books by local authors; materials on the history of Plymouth; photographs of all houses in Plymouth taken during the 1930's; and college memorabilia.

SEE: Meckler and McMullin; Robbins.

SEE ALSO: a mimeographed list of holdings in the George H. Browne-Robert Frost collection through 1972, available from the Library.

PORTSMOUTH

NH784-620
Pearl Harbor Survivors Association, Inc.
Granite State Chapter No. 1 N.H.
1106 Maplewood Avenue
Portsmouth NH 03801

(603) 436-5835

OPEN: by appointment only
COPYING FACILITIES: yes
MATERIALS SOLICITED: Diaries, logbooks, correspondence, audiovisual materials, photographs, microfilmed documents, and other archival materials relating to the Japanese attack on Pearl Harbor. Will also accept materials documenting U.S. military history during the period of the Pearl Harbor attack.

HOLDINGS:
Total volume: 8 l.f.
Inclusive dates: 1940 - 1945
Description: Personal narratives, letters, manuscripts of magazine articles, and photographs concerning the Japanese raid on Pearl Harbor.

NH784-630
Portsmouth Athenaeum
Library
9 Market Square
Portsmouth NH

MAILING ADDRESS:
P.O. Box 848
Portsmouth NH 03801

(603) 431-2538

OPEN: M-F 9-4 by appointment; closed weekends and holidays
COPYING FACILITIES: yes
MATERIALS SOLICITED: Local, nautical, genealogical, and colonial history; 18th and 19th century shipping information.

HOLDINGS:
Total volume: 800 items; 2,300 photographs
Inclusive dates: 1690 - 1850
Description: 18th and 19th century manuscripts relating to local history, politics, military affairs, and shipping; and records of the New Hampshire Fire and Marine Insurance Company, 1803-23.
Also includes the papers of Thomas Larkin and Daniel and John Peirce.

SEE: NUCMC, 1959-61.

SEE: Ingram; Leventhal and Mooney - I.

NH784-700
St. John's Church
101 Chapel Street
Portsmouth NH 03801

(603) 436-8283, 7416

OPEN: M-F 9-4 (building open), Tu, W 9-3, Th 9-12 Sept.-June (office open) by appointment
ACCESS: identification required; advance appointment requested
COPYING FACILITIES: no
MATERIALS SOLICITED: Will accept manuscripts pertaining to St. John's Church or its Rectors.

HOLDINGS:
Total volume: 24 l.f.
Inclusive dates: 1736 -
Description: Records of St. John's Church, an Episcopal church known as Queen's Chapel until 1791, relating to New Hampshire and southwestern Maine. Included are correspondence, account books, genealogical records, and biographical material relating to clergy and lay people active in the church.

SEE: Leventhal and Mooney - I.

NH784-720
Strawbery Banke, Inc.
46 Jefferson Street
Portsmouth NH

MAILING ADDRESS:
P.O. Box 300
Portsmouth NH 03801

(603) 436-8010

OPEN: Tu, Th by appointment, W all day
ACCESS: by appointment only, to scholars
COPYING FACILITIES: no
MATERIALS SOLICITED: Historical records relating to Portsmouth and the Piscataqua River area.

HOLDINGS:
Total volume: 7,000 items
Inclusive dates: 1689 - 1935
Description: A collection of materials relating to Portsmouth, the Piscataqua area, and the Portsmouth Naval Shipyard. Included are documents and account books of Stephen Chase, 1775-1805; materials of a local nature,

1689-1880; and a collection of glass plate and cellulose negatives and some prints of the Portsmouth area, including scenes of the original site of Hill, NH, which was submerged by water in 1931 to make way for a flood control project.

SEE: Allard, Crawley, and Edmison.

SEE ALSO: James L. Garvin, *Historic Portsmouth: Early Photographs from the Collections of Strawbery Banke, Inc.* (New Hampshire Publishing Co., 1974).

RAYMOND

NH796-690
Raymond Historical Society, Inc.
Railroad Depot
Raymond NH

MAILING ADDRESS:
P.O. Box 1764
Raymond NH 03077

no telephone

OPEN: by appointment only
ACCESS: prior authorization required
COPYING FACILITIES: yes
MATERIALS SOLICITED: Materials pertaining to the history of Raymond and its environs. Will also accept other historical materials of value.

HOLDINGS:
   Total volume: not specified
   Inclusive dates: 18th century -
   Description: Account books, town records, manuscripts, and photographs relating to the Raymond and Freetown area.

ROCHESTER

NH820-690
Rochester Public Library
65 South Main Street

MAILING ADDRESS:
P.O. Box 1270
Rochester NH 03867

(603) 332-1428

OPEN: Winter, M-Th 9:30-9, F 9:30-4, Sa 9:30-4, Su 1-4 closed holidays
COPYING FACILITIES: yes
MATERIALS SOLICITED: Will accept materials suitable for the collection.

HOLDINGS:
   Total volume: 3 l.f.; 14 items
   Inclusive dates: 1747 - 1825
   Description: Sermons of Joseph Haven, Rochester, NH, minister, and records of two community organizations.

SEE: Hamer; NUCMC, 1966.

SEE: Hinding.

SALEM

NH832-720
Salem Historical Society
43 Lake Shore Road
Salem NH 03079

(603) 898-5660

OPEN: 2nd Tu 2-4
COPYING FACILITIES: yes

HOLDINGS:
   Total volume: 150 items
   Inclusive dates: 18th century -
   Description: Salem town records since the 18th century, deeds for the period 1845 to 1936, a 19th century travel diary,

pension forms and other records of the Civil War, and research materials used in preparing a history of Salem for the period 1900 to 1975, including bills and other manuscripts.

TILTON

NH904-760
Tilton School
School Street
Tilton NH 03276

(603) 286-4342

OPEN: M-F 8-4, Sa 8-noon, evenings 8-10; closed Sundays
COPYING FACILITIES: no

HOLDINGS:
   Total volume: 3 vols.
   Inclusive dates: 1845 -
   Description: Materials pertaining to the history of the Tilton School, including minutes of trustees' meetings from the School's founding in 1845, photographs, correspondence, and a collection of speeches and papers of Daniel Knowles, former headmaster.

NEW JERSEY

Since 1953 the Bureau of Archives and History of the New Jersey State Library has administered a statewide program for preserving local public records. Permanently valuable local public records have normally remained in the custody of local officials, but the Bureau of Archives and History in Trenton holds some pre-20th century records. The Bureau also makes available to researchers some 12,000 reels of microfilm of county vital, probate, and land records; town minutes; and other local public records that were filmed by the Genealogical Society of Utah.

ALLAIRE

NJ8-160
Deserted Village at Allaire
Allaire Village Auxiliary Library
Allaire State Park
Route 524
Allaire NJ 07727

(201) 938-2253

OPEN: M-F 9-4; closed weekends and holidays
ACCESS: by appointment only
COPYING FACILITIES: yes
MATERIALS SOLICITED: Materials relating to James P. Allaire and his family, the Howell Works, the Allaire Works, the New York and Charleston Steam Packet Co., the Southern Steam Packet Co., southern Monmouth County, and New Jersey iron production in the 19th century. Will also accept materials on the bog iron industry in general and early steamship manufacturing.

HOLDINGS:
   Total volume: 500 items
   Inclusive dates: 1810 -
   Description: Materials relating chiefly to James P. Allaire and his several businesses, the Howell Works, and the Allaire family. Included are letters, account and record books, a photograph collection, archaeological information, architectural drawings, and manuscripts.

ATLANTIC CITY

NJ20-40
Atlantic City Free Public Library
Alfred M. Heston Collection
1 N. Tennessee Avenue
Atlantic City NJ 08401

(609) 345-2269

OPEN: M, Tu, Th, F 10-4; closed Wednesdays, weekends, and holidays
ACCESS: advance arrangements suggested
COPYING FACILITIES: yes
MATERIALS SOLICITED: Materials pertaining to Atlantic City, Absecon Island, and Atlantic County, NJ. Will also accept materials on New Jersey, particularly southern New Jersey.

HOLDINGS:
   Total volume: not specified
   Inclusive dates: 1700's -
   Description: Materials concerning the history of Atlantic City and its environs, including oral history recordings, photographs, scrapbooks, typescript histories, hotel registers, organization records, genealogical materials, and records of the library and its predecessor, the Woman's Research Club.

BAYONNE

NJ46-560
National Archives and Records
   Administration
Federal Archives and Records Center
Archives Branch
Building 22 MOT - Bayonne
Bayonne NJ 07002

(201) 823-7252

OPEN: M-F 8-4:30; closed weekends and holidays
ACCESS: Records are open, subject to Federal agency restrictions and restrictions based upon current legislation relevant to confidentiality and security classification. See General Information Leaflet No. 2, 'Regulations for the Public Use of Records in the National Archives.'
COPYING FACILITIES: yes
MATERIALS SOLICITED: Records from field offices of Federal agencies located in New York, New Jersey, Puerto Rico, and the Virgin Islands.

HOLDINGS:
   Total volume: 47,118 c.f.
   Inclusive dates: 1792 - 1946
   Description: Records of Federal agencies located in New York, New Jersey, and Puerto Rico. Included are records of

the U.S. Court of Appeals for the Second Circuit; the U.S. District Courts for the Southern, Eastern, Northern, and Western Districts of New York; the U.S. District Courts for the District of New Jersey and for Puerto Rico; the Immigration and Naturalization Service; the Bureau of Customs; and the Internal Revenue Service.

GUIDES: A guide, *Holdings of the Archives Branch of the Federal Archives and Records Center,* is available from the repository.

SEE: Davis.

BERNARDSVILLE

NJ66-80
Bernardsville Public Library
Spinning Room
2 Morristown Road
Bernardsville NJ 07924

(201) 766-0118

OPEN: Th 10-5 or by prior arrangement
ACCESS: prior arrangements are recommended
COPYING FACILITIES: yes
MATERIALS SOLICITED: Materials relating to the history of Bernardsville, Basking Ridge, and the Somerset Hills area, especially biographical information; photographs and documents pertaining to area homes, buildings, and institutions; and data on the Revolutionary War period and the 'mountain' era around 1900. Will also accept genealogical materials.

HOLDINGS:
   Total volume: 9 file drawers
   Inclusive dates: colonial period -
   Description: Materials relating to the Somerset Hills area, including some gathered for a history of Bernardsville. Other holdings include historical society papers, memoirs, reminiscences of early settlers about their life and the Revolutionary War period, and materials relating to the 'mountain' era (1890-1920), when Bernardsville was a fashionable summer colony for New Yorkers.

BLOOMFIELD

NJ76-70
Bloomfield College
Library
467 Franklin Street
Bloomfield NJ 07003

(201) 748-9000, Ext. 332

OPEN: M-Th 8:30-10:30, F 8:30-6:30, Sa 10-4; closed Sundays and holidays
COPYING FACILITIES: yes
MATERIALS SOLICITED: Materials relating to the history of Bloomfield College and the town of Bloomfield; and to the Presbyterian church, especially in New Jersey and Pennsylvania.

HOLDINGS:
Total volume: several boxes
Inclusive dates: 1778 -
Description: Materials relating to Bloomfield College, the town of Bloomfield, and the Presbyterian church. Included are registration, financial, and enrollment data; minutes and notes of meetings; and other materials.

BOONTON

NJ84-320
Historical Society of Boonton Township, Inc.
Boonton NJ

MAILING ADDRESS:
R.D. 2, Box 152
Boonton NJ 07005

no telephone

OPEN: by appointment only
MATERIALS SOLICITED: Materials pertaining to the history of Boonton Township.

HOLDINGS:
Total volume: not specified
Inclusive dates: 1900 -
Description: Photographs of historic sites and other subjects in Boonton Township and the surrounding area.

BOUND BROOK

NJ92-80
Bound Brook Memorial Library
402 East High Street
Bound Brook NJ 08805

(201) 356-0043

OPEN: M-F 10-9, Sa 10-5; closed Sundays and holidays; shorter summer hours
COPYING FACILITIES: yes
MATERIALS SOLICITED: Materials relating to the history of Bound Brook.

HOLDINGS:
Total volume: 10 l.f.; 30 items
Inclusive dates: 1800's -
Description: Materials relating to the history of Bound Brook, including borough minutes, photographs, maps, oral history tapes, and data on local Revolutionary War tombstones.

BURLINGTON

NJ100-80
Burlington County Historical Society
457 High Street
Burlington NJ 08016

(609) 386-4773

OPEN: W 1-4, Th, F 10-12, Su 2-4 or by appointment; closed holidays
COPYING FACILITIES: yes
MATERIALS SOLICITED: Materials relating to Burlington County. Will also accept materials related to areas surrounding Burlington County.

HOLDINGS:
Total volume: not specified
Inclusive dates: 1700 - 1900
Description: A collection of personal letters and papers, organization records (including materials relating to the Burlington County Abolition Society and the New Jersey Abolition Society), business records, government records, indentures, deeds, wills, marriage certificates, and other materials relating to Burlington County and the surrounding region.

SEE: Hamer.

CALIFON

NJ108-120
Califon Historical Society
Califon NJ

MAILING ADDRESS:
P.O. Box 374
Califon NJ 07830

no telephone

OPEN: M-F by appointment only; closed weekends
COPYING FACILITIES: no
MATERIALS SOLICITED: Materials pertaining to the history of Califon and its environs.

HOLDINGS:
Total volume: 4 vols.; 5 oral histories; 34 items; additional materials
Inclusive dates: 1861 -
Description: Materials that document the history of Califon, including account books of a general store, 1861-71; a medical student's diary, 1873; oral history interviews; receipts; indentures; and other papers.

CAMDEN

NJ112-120
Camden County Historical Society
Park Boulevard and Euclid Avenue
Camden NJ 08103

(609) 964-3333

OPEN: Su 2-4:30, M-Th 12:30-4:30; closed Fridays, Saturdays, and holidays
COPYING FACILITIES: yes
MATERIALS SOLICITED: Camden County materials. Will also accept materials relating to southern New Jersey and the surrounding region.

HOLDINGS:
Total volume: 23 drawers; several bookcases
Inclusive dates: 1800 -
Description: Camden County historical materials, including journals, financial records, deeds, genealogical data, and manuscript maps.

SEE: Davis; Hinding; Robbins.

NJ112-880
Walt Whitman Association
330 Mickle Street
Camden NJ

MAILING ADDRESS:
46 Centre Street
Haddonfield NJ 08033

(609) 964-5383

OPEN: W-Su 9-5; closed M, Tu, Christmas, New Year's Day
SEE: Hamer.

Questionnaire not returned.

CAPE MAY COURT HOUSE

NJ120-120
Cape May County Historical and Genealogical Society
Route 9
Cape May Court House NJ 08210

(609) 465-3535

OPEN: June 15-Sept. 15, M-Sa 10-4; Sept. 15-June 15, Tu-Sa 10-4; closed other days and holidays
USER FEES: one dollar for nonmembers
COPYING FACILITIES: yes

HOLDINGS:
Total volume: 54 l.f.; 2 file cabinets
Inclusive dates: 17th century -
Description: Materials relating to the history and genealogy of Cape May County and its families.

SEE: Hamer.

CARLSTADT

NJ124-240
William E. Dermody Free Public Library
420 Hackensack Street
Carlstadt NJ 07072

(201) 438-8866

OPEN: M-Th 10-9, F 10-5:30, Sa 10-noon; closed Sundays and holidays
ACCESS: with permission of Library Director
COPYING FACILITIES: yes
MATERIALS SOLICITED: Local historical materials.

HOLDINGS:
Total volume: 28 items
Inclusive dates: 1872 -
Description: Records of the Volunteer Fire Department of Carlstadt.

CEDAR GROVE

NJ128-120
Cedar Grove Historical Society
Public Library
Cedar Grove NJ 07009

(609) 239-5264

OPEN: M-F 9-5:30, Sa 9-1; closed
Sundays, Christmas, and New Year's
COPYING FACILITIES: yes
MATERIALS SOLICITED: Historical materials relating to the Cedar Grove area.

HOLDINGS:
Total volume: 18 l.f.
Inclusive dates: 1773 -
Description: A collection of manuscripts, photographs, archives of organizations, sound recordings, cemetery records, maps, and genealogical records.

CHERRY HILL

NJ138-120
Cherry Hill Free Public Library
1100 Kings Highway, North
Cherry Hill NJ 08034

(609) 667-0300

OPEN: M-F 9:30-9, Sa 9:30-5, Su 1-5;
closed Sundays, June - Sept., and
holidays
COPYING FACILITIES: yes
MATERIALS SOLICITED: Materials relating to Cherry Hill history, including its families and businesses. Will also accept materials relating to the history of Camden County and the South Jersey area.

HOLDINGS:
Total volume: 20 c.f.
Inclusive dates: 1925 -
Description: Cherry Hill Township records, including records of the Planning Board, Zoning Board, Board of Education, and Cherry Hill Free Public Library. Other materials concerning Cherry Hill include personal papers and genealogical materials of residents, Parent-Teacher Association records, slides of historic homes, and oral history recordings.

CLIFTON

NJ154-690
Roman Catholic Diocese of Paterson
Archives
775 Valley Road
Clifton NJ 07013

(201) 777-8818

OPEN: by appointment only
ACCESS: approval based on nature of
research
COPYING FACILITIES: yes
MATERIALS SOLICITED: Materials relating to the Diocese and its schools, parishes, and major offices. Will also accept general materials relating to the Roman Catholic church in northern New Jersey and its prominent members.

HOLDINGS:
Total volume: not specified
Inclusive dates: 19th century -
Description: Records of the Diocese of Paterson, which encompasses Morris, Passaic, and Sussex counties. Included are correspondence of diocesan officers and institutions, 1937 to date, and 19th and 20th century parish records, such as correspondence, deeds, blueprints, commemorative booklets, journals, and genealogical materials.

COLLINGSWOOD

NJ162-110
Collingswood Free Public Library
New Jersey Room
Collingswood Collection
Haddon and Frazer Avenues
Collingswood NJ 08108

(609) 858-0649

OPEN: M-Sa 10-9; closed Sundays,
holidays, and Saturdays in July and
Aug.
COPYING FACILITIES: yes
MATERIALS SOLICITED: Materials relating to Collingswood history, including account books, diaries, journals, genealogical materials, maps, charts, photographs, slides, oral history interviews, and records of local institutions, organizations, and community groups. Will also accept architectural drawings.

HOLDINGS:
Total volume: 6 l.f.
Inclusive dates: 1850 -
Description: Collections on the history of Collingswood and its parent settlements Newton Township and Newton Colony. Included are correspondence, account books, genealogical source data, oral history tapes and transcripts, photographs, and slides, all relating to the early history and development of the community and its institutions.

COLTSNECK

NJ175-333
Pleasant Valley Preservation Society
15 The Enclosure
Coltsneck NJ 07722

no telephone

OPEN: by appointment only
COPYING FACILITIES: no
MATERIALS SOLICITED: Materials relating to the American Revolutionary War signal system. Will also accept genealogical sources of Pleasant Valley families.

HOLDINGS:
Total volume: 2 c.f.
Inclusive dates: early 19th century -
Description: Copies of manuscripts and a collection of slides concerning the establishment of the American Revolutionary War signal system; 19th century letters, diaries, and business papers of the Gordon family, including some copies; letters and other papers pertaining to the Pleasant Valley Preservation Society; and copies of early deeds of families from Pleasant Valley.

CONVENT STATION

NJ178-110
College of Saint Elizabeth
Archives
Convent Station NJ 07961

(201) 539-1600, Ext. 352, 365

OPEN: M-F by appointment; closed
weekends and holidays
COPYING FACILITIES: no

HOLDINGS:
Total volume: 7 file cabinets; 9 boxes
Inclusive dates: 1899 -
Description: Archives of the College, including records of its administrative and academic departments and activities, as well as other materials pertaining to its history. Photographs include views of persons and activities, and other scenes of the College's history.
Also included is material on the Great Swamp and the Morris County jetport.

SEE: Hinding.

NJ178-115
College of Saint Elizabeth
Mahoney Library
Phillips Rare Books and Manuscripts
Library
Convent Station NJ 07961

(201) 539-1600, Ext. 365

OPEN: M-F 9-4; closed weekends,
Thanksgiving, and Christmas week
ACCESS: advance arrangements required
COPYING FACILITIES: yes
MATERIALS SOLICITED: Will accept correspondence of Henry Cutler Wolfe.

HOLDINGS:
Total volume: 2 c.f.
Inclusive dates: 1914 - 1975
Description: Henry Cutler Wolfe correspondence and photographs and negatives of the American Field Service; and the World War I American Relief Service.

SEE: Robbins.

CRANBURY

NJ182-110
Cranbury Historical and Preservation
Society, Inc.
Museum Research Center
4 Park Place
Cranbury NJ 08512

no telephone

OPEN: Sa, Su 2-5; closed other days
except by special appointment
COPYING FACILITIES: no
MATERIALS SOLICITED: Materials documenting the history of Cranbury and its residents, churches, businesses, and historic sites.

HOLDINGS:
Total volume: 2 file cabinets
Inclusive dates: 1745 -
Description: Documents from Cranbury and its environs, primarily dating from the 18th and 19th centuries. Included are Revolutionary War service records, indexes of the South Brunswick militia of 1793, genealogical data, photographs, oral histories, and church records containing information on births, deaths, and marriages.

CRANFORD

NJ186-110
Cranford Historical Society
Museum
124 North Union Avenue
Cranford NJ 07016

(201) 276-0082

OPEN: Su, Th 2-4 by appointment; closed holidays
COPYING FACILITIES: no
MATERIALS SOLICITED: Memorabilia, photographs, oral histories, and other documents relating to the history of Cranford.

HOLDINGS:
Total volume: 2,000 items
Inclusive dates: not specified
Description: Photographs and oral history tapes relating to the history of Cranford.

SEE: Meckler and McMullin.

EAST ORANGE

NJ212-200
East Orange Public Library
Reference Department
21 South Arlington Avenue
East Orange NJ 07018

(201) 266-5612

OPEN: M-Th 9-9, F 10-6, Sa 9-5, Su 1-5; closed holidays; variable summer hours
COPYING FACILITIES: yes
MATERIALS SOLICITED: Materials concerning East Orange.

HOLDINGS:
Total volume: 15 file drawers
Inclusive dates: 1870's -
Description: Archives and noncurrent records of local and city organizations, including the now defunct East Orange Historical Society. Also included are photographs and slides of the city of East Orange.

EDGEWATER

NJ220-200
Edgewater Free Public Library
Undercliff and Hudson Avenues
Edgewater NJ 07020

(201) 943-1778

SEE: Hamer.

Questionnaire not returned.

ELMWOOD PARK

NJ222-333
American Leprosy Missions, Inc.
One Broadway
Elmwood Park NJ 07407

(201) 794-8650

OPEN: M-F 8:30-4:30; closed weekends, legal and religious holidays
ACCESS: appointment required
COPYING FACILITIES: yes

HOLDINGS:
Total volume: 100 c.f.; 25 file drawers
Inclusive dates: 1906 -
Description: Records dealing with the work of American Leprosy Missions in Asia, Africa, and South America. Focus is on leprosy patients, their care, organization of personnel and institutions, research and treatment methods, and relationships with other private voluntary organizations, especially Christian groups. Also included are records dealing with donors, donations, solicitations, and finances.

FORT LEE

NJ266-240
Fort Lee Free Public Library
Silent Film Photo Collection
320 Main Street
Fort Lee NJ 07024

(201) 592-3614

OPEN: M-Th 10-9, F, Sa 10-5; closed Sundays, holidays, and Saturdays in July and Aug.
COPYING FACILITIES: yes
MATERIALS SOLICITED: Material relating to the silent film period in Fort Lee history.

HOLDINGS:
Total volume: 930 items
Inclusive dates: 1907 - 1920
Description: Photographs of productions, sets, and backgrounds of silent films made in Fort Lee and the surrounding area.
Also silent films made in Fort Lee.

NJ266-520
Madonna Cemetery and Mausoleum
2070 Hoefley's Lane
Fort Lee NJ 07024

(201) 944-7723

OPEN: M-F 8:30-4, Sa 8:30-noon; closed Sundays, Thanksgiving, Christmas, and New Year's
COPYING FACILITIES: yes

HOLDINGS:
Total volume: not specified
Inclusive dates: 1855 -
Description: Records and personal papers relevant to the history of Madonna Church and Cemetery. Included are journals of pastors active in their establishment, business records, burial records, architectural plans and drawings, and photographs dating from the 1930's to the present, including aerial photographs.

FORT MONMOUTH

NJ270-800
United States Army
   Communications-Electronics Museum
Myer Hall
Avenue of Memories
Fort Monmouth NJ 07703

(201) 532-2445

OPEN: M-F 8-4; closed weekends and holidays
COPYING FACILITIES: yes
MATERIALS SOLICITED: Background papers and manuscripts on the development of electronics equipment. Will also accept materials pertaining to the development of communications and electronics equipment used by the U.S. Army.

HOLDINGS:
Total volume: 60 l.f.
Inclusive dates: 1860 -
Description: A collection of manuscripts, audio-visual material, and correspondence relating chiefly to the development of communications and electronics equipment in the U.S. Army. Included are logbooks, journals, and correspondence pertaining to the U.S. Veterans Signal Corps Association; records of the 1st Telegraph Battalion, World War I; a few diaries; some reminiscences of radio pioneers; and documents and photographs describing many obsolete and rare items of equipment.

SEE: Hamer; NUCMC, 1967 (as U.S. Army Signal Corps Museum).

SEE: Paszek.

FRANKFORD TOWNSHIP

NJ273-740
Sussex County Library
Sussex County History Room
Route 655
Frankford Township NJ

MAILING ADDRESS:
R.D. 3, Box 76
Newton NJ 07860

(201) 948-3660

OPEN: M-Th 8:30-8:30, F 8:30-6, Sa 9-5; closed Sundays and holidays
COPYING FACILITIES: yes
MATERIALS SOLICITED: Information related to Sussex County history. Will also accept local genealogy files.

HOLDINGS:
Total volume: 5 l.f.
Inclusive dates: 1860 -
Description: A local history collection, primarily 20th century, including genealogy files, church and cemetery records, a ledger, and several photocopies of manuscript genealogical works.

FREEHOLD

NJ276-510

Monmouth County Historical
  Association
Library
70 Court Street
Freehold NJ 07728

(201) 462-1466

OPEN: W-Sa 10-4; closed other days and
  holidays
USER FEES: one dollar
COPYING FACILITIES: yes
MATERIALS SOLICITED: Records of Monmouth County business, industrial, and
  mercantile concerns of the 18th and
  19th centuries; local history collections
  for the various communities of the
  county; papers of local political and
  labor groups and leaders; genealogical
  manuscripts; and papers and records of
  the county's ethnic and racial minorities. Will also accept photographs;
  records of county steamboat companies; and diaries and collections of family papers.

HOLDINGS:
> *Total volume:* 30,000 items
> *Inclusive dates:* 1660 -
> *Description:* Materials relating to Monmouth County and central New Jersey.
> Included are personal and business papers
> and records; records of the North American Phalanx, a mid-19th century communal group; records of the Monmouth
> County Historical Association; church
> records; records of 19th and early 20th
> century steamboat companies; and materials documenting shipwrecks along the
> county's coast in the 19th century.
>
> Also included are other materials relating to the American Revolution, especially the Battle of Monmouth, the Civil
> War, 17th-19th century ironworks, 19th
> century women's education, and local history.

SEE: Hinding; Leventhal and Mooney - I.

GLASSBORO

NJ280-270

Glassboro State College
Savitz Library
Stewart Room
Glassboro NJ 08028

(609) 863-6302

OPEN: M-F 8-4; closed weekends and
  holidays
ACCESS: identification required; an
  appointment is advised
COPYING FACILITIES: yes
MATERIALS SOLICITED: New Jersey history. Will also accept materials in specific areas of U.S. history, especially
  the Revolutionary War period; Quaker
  history; genealogy; Indian lore; nearby
  localities, such as Pennsylvania; and
  Glassboro State College.

HOLDINGS:
> *Total volume:* 7,000 items
> *Inclusive dates:* 18th century - 19th
> century
> *Description:* Manuscript collections
> consisting primarily of papers from such
> southern New Jersey families as the
> Howells, Ladds, Brownings, Leamings,
> Haines, Innskeeps, and Lippincotts.
> There are also about 60 items relating to
> the Rush-Boudinot U.S. Mint controversy; Quaker materials, including minutes
> of the Haddonfield Women's Meeting,
> 1725-76, kept by Elizabeth Haddon;
> manumission papers freeing slaves owned
> by members of the Society of Friends;
> and 500 original deeds of old West Jersey.

SEE: NUCMC, 1967.

SEE: Schatz; Robbins.

HACKENSACK

NJ304-80

Bergen County Historical Society
Johnson Public Library
275 Moore Street
Hackensack NJ

MAILING ADDRESS:
P.O. Box 55
River Edge NJ 07661

(201) 343-4781

OPEN: M-Th 9-9, F, Sa 9-5; closed
  Sundays and holidays
ACCESS: 18 years old or older
COPYING FACILITIES: yes

HOLDINGS:
> *Total volume:* 11,000 pages
> *Inclusive dates:* 1680 - 19th century
> *Description:* Local government records
> and private manuscripts, including court
> records, vital statistics, reports, tax books,
> journals, account books, letters, photographs, genealogical materials, and other
> papers related to the history of Bergen
> County.

GUIDES: Hackensack-Ridgewood Local
  History Service, Manuscript Microfilm
  Project, *Manuscripts on Microfilm*
  (Johnson Free Public Library, 1976).

SEE: NUCMC, 1962.

HACKETTSTOWN

NJ308-120

Centenary College
Taylor Memorial Library Learning
  Resource Center
Centenariana Collection
400 Jefferson Street
Hackettstown NJ 07840

(201) 852-1400, Ext. 243

OPEN: M-Th 9-10, F 9-5, Sa 9-1, Su
  1:30-9; special summer and holiday
  hours
ACCESS: appointment by letter or
  telephone call
COPYING FACILITIES: yes

MATERIALS SOLICITED: Papers, programs, pictures, and news clippings of
  Centenary College alumnae concerning
  its history.

HOLDINGS:
> *Total volume:* 12 file drawers
> *Inclusive dates:* 1700 -
> *Description:* Letters, deeds, account
> books, ledgers, cemetery records, and other documents relating to Warren and Sussex counties and northwestern New Jersey. There is also a collection of correspondence, photographs, and other papers of Centenary College alumnae,
> dating from 1874 to the present.

SEE: Hinding.

NJ308-320

Hackettstown Historical Society
Museum
106 Church Street
Hackettstown NJ 07840

(201) 852-8797

OPEN: M-W, F 9-4, Sa by appointment;
  closed Thursdays, Sundays, and
  holidays
COPYING FACILITIES: no
MATERIALS SOLICITED: Letters, public
  records, photographs, and other materials relating to the Hackettstown area.

HOLDINGS:
> *Total volume:* 8,500 items; 10 file
> drawers
> *Inclusive dates:* 1751 -
> *Description:* Letters, deeds, maps, and
> photographs relating to people, buildings,
> and areas of interest in and around
> Hackettstown.

HADDON HEIGHTS

NJ312-320

Haddon Heights Public Library
608 Station Avenue
Haddon Heights NJ 08035

(609) 547-7132

OPEN: M-F 10-9, Sa 10-2; closed
  Sundays, holidays, and Saturdays, July
  - Aug.
COPYING FACILITIES: yes
MATERIALS SOLICITED: History of Haddon Heights, including photographs.

HOLDINGS:
> *Total volume:* 10 l.f.; 200 items
> *Inclusive dates:* 1875 -
> *Description:* Materials pertaining to
> Haddon Heights, including diaries,
> reminiscences, documents, oral history recordings, and photographs of homes,
> buildings, and events.

HADDONFIELD

NJ316-310
Haddonfield Public Library
Haddon Avenue and Tanner Street
Haddonfield NJ 08033

(609) 429-1304

OPEN: M-F 10-9, Sa 10-5, Su 1-5; closed
holidays
COPYING FACILITIES: yes
MATERIALS SOLICITED: Material relating
to Haddonfield. Will also accept material relating to the history and genealogy of southern New Jersey.

HOLDINGS:
> *Total volume:* 16 vols.; 3 boxes; 25
> items
> > *Inclusive dates:* 1900 -
> > *Description:* Minutes, correspondence,
> and special files of the Haddonfield Civic
> Association; Harvard Law School note-
> books of Alfred E. Driscoll, Governor of
> New Jersey; and a series of interview
> tapes and transcripts with Haddonfield
> senior citizens, emphasizing their recollec-
> tions of life in Haddonfield and informa-
> tion about local organizations or groups
> with which they were affiliated.

NJ316-330
Historical Society of Haddonfield
Greenfield Hall
343 King's Highway East
Haddonfield NJ 08033

no telephone

SEE: Hamer.

Questionnaire not returned.

HAMBURG

NJ318-320
Hardyston Heritage Society, Inc.
Old Monroe Schoolhouse Museum
Hamburg NJ

MAILING ADDRESS:
RD 1, Box 599
Hamburg NJ 07419

no telephone

OPEN: May - Oct., Su 1-4; closed other
times
ACCESS: appointment required
COPYING FACILITIES: no
MATERIALS SOLICITED: Materials relating
to rural education in one-room schools
in New Jersey, 1800-1930, and particularly to the Old Monroe Schoolhouse.

HOLDINGS:
> *Total volume:* 230 items
> *Inclusive dates:* 1819 - 1930
> *Description:* Photographs, diplomas,
student notebooks, diaries, account
books, registers, correspondence, and 30
oral history recordings, relating to the Old
Monroe Schoolhouse and its students and
teachers.

HIBERNIA

NJ330-320
Historical Society of the Rockaways
Rockaway Township Free Public
Library
Green Pond Road
Hibernia NJ

MAILING ADDRESS:
Box 100
Hibernia NJ 07842

(201) 627-2344

OPEN: M, W, F 10-9, Tu, Th 9-5, Sa
10-4; closed Sundays and holidays
ACCESS: appointment required
COPYING FACILITIES: yes
MATERIALS SOLICITED: Materials per-
taining to Old Rockaway Township.

HOLDINGS:
> *Total volume:* 2 file cabinets
> *Inclusive dates:* 1800 -
> *Description:* Materials relating to the
history of Rockaway Township, including
manuscripts, documents, photographs,
oral history interviews, reminiscences, letters, genealogical information, and research papers relating to the history of
iron mines, forges, and blast furnaces.

SEE: Hinding.

HIGHTSTOWN

NJ339-40
The Aaron Burr Association
R. D. 1
Route 33, Box 429
Hightstown NJ 08520

(609) 448-2218

OPEN: by appointment only
COPYING FACILITIES: no
MATERIALS SOLICITED: Any materials
having to do with Aaron Burr, members of his immediate family, allied
families, close associates, and on the
political and economic situation during
Burr's active life. Will also accept any
genealogical material on the Burr family in America, chiefly the Reverend
Aaron Burr, Col. Aaron Burr's daughter, and Theodosia Burr Alston, as well
as the Reverend John Bartow and descendants.

HOLDINGS:
> *Total volume:* 4 file drawers
> *Inclusive dates:* 1750 -
> *Description:* Primarily genealogical ma-
terial on the Burr family in America,
chiefly Aaron Burr, his daughter
Theodosia Burr Alston, his first wife
Theodosia Bartow Prevost, and his second wife Eliza Boweb Jumel. There is
also correspondence of The Aaron Burr
Association, 1946- .

SEE: Hamer.

HOBOKEN

NJ346-720
Stevens Institute of Technology
Library
Hoboken NJ

MAILING ADDRESS:
Castle Point Station
Hoboken NJ 07030

no telephone

SEE: Hamer; NUCMC, 1959-61.

Questionnaire not returned.

HOPEWELL

NJ358-320
Hopewell Museum
28 East Broad Street
Hopewell NJ 08525

(609) 466-0103

OPEN: M, W, Sa 2-5; closed other days
and holidays
COPYING FACILITIES: yes
MATERIALS SOLICITED: Will accept
church and business records relating to
local history and genealogy.

HOLDINGS:
> *Total volume:* 2 file cabinets; 9 l.f.
> *Inclusive dates:* 1715 -
> *Description:* Local history materials, in-
cluding farm and store account books;
medical daybooks and account books of
Dr. James H. Baldwin and Dr. Benjamin
Van Kirk, school copy books, the Hopewell Township Poor Book, including
town minutes, 1801-61; lawyers' docket
books; ledgers of Rosedale Mills; Somerset Town Book, 1772-1841; family papers; and church records.

IRVINGTON

NJ376-360
Irvington Public Library
Civic Square
Irvington NJ 07111

(201) 372-6400

OPEN: M-Th 9-9, F 9-5:30, Sa 9-5;
closed Sundays, holidays, and
Saturdays in summer
COPYING FACILITIES: yes
MATERIALS SOLICITED: Items relating to
Olympic Park, Irvington, NJ.

HOLDINGS:
> *Total volume:* 24 items; 1,000
> photographs
> > *Inclusive dates:* 1769 -
> > *Description:* A small collection focusing
> on the history of Irvington, including led-
> gers, records of organizations, letters from
> members of the armed forces during
> World War II, audio-visual materials, and
> photographs, many from the 19th cen-
> tury.

JERSEY CITY

NJ386-380
Jersey City Public Library
New Jersey Room
472 Jersey Avenue
Jersey City NJ 07302

(201) 547-4503

OPEN: M-Sa 10-5; closed Saturdays and
  Sundays in summer
ACCESS: prior notice for use of
  manuscripts required
COPYING FACILITIES: yes
MATERIALS SOLICITED: Jersey City and
  Hudson County history and railroad
  history materials dealing with the New
  York-New Jersey area. Will also accept
  other New Jersey history materials and
  personal genealogies.

HOLDINGS:
  Total volume: 92 l.f.; other items
  Inclusive dates: 1700 - 1970
  Description: Manuscripts of the Hudson County Historical Society, including
  legal materials from the files of former
  State Chancellor A. Zabriskie, manuscripts relating to railroad transactions,
  and other local items; records of the Jersey City municipal government; scrapbooks and ledgers of the Jersey City Fire
  Department; maps; photographs; and
  miscellaneous manuscripts.

SEE: Hamer.

KEYPORT

NJ398-440
Keyport Historical Society
Broad Street
Keyport NJ

MAILING ADDRESS:
P.O. Box 312
Keyport NJ 07735

(201) 264-2102, 6119

OPEN: June-Sept. Su 2-5; closed other
  times
COPYING FACILITIES: no
MATERIALS SOLICITED: Materials pertaining to the history of Keyport and
  the surrounding area, including the oyster and shipbuilding industries. Will
  also accept organization records.

HOLDINGS:
  Total volume: 3 boxes
  Inclusive dates: 1820 -
  Description: A collection of ledgers, let-
  ters, photographs, maps, and deeds relat-
  ing to the founding and development of
  Keyport.

LAKEWOOD

NJ408-280
Georgian Court College
Farley Memorial Library
Lakewood NJ 08701

SEE: Hamer.

Questionnaire not returned.

LAMBERTVILLE

NJ412-480
Lambertville Historical Society
The Marshall House Museum
52 Bridge Street
Lambertville NJ

MAILING ADDRESS:
P.O. Box 2
Lambertville NJ 08530

(609) 397-0770

OPEN: by appointment only
COPYING FACILITIES: yes
MATERIALS SOLICITED: Materials on
  Lambertville, particularly the James
  Marshall family. Will also accept ma-
  terials relating to the Lambertville-
  Delaware Valley area.

HOLDINGS:
  Total volume: 10 l.f.
  Inclusive dates: 1750's -
  Description: Materials relating to the
  Lambertville area, including account
  books, logbooks, journals, genealogical
  source data, public documents, maps, and
  aerial photographs.

LAWRENCEVILLE

NJ420-490
The Lawrenceville School
The John Dixon Library
Archives Collection
Lawrenceville NJ 08648

(609) 896-0076

OPEN: M-F 8-5; closed weekends,
  holidays, Dec. 10 - Jan. 1, March, and
  June 1 - Sept. 15
ACCESS: serious scholars only
COPYING FACILITIES: yes
MATERIALS SOLICITED: Materials relating
  to the history and operation of The
  Lawrenceville School. Will also accept
  materials relating to the local area and
  its history.

HOLDINGS:
  Total volume: 30 l.f.
  Inclusive dates: 1826 -
  Description: Correspondence, reports,
  addresses, minutes, diaries, literary manu-
  scripts, photographs, and sound record-
  ings relating to the history of The
  Lawrenceville School and the papers of
  James C. MacKenzie, headmaster,
  1883-99.

SEE: NUCMC, 1972.

SEE ALSO: a typescript guide to the Mac-
  Kenzie papers available at the Library.

LITTLE FALLS

NJ440-490
Little Falls Township Historical
  Society
95 Jacobus Avenue
Little Falls NJ

MAILING ADDRESS:
c/o Mrs. John J. Curreri, President
Little Falls NJ 07424

no telephone

OPEN: M-F 10-8, variable weekend
  hours; closed holidays
COPYING FACILITIES: yes
MATERIALS SOLICITED: Materials per-
  taining to the history of Little Falls,
  including its railroad, cemetery, houses,
  Grandview Park, and Historic Colonial
  Inn.

HOLDINGS:
  Total volume: 3 file cabinets
  Inclusive dates: 1753 -
  Description: Materials pertaining to the
  history of Little Falls and its homes,
  churches, and other buildings, as well as
  records of its Bicentennial parade.

LIVINGSTON

NJ444-240
Free Public Library of Livingston
Memorial Park
Livingston NJ 07039

(201) 992-4600

OPEN: M, W, Th 10-9, Tu, F 10-6, Sa
  10-5; closed Sundays, holidays, and
  Saturdays during July and Aug.
COPYING FACILITIES: yes
MATERIALS SOLICITED: Materials relating
  to the history of Livingston and New
  Jersey.

HOLDINGS:
  Total volume: 70 l.f.; 2 file cabinets
  Inclusive dates: 1813 -
  Description: Materials that describe the
  history of Livingston Township, including
  a police journal, 1907-29; a photographic
  history of Livingston, 1926-46; minutes
  of township meetings, 1813-77; and ten
  oral histories covering local government,
  transportation, education, planning, and
  land development.

SEE: Hinding; Robbins.

MADISON

NJ464-150
Drew University
Library
Madison NJ 07940

no telephone

SEE: Hamer.

Questionnaire not returned.

NJ464-240
Fairleigh Dickinson University
Friendship Library
285 Madison Avenue
Madison NJ 07940

(201) 377-4728

OPEN: M-Th 8:30-10, F 8:30-5, Sa 11-5,
Su 2-10; closed holidays
ACCESS: permission of Library Director
required for use of outdoor advertising
collection
COPYING FACILITIES: yes
MATERIALS SOLICITED: Outdoor advertising materials and manuscripts of cartoonists.

HOLDINGS:
Total volume: 600 l.f.
Inclusive dates: 17th century -
Description: Outdoor advertising collection consisting of slides, photographs,
film footage of highway billboards, correspondence, blueprints, records, ledgers,
legislation, minutes, proceedings, reports
of national and regional committee meetings, and speeches; the Harry 'A' Chesler
collection of original comic art and preliminary sketches (emphasis on 1930's
and 1940's) including cartoonists' manuscripts.
Original graphics from the 17th to
mid-20th century; and material relating
to anthropology, geology, and the group
psychotherapy movement.

SEE: Robbins.

NJ464-510
Madison Historical Society
Madison Public Library
39 Keep Street
Madison NJ

MAILING ADDRESS:
P.O. Box 148
Madison NJ 07940

(201) 377-0722

OPEN: M, Tu, Th 9-9, W, F 9-6, Sa 9-5,
Su 2-5; closed holidays
COPYING FACILITIES: yes
MATERIALS SOLICITED: Materials per-
taining to the history of Madison. Will
also accept materials relating to New
Jersey history.

HOLDINGS:
Total volume: 2 file drawers
Inclusive dates: 1776 -
Description: A local history collection
concentrating on the early development
of Madison, including correspondence,
diaries, account books, school and organization records, oral history recordings,
and photographs.

SEE: Hamer.

SEE: Hinding.

NJ464-666
United Methodist Church
General Commission on Archives and
History
36 Madison Avenue
Madison NJ

MAILING ADDRESS:
P.O. Box 127
Madison NJ 07940

(201) 822-2787

OPEN: M-F 9-5; closed weekends and
holidays
ACCESS: advance permission required
for access to missionary
correspondence
COPYING FACILITIES: yes
MATERIALS SOLICITED: Records of the
United Methodist church, as well as
personal papers of pastors, missionaries, and church administrators. Will
also accept ecumenical records that reflect United Methodist cooperation.

HOLDINGS:
Total volume: 6,000 c.f.
Inclusive dates: 1784 -
Description: Records of the United
Methodist church and its antecedents: the
Methodist Episcopal church; the Methodist Episcopal Church, South; the Methodist Protestant church; the Methodist
church; the Evangelical Association; the
United Evangelical church; the Evangelical church; the Church of the United
Brethren in Christ; and the Evangelical
United Brethren church. Included are the
records of various boards, agencies, and
institutions, as well as the papers of bishops, pastors, denominational executives,
and missionaries.The repository also
holds the records of the Primitive Methodist Church of America (1829-).

SEE: NUCMC, 1967.

SEE: Hinding.

SEE ALSO: Robert B. Downs, ed., Re-
sources of North Carolina Libraries
(Governor's Commission on Library
Resources, 1965).

In 1983, the United Methodist
church's archives moved from 39
Lake Shore Drive, Lake Junaluska,
NC 28745.

MAPLEWOOD

NJ482-520
Maplewood Memorial Library
51 Baker Street
Maplewood NJ 07040

(201) 762-1622

OPEN: M, W 10-9, Tu, Th 10-6, F, Sa
10-5; closed Sundays, holidays,
Saturdays in Summer
COPYING FACILITIES: yes
MATERIALS SOLICITED: Correspondence,
journals, photographs, deeds, and other
materials relating to the history of the
township of Maplewood.

HOLDINGS:
Total volume: 6 c.f.
Inclusive dates: 1870's -
Description: Minutes, financial records,
and librarian's reports of Maplewood Memorial Library; a scrapbook of township
history; photographs; and slides.

MENDHAM

NJ502-520
Mendham Free Public Library
10 Hilltop Road
Mendham NJ 07945

(201) 543-4152

OPEN: M-Th 9-9, F 9-5, Sa 9-4, Su 2-4;
closed Sa, Su July-Aug. and holidays

SEE: Hamer.

Questionnaire not returned.

NJ502-690
Ralston Historical Association
N.J. Route 24
Mendham NJ

MAILING ADDRESS:
Box 301
Mendham NJ 07945

(201) 543-4347

OPEN: by appointment only
COPYING FACILITIES: no
MATERIALS SOLICITED: Records, deeds,
and any other materials pertaining to
local history.

HOLDINGS:
Total volume: 24 c.f.
Inclusive dates: 1784 - 1942
Description: Account books and other
financial records, deeds, indentures, and
correspondence, 1784-1820, of John
Ralston, as well as of those who later
operated his mill and store.

MONTCLAIR

NJ532-515
Montclair Public Library
50 South Fullerton Avenue
Montclair NJ 07042

(201) 744-0500

OPEN: M, W, Th 9-9, Tu 9-6, F 9-5, Sa
10-5; closed Sundays, holidays, and
Saturdays in summer
ACCESS: advance appointment suggested
COPYING FACILITIES: yes
MATERIALS SOLICITED: Materials relating
to Montclair.

HOLDINGS:
Total volume: 7 file drawers;
additional items
Inclusive dates: 1860 -
Description: A collection of photo-
graphs, some diaries, and other manu-
scripts pertaining to the history of
Montclair.

SEE: Novotny; Hinding.

MORRISTOWN

NJ548-400

Joint Free Public Library of
  Morristown and Morris Township
1 Miller Road
Morristown NJ 07960

(201) 538-6161

OPEN: Su 2-5, M-F 9-9, Sa 9-5; closed
  holidays
COPYING FACILITIES: yes
MATERIALS SOLICITED: Material relating
  to Morris County. Will also accept material relating to New Jersey.

HOLDINGS:
  Total volume: 250 items
  Inclusive dates: 1740 - 1880
  Description: A manuscript collection
  relating chiefly to political, religious, and
  business life in Morristown, Morris
  Township, and Morris County, including
  papers of organizations and individuals.

SEE: Hamer (as Morristown Library).

SEE: Robbins; Davis.

NJ548-520

Morris County Historical Society
68 Morris Avenue
Morristown NJ

MAILING ADDRESS:
Box 170
Morristown NJ 07960

(201) 267-3465

OPEN: M-W 9-2, Th 9-4; closed other
  days and holidays, except by
  appointment
ACCESS: advance arrangements requested
COPYING FACILITIES: no
MATERIALS SOLICITED: Materials from
  the Victorian-Edwardian period, with
  emphasis on photography, women, children, architecture, decorative and applied arts, costume, textiles, landscape
  gardening, horticulture, music, and general social and cultural history; materials relating to social and cultural history, architecture, and the decorative
  arts in Morris County; and related New
  Jersey material. Will also accept late
  18th century items from these subject
  areas.

HOLDINGS:
  Total volume: 36 l.f.
  Inclusive dates: 1790 - 1970
  Description: Papers of the Crane family, 1850-1970, relating to 'Acorn Hall'
  and Morris County; photographs of Morris County, New York City, and other
  locations; oral history tapes and transcripts; manuscript school books; diaries;
  and autograph books.

SEE: Hamer.

NJ548-530

Morristown National Historical Park
230 Morris Street
Morristown NJ

MAILING ADDRESS:
P.O. Box 1136 R
Morristown NJ 07960

(201) 539-2016

OPEN: M-F 8-5, Sa 9-5; closed Sundays,
  Christmas, and New Year's
COPYING FACILITIES: yes

HOLDINGS:
  Total volume: 25,000 items
  Inclusive dates: 1700 - 1930
  Description: Materials pertaining to
  American history, especially the American Revolution and its impact on New
  Jersey. Revolutionary War materials include 100 letters, account books and other papers of George Washington, letters
  of prominent political figures, American
  and British army journals and orderly
  books, and 19th century transcripts of
  Hessian soldiers' manuscripts. There is
  also a collection concerning the economic, social, and legal history of 18th and
  19th century Morris County, with emphasis on the iron industry.

SEE: Hamer; NUCMC, 1959-62.

SEE: Gehring; Leventhal and Mooney - I;
  Robbins.

SEE ALSO: Bruce W. Stewart and Joan
  Reilly, eds., *A Guide to the Manuscript
  Collection* (Morristown National His-
  torical Park, 1967); Richard C. Davis,
  *North American Forest History: A
  Guide to Archives and Manuscripts in
  the United States and Canada* (Clio
  Books, 1977).

NJ548-720

The Speedwell Village (Historic
  Speedwell)
333 Speedwell Avenue
Morristown NJ 07960

(201)540-0211

OPEN: Th-Su afternoons by appointment
COPYING FACILITIES: no
MATERIALS SOLICITED: Materials relating
  to the fabrication of iron, the development of the telegraph, and the Vail
  family at Speedwell.

HOLDINGS:
  Total volume: 2 file cabinets; 4
shelves
  Inclusive dates: 1742- 1885
  Description: Papers of Stephen Vail,
  including his journal, business papers,
  and family correspondence, and emphasizing his entrepreneurial activities regarding the Speedwell Iron Works; papers
  of Alfred Vail, who assisted Samuel F. B.
  Morse in developing the telegraph at
  Speedwell Village; and photocopies of
  some of the records of the First Presbyterian Church of Morristown.

SEE: Hinding.

MOUNT HOLLY

NJ552-70

Burlington County Library
West Woodlane Road
Mount Holly NJ 08060

(609) 267-9660

OPEN: M-F 8:30-8:30, Sa 9-5; closed
  Sundays, holidays, and Saturdays July -
  Aug.
COPYING FACILITIES: yes
MATERIALS SOLICITED: Materials relating
  to Burlington County. Will also accept
  materials relating to New Jersey.

HOLDINGS:
  Total volume: not specified
  Inclusive dates: 1777 -
  Description: Materials pertaining to
  Burlington County and New Jersey, including genealogical data, account books
  and ledgers, correspondence, oral histories, photographs, scrapbooks, maps, and
  slides.

SEE: Meckler and McMullin.

NJ552-80

Burlington County Lyceum of History
  and Natural Sciences (Mount Holly
  Library)
307 High Street
Mount Holly NJ 08060

(609) 267-7111

OPEN: M, Tu, Th, F 10-5, W 12-8;
  closed weekends and holidays
ACCESS: identification required
COPYING FACILITIES: yes
MATERIALS SOLICITED: Materials relating
  to the history of Mount Holly,
  Burlington County, and New Jersey.

HOLDINGS:
  Total volume: 600 items
  Inclusive dates: 1765 -
  Description: The original charter of the
  Library, signed in 1765 by King George
  III; original papers by members of the
  Lyceum, dating from 1860; genealogical
  data; maps; deeds; diaries; and correspon-
  dence pertaining to the Burlington Coun-
  ty area, 1800-1920.

SEE: Hamer.

SEE: Meckler and McMullin.

NEPTUNE

NJ564-560

Neptune Historical Museum
25 Neptune Boulevard
Neptune NJ 07753

(201) 775-8241

OPEN: Tu, F 10-5:30, Th 1-9; closed
  other days and holidays
COPYING FACILITIES: yes
MATERIALS SOLICITED: Photographs of
  the Neptune and Ocean Grove, NJ,
  shore area. Will also accept manuscripts of the area.

HOLDINGS:
Total volume: 1 file cabinet
Inclusive dates: 1793 -
Description: Manuscripts, photographs, post cards, oral history recordings, and motion pictures relating to Neptune.

SEE: Hinding.

NEW BRUNSWICK

NJ568-540
New Brunswick Historical Club
Special Collections Department
Alexander Library
Rutgers University
New Brunswick NJ 08901

(201) 932-7006, 7510

OPEN: M-Sa 9-5; closed Sundays, holidays, and Saturdays during summer
COPYING FACILITIES: yes

HOLDINGS:
Total volume: 8 file drawers
Inclusive dates: 1730 -
Description: Manuscript or typescript copies of addresses given before the New Brunswick Historical Club, 1870-1938; records of the Club, including correspondence; 18th and 19th century manuscripts relating to New Brunswick and other parts of New Jersey; and other items.

NJ568-570
Reformed Church in America
Archives
21 Seminary Place
New Brunswick NJ 08901

(201) 246-1779

OPEN: by appointment only
ACCESS: prior arrangements should be made
COPYING FACILITIES: yes
MATERIALS SOLICITED: Papers relating to the Reformed Church in America, including correspondence; records of congregations, judicatories, and agencies; and architectural data regarding its church buildings. Will also accept materials of organizations or individuals connected with the Reformed Church in America and its mission fields.

HOLDINGS:
Total volume: 570 l.f.
Inclusive dates: 1628 -
Description: Records of the Reformed Church in America, General Synod, including some correspondence of Dutch churches in North America with Holland; missionary correspondence and reports from China, India, Japan, the Persian Gulf, and parts of the American West; records of the New Brunswick Theological Seminary; and personal papers of Reformed Church ministers and others affiliated with the Church's work.

SEE: Hamer; NUCMC, 1962 (as New Brunswick Theological Seminary, Library).

SEE: Martin; Hinding; Gehring.

NJ568-625
Rutgers, the State University of New Jersey
Douglass College
American Studies Department
New Jersey Folklore Archive
Hickman Hall 413
George Street
New Brunswick NJ 08901

(201) 932-9179

OPEN: M-F 8:30-12 noon; closed weekends and holidays
ACCESS: serious researchers only
COPYING FACILITIES: yes
MATERIALS SOLICITED: Folklore materials relating to New Jersey.

HOLDINGS:
Total volume: 2 file cabinets
Inclusive dates: 1975 -
Description: Folklore collections relating to academic lore, religious lore, drug lore, agricultural lore, belief tales, children's folklore, clothing, cookery, cults and sects, death lore, calendar customs, epitaphs, fables, family legends, folk architecture, folk crafts, folk dance, folk medicine, folk music, folk poetry, folk song, folk tales, fraternity lore, games, ghost stories, graffiti, holidays, jewelry, jokes, jump rope rhymes, legends, medical lore, plant lore, occupational lore, proverbs, quilts, scatology, superstitions, and witchcraft.

NJ568-670
Rutgers, the State University of New Jersey
University Libraries
Special Collections Department
Alexander Library
169 College Avenue
New Brunswick NJ 08903

(201) 932-7510, 7527

OPEN: M-Sa 9-5; closed Sundays, Saturdays during summer, and holidays
COPYING FACILITIES: yes
MATERIALS SOLICITED: Materials relating to New Jersey. Will also accept other materials.

HOLDINGS:
Total volume: 8,000,000 items
Inclusive dates: 14th century -
Description: Materials relating largely to New Jersey, but with national and international coverage. Photographs include 3,000 views of New Brunswick and 18,000 postcards, with about 10,000 of New Jersey scenes. Manuscript collections include papers of the Morris family, Clifford P. Case, Walt Whitman, William Dean Howells, and William Eliot Griffis, organizer of the American system of education in Japan.

Archives include records of the Consumers' League of New Jersey, the New Jersey League of Women Voters, and the Sheltering Arms Children's Service. Other holdings include manuscript maps, records of the Genealogical Society of New Jersey, and a 7,500 item collection on New Brunswick history.

GUIDES: Herbert F. Smith, *A Guide to the Manuscript Collection of the Rutgers University Library* (Rutgers University, 1964).

SEE: Hamer; NUCMC, 1965-66.

SEE: Allard, Crawley, and Edmison; Davis; Duignan; Hinding; Hines; Hounshell; Novotny; Robbins; Schatz; Leventhal and Mooney - I.

NJ568-680
Rutgers, the State University of New Jersey
University Libraries
University Archives
New Brunswick NJ 08903

(201) 932-7006, 7510

OPEN: M, Tu, Th, F 9-5, W 9-9, Sa 12-6 academic year; W, Sa 9-5 Summer; closed Sundays
COPYING FACILITIES: yes
MATERIALS SOLICITED: Records of all branches of the University, of faculty, staff, students, alumni/alumnae and their organizations, and other materials that serve to document the history of the institution.

HOLDINGS:
Total volume: 3,800 c.f.
Inclusive dates: 1770 -
Description: Records of major offices, branches, governing bodies and faculties, and the records, papers and memorabilia of individuals and organizations associated with the University. Included are an extensive collection of photographs, material relating to Paul Robeson, class of 1919, and the records of the International Union of Electrical, Radio and Machine Workers.

SEE: Hamer.

SEE: Hinding.

NEW PROVIDENCE

NJ574-560
New Providence Historical Society
Museum and Library
1350 Springfield Avenue
New Providence NJ

MAILING ADDRESS:
P.O. Box 661
New Providence NJ 07974

(201) 464-5798

OPEN: Su 2-4, Th 10-12 or by appointment
COPYING FACILITIES: no
MATERIALS SOLICITED: Materials relating to the history of New Providence and its people, including diaries, photographs, and tape recordings.

HOLDINGS:
Total volume: 3 file cabinets; 130 vols.; 60 oral histories; 60-70 ledgers
Inclusive dates: 1600 -
Description: Materials relating to the history and genealogy of New Providence. Included are items on local government, churches, schools, buildings, the police and fire departments, floods, and zoning. There are also photographs,

maps, oral history interviews with local people, ledgers and account books of a local general store, club minutes, and manuscript voting lists.

SEE: Hinding.

NEWARK

NJ578-510
The New Jersey Historical Society
Library
230 Broadway
Newark NJ 07104

(201) 483-3939

OPEN: Tu-Sa 9:30-4:15; closed other days and holidays
COPYING FACILITIES: yes
MATERIALS SOLICITED: Manuscripts relating to New Jersey history, including personal papers; business, public, and institutional records; literary manuscripts; maps; and early architectural drawings and records. Will also accept, selectively, manuscripts concerning the mid-Atlantic States and copies and transcripts of inaccessible historical material.

HOLDINGS:
Total volume: 1,250 l.f.
Inclusive dates: 1644 -
Description: Materials relating to the history of New Jersey, especially northern New Jersey in the 18th and 19th centuries, and including papers of colonial and Revolutionary War era figures and political, business, and religious leaders.

SEE: Hamer; NUCMC, 1959-61.

SEE: Allard, Crawley, and Edmison; Davis; Gehring; Hinding; Hounshell; Krichmar; Leventhal and Mooney - I; Novotny; Schatz.

NJ578-515
New Jersey Institute of Technology
Archives
323 Dr. Martin Luther King, Jr.
Boulevard
Newark NJ 07102

(201) 596-3110

OPEN: M-F 9-4; closed weekends, Christmas, Thanksgiving, and Easter
COPYING FACILITIES: yes
MATERIALS SOLICITED: Material related to scientist and inventor Edward Weston.

HOLDINGS:
Total volume: 200 boxes
Inclusive dates: 1860 -
Description: Archives of the New Jersey Institute of Technology, 1880 - , including printed material, microfiche, blueprints, and photographs. There are also 40 boxes of materials on the inventor Edward Weston, including laboratory books, letters, court proceedings, and memorabilia.

NJ578-530
The Newark Museum
49 Washington Street
Newark NJ

MAILING ADDRESS:
P.O. Box 540
Newark NJ 07101

(201) 733-6600

OPEN: daily 12-5 by appointment only; closed holidays
ACCESS: advance written request required
COPYING FACILITIES: yes
MATERIALS SOLICITED: Will accept materials relating to Newark and New Jersey (including fire fighting), and Tibet.

HOLDINGS:
Total volume: 3,529 items
Inclusive dates: 1619 -
Description: American and European documents, 1619-1960, consisting mainly of indentures, business records, papers of prominent New Jersey residents, artists' correspondence, and materials relating to fire fighting. There are Oriental materials, including religious manuscripts, correspondence, and maps from India, China, Southeast Asia, Japan, and especially Tibet. Visual documents include photographs, slides, and films of Tibet, and photographs of New Jersey and Africa.

SEE: Hamer.

SEE: Martin; Spalek.

SEE ALSO: Ann Novotny, ed., *Picture Sources 3* (Special Libraries Assn., 1975); 'Fires and Firefighters of Newark,' *The Museum* 20 (Fall 1968); 'The Western Experience in Tibet, 1327-1950,' *The Museum* 24 (Spring and Summer 1972); 'Newark Long Ago: 19th Century Photographs,' *The Museum* 26 (Fall 1975).

NJ578-540
Newark Public Library
Art and Music Department
5 Washington Street
Newark NJ 07101

(201) 733-7828

OPEN: M, W, Th 9-9, Tu, F 9-5:30, Sa 9-5; closed Sundays and holidays
COPYING FACILITIES: yes
MATERIALS SOLICITED: Autograph letters and documents of literary, art, and music figures with New Jersey connections. Will also accept New Jersey historical manuscripts and documents.

HOLDINGS:
Total volume: 3.5 file drawers
Inclusive dates: 1880's -
Description: Autograph letters, documents, typescripts, manuscript scores, and memorabilia relating to literary and music figures, some with New Jersey connections.

SEE: Hamer; NUCMC, 1960.

SEE: Robbins; Hinding; Novotny.

NEWTON

NJ586-720
Sussex County Historical Society
Manuscripts Collection
82 Main Street
Newton NJ 07860

SEE: Hamer; NUCMC, 1979.

Questionnaire not returned.

OLD BRIDGE TOWNSHIP

NJ622-690
Madison Township Historical Society
Thomas Warne Historical Museum
and Library
Route 516
Old Bridge Township NJ

MAILING ADDRESS:
Box 150, R.D. 1
Matawan NJ 07747

(201) 566-0348

OPEN: W 9:30-noon, 1st Sunday of each month 1-4 or by appointment
COPYING FACILITIES: yes
MATERIALS SOLICITED: Any materials including diaries, music, photographs, and maps, pertaining to New Jersey history, Middlesex County, South Amboy Township before 1869, and Madison Township after 1869.

HOLDINGS:
Total volume: not specified
Inclusive dates: 1700 - 1930
Description: Materials related to the Revolutionary War, churches, cemeteries, businesses, genealogy, land holdings, schools, and Indians in Middlesex and Monmouth counties.

SEE: Hinding.

PARAMUS

NJ630-40
Armenian Missionary Association of
America, Inc.
A. A. Bedikian Library
140 Forest Avenue
Paramus NJ 07652

(201) 265-2608 (days); (201) 265-2607 (evenings)

OPEN: M-F 9-5; closed weekends and holidays
ACCESS: appointment required
COPYING FACILITIES: yes
MATERIALS SOLICITED: Will accept manuscripts dealing with Armenian evangelical history.

HOLDINGS:
Total volume: 2,000 vols.
Inclusive dates: 1919 -
Description: Minutes, annual reports, newsletters, and correspondence of the Association.

PATERSON

NJ646-630
Passaic County Historical Society
Paterson NJ

MAILING ADDRESS:
Box 1729
Paterson NJ 07509

(201) 881-2761

SEE: Hamer.

Questionnaire not returned.

NJ646-660
Paterson Public Library
250 Broadway
Paterson NJ 07501

(201) 881-7038, 7056, 8014

OPEN: M-W 8-8, Th, F 10-6, Sa 9-5;
closed Sundays and holidays
ACCESS: advance arrangements advisable
COPYING FACILITIES: yes

HOLDINGS:
Total volume: 8 file drawers; 100,000
photographs; 200 items
Inclusive dates: 1791 -
Description: Correspondence, leases,
deeds, maps, and engineering drawings of
the Society for Establishing Useful Manufactures, 1791-1946, and 100,000 photographs, mostly negatives, documenting local history, including many taken by
Charles Heinrichs, Sr., and his son Alben
and daughter Dorothy. There are also letters, sketches, blueprints, and historical
notes, 1875-1900, of John P. Holland
concerning his submarine invention.
Includes daybooks of Jacob Rogers.

SEE: Hinding.

PENNINGTON

NJ658-840
The United Methodist Church
Southern New Jersey Conference
Historical Society
Meckler Library
Pennington School
112 West Delaware Avenue
Pennington NJ 08534

(609) 737-1838

OPEN: M-F 9-5, summer hours by
appointment only; closed weekends,
holidays, and school vacations
COPYING FACILITIES: yes
MATERIALS SOLICITED: Materials relating
to United Methodism and its antecedent bodies in southern New Jersey.
Will also accept materials relating to
United Methodism in other areas.

HOLDINGS:
Total volume: not specified
Inclusive dates: 1790's -
Description: Materials relating to the
United Methodist church in southern
New Jersey, such as records of closed
churches, ministers' diaries and other pa-
pers, records of conference institutions,
agencies, and personnel, and miscella-

neous historical data regarding conference
churches.

PERTH AMBOY

NJ666-650
Proprietary House Association
272 High Street
Perth Amboy NJ

MAILING ADDRESS:
P.O. Drawer 868
Perth Amboy NJ 08862

(201) 826-2100

OPEN: by appointment only
COPYING FACILITIES: yes
MATERIALS SOLICITED: Materials related
to William Franklin, Colonial Governor of New Jersey; his associates; the
Proprietary House; and Perth Amboy
prior to 1820.

HOLDINGS:
Total volume: 340 items
Inclusive dates: 1680's -
Description: Materials relating to Wil-
liam Franklin, the New Jersey Assembly,
the Proprietary House, and the city of
Perth Amboy, 1762-1820.

PLAINFIELD

NJ674-720
Seventh Day Baptist Historical
Society
510 Watchung Avenue
Plainfield NJ 07061

no telephone

SEE: Hamer; NUCMC, 1972.

Questionnaire not returned.

PRINCETON

NJ692-190
E. R. Squibb & Sons
Lawrenceville-Princeton Road
Princeton NJ

MAILING ADDRESS:
P.O. Box 4000
Princeton NJ 08540

(609) 921-4000

OPEN: by appointment only
COPYING FACILITIES: yes
MATERIALS SOLICITED: Materials relating
to the history of Squibb. Will also accept significant materials in the history
of pharmacy and medicine.

HOLDINGS:
Total volume: 104 file drawers
Inclusive dates: 1850 -
Description: Records and memorabilia
directly associated with or about E. R.
Squibb & Sons, its founder, and its asso-
ciated or subsidiary enterprises in the
United States and abroad.

NJ692-210
Educational Testing Service
Archives
Rosedale Road
Princeton NJ

MAILING ADDRESS:
B-008
Princeton NJ 08541

(609) 734-5744

OPEN: M-F 8:30-4:45; closed weekends
and holidays
ACCESS: prior arrangements are advised
COPYING FACILITIES: yes
MATERIALS SOLICITED: Corporate
records and publications of Educational
Testing Service and related material.

HOLDINGS:
Total volume: 1,000 l.f.
Inclusive dates: 1899 -
Description: Materials pertaining to the
educational, research, and testing activities of Educational Testing Service (1948
-), and, to a lesser degree, to the earlier
testing activities of its founding organizations, the American Council on Education, the Carnegie Foundation for the Advancement of Teaching, and the College
Entrance Examination Board. Included
are corporate records and papers of staff
members; corporate publications and research reports; journal articles and
speeches; and photographs, tapes, and
other audio-visual material.

SEE: Hinding.

SEE ALSO: preliminary inventories of
some record groups available to qualified researchers at the repository.

NJ692-320
Historical Society of Princeton
Library
Bainbridge House
158 Nassau Street
Princeton NJ 08540

(609) 921-6748

OPEN: W, F 12-4 or by appointment
COPYING FACILITIES: yes
MATERIALS SOLICITED: Materials per-
taining to the history of the town of
Princeton and the surrounding area.

HOLDINGS:
Total volume: 90 l.f.
Inclusive dates: 1669 -
Description: Materials documenting the
history of the town of Princeton, including approximately 1,000 manuscripts; 75
ledgers, account books, and minute
books; 7,000 glass plate negatives; and 3
trunks of papers regarding Richard Stockton and his family.

GUIDES: Joseph J. Felcone, Guide to the
Manuscript Collections in the Historical
Society of Princeton, New Jersey (1980).

NJ692-610

Princeton Theological Seminary
Speer Library
Mercer Street and Library Place
Princeton NJ

MAILING ADDRESS:
P.O. Box 111
Princeton NJ 08540

(609) 921-8092

OPEN: M-Th 8-11, F 8-5, Sa 9-5, Su
7-11; closed holidays; shorter hours
during vacations
COPYING FACILITIES: yes
MATERIALS SOLICITED: Materials relevant to the theological enterprise. Will
also accept materials with some historical connection with Princeton Seminary.

HOLDINGS:
Total volume: 1,500 items; 28 l.f.
Inclusive dates: 1767 -
Description: Materials relating to
Princeton Theological Seminary and the
Presbyterian church. Included are papers
of such faculty-clergy as Archibald
Alexander, Charles Hodge, Samuel Mill-
er, and Benjamin B. Warfield, and the
papers of alumni-missionaries Robert
Hamill Nassau and Sheldon Jackson. Of
special interest are the papers of Robert
E. Speer (28 l.f.), onetime General Sec-
retary of the Board of Foreign Missions
of the Presbyterian Church in the U.S.A.;
the papers of Revolutionary War chaplain
David Avery; and records of local
churches within the bounds of the former
Synod of New Jersey.

SEE: Hamer; NUCMC, 1959-62.

SEE: Robbins.

SEE ALSO: Peter Duignan, *Handbook of
American Resources for African Studies*
(Hoover Institution, 1967); Robert O.
Collins and Peter Duignan, *Americans
in Africa* (Hoover Institution, 1963).

NJ692-620

Princeton University
Art Museum
Princeton NJ 08544

(609) 452-3788

OPEN: M-F 9-5; closed weekends and
holidays
ACCESS: by appointment only
COPYING FACILITIES: no

HOLDINGS:
Total volume: 1 item
Inclusive dates: 1783
Description: A letter from George
Washington to Elisha Boudinot.

NJ692-660

Princeton University
Library
Department of Rare Books and
Special Collections
Manuscript Division
Princeton NJ 08544

(609) 452-3184

OPEN: M-F 9-5; closed weekends and
holidays

COPYING FACILITIES: yes
MATERIALS SOLICITED: Materials that
build upon existing areas of strength
and that support the University's teaching programs, with special attention to
papers of American authors and public
officials. Will also accept other materials of significance to potential researchers.

HOLDINGS:
Total volume: 20,500 l.f.
Inclusive dates: Babylonian period -
Description: Materials representing a
broad range in time, area, and subject
interest. Most of the material is of American origin, with particular emphasis on
papers of 20th century authors and persons in government and public life. Other
areas of strength include documents of
the ancient world such as cuneiform tablets and papyri, medieval and Renaissance manuscripts, Middle Eastern manuscripts (Arabic, Persian, Indic, Turkish),
Chinese manuscripts, manuscripts in the
indigenous languages of Middle America,
and English literary manuscripts of the
19th century.

SEE: Hamer; NUCMC, 1959-62, 71-72.

SEE: Meckler and McMullin; Allard,
Crawley, and Edmison; Martin; Spalek;
Robbins; Hinding.

SEE ALSO: Articles in *The Princeton University Library Chronicle* (see its
25-year index, 1969); Lawrence J.
Paszek, comp., *United States Air Force
History: A Guide to Documentary
Sources* (Office of Air Force History,
1973); C. U. Faye and W. H. Bond,
eds., *Supplement* to Seymour De Ricci
and J. W. Wilson, *Census of Medieval
and Renaissance Manuscripts in the
United States and Canada* (The Bib-
liographic Society of America, 1962);
Rudolph Mach, *Catalogue of Arabic
Manuscripts (Yahuda Section) in the
Garrett Collection in the Princeton Uni-
versity Library* (Princeton Univ. Press,
1977); Robert Wauchope, Howard F.
Cline, and others, *Handbook of Middle
American Indians: Guide to
Ethnohistorical Sources* (Univ. of Texas
Press, 1975).

Howard C. Rice, Jr., and Anne S. K. Brown,
trans. and eds., *The American Campaigns
of Rochambeau's Army, 1780, 1781, 1782,
1783* (Princeton Univ. Press and Brown
Univ. Press, 1972); *Map Collections in
the United States and Canada, A Direc-
tory* (Special Libraries Assn., 1970);
*Source Materials for the Recent History of
Astronomy and Astrophysics: A Checklist
of Manuscript Collections in the United
States* (American Institute of Physics,
1971); Thomas S. Kuhn, John L.
Heilbron, Paul Forman, and Lini Allen,
*Sources for History of Quantum Physics:
An Inventory and Report* (American
Philosophical Society, 1967); Joan Nelson
Warnow, *A Selection of Manuscript Col-
lections at American Repositories*
(American Institute of Physics, 1969).

James M. Merrill, 'The Naval Historian and
His Sources,' *American Archivist* 32 (July
1969); Alan M. Meckler and Ruth
McMullin, comps., *Oral History Collections* (Bowker, 1975); *The Mendel Newsletter* 1 (April 1968); Walter Schatz, ed.,
Directory of Afro-American Resources

(Bowker, 1970); Peter Duignan, *Handbook of American Resources for African
Studies* (Hoover Institution, 1967); and
the following publications of Princeton
University Library: Nancy Bressler, *A Descriptive Catalogue of Papers in the Area
of Twentieth Century American Statecraft
and Public Policy* (1974); *New Jersey
Road Maps in the 18th Century* (1970);
*The John Foster Dulles Oral History Col-
lection, A Descriptive Catalogue* (1974).

NJ692-880

Westminster Choir College
Talbott Library
College Archives
Hamilton Avenue at Walnut Lane
Princeton NJ 08540

(609) 921-3658

OPEN: by appointment only
COPYING FACILITIES: yes
MATERIALS SOLICITED: Materials relating
to the College (located in Dayton, OH,
1920-29; Ithaca, NY, 1929-32; and
Princeton, 1932-) and its founders
(Dr. and Mrs. John F. Williamson), its
early benefactors (Mrs. Katherine H.
Talbott and Mrs. Sophia S. Taylor),
and tours and performances of its
choirs, faculty members, and graduates.

HOLDINGS:
Total volume: 10 file cabinets
Inclusive dates: 1920 -
Description: Correspondence, diaries,
and minute books of faculty and trustee
meetings, alumni newsletters, college catalogs, concert programs, newspaper
clippings, sound recordings of interviews
with early students and of other subjects,
photographs, motion pictures, video
tapes, and scrapbooks, all relating to
Westminster Choir College.

RANDOLPH

NJ708-690

Randolph Township Public Library
Historical Room
526 Millbrook Avenue
Randolph NJ 07081

(201) 895-3556

OPEN: M-W 9-9, Th-Sa 9-5, Su noon-4;
closed holidays
COPYING FACILITIES: yes
MATERIALS SOLICITED: Materials pertaining to local history.

HOLDINGS:
Total volume: 30 items
Inclusive dates: 1767 - 1905
Description: Materials relating to Randolph local history, including a deed,
dated 1767, to the land now occupied by
the County College of Morris; a copy of
the minutes of the Randolph Township
Committee Meeting, 1806-35; and a
number of photographs, school notebooks, and account ledgers from the late
19th century.

RIVERTON

NJ736-690
Riverton Free Library
306 Main Street
Riverton NJ 08077

(609) 829-2476

OPEN: M, Tu, Th 2:30-8:30, F 2:30-5, Sa 10-2; closed Sundays and holidays
COPYING FACILITIES: yes
MATERIALS SOLICITED: Will accept materials of local interest.

HOLDINGS:
Total volume: 27 items
Inclusive dates: 1899 -
Description: Minute books, cash books, circulation records, and visitors' registry books of Riverton Free Library; two minute books of the Riverton Yacht Club, 1901-32; two minute books of the Riverton Improvement Company, 1853-64; hand drawn maps of area recording land sales; and a few invoices and other miscellaneous business papers.

RUMSON

NJ751-520
Moss Archives
39 Rumson Road
Rumson NJ

MAILING ADDRESS:
Box 336
Sea Bright NJ 07760

(201) 842-0336

OPEN: by appointment only
ACCESS: letter of introduction and written request for appointment required
COPYING FACILITIES: no
MATERIALS SOLICITED: Material relating to Monmouth County. Will also accept early New Jersey photographic collections.

HOLDINGS:
Total volume: 10,000 items
Inclusive dates: 1680 - 1930
Description: Materials relating to the history of Monmouth County, documenting social and historical change on the Jersey shore. Included are 5,000 glass negatives, 1,000 other photographs, other pictures, maps, logbooks, ledgers, deeds, and letters.

RUTHERFORD

NJ756-240
Fairleigh Dickinson University
Messler Library
New Jersey Room
Rutherford NJ 07070

(201) 460-5074

OPEN: M-W 9-10, Th, F 8:30-4:30; closed weekends and holidays; no evening hours during summer intercessions

ACCESS: letter of request to Librarian required from persons outside University
COPYING FACILITIES: yes

HOLDINGS:
Total volume: 37 boxes
Inclusive dates: 1694 - 1968
Description: Manuscripts relating to the State and local history of New Jersey, principally during the 19th century. The largest single collection contains political papers of Fairleigh S. Dickinson, Jr. Other collections of importance include the Rutherford-Russell-Watts family, Garret A. Hobart, and John S. Schultze papers, the latter containing materials on iron mines in Morris County in the 1880's. Also included are manuscript public documents, as well as materials of economic interest, such as land surveys, day books, and receipts relating to medicine, law, agriculture, and trade.

GUIDES: Hackensack-Ridgewood Local History Service, Manuscript Microfilm Project, *Manuscripts on Microfilm* (Johnson Free Public Library, 1976).

SEE: Robbins.

SALEM

NJ760-720
Salem County Historical Society
79-83 Market Street
Salem NJ 08079

(609) 935-5004

OPEN: Tu-F 12-4, Sa-M by appointment; closed holidays

SEE: Hamer.

Questionnaire not returned.

SERGEANTSVILLE

NJ766-160
Delaware Township Committee
Township Hall
Sergeantsville Road
Sergeantsville NJ 08557

(609) 397-3240

OPEN: M-F by appointment; closed weekends and holidays
COPYING FACILITIES: yes

HOLDINGS:
Total volume: 312 l.f.
Inclusive dates: 1847 - 1921
Description: Delaware Township public records, including minutes of Township meetings.

SOMERS POINT

NJ786-40
Atlantic County Historical Society
907 Shore Road
Somers Point NJ

MAILING ADDRESS:
P.O. Box 301
Somers Point NJ 08244

(609) 927-5218

OPEN: W-Sa 10-4; closed other days and holidays
COPYING FACILITIES: yes
MATERIALS SOLICITED: Records of southern New Jersey, including family Bible records, genealogies, and other family papers.

HOLDINGS:
Total volume: 25 manuscript boxes; additional materials
Inclusive dates: late 1600's -
Description: Materials pertaining to southern New Jersey, particularly Atlantic County, often relating to ships and shipping. Included are genealogical materials, account books, logbooks, legal papers, oral history interviews, materials regarding local folklore, church papers, hotel registers, journals, photographs, survey books, and other materials.

SEE: Hamer; NUCMC, 1975.

SEE: Hinding.

SOMERVILLE

NJ792-720
Somerset County Historical Society
Somerville NJ

MAILING ADDRESS:
P.O. Box 632
Somerville NJ 08876

OPEN: Tu 10-2, 7-9

SEE: Hamer.

Questionnaire not returned.

SOUTH ORANGE

NJ798-720
Seton Hall University
McLaughlin Library
Archives & Special Collections
South Orange NJ 07079

(201) 762-7052

OPEN: M-F 9-5, Sa by appointment; closed federal holidays and some holy days
COPYING FACILITIES: yes
MATERIALS SOLICITED: Material documenting the history and development of New Jersey Roman Catholicism and Seton Hall University.

HOLDINGS:
Total volume: 500 l.f.
Inclusive dates: 1770 -
Description: Archives of the Archdiocese of Newark, bishops' papers, annual parish reports, some parish sacramental

registers, administrative records of Seton Hall University, manuscript collections of New Jersey lay Catholics, priests' personal papers, and records of Catholic benevolent and charitable institutions. Included are manuscripts, oral history tapes, video cassettes, sound recordings, photographs, correspondence, and financial records.

SEE: NUCMC, 1980.

SPRINGFIELD

NJ800-720

Springfield Historical Society
126 Morris Avenue
Springfield NJ 07081

no telephone

OPEN: Su 2-5; closed other days and holidays
COPYING FACILITIES: no
MATERIALS SOLICITED: Materials relating to New Jersey, Union County, and Springfield Township.

HOLDINGS:
Total volume: 1,000 vols.
Inclusive dates: 17th century - 20th century
Description: Material on Springfield and Union County.

STANHOPE

NJ804-120

Canal Society of New Jersey Museum
Waterloo Village Restoration
Stanhope NJ

MAILING ADDRESS:
P.O. Box 737
Morristown NJ 07960

(201) 347-0900

OPEN: by appointment only
ACCESS: appointment required
COPYING FACILITIES: no
MATERIALS SOLICITED: Material relating to New Jersey canals. Will also accept materials related to other canals and inland waterways.

HOLDINGS:
Total volume: 1 filing cabinet
Inclusive dates: 1824 - 1900
Description: Legislative documents, photographs, glass slides, engineering drawings, a ledger recording the passage of boats, and other written records, all relating to canals.

SUMMIT

NJ812-710

Summit Free Public Library
75 Maple Street
Summit NJ 07901

(201) 273-0350

OPEN: M-Th 9-9, F, Sa 9-5:30; closed Sundays and holidays
COPYING FACILITIES: yes

HOLDINGS:
Total volume: 10 l.f.
Inclusive dates: 1797 -
Description: Collections include a letter of George Washington; a letter of Thomas Pinckney to Washington; records of the Summit Atheneum, 1908-53; records and account books of the Summit Free Public Library, 1854 to date; and a manuscript history of the Summit Library.

TEANECK

NJ816-760

Teaneck Public Library
Oral History Project and Local History Project
840 Teaneck Road
Teaneck NJ 07666

(201) 837-4171

OPEN: M-F 9-9, Sa 9-5; also open Sundays and most holidays in the fall and winter
ACCESS: advance arrangements should be made
COPYING FACILITIES: yes
MATERIALS SOLICITED: Local history. Will also accept photographs and memorabilia dealing with the history of Teaneck.

HOLDINGS:
Total volume: 480 items
Inclusive dates: 1900 -
Description: Oral history tapes and questionnaire interviews with members of the Teaneck Jewish community and others, recalling the town's history since 1900. There are also some manuscript notebooks and file cards dealing with the town's history, as well as a collection of photographs.

TENNENT

NJ822-80

Battleground Historical Society
Route 522
Tennent NJ

MAILING ADDRESS:
P.O. Box 1776
Tennent NJ 07763

(201) 431-0649

OPEN: summer, Sa, Su 2-4; other times by appointment
COPYING FACILITIES: no
MATERIALS SOLICITED: Materials pertaining to the Battle of Monmouth, June 28, 1778, and to life in western Monmouth County during the colonial and Victorian periods. Will also accept material on New Jersey life in general, local Indians, and personalities related to the Battle of Monmouth.

HOLDINGS:
Total volume: 10 boxes; hundreds of photographs
Inclusive dates: 1880 -
Description: Public documents related to real estate in Tennent and its environs, including mortgages, deeds, title searches, surveys, and photographs of historic sites

and buildings, including one constructed in 1670.

TRENTON

NJ838-240

Free Public Library
120 Academy Street
Trenton NJ 08608

(609) 392-7188

OPEN: M, W, Th 9-9, Tu, F, Sa 9-5; closed Sundays and holidays

SEE: Hamer; NUCMC, 1959-61.

Questionnaire not returned.

NJ838-530

The Meredith Havens Fire Museum of Trenton
Fire Headquarters
244 Perry Street
Trenton NJ 08618

(609) 989-4038

OPEN: daily 10-8; closed Christmas
COPYING FACILITIES: no
MATERIALS SOLICITED: Materials pertaining to fires and fire fighting, especially of local significance. Will also accept material pertaining to the Civil War.

HOLDINGS:
Total volume: 450 vols.; 200 photographs
Inclusive dates: 1890 -
Description: Photographs of fires and fire fighting, fire company logbooks, minute books of the Board of Fire Commissioners, photographs of Civil War related subjects, minute books of local branches of the Grand Army of the Republic and the 2nd New Jersey Cavalry Association, Civil War sketch books, and photographs of activities of the G.A.R. and the Sons of Union Veterans of the Civil War.

NJ838-550

New Jersey Department of Conservation and Economic Development
520 East State Street
Trenton NJ 08609

no telephone

SEE: Hamer.

Questionnaire not returned.

NJ838-580

New Jersey Department of State
Bureau of Archives and Records
    Preservation
Division of Archives and Records
    Management
185 W. State Street
Trenton NJ

MAILING ADDRESS:
P.O. Box 1898
Trenton NJ 08625

(609) 292-6260

OPEN: M-F 8:30-4:30, Sa 9-5; closed
    Sundays and holidays
COPYING FACILITIES: yes
MATERIALS SOLICITED: State government
    record groups. Will also accept county
    and municipal records and, selectively,
    materials relating to New Jersey his-
    tory.

HOLDINGS:
    Total volume: 10,600 c.f.
    Inclusive dates: 1663 -
    Description: The official archives of
    the State of New Jersey, including record
    groups relating to the executive, legisla-
    tive, and judicial activities of the govern-
    ment, and some county and municipal
    records. These are supplemented by a
    small manuscript collection dealing with
    New Jersey history.
        Major groups include military records
    from the and colonial period to World
    War I; judicial records, 1681-1865; state
    censuses, 1855-1915; records of the gov-
    ernors, 1878-1974; and colonial deeds
    and wills to 1900. Land, marriage, pro-
    bate, and other records for most counties
    to 1900 are available on microfilm.

SEE: Hamer; NUCMC, 1959-61.

SEE: Davis; Hinding; Leventhal and Moo-
    ney - I.

SEE ALSO: Ann Novotny, ed., *Picture
    Sources 3* (Special Libraries Assn.,
    1975) and the following publications of
    the Bureau: *Genealogical Research*
    (1971); *Guide to County Archives in the
    Archives and History Bureau* (1963);
    *Guide to Municipal Archives in the Ar-
    chives and History Bureau* (1963). Ad-
    ditional finding aids are available at
    the institution.

NJ838-600

New Jersey State Museum
Bureau of Archaeology and Ethnology
205 West State Street
Trenton NJ 08625

(609) 292-8594

OPEN: Tu-F 9-4 by appointment only;
    closed weekends, Mondays, and
    holidays
COPYING FACILITIES: yes
MATERIALS SOLICITED: Materials per-
    taining to the archaeology and
    ethnology of New Jersey, particularly of
    the Lennilenape Indians.

HOLDINGS:
    Total volume: more than 200 items
    Inclusive dates: 1870's -
    Description: Reports regarding archae-
    ological sites, surveys, and excavations in
    New Jersey, including some of Museum-
    sponsored work.

SEE: Hamer.

The archives of the Archaeological
Society of New Jersey and of the Eastern States Archaeological Federation,
listed in Hamer, are no longer stored
at the Museum, and should be sought
through those organizations directly.

NJ838-610

New Jersey State Museum
Bureau of Cultural History
205 West State Street
Trenton NJ 08625

(609) 292-5421

OPEN: M-F 9-4; closed weekends and
    holidays
ACCESS: by appointment only
COPYING FACILITIES: yes

HOLDINGS:
    Total volume: 4 items
    Inclusive dates: 1662 - 1904
    Description: A land grant to E.
    Steenhuysen from Peter Stuyvesant, 1662;
    a 34-page land survey exercise book in
    ink and watercolor by William Parrish,
    1784-90; a letter by Dorothea Dix; and a
    handwritten illuminated book honoring
    John R. Curran at the time of his retire-
    ment from the Phoenix Manufacturing
    Company, 1904.

NJ838-630

Old Barracks Association
Old Barracks
Barrack Street
Trenton NJ 08608

(609) 396-1776

OPEN: M-F 10-4 by appointment only;
    closed weekends and holidays
USER FEES: fifty cents
ACCESS: access limited to scholars and
    researchers
COPYING FACILITIES: no
MATERIALS SOLICITED: Will accept ac-
    count books, journals, diaries, and let-
    ters relating to early New Jersey state
    history, and to Trenton during the
    American Revolution.

HOLDINGS:
    Total volume: 106 items
    Inclusive dates: 1691 - 1915
    Description: Letters, indentures, deeds,
    and muster rolls, primarily for the 18th
    century and Revolutionary War era, relat-
    ing to political and military affairs in
    New Jersey. Also included are ledger
    books of Trenton-area craftsmen and
    merchants, 1758-79 and 1872-74, and fif-
    teen early 19th century illustrated copy-
    books done by Trenton-area children.

NJ838-730

Trenton Psychiatric Hospital
Sullivan Way
Station A
Trenton NJ

MAILING ADDRESS:
P.O. Box 7500
West Trenton NJ 08628

(609) 396-8261

OPEN: by appointment only
COPYING FACILITIES: yes

HOLDINGS:
    Total volume: not specified
    Inclusive dates: 1840 -
    Description: Photographs, letters, re-
    ports, patient histories, and other materi-
    als related to Dorothea L. Dix and to the
    history of the Trenton Psychiatric Hos-
    pital.

NJ838-740

Trenton State College
Department of Geography
Trenton NJ

MAILING ADDRESS:
Hillwood Lakes
P.O. Box 940
Trenton NJ 08625

(609) 771-2415

OPEN: M-F 9:30-4:30, Sa, Su by
    appointment
ACCESS: appointment advised
COPYING FACILITIES: no
MATERIALS SOLICITED: Aerial photo-
    graphs and New Jersey planning and
    land use maps.

HOLDINGS:
    Total volume: 250 map case drawers
    Inclusive dates: 1900 -
    Description: 10,000 individual and
    map set sheets. The collection includes
    geologic survey maps, early aerial pho-
    tographs of selected areas of New Jersey,
    and geographic educational materials.

NJ838-750

Trenton State College
Library
Special Collections
Pennington Road
Trenton NJ

MAILING ADDRESS:
Hillwood Lakes
P.O. Box 940
Trenton NJ 08625

(609) 771-2346

OPEN: M-Th 9-5, F 9-noon preferably by
    appointment; closed weekends and
    holidays
ACCESS: appointment recommended
COPYING FACILITIES: yes
MATERIALS SOLICITED: Trenton State
    College materials. Will also accept ma-
    terials relating to New Jersey history.

HOLDINGS:
Total volume: 72 c.f.; 1,000 items
Inclusive dates: 1709 -
Description: Reports, photographs, master's theses, research projects, and other materials relating to Trenton State College, particularly since 1950. There are also the archives of the Ewing Presbyterian Church, 1709 to date, and two dozen manuscript acts of the New Jersey legislature during the Revolutionary War period.

Includes oral histories relating to the U.S. Steel plant in Fairless Hill, PA.

SEE ALSO: *The Sol Feinstone Collection of the American Revolution in the Roscoe L. West Library* (Trenton State College, 1968); a guide to the archives of the Ewing Presbyterian Church available on request.

UNION

NJ844-800
Union Township Historical Society
Caldwell Parsonage Museum
909 Caldwell Avenue
Union NJ 07083

(201) 688-5370

OPEN: fourth Sunday of month 2-4 and by appointment
COPYING FACILITIES: no
MATERIALS SOLICITED: Materials pertaining to Union Township history.

HOLDINGS:
Total volume: 50 items
Inclusive dates: 1800 - 1900
Description: Account books, deeds, business letters, and orders of early settlers in the Connecticut Farms area and their descendants.

VINELAND

NJ874-840
Vineland Historical and Antiquarian Society
108 South 7th Street
Vineland NJ 08360

(609) 691-1111

OPEN: Tu-Sa 1-4; closed Su, M, holidays and Aug.

SEE: Hamer.

Questionnaire not returned.

WEST ORANGE

NJ910-200
Edison National Historic Site
Main Street and Lakeside Avenue
West Orange NJ 07052

(201) 736-0550

OPEN: M-Sa 9-4 by appointment only; closed Sundays and holidays
ACCESS: researchers should contact the institution a week before their expected arrival date
COPYING FACILITIES: yes

HOLDINGS:
Total volume: 5,000 c.f.
Inclusive dates: 1869 - 1931
Description: Document and photographic files, consisting of Thomas A. Edison's laboratory and business records, and including his Menlo Park and West Orange laboratory experimental notebooks. The collection also contains 7,000 photographic negatives of Edison inventions, portraits of Edison, and group pictures, as well as 2,000 positive prints of still shots from Edison motion pictures, 1915-17. Edison's 1,093 U.S. patents are also included in the collection.

SEE: Hamer; NUCMC, 1966.

SEE: Hounshell.

WEST TRENTON

NJ918-520
Motor Bus Society, Inc.
West Trenton NJ

MAILING ADDRESS:
P.O. Box 7058
West Trenton NJ 08628

no telephone

OPEN: by appointment
COPYING FACILITIES: no
MATERIALS SOLICITED: Material relating to the manufacture and operation of motor buses and trolley buses in North America, including photographs and vehicle construction/operational data. Will also accept other historical documents of a selected nature.

HOLDINGS:
Total volume: 90,000 items
Inclusive dates: 1920 -
Description: Primarily photographs and negatives of buses, bus terminals, and other subjects relating to the history and operation of motor buses in North America.

WESTFIELD

NJ926-840
Union County Cultural and Heritage Programs Advisory Board
300 North Avenue East
Westfield NJ 07090

(201) 233-7906

OPEN: M-F 9-4 by appointment only; closed weekends and holidays
ACCESS: advance arrangements required
COPYING FACILITIES: yes
MATERIALS SOLICITED: New Jersey history, specifically the history of Union County and its municipalities. Will also accept source materials relating to grants.

HOLDINGS:
Total volume: 5 boxes; 1 map storage case
Inclusive dates: 19th century -
Description: Photographs, including Historic American Buildings Survey materials and a 1937 aerial survey; one video tape presentation on architecture; oral

history material; and scrapbooks on local history.

WHIPPANY

NJ950-520
Morris County Free Library
New Jersey Room
30 East Hanover Avenue
Whippany NJ 07981

(201) 829-0505, Ext. 41

OPEN: M-Th 9-9, F-Sa 9-5; closed Sundays and holidays
COPYING FACILITIES: yes
MATERIALS SOLICITED: Manuscripts, maps, oral histories, microfilms of documents, photographs, and other items pertaining to New Jersey, with emphasis on Morris County. Will also accept genealogical materials from any area.

HOLDINGS:
Total volume: 5 file drawers
Inclusive dates: late 18th century -
Description: Manuscript and typescript materials relating to the history of New Jersey, with emphasis on Morris County, from the late 18th century. Included are family genealogical materials, account books, cemetery records, legal documents, and maps.

SEE: NUCMC, 1971.

WOODBURY

NJ982-280
Gloucester County Historical Society Library
17 Hunter Street
Woodbury NJ

MAILING ADDRESS:
P.O. Box 409
Woodbury NJ 08096

(609) 845-4771

OPEN: M-Th 1-4, F 1-4, 7-9:30, last Sunday of month 2-5; closed other days and holidays
COPYING FACILITIES: yes
MATERIALS SOLICITED: Genealogical materials on families in New Jersey and eastern Pennsylvania, and Gloucester County and New Jersey historical materials. Will also accept materials pertinent to American history.

HOLDINGS:
Total volume: 94 file drawers
Inclusive dates: 1686 -
Description: The genealogical collections contain manuscripts, photographs, Bible records, family group sheets and charts, and other materials pertaining to South Jersey and Delaware Valley families. There are also 70,000 Gloucester County government documents, including marriage records, Civil War and Revolutionary War records, slave documents, court proceedings, tavern petitions, death inquisitions, and other items.

SEE: NUCMC, 1978.

SEE: Hinding; Robbins.

WOODCLIFF LAKE

NJ990-322
Witco Chemical Corporation
155 Tice Boulevard
Woodcliff Lake NJ 07675

(201) 573-2800

OPEN: M-F 9-5; closed weekends and
   holidays
ACCESS: prior authorization required

COPYING FACILITIES: no

HOLDINGS:
   Total volume: 6,411 c.f.
   Inclusive dates: 1901 -
   Description: Financial records, general
ledgers, journal entries, and other records
of the Witco Chemical Corporation.

NEW MEXICO

Since 1963 the New Mexico State Records Center and Archives has assisted county and municipal officials in developing disposition schedules for their records as part of a statewide preservation program. Most local public agencies retain custody of their permanently valuable records, but some 215 cubic feet of county records, primarily from the Territorial period (1846-1912), have been deposited at the State Records Center and Archives in Santa Fe. Along with these county records, there are also 745 cubic feet of Territorial court records housed in Santa Fe.

ALBUQUERQUE

NM114-35

Albuquerque Museum of Art, History and Science
2000 Mountain Road N.W.
Albuquerque NM

MAILING ADDRESS:
P.O. Box 1293
Albuquerque NM 87103

(505) 766-7878

OPEN: Tu-F 10-5; closed other days, Christmas, Thanksgiving, and New Year's
COPYING FACILITIES: yes
MATERIALS SOLICITED: Photographs relating to the history of Albuquerque and New Mexico. Will also accept documents relating to the Museum's historical collections.

HOLDINGS:
Total volume: 44,000 photographs
Inclusive dates: 1866 - 1960
Description: A collection of photographs relating to Native Americans in New Mexico, the history of Albuquerque, and the development of air transportation in the region.

SEE: Hinding; Paszek.

NM114-50

Archdiocese of Santa Fe
Archives
202 Morningside Drive, S.E.
Albuquerque NM 87108

(505) 345-7727, Ext. 25

OPEN: F 9-3; closed other days
COPYING FACILITIES: no

MATERIALS SOLICITED: Regional material pertaining to the Archdiocese, including documents and photographs.

HOLDINGS:
Total volume: 40 l.f.; 30 file cabinets
Inclusive dates: 1678 - 1980
Description: Mission records, 1678-1851, relating to all of New Mexico; and Diocesan records, 1851-1980, relating to the Archdiocese of Santa Fe only.

SEE: Beers - Southwest.

The Archives generally are not open to the public, due to lack of staff. For microfilms of most records, 1678-1851, researchers are referred to the New Mexico State Records Center and Archives in Santa Fe, NM. Microfilms of genealogical records, 1700-1850, are at the Church of Jesus Christ of Latter-day Saints, Genealogical Society of Utah, Library, in Salt Lake City, UT.

NM114-525

Menaul School
Menaul Historical Library
301 Menaul Boulevard, NE
Albuquerque NM 87107

(505) 345-7727

OPEN: M-F 8:30-4:30 preferably by appointment; closed weekends, holidays, and during school vacations
COPYING FACILITIES: yes
MATERIALS SOLICITED: Materials concerning 19th century missionary activities of Presbyterians and other Protestant denominations in Arizona, Colorado, New Mexico, and Utah, especially among Spanish people. Will also accept any historical materials on Presbyterianism and the southwestern United States.

HOLDINGS:
Total volume: 90 l.f.; 15 file drawers; 12 boxes; other items
Inclusive dates: 1838 -
Description: Materials pertaining to Presbyterian mission work in New Mexico, Colorada, Arizona, and Utah, including medical, educational, and church records, unpublished manuscripts, oral history tapes, and photographs. There are also some records of other religious denominations.

NM114-760

Telephone Pioneers of America
Zia Council
Telephone Pioneer Museum
1209 Mountain Road, N.E.
Albuquerque NM 87110

(505) 256-2105

OPEN: M-F 8-5; closed weekends and holidays
COPYING FACILITIES: no
MATERIALS SOLICITED: Materials relating to the growth and development of the telephone in territorial New Mexico. Will also accept materials relating to the growth and development of the telephone in the Southwest from 1876 to the present.

HOLDINGS:
Total volume: 1,350 items
Inclusive dates: 1876 -
Description: Written, photographic, and oral history materials relating to the growth and development of the telephone in territorial New Mexico.

NM114-800

University of Albuquerque
Center for Learning and Information Resources
St. Joseph Place, N.W.
Albuquerque NM 87140

(505) 277-5340

OPEN: M-F 8-4; closed weekends and holidays
ACCESS: limited access until adequate housing is provided
COPYING FACILITIES: yes

HOLDINGS:
Total volume: 469,200 items
Inclusive dates: 1927 - 1962
Description: Correspondence and memo files of U.S. Senator Dennis E. Chavez.

NM114-825

University of New Mexico
Department of Biology
Museum of Southwestern Biology
Herbarium and Museum of Botany
Albuquerque NM 87131

(505) 277-3838

OPEN: by appointment only
COPYING FACILITIES: yes
MATERIALS SOLICITED: Materials relating to the flora of the southwestern United States. Will also accept materials relating to plant systematics.

HOLDINGS:
Total volume: 8 l.f.
Inclusive dates: 1930's -
Description: Collection consists of manuscripts of floristic analyses of various locales, generic monographs, personal field collection notebooks, and materials relating to the Threatened and Endangered Species Survey of New Mexico and Arizona.

NM114-870

University of New Mexico
Jonson Gallery
1909 Las Lomas Road, N.E.
Albuquerque NM 87106

(505) 277-4967

OPEN: Tu-F 10-5, Sa, Su 1-5 by appointment only; closed Mondays
ACCESS: application to and permission of the Director is required
COPYING FACILITIES: no
MATERIALS SOLICITED: Will accept Raymond Jonson correspondence.

HOLDINGS:
Total volume: 13,000 items
Inclusive dates: 1910 -
Description: Materials relating to artist Raymond Jonson, including correspondence, diaries, photographs, typescripts of lectures, and other materials.

SEE: Hinding.

NM114-880

University of New Mexico
Maxwell Museum of Anthropology
Roma & University, N.E.
Albuquerque NM 87131

(505) 277-4404

OPEN: by appointment only
COPYING FACILITIES: yes
MATERIALS SOLICITED: Archaeology and ethnology of the Southwest.

HOLDINGS:
Total volume: 2 file cabinets; 50 l.f.
Inclusive dates: 1870 -
Description: Field notes and photographs on southwestern U.S. archaeology and ethnology, as well as photographs of artifacts. Of particular interest are materials relating to Frances Newcomb, and the papers of Dorothy Luhrs, which include her field notes on Indians in northern Mexico.

NM114-900

University of New Mexico
Zimmerman Library
Special Collections Department
Albuquerque NM 87131

(505) 277-6451

OPEN: M-F 8-4:30, also Wednesday evenings 6:30-9 during school sessions; closed weekends and holidays
COPYING FACILITIES: yes
MATERIALS SOLICITED: Will accept materials relating to New Mexico and the Southwest.

HOLDINGS:
Total volume: 2,052 l.f.
Inclusive dates: 1462 -
Description: Collections focusing primarily on New Mexico and the Southwest. Materials include maps, literary manuscripts, correspondence, diaries, private papers, business records, legal documents, theses and dissertations, photographs, oral history tapes, sound recordings, videotapes, microfilm, and photocopies of manuscripts, typescripts, and architectural records.

SEE: NUCMC, 1966-67, 70, 74, 77-78.

SEE: Beers - Southwest; Hinding; Parkinson; Robbins.

SEE ALSO: Alan M. Meckler and Ruth McMullin, comps., *Oral History Collections* (Bowker, 1975); *Map Collections in the United States and Canada: A Directory* (Special Libraries Assn., 1970); Albert James Diaz, *A Guide to the Microfilm of Papers Relating to New Mexico Land Grants* (Univ. of New Mexico Press, 1960).

Richard C. Davis, *North American Forest History: A Guide to Archives and Manuscripts in the United States and Canada* (Clio Books, 1977).

CARLSBAD

NM200-800

The United Methodist Church
New Mexico Annual Conference
  Archives
Historical Library
c/o Willard Steinsiek, Chairman
2301 W. Texas
Carlsbad NM 88220

(505) 885-4754

OPEN: by appointment only
ACCESS: advance arrangements required
COPYING FACILITIES: yes
MATERIALS SOLICITED: Letters and papers of ministers who have served in the New Mexico Annual Conference and historical materials relating to the New Mexico Conference or constituent churches. Will also accept materials relating to the history of the United Methodist church in America, and its constituent denominations.

HOLDINGS:
Total volume: 70 l.f.
Inclusive dates: 1890 -
Description: The records of the New Mexico Annual Conference, the United Methodist church, and the constituent denominations of the United Methodist church, including the Methodist Episcopal church, the Methodist Episcopal Church South, and the Evangelical United Brethren church, the merger of which, in 1968, formed the United Methodist church. The New Mexico Annual Conference embraces all of the State of New Mexico, together with the western-most portion of Texas.
Included in the collection are Annual Conference journals, financial records, minutes of Conference Boards, Commissions, and Committees; a limited number of private collections from Methodist

ministers; and some items from local churches and ministers.

CIMARRON

NM266-720

Seton Memorial Library and Museum
Philmont Scout Ranch
Cimarron NM 87714

(505) 376-2281, Ext. 46

OPEN: Tu-Sa 8-5; closed Sundays, Mondays, and holidays
COPYING FACILITIES: no
MATERIALS SOLICITED: Materials relating to Ernest Thompson Seton. Will also accept materials relating to the history of the Southwest.

HOLDINGS:
Total volume: 9.75 l.f.
Inclusive dates: 1870 - 1967
Description: Correspondence, manuscripts, journals, and business records of artist, naturalist, and writer Ernest Thompson Seton and his second wife, Julia M. Butree Seton.

CLOVIS

NM304-320

High Plains Historical Foundation, Inc.
Route 2
Clovis NM

MAILING ADDRESS:
P.O. Box 152
Clovis NM 88101

(505) 985-2479

OPEN: by appointment
ACCESS: at the discretion of the Foundation; prior arrangements must be made
COPYING FACILITIES: yes
MATERIALS SOLICITED: Documents relating to the history of central eastern New Mexico, specifically Curry, Roosevelt, Quay, and DeBaca counties. Material relating to the open range period (1880-1910) of this area is particularly sought. Will also accept materials relating to the Santa Fe Railroad, businesses of the area, agriculture, and personal histories and documents.

HOLDINGS:
Total volume: 24 c.f.
Inclusive dates: 1883 -
Description: Personal histories of area pioneers; miscellaneous manuscripts; scrapbooks; 25 cassette interviews dealing with the area during 1907-20; correspondence and postcards; a cemetery list from Curry, Roosevelt, Quay, and DeBaca counties; and over 2,000 photographs relating to the area.

FARMINGTON

NM398-720
San Juan County Museum Association
San Juan County Archaeological
  Research Center and Library at
  Salmon Ruin
Route 3, Box 169
Farmington NM 87401

(505) 632-2013

OPEN: daily 9-5; closed Thanksgiving,
  Christmas, and New Year's
COPYING FACILITIES: yes
MATERIALS SOLICITED: Archives and
  manuscripts of all types relating to the
  Four Corners area of the Southwest.
  Will also accept microfilms and other
  copies of manuscripts relating to this
  area.

HOLDINGS:
> Total volume: 30 l.f.
> Inclusive dates: 1876 -
> Description: Archives and manuscript
> materials, including photographs, relating
> to the Four Corners area of the South-
> west.

LAS CRUCES

NM494-570
New Mexico State University
Library
Rio Grande Historical
  Collections/Hobson-Huntsinger
  University Archives
Las Cruces NM

MAILING ADDRESS:
Box 3475
Las Cruces NM 88003

(505) 425-7511, Ext. 404

OPEN: M-F 8-5; closed weekends,
  holidays, and Christmas vacation
COPYING FACILITIES: yes
MATERIALS SOLICITED: Agriculture, business, industries, trades, churches and
  religious affairs, cultural affairs, education, family and personal papers, Indians and Indian agents, irrigation,
  government, labor, land, medical affairs, military affairs, mining, natural
  resources, organizations and societies,
  pioneer life, politics, recreation and
  sports, science, social life and conditions, and transportation. Will also accept other materials related to New
  Mexico and the Southwest.

HOLDINGS:
> Total volume: 2,250 c.f.
> Inclusive dates: 1820 -
> Description: Noncurrent records of
> New Mexico State University and collec-
> tions of documentary materials relating
> primarily to New Mexico. Included are
> records of organizations, papers of
> individuals and families, ephemera, and
> audio-visual materials documenting edu-
> cation, farming, ranching and related ac-
> tivities, water resources management,
> mining, transportation, business and
> commerce, politics and government, so-
> cial and cultural affairs, and pioneer life.

SEE: Robbins.

SEE ALSO: Mildred A. Barrett and J. Lawrence McConville, 'The Amador Collection at New Mexico State University,'
Password 17 (Winter 1972); *Map Collections in the United States and
Canada: A Directory* (Special Libraries
Assn., 1970).

LAS VEGAS

NM513-560
New Mexico Highlands University
Library
Arrott Collection and Spanish and
  Mexican Archives
Las Vegas NM 87701

(505) 425-7511

OPEN: M-Th 8-10, F 8-5; closed
  weekends, holidays, and Christmas
  vacation
COPYING FACILITIES: yes
MATERIALS SOLICITED: Materials relating
  to military history and New Mexico.

HOLDINGS:
> Total volume: 18 c.f.
> Inclusive dates: 1851 - 1891
> Description: 50,000 items pertaining to
> New Mexico military history, particularly
> to Fort Union. Included are post returns,
> materials relating to medical history, per-
> sonal diaries, journals, recollections, and
> miscellaneous materials pertaining to oth-
> er New Mexico forts.

SEE: Hamer.

LINCOLN

NM532-520
Museum of New Mexico
Monument Division
Lincoln State Monument
Lincoln NM

MAILING ADDRESS:
P.O. Box 2087
Santa Fe NM 87503

(505) 827-8940

OPEN: Tu-Sa 9-5; closed Sundays
USER FEES: 25 cents
COPYING FACILITIES: no
MATERIALS SOLICITED: Will accept ma-
  terials for the 1875-1900 era.

HOLDINGS:
> Total volume: not specified
> Inclusive dates: 1882 - 1957
> Description: Account books and ledgers
> from the local area.

LOS ALAMOS

NM570-80
Bandelier National Monument
Library and Photo File
Los Alamos NM 87544

(505) 672-3861

OPEN: by appointment only; closed
  weekends and holidays
ACCESS: researchers by appointment
  with Chief of Interpretation
COPYING FACILITIES: no
MATERIALS SOLICITED: Will accept materials relating to archaeology, especially of the southwestern United States;
  the wilderness; resources management;
  New Mexico history; National Park
  Service areas; environmental education;
  anthropology; ethnology; and photographs pertaining to the early years of
  Bandelier.

HOLDINGS:
> Total volume: 5,000 items
> Inclusive dates: 1880 -
> Description: Original Civilian Conser-
> vation Corps work reports pertaining to
> construction in Frijoles Canyon; records
> of the Monument; excavation and sta-
> bilization reports on work on Monument
> ruins; and photographs of excavations,
> stabilization, and other aspects of the
> Monument.

NM570-480
Los Alamos County Historical
  Museum and Society
1921 Juniper Street
Los Alamos NM

MAILING ADDRESS:
P.O. Box 43
Los Alamos NM 87544

(505) 662-6272

OPEN: M-Sa 10-4; closed Sundays and
  holidays
COPYING FACILITIES: yes
MATERIALS SOLICITED: Materials related
  to all periods of local history.

HOLDINGS:
> Total volume: 3,000 items
> Inclusive dates: 20th century
> Description: Materials relating to the
> Ranch School era (1917-43), including fi-
> nancial, architectural, administrative, and
> personal records; maps; photographs;
> audiotapes; and letters; some produced in
> modern times by alumni and former
> teachers. Other holdings relate to the
> Manhattan Project and development of
> the atomic bomb; local government sys-
> tems implemented by the military and
> the Atomic Energy Commission; and the
> history of the county and its government.

MOUNTAINAIR

NM646-280
Gran Quivira National Monument
Library
Mountainair NM

MAILING ADDRESS:
P.O. Box 496
Mountainair NM 87036

(505) 847-2585

OPEN: daily 8-5; closed Christmas
ACCESS: contingent upon authorization
from Area Superintendent; outside
researchers may utilize library only if
personnel are available and research
will not interfere with area operations.
COPYING FACILITIES: yes
MATERIALS SOLICITED: Materials relating
to pre-18th century history and
archaeology of Gran Quivira National
Monument and the surrounding region.
Will also accept materials relating to
later time periods.

HOLDINGS:
   Total volume: 20 l.f.
   Inclusive dates: late 16th century -
   Description: Archaeological and histori-
   cal material on Gran Quivira National
   Monument and the surrounding region,
   including stabilization records on cultural
   resources at the Monument.

PORTALES

NM668-210
Eastern New Mexico University
Golden Library
Special Collections and Archives
Portales NM 88130

(505) 526-2636

OPEN: M-F 8-5; closed weekends and
holidays
COPYING FACILITIES: yes
MATERIALS SOLICITED: Materials on sci-
ence fiction, southwestern history, and
Roosevelt County history.

HOLDINGS:
   Total volume: 80 c.f.
   Inclusive dates: 1900 -
   Description: A collection of manuscripts, oral histories, and other materials
   relating to science fiction, chiefly after
   1925. There are also records of organizations, oral histories, clippings, and other
   materials relating to southwestern and local history.

SEE: NUCMC, 1979.

SEE ALSO: registers to some collections
available at the repository.

ROSWELL

NM684-120
Chaves County Historical Society
Chaves County Historical Museum
Pecos Valley Collection
200 North Lea Avenue
Roswell NM 88201

(505) 622-8333

OPEN: by appointment only
ACCESS: advance appointment requested
COPYING FACILITIES: no
MATERIALS SOLICITED: Personal papers,
business and organizational records,
manuscripts, photographs and oral history tapes pertaining to the history of
the Pecos Valley region.

HOLDINGS:
   Total volume: 300 l.f.
   Inclusive dates: 1890 -
   Description: Materials pertaining to the
   post-Civil War history of Roswell, Chavez County, the Pecos Valley, New Mexico, and the Southwest in general.

NM684-690
Roswell Museum and Art Center
100 West 11th Street
Roswell NM 88201

(505) 624-6744

OPEN: M-F 9-4:30; closed weekends and
holidays
ACCESS: research students, scholars, and
other qualified individuals
COPYING FACILITIES: no
MATERIALS SOLICITED: Materials relating
to Robert H. Goddard and his work in
Roswell.

HOLDINGS:
   Total volume: 1.5 c.f.
   Inclusive dates: 1920 - 1942
   Description: Materials relating to the
   work of Robert H. Goddard, including
   notes on theoretical aspects of solar and
   atomic energy sources, graphs on problems and situations of rocket motor performance and flight research, drawings of
   rocket components, blueprints of rocket
   motor components, and photographs of
   Goddard's rocket research.

SEE: Hamer.

SANTA FE

NM722-30
Anthropology Film Center
Visual Anthropology Resource
   Collection
1626 Canyon Road
Santa Fe NM

MAILING ADDRESS:
P.O. Box 493
Santa Fe NM 87501

(505) 983-4127

OPEN: M-F 9-5; closed weekends and
holidays
USER FEES: variable
ACCESS: prior arrangements necessary
COPYING FACILITIES: yes

MATERIALS SOLICITED: Manuscript material relating to photographs, films,
and audiotapes that document natural-
ly occurring human behavior in con-
text, and photographs, films, and
audiotapes with accompanying documentation. Will also accept films, photographs, and audiotapes of historic or
cultural subjects without documentation, as well as manuscripts, field
notes, camera reports and logs, and
transcriptions without accompanying
audio-visual material.

HOLDINGS:
   Total volume: 30 l.f.
   Inclusive dates: 1930 -
   Description: Manuscript papers, proposals, scripts, logs, transcriptions, and
   annotations relating to documentary and
   research film in anthropology; slide and
   film 'notes' on Ixil Maya of Guatemala
   (1965); records and conference schedules
   of the 1972 'Programs in Ethnographic
   Film' and of the Society for the Anthropology of Visual Communications
   (SAVICOM), as well as audio tapes of
   various conferences on visual anthropology.

SEE ALSO: Munro S. Edmunson, review of
film 'An Ixil Calendrical Divination,'
American Anthropologist 69 (1967).

NM722-360
Institute of American Indian Arts
Museum
Cerrillos Road
Santa Fe NM 87501

(505) 988-6281

OPEN: M-F 8-5; closed weekends and
holidays
ACCESS: advance arrangements required
COPYING FACILITIES: yes
MATERIALS SOLICITED: Videotapes, photographs, and other materials pertaining to Native American culture, especially in the fields of arts and crafts,
drama, and dance. Will also accept videotapes of world interest dealing with
artists, craftspersons, architecture, music, dance, drama, literature, comparative religions, and cultures, as well as
photographs of ethnic and other cultural groups.

HOLDINGS:
   Total volume: 2 slide cabinets; 4 file
cabinets; 600 videotapes
   Inclusive dates: 1962 -
   Description: Videotapes (1976 to the
   present) of contemporary Native American concerns, including politics, economics, arts and crafts, oral history, record
   keeping, fairs, rodeos, ethnic celebrations,
   powwows, educational programs, and Native American art programs. Also included are videotapes pertaining to various
   ethnic cultures throughout the world and
   a photograph collection documenting the
   activities of the Institute of American Indian Arts (1962).

NM722-510
Museum of Navaho Ceremonial Art
Santa Fe NM

MAILING ADDRESS:
P.O. Box 5153
Santa Fe NM 87501

no telephone

SEE: Hamer; NUCMC, 1969.

Questionnaire not returned.

NM722-530
Museum of New Mexico
History Bureau
History Library
118 Washington Avenue
Santa Fe NM

MAILING ADDRESS:
P.O. Box 2087
Santa Fe NM 87503

(505) 827-6470, 6451

OPEN: Tu-F 9-4:45, Sa 9-12; closed
    Sundays, Mondays, and state holidays
COPYING FACILITIES: yes
MATERIALS SOLICITED: Private records,
    regardless of medium or characteristic,
    that pertain directly or indirectly to the
    political, economic, social, cultural, and
    religious history of New Mexico, the
    Southwest, and the West. Will also ac-
    cept records pertaining to the history of
    the United States and Mexico.

HOLDINGS:
    Total volume: 200 l.f.; 3,000 items
    Inclusive dates: 1729 -
    Description: Collections pertaining
    chiefly to New Mexico history and secon-
    darily to southwestern and western his-
    tory, with special emphasis upon political,
    economic, social, cultural, and religious
    affairs in New Mexico during the Span-
    ish, Mexican, territorial, and statehood
    periods. Included are manuscripts, docu-
    ments, scrapbooks, and audible,
    microform, photographic, and cartograph-
    ic records.

SEE: Hamer.

SEE: Hinding; Robbins.

NM722-535
Museum of New Mexico
Laboratory of Anthropology
708 Camino Lejo
Santa Fe NM

MAILING ADDRESS:
Box 2087
Santa Fe NM 87503

(505) 827-8940

OPEN: M-F 8-5; closed weekends and
    holidays
ACCESS: location information is
    available only to qualified individuals,
    agencies, or institutions in accordance
    with the Archeological Resources
    Protection Act of 1979 and managed
    under provisions of NMSA 18-6-11.1 a
    and b; other materials are available to
    the public
COPYING FACILITIES: yes

MATERIALS SOLICITED: Materials de-
    scribing, interpreting, and evaluating
    the archaeology and ethnology of New
    Mexico. Will also accept materials de-
    scribing, interpreting, and evaluating
    the archaeology and ethnology of the
    Southwest.

HOLDINGS:
    Total volume: 45 l.f.; 42 file drawers
    Inclusive dates: 1900 -
    Description: Documents relating to 50
    years of archaeological work in the South-
    west, including primary records, field
    journals, photographs, site maps, and fea-
    ture descriptions. Included are reports
    and site survey forms for archaeological
    work currently being conducted in the
    state. Approximately 26,000 archaeologi-
    cal sites are covered in the entire collec-
    tion, which is being coded to an auto-
    mated data base. There are also manu-
    scripts of works dealing with the
    archaeology and ethnology of New Mexi-
    co and Middle America.

NM722-570
New Mexico State Records Center
    and Archives
Historical Services Division
404 Montezuma
Sante Fe NM 87503

(505) 827-8860

OPEN: M-F 8-5; closed weekends and
    holidays
COPYING FACILITIES: yes
MATERIALS SOLICITED: Public and pri-
    vate records containing historical, legal,
    financial, and administrative informa-
    tion relating to New Mexico.

HOLDINGS:
    Total volume: 3,375 c.f.
    Inclusive dates: 1621 -
    Description: Records, private papers,
    and collections relating to New Mexico
    history. Included are the Spanish and
    Mexican archives (1621-1846), consisting
    of official records of governing agencies
    and administrators, correspondence, de-
    crees, ordinances, military records, and
    papers relating to church matters; territo-
    rial and State records, consisting of ex-
    ecutive, legislative, and judicial materials,
    records of constitutional conventions, and
    county records; and personal and busi-
    ness papers of prominent New Mexicans
    from the Spanish period to the present,
    as well as other materials relating to New
    Mexican history.

SEE: NUCMC, 1975.

SEE: Beers - Southwest; Hinding; Mehr;
    Parkinson.

SEE ALSO: *State of New Mexico Historical
    Film Collection* (New Mexico State
    Records Center and Archives, 1974);
    guides to microfilm editions available
    from the institution.

NM722-730
Southwest Foundation for
    Audio-Visual Resources
Southwest Audio-Visual Collection
Anthropology Film Center
1626 Canyon Road
Santa Fe NM

MAILING ADDRESS:
P.O. Box 522
Santa Fe NM 87501

(505) 983-4127

OPEN: F 9-5, and by appointment;
    closed holidays
USER FEES: variable
ACCESS: prior arrangements required
COPYING FACILITIES: yes
MATERIALS SOLICITED: Films and pho-
    tographs, especially 35mm color slides,
    of southwestern arts, crafts, and tradi-
    tional lifestyles, with description. Will
    also accept films, photographs, and
    video- and audiotapes on any south-
    western subject matter of historic or
    cultural significance.

HOLDINGS:
    Total volume: 6,000 items
    Inclusive dates: 1939 -
    Description: 35mm color slides of arts,
    crafts, artists, and craftspeople of the tra-
    ditional cultures of the Southwest; slides
    of the environment, landscape, and
    lifeways of the Southwest, especially New
    Mexico; aerial photographs of culturally
    significant landscapes; aerial views of
    pueblos; and early views of Los Alamos,
    NM, and its ranch school (1939-).

SILVER CITY

NM760-280
Gila National Forest
2610 North Silver Street
Silver City NM 88061

(505) 388-8201

OPEN: M-F 8-5; closed weekends and
    holidays
COPYING FACILITIES: no

HOLDINGS:
    Total volume: 50 items; 7 vols.
    Inclusive dates: 1905 - 1950
    Description: Photographs taken on and
    near the Gila National Forest.

NM760-720
Silver City Museum
312 West Broadway
Silver City NM 88061

(505) 538-5921

OPEN: Tu-F 9-4:30, Sa 9-1, Su 1-4;
    closed Mondays and holidays
COPYING FACILITIES: yes
MATERIALS SOLICITED: Materials relating
    to the Grant County area prior to 1920
    and to families who lived there, espe-
    cially prior to 1900. Will also accept
    other research materials, including
    items relating to the history of the
    Southwest, as well as genealogical
    source material.

HOLDINGS:
Total volume: 100 l.f.
Inclusive dates: 1870 -
Description: Materials relating to Silver City and Grant County, including records of a hardware store and a mortuary, county court records and sheriff's record books; 19th century mining documents, Silver City tax rolls and other town records, hotel registers, and photographs.

NM760-900
Western New Mexico University
Museum
Silver City NM 88061

(505) 538-6386

OPEN: M-F 8-5 preferably by appointment; closed weekends and holidays
ACCESS: advance arrangements required
COPYING FACILITIES: yes
MATERIALS SOLICITED: Materials of all kinds dealing with history of the American Southwest, especially New Mexico.

HOLDINGS:
Total volume: 7,500 items
Inclusive dates: 1880 -
Description: Collections of manuscript and visual materials dealing with the history of New Mexico and the Southwest, including the papers of Alvan White, longtime Speaker of the House in the New Mexico State Legislature, first state school superintendent, and attorney in Silver City, 1895-1945.

TAOS

NM874-440
Kit Carson Memorial Foundation, Inc.
Historical Research Library and Archives
Old Kit Carson Road
Taos NM

MAILING ADDRESS:
P.O. Drawer B
Taos NM 87571

(505) 758-4741

OPEN: M-F 8-5 by appointment only; closed weekends, Thanksgiving, Christmas, and New Year's
COPYING FACILITIES: yes
MATERIALS SOLICITED: Materials relating to Taos and the Southwest. Will also accept materials on the trans-Mississippi West.

HOLDINGS:
Total volume: 100 l.f.
Inclusive dates: 1800 -
Description: Materials relating to the history, geography, and archaeology of New Mexico and the Southwest; biographies of early pioneers; a photograph collection; and oral history interviews.

TRUTH OR CONSEQUENCES

NM912-280
Sierra County Historical Society
Geronimo Springs Museum
325 Main Street
Truth or Consequences NM

MAILING ADDRESS:
P.O. Box 1029
Truth or Consequences NM 87901

(505) 894-6600

OPEN: M-Sa 9-5; closed Sundays and holidays
ACCESS: advance arrangements required
COPYING FACILITIES: no
MATERIALS SOLICITED: Will accept maps and photographs of Sierra County and outlying areas, especially of military outposts and mining installations before 1930.

HOLDINGS:
Total volume: 30 l.f.
Inclusive dates: 1860 - 1960's
Description: Local history collection including school records of Hot Springs and Sierra County, church records, diaries, photographs of pioneer life and mining, Civil War discharge papers, voters lists, club minutes, and hotel registers.

TUCUMCARI

NM950-270
Tucumcari Historical Research Institute
Museum
416 South Adams Street
Tucumcari NM 88401

(505) 461-4201

OPEN: June 2 - Sept. 2, M-Sa 9-8, Su 1-8; Sept. 3 - June 1, Tu-Sa 9-5, Su 1-5; closed other days and holidays
USER FEES: one dollar
ACCESS: permission required
COPYING FACILITIES: no

HOLDINGS:
Total volume: not specified
Inclusive dates: late 1800's -
Description: Two 1912 hotel registers, attorneys' letters, a record book from a Methodist church, bank records, photographs of railroad personnel and stations, and family letters.

NEW YORK

In 1976 the New York State Archives, State Education Department, assumed responsibility for supervising local government records, continuing a statewide program that had been carried out by various Education Department offices since 1912. Most historically valuable local government records are retained by local governments themselves, and a number of municipalities have established their own archival programs. Some of these materials have been deposited at various local repositories including historical societies, libraries, and educational institutions.

The State Archives holds a few local government records but does not collect records in this area. The Archives also has microfilm copies of selected early records of some 150 local governments.

ADDISON

NY5-40
Addison Public Library
Addison NY 14801

(607) 359-3888

OPEN: M, W 6-9, Tu, F noon-3, Th, Sa 2-5; closed Sundays and holidays
COPYING FACILITIES: no

HOLDINGS:
Total volume: 2.5 c.f.
Inclusive dates: 1847 -
Description: Photographs, business records, and other materials relating to the history of Addison.

SEE: Steuben County Guide.

AFTON

NY6-40
Afton Free Library
154 Main Street
Afton NY 13730

(607) 639-1212

OPEN: M, Tu, Th, F 1:30-5, Sa 9-1; closed Sundays, Wednesdays, and holidays

COPYING FACILITIES: no
MATERIALS SOLICITED: Materials concerning the history of Afton.

HOLDINGS:
Total volume: 10 vols.; 0.5 c.f.
Inclusive dates: 1855 - 1965
Description: Scrapbooks, essays, and cemetery records concerning Afton local history and genealogy.

SEE: Chenango County Guide.

NY6-400
Jericho Historical Society
Main Street
Afton NY

MAILING ADDRESS:
c/o Charles J. Decker
East River Road
Afton NY 13730

(607) 639-2720

OPEN: Sa 9-12, Su 2-5; closed weekdays
COPYING FACILITIES: no
MATERIALS SOLICITED: Materials dealing with the history and genealogy of Afton.

HOLDINGS:
Total volume: 106 items; 4 vols.
Inclusive dates: 1820 - 1945
Description: Business records, military records, and photographs of Afton and Chenango County, NY, chiefly during the 19th century.

SEE: Chenango County Guide.

ALBANY

NY10-60
Albany Department of Human Resources
Bureau for Historical Services
City Records Library
27 Western Avenue
Albany NY 12203

no telephone

OPEN: M-F 9-3:30; closed weekends and holidays
COPYING FACILITIES: no
MATERIALS SOLICITED: Will accept municipal records from any of the Albany city departments.

HOLDINGS:
Total volume: not specified
Inclusive dates: 1800 -
Description: Materials relating chiefly to the municipal history of Albany. Included are extensive records of the city's Common Council and its committees; various government agencies; inter-agency correspondence; financial accounts; manuscripts of public documents, such as petitions and ordinances; tax records; and a limited collection of maps. Records of defunct city departments are also included.

NY10-80
Albany Institute of History and Art
McKinney Library
125 Washington Avenue
Albany NY 12210

(518) 463-4478

OPEN: M-Sa 8:30-4; closed Sundays and holidays
COPYING FACILITIES: yes
MATERIALS SOLICITED: Historical materials for the social, political, and cultural history of the city and county of Albany and the upper Hudson region of New York State, and sources relating to the fine and decorative arts of the area.

HOLDINGS:
Total volume: 500,000 items
Inclusive dates: 1635 -
Description: Collections covering the history of the city and county of Albany and the Manor of Rensselaerswyck from the early Dutch period through the present. Included are Dutch and English colonial manuscripts, records of organizations and businesses, private papers, memoirs and journals, and ephemera. Major collections document 19th and 20th century economic, political, and social interests in Albany, and special collections consist of photographs, deeds and indentures, and maps.

SEE: Hamer; NUCMC, 1959-61, 75.

SEE: Gehring; Hinding; Leventhal and Mooney - I; Robbins.

SEE ALSO: Walter Schatz, ed., *Directory of Afro-American Resources* (Bowker, 1970); Ann Novotny, ed., *Picture Sources 3* (Special Libraries Assn., 1975).

NY10-100
Albany Public Library
161 Washington Avenue
Albany NY 12210

(518) 449-3380

OPEN: M-F 9-9, Sa 9-5, Su 1-5; closed
holidays

SEE: Hamer; NUCMC, 1966.

Questionnaire not returned.

NY10-150
College of St. Rose
Library
Archives
432 Western Avenue
Albany NY 12203

(518) 454-5180

OPEN: M-F 8:15-11, Sa 9-5, Su 1-10:30;
closed Thanksgiving and Christmas
vacations
ACCESS: advance arrangements required
COPYING FACILITIES: yes
MATERIALS SOLICITED: Materials relating
to the history of the College of St.
Rose.

HOLDINGS:
> Total volume: 280 items; 3 file
> drawers
> Inclusive dates: 1920 -
> Description: Materials relating to the
history of the College of St. Rose, including blueprints and photographs of the
buildings, oral histories, and sodality and
faculty meeting minutes.

SEE: Hinding.

NY10-160
Daughters of Charity
Northeast Province
Archives
96 Menands Road
Albany NY 12204

(518) 462-5593

OPEN: M-F 8-5, Sa-Su by appointment;
closed holidays
ACCESS: appointment recommended
COPYING FACILITIES: yes
MATERIALS SOLICITED: Administrative
records, historical materials, correspondence, and photographs of all establishments or programs in which members
of the Daughters of Charity are involved, including materials from foreign missions and publications and oral
history by or about members of the
order.

HOLDINGS:
> Total volume: 250 l.f.
> Inclusive dates: 1753 -
> Description: Historical manuscripts,
adminstrative records, and correspondence relating to the Daughters of
Charity and their health, education, and
social service programs, such as schools,
orphanages, and hospitals, in the New
England and Middle Atlantic states.
There are also account books, mortgages,
legal records, title searches, and deeds to
property.

Topics covered include the service of
the order during epidemics, 1828-1918, at
Satterlee Hospital, Philadelphia, and in
the Spanish-American War; travel in
stagecoaches and canal boats; anti-
Catholic and anti-Irish prejudice, especially in Boston and Philadelphia; and
contemporary refugee programs for Viet-
namese, Cubans, and Cambodians.

NY10-320
Historic Cherry Hill
523-1/2 South Pearl Street
Albany NY 12202

(518) 434-4791

OPEN: Su 1-4, M-Sa 10-4; closed
Mondays and holidays
USER FEES: one dollar
COPYING FACILITIES: no
MATERIALS SOLICITED: Materials that
belonged to or help to interpret the
Van Rensselaer/Rankin family.

HOLDINGS:
> Total volume: 12 l.f.
> Inclusive dates: 1787 - 1963
> Description: Materials relating to the
Van Rensselaer/Rankin family, which
lived at Cherry Hill. Included are diaries,
archives, and noncurrent records of Historic Cherry Hill; photographs, architectural drawings; postcards; scrapbooks;
and correspondence.

NY10-570
New York State Department of State
Community Affairs Library
162 Washington Avenue
Albany NY 12231

(518) 474-7144

OPEN: M-F 8-5:15; closed weekends and
holidays
COPYING FACILITIES: yes
MATERIALS SOLICITED: Copies of New
York State laws, materials concerning
Federal programs that affect the State,
and materials pertaining to State public
administration and economic opportu-
nity and planning, including land use,
housing, and coastal zone management.

HOLDINGS:
> Total volume: not specified
> Inclusive dates: 1960 -
> Description: Planning documents pre-
pared for or by the counties and municipalities of New York State. Included are
zoning ordinances, county statistical reports and master plans, housing studies,
transportation plans, industrial resources
surveys, land classification maps,
recreation plans, capital improvement
programs, soil surveys, and reports pertaining to water supplies, natural resources, glacial geology, human resources,
historic preservation, public buildings,
and sewage works.

NY10-580
New York State Department of
Transportation
Map Information Unit
Room 105
State Office Campus Building 4
Albany NY 12232

(518) 457-3555

OPEN: M-F 7-4; closed major holidays
and weekends
COPYING FACILITIES: no
MATERIALS SOLICITED: Recent aerial
photographs of New York State.

HOLDINGS:
> Total volume: 60 l.f.
> Inclusive dates: 1968 -
> Description: Black and white aerial
photographs of New York State, with
multiple coverage at different dates available for many areas.

SEE ALSO: *Inventory of Aerial Photography
and Other Remotely Sensed Imagery of
New York State* (New York State Dept.
of Transportation, 1979).

NY10-640
New York State Library
Manuscripts and Special Collections
Cultural Education Center
Empire State Plaza
Albany NY 12230

(518) 474-8955, 6282, 4461

OPEN: M-F 9-5; closed weekends and
holidays
ACCESS: not open to school children; for
undergraduates, instructor must
indicate a necessity
COPYING FACILITIES: yes
MATERIALS SOLICITED: Materials documenting New York State history, including its political, military,
mercantile, scientific, technological, agricultural, religious, social, and ethnic
aspects. Will also accept materials concerning American history topics that
significantly relate to New York State.

HOLDINGS:
> Total volume: 8,500 l.f.
> Inclusive dates: 1630 -
> Description: Some 600 collections and
17,000 items consisting of personal papers and other manuscripts relating to the
history of New Netherlands and the colony and State of New York.

GUIDES: Jamie Messmer and Peter
Christoph, eds., *Guide to the Manu-
script Collections of the New York State
Library* (Univ. of the State of New
York, 1982).

SEE: Hamer; NUCMC, 1962, 73, 76, 79.

SEE: Gehring; Hinding; Hines; Ingram;
Leventhal and Mooney - I; Robbins.

SEE ALSO: Walter Schatz, ed., *Directory of
Afro-American Resources* (Bowker,
1970); Ann Novotny, ed., *Picture
Sources 3* (Special Libraries Assn.,
1975); *A Guide to Revolutionary War
Manuscripts in the New York State Li-
brary* (N.Y. State American Revolution
Bicentennial Commission, 1976).

Richard C. Davis, *North American Forest History: A Guide to Archives and Manuscripts in the United States and Canada* (Clio Books, 1977).

NY10-675

Roman Catholic Diocese of Albany
Archives
465 State Street
Albany NY

MAILING ADDRESS:
P.O. Box 6297
Albany NY 12206

(518) 462-5476

OPEN: M-F 9-4:30; closed weekends and holidays
ACCESS: by appointment
COPYING FACILITIES: yes
MATERIALS SOLICITED: Church records and other materials relating to the history of the parishes in the 14 counties of the Diocese. Will also accept letters, diaries, journals of clergy, laymen and laywomen active in church circles of the Diocese, along with logbooks and minutes of various related associations.

HOLDINGS:
> *Total volume:* 105 l.f.; 20 file cases
> *Inclusive dates:* 1800 -
> *Description:* The correspondence of John Cardinal McCloskey, first American cardinal, and of Bishop John Joseph Conroy; correspondence, journals, and diaries of Bishops Francis J. McInerney and Thomas M. A. Burke; and miscellaneous uncataloged material of Bishop Edmund F. Gibbons. Also included are financial records, clergy records, parochial records (nonsacramental), histories of parishes, and architectural and engineering drawings.

NY10-710

Sisters of Mercy
Archives
634 New Scotland Avenue
Albany NY 12208

(518) 489-8341

OPEN: M-Th 9-4, F 9-noon; other times by special appointment
COPYING FACILITIES: yes
MATERIALS SOLICITED: Records of the Sisters of Mercy, including their missions in Alaska, the Virgin Islands, and Beirut, Lebanon. Will also accept other materials relating to the order, such as private papers of pastors, hospital administrators, and doctors.

HOLDINGS:
> *Total volume:* 75 l.f.; 4 file cabinets
> *Inclusive dates:* 1831 -
> *Description:* Two histories of the establishment of the Sisters of Mercy in Albany in the 1860's; letters of Sisters; official journals, financial records, blueprints and plans of churches and other institutions operated by the Sisters, mainly in the Albany Diocese; and numerous photographs of church-related subjects.

NY10-770

State University of New York at Albany
University Libraries
Special Collections
1400 Washington Avenue
Albany NY 12222

(518) 442-3543

OPEN: M-F 9-4; closed weekends and holidays
COPYING FACILITIES: yes
MATERIALS SOLICITED: Papers of eastern European exiles, especially Austrian and German exiles since 1933; German youth movement; German resistance movement; materials relating to the Albany, NY, Jewish community; and materials relating to the New School for Social Research (of New York City). Will also accept materials in fields relevant to the curriculum of the University.

HOLDINGS:
> *Total volume:* 179 l.f.
> *Inclusive dates:* 1777 -
> *Description:* Day books, account books, and financial records of general stores, banks, railroads, and insurance firms in New York and New England, with concentration in the 19th century; Exile Literature Collection (originals and photocopies) consisting of papers of individuals and groups.
> Case studies of Community Research Associates (1954-55); scrapbook and press releases of New York Senator Thomas C. Desmond; and personal papers of Fred R. Brown, Howard Palfrey Jones, and Edwin Robert Van Kleeck.
> Also included are the University archives.

SEE: NUCMC, 1977.

SEE: Hinding.

SEE ALSO: Ann Novotny, ed., *Picture Sources 3* (Special Libraries Assn., 1975); Albert Krichmar, *The Women's Rights Movement in the United States, 1848-1970: A Bibliography and Sourcebook* (Scarecrow Press, 1972).

NY10-800

Union University
Albany Medical College
Schaffer Library of Health Sciences
New Scotland Avenue
Albany NY 12208

(518) 445-5534

OPEN: Su 2-10, M-Th 8-midnight, F 8-9, Sa 10-6; closed holidays
ACCESS: appointment required
COPYING FACILITIES: yes
MATERIALS SOLICITED: Materials pertaining to the history of Albany Medical College.

HOLDINGS:
> *Total volume:* 62 vols.; 180 boxes
> *Inclusive dates:* 1820 -
> *Description:* Personal papers, diaries, account books, lectures, and case records of Dr. Alden March, founder of Albany Medical College, archival material pertaining to the institution, and handwritten theses of its graduates, 1839-91.

SEE: NUCMC, 1962 (as Albany Medical College).

ALBION

NY12-720

Swan Library
4 North Main Street
Albion NY 14411

(716) 589-4246

OPEN: M-F 12-8, Sa 10-3; closed Sundays and holidays
ACCESS: an appointment is advised
COPYING FACILITIES: yes
MATERIALS SOLICITED: Orleans County history and genealogy. Will also accept other materials pertaining to Orleans County.

HOLDINGS:
> *Total volume:* 10 c.f.
> *Inclusive dates:* 1837 -
> *Description:* A collection of manuscripts, photographs, diaries, and other materials relating to the history of Orleans County.

SEE: Hinding.

ALFRED

NY18-40

Alfred University
Herrick Library
Alfred NY 14802

(607) 871-2184

OPEN: M-F 9-5; by appointment May 15-Aug. 20; closed weekends and Christmas week
COPYING FACILITIES: yes

HOLDINGS:
> *Total volume:* 100 c.f.
> *Inclusive dates:* 1813 -
> *Description:* Records and memorabilia of Alfred University; the papers of the Howells-Frechette family, including letters of William Dean Howells; the Waid collection of materials concerning the Nazis and the U.S. occupation of Germany; and local photographs, organization records, and family papers.

SEE: Allegany County Guide.

NY18-720

State University of New York at Alfred
Agricultural and Technical College
Walter C. Hinkle Memorial Library
College Archives and Western New York Historical Collections
Alfred NY 14802

(607) 871-6313

OPEN: M-Th 8-10:30, F 8-5, Sa 1-9, Su 1-10:30 during school session, daily 8-4 during school breaks; closed holidays
COPYING FACILITIES: yes
MATERIALS SOLICITED: Archives of the College, as well as other materials documenting the history of New York State west of Syracuse.

HOLDINGS:
Total volume: 40 c.f.
Inclusive dates: 1830's -
Description: College archives, including rosters and annual reports, as well as a small collection of private papers, legal documents, photographs, oral histories, and genealogical records pertaining to families and local governments in western New York, 1830's to date. There are also U.S. Weather Bureau records for the town of Alfred.
Included are the holdings of the Alfred Historical Society, including genealogical materials, deeds and legal papers, records of local businesses and organizations, and other papers relating to the history of Alfred and Allegany.

SEE: Allegany County Guide.

ALMOND

NY20-40
Almond Historical Society
110 North Main Street
Almond NY 14804

(607) 276-6166

OPEN: by appointment only
COPYING FACILITIES: no
MATERIALS SOLICITED: Materials concerning the history and genealogy of Almond.

HOLDINGS:
Total volume: 30 c.f.
Inclusive dates: 1800 -
Description: Family papers, town and school records, diaries, photographs, scrapbooks, and a vertical file concerning individuals and institutions in Almond.

SEE: Allegany County Guide.

NY20-760
Twentieth Century Club Library
Almond NY 14804

no telephone

OPEN: Tu 3-9, Th 2-9, Sa 2-5; closed other days
COPYING FACILITIES: no

HOLDINGS:
Total volume: 1.5 c.f.
Inclusive dates: 1901 -
Description: Records of the library and the club that sponsors it.

SEE: Allegany County Guide; Hinding.

AMHERST

NY24-720
State University of New York at Buffalo
Libraries
University Archives
420 Capen Hall
Amherst NY 14260

(716) 636-2916

OPEN: M-F 9-5; closed weekends and holidays
COPYING FACILITIES: yes

MATERIALS SOLICITED: Archives of the State University of New York at Buffalo and its predecessor, the University of Buffalo; personal and organizational papers of its administrators, faculty, students, and alumni; documentation of Frank Lloyd Wright buildings in Buffalo, especially the Darwin D. Martin House; and records of selected professional and other local organizations.

HOLDINGS:
Total volume: 5,000 c.f.
Inclusive dates: 1846 -
Description: Archives of the State University of New York at Buffalo and its predecessor, the University of Buffalo, 1846 to date, including official records, papers of faculty members and others associated with the University, and audiovisual records. The University Archives also contains manuscript collections relating to Buffalo history and documents pertaining to the Darwin D. Martin House and other Buffalo buildings designed by Frank Lloyd Wright.

SEE: NUCMC, 1971, 77, 80.

SEE: Hinding.

SEE ALSO: *Manuscripts for Research* (Five Associated University Libraries, 1969).

NY24-725
State University of New York at Buffalo
Lockwood Library
Polish Collection
Amherst NY 14260

(716) 636-2818

OPEN: M-F 8-11, Sa 10-5, Su 11-6; closed holidays
COPYING FACILITIES: yes
MATERIALS SOLICITED: Scientific materials relating to Poland.

HOLDINGS:
Total volume: not specified
Inclusive dates: 16th century -
Description: Photographs, royal documents, and other materials relating to Poland.

NY24-735
State University of New York at Buffalo
Libraries
Poetry/Rare Books
420 Capen Hall
Amherst NY 14260

(716) 636-2917

OPEN: M-F 9-5; closed weekends and holidays
ACCESS: written permission of the appropriate author, heir, or estate required for access to all letters and some manuscript material
COPYING FACILITIES: yes
MATERIALS SOLICITED: 20th century poetry written or translated into English, and prose by poets represented in the collection.

HOLDINGS:
Total volume: 60,000 items
Inclusive dates: 20th century -
Description: Photographs, letters, and 14,642 manuscript titles of British and American poets, including James Joyce, Robert Graves, Dylan Thomas, Wyndham Lewis, and William Carlos Williams.

SEE: Robbins.

SEE ALSO: Peter Spielberg, comp., *James Joyce's Manuscripts and Letters at the University of Buffalo: A Catalogue* (Univ. of Buffalo, 1962); Neil Baldwin and Steven L. Meyers *The Manuscripts and Letters of William Carlos Williams in the Poetry Collection of the Lockwood Memorial Library, State University of New York at Buffalo: A Descriptive Catalogue* (G. K. Hall, 1978).

AMITYVILLE

NY26-40
Amityville Historical Society
Museum
Research Library
170 Broadway
Amityville NY

MAILING ADDRESS:
Box 764
Amityville NY 11701

(516) 598-1486

OPEN: Su, Tu, F afternoon by appointment; closed other days and holidays
COPYING FACILITIES: no
MATERIALS SOLICITED: Materials relating to Amityville, Copiague, and Massapequa, NY. Will also accept other materials relating to Long Island history.

HOLDINGS:
Total volume: not specified
Inclusive dates: 1850 -
Description: Maps, photographs, records of organizations, and slides relating to the history of the Amityville, Copiague, and Massapequa, Long Island area.

ANDOVER

NY29-40
Andover Free Library
Andover NY 14806

(607) 478-8442

OPEN: M noon-9, W 6-9, F 11-3; closed other days and holidays
COPYING FACILITIES: no
MATERIALS SOLICITED: History of the town of Andover and Allegany County, NY.

HOLDINGS:
Total volume: 2 c.f.
Inclusive dates: 1857 -
Description: Photographs, library records, clippings, and reports of the town historian of Andover.

SEE: Allegany County Guide.

ANGELICA

NY32-50
Angelica Free Library
55 West Main Street
Angelica NY 14709

no telephone

OPEN: Tu 1-5, 7-9, Th 2-4, 7-9, Sa
10-12; closed Su, M, W, F and holidays
COPYING FACILITIES: no

HOLDINGS:
Total volume: 6.5 c.f.
Inclusive dates: 1793 -
Description: Holdings of account
books, deeds, and other items relating to
the Church tract in Allegany County, NY,
owned by John Barker Church, his son
Philip, and others. Also included are
copies of letters of Marie d'Ohent
d'Autremont, a French exile in Angelica,
as well as photographs, documents, and
letters.

SEE: Allegany County Guide.

ANNANDALE-ON-HUDSON

NY35-80
Bard College
Library
Annandale-on-Hudson NY 12504

(914) 758-6822

SEE: Hamer.

Questionnaire not returned.

ARMONK

NY40-360
International Business Machines
Corporation
Archives
Old Orchard Road
Armonk NY 10504

(914) 765-3144

OPEN: by appointment only
ACCESS: prior approval required
COPYING FACILITIES: yes
MATERIALS SOLICITED: IBM corporate
records that are useful to company operations, important to its history, and
contain unique information. Will also
accept company-related employee
memorabilia.

HOLDINGS:
Total volume: 4,500 c.f.
Inclusive dates: 1880's - 1975
Description: Records of IBM including
publications, samples of advertising,
product announcements, marketing reports, financial statements, minutes of
board of directors' meetings and
stockholders' meetings, patents and copy-
rights, employee benefits plans, and photographs.

ATTICA

NY50-40
Attica Historical Society
130 Main Street
Attica NY

MAILING ADDRESS:
90 East Avenue
Attica NY 14011

(716) 591-2161

OPEN: by appointment only Su, W 3-5
COPYING FACILITIES: no

HOLDINGS:
Total volume: 40 c.f.
Inclusive dates: 1820 - 1970
Description: Primarily 19th century
materials relating to Attica and the sur-
rounding area of Wyoming County, NY.

SEE: Wyoming County Guide.

AUBURN

NY51-90
Cayuga County Community College
Library
Franklin Street
Auburn NY 13021

(315) 255-1743, Ext. 296

OPEN: Su 3-10, M-Th 8-10, F 8-5, Sa
10-5; closed holidays
COPYING FACILITIES: yes

HOLDINGS:
Total volume: 35 c.f.; 13 vols.
Inclusive dates: 1917 -
Description: College archives, chiefly
publications such as handbooks, literary
magazines and catalogs; papers of author
Earl Conrad, including manuscripts, galleys, research materials, correspondence,
and clippings; and papers of George
Metcalf, including press clippings and
some notes and outlines relating to black
studies.

SEE: NUCMC, 1972.

SEE: Cayuga County Guide.

NY51-100
Cayuga County Historian
County Office Building
Auburn NY 13021

(315) 253-1300

OPEN: M-F 9-5; closed weekends and
holidays
COPYING FACILITIES: yes
MATERIALS SOLICITED: Cayuga County
history, especially genealogical materials.

HOLDINGS:
Total volume: 100,000 cards; 500
items; 20 vols.
Inclusive dates: early 19th century -
Description: Census records; family
histories; cemetery records; data compiled
about Revolutionary War soldiers; a card
file pertaining to early settlers, businesses,
and events; and other materials tracing
the history of Cayuga County.

SEE: Hinding.

NY51-140
Cayuga Museum of History and Art
203 Genesee Street
Auburn NY 13021

(315) 253-8051

OPEN: by appointment; closed Mondays
and holidays
ACCESS: by permission of museum
director
COPYING FACILITIES: no

HOLDINGS:
Total volume: 10 c.f.; 3 vols.
Inclusive dates: 1780 - 1875
Description: American Revolution
military orderly books of George Fleming
and John L. Hardenburgh; a diary of
William Gifford, 1875; miscellaneous
19th century legal records; and manuscript research notes of John S. Clark,
relating chiefly to history and genealogy.

SEE: Hamer.

SEE: Cayuga County Guide.

This repository is also known as the
Cayuga County Historical Society.

NY51-240
Foundation Historical Association,
Inc.
33 South Street
Auburn NY 13021

(315) 252-1283

OPEN: March - Dec., M-Sa 1-5; closed
Sundays, holidays, and Jan. - Feb.
COPYING FACILITIES: no

HOLDINGS:
Total volume: 95 vols.; 8 c.f.; 408
items
Inclusive dates: 1820's - 1951
Description: Collections relating solely
to Seward family members, including personal and financial records, photographs,
and the Civil War military papers of William Henry Seward.

SEE: Cayuga County Guide; Robbins.

NY51-730
Seymour Library
Case Memorial Building
176 Genesee Street
Auburn NY 13021

(315) 252-2571

OPEN: M, W 2-9, Tu, Th, F 2-5; closed
weekends
COPYING FACILITIES: yes

HOLDINGS:
Total volume: 4 c.f.; 45 vols.; 11
items
Inclusive dates: 1706 -
Description: Materials, chiefly photo-
copies, compiled by Ellen Jean Mahoney
about artist George Lafayette Clough,
Harriet Tubman, and the Auburn State
Prison; a clipping file of local interest;
and scrapbooks, 1878-1930.

SEE: Cayuga County Guide.

AURORA

NY53-880
Wells College
Louis Jefferson Long Library
Aurora NY 13026

(315) 364-3351, 3356

OPEN: M-F 8:30-4:30, Sa 10-2; closed
  Sundays and holidays
ACCESS: appointment with Director of
  Library required
COPYING FACILITIES: yes
MATERIALS SOLICITED: Materials relating
  to Wells College and the town of Au-
  rora. Will also accept other materials.

HOLDINGS:
  Total volume: 736 items; 322 vols.;
  84 c.f.
    Inclusive dates: 1790 -
    Description: Materials dealing with
  Wells College; Morgan family papers; the
  E. D. Palmer collection, 1856-90; the
  Henry Wells collection, 1840-78; materials relating to Cayuga Lake Academy,
  1830-1945; Helen Fairchild Smith letters
  and diaries, 1864-1926; the Aurora Electric Light Company collection,
  1874-1923; maps and blueprints,
  1840-1934; and other materials relating
  to the Aurora area.

SEE: NUCMC, 1980.

SEE: Cayuga County Guide.

AVOCA

NY54-40
Avoca Free Library
Griswold Street
Avoca NY 14809

no telephone

OPEN: W, F 2-9; closed other days and
  holidays
COPYING FACILITIES: no
MATERIALS SOLICITED: The history and
  genealogy of Avoca and the vicinity.

HOLDINGS:
  Total volume: 1 c.f.
  Inclusive dates: 1834 -
  Description: Genealogical materials
  and school records relating to Avoca.

SEE: Steuben County Guide.

BABYLON

NY56-80
Babylon Public Library
24 South Carll Avenue
Babylon NY 11702

(516) 669-1624

OPEN: M-Th 9:30-9, F, Sa 9:30-5; closed
  Sundays

SEE: Hamer.

Questionnaire not returned.

BAINBRIDGE

NY59-80
Bainbridge Free Library
13 North Main Street
Bainbridge NY 13733

no telephone

OPEN: M 6:30-9, Tu 9:30-9, Th 1-9, Sa
  9-12:30; closed other days, holidays,
  and Saturdays July - Aug.
COPYING FACILITIES: no
MATERIALS SOLICITED: Bainbridge history and genealogy.

HOLDINGS:
  Total volume: 6 vols.
  Inclusive dates: 1930 -
  Description: Scrapbooks of clippings
  concerning the Rotary Club and Library,
  and a photocopied typescript on the history of the Stockwell family.

SEE: Chenango County Guide.

BALLSTON SPA

NY66-720
Saratoga County Historical Society
Brookside
Ballston Spa NY 12020

(518) 885-4000

OPEN: Tu-F 1-5; closed Sa-M
ACCESS: appointment advisable
COPYING FACILITIES: no
MATERIALS SOLICITED: Materials relating
  to the history of Saratoga County.

HOLDINGS:
  Total volume: 48 l.f.
  Inclusive dates: 1789 -
  Description: The collection relates to
  Saratoga County, including school trust-
  ees' reports, business records, court
  records, family papers, and account
  books.

BATAVIA

NY69-280
Genesee County Department of
  History
Library
Holland Land Office
131 West Main Street
Batavia NY 14020

(716) 344-2550, Ext. 275

OPEN: M-F 9-5; closed weekends and
  holidays
COPYING FACILITIES: no
MATERIALS SOLICITED: Historical materials concerning western New York,
  particularly Genesee County.

HOLDINGS:
  Total volume: 14 c.f.; 1,303 vols.
  Inclusive dates: 1801 -
  Description: Land records, scrapbooks,
  notes, diaries, clippings, and photographs
  relating to the history of Genesee County
  and western New York State.

SEE: Hamer.

The manuscript collections of the
Holland Purchase Historical Society
are located at the Library.

BATH

NY71-715
Steuben County Agricultural Society
Memorial Pioneer Log Cabin and
  Museum
15 East Washington Street
Bath NY 14810

(607) 776-4801

OPEN: M-F 10-4 July 4-Sept. 5; closed
  other times
USER FEES: admission fee
COPYING FACILITIES: no

HOLDINGS:
  Total volume: 100 items
  Inclusive dates: 1848 -
  Description: Materials include photographs, broadsides, memorabilia, and other items relating to activities of the Steuben County Agricultural Society and history of Steuben County.

SEE: Steuben County Guide.

NY71-720
Steuben County Historical Society
Steuben County Clerk's Office
Pulteney Square
Bath NY

MAILING ADDRESS:
P.O. Box 349
Bath NY 14810

(607) 583-4439

OPEN: M-F 8:30-5; July and Aug., M-F
  8:30-4; closed weekends and holidays
COPYING FACILITIES: yes
MATERIALS SOLICITED: Genealogical material relating to Steuben County, NY,
  and adjacent counties.

HOLDINGS:
  Total volume: 6 c.f.
  Inclusive dates: 1796 -
  Description: Steuben County records,
  including indexed cemetery records; the
  indexed state census (1825-1925); Bible,
  family, and church records; and early vital record abstracts.

SEE: Steuben County Guide.

BEAVER DAMS

NY78-320
Hornby Historical Society
R.D. 3
Beaver Dams NY 14812

no telephone

OPEN: by appointment only
COPYING FACILITIES: no
MATERIALS SOLICITED: History of
  Hornby and Steuben County, NY.

HOLDINGS:
  Total volume: 3 c.f.
  Inclusive dates: 1836 -
  Description: Photographs, account books, school records, cemetery transcriptions, and other materials relating to the town of Hornby.

SEE: Steuben County Guide.

BELFAST

NY82-80
Belfast Public Library
Belfast NY 14711

(716) 365-2072

OPEN: Tu 2-5, Th 2-9, Sa 10-5; closed other days and holidays
COPYING FACILITIES: no

HOLDINGS:
  Total volume: 11 c.f.
  Inclusive dates: 1823 -
  Description: Records of the town of Belfast and local schools, clippings and photographs relating to Belfast history, and the diaries and papers of Lucinda E. Ford.

SEE: Allegany County Guide.

BELMONT

NY87-40
Allegany County Department of
  History
Allegany County Museum
11 Wells Street
Belmont NY

MAILING ADDRESS:
Court House
Belmont NY 14813

(716) 268-7612

OPEN: M-F 9-5; closed weekends and holidays
COPYING FACILITIES: yes
MATERIALS SOLICITED: Material relating to Allegany County genealogy and land records. Will also accept artifacts relating to Allegany County history, geography, and industry.

HOLDINGS:
  Total volume: 2 file cabinets
  Inclusive dates: 1802 - 1910
  Description: Land records of Philip Church and his surveyor, Van Campen, including 3 ledgers and 1,500 documents (1803-45). Also included are various genealogical records and photographs of Allegany County in the late 19th and early 20th centuries.

SEE: Allegany County Guide.

NY87-50
Allegany County Historical Society
20 Willets Avenue
Belmont NY 14813

(716) 268-7612

OPEN: M-F 10-5; closed weekends and holidays
COPYING FACILITIES: yes

MATERIALS SOLICITED: Materials relating to the history and genealogy of Allegany County.

HOLDINGS:
  Total volume: 25 c.f.
  Inclusive dates: 1803 -
  Description: Collections include account books, photographs, maps, church and school records, cemetery and census transcriptions and indices, architectural survey records, and vertical files of genealogical data relating to Allegany County.

SEE: Allegany County Guide.

NY87-80
Belmont Literary and Historical
  Society Free Library
Belmont NY 14813

(716) 268-5308

OPEN: Th, F 2-9, Sa 1-9; closed other days and holidays
COPYING FACILITIES: no

HOLDINGS:
  Total volume: 1.5 c.f.
  Inclusive dates: 1856 -
  Description: Records of the library and items concerning the history of Belmont and Allegany County, NY.

SEE: Allegany County Guide.

NY87-900
Villa Belvidere
Belmont NY

MAILING ADDRESS:
c/o Bromeley
R.D.
Belmont NY 14813

no telephone

OPEN: by appointment
ACCESS: qualified researchers only; advance arrangements required
COPYING FACILITIES: no

HOLDINGS:
  Total volume: 100 items
  Inclusive dates: 1804 - 1943
  Description: Materials relating to development of the Church Tract, including letters of Philip Church, John Barker Church, Robert Troup, Dugald Cameron, and others; land records, deeds, and business records from Allegany County; and maps of Allegany County, the Holland Land Purchase, and the Morris Reserve.

SEE: Allegany County Guide.

BERKSHIRE

NY91-80
Berkshire Free Library
Route 38
Berkshire NY 13736

no telephone

OPEN: M 2-5, W 9-noon, Th 1-5, F 7-9; closed other days and holidays
COPYING FACILITIES: no
MATERIALS SOLICITED: Berkshire history.

HOLDINGS:
  Total volume: 10 items
  Inclusive dates: 1855 -
  Description: Writings by Berkshire residents concerning local history.

SEE: Tioga County Guide.

BETHPAGE

NY95-280
Grumman Corporation
History Center
Bethpage NY 11714

(516) 575-2401

OPEN: by appointment only; closed weekends and holidays
COPYING FACILITIES: yes
MATERIALS SOLICITED: Documents pertaining to the history of the Grumman Aerospace Corporation. Will also accept selected aerospace documents.

HOLDINGS:
  Total volume: 1,200 l.f.
  Inclusive dates: 1930 -
  Description: Photographs and documents relating to Grumman products, people, and facilities.

SEE ALSO: Ann Novotny, ed., *Picture Sources 3* (Special Libraries Assn., 1975).

BIG FLATS

NY98-80
Big Flats Historical Society
3252 Sing Sing Road
Big Flats NY

MAILING ADDRESS:
P.O. Box 232
Big Flats NY 14814

(607) 562-3101

OPEN: Tu 9:30-3:30, Su 2-5, other times by appointment
ACCESS: appointment required, by calling Big Flats Town Historian at (607) 562-8523
COPYING FACILITIES: no
MATERIALS SOLICITED: Big Flats history. Will also accept materials relating to history of Chemung County.

HOLDINGS:
  Total volume: 8 c.f.; 43 vols.; 3,050 items
  Inclusive dates: 1810 -
  Description: Materials dealing with the history of Big Flats, including documents for the period 1810-60, photographs, newspaper clippings, and a complete file on cemeteries.

SEE: Chemung County Guide.

BINGHAMTON

NY101-70
Binghamton Public Library
78 Exchange Street
Binghamton NY 13901

(607) 723-6457

OPEN: M-F 9-9, Sa 9-5; closed
　Saturdays, July - Aug., and Sundays
COPYING FACILITIES: yes

HOLDINGS:
　　Total volume: 29.4 c.f.; 71 items; 179
　vols.
　　Inclusive dates: 1806 -
　　Description: A clipping and subject file
on Binghamton and Broome County, late
1800's- ; the journal of John McComb,
Jr., 1833; 8 vols. of scrapbooks, chiefly
concerning library activities, 1949- ; an
autograph letter collection, 1817-73; a
transcript of a Civil War diary of two
privates held prisoner at Andersonville,
1864; photographs; account books,
1806-52; and the Putnam collection of
126 vols. of scrapbooks documenting
Broome County history.

SEE: Broome County Guide.

NY101-80
Broome Community College
Cecil C. Tyrrell Library
905 Front Street
Binghamton NY 13902

(607) 771-5045

OPEN: M-Th 8-10, F 8-5, Su 4-10; closed
　Saturdays and holidays; summer, M,
　W, Th 8-9, Tu 8-5, F 8-4:30
COPYING FACILITIES: yes
MATERIALS SOLICITED: Broome Commu-
　nity College and State University of
　New York archives.

HOLDINGS:
　　Total volume: 10 c.f.
　　Inclusive dates: 1949 -
　　Description: Archives of Broome Com-
munity College and the State University
of New York.

SEE: Broome County Guide.

NY101-90
Broome County Historical Society
Roberson Center for the Arts and
　Sciences
30 Front Street
Binghamton NY 13902

(607) 772-0660

OPEN: Tu-F 10-5, M by appointment;
　closed weekends and holidays
COPYING FACILITIES: yes
MATERIALS SOLICITED: History of Bing-
　hamton and Broome County, NY.

HOLDINGS:
　　Total volume: 119 c.f.
　　Inclusive dates: 1727 -
　　Description: Papers of Joshua Whitney,
William Bingham, Clement Bowers, J.
Stuart Wells, Daniel S. Dickinson, Wil-
liam L. Ford, John C. Rankin, Foster
Disinger, and others; organization
records; cemetery records; diaries; maps;

photographs, including Robert Garvin aerial photographs and Gilbert deClerque
glass negatives; chattel mortgages; scrapbooks; military records compiled by Hilton M. LeCouver for World War II area
military personnel; and a large file of
photocopied town, church, and genealogical records from Broome County and
Binghamton.

SEE: NUCMC, 1959-61, 75.

SEE: Broome County Guide.

NY101-690
Roberson Center for the Arts and
　Sciences
30 Front Street
Binghamton NY 13902

(607) 772-0660

OPEN: M-F 9-5; closed weekends and
　holidays
COPYING FACILITIES: yes

HOLDINGS:
　　Total volume: 6 c.f.
　　Inclusive dates: 1837 -
　　Description: Materials on circuses and
on the Roberson Center for the Arts and
Sciences.

SEE: Broome County Guide.

NY101-720
State University of New York at
　Binghamton
Glenn G. Bartle Library
Special Collections
Vestal Parkway East
Binghamton NY 13901

(607) 777-4844

OPEN: M-F 1-5; closed weekends and
　holidays
COPYING FACILITIES: yes
MATERIALS SOLICITED: Broome County
　local history documents; Padraic Col-
　um primary materials; records dealing
　with Max Reinhardt, 1873-1943, Aus-
　trian theatrical director; and records
　concerning the State University of New
　York at Binghamton and its faculty.

HOLDINGS:
　　Total volume: 350 l.f.
　　Inclusive dates: 1806 -
　　Description: Literary papers include
manuscripts, play scripts, notebooks, cassettes, pictures, and letters of Padraic
Colum, in addition to papers of Mary
Colum. The Mary Lavin Collection represents her twenty-year correspondence begun in 1943 with Lord and Lady Dunsany and other Irish writers. There are
also papers of Edwin A. Link concerning
aviation and underwater archaeology;
business and private papers of L. M.
Bowers, Broome County inventor and
manufacturer; papers of David Bernstein,
editor of the Binghamton *Sun-Bulletin*;
archives of the Associated Colleges of
Upper New York, 1946-50; and Broome
County Medical Society records,
1806-1935.

SEE: NUCMC, 1981.

SEE: Hinding; Martin; Robbins; Broome
　County Guide.

SEE ALSO: *Map Collections in the United
States and Canada, A Directory*
(Special Libraries Assn., 1970). Catalogs of the Colum and Lavin materials
have been published by the University.

Finding aids to the papers of Mary Colum,
Mary Lavin, and Lamont Montgomery
Bowers have been published by the Uni-
versity.

BLUE MOUNTAIN LAKE

NY104-40
Adirondack Historical Association
Blue Mountain Lake NY 12812

(518) 352-7311

OPEN: by appointment only

SEE: NUCMC, 1962, 71 (as Adirondack
　Museum).

　Questionnaire not returned.

BOLIVAR

NY106-80
Bolivar Free Library
Bolivar NY 14715

no telephone

OPEN: Tu-F 9-4, Sa 9-noon; closed
　Sundays, Mondays, and holidays
COPYING FACILITIES: no

HOLDINGS:
　　Total volume: 1.5 c.f.
　　Inclusive dates: 1826 -
　　Description: Library records, photo-
graphs, a Civil War draft list, and other
materials.

SEE: Allegany County Guide.

NY106-640
Pioneer Oil Museum of New York
Main Street
Bolivar NY

MAILING ADDRESS:
121 South Street
Bolivar NY 14715

(716) 928-1433

OPEN: Tu, Th, F afternoon, Sa morning,
　or by appointment; closed holidays
COPYING FACILITIES: no

HOLDINGS:
　　Total volume: 4 c.f.
　　Inclusive dates: 1860 -
　　Description: Photographs, clippings,
and other items relating to the history of
Bolivar and the oil industry in Allegany
County, NY.

SEE: Allegany County Guide.

BOONVILLE

NY107-200

Erwin Library and Institute
Schuyler Street
Boonville NY 13309

(315) 942-4834

OPEN: Tu, Th 10-9, W, F 1-9, Sa 10-12; closed Su, M
COPYING FACILITIES: yes
MATERIALS SOLICITED: Will accept genealogies and local history materials.

HOLDINGS:
Total volume: 96 l.f.; 2 file cabinets
Inclusive dates: 1865 -
Description: Family genealogies, cemetery records, records of servicemen, Civil War materials, and photographs of local scenes and people.

SEE: Hamer.

BOVINA CENTER

NY111-60

Bovina Historical Society
Museum
Bovina Center NY 13740

no telephone

OPEN: by appointment only
COPYING FACILITIES: no
MATERIALS SOLICITED: Materials relating to Bovina Center and surrounding areas.

HOLDINGS:
Total volume: 3 vols.
Inclusive dates: 1884 - 1921
Description: Ledger of Andrew T. Strangeway, owner of general store in Bovina Center, 1884-1907; town clerk's memoranda of town charges, 1899-1921; and a doctor's medical almanac, 1907.

SEE: Delaware County Guide.

NY111-80

Bovina Public Library
Bovina Center NY 13740

no telephone

OPEN: Tu, Th 1-9; closed other days
COPYING FACILITIES: no

HOLDINGS:
Total volume: 4 vols.
Inclusive dates: 1973
Description: A typescript of original diaries of James H. Thomson, recording farm life in Bovina Center, 1832-1903.

SEE: Delaware County Guide.

The original Thomson diaries are at the New York State Historical Association, Library, in Cooperstown, NY.

BRANCHPORT

NY112-80

Branchport Free Library
Branchport NY 14418

no telephone

OPEN: Tu, F, Sa 2-5; closed other days and holidays
COPYING FACILITIES: no
MATERIALS SOLICITED: The history of Branchport and vicinity.

HOLDINGS:
Total volume: 2 c.f.
Inclusive dates: 1812 -
Description: Scrapbooks, photographs, a diary, a school minute book, and other materials on the history of Branchport and vicinity.

SEE: Yates County Guide.

BRENTWOOD

NY115-720

Sisters of St. Joseph
Archives Department
St. Joseph Convent
Brentwood NY 11717

(516) 273-4531

OPEN: M-F 9-4; closed weekends and holidays
ACCESS: qualified researchers according to congregational policy
COPYING FACILITIES: yes
MATERIALS SOLICITED: Records of administrative units of Congregation of Sisters of St. Joseph and records of defunct institutions staffed by members of the order. Will also accept annals and photographs from local communities of Sisters, accounts of celebrations and jubilees, and papers of Sisters.

HOLDINGS:
Total volume: 150 c.f.
Inclusive dates: 1856 -
Description: Materials relating to the history of the Congregation of Sisters of St. Joseph, including papers of major superiors, rules, customs, and annals, as well as personnel, formation, and financial records. Among the papers of deceased Sisters are those of Mother de Chantal Keating, an Army nurse during 1864-65. Administrative records include proceedings of general chapters and committees, and accounts of educational and other institutions on Long Island and in Puerto Rico staffed by the members of the congregation.

BRISTON CENTER

NY124-60

Briston Historical Society
Briston Center NY 14419

no telephone

OPEN: by appointment only
COPYING FACILITIES: no

HOLDINGS:
Total volume: 9 c.f.
Inclusive dates: 1800 -
Description: Town records, diaries, account books, scrapbooks, church records, Grange records, and genealogical materials from Bristol Center and vicinity.

BROCKPORT

NY125-700

Seymour Library
49 State Street
Brockport NY 14420

(716) 637-4140

OPEN: Th noon-9, F 9-9, Sa 9-5; closed other days
COPYING FACILITIES: yes

HOLDINGS:
Total volume: 3 c.f.
Inclusive dates: 1890 -
Description: Papers on the history of Brockport, the reaper industry, and Daniel and Mary Jane Holmes.

NY125-720

State University of New York
College at Brockport
Drake Memorial Library
Brockport NY 14420

(716) 395-2145

OPEN: M-F 8:30-4:30; closed weekends, holidays, and Saturdays during College vacations
COPYING FACILITIES: yes
MATERIALS SOLICITED: Materials relating to the College, western Monroe County, and Orleans County.

HOLDINGS:
Total volume: 25 l.f.
Inclusive dates: 1841 -
Description: Archives of the State University of New York College at Brockport and its predecessor institutions, including minutes of meetings of governing bodies, 1841-1962; student academic records, 1864-1900; records of faculty meetings, 1881-1914 and 1970- ; scrapbooks; photographs; student papers; and masters' theses. Manuscript collections include records of the D. S. Morgan Company, manufacturers of agricultural implements; correspondence, 1888-1939, between Sara Morgan Manning and her mother, Susan Joslyn Morgan; and materials relating to a New York cavalry company in the Civil War.

SEE: Hamer.

SEE: Hinding.

NY125-740
State University of New York
College at Brockport
Educational Communications Center
Brockport NY 14420

(716) 395-2348

OPEN: M-F 8-5 by appointment; closed
  weekends and holidays
ACCESS: advance arrangements required
COPYING FACILITIES: yes
MATERIALS SOLICITED: Will accept vid-
  eotapes prepared at the College.

HOLDINGS:
  Total volume: 196 items
  Inclusive dates: 1968 -
  Description: Videotapes prepared by
  the Center for Philosophic Exchange and
  the Writers Forum. The Center's tapes
  relate to matters of both academic and
  public concern and include discussions of
  such topics as technology and ethics, the
  equality of animals, moral aspects of euthanasia, infinity and the double language
  of mathematics, and the philosophy of
  medicine. Major participants have included Sir Alfred J. Ayer, Brand Blandshard,
  Phillipa Foot, R. M. Hare, Paul Ricoeur,
  Kurt Baier, and Norman Malcolm.
  The Writers Forum tapes include styl-
  istics, formal aesthetics, literary trends in
  contemporary fiction and poetry, and the
  teaching of creative writing. Discussants
  include Archibald MacLeish, Richard
  Wilbur, Maxine Kumin, Donald Justice,
  James T. Farrell, Ihab Hassan, Joyce Carol Oates, John Berryman, James Dickey,
  Denise Levertov, and Stephen Spender.

SEE: Robbins.

NY125-880
Western Monroe Historical Society
151 Main Street
Brockport NY

MAILING ADDRESS:
P.O. Box 217
Brockport NY 14420

(716) 637-3645

OPEN: weekdays by appointment only;
  closed weekends and holidays
COPYING FACILITIES: no
MATERIALS SOLICITED: Materials relating
  to the Morgan and Manning families.

HOLDINGS:
  Total volume: 3 c.f.
  Inclusive dates: 1855 - 1950
  Description: Correspondence, diaries,
  and financial papers of Sara Morgan
  Manning and the Morgan family of
  Brockport.

BRONXVILLE

NY128-480
Lutheran Church-Missouri Synod
Atlantic District
Archives
Concordia College
171 White Plains Road
Bronxville NY

MAILING ADDRESS:
360 Park Avenue S.
New York NY 10010

(914) 337-9300, Ext. 138

OPEN: by appointment with archivist
COPYING FACILITIES: yes
MATERIALS SOLICITED: Materials relating
  to church members, congregations, and
  auxiliary organizations of the Atlantic
  District.

HOLDINGS:
  Total volume: 3,776 items
  Inclusive dates: 1840 -
  Description: Records of the Lutheran
  Church-Missouri Synod for the area from
  Maine to New Jersey, including corre-
  spondence, account books, financial
  records, genealogical source data, and bio-
  graphical information relating to clergy
  and lay people active in the church.

SEE ALSO: a mimeographed guide to holdings available by request.

NY128-720
Sarah Lawrence College
Esther Raushenbush Library
Glen Washington Road
Bronxville NY 10708

(914) 337-0700

OPEN: M-F 9-5; closed weekends and
  holidays
ACCESS: librarian's permission required
COPYING FACILITIES: yes
MATERIALS SOLICITED: Materials relating
  to the College, continuing education,
  and the history of education and of
  women.

HOLDINGS:
  Total volume: 1,072 vols.; 344
  cassettes and tapes; 17 cabinets; 59 boxes;
  16 scrapbooks
  Inclusive dates: 1928 -
  Description: Records and other materials relating to Sarah Lawrence College
  and its association with women's history,
  the history of education, and continuing
  education. Included are College presidents' reports, faculty publications, interviews with College founders, and papers
  of faculty members and those involved in
  the progressive education movement.

SEE: Hinding.

BUFFALO

NY134-50
Buffalo and Erie County Historical
  Society
Iconography Department
25 Nottingham Court
Buffalo NY 14216

(716) 873-9644

OPEN: M-F 10-5; closed weekends and
  holidays
COPYING FACILITIES: yes
MATERIALS SOLICITED: Work of local
  photographers and architectural plans
  of local interest.

HOLDINGS:
  Total volume: 50,000 items
  Inclusive dates: 18th century - 20th
  century
  Description: Visual materials relating
  to the history of the Niagara frontier,
  consisting of maps, photographs, architectural and engineering drawings, films,
  broadsides, posters, prints, and local television news footage.

SEE ALSO: Ann Novotny, ed., *Picture
  Sources 3* (Special Libraries Assn.,
  1975); *Map Collections in the United
  States and Canada, A Directory*
  (Special Libraries Assn., 1970).

Available upon request are inventories of
various collections and a brochure,
'Pictorial Resources,' describing the holdings.

NY134-60
Buffalo and Erie County Historical
  Society
Manuscripts Department
25 Nottingham Court
Buffalo NY 14216

(716) 873-9644

OPEN: M-F 10-5; closed weekends and
  holidays
COPYING FACILITIES: yes
MATERIALS SOLICITED: Material pertaining to Buffalo and the Niagara frontier.
  Will also accept materials relating to
  genealogy and Great Lakes and military history, and papers of Presidents
  and New York State political figures.

HOLDINGS:
  Total volume: 1,000,000 items
  Inclusive dates: 1767 -
  Description: Papers relating chiefly to
  Buffalo and the Niagara frontier with spe-
  cial emphasis on military and Great
  Lakes history.

SEE: Hamer; NUCMC, 1962, 64, 75.

SEE: Allard, Crawley, and Edmison; Martin; Hinding; Robbins.

SEE ALSO: Morris Rieger, 'Africa-Related
  Papers of Persons and Organizations in
  the United States,' *African Studies Bul-
  letin* 8 (Dec. 1965); Peter Duignan,
  *Handbook of American Resources for
  African Studies* (Hoover Institution,

1967); Alan M. Meckler and Ruth McMullin, comps., *Oral History Collections* (Bowker, 1975); and the Society's publications: *Niagara Frontier* and the *Buffalo and Erie County Historical Society Publications*.

Guides to microfilm editions of several collections have been published.

NY134-85
Buffalo and Erie County Public
   Library
North Jefferson Branch Library
Center for Local Afro-American
   History & Research
332 E. Utica Street
Buffalo NY

MAILING ADDRESS:
P.O. Box 1663
Buffalo NY 14216

(716) 883-4418

OPEN: M, Th 12-8, Tu, F 9:30-5:30, W
   1-5:30; closed weekends and holidays
COPYING FACILITIES: yes
MATERIALS SOLICITED: Manuscript collections pertaining to the life and history of Afro-Americans in Buffalo and the Niagara Frontier region. The Center microfilms such collections for housing in the repository.

HOLDINGS:
   Total volume: 50 reels of microfilm
   Inclusive dates: 1860's - 1970's
   Description: Microfilms of records and papers pertaining to the black community in Buffalo. Included are materials pertaining to the Colored Musicians of Buffalo, 1917-61; the Buffalo Cooperative Economic Society, 1929-60; the Bethel A. M. E. Church, 1930's-1970's; B.U.I.L.D., a federation of 143 black community organizations; and Carolyn B. McClester Thomas, a local social worker, community activist, and church worker.

NY134-90
Buffalo and Erie County Public
   Library
Rare Book Room
Lafayette Square
Buffalo NY 14203

(716) 856-7525

OPEN: by appointment only
COPYING FACILITIES: yes
MATERIALS SOLICITED: Manuscripts by local authors and musicians. Will also accept letters and autographs by famous persons and some materials relating to local history.

HOLDINGS:
   Total volume: 2,000 items; additional materials
   Inclusive dates: 1592 -
   Description: The collection contains some 2,000 letters and literary manuscripts, representing many of the most eminent authors of 19th century America and Great Britain. Among the more significant manuscripts are Mark Twain's *Huckleberry Finn,* Ralph Waldo Emerson's *Representative Men,* and Elbert Hubbard's *A Message to Garcia.* The modern local authors collection includes

manuscripts by Taylor Caldwell, Julius W. Pratt, Sloan Wilson, and many others. There are also local history materials, including some church and organization records and a large quantity of genealogical materials.

SEE: Hamer.

SEE: Spalek; Martin; Robbins.

SEE ALSO: Andrea Hinding and Rosemary Richardson, comps., *Archival and Manuscript Resources for the Study of Women's History: A Beginning* (Univ. of Minnesota Libraries, Social Welfare History Archives Center, 1972); Walter Schatz, ed., *Directory of Afro-American Resources* (Bowker, 1970); Ann Novotny, *Picture Sources 3* (Special Libraries Assn., 1975).

NY134-120
Canisius College
Archives
Buffalo NY 14208

(716) 883-7000, Ext. 433

OPEN: M-F 1-5; closed weekends and holidays
COPYING FACILITIES: yes
MATERIALS SOLICITED: Materials relating to the history of Canisius College. Will also accept materials relating to history of Buffalo, the Roman Catholic Diocese of Buffalo, and the Society of Jesus.

HOLDINGS:
   Total volume: 260 l.f.
   Inclusive dates: 1848 -
   Description: Materials relating to the history of Canisius College, including diaries, financial records, bulletins describing courses, award presentations, news releases, and materials concerning alumni careers.

NY134-170
D'Youville College
Archives
320 Porter Avenue
Buffalo NY 14201

(716) 881-6708

OPEN: M-Th 8-10, F 8-5, Sa 1-5, Su
   1-10; closed holidays
COPYING FACILITIES: yes
MATERIALS SOLICITED: Materials pertaining to the history of D'Youville College, its former and current faculty, and its alumni.

HOLDINGS:
   Total volume: 490 c.f.; 8 file drawers; one blueprint case
   Inclusive dates: 1874 -
   Description: Materials relating to the history of D'Youville College, including college and faculty publications and manuscripts of publications; photo and clipping files; data on former faculty, trustees, honorary degree recipients, and alumni; tapes of campus lectures; blueprints of college buildings; and other materials.

SEE: Hamer; NUCMC, 1968.

NY134-510
E. J. Meyer Memorial Hospital
Central Photo Lab
462 Grider Street
Buffalo NY 14215

(716) 898-3000

OPEN: M-F 9-4; closed weekends and holidays
ACCESS: permission from Assistant Medical Director
COPYING FACILITIES: no
MATERIALS SOLICITED: Photographs relating to medicine.

HOLDINGS:
   Total volume: 70,000 items
   Inclusive dates: 1950 -
   Description: Medical photographs of various subjects.

NY134-660
Protestant Episcopal Diocese of
   Western New York
1114 Delaware Avenue
Buffalo NY 14209

(716) 881-0660

OPEN: M-F 9-5; closed weekends and holidays
COPYING FACILITIES: yes
MATERIALS SOLICITED: Records of the Diocese, records of defunct churches in the Diocese, and bishops' papers.

HOLDINGS:
   Total volume: 253 c.f.
   Inclusive dates: 1833 - 1977
   Description: Archives of the Diocese, records of defunct churches in the Diocese, and diaries and other personal papers of bishops.

NY134-710
State University of New York
College at Buffalo
Burchfield Center, Western New York
   Forum for American Art
1300 Elmwood Avenue
Buffalo NY 14222

(716) 878-6011

OPEN: M-Sa 10-5, Su 1-5; closed holidays
ACCESS: advance arrangements suggested
COPYING FACILITIES: yes
MATERIALS SOLICITED: Items pertaining to Charles Burchfield and to outstanding western New York State artists, including architects, sculptors, photographers, and craftspeople. Will also accept materials relating to art organizations, movements, critics, collectors, dealers, and schools, both contemporary and historical, in the eight western New York counties.

HOLDINGS:
   Total volume: 560 items
   Inclusive dates: 1903 -
   Description: A collection of items relating chiefly to American artist Charles Burchfield but also containing items relating to other artists from western New York State. Burchfield materials include his writings, notebooks, letters, and slides of him and his studio. Notebooks of art-

ist and teacher George William Eggers also are represented.

Other materials include records of various local art organizations, such as the Patteran Society and the Buffalo Society of Artists.

NY134-730
State University of New York
College at Buffalo
E. H. Butler Library
Archives/Special Collections
1300 Elmwood Avenue
Buffalo NY 14222

(716) 878-6304

OPEN: M-F 8:30-4; weekends and holidays by appointment only
COPYING FACILITIES: yes
MATERIALS SOLICITED: Polish manuscripts and archives of the State University of New York College at Buffalo.

HOLDINGS:
> *Total volume:* 1,292 l.f.
> *Inclusive dates:* 1640 -
> *Description:* Archives of the State University of New York College at Buffalo; illustrations and book manuscripts by author Lois Lenski; and correspondence, photographs, and other material relating to physician Francis E. Fronczak.

SEE: NUCMC, 1977.

SEE: Hinding.

SEE ALSO: guides to the Lenski and Fronczak collections available at the institution.

CALEDONIA

NY139-80
Big Springs Historical Society
Main Street
Caledonia NY

MAILING ADDRESS:
1067 Main Street
Mumford NY 14511

(716) 538-4473

OPEN: F 1-4 May-July and Sept.-Nov., Su 2-5 Dec.-Apr.; closed holidays
COPYING FACILITIES: no

HOLDINGS:
> *Total volume:* 59 vols.; 6 c.f.
> *Inclusive dates:* 1840's -
> *Description:* Scrapbooks of local events, Caledonia trout ponds, and obituaries of the Caledonia area. Also included are photographs of people, places, and events of Caledonia and vicinity.

SEE: Livingston County Guide.

NY139-120
Caledonia Library Association
3108 Main Street
Caledonia NY 14423

(716) 538-4512

OPEN: M 2-9, Tu 10-5, Th-Sa 2-5; closed Sundays and Wednesdays
COPYING FACILITIES: no

HOLDINGS:
> *Total volume:* 23 vols.; 4.5 c.f.
> *Inclusive dates:* 1860 -
> *Description:* Genealogical materials on families of the Caledonia area and scrapbooks and clippings on local people, places, and events.

SEE: Hamer.

SEE: Davis; Livingston County Guide.

CANANDAIGUA

NY147-280
Granger Homestead Society
295 North Main Street
Canandaigua NY 14424

(716) 394-1472

OPEN: M-F 9-5; closed weekends and holidays
USER FEES: one dollar for adults
COPYING FACILITIES: no

HOLDINGS:
> *Total volume:* 3.5 c.f.
> *Inclusive dates:* 1820 -
> *Description:* Photographs of the Granger Homestead, related historical data, and an unpublished biography of Gideon Granger.

NY147-595
Ontario County Historian's Office
120 North Main Street
Canandaigua NY 14424

(716) 394-7070

OPEN: Tu, Th 3-5 by appointment; closed holidays
COPYING FACILITIES: no

HOLDINGS:
> *Total volume:* 1 c.f.
> *Inclusive dates:* 1974 -
> *Description:* Cemetery transcriptions of Ontario County, NY.

NY147-600
Ontario County Historical Society
55 North Main Street
Canandaigua NY 14424

(716) 394-4975

OPEN: Tu-Sa 1-5; closed Sundays, Mondays, and holidays
COPYING FACILITIES: no
MATERIALS SOLICITED: Ontario County history.

HOLDINGS:
> *Total volume:* 25,000 items
> *Inclusive dates:* 1780 -
> *Description:* Manuscripts, archives, maps, and photographs, chiefly relating to Ontario County and western New York. Major subject focuses include land transactions, business, the Civil War, community groups (especially in Canandaigua), and local historians.

SEE: Hamer; NUCMC, 1959-61.

SEE: Robbins.

NY147-720
Sonnenberg Gardens
151 Charlotte Street
Canandaigua NY 14424

(716) 394-4922

OPEN: by appointment only
USER FEES: $4 for adults
COPYING FACILITIES: no

HOLDINGS:
> *Total volume:* 1.5 c.f.
> *Inclusive dates:* 1885 -
> *Description:* Photographs of Sonnenberg Gardens.

NY147-880
Wood Library
134 North Main Street
Canandaigua NY 14424

(716) 394-1381

OPEN: M-F 10-9, Sa 1-5; closed Sundays and holidays
COPYING FACILITIES: yes

HOLDINGS:
> *Total volume:* 2 c.f.
> *Inclusive dates:* 1900 -
> *Description:* Photographs of Canandaigua and Sonnenberg Gardens, genealogical data, and typescript materials on local history.

CANASERAGA

NY148-200
Essential Club Free Library
Canaseraga NY 14822

(607) 545-6443

OPEN: M 2-5, W 2-7:30, Sa 10-1; closed other days and holidays
COPYING FACILITIES: no
MATERIALS SOLICITED: History of Canaseraga village and the towns of Burns and Ossian, NY.

HOLDINGS:
> *Total volume:* 12 c.f.
> *Inclusive dates:* 1811 -
> *Description:* Genealogical materials, cemetery transcriptions, photographs, scrapbooks, lists of veterans, school records, clippings, tape recordings, and other mateials on the history of Canaseraga and vicinity.

SEE: Allegany County Guide.

CANDOR

NY148A-12
Candor Free Library
Main and Bank Streets
Candor NY 13743

(607) 659-7258

OPEN: M, W 2-5, Tu, F 2-8, Th 10-5, Sa 10-4; closed Sundays and holidays
COPYING FACILITIES: yes
MATERIALS SOLICITED: Candor history.

HOLDINGS:
> *Total volume:* 2.5 c.f.; 57 vols.; 41 items
> *Inclusive dates:* 1808 -
> *Description:* Scrapbooks, photographs, and business, church, school, and town records of Candor, primarily for the 19th and early 20th centuries.

SEE: Tioga County Guide.

CANISTEO

NY148B-88

Wimodaughsian Free Library
Canisteo NY 14823

(607) 698-4445

OPEN: M, F 1:30-5:30, Th 7-9, Sa 10-5; closed other days and holidays
COPYING FACILITIES: no
HOLDINGS:
> *Total volume:* 4.5 c.f.
> *Inclusive dates:* 1818 -
> *Description:* Library records, records of the Woman's Christian Temperance Union, photographs of Canisteo, and family papers.

SEE: Steuben County Guide.

CANTON

NY150-700

St. Lawrence County Historical Association
3 East Main Street
Canton NY

MAILING ADDRESS:
P.O. Box 8
Canton NY 13617

(315) 386-8118, 8133

OPEN: M-Sa 1-5; closed Sundays and holidays
COPYING FACILITIES: yes
MATERIALS SOLICITED: Photographs, records of organizations, diaries, and other documents pertaining to the history of New York State's north country, especially St. Lawrence County. Will also accept materials relating to prominent national and state figures native to St. Lawrence County.

HOLDINGS:
> *Total volume:* 600 items, 3,000 vols.
> *Inclusive dates:* 1749 - 1847
> *Description:* Correspondence and other personal papers of Silas Wright, U.S. Senator and New York Governor.
>   Materials relating to northern New York, especially St. Lawrence County, the St. Lawrence River, the Adirondack Mountains and the Mohawk Indians. Collections include diaries (1820-1925), merchant account books (1809-1900), member and minute books of early churches and organizations, county government records, Civil War correspondence and records, genealogical records, photographs, and tape recordings of reminiscences.

NY150-740

St. Lawrence University
Archives
Herring Cole
Canton NY 13617

(315) 379-5476

OPEN: M-F 9-5; closed weekends and holidays
COPYING FACILITIES: yes
MATERIALS SOLICITED: Material relating to St. Lawrence University, the area that it serves culturally, and the northern counties of New York State. Will also accept materials relating to education and 19th century farm, village, and family life.

HOLDINGS:
> *Total volume:* 150 l.f.
> *Inclusive dates:* 19th century -
> *Description:* Manuscripts, documents, and other materials illustrating the history of the northern New York area, with special relevance to St. Lawrence University and the persons and ideas associated with its history (1856-).

SEE: Hamer (as St. Lawrence University Museum); NUCMC, 1962, 71.

SEE: Hinding; Robbins.

NY150-760

State University of New York, Agricultural and Technical College
Southworth Library
Merritt-Wright Room
Canton NY 13617

(315) 386-7228

OPEN: Su 1-10, M-Th 8-11, F 8-5, Sa 12-5; closed holidays and weekends when College not in session
COPYING FACILITIES: yes
MATERIALS SOLICITED: Historical materials relating to the College.

HOLDINGS:
> *Total volume:* 450 l.f.
> *Inclusive dates:* 1911 -
> *Description:* Historical materials relating to the College, oral history recordings of its past employees and students, and agricultural materials relating to New York.

CASTILE

NY156-120

Castile Historical Society
17 East Park Road
Castile NY

MAILING ADDRESS:
Box 256
Castile NY 14427

(716) 493-2807, 5370

OPEN: Tu, Th 9-3 and by appointment
COPYING FACILITIES: no

HOLDINGS:
> *Total volume:* 90 c.f.
> *Inclusive dates:* 1790 - 1970
> *Description:* Manuscript materials concerning the Castile area, including materials on a local sanitarium, 1850-1950, and a diary collection, 1850-1930.

SEE: Wyoming County Guide.

NY156-140

Cordelia A. Greene Library
11 South Main
Castile NY

MAILING ADDRESS:
P.O. Box 208
Castile NY 14427

(716) 493-5466

OPEN: Tu 10-5:30, Th-Sa 3-9; closed Su, M, W and holidays
COPYING FACILITIES: no

HOLDINGS:
> *Total volume:* 7 vols.; 0.5 c.f.
> *Inclusive dates:* 1870 - 1960
> *Description:* Personal papers of Dr. Cordelia A. Greene and records of the library.

SEE: Wyoming County Guide.

NY156-480

Letchworth State Park Museum
Castile NY 14427

(716) 493-2611

OPEN: May-Oct., Tu-F, 11-5, Sa, Su, 10-6; closed other times
ACCESS: advance arrangements with Park Superintendent required
COPYING FACILITIES: no

HOLDINGS:
> *Total volume:* 75 c.f.
> *Inclusive dates:* 19th century - 1920
> *Description:* Materials concerning Indians of Wyoming County, NY, before 1900.

SEE: Wyoming County Guide.

CATLIN

NY159-120

Catlin Historical Society
Catlin Town Hall
Chamber Road
Catlin NY

MAILING ADDRESS:
c/o President
4373 Murphy Hill Road
Catlin NY 14845

no telephone

OPEN: by appointment only
COPYING FACILITIES: no
MATERIALS SOLICITED: Catlin history. Will also accept historical materials from Chemung and Steuben counties that concern Catlin.

HOLDINGS:
Total volume: 5 c.f.; 10 vols.
Inclusive dates: 1830 -
Description: Catlin history materials, including burial records, 1839-1930, and scrapbooks of clippings, photographs, and historical notes.

SEE: Chemung County Guide.

CATO

NY160-120
Cato Free Library
Cato NY 13033

(315) 626-2101

OPEN: M, W, Sa 1-5; closed other days and holidays
COPYING FACILITIES: no

HOLDINGS:
Total volume: 16 vols.; 75 items
Inclusive dates: mid-1800's - 1974
Description: Photographs of Cato and scrapbooks concerning World War II personnel from Cato, the clean-up and beautification of Cato, and national baseball.

SEE: Cayuga County Guide.

CATTARAUGUS

NY163-120
Cattaraugus Area Historical Society
Cattaraugus Historical Center
23 Main Street
Cattaraugus NY 14719

(716) 257-9012

OPEN: Su 2-5 Memorial-Labor Day, other times by appointment
COPYING FACILITIES: no
MATERIALS SOLICITED: Materials relating to the Cattaraugus area, including account books, business and financial records, diaries, journals, records of businesses and community groups, photographs, scrapbooks, and aerial photographs.

HOLDINGS:
Total volume: not specified
Inclusive dates: 1800 -
Description: Materials relating to the Cattaraugus area.

CAZENOVIA

NY164-570
New York State Parks and Recreation
Lorenzo State Historic Site
Cazenovia NY 13035

(315) 655-3200

OPEN: Tu-F 9-4:30, Sa 10-4:30; closed Su, M, holidays, Sa during winter
ACCESS: appointment required
MATERIALS SOLICITED: Records relating to the Lincklean-Ledyard family, Cazenovia, the Holland Land Company, and the Third Great Western Turnpike.

HOLDINGS:
Total volume: 80 l.f.
Inclusive dates: 1759 - 1967
Description: Materials relating to John Lincklean, agent of the Holland Land Company, founder of Cazenovia, and President of the Third Great Western Turnpike; Samuel Forman, his assistant; the mercantile dealing of the Forman family, 1759-1823; local political, militia, business, and social matters; and the papers of John Lincklean's successors descended from his brother-in-law, Jonathan D. Ledyard, including Charles S. Fairchild, Secretary of the Treasury under President Grover Cleveland.

CEDARHURST

NY166-80
The New York Bartok Archive
2 Tulip Street
Cedarhurst NY

MAILING ADDRESS:
P.O. Box 717
Lynbrook NY 11563

no telephone

OPEN: Sa 10-4; closed other days
ACCESS: qualified scholars with specific research problems or projects related to the life and music of Bela Bartok
COPYING FACILITIES: no
MATERIALS SOLICITED: Materials related to the life and works of Bela Bartok. Will also accept materials related to Bartok's family, friends, colleagues, teachers, and other associates.

HOLDINGS:
Total volume: 300 l.f.
Inclusive dates: 1881 -
Description: A collection focusing on the life and work of composer Bela Bartok. Included are manuscripts of Bartok compositions and of his folk music collections (Hungarian, Rumanian, Slovak, Yugoslav, Arab, Turkish, and Ruthenian), correspondence, essays, iconographic sources, tapes, films, microfilms, and other materials.

GUIDES: Victor Bator, *The Bela Bartok Archives: History and Catalogue* (Boosey & Hawkes, 1963).

SEE: NUCMC, 1966.

CENTER MORICHES

NY169-120
Center Moriches Free Public Library
529 Main Street
Center Moriches NY 11934

(516) 878-0940

OPEN: M 2-5:30, T, Th 2-9, W 10-9, F 10-5:30, Sa 10-5; closed Sundays and holidays
COPYING FACILITIES: yes
MATERIALS SOLICITED: Materials pertinent to the Moriches area, including oral histories and manuscripts of local historians and authors.

HOLDINGS:
Total volume: 104 items
Inclusive dates: 1964 -
Description: Two manuscripts of local author James Poling, two taped interviews with an area resident, and slides of local buildings and landmarks.

CHAPPAQUA

NY172-120
New Castle Historical Society
185 S. Greeley Avenue
Chappaqua NY

MAILING ADDRESS:
P.O. Box 55
Chappaqua NY 10514

(914) 238-4666

OPEN: W 1-4 and by appointment
COPYING FACILITIES: yes

HOLDINGS:
Total volume: not specified
Inclusive dates: 1791 -
Description: Fifty letters by Horace Greeley to family and friends; materials relating to Quakers, especially in the Chappaqua area, including genealogical data, information on the Chappaqua Mountain Institute, and photographs; and oral history tapes of local residents. There are also facsimile copies of the town minutes of New Castle, NY (1791-1850).

CHATHAM

NY178-120
Chatham Public Library
Woodbridge Avenue
Chatham NY 12037

(518) 392-3666

OPEN: M-F 11:30-4:30, Sa 9-noon; closed Sundays and holidays
ACCESS: advance arrangements recommended
COPYING FACILITIES: yes
MATERIALS SOLICITED: Originals and photocopies of materials relating to the Chatham area, including diaries, journals, business records, school district records, club and organization records, church records, and cemetery records. Will also accept photographs and materials dealing with the library.

HOLDINGS:
Total volume: 2 file drawers
Inclusive dates: 1797 - 1920's
Description: Original and photocopies of documents relating to Chatham, Columbia County, and western Massachusetts. Included are school district minutes; records of organizations such as the Tau Alpha Kappa Society, the Chatham Village Literary Society, the Ladies Temperance Society, the Telephone Co-operative, the Sunday School Teachers Union, and the Austerlitz Cemetery Association; a record book from the Chatham Turnpike; church records; business cash books; and cemetery records.

SEE: Hamer.

CHAUTAUQUA

NY179-120
Chautauqua Institution
Smith Memorial Library
Chautauqua Collection
Chautauqua NY

MAILING ADDRESS:
Box 1093
Chautauqua NY 14722

(716) 357-6296

OPEN: M, W, F 10-5, Sa 10-1; closed
other days and holidays
ACCESS: advance arrangements advised;
some materials restricted
COPYING FACILITIES: yes
MATERIALS SOLICITED: Materials relating
to the Chautauqua Institution and its
administration and board of trustees.

HOLDINGS:
Total volume: not specified
Inclusive dates: 1874 -
Description: Historical materials relating to the founding of the Chautauqua
Institutions, including manuscripts, minutes of board of trustees meetings, and
publications. There is also a photograph
and slide collection.

CHERRY VALLEY

NY187-120
Cherry Valley Historical Society
49 Main Street
Cherry Valley NY 13320

(607) 264-3318, 3303

OPEN: daily 10-5; closed Oct.
15-Memorial Day
COPYING FACILITIES: no
MATERIALS SOLICITED: Materials relating
to Cherry Valley and the surrounding
areas.

HOLDINGS:
Total volume: 2.6 c.f.; 76 vols.; 186
items
Inclusive dates: 1777 -
Description: Account books,
1797-1898; scrapbooks, late 1700's- ;
minute books of local organizations,
1815-1904; photographs, mid-
1800's-mid-1900's; the papers of Joseph
Phelon, 1829-79, newspaper editor J. N.
Van Dyke, 1950's-60's, playwright Abraham B. Cox, late 1800's-early 1900's, and
minister Henry Ulyate Swinnerton, mid-
1800's-mid-1900's; military records,
1777-1915; church and religious records,
1799-1900; town records, 1800-89; and
other materials.

CLAYTON

NY194-760
Thousand Islands Shipyard Museum
750 Mary Street
Clayton NY 13624

(315) 686-4104

OPEN: June - Sept., daily 9-8, Oct. -
May, M-F 9-5; closed weekends and
holidays
ACCESS: advance arrangements required
COPYING FACILITIES: no
MATERIALS SOLICITED: Thousand Islands
materials. Will also accept materials
concerning Jefferson County and New
York State.

HOLDINGS:
Total volume: 8 file drawers; 500
pages; 1,500 photographs
Inclusive dates: early 1800's -
Description: Ledgers and diaries, business records, and photographs concerning
the history of the Thousand Islands area.

CLIFTON SPRINGS

NY195-120
Clifton Springs Library
Clifton Springs NY 14432

(315) 462-7371

OPEN: M 2:30-5:30, Tu 2:30-9, W
10-5:30, Th 10-9, F 2:30-5:30 June
15-Sept. 15, Sa 9-1 Sept. 16-June 14;
closed Sundays and holidays
COPYING FACILITIES: no

HOLDINGS:
Total volume: 1.5 c.f.
Inclusive dates: 1867 -
Description: Photographs of Clifton
Springs and records of the Library.

CLINTON

NY197-120
Clinton Historical Society
Kirkland Town Library
College Street
Clinton NY

MAILING ADDRESS:
P.O. Box 42
Clinton NY 13323

no telephone

OPEN: by appointment only
COPYING FACILITIES: no
MATERIALS SOLICITED: Will accept material of historic interest to the village
of Clinton.

HOLDINGS:
Total volume: not specified
Inclusive dates: 1790 -
Description: Photographs, motion pictures of local high school activities,
records of street numbers of houses and
their dates of construction, ledgers of a
local business (Split Rock Spring,
1911-29), and genealogical records.

NY197-310
Hamilton College
The Burke Library
Clinton NY 13323

(315) 859-4475

OPEN: M-F 8:30-midnight, Sa 8:30-5, Su
12-12; summer M-F 8:30-4:30; closed
holidays
COPYING FACILITIES: yes
MATERIALS SOLICITED: Material relating
to Ezra Pound and Alexander Woollcott. Will also accept material relating
to the history of Hamilton and
Kirkland Colleges, papers of alumni
and faculty, and central New York history items.

HOLDINGS:
Total volume: 150 l.f.
Inclusive dates: 1750 - 1950
Description: Manuscripts relating to
the history of Hamilton College, and letters and papers of alumni. In addition,
papers of Samuel Kirkland (founder of
Hamilton College), as well as special collections relating to distinguished alumni
and faculty and the history of central
New York.

SEE: Hamer; NUCMC, 1966, 75, 77, 79.
SEE: Robbins.

CLYDE

NY198-280
Galen Free Library
31 North Park Street
Clyde NY 14433

(315) 923-7767

OPEN: M-Sa 2-9; closed Sundays
COPYING FACILITIES: no

HOLDINGS:
Total volume: not specified
Inclusive dates: not specified
Description: Newspaper clippings and
photographs relating to the town of Galen
and Wayne County, NY.

SEE: Wayne County Guide.

COBLESKILL

NY200-120
Cobleskill Public Library
Box 219
Union Street
Cobleskill NY 12043

(518) 234-7897

OPEN: Tu, F 11-8, W, Th 2-6, Sa 9-1;
closed Su, M and holidays
COPYING FACILITIES: yes
MATERIALS SOLICITED: Town of
Cobleskill genealogical studies.

HOLDINGS:
Total volume: 50 l.f.
Inclusive dates: 1800 -
Description: Materials relating to the
history of the town of Cobleskill.

SEE: Hamer

NY200-720
State University of New York at
   Cobleskill
Agriculture and Technical College
Learning Resources Center
Van Wagenen, Jr., Hall
Cobleskill NY 12043

(518) 234-5841

OPEN: M-Th 9:30-3:30, 6-9:30, F
   9:30-3:30, Sa 1-4:30, Su 2-9:30; during
   summers and intersession, M-F 9-4
   only; closed holidays
ACCESS: appointment requested
COPYING FACILITIES: yes
MATERIALS SOLICITED: Records dealing
   with the College, its faculty, and its
   alumni. Will also accept materials relating to agriculture, caves, and children's
   literature.

HOLDINGS:
   Total volume: 45 l.f.
   Inclusive dates: 1840 -
   Description: Manuscripts relating chiefly to Schoharie County, including biographies of early settlers, photographs,
   maps, histories, and folklore materials.
   Also included are historical materials relating to caves and agriculture, and
   records of the College, its faculty, and its
   alumni.

COHOCTON

NY201-120
Cohocton Historical Society
6 Maple Avenue
Cohocton NY

MAILING ADDRESS:
P.O. Box 177
Cohocton NY 14826

(716) 384-5572, 5188

OPEN: by appointment only
COPYING FACILITIES: no

HOLDINGS:
   Total volume: 3 c.f.
   Inclusive dates: 1839 -
   Description: Account books, photo-
   graphs, and genealogical data on local
   families.

SEE: Steuben County Guide.

COLD SPRING HARBOR

NY205-120
Cold Spring Harbor Laboratory
Main Library
Cold Spring Harbor NY

MAILING ADDRESS:
Box 100
Cold Spring Harbor NY 11721

(516) 367-8350, 8351

OPEN: M-F 9-5; closed weekends and
   holidays
ACCESS: appointment required
COPYING FACILITIES: yes
MATERIALS SOLICITED: Material relating
   to the history of Cold Spring Harbor
   Laboratory, including genetics, eugen-

ics, biochemistry, and cancer research.
Will also accept materials in Long Island history and in the history of science as it relates to work done at the
Laboratory.

HOLDINGS:
   Total volume: 85 l.f.
   Inclusive dates: 1890 -
   Description: A collection of manu-
   scripts, noncurrent records of the Cold
   Spring Harbor Laboratory, and photo-
   graphs related to the history of Cold
   Spring Harbor Laboratory, its scientific
   work and personnel.

NY205-880
Whaling Museum Society, Inc.
Main Street
Cold Spring Harbor NY

MAILING ADDRESS:
P.O. Box 25
Cold Spring Harbor NY 11724

(516) 692-6499

OPEN: Tu-Su 11-5; closed Mondays and
   holidays
ACCESS: prior application by written
   letter must be approved by Museum's
   curator
COPYING FACILITIES: no
MATERIALS SOLICITED: Material relating
   to whaling, the natural history of
   whales, and Cold Spring Harbor.

HOLDINGS:
   Total volume: 26 vols.; 2,800 items
   Inclusive dates: 1836 - 1862
   Description: A collection focusing on
   whaling, especially the Cold Spring Whaling Company. Included are logbooks, account books, financial records, diaries,
   photographs, and letters providing genealogical information on local families.

CONSTABLEVILLE

NY208-120
Constable Hall Association
John Street
Constableville NY 13325

(516) 367-3418

OPEN: Tu-Sa 10-5, Su 1-5; closed
   Mondays, except holidays, and Nov. -
   April
USER FEES: $1.50
COPYING FACILITIES: no
MATERIALS SOLICITED: Northern New
   York history related to the William
   Constable family.

HOLDINGS:
   Total volume: not specified
   Inclusive dates: 1790 - 1945
   Description: A collection of correspondence and other papers relating to the
   Constable family, descendants of William
   C. Constable, late 18th and early 19th
   century New York land magnate. Included are letters of Gouverneur Morris and
   materials relating to business and commerce in New York and Europe.

SEE: Hamer.

COOPERSTOWN

NY211-540
National Baseball Hall of Fame and
   Museum
National Baseball Library
Cooper Park
Cooperstown NY 13326

(607) 547-9988

OPEN: M-F 9-5; closed weekends
ACCESS: appointment required
COPYING FACILITIES: yes
MATERIALS SOLICITED: Materials dealing
   with the past and present history of
   baseball.

HOLDINGS:
   Total volume: 400 c.f.; 550 vols.; 450
   items
   Inclusive dates: 1850 -
   Description: Audiotapes, films, clippings, photographs, scrapbooks, notebooks, daily record sheets, rosters,
   scorebooks, scorecards, and other records
   of America's national pastime. Also included are the papers of baseball officials,
   including August Herrman and Abraham
   G. Mills.

SEE: Hamer; NUCMC, 1966.

SEE ALSO: Ann Novotny, ed., *Picture
   Sources 3* (Special Libraries Assn.,
   1975).

NY211-580
New York State Historical Association
Special Collections
Cooperstown NY 13326

(607) 547-2509

OPEN: M-F 9-5; closed weekends and
   holidays
COPYING FACILITIES: yes
MATERIALS SOLICITED: Materials relating
   to the development of upstate New
   York.

HOLDINGS:
   Total volume: 500,000 items; 4,000
   vols.
   Inclusive dates: 1734 - 1960
   Description: Materials relating to upstate New York, with emphasis on agriculture and economics. Included are account books, business records, diaries,
   and collections of correspondence.

SEE: Hamer.

SEE: Allard, Crawley, and Edmison;
   Leventhal and Mooney - I; Robbins.

SEE ALSO: Walter Schatz, ed., *Directory of
   Afro-American Resources* (Bowker,
   1970); Ann Novotny, ed., *Picture
   Sources 3* (Special Libraries Assn.,
   1975).

Richard C. Davis, *North American Forest
   History: A Guide to Archives and Manu-
   scripts in the United States and Canada*
   (Clio Books, 1977).

CORNING

NY214-100

Corning Community College
Arthur A. Houghton, Jr., Library
Corning NY 14830

(607) 962-9251

OPEN: M-Th 8-5, F 8-4; closed weekends and holidays
COPYING FACILITIES: yes

HOLDINGS:
Total volume: 40 c.f.
Inclusive dates: 1300 -
Description: Records of the College, letters, leaves of medieval manuscripts, and materials dealing with local history.

SEE: Steuben County Guide; Hinding.

NY214-120

Corning Glass Works
The Archives
Corning NY

MAILING ADDRESS:
MP-CH-2
Corning NY 14830

(607) 974-7670, 4257

OPEN: M-F 8:15-5; closed weekends and holidays
ACCESS: appointment required
COPYING FACILITIES: yes
MATERIALS SOLICITED: Records dealing with Corning Glass Works plants, personnel, plant towns, products, manufacturing processes, product research, and machinery. Will also accept records relating to other glass companies, company employees, and plant towns.

HOLDINGS:
Total volume: 7,150 l.f.
Inclusive dates: 1851 -
Description: Materials relating to the history of Corning Glass Works, including its employees, production procedures, specialty glass manufacturing in 24 countries, and life in 78 plant towns. Included are 7,000 l.f. of personnel, financial, purchasing, legal, product development, research, stockholder, subsidiary, and executive records. There are also 150 l.f. of photographs, including 150,000 computer-indexed negatives, prints, and slides; 5,000 historic blueprints, tracings, and sketches of company sites, products, tools, and machines; and motion picture films.

SEE: Hinding.

NY214-140

Corning Museum of Glass
Corning Glass Center
Corning NY 14830

(607) 974-4257

OPEN: M-F 8-5; closed weekends and holidays
COPYING FACILITIES: yes
MATERIALS SOLICITED: History and art of glass.

HOLDINGS:
Total volume: 100 c.f.
Inclusive dates: 1150 -
Description: The papers and/or records of Richard M. Atwater, as well as Pairpoint Manufacturing Co., Thomas G. Hawkes & Co. and other firms and individuals involved in the production of glass. Collections also include medieval manuscripts relating to glass, and videotapes and recordings of lectures/talks concerning glass. There are also vertical files containing documents, letters, clippings, photographs, and other materials dealing with the history and technology of glass uses in the United States, Europe, the Middle East, and other parts of the world.

SEE: Hamer.

SEE: Steuben County Guide.

NY214-150

Corning Public Library
Civic Center Plaza
Corning NY 14830

(607) 936-3713

OPEN: Su 2-5, M-F 9:30-9, Sa 9:30-5; closed weekends in summer
COPYING FACILITIES: yes
MATERIALS SOLICITED: History of Corning, Painted Post, and vicinity.

HOLDINGS:
Total volume: 7 c.f.
Inclusive dates: 1773 -
Description: Scrapbooks, maps, newspaper clippings, photographs, and other materials concerning local history.

SEE: Steuben County Guide.

NY214-160

Corning-Painted Post Historical Society
59 West Pulteney Street
Corning NY 14830

(607) 937-5281

OPEN: M-F 10-4; closed weekends and holidays
COPYING FACILITIES: no
MATERIALS SOLICITED: Materials dealing with the history of Corning, Painted Post and the vicinity.

HOLDINGS:
Total volume: 25 c.f.; 20,000 items
Inclusive dates: 1796 -
Description: Civil War materials, color slides of the Corning area, Historical Society records, photograph albums and scrapbooks of Margaret T. Drake, papers of Robert F. McNamara, material on the history and restoration of Benjamin Patterson Inn, 20,000 glass negatives by Frank L. Hewitt, account books, and other items of local interest.

SEE: Steuben County Guide.

CORTLAND

NY216-120

Cortland County Historical Society Library
25 Homer Avenue
Cortland NY 13045

(607) 756-6071

OPEN: Tu-F 1-5, Sa 1-4; closed Sundays, Mondays, Christmas, New Year's, and July 4
COPYING FACILITIES: yes
MATERIALS SOLICITED: History of Cortland County.

HOLDINGS:
Total volume: 622 c.f.
Inclusive dates: 1794 -
Description: Materials pertaining to the history of Cortland County; including business and organization records; personal papers; church; cemetery; genealogical and vital records; town and village records; photographs; a small collection of oral history recordings; manuscript maps; and architectural drawings.

SEE: Hamer; NUCMC, 1965, 69-70.

SEE: Cortland County Guide; Hinding.

NY216-130

Cortland Free Library
32 Church Street
Cortland NY 13045

(607) 753-1042

OPEN: M-Th 10-9, F, Sa 10-5:30; closed Sundays and holidays
COPYING FACILITIES: yes
MATERIALS SOLICITED: Cortland and Cortland County history.

HOLDINGS:
Total volume: 10 items
Inclusive dates: 1934 - 1970
Description: Typescript essays concerning the history of Cortland and Cortland County from 1800 to 1950.

SEE: Cortland County Guide.

NY216-720

State University of New York
College at Cortland
Memorial Library
Cortland NY 13045

(607) 753-2525

OPEN: M-Th 8:30-11, F 8:30-5; closed weekends and holidays
COPYING FACILITIES: yes
MATERIALS SOLICITED: Materials pertaining to the State University of New York, College at Cortland.
Total Volume: 147 l.f.; 3 file cabinets
Inclusive dates: mid-1800's -
Description: Library records; minutes of the Delphi fraternity; records of divisions of the College; faculty, alumni, and student records; other materials relating to the College; writings of mathematician David Eugene Smith; and other materials.

SEE: Cortland County Guide.

COXSACKIE

NY219-290
Greene County Historical Society
Vedder Memorial Library
Coxsackie NY

MAILING ADDRESS:
Rural Delivery
Coxsackie NY 12051

(518) 731-6822

OPEN: Open Tuesdays, May-September;
  appointment suggested if coming from
  afar
COPYING FACILITIES: no
MATERIALS SOLICITED: Material on
  Greene County, New York, the Cats-
  kills, and the mid-Hudson Valley. Will
  also accept other historical materials.

HOLDINGS:
  Total volume: not specified
  Inclusive dates: 17th century -
  Description: A collection of manuscript
  material relating to the Coxsackie area,
  Greene County, the Hudson River area
  around Greene County, and the Catskill
  Mountains. Included are court records,
  county archives, and approximately 700
  miscellaneous handwritten volumes.

SEE: Hamer; NUCMC, 1959-61, 78.

SEE: Hinding.

SEE ALSO: Ann Novotny, ed., *Picture
  Sources 3* (Special Libraries Assn.,
  1975).

CROTON-ON-HUDSON

NY222-110
Croton Free Library
Historical Reference Room
171 Cleveland Drive
Croton-on-Hudson NY

MAILING ADDRESS:
226 Mount Airy Road
Croton-on-Hudson NY 10520

(914) 271-8159

OPEN: Tu 10-12 or by appointment
ACCESS: advance arrangements preferred
COPYING FACILITIES: yes
MATERIALS SOLICITED: Materials relating
  to Croton-on-Hudson, the Hudson River, and Van Cortlandt Manor. Will also
  accept materials concerning Westchester County, the New York Central
  Railroad, and Croton Dam.

HOLDINGS:
  Total volume: 500 items
  Inclusive dates: 1758 - 1925
  Description: 400 photographs and
  some records of the building of Croton
  Dam, 1895-1907; 48 deeds of land in
  Van Cortlandt Manor, 1760-1902; letters;
  unpublished histories, and village government and organization minutes,
  1898-1925; local justice of the peace and
  recorder of deeds records; oral histories
  of area residents; a 1758 journal of a
  local weaver; and 8 photographs of Theodore Roosevelt, taken in 1898.

SEE ALSO: Typescript index to historical
  material, available for use at the institution.

CUBA

NY228-110
Cuba Circulating Library Association
39 East Main Street
Cuba NY 14727

(716) 968-1668

OPEN: Tu-F 2-9, Sa 10-5; closed
  Sundays, Mondays, and holidays
COPYING FACILITIES: no
MATERIALS SOLICITED: The history of
  Cuba and Allegany County, NY.

HOLDINGS:
  Total volume: 8.5 c.f.
  Inclusive dates: 1840 -
  Description: The Philip Church estate
  land sales book, photographs of Cuba and
  the vicinity, Civil War letters, school
  records, scrapbooks, clippings, miscellaneous documents, and telegrams dating
  from the turn of the century.

SEE: Allegany County Guide.

CUDDEBACKVILLE

NY229-560
Neversink Valley Area Museum
D&H Canal Park
Hoag Road
Cuddebackville NY 12729

MAILING ADDRESS:
Box 263
Cuddebackville NY 12729

(914) 754-8870

OPEN: W-Su 10-4; closed M-Tu,
  Thanksgiving, Christmas, New Year's
ACCESS: appointment required
COPYING FACILITIES: no
MATERIALS SOLICITED: Manuscripts, ac-
  count books, business records, letters,
  diaries, and journals relating to the
  Delaware and Hudson Canal and the
  Neversink Valley region. Will also ac-
  cept genealogical materials and regional
  family and business records.

HOLDINGS:
  Total volume: 25 items
  Inclusive dates: 1830 - 1898
  Description: Records relating to the
  Delaware and Hudson Canal; associated
  people, businesses, and developments;
  and the social history, people, and tech-
  nology of the Neversink Valley region.

DANSVILLE

NY234-165
Dansville Public Library
200 Main Street
Dansville NY 14437

(716) 335-6720

OPEN: M, W 10-9, Tu, F 1-9, Th 1-5, Sa
  1-4:30 except July-Aug.; closed Sundays
  and holidays

COPYING FACILITIES: no
HOLDINGS:
  Total volume: 4.7 c.f.; 5 vols.
  Inclusive dates: 1852 -
  Description: Records of Dansville Pub-
  lic Library, papers and correspondence of
  Charles McCormick Reeve, records of the
  Dansville Shakespeare Club, a notebook
  of various Dansville family pedigrees,
  and letters and papers relating to local
  history.

SEE: Livingston County Guide.

DAVENPORT

NY235-160
Davenport Historical Society
Town Clerk's Office
2nd Floor
Davenport Town Hall
Davenport NY

MAILING ADDRESS:
Davenport Center NY 13751

(607) 278-5600

OPEN: by appointment only
COPYING FACILITIES: yes
MATERIALS SOLICITED: Davenport and
  the vicinity.

HOLDINGS:
  Total volume: 40 items; 250 vols.; 57
  c.f.
  Inclusive dates: 1816 -
  Description: Records of the town of
  Davenport, 1816-1922, including justice
  dockets, assessment rolls, highway accounts, and other records. Also included
  are the records of the Davenport Methodist Church; a transcript of early church
  records from the mid-1800's; cemetery
  records, 1876- ; minutes of the Ladies
  Aid Society, 1917-34; a video tape of
  town history; photographs of town residents, mid-1800's-early 1900's; architectural slides of Davenport residences and
  businesses; and the Ferguson-Jayne family papers, 1826-1930.

DELHI

NY240-160
Delaware County Historical
  Association
Frisbee House
R.D. 2
Delhi NY 13753

(607) 746-3849

OPEN: M-F 8:30-4; closed weekends and
  holidays
ACCESS: appointment with Director
  required
COPYING FACILITIES: no
MATERIALS SOLICITED: Materials relating
  to Delaware County.

HOLDINGS:
  Total volume: 37 c.f.; 208 vols.; 9,200
  items
  Inclusive dates: 1779 -
  Description: The papers of writer John
  Vandercook, attorney Daniel Arbuckle,
  writer and attorney John D. Monroe,
  general store owner Matthew Griffin,

George H. Redmond, Clark K. Adams, the Thomas Gordon family, and the Sherwood family. Also held are records of local schools, the town of Delhi, churches in Delhi, local organizations, the county fair, the Ben Marvin Post 209 of the Grand Army of the Republic, the Delaware County Historical Association, the Delhi Tourist Club, the Monday Night Club, local woolen manufacturers, and the Delhi railroad station. Other collections include land records, military records, a Bicentennial collection, photographs, lantern slides, Robert Wyer's studio negative file, scrapbooks, newspaper clippings, genealogical materials, post cards, diaries, and other materials.

SEE: Delaware County Guide.

NY240-720
State University of New York
Agricultural and Technical College at Delhi
Library
Delhi NY 13753

(607) 746-4107

OPEN: Su 2-10, M-Th 8-10, F 8-5, Sa 9-5; closed holidays; M-F 8-4 during University vacations
ACCESS: appointment required
COPYING FACILITIES: yes
MATERIALS SOLICITED: Materials related to the University.

HOLDINGS:
Total volume: 3 c.f.; 1 item
Inclusive dates: 1856 -
Description: College archives, 1915- , including College catalogs, handbooks, newsletters, brochures, memorandums, weekly bulletins, commencement materials, open house materials, literary and other student publications, and other items documenting statutes, academic affairs, State University of New York faculty-senate, faculty meetings, and other University-related subjects. The holdings also include a navy register, 1856.

SEE: Delaware County Guide.

DEPOSIT

NY241-160
Deposit Free Library
165 Front Street
Deposit NY 13754

(607) 467-2577

OPEN: Tu, Th, F 1-9, Sa 10-5; closed other days and holidays
COPYING FACILITIES: no
MATERIALS SOLICITED: Materials relating to the town of Deposit and its surrounding areas.

HOLDINGS:
Total volume: 59 vols.; 591 items
Inclusive dates: 1799 - 1969
Description: Collections relating chiefly to Deposit and the surrounding area, including church, school, and business materials; literary club records; papers of prominent residents among whom are William Butler, Martial Hulce, and Clark H. Miror; and early 20th century photographs.

SEE: Broome County Guide.

DOLGEVILLE

NY245-720
Salisbury Historical Society
Dolgeville NY 13329

(315) 429-3330

OPEN: daily 9-6
COPYING FACILITIES: no
MATERIALS SOLICITED: Local history of Salisbury and Herkimer County, NY. Will also accept records relating to the Century School, Fairfield Academy, and Fairfield, NY.

HOLDINGS:
Total volume: 4-drawer file cabinet
Inclusive dates: 19th century -
Description: Cemetery records, photographs, and scrapbooks relating to Salisbury, NY.

DRYDEN

NY246-720
Southworth Library Association
24 West Main Street
Dryden NY

MAILING ADDRESS:
P.O. Box 45
Dryden NY 13053

(607) 844-4782

OPEN: M, Th 2-5, Tu, F 2-8, Sa 10-5; closed Sundays, Wednesdays, and holidays
COPYING FACILITIES: no

HOLDINGS:
Total volume: 0.2 c.f.; 200 items; 30 vols.
Inclusive dates: 1775 -
Description: Records of the Southworth Library Association, Dryden school district 26, 1910-35, the Dryden Fair, 1854-1917, and the town of Dryden, 1775-1954; papers collected by Emil Premru, 1818-1915; a map and blueprint collection; scrapbooks, 1845-1965; biographies; genealogies; and other materials relating to the history of Dryden.

SEE: Tompkins County Guide.

NY246-760
Tompkins Cortland Community College
Division of Instructional and Learning Resources
Dryden NY 13053

(607) 844-8211

OPEN: M-F 9-4; closed weekends and holidays
COPYING FACILITIES: yes
MATERIALS SOLICITED: Materials relating to the history and activities of the College.

HOLDINGS:
Total volume: 7 c.f.
Inclusive dates: 1968 -
Description: Materials concerning the College, including records, a chronological file, minutes of selected committee meetings, and College history.

SEE: Tompkins County Guide.

DUNDEE

NY247-160
Dundee Area Historical Society
Seneca Street
Dundee NY 14837

(607) 243-7047

OPEN: W, F 10:30-5; closed other days and holidays
COPYING FACILITIES: no
MATERIALS SOLICITED: History of Dundee and Yates County, NY.

HOLDINGS:
Total volume: 17 c.f.
Inclusive dates: 1804 -
Description: Account books, diaries, genealogical materials, letters from soldiers in the Civil War and World War II, and papers of James M. Letts, U.S. Consul to Haiti, 1865. Also included are photographs, school records, scrapbooks, photographs and other materials concerning Starkey Seminary, and other materials on the history of Dundee.

SEE: Yates County Guide.

NY247-880
Women's Study Club and Library
Dundee NY 14837

no telephone

OPEN: M-F 2-5:30; closed weekends and holidays
COPYING FACILITIES: no
MATERIALS SOLICITED: History of Dundee and Yates County.

HOLDINGS:
Total volume: 2.5 c.f.
Inclusive dates: 1832 -
Description: Scrapbooks, maps, reminiscences, photographs, and other documents of local interest.

SEE: Yates County Guide.

EAST AURORA

NY250-50
Aurora Historical Society and Aurora Town Historian
5 South Grove Street
East Aurora, NY 14052

(716) 652-3280

OPEN: Summer, W 1-4, Sa, Su 2-4; by appointment rest of year
COPYING FACILITIES: yes
MATERIALS SOLICITED: Iconography pertaining to the history of the town of Aurora.

HOLDINGS:
  Total volume: 1 file cabinet
  Inclusive dates: 1820 - 1976
  Description: Aurora town records, photographs, and genealogy files.

SEE: Hinding.

NY250-212
Elbert Hubbard Library-Museum
Village Hall
Main Street at Paine
East Aurora NY 14052

(716) 652-6000

OPEN: June - Oct., W, Sa, Su 2:30-4:30;
  by appointment other times
COPYING FACILITIES: yes

HOLDINGS:
  Total volume: 5 c.f.
  Inclusive dates: 1895 - 1938
  Description: Manuscripts, photographs, and cassette tapes concerning Elbert Hubbard and the Roycrofters.

SEE: Hinding; Robbins.

EAST BLOOMFIELD

NY251-80
Bloomfield Public Library
Main Street
East Bloomfield NY 14443

(716) 657-6264

OPEN: M, W, Th 2:30-8:30, Tu 10-noon,
  2:30-8:30, F 2:30-4:30, Sa 10-noon;
  closed Saturdays, July - Aug., and
  Sundays
COPYING FACILITIES: no

HOLDINGS:
  Total volume: 1 c.f.
  Inclusive dates: 1857 -
  Description: Local scrapbooks.

NY251-320
Historical Society of the Town of East
  Bloomfield
South Avenue
East Bloomfield NY 14443

(716) 657-7244

OPEN: by appointment only
COPYING FACILITIES: no

HOLDINGS:
  Total volume: 8 c.f.
  Inclusive dates: 1793 -
  Description: Highway surveys of the town of East Bloomfield, local account books, photographs, scrapbooks, school materials, Grange records, and diaries of Thayer Gauss and Stephen W. Clark.

EAST DURHAM

NY254-160
Durham Center Museum, Inc.
Route 145
East Durham NY 12423

(518) 239-8461

OPEN: Memorial Day - Labor Day, W,
  Th, Sa, Su 9-5; other times by
  appointment
USER FEES: 50 cents Museum admission
  and 50 cents per hour researcher fee
COPYING FACILITIES: yes

HOLDINGS:
  Total volume: 40 l.f.; 45 c.f.; 40 vols.;
  14 drawers; additional materials
  Inclusive dates: 1760 -
  Description: 19th century records of the Susquehanna Turnpike and the Catskill-Canajoharie Railroad; militia records; records of local schools and churches; extensive local genealogical materials; 160 ledgers of local businesses, farmers, and professionals; and 18th-century indentures and other papers of the Van Rensselaers, Schuylers, and other families.

SEE: Hinding.

EAST HAMPTON

NY257-190
East Hampton Free Library
Long Island Collection
159 Main Street
East Hampton NY 11937

(516) 324-0222

OPEN: Tu, 1-5, 7-9, W, Th, Sa 1-5;
  closed other days and holidays;
  extended hours in summer
COPYING FACILITIES: yes
MATERIALS SOLICITED: Materials concerning Long Island and Thomas Moran.

HOLDINGS:
  Total volume: not specified
  Inclusive dates: 17th century -
  Description: Letters, journals, whaling logbooks, account books, and genealogical material relating to Long Island, with emphasis on eastern Long Island. There are also records of several East Hampton community organizations and photographs and oral history tapes of the East Hampton area. The Thomas Moran biographical art collection contains correspondence, photographs, biographical materials, and other items relating to members of the Moran family and their artistic interests.

SEE: Hamer; NUCMC, 1966, 68.

SEE ALSO: Leventhal and Mooney - I;
  Robbins.

EAST MEADOW

NY260-560
Nassau County Museum
Reference Library
Eisenhower Park
East Meadow NY 11554

(516) 542-4516

OPEN: M-F 9-4:45; closed weekends and
  holidays
ACCESS: serious mature students
COPYING FACILITIES: yes
MATERIALS SOLICITED: Nassau County and Long Island history. Will also accept materials in aviation, architecture, archaeology, and agriculture.

HOLDINGS:
  Total volume: 100,000 items
  Inclusive dates: 1670 -
  Description: A collection of manuscripts, account books, and ephemera relating to Nassau County and Long Island history and genealogy.

SEE: Hamer (as Nassau County Historical Museum and Library); NUCMC, 1966-68.

SEE: Duignan; Leventhal and Mooney - I;
  Robbins.

EAST MEREDITH

NY261-320
Hanford Mills Museum
East Meredith NY 13757

(607) 278-5744

OPEN: April 15 - Oct. 15, daily 10-5;
  closed rest of year and holidays
ACCESS: appointment with Director
  advisable
COPYING FACILITIES: no
MATERIALS SOLICITED: Business records and other materials relating to Hanford Mills. Will also accept materials relating to East Meredith.

HOLDINGS:
  Total volume: 8 c.f.; 147 vols.; 204
  items
  Inclusive dates: 1884 -
  Description: East Meredith historical materials, including business records of the Hanford Brothers, mill owners and agricultural suppliers, 1884-1945; and their successors the Pizza Brothers, 1945-68; photographs, 1914; and voter registration lists, 1977.

SEE: Delaware County Guide.

EAST ROCHESTER

NY262-200
East Rochester Village Historian
Local History Rooms
Fryatt Memorial Building
901 Main Street
East Rochester NY 14445

(716) 381-3023

OPEN: M-F 1:30-5:00; closed weekends
  and holidays

COPYING FACILITIES: no

HOLDINGS:
Total volume: 27 c.f.; 63 vols.
Inclusive dates: 1895 -
Description: Newspaper clippings, scrapbooks, photographs, local histories, and genealogical information pertaining to East Rochester.

NY262-280
General James Clinton Free Library
East Springfield NY 13333

no telephone

OPEN: W noon-4, Sa 2-5; closed other days and holidays
COPYING FACILITIES: no
MATERIALS SOLICITED: Will accept East Springfield area history.

HOLDINGS:
Total volume: 6 c.f.; 1 vol.
Inclusive dates: 1880 -
Description: Records of the local Daughters of the American Revolution chapter, 1880- , and of the local Home Demonstration Unit, 1955-59.

EDEN

NY263-210
Eden Historical Society
Town Historian's Office
8484 South Main Street
Eden NY

MAILING ADDRESS:
2577 West Church Street
Eden NY 14057

(716) 992-9141

OPEN: weekdays by appointment
COPYING FACILITIES: no
MATERIALS SOLICITED: Materials relating to Eden or Eden families.

HOLDINGS:
Total volume: 70 c.f.
Inclusive dates: 1809 -
Description: Records of the town of Eden, including town meeting records, cattle marks, tax rolls, road warrants, tavern licenses, school district rolls, election and jury lists, and 1847-51 vital records; Baptist, Congregational, Evangelical and Reformed, and Methodist church records; account books; Bible records; cemetery records; family genealogies; letters; memoirs; reminiscences; photographs; and scrapbooks.

SEE: Hinding.

EDMESTON

NY264-200
Edmeston Free Library and Museum
4 West Street
Edmeston NY 13335

(607) 965-8208

OPEN: Tu-Th 3-9, Sa 2-6; closed other days and holidays
COPYING FACILITIES: no
MATERIALS SOLICITED: Edmeston history.

HOLDINGS:
Total volume: 175 vols.; 15 c.f.; 8 items
Inclusive dates: 1809 -
Description: Documentation of Edmeston history, including photographs, subject files, and business, cemetery, organization, school, and town records.

ELLENVILLE

NY269-200
Ellenville Public Library and Museum
126 Canal Street
Ellenville NY

MAILING ADDRESS:
40 Center Street
Ellenville NY 12428

(914) 647-5530

OPEN: M, W, F 1-4 or by appointment; closed weekends and holidays
COPYING FACILITIES: no
MATERIALS SOLICITED: Documents relating to the history of the Ellenville Central School District area or the town of Wawarsing, NY. Will also accept materials regarding Ulster County history.

HOLDINGS:
Total volume: 1,400 maps; 6 file cabinets; additional materials
Inclusive dates: 1800 -
Description: Collections devoted to Ellenville area history, including photographs and copies of annual reports, contracts, bills of lading, and other records of the Delaware and Hudson Canal; oral history interviews with people who worked or traveled on the Canal; records of a glass company; surveyors' maps, field books, and related documents, dating from the 1930's and 1940's; and letters and other manuscripts.

SEE: Hamer.

ELMIRA

NY272-40
Arnot Art Museum
235 Lake Street
Elmira NY 14901

(607) 734-3697

OPEN: Tu-F by appointment; closed weekends, M, and holidays
COPYING FACILITIES: yes
MATERIALS SOLICITED: Materials relating to the Arnot family or the Museum.

HOLDINGS:
Total volume: 18 c.f.; 50 vols.
Inclusive dates: 1848 -
Description: The records of the Arnot Art Museum and the papers of Matthias H. Arnot.

SEE: Chemung County Guide.

NY272-120
Chemung County Historical Society
304 William Street
Elmira NY 14901

(607) 737-2900

OPEN: M-F 9-4; closed weekends and holidays
COPYING FACILITIES: yes
MATERIALS SOLICITED: Will accept manuscripts and other materials pertinent to Chemung County and the immediate vicinity.

HOLDINGS:
Total volume: 70 l.f.
Inclusive dates: 1798 -
Description: Collections relating to Chemung County and the immediate area, including family history collections, records of the John Sullivan campaign against the Indians in 1779, other materials concerning Indian history, Civil War diaries and papers, Mark Twain memorabilia, oral histories, and photographs.

SEE: Hamer.

SEE: Hinding; Robbins; Allard, Crawley, and Edmison; Chemung County Guide.

SEE ALSO: Alan M. Meckler and Ruth McMullin, comps., *Oral History Collections* (Bowker, 1975).

NY272-200
Elmira College
Archives
Gannett-Tripp Learning Center
Elmira College
Elmira NY 14901

(607) 734-3911

OPEN: by appointment only
ACCESS: by arrangement with Public Services Coordinator, Gannett-Tripp Learning Center
COPYING FACILITIES: yes
MATERIALS SOLICITED: Elmira College history. Will also accept materials relating to Charles T. Griffes, Mark Twain, and women's history.

HOLDINGS:
Total volume: 300 vols.; 92 c.f.; 140 items
Inclusive dates: 1847 -
Description: Records of Elmira College, consisting primarily of financial records and records of student organizations; small collections relating to author Mark Twain and composer Charles T. Griffes; and records of the New York State Federation of Women's Clubs, 1898-1962.

SEE: Hamer; NUCMC, 1959-61.

SEE: Hinding; Robbins; Chemung County Guide.

NY272-640
Park Congregational Church
Archives
208 West Gray Street
Elmira NY 14901

(607) 733-9104

OPEN: by appointment only
ACCESS: appointment with Secretary required

COPYING FACILITIES: yes
MATERIALS SOLICITED: Materials concerning the history of Park Church and its ministers, including Thomas K. Beecher, Samuel E. and Annis Ford Eastman, Albert G. Cornwell, John F. Stearns, and Richard F. Lester.

HOLDINGS:
Total volume: 21 c.f.; 1 vol.
Inclusive dates: 1714 -
Description: Materials concerning the Park Church, including church records and ministers' papers.

SEE: Chemung County Guide.

NY272-720
Steele Memorial Library
Lake and Church Streets
Elmira NY 14901

(607) 733-9173

OPEN: M-Th 9-9, F, Sa 9-6, Su 2-6; closed holidays
COPYING FACILITIES: yes

HOLDINGS:
Total volume: 11 c.f.
Inclusive dates: 1920 -
Description: Materials relating to local topics in Elmira and Chemung County, including bridges, education, floods, and politics.

SEE: Chemung County Guide.

ENDICOTT

NY273-280
George F. Johnson Memorial Library
1001 Park Street
Endicott NY 13760

(607) 754-1746

OPEN: M-F 9-9, Sa 9-4; closed Sundays and holidays
COPYING FACILITIES: yes
MATERIALS SOLICITED: Materials pertaining to Endicott local history, the Endicott-Johnson Corporation, and George F. Johnson.

HOLDINGS:
Total volume: 6 c.f.; 5 vols.; 190 items
Inclusive dates: 1546 -
Description: Materials concerning George F. Johnson, the Endicott-Johnson Corporation, the Endicott area, and Broome County.

SEE: Broome County Guide.

NY273-800
Union Presbyterian Church of Endicott
John Mark Chapel Museum
200 East Main Street
Endicott NY 13760

(607) 748-9651

OPEN: by appointment only
COPYING FACILITIES: no

HOLDINGS:
Total volume: 3 c.f.
Inclusive dates: 1795 -
Description: Records of the Union Presbyterian Church, and scrapbooks and photographs relating to the Church, the town of Union, NY, and the city of Endicott.

SEE: Broome County Guide.

ERIN

NY274-200
Erin Historical Society
Route 223
Erin NY

MAILING ADDRESS:
c/o Kitty Schanbacher
R.D. 1
Marsh Road
Erin NY 14838

(607) 739-4086

OPEN: summer, Su 1-5 and by appointment; closed rest of year
COPYING FACILITIES: no
MATERIALS SOLICITED: Materials concerning Erin. Will also accept materials concerning Chemung County.

HOLDINGS:
Total volume: 14 c.f.; 324 vols.; 23 items
Inclusive dates: 1802 -
Description: Materials relating to the history of Erin, including town records and records of the Rodbaurn store and sawmill.

SEE: Chemung County Guide.

ESPERANCE

NY277-200
Esperance Historical Society
Church Street
Esperance NY

MAILING ADDRESS:
Kenneth M. Jones
Box 143
Esperance NY 12066

(518) 875-6417

OPEN: Sa, Su 1-5, other times by appointment
COPYING FACILITIES: no
MATERIALS SOLICITED: Genealogical records. Will also accept other materials.

HOLDINGS:
Total volume: 2 file drawers
Inclusive dates: 1800 -
Description: Diaries, chiefly of natives to the Esperance area in the late 19th century, records of the Presbyterian (Old Stone) Church and the local academy and schools, and letters, business records, and photographs concerning Esperance and vicinity.

FAIRPORT

NY281-640
Perinton Historical Society
18 Perrin Street
Fairport NY 14450

(716) 223-3989

OPEN: Su, Tu 2-4, Th 7-9; other times by appointment; closed holidays
COPYING FACILITIES: no

HOLDINGS:
Total volume: 96 vols; 25 c.f.
Inclusive dates: 1828 -
Description: Scrapbooks, photographs, business records, articles, notes, and abstracts of history concerning Perinton, NY.

FAYETTEVILLE

NY286-240
Fayetteville Free Library
111 East Genesee Street
Fayetteville NY 13066

(315) 637-6374

OPEN: M-F 10-9, Sa 11-4, Su 1-3; closed July and Aug.
COPYING FACILITIES: yes
MATERIALS SOLICITED: Fayetteville history.

HOLDINGS:
Total volume: 1 l.f.
Inclusive dates: 1830 - 1940's
Description: An account book and correspondence of John McViccar, including correspondence relating to Ledyard Dyke; a scrapbook of feminist Matilda Joslyn Gage; and scrapbooks of local families relating to vacations and local war news.

FILLMORE

NY287-880
Wide Awake Club Library
Main Street
Fillmore NY 14735

(716) 567-8301

OPEN: Th 1-9, Sa 9-3, longer hours in summer; closed other days and holidays
COPYING FACILITIES: yes

HOLDINGS:
Total volume: 6.5 c.f.
Inclusive dates: 1800 -
Description: Scrapbooks, photographs, clippings, organization records, and other materials relating to the village of Fillmore, town of Hume, and Allegany County, NY.

SEE: Allegany County Guide.

FISHERS

NY288-840
Victor Historical Society
Valentown Museum
Valentown Square
Fishers NY 14453

(716) 924-2645

OPEN: by appointment only
USER FEES: one dollar for adults
COPYING FACILITIES: no

HOLDINGS:
Total volume: 20 c.f.
Inclusive dates: 1703 -
Description: Letters of Nathaniel Gorham and Joseph Fellows concerning land sales in western New York; historical and genealogical files on Fishers and Victor; papers of Charles Fisher and Henry Pardee, mid-19th century investors in New York railroads; papers of Dr. Charles Came, physician and travelling showman; Civil War letters and memorabilia; photographs; scrapbooks; records of the projected city of Valentown; journals of John W. Davis, seaman on the Perry Expedition to Japan; letters of James Dewey Egbert concerning the Republic of Texas and the California gold rush; and documents of the Lewis family of Virginia.

FISHKILL

NY289-240
Fishkill Historical Society
Van Wyck Homestead Museum
Routes 9 and I84
Fishkill NY

MAILING ADDRESS:
P.O. Box 133
Fishkill NY 12524

(914) 896-9560

OPEN: Su, W 1-5, Sa 10-5; closed other days
ACCESS: advance arrangements required
COPYING FACILITIES: no
MATERIALS SOLICITED: Manuscripts concerning American history, especially the Revolutionary War, early American crafts, and archaeology. Will also accept related photographs and maps.

HOLDINGS:
Total volume: 575 items
Inclusive dates: 1750 - 1890
Description: Diaries, genealogical source data, and other manuscripts of Dutch settlers in the mid-Hudson area, including papers relating to grist mills, transportation, military history, and family history.

FONDA

NY292-520
Montgomery County Department of History and Archives
Fonda NY 12068

(518) 853-3431, Ext. 291, 293

OPEN: M-F 9-5; July - Aug., M-F 9-4; closed weekends and holidays
USER FEES: $1 daily fee for nonresidents of Montgomery County; $3 daily fee for nonresidents of New York State
COPYING FACILITIES: yes
MATERIALS SOLICITED: Materials relating to New York history, including church, cemetery, genealogy, maps, and any other pertinent material.

HOLDINGS:
Total volume: 7,854 sq.f.
Inclusive dates: 1720-
Description: Genealogical source data, including church records, tombstone records, town records of vital statistics, abstracts of wills, and land records, primarily for Montgomery County and east central New York State, but also for other New York localities. In addition, there are unpublished family histories, local highway records, town clerks' and town officers' records, court documents, and photographs.
Other records pertain to the New York State census, Civil War, tax assessments, New York State Society of the Daughters of 1812, and the American Revolution.

SEE: Hamer.

SEE: Leventhal and Mooney - I.

SEE ALSO: *Catalogue of Genealogical Material in the Montgomery County Department of History and Archives* (1973).

FORT JOHNSON

NY297-520
Montgomery County Historical Society
Fort Johnson Mansion
Fort Johnson NY 12070

(518) 843-0683

OPEN: M-F 10-5; closed November 1 through April 30 and weekends
COPYING FACILITIES: no
MATERIALS SOLICITED: Materials relating to Sir William Johnson, Sir John Johnson, Daniel Claus, the 18th century settlement of Montgomery (Tryon) County especially as it pertains to the Johnsons and their land, the colonial wars in the Mohawk Valley, and William Johnson's dealings with the Iroquois. Will also accept materials relating to the inhabitants and settlement of Montgomery County.

HOLDINGS:
Total volume: not specified
Inclusive dates: 1700 - 1900
Description: Manuscripts, deeds, letters, and account books pertaining to the settlement of Montgomery County, NY, and 18th and 19th century residents of Montgomery County. Included are business records of the Fonda family, detailed surveys of 19th century land holdings in southern Montgomery County, and the Voorhees collection on female writing and education at Litchfield, CT.

SEE: Hamer; NUCMC, 1966.

SEE: Leventhal and Mooney - I.

FRANKLIN

NY303-600
Oulehoudt Valley Historical Society
66 Main Street
Franklin NY 13775

no telephone

OPEN: by appointment only
ACCESS: appointment required by calling Director at (607) 829-3471
COPYING FACILITIES: no
MATERIALS SOLICITED: Materials relating to Franklin and Delaware County.

HOLDINGS:
Total volume: 40 vols.; 185 items
Inclusive dates: 1810 - 1960
Description: Materials concerning Franklin, including account books of C. J. Bush, papers of physician F. N. Winans, 100 photographs, and the Excelsior Society collection.

SEE: Delaware County Guide.

FREDONIA

NY310-160
Darwin R. Barker Library
Historical Museum
20 East Main Street
Fredonia NY 14063

(716) 672-2114

OPEN: Tu, Sa 2:30-4:30, Th 2:30-4:30, 7-9; closed other days and holidays
COPYING FACILITIES: yes
MATERIALS SOLICITED: Materials relating to the history, culture, educational institutions, businesses, and military service of the people of the Fredonia area.

HOLDINGS:
Total volume: 31 c.f.; 130 vols.; 5,184 items; 18 oral tapes
Inclusive dates: 1776-
Description: A varied collection pertaining chiefly to the history of Fredonia and its environs. Included is material on the Fredonia Academy, local churches and organizations, genealogical data, and letters of Horace Greeley, DeWitt Clinton, Henry Ward Beecher, Washington Irving, Booker T. Washington, and Samuel Langhorne Clemens, as well as correspondence and legal papers pertaining to the early history of the region.

SEE: Hamer; NUCMC, 1968.

NY310-720
State University of New York
College at Fredonia
Reed Library
Fredonia NY 14063

(716) 673-3183

OPEN: M-F 8:30-5; closed weekends and
holidays
COPYING FACILITIES: yes
MATERIALS SOLICITED: Materials relating
to Stefan Zweig and local history.

HOLDINGS:
Total volume: 101.8 c.f.; 41 l.f.; 45
vols.; 36 microfilm reels; 117 items
Inclusive dates: 1828-
Description: Substantial collections on
Austrian writer Stefan Zweig, local novel-
ist Grace Richmond, and local history.
Other collections include Fredonia gradu-
ates and teachers, and some materials on
Congressman Daniel Reed and Judge
John S. Lamber.

SEE: NUCMC, 1974.

SEE: Spalek.

FRIENDSHIP

NY313-240
Friendship Free Library
40 W. Main Street
Friendship NY 14739

(716) 973-7724

OPEN: M 1-5, Tu 2-8, W 2-5, Sa 10-1;
closed Su, Th, F and holidays
COPYING FACILITIES: no

HOLDINGS:
Total volume: 5 c.f.
Inclusive dates: 1868 -
Description: Photographs, scrapbooks,
organization records, and other items re-
lating to the history of Friendship.

SEE: Allegany County Guide.

GARDEN CITY

NY315-30
Adelphi University
Libraries
Special Collections
Garden City NY 11530

(516) 663-1042

OPEN: by appointment; closed holidays,
Thanksgiving and Christmas vacations
ACCESS: identification required
COPYING FACILITIES: yes
MATERIALS SOLICITED: Materials relating
to Adelphi University, Americana, Wil-
liam Cobbett, Spanish Civil War, expa-
triate writers, Cuala Press, Gerhart
Hauptmann, and William Blake.

HOLDINGS:
Total volume: 45 l.f.; 35 file drawers
Inclusive dates: 1772 -
Description: Historic material relating
to Adelphi University; papers and bio-
graphical information about William
Cobbett; collections covering the political,
social, and economic history of the Unit-

ed States, especially New York; materials
pertaining to the International Brigade in
the Spanish Civil War; clippings, letters,
photographs, and miscellany relating to
the life and works of Gerhart Hauptmann.

NY315-200
Episcopal Diocese of Long Island
36 Cathedral Avenue
Garden City NY 11530

(516) 248-4800

OPEN: M-F 9-4:30 by appointment;
closed weekends
USER FEES: $10 per hour for staff
research for genealogical inquiries
ACCESS: appointment required
COPYING FACILITIES: yes

HOLDINGS:
Total volume: not specified
Inclusive dates: 1784 -
Description: Diocesan records, including registers of defunct churches; trustees'
minutes pertaining to an estate owned by
the Diocese; the diocesan constitution,
canons, and statutes; and journals of conventions. Also included is an original
manuscript of 'Death of a Salesman,' by
Arthur Miller.

GARRISON

NY318-240
Franciscan Sisters of the Atonement
St. Francis Convent
Graymoor
Garrison NY 10524

(914) 424-3671

OPEN: M-Sa 9-4; closed Sundays and
holidays
COPYING FACILITIES: yes
MATERIALS SOLICITED: Correspondence,
diaries, financial records, photographs,
business records, and account books
pertaining to the Franciscan Sisters of
the Atonement. Will also accept related
oral history tapes and copies of manuscripts from foreign missions.

HOLDINGS:
Total volume: 150 l.f.
Inclusive dates: 1895 -
Description: Manuscripts relating to
the community of the Franciscan Sisters
of the Atonement, its missions, and its
affiliated institutions that have closed. Included is correspondence between two
founders of the community prior to its
establishment in 1898.

SEE: Hinding.

NY318-260
Friars of the Atonement
Graymoor
Garrison NY 10524

(914) 424-3671 or (212) 562-6522

OPEN: M-F 9-4; Saturdays by
appointment; closed Sundays and
holidays
COPYING FACILITIES: yes

MATERIALS SOLICITED: Correspondence,
diaries, journals, logbooks, financial
records, photographs, and business
records pertaining to the Friars of the
Atonement and the Society of the
Atonement; manuscripts, correspondence and writings of Rev. Paul James
Francis Wattson (Lewis Wattson),
founder of the Society of the
Atonement; and materials pertaining to
the ecumenical movement, especially
the Church Unity Octave and Week of
Prayer for Christian Unity. Will also
accept oral history interviews of members, former members, and associates
of the Friars of the Atonement.

HOLDINGS:
Total volume: 560 l.f.
Inclusive dates: 1865 -
Description: A collection relating chiefly to the history, foundation, and works
of the Friars of the Atonement. Among
the materials are manuscripts and correspondence of the Rev. Paul James
Francis Wattson (Lewis Wattson),
founder of the Society of the Atonement;
documents relating to the Church Unity
Octave and the Week of Prayer for Christian Unity; records, tapes, and scripts of
the 'Ave Maria' radio programs; documents relating to the ecumenical movement in the United States and Europe,
specifically involvement in that movement by the Society of the Atonement;
and materials on the Anglo-Roman
Union, the Catholic Near East Welfare
Association, the Catholic Medical Board,
and Baroness Catherine de Hueck.

GENESEO

NY321-480
Livingston County Historian's Office
30 Center Street
Geneseo NY 14454

(716) 243-2311

OPEN: M-F 1-5; closed weekends and
holidays
COPYING FACILITIES: no

HOLDINGS:
Total volume: 7 file cabinets
Inclusive dates: 19th century
Description: Clippings, photographs,
and other materials relating to the history
of Livingston County and vicinity. Also
included are veterans' records, genealogical materials, and census records of Livingston County.

SEE: Hamer (as Livingston County Historical Society).

SEE: Livingston County Guide.

NY321-720
State University of New York
College at Geneseo
Milne Library
Geneseo NY 14454

(716) 245-5595

OPEN: Su 2-10, M-Th 8-10, F 8-5, Sa
9-5; closed holidays
ACCESS: advance arrangements required
COPYING FACILITIES: yes

MATERIALS SOLICITED: Materials relating to the history of the Genesee Valley, the State University of New York College at Geneseo, and local families.

HOLDINGS:
Total volume: 325 l.f.; 12 files
Inclusive dates: 1780 -
Description: Collections relating chiefly to the history of the Genesee River Valley in New York State. Among the materials are the papers of the Wadsworth family, pioneer settlers of the Valley; philanthropist William Pryor Letchworth; architectural historian Carl Schmidt; and the archives of the College.

SEE: NUCMC, 1974, 79.

SEE: Livingston County Guide; Hinding; Robbins.

SEE ALSO: William T. Lane, *The Genesee Valley Historical Collection* (Milne Library, 1972); Rochester Regional Research Library Council, *RRRLC Union List of Historical Maps* (n.d.).

GENEVA

NY323-280
Geneva Historical Society
Archives
543 South Main Street
Geneva NY 14451

(315) 789-5151

OPEN: M-F 1-5 by appointment, Sa by appointment; closed Sundays and holidays
COPYING FACILITIES: yes
MATERIALS SOLICITED: Materials relating to the history and industry of the Geneva area, and genealogical resources. Will also accept 19th century diaries and correspondence.

HOLDINGS:
Total volume: 300 l.f.; 4 file cabinets
Inclusive dates: 1787 -
Description: Materials relating to Geneva and the surrounding area, including photographs, glass plate negatives, diaries, correspondence, church records, organization records, scrapbooks, business ledgers, genealogical materials, maps, cemetery records, 19th century censuses of Ontario County on microfilm, and miscellaneous other items.

SEE: NUCMC, 1959-61 (as Geneva Historical Museum).

NY323-320
Hobart and William Smith Colleges
Warren Hunting Smith Library
Geneva NY 14456

(315) 789-5500, Ext. 349

OPEN: M-Th 8:30-11:30, F, Sa 8:30-11, Su 10-11:30; closed holidays
COPYING FACILITIES: yes
MATERIALS SOLICITED: Material concerning Hobart and William Smith Colleges and the history of the Geneva area.

HOLDINGS:
Total volume: 5,000 items
Inclusive dates: 1798 -
Description: Primarily the archives of Hobart and William Smith Colleges, including charters, minutes, letters, photographs, records of student organizations, and student and faculty manuscripts. There are also materials concerning early Geneva history; papers of U.S. Senator James Rood Doolittle; papers of Benjamin Hale, president of Hobart College; and correspondence of Thornton Wilder and Mrs. Adaline Glasheen concerning James Joyce's *Finnegans Wake.*

SEE: Hamer; NUCMC, 1962.

SEE: Hinding; Robbins.

GILBERTSVILLE

NY326-280
Gilbertsville Free Library
Historical Section
Gilbertsville NY 13776

(607) 783-2405

OPEN: M, Tu, F, Sa 2:45-5:15, W 2:45-5:15, 7-8:30; closed Sundays, Thursdays, and legal holidays
COPYING FACILITIES: no
MATERIALS SOLICITED: Materials relating to the history of Gilbertsville.

HOLDINGS:
Total volume: 30 c.f.; 315 vols.; 85 items
Inclusive dates: 1787 -
Description: Materials relating to the history of Gilbertsville, including documents, letters, diaries, scrapbooks, photographs, church records, organization records, and genealogical source data.

SEE: Hinding.

GLEN COVE

NY327-880
Webb Institute of Naval Architecture
Livingston Library
Crescent Beach Road
Glen Cove NY 11542

(516) 671-0439

OPEN: M-F 9-4; closed weekends, holidays, and summer recess
ACCESS: appointment required
COPYING FACILITIES: yes
MATERIALS SOLICITED: Will accept ship plans and photographs.

HOLDINGS:
Total volume: not specified
Inclusive dates: 1815 - 1900
Description: Records of Webb Shipyards, including a book of abstracts; roll books; receipt books; photographs; William H. Webb's scrapbook, correspondence, and deeds to real estate; and ship plans, pictures, and logbooks, mostly of Webb ships.

GLENS FALLS

NY331-120
Crandall Library
Local History Collection
City Park
Glens Falls NY 12801

(518) 792-6508

OPEN: M-Th 9-9, F, Sa 9-5; closed Sundays, holidays, and Saturdays during summer
COPYING FACILITIES: yes
MATERIALS SOLICITED: Local pictures, scrapbooks, and genealogical material such as old wills and deeds.

HOLDINGS:
Total volume: not specified
Inclusive dates: 1830 -
Description: A collection of photographs of buildings, fires, transportation, and other subjects in Glens Falls and the surrounding area, including scenes of Lake George and the Adirondack Mountains. Glass plate negatives from which some of these photographs were made are also in the possession of the Library.

Materials cited in Hamer are no longer in possession of the Library.

NY331-280
Glens Falls - Queensbury Historical Association
Chapman Historical Museum
348 Glen Street
Glens Falls NY 12801

(518) 793-2826

OPEN: M-Sa 9-5 by appointment; closed Sundays and holidays
ACCESS: appointment required
COPYING FACILITIES: yes
MATERIALS SOLICITED: Materials relating to Glens Falls and Queensbury area history, particularly the period from the mid-1800's to 1918, with special interest in social and business history. Will also accept materials since 1918; materials relating to the Adirondack mountain region of New York State; and materials relating to 19th and early 20th century photography.

HOLDINGS:
Total volume: 300 l.f.
Inclusive dates: 1760's -
Description: Over 20,000 photographs, including a large collection of photos, scrapbooks and memorabilia of Glens Falls photographer Seneca Ray Stoddard (1843-1917). Other special collections include the archives of the Glens Falls Insurance Company and letters, ledgers, minute books, and private scholarly collections dealing with Glens Falls history (the Miller collection), the Glens Falls YMCA, the Glens Falls City School system, and the Broad Street School.

GLOVERSVILLE

NY334-240

Fulton County Museum
237 Kingsboro Avenue
Gloversville NY 12078

(518) 725-2203

OPEN: Sept. - June, Tu-Sa 12-4; closed
Sundays and Mondays; July - Aug.,
Tu-Sa 10-4, Su 12-4; closed Mondays
COPYING FACILITIES: no
MATERIALS SOLICITED: Manuscripts and
documents related to the history of
Fulton County.

HOLDINGS:
Total volume: 2,500 vols.
Inclusive dates: 1770's -
Description: Photographs relating to
early county history, including the
Sacandaga Reservoir; scrapbooks con-
cerning local history and Parent-Teacher
Associations; and local cemetery records.

NY334-280

Gloversville Free Library
58 East Fulton Street
Gloversville NY 12078

(518) 725-2819

OPEN: Tu-F 10-8, Sa 10-5; closed Su, M,
holidays
COPYING FACILITIES: yes

HOLDINGS:
Total volume: 10 l.f.
Inclusive dates: 1796 -
Description: Materials relating chiefly
to Fulton County, including diaries, ser-
mons, letters, and other papers of Elisha
Yale, New York Congregational minister,
1803-54.

SEE: Hamer; NUCMC, 1968.

GOSHEN

NY340-280

Goshen Library and Historical Society
203 Main Street
Goshen NY 10924

(914) 294-6606

OPEN: M-F 10-5, Sa 10-4; closed
Sundays and holidays
ACCESS: qualified researchers
COPYING FACILITIES: yes
MATERIALS SOLICITED: Manuscripts per-
taining to Orange County. Will also ac-
cept items of state and national inter-
est.

HOLDINGS:
Total volume: 11,000 items
Inclusive dates: 1703 - 1945
Description: Materials relating to Orange County and to individuals from Orange County prominent in state or national affairs. The majority of the holdings are from the 18th and early 19th
centuries, with nearly 1,000 items from
the pre-Revolutionary period.

SEE: Hamer; NUCMC, 1962.

NY340-320

Hall of Fame of the Trotter
240 Main Street
Goshen NY 10924

(914) 294-6330

OPEN: M-Sa 10-5, Su 1:30-5; closed
Thanksgiving, Christmas, and New
Year's; other holidays open 1:30-5
COPYING FACILITIES: yes
MATERIALS SOLICITED: Photographs,
motion pictures, and audible documents concerning the standardbred
horse in America. Will also accept related manuscripts and genealogical
source data.

HOLDINGS:
Total volume: not specified
Inclusive dates: late 1700's -
Description: A collection of photographs, films, diaries, business records,
and genealogical source data relating to
the development of the standardbred
horse in America, primarily 1849-1900.

GRANVILLE

NY347-640

Pember Library and Museum
Granville NY 12832

(518) 642-1515

SEE: Hamer.

Questionnaire not returned.

GREENE

NY353-520

Moore Memorial Library
59 Genesee Street
Greene NY 13778

(607) 656-9349

OPEN: M-W, F, Sa 9-5:30, Th 9-9; closed
Sundays and holidays
COPYING FACILITIES: yes
MATERIALS SOLICITED: Materials of local
historical interest.

HOLDINGS:
Total volume: 100 items
Inclusive dates: 19th century -
Description: Records of local organizations, such as early fire brigades, businesses, and clubs, as well as cemetery
records and local family genealogies.

SEE: Chenango County Guide.

GREENPORT

NY354-480

Lightfoot Collection
222 4th Avenue
Greenport NY

MAILING ADDRESS:
P.O. Box A-F
Greenport NY 11944

(516) 477-2589

OPEN: by appointment only

COPYING FACILITIES: no
MATERIALS SOLICITED: Photographs,
particularly stereographs. Will also accept 19th century U.S. prints and local
histories.

HOLDINGS:
Total volume: 30,000 items
Inclusive dates: 1860 - 1910
Description: Stereographic images
(originals and copy negatives) and other
photographs and prints relating to all aspects of American life, as well as lighter
coverage worldwide.

GREENVALE

NY355-480

Long Island University
C. W. Post Center
Library
Special Collections
Greenvale NY 11548

(516) 299-2880

OPEN: M-F 8-5; closed weekends,
holidays, and spring and winter recess
COPYING FACILITIES: yes
MATERIALS SOLICITED: Any material issued by or about the C. W. Post Center
of Long Island University.

HOLDINGS:
Total volume: 246 l.f.; additional
materials
Inclusive dates: 1955 -
Description: Archives of the C. W.
Post Center, including school publications, memorandums, photographs, oral
history tapes, building plans, budgets,
minutes, newspapers, theses, brochures,
and like material.

GROTON

NY358-280

Groton Public Library
112 East Cortland Street
Groton NY 13073

(607) 898-5055

OPEN: M-Th 2-9, F 10-9, Sa 10-5:30;
closed Sundays
COPYING FACILITIES: no
MATERIALS SOLICITED: Will accept materials relating to Groton history and
genealogy.

HOLDINGS:
Total volume: 7 vols.; 1.5 c.f.; 16
items
Inclusive dates: 1800 -
Description: Subject files, cemetery
records, and other materials relating to
Groton and Tompkins County, NY.

SEE: Tompkins County Guide.

NY358-760
Town of Groton Historical
    Association
Main Street
Groton NY

MAILING ADDRESS:
c/o Dykeman
120 Corona Avenue
Groton NY 13073

(607) 898-3334

OPEN: Su 1:30-4, other days by
    appointment
COPYING FACILITIES: no
MATERIALS SOLICITED: Manuscripts;
    noncurrent records of businesses,
    schools, and other institutions; and vi-
    sual and audible documents pertaining
    to Groton and its vicinity.

HOLDINGS:
    Total volume: 4.5 c.f.; 750 items
    Inclusive dates: 1818 -
    Deand scription: Cemetery and church
    records from Groton and surrounding
    towns; records of Groton Savings and
    Loan Association; materials on local in-
    dustries, clubs, and organizations; pho-
    tographs, maps, scrapbooks; and 5 vol-
    umes of histories of families in the
    Groton area.

SEE: Tompkins County Guide.

HAMLIN

NY365-340
Hamlin Town Historian's Office
1658 Lake Road
Hamlin NY 14464

(716) 964-2101

OPEN: by appointment only
COPYING FACILITIES: no

HOLDINGS:
    Total volume: not specified
    Inclusive dates: 1810 -
    Description: Materials, including
    church, cemetery, and business records,
    articles, photographs, slides, sound re-
    cordings, scrapbooks, and news clippings
    relating to the history of Hamlin and
    western Monroe County.

HAMMONDSPORT

NY367-270
Glenn H. Curtiss Museum of Local
    History
Lake and Main Streets
Hammondsport NY 14840

(607) 569-2160

OPEN: M-Sa 10-3:30; closed Sundays and
    Nov. - April
ACCESS: appointment required
COPYING FACILITIES: no
MATERIALS SOLICITED: Materials con-
    cerning Glenn H. Curtiss and his asso-
    ciates, Curtiss aircraft and engines,
    Thomas Brothers and Kirkham Broth-
    ers aircraft and engines, early aviation
    (1900-29), and the history of Keuka
    Lake and Hammondsport and vicinity.

Will also accept materials concerning
aviation history.

HOLDINGS:
    Total volume: 8 l.f.; 12 tapes
    Inclusive dates: 1870 - 1940
    Description: Primarily a collection of
    photographs of Curtiss, his aircraft, and
    local historical subjects. There are also 12
    tape-recorded interviews with early avi-
    ators and a manuscript of a biography of
    Curtiss.

SEE: Steuben County Guide.

NY367-290
Greyton H. Taylor Wine Museum
R.D. 2
Bully Hill Road
Hammondsport NY 14840

no telephone

OPEN: May - Oct., M-Sa 9-5; closed
    Sundays and rest of year
COPYING FACILITIES: no
MATERIALS SOLICITED: The history and
    science of grape growing and wine
    making in the United States and other
    countries, and the history of
    Hammondsport and vicinity.

HOLDINGS:
    Total volume: 28 c.f.
    Inclusive dates: 1848 -
    Description: Correspondence, photo-
    graphs, and other materials relating to the
    Hammondsport wineries, the wine indus-
    try in general, and the history of
    Hammondsport.

SEE: Steuben County Guide.

NY367-320
Hammondsport Public Library
41 Lake Street
Hammondsport NY

MAILING ADDRESS:
P.O. Box 395
Hammondsport NY 14840

(607) 569-2045

OPEN: M, W 6-9, Tu, Th, F 1-5; closed
    weekends and holidays
COPYING FACILITIES: no
MATERIALS SOLICITED: History of
    Hammondsport and vicinity and ma-
    terials on Glenn H. Curtiss and avi-
    ation history.

HOLDINGS:
    Total volume: 6 c.f.
    Inclusive dates: 1804 -
    Description: Photographs and other
    materials concerning Glenn H. Curtiss
    and the history of American aviation, as
    well as documents, photographs, and oth-
    er materials dealing with the history of
    Hammondsport.

SEE: Steuben County Guide.

HARPURSVILLE

NY368-600
Old Onaquaga Historical Society
St. Luke's Museum
Harpursville NY

MAILING ADDRESS:
P.O. Box 24
Onaquaga NY 13826

(607) 693-1298

OPEN: summer, Sa, Su 2-5; other times
    by appointment
COPYING FACILITIES: no

HOLDINGS:
    Total volume: 10 c.f.
    Inclusive dates: 1755 -
    Description: Photographs, genealogical
    data, business records, and other materi-
    als relating to the history of the towns of
    Windsor and Colesville, NY.

SEE: Broome County Guide.

HARTWICK

NY373-320
Hartwick Historical Society
Hartwick NY

MAILING ADDRESS:
c/o Mrs. Gladys Harrison
R.D. 1, P.O. Box 124
Oneonta NY 13820

(607) 432-6858

OPEN: by appointment only
COPYING FACILITIES: no
MATERIALS SOLICITED: Hartwick history
    and genealogy.

HOLDINGS:
    Total volume: 18 vols.; 7 items
    Inclusive dates: 1796 -
    Description: Court records, school
    records, scrapbooks, and maps relating to
    the Hartwick area, chiefly during the 19th
    and early 20th centuries.

NY373-440
Kinney Memorial Library
East Main Street
Hartwick NY 13348

(607) 293-6600

OPEN: M, W 2-9, F, Sa 2-5; closed other
    days and holidays
COPYING FACILITIES: no
MATERIALS SOLICITED: Will accept
    Hartwick area history.

HOLDINGS:
    Total volume: 18 vols.; 14 items
    Inclusive dates: 1790 -
    Description: Historical and genealogical
    materials concerning Hartwick, chiefly in
    the 19th century.

HASTINGS-ON-HUDSON

NY376-320
Hastings Historical Society
Municipal Bldg.
Hastings-on-Hudson NY 10706

(914) 478-4141

OPEN: by appointment only
COPYING FACILITIES: yes
MATERIALS SOLICITED: Correspondence, diaries, photographs, maps, organization records, motion pictures, and oral history tapes of local interest.

HOLDINGS:
Total volume: 73 l.f.
Inclusive dates: 1800 -
Description: Village-related correspondence and photographs.

HEMPSTEAD

NY382-310
Hempstead Public Library
115 Nichols Court
Hempstead NY 11550

(516) 481-6990

OPEN: M-F 10-5; closed weekends and holidays
COPYING FACILITIES: yes

HOLDINGS:
Total volume: 800 vols.; 200 photographs
Inclusive dates: 1805 -
Description: Materials tracing the history and genealogy of Long Island, chiefly Hempstead and North Hempstead. Included are 19th century account books of a church, school district, town government, physician, and the Jericho Plank Road Company. There are additional church and cemetery records, as well as photographs, including many views of people and homes in Hempstead around the turn of the century.

SEE: Hamer.

HENRIETTA

NY383-560
New York Museum of Transportation
East River Road
Henrietta NY

MAILING ADDRESS:
P.O. Box 136
West Henrietta NY 14586

(716) 533-1113

OPEN: Sa, Su 11-5 and by appointment; closed Christmas
USER FEES: one dollar
COPYING FACILITIES: no

HOLDINGS:
Total volume: 16 c.f.
Inclusive dates: 1878 -
Description: Photographs of trolley cars in Rochester and other cities of New York State; scrapbooks on Rochester transit history; correspondence of the Rochester Division of the New York Central Railroad Company; and other material on transit systems.

The repository has moved to East River Road at Town Line Road, Rush, NY.

HERKIMER

NY385-320
Herkimer County Historical Society
400 North Main Street
Herkimer NY 13350

(315) 866-6413

OPEN: June - Aug., M-F 11-4, Sa 10-2; Sept. - May, Tu 11-5 and by appointment; closed Sundays and holidays
USER FEES: one dollar for non-members
ACCESS: an appointment is advised
COPYING FACILITIES: no
MATERIALS SOLICITED: Materials relating to the settlement, development, transportation, industries, and social and civic affairs of Herkimer County.

HOLDINGS:
Total volume: 3,500 items
Inclusive dates: 1683 -
Description: A collection of manuscripts, journals, correspondence, account books, business records, manuscript public documents, maps, architectural drawings, and noncurrent records of schools, churches, government agencies, businesses, associations, and community groups, relating to the exploration, settlement, and growth of Herkimer County.

SEE: Hamer.

HILTON

NY393-320
Hilton Village Historian
24 Main Street
Hilton NY 14468

(716) 392-4144

OPEN: by appointment only
COPYING FACILITIES: yes

HOLDINGS:
Total volume: 20 c.f.; 22 vols.
Inclusive dates: 1823 -
Description: Clippings, photographs, genealogies, business, organization, government, and church records, and other materials relating to the history of Hilton and Parma, NY.

NY393-640
Parma Town Historian
1300 Hilton Parma Road
Hilton NY 14468

(716) 392-9461, 9156

OPEN: by appointment only
COPYING FACILITIES: yes

HOLDINGS:
Total volume: 17 c.f.; 50 vols.
Inclusive dates: 1822 -
Description: Scrapbooks, photographs, reminiscences, and government and organization records relating to the history of Parma and vicinity. Also included are genealogical materials concerning families of the Parma area.

HOLCOMB

NY396-40
Antique Wireless Association, Inc.
Electronic Communication Museum
Main Street
Holcomb NY 14469

(716) 657-7489

OPEN: Su 2-5, W 7-9
ACCESS: advance arrangements required
COPYING FACILITIES: no
MATERIALS SOLICITED: Materials relating to electronic communication, including radio, television, telegraphy, and facsimile. Will also accept materials relating to electrical measurement, electric motors, and electric lights.

HOLDINGS:
Total volume: not specified
Inclusive dates: not specified
Description: Documents, pictures, magnetic tapes, slides, and motion pictures relating to radio history, development, and equipment.

HOLLAND PATENT

NY398-320
Holland Patent Free Library
Holland Patent NY 13354

(315) 865-5034

OPEN: Tu, F 6-9, W, Th 2-5, Sa 9-noon; closed Sundays, Mondays, and holidays
COPYING FACILITIES: no

HOLDINGS:
Total volume: 5 vols.; 24 items
Inclusive dates: 1805 -
Description: Materials relating chiefly to the Holland Patent area.

SEE: Hamer.

HOMER

NY404-640
Phillips Free Library
37 South Main Street
Homer NY 13077

(607) 749-4616

OPEN: M-F 2-9, Sa 2-6; closed Sundays
   and holidays
COPYING FACILITIES: no
MATERIALS SOLICITED: Homer history
   and genealogy.

HOLDINGS:
   Total volume: 18 vols.; 0.5 c.f.; 1
   item
   Inclusive dates: 1800 -
   Description: Historical essays and organization, school, town, and cemetery
records relating to Homer, chiefly in the
19th century.

SEE: Cortland County Guide.

HONEOYE

NY406-320
Honeoye Public Library
Main Street
Honeoye NY 14471

(716) 229-5020

OPEN: M, Tu, Th 2-9, Sa 10-1; closed
   other days and holidays
COPYING FACILITIES: no

HOLDINGS:
   Total volume: 6 c.f.
   Inclusive dates: 1789 -
   Description: Genealogical data, account
books, photographs, and other materials
relating to Richmond, NY.

HONEOYE FALLS

NY407-320
Honeoye Falls Village Historian
Village Hall
Honeoye Falls NY 14472

(716) 624-1711, 1705

OPEN: by appointment only
COPYING FACILITIES: yes

HOLDINGS:
   Total volume: 131 vols.; 2 items
   Inclusive dates: 1796 -
   Description: Early deeds to land which
is now the Village of Honeoye Falls; minutes of Village meetings; and tax records
of the Village.

NY407-520
Mendon Town Historian
5 East Street
Honeoye Falls NY 14472

(716) 624-1711

OPEN: Th 12-4 and by appointment
COPYING FACILITIES: no

HOLDINGS:
   Total volume: 7.5 c.f.
   Inclusive dates: 1900 -
   Description: Materials include
clippings, photographs, historical sketches,
abstracted records, maps, and various
other materials pertaining to the history
of Mendon, NY, and vicinity.

HORNELL

NY410-320
Hornell Public Library

MAILING ADDRESS:
Hornell NY 14843

(607) 324-1210

OPEN: M-F 10-9, Sa 10-5; closed
   Saturdays in summer, Sundays, and
   holidays
COPYING FACILITIES: yes
MATERIALS SOLICITED: The history of
   Hornell and nearby communities in
   Steuben and Allegany counties.

HOLDINGS:
   Total volume: 11 c.f.
   Inclusive dates: 1797 -
   Description: Collections including the
records of the library, materials on local
history and genealogy, and the papers of
the Hornell family.

SEE: Hamer.

SEE: Steuben County Guide.

HORSEHEADS

NY411-320
Horseheads Cultural Center and
   Historical Society, Inc.
Zim Center, Grand Central and Broad
Horseheads NY 14845

(607) 739-3938

OPEN: M-F 10-4, weekends 2-4; closed
   holidays and holiday weekends
COPYING FACILITIES: yes
MATERIALS SOLICITED: Materials dealing
   with the town of Horseheads and Eugene (Zim) Zimmerman. Will also accept materials dealing with Chemung
   County.

HOLDINGS:
   Total volume: 31 c.f.; 59 vols.; 126
   items
   Inclusive dates: 1805 -
   Description: Collections relating chiefly
to the town of Horseheads, including
records of the town government, businesses, and schools, as well as cartoons,
correspondence, and other papers of local
cartoonist Eugene (Zim) Zimmerman.

SEE: Chemung County Guide.

HOUGHTON

NY413-320
Houghton College
Willard J. Houghton Library
Houghton NY 14744

(716) 567-2211, Ext. 240

OPEN: M-Th 7:50-11, F, Sa 7:50-10,
   shorter hours on holidays; closed
   Sundays
COPYING FACILITIES: yes

HOLDINGS:
   Total volume: 8 c.f.
   Inclusive dates: 1450 -
   Description: Photographs and records
of Houghton College, local church
records, and conference minutes of the
Wesleyan Methodist church in central
and western New York State.

SEE: Allegany County Guide.

HOWARD

NY414-320
Howard Public Library
Howard NY

MAILING ADDRESS:
R.D. 1
Avoca NY 14809

no telephone

OPEN: M 6-9, Tu, Th 2-5, Sa 9-12;
   closed other days and holidays
COPYING FACILITIES: no
MATERIALS SOLICITED: Materials on the
   history of Howard and Steuben County.

HOLDINGS:
   Total volume: 1.0 l.f.
   Inclusive dates: 1857 -
   Description: The charter and records of
the library, 19th century maps, and local
history materials.

SEE: Steuben County Guide.

HUDSON

NY416-320
Hendrick Hudson Chapter House
113 Warren Street
Hudson NY 12534

(518) 828-9764, 7288

OPEN: W 1-4 July-Aug., other times by
   appointment

SEE: Hamer.

Questionnaire not returned.

NY416-600
Olana State Historic Site
Hudson NY

MAILING ADDRESS:
R.D. 2
Hudson NY 12534

(518) 828-0135

OPEN: M-F 9-5; closed weekends and
holidays
ACCESS: parts of the collection are
available only to researchers at the
graduate level or above
COPYING FACILITIES: no
MATERIALS SOLICITED: Materials relating
to Frederic Edwin Church. Will also
accept other 19th century materials
pertaining to Olana and the surrounding area, and 19th century American
art.

HOLDINGS:
Total volume: 24 c.f.
Inclusive dates: 1790's - 1900
Description: Materials relating to 19th
century American landscape artist
Frederic Edwin Church and his home,
Olana, including complete documentation
of the house and landscaped grounds, as
well as letters, diaries, bills, accounts, architectural drawings, and a photograph
collection.

HUNTINGTON

NY419-310
Huntington Historical Society
Library
209 Main Street
Huntington NY

MAILING ADDRESS:
P.O. Box 506
Huntington NY 11743

(516) 427-7045

OPEN: Tu-F 1-4:30 and by appointment
mornings after 9:30; closed Mondays,
weekends, and holidays
COPYING FACILITIES: yes
MATERIALS SOLICITED: Family papers,
records of institutions, architectural
drawings, and other materials bearing
on the history of Huntington Township, as well as genealogical records for
Long Island, New York State, and New
England.

HOLDINGS:
Total volume: 30 l.f.; 2,500
photographs
Inclusive dates: mid-1700's -
Description: Materials relating primarily to the history of Huntington Township, including photographs dating from
the mid-19th century; business, church,
school, and organization records; personal
papers; legal documents; architectural
drawings, and a few manuscript maps.
There is a large genealogical collection
covering families in Long Island, New
York State, and New England.

SEE: Hamer.

SEE: Davis.

SEE ALSO: unpublished guides to some
collections available on request.

NY419-330
Huntington Public Library
338 Main Street
Huntington NY 11743

(516) 427-5165

OPEN: M-F 10-4; closed weekends and
holidays

SEE: Hamer.

Questionnaire not returned.

NY419-350
Huntington Town Historian
228 Main Street
Huntington NY 11743

(516) 351-3244

OPEN: M-F 10-4; closed weekends and
holidays
COPYING FACILITIES: yes
MATERIALS SOLICITED: Will accept any
material relating to the town of Huntington.

HOLDINGS:
Total volume: 88 l.f.
Inclusive dates: 1653 -
Description: All town records including
deeds, minutes of the Town Board and
Town Trustees, highway records, justices'
records, overseer of the poor records,
maps, and genealogical records.

SEE: Leventhal and Mooney - I.

HUNTINGTON STATION

NY421-880
Walt Whitman Birthplace Association
246 Old Walt Whitman Road
Huntington Station NY 11746

(516) 427-5240

OPEN: daily 10-4; closed holidays
COPYING FACILITIES: no
MATERIALS SOLICITED: Materials con-
cerning Walt Whitman.

HOLDINGS:
Total volume: not specified
Inclusive dates: 19th century -
Description: Materials relating to Walt
Whitman, including recordings and tapes
of Whitman readings and musical
settings, photographs, and reproductions
of letters and manuscripts.

SEE: Robbins.

HURLEYVILLE

NY424-720
Sullivan County Historical Society
Main Street
Hurleyville NY

MAILING ADDRESS:
P.O. Box 247
Hurleyville NY 12747

(914) 434-8044

OPEN: Su 1-4, M-Sa 10-4; closed
holidays

USER FEES: no charge for first visit;
membership fee for subsequent visits
COPYING FACILITIES: yes
MATERIALS SOLICITED: Material pertaining to Sullivan County.

HOLDINGS:
Total volume: not specified
Inclusive dates: 1790 -
Description: Material relating to Sullivan County, including church and cemetery records, photos, surveys, maps, and
general memorabilia.

HYDE PARK

NY427-240
Franklin D. Roosevelt Library
Hyde Park NY 12538

(914) 229-8114

OPEN: M-F 9-4:45; in July and August
M-F 8-4:45, Sa 9-4:45; closed weekends
and holidays
ACCESS: Applicants for research must
complete an application providing
detailed information on their topics.
Regulations governing the use of
materials are outlined in National
Archives General Information Leaflet
No. 2, 'Regulations for the Public Use
of Records in the National Archives.'
COPYING FACILITIES: yes
MATERIALS SOLICITED: Papers of the
family, friends, and associates of
Franklin D. and Eleanor Roosevelt,
and of prominent persons outside the
Federal sector who were active during
the Roosevelt era.

HOLDINGS:
Total volume: 16,000,000 pages;
126,000 photographs; 303,000 l.f. motion
picture film; 2,000 discs and tapes; 2,500
pages of oral history transcripts; 50
manuscript maps
Inclusive dates: 16th century -
Description: About 150 collections
dealing primarily with the life, career,
and times of Franklin D. Roosevelt and
his associates. The papers of Franklin D.
Roosevelt comprise 55 percent of the volume of the Library's holdings. Other collections include those of Eleanor Roosevelt, Harry L. Hopkins, Henry M. Morgenthau, Jr., and Adolf A. Berle. The
Library has a few collections dealing with
the history of the Hudson Valley from
the 16th through the 20th centuries, most
notably the papers of the Livingston,
Hall, Delano, and Roosevelt families, and
the President's collection of Hudson Valley and Dutchess County, NY, manuscripts. The Library also has the President's collection of naval and marine
manuscripts, which spans the period
1731 to 1942.

GUIDES: *Historical Materials in the
Franklin D. Roosevelt Library* (July
1979) is available from the institution.

SEE: Hamer; NUCMC, 1965, 72, 74-75,
77-78, 80.

SEE: Robbins; Hinding; Allard, Crawley,
and Edmison; Parkinson; Bean and
Vane; Spalek; Ingram; Paszek; Gehring;
Zobrist.

SEE ALSO: Ann Novotny, ed., *Picture Sources 3* (Special Libraries Assn., 1975); Albert Krichmar, *The Women's Rights Movement in the United States, 1848-1970: A Bibliography and Sourcebook* (Scarecrow Press, 1972); Walter Schatz, ed., *Directory of Afro-American Resources* (Bowker, 1970); David A. Hounshell, comp., *Manuscripts in U.S. Depositories Relating to the History of Electrical Science and Technology* (Smithsonian Institution, n.d.); Richard C. Davis, *North American Forest History: A Guide to Archives and Manuscripts in the United States and Canada* (Clio Books, 1977).

INTERLAKEN

NY433-350

Interlaken Historical Society
Main Street
Interlaken NY 14847

no telephone

OPEN: by appointment only; closed winters
COPYING FACILITIES: no
MATERIALS SOLICITED: Records relating to Interlaken and surrounding areas.

HOLDINGS:
Total volume: 6.7 c.f.
Inclusive dates: 1750 - 1977
Description: Scrapbooks, account books, school records, photographs, and maps relating to the Interlaken area. Also included are records of the Interlaken Historical Society, Interlaken Business Men's Association, Interlaken Fire Department, and Seneca Lodge No. 694 of the International Order of Odd Fellows.

SEE: NUCMC, 1978.

SEE: Seneca County Guide.

NY433-370

Interlaken Public Library
Main Street
Interlaken NY 14847

(607) 532-4341

OPEN: Sa 2-5 and by appointment
COPYING FACILITIES: no
MATERIALS SOLICITED: Local history and scrapbooks.

HOLDINGS:
Total volume: 1 vol.
Inclusive dates: 1934
Description: Biographical sketches of 25 early settlers in southern Seneca County, 1790-1815, written by Wheeler A. Bassett.

ITHACA

NY439-120

Cornell University
Libraries
Department of Manuscripts and
    University Archives
101 Olin Library
Ithaca NY 14853

(607) 256-3530, 2342

OPEN: M-F 8-5, Sa 9-1; closed Sundays and holidays
COPYING FACILITIES: yes
MATERIALS SOLICITED: Materials concerning Cornell University, upstate New York, and U.S. agriculture, political activities, architecture and planning, medical services, land utilization, and family studies.

HOLDINGS:
Total volume: 24,000 c.f.
Inclusive dates: 1490 -
Description: More than 6,000 collections relating to Cornell University and to U.S. history, both domestic and foreign, especially in the 19th and 20th centuries. There is also extensive documentation relating to upstate New York. Holdings include individuals' papers and organization records, as well as audiotape recordings, photographs, and architectural drawings.

SEE: Hamer (as Collection of Regional History and Cornell University Archives, Cornell University Library); NUCMC, 1959-64, 66, 70-71, 73, 77.

SEE: Bean and Vane; Spalek; Allard, Crawley, and Edmison; Ingram; Hinding.

SEE ALSO: Peter Duignan, *Handbook of American Resources for African Studies* (Hoover Institution, 1967); Walter Schatz, ed., *Directory of Afro-American Resources* (Bowker, 1970); Albert Krichmar, *The Women's Rights Movement in the United States, 1848-1970: A Bibliography and Sourcebook* (Scarecrow Press, 1972); Andrea Hinding and Rosemary Richardson, comps., *Archival and Manuscript Resources for the Study of Women's History: A Beginning* (Univ. of Minnesota Libraries, Social Welfare History Archives Center, 1972); David A. Hounshell, comp., *Manuscripts in U.S. Depositories Relating to the History of Electrical Science and Technology* (Smithsonian Institution, n.d.).

Joan Nelson Warnow, *A Selection of Manuscript Collections at American Repositories* (American Institute of Physics, 1969); Thomas S. Kuhn, John L. Heilbron, Paul Forman, and Lini Allen, *Sources for History of Quantum Physics: An Inventory and Report* (American Philosophical Society, 1967); Alan M. Meckler and Ruth McMullin, comps., *Oral History Collections* (Bowker, 1975); Gould P. Colman, 'Oral History at Cornell,' *Wilson Library Bulletin* 40 (March 1966); Ann Novotny, ed., *Picture Sources 3* (Special Libraries Assn., 1975); Richard C. Davis, *North American Forest History: A Guide to Archives and Manuscripts in the United States and Canada* (Clio Books, 1977); Lawrence J. Paszek, comp., *United States Air Force History: A Guide to Documentary Sources* (Office of Air Force History, 1973).

Manuscripts for Research (Five Associated University Libraries, 1969); the following publications of the University: Douglas Bakken, ed., *The William R. George Junior Republic Papers, 1895-1970* (1970); Deborah A. Wood, *Directed Cultural Change in Peru: A Guide to the Vicos Collection* (1975); and the *Documentation Newsletter* (and two previous series, *Re-*

port of the Curator and Archivist of the Collection of Regional History and University Archives and *Newsletter of the Cornell Program in Oral History*, which it replaced). The University has published guides to several microfilmed collections of personal papers. Copies of unpublished finding aids for many collections also are available on request.

NY439-140

Cornell University
Libraries
Department of Rare Books
Ithaca NY 14853

(607) 256-5281

OPEN: M-F 9-5 and by appointment; closed Christmas and New Year's
COPYING FACILITIES: yes
MATERIALS SOLICITED: Modern literature.

HOLDINGS:
Total volume: 873 l.f.; 1,367 vols.
Inclusive dates: 10th century -
Description: Literary papers and manuscripts, letters and diaries of writers, and other related materials, chiefly of the 19th and 20th centuries.

SEE: Hamer (as Cornell University Library); NUCMC, 1964-65.

SEE: Robbins; Martin.

SEE ALSO: Mary F. Daniels, comp., *Wyndham Lewis: A Descriptive Catalogue of the Manuscript Material in the Department of Rare Books, Cornell University Library* (Cornell Univ. Library, 1972); Robert E. Scholes, *The Cornell Joyce Collection, A Catalogue* (Cornell Univ. Library, 1961); Andrea Hinding and Rosemary Richardson, comps., *Archival and Manuscript Resources for the Study of Women's History: A Beginning* (Univ. of Minnesota Libraries, Social Welfare History Archives Center, 1972); Mary F. Daniels, *The Lafayette Collection at Cornell* (Cornell Univ. Libraries, n.d.), reprinted from *The Quarterly Journal of the Library of Congress* (April 1972).

Louis Gottschalk, Phyllis S. Pestieau, and Linda J. Pike, eds., *Lafayette: A Guide to the Letters, Documents, and Manuscripts in the United States* (Cornell Univ. Press, 1975). Unpublished guides are available, on request, for most collections.

NY439-145

Cornell University
Libraries
History of Science Collections
Ithaca NY 14853

(607) 256-4033

SEE: NUCMC, 1977.

Questionnaire not returned.

NY439-150
Cornell University
Libraries
M. P. Catherwood Library
Labor-Management Documentation
	Center
144 Ives Hall
Ithaca NY 14850

(607) 256-3183

OPEN: M-F 8-4; closed weekends,
	holidays, and Christmas week
COPYING FACILITIES: yes
MATERIALS SOLICITED: Union records;
	management records related to indus-
	trial relations; personal papers of
	individuals related to the labor move-
	ment or active in labor and industrial
	relations, management theory, and per-
	sonnel theory; and oral history materi-
	als. Particularly interested in New York
	State based groups.

HOLDINGS:
	Total volume: 5,702 l.f.; 253 oral
	histories; 2,350 microfilm reels
	Inclusive dates: 1776 -
	Description: Over 8,000,000 manu-
	script items and 32,000 collective bar-
	gaining agreements, plus other materials
	relating to industrial and labor relations.
	Included are the records of 6 national
	labor unions, 5 New York State labor
	organizations, several labor education and
	labor legislation groups, and individuals
	with significant careers in industrial and
	labor relations. Principal subject areas re-
	presented include New York State indus-
	trial relations, labor education, arbitra-
	tion, labor legislation, rail transportation,
	public employment, the garment industry,
	and the history of the National Labor
	Relations Board.

SEE: NUCMC, 1959-62 (as Cornell Uni-
	versity, New York State School of In-
	dustrial and Labor Relations).

SEE: Hinding; Parkinson.

SEE ALSO: Richard C. Davis, *North
	American Forest History: A Guide to
	Archives and Manuscripts in the United
	States and Canada* (Clio Books, 1977);
	and the following publications of the
	Labor-Management	Documentation
	Center: *Guide to the Records* (1963);
	M. Constance Bulkley, comp., *Agricul-
	tural Labor: A Preliminary Guide to
	Primary Sources* (1975); M. Constance
	Bulkley, comp., *Women and Work: A
	Preliminary Guide to Primary Sources*
	(1975); *Checklist of Non-Current
	Collective Bargaining Agreements Held
	by the Labor-Management Documenta-
	tion Center* (1975); Richard Strassberg
	and M. Constance Bulkley, comps.,
	*Radicals and Reactionaries: A Prelimi-
	nary Guide to Primary Sources* (1974).

A guide to the manuscript holdings of the
Documentation Center is available at the
institution.

NY439-156
Cornell University
Libraries
Wason Collection
Ithaca NY 14853

(607) 256-4357

OPEN: M-Th 9-5, F 9-4; closed weekends
	and Christmas-New Year's
ACCESS: appointment requested
COPYING FACILITIES: yes
MATERIALS SOLICITED: Will accept ma-
	terials from or on East and Southeast
	Asia in the humanities and social sci-
	ences.

HOLDINGS:
	Total volume: 42 l.f.
	Inclusive dates: 17th century -
	Description: Memoirs, letters, journals,
	and papers relating to countries of East
	and Southeast Asia in various western
	and Asian languages. Included are records
	of early diplomatic and missionary mis-
	sions to China, parts of a manuscript
	encyclopedia in Chinese, ephemera, and
	photographs relating to the life of natives
	and foreign visitors in Asia.

NY439-180
DeWitt Historical Society of
	Tompkins County
Clinton House
116 North Cayuga Street
Ithaca NY 14850

(607) 273-8284

OPEN: Tu-Sa 12:30-5; closed Sundays,
	Mondays, and holidays
COPYING FACILITIES: yes

HOLDINGS:
	Total volume: 450 c.f.
	Inclusive dates: 1784 -
	Description: Papers of Douglas
	Boardman, Dorothy Cornell, Simeon
	DeWitt, John C. Gauntlett, D. Boardman
	Lee, Jennie McGraw Fiske, Robert
	Mynderse, G. H. Speed, Charles E. Van
	Cleef, and Josiah B. Williams. Other ma-
	terials include account books, scrapbooks,
	clippings, photographs (including glass
	plates), diaries, school, church, and or-
	ganization records, Civil War materials,
	records of Tompkins County, oral history
	tapes, and genealogical materials, mostly
	relating to Ithaca and Tompkins County.

SEE: Hamer.

SEE: Tompkins County Guide; Davis;
	Hinding; Robbins.

NY439-310
Hinckley Foundation Museum
410 East Seneca Street
Ithaca NY 14850

(607) 273-7053

OPEN: Tu, Th, Sa 1-4:30; closed other
	days, Thanksgiving, and Christmas
COPYING FACILITIES: no
MATERIALS SOLICITED: Materials relating
	to Ithaca, NY, and the Tompkins
	County area, primarily in the 19th cen-
	tury.

HOLDINGS:
	Total volume: 100 l.f.
	Inclusive dates: 1800 - 1920
	Description: A collection of manu-
	scripts relating to Ithaca, Tompkins
	County, and the surrounding area, pri-
	marily in the 19th century. Included are
	diaries, deeds, record and account books
	of individuals and organizations, personal
	correspondence, family histories, maps,
	photographs and photographic negatives,
	and ephemera.

SEE: Tompkins County Guide.

NY439-360
Ithaca College
Library
Danby Road
Ithaca NY 14850

(607) 274-3206

OPEN: M-Th 8:30-midnight, F 8:30-10,
	Sa 12-10, Su 12:30-midnight; closed
	Thanksgiving, Christmas, and
	weekends during College vacations;
	shorter hours during College vacations
COPYING FACILITIES: yes
MATERIALS SOLICITED: Materials relating
	to Roberta Peters and Ithaca College
	history.

HOLDINGS:
	Total volume: 1,392 c.f.
	Inclusive dates: 1893 -
	Description: The College's holdings
	consist of 4 major collections. The Ro-
	berta Peters Collection consists of
	clippings, diaries, tapes, records, corre-
	spondence, photographs, and other items
	relating to the life and career of this Me-
	tropolitan Opera star. The Gustave
	Haenschen Collection contains arrange-
	ments made for radio of classical and
	popular music during 1925-52. Included
	are approximately 10,000 manuscript
	scores and parts. The Donald Voorhees
	Collection contains materials formerly
	used by the Bell Telephone Hour
	radio/television program, 1940-50. The
	Ithaca College History Archives includes
	photographs, minutes of meetings, class
	lists, and other materials relating to the
	history of the Ithaca Conservatory of Mu-
	sic and Affiliated Schools, as well as Itha-
	ca College, the present institution into
	which the Conservatory grew.

SEE: Hinding; Tompkins County Guide.

SEE ALSO: brochures describing some of
	the collections available from the re-
	pository.

NY439-640
Paleontological Research Institution
1259 Trumansburg Road
Ithaca NY 14850

(607) 273-6623

OPEN: M-F 9-4; closed weekends and
	holidays
COPYING FACILITIES: yes

HOLDINGS:
	Total volume: 21.5 c.f.
	Inclusive dates: 1840 -
	Description: Papers of paleontologists
	Gilbert D. Harris, Frederick B. and
	Helen Jeanne Plummer, and others; glass
	plate negatives of New York State and

Louisiana; data on American and foreign paleontologists; and records of the Paleontological Research Institution and its publications.

SEE: Tompkins County Guide.

NY439-760
Tompkins County Public Library
312 North Cayuga Street
Ithaca NY 14850

(607) 272-4555

OPEN: M-Th 10-9, F 10-6, Sa 9-5; closed Sundays and holidays
COPYING FACILITIES: yes
MATERIALS SOLICITED: Will accept materials pertaining to Tompkins County history.

HOLDINGS:
  Total volume: 0.5 c.f.; 17 vols.
  Inclusive dates: 1800 -
  Description: Transcriptions of 19th century Tompkins County deeds and wills, as well as scrapbooks and library records.

SEE: Hamer.

SEE: Tompkins County Guide.

JAMESTOWN

NY442-230
Fenton Historical Society
Library
67 South Washington
Jamestown NY 14701

(716) 483-7521

OPEN: M-Sa 10-4; closed Sundays, holidays, and Jan. 1-15
COPYING FACILITIES: yes
MATERIALS SOLICITED: Genealogy and records of Jamestown and southern Chautauqua County and Chautauqua Lake.

HOLDINGS:
  Total volume: 5,000 items
  Inclusive dates: 1800 -
  Description: A collection of manuscripts, archives, visual documents, and audible documents relating to the history of Jamestown and southern Chautauqua County and Chautauqua Lake.

NY442-250
Fluvanna Free Library
Jamestown NY

MAILING ADDRESS:
R.D. 1
Jamestown NY 14701

(716) 487-1773

SEE: Hamer.

Questionnaire not returned.

JASPER

NY443-400
Jasper Free Library
Jasper NY

MAILING ADDRESS:
P.O. Box 53
Jasper NY 14855

no telephone

OPEN: M 7-9:30, Tu, Th 12:30-4, Sa 10-12:30; closed other days and holidays
COPYING FACILITIES: no
MATERIALS SOLICITED: History of Jasper.

HOLDINGS:
  Total volume: 1 c.f.
  Inclusive dates: 1827 -
  Description: Minutes of town government, library records, and other items.

SEE: Steuben County Guide.

JOHNSON CITY

NY446-920
Your Home Public Library
107 Main Street
Johnson City NY 13790

(607) 797-4816

OPEN: M-F 10-8:30, Sa 10-5; closed Sundays, holidays, and Saturdays July - Aug.
COPYING FACILITIES: yes
MATERIALS SOLICITED: Materials dealing with local history, George F. Johnson, and the Endicott-Johnson Corporation. Will also accept materials concerning Broome County history.

HOLDINGS:
  Total volume: 4 c.f.; 75 items
  Inclusive dates: 1876 -
  Description: Photographs, clippings, and other materials concerning the history of Broome County, Johnson City, and the Endicott-Johnson Corporation.

SEE: Broome County Guide.

JOHNSTOWN

NY447-400
The Johnstown Historical Society
17 North William Street
Johnstown NY 12095

(518) 762-7076

OPEN: Tu-Sa 1:30-5; also open by appointment; closed Sundays, Mondays, and holidays
USER FEES: donations requested
COPYING FACILITIES: no
MATERIALS SOLICITED: Significant materials covering the history of Fulton County and adjacent counties in New York State.

HOLDINGS:
  Total volume: 1,000 books and manuscripts
  Inclusive dates: 17th century - 1965
  Description: Manuscripts relating to the area of the central Mohawk River and the Adirondack Mountains in New York State. The subject matter covers local businesses and industries, including leather manufacturing, as well as Sir William Johnson, Elizabeth Cady Stanton, and other local residents.

    Also included are materials pertaining to the family of Washington Irving; Grace Livingston Hill; Rose Knox; and E. L. Henry.

SEE: Hamer.

JORDANVILLE

NY450-760
Town of Warren Historical Association
Jordanville Public Library
Main Street
Jordanville NY

MAILING ADDRESS:
R.D. 2
Richfield Springs NY 13439

(315) 858-1089

OPEN: Th 7:30-9:30, F, Sa 2-5; closed other days and holidays
ACCESS: Users wishing access during other than regular hours should contact Mrs. Gordon Hoke, Hoke Construction & Supply Company, Jordanville, NY 13361.
COPYING FACILITIES: yes
MATERIALS SOLICITED: Historical data relating to the town of Warren. Will also accept historical data relating to the general Jordanville-Warren area.

HOLDINGS:
  Total volume: not specified
  Inclusive dates: 1800 - 1900
  Description: Genealogies of local citizens; daily journals and diaries, 1820-1900; and photographs of historic buildings in the Jordanville-Warren area.

KEENE VALLEY

NY456-440
Keene Valley Public Library
Keene Valley NY 12943

no telephone

SEE: Hamer; NUCMC, 1968.

Questionnaire not returned.

KENMORE

NY459-520

Sisters of St. Mary of Namur
Archives
Mount St. Mary
3756 Delaware Avenue
Kenmore NY 14217

(716) 875-4705

OPEN: M-F 8-5; closed weekends
COPYING FACILITIES: yes
MATERIALS SOLICITED: Diaries and other
manuscripts relating to the history of
the Sisters of St. Mary of Namur. Will
also accept records of schools operated
by the Sisters of St. Mary, including
reminiscences of former students and
photographs.

HOLDINGS:
    Total volume: 110 l.f.
    Inclusive dates: 1819 -
    Description: Records of the Sisters, of
St. Mary of Namur in the United States,
Canada, Belgium, Great Britain, the Congo, Rwanda, and Cameroon, including
documentation on schools, missions, and
other institutions that they operate. General Superiors' letters, treasurers' reports,
legal documents, blueprints, photographs,
biographies of Sisters, and annals are
among the records held.

KEUKA PARK

NY462-440

Keuka College
Lightner Library
Keuka Park NY 14478

(315) 536-4411

OPEN: Su 2-11, M-Th 8:30-11, F 8:30-9,
Sa 8:30-5; closed holidays
COPYING FACILITIES: yes
MATERIALS SOLICITED: History of Keuka
College and Yates County.

HOLDINGS:
    Total volume: 30 c.f.
    Inclusive dates: 1822 -
    Description: Records and memorabilia
of the College, and photographs, diaries,
scrapbooks, and other materials relating
to Yates County history.

SEE: Yates County Guide.

KINDERHOOK

NY466-120

Columbia County Historical Society
Broad Street
Kinderhook NY 12106

(518) 758-9265

OPEN: Memorial Day - Labor Day Tu-Sa
10:30-4:30, Su 1:30-4:30; rest of year
M-F 10:30-4:30; closed other days
COPYING FACILITIES: yes
MATERIALS SOLICITED: Materials relating
to Columbia County and the Hudson
Valley region.

HOLDINGS:
    Total volume: not specified
    Inclusive dates: 1713 -
    Description: Materials relating to Co-
lumbia County and the Hudson River
Valley. Included are genealogical data;
deeds; 19th century manuscripts; documents relating to the Van Alstyne, Van
Buren, Merwin, Vanderpoel, McKinstry,
Clarkson, and Van Santvoord families;
and other items.

SEE: Hamer; NUCMC, 1962.

SEE: Schatz.

KINGSTON

NY469-600

Reformed Protestant Dutch Church of
Kingston, NY
Heritage Committee
Museum Subcommittee
272 Wall Street
Kingston NY

MAILING ADDRESS:
U.P.O. Box 3006
Kingston NY 12401

(914) 338-6759

OPEN: M-F 10-2; closed weekends and
holidays
ACCESS: appointment required
COPYING FACILITIES: yes
MATERIALS SOLICITED: Records pertaining to the church. Will also accept
records relating to early church history
or history of the local area, particularly
for the early Dutch settlement period.

HOLDINGS:
    Total volume: 57.5 c.f.
    Inclusive dates: 1660 -
    Description: Records of the Reformed
Dutch Protestant Church of Kingston; including account books, baptism and marriage records, 1660- ; and consistory minutes.

SEE: Gehring.

NY469-720

Senate House State Historic Site
Fair Street
Kingston NY 12401

(914) 338-2786

OPEN: W-Sa 9-5; closed other days and
holidays
ACCESS: advance arrangements
recommended
COPYING FACILITIES: yes
MATERIALS SOLICITED: Materials relating
to the mid-Hudson region from the
17th to the 19th centuries.

HOLDINGS:
    Total volume: 40 l.f.
    Inclusive dates: 1650 - 1900
    Description: A collection of manu-
scripts, primarily from 1750 to 1875, relating to the mid-Hudson region, emphasizing social, economic, and political
themes. Major holdings include the papers of John Vanderlyn and Peter Van
Gaasbeek. There are also ledgers and
business records relating to the Hudson

Valley area, as well as a variety of other
materials.

SEE: Hamer; NUCMC, 1966.

SEE: Gehring.

SEE ALSO: Michael D'Innocenzo and John
Turner, 'The Peter Van Gaasbeek Papers: A Resource for Early New York
History, 1771-97,' *New York History* 47
(1966).

LACKAWANNA

NY472-480

Lackawanna Public Library
560 Ridge Road
Lackawanna NY 14218

(716) 823-0630

OPEN: M, W 1-8, Tu, Th, F 11-6, Sa
11-4; closed Sundays and holidays
COPYING FACILITIES: no

HOLDINGS:
    Total volume: 3 items
    Inclusive dates: 1935
    Description: Papers relating to the his-
tory and development of Lackawanna.

SEE: Hamer.

LATHAM

NY481-720

Sisters of St. Joseph of Carondelet
Albany NY Province
Archives
St. Joseph Provincial House
Watervliet Shaker Road
Latham NY 12110

(518) 785-4575

OPEN: M-F 9-4; closed weekends and
holidays
ACCESS: appointment required
COPYING FACILITIES: yes
MATERIALS SOLICITED: Documentation
of the lives of members of the Sisters
of St. Joseph of Carondelet in New
York State.

HOLDINGS:
    Total volume: 178 c.f.
    Inclusive dates: 1858 -
    Description: Manuscripts relating pri-
marily to 2,000 Roman Catholic Sisters
of St. Joseph in central New York State
and their service in education, support of
orphans, and health care. There are some
materials concerning the order's foundations in St. Paul, MN; Los Angeles, CA;
and St. Louis, MO; and its missions in
Peru, Japan, and Hawaii. Materials include correspondence, diaries, account
books, unpublished memoirs and histories, periodic reports, and records of
schools founded in upstate New York between 1858 and 1862.

SEE: Hinding.

LEROY

NY484-160
Daughters of the American
Revolution
LeRoy NY 14482

no telephone

SEE: Hamer.

Questionnaire not returned.

NY484-480
LeRoy Historical Society
23 East Main
LeRoy NY

MAILING ADDRESS:
26 Lincoln Avenue
LeRoy NY 14482

(716) 768-7433

OPEN: Su 2-5, Th, F 10-4, Sa 10-1;
closed other days and holidays
COPYING FACILITIES: yes
MATERIALS SOLICITED: Materials relating
to the town of LeRoy.

HOLDINGS:
Total volume: 30 c.f.; 200 vols.
Inclusive dates: 1800 -
Description: Materials relating to Le-
Roy, including genealogical records,
1800-1940, and records of a local Baptist
church and its societies, 1816-1927.

SEE: Hamer; NUCMC, 1980.

LIMA

NY488-480
Lima Public Library
1872 Genesee Street
Lima NY 14485

(716) 582-1311

OPEN: M-W 1-9, Th 10-5, F 1-9; closed
other days and holidays
COPYING FACILITIES: no

HOLDINGS:
Total volume: 3.5 c.f.
Inclusive dates: 1914 -
Description: Records of the library and
local history papers.

SEE: Livingston County Guide.

LINDENHURST

NY490-480
Lindenhurst Historical Society
Old Village Hall Museum
215 S. Wellwood Avenue
Lindenhurst NY

MAILING ADDRESS:
Lindenhurst Historical Society
Box 296
Lindenhurst NY 11757

(516) 957-4385

OPEN: by appointment; closed Sundays
and holidays

ACCESS: researchers with permission of
Museum Board
COPYING FACILITIES: no
MATERIALS SOLICITED: Materials relating
to Lindenhurst.

HOLDINGS:
Total volume: 42.5 l.f.
Inclusive dates: 1860 -
Description: Materials relating to the
history of Lindenhurst, including letters,
papers, account books, photographs,
maps, and records of organizations and
institutions such as churches, schools,
municipal agencies, businesses, associations, and community groups.
Collection also includes architectural
drawings.

LISLE

NY491-480
Lisle Free Library
Main Street
Lisle NY

MAILING ADDRESS:
Box 32
Lisle NY 13797

(607) 692-3115

OPEN: M, W, Sa 1:30-5, Tu, F 1:30-8;
closed Thursdays, Sundays, and
holidays
COPYING FACILITIES: no
MATERIALS SOLICITED: Materials dealing
with the history of Lisle.

HOLDINGS:
Total volume: 1 c.f.; 26 vols.
Inclusive dates: 1820 - 1958
Description: Church; school; and organization records; scrapbooks; clippings;
and other materials concerning the village
of Lisle.

SEE: Broome County Guide.

LITTLE FALLS

NY493-320
Herkimer Home State Historic Site
Route 169
Little Falls NY

MAILING ADDRESS:
P.O. Box 631
Little Falls NY 13365

(315) 823-0398

OPEN: W-Sa 9-5, Su 1-5; closed other
days and mid-April through mid-Oct.
COPYING FACILITIES: yes
MATERIALS SOLICITED: Materials relating
to General Herkimer's home, the Herkimer family, and the American Revolution in the Mohawk Valley. Will also
accept material relating to Palatine
German immigration and settlement in
New York in the 18th century.

HOLDINGS:
Total volume: 2 l.f.
Inclusive dates: 1750 -
Description: Deeds, maps, accounts, ge-
nealogical, and other material relating to
General Herkimer and the Herkimer
family. Other materials relate to Palatine

Germans in the Mohawk Valley and the
Revolutionary War.

LITTLE GENESEE

NY494-280
Genesee Public Library
Main Street
Little Genesee NY 14754

no telephone

OPEN: M, W 7-9, F 3-5; closed other
days and holidays
COPYING FACILITIES: no
MATERIALS SOLICITED: History of the
town of Genesee and Allegany County,
NY.

HOLDINGS:
Total volume: 1 c.f.
Inclusive dates: 1869 -
Description: Library records and local
history materials.

SEE: Allegany County Guide.

LITTLE VALLEY

NY496-120
Cattaraugus County Historian
County Memorial and Historical
Building
Little Valley NY 14755

(716) 938-9111, Ext. 440

OPEN: M, W, F 10-4:30, Sa 1-4:30
Apr.-Oct.; closed other days and
holidays

SEE: Hamer.

Questionnaire not returned.

LIVERPOOL

NY499-720
The Salt Museum
Liverpool NY

MAILING ADDRESS:
P.O. Box 146
Liverpool NY 13088

(315) 457-2990

OPEN: M-F 8:30-4:30; closed weekends
COPYING FACILITIES: yes
MATERIALS SOLICITED: Photographs, diaries, and company records relating to
the Onondaga County salt industry.
Will also accept materials concerning
salt manufacture in general and 19th
century industries such as harness making, wagon making, coopering, and log
pipe boring.

HOLDINGS:
Total volume: 12 Hollinger boxes
Inclusive dates: 1840's - 1926
Description: Records of salt manufacture in Onondaga County, NY, including
company account books and records,
1880-1926; town assessors' records concerned with salt-producing plants beginning in the 1840's; company time books
and business correspondence from the

early 20th century; and photographs, 1870-1926.

LIVONIA

NY500-480
Livonia Public Library
2 Washington Street
Livonia NY 14487

(716) 346-3450

OPEN: M 2:30-5:30, Tu 2:30-9, Th 10-12, 2:30-5:30, F 2:30-9, Sa 2:30-5:30; closed other times
COPYING FACILITIES: no

HOLDINGS:
Total volume: 0.3 c.f.
Inclusive dates: 1861 - 1942
Description: Genealogical materials relating to various families of the Livonia area.

SEE: Livingston County Guide.

LYONS

NY510-480
Lyons School District Public Library
67 Canal Street
Lyons NY 14489

(315) 946-9262

OPEN: M-Th 1-9, F 12-5:30, Sa 10-3; closed Sundays and holidays
COPYING FACILITIES: yes

HOLDINGS:
Total volume: 8 vols.; 11 c.f.
Inclusive dates: 1874 -
Description: Library records; essays on Wayne County, NY, history; architectural and historical slides; and scrapbooks and clippings file of people, places; and events in Lyons and vicinity.

SEE: Wayne County Guide.

NY510-880
Wayne County Historian's Office
21 Butternut Street
Lyons NY 14489

(315) 946-6191

OPEN: M-F 9-5; closed weekends and holidays
COPYING FACILITIES: no

HOLDINGS:
Total volume: 62 c.f.; 340 vols.
Inclusive dates: 1800 -
Description: Genealogical materials relating to Wayne County families; business and school records; scrapbooks, clippings, papers, photos, etc., relating to local people, places, events, organizations and businesses; records of local servicemen; and local government records.

SEE: Wayne County Guide.

LYONS FALLS

NY511-480
Lewis County Historical Society
Box 306
High Street
Lyons Falls NY 13368

(315) 348-8089

OPEN: by appointment only; closed from Oct. 15-Apr. 30
ACCESS: appointment required
COPYING FACILITIES: no
MATERIALS SOLICITED: Materials relating to Lewis County, NY.

HOLDINGS:
Total volume: not specified
Inclusive dates: 1790's -
Description: Manuscripts relating chiefly to Lewis County, NY; maps of county towns and villages; photographs; manuscripts relating to county organizations; diaries; business ledgers; correspondence; land deeds; and scrapbooks.

MAMARONECK

NY519-200
ESTO Photographics, Inc.
222 Valley Place
Mamaroneck NY 10543

(914) 698-4060

OPEN: M-F 9:30-5
USER FEES: research fee for general requests; no charge for specific projects
ACCESS: publishers and architectural researchers; appointment is advised
COPYING FACILITIES: yes

HOLDINGS:
Total volume: 450 l.f.
Inclusive dates: 1939 -
Description: Photographs of architecture. Most of the collection is the work of Ezra Stoller, but also includes photographs by Peter Aaron, Wolfgang Hoyt, Paul Warchol, and David Franzen. The collection includes, but is not limited to, industrial, corporate, and residential installations. Urban scenes and adaptive use are also included. Most of the work is contemporary and in the United States.

SEE: Novotny.

MARATHON

NY524-640
Peck Memorial Library
Main Street
Marathon NY 13803

(607) 849-6135

OPEN: M, Th, F 2-8:30, W, Sa 9:30-12:30; closed Sundays, Tuesdays, and holidays
COPYING FACILITIES: no
MATERIALS SOLICITED: Marathon area history.

HOLDINGS:
Total volume: 3 items
Inclusive dates: 1876 - 1926
Description: Materials including a handwritten notebook, with photographs, on the history of the town of Lapeer and Cortland County, NY.

SEE: Cortland County Guide.

MARCELLUS

NY525-520
Marcellus Historical Society
Museum
4 Slocombe Street
Marcellus NY

MAILING ADDRESS:
1 Park Street
Marcellus NY 13108

no telephone

OPEN: first Sunday of month, 1-4, and by appointment
COPYING FACILITIES: no
MATERIALS SOLICITED: Marcellus area account books.

HOLDINGS:
Total volume: not specified
Inclusive dates: 19th century -
Description: Records relating to the history of Marcellus.

MARYKNOLL

NY529-530
Maryknoll Sisters of St. Dominic
Archives
Maryknoll NY 10545

(914) 941-7575

OPEN: M-F 9-5, weekends and holidays by appointment only
ACCESS: approval is required from the Community Secretary of the Maryknoll Sisters
COPYING FACILITIES: yes
MATERIALS SOLICITED: Materials dealing with the history or current administration and activities of the Maryknoll Sisters.

HOLDINGS:
Total volume: 500 l.f.
Inclusive dates: 1912 -
Description: Records of the missionary activities of the Maryknoll Sisters in Africa, Asia, Latin America, the Pacific islands, and the United States, including records of their educational, social, medical, and pastoral work. The collection contains diaries, correspondence, minutes of meetings, reports, records of conferences, financial records, motion pictures, photographs, oral recordings, personal accounts of significant events, literary manuscripts, and the archives of Rogers College and its predecessor, Maryknoll Teachers College in Maryknoll, NY.

SEE: Hinding.

SEE ALSO: Robert O. Collins and Peter Duignan, *Americans in Africa* (Hoover Institution, 1963).

MASTIC

NY536-520
Manor of St. George Museum
William Floyd Parkway
Mastic NY

MAILING ADDRESS:
P.O. Box 349
Patchogue NY 11772

(516) 475-0327

OPEN: May 1-October 31, W-F 9-5
ACCESS: permission of trustees required
COPYING FACILITIES: no

HOLDINGS:
Total volume: 21 l.f.
Inclusive dates: 1658 - 1954
Description: Materials relating to William 'Tangier' Smith and his family and descendants.

SEE: Hamer; NUCMC, 1966.

SEE ALSO: Morris Rieger, 'Africa-related Papers of Persons and Organizations in the United States,' *African Studies Bulletin* 8 (Dec. 1965).

MCGRAW

NY537E-60
Lamont Memorial Free Library
5 Main Street
McGraw NY 13101

(607) 836-6767

OPEN: M, Tu, Th, F 3-9, Sa 1-4; closed Sundays, Wednesdays, and holidays
COPYING FACILITIES: no
MATERIALS SOLICITED: McGraw history.

HOLDINGS:
Total volume: 3 c.f.; 3 vols.
Inclusive dates: 1835 -
Description: Subject files and 19th century school and business records from McGraw.

MERRICK

NY537-320
The Historical Society of the Merricks
The Merrick Library
2279 South Merrick Avenue
Merrick NY 11566

(516) 378-1235

OPEN: M-F 9:30-9, Sa 9:30-5; closed Sundays and holidays
COPYING FACILITIES: yes
MATERIALS SOLICITED: Genealogical source data, manuscript maps, and oral histories relating to the history of Merrick. Will also accept literary manuscripts and music scores in manuscript.

HOLDINGS:
Total volume: 300 c.f.
Inclusive dates: 1641 -
Description: Genealogical records for the Merrick area (1641-1950), oral history recordings documenting local events since 1897, bills of sale, 19th century bank records, photographs, and other local historical data.

MIDDLEFIELD

NY540-760
Town of Middlefield Historical Association
Middlefield NY

MAILING ADDRESS:
P.O. Box 348
Cooperstown NY 13326

no telephone

OPEN: summer, Sa 10-3; other times by appointment
COPYING FACILITIES: no
MATERIALS SOLICITED: Materials dealing with the town of Middlefield. Will also accept Oswego County materials.

HOLDINGS:
Total volume: 15 c.f.; 96 vols.; 53 items
Inclusive dates: 1780 -
Description: Collections dealing with the town of Middlefield, with special emphasis on agriculture, education, and genealogy.

MIDDLETOWN

NY542-320
Historical Society of Middletown and the Wallkill Precinct
25 East Avenue
Middletown NY 10940

(914) 342-0941

OPEN: W 1-5, 7-9; other days by appointment
COPYING FACILITIES: no
MATERIALS SOLICITED: Local documents and photographs of historical value.

HOLDINGS:
Total volume: 8 filing cabinets; 15 shelves
Inclusive dates: 1750 -
Description: Materials from the Middletown area, including letters, diaries, wills, business records, genealogical source data, public documents, histories of churches and cemeteries, architectural drawings, photographs, and tax and school assessment rolls.

MINERVA

NY550-520
Minerva Historical Society
Town Historian
Minerva NY

MAILING ADDRESS:
P.O. Box 257
Minerva NY 12851

(518) 251-2146

OPEN: Tu 9-4
COPYING FACILITIES: no
MATERIALS SOLICITED: Genealogical materials relating to the Minerva area.

HOLDINGS:
Total volume: 10 l.f.
Inclusive dates: 1817 -
Description: Materials relating to the Minerva area. Included are store and school account books, diaries, census records, wills, deeds, genealogies of local families, scrapbooks, Minerva town records, and correspondence.

MOHAWK

NY553-880
Weller Library
41 West Main Street
Mohawk NY 13407

no telephone

SEE: Hamer.

Questionnaire not returned.

MONROE

NY558-520
Museum Village in Orange County
Museum Village Road
Monroe, NY 10950

(914) 782-8247

OPEN: Tu-Su 10-5; closed Mondays and holidays
ACCESS: advance arrangements required
COPYING FACILITIES: yes
MATERIALS SOLICITED: Will accept local business records and papers of local residents.

HOLDINGS:
Total volume: 70 l.f.
Inclusive dates: 1820 - 1900
Description: Legal papers, correspondence, and business records of New York residents, particularly of Orange County in the 19th century.

MONTOUR FALLS

NY562-510
Montour Falls Memorial Library
406 Main Street
Montour Falls NY 14865

(607) 535-7489

OPEN: M-Sa 2:30-5, Sa 7-9; closed Sundays and holidays
COPYING FACILITIES: no

HOLDINGS:
Total volume: 265 vols.; 20 l.f.
Inclusive dates: 1781 -
Description: Diaries and papers of local residents, including papers of the Clawson family and of Jane A. Delano; accounts and ledgers of local businesses; records of town governments of Catherine and Montour Falls; records of Cook Academy, the Montour Falls Historical Society, and other local schools and organizations; church records; genealogical materials; military records from the 19th and 20th centuries; photographs; maps; and scrapbooks

SEE: Hamer; NUCMC, 1959-61.

SEE: Schuyler County Guide.

NY562-720
Schuyler County Historical Society
Dr. Charles DeLand Clawson Medical
  Collection
108 North Catherine Street
Montour Falls NY 14865

(607) 535-9741

OPEN: M-F 8-4:30; closed weekends and
  holidays
COPYING FACILITIES: no
MATERIALS SOLICITED: Materials relating
  to Dr. Charles DeLand Clawson, such
  as correspondence, photographs, and
  other materials relating to Schuyler
  County. Will also accept materials relating to the Bethesda Sanitarium.

HOLDINGS:
    Total volume: 4 file drawers; other
    items
    Inclusive dates: 1895 -
    Description: 500 photographs of Schuy-
    ler County, cemetery records, genealogical
    charts, and papers of Dr. Charles DeLand
    Clawson.

GUIDES: *Organization,* available from the
  Society.

SEE: Schuyler County Guide.

MORAVIA

NY563-120
Cayuga Owasco Lakes Historical
  Society
History House
15 South Main Street
Moravia NY

MAILING ADDRESS:
P.O. Box 241
Moravia NY 13118

no telephone

OPEN: May - Nov., M, Sa 1-4 and by
  appointment; closed rest of year
COPYING FACILITIES: no
MATERIALS SOLICITED: Materials pertaining to the town of Moravia and the
  vicinity.

HOLDINGS:
    Total volume: 4 c.f.; 90 vols.; 114
    items
    Inclusive dates: late 1700's -
    Description: Records of the Cayuga
    County Chapter of the American Red
    Cross, the Moravia Junior Unit of the
    Veterans of Foreign Wars, and the
    Moravia Water Works Company. Other
    materials include records of the town,
    such as school records and tax assessment
    rolls, 1859-1942; a cemetery census;
    Moravia vital statistics; the papers of
    William Slade, Carlon Saxton, G. W.
    Peck, Captain E. C. Pulver, and Lester
    and Bertha Luther; the manuscripts of
    Moses Little; account books, 1827-1911;
    scrapbooks, 1850's -1960's; photographs;
    and other materials.

SEE: Cayuga County Guide.

NY563-322
Powers Library Association
Moravia NY 13118

(315) 497-1955

OPEN: M, Tu, Th, F, Sa by appointment;
  closed W, Su, and Sa during July and
  August
COPYING FACILITIES: no
MATERIALS SOLICITED: Materials relating
  to the town of Moravia and vicinity.

HOLDINGS:
    Total volume: 12 vols.
    Inclusive dates: 1813 - 1946
    Description: Account book of Isaac
    Cady, 1834-91; unidentified account
    book, 1841-54; records of the Powers Li-
    brary Association, 1913-46; records of the
    Lookabout Club, 1908-32; register of
    school attendance, 1878-86; minutes of
    the Moravia Calliopean Society; Moravia
    Union School registry of voters,
    1878-1937; and minutes of public meet-
    ings of the village of Moravia and town
    of Sempronius, 1813-39.

SEE: Cayuga County Guide

MORRIS

NY564-840
Village Library of Morris
East Main Street
Morris NY 13808

no telephone

OPEN: Tu, Th 3-9, Sa 1-5; closed other
  days and holidays
COPYING FACILITIES: no

HOLDINGS:
    Total volume: 11 vols.
    Inclusive dates: 1906 - 1967
    Description: Scrapbooks, including that
    of Lucinda Johnson, 1906-36, and the
    manuscript poetry of Vivian Curtis.

MT. MORRIS

NY566-540
Mt. Morris Library
119 Main Street
Mt. Morris NY 14510

no telephone

OPEN: Tu, Th, F 2:30-9, Sa 1-5; closed
  other days and legal holidays
COPYING FACILITIES: no

HOLDINGS:
    Total volume: 7 c.f.
    Inclusive dates: 1850 -
    Description: Clippings, pamphlets, pa-
    pers on local people, places, and events,
    including files on the Bellamy and Par-
    sons families, Mary Jemison, Letchworth
    Park, Shakers, the Sullivan-Clinton Cam-
    paign, the Civil War, local genealogy, and
    library records.

SEE: Livingston County Guide.

MOUNT VERNON

NY569-120
Consumers Union Foundation, Inc.
Center for the Study of the Consumer
  Movement
256 Washington Street
Mount Vernon NY 10550

(914) 667-9400

OPEN: by appointment only
COPYING FACILITIES: yes
MATERIALS SOLICITED: Materials relating
  to the consumer movement, individuals
  identified with the movement, and con-
  sumer organizations, especially the
  Consumers Union of United States,
  Inc.

HOLDINGS:
    Total volume: 398 l.f.
    Inclusive dates: 1920 -
    Description: Materials of Consumers
    Union of United States, Inc.; Colston E.
    Warne, economist and president of Con-
    sumer's Union, 1936- ; Persia Campbell,
    economist and consumer counsel of the
    State of New York; and Consumer-
    Farmer Milk Cooperative, Inc.

SEE: Hinding.

NAPLES

NY569A-56
Naples Library
118 Main Street
Naples NY 14512

(716) 374-2757

OPEN: M 2-9, Tu, Th 2-5:30, F 10-9, Sa
  10-12; closed Sundays, Wednesdays,
  and holidays
COPYING FACILITIES: no

HOLDINGS:
    Total volume: 30 c.f.
    Inclusive dates: 1795 -
    Description: Journal of local Presbyte-
    rian minister, 1830's and 1840's; account
    books; photographs; diaries; Civil War
    letters; maps; and photographs of local
    interest.

NEW BERLIN

NY570-560
New Berlin Library
South Main Street
New Berlin NY 13411

(607) 847-8564

OPEN: M, W 2-9, F 10-5; closed other
  days and holidays
COPYING FACILITIES: no
MATERIALS SOLICITED: New Berlin history and genealogy. Will also accept
  materials concerning Chenango County
  history.

HOLDINGS:
    Total volume: 8.5 c.f.
    Inclusive dates: 1800 -
    Description: Holdings include genea-
    logical data, photographs, and personal
    papers relating to the New Berlin area,

1850- . There are also cemetery files of persons buried in New Berlin, 1800-1950.

SEE: Chenango County Guide.

NEW PALTZ

NY574-320
Huguenot Historical Society
New Paltz NY

MAILING ADDRESS:
P.O. Box 339
New Paltz NY 12561

(914) 255-1660

OPEN: May 15-Oct. 30; library open all year by appointment
USER FEES: membership requested
ACCESS: open access to members; others by appointment only
COPYING FACILITIES: yes
MATERIALS SOLICITED: French Huguenot documents and documents pertaining to Ulster County, chiefly from the period 1652-1850; genealogical materials; manuscript term papers by college students; and manuscripts pertaining to New York State history. Will also accept Civil War material.

HOLDINGS:
Total volume: 1,000 items
Inclusive dates: 1662 - 1865
Description: The collection focuses on documents relating to the French Huguenots in the United States. Other parts of the collection include letters and other material relating to political life in the District of Columbia, Albany, and Ulster County; papers of Josiah and Levi Hasbrouck; ledgers, wills, and deeds, chiefly from Ulster County; and slides and manuscripts relating to period and marked furniture.

SEE: Hamer (as Jean Hasbrouck Memorial House); NUCMC, 1959-61, 72.

NY574-710
State University of New York
College at New Paltz
Center for Catskill Mountain and Hudson River Studies
English Department
College Hall, Room 202E
New Paltz NY 12561

(914) 257-2383

OPEN: M-F by appointment only; closed weekends and holidays
COPYING FACILITIES: yes

HOLDINGS:
Total volume: 1,500 slides
Inclusive dates: late 19th century -
Description: A collection of 35mm transparencies concerning natural landmarks, railroads, architecture, folklore, paintings, and other aspects of the Catskill Mountain and Hudson River Valley region. Included are reproductions of historical photographs and of railroad records.

NY574-730
State University of New York
College at New Paltz
Sojourner Truth Library
New Paltz NY 12561

(914) 257-2200

OPEN: M-Th 8:30-11, F 8-10, Sa 8-5; closed Sundays and holidays; shorter summer hours
ACCESS: permission of donor required
COPYING FACILITIES: yes
MATERIALS SOLICITED: Will accept materials relating to the history of the College and the Hudson River - Catskill Mountain region.

HOLDINGS:
Total volume: 75 l.f.
Inclusive dates: 1890 -
Description: Papers of William J. Haggerty, President of the College; photographs and other materials relating to Sojourner Truth; and materials relating to the Hudson River and the Catskill Mountain region.

NEW ROCHELLE

NY577-330
Huguenot-Thomas Paine Historical Association
Hufeland Memorial Library
983 North Avenue
New Rochelle NY 10804

(914) 632-5376

OPEN: F, Sa, Su 2-5, other times by appointment; closed winter
ACCESS: permission of Curator required
COPYING FACILITIES: no

HOLDINGS:
Total volume: 3,310 items
Inclusive dates: 18th century - 19th century
Description: A collection relating to the Revolutionary War era and to 18th and 19th century Westchester County, NY. Significant American Revolution materials are letters of Thomas Paine and the McDonald interviews, 8 volumes of interviews conducted in the 1840's with participants in the American Revolution. Items of local interest include lists of slaves owned by wealthy families, land records, grocery lists and prices, the original deed of the city of New Rochelle, photographs, and other materials.

SEE: Hamer (as Thomas Paine Memorial House).

NEW YORK CITY

NY586-180
American Academy and Institute of Arts and Letters
Library and Archives
633 West 155th Street
New York NY 10032

(212) 368-5900

OPEN: M-F 9:30-5; July and Aug. M-F 10-4; closed weekends and holidays

ACCESS: by appointment only
COPYING FACILITIES: yes

HOLDINGS:
Total volume: 1,500 c.f.
Inclusive dates: 1898 -
Description: Collections relate solely to members of the National Institute of Arts and Letters, (founded 1898) and the American Academy of Arts and Letters (founded 1904), now the American Academy and Institute of Arts and Letters (merged 1976). Collections contain correspondence (most of which relates to Academy-Institute business), manuscripts, musical scores, sound recordings, photographs, and related data having to do with the artists, writers, and composers who are and who have been members, as well as with the activities of the organization.

SEE: Hamer; NUCMC, 1959-62.

SEE: Schatz; Davis; Robbins; Hinding; Spalek.

NY586-220
The American Alpine Club
The American Alpine Library
113 East 90th Street
New York NY 10028

(212) 722-1628

OPEN: M-F 9-5; closed weekends and holidays
COPYING FACILITIES: yes
MATERIALS SOLICITED: Correspondence, diaries, logbooks, maps and charts, motion pictures, and literary manuscripts concerning ascents of high altitude mountains and Arctic and Antarctic exploration. Will also accept photographs and slides of identifiable people, and aerial photographs, all relating to high altitude mountaineering.

HOLDINGS:
Total volume: 125 l.f.; 100 boxes; 4 file cabinets
Inclusive dates: 1850's -
Description: Letters, logbooks, diaries, maps, and other manuscripts of 19th and 20th century explorers of mountain areas in North America and other parts of the world; 5,000 photographs and 3,000 lantern slides of mountain exploration; and 2,000 negatives of North American glaciers, covering a sufficient time span to show movement and other changes. There are also hundreds of items relating to the history of the Club since 1902.

NY586-280
American Bible Society
Library
1865 Broadway
New York NY 10023

(212) 581-7400, Ext. 203

OPEN: M-F 9-4:30; closed weekends and holidays
ACCESS: appointment is appreciated for any extensive research
COPYING FACILITIES: yes
MATERIALS SOLICITED: Documents concerning the history of the Bible Society movement in the United States and other countries. Will also accept docu-

ments concerning the history and use of the Bible and its translations.

HOLDINGS:
> *Total volume:* not specified
> *Inclusive dates:* 1815 -
> *Description:* A collection of manuscripts, chiefly consisting of correspondence of the American Bible Society with persons engaged in Bible translation, promotion, and distribution, but also including minutes, reports, and other records of the Society and unpublished histories and audiovisual materials concerning the Bible.

SEE: Hamer; NUCMC, 1975.

SEE ALSO: Harry J. Carman and Arthur W. Thompson, *A Guide to the Principal Sources for American Civilization, 1800-1900, in the City of New York: Manuscripts* (Columbia Univ. Press, 1960).

NY586-330
American Council for the Arts
Library
570 7th Avenue
New York NY 10018

(212) 354-6655

OPEN: M-F 9-5; closed weekends and holidays
COPYING FACILITIES: yes
MATERIALS SOLICITED: Materials dealing with the status of and support for the arts, arts management, economics and demographics of the arts in the U.S., arts service agencies, and funding for the arts.

HOLDINGS:
> *Total volume:* 10 l.f.
> *Inclusive dates:* 1960 -
> *Description:* Manuscripts and unpublished studies on the status and characteristics of various art fields in the U.S.; source papers for a Rockefeller Brothers study, 'The Performing Arts;' and an archive on the history and activities of ACA.

NY586-360
American Craft Council
Library
44 West 53rd Street
New York NY 10019

(212) 869-9462

OPEN: Tu, W, F, Sa 12-4:30; closed other days and holidays
USER FEES: admission fee for nonmembers
ACCESS: open only to members on Tuesdays, Wednesdays, and Fridays, and to nonmembers on Saturdays
COPYING FACILITIES: no
MATERIALS SOLICITED: Materials pertaining to American craft in all media from 1943 to the present, including visual materials, exhibition catalogs, exhibition checklists, and related items.

HOLDINGS:
> *Total volume:* 80 l.f.
> *Inclusive dates:* 1943 -
> *Description:* Portfolio files consist of biographical material, clippings, related materials, and slides and/or black and white photographs for approximately

2,500 contemporary American craftspeople working in all media.

Other holdings include the Photo-Archives of the American Craft Museum (formerly Museum of Contemporary Crafts, New York City) consisting of over 8,000 photographs of objects in exhibitions held in the museum since 1956.

SEE ALSO: Ann Novotny, ed., *Picture Sources 3* (Special Libraries Assn., 1975).

Indexes are available at the institution.

NY586-440
American Foundation for the Blind
Helen Keller Archives
15 West 16th Street
New York NY 10011

no telephone

OPEN: by appointment only
COPYING FACILITIES: yes
MATERIALS SOLICITED: Manuscripts, photographs, sound recordings, films, and slides about Helen Keller, her teacher Anne Sullivan Macy, her companion Polly Thomson, and John Albert Macy, husband of Anne Sullivan Macy.

HOLDINGS:
> *Total volume:* 65,000 items
> *Inclusive dates:* 1887 -
> *Description:* A collection relating to Helen Adams Keller. Included are correspondence with friends and admirers, speeches, literary manuscripts, legal and genealogical material, photographs, sound recordings, and one film. Among the subjects represented are work on behalf of the blind, deaf-blind, and deaf; children and women in factories; planned parenthood; labor movements; peace; and suffrage.

SEE: Hinding; Robbins.

NY586-443
American Foundation for the Blind
Records Center/Archives
15 West 16th Street
New York NY 10011

no telephone

OPEN: by appointment only
COPYING FACILITIES: yes
MATERIALS SOLICITED: Will accept personal papers of important personalities in the field of blindness.

HOLDINGS:
> *Total volume:* 1,002 l.f.
> *Inclusive dates:* 1921 -
> *Description:* A collection of manuscripts and photographs reflecting nonmedical activities in behalf of the blind in the United States.

SEE: Hinding.

NY586-520
American Institute for Marxist Studies
20 East 30th Street
New York NY 10016

no telephone

SEE: NUCMC, 1974.

Questionnaire not returned.

NY586-580
American Institute of Physics
Center for History of Physics
Niels Bohr Library
335 East 45th Street
New York NY 10017

(212) 661-9404

OPEN: M-F 8:45-4:45; closed weekends and holidays
ACCESS: individuals whose applications for access have been approved by the Institute
COPYING FACILITIES: yes
MATERIALS SOLICITED: Materials relating to modern physics and astronomy, including the records of the American Institute of Physics and its member societies, photographs, film footage, sound recordings, manuscript autobiographies, microfilms of personal papers and institutional records, and oral history interviews. Will also accept personal papers and institutional records for which there is no more appropriate repository.

HOLDINGS:
> *Total volume:* 900 l.f.
> *Inclusive dates:* 1870 -
> *Description:* Materials relating to historical, philosophical, biographical, and social aspects of physics in the late 19th and 20th centuries, particularly in the United States, and including such subjects as physics, education and personnel, physics in the academic community and in industry, scientific societies, and theoretical and experimental developments in various subfields of physics and astronomy. Included are personal papers and records, microfilms of correspondence, manuscript autobiographies, oral history interviews, sound recordings, original film footage, and photographs, mostly of physicists.

GUIDES: Joan N. Warnow, *A Selection of Manuscript Collections at American Repositories* (American Institute of Physics, 1969).

SEE: NUCMC, 1965, 68, 70.

SEE: Spalek; Hinding.

SEE ALSO: Alan M. Meckler and Ruth McMullin, comps., *Oral History Collections* (Bowker, 1975); Thomas S. Kuhn, et al., *Sources for History of Quantum Physics: An Inventory and Report* (American Philosophical Society, 1967); Lawrence Badash, *Rutherford Correspondence Catalog* (American Institute of Physics, 1974); Center for History of Physics *Newsletter* available on request.

NY586-600

American Irish Historical Society
991 Fifth Avenue
New York NY 10028

(212) 288-2263

OPEN: Tu-F 12-7, Sa 10-5; closed
Sundays, Mondays, and holidays
COPYING FACILITIES: no
MATERIALS SOLICITED: Materials pertaining to the history of the Irish in
Ireland and America. Will also accept
materials relating to U.S. and British
history in general.

HOLDINGS:
Total volume: not specified
Inclusive dates: 1700 -
Description: Manuscript collections
and archival materials relating to Irish-
American individuals, families, and organizations, chiefly of the 19th and 20th
centuries.

SEE: Hamer.

NY586-640

American Jewish Committee
Blaustein Library
165 East 56th Street
New York NY 10022

(212) 751-4000, Ext. 297

OPEN: M-F 9:30-5:30; closed weekends
and holidays
ACCESS: qualified scholars and
researchers
COPYING FACILITIES: no

HOLDINGS:
Total volume: 40 file drawers
Inclusive dates: 20th century
Description: Materials on intergroup
relations, including such topics as prejudice and discrimination, civil rights and
civil liberties, and the status of religious
and ethnic minorities in American society. There is also a special collection of
propaganda materials produced by foreign and domestic hate groups and other
extremist organizations.

NY586-650

The American Jewish Committee
William E. Wiener Oral History
Library
165 East 56th Street
New York NY 10022

(212) 751-4000

OPEN: M-F 10-5; closed weekends and
legal and Jewish holidays
ACCESS: historians, scholars, authors,
and students by appointment
COPYING FACILITIES: no
MATERIALS SOLICITED: Tape-recorded
interviews and transcripts with
individuals whose lives and careers reflect the American Jewish experience in
the 20th century. Special projects include Jews in sports and the changing
role of the American Jewish woman.
Will also accept photographs, letters,
and other supportive materials submitted by interviewees.

HOLDINGS:
Total volume: 1,000 items
Inclusive dates: 1969 -
Description: Oral history materials on
the American Jewish experience in the
20th century. Subjects covered include
general biography, Jacob Blaustein,
Negro-Jewish relations in the civil rights
movement, east European Jewish communities, Jewish political behavior in
Presidential campaigns, and Holocaust
survivors and their adaptation to life in
the United States.
Collections include materials on recent
Soviet Union émigrés in America.

SEE: Hinding.

SEE ALSO: *Midpoint in a Decade: A
Progress Report of the William E. Wiener Oral History Library, 1974-1975*
(American Jewish Committee, n.d.).

NY586-720

American Museum of Natural History
Library Services Department
Archives and Photographic Collection
Central Park West at 79th Street
New York NY 10024

(212) 873-1300, Ext. 541

OPEN: M-F 11-4 by appointment; closed
weekends and holidays
ACCESS: appointment required for use of
archives; photographic collections open
for use without an appointment
COPYING FACILITIES: yes
MATERIALS SOLICITED: Manuscripts and
historical photographs in all areas of
natural history. Will also accept memorabilia pertinent to the history of natural history.

HOLDINGS:
Total volume: 1,000 l.f.; 240 reels
microfilm; 800,000 items
Inclusive dates: 1850's -
Description: Materials relating to zoology, anthropology, geology, paleontology,
the history of natural history, museology,
travel, expeditions, marine science, and
astronomy. Included are records of the
Museum and other organizations, papers
of individuals, unpublished memoirs and
histories, memorabilia, films, and an
800,000 item photograph collection.

SEE: Hamer.

SEE: Novotny; Bean and Vane; Allard,
Crawley, and Edmison.

NY586-770

American Numismatic Society
Library
Broadway at 155th Street
New York NY 10032

(212) 234-3130

OPEN: Tu-Sa 9-4:30; closed Sundays,
Mondays, and holidays
COPYING FACILITIES: yes
MATERIALS SOLICITED: All materials
dealing with numismatics.

HOLDINGS:
Total volume: 70 l.f.
Inclusive dates: 1557 -
Description: Manuscripts, collections of
photographs and rubbings, dissertations,
card files, and slides dealing with coins,
medals, tokens, and paper money in all
areas of the world. In addition, there are
hundreds of auction catalogs, 18th-20th
centuries, which contain handwritten indication of prices realized and names of
purchasers of coins sold.

SEE: Hamer.

NY586-880

American Sephardi Federation
Research Department
521 Fifth Avenue
Suite 1404
New York NY 10017

no telephone

OPEN: M-Th 11-4, F 11-2; closed
weekends, holidays, and Jewish holy
days
ACCESS: advance arrangements required
COPYING FACILITIES: yes
MATERIALS SOLICITED: Materials relating
to the history of early Jewish settlement in the United States and the
Western Hemisphere; cultural, social
and religious institutions of non-
European Jewry; social integration policies in Israel; problems affecting non-
European Jewry in Israel; and non-
European Jewish linguistics. Will also
accept materials relating to Jews in
general.

HOLDINGS:
Total volume: 4 file cabinets; 20 l.f.
Inclusive dates: 1950 -
Description: Materials on Jews from
non-European countries (Sephardim),
with emphasis on social integration of
Sephardim in Israel, as well as clippings
from the American and international
press on related subjects.

NY586-910

American Society for Psychical
Research
5 West 73rd Street
New York NY 10023

(212) 799-5050

OPEN: M-F 10-4; closed weekends and
holidays
ACCESS: restricted to serious scholars
with approval of the Society
COPYING FACILITIES: yes

HOLDINGS:
Total volume: 44 l.f.
Inclusive dates: 1885 - 1940
Description: Manuscripts relating to
psychical research and parapsychology,
chiefly consisting of correspondence of
psychic researchers, but also including
case reports of witnesses to psychic
events.

SEE: Hamer.

NY587-80

Anonymous Arts Recovery Society
383 West Broadway
New York NY

MAILING ADDRESS:
380 West Broadway
New York NY 10012

(212) 431-3600

OPEN: by appointment only
ACCESS: specialists in the field
COPYING FACILITIES: no
MATERIALS SOLICITED: Late 19th century documents and photographs relating to the ornamental arts as applied to buildings.

HOLDINGS:
   Total volume: 500 items
   Inclusive dates: 1850 - 1910
   Description: Original slide collection of ornamentation on New York buildings.

NY587-180

Archaeological Institute of America
53 Park Place
New York NY 10007

(212) 732-6677

OPEN: M-F 9-4:30; closed weekends and holidays
ACCESS: by appointment with Executive Director
COPYING FACILITIES: yes
MATERIALS SOLICITED: Materials relating to American and classical archaeology, as well as to the history of the Institute.

HOLDINGS:
   Total volume: 10,000 items
   Inclusive dates: 1950 -
   Description: Photographs and color slides relating to classical and American archaeology, the latter chiefly concerning the southwestern United States and Mexico.

SEE: Novotny.

NY587-190

The Architectural League of New York
Archive of Women in Architecture
457 Madison Avenue
New York NY 10022

(212) 753-1722

OPEN: by appointment only
COPYING FACILITIES: yes
MATERIALS SOLICITED: Biographical and project data from women architects, and historical materials relating to women architects.

HOLDINGS:
   Total volume: 300 biographies
   Inclusive dates: 1850 -
   Description: Biographical materials relating to 19th and 20th century women architects and women involved in historic preservation.

SEE ALSO: *Women in American Architecture: A Historical and Contemporary Perspective* (Whitney Library of Design/Watson-Guptill, 1977).

NY587-300

Association of Child Psychoanalysis
40 East 89th Street
New York NY 10028

no telephone

OPEN: M-F by appointment only; closed weekends and holidays
COPYING FACILITIES: no

MATERIALS SOLICITED: Historical and scientific data relating to child psychoanalysis. Will also accept reports of annual meetings of the Association.

HOLDINGS:
   Total volume: 8 vols.; 10 tapes
   Inclusive dates: 1966 -
   Description: Tape-recorded reports by Anna Freud relating to the history and development of child analysis, and reports of the Association's annual scientific meetings.

NY587-340

Association of the Bar of the City of New York
Library
42 West 44th Street
New York NY 10036

no telephone

SEE: Hamer.

Questionnaire not returned.

NY587-460

Bank of New York
Archives
48 Wall Street
New York NY 10005

no telephone

SEE: Hamer.

Questionnaire not returned.

NY587-500

Barco Photo Agency
100 Beekman Street
Suite IK
New York NY 10038

no telephone

OPEN: by appointment only
COPYING FACILITIES: no
MATERIALS SOLICITED: Photographs and 16mm film relating to New York City.

HOLDINGS:
   Total volume: 2,000 photographs; 8,000 ft. 16mm film
   Inclusive dates: 1965 -
   Description: Photographs and film relating to New York City with specific concentration on Brooklyn. Special subjects covered include the Myrtle Avenue elevated line before demolition, the Brooklyn Music School, and specific geographical locations.

SEE: Novotny.

NY587-510

Barnard College
Archives
606 West 120th Street
New York NY 10027

(212) 280-4079, 3953

OPEN: M-F 9-5 by appointment; closed weekends, holidays, mid-June-late Aug.
ACCESS: appointment recommended
COPYING FACILITIES: yes
MATERIALS SOLICITED: Materials created by Barnard College administration, faculty, and undergraduates.

HOLDINGS:
   Total volume: 300 l.f.
   Inclusive dates: 1880 -
   Description: A collection of records, correspondence, photographs, memorabilia, and other materials relating to Barnard College.

SEE: Robbins; Hinding.

NY587-720

Bronx County Historical Society
Research Library
3309 Bainbridge Avenue
Bronx NY 10467

(212) 881-8900

OPEN: M-F 9:30-4; closed weekends and holidays
ACCESS: by appointment with Librarian
COPYING FACILITIES: yes
MATERIALS SOLICITED: Materials pertaining to the Bronx. Will also accept materials relating to early Westchester County history and New York City.

HOLDINGS:
   Total volume: 15,000 c.f.
   Inclusive dates: 1880 -
   Description,: Bronx County government records; police, fire, school, association, and business records; oral history recordings; motion pictures of recreated Revolutionary battles; radio tapes of the Society's 'Out of the Past' series; aerial photographs; negatives; and other materials relating chiefly to the history of the Bronx.

SEE: Hinding.

SEE ALSO: *Architectural Research Materials in New York City: A Guide to Resources in All Five Boroughs* (Committee for the Preservation of Architectural Records, Inc., 1977).

NY587-740

Brooklyn Botanic Garden
Library
Brooklyn NY 11225

no telephone

SEE: Hamer; NUCMC, 1966.

Questionnaire not returned.

NY587-780

Brooklyn Museum
Libraries
188 Eastern Parkway
Brooklyn NY 11238

(718) 638-5000

OPEN: M-F by appointment only
COPYING FACILITIES: yes
MATERIALS SOLICITED: Materials relating to the Brooklyn Institute of Arts and Sciences, the Brooklyn Museum, and Brooklyn artists.

HOLDINGS:
   Total volume: 4 boxes; 32 vols.; other items
   Inclusive dates: 1826 - 1923
   Description: Reports by Stewart Culin on collecting in the Orient, the southwestern U.S., and in Europe, and papers of

Charles Edwin Wilbour and Gustavus Seyffarth.

SEE: Hamer.

SEE: Bean and Vane; Leventhal and Mooney - I.

NY587-800

Brooklyn Public Library
History Division
Brooklyn Collection
Grand Army Plaza
Brooklyn NY 11238

(718) 780-7700

OPEN: Su 1-5, M-Th 9-8, F, Sa 10-6; closed holidays and Sundays in summer
ACCESS: appointment and identification required
COPYING FACILITIES: yes
MATERIALS SOLICITED: Photographs, scrapbooks, diaries, archives, and noncurrent records of institutions and organizations related to Brooklyn.

HOLDINGS:
  Total volume: 1,000 l.f.; 50,000 photographs
  Inclusive dates: 1850 -
  Description: Photographs, unpublished theses, 1930-60, diaries, and manuscripts on Brooklyn. Also included are papers of businesspersons and historians, the Gertrude Hoffman dance collection, institutional archives of the Brooklyn Public Library, and card files on street and school name origins and Brooklyn notables.

SEE: Hamer.

SEE: Hinding; Leventhal and Mooney - I; Robbins.

SEE ALSO: Harry J. Carman and Arthur W. Thompson, *A Guide to the Principal Sources for American Civilization, 1800-1900, in the City of New York: Manuscripts* (Columbia Univ. Press, 1960); Ann Novotny, ed., *Picture Sources 3* (Special Libraries Assn., 1975); Walter Schatz, ed., *Directory of Afro-American Resources* (Bowker, 1970).

NY587-820

Bund Archives for the Jewish Labor Movement
25 E. 21st Street
New York NY 10021

(212) 473-5101

OPEN: M-F 10-5; closed weekends, national, and Jewish holidays
ACCESS: advance arrangements required
COPYING FACILITIES: no
MATERIALS SOLICITED: Materials relating to the history of the Jewish labor movement with special emphasis on eastern Europe from the late 19th century to date and on Yiddish language materials. Will also accept materials relating to the international socialist movement, Yiddish culture, eastern European Jews in the 19th and 20th centuries, and the Holocaust and Jewish resistance.

HOLDINGS:
  Total volume: 2,500 l.f.
  Inclusive dates: 1870 -
  Description: Materials relating to the history of the Jewish labor movement in its various aspects (Bundist, Zionist, anarchist, communist), the labor movement in eastern Europe, socialism, Yiddish culture, eastern European Jews in the 19th and 20th centuries, the Holocaust, and the Jewish labor movement and socialism in America.
  Included are letters of leading Bundists and socialists, correspondence of Yiddish writers and Yiddish language institutions, underground leaflets from Tsarist Russia, diaries and leaflets from the underground in Nazi-occupied Poland, newspaper clippings, photographs, and other items.

SEE: Hamer.

NY587-840

Butterick Archives/Library
161 Sixth Avenue
New York NY 10013

(212) 620-2570

OPEN: M-F 8:45-4:30; closed weekends and holidays
ACCESS: available to researchers as staff time permits; prior inquiry by mail advised
COPYING FACILITIES: yes
MATERIALS SOLICITED: Materials relating to the history of costume, fashion, the home sewing industry, Butterick patterns, and Vogue patterns.

HOLDINGS:
  Total volume: 2,000 c.f.
  Inclusive dates: 1851 -
  Description: Materials documenting the history of fashion in dress, the home sewing industry, and the development and improvement of dress patterns. Included are records of advertising and marketing relating to consumer goods, original pattern drafts, models' proofs, and other materials.

SEE: Novotny; Hinding.

NY587-880

The Carl and Lily Pforzheimer Foundation, Inc.
The Carl H. Pforzheimer Library
41 East 42nd Street
Room 815
New York NY 10017

(212) 697-7217

OPEN: M-F 9:30-4:30; closed weekends and holidays
ACCESS: qualified researchers by prior application and appointment
COPYING FACILITIES: no
MATERIALS SOLICITED: English literature from 1475 to 1700; correspondence, diaries, journals, and literary manuscripts concerning Percy Bysshe Shelley and his circle (Godwin, Byron, Leigh Hunt, Peacock, etc.); women writers 1790-1840 (Mary Wollstonecraft, Mary Shelley, Mary Hays, Lady Blessington, Jane and Anna Maria Porter, etc.); George Gissing; and Bruce Rogers.

HOLDINGS:
  Total volume: not specified
  Inclusive dates: late 18th century - late 19th century
  Description: Literary and other manuscripts related to Percy Shelley and his circle of friends, George Gissing, and feminists of the 18th and 19th centuries.

SEE: Robbins.

NY587-930

Catholic Diocese of Brooklyn
The Chancery
75 Greene Avenue
Brooklyn NY

MAILING ADDRESS:
P.O. Box C
Brooklyn NY 11202

(718) 596-5500

OPEN: by appointment; closed weekends, holidays, and holy days
ACCESS: written requests for access must be made in advance of visit
COPYING FACILITIES: yes

HOLDINGS:
  Total volume: 300 l.f.
  Inclusive dates: 1820 - 1964
  Description: Correspondence of the first two bishops of Brooklyn, 1853-1921; administrative records of the Chancery, especially marriage dispensations, deeds of church property, and records of baptisms and marriages in defunct parishes; and annual reports of parishes, including those of some formerly in the Diocese of Brooklyn but now in the Diocese of Rockville Centre.

NY587-940

Center for Migration Studies
Archives
209 Flagg Place
Staten Island NY 10304

(718) 351-8800

OPEN: M-F 9-5; closed weekends and holidays
ACCESS: qualified researchers upon written request
COPYING FACILITIES: yes
MATERIALS SOLICITED: Materials dealing with all aspects of the immigrant and ethnic experience in the United States.

HOLDINGS:
  Total volume: 650 c.f.
  Inclusive dates: 1880 -
  Description: Materials relating to the immigrant experience in America, primarily that of Italian-Americans, as well as documentation of the role of the Catholic church in the immigration and assimilation process. Included are records of social welfare organizations, labor unions, educational institutions, religious orders, and Catholic church organizations, as well as unpublished memoirs of immigrants and private papers of individuals prominent in 20th century immigration and ethnic history.

GUIDES: Oha della Cava, *A Guide to the Archives* 3 vols. (1974, 1977, 1979).

SEE: Hinding.

NY588-60

The Chase Manhattan Bank, N.A.
Archives
1 Chase Manhattan Plaza
23rd Floor
New York NY 10081

(212) 552-6658

OPEN: M-F 9-5; closed weekends and holidays
ACCESS: Researchers who are not Bank employees must submit letter detailing topic, purpose, scope of work, and institutional or professional affiliation.
COPYING FACILITIES: no
MATERIALS SOLICITED: Records of the Bank, including executive correspondence, interoffice communications relating to policy making, financial summaries, photographs, department records, files on bank services, oral histories, and motion pictures.

HOLDINGS:
  Total volume: 650 c.f.
  Inclusive dates: 1799 -
  Description: Collections relating to the history of the Chase Manhattan Bank and its predecessors in the New York City area, including the Chase National Bank, the Equitable Trust Company, and the Bank of the Manhattan Company. Some materials document the early years of the Manhattan Company (founded in 1799) and its operations as water supplier for New York City. Photographs show banking facilities, employees' work and activities, and major figures in the Bank's development.

SEE: Novotny.

NY588-300

City University of New York
Brooklyn College
Library
Special Collections Division
Bedford Avenue and Avenue H
Brooklyn NY 11210

(718) 780-5346

OPEN: M-F 9-5; closed weekends and holidays
ACCESS: unrestricted to faculty and students of Brooklyn College; to other qualified scholars by prior arrangement only
COPYING FACILITIES: yes
MATERIALS SOLICITED: Book manuscripts by distinguished alumni; minutes and records of the New York City Board of Higher Education and the Chancellor of the City University of New York; official publications and reports of Brooklyn College; student publications; Brooklyn College masters' theses; and oral history tapes on the early development of the College. Will also accept publications, pictures, and memorabilia of quasi-official groups, such as the Faculty Club, the Professional Staff Congress, and the Alumni Association of Brooklyn College.

HOLDINGS:
  Total volume: 700 l.f.
  Inclusive dates: 1930 -
  Description: Materials relating to Brooklyn College. Included are official publications, oral history tapes, and other materials, including papers of alumni William Alfred, Oscar Brand, Oscar Handlin, Sam Levenson, Arthur Mann, and Richard and Clara Winston. There are also non-University related manuscript collections, including the papers of Lauretta Bender, Paul F. Schilder, Norman Cousins, Dorothy Salisbury Davis, James M. Pettit, and Roy D. Richardson.

SEE: NUCMC, 1965, 75.

SEE: Meckler and McMullin; Robbins; Hinding.

NY588-340

City University of New York
City College
Library
Archives/Special Collections
307 Cohen Library
Convent Avenue and 138th Street
Brooklyn NY 10031

(212) 690-5367

OPEN: M-F 1-5; closed weekends and holidays
COPYING FACILITIES: yes
MATERIALS SOLICITED: Materials relating to the history and current operation of the New York City Board of Higher Education, the City University of New York, and City College, and collections of manuscripts and memorabilia of alumni and faculty.

HOLDINGS:
  Total volume: 1,600 l.f.
  Inclusive dates: 1847 -
  Description: Materials relating to the history of City College, including the records of the College, the City University of New York, and the New York City Board of Higher Education. Also included are papers of outstanding alumni and faculty, as well as records of student organizations, and a collection of taped interviews with black artists and other original sound recordings of American poets.
    Included are the papers of Townsend Harris, first U.S. Envoy to Japan.

SEE: Hamer (as City College Library); NUCMC, 1974 (as City College of New York Archives).

SEE: Robbins.

NY588-380

City University of New York
Graduate School and University Center
Library
33 West 42nd Street
New York NY 10036

(212) 790-4541

OPEN: Su 1-6, M-Th 9-9, F, Sa 9-5; closed holidays
ACCESS: serious scholars, by appointment with Music Librarian
COPYING FACILITIES: yes

MATERIALS SOLICITED: Microfilms of music manuscripts and thematic catalogs. Will also accept research materials in the field of music history and musicology.

HOLDINGS:
  Total volume: 910 microfilm reels
  Inclusive dates: 1100 - 1900
  Description: 2,140 music titles, including significant music scores in manuscript and early thematic catalogs, mostly from Europe.

SEE ALSO: Bruce Saylor, 'City University of New York,' *Current Musicology* 17 (1974).

NY588-420

City University of New York
Hunter College
Library
Archives
695 Park Avenue
New York NY

MAILING ADDRESS:
P.O. Box 1217
New York NY 10021

(212) 772-4149, 4146

OPEN: M, W, Th 9-5; closed other days and holidays
COPYING FACILITIES: yes
MATERIALS SOLICITED: Personal papers of Hunter College alumni and faculty. Will also accept other items associated with the history of the College and its alumni.

HOLDINGS:
  Total volume: 423 l.f.
  Inclusive dates: 1870 - 1964
  Description: Records, photographs, tape recordings, and some manuscripts covering the history of Hunter College during its administration as a women's college, 1870 to 1964. There are also records of the Alumni Association of Hunter College, founded in 1872.

SEE: Hinding; Robbins.

NY588-440

City University of New York
John Jay College of Criminal Justice
Library
445 West 59th Street
New York NY 10019

(212) 489-5169

OPEN: M-Th 9-9, F 9-5, Sa 11-4; closed Sundays and holidays
COPYING FACILITIES: yes
MATERIALS SOLICITED: Materials related to the criminal justice system and to fire service administration.

HOLDINGS:
  Total volume: 3,000 vols.; 75 l.f.; 26 video tapes
  Inclusive dates: 1819 -
  Description: Materials relating to the U.S. criminal justice system, including a letter by John Jay; 3,000 volumes of trial transcripts from New York City criminal courts, 1890's-1920's; 2 cartons of papers, scrapbooks, photographs and letters of Lewis E. Lawes, warden of Sing Sing prison from 1920 to 1941; and 26 videotapes

documenting the 'Theater for the Forgotten' program involving juveniles in criminal justice agencies.

Included are records of the Center for Knowledge in Criminal Justice Planning (60 l.f.), an agency involved in a massive study of the effectiveness of the penal system.

NY588-520
City University of New York
Queens College
Historical Documents Collection
Paul Klapper Library
Flushing NY 11367

(718) 520-7023

OPEN: M-F 9-4; closed weekends, except by appointment, and holidays
COPYING FACILITIES: yes
MATERIALS SOLICITED: Legal records relating to New York City and New York State. Will also accept any historically important materials relating to New York City or New York State.

HOLDINGS:
   Total volume: 18,000 c.f.
   Inclusive dates: 1650 - 1950
   Description: Chiefly legal materials relating to the State of New York. Included are the records of the Court of Appeals, including Chancery, the Supreme Court, and the Court of Errors. There are also wills, inventories, administrative papers, and criminal court records.

SEE: NUCMC, 1974.

SEE: Hinding; Leventhal and Mooney - I; Robbins.

NY588-560
City University of New York
Queensborough Community College
56th Avenue and Springfield
   Boulevard
Bayside NY 11364

(718) 631-6226, 6227

OPEN: M-Th 9-9, F 9-5; closed weekends and holidays
COPYING FACILITIES: yes
MATERIALS SOLICITED: Records and other materials relating to the operation and history of Queensborough Community College. Will also accept relevant records from the Board of Higher Education, State University of New York, and New York State Department of Education.

HOLDINGS:
   Total volume: 475 document cases
   Inclusive dates: 1959 -
   Description: Records and documents relating to the operation, activities, and history of Queensborough Community College.

NY588-700
Collegiate Reformed Dutch Church
45 John Street
New York NY 10038

(212) 233-1960

OPEN: M-F 9-5; closed weekends and holidays
ACCESS: prior arrangements advisable
COPYING FACILITIES: yes

HOLDINGS:
   Total volume: 20 l.f.
   Inclusive dates: 1639 -
   Description: Minute books, and baptismal, marriage, death and membership listings for the Church since its founding in New Amsterdam.

SEE: Gehring.

NY588-780
Columbia University
Department of Art History and
   Archaeology
Photograph Collection
New York NY 10027

(212) 280-5203

OPEN: M-F 10-5; closed weekends and holidays
COPYING FACILITIES: yes
MATERIALS SOLICITED: Photographs and microfiche images relating to the history of architecture and to architecture, sculpture, paintings, drawings, prints, and decorative arts in the primitive, pre-Columbian, ancient Near Eastern, Far Eastern, Greek, Roman, early Christian, Medieval, Renaissance, Baroque, and Modern periods and styles.

HOLDINGS:
   Total volume: 185,100 items
   Inclusive dates: 1900 -
   Description: Photographs relating to the history of architecture and to architecture, sculpture, paintings, drawings, prints, and decorative arts in the fields of primitive, pre-Columbian, ancient Near Eastern, Far Eastern, Greek, Roman, early Christian, Medieval, Renaissance, Baroque, and Modern art. Special collections include the Marburger index of art in Germany, on microfiche; the Ware collection of architectural photographs; and the Courtauld Institute illustration archives.

NY588-820
Columbia University
Libraries
Avery Architectural and Fine Arts
   Library
New York NY 10027

(212) 280-4110

OPEN: M-F 9-5 by appointment; closed weekends and holidays
ACCESS: qualified researchers upon application
COPYING FACILITIES: yes
MATERIALS SOLICITED: Original architectural drawings and architects' diaries, journals, and logbooks. Will also accept account books and correspondence of architects.

HOLDINGS:
   Total volume: 30,000 items
   Inclusive dates: 16th century -
   Description: A number of extensive collections concerning American architecture from the late 18th century to the 20th century, including files, drawings, blueprints, and photographs. There are also small collections of English, French, and Italian architectural drawings of the 16th to 19th centuries.

GUIDES: *Catalog of the Avery Memorial Architectural Library* (G. K. Hall, 1968), and *Supplements* (1973, 1975).

SEE: Hamer.

SEE: Hinding.

SEE ALSO: *Architectural Research Materials in New York City: A Guide to Resources in All Five Boroughs* (Committee for the Preservation of Architectural Records, 1977); Harry J. Carman and Arthur W. Thompson, *A Guide to the Principal Sources for American Civilization, 1800-1900, in the City of New York: Manuscripts* (Columbia Univ. Press, 1960).

NY588-825
Columbia University
Libraries
Bakhmeteff Archive of Russian and
   East European History and Culture
535 W. 114th Street
New York NY 10027

(212) 280-3986

OPEN: M-F 9-5; closed weekends and holidays
ACCESS: to qualified scholars on application
COPYING FACILITIES: yes
MATERIALS SOLICITED: Correspondence, manuscripts, documents, and photographs pertaining to Russia, the Soviet Union, and other east European countries; émigrés from these countries; U.S. relations with these countries; and Slavic and east European scholarship in western Europe and America.

HOLDINGS:
   Total volume: 700,000 items
   Inclusive dates: 1600 -
   Description: Materials on Russian history and literature, chiefly in the 19th and 20th centuries; World War I and the revolutionary period in Russia; the cultural, political, and social life of the post-1917 Russian emigrations, particularly in Europe and the U.S.; the development of the Soviet Union; U.S.-Soviet relations; and American and western European scholarship concerning Russia and east Europe. There are also major collections on Poland, Czechoslovakia, Hungary, Yugoslavia, and the Ukraine.

NY588-830
Columbia University
Libraries
Columbiana Collection
210 Low Memorial Library
New York NY 10027

(212) 280-3786

OPEN: M-F 1-5; closed weekends and
holidays
COPYING FACILITIES: yes
MATERIALS SOLICITED: Materials pertaining to the history of Columbia University, and people, projects, and
events associated with it. Will also accept materials relating to affiliated institutions, such as Barnard College and
Teachers College, as well as to New
York City and State.

HOLDINGS:
> *Total volume:* 14,500 vols.; 80 file
cabinets; 24,000 photographs
> *Inclusive dates:* 1754 -
> *Description:* Diaries, records, manu-
scripts, catalogs, faculty and administrators' letters, registers, maps, and photographs dealing with the history and
record of Columbia University from its
founding in 1754 as King's College to its
current administration as Columbia University and affiliated institutions.

SEE: Hamer.

SEE: Hinding.

SEE ALSO: Harry J. Carman and Arthur
W. Thompson, *A Guide to the Principal
Sources for American Civilization,
1800-1900, in the City of New York:
Manuscripts* (Columbia Univ. Press,
1960).

NY588-850
Columbia University
Libraries
Herbert H. Lehman Papers
406 International Affairs Building
420 West 118th Street
New York NY 10027

(212) 280-3060

OPEN: M-F 9-4:30; closed weekends and
holidays
COPYING FACILITIES: yes
MATERIALS SOLICITED: Materials concerning the life and times of Herbert
H. Lehman and the people and institutions with which he was associated.
Will also accept special materials concerning immigration, refugees, civil
rights and liberties, McCarthyism, and
philanthropy.

HOLDINGS:
> *Total volume:* 2,500,000 items
> *Inclusive dates:* 1875 -
> *Description:* Manuscripts, correspon-
dence, films, recordings, oral history transcripts, and other materials regarding
Herbert H. Lehman, including materials
relating to New York government and
politics, civil rights, McCarthyism, and
refugee immigration. Also included are
papers of James G. McDonald and
Charles Poletti, as well as the UN Relief
and Rehabilitation Administration papers
of Sir Robert G. A. Jackson, Hugh Jack-

son, Marshall MacDuffie, and Richard B.
Scandrett.

GUIDES: William B. Liebmann, *The Herbert H. Lehman Papers, An Introduction, Checklist and Guide* (School of
International Affairs, Columbia Univ.,
1968).

SEE: NUCMC, 1974, 78.

SEE: Hinding.

NY588-860
Columbia University
Libraries
Law Library
435 West 116th Street
New York NY 10027

(212) 280-3737

OPEN: M-F 9-4; closed weekends and
holidays
ACCESS: advance arrangements required
COPYING FACILITIES: yes
MATERIALS SOLICITED: Materials per-
taining to the history of the Columbia
University Law School and to interna-
tional war crimes.

HOLDINGS:
> *Total volume:* 370 l.f.
> *Inclusive dates:* not specified
> *Description:* Miscellaneous materials,
including the Patterson papers on New
York insurance law, materials on German and Japanese war crimes during
World War II, papers of John Bassett
Moore relating to international boundary
disputes, and materials documenting the
history of the Columbia University Law
School.

SEE: Hamer.

NY588-900
Columbia University
Libraries
Rare Book and Manuscript Library
801 Butler Library
New York NY 10027

(212) 280-2231, 2232

OPEN: M-F 9-5; closed weekends and
holidays
ACCESS: open to qualified scholars
COPYING FACILITIES: yes
MATERIALS SOLICITED: Materials relating
to American publishing, including literary agents, international relations,
American literature and history, English literature and history, New York
history, history of libraries and librarianship, and New York dramatists and
theater.

HOLDINGS:
> *Total volume:* 10,400,000 items
> *Inclusive dates:* 1450 -
> *Description:* Manuscripts, papers, and
archives relating chiefly to American authors, American publishers and literary
agents, English authors, international affairs organizations, New York political
figures, and émigrés and authors. Included are records of organizations, papers of
individuals, unpublished memoirs, oral
histories, and audiovisual materials.

SEE: Hamer (as Columbia University Libraries, Department of Special Collections); NUCMC, 1959-67, 69-71,
73-75, 77-78, 80.

SEE: Allard, Crawley, and Edmison; Beers
- Confederate; Hinding; Ingram;
Leventhal and Mooney - I; Martin;
Parkinson; Robbins; Spalek.

SEE ALSO: Robert O. Collins and Peter
Duignan, *Americans in Africa* (Hoover
Institution, 1963); Roland Baughman,
'Columbia University's Department of
Special Collections,' *Manuscripts* 15
(Winter 1963); Walter Schatz, ed., *Di-
rectory of Afro-American Resources*
(Bowker, 1970); Peter Duignan, *Hand-
book of American Resources for African
Studies* (Hoover Institution, 1967); David A. Hounshell, comp., *Manuscripts
in U.S. Depositories Relating to the History of Electrical Science and Technology* (Smithsonian Institution, n.d.); Albert Krichmar, *The Women's Rights
Movement in the United States,
1848-1970: A Bibliography and
Sourcebook* (Scarecrow Press, 1972);
*Source Materials for the Recent History
of Astronomy and Astrophysics: A
Checklist of Manuscript Collections in
the United States* (American Institute
of Physics, 1971).

Gerald Friedberg, 'Sources for the Study of
Socialism in America, 1901-1919,' *Labor
History* 6 (Spring 1965); Harry J. Carman
and Arthur W. Thompson, eds., *A Guide
to the Principal Sources for American
Civilization in the City of New York,
1800-1900: Manuscripts* (Columbia Univ.
Press, 1960).

Columbia Library Columns, issued three
times each year, describes recent accessions.

The number of items given above
for the volume of this Library includes the holdings of the Columbiana
Collection, **(NY588-830).**

NY588-940
Columbia University
The Oral History Collection
Box 20
Butler Library
New York NY 10027

(212) 280-2273

OPEN: M-F 9-5; closed weekends and
holidays
COPYING FACILITIES: yes
MATERIALS SOLICITED: United States
National and international affairs,
1940's-1960's; materials relating to
20th century American literature, law,
medicine, music, business, and labor.
Will also accept oral history tapes and
transcripts generated independently if
they are relevant to the Collection's
subject areas of interest.

HOLDINGS:
> *Total volume:* 501,962 pages
> *Inclusive dates:* 1948 -
> *Description:* Oral history relating chief-
ly to United States political, social, and
intellectual history in the 20thcentury.
Major subject areas include Franklin D.
Roosevelt and the New Deal; the Eisenhower administration; the Social Security

system; the development of aviation and broadcasting; organized labor; diplomacy and international affairs; leaders in civil rights, law, medicine, education, and religion; and women pioneers and professionals. Special subject focuses include American historians, Argentina in the 1930's, the Book of the Month Club, the Carnegie Corporation, the League of Nations, the U.S. occupation of Japan, and the World Bank.

GUIDES: Elizabeth B. Mason and Louis M. Starr, eds., *The Oral History Collection of Columbia University* (Oral History Research Office, 1979).

SEE: Hamer (as Columbia University Libraries, Department of Special Collections); NUCMC, 1970, 75.

SEE: Meckler and McMullin; Davis; Schatz; Hinding; Parkinson.

NY588-970
Columbia University
Teachers College
Milbank Memorial Library
Special Collections
525 West 120th Street
New York NY 10027

(212) 678-3031

OPEN: M-F 10-6; closed weekends and holidays
ACCESS: prior arrangements should be made
COPYING FACILITIES: yes
MATERIALS SOLICITED: Education and the history of education and materials related to Teachers College, Columbia University. Will also accept materials concerning nursing and nursing education.

HOLDINGS:
Total volume: 2,700 l.f.
Inclusive dates: 1400 -
Description: Manuscripts, Teachers College Archives teaching materials, scrapbooks, photographs, films, videotapes, audiotapes, and phonograph records. The collection encompasses manuscripts dating back to the Middle Ages, as well as substantial holdings on modern international education.
Teachers College Press is represented by documents relating to authors and publications.
The Nursing Archives and the M. Adelaide Nutting book collection constitute one of the nation's most extensive sources dealing with the development of nursing and nursing education in the United States.

SEE: Hamer; NUCMC, 1979.

SEE: Hinding.

SEE ALSO: *Preliminary Checklist to the Records of the Board of Education of the City of New York* (Teachers College Library, Archives, 1977).

NY589-100
The Cooper Union for the
Advancement of Science and Art
Library
Cooper-Hewitt Collection
Cooper Square
New York NY 10003

(212) 254-6300, Ext. 329

OPEN: M, Tu 9-10, W-F 9-6; closed weekends, holidays, and June-Aug.
ACCESS: graduate students or other legitimate researchers; a letter describing the intended research or a personal interview with the librarian is a prerequisite
COPYING FACILITIES: yes
MATERIALS SOLICITED: Materials by or about the Cooper-Hewitt family, Cooper Union, or its faculty.

HOLDINGS:
Total volume: 15,000 items; 5 l.f.
Inclusive dates: 1783 -
Description: Papers of Peter Cooper and Abram S. Hewitt; partial archives and historical materials on Cooper Union and its students, alumni, and faculty; recordings of addresses and convocations at Cooper Union; and the archives of the People's Institute of New York City, 1910-26.

SEE: Hamer.

NY589-160
Council on Foreign Relations, Inc.
Archives
58 East 68th Street
New York NY 10021

(212) 734-0400

OPEN: M-F 9-5, by appointment; closed weekends, holidays, and Fridays mid-June through Labor Day.
COPYING FACILITIES: yes

HOLDINGS:
Total volume: 23 l.f.
Inclusive dates: 1920 - 1955
Description: Records of the Council's study and discussion groups, meetings with individual speakers, and conferences covering discussions of all aspects of U.S. foreign relations and associated topics.

NY589-200
Culver Pictures, Inc.
150 W. 22nd Street
New York NY 10011

(212) 684-5054

OPEN: M-F 9-5; closed weekends and holidays
USER FEES: sliding scale according to use
ACCESS: appointment required
COPYING FACILITIES: no
MATERIALS SOLICITED: Historic photographs.

HOLDINGS:
Total volume: 9,500,000 items
Inclusive dates: not specified
Description: Photographs, including motion picture stills, and other visual materials dealing with all aspects of human

history. Materials include the Seidman collection.

SEE: Novotny.

NY589-340
Donaldson, Lufkin & Jenrette
Securities Corporation
140 Broadway
New York NY 10005

(212) 504-3000

OPEN: M-F 9-5; closed weekends and holidays
ACCESS: students and scholars
COPYING FACILITIES: yes
MATERIALS SOLICITED: Financial history of the American Revolution.

HOLDINGS:
Total volume: 320 items
Inclusive dates: 1740 - 1790
Description: Materials dealing with the financial history of the American Revolution, including colonial money and examples of bonds used to finance the war.

NY589-460
Engineering Societies Library
345 East 47th Street
New York NY 10017

(212) 705-7611

OPEN: M-Th 9-7, F 9-5; closed weekends and holidays
COPYING FACILITIES: yes
MATERIALS SOLICITED: All fields of engineering, with emphasis on the interests of societies supporting the Library.

HOLDINGS:
Total volume: 250,000 vols.
Inclusive dates: 1473 -
Description: Papers and records, mainly from the American Engineering Council, the American Society of Civil Engineers, the American Society of Mechanical Engineers, and the Tripartite Committee, including unpublished papers presented at meetings of these societies.

SEE: Hamer; NUCMC, 1971.

SEE: Robbins.

SEE ALSO: *Engineering Societies Library Classed Subject Catalog* (G. K. Hall, various dates).

NY589-500
Explorers Club
46 East 70th Street
New York NY 10021

(212) 628-8383

OPEN: by appointment only
COPYING FACILITIES: yes
MATERIALS SOLICITED: Will accept materials of or about Explorers Club members.

HOLDINGS:
Total volume: not specified
Inclusive dates: 1900 -
Description: Papers and correspondence of Explorers Club members; photographs dating from 1900; and a map collection that is concerned with the routes of Club members' explorations.

NY589-560
Ford Foundation
Archives
320 East 43rd Street
New York NY 10017

(212) 573-5231

OPEN: M-F 9-5; closed weekends and
holidays
ACCESS: by written application and
subject to restrictions established by
the Ford Foundation
COPYING FACILITIES: yes
MATERIALS SOLICITED: Ford Foundation
records. Will also accept some records
of organizations previously created by
the Ford Foundation.

HOLDINGS:
Total volume: 1,000 c.f.
Inclusive dates: 1949 -
Description: Records of the Ford
Foundation, consisting of grant records,
logs, correspondence, office files of the
Foundation's programs, reports, and pub-
lications. The materials relate to activities
in the United States, Europe, Asia, Af-
rica, the Middle East, and Latin America.

SEE: Novotny; Robbins.

NY589-580
Fordham University
Library
Bronx NY 10458

(212) 579-2414

OPEN: M-F 9-5; closed weekends and
holidays
ACCESS: advance arrangements with
Reference Department required
COPYING FACILITIES: yes

HOLDINGS:
Total volume: 46 items
Inclusive dates: 1684 - 1877
Description: Materials relating to the
Revolutionary War and early Federal
America, including letters and orderly
books of Revolutionary War leaders.

SEE: Hamer; NUCMC, 1966.

SEE: Robbins.

SEE ALSO: a checklist to the collection is
available in the Library.

NY589-620
Franciscan Friars
Province of the Immaculate
Conception
Archives
147 Thompson Street
New York NY 10012

no telephone

SEE: Hamer.

Questionnaire not returned.

NY589-640
Frederic Lewis, Inc.
134 W. 29th Street
New York NY 10001

(212) 594-8816

OPEN: M-F 9:30-4:30; closed weekends
and holidays
ACCESS: by appointment only
COPYING FACILITIES: no
MATERIALS SOLICITED: Photographs and
other visual documents in all fields.

HOLDINGS:
Total volume: 1,000,000 items
Inclusive dates: ancient times -
Description: Photographs, drawings,
and other visual materials providing gen-
eral subject coverage for the United
States and the world.

SEE: Novotny.

SEE ALSO: A subject index (1980) has
been issued by the institution.

NY589-680
Frick Art Reference Library
10 East 71st Street
New York NY 10021

(212) 288-8700

OPEN: M-F 10-4, Sa 10-12; closed Sa
June-Aug., Su and holidays
ACCESS: students on the graduate level
and adults with a serious interest in art
COPYING FACILITIES: yes

HOLDINGS:
Total volume: 2,398 l.f.
Inclusive dates: 19th century -
Description: Photographs (with documentation) of paintings, drawings, sculpture, and illuminated manuscripts of
western Europe and the United States
from the 4th century A.D. to the 1930's.
There are also diaries of artists G. P. A.
Healy, J. F. Kensett, and Theodore Robinson; a sketchbook of original drawings
by Anton Mauve; and numerous typescripts of publications on art, including
materials relating to the Codman Collection, William Hogarth, and William
Dunlap.

SEE: Hamer.

NY589-690
Gabriel D. Hackett
Photography and Picture Archives
130 West 57th Street
New York NY 10019

(212) 265-6842

OPEN: M-F by appointment only; closed
holidays
ACCESS: by appointment only
COPYING FACILITIES: yes
MATERIALS SOLICITED: U.S. and European history; Czarist and Soviet Russia; historical documentation of music
and arts; religions, especially Jewish
history; American Indians; etc.

HOLDINGS:
Total volume: 150,000 items
Inclusive dates: ancient times -
Description: Photographs and negatives
dealing with historical and social events
and personalities in the United States and
Europe.

SEE: Novotny.

NY589-710
General Theological Seminary
St. Mark's Library
175 Ninth Avenue
New York NY 10011

(212) 243-5150, Ext. 264

OPEN: M-F 9-4; closed weekends,
holidays, and summers
ACCESS: letters of recommendation from
2 bona fide libraries or research
advisors
COPYING FACILITIES: yes
MATERIALS SOLICITED: Materials relating
to the history and theology of the Episcopal church in the United States, including items concerning bishops,
priests, scholars, musicians, and others
active in the church.

HOLDINGS:
Total volume: not specified
Inclusive dates: 1740 - 1960's
Description: A collection of letters, sermons, diaries, and other papers of bishops and other clergy of the American
Episcopal church, as well as papers pertaining to the General Theological Seminary and, more broadly, to the Episcopal
church in the United States.

SEE: Hamer; NUCMC, 1959-62, 65, 76.

SEE: Hinding; Leventhal and Mooney - I.

SEE ALSO: Harry J. Carman and Arthur
W. Thompson, *A Guide to the Principal
Sources for American Civilization,
1800-1900, in the City of New York:
Manuscripts* (Columbia Univ. Press,
1960).

NY589-720
Girl Scouts of the U.S.A.
Library/Archives
830 Third Avenue
New York NY 10022

(212) 940-7500

OPEN: M-F 8:30-4:30; closed weekends
and holidays
ACCESS: academic or literary credentials
required for extensive access to
materials
COPYING FACILITIES: yes
MATERIALS SOLICITED: Will accept all
materials related to Girl Scout history
on a national level and to persons
prominent in scouting, especially Juliette Low.

HOLDINGS:
Total volume: 2,500 l.f.
Inclusive dates: 1912 -
Description: Records of the Girl Scout
organization, including official minutes.
In addition, there are papers of
individuals, oral history tapes, photo-
graphs, and other audiovisual material
documenting the history of the Girl
Scouts as an organization and as a social

movement. Many items relate to Juliette Low, founder of the organization, and to Girl Scout relationships with other youth groups.

SEE: Hinding.

NY589-800
The Granger Collection
1841 Broadway
New York NY 10023

(212) 586-0971

OPEN: M-F 9-5; closed weekends and holidays
ACCESS: qualified researchers by appointment
COPYING FACILITIES: yes
MATERIALS SOLICITED: Pictures of every description relating to political, cultural, and social history.

HOLDINGS:
Total volume: 4,000,000 items
Inclusive dates: 1860 -
Description: Photographs and other visual items covering a broad subject range from prehistoric times to the present.

SEE: Novotny.

NY589-840
The Grolier Club
Library
47 East 60th Street
New York NY 10022

no telephone
SEE: Hamer.

Questionnaire not returned.

NY589-900
Hadassah Women's Zionist Organization of America and Hadassah Medical Relief Association
50 West 58th Street
New York NY 10019

(212) 355-7900

OPEN: M-Th 9-5, F 9-2; closed weekends and holidays, including Jewish holidays
ACCESS: serious researchers, by appointment only
COPYING FACILITIES: yes
MATERIALS SOLICITED: Materials pertaining to Hadassah history, youth activities and Youth Aliyah, the Hadassah Hospital and Medical Center, Henrietta Szold and other leaders of Hadassah, Hadassah Israel Education Services, Hebrew University-Hadassah Medical School, and Hadassah's relationship to the Zionist movement.

HOLDINGS:
Total volume: 600 l.f.; 300 vols.; 300 microfilm reels; 110,000 photographs
Inclusive dates: 1889 -
Description: A collection of letters and other manuscripts, documents, publications, microfilm reels, motion pictures, and audio recordings covering the history of Hadassah's activities in Palestine, Israel, and the United States, and of its chapters, founders, and presidents, including the first president Henrietta Szold. Also included are letters and records relating to Hadassah's youth or-

ganizations and medical organizations, the Jewish National Fund, Hadassah Israel Education Services, Machon Szold, Zionism, Hadassah's relationship to the U.S. government, Arab-Jewish relations, and the British mandate government in Palestine. The picture archives consists of 75,000 color slides and 35,000 black-and-white photographs, mainly of Hadassah personalities and projects.

SEE: Hinding.

NY590-40
Hispanic Society of America
Manuscripts and Rare Books
613 West 155th Street
New York NY 10032

no telephone
SEE: Hamer; NUCMC, 1968-69.

Questionnaire not returned.

NY590-80
The Holland Society of New York
122 East 58th Street
New York NY 10022

(212) 758-1675

OPEN: F 11-4; closed other days, holidays, and during August
COPYING FACILITIES: yes
MATERIALS SOLICITED: Genealogies and historical source materials relating to the Dutch in America. Will also accept manuscripts of scholarly studies and local histories concerning Dutch colonization of New York and New Jersey.

HOLDINGS:
Total volume: 180 l.f.
Inclusive dates: 1630's -
Description: Church records, genealogical materials, and other manuscripts chiefly relating to early Dutch settlers and their descendants in New York, New Jersey, Pennsylvania, and Delaware.

SEE: Hamer.

SEE ALSO: Harry J. Carman and Arthur W. Thompson, *A Guide to the Principal Sources for American Civilization, 1800-1900, in the City of New York: Manuscripts* (Columbia Univ. Press, 1960).

NY590-360
The International Art Registry, Ltd.
111 John Street
New York NY 10038

no telephone

OPEN: M-F 9-5; closed weekends and holidays
COPYING FACILITIES: yes
MATERIALS SOLICITED: Technical information regarding art, antiques, and crafts, including reports about stolen art objects.

HOLDINGS:
Total volume: not specified
Inclusive dates: 1968 -
Description: Photographs, slides, and documentary information relating to 2,500 paintings, sculptures, prints, drawings, antiques, pieces of furniture,

porcelains, and other art objects for which the Registry maintains data files. There are also collections of the International Association of Art Security, Inc., ARTCENTRAL division, containing 12,000 reports about stolen art objects and antiques, compiled by Interpol, the Art Dealers' Association, police agencies, and insurance firms.

NY590-430
International Ladies' Garment Workers' Union
Archives
275 Seventh Avenue
New York NY 10001

(212) 675-4771

OPEN: M-Th 10-4; closed Fridays, weekends, and holidays
ACCESS: appointment required
COPYING FACILITIES: yes
MATERIALS SOLICITED: Materials originated by the ILGWU and its local affiliates, such as correspondence, minutes, photographs, and oral histories. Will also accept manuscripts and other materials relating to the ILGWU.

HOLDINGS:
Total volume: 625 l.f.
Inclusive dates: 1877 -
Description: Materials created by and relating to the International Ladies' Garment Workers' Union. Included are correspondence of Union Presidents, 1914- ; records of affiliated bodies of the Union, such as the New York Cloak Joint Board, the New York Dress Joint Board, the Chicago Area, the Canadian Area, and New York City locals.

Also included are minutes of the General Executive Board, 1900-75; Union publications; oral history interviews; collections pertaining to the Union and to the ladies' garment industry; and materials on Union activities in law and legislation, political action, and international affairs.

NY590-535
J. Walter Thompson Company
Archives
466 Lexington Avenue
New York NY 10017

(212) 210-7124

OPEN: M-F 9-5 by appointment; closed weekends and holidays
COPYING FACILITIES: yes

HOLDINGS:
Total volume: 1,000 l.f.
Inclusive dates: 1864 -
Description: Archives of the J. Walter Thompson Company, one of the oldest and largest advertising agencies in the world. Included are records documenting the history of the company; biographical information on and speeches and writings of former executives and staff members; microfilmed records; proofs of advertisements; company newsletters and publications; photographs; and scrapbooks.

NY590-680

Jewish Theological Seminary of
    America
Library
3080 Broadway
New York NY 10027

(212) 678-8075

OPEN: M-F 9-5; closed weekends and
    Jewish and legal holidays
ACCESS: serious researchers
COPYING FACILITIES: yes
MATERIALS SOLICITED: Materials dealing
    with the history of the Conservative
    Jewish movement and the Jewish The-
    ological Seminary. Will also accept re-
    lated historical material, particularly
    that dealing with the history of Jewish
    scholarship in the 19th and 20th cen-
    turies.

HOLDINGS:
    Total volume: 115 file drawers; 200
    boxes
        Inclusive dates: 1450 -
        Description: Personal files and materi-
        als of Jewish scholars, rabbis, writers, and
        other individuals; materials relating to
        Jewish communities, communal organiza-
        tions, and family history in Europe, the
        Middle East, and the United States; cor-
        respondence of key figures in the
        German-Jewish Wissenschaft of the 19th
        century; and photographs, maps, and
        drawings relating to Jewish subjects.

SEE: Hamer.

SEE: Ingram; Martin.

SEE ALSO: Philip P. Mason, ed., *Directory
    of Jewish Archival Institutions* (Wayne
    State Univ. Press, 1975).

NY590-700

Joseph Pilsudski Institute of America
    for Research in Modern History of
    Poland, Inc.
381 Park Avenue South
New York NY 10016

(212) 683-4342

OPEN: M-F 10-3; closed weekends and
    holidays
COPYING FACILITIES: yes
MATERIALS SOLICITED: Materials relating
    to the history of Poland after 1861, the
    Polish-American community, and the
    history of the Ukraine, Lithuania, Lat-
    via, Byelorussia, and Czechoslovakia.
    Will also accept materials relating to
    20th century history and international
    relations and the history of Russia and
    Germany.

HOLDINGS:
    Total volume: 570 l.f.; 708 microfilm
    reels
        Inclusive dates: 1861 -
        Description: Records and documents
        relating to late 19th century and 20th
        century political and social history of Po-
        land, the Polish-American community,
        and some eastern European nations
        neighboring Poland. Included are records
        of organizations, state agencies, embas-
        sies, photographs, maps, films, and pa-
        pers of individuals documenting military
        and political developments, international
        relations, political ideologies, migrations,

revolutionary upheavals, resistance movements, and war relief.

SEE: NUCMC, 1972.

SEE ALSO: K. Szwedowicz,
'Trzydziestolecie Instytutu Jozefa
Pilsudskiego w Nowym Jorku,' *Kultura*
12 (1973); M. Fudala, 'Polacy w
rozwoju nauki amerykamskiej,' *Numer
specjalny* (Krajowa Agencja
Informacyjna, 1976). The Institute issues an annual report and has prepared
an historical outline of its work covering the years 1943 to 1973. A mimeographed guide to the holdings will be
sent upon request.

NY590-720

The Juilliard School
The Lila Acheson Wallace Library
Lincoln Center
New York NY 10023

(212) 799-5000

OPEN: M-Th 9-9, F 9-5, Sa 9-4; closed
    Sundays, holidays, and July - Aug.
ACCESS: qualified researchers, by
    permission of librarian
COPYING FACILITIES: yes
MATERIALS SOLICITED: Materials per-
    taining to music, drama and theater,
    and dance. Will also accept fine arts
    and humanities materials.

HOLDINGS:
    Total volume: 30 l.f.
    Inclusive dates: 1750 -
    Description: Manuscripts, including
    correspondence of European and Ameri-
    can musicians, chiefly of the 19th and
    20th centuries, and holograph music
    scores, principally 20th century Ameri-
    can; the archives of the Institute of Musi-
    cal Art, predecessor of the Juilliard
    School, 1905-45, including catalogs,
    records of enrollment and grades, pro-
    grams of music concerts, brochures, and
    master's theses in music education; and
    photographs of late 19th century German
    and German-American musicians and of
    American musicians of the 20th century,
    primarily New York artists and the fac-
    ulty of the Institute of Musical Art and
    the Juilliard School.

SEE: Hinding; Robbins.

NY590-740

Archive for Research in Archetypal
    Symbolism
28 East 39th Street
New York NY 10016

(212) 697-3480

OPEN: M 1:15-8:45, Tu-F 10:15-5:45;
    closed weekends and holidays
COPYING FACILITIES: yes

HOLDINGS:
    Total volume: 13,000 items
    Inclusive dates: 20th century
    Description: Photographs and clippings
    of photographs of works of art created
    from paleolithic times to the present day
    having archetypal imagery and relating to
    C. G. Jung's concept of the collective
    unconscious.

NY590-760

Kingsborough Historical Society
Kingsborough Community College
2001 Oriental Boulevard
Brooklyn NY 11235

no telephone

OPEN: M-Th 11-4 and by appointment;
    closed F-Su
ACCESS: appointments preferred
COPYING FACILITIES: yes
MATERIALS SOLICITED: Photographs and
    memorabilia on Coney Island, Manhat-
    tan Beach, Gravesend, Sheepshead Bay,
    Gerritsen Beach, and Floyd Bennett
    Field. Will also accept newspaper
    clippings, music, and motion pictures
    relating to these areas.

HOLDINGS:
    Total volume: 3,000 items
    Inclusive dates: 1890 -
    Description: Photographs tracing
    changes in the southern Brooklyn shore
    area, showing the rise and fall of Coney
    Island; the progressive change of Manhat-
    tan Beach from an exclusive resort to
    baths to use as a military installation to
    its current community status; the devel-
    opment of Sheepshead Bay as a fishing
    community; and the transition of
    Gravesend from a colony to a commu-
    nity.

NY590-840

Leo Baeck Institute, Inc.
Archives Division
129 East 73rd Street
New York NY 10021

(212) 744-6400

OPEN: M 9:30-8, Tu-Th 9:30-4:30, F
    9:30-3; closed weekends, holidays, and
    during August except by appointment
COPYING FACILITIES: yes
MATERIALS SOLICITED: Materials per-
    taining to the history, literature, and
    political, economic, and intellectual life
    of German-speaking Jewry in Central
    Europe from the 17th century to the
    period immediately after World War II.
    Will also accept materials pertaining to
    German-speaking Jews of Central
    Europe during other periods.

HOLDINGS:
    Total volume: 900 l.f.
    Inclusive dates: 1480 -
    Description: About 2,500 collections
    concerning the history and literature of
    Jews in German-speaking central Europe.
    The collections are especially strong in
    genealogy, the history of Jewish commu-
    nities, and literary and intellectual life of
    the 19th and 20th centuries. Included are
    personal and family papers, communal
    records and government documents, and
    family trees and other genealogical ma-
    terials. There are also several hundred
    memoirs, literary manuscripts, large col-
    lections of photographs, music-related col-
    lections, and architectural plans.

SEE: NUCMC, 1970-72, 75, 78.

SEE: Spalek.

SEE ALSO: Max Kreutzberger and Irmgard Foerg, *Leo Baeck Institut, New York, Bibliothek und Archiv: Katalog* (1970); Philip P. Mason, ed., *Directory of Jewish Archival Institutions* (Wayne State Univ. Press, 1975); *Inventory List of Archival Collections* (Leo Baeck Institute, 1971 and 1976); Margarete Edelheim-Muehsam, 'Das Archiv des Leo Baeck Instituts, New York,' *Bulletin des Leo Baeck Instituts* 3 (1960); Max Kreutzberger, 'The Library and Archives of the Leo Baeck Institute in New York,' *Jewish Book Annual* 29 (1971-72); Sybil Milton, 'Die Quellen zur Geschichte der Deutschen Arbeiterbewegung im Leo Baeck Institut, New York,' *Internationale Wissenschaftliche Korrespondenz zur Geschichte der Deutschen Arbeiterbewegung* 2 (June 1975).

Architectural Research Materials in New York City: A Guide to Resources in All Five Boroughs (Committee for the Preservation of Architectural Records, 1977); Janet Hadda, 'The Leo Baeck Institute,' *The Germanic Review* 1 (Nov. 1975); Ernest Hamburger, 'Das Leo Baeck Institute,' *Geschichte in Wissenschaft und Unterricht* (1970); Jacob Robinson and Philip Friedman, *Guide to Jewish History Under Nazi Impact* (YIVO Institute for Jewish Research and Yad Vashem Martyrs' and Heroes' Memorial Authority, Joint Documentary Projects, 1960); and many articles in *LBI Library and Archive News*.

NY590-940

The Long Island Historical Society
128 Pierrepont Street
Brooklyn NY 11201

(718) 624-0890

OPEN: Tu-Sa 9-5; closed Sundays, Mondays, and holidays
USER FEES: one dollar per day
ACCESS: graduate level students or researchers with credentials
COPYING FACILITIES: yes
MATERIALS SOLICITED: Materials reflecting Brooklyn and Long Island history and personalities, early Indian deeds, Brooklyn commercial and business records, and genealogical materials. Will also accept records or manuscripts relating to New York City and State, New England, and other adjacent areas that have some bearing on Long Island families or institutions.

HOLDINGS:
 Total volume: 600 l.f.
 Inclusive dates: 1650 -
 Description: A collection primarily covering the history of Brooklyn and Long Island, including papers and journals of individuals; early deeds; manuscript maps; genealogical manuscripts; architectural drawings; photographs; records of organizations, churches, and businesses; and oral history tapes.

SEE: Hamer.

SEE: Gehring; Leventhal and Mooney - I; Hinding; Spalek; Robbins.

SEE ALSO: Ann Novotny, ed., *Picture Sources 3* (Special Libraries Assn., 1975); *Map Collections in the United States and Canada, A Directory* (Special Libraries Assn., 1970); Harry J. Carman and Arthur W. Thompson, *A Guide to the Principal Sources for American Civilization, 1800-1900, in the City of New York: Manuscripts* (Columbia Univ. Press, 1960); Walton H. Rawls, ed., *The Century Book of the Long Island Historical Society* (Long Island Historical Society, 1964); and accession notices in *The Journal of Long Island History* (1961-69, 1973-).

NY590-960

Long Island University
Brooklyn Center
Library
Archives Department
University Plaza
Brooklyn NY 11201

(718) 834-6000, Ext. 2186, 2187

OPEN: Su 1-5, M, Tu 9-10, W, Th 9-9, F 9-5, Sa 10-4; closed holidays, Fridays, and some weekends in summer
COPYING FACILITIES: yes
MATERIALS SOLICITED: Archives of Brooklyn institutions. Will also accept letters, diaries, tape recordings, photographs, drawings, and maps relating to the New York metropolitan area.

HOLDINGS:
 Total volume: 300 c.f.
 Inclusive dates: 1895 -
 Description: The Robert Weinberg papers relating to architecture and urban design, 1945-74, and the Heller Collection of 3,000 photographs of the construction of railroad and rapid transit lines in the New York metropolitan area, 1895-1943.

SEE: Hinding.

NY591-35

Lutheran Church in America
Metropolitan New York Synod
Archives
Wagner College
360 Park Avenue South
New York NY 10010

(212) 532-6350

OPEN: by appointment only
ACCESS: serious researchers
COPYING FACILITIES: yes
MATERIALS SOLICITED: Records and papers of the Metropolitan New York Synod and its congregations and pastors. Will also accept important items relating to the Lutheran church in New York.

HOLDINGS:
 Total volume: 400 l.f.
 Inclusive dates: 1649 -
 Description: Materials relating to the Lutheran church in New Netherland, New York, New Jersey, and New England from the colonial period to 1960, and in the New York City metropolitan area after 1960. Included are biographical and historical items concerning clergy and congregations, records of defunct congregations, minutes of the Synod and

its committees, manuscript research studies, Synod correspondence, and diaries of church leaders.

NY591-40

Lutheran Council in the USA
Archives of Cooperative Lutheranism
360 Park Avenue South
New York NY 10010

(212) 532-6350

OPEN: M-F 8:30-4:30; closed weekends and holidays
ACCESS: restricted to scholars and students
COPYING FACILITIES: yes
MATERIALS SOLICITED: Archives of Lutheran cooperative organizations apart from the church bodies themselves.

HOLDINGS:
 Total volume: 750 l.f.
 Inclusive dates: 1910 -
 Description: Minutes, reports, documents, correspondence, publications, photographs, films, biographies of 33 record groups of cooperative inter-Lutheran work such as the Lutheran Council and Lutheran World Relief. An oral history collection of 65 memoirs, with the program still continuing, covers all the record groups.

NY591-100

Manhattan College
Cardinal Hayes Library
Manhattan College Parkway
Bronx NY 10471

no telephone

SEE: Hamer; NUCMC, 1966.

Questionnaire not returned.

NY591-140

Mannes College of Music
Library
150 W. 85th Street
New York NY 10024

(212) 580-0210, Ext. 31, 32

OPEN: M-F 9-6, Sa 9-3; closed Sundays, holidays, and August
COPYING FACILITIES: no
MATERIALS SOLICITED: Music manuscripts of Leopold Mannes.

HOLDINGS:
 Total volume: 3 l.f.
 Inclusive dates: early 1900's - 1959
 Description: Music manuscripts of David Mannes.

NY591-240

Medical Research Library of Brooklyn
450 Clarkson Avenue
Brooklyn NY 11203

no telephone

SEE: Hamer; NUCMC, 1966 (as Academy of Medicine of Brooklyn, Library).

Questionnaire not returned.

NY591-350

The Metropolitan Museum of Art
Department of Prints and
  Photographs
Fifth Avenue and 82nd Street
New York NY 10028

(212) 570-3920

OPEN: Tu-F 2-5; closed Mondays,
  weekends, and holidays
ACCESS: by appointment only to
  qualified researchers
COPYING FACILITIES: yes
MATERIALS SOLICITED: Drawings and
  photographs in the subject area of the
  collection.

HOLDINGS:
> Total volume: not specified
> Inclusive dates: 1465 -
> Description: A small collection of pho-
> tographs and drawings relating to Ameri-
> can and European architecture, interior
> design, furniture, costume, industrial de-
> sign, and transportation.

SEE: Novotny.

SEE ALSO: Architectural Research Materials in New York City: A Guide to Resources in All Five Boroughs
(Committee for the Preservation of Architectural Records, 1977).

NY591-380

The Metropolitan Museum of Art
Thomas J. Watson Library
Fifth Avenue and 82nd Street
New York NY 10028

(212) 879-5500

OPEN: Tu-F 10-4:45; closed weekends,
  Mondays, and holidays
ACCESS: qualified scholars and graduate
  students; appointment required
COPYING FACILITIES: yes

HOLDINGS:
> Total volume: not specified
> Inclusive dates: 18th century -
> Description: Miscellaneous personal pa-
> pers of artists and architects, American
> and foreign, including letters, diaries,
> sketchbooks, and notebooks, as well as
> papers pertaining to the history of the
> Museum.

SEE: Hamer; NUCMC, 1959-61, 68.

SEE: Robbins.

NY591-420

Metropolitan Opera Association
Metropolitan Opera Archives
Metropolitan Opera House
Lincoln Center, B9
New York NY 10023

(212) 799-3100, Ext. 2525

OPEN: Tu-Th 11-5:30 by appointment;
  closed other days and holidays
ACCESS: advanced students, authors,
  publishers, and serious fans;
  identification required
COPYING FACILITIES: yes
MATERIALS SOLICITED: Information on
  names, roles, and performance dates of
  Metropolitan Opera singers and musicians. Will also accept other items, including photographs and clipping books
of former Metropolitan Opera singers.

HOLDINGS:
> Total volume: 1,000 l.f.; 165 file
> drawers
> Inclusive dates: 1883 -
> Description: Archival materials relating
> to the history of the Metropolitan Opera,
> including card files on all Metropolitan
> artists, orchestra players, dancers, and
> choristers; performance programs and
> press clippings; and floor plans.

SEE: Spalek; Hinding.

SEE ALSO: Mary Ellis Peltz, 'The Metropolitan Opera Archives,' American Archivist 30 (July 1967); Ann Novotny,
ed., Picture Sources 3 (Special Libraries
Assn., 1975).

NY591-500

Missionary Research Library
3041 Broadway
New York NY 10027

SEE: Hamer; NUCMC, 1967.

Questionnaire not returned.

NY591-600

Mount Sinai School of Medicine
Archive
Annenberg Building 10-31
One Gustave Levy Place
New York NY 10029

(212) 860-9544

OPEN: M-F by appointment only; closed
  weekends and holidays
ACCESS: advance arrangement required
COPYING FACILITIES: yes
MATERIALS SOLICITED: Materials relating
  to the history of Mount Sinai Medical
  Center, including documents on the
  history of medicine and medical education, such as photographs, public documents, letters, and audiovisual materials, and materials relating to the teaching of the history of medicine, including slides, films, and bibliographic materials.

HOLDINGS:
> Total volume: not specified
> Inclusive dates: 1852 -
> Description: Materials relating to the
> history of Mount Sinai Hospital and
> School of Medicine and to the teaching
> of the history of medicine. Included are
> oral history tapes and transcripts.

SEE: Meckler and McMullin.

NY591-690

The Museum of Broadcasting
1 East 53rd Street
New York NY 10022

(212) 752-4690

OPEN: Tu-Sa noon-5; closed Sundays,
  Mondays, and holidays
USER FEES: membership (variable rates)
  suggested, or nonmember contribution
  of $1.50
COPYING FACILITIES: no
MATERIALS SOLICITED: Landmark network broadcasts, 1920's to date. Will
also accept other radio and television
scripts and transcripts.

HOLDINGS:
> Total volume: 4,215 videotapes;
> 3,648 audiotapes
> Inclusive dates: 1918 -
> Description: Radio and television pro-
> grams, including full broadcast days, such
> as V-J Day and President Jimmy Carter's
> inauguration day. There are propaganda
> broadcasts made by Americans and Eng-
> lish working for the Axis powers;
> 'Columbia Workshop' and 'One World
> Flight' series; examples of the 1937
> 'Shakespeare War;' the earliest 'Amos 'n'
> Andy' program; radio coverage of Lind-
> bergh's return to the U.S. in 1927; and a
> sampling of popular comedy and musical
> variety programs of the 1930's and
> 1940's.
>
> Television programs include many
> drawn from the first five years of net-
> work television broadcasting, 1948-53,
> such as 'Studio One,' and 'Omnibus,' as
> well as classic comedy routines of Bert
> Lahr, Lucille Ball, Beatrice Lillie, Ernie
> Kovacs, and Jack Benny.

NY591-700

The Museum of Modern Art
Photographic Archives
11 West 53rd Street
New York NY 10019

(212) 708-9459

OPEN: M-F 11-5; closed weekends
ACCESS: serious scholars, authors,
  publishers, and photographic
  researchers
COPYING FACILITIES: no

HOLDINGS:
> Total volume: 175,000 photographs
> Inclusive dates: 1880 -
> Description: Photographs documenting
> the Museum's collections and exhibitions
> of 20th century art, including photo-
> graphs of Museum exhibitions.

SEE: Novotny.

NY591-760

Museum of Modern Art
Film Study Center
11 West 53rd Street
New York NY 10019

(212) 708-9614

OPEN: M-F 1-5; closed weekends and
  holidays
USER FEES: fee for projection of films
ACCESS: qualified researchers; by
  appointment
COPYING FACILITIES: yes
MATERIALS SOLICITED: Materials per-
  taining to motion pictures.

HOLDINGS:
> Total volume: not specified
> Inclusive dates: 1890 -
> Description: Manuscripts relating to
> motion pictures, including personal pa-
> pers of D. W. Griffith and some of his
> associates, correspondence and manu-
> scripts of Merritt Crawford on early film
> pioneers, and some scripts. Included is a

major collection of original motion pictures and still photographs.

SEE ALSO: Charles Silver, 'Using MOMA,' *American Film* 1 (May 1976); Ann Novotny, ed., *Picture Sources 3* (Special Libraries Assn., 1975).

NY591-780
Museum of Modern Art
Library
11 West 53rd Street
New York NY 10019

(212) 708-9431

OPEN: M-F 1-5; closed weekends and holidays
ACCESS: accredited scholars upon written application, and with donor's written permission
COPYING FACILITIES: yes
MATERIALS SOLICITED: Material pertaining to contemporary art and artists.

HOLDINGS:
> *Total volume:* not specified
> *Inclusive dates:* 1880 -
> *Description:* Collection of manuscripts, correspondence, and photographs relating to modern art, American as well as international.
> There are also over 600 audiotapes dating from 1952 that include interviews with artists, symposia, and lectures.

SEE: Spalek.

NY591-820
Museum of the American Indian, Heye Foundation
Huntington Free Library and Reading Room
9 Westchester Square
Bronx NY

MAILING ADDRESS:
Broadway and 155th Street
New York NY 10032

(212) 829-7770

OPEN: M-Sa by appointment
ACCESS: call one day in advance for appointment
COPYING FACILITIES: yes
MATERIALS SOLICITED: Archaeology and ethnology of Native Americans in the Western Hemisphere. Will also accept photographs, manuscripts, and records relating to New York City history, and photographs of and manuscripts relating to American Indians.

HOLDINGS:
> *Total volume:* 300 items
> *Inclusive dates:* 1800 - 1965
> *Description:* Manuscripts relating to American Indians, Eskimos, and Aleuts, especially in the fields of archaeology, history, ethnology, and current events. Also included are anthropological papers from major university studies.

SEE: NUCMC, 1962.

SEE: Ingram; Bean and Vane.

SEE ALSO: *Dictionary Catalog of the American Indian Collection in the Huntington Free Library and Reading Room* 4 vols. (G. K. Hall, 1977).

NY591-840
Museum of the City of New York
Library
Fifth Avenue and 103rd Street
New York NY 10029

(212) 534-1672

OPEN: M-F by appointment; closed weekends and holidays
COPYING FACILITIES: yes

HOLDINGS:
> *Total volume:* 40,000 items
> *Inclusive dates:* 1626 -
> *Description:* A collection of letters, deeds, certificates, bills, account books, and other papers dealing with the history of New York City, with emphasis on prominent families of the 18th and 19th centuries.

SEE: Hamer; NUCMC, 1959-61, 70.

SEE: Robbins; Hinding; Spalek; Gehring; Leventhal and Mooney - I.

NY591-850
Museum of the City of New York
Theatre and Music Collection
Fifth Avenue at 103rd Street
New York NY 10029

(212) 534-1672

OPEN: Tu-F 10-4:45; closed Mondays, weekends, and holidays
USER FEES: by donation only
ACCESS: qualified researchers by appointment only
COPYING FACILITIES: yes
MATERIALS SOLICITED: Photographs documenting the history of the theater in New York City. Will also accept related personal papers and records, scripts, music scores in manuscript, and correspondence.

HOLDINGS:
> *Total volume:* not specified
> *Inclusive dates:* 1785 -
> *Description:* Materials tracing the history of the theater in New York City, including files pertaining to theatrical productions and personnel, a special Yiddish theater collection, the Dazian Library of Theatrical Design, playscripts, and several hundred thousand photographs.

SEE: Novotny.

NY591-920
National Academy of Design
1083 Fifth Avenue
New York NY 10028

(212) 369-4880

OPEN: by appointment only
COPYING FACILITIES: yes

HOLDINGS:
> *Total volume:* not specified
> *Inclusive dates:* 1825 -
> *Description:* Materials relating to the history of the National Academy of Design and its members and exhibitions, such as administrative records, exhibition records, and biographical data. There are also materials relating to other aspects of American art, specifically painting, sculpture, and the graphic arts.

SEE: Hinding.

NY592-20
National Audubon Society
Library
950 Third Avenue
New York NY 10022

(212) 546-9100, 832-3200

OPEN: M-F by appointment; closed weekends and holidays

SEE: Hamer; NUCMC, 1959-61.

Questionnaire not returned.

NY592-30
National Board of the Young Women's Christian Association of the United States of America
Archives
726 Broadway
New York NY 10003

(212) 614-2716

OPEN: M-F 9:30-4; closed weekends and holidays
ACCESS: by appointment
COPYING FACILITIES: no
MATERIALS SOLICITED: Official records of the National Board YWCA, personal papers of National Board members that relate to the YWCA and its purpose, and personal papers of National Board staff members. Will also accept papers that relate to the programs of the YWCA and its place in the United States and the world, and community papers within specified limitations.

HOLDINGS:
> *Total volume:* 345 microfilm reels
> *Inclusive dates:* 1875 - 1970
> *Description:* Records of the National Board of the Young Women's Christian Association of the United States of America. Included are personal papers of and material relating to the National Board's members and staff. The holdings document the development of the YWCA and its work in the United States and abroad, especially Africa, China, Japan, the Middle East, Central America, and South America, in the areas of employment of women, health, housing, human relations, immigration, labor and industrial relations, family relations, public affairs, racial justice, social work, the United Service Organization, vocational guidance, volunteer training, and women's service during World Wars I and II.

SEE: Schatz.

NY592-260
The New York Academy of Medicine
Library
Malloch Rare Book and History of Medicine Room
2 East 103rd Street
New York NY 10029

(212) 876-8200

OPEN: M-F 9-5; closed weekends and holidays

ACCESS: for access to records of a medical society, written permission of an officer required
COPYING FACILITIES: yes
MATERIALS SOLICITED: Materials concerning medicine, public health, dentistry, and nursing. Will also accept allied health sciences material.

HOLDINGS:
Total volume: 6,535 items
Inclusive dates: 9th century -
Description: Manuscript collection relating chiefly to medicine in Europe and the United States. Included are 18 medieval and Renaissance medical manuscripts, diaries, and correspondence, as well as lecture notes, collections of recipes, case books, diplomas, and records of medical societies and hospitals, especially of the New York area.

GUIDES: *Subject Catalog of the Library of the New York Academy of Medicine* (G. K. Hall, 1969) and *First Supplement* (1974); *Author Catalog of the New York Academy of Medicine* (G. K. Hall, 1969) and *First Supplement* (1974); and *Illustration Catalog of the New York Academy of Medicine* (G. K. Hall, 1976).

SEE: Hamer; NUCMC, 1959-61, 68.

SEE: Hinding; Leventhal and Mooney - I.

SEE ALSO: Ann Novotny, ed., *Picture Sources 3* (Special Libraries Assn., 1975); Harry J. Carman and Arthur W. Thompson, *A Guide to the Principal Sources for American Civilization, 1800-1900, in the City of New York: Manuscripts* (Columbia Univ. Press, 1960).

NY592-280

New York Academy of Sciences
2 East 63rd Street
New York NY 10021

(212) 838-0230

OPEN: M-F 10-4; closed weekends and holidays
COPYING FACILITIES: yes

HOLDINGS:
Total volume: 160 vols.
Inclusive dates: 1817 -
Description: Minutes, correspondence, and other materials relating to the history of the Academy and of science in New York.

NY592-320

The New York Botanical Garden
Library
Manuscripts and Archives
Bronx NY 10548

(212) 220-8749

OPEN: M-F 1-4; closed weekends and holidays
ACCESS: advance arrangements suggested
COPYING FACILITIES: yes
MATERIALS SOLICITED: Botany, horticulture, gardening, greenhouse/conservatory technology and history, landscape architecture.

HOLDINGS:
Total volume: 400,681 items
Inclusive dates: 1700 -
Description: Materials relating chiefly to the institutional history of the New York Botanical Garden and to 20th century botanical researchers, but also including letters and manuscripts of John Torrey, Charles Darwin, and other 19th century scientists and botanists.
Included are noninstitutional collections, such as records of the Torrey Botanical Club, the American Society of Plant Taxonomists, and the Society for Economic Botany; and business and architectural records (1880-1930) of The Lord and Burnham Corporation, manufacturers of conservatories. The collections include botanical artworks and glass plate negatives.

GUIDES: Steven P. Johnson and Terry Collins, comps., *Guide to the Archives and Manuscripts of the New York Botanical Garden* (Nicholas T. Smith and New York Botanical Garden, 1982); Sara Lenley, et al., *Catalog of the Manuscript and Archival Collection and Index to the Correspondence of John Torrey* (G. K. Hall, 1973).

SEE: Hamer.

SEE: Davis; Hinding.

SEE ALSO: Harry J. Carman and Arthur W. Thompson, *A Guide to the Principal Sources for American Civilization, 1800-1900, in the City of New York: Manuscripts* (Columbia Univ. Press, 1960); Ann Novotny, ed., *Picture Sources 3* (Special Libraries Assn., 1975).

NY592-350

New York City Department of Records and Information Services
Division of Municipal Archives
31 Chambers Street
New York NY 10007

(212) 566-5292

OPEN: M-F 9:30-4:30; closed weekends and holidays
COPYING FACILITIES: yes
MATERIALS SOLICITED: Official records of the government of the City of New York having historic, cultural, or social import, including mayoral campaign materials, working papers of charter revisions, and selected collections of organizations or individuals closely related to city government.

HOLDINGS:
Total volume: 75,000 c.f.
Inclusive dates: 17th century -
Description: Official records of the City of New York including, Mayors' papers, 1838 to present; records of agencies, such as Almshouse, Department of Building, and Board of Education; financial records of the City of New York generated by the Office of the Comptroller; records of the Common Council/Board of Aldermen/City Council; and records of the Police Court, Magistrates' Court, Special and General Sessions Courts, and Manhattan and Brooklyn District Attorney's Office papers.

Special collections include the Brooklyn Bridge Drawings Collections, 1875 to 1920; manuscripts of the New York City Unit of the Federal Writers Project of the WPA; vital records (birth, death, and marriage, 1795 to 1898); police census, Manhattan only, 1890; and photographic collections.

SEE: Hamer.

NY592-420

New York County
County Clerk and Clerk of the Supreme Court
Division of Old Records
31 Chambers Street
New York NY

MAILING ADDRESS:
60 Centre Street
Room 161
New York NY 10007

(212) 374-4376, 4781

OPEN: M, W, F by appointment, Tu, Th 9-5; closed weekends and holidays
COPYING FACILITIES: yes
MATERIALS SOLICITED: Records of the Supreme Court, Civil and Criminal, in New York County and the six predecessor courts whose jurisdiction was merged into that of the Supreme Court; and business records of New York-based firms that should have been filed with the County Clerk since the inception of that requirement, ca. 1785.

HOLDINGS:
Total volume: 17,000 c.f.
Inclusive dates: 1674 - 1910
Description: Primarily records generated by the Supreme Court, Civil and Criminal, in New York County (New York City before 1898, Manhattan after 1898) and its six predecessor courts whose jurisdiction was merged into that of the Supreme Court. Spanning the years 1674 to 1910, these predecessor courts included: Mayor's Court, Supreme Court of Judicature, Court of Chancery, Superior Court, Court of Oyer and Terminer, and Court of General Sessions of the Peace.
Among the record series of these courts are minute books, judgments, pleas, affidavits, bonds, various motions, and naturalization papers. In addition, certificates of incorporation, business partnerships, bankruptcies, and other business papers filed with the County Clerk since 1785 are included among the record groups.

NY592-440

New York Genealogical and Biographical Society
122 East 58th Street
New York NY 10022

(212) 755-8532

OPEN: M-F 9:30-5, Sa 9:30-5 Oct.-May; closed Sundays, holidays, Aug.
ACCESS: members only
COPYING FACILITIES: yes
MATERIALS SOLICITED: Materials pertaining to genealogy and local history, especially that of New York City and State and surrounding areas; early

church records; family Bible records; and family histories.

HOLDINGS:
Total volume: 22,811 items
Inclusive dates: 17th century -
Description: Manuscripts consist of bound church, cemetery, family, and town records; a vertical file of family, Bible, and miscellaneous genealogical data; and archival collections of family research. The geographical emphasis is on New York City and New York State, with representation in essentially eastern states, from the 17th through 19th centuries in America.

SEE: Hamer; NUCMC, 1976.

SEE: Gehring; Leventhal and Mooney - I.

NY592-460
New-York Historical Society
Manuscript Department
170 Central Park West
New York NY 10024

(212) 873-3400

OPEN: Tu-Sa 10-5; closed Sundays, Mondays, and holidays
USER FEES: one dollar for nonmembers
ACCESS: graduate students and other scholars with approval of curator
COPYING FACILITIES: yes
MATERIALS SOLICITED: Materials pertaining to all aspects of the history of New York City and State.

HOLDINGS:
Total volume: 1,000,000 items
Inclusive dates: 1492 -
Description: Materials pertaining to the history of New York City and State, including art and architecture, religion and church history, law, daily urban and rural life, trade, slavery, Indians, entertainment, shipping, education, banking and finance, poetry and literature, trades and crafts, politics, Americans abroad, military and naval history, and many other areas.

GUIDES: Arthur J. Breton, *A Guide to the Manuscript Collections of the New York Historical Society* (Greenwood Press, 1972).

SEE: Hamer; NUCMC, 1959-67, 69-74, 76-77, 80.

SEE: Davis; Hinding; Robbins; Allard, Crawley, and Edmison; Parkinson; Bean and Vane; Ingram; Beers - Southwest; Beers - Confederate; Gehring; Levanthal and Mooney - I.

SEE ALSO: Harry J. Carman and Arthur W. Thompson, *A Guide to the Principal Sources for American Civilization, 1800-1900, in the City of New York: Manuscripts* (Columbia Univ. Press, 1960); James M. Merrill, 'The Naval Historian and His Sources,' *Source Materials for the Recent History of Astronomy and Astrophysics: A Checklist of Manuscript Collections in the United States* (American Institute of Physics, 1971).

NY592-480
New York Hospital-Cornell Medical Center
Medical Archives
1300 York Avenue
New York NY 10021

(212) 472-5759, 5760

OPEN: M-F 9-5; closed weekends and holidays
COPYING FACILITIES: yes
MATERIALS SOLICITED: Records of the institutions that make up the Medical Center and of people associated with the Center. Will also accept materials on the history of medicine in America, particularly New York, or that support the Archives collection.

HOLDINGS:
Total volume: 2,300 l.f.
Inclusive dates: 1769 -
Description: Records of member institutions of the New York Hospital-Cornell Medical Center, including the New York Hospital, the Cornell University Medical College, the Cornell University-New York Hospital School of Nursing, the Lying-In Hospital of New York, and the Manhattan Maternity and Dispensary, as well as papers of physicians and researchers connected with these institutions. Included are administrative records, financial data, medical case books, architectural specifications, student notebooks, minute books, photographs, oral history tapes, and motion pictures.
Also held are records of the New York Asylum for Lying-In Women, the New York Infant Asylum, and the New York Nursery and Child's Hospital.

GUIDES: Adele A. Lerner, *An Introduction to the Medical Archives, the New York Hospital-Cornell Medical Center* (1976).

SEE: NUCMC, 1980.

SEE: Hinding.

SEE ALSO: *Architectural Research Materials in New York City: A Guide to Resources in All Five Boroughs* (Committee for the Preservation of Architectural Records, 1977).

NY592-540
New York Law Institute
Library
120 Broadway
New York NY 10005

(212) 732-8720

SEE: Hamer; NUCMC, 1965.

Questionnaire not returned.

NY592-580
New York Life Insurance Company
Archives
51 Madison Avenue
New York NY 10010

(212) 576-5036

OPEN: M-F 9-4:30; closed weekends and holidays
ACCESS: qualified researchers with permission; appointment required
COPYING FACILITIES: yes

MATERIALS SOLICITED: Materials relating to the New York Life Insurance Company.

HOLDINGS:
Total volume: 500 l.f.
Inclusive dates: 1845 -
Description: Materials relating to the history of the New York Life Insurance Company, including business records (U.S. and foreign), policy forms, claims, photographs, and motion pictures.

NY592-640
New York Psychoanalytic Institute
Abraham A. Brill Library
247 East 82nd Street
New York NY 10028

(212) 879-6900

OPEN: weekday afternoons and evenings by appointment only; closed weekends, holidays, and Aug. through Labor Day
USER FEES: $25 annual fee for regular users (does not apply to college students or one-time users)
ACCESS: application forms must be submitted in advance
COPYING FACILITIES: yes
MATERIALS SOLICITED: Papers and oral history relating to the members of the New York Psychoanalytic Society, to Sigmund Freud, and to pioneer figures in psychoanalysis. Will also accept other material relating to the history of psychoanalysis or the Society.

HOLDINGS:
Total volume: 60 l.f.
Inclusive dates: 1880 -
Description: Correspondence of Sigmund Freud; correspondence, book manuscripts, and papers of members of the New York Psychoanalytic Society and other psychoanalysts (Anna Freud, Smith Ely Jelliffe, Theodor Reik, Fritz Wittels, Berta Bornstein); archives and noncurrent records of the New York Psychoanalytic Society; photographs of individual analysts and Society events; and tapes and transcripts of oral history interviews with and lectures by psychoanalysts.

SEE ALSO: Alan M. Meckler and Ruth McMullin, comps., *Oral History Collections* (Bowker, 1975); Bernice Ennis, *Guide to the Literature in Psychiatry* (Partridge Press, 1971).

NY592-680
The New York Public Library
Arents Collections
Room 324
Fifth Avenue and 42nd Street
New York NY 10018

(212) 930-0801

OPEN: M-W, F, Sa 10-6; closed Thursdays, Sundays, and holidays
ACCESS: graduate students or other adults with a serious research project or inquiry
COPYING FACILITIES: yes
MATERIALS SOLICITED: Manuscripts related to tobacco and to books published in parts.

HOLDINGS:
> *Total volume:* 600 items
> *Inclusive dates:* 1564 -
> *Description:* Materials relating to the history, production, consumption, and distribution of tobacco products in the United States and abroad, including accounts, receipts, and correspondence of a literary and nonliterary nature. There are also materials relating to books in parts, including 19th century English and American literary manuscripts and correspondence of authors and illustrators connected with such works.

SEE: Novotny.

SEE ALSO: Sam P. Williams, comp., *Guide to the Research Collections of the New York Public Library* (American Library Assn., 1975); *Tobacco, A Catalog of the Books, Manuscripts and Engravings Acquired Since 1942* (New York Public Library, 1961-69).

NY592-760
The New York Public Library
Jewish Division
Room 84
Fifth Avenue and 42nd Street
New York NY 10018

(212) 930-0601

OPEN: M, W, F, Sa 10-6, Tu 10-9; closed Thursdays, Sundays, and holidays
ACCESS: Qualified, experienced researchers and students engaged in advanced graduate study. Readers are expected to present evidence that preliminary bibliographic preparation and literature searching have been completed and that the materials being sought are directly relevant to their research.
COPYING FACILITIES: yes
MATERIALS SOLICITED: Will accept manuscripts and archives considered of potential value for the study of Jewish life.

HOLDINGS:
> *Total volume:* 500 pieces
> *Inclusive dates:* 15th century -
> *Description:* Materials relating to Jewish history, including a 15th century Italian mahzor (festival prayer book); 30 ketubot (marriage contracts); letters; kabbalistic works; Yemenite liturgical works; the Thomashefsky collection related to the Yiddish theater; papers of Joseph Judah Lob Sossnitz, a 19th century Talmudic scholar, mathematician, and scientific author; and the diary of Abraham Jona, last rabbi of the Venetian ghetto, for the years 1797-1814.

SEE ALSO: Ann Novotny, ed., *Picture Sources 3* (Special Libraries Assn., 1975); Sam P. Williams, comp., *Guide to the Research Collections of the New York Public Library* (American Library Assn., 1975).

NY592-800
The New York Public Library
Manuscripts and Archives Division
Room 319
5th Avenue and 42nd Street
New York NY 10018

(212) 930-0804, 0805

OPEN: M, Tu, Th-Sa 10-6; closed Sundays, Wednesdays, and holidays
ACCESS: qualified researchers only
COPYING FACILITIES: yes
MATERIALS SOLICITED: Materials relating to all aspects of American history, particularly literature, business, printing, publishing, the Revolutionary War, and New York.

HOLDINGS:
> *Total volume:* 21,249 l.f.
> *Inclusive dates:* 3000 B.C. -
> *Description:* The holdings include samples of the recorded word in most periods and media, with notable collections of clay tablets and stelae, medieval and Renaissance manuscripts, documents relating to early Spanish America and the American Revolution, diaries, logbooks, account books, and U.S. Presidential papers. Included are numerous collections of personal and organization papers relating to American history, politics, literature, art, science, printing, and publishing, with emphasis on New York City and State.

GUIDES: *Dictionary Catalog of the Manuscript Division* (G. K. Hall, 1967).

SEE: Hamer; NUCMC, 1963-64, 68-74, 76.

SEE: Davis; Schatz; Duignan; Hounshell; Krichmar; Hinding; Bean and Vane; Allard, Edmison, and Crawley; Spalek; Ingram; Parkinson; Beers - Southwest; Beers - Confederate.

SEE ALSO: Gerald Friedberg, 'Sources for the Study of Socialism in America, 1901-1919,' *Labor History* 6 (Spring 1965); Harry J. Carman and Arthur W. Thompson, *A Guide to the Principal Sources for American Civilization, 1800-1900, in the City of New York: Manuscripts* (Columbia Univ. Press, 1960); Ann Novotny, ed., *Picture Sources 3* (Special Libraries Assn., 1975); *Map Collections in the United States and Canada, A Directory* (Special Libraries Assn., 1970); *Bulletin of the New York Public Library* (1897-).

NY592-860
The New York Public Library
Oriental Division
Room 219
5th Avenue and 42nd Street
New York NY 10018

(212) 930-0716

OPEN: M, W, F, Sa 10-6, Tu 10-9; closed Sundays, Thursdays, and holidays
COPYING FACILITIES: yes

HOLDINGS:
> *Total volume:* 250 items
> *Inclusive dates:* 12th century - 19th century
> *Description:* Manuscripts, mostly Arabic, but also Persian and Turkish, chiefly pertaining to the Islamic religious sciences, with some coverage of the natural sciences.

GUIDES: *Dictionary Catalog of the Oriental Collection* (G. K. Hall, 1960).

SEE ALSO: Sam P. Williams, comp., *Guide to the Research Collections of the New York Public Library* (American Library Assn., 1975); Peter Duignan, *Handbook of American Resources for African Studies* (Hoover Institution, 1967).

NY592-870
The New York Public Library
Performing Arts Research Center
Dance Collection
111 Amsterdam Avenue
New York NY 10023

(212) 870-1657, 1658

OPEN: June-Aug., M-Sa 12-5:45; Sept.-May, M, Th 12-7:45, Tu, W, F, Sa 12-5:45; closed Sundays and holidays
COPYING FACILITIES: yes
MATERIALS SOLICITED: Historical documents, individual letters, major collections of correspondence, business records, diaries, journals, notebooks, unpublished book manuscripts, and memorabilia pertaining to the field of dance. Will also accept related institutional archives, oral recordings, motion pictures, and videotapes.

HOLDINGS:
> *Total volume:* 300,000 items
> *Inclusive dates:* 1460 -
> *Description:* Over 50 major manuscript collections and several hundred individual manuscripts, book manuscripts, historical documents, and notebooks related to all aspects of dance since the 15th century. Major figures represented include Isadora Duncan, Gordon Craig, Sergei Diaghilev, Vaslav Nijinsky, Ruth St. Denis, Ted Shawn, Doris Humphrey, Jose Limon, Agnes de Mille, Ruth Page, and Helen Tamiris. Major archival collections include the records of the American Ballet Theatre, the Royal Academy of Dance (London), and the Jerome Robbins' Ballets: U.S.A. Historical documents include a manuscript of Giorgia Ebreo, dancing master of 15th century Italy; a 1698 edict of Louis XIV; and the black notebook of Diaghilev.

GUIDES: *Dictionary Catalog of the Dance Collection* (G. K. Hall, 1974) and *Supplements* (1976 and 1977).

SEE: NUCMC, 1972.

SEE: Hinding.

SEE ALSO: Sam P. Williams, comp., *Guide to the Research Collections of the New York Public Library* (American Library Assn., 1975); Genevieve Oswald, 'Creating Tangible Records for an Intangible Art,' *Special Libraries* 59 (March 1968); Ann Novotny, ed., *Picture Sources 3* (Special Libraries Assn., 1975).

NY592-875

The New York Public Library
Performing Arts Research Center
Music Division
111 Amsterdam Avenue
New York NY 10023

(212) 799-2200

OPEN: M-Sa 12-6; closed Sundays and
holidays
ACCESS: no one under 18 years old
COPYING FACILITIES: yes
MATERIALS SOLICITED: Materials pertaining to all aspects of music and musicians excluding primary music education and music therapy.

HOLDINGS:
Total volume: 22,000 items; 10,000
tapes
Inclusive dates: 10th century -
Description: Music scores and manuscripts and other papers of musicians and
composers, as well as recorded music of
all types.

GUIDES: *Dictionary Catalog of the Music
Collection* (G. K. Hall,1964) and *Supplement* (1973); *Dictionary Catalog of
the Manuscript Division* (G. K. Hall,
1967).

SEE: Hamer; NUCMC, 1976.

SEE ALSO: Sam P. Williams, comp., *Guide
to the Research Collections of the New
York Public Library* (American Library
Assn., 1975); Frank C. Campbell, 'The
Music Division of the New York Public Library,' *Fontes Artis Musicae* (July
- Dec. 1969); Ann Novotny, ed., *Picture Sources 3* (Special Libraries Assn.,
1975); and frequent articles in the *Bulletin of the New York Public Library.*

NY592-878

The New York Public Library
Performing Arts Research Center
Rodgers and Hammerstein Archives
of Recorded Sound
111 Amsterdam Avenue
New York NY 10023

(212) 870-1651

OPEN: M-Sa 12-6; closed Sundays and
holidays
ACCESS: Persons 18 years of age or
above, or performing arts
professional-level students
COPYING FACILITIES: yes
MATERIALS SOLICITED: Sound recordings
of potential historic-cultural significance, recordings and record industry
iconography and documents, and
discographies.

HOLDINGS:
Total volume: 403,200 items
Inclusive dates: 1877 -
Description: Sound recordings and other materials relating primarily to the performing arts, with some documentation
in ethnography and politics. Areas of special strength include the American musical theater, film sound tracks, classical
music, and jazz and popular music.

NY592-880

The New York Public Library
Performing Arts Research Center
The Billy Rose Theatre Collection
111 Amsterdam Avenue
New York NY 10023

(212) 870-1639

OPEN: M, Th 12-7:45, Tu, W, F, Sa
12-5:45; M-Sa 12-5:45 Memorial
Day-Labor Day; closed Sundays and
holidays
ACCESS: 18 years of age or older, or
college students
COPYING FACILITIES: yes
MATERIALS SOLICITED: Materials pertaining to the theater, motion pictures,
radio, television, circuses, magic,
marionettes, carnivals, fairs, and
amusement parks.

HOLDINGS:
Total volume: not specified
Inclusive dates: 1707 -
Description: Materials concerning theater and popular entertainment of all
periods. Included are typescripts, scrapbooks, playbills, programs, designs, organization records, letters, contracts, diaries,
and other papers, as well as an extensive
photograph collection.

GUIDES: *Catalog of the Theatre and Dra-
ma Collections, Parts I and II* (G. K.
Hall, 1967), *Supplement* (1973), and
Part III (1976).

SEE: NUCMC, 1965.

SEE: Hinding.

SEE ALSO: Sam P. Williams, comp., *Guide
to the Research Collections of the New
York Public Library* (American Library
Assn., 1975); Alan M. Meckler and
Ruth McMullin, comps., *Oral History
Collections* (Bowker, 1975); Ann
Novotny, ed., *Picture Sources 3* (Special
Libraries Assn., 1975); *Architectural
Research Materials in New York City:
A Guide to Resources in All Five Bor-
oughs* (Committee for the Preservation
of Architectural Records, 1977); and
frequent articles in the *Bulletin of the
New York Public Library.*

NY592-930

The New York Public Library
Schomburg Center for Research in
Black Culture
515 Lenox Avenue
New York NY 10037

(212) 862-4000

OPEN: M-W 12-5:30, Th-Sa 10-5:30;
closed Sundays and holidays
COPYING FACILITIES: yes
MATERIALS SOLICITED: Manuscripts,
photographs, audio recordings, motion
pictures, and other materials relating to
black people and their culture.

HOLDINGS:
Total volume: 2,500 c.f.
Inclusive dates: 1717 -
Description: Archives and manuscripts
devoted to the history and culture of
black people throughout the world. Included are papers of individuals, records
of organizations, typescripts, photographs,
and audiovisual materials. The collections

relate to black literature, the Harlem Renaissance, black music, slavery and the
abolition of the slave trade, Caribbean
(notably Haitian) history, and various social and political organizations and movements.

GUIDES: *Dictionary Catalog of the
Schomburg Collection of Negro Litera-
ture and History* (G. K. Hall, 1962);
First Supplement (1967), and *Second
Supplement* (1972).

SEE: Hamer; NUCMC, 1972, 79.

SEE: Hinding; Robbins.

SEE ALSO: Sam P. Williams, comp., *Guide
to the Research Collections of the New
York Public Library* (American Librar-
ies Assn., 1975); Walter Schatz, ed., *Di-
rectory of Afro-American Resources*
(Bowker, 1970); Peter Duignan, *Ameri-
can Resources for African Studies*
(Hoover Institution, 1967); Robert O.
Collins and Peter Duignan, *Americans
in Africa* (Hoover Institution, 1963);
Harry J. Carman and Arthur W.
Thompson, *A Guide to the Principal
Sources for American Civilization,
1800-1900, in the City of New York:
Manuscripts* (Columbia Univ. Press,
1960); Ann Novotny, ed., *Picture
Sources 3* (Special Libraries Assn.,
1975); Stanton F. Biddle, 'The
Schomburg Center for Research in
Black Culture: Documenting the Black
Experience,' *Bulletin of the New York
Public Library* 76 (1972).

NY592-970

The New York Public Library
Spencer Collection
Room 313
5th Avenue and 42nd Street
New York NY 10018

(212) 930-0834, 0835

OPEN: M-W, F, Sa 10-6; closed
Thursdays, Sundays, and holidays
ACCESS: qualified, experienced
researchers and graduate students
COPYING FACILITIES: yes
MATERIALS SOLICITED: Illustrated manu-
script books.

HOLDINGS:
Total volume: 800 items
Inclusive dates: 12th century -
Description: Manuscript books illus-
trated with original graphics representa-
tive of the history of illustration. Included
are medieval, Renaissance, later western
European, Japanese, Persian, Indian, and
Thai examples.

NY593-10

New York Society
Library
53 East 79th Street
New York NY 10021

no telephone

SEE: Hamer; NUCMC, 1959-61.

Questionnaire not returned.

NY593-040

New York Stock Exchange
Office of the Secretary
Archives
11 Wall Street
New York NY 10005

(212) 623-2252

OPEN: by appointment only M-F; closed weekends and holidays
ACCESS: serious researchers only
COPYING FACILITIES: yes
MATERIALS SOLICITED: Original manuscript materials, both organizational and personal, pertaining to the New York Stock Exchange and stock trading. Will also accept visual and audible documents about the Exchange and its activities.

HOLDINGS:
Total volume: 2,000 l.f.
Inclusive dates: late 18th century -
Description: Materials relating to the history of the New York Stock Exchange, its subsidiary companies, the financial district of New York, and stock trading in the U.S. and Europe. Included are the continuous operating records of the organization and the daily stock transactions since 1817, scrapbooks, and visual and audible documents.

NY593-60

The New York Times
NYT Pictures-The New York Times Photo Syndicate
229 West 43rd Street
New York NY 10036

(212) 556-1243

OPEN: M-F 9-5; closed weekends, July 4, Christmas, and New Year's
ACCESS: collections closed to public; research performed by staff of NYT Pictures or the New York Times at $25 per hour or fraction thereof
COPYING FACILITIES: yes
MATERIALS SOLICITED: Black-and-white photographs of news events, personalities, sports, history, and other topics of interest.

HOLDINGS:
Total volume: 3,000,000 items
Inclusive dates: 1875 -
Description: Black-and-white still photographs, worldwide in scope.

SEE: Novotny.

NY593-90

New York University
Fales Library
70 Washington Square South
New York NY 10012

(212) 598-3756

OPEN: M-F by appointment; closed weekends and holidays
COPYING FACILITIES: yes
MATERIALS SOLICITED: Materials pertaining to 19th and 20th century American and English literature.

HOLDINGS:
Total volume: 30,000 items
Inclusive dates: 19th century -
Description: Letters, literary manuscripts, and other papers of English and American authors of the 19th and 20th centuries, including Lewis Carroll, as well as papers of Henry Barnard, American educator.

SEE: Hamer; NUCMC, 1959-61, 68.

SEE: Robbins; Hinding.

NY593-100

New York University
Institute of Fine Arts
Photographic Archives
1 East 78th Street
New York NY 10021

(212) 772-5800

OPEN: M-F 9-5; closed weekends, legal and University holidays
ACCESS: by appointment to students and scholars in field of art history
COPYING FACILITIES: no
MATERIALS SOLICITED: Photographic collections and research materials dealing with all areas of art and architecture.

HOLDINGS:
Total volume: 250,000 items
Inclusive dates: 19th century -
Description: 250,000 photographs dealing with the history of art, mainly European, and including the Gernsheim Corpus Photographicum of drawings in European collections, the Offner Collection of photographs of Italian 13th to 19th century painting, an iconographic index to painting and drawing of the Low Countries, a copy of the photographic resources of the Berenson Library in Italian painting and drawing, and a census of antique works of art known at the time of the Renaissance.

SEE: Novotny.

NY593-120

New York University
Libraries
Tamiment Library
70 Washington Square South
New York NY 10012

(212) 598-3708

OPEN: M-F 10-5:45; closed weekends and holidays
ACCESS: must give evidence of research need for materials unique to Tamiment collection
COPYING FACILITIES: yes
MATERIALS SOLICITED: Materials pertaining to 19th and 20th century American labor and socialist movements. Will also accept materials relating to the New Left, anarchism, utopian movements, and left-wing fringe groups.

HOLDINGS:
Total volume: 811 l.f.; 550 microfilm reels
Inclusive dates: 1840 -
Description: Records of trade unions and Old and New Left groups, personal papers and records of individuals associated with the Rand School of Social Sciences and with trade unionism, and 4 l.f. of related photographs.

SEE: Hamer (as Tamiment Institute Library).

SEE: Hinding; Spalek.

SEE ALSO: Daniel Bell, *The Tamiment Library,* Bibliographical Series, no. 6 (New York Univ. Libraries, 1969); Walter Schatz, ed., *Directory of Afro-American Resources* (Bowker, 1970); Gerald Friedberg, 'Sources for the Study of Socialism in America, 1901-1919,' *Labor History* 6 (Spring 1965); Andrea Hinding and Rosemary Richardson, comps., *Archival and Manuscript Resources for the Study of Women's History: A Beginning* (Univ. of Minnesota Libraries, Social Welfare History Archives Center, 1972); Harry J. Carman and Arthur W. Thompson, *A Guide to the Principal Sources for American Civilization, 1800-1900, in the City of New York: Manuscripts* (Columbia Univ. Press, 1960); and articles in *Tamiment Library Bulletin* and *Labor History.*

NY593-130

New York Zoological Society
Archives
New York Zoological Park
Bronx NY 10460

(212) 220-6874

OPEN: M-F 10-4 by appointment; closed weekends and holidays
ACCESS: accredited scholars and researchers upon written application; appointments must be scheduled two weeks in advance and confirmed 24 hours before visit.
COPYING FACILITIES: yes
MATERIALS SOLICITED: Materials dealing with wildlife conservation, habitat research, and the preservation and propagation of animal species, including the records of individuals and organizations.

HOLDINGS:
Total volume: 740 l.f.
Inclusive dates: 1880 -
Description: Records of the New York Zoological Society, 1895- , and its main divisions: the New York Zoological Park, New York Aquarium, Osborn Laboratories of Marine Sciences, and international field science and conservation, programs. Holdings document the development of zoo and aquarium exhibits, management and propagation of wild animals, basic research, habitat preservation, and environmental education.

Major figures represented include C. William Beebe, W. Reid Blair, Lee S. Crandall, Raymond L. Ditmars, Myron Gordon, Madison Grant, William T. Hornaday, Henry Fairfield Osborn, John Tee-Van, and Charles H. Townsend. There are also records of affiliated organizations, such as the American Committee for International Protection of Wild Life, American Bison Society, Camp Fire Club, Conservation Foundation, and Permanent Wild Life Protection Fund.

NY593-132
92nd Street Young Men's and Young
  Women's Hebrew Association
Archives
1395 Lexington Avenue
New York NY 10028

(212) 427-6000

OPEN: M-F 9-5; closed weekends,
  holidays, and Jewish holy days
COPYING FACILITIES: yes
MATERIALS SOLICITED: Materials relating
  to The Young Men's Hebrew Associ-
  ation,, The Young Women's Hebrew
  Association, The Clara de Hirsch
  Home for Working Girls, The Young
  Men's and Young Women's Hebrew
  Association, Surprise Lake Camp of the
  Educational Alliance, and Young Men's
  Hebrew Association, and to personal-
  ities associated with these organiza-
  tions.

HOLDINGS:
  Total volume: 900 c.f.; 1,000 items
  Inclusive dates: 1874 -
  Description: Records of the Young
  Men's Hebrew Association, 1874-1945;
  The Young Women's Hebrew Association, 1902-45; The Clara de Hirsch
  Home for Working Girls, 1897-1962; The
  Young Men's and Young Women's Hebrew Association, 1945- ; and The Surprise Lake Camp of the Educational Alliance.
    Included are minutes, correspondence,
  financial records, printed materials, photographs, oral history tapes, reports, and
  sound recordings of events held at the
  92nd Street YM-YWHA. Of special note
  are the recordings of the Y's Poetry Center since 1949 and of concerts in the Y's
  Kaufman Concert Hall since 1976.

NY593-290
The Parish of Trinity Church
Office of Parish Archives
74 Trinity Place
New York NY 10006

(212) 602-0847

OPEN: M-F 9:30-3:30 by appointment;
  closed weekends and holidays
COPYING FACILITIES: yes
MATERIALS SOLICITED: Materials relating
  to the Parish's history.

HOLDINGS:
  Total volume: 1,200 l.f.
  Inclusive dates: 1644 -
  Description: Records of the Parish of
  Trinity, Church in New York City, including correspondence, financial records,
  vestry committee minutes, deeds, leases,
  indentures, maps, photographs, account
  books, diaries, sermons, genealogical
  source data, biographical information, architectural and engineering drawings,
  films, tapes, and scrapbooks. The records
  relate to the history of the Parish; its land
  holdings, lay people, and clergy, including
  those buried in the churchyards and
  cemetery; chapels and other institutions
  in Manhattan; and churches worldwide
  aided by Trinity.

NY593-380
Phelps-Stokes Fund
Archives
10 East 87th Street
New York NY 10028

(212) 427-8100

OPEN: by appointment only; closed
  holidays
ACCESS: by appointment only
COPYING FACILITIES: no
MATERIALS SOLICITED: Manuscripts pertaining to the history and present activities of the Phelps-Stokes Fund. Will
  also accept materials related to education in Africa; the education of Indians, blacks, and low-income whites in
  the United States; and housing facilities for the poor and elderly in New
  York City.

HOLDINGS:
  Total volume: 800 boxes
  Inclusive dates: 1822 -
  Description: Records of the Phelps-
  Stokes Fund's programs since the 1910's,
  including American Indian and black
  education, low-income housing, African
  student scholarships in the United States,
  and education in Liberia, western Africa,
  and other areas of Africa. There are also
  records of U.S. government aid for African scholarships and of the New York
  State Colonization Society's educational
  programs in Liberia since 1822.

GUIDES: Toni Trent Parker, *Phelps-Stokes
Fund Annotated Bibliography* (1976).

SEE: Schatz.

NY593-420
Photo Trends
1472 Broadway
New York NY 10036

(212) 279-2130

OPEN: M-Sa 10-4; closed Sundays and
  holidays
ACCESS: advance arrangements should
  be made
COPYING FACILITIES: no

HOLDINGS:
  Total volume: 500,000 items
  Inclusive dates: 1920 -
  Description: Black-and-white and color
  photographs from the Harris and Ewing
  collection, which includes many Washington, DC, and U.S. government personalities. There are also photographs of Hollywood personalities since 1960 and of
  well-known people of Great Britain since
  1920, as well as collections relating to
  nature, geography, and science around the
  world.

SEE: Novotny.

NY593-460
Pierpont Morgan Library
29 East 36th Street
New York NY 10016

no telephone

SEE: Hamer.

Questionnaire not returned.

NY593-485
The Players
The Hampden-Booth Theatre Library
16 Gramercy Park, S.
New York NY 10003

(212) 228-7610

OPEN: M-F 10-5 by appointment; closed
  weekends and holidays
ACCESS: advance arrangements required
COPYING FACILITIES: yes
MATERIALS SOLICITED: Original manuscripts, documents, and archival materials on The Players and its founder,
  Edwin Booth, and his contemporaries;
  the 19th century American and English
  theater; Walter Hampden (late 19th -
  mid-20th century); and historical and
  scholarly materials on conjuring for the
  John Mulholland Magic Collection.
  Will also accept additions to existing
  collections.

HOLDINGS:
  Total volume: not specified
  Inclusive dates: early 1800's -
  Description: Collections covering the
  history of the American and English stage
  with emphasis on the 19th century. In-
  cluded among the holdings are papers,
  records, and memoirs of Max Gordon,
  Robert B. Mantell, Tallulah Bankhead,
  Newman Levy, Maurice Evans, Franklin
  Heller, Muriel Kirkland, the British Ac-
  tors Orphanage Fund, the Union Square
  Theatre, La Mama Experimental Theatre
  Club (off-off-Broadway theater), bur-
  lesque, Edwin Booth, Walter Hampden,
  The Players, and the John Mulholland
  Magic Collection.

SEE: Hamer; NUCMC, 1966, 69.

SEE: Robbins.

NY593-500
The Polish Institute of Arts and
  Sciences of America
New York NY 10021

(212) 988-4338

OPEN: M-F 10-4; closed weekends and
  holidays
ACCESS: advance arrangements required
COPYING FACILITIES: yes
MATERIALS SOLICITED: Audiovisual material concerning Poland, the Poles, and
  the Polonia with an emphasis on history, political science, literature, culture, sociology, and education. Will
  also accept other materials dealing with
  these subjects.

HOLDINGS:
  Total volume: 80 file drawers
  Inclusive dates: 16th century -
  Description: Materials relating to Poland, the Poles, and the Polonia, with an
  emphasis on history, political science, literature, culture, sociology, and education.

NY593-560

Pratt Institute
Library
215 Ryerson Street
Brooklyn NY 11205

(718) 636-3532

OPEN: M-F 9-5; closed weekends and
holidays
ACCESS: prior arrangements
recommended
COPYING FACILITIES: yes

HOLDINGS:
Total volume: 25 l.f.; 170,000 items
Inclusive dates: 1850 -
Description: Papers of Charles Pratt
and his son Frederic, pertaining chiefly to
both men's service as President of Pratt
Institute. There are also art-related photographs, color transparencies, and other
visual documents.

SEE: NUCMC, 1967.

SEE: Novotny; Hinding; Robbins.

NY593-590

Protestant Episcopal Church
Diocese of New York
Archives
1047 Amsterdam Avenue
New York NY 10025

(212) 316-7419

OPEN: M-F 9-5; closed weekends and
holidays
ACCESS: prior arrangements should be
made
COPYING FACILITIES: yes
MATERIALS SOLICITED: Materials pertaining to diocesan departments and
organizations, churches in union with
convention, and bishops and other
prominent people within the Diocese.
Will also accept National Episcopal
church materials, records of churches
formerly affiliated with the Diocese of
New York, and materials pertinent to
Episcopal church history in general.

HOLDINGS:
Total volume: 1,022 c.f.
Inclusive dates: 1789 -
Description: Correspondence, records,
photographs, audible recordings, and other materials relating to the history of the
Diocese and its individual churches, and,
for the early period, to New York City
and State.

SEE: Hinding.

NY593-600

Queens Borough Public Library
Long Island Division
89-11 Merrick Boulevard
Jamaica NY 11432

(718) 990-0700

OPEN: Tu-Th 10-6, Sa 10-5:30; closed
other days and holidays
ACCESS: researchers should be of college
level
COPYING FACILITIES: yes
MATERIALS SOLICITED: Manuscripts re-
lating to the four Long Island counties:
Kings, Queens, Nassau, and Suffolk.

HOLDINGS:
Total volume: 36,000 items
Inclusive dates: 1642 -
Description: Materials relating to the
Long Island area, chiefly from the 19th
century. Included are personal papers and
records of institutions, with subject emphasis on whaling, churches, and genealogy.

SEE: Hamer; NUCMC, 1968, 76 (listed
under Jamaica, NY).

SEE: Gehring; Hinding; Leventhal and
Mooney - I; Novotny; Robbins.

NY593-710

Religious Society of Friends
New York Yearly Meeting
Records Committee
Haviland Records Room
15 Rutherford Place
New York NY 10003

(212) 777-8866

OPEN: W, Th 10-4 and by appointment;
closed holidays
USER FEES: $2 per day for nonmembers;
no charge for students and scholars
ACCESS: advance arrangements required
COPYING FACILITIES: no
MATERIALS SOLICITED: Minute books
and registers of the Religious Society of
Friends. Will also accept personal papers and memorabilia of members,
photographs, and audiovisual records
of the New York Yearly Meeting and
its constituent meetings.

HOLDINGS:
Total volume: 1,380 l.f.; 6 file
cabinets; 1 map case
Inclusive dates: 1670 -
Description: Records and other materials pertaining to the New York Yearly
Meeting of the Religious Society of
Friends and pertaining to Friends meetings in New York State, western Connecticut, northern New Jersey, and southern Vermont.

SEE: Hamer (as Society of Friends
Records Committee).

SEE: Schatz.

NY593-720

Research Foundation for Jewish
    Immigration, Inc.
570 7th Avenue
New York NY 10018

(212) 921-3871

OPEN: by appointment only
COPYING FACILITIES: yes
MATERIALS SOLICITED: Biographical
source data, oral history tapes, reports
and transcripts, and other manuscripts
and archival materials pertinent to
Jewish emigration and resettlement,
1933-45.

HOLDINGS:
Total volume: 125 l.f.
Inclusive dates: 1933 -
Description: Collections relating to the
immigration, resettlement, and acculturation of central European refugees from
1933 to 1945. Included are the International Biographical Archives of Central
European Emigres, 1933-45, archives of

the American Federation of Jews from
Central Europe, oral history interviews
with leaders of German Jewish immigrant communities in the United States,
and other materials documenting central
European emigration of the Nazi period.

NY593-840

The Rockefeller University
Archives
1230 York Avenue
New York NY

MAILING ADDRESS:
P.O. Box 263
New York NY 10021-6399

(212) 570-8912

OPEN: M-Th 9-5, F 9-2; closed weekends
and holidays
ACCESS: qualified scholars
COPYING FACILITIES: yes
MATERIALS SOLICITED: Institutional
records of The Rockefeller University
(formerly The Rockefeller Institute for
Medical Research) and manuscript collections of the scientists who have been
affiliated with the University. The
range and variety of the scientific work
at the University includes animal behavior; bacteriology; and immunology;
biochemical cytology; biochemistry;
biophysics; cardiac physiology; cell biology, biochemistry, physiology, and
immunology; experimental high energy
physics; experimental psychology; and
genetics.

HOLDINGS:
Total volume: 1,000 l.f.
Inclusive dates: 1901 -
Description: The institutional records
of the University from its founding in
1901 as The Rockefeller Institute for
Medical Research include minutes of
boards, annual reports of the business
manager and of the scientists, records of
the treasurer and the various supportive
departments, and a large collection of
photographs of scientific and auxiliary
personnel, buildings, laboratories, and
special events.
    Manuscript collections include corre-
spondence, laboratory notes and records,
slides, drawings, and assorted memorabilia. The collection documents biomedical research in the United States in
the 20th century, as well as developments
in public health and medicine and medical education.

SEE: Spalek.

Additional institutional records and
papers of other University scientists
are located at the Rockefeller University, Rockefeller Archives Center, in
North Tarrytown, NY.

NY593-900

St. Francis College
James A. Kelly Local Historical
    Studies Institute
180 Remsen Street
Brooklyn NY 11201

(718) 522-2300

OPEN: M-F 9-5; closed weekends and
holidays

COPYING FACILITIES: no
MATERIALS SOLICITED: Documentary materials and memorabilia concerning the history of Brooklyn and its institutions and personalities. Will also accept similar materials regarding New York City and State.

HOLDINGS:
>*Total volume:* 3 million pages
>*Inclusive dates:* 1643 -
>*Description:* Collections include records of the six original towns of Kings County: Gravesend, Flatbush, New Utrecht, Flatlands, Bushwick, and Brooklyn, dating from 1645 to 1898. There are records of the Common Council of Brooklyn City, 1834-98, and Supervisors' minutes of Kings County, 1701-1896. Materials pertaining to varied areas of local history, including transit, politics, and churches, are also included.

SEE: Gehring; Leventhal and Mooney - I.

NY593-940

St. John's University
Library
Grand Central and Utopia Parkways
Jamaica NY 11432

(212) 990-6161

OPEN: by appointment only

SEE: NUCMC, 1975.

Questionnaire not returned.

NY593-970

St. Mark's Church In-the-Bowery
Archives
10th Street at Second Avenue
New York NY 10003

(212) 674-6377

OPEN: Tu-F 10-5; closed weekends, Mondays, and holidays
COPYING FACILITIES: yes
MATERIALS SOLICITED: Will accept materials relating to the history of the Lower East Side.

HOLDINGS:
>*Total volume:* not specified
>*Inclusive dates:* 1799 -
>*Description:* Church manuscripts and records. Included are marriage, baptism and burial records, vestry and church committee documents, parish registers, rectors' papers and correspondence, property histories, and a photograph collection. There are also records of the St. Mark's Arts Projects (The Poetry Project, Danspace, Theatre Genesis) and oral history interviews relating to the Lower East Side community.

NY594-20

The Salvation Army
Archives and Research Center
145 West 15th Street
New York NY 10011

(212) 620-4392

OPEN: M-F 8:30-4; closed weekends and holidays
COPYING FACILITIES: yes

MATERIALS SOLICITED: All types of historical materials and records concerning the Salvation Army.

HOLDINGS:
>*Total volume:* 1,000 c.f.
>*Inclusive dates:* 1880 -
>*Description:* A collection of materials concerning various aspects of the social work of The Salvation Army including seasonal relief work; cafeterias and food depots; industrial homes; working men's and women's hotels; rescue homes for single mothers; work with abandoned, abused, and delinquent children; children's homes; nurseries and day care centers; slum work and settlement houses; farm colonies; labor bureaus; work with immigrants and various ethnic groups; services to the Armed Forces; correctional services; emergency disaster services; missing persons; relief work during the Depression; general and maternity hospitals; and specialized work with alcoholics, drug addicts, the handicapped, and the mentally ill.

>There are also organizational materials on the internal structure of The Salvation Army, materials regarding the incorporation of The Salvation Army in New York State in 1899, correspondence, scrapbooks, journals and diaries, briefs, minutes, annual reports, financial ledgers, legal records, architectural plans, and photographs.

>Included are personal papers of General Evangeline Booth and composer Erik Leidsen.

SEE: NUCMC, 1981.

SEE: Hinding.

NY594-060

Seamen's Church Institute of New York
50 Broadway
New York NY 10004

(212) 269-2710

OPEN: M-Th 11-9, F 11-6, Sa-Su 2-9
ACCESS: advance arrangements required
COPYING FACILITIES: yes
MATERIALS SOLICITED: Diaries, logbooks, and journals relating to maritime voyages; ship photographs; scrapbooks about ships; ship plans and blueprints; sea charts and maps; and oral history tapes and interviews with merchant seamen. Will also accept records of shipping companies and material relating to the history of the port of New York.

HOLDINGS:
>*Total volume:* 100 vols.; 24 file cabinets
>*Inclusive dates:* 19th century -
>*Description:* Scrapbooks, photographs, and manuscripts relating to the history of merchant shipping, working conditions of seafarers, and the history of the port of New York.

NY594-080

The Shevchenko Scientific Society
63 4th Avenue
New York NY 10003

(212) 929-7622

OPEN: M-F 8-5; closed weekends and holidays
ACCESS: by appointment only
COPYING FACILITIES: no
MATERIALS SOLICITED: Material on Ukrainian culture. Will also accept material dealing with the Slavic world.

HOLDINGS:
>*Total volume:* 10,000 pages
>*Inclusive dates:* 1900 -
>*Description:* Manuscripts of scholarly works, memoirs, and letters by prominent Ukrainian scholars, humanists, writers, and journalists, the majority pertaining to Ukrainian culture and the history of the Ukraine.

NY594-220

Sons of the Revolution in the State of New York
Fraunces Tavern Museum
54 Pearl Street
New York NY 10004

(212) 425-1778

OPEN: by appointment only; closed holidays
ACCESS: by appointment only
COPYING FACILITIES: yes
MATERIALS SOLICITED: Materials relating to the American Revolution. Will also accept original papers and typed versions of speeches of scholarly value.

HOLDINGS:
>*Total volume:* 99 items
>*Inclusive dates:* 1703 - 1905
>*Description:* Documents and other items relating to the American Revolution and its participants. There is an emphasis on New York City and New York State materials, but there are also items concerning George Washington, John Adams, Thomas Jefferson, and the Laurens family.

SEE: Hamer.

NY594-240

South Street Seaport Museum
Library
213 Water Street
New York NY

MAILING ADDRESS:
207 Front Street
New York NY 10038

(212) 669-9438

OPEN: M-F 10-6; closed weekends, Thanksgiving, and Christmas
COPYING FACILITIES: yes
MATERIALS SOLICITED: Materials relating to 19th and 20th century shipping, history of the port of New York, the waterways of New York State, and the general history of New York City.

HOLDINGS:
Total volume: 60 l.f.
Inclusive dates: 1790's -
Description: A collection of photographs, clippings, and a few manuscripts and documents dealing with ships of all types and their operation, and with the development of the port of New York.

NY594-340
State University of New York
Maritime College
Stephen B. Luce Library
Archives
Fort Schuyler
Bronx NY 10465

(212) 409-7231

OPEN: M-F 9-4; closed weekends and holidays
ACCESS: bona fide researchers; prior appointment necessary
COPYING FACILITIES: yes
MATERIALS SOLICITED: Institutional papers, personal papers and other materials pertaining to SUNY Maritime College, its training ships U.S.S. *St. Mary's*; U.S.S. *Newport; Empire State I, II, III, IV*; and *Empire State*, 1874- , and its alumni. Will also accept materials related to the maritime history of New York City including the Marine Society of the City of New York, 1769- ; Sailors' Snug Harbor, the Society's home for retired seamen, 1833- ; and the Sandy Hook Pilots' Association, 1854-1964.

HOLDINGS:
Total volume: 354 l.f.
Inclusive dates: late 18th century -
Description: Records and papers relating to the Maritime College and its alumni. Included are data relating to Fort Schuyler; a photograph collection, emphasizing life aboard the early training ships; records of the Marine Society of the City of New York; and logbooks of the Sandy Hook Pilots' Association.

NY594-360
Staten Island Historical Society
441 Clarke Avenue
Staten Island NY 10306

(718) 351-1611

OPEN: by appointment only; closed holidays
USER FEES: fifty cents (waived for qualified students)
ACCESS: appointment required
COPYING FACILITIES: yes
MATERIALS SOLICITED: Materials relating to the history of Staten Island.

HOLDINGS:
Total volume: 400 c.f.; 25,000 photographs; 250 architectural drawings
Inclusive dates: 1640 -
Description: Legal papers; town and county government records; papers of Staten Island families, trades, industries, organizations, and churches; microfilmed diaries of Hessian soldiers in America during the Revolutionary War; and other papers relating to the history of Staten Island and its residents.

SEE: Hamer.

SEE: Leventhal and Mooney - I.

SEE ALSO: Harry J. Carman and Arthur W. Thompson, *A Guide to the Principal Sources for American Civilization, 1800-1900, in the City of New York: Manuscripts* (Columbia Univ. Press, 1960); Ann Novotny, ed., *Picture Sources 3* (Special Libraries Assn., 1975).

NY594-380
Staten Island Institute of Arts and Sciences
Archives and Library
51 Stuyvesant Place
Staten Island NY

MAILING ADDRESS:
75 Stuyvesant Place
Staten Island NY 10301

(718) 727-1135

OPEN: M-F 10-4; closed weekends and holidays
COPYING FACILITIES: yes
MATERIALS SOLICITED: Will accept manuscripts and supportive materials that complement the collections.

HOLDINGS:
Total volume: 1,500 c.f.
Inclusive dates: 1450 -
Description: Materials related to Staten Island history and to science and natural history. There are 23 manuscript collections, including personal papers, genealogical source data, and literary manuscripts; archives of the Institute; drawings and manuscript maps; aerial photographs; photographs, daguerrotypes, ambrotypes, and glass negatives; and oral history tapes and transcripts.

SEE: Hamer.

SEE: Hinding; Robbins.

SEE ALSO: Richard C. Davis, *North American Forest History: A Guide to Archives and Manuscripts in the United States and Canada* (Clio Books, 1977); Ann Novotny, ed., *Picture Sources 3* (Special Libraries Assn., 1975); *Map Collections in the United States and Canada, A Directory* (Special Libraries Assn., 1970). Inventories and descriptions of many collections have been published in the Institute's *Proceedings,* and in the following publications by Gail Schneider: *The Community of the Press on Staten Island* (The Library, Staten Island Institute of Arts and Sciences, 1966), *The Print, Map, and Photograph Collections of the Staten Island Institute of Arts and Sciences* (1968), and 'Developing a Small Resource Collection on Local Black History: The Staten Island Project,' *Afro-Americans in New York Life and History* 1 (1977).

NY594-390
Statue of Liberty National Monument
American Museum of Immigration
Library
Liberty Island
New York NY 10004

(212) 964-3451

OPEN: M-Th 9:30-5 by appointment; closed F, Sa, Su and holidays
USER FEES: $1.50 fee to reach island
ACCESS: advance arrangements with librarian required
COPYING FACILITIES: yes
MATERIALS SOLICITED: Historic photographs, film, and oral history tapes.

HOLDINGS:
Total volume: 10 l.f.; 304 items; other materials
Inclusive dates: 1891 -
Description: Oral history tapes and transcripts recording the history of immigration and the history of Ellis and Liberty islands; 174 original Augustus F. Sherman photographs of Ellis Island immigrants; miscellaneous photographs of the Statue of Liberty and Ellis Island; Holland America Line passenger lists, 1891-1961, to New York and Hoboken; and Ellis Island records, such as financial records, account books, and literacy cards, largely from the late 1940's and 1950's.

NY594-640
Time Inc.
Archives
Time & Life Building, Room 21-20
Rockefeller Center
New York NY 10020

(212) 841-1033, 1400

OPEN: M-F 9-5; closed weekends and holidays
ACCESS: pre-1960 materials at the discretion of Time Inc.; post-1960 materials are closed
COPYING FACILITIES: yes
MATERIALS SOLICITED: Materials relating to the business activities of Time Inc.

HOLDINGS:
Total volume: 540 c.f.; 335 l.f.
Inclusive dates: 1922 -
Description: Business and editorial records consisting of memorandums, correspondence, promotional materials, and publicity generated by or pertaining to Time Inc., a communications and forest products company. Also included are published material reflecting the company's activities as well as tapes of the March of Time radio shows and March of Time Films.

NY594-680
Tobacco Merchants Association of the United States
Howard S. Cullman Library
Suite 705
1220 Broadway
New York NY 10001

(212) 239-4435

OPEN: M-F 9-5 by appointment; closed weekends and holidays

ACCESS: by appointment only
COPYING FACILITIES: yes
MATERIALS SOLICITED: Information on tobacco and tobacciana.

HOLDINGS:
   Total volume: 135 drawers; other items
   Inclusive dates: 1870 -
   Description: A card collection of all brand names and registered trademarks used for tobacco products and smokers' articles in the United States since the 1870's and the records and correspondence of the Tobacco Merchants Association of the United States.

NY594-860

Union Theological Seminary
Library
3041 Broadway
New York NY 10006

(212) 662-7100, Ext. 274

OPEN: M-F 9-5; closed weekends and holidays

SEE: Hamer; NUCMC, 1959-61.

Questionnaire not returned.

NY594-880

United Board for Christian Higher Education in Asia
475 Riverside Drive
Room 1221
New York NY 10115

no telephone

The archives of the United Board have been deposited at Yale University, Libraries, Divinity School Library, **CT505-900.**

NY595-20

United Nations
Archives
345 Park Avenue South
New York NY 10010

MAILING ADDRESS:
PK1200
United Nations
New York NY 10017

(212) 754-8683

OPEN: M-F 9-5; closed weekends and holidays
ACCESS: by appointment; files less than 20 years old are closed
COPYING FACILITIES: yes
MATERIALS SOLICITED: Records of the United Nations and its organizations.

HOLDINGS:
   Total volume: 29,745 l.f.
   Inclusive dates: 1893 -
   Description: Archival and semicurrent records of the United Nations Secretariat, including those of the Office of the Secretary General, the several Secretariat Departments, and the Registries; and predecessor bodies such as the International Penal and Penitentiary Commission, UN Relief and Rehabilitation Administration, and the UN Preparatory Commission.

Related agencies such as the UN Children's Fund, International Refugee Organization, and the UN Korean Reconstruction Agency; and missions, such as the UN Emergency Force and the UN Organization in the Congo.

SEE: Hamer.

SEE ALSO: 'Establishment and Organization of United Nations Archives,' *Actes de la Sixième Table Ronde Internationale des Archives, Warsaw, 1961* (Imprimerie Nationale, 1963).

Hinding.

NY595-40

United Nations
Dag Hammarskjold Library
Map Collection
New York NY 10017

(212) 754-7425

OPEN: M-F 9-5; closed weekends and holidays
ACCESS: prior arrangements necessary
COPYING FACILITIES: yes
MATERIALS SOLICITED: Armistice and cease-fire maps, including signed originals.

HOLDINGS:
   Total volume: 25 items
   Inclusive dates: 1946 -
   Description: Copies or original manuscripts of armistice or cease-fire maps in such areas as Cyprus, Indonesia, Kashmir, and Palestine.

NY595-130

United Negro College Fund
Archives
500 East 62nd Street
New York NY 10021

(212) 644-9672

OPEN: M-F 8:30-4:30; closed weekends and holidays
ACCESS: by appointment prior to visit
COPYING FACILITIES: yes
MATERIALS SOLICITED: Materials relating to the history of the United Negro College Fund. Will also accept materials relating to the history of black, private higher education in America.

HOLDINGS:
   Total volume: 450 c.f.
   Inclusive dates: 1935 -
   Description: Records of the United Negro College Fund, including correspondence, minutes, financial records, photographs, videotapes, sound recordings, and oral history tapes and transcripts. The UNCF Archives also contain a limited amount of information about its member institutions (private, fully-accredited, four year, predominantly black colleges and universities), and general information about the history of black higher education in the United States.

The records reflect the UNCF's dealings with government agencies and officials, private foundations, the business community, fraternal and labor organizations, individual donors and volunteers, and, most importantly, the member institutions and their students.

SEE: Hinding.

NY595-180

United States Committee for UNICEF
Information Center on Children's Cultures
331 East 38th Street
New York NY 10016

(212) 686-5522

OPEN: M-F 9-5; closed weekends and holidays
COPYING FACILITIES: yes
MATERIALS SOLICITED: Photographs of children in developing countries and of children in the U.S. involved in UNICEF 'trick-or-treat' or other fund-raising operations.

HOLDINGS:
   Total volume: 12,000 photographs
   Inclusive dates: 1949 -
   Description: Photographs relating to children in developing countries and how they have been assisted by UNICEF and photographs of U.S. children participating in 'trick-or-treat' or other fund-raising activities for UNICEF.

NY595-360

Wagner College
The Horrmann Library
631 Howard Avenue
Staten Island NY 10301

(718) 390-3401

OPEN: M-F 9-4:30; closed weekends and holidays
USER FEES: free for one-time use; $60 deposit and $15 annual fee for regular use
COPYING FACILITIES: yes
MATERIALS SOLICITED: Materials pertaining to the history of the College and of Lutheran churches in the Northeast, diaries of Hessian soldiers who served in the American Revolution, and materials concerning Edwin Markham and Thomas Lake Harris.

HOLDINGS:
   Total volume: 840 l.f.
   Inclusive dates: 1776 -
   Description: An extensive collection of poems, letters, and other papers of Edwin Markham, as well as four boxes of papers of Thomas Lake Harris, with editorial notes by Markham. There are also nine manuscripts on the history of Wagner College and four diaries, on microfilm, of Hessians stationed in America during the Revolutionary War.

SEE: Hamer; NUCMC, 1967.

SEE ALSO: 'The Thomas Lake Harris Collection of the Markham Archives', *The Markham Review* (Feb. 1969).

NY595-480

Wide World Photos, Inc.
50 Rockefeller Plaza
New York NY 10020

(212) 621-1930

OPEN: M-F 9-5; closed weekends and holidays
ACCESS: must work with staff researcher
COPYING FACILITIES: yes

MATERIALS SOLICITED: Photographs of feature personalities in news and sports.

HOLDINGS:
Total volume: 50,000,000 items
Inclusive dates: 19th century -
Description: Photographs of feature personalities in news and sports.

SEE: Novotny.

NY595-660

Yeshiva University
Division of Archives and Manuscript
Collections
2520 Amsterdam Avenue
New York NY 10033

(212) 960-5451

OPEN: M-Th 9-5:30, F 9-12:30; closed weekends, holidays, Jewish holidays, and 2-4 weeks in summer
ACCESS: appointment required
COPYING FACILITIES: yes
MATERIALS SOLICITED: Records of orthodox Jewish synagogues in the New York City area. Will also accept organization records and individuals' papers relating to the lives of Jews in America, particularly orthodox Jews.

HOLDINGS:
Total volume: 825 c.f.
Inclusive dates: 1800 - 1969
Description: 25 collections relating to different aspects of Jewish life in America, central and eastern Europe, and Israel. Subject matter includes immigration to the United States, war and rehabilitation relief of World I and II, the Holocaust, activities of New York Jewry, education and cultural life, and communes in eastern Poland in the 19th century. Included are papers of individuals, genealogical records, photographs, and records of American Jewish organizations, including extensive documentation of European and Palestinian Jewry before 1945.

SEE: NUCMC, 1980.

SEE ALSO: Jacob F. Dienstag, 'The Mendel Gottesman Library of the Yeshiva University,' Jewish Book Annual 22 (1964-65); Harry J. Carman and Arthur W. Thompson, A Guide to the Principal Sources for American Civilization, 1800-1900, in the City of New York: Manuscripts (Columbia Univ. Press, 1960).

NY595-670

Yeshiva University
Museum
2520 Amsterdam Avenue
New York NY 10033

(212) 535-6700, Ext. 31

OPEN: M-Th 9-5:30; July and Aug. by appointment only; closed Fridays, weekends, Jewish and other holidays
ACCESS: students and researchers with special permission from Museum Director
COPYING FACILITIES: yes
MATERIALS SOLICITED: Manuscripts and documents reflecting the attitudes and folkways of the Jewish people, as well

as photographs that document Jewish history.

HOLDINGS:
Total volume: 800 items
Inclusive dates: 1700 -
Description: 19th century marriage documents from the Middle East, central Europe, and the United States; photographs relating to Jewish communities around the world; slides of ancient synagogues, historical synagogues of Europe, and ceremonial objects and textiles dating back to the early 1700's; and 500 photographs and primary materials from pre-World War II Europe and Israel.

NY595-700

YIVO Institute for Jewish Research
Archives
1048 Fifth Avenue
New York NY 10028

(212) 535-6700

OPEN: M, Tu, Th, F 9:30-5:30; closed Wednesdays, weekends, Jewish and other holidays
COPYING FACILITIES: yes
MATERIALS SOLICITED: Materials pertaining to modern Jewish history and cultural life throughout the world, including institutional records, private papers, subject collections, photographs, sound recordings, films, and microfilms.

HOLDINGS:
Total volume: 8,500 l.f.
Inclusive dates: 15th century -
Description: Over 800 collections relating to Jewish history and culture, and more specifically to immigration and resettlement, especially in the Western Hemisphere; labor movements; the Holocaust and its aftermath; prominent personalities; art; Yiddish culture, including language, literature, theater, press, education, and folklore; and eastern European Jewry. Included are records of institutions and organizations, private papers, photographs, and special subject collections.

GUIDES: Mimeographed copies of Guide to Major Collections in the YIVO Archives (1972) are available on request.

SEE: Hamer; NUCMC, 1959-62, 64, 68-69.

SEE: Spalek; Robbins.

SEE ALSO: Philip P. Mason, ed., Directory of Jewish Archival Institutions (Wayne State Univ. Press, 1975); Jacob Robinson and Philip Friedman, Guide to Jewish History Under Nazi Impact (YIVO Institute for Jewish Research and Yad Vashem Martyrs' and Heroes' Memorial Authority, Joint Documentary Projects, 1960); Gerald Friedberg, 'Sources for the Study of Socialism in America, 1901-1919,' Labor History 6 (Spring 1965); Alan M. Meckler and Ruth McMullin, comps., Oral History Collections (Bowker, 1970); Ann Novotny, ed., Picture Sources 3 (Special Libraries Assn., 1975); Walter Schatz, ed., Directory of Afro-American Resources (Bowker, 1970).

NY595-740

Young Women's Christian Association
City of New York
Laura Parson Pratt Archives and
Research Center
610 Lexington Avenue
New York NY 10022

(212) 755-4500

OPEN: by appointment only
COPYING FACILITIES: yes
MATERIALS SOLICITED: Materials relating to the programs of the YWCA of the City of New York and its involvement in the history of women in the New York City community. Will also accept papers of and materials relating to former leaders of the YWCA.

HOLDINGS:
Total volume: 1,000 l.f.; other items
Inclusive dates: 1870 -
Description: Materials relating chiefly to the history of the YWCA of New York City. Included are legal documents, correspondence, reports, articles, statistical information, manuals, handbooks, policy statements, program materials, budgets, clippings, photographs, course curricula, catalogs, and other items.

NY595-760

Zionist Library and Archives
515 Park Avenue
New York NY 10022

(212) 753-2167

OPEN: M-Th 10-5:15, F 10 until two hours before sundown; closed weekends and Jewish holy days
COPYING FACILITIES: yes
MATERIALS SOLICITED: Materials relating to Israel, Palestine, Zionism, and American Jewish history.

HOLDINGS:
Total volume: 721 l.f.; 117 reels microfilm
Inclusive dates: 1896 -
Description: Materials dealing with Zionism, Palestine, Israel, other Middle Eastern countries, and Jewish history from the late 19th and 20th centuries. Holdings consist of correspondence, memorandums, minutes of meetings of organizations, microfilm, manuscripts, photographs, collections of ephemera, and audiovisual materials.

SEE: Hamer.

SEE: Hinding; Novotny.

NEWARK

NY597-130

Daughters of the American
Revolution
Colonel William Prescott Chapter
119 High Street
Newark NY 14513

(315) 331-2027

OPEN: by appointment only
COPYING FACILITIES: no

HOLDINGS:
Total volume: 10 c.f.; 80 vols
Inclusive dates: 1845 -
Description: Scrapbooks of DAR and genealogical materials and papers prepared by DAR members on various topics of local historical interest.

SEE: Wayne County Guide.

NY597-520
Newark Public Library
High Street
Newark NY 14513

(315) 331-4370

OPEN: M-F 9:30-9, Sa 9:30-5:30; closed Sundays, Saturdays during July and Aug., and legal holidays
COPYING FACILITIES: yes

HOLDINGS:
Total volume: 50 vols.; 2 c.f.
Inclusive dates: 1819 -
Description: Records of the library; travel scrapbooks of Henry C. Rew, ca. 1900; and scrapbooks of local people, places, and events.

SEE: Wayne County Guide.

NEWARK VALLEY

NY598-560
Newark Valley Historical Society
Newark Valley NY

MAILING ADDRESS:
Box 222
Newark Valley NY 13811

no telephone

OPEN: by appointment only
COPYING FACILITIES: no
MATERIALS SOLICITED: Newark Valley history and genealogy. Will also accept materials pertaining to Tioga County history.

HOLDINGS:
Total volume: 5 vols.; 3 items
Inclusive dates: 1836 - 1909
Description: The daybook from Joseph Cookson's dry goods store, 1836-39; the records of the Woman's Christian Temperance Union, 1889-1909; and other materials dealing with Tioga County and Newark Valley.

SEE: Tioga County Guide.

NEWBURGH

NY599-320
Historical Society of Newburgh Bay
and the Highlands
Library
Crawford House
189 Montgomery Street
Newburgh NY 12550

(914) 561-2585

OPEN: Tu-Th 2-4; closed other days, holidays, Jan and Feb
ACCESS: appointments requested
COPYING FACILITIES: no

MATERIALS SOLICITED: Materials relating to the towns of Newburgh and New Windsor, including early records of the Provincial Congress and the State Congress. Will also accept, space permitting, materials relating to other area towns, Orange County, New York, and American history.

HOLDINGS:
Total volume: 6 file cabinets
Inclusive dates: 18th century -
Description: Historical materials relating to Newburgh and the surrounding area.

SEE: Hamer.

NY599-560
Newburgh Free Library
124 Grand Street
Newburgh NY 12550

(914) 561-1836

OPEN: winter, M-Th 9-9, F, Sa 9-5, Su 1-5; summer, M 9-9, Tu-F 9-5; closed weekends July-Aug. and holidays
COPYING FACILITIES: yes
MATERIALS SOLICITED: Materials that relate to the history of Newburgh and Orange County.

HOLDINGS:
Total volume: 12 l.f.
Inclusive dates: 18th century -
Description: Materials relating to Orange County, Ulster County, and Newburgh history, especially the Revolutionary War and Civil War periods. Included are literary manuscripts, correspondence, genealogical charts and family histories, church and cemetery records, reports, records of associations and government agencies, a manuscript atlas of Newburgh, photographs, and tapes of meetings and speeches.

NY599-880
Washington's Headquarters State
Historic Site
84 Liberty Street
Newburgh NY

MAILING ADDRESS:
P.O. Box 1783
Newburgh NY 12550

(914) 562-1195

OPEN: W-Su 9-5, M, Tu by appointment only; closed Thanksgiving, Christmas, and New Year's
ACCESS: appointment required
COPYING FACILITIES: no
MATERIALS SOLICITED: Manuscripts relating to the American Revolution, George Washington, and local colonial history.

HOLDINGS:
Total volume: 1,750 items; 24 vols.
Inclusive dates: 1648 - 1900
Description: Materials relating to the colonial and revolutionary period in New York State. Included are papers relating to George Washington, Timothy Pickering, DeWitt Clinton, George Clinton, the New York Convention's 1776 committee to obstruct the Hudson River, and privateering and other military and naval

materials from the late 18th and 19th centuries.

SEE: NUCMC, 1966.

NIAGARA FALLS

NY602-570
Niagara Falls Public Library
Local History Department
1425 Main Street
Niagara Falls NY 14305

(716) 278-8229

OPEN: by appointment only
COPYING FACILITIES: yes
MATERIALS SOLICITED: Materials concerning the Niagara frontier area, including Niagara County and Niagara Falls. Will also accept western New York materials.

HOLDINGS:
Total volume: 10,000 items
Inclusive dates: 19th century -
Description: Materials dealing with the Niagara frontier and Niagara Falls, including manuscripts, 1,000 photographs, and 5,000 postcards, in addition to deeds, relief records of the 1930's-40's, and other records of the town of Pendleton.
Materials relating to Niagara Falls, including visitors' descriptions; hotel registers; letters, papers, and other memorabilia of the Porter, Whitney, and other early families in the area; cemetery and church records; vital statistics and census data; and manuscripts relating to electric power development.

SEE: Hinding.

SEE ALSO: a subject guide to the photograph collection available upon request.

The repository holds materials previously listed separately under Niagara Falls Historical Society, Inc., **(NY602-550)** in the first edition.

NIAGARA UNIVERSITY

NY604-560
Niagara University
Archives
Niagara University NY 14109

(716) 285-1212, Ext. 380

OPEN: Su 1-12, M-Th 8-12, F 8-9, Sa 10-8; closed holidays; hours vary during academic recesses
ACCESS: at the discretion of the archivist
COPYING FACILITIES: yes
MATERIALS SOLICITED: Materials pertaining to the University and the Vincentian Fathers. Will also accept materials concerning the history of the Niagara frontier and western New York.

HOLDINGS:
Total volume: 5.5 c.f.
Inclusive dates: 1856 -
Description: Materials relating to the history of Niagara University and the Vincentian Fathers. Holdings consist of diaries predating 1907, photographs, charters from the New York Board of

Regents, letters from Roman Catholic church officials, and University records, including student transcripts and financial accounts, yearbooks and other student publications, minutes of organizations, catalogs, and treasurer's reports.

SEE: Hamer.

NICHOLS

NY605-280

George P. and Susan Platt Cady
  Library
18 River Street
Nichols NY

MAILING ADDRESS:
P.O. Box 70
Nichols NY 13812

(607) 699-3835

OPEN: M, Tu, Th 3-9, W, F 3-5; closed weekends and holidays
COPYING FACILITIES: no
MATERIALS SOLICITED: Will accept materials dealing with the Cady family and the town of Nichols.

HOLDINGS:
    Total volume: 65 items
    Inclusive dates: 1851 - 1910
    Description: An account book, scrapbooks, photographs, and other materials pertaining to the Cady and Platt families of Nichols.

SEE: Tioga County Guide.

NORTH TARRYTOWN

NY612-690

Rockefeller University
Rockefeller Archive Center
Hillcrest, Pocantico Hills
North Tarrytown NY 10591

(914) 631-4505

OPEN: M-F 9-5; closed weekends and holidays
ACCESS: qualified scholars
COPYING FACILITIES: yes
MATERIALS SOLICITED: Rockefeller Foundation, Rockefeller University, and Rockefeller family records, and those of associated individuals and institutions.

HOLDINGS:
    Total volume: 7,832 c.f.
    Inclusive dates: 1877 -
    Description: Archives and manuscripts relating to world-wide programs in education, research, public health, medicine, the arts, humanities, social science, social welfare, agricultural development, public administration, business, and philanthropy. Institutions and individuals represented include the Rockefeller Foundation, Rockefeller University, General Education Board, Bureau of Social Hygiene, China Medical Board, International Education Board, Laura Spelman Rockefeller Memorial, Rockefeller Sanitary Commission for the Eradication of Hookworm Disease, Spelman Fund of New York, Claude W. Barlow, Wallace Buttrick, Lawrence B. Dunham, John A. Ferrell,

Frederick T. Gates, Wickliffe Rose, and John D. Rockefeller.

GUIDES: *Archives and Manuscripts in the Rockefeller Archive Center* (1979).

SEE: NUCMC, 1974 (listed under New York City, NY, as Rockefeller Foundation Archives and Rockefeller University Library-Archives), 75-76, 77, 80.

SEE: Parkinson; Hinding.

NORTHPORT

NY615-560

Northport Public Library
Reference Department
151 Laurel Avenue
Northport NY 11768

(516) 261-6930

OPEN: M-F 9-9, Sa 9-5, Su 1-5; closed Sundays, June-Aug.; closed holidays
ACCESS: identification is required
COPYING FACILITIES: yes
MATERIALS SOLICITED: Material relating to local history, personalities, and organizations, including photographs, slides, and oral history tapes. Will also accept some materials relating to Suffolk County, as well as supporting documentation from New York State and Connecticut.

HOLDINGS:
    Total volume: 20 oral history tapes; other materials
    Inclusive dates: 1800's -
    Description: Materials relating to Northport, including original manuscripts of writers who live or have lived in the community, photographs, and oral history interviews with local citizens.

SEE: Robbins.

NORWICH

NY618-115

Chenango County Historian's Office
Chenango County Historical Society
  Museum
Rexford and Silver Streets
Norwich NY 13815

(607) 334-9227

OPEN: M-F 9-5; closed weekends and holidays
COPYING FACILITIES: yes
MATERIALS SOLICITED: Materials concerning Chenango County history and genealogy.

HOLDINGS:
    Total volume: 260 c.f.; 230 vols.; 175 items
    Inclusive dates: 1790 -
    Description: County records, school records, business records, genealogical records, photographs, scrapbooks, and subject files concerning Chenango County, primarily from the 19th century.

SEE: Chenango County Guide.

NY618-120

Chenango County Historical Society
Rexford and Silver Streets
Norwich NY 13815

(607) 334-9227

OPEN: summer, Su, W, Sa 2-5; other times by appointment only
COPYING FACILITIES: yes
MATERIALS SOLICITED: Chenango County history and genealogy.

HOLDINGS:
    Total volume: 35 c.f.; 600 vols.; 100 items
    Inclusive dates: 1798 -
    Description: Assessment rolls and church, court, business, school, organization, and railroad records from towns in Chenango County. Also included are Civil War papers, diaries, scrapbooks, photographs, subject files, and genealogical data, chiefly from the 19th century.

SEE: Chenango County Guide.

NY618-280

Guernsey Memorial Library
3 Court Street
Norwich NY 13815

(607) 334-4034

OPEN: M-F 10-9, Sa 10-5; Saturdays 10-1 July - Aug.; closed Sundays and holidays
COPYING FACILITIES: yes
MATERIALS SOLICITED: Materials dealing with the history and genealogy of Norwich and Chenango County.

HOLDINGS:
    Total volume: 25 c.f.; 80 vols.; 225 items
    Inclusive dates: 1656 -
    Description: Local business records, Civil War records, genealogical data, photographs, personal papers, and subject files dealing with the city of Norwich and Chenango County, chiefly during the 19th and early 20th centuries.

SEE: Chenango County Guide.

OGDENSBURG

NY634-160

Diocese of Ogdensburg
Archives
622 Washington Street
Ogdensburg NY 13669

(315) 393-2920

OPEN: M-F 9-4; closed weekends and holidays
COPYING FACILITIES: yes
MATERIALS SOLICITED: Materials of special interest to the Diocese, to Ogdensburg, and to northern New York.

HOLDINGS:
    Total volume: not specified
    Inclusive dates: 1751 -
    Description: Materials concerning the history of the Roman Catholic Diocese of Ogdensburg since 1872, with emphasis on the post-1940 period, including information on its constituent parishes and or-

ganizations. Of special interest are mid-18th century records of Fort La Presentation, a French and Indian settlement at Ogdensburg.

NY634-600

Ogdensburg Public Library
312 Washington Street
Ogdensburg NY 13669

(315) 393-4325

OPEN: M-F 10-8, Sa 10-5; closed Sundays, holidays, and Saturdays during the summer
COPYING FACILITIES: yes
MATERIALS SOLICITED: Historical and genealogical materials relating to Ogdensburg, the St. Lawrence Seaway, and St. Lawrence County, NY. Will also accept materials relating to northern New York history or geneaology.

HOLDINGS:
   Total volume: 3,000 items; 15 l.f.
   Inclusive dates: 1750 -
   Description: Manuscripts, maps, charts, account books, photographs, diaries, oral history interviews, scrapbooks, and other materials relating to the history of the St. Lawrence Seaway, St. Lawrence County, NY, and especially Ogdensburg.

OLD CHATHAM

NY637-720

The Shaker Museum
Emma B. King Library
95 Shaker Museum Road
Old Chatham NY 12136

(518) 794-9100

OPEN: by appointment Tu-Th; closed holidays
ACCESS: by application to Director
COPYING FACILITIES: yes
MATERIALS SOLICITED: Materials relating to the United Society of Believers in Christ's Second Appearing (Shakers) plus items relating to local history, folklore, and 18th and 19th century crafts and technology.

HOLDINGS:
   Total volume: 117 file drawers; 4,990 books
   Inclusive dates: 1794 -
   Description: A wide range of Shaker writings and related materials, including a large records and manuscript collection.

GUIDES: Robert F. W. Meader, comp., *Catalogue of the Emma B. King Library of The Shaker Museum* (1970).

SEE: NUCMC, 1966.

SEE: Novotny; Robbins.

ONEIDA

NY646-520

Madison County Historical Society
435 Main Street
Oneida NY

MAILING ADDRESS:
P.O. Box 415
Oneida NY 13421

(315) 363-4136

OPEN: W 9-5, Th, F noon-5; closed other days and holidays
COPYING FACILITIES: no
MATERIALS SOLICITED: Manuscripts relating to central New York. Will also accept other manuscripts.

HOLDINGS:
   Total volume: 15,500 items
   Inclusive dates: 1638 -
   Description: Approximately 300 manuscript items relating to Madison County and central New York, including correspondence, genealogical material, diaries, and business and church records. There is also the Traditional Crafts Archive, containing 15,000 slides, 150 tapes, and 30 motion pictures.

SEE: Hamer.

SEE: Schatz; Hinding.

ONEONTA

NY648-310

Hartwick College
Archives
Oneonta NY 13820

(607) 432-4200, Ext. 402

OPEN: summer M-F 9-4:30
ACCESS: advance arrangements suggested
COPYING FACILITIES: yes
MATERIALS SOLICITED: Materials relating to Hartwick Seminary and Hartwick College.

HOLDINGS:
   Total volume: 300 l.f.; 16 file cabinets
   Inclusive dates: 1700's -
   Description: Manuscripts relating to John C. Hartwick and his business affairs, in addition to photographs, videotapes, yearbooks, and other records of Hartwick Seminary and Hartwick College.

SEE: Meckler and McMullin; Hinding.

NY648-330

Huntington Memorial Library
62 Chestnut Street
Oneonta NY 13820

(607) 432-1980

OPEN: M-F 9-9, Sa 9-5:30; summer, M-F 9-9, Sa 9-noon; closed Sundays and holidays
COPYING FACILITIES: yes
MATERIALS SOLICITED: Materials dealing with the history and genealogy of Oneonta.

HOLDINGS:
   Total volume: 22.5 c.f.; 57 vols.
   Inclusive dates: 19th century -
   Description: Census, church, and organization records. Other collections include historical notes, genealogical data, scrapbooks, and subject files concerning Oneonta and Otsego County history.

NY648-720

State University of New York
College at Oneonta
James M. Milne Library
Special Collections Center
Oneonta NY 13820

(607) 431-3500

OPEN: M-F 1:30-4:30; closed weekends and holidays
COPYING FACILITIES: yes
MATERIALS SOLICITED: Noncurrent records of the State University College at Oneonta, and related photographs, oral history tapes and transcripts, and faculty papers. Will also accept manuscripts, visual documents, and oral histories relating to Oneonta local history.

HOLDINGS:
   Total volume: 200 items; 184 l.f.
   Inclusive dates: 1889 -
   Description: Correspondence, minutes, official reports, publications, faculty papers, audiovisual materials, oral history tapes and transcripts, and other records of the State University College at Oneonta.

NY648-800

Upper Susquehanna Historical Society
Historical Museum
11 Ford Avenue
Oneonta NY

MAILING ADDRESS:
203 River Street
Oneonta NY 13820

(607) 432-2888

OPEN: by appointment only
COPYING FACILITIES: no
MATERIALS SOLICITED: Materials pertaining to Oneonta and Otsego County.

HOLDINGS:
   Total volume: 3 file drawers
   Inclusive dates: 18th century -
   Description: Materials relating to Oneonta and Otsego County, including diaries, early city records, account books, land grants, and military records.

ORIENT

NY654-600

Oysterponds Historical Society
Village Lane
Orient NY 11957

(516) 323-2480

OPEN: by appointment
COPYING FACILITIES: no
MATERIALS SOLICITED: Local historical documents.

HOLDINGS:
> *Total volume:* 80 l.f.
> *Inclusive dates:* 1640 -
> *Description:* Materials relating to Orient (formerly Oyster-ponds), a fishing, agricultural, and resort area. Included are diaries; hotel, school, and church registers; account books and ledgers pertaining to farming and shopkeeping; ships' logs; minute books of social clubs; jury lists; legal documents such as wills, deeds, and contracts; personnel and business correspondence; military records; and 'Griffin's Journal,' a history of the area.

There is also the Clarence Ashton Wood Collection, consisting of 25 l.f. of his research notes and manuscripts of articles published locally and relating to the North Fork of Long Island from Riverhead to Orient Point, including Shelter Island.

OSSINING

NY657-600

Ossining Historical Society
Museum
196 Croton Avenue
Ossining NY 10562

(914) 941-0001

OPEN: Su, M, W 2-4; other days by appointment
ACCESS: qualified students with permission of Museum director
COPYING FACILITIES: no
MATERIALS SOLICITED: Materials on the history of the Ossining area. Will also accept literary manuscripts by local authors.

HOLDINGS:
> *Total volume:* 30 l.f.
> *Inclusive dates:* 1750 -
> *Description:* Correspondence, business records, genealogical source data, institutional records, aerial photographs and other pictorial items, audio recordings, and other materials concentrating on the social and economic history of the town of Ossining.

SEE: NUCMC, 1959-61.

SEE: Hinding.

OSWEGO

NY660-600

Oswego County Historical Society
135 East Third Street
Oswego NY 13126

(315) 343-1342

OPEN: by appointment only Tu-F 10-5; closed weekends, Mondays, and holidays
COPYING FACILITIES: yes
MATERIALS SOLICITED: Materials related to the history of Oswego County.

HOLDINGS:
> *Total volume:* 90 l.f.
> *Inclusive dates:* not specified
> *Description:* Manuscripts, chiefly from the 19th century, including Civil War correspondence, diaries, and accounts; records of local businesses, churches, and

schools; and music scores, maps, and photographs.

SEE: Hamer; NUCMC, 1959-61.

SEE: Novotny; Hinding.

NY660-720

State University of New York
College at Oswego
Penfield Library
SUCO Special Collections
Oswego NY 13126

(315) 341-3122

OPEN: M-Th 1-4:30; by appointment during school vacations; closed Fridays, weekends, and holidays
COPYING FACILITIES: yes
MATERIALS SOLICITED: Archival materials relating to the State University of New York, College at Oswego, and manuscripts and oral history tapes relating to Oswego County. Will also accept materials relating to New York State history.

HOLDINGS:
> *Total volume:* 513 l.f.
> *Inclusive dates:* 1762 -
> *Description:* Manuscripts, photographs, and other materials relating to the city and county of Oswego. Included are 100 oral histories documenting early 20th century economic and social history, papers of Millard Fillmore and other prominent 19th century figures of Buffalo, NY, and the archives of the College, 1850 to date.

SEE: NUCMC, 1970, 74, 76.

SEE: Hinding.

SEE ALSO: Donald W. Barden and Charles W. Brownson, *Guide to the Marshall Family Papers (1762-1908)* (SUCO Special Collections, 1975). Other guides, both published and unpublished, are available at the Library.

OTEGO

NY661-620

Otego Historical Society
Harris House
67 Main Street
Otego NY 13825

no telephone

OPEN: by appointment only
COPYING FACILITIES: no
MATERIALS SOLICITED: Otego history.

HOLDINGS:
> *Total volume:* 2 c.f.; 24 vols.; 7 items
> *Inclusive dates:* 1843 -
> *Description:* Business records, school records, and photographs of Otego.

OVID

NY664-200

Edith B. Ford Memorial Library
Ovid NY 14521

(607) 869-3031

OPEN: Tu 2-8, W 2-4, F 2-5, Sa 9-noon; closed other days and holidays
COPYING FACILITIES: no

HOLDINGS:
> *Total volume:* 3 vols.; 2 c.f.
> *Inclusive dates:* 1840 - 1968
> *Description:* Materials related to the town of Ovid.

SEE: Seneca County Guide.

OWEGO

NY665-760

Tioga County Historical Society
Museum
110-112 Front Street
Owego NY 13827

(607) 687-2460

OPEN: Sa, Su 1:30-4:30, Tu 10-4:30, W 10-4:30, 7-9, Th, F 10-4:30; closed Mondays and holidays
COPYING FACILITIES: yes
MATERIALS SOLICITED: Materials relating to Tioga County history.

HOLDINGS:
> *Total volume:* 2,000 items
> *Inclusive dates:* 1790 -
> *Description:* Material relating to Tioga County, including public documents, church records, merchants' and artisans' journals, club records, letters, docket books, and logbooks. There are also genealogical materials, photographs, and oral history tapes.

SEE: Tioga County Guide.

OXFORD

NY667-580

Oxford Historical Society
Oxford Memorial Library
Fort Hill Park
Oxford NY 13830

(607) 843-4021

OPEN: Tu 2-4 and 7-9; closed other days and holidays
COPYING FACILITIES: no
MATERIALS SOLICITED: Oxford history. Will also accept Chenango history.

HOLDINGS:
> *Total volume:* 4 c.f.; 35 vols.; 175 items
> *Inclusive dates:* 1808 -
> *Description:* Collections including legal documents, school records, business records, photographs, and scrapbooks concerning local history.

SEE: Chenango County Guide.

NY667-600
Oxford Memorial Library
Fort Hill Park
Oxford NY 13830

(607) 843-4021

OPEN: Tu-Th 1-9, F 1-5; Saturdays
9-noon May - Oct. and 2-5 Nov. -
April; closed Sundays, Mondays, and
holidays
COPYING FACILITIES: no
MATERIALS SOLICITED: Oxford town history and genealogy. Will also accept
materials relating to Chenango County.

HOLDINGS:
Total volume: 2 c.f.; 86 vols., 55
items
Inclusive dates: 1577 - 1972
Description: Genealogical materials,
photographs, scrapbooks, and church,
school, military, business, library, organization, and town records, concerning Oxford, primarily in the 19th and early 20th
centuries.

SEE: Hamer.

SEE: Chenango County Guide.

PAINTED POST

NY670-760
Town of Erwin Museum
Building 3, Village Square
Painted Post NY 14870

no telephone

OPEN: July - Aug., M-Sa 10-4; other
times by appointment
COPYING FACILITIES: no
MATERIALS SOLICITED: History of Painted Post and the town of Erwin, NY.

HOLDINGS:
Total volume: 14 c.f.
Inclusive dates: 1786 -
Description: Account books, photographs, diaries, tax rolls, and other materials relating to Painted Post, Corning,
and the vicinity.

SEE: Steuben County Guide.

PALMYRA

NY672-440
King's Daughters Free Library
127 Cuyler Street
Palmyra NY 14522

(315) 597-5276

OPEN: M 12-9, Tu, W 12-5, Th 10-5, F
12-9, Sa 2-5; closed Sundays and
weekends in July and August
COPYING FACILITIES: yes

HOLDINGS:
Total volume: 20 c.f.; 24 vols.; 100
items
Description: Material includes legal papers; reminiscences and papers on local
history; letters of Justin Perkins, missionary in Persia, 1830's; scrapbooks relating
to people, places, and events in the Palmyra area; papers of the Harrison and
Lakey families of Palmyra; service
records of World Wars I and II of Pal-

myra residents; and materials relating to
the Civil War, local Civil War veterans,
and the Grand Army of the Republic;
and material on various families of the
Palmyra area.

SEE: Wayne County Guide.

PAUL SMITH'S

NY675-640
Paul Smith's College
Library
Paul Smith's NY 12970

(518) 327-6313

OPEN: M-Th 8-10:30, F 8-4:30, Sa, Su
2-10; summer, M-F 8-8; closed
weekends during summer and for
school vacations
COPYING FACILITIES: yes
MATERIALS SOLICITED: Paul Smith's area
history and old photographs of the area
and its people. Will also accept materials on the town of Brighton, Franklin
County, and the state of New York.

HOLDINGS:
Total volume: 8 c.f.
Inclusive dates: 19th century -
Description: Photographs of the
Adirondacks area, depicting logging,
hunting and fishing activities, as well as
old resorts, guides, and famous guests.

PAWLING

NY681-320
Historical Society of Quaker Hill
Wilkinson Hollow Road
Pawling NY

MAILING ADDRESS:
P.O. Box 40
Pawling NY 12564

(914) 855-5891

OPEN: June - Sept., Tu, Th, Sa 2-4:30;
closed other days; open rest of year by
appointment only
COPYING FACILITIES: no
MATERIALS SOLICITED: Materials pertaining to the history of Pawling and
Quaker Hill.

HOLDINGS:
Total volume: not specified
Inclusive dates: 1700 -
Description: Materials focusing on the
history of Quaker Hill and its people.
Included are account books, deeds, and
genealogical records.

PEEKSKILL

NY687-120
The Community of St. Mary
Convent of St. Mary
John Street
Peekskill NY 10566

(914) 737-0113

OPEN: by appointment only
ACCESS: consent of the Mother Superior
required

COPYING FACILITIES: no
MATERIALS SOLICITED: Material relating
to the Community of St. Mary.

HOLDINGS:
Total volume: 15 l.f.
Inclusive dates: 1865 -
Description: A collection of letters, pic-
tures, diaries, chronicles, and manuscripts
dealing with the Anglican Community of
St. Mary, which was founded in 1865.
Some materials deal with St. Mary's Free
Hospital for Children in New York,
which was founded by the order in 1868.

PENN YAN

NY693-640
Penn Yan Public Library
Main Street
Penn Yan NY 14527

(315) 536-6114

OPEN: M, F 10-8:30, Tu-Th 2-8:30, Sa
noon-5; closed Sundays, holidays, and
Wednesdays in summer
COPYING FACILITIES: yes
MATERIALS SOLICITED: History of Penn
Yan and Yates County, NY.

HOLDINGS:
Total volume: 2.5 c.f.
Inclusive dates: 1831 -
Description: A collection of local dia-
ries and scrapbooks.

SEE: Hamer; NUCMC, 1970.

SEE: Yates County Guide.

NY693-920
Yates County Genealogical and
Historical Society
200 Main Street
Penn Yan NY 14527

(315) 536-7318

OPEN: M-F 10-5; closed evenings and
weekends
COPYING FACILITIES: yes
MATERIALS SOLICITED: Will accept docu-
ments pertaining to the history of
Yates County and western New York.

HOLDINGS:
Total volume: 65 c.f.; 370 vols.
Inclusive dates: 1771 -
Description: Papers and diaries of local
residents, including Jemima Wilkinson
(and writings about her) and Fred S.
Hollowell; writings and photographs relating to Marcus Whitman; records of local
businesses, schools, churches, and organizations; an architectural survey of Yates
County; photographs, maps, prints, and
broadsides; genealogical materials; and
records of various local governments.

SEE: Hinding; Yates County Guide.

PERRY

NY694-640
Perry Public Library
70 North Main Street
Perry NY 14530

(716) 237-2243

OPEN: M-F 2-9, Sa 2-5; closed Sundays
  and holidays
COPYING FACILITIES: yes

HOLDINGS:
  Total volume: 14 c.f.; 29 vols.
  Inclusive dates: 1850 -
  Description: Materials relating to Perry
  local history.

SEE: Wyoming County Guide.

PHELPS

NY695-640
Phelps Community Memorial Library
Church Street
Phelps NY 14532

(315) 548-3120

OPEN: M 2-8:30, Tu 10-8:30, W 10-12,
  6:30-8:30, Th 10-8:30, F 10-12,
  6:30-8:30, Sa 2-5; closed Sundays,
  Saturdays in July and Aug., and legal
  holidays
COPYING FACILITIES: no

HOLDINGS:
  Total volume: 2.0 c.f.
  Inclusive dates: 1839 -
  Description: Records of the library, pa-
  pers of local historian Maebel E. Oaks,
  photographs, and maps.

NY695-650
Phelps Historical Society
Phelps NY 14532

no telephone

OPEN: by appointment only
COPYING FACILITIES: no

HOLDINGS:
  Total volume: 1 c.f.
  Inclusive dates: 1850 -
  Description: Maps of Phelps, grave-
  stone rubbings, a school register, and
  photographs.

PIKE

NY698-650
Pike Library
Main Street
Pike NY 14130

no telephone

OPEN: M 2-5, W 1:30-5, Sa 2-5; closed
  other days and holidays
COPYING FACILITIES: no

HOLDINGS:
  Total volume: 6 vols.
  Inclusive dates: 1879 -
  Description: Minutes and records of
  the Emersonian Reading Club,
  1879-1906, and the Pike Reading Room
  and Library Associates (1908-).

SEE: Wyoming County Guide.

PINE PLAINS

NY699-480
Little Nine Partners Historical
  Society, Inc.
Pine Plains NY

MAILING ADDRESS:
Box 243
Pine Plains NY 12567

(518) 398-7213, 1955

OPEN: by appointment only
COPYING FACILITIES: no
MATERIALS SOLICITED: Local history
  materials.

HOLDINGS:
  Total volume: 3 trunks
  Inclusive dates: 1790 -
  Description: Historical records of the
  area of the Little Nine Partners grant,
  now comprised of the towns of Pine
  Plains, North East, and Milan. Included
  are photographs, account books, two
  Quaker marriage certificates, oral histories, and a journal of Isaac Huntting, including genealogical information and an
  account of his Civil War service.

PITTSFORD

NY702-660
Pittsford Town Historian
Pittsford Town Hall
11 South Main Street
Pittsford NY 14534

(716) 381-7560

OPEN: Th 1-5; other times by
  appointment
COPYING FACILITIES: no

HOLDINGS:
  Total volume: 9 c.f.; 265 vols.; 5
  items
  Inclusive dates: 1826 -
  Description: Materials relating to the
  history of the town of Pittsford, including
  town and business records, architectural/
  historical surveys, and scrapbooks.

PLAINVIEW

NY705-560
Mergenthaler Linotype Company
Mergenthaler Drive
Plainview NY 11803

no telephone

OPEN: M-F 8:30-5; closed weekends and
  holidays
ACCESS: appointment required
COPYING FACILITIES: no

MATERIALS SOLICITED: Materials relating
  to the history of the Linotype machine
  and its typeface.

HOLDINGS:
  Total volume: 56 c.f.
  Inclusive dates: 1890 -
  Description: Materials concerning the
  invention of the Linotype and of the
  typewriter, as well as account records of
  the Mergenthaler Linotype Company
  (1890-1924) and information covering the
  development of the Mergenthaler library
  of typefaces (1920-).

PLATTSBURGH

NY708-120
Clinton County Historical Association
Clinton County Historical Museum
City Hall
Plattsburgh NY

MAILING ADDRESS:
P.O. Box 332
Plattsburgh NY 12901

(518) 561-0340

OPEN: by appointment only M-F 10-4;
  closed weekends, Christmas, New
  Year's, and July 4
ACCESS: Prior arrangements
  recommended
COPYING FACILITIES: no
MATERIALS SOLICITED: Materials relating
  to the history of Clinton County.

HOLDINGS:
  Total volume: not specified
  Inclusive dates: 1733 -
  Description: 17,000 glass negatives,
  1884-1920, mostly portraits of Clinton
  County residents, in addition to land
  grants, company records, private ledgers,
  and other documents relating to the settlement and growth of Clinton County.

NY708-440
Kent-Delord Museum
17 Cumberland Avenue
Plattsburgh NY 12901

(518) 561-1035

OPEN: Tu-Sa 9-5; closed Sundays,
  Mondays, and holidays
ACCESS: serious researchers; advance
  arrangements required
COPYING FACILITIES: no
MATERIALS SOLICITED: Will accept
  archival materials concerning the
  DeLord, Swetland, Ketchum, and
  Webb families and their descendants.

HOLDINGS:
  Total volume: 1,000 items
  Inclusive dates: 1776 - 1914
  Description: Correspondence, ledgers,
  maps, photographs, genealogical materials, architectural drawings, and scrapbooks pertaining to the Delord, Ketchum,
  Swetland, Webb, Mooers, Sailly,
  Walworth, Platt, and other early families
  of Clinton County, including their connections with military figures and events
  of the War of 1812 in the Champlain
  Valley.

SEE: Hamer.

15,000 additional items are on loan to the Special Collections Department, Feinberg Library, State University of New York College at Plattsburgh.

NY708-640

Plattsburgh Public Library
Local Collection
15 Oak Street
Plattsburgh NY

MAILING ADDRESS:
P.O. Box 570
Plattsburgh NY 12901

(518) 563-0921

OPEN: M, W-F 10-9, Tu 10-5, Sa 9-5; closed Sundays and holidays
COPYING FACILITIES: yes
MATERIALS SOLICITED: Materials relating to the city of Plattsburgh and Clinton County. Will also accept materials relating to Essex, and Franklin counties.

HOLDINGS:
Total volume: not specified
Inclusive dates: not specified
Description: Materials relating to the history of Plattsburgh and the counties of Clinton, Essex, and Franklin, including genealogies of North Country families, cemetery records, church records, and maps.

SEE: Hamer.

NY708-720

State University of New York
College at Plattsburgh
Feinberg Library
Special Collections Department
North Country History Center
Plattsburgh NY 12901

(518) 564-5206

OPEN: M 9-7, Tu-F 9-5; closed weekends and holidays
COPYING FACILITIES: yes
MATERIALS SOLICITED: Archival materials relating to the history of Clinton, Essex, and Franklin counties, with special emphasis on the Adirondacks and the Lake Champlain Valley. Will also accept materials relating to St. Lawrence, Jefferson, Lewis, Herkimer, Hamilton, Warren, and Washington counties.

HOLDINGS:
Total volume: 300 l.f.
Inclusive dates: 1776 -
Description: Manuscripts and other materials relating to the history of Clinton, Essex, and Franklin counties; the Adirondack Mountains; and the Lake Champlain Valley. Subject matter includes the military history of Lake Champlain, the iron ore and logging industries, North Country folklore and music, and genealogy. Included are more than 2,000 maps, surveys, and architectural drawings; 259 oral history tapes; and 3,500 photographs.

GUIDES: George Glyndon Cole, *Manuscripts for Research: Report of the Director, 1961-1974, North Country History Center* (1974).

SEE: NUCMC, 1977.

SEE: Meckler and McMullin; Hinding; Robbins.

PORT CHESTER

NY71S-720

Port Chester Public Library
1 Haseco Avenue
Port Chester NY 10573

no telephone
SEE: NUCMC, 1976.

Questionnaire not returned.

PORT JERVIS

NY714-560

Minisink Valley Historical Society
Library Building
138 Pike Street
Port Jervis NY

MAILING ADDRESS:
P.O. Box 659
Port Jervis NY 12771

(914) 856-2375

OPEN: Th 1-4 and by appointment
COPYING FACILITIES: yes
MATERIALS SOLICITED: Materials relating to American history, geography, and genealogy, 1600 to date, with emphasis on New York State and Orange and Ulster counties.

HOLDINGS:
Total volume: 10,000 items
Inclusive dates: 1700 -
Description: Materials relating chiefly to western Orange County, including the archives of the town of Deerpark and the village of Port Jervis, local records of the Delaware and Hudson Canal (1700-1910), 2,000 photographs, genealogical records, and Work Projects Administration files.

PORT WASHINGTON

NY717-640

Port Washington Public Library
Ernie Simon Collection
245 Main Street
Port Washington NY 11050

(516) 883-4400, Ext. 111

OPEN: M-F 9-9, Sa 9-5; closed Sundays and holidays
COPYING FACILITIES: yes
MATERIALS SOLICITED: Materials related to local history.

HOLDINGS:
Total volume: 25 l.f.
Inclusive dates: 1908 -
Description: The papers of Ernest Simon, editor of the *Port Washington News* for 50 years, who wrote a weekly series 'Port Remembered.' The collection, which is indexed, includes video-tapes of Mr. Simon on his 85th birthday, signed articles, photographs, correspondence, and memorabilia.

SEE: NUCMC, 1979.

PORTVILLE

NY720-640

Portville Free Library
1 North Main Street
Portville NY 14770

(716) 933-8441

OPEN: by appointment only; closed holidays
COPYING FACILITIES: yes

HOLDINGS:
Total volume: 4.25 c.f.; 76 vols.
Inclusive dates: 1837 -
Description: Accounts of J. E. Dusenbury's general store, 1842-83; Portville post office records, 1837-49; Portville justice dockets, 1895-1918; library records, 1857-1969; and other materials on local organizations, especially the Woman's Christian Temperance Union, schools, churches, families, and events.

SEE: Hamer; NUCMC, 1968.

SEE: Davis.

POTSDAM

NY723-640

Potsdam Public Museum
Civic Center
Park Street
Potsdam NY 13676

(315) 265-6910

OPEN: Tu-Sa 2-5, other hours by appointment; closed Sundays, Mondays, and holidays
COPYING FACILITIES: no
MATERIALS SOLICITED: Materials relating to the history of Potsdam. Will also accept historical material on St. Lawrence County.

HOLDINGS:
Total volume: not specified
Inclusive dates: 1806 -
Description: Materials dealing with the history of Potsdam and surrounding communities. Included are 10 file drawers and 60 volumes of assessment books and poll records, in addition to diaries, business records, and correspondence.

NY723-715
State University of New York
College at Potsdam
Crane School of Music
Library
Potsdam NY 13676

(315) 267-2451

SEE: NUCMC, 1980.

Questionnaire not returned.

NY723-720
State University of New York
College at Potsdam
Frederick W. Crumb Memorial
  Library
Pierrepont Avenue
Potsdam NY 13676

(315) 267-2486

OPEN: M-F 8-11, Sa, Su 10-11; closed
  Christmas, New Year's, and
  Thanksgiving
COPYING FACILITIES: yes
MATERIALS SOLICITED: College archives
  and Congressional papers for New
  York's 30th Congressional district.

HOLDINGS:
  Total volume: 356 l.f.
  Inclusive dates: 1869 -
  Description: Letters and papers of U.S.
Representative from New York Bertrand
Snell, and the archives of the College and
its predecessors.

SEE: NUCMC, 1969, 80.

SEE: Hinding.

POUGHKEEPSIE

NY726-40
Adriance Memorial Library
Local History Collection
93 Market Street
Poughkeepsie NY 12601

(914) 485-3445

OPEN: M, W, F, Sa 9-5, Tu, Th 9-9;
  closed Sundays, holidays, and
  Saturdays from Memorial Day through
  Labor Day
ACCESS: restricted access to local history
  collection; appointment preferred
COPYING FACILITIES: yes
MATERIALS SOLICITED: Genealogy and
  history of Dutchess, Putnam, Columbia, Orange, Ulster, and Greene counties. Will also accept materials relating
  to the history and genealogy of neighboring States.

HOLDINGS:
  Total volume: 300 l.f.
  Inclusive dates: 1697 - 1900
  Description: A collection pertaining to
the genealogy and history of Dutchess,
Putnam, Columbia, Orange, Ulster, and
Greene counties in New York State. Included are family genealogies and church
records, early records of Poughkeepsie
and other towns in Dutchess County
from the 1700's, and Poughkeepsie Common Council minutes from 1803 to the
present. Also included are materials on

deposit from the Dutchess County Historical Society.
  Included are papers of the Livingstone
family; Robert Newlin Verplanck; diaries
of Matthew Vassar, Jr.; musical compositions of Charles Gilbert Spross; correspondence of Franklin D. Roosevelt and
Helen Wilkinson Reynolds; manuscript
maps; records of the Woman's Christian
Temperance Union and various women's
clubs; and papers of Benson J. Lossing.

SEE: Hamer.

NY726-850
Vassar College
Library
Poughkeepsie NY 12601

(914) 452-7000, Ext. 2135

OPEN: M-F 8:30-5; closed weekends,
  Christmas, New Year's, July 4;
  irregular hours during College
  vacations
COPYING FACILITIES: yes
MATERIALS SOLICITED: History of wom-
  en and the women's rights movement;
  papers of Vassar writers and scholars;
  black studies materials; and manuscripts of major composers. Will also
  accept materials relating to European
  and American literature and history.

HOLDINGS:
  Total volume: 700 l.f.; 3,500 vols.
  Inclusive dates: 15th century -
  Description: Materials relating to the
social sciences, history and literature,
Vassar College archives, and papers of
Vassar faculty and alumnae.

SEE: Hamer; NUCMC, 1966, 78.

SEE: Martin; Armstrong; Robbins.

SEE ALSO: Albert Krichmar, *The Women's
Rights Movement in the United States,
1848-1970: A Bibliography and
Sourcebook* (Scarecrow Press, 1972);
*Source Materials for the Recent History
of Astronomy and Astrophysics: A
Checklist of Manuscript Collections in
the United States* (American Institute
of Physics, 1971).

PULTENEY

NY728-640
Pulteney Free Library
Pulteney NY 14874

(607) 868-3652

OPEN: Tu, Th, Sa 2-5; closed other days
  and holidays
COPYING FACILITIES: no
MATERIALS SOLICITED: History of the
  town of Pulteney and vicinity.

HOLDINGS:
  Total volume: 2.5 c.f.
  Inclusive dates: 1814 -
  Description: Photographs, church
records, clippings, account books, and
diaries from Pulteney.

SEE: Steuben County Guide.

PURCHASE

NY732-520
Manhattanville College
Library
Rare Books (Special Collections) and
  Archives
Purchase NY 10577

(914) 694-2200, Ext. 546

OPEN: by appointment only
ACCESS: College community and
  accredited scholars
COPYING FACILITIES: yes
MATERIALS SOLICITED: Rare and unusu-
  al materials of significance to the lib-
  eral arts curriculum of the College, and
  College records and other related ma-
  terial from offices, alumni, and friends.
  Will also accept diaries, letters, and
  other materials of historic, literary, and
  religious interest; and materials on
  New York City, especially the Houston
  Street and Convent Avenue areas in
  the 19th century, and on Westchester
  County, especially the Harrison area.

HOLDINGS:
  Total volume: 50 l.f.; 350,500 items
  Inclusive dates: 1800 -
  Description: A collection of correspondence; reminiscences, chiefly of historical
figures of the Civil War period; miscellaneous materials relating to 20th century
American religious history; College and
Academy records dating from 1841; and
related correspondence and other materials.

SEE: Hamer; NUCMC, 1977.

NY732-730
State University of New York
College at Purchase
Library
Purchase NY 10577

(914) 253-5085

OPEN: M-F 8:30-5; closed weekends and
  holidays
COPYING FACILITIES: yes
MATERIALS SOLICITED: Materials pertaining to the history of the College.
  Will also accept materials about the
  community of Purchase.

HOLDINGS:
  Total volume: 29 l.f.
  Inclusive dates: 1967 -
  Description: Records of the College
and related institutions, such as the
Neuberger Museum and the Performing
Arts Center.

RENSSELAER

NY741-720
St. Anthony-on-Hudson Library
Rensselaer NY 12144

(518) 463-2261

OPEN: by appointment only
ACCESS: qualified scholars approved by
  institution
COPYING FACILITIES: yes

MATERIALS SOLICITED: History of the order of Friars Minor Conventual in the United States. Will also accept materials relating to local church history in Albany and the surrounding area.

HOLDINGS:
Total volume: 250 items
Inclusive dates: 1840 -
Description: Financial and academic records of St. Anthony-on-Hudson; materials relating to the Friars Minor Conventual in the United States and Canada, including sermons, lectures, class lectures, parochial records, chronicles, 19th century American diaries, 20th century Canadian diaries, and photograph albums; and financial records of St. Mary's Parish, Albany (1840-50).

RENSSELAERVILLE

NY742-690
Rensselaerville Historical Society
Grist Mill
Main Street
Rensselaerville NY

MAILING ADDRESS:
Box 8
Rensselaerville NY 12147

(518) 797-5154

OPEN: by appointment only
COPYING FACILITIES: yes
MATERIALS SOLICITED: Material of all types relating to the town of Rensselaerville and its vicinity.

HOLDINGS:
Total volume: 12 boxes; 5 file cabinets
Inclusive dates: 1787 -
Description: Collections covering the history of the town of Rensselaerville, from its establishment in 1787 to the present day. Included are correspondence, account books, finance records, genealogical source data, biographical information photos, family and business papers, and literary manuscripts.

RICHBURG

NY744-680
Richburg Colonial Library
Main Street
Richburg NY 14774

no telephone

OPEN: M, Th 10-5, Tu 10-5 when Monday is holiday; closed other days
COPYING FACILITIES: no

HOLDINGS:
Total volume: 3 c.f.
Inclusive dates: 1774 -
Description: Library records, photographs, scrapbooks, genealogical data, and other items relating to the history of Richburg and Allegany County, NY.

SEE: Allegany County Guide.

RICHFIELD SPRINGS

NY745-690
Richfield Springs Public Library
59 Main Street
Richfield Springs NY

MAILING ADDRESS:
P.O. Box 271
Richfield Springs NY 13439

(315) 858-0230

OPEN: M 11:30-4:30, 7-9, Tu-F 11:30-4:30; closed weekends and holidays
COPYING FACILITIES: yes
MATERIALS SOLICITED: Will accept materials relating to Richfield Springs history and genealogy.

HOLDINGS:
Total volume: 5 c.f.
Inclusive dates: 1868 - 1920
Description: Photographs of Richfield Springs, 1870-1920.

RIVERHEAD

NY749-720
Suffolk County Historical Society
300 West Main Street
Riverhead NY 11901

(516) 727-2881

OPEN: M-Sa 12:30-4:30; closed Sundays and holidays
COPYING FACILITIES: yes
MATERIALS SOLICITED: Material relating to the history of Suffolk County. Will also accept other material pertaining to Long Island.

HOLDINGS:
Total volume: 3,500 items
Inclusive dates: 1640 -
Description: Materials relating to the human and natural history of Suffolk County.

SEE: Hamer; NUCMC, 1962.

SEE: Hinding; Leventhal and Mooney - I.

ROCHESTER

NY752-40
American Baptist-Samuel B. Colgate Historical Library
1106 South Goodman Street
Rochester NY 14620

(716) 473-1740

OPEN: M-F 9-4:30; closed weekends and holidays
COPYING FACILITIES: yes
MATERIALS SOLICITED: Materials relating to the Baptist faith and life. Will also accept materials against the Baptist position.

HOLDINGS:
Total volume: 800 l.f.
Inclusive dates: 1687 -
Description: Papers of Baptist leaders including Horatio Jones, Sr., and Jr., Walter Rauschenbusch, John Roach

Straton, Justin Wroe Nixon, Albert W. Beaven, and others. Also archives of the American Baptist Churches in the U.S., including American Baptist Home and Foreign Mission societies; records of New York, Pennsylvania, and New Jersey churches; archives of the Danish Baptist Churches in America and of the Free Baptist church.

SEE: Hamer; NUCMC, 1971.

SEE: Hinding; Robbins.

NY752-60
Asbury First Methodist Church Library
1050 East Avenue
Rochester NY 14607

(716) 271-1050

OPEN: by appointment
COPYING FACILITIES: no

HOLDINGS:
Total volume: 7.5 c.f.; 66 vols.
Inclusive dates: 1836 -
Description: Records of and materials relating to the history of First Methodist, Asbury Methodist, and Asbury First Methodist churches. Most records relate to Sunday schools, missionary societies, and church government. There are also financial and government records of the East Methodist Society and membership, marriage and birth records of the Frank Street Methodist Church, both of Rochester.

NY752-100
Chili Town Historian
3235 Chili Avenue
Rochester NY 14624

(716) 889-4676, 3550

OPEN: by appointment only
COPYING FACILITIES: no

HOLDINGS:
Total volume: 14.5 c.f.
Inclusive dates: 1940 -
Description: Clippings, photographs, pamphlets, brochures, etc., pertaining to the history of Chili, NY.

NY752-110
Colgate Rochester/Bexley Hall/Crozer Theological Seminaries
Ambrose Swasey Library
1100 South Goodman Street
Rochester NY 14620

(716) 271-1320

OPEN: M-F 9-5; closed weekends and other days designated by the institution
ACCESS: appointment and permission required; applicants should state the objective of their research
COPYING FACILITIES: yes
MATERIALS SOLICITED: Materials related to the history and administration of the schools involved in this center of theological studies, to faculty and alumni, and to Rochester area church life and religious movements. Will also accept correspondence, papers, and sermons of prominent religious leaders.

HOLDINGS:
>*Total volume:* 40 l.f.
>*Inclusive dates:* 1805 -
>*Description:* Manuscripts, official records, correspondence, and congregational records of several Baptist churches in western New York; and faculty and trustee minutes, student records, financial accounts, and alumni papers of Colgate Rochester Divinity School and its predecessors: Rochester Theological Seminary, Colgate Theological Seminary, Baptist Missionary Training School, Bexley Hall, and Crozer Theological Seminary.

SEE: Hamer (as Colgate Rochester Divinity School Library); NUCMC, 1976.

SEE: Robbins.

NY752-200
Eastman Kodak Company
Archives
343 State Street
Rochester NY 14650

(716) 724-3041

OPEN: by appointment
ACCESS: prior approval required
COPYING FACILITIES: yes

HOLDINGS:
>*Total volume:* not specified
>*Inclusive dates:* 1876 -
>*Description:* Archives of Eastman Kodak Company, including photographs, slides, motion pictures, annual reports, press clippings, training materials, company publications, memorabilia, correspondence, news releases, financial records, advertising materials, and biographical files.

NY752-220
Episcopal Diocese of Rochester, New York
Archives
935 East Avenue
Rochester NY 14607

(716) 473-2977

OPEN: by appointment only
COPYING FACILITIES: yes
MATERIALS SOLICITED: Anglicanism in western New York, official records of the Diocese of Rochester, 1931- , and architecture and architects of Episcopal churches in western New York.

HOLDINGS:
>*Total volume:* not specified
>*Inclusive dates:* 1792 -
>*Description:* Official records, papers of bishops, journals, and other materials relating to the Episcopal church in western New York, including the counties of Monroe, Livingston, Allegany, Steuben, Schuyler, Yates, Ontario, and Wayne. The bulk of materials dates from the establishment of the Diocese of Rochester in 1931, but items concerning western New York under the Diocese of New York, 1785-1837, and the Diocese of Western New York, 1838-1931, also are held.

NY752-250
Greece Town Historian
Historical Center
1077 English Road
Rochester NY 14616

(716) 225-0293

OPEN: by appointment only
COPYING FACILITIES: no

HOLDINGS:
>*Total volume:* 9 c.f.; 350 items
>*Inclusive dates:* 1797 - 1969
>*Description:* Letters, account books, legal documents, church records, and public records relating to the history of Greece and Charlotte, NY.

NY752-330
International Museum of Photography at George Eastman House
900 East Avenue
Rochester NY 14607

(716) 271-3361

OPEN: by appointment only
ACCESS: appointment should be made 1 or 2 weeks in advance
COPYING FACILITIES: yes
MATERIALS SOLICITED: Historic and contemporary photography and cinema; history of cameras and photographic apparatus and processes; and literature pertaining to any of the above. Will also accept George Eastman effects and papers.

HOLDINGS:
>*Total volume:* 450,000 photographs; 1,225 items
>*Inclusive dates:* 1800 -
>*Description:* Materials documenting the history of photography. There are extensive collections of 19th century daguerreotypes, tintypes, and Kodak snapshots; many later photographs; 1,200 letters, diaries, and other manuscripts; and 25 audio recordings of symposia and of interviews with photographers.

SEE: Hinding; Robbins.

SEE ALSO: Ann Novotny, ed., *Picture Sources 3* (Special Libraries Assn., 1975); Steven Lewis, James McQuaid, and David Tait, *Photography Source and Resource* (Turnip Press, 1973); Norman Snyder, ed., *The Photography Catalog* (Harper and Row, 1976); and issues of the Museum's periodical, *Image.*

NY752-480
Landmark Society of Western New York, Inc.
Wenrich Memorial Library
130 Spring Street
Rochester NY 14608

(716) 546-7029

OPEN: M-F 9-5; closed weekends and holidays
COPYING FACILITIES: yes
MATERIALS SOLICITED: Materials concerning architecture, preservation, the decorative arts, and local history.

HOLDINGS:
>*Total volume:* 3,000 slides; 5,500 photographs; 150 drawings; 1 file cabinet
>*Inclusive dates:* 19th century -
>*Description:* A collection of photographs, slides, building files, survey books, and drawings relating to architecture, chiefly in New York State, Rochester, and Monroe County. Included are drawings sponsored by the Historic American Buildings Survey, as well as drawings by Walter Cassebeer and Claude Bragdon.

NY752-525
Monroe Community College
LeRoy V. Good Library
1000 East Henrietta Road
Rochester NY 14623

(716) 424-5200

OPEN: M-F 9-5; closed weekends and legal holidays
ACCESS: approval of head librarian necessary
COPYING FACILITIES: yes

HOLDINGS:
>*Total volume:* 18 c.f.
>*Inclusive dates:* 1831 -
>*Description:* Memoranda, reports, organization meeting minutes, newsletters, brochures, pamphlets, etc., of Monroe Community College administration, student body, and various departments. Also early legal papers relating to M.C.C. campus land, plans of the campus and buildings, and photographs of campus events.

NY752-530
Monroe County Historian's Office
Rundel Library
115 South Avenue
Rochester NY 14604

(716) 428-7375

OPEN: M-F 9-5; closed weekends and holidays
COPYING FACILITIES: yes
MATERIALS SOLICITED: Materials pertaining to Monroe County. Will also accept materials on New York State, New Jersey, Pennsylvania, and New England.

HOLDINGS:
>*Total volume:* 8,000 items
>*Inclusive dates:* 1789 -
>*Description:* Materials relating to Monroe County, including manuscripts; a file on place names; diaries; slides; barge canal construction photographs; a biography file; manuscript indexes to Federal censuses and county histories; records of veterans buried within the county; microfilms of State censuses; and school records.

SEE: Hinding.

NY752-560
Nazareth College
Lorette Wilmot Library
4245 East Avenue
Rochester NY 14610

(716) 586-2525, Ext. 458

OPEN: M-Th 8-11, F 8-10, Sa 9-5, Su
  1-11; recess and summer hours vary;
  closed legal holidays.
ACCESS: prior arrangements with
  director necessary
COPYING FACILITIES: yes

HOLDINGS:
  Total volume: 30 c.f.
  Inclusive dates: 1903 -
  Description: Personal letters by Thom-
  as A. Hendrick, written 1903-09 during
  his tenure as first American Roman
  Catholic Bishop of Cebu, Philippines.
  Also, materials relating to history of
  Nazareth College and its departments, or-
  ganizations, and administration.

NY752-660
Roberts Wesleyan College
Archives
2301 Westside Drive
Rochester NY 14624

(716) 594-9471, Ext. 118

OPEN: M-F 9-4; closed weekends and
  holidays
ACCESS: appointment required
COPYING FACILITIES: yes
MATERIALS SOLICITED: Archival materials relating to early Methodism and the
  founding and history of Roberts Wesleyan College (formerly Chili Seminary,
  A. M. Chesbrough Seminary, and Roberts Junior College), as well as materials relating to the history of the Free
  Methodist church. Will also accept selected materials of general historical interest.

HOLDINGS:
  Total volume: 45 c.f.; 200 vols.
  Inclusive dates: 1860 -
  Desphs,ription: Materials relating to the
  history and development of Roberts Wesleyan College, including records of organizations, administration, college and
  faculty publications, photographs and a
  small audiovisual collection. There are
  also manuscripts, photographs, diaries,
  and ephemera covering the life and work
  of Benjamin Titus Roberts, founder of
  Roberts Wesleyan College and principal
  founder of the Free Methodist church.

NY752-665
Rochester Business Institute
Betty Cronk Memorial Library
107 Clinton Avenue North
Rochester NY 14604

(716) 325-7290

OPEN: daily 9-5; closed legal holidays
COPYING FACILITIES: yes

HOLDINGS:
  Total volume: 8 c.f.
  Inclusive dates: 1832 -
  Description: Records and memorabilia
  of Rochester Business Institute and its
  predecessors, as well as photographs.

NY752-700
Rochester Institute of Technology
Wallace Memorial Library
Archives and Special Collections
1 Lomb Memorial Drive
Rochester NY 14623

(716) 475-2557, 2564

OPEN: M-F 8:30-4:30; closed weekends,
  holidays, and breaks between terms
COPYING FACILITIES: yes
MATERIALS SOLICITED: Materials relating
  to the history and development of the
  Rochester Institute of Technology, its
  predecessors, and its various colleges.

HOLDINGS:
  Total volume: 366 l.f.; 140 file
  drawers
  Inclusive dates: 1885 -
  Description: Materials relating to the
  history of the Rochester Institute of Technology from its origins as the Mechanics
  Institute and the Rochester Athenaeum
  and Mechanics Institute. Included is a
  photograph collection.

SEE: Robbins.

SEE ALSO: a brochure available from the
  institution.

NY752-720
Rochester Museum and Science
  Center
Library
657 East Avenue
Rochester NY

MAILING ADDRESS:
P.O. Box 1480
Rochester NY 14603

(716) 271-4320, Ext. 30

OPEN: daily M-Sa; closed Sundays and
  holidays
COPYING FACILITIES: yes
MATERIALS SOLICITED: Manuscript and
  audiovisual material relating to the history, natural history, and archaeology
  of the Genesee Country with special
  emphasis on Monroe County and the
  Rochester area.

HOLDINGS:
  Total volume: 16,000 items
  Inclusive dates: 1790's -
  Description: Twelve collections and additional single items relating primarily to
  the history of the Genesee Country. Included are records of several local business firms; letters and other papers of
  Susan B. Anthony, Freeman Johnson,
  and Sir William Pulteney; records and
  papers relating to the Erie and Genesee
  Valley canals; 19th century account
  books; Civil War letters and documents;
  a photograph collection for the period
  1900-30; and 19th century police and
  coroner's records.

SEE: Hamer.

SEE: Hinding; Robbins.

SEE ALSO: guides and inventories to parts
  of the collection available at the institution.

NY752-740
Rochester Public Library
Local History Division
115 South Avenue
Rochester NY 14612

(716) 428-7338

OPEN: M-Th 9-9, F 9-6, Sa 10-4; closed
  Saturdays June-Sept.; closed Sundays
  and holidays
COPYING FACILITIES: yes
MATERIALS SOLICITED: not actively so-
  liciting materials

HOLDINGS:
  Total volume: 300 l.f.; 24 file drawers
  Inclusive dates: 1788 -
  Description: A collection of material
  relating to the history of Rochester and
  Monroe County, largely from the 19th
  century. Included are letters, diaries, and
  journals of early pioneers; account books;
  a few literary manuscripts; other
  unpublished manuscripts; manuscript
  maps; photographs; municipal documents; association records; and genealogical source data.

SEE: Hamer; NUCMC, 1966.

SEE: Hounshell; Schatz; Hinding; Robbins.

NY752-760
St. Bernard's Institute
Library
1100 South Goodman Street
Rochester NY 14620

(716) 271-1320, Ext. 225

OPEN: M-F 9-5; closed weekends and
  holidays
COPYING FACILITIES: yes
MATERIALS SOLICITED: Roman Catholicism in western New York; materials
  relating to the Diocese of Rochester
  and its institutions and parishes; materials by and about Archbishop Fulton
  John Sheen; radio and television history; and communism and the Catholic
  church.

HOLDINGS:
  Total volume: 7,700 items
  Inclusive dates: 1615 -
  Description: Materials relating to the
  Roman Catholic Diocese of Rochester
  and its bishops. Included are papers of
  Bernard J. McQuaid, first bishop, relating
  to Vatican I, the New York public school
  controversy, and diocesan business; materials relating to Frederick Zwierlein,
  editor of McQuaid's papers; and papers
  on the life and ministry of Fulton John
  Sheen, including records, radio and television tapes, photographs, clippings, and
  other materials.

SEE: Hamer; NUCMC, 1959-61.

SEE ALSO: Jasper Green Pennington, *Fulton John Sheen: A Chronology and Bibliography* (St. Bernard's Seminary,
  1976).

NY752-780

St. John Fisher College
Lavery Library
3690 East Avenue
Rochester NY 14618

(716) 385-8141

OPEN: M-F 8:30-4:30; closed weekends
and holidays
ACCESS: by appointment, and with
permission of Library director
COPYING FACILITIES: yes
MATERIALS SOLICITED: Materials relating
to the history and geology of the Genesee Country, Jesuit missionaries and
early French contacts, Seneca Indians,
the Erie Canal, Frederick Douglass and
the antislavery movement, women's
rights, religious movements in western
New York, early area settlers, genealogy, music, and business. Will also accept amateur films.

HOLDINGS:
  Total volume: 5,000 items
  Inclusive dates: 1640 - 1960
  Description: Materials relating to the
history of Rochester and the Genesee
Country, including archaeological field
notes, diaries, account books, letters, personal papers, genealogical data on local
families, photographs, reels of amateur
films, and tapes of interviews with local
people.

NY752-790

Susan B. Anthony Memorial, Inc.
52 Kimbark Road
Rochester NY 14610

no telephone

SEE: Hamer.

Questionnaire not returned.

NY752-800

Temple B'rith Kodesh
Museum
2131 Elmwood Avenue
Rochester NY 14618

(716) 244-7060

OPEN: by appointment only; closed
Jewish holy days and festivals
COPYING FACILITIES: yes
MATERIALS SOLICITED: Materials relating
to Jewish history and folklore. Will
also accept Jewish family records and
papers.

HOLDINGS:
  Total volume: 500 items
  Inclusive dates: 1834 -
  Description: Materials relating to the
history of the Rochester Jewish commu-
nity, including the history of Temple
B'rith Kodesh.

NY752-820

Town of Irondequoit Historian
1280 Titus Avenue
Rochester NY 14617

(716) 467-8840

OPEN: M-F 9-11:30; closed weekends
and holidays
COPYING FACILITIES: yes

MATERIALS SOLICITED: Photographs of
any aspect of life in Irondequoit. Will
also accept documents relating to
Irondequoit.
HOLDINGS:
  Total volume: 4,000 items
  Inclusive dates: 1839 -
  Description: Photographs of
Irondequoit places, people, and activities.

NY752-840

The University of Rochester
Eastman School of Music
Sibley Music Library
Rochester NY 14604

(716) 275-3046

OPEN: M-F 9-5; closed weekends and
holidays

SEE: Hamer.

Questionnaire not returned.

NY752-880

The University of Rochester
Rush Rhees Library
Department of Rare Books,
  Manuscripts and Archives
Rochester NY 14627

(716) 275-4477, 4494

OPEN: M-F 9-5; closed weekends and
holidays
ACCESS: serious researchers
COPYING FACILITIES: yes
MATERIALS SOLICITED: American political and social history, especially 19th
and 20th centuries; upstate New York
materials; and English and American
literary material, especially 19th and
20th centuries.

HOLDINGS:
  Total volume: 6,000 l.f.
  Inclusive dates: 1750 -
  Description: 250 collections relating to
such topics as 19th and 20th century
American history, especially that of up-
state New York; 19th and 20th century
American anthropology; and American
and English literature.

SEE: Hamer; NUCMC, 1959-62, 68-69,
76.

SEE: Duignan; Schatz; Krichmar; Davis;
Parkinson; Robbins; Hinding.

NY752-885

University of Rochester
School of Medicine and Dentistry
Edward G. Miner Library
601 Elmwood Avenue
Rochester NY 14642

(716) 275-3361

OPEN: M-Th 8-midnight, F, Sa 8-10, Su
1-midnight; variable summer hours
COPYING FACILITIES: yes

HOLDINGS:
  Total volume: 150 c.f.
  Inclusive dates: 1632 -
  Description: Papers of Sarah Adamson
Dolley, George Hoyt Whipple, and other
physicians; archives of the Rochester
Academy of Medicine and University of

Rochester School of Medicine and Dentistry; medical lecture notes, 18th-19th
centuries; medical photographs; and letters and manuscripts on cholera, yellow
fever, and other subjects.

SEE: Hinding.

NY752-890

Visual Studies Workshop
31 Prince Street
Rochester NY 14607

(716) 442-8676

OPEN: M, Tu 9-9, W-F 9-5; closed
weekends, Thanksgiving, and
Christmas
ACCESS: appointment required
COPYING FACILITIES: yes

HOLDINGS:
  Total volume: 75 c.f.
  Inclusive dates: 1850 -
  Description: Collection includes daguerreotypes, ambrotypes, tintypes,
cartes-de-visite, stereographs, postcards,
cabinet cards, snapshots, photo albums,
books illustrated with photographs,
35mm slides, lantern slides, and prints by
about 600 contemporary American photographers, many of them associated with
the Visual Studies Workshop.

SEE: Hinding.

ROME

NY757-400

Jervis Public Library
613 North Washington Street
Rome NY 13440

(315) 336-4570

OPEN: by appointment only; closed
Saturdays July-Aug.; closed Sundays
and holidays
ACCESS: doctoral candidates or scholars;
query in advance by letter advisable
COPYING FACILITIES: yes

HOLDINGS:
  Total volume: not specified
  Inclusive dates: 1689 - 1897
  Description: Materials relating chiefly
to canals and railroads, including the papers of John Bloomfield Jervis. There are
also two autograph collections, including
letters written during the Revolutionary
War era, deeds, indentures, leases, letters
concerning the feasibility of constructing
the Erie Canal, and papers relating to
slavery and apprenticeships.

SEE: Hamer; NUCMC, 1966, 72, 74 (as
Jervis Library Association).

SEE: Robbins.

SEE ALSO: guides to specific parts of the
collection available at the institution.

ROSLYN

NY760-90
Bryant Library
Local History Collection
Paper Mill Road
Roslyn NY 11576

(516) 621-2240

OPEN: M, Tu, Th, F 10-6, W 10-9, Sa
9-5; closed Sundays and holidays
COPYING FACILITIES: yes
MATERIALS SOLICITED: Materials relating
to Long Island history, William Cullen
Bryant, Christopher Morley, the Clarence Mackay family, New York participation in the Civil War, and Roslyn
artists and authors. Will also accept
materials relating to architecture and
the State of New York.

HOLDINGS:
Total volume: 250 boxes; 5,000 vols.
Inclusive dates: 1732 -
Description: Manuscripts, account
books, maps, photographs, correspondence, news clippings, and other materials relating to Roslyn and Long Island
history. Included are items relating to
William Cullen Bryant, Christopher Morley, Clarence H. Mackay, and the Daniel
Bogart family, as well as 35 oral history
tapes.

SEE: NUCMC, 1975, 78.

SEE: Robbins; Hinding.

NY760-690
Roslyn Landmark Society
William M. Valentine House
Paper Mill Road
Roslyn NY 11576

(516) 621-3040

OPEN: by appointment only
COPYING FACILITIES: yes
MATERIALS SOLICITED: Materials relating
to the architectural history of Roslyn.

HOLDINGS:
Total volume: not specified
Inclusive dates: late 18th century -
late 19th century
Description: Materials relating to the
architectural history of Roslyn, including
diaries, photographs, maps, and shop
records.

ROXBURY

NY763-680
Roxbury Public Library
Main Street
Roxbury NY 12474

(607) 326-7901

OPEN: M-Th 9:30-4, 7-9, Sa 9:30-11:30;
closed Sundays, Fridays, and holidays
COPYING FACILITIES: no
MATERIALS SOLICITED: Materials relating
to the town of Roxbury and surrounding areas.

HOLDINGS:
Total volume: 49 vols.; 21 items
Inclusive dates: 1799 -
Description: Church records, business
records, records of cattle and sheep trans-
actions, and other records documenting
Roxbury history, 1799-1880's; photo-
graphs; records of the Roxbury Public
Library, 1816-1975; and other materials.

SEE: Delaware County Guide.

RUSH

NY763-690
Rush Town Historian
Rush Town Hall
5977 East Henrietta Road
Rush NY 14543

(716) 533-1312

OPEN: Tu 1-5; other times by
appointment
COPYING FACILITIES: yes

HOLDINGS:
Total volume: not specified
Inclusive dates: 1807 - 1960
Description: Scrapbooks, some school
records, marriage certificates, clippings,
pamphlets, and papers relating to the history of Rush, NY.

RUSHFORD

NY764-690
Rushford Historical Society
Rushford NY 14777

no telephone

OPEN: by appointment only
COPYING FACILITIES: no

HOLDINGS:
Total volume: 2 c.f.
Inclusive dates: 1816 -
Description: Local account books,
school records, and photographs.

SEE: Allegany County Guide.

RYE

NY766-690
Rye Historical Society
1 Purchase Street
Rye NY 10580

(914) 967-7588

OPEN: M-F 10-4:30; closed weekends
and holidays
COPYING FACILITIES: no
MATERIALS SOLICITED: Family records.
Will also accept anything relating to
the early history of the Rye area.

HOLDINGS:
Total volume: 1,600 items
Inclusive dates: 1683 - 1863
Description: Two collections of family
papers from the Rye area; diaries recording primarily weather observations;
manuscript maps showing the location of
local Indian villages; and vestry records
of Christ's Church, Rye.

SEE: NUCMC, 1976.

SEE: Robbins.

SACKETS HARBOR

NY769-640
Pickering-Beach Historical Museum
503 West Main Street
Sackets Harbor NY 13685

(315) 646-2052, 3868

OPEN: Memorial Day-Labor Day, daily
10-5; closed rest of year
USER FEES: one dollar
ACCESS: advance arrangements
recommended
COPYING FACILITIES: no
MATERIALS SOLICITED: Will accept materials concerned with 19th century
Sackets Harbor and family records relating to the Pickering and Beach families of Sackets Harbor.

HOLDINGS:
Total volume: not specified
Inclusive dates: 1800 - 1940
Description: Manuscripts and photo-
graphs dealing with the Pickering and
Beach families and their descendants, and
manuscripts, noncurrent records of insti-
tutions and organizations, manuscript
maps, and photographs relating to the
Sackets Harbor area in the 19th century.

SEE: Hamer.

SAG HARBOR

NY772-720
Suffolk County Whaling Museum of
Sag Harbor, Long Island
Main Street
Sag Harbor NY

MAILING ADDRESS:
P.O. Box 1327
Sag Harbor NY 11963

(516) 725-0770

OPEN: Wednesdays 12-4
USER FEES: adults one dollar, children
(6-13), and senior citizens fifty cents
ACCESS: advance written reservation
required
COPYING FACILITIES: no
MATERIALS SOLICITED: Whaling materials of the mid-19th century. Will also
accept other materials relating to the
period.

HOLDINGS:
Total volume: 20 vols.; other
materials
Inclusive dates: 1800 - 1870
Description: Materials relating to Sag
Harbor as the first port of customs entry
in New York State and as a whaling
center. Included are 14 logbooks of whaling vessels.

SEE: Hamer.

St. Bonaventure

NY775-720
St. Bonaventure University
Library
Archive Collection
St. Bonaventure NY 14778

(716) 375-2323, Ext. 2322

OPEN: M-F 8-4; closed weekends and holidays
ACCESS: qualified researchers
COPYING FACILITIES: yes
MATERIALS SOLICITED: Materials related to Archives' holdings and in areas of scholastic interest. Will also accept other materials related to the University's educational and religious history.

HOLDINGS:
Total volume: 75 l.f.; 130 vols.
Inclusive dates: 1450 -
Description: Late medieval and Renaissance European manuscripts and materials relating to St. Bonaventure University, the St. Bonaventure cemetery, the Devereux family, and various aspects of Roman Catholic church history. There are also literary manuscripts by such authors as Jim Bishop and Thomas Merton, sound recordings, and microfilm reels relating to the assassination of John F. Kennedy.

SEE: Hamer.

SEE: Robbins.

SEE ALSO: W. H. Bond, ed., *Census of Medieval and Renaissance Manuscripts in the United States and Canada, Supplement* (Bibliographical Society of America, 1962); Thomas T. McAvoy, 'Catholic Archives and Manuscript Collections,' *American Archivist* 24 (Oct. 1961). Additional descriptions and finding aids are available at the repository.

Saratoga Springs

NY795-120
City of Saratoga Springs
Archives
297 Broadway
Saratoga Springs NY 12866

(518) 587-2358

OPEN: M-F by appointment; closed weekends and holidays
ACCESS: by appointment with City Historian or City Clerk in Commissioner of Accounts Office
COPYING FACILITIES: yes
MATERIALS SOLICITED: Inactive city records.

HOLDINGS:
Total volume: 230 c.f.
Inclusive dates: 1820 -
Description: Municipal records of Saratoga Springs since its establishment, including records of the town, village, and city of Saratoga Springs; records of the board of education; maps; and other materials.

GUIDES: 'Guide to the Archives, City of Saratoga Springs, N.Y.' (1978).

SEE: Hinding.

NY795-320
Historical Society of Saratoga Springs
Museum
Beatrice S. Sweeney Library
The Casino
Congress Park
Saratoga Springs NY

MAILING ADDRESS:
P.O. Box 216
Saratoga Springs NY 12866

(518) 584-6920

OPEN: by appointment only M-F 9-5; closed weekends and holidays
ACCESS: appointment required
COPYING FACILITIES: no
MATERIALS SOLICITED: Saratoga Springs local history materials. Will also accept materials related to American Victorian history.

HOLDINGS:
Total volume: 40 c.f.
Inclusive dates: 18th century -
Description: Collections of Walworth and Batcheller family papers; diaries, reminiscences, and other papers related to Saratoga Springs history, including gambling, hotels, horse racing, and springs; financial records of some local businesses; papers of humorist Frank Sullivan; photographs; and oral history recordings and transcripts.

SEE: Hinding.

NY795-710
Saratoga County Historian's Office
31 Woodlawn Avenue
Saratoga Springs NY 12866

(518) 584-3690

OPEN: M-F 9-5; closed weekends and holidays
COPYING FACILITIES: yes
MATERIALS SOLICITED: Saratoga County documents, manuscripts, and pictures, with special attention to records of Century Farms and of the Champlain and Erie Canals.

HOLDINGS:
Total volume: 33 c.f.
Inclusive dates: 1790 - 1900
Description: Materials pertaining chiefly to Saratoga County history, including photographs, church records, genealogical data, military records, local government documents, and personal papers.

SEE: Hamer; NUCMC, 1966.

SEE: Hinding.

NY792-720
Saratoga Springs Public Library
Broadway
Saratoga Springs NY 12866

(518) 584-7860

OPEN: M-Sa 9-5; closed Sundays and holidays
ACCESS: advance arrangements required
COPYING FACILITIES: yes

MATERIALS SOLICITED: Materials relating to the history of Saratoga Springs. Will also accept material relating to Saratoga County, the Adirondacks, and the Battle of Saratoga, 1777, and to the history, study, and use of mineral springs.

HOLDINGS:
Total volume: 50 items; 1 file cabinet
Inclusive dates: 1840 -
Description: Diaries, records, scrapbooks, and papers relating mainly to the history of Saratoga Springs and papers of Dr. Walter S. McClellan, medical director at the Saratoga Springs Reservation, 1931-53, dealing with mineral waters.

SEE: Hinding.

Savona

NY797-720
Savona Free Library
McCoy Street
Savona NY 14879

(607) 583-4426

OPEN: M, W 6-9, F 1-5; closed other days and holidays
COPYING FACILITIES: no

HOLDINGS:
Total volume: 1 c.f.
Inclusive dates: 1925 -
Description: Records of the library.

SEE: Steuben County Guide.

Schenectady

NY804-280
General Electric Company
Main Library
Room B-15
Building 2
1 River Road
Schenectady NY 12345

(518) 385-3652

OPEN: M-F 8-5; closed weekends and holidays
ACCESS: advance arrangements required
COPYING FACILITIES: yes

HOLDINGS:
Total volume: 12 l.f.
Inclusive dates: 1878 - 1930
Description: Newspaper and magazine clippings, correspondence, news releases, and miscellaneous resource materials used by John W. Hammond in preparation of the book *Men and Volts*, a history of the General Electric Company, U.S.A. Included is information on such subjects as alternating current versus direct current, electric railways, electric vehicles, electric power development, labor relations, and other aspects of early industrial development.

SEE ALSO: Index available at the library.

NY804-560
National Railway Historical Society
Mohawk and Hudson Chapter
Alco Historic Photos
Schenectady NY

MAILING ADDRESS:
P.O. Box 655
Schenectady NY 12301

(518) 374-0153

OPEN: by appointment only
ACCESS: authorized persons whose names are approved by the Chairman, Board of Trustees, Alco Historic Photos, and are on file with the Library
COPYING FACILITIES: yes
MATERIALS SOLICITED: Builder's photograph negatives and prints by Alco and its predecessors, especially those taken between 1954 and 1969. Will also accept photographs of Alco locomotives and other products, and other railroad-related materials.

HOLDINGS:
Total volume: 26,000 items
Inclusive dates: 1880 - 1967
Description: 25,000 photographic negatives of locomotives built between 1880 and 1967 by Alco and its predecessor companies. There are also about 1,000 photographic records of 'erecting card' drawings. Both steam and diesel locomotives are represented.

NY804-700
Schenectady City History Center
City Hall
Schenectady NY 12305

no telephone

SEE: Hamer.

Questionnaire not returned.

NY804-720
Schenectady County Historical Society
32 Washington Avenue
Schenectady NY 12305

(518) 374-0263

OPEN: M-F 1-5; closed weekends and holidays
USER FEES: one dollar for nonmembers, $5 for genealogical research done by society staff
COPYING FACILITIES: yes
MATERIALS SOLICITED: Materials relating to the history of Schenectady County and local genealogies.

HOLDINGS:
Total volume: 16,000 items
Inclusive dates: 1690 -
Description: Materials relating to Schenectady County, including account books, many in Dutch; church records; colonial broadsides, commissions, and deeds; 383 letters of the Glen family, 1777-1818; diaries, journals, and logbooks; archives of local institutions; photographs; scrapbooks; and genealogical materials on over 1,000 local families.

SEE: Hamer.

SEE: Leventhal and Mooney - I; Novotny; Schatz.

NY804-740
Schenectady County Public Library
Liberty and Clinton Streets
Schenectady NY 12305

(518) 382-3500

OPEN: M, Tu, Th 9-9, W, F, Sa 9-5; summer, M-F 9-9, closed Saturdays; closed Sundays
COPYING FACILITIES: yes
MATERIALS SOLICITED: Schenectady County material. Will also accept materials relating to Fulton, Montgomery, and Schoharie counties.

HOLDINGS:
Total volume: 30 vols.; 37 items
Inclusive dates: 1850 -
Description: Materials relating to Schenectady County history, including records compiled from cemeteries, churches, and local newspapers and periodicals; photographs of Schenectady; and other documents relating to local history.

SEE: Hamer.

NY804-800
Union College
Schaffer Library
Special Collections
Schenectady NY 12308

(518) 370-6278, 6279

OPEN: M, Tu, Th, F 8:30-4:30; closed weekends, Wednesdays, and holidays
ACCESS: an appointment is advised
COPYING FACILITIES: yes
MATERIALS SOLICITED: Letters of Union College alumni and English Pre-Raphaelites and their associates, and scientific and technical papers produced in the Schenectady area. Will also accept materials relating to Union College's curriculum in the sciences and humanities; New York State colonial history; the history of the Schenectady area; and the Erie Canal.

HOLDINGS:
Total volume: 800 l.f.
Inclusive dates: 1647 -
Description: Union College Archives, and papers of Schenectady scientists and engineers, including technical papers. Specific collections relate to Ernst F. W. Alexanderson, Andrew Yates, Charles Proteus Steinmetz, and the American Locomotive Company.

SEE: Hamer; NUCMC, 1967, 74, 76-77, 80.

SEE: Gehring; Robbins.

SEE ALSO: Frances Miller, *Catalogue of the William James Stillman Collection* (Friends of the Union College Library, 1974); David A. Hounshell, comp., *Manuscripts in U.S. Depositories Relating to the History of Electrical Science and Technology* (Smithsonian Institution, n.d.); Walter Schatz, ed., *Directory of Afro-American Resources* (Bowker, 1970).

SCHOHARIE

NY807-730
Schoharie County Historical Society
Reference Library
Old Stone Fort Museum
N. Main Street
Schoharie NY

MAILING ADDRESS:
P.O. Box 69
Schoharie NY 12157

(518) 295-7192

OPEN: W-Sa 10-5, Su 1-5; closed Mondays and Tuesdays
USER FEES: $1.50
COPYING FACILITIES: yes
MATERIALS SOLICITED: Material, pertaining to the economic, social, and political development of Schoharie County, and genealogical material.

HOLDINGS:
Total volume: 4 file drawers
Inclusive dates: 1730 -
Description: Materials relating to Schoharie County, including early land patents and grants; indentures; deeds; canvass and voter registers; proceedings of county, town, and village boards; logbooks; scrapbooks; hotel registers; school records; church and cemetery records; and unpublished genealogies.

SEE: Hamer.

SCHUYLER LAKE

NY811-200
Exeter Historical Society
Old Stone Church
Schuyler Lake NY 13457

no telephone

OPEN: by appointment only
COPYING FACILITIES: no
MATERIALS SOLICITED: Documents, manuscripts, correspondence, and journals relating particularly to Exeter Township.

HOLDINGS:
Total volume: not specified
Inclusive dates: 1799 -
Description: Materials relating to Exeter Township including account books, business records, correspondence, diaries, journals, genealogical source data, photographs, and maps.

SCIO

NY813-720
Scio Free Library
West Sciota Street
Scio NY 14880

no telephone

OPEN: Tu, Th, Sa 1-4; closed holidays
COPYING FACILITIES: no

HOLDINGS:
Total volume: 2.5 c.f.
Inclusive dates: 1905 -
Description: Records of Scio Free Library and other local materials.

SEE: Allegany County Guide.

SCOTIA

NY814-720
Scotia History Center
4 North Ten Broeck Street
Scotia NY 12302

(518) 374-1071

OPEN: by appointment
COPYING FACILITIES: yes
MATERIALS SOLICITED: Materials relating to the history of the village of Scotia. Will also accept oral histories of people living in the area and materials relating to the Glen-Sanders family.

HOLDINGS:
Total volume: 533 items
Inclusive dates: 17th century
Description: Materials relating to the history of Scotia.

SELKIRK

NY818-760
Town of Bethlehem Historical
Association
Clapper Road and Route 144
Selkirk NY 12158

(518) 767-9432

OPEN: Su 2-5, other days by appointment; closed Nov. - May
ACCESS: advance arrangements required
COPYING FACILITIES: no
MATERIALS SOLICITED: Materials concerning the history of Bethlehem and surrounding townships, especially before 1930, with special attention to the 1735 Bethlehem House.

HOLDINGS:
Total volume: 400 items
Inclusive dates: 1773 -
Description: Local history materials, including logbooks and papers of a Hudson River light tender, 1885-1930; papers of the Bethlehem Protective Association, concerning horse thievery, 1927-31; a few early indentures; deeds and mortgages, 1773-1914; business receipts of brickyards and river barges; photographs of churches, schools, railroad stations, and residents dating from 1900 to the present; and some oral history recordings.

SENECA FALLS

NY821-520
Mynderse Public Library
31 Fall Street
Seneca Falls NY 13148

(315) 568-8265

OPEN: M, Th, F 2-9, W 10-9, Sa 2-5; July - Aug., M 7-9, Tu, Th, Sa 2-5; closed other days and holidays
COPYING FACILITIES: no

HOLDINGS:
Total volume: 13 vols.
Inclusive dates: 1839 - 1859
Description: Records of the Cayuga and Seneca Canal.

SEE: Seneca County Guide.

NY821-720
Seneca Falls Historical Society
Museum
55 Cayuga Street
Seneca Falls NY 13148

(315) 568-8412

OPEN: M-F 9-5, Sa 9-4; Su 1-4 June 1-Aug. 31; closed holidays, and Sundays rest of year
ACCESS: appointment suggested
COPYING FACILITIES: yes
MATERIALS SOLICITED: Women's rights material and Victoriana. Will also accept materials of local historical importance.

HOLDINGS:
Total volume: 180 boxes
Inclusive dates: 1800 -
Description: Materials relating to Seneca County and Seneca Falls. Included are holdings relating to family history, industrial history, women's rights, and local church records, with particular emphasis on the correspondence of early industrialists.

SEE: Hamer.

SEE: Hinding; Seneca County Guide.

SETAUKET

NY824-200
Emma S. Clark Memorial Library
Three Village Local History Collection
120 Main Street
Setauket NY 11733

(516) 941-4080

OPEN: by appointment only M-F
COPYING FACILITIES: yes
MATERIALS SOLICITED: Historical materials relating to the Three Village area of Long Island.

HOLDINGS:
Total volume: not specified
Inclusive dates: 1691 -
Description: Historical materials related to people, places, and events in the Three Village area of Long Island. Included are thousands of letters, deeds, diaries, account books and ledgers, bills, and photographs pertaining to Setauket, Stony Brook, Old Field, Poquott, and adjoining areas of the north shore of Long Island.

SEE ALSO: Finding aid available at the institution.

NY824-720
Society for the Preservation of Long
Island Antiquities
93 North Country Road
Setauket NY 11733

(516) 941-9444

OPEN: M-F 9-5; closed weekends and holidays
COPYING FACILITIES: yes
MATERIALS SOLICITED: Manuscript material connected with the Society's properties and visual documents pertaining to Long Island architecture and decorative arts.

HOLDINGS:
Total volume: 20 l.f.
Inclusive dates: 1750 -
Description: Manuscripts relating to the Society's properties and visual documents pertaining to Long Island architecture and decorative arts. Included are diaries, journals, correspondence, logbooks, account books, genealogical source data, manuscript maps, charts, and photographs.

SHELTER ISLAND

NY827-720
Shelter Island Historical Society
Documents Committee
Havens House
Route 114
Shelter Island NY

MAILING ADDRESS:
P.O. Box 1591
Shelter Island NY 11964

(516) 749-0826

OPEN: Tu 10-12; summer, Sa 10-12; closed other days
COPYING FACILITIES: yes
MATERIALS SOLICITED: Material documenting the history of Shelter Island.

HOLDINGS:
Total volume: 5,000 items
Inclusive dates: 1600 -
Description: Material relating to the history of Shelter Island, including diaries, logbooks, ledgers, letters, deeds, photographs, and postcards. Also of interest are records of churches, social groups, schools, and local government agencies.

SEE: NUCMC, 1976.

SHERBURNE

NY829-720
Sherburne Public Library
10 East State Street
Sherburne NY 13460

(607) 674-4242

OPEN: M, F 1-9, Tu-Th 1-5, Sa 10-4;
closed Sundays, holidays, and
Saturdays in summer
COPYING FACILITIES: yes
MATERIALS SOLICITED: Materials dealing
with the history and genealogy of
Sherburne. Will also accept materials
dealing with Chenango County history.

HOLDINGS:
Total volume: 11.5 c.f.; 19 vols.; 375
items
Inclusive dates: 1700 -
Description: Church records, genealogical data, maps, scrapbooks, subject files, and historical articles concerning the history of Sherburne and other areas in Chenango County, chiefly during the 19th and 20th centuries.

SEE: Chenango County Guide.

SHERMAN

NY830-520
Minerva Free Library
Sherman NY 14781

(716) 761-6378

OPEN: Tu, Sa 2-5, 7-9, Th 12:30-4:30;
closed other days
COPYING FACILITIES: yes

HOLDINGS:
Total volume: 30 vols.; 3 items
Inclusive dates: 19th century -
Description: Civil War documents, census records, and other materials pertaining to the history of Sherman.

SEE: Hamer.

SIDNEY

NY839-720
Sidney Historical Society
Civic Center
Liberty Street
Sidney NY

MAILING ADDRESS:
Box 217
Sidney NY 13838

(607) 563-2134

OPEN: Tu 2-5
COPYING FACILITIES: no
MATERIALS SOLICITED: Materials relating
to Sidney and surrounding areas.

HOLDINGS:
Total volume: 13 c.f.; 60 vols., 160
items
Inclusive dates: 1807 -
Description: A photograph collection of local interest, 1875- ; records of the Sidney chapter of the Daughters of the American Revolution, 1917-68; a local history manuscript collection; scrapbooks,

account books, and store records; and other materials.

SEE: Delaware County Guide.

SMITHTOWN

NY842-720
Smithtown Historical Society
Route 25A
Smithtown NY

MAILING ADDRESS:
P.O. Box 69
Smithtown NY 11787

(516) 265-6768

OPEN: Th 2-5, Sa 2-5, other days by
appointment; closed holidays
USER FEES: 50 cents donation
ACCESS: by appointment
COPYING FACILITIES: yes
MATERIALS SOLICITED: Documents pertaining to Smithtown history.

HOLDINGS:
Total volume: 60 c.f.
Inclusive dates: 1600's -
Description: Personal letters, diaries, logbooks, account books, genealogical records, deeds to property, and other historical materials from the Smithtown area.

NY842-730
Smithtown Library
Long Island Room
1 North Country Road
Smithtown NY 11787

(516) 265-2072

OPEN: Tu 1-5, 6-9, W-F 10-6, Sa 9-5;
closed Sundays, Mondays, and holidays
USER FEES: $10 fee for extended mail
inquiries
COPYING FACILITIES: yes
MATERIALS SOLICITED: Materials relating
to eastern Long Island.

HOLDINGS:
Total volume: 41.5 l.f.
Inclusive dates: 1700 -
Description: Materials relating to early land development and the political, social, and economic history of Smithtown Township and the surrounding area. Included are papers pertaining to the founding Smith family, Democratic political and economic affairs on Long Island, and the career of J. Lawrence Smith as attorney and judge in Suffolk County during the 1830's to 1880's. There are also school board and other institutional records from the 20th century.

SEE: Hamer.

SEE: Leventhal and Mooney - I.

SODUS

NY844-720
Sodus Free Library
17 Maple Avenue
Sodus NY 14551

(315) 483-9292

OPEN: M 9:30-1, Tu, Th 1-9, F 1-5:30,
Sa 10-5, Su 2-4; closed legal holidays
COPYING FACILITIES: yes

HOLDINGS:
Total volume: 41 vols.; 150 items
Inclusive dates: 1776 -
Description: Organization records, a scrapbook, slides, and photographs of Sodus and vicinity. Includes one letter each of Anthony Wayne and artist Norman Rockwell.

SEE: Wayne County Guide.

SOMERS

NY845-720
Somers Historical Society
Elephant Hotel
Somers NY

MAILING ADDRESS:
Box 336
Somers NY 10589

(914) 277-4977

OPEN: F 2-4; closed other days
ACCESS: by appointment only
COPYING FACILITIES: yes
MATERIALS SOLICITED: Materials relating
to early circuses and the history of
Somers.

HOLDINGS:
Total volume: 100 items
Inclusive dates: 1780 - 1900
Description: Manuscripts relating to early circuses in America, including agreements, bills of sale, correspondence, journals, route books, account books, and records. There are also materials relating to the history of the Somers area, including correspondence, diaries, unrecorded deeds, family records, local church and school records, and photographs.

SEE: Hinding; Robbins.

SOUTH NEW BERLIN

NY847-560
Nathan Taylor Yorkers Museum
North Main Street
South New Berlin NY 13843

no telephone

OPEN: by appointment only
COPYING FACILITIES: no
MATERIALS SOLICITED: South New Berlin history.

HOLDINGS:
Total volume: 27 vols.; 100 items
Inclusive dates: 1808 -
Description: Business records, school records, family papers, photographs, postcards, and scrapbooks of South New Ber-

lin and vicinity, chiefly during the 19th century.

SEE: Chenango County Guide.

NY847-720
South New Berlin Free Library
North Main Street
South New Berlin NY 13843

no telephone

OPEN: M, Th 2:30-9; closed other days and holidays
COPYING FACILITIES: no
MATERIALS SOLICITED: South New Berlin history and genealogy.

HOLDINGS:
> *Total volume:* 1 c.f.; 14 vols.; 25 items
> *Inclusive dates:* 1841 -
> *Description:* School records, photographs, scrapbooks, and other materials dealing with the history of the South New Berlin area.

SEE: Chenango County Guide.

SOUTHPORT

NY851-720
Southport Historical Society
Southport NY

MAILING ADDRESS:
P.O. Box 146
Pine City NY 14871

(607) 734-6623, 3563; 733-2660

OPEN: by appointment only
COPYING FACILITIES: no
MATERIALS SOLICITED: Southport history and genealogy.

HOLDINGS:
> *Total volume:* 18 items
> *Inclusive dates:* 1822 - 1933
> *Description:* The papers of Theron A. Morris, the Southport postmaster, 1875-1904; the cashbooks of William G. Snyder's building supplies store, 1924-27; and other business records and photographs, 1822-1933.

SPENCER

NY852-720
Spencer Historical Society
Museum
Center Street
Spencer NY

MAILING ADDRESS:
P.O. Box 71
Spencer NY 14883

(607) 589-6906, 4916

OPEN: summer, Sunday afternoons; other times by appointment
COPYING FACILITIES: no
MATERIALS SOLICITED: Spencer local history. Will also accept Tioga County history.

HOLDINGS:
> *Total volume:* 6.5 c.f.; 22 vols.; 20 items
> *Inclusive dates:* 1600 -
> *Description:* Business and school records, genealogical data, photographs, maps, and postcards concerning Spencer history, primarily in the 19th and 20th centuries.

SEE: Tioga County Guide.

NY852-730
Spencer Library
North Main Street
Spencer NY 14883

(607) 589-4496

OPEN: M 1-5, Th 4-8, F 5-8, Sa 9-noon; closed other days and holidays
COPYING FACILITIES: no
MATERIALS SOLICITED: Spencer history. Will also accept Tioga County history.

HOLDINGS:
> *Total volume:* 6 items
> *Inclusive dates:* 1869 - 1967
> *Description:* Materials dealing with various aspects of the history of Spencer.

SEE: Tioga County Guide.

SPRINGVILLE

NY855-120
Concord Historical Society
98 East Main Street
Springville NY 14141

no telephone

SEE: Hamer.

Questionnaire not returned.

STAMFORD

NY858-720
Stamford Village Library
117 Main Street
Stamford NY 12167

(607) 652-5001

OPEN: M, Th, F 2-5, M 7-9, W 2-4, Sa 10-noon; summer only, Th 7-9; closed Tuesdays, Sundays, and holidays
COPYING FACILITIES: yes

HOLDINGS:
> *Total volume:* 3 c.f.; 191 vols.; 1,816 items
> *Inclusive dates:* 1832 -
> *Description:* Included are the records of the Stamford Seminary and Union Free School, the Stamford Village Library, Stamford Women's Club, and the Stamford Fire Department's L. H. Maynard Hose Company, 1894-1960. There are also cemetery, census, and genealogical records; photographs; maps; scrapbooks and letters to S. B. Campion, 1865-97.

SEE: Delaware County Guide.

STELLA NIAGARA

NY859-720
Sisters of St. Francis of Penance and Christian Charity
Sisters of St. Francis of Holy Name Province
Archives
4421 Lower River Road
Stella Niagara NY 14144

(716) 754-4311, 693-6846

OPEN: M-F 9-4; closed weekends, holidays, and summer break
ACCESS: advance arrangements required
COPYING FACILITIES: yes
MATERIALS SOLICITED: Materials relating to the history, life, and work of Sisters of St. Francis of Penance and Christian Charity.

HOLDINGS:
> *Total volume:* 200 l. f.
> *Inclusive dates:* 1874 -
> *Description:* Records of the Sisters of St. Francis of Penance and Christian Charity in the United States, 1874-1939, and in New York, New Jersey, Ohio, West Virginia, and South Carolina, 1939. Included are administrative and financial records, correspondence, chronicles, architectural drawings, photographs, and scrapbooks relating to the sisters and those served through various forms of ministry.

SEE: Hinding.

STILLWATER

NY861-720
Saratoga National Historical Park Library
Stillwater NY

MAILING ADDRESS:
R. D. 2 Box 33
Stillwater NY 12170

(518) 664-9821

OPEN: by appointment only; closed Thanksgiving, Christmas, and New Year's
ACCESS: letter of notification addressed to Park Superintendent
COPYING FACILITIES: yes
MATERIALS SOLICITED: Materials related to the Burgoyne campaign (1777).

HOLDINGS:
> *Total volume:* 268 items
> *Inclusive dates:* late 18th century - 1830
> *Description:* Personal papers of local residents, including 100 items relating to the domestic life of John Neilson and his family, 1800-30.

SEE: Hamer.

NY861-740
Stillwater Town Historian
Stillwater Free Library
72 South Hudson Avenue
Stillwater NY 12170

(518) 664-4489, 6255

OPEN: Th 1-5 and other times by appointment; closed holidays
COPYING FACILITIES: yes
MATERIALS SOLICITED: Manuscripts, maps, family records, photographs, and other materials relating to local history.

HOLDINGS:
Total volume: 8 file drawers; other materials
Inclusive dates: 1797 -
Description: Local merchants' account books, photographs, early school and church records, scrapbooks, oral history interviews, and genealogical research materials pertaining to Stillwater.

SEE: Hinding.

STONY BROOK

NY866-520
The Museums at Stony Brook
Archives
1208 Route 25A
Stony Brook NY 11790

(516) 751-0066, Ext. 32

OPEN: M-F 9-5; closed weekends and holidays
ACCESS: advance arrangements required
COPYING FACILITIES: yes
MATERIALS SOLICITED: Materials relating to 19th century American art, especially on Long Island; carriage building, coaching, and transportation; Long Island history, especially Suffolk County in the 19th century; the history of costume and dress, especially in America; and wildfowl decoys and related hunting material. Will also accept other materials relating to 19th century American life.

HOLDINGS:
Total volume: 200 l.f.
Inclusive dates: mid-17th century - early 20th century
Description: Papers of artist William Sidney Mount, including notebooks, journals, diaries, photographs, correspondence, and manuscript sheet music collected by Mount, as well as papers of other Mount family members, including Shepard Alonzo Mount and Micah Hawkins. There are also local history materials, mid-17th century-early 20th century, including several hundred photographs. Additional materials relate to the Museum's major exhibiting collections of horse-drawn vehicles, costume (especially 19th century American), and wildfowl decoys, especially those from Long Island.

SEE: Hamer (as Suffolk Museum and Carriage House).

NY866-710
State University of New York at Stony Brook
Frank Melville, Jr., Memorial Library
Department of Special Collections
Stony Brook NY 11794-3323

(516) 246-3615

OPEN: M-F 11-5; closed weekends and holidays
ACCESS: advance arrangements recommended
COPYING FACILITIES: yes
MATERIALS SOLICITED: Long Island civic, civil liberties, energy, environmental, political, social services, and women's personal papers and organizational records. Contemporary literary manuscripts and press files; national environmental records; University records.

HOLDINGS:
Total volume: 950 l.f.
Inclusive dates: 1774-
Description: Manuscripts, documents, maps, photographs, and ephemera relating to Long Island history. Literary manuscripts, including Carrera Andrade, Perishable Press, and Black Mountain poets and writers; records of the Environmental Defense Fund, Long Island Railroad (track drawings and photographs), and the Suffolk County chapter of the NY Civil Liberties Union; personal papers of Oakley C. Johnson and Clarence Weston Hansell; and University records.

SEE: NUCMC, 1971, 77-78.

SEE: Hinding; Robbins.

SEE ALSO: Alex Baskin, *The American Civil Liberties Union Papers: A Guide to the Records: A.C.L.U. Cases 1912-1946* (Archives of Social History, 1971); David A. Hounshell, comp., *Manuscripts in U.S. Depositories Relating to the History of Electrical Science and Technology* (Smithsonian Institution, n.d.).

NY866-730
State University of New York at Stony Brook
Frank Melville, Jr., Memorial Library
William Butler Yeats Memorial Manuscript Collection
Stony Brook NY 11794-3323

(516) 246-3615

OPEN: M-F 1-4; closed weekends and holidays
ACCESS: advance arrangements required
COPYING FACILITIES: yes
MATERIALS SOLICITED: Originals or copies, preferably on microfilm, of manuscript materials relating to the life and work of William Butler Yeats and members of the Yeats family. Will also accept originals or copies of manuscripts relating to the lives and works of modern Irish literary personalities such as George Bernard Shaw, John Millington Synge, James Joyce, Samuel Beckett, George Russell, and Lady Augusta Gregory.

HOLDINGS:
Total volume: 80,000 frames
Inclusive dates: late 19th - 20th century
Description: Microfilms of manuscripts in the possession of Michael Butler Yeats and the National Library of Ireland in Dublin. The collection contains manuscripts, typescripts, and publishers' proofs of published as well as unpublished poems, plays, fiction, and essays from Yeats's entire creative career. In addition, there are unpublished diaries, journals, and notebooks pertaining to Yeats's varied interests, and Yeats's correspondence with fellow writers, occultists, political figures, and friends. Also included are works and letters by other members of the Yeats family.

SYOSSET

NY870-600
Orthodox Church in America
Department of History and Archives
Syosset NY

MAILING ADDRESS:
Route 25A, Box 675
Syosset NY 11791

(516) 922-0550

OPEN: M-F 9-5; closed weekends, and church and other holidays
ACCESS: permission required
COPYING FACILITIES: yes
MATERIALS SOLICITED: Records of Orthodox church institutions, such as monasteries, dioceses and parishes, and papers of retired clergy and lay people. Will also accept any materials connected with Orthodox church history.

HOLDINGS:
Total volume: 225,000 items
Inclusive dates: 1799 -
Description: Records of Orthodox churches in the Middle East and in eastern Europe, since the early 19th century; and records of the American Orthodox church beginning with the Alaskan Diocese in 1799 through its organization in the continental United States, Canada, Mexico, and South America. Materials include reports of synods and dioceses; diaries and reminiscences of parish priests; early alphabets and translations of Alaskan native languages; official correspondence with U.S. government agencies; and materials concerning the ethnic groups that comprise the church.

SYRACUSE

NY872-120
Erie Canal Museum
Library
318 Erie Boulevard E.
Syracuse NY 13202

(315) 471-0593

OPEN: M-F 9-5; closed weekends and holidays
ACCESS: by appointment only
COPYING FACILITIES: no

MATERIALS SOLICITED: Materials relating to New York State canals and other United States canals. Will also accept materials on foreign canals and on Syracuse and Onondaga County.

HOLDINGS:
> *Total volume:* 47,000 items; 650 l.f.
> *Inclusive dates:* 1840 - 1920
> *Description:* A collection of material on the Erie Canal, the New York State Barge Canal, and other New York canals, focusing primarily on their construction. Included are maps, estimates, journals, letters, contracts, field books, and photographs.

SEE: Hinding.

NY872-150

Diocese of Central New York
310 Montgomery Street, Suite 200
Syracuse NY 13202

(315) 474-6596

OPEN: M-F 8:30-4:30; closed weekends and holidays
COPYING FACILITIES: yes
MATERIALS SOLICITED: Records of general programs of the Episcopal church in the Diocese of Central New York. Will also accept records of parishes closed due to inactivity or merger.

HOLDINGS:
> *Total volume:* 300 l.f.
> *Inclusive dates:* 1819 -
> *Description:* Diocesan records, including files of bishops; records of defunct parishes; a complete set of periodicals, the 'Messenger,' and the diocesan 'Newsletter'; and a complete file of diocesan journals since 1819 for the geographic area covered by the Diocese of Central New York. The diocesan journals contain annual reports to conventions, records of convention activities, minutes, and lists of clergy.

NY872-590

Onondaga County Public Library
Local History and Genealogy Department
335 Montgomery Street
Syracuse NY 13202

(315) 473-6801

OPEN: M-Sa 8:30-4:30; closed Sundays and holidays
COPYING FACILITIES: yes
MATERIALS SOLICITED: Genealogical source data and family histories, especially of the northeastern United States, and Syracuse and Onondaga County historical material.

HOLDINGS:
> *Total volume:* 1,550 vols.; 250 items; 5 file drawers
> *Inclusive dates:* 19th century -
> *Description:* Materials relating primarily to Syracuse and Onondaga County history and genealogy in the 19th century. Included are copied church, cemetery, census, Bible, and family records; genealogical information about local and out-of-area families; and 30,000 file cards listing residents of Onondaga County before 1850.

SEE: Hamer (as Syracuse Public Library).

NY872-610

Onondaga Historical Association
311 Montgomery Street
Syracuse NY 13202

no telephone
SEE: Hamer.

Questionnaire not returned.

NY872-720

State University of New York
College of Environmental Science and Forestry
Franklin Moon Library
Terence J. Hoverter Memorial Archives
Moon Library, Room 102
Syracuse NY 13210

(315) 470-6715, 6719

OPEN: M-F 9-5; closed weekends and holidays
ACCESS: approval required
COPYING FACILITIES: yes
MATERIALS SOLICITED: Materials relating to the history of the College, its faculty, staff, and students.

HOLDINGS:
> *Total volume:* 334 l.f.; 54 file drawers
> *Inclusive dates:* 1912 -
> *Description:* College records of all types; administrative records of Empire State Forest Products Association, the Society of American Foresters-New York Section, the New York Forest Owners Association, the Natural Resources Council of Onondaga County, and the New York State Forestry and Park Association; and personal papers, business records, etc. of Fletcher Steele.

SEE: Davis.

NY872-760

Syracuse University
Libraries
Belfer Audio Laboratory and Archives
222 Waverly Avenue
Syracuse NY 13210

(315) 423-3477

OPEN: M-F 8:30-5; closed weekends and holidays
ACCESS: an appointment is required
COPYING FACILITIES: no
MATERIALS SOLICITED: Sound recordings to complement and complete existing collection.

HOLDINGS:
> *Total volume:* 300,000 items
> *Inclusive dates:* 1888 -
> *Description:* Sound recordings, including such varied subjects as air checks of radio broadcasts, interviews with visitors to the Syracuse area, master molds for Edison disc records, test pressings of vocal classical and operatic performances, and popular and folk music from Europe and South America. All types of recording media are represented.

SEE ALSO: a brochure, 'The Syracuse University Audio Archives and Thomas Alva Edison Foundation Re-recording Laboratory at Syracuse University, Syracuse, New York,' available from the institution.

NY872-800

Syracuse University
Libraries
George Arents Research Library
Manuscript Collections
E.S. Bird Library
Syracuse NY 13210

(315) 423-2697

OPEN: M-F 8:30-5; closed weekends and holidays
ACCESS: advance arrangements recommended
COPYING FACILITIES: yes

HOLDINGS:
> *Total volume:* 30,000 l.f.
> *Inclusive dates:* 1551 -
> *Description:* Materials relating to the following fields: art; business; government and public administration; literature, including science fiction; mass communications; religion, especially that of the Methodist church in America; American history, particularly that of the state of New York; education and continuing education; and local history.

SEE: Allard, Crawley, and Edmison; Davis; Duignan; Hinding; Hounshell; Krichmar; Parkinson; Paszek; Robbins; Schatz; Spalek; Ingram.

NY872-810

Syracuse University
Libraries
George Arents Research Library
University Archives
E. S. Bird Library
Syracuse NY 13210

(315) 423-3335

OPEN: M-F 8:30-5; closed weekends and holidays
COPYING FACILITIES: yes
MATERIALS SOLICITED: Any materials relating directly to Syracuse University, including printed items, manuscripts, and photographs.

HOLDINGS:
> *Total volume:* 11,386 l.f.
> *Inclusive dates:* 1856 -
> *Description:* Archives of Syracuse University, including non-current administrative records, records of schools and departments, personal papers of faculty, University publications, theses and dissertations, photographs, memorabilia, and other items.

SEE: Hamer (as Syracuse University, Library).

SEE: Hinding.

TARRYTOWN

NY878-320

The Historical Society of the
Tarrytowns, Inc.
1 Grove Street and 19 Grove Street
Tarrytown NY 10591

(914) 631-8374

OPEN: Tu-Sa 2-4; closed Sundays,
Mondays, and holidays
USER FEES: contributions welcome
ACCESS: special arrangements by
advance appointment only
COPYING FACILITIES: no
MATERIALS SOLICITED: Materials relating
to the capture of Major John Andre on
September 23, 1780; including materi-
als on his captors, John Paulding, Isaac
VanWart, and David Williams; and on
the history of his involvement with
Benedict Arnold. Also, materials relat-
ing to the history of the Tarrytowns,
Westchester County, and the Hudson
River Valley.

HOLDINGS:
Total volume: 40 file drawers; 500
items
Inclusive dates: 1600's -
Description: Materials relating to the
capture of Major John Andre in
Tarrytown, September 23, 1780; to the
history of his involvement with Benedict
Arnold; and to his captors, John
Paulding, Isaac Van Wart, and David
Williams. There are also other materials
relating to the history of the Tarrytowns
and the United States, with emphasis on
land use changes, architectural history,
and individuals and families of the area.

SEE: NUCMC, 1962.

SEE: Robbins; Schatz.

NY878-510

Marymount College
Archives
Tarrytown NY 10591

(914) 631-3200

OPEN: by appointment only M-Th
COPYING FACILITIES: yes

HOLDINGS:
Total volume: 432 l.f.
Inclusive dates: 1920 -
Description: Materials relating to the
history of the College, including biographical information on the founders;
constitutions and bylaws; reports; minutes
of trustees' meetings; correspondence; student activities and publications; news releases; and photographs.

SEE: Hinding.

NY878-720

Sleepy Hollow Restorations
Library
150 White Plains Road
Tarrytown NY 10591

(914) 631-8200

OPEN: by appointment only
ACCESS: serious scholars, by
appointment only
COPYING FACILITIES: yes

MATERIALS SOLICITED: Materials relating
to the three sites administered by
Sleepy Hollow Restorations: Sunnyside,
Philipsburg Manor, and Van Cortlandt
Manor.

HOLDINGS:
Total volume: 30,000 items
Inclusive dates: 17th century - 19th
century
Description: A collection relating to
New York State, specifically Westchester
County. Included are materials relating to
Washington Irving; the Irving, Van
Cortlandt, Philipse, Beekman,
Chadeayne, Conklin, Hamilton, Schuyler,
and Van Wyck families; and Henry
Brevoort. There are also manuscript
maps and architectural plans of the Res-
toration sites, as well as documentation
of the restoration process.

SEE: Leventhal and Mooney - I; Robbins.

TICONDEROGA

NY881-260

Fort Ticonderoga Museum
Ticonderoga NY

MAILING ADDRESS:
Box 390
Ticonderoga NY 12883

no telephone

SEE: Hamer.

Questionnaire not returned.

NY881-750

Ticonderoga Historical Society
Hancock House
Moses Circle
Ticonderoga NY 12883

(518) 585-7868

OPEN: July - Aug., daily 10-4; rest of
year, W-Sa 10-4
COPYING FACILITIES: no
MATERIALS SOLICITED: Material relating
to history and family life in the
Ticonderoga-Champlain Valley area.
Will also accept materials relating to
the Hancock House, such as information about the original house and its
inhabitants.

HOLDINGS:
Total volume: 2,000 items
Inclusive dates: 1609 -
Description: Materials relating to the
Ticonderoga-Champlain Valley area. Included are correspondence, diaries, journals, logbooks, account books, business
records, financial records, genealogical
materials, public documents, maps, and
photographs.

SEE: Hamer (as Hancock House, Fort
Ticonderoga Association).

NY881-770

Troy Conference Historical Society
First Methodist Church
Ticonderoga NY 12883

no telephone

SEE: Hamer.

Questionnaire not returned.

TROY

NY890-200

Emma Willard School
285 Pawling Avenue
Troy NY 12180

(518) 274-4440

OPEN: M-F 9-5; closed weekends,
holidays, and school vacations
COPYING FACILITIES: yes
MATERIALS SOLICITED: Archives, manuscripts, photographs, and recordings of
the Emma Willard School and its
board of trustees, faculty, staff, and
students. Will also accept papers of
alumnae, particularly those relating to
the School.

HOLDINGS:
Total volume: 320 vols.; 170 l.f.
Inclusive dates: 1814 -
Description: Archives of the Emma
Willard School, and papers of trustees,
staff, students, and alumnae. Individuals
who are represented include Emma Hart
Willard, the School's founder; Margaret
Olivia Slocum Sage; Eliza Kellas; and
William M. Dietel. There is also a collec-
tion of photographs relating to the
School.

SEE: Hamer.

SEE: Hinding.

NY890-680

Rensselaer County Historical Society
Library
59 Second Street
Troy NY 12180

(518) 272-7232

OPEN: Tu-Sa 10-4; closed Sundays,
Mondays, and holidays
COPYING FACILITIES: yes
MATERIALS SOLICITED: Materials relating
to Rensselaer County history and
American decorative arts.

HOLDINGS:
Total volume: 75 l.f.
Inclusive dates: 1800 -
Description: Personal papers and business records of local individuals and
firms, including correspondence, diaries,
account books, and financial and legal
materials. There are also manuscript
maps, genealogical source materials, and
a collection of photographs, including
prints, negatives, and glass plate negatives
of local scenes, buildings, and people.

NY890-700
Rensselaer Polytechnic Institute
Archives
Troy NY 12180

(518) 266-8340

OPEN: M-F 9-5; closed weekends and
holidays
COPYING FACILITIES: yes
MATERIALS SOLICITED: Materials relating
to the history of applied science and
engineering, Institute alumni, and local
history. Will also accept materials relating to American history and the history
of science.

HOLDINGS:
Total volume: 1,050 l.f.
Inclusive dates: 1524 -
Description: Materials relating chiefly
to Rensselaer Polytechnic Institute, its
alumni, northern New York, and the history of engineering and applied science in
the United States. Included are the archives of the Institute as well as collections related to 19th century chemistry,
railroads, and the Brooklyn Bridge.

SEE: NUCMC, 1976.

SEE: Allard, Crawley, and Edmison.

NY890-740
Russell Sage College
Library
46 Ferry Street
Troy NY 12180

no telephone

SEE: Hamer; NUCMC, 1959-61, 70.

Questionnaire not returned.

TRUMANSBURG

NY891-800
Ulysses Philomathic Library
Trumansburg NY 14886

(607) 387-5623

OPEN: M, Tu 3-5, W 3-9, Th 3-5, F, Sa
12-5; closed Sundays and holidays
COPYING FACILITIES: no

HOLDINGS:
Total volume: 2 vols.
Inclusive dates: 1954 - 1962
Description: Two scrapbooks of news-
paper columns written by Lydia Sears on
local history and published in the
Trumansburg *Free Press.*

SEE: Tompkins County Guide.

UNADILLA

NY894-800
Unadilla Public Library
Main Street
Unadilla NY 13849

(607) 369-7500

OPEN: Tu, Th 2-5, 7-9, Sa 3-5; variable
summer hours; closed other days and
holidays
COPYING FACILITIES: no

HOLDINGS:
Total volume: 1 vol.
Inclusive dates: 1921 - 1942
Description: Minutes of the meetings
of the Unadilla Public Library, with some
financial data and copies of correspondence.

UNION SPRINGS

NY895-240
Frontenac Historical Society
Municipal Building
Factory Street
Union Springs NY 13160

no telephone

OPEN: by appointment
COPYING FACILITIES: no
MATERIALS SOLICITED: Materials on the
town of Union Springs and vicinity.

HOLDINGS:
Total volume: 5.6 c.f.; 34 vols.; 328
items
Inclusive dates: 1817 -
Description: Legal papers, 1817-68; ge-
nealogical files; and records of the Union
Springs High School, town of Union
Springs, churches, Methodist and Baptist
Young People's Societies, the Oakmont
Club and the Red Cross. Collections also
include photographs, business receipts,
personal and business records, and other
materials.

SEE: Cayuga County Guide.

UTICA

NY899-520
Munson-Williams-Proctor Institute
310 Genesee Street
Utica NY 13502

(315) 797-0000, Ext. 59

OPEN: Tu-Sa 10-5, Su 1-5; closed
Mondays and holidays
ACCESS: Saturday use requires prior
notice
COPYING FACILITIES: yes
MATERIALS SOLICITED: Will accept items
relating to areas of collecting that may
enrich the exhibition program or local
areas of research.

HOLDINGS:
Total volume: 6 boxes
Inclusive dates: 18th century -
Description: A collection of autographs;
papers relating to Ulysses S. Grant, Roscoe Conkling, Sarah Orne Jewett, Jacob
Riis, Irving Bacheller, Lyonel Feininger,
and Albert Bloch; and miscellaneous artists' letters.
Included are plans, specifications, bills,
memorandums, and correspondence concerning the building of Fountain Elms,
the home of James Watson Williams, by
architect William L. Woollett, Jr.

SEE: NUCMC, 1968.

NY899-600
Oneida Historical Society
318 Genesee Street
Utica NY 13502

(315) 735-3642

OPEN: T-Sa 10-5; closed Sundays,
Mondays, and holidays
ACCESS: advance arrangements preferred
COPYING FACILITIES: yes
MATERIALS SOLICITED: Manuscripts, archives, visual documents, audible documents, and scrapbooks relating to
Oneida County and especially to the
city of Utica and environs; also manuscripts relating to the Mohawk Valley
in the colonial and Revolutionary period.

HOLDINGS:
Total volume: 63.5 l.f.; 8 file cabinets;
521 boxes
Inclusive dates: 1750 - 1950
Description: Materials relating to the
history of Oneida County and Utica and
to the Mohawk Valley and central New
York in the colonial and Revolutionary
War periods. Included are the Munson,
Williams, and Proctor family papers;
records of the New York Mills textile
company; records of Oneida County
Home Defense, a World War I organization; records of the Overseas Friendship
Center; and the Frank Deuel collection of
genealogical notes on Palatine German
settlers of the Mohawk Valley.

SEE: Hamer.

SEE: Novotny.

NY899-800
Utica Public Library
303 Genesee Street
Utica NY 13501

(315) 735-2279

OPEN: M-F 2-4; closed weekends and
holidays

SEE: Hamer; NUCMC, 1968.

Questionnaire not returned.

VAILS GATE

NY902-560
National Temple Hill Association
Vails Gate NY

MAILING ADDRESS:
P.O. Box 315
Vails Gate NY 12584

(914) 562-6397

OPEN: by appointment
COPYING FACILITIES: no

HOLDINGS:
Total volume: 500 items
Inclusive dates: 1800 - 1850
Description: Records of the town clerk
of New Windsor, NY, mostly receipts
and letters.

VALHALLA

NY893-890
Westchester County Historical Society
Library
75 Grasslands Road
Valhalla NY 10595

(914) 592-4323, 4338

OPEN: Tu, F 10-5; closed other days and
holidays
COPYING FACILITIES: yes
MATERIALS SOLICITED: Material relating
to the history of Westchester County.

HOLDINGS:
Total volume: 60 l.f.
Inclusive dates: 17th century - 20th
century
Description: Materials relating to Westchester County, including records of municipalities, churches, schools, associations, businesses, and professions; diaries; letters; deeds; contracts; maps; genealogical materials; and photographs.

SEE: Hamer (in White Plains); NUCMC,
1967.

VAN HORNESVILLE

NY905-840
Van Hornesville Community
Corporation
Van Hornesville NY 13475

(315) 858-0030

OPEN: by appointment
ACCESS: Graduate students are asked to
submit a letter of recommendation
from their faculty advisors.
COPYING FACILITIES: yes
MATERIALS SOLICITED: Materials relating
to Owen D. Young.

HOLDINGS:
Total volume: 1,085 boxes
Inclusive dates: 1880 - 1962
Description: Papers of Owen D.
Young, including materials on the Radio
Corporation of America, reparations, and
Young's activities as a rare book collector
and breeder of Holstein-Friesian cattle.
Included are correspondence, bills, pho-
tographs, and a collection of clippings.

VESTAL

NY909-840
Vestal Historical Society
Museum
Vestal Parkway East
Vestal NY

MAILING ADDRESS:
P.O. Box 114
Vestal NY 13850

(607) 748-1432

OPEN: Sa 1-4, Su 2-5; closed other days
and holidays.
COPYING FACILITIES: no
MATERIALS SOLICITED: Vestal town history. Will also accept materials concerning Broome County history.

HOLDINGS:
Total volume: 5.5 c.f.; 6 vols.; 1 item
Inclusive dates: 1840 -
Description: Photographs, business
records, and family papers of the Vestal
area, chiefly during the 19th and early
20th centuries.

SEE: Broome County Guide.

NY909-850
Vestal Public Library
320 Vestal Parkway East
Vestal NY 13850

(607) 754-4243

OPEN: M-F 9-9, Sa 9-5, Su 1-7; closed
holidays, and weekends during summer
COPYING FACILITIES: yes
MATERIALS SOLICITED: Vestal & Broome
County history and genealogy.

HOLDINGS:
Total volume: 24 c.f.; 1 folder
Inclusive dates: 1800 -
Description: Subject files and topo-
graphical maps relating to Vestal, Broome
County, and other regions of New York.
There are also 1860 census records for
Vestal.

SEE: Broome County Guide.

VICTOR

NY910-840
Victor Free Library
91 Maple Avenue
Victor NY 14564

(716) 924-2637

OPEN: M, W 1-9, Tu, Th 10-9, F 1-5, Sa
10-4 (summer, 10-1); closed Sundays
and holidays
COPYING FACILITIES: yes

HOLDINGS:
Total volume: 3 c.f.
Inclusive dates: 1732 -
Description: Photographs of Victor,
Boughton family papers, scrapbooks,
maps, a farm ledger, documents, and
printed material relating to Victor, NY.

NY910-860
Victor Town Historian
Town Hall
85 East Main Street
Victor NY 14564

no telephone

OPEN: by appointment only
COPYING FACILITIES: yes

HOLDINGS:
Total volume: 2 c.f.
Inclusive dates: 1830 -
Description: Scrapbooks, photographs,
pamphlets, clippings, society and school
records, and other materials relating to
the town of Victor.

WADING RIVER

NY911-880
Wading River Historical Society
Wading River NY 11792

no telephone

SEE: NUCMC, 1959-61.

Questionnaire not returned.

WALTON

NY915-870
Walton Historical Society
William B. Ogden Free Library
North Street & Gardiner Place
Walton NY

MAILING ADDRESS:
16 Meade Street
Walton NY 13856

(607) 865-5929

OPEN: M 7-9, Tu-F 2-9, Sa 1-3; closed
Sundays and Saturdays, July-Labor
Day.
ACCESS: an appointment is
recommended
COPYING FACILITIES: no
MATERIALS SOLICITED: Any materials re-
lating to the town of Walton and near-
by surrounding areas.

HOLDINGS:
Total volume: .4 c.f.; 84 vols.; 627
items
Inclusive dates: 1805 -
Description: Military records from the
Civil War and World War II; Civil War
letters of Nelson L. Fox; records of the
Mary Weed Martin Chapter of the
Daughters of the American Revolution;
library records; Walton High School
records; tax assesssment rolls; church
records; account books, chiefly from gen-
eral stores; records of the Delaware Plank
Road Company; records of the Walton
Civic Club; scrapbooks; photographs; and
other materials of local interest.

SEE: Delaware County Guide.

NY915-880
William B. Ogden Free Library
North Street and Gardiner Place
Walton NY 13856

(607) 865-5929

OPEN: M 7-9, Tu-F 2-9, Sa 1-3; closed
Sundays and Saturdays, July-Labor
Day
COPYING FACILITIES: no

HOLDINGS:
Total volume: 2 vols.
Inclusive dates: 1859 - 1877
Description: A typescript diary of a
Mrs. Mead, 1859-61, and a real estate
ledger, 1869-77, of William B. Ogden.

SEE: Delaware County Guide.

WARSAW

NY923-880
Warsaw Historical Society
15 Perry Avenue
Warsaw NY

MAILING ADDRESS:
P.O. Box 245
Warsaw NY 14569

(716) 796-3422

OPEN: June-Oct., M, Tu, Th 10-3 or by
appointment; closed other days and
holidays
COPYING FACILITIES: yes
MATERIALS SOLICITED: Materials relating
to Warsaw and the surrounding area.

HOLDINGS:
    Total volume: 40 c.f.
    Inclusive dates: 1790 - 1960
    Description: Primarily materials relat-
ing to the town of Warsaw and Wyoming
County, including records of organizations, churches, schools, and the Historical Society; personal papers; assessment
rolls; a physician's and undertaker's register; and records of the local water works.
Also included are documents relating to
the French and Indian, Revolutionary,
and Civil wars.

SEE: Hamer; NUCMC, 1959-61.

SEE: Wyoming County Guide.

NY923-890
Warsaw Public Library
130 North Main Street
Warsaw NY 14569

(716) 226-2770

OPEN: M 2-9, Tu 10-9, W-F 2-9, Sa 2-5;
closed Sundays
COPYING FACILITIES: yes

HOLDINGS:
    Total volume: 1.2 c.f.
    Inclusive dates: 1890 - 1950
    Description: Minutes of three clubs in
Warsaw.

SEE: Wyoming County Guide.

NY923-910
Wyoming County Historical Center
26 Linwood Street
Warsaw NY 14569

(716) 786-2440

OPEN: M, W, F 9-5; closed other days
COPYING FACILITIES: no

HOLDINGS:
    Total volume: 50 c.f.
    Inclusive dates: 1790 - 1960
    Description: Material on Wyoming
County, NY; mostly 19th and early 20th
centuries, primarily arranged for genealogical purposes.

SEE: Wyoming County Guide.

WATERLOO

NY928-880
Waterloo Library and Historical
Society
31 East Williams Street
Waterloo NY 13165

(315) 539-3313

OPEN: M-Sa 2-5, M, W, F 7-9; closed
Saturdays in July, Sundays, and
holidays
ACCESS: appointment required
COPYING FACILITIES: no
MATERIALS SOLICITED: Materials relating
to the history of Waterloo.

HOLDINGS:
    Total volume: 4 c.f.; 130 vols.; 260
items
    Inclusive dates: 1777 - 1970
    Description: Daybooks and ledgers of
local businesses; papers of George Story;
records of the Christ Reformed Church
of Bearytown, NY, the Waterloo Female
Temperance Society, and the General
Missionary Society of Western New
York; genealogical materials; and other
church and business records.

SEE: Hamer; NUCMC, 1963-64.

SEE: Hinding; Seneca County Guide.

WATERTOWN

NY930-410
Jefferson County Historical Society
228 Washington Street
Watertown NY 13601

no telephone

SEE: Hamer.

Questionnaire not returned.

WATERVILLE

NY932-880
Waterville Historical Society
322 White Street
Waterville NY

MAILING ADDRESS:
P.O. Box 67
Waterville NY 13480

no telephone

OPEN: by appointment
COPYING FACILITIES: yes
MATERIALS SOLICITED: Materials pertaining to the history of Waterville and
the surrounding area, with emphasis on
hops growing and marketing.

HOLDINGS:
    Total volume: 10 vols.; 200 slides
    Inclusive dates: 1800 -
    Description: Account books of local
stores, a hotel register from the late 19th
century, township tax and election
records, and copies of photographs in private collections depicting local historical
events.

WAYLAND

NY936-280
Gunlocke Memorial Library
101 West Naples Street
Wayland NY 14572

(716) 728-5380

OPEN: M, W 1:30-9, Tu, Th, Sa 1:30-5,
F 10:30-5; closed Sundays and holidays
COPYING FACILITIES: yes
MATERIALS SOLICITED: History of
Wayland and vicinity.

HOLDINGS:
    Total volume: 1.5 c.f.
    Inclusive dates: 1870 -
    Description: Scrapbooks, photographs,
and other materials concerning the history of Wayland.

SEE: Steuben County Guide (as Wayland
Free Library).

WEBSTER

NY938-890
Webster Town Historian
1000 Ridge Road
Webster NY 14580

(716) 872-1000, 265-3939

OPEN: by appointment
COPYING FACILITIES: no

HOLDINGS:
    Total volume: 20 c.f.
    Inclusive dates: 1815 -
    Description: Photos, clippings, pam-
phlets, scrapbooks, histories, genealogies,
and other materials relating to the history
of Webster, NY.

NY938-900
Webster Village Historian
28 West Main Street
Webster NY 14580

(716) 265-3939

OPEN: by appointment
COPYING FACILITIES: no

HOLDINGS:
    Total volume: 6 c.f.
    Inclusive dates: 1890 -
    Description: Photos, sound recordings,
articles, clippings, pamphlets, and other
materials relating to the history of the
village of Webster.

WEEDSPORT

NY941-600
Old Brutus Historical Society, Inc.
8943 North Seneca Street
Weedsport NY 13166

(315) 834-6779

OPEN: Su, W 1-4; closed other days and
Nov. - April except by appointment
COPYING FACILITIES: no
MATERIALS SOLICITED: Genealogical and
historical materials relating to
Weedsport, Cayuga County, and the

Erie Canal, including business, farm, and Indian records.

HOLDINGS:
Total volume: 40 file drawers; 260 l.f.
Inclusive dates: 1794 -
Description: Materials relating to Weedsport, Cayuga County, and the Erie Canal, including documents, genealogical charts, maps, and photographs.

SEE: Cayuga County Guide.

WELLSVILLE

NY942-160
David A. Howe Public Library
155 North Main Street
Wellsville NY 14895

(716) 593-3410

OPEN: M, Th 10-9, Tu, F, Sa 10-5; closed Sundays, Wednesdays, and holidays; summer, closed Saturdays and open Wednesdays 10-5
COPYING FACILITIES: yes
MATERIALS SOLICITED: History of Wellsville and Allegany County.

HOLDINGS:
Total volume: 40 c.f.
Inclusive dates: 1806 -
Description: Pictures and other materials concerning Abraham Lincoln, account books, organization records, photographs, records of the Howe Library, diaries, scrapbooks, and vertical files concerning Wellsville and Allegany County.

SEE: Allegany County Guide.

NY945-760
Thelma Rogers Genealogical and Historical Society
Dyke Street
Wellsville NY 14895

(716) 593-4704

OPEN: W 1-4; closed other days
COPYING FACILITIES: no
MATERIALS SOLICITED: History and genealogy of Wellsville and Allegany County, NY.

HOLDINGS:
Total volume: 30 c.f.
Inclusive dates: 1799 -
Description: Collections include account books for Allegany County, cemetery transcriptions, genealogical materials, local church records, diaries, photographs, assessment rolls for Wellsville and Willing, scrapbooks of local interest, and other materials relating to Wellsville. Also included are scrapbooks, photographs, and Methodist church records pertaining to central and northern New York State.

SEE: Allegany County Guide.

WEST POINT

NY949-120
Constitution Island Association, Inc.
Warner House
Constitution Island
West Point NY

MAILING ADDRESS:
P.O. Box 41
West Point NY 10996

(914) 446-8676, 5029

OPEN: by appointment only M-F 10-11:30 mid-May - Oct.; closed Oct. - mid-May
ACCESS: at the discretion of the Association
COPYING FACILITIES: no
MATERIALS SOLICITED: Documents written by or relating to Susan Bogert Warner and Anna Bartlett Warner.

HOLDINGS:
Total volume: 11 file drawers
Inclusive dates: 1800 -
Description: Manuscripts and documents owned by or related to 19th century writers Susan Bogert Warner and Anna Bartlett Warner and their family.

SEE: Hinding.

NY949-780
United States Military Academy
Archives
West Point NY 10996

(914) 938-2017, 2518

OPEN: M-F 7:45-4:30; closed weekends and holidays
USER FEES: fees for extensive, nonroutine reference searches by staff members, as prescribed in Army Regulation 37-30
ACCESS: Academy staff members, cadets, officials of other Federal agencies, and bona fide scholars and researchers
COPYING FACILITIES: yes
MATERIALS SOLICITED: Official records documenting the history and functioning of the U.S. Military Academy, the U.S. Corps of Cadets, and, to some extent, the post of West Point. Will also accept other materials closely related to the Academy, such as photographs of and articles on the Academy or its noted graduates, and records of quasi-official organizations, such as the Army Athletic Association and the Association of Graduates, U.S.M.A.

HOLDINGS:
Total volume: 1,538 l.f.
Inclusive dates: 1802 -
Description: Textual and nontextual records of the Academy, including materials relating to Academy and Post administration, courses of instruction, the activities of special boards and committees, special events, and organizations. There are also photographs of West Point, sound recordings of speeches and lectures given at the Academy, and alumni files of the Association of Graduates, U.S.M.A. The majority of the holdings date from after 1838.

GUIDES: Stanley P. Tozeski, comp., *Preliminary Inventory of the Records of the U.S. Military Academy* (National Archives and Records Service, 1976).

SEE: Allard, Crawley, and Edmison.

SEE ALSO: *Guide to the National Archives of the United States* (GPO, 1974).

Although the U.S.M.A. Archives are housed at West Point, they are also considered to be Record Group 404 in the National Archives and Records Service, Office of the National Archives.

NY949-830
United States Military Academy
Library
Special Collections Division
West Point NY 10996

(914) 938-2954

OPEN: M-F 8-4:30; closed weekends and holidays
ACCESS: an appointment is requested
COPYING FACILITIES: yes
MATERIALS SOLICITED: Material on the military history of the United States, with emphasis on the papers of the graduates of the Academy and information concerning the environs of West Point; and material on military art and science, with emphasis on fortifications. Will also accept other materials on an individual basis.

HOLDINGS:
Total volume: 250,000 items
Inclusive dates: 16th century -
Description: Primarily the papers of graduates of the Academy and material on West Point and its environs. There is material on American military history; European and American military art and science, with emphasis on fortifications; and the Revolutionary War at West Point and in the Hudson Highlands. A photograph collection includes items on the Philippine War (1899-1900), the China Relief Expedition (1900-01), and the Panama Canal (1887-1916).

SEE: Hamer; NUCMC, 1965, 70, 72.

SEE: Leventhal and Mooney - I; Robbins; Hines.

SEE ALSO: *Subject Catalog of the Military Art and Science Collection: Including a Preliminary Guide to the Manuscript Collection* (Greenwood Press, 1971); Walter Schatz, ed., *Directory of Afro-American Resources* (Bowker, 1970); Ann Novotny, ed., *Picture Sources 3* (Special Libraries Assn., 1975); *Map Collections in the United States and Canada, A Directory* (Special Libraries Assn., 1970); and the following publications of the Academy: J. Russell Thomas, comp., *Preliminary Guide to the Manuscript Collection of the U.S. Military Academy Library* (1968); *The Library Map Collection: Period of the American Revolution, 1753-1800* (1971).

WEST SAYVILLE

NY952-720
Suffolk Marine Museum
Montauk Highway
West Sayville NY 11796

(516) 567-1733

OPEN: M-Sa 10-3, Su 12-4 by
  appointment; closed holidays
ACCESS: appointment required
COPYING FACILITIES: no
MATERIALS SOLICITED: Maps, logs, photographs, and records related to Long
  Island small craft, life saving, the
  shellfishing industry, ship wrecks, and
  groundings. Will also accept other nautical materials related to Long Island.

HOLDINGS:
  Total volume: not specified
  Inclusive dates: 1880's - 1930
  Description: Historical records relating
  to maritime history on the Long Island
  southern shore. Included are records of
  local participation in the America's Cup
  races, as well as papers of ship captains,
  wreckmasters, lighthouses, and lighthouse
  keepers.

WESTFIELD

NY958-640
Patterson Library
40 South Portage Street
Westfield NY 14787

(716) 326-2154

OPEN: M-W 9-8, Th-Sa 9-5; closed
  Sundays and holidays
COPYING FACILITIES: yes
MATERIALS SOLICITED: Material relating
  to Westfield, Chautauqua County, and
  western New York. Will also accept genealogical materials, literary manuscripts, and photographs.

HOLDINGS:
  Total volume: 75 c.f.
  Inclusive dates: 1803 -
  Description: Photographs of Westfield
  people, places, and events, 1880-1940;
  personal papers and diaries of local residents; manuscript maps; oral history
  tapes; and county records from the 19th
  century, including deed books, ledgers,
  and field notes.
    Included are local records of the Hol-
  land Land Company (1803-70) and glass
  plate negatives of William Sherman.

SEE: Hamer.

WHITE PLAINS

NY964-322
Texaco, Inc.
Archives
2000 Westchester Avenue
White Plains NY 10650

(914) 253-7129

OPEN: M-F 9-3; closed weekends and
  holidays

ACCESS: advance appointments required;
  all requests for research must be in
  writing
COPYING FACILITIES: yes
MATERIALS SOLICITED: Materials relating
  to Texaco, The Texas Company, and
  major subsidiaries.

HOLDINGS:
  Total volume: 1,500 c.f.; 200 vols.
  Inclusive dates: 1902 -
  Description: Records of The Texas
  Company, Texaco, Inc., and their major
  subsidiaries.

WHITESVILLE

NY967-880
Whitesville Public Library
Whitesville NY 14897

no telephone

OPEN: M 7-9, F 2-5:30; closed holidays
COPYING FACILITIES: no
MATERIALS SOLICITED: History of
  Whitesville and vicinity.

HOLDINGS:
  Total volume: 1 c.f.
  Inclusive dates: 1860 - 1965
  Description: Records of Whitesville
  Union School and Academy and of The
  Whitesville and Beech Hill Telephone
  Company, local election records, a scrap-
  book of material on the Spanish-
  American War, and poetry by a local
  resident.

SEE: Allegany County Guide.

WHITNEY POINT

NY968-520
Mary Wilcox Memorial Library
Main Street
Whitney Point NY 13862

(607) 692-3159

OPEN: Tu-Th 11-5, F 1-9, Sa 11-3;
  closed Sundays, Mondays, and holidays
COPYING FACILITIES: no
MATERIALS SOLICITED: Whitney Point
  history.

HOLDINGS:
  Total volume: 4 c.f.; 30 vols.
  Inclusive dates: 1830 -
  Description: Collection consists chiefly
  of local school records, 1881-1936, and
  subject files concerning the history of the
  village of Whitney Point.

SEE: Broome County Guide.

WILLIAMSVILLE

NY970-840
The United Methodist Church
Western New York United Methodist
  Conference
Archives Center
5681 Main Street
Williamsville, NY 14221

(716) 634-4800

OPEN: M-F 9-4; closed weekends and
  holidays
COPYING FACILITIES: yes
MATERIALS SOLICITED: Materials related
  to the United Methodist church in
  western New York.

HOLDINGS:
  Total volume: 31 l.f.
  Inclusive dates: 1792 -
  Description: Historical records and other materials on the United Methodist
  church and antecedent churches in western New York. Included are local church
  files, original minutes of the Genesee
  Conference, early manuscripts, conference
  minutes, disciplines, and conference history materials.

WINDSOR

NY973-600
Old Stone Museum
10 Chestnut Street
Windsor NY 13865

(607) 655-1443

OPEN: by appointment only
COPYING FACILITIES: no
MATERIALS SOLICITED: Military history
  of Windsor and Broome County, NY.

HOLDINGS:
  Total volume: 11 c.f.
  Inclusive dates: 1807 -
  Description: Primarily Civil War letters
  and documents, papers of local families,
  and photographs and memorabilia relating to Broome County participation in
  various wars.

SEE: Broome County Guide.

WOLCOTT

NY974-890
Wolcott Town Historian
Wolcott Town Hall
Wolcott NY 14590

(315) 594-9431

OPEN: by appointment only
COPYING FACILITIES: no

HOLDINGS:
  Total volume: 5 c.f.
  Inclusive dates: 1870 -
  Description: Photographs, motion pic-
  tures, reminiscences, and business papers
  relating to the history of Wolcott, NY.

SEE: Wayne County Guide.

WOODSTOCK

NY975-890
Woodstock Library
5 Library Lane
Woodstock NY 12498

(914) 679-2213

OPEN: Tu 10-6, W 1-8, Th 10-6, F 1-6,
  Sa 10-5; closed Sundays, Mondays, and
  holidays
COPYING FACILITIES: yes

MATERIALS SOLICITED: Materials relating to Woodstock.

HOLDINGS:
Total volume: 350 items
Inclusive dates: 1900 - 1950
Description: Accounts and minutes of the Library; local church records; and a few manuscripts by or about local residents.

WORCESTER

NY978-870
Worcester Free Library
Main Street
Worcester NY 12197

no telephone

OPEN: Th, Sa, noon-6; summer, Tu, Th 1-5:30, Sa 5-8; closed other days and holidays
COPYING FACILITIES: no

HOLDINGS:
Total volume: 4 vols.
Inclusive dates: 1868 - 1970
Description: A 1970 manuscript by Howson H. Hartley entitled 'A History of South Worcester, New York' and other materials.

NY978-880
Worcester Historical Society
Worcester NY 12197

no telephone

OPEN: M-W, F 10-4, Sa 10-1; closed Thurdays, Sundays, and holidays
COPYING FACILITIES: no
MATERIALS SOLICITED: Materials relating to Worcester and vicinity.

HOLDINGS:
Total volume: 98 vols.; 1.6 c.f.; 1,800 items
Inclusive dates: 1808 -
Description: Worcester town records, 1808-1942, including criminal justice dockets, tax records, and utility records; cemetery and school records, including basketball scores for Worcester High School; diaries and papers of banker Fern Ferguson; papers of Richard Tandler; photographs; correspondence; account books; and other materials.

YONKERS

NY984-200
Elizabeth Seton College Library
1061 North Broadway
Yonkers NY 10701

(914) 969-4000

OPEN: M-Th 8:30-10, F 8:30-5, Sa 12:30-8, Su 12:30-5, holidays 1-5; closed Christmas and Easter vacations
ACCESS: restrictions statement available upon request
COPYING FACILITIES: yes
MATERIALS SOLICITED: Materials relating to the history of the College. Will also accept music manuscripts and materials relating to local history.

HOLDINGS:
Total volume: 550 items
Inclusive dates: 1951 -
Description: Materials relating to Elizabeth Seton School and Junior College, and Irish music manuscripts.

NY984-320
Hudson River Museum
511 Warburton Avenue
Trevor Park-on-Hudson
Yonkers NY 10701

no telephone

SEE: Hamer.

Questionnaire not returned.

NY984-710
St. Joseph's Seminary
Archbishop Corrigan Memorial Library
Dunwoodie
Yonkers NY 10704

no telephone

SEE: Hamer.

Questionnaire not returned.

YOUNGSTOWN

NY990-600
Old Fort Niagara Association, Inc.
Fort Niagara State Park
Youngstown NY

MAILING ADDRESS:
P.O. Box 169
Youngstown NY 14174

(716) 745-7611

OPEN: daily with variable closing hours; closed Thanksgiving, Christmas, and New Year's
COPYING FACILITIES: no

HOLDINGS:
Total volume: 18 pieces; 6 vols.
Inclusive dates: 1813 - 1901
Description: Miscellaneous records of the fort, including items relating to the restoration, and a diary of a California '49er.

NORTH CAROLINA

Since 1959 the Division of Archives and History of North Carolina's Department of Cultural Resources has administered a statewide program for preserving local public records. All permanently valuable county records, with the exception of recordings of wills and deeds, are transferred to the State Archives in Raleigh, usually about 60 years after their creation. In addition, the State Archives makes available to researchers more than 22,000 reels of microfilm of county and municipal records. Included are the minutes of the governing body of many municipalities.

ALBEMARLE

NC30-715
Stanly County Historic Properties Commission
112 North Third Street
Albemarle NC 28001

(704) 983-1623

OPEN: M-F 1-3; closed weekends, legal holidays, and during vacation week
COPYING FACILITIES: no
MATERIALS SOLICITED: Materials relating to Stanly County people, historic sites, and structures, including surveys, land grant records, deeds of property, photographs, cemetery and family records, business records, diaries, journals, ledgers, and logbooks.

HOLDINGS:
    Total volume: 970 items
    Inclusive dates: 1790 -
    Description: Historical manuscripts and other materials relating to the history of the geographical area of Stanly County. Included are land grants, property deeds, mortgage bonds, Civil War and Reconstruction records, family history materials, photographs, government and business ledgers and other records, and records relating to hydroelectric development along the Yadkin and Pee Dee rivers.

ASHEVILLE

NC60-160
National Oceanic and Atmospheric Administration
Environmental Data Information Service
National Climatic Data Center
Federal Building
Asheville NC 28801-2696

(704) 259-0682

OPEN: M-F 8-4:30; closed weekends and holidays
COPYING FACILITIES: yes
MATERIALS SOLICITED: Weather records produced by the National Weather Service, the Federal Aviation Administration, the Air Force, the Coast Guard, and the Navy.

HOLDINGS:
    Total volume: 67,228 c.f.
    Inclusive dates: 19th century -
    Description: 73,500,000 original records documenting the climate of the United States, other world areas, and the upper atmosphere. Many records have been placed on microfilm and microfiche. The collection also includes 18,000 reels depicting radar echoes; 11,000 reels containing meteorological satellite imagery; 40,000 reels of magnetic tape; and 30,114 reels of FOSDIC film representing around 361,400,000 punched card images of coded meteorological data. Some of the holdings include reports filed with the Department of Agriculture in the 19th century.

SEE: Hamer (as National Weather Records Center).

SEE: Paszek.

SEE ALSO: National Weather Records Center, *Selective Guide to Climatic Data Sources: 4.11* (GPO, 1969); National Oceanic and Atmospheric Administration, *The National Climatic Center, Asheville, N.C.* (U.S. Dept. of Commerce, 1970).

NC60-240
Forest Service
National Forests in North Carolina
Post and Otis Streets
Asheville NC

MAILING ADDRESS:
P.O. Box 2750
Asheville NC 28802

(704) 257-4200

OPEN: M-F 8-4:30; closed weekends and holidays

COPYING FACILITIES: yes
MATERIALS SOLICITED: Materials relating to the history of National Forests in North Carolina, including such topics as land acquisition and development, forestry procedures, forest fires, Gifford Pinchot, Carl Alwyn Schenck, and the Biltmore Forest School. Will also accept materials relating to land use in North Carolina, including such topics as forestry and logging.

HOLDINGS:
    Total volume: not specified
    Inclusive dates: 1890 -
    Description: Materials relating to the National Forests in North Carolina, including land records, land surveys, manuscript maps, tape recordings on such topics as methods of fire fighting and the Civilian Conservation Corps, and correspondence of Carl Schenck, founder of the Biltmore Forest School.

NC60-640
Pack Memorial Public Library
North Carolina Collection and Thomas Wolfe Collection
67 Haywood Street
Asheville NC 28801

(704) 252-8701

OPEN: M-F 9-9, Sa 9-6, Su 2-5; closed holidays, and Sundays during July and August
USER FEES: small handling fees for mail requests
COPYING FACILITIES: yes
MATERIALS SOLICITED: Materials relating to Asheville, Buncombe County, western North Carolina, and Thomas Wolfe.

HOLDINGS:
    Total volume: 60 l.f.
    Inclusive dates: 1730 -
    Description: Materials focusing on Thomas Wolfe, Asheville history, natural history, and southeastern Indians. Included are maps of North Carolina and the eastern United States; 7,000 photographs, 1865- , dealing mainly with Asheville and western North Carolina; records of local and regional institutions; unpublished family histories; sound recordings; correspondence; and other items.

SEE: Hamer; NUCMC, 1959-61.

SEE: Davis; Robbins.

NC60-720

Southeastern Forest Experiment
    Station
200 Weaver Boulevard
Asheville NC

MAILING ADDRESS:
P.O. Box 268
Asheville NC 28802

(704) 259-0758

OPEN: M-F 8-4:30 by appointment only;
    closed weekends and holidays
COPYING FACILITIES: yes
MATERIALS SOLICITED: Materials per-
    taining to the history of the Station.

HOLDINGS:
    Total volume: 11 l.f.
    Inclusive dates: 1921 -
    Description: Records of the research
    and administrative activities of the Ex-
    periment Station, including annual re-
    ports, 1921-65, tape-recorded interviews,
    and photographs.

NC60-810

University of North Carolina at
    Asheville
Southern Highlands Research Center
P.O. Box 8467
University Heights
Asheville NC 28814

(704) 258-6414

OPEN: M-F 1-4; closed weekends and
    holidays
COPYING FACILITIES: yes
MATERIALS SOLICITED: Materials related
    to western North Carolina, especially
    its urban areas, including family and
    genealogy materials, business and com-
    mercial records, records of religious or-
    ganizations, historical materials concern-
    cerning black highlanders, records of
    organizations dealing with regional is-
    sues, oral history collections, and pho-
    tographic materials. Will also accept
    Appalachian materials and general ge-
    nealogical materials.

HOLDINGS:
    Total volume: 80 l.f.
    Inclusive dates: 1790 -
    Description: Oral history recordings
    pertinent to western North Carolina, a
    photograph collection related largely to
    Asheville and Buncombe County, and pa-
    pers of U.S. Representative Roy A.
    Taylor concerning the proposed Mount
    Mitchell National Park.
        Includes materials on the beginning of
    the U.S. Forest Service and the Blue
    Ridge Parkway and extensive records per-
    taining to Jews, Greeks, blacks, and other
    ethnic groups in the area.

NC60-880

Western North Carolina Historical
    Association
346 Montford Avenue
Asheville NC 28801

no telephone

SEE: NUCMC, 1962.

Questionnaire not returned.

BELMONT

NC090-080

Belmont (Mary Help of Christians)
    Abbey
Belmont Abbey College
Belmont NC 28012

(704) 825-3711

OPEN: by appointment only
COPYING FACILITIES: yes
MATERIALS SOLICITED: Materials related
    to Belmont Abbey; Belmont Abbey
    Nullius; St. Mary's College and Semi-
    nary; Belmont Abbey College, Semi-
    nary, and Preparatory School; St. Bene-
    dict Priory and Benedictine High
    School, Richmond, VA; Sacred Heart
    Priory and Benedictine High School,
    Savannah, GA (through 1961); St. Leo
    Priory, FL (through 1894); St. Maur
    Priory and St. Joseph Institute, Bristol,
    VA; and the Vicariate Apostolic of
    North Carolina, 1887-1924. Will also
    accept materials related to the history
    of the Roman Catholic church in
    North Carolina.

HOLDINGS:
    Total volume: not specified
    Inclusive dates: 1876 -
    Description: Materials relating to the
    history and work of Belmont Abbey. In-
    cluded are records from the Nullius dio-
    cese, 1910-77, the final years of the
    Vicariate Apostolic of North Carolina,
    1887-1924, and several priories and
    schools directed by Belmont Abbey.
    There are also records of Belmont Abbey
    College through 1976, and the papers of
    Bishop Leo Haid, O.S.B., Abbot-Nullius
    Vincent Taylor, O.S.B., and Abbot-
    Nullius Walter Coggin, O.S.B.

BOILING SPRINGS

NC100-280

Gardner-Webb College
Dover Library
Special Collections
Boiling Springs NC

MAILING ADDRESS:
P.O. Box 836
Boiling Springs NC 28017

(704) 434-2361, Ext. 301

OPEN: M-Th 7:45-midnight, F 7:45-5, Sa
    9-5, Su 6-10; closed holidays,
    Christmas vacation, and evenings and
    weekends during semester and summer
    breaks
ACCESS: serious researchers only
COPYING FACILITIES: yes
MATERIALS SOLICITED: Records and
    publications of Gardner-Webb College
    and its faculty and alumni. Will also
    accept works and papers of Thomas
    Dixon.

HOLDINGS:
    Total volume: 314 l.f.
    Inclusive dates: 1782 -
    Description: Scrapbooks, diaries, and
    photographs concerning Fay Webb and
    former North Carolina governor Oliver
    Max Gardner and their families; records
    from churches in the King's Mountain

Baptist Association; and papers of author
Thomas Dixon.

SEE: Schatz.

BUIES CREEK

NC130-120

Campbell University
Carrie Rich Memorial Library
Buies Creek NC

MAILING ADDRESS:
P.O. Box 98
Buies Creek NC 27506

(919) 893-4111, Ext. 2407

OPEN: M-F 7:50-4:30; closed weekends
    and holidays
COPYING FACILITIES: yes
MATERIALS SOLICITED: Will accept ma-
    terial dealing with Campbell College or
    with the genealogy of North Carolin-
    ians.

HOLDINGS:
    Total volume: 30,000 items
    Inclusive dates: 1887 -
    Description: Materials tracing the
    founding and growth of Campbell Col-
    lege, including papers of two former
    presidents, as well as a small collection of
    Harnett County historical materials.

CHAPEL HILL

NC150-780

University of North Carolina at
    Chapel Hill
Geology Library
Chapel Hill NC

MAILING ADDRESS:
Mitchell Hall 029-A
Chapel Hill NC 27514

(919) 962-2386

OPEN: M-Th 8-9, F 8-5, Su 3-9; during
    summer and intersessions M-F 8-5;
    closed holidays
COPYING FACILITIES: yes

HOLDINGS:
    Total volume: not specified
    Inclusive dates: 20th century -
    Description: Annual reports of the Ge-
    ology Department Library, a term paper
    covering the life and work of Elisha
    Mitchell, and 35 manuscript maps show-
    ing the geology of Orange County, NC.

NC150-790

University of North Carolina at
    Chapel Hill
Institute of Outdoor Drama
Chapel Hill NC

MAILING ADDRESS:
202 Graham Memorial 052-A
Chapel Hill NC 27514

(919) 962-1328

OPEN: M-F 8-5; closed weekends and
    holidays
ACCESS: permission of the Director of
    the Institute required

COPYING FACILITIES: yes
MATERIALS SOLICITED: Materials concerning historic outdoor dramas, including photographs, blueprints, scripts, and information on employment, casts, finances, publicity, sets, and costume design.

HOLDINGS:
> *Total volume:* 120 c.f.; 65 items
> *Inclusive dates:* 1937 -
> *Description:* Records of 60 historic outdoor dramas, including scripts, photographs, blueprints and publicity materials. There are also five films concerning the Institute's history, playwright Paul Green, the historic English lost colony on Roanoke Island, NC, and the outdoor dramas *Texas* and *Unto These Hills.*

NC150-800

University of North Carolina at
    Chapel Hill
Library
Manuscripts Department and
    Southern Historical Collection
Chapel Hill NC

MAILING ADDRESS:
Wilson Library 024-A
Chapel Hill NC 27514

(919) 962-1345

OPEN: M-F 8-5, Sa 9-1; closed Sundays; building renovations may cause temporary closures
ACCESS: User must complete application, show driver's license or other proof of identity, and have a serious purpose; special permission required for a few restricted manuscript groups.
COPYING FACILITIES: yes
MATERIALS SOLICITED: Materials relating to Southern history and literature, the University of North Carolina, George Bernard Shaw, and John Ruskin. Will also accept other materials depending on faculty interest.

HOLDINGS:
> *Total volume:* 8,168,051 items
> *Inclusive dates:* 1750 -
> *Description:* The Southern Historical Collection consists of private papers relating to the history of North Carolina, other Southern States, and the South as a region. Included are correspondence, business papers, church records, diaries, account books, and other miscellaneous manuscripts, microfilm, photographs, and audio-visual records. There are also general and literary manuscripts, including some relating to Europe and Latin America, as well as the University of North Carolina archives, containing official records of the University at Chapel Hill since 1789 and of the general administration of the State university system.
> Also includes the holdings of the Chapel Hill Historical Society (see separate listing in first edition).

SEE: Hamer; NUCMC, 1959-65, 68, 70, 72, 74, 77-78, 80.

SEE: Davis; Beers - Confederate; Ingram; Parkinson; Hinding; Robbins.

SEE ALSO: Susan S. Blosser and Clyde Norman Wilson, Jr., eds., *The Southern Historical Collection: A Guide to Manuscripts* (1970); Everard H. Smith, III, comp., *The Southern Historical Collection: Supplementary Guide to Manuscripts, 1970-75* (1976); Carolyn A. Wallace, 'The Southern Historical Collection,' *North Carolina Libraries* 19 (Winter 1961); Carolyn A. Wallace, 'The Southern Historical Collection,' *American Archivist* 28 (July 1965); Clyde Edward Pitts, ed., *The Christopher Gustavus Memminger Papers in the Southern Historical Collection of the University of North Carolina Library* (1966).

Ellen B. Neal, 'Resources for Georgia Studies in the Southern Historical Collections,' *Georgia Archive* (Winter 1974); James M. Merrill, 'The Naval Historian and His Sources,' *American Archivist* 32 (July 1969); Walter Schatz, ed., *Directory of Afro-American Resources* (Bowker, 1970); Peter Duignan, *Handbook of American Resources for African Studies* (Hoover Institution, 1967); David A. Hounshell, comp., *Manuscripts in U.S. Depositories Relating to the History of Electrical Science and Technology* (Smithsonian Institution, n.d.).

NC150-810

University of North Carolina at
    Chapel Hill
Wilson Library
North Carolina Collection
Chapel Hill NC

MAILING ADDRESS:
Wilson Library 024-A
Chapel Hill NC 27514

(919) 962-1172

OPEN: M-F 8-5; closed weekends and holidays
ACCESS: identification is required
COPYING FACILITIES: yes
MATERIALS SOLICITED: Material relating to North Carolina and North Carolinians.

HOLDINGS:
> *Total volume:* 6,663 items
> *Inclusive dates:* 1570 -
> *Description:* Manuscripts relating to North Carolina or North Carolinians. Included are 1,500 pieces relating to Thomas Wolfe and his family; 11 pieces concerning Sir Walter Raleigh; and 425 manuscripts of books by authors. There are many single items relating to North Carolinians; manuscript maps; and microfilm and photostats of manuscripts relating to North Carolina in other repositories.

SEE: Hamer; NUCMC, 1959-62, 68, 79 (as University of North Carolina Library).

SEE ALSO: Robert B. Downs, ed., *Resources of North Carolina Libraries* (Governor's Commission on Library Resources, 1965).

NC150-860

University of North Carolina at
    Chapel Hill
Library
Rare Book Collection
Chapel Hill NC

MAILING ADDRESS:
Wilson Library 024-A
Chapel Hill NC 27514

(919) 962-1143

OPEN: M-F 8-5; closed weekends and holidays
ACCESS: users must have a legitimate scholarly purpose
COPYING FACILITIES: yes
MATERIALS SOLICITED: European manuscripts from the medieval and Renaissance periods, as well as from the 17th and 18th centuries.

HOLDINGS:
> *Total volume:* 40 l.f.
> *Inclusive dates:* 1250 - 1800
> *Description:* A collection of European manuscripts, mostly from Italy, including 435 items from prior to 1600. They include legal documents and private agreements, business and personal letters, and church and theological documents.

CHARLOTTE

NC160-120

Charlotte and Mecklenburg County
    Library
Special Collections
310 North Tryon Street
Charlotte NC 28202

no telephone

SEE: Hamer.

Questionnaire not returned.

NC160-520

Mint Museum
2730 Randolph Road
Charlotte NC 28207

(704) 337-2000

OPEN: Tu-F 10-5, Sa, Su 2-5; closed Mondays and holidays
ACCESS: serious researchers only
COPYING FACILITIES: yes
MATERIALS SOLICITED: Items relating to the history of Charlotte and Mecklenburg County.

HOLDINGS:
> *Total volume:* not specified
> *Inclusive dates:* 1760 -
> *Description:* Materials relating to the history of Charlotte and Mecklenburg County, with emphasis on government, commerce, transportation, business, culture, education, medicine, and religion. Included are papers of Mecklenburg County families, such as the Alexanders, Osbornes, and Shells; and a photograph collection documenting county growth, with major emphasis on administrative units of the city government such as the fire department and traffic engineering.

NC160-800
University of North Carolina at
    Charlotte
Atkins Library
Special Collections
Charlotte NC 28223

(704) 597-2369

OPEN: M-F 8-5; closed weekends and
    holidays
COPYING FACILITIES: yes
MATERIALS SOLICITED: Official records of
    the University, papers of individuals as-
    sociated with the University, and papers
    of individuals and organizations which
    document the history and culture of
    North and South Carolina (with a con-
    centration on the Metrolina region). Will
    also accept materials which support the
    academic programs or research needs of
    the University.

HOLDINGS:
    Total volume: 460 l.f.
    Inclusive dates: 1770 -
    Description: Records of the University
    comprise about 55 percent of the collec-
    tions. Additional holdings include manu-
    scripts, photographs, and oral history re-
    cordings and transcripts emphasizing
    Mecklenburg County, NC, and the pied-
    mont area of North and South Carolina,
    primarily in the 20th century.

SEE: NUCMC, 1980.

SEE: Meckler and McMullin.

CONCORD

NC200-120
Charles A. Cannon Memorial Library
27 Union Street, North
Concord NC 28025

(704) 788-3167

OPEN: Tu, Th 9-5; closed other days and
    holidays
COPYING FACILITIES: yes
MATERIALS SOLICITED: Materials per-
    taining to the history of Concord,
    Cabarrus County, and Mecklenburg
    County.

HOLDINGS:
    Total volume: 20 vols.; 4 reels; 70
    slides
    Inclusive dates: 1750's -
    Description: Birth, marriage and death
    records of Cabarrus and Mecklenburg
    counties, local Rotary Club minutes
    (1951-), 16 mm film of Concord and its
    vicinity (1938-41), and color slides of
    Cabarrus County in 1975, including
    views of historic homes, churches, indus-
    trial sites, and agriculture.

CULLOWHEE

NC210-870
Western Carolina University
Hunter Library
Special Collections
Cullowhee NC 28723

(704) 227-7474

OPEN: M-F 8-5; closed weekends and
    holidays
COPYING FACILITIES: yes
MATERIALS SOLICITED: Materials relating
    to the Appalachian wilderness, the Chero-
    kee Indians, the Great Smoky Mountains
    National Park, Western Carolina Univer-
    sity, and the history and culture of Ap-
    palachia, especially western North Caro-
    lina. Will also accept Americana and spe-
    cial subjects in support of faculty re-
    search.

HOLDINGS:
    Total volume: 600 l.f.
    Inclusive dates: 1830 -
    Description: Manuscripts and archives
    relating to the history and culture of Ap-
    palachia, especially western North Caro-
    lina, and to changing attitudes toward
    wilderness use in the eastern mountains.
    There are also 120 reels of microfilm of
    Cherokee Indian material from repositor-
    ies in Great Britain, France, and Spain,
    and the archives of Western Carolina
    University.

SEE: NUCMC, 1972.

SEE: Davis.

DAVIDSON

NC240-160
Davidson College
Library
Archives Department
Davidson NC 28036

(704) 892-2000, Ext. 331

OPEN: M-F 8-1 a.m., Sa 8-6, Su 2-1;
    during vacations and summer, M-F
    8-5, Sa 8-noon, Su 2-5; closed holidays
COPYING FACILITIES: yes
MATERIALS SOLICITED: Materials relating
    to Davidson College.

HOLDINGS:
    Total volume: 123 file drawers
    Inclusive dates: 1820 -
    Description: 30 file drawers of David-
    son College historical materials, com-
    posed of faculty minutes from 1820,
    trustee minutes from 1836, literary soci-
    ety minutes, 1837-1900, and student let-
    ters, addresses, and notebooks, 1837 to
    date. Also included are the Peter S. Ney
    Collection, containing photographs of
    Ney, his holograph poems, a mathematics
    notebook in his hand, and a scrapbook,
    and the Woodrow Wilson Collection,
    consisting of 4 signed letters, his personal
    notebook kept while a freshman at Da-
    vidson College, and 4 scrapbooks.

SEE: Hamer; NUCMC, 1959-61.

SEE: Robbins.

SEE ALSO: Robert B. Downs, ed., *Re-
    sources of North Carolina Libraries*
    (Governor's Commission on Library
    Resources, 1965).

DOBSON

NC250-720
Surry Community College
Learning Resources Center
Surry County Local History Collection
Dobson NC

MAILING ADDRESS:
P.O. Box 304
Dobson NC 27017

(919) 386-8121, Ext. 52

OPEN: M-Th 8-9, F 8-4:30; closed
    weekends, Thanksgiving, and
    Christmas
COPYING FACILITIES: yes
MATERIALS SOLICITED: Photographs, dia-
    ries, letters, journals, genealogical
    records, and maps of Surry County and
    the surrounding area.

HOLDINGS:
    Total volume: 280 l.f.; 3 drawers
    microfilm
    Inclusive dates: 1741 -
    Description: Materials relating to Surry
    County, including manuscripts, maps, let-
    ters, and microfilmed genealogical
    records.

DURHAM

NC260-150
Duke University
Archives
341 Perkins
Duke University
Durham NC 27706

(919) 684-5637

OPEN: M-F 8-5; closed weekends and
    holidays
COPYING FACILITIES: yes
MATERIALS SOLICITED: Institutional
    records of the University including stu-
    dent organizations; personal papers of
    faculty, administrators, and staff.

HOLDINGS:
    Total volume: not specified
    Inclusive dates: 1838 -
    Description: Institutional archives of
    Duke University (formerly Trinity Col-
    lege, Normal College, Union Institute,
    and Brown's Schoolhouse). In addition to
    institutional record groups the collection
    includes personal papers of faculty and
    administrators, publications of and about
    the University, records of student groups,
    and a motion picture and photographic
    file. The repository also contains a signifi-
    cant amount of material pertaining to the
    Methodist church as well as the archives
    of the *Hispanic American Historical Re-
    view* and the Triangle Universities Com-
    putation Center.

SEE: Davis; Hinding.

SEE ALSO: Thomas S. Kuhn, John L. Heilbron, Paul Forman, and Lini Allen, *Sources for History of Quantum Physics: An Inventory and Report* (American Philosophical Society, 1967); Joan Nelson Warnow, *A Selection of Manuscript Collections at American Repositories* (American Institute of Physics, 1969).

NC260-160
Duke University
Medical Library
Trent Collection
Duke University Medical Center
Durham NC 27706

(919) 684-3325

SEE: Hamer (as Duke Hospital Library).

Questionnaire not returned.

NC260-170
Duke University
William R. Perkins Library
Manuscript Department
Durham NC 27706

(919) 684-3372

OPEN: M-F 8-5:30, Sa 9-12:30; closed Sundays and holidays
COPYING FACILITIES: yes
MATERIALS SOLICITED: Materials relating to Southern history; the British Empire and Commonwealth; business history, especially textiles, tobacco, lumber, and furniture; labor unions in the Middle Atlantic States; literature; the Methodist church; public affairs; and economic, social, military, and political history of the United States.

HOLDINGS:
    Total volume: 5,000,000 items; 15,000 vols.
    Inclusive dates: 1750 -
    Description: Materials relating primarily to the southern States, as well as other areas of the United States and foreign countries. Subject focuses include the antebellum South, the Civil War and Reconstruction, Afro-American history, the antislavery movement in the United States and the British Empire, religion, education, public affairs of the 19th and 20th centuries, the Socialist Party of America, agriculture, business and economic history, social life, women, the labor movement, southern literature, and Great Britain and the British Empire.

GUIDES: Richard C. Davis and Linda Angle Miller, eds., *Guide to the Catalogued Collections in the Manuscript Departmnt of the William R. Perkins Library, Duke University* (1980).

SEE: Hamer; NUCMC, 1959-64, 68-72, 75, 77, 79.

SEE: Allard, Crawley, and Edmison; Beers - Confederate; Davis; Hinding; Leventhal and Mooney - III; Paszek.

SEE ALSO: Mattie Russell, 'The Manuscript Department in Duke University Library,' *American Archivist* 28 (July 1965); Alan M. Meckler and Ruth McMullin, comps., *Oral History Collections* (Bowker, 1975); Ann Novotny, ed., *Picture Sources 3* (Special Libraries

Assn., 1975); David A. Hounshell, comp., *Manuscripts in U.S. Depositories Relating to the History of Electrical Science and Technology* (Smithsonian Institution, n.d.); Albert Krichmar, *The Women's Rights Movement in the United States, 1848-1970: A Bibliography and Sourcebook* (Scarecrow Press, 1972).

Robert O. Collins and Peter Duignan, *Americans in Africa* (Hoover Institution, 1963); Peter Duignan, *Handbook of American Resources for African Studies* (Hoover Institution, 1967); Walter Schatz, ed., *Directory of Afro-American Resources* (Bowker, 1970); Robert B. Downs, ed., *Resources of North Carolina Libraries* (Governor's Commission on Library Resources, 1965); Gerald Friedberg, 'Sources for the Study of Socialism in America,' *Labor History* 6 (Spring 1965); William Rector Erwin, *Sources for the History of India and Adjacent Areas in the Manuscript Department at the William R. Perkins Library of Duke University* (1971).

Richard C. Davis, *North American Forest History: A Guide to Archives and Manuscripts in the United States and Canada* (Clio Books, 1977).

EDENTON

NC290-120
Cupola House Association, Inc.
S. Broad Street
Edenton NC

MAILING ADDRESS:
P.O. Box 474
Edenton NC 27932

(919) 482-3663

OPEN: by appointment only

SEE: Hamer.

Questionnaire not returned.

ELON COLLEGE

NC310-200
Elon College
Library
Christian Church History Collection
P.O. Box 187
Elon College NC 27244

(919) 584-2338

OPEN: W 9-12, other times by appointment; closed New Year's, July 4th, Thanksgiving, and December
COPYING FACILITIES: yes
MATERIALS SOLICITED: Materials related to the history of the Christian church.

HOLDINGS:
    Total volume: 50 l.f.
    Inclusive dates: 1840 -
    Description: Records of the Christian church up to 1931, and materials relating to the Congregational Christian church and the United Church of Christ after 1931. Most of the materials relate to Virginia and North Carolina. The collection includes records of local churches and

minutes of various meetings, as well as a small number of other manuscripts.

NC310-640
The Primitive Baptist Library and Archives
Highway 87
Elon College NC

MAILING ADDRESS:
Route 2, P.O. Box 422
Elon College NC 27244

(919) 584-8531

OPEN: M-Sa 8-6, and by appointment; closed Sundays and holidays
COPYING FACILITIES: no
MATERIALS SOLICITED: Church records and minutes, association minutes, and personal papers of religious or historical value, with emphasis on the Baptist church.

HOLDINGS:
    Total volume: 50,000 items
    Inclusive dates: 1600 -
    Description: Church records and minutes, journals, correspondence, church histories, and other materials relating to religious history, chiefly of the Baptist church.

SEE ALSO: Robert B. Downs, ed., *Resources of North Carolina Libraries* (Governor's Commission on Library Resources, 1965).

FAYETTEVILLE

NC330-520
Methodist College
Davis Memorial Library
Lafayette Room
Fayetteville NC 28301

(919) 488-7110

OPEN: Su 5-9, M-Th 8-10, F 8-5, Sa 12-4; closed Thanksgiving and Christmas week
COPYING FACILITIES: yes

HOLDINGS:
    Total volume: 28 items
    Inclusive dates: 1729 -
    Description: 16 letters and memos written by the Marquis de Lafayette, and other letters by Varina Davis, Letitia Tyler Semple, G. W. Custis Lee, and Mary Ann Morrison Jackson.

SEE: NUCMC, 1980.

SEE ALSO: Louis Gottschalk, Phyllis S. Pestieau, and Linda J. Pike, eds., *Lafayette: A Guide to the Letters, Documents and Manuscripts in the United States* (Cornell Univ. Press, 1975).

GREENSBORO

NC380-80

Bennett College
Thomas F. Holgate Library
Macon and Washington Streets
Greensboro NC 27420

(919) 273-4431, Ext. 187

OPEN: M-Th 8-9:30, F 9-5, Sa 9-1;
closed Sundays and holidays
COPYING FACILITIES: yes
MATERIALS SOLICITED: Bennett College
history, information pertaining to faculty, staff, student, and alumni activities. Will also accept correspondence,
papers, reports, and other materials of
terminated projects on Bennett's campus.

HOLDINGS:
Total volume: 51 boxes; 4 file
cabinets; 3 display cases; 1 bookcase
Inclusive dates: 1879 -
Description: Records of the College,
consisting of reports, letters, papers, photographs, books, newspaper clippings,
scrapbooks, student publications, and biographical information and documents relating to former presidents.

SEE: Hamer; NUCMC, 1967.

SEE: Hinding.

SEE ALSO: Walter Schatz, ed., *Directory of
Afro-American Resources* (Bowker,
1970); Andrea Hinding and Rosemary
Richardson, comps., *Archival and
Manuscript Resources for the Study of
Women's History: A Beginning* (Univ.
of Minnesota Libraries, Social Welfare
History Archives Center, 1972); Robert
B. Downs, ed., *Resources of North
Carolina Libraries* (Governor's Com-
mission on Library Resources, 1965).

NC380-280

Greensboro Public Library
Caldwell-Jones Collection
201 North Greene Street
Greensboro NC

MAILING ADDRESS:
Drawer X-4
Greensboro NC 27402

(919) 373-2471

OPEN: M-Th 9-9, F, Sa 9-6, Su 2-6;
closed holidays
ACCESS: advance arrangements
recommended; use during weekdays
suggested
COPYING FACILITIES: yes
MATERIALS SOLICITED: Materials relating
to Greensboro and North Carolina history, O. Henry, the South, and genealogy, especially of Guilford County, NC,
families. Will also accept archival
records of local organizations and governments.

HOLDINGS:
Total volume: 12 l.f.; 3 file drawers;
65 items
Inclusive dates: 1902 -
Description: Collections relating chiefly
to Greensboro and Guilford County. Included are manuscripts of books by local
authors, oral history interviews, photographs of local homes and public buildings, and records of community clubs and
organizations.

SEE: Hinding.

NC380-290

Guilford College
Library
Friends Historical Collection
5800 West Friendly Avenue
Greensboro NC 27410

MAILING ADDRESS:
5800 W. Friendly Avenue
Greensboro NC 27410

(919) 292-5511, Ext. 264

OPEN: M-F 10-4; closed weekends,
Thanksgiving, and Christmas vacation
USER FEES: $10 for one day; $15 for two
successive days; $20 for three or more
successive days. Members of the
Society of Friends and certain others
exempt.
COPYING FACILITIES: yes
MATERIALS SOLICITED: Quaker records,
private papers of Quakers, and oral his-
tory from North Carolina Quakers and
National Quaker leaders.

HOLDINGS:
Total volume: 600 vols.; 66 l.f.
Inclusive dates: 1680 -
Description: Records of the Society of
Friends in North Carolina, New Garden
Boarding School, and Guilford College;
private papers of North Carolina Quakers; and oral history of Quaker National
leaders and local Quaker residents. There
are also 310 single papers of Quakers or
collections of less than 10 items.

SEE: Hamer; NUCMC, 1969.

SEE ALSO: J. Floyd Moore, *Sources of
Quaker History in North Carolina*
(Guilford College, 1967); Robert B.
Downs, ed., *Resources of North Caro-
lina Libraries* (Governor's Commission
on Library Resources, 1965).

NC380-800

University of North Carolina at
Greensboro
The Walter Clinton Jackson Library
Special Collections
Greensboro NC 27412

(919) 379-5246

OPEN: M-F 8-5; closed weekends and
holidays
COPYING FACILITIES: yes
MATERIALS SOLICITED: Papers of prominent public figures, especially North
Carolina women in public office; literary figures, especially women; papers
of the past presidents and chancellors
of the University and its predecessor
institution, and some faculty and alumni manuscripts. Will also accept papers
of North Carolina organizations, especially those which are related to various activities of this University, such
as home economics, physical education,
drama, art, and creative writing.

HOLDINGS:
Total volume: 450 l.f.
Inclusive dates: 1891 -
Description: Collections relating chiefly
to the University, its former role as the
Woman's College of the University of
North Carolina, North Carolina, and
North Carolinians. Included are the University and College archives; papers of
Charles Duncan McIver, founder of the
College, and Julius I. Foust, its second
president; records of faculty and student
activities; presidents' and chancellors'
files; and photographs. Manuscript collections relate to women in North Carolina,
and include the papers of Ellen Winston
and Harriet Elliott. There are literary
manuscripts by authors, such as Randall
Jarrell, associated with North Carolina;
music manuscripts by North Carolina
composers; and records of such organizations as the Southeastern Theatre Conference, the Southern Association of
Physical Education for Women, and the
North Carolina Council of Women's Organizations.

SEE: Hamer (as Woman's College Library,
University of North Carolina);
NUCMC, 1968, 70.

SEE: Hinding; Robbins.

SEE ALSO: An unedited, manuscript guide
to the holdings is available at the institution.

GREENVILLE

NC390-200

East Carolina University
East Carolina Manuscript Collection
J. Y. Joyner Library
Greenville NC 27834

(919) 757-6671

OPEN: M-F 8-5; closed weekends and
holidays
COPYING FACILITIES: yes
MATERIALS SOLICITED: Materials relating
to North Carolina history, military history, missionaries, and tobacco. Will
also accept other materials when they
will complement areas of solicitation.

HOLDINGS:
Total volume: 1,500,000 items
Inclusive dates: 1715 -
Description: Collections relating to
North Carolina history since 1800; military history; missionaries in the 20th century in Africa, China, Japan, and Latin
America; and agricultural, manufacturing,
and marketing aspects of tobacco in the
20th century. There are also oral history
tapes which complement these areas of
specialization.
Also included is the University Archives.

SEE: NUCMC, 1970, 73, 77, 79, 80.

SEE: Paszek; Allard, Crawley, and
Edmison; Hinding; Robbins.

SEE ALSO: *East Carolina Manuscript Collection Bulletin* (1969-).

HERTFORD

NC405-640
Perquimans County Historical Society
Hertford NC

MAILING ADDRESS:
P.O. Box 652
Hertford NC 27944

no telephone

OPEN: by appointment only
COPYING FACILITIES: no
MATERIALS SOLICITED: Manuscripts and visual documents related to Perquimans County. Will also accept other materials related to the county.

HOLDINGS:
Total volume: 1 c.f.
Inclusive dates: 1800 - 1900
Description: A collection on Perquimans County, including miscellaneous letters, merchants' account books, and photographs of historic buildings.

Parts of the collection are occasionally transferred to the East Carolina Manuscript Collection, East Carolina University, Greenville, NC.

HICKORY

NC410-200
Elbert Ivey Memorial Library
North Carolina Room
420 3rd Avenue, N.W.
Hickory NC 28601

(704) 322-2905

OPEN: Su 2-5, M-Sa 9-5; closed Sundays June - Aug. and holidays
COPYING FACILITIES: yes
MATERIALS SOLICITED: Historical and genealogical materials relating to the Hickory area or to North Carolina.

HOLDINGS:
Total volume: 15 file drawers
Inclusive dates: 18th century - 1940
Description: Genealogical materials relating to local families.

HIGH POINT

NC420-310
High Point College
Library
High Point NC 27262

no telephone

SEE: Hamer.

Questionnaire not returned.

HILLSBOROUGH

NC430-340
Historic Hillsborough Commission
Burwell School
Collections on Women's Education in Early North Carolina
319 North Churton Street
Hillsborough NC

MAILING ADDRESS:
P.O. Box 922
Hillsborough NC 27278

(919) 732-7451

OPEN: W, Su 1:30-4:30 and by appointment; closed Thanksgiving and Christmas
COPYING FACILITIES: yes
MATERIALS SOLICITED: Materials on women's education in North Carolina, 1752-ca. 1880, particularly concerning the Burwell School, 1837-57, and its derivative schools; materials relating to the achievement of educated women before the Civil War; and genealogical records of the students and teachers of the Burwell School.

HOLDINGS:
Total volume: 48 l.f.; 10 boxes; 3 file cabinets
Inclusive dates: 1752 - 1880
Description: Materials relating to women's education in early North Carolina. Included are records of the Burwell School and its teachers and students, plus photographs, slides, diaries, letters, account books, and other materials. Sixteen other collections focus on institutions derivative from the Burwell School--Reidsville Seminary, the Nash and Rollock School, Queens College, Peace College, and Mitchell College--as well as other area academies.

There are also genealogical collections, and records of colonial and early 19th century Hillsborough, including materials on early Quakers, mill records, and cemetery records.

LUMBERTON

NC540-690
Robeson County Public Library
101 North Chestnut Street
Lumberton NC

MAILING ADDRESS:
P.O. Box 988
Lumberton NC 28358

(919) 738-4859

OPEN: M, Tu, Th-Sa 9-6, W 1-6; closed Sundays and holidays
COPYING FACILITIES: yes
MATERIALS SOLICITED: Materials relating to Robeson County history and genealogy, and similar material for adjacent counties.

HOLDINGS:
Total volume: 30 l.f.
Inclusive dates: 1800 -
Description: A collection of unpublished material relating chiefly to Robeson and Bladen counties. Included

are diaries, cemetery records, memoirs, and family and church histories.

MARS HILL

NC570-530
Mars Hill College
Memorial Library
Appalachian Room
Mars Hill NC 28754

(704) 689-1244

OPEN: M-F 8-5; closed weekends and holidays
COPYING FACILITIES: yes
MATERIALS SOLICITED: Manuscripts, diaries, and photographs pertaining to Mars Hill College and vicinity; material on folk music of the region. Will also accept papers of notable Mars Hill College alumni.

HOLDINGS:
Total volume: 72 l.f.
Inclusive dates: 1856 -
Description: Materials relating chiefly to the culture of southern Appalachia. Included are correspondence, memoirs, music recordings, photographs, and 3,000 manuscript texts of folk songs. There are also local Baptist church records, and records of Mars Hill College and its founders, including genealogical source material.

SEE: NUCMC, 1972.

SEE: Hinding.

MONTREAT

NC590-320
Historical Foundation of the Presbyterian and Reformed Churches
318 Georgia Terrace
Montreat NC 28757

MAILING ADDRESS:
Box 847
Montreat NC 28757

(704) 669-7061

OPEN: M-F 8:30-4:30, Sa 9-1:30; closed Sundays and holidays, and Saturdays during Oct. - March
COPYING FACILITIES: yes
MATERIALS SOLICITED: Materials pertaining to Presbyterian and Reformed church history.

HOLDINGS:
Total volume: 3,500 l.f.; 5,000 vols.; 3,500 tapes; 300 discs; 200 reels of film
Inclusive dates: 1638 -
Description: Records of the Presbyterian and Reformed churches of the world, particularly in the United States, especially the South. Included are records of synods and presbyteries of the Presbyterian, Associate Presbyterian, and Cumberland Presbyterian churches of the south Atlantic, southern, and certain other States. There are also records of Presbyterian organizations in Brazil, Canada, China, Cuba, England, France, Japan, Korea, Mexico, Zaire, The Netherlands, Northern Ireland, and Scotland; some papers relating to Greece and Asia Minor

during the 19th century; and papers concerning early missionary activities in China, Mexico, Africa, and Japan. Numerous items are associated with the organization of the Presbyterian church in the United States in 1861, and its subsequent reorganizations.

SEE: Hamer; NUCMC, 1959-62, 66, 76, 77, 78, 80.

SEE ALSO: Thomas H. Spence, *The Historical Foundation and Its Treasures* (Historical Foundation Publications, 1960); Robert B. Downs, ed., *Resources of North Carolina Libraries* (Governor's Commission on Library Resources, 1965); Walter Schatz, ed., *Directory of Afro-American Resources* (Bowker, 1970); Albert Krichmar, *The Women's Rights Movement in the United States, 1848-1970: A Bibliography and Sourcebook* (Scarecrow Press, 1972).

MOUNT OLIVE

NC610-520
Mount Olive College
Moye Library
The Free Will Baptist Historical
Collection
Mount Olive NC 28365

(919) 658-2502, Ext. 26

OPEN: M-Th 8-10, F 8-5; closed weekends, holidays, and College vacations
COPYING FACILITIES: yes
MATERIALS SOLICITED: Pre-1850 materials relating to the Free Will Baptist denomination. Will also accept other denominational materials related to the Free Will Baptists.

HOLDINGS:
  Total volume: 3,500 items
  Inclusive dates: 1835 -
  Description: A collection relating to the Free Will Baptist denomination with specific concentration in North Carolina and the South. Included is a manuscript collection of over 500 pieces containing minutes of churches and conferences, diaries, letters, and deeds; a microfilm collection (mostly church records); a photograph collection; papers of church leaders; and some audio-visual materials and memorabilia.

MURFREESBORO

NC620-520
The Murfreesboro Historical
  Association, Inc.
Roberts Vaughn Village Center
Murfreesboro NC

MAILING ADDRESS:
P.O. Box 3
Murfreesboro NC 27855

(919) 398-4886

OPEN: M-Sa 9-5; closed Sundays and holidays
COPYING FACILITIES: yes

MATERIALS SOLICITED: Materials pertaining to the early history of Murfreesboro and of Hertford, Bertie, Northampton, and Gates counties, NC.

HOLDINGS:
  Total volume: 70,000 items
  Inclusive dates: 1707 - 1950
  Description: Materials documenting the political, social, and economic history of the Roanoke-Chowan region of North Carolina. Holdings consist of over 20,000 photographs depicting the early architecture of Murfreesboro and surrounding areas and over 50,000 manuscripts, including letters, legal and business papers, diaries, and account books.

NEWTON

NC650-120
Catawba County Historical Museum
1716 South College Drive
Newton NC

MAILING ADDRESS:
P.O. Box 73
Newton NC 28658

(704) 465-0383

OPEN: Tu-Su 1-5; closed Mondays and holidays
COPYING FACILITIES: no
MATERIALS SOLICITED: Genealogical and family history materials; records dealing with pioneer families; and materials relating to the history of Catawba County and the western Piedmont section of North Carolina.

HOLDINGS:
  Total volume: 4 l.f.
  Inclusive dates: 1780 -
  Description: Materials relating to the history of Catawba County and the western Piedmont area of North Carolina. Included are letters and manuscripts of Dr. J. E. Hodges, the genealogical works of D. M. Eaton, the Long Island papers, and a collection of original documents: deeds, land grants, legal records, and letters. There are also a number of 16mm silent films dealing with local people and events and a photograph collection.

SEE: Hinding.

OTTO

NC656-720
Southeastern Forest Experiment
  Station
Coweeta Hydrologic Laboratory
999 Coweeta Lab Road
Otto NC 28763

(704) 524-2128

OPEN: M-F 7:30-4; closed weekends and holidays
COPYING FACILITIES: no
MATERIALS SOLICITED: Hydrologic data for the Coweeta drainage. Will also accept related geological information.

HOLDINGS:
  Total volume: not specified
  Inclusive dates: 1933 -
  Description: Hydrologic data about water quality, stream flow, rainfall, climate, soil moisture, and vegetation in the 5,400 acre Coweeta drainage of the Little Tennessee River in North Carolina.

RALEIGH

NC680-200
Episcopal Church
Diocese of North Carolina
G-111 D. H. Hill Library
Raleigh NC

MAILING ADDRESS:
P.O. Box 17025
Raleigh NC 27619

(919) 787-6313

OPEN: M-Th 8-5, F 8-6; closed weekends and holidays
COPYING FACILITIES: yes

HOLDINGS:
  Total volume: 320 l.f.
  Inclusive dates: 1900 -
  Description: Official correspondence of the bishops of North Carolina, minutes of the Diocesan Council, 1922- , and correspondence related to diocesan institutions and agencies.

NC680-460
North Carolina Department of
  Cultural Resources
North Carolina State Archives
109 East Jones Street
Raleigh NC 27611

(919) 733-3952

OPEN: Tu-Sa 8-5:30; closed Sundays and holidays, Saturdays after Friday holidays, and Saturdays before Easter and Labor Day
ACCESS: identification required
COPYING FACILITIES: yes
MATERIALS SOLICITED: Public records of State and local government agencies and institutions, and manuscripts relating to North Carolina and North Carolinians. Will also accept iconographic materials, maps, and sound recordings.

HOLDINGS:
  Total volume: 24,000 l.f.
  Inclusive dates: 1535 -
  Description: Official records of the colony and State of North Carolina, including legislative, executive, and judicial records of State agencies; original and microfilmed records of the North Carolina counties; and private papers relating primarily to North Carolina and neighboring States. There are also records of various organizations, hundreds of North Carolina account books from the 18th through the 20th century, copies of family Bible records, a collection of maps dealing primarily with North Carolina but including some general maps, and papers relating to wars in which the United States has been involved. Significant audio-visual and iconographic materials include 80 motion picture films, the Archives and History and the Raleigh *News*

and Observer photographic negative collections, and sound recordings.

SEE: Hamer (as State Department of Archives and History).

SEE: Allard, Crawley, and Edmison; Davis; Ingram; Beers - Confederate; Hinding; Robbins.

SEE ALSO: Walter Schatz, ed., *Directory of Afro-American Resources* (Bowker, 1970); H. G. Jones, 'State Department of Archives and History,' *North Carolina Libraries* 19 (Winter 1961); Robert B. Downs, ed., *Resources of North Carolina Libraries* (Governor's Commission on Library Resources, 1965); David A. Hounshell, comp., *Manuscripts in U.S. Depositories Relating to the History of Electrical Science and Technology* (Smithsonian Institution, n.d.); Richard C. Davis, *North American Forest History: A Guide to Archives and Manuscripts in the United States and Canada* (Clio Books, 1977).

Publications of the Department (and of the former Department of Archives and History) include: Beth Crabtree, *Guide to Private Manuscript Collections in the North Carolina State Archives* (1964); *Guide to Research Materials in the North Carolina State Archives, Section B: County Records* (1975); *Guide to Civil War Records in the North Carolina State Archives* (1966); *A Select Bibliography for Genealogical Research in North Carolina* (Archives Information Circular No. 10).

Other Department publications include: *Military Personnel Records in the North Carolina State Archives, 1918-1964* (Archives Information Circular No. 11); W. P. Cumming, ed., *North Carolina in Maps* (n.d.); *Summary Guide to Research Materials in the North Carolina State Archives, Section A: Records of State Agencies* (1963); Ellen A. McGrew, *North Carolina Census Records, 1787-1890* (Archives Information Circular No. 2, 1967); Donald R. Lennon, *North Carolina's Revolutionary War Pay Records* (Archives Information Circular No. 1, 1966); *Colonial Records of North Carolina* (1972); C. F. W. Coker, *Records Relating to Tennessee in the North Carolina State Archives* (Archives Information Circular No. 3, 1973); *Surry County Records Inventory* (1963).

NC680-550

North Carolina State University
Archives
Room G-111, D. H. Hill Library
Raleigh NC

MAILING ADDRESS:
Campus Box 7111
Raleigh NC 27695-7111

(919) 737-2273

OPEN: M-F 8-5; closed weekends, holidays, and Christmas vacation
COPYING FACILITIES: yes
MATERIALS SOLICITED: Noncurrent official records of University schools, departments, and divisions; University committees; faculty and student organizations; and papers of retired and deceased faculty and staff.

HOLDINGS:
    Total volume: 1,014 c.f.; 1,648 color slides; 1,004 vols.; 792 microfilm reels; 312 sound records and tapes; 908 motion picture reels and video tapes
    Inclusive dates: 1859 -
    Description: Non-current official records of University schools, departments and divisions; University committees; faculty and student organizations; and papers of retired and deceased faculty and staff. Included are paper records, microfilm, motion pictures and video tapes, sound recordings, and audio tapes. There are also the papers of Carl Alwyn Schenck, and the records of the Biltmore Forest School.

SEE: Hamer.

SEE: Davis.

NC680-720

St. Mary's College
Library
900 Hillsborough Street
Raleigh NC 27603

(919) 828-2521, Ext. 313

OPEN: M-F 8-5; closed weekends and holidays
ACCESS: approval of College president, College historian, and head librarian required
COPYING FACILITIES: yes
MATERIALS SOLICITED: Materials pertaining to St. Mary's School, Junior College, and College. Will also accept materials relating to the history of women's education in the South.

HOLDINGS:
    Total volume: not specified
    Inclusive dates: 1842 -
    Description: Diaries, letters, minutes, school publications, memorabilia, photographs, and other records of St. Mary's College, in addition to some items concerning women's education in the South.

SEE: Hinding.

ROCKY MOUNT

NC710-540

Nash County Historical Association
Stonewall
1325 Falls Road Ext.
Rocky Mount NC

MAILING ADDRESS:
4009 Lochinvar Lane
Rocky Mount NC 27801

(919) 443-6708

OPEN: by appointment only
COPYING FACILITIES: no
MATERIALS SOLICITED: Materials pertaining to the history of Nash County and of Stonewall, a historic home built in 1830.

HOLDINGS:
    Total volume: 10 l.f.
    Inclusive dates: 1820's -
    Description: Journals, doctors' and store ledgers, and family cemetery records of Nash County, as well as the original

inventory of sale of the Bennett Bunn estate.

SALISBURY

NC730-120

Catawba College
Library
Salisbury NC 28144

no telephone

SEE: Hamer.

Questionnaire not returned.

NC730-480

Livingstone College
Andrew Carnegie Library
Afro-American Studies
Salisbury NC 28144

(704) 633-7960, Ext. 62

OPEN: M-Th 8-10:30, F 8-5:30, Su 6:30-10:30; closed Saturdays and holidays
ACCESS: appointment required
COPYING FACILITIES: yes
MATERIALS SOLICITED: Papers and other materials concerning Livingstone College and the African Methodist Episcopal Zion church. Will also accept materials related to American Negroes, Africa, and the Caribbean.

HOLDINGS:
    Total volume: 700 sq. ft.
    Inclusive dates: 1882 - 1979
    Description: Collections include letters of Sylvia P. L. Dannett; Livingstone College Centennial memorabilia; civil rights files of the 1960's; papers of most college presidents; materials pertaining to the A. M. E. Zion church; and papers of Elizabeth D. Koontz.

SEE ALSO: Louise M. Rountree, comp., *The American Negro and African Studies: A Bibliography on the Special Collections in Carnegie Library, Livingstone College* (Carnegie Library, Livingstone College, 1968); Walter Schatz, ed., *Directory of Afro-American Resources* (Bowker, 1970). Several guides to parts of the collection are available.

NC730-500

Lutheran Church in America
North Carolina Synod
Archives
1950 Holiday Inn Drive
Salisbury NC

MAILING ADDRESS:
P.O. Box 2049
Salisbury NC 28145-2049

(704) 633-4861

OPEN: M-F 9-5; closed weekends and holidays
COPYING FACILITIES: yes
MATERIALS SOLICITED: Congregation records of the North Carolina Lutheran Synod and its predecessors, including parish registers, minutes, journals, blueprints, and photographs. Will also accept related personal papers of congregation members.

HOLDINGS:
Total volume: 95 l.f.
Inclusive dates: 1740 -
Description: Official minutes and proceedings of the Synod and predecessor bodies from 1803 to date; minutes and proceedings of the Tennessee Synod, a splinter group which was reinstated in 1921; files of Synod presidents of the 20th century; records of Mt. Pleasant Institute and Mont Ameona Seminary, both in Mt. Pleasant, NC; records of defunct congregations; parish registers of numerous churches; 18th and 19th century journals of pastors; and biographical data for all pastors in the Synod since 1773.

NC730-710
Rowan Public Library
History Room
201 West Fisher Street
Salisbury NC

MAILING ADDRESS:
P.O. Box 4039
Salisbury NC 28144

(704) 633-5578

OPEN: Sept.-May, Su 2-5, M-F 9-9, Sa 9-5; closed holidays, and Sundays June - Aug.
COPYING FACILITIES: yes
MATERIALS SOLICITED: Historical and genealogical materials of the Piedmont area of North Carolina, especially 'Old Rowan County.' Will also accept any materials of a genealogical nature.

HOLDINGS:
Total volume: 229 l.f.
Inclusive dates: 1720 - 1950
Description: The McCubbins and Smith collections of court records, wills, deeds, Bible records, correspondence, and family charts.

SEE ALSO: Robert B. Downs, ed., *Resources of North Carolina Libraries* (Governor's Commission on Library Resources, 1965).

SANFORD

NC740-690
Railroad House Historical Association
Charlotte and Hawkins Avenues
Sanford NC

MAILING ADDRESS:
P.O. Box 519
Sanford NC 27330

(919) 775-7341

OPEN: M-F 9-5; closed weekends and holidays
COPYING FACILITIES: yes
MATERIALS SOLICITED: Materials relating to the Sanford - Lee County area, or to railroading. Will also accept materials dating from the immediate post-Civil War era, when Sanford was formed.

HOLDINGS:
Total volume: 1,000 items
Inclusive dates: 1800 -
Description: Materials relating to the Sanford - Lee County area, railroading, and to the immediate post-Civil War period.

SOUTHERN PINES

NC760-520
Moore County Historical Association, Inc.
Weymouth Center
E. Vermont Avenue
Southern Pines NC

MAILING ADDRESS:
P.O. Box 324
Southern Pines NC 28387

(919) 949-3274

OPEN: by appointment only
COPYING FACILITIES: no
MATERIALS SOLICITED: Materials pertaining to the history of Moore County.

HOLDINGS:
Total volume: 8 file drawers
Inclusive dates: 1780 -
Description: A collection of manuscripts, records of local organizations, and other documents relating primarily to Moore County, but including material relating to adjacent counties.

WAKE FOREST

NC840-720
Southeastern Baptist Theological Seminary
Library
North Wingate Street
Wake Forest NC

MAILING ADDRESS:
P.O. Box 752
Wake Forest, NC 27587

(919) 556-3101

OPEN: by appointment
COPYING FACILITIES: yes
MATERIALS SOLICITED: Materials related to the history of Southeastern Seminary, to persons who have been involved in the life of the Seminary, and to other persons who have been creative or influential in theological education or in the mission and ministry of the Christian religion.

HOLDINGS:
Total volume: not specified
Inclusive dates: 1900 -
Description: Manuscript collections of missionaries Arthur Raymond Gallimore, Everett Gill, and John Burder Hipps; manuscripts of published and unpublished writings of Walter Nathan Johnson; correspondence and other papers of Edward Allison McDowell, Jr.; sermons of John Clyde Turner; and papers and tape recordings of Theodore Floyd Adams. There are also archives of Southeastern Baptist Theological Seminary.

SEE: NUCMC, 1962.

NC840-880
Wake Forest College Birthplace Society
North Main Street
Wake Forest NC

MAILING ADDRESS:
P.O. Box 494
Wake Forest NC 27587

no telephone

OPEN: by appointment
COPYING FACILITIES: no
MATERIALS SOLICITED: Historical manuscripts relating to Wake Forest College from its founding in 1834 to its relocation in Winston-Salem, NC, in 1956. Will also accept materials relating to the town of Wake Forest during this same period.

HOLDINGS:
Total volume: not specified
Inclusive dates: 1834 - 1956
Description: Diaries, letters, account books, and photographs relating to Wake Forest College and the town of Wake Forest.

WASHINGTON

NC850-120
George H. and Laura E. Brown Library
Local History Room
122 Van Norden Street
Washington NC 27889

(919) 946-4300

OPEN: M-Th 9-9, F 9-5, Sa 9-1; closed Sundays and holidays
COPYING FACILITIES: yes
MATERIALS SOLICITED: Manuscript or ledger collections relating to the history of Washington and Beaufort County. Will also accept North Carolina historical papers or ledgers.

HOLDINGS:
Total volume: 2 file cabinets; 16 cassettes; 150 pictures
Inclusive dates: 1825 - 1905
Description: Letters and papers of lawyers E. J. Warren and Charles F. Warren, bankers B. F. and Jonathan Havens, and other individuals and businesspersons. Included are ledgers for the Havens business and banking enterprises, as well as a Beaufort County World War I enrollment list, a similar list from the Civil War, and a World War II Red Cross scrapbook.

Also includes minutes of local book clubs; Dunstan-Bellamy collection of papers; genealogical holdings and cemetery registers.

WAYNESVILLE

NC860-320
Haywood County Public Library
402 South Haywood Street
Waynesville NC 28786

(704) 452-5169

OPEN: M, W, F 8:30-6, Tu, Th 8:30-9,
Sa 8:30-5; closed Sundays and holidays
COPYING FACILITIES: yes

HOLDINGS:
Total volume: 15 boxes; 5 notebooks
Inclusive dates: 1919 - 1962
Description: Papers of Hiram C.
Wilburn, including correspondence, personal papers, scrapbooks relating to the
Great Smoky Mountains National Park,
and papers prepared for publication in
newspapers and magazines.

WENTWORTH

NC870-690
Rockingham Community College
Learning Resources Center
Wentworth NC 27375

(919) 342-4261, Ext. 245

OPEN: M-Th 7:45-9:45, F 7:45-5; closed
weekends and holidays
COPYING FACILITIES: yes
MATERIALS SOLICITED: Material on
Rockingham County. Will also accept
materials on North Carolina.

HOLDINGS:
Total volume: 2 file drawers; 1 shelf
Inclusive dates: 1900 -
Description: Materials on Rockingham
County. Included are pictures, oral history cassette tapes, and graveyard records.

WHITEVILLE

NC880-720
Southeastern Community College
Library
Whiteville NC

MAILING ADDRESS:
P.O. Box 151
Whiteville NC 28472

(919) 642-7141

OPEN: M-Th 8:30-10, F 8:30-5; closed
weekends and holidays
COPYING FACILITIES: yes
MATERIALS SOLICITED: Genealogical
records of Columbus County, NC, and
materials relating to the Cape Fear region of North Carolina.

HOLDINGS:
Total volume: not specified
Inclusive dates: 1820 - 1900
Description: Genealogical records of
Columbus County, NC.

WILKESBORO

NC890-880
Wilkes Community College
Learning Resources Division
Wilkesboro NC

MAILING ADDRESS:
P.O. Drawer 120
Wilkesboro NC 28697

(919) 667-7136

OPEN: M-Th 8-9, F 8-5; closed weekends
and holidays
COPYING FACILITIES: yes
MATERIALS SOLICITED: Wilkes County
history and genealogy. Will also accept
other materials.

HOLDINGS:
Total volume: 225 items
Inclusive dates: 1800 -
Description: Oral history tapes relating
to Wilkes County industry, schools, and
people, as well as microfilms of original
County records.

WILMINGTON

NC900-120
Cape Fear Technical Institute
Library Learning Resource Center
411 North Front Street
Wilmington NC 28401

(919) 343-0481

OPEN: M-F 7:30-10; closed weekends
and holidays
ACCESS: identification required
COPYING FACILITIES: yes
MATERIALS SOLICITED: Materials related
to southeastern North Carolina, particularly the greater Wilmington area.

HOLDINGS:
Total volume: 20 l.f.
Inclusive dates: mid-18th century
Description: The Simpson family library, which includes the family pedigree
inscribed in a Bible and other manuscript
inscriptions.

NC900-810
University of North Carolina at
Wilmington
William Madison Randall Library
Special Collections
601 S. College Road
Wilmington NC 28403

(919) 794-3140, 4738

OPEN: M-F 8-5; closed weekends and
holidays
COPYING FACILITIES: yes
MATERIALS SOLICITED: Manuscripts and
archives of persons and organizations
related to the lower Cape Fear area
(Brunswick, Columbus, New Hanover,
and Pender counties) of North Carolina.

HOLDINGS:
Total volume: 265 l.f.
Inclusive dates: 1700 -
Description: About 25 collections, including the papers of Congressman Alton
Lennon and the papers of Thomas J.
Armstrong, consisting largely of letters
written by his son during the Civil War.
There are also other local history materials, including land grants from George II,
as well as other property documents.

WINDSOR

NC915-320
Historic Hope Foundation
Hope Plantation
Highway 308
Windsor NC

MAILING ADDRESS:
P.O. Box 601
Windsor NC 27983

(919) 794-3140

OPEN: Tu-Sa 10-4, Su 2-5; closed
Mondays, Thanksgiving, Christmas,
and New Year's
USER FEES: $1.50
ACCESS: advance arrangements required
COPYING FACILITIES: no
MATERIALS SOLICITED: Records relating
to David Stone and William King, both
of Bertie County, NC. Will also accept
other historical and genealogical materials pertaining to Bertie County.

HOLDINGS:
Total volume: not specified
Inclusive dates: 17th century -
Description: Records of the now defunct Bertie County Historical Society,
1950-78; genealogical information on David Stone, as well as two manuscripts
about his life and politics; and genealogical information on William King.

WINSTON-SALEM

NC930-510
Moravian Church in America,
Southern Province
Moravian Archives
4 E. Bank Street
Winston-Salem NC 27101

(919) 722-1742

OPEN: M-F 9-4:30; closed weekends and
church holidays
USER FEES: project fee for research;
geneological fee for service
ACCESS: advance notice requested
COPYING FACILITIES: no
MATERIALS SOLICITED: Materials related
to the Moravian Church in America,
Southern Province.

HOLDINGS:
Total volume: 2,500 vols.; 15,000
pages
Inclusive dates: 1753 -
Description: Records of the Moravian
Church in America, Southern Province.
Included are church records, official
board minutes, congregation diaries, mission diaries, and correspondence. All

manuscripts are in handwritten German script up to 1854.

SEE: Hamer.

Much of the German script material has been translated and published in the 11-volume *Records of the Moravian Church in North Carolina,* published by the North Carolina Historical Commission.

NC930-530

The Moravian Music Foundation, Inc.
20 Cascade Avenue
Winston-Salem NC 27107

(919) 725-0651

OPEN: M-F 8:30-4:30; closed weekends and holidays
COPYING FACILITIES: yes
MATERIALS SOLICITED: Materials relating to 18th and 19th century music, American music, hymnology, and the Moravians. Will also accept 20th century music materials.

HOLDINGS:
   Total volume: 10,000 items
   Inclusive dates: 1760 - 1900
   Description: Music manuscripts used in the Moravian towns of Lititz, Bethlehem, and Nazareth, PA, and Salem, NC, during the 18th and 19th centuries. Included is American and European sacred, secular, instrumental, and vocal music.

SEE ALSO: M. Gombosi, *Catalog of the Johannes Herbst Collection* (Univ. of North Carolina Press, 1970).

NC930-840

Wake Forest University
North Carolina Baptist Historical Collection and
University Archives
Winston-Salem NC

MAILING ADDRESS:
P.O. Box 7777, Reynolds Station
Winston-Salem NC 27109

(919) 761-5472

OPEN: M-F 8:30-4:30; closed weekends and holidays
ACCESS: permission to use University Archives required from the President's office
COPYING FACILITIES: yes
MATERIALS SOLICITED: North Carolina Baptist church, association, and union records; and manuscript collections of alumni and Baptist leaders and institutions. Will also accept local history materials and non-Baptist manuscript collections.

HOLDINGS:
   Total volume: 235 l.f.; 300 microfilm reels
   Inclusive dates: 1770 -
   Description: North Carolina Baptist association and church records, and collections relating to North Carolina Baptists, including Southern, Primitive, and black Baptists. Also included are the archives of Wake Forest University.

SEE: Hamer; NUCMC, 1972.

SEE ALSO: Robert B. Downs, ed., *Resources of North Carolina Libraries* (Governor's Commission on Library Resources, 1965); *A Preliminary Inventory of Church Records in the Ethel T. Crittenden Collection, in Baptist History* (1972), *Supplement* (1973); Richard C. Davis, *North American Forest History: A Guide to Archives and Manuscripts in the United States and Canada* (Clio Books, 1977).

YADKINVILLE

NC950-940

Yadkin County Public Library and Yadkin County Historical Society
History Room
East Main Street
Yadkinville NC

MAILING ADDRESS:
P. O. Box 1250
Yadkinville NC 27055

(919) 679-2795

OPEN: M-W, F 9-5, Th 9-8:30, Sa 9-1; closed Sundays and holidays
COPYING FACILITIES: yes
MATERIALS SOLICITED: Historical and genealogical material about Yadkin County and the state of North Carolina.

HOLDINGS:
   Total volume: 6 file cabinets; other items
   Inclusive dates: 1800 -
   Description: Newspaper clippings on local people and events; store account books; church history materials; a scrapbook on the Richmond Hill Law School; slides of historic sites in Yadkin County; microfilmed census records; a manuscript land grant map for the period 1750-1800; and photographs of the county.

NORTH DAKOTA

In 1977 the North Dakota State Archives was created as a division of the State Historical Society and was delegated the existing statutory authority to preserve North Dakota local public records. Most county and municipal records of permanent value remain in local jurisdictions, but several hundred cubic feet have been transferred to the State Archives in Bismarck.

BISMARCK

ND43-730
State Historical Society of North
  Dakota
North Dakota Heritage Center
Bismarck ND 58505

(701) 224-2666

SEE: Hamer; NUCMC, 1965.

Questionnaire not returned.

BOTTINEAU

ND80-560
North Dakota State University at
  Bottineau
Library
First and Simrall Boulevards
Bottineau ND 58318

no telephone

SEE: Hamer (as North Dakota School of
  Forestry).

Questionnaire not returned.

CARRINGTON

ND117-240
Foster County Historical Society
175 17th Avenue
South Carrington ND

MAILING ADDRESS:
P.O. Box 512
Carrington ND 58421

no telephone

OPEN: Su 2-5 and by appointment;
  closed Dec. - April
COPYING FACILITIES: no
MATERIALS SOLICITED: Materials relating
  to Foster County, including recorded
  interviews, writings, and clippings.

HOLDINGS:
  Total volume: 4 file drawers
  Inclusive dates: 1872 -
  Description: Materials relating to Foster County, including county, township, and school district records; land ownership maps; manuscript pioneer histories; a card index to significant historic events described in local newspapers, 1894-1920; and a few oral history interviews.

FARGO

ND375-570
North Dakota State University
North Dakota Institute for Regional
  Studies
Fargo ND 58105

(701) 237-8914

OPEN: M-F 8-5; summer M-F 7:30-4;
  closed weekends and holidays
COPYING FACILITIES: yes
MATERIALS SOLICITED: Agriculture and land development, business records, the Nonpartisan League, literary materials, local history collections, family history, organizations, photographs, North Dakota maps, and North Dakota State University. Will also accept other historically significant records relating to North Dakota.

HOLDINGS:
  Total volume: 765 c.f.
  Inclusive dates: 1860's -
  Description: Approximately 1,500 manuscript collection,s related mainly to North Dakota, especially the Red River Valley, and western Minnesota. The photograph collection includes early scenes from northeastern North Dakota (including sod houses), farms and people in Griggs County, Bonanza farming scenes, and steamboats on the Red River. The Institute also houses the archives of North Dakota State University, 1890- , formerly North Dakota Agricultural College, which includes presidential correspondence, a photograph collection, and files on faculty and alumni.

SEE: NUCMC, 1981.

SEE ALSO: John E. Bye, comp., *Guide to the Small Collection Manuscripts of the North Dakota Institute for Regional Studies* (North Dakota Institute for Regional Studies, 1977).

GRAND FORKS

ND486-770
United Methodist Church
North Dakota Conference
Wesley United Methodist Church
1600 4th Avenue North
Grand Forks ND 58201

(701) 772-1869

OPEN: by appointment
COPYING FACILITIES: no
MATERIALS SOLICITED: Records of Methodist churches in North Dakota which have closed, and manuscript church histories.

HOLDINGS:
  Total volume: 8 file drawers; 4 l.f.
  Inclusive dates: 1890 -
  Description: Records and photographs concerning Methodist churches in North Dakota. Included are board minutes; minutes of women's organizations; baptismal, funeral, and marriage records; and manuscript church histories.

ND486-800
University of North Dakota
Chester Fritz Library
Department of Special Collections
Grand Forks ND 58202

(701) 777-4625

OPEN: M, Tu, Th, F 8-5, W 8-11; closed
  weekends
COPYING FACILITIES: yes
MATERIALS SOLICITED: Materials relating to the northern Great Plains, especially those on coal, politics, women, and social and oral history; and the archives of the University of North Dakota.

HOLDINGS:
  Total volume: 5,000 l.f.
  Inclusive dates: 1880 -
  Description: Records of 12 North Dakota governors, several Congressmen and Senators, the Nonpartisan League, the Farmer's Union, and North Dakota businesses. Also included are oral history tapes on politics and energy development and extensive University archives.

GUIDES: John B. Davenport, comp., *Guide to the Orin G. Libby Manuscript Collection and Related Research Collections at the University of North Dakota* (1975).

SEE: Hamer; NUCMC, 1959-62, 70-71.

SEE: Hounshell; Svoboda and Dunning; Robbins; Hinding.

ND486-810
University of North Dakota
Geography Department
Grand Forks ND

MAILING ADDRESS:
8274 University Station
Grand Forks ND 58202-8274

(701) 777-4246

OPEN: M-F 8:30-4:30; closed weekends,
holidays, and University vacations
COPYING FACILITIES: yes
MATERIALS SOLICITED: Records created
by the Department.

HOLDINGS:
Total volume: 120 l.f.
Inclusive dates: 1890 -
Description: Meteorological data gathered at the weather station maintained by the Department since 1890 about temperature, precipitation, wind speed, cloud cover and type of clouds, relative humidity, and evaporation statistics. Also included are manuscript maps and photographs.

HOPE

ND523-720
Steele County Historical Society
Archives and Library
Steele Avenue
Hope ND 58046

(701) 945-2394

OPEN: M-F 10-4; closed weekends and
holidays except by prior appointment
COPYING FACILITIES: yes
MATERIALS SOLICITED: Diaries, journals,
business records, and genealogical source data pertaining to local history.

HOLDINGS:
Total volume: 860 items
Inclusive dates: 1882 -
Description: A collection of Steele County manuscripts, including individuals' diaries, reminiscences, and other papers, as well as records of clubs, businesses, schools, and local governments. In addition, there are collections

of photographs dating from the 1880's and of oral history recordings.

MINOT

ND652-520
Minot State College
Memorial Library
Minot ND 58701

(701) 857-3200

OPEN: Su 6-10, M-Th 7:30-10, F
7:30-4:30, Sa 1-5; closed holidays and weekends during summer
ACCESS: serious researchers
COPYING FACILITIES: yes

HOLDINGS:
Total volume: 30 l.f.
Inclusive dates: 1880's - 1940's
Description: Photographs, clippings, and miscellaneous manuscript material concerning Minot State College, and to a lesser extent the city of Minot and the State of North Dakota.

RICHARDTON

ND824-40
Assumption Abbey
Archives
Richardton ND 58652

(701) 974-3315

OPEN: by appointment
COPYING FACILITIES: yes
MATERIALS SOLICITED: Regional history,
especially pertaining to Catholic institutions.

HOLDINGS:
Total volume: 5,000 c.f.
Inclusive dates: 1800 -
Description: Records of the Abbey and other Catholic institutions in the region. There are also secular history materials of the region, including the James McLaughlin papers on Indian tribes.

SEE: NUCMC, 1975.

SEE ALSO: a guide to the McLaughlin collection available at the Archives.

VALLEY CITY

ND876-80
Barnes County Historical Society
Barnes County Court House
Valley City ND

MAILING ADDRESS:
P.O. Box 188
Valley City ND 58072

(701) 845-0966

OPEN: M-F 2-4, mornings by
appointment; closed weekends and holidays
COPYING FACILITIES: yes

HOLDINGS:
Total volume: not specified
Inclusive dates: not specified
Description: Brief biographical histories of over 800 local families and account books and minutes of local community organizations, including the American Legion Auxiliary, Tuesday Club, Women's Relief Corps, Daughters of the American Revolution, and Pioneer Daughters.

ND876-830
Valley City State College
Allen Memorial Library
College Street
Valley City ND 58072

(701) 845-7276

OPEN: Su 4-9, M-Th 8-9, F 8-4; closed
weekends and holidays
ACCESS: advance appointment required;
qualified researchers only
COPYING FACILITIES: yes
MATERIALS SOLICITED: Will accept materials related to the College or collected by its alumni.

HOLDINGS:
Total volume: 110 c.f.
Inclusive dates: 1890 -
Description: Personal papers of E. C. and Audrey Woiwode, including diaries, letters, and photographs. Also included are correspondence, literary manuscripts, and holograph drafts of Larry Woiwode.

OHIO

Since 1975 the Ohio Historical Society has actively administered a statewide program for preserving local public records. As space becomes available, permanently valuable local records are transferred to the appropriate regional research center in the Ohio Network of American History Research Centers. There are eight centers: the University of Akron, Bowling Green State University, the University of Cincinnati, Kent State University, the Ohio Historical Society, the Western Reserve Historical Society, Ohio University, and Wright State University. More than 5,000 cubic feet of permanently valuable local public records have been transferred to the centers, but most records, including over 600,000 cubic feet of county records, remain in the custody of local officials. The Ohio Historical Society has recently completed an inventory of all county records, which is available on microfilm from the Society.

AKRON

OH11-240

The Firestone Tire & Rubber
  Company
Archives Department
2930 West Market Street
Akron OH

MAILING ADDRESS:
1200 Firestone Parkway
Akron OH 44317

(216) 379-6650

OPEN: M-F 7:45-4:45; closed weekends and holidays
ACCESS: generally restricted to Firestone executives and certain other employees; others by appointment
COPYING FACILITIES: yes
MATERIALS SOLICITED: Company mailings to the field, Public Relations Department press releases on personnel changes, new plants, new products, and price increases, and proofs of magazine advertisements.

HOLDINGS:
  Total volume: 750,000 items
  Inclusive dates: 19th century -
  Description: Personal papers and records of Harvey S. Firestone and his family, and his business papers from the founding of the Company to his death in 1938; business correspondence, speeches, photographs, and other materials of Har-

vey S. Firestone, Jr. (1920-73); and non-current Company records of archival value.

SEE: Hamer.

OH11-290

Goodyear Tire & Rubber Company
Archives
1144 East Market Street
Akron OH 44316

(216) 796-8928

OPEN: by appointment only
COPYING FACILITIES: no
MATERIALS SOLICITED: Materials relating to the Goodyear Company.

HOLDINGS:
  Total volume: 100 l.f.
  Inclusive dates: 1898 -
  Description: A collection of materials relating to the formation, history, and growth of the Goodyear Tire & Rubber Company. There are also some materials on Charles Goodyear, discoverer of the process of vulcanization.

OH11-800

University of Akron
Archives of the History of American
  Psychology
Akron OH 44325

(216) 375-7285

OPEN: M-F 8-5; closed weekends and holidays
COPYING FACILITIES: yes
MATERIALS SOLICITED: Materials relating to American psychology. Will also accept materials in psychology adjunctive to the United States, and in disciplines adjunctive to psychology.

HOLDINGS:
  Total volume: 1,350 l.f.; 2,000 items
  Inclusive dates: 1833 -
  Description: Papers of individual psychologists and the records of journals, organizations, and institutions. There are also photographs, films, audio tapes, early tests, and oral histories, all relating to psychology in America.

SEE: NUCMC, 1970, 72, 76.

SEE ALSO: John A. Poppleston and Marion W. McPherson, 'The Archives of the History of American Psychology,' *American Archivist* 34 (Jan. 1971).

OH11-810

University of Akron
Bierce Library
Archival Services
Akron OH 44325

(216) 375-7670

OPEN: M-F 8-5; closed weekends and holidays
COPYING FACILITIES: yes
MATERIALS SOLICITED: Materials relating to an eight-county region in northeastern Ohio with special emphasis on the rubber industry and lighter-than-air materials; and materials by and about the University of Akron.

HOLDINGS:
  Total volume: 4,500 c.f.
  Inclusive dates: 1827 -
  Description: The American History Research Center contains more than 50 collections measuring 2,200 cubic feet and dating from 1827. Included are personal papers and records of local governments, businesses, churches, labor unions, and civic organizations, relating to an eight-county area, consisting of Ashland, Coshocton, Holmes, Richland, Stark, Summit, Tuscarawas, and Wayne counties. Special collecting areas, including materials from outside the eight-county region, are the rubber industry and lighter-than-air flight. The University Archives, 1,600 cubic feet (1870-), consists of administrative, faculty, student, and alumni records pertaining to the University of Akron and its predecessor, Buchtel College.

SEE: NUCMC, 1968.

SEE ALSO: David R. Larson, ed., *Guide to Manuscripts Collections and Institutional Records in Ohio* (Society of Ohio Archivists, 1974); Andrea Hinding and Rosemary Richardson, comps., *Archival and Manuscript Resources for the Study of Women's History: A Beginning* (Univ. of Minnesota Libraries, Social Welfare History Archives Center, 1972); David Kyvig, 'University of Akron Opens Library and Learning Resources Center,' *Ohio Archivist* 4 (Spring 1973); Daniel Nelson, 'Oral History of Rubber Industry Recorded at University of Akron,' *Ohio Archivist* 4 (Spring 1973).

OH11-840

University of Akron
Child Development Film Archives
Akron OH 44325

(216) 375-7285

OPEN: M-F 8-5; closed weekends and holidays
COPYING FACILITIES: yes
MATERIALS SOLICITED: Motion picture films relating to child development, preferably experimentally produced footage. Will also accept tapes relating to child development.

HOLDINGS:
Total volume: 3,500 reels
Inclusive dates: 1914 -
Description: Film collections of Arnold Gesell, L. Joseph Stone, Margaret Mahler, and others dealing primarily with North American children. Also included are films of Greek and Nigerian children.

ALLIANCE

OH16-30

Alliance Historical Society
Alliance OH

MAILING ADDRESS:
Box 42
Alliance OH 44601

no telephone

OPEN: by appointment only
ACCESS: scholarly researchers
COPYING FACILITIES: yes

HOLDINGS:
Total volume: 25 l.f.
Inclusive dates: 1850 -
Description: Records of institutions and organizations in Alliance, as well as photographs, oral history tapes, and transcripts.

OH16-520

Mount Union College
Library
Alliance OH 44601

(216) 821-5320, Ext. 260

OPEN: Su 2-11, M-Th 8-11, F 8-9, Sa 8:30-5; closed holidays and Aug. 20 - Sept. 9
ACCESS: permission of Librarian required
COPYING FACILITIES: yes
MATERIALS SOLICITED: Materials relating to Mount Union College.

HOLDINGS:
Total volume: 147 l.f.
Inclusive dates: 1846 -
Description: A collection of manuscripts, memorabilia, business records, official records, and photographs relating to the history of Mount Union College (1846-) and Scio College (1857-1911).

OH16-690

Rodman Public Library
Oral History Division
215 East Broadway
Alliance OH 44601

(216) 821-2665

OPEN: M-Th 9-9, F, Sa 9-5:30; closed Sundays, holidays, and Saturdays in summer
COPYING FACILITIES: yes

HOLDINGS:
Total volume: 50 tapes
Inclusive dates: 1953 -
Description: Oral history tapes and transcripts dealing with the Alliance area encompassing education, newspaper, radio, ethnic groups, local businesses, industry, and the railroads.

ANTWERP

OH21-600

Otto E. Ehrhart - Paulding County Historical Society
City Hall
North Main Street
Antwerp OH 45813

(419) 258-2212, 8161

OPEN: W 2-4, Sa 1-5; closed other days, Thanksgiving, Christmas, and Easter
COPYING FACILITIES: no
MATERIALS SOLICITED: Local historical and genealogical manuscripts.

HOLDINGS:
Total volume: not specified
Inclusive dates: 19th century -
Description: Manuscripts of Otto E. Ehrhart on business, industry, and families of Antwerp and the surrounding area, as well as photographs, slides, unpublished histories, records of organizations, and early logbooks, covering local history.

ASHLAND

OH26-40

Ashland College
Library
John W. Brown Center for Current Government Studies
Ashland OH 44805

(419) 289-4142, Ext. 5400

OPEN: Sept. - June, M-F 8-5; closed rest of year and holidays
COPYING FACILITIES: yes
MATERIALS SOLICITED: Papers of governmental or political significance. Will also accept materials relating to Ashland College.

HOLDINGS:
Total volume: 75 l.f.
Inclusive dates: 1950 -
Description: Papers relating to the political and governmental career of John W. Brown, Lieutenant Governor of Ohio, 1952-74.

ATHENS

OH35-40

Athens County Museum
65 N. Court Street
Athens OH 45701

(614) 593-6216

OPEN: W-F 1-4 and by appointment
COPYING FACILITIES: yes
MATERIALS SOLICITED: Materials relating to Athens County, specifically its geology, Indians, pioneers, industry, education, ethnic groups, and military history. Will also accept materials in these subject areas relating to surrounding counties.

HOLDINGS:
Total volume: 533 items
Inclusive dates: 19th century -
Description: Materials relating to Athens County, including account books, ledgers, scrapbooks, and photographs. Special subject emphases include the coal industry and ethnic groups.

OH35-610

Ohio University
Library
Special Collections and University Archives
Athens OH 45701

(614) 594-5755

OPEN: M-F 8-5; closed weekends and holidays
COPYING FACILITIES: yes

HOLDINGS:
Total volume: 4,330 l.f.
Inclusive dates: 1790's -
Description: The Ohio University Archives, manuscript collections relating especially to southeastern Ohio, and local government records from southeastern Ohio. Materials focus on Ohio University and the surrounding region, with most dating from after 1920.

SEE: NUCMC, 1966.

SEE: Davis; Robbins; Hinding.

BARBERTON

OH54-80

Barberton Public Library
602 West Park Avenue
Barberton OH 44203

(216) 745-1194

OPEN: M-F 10-9, Sa 10-6; closed Sundays and holidays; shorter summer hours
ACCESS: 18 years of age or older, with Librarian's permission
COPYING FACILITIES: yes
MATERIALS SOLICITED: Materials relating to Barberton history.

HOLDINGS:
Total volume: 1 l.f.
Inclusive dates: 1864 - 1946
Description: Papers of William Alexander Johnston, the civil engineer who planned Barberton in the 1890's,

and other materials relating to Johnston and Barberton history.

BATAVIA

OH63-110
Clermont County Historical Society
Batavia OH

MAILING ADDRESS:
Box 14
Batavia OH 45103

(513) 724-2923

SEE: NUCMC, 1968.

Questionnaire not returned.

OH63-130
Clermont County Public Library
180 South Third Street
Batavia OH

MAILING ADDRESS:
Box 137
Batavia OH 45103

(513) 732-2128

SEE: NUCMC, 1976.

Questionnaire not returned.

BELLEVUE

OH77-330
Historic Lyme Village
Library
5451 Strongs Ridge Road
S.R. 113
Bellevue OH

MAILING ADDRESS:
P.O. Box 342
Bellevue OH 44811

(419) 483-4949, 6052

OPEN: Tu-Su 1-5; closed Mondays and
    Labor Day to Memorial Day
ACCESS: advance arrangements required
COPYING FACILITIES: no
MATERIALS SOLICITED: Local history
    materials relating to Huron, Erie, Sen-
    eca, and Sandusky counties and the
    Bellevue area. Will also accept other
    historical sources.

HOLDINGS:
    Total volume: 2 file cabinets
    Inclusive dates: 19th century -
    Description: Manuscript histories of
    the Bellevue area; oral history interviews
    of older residents; and genealogical source
    materials.

BEREA

OH82-50
Baldwin-Wallace College
Library
Berea OH 44017

no telephone

SEE: Hamer.

Questionnaire not returned.

BLUFFTON

OH92-520
Mennonite Historical Library
Bluffton College
Bluffton OH 45817

(419) 358-8015, Ext. 271

OPEN: by appointment
COPYING FACILITIES: yes
MATERIALS SOLICITED: Materials relating
    to Mennonites, Anabaptists, Amish,
    peace, the Apostolic Christian church,
    the Hutterian Brethren, and the Breth-
    ren in Christ.

HOLDINGS:
    Total volume: 150 l.f.; 10 microfilm
rolls
    Inclusive dates: 1525 -
    Description: Materials relating primar-
    ily to Mennonites and Anabaptists in the
    eastern United States, Canada, Switzer-
    land, eastern France, and Germany. In-
    cluded are church records, bulletins, min-
    utes, local history materials on settlers in
    the Bluffton area, and the archives of
    Bluffton College.
    The Library is the official depository
    for the Central District of the General
    Conference Mennonite Church and the
    Africa Inter-Mennonite Mission.

SEE: Hamer; NUCMC, 1976.

SEE: Larson; Hinding.

BOWLING GREEN

OH97-80
Bowling Green State University
Libraries
Center for Archival Collections
5th Floor, University Library
Bowling Green OH 43403

(419) 372-2411

OPEN: M-F 8:30-4:30; closed weekends
    and holidays
COPYING FACILITIES: yes
MATERIALS SOLICITED: Local history
    (northwest Ohio), Great Lakes history,
    university archives: manuscripts, ar-
    chives, visual documents, audible docu-
    ments, microforms, scrapbooks, etc.

HOLDINGS:
    Total volume: 10,000 l.f.
    Inclusive dates: 1814 -
    Description: Materials on the history of
    19 northwestern Ohio counties: records of
    county and municipal governments,
    churches, businesses, railroads, and
    voluntary and charitable associations.

The Center also maintains an extensive
Great Lakes collection of photographs,
diaries, ships' logs, correspondence,
shipbuilding records, and port development materials.
    The University Archives maintains
records documenting the history and development of the University. Included are
copies of theses, dissertations, University
bulletins, yearbooks, other publications,
photographs, and tape recordings.

SEE: Robbins; Allard, Crawley, and
    Edmison.

SEE ALSO: David R. Larson, ed., *Guide to
    Manuscripts Collections and Institution-
    al Records in Ohio* (Society of Ohio
    Archivists, 1974); Paul D. Yon, *Guide
    to Ohio County and Municipal Govern-
    ment Records for Urban Research* (Ohio
    Historical Society, 1973); Richard C.
    Davis, *North American Forest History:
    A Guide to Archives and Manuscripts in
    the United States and Canada* (Clio
    Books, 1977).

OH97-890
Wood County Historical Society
13660 County Home Road
Bowling Green OH 43402

(419) 352-0967

OPEN: Su 1-4, M-F 9-4; closed Saturdays
    and holidays
COPYING FACILITIES: yes
MATERIALS SOLICITED: Research materi-
    als on the history of Wood County.

HOLDINGS:
    Total volume: 11 l.f.
    Inclusive dates: 1800 -
    Description: Materials relating to the
    history of Wood County, including genea-
    logical data on 6 families and documents
    relating to the history of a local infir-
    mary.

SEE: NUCMC, 1970.

BURTON

OH112-80
Burton Public Library
14588 West Park
Burton OH 44021

(216) 834-4466

OPEN: M-F 9-9, Sa 9-6; closed Sundays
    and holidays
COPYING FACILITIES: no
MATERIALS SOLICITED: Local history
    materials. Will also accept materials re-
    lating to Ohio history and the Amish.

HOLDINGS:
    Total volume: 51 fiche
    Inclusive dates: 1808 - 1967
    Description: Microfiche copies of
    records of the Burton Congregational
    Church, including Marimon Cook's book
    of records, transfers and requests, dis-
    missal papers, sermons, letters to Wilmot
    E. Stevens, newspaper clippings, and an-
    niversary proceedings.

SEE: Larson.

OH112-280
Geauga County Historical Society
14653 East Park Street
Burton OH

MAILING ADDRESS:
Box 153
Burton OH 44021

(216) 834-1492

OPEN: Tu-Sa 10-5, Su 1-5; closed
Mondays and holidays
COPYING FACILITIES: no
MATERIALS SOLICITED: Any items related to the history of Geauga County and genealogical material concerning Geauga County families. Will also accept materials relating to the history of the Western Reserve and Ohio.

HOLDINGS:
Total volume: 275 l.f.
Inclusive dates: 1795 -
Description: Manuscripts and documents relating to the history of Geauga County. Included are materials relating to settlement and development of the County; original land grants from the Connecticut Land Company; account books of early merchants and doctors; records of townships and institutions, such as the Agricultural Society (County Fair Board); and church records. Most materials date from the 19th century.

SEE: Larson.

CANTON

OH137-520
Malone College
Library
Canton OH 44709

no telephone

SEE: NUCMC, 1973.

Questionnaire not returned.

OH137-730
Stark County Historical Society
McKinley Museum of History,
Science, and Industry
Ramsayer Library
749 Hazlett Avenue, NW
Canton OH

MAILING ADDRESS:
P.O. Box 483
Canton OH 44701

(216) 455-7043

OPEN: Tu-F 10-4; closed weekends,
Mondays, and holidays
USER FEES: $2 per visit
COPYING FACILITIES: yes

HOLDINGS:
Total volume: not specified
Inclusive dates: 1820 -
Description: Historic photographs, scrapbooks, and a newspaper clipping file.

SEE: Larson.

CELINA

OH147-520
Mercer County Historical Museum
The Riley Home
Archives
130 East Market Street
Celina OH 45822

(419) 586-6065

OPEN: Su 1-4, Tu-F 8:30-4; closed
Mondays, Saturdays, and holidays
ACCESS: advance arrangements required
COPYING FACILITIES: no
MATERIALS SOLICITED: Materials relating to Mercer County and western Ohio, including settlement by Indians and by German immigrants; James Riley and his son James Watson Riley; and genealogy. Will also accept materials relating to settlement of other areas of Ohio and the Northwest Territory.

HOLDINGS:
Total volume: 20 c.f.
Inclusive dates: 1830 -
Description: A collection relating primarily to Mercer County history. Subjects include James Riley and James Watson Riley; settlement by blacks and by German immigrants via the Miami-Erie Canal; and John Randolph's slaves' land dispute. Included are correspondence and diaries; business, church, and school records; genealogical source material; photographs; and oral histories.

SEE ALSO: Unpublished guide to holdings available at museum.

CENTERVILLE

OH152-120
Centerville Historical Society
89 West Franklin Street
Centerville OH 45459

(513) 433-0123

OPEN: Th 1-5; closed other days and holidays
USER FEES: 50 cents
COPYING FACILITIES: no
MATERIALS SOLICITED: Family histories and historical photographs.

HOLDINGS:
Total volume: 3 l.f.
Inclusive dates: 1799 -
Description: Local history collection of genealogical data, as well as deeds, tax records, photographs, and materials relating to homes built before 1876.

CHAGRIN FALLS

OH157-120
Chagrin Falls Historical Society
Shute Memorial Building
21 Walnut Street
Chagrin Falls OH

MAILING ADDRESS:
P.O. Box 15
Chagrin Falls OH 44022

(215) 247-6306

OPEN: Th 2-4; closed other days
ACCESS: by appointment
COPYING FACILITIES: no

HOLDINGS:
Total volume: not specified
Inclusive dates: 1816 -
Description: Manuscripts relating to Chagrin Falls, primarily in the 19th century. Materials consist of village records, diaries and other personal papers, records of businesses and social organizations, and photographs.

SEE: NUCMC, 1977.

SEE: Larson.

CHARDON

OH161-240
Geauga County Public Library
110 East Park Street
Chardon OH 44024

no telephone

SEE: NUCMC, 1977.

Questionnaire not returned.

CHILLICOTHE

OH166-590
Ohio Historical Society
Adena State Memorial
Allen Avenue Extension
Chillicothe OH

MAILING ADDRESS:
P.O. Box 831-A
Chillicothe OH 45601

(614) 772-1500

OPEN: Apr. 15-June 14, Tu-Su 9:30-5;
June 15-Labor Day, Tu-Su 10-6; Labor Day-Oct. 31, Tu-Su 9:30-5; closed Mondays and Nov. 1-April 14
ACCESS: advance arrangements required
COPYING FACILITIES: no
MATERIALS SOLICITED: Materials pertaining to the Thomas Worthington family or to the Adena mansion, especially 1773-1848. Will also accept materials pertaining to early Chillicothe and to Ohio in the territorial and early statehood periods.

HOLDINGS:
Total volume: 1 box
Inclusive dates: 1800 -
Description: A collection of Worthington family papers, including correspondence, diaries, account books, and genealogical data; and photographs of the Adena mansion dating from 1868.

OH166-690
Ross County Historical Society
45 West 5th Street
Chillicothe OH 45601

(614) 772-1936

SEE: Hamer.

Questionnaire not returned.

CINCINNATI

OH171-20
American Jewish Archives
3101 Clifton Avenue
Cincinnati OH 45220

(513) 221-1875

OPEN: M-F 8:30-5; closed weekends,
 holidays, and Jewish holidays
COPYING FACILITIES: yes
MATERIALS SOLICITED: Manuscripts, institution and organization records, photographs, and oral history tapes and
 transcripts, relating to Jewish history.

HOLDINGS:
 Total volume: 5,000,000 pages
 Inclusive dates: 1592 -
 Description: Materials relating to Jewish history in the Western Hemisphere.
 The primary focus is on the United
 States, including such topics as anti-
 Semitism, civil rights, immigration, and
 social welfare activities. Included are personal papers, organization records, Yiddish plays in manuscript, memoirs, diaries, genealogical data, photographs, and
 oral history recordings.

GUIDES: *Manuscript Catalog of the
 American Jewish Archives* (G. K. Hall,
 1971).

SEE: Hamer; NUCMC, 1965-68, 80.

SEE: Ingram; Allard, Crawley, and
 Edmison; Hinding.

SEE ALSO: Walter Schatz, ed., *Directory of
 Afro-American Resources* (Bowker,
 1970); Alan M. Meckler and Ruth
 McMullin, comps., *Oral History Collections* (Bowker, 1975); Andrea Hinding
 and Rosemary Richardson, comps.,
 *Archival and Manuscript Resources for
 the Study of Women's History: A Beginning* (Univ. of Minnesota Libraries, Social Welfare History Archives Center,
 1972); Philip P. Mason, ed., *Directory
 of Jewish Archival Institutions* (Wayne
 State Univ. Press, 1975).

OH171-50
Archdiocese of Cincinnati
Archdiocesan Archives
Mount St. Mary's Seminary
6616 Beechmont Avenue
Cincinnati OH 45230

(513) 231-0810

OPEN: by appointment
COPYING FACILITIES: yes
MATERIALS SOLICITED: Records and
 manuscripts of parishes and institu-
 tions of the Archdiocese of Cincinnati.
 Will also accept memorabilia and
 manuscripts relating to Cincinnati and
 Ohio history.

HOLDINGS:
 Total volume: 190 l.f.
 Inclusive dates: 1800 - 1925
 Description: A collection of manuscripts and memorabilia concerning the
 Catholic church in the Midwest, especially in Ohio. The bulk of the collection
 consists of correspondence of the bishops
 and archbishops of Cincinnati. Also included are diaries, ledgers, statistical re-

ports, registers of defunct parishes, and
records of Mount St. Mary's Seminary.

SEE: NUCMC, 1978.

SEE: Larson.

OH171-95
Church of the New Jerusalem
New Church Library
5008 Whetsel Avenue
Cincinnati OH 45227

no telephone

SEE: NUCMC, 1959-61, 65.

Questionnaire not returned.

OH171-100
Cincinnati Art Museum-Art Academy
 of Cincinnati
Archives
Eden Park
Cincinnati OH 45202

(513) 721-5204

OPEN: Tu-F 10-4:45; closed other days
 and holidays
USER FEES: one dollar for non-members
ACCESS: at the discretion of the Museum
COPYING FACILITIES: yes
MATERIALS SOLICITED: Correspondence
 and other papers, photographs of administrators, curators, and trustees of
 the Cincinnati Art Museum; and similar materials of deans and instructors
 of the Art Academy of Cincinnati. Will
 also accept manuscripts, photographs,
 biographical information, clippings,
 and exhibition information of artists
 who have lived or worked in Cincinnati.

HOLDINGS:
 Total volume: 324 c.f.
 Inclusive dates: 1880 - 1977
 Description: Records of the Cincinnati
 Art Museum, including correspondence,
 exhibition documents, financial ledgers,
 photographs, and scrapbooks. Also,
 records of the Art Academy of Cincinnati
 consisting of student records, faculty biographical information, and photographs
 of student and faculty art work.

SEE: Larson; Novotny; Martin; Hinding.

SEE ALSO: Typewritten records inventory
 available at the institution.

OH171-110
Cincinnati Historical Society
Eden Park
Cincinnati OH 45202

(513) 241-4622

OPEN: Tu-Sa 9-4:30; closed Sundays and
 holidays
COPYING FACILITIES: yes
MATERIALS SOLICITED: Materials dealing
 with Cincinnati and southwestern
 Ohio. Will also accept materials dealing
 with American history in general.

HOLDINGS:
 Total volume: 4,800 l.f.
 Inclusive dates: 1775 -
 Description: A collection of personal
 and family papers, institutional records,
 architectural drawings, scrapbooks, photographs, oral history tapes, and motion
 pictures dealing with all aspects of American history, with primary emphasis on
 Cincinnati and the surrounding area. Also
 includes a special collection of manuscripts and photographs relating to German Methodism with some unpublished
 translations.

SEE: Hamer (as Historical and Philosophical Society of Ohio); NUCMC,
 1962-65, 71-72.

SEE: Hinding; Robbins; Allard, Crawley,
 and Edmison.

SEE ALSO: Walter Schatz, ed., *Directory of
 Afro-American Resources* (Bowker,
 1970); Ann Novotny, ed., *Picture
 Sources 3* (Special Libraries Assn.,
 1975); Edwin T. Layton, Jr., ed., *A Re-
 gional Union Catalog of Manuscripts
 Relating to the History of Science and
 Technology Located in Indiana, Michi-
 gan, and Ohio* (Case Western Reserve
 Univ., 1971); Andrea Hinding and
 Rosemary Richardson, comps., *Archival
 and Manuscript Resources for the Study
 of Women's History: A Beginning*
 (Univ. of Minnesota Libraries, Social
 Welfare History Archives, 1972); Louis
 Leonard Tucker, 'The Historical and
 Philosophical Society of Ohio: Its Re-
 sources,' *Ohio History* 71 (1962); Rich-
 ard C. Davis, *North American Forest
 History: A Guide to Archives and Manu-
 scripts in the United States and Canada*
 (Clio Books, 1977).

OH171-130
Cincinnati Observatory
Observatory Place
Cincinnati OH 45208

no telephone

SEE: NUCMC, 1975.

Questionnaire not returned.

OH171-165
The Diocese of Southern Ohio
412 Sycamore Street
Cincinnati OH45202

(513) 421-0311

OPEN: M-F 9-5; closed weekends and
 holidays
COPYING FACILITIES: yes
MATERIALS SOLICITED: Records relating
 to the Episcopal Diocese of Southern
 Ohio.

HOLDINGS:
 Total volume: 120 microfilm reels
 Inclusive dates: 1804 -
 Description: Records and personal papers relating to the Episcopal church in
 southern Ohio, including diaries of bishops, diocesan financial records, records of
 congregations, and records of baptisms,
 confirmations, and burials.

OH171-320

Hebrew Union College-Jewish
  Institute of Religion
Klau Library
3101 Clifton Avenue
Cincinnati OH 45220

(513) 221-1875

OPEN: M-F 8:30-5; closed weekends,
  holidays, and Jewish holidays
ACCESS: serious scholars
COPYING FACILITIES: yes
MATERIALS SOLICITED: Judaica.

HOLDINGS:
  Total volume: 380 l.f.
  Inclusive dates: medieval period -
  Description: Literary manuscripts of
  Biblical, liturgical, philosophical, legal,
  and other books; music manuscripts; collections from European and Near Eastern
  sources; community records; microfilms
  of Hebrew manuscripts from other repositories; photographs of Jewish personalities, archaeological artifacts from Palestine, and other subjects.
    Also includes sound recordings and
  microfilm manuscripts from other repositories.

SEE: Hamer.

SEE ALSO: David R. Larson, ed., *Guide to
  Manuscripts Collections and Institution-
  al Records in Ohio* (Society of Ohio
  Archivists, 1974); Philip P. Mason, *Di-
  rectory of Jewish Archival Institutions*
  (Wayne State Univ. Press, 1975).

OH171-470

Lloyd Library and Museum
917 Plum Street
Cincinnati OH 45202

no telephone
SEE: Hamer.

Questionnaire not returned.

OH171-530

Miami Purchase Association for
  Historic Preservation
812 Dayton Street
Cincinnati OH 45214

(513) 721-4506

OPEN: M-F 9-5; closed weekends and
  holidays
COPYING FACILITIES: yes
MATERIALS SOLICITED: Materials pertaining to architecture, archaeology,
  and historic preservation in southwestern Ohio.

HOLDINGS:
  Total volume: 2,000 items
  Inclusive dates: 1830's -
  Description: Notes, photographs, and
  research reports concerning historic buildings and neighborhoods in Cincinnati
  and southwestern Ohio.

OH171-650

Public Library of Cincinnati and
  Hamilton County
Department of Rare Books and
  Special Collections
800 Vine Street
Cincinnati OH 45202

(513) 369-6957

OPEN: M-Sa 9-5; closed Sundays and
  holidays
COPYING FACILITIES: yes
MATERIALS SOLICITED: Inland rivers materials.

HOLDINGS:
  Total volume: not specified
  Inclusive dates: 12th century -
  Description: A collection relating chiefly to Ohio and inland water navigation.
  Included are diaries of inland river captains and pilots; and account books,
  freight books, landing lists, lock books,
  logbooks, passenger lists, wharfboat books
  and logs, photographs, and other records
  of steamboats, packet lines, and individual boat operators. The collection also
  includes papers of several Ohio families;
  papers of political and artistic figures; aerial photographs; and several Renaissance, medieval, and Oriental manuscripts.
    Includes special collections of Cincin-
  nati imprints and authors; English language dictionaries prior to 1870, etc.

SEE: Hamer; NUCMC, 1962, 68.

SEE: Allard, Crawley, and Edmison; Robbins.

SEE ALSO: David R. Larson, ed., *Guide to
  Manuscripts Collections and Institution-
  al Records in Ohio* (Society of Ohio
  Archivists, 1974); Edwin T. Layton, Jr.,
  ed., *A Regional Union Catalog of
  Manuscripts Relating to the History of
  Science and Technology Located in In-
  diana, Michigan, and Ohio* (Case West-
  ern Reserve Univ., 1971); Ann
  Novotny, ed., *Picture Sources 3* (Special
  Libraries Assn., 1975); Clyde N.
  Bowden, comp., *Catalog of the Inland
  Rivers Library* (1968).

OH171-730

Sisters of Notre Dame de Namur
Ohio Province
Archives
Provincial House
701 East Columbia Avenue
Cincinnati OH 45215

(513) 821-7448

OPEN: M-F 9-4; closed weekends and
  holidays
ACCESS: permission required
COPYING FACILITIES: yes
MATERIALS SOLICITED: Anything relative
  to the houses, institutions, and works
  of the Ohio Province of the Sisters of
  Notre Dame de Namur with emphasis
  on the work of St. Julie Billiart. Will
  also accept letters, diaries, photographs,
  programs, and educational materials of
  former pupils and associates of the Sisters of Notre Dame in their many educational institutions.

HOLDINGS:
  Total volume: 550 c.f.
  Inclusive dates: 1840 -
  Description: Materials dealing with the
  history of the Sisters of Notre Dame de
  Namur in the Ohio Province since its
  founding in 1840, including records of
  affiliated convents and schools across the
  country east of the Rocky Mountains.
    Manuscript items consist of original
  and copied letters of church officials, the
  sisters in the United States and their
  Generalates in Europe, as well as in the
  foreign mission: annals of convents and
  schools, membership registers, biographies and memoirs of the sisters, proceedings of general and provincial chapters of affairs, educational organizations,
  institutional histories, rules and constitutions, cemetery records, and necrologies.

SEE ALSO: guides to parts of the collection
  available from the institution.

Guide to holdings available at institution.

OH171-800

University of Cincinnati
Libraries
Archives and Rare Books Department
Blegan Library
Cincinnati OH 45221-0113

(513) 475-6459

OPEN: M-F 8-5; closed weekends and
  holidays
COPYING FACILITIES: yes
MATERIALS SOLICITED: Materials relating
  to the University of Cincinnati, urban
  studies, medical history, and county
  and local government, and other
  records and manuscripts from an eight
  county region in southwestern Ohio.

HOLDINGS:
  Total volume: 2,527 l.f.
  Inclusive dates: 1000 B.C. -
  Description: The University of Cincinnati archives, including official and administrative records, as well as personal
  paper collections; materials relating to urban studies, with emphasis on 20th century Cincinnati; materials in medical history, with emphasis on 19th and 20th
  century Cincinnati medical records and
  papers; county and local government
  records and other manuscripts and audio-
  visual materials from an 8 county area in
  southwestern Ohio; and other materials,
  including literary manuscripts from the
  medieval period, as well as the 20th century. Among the individuals on whom
  collections focus are Alfred Bettman, Gilbert Bettman, Martha Ransohoff, and Albert Sabin.

SEE: Hamer.

SEE: Spalek; Martin; Hinding; Robbins.

SEE ALSO: David R. Larson, ed., *Guide to
  Manuscripts Collections and Institutional Records in Ohio* (Society of Ohio
  Archivists, 1974); 'Archival Programs
  at University of Cincinnati,' *Ohio Archivist* 3 (Spring 1972).

OH171-920
Xavier University
McDonald Memorial Library
Victory Parkway and Dana Avenue
Cincinnati OH 45207

(513) 745-3881

OPEN: M-F 9-5; closed weekends and
  holidays
ACCESS: by special arrangement
COPYING FACILITIES: yes
HOLDINGS:
  Total volume: 108 l.f.; 206 items
  Inclusive dates: 1826 -
  Description: Collection of 200 political
  letters of the Jacksonian period, 1826-44,
  written to Moses Dawson, editor of the
  Cincinnati *Advertiser*, from Andrew Jack-
  son, Levi Woodbury, Martin Van Buren,
  Thomas Hart Benton, William Henry
  Harrison, and James K. Polk; literary
  manuscripts of Francis J. Finn, Jr.; Xa-
  vier University archives, including papers
  of presidents and boards of trustees, and
  departmental histories; and photographs.

SEE: Larson; Robbins.

CIRCLEVILLE

OH176-650
Pickaway County Historical Society
Ted Lewis Museum
Historical and Genealogical Library
133 West Main Street
Circleville OH

MAILING ADDRESS:
P.O. Box 85
Circleville OH 43113

no telephone

OPEN: by appointment only
COPYING FACILITIES: yes
MATERIALS SOLICITED: Will accept ma-
  terials pertaining to Pickaway County
  or to Ted Lewis.
HOLDINGS:
  Total volume: not specified
  Inclusive dates: 1803 -
  Description: A collection of journals,
  land and probate records, genealogical
  data, and scrapbooks concerned primarily
  with Pickaway County history.

SEE: Larson.

CLEVELAND

OH181-80
Blessed Sacrament Seminary
Library
5384 Wilson Mills Road
Cleveland OH 44143

no telephone

SEE: NUCMC, 1959-61.

Questionnaire not returned.

OH181-110
Case Western Reserve University
Archives
Quail Building, Room 317
Cleveland OH 44106

(216) 368-3370

OPEN: M-F 8:30-4:30; closed weekends
  and holidays
ACCESS: at discretion of Archivist
COPYING FACILITIES: yes
MATERIALS SOLICITED: Materials concerning Case Western Reserve University.

HOLDINGS:
  Total volume: 4,265 l.f.
  Inclusive dates: 1826 -
  Description: Records of the University,
  including publications, minutes, office
  files, student records, theses and dissertations, photographs, microfilm, audio and
  video tapes, blueprints, personal papers of
  faculty, staff, and trustees, and any other
  materials relating to Western Reserve
  College, 1826-82, Western Reserve University, 1884-1967, Case School of Applied Science and Case Institute of Technology, 1880-1967, and Case Western Reserve University, 1967- .

SEE: Hamer (as Western Reserve University Library); NUCMC, 1968, 74, 80.

SEE: Hinding.

SEE ALSO: David R. Larson, ed., *Guide to
  Manuscripts Collections and Institutional Records in Ohio* (Society of Ohio
  Archivists, 1974); Edwin T. Layton, Jr.,
  ed., *A Regional Union Catalog of
  Manuscripts Relating to the History of
  Science and Technology Located in Indiana, Michigan, and Ohio* (Case Western Reserve Univ., 1971); *Source Materials for the Recent History of Astronomy and Astrophysics: A Checklist of
  Manuscript Collections in the United
  States* (American Institute of Physics,
  1971).

OH181-130
Case Western Reserve University
Libraries
Special Collections
11161 East Blvd.
Cleveland OH 44106

(216) 368-2993

OPEN: M-F 9-5; closed weekends and
  holidays
COPYING FACILITIES: yes
MATERIALS SOLICITED: Materials relating
  to the University's academic programs
  and present collections.

HOLDINGS:
  Total volume: 60,000 items
  Inclusive dates: 1650 -
  Description: Rare books, manuscripts,
  and special collections. Collections include history of science, housing, and
  planning library, Henry David Thoreau
  collection, film book collection (Sylvia
  Plath, Ted Hughes, W. S. Merwin, Galway Kinnell, and John Berryman), letter
  collections of H. Jack Lang and John
  Masefield, etc.

SEE: Hamer (as Western Reserve University Library); NUCMC, 1959-61, 68-69,
  71 (latter years as Case Western Reserve University, Sears Library, Archive of Science and Technology).

SEE: Robbins.

SEE ALSO: David A. Hounshell, comp.,
  *Manuscripts in U.S. Depositories Relat-
  ing to the History of Electrical Science
  and Technology* (Smithsonian Institu-
  tion, n.d.); Edwin T. Layton, Jr., ed., *A
  Regional Union Catalog of Manuscripts
  Relating to the History of Science and
  Technology Located in Indiana, Michi-
  gan, and Ohio* (Case Western Reserve
  Univ., 1971); David R. Larson, ed.,
  *Guide to Manuscripts Collections and
  Institutional Records in Ohio* (Society
  of Ohio Archivists, 1974): as Case
  Western Reserve University Archive of
  Science and Technology.

OH181-180
Cleveland Health Sciences Library
Historical Division
11000 Euclid Avenue
Cleveland OH 44106

(216) 368-3648, 3649

OPEN: M-F 10-5; closed weekends and
  holidays
COPYING FACILITIES: yes
MATERIALS SOLICITED: Papers of physicians, especially in the Western Reserve
  area and Ohio, and archives of medical
  societies, hospitals, and other medically
  related institutions.

HOLDINGS:
  Total volume: 500 l.f.
  Inclusive dates: 1742 -
  Description: Materials relating to the
  medical profession in Ohio, especially
  Cleveland, Cuyahoga County, and the
  Western Reserve. Major subject areas include thyroid and goiter, diabetes, surgery, arthritis, pathology, forensic medicine, and military medicine, especially in
  the Spanish-American War and World
  War I. Included are a special collection
  relating to Charles Darwin, papers of
  Cleveland physicians, and records of such
  organizations as the Cleveland Medical
  Library Association, the Hospital Obstetrical Society of Ohio, the Pasteur Club,
  the Woman's General Hospital, the
  Cleveland Clinical Club, and the Cleveland Clinic.

SEE ALSO: David R. Larson, ed., *Guide to
  Manuscripts Collections and Institutional Records in Ohio* (Society of Ohio
  Archivists, 1974); Ann Novotny, ed.,
  Picture Sources 3 (Special Libraries
  Assn., 1975); Edwin T. Layton, Jr., ed.,
  *A Regional Union Catalog of Manu-
  scripts Relating to the History of Science and Technology Located in Indiana, Michigan, and Ohio* (Case Western Reserve Univ., 1971).

OH181-240

Cleveland Museum of Natural History
Harold Terry Clark Library
Wade Oval, University Circle
Cleveland OH 44106

(216) 231-4600

OPEN: Tu-Sa 10-5; closed Sundays, Mondays, and holidays
USER FEES: admission fee; free Tu 1-5
ACCESS: appointment required
COPYING FACILITIES: yes
MATERIALS SOLICITED: Will accept manuscripts of local and well-known naturalists; archives of local nature-oriented clubs and organizations; and field notes and maps of local natural history studies.

HOLDINGS:
Total volume: 6 l.f.
Inclusive dates: 1840 -
Description: A collection of about 350 letters by well-known naturalists, and local scientists and naturalists, 1840-1900; and archives of local nature-oriented clubs and organizations, 1920 to date.

SEE: Larson.

OH181-270

Cleveland Public Library
325 Superior Avenue
Cleveland OH 44114

(216) 623-2800

OPEN: M-Sa 9-6; closed Sundays and holidays
ACCESS: identification may be required and held during use
COPYING FACILITIES: yes
MATERIALS SOLICITED: Manuscripts relating to chess. Will also accept other materials.

HOLDINGS:
Total volume: 2,718 l.f.
Inclusive dates: 1450 -
Description: Manuscript holdings consist of about 500 European and oriental works on folklore, travel, literature, and religion; about 1,000 chess manuscripts in Western and Middle Eastern languages; 250 vols. of documents and correspondence relating to British affairs in India and Central Asia, 1741-1859; 9 Billy Bryant plays; literary works of Charles Waddell Chesnutt; 25 vols. of Charles V. Rychlie's encyclopedia of violin techniques.

Theatrical memorabilia; facsimiles of Mexican and Mayan codices; records of the Library; manuscript and photographic materials pertaining to Cleveland history; the May Augusta Klipple African folktale collection of translations; and folklore materials collected by Newbell N. Puckett.

SEE: Hamer; NUCMC, 1959-61, 70.

SEE: Larson; Schatz; Krichmar; Novotny; Martin; Hinding; Robbins.

OH181-290

Cleveland State University
Archives
1860 E. 22nd Street
Cleveland OH 44115

(216) 687-3529

OPEN: M-F 8:30-5:30; closed weekends and holidays
COPYING FACILITIES: yes
MATERIALS SOLICITED: Departmental files of Fenn College, Cleveland Law School, John Marshall Law School, Cleveland-Marshall Law School, Cleveland-Marshall College of Law, and Cleveland State University; and papers of people prominent in the history of the University; master's degree theses and doctoral dissertations.

HOLDINGS:
Total volume: 600 l.f.; 1,000 vols.
Inclusive dates: 1898 - Law School, Cleveland-Marshall Law School, and Cleveland-Marshall College of Law.
Description: Departmental files; publications; minutes of the board of trustees; faculty, student, and alumni records; and records of ceremonies and social events of Cleveland State University, 1965- , and its predecessors Fenn College, 1930-65, and the YMCA School of Technology, School of Commerce, and Preparatory School, 1923-30.

Includes records of Cleveland Law School, John Marshall

SEE: Larson.

OH181-310

Cleveland State University
Libraries
Audio/Music Services
1860 E. 22nd Street
Cleveland OH 44115

(216) 687-2483, 2486

OPEN: M-Th 8-8, F 8-5, Sa noon-5; closed Sundays, holidays, and weekends between quarters
COPYING FACILITIES: yes
MATERIALS SOLICITED: Materials relating to the Cleveland City Club weekly forums, Balkan Slavic music, and the musical career of Herbert Elwell.

HOLDINGS:
Total volume: 579 items; 6 l.f.
Inclusive dates: 1950 -
Description: Audio tapes of the weekly Friday forums of the Cleveland City Club which feature speakers of national and local prominence on a wide variety of political and social issues; audio tapes of music and oral commentaries documenting the musical traditions of southern European peoples; and papers of Herbert Elwell documenting his musical career.

SEE: Meckler and McMullin.

OH181-325

Cuyahoga County Archives
2905 Franklin Boulevard, N.W.
The Robert Russell Rhodes House
Cleveland OH 44113

(216) 443-7250

OPEN: M-F 8:30-4:30; closed weekends and holidays; open on these days by special request
COPYING FACILITIES: yes
MATERIALS SOLICITED: Materials relating to Cuyahoga County and northeastern Ohio, including cartographic and survey materials and Cuyahoga County township and village records, and architectural and engineering drawings and records. Will also accept personal and public papers from Cuyahoga County municipal, township, and county officials; collections documenting the history of the northeastern Ohio area; neighborhood redevelopment and historic preservation guides; genealogical records and family compilations; and miscellaneous materials.

HOLDINGS:
Total volume: 23,500 square feet
Inclusive dates: 1750 -
Description: Chiefly non-current records of Cuyahoga County government offices and agencies. There are also architectural records collected as part of a joint project with the Western Reserve Historical Society, including documents from such individuals and firms as John H. Edelmann, John Eisenmann, Joseph Ireland, Charles Schweinfurth, Levi Scofield, Briggs and Nelson, Coburn and Barnum, Hubbell and Benes, and Walker and Weeks. Also included is a photo collection focusing on northeastern Ohio architecture.

OH181-400

Dyke College
Library Resource Center
Archival Collection
112 Prospect Avenue
Cleveland OH 44115

(216) 696-9000, Ext. 731

OPEN: M-Th 8-8, F 8-5; closed weekends and holidays; shorter hours in summer
USER FEES: $20 annual fee for those not affiliated with Dyke College or reciprocal lending institutions
COPYING FACILITIES: yes
MATERIALS SOLICITED: Materials relating to early business education, Platt Rogers Spencer and family, Spencerian penmanship, and Dyke College and other Spencerian colleges. Will also accept materials relating to calligraphy and to the history of Cleveland, the Western Reserve, and Ohio.

HOLDINGS:
Total volume: 35 c.f.
Inclusive dates: 1848 -
Description: A collection relating to the history of Dyke College, its founders, and business education. Included are letters of Platt Rogers Spencer and his descendants, specimens of Spencerian script, photographs, and the College archives.

SEE: Larson; Novotny.

OH181-430
Episcopal Diocese of Ohio
Archives
2230 Euclid Avenue
Cleveland OH 44115

(216) 771-4815

OPEN: M-F by appointment; closed
Saturdays, Sundays, and holidays
COPYING FACILITIES: yes
MATERIALS SOLICITED: Historical and
current records relating to the Diocese
of Ohio. Will also accept historical materials relating to the Episcopal church
outside of the Diocese and to member
churches of the Anglican Communion,
worldwide.

HOLDINGS:
    Total volume: 107 l.f.; 90 microfilm
reels; 37 drawers
    Inclusive dates: 18th century -
    Description: Parish records of the Dio-
cese of Ohio, both original and microfilm; registers of baptisms, confirmations,
marriages, and burials; architectural plans
for some churches and parish houses;
photographs; vertical files of miscellaneous records; minutes of diocesan administrative bodies and committees; and
letters and papers of early bishops of
Ohio.

SEE: Larson.

OH181-630
Plain Dealer
Library
1801 Superior Avenue
Cleveland OH 44114

(216) 344-4195, 4500

OPEN: by appointment
USER FEES: variable photograph
reproduction fees
ACCESS: The Library is closed to the
general public. Researchers must write
to the Public Service Department
stating subject of interest; staff will
perform research and provide
reproductions for a fee.
COPYING FACILITIES: yes

HOLDINGS:
    Total volume: 3,450,000 items
    Inclusive dates: 1855 -
    Description: A collection of photo-
graphs, daguerreotypes, drawings, and
other pictures, containing many early
views of Cleveland and its people; and a
necrology file of death notices from
Cleveland-area newspapers and cemetery
records.

SEE: Hinding.

SEE ALSO: Ann Novotny, ed., *Picture
Sources 3* (Special Libraries Assn.,
1975); David R. Larson, ed., *Guide to
Manuscripts Collections and Institution-
al Records in Ohio* (Society of Ohio
Archivists, 1974); Grace D. Parch, ed.,
*Directory of Newspaper Libraries in the
U.S. and Canada* (Special Libraries
Assn., 1976). The Library maintains a
subject index to 1,000,000 of its pho-
tographs, for use by staff members.

OH181-660
The Sherwin-Williams Company
101 Prospect Avenue, N.W.
Cleveland OH 44115

(216) 566-3082, 2334

OPEN: by appointment only; closed
weekends and holidays
COPYING FACILITIES: yes
MATERIALS SOLICITED: Materials pertaining to the history of The Sherwin-
Williams Company. Will also accept
materials pertaining to the paint industry.

HOLDINGS:
    Total volume: 40 l.f.
    Inclusive dates: late 1800's -
    Description: A collection of manu-
scripts and photographs relating to The
Sherwin-Williams Company and people
who have been associated with it.

OH181-730
The Temple
Library
Abba Hillel Silver Memorial Archives
University Circle and Silver Park
Cleveland OH 44106

(216) 791-7755

OPEN: M-F 9-5; closed weekends and
holidays
ACCESS: scholars only
COPYING FACILITIES: yes

HOLDINGS:
    Total volume: 320 l.f.
    Inclusive dates: 1915 -
    Description: Materials relating to Abba
Hillel Silver, including personal papers,
correspondence, sermons, speeches, photographs, and tape recordings of public
addresses. Subjects covered include Zionist organizations, the Central Conference
of American Rabbis, and Israel. There
are also archives of The Temple, such as
annual reports, graduation programs, and
other records of this religious institution
and its affiliated school system.

SEE: NUCMC, 1970.

SEE: Larson.

OH181-780
Ukrainian Museum
Archives
1202 Kenilworth Avenue
Cleveland OH 44113

(216) 741-4537

OPEN: Sa 9-1; other times by
appointment
COPYING FACILITIES: no
MATERIALS SOLICITED: Materials pertaining to the cultural, social, religious,
and political life of Ukrainian immigrants. Will also accept materials pertaining to Ukrainian life outside the
United States.

HOLDINGS:
    Total volume: 2,500 items
    Inclusive dates: 1905 -
    Description: Materials relating to
prominent Ukrainian-Americans, as well
as Ukrainian organizations in Cleveland,
primarily Plast, a Ukrainian youth association. There are photographs as well as
written records, and all materials are in
the Ukrainian language.

SEE: Larson.

OH181-790
University Hospitals of Cleveland
Hospital Archives
Lowman House 330
2065 Adelbert Road
Cleveland OH 44106

(216) 844-1000

OPEN: M-F 8-5; closed weekends and
holidays
ACCESS: appointment recommended
COPYING FACILITIES: yes
MATERIALS SOLICITED: Archives of the
University Hospitals of Cleveland and
personal papers of professional and ad-
ministrative staff members. Will also
accept other materials related to the
University Hospitals of Cleveland.

HOLDINGS:
    Total volume: 3,000 l.f.
    Inclusive dates: 1865 -
    Description: Materials relating to the
history of the University Hospitals. Included is documentation of such subjects
as hospital room rates, as well as scientific manuscripts and oral history tapes
and transcripts. Much of the material relates to the history of medicine in the city
of Cleveland as a whole.

SEE: Meckler and McMullin.

OH181-880
Western Reserve Historical Society
History Library
10825 East Boulevard
Cleveland OH 44106

(216) 721-5722

OPEN: Tu-Sa 9-5; closed Sundays,
Mondays, and holidays
USER FEES: $2 per day
COPYING FACILITIES: yes
MATERIALS SOLICITED: History of
northeastern Ohio and the greater
Cleveland area, especially political, so-
cial welfare, and ethnic history. Will
also accept materials relating to the
Shakers, the Civil War, slavery and
abolitionism, the American Revolution,
and American genealogy.

HOLDINGS:
    Total volume: 10,000 l.f.
    Inclusive dates: 1636 -
    Description: More than 1,500 collec-
tions, relating chiefly to the exploration,
growth, and development of the State of
Ohio and the Old Northwest, with emphasis on the northeastern section of
Ohio known as the Western Reserve.
Special interest areas include Cleveland
urban, black, ethnic, and Jewish history,
and American genealogy. Also included
are collections dealing with the Civil
War, the antislavery movement, the
Shakers, and the era of the American
Revolution, as well as the personal papers
of nationally prominent men and women
who resided in northeastern Ohio.

GUIDES: Kermit J. Pike, *A Guide to the Manuscripts and Archives of the Western Reserve Historical Society* (1972).

SEE: Hamer; NUCMC, 1962, 67, 69, 75.

SEE: Schatz,; Hounshell; Davis; Paszek; Parkinson; Hines; Allard, Crawley, and Edmison; Robbins; Hinding.

SEE ALSO: Kermit J. Pike, *A Guide to Shaker Manuscripts in the Library of the Western Reserve Historical Society, with an Inventory of its Shaker Photographs* (The Society, 1974); Ann Novotny, ed., *Picture Sources 3* (Special Libraries Assn., 1975); Edwin T. Layton, Jr., ed., *A Regional Union Catalog of Manuscripts Relating to the History of Science and Technology Located in Indiana, Michigan, and Ohio* (Case Western Reserve Univ., 1971); Meredith B. Colkett, Jr., 'The Western Reserve Historical Society,' *Ohio History* 72 (April 1963); John J. Grabowski, 'Ethnic Collections of the Western Reserve Historical Society,' *Illinois Libraries* 57 (March 1975).

CLYDE

OH194-120
Clyde Public Library
222 West Buckeye Street
Clyde OH 43410

(419) 547-7174

OPEN: M-Th 10-8:30, F, Sa 9:30-5:30; closed Sundays and holidays
COPYING FACILITIES: yes

HOLDINGS:
> *Total volume:* 6 vols.
> *Inclusive dates:* 1931 -
> *Description:* Minutes of the Library Board of Trustees, and the Clyde Progress Club, a literary association; and two volumes of genealogical charts of local families.

COLUMBIANA

OH199-320
Historical Society of Columbiana and Fairfield Township
Log House, on the Square
Columbiana OH

MAILING ADDRESS:
P.O. Box 101
Columbiana OH 44408

no telephone

OPEN: Sa, Su 2-4; closed other days and Sept. - May; open on holidays; also open by appointment
COPYING FACILITIES: no
MATERIALS SOLICITED: Letters of General Ephraim S. Holloway during the Civil War.

HOLDINGS:
> *Total volume:* 6 vols.
> *Inclusive dates:* 1861 - 1895
> *Description:* Correspondence and diary of General Ephraim S. Holloway, primarily relating to his experiences during the Civil War.

SEE: NUCMC, 1959-61.

COLUMBUS

OH203-100
Capital University
Archives
Columbus OH 43209

(614) 236-6351, 6615

OPEN: by appointment
COPYING FACILITIES: yes
MATERIALS SOLICITED: Materials relating to the history of Capital University.

HOLDINGS:
> *Total volume:* 30 l.f.
> *Inclusive dates:* 1850 -
> *Description:* A collection relating chiefly to the University, including minute books, committee records, board reports, photographs, printed programs, and catalogs.

SEE: NUCMC, 1976.

SEE: Larson.

OH203-170
Diocese of Columbus
Archives
198 East Broad Street
Columbus OH 43215

(614) 224-2251

OPEN: M-F 10-4; closed weekends, holidays, and Holy Week
COPYING FACILITIES: yes

HOLDINGS:
> *Total volume:* 96 l.f.; 85 file drawers
> *Inclusive dates:* 1818 -
> *Description:* Microfilmed parish records of the Diocese of Columbus; parish financial and census reports; pastoral letters of bishops; some correspondence of early bishops; clergy records; death and burial records; photographs; scrapbooks; architectural drawings; materials relating to diocesan organizations; and materials relating to various religious, charitable, social, and educational institutions.

OH203-600
The Ohio Historical Society
Archives-Manuscripts Division
I-71 and 17th Avenue
Columbus OH 43211

(614) 466-1500

OPEN: M-Sa 9-5; closed Sundays and holidays
COPYING FACILITIES: yes
MATERIALS SOLICITED: Ohio history in general, including archival material, with special emphasis on women's history, black history, and labor history. Will also accept materials of general historical value that relate to collections already possessed by the Society.

HOLDINGS:
> *Total volume:* 21,000 l.f.
> *Inclusive dates:* 1731 -
> *Description:* A collection of manuscripts, State government records, local government records, and audio-visual materials relating to Ohio. Included are

the papers of prominent individuals such as Warren G. Harding and Paul Laurence Dunbar, and of institutions such as the Anti-Saloon League of America. The Society is also the official State archives and holds county and municipal records for central Ohio.

SEE: Hamer; NUCMC, 1959-64, 68, 73, 75-76.

SEE: Allard, Crawley, and Edmison; Parkinson; Hinding; Robbins.

SEE ALSO: Andrea Lentz, ed., *A Guide to Manuscripts at the Ohio Historical Society* (The Society, 1972); David A. Hounshell, comp., *Manuscripts in U.S. Depositories Relating to the History of Electrical Science and Technology* (Smithsonian Institution, n.d.); Paul D. Yon, *A Guide to Ohio County and Municipal Records for Urban Research* (The Society, 1973); Donald E. Pitzer, 'An Introduction to the Harding Papers,' *Ohio History* 75 (Spring and Summer 1966); Charles M. Cummings, 'The Scott Papers: An Inside View of Reconstruction,' *Ohio History* 79 (Spring 1970); Andrea Hinding and Rosemary Richardson, comps., *Archival and Manuscript Resources for the Study of Women's History: A Beginning* (Univ. of Minnesota Libraries, Social Welfare History Archives Center, 1972).

Walter Schatz, ed., *Directory of Afro-American Resources* (Bowker, 1970); Alan M. Meckler and Ruth McMullin, comps., *Oral History Collections* (Bowker, 1975); Albert Krichmar, *The Women's Rights Movement in the United States, 1848-1970: A Bibliography and Sourcebook* (Scarecrow Press, 1972); Ann Novotny, ed., *Picture Sources 3* (Special Libraries Assn., 1975); Edwin T. Layton, Jr., ed., *A Regional Union Catalog of Manuscripts Relating to the History of Science and Technology Located in Indiana, Michigan, and Ohio* (Case Western Reserve Univ., 1971); Richard C. Davis, *North American Forest History: A Guide to Archives and Manuscripts in the United States and Canada* (Clio Books, 1977). Unpublished inventories, other finding aids, and guides to microfilm editions are available at the repository.

OH203-630
Ohio State University
Department of Photography and Cinema
156 West 19th Avenue
Columbus OH 43210

(614) 422-1766

OPEN: M-F 9-5; closed weekends and holidays
COPYING FACILITIES: yes
MATERIALS SOLICITED: Photographs illustrating the history and/or creative use of the medium.

HOLDINGS:
> *Total volume:* 6,000 items
> *Inclusive dates:* 1839 -
> *Description:* Photographs, including portraits of Indians, blacks, the aged, notable persons, and other individuals. There are also studies of the outdoors, occupations, hobbies, and afflictions.

Manuscript materials relating to the photographs include patents and biographical notes on 1,700 early daguerreotypists and 200 jobbers and manufacturers of photographic equipment.

GUIDES: *A Reference Guide to the Floyd and Marion Rinhart Collection of Daguerreian Art and Other Rare Photographic Images* (n.p., 1972).

SEE ALSO: Ann Novotny, ed., *Picture Sources 3* (Special Libraries Assn., 1975); Walter Johnson, 'Ohio State Acquires Pioneer Photo Collection,' *Ohio Archivist* 4 (Spring 1973).

OH203-650
Ohio State University
Libraries
Division of Special Collections
1858 Neil Avenue
Columbus OH 43210

(614) 422-5938

OPEN: M-F 9-5; closed weekends and holidays
COPYING FACILITIES: yes
MATERIALS SOLICITED: Literary and scientific papers. Will also accept faculty papers and similar materials with potential research interest.

HOLDINGS:
> *Total volume:* 600 l.f.
> *Inclusive dates:* 1830 -
> *Description:* Manuscripts, primarily literary and scientific in nature. Subjects covered include agriculture, botany, education, geology, and bibliography, primarily in 20th century Ohio.

SEE: Hamer; NUCMC, 1959-62.

OH203-670
Ohio State University
Jerome Lawrence and Robert E. Lee
  Theatre Research Institute
1089 Drake Union
1849 Cannon Drive
Columbus OH 43210

(614) 292-6614

OPEN: M-F 9-5; closed weekends, holidays, and between quarters
COPYING FACILITIES: yes
MATERIALS SOLICITED: American and European theater documents. Will also accept materials pertaining to local Columbus or Ohio theaters.

HOLDINGS:
> *Total volume:* 10,000 items
> *Inclusive dates:* 1450 -
> *Description:* Primarily microfilm copies of European theater documents, with heavy concentrations in English theater, 18th-19th centuries, and Italian and French theater, 15th-18th centuries. Included are reproductions of scene and costume designs; promptbooks; and materials on the Comedie-Francaise, Sadler's Wells, and the Burgtheater. Nonmicrofilm collections cover such former theatrical institutions in Ohio as the Harmount's Uncle Tom's Cabin Company, the Hartman Theatre of Columbus, and the scenic designs and records of the Armbruster Scenic Studio.

SEE ALSO: Alan Woods, 'A Survey of the Ohio State University Theatre Research Institute,' in Ted Perry, ed., *Performing Arts Resources* (Drama Book Specialists, 1975); articles and lists in *Theatre Studies*, 1954- , published by the Institute.

OH203-680
Ohio State University
University Archives
Converse Hall, Room 169
2121 Tuttle Park Place
Columbus OH 43210

(614) 422-2409

OPEN: M-F 8-5; closed weekends and holidays
COPYING FACILITIES: yes
MATERIALS SOLICITED: Materials relating to the history of Ohio State University, including its administration, faculty, students, and ancillary organizations. Will also accept materials relating to Starling Medical College, Ohio Medical University, Mortarboard, the Ohio Dietetic Association, the Columbus Dietetic Association, the Ohio State University Marching Band Alumni Association, and the North Central Sociological Association.

HOLDINGS:
> *Total volume:* 2,750 c.f.; 275,000 items
> *Inclusive dates:* 1848 -
> *Description:* Minutes, reports, office files, personal papers, sound recordings, publications, 275,000 photographs, and architectural drawings relating to Ohio State University and its involvement in education, research, and public service, 1870 to date. Also included are some registration records of Starling Medical College and the Ohio Medical University, precursors of Ohio State University's College of Medicine.

SEE: Hamer (as Ohio State University, Libraries).

SEE: Davis; Hinding; Larson; Novotny; Robbins.

DAYTON

OH223-160
Dayton and Montgomery County
  Public Library
Dayton Collection
215 East Third Street
Dayton OH 45402

(513) 224-1651

OPEN: M-F 9-9, Sa 9-6; closed Sundays and holidays
COPYING FACILITIES: yes

HOLDINGS:
> *Total volume:* 5,100 items
> *Inclusive dates:* 1728 - 1960
> *Description:* A collection of manuscripts relating chiefly to the economic, social, and political history of Dayton and Ohio in the 19th century. The collection includes diaries; correspondence; records of local government, businesses, and churches; and 2,100 photographs of the Dayton area, 1857-1960.

SEE: Hamer; NUCMC, 1966.

SEE ALSO: David R. Larson, ed., *Guide to Manuscripts Collections and Institutional Records in Ohio* (Society of Ohio Archivists, 1974); Edwin T. Layton, Jr., ed., *A Regional Union Catalog of Manuscripts Relating to the History of Science and Technology Located in Indiana, Michigan, and Ohio* (Case Western Reserve Univ., 1971); Albert Krichmar, *The Women's Rights Movement in the United States, 1848-1970: A Bibliography and Sourcebook* (Scarecrow Press, 1972).

OH223-520
Montgomery County Historical
  Society
7 North Main Street
Dayton OH 45402

(513) 228-6271

OPEN: Tu-F 10-4; closed weekends, Mondays, and holidays
ACCESS: advance arrangements required
COPYING FACILITIES: yes
MATERIALS SOLICITED: Dayton and Montgomery County items including manuscripts, papers from individuals, archives from non-governmental agencies, maps, photographs, motion pictures, and scrapbooks. Will also accept similar materials relating to the Miami Valley, as well as oral history tapes, sound recordings, and videotapes.

HOLDINGS:
> *Total volume:* 325 l.f.
> *Inclusive dates:* 1780 -
> *Description:* Materials relating to the Dayton and Montgomery County area. Included are records of organizations, such as social clubs and schools; papers of individuals; unpublished memoirs and diaries; and ephemera and photographs. Of particular interest are the Patterson Family Papers, records of the Dayton Manufacturing Company, and records of the Frigidaire Company.

SEE: NUCMC, 1959-61, 78 (as Associated Dayton and Montgomery County Historical Societies).

SEE: Hinding; Larson.

OH223-710
Sisters of the Precious Blood
Salem Heights Archives
4960 Salem Avenue
Dayton OH 45416

(513) 278-0871, Ext. 31

OPEN: M-F 9-3; closed weekends and holidays
ACCESS: appointment advisable
COPYING FACILITIES: yes
MATERIALS SOLICITED: Records and materials associated with the history, mission, and apostolate of the Sisters of the Precious Blood in the various areas in which they served.

HOLDINGS:
Total volume: 300 l.f.
Inclusive dates: 1833 -
Description: A collection of manuscripts and records on the founding of this religious community in Switzerland, its removal to America, and its work, especially in schools in Ohio and the Midwest.

SEE: Hinding.

OH223-720

Society of Mary
Province of Cincinnati
Archives
Box 472
University of Dayton
Dayton OH 45469

(513) 229-2724

OPEN: M-F 9-4; closed weekends, holidays, and vacations
COPYING FACILITIES: yes
MATERIALS SOLICITED: Records of Provincial offices. Will also accept material which deals with the Society of Mary or activities related to it.

HOLDINGS:
Total volume: 2,530 boxes
Inclusive dates: 1790 -
Description: Records and documents of the Province of Cincinnati, as well as missions overseas. Materials relating to missions include newsletters, reports from superiors, statistics, and records, covering such areas as France, Italy, Spain, Switzerland, Austria, Kenya, Australia, Peru, Argentina, Chile, Colombia, Japan, Korea, and Canada. Provincial materials include reports of meetings and documents on Marianist schools such as the University of Dayton. There are also microfilms, photographs, and letters relating to William Chaminade.

SEE: Duignan.

OH223-790

United Theological Seminary
Library
1810 Harvard Boulevard
Dayton OH 45406

(513) 278-5817, Ext. 118

OPEN: M-Th 8-10, F 8-5, Sa 12-4; closed Sundays and holidays; shorter hours June - Sept.
COPYING FACILITIES: yes
MATERIALS SOLICITED: Materials concerning the Evangelical United Brethren church and its predecessors, Methodist church materials, non-current records of the United Theological Seminary, and sound recordings of speeches made at the Seminary.

HOLDINGS:
Total volume: 100 l.f.
Inclusive dates: 1784 -
Description: The archives of the Evangelical United Brethren church and its predecessors, and materials relating to the several branches of the Methodist church, mainly in the United States. The collection contains periodicals; conference journals; annual yearbooks; records of the United Theological Seminary, colleges, overseas missions, hospitals, and other church institutions; sermons, diaries, correspondence, and other papers of clergy and educators; photographs; and tape recordings of speeches.

SEE: Hamer; NUCMC, 1966-67.

SEE: Larson; Schatz.

OH223-800

University of Dayton
Roesch Library
University Archives
College Park Avenue
Dayton OH 45469

(513) 229-4267, 4221

OPEN: M-F 8:30-4:30; closed weekends and holidays
COPYING FACILITIES: yes
MATERIALS SOLICITED: Materials relating to the University of Dayton, its faculty, students, and alumni.

HOLDINGS:
Total volume: 500 l.f.
Inclusive dates: 1850 -
Description: A collection of records of the University of Dayton, including departmental records; personal papers of faculty; publications of faculty, students, and departments; and other printed and manuscript materials. Most of the material is from the 20th century. There is also a collection of photographs of the University and oral history tapes of people connected with the University.

Also includes the archives of the Academic Library Association of Ohio and the Association for Creative Change.

SEE: NUCMC, 1978.

SEE: Robbins.

OH223-810

University of Dayton
Roesch Library
Wright Brothers-Charles F. Kettering Oral History Project
College Park Avenue
Dayton OH 45469-0001

(513) 229-4267, 4221

OPEN: M-F 8:30-4:30; closed weekends except by appointment, holidays, and holy days
COPYING FACILITIES: yes
MATERIALS SOLICITED: Will accept materials relating to the Wright brothers or Charles F. Kettering.

HOLDINGS:
Total volume: 1 l.f.
Inclusive dates: 1966 - 1967
Description: Tapes and typed transcripts of interviews with 22 associates of Orville and Wilbur Wright and Charles F. Kettering.

GUIDES: A master index to the collection is available at the Library.

OH223-880

Wright State University
Library
Department of Archives and Special Collections
Greater Miami Valley Research Center
Dayton OH 45435

(513) 873-2092

OPEN: M, Th, F 8-5, Tu, W 8-10, Su 2-5; closed Saturdays and holidays
COPYING FACILITIES: yes
MATERIALS SOLICITED: Materials relating to the history of the 11 county Miami Valley area of southwestern Ohio, and materials on early aviation and aeronautics prior to World War I. Will also accept aviation collections dealing with the post-World War I period.

HOLDINGS:
Total volume: 2,000 l.f.
Inclusive dates: 1750 -
Description: Over 150 collections, including archives of Wright State University; correspondence, diaries, scrapbooks and other private papers of individuals; records of businesses and service establishments; documents from commercial, civic, social, farm, and labor organizations; and photographs and maps concerning the history of aeronautics, the Miami Valley, and Ohio. Included are papers of the Wright brothers and James M. Cox; county and local government records from Montgomery, Greene, Clark, Champaign, Darke, Preble, Mercer, Shelby, Auglaize, Miami, and Logan counties; and records of 19th century agricultural equipment manufacturers and flood control projects.

Also records of several posts of the G.A.R., local unions of the International Union of Electrical Workers, Stereotypers & Electrotypers Union, Typographical Union, Barber's Union, Machinist's Union, and Teamsters Union.

Also papers of the Dayton Ballet Company, Dayton Council on World Affairs, Dayton-area Red Cross, Dayton Philharmonic, Dayton Socialist Party, the O. S. Kelly Co., the James Leffel & Co., Dayton Malleable Inc., and the Dayton and Springfield Urban Leagues.

SEE: NUCMC, 1978, 80.

SEE: Hinding.

SEE ALSO: David R. Larson, ed., *Guide to Manuscripts Collections and Institutional Records in Ohio* (Society of Ohio Archivists, 1974); *The Ohio Black History Guide* (Ohio Historical Society, 1975); Stephen E. Haller and Patrick B. Nolan, comps., *First Stop for Local History Research: A Guide to County Records Preserved at the Wright State Greater Miami Valley Research Center* (Wright State Univ., Greater Miami Valley Research Center, 1976).

DELAWARE

OH232-600
Ohio Wesleyan University
Library
Delaware OH 43015

no telephone

SEE: NUCMC, 1968.

Questionnaire not returned.

DOVER

OH237-160
Dover Historical Society
J. E. Reeves Home and Museum
325 East Iron Avenue
Dover OH 44622

(216) 343-7040

OPEN: June-Sept., Tu-Su 1-4; closed
   Mondays and rest of year
ACCESS: advance arrangements required
COPYING FACILITIES: no
MATERIALS SOLICITED: Manuscripts,
   records of institutions and organiza-
   tions, visual documents, audible docu-
   ments, and scrapbooks relating to
   Tuscarawas County.

HOLDINGS:
   Total volume: 16 l.f.
   Inclusive dates: 18th century -
   Description: Records, correspondence,
   account books, maps, deeds, manuscripts,
   pictures, and other materials pertaining to
   Tuscarawas County, OH.

SEE: Larson.

EAST CLEVELAND

OH246-200
East Cleveland Public Library
Main Branch
14101 Euclid Avenue
East Cleveland OH 44112

(216) 541-4128

OPEN: M-Th 9-8, F, Sa 9-5, Su
   1:30-5:30; closed holidays; different
   summer hours
COPYING FACILITIES: yes
MATERIALS SOLICITED: Will accept materials relating to East Cleveland history, organizations, agencies, and city
   government.

HOLDINGS:
   Total volume: one file cabinet
   Inclusive dates: 1867 - 1940
   Description: Typewritten compilations
   and transcripts of materials relating to
   East Cleveland history prepared by the
   Works Progress Administration. Included
   is information on early settlement and
   land titles, religious groups, organizations,
   educational institutions, libraries, city
   government, arts and crafts, authors,
   banking, cemeteries, hospitals, hotels, industry, commerce, development, merchants, military history, political history,
   and individuals' biographies.

SEE: Larson.

ELYRIA

OH266-200
Elyria Public Library
320 Washington Avenue
Elyria OH 44035

(216) 323-5747

OPEN: M-Th 9-8:30, F, Sa 9-5, Su 1-4;
   summers only, shorter Saturday hours
   and closed Sundays
ACCESS: advance arrangements required
COPYING FACILITIES: yes

HOLDINGS:
   Total volume: 15 l.f.
   Inclusive dates: 1798 - 1897
   Description: Record books of land
   transactions in early Elyria and personal
   papers of Herman Ely, consisting of
   record books, correspondence and genealogies. There are also photographs and
   maps relating to the history of Elyria.

SEE: NUCMC, 1959-61.

OH266-480
Lorain County Historical Society
509 Washington Avenue
Elyria OH 44035

(216) 322-3341

SEE: NUCMC, 1959-61.

Questionnaire not returned.

OH266-490
Lorain County Metropolitan Park
   District
8847 W. Ridge Road
Elyria OH 44035

(216) 322-7800

OPEN: M-F 8-5; closed weekends and
   holidays
COPYING FACILITIES: yes
MATERIALS SOLICITED: Will accept materials relating to local or State history.

HOLDINGS:
   Total volume: 5 l.f.
   Inclusive dates: 1800 -
   Description: Family papers, business
   records, and photographs documenting
   the history of Lorain County parklands.

FINDLAY

OH281-240
Findlay College
Library
100 North Main Street
Findlay OH 45840

no telephone

SEE: NUCMC, 1975.

Questionnaire not returned.

FREMONT

OH301-690
Rutherford B. Hayes Presidential
   Center
Rutherford B. Hayes Library
1337 Hayes Avenue
Fremont OH 43420

(419) 332-2081

OPEN: M-Sa 9-5; closed Sundays,
   Thanksgiving, Christmas, and New
   Year's
COPYING FACILITIES: yes
MATERIALS SOLICITED: Materials pertaining to Rutherford B. and Lucy W.
   Hayes and family members; other 19th
   century and early 20th century
   individuals in political, civil, or military life; and materials relating to State
   and local history, especially Fremont
   and the Sandusky Valley, and to existing special collections: the Frohman
   Theatre Collection, a Great Lakes collection, and a collection on William
   Dean Howells.

HOLDINGS:
   Total volume: 1,000,000 items;
   55,000 photographs
   Inclusive dates: 1676 -
   Description: Materials relating to the
   history of the United States during the
   second half of the 19th and early 20th
   centuries, focusing on such areas as the
   Civil War and Reconstruction, the
   Spanish-American War, civil service reform, transportation, cityscapes, monetary and prison reform, education, blacks,
   and Indians. Also materials relating to
   William Dean Howells, Ohio and local
   history, especially the Sandusky River
   Valley, and the Great Lakes.

SEE: Hamer; NUCMC, 1959-62, 69, 72,
   75.

SEE: Bean and Vane; Hines; Allard,
   Crawley, and Edmison; Parkinson;
   Robbins; Hinding.

SEE ALSO: Walter Schatz, ed., *Directory of
   Afro-American Resources* (Bowker,
   1970); Andrea D. Lentz, ed., *A Guide
   to Manuscripts at the Ohio Historical
   Society* (Ohio Historical Society, 1972);
   Ann Novotny, ed., *Picture Sources 3*
   (Special Libraries Assn., 1975); Edwin
   T. Layton, Jr., ed., *A Regional Union
   Catalog of Manuscripts Relating to the
   History of Science and Technology Lo-
   cated in Indiana, Michigan, and Ohio*
   (Case Western Reserve Univ., 1971).

GAMBIER

OH320-430
Kenyon College
Archives
Gambier OH 43022

(614) 427-2244

OPEN: M-F 9-noon; closed weekends,
   College vacations, and holidays
ACCESS: scholarly researchers
COPYING FACILITIES: yes

MATERIALS SOLICITED: Historical material relating to Kenyon College and Gambier.

HOLDINGS:
Total volume: 150 file drawers
Inclusive dates: 1796 -
Description: Manuscripts, photographs, records, and publications relating to Kenyon College, its divinity school Bexley Hall, other educational institutions in Gambier, and the village of Gambier; papers of Philander Chase and Charles Pettit McIlvaine; a complete file of manuscripts and other records of the *Kenyon Review;* tape recordings of readings by such poets as Robert Frost, Robert Lowell, and John Crowe Ransom; and materials on the early Episcopal church in Ohio.

SEE: Hamer; NUCMC, 1959-61.

SEE: Larson.

GRANVILLE

OH350-170
Denison University
W. H. Doane Library
Granville OH 43023

(614) 587-6215

OPEN: by appointment
ACCESS: permission of Library Director or University Archivist
COPYING FACILITIES: yes
MATERIALS SOLICITED: Records and memorabilia relating to the history of Denison University. Will also accept papers of alumni, particularly as they pertain to their lives at Denison.

HOLDINGS:
Total volume: 1,000 l.f.
Inclusive dates: 1830 -
Description: Letters and journals of alumni, and institutional records of Denison University.

SEE: NUCMC, 1959-61, 77.

SEE: Larson.

Diaries of Thomas Price and his sons, listed in NUCMC, 1961, have been transferred to the Ohio Historical Society in Columbus.

HAMILTON

OH360-80
Butler County Historical Society
Museum
327 North 2nd Street
Hamilton OH 45011

(513) 898-7111

SEE: NUCMC, 1962.

Questionnaire not returned.

OH360-480
Lane Public Library
Reference Department
North Third and Buckeye
Hamilton OH 45011

(513) 894-7156

OPEN: M-Th 9-9, F, Sa 9-5; closed holidays and Sundays
ACCESS: adult card holders
COPYING FACILITIES: yes
MATERIALS SOLICITED: Materials relating to Butler County.

HOLDINGS:
Total volume: not specified
Inclusive dates: 1800 -
Description: Biographical, legal, historical, and genealogical materials on Hamilton and Butler County, including manuscripts, diaries, and photographs.

HIRAM

OH370-310
Hiram College
Teachout-Price Memorial Library
College Archives
Hiram OH 44234

(216) 569-5361

OPEN: M-Th 9-4; closed Fridays, weekends, and holidays
ACCESS: permission of Archivist required; advance arrangements recommended
COPYING FACILITIES: yes
MATERIALS SOLICITED: Materials relating to Hiram College, Hiram Village and Township, James A. Garfield, Nicholas Vachel Lindsay, John S. Kenyon, and history of the Disciples of Christ in northeastern Ohio. Will also accept materials relating to the Western Reserve and to the Civil War in northeastern Ohio.

HOLDINGS:
Total volume: 336 l.f.
Inclusive dates: 1800 -
Description: Collections relating primarily to Hiram College, the village of Hiram, and Hiram Rapids. Included are journals, correspondence, papers, book manuscripts, records of churches and organizations, and materials on pioneers in the Western Reserve, an 1870 geologic survey, and the Civil War.

SEE: Hamer; NUCMC, 1966.

SEE: Larson; Robbins.

OH370-330
Hiram Township Historical Society
Hiram OH

MAILING ADDRESS:
P.O. Box 444
Hiram OH 44234

no telephone
SEE: NUCMC, 1976.

Questionnaire not returned.

JEFFERSON

OH394-320
Henderson Memorial Public Library
54 East Jefferson Street
Jefferson OH 44047

(216) 576-3761

OPEN: M, Tu, Th 9-8, W, F, Sa 9-5; closed Sundays and holidays
COPYING FACILITIES: yes
MATERIALS SOLICITED: Materials relating to the village of Jefferson and Jefferson Township, and Ashtabula County.

HOLDINGS:
Total volume: 4 l.f.; 26 microfilm reels
Inclusive dates: 1822 -
Description: Microfilm of local history and genealogical materials from Ashtabula County, including family papers, inscriptions in Bibles, and birth and death records; microfilm of estate records of the County probate court; and original tax records, photographs of Jefferson, and the daybook of the Warner Inn, 1822-23.

KALIDA

OH397-640
Putnam County Historical Society
Museum
Kalida OH

MAILING ADDRESS:
P.O. Box 264
Kalida OH 45853

(419) 453-3143

OPEN: W 9-10; June 1 - Sept. 15 Su 2-4; closed other days
ACCESS: appointment required
COPYING FACILITIES: yes
MATERIALS SOLICITED: Account books, record books, correspondence, diaries, journals, logbooks, genealogical information, and other manuscripts relating to the history of Putnam County. Will also accept other materials relating to Putnam County.

HOLDINGS:
Total volume: 5 l.f.
Inclusive dates: 1830 - 1900
Description: Materials relating to the early history of Putnam County, including correspondence, genealogical materials, account books, minute books of school board meetings, and other records.

SEE ALSO: Card file available at the institution.

KENT

OH399-420
Kent State University
Libraries
American History Research Center
Kent OH 44242

(216) 672-2411

OPEN: M-F 8-5; closed weekends and holidays
COPYING FACILITIES: yes

MATERIALS SOLICITED: Materials relating to local, State, and National history in the eight county area in the Center's jurisdiction.

HOLDINGS:
Total volume: 2,000 c.f.
Inclusive dates: 1792 -
Description: Materials relating to the eight county area in northeastern Ohio served by the Center. Included are records of the International Brotherhood of Pottery and Allied Workers, the Diocese of Youngstown, and county governments within the area. There are also papers of Representative Charles A. Mosher.
Also included are papers of the Parsons Lumber Company, Charles A. Mosher, Marcus A. Roberto, Jack Stukas, the Fuller Family, Giles Hooker Cowles, Betsy Mix Cowles, Edward A. Schultz, Joseph J. Craciun, and John Begala.

SEE: NUCMC, 1971.

SEE: Schatz; Parkinson; Hinding.

OH399-440
Kent State University
Libraries
Department of Special Collections
Kent OH 44242

(216) 672-2270

OPEN: M-F 8-5; closed weekends and holidays
COPYING FACILITIES: yes
MATERIALS SOLICITED: English and American literature in the 19th and 20th centuries, and theater and motion picture history. Will also accept other materials.

HOLDINGS:
Total volume: 280 l.f.
Inclusive dates: 1800 -
Description: Materials relating to English literature, American literature, the theater, cryptography, and Queen Marie of Romania. Included are papers relating to Hector Bolitho, Constance Holme, James Stephens, Hart Crane, Robert Duncan, Logan Pearsall Smith, Gary Snyder, William Carlos Williams, Joseph Chaiken, Jean Claude van Itallie, the Open Theater, and the Cincinnati Playhouse in the Park.

SEE: NUCMC, 1971.

SEE: Larson; Robbins.

OH399-450
Kent State University
Libraries
University Archives
Kent OH 44242

(216) 672-2411

OPEN: M-F 8-5; closed weekends and holidays
COPYING FACILITIES: yes
MATERIALS SOLICITED: History of Kent State University and the history of student unrest.

HOLDINGS:
Total volume: 1,175 c.f.
Inclusive dates: 1910 -
Description: Materials pertaining to the history of the University, and to student unrest at other universities in 1969 and 1970. Holdings are primarily non-printed materials such as office files and the personal papers of faculty members.
May 4th Collection consists principally of sources such as personal papers, committee files, and ephemera.

SEE: Larson; Hinding.

LAKEWOOD

OH426-470
Lakewood Historical Society
Old Stone House Museum
14710 Lake Avenue
Lakewood OH

MAILING ADDRESS:
1200 Andrews Avenue
Lakewood OH 44107

(216) 221-7343

OPEN: W, Su 2-5; closed other days and holidays
ACCESS: by appointment to qualified researchers
COPYING FACILITIES: no
MATERIALS SOLICITED: Lakewood history. Will also accept genealogical materials on early Lakewood families.

HOLDINGS:
Total volume: 3 c.f.
Inclusive dates: 1850 -
Description: Correspondence relating to the formation of the Lakewood Historical Society, and publication of two books on Lakewood and the Western Reserve; reminiscences of early Lakewood families; account books; personal letters relating to the settling of Rockport; photographs; and oral history tapes.

SEE: Larson.

OH426-490
Lakewood Public Library
15425 Detroit Avenue
Lakewood OH 44107

(216) 226-8275

OPEN: M-F 9-9, Sa 9-6; closed Sundays and holidays
COPYING FACILITIES: yes
MATERIALS SOLICITED: Materials relating to Lakewood.

HOLDINGS:
Total volume: 1.5 l.f.
Inclusive dates: 19th century -
Description: Photographs of the city of Lakewood and Rockport Township in Cuyahoga County.

SEE: Larson.

LEBANON

OH436-880
Warren County Historical Society Museum
Historical and Genealogical Library
105 South Broadway
Lebanon OH

MAILING ADDRESS:
P.O. Box 223
Lebanon OH 45036

(513) 932-1817

OPEN: Tu-Sa 9-4, Su 12-4; closed Mondays and holidays
USER FEES: one dollar daily or $5 annually
COPYING FACILITIES: yes
MATERIALS SOLICITED: Manuscripts relating to Warren County and surrounding areas, especially genealogical and cemetery records. Will also accept photographs of local historical interest.

HOLDINGS:
Total volume: 177 c.f.
Inclusive dates: 1790 -
Description: Materials relating primarily to Warren County, including vital, land, and probate records; genealogical and cemetery records; church, school, and other organization records; diaries; ledgers; and photographs.

SEE: NUCMC, 1959-61.

SEE ALSO: David R. Larson, ed., *Guide to Manuscripts Collections and Institutional Records in Ohio* (Society of Ohio Archivists, 1974); Edwin T. Layton, Jr., ed., *A Regional Union Catalog of Manuscripts Relating to the History of Science and Technology Located in Indiana, Michigan, and Ohio* (Case Western Reserve Univ., 1971).

LEETONIA

OH441-480
Leetonia Public Library
24 East Walnut Street
Leetonia OH 44431

no telephone
SEE: NUCMC, 1976.

Questionnaire not returned.

LEXINGTON

OH446-690
Richland County Genealogical Society
Richland County Museum
51 West Church Street
Lexington OH

MAILING ADDRESS:
P.O. Box 3154
Lexington OH 44904

no telephone

OPEN: May 1 - Oct. 31, Sa, Su 1-4; closed other days
COPYING FACILITIES: no

HOLDINGS:
Total volume: not specified
Inclusive dates: not specified
Description: Photographs of County life in the 19th and 20th centuries and genealogical source data, including notations taken from tombstones throughout the County.

LIMA

OH451-40

Allen County Historical Society
Allen County Museum
620 West Market Street
Lima OH 45801

(419) 222-9426

OPEN: Tu-Su 1:30-5; closed Mondays and holidays
COPYING FACILITIES: yes
MATERIALS SOLICITED: Materials relating to Allen County and Ohio history, railroads and inter-urban transportation, railroad labor unions, and the Lima Locomotive Works.

HOLDINGS:
Total volume: not specified
Inclusive dates: 1840 -
Description: Materials relating to the history of Allen County and Ohio, including genealogical items. Special emphases include records, photographs, and other documents of the Lima Locomotive Works, as well as materials relating to railroads and railroad labor unions within the United States.

SEE: Larson.

LORAIN

OH471-480

Lorain Public Library
351 Sixth Street
Lorain OH 44052

(216) 244-1192

OPEN: M-Th 9-8:30, F, Sa 9-6; closed Sundays and holidays
COPYING FACILITIES: yes
MATERIALS SOLICITED: Typewritten manuscripts pertaining to the history, genealogy, and ethnic heritage of the Lorain area, local history scrapbooks, and Lorain area photographs. Will also accept literary manuscripts of local authors, visual and audible documents of research value pertaining to Lorain County, and Lorain area genealogical source data.

HOLDINGS:
Total volume: 33 c.f.
Inclusive dates: 1900 -
Description: Historical and genealogical materials relating to Lorain County and the city of Lorain.

SEE: Larson.

MANSFIELD

OH481-530

Mansfield-Richland County Public Library
43 West Third Street
Mansfield OH 44902

(419) 524-1041

OPEN: M-F 9-9, Sa 9-5:30; closed Sundays, holidays, and Saturdays June - Aug.
COPYING FACILITIES: yes
MATERIALS SOLICITED: Materials relating to John Sherman and local history and genealogy.

HOLDINGS:
Total volume: not specified
Inclusive dates: 1839 - 1950
Description: Papers of John Sherman, including correspondence with William Tecumseh Sherman, Nelson A. Miles, James A. Garfield, and William McKinley relating to the election of 1872, politics, slavery, social affairs, and personal business; correspondence relating to the gift of Sherman materials to the Library; drafts of Sherman's speeches on Andrew Johnson's impeachment; student compositions on mathematics; and checks. There are also circuit court records; records of the Greystone Night Club; minutes of the Security Savings and Loan Company; and minutes and annual reports of the Library.

OH481-610

Ohio Genealogical Society
Library
419 West Third Street
Mansfield OH

MAILING ADDRESS:
P.O. Box 2625
Mansfield OH 44906

(419) 522-9077

OPEN: Tu, Th, Sa 9-3; closed other days and holidays
COPYING FACILITIES: yes
MATERIALS SOLICITED: Genealogical material, including manuscripts, family generation charts, county court records, and deeds.

HOLDINGS:
Total volume: not specified
Inclusive dates: 1820 -
Description: Genealogical source data on Ohio families, and court records from Crawford and Richland counties.

MARIETTA

OH486-510

Marietta College
Dawes Memorial Library
Marietta OH 45750

(614) 374-4757

OPEN: by appointment only
COPYING FACILITIES: yes
MATERIALS SOLICITED: Materials on the history of Marietta, and the Ohio Company of Associates (1786-95). Will also accept literary manuscripts and other materials, especially from local individuals and alumni.

HOLDINGS:
Total volume: 35,000 items
Inclusive dates: 1475 -
Description: Materials, chiefly 1760-1865, relating for the most part to the Northwest Territory and Ohio, especially the Marietta region. Included are the records of the Ohio Company of Associates and the papers of such individuals as Rufus Putnam, Samuel Prescott Hildreth, and Ephraim and William Parker Cutler. The Library also houses the Charles Gates Dawes and Charles Goddard Slack collections of autograph letters, as well as the College archives. Also included are 14,000 photographic plates of Ohio steamboats and early 20th century Marietta scenes and persons, and a mid-20th century photograph collection.

SEE: Hamer.

SEE ALSO: George Jordan Blazier, *The Cutler Collection of Letters and Documents: 1748-1925* (Marietta College, 1963).

OH486-660

Ohio Historical Society
Campus Martius Museum
601 Second Street
Marietta OH 45750

(614) 373-3750

OPEN: M-Sa 10-4:30; closed Sundays and holidays
USER FEES: $1.50; members of Ohio Historical Society free
ACCESS: advance arrangements requested
COPYING FACILITIES: yes
MATERIALS SOLICITED: Materials pertinent to the early settlement of Marietta and the Northwest Territory, as well as materials relating to the history of the Ohio River.

HOLDINGS:
Total volume: 1,000 items
Inclusive dates: 1720 -
Description: Collections consist primarily of documents and correspondence pertaining to the early settlement of Marietta, Ohio, in 1788, and material pertaining to Blennerhassett Island.

SEE: Hamer.

OH486-890

Washington County Public Library
615 Fifth Street
Marietta OH 45750

(614) 373-1057

OPEN: M-F 9-8:30, Sa 9-5; closed Sundays and holidays
COPYING FACILITIES: yes
MATERIALS SOLICITED: Materials relating to southeastern Ohio, especially Marietta and Washington County. Will also accept certain family genealogies.

HOLDINGS:
Total volume: 250 sq. f.
Inclusive dates: 19th century -
Description: Records and accounts of the Marietta Library Association; a manuscript map of Washington County cemeteries where Revolutionary War veterans are buried; photographs of early Marietta and Washington County; and scrapbooks relating to local events of historical and current interest, compiled 1950-74.

Martins Ferry

OH495-510
Martins Ferry Area Historical Society
Sedgwick Museum
627 Hanover Street
Martins Ferry OH 43935

no telephone

OPEN: Su 2-5 or by appointment; closed other days and holidays
USER FEES: 50 cents for non-members
COPYING FACILITIES: no
MATERIALS SOLICITED: Materials pertaining to Martins Ferry and environs: photographs, organization and business records. Will also accept similar materials pertaining to other parts of the county and to southern Jefferson County.

HOLDINGS:
Total volume: not specified
Inclusive dates: 1830 -
Description: A small collection concerned with the Martins Ferry area, consisting of letters, photographs, records of a stove manufacturing company (1880-1937), and a drugstore prescription file from the early 1900's.

Marysville

OH500-800
Union County Historical Society
246 West 6th Street
Marysville OH 43040

no telephone

SEE: NUCMC, 1976.

Questionnaire not returned.

Massillon

OH505-510
The Massillon Museum
212 Lincoln Way East
Massillon OH 44646

(216) 833-4061

OPEN: Su 2-5, Tu-Sa 9:30-5; closed Mondays and holidays
ACCESS: scholarly researchers; by appointment only
COPYING FACILITIES: yes
MATERIALS SOLICITED: Massillon history.

HOLDINGS:
Total volume: 40 l.f.
Inclusive dates: 1800 -
Description: A collection of manuscripts related to the history of Massillon business, families, and social and political growth. Included are business records, papers and journals of individuals, genealogical information, records of organizations and schools, city government records, and photographs encompassing all above areas.

SEE: Hinding.

SEE ALSO: David R. Larson, ed., *Guide to Manuscripts Collections and Institutional Records in Ohio* (Society of Ohio Archivists, 1974); David W. Palmquist, 'Jacob Coxey Marches Again in Massillon,' *The Ohio Archivist* 3 (Fall 1972).

OH505-520
Massillon Public Library
208 Lincoln Way East
Massillon OH 44646

(216) 832-9831

OPEN: M-Sa 9:30-9; closed Sundays and holidays
ACCESS: restricted to upper class college students, graduate students, and other serious scholars; advance arrangements required
COPYING FACILITIES: yes
MATERIALS SOLICITED: Will accept material relating to history of Massillon and Stark County.

HOLDINGS:
Total volume: 22 l.f.
Inclusive dates: 1780 - 1882
Description: Family papers of Thomas Rotch, Arvine Wales, and his son, Arvine C. Wales, including materials pertaining to Quakers and antislavery activities; whaling and shipping in Nantucket and New Bedford, MA; sheep raising and woolen manufacturing in Hartford, CT; and the founding and early history of Kendal (now Massillon). The Library also has the minutes of the Kendal Society, a local Owenite community (1826-1829).

SEE: NUCMC, 1972.

SEE ALSO: Edwin T. Layton, Jr., ed., *A Regional Union Catalog of Manuscripts Relating to the History of Science and Technology Located in Indiana, Michigan, and Ohio* (Case Western Reserve Univ., 1971).

Medina

OH530-240
Medina District Public Library
210 South Broadway
Medina OH

MAILING ADDRESS:
P.O. Box 306
Medina OH 44256

(216) 725-0588

OPEN: M 9-8:30, Sa 9-4; closed other times
COPYING FACILITIES: yes

MATERIALS SOLICITED: Materials pertaining to Medina County including photographs, letters, diaries, maps, advertising, newspapers, personal accounts, genealogical material, public records, and documents.

HOLDINGS:
Total volume: 25 c.f.; 2 file cabinets
Inclusive dates: 1818 -
Description: Correspondence, journals, genealogical source data, photographs, and oral history tapes dealing with Medina County history.

The collections belong to the Medina County Historical Society and are on deposit at the Sylvester Public Library.

Middletown

OH545-530
Middletown Public Library
Ohio Section
Genealogy Room
125 South Broad
Middletown OH 45044

(513) 424-1251

OPEN: M-F 9-8:30, Sa 9-4; closed Sundays and holidays
COPYING FACILITIES: yes
MATERIALS SOLICITED: Materials relating to Middletown and Butler County. Will also accept materials relating to Ohio.

HOLDINGS:
Total volume: 4 l.f.
Inclusive dates: 1830 -
Description: A collection relating chiefly to the history of Butler County and the Middletown area. Included are photographs of the 1913 flood, material on the Miami-Erie Canal, historical papers on nearby towns, business records, local church histories, family histories, and unpublished memoirs.

SEE: Larson.

Milan

OH550-200
Edison Birthplace Museum
9 North Edison Drive
Milan OH 44846

(419) 499-2135

SEE: Hamer; NUCMC, 1976.

Questionnaire not returned.

MOUNT PLEASANT

OH588-520

Mount Pleasant Historical Center
Mount Pleasant OH 43939

(614) 769-2921

OPEN: summer, Su 12-5; other times by appointment
COPYING FACILITIES: no
MATERIALS SOLICITED: Materials relating to Quakers; the first silk mill in Ohio; the underground railroad; the antislavery newspaper *The Philanthropist* and its printer, Benjamin Lundy; the Free Labor Association; and the Mount Pleasant area.

HOLDINGS:
> *Total volume:* several hundred items
> *Inclusive dates:* 1795 -
> *Description:* Materials relating chiefly to the Mount Pleasant area. Included are land deeds and charters, letters and diaries of local residents, photographs, school records, genealogical materials, and ledgers and account books relating to coal mining, medical practice, industry, and disease cures for both humans and animals.

SEE ALSO: David R. Larson, ed., *Guide to Manuscripts Collections and Institutional Records in Ohio* (Society of Ohio Archivists, 1974): as Mount Pleasant Historical Society; Edwin T. Layton, Jr., ed., *A Regional Union Catalog of Manuscripts Relating to the History of Science and Technology Located in Indiana, Michigan, and Ohio* (Case Western Reserve Univ., 1971): as The Historical Society of Mount Pleasant.

MT. ST. JOSEPH

OH593-720

Sisters of Charity of Cincinnati, Ohio
Mt. St. Joseph Motherhouse
Delhi Road
Mt. St. Joseph OH 45051

(513) 244-4624

OPEN: M-F 8:30-4; closed weekends, holidays, and holy days
ACCESS: advance arrangements and identification required
COPYING FACILITIES: yes
MATERIALS SOLICITED: Materials relating to the Sisters of Charity in Ohio, Michigan, Colorado, and New Mexico.

HOLDINGS:
> *Total volume:* 500 l.f.
> *Inclusive dates:* 1829 -
> *Description:* Manuscripts relating to the Sisters of Charity in Ohio, Michigan, Colorado, and New Mexico. Included are biographies of individual sisters, a photograph collection, and research papers on early education and health care in these states.

SEE: Larson.

NAVARRE

OH603-560

Navarre-Bethlehem Township Historical Society
Archives
8561 Bender Street
Navarre OH

MAILING ADDRESS:
P.O. Box 491
Navarre OH 44662

no telephone

OPEN: by appointment
COPYING FACILITIES: yes
MATERIALS SOLICITED: Correspondence, diaries, oral histories, photographs, manuscript maps, and engineering drawings relating to the history of Navarre, Bethlehem Township, or Stark County; and records and papers concerning Christian Frederick Post, a Moravian missionary, and William McKinley's law practice in Navarre, beginning in 1869.

HOLDINGS:
> *Total volume:* 4 items
> *Inclusive dates:* 1761 - 1939
> *Description:* Material relating to the history of the Navarre area, including a family history, voting records, and records of social organizations.
> Also includes photographs by William Bennett (1850's-1900's).

NORTH BALTIMORE

OH646-560

North Baltimore Public Library
230 North Main Street
North Baltimore OH 45872

(419) 257-3621

OPEN: M, W 9-9, Tu, Th-Sa 10-6; closed Sundays and holidays
COPYING FACILITIES: yes
MATERIALS SOLICITED: History of the late 19th and early 20th century oil boom in northwestern Ohio. Will also accept any oral history related items dealing with northwestern Ohio.

HOLDINGS:
> *Total volume:* 64 items
> *Inclusive dates:* not specified
> *Description:* Oral history tapes and transcripts documenting life in the oil boom days of northwestern Ohio during the late 19th and early 20th centuries.

SEE: Larson.

NORWALK

OH660-240

Fire Lands Historical Society
4 Case Street
Norwalk OH 44857

(419) 668-6038

SEE: Hamer.

Questionnaire not returned.

OH660-560

Norwalk Public Library
46 West Main
Norwalk OH 44857

(419) 668-6063

OPEN: M-Th 9:30-8:30, F 9:30-5:30, Sa 9:30-5; closed Sundays and holidays
COPYING FACILITIES: yes
MATERIALS SOLICITED: Materials on Norwalk and Huron County. Will also accept other materials.

HOLDINGS:
> *Total volume:* 15 items
> *Inclusive dates:* 1905 -
> *Description:* Typewritten manuscripts on family and local history, and photographs of the library building and personnel.

OBERLIN

OH665-580

Oberlin College
Archives
420 Mudd Learning Center
Oberlin OH 44074

(216) 775-8285, Ext. 247

OPEN: M-F 8-4:30; closed weekends and holidays
COPYING FACILITIES: yes
MATERIALS SOLICITED: Records reflecting the development of Oberlin College and the town of Oberlin. Will also accept records of persons connected with Oberlin and some records relating to the Oberlin area.

HOLDINGS:
> *Total volume:* 1,600 c.f.
> *Inclusive dates:* 1800 -
> *Description:* Records relating to Oberlin College and the town of Oberlin. Included are materials on movements with which Oberlin has been associated, such as missions, the antislavery movement, and temperance. There are also personal papers of faculty, graduates, and other Oberlin-related individuals; municipal government records of the town of Oberlin; and photographs of the College and the town.

SEE: Hamer (as Oberlin College Library); NUCMC, 1962, 66, 70-71, 74, 76, 80.

SEE: Schatz; Larson; Novotny; Hinding.

OH665-590

Oberlin College
Library
Oberlin OH 44074

(216) 775-8285

OPEN: winter, M-F 8-4:30; summer, M-F 12-4:30; closed weekends and holidays
COPYING FACILITIES: yes
MATERIALS SOLICITED: Will accept all materials, especially those relating to the antislavery movement and Oberlin College.

HOLDINGS:
Total volume: 5 l.f.
Inclusive dates: 19th century -
Description: Journals of Dan Beach Bradley, missionary to Siam, and records of Congregational churches in Ohio.

SEE: NUCMC, 1962 (Dan Beach Bradley papers only).

SEE: Spalek; Robbins.

OTTAWA

OH675-640
Putnam County District Library
364 East Main Street
Ottawa OH 45875

(419) 523-3747

OPEN: M-Th 10-8, F 10-6, Sa 9-5; closed Sundays and holidays
COPYING FACILITIES: yes

HOLDINGS:
Total volume: not specified
Inclusive dates: 1924 -
Description: Minute books and ledgers of the board of trustees of the Putnam County District Library, and a few local family histories.

SEE: Larson.

OXFORD

OH680-540
Miami University
King Library
Walter Havighurst Special Collections
Oxford, OH 45056

(513) 529-2537

OPEN: M-F 9-4; closed weekends and holidays; variable hours during university vacations
ACCESS: advance arrangements recommended
COPYING FACILITIES: yes
MATERIALS SOLICITED: Materials relating to Benjamin Harrison, William Henry Harrison, and their associates. Will also accept any items relating to current holdings.

HOLDINGS:
Total volume: 84 l.f.
Inclusive dates: 1810 - 1953
Description: Railroad scrapbooks, and collections relating to the following individuals: Robert C. Schenck, William H. McGuffey, John H. James, Robert H. Bishop, Samuel F. Covington, Jefferson Davis, William Dean Howells, Matthew Prior, and Burton L. French.

SEE: Hamer; NUCMC, 1959-61, 71.

SEE: Larson; Robbins.

PAINESVILLE

OH684-520
Morley Library
Genealogical Collection
184 Phelps Street
Painesville OH 44077

(216) 352-3383

OPEN: M-Th 9:30-8:30, F 9:30-6, Sa 9:30-5; closed Sundays and holidays, and Saturdays in summer
COPYING FACILITIES: yes
MATERIALS SOLICITED: Materials on Ohio and genealogy.

HOLDINGS:
Total volume: not specified
Inclusive dates: 19th century -
Description: Family histories and personal reminiscences, cemetery records, marriage records, and township records, relating to Lake County and the surrounding area.

SEE: Larson.

PIQUA

OH709-240
Flesh Public Library
124 West Greene
Piqua OH 45356

(513) 773-6753

OPEN: M-Th 9-8:30, F, Sa 9-5:30; closed Sundays and holidays
COPYING FACILITIES: yes
MATERIALS SOLICITED: Family genealogies relating to the Piqua area.

HOLDINGS:
Total volume: 9 c.f.
Inclusive dates: 1847 -
Description: Materials relating to Piqua, including oral history tapes, diaries, correspondence, photographs, and family genealogies.

SEE: NUCMC, 1976.

SEE: Larson.

POMEROY

OH714-510
Meigs County Pioneer and Historical Society
Meigs County Museum
144 Butternut Avenue
Pomeroy OH

MAILING ADDRESS:
Box 145
Pomeroy OH 45769

(614) 992-3810, 2264

OPEN: by appointment only
USER FEES: one dollar or membership
ACCESS: advance permission required
COPYING FACILITIES: no
MATERIALS SOLICITED: History and genealogy of Meigs County.

HOLDINGS:
Total volume: 30 l.f.; 1 file cabinet
Inclusive dates: 1850 -
Description: Materials documenting the history of Meigs County, including a manuscript history of the area around the Pomeroy Bend of the Ohio River; a manuscript history of local churches; a list of cemeteries; diaries; county government and business records; and 400 photographs.

PORTSMOUTH

OH724-630
Portsmouth Public Library
1220 Gallia Street
Portsmouth OH 45662

(614) 354-5688

OPEN: M-F 9-8, Sa 9-5:30; closed Sundays and holidays
COPYING FACILITIES: yes
MATERIALS SOLICITED: Will accept local history, Ohio history, and Northwest Territory materials.

HOLDINGS:
Total volume: 15 l.f.
Inclusive dates: 1846 -
Description: A collection of institutional records, personal manuscripts, and scrapbooks relating chiefly to Scioto County.

SEE: Larson.

RAVENNA

OH733-690
Reed Memorial Library
167 East Main Street
Ravenna OH 44266

(216) 296-2827

OPEN: M-F 10-9, Sa 10-6; closed Sundays and holidays
COPYING FACILITIES: yes

HOLDINGS:
Total volume: 3 items
Inclusive dates: 1830 -
Description: Proceedings of the Ravenna Temperance Society (1830-34); board minutes of the Reed Memorial Library; and a history of the Reed Memorial Library.

SALEM

OH753-720
Salem Public Library
821 East State Street
Salem OH 44460

no telephone

SEE: NUCMC, 1977.

Questionnaire not returned.

SIDNEY

OH778-40

Amos Memorial Public Library
230 East North Street
Sidney OH 45365

(513) 492-8354

OPEN: M-F 9-9, Sa 9-6; summers, M-Th, Sa 9-6, F 9-9; closed Sundays, New Year's, and Martin Luther King's birthday
COPYING FACILITIES: yes
MATERIALS SOLICITED: Photographs and oral history pertaining to Shelby County, and materials relating to west-central Ohio counties and people. Will also accept family histories and genealogies of the Shelby County area.

HOLDINGS:
Total volume: 3,500 items
Inclusive dates: 1620 -
Description: Materials relating to Ohio, focusing on west-central Ohio and Shelby County. Included are manuscripts, census records, military records, court records, ship passenger lists, and genealogical materials. Some of the genealogical material contains information on Pennsylvania, Virginia, New England, and New Jersey.

SEE: NUCMC, 1976.

SPRINGFIELD

OH788-120

Clark County Historical Society
Memorial Hall
300 West Main Street
Springfield OH 45504

(513) 324-0657

OPEN: Tu-F 9-4, Sa 9-1; closed Sundays, Mondays, and holidays
USER FEES: 50 cents per item removed from storage
COPYING FACILITIES: yes
MATERIALS SOLICITED: Anything pertaining to Clark County history. Will also accept other materials if they pertain to a long-established family of the area.

HOLDINGS:
Total volume: 150 l.f.
Inclusive dates: 1730 -
Description: Materials relating chiefly to Clark County, including 18th century land grants, diaries, letters, deeds, recipes for home remedies, and documents on the Civil War.

SEE: NUCMC, 1976.
SEE: Larson.

OH788-600

Lutheran Church in America
Ohio Synod
Archives
Thomas Library
Wittenberg University
Springfield OH

MAILING ADDRESS:
P.O. Box 720
Springfield OH 45501

(513) 327-7528, 7511

OPEN: by appointment only
COPYING FACILITIES: yes
MATERIALS SOLICITED: Materials on all defunct Lutheran congregations in Ohio and on pastors sometime active in Ohio. Will also accept materials on Lutheran history in Ohio, Indiana, Kentucky, and Michigan, particularly early hymnbooks.

HOLDINGS:
Total volume: 58 l.f.
Inclusive dates: 1847 -
Description: Records of Lutheran congregations and synodical bodies of Ohio, particularly those that formed the Ohio Synod of the Lutheran Church in America. Included are congregational record books, congregational histories, synodical histories, and minutes of the East Ohio Synod, Miami Synod, Wittenberg Synod, and Ohio Synod.

SEE: Larson.

OH788-870

Warder Public Library
137 East High Street
Springfield OH 45501

(513) 323-8616

OPEN: Su 1-5, M-F 9-9, Sa 9-6; closed holidays
COPYING FACILITIES: yes
MATERIALS SOLICITED: Lois Lenski materials.

HOLDINGS:
Total volume: 7 l.f.
Inclusive dates: 20th century
Description: Materials relating to or by Lois Lenski, including manuscripts, papers, drawings, and Christmas cards.

SEE: NUCMC, 1970.
SEE: Robbins.

OH788-880

Wittenberg University
Archives
Thomas Library
Springfield OH

MAILING ADDRESS:
P.O. Box 720

(513) 327-7514, 7511

OPEN: M-F 8-5; closed weekends and holidays
COPYING FACILITIES: yes

HOLDINGS:
Total volume: 150 l.f.
Inclusive dates: 1845 -
Description: Diaries, scrapbooks, sermons, and correspondence of early Wittenberg presidents; miscellaneous minutes, record books, and correspondence of early organizations and departments on campus; photographs of buildings, grounds, individuals, and organizations; and official records of Wittenberg College, 1845-1900.

SEE ALSO: David R. Larson, ed., Guide to Manuscripts Collections and Institutional Records in Ohio (Society of Ohio Archivists, 1974).

SWANTON

OH803-720

Swanton Public Library
305 Chestnut Street
Swanton OH 43558

(419) 826-2760

OPEN: M, W, F 12-8:30, Tu 10-4:30, Th 10-1, Sa 10-3:30; closed Sundays and holidays
COPYING FACILITIES: yes

HOLDINGS:
Total volume: 3 vols.; 1 file drawer
Inclusive dates: 1841 -
Description: Civil court dockets for Swanton and Fulton townships, 1841-90, and photographs of Fulton and Lucas counties.

TALLMADGE

OH808-760

Tallmadge Historical Society
594 North East Avenue
Tallmadge OH 44278

no telephone

SEE: NUCMC, 1962.

Questionnaire not returned.

TIFFIN

OH813-310

Heidelberg College
Archives
Tiffin OH 44883

(419) 448-2269, 2000

OPEN: by appointment during academic year
COPYING FACILITIES: yes
MATERIALS SOLICITED: Materials on the history of Heidelberg College, 1850 to present.

HOLDINGS:
Total volume: 250 c.f.
Inclusive dates: 1820 -
Description: Church records relating to the German Reformed church, other Reformed churches, and the Evangelical church in the United States, including classis minutes, statistical reports, yearbooks, mission reports, and correspon-

dence; and materials relating to Heidelberg College, including photographs, presidential papers, records of student activities, financial records, student theses, materials relating to the 1950 College centennial celebration, library records, student personnel records, and publications. Some of the early material is in German.

TOLEDO

OH823-750

Toledo-Lucas County Public Library
Local History Department
325 Michigan Street
Toledo OH 43624

(419) 255-7055, Ext. 233

OPEN: M-Th 9-9, F, Sa 9-5:30; closed Sundays, holidays, and Saturdays during summer
COPYING FACILITIES: yes
MATERIALS SOLICITED: Materials relating to Toledo and Lucas County history, 1815- , and regional Ohio history. Will also accept genealogical materials.

HOLDINGS:
    Total volume: 300 l.f.
    Inclusive dates: 1800 -
    Description: Personal papers, organization records, and other materials, relating chiefly to the development of the Toledo area. Collections focus on pioneer history, the War of 1812, the Civil War, and 19th and early 20th century urban development. Progressive reform materials, including the papers of Samuel 'Golden Rule' Jones, are of special interest. Some 3,000 photographs and 19th century manuscript maps document urban growth. About 35 oral history interviews relate to social, ethnic, industrial, and black history of the Maumee Valley area.

SEE: Hamer; NUCMC, 1966-67, 75, 77.

SEE: Hinding; Robbins.

SEE ALSO: unpublished manuscript and oral history inventories available from the Library.

OH823-770

Toledo Museum of Art
George W. Stevens Collection
2445 Monroe Street
Toledo OH

MAILING ADDRESS:
Box 1013
Toledo OH 43697

(419) 255-8000

OPEN: Su 1-5, Tu-Sa 9-5; closed Mondays and holidays
ACCESS: appointment required
COPYING FACILITIES: yes

HOLDINGS:
    Total volume: 54 items
    Inclusive dates: 1780 - 1908
    Description: Autograph letters and notes of various American and European artists and of George Washington. Included is the manuscript of Charles Meryon's *Mes observations* and over 30 letters by

Meryon contained in *Journal et correspondence artistique*, 1865-67.

SEE: Hamer; NUCMC, 1963-64.

SEE: Martin.

OH823-800

University of Toledo
William S. Carlson Library, Ward M. Canaday Center, and University of Toledo Archives
2801 West Bancroft Street
Toledo OH 43606

(419) 537-2170, 2443

OPEN: M-F 8-5; closed weekends and holidays
COPYING FACILITIES: yes
MATERIALS SOLICITED: Local history items; manuscripts of political, literary, and business leaders; papers of black poets; and archival materials of the University of Toledo. Will also accept veterans' materials, such as papers of Lucas County war veterans.

HOLDINGS:
    Total volume: 677 l.f.
    Inclusive dates: 1497 -
    Description: Letters of American historical figures, such as colonial governors, signers of the Declaration of Independence, Presidents, military leaders in the Revolutionary War, scientists, leaders in the women's rights movement, writers, and black poets. Also included are the archives of the University of Toledo.

SEE: Robbins.

SEE ALSO: *University Archives: Report of Holdings* (Univ. of Toledo Libraries, 1970).

UNIVERSITY HEIGHTS

OH843-400

John Carroll University
Grasselli Library
20700 North Park Boulevard
University Heights OH 44118

(216) 397-4234

OPEN: daily 8-5; closed weekends and holidays during vacations; shorter summer hours
ACCESS: permission of Director required
COPYING FACILITIES: yes
MATERIALS SOLICITED: Memorabilia, autographs, and correspondence relating to G. K. Chesterton. Will also accept materials relating to Hilaire Belloc, the Jesuit community in Cleveland, and John Carroll University.

HOLDINGS:
    Total volume: 1,050 items; 42 l.f.
    Inclusive dates: 1869 -
    Description: Materials relating to G. K. Chesterton, including correspondence, notebooks, manuscripts, typescripts, drawings, sketches, and a tape recording of a speech. There are also manuscripts of Frederick Louis Odenbach, and the University archives, including academic records and alumni and administrative files.

SEE: NUCMC, 1975.
SEE: Larson.

URBANA

OH853-130

Champaign County Library
160 West Market
Urbana OH 43078

(513) 653-3811

OPEN: M-Th 9-9, F, Sa 9-5; closed Sundays and holidays
COPYING FACILITIES: yes
MATERIALS SOLICITED: Champaign County history.

HOLDINGS:
    Total volume: 4 vols.; 13 envelopes
    Inclusive dates: 1782 -
    Description: Genealogical records of John Wiant of Albemarle County, VA, his descendants, and various families related to the Wiants by marriage. Included are photographs, maps, deeds, letters, and birth, death, and marriage records. Most are photocopies.

OH853-800

Urbana College
Swedenborg Memorial Library
Urbana OH 43078

(513) 652-1301, Ext. 337

OPEN: Su 2-10, M-Th 8-10, F 8-5, Sa 9-5; closed holidays and weekends during summer
COPYING FACILITIES: yes
MATERIALS SOLICITED: Archival materials of Urbana College. Will also accept materials relating to the Swedenborgian church.

HOLDINGS:
    Total volume: 150 l.f.
    Inclusive dates: 1850 -
    Description: The archives of Urbana College, including fraternity and sorority records; student literary manuscripts; photographs dating from the 19th and early 20th centuries; account books and business records; and papers of Milo Williams, first president of the College.

SEE: Larson.

VERMILION

OH863-280

Great Lakes Historical Society
Clarence Metcalf Research Library
480 Main Street
Vermilion OH 44089

(216) 967-3467

OPEN: daily 10-5; closed Christmas
USER FEES: Society membership fee of $12 per year
ACCESS: by appointment
COPYING FACILITIES: yes
MATERIALS SOLICITED: Personal papers, and materials relating to companies engaged in trade and commerce in the Great Lakes region. Will also accept photographs and genealogical data pertaining to the region.

HOLDINGS:
Total volume: 418 l.f.
Inclusive dates: 1826 -
Description: Materials relating to the Great Lakes. Included are items relating to ships and shipping, including logbooks, account books, diaries, lighthouse logbooks, yachting records, lifesaving documents, and material on wrecks, disasters, and storms. There are photographs of Great Lakes ships, harbors, lighthouses, and individuals connected with the area, and ship plans from the American Shipbuilding Co., 1890's-1920.

WARREN

OH878-720

Sutliff Museum
Warren Public Library
444 Mahoning Avenue, N.W.
Warren OH 44483

(216) 399-8807

OPEN: Tu, Th 2:30-4:30, W 7-8:30;
closed other days and holidays
ACCESS: prior arrangement with Curator required
COPYING FACILITIES: yes

HOLDINGS:
Total volume: 4 l.f.
Inclusive dates: 1790 - 1953
Description: Papers of the Sutliff family, prominent locally in farming and law. Included are personal and business correspondence, diaries, deeds, promissory notes, tax receipts, and military papers. There is an account of the Marvin family's migration from Connecticut to Bazetta, OH, in 1821, by Phebe Lord Marvin Sutliff, as well as her diaries; letters, 1833-42, of the Plumb and Marvin families; correspondence, 1839-42, with U.S. Representative Joshua Reed Giddings; and papers, 1834-40, relating to the American Anti-Slavery Society.

SEE: NUCMC, 1976.

OH878-880

Warren Public Library
444 Mahoning Avenue, N.W.
Warren OH 44483

(216) 399-8807

OPEN: M-Th 9-9, F 9-6, Sa 9-5; closed Sundays and holidays; closed Saturdays in July and August
COPYING FACILITIES: yes

HOLDINGS:
Total volume: 3 l.f.; 85 microfilm reels
Inclusive dates: 1803 -
Description: Minutes, 1968- , of the Board of Education of Warren; minutes, 1930-40, of the City Federation of Women's Clubs; ledgers, 1845-55, of Perkins Realty Company; and microfilm of Trumbull County Probate Court records, 1803-1921.

SEE: NUCMC, 1976.

WASHINGTON COURT HOUSE

OH883-880

Washington Carnegie Public Library
127 South North Street
Washington Court House OH 43160

(614) 335-2540

OPEN: M-Th 9-8, F, Sa 9-5; closed Sundays and holidays
COPYING FACILITIES: yes
MATERIALS SOLICITED: Materials relating to local and State history, with special attention to the temperance movement in Washington Court House. Will also accept genealogical material, and films, photographs, and sound recordings concerned with Ohio history.

HOLDINGS:
Total volume: 20 vols.
Inclusive dates: 1920 - 1960
Description: Manuscript genealogical histories relating primarily to families that settled in southern Ohio after the Revolutionary War.

WELLINGTON

OH906-320

Herrick Memorial Public Library
101 Public Square
Wellington OH 44090

(216) 647-2120

OPEN: M, Tu, Th 12-8, F 12-5, Sa 9:30-5; closed Sundays, Wednesdays, and holidays
COPYING FACILITIES: yes
MATERIALS SOLICITED: Will accept materials relating to Archibald M. Willard, Myron T. Herrick, and Lorain County-Wellington Township history.

HOLDINGS:
Total volume: 30 c.f.
Inclusive dates: 1870 - 1930
Description: Correspondence, 1895-1901, relating to Archibald M. Willard, Wellington artist and painter of 'The Spirit of '76'; photographs of Myron T. Herrick, U.S. Ambassador to France; and minute books of the Lorain County Agricultural Society, 1870-90.

WESTERVILLE

OH925-600

Otterbein College
Courtright Memorial Library
Westerville OH 43081

(614) 898-1414, 1164

OPEN: M-Th 7:45-10, F 7:45-5, Sa 10-5, Su 2-10; closed holidays
ACCESS: serious scholars only
COPYING FACILITIES: yes
MATERIALS SOLICITED: Diaries and other manuscript sources about Westerville, Otterbein College, and the United Brethren church in Ohio.

HOLDINGS:
Total volume: 185 l.f.
Inclusive dates: 1815 -
Description: The archives of Otterbein College, consisting of papers of College presidents, 1909-71; faculty minutes, 1856- ; trustee minutes, 1847- ; Literary Society papers; and other materials.

SEE: Hamer; NUCMC, 1968.

SEE: Hinding.

SEE ALSO: David R. Larson, ed., *Guide to Manuscripts Collections and Institutional Records in Ohio* (Society of Ohio Archivists, 1974); Edwin T. Layton, Jr., ed., *A Regional Union Catalog of Manuscripts Relating to the History of Science and Technology Located in Indiana, Michigan, and Ohio* (Case Western Reserve Univ., 1971). An inventory to the College presidents' correspondence is available at the Library.

WILBERFORCE

OH939-860

Wilberforce University
Archives and Special Collections
Rembert E. Stokes Learning Resources Center
Wilberforce OH 45384-1003

(513) 376-2911, Ext. 628

OPEN: M-F 8-4:30, other times by request; closed weekends and holidays
ACCESS: proper identification required
COPYING FACILITIES: yes
MATERIALS SOLICITED: Materials relating to the University and the history of the African Methodist Episcopal church. Will also accept materials on bishops and outstanding lay leaders of the AME church.

HOLDINGS:
Total volume: 106 l.f.
Inclusive dates: 1856 - 1950
Description: Materials relating to the history of Wilberforce University and the growth of the African Methodist Episcopal church in the 19th century. Individual collections include papers of Bishop Reverdy Cassius Ransome; papers of W. S. Scarbrough, University president; and papers of Milton S. J. Wright, Wilberforce professor.

SEE: NUCMC, 1959-61.

SEE: Schatz; Duignan; Larson.

SEE ALSO: Guides to individual collections are available from the institution.

WILMINGTON

OH953-120

Clinton County Historical Society
149 East Locust Street
Wilmington OH

MAILING ADDRESS:
P.O. Box 529
Wilmington OH 45177

(513) 382-4684

OPEN: Tu-F 1:30-5, Su 2-4; closed
   Mondays, Saturdays, holidays, and
   during Jan. and Feb.
COPYING FACILITIES: yes

HOLDINGS:
   Total volume: not specified
   Inclusive dates: 19th century -
   Description: Genealogical data, correspondence, photographs, and other materials pertaining to Clinton County history.

OH953-870
Wilmington College
S. Arthur Watson Library
Quaker Collection/College Archives
Wilmington OH

MAILING ADDRESS:
Pyle Center Box 1227
Wilmington OH 45177

(513) 382-6661, Ext. 207

OPEN: M-F 10-5; closed weekends,
   holidays, and last two weeks of August
   and December
ACCESS: advance arrangements requested
COPYING FACILITIES: yes
MATERIALS SOLICITED: Quaker meeting
   records for the Orthodox branch in
   Ohio and the Hicksite branch in Indiana and Ohio; journals, diaries, and
   logbooks of Quakers in Ohio; materials
   related to Wilmington College and its
   graduates; materials related to the
   Lebanon (Ohio) National Normal University; and personal papers of Quakers. Will also accept materials relating
   to Gerald Doan McDonald and personal papers of literary figures and Underground Railroad materials relating
   to southwestern Ohio.

HOLDINGS:
   Total volume: 100 l.f.; 8 file cabinets
   Inclusive dates: 1790's -
   Description: Records of the Religious
   Society of Friends (Quakers) for the
   Orthodox branch in southwestern Ohio
   (now Wilmington Yearly Meeting) and
   for the Hicksite branch in Indiana and
   Ohio (now Ohio Valley Yearly Meeting),
   including minutes of yearly, quarterly,
   and monthly meetings, genealogical
   source data, correspondence, and diaries.
      There are also a photograph collection
   relating to early Quaker mission work in
   Alaska; personal papers of Gerald Doan
   McDonald; diaries of John Michener
   Watson relating to work with the Freedmen's Bureau and with schools in the
   Indian Territory; academic and financial
   records of Lebanon (Ohio) National Normal University; and archives of Wilmington College, consisting of trustee minutes,
   1870- , faculty minutes, papers of literary
   societies and other student organizations,
   photographs, and sound recordings of lec-
   turers.

SEE: NUCMC, 1967.

SEE: Larson; Schatz.

WOOSTER

OH968-120
College of Wooster
Library
East University Street
Wooster OH 44691

no telephone
SEE: NUCMC, 1959-61.

   Questionnaire not returned.

OH968-600
Ohio Agricultural Research and
   Development Center
1680 Madison Avenue
Wooster OH 44691

(216) 263-3700

OPEN: M-F 8-5; closed weekends and
   holidays
COPYING FACILITIES: yes

HOLDINGS:
   Total volume: 25 c.f.
   Inclusive dates: 1887 - 1965
   Description: Records of the Center, in-
   cluding those of its predecessor, the Ohio
   Agricultural Experiment Station. Included
   are photographs of the first application of
   pesticides by airplane.

SEE ALSO: Edwin T. Layton, Jr., ed., *A
   Regional Union Catalog of Manuscripts
   Relating to the History of Science and
   Technology Located in Indiana, Michi-
   gan, and Ohio* (Case Western Reserve
   Univ., 1971).

OH968-880
Wayne County Historical Society
546 East Bowman Street
Wooster OH 44691

(216) 264-8856

OPEN: Su, Tu-Sa afternoons; closed
   Mondays and holidays
COPYING FACILITIES: yes
MATERIALS SOLICITED: Will accept his-
   torical materials relating to Wayne
   County.

HOLDINGS:
   Total volume: 110 c.f.
   Inclusive dates: 1812 - 1950
   Description: Materials pertaining to
   Wayne County history, including township, school, and draft board records,
   fireman's association records, ordinances
   of the city of Wooster, and 29 volumes of
   court records.
      Also includes land deeds (1810-1930),
   marriage records of Wayne County
   (1813-1888) and burial records.

SEE: Larson.

WRIGHT-PATTERSON AFB

OH978-120
U.S. Air Force Museum
Research Division
Wright-Patterson Air Force Base OH
   45433

(513) 255-4644

OPEN: M-F 9-4; closed weekends and
   holidays
COPYING FACILITIES: yes
MATERIALS SOLICITED: Materials relating
   to the history of the U.S. Air Force.

HOLDINGS:
   Total volume: 1,500 l.f.
   Inclusive dates: 1900 -
   Description: Documentary materials relating to the history of the U.S. Air Force
   and its predecessor organizations. Holdings include technical orders and manuals
   relating to aircraft and associated systems; aircraft drawings; and photographs.

SEE: Hamer.

SEE: Paszek; Hinding.

XENIA

OH982-290
Greene County District Library
Greene County Room
Local History Department
76 E. Market Street
Xenia OH 45385

(513) 376-2995

OPEN: M-Sa 9-5; closed Sundays and
   holidays
COPYING FACILITIES: yes
MATERIALS SOLICITED: Materials relating
   to the history of Greene County, and
   family histories. Will also accept historical materials relating to Ohio and
   genealogical items relating to the Xenia
   area.

HOLDINGS:
   Total volume: 200 l.f.
   Inclusive dates: late 1700's -
   Description: Materials collected by William A. Galloway, including memoirs of
   the Civil War, documents relating to the
   Shawnee Indians and Tecumseh, legal papers, family papers, and materials relating
   to Antioch College and Wilberforce University; a collection focusing around the
   Xenia tornado of April 3, 1974; genealogical materials; miscellaneous diaries,
   journals, and letters; and church records.

SEE: Hinding.

YELLOW SPRINGS

OH986-40
Antioch College
Antiochiana
Yellow Springs OH 45387

(513) 767-7331, Ext. 200

OPEN: M, W, F 1-4:30; closed other
   days, holidays, and between terms
COPYING FACILITIES: yes

MATERIALS SOLICITED: Materials relating to Antioch College or Horace Mann.

HOLDINGS:
Total volume: 440 c.f.
Inclusive dates: 1750 - 1950
Description: Materials relating to the history of Antioch College, including manuscripts, tapes, films, and enrollment and financial ledgers; papers of and relating to Horace Mann; copies of letters of the Peabody, Mann, and related families, 1790-1953; and an unpublished biography of Olympia Brown.

SEE: Hamer.

SEE: Robbins; Hinding.

YOUNGSTOWN

OH990-510

Mahoning Valley Historical Society
The Arms Museum
648 Wick Avenue
Youngstown OH 44502-1289

(216) 743-2589

OPEN: Tu-F 9-4; closed other days and holidays
ACCESS: prior appointment required
COPYING FACILITIES: yes
MATERIALS SOLICITED: Will accept materials pertinent to the history of the Mahoning Valley.

HOLDINGS:
Total volume: 1,300 collections
Inclusive dates: 1770's -
Description: Collections covering the history and settlement of the Mahoning Valley. Included are records of organizations and businesses, diaries, correspondence, public documents, maps, photographs, and papers of individuals notable in the history of the Mahoning Valley area.

SEE ALSO: David R. Larson, ed., *Guide to Manuscripts Collections and Institutional Records in Ohio* (Society of Ohio Archivists, 1974); Edwin T. Layton, Jr., ed., *A Regional Union Catalog of Manuscripts Relating to the History of Science and Technology Located in Indiana, Michigan, and Ohio* (Case Western Reserve Univ., 1971).

OH990-640

Public Library of Youngstown and Mahoning County
305 Wick Avenue
Youngstown OH 44503

(216) 744-8636

OPEN: M, Tu 9-8, W-Sa 9-5:30; closed Sundays, holidays, and Dec. 24 and 31
COPYING FACILITIES: yes
MATERIALS SOLICITED: Materials relating to the history of Youngstown and Mahoning County, as well as government and cultural records.

HOLDINGS:
Total volume: 75 l.f.
Inclusive dates: 1825 -
Description: Genealogical data relating to western Pennsylvania and eastern Ohio; materials relating to water use in northeastern Ohio, including the Lake Erie-Ohio River Canal, reservoir development, flood control, industrial water supplies, and the planning of the St. Lawrence Seaway; records of cultural, political, and other civic organizations in Youngstown; and oral histories of the local black community.

SEE: Hamer; NUCMC, 1966, 79.

SEE: Larson.

ZANESVILLE

OH996-520

Muskingum County Pioneer and Historical Society
The Dr. Increase Mathews House
304 Woodlawn Avenue
Zanesville OH

MAILING ADDRESS:
Box 2201
Zanesville OH 43701

no telephone

OPEN: May 1 - Oct. 30 Sa, Su 2-4:30; closed other days and rest of year
USER FEES: one dollar for non-members
ACCESS: by arrangement with Director
COPYING FACILITIES: no
MATERIALS SOLICITED: Materials relating to early Muskingum County and Ohio. Will also accept materials relating to the time period 1776-1876.

HOLDINGS:
Total volume: 8 l.f.
Inclusive dates: 1800 - 1920
Description: Materials relating to early Muskingum County and Ohio history, inlcuding family histories, clippings, records of mercantile establishments, and records of clubs.

OKLAHOMA

Oklahoma does not have a statewide program for preserving local public records. County and municipal records normally remain in the custody of local officials.

ALVA

OK42-560
Northwestern Oklahoma State
University
Library
Alva OK 73717

(405) 327-1700, Ext. 219

OPEN: Su 5-10, M-Th 8-10, F 8-5, Sa 9-noon; closed holidays and University vacations
COPYING FACILITIES: yes
MATERIALS SOLICITED: Genealogy; local history; and history of Northwestern Oklahoma State University. Will also accept other materials.

HOLDINGS:
Total volume: 25 l.f.
Inclusive dates: 1895 -
Description: Materials relating chiefly to Northwestern Oklahoma State University. The collection contains photographs; correspondence and reminiscences of William J. Mellor and other alumni; a speech delivered on campus by Eleanor Roosevelt; letters of Ernest Tyler; records of the Sequoyah Children's Book Award; and University records, 1895- .

BARTLESVILLE

OK118-70
Bartlesville Public Library
History Room
6th and Johnstone
Bartlesville OK 74003

(918) 337-5217

OPEN: M-F 9-5, Sa 9-1;closed Sundays and holidays
COPYING FACILITIES: yes
MATERIALS SOLICITED: Biographies of local pioneers. Will also accept other materials relating to local history or the Delaware Indians.

HOLDINGS:
Total volume: 7,000 items
Inclusive dates: 1880's -
Description: A collection of manuscripts, photographs, and lists and rolls relating to the Delaware Indians and to local white settlers, businesses, and industries in the late 19th and early 20th centuries.

SEE: Hinding.

CHICKASHA

OK228-610
University of Science and Arts of
Oklahoma
Nash Library
Chickasha OK 73018

(405) 224-3140, Ext. 260

OPEN: Su 3-10, M-Th 8-10, F 8-5; closed Saturdays and holidays
COPYING FACILITIES: yes
MATERIALS SOLICITED: University history and materials on American Indians of the area. Will accept other materials.

HOLDINGS:
Total volume: 31 l.f.; 10 boxes; 1 cabinet
Inclusive dates: 1908 - 1973
Description: Materials relating to the University including college catalogs, yearbooks, issues of the school newspaper, programs of events, photographs, and other records. Also included are manuscripts of the book, *Comanche and Kiowa Captives in Oklahoma*, and articles about Kiowa and other Indians, by Hugh D. Corwin, field notes of talks with elderly Indians, and galley proofs of a journal edited by Corwin.

SEE: Hinding.

CLAREMORE

OK245-880
The Will Rogers Memorial
Will Rogers Memorial Library
Office of the Curator
West Will Rogers Boulevard
Claremore OK

MAILING ADDRESS:
Box 157
Claremore OK 74017

(918) 341-0719

OPEN: daily 8-5
ACCESS: appointment required
COPYING FACILITIES: yes
MATERIALS SOLICITED: Memorabilia pertaining to the life of Will Rogers.

HOLDINGS:
Total volume: 6,635 items
Inclusive dates: 1879 - 1935
Description: A collection of manuscripts and visual and audible documents relating to the public and private life of Will Rogers.

SEE: NUCMC, 1975.
SEE: Robbins.

EL RENO

OK338-120
Canadian County Historical Museum
300 South Grand
El Reno OK 73036

(405) 262-5121

OPEN: Tu-F 10-5, Su 1:30-5; closed Mondays, Saturdays, and holidays
ACCESS: advance arrangements requested
COPYING FACILITIES: no
MATERIALS SOLICITED: Materials relating to the history of the Cheyenne and Arapahoe Indians, Darlington Agency, and Fort Reno. Will also accept materials on local and county history.

HOLDINGS:
Total volume: 6 file drawers
Inclusive dates: 1870 - 1970
Description: Historical materials relating to the Rock Island Railroad, early lawmen, churches, schools, towns, businesses, and medicine of Canadian County. Also included are oral history interviews with local residents.

OK338-200
El Reno Carnegie Library
215 East Wade
El Reno OK 73036

(405) 262-2409

OPEN: M-Th 10-7, F 10-6, Sa 10-4; closed Sundays and holidays
COPYING FACILITIES: yes
MATERIALS SOLICITED: Will accept correspondence, photographs, and other materials with an emphasis on the history of Oklahoma and Canadian County.

HOLDINGS:
Total volume: 45 boxes; 30 drawers
Inclusive dates: 1878 -
Description: Collections pertaining to the history of Oklahoma, especially Canadian County. Included are a letterbook of a Darlington Indian agent, 1878; a manuscript history of Fort Reno; written and oral reminiscences of Fort Reno; police dockets for El Reno, 1902-03; and photographs of the Darlington Indian office and other subjects.
Also includes City Council minute books (1889 -).

ENID

OK355-640
Phillips University
Graduate Seminary Library
Enid OK 73701

no telephone

SEE: NUCMC, 1969-70.

Questionnaire not returned.

FORT SILL

OK372-240
Field Artillery and Fort Sill Museum
Museum Archival Library
Building 441
Fort Sill OK 73503

(405) 351-5224

OPEN: M-F 7:30-4; closed weekends and
holidays
COPYING FACILITIES: yes
MATERIALS SOLICITED: Materials on
Fort Sill history and field artillery.

HOLDINGS:
Total volume: 20,000 items
Inclusive dates: 1700 -
Description: Materials, including maps
and photographs, pertaining to the history of Fort Sill and the surrounding
area. These materials focus on military
history, American Indians, and pioneer
life. The collection also includes materials
on field artillery.

GOODWELL

OK389-560
No Man's Land Historical Museum
Sewell Street
Goodwell OK 73939

MAILING ADDRESS:
P.O. Box 278
Goodwell OK 73939

(405) 349-2670

OPEN: Tu-F 9-5; closed other days,
Thanksgiving, and Christmas
COPYING FACILITIES: yes
MATERIALS SOLICITED: Family, church,
business, post office, and town history
of the Oklahoma panhandle (No Man's
Land). Will also accept other information concerning the Oklahoma
panhandle.

HOLDINGS:
Total volume: 1,500 items
Inclusive dates: 1886 -
Description: Materials relating to the
Oklahoma panhandle (No Man's Land),
including diaries, letters, business records,
hotel registers, ledgers, photographs of
buildings and people, and oral history
tapes of local residents, such as ranchers
and railroad workers.

SEE: Hinding.

GUTHRIE

OK406-600
Oklahoma Historical Society
Oklahoma Territorial Museum
402-406 East Oklahoma Avenue
Guthrie OK 73044

(405) 282-1889

OPEN: Tu-F 9-5, Sa, Su 2-5; closed
Mondays and holidays
ACCESS: students and researchers
COPYING FACILITIES: no
MATERIALS SOLICITED: Material relating
to the Oklahoma Territory, 1889-1907.

HOLDINGS:
Total volume: 64 c.f.
Inclusive dates: 1889 - 1907
Description: Material relating to the
territorial era of Oklahoma, and geo-
graphically to that area of the State
known as the Oklahoma Territory.

KINGFISHER

OK456-120
Chisholm Trail Museum and
Governor A. J. Seay Mansion
605 Zellers Avenue
Kingfisher OK 73750

(405) 375-5176

OPEN: Su 1-5, M-Sa 9-5; closed
Thanksgiving, Christmas, and New
Year's
COPYING FACILITIES: no

HOLDINGS:
Total volume: not specified
Inclusive dates: 1889 - 1921
Description: Early photographs of
Kingfisher County and archival material
pertaining to Kingfisher College,
1895-1921, including photographs, scrap-
books, and yearbooks.

LAWTON

OK490-520
Museum of the Great Plains
Library and Archives
601 Ferris
Lawton OK

MAILING ADDRESS:
P.O. Box 68
Lawton OK 73502

(405) 353-5675

OPEN: M-F 8-5; closed weekends and
holidays
COPYING FACILITIES: yes
MATERIALS SOLICITED: Manuscript and
photograph collections relating primarily to the settlement of Oklahoma, with
special emphasis on Lawton history.
Will also accept other historical and
political materials concerning the Great
Plains, with special emphasis on Oklahoma.

HOLDINGS:
Total volume: 180,000 items
Inclusive dates: 1875 - 1965
Description: Political papers of Fred
Harris, L. M. Gensman, T. P. Gore, and
Scott Ferris, as well as a collection relat-
ing to Ophelia Vestal and her work gath-
ering information on the Plains Indians
in Oklahoma for the WPA during the
1930's.

SEE: NUCMC, 1966.
SEE: Novotny; Hinding.

MEDFORD

OK524-280
Grant County Historical Society
Grant County Museum
104 East Cherokee Street
Medford OK

MAILING ADDRESS:
P.O. Box 127
Medford OK 73759

(405) 395-2888

OPEN: by appointment only M, W, F 2-4
COPYING FACILITIES: yes
MATERIALS SOLICITED: Materials relating
to the history of Grant County and its
residents and the history of the
'Cherokee Outlet.'

HOLDINGS:
Total volume: not specified
Inclusive dates: 1890 -
Description: Material concentrating on
the history of Grant County, 1890-1920.
Included are family history data, notes of
tombstone inscriptions, County government records, newspaper clipping files,
photographs, and oral history recordings.

SEE: Hinding.

MUSKOGEE

OK541-240
Five Civilized Tribes Museum
Agency Hill
Honor Heights Drive
Muskogee OK 74401

(918) 683-1701

OPEN: M-Sa 10-5, Su 1-5; closed
Thanksgiving, Christmas, and New
Year's
USER FEES: fifty cents; students
twenty-five cents
COPYING FACILITIES: yes
MATERIALS SOLICITED: Materials per-
taining to Cherokee, Choctaw, Chicka-
saw, Creek and Seminole Indians.

HOLDINGS:
Total volume: 3,500 items
Inclusive dates: 1700's -
Description: Materials from the southeastern United States and Indian Territory pertaining to Cherokee, Chickasaw,
Choctaw, Creek, and Seminole Indians,
primarily 1820-1900. Also included are
roll books of the Dawes Commission,
1896-1906, and correspondence of Elias
Boudinot.

NORMAN

OK558-790

University of Oklahoma
Libraries
Western History Collections
Division of Manuscripts
630 Parrington Oval
Norman OK 73019

(405) 325-3641

OPEN: M-F 8-5; closed weekends and
holidays
COPYING FACILITIES: yes
MATERIALS SOLICITED: Materials relating
to the history and culture of the American West, with emphasis on Oklahoma,
the Southwest, and North American Indians; papers of U.S. Representatives
and Senators and other public figures;
and archives of the University and various organizations. Will also accept collections relating to literary figures,
business and industry (such as oil),
government agencies, churches, and
professional and social organizations,
or other items of significant research
value.

HOLDINGS:
Total volume: 13,500 l.f.; 259,000
items
Inclusive dates: 1600 -
Description: Materials relating to the
American West, including documents on
exploration, military activities, settlements, and political, economic, social,
and cultural development. Emphasis is on
the history and culture of Oklahoma, the
American Southwest, North American Indians, and collections of 20th century political figures who served in the U.S. Congress and other State and National offices.
Also includes the collections of the
Carl Albert Congressional Research and
Studies Center.

GUIDES: A. M. Gibson, *A Guide to Regional Manuscript Collections in the Division of Manuscripts, University of
Oklahoma Library* (Univ. of Oklahoma
Press, 1960).

SEE: Hamer; NUCMC, 1962-64.

SEE: Schatz; Meckler and McMullin;
Novotny; Davis; Paszek; Bean and
Vane; Parkinson; Allard, Crawley, and
Edmison; Svoboda and Dunning; Rob-
bins.

OKLAHOMA CITY

OK592-570

The Ninety-Nines, Inc.
Library and Archives
Amelia Earhart Lane and East
Terminal Drive
Will Rogers World Airport
Oklahoma City OK

MAILING ADDRESS:
P.O. Box 59965
Will Rogers World Airport
Oklahoma City OK 73159

(405) 685-7969, 682-4425

OPEN: M-Th 10-5; closed other days
COPYING FACILITIES: yes
MATERIALS SOLICITED: Materials related
to women in aviation, including newspaper clippings, photographs, and personal memoirs.

HOLDINGS:
Total volume: not specified
Inclusive dates: 1900 -
Description: Collection relating to
women in aviation, including photographs, periodical clippings, letters, journals, records, and scrapbooks.

OK592-580

Oklahoma Christian College
Oklahoma Living Legends
North Eastern and Memorial
Oklahoma City OK 73111

(405) 478-1661

OPEN: M-F 8-5; closed weekends and
holidays
COPYING FACILITIES: yes
MATERIALS SOLICITED: Items on Oklahoma in general, including both state
and local historical reminiscences. Will
also accept photographs, slides, and
motion pictures related to Oklahoma.

HOLDINGS:
Total volume: 1,100 tapes
Inclusive dates: 1960 -
Description: A general collection relating to Oklahoma, including reminiscences
dealing with the State, its communities,
and its industries.

SEE: Meckler and McMullin; Hines;
Hinding.

OK592-620

Oklahoma Department of Libraries
Archives and Records Division
200 Northeast 18th Street
Oklahoma City OK 73105

(405) 521-2502, Ext. 61

OPEN: M-F 8-5; closed weekends and
holidays
COPYING FACILITIES: yes
MATERIALS SOLICITED: Oklahoma State
records. Will also accept private papers
related to Oklahoma government and
culture.

HOLDINGS:
Total volume: 25,500 c.f.
Inclusive dates: 1890 -
Description: Chiefly records of the legislative, judicial, and executive branches
and agencies of the State government of
Oklahoma since 1907, and to a lesser
extent of the territorial government,
which preceded it from 1890 to 1907.
There are also manuscript collections, including the records of the Oklahoma Historical Records Survey.

GUIDES: Thomas W. Kremm, comp.,
*Guide to Oklahoma State Archives, Vol-
ume I* (Oklahoma Department of Libraries, 1980); Thomas W. Kremm,
comp., *Guide to Special Collections of
the Oklahoma State Archives*
(Oklahoma Department of Libraries).

SEE: Hamer; NUCMC, 1970-71.

SEE: Davis; Parkinson; Hinding.

OK592-630

Oklahoma Heritage Association
Archives Division
201 Northwest 14th Street
Oklahoma City OK 73103

(405) 232-7338

OPEN: M-F 9-4; closed weekends and
holidays
ACCESS: appointment required
COPYING FACILITIES: yes
MATERIALS SOLICITED: Will accept materials relevant to the history of Oklahoma.

HOLDINGS:
Total volume: 5 file drawers
Inclusive dates: 1889 -
Description: Chiefly biographical data,
correspondence, and other manuscripts
relating to 425 prominent Oklahomans
inducted into the Oklahoma Hall of
Fame since 1928. There are also newspaper clippings and other materials concerning Oklahoma State and local history.

SEE: Hinding.

OK592-640

Oklahoma Historical Society
Indian Archives Division
Historical Building
Oklahoma City OK 73152

(405) 521-2492

OPEN: M-Sa 9-5; closed Sundays and
holidays
COPYING FACILITIES: yes
MATERIALS SOLICITED: Materials pertaining to Indian history and culture,
including Federal documents and correspondence and papers of individuals
involved in Indian affairs.

HOLDINGS:
Total volume: 7,000,000 pages
Inclusive dates: 1830's -
Description: Primarily Federal Indian
agency records, 1870's-1920's, for Oklahoma and the Indian Territory. Also included are records kept by the Cherokee,
Choctaw, Chickasaw, Creek, and Seminole Nations prior to Oklahoma statehood. There are also other collections focusing on Indian affairs, and including
letters, diaries, account books, and church
and missionary correspondence; and 112
volumes of transcribed interviews prepared by a WPA project, 1936-38.

GUIDES: John Stewart and Kenny A.
Franks, *State Records, Manuscripts and
Newspapers at the Oklahoma State Ar-
chives and Oklahoma Historical Society*
(Oklahoma Dept. of Libraries and
Oklahoma Historical Society, 1975).

SEE: Hamer.

SEE: Davis; Bean and Vane; Hinding.

SEE ALSO: Unpublished finding aids available at the repository.

OK592-650

Oklahoma Historical Society
Library Resources Division, Reference
  Library
2100 North Lincoln Boulevard
Oklahoma City OK

MAILING ADDRESS:
Historical Building
Oklahoma City OK 73105

(405) 521-2491

OPEN: M-F 9-9, Sa 9-5; closed Sundays
  and holidays
COPYING FACILITIES: yes
MATERIALS SOLICITED: Materials relating
  to the history and culture of Oklahoma,
  in particular, and the Southwest as it
  relates to Oklahoma.

HOLDINGS:
  Total volume: 20,000 photographs;
  400 c.f.; 500 maps
  Inclusive dates: 1880 -
  Description: Personal papers, government records, and other materials documenting the State and local history of
  Oklahoma. Included are the papers of
  Robert L. Williams, member of the Oklahoma Constitutional Convention and
  Governor of Oklahoma; papers of Amiel
  Weeks Whipple, Chief Topographical Engineer for the United States Army ca.
  1850; official reports and personal correspondence of W. S. Harn, a federal
  investigator for the 1889 Oklahoma land
  run; papers of David L. Payne, leader of
  the Oklahoma Boomer Movement;
  Sanborn Fire Maps ca. 1910 for Oklahoma.

GUIDES: John Stewart and Kenny A.
  Franks, *State Records, Manuscripts and
  Newspapers at the Oklahoma State Ar-
  chives and Oklahoma Historical Society*
  (Oklahoma Dept. of Libraries and
  Oklahoma Historical Society, 1975).

SEE: Hamer.

OK592-780

United Methodist Church
Oklahoma Annual Conference
Commission on Archives and History
Conference Archives
Oklahoma City University Library
2501 North Blackwelder
Oklahoma City OK 73106

(405) 521-5072, 5068

OPEN: M-F 8:30-5; closed weekends,
  holidays, and school vacations
USER FEES: $10 initial fee for outside
  researchers
ACCESS: advance arrangements required
COPYING FACILITIES: yes
MATERIALS SOLICITED: Personal papers
  of Methodist ministers, records of individual churches and of Methodist organizations and administrative offices,
  all in Oklahoma. Will also accept other
  materials connected with the United
  Methodist church in Oklahoma.

HOLDINGS:
  Total volume: 4,660 vols.; 30 l.f.
  Inclusive dates: 1817 -
  Description: Materials relating to the
  history of the United Methodist church
  in Oklahoma and its affiliated denominations and associations. Documents include church records; journals and other
  writings of ministers; and records of an
  Indian missionary organization,
  1831-1907.

OKMULGEE

OK609-120

Creek Council House Museum
Archives
Town Square
Okmulgee OK 74447

(918) 756-2324

OPEN: Tu-Sa 9-5; closed Sundays,
  Mondays, and holidays
ACCESS: advance arrangements required
COPYING FACILITIES: no
MATERIALS SOLICITED: Materials, including maps, relating to Creek (Muscogee)
  culture and history and to Creek governmental affairs before 1907. Will also
  accept materials relating to the local
  area or to Native Americans.

HOLDINGS:
  Total volume: 20 vols.
  Inclusive dates: 1828 - 1907
  Description: Records from Creek Nation removal and the governmental period in Oklahoma, including probate
  records, trial records, removal land sales
  ledgers, Chief's letter press book, letters,
  and other documents.

PONCA CITY

OK634-640

Ponca City Cultural Center Museum
1000 East Grand
Ponca City OK 74601

(405) 762-6123

OPEN: Sundays and holidays 1-5, M,
  W-Sa 10-5; closed Tuesdays,
  Thanksgiving, Christmas, and New
  Year's
USER FEES: one dollar for non-resident
  adults
ACCESS: appointment required
COPYING FACILITIES: no
MATERIALS SOLICITED: Materials relating
  to E. W. Marland, prior to 1928;
  American Indian tribes, particularly
  Ponca, Kaw, Otoe, Osage, and
  Tonkawa; the 101 Ranch; Bryant Ba-
  ker; and the Pioneer Woman Statue.

HOLDINGS:
  Total volume: 5 file cabinents
  Inclusive dates: 19th century -
  Description: Materials, including
  manuscripts, photographs, and sound recordings, relating to E. W. Marland, prior
  to 1928; American Indian tribes, particularly Ponca, Kaw, Otoe, Osage, and
  Tonkawa; the 101 Ranch; Bryant Baker;
  and the Pioneer Woman Statue.

SAPULPA

OK685-710

Sapulpa Historical Society, Inc.
Sapulpa Historical Museum
100 East Lee
Sapulpa OK

MAILING ADDRESS:
Box 278
Sapulpa OK 74066

(918) 224-4871

OPEN: Tu-Su 1-4; closed Mondays and
  holidays
COPYING FACILITIES: no
MATERIALS SOLICITED: Materials relating
  to early Sapulpa businesses and those
  in neighboring towns, as well as materials and photographs documenting all
  aspects of the history of this area.

HOLDINGS:
  Total volume: 1 file cabinet
  Inclusive dates: 1856 -
  Description: Local historical materials
  including oral history tapes and transcripts, photographs, slides, maps, books,
  store accounts, and club minutes.

SEE: Svoboda and Dunning.

OK685-720

Sapulpa Public Library
27 West Dewey
Sapulpa OK 74066

(918) 224-5624

OPEN: M, Tu, Th 9-8, W 9-6, F 9-5, Sa
  9-1; closed Sundays and holidays
COPYING FACILITIES: yes
MATERIALS SOLICITED: Will accept ma-
  terials pertaining to Sapulpa, Creek
  County, and Creek Nation history.

HOLDINGS:
  Total volume: 3 file drawers
  Inclusive dates: 1890 -
  Description: Genealogical data, manu-
  script histories, correspondence, and pho-
  tographs relating to local families.

SHAWNEE

OK736-600

Oklahoma Baptist University
Library
Oklahoma Baptist Collection
Shawnee OK 74801

(405) 275-2850, Ext. 2251

OPEN: by appointment
COPYING FACILITIES: yes
MATERIALS SOLICITED: Materials relating
  to the Baptist church in Oklahoma and
  Baptist associations, and records of
  Oklahoma Baptist University. Will also
  accept biographical material on Okla-
  homa Baptist leaders.

HOLDINGS:
  Total volume: 1,200 l.f.
  Inclusive dates: 1830 -
  Description: Minutes and reports of the
  Baptist General Convention of Oklahoma
  and 42 Baptist regional associations; ar-
  chives of Oklahoma Baptist University;

12 personal paper collections of Baptist leaders in Oklahoma; oral history tapes of older Baptists in the State and addresses given at various churches; and other materials relating to Baptist life in Oklahoma.

SEE ALSO: inventories, checklists, and other finding aids available at the institution.

OK736-640
Pottawatomie County Historical Society
Santa Fe Depot Museum
E. Main Street
Shawnee OK 74801

MAILING ADDRESS:
431 West Midland
Shawnee OK 74801

(405) 273-8412, 7957

OPEN: Sunday afternoons, and by appointment
COPYING FACILITIES: no
MATERIALS SOLICITED: Family histories pertaining to Pottawatomie County, and State and local railroad records. Will also accept other materials pertaining to Pottawatomie County.

HOLDINGS:
    Total volume: not specified
    Inclusive dates: 19th century -
    Description: A collection of photographs, diaries, pioneer reminiscences, legal documents, and other papers pertaining to Pottawatomie County history.

STILLWATER

OK753-600
Oklahoma State University
Library
Special Collections and Map Room
Stillwater OK 74078

(405) 624-6311

OPEN: M-F 8-5; closed weekends and University holidays
COPYING FACILITIES: yes
MATERIALS SOLICITED: History of Oklahoma State University, papers of Oklahoma public figures, and local history. Will also accept materials relating to State and regional history.

HOLDINGS:
    Total volume: 300 c.f.; 6,600 items
    Inclusive dates: 1889 -
    Description: Papers of two Oklahoma governors, Will Rogers manuscripts, and University records, including papers of Oliver Willham, former president, and materials on athletics. The Map Room contains aerial photographs covering Oklahoma.

SEE: NUCMC, 1975.

SEE: Svoboda and Dunning; Robbins; Hinding.

TAHLEQUAH

OK778-120
Cherokee National Historical Society
Cherokee National Historical Museum
Tahlequah OK

MAILING ADDRESS:
Box 515
Tahlequah OK 74465

(918) 456-5511, Ext. 3220

OPEN: M-F 8-5; closed weekends, Thanksgiving, Christmas, and New Year's
ACCESS: permission of Executive Vice President should be obtained
COPYING FACILITIES: yes
MATERIALS SOLICITED: Any material related to the Cherokee Indians or to persons and places involved in their history. Will also accept material concerning other tribes.

HOLDINGS:
    Total volume: 500 c.f.
    Inclusive dates: 1850 -
    Description: Several collections of manuscripts that outline the history of the Cherokee Indians. Included are the papers of principal chiefs W. W. Keeler, John Ross, and William P. Ross.

OK778-560
Northeastern Oklahoma State University
Library/Learning Resources Center
Tahlequah OK 74464

(918) 456-5511, Ext. 304

OPEN: M-F 8-5; closed weekends, holidays, and between semesters
COPYING FACILITIES: yes
MATERIALS SOLICITED: Materials concerning the Cherokee Indians, Oklahoma, and Tahlequah local history.

HOLDINGS:
    Total volume: 504 l.f.
    Inclusive dates: 1840 -
    Description: Materials relating chiefly to the Cherokee Indians, but also to Oklahoma politics, the city of Tahlequah, the Civil War, and the experiences of early settlers. Included are correspondence, school records, business records, diaries, ledgers, photographs, sound recordings, and video tape recordings.

SEE: Hamer; NUCMC, 1966 (as Northeastern State College Library).

TONKAWA

OK812-560
Northern Oklahoma College
Library
1220 East Grand
Tonkawa OK 74653

(405) 628-2581, Ext. 250

OPEN: Su 5:30-9, M-Th 7:45-9:30, F 7:45-4:30; closed Saturdays, Labor Day, Thanksgiving, Christmas, and College vacations
COPYING FACILITIES: yes

MATERIALS SOLICITED: Indian oral history.
HOLDINGS:
    Total volume: 15 items
    Inclusive dates: 1972
    Description: Interviews with Native Americans concerning major Indian settlements in northern Oklahoma before statehood: Nez Perce, Osage, Otoe and Missouria, Pawnee, Ponca, Quapaw, and Tonkawa.

TULSA

OK829-520
Thomas Gilcrease Institute of American History and Art
1400 North 25th West Avenue
Tulsa OK 74127

(918) 582-3122

OPEN: M-F 9-5; closed weekends and holidays
ACCESS: advance arrangements requested
COPYING FACILITIES: yes
MATERIALS SOLICITED: Materials relating to American history and art with emphasis on Indian cultures and the development and growth of the west.

HOLDINGS:
    Total volume: 150 l.f.
    Inclusive dates: 1512 - 1900
    Description: Hispanic documents, including letters from early Spanish explorers, land grants, church records, heresy charges, and lawsuits. Letters include those from Diego Columbus, De Soto, and Ponce de Leon. American documents include a 1777 certified copy of the Declaration of Independence sent to Frederick the Great of Prussia, the letters of Josiah Gregg, the Benteen-Goldin papers, several letters of Andrew Jackson, letters and journals of artist Thomas Moran, and papers of other artists. Also includes journals, correspondence and records from several members of the Five Civilized Tribes and other Indian Tribes of the Oklahoma region.

SEE: Hamer; NUCMC, 1967.

SEE: Schatz; Robbins; Bean and Vane; Beers-Southwest.

OK829-770
Tulsa County Historical Society
250 W. Newton Street
Tulsa OK

MAILING ADDRESS:
P.O. Box 27303
Tulsa OK 74149

(918) 585-5520

OPEN: M, Th 9-4, W, F 10-4; closed Tuesdays, weekends, and holidays
COPYING FACILITIES: yes
MATERIALS SOLICITED: Materials relating to Oklahoma, especially Tulsa County.

HOLDINGS:
    Total volume: 600 c.f.
    Inclusive dates: 1880 -
    Description: Materials relating to the history of Oklahoma, especially Tulsa County. Included are reminiscences of

pioneers, oral history tapes, diaries, business records, public documents, manuscript maps, and photographs.

SEE: Hinding.

OK829-790
University of Tulsa
Library
600 South College Avenue
Tulsa OK 74104

(918) 592-6000, Ext. 2351

SEE: Hamer; NUCMC, 1959-61.

Questionnaire not returned.

VINITA

OK854-840
Vinita Public Library
Archives Division
215 West Illinois
Vinita OK

MAILING ADDRESS:
P.O. Box 963
Vinita OK 74301

(918) 256-2115

OPEN: M, Th 1-9, Tu, W, F, Sa 1-5; closed Sundays and holidays
COPYING FACILITIES: yes
MATERIALS SOLICITED: Materials on Cherokee, Delaware, and Shawnee Indians; pioneer family histories; and local historical materials. Will also accept other historical materials pertaining to Oklahoma.

HOLDINGS:
Total volume: 6 file drawers
Inclusive dates: 1870 -
Description: Materials relating to local settlement and institutions, including a minute book of the Congregational Church in Vinita; a census of the Cherokee Nation, 1880 and 1890; Craig County courthouse records, 1902-35; the school census, 1915-36; records of grave removals during construction of the Pensacola Dam on the Grand River; and materials concerning homes in Vinita, 1882-1911.

Also included are interviews with pioneer residents; scrapbooks on the early history of Vinita and the Cherokee Nation; diaries, 1870 and 1888, by a Cherokee Nation pioneer; a minute book of Willie Halsell College; letters from the first Craig County superintendent, 1907; religious tracts in the Cherokee language; a history of Worcester Academy; and photographs of Plains Indians and early Vinita people and places.

WEWOKA

OK922-720
The Seminole Nation Museum
524 South Wewoka Avenue
Wewoka OK

MAILING ADDRESS:
P.O. Box 1532
Wewoka OK 74884

(405) 257-5580

OPEN: daily 1-5; closed Christmas, Dec. 24, and all January
COPYING FACILITIES: no
MATERIALS SOLICITED: Will accept material relating to the Seminole Nation after 1832, especially the removal from Florida and the period afterward.

HOLDINGS:
Total volume: 6 c.f.
Inclusive dates: 1850 - 1920
Description: Letters, business journals, roll books of Seminoles and black freedmen, an allotment map, and photographs, all pertaining to the Seminole Nation.

WOODWARD

OK956-640
Plains Indians and Pioneer Historical Foundation
Pioneer Museum and Art Center
2009 Williams Avenue
Woodward OK

MAILING ADDRESS:
Box 1167
Woodward OK 73801

(405) 256-6136

OPEN: Su 1-4, Tu-Sa 10-5; closed Mondays, Christmas, and Easter
COPYING FACILITIES: yes
MATERIALS SOLICITED: Will accept pictures, papers, and artifacts pertaining to northwestern Oklahoma.

HOLDINGS:
Total volume: 2 c.f.; 5 file cabinets
Inclusive dates: 1870 - 1980
Description: Collections cover the opening of the Cherokee Strip; political, social, and economic growth of northwestern Oklahoma. Included are records of organizations, papers of individuals, unpublished and published memoirs and histories, photographs, maps, and books.

OREGON

Since 1945 the Archives Division of the Oregon Secretary of State has administered a statewide program for preserving local public records of lasting value. Such records normally remain in the custody of local officials, but some 1,500 cubic feet of county and municipal records have been transferred to the Archives Division in Salem. The Division maintains 55,600 reels of security copy microfilm, primarily of county land and tax records filmed by local government units.

The Division will produce working copies of films for researchers at a fee, and also make available lists of its microfilm holdings.

ALBANY

OR16-40
Albany Public Library
1390 Waverly Drive, S.E.
Albany OR 97321

(503) 967-4307

OPEN: M-F 10-9, Sa 10-5; closed Sundays
COPYING FACILITIES: yes
MATERIALS SOLICITED: Materials relating to the history and geography of Albany, Linn County, and Oregon, including genealogical source materials, materials on Northwest volcanic activity, school records, church records, and community organization meeting records and membership lists. Will also accept business and agricultural records of the local area and materials on Indian tribes and culture.

HOLDINGS:
Total volume: 2 file cabinets
Inclusive dates: 19th and early 20th centuries
Description: Manuscripts relating to early history of the city and county, including records of the library, scrapbooks of clubs and organizations, and photographs by early photographers.

ASHLAND

OR32-720
Southern Oregon State College Library
1251 Siskiyou Blvd.
Ashland OR 97520

(503) 482-6445

OPEN: M-F 9-noon; closed weekends and holidays
COPYING FACILITIES: yes
MATERIALS SOLICITED: Archival materials of Southern Oregon State College. Will also accept materials relating to southern Oregon history and William Shakespeare.

HOLDINGS:
Total volume: 164 l.f.
Inclusive dates: 1868 -
Description: Official records of Southern Oregon State College and its predecessor institutions, and a few manuscripts relating to the history of southern Oregon.

ASTORIA

OR48-40
Astoria Public Library
450 Tenth Street
Astoria OR 97103

(503) 325-7323

OPEN: Su 2-5, Oct.-April, M-F 9-9, Sa 9-6; closed holidays
COPYING FACILITIES: yes
MATERIALS SOLICITED: Materials relating to local history and genealogy.

HOLDINGS:
Total volume: 500 l.f.
Inclusive dates: 1873 -
Description: Files of Columbia River Packers Association correspondence, 1898-1920, records of the Columbia River fish harvest, 1910-65, and Finnish-American folklore tapes by Elli Kongas Maranda.

SEE: Winroth.

AURORA

OR56-40
Aurora Colony Historical Society
Ox Barn Museum
Aurora OR

MAILING ADDRESS:
P.O. Box 202
Aurora OR 97002

(503) 678-5754

OPEN: W-Su 1-5; closed Mondays, Tuesdays, holidays, and Jan.
ACCESS: appointment required
COPYING FACILITIES: no
MATERIALS SOLICITED: Historical materials pertaining to Aurora and Bethel colonies. Will also accept materials on early Oregon history.

HOLDINGS:
Total volume: 18 l.f.; 1 file cabinet
Inclusive dates: 1835 - 1890
Description: Records of Bethel and Aurora colonies including genealogical source data, account books, ledgers, correspondence, music scores in manuscript, school books, photographs, oral history tapes, sound recordings, and unpublished manuscripts.

SEE: Hinding; Winroth.

BAKER

OR64-80
Baker County Public Library
Oregon Room Collection
2400 Resort Street
Baker OR 97814

(503) 523-6414

OPEN: Su 1-5, M-Th 10-9, F, Sa 9-5; closed holidays
COPYING FACILITIES: yes
MATERIALS SOLICITED: Materials relating to Baker County history. Will also accept materials relating to eastern Oregon history.

HOLDINGS:
Total volume: 30 l.f.
Inclusive dates: 19th century -
Description: A collection documenting Baker County history, including maps, diaries, manuscripts, mining reports, photographs, and oral history transcripts.

OR64-120
Catholic Diocese of Baker
Chancery Office
2215 First Street
Baker OR

MAILING ADDRESS:
P.O. Box 826
Baker OR 97814

(503) 523-2373

OPEN: by appointment
ACCESS: restricted to serious researchers
COPYING FACILITIES: yes

HOLDINGS:
Total volume: not specified
Inclusive dates: 1903 -
Description: Photographs, church building plans and specifications, newspaper clippings, and research notes, all pertaining to the Roman Catholic church in eastern Oregon.

BANDON

OR72-80
Bandon Historical Society
390 Southwest First Street
Bandon OR

MAILING ADDRESS:
P.O. Box 737
Bandon OR 97411

(503) 347-2164

OPEN: Su-F 1-4, Sa 11-4; closed holidays
COPYING FACILITIES: yes
MATERIALS SOLICITED: Materials relating to Bandon and Coos & Curry counties, including the Bandon fires, Indians, ship builders, and photographs relating to the Coos & Curry counties.

HOLDINGS:
Total volume: not specified
Inclusive dates: 1900 -
Description: Historic materials and photographs relating to Coos and Curry counties, primarily of Bandon, covering the fires that occurred in 1914 and 1936. Materials relating to shipbuilding along the coast from Gold Beach to Prosper.

SEE: Winroth.

BEND

OR96-120
Central Oregon Community College
Library
N.W. College Way
Bend OR 97701

(503) 385-5512

OPEN: Su 3-9, M-Th 8-9, F 8-4; closed Saturdays and holidays; summers, M-Th 10-6 and closed other days
COPYING FACILITIES: yes
MATERIALS SOLICITED: Materials pertaining to central Oregon. Will also accept materials relating to the Pacific Northwest.

HOLDINGS:
Total volume: 541 items
Inclusive dates: 1880 -
Description: A photograph collection depicting Oregon and northern California Indians and the logging industry and pioneer life in the Bend area; and oral history interviews with early settlers of central Oregon.

SEE: Hines.

OR96-150
Deschutes County Library
Bend OR 97701

no telephone

SEE: Hamer.

Questionnaire not returned.

BROWNSVILLE

OR104-640
Pioneer Picture Gallery
City Park
Brownsville OR

MAILING ADDRESS:
33364 White Oak Road
Corvallis OR 97330

no telephone

OPEN: by appointment only
COPYING FACILITIES: yes
MATERIALS SOLICITED: Photographs of Linn County, OR.

HOLDINGS:
Total volume: 1,000 items
Inclusive dates: 1890's -
Description: Visual documents pertaining to all aspects of the history of Linn County, OR.

SEE: Winroth.

BURNS

OR112-335
Harney County Library
80 West D Street
Burns OR 97720

(503) 573-6670

OPEN: M-Th 12:30-9, F 12:30-5:30; closed weekends
COPYING FACILITIES: yes
MATERIALS SOLICITED: Historical materials pertaining to Harney County.

HOLDINGS:
Total volume: 2 file cabinets
Inclusive dates: 1910 - 1930
Description: Historical materials pertaining to Harney County, including photographs and oral history tapes of local settlers.

SEE: Winroth.

COOS BAY

OR128-720
Southwestern Oregon Community
College
Learning Resource Center
Coos Bay OR 97420

(503) 888-7431

OPEN: Su 1-5, M-F 7:30-10; closed Saturdays and holidays
COPYING FACILITIES: yes
MATERIALS SOLICITED: Materials pertaining to the history of the Coos Bay area.

HOLDINGS:
Total volume: 500 items
Inclusive dates: 1870's -
Description: Oral history interviews, some with accompanying sets of photographic slides, of residents of the Coos County area. Described are the establishment and growth of southwestern Oregon, lumbering and other industries, experiences in early schools, social activities, and other local events. There are also 25 survey maps of Coos and Curry counties, 1870's-80's, and aerial photographs of the estuary of Coos Bay, 1972.

SEE: Hinding.

SEE ALSO: Besse L. Guthrie, *Index to Living History Series* (Southwestern Oregon Community College, 1976).

CORVALLIS

OR144-600
Oregon State University
Archives
Corvallis OR 97331

(503) 754-2165

OPEN: M-F 8-5; closed weekends and holidays
COPYING FACILITIES: yes
MATERIALS SOLICITED: Records of the University of archival value. Will also accept photographs and oral history tapes.

HOLDINGS:
Total volume: 120,000 photographs; 4,500 microfilm reels
Inclusive dates: 1868 -
Description: Materials relating to the history and development of the University, including approximately 200 microfilmed groups of records from schools, departments, and administrative offices, including student and faculty organizations. There are also photographs, covering a variety of subject areas, including the University, and some oral history tapes.

SEE: NUCMC, 1968.

SEE: Hinding.

SEE ALSO: *Guide to the Microfilmed Collections in the Oregon State University Archives* (Oregon State Univ., 1976); Richard C. Davis, *North American Forest History: A Guide to Archives and Manuscripts in the United States and Canada* (Clio Books, 1977); individual guides to collections available upon request.

OR144-610

Oregon State University
Horner Museum
Gill Coliseum
Oregon State University
Corvallis OR 97331

(503) 754-2951

OPEN: winter, Tu-F 10-5; summer, M-F 10-5; closed weekends and holidays
ACCESS: advance arrangements required
COPYING FACILITIES: yes
MATERIALS SOLICITED: Manuscripts, photographs, and oral history tapes pertaining to the history of Oregon Territory and State, especially agriculture, forestry, pharmacy, shipping, other commercial development, and daily life of residents.

HOLDINGS:
> *Total volume:* 80 l.f.
> *Inclusive dates:* 1870 - 1970
> *Description:* Photographs and other materials relating to the Corvallis area and Oregon, with emphasis on lumbering and forestry history.

SEE: Winroth.

OR144-620

Oregon State University
William Jasper Kerr Library
Corvallis OR 97331

(503) 754-3432

SEE: NUCMC, 1972.

Questionnaire not returned.

CRATER LAKE

OR176-120

Crater Lake National Park
Crater Lake Library
Crater Lake OR

MAILING ADDRESS:
P.O. Box 7
Crater Lake OR 97604

(503) 594-2211

OPEN: M-F 8-5; closed weekends and holidays
ACCESS: serious researchers
COPYING FACILITIES: no
MATERIALS SOLICITED: Materials relating to the natural history of the Cascade Mountains, the geology of volcanos, and the human history of the area.

HOLDINGS:
> *Total volume:* not specified
> *Inclusive dates:* 1885 -
> *Description:* Correspondence, reports, diaries, and other papers relating to the human history, environment, visitor use,

and administration of Crater Lake National Park. There are also slides, photographs, and glass negatives relating to the Park.

SEE: Hamer; NUCMC, 1966.

SEE: Davis.

EUGENE

OR224-480

Lane County Historical Museum
740 West 13th Avenue
Eugene OR 97402

(503) 687-4239

OPEN: by appointment only
ACCESS: advance arrangements recommended
COPYING FACILITIES: yes
MATERIALS SOLICITED: Materials concerning Lane County history, 1846-1920. Will also accept materials that have unique value or pertain to Lane County after 1920.

HOLDINGS:
> *Total volume:* 210 l.f.; 40,000 photographs
> *Inclusive dates:* 1846 -
> *Description:* A collection of diaries, correspondence, land patents, genealogies, account books and other business records, county records, and photographs that document the development of Lane County, with special focus on the pioneer period, 1846-1920.

GUIDES: Edward Nolan, *Catalogue of Manuscripts in the Lane County Museum Library* (1980).

SEE: NUCMC, 1959-61.

SEE: Novotny; Hinding.

OR224-800

University of Oregon
Library
Eugene OR 97403

(503) 686-3068

OPEN: M-F 8-5; closed weekends and holidays
ACCESS: qualified researchers
COPYING FACILITIES: yes
MATERIALS SOLICITED: Materials on American authors and illustrators with special emphasis on children's books and western fiction, missionary movements especially in the Far East, political conservatism, 20th century American history, and the Pacific Northwest.

HOLDINGS:
> *Total volume:* 2,490,000 items
> *Inclusive dates:* 1500 -
> *Description:* Materials emphasizing political, social, economic, and literary history of the United States in the 20th century. Special strengths include papers of political conservatives, missionaries, artists and illustrators, and Pacific Northwest political figures. There are also photographs relating mainly to Oregon and Washington.

GUIDES: Martin Schmitt, comp., *Catalogue of Manuscripts in the University of Oregon Library* (1971).

SEE: Hamer; NUCMC, 1959-64, 66, 69-72, 74, 76, 78.

SEE: Allard, Crawley, and Edmison; Parkinson; Mehr; Martin; Hinding; Robbins.

SEE ALSO: Peter Duignan, *Handbook of American Resources for African Studies* (Hoover Institution, 1967); Walter Schatz, ed., *Directory of Afro-American Resources* (Bowker, 1970); Andrea Hinding and Rosemary Richardson, comps., *Archival and Manuscript Resources for the Study of Women's History: A Beginning* (Univ. of Minnesota Libraries, Social Welfare History Archives Center, 1972); Joan Hoff Wilson and Lynn B. Donovan, 'Women's History: A Listing of West Coast Archival and Manuscript Sources, Part II,' *California Historical Quarterly* 55 (Summer 1976); David A. Hounshell, comp., *Manuscripts in U.S. Depositories Relating to the History of Electrical Science and Technology* (Smithsonian Institution, n.d.).

Ann Novotny, ed., *Picture Sources 3* (Special Libraries Assn., 1975); G. Q. Flynn, 'The New Deal and Local Archives: The Pacific Northwest,' *American Archivist* 33 (Jan. 1970); Terry Abraham, comp., *A Union List of the Papers of Members of Congress from the Pacific Northwest* (Washington State Univ. Library, 1976); Richard C. Davis, *North American Forest History: A Guide to Archives and Manuscripts in the United States and Canada* (Clio Books, 1977). Inventories to individual collections are available from the Library.

OR224-810

University of Oregon
Map Library
165 Condon Hall
Eugene OR 97403

(503) 686-3051

OPEN: Su 1-5, M-Th 8-9, F 8-5; closed Saturdays and holidays
COPYING FACILITIES: yes
MATERIALS SOLICITED: Oregon and Pacific Northwest aerial photographs. Will also accept maps of the world.

HOLDINGS:
> *Total volume:* 200,000 items
> *Inclusive dates:* 1938 -
> *Description:* Aerial photographs of Oregon and the Pacific Northwest, and manuscript maps drawn by students on field trips and other assignments.

OR224-880

Willamette National Forest
Historical Collection
Eugene Federal Building
Eugene OR

MAILING ADDRESS:
P.O. Box 10607
Eugene OR 97440

(503) 687-6539

OPEN: M-F 7:45-4:30; closed weekends and holidays
ACCESS: restricted to serious researchers
COPYING FACILITIES: yes

MATERIALS SOLICITED: Materials pertinent to the history of the Willamette National Forest.

HOLDINGS:
Total volume: 8 c.f.
Inclusive dates: 1890 -
Description: Materials pertaining to the history of the Willamette National Forest, consisting of research notes, unpublished monographs, oral interviews, field diaries, newspaper clippings, correspondence, black and white photographs, and 35mm and lantern slides.

FLORENCE

OR240-240
Siuslaw Public Library
250 Highway 101
Florence OR

MAILING ADDRESS:
P.O. Box A
Florence OR 97439

(503) 997-3132

OPEN: M, F, Sa 1-5, Tu-Th 1-9; closed Sundays and holidays
COPYING FACILITIES: no
MATERIALS SOLICITED: Oral history interviews of people who grew up in the Florence - Mapleton area.

HOLDINGS:
Total volume: 60 tapes
Inclusive dates: 1974 -
Description: A collection of oral history interviews with 41 residents of the Florence - Mapleton area, particularly relating to early settlement. The focus is on family history, with particular attention to the role of families in the growth and development of communities in the western section of Lane County.

FOREST GROVE

OR256-650
Pacific University
Museum
Forest Grove OR 97116

(503) 357-6151

OPEN: W afternoon; closed other days
COPYING FACILITIES: yes
MATERIALS SOLICITED: Local history documents.

HOLDINGS:
Total volume: 2 filing cabinets
Inclusive dates: 1840 -
Description: A collection of manuscripts and photographs concerning the history of Forest Grove, Washington County, and Pacific University.

SEE: Hamer (as Pacific University, Library).

GRANTS PASS

OR288-400
Josephine County Historical Society
508 S.W. 5th Street
Grants Pass OR 97526

MAILING ADDRESS:
P.O. Box 742
Grants Pass OR 97526

(503) 479-7827, 476-5898

OPEN: M-F 10-4; closed weekends and holidays
COPYING FACILITIES: no
MATERIALS SOLICITED: Early maps of trails and roads. Will also accept historical materials pertaining to Oregon and Josephine County, in particular.

HOLDINGS:
Total volume: not specified
Inclusive dates: 1890's -
Description: A collection of glass negatives of local subjects, slides of County historical sites, and Josephine County court records, 1895- .

SEE: Winroth.

HILLSBORO

OR352-900
Washington County Museum
641 East Main
Hillsboro OR 97123

(503) 648-8601

OPEN: M-F 10-4:30, Sa, Su noon-4:30; closed holidays
COPYING FACILITIES: yes
MATERIALS SOLICITED: Materials related to the history of Washington County and its people.

HOLDINGS:
Total volume: 250 c.f.
Inclusive dates: 1839 -
Description: Materials relating to the history of Washington County, including maps, photographs, oral history tapes, ephemera, records of local organizations and businesses, and papers of local citizens, business leaders, and politicians.

SEE: Hamer (as Washington County Historical Society Museum).

SEE: Winroth.

JACKSONVILLE

OR400-720
Southern Oregon Historical Society
Jacksonville Museum
Research Library
206 North 5th Street
Jacksonville OR

MAILING ADDRESS:
Box 480
Jacksonville OR 97530

(503) 899-1847

OPEN: by appointment Tu-Sa 9-5; closed Sundays and Mondays, except M 9-5 June-Aug.
COPYING FACILITIES: yes
MATERIALS SOLICITED: Materials relating to southwestern Oregon, especially Jackson County.

HOLDINGS:
Total volume: 1,000 l.f.
Inclusive dates: 1845 -
Description: Materials relating to southwestern Oregon, especially Jackson County, 1850-1920. Included are diaries and letters; archival materials of Jackson County, the city of Jacksonville, and numerous firms and organizations; photographs; motion picture films; oral histories; and glass plate negatives.

GUIDES: Richard H. Engeman, comp., *Preliminary Guide to Local History Materials: Jacksonville Museum Library* (1978).

SEE: NUCMC, 1959-61.

SEE: Novotny; Davis; Hinding.

JOSEPH

OR424-322
Oregon Electric Railway Historical Society, Inc.
Main Street
Joseph OR 97846

(503) 357-3574

OPEN: by appointment
COPYING FACILITIES: yes
MATERIALS SOLICITED: Photographs of people using trolleys and of workmen in the trolley barns and shops. Will also accept trolley memorabilia.

HOLDINGS:
Total volume: 15 c.f.
Inclusive dates: 1902 -
Description: Company letters, tax records, employment records, accident files from Portland Traction Company and related firms; photograph and negatives relating to electric interurban and street railways.

OR424-880
Wallowa County Museum
Joseph OR

MAILING ADDRESS:
Grace Bartlett
Wallowa County Museum
Joseph OR 97846

no telephone

OPEN: by appointment only
COPYING FACILITIES: no
MATERIALS SOLICITED: Historical materials pertaining to Wallowa County, including photographs before the mid-1930's, diaries, personal stories, early survey data, and business records. Will also accept scrapbooks if pertinent.

HOLDINGS:
Total volume: not specified
Inclusive dates: 1870's - 1930's
Description: Letters, scrapbooks, and photographs collected by historian J. H. Horner, diaries and photographs of D.

W. Mote, 1877-1922, diaries of Caroline Wasson Thomason, and sales records of F. D. McCully's general store in Joseph from the early 1900's. Also included are photographs, glass negatives, scrapbooks, survey books, and oral history pertaining to Wallowa County.

SEE: Winroth.

KLAMATH FALLS

OR448-450

Klamath County Museum
Research Library
1451 Main Street
Klamath Falls OR 97601

(503) 882-2501, Ext. 208

OPEN: Tu-Sa 9-5, Su 1-5; closed Mondays and holidays
ACCESS: by appointment only
COPYING FACILITIES: yes
MATERIALS SOLICITED: Materials relating to Klamath County history. Will also accept significant research materials on Oregon.

HOLDINGS:
> *Total volume:* not specified
> *Inclusive dates:* late 1800's -
> *Description:* Manuscripts, documents, letters, photographs, dry negatives, and oral histories relating chiefly to Klamath County history, with significant holdings on the Modoc Indian War, 1872-73.

SEE: Bean and Vane.

LA GRANDE

OR464-200

Eastern Oregon State College
Walter M. Pierce Library
La Grande OR 97850

(503) 963-1540

OPEN: M-Th 8-10, F 8-5, Sa 1-5, Su 7-10; schedule varies with academic year; closed holidays
COPYING FACILITIES: yes
MATERIALS SOLICITED: Materials relating to Oregon, especially eastern Oregon, as well as the Pacific Northwest, the Oregon Trail, Oregon authors, and Indians. Will also accept materials relating to genealogy and western exploration.

HOLDINGS:
> *Total volume:* 750 l.f.; 30 c.f.
> *Inclusive dates:* 1850 -
> *Description:* Materials relating principally to eastern Oregon, including manuscripts, diaries, pioneer reminiscences, and photographs.

SEE: Winroth.

SEE ALSO: John W. Evans, *Genealogical Material and Other Records of Genealogical Interest in Walter M. Pierce Library, Eastern Oregon State College* (n.p., 1976).

OR464-322

Episcopal Diocese of Eastern Oregon
Office of the Historiographer
2102 Cove Avenue
La Grande OR

MAILING ADDRESS:
P.O. Box 1091
La Grande OR 97850

(503) 963-5521

OPEN: by appointment
COPYING FACILITIES: no
MATERIALS SOLICITED: Materials relating to the Episcopal church in eastern Oregon since 1870.

HOLDINGS:
> *Total volume:* 250 c.f.
> *Inclusive dates:* 1855 -
> *Description:* Records of the Episcopal Diocese of eastern Oregon, including parish records, and records of marriages, births, and confirmations; personal papers, including reports and correspondence of clergy; and photographs of churches, people, and places related to the Episcopal church in eastern Oregon.

OR464-470

La Grande Public Library
Fourth and Pennsylvania Streets
La Grande OR 97850

no telephone

SEE: NUCMC, 1959-61.

Questionnaire not returned.

OR464-490

Pacific Northwest Forest and Range Experiment Station
Forestry and Range Sciences Laboratory
La Grande OR

MAILING ADDRESS:
P.O. Box 2315, Route 2
La Grande OR 97850

(503) 963-7122

OPEN: M-F 7:30-4:30; closed weekends and holidays
COPYING FACILITIES: yes
MATERIALS SOLICITED: Manuscripts, photographs, maps, and drawings related to management and research on forest and range lands in the Pacific Northwest, with emphasis on the period before 1920. Will also accept diaries, botanical survey notes, charts, and maps of early Forest Service employees, botanists, biologists, and government trappers.

HOLDINGS:
> *Total volume:* 150 items
> *Inclusive dates:* 1878 - 1942
> *Description:* Photographs of forest and range conditions in eastern Oregon, 1890's-1911, by Gifford Pinchot, George B. Sudsworth, Arthur W. Sampson, J. T. Jardine, and others. Also included are ink drawings of plant parts and several plants by botanist W. T. Webber, and copies of letters, diaries, notes, maps, and plant lists by William Conklin Cusick, eastern Oregon botanical explorer, plant hunter,

taxonomist, and Grande Ronde Valley rancher, 1878-1910.

LAFAYETTE

OR480-940

Yamhill County Historical Museum
6th & Market Streets
Lafayette OR

MAILING ADDRESS:
P.O. Box 484
Lafayette OR 97127

no telephone

OPEN: Sa-Su 1-4:30; closed weekdays and holidays
COPYING FACILITIES: no
MATERIALS SOLICITED: Historical materials pertaining to Yamhill County, OR, especially school pictures and records. Will also accept materials pertaining to early Yamhill County pioneers and settlers after they left the county.

HOLDINGS:
> *Total volume:* 40 c.f.
> *Inclusive dates:* 1854 - 1970
> *Description:* Material relating to Yamhill County's history, including account books, day books, letters, diaries, and genealogical materials on early settlers. Also included are school records dating to 1854, records of businesses, community groups, and churches; photographs, scrapbooks, and oral history tapes.

SEE: Winroth.

LAKEVIEW

OR512-480

Lake County Library
Lakeview OR 97630

(503) 947-2321

OPEN: M-Th 8:30-9, F 8:30-6, Sa 12-4; closed Sundays and holidays
COPYING FACILITIES: yes
MATERIALS SOLICITED: Local family histories. Will also accept other local materials.

HOLDINGS:
> *Total volume:* 6 folders; 100 items
> *Inclusive dates:* 1851 -
> *Description:* Diaries, correspondence, and genealogical data pertaining to 6 pioneer families in eastern Oregon; and a photograph collection depicting Lake County subjects at the turn of the century.

SEE: Winroth.

OR512-720

Schminck Memorial Museum
128 South E Street
Lakeview OR 97630

(503) 947-3134

OPEN: Tu-Sa 1-5 or by appointment; closed Sundays, Mondays, holidays, December, and January
COPYING FACILITIES: no

HOLDINGS:
Total volume: 500 items
Inclusive dates: 1875 - 1930
Description: Photographs of early business buildings, homes, schools, ranches, Indians, families, livestock, and teams portraying life in early Lake County, OR.

SEE: Winroth.

MARYLHURST

OR528-718
Sisters of the Holy Names of Jesus
  and Mary
Oregon Province
Archives
Convent of the Holy Names
Marylhurst OR

MAILING ADDRESS:
P.O. Box 214
Marylhurst OR 97036

(503) 636-8105

OPEN: M-F 9-3; other times by
  appointment
COPYING FACILITIES: yes
MATERIALS SOLICITED: Materials relating to the Sisters of the Holy names and their educational institutions in the Pacific Northwest, 1859- .

HOLDINGS:
Total volume: 380 c.f.
Inclusive dates: 1859 -
Description: A collection of materials relating to the Sisters of the Holy Names of Jesus and Mary in the Pacific Northwest, with special emphasis in the field of education. Included are letters, journals, diaries, maps, architectural plans, photographs, and other items relating to this community.

SEE: Hinding; Winroth.

MEDFORD

OR560-690
Rogue River National Forest
Supervisor's Office
333 W. 8th Street
Federal Building, Room 308
Medford OR

MAILING ADDRESS:
P.O. Box 520
Medford OR 97501

(503) 776-3639

OPEN: M-Th 8-4:30; closed other days
  and holidays
ACCESS: advance arrangements required
COPYING FACILITIES: yes
MATERIALS SOLICITED: Records, personal memoirs, and photographs pertaining to the history, especially administrative history, of the Rogue River National Forest prior to 1960.

HOLDINGS:
Total volume: 10 l.f.
Inclusive dates: 1900 - 1960
Description: A collection focusing on the administrative history and past personnel of the Rogue River National For-

est, including Forest Service documents, correspondence, diaries, maps, and photographs. Documented are such activities as timber, fire, and range management, watershed and wildlife management, recreational use, homestead entry and mining claim examinations, and Civilian Conservation Corps projects.

MONMOUTH

OR576-600
Oregon College of Education
Library
234 North Monmouth Street
Monmouth OR 97361

(503) 838-1220, Ext. 240

OPEN: M-Th 8-10, F 8-5; closed
  weekends, July 4th, Labor Day, and
  Christmas vacation; shorter hours in
  summer and between semesters
COPYING FACILITIES: yes
MATERIALS SOLICITED: Records and audio-visual materials relating to the Oregon College of Education, the Oregon State System of Higher Education, and the history and culture of the Pacific Northwest. Will also accept materials relating to local communities of the area and to OCE's activities in Micronesia and Alaska.

HOLDINGS:
Total volume: 25 c.f.
Inclusive dates: 1854 -
Description: Materials pertaining to the history of the College and local communities, including correspondence, photographs, slides, audio tapes, and clippings. Also included is the John C. Higgins Memorial Collection of historical materials on the Pacific Northwest.

NEWPORT

OR624-480
Lincoln County Historical Museums
545 S. W. 9th
Newport OR 97365

(503) 265-7509

OPEN: Tu-F 11-4, Sa 11-1; closed
  Sundays, Mondays, Thanksgiving,
  Christmas, and New Year's
COPYING FACILITIES: yes
MATERIALS SOLICITED: Records, documents, diaries, photographs, and other materials pertaining to the history of Lincoln County.

HOLDINGS:
Total volume: 15 c.f.
Inclusive dates: 1866 -
Description: Collections of records, diaries, reports, and correspondence from the Siletz Indian Reservation; diaries and records of early exploration; memorabilia of the area's early days as a tourist resort; deeds, maps, and abstracts of early real estate transactions; oral history tapes; school record books; and ledgers from early resort hotels.

SEE: Winroth.

PENDLETON

OR688-810
Umatilla County Library
214 North Main
Pendleton OR 97801

(503) 276-1881

OPEN: M 1-8, Tu-Sa 10-5; closed
  Sundays and holidays
COPYING FACILITIES: yes
MATERIALS SOLICITED: Historical documents of the Pacific Northwest, specifically eastern Oregon.

HOLDINGS:
Total volume: 1,000 items
Inclusive dates: 1850 -
Description: Lee Moorehouse glass negatives, the original manuscript of *Let'er Buck* by Charles Wellington Furlong, Dr. William McKay correspondence, a logbook of the Umatilla Indian Agency, and 16mm film of the Pendleton roundup, 1912 and 1952.

OR688-820
Umatilla National Forest
2517 S.W. Hailey Avenue
Pendleton OR 97801

(503) 276-3811, Ext. 424

OPEN: M-F 7:45-4:30; closed weekends
  and holidays
COPYING FACILITIES: yes
MATERIALS SOLICITED: Diaries, journals, correspondence, photographs, unpublished histories, records of early grazing and homesteading, and records of early roads and trails, relating to the Umatilla National Forest.

HOLDINGS:
Total volume: 2 c.f.
Inclusive dates: 1905 - 1968
Description: A collection of memoranda, letters, diaries, reminiscences, unpublished histories, and reports, primarily concerning Umatilla National Forest, located in eastern Oregon and southeastern Washington.

PHILOMATH

OR704-80
Benton County Historical Society
Benton County Historical Museum
1101 Main Street
Philomath OR

MAILING ADDRESS:
P.O. Box 47
Philomath OR 97370

(503) 929-6230

OPEN: by appointment only
COPYING FACILITIES: no
MATERIALS SOLICITED: Materials relating to Benton County and its residents.

HOLDINGS:
Total volume: 1,350 items
Inclusive dates: 1850 -
Description: Manuscripts, maps, and photographs relating to Benton County and its residents, including records of

businesses, churches, schools, and individuals.

PORTLAND

OR720-40

Archdiocese of Portland in Oregon
History and Archives Department
2838 E. Burnside
Portland OR 97214

(503) 234-5334

OPEN: by appointment only M-F 8:15-4:45; closed weekends, and religious and other holidays
COPYING FACILITIES: no
MATERIALS SOLICITED: Roman Catholic church history in Oregon and the Pacific Northwest.

HOLDINGS:
    Total volume: not specified
    Inclusive dates: 1840 -
    Description: Correspondence of archbishops; account books, business records, and financial records of the Archdiocese and its parishes; genealogical source data from records of parishes; archives and non-current records of churches, schools, and the Archdiocese; copies of plans of churches, schools, and other buildings; photographs of churches, schools, and people connected with the Archdiocese; and oral history tapes and transcripts.

OR720-200

Episcopal Diocese of Oregon
11800 S.W. Military Lane
Portland OR 97219

(503) 636-5613

OPEN: M-F 9-5; closed weekends and holidays
COPYING FACILITIES: yes

HOLDINGS:
    Total volume: 75 items
    Inclusive dates: 1841 -
    Description: Birth and marriage records from defunct parishes, and diaries of bishops of the diocese.

OR720-400

Jewish Historical Society of Oregon, Inc.
6651 S.W. Capitol Highway
Portland OR 97219

(503) 246-9844

OPEN: by appointment only
COPYING FACILITIES: no
MATERIALS SOLICITED: Documents and memorabilia of Jewish interest, pertaining to the history and settlement of the area.

HOLDINGS:
    Total volume: 180 l.f.; 8 file drawers
    Inclusive dates: 1858 -
    Description: Documents, photographs, and record books pertaining to Jewish life in Oregon, including a record book of the Committee on Emigres, 1936-49; minutes of the Synagogue Ahavai Sholom, 1912-20; minutes of the Hebrew School, 1916-34; record books of the Jewish Edu-

cation Association, 1927-53; The B'nai Brith Building Association, 1910-17; and transcripts of interviews with over 90 members of the local Jewish community.

OR720-440

Lewis and Clark College
Watzek Library
College Archives
0615 S.W. Palatine Hill Road
Portland OR 97219

(503) 293-2761

OPEN: M-F 8-12 or by appointment; closed weekends and holidays
ACCESS: advance arrangements required
COPYING FACILITIES: yes
MATERIALS SOLICITED: Administrative records of the college as well as materials throwing light on the various dimensions of college life.

HOLDINGS:
    Total volume: 500 c.f.
    Inclusive dates: 1867 -
    Description: Materials related to Albany College, Albany, Oregon (1867 - 1942) and its successor, Lewis and Clark College (1942 -), including administrative records, college publications, faculty and student manuscripts, architectural drawings, photographs, motion pictures, video tapes, oral history tapes, sound recordings, and scrapbooks.

OR720-450

Library Association of Portland
801 S.W. Tenth Avenue
Portland OR 97205

(503) 223-7201

OPEN: Tu-Th 10-9, F, Sa 10-5:30; closed Sundays, Mondays, and holidays
COPYING FACILITIES: yes

HOLDINGS:
    Total volume: not specified
    Inclusive dates: not specified
    Description: Charles Bulkley's journal of the Russo-American telegraph expedition, the official records of the Lewis and Clark centennial exposition, several medieval and Renaissance manuscripts, and meteorological records for Portland, 1870-74.

SEE: Hamer; NUCMC, 1973.

OR720-470

Lutheran Church-Missouri Synod
Northwest District
1700 N.E. Knott
Portland OR 97212

(503) 288-8383

OPEN: M-F 8:30-5; closed weekends and holidays
COPYING FACILITIES: yes
MATERIALS SOLICITED: Materials pertaining to the congregations, professional workers, organizations, and District Board of Directors of the Lutheran Church-Missouri Synod Northwest District in Alaska, Idaho, Oregon, and Washington.

HOLDINGS:
    Total volume: 100 l.f.
    Inclusive dates: 1890 -
    Description: Materials relating to the history of the Northwest District of the Lutheran Church-Missouri Synod, including records of the Lutheran Laymen's League, the Lutheran Women's Missionary League, the Walther League, and youth organizations; reports; correspondence; minutes; biographical material; congregational records; and anniversary booklets.

OR720-560

National Railway Historical Society
Pacific Northwest Chapter
Room 1, Union Street
Portland OR 97209

(503) 226-6747

OPEN: by appointment only
COPYING FACILITIES: no
MATERIALS SOLICITED: Materials pertaining to railroading in Oregon, Washington, and British Columbia. Will also accept materials on general railroad subjects.

HOLDINGS:
    Total volume: 2,000 c.f.
    Inclusive dates: 1870's -
    Description: The collection consists of the vice-presidential files of the Spokane, Portland and Seattle Railway, as well as mechanical records for equipment, authorizations for expenditures, manuscript maps, charts, and architectural, engineering, and technical drawings. Similar items from other railroads are also collected.

OR720-580

Oregon Department of Geology and Mineral Industries
Library
1005 State Office Building
Portland OR 97201

(503) 229-5580

OPEN: M-F 8-5; closed weekends and holidays
COPYING FACILITIES: yes
MATERIALS SOLICITED: Will accept materials relating to the early history of the mining industry in Oregon.

HOLDINGS:
    Total volume: not specified
    Inclusive dates: late 19th century -
    Description: A collection relating to the history of mining and geology in Oregon. Included are 2,500 maps; research reports; and materials concerning early geologists.

SEE: Parkinson.

OR720-590

Oregon Historical Society
Library
1230 S.W. Park Avenue
Portland OR 97205

(503) 222-1741

OPEN: M-Sa 10-4:45; closed Sundays and holidays
ACCESS: researchers should be at least college level

COPYING FACILITIES: yes
MATERIALS SOLICITED: Pioneer diaries
and reminiscences; architectural plans,
renderings, and specifications for buildings and homes in Oregon; lumber,
shipping, railroad, and other business
papers; and materials relating to wom-
en in the Pacific Northwest, ethnic
groups, and the performing arts. Will
also accept other materials relating to
Oregon, the Oregon Territory, the Pacific Northwest, and the Pacific Rim.

HOLDINGS:
    Total volume: 5,400 l.f.
    Inclusive dates: 1785 -
    Description: Materials relating to early
coastal explorations by the British, Spanish, and Russians; the fur trading period,
including documents of the Hudson's Bay
Company and its factors; Protestant and
Catholic missionaries; and overland jour-
neys to the Pacific Ocean. There are also
Oregon provisional and territorial government records; regional church, business,
and association records; personal papers
of State and local politicians, business
leaders, suffragists, writers, and educators;
records documenting lumber and fishing
industries in the Pacific Northwest; and
microfilm holdings of manuscripts from
other institutions, such as the British Museum, the Public Record Office in London, and the Huntington Library.

SEE: Hamer; NUCMC, 1959-64, 66, 68,
72-74, 76, 77, 78, 80.

SEE: Hinding; Mehr; Robbins.

SEE ALSO: Ann Novotny, ed., *Picture
Sources 3* (Special Libraries Assn.,
1975); Terry Abraham, comp., *A Union
List of the Papers of Members of Con-
gress from the Pacific Northwest*
(Washington State Univ. Library,
1976); Joan Hoff Wilson and Lynn B.
Donovan, 'Women's History: A Listing
of West Coast Archival and Manuscript
Sources, Part II,' *California Historical
Quarterly* 55 (Summer 1976); Richard
C. Davis, *North American Forest History: A Guide to Archives and Manuscripts in the United States and Canada*
(Clio Books, 1977); and the following
publications of the Society: *Guide to
the Manuscripts Collections* (1971);
*Supplement to the Guide to the Manu-
scripts Collections* (1974-75); and *Oregon Historical Society Microfilm Guide*
(1973).

OR720-660
Oregon Art Institute
Portland Art Museum
1219 S.W. Park Avenue
Portland OR 97205

(503) 226-2811

OPEN: by appointment only
ACCESS: by appointment only, for those
with legitimate scholarly intent
COPYING FACILITIES: no
MATERIALS SOLICITED: Will accept materials pertaining to the Portland Art
Association, artists whose work is in
the Museum collection, or faculty and
students of the Museum Art School.

HOLDINGS:
    Total volume: not specified
    Inclusive dates: 1900 -
    Description: Records of the Portland
Art Association, photographs of early
Portland architecture, and papers of art
collectors, including Axel Rasmussen,
whose specialty was Northwest American
Indian art.

SEE: Mehr.

OR720-670
Portland State University
Department of Geography
Map Room
Montgomery Street
Portland OR

MAILING ADDRESS:
P.O. Box 751
Portland OR 97207

(503) 229-3916

OPEN: M-F 8-5; closed weekends and
holidays
COPYING FACILITIES: yes
MATERIALS SOLICITED: Maps of Portland, Oregon, and the Pacific Northwest; aerial photographs; and other geographical materials. Will also accept
cartographic teaching or research materials.

HOLDINGS:
    Total volume: 16,000 items
    Inclusive dates: 1930's -
    Description: A collection of 15,000 ae-
rial photographs of Oregon and 1,000
manuscript maps showing land use in the
Portland area.

OR720-700
Reed College
Library
3203 S.E. Woodstock Blvd.
Portland OR 97211

(503) 771-1112, Ext. 338

OPEN: M-F 9-5; closed weekends and
holidays
COPYING FACILITIES: yes
MATERIALS SOLICITED: Will accept materials relating to Reed College and its
faculty and alumni.

HOLDINGS:
    Total volume: 81.5 l.f.
    Inclusive dates: 1854 -
    Description: Personal papers relating
primarily to Oregon and Reed College.
The papers of Simeon Gannett Reed,
concerning Oregon business interests in
the 19th century, comprise the bulk of
the collection. Also represented are the
papers of Edouard Chambreau, Indian
scout; Thomas Lamb Elliot, Portland religious leader and a founder of Reed College; and Philip Whalen, poet.

SEE: Hamer.

SEE: Davis.

OR720-740
University of Portland
Archives
5000 North Willamette Boulevard
Portland OR 97203

(503) 283-7116

OPEN: M-Th 8:30-4:30; closed other days
and holidays
ACCESS: by appointment
COPYING FACILITIES: no
MATERIALS SOLICITED: Material relating
to the history of the University of Portland and the north Portland area. Will
also accept documents and correspondence from University offices.

HOLDINGS:
    Total volume: 284 l.f.
    Inclusive dates: 1901 -
    Description: Materials relating to the
University of Portland and its early history. Included are manuscripts, University publications, oral history interviews
and transcripts, and a photograph collection.

PRINEVILLE

OR736-40
A. R. Bowman Memorial Museum
246 North Main Street
Prineville OR 97754

(503) 447-3715

OPEN: W-Sa noon-5; closed other days,
holidays, and Jan. - Feb.; open Sundays
in summer
COPYING FACILITIES: no

HOLDINGS:
    Total volume: not specified
    Inclusive dates: 1880 -
    Description: Materials pertaining to the
history of Prineville and Crook County,
including post office ledgers, business
records, family histories, and photographs
of settlers.

SEE: Winroth.

ROSEBURG

OR768-170
Douglas County Museum of History
and Natural History
History Center Library
County Fairgrounds
Roseburg OR

MAILING ADDRESS:
P.O. Box 1550
Roseburg OR 97470

(503) 440-4507

OPEN: Tu-F 10-4; closed weekends,
Mondays, and holidays
COPYING FACILITIES: yes
MATERIALS SOLICITED: Douglas County
pioneer history. Will also accept materials relating to the genealogy of local
pioneer families.

HOLDINGS:
> *Total volume:* 419 l.f.
> *Inclusive dates:* 1700's -
> *Description:* A collection of Douglas County historical materials, consisting of letters, unpublished reminiscences, other manuscripts, and 6,000 copy negatives of early photographs.

SEE: Paszek; Hinding; Winroth.

SALEM

OR816-530
Mission Mill Museum Association
1313 Mill Street, S.E.
Salem OR 97301

(503) 585-7012

OPEN: June-Oct., W-Su 1:30-4:30; Nov.-May, W-Sa 1:30-4:30; closed Mondays, Tuesdays, and holidays, including Christmas week
COPYING FACILITIES: no
MATERIALS SOLICITED: Original papers of early settlers of the Salem area and documents pertaining to the management of the Methodist Mission. Will also accept materials pertaining to Marion County.

HOLDINGS:
> *Total volume:* 1.5 c.f.
> *Inclusive dates:* 1860 - 1972
> *Description:* Letters to Robert Thomas Judson and his wife pertaining to the writer's activities, receipts for payment of taxes, photographs of the Salem area, including the Thomas Kay Woolen Mill and the Jefferson Woolen Mill, and an original manuscript of master's thesis on the history of the Willamette Mission.

OR816-590
Oregon Secretary of State
Archives Division
Oregon State Archives and Records Center
1005 Broadway N.E.
Salem OR 97310

(503) 378-4240

OPEN: M-F 8-5; closed weekends and holidays
COPYING FACILITIES: yes
MATERIALS SOLICITED: Records of Oregon State agencies. Will also accept, to a limited degree, records of counties and other political subdivisions.

HOLDINGS:
> *Total volume:* 75,596 c.f.
> *Inclusive dates:* 1843 -
> *Description:* Oregon State government records, and related materials, including files of the provisional and territorial governments, the governor's office, the Legislative Assembly, the Supreme Court, the Secretary of State's office, the Justice Department, the Treasurer, the Lands Division, the Labor Bureau, the Military Department, the Highway Division, and such defunct State agencies as the Board of Control, the Capitol Reconstruction Commission, the Defense Council, the Finance and Administration Department, the Planning Board, and the World War I Veterans State Aid Commission. Records

from 28 counties and 9 cities are also included.

SEE: Hamer.

SEE ALSO: Richard C. Davis, *North American Forest History: A Guide to Archives and Manuscripts in the United States and Canada* (Clio Books, 1977); Ann Novotny, ed., *Picture Sources 3* (Special Libraries Assn., 1975); G. Q. Flynn, 'The New Deal and Local Archives: The Pacific Northwest,' *American Archivist* 33 (Jan. 1970); David C. Duniway, 'How Does One Collect Archives?--The Oregon Experience,' *Indian Archives* 17 (Jan. 1967/Dec. 1968); and the following publications of the Archives: *Guide to Legislative Records in the Oregon State Archives* (1968); *Members of the Legislature of Oregon, 1843-1967* (1968); *Records of Agricultural Agencies in the Oregon State Archives* (1968); *Have You an Oregon Ancestor?* (1962); and biennial reports listing accessions.

OR816-890
Willamette University
Library
Salem OR 97301

no telephone
SEE: Hamer.

Questionnaire not returned.

THE DALLES

OR848-40
Western America Institute for Exploration, Inc.
Aleutian-Bering Sea Expeditions Research Library
1821 East 9th Street
The Dalles OR 97058

(503) 296-9414

OPEN: by appointment
USER FEES: $5 per hour for assistance from staff member
ACCESS: qualified scholars; advance appointment required
COPYING FACILITIES: no
MATERIALS SOLICITED: Field journals, manuscript maps and charts, and historical documents relating to exploration in general, and more specifically to Aleut-Eskimo culture, prehistoric cultural contacts between Alaska and Asia, Aleutian-Bering Sea history, land use and conservation in western Alaska, and the history and culture of Hokkaido, Japan, northeast Asia, and the North Pole region. Will also accept contemporary research materials on scientific expeditions and on technological innovations of application to exploration.

HOLDINGS:
> *Total volume:* 7 file cabinets
> *Inclusive dates:* 1800's -
> *Description:* Manuscripts, field journals, diaries, rough field data, photographs, and native-produced texts resulting from field research of Jay Ellis Ransom in Alaska and the Aleutian Islands, primarily in anthropology, linguistics,

ethnobotany, geology, and general ecology; and similar materials relating to Ransom's field work in the mountain and desert regions of the American West, primarily in anthropology, linguistics, archaeology, and geology, all material dating from 1930 to the present. There are also some original manuscripts and field data compiled by other explorers in Alaska and the American West dating from the 1800's.

OR848-160
The Dalles-Wasco County Public Library
722 Court Street
The Dalles OR 97058

(503) 296-2815

OPEN: Tu-Th 10-9, F, Sa 10-6; closed Sundays, Mondays, and holidays
COPYING FACILITIES: yes

HOLDINGS:
> *Total volume:* 57 vols.
> *Inclusive dates:* 1907 - 1956
> *Description:* Manuscript of *Swift Flows the River* by Nard Jones, and the 56-volume diary of George Vause.

SEE: Hamer (as Wasco County Library).

TILLAMOOK

OR880-760
Tillamook County Pioneer Museum
2106 Second Street
Tillamook OR 97141

(503) 842-4553

OPEN: M-Sa 8:30-5, Su 1-5; closed holidays
COPYING FACILITIES: yes
MATERIALS SOLICITED: Materials relating to State and local history, particularly to Tillamook County pioneers.

HOLDINGS:
> *Total volume:* not specified
> *Inclusive dates:* 1851 -
> *Description:* Photographs, oral histories, pioneer diaries, ship logbooks, Tillamook city records, a Spanish-American War diary, early church records, Indian land claim records, and other materials relating mainly to Tillamook County history.

SEE: Hamer; NUCMC, 1968.

SEE: Winroth.

TROUTDALE

OR901-760
Troutdale Historical Society
104 Kibling Street
Troutdale OR 97060

(503) 665-5175

OPEN: by appointment only
COPYING FACILITIES: yes
MATERIALS SOLICITED: Historical materials relating to development of business, cultural, and social life of Troutdale, the Sandy and Columbia rivers, and nearby areas. Will also ac-

cept photographs of the Columbia River Gorge and pioneer diaries.

HOLDINGS:
Total volume: 6 l.f.
Inclusive dates: 1850 - 1976
Description: Photographs and documents relating to development of Troutdale and nearby areas with emphasis on smelt runs, railroads, and the Columbia River Gorge.

SEE: Winroth.

UNION

OR907-800

Union County Museum
311 South Main Street
Union OR

MAILING ADDRESS:
P.O. Box 190
Union OR 97883

(503) 562-6163

OPEN: M-F 8-5:00; closed weekends and holidays

ACCESS: advance arrangements requested
COPYING FACILITIES: no
MATERIALS SOLICITED: Materials relating to the history and environment of Union County.

HOLDINGS:
Total volume: 40 l.f.
Inclusive dates: 1860 -
Description: Photographs, non-current records, and oral history tapes relating to the development of Union County and northeastern Oregon.

SEE: Winroth.

PENNSYLVANIA

The Division of Archives and Manuscripts (State Archives) of the Pennsylvania Historical and Museum Commission is responsible for preserving the records of the Commonwealth's political subdivisions and, since its creation, has been empowered to accept historically valuable local public records.

Acting under the authority of legislation passed in 1963 and 1968, the Commission administers a records management program for county and municipal offices and has approved the transfer of large quantities of local public records to the State Archives in Harrisburg and to other historical depositories. Original records of permanent administrative value may not be transferred from a courthouse unless they have been microfilmed. The State Archives also makes available to researchers some 5,000 reels of microfilm of county and municipal records.

ALLENTOWN

PA25-60
Archives of Lehigh County
Lehigh County Courthouse
5th and Hamilton Streets
Allentown PA 18101

(215) 435-4664

OPEN: M-F 8-4; closed weekends and holidays
COPYING FACILITIES: yes

HOLDINGS:
  Total volume: 25,000 square ft.
  Inclusive dates: 1812 -
  Description: Records of County government offices, including minutes of the Board of County Commissioners' meetings, dating from 1850; miscellaneous records of the Board of Prison Inspectors; tax assessment lists, dating from 1847; court records; record books of the County controller's office; and scattered probate, justice of the peace, and County treasurer's records.

PA25-480
Lehigh County Historical Society
Scott Andrew Trexler II Memorial
  Library
Old Court House
Hamilton Street at Fifth
Allentown PA 18101

(215) 435-1074

OPEN: M-F 10-4, Sa 1-4; closed Sundays and holidays
USER FEES: $2
COPYING FACILITIES: yes
MATERIALS SOLICITED: Materials on the Lehigh Valley of Pennsylvania and surrounding counties.

HOLDINGS:
  Total volume: 1,500 titles
  Inclusive dates: 1770's - 1900's
  Description: Materials relating to Lehigh and Northampton counties and adjacent areas. Included are correspondence, church records, business records, Civil War army discharge papers, copies of tombstone inscriptions, genealogical materials, a letterbook of an officer during the Revolutionary War, 1778-81, a manuscript map of Lehigh County land holdings drawn in 1816, and baptismal, burial, and marriage records.

SEE: Hamer; NUCMC, 1966.

PA25-520
Muhlenberg College
Haas Library
Allentown PA 18104

(215) 433-3191, Ext. 214

OPEN: M-F 8-11:30, Sat 9-5, Su noon-11:30; closed school holidays
COPYING FACILITIES: yes
MATERIALS SOLICITED: 18th and 19th century manuscripts and correspondence by and pertaining to the Henry Melchior Muhlenberg family. Will also accept materials on Germans in Pennsylvania, particularly materials in the Pennsylvania German dialect.

HOLDINGS:
  Total volume: 12 l.f.
  Inclusive dates: 1770 - 1850
  Description: Letters, manuscripts of speeches and articles by and to members of the Muhlenberg family, 1770- , including a journal of Frederick Augustus Conrad Muhlenberg, Lutheran clergyman and U.S. Congressman. The bulk of the material consists of the papers of Henry Augustus Philip Muhlenberg, describing national, Pennsylvania, and Berks County politics in the 1830's and 1840's. Also includes materials on Germans in Pennsylvania, many in the Pennsylvania German dialect.

SEE: Hamer; NUCMC, 1959-61.

ALLISON PARK

PA30-720
Sisters of Divine Providence
Providence Heights Archives
9000 Babcock Boulevard
Allison Park PA 15101

(412) 931-5241

OPEN: M-F 8:30-11, 12:30-4; closed Sundays and holidays
ACCESS: collections are open to scholars interested in the life and work of Bishop Emmanuel von Ketteler, social reformer and founder of the congregation in Mainz, Germany, in 1851, and to members of religious congregations of women
COPYING FACILITIES: yes
MATERIALS SOLICITED: Manuscripts related to Bishop William E. von Ketteler and the founding of parishes and institutions served by the Sisters of Divine Providence since 1876. Will also accept materials relating to important movements in the Catholic church since the second Vatican Council.

HOLDINGS:
  Total volume: 132 l.f.
  Inclusive dates: 1851 - 1980
  Description: An account of the foundation of the Sisters of Divine Providence congregation in Germany in 1851 by Bishop William E. von Ketteler; unpublished biographies of Bishop von Ketteler; histories of the congregation and its affiliated schools and hospitals in the United States and abroad; and newsletters, photographs, correspondence, and news clippings.

ALTOONA

PA35-40
Altoona Area Public Library
Pennsylvania Room
1600 Fifth Avenue
Altoona PA 16602

(814) 946-0417

OPEN: M, Tu, Th 8:30-9, W, F 8:30-5, Sa 9-5, Su 2-5; closed holidays
ACCESS: persons under 16 are to be accompanied by adult unless doing school assignments
COPYING FACILITIES: yes
MATERIALS SOLICITED: Materials relating to Altoona and Blair County, especially genealogical source data, photographs, and oral histories. Will also accept

manuscripts and non-current records of institutions and organizations.

HOLDINGS:
>*Total volume:* 1 l.f.; 13,000 items
>*Inclusive dates:* 1899 -
>*Description:* A collection of 13,000 Pennsylvania Railroad photograph negatives, 1899-1960, depicting trains and equipment and Altoona and its people. A vertical file, including photographs and unpublished reports, relates to local and State history.

PA35-80

Blair County Historical Society
3501 Oak Lane
Altoona PA

MAILING ADDRESS:
Box 1083
Altoona PA 16603

(814) 942-3916

SEE: Hamer; NUCMC, 1977.

Questionnaire not returned.

AMBRIDGE

PA40-600

Old Economy Village
14th and Church Streets
Ambridge PA 15003

(412) 266-4500

OPEN: Tu-Sa 8:30-5, Su 1-5; closed Mondays and winter holidays
ACCESS: except for the music records of the Harmony Society, the collection is deposited at the Pennsylvania State Archives in Harrisburg; scholars must write in advance for an appointment to use the music records
COPYING FACILITIES: yes
MATERIALS SOLICITED: Material on the Harmony Society.

HOLDINGS:
>*Total volume:* 400 c.f.
>*Inclusive dates:* 1785 - 1951
>*Description:* Archives of the Harmony Society, including religious, business, and personal records, music, correspondence, accounts, legal documents, maps, plans, and other materials concerning the Society's activities in Wuertemberg (Germany), Pennsylvania, and Indiana.

SEE: NUCMC, 1962.

SEE ALSO: Richard D. Wetzel, *Music of George Rapp's Harmony Society: 1805-1905* (unpublished Ph.D. dissertation, Univ. of Pittsburgh, 1970); Richard C. Davis, *North American Forest History: A Guide to Archives and Manuscripts in the United States and Canada* (Clio Books, 1977).

As of 1983, the archives of the Harmony Society have been transferred to the Pennsylvania Historical and Museum Commission, Division of Archives and Manuscripts, **PA380-650.** Some other manuscripts have been retained at Old Economy.

ANNVILLE

PA45-480

Lebanon Valley College
Library
Annville PA 17003

SEE: Hamer; NUCMC, 1959-61.

Questionnaire not returned.

ASTON

PA50-720

The Sisters of St. Francis of Philadelphia
Our Lady of Angels Convent - Glen Riddle
Aston PA 19014

(215) 459-4125

OPEN: M-F 9-4, Sa 9-noon; closed Sundays and holidays
ACCESS: appointment required
COPYING FACILITIES: no
MATERIALS SOLICITED: Tape recordings, photographs, and slides relating to the history of the apostolic missions maintained by the Sisters of St. Francis.

HOLDINGS:
>*Total volume:* 26 cabinets
>*Inclusive dates:* 1855 -
>*Description:* Correspondence, manuscript histories, financial records, blueprints, and photographs of the apostolic missions under the jurisdiction of the Sisters of St. Francis of Philadelphia. Complete records are held for the numerous missions that are no longer functioning, and incomplete materials for operational missions. Also included are the institutional records of the Sisters' headquarters (Our Lady of Angels Convent), including ecclesiastical directives, correspondence, financial records, and films.

ATHENS

PA55-760

Tioga Point Museum
724 South Main Street
Athens PA

MAILING ADDRESS:
P.O. Box 143
Athens PA 18810

(717) 888-7225

OPEN: M 7-9, W, Sa 2-5, or by appointment; closed holidays
COPYING FACILITIES: yes
MATERIALS SOLICITED: Materials relating to local history, Indians, Sullivan's campaign, the French colony of Azilum, Stephen Foster, canals, and railroads.

HOLDINGS:
>*Total volume:* not specified
>*Inclusive dates:* 18th century-
>*Description:* Primarily local history papers, including papers pertaining to claims of Pennsylvania and Connecticut to lands along the Susquehanna River,

1780-1840; items concerning the Asylum Company and the French colony of Azilum; merchants' account books; railroad and canal papers; church records; records of the Athens Academy, 1797-1876; Revolutionary War letters of George Washington, John Hancock, and others; Civil War letters; and other materials.

SEE: Hamer.

BELLEFONTE

PA80-110

Centre County Library and Historical Museum
203 North Allegheny Street
Bellefonte PA 16823

(814) 355-1516

OPEN: M-Th 9-9, F, Sa 9-5; closed Sundays and holidays
COPYING FACILITIES: yes
MATERIALS SOLICITED: Historical, genealogical, and biographical materials relating to Centre County and to Pennsylvania.

HOLDINGS:
>*Total volume:* 722 c.f.
>*Inclusive dates:* 1600 -
>*Description:* A collection of unpublished manuscripts, correspondence, surveys, and other materials relating to early central Pennsylvania history and development; numerous account books, ledgers and journals dealing with Centre County; notebooks of early Centre County school minutes and teachers institute records; 65 oral history interviews relating to Centre County; numerous notebooks of unpublished, indexed Centre County genealogical data; Centre County courthouse records, including marriage records, 1885-1973; and wills and intestate records, 1800-1970.

Also included are tax assessments, 1802-1930; Orphan Court dockets, 1801-1970; civil and criminal court records, 1800-50, and road applications, 1800-1950.

BENSALEM

PA85-730

Sisters of the Blessed Sacrament Archives
St. Elizabeth Convent
1663 Bristol Pike
Bensalem PA 19020

(215) 244-9900

OPEN: M-F 9-4; closed weekends, holidays, and holy days
ACCESS: advance arrangements required
COPYING FACILITIES: yes
MATERIALS SOLICITED: Historical materials from the various missions of the Sisters of the Blessed Sacrament and letters and documents from the congregation. Will also accept materials concerning American Blacks or Native Americans.

HOLDINGS:
Total volume: 228 l.f.; 10 file cabinets
Inclusive dates: 1863 -
Description: Materials relating to the order's work with American Blacks and Native Americans throughout the United States including administrative documents, correspondence,, annals and photographs. Also includes materials concerning the Drexel family, such as genealogies, journals, diaries, correspondence and photographs.

BETHLEHEM

PA90-30

American Mathematical Society
Building 14
Lehigh University
Bethlehem PA 18015

(215) 865-4121

OPEN: by appointment only
ACCESS: by application and at the convenience of the secretary
COPYING FACILITIES: yes

HOLDINGS:
Total volume: 10 l.f.; 40 file drawers
Inclusive dates: 1888 -
Description: Archives of the American Mathematical Society, including minutes of the council and board of trustees, correspondence of the secretary, copies of correspondence of other officers, and some group photographs.

SEE: Hamer (listed under Los Angeles, CA).

PA90-40

Annie S. Kemerer Museum
427 North New Street
Bethlehem PA 18018

(215) 868-6868

OPEN: M-F 9-4
COPYING FACILITIES: no

HOLDINGS:
Total volume: not specified
Inclusive dates: 18th century - 19th century
Description: Deeds, letters, and business records relating to families of Lower Saucon Township, Northampton County. Also included are a few Fraktur documents.

PA90-80

Bethlehem Public Library
11 West Church Street
Bethlehem PA 18018

(215) 867-3761

OPEN: M-Th 9-9, F 9-6; Sa 9-5 Sept.-May; closed Sundays and holidays
ACCESS: use limited to adults
COPYING FACILITIES: yes
MATERIALS SOLICITED: Materials relating to local history. Will also accept some family histories.

HOLDINGS:
Total volume: 65 vols.
Inclusive dates: 1742 - 1937
Description: Volumes of typed transcripts of original church, pastoral, and cemetery records from the Bethlehem area.

SEE: Hamer; NUCMC, 1966.

PA90-160

Diocese of Bethlehem of the Episcopal Church
333 Wyandotte Street
Bethlehem PA 18015

(215) 691-5655

OPEN: M-F 9-4:30; closed weekends and holidays
ACCESS: arrangements should be made with Historiographer
COPYING FACILITIES: yes
MATERIALS SOLICITED: Diocesan materials, including general convention and other diocesan journals.

HOLDINGS:
Total volume: 18 file drawers
Inclusive dates: 1871 -
Description: Journals, correspondence, photographs, and other papers concerning Episcopal churches, institutions, and committees of the Diocese of Bethlehem, comprised of 14 counties of northeastern Pennsylvania.

PA90-320

Historic Bethlehem, Inc.
501 Main Street
Bethlehem PA 18018

(215) 868-6311, 691-5300

OPEN: M-F 9-5; closed weekends and holidays
COPYING FACILITIES: yes
MATERIALS SOLICITED: Moravian and Bethlehem history, 1740's to date, and history of technology in the 18th and 19th centuries.

HOLDINGS:
Total volume: 75 l.f.
Inclusive dates: 1740's -
Description: A collection relating to Bethlehem, the Moravian church, and 18th and 19th century industrial technology. Included are microfilm copies of documents in the Moravian Archives in Herrnhut, Germany; plans and drawings of waterwheels, grist mills, and residential and religious structures; 4,000 photographs of the Bethlehem area; and a collection of correspondence, photographs, and other materials pertaining to William H. Rice, Moravian minister of the 19th century.

SEE: NUCMC, 1977.

SEE ALSO: unpublished finding aids to individual collections available from the institution.

PA90-480

Lehigh University
Libraries
Bethlehem PA 18015

(215) 861-3026

OPEN: M-F 9-4; closed weekends and holidays
COPYING FACILITIES: yes
MATERIALS SOLICITED: Lehigh University records. Will also accept other materials.

HOLDINGS:
Total volume: not specified
Inclusive dates: 18th century -
Description: A collection relating to Pennsylvania, the Northeast, and the United States, including papers of political figures, scientists, and authors. A group of 500 autograph letters represents all Presidents of the United States. Also included are Congressional files of Francis E. Walter and Fred C. Rooney, Lehigh University archival material, and maps and drawings of the Lehigh Coal and Navigation Company.

SEE: Hamer; NUCMC, 1967.

SEE: Martin; Robbins.

SEE ALSO: Irwin Richman, comp., *Historical Manuscript Depositories in Pennsylvania* (Pennsylvania Historical and Museum Commission, 1965).

PA90-500

The Moravian Archives
41 West Locust Street
Bethlehem PA 18018

(215) 866-3255

OPEN: M-F 9-5; closed weekends and holidays
COPYING FACILITIES: yes
MATERIALS SOLICITED: Records of the Northern Province of the Moravian church in America, and its related mission fields in the Caribbean and Alaska. Will also accept personal papers of Moravian ministers or their families.

HOLDINGS:
Total volume: 2,900 l.f.
Inclusive dates: 1450 -
Description: Diaries, travel diaries, membership data, letters, minutes, biographies, music, pictures, photographs, maps, architectural drawings, school records, and business and economic materials, relating to the Moravian church, especially in North America, but also in the Caribbean, Alaska, Labrador, and to some extent Europe. Subjects covered include Indians (especially the Delawares), music, architecture and town planning, cultural anthropology, and sociology.

SEE: Hamer (as Archives of the Moravian Church); NUCMC, 1962.

SEE: Ingram.

SEE ALSO: Kenneth G. Hamilton, 'The Moravian Archives at Bethlehem, Pennsylvania,' *American Archivist* 24 (Oct. 1961); Kenneth G. Hamilton, 'The Resources of the Moravian Church Archives,' *Pennsylvania History* 27 (July 1960); *Guide to the Records of the Moravian Mission Among the In-*

dians of North America (Research Publications, 1970); Richard C. Davis, *North American Forest History: A Guide to Archives and Manuscripts in the United States and Canada* (Clio Books, 1977).

BLOOMSBURG

PA100-80

Bloomsburg State College
H. A. Andruss Library
College Archives
Bakeless Center for the Humanities
Bloomsburg PA 17815

(717) 389-4224

OPEN: M-Th 10-12; closed Fridays, weekends, and when the College is not in session
COPYING FACILITIES: no
MATERIALS SOLICITED: Materials relating to the College and the people connected with it.

HOLDINGS:
> *Total volume:* 35 file drawers
> *Inclusive dates:* 1867 -
> *Description:* Materials relating to the College including Board of Trustees minutes, materials relating to Presidents, minutes of departmental and college-wide committees, student and faculty organization materials, scrapbooks, diaries, blueprints, maps, and photographs.

PA100-320

Columbia County Historical Society
Bloomsburg State College
Bloomsburg PA

MAILING ADDRESS:
P.O. Box 197
Orangeville PA 17859

(717) 683-6011

OPEN: M-F 9-4; closed weekends, holidays, and Christmas vacation
COPYING FACILITIES: yes
MATERIALS SOLICITED: Columbia County materials. Will also accept materials relating to Luzerne, Lycoming, Montour, Northumberland, Schuylkill, and Sullivan counties.

HOLDINGS:
> *Total volume:* 20 l.f.
> *Inclusive dates:* 1800 -
> *Description:* Diaries, correspondence, business records, family histories, photographs, and other materials concerning Columbia County, with emphasis on businesses, government, and genealogy.

SEE: Hamer; NUCMC, 1965, 75.

SEE ALSO: Irwin Richman, comp., *Historical Manuscript Depositories in Pennsylvania* (Pennsylvania Historical and Museum Commission, 1965).

BLUE BELL

PA105-520

Montgomery County Community College
Learning Resources Center
340 DeKalb Pike
Blue Bell PA 19422

no telephone
SEE: NUCMC, 1980.

Questionnaire not returned.

BRYN ATHYN

PA130-30

Academy of the New Church
Archives
2815 Huntingdon Pike
Bryn Athyn PA

MAILING ADDRESS:
Box 278
Bryn Athyn PA 19009

(215) 947-4200, 9919

OPEN: M-F 8-5 by appointment only; closed weekends and holidays
ACCESS: bona fide researchers and scholars
COPYING FACILITIES: yes
MATERIALS SOLICITED: Will accept materials relating to activities and achievements of members of the Church of the New Jerusalem.

HOLDINGS:
> *Total volume:* 1,000 c.f.
> *Inclusive dates:* late 18th century -
> *Description:* Records of the General Church of the New Jerusalem in the United States and abroad, and records of the Academy of the New Church. There are also papers of prominent church members and records of the borough of Bryn Athyn.

SEE: Hamer.

SEE: Hinding.

SEE ALSO: Irwin Richman, comp., *Historical Manuscript Depositories in Pennsylvania* (Pennsylvania Historical and Museum Commission, 1965).

PA130-50

Academy of the New Church
Swedenborgiana Library
2815 Huntingdon Pike
Bryn Athyn PA

MAILING ADDRESS:
Box 278
Bryn Athyn PA 19009

(215) 947-4200, Ext. 26

OPEN: M-F 8-5; closed weekends and holidays
COPYING FACILITIES: yes
MATERIALS SOLICITED: Manuscripts by or relating to Emanuel Swedenborg.

HOLDINGS:
> *Total volume:* 21 l.f.
> *Inclusive dates:* 18th century -
> *Description:* Original manuscripts by Emanuel Swedenborg, in addition to copies of all known extant Swedenborg manuscripts and letters, and many related documents. Three manuscript Coptic New Testaments, which are undated, are also housed at the Library.

SEE: Hamer.

BRYN MAWR

PA135-40

The American College of Life Underwriters
Oral History Center
270 Bryn Mawr Avenue
Bryn Mawr PA 19010

(215) 896-4498

OPEN: M-F 8:45-4:30; closed weekends and holidays
COPYING FACILITIES: yes
MATERIALS SOLICITED: Oral history materials related to the history of the life insurance business, education on life insurance, the American College of Life Underwriters, and women in the life insurance business. Will also accept materials pertaining to famous individuals who have been connected with life insurance, such as the composer Charles Ives.

HOLDINGS:
> *Total volume:* 100 c.f.; 100 items
> *Inclusive dates:* 1927 -
> *Description:* Oral history tapes and archival materials on the history of the life insurance business, life insurance education, and the American College of Life Underwriters. Included is a collection of oral history interviews with women professionals in life insurance.

PA135-80

Bryn Mawr College
Archives
Bryn Mawr PA 19010

(215) 645-5285, 5289

OPEN: M-F 9-5; closed weekends and holidays
COPYING FACILITIES: yes
MATERIALS SOLICITED: Papers of Bryn Mawr faculty and alumni, and other materials relating to the College; and manuscripts relating to English and American studies and women's studies.

HOLDINGS:
> *Total volume:* archives 1,572 l.f.; manuscripts 56 l.f.; photographs 114 l.f.
> *Inclusive dates:* 19th century - 20th century
> *Description:* Records of Bryn Mawr College, papers of its faculty and alumni, and materials relating to the College, 1884- ; and papers of American and English literary figures.
> Women's studies materials; medieval and Renaissance manuscripts; photographs illustrating architecture, sculpture, painting, and minor arts; U.S.G.S. photographs; and works by modern and con-

temporary photographers, including Eakins and Jacobi.

SEE: NUCMC, 1965.

SEE: Meckler and McMullin; Hinding; Robbins.

CALIFORNIA

PA145-120

California State College
Louis L. Manderino Library
Archives
California PA 15419

(412) 938-4091

OPEN: M-F 8-4; closed weekends and Dec. 23 - Feb. 1
COPYING FACILITIES: yes
MATERIALS SOLICITED: Records relating to the College and its faculty and students. Will also accept materials pertaining to the social, cultural, political, and economic history of the Monongahela Valley and Washington, Fayette, Greene, Westmoreland, and Allegheny counties of Pennsylvania.

HOLDINGS:
   Total volume: 345 l.f.
   Inclusive dates: 1814 -
   Description: Records of faculty, administration, and students of the College, which was founded as a seminary, including charters, stocks, land deeds, and administrative documents, 1852- , and student records, 1865- . Also included is the Henry D. Wilkins collection, 15 l.f., relating to the growth and development of the steamboat trade on the Monongahela River to New Orleans, 1814-1912, including photographs, histories of boats and shipbuilding plants, and biographical information about boatmen.

CARLISLE

PA160-120

Cumberland County Historical Society and
Hamilton Library Association
21 North Pitt Street
Carlisle PA

MAILING ADDRESS:
P.O. Box 626
Carlisle PA 17013

(717) 249-7610

OPEN: M 7-9, Tu-F 1-4; closed weekends and holidays
COPYING FACILITIES: yes
MATERIALS SOLICITED: Manuscript materials which relate to the history of Cumberland County and adjacent areas in Pennsylvania; non-current records of local organizations and of local and county government; genealogical materials relating to Cumberland County families; and photographs and maps which deal with the above-mentioned areas.

HOLDINGS:
   Total volume: 50 c.f.; 50 l.f.
   Inclusive dates: 1750 -
   Description: Materials relating to Cumberland County. Included are correspondence, deeds, genealogical materials, business records, Cumberland County records, Carlisle borough minutes, Revolutionary War era loyalty oaths, draft records from the Civil War, and records of local organizations. There are also papers of Robert Whitehill, photographs of the Carlisle Indian School, aerial photographs of Cumberland County, and miscellaneous photographic prints and glass negatives.
   Included are papers of James Hamilton (1751-1819), Samuel Postelthwaite, and George Stevenson.

SEE: Hamer; NUCMC, 1980.

SEE: Hinding.

PA160-160

Dickinson College
Library
Special Collections
Carlisle PA 17013

(717) 245-1399

OPEN: M, W-F 8-4, Tu 8-10; closed weekends and holidays
COPYING FACILITIES: yes
MATERIALS SOLICITED: Dickinson College archival materials and manuscripts relating to Pennsylvania and United States history.

HOLDINGS:
   Total volume: 600 l.f.
   Inclusive dates: 1482 -
   Description: Over 350 manuscript collections and 700,000 pieces, including the College archives, 1773- , principally relating to the history of the College and figures associated with the College. Included are collections of papers of James Buchanan, Joseph Priestley, Roger Brooke Taney, Benjamin Rush, Moncure Conway, Carl Sandburg, and John Drinkwater. The collection's focus is on Pennsylvania and the College's 18th century origins, with records from local Methodist, Presbyterian, and Evangelical United Brethren churches.

GUIDES: Charles Coleman Sellers and Martha Calvert Slotten, comps., *Archives and Manuscript Collections of Dickinson College* (1972).

SEE: Hamer; NUCMC, 1966, 73.

SEE: Parkinson; Allard, Crawley, and Edmison; Robbins; Hinding.

SEE ALSO: Walter Schatz, ed., *Directory of Afro-American Resources* (Bowker, 1970); Peter Duignan, *Handbook of American Resources for African Studies* (Hoover Institution, 1967); Robert O. Collins and Peter Duignan, *Americans in Africa* (Hoover Institution, 1963); Richard C. Davis, *North American Forest History: A Guide to Archives and Manuscripts in the United States and Canada* (Clio Books, 1977); Irwin

Richman, comp., *Historical Manuscript Depositories in Pennsylvania* (Pennsylvania Historical and Museum Commission, 1965). Published guides to individual collections are available at the Library.

CARLISLE BARRACKS

PA165-790

U.S. Army Military History Institute
Carlisle Barracks PA 17013

(717) 245-3601, 3434

OPEN: M-F 8-4:30; closed weekends and holidays
ACCESS: Classified papers may only be made available to persons with appropriate security clearance. A few unclassified memoirs are under personal restrictions on access; most unclassified material is available for study by serious researchers and scholars.
COPYING FACILITIES: yes
MATERIALS SOLICITED: Personal papers, photographs, pictures, maps, films, and tapes and retained copies of official papers of officers and enlisted men of Regular, Volunteer, and Militia land forces of the United States in peace and war, 1600 to the present.

HOLDINGS:
   Total volume: 6,632 l.f.
   Inclusive dates: 1600 -
   Description: Non-official Army historical source materials. Included are personal letters, diaries, memoirs, retained copies of official papers, photographs, maps, motion pictures, and taped interviews, speeches, and lectures, principally covering Regular, Volunteer, and Militia land forces in American military history. Military leaders whose papers are held, and who have participated in the Institute's oral history program, include Matthew B. Ridgway, Harold K. Johnson, and Lewis B. Hershey. There are also materials from other United States military services, as well as foreign forces, and the institutional archives of the Army War College.

GUIDES: *Manuscript Holdings of the Military History Research Collection* (1972-75).

SEE: NUCMC, 1975-77.

SEE: Paszek.

SEE ALSO: *Manuscript Holdings of the Military History Research Collection* (1972-75), *A Suggested Guide to the Curricular Archives of the U.S. Army War College, 1907-40* (1973), *The U.S. Army and the Spanish-American War; Volume I: Manuscripts* (1974), *Oral History* (1976-77), *The United States Army and the Indian Wars in the Trans-Mississippi West, 1860-98* (1978).

Audio-Visual Archives (1981-82), *World War One; Volume I: Manuscripts* (1986).

The Institute was formerly known as the U.S. Army Military History Research Collection.

CHADDS FORD

PA175-80
Brandywine River Museum
Brandywine Conservancy, Inc.
U.S. Route 1
Chadds Ford PA

MAILING ADDRESS:
Box 141
Chadds Ford PA 19317

(215) 388-7601, 459-1900

OPEN: by appointment
COPYING FACILITIES: yes
MATERIALS SOLICITED: Manuscript material related to artists of the Brandywine Valley, including Howard Pyle, his students, and members of the Wyeth family, as well as material relating to American illustration. Will also accept materials relative to the history of the Brandywine Valley.

HOLDINGS:
Total volume: 360 l.f.
Inclusive dates: 1830 -
Description: Collections of manuscripts and ephemera relating to American illustration, with special areas of emphasis on Scribner's publications and the artists of the Howard Pyle tradition, including collections relating to the careers of N. C. Wyeth, Thornton Oakley, Stanley Arthurs, and F. E. Schoonover. Included are publishers' card indexes, diaries, daybooks, correspondence, and autobiographical materials.
Also included are complete runs of *Harper's Monthly, Scribner's,* and *Century,* as well as miscellaneous bound volumes of other periodicals. Collection of books illustrated by Howard Pyle and his students, including N.C. Wyeth, F.E. Schoonover, and Thornton Oakley.

CHAMBERSBURG

PA180-120
Conococheague District Library
Franklin County Library
102 N. Main Street
Chambersburg PA 17201

(717) 263-1054

OPEN: M-F 10-8:30, Sa 9:30-5; closed Sundays and holidays
COPYING FACILITIES: yes
MATERIALS SOLICITED: Local history of Cumberland and Franklin counties. Will also accept other materials.

HOLDINGS:
Total volume: 1 vol.
Inclusive dates: 1795 - 1798
Description: A general store account book, from Upper Strasburg, PA.

CHESTER

PA185-160
Delaware County Historical Society
Widener University
Wolfgram Memorial Library
15th and Walnut Streets
Chester PA

MAILING ADDRESS:
Box 1036
Widener University
Chester PA 19013

(215) 874-6444

OPEN: M, F 10-3, Tu-Th 10-4; closed weekends and during August.
COPYING FACILITIES: yes
MATERIALS SOLICITED: Materials relating to Delaware County history and genealogy.

HOLDINGS:
Total volume: 12 file drawers; 50 boxes
Inclusive dates: 1682 -
Description: Collection concentrates on Delaware County history and includes legal documents (deeds, etc.), family and business papers, diaries and correspondence, genealogies, photographs, and manuscripts. Items of interest include: Dr. Anna Broomall's scrapbooks, Chester F. Baker's scrapbooks, Chester Rural Cemetery records, and records of the Chester United Methodist Church.

SEE: Hamer.

CLARION

PA200-110
Clarion County Historical Society
18 Grant Street
Clarion PA 16214

(814) 226-4450

OPEN: mid-March-Dec., Tu, F 1-4, Su 2-4 (during April, May, Nov., Dec. 1st and 3rd Su); other days and holidays by appointment
COPYING FACILITIES: yes
MATERIALS SOLICITED: Materials, such as genealogical source data, church and business records, and photographs, related to Clarion County history. Will also accept similar materials relating to Pennsylvania history.

HOLDINGS:
Total volume: 12 l.f.; 4 file drawers
Inclusive dates: 18th century - 1945
Description: Records of Clarion County, including church histories, genealogical source data, business records, community histories, and photographs.

COLLEGEVILLE

PA210-800
Ursinus College
Library
Collegeville PA 19426

(215) 489-4111

OPEN: M-F 9-5; closed weekends and holidays
COPYING FACILITIES: yes
MATERIALS SOLICITED: Materials on Pennsylvania German culture and the German Reformed church.

HOLDINGS:
Total volume: 179,500 items
Inclusive dates: 1750 -
Description: A collection of manuscripts, photographs, oral histories, and video tapes relating primarily to Pennsylvania, with emphasis on the German Reformed church and Pennsylvania German culture. Also included are the diplomatic papers, 1897-1913, of Francis Mairs Huntington Wilson.

SEE ALSO: Irwin Richman, comp., *Historical Manuscript Depositories in Pennsylvania* (Pennsylvania Historical and Museum Commission, 1965).

COLUMBIA

PA215-560
National Association of Watch and Clock Collectors, Inc.
Museum
Library
514 Poplar Street
Columbia PA

MAILING ADDRESS:
Box 33
Columbia PA 17512

(717) 684-8261

OPEN: M-F 9-4, Sa 9-5; closed Sundays and holidays
USER FEES: admission free to members; non-member fees: adults, 1.50; senior citizens, seventy-five cents; children 8-17, fifty cents
COPYING FACILITIES: yes
MATERIALS SOLICITED: Materials relating to horology, including timekeeping in general, clock, and watch repair, and to people and companies relating to horology.

HOLDINGS:
Total volume: not specified
Inclusive dates: 1718 -
Description: Records of the Hamilton Watch Company.

COUDERSPORT

PA235-640
Potter County Historical Society
308 North Main Street
Coudersport PA 16915

(814) 274-8124

OPEN: M, F 2-4; closed other days and
  holidays
COPYING FACILITIES: yes
MATERIALS SOLICITED: Materials relating
  to Potter County and surrounding
  areas, including genealogical and business records.

HOLDINGS:
    Total volume: 25 l.f.
    Inclusive dates: Early 1800's -
    Description: Records and account
  books from early Potter County businesses and hotels; letters; church and
  school records; and diaries. Also included
  are some hand-drawn maps, photographs
  of Potter County, and two films, 1940
  and 1948.

SEE: Hamer.

DALLAS

PA240-710
Sisters of Mercy
Province of Scranton
Province Archives
Mercy Center
Dallas PA

MAILING ADDRESS:
P.O. Box 370
Dallas PA 18612

(717) 675-2131

OPEN: M-F 10-3; closed weekends and
  holidays
COPYING FACILITIES: yes
MATERIALS SOLICITED: Materials pertaining to the Sisters of Mercy, particularly in Pennsylvania, Long Island, and
  Guyana.

HOLDINGS:
    Total volume: 300 l.f.
    Inclusive dates: 1852 -
    Description: Non-current records of ad-
  ministrative officers, institutions, organizations, and individuals of the Scranton
  Province of the Sisters of Mercy, including reports, correspondence, and community newsletters. Also included are materials, such as chronicles, annals, scrapbooks, minutes of meetings and conferences, oral history tapes, and photographs.

DOYLESTOWN

PA260-80
Bucks County Historical Society
Pine and Ashland Streets
Doylestown PA

MAILING ADDRESS:
P.O. Box 1092
Doylestown PA 18901

(215) 345-0210

SEE: Hamer; NUCMC, 1959-62, 70.

Questionnaire not returned.

EASTON

PA270-200
Easton Area Public Library
Sixth and Church Streets
Easton PA 18042

(215) 258-2917

OPEN: M-F 8-9, Sa 9-5; closed Sundays
  and holidays
COPYING FACILITIES: yes
MATERIALS SOLICITED: Genealogical
  source data relating to Pennsylvania,
  primarily Northampton County, including scrapbooks, family histories, old
  maps, photographs, and church records.

HOLDINGS:
    Total volume: 45 l.f.
    Inclusive dates: 1740 -
    Description: Materials relating to
  Northampton County, including scrapbooks, family histories, maps, photographs, church records of an iron company, Civil War diaries, oaths of alle-
  giance, 1774-84, tax lists, 1761-1806,
  tombstone inscriptions, and translations
  of German wills.

SEE: Hamer; NUCMC, 1966.

PA270-320
Hugh Moore Park
Canal Museum
Research Library
200 South Delaware Drive
Easton PA

MAILING ADDRESS:
P.O. Box 877
Easton PA 18042

(215) 250-6700, 6703

OPEN: by appointment
COPYING FACILITIES: yes
MATERIALS SOLICITED: American canals.
  Will also accept materials on canal-
  related industries.

HOLDINGS:
    Total volume: 5,000 items
    Inclusive dates: 1790 -
    Description: A collection of documents,
  books, photographs, and oral histories relating to American tow path canals, with
  a particular emphasis on those of Pennsylvania and New Jersey.

PA270-470
Lafayette College
David Bishop Skillman Library
Easton PA 18042

(215) 250-5000

OPEN: M-Sa 8:30-midnight, Su
  1-midnight; closed holidays and
  weekends July-Aug.; shorter hours
  during college vacations.
COPYING FACILITIES: yes
MATERIALS SOLICITED: Materials relating
  to Lafayette College and the Marquis
  de Lafayette.

HOLDINGS:
    Total volume: 1700 l.f.
    Inclusive dates: 1774 -
    Description: Materials including the ar-
  chives of the College and manuscripts of
  the Marquis de Lafayette.

SEE: Hamer; NUCMC, 1966.

SEE: Robbins; Martin.

For Lafayette manuscripts, see
Gottschalk, *Lafayette, Guide to
the Letters,* etc. Cornell, 1975.

PA270-480
Lafayette College
Kirby Political Science Museum
Easton PA 18042

no telephone

SEE: Hamer.

Questionnaire not returned.

PA270-560
Northampton County Historical and
  Genealogical Society
107 S. 4th Street
Easton PA 18042

(215) 253-1222

OPEN: F, Sa 1-3; closed other days and
  holidays
COPYING FACILITIES: no
MATERIALS SOLICITED: Historical and
  genealogical information about Northampton County.

HOLDINGS:
    Total volume: not specified
    Inclusive dates: 1755 -
    Description: Maps, deeds, letters,
  unpublished manuscripts, photographs,
  and slides relating to local history.

SEE: Hamer; NUCMC, 1966.

EBENSBURG

PA275-120
Cambria County Historical Society
Museum and Library
521 West High Street
Ebensburg PA 15931

(814) 472-6674

OPEN: M-F 10:30-4:30; closed weekends
  and holidays
COPYING FACILITIES: no

MATERIALS SOLICITED: Materials pertaining to Cambria County. Will also accept related materials from other areas.

HOLDINGS:
  Total volume: 400 items
  Inclusive dates: 1820's - 1936
  Description: Materials pertinent to Cambria County, including a Civil War diary, correspondence, business ledgers, records of social and voluntary organizations, photographs, and genealogies.

SEE: Hamer.

ELIZABETHTOWN

PA285-200
Elizabethtown College
Zug Memorial Library
Elizabethtown PA 17022

(717) 367-1151, Ext. 222

OPEN: M-F 8:30-5 by appointment only; closed weekends and holidays
COPYING FACILITIES: yes
MATERIALS SOLICITED: Church of the Brethren history and publications of the College.

HOLDINGS:
  Total volume: 60 boxes; 10 drawers; 20 l.f.
  Inclusive dates: 1852 -
  Description: Archives of the College, 1897- , consisting of office records, publications, correspondence concerning the establishment of the College, photographs, and oral history recordings of faculty members and convocation speakers. There are also materials relating to the Church of the Brethren in southeastern Pennsylvania, including financial records and minutes of congregations, and letters and diaries of ministers and lay workers affiliated with the church.

EMPORIUM

PA295-130
Cameron County Public Library
1 East 4th Street
Emporium PA

MAILING ADDRESS:
P.O. Box 430
Emporium PA 15834

(814) 486-8011

OPEN: M, Tu, Th, F 12:30-8:30, W 10-1, Sa 9-1; closed Sundays and holidays; shorter summer hours
COPYING FACILITIES: yes
MATERIALS SOLICITED: Cameron County history and genealogy. Will also accept materials on Pennsylvania history.

HOLDINGS:
  Total volume: 1 l.f.
  Inclusive dates: 1939 -
  Description: Manuscripts relating to Cameron County history and genealogy, including 2 volumes of records of tombstone inscriptions dating to about 1800; reminiscences of founders and employees of Sylvania Electronic Products, Inc.; and

an unpublished history of the Methodist church in Cameron County.

ERIE

PA305-190
Erie County Historical Society
407 State Street
Erie PA 16501

SEE: Hamer.

Questionnaire not returned.

PA305-210
Erie Historical Museum and Planetarium
356 West 6th Street
Erie PA 16507

(814) 453-5811

OPEN: by appointment only
COPYING FACILITIES: yes

HOLDINGS:
  Total volume: not specified
  Inclusive dates: 16th century -
  Description: Collections concentrating on Erie and northwestern Pennsylvania, primarily in the 18th and 19th centuries. Items include Lake Erie shipping ledgers; autograph letters of Presidents and other notable Americans; records of the Pennsylvania Population Company; business and family papers; land records; and photographs.

SEE: Hamer.

SEE ALSO: Irwin Richman, comp., *Historical Manuscript Depositories in Pennsylvania* (Pennsylvania Historical and Museum Commission, 1965).

PA305-510
Mercyhurst College
Mercyhurst Hammermill Library
Mercyhurst College Archives and Center for Erie Studies
501 East 38th Street
Erie PA 16546

(814) 825-0237

OPEN: M-F 9-5; closed weekends and holidays
ACCESS: advance arrangements requested
COPYING FACILITIES: yes
MATERIALS SOLICITED: Manuscripts; archives; and non-current records, visual and audible documents, microfilms, and scrapbooks pertinent to the development of the Erie County area of northwestern Pennsylvania. Will also accept materials from outside the Erie County area that complement the collections.

HOLDINGS:
  Total volume: 298 l.f.; 211 microfilm reels; 137 tape recordings
  Inclusive dates: 1880 -
  Description: 200 collections documenting the development of Erie and surrounding communities, primarily 1880-1950. Included are personal papers, records of businesses and social and ethnic organizations, and Mercyhurst College materials.

Also included are Erie County government records (1947-1971), tax records (1890-1974), and official election records (1922-59).

GUIDES: *Catalogue of Manuscript Collection* (Mercyhurst College Archives, 1980).

SEE: NUCMC, 1976.

SEE: Hinding.

PA305-720
Sisters of Mercy of Erie County Archives
444 East Grandview Blvd.
Erie PA 16504

(814) 454-4476

OPEN: M, W, F 3-5 by appointment only; closed other days and holidays
ACCESS: appointment required
COPYING FACILITIES: yes
MATERIALS SOLICITED: Records of branchhouses or missions of the Sisters of Mercy, photographs, slides, and oral history tapes. Will also accept correspondence, diaries, literary manuscripts, and doctoral theses pertaining to the Sisters of Mercy.

HOLDINGS:
  Total volume: 46 c.f.
  Inclusive dates: 1870 -
  Description: Correspondence, chronicles, diaries, financial and business records, genealogical data, photographs and slides, architectural drawings and blueprints, oral history tapes, and non-current records of the Sisters of Mercy of Erie County and the communities, churches, and schools they have served in northwestern Pennsylvania since their foundation in Titusville, PA, in 1870.

SEE: Hinding.

FALLSINGTON

PA308-320
Historic Fallsington, Inc.
4 Yardley Avenue
Fallsington PA 19054

(215) 295-6567

OPEN: W-Su 1-5; closed Tuesdays, Mondays except when a holiday, and Nov. 15 - March 15
ACCESS: appointment required
COPYING FACILITIES: yes
MATERIALS SOLICITED: Material relating to the local history of Fallsington.

HOLDINGS:
  Total volume: 35 items
  Inclusive dates: 18th century - 20th century
  Description: Materials relating to the Fallsington area, including deeds, scrapbooks, and a minute book of a local lodge.

FORT WASHINGTON

PA315-320
Historical Society of Fort Washington
473 Bethlehem Pike
Fort Washington PA 19034

no telephone

SEE: Hamer.

Questionnaire not returned.

GETTYSBURG

PA325-40
Adams County Historical Society
Confederate Avenue
Lutheran Theological Seminary
   Campus
Gettysburg PA

MAILING ADDRESS:
Drawer A
Gettysburg PA 17325

(717) 334-4723

OPEN: W 1-5, Sa 9-5; closed other days,
   holidays, and last week of Aug. and
   Dec.
COPYING FACILITIES: yes
MATERIALS SOLICITED: Material relating
   to Adams County.

HOLDINGS:
   Total volume: not specified
   Inclusive dates: 1730 -
   Description: Estate records, and other
   County records, primarily from the clerks
   of courts and registrars of wills' offices;
   land surveys; records of local churches,
   businesses, professional people, public
   schools, and families; indexes to newspaper notices of marriages and deaths,
   1800-85; an index to 30,000 tombstone
   inscriptions; and photographs.

SEE: NUCMC, 1959-62.

SEE ALSO: Irwin Richman, comp., *Historical Manuscript Depositories in Pennsylvania* (Pennsylvania Historical and Museum Commission, 1965).

PA325-280
Gettysburg College
Musselman Library/Learning
   Resources Center
Gettysburg PA 17325

(717) 337-7000

OPEN: M-Th 8:30-11:30, F 8:30-11, Sa
   9:30-10, Su 12-11:30; closed holidays,
   and weekends when College is not in
   session
ACCESS: at discretion of Librarian
COPYING FACILITIES: yes
MATERIALS SOLICITED: Materials relating
   to Gettysburg, the Civil War, Lutheran
   church history, H. L. Mencken, F.
   Scott Fitzgerald and his
   contemporaries, and the Vietnam War
   peace movement, as well as manuscript
   correspondence.

HOLDINGS:
   Total volume: 160 l.f.
   Inclusive dates: 1800 -
   Description: Archives of Gettysburg
   College, including account books, motion
   pictures, and oral history recordings; letters, sermons, and diaries of College-
   associated Lutheran families describing
   their travels and church work during the
   19th century; manuscript maps of America and Europe, 16th-18th centuries; and
   materials relating to the Civil War, Douglas MacArthur's World War II and Korean War commands, H. L. Mencken and
   his contemporaries, Franklin D. Roosevelt's Presidential administration and
   economic affairs in Latin America, and
   the Vietnam War peace movement.

SEE: NUCMC, 1965.

SEE: Robbins.

SEE ALSO: Irwin Richman, comp., *Historical Manuscript Depositories in Pennsylvania* (Pennsylvania Historical and Museum Commission, 1965).

PA325-470
Lutheran Historical Society
Library
West Confederate Avenue
Gettysburg PA 17325

no telephone

SEE: Hamer.

Questionnaire not returned.

PA325-490
Lutheran Theological Seminary
Abdel Ross Wentz Library
66 West Confederate Avenue
Gettysburg PA 17325

(717) 334-6286

OPEN: M-F 9-4; closed weekends and
   holidays
ACCESS: genealogical research is not
   permitted
COPYING FACILITIES: yes
MATERIALS SOLICITED: Will accept correspondence, diaries, journals, and
   logbooks relating to the Lutheran
   church and its pastors.

HOLDINGS:
   Total volume: 260 l.f.
   Inclusive dates: 1700's -
   Description: Papers relating to the early
   Lutheran church and its pastors, primarily in the eastern United States and particularly in Pennsylvania. Included are
   central Pennsylvania synod archives and
   early Seminary archives.

SEE: Hamer; NUCMC, 1966.

SEE: Hinding.

SEE ALSO: Irwin Richman, comp., *Historical Manuscript Depositories in Pennsylvania* (Pennsylvania Historical and Museum Commission, 1965); Robert O.
Collins and Peter Duignan, *Americans
in Africa* (Hoover Institution, 1963).
Preliminary listings and other finding
aids to the collections are available at
the Library.

GLADWYNE

PA330-160
Deaconess Community of the
   Lutheran Church in America
Archives
801 Merion Square Road
Gladwyne PA 19035

(215) 642-8838

OPEN: by appointment only
COPYING FACILITIES: yes
MATERIALS SOLICITED: Materials rel-
   evant to deaconess work in North
   America, especially those related to the
   Lutheran Church in America and its
   predecessor bodies.

HOLDINGS:
   Total volume: 180 l.f.
   Inclusive dates: 1881 -
   Description: Records of Lutheran deaconess motherhouses in Baltimore, Philadelphia, and Omaha, including letters,
   minutes, handbooks, financial records,
   and personal histories. Also included are
   records of ecumenical deaconess organizations, records of institutions related to
   the Lutheran motherhouses, papers on
   deaconess work, and photographs of persons concerned with deaconess work.

GRANTHAM

PA340-520
Messiah College
Archives of the Brethren in Christ
   Church and Messiah College
Grantham PA 17027

(717) 766-2511, Ext. 388

OPEN: M-Sa 8-5 or by appointment
COPYING FACILITIES: yes
MATERIALS SOLICITED: Materials relating
   to the Brethren in Christ Church
   (formerly River Brethren).

HOLDINGS:
   Total volume: 1,082 boxes; 75 l.f.
   Inclusive dates: 1780 -
   Description: Records of the Brethren in
   Christ Church, Messiah College, and Upland College, including correspondence,
   minute books, diaries, journals, financial
   records, papers of individuals, genealogical source data, missionary correspondence and diaries, oral history tapes, and
   transcripts.

GREEN LANE

PA345-280
Goschenhoppen Historians, Inc.
Folk Life Library and Museum
Red Men's Hall
Green Lane PA 18054

(215) 234-8953

OPEN: Sundays 1:30-4; closed other days
   and Dec. 15 - Jan. 15
ACCESS: advance arrangements required
COPYING FACILITIES: no
MATERIALS SOLICITED: Manuscripts per-
   taining to the folk life of the
   Goschenhoppen area.

HOLDINGS:
Total volume: 22 l.f.
Inclusive dates: 1720 - 1900
Description: Records pertaining to the folklife of the Goschenhoppen area, an 18th century geographical designation, which includes the northeast corner of Montgomery County, PA and adjoining areas in Berks, Lehigh, and Bucks counties. Materials include account books, business and financial records, correspondence, diaries, journals, wills and estate inventories, music scores, and genealogical source data. Materials are primarily in the Pennsylvania High German language in the old German script.

GREENSBURG

PA350-160

Catholic Diocese of Greensburg
Diocesan Archives
723 E. Pittsburgh Street
Greensburg PA 15601

(412) 837-0901

OPEN: M-W, F 10-noon; closed other days and holidays
COPYING FACILITIES: yes
MATERIALS SOLICITED: Records of the Diocese of Greensburg and its member parishes and institutions. Will also accept other materials that broadly relate to Diocesan activities.

HOLDINGS:
Total volume: not specified
Inclusive dates: 1799 -
Description: The archives of the Diocese and its constituent parishes, consisting of newspapers, manuscript histories, official records, and vital records of parishioners.

PA350-720

Seton Hill College
Reeves Library
College Archives
Greensburg PA 15601

(412) 834-4291, 2200

OPEN: M, W, F 9-3, Tu, Th 9-11; closed weekends
ACCESS: identification must be presented
COPYING FACILITIES: yes
MATERIALS SOLICITED: Non-current College records, especially records of department offices, administrative offices, and faculty members and alumnae.

HOLDINGS:
Total volume: 200 boxes, plus scrapbooks and account books
Inclusive dates: 1883 -
Description: Non-current records of Seton Hill College, and related historical materials.

PA350-880

Westmoreland County Historical Society
102 N. Main Street
Greensburg PA 15601

(412) 836-1800

OPEN: Tu-F 10-4:45, Sa 10-1; closed Sundays, Mondays and holidays
COPYING FACILITIES: yes
MATERIALS SOLICITED: Documents relating to Westmoreland County and the surrounding area in southwestern Pennsylvania. Will also accept other materials on Pennsylvania history.

HOLDINGS:
Total volume: 100 l.f.
Inclusive dates: 1750's -
Description: Materials relating to southwestern Pennsylvania, including church records, genealogical materials, ledgers, letters, miscellaneous documents, and materials on local Indians.

GREENVILLE

PA355-760

Thiel College
College Archives
Archives of Lutheran Church of America
Western Pennsylvania-West Virginia Synod
Greenville PA 16125

(412) 588-7700, Ext. 235

OPEN: M-F 2-6; closed weekends
COPYING FACILITIES: yes
MATERIALS SOLICITED: Materials relating to the life of Thiel College and congregational and pastoral records of parishes of the synod.

HOLDINGS:
Total volume: 261 l.f.; 18 file cabinets
Inclusive dates: 1787 -
Description: The College archives, 1872- , contains records of the institution's founding, student enrollments, endowments, and fund raising campaigns; financial records of tuitions and gifts; faculty and trustee minutes; curricula records; literary society papers; the college paper, *The Thielensian*; the college yearbook, *Endymion*; college catalogues; sports records; alumni records; scrapbooks; newspaper scrapbooks, 1930- ; and presidential papers and materials.
The archives of the Western Pennsylvania-West Virginia Synod of the Lutheran Church of America and its predecessor bodies, 1787- , includes original minutes of convention proceedings; congregational records with genealogical data; periodicals; and conference or district records.

HANOVER

PA370-310

Hanover Area Historical Society
113 West Chestnut Street
Hanover PA 17331

(717) 632-3207

OPEN: M, W, F 9-noon; closed other days and Christmas
COPYING FACILITIES: no

HOLDINGS:
Total volume: 1 file cabinet; 300 items
Inclusive dates: late 1800's -
Description: Photographs and copies of tombstone inscriptions concerning Hanover and the surrounding area.

PA370-330

Hanover Public Library
Library Place
Hanover PA 17331

(717) 632-5183

OPEN: M-F 10-9, Sa 9-5; closed Sundays and holidays; shorter hours in summer
COPYING FACILITIES: yes
MATERIALS SOLICITED: Hanover history.

HOLDINGS:
Total volume: 36 l.f.
Inclusive dates: 1720 -
Description: Manuscripts, records, and visual material pertaining to the history of Hanover. The collections consist of journals and literary manuscripts; genealogical data, including church and cemetery records of births, marriages, deaths, and baptisms; church histories; Hanover borough minutes; blueprints of wooden water wheels and mills; maps; and photographs.

HARRISBURG

PA380-320

Historical Society of Dauphin County
219 South Front Street
Harrisburg PA 17104

(717) 233-3462

OPEN: M 1-4, 7-9, Tu-F 1-4; closed weekends and holidays
COPYING FACILITIES: yes
MATERIALS SOLICITED: Materials by or about Simon Cameron or Casper Dull, and materials concerning Dauphin County.

HOLDINGS:
Total volume: 24 c.f.
Inclusive dates: 1742 - 1892
Description: Materials relating to Pennsylvania, particularly Dauphin County. Included are early court records of Dauphin, Lancaster, and Cumberland counties; business papers, such as those of Frederick Kelker, hardware merchant, and his family; personal papers of such individuals as politician Simon Cameron and William R. De Witt; and a collection of genealogical materials.

SEE: Hamer; NUCMC, 1964.

SEE: Hinding.

SEE ALSO: Walter Schatz, ed., *Directory of Afro-American Resources* (Bowker, 1970); Irwin Richman, comp., *Historical Manuscript Depositories in Pennsylvania* (Pennsylvania Historical and Museum Commission, 1965).

PA380-650

Pennsylvania Historical and Museum Commission
Division of Archives and Manuscripts
Third and Forster Streets
William Penn Memorial Museum and Archives Building
Harrisburg PA

MAILING ADDRESS:
P.O. Box 1026
Harrisburg PA 17108-1026

(717) 787-2701

OPEN: M-F 8:30-5; closed weekends and holidays
ACCESS: responsible researchers, who must register at the search room, and adhere to State regulations pertaining to the use of records
COPYING FACILITIES: yes
MATERIALS SOLICITED: Public records of the Commonwealth of Pennsylvania, with particular emphasis on the records of State government; and papers of Pennsylvania governors and other State officials. Will also accept private papers relevant to Pennsylvania history.

HOLDINGS:
  Total volume: 23,000 c.f.
  Inclusive dates: 1664 -
  Description: Primarily records of the executive, legislative, and judicial branches of State and provincial government. Major record groups include records from most departments, boards, and commissions of the executive branch, and records of Pennsylvania's proprietary and Revolutionary War governments. The 257 manuscript groups contain the records and papers of prominent individuals and families, business concerns, and numerous social, cultural, political, and military organizations, relating to almost every aspect of Pennsylvania history. Included among these records are special collections of maps, posters, postcards, photographs, and motion picture films.

GUIDES: Harry E. Whipkey, *Guide to the Manuscript Groups in the Pennsylvania State Archives* (1976), and *Guide to the Record Groups in the Pennsylvania State Archives* (1977).

SEE: Hamer; NUCMC, 1959-61, 66, 68, 74, 76-77.

SEE: Meckler and McMullin; Davis; Parkinson; Hinding; Robbins; Allard, Crawley, and Edmison.

SEE ALSO: Walter Schatz, ed., *Directory of Afro-American Resources* (Bowker, 1970); Frank B. Evans, 'The Many Faces of the Pennsylvania Archives,' *American Archivist* 27 (April 1964); Martha L. Simonetti, comp., *Descriptive List of the Map Collection in the Pennsylvania State Archives*

(Pennsylvania Historical and Museum Commission, 1976); David A. Hounshell, comp., *Manuscripts in U.S. Depositories Relating to the History of Electrical Science and Technology* (Smithsonian Institution, n.d.).

PA380-665

Pennsylvania Historical and Museum Commission
Division of Land Records
Third and Forster Street
William Penn Memorial Museum and Archives Building
Harrisburg PA

MAILING ADDRESS:
Box 1026
Harrisburg PA 17120

(717)787-5989, 7180

OPEN: M-F 8:30-4:45; closed weekends and holidays
ACCESS: responsible researchers, who must register at the research room, and adhere to state regulations pertaining to the use of records
COPYING FACILITIES: yes
MATERIALS SOLICITED: Documents dealing with land titles.

HOLDINGS:
  Total volume: 2,000,000 items
  Inclusive dates: 1681 -
  Description: Documents relating to original land titles in Pennsylvania, including early records of William Penn; charters of churches, towns, and fraternal organizations; Letter of Attorney books; survey or general correspondence; records of military land grants (Revolutionary War); and related maps.

PA380-700

Roman Catholic Diocese of Harrisburg
Bureau of History and Archives
4800 Union Deposit Road
Harrisburg PA

MAILING ADDRESS:
P.O. Box 2153
Harrisburg PA 17105

(717) 657-4804, Ext. 214

OPEN: M-F 9-noon; closed weekends, Good Friday, Aug. 15, and Nov. 1
COPYING FACILITIES: yes
MATERIALS SOLICITED: Materials relating to histories of 15 counties in east-central Pennsylvania; social histories of ethnic groups immigrating to the Harrisburg - Steelton area; materials concerning area anthracite coal fields; and data on Irish immigrants engaged in building the Pennsylvania Canal, 1825. Will also accept early maps of east-central Pennsylvania, identified early photographs of Roman Catholic clergy and biographies of clergy of all faiths.

HOLDINGS:
  Total volume: 180 l.f.; 14 file cabinets
  Inclusive dates: 1750 -
  Description: Materials relating to the history of the Roman Catholic church and associated institutions in east-central Pennsylvania, including the foundation of churches, schools, orphanages, and hos-

pitals, and the clerical and lay personnel engaged in this work. Included are papers and letters of Bishop Philip R. McDevitt, 1916-35; papers of historian George D. Mulcahy, papers of Sylvan Heights Home for Girls, 1901-79, pastoral letters of bishops, 1879- , spiritual and temporal reports of parishes, 1890-1979, and papers of historian Anna Dill Gamble.

HAVERFORD

PA395-320

Haverford College
James P. Magill Library
Treasure Room
Haverford PA 19041

(215) 896-1284

OPEN: M-F 9-4:30; closed weekends and holidays
COPYING FACILITIES: yes
MATERIALS SOLICITED: Quaker records and papers. Will also accept other materials consistent with the scope of collections.

HOLDINGS:
  Total volume: 250,000 items
  Inclusive dates: 1527 -
  Description: Records of the Philadelphia and Baltimore Yearly Meetings of the Society of Friends; papers of Quaker families and individuals, mainly from Pennsylvania and surrounding areas, concerning the Society of Friends, Indians, and other topics; the Charles Roberts collection of autograph letters of distinguished authors, scientists, royalty, statesmen, and others; archives of Haverford College, including manuscripts, maps, and photographs; and Treasure Room manuscript collections of prominent persons.

SEE: NUCMC, 1962-65, 67, 69-72, 74.

SEE: Allard, Crawley, and Edmison; Hinding; Robbins; Schatz; Duignan; Meckler and McMullin; Krichmar; Bean and Vane; Martin.

SEE ALSO: Herbert Leventhal and James E. Mooney, 'A Bibliography of Loyalist Source Material in the United States, Part I,' *American Antiquarian Society Proceedings* 85 (April 1975); *Source Materials for the Recent History of Astronomy and Astrophysics: A Checklist of Manuscript Collections in the United States* (American Institute of Physics, 1971).

Finding aids to individual collections are available at the institution.

HONESDALE

PA410-880

Wayne County Historical Society
810 Main Street
Honesdale PA

MAILING ADDRESS:
P.O. Box 446
Honesdale PA 18431

(717) 253-3240

OPEN: M-Sa 10-4; closed Sundays, holidays, and Saturday mornings Oct. - May
USER FEES: 50¢ entrance fee
ACCESS: advance arrangements requested
COPYING FACILITIES: yes
MATERIALS SOLICITED: Materials relating to Wayne County and surrounding counties.

HOLDINGS:
Total volume: 30 l.f.
Inclusive dates: not specified
Description: Account books, letters, journals, church, and cemetery records. Also includes materials relating to the Delaware and Hudson Canal and a gravity railroad.

SEE: Hamer.

HUNTINGDON

PA415-320

Huntingdon County Historical Society
106 Fourth Street
Huntingdon PA

MAILING ADDRESS:
P.O. Box 305
Huntingdon PA 16652

(814) 643-5449

OPEN: Tu, Th 8-4; closed holidays
USER FEES: non-members $2
COPYING FACILITIES: yes
MATERIALS SOLICITED: Materials documenting Huntingdon County history, including genealogical materials, photographs of buildings, townscapes, and other subjects, and non-current county records, such as tavern licenses, divorce papers, and tax records.

HOLDINGS:
Total volume: 70 l.f.; 12 file drawers
Inclusive dates: 1750 -
Description: Materials documenting the history of Huntingdon County and its people, buildings, businesses, and institutions. Included are manuscripts, photographs, and scrapbooks.

PA415-400

Juniata College
Library
Huntingdon PA 16652

(814) 643-4310

OPEN: by appointment only
COPYING FACILITIES: yes
MATERIALS SOLICITED: Materials concerning the Church of the Brethren and German settlement in Pennsylvania. Will also accept genealogies, diaries, and records of early Huntingdon County residents.

HOLDINGS:
Total volume: 48 file drawers
Inclusive dates: 1700 - 1930
Description: Manuscripts related chiefly to Huntingdon, Juniata College, and the Church of the Brethren in America. Included are early records of the Church and College; hymns of Johann Conrad Beissel; papers of Martin Grove Brumbaugh, College president and Pennsylvania governor; and letters of Abra-

ham Harley Cassel, 19th century book collector.

SEE: Hamer.

SEE ALSO: Irwin Richman, comp., *Historical Manuscript Depositories in Pennsylvania* (Pennsylvania Historical and Museum Commission, 1965).

PA415-720

The Swigart Museum
Library
U.S. Route 22
Huntingdon PA 16652

MAILING ADDRESS:
P.O. Box 214
Huntingdon PA 16652

(814) 643-0885, 3000

OPEN: June - Aug., daily 9-5; May, Sept., Oct., Sa, Su 10-5; closed rest of year
ACCESS: advance appointment required
COPYING FACILITIES: yes
MATERIALS SOLICITED: History of the automobile.

HOLDINGS:
Total volume: not specified
Inclusive dates: late 1800's -
Description: Manuscripts and photographs relating to the history and development of the automobile and related fields, such as license plates, development of horns, ignition, and modes of dress.

IMMACULATA

PA420-720

Sisters, Servants of the Immaculate Heart of Mary
Villa Maria House of Studies
Immaculata PA 19345

(215) 647-2160

OPEN: M-Th 9-3, F 9-noon; closed weekends and holidays
COPYING FACILITIES: yes
MATERIALS SOLICITED: Materials related to the congregation and its history.

HOLDINGS:
Total volume: 160 c.f.
Inclusive dates: 1840 -
Description: Correspondence, journals, financial records, architectural drawings, and photographs relating to the congregation of the Sisters, Servants of the Immaculate Heart of Mary. Early materials refer to Monroe, MI, and Susquehanna and Reading, PA. Later materials cover many areas of the eastern United States, as well as Chile and Peru.

SEE: Hinding.

INDIANA

PA425-320

The Historical and Genealogical Society of Indiana County
6th Street and Wayne Avenue
Indiana PA 15701

(412) 463-9600

OPEN: M-F 10-3; closed weekends and holidays
COPYING FACILITIES: yes
MATERIALS SOLICITED: Materials relating to Indiana County: personal and family records; business accounts; church and school records; local government and judicial records; organization records; manuscript maps and land records; and photographs. Will also accept machine-readable records; literary manuscripts; and military and veterans' records.

HOLDINGS:
Total volume: not specified
Inclusive dates: 1803 -
Description: Materials relating to the history of Indiana County, including 38 cubic feet of genealogical source data.

SEE ALSO: Irwin Richman, comp., *Historical Manuscript Depositories in Pennsylvania* (Pennsylvania Historical and Museum Commission, 1965).

PA425-360

Indiana University of Pennsylvania
Library
Special Collections
Indiana PA 15701

(412) 357-3039

OPEN: M-F 8:30-4:30, Sa 1:30-4:30, Su 2-5; closed holidays, and weekends between terms
COPYING FACILITIES: yes
MATERIALS SOLICITED: Pennsylvania and local government and history. Will also accept other materials.

HOLDINGS:
Total volume: 30 c.f.
Inclusive dates: 1871 -
Description: 20 volumes of memorabilia, correspondence, photographs, speeches, and scrapbooks of U.S. Representative John P. Saylor; two file drawers of correspondence and manuscripts of Pittsburgh journalist and local historian George A. Swetnam; two drawers of correspondence of Williamsport, PA, businessman George L. Sanderson; and one drawer of correspondence and personal papers of State Senator Albert R. Pechan.

SEE: Robbins.

JENKINTOWN

PA430-600

The Old York Road Historical Society
Jenkintown Library
York and Vista Roads
Jenkintown PA 19046

(215) 887-2122

OPEN: by appointment
COPYING FACILITIES: no

MATERIALS SOLICITED: Photographs, manuscripts, deeds, and memorabilia connected with the section of southeastern Montgomery County known as the Old York Road area. Will also accept non-current records of businesses and associations, as well as scrapbooks connected with local families and events.

HOLDINGS:
> Total volume: 20 l.f.
> Inclusive dates: 1681 -
> Description: Photographs and other local history materials, including real estate deeds and maps of the 17th-19th centuries.

JOHNSTOWN

PA435-400
Johnstown Flood Museum Association
Johnstown Flood Museum
304 Washington Street
Johnstown PA 15901

(814) 539-1889

OPEN: Tu-F 10-4, Sa 11-4, Su 12:30-4:30; closed Mondays and holidays
ACCESS: arrangements should be made in writing one week prior to visit
COPYING FACILITIES: no
MATERIALS SOLICITED: Johnstown history, with emphasis on floods. Will also accept materials relating to the Pennsylvania Main Line Canal, the Allegheny Portage Railroad, Clara Barton and the Red Cross, the iron and steel industry, and the coal industry.

HOLDINGS:
> Total volume: 3,000 items
> Inclusive dates: 1700 -
> Description: A collection of manuscripts, non-current records of organizations, and visual and audible documents. Included are correspondence, diaries, account books, business records, financial records, photographs, maps, technical drawings, and taped oral interviews with 1889 flood survivors.

SEE: Hinding.

KENNETT SQUARE

PA440-80
Bayard Taylor Memorial Library
East State Street
Kennett Square PA 19348

(215) 444-2702

OPEN: M, W 9-8, Tu, Th, F 9-5, Sa 9-3; closed Sundays and holidays
COPYING FACILITIES: yes
MATERIALS SOLICITED: Materials relating to Bayard Taylor and local history.

HOLDINGS:
> Total volume: 150 items
> Inclusive dates: 1840's - 1880's
> Description: A small collection of various items primarily related to the life of Bayard Taylor, including an original manuscript of one of his plays, a wallet-passport used while traveling abroad, and

various musical scores, letters, drawings, and photographs.

SEE: Hamer.

LANCASTER

PA470-40
Armstrong World Industries, Inc.
Management Reference Service
Liberty and Charlotte Streets
Lancaster PA 17604

(717) 397-0611

OPEN: M-F 8:15-5; closed weekends and holidays
ACCESS: advance appointment required
COPYING FACILITIES: yes
MATERIALS SOLICITED: Company publications. Will also accept materials of employees.

HOLDINGS:
> Total volume: 650 l.f.; 944 boxes
> Inclusive dates: 1870 -
> Description: Records of the Armstrong Cork Company from its founding in Pittsburgh in 1870 to the present, including data on all factories, foreign and domestic subsidiaries, and companies acquired. Materials consist of annual reports, minutes, correspondence, company publications, photographs, and other materials.

SEE: Davis.

PA470-240
Franklin and Marshall College
Library
College Avenue
Lancaster PA

MAILING ADDRESS:
P.O. Box 3003
Lancaster PA 17604

(717) 291-4216

OPEN: M-Sa 8-midnight, Su 1-midnight; closed holidays
COPYING FACILITIES: yes
MATERIALS SOLICITED: Pennsylvania-German materials; materials relating to the history of Franklin and Marshall College; and papers of literary and political figures.

HOLDINGS:
> Total volume: 1,000 items
> Inclusive dates: 1774 -
> Description: Manuscripts relating mainly to Pennsylvania political, scientific, and artistic figures, including some letters of President James Buchanan. The collection also contains records of Franklin and Marshall College and its predecessors, 1785- .

SEE: Hamer; NUCMC, 1959-61.

SEE: Allard, Crawley, and Edmison; Hinding; Robbins.

SEE ALSO: Irwin Richman, comp., *Historical Manuscript Depositories in Pennsylvania* (Pennsylvania Historical and Museum Commission, 1965).

PA470-460
Lancaster County Historical Society
Willson Memorial Building
230 North President Avenue
Lancaster PA 17603

(717) 392-4633

OPEN: Tu-Sa 9:30-4:30; closed Sundays, Mondays, holidays, and the first two weeks of Sept.
USER FEES: free to members; students one dollar per day or $2 per year; adults one dollar per day or $5 per year
COPYING FACILITIES: yes
MATERIALS SOLICITED: Materials relating to Lancaster County and southeastern Pennsylvania history and people, including business and economic records, institutional records, early public records, 1729-1850, religious records, technological records, and social history regardless of form.

HOLDINGS:
> Total volume: 9,100 vols.; 320 c.f.
> Inclusive dates: 1729 -
> Description: Collections consist primarily of public and private (personal, professional, and commercial) records, account books, inventories, letterbooks, diaries, maps, charts, and genealogical papers. Among the public records are Lancaster County tax assessment records, 1750-1940; estate records and inventories, 1729-1850; criminal and civil court records, 1729-1850; and U.S. direct tax records, 1815-16.

SEE: Hamer; NUCMC, 1966.

SEE: Schatz; Hinding.

PA470-470
Lancaster County Library
125 North Duke Street
Lancaster PA 17602

(717) 394-2651

OPEN: M-F 9-9, Sa 9-5:30; closed Sundays and holidays
COPYING FACILITIES: yes
MATERIALS SOLICITED: Church records, recordings of church services, correspondence, personal papers, charters, records, dispatches, and oral history tapes. Will also accept any other local materials.

HOLDINGS:
> Total volume: 240 items
> Inclusive dates: 1744 -
> Description: A collection primarily of local history materials, some on microfilm, including personal papers, church records, and library records. Audio materials include recordings of church services and 70 interviews with Lancaster County residents.

SEE ALSO: *A Directory of Resources for Lancaster County* (Lancaster County Library, 1975).

PA470-480
Lancaster Mennonite Historical
   Society
2215 Millstream Road
Lancaster PA 17602

(717) 393-9745

OPEN: Tu-Sa 8:30-4:30; closed Sundays,
   Mondays, holidays, and the Saturday of
   the last weekend in June
USER FEES: suggested donation by
   non-Society members; genealogical
   research fees for surname searches
COPYING FACILITIES: yes
MATERIALS SOLICITED: Materials relating
   to Mennonite and Amish history and
   genealogy, including correspondence,
   diaries, journals, and account books of
   individuals in the Lancaster Mennonite
   Conference; genealogical data on southeastern Pennsylvania names; archives
   of Lancaster Mennonite Conference institutions; maps; charts; photographs;
   and oral history tapes of Mennonite-
   related groups. Will also accept materials relating to the history of
   Mennonite-related groups, as well as local historical or theological items.

HOLDINGS:
   Total volume: 1,000 c.f.
   Inclusive dates: 1660 -
   Description: Records of Lancaster
   Mennonite Conference congregations,
   individuals, and institutions, primarily in
   southeastern Pennsylvania, but also in the
   eastern United States in general, as well
   as Ontario, Canada. There are also genealogical materials relating to southeastern
   Pennsylvania families, primarily Mennonite, and a collection of theologically-
   related materials.

SEE: Hinding.

PA470-640
Pennsylvania Farm Museum of
   Landis Valley
2451 Kissel Hill Road
Lancaster PA 17601

(717) 569-0401

SEE: Hamer; NUCMC, 1969.

Questionnaire not returned.

PA470-800
United Church of Christ
Historical Council
Lancaster Archives
555 West James Street
Lancaster PA 17603

(717) 393-0654, Ext. 29

OPEN: M-F 8:30-5; closed weekends and
   holidays; shorter hours in summer
COPYING FACILITIES: yes
MATERIALS SOLICITED: Pastoral records
   of local churches and historical ecclesiastical material. Will also accept local
   church histories, biographical material
   of pastors, out-of-print publications of
   the Reformed church in the U.S. and
   the Evangelical and Reformed church.

HOLDINGS:
   Total volume: 12,000 vols.; 300 l.f.;
   181 c.f.
   Inclusive dates: 1710 -
   Description: Official records of the
   German Reformed Church,, the Reformed church in the U.S., the Evangelical and Reformed church, and the United
   Church of Christ. Over 700 pastoral
   records of early colonial churches, mostly
   in Pennsylvania, Maryland, Virginia, and
   North Carolina. Large collection of early
   hymnbooks in German and English,
   catechisms, pastors' diaries, and sermons.

SEE: Hamer; NUCMC, 1959-61, 70 (as
   Evangelical and Reformed Historical
   Society).

LANSDALE

PA478-530
Mennonite Historians of Eastern
   Pennsylvania
Mennonite Historical Library and
   Archives of Eastern Pennsylvania
1000 Forty Foot Road
Lansdale PA 19446

(215) 362-0304

OPEN: M, Tu, Th-Sa 10-5; closed
   Sundays, Wednesdays, and holidays
COPYING FACILITIES: yes
MATERIALS SOLICITED: Materials relating
   to Mennonites, other people of Pennsylvania, and the local history of Montgomery, Berks, and Bucks counties.

HOLDINGS:
   Total volume: 75 l.f.
   Inclusive dates: 1700 -
   Description: Records of congregations
   since 1738; personal diaries, the earliest
   from 1828; microfilm copies of 2,200 letters received by five Mennonite families
   from the Franconia Mennonite Conference, 1850-1920; family records and genealogies; and cemetery records for area
   churches.

LATROBE

PA485-720
St. Vincent Archabbey and College
Latrobe PA 15650

(412) 539-9761

OPEN: by appointment
COPYING FACILITIES: no
MATERIALS SOLICITED: Will accept ma-
   terials pertaining to the history of the
   Archabbey and College or to the Bene-
   dictine order.

HOLDINGS:
   Total volume: 220 l.f.
   Inclusive dates: 1846 -
   Description: Archives of the Archabbey
   and College and other materials documenting the history of the Benedictine
   order. Included are papers of Boniface
   Wimmer and his successors as archabbot;
   papers of monks, 1846 to date; records of
   foundations, missions, parishes, and
   schools of the Archabbey; 40 linear feet
   of photographs; and archives of the

American Cassinese Federation of the Order of Saint Benedict.

SEE: Hamer; NUCMC, 1967.

LEBANON

PA490-480
Lebanon County Historical Society
   Library
924 Cumberland Street
Lebanon PA 17042

(717) 272-1473

OPEN: M 1-4:30, 7-9, W, F, Su 1-4:30;
   closed other days and holidays
ACCESS: identification required
COPYING FACILITIES: yes
MATERIALS SOLICITED: Will accept materials relating to the Lebanon County
   region.

HOLDINGS:
   Total volume: 5,000 items
   Inclusive dates: 1750 -
   Description: Materials relating to Lebanon County, as well as the adjacent counties of Lancaster, Berks, and Dauphin.
   There are also records of local churches
   and organizations, and a photograph collection focusing on the Lebanon County
   area.

SEE ALSO: Irwin Richman, comp., *Historical Manuscript Depositories in Pennsylvania* (Pennsylvania Historical and Museum Commission, 1965).

LENHARTSVILLE

PA495-640
Pennsylvania Dutch Folk Culture
   Society, Inc.
Lenhartsville PA 19534

(215) 562-4803

OPEN: M-Sa 10-5, Su 1-5
USER FEES: one dollar
COPYING FACILITIES: no
MATERIALS SOLICITED: Materials pertaining to folklore, especially from the
   late 19th and early 20th centuries. Will
   also accept old school compositions
   and other materials pertaining to one-
   room schools. Also accept records of
   value to anyone doing genealogical research, such as church and cemetery
   records, family surname records, etc.

HOLDINGS:
   Total volume: 1,000 items
   Inclusive dates: mid-18th century -
   1900
   Description: A collection of Pennsylvania church records documenting births,
   deaths, baptisms, and marriages.
      Also included are various items on
   folklore and local history.

LEWISBURG

PA500-70
Bucknell University
Library
Archives
Lewisburg PA

MAILING ADDRESS:
P.O. Box A-417
Lewisburg PA 17837

(717) 524-3101, 1493

OPEN: M-F 8:30-noon, afternoons by appointment; closed weekends and holidays
COPYING FACILITIES: yes
MATERIALS SOLICITED: All non-current records of the University; minutes of faculty, senate, and student groups; publications of students and the University; trustee correspondence; and faculty and alumni publications. Will also accept items of local historical value.

HOLDINGS:
    Total volume: 480 l.f.; 20 cabinets; 1 map case
    Inclusive dates: 1846 -
    Description: Records of the University, including minutes of the board of trustees, faculty, Christian Association, senate, and various other campus organizations; presidents' papers and reports; records of the treasurer and other administrative offices; a photograph collection of campus scenes, personnel, and the local community; literary manuscripts; scrapbooks; Civil War letters and diaries; old ledgers and businesspapers of local businesses; Daughters of the American Revolution papers; unpublished memoirs and histories; and correspondence of presidents, trustees, deans, and other University officers.

SEE: NUCMC, 1959-61 (as Bucknell University Library), 75.

SEE ALSO: David A. Hounshell, comp., *Manuscripts in U.S. Depositories Relating to the History of Electrical Science and Technology* (Smithsonian Institution, n.d.); Irwin Richman, comp., *Historical Manuscript Depositories in Pennsylvania* (Pennsylvania Historical and Museum Commission, 1965).

PA500-80
Bucknell University
Ellen Clarke Bertrand Library
Lewisburg PA 17837

(717) 524-1557

OPEN: M-F 1-3 and by appointment
COPYING FACILITIES: yes
MATERIALS SOLICITED: Materials on late 19th and 20th century Irish literature and local history.

HOLDINGS:
    Total volume: 10,000 items; 5,000 vols.
    Inclusive dates: 1850 -
    Description: Over 2,000 manuscripts, letters, and memorabilia items of Oliver St. John Gogarty; over 2,000 manuscripts, letters, and memorabilia items of George Bernard Shaw; and correspon-

dence, speeches, scrapbooks, and memorabilia items of Congressman Benjamin K. Focht.

SEE: NUCMC, 1969.

SEE ALSO: Irwin Richman, comp., *Historical Manuscript Depositories in Pennsylvania* (Pennsylvania Historical and Museum Commission, 1965).

PA500-640
The Packwood House Museum
10 Market Street
Lewisburg PA

MAILING ADDRESS:
15 North Water Street
Lewisburg PA 17857

(717) 524-0323

OPEN: by appointment only
ACCESS: serious researchers; appointments must be made one week in advance
COPYING FACILITIES: no
MATERIALS SOLICITED: Manuscripts, photographs, diaries, and other primary documents on domestic, agricultural, or industrial arts relating to the central Susquehanna Valley.

HOLDINGS:
    Total volume: 500 items
    Inclusive dates: 1785 - 1972
    Description: Manuscripts relating chiefly to the central Susquehanna Valley. Included are materials from the John T. Fetherston papers, local account books, diaries, and biographical materials.

LIMA

PA512-400
The John J. Tyler Arboretum
Painter Library
515 Painter Road
Lima PA

MAILING ADDRESS:
P.O. Box 216
Lima PA 19037

(215) 566-5431

OPEN: by appointment only
COPYING FACILITIES: yes
MATERIALS SOLICITED: Will accept material relating to the Minshall, Painter, and Tyler families.

HOLDINGS:
    Total volume: not specified
    Inclusive dates: 1800's - 1930's
    Description: Account books, including those referring to farm or personal loans; photographs of local structures; maps and notations concerning local areas; and letters and records pertaining to development of the arboretum.

LINCOLN UNIVERSITY

PA516-480
Lincoln University
Library
Lincoln University PA 19352

no telephone
SEE: Hamer.

Questionnaire not returned.

LOCK HAVEN

PA520-470
Lock Haven University
Archives and Records Centre
Lock Haven PA 17745

(717) 893-2371, 2309

OPEN: M-F 3-6, weekends by appointment; closed holidays
COPYING FACILITIES: yes
MATERIALS SOLICITED: Records of Lock Haven State College, including materials on alumni, former faculty, and administrators; records of the lumber industry in the Lock Haven area; and records of area industries and cultural activities. Will also accept other materials relating to the history of the region.

HOLDINGS:
    Total volume: 500 c.f.
    Inclusive dates: 1869 -
    Description: Materials relating to the Lock Haven area and Lock Haven State College. Archives of the College, in addition to College records, include faculty and student publications, alumni records, union records, and records of the board of trustees. Manuscript materials focus on local and area industries, the lumber trade, churches, fraternal organizations, civic clubs, attorneys, and flood control.

GUIDES: *Guide to the Lock Haven State Archives and Records Centre* (Lock Haven State College, Stevenson Library, 1979).

MCCONNELLSBURG

PA540-240
Fulton County Historical Society, Inc.
Fulton House
McConnellsburg PA

MAILING ADDRESS:
Box 115
McConnellsburg PA 17233

(717) 485-3207

OPEN: Th 7-9; closed other days
COPYING FACILITIES: no
MATERIALS SOLICITED: Materials relating to Fulton County, including genealogies, church records and photographs.

HOLDINGS:
    Total volume: 100 l.f.
    Inclusive dates: 1790 -
    Description: Daniel McConnell deed to the town; subscription list for the erection of the first county courthouse; Floyd

Sipes genealogical notebooks; cemetery file; family and church histories.

SEE: Hamer.

MEADVILLE

PA555-40
Allegheny College
Pelletier Library
North Main Street
Meadville PA 16335

(814) 724-3769

OPEN: by appointment only
COPYING FACILITIES: yes
MATERIALS SOLICITED: Materials relating to Allegheny College and its first president Timothy Alden, and to Ida Tarbell.

HOLDINGS:
Total volume: 500 vols.; 13,000 items
Inclusive dates: 1815 -
Description: Collections relating chiefly to Allegheny College, Meadville, and Pennsylvania in the 19th century. Included are the College archives, and papers concerning the early history of the College, Meadville, and the Atlantic and Great Western Railway. There also are collections of papers of author Ida Tarbell, Methodist clergyman James Matthew Thoburn, and Civil War officer George W. Cullum.
Also included are the Archives of the Western Pennsylvania Conference of the United Methodist Church, which consist of 90 linear feet of archival material, 591 volumes, and 61 periodical runs.

GUIDES: Laura A. Grotzinger, *Guide to the Archives of the Western Pennsylvania Conference of the United Methodist Church* (Allegheny College, 1980).

SEE: Hamer; NUCMC, 1966.

SEE: Robbins; Hinding.

SEE ALSO: Walter Schatz, ed., *Directory of Afro-American Resources* (Bowker, 1970); Irwin Richman, comp., *Historical Manuscript Depositories in Pennsylvania* (Pennsylvania Historical and Museum Commission, 1965).

PA555-120
Crawford County Historical Society
848 North Main Street
Meadville PA 16335

(814) 724-6080

OPEN: M-F 1-5, Sa 10-2; closed Sundays and holidays
COPYING FACILITIES: yes
MATERIALS SOLICITED: Materials regarding Crawford County history.

HOLDINGS:
Total volume: 32 c.f.
Inclusive dates: 1792 -
Description: Manuscript and typescript materials relating to Crawford County, including David Dick letters, 1809-72; Bank of Western Pennsylvania papers, 1814-25; Holland Land Company papers, 1795-1835; Huidekoper family papers, 1800-95; the John E. Reynolds collection, 1795-1846; and a genealogical collection.

SEE: Hamer; NUCMC, 1959-61, 80.

SEE ALSO: Irwin Richman, comp., *Historical Manuscript Depositories in Pennsylvania* (Pennsylvania Historical and Museum Commission, 1965).

MECHANICSBURG

PA560-690
Rolls-Royce Owners' Club Foundation
Library
Hempt Road
Mechanicsburg PA

MAILING ADDRESS:
P.O. Box 2001
New Kingstown PA 17072

(717) 697-4671

OPEN: M-F 9-4; closed weekends and holidays
ACCESS: members of the Rolls-Royce Owners' Club Foundation and interested researchers by prior arrangement
COPYING FACILITIES: yes
MATERIALS SOLICITED: Materials relating to Rolls-Royce and Bentley automobiles. Will also accept data on British and American automobile body builders whose bodies were fitted to Rolls-Royce and Bentley automobiles.

HOLDINGS:
Total volume: 16,000 items
Inclusive dates: 1904 -
Description: Materials relating to Rolls-Royce and Bentley automobiles, their factories in Great Britain and America, their designers and builders, and other products made by the companies. Included are correspondence, drawings and specifications, films, photographs, and other records.

MEDIA

PA565-160
Delaware County Institute of Science
11 South Avenue
Media PA 19063

(215) 566-5126

SEE: Hamer.

Questionnaire not returned.

PA565-640
Pennsylvania State University
Delaware County Campus
The Papers of Martin Van Buren
25 Yearsley Mill Road
Media PA 19063

(215) 565-3300

OPEN: by appointment only
ACCESS: qualified academic scholars only, with prior arrangements required
COPYING FACILITIES: yes
MATERIALS SOLICITED: Material from or to Martin Van Buren. Will also accept material on the Van Buren family.

HOLDINGS:
Total volume: 13,00 items
Inclusive dates: 1802 - 1868
Description: Photocopies of all available manuscript Martin Van Buren materials from over 260 locations, compiled for the microfilm publication of Van Buren's papers. There is also the Alexander Duer Harvey collection of 92 letters written by John Van Buren, second son of Martin Van Buren, and other members of the immediate family, usually to Martin Van Buren, plus a small collection of memorabilia.

MERCER

PA570-520
Mercer County Historical Society
119 South Pitt Street
Mercer PA 16137

(412) 662-3490

OPEN: Tu-Th, Sa 11-4:30, F 7-9; closed Sundays, Mondays, and holidays
COPYING FACILITIES: yes
MATERIALS SOLICITED: Any subject matter pertaining to the history of Mercer County and nearby areas. Will also accept some materials pertaining to Pennsylvania, particularly the western section of the State, and nearby Ohio.

HOLDINGS:
Total volume: 200 c.f.
Inclusive dates: 1750 -
Description: Historical material focusing chiefly on Mercer County and surrounding areas. Included are manuscripts, diaries, account and ledger books, letters, and a collection of old maps.
Also included are old newspapers and cemetery records.

SEE: NUCMC, 1966.

SEE ALSO: Irwin Richman, comp., *Historical Manuscript Depositories in Pennsylvania* (Pennsylvania Historical and Museum Commission, 1965).

MERION STATION

PA575-80
Buten Museum
246 North Bowman Avenue
Merion Station PA 19066

(215) 664-6601

OPEN: Tu-Th 2-5, Sa 10-1; closed other days and holidays
ACCESS: by appointment
COPYING FACILITIES: yes
MATERIALS SOLICITED: Materials on Wedgwood, related companies, and English ceramics. Will also accept 18th-20th century materials relating to the study of ceramic development.

HOLDINGS:
Total volume: 10,000 items
Inclusive dates: 1775 -
Description: Correspondence and photographs about the Wedgwood Company in originals and copies, especially correspondence between the United States sales organization and the English parent company.

SEE ALSO: Gisela Heilpern, *Josiah Wedgwood, 18th Century Potter: Bibliography* (Southern Illinois Univ., 1967).

MILFORD

PA590-640
Pike County Historical Society
Community House
Milford PA 18337

no telephone

SEE: Hamer; NUCMC, 1967.

Questionnaire not returned.

MILLERSVILLE

PA595-530
Millersville University of
     Pennsylvania
Ganser Library
Archives and Special Collections
Millersville PA 17551

(717) 872-3624

OPEN: M-Th 8:30-9, F 8:30-4:30, Sa 2-5,
     Su 7-9; closed College holidays
COPYING FACILITIES: yes
MATERIALS SOLICITED: Archives of the
American Industrial Arts Association,
the Pennsylvania State Modern Language Association, the Pennsylvania
Sociological Association, the National
Council of State Sociological Associations, and manuscripts and oral history materials relating to the
Millersville area. Will also accept materials relating to Leo Ascher and his
contemporaries.

HOLDINGS:
     Total volume: 210 l.f.
     Inclusive dates: 1739 -
     Description: Archives of the American
Industrial Arts Association and the Pennsylvania State Modern Language Association. There are also the College archives
and a local manuscript collection containing unpublished diaries, reminiscences of
students and members of the community,
inventories of 19th century farms, and
manuscripts of local authors.
     Also included are archives of the
Pennsylvania Sociological Association
and the National Council of State Sociological Associations. The Leo Ascher
Center for the Study of Operetta contains
works by Leo Ascher and his
contemporaries.

SEE: NUCMC, 1980.

MONTROSE

PA615-720
Susquehanna County Historical
     Society and Free Library
     Association
Monument Square
Montrose PA 18801

(717) 278-1881

OPEN: Oct. 1-May 31 M, Tu, F 10-5;
     June 1-Sept. 30 M, Tu, F 10-5, W, Th
     1-5, Sa 10-1; closed Sundays and
     holidays
USER FEES: one dollar per person per
     day, or $4 per person per year; written
     inquiries $5 for first surname, $2 for
     each additional surname
COPYING FACILITIES: yes
MATERIALS SOLICITED: Materials relating
     to Susquehanna County history.

HOLDINGS:
     Total volume: not specified
     Inclusive dates: 1790's - 1890's
     Description: Account books, correspondence, diaries, journals, church and
school histories, photographs, local DAR
records, family genealogies, and oral history tapes.

SEE: Hamer.

MUNCY

PA625-520
Muncy Historical Society
44 N. Main Street
Muncy PA

MAILING ADDRESS:
131 S. Main Street
Muncy PA 17756

no telephone

SEE: Hamer.

Questionnaire not returned.

NAZARETH

PA640-570
Nazareth Moravian Historical Society
216 E. Center Street
Nazareth PA

MAILING ADDRESS:
P.O. Box 251
Nazareth PA 18064

(215) 759-5070

OPEN: Tu, F, Sa 2-5; closed other days,
     holidays, and Dec. 1 - April 1
ACCESS: prior approval of Board
     required
COPYING FACILITIES: no

HOLDINGS:
     Total volume: 5,000 pages
     Inclusive dates: 1743 - 1857
     Description: Overseers' accounts of the
Moravian community and original translations of church and town records.

SEE: Hamer; NUCMC, 1968.

NEW CASTLE

PA645-560
New Castle Free Public Library
207 E. North Street
New Castle PA 16101

(412) 658-6659

OPEN: M-Th 8:30-9, F 8:30-5:30, Sa
     8:30-5; closed Sundays and holidays
COPYING FACILITIES: yes
MATERIALS SOLICITED: Materials relating
     to New Castle and the local area.

HOLDINGS:
     Total volume: 3 vols.
     Inclusive dates: 1861 - 1879
     Description: Correspondence of Oscar
L. Jackson, U.S. Representative, 1875-79;
Civil War letters; letters and sermons of
Ira D. Sankey and Dwight L. Moody,
evangelists, and miscellaneous materials
of local interest.

SEE: Hamer.

NORRISTOWN

PA690-320
Historical Society of Montgomery
     County
1654 DeKalb Street
Norristown PA 19401

(215) 272-0297

SEE: Hamer.

Questionnaire not returned.

PA690-520
Montgomery County-Norristown
     Public Library
Steinbright Local History Collection
Swede and Elm Streets
Norristown PA 19401

(215) 277-3355

OPEN: M-F 9-9, Sa 9-1; closed Sundays
     and holidays
COPYING FACILITIES: yes
MATERIALS SOLICITED: Manuscripts,
manuscript maps, photographs, motion
pictures, audible documents, and
microforms concerning or originating
in Montgomery County or Pennsylvania. Will also accept archives and noncurrent records of institutions and organizations in Montgomery County and
Pennsylvania.

HOLDINGS:
     Total volume: 10 l.f.
     Inclusive dates: 1794 - 1952
     Description: Manuscripts, recordings,
and visual documents relating to Montgomery County and Pennsylvania. Included are records of the Library, such as
the circulation records of the Norristown
Library Company, 1794-1834, and the
Company's first catalog; photographs of
the area; and recordings of a Library-sponsored radio interview program.

OIL CITY

PA705-320

Heritage Society of Oil City
c/o Heritage Room
Oil City Library
Central Avenue and West Front Street
Oil City PA

MAILING ADDRESS:
P.O. Box 962
Oil City PA 16301

(814) 677-4057

OPEN: M-Sa 1-5; closed Sundays and
holidays; other times by appointment
only
ACCESS: advance notice requested
COPYING FACILITIES: yes
MATERIALS SOLICITED: Materials relating
to Venango County and the oil industry, including photographs, maps, general store ledgers, church records of Oil
City, National Transit Company
(Standard Oil Company) materials, and
early railroad materials.

HOLDINGS:
Total volume: not specified
Inclusive dates: 1800 -
Description: Lists of cemeteries and
burials in Venango County, PA, 1802- ;
Oil City birth and marriage records,
1882-1904; 200 photographs from an art
noveau studio, 1904-06; records of Christ
Lutheran Church, 1864-1900; account
books of Derrick Publishing Company,
1871-1925; copies of Oil City borough
records, 1864-84; and pipeline records of
the National Transit Company.

PENNSBURG

PA715-720

Schwenkfelder Library
1 Seminary Street
Pennsburg PA 18073

(215) 679-3103

OPEN: M-F 10-4; closed weekends and
holidays
COPYING FACILITIES: yes
MATERIALS SOLICITED: Materials relating
to the history of the Schwenkfelders,
the Radical Reformation, Silesia, and
the Upper Perkiomen Valley of Montgomery County.

HOLDINGS:
Total volume: 2,500 items; 500 vols.
Inclusive dates: 1543 -
Description: Materials relating to the
Schwenkfelder movement in Germany,
1525-1734, and America, 1734- , local
history, Mennonites, and the founder of
the local Universalist church.

SEE: Hamer; NUCMC, 1972.

SEE ALSO: Irwin Richman, comp., *Historical Manuscript Depositories in Pennsylvania* (Pennsylvania Historical and Museum Commission, 1965).

PHILADELPHIA

PA725-15

Academy of Natural Sciences of
Philadelphia
Library
19th Street and the Parkway
Philadelphia PA 19103

(215) 299-1040

OPEN: M-F 9-5; closed weekends and
holidays
COPYING FACILITIES: yes
MATERIALS SOLICITED: Academy records
and personal papers of scientists connected with the Academy. Will also accept notebooks, diaries, letters, and
other materials relating to either members of the Academy or scientists
prominent in areas of natural history.

HOLDINGS:
Total volume: 570 l.f.; 50 cartons
Inclusive dates: 1681 -
Description: Approximately 250,000
items relating to the natural sciences. Included are the archives of the Academy
and the American Entomological Society;
personal collections of letters, journals,
field notebooks, diaries, and speeches;
and letters signed by prominent naturalists. Two major series are the official correspondence of the Academy, 1812-1920,
and the correspondence of the American
Entomological Society, 1866-1920. Photographs of famous naturalists and of expeditions involving Academy personnel
also comprise part of the collection.

Also included: the Witmer Stone correspondence on ornithology; the Tryon-
Pilsbry malacological correspondence; the
papers and memorabilia of Joseph Leidy;
the Brooke Dolan diaries of Tibetan expeditions; the correspondence of
Zaccheus Collins; Richard Kern paintings
of the West; letters and scientific writings
of Thomas Say; papers of L. D. von
Schweinitz; a 17th century album of
insect paintings ascribed to Alexander
Marshall; and papers and drawings of C.
A. Lesueur.

GUIDES: Venia T. and Maurice E. Phillips, *Guide to the Manuscript Collections in the Academy of Natural Sciences of Philadelphia* (1963).

SEE: Hamer; NUCMC, 1966.

SEE: Parkinson; Allard, Crawley, and
Edmison; Hinding.

SEE ALSO: Venia T. and Maurice E. Phillips, *Minutes and Correspondence of the
Academy of Natural Sciences of Philadelphia, 1812-1924, Microfilm Publication Guide* (Academy of Natural Sciences of Philadelphia, 1967).

PA725-45

American Catholic Historical Society
of Philadelphia
Historical Collections
St. Charles Seminary
Philadelphia PA 19151

(215) 839-3760, Ext. 283

OPEN: by appointment only
COPYING FACILITIES: yes

MATERIALS SOLICITED: Papers of prominent Catholic citizens and members of
the Church hierarchy. Will also accept
any materials of historical interest.
HOLDINGS:
Total volume: 240 l.f.
Inclusive dates: 1759 -
Description: Manuscripts dealing with
prominent Catholic citizens, their families, businesses, and religious and social,
activities from the late 1700's to the early
1900's, consisting almost entirely of correspondence, and concerning the role of
Catholics, both laymen and clergy, in
American history. Included in the collection are account books, business and financial records, diaries and journals, literary manuscripts, legal papers, music
scores, manuscript maps, records of the
Society, and photographs.

Subjects include the history of the Roman Catholic church in America, the
Temperance Movement, the slave
uprisings in St. Domingue, the introduction of shorthand in the U.S.A., diplomatic relations between the U.S. and various foreign countries, and Church attitudes on many subjects.

SEE: Hamer.

PA725-60

American Friends Service Committee
Archives
1501 Cherry Street
Philadelphia PA 19102

(215) 241-7044

OPEN: M-F 8:30-4:30; closed weekends
and holidays
COPYING FACILITIES: yes
MATERIALS SOLICITED: Archives of the
American Friends Service Committee.
Will also accept papers of individuals
who have served with the Committee.

HOLDINGS:
Total volume: 900 l.f.
Inclusive dates: 1917 -
Description: Material pertaining to the
work of the American Friends Service
Committee in the United States and other parts of the world. Documents relate
to the organization and implementation
of relief, social, and reconciliation efforts,
and work with conscientious objectors
from the time of the Committee's
founding in 1917. Included are letters,
reports, minutes, photographs, slides, motion pictures, and personal diaries and
letters of individuals who have served
with the Committee.

SEE: Parkinson.

PA725-75

American Philosophical Society
Library
105 South Fifth Street
Philadelphia PA 19106

(215) 627-0706

OPEN: M-Sa 9-5; closed weekends and
holidays
COPYING FACILITIES: yes
MATERIALS SOLICITED: American Indian
linguistics; Benjamin Franklin and his
circle; Charles Robert Darwin, his circle and the evolution crisis; natural his-

tory; quantum physics; genetics; biochemistry; and medicine. Will also accept institutional archives and materials in archaeology; geography; and psychology.

HOLDINGS:
> *Total volume:* 7,000,000 pieces
> *Inclusive dates:* 1700 -
> *Description:* Manuscripts pertaining primarily to the history of science in America: 18th and 19th century manuscripts, which consist primarily of correspondence, relate to science in general, including botany, entomology, geology, electricity, evolution, and medicine; and 20th century documents, which include correspondence, diaries, laboratory notes, research reports, tape recordings, and photographs, concern chiefly genetics, biochemistry, quantum physics, and medicine. In addition, there are the archives of the Society and several scientific societies, as well as a collection of manuscripts documenting the history, customs, and languages of the American Indian.

GUIDES: Whitfield J. Bell, Jr., and Murphy D. Smith, comps., *Guide to the Archives and Manuscript Collections of the American Philosophical Society* (1966).

SEE: Hamer; NUCMC, 1959-64, 68-69, 76.

SEE: Allard, Crawley, and Edmison; Bean and Vane; Hinding; Ingram; Leventhal and Mooney - I; Parkinson; Robbins; Spalek.

SEE ALSO: Richard C. Davis, *North American Forest History: A Guide to Archives and Manuscripts in the United States and Canada* (Clio Books, 1977); Ann Novotny, ed., *Picture Sources 3* (Special Libraries Assn., 1975); Alan M. Meckler and Ruth McMullin, comps., *Oral History Collections* (Bowker, 1975); G. Bhagat, 'Materials Relating to Eighteenth and Nineteenth Century Indo-American Trade and Consular Relations in Private Archives in the United States,' *Indian Archives* 17 (Jan. 1967/Dec. 1968); Whitfield J. Bell, Jr., 'Papers for the History of Science,' *Library of Congress Quarterly Journal* 24 (July 1967); David A. Hounshell, comp., *Manuscripts in U.S. Depositories Relating to the History of Electrical Science and Technology* (Smithsonian Institution, n.d.); Peter Duignan, *Handbook of American Resources for African Studies* (Hoover Institution, 1967).

Walter Schatz, ed., *Directory of Afro-American Resources* (Bowker, 1970); Lisabeth M. Holloway, comp., *Philadelphia Resources in the History of the Health Sciences* (n.p., 1975); *Source Materials for the Recent History of Astronomy and Astrophysics: A Checklist of Manuscript Collections in the United States* (American Institute of Physics, 1971); John Finley Freeman, 'The American Indian in Manuscript: Preparing A Guide to Holdings in the Library of the American Philosophical Society,' *Ethnohistory* 8 (Spring 1961); Murphy D. Smith, 'Preparing a Manuscripts Guide for a Learned Society,' *American Archivist* 25 (July 1962).

American Philosophical Society, *Catalog of Manuscripts, and Archival Shelflist* (Greenwood Press, 1971); and the following publications of the Society: John Finley Freeman, comp., *A Guide to Manuscripts Relating to the American Indian in the Library of the American Philosophical Society* (1966); Thomas S. Kuhn, John L. Heilbron, Paul Forman, and Lini Allen, *Sources for History of Quantum Physics: An Inventory and Report* (1967).

PA725-120
American Swedish Historical Museum
1900 Pattison Avenue
Philadelphia PA 19145

(215) 389-1776

OPEN: Tu-F 10-4, Sa 12-4; closed Sundays, Mondays, and holidays
COPYING FACILITIES: no
MATERIALS SOLICITED: Materials relating to John Ericsson.

HOLDINGS:
> *Total volume:* 8 c.f.
> *Inclusive dates:* 1836 - 1911
> *Description:* Papers of John Ericsson, Swedish-American engineer, inventor, designer of the *Monitor* and other naval vessels, and pioneer in solar energy.

GUIDES: Esther Chilstrom Meixner, *Guide to the Microfilm Edition of the John Ericsson Papers* (1970).

SEE: Hamer; NUCMC, 1972, 74.

SEE: Hinding.

SEE ALSO: Irwin Richman, comp., *Historical Manuscript Depositories in Pennsylvania* (Pennsylvania Historical and Museum Commission, 1965).

PA725-150
Athenaeum of Philadelphia
219 South Sixth Street
Philadelphia PA 19106

(215) 925-2688

OPEN: M-F 9-5; closed weekends and holidays
ACCESS: advance arrangements required
COPYING FACILITIES: yes
MATERIALS SOLICITED: Drawings, correspondence, ledgers, trade catalogues, and photographs relating to architecture and the decorative arts of the 19th century up to 1930. Will also accept business records and drawings from crafts related to architecture and the decorative arts, including stained glass, ironwork, woodworking.

HOLDINGS:
> *Total volume:* 230 c.f.
> *Inclusive dates:* 1814 - 1945
> *Description:* Papers of Charles Wharton Stork, American poet; Curwen family papers; miscellaneous manuscript collections relating to the 19th and early 20th century, including architectural drawings, photographs, ledgers, drawings, registers, and correspondence.
>
> Architects represented in the collection include Mellor, Meigs and Howe; Willing, Sims and Talbutt; Zantzinger, Borie and Medary; Horace Trumbauer; Louis Magaziner; Paul Cret; John Notman; John Carver; John Haviland; Thomas S.

Stewart; Thomas Ustick Walter; John Harbeson; Collins and Autenrieth; Rankin and Kellogg; Hazlehurst and Huckel. Items relating to the decorative arts include collections from the D'Ascenzo Stained Glass Studio, the William Reith Stained Glass Studio, and manuscripts relating to silversmith Thomas Fletcher.

SEE: NUCMC, 1959-61, 69.

PA725-165
The Balch Institute for Ethnic Studies Library
18 South Seventh Street
Philadelphia PA 19106

(215) 925-8090

OPEN: M-Sa 9-5; closed Sundays and holidays
COPYING FACILITIES: yes
MATERIALS SOLICITED: Materials relating to North American immigration history and ethnicity. Will also accept material relating to American nativism, U.S. immigration policy, the American labor movement, and American radicalism.

HOLDINGS:
> *Total volume:* 1,000 l.f.
> *Inclusive dates:* 1750 -
> *Description:* Materials relating to more than 40 ethnic groups, with special emphasis on the Middle Atlantic region of the United States. Included are collections of personal papers, organization and business records, a photograph collection, and sound recordings.

SEE: Hinding.

PA725-195
Chestnut Hill College
Logue Library
Germantown & Northwestern Avenue
Philadelphia PA 19118

(215) 248-7050

OPEN: by appointment only; closed holidays
ACCESS: qualified researchers only
COPYING FACILITIES: yes

HOLDINGS:
> *Total volume:* 20 items; other materials
> *Inclusive dates:* 1850 -
> *Description:* Two versions of the original manuscript of the *Rubaiyat of Doc Sifers*, by James Whitcomb Riley; letters from George Bernard Shaw to James G. Huneker; and some Eugene Field manuscripts. Also included are photographs and records of the College.

PA725-208
The Philadelphia Contributionship
212 South Fourth Street
Philadelphia PA 19106

(215) 627-1752

OPEN: by appointment only
ACCESS: restricted to serious researchers
COPYING FACILITIES: yes
MATERIALS SOLICITED: Materials pertaining to the Philadelphia Contributionship, its directors, officers, and early policyholders.

HOLDINGS:
> *Total volume:* 345 l.f.
> *Inclusive dates:* 1752 -
> *Description:* Administrative, legal, financial, and underwriting records of The Philadelphia Contributionship, the nation's oldest fire insurance company. Also includes architectural surveys of insured properties done by company surveyors, 1752- .

PA725-240

City Archives of Philadelphia
523 City Hall Annex
Philadelphia PA

MAILING ADDRESS:
Department of Records
156 City Hall
Philadelphia PA 19107

(215) 686-2276

OPEN: M-F 8:30-5; closed weekends and holidays
COPYING FACILITIES: yes
MATERIALS SOLICITED: Records originating from the activities of the City and County governments of Philadelphia, and records of the Centennial Exhibition of 1876 and the Sesquicentennial Exhibition of 1926.

HOLDINGS:
> *Total volume:* 16,000 c.f.
> *Inclusive dates:* 1683 -
> *Description:* Among the archives of the City of Philadelphia are correspondence and files of the Mayor's Office and of cabinet officers; records of police, fire, health, and other departments; City Council records and ordinances; and judicial records. Philadelphia County archives include records of the following offices: County Commissioners (holdings include extensive tax records), County Treasurer, District Attorney, Recorder of Deeds, all County Courts (18th to 20th centuries), Board of Health, overseers of the poor, prison inspectors, and the jurisdictions of Philadelphia County which were consolidated into the City of Philadelphia in 1854. There are also extensive records of the Centennial and Sesquicentennial Exhibitions of 1876 and 1926.
> Also included are records of Philadelphia's Bicentennial celebration of 1976.

GUIDES: John Daly and Allen Weinberg, *Descriptive Inventory of the Archives of the City and County of Philadelphia* (1970).

SEE: Hamer.

SEE: Davis; Hinding; Leventhal and Mooney - I.

SEE ALSO: Lisa Eizen and Allen Weinberg, *Subject Index to the Photograph Collection of the Philadelphia City Archives* (1976); Allen Weinberg, 'Publication Program of the Philadelphia Archives,' *American Archivist* 25 (April 1962).

PA725-285

College of Physicians of Philadelphia
Library
Historical Collections
19 South 22nd Street
Philadelphia PA 19103

(215) 561-6050, Ext. 75

OPEN: M-F 9-5; closed weekends and holidays
COPYING FACILITIES: yes
MATERIALS SOLICITED: Manuscripts, archives, photographs, and microforms relating to the history of medicine, particularly American and European medicine, 18th century to present, with emphasis on the Philadelphia area. Will also accept audible documents and motion pictures.

HOLDINGS:
> *Total volume:* 800 l.f.
> *Inclusive dates:* 1348 -
> *Description:* About 1,000 collections, nearly all on medicine and related subjects, with emphasis on medicine in Philadelphia and Pennsylvania. Included are 18th and 19th century student lecture notes; archives of organizations and institutions, including the College of Physicians; personal and professional papers of physicians; case histories; ledgers; fee books; manuscripts of published and unpublished books and articles; prescription and remedy books; scrapbooks; a 20,000 item autograph collection; and 12,000 visual documents.

SEE: Hamer; NUCMC, 1966, 68.

SEE: Hinding; Ingram;; Leventhal and Mooney - I; Robbins.

SEE ALSO: Lisabeth M. Holloway, 'The Historical Collections of the Library of the College of Physicians of Philadelphia: A Survey of Their Extent in 1973 and a Chronicle of Major Acquisitions,' *Transactions and Studies of the College of Physicians of Philadelphia* 41 (Jan. 1974); Lisabeth M. Holloway, comp., *Philadelphia Resources in the History of the Health Sciences* (n.p., 1975); Irwin Richman, comp., *Historical Manuscript Depositories in Pennsylvania* (Pennsylvania Historical and Museum Commission, 1965).

PA725-330

Congregation Mikveh Israel
Archives
44 N. 4th Street
Philadelphia PA 19106

(215) 922-5446

OPEN: M-Th 10-4, Su 10-1; closed Fridays, Saturdays, and Jewish holy days
ACCESS: by appointment
COPYING FACILITIES: no
MATERIALS SOLICITED: Will accept documents pertaining to the Jewish communities of the 18th and 19th centuries.

HOLDINGS:
> *Total volume:* 120 c.f.
> *Inclusive dates:* 1770 - 1969
> *Description:* A manuscript collection of 40,000 items relating to the origins and development of the Philadelphia Jewish community, in the religious, social, and economic spheres. Included are minute books of Congregation Mikveh Israel, inter- and intra-community correspondence, statistics on birth, marriage, and death, accounts, demographic information, and genealogical source data.

SEE ALSO: Irwin Richman, comp., *Historical Manuscript Depositories in Pennsylvania* (Pennsylvania Historical and Museum Commission, 1965).

PA725-345

Curtis Institute of Music
Library
1720 Locust Street
Philadelphia PA 19103

(215) 893-5265

OPEN: M-F 9-5; closed weekends and holidays
ACCESS: by appointment
COPYING FACILITIES: no
MATERIALS SOLICITED: Holographs and memorabilia of alumni and faculty of the Curtis Institute.

HOLDINGS:
> *Total volume:* 128 l.f.
> *Inclusive dates:* primarily 1800 -
> *Description:* Materials relating to Richard Wagner, including letters, manuscripts, documents, and biographical material; and manuscripts and letters of Franz Liszt, Samuel Barber, Johannes Brahms, Gian-Carlo Menotti, Wolfgang Amadeus Mozart, Franz Schubert, and Robert Schumann.
> Also included are the following: archives of the Institute, including scrapbooks and clippings, concert programs, annual catalogues, a complete run of the Institute's periodical, *Overtones*; sound recordings of recital, with the 1930's-40's on 78-rpm discs, the 1960's-present on tapes, and opera productions of the 1970's on video tapes.
> Scrapbooks and other memorabilia of Lynnwood Farnam; holograph compositions and transcriptions for harp of Carlos Salzedo; orchestral transcriptions of Leopold Stokowski; holograph compositions and transcriptions of William Strasser; holograph editions of music for contrabass of Anton Torello.
> Personal papers of Mary Louise Curtis Bok Zimbalist, including correspondence, photographs, and memorabilia; single holograph letters and music manuscripts of many well-known composers and distinguished alumni and faculty of the Institute.

SEE: NUCMC, 1966.

SEE ALSO: John N. Burk, ed., *Letters of Richard Wagner: The Burrell Collection* (Vienna House, 1972).

PA725-375

Drexel University
Libraries
Drexel Collection
32nd and Chestnut Streets
Philadelphia PA 19104

(215) 895-2755

OPEN: M-F 9-5; closed weekends and holidays

COPYING FACILITIES: yes
MATERIALS SOLICITED: Materials dealing with the Drexel family and with Drexel University.

HOLDINGS:
Total volume: 120 l.f.
Inclusive dates: 1885 -
Description: Correspondence and other manuscripts of Anthony Joseph Drexel and other members of the Drexel family; papers of George W. Childs and Pennsylvania Railroad executive Frank Thomson; archives of the Delaware Valley Chapter of the Association of College and Research Libraries, Information Science Abstracts, and the Pennsylvania Library Club; documents relating to the University and its faculty, students, alumni, and activities; and photographs of the Drexel family and the University.

SEE: Hinding.

PA725-405

The Dropsie University
Library
Broad and York Streets
Philadelphia PA 19132

no telephone

OPEN: M-F 9-4:30; closed weekends, holidays, and Jewish holy days
COPYING FACILITIES: yes
MATERIALS SOLICITED: Hebraica, Judaica, and materials relating to the Bible. Will also accept materials relating to Arabian and Semitic history.

HOLDINGS:
Total volume: 50,000 items
Inclusive dates: 8th century -
Description: Materials dealing both with medieval Middle Eastern history and modern Jewish-American history. Included are 256 Oriental manuscripts in Arabic, Ethiopic, Hebrew, Samaritan, and Coptic; 450 fragments from the *Cairo Genizah* in Hebrew and Arabic; and a large collection of correspondence and papers of prominent Jewish-American figures in the 19th and 20th centuries.

SEE: Hamer.

SEE: Ingram; Martin.

SEE ALSO: Philip P. Mason, ed., *Directory of Jewish Archival Institutions* (Wayne State Univ. Press, 1975).

PA725-430

St. Clement Ukrainian Catholic
   University in Rome
Philadelphia Center
Institute for the Study of Religious
   Dimensions
in Ukrainian Culture
7911 Whitewood Road, Elkins Park
Philadelphia PA 19126

(215) 635-1555

OPEN: M-Th 9-2, F, Sa by appointment; closed weekends, holidays, and holy days
ACCESS: advance arrangements requested
COPYING FACILITIES: no

MATERIALS SOLICITED: Materials relating to Ukrainian culture in the Ukraine and the United States, especially concerning religious life.

HOLDINGS:
Total volume: 270 items
Inclusive dates: 19th century -
Description: Primarily an audio-tape collection of weekly radio broadcasts of 'The Voice of the Ukrainian Community.' Also includes video-tapes of television programs dealing with Ukrainian life in the United States; manuscripts of unpublished materials on the life and works of Archbishop Andrew Sheptytzky; archives of the Patriarchal Society; materials on the violations of human and religious rights in the Ukraine by the government of the USSR; and the archives of the St. Sophia Religious Association of Ukrainian Catholics, Inc., 1976- .

PA725-495

The Franklin Institute
Historical Collections
20th Street and Benjamin Franklin
   Parkway
Philadelphia PA 19103

(215) 448-1143

OPEN: M-F 10-5; closed weekends and holidays
ACCESS: by appointment
COPYING FACILITIES: yes
MATERIALS SOLICITED: Franklin Institute history and history of American physical science and technology, especially that relating to industrial civilization. Will also accept documents relating to Benjamin Franklin.

HOLDINGS:
Total volume: 175 l.f.; 10,000 items
Inclusive dates: 1824 -
Description: Materials relating chiefly to the Franklin Institute and to science and technology in American culture, including the introduction of experimental science to technological research in the pre-Civil War period, the rise of engineering and industrial standards in the last half of the 19th century, and the creation of science museums and laboratories in basic physical research and military-industrial research since World War I. Included is information on such National scientific and technological leaders as William Strickland, Alexander Dallas Bache, William Sellers, Elihu Thomson, Lee De Forest, and William F. G. Swann, and on mechanics, industrialists, and scientists in the Philadelphia area, 1824-1924.

SEE: NUCMC, 1959-61, 63-64, 71.

SEE: Spalek; Hinding; Allard, Crawley, and Edmison.

SEE ALSO: *For the Promotion of Technology: A Guide to the Nineteenth Century Records of the Franklin Institute's Committee on Science and the Arts* (Scholarly Resources, 1976); David A. Hounshell, comp., *Manuscripts in U.S. Depositories Relating to the History of Electrical Science and Technology* (Smithsonian Institution, n.d.); Law-

rence J. Paszek, comp., *United States Air Force History: A Guide to Documentary Sources* (Office of Air Force History, 1973); Eugene S. Ferguson, *Bibliography of the History of Technology* (MIT Press, 1968).

PA725-510

Free Library of Philadelphia
Rare Book Department
Logan Square
Philadelphia PA 19103

(215) 686-5416

OPEN: M-Sa 9-5; closed Sundays, holidays, and Saturdays June-Aug.
COPYING FACILITIES: yes
MATERIALS SOLICITED: Materials relating to any areas covered in the current collections.

HOLDINGS:
Total volume: not specified
Inclusive dates: 3,000 B.C. -
Description: The John Frederick Lewis collections of cuneiform tablets, European manuscripts, and Oriental manuscripts; British and American manuscripts and letters pertaining to the growth and development of the common law; letters and manuscripts of authors Charles Dickens, Edgar Allan Poe, and A. Edward Newton; letters of authors Beatrix Potter, Arthur Rackham, Kate Greenaway, and Oliver Goldsmith; Pennsylvania German Fraktur; and a collection of letters of the Presidents.

SEE: Hamer; NUCMC, 1959-61, 70.

SEE: Novotny; Martin; Robbins.

PA725-525

Friends Hospital
Weiner Professional Library
Archives
Roosevelt Blvd. at Adams Avenue
Philadelphia PA 19124

(215) 831-4763

OPEN: M, Tu 8:30-4:30, W-F 8:30-8:30; closed weekends and holidays
ACCESS: advance permission required
COPYING FACILITIES: yes

HOLDINGS:
Total volume: 1,000 c.f.
Inclusive dates: 1813 - 1930
Description: Records of Friends Hospital, which was titled Friends Asylum from 1813 to 1900, including account books, financial reports, patient records, and the daily diary of the superintendents of the Asylum.

PA725-540

Friends Free Library of Germantown
5418 Germantown Avenue
Philadelphia PA 19144

(215) 438-6023

OPEN: M-Th 9-4, F 9-3, Sa 9-noon; closed Sundays, holidays, and the week before Labor Day; shorter summer hours
COPYING FACILITIES: yes

MATERIALS SOLICITED: Historical materials regarding Germantown Friends School.

HOLDINGS:
> Total volume: 250 vols.; 20 l.f.
> Inclusive dates: 1845 -
> Description: The archives of the Germantown Friends School, including early grade books, account records, photographs, yearbooks, and minutes. There is also the Irvin C. Poley Collection of 250 scrapbooks relating to theater in Philadelphia, 1906-74.

SEE: Martin; Robbins.

PA725-585
German Society of Pennsylvania
Joseph Horner Library
611 Spring Garden Street
Philadelphia PA 19123

(215) 627-4365

SEE: Hamer.

Questionnaire not returned.

PA725-600
Germantown Historical Society
Library
5214 Germantown Avenue
Philadelphia PA 19144

(215) 844-0514

OPEN: Tu 1-5, other days by appointment
COPYING FACILITIES: yes
MATERIALS SOLICITED: Materials relating to Germantown and Philadelphia.

HOLDINGS:
> Total volume: 700 c.f.
> Inclusive dates: 1683 -
> Description: A collection of business records, family papers, deeds, wills, genealogical data, and photographs, chiefly pertaining to Germantown and Philadelphia history. The Library also holds the manuscripts of horticulturists Edwin C. Gellett and Thomas Meehan.

SEE: Hamer.

SEE: Hinding; Leventhal and Mooney - I.

SEE ALSO: Irwin Richman, comp., *Historical Manuscript Depositories in Pennsylvania* (Pennsylvania Historical and Museum Commission, 1965).

PA725-608
Germantown Mennonite Church Corporation
Archives
6133 Germantown Avenue
Philadelphia PA

MAILING ADDRESS:
6117 Germantown Avenue
Philadelphia PA 19144

(215) 843-0943

OPEN: M-F 10-4; closed weekends
ACCESS: appointment required
COPYING FACILITIES: no
MATERIALS SOLICITED: Papers and documents originated by, or concerning the Mennonites of Germantown.

HOLDINGS:
> Total volume: 4 file drawers; 1 box
> Inclusive dates: 1822 -
> Description: Materials related to the Germantown Mennonite congregation, including the papers of Philadelphia Student services, 1971-75; the Charles Longmire collection of letters to Germantown Mennonites, 1820-60; and congregation records, 1970- .

Congregation records older than 10 years are deposited at the Mennonite Historians of Eastern Pennsylvania, Mennonite Historical Library, and Archives of Eastern Pennsylvania, in Lansdale, PA.

PA725-615
Girard College
Stephen Girard Papers
Founder's Hall
Girard and Corinthian Avenues
Philadelphia PA 19121

(215) 787-2680, 2626

OPEN: Th 2-4; closed other days and holidays
ACCESS: permission through application to the President of Girard College
COPYING FACILITIES: yes
MATERIALS SOLICITED: Documents relating to Stephen Girard. Will also accept material relating to Girard College.

HOLDINGS:
> Total volume: 150,000 pieces; other items
> Inclusive dates: 1780 - 1831
> Description: Correspondence of Stephen Girard, including among the correspondents U.S. Presidents, statesmen, naval officers, diplomats, Simon Bolivar, Toussaint L'Ouverture, and members of the Bonaparte family; business papers, such as bills and receipts, business statements, memoranda, law proceedings, and items on real estate, ships, and shipping; bank records; and material on yellow fever epidemics.
> Also includes records on China trade, navigation, ships' logs, horticulture, agriculture, and the French Revolution.

Microfilms of the papers are on deposit at the American Philosophical Society.

PA725-660
Fleisher Art Memorial
715 Catherine Street
Philadelphia PA 19147

(215) 922-3456

SEE: Hamer.

Questionnaire not returned.

PA725-690
Hahnemann University
Archives and History of Medicine Collections
Room 2255, Medical College, Hahnemann University
245 N. 15th Street
Philadelphia PA

MAILING ADDRESS:
Mail Stop 912
245 North 15th Street
Philadelphia PA 19102

(215) 448-7811, 7184

OPEN: M-F 9-5 by appointment only; closed weekends and holidays
COPYING FACILITIES: yes
MATERIALS SOLICITED: History of Hahnemann Medical College. Will also accept materials in the history of medicine.

HOLDINGS:
> Total volume: 77 l.f.
> Inclusive dates: 1849 -
> Description: Archives of the College and Hospital, including 250 letters and documents of the College, 1860-70; 43 l.f. of M.D. and B.S. theses, 1849- ; and 15 l.f. of biographical material on homeopathic physicians, compiled by T. L. Bradford.

SEE ALSO: Lisabeth M. Holloway, comp., *Philadelphia Resources in the History of the Health Sciences* (n.p., 1975).

PA725-700
Historic St. George's United Methodist Church
Museum and Library Complex
235 North 4th Street
Philadelphia PA 19106

(215) 925-7788

OPEN: M-F 9:30-4; closed weekends and holidays
COPYING FACILITIES: no
MATERIALS SOLICITED: Materials pertaining to the history of Methodism in America.

HOLDINGS:
> Total volume: 140 c.f.
> Inclusive dates: 1773 -
> Description: Materials primarily oriented towards the history of Methodism and Christianity in general, including biographical, missionary, geographical, and general church information, chiefly pertaining to the growth of Methodism in America.

SEE: Hamer (as Historical Society of the Philadelphia Annual Conference of the Methodist Episcopal Church).

SEE ALSO: Irwin Richman, comp., *Historical Manuscript Depositories in Pennsylvania* (Pennsylvania Historical and Museum Commission, 1965): as Historical Society of the Philadelphia Methodist Conference.

PA725-710
Historical Society of Frankford
14078 Kelvin Avenue
Philadelphia PA 19116

no telephone

SEE: Hamer.

Questionnaire not returned.

PA725-720
Historical Society of Pennsylvania
Manuscripts Department
1300 Locust Street
Philadelphia PA 19107

(215) 732-6200

OPEN: M 1-9, Tu-F 9-5; closed weekends
and holidays
USER FEES: non-members, one dollar per
day
ACCESS: only for research work by
qualified and experienced persons, and
not for undergraduate study, prize
competitions, genealogical research or
secondary school work; application,
positive identification, and letter of
introduction required
COPYING FACILITIES: yes
MATERIALS SOLICITED: Materials
strengthening existing 18th and 19th
century collections, and 19th and 20th
century materials relating to political,
social, and economic history of the
Delaware Valley and southeastern
Pennsylvania. Will also accept other
materials relating to southeastern Pennsylvania.

HOLDINGS:
    Total volume: 34,000 l.f.
    Inclusive dates: 1460 -
    Description: Over 2,500 collections
documenting the economic, social, and
political history of the middle colonies
and states from the 1650's to the present.
Papers of William Penn and the Penn
family, John Dickinson, James Buchanan,
George Mifflin Dallas, Jay Cooke, James
Logan, Salmon P. Chase, and Joel R.
Poinsett.
    Autograph collections include Ameri-
can and European authors, artists, scientists, musicians, politicians, and other
public figures, 1456-1963. Also prints,
photographs, architectural drawings, and
maps, especially Delaware Valley materials. Organizational archives of the Indian
Rights Association, the Pennsylvania
Abolition Society, the Print Club of
Philadelphia, etc.

GUIDES: Guide to the Manuscript Collections of the Historical Society of Pennsylvania (1949).

SEE: Hamer; NUCMC, 1959-72, 74,
76-77, 79.

SEE: Hinding; Bean and Vane; Hines;
Allard, Crawley, and Edmison;
Gehring; Leventhal and Mooney - I;
Robbins.

SEE ALSO: Jerome S. Handler, A Guide to
Source Materials for the Study of Bar-
bados History, 1627-1834 (Southern Il-
linois Univ. Press, 1971); G. Bhagat,
'Materials Relating to Eighteenth and
Nineteenth Century Indo-American
Trade and Consular Relations in Pri-
vate Archives in the United States,' In-
dian Archives 17 (Jan. 1967/Dec. 1968);
Lisabeth M. Holloway, comp., Philadel-
phia Resources in the History of the
Health Sciences (n.p., 1975); Walter
Schatz, ed., Directory of Afro-American
Resources (Bowker, 1970); Peter
Duignan, Handbook of American Re-
sources for African Studies (Hoover In-
stitution, 1967); Robert O. Collins and
Peter Duignan, Americans in Africa
(Hoover Institution, 1963).

Morris Rieger, 'Africa-Related Papers of
Persons and Organizations in the United
States,' African Studies Bulletin 8 (Dec.
1965); Ann Novotny, ed., Picture Sources
3 (Special Libraries Assn., 1975); David
A. Hounshell, comp., Manuscripts in U.S.
Depositories Relating to the History of
Electrical Science and Technology
(Smithsonian Institution, n.d.); Lawrence
J. Paszek, comp., United States Air Force
History: A Guide to Documentary Sources
(Office of Air Force History, 1973); Rich-
ard C. Davis, North American Forest His-
tory: A Guide to Archives and Manuscripts
in the United States and Canada (Clio
Books, 1977). Finding aids to some in-
dividual collections are available at the
institution.

PA725-765
Holy Family College
The Archives
Grant and Frankford Avenues
Philadelphia PA 19114

(215) 637-7700, Ext. 53

OPEN: M-F 10-3, other days by
appointment
COPYING FACILITIES: yes
MATERIALS SOLICITED: Materials relating
to Holy Family College, the Torresdale
area of Philadelphia, and the history
and culture of American Poles. Will
also accept papers of faculty and College personnel and of outstanding men
and women in subject areas of interest
to the College.

HOLDINGS:
    Total volume: 21 l.f.; 131 items
    Inclusive dates: 1911 -
    Description: Non-current records of
Holy Family College, including account
books, business and financial records,
correspondence, literary manuscripts, architectural and engineering drawings of
campus buildings, photographs, and
ephemera. There are also several collections of papers on the history of Polish
parishes, organizations, and customs,
1911- , including materials documenting
war relief, political and civic activities,
and educational, cultural, and scientific
accomplishments of American Poles and
the Polish people.

SEE: NUCMC, 1978, 80.

PA725-780
INA Corporation
Archives
1600 Arch Street
Philadelphia PA

MAILING ADDRESS:
P.O. Box 7728
Philadelphia PA 19101

(215) 241-3293, 4386

OPEN: M-F 8:30-4:45; closed weekends
and holidays
ACCESS: by appointment
COPYING FACILITIES: yes
MATERIALS SOLICITED: Materials gener-
ated by the Insurance Company of
North America and its subsidiaries and
affiliates.

HOLDINGS:
    Total volume: 2,300 l.f.; 390
microfilm rolls; 2.5 l.f. microfiche; 250
artifacts; 112 audio discs and tapes
    Inclusive dates: 1791 -
    Description: The 18th and 19th cen-
tury records consist almost entirely of fire
and marine insurance records, minutes,
and some executive correspondence. The
20th century records also include documentation of other aspects of company
activity: publications, reports and evaluations, advertising, subsidiaries, real
estate, international expansion, and legal
and regulatory activity.

GUIDES: Mary Elizabeth Ruwell, Guide to
the INA Corporation Archives (1975).

SEE ALSO: M. J. McCosker, The Historical
Collection of the Insurance Company of
North America, 1792-1967 (Insurance
Company of North America, 1967).

PA725-795
Independence National Historical
Park
311-313 Walnut Street
Philadelphia PA 19106

SEE: Hamer; NUCMC, 1965.

Questionnaire not returned.

PA725-810
Inter-Church Child Care Society
125 South 22nd Street
Philadelphia PA 19103

SEE: Hamer.

Questionnaire not returned.

PA725-870
The Library Company of Philadelphia
1300 Locust Street
Philadelphia PA

MAILING ADDRESS:
1314 Locust Street
Philadelphia PA 19107

(215) 732-6200

OPEN: M-F 9-4:45; closed weekends and
holidays
USER FEES: Historical Society of
Pennsylvania members free;
non-members, one dollar per day or
$7.50 for six-month reader's ticket

ACCESS: only for research work by qualified and experienced persons, and not for undergraduate study, prize competitions, genealogical, or secondary school work
COPYING FACILITIES: yes
HOLDINGS:
Total volume: 342 c.f.
Inclusive dates: 1678 - 1896
Description: 16 major collections and approximately 150 minor collections covering mainly 18th and 19th century political, economic, social, and scientific (especially medical) history for Philadelphia.
SEE: Hamer; NUCMC, 1959-62, 74.
SEE: Martin.

SEE ALSO: Walter Schatz, ed., *Directory of Afro-American Resources* (Bowker, 1970); Lisabeth M. Holloway, comp., *Philadelphia Resources in the History of the Health Sciences* (n.p., 1975); Irwin Richman, comp., *Historical Manuscript Depositories in Pennsylvania* (Pennsylvania Historical and Museum Commission, 1965).

PA725-885

The Lutheran Archives Center at Philadelphia
7301 Germantown Avenue
Philadelphia PA 19119

(215) 248-4616, Ext. 34

OPEN: by appointment only
USER FEES: $5 per year for non-members of constituent synods
COPYING FACILITIES: yes
MATERIALS SOLICITED: Records of supporting Lutheran synods and member congregations and records of Lutheran pastors and scholars. Will also accept other materials of historical interest to Lutherans and Pennsylvanians.

HOLDINGS:
Total volume: 633 l.f.; 150 file drawers
Inclusive dates: 1740 -
Description: A collection of documents and records of the Ministerium of Pennsylvania, the General Council, the Eastern Pennsylvania Synod, the Southeastern Pennsylvania Synod, the Northeastern Pennsylvania Synod, the New Jersey Synod, the Upper New York Synod, and the Slovak-Zion Synod of the Lutheran Church in America. Included are records of all auxiliary committees, societies, and missions, as well as of individual congregations.
There are also journals of Lutheran patriarchs, including Henry Melchior Muhlenberg, as well as manuscripts and papers from Lutheran pastors, missionaries, and scholars. Special collections include liturgical materials, records of the Lutheran Children's & Family Services, and records from the Lutheran Theological Seminary.
SEE: Hamer; NUCMC, 1959-64, 75.
SEE: Ingram.

PA725-900

Medical College of Pennsylvania
Archives and Special Collections on Women in Medicine
3300 Henry Avenue
Philadelphia PA 19129

(215) 842-7124

OPEN: M-F 8-4; closed weekends and holidays
ACCESS: advance notice desirable
COPYING FACILITIES: yes
MATERIALS SOLICITED: Materials on and papers of women physicians and women's medical organizations. Will also accept papers and manuscripts of women and men who are not physicians but who are closely related to women physicians or the subject area.

HOLDINGS:
Total volume: 600 l.f.; 4,000 photographs
Inclusive dates: 1848 -
Description: Archives of the Medical College of Pennsylvania, formerly Woman's Medical College of Pennsylvania. In addition, the Special Collections of Women in Medicine includes the following: papers of primarily U.S. women physicians; records of defunct women's medical schools in the United States; records of defunct women's hospitals in the United States.
Manuscripts of published and unpublished works on and by women physicians throughout the world; papers of Kate Hurd-Mead, Rhoda Truax, and Lida Poynter; American Medical Women's Association historical collection; American Women's Hospitals Service records; records of other medical women's organizations and associations in the United States; Oral History Project on Women in Medicine, tapes and transcripts of 43 interviews.
The non-print collection (photographs, slides, films, etc.) documents the education, administration, practice patterns, and leisure activities of women physicians throughout the world.
SEE: Hinding.

SEE ALSO: Lisabeth M. Holloway, comp., *Philadelphia Resources in the History of the Health Sciences* (n.p., 1975).

PA725-908

Medical Mission Sisters (Society of Catholic Medical Missionaries)
8400 Pine Road
Philadelphia PA 19111

(215) 742-6100

OPEN: by appointment only
ACCESS: advance arrangements required
COPYING FACILITIES: yes
MATERIALS SOLICITED: Materials relating to the Medical Mission Sisters and their institutions and activities.

HOLDINGS:
Total volume: 2,275 l.f.
Inclusive dates: 1925 -
Description: Materials relating to the Medical Mission Sisters, including correspondence, financial records, administration records, chapter assemblies, photographs, scrapbooks, letters from sisters at missions, and records of hospitals in Africa, Asia, South America, and the United States. Also included are materials relating to the midwifery institute in Santa Fe, NM, 1944-70, including birth and medical records and project studies in nurse midwifery.
SEE: Duignan.

PA725-930

Military Order of the Loyal Legion of the United States
War Library and Museum
1805 Pine Street
Philadelphia PA 19103

(215) 735-8196

OPEN: M-F 10-4; closed weekends and holidays
COPYING FACILITIES: no
MATERIALS SOLICITED: Material concerning events leading up to the Civil War, the War itself, and early Reconstruction to 1875. Will also accept material concerning U.S. military forces.

HOLDINGS:
Total volume: 10,000 vols.
Inclusive dates: 1840 - 1875
Description: Correspondence, diaries, journals, logbooks, and photographs of Civil War officers and enlisted men, and genealogical source data and records of Civil War officers.

PA725-980

Museum of American Jewish History
55 North 5th Street
Philadelphia PA 19106

(215) 923-3811

OPEN: Su 11-4, M-F 10-4; closed Saturdays, holidays, and Jewish holy days
USER FEES: adults $1.50; students and senior adults $1.25
COPYING FACILITIES: no
MATERIALS SOLICITED: Documents pertaining to the Jewish population in the United States.

HOLDINGS:
Total volume: not specified
Inclusive dates: 1762 -
Description: Documents and manuscripts relating to the first Jewish families of Philadelphia.

PA725-990

The Mutual Assurance Company
240 South 4th Street
Philadelphia PA 19106

(215) 925-0609

OPEN: M-F by appointment; closed weekends and holidays
COPYING FACILITIES: yes
MATERIALS SOLICITED: Mutual Assurance Company business records and correspondence. Will also accept papers relating to Company history, or the insured houses and owners of the original policies.

HOLDINGS:
Total volume: 155 c.f.
Inclusive dates: 1784 -
Description: A collection of business records and related papers, dating from the formation of The Mutual Assurance Company, familiarly known as The Green Tree, in 1784. The major part consists of financial accounts and receipts, cancelled insurance surveys and policies, and minutes of meetings. Other related records include correspondence, Company histories, and miscellaneous material.

PA726-7

National Archives and Records
  Administration
Federal Archives and Records Center
Archives Branch
5000 Wissahickon Avenue
Philadelphia PA 19144

(215) 951-5696

OPEN: M-F 7:30-4; closed weekends and holidays
ACCESS: Records are open, subject to Federal agency restrictions and restrictions based upon current legislation relevant to confidentiality and security classification. See General Information Leaflet No. 27, 'General Restrictions on Access to Records in the National Archives of the United States.'
COPYING FACILITIES: yes
MATERIALS SOLICITED: Non-current records of agencies of the Federal government in Pennsylvania, Delaware, Maryland, Virginia, and West Virginia. Will also accept other materials subject to appropriate guidelines of the National Archives and Records Service.

HOLDINGS:
Total volume: 27,000 c.f.
Inclusive dates: 1789 -
Description: Federal records, primarily for Pennsylvania, Delaware, Maryland, Virginia, and West Virginia. Represented are records of District Courts, the Court of Appeals for the 3rd Circuit, the Army Corps of Engineers, the Bureau of Customs, the National Park Service, the Chief of Ordnance, and the Office of the Quartermaster General.

SEE: Hamer.

PA726-37

Old Christ Church in Philadelphia
Archives
2nd Street above Market
Philadelphia PA

MAILING ADDRESS:
20 N. American Street
Philadelphia PA 19106

(215) 922-1695

OPEN: by appointment only
USER FEES: $3 annually
ACCESS: advance written arrangements with the Rector's office
COPYING FACILITIES: yes
MATERIALS SOLICITED: Will accept manuscripts and photographs relating to Old Christ Church in Philadelphia, 1695- , Bishop William White,

1742-1836, rectors of the church, and associated 19th century missions and institutions.

HOLDINGS:
Total volume: 12 c.f.; 264 vols.
Inclusive dates: 1695 -
Description: Materials relating to Christ Church in Philadelphia and related institutions such as Christ Church Hospital, St. Peters Church, St. James Church, Calvary Mission, and the Episcopal Academy. Included are finanical records, genealogical source data, building records for Philadelphia for the 17th through 19th centuries, and bibliographical material and correspondence of Bishop William White and other rectors of Christ Church.

Also held is material on the formation and development of the Episcopal church in America, social programs of the Episcopal church in Philadelphia in the 19th century, early 20th century, and Depression, and Bicentennial activities, 1976.

SEE: Hamer (as Christ Church, Library).

SEE: Leventhal and Mooney - I.

PA726-43

The Pennsylvania Academy of the
  Fine Arts
Broad and Cherry Streets
Philadelphia PA 19102

(215) 972-7641

OPEN: M-F by appointment only; closed weekends and holidays
COPYING FACILITIES: yes
MATERIALS SOLICITED: Academy records, photographs, memorabilia, and reminiscences of former students and faculty of the Academy.

HOLDINGS:
Total volume: 300 c.f.
Inclusive dates: 1795 -
Description: Records of the Pennsylvania Academy of the Fine Arts museum and school, including correspondence, minutes, photographs, exhibition records, student records, and biographical information about faculty and board members.

PA726-057

Pennsylvania Free and Accepted
  Masons
R. W. Grand Lodge
1 North Broad Street
Philadelphia PA 19107

no telephone

SEE: Hamer.

Questionnaire not returned.

PA726-60

Pennsylvania Hospital
Medical Library
Eighth and Spruce Streets
Philadelphia PA 19107

no telephone

SEE: Hamer.

Questionnaire not returned.

PA726-105

Philadelphia Archdiocesan Archives
222 North 17th Street
Philadelphia PA 19103

(215) 875-1111

OPEN: by appointment only
ACCESS: qualified researchers; by appointment only
COPYING FACILITIES: yes
MATERIALS SOLICITED: Parish and institution records and administrative records of the Philadelphia Archdiocese.

HOLDINGS:
Total volume: 15,117 items
Inclusive dates: 1808 -
Description: Collections of correspondence of bishops of Philadelphia. The early part of the collection deals with many areas of the State of Pennsylvania which originally comprised the Diocese of Philadelphia, while other materials deal with the establishment of various institutions, schools, and parishes. The Kenrick diary and journal and the Neumann visitation diary are prominent items in the collection.

SEE: Hinding.

PA726-135

Philadelphia College of Art
Library
330 S. Broad
Philadelphia PA 19102

(215) 893-3126

OPEN: M-F 9-10, Sa 9-4; summer, M-F 9-4; closed Sundays, holidays, and Christmas vacation
COPYING FACILITIES: yes
MATERIALS SOLICITED: Materials relating to the Philadelphia College of Art and its predecessors, the Pennsylvania Museum and School of Industrial Art, the Philadelphia Museum and School of Industrial Art, the Philadelphia Museum School of Art, and the Philadelphia Museum College of Art.

HOLDINGS:
Total volume: 20 l.f.
Inclusive dates: 1876 -
Description: Archives of the Philadelphia College of Art, dating from its founding in 1876 as an integral part of the Pennsylvania Museum and School of Industrial Art, and covering the history of the College, its art education and curriculum, and records of some faculty and students. Included are some photographs documenting art instruction.

GUIDES: A guide to the College archives is available at the institution.

PA726-225

Philadelphia Jewish Archives Center
18 S. 7th Street
Philadelphia PA 19106

(215) 925-8090

OPEN: M-F 8-4; closed weekends, holidays, and Jewish holy days
COPYING FACILITIES: yes

MATERIALS SOLICITED: Materials on the Philadelphia-area Jewish community and individuals, including records of organizations, community agencies, and congregations.

HOLDINGS:
Total volume: 2,000 c.f.
Inclusive dates: 1820's -
Description: Records of Jewish voluntary organizations in the Philadelphia area, such as social welfare agencies, religious organizations, labor unions, and educational and fraternal societies. Also included are correspondence and photographs of individuals, with emphasis on the immigrant experience.

GUIDES: Lindsay B. Nauen, ed., *Guide to Philadelphia Jewish Archives Center* (1977).

SEE ALSO: a newsletter describing parts of the collection available from the Center.

PA726-240
Philadelphia Maritime Museum
Library
321 Chestnut Street
Philadelphia PA 19106

(215) 925-5439

OPEN: M-F 9-5 by appointment only; closed weekends and holidays
ACCESS: by appointment
COPYING FACILITIES: yes
MATERIALS SOLICITED: Materials relating to the maritime history of the port of Philadelphia and the Delaware Bay and River area.

HOLDINGS:
Total volume: 200 vols.; 10,000 leaves; 5,500 photos; 81 microfilm reels
Inclusive dates: 1770 - 1950
Description: A collection of manuscripts and photographs related to the maritime history of Philadelphia and the Delaware River area. Included are correspondence, public documents, journals, logbooks, business records, and personal papers. Special collections include business and personal papers of John Barry and Patrick Hayes, and photographs of vessels constructed by the New York Shipbuilding Company.
Also included are business records of Cramp Shipbuilding Company and papers of the estate of Robert Morris.

SEE: Davis; Allard, Crawley, and Edmison; Hinding.

PA726-255
Philadelphia Museum of Art
Archives
26th Street and the Parkway
Philadelphia PA

MAILING ADDRESS:
P.O. Box 7646
Philadelphia PA 19101

(215) 787-5419, 763-8100

OPEN: Tu, Th 9-5 by appointment only; closed holidays

ACCESS: archival materials may be used only by graduate students or identified scholars or researchers; advance arrangement required
COPYING FACILITIES: yes
MATERIALS SOLICITED: Museum history, and materials related to Museum collections and holdings. Will also accept Marie and Fiske Kimball papers.

HOLDINGS:
Total volume: 450 l.f.
Inclusive dates: 1876 -
Description: Correspondence and records of the Philadelphia Museum of Art from the time of its founding in 1876 as the Pennsylvania Museum and School of Industrial Art, an outgrowth of the Centennial Exhibition. There are materials concerning other affiliated institutions, including the Rodin Museum and the Fleisher Art Memorial, as well as personal files of Fiske Kimball, Philadelphia Museum of Art director from 1925 to 1955.
Also included are the George Grey Barnard papers, the research files of Francis Henry Taylor, and materials related to the Park Houses.

PA726-270
Philadelphia Museum of Art
Department of Prints, Drawings, and Photographs
26th Street and the Parkway
Philadelphia PA

MAILING ADDRESS:
P.O. Box 7646
Philadelphia PA 19101

(215) 787-5402

OPEN: by appointment only
ACCESS: by appointment
COPYING FACILITIES: yes
MATERIALS SOLICITED: Papers relating to artists, especially American. Will also accept photographs, rare documents and ephemera.

HOLDINGS:
Total volume: 3 file drawers
Inclusive dates: 14th century -
Description: Letters and manuscripts to, from, and about artists, 1880- . There is also a small collection of illuminated manuscripts, 14th-19th centuries.

SEE: Hamer; NUCMC, 1966.

PA726-412
The Rosenbach Museum and Library
2010 Delancey Place
Philadelphia PA 19103

(215) 732-1600

OPEN: M-F 9-5; closed weekends, holidays, and month of Aug.
ACCESS: by appointment
COPYING FACILITIES: yes
MATERIALS SOLICITED: Correspondence, diaries, journals, logbooks, and literary manuscripts of English and American authors already represented in the collection, and of selected historical figures. Will also accept manuscripts, maps, and photographs in subject areas already represented in the collection.

HOLDINGS:
Total volume: 130,000 pieces
Inclusive dates: 1200 -
Description: A collection of literary manuscripts and correspondence of major English and American authors, including the Marianne Moore Archive. There are also correspondence, diaries, journals, logbooks, financial records, and manuscript public documents of American historical persons and activities, including 3,000 manuscript documents and letters pertaining to early Mexican and Peruvian history. Also included are materials relating to western exploration and settlement, chiefly in the Oregon Territory.

SEE: Hinding; Robbins.

SEE ALSO: David M. Szewczyk, *A Calendar of the Peruvian and Other South American Manuscripts in the Philip H. & A. S. W. Rosenbach Foundation, 1536-1914* (Rosenbach Foundation, 1977).

PA726-480
Sisters of St. Joseph of Philadelphia
Archives
Mount St. Joseph Convent
Germantown and Northwestern Avenues
Chestnut Hill
Philadelphia PA 19118-2693

(215) 248-7275

OPEN: M-F 8:30-3; closed weekends and holidays
ACCESS: appointment required
COPYING FACILITIES: yes
MATERIALS SOLICITED: Materials concerning the Sisters of St. Joseph of Philadelphia which are now held by its affiliated institutions or by other religious communities. Will also accept materials related to the history of areas served by the Philadelphia congregation and to the activities of its members.

HOLDINGS:
Total volume: 329 c.f.
Inclusive dates: late 1600's -
Description: Records and photographs of the Sisters of St. Joseph of Philadelphia, dating from the congregation's American founding in Philadelphia in 1847, including materials relating to affiliated institutions and membership in the mid-Atlantic region. A small collection of records dating from the 17th century, mostly copies, concerns the congregation in France.

PA726-495
Sisters of the Holy Family of Nazareth
Immaculate Conception Province Archives
Grant and Frankford Avenues
Philadelphia PA 19114

(215) 637-6464

OPEN: by appointment
COPYING FACILITIES: yes
MATERIALS SOLICITED: Materials pertaining to the congregation of the Sisters of the Holy Family of Nazareth, Catholic educational trends, Catholic hospital trends, and family life. Will

also accept papers of the members of the congregation and materials relating to the Catholic church in Philadelphia.

HOLDINGS:
>   *Total volume:* 14 l.f.
>   *Inclusive dates:* 1918 -
>   *Description:* Records and manuscripts relating chiefly to the Immaculate Conception Province of the Sisters of the Holy Family of Nazareth. Included are records of convents; correspondence of Provincial superiors; and documents on members and their apostolic labor. The collection contains information on Catholic schools; convent life in parishes, hospitals, and other institutions; and the religious, educational, cultural, and civic activities of Catholic parishes in the eastern United States, especially New Jersey, Pennsylvania, Maryland, Florida, and Puerto Rico.

SEE: Hinding.

SEE ALSO: the following two works compiled by Mary Jane Menzenska and published by the congregation in 1975: *Guide to Nazareth Literature, 1873-1973* and *Works by and about the Sisters of the Holy Family of Nazareth.*

PA726-508

Sons of Union Veterans of the Civil War
Philadelphia Camp 200
GAR Memorial Hall
Library
4278-80 Griscom Street
Philadelphia PA 19124

no telephone

OPEN: by appointment
COPYING FACILITIES: no
MATERIALS SOLICITED: Original material related to the Grand Army of the Republic and Civil War related material. Will also accept Pennsylvania historical material and genealogical source material that gives information on Union and Confederate personnel after the Civil War.

HOLDINGS:
>   *Total volume:* 100 c.f.
>   *Inclusive dates:* 1861 - 1949
>   *Description:* 75 cubic feet of journals, account books, financial records, and meeting minutes of Grand Army of the Republic (Civil War veterans organization) posts, camps, and State departments, mostly from Pennsylvania, but also from other States; over 5,000 membership applications from GAR posts; a photograph file of 1,000 items depicting Civil War veterans, mostly GAR members; 20 cubic feet of Sons of Union Veterans' records, photographs, and membership applications; Civil War period letters and diaries; and some Pennsylvania and Philadelphia historical records.

PA726-600

Temple University
Libraries
Conwellana-Templana Collection
Samuel Paley Library
13th and Berks Streets
Philadelphia PA 19122

(215) 787-8240

OPEN: M-Sa 9-5; closed Sundays and holidays
COPYING FACILITIES: yes
MATERIALS SOLICITED: History of Temple University and the University area; life, activities, and writings of Russell Herman Conwell and his family; and manuscripts and other creative or scholarly works of Temple University faculty, alumni, administrators, and trustees. Will also accept publications (including periodical articles), photographs, tape and sound recordings, microforms, formal documents (such as diplomas), and memorabilia originating with or related to Temple University and its units, personnel, alumni, and students.

HOLDINGS:
>   *Total volume:* 428 l.f.; 4,600 audible and visual documents
>   *Inclusive dates:* 1862 -
>   *Description:* Archives of Temple University and the personal papers of its personnel. Included are writings, correspondence, and memorabilia of the founder of the University, Russell Herman Conwell, covering his Civil War service and his career as a Baptist minister, educator, and Chautauqua lecturer; records of the University Theater, 1930-69; and papers of faculty and alumni, including criminologist Negley Teeters, sociologist Herbert A. Miller, surgeon W. Wayne Babcock, and California writer Miriam Allen DeFord.
>   Also included are papers of poet and artist Frank Ankenbrand, linguist Henry Dexter Learned, journalist Frank Brookhouser, physicist Melville S. Green, playwright and novelist Richard E. Peck, French language scholar Raymond J. Cormier, and popular novelist Mary Wallace (including extensive correspondence with her literary agent, Muriel Fuller); the postcard correspondence of surgeon Chevalier Jackson; and the Barrows Dunham-Fred Zimring collection of oral history on academic freedom in higher education, particularly in the 1950's.

SEE: Hamer; NUCMC, 1961, 74.

SEE: Meckler and McMullin; Robbins.

PA726-615

Temple University
Libraries
Rare Book and Manuscript Collection
Paley Library
Philadelphia PA 19122

(215) 787-8230

OPEN: M-F 9-5; closed weekends and holidays
COPYING FACILITIES: yes
MATERIALS SOLICITED: Materials relating to English and American literature; the alternative press; science fiction; print-

ing, publishing, and bookselling; and business history. Will also accept other materials.

HOLDINGS:
>   *Total volume:* 350 l.f.
>   *Inclusive dates:* 1450 -
>   *Description:* Manuscript collections relating to Walter de la Mare, Richard Aldington, French poet Charles Morice, Constable & Company, Carlton E. Morse and the history of radio and television, Ben Bova and science fiction, the William Campbell and Leary & Company bookstores, and business history, especially medieval Italian business records.

SEE: Hamer; NUCMC, 1959-62, 69-71, 74, 76.

SEE: Davis.

PA726-630

Temple University
Libraries
Urban Archives Center
Paley Library
Philadelphia PA 19122

(215) 787-8257

OPEN: M-F 9-5; closed weekends and holidays
COPYING FACILITIES: yes
MATERIALS SOLICITED: Materials relating to the Philadelphia metropolitan area after 1850, including such topics as social services, education, labor, urban planning, neighborhood activities, housing, politics, criminal justice, and economic development.

HOLDINGS:
>   *Total volume:* 2,500 c.f.
>   *Inclusive dates:* 1835 -
>   *Description:* Records of 60 private agencies and organizations and 12 individuals involved in the development of the Philadelphia metropolitan area since 1850. Major subject concentrations are social services, housing, planning, politics, education, criminal justice, and labor. Most of the holdings are large organization collections including minutes, reports, correspondence, financial records, program files, and general office files. Depositors include social service agencies, reform organizations, labor unions, settlements, and pressure groups. The Archives also has photograph and audio tape collections relating to the social history of the Philadelphia area.

SEE: NUCMC, 1969-72, 76.

SEE: Hinding.

SEE ALSO: Walter Schatz, ed., *Directory of Afro-American Resources* (Bowker, 1970); and the following publications of the Center: *Private Social Services in Philadelphia: A Survey of the Records* (1973); Barbara Howe, Fredric Miller, and Peter Silverman, comps., *Guide to Philadelphia Social Service Collections at the Urban Archives Center* (1976); and Sheryl Dams Pendzich, Fredric Miller, and Peter Silverman, comps., *Housing Association of Delaware Valley: A Guide to the Collection* (1976). The Center's newsletter, *Urban Archives Notes,* contains lists of new accessions in its fall issue.

PA726-690
Thomas Jefferson University
Scott Memorial Library
1020 Walnut Street
Philadelphia PA 19107

(215) 928-7769

OPEN: M-F 9-5; closed weekends and holidays
ACCESS: prior approval required
COPYING FACILITIES: yes
MATERIALS SOLICITED: Records of Thomas Jefferson University.

HOLDINGS:
Total volume: 31 vols.; other items
Inclusive dates: 1824 -
Description: Minutes of the Jefferson Medical College board of trustees; hospital minutes; and the University president's papers and memorabilia, 1969- .

PA726-705
Union League of Philadelphia
140 South Broad Street
Philadelphia PA 19102

no telephone

SEE: Hamer.

Questionnaire not returned.

PA726-713
Presbyterian Church (U.S.A.)
Presbyterian Historical Society
425 Lombard Street
Philadelphia PA 19147

(215) 627-1852

OPEN: M-F 9-5; closed weekends and holidays
COPYING FACILITIES: yes
MATERIALS SOLICITED: Materials related to the Presbyterian church in America and organizations in which Presbyterians played a key role, such as the American Sunday School Union and the National Council of Churches.

HOLDINGS:
Total volume: 13,800 vols.; 40,732 l.f.
Inclusive dates: 1743 -
Description: Archives of the United Presbyterian Church in the United States of America and its predecessor bodies, including minutes, correspondence, and judicial records. Special collections focus on Sheldon Jackson, John D. Shane, domestic and foreign missions, the American Sunday School Union, the National Council of Churches, Eugene C. Blake, Lewis S. Mudge, expansion of the church, and Christian education in the 19th and 20th centuries.

SEE: Hamer; NUCMC, 1961, 66, 69-75, 81.

SEE ALSO: Lisabeth M. Holloway, comp., *Philadelphia Resources in the History of the Health Sciences* (n.p., 1975); Peter Duignan, *Handbook of American Resources for African Studies* (Hoover Institution, 1967); Walter Schatz, ed., *Directory of Afro-American Resources* (Bowker, 1970); Gerald W. Gillette, 'Piety, Papers and Print: The Presbyterian Historical Society,' *Drexel Library Quarterly* 6 (Jan. 1970); Robert O. Collins and Peter Duignan, *Americans in Africa* (Hoover Institution, 1963); Alan M. Meckler and Ruth McMullin, comps., *Oral History Collections* (Bowker, 1975).

PA726-725
University of Pennsylvania
Archives
North Arcade
Franklin Field E6
Philadelphia PA 19104

(215) 898-7024, 7025

OPEN: M-F 9-5; closed weekends, holidays, and Christmas vacation
COPYING FACILITIES: yes
MATERIALS SOLICITED: Material relating to the University of Pennsylvania. Will also accept some other materials relating to Philadelphia and Pennsylvania.

HOLDINGS:
Total volume: 9,000 c.f.
Inclusive dates: 1740 -
Description: Archives of the University of Pennsylvania, including records of administrative, academic, and social divisions of the University, visual documents, and manuscripts relating to alumni, faculty, and trustees. Included are documents relating to the founding of the University, journals, trustees' records, matriculation and tuition registers, diplomas, archives of the Medical School, letters and manuscripts of signers of the Declaration of Independence, 18th century manuscript maps, 19th and 20th century architectural plans and drawings and photographs of University buildings and scenes, groups, and individuals, and University-related motion pictures. Genealogical source data can be found in some 85,000 individual biographical folders which, in some instances, also contain minor manuscript material relating to literary figures.

GUIDES: Francis James Dallett, *Guide to the Archives of the University of Pennsylvania from 1740 to 1820* (1978).

SEE: Hamer.

SEE ALSO: Lisabeth M. Holloway, comp., *Philadelphia Resources in the History of the Health Sciences* (n.p., 1975).

PA726-750
University of Pennsylvania
Law School
Biddle Law Library
3400 Chestnut Street
Philadelphia PA 19104-6279

(215) 898-7478

OPEN: M-F 8:30-midnight, Sa 9-9, Su 12-12; closed holidays
COPYING FACILITIES: yes

HOLDINGS:
Total volume: 46 vols.; 305 items
Inclusive dates: 1377 - 1860
Description: English and American deeds, indentures, and other legal documents, Law School lecture notes, and miscellaneous legal manuscripts.

SEE: Hamer.

PA726-765
University of Pennsylvania
Van Pelt Library
Edgar Fahs Smith Collection in the History of Chemistry
3420 Walnut Street
Philadelphia PA 19104

(215) 898-7088

OPEN: M-F 1-5; closed weekends and holidays
ACCESS: advance arrangements preferred
COPYING FACILITIES: yes
MATERIALS SOLICITED: History of chemistry and pharmacy, especially post-1800, including both institutional and individual records. Will also accept material in disciplines related to chemistry and pharmacy, such as spectroscopy, atomic physics, medical chemistry, and biochemistry.

HOLDINGS:
Total volume: 74 vols.; 25 l.f.
Inclusive dates: early 15th century -
Description: Letters, lecture notes, and early chemical and alchemical tracts pertaining to various aspects of the history of chemistry and allied disciplines in western Europe and North America since the Renaissance. Also, a collection of 200-300 letters pertaining to Revolutionary War era Philadelphia and Pennsylvania, and the early history of the University of Pennsylvania, and archives of the Division of Chemical Education, American Chemical Society.

SEE: Hamer (under University of Pennsylvania Library).

SEE ALSO: Norman P. Zacour and Rudolf Hirsch, comps., *Catalogue of Manuscripts in the Libraries of the University of Pennsylvania to 1800* (Univ. of Pennsylvania Press, 1965); Rudolf Hirsch, 'Catalogue of Manuscripts in the Libraries of the University of Pennsylvania to 1800: Supplement A(5),' *Library Chronicle* 37 (1971); Lisabeth M. Holloway, comp., *Philadelphia Resources in the History of the Health Sciences* (n.p., 1975); Irwin Richman, comp., *Historical Manuscript Depositories in Pennsylvania* (Pennsylvania Historical and Museum Commission, 1965).

PA726-770
University of Pennsylvania
Van Pelt Library
Henry Charles Lea Library of Medieval History
3420 Walnut Street
Philadelphia PA 19104

(215) 898-7088

OPEN: M-F 1-5; closed weekends and holidays
COPYING FACILITIES: yes
MATERIALS SOLICITED: Medieval and Renaissance history.

HOLDINGS:
Total volume: 600 vols.; 75 l.f.
Inclusive dates: 1000 - 1900
Description: Text manuscripts, 1000 - 1800, and notes and personal papers of H. C. Lea.

SEE: Hamer (as University of Pennsylvania Library); NUCMC, 1968, 70, 73.

PA726-775

University of Pennsylvania
Van Pelt Library
Special Collections
3420 Walnut Street
Philadelphia PA 19104

(215) 898-7088

OPEN: M-F 9-5; closed weekends and holidays
ACCESS: serious researchers; identification and interview required
COPYING FACILITIES: yes
MATERIALS SOLICITED: Literary papers and other materials in the humanities. Will also accept any materials pertinent to areas of research at the University, subject to space and staff available.

HOLDINGS:
> *Total volume:* 19,000 l.f.
> *Inclusive dates:* 1450 -
> *Description:* Manuscripts, correspondence, and other documents of 20th century literary figures; other collections of miscellaneous items, literary and historical, 18th-20th centuries; and text manuscripts, pre-1450-1800.
> Also included are 800 microfilms of medieval manuscripts in European libraries.

SEE: Hamer; NUCMC, 1960, 62, 68, 70, 73.

SEE ALSO: Norman P. Zacour and Rudolf Hirsch, comps., *Catalogue of Manuscripts in the Libraries of the University of Pennsylvania to 1800* (Univ. of Pennsylvania Press, 1965); Walter Schatz, ed., *Directory of Afro-American Resources* (Bowker, 1970); articles in the *Library Chronicle*, publication of the Friends of the University of Pennsylvania Library.

PA726-795

University of Pennsylvania
Museum
33rd and Spruce Streets
Philadelphia PA 19174

no telephone

SEE: Hamer.

Questionnaire not returned.

PA726-810

University of Pennsylvania
School of Dental Medicine
Library
4001 Spruce Street A1
Philadelphia PA 19104

(215) 898-8978

OPEN: Su-F 9-9:45, Sa 9-3:45; closed holidays, Christmas, and summer weekends; archive section closed winter weekends
ACCESS: by appointment for initial visit
COPYING FACILITIES: yes
MATERIALS SOLICITED: Materials dealing with dentistry and oral biology, including correspondence, record books, fee bills, pictures, photographs, and espe-

cially letters and papers of Dr. Thomas W. Evans.

HOLDINGS:
> *Total volume:* 250 l.f.
> *Inclusive dates:* 1800 - 1950
> *Description:* Manuscripts, letters, and photographs of Dr. Thomas W. Evans; papers, records, and letters of alumni of the Dental School; a collection of U.S. dental patents, 1797-1966; foreign dental patents; the S. S. White collection of dentistry-related materials; records of the Pennsylvania College of Dental Surgery, 1856-1909; and visual documents on dentistry and its history.

SEE ALSO: Lisabeth M. Holloway, comp., *Philadelphia Resources in the History of the Health Sciences* (n.p., 1975).

PA726-855

Wagner Free Institute of Science
Montgomery Avenue and 17th Street
Philadelphia PA 19121

(215) 763-6529

OPEN: M-F 10-5; closed weekends and holidays
ACCESS: advance request by letter giving purpose of research required
COPYING FACILITIES: no
MATERIALS SOLICITED: Archives of the Institute.

HOLDINGS:
> *Total volume:* 42 c.f.
> *Inclusive dates:* 1814 -
> *Description:* A collection of letters and business records of William Wagner, founder of the Wagner Institute, concerning the lumber trade between North Carolina and Philadelphia, 1814-40, and the coal trade between Pottsville, PA, and Philadelphia and the sawed-lumber business between Columbia, PA, and Philadelphia, 1840-55; and the archives of the Wagner Institute, a free science educational institution, 1855- .

SEE: Hamer; NUCMC, 1966.

SEE: Davis.

PA726-870

Westminster Theological Seminary
Library
Chestnut Hill
Philadelphia PA 19118

no telephone

SEE: Hamer.

Questionnaire not returned.

PA726-895

Willet Stained Glass Studios
10 East Moreland Avenue
Philadelphia PA 19118

(215) 247-5721

OPEN: M-F 8-4:30, Sa 9-11:30; closed Sundays, Christmas Eve, Christmas, New Year's, last week in July, and first week in Aug.
ACCESS: by appointment only
COPYING FACILITIES: yes
MATERIALS SOLICITED: Records of the Willet Stained Glass Studios.

HOLDINGS:
> *Total volume:* 116 file drawers; 35,000 items
> *Inclusive dates:* 1885 -
> *Description:* Slides, photographs, drawings, and descriptions of stained glass, especially windows and their installation, as well as of church architecture; and correspondence relating to the Willet stained glass business and the Willet family.

SEE: Novotny.

PHOENIXVILLE

PA730-640

Phoenixville Public Library
Main Street and Second Avenue
Phoenixville PA 19460

SEE: Hamer.

Questionnaire not returned.

PITTSBURGH

PA735-110

Carnegie Library of Pittsburgh
Pennsylvania Division
4400 Forbes Avenue
Pittsburgh PA 15213

(412) 622-3154

OPEN: M, Tu, F, Sa 9-9, W, Th 9-5:30, Su 2-5; closed holidays; shorter summer hours
ACCESS: identification and prior notice required for use of original manuscripts
COPYING FACILITIES: yes
MATERIALS SOLICITED: Will accept materials in Pennsylvania history at the discretion of the Library Director.

HOLDINGS:
> *Total volume:* 25,000 items
> *Inclusive dates:* 1768 -
> *Description:* Materials relating chiefly to Pittsburgh and western Pennsylvania, with special focus on the period 1791-1906, when Pittsburgh was a military supply base, and including papers relating to the Whiskey Rebellion.

SEE: Hamer; NUCMC, 1959-61, 72.

SEE: Novotny; Allard, Crawley, and Edmison; Hines; Robbins.

Many manuscripts have been microfilmed and may be examined whenever the Library is open.

PA735-140

Carnegie-Mellon University
Hunt Institute for Botanical Documentation
Hunt Library
Pittsburgh PA 15213

(412) 578-2437, 2434

OPEN: M-F 9-5; closed weekends and holidays
COPYING FACILITIES: yes
MATERIALS SOLICITED: Papers and records of botanical societies; papers of botanists and other researchers in the

plant sciences and of botanical artists and illustrators; portraits of the latter individuals. Will also accept taped interviews with botanists and botanical artists.

HOLDINGS:
> *Total volume:* 200 l.f.
> *Inclusive dates:* 1706 -
> *Description:* Approximately 200 collections including correspondence, scientific manuscripts, notes, reports, and journals of botanists, botanical artists, and horticulturists from various nations, particularly the United States, as well as records of botanical societies. Included are papers and library of Michel Adanson, and the papers of Francis Boott, Chretien Lamoignon de Malesherbes, Franz Carl Mertens, Frederick Wilson Popenoe, Pierre Joseph Redoute, and Joseph Rock, among others.

> Also included are over 50 oral history interviews and transcriptions with persons in the plant sciences, an autograph collection of over 2,000 letters written by several hundred botanists, and over 21,000 photographs or other likenesses of persons in the plant sciences. A recent acquisition is that of selected correspondence and papers of Kate Greenaway.

SEE: NUCMC, 1972, 74.

SEE ALSO: Richard C. Davis, *North American Forest History: A Guide to Archives and Manuscripts in the United States and Canada* (Clio Books, 1977); guides to the papers of Michel Adanson and Pierre-Joseph Redoute, published by the Institute.

PA735-150
Carnegie-Mellon University
Hunt Library
Fine and Rare Book Rooms
Schenley Park
Pittsburgh PA 15213

(412) 578-6622

OPEN: M-F 1:30-4:30 and by appointment; closed weekends and holidays
COPYING FACILITIES: yes
MATERIALS SOLICITED: Materials relating to English and American literature and American history. Will also accept materials in science and music.

HOLDINGS:
> *Total volume:* 100 l.f.
> *Inclusive dates:* 1684 -
> *Description:* Included are letters of the writer on Pittsburgh and the American Southwest Haniel Long, 1917-56; papers of the novelist and poet Gladys Schmitt, 1925-72; and ledgers of ironmaster Isaac Meason's Mount Vernon Furnace Company in Fayette County, PA, 1797-1825.

> Also included are papers of poet Sara Henderson Hay, 1939-1966; papers of playwright and short story writer Rosemary Casey, 1925-1967; and architectural drawings of American architect Peter Berndtson from 1942 to 1972.

SEE: NUCMC, 1971, 79.

SEE: Robbins.

PA735-160
Catholic Diocese of Pittsburgh
Diocesan Historical Archives
125 North Craig Street
Pittsburgh PA 15213

(412) 621-6217

OPEN: M-F by appointment; closed weekends and holidays
ACCESS: at the discretion of the Archivist
COPYING FACILITIES: yes
MATERIALS SOLICITED: Materials relating to the history of Roman Catholic parishes in Pittsburgh, as well as the Catholic church in western Pennsylvania.

HOLDINGS:
> *Total volume:* 18 c.f.
> *Inclusive dates:* 1750 - 1921
> *Description:* A collection of manuscripts, documents, and letters relating chiefly to the history of Roman Catholicism in western Pennsylvania and more specifically to the Catholic Diocese of Pittsburgh, established in 1843.

PA735-170
Central Council of Polish
  Organizations of Pittsburgh
Polish Historical Commission
4291 Stanton Avenue
Pittsburgh PA 15201

(412) 355-0710

The manuscript collections of the Polish Historical Commission are held at present by the Archives of Industrial Society, Hillman Library, University of Pittsburgh, Pittsburgh, PA 15260 (**PA735-790**).

PA735-200
Duquesne University
Library
Locust and Colbert Streets
Pittsburgh PA 15219

(412) 434-6130

SEE: Hamer.

Questionnaire not returned.

PA735-320
Historical Society of Western
  Pennsylvania
4338 Bigelow Boulevard
Pittsburgh PA 15213

(412) 681-5533

SEE: Hamer; NUCMC, 1970-71.

Questionnaire not returned.

PA735-515
Mercy Hospital of Pittsburgh
Archives
1400 Locust Street
Pittsburgh PA 15219

(412) 232-7653

OPEN: M-F 9-4 by appointment only; closed weekends and holidays
ACCESS: advance arrangements required
MATERIALS SOLICITED: Will accept papers, photographs, and correspondence from the Doctors, School of Nursing, and hospital personnel who have made contributions to their respective fields.

HOLDINGS:
> *Total volume:* 130 l.f.
> *Inclusive dates:* 1847 -
> *Description:* Records of the hospital, including correspondence, minutes of meetings of the medical board, board of trustees, and other groups, 1871- ; hospital registers, 1847-90; annual reports, 1848- ; department histories; hospital publications, architects' drawings and floor plans, and photographs of the hospital and staff, 1847- ; videotapes of special hospital events; and taped interviews of administrators and medical staff.

PA735-630
Pittsburgh Theological Seminary
Clifford E. Barbour Library
616 North Highland Avenue
Pittsburgh PA 15206

(412) 362-5610

OPEN: M-F 9-4:30; closed weekends and holidays
COPYING FACILITIES: yes
MATERIALS SOLICITED: Minutes and correspondence of boards of directors and trustees of Pittsburgh Theological Seminary and its antecedent seminaries, minutes of faculty and faculty committee meetings, and manuscripts of leading clergy in the early history of the Presbyterian-Reformed tradition. Will also accept historical items concerning the antecedent denominations of the United Presbyterian Church (USA), 1793-1958, and tapes of lectures and convocations held at Pittsburgh Theological Seminary.

HOLDINGS:
> *Total volume:* 158 l.f.
> *Inclusive dates:* 1751 -
> *Description:* Lectures by professors at the antecedent seminaries of Pittsburgh Theological Seminary, class notes, and sermons. Emphasis is on the western Pennsylvania area and Pittsburgh in particular.

SEE: Hamer; NUCMC, 1959-61.

PA735-720
Sisters of St. Francis of Millvale
146 Hawthorne Road
Pittsburgh PA 15209

(412) 821-2200

OPEN: daily by appointment; closed holidays
COPYING FACILITIES: yes

MATERIALS SOLICITED: Material on schools and hospitals staffed by the Sisters of St. Francis of Millvale, and material pertaining to St. John Nepomucene Neumann, Bishop of Philadelphia.

HOLDINGS:
Total volume: 105 boxes; 40 volumes of the houses of the community
Inclusive dates: 1855 -
Description: Annals of the community of the Sisters of St. Francis; 9 drawers of photograph albums relating to the work of the Sisters; some fiscal records; 26 tapes of oral history of the community; records of chapter activity; theses written by Sisters of St. Francis; a showcase and drawer of articles pertaining to the missions; a drawer of diplomas; 1 box of engravings; 15 drawers of blueprints; 4 file drawers of community papers.

SEE: Hinding.

PA735-730
Soldiers & Sailors Memorial Hall
County of Allegheny
Fifth and Bigelow
Pittsburgh PA 15213

(412) 621-4253

OPEN: Su 1-4, M-Sa 9-4; closed New Year's, Thanksgiving, and Christmas
ACCESS: advance arrangements required
COPYING FACILITIES: yes
MATERIALS SOLICITED: Materials relating to all wars.

HOLDINGS:
Total volume: 27 items
Inclusive dates: 1865 - 1935
Description: Records of the Allegheny County Grand Army of the Republic (GAR) post including minute books and correspondence.

PA735-760
University of Pittsburgh
Stephen Foster Memorial
Pittsburgh PA 15260

(412) 624-4100

SEE: Hamer.

Questionnaire not returned.

PA735-780
University of Pittsburgh
University Libraries
University Archives
Pittsburgh PA 15260

(412) 624-4430

OPEN: M-F 8:30-5; closed weekends and holidays
COPYING FACILITIES: yes
MATERIALS SOLICITED: Records and publications of the University of Pittsburgh and its forerunners.

HOLDINGS:
Total volume: 4882 l.f.
Inclusive dates: 1787 -
Description: The University of Pittsburgh Archives contains only records pertaining to the institution, including correspondence and campus memos, minutes of meetings of official bodies and

committees, reports and policy and procedure documents, financial records, speeches, news clippings, scrapbooks, subject and personnel files, audiovisual items, University faculty and student publications, building plans, class instructional material, research project studies, student records, and University history.

SEE: Hinding.

SEE ALSO: Robert E. Wilson and Frank Zabrosky, *Resources on the Ethnic and the Immigrant in the Pittsburgh Area* (Pittsburgh PA, 1979).

PA735-790
University of Pittsburgh
Libraries
Archives of Industrial Society
Hillman Library
Pittsburgh PA 15260

(412) 624-4430

OPEN: M-F 8:30-5; closed weekends and holidays
COPYING FACILITIES: yes
MATERIALS SOLICITED: Records and manuscripts reflecting the growth and development of urban-industrial society as represented by Pittsburgh and western Pennsylvania. Will also accept maps, photographs, and oral history.

HOLDINGS:
Total volume: 5,333 l.f.; 11,082 vols.
Inclusive dates: 1772 -
Description: Approximately 211 collections concentrating on the post-Civil War period, primarily in Pittsburgh and western Pennsylvania. Included are the personal papers of political figures, labor union representatives, businesspersons, political and social activists, and the records of companies, institutions, organizations, societies, labor unions, schools, and churches, as well as various government records of the cities of Allegheny and Pittsburgh and Allegheny County, such as tax records, inactive voters' registration cards, voting return books, building permits, and birth, death, and marriage records.

Also included are the materials which were previously held by the Central Council of Polish Organizations of Pittsburgh, Polish Historical Commission (entry PA 735 - 170 in first edition of *Directory*).

SEE: NUCMC, 1965, 69-72, 74, 77, 80.

SEE: Parkinson; Allard, Crawley, and Edmison; Hinding.

SEE ALSO: Walter Schatz, ed., *Directory of Afro-American Resources* (Bowker, 1970); David A. Hounshell, comp., *Manuscripts in U.S. Depositories Relating to the History of Electrical Science and Technology* (Smithsonian Institution, n.d.); Albert Krichmar, *The Women's Rights Movement in the United States, 1848-1970: A Bibliography and Sourcebook* (Scarecrow Press, 1972); *Source Materials for the Recent History of Astronomy and Astrophysics: A Checklist of Manuscript Collections in the United States* (American Institute of Physics, 1971); Robert Wilson and Frank A. Zabrosky, *Resources on the*

Ethnic and the Immigrant in the Pittsburgh Area: A Preliminary Guide (Pittsburgh Council on Higher Education, 1976); Frank A. Zabrosky, 'The Archives of Industrial Society at the University of Pittsburgh,' *Records Management Quarterly* 3 (April 1969).

The Archives of Industrial Society has acquired the 2,000 reels of news film listed under the holdings of Point Park College, **PA735-640**, in the 1978 edition of the *Directory*.

PA735-800
University of Pittsburgh
Libraries
Darlington Memorial Library
601 Cathedral of Learning
Fifth Avenue and Bigelow Boulevard
Pittsburgh PA 15260

(412) 624-4491, 4428

OPEN: M-F 1-5; closed weekends and holidays; schedule subject to change
COPYING FACILITIES: yes

HOLDINGS:
Total volume: 40 vols.; 31 l.f.
Inclusive dates: 1680 - 1900
Description: Manuscripts focusing on the Revolutionary War. Also included are papers concerning H. H. Brackenridge, H. M. Brackenridge, Robert McKnight, Charles Nisbet, Joseph Leger d'Happart, and the Pitt family, including William Pitt the elder and William Pitt the younger.

SEE: Hamer; NUCMC (as University of Pittsburgh Libraries), 1959-64, 68-70.

SEE ALSO: Irwin Richman, comp., *Historical Manuscript Depositories in Pennsylvania* (Pennsylvania Historical and Museum Commission, 1965); Walter Schatz, ed., *Directory of Afro-American Resources* (Bowker, 1970); Ruth Salisbury, 'Survey of the Darlington Library,' *Western Pennsylvania Historical Magazine* 48 (Jan. 1964).

PA735-825
University of Pittsburgh
Nationality Rooms & Intercultural Exchange Programs
Nationality Room Archives
Pittsburgh PA 15260

(412) 624-6150

OPEN: M-F 9-5; closed weekends and University holidays
ACCESS: advance arrangements required
COPYING FACILITIES: yes
MATERIALS SOLICITED: Manuscripts, archival materials, and audio and visual materials documenting the nationalities represented in the collections. Will also accept materials concerning Africans, Americans, Austrians, Israelis, and Ukrainians.

HOLDINGS:
Total volume: 150 l.f.
Inclusive dates: 1925 -
Description: The collections concern the 18 Nationality Classrooms at the University of Pittsburgh. Eighteen ethnic groups: Chinese, Czechoslovak, English,

French, German, Greek, Hungarian, Irish, Italian, Lithuanian, Norwegian, Polish, Romanian, Russian, Scottish, Swedish, Syria-Lebanese, Yugoslav, plus Early American cultures are represented by period or folk classrooms designed by architects from abroad and executed in authentic materials. The periods of the Rooms range from 5th century Athens to Victorian England.

Archives are bound in volumes containing architectural drawings, correspondence, photographs, publicity, and documents. The archives and files document the process of each ethnic committee (in Pittsburgh and abroad) evolving a classroom design that represents a highly creative period of their culture. The history of each room dramatically reflects the pride and devotion of each group as they raised funds during the Depression; the impact of World War II on many room plans; and the essence of each heritage as portrayed in the rooms' concepts.

POTTSVILLE

PA740-320

The Historical Society of Schuylkill County
14 North Third Street
Pottsville PA 17901

(717) 622-7540

OPEN: Tu-Sa 10-4; closed Sundays, Mondays, and holidays
USER FEES: $2 per day for non-members to use research materials
COPYING FACILITIES: yes
MATERIALS SOLICITED: Photographs of the local area; maps of local mining, railroad and canal development; diaries and histories of the area; and genealogical information on families of the area.

HOLDINGS:
Total volume: 70 c.f.
Inclusive dates: 1807 - 1860
Description: Papers of Christopher Loeser, 1815-60, relating to land transactions, legal practice, railroads, and canals; papers of Edwin Owen Parry, a Schuylkill County judge; papers of George C. Wynkoop, a Civil War general; papers of Daniel Yost, relating to legal matters, land, lumbering, mining, labor, and the Civil War. Also, 50 manuscript maps of coal lands and mining, railroads, and canals; photographs of area street scenes, celebrations, buildings, canals, and railroads.

SEE: Hamer.
SEE: Davis.

READING

PA755-40

Albright College
Library
13th and Exeter Streets
Reading PA 19604

(215) 921-2381, Ext. 470

OPEN: Sept. - May, M-F 8-midnight, Sa 9-5, Su 2-10; June - Aug., M-F 8-5; closed holidays
COPYING FACILITIES: yes
MATERIALS SOLICITED: Materials relating to Albright College and its predecessors.

HOLDINGS:
Total volume: 50 vols.
Inclusive dates: 1854 -
Description: Minutes of the board of trustees and the literary society of Albright College.

PA755-320

Historical Society of Berks County
940 Centre Avenue
Reading PA 19601

(215) 375-4375

OPEN: Tu-Sa 9-2; closed Sundays, Mondays, and holidays
USER FEES: $2 for non-members
COPYING FACILITIES: yes
MATERIALS SOLICITED: Materials relating to Berks County and local families.

HOLDINGS:
Total volume: not specified
Inclusive dates: not specified
Description: Materials of local interest, including family, church, and government records.

SEE: Hamer.

SEE: Davis; Novotny.

SCRANTON

PA795-120

Congregation of the Sisters, Servants of the Immaculate Heart of Mary
Generalate of Immaculate Heart of Mary
2300 Adams Avenue
Marywood
Scranton PA 18509

(717) 342-2866

OPEN: by appointment only
ACCESS: arrangements to be made with the Secretary General
COPYING FACILITIES: yes
MATERIALS SOLICITED: Annals of the Order's mission houses.

HOLDINGS:
Total volume: 152 vols.
Inclusive dates: 1845 -
Description: Correspondence and journals relating to the foundation and early history of the Sisters, Servants of the Immaculate Heart of Mary.

SEE: Hinding.

PA795-480

Lackawanna Historical Society
The Catlin House
232 Monroe Avenue
Scranton PA 18510

(717) 344-3841

OPEN: M-F 10-5; closed weekends and holidays
USER FEES: One dollar per day research fee
COPYING FACILITIES: yes
MATERIALS SOLICITED: Materials relating to the city of Scranton, Lackawanna County, and northeastern Pennsylvania.

HOLDINGS:
Total volume: not specified
Inclusive dates: 1800 -
Description: Photographs, maps, manuscripts, and documents relating to the history of Scranton and Lackawanna County.

SEE: Hamer.

PA795-710

Scranton Public Library
Vine Street and Washington Avenue
Scranton PA 18503

SEE: Hamer.

Questionnaire not returned.

PA795-800

University of Scranton
Alumni Memorial Library
Special Collections
Scranton PA 18510

(717) 961-7525

OPEN: M-F 8:30-4:30; closed weekends and holidays
COPYING FACILITIES: yes
MATERIALS SOLICITED: Materials relating to the history of the University of Scranton.

HOLDINGS:
Total volume: 50 l.f.
Inclusive dates: 1250 -
Description: Records, including photographs, of the University of Scranton and its faculty; manuscripts of Medieval and Renaissance missals, antiphonals, and breviaries; and manuscripts and correspondence of the Roosevelt family, including several letters by Franklin Delano Roosevelt.

SELINSGROVE

PA800-720

Susquehanna University
Roger M. Blough Learning Center
Selinsgrove PA 17870

(717) 374-010, Ext. 320

OPEN: M-F 9-10, Sa 10-4, Su 1-10; closed holidays, and weekends and evenings during summer vacation
COPYING FACILITIES: yes
MATERIALS SOLICITED: University-related manuscripts and non-current records of the University. Will also ac-

cept audible documents of research or archival value.

HOLDINGS:
Total volume: several thousand items
Inclusive dates: 1858 -
Description: A collection of president's reports, board minutes, and letters related to the founding of the University. Also included are copies of personal papers of Vidkun Quisling.

SHIPPENSBURG

PA810-700
Shippensburg Historical Society
73 West King Street
Shippensburg PA 17257

no telephone

OPEN: M-F 10-9, Sa 9-noon; closed Sundays and holidays
COPYING FACILITIES: yes
MATERIALS SOLICITED: Items pertaining to the history of the Shippensburg area, and genealogical material. Will also accept scrapbooks and old deeds.

HOLDINGS:
Total volume: 30 l.f.
Inclusive dates: 1800 -
Description: A photograph collection of the Shippensburg area, records of local organizations and local industries, and personal papers, some dating from 1800.

SLIPPERY ROCK

PA815-710
Slippery Rock State College
Library
College Archives
Slippery Rock PA 16057

(412) 794-7242

OPEN: M-F 9-4; closed weekends, holidays, and College vacations; shorter summer hours
ACCESS: by appointment
COPYING FACILITIES: yes
MATERIALS SOLICITED: Materials concerning the College, the surrounding Butler County area, and western Pennsylvania. Will also accept materials relating to the State college system in Pennsylvania.

HOLDINGS:
Total volume: 90 l.f.; 28 c.f.
Inclusive dates: 1889 -
Description: Materials relating to Slippery Rock State College since its founding in 1889, including unpublished masters theses, minutes of the board of trustees and of various faculty organizations, photographs, and student papers. There is also a small collection of letters and memorabilia, 1862-1913, relating to the locally prominent Kiester family.
Also included are materials relating to Emma Guffey Miller (1875-1970), active in Democratic Party affairs, and to the Arthur P. Vincent family.

SMETHPORT

PA820-520
McKean County Historical Society
McKean County Courthouse
Smethport PA 16749

(814) 887-5142

OPEN: Tu, Th 1-4; closed holidays and election days
COPYING FACILITIES: yes
MATERIALS SOLICITED: Will accept photographs of early McKean County, correspondence relating to settlement in the County and surrounding counties, biographies of early settlers, and related documents.

HOLDINGS:
Total volume: not specified
Inclusive dates: 1743 -
Description: Historical documents relating chiefly to McKean County. Included are early correspondence of land agents; deeds; journals; several dozen letters from famous persons, such as Benjamin Franklin, mid-18th to late-19th century; photographs; and other materials.

SOMERSET

PA825-720
Pennsylvania Historical and Museum Commission
Somerset Historical Center
Somerset PA

MAILING ADDRESS:
R.D. 2, P.O. Box 238
Somerset PA 15501

(814) 445-6077

SEE: NUCMC, 1976.

Questionnaire not returned.

STATE COLLEGE

PA837-720
Schlow Memorial Library
100 East Beaver Avenue
State College PA 16801

no telephone

SEE: NUCMC, 1980.

Questionnaire not returned.

STRASBURG

PA840-690
Railroad Museum of Pennsylvania
Strasburg PA

MAILING ADDRESS:
Route 741, P.O. Box 15
Strasburg PA 17579

(717) 687-8628

SEE: NUCMC, 1976.

Questionnaire not returned.

STROUDSBURG

PA850-520
Monroe County Historical Society
Library
Stroud Community House
900 Main Street
Stroudsburg PA

MAILING ADDRESS:
P.O. Box 488
Stroudsburg PA 18360

(717) 421-7703

OPEN: Tu, Th, and 1st and 3rd Su 1-4 or by appointment; closed holidays
COPYING FACILITIES: yes

HOLDINGS:
Total volume: not specified
Inclusive dates: 1743 -
Description: Manuscript materials relating primarily to families and businesses in Monroe County, especially in the 19th century. Included are typed family genealogies; church and cemetery records; docket books and ledgers; township tax lists; deeds; wills; and correspondence. There is also a collection of local history research papers.

SEE: Hamer.

SEE ALSO: Irwin Richman, comp., *Historical Manuscript Depositories in Pennsylvania* (Pennsylvania Historical and Museum Commission, 1965). A guide to the collection is available at the Library.

SUNBURY

PA855-560
Northumberland County Historical Society
Public Library
228 Arch Street
Sunbury PA 17801

no telephone

SEE: Hamer.

Questionnaire not returned.

SWARTHMORE

PA860-710
Swarthmore College
Friends Historical Library
Swarthmore PA 19081

(215) 447-7557

OPEN: M-F 8:30-4:30, and Sa 9-noon when College is in session; closed Sundays, holidays, and during Aug.
COPYING FACILITIES: yes
MATERIALS SOLICITED: Material on the history of the Society of Friends. Of particular interest are records of Friends meetings and organizations, personal papers of significant individual Friends, and material on the history of Swarthmore College. Will also accept genealogical material concerning families with Quaker ancestry, and pic-

tures of Friends meeting houses, individual Friends, and activities of Friends organizations.

HOLDINGS:
Total volume: 1,400 l.f.
Inclusive dates: 1650 -
Description: Records and manuscripts tracing the history of the Society of Friends. Included are original records of Friends meetings in Pennsylvania, New Jersey, Delaware, Maryland, Ohio, and Illinois, many containing membership information and vital statistics. There are also journals of prominent Quaker ministers; papers of individuals and organizations active in the social concerns of Friends, including peace, race relations, education, prison reform, abolitionism, mental health, Indian rights, and temperance; a card index to Quaker genealogical data in the United States; and records and manuscripts documenting the history of Swarthmore College.

GUIDES: *Friends Historical Library of Swarthmore College* (1969).

SEE: Hamer; NUCMC, 1959-62, 66-67, 69-72, 74.

SEE: Hinding; Ingram; Leventhal and Mooney - I; Robbins; Spalek.

SEE ALSO: Irwin Richman, comp., *Historical Manuscript Depositories in Pennsylvania* (Pennsylvania Historical and Museum Commission, 1965); Walter Schatz, ed., *Directory of Afro-American Resources* (Bowker, 1970); Gerald Friedberg, 'Sources for the Study of Socialism in America, 1901-1919,' *Labor History* 6 (Spring 1965); Albert Krichmar, *The Women's Rights Movement in the United States, 1848-1970: A Bibliography and Sourcebook* (Scarecrow Press, 1972); Peter Duignan, *Handbook of American Resources for African Studies* (Hoover Institution, 1967); Dorothy G. Harris, 'Manuscript Resources of Friends Libraries: Friends Historical Library, Swarthmore College,' in Anna Brinton, ed., *Then and Now: Quaker Essays, Historical and Contemporary* (Univ. of Pennsylvania Press, 1960).

Richard C. Davis, *North American Forest History: A Guide to Archives and Manuscripts in the United States and Canada* (Clio Books, 1977).

PA860-730
Swarthmore College
Peace Collection
Swarthmore PA 19081

(215) 447-7557

OPEN: M-F 8:30-4:30, Sa 9-noon, preferably by appointment; closed Sundays and college holidays
ACCESS: scholarly researchers
COPYING FACILITIES: yes
MATERIALS SOLICITED: Records and papers of peace organizations and leaders, as well as materials relating to amnesty, conscription, war tax refusal, peace research, pacifism, nonviolence, conscientious objection, disarmament, civil rights, civil liberties, women and peace, anti-war protest, international relations, peace-keeping, and race relations. Will also accept materials relating to inten-

tional communities, capital punishment, the military-industrial complex, chemical, biological, and radiological warfare, civil defense, international law, vegetarianism, and the antislavery movement.

HOLDINGS:
Total volume: 6,400 boxes
Inclusive dates: 1642 -
Description: 107 major document groups covering largely 19th and 20th century historical records of the peace movement and its leaders, for the most part North American, but including materials on a worldwide scope. Included are the records of organizations and the papers of individuals in the peace movement opposing war and injustice through nonviolent methods, unpublished diaries, posters, and audio-visual materials.

SEE: Hamer (as Friends Historical Library); NUCMC, 1960-62.

SEE: Hinding.

SEE ALSO: Irwin Richman, comp., *Historical Manuscript Depositories in Pennsylvania* (Pennsylvania Historical and Museum Commission, 1965).

TITUSVILLE

PA870-160
Drake Well Museum
Titusville PA

MAILING ADDRESS:
R.D. 3
Titusville PA 16354

(814) 827-2797

OPEN: M-Sa 9-5, Su 1-5; closed holidays
COPYING FACILITIES: yes
MATERIALS SOLICITED: American oil industry and related subject areas. Will also accept materials in regional history.

HOLDINGS:
Total volume: 850 l.f.
Inclusive dates: 1859 - 1900
Description: Materials relating to the birth and development of the American oil industry. Included are manuscript collections, stock certificates, company records, and photographs. There are also some papers of Edwin L. Drake, Ida M. Tarbell, and James H. Townsend.

SEE: Hamer.

SEE: Novotny; Hinding.

TOWANDA

PA875-80
Bradford County Historical Society
21 Main Street
Towanda PA 18848

(717) 265-2240

OPEN: M, F 7-9, Th, Sa 2-4; closed other days and holidays
USER FEES: $5 annual membership fee; non-member contribution requested
COPYING FACILITIES: yes

MATERIALS SOLICITED: Items pertaining to genealogy and industrial and agricultural history, and personal journals kept by individuals from the Bradford County area.

HOLDINGS:
Total volume: 30 l.f.
Inclusive dates: 1780 -
Description: Daybooks and ledgers dating from 1800 concerning local commerce and canal construction, dockets kept by an area justice of the peace, 1830-50, photographs dating from 1880 to the present, and other local history materials.

SEE: Hamer.

TRAPPE

PA880-320
Historical Society of Trappe
Library
303 Main Street
Trappe PA 19426

(215) 539-9065

OPEN: by appointment only
ACCESS: appointment required
COPYING FACILITIES: no
MATERIALS SOLICITED: Manuscript and photographic materials on the Upper Providence area of Montgomery County, Pennsylvania. Will also accept manuscript and photographic material on the larger southeastern Pennsylvania area.

HOLDINGS:
Total volume: 9 boxes
Inclusive dates: 1840 - 1960
Description: Records relating to the Trappe area of Montgomery County including family correspondence, school records, diaries, church records, maps, photographs, drawings, taped interviews, and borough records, 1900-20.

UNIONTOWN

PA890-800
Uniontown Public Library
24 Jefferson Street
Uniontown PA 15401

(412) 437-1165

OPEN: M-Th 12-9, F, Sa 9:30-5; closed Sundays and holidays; shorter summer hours
COPYING FACILITIES: yes
MATERIALS SOLICITED: Materials pertaining to Fayette County and southwestern Pennsylvania.

HOLDINGS:
Total volume: 500 items
Inclusive dates: 1788 - 1930's
Description: Records of institutions in Fayette County and the surrounding area, such as local businesses, including an iron foundry; copies of church records, 1770-1930; and records of justices of the peace, road commissioners, and other local government agencies. There are also papers relating to the Whiskey Rebellion.

SEE: Hamer.

UNIVERSITY PARK

PA895-680

Pennsylvania State University
Agricultural Extension Service
104 Agricultural Administration
   Building
University Park PA 16802

(814) 865-3407

OPEN: by appointment; closed weekends,
   holidays, and Christmas vacation
COPYING FACILITIES: yes
MATERIALS SOLICITED: Photographs relating to agriculture and homemaking
   in Pennsylvania, 1912- .

HOLDINGS:
   Total volume: 10,000 items
   Inclusive dates: 1912 -
   Description: Photographs of agricultur-
   al and homemaking activities in Penn-
   sylvania.

SEE: Novotny.

PA895-710

Pennsylvania State University
Libraries
Special Collections Division
W342 Pattee Library
University Park PA 16802

(814) 865-1793, 7931

OPEN: M-F 8-5; closed weekends, and
   holidays when University is not in
   session
COPYING FACILITIES: yes
MATERIALS SOLICITED: Modern American and English literary manuscripts,
   especially papers of Pennsylvania authors and materials relating to American and English literary relations with
   Germany; records of labor unions and
   papers relating to labor history and
   Pennsylvania history, particularly central Pennsylvania; and records of Penn
   State University and papers of its faculty.

HOLDINGS:
   Total volume: 5,105 l.f.
   Inclusive dates: 1450 -
   Description: Materials relating primarily to 19th and 20th century American
   and English literary history; American
   and Pennsylvania political, economic, labor, and social history; and the history of
   the Pennsylvania State University. Literary manuscripts are complemented by
   the papers of authors John O'Hara,
   Vance Packard, Kenneth Burke, and
   Theodore Roethke. There are also records
   of the United Steelworkers of America,
   the Graphic Arts International Union,
   and the Pennsylvania AFL-CIO; papers
   of Pennsylvania political figures and central Pennsylvania industries and families;
   the University archives, as well as faculty
   and organization papers; photographs and
   audio-visual materials; and a labor oral
   history project focusing primarily on the
   United Steelworkers of America.

SEE: Hamer; NUCMC, 1962, 69-71,
   73-74, 76.

SEE: Hinding.

SEE ALSO: Ronald L. Filippelli, 'Labor
Manuscripts in the Pennsylvania State
University Library,' *Labor History* 13
(Winter 1972); Leon J. Stout,
'Pennsylvania Town Views, 1850-1922:
A Union Catalogue,' *Western Pennsyl-
vania Historical Magazine* 58 and 59
(July, Oct. 1975, Jan. 1976); Richard
C. Davis, *North American Forest His-
tory: A Guide to Archives and Manu-
scripts in the United States and Canada*
(Clio Books, 1977); Alan M. Meckler
and Ruth McMullin, comps., *Oral His-
tory Collections* (Bowker, 1975).

Albert Krichmar, *The Women's Rights
Movement in the United States,
1848-1970: A Bibliography and
Sourcebook* (Scarecrow Press, 1972); Walter Schatz, ed., *Directory of Afro-American
Resources* (Bowker, 1970); and the following publications of the University Libraries: *Manuscript Materials in the Rare
Books and Special Collections Division*
(1970); and *Voices and Events, A Catalog
of Audio Tapes Recorded on the University Park Campus of the Pennsylvania
State University* (1975). Guides to some
individual collections are available from
the repository.

VALLEY FORGE

PA905-60

American Baptist Churches in the
   U.S.A.
International Ministries Library and
   Central Files
Valley Forge PA 19481

(215) 768-2365

OPEN: M-F 8-4:15; closed weekends and
   holidays
ACCESS: by permission of the Overseas
   Secretary
COPYING FACILITIES: yes
MATERIALS SOLICITED: Historical American Baptist material related to foreign
   missions work. Will also accept historical or general background information
   on the countries in which the Ministries work, and on the Ministries'
   missionaries.

HOLDINGS:
   Total volume: 1,800 c.f.
   Inclusive dates: 1813 -
   Description: Approximately 5,500
   books and bound periodicals; 615 microfilm reels of correspondence; geographic
   files on 53 countries; subject files with 65
   classifications; 105 cubic feet of biographical files covering the history of
   American Baptist Foreign Missions from
   1813 to the present. Also included is a
   special collection of biographical material
   on Adoniram Judson and his wives.

PA905-840

Valley Forge Historical Society
P.O. Box 122
Valley Forge PA 19481

(215) 783-0535

OPEN: M-Sa 9:30-5, Su 1-5 by
   appointment only; closed Christmas
ACCESS: researchers must contact the
   Society beforehand and request an
   officer of the Society to open files
COPYING FACILITIES: no
MATERIALS SOLICITED: Materials relating
   to the Revolutionary War, George
   Washington, and the Pennsylvania
   Campaign of 1777, in particular Valley
   Forge. Will also accept Presidential
   items.

HOLDINGS:
   Total volume: 100 items
   Inclusive dates: 1775 - 1783
   Description: Materials chiefly relating
   to Valley Forge before, during, and after
   the Continental Army's encampment. In-
   cluded are George Washington letters, let-
   ters and other papers written by other
   American leaders, and original Valley
   Forge orderly books.

SEE ALSO: NUCMC, 1959-61.

VILLA MARIA

PA908-720

Sisters of the Humility of Mary
Villa Maria Community Center
Archives Office
Villa Maria Road
Villa Maria PA

MAILING ADDRESS:
P.O. Box 212
Villa Maria, PA 16155

(412) 964-8861

OPEN: M-F 9:30-3:30 by appointment
   only; closed weekends and holidays
ACCESS: open to authorized members of
   the Community; for others,
   identification and advance
   arrangements are required.
COPYING FACILITIES: no
MATERIALS SOLICITED: Seek only material pertinent to the settling and establishment of Villa Maria, and to the
   members and works of the Community, particularly regarding earliest days
   in Lawrence County, Pennsylvania, and
   in the towns of the western
   Pennsylvania-eastern Ohio area since
   the community emigrated from France
   to the Diocese of Cleveland in 1864.
   Will also accept items associated with
   the sisters and their endeavors.

HOLDINGS:
   Total volume: 24 l.f.
   Inclusive dates: 1727 - 1962
   Description: Records of the Sisters of
   the Humility of Mary since the foundation of the community in 1854 in the
   diocese of Nancy, France, including biographical material on the founders, particularly John J. Begel; personal and business correspondence; early financial
   records; old account books; journals;
   memoirs; music; book manuscripts; contracts and legal documents; photographs;

and memorabilia. Also includes material on schools, hospitals, social work, and the founding of a parish in pioneer days.

SEE: Hinding.

VILLANOVA

PA910-840
Villanova University
Falvey Memorial Library
Villanova PA 19085

(215) 645-4271

OPEN: M-F 8-midnight, Sa 9-5, Su 2-midnight; closed holidays
COPYING FACILITIES: yes
MATERIALS SOLICITED: Will accept significant materials.

HOLDINGS:
Total volume: 29 vols.; 420 items
Inclusive dates: 14th century -
Description: European medieval and Renaissance documents, private papers relating to Pennsylvania and Villanova University, and other manuscripts.

SEE: Hamer; NUCMC, 1959-61.

SEE: Robbins.

SEE ALSO: Irwin Richman, comp., *Historical Manuscript Depositories in Pennsylvania* (Pennsylvania Historical and Museum Commission, 1965).

WARREN

PA915-870
Warren County Historical Society
Archives
210 Fourth Avenue
Warren PA

MAILING ADDRESS:
P.O. Box 427
Warren PA 16365

(814) 723-1795

OPEN: M, Tu, F 1-5, W, Th 9-5; closed weekends and holidays
COPYING FACILITIES: yes
MATERIALS SOLICITED: Primarily material relating to Warren County.

HOLDINGS:
Total volume: 370 boxes; 250 tapes; 327 miscellaneous volumes; 30 l.f. other material
Inclusive dates: 1795 -
Description: Materials relating chiefly to Warren County and its people, including manuscripts, genealogical data, maps, photographs, clippings, census and cemetery records, oral history interviews with local people, recordings of talks given to the Society, and a series of recorded talks given by one of the Society's members over a local radio station about local history and geography.
Also included is material on the Indian Cornplanter.

SEE: Davis.

WASHINGTON

PA920-870
Washington County Historical Society
LeMoyne House
49 East Maiden Street
Washington PA 15301

(412) 225-6740

OPEN: Tu-F 1-5, Su 2-4; closed Mondays, Saturdays, holidays, and Sundays Dec. 15 - Apr. 1
USER FEES: one dollar donation
COPYING FACILITIES: no
MATERIALS SOLICITED: Materials on the history of Washington County and the local western Pennsylvania area.

HOLDINGS:
Total volume: 3,000 items
Inclusive dates: 1750 -
Description: Materials relating to Washington County, including letters, deeds, manuscripts, maps, photographs, genealogies, church histories, and clippings. The collection includes Virginia court records, Ulysses S. Grant correspondence, regimental rosters for the War of 1812 and the Civil War, National Pike toll records, LeMoyne family correspondence, physicians' day books, Duncan Glass records, early school records, records of the building and use of the first crematory in the U.S., and documents and letters concerning the early settlement of the county and town.

SEE: Hamer; NUCMC, 1959-61.

PA920-890
Washington and Jefferson College Library
Historical Collection
Lincoln and Wheeling Streets
Washington PA 15301

(412) 225-8304

OPEN: M-F 9-5; closed weekends and holidays
COPYING FACILITIES: yes
MATERIALS SOLICITED: Will accept College archives and materials on western Pennsylvania and upper Ohio River Valley history.

HOLDINGS:
Total volume: 8,500 items
Inclusive dates: 1740 -
Description: Washington and Jefferson College archives and manuscript materials relating to American history. Included are papers of Thaddeus Dod, founder of the school from which Washington and Jefferson College developed; trustees' minutes, 1787- ; literary society records; and other records of the College.
There are also materials relating to the Revolutionary War in the West; minute books and other records of Virginia courts in what is now southwestern Pennsylvania; papers on the boundary controversy between Pennsylvania and Virginia; records of the North American Land Company and papers of John Hoge relating to the Company; records of the Indiana Land Company; other papers relating to land; papers of Henry Willson Temple and Joseph F. Guffey; materials on the Whiskey Rebellion in 1794; early

church and school records; local materials on the War of 1812, the Mexican War, and the Civil War, including letters and diaries; and manuscripts documenting activities of the Molly Maguires in the western Pennsylvania coal fields, 1870-75, including some letters of Allan Pinkerton.

SEE: Hamer.

SEE ALSO: Irwin Richman, comp., *Historical Manuscript Depositories in Pennsylvania* (Pennsylvania Historical and Museum Commission, 1965).

WASHINGTON CROSSING

PA925-160
David Library of the American Revolution
River Road (Route 32)
Washington Crossing PA

MAILING ADDRESS:
P.O. Box 48
Washington Crossing PA 18977

(215) 493-6776

OPEN: Tu-Sa 10-5; closed Sundays, Mondays, and holidays
COPYING FACILITIES: yes
MATERIALS SOLICITED: America, 1764-1789, and the American Revolution.

HOLDINGS:
Total volume: 3,000 items; 10,000 reels microfilm
Inclusive dates: 1764 - 1820
Description: The collections are devoted solely to the period of the American Revolution. The chief manuscript collection is the Sol Feinstone Collection of the American Revolution. Many other important Revolutionary War-period manuscript collections, in America and abroad, are available on over 7,000 reels of microfilm.

GUIDES: *The Sol Feinstone Collection of the American Revolution: Guide to the Microfilm Edition* (Rhistoric Publications, 1969); *Supplement to the Sol Feinstone Collection of the American Revolution: Guide to the Microfilm Edition* (Scholarly Resources, 1975).

SEE ALSO: Joseph J. Felcone, comp., *Abstracts of New Jersey Manuscripts in the Sol Feinstone Collection of the American Revolution* (David Library of the American Revolution, 1976).

Manuscript materials are available on microfilm.

WATERFORD

PA930-240
Fort LeBoeuf Museum
Amos Judson Library
123 South High Street
Waterford PA 16441

(814) 732-2573, 796-4113

OPEN: by appointment only
ACCESS: by appointment only
COPYING FACILITIES: no

MATERIALS SOLICITED: Erie County history, particularly that of Waterford Township and the borough of Waterford.

HOLDINGS:
Total volume: 12 l.f.
Inclusive dates: 1795 - 1950
Description: A manuscript collection relating chiefly to the history of the Waterford area. The collection includes diaries of early settlers, business records of local firms, early church records and deeds, pictures and minutes of community groups, and genealogical records.

The Museum's manuscripts are in the custody of Edinboro University of Pennsylvania. Further information is available by calling (814) 732-2573.

WAYNE

PA935-690
Radnor Historical Society
113 West Beechtree Lane
Wayne PA 19087

(215) 688-2668

OPEN: Tu 2-5, or by appointment
COPYING FACILITIES: yes
MATERIALS SOLICITED: Materials on Radnor Township history. Will also accept items on neighboring areas.

HOLDINGS:
Total volume: 25 l.f.
Inclusive dates: 1725 - 1976
Description: Manuscripts relating to Radnor Township, including correspondence, deeds, and tavern licenses; early records of the overseer of the poor; tax assessment records; mill and farm records; and minute books of social organizations. There is also a collection of 19th century photographs of local subjects.

SEE: NUCMC, 1962.

SEE ALSO: Irwin Richman, comp., *Historical Manuscript Depositories in Pennsylvania* (Pennsylvania Historical and Museum Commission, 1965).

WAYNESBURG

PA940-120
Cornerstone Genealogical Society
Eva K. Bowlby Public Library
311 North West Street
Waynesburg PA

MAILING ADDRESS:
P.O. Box 547
Waynesburg PA 15370

(412) 627-9776, 5255; 852-1878

OPEN: Su 1-4, M-F 10-9, Sa 10-4; closed holidays and Sundays June - Aug.
COPYING FACILITIES: yes
MATERIALS SOLICITED: Materials relating to genealogy and local history of southwestern Pennsylvania and surrounding areas.

HOLDINGS:
Total volume: not specified
Inclusive dates: 1700's -
Description: Manuscripts, ledgers, day books, church records, court records, and family histories relating to Greene County.

PA940-280
Greene County Historical Society
Waynesburg PA

MAILING ADDRESS:
R.D. 2
Waynesburg PA 15370

no telephone

SEE: Hamer.

Questionnaire not returned.

PA940-300
Greene County Library System
Eva K. Bowlby Public Library
Oral History Collection
311 North West Street
Waynesburg PA 15370

(412) 627-9776; 852-1876

OPEN: M, W, F 1-9, Tu, Th 10-9, Sa 9-4, Su 2-5; closed holidays, and Sundays June - Aug.
COPYING FACILITIES: no
MATERIALS SOLICITED: Materials related to the history and life style of Greene County as recalled by senior citizens.

HOLDINGS:
Total volume: 33 cassettes
Inclusive dates: 1977 -
Description: Oral history recordings relating to life in late 19th and 20th century Greene County as recalled by senior citizens.

WELLSBORO

PA943-760
Tioga County Historical Society
Robinson House Museum
120 Main Street
Wellsboro PA

MAILING ADDRESS:
Box 724
Wellsboro PA 16901

(717) 724-6116

OPEN: Su, Tu, Sa 2-5; closed Thanksgiving, Christmas, and New Year's
COPYING FACILITIES: yes
MATERIALS SOLICITED: Materials relating to the history and families of Tioga County. Will also accept family records and historical records of surrounding counties including Steuben and Chemung counties in New York.

HOLDINGS:
Total volume: 150 items
Inclusive dates: 1795 -
Description: Manuscripts, minute books, veterans records, account books, family records, wills, deeds, Bible records, and cemetery records relating to Tioga County.

WEST CHESTER

PA945-120
Chester County Historical Society Library
225 North High Street
West Chester PA 19380

(215) 692-4800

OPEN: W 1-8, Th, F 10-4; closed weekends, Mondays, Tuesdays, and holidays
USER FEES: $2 per day for non-members
COPYING FACILITIES: yes
MATERIALS SOLICITED: Materials relating to Chester County and its people.

HOLDINGS:
Total volume: 140 file drawers
Inclusive dates: 1600's -
Description: Records relating to Chester County people, businesses, churches, and schools, including deeds, title searches, clipping files, daybooks, account books, minute books, correspondence, and manuscripts. Also, includes materials dealing with Indians, Quakers, and Blacks in the county.

SEE: Hamer.

SEE: Davis; Hinding; Leventhal and Mooney - I.

PA945-880
West Chester State College
Francis Harvey Green Library
West Chester PA 19380

(215) 436-2946

OPEN: M-F 8-4:30; closed weekends and holidays
ACCESS: qualified researchers; appointment recommended
COPYING FACILITIES: yes
MATERIALS SOLICITED: Materials relating to the West Chester area.

HOLDINGS:
Total volume: 102 vols.; 10,100 pieces
Inclusive dates: 1776 - 1898
Description: Papers of William Darlington; several letters from pre-Civil War military and political leaders to Persifer F. Smith; letters to and from Anthony Wayne; some autograph letters of the signers of the Declaration of Independence; several thousand items relating to the history and development of West Chester State College; and letters and writings of William Goddell.

SEE: Hamer.

SEE: Robbins.

SEE ALSO: Irwin Richman, comp., *Historical Manuscript Depositories in Pennsylvania* (Pennsylvania Historical and Museum Commission, 1965).

WESTTOWN

PA950-880

Westtown School
Historical Library
Westtown PA 19395

(215) 399-0123

OPEN: by appointment only
ACCESS: researchers should contact
Headmaster of Westtown School
COPYING FACILITIES: yes
MATERIALS SOLICITED: Letters and correspondence relating to the history of Westtown School.

HOLDINGS:
Total volume: 39 boxes; 50 l.f.
Inclusive dates: 1780 -
Description: Materials relating to Westtown School, people connected with the School, and the Society of Friends, Philadelphia Yearly Meeting School Committee, which runs the School. Included are letters, diaries, literary society essays, ledgers, account books, student registers, minute books of committees and alumni groups, deeds, plans of the early School grounds and arboretum, architectural plans and drawings of the School buildings, and photographs.

SEE: Hamer.

WILKES-BARRE

PA960-440

King's College
D. Leonard Corgan Library
Special Collections
14 West Jackson Street
Wilkes-Barre PA 18711

(717) 826-5840, Ext. 649

OPEN: Tu, Th 9-5; closed other days and holidays
ACCESS: permission of special collections librarian required; schedule subject to change; prospective researchers advised to write
COPYING FACILITIES: yes
MATERIALS SOLICITED: Materials relating to the Wyoming Valley and the anthracite mining region of Pennsylvania.

HOLDINGS:
Total volume: 1,000 l.f.
Inclusive dates: 1801 -
Description: Manuscripts and tape recordings relating to the history, politics, religion, social life, and culture of the Wyoming Valley and the anthracite mining region of Pennsylvania. Included are papers and tapes on the art, folklore, ethnic groups, churches, and political activities of the area, as well as papers of local U.S. Representative Daniel J. Flood.

SEE ALSO: The following King's College Press publications by Judith Tierney: *A Description of the George Korson Folklore Archives* (1973); *Daniel J. Flood: A Register of His Papers* (1974).

PA960-870

Wilkes College
Eugene Shedden Farley Library
South Franklin and South Streets
Wilkes-Barre PA 18766

(717) 824-4651

OPEN: M-Th 8-10, F 8-5, Sa 9-5, Su 2-10; closed holidays, and Sundays in summer
ACCESS: permission of Curator required; schedule varies; prospective users advised to write
COPYING FACILITIES: yes
MATERIALS SOLICITED: History of transportation, particularly urban and interurban railways. Will also accept materials on the history of mining and mining technology.

HOLDINGS:
Total volume: 450 items; 1,600 l.f.
Inclusive dates: 1549 -
Description: The McClintock collection, 1549-1959, containing papers relating to the American Revolution, correspondence of U.S. Presidents, documents of the kings of France and England, correspondence of noted literary figures, and papers concerning the history of northeastern Pennsylvania, particularly during the Revolutionary War period. There are also 1,600 linear feet, 1804-1970, of correspondence, minute books, maps and other papers relating to the history of transportation, particularly urban and interurban railways, and to the history of mining and mining technology.

SEE: Hamer.

SEE ALSO: Fred Walters, ed., *The McClintock Papers Index* (Wilkes College, 1973).

PA960-910

Wyoming Historical and Geological Society
49 South Franklin Street
Wilkes-Barre PA 18701

(717) 823-6244

OPEN: Tu-F 10-5, Sa 10-4; closed Sundays, Mondays, and holidays
USER FEES: one dollar per day or $3 per year, for non-members
COPYING FACILITIES: yes
MATERIALS SOLICITED: Manuscripts, non-current records and visual documents pertaining to the industries, labor organizations, government, ethnic groups, churches, schools and community organizations of Luzerne County, PA, especially correspondence and financial records of anthracite companies and secondary industry, and any material on ethnic migration, life and culture. Will also accept audio material and microforms related to these areas.

HOLDINGS:
Total volume: 1,300 c.f.
Inclusive dates: 1750 - 1950
Description: Materials relating chiefly to the Wilkes-Barre region and the Wyoming Valley. Included are early township proprietors' books, land records, tax lists, church records, turnpike, canal, and railroad papers, and photographs relating to local history. There are also records of

the Albert B. Lewis Lumber Company, the Bear Creek Ice Company, the Lehigh and Wilkes-Barre Coal Company, and the Sharpe, Weiss Coal Company, and papers of Zebulon Butler, Edmund N. Carpenter, Isaac A. Chapman, Jacob Cist, Edmund L. Dana, Matthias and George Hollenback, Henry M. Hoyt, Volney Maxwell, Samuel Meredith, Charles Miner, Timothy Pickering, Victor E. Piolett, Jason Torry, and Hendrik B. Wright.

SEE: Hamer; NUCMC, 1971.

SEE ALSO: Irwin Richman, comp., *Historical Manuscript Depositories in Pennsylvania* (Pennsylvania Historical and Museum Commission, 1965); Richard C. Davis, *North American Forest History: A Guide to Archives and Manuscripts in the United States and Canada* (Clio Books, 1977).

WILLIAMSPORT

PA965-400

James V. Brown Library
19 East Fourth Street
Williamsport PA 17701

(717) 326-0536

SEE: Hamer.

Questionnaire not returned.

PA965-470

Lycoming College
Library
Williamsport PA 17701

(717) 326-1951

OPEN: Su 1-11, M-Th 8-11, F 8-4:30, Sa 10-5; closed holidays
COPYING FACILITIES: yes
MATERIALS SOLICITED: Materials relating to Lycoming College and to Williamsport and Lycoming County, Pennsylvania.

HOLDINGS:
Total volume: not specified
Inclusive dates: early 19th century -
Description: Materials relating to the history of Lycoming College and the surrounding area.

PA965-490

Lycoming County Historical Society
Lycoming County Historical Museum
858 West Fourth Street
Williamsport PA 17701

(717) 326-3326

OPEN: Tu-F 10-4, Su 2-5; closed Mondays, Saturdays, and holidays
USER FEES: $3
COPYING FACILITIES: no
MATERIALS SOLICITED: History of Williamsport and central Pennsylvania.

HOLDINGS:
Total volume: 40,000 items
Inclusive dates: 1760 -
Deses, dription: The collections emphasize the economic history of Williamsport and central Pennsylvania. Business records include railroad and canal maps and deeds, as well as records of lumber

companies. There are also minutes of farmers' organizations, a large collection of photographs of farming and natural scenes dating from 1865, and oral history recordings, chiefly of farmers and school teachers.

YORK

PA975-320

The Historical Society of York County
Library and Archives
250 East Market Street
York PA 17403

(717) 848-1587

OPEN: M, W, F, Sa 9-5, Tu, Th 1-5; closed Sundays and holidays
USER FEES: one dollar per day for non-members
COPYING FACILITIES: yes
MATERIALS SOLICITED: Materials relating to York and York County, including manuscripts, business records, oral history, genealogical source data, and church records. Will also accept photographs and ephemera.

HOLDINGS:
   Total volume: 180 l.f.
   Inclusive dates: 1733 -
   Description: Materials relating to the history of York and York County. Included are city and County records, personal papers of individuals and families, business records, records of unincorporated organizations and military units, audio-visual materials, and ephemera.

SEE: Hamer; NUCMC, 1959-61, 70.

SEE ALSO: Irwin Richman, comp., *Historical Manuscript Depositories in Pennsylvania* (Pennsylvania Historical and Museum Commission, 1965).

ZELIENOPLE

PA986-960

Zelienople Historical Society
243 South Main Street
Zelienople PA

MAILING ADDRESS:
P.O. Box 45
Zelienople PA 16063

(412) 452-9457

OPEN: M-Th 9-4, Sa 10-2; closed Fridays, Sundays and holidays, except for special appointments
COPYING FACILITIES: no
MATERIALS SOLICITED: Materials relating to William A. Passavant; the Buhl family; early settlers of southwestern Pennsylvania, especially Butler, Beaver, Lawrence, and Allegheny counties; the early oil industry; and the Empire Glass Company. Also, institutional records, church records, genealogies, and court cases and medical informaton pertaining to southwestern Butler County.

HOLDINGS:
   Total volume: 5,000 items
   Inclusive dates: 1785 -
   Description: Basse-Passavant-Jennings family letters, 1785-1900, including materials written in Germany and France; genealogical data; materials relating to travel; records of an orphanage; diaries and letters of early clergy; correspondence relating to Presbyterian and Lutheran churches; scrapbooks and letters of the Buhl family; architectural plans for the Boggs and Buhl department store in Pittsburgh; photographs; aerial views of the Zelienople area; papers of a disbanded League of Women Voters chapter; oral history interviews; literary manuscripts; and other items.

PUERTO RICO

Legislation enacted in 1955 empowers the General Archives of Puerto Rico to accession permanently valuable local public records. The General Archives has acquired records, 1730 to date, from all but five municipalities.

RIO PIEDRAS

PR600-800

University of Puerto Rico at Rio Piedras
Historical Research Center
Rio Piedras PR

MAILING ADDRESS:
P.O. Box 22802, U.P.R. Station
Rio Piedras PR 00931

(809) 764-0000, Ext. 3274

OPEN: M-Th 8-4:30, F 8-noon; closed weekends and holidays
COPYING FACILITIES: no
MATERIALS SOLICITED: Puerto Rico historical documents, 16th to 19th centuries.

HOLDINGS:
Total volume: not specified
Inclusive dates: 16th century -
Description: Manuscripts related to the development of Puerto Rico under Spanish rule, and a collection of papers of Juan Ramon Jimenez and other Spanish literary figures.

SEE: Hamer; NUCMC, 1967.

SAN JUAN

PR720-360

Instituto de Cultura Puertorriquena
Archivo General de Puerto Rico
Ponce de Leon 500
Puerta de Tierra
San Juan PR

MAILING ADDRESS:
Apartado 4184
San Juan PR 00905

(809) 724-2680

OPEN: M-F 8:30-5; closed weekends and holidays
COPYING FACILITIES: yes
MATERIALS SOLICITED: Puerto Rican government records of archival quality. Will also accept notarial records, private collections, and music manuscripts.

HOLDINGS:
Total volume: 32,000 c.f.
Inclusive dates: 1730 -
Description: Records of central and local Puerto Rican governments created during Spanish, United States colonial, and commonwealth rule. Included are records of courts, public works, the public treasury, municipalities, public utilities, and other government agencies. Materials relate to or include wills, divorce proceedings, highways, waterways and railroad construction, public and religious buildings, property tax, municipal acts, and the organization and functions of public agencies.

SEE: Hamer.

SEE: Hinding.

SEE ALSO: the following publications of the Instituto: *Guia al Archivo General de Puerto Rico* (1964); Lino Gomez Canedo, *Los Archivos Historicos de Puerto Rico* (1964); and Ricardo E. Alegria, *El Instituto de Cultura Puertorriquena: Los Primeros Cinco Anos* (1960).

RHODE ISLAND

In 1981 the Rhode Island General Assembly enacted the Rhode Island Public Records Administration Act, which establishes an administration program for state and local records.

BRISTOL

RI105-320
Brown University
Haffenreffer Museum of Anthropology
Mt. Hope Grant
Bristol RI 02809

(401) 253-8388

OPEN: Tu-Su 1-5; closed Mondays and holidays
ACCESS: prior arrangements required
COPYING FACILITIES: yes
MATERIALS SOLICITED: Photographs relating to the archaeology and ethnology of North, Central and South America. Will also accept photographs relating to Old World archaeology and ethnology.

HOLDINGS:
Total volume: 25,000 items
Inclusive dates: 1879 - 1960
Description: The Spinden Collection consists of photographic prints, negatives, drawings, fieldnotes and manuscript materials from the lifework of archaeologist and Mayanist Herbert J. Spinden, relating primarily to the archaeology and ethnology of Western North America, Central and South America.

CUMBERLAND

RI210-720
Sisters of Mercy
Province of Providence
Provincial Archives
Cumberland RI

MAILING ADDRESS:
RD 3
Cumberland RI 02864

(401) 333-6333

OPEN: M-F 9-3; closed weekends and holy days
COPYING FACILITIES: yes
MATERIALS SOLICITED: Materials pertaining to the Order of Sisters of Mercy, including its affiliated institutions.

HOLDINGS:
Total volume: 150 l.f.
Inclusive dates: 1831 -
Description: Records of the Sisters of Mercy Provincialate and its affiliated institutions in the Providence area, and in

Belize and Honduras. Material consists of official correspondence; records of meetings; journals; manuscript writings, academic theses, and musical compositions by Sisters of Mercy and other Catholic clergy; genealogical source data; and 1,000 photographs.

SEE: Hinding.

KINGSTON

RI420-440
Kingston Free Library
Little Rest Archives
1329 Kingstown Road
Kingston RI 02881

(401) 792-2653

OPEN: M-F 10-5, Sa 9-5; closed Sundays and holidays
COPYING FACILITIES: yes

HOLDINGS:
Total volume: 37 square ft.
Inclusive dates: late 18th century -
Description: A collection focusing on Kingston and South Kingstown history. Included are photographs, Library records, and other organization records.

RI420-800
University of Rhode Island
Library
Kingston RI 02881

no telephone

SEE: Hamer.

Questionnaire not returned.

NEWPORT

RI560-360
International Tennis Hall of Fame
and Tennis Museum
194 Bellevue Avenue
Newport RI 02840

(401) 849-3990

OPEN: daily 10-5, May - Oct.; daily 11-4, Nov. - April
ACCESS: permission of Executive Director required
COPYING FACILITIES: yes
MATERIALS SOLICITED: Materials relating to tennis. Will also accept materials relating to other racquet sports.

HOLDINGS:
Total volume: 2 file drawers; 73 vols.
Inclusive dates: 1880 -
Description: A collection of photographs of prominent tennis players and others associated with the sport and of the Newport Casino and tennis tournaments held there, 1881-1914. A manuscript collection includes journals of the Casino Superintendent, 1885-1957.

SEE: Hinding.

RI560-510
Naval War College
Naval Historical Collection
Newport RI 02840

(401) 841-2435

OPEN: M-F 8-4:30; closed weekends and holidays
ACCESS: scholarly researchers; advance appointment required
COPYING FACILITIES: yes
MATERIALS SOLICITED: History of naval warfare, the Naval War College, and the U.S. Navy in the Narragansett Bay region.

HOLDINGS:
Total volume: 1,350 l.f.
Inclusive dates: 1807 -
Description: Manuscripts and Naval War College archival records concerning the history of naval warfare, in particular, theories and concepts of strategy and tactics, as well as materials in related areas such as foreign diplomacy and naval technology, and manuscripts concerning the history of the U.S. Navy in the Narragansett Bay region. The manuscript collection consists of corporate records and papers of naval and non-naval persons associated with the College or naval warfare. Included are papers of Stephen B. Luce, Alfred Thayer Mahan, Raymond Ames Spruance, and William Veazie Pratt.
The College archives consists chiefly of administrative and academic records relating to the founding and development of the College. An oral history collection includes interviews with officers and covers the history of the College, naval war gaming, and Milton Miles and the Rice Paddy War. Photographs concentrate on the period 1900 - present.

GUIDES: *A Guide to Research Source Materials in the Naval War College Naval Historical Collection* (1980).

SEE: NUCMC, 1977.

SEE: Allard, Crawley, and Edmison.

SEE ALSO: David F. Trask and Thomas H. Etzold, 'The Archives and Manuscripts of the United States Naval War College,' *The Society of Historians of American Foreign Relations Newsletter* 7 (June 1975); Alan M. Meckler and Ruth McMullin, comps., *Oral History Collections* (Bowker, 1975); unpublished guides to specific collections available at the College.

RI560-570
Newport Historical Society
82 Touro Street
Newport RI 02840

(401) 846-0813

OPEN: Tu-F 9:30-4:30, Sa 9:30-noon; closed Sundays, Mondays, and holidays
USER FEES: for non-members, fee of one dollar per day or $5 for extended period of one week to one month
COPYING FACILITIES: yes
MATERIALS SOLICITED: Items of historical interest pertaining to the city of Newport and Newport County.

HOLDINGS:
Total volume: 700 c.f.
Inclusive dates: 1650 - 1900
Description: A collection relating to the history of Newport and Rhode Island. Included are the earliest municipal records of Newport; early church records, particularly those of New England Friends; 18th and 19th century business records; diaries, journals, and logbooks of prominent Newport families; probate and customhouse records; ships' logs; genealogical data; and photographs of Newport houses and people.

SEE: Hamer; NUCMC, 1966.

SEE ALSO: Freda Egnal, comp. and ed., 'An Annotated Critical Bibliography of Materials Relating to the History of the Jews in Rhode Island Located in Rhode Island Depositories (1678-1966),' *Rhode Island Jewish Historical Notes* 4 (Nov. 1966); Walter Schatz, ed., *Directory of Afro-American Resources* (Bowker, 1970); Peter Duignan, *Handbook of American Resources for African Studies* (Hoover Institution, 1967).

The repository holds materials previously held by the now defunct Oldport Association, Inc.

PROVIDENCE

RI700-45
Brown University
Annmary Brown Memorial
21 Brown Street
Providence RI

MAILING ADDRESS:
P.O. Box 1905
Brown University
Providence RI 02912

(401) 863-2429

OPEN: M-F 9-5; closed weekends and holidays
ACCESS: qualified scholars with proper identification

COPYING FACILITIES: no
HOLDINGS:
Total volume: 7,900 items
Inclusive dates: 1400 - 1920
Description: Papers of Rush C. Hawkins, relating to the Civil War and other topics; papers of George Weedon, Revolutionary War officer; Samuel Wyllys papers, consisting of colonial Connecticut legal documents, many relating to witchcraft trials and Indian relations; and Civil War papers, primarily Confederate.

SEE: Hamer; NUCMC, 1959-61, 63-64.

SEE ALSO: Stuart C. Sherman and Dorothy A. Hill, *Guide to the Manuscript Collections in the Brown University Library* (Brown Univ. Library, 1974).

RI700-50
Brown University
Archives
John Hay Library
Prospect Street
Providence RI

MAILING ADDRESS:
Box A, Brown University
Providence RI 02912

(401) 863-2148

OPEN: M-F 8:30-5; closed weekends and holidays
ACCESS: qualified scholars on application
COPYING FACILITIES: yes
MATERIALS SOLICITED: Personal papers of University faculty, and office files of University officials. Will also accept papers of prominent alumni.

HOLDINGS:
Total volume: 450 l.f.; 122,000 items
Inclusive dates: 1764 -
Description: Materials relating to Brown University history, including papers of presidents James Manning, Francis Wayland, and William Herbert Perry Faunce; professors C. J. Ducasse, H. E. Walter, and Carl Barus; and alumni Solomon Drowne and William Williams Keen. Other holdings consist of University records, theses, films, tapes, prints and photographs.

SEE: Allard, Crawley, and Edmison; Martin; Robbins.

RI700-70
Brown University
John Carter Brown Library
Providence RI

MAILING ADDRESS:
Box 1894
Providence RI 02912

(401) 863-2725

OPEN: M-F 8:30-5, Sa 9-5; closed Sundays, holidays, and Saturdays in summer
COPYING FACILITIES: yes
MATERIALS SOLICITED: Textual manuscripts (not correspondence, autograph letters, or similar papers) which were written in the colonial period concerning the Americas. Will also accept business papers relating to the Providence

firm of Brown and Ives, and to Welcome Arnold and John Russell Bartlett.

HOLDINGS:
Total volume: 960 l.f.
Inclusive dates: 1492 -
Description: Journals, ships' logs, Indian grammars, personal narratives, and other manuscripts relating chiefly to the colonization of America, but also to Rhode Island history in the 18th and 19th centuries. There is also the archives of the Library, 1840- .

SEE: Hamer; NUCMC, 1959-62, 66.

SEE: Beers - Southwest; Ingram; Allard, Crawley, and Edmison.

SEE ALSO: *Opportunities for Research in the John Carter Brown Library* (1968); G. Bhagat, 'Materials Relating to Eighteenth and Nineteenth Century Indo-American Trade andConsular Relations in Private Archives in the United States,' *Indian Archives* 17 (Jan. 1967/Dec. 1968); Jerome S. Handler, *A Guide to Source Materials for the Study of Barbados History, 1627-1834* (Southern Illinois Univ. Press, 1971).

Some materials listed in Hamer and NUCMC relating to Rhode Island history have been transferred to the Rhode Island Historical Society in Providence.

RI700-100
Brown University
John Hay Library
20 Prospect Street
Providence RI 02912

MAILING ADDRESS:
Box A, Brown University
Providence RI 02912

(401) 863-2148

OPEN: M-F 9-4:30; closed weekends and holidays
ACCESS: qualified scholars presenting proper identification
COPYING FACILITIES: yes
MATERIALS SOLICITED: American plays and poetry, and materials on Abraham Lincoln, his family and associates, John Hay, Emile Zola, Howard P. Lovecraft, and John B. Wheelwright. Will also accept materials on American diplomatic history, American literature, Rhode Island history, the Baptist church in New England, the American Civil War, American whaling, the history of science, book collecting, and bibliography.

HOLDINGS:
Total volume: 166,000 items
Inclusive dates: 1300 B.C. -
Description: Manuscript collections focusing chiefly on American history and literature in the 18th and 19th centuries. Correspondence and personal papers predominate, although there are also legal and military documents, unpublished works, and records of organizations. Subject strengths include Abraham Lincoln, John Hay, and the Civil War; American plays and poetry; and Rhode Island history.

SEE: Hamer; NUCMC, 1959-62, 73, 78.

SEE ALSO: *Dictionary Catalog of the Harris Collection of American Plays and Poetry, Brown University, Providence, Rhode Island* (G. K. Hall, 1972); Stuart C. Sherman and Dorothy A. Hill, *Guide to the Manuscript Collections in the Brown University Library* (Brown Univ. Library, 1974); Walter Schatz, ed., *Directory of Afro-American Resources* (Bowker, 1970).

RI700-160

Diocese of Providence
Archives
1 Cathedral Square
Providence RI 02903

(401) 278-4546

OPEN: by appointment only
ACCESS: advance arrangements required
COPYING FACILITIES: yes

HOLDINGS:
   Total volume: not specified
   Inclusive dates: 1870's -
   Description: Account books, financial records, correspondence, diaries, scrapbooks, and other materials relating to the churches, institutions, schools, organizations, and community groups of the Roman Catholic Diocese of Providence.

RI700-240

First Baptist Church in America
Rhode Island Historical Society
   Library
121 Hope Street
Providence RI 02906

(401) 331-0448

OPEN: Sept.-May, Tu-Sa 10-4, June-Aug., M-F 10-4; closed holidays and Saturdays before Monday holidays
ACCESS: written permission of the Historical Committee required
COPYING FACILITIES: yes

HOLDINGS:
   Total volume: 54 l.f.
   Inclusive dates: 1638 - 1965
   Description: Records of the First Baptist Church in America including correspondence, annual reports, minutes of meetings, women's societies, financial records, missions, genealogical data, and biographical information relating to clergy.

RI700-620

Providence Athenaeum
251 Benefit Street
Providence RI 02903

(401) 421-6970

OPEN: M-Sa 8:30-5:30; closed Sundays, holidays, and Saturdays in summer
COPYING FACILITIES: yes

HOLDINGS:
   Total volume: 1 l.f.
   Inclusive dates: 14th century - 19th century
   Description: One illuminated Latin manuscript and individual letters of several American literary and political figures.

SEE: Robbins.

RI700-630

Providence College
Phillips Memorial Library
College Archives
Eaton Street and River Avenue
Providence RI 02918

(401) 865-2377

OPEN: M-F 9-5:30; closed weekends and holidays, except by special appointment
COPYING FACILITIES: yes
MATERIALS SOLICITED: 20th century Rhode Island political, social, economic, ethnic and literary history. Will also accept collections relating to individuals of New England regional importance.

HOLDINGS:
   Total volume: 2,700 l.f.
   Inclusive dates: 1864 -
   Description: Papers of Rhode Island political leaders of National significance such as Dennis J. Roberts, John E. Fogarty, John O. Pastore, Joseph A. Doorley, Jr., Aime J. Forand and Robert E. Quinn. Also included are institutional collections, such as the records of the Urban League of Rhode Island, and material relating to several ethnic communities. Other holdings include the papers of Louis F. Budenz and William H. Chamberlin, and a machine-readable collection of English and colonial 18th century trade statistics.
   Also included are papers of Thomas M. McGlynn, O.P., Cornelius Moore, John J. Fawcett, J. Lyons Moore, Alice Lafond Altieri, and J. Howard McGrath. Rhode Island records include the Constitutional Conventions of 1964-69 and 1973, the Quonset Point Naval Air Station and court records.

SEE: NUCMC, 1971.

SEE: Hinding.

SEE ALSO: inventories to several collections available at the Library.

RI700-640

Providence Public Library
Special Collections
150 Empire Street
Providence RI 02903

(401) 521-8731, 7722

OPEN: M-F 8:30-5; closed weekends and holidays
COPYING FACILITIES: yes
MATERIALS SOLICITED: Will accept materials relating to the existing collections.

HOLDINGS:
   Total volume: 100 l.f.
   Inclusive dates: 1700 - 1941
   Description: Logbooks, journals, and account books recording over 1,000 whaling voyages, as well as business records and correspondence relating to the American whaling industry, 1762-1922; approximately 800 letters and documents, late 17th to mid-19th centuries, with emphasis on Rhode Island history and politics; 100 music scores by David Wallace Reeves; correspondence of Daniel Berkeley Updike; letters and diaries of Rhode Islanders in the Civil War; and photographs and negatives of Rhode Island and whaling interest.

SEE: Hamer; NUCMC, 1971.

SEE: Novotny.

RI700-660

Rhode Island College
James P. Adams Library
Archives
600 Mt. Pleasant Avenue
Providence RI 02908

(401) 456-9653

OPEN: M-F 8:30-4:30; closed weekends and holidays
COPYING FACILITIES: yes
MATERIALS SOLICITED: Material pertaining to the history of Rhode Island College and collections concerning Rhode Island's ethnic heritage. Will also accept collections related to education in Rhode Island, as well as Rhode Island social and political history.

HOLDINGS:
   Total volume: 325 l.f.
   Inclusive dates: 1780's -
   Description: College archives and manuscript collections related to Rhode Island history. Included are papers on subjects such as ethnic history, higher education, black history, and business history.

SEE: NUCMC, 1977, 79.

SEE: Hinding; Robbins.

SEE ALSO: registers to individual collections available at the institution.

RI700-680

The Rhode Island Historical Society
Library
121 Hope Street
Providence RI 02906

(401) 331-8575

OPEN: winter, Tu-Sa 10-5; closed Sundays, Mondays, and holidays; summer, M 1-9, Tu-F 10-5; closed weekends and holidays
USER FEES: non-members, one dollar per day or $5 for 4 months; annual membership $15
COPYING FACILITIES: yes
MATERIALS SOLICITED: Any manuscript or graphic material relating to Rhode Island.

HOLDINGS:
   Total volume: 1,000 l.f.
   Inclusive dates: 1636 -
   Description: Over 1,000 manuscript collections numbering 1,000,000 pieces, relating primarily to Rhode Island. The collections are particularly strong in records of businesses and social organizations, as well as personal papers. Included are materials on the Revolutionary and Civil Wars; city, town, and State records; and a graphics collection containing photographs, architectural drawings, manuscript maps, feature films, newsreels, and television newsfilm, all relating specifically to Rhode Island.

SEE: Hamer; NUCMC, 1971-74, 76.

SEE: Ingram; Robbins; Hinding; Allard, Crawley, and Edmison.

SEE ALSO: Walter Schatz, ed., *Directory of Afro-American Resources* (Bowker, 1970); Ann Novotny, ed., *Picture Sources 3* (Special Libraries Assn., 1975); Kathleen Karr, 'The Rhode Island Historical Society Film Archive: A Progress Report,' *Rhode Island History* 28 (Nov. 1969); Freda Egnal, comp. and ed., 'An Annotated Critical Bibliography of Materials Relating to the History of the Jews in Rhode Island Located in Rhode Island Depositories (1678-1966),' *Rhode Island Jewish Historical Notes* 4 (Nov. 1966); inventories of individual collections available at the Society.

RI700-690

Rhode Island Jewish Historical
Association
130 Sessions Street
Providence RI 02906

(401) 331-1360

OPEN: by appointment only
COPYING FACILITIES: no
MATERIALS SOLICITED: Personal papers, minutes of organizations, photographs, and other historical materials pertaining to the Jewish population of Rhode Island.

HOLDINGS:
    Total volume: 118 c.f.; 46 vols.
    Inclusive dates: 1658 -
    Description: Materials documenting the history of Jewish people in Rhode Island. Significant collections include family papers and institutional records, 1850-1960, and copies of papers of prominent Jewish families in Newport, 1658-1750. There are also photographs of individuals, organizations, and social events.

SEE ALSO: Freda Egnal, comp. and ed., 'An Annotated Critical Bibliography of Materials Relating to the History of the Jews in Rhode Island Located in Rhode Island Depositories (1678-1966),' *Rhode Island Jewish Historical Notes* 4 (Nov. 1966).

RI700-710

Rhode Island Medical Society
Library
106 Francis Street
Providence, RI 02903

(401) 331-3208

OPEN: M-F 8:15-4:30; closed weekends and holidays
COPYING FACILITIES: yes
MATERIALS SOLICITED: Materials relating to medical history and manuscripts of Charles V. Chapin. Will also accept historical and genealogical materials relating to medicine and physicians in the state of Rhode Island.

HOLDINGS:
    Total volume: 50,000 items
    Inclusive dates: 19th century
    Description: Materials relating to medicine and physicians in Rhode Island.

SEE: NUCMC, 1959-62.

RI700-740

Rhode Island Secretary of State
Archives Division
Room 43, State House
Smith Street
Providence RI 02903

(401) 277-2353

OPEN: M-F 9-4:30; closed weekends and holidays
COPYING FACILITIES: yes
MATERIALS SOLICITED: Will accept historical, genealogical or other materials pertinent to the colony or State of Rhode Island.

HOLDINGS:
    Total volume: 2,700 vols.
    Inclusive dates: 1636 -
    Description: Primarily legislative archives of the State and colony of Rhode Island, but also including State censuses and records of the executive and judicial branches of the State government. A small collection of private manuscripts concerning Rhode Island contains maps, business ledgers, and papers of political leaders from the Revolutionary War period.

SEE: Hamer; NUCMC, 1959-61.

SEE: Allard, Crawley, and Edmison; Hinding; Ingram; Leventhal and Mooney - I; Robbins.

SEE ALSO: Freda Egnal, comp. and ed., 'An Annotated Critical Bibliography of Materials Relating to the History of the Jews in Rhode Island Located in Rhode Island Depositories (1678-1966),' *Rhode Island Jewish Historical Notes* 4 (Nov. 1966). The Archives Division will provide researchers with copies of an unpublished guide to most of its holdings.

WARWICK

RI875-880

Warwick Historical Society
22 Roger Williams Avenue
Warwick RI 02888

(401) 467-7647

OPEN: Su 2-4, Tu, W 9-12; open holidays in summer
COPYING FACILITIES: no
MATERIALS SOLICITED: Letters, documents, ledgers and photographs pertaining to Warwick and Kent County.

HOLDINGS:
    Total volume: 4 c.f.; 2 cabinets
    Inclusive dates: 1642 -
    Description: A collection of family papers, ledgers, shipping invoices and letters concerning early settlers and Indians in the Warwick area and depicting the social evolution of this seashore community. Included are slides of Warwick dating from 1898, photographs of the history of manufacturing in Kent County, and oral history recordings.

WESTERLY

RI910-730

Seventh Day Baptist Missionary
Society
401 Washington Trust Building
Westerly RI 02891

(401) 596-4326

OPEN: M-F 8-4:30; closed weekends and holidays
ACCESS: by appointment
COPYING FACILITIES: yes
MATERIALS SOLICITED: Minutes, records of meetings, publications, correspondence and reports pertaining to missionary work of the Seventh Day Baptist General Conference and related conferences.

HOLDINGS:
    Total volume: 4 file cabinets
    Inclusive dates: 1842 -
    Description: Minute books of the Seventh Day Baptist Missionary Society, and correspondence and reports of missionaries active in Malawi, Guyana, and Jamaica. Slides, filmstrips, and photographs supplement the manuscript collection, particularly for the period since 1950.

SEE ALSO: Peter Duignan, *Handbook of American Resources for African Studies* (Hoover Institution, 1967); Robert O. Collins and Peter Duignan, *Americans in Africa* (Hoover Institution, 1963).

RI910-880

Westerly Public Library
Broad Street
Westerly RI 02891

(401) 596-2877

OPEN: M-W 8-9, Th 8-5, F-Sa 8-2; closed Sundays and holidays
COPYING FACILITIES: yes
MATERIALS SOLICITED: Any historical, genealogical or graphic material relating to Westerly.

HOLDINGS:
    Total volume: 2,500 items
    Inclusive dates: 1661 -
    Description: Historical and genealogical manuscript material relating primarily to Westerly as well as neighboring Hopkinton and Stonington. Collection includes Indian-colonial deeds and land disputes, account books, business records, diaries, letters, military commissions, tax and school records, whaling logs, family papers and genealogies. Includes materials of the Noyes family, Steadman family, and related Dorr Rebellion material, the Frederick Denison collection and the records of the Westerly Rifle Company; also letters and manuscripts of Margaret Wise Brown and glass plate negatives (1895-1925) of local photographer J. H. Burk.

SEE: Hinding.

WOONSOCKET

RI945-760

The Pilgrim John Howland Society, Inc.
73 Pound Hill Road
North Smithfield
Woonsocket RI 02895

(401) 762-0162

OPEN: by appointment
COPYING FACILITIES: no
MATERIALS SOLICITED: Genealogical materials relating to new members of the Society, who must be descendants of John Howland.

HOLDINGS:
Total volume: 1,650 items
Inclusive dates: 1680 -
Description: Genealogical materials relating to members of the Society, all descendants of John Howland; correspondence and land deeds of the Howland family, 1680-early 1700's; and business records of the Society, 1897- .

The above address is the mailing address. The repository is located at Howland House, 33 Sandwich Street, Plymouth, MA 02360

RI945-800

Union Saint-Jean-Baptiste
Bibliotheque Mallet
1 Social Street
Woonsocket RI 02895

(401) 769-0520

OPEN: M-F 8:30-4:30; closed weekends and holidays
COPYING FACILITIES: no
MATERIALS SOLICITED: Materials relating to Franco-American history, biography, and societies. Will also accept papers and theses dealing with Franco-American, French Canadian and French topics, and copies of genealogies of French ancestry.

HOLDINGS:
Total volume: 800 items
Inclusive dates: 1870 -
Description: Letters and manuscript notes relating to the French ethnic *survivance* in the United States; Roman Catholic missionary work in the Northwest; the Oregon missions and the Whitman Massacre; Archbishop J. B. Lamy's history of the Pueblos of New Mexico; Louis Riel; Gabriel Dumont; and the Metis. Also included are reports of U.S. Indian Inspector Edmond Mallet to the Department of the Interior.

SOUTH CAROLINA

Since 1968 the South Carolina Department of Archives and History in Columbia has administered a statewide program for preserving local public records. Local governments may retain custody of their records, but the Archives Department is acquiring microfilm copies or originals of all permanently valuable records generated by counties prior to 1900 (1920 for land records). It now has substantial holdings for many of the State's 46 counties.

County and municipal records at the Archives Department total more than 3,600 cubic feet of original documents and 9,000 reels of microfilm copies. Microfilm holdings include pre-1920 land and pre-1920 probate records of counties, some of which were filmed by the Church of Jesus Christ of Latter-day Saints. The Archives Department's holdings of local public records are described in its publication, revised in 1976: *The South Carolina Archives: A Temporary Summary Guide.*

BEAUFORT

SC54-80
Beaufort County Library
710 Craven Street
Beaufort SC 29902

(803) 525-7279

OPEN: M-F 9-8, Sa 10-5; closed Sundays and holidays
COPYING FACILITIES: yes
MATERIALS SOLICITED: Items pertaining to the history of Beaufort and Beaufort County. Will also accept materials relevant to South Carolina history and local genealogy.

HOLDINGS:
Total volume: not specified
Inclusive dates: 1795 -
Description: A collection of materials relating to the history of Beaufort and Beaufort County. Included are 19th century letters of a local family, copies of papers presented before the Beaufort County Historical Society, minutes of the city of Beaufort, records of two fire companies, records of the Beaufort College and Female Seminary, and photographs and scrapbooks on the history of the community.

BENNETTSVILLE

SC72-510
Marlborough County Library
Market Street
Bennettsville SC 29512

(803) 479-6201

OPEN: M 1-9, Tu-Sa 9-5; closed Sundays and holidays and Dec. 24 and 26
COPYING FACILITIES: yes
MATERIALS SOLICITED: Materials on the history of Marlboro County. Will also accept government reports in such fields as zoning and statistics.

HOLDINGS:
Total volume: 21 l.f.
Inclusive dates: 1800's -
Description: Materials relating to Marlboro County, including genealogical data on County families; church histories and records; minutes of school board meetings; minutes of local organization meetings; cemetery records; materials on County pioneers and early homes; sketches of County citizens; ministers' daybooks; papers and addresses prepared by local residents; marriage and death notices; and probated wills.

SEE ALSO: John Hammond Moore, *Research Materials in South Carolina: A Guide* (Univ. of South Carolina Press, 1967).

CAMDEN

SC108-100
Camden Archives
1314 Broad Street
Camden SC 29020

(803) 432-3242

OPEN: M-F 8-5, Sa, Su 1-5; closed holidays
COPYING FACILITIES: yes
MATERIALS SOLICITED: Historical and genealogical materials regarding Camden, Kershaw County, and the State of South Carolina. Will also accept some materials of National interest.

HOLDINGS:
Total volume: 2,800 items
Inclusive dates: 1690 -
Description: Materials relating primarily to local and state history. Included are government records, such as a Charleston ledger, 1796-1800; Camden city ordinances, 1792-1886; Camden City Council minutes, 1865-1890; and records of wills in Kershaw County, 1770-1853. There are papers of Revolutionary War Colonel Joseph Kershaw and of Confederate General Joseph Brevard Kershaw.

Early records of the Kershaw County Medical Society, 1866-1951; early insurance records of the Kennedy Insurance Agency, 1876-1942; a weather book of Major J. M. DeSaussure, 1858-1876; and a minute book of The Hebrew Benevolent Association of Camden, 1877-1935.

CHARLESTON

SC144-70
Bethel United Methodist Church
57 Pitt Street
Charleston SC 29401

(803) 723-4587

OPEN: by appointment only
ACCESS: serious researchers interested in church history
COPYING FACILITIES: yes
MATERIALS SOLICITED: Materials relating to Bethel United Methodist Church and to persons currently or formerly members, clergy, or officers of the church.

HOLDINGS:
Total volume: 8 l.f.
Inclusive dates: 1824 -
Description: Papers and records pertaining to the history of Bethel United Methodist Church, including volumes of minutes, 1848- , and membership records, 1851- .

SC144-90
Carolina Art Association
Gibbes Art Gallery
135 Meeting Street
Charleston SC 29401

(803) 722-2706

OPEN: Tu-F 10-4:30; closed other days
ACCESS: appointment required to see anything not on display
COPYING FACILITIES: yes
MATERIALS SOLICITED: Miniatures reference materials; other archival material relating to collection, especially Charleston artists, and photographs of Charleston.

HOLDINGS:
Total volume: 6 file drawers
Inclusive dates: 1800 -
Description: Journals of Alice Ravenel Huger Smith, an account book of Charles Fraser, a collection of approximately 500 glass negatives and photographs by Charleston photographer George Johnson, records of the Dock Street Theater, and records of the Carolina Art Association.

SEE: Hinding.

SC144-100
Charleston County Library
South Carolina Room
404 King Street
Charleston SC 29403

(803) 723-1645

OPEN: Sept. - May, Su 3-6, M-Th 10-9,
F, Sa 10-6; closed holidays and
Sundays June - Aug.
ACCESS: college age or older
COPYING FACILITIES: yes
MATERIALS SOLICITED: Materials relating
to the Charleston area and South Caro-
lina history, genealogy, law, arts or bi-
ography.

HOLDINGS:
Total volume: 400 l.f.; 60 file drawers
Inclusive dates: 1670 -
Description: Materials relating to the
history of South Carolina and its laws,
culture, institutions, and people. Included
are transcriptions of wills, birth and
death records, newspaper clippings, and
reports.

SC144-105
Charleston Division of Archives and
Records
100 Broad Street, Suite 300
Charleston SC 29401

MAILING ADDRESS:
Box 304
Charleston SC 29402

(803) 724-7302

OPEN: M-F 9-5; closed weekends and
holidays
COPYING FACILITIES: yes
MATERIALS SOLICITED: Records relating
to the history and current administration of the municipal government of
Charleston. Will also accept records
pertaining to the history and culture of
the Charleston area.

HOLDINGS:
Total volume: 275 c.f.
Inclusive dates: 1671 -
Description: Collections covering the
history and current administration of the
City of Charleston's government, its department, and outside interests. Included
are papers of the mayors of the city,
1800- ; Clerk of the Council records, including ordinances, 1773- ; yearbooks of
the City of Charleston, 1881-1951; scrapbooks, 1930-79; deeds to and from the
city council, 1800-1960.
Assessor's Office records, including
ward books, 1852-1956; list of the tax-
payers of the City of Charleston, 1858;
business licenses, 1872-1976; Department
of Public Service records, including City
Engineer's plat book, 1691-1951; maps
and plats, pre-1900; journal of Commissioners of Streets and Lamps, 1806-66;
building permits, 1832- .
Department of Administrative Service
records, including audit reports, 1923-73;
annual budgets, 1958- ; annual reports of
the Controller, 1924-79; materials relating
to the 1886 earthquake; Charleston Orphan House records, including minutes,
1790-1964; registers and indenture books,
1790-1949; medical reports, 1862-1957;
financial records, 1790-1970; Poor House

records, including minutes, 1801-1916;
records of other city departments; and
general files on the history of Charleston,
1670- .

SEE: Hinding.

SC144-130
Charleston Library Society
164 King Street
Charleston SC 29401

(803) 723-9912

OPEN: M-F 9:30-5:30, Sa 9:30-2; closed
Sundays and holidays
USER FEES: one dollar per day, $3 for
two weeks, or $5 per month for
non-members
COPYING FACILITIES: yes
MATERIALS SOLICITED: Will accept materials pertaining to South Carolina, the
colonial period, or the Civil War.

HOLDINGS:
Total volume: 30 l.f.; 2 file cabinets
Inclusive dates: 16th century - 20th
century
Description: Collections covering all as-
pects of life in South Carolina. Included
are records of the Huguenots and the
Protestant Episcopal Diocese of South
Carolina, Charleston tax and police
records, minute books and papers of
Charleston organizations, and literary
manuscripts, including Porgy, by DuBose
Heyward. There are also diaries, account
books, and letters of such men as George
Washington, John Paul Jones, John C.
Calhoun, John Rutledge, and Wade
Hampton, III.

SEE: Hamer.

SEE: Martin; Hinding; Robbins.

SC144-140
Charleston Museum
121 Rutledge Street
Charleston SC 29401

no telephone

SEE: Hamer.

Questionnaire not returned.

SC144-150
The Citadel
Archives-Museum
Charleston SC 29409

(803) 792-6846

OPEN: M-F 8:30-5; closed weekends and
holidays
ACCESS: prior arrangements preferred
COPYING FACILITIES: yes
MATERIALS SOLICITED: Materials pertaining to The Citadel. Will also accept
historical and literary materials pertaining to South Carolina history and military history.

HOLDINGS:
Total volume: 1,200 c.f.
Inclusive dates: 1842 -
Description: Archives of The Citadel;
Civil War diaries; materials relating to
the South Carolina Poetry Society; photographs; microfilm; film; videotapes; and
research papers of historian Bruce Catton. Personal paper collections include

those of military leaders Mark W. Clark,
Hugh P. Harris, Charles P. Summerall,
William C. Westmoreland, and Friedrich
Ruge (including Erwin Rommel diaries),
as well as L. Mendel Rivers.

SEE: NUCMC, 1971.

SEE: Allard, Crawley and Edmison;
Paszek; Meckler and McMullin.

SC144-170
College of Charleston
Library
Department of Archives and
Manuscripts
Charleston SC 29424

(803) 792-8016

OPEN: M-F 8-5; closed weekends,
holidays, and University breaks
COPYING FACILITIES: yes
MATERIALS SOLICITED: Manuscript material concerning College history, including papers of the faculty, alumni,
trustees, administrators, and friends of
the College; materials relating to the
history of the South Carolina Low
Country, particularly its cultural and
social development, and its black communities.

HOLDINGS:
Total volume: 600 l.f.
Inclusive dates: 1667 -
Description: A collection of 19th century musicians' letters, materials on
camellia culture, papers pertaining to
prominent South Carolina families, faculty papers, meteorological records, architectural drawings, photographs,
1886-1974, oral history tapes concerning
black history, and the College archives.

GUIDES: Ralph Melnick, 'College of
Charleston Special Collections: A
Guide to its Holdings,' South Carolina
Historical Magazine 81 (April 1980).

SEE: Hamer.

SEE: Robbins.

SEE ALSO: Lorenzo J. Greene,
'Manuscripts,' Negro History Bulletin
30 (Oct. 1967).

SC144-190
Diocese of Charleston
Charleston Diocesan Archives
114 (rear) Broad Street
Charleston SC 29401

MAILING ADDRESS:
P.O. Box 818
Charleston SC 29402

(803) 722-8153

OPEN: M-F 9:30-4; closed weekends and
holidays
ACCESS: by appointment
COPYING FACILITIES: no

HOLDINGS:
Total volume: 52 c.f.
Inclusive dates: 1790 - 1969
Description: Correspondence of bish-
ops of the Diocese of Charleston, and
materials relating to the history of 200
Roman Catholic parishes and missions in
South Carolina.

SC144-520

Medical University of South Carolina
Health Affairs Library
Waring Historical Library
80 Barre Street
Charleston SC 29401

(803) 792-2288

OPEN: M-F 9-5; closed weekends and
holidays
COPYING FACILITIES: yes
MATERIALS SOLICITED: Materials concerning the history of South Carolina
medicine.

HOLDINGS:
Total volume: 65 l.f.
Inclusive dates: 1736 -
Description: Manuscripts, including
doctors' daybooks, account books, prescription books, scrapbooks, letters, lecture notes, theses, and diplomas. Hospital
admission books and photographs of
South Carolina physicians are also included.

SEE: NUCMC, 1959-62, 70.

SEE: Hinding.

SC144-710

St. Michael's Episcopal Church
14 St. Michael's Alley
Charleston SC 29401

(803) 723-0603

OPEN: by appointment only
MATERIALS SOLICITED: Will accept
manuscript and printed material pertaining to the history of St. Michael's
Episcopal Church and its clergy and
members.

HOLDINGS:
Total volume: 20 l.f.
Inclusive dates: 1751 -
Description: Records including parish
registers, 1862- ; private registers of the
Rev. Paul Trapier, 1827-64 and the Rev.
Thomas Young, 1843-51; minutes of the
vestry, 1758- ; financial records, including
pew indentures and payments, vouchers
and bills for building the church,
1751-61, and glebe property leases,
1771-1841; service records; Sunday
school records; parish reports.
Scrapbooks; minutes of church organizations; manuscripts of hymns and songs
composed by Jacob Eckherd, organist,
1809-33; Robert Mills's plan for contem-
plated additions to the church, 1804; and
miscellaneous correspondence and photographs.

SC144-730

South Carolina Historical Society
100 Meeting Street
Charleston SC 29401

(803) 723-3225

OPEN: M-F 8:30-4; closed weekends and
holidays
USER FEES: free to members ($20 annual
fee) and scholars; $5 daily fee for
non-members
ACCESS: no students under 18 without
special permission
COPYING FACILITIES: yes

MATERIALS SOLICITED: Manuscripts,
photographs, and other materials relating to the history of South Carolina.

HOLDINGS:
Total volume: 1,200 l.f.
Inclusive dates: 1520 -
Description: Materials relating chiefly
to South Carolina, especially Charleston
and the coastal region, with emphasis on
the 18th and 19th centuries. Included are
correspondence, diaries, travel journals,
and related papers of planters,
businesspersons, scientists, artistic and literary figures, and government officials;
records of local governments, churches,
businesses, plantations, and social organizations; genealogical data; manuscript
maps and plats; architectural drawings;
and photographs.

GUIDES: David Moltke-Hansen and Sallie
Dosher, *South Carolina Historical Society Manuscript Guide* (1979).

SEE: Hamer; NUCMC, 1963-65.

SEE: Ingram; Allard, Crawley, and
Edmison; Hinding; Robbins.

SEE ALSO: John Hammond Moore, *Re-
search Materials in South Carolina: A
Guide* (Univ. of South Carolina Press,
1967); Walter Schatz, ed., *Directory of
Afro-American Resources* (Bowker,
1970); 'Manuscript Collections of the
South Carolina Historical Society,'
South Carolina Historical Magazine 78
(July 1977).

CLEMSON

SC185-120

Clemson University
Robert Muldrow Cooper Library
Special Collections
Clemson SC 29631

(803) 656-3031

OPEN: M-F 8-4:30; closed weekends,
holidays, and University breaks
COPYING FACILITIES: yes
MATERIALS SOLICITED: Will accept material relating to South Carolina.

HOLDINGS:
Total volume: 503 l.f.
Inclusive dates: 1762 -
Description: Manuscript collections relating chiefly to South Carolina. The
greater proportion consists of collections
of papers of South Carolinians distinguished for their service in official
capacities, such as John C. Calhoun, Benjamin R. Tillman, Edgar A. Brown,
James F. Byrnes, and Strom Thurmond.
Also included are papers of several State
agricultural societies.

SEE: Hamer; NUCMC, 1959-62 (as
Clemson Agricultural College), 77.

SEE: Allard, Crawley, and Edmison; Robbins.

SEE ALSO: John Hammond Moore, *Research Materials in South Carolina: A
Guide* (Univ. of South Carolina Press,
1967); David A. Hounshell, comp.,
*Manuscripts in U.S. Depositories Relat-
ing to the History of Electrical Science
and Technology* (Smithsonian Institution, n.d.).

COLUMBIA

SC216-110

Columbia Bible College
7435 Monticello Road
Columbia SC

MAILING ADDRESS:
P.O. Box 3122
Columbia SC 29203

(803) 754-4100

OPEN: M-F 8-10, Sa 9-5; closed Sundays,
Christmas, and New Year's
ACCESS: Columbia Bible College
students and alumni; others by special
permission only
COPYING FACILITIES: yes
MATERIALS SOLICITED: College history
and files.

HOLDINGS:
Total volume: not specified
Inclusive dates: 1920 -
Description: Records of Columbia Bi-
ble College, including information on
alumni activities.

SC216-720

South Carolina Department of
Archives and History
1430 Senate Street
Columbia SC 29201

MAILING ADDRESS:
P.O. Box 11669, Capitol Station
Columbia SC 29211

(803) 758-5816

OPEN: M-Sa 9-9, Su 1-9; closed holidays
COPYING FACILITIES: yes
MATERIALS SOLICITED: Official records
of South Carolina State and local government. Will also accept microfilm of
Federal records relating to South Carolina; microfilm of records relating to
the American Revolution and the Civil
War; and maps of South Carolina and
neighboring States.

HOLDINGS:
Total volume: 12,375 c.f.
Inclusive dates: 1671 -
Description: Almost all known public
records of South Carolina before 1785,
and nearly complete records of the State
government to 1940, as well as many
more recent records. Included are all pre-
1900 documents of permanent value, either in original form or on microfilm,
from 10 of 46 county courthouses. Holdings of other local government records,
although sometimes large, are less systematic.

GUIDES: Marion C. Chandler and Earl W.
Wade, *The South Carolina Archives: A
Temporary Summary Guide* (1976).

SEE: Hamer.

SEE: Allard, Crawley, and Edmison; Beers
- Confederate; Hinding; Ingram;
Leventhal and Mooney - III.

SEE ALSO: Walter Schatz, ed., *Directory of
Afro-American Resources* (Bowker,
1970); Richard C. Davis, *North American Forest History: A Guide to Archives
and Manuscripts in the United States
and Canada* (Clio Books, 1977); John

Hammond Moore, *Research Materials in South Carolina: A Guide* (Univ. of South Carolina Press, 1967); Charles E. Lee and Ruth S. Green, 'A Guide to the Upper House Journals of the South Carolina General Assembly, 1721-1775,' 'A Guide to South Carolina Council Journals, 1671-1775,' 'A Guide to the Commons House Journals of the South Carolina General Assembly, 1692-1721,' and 'A Guide to the Commons House Journals of the South Carolina General Assembly, 1721-1775,' *The South Carolina Historical Magazine* 67 (Oct. 1966), 68 (Jan., April, and July 1967).

SC216-800

University of South Carolina
Museums and Archives
Department of Archives and Records
  Management
McKissick Museums
Columbia SC 29208

(803) 777-7251

OPEN: M-F 9-4; Sept.-May, Su 1-5; closed other days and holidays
COPYING FACILITIES: yes
MATERIALS SOLICITED: University archives and papers of distinguished University alumni, faculty, staff, and trustees. Will also accept University-related records and manuscripts.

HOLDINGS:
  Total volume: 1,500 c.f.
  Inclusive dates: 1801 -
  Description: Trustee minutes, faculty minutes, presidential archives, other university records, and related manuscripts and photographs.

SEE ALSO: A preliminary guide is available from the institution.

SC216-820

University of South Carolina
South Caroliniana Library
Manuscripts Division
Columbia SC 29208

(803) 777-5183

OPEN: M-F 8:30-5, Sa 8:30-1; closed Sundays and holidays
COPYING FACILITIES: yes
MATERIALS SOLICITED: Materials relating to South Carolina.

HOLDINGS:
  Total volume: 2,200,000 items
  Inclusive dates: 1670 -
  Description: A collection relating chiefly to South Carolina persons, families, institutions and organizations, including diaries, plantation and business account books, and original and typescript copies of church records and epitaphs.

SEE: Hamer; NUCMC, 1959-62, 66-67, 69-72, 74, 76, 78, 81.

SEE: Allard, Crawley, and Edmison; Beers - Confederate; Hinding; Leventhal and Mooney - III; Robbins.

SEE ALSO: Thomas H. English, *Roads to Research: Distinguished Library Collections of the Southeast* (Univ. of Georgia Press, 1968); John Hammond Moore, *Research Materials in South Carolina: A Guide* (Univ. of South Carolina Press, 1967); Walter Schatz, ed., *Directory of Afro-American Resources* (Bowker, 1970); Richard C. Davis, *North American Forest History: A Guide to Archives and Manuscripts in the United States and Canada* (Clio Books, 1977); Ann Novotny, ed., *Picture Sources 3* (Special Libraries Assn., 1975); John R. Welsh, 'The Charles Carroll Sims Collection,' *South Atlantic Bulletin* (Nov. 1966).

DARLINGTON

SC270-160

Darlington County Historical
  Commission
Room 307, Darlington County
  Courthouse
Darlington SC 29532

(803) 393-8106

OPEN: M-F 9-5; closed weekends and holidays
COPYING FACILITIES: yes
MATERIALS SOLICITED: Photographs, documents, and manuscripts concerning Darlington County. Will also accept maps of the region showing the Darlington County area.

HOLDINGS:
  Total volume: 800 c.f.
  Inclusive dates: 1735 -
  Description: Unpublished histories, diaries, farm and business journals, private and business letters, and lodge and society minute books, all relating to Darlington County.

SEE: Hinding.

DUE WEST

SC306-200

Erskine College
McCain Library
Due West SC 29639

(803) 379-8898

OPEN: M-F 8:30-4:30; closed weekends and holidays
ACCESS: qualified researchers; appointment required
COPYING FACILITIES: yes
MATERIALS SOLICITED: Associated Reformed Presbyterian church records, Erskine College records, memoirs and family histories of persons and families associated with the Associated Reformed Presbyterian church, Erskine College, or Abbeville County.

HOLDINGS:
  Total volume: 46 l.f.
  Inclusive dates: 1733 -
  Description: Associated Reformed Presbyterian church and Erskine College records; the diary of John Pratt, a Leveland, SC, farmer; genealogical records of several South Carolina families; and memoirs and sermons of various individuals associated with the Associated Reformed Presbyterian church.

FLORENCE

SC378-250

Francis Marion College
Rogers Library
Archives
Florence SC 29501

(803) 669-4121

OPEN: M-F 8:30-5; closed weekends and holidays
COPYING FACILITIES: yes
MATERIALS SOLICITED: Materials relating to the college, including official records and papers of the faculty, staff and trustees. Will also accept papers of private citizens and community organizations relating to the founding or development of the College.

HOLDINGS:
  Total volume: 100 c.f.
  Inclusive dates: 1956 -
  Description: Archives of the College, including correspondence, administrative records, publications, scrapbooks, tapes, and slides.

GAFFNEY

SC414-110

Cherokee County Public Library
300 East Rutledge Street
Gaffney SC 29340

(803) 489-4381

OPEN: M-F 10-8, Sa 10-4; closed Sundays and holidays
COPYING FACILITIES: yes

HOLDINGS:
  Total volume: 200 photographs
  Inclusive dates: 1890 - 1940
  Description: Photographic work of Mr. June H. Carr, a professional photographer, recording life in Gaffney and Cherokee county.

GREENVILLE

SC450-240

Furman University
Library
Special Collections
Greenville SC 29613

(803) 294-2194

OPEN: M-F 8:30-4:30; closed weekends and holidays
COPYING FACILITIES: yes
MATERIALS SOLICITED: South Carolina Baptist materials and materials related to Furman University.

HOLDINGS:
  Total volume: 15,000 items
  Inclusive dates: 1730's -
  Description: Manuscripts relating to the history of Baptists in South Carolina, and Furman University archives. Included are files of the printed minutes of the

Baptist associations and annals of the South Carolina Baptist Convention, microfilmed records of South Carolina Baptist churches, biographical files on South Carolina Baptists and Furman alumni and faculty, files on individual Baptist churches, photographs, and a few oral history tapes.

SEE: NUCMC, 1963-66, 68.

SEE: Schatz.

LATTA

SC540-200

Ebenezer Memorial and Historical Association
Old Ebenezer Church
Junction of Highways 501 and 38
Latta SC

MAILING ADDRESS:
P.O. Box 281
Latta SC 29565

(803) 271-7901

OPEN: third Sunday in June, other times by appointment
COPYING FACILTIES: no
MATERIALS SOLICITED: Records of Old Ebenezer Church. Will also accept materials relating to Marion County churches and families.

HOLDINGS:
Total volume: 10 c.f.
Inclusive dates: 1786 -
Description: Records of Old Ebenezer Church and local cemetery records and genealogical materials.

LEXINGTON

SC576-480

Lexington County Museum
230 Fox Street
Lexington SC

MAILING ADDRESS:
P.O. Box 637
Lexington SC 29072

(803) 359-8369

OPEN: Tu-Sa 10-4, Su 2-4; closed Mondays and holidays
ACCESS: Museum must be notified at least 30 days prior to arrival of researcher
COPYING FACILITIES: no
MATERIALS SOLICITED: Manuscripts dealing with the history of Lexington County.

HOLDINGS:
Total volume: 1,495 items
Inclusive dates: 1820 - 1880's
Description: Personal papers of John Fox, planter, county official and lawyer of Lexington County. Included are copies of official legal documents, court records, estate records, receipts, and inventories and business records of the management of plantation and civic affairs, relating primarily to socio-economic conditions in Lexington County before the Civil War.

NEWBERRY

SC684-550

Newberry College
Wessels Library
Special Collection
Newberry SC 29108

(803) 276-5010

OPEN: Su 2-10, M-Th 8:30-10:30, F 8:30-5, Sa 10-4; closed holidays; variable summer hours
COPYING FACILITIES: yes
MATERIALS SOLICITED: Local family histories. Will also accept South Caroliniana and Lutheran church histories and records.

HOLDINGS:
Total volume: 100 l.f.
Inclusive dates: 1690 -
Description: College records, including correspondence, account books, and financial records, as well as local history and genealogy.

ORANGEBURG

SC720-120

Claflin College
H. V. Manning Library
Orangeburg SC 29115

(803) 534-2710, Ext. 56

OPEN: by appointment; closed holidays and June-Aug.
ACCESS: researchers must notify Librarian a day in advance of visit
COPYING FACILITIES: yes
MATERIALS SOLICITED: Materials concerning Claflin College, its students, alumni, and faculty, and the United Methodist church. Will also accept faculty dissertations, manuscripts of well-known writers, and materials concerning persons associated with the College.

HOLDINGS:
Total volume: not specified
Inclusive dates: 1888 -
Description: Photographs of the College's six presidents and their administrations, 1869- , including faculty, students, and buildings, in addition to a collection of catalogs, yearbooks, newspaper clippings, school programs, minutes of faculty meetings, alumni bulletins, and other Claflin College records.

SEE: Schatz.

SC720-710

South Carolina State College
Miller F. Whittaker Library
South Carolina State College Historical Collection
Orangeburg SC

MAILING ADDRESS:
P.O. Box 1991
Orangeburg SC 29117

(803) 536-7045, 7046

OPEN: M-Th 8:30-10, F 8:30-6, Sa 8:30-5, Su 12-8; shorter hours between academic sessions; closed holidays

COPYING FACILITIES: yes
MATERIALS SOLICITED: Papers of graduates, faculty, and staff. Will also accept materials pertaining to history of blacks in South Carolina, with special emphasis on Orangeburg.

HOLDINGS:
Total volume: not specified
Inclusive dates: 1896 -
Description: College records, presidential papers, photographs, blueprints, College publications such as newspapers and yearbooks, oral history recordings, and other materials documenting the development of South Carolina State College.

SEE: Schatz.

PENDLETON

SC738-640

Pendleton District Historical and Recreational Commission
Research Division
125 East Queen Street
Pendleton SC

MAILING ADDRESS:
P.O. Box 234
Pendleton SC 29670

(803) 646-3782

OPEN: M-F 9-4:30; closed weekends and holidays
COPYING FACILITIES: yes
MATERIALS SOLICITED: Materials relating to the Cherokee Indian tribe before 1812, the American Revolution in the South Carolina upcountry, the Pendleton District in northwestern South Carolina, and Anderson, Oconee, and Pickens counties, which were formed from the District in 1826. Will also accept other materials pertinent to South Carolina history.

HOLDINGS:
Total volume: 250 l.f.
Inclusive dates: 1750 -
Description: Documents relating primarily to the area of the Pendleton District. Materials consist of 2,000 photographs, 1860 to date, as well as letters, diaries, and a manuscript history of agriculture in South Carolina.

SEE: Hinding.

ROCK HILL

SC774-880

Winthrop College
Dacus Library
Archives and Special Collections Department
Rock Hill SC 29733

(803) 323-2131, Ext. 28

OPEN: M-F 8:30-5; closed weekends, Thanksgiving, Christmas, and July 4
COPYING FACILITIES: yes
MATERIALS SOLICITED: Non-current records of Winthrop College; personal and professional papers of faculty, alumni and administrative offices; local history related to York County, SC;

and women's history, especially 20th century clubs and organizations. Will also accept papers and records which may have historical importance, but which would otherwise be lost without an attempt to preserve them.

HOLDINGS:
    Total volume: 701 l.f.; 1,320 vols.; 184 oral history tapes
    Inclusive dates: 1785 -
    Description: Official and quasi-official records of Winthrop College, documenting its history from 1886 to date. Included is information on higher education, especially that of women. There are also manuscripts and related documents on individuals, families, and organizations in York County and the surrounding area, as well as on the history of women in South Carolina.

GUIDES: Ron Chepesink, *The Winthrop College Archives and Special Collections: A Guide to the Records Relating to the History of Winthrop College* (1979).

SEE: NUCMC, 1974, 76-77, 79.

SEE: Hinding.

SEE ALSO: inventories to each collection available upon request.

ST. MATTHEWS

SC792-120
Calhoun County Museum
Archives and Research
303 Butler Street
St. Matthews SC 29135

(803) 874-3964

OPEN: M-F 10-5; closed weekends and holidays
COPYING FACILITIES: yes
MATERIALS SOLICITED: Records relating to Calhoun County, particularly before 1865, including court house records, ledgers, diaries, letters and family Bible records.

HOLDINGS:
    Total volume: not specified
    Inclusive dates: 1732 -
    Description: Materials relating to the original Orangeburg District and genealogical data pertaining to the entire state of South Carolina.

SEE: Hinding.

SPARTANBURG

SC846-730
Spartanburg County Public Library
333 South Pine Street
Spartanburg SC 29302

MAILING ADDRESS:
Box 2409
Spartanburg SC 29302

(803) 596-3505

OPEN: M-F 9-9, Sa 9-6, Su 2-5; closed June-August and holidays

SEE: Hamer.

Questionnaire not returned.

SC846-890
Wofford College
Sandor Teszler Library
Archives Department
Spartanburg SC 29301

(803) 585-4821

OPEN: M-F 9-3:30; closed weekends and holidays
COPYING FACILITIES: yes
MATERIALS SOLICITED: Material relevant to the history of Wofford College and the South Carolina Conference of the United Methodist church.

HOLDINGS:
    Total volume: 690 l.f.; 1,575 vols.
    Inclusive dates: 1795 -
    Description: Records of the Historical Society of the South Carolina Conference of the United Methodist Church, including minutes, reports, journals, letters, and other papers; archives of Wofford College, including papers of some of its presidents and faculty members, financial records, photographs, records of literary societies, and oral history; and the rough draft manuscript of *Scarlet Sister Mary,* by Julia Peterkin.

SEE: Hamer; NUCMC, 1966.

SEE: Hinding.

SEE ALSO: John Hammond Moore, *Research Materials in South Carolina: A Guide* (Univ. of South Carolina Press, 1967).

SULLIVAN'S ISLAND

SC860-600
Old Slave Mart Museum
Black Heritage Research Center
412 Station 14 Street
Sullivan's Island SC

MAILING ADDRESS:
P.O. Box 446
Sullivan's Island SC 29482

(803) 883-3797

OPEN: by appointment; closed June - Sept.
ACCESS: serious scholars at the discretion of the institution
COPYING FACILITIES: yes
MATERIALS SOLICITED: Materials pertinent to the cultural history of Afro-Americans and slavery, especially slave craftspeople. Will also accept materials on South Carolina and Charleston history, including photographs and data concerning Charleston architecture.

HOLDINGS:
    Total volume: 3,000 items; 50 boxes
    Inclusive dates: 1765 -
    Description: Materials concerned with Afro-American and African cultural history, particularly slavery; South Carolina history; Charleston architecture; and the history of the Old Slave Mart Museum. Included are correspondence, diaries, logbooks, business and financial records, genealogical source data, literary manuscripts, and public documents. Audio-visual items consist of manuscript maps, photographs, motion pictures, oral history recordings and transcripts, and recorded music.

GUIDES: *Catalog of the Old Slave Mart Museum and Library* (G. K. Hall, 1977).

SEE: Novotny; Schatz.

SOUTH DAKOTA

Since 1974 authority for local public records preservation in South Dakota has rested with the Archives Resource Center of the Department of Education and Cultural Affairs in Pierre. Local governments normally retain custody of their permanently significant records, but the Archives holds a substantial amount of probate, tax, and other county records.

ABERDEEN

SD18-40
Alexander Mitchell Public Library
South Dakota Collection
519 South Kline Street
Aberdeen SD 57401

(605) 225-4186

OPEN: M-Th 9-9, F 9-6, Sa 9-5; closed Sundays and holidays
COPYING FACILITIES: yes
MATERIALS SOLICITED: Items dealing with the history of Aberdeen and Brown County, including family histories. Will also accept historical or genealogical materials from surrounding counties in North and South Dakota, and items of importance to Dakota Territory history.

HOLDINGS:
Total volume: 20 l.f.
Inclusive dates: 1880 -
Description: Photographs, oral history recordings, club minute books and scrapbooks, correspondence, unpublished manuscripts and early township school records, all relating to Aberdeen and Brown County history.

SD18-160
Dacotah Prairie Museum
21 South Main Street
Aberdeen SD

MAILING ADDRESS:
P.O. Box 395
Aberdeen SD 57401

(605) 229-1608

OPEN: M-F 9-5, Sa, Su 1-4; closed holidays
ACCESS: by appointment
COPYING FACILITIES: yes
MATERIALS SOLICITED: Materials concerning early Brown County history and regional history, 1800-1930, including school records, diaries, oral histories, business account books, and photographs. Will also accept correspondence, manuscript documents, and church and organization records relating to the plains-prairie region.

HOLDINGS:
Total volume: not specified
Inclusive dates: 1797 - 1930
Description: Materials relating to northeastern South Dakota. Included are ledgers, photographs, school records, oral histories, records of organizations and businesses, and letters and manuscripts of missionaries in the area, 1860-80.
Also includes blueprints of Brown County public and private buildings.

SEE: Hinding.

BRANDT

SD41-160
Deuel County Historical Museum
Brandt SD 57218

(605) 876-3461

OPEN: by appointment only
COPYING FACILITIES: no
MATERIALS SOLICITED: Materials relating to Brandt County, to South Dakota, and to the territories of Minnesota, Iowa, and South Dakota.

HOLDINGS:
Total volume: not specified
Inclusive dates: 1870's - 1960's
Description: A small photograph collection of homesteads, Dakota Territory legislators, and Brandt (District 50) School buildings and people.

BROOKINGS

SD54-715
South Dakota State University
Hilton M. Briggs Library
Archives
Brookings SD 57007

(605) 688-5106

OPEN: by appointment only
COPYING FACILITIES: yes
MATERIALS SOLICITED: Records of South Dakota State University and associated organizations, including student clubs, and the papers of outstanding faculty and alumni. Will also accept collections of regional interest.

HOLDINGS:
Total volume: 20 c.f.
Inclusive dates: 1880's - 1970's
Description: Records of South Dakota State University, including its extension service and experiment station. Materials include faculty meeting minutes, early photographs of the university, and locally produced films and manuscripts of alumnus outdoor writer, Bert Popowski.

DE SMET

SD126-480
Laura Ingalls Wilder Memorial Society Inc.
De Smet SD

MAILING ADDRESS:
Box 344
De Smet SD 57231

(605) 584-2013

OPEN: daily 9-5; closed Sept. 16-May 29
USER FEES: $1.50
COPYING FACILITIES: no

HOLDINGS:
Total volume: not specified
Inclusive dates: 1930's - 1957
Description: Records relating to Laura Ingalls Wilder and her family including correspondence, maps, and the manuscript of Wilder in the West.

DEADWOOD

SD144-160
Deadwood Public Library
Centennial Archives
435 Williams Street
Deadwood SD 57732

(605) 578-2821

OPEN: M-F 12:30-8:30, Sa 12:30-5; closed Sundays and holidays
COPYING FACILITIES: yes
MATERIALS SOLICITED: Photographs and manuscript material on Deadwood, Lead, and the northern Black Hills of South Dakota. Will also accept oral history tapes.

HOLDINGS:
Total volume: 4,000 items; 1 box; 1 l.f.
Inclusive dates: 1875 -
Description: Photographs and manuscripts on Deadwood, Lead, and the northern Black Hills of South Dakota. Included are photographs relating to railroads, family records, memoirs of members of the Society of Black Hills Pioneers, and other recollections and reminiscences.

EUREKA

SD153-200
Eureka Pioneer Museum of
  McPherson County
1610 J Avenue
Eureka SD 57437

(605) 284-2711

OPEN: W-F 9-5, Sa, Su 2-5; closed M,
  Tu and Nov. 15 to Apr. 15
COPYING FACILITIES: no
MATERIALS SOLICITED: History of local
  organizations. Will also accept other
  material relating to the area, including
  pictures.

HOLDINGS:
  Total volume: 126 sq. ft.
  Inclusive dates: not specified
  Description: Records relating to
  McPherson County, especially schools.

FREEMAN

SD234-250
Freeman Junior College
Library
Historical Library
748 South Main Street
Freeman SD 57029

(605) 925-4237

OPEN: M, W, F 8-5, Tu, Th 8-10; closed
  weekends, Easter, Thanksgiving, and 2
  weeks at Christmas; summer hours by
  appointment only
COPYING FACILITIES: yes
MATERIALS SOLICITED: Manuscripts relating to pioneer Mennonites and
  Hutterian Brethren, primarily in South
  Dakota.

HOLDINGS:
  Total volume: 100 items
  Inclusive dates: 1876 -
  Description: Diaries, correspondence,
  pioneer reminiscences, genealogies, and
  church records relating to Mennonites
  and Hutterian Brethren in South Dakota
  and adjacent States.

LEAD

SD414-640
Phoebe Apperson Hearst Free Library
Box 880-309 West Main Street
Lead SD 57754

(605) 584-2013

OPEN: Tu-Th 1-9, F, Sa 1-5; closed
  Sundays, Mondays, and holidays
COPYING FACILITIES: yes

HOLDINGS:
  Total volume: 11 boxes
  Inclusive dates: 1919 -
  Description: The Ralph G. Cartwright
  collection, consisting of correspondence,
  photographs, and other materials related
  to research on George Armstrong Custer
  and the Battle of the Little Big Horn in
  1876.

MADISON

SD450-150
Dakota State College
Karl E. Mundt Library
Karl E. Mundt Archives
Madison SD 57042

(605) 256-5205

OPEN: M-F 8-5; closed weekends and
  holidays
COPYING FACILITIES: yes
MATERIALS SOLICITED: Will accept ma-
  terials relating to Senator Karl E.
  Mundt's career.

HOLDINGS:
  Total volume: 640 l.f.; 3,300 items
  Inclusive dates: 1924 -
  Description: A collection relating to
  Karl E. Mundt, U.S. Senator from South
  Dakota, including Mundt's office files
  and personal papers, his manuscript book
  on the Army-McCarthy hearings, photographs, oral history interviews with colleagues, and films and recordings of political speeches and hearings. The materials focus on Mundt's Congressional career, 1939-73, relating most strongly to
  the United Nations and foreign affairs,
  anti-Communist activities, and election
  campaigns.

SEE: NUCMC, 1978.

SEE ALSO: William Frank Zornow, 'The
  Karl E. Mundt Library, Dakota State
  College, Madison, South Dakota: A
  New Repository of Historical Material
  in the Great Plains Region,' *Serif* 9
  (Fall 1972); Richard C. Davis, *North
  American Forest History: A Guide to
  Archives and Manuscripts in the United
  States and Canada* (Clio Books, 1977).
  Indexes and inventories to the collec-
  tion are available at the Library.

MITCHELL

SD522-160
Dakota Wesleyan University
Layne Library
University Drive
Mitchell SD 57301

(605) 996-6511, Ext. 618

OPEN: M-F 8-5; closed holidays and
  weekends
COPYING FACILITIES: yes
MATERIALS SOLICITED: Materials relating
  to the early history of the region, including the Dakotas, Minnesota, Nebraska, Iowa, Montana, Wyoming, and
  south central Canada; and the political
  career of Senator Francis Case. Will
  also accept materials relating to poet
  Badger Clark and the history of the
  Methodist church in South Dakota.

HOLDINGS:
  Total volume: 250 file drawers
  Inclusive dates: 1745 -
  Description: Personal and professional
  papers of Senator Francis Case of South
  Dakota; oral history and manuscript collections covering the history of the Dakotas region, including maps and photographs; letters and manuscripts by Badger

Clark; and historical materials concerning
the United Methodist church in South
Dakota.

SD522-800
United Methodist Church
South Dakota Conference
Commission on Archives and History
1331 West University Avenue
Mitchell SD 57301

(605) 996-6552

OPEN: M-F 9-noon; closed weekends and
  holidays
COPYING FACILITIES: yes
MATERIALS SOLICITED: Secretarial
  records of Conference committees,
  records of defunct Methodist churches
  in South Dakota, and archives of Dakota Wesleyan University. Will also accept photographs.

HOLDINGS:
  Total volume: 20 l.f.
  Inclusive dates: 1636 -
  Description: The archives of the South
  Dakota Conference of the United Meth-
  odist church and of Dakota Wesleyan
  University.

OLDHAM

SD550-600
Oldham Library and Historical
  Association
Emil Loriks Heritage House
Oldham SD 57051

(605) 482-8659

OPEN: Su and Memorial Day 2-5, by
  appointment other times
ACCESS: advance arrangements required
COPYING FACILITIES: no
MATERIALS SOLICITED: Genealogical
  source data. Will also accept literary
  manuscripts, public documents, proclamations, petitions, diaries, journals and
  logbooks.

HOLDINGS:
  Total volume: 30 c.f.
  Inclusive dates: 1919 -
  Description: Materials concerning
  cooperatives, farm organizations, and the
  South Dakota state legislature; scrapbooks
  of Emil Loriks concerning cooperatives
  and other subjects; and World War I photographs.

PIERRE

SD558-710
South Dakota State Library &
  Archives
State Archives
800 North Illinois Avenue
Pierre SD 47501

(605) 773-3173

OPEN: M-F 8-5; closed weekends and
  holidays
COPYING FACILITIES: yes
MATERIALS SOLICITED: City, county, and
  State government records.

HOLDINGS:
Total volume: 1,000 c.f.
Inclusive dates: 1860 -
Description: State and local government records, primarily post-1900 materials.

GUIDES: Dennis F. Walle, *Guide to the South Dakota Archives Resource Center* (1979).

SEE: Svoboda and Dunning.

SD558-720

South Dakota Office of History
Historical Resource Center
Soldiers' Memorial Building
E. Capitol Avenue
Pierre SD 57501

(605) 773-3615

OPEN: M-F 8-5; closed weekends and holidays
COPYING FACILITIES: yes
MATERIALS SOLICITED: South Dakota history and related fields, such as the fur trade, cattle industry and Sioux Indians. Will also accept materials dealing with Dakota families or businesses.

HOLDINGS:
Total volume: 400 l.f.
Inclusive dates: 1840 -
Description: Manuscript collections relating chiefly to South Dakota and Dakota territorial history. Major topics include social, political and religious history, the fur trade, Sioux Indians and pioneer experiences. Included are the papers of individuals, records of organizations, official State government records, and several collections of ephemera. In addition, there are approximately 44,000 photographic images (photographs, glass plates and other negatives).

SEE: Hamer (as South Dakota State Historical Society); NUCMC, 1976-77, 79.

SEE: Hinding.

SEE ALSO: Clifton H. Jones, 'Manuscript Sources in Women's History at the Historical Resource Center,' *South Dakota History* 7 (Winter 1976), and 'Manuscript Sources on Religious History at the Historical Resource Center,' *South Dakota History* 8 (Summer 1977); Ann Novotny, ed., *Picture Sources 3* (Special Libraries Assn., 1975); Richard C. Davis, *North American Forest History: A Guide to Archives and Manuscripts in the United States and Canada* (Clio Books, 1977).

Collections are held jointly with the South Dakota State Historical Society.

RAPID CITY

SD648-690

Rapid City Public Library
610 Quincy
Rapid City SD

MAILING ADDRESS:
Box 3090
Rapid City SD 57701

(605) 394-4171

OPEN: M-Th 9-9, F, Sa 9-5:30; Su 1-5, Nov. - April; closed other days and holidays
COPYING FACILITIES: yes

HOLDINGS:
Total volume: 100 items
Inclusive dates: 1972
Description: Slides of the Rapid City flood of June 9, 1972.

SD648-710

South Dakota School of Mines and Technology
Devereaux Library
Rapid City SD 57701

(605) 394-2419

OPEN: Su 1-12, M-Th 7-12, F 7-5, Sa 10-4; closed holidays; shorter hours during summer, semester breaks, and vacations
USER FEES: non-faculty, students or staff $3 for two years
ACCESS: by permission of staff or Library Director
COPYING FACILITIES: yes
MATERIALS SOLICITED: Materials relating to the Black Hills of South Dakota and Wyoming; the West River area of South Dakota, including the Badlands; South Dakota history; and mining and related activities in the Black Hills area; and similar materials in connection with the Powder River Basin area. Will also accept materials pertaining to aviation and aerospace; caves and caving; and weather modification efforts.

HOLDINGS:
Total volume: 130 l.f.; 12 file drawers
Inclusive dates: mid-19th century -
Description: Materials relating to the history of South Dakota, including territorial papers, legislative and other State documents, journals, and diaries. Also included are documents relating to the South Dakota School of Mines and Technology, as well as the history of the Black Hills area.

SEE: Meckler and McMullin.

SIOUX FALLS

SD684-200

Episcopal Diocese of South Dakota
17th Street
Sioux Falls SD 57105

(605) 338-9751

OPEN: by appointment
COPYING FACILITIES: yes
MATERIALS SOLICITED: Correspondence, journals, and other materials pertinent to the Episcopal church in South Dakota.

HOLDINGS:
Total volume: not specified
Inclusive dates: 1860's -
Description: The archives of the Diocese, including sermons of Bishop Hobart Hare, dating from the 1860's; parish registers; records of Diocesan schools; and journals of Diocesan field workers, lay and clergy, mostly in South Dakota, dating from the 1860's.

SD684-280

Geological Survey
Earth Resources Observation Systems Data Center
Karl Mundt Federal Building
Sioux Falls SD 57198

(605) 594-6511

OPEN: M-F 7:45-4:15; closed weekends and holidays
COPYING FACILITIES: yes

HOLDINGS:
Total volume: 6,356,000 photographic images
Inclusive dates: 1950 -
Description: Archival data includes NASA research aircraft photography; Department of the Interior aerial mapping photography; Landsat satellite data; Skylab imagery; and Apollo and Gemini space photography. Approximately 20,000 frames of spacecraft and aircraft imagery are added to the data base each month.
Landsat coverage is available over most of the Earth's ground areas; Skylab coverage over selected areas between latitudes 50 degrees North and 50 degrees South; and aerial photography over United States areas only. About 95 percent of the material is available on microfilm for research at the repository.

SEE: Novotny.

SEE ALSO: The institution maintains a computerized geographic index to its holdings.

SD684-480

Lutheran Church-Missouri Synod
South Dakota District Archives
101 East 38th Street
Sioux Falls SD 57105

(605) 336-0811

OPEN: M-F 1:30-4:30; closed weekends and holidays
COPYING FACILITIES: yes
MATERIALS SOLICITED: Items dealing with the history of the Lutheran Church-Missouri Synod in South Dakota since 1875.

HOLDINGS:
Total volume: 70 c.f.
Inclusive dates: 1875 -
Description: The archives of the South Dakota District includes publications, convention proceedings, histories of congregations, photographs, and a biographical file on 2,000 pastors and parochial school teachers.

SD684-640

Pettigrew Museum of Natural Arts and History
131 North Duluth
Sioux Falls SD 57104

(605) 339-7097

OPEN: M-F 9-5; closed weekends and holidays

SEE: NUCMC, 1962.

Questionnaire not returned.

SISSETON

SD702-690

Roberts County Historical Society
Sisseton Library
305 East Maple Street
Sisseton SD 57262

(605) 698-7391

OPEN: M-F 9-5; closed weekends and
  holidays
COPYING FACILITIES: yes
MATERIALS SOLICITED: Roberts County
  and South Dakota historical materials.
  Will also accept items relating to regional and National history.

HOLDINGS:
    Total volume: not specified
    Inclusive dates: 1880's -
    Description: Correspondence, family
  histories, and other manuscripts of significance to Roberts County history.

SPEARFISH

SD720-80

Black Hills State College
E. Y. Berry Library/Learning Center
Leland D. Case Library for Western
  Historical Studies and
E. Y. Berry Manuscript Collection
1200 University Avenue
Spearfish SD 57783

(605) 642-6833

OPEN: M-F 8-5; closed weekends,
  holidays, semester and spring vacations
COPYING FACILITIES: yes
MATERIALS SOLICITED: Materials pertaining to the American West, northern
  Great Plains, and regional history of
  the Black Hills.

HOLDINGS:
    Total volume: 677 c.f.
    Inclusive dates: 1875 -
    Description: A photograph collection
  on the Black Hills area and Black Hills
  State College; papers of U.S. Representative E. Y. Berry, 1951-71, including correspondence, photographs, and recordings; and unpublished manuscripts, diaries, scrapbooks, maps, and other items
  pertaining to the Black Hills area.

STURGIS

SD756-720

Sturgis Public Library
1040 Second Street
Sturgis SD 57785

(605) 347-2740

OPEN: M-Th 9-7, F, Sa 9-4; closed
  Sundays and holidays
USER FEES: nonresident fee $2
COPYING FACILITIES: yes
MATERIALS SOLICITED: Manuscripts per-
  taining to Dakota and western history
  and oral history tapes relating to
  Sturgis and Meade County history. Will
  also accept microfilm church, school,
  business, death and cemetery records.

HOLDINGS:
    Total volume: 10 manuscripts; 28
  tapes; 6 microfilm reels
    Inclusive dates: 1900 -
    Description: Manuscripts relating chief-
  ly to Meade County including biographies
  of early settlers; oral history interviews
  relating to the county; reminiscences of
  pioneers; the pioneer era; the history of
  the Sturgis Public Library; church baptismal records; school, business, death, and
  cemetery records.

VERMILLION

SD792-800

University of South Dakota
American Indian Research Project
16 Dakota Hall
Vermillion SD 57069

(605) 677-5208

OPEN: M-F 8-5; closed weekends and
  holidays
ACCESS: scholarly use
COPYING FACILITIES: yes
MATERIALS SOLICITED: Interviews con-
  cerning Indian history collected from
  South Dakota, Minnesota, Wisconsin,
  Montana, Idaho, Washington, and
  Canada.

HOLDINGS:
    Total volume: 1,114 items
    Inclusive dates: 1968 -
    Description: Oral history tapes con-
  cerning Indian culture, religion, and history in South Dakota, Minnesota, Wisconsin, Montana, Idaho, Washington, and
  Canada. Also included in the project is
  the Jurrens collection of American Indian
  music on tape.

GUIDES: Ramon Harris, ed., *Oyate
  Iyechinka Woglakapi: An Oral History
  Collection* (Institute of Indian Studies,
  1970-73).

SEE: Meckler and McMullin.

SEE ALSO: Suzanne Julin, Judy Zabdyr,
  Herbert T. Hoover, and Gerald W.
  Wolff. *American Indian Research
  Project Index* (1979).

SD792-820

University of South Dakota
I. D. Weeks Library
Richardson Archives
Vermillion SD 57069

(605) 677-5371

OPEN: M-F 8-5; closed weekends and
  holidays
COPYING FACILITIES: yes
MATERIALS SOLICITED: South Dakota
  history, politics, and business, and Indians of South Dakota and the northern Great Plains.

HOLDINGS:
    Total volume: 690 l.f.
    Inclusive dates: 1860 -
    Description: Papers of South Dakotans
  prominent in politics, law, education,
  business, and other fields, such as Paul E.
  Bellamy, Peter Norbeck, Ralph Herseth,
  James Abourezk, and Richard F. Kneip;
  records of the Federal Writers' Project

and the Historical Records Survey of the
Work Projects Administration, 1935-45;
and materials relating to Indians of South
Dakota and the northern Great Plains.

SEE: Hamer; NUCMC, 1959-61, 71, 74.

SEE: Davis; Hinding.

SD792-830

University of South Dakota
School of Medicine
Health Science Library
East Clark and Dakota
Vermillion SD 57069

(605) 677-5347

OPEN: M-F 8-5; closed weekends and
  holidays
COPYING FACILITIES: yes
MATERIALS SOLICITED: Archival material
  relating to the University of South Dakota School of Medicine. Will also accept materials relating to the history of
  medicine in South Dakota.

HOLDINGS:
    Total volume: 1,216 items
    Inclusive dates: 1756 -
    Description: A collection of materials
  relating to the University of South Dakota School of Medicine. Included are
  photographs, scrapbooks, unpublished
  memoirs, and some correspondence.

SD792-850

University of South Dakota
South Dakota Oral History Project
16 Dakota Hall
Vermillion SD 57069

(605) 677-5208

OPEN: M-F 8-5; closed weekends and
  holidays
ACCESS: scholarly use
COPYING FACILITIES: yes
MATERIALS SOLICITED: Oral history on
  all aspects of South Dakota history.
  Will also accept any material relevant
  to South Dakota history.

HOLDINGS:
    Total volume: 2,115 items
    Inclusive dates: 1970 -
    Description: Oral history tapes dealing
  with the history of South Dakota, with
  special emphasis on recollections of early
  statehood, homesteading, and the pioneer
  experience. There are also interviews on
  ranching, rural life, the Depression, politics, and the Black Hills flood of 1972.

GUIDES: *The South Dakota Experience:
  An Oral History Collection of its People*
  (1972-75).

SEE ALSO: Stephen R. Ward, 'An Early
  Assessment of the South Dakota Oral
  History Project,' *South Dakota History*
  1 (Winter 1970); Alan M. Meckler and
  Ruth McMullin, comps., *Oral History
  Collections* (Bowker, 1975).

SD792-880
W. H. Over Museum
University of South Dakota
Vermillion SD 57069

(605) 677-5228

OPEN: M-F 8-4:30, Sa 10-4:30, Su
2-4:30; closed holidays
ACCESS: appointment suggested for
viewing original photographs
COPYING FACILITIES: yes
MATERIALS SOLICITED: Stereographs of
Yankton and Dakota Territory produced by Stanley J. Morrow, and original photographs of Dakota (Sioux) Indians, the University of South Dakota,
and South Dakota in general. Will also
accept original photographs of the upper Great Plains region in the 19th
century.

HOLDINGS:
Total volume: 15 l.f.
Inclusive dates: 1860 -
Description: A photograph collection
including original prints, negatives, and
copies of early pictures. Emphasis is on
regional history, especially Dakota (Sioux)
Indians, Vermillion, and the University
of South Dakota, 1860- . The Stanley J.
Morrow collection contains approximately 300 stereographs, 1869-83, of the Dakota and Montana territories. Subjects
covered are Indians, forts, towns,
railroads, steamboats, and the Yankton
flood of 1881.

SEE: Novotny.

YANKTON

SD936-930
Yankton College
Library
Archive Collection
1016 Douglas
Yankton SD 57078

(605) 665-3661

OPEN: M-Th 8:30-9:45, F 8:30-5, Sa 1-3,
Su 2-9:45; summer, M-F 8:30-4; closed
holidays
COPYING FACILITIES: yes
MATERIALS SOLICITED: Will accept materials relating to Yankton College and
its students, faculty, and graduates, and
to South Dakota history and literature.

HOLDINGS:
Total volume: 3,272 c.f.
Inclusive dates: early 1800's -
Description: The collection includes
yearbooks, council minutes, and other
materials from the Congregational church
in South Dakota; correspondence, photographs, and other papers of the Riggs
family, which administered schools for
Indians in Santee, NE, and Oahe, SD;
and archives of Yankton College,
Redfield College, and Fargo College.

SEE: Hinding.

SD936-950
Dakota Territorial Museum
Yankton County Historical Society
West Side Park
Yankton SD

MAILING ADDRESS:
P.O. Box 1033
Yankton SD 57078

(605) 665-3898

OPEN: Memorial Day - Labor Day Su,
M 1-5, W-Sa 1-5; closed Tuesdays and
Labor Day - Memorial Day
COPYING FACILITIES: no
MATERIALS SOLICITED: Materials relating
to steamboats, early Dakota Territory
history, and western history.

HOLDINGS:
Total volume: not specified
Inclusive dates: not specified
Description: Photographs and manu-
scripts of early settlement; recordings,
original songs, poems, and manuscripts of
George B. German, radio entertainer on
WNAX; and records of Felix Villiet
Vinatieri, musician with Custer's Seventh
Cavalry.

TENNESSEE

Since 1964 the Tennessee State Library and Archives has administered a statewide program for preserving local public records. Local officials have retained custody of permanently valuable county and municipal records, but microfilm copies of many county records are available to researchers at the State Archives in Nashville. For approximately half the counties the State Archives has filmed permanently valuable bound records extant at the time of filming (1964-72), and has prepared an inventory for each county's records.

For nearly all remaining counties permanently valuable bound records dated prior to 1900 have been microfilmed.

ATHENS

TN15-760
Tennessee Wesleyan College
Merner-Pfeiffer Library
Athens TN

MAILING ADDRESS:
P.O. Box 40
Athens TN 37303

(615) 745-2363

OPEN: M-Th 8-9, F 8-5, Sa 9-1, Su 2-5:30; closed holidays
ACCESS: prefer use M-F 8-5
COPYING FACILITIES: yes
MATERIALS SOLICITED: Will accept journals or diaries relating to Tennessee Wesleyan College.

HOLDINGS:
Total volume: 8 l.f.
Inclusive dates: 1759 - 1928
Description: A collection of diaries and journals relating to Holston Conference Methodism and Tennessee Wesleyan College. There is also a small collection of papers relating to the Moddox, Mattox or Maddux family of eastern Tennessee.

CHATTANOOGA

TN60-120
Chattanooga-Hamilton County
  Bicentennial Library
1001 Broad Street
Chattanooga TN 37402

(615) 757-5317

OPEN: M-Th 9-9, F, Sa 9-6; closed Sundays and holidays
COPYING FACILITIES: yes
MATERIALS SOLICITED: Materials relating to the history of Chattanooga and vicinity.

HOLDINGS:
Total volume: 236 collections
Inclusive dates: 1600 -
Description: Papers of local political figures and other prominent individuals; scrapbooks of organizations; and records of governmental bodies, dating primarily from the 1860's to present day.

SEE: Hamer; NUCMC, 1959-62, 65 (as Chattanooga Public Library).

SEE: Parkinson.

CLARKSVILLE

TN75-50
Austin Peay State University
Felix G. Woodward Library
Clarksville TN 37040

(615) 648-7346

OPEN: Su 3-10, M-Th 7:30-10, F 7:30-4:30, Sa 10-5; closed holidays, weekends between quarters, and Christmas vacation.
COPYING FACILITIES: yes
MATERIALS SOLICITED: Materials relating to the history of the Clarksville area and upper middle Tennessee.

HOLDINGS:
Total volume: 24 l.f.
Inclusive dates: 1877 -
Description: Letters, newspaper clippings, and travel diaries, 1919-33, of Elizabeth Meriwether Gilmer (Dorothy Dix), and archives of Austin Peay State University, 1929- .
Also includes research materials of Milton Henry; records of the Hillman Land & Iron Company and its successor; and University archives.

SEE: NUCMC, 1979.

SEE: Hinding.

CLEVELAND

TN90-80
Bradley County Historical Society
Cleveland Public Library
Ocoee Street
Cleveland TN

MAILING ADDRESS:
P.O. Box 1035
Cleveland TN 37311

(615) 472-2163, 4222

OPEN: M 9-9, Tu, W 9-5, Th 9-9, F, Sa 9-5; closed Sundays and holidays
COPYING FACILITIES: yes
MATERIALS SOLICITED: Genealogical materials and materials relating to the Cherokee Indians. Will also accept Tennesseeana and materials relating to the stove and furniture industries.

HOLDINGS:
Total volume: 1,000 items
Inclusive dates: 1834 -
Description: Records of early county businesses; court records; genealogical files on area families; and the James F. Corn collection on Cherokee Indians.

TN90-130
Cleveland State Community College
Library
Cleveland TN

MAILING ADDRESS:
Box 1205
Cleveland TN 37311

(615) 472-7141

OPEN: M-Th 7-10:30, Sa 9-1; closed F, Su and holidays
COPYING FACILITIES: yes
MATERIALS SOLICITED: Materials relating to the Church of God, A. J. Tomlinson, Grady Kent, and Pentecostal history. Will also accept materials on Sabbatarianism.

HOLDINGS:
Total volume: not specified
Inclusive dates: 1835 - 1940
Description: Records relating to Polk and Bradley counties, TN, including scrapbooks of J. D. Clemmer, a journal of Col. R. M. Edwards, the diary of Myra Inman Carter, and microfilm of the Wooten scrapbooks.

TN90-440

Kent College
Library
Jerusalem Acres
Cleveland TN

MAILING ADDRESS:
P.O. Box 1207
Cleveland TN 37311

no telephone

OPEN: M-F 9-5; closed weekends and
holidays
COPYING FACILITIES: yes
MATERIALS SOLICITED: Materials relating
to the Church of God, A. J.
Tomlinson, Grady Kent and Pentecostal history. Will also accept materials
on Sabbatarianism.

HOLDINGS:
Total volume: 5,000 items
Inclusive dates: not specified
Description: Materials on religion with
an emphasis on Sabbatarianism, Pente-
costalism and Jewish traditions.

COLUMBIA

TN120-120

Columbia State Community College
John W. Finney Memorial Library
Highway 99 West
Columbia TN

MAILING ADDRESS:
P.O. Box 1315
Columbia TN 38401

(615) 388-0120, Ext. 234

OPEN: M-Th 7:45-9, F 7:45-4:15; closed
weekends and holidays
COPYING FACILITIES: yes
MATERIALS SOLICITED: Materials relating
to Maury and surrounding counties
and Tennessee. Will also accept pictures of Tennessee landmarks and middle Tennessee family histories.

HOLDINGS:
Total volume: 200 vols.; 1 file cabinet
Inclusive dates: 1862 -
Description: Diaries, correspondence,
church records, manuscripts and other
material relating to middle Tennessee.

GATLINBURG

TN285-280

Great Smoky Mountains National
Park
Gatlinburg TN 37738

(615) 436-5615

OPEN: M-Th 8-4:30; closed other days
and holidays
COPYING FACILITIES: no
MATERIALS SOLICITED: Materials relating
to the history of the Great Smoky
Mountains area in eastern Tennessee
and western North Carolina, the development of the Great Smoky Mountains
National Park, and the Civilian Conservation Corps in the Great Smoky
Mountains National Park, as well as
photographs of early residents, their

homes and families, farms and farming
activities. Will also accept botanical,
geological, and zoological studies of the
area.

HOLDINGS:
Total volume: 130 l.f.
Inclusive dates: 1900 -
Description: Materials relating primarily to the Great Smoky Mountain area
prior to the establishment of the Great
Smoky Mountains National Park. Included are materials on lumber company operations, railroads, and land development
plans; records of land acquisition by state
commissions; scrapbooks; the Colonel
David Chapman collection of correspondence and scrapbooks, 1900-35; vegetation studies; and a 16,000 item photograph collection.

SEE: Hamer.

SEE: Davis.

GREENEVILLE

TN300-760

Tusculum College
Archives
Greeneville TN 37743

(615) 638-1111

OPEN: by appointment
COPYING FACILITIES: yes
MATERIALS SOLICITED: Material relating
to Tusculum College and selected types
of manuscripts of persons related to
Tusculum College. Will also accept endangered material of archival value relating to Greene County and eastern
Tennessee.

HOLDINGS:
Total volume: 300 c.f.
Inclusive dates: 1794 -
Description: Archival materials relating
to Tusculum College. Included are
charters, board of trustee minutes, papers
of the presidents, faculty minutes, student
publications, records of student societies,
and College publications. Some of the
records relate to the Presbyterian church.

SEE: Hinding.

SEE ALSO: guide to archives available at
institution.

HARROGATE

TN315-480

Lincoln Memorial University
Harrogate TN 37752

(615) 869-3611

OPEN: M-Sa 9-6, Su 1-4; closed Dec.,
Jan.

SEE: Hamer; NUCMC, 1963-64.

Questionnaire not returned.

HERMITAGE

TN345-480

Ladies' Hermitage Association
Rachel's Lane, Route 4
Hermitage TN

MAILING ADDRESS:
Box D
Hermitage TN 37076

(615) 889-2941

OPEN: daily 9-5 by appointment; closed
Christmas

SEE: Hamer; NUCMC, 1962, 71 (as The
Hermitage).

Questionnaire not returned.

JACKSON

TN390-390

Jackson - Madison County Library
433 East Lafayette Street
Jackson TN 38301

(901) 423-0225

OPEN: M-Th 9:30-9, F, Sa 9:30-5:30;
closed Sundays and holidays
COPYING FACILITIES: yes
MATERIALS SOLICITED: Local and State
history and genealogy and information
on nationally known local persons.

HOLDINGS:
Total volume: 100 vols.
Inclusive dates: 1850 - 1930
Description: A collection of manuscripts and microfilmed papers from private collections focusing on local and
Tennessee history. Included are diaries,
records of early pioneers and soldiers,
church records, land grants, diplomas
signed by prominent Tennessee residents,
photographs of early Jackson, oral history
tapes, and clipping files on genealogy and
funeral notices, 1860-80.

JOHNSON CITY

TN435-220

East Tennessee State University
The Sherrod Library
Archives of Appalachia
Johnson City TN 37601

(615) 929-4338, 4365

OPEN: M-F 8-4:30; closed weekends and
holidays
ACCESS: serious scholars; graduate
students working under scholar's
supervision; community organizations
by special arrangement
COPYING FACILITIES: yes
MATERIALS SOLICITED: Materials documenting southern Appalachia and its
people or organizations active in political, economic, and cultural development, with emphasis on grass-roots or
self-help organizations which served as
innovators or models; and East Tennessee State University archives relating to the history of Tennessee, Appalachia, and southeastern United States.

HOLDINGS:
> *Total volume:* 2,000 l.f.
> *Inclusive dates:* 1780 -
> *Description:* Files of community organizations of the southern Appalachia region, including craft guilds, religious groups, educational institutions, and business, development, and farming cooperatives, primarily 1900-25. Also held are manuscripts of individuals involved in the region's politics and business; Washington County court, tax, and administrative records, 1780- ; video tapes; the University archives; and southern Appalachian photographs, 1880's- , primarily dating from the mid-1930's to the present.

SEE ALSO: collection descriptions in *Archives of Appalachia Newsletter*.

KNOXVILLE

TN465-440
Knoxville-Knox County Public Library
McClung Historical Collection
600 Market Street
Knoxville TN

MAILING ADDRESS:
500 West Church Avenue
Knoxville TN 37902

(615) 523-0781, Ext. 144

OPEN: M, Tu 9-8:30, W-F 9-5:30; closed weekends and holidays
SEE: Hamer; NUCMC, 1976.

Questionnaire not returned.

TN465-760
Tennessee Valley Authority
Technical Library
400 W. Summit Hill Drive, E2 B7
Knoxville TN 37902

(615) 632-3466

OPEN: M-F 8-4:45; closed weekends and holidays
ACCESS: Researchers should write to the Technical Library in Knoxville for access to materials housed at Chattanooga and Norris, TN, and at Muscle Shoals, AL.
COPYING FACILITIES: yes
MATERIALS SOLICITED: Reports, memoranda, news releases, and other archives of the TVA. Will also accept other materials documenting TVA history, including personal papers of staff members, photographs, poems, songs, plays, and other manuscripts.

HOLDINGS:
> *Total volume:* not specified
> *Inclusive dates:* 1933 -
> *Description:* Records of the Authority, including minutes of the TVA Board, administrative files, records concerning accounting, personnel, and labor relations, and records of the management of reservoirs and other projects. Available at Chattanooga, TN, are more than 500,000 manuscript maps, navigation charts, and aerial photographs pertaining to the Tennessee Valley region, as well as TVA records of electric power generation, real

estate, and health and safety programs. TVA forestry, soil erosion, wildlife and fishery records are housed at Norris, TN, and there are records pertaining to chemical engineering, agriculture, fertilizer, and soil erosion at Muscle Shoals, AL.

Approved archival records stored at the Federal Records Center, NARA Branch Archives, East Point, Georgia. Contact agency representative: Asst. TVA Archivist, 205 Krystal Building, Chattanooga, TN 37401.

SEE: Hamer.

SEE: Novotny.

TN465-800
University of Tennessee at Knoxville Library
Special Collections
Knoxville TN 37996

(615) 974-4480

OPEN: M-F 9-5:30; closed weekends and holidays
COPYING FACILITIES: yes
MATERIALS SOLICITED: Materials relating to Tennessee, the Southeast, and radiation biology. Will also accept appropriate materials supporting research in any of the University's graduate programs.

HOLDINGS:
> *Total volume:* 2,041,000 items
> *Inclusive dates:* 1689 -
> *Description:* Over 800 collections dealing mostly with Tennessee and the Southeast. Included are papers of political figures, literary figures, historians, educators, scientists, and businesspersons, as well as business records, cemetery records, diaries, and other private papers.

SEE: Hamer; NUCMC, 1959-64, 69, 71, 78.

SEE: Schatz; Parkinson; Hinding; Robbins.

LEBANON

TN495-120
Cumberland College
Mitchell Library
Archives
South Greenwood Street
Lebanon TN 37087

(615) 444-2562, Ext. 274, 259

OPEN: M-F 8-4; closed holidays and Christmas and spring breaks
COPYING FACILITIES: yes
MATERIALS SOLICITED: Materials relating to Cumberland University, past faculty members, Wilson County, TN, and Wilson countians.

HOLDINGS:
> *Total volume:* not specified
> *Inclusive dates:* 19th century -
> *Description:* Materials relating to Cumberland University.

MEMPHIS

TN630-120
Christian Brothers College
Archives
650 East Parkway South
Memphis TN 38104

(901) 278-0100

OPEN: M-F 9-3, Sa by appointment; closed Sundays and holidays
COPYING FACILITIES: yes
MATERIALS SOLICITED: Christian Brothers College archival materials. Will also accept family diaries and news clippings relevant to the College and its alumni.

HOLDINGS:
> *Total volume:* 75 l.f.
> *Inclusive dates:* 1871 -
> *Description:* Manuscripts, institutional records, photographs, clippings, oral documents, and unpublished translations pertaining to the history of Christian Brothers College and of the Christian Brothers Roman Catholic religious order in the United States and abroad.

TN630-200
Episcopal Diocese of Tennessee
700 Poplar Avenue
Memphis TN

MAILING ADDRESS:
692 Poplar Avenue
Memphis TN 38105

(615) 356-6107

OPEN: by appointment
COPYING FACILITIES: no
MATERIALS SOLICITED: Materials pertaining to the Episcopal church in the State of Tennessee.

HOLDINGS:
> *Total volume:* not specified
> *Inclusive dates:* 19th century -
> *Description:* Diocesan records; parish records; correspondence of bishops, 1938 - ; and records of diocesan and local institutions.

TN630-510
Memphis Pink Palace Museum
3050 Central Avenue
Memphis TN 38111

(901) 458-8587

OPEN: M-F 9-5; closed weekends and holidays
ACCESS: by appointment
COPYING FACILITIES: yes
MATERIALS SOLICITED: Materials relating to the South within a 150-mile radius of Memphis. Will also accept materials relating to southern history in general.

HOLDINGS:
> *Total volume:* 5 l.f.
> *Inclusive dates:* 1603 -
> *Description:* Materials relating chiefly to the history of the South, but also to Europe and North America in general. Collections date principally from the 19th century and include photographs, correspondence, diaries, business records, genealogical data, literary works, and public

documents. There are also the archives of the Museum from its founding in 1929.

TN630-530
Memphis State University
Libraries
Mississippi Valley Collection/Special
Collections Department
Memphis TN 38152

(901) 454-2210

OPEN: M 8-9, Tu-F 8-5; closed weekends and holidays
ACCESS: researchers must be of post-high school age
COPYING FACILITIES: yes
MATERIALS SOLICITED: Materials concerning the history and culture of the lower Mississippi Valley, especially 20th century literature, politics, and social action, and including photographs and oral history.

HOLDINGS:
   Total volume: 2,800 l.f.
   Inclusive dates: 15th century -
   Description: Approximately 100 collections focusing on Memphis and the lower Mississippi Valley, with particular strengths in late 19th and 20th century political and literary movements and personalities. Included are records of organizations, papers of individuals, records of Memphis State University, oral history, and materials documenting the 1968 sanitation workers' strike in Memphis, during which Dr. Martin Luther King, Jr., was assassinated.

SEE: NUCMC, 1969, 78.

SEE: Hinding; Robbins.

SEE ALSO: Alan M. Meckler and Ruth McMullin, comps., *Oral History Collections* (Bowker, 1975); Richard C. Davis, *North American Forest History: A Guide to Archives and Manuscripts in the United States and Canada* (Clio Books, 1977). The *Mississippi Valley Collection Bulletin,* published occasionally, contains annotated checklists of manuscript collections.

TN630-570
Memphis/Shelby County Public
  Library and Information Center
Memphis Room
1850 Peabody Avenue
Memphis TN 38104

(901) 725-8820

OPEN: M-Th 9-9, F, Sa 9-6; closed Sundays and holidays
COPYING FACILITIES: yes
MATERIALS SOLICITED: Memphis and Shelby County materials. Will also accept materials relating to the Mississippi River, Arkansas, Mississippi, Tennessee, genealogy, the Civil War, World War I, and World War II.

HOLDINGS:
   Total volume: 6,000 l.f.
   Inclusive dates: 1820 -
   Description: A collection emphasizing Tennessee State history and Memphis and Shelby County local history. The Senator Kenneth D. McKellar papers, 876 linear feet, cover his Congressional career from 1911 to 1953. Local history collections consist of papers of prominent civic and literary figures; records of social events and the yellow fever epidemic; 6,000 photographs; and the Memphis - Shelby County archives, dating primarily from the 19th century and including personal papers of elected officials. 300 hours of oral history interviews concentrate on political and cultural topics.

SEE: Hamer; NUCMC, 1963-64, 81.

SEE ALSO: Alan M. Meckler and Ruth McMullin, comps., *Oral History Collections* (Bowker, 1975); Nathan A. Josel, 'Special Collections of the Memphis and Shelby County Public Library,' *Tennessee Librarian* 22 (Summer 1970); Joseph H. Riggs, 'The McKellar Collection,' *Tennessee Librarian* 14 (Jan. 1962). Finding aids to individual collections are available at the Library.

TN630-590
National Cotton Council of America
1918 North Parkway
Memphis TN

MAILING ADDRESS:
P.O. Box 12285
Memphis TN 38112

(901) 274-9030

OPEN: M-F 8:30-5; closed weekends and holidays
COPYING FACILITIES: yes

HOLDINGS:
   Total volume: 16 file drawers
   Inclusive dates: 1938 -
   Description: A collection of speeches, legislative testimony, and annual reports dating from the inception of the National Cotton Council of America in 1938.

TN630-730
Southern College of Optometry
William P. MacCracken, Jr.,
  Memorial Library
1245 Madison Avenue
Memphis TN 38104

(901) 725-0180, Ext. 237

OPEN: M-F 8:30-4:30; closed weekends and holidays
ACCESS: advance arrangements requested
COPYING FACILITIES: yes
MATERIALS SOLICITED: History of optometry, pioneers in optometry and visual science.

HOLDINGS:
   Total volume: 60 l.f.; 63 oral history tapes
   Inclusive dates: 1917 - 1967
   Description: Primarily papers of William P. MacCracken, Jr., for the period 1947-67, when he served as attorney for the American Optometric Association. There are also oral history tapes and materials relating to the early historyof aviation in America.

TN630-740
Rhodes College
Burrow Library
2000 North Parkway
Memphis TN 38112

(901) 276-3900

OPEN: M-F 8:30-5; closed weekends and holidays
COPYING FACILITIES: no
MATERIALS SOLICITED: Will accept materials relating to the Memphis area or the needs and interests of the College.

HOLDINGS:
   Total volume: 2,000 items
   Inclusive dates: 1805 -
   Description: Robertson Topp papers, including correspondence, biographical and genealogical data, diaries, memoirs, and local papers pertinent to Memphis and its environs; data on the cotton trade during the Civil War and immediately after; and a collection of manuscripts and notebooks of Joan Williams, southern novelist.

SEE: Hamer; NUCMC, 1966.

SEE: Schatz.

The materials listed in Hamer concerning the Presbyterian church and Protestantism have been transferred to the Historical Foundation of the Presbyterian and Reformed Churches, Montreat, NC.

MURFREESBORO

TN675-720
Stones River National Battlefield
Route 10, Box 401
Old Nashville Highway
Murfreesboro TN 37130

(615) 893-9501

OPEN: daily 8-4:45; closed Christmas
COPYING FACILITIES: yes
MATERIALS SOLICITED: Materials on the Civil War, especially Stones River. Will also accept materials relating to environmental education and natural history.

HOLDINGS:
   Total volume: 2 l.f.
   Inclusive dates: 1861 - 1865
   Description: Records of regiments that participated in the Battle of Stones River.

NASHVILLE

TN690-110
Country Music Foundation, Inc.
Library and Media Center
4 Music Square East
Nashville TN 37203

(615) 256-1639

OPEN: M-F 9-5; closed weekends and holidays
ACCESS: advance arrangements required
COPYING FACILITIES: yes

MATERIALS SOLICITED: Materials relating to country music and related fields; sound recording history and technology; the music industry; entertainment law and Anglo-American folksongs and ballads. Will also accept materials relating to the popular music industry.

HOLDINGS:
Total volume: 88,000 items; 56 file drawers
Inclusive dates: 1922 -
Description: Audio-visual collection of 88,000 items including photographs, audiotapes and videotapes. Vertical file materials relate to Country and Western music, singers, and musicians.

TN690-170
Disciples of Christ Historical Society
Library and Archives
1101 19th Avenue South
Nashville TN 37212

(615) 327-1444

OPEN: M-F 8-4:30; closed weekends and holidays
USER FEES: Use permit $5 per quarter
COPYING FACILITIES: yes
MATERIALS SOLICITED: Material dealing with organizations and individuals connected with the Christian church (Disciples of Christ).

HOLDINGS:
Total volume: 1,005 accession groups; 21,293 vols.
Inclusive dates: 1800 -
Description: Manuscripts, archival records, and audio-visual material relating to, generated by or written by members and organizations connected with the Christian Church (Disciples of Christ), Christian Churches, and Churches of Christ.

SEE: Hamer; NUCMC, 1965, 68, 70.

SEE: Hinding.

SEE ALSO: Walter Schatz, ed., Directory of Afro-American Resources (Bowker, 1970); Peter Duignan, Handbook of American Resources for African Studies (Hoover Institution, 1967); Clifton H. Johnson, 'Some Archival Sources on Negro History in Tennessee,' Tennessee Historical Quarterly 28 (Winter 1969). Available from the Disciples of Christ Historical Society are Preliminary Guide to Black Materials in the Disciples of Christ Historical Society (n.d.) and several registers of individual collections.

TN690-220
Fisk University
Library and Media Center
Special Collections
17th Avenue North at Jackson Street
Nashville TN 37203

(615) 329-8646

OPEN: M-F 8-5; closed weekends, academic holidays, and June - Aug.
ACCESS: serious researchers; identification required; advance arrangements preferred
COPYING FACILITIES: yes

MATERIALS SOLICITED: Materials relating to Afro-Americans and Africans.

HOLDINGS:
Total volume: 2,000 boxes; 25 file cabinets; 76 collections
Inclusive dates: 1698 -
Description: Over 70 collections covering all phases of Afro-American history, life, and culture, dating primarily from 1866 to the present. Included are records of organizations, the University archives, papers of individuals, unpublished manuscripts, memoirs, ephemera, memorabilia, 500 oral history interviews, interview transcripts, sketches, drawings, photographs, and sound recordings.

SEE: Hamer; NUCMC, 1959-62, 68-69, 72-73, 76.

SEE: Robbins; Hinding.

SEE ALSO: Walter Schatz, ed., Directory of Afro-American Resources (Bowker, 1970); Peter Duignan, Handbook of American Resources for African Studies (Hoover Institution, 1967); Dictionary Catalog of the Negro Collection of the Fisk University Library (G. K. Hall, 1974); Alan M. Meckler and Ruth McMullin, comps., Oral History Collections (Bowker, 1975); John Dobson, 'Preservation of Historical Materials in Tennessee College and University Libraries,' Tennessee Librarian 14 (Jan. 1962). BANC, a publication of Special Collections, 1970-75, describes individual collections.

TN690-240
Free Will Baptist Bible College
Welch Library
Free Will Baptist Historical Collection
3606 West End Avenue
Nashville TN 37205

(615) 383-1340

OPEN: M-F 8-4:30, Sa by appointment; closed Sundays and holidays
COPYING FACILITIES: yes
MATERIALS SOLICITED: Free Will Baptist history.

HOLDINGS:
Total volume: not specified
Inclusive dates: 1800 -
Description: Records of the Free Will Baptist church in the U.S. In addition to minutes, periodicals, and records of individual churches and associations, holdings include correspondence, diaries, photographs, and oral histories.

TN690-360
Jewish Federation of Nashville and Middle Tennessee
3500 West End Avenue
Nashville TN 37205

(615) 356-3242

OPEN: M-F 9-1; closed weekends, holidays and holy days
COPYING FACILITIES: yes
MATERIALS SOLICITED: Materials pertaining to the Jewish communities of Nashville or middle Tennessee.

HOLDINGS:
Total volume: 90 c.f.
Inclusive dates: late 19th century -
Description: Records of the Jewish Federation of Nashville and Middle Tennessee, Jewish Community Center, and Jewish Family Services, including annual reports, correspondence, minutes, microfilm, photographs, slides, tapes, scrapbooks, unpublished memoirs and histories, and biographical information related to professionals, staff and lay people active in these agencies. Also included are papers, photographs, and oral histories of Jewish residents of Nashville, and records of three Jewish congregations, Akiva (Jewish day school), and local Jewish businesses and organizations.

TN690-510
Meharry Medical College
Library
Kresge Learning Resources Center
Meharry Medical College Archives
1005 D. B. Todd Boulevard
Nashville TN 37208

(615) 327-6470, 6318

OPEN: M-F 9-5; closed weekends and holidays
COPYING FACILITIES: yes
MATERIALS SOLICITED: Materials on Meharry Medical College and the Meharry schools of dentistry, pharmacy, nursing, and dental hygiene, and Hubbard Hospital. Will also accept oral history tapes.

HOLDINGS:
Total volume: not specified
Inclusive dates: 1876 -
Description: Materials relating to Meharry Medical College and associated schools, including records of organizations, papers of individuals, unpublished memoirs and histories, and collections of ephemera.

SEE: Schatz.

TN690-600
Public Library of Nashville and Davidson County
The Nashville Room
8th and Union
Nashville TN 37203

(615) 244-4700, Ext. 66

OPEN: Su 2-5, M-F 9-8, Sa 9-5; closed holidays and Sundays in summer
COPYING FACILITIES: yes
MATERIALS SOLICITED: Material pertaining to local authors and history, including oral histories and photographs.

HOLDINGS:
Total volume: 50 l.f.
Inclusive dates: 1880 -
Description: School diaries of the 1890's, manuscripts of local authors, taped interviews with local authors, and photographs and slides of Nashville and its people.

TN690-690
Roman Catholic Diocese of Nashville
2400 Twenty-first Avenue, South
Nashville TN 37212

(615)383-6393

OPEN: M-F 8:30-4:30; closed weekends,
National and church holidays
COPYING FACILITIES: yes

HOLDINGS:
> *Total volume:* 96 c.f.
> *Inclusive dates:* 1837 -
> *Description:* General correspondence of
> bishops and other officers of the diocese,
> 1837- ; financial records of churches,
> 1837- . Also includes microfilm of sac-
> ramental records for all parishes in Ten-
> nessee, 1837-1952.

TN690-740
Southern Baptist Convention
Historical Commission
E. C. Dargan Library
127 9th Avenue N.
Nashville TN 37234

(615) 244-4344

OPEN: M-F 7:30-4; closed weekends and
holidays
COPYING FACILITIES: yes
MATERIALS SOLICITED: Materials pertaining to the history, biography, doc-
trine, life, and work of Baptists. Will
also accept other materials by or about
Baptists.

HOLDINGS:
> *Total volume:* 1,400 l.f.
> *Inclusive dates:* 1692 -
> *Description:* Over 300 manuscript col-
> lections; records of more than 800 Baptist
> churches, 1,250 Baptist associations, 50
> State Baptist conventions, the Southern
> Baptist Convention, and other National
> groups of Baptists in the United States,
> particularly in the South. There are also
> records of Baptist groups in Mexico, Bra-
> zil, Argentina, and other foreign coun-
> tries, as well as records of 19th century
> missionary activities in Nigeria. Also in-
> cluded are personal papers, diaries, and
> journals of Baptist leaders; audio-visual
> materials; and microfilm of local church
> and organization records and manuscript
> collections.

SEE: NUCMC, 1959-61, 63-64, 66, 68, 73.

SEE ALSO: *Microfilm Catalog of Basic
Baptist Historical Materials on Micro-
film* (Southern Baptist Convention,
Historical Commission, 1969), and an-
nual supplements through 1976; Mrs.
G. Kearnie Keegan, 'The Archival Re-
sources of Dargan-Carver Library,'
Baptist History and Heritage 6 (July
1971); 'A Baptist Research Center: The
Dargan-Carver Library,' *Baptist History
and Heritage* 6 (Oct. 1971); Clifton H.
Johnson, 'Some Archival Sources on
Negro History in Tennessee,' *Tennessee
Historical Quarterly* 28 (Winter 1969);
Walter Schatz, ed., *Directory of Afro-
American Resources* (Bowker, 1970);
Peter Duignan, *Handbook of American
Resources for African Studies* (Hoover
Institution, 1967).

TN690-750
Southern Baptist Convention
Sunday School Board
E. C. Dargan Library
127 9th Avenue N.
Nashville TN 37234

(615) 251-2133

OPEN: M-F 7:30-4; closed weekends and
holidays
COPYING FACILITIES: yes
MATERIALS SOLICITED: Baptist materials
of both national and international
scope relating to Sunday schools,
churches, and associations.

HOLDINGS:
> *Total volume:* 2,328 l.f.
> *Inclusive dates:* 1776 -
> *Description:* Manuscript collections fo-
> cusing on people active in the Sunday
> School Board, including papers of past
> Board presidents; tapes of Board proceed-
> ings since 1954; association minutes and
> church histories from the United States,
> England, Germany, Russia, Brazil, Israel,
> and other countries; oral histories; and
> departmental archives.

SEE ALSO: registers to major collections
available at the institution.

TN690-770
Tennessee State Museum
James K. Polk Building
Nashville TN 37219

(615) 741-2692

OPEN: Su, M 1-5, T-Sa 8-5; closed
Christmas Day
ACCESS: advance arrangements required
COPYING FACILITIES: yes
MATERIALS SOLICITED: Materials relating
to American art and antiques, and to
Tennessee, Southern, and American
history.

HOLDINGS:
> *Total volume:* 4500 items
> *Inclusive dates:* 1770 -
> *Description:* Correspondence; invita-
> tions to funerals and political picnics;
> campaign literature; and illustrations and
> photographs of various subjects.

TN690-780
Tennessee State Library and Archives
Archives and Manuscripts Section
403 7th Avenue North
Nashville TN 37219

(615) 741-2561

OPEN: M-Sa 8-4:30; closed Sundays and
holidays
COPYING FACILITIES: yes
MATERIALS SOLICITED: Tennessee executive, legislative, and judicial records,
county records, and ethics records, including sound recordings and maps, as
well as traditional materials.

HOLDINGS:
> *Total volume:* 7,000 c.f.; 1,070 vols.;
> 14,300 microfilm reels; 6,395 hours of
> recordings; 3,000,000 manuscript items
> *Inclusive dates:* 1777 -
> *Description:* Government and related
> records of Tennessee, including 600 vol-
> umes of land records, 1777-1903; State

agency records and governors papers,
1796- ; legislative records and recordings,
1796- ; State Supreme Court records,
1815-1955; ethics records, 1975- ; and
county records on microfilm.

Manuscript materials relating primarily to Tennessee and secondarily to the
South. Included are personal papers;
records of organizations, institutions and
associations; church, cemetery, and Bible
records; and genealogical data.

Holdings are particularly strong for the
Jacksonian and Civil War periods, and in
such areas of interest as politics, military
history, medicine and dentistry, religion,
art, music, education, business, industry,
mining, geology, turnpikes, county and
local history, women's suffrage, Indians,
U.S. diplomacy, and the Reconstruction
era.

SEE: Hamer (also as Tennessee Historical
Society and Tennessee State Library
and Archives); NUCMC, 1959-67,
68-76, 79.

SEE: Davis; Schatz; Hounshell; Paszek;
Novotny; Krichmar; Parkinson; Hines;
Robbins; Hinding; Allard, Crawley, and
Edmison.

SEE ALSO: Richard C. Davis, *North
American Forest History: A Guide to
Archives and Manuscripts in the United
States and Canada* (Clio Books, 1977);
Clifton H. Johnson, 'Some Archival
Sources on Negro History in Tennes-
see,' *Tennessee Historical Quarterly* 28
(Winter 1969); Walter Schatz, ed., *Di-
rectory of Afro-American Resources*
(Bowker, 1970). Pamphlets and other
materials describing specific aspects of
the Archives Section's holdings are
available from the institution.

Additional citations listed in 1st edition of
the *Directory* under TN690-780 and
TN690-790.

TN690-850
Trevecca Nazarene College
Library
Trevecca Archives
333 Murfreesboro Road
Nashville TN 37210

(615) 248-1339, 1200

OPEN: M, W-F 10-11, 4-5; Tu 4-5;
closed weekends, holidays, Dec. and
Aug.
COPYING FACILITIES: yes
MATERIALS SOLICITED: Materials relating
to Trevecca Nazarene College and the
Church of the Nazarene in the South-
east.

HOLDINGS:
> *Total volume:* 150 items
> *Inclusive dates:* 1900 -
> *Description:* A collection of manu-
> scripts relating to Trevecca Nazarene Col-
> lege and the Church of the Nazarene in
> the southeastern United States. Included
> are internal publications, correspondence,
> logbooks, and ephemera.

SEE: Meckler and McMullin.

TN690-880

The United Methodist Church
Board of Higher Education and
　Ministry
1001 19th Avenue
Nashville TN

MAILING ADDRESS:
P.O. Box 871
Nashville TN 37202

(615) 327-2700

OPEN:　M-F 9-4; closed weekends and
　holidays
ACCESS:　subject to permission of the
　Office of the General Secretary
COPYING FACILITIES:　yes
MATERIALS SOLICITED: Archival materi-
　als from offices within the Board. Will
　also accept materials pertaining to
　United Methodist higher education, if
　judged useful for archival purposes.

HOLDINGS:
　Total volume:　300 l.f.
　Inclusive dates:　1840 -
　Description: Materials relating to the
　educational work of the United Meth-
　odist church, including predecessor de-
　nominations and their agencies, with
　some materials focused specifically on the
　South. Included are financial records;
　minutes; charters and historical materials
　pertaining to colleges, universities, the-
　ological schools, and other educational in-
　stitutions; and materials relating to Unit-
　ed Methodist work with American mi-
　nority groups, such as records of the
　Freedman's Aid and Southern Education
　Society, 1886-1925, and documents on
　the relocation of Japanese-American stu-
　dents, 1943-46.

GUIDES: A typewritten guide is available
　from the Office of the General Sec-
　retary.

SEE: Schatz.

TN690-885

United Methodist Church
General Board of Discipleship
The Upper Room Devotional Library
1908 Grand Avenue
Nashville TN 37202

(615) 327-2700, Ext. 443, 444

OPEN:　M-F 8-4:30; closed weekends and
　holidays
ACCESS:　bona fide students and scholars
COPYING FACILITIES:　yes
MATERIALS SOLICITED: Materials relating
　to Methodist church history, worship,
　and devotions. Will also accept materi-
　als of general interest to Christian wor-
　ship and church history.

HOLDINGS:
　Total volume:　not specified
　Inclusive dates:　1763 -
　Description: Letters of John Wesley; a
　journal of Methodist preacher Noah
　Fidler, 1801-05; copies of Francis Asbury
　letters; photographs of the Board of Evan-
　gelism of the Methodist church, and of
　people and events in The Upper Room;
　minutes of the Board of Evangelism;
　sound recordings of The Upper Room
　Chapel Messages; miscellaneous tapes and

cassettes; and single letters from writers
of Protestant hymns.

TN690-890

United Methodist Publishing House
Library
201 Eighth Avenue, South
Nashville TN 37202

(615) 749-6437

OPEN:　M-F 8-4:15; closed weekends and
　holidays
COPYING FACILITIES:　yes
MATERIALS SOLICITED: Materials on
　Methodism, especially those relating to
　the publishing interests of the United
　Methodist church and its predecessor
　denominations. Will also accept other
　materials.

HOLDINGS:
　Total volume:　15 l.f.
　Inclusive dates:　1770's -
　Description: A collection of correspon-
　dence and manuscripts relating to Meth-
　odists and Methodism. Included is cor-
　respondence of editors of Methodist pub-
　lishing interests, bishops, and other
　church leaders.

SEE: Hamer; NUCMC, 1964 (as Meth-
　odist Publishing House).

SEE ALSO: Walter Schatz, ed., *Directory of
　Afro-American Resources* (Bowker,
　1970); Clifton R. Johnson, 'Some
　Archival Sources on Negro History in
　Tennessee,' *Tennessee Historical Quar-
　terly* 28 (Winter 1969); Peter Duignan,
　*Handbook of American Resources for
　African Studies* (Hoover Institution,
　1967).

TN690-950

Vanderbilt University
Education Library
George Peabody College of Vanderbilt
　University
Nashville TN

MAILING ADDRESS:
Box 325, George Peabody College of
　Vanderbilt University
Nashville TN 37203

(615) 322-2807

　Materials formerly held by the Educational Library, **TN690-390** in the
1978 edition of the *Directory,* are now
in custody of Special Collections and
Vanderbilt University Archives,
TN690-975.

TN690-960

Vanderbilt University
Medical Center Library
Special Collections
Nashville TN 37232

(615) 322-0008

OPEN:　M-F 8-4:30; closed weekends and
　holidays
COPYING FACILITIES:　yes
MATERIALS SOLICITED: Materials relating
　to the history of medicine and nutri-
　tion; papers of Vanderbilt University

Medical School faculty and alumni and
papers of local physicians.

HOLDINGS:
　Total volume:　not specified
　Inclusive dates:　not specified
　Description: Materials relating to the
　history of medicine, primarily American
　medicine with a special subject focus on
　the history of nutrition. The collection
　includes the archives of Vanderbilt Uni-
　versity Medical School, personal papers,
　faculty, publications of and about the
　medical school, and a photographic file.

TN690-975

Vanderbilt University
Library
Special Collections and Vanderbilt
　University Archives
419 21st Avenue South
Nashville TN 37203

(615) 322-2807

OPEN:　M-F 8-4:30; closed weekends and
　holidays
COPYING FACILITIES:　yes
MATERIALS SOLICITED: Fugitive/Agrarian
　movement materials, Vanderbilt Uni-
　versity faculty papers, and regional lit-
　erary manuscripts. Will also accept ma-
　terials concerning Tennessee history,
　Vanderbilt University, and private sec-
　ondary schools of the region.

HOLDINGS:
　Total volume:　12,000 l.f.
　Inclusive dates:　1800 -
　Description: A diverse collection that is
　especially strong in the social and cultural
　history of Tennessee and the South.
　There is an extensive collection of letters,
　literary manuscripts, and other materials
　relating to the Fugitive/Agrarian period,
　1920-30. Other significant materials in-
　clude archives of Vanderbilt University,
　George Peabody College for Teachers,
　and University of Nashville, including
　faculty papers; Peabody Education Fund
　papers; antebellum and Civil War papers
　(many on microfilm); and papers of as-
　tronomer Edward E. Barnard.

SEE: Hamer; NUCMC, 1966, 68-73.

SEE: Schatz; Krichmar.

SEE ALSO: *Source Materials for the Recent
　History of Astronomy and Astrophysics:
　A Checklist of Manuscript Collections in
　the United States* (American Institute
　of Physics, 1971); Thomas H. English,
　*Roads to Research: Distinguished Li-
　brary Collections of the Southeast*
　(Univ. of Georgia Press, 1968); Martha
　Emily Cook and Thomas Daniel
　Young, 'Fugitive/Agrarian Materials at
　Vanderbilt University,' *Resources for
　American Literary Study* 1 (Spring
　1971).

TN690-980
Vanderbilt University
Library
Vanderbilt Television News Archive
419 21st Avenue South
Nashville TN 37203

MAILING ADDRESS:
Nashville TN 37240

(615) 322-2927

OPEN: M-F 8:30-5; closed weekends and
holidays
USER FEES: $3 per viewing hour
COPYING FACILITIES: yes
MATERIALS SOLICITED: Television news,
telecasts.

HOLDINGS:
Total volume: 7,000 hours
Inclusive dates: 1968 -
Description: The collection consists of
videotapes of national television news
broadcasts.

SEE ALSO: Emily Wheeler, 'TV News Archives,' *Tennessee Librarian* 23
(Summer 1971); *Television News Index
and Abstracts,* published monthly by
the Archive.

NORRIS

TN705-560
Norris City Archives
Norris TN

MAILING ADDRESS:
P.O. Drawer G
Norris TN 37828

(615) 494-7645

OPEN: M-F 9-4, Sa 9-11; closed Sundays
and holidays
ACCESS: advance arrangements required
COPYING FACILITIES: no
MATERIALS SOLICITED: Reports, photographs and other materials from
churches and community organizations,
such as civic and service clubs, and
business records. Will also accept any
materials related to the history of the
area within the Norris city limits.

HOLDINGS:
Total volume: 12.75 l.f.; 42 maps and
drawings
Inclusive dates: 1933 -
Description: Materials relating to the
history of Norris since the city's founding
in 1933. Included are reports, letters,
photographs, tapes, maps, lists of residents, historical manuscripts, a genealogy,
and minutes of citizen council meetings
prior to incorporation of the city.

PINEY FLATS

TN750-690
Rocky Mount Historical Association
Massengill Museum of Overmountain
History
Rt. 11-E
Piney Flats TN

MAILING ADDRESS:
Rt. 2, Box 70
Piney Flats TN 37686

(615) 538-7396

OPEN: M-Sa 10-5, Su 2-6; closed
Thanksgiving Day, weekends in Jan.
and Feb., Dec. 21-Jan. 5
ACCESS: advance arrangements required
COPYING FACILITIES: yes
MATERIALS SOLICITED: Deeds, diaries,
account books, journals, petitions,
maps, land grants and tax receipts relating to upper east Tennessee.

HOLDINGS:
Total volume: 500 items
Inclusive dates: 1791 - 1894
Description: Materials relating to
Washington and Sullivan counties, TN,
including diaries, summonses, deeds, land
grants, tax receipts, notes, and account
books of the Bean, Patton, Miller, Cobb,
Devault, and Massengill families.

SEE: Hinding.

PULASKI

TN765-280
Giles County Historical Society
122 S. 2nd Street
Pulaski TN

MAILING ADDRESS:
Box 693
Pulaski TN 38478

(615) 363-2720

OPEN: M-Th 10-5, Sa 10-4, Su 2-4;
closed Fridays and holidays
COPYING FACILITIES: yes
MATERIALS SOLICITED: Will accept any
records relating to Giles County, TN,
and the area.

HOLDINGS:
Total volume: 87 l.f.; 2 file cabinets
Inclusive dates: 19th century
Description: Biographies, photographs,
oral histories, and cemetery and census
records relating to Giles County, local
Jewish and Black history, the Ku Klux
Klan, and Civil War.

TN765-800
United Methodist Church, Tennessee
Conference
Commission on Archives and History
Martin College
Pulaski TN

MAILING ADDRESS:
Rev. William H. Moss
Route 2
Prospect TN 38477

(615) 363-7456, Ext. 103

OPEN: by appointment during normal
college hours
ACCESS: advance written arrangements
required
COPYING FACILITIES: yes
MATERIALS SOLICITED: Materials relating
to Methodism in middle Tennessee.

HOLDINGS:
Total volume: 500 vols.; 50 l.f.
Inclusive dates: 1786 -
Description: Records of the Tennessee
Conference, Methodist Episcopal Church,
1786-1844; Tennessee Conference, Meth-
odist Episcopal Church, South,
1845-1939; Tennessee Conference, the
Methodist Church, 1939-67; Tennessee
Conference, United Methodist Church,
1968- ; as well as materials from local
congregations, conference agencies, and
individuals, and materials about other
Methodist groups.

RUGBY

TN825-690
Historical Rugby, Inc.
Board of Aid to Landownership
Office
Highway 52
Rugby TN

MAILING ADDRESS:
P.O. Box 8
Rugby TN 37733

(615) 628-2441

OPEN: daily March 1-Nov. 15 by
appointment
ACCESS: The collection was destroyed by
fire in 1977. Much of the material is
on deposit on microfilm and in
photocopy at the Tennessee State
Library.
MATERIALS SOLICITED: Documents on
the Tabard Hotel in Rugby, land
records, architectural materials, materials in social history, and manuscripts
relating to Rugby, TN, or to the life of
Thomas Hughes. Will also accept materials relating to the Rugby School and
British public school education.

HOLDINGS:
Total volume: 30 boxes
Inclusive dates: 1830 - 1945
Description: Records of the Board of
Aid to Landownership, Ltd., and materi-
als relating to the English colony of
Rugby, TN, founded by Thomas Hughes.

SEWANEE

TN840-800
The University of the South
Jessie Ball duPont Library
Sewanee TN 37375-4005

(615) 598-1387

OPEN: M-F 8-4:30; closed weekends and
holidays
COPYING FACILITIES: yes
MATERIALS SOLICITED: Materials relating
to the history of The University of the
South and to the Protestant Episcopal
church in the United States (especially
southern dioceses); and papers of

individuals associated with this general area of the South, and southern literary figures.

HOLDINGS:
Total volume: 1,500 l.f.
Inclusive dates: 1858 -
Description: Records of The University of the South and the town of Sewanee (which was founded on University-owned land and is governed by the University), dating from 1858. Also included are family papers dating from the 18th century, church records, and materials concerning political and literary figures of the area.

SEE: Hamer; NUCMC, 1962, 71.

SEE: Schatz; Davis; Allard, Crawley, and Edmison; Hinding.

SHILOH

TN870-720
Shiloh National Military Park
Shiloh TN 38376

(901) 689-5275

OPEN: M-F 8-5; closed weekends and holidays

SEE: Hamer.

Questionnaire not returned.

TEXAS

Since 1972 the Texas State Library has administered a statewide program for preserving local public records. Most permanently valuable local public records remain in the custody of local officials, but some records have been transferred to the 24 regional depositories which participate in the Regional Historical Resource Depository program.

Each depository also makes available to researchers microfilm copies of county vital, probate, and land records filmed by the Church of Jesus Christ of Latter-day Saints and microfilms of county tax rolls. Inventories of county records have been published for more than a quarter of Texas's 254 counties.

ABILENE

TX7-320
Hardin Simmons University
Richardson Library
Richardson Research Center
2200 Hickory Street
Abilene TX 79698

(915) 677-7281, Ext. 239, 236

OPEN: Library hours, by appointment only
COPYING FACILITIES: yes
MATERIALS SOLICITED: Materials relating to the American Southwest and Texas.

HOLDINGS:
  Total volume: 150 c.f.
  Inclusive dates: 1880 - 1920
  Description: Correspondence, case records, and office files of R. C. Crane and Henry Sayles, lawyers; correspondence, diaries, journals, and accounts of two ranches in Arizona and Texas; miscellaneous records including 17th century indentures relating to the area, and a Civil War diary.

TX7-800
United Methodist Church
Northwest Texas Annual Conference
Archives Depository
McMurry College
Abilene TX 79605

MAILING ADDRESS:
Box 296
McMurry College
Abilene TX 79697

(915) 698-1841

OPEN: Su 3-10, M-F 7:45-5, Sa 12-5; closed holidays and school vacations
ACCESS: advance arrangements recommended
COPYING FACILITIES: yes
MATERIALS SOLICITED: Materials relating to the Methodist church in the Northwest Texas Conference and its predecessor conference.

HOLDINGS:
  Total volume: 150 l.f.
  Inclusive dates: 1881 -
  Description: Materials relating to the Methodist church in the northwest quadrant of Texas. Included are conference journals, official church records, photographs, biographical materials on pioneer preachers, records of youth and women's groups, and other materials.

ALPINE

TX14-720
Sul Ross State University
Bryan Wildenthal Memorial Library
Archives of the Big Bend
Alpine TX 79830

(915) 837-8127

OPEN: M-W, F 8-5, Th 1-10; closed weekends, University holidays, and spring vacation
COPYING FACILITIES: yes
MATERIALS SOLICITED: Manuscripts, University and business records, maps, photographs, and oral histories pertaining to history of the Big Bend region of Texas. Special attention is given to Spanish language materials and Mexican-American photographs.

HOLDINGS:
  Total volume: 640 c.f.
  Inclusive dates: 1820 -
  Description: Manuscripts and business records concerned primarily with colonization and development of the Big Bend area, 1870-1930. Collections focus on ranching, mining, small businesses, and domestic life. Included are photographs dating from the 19th century and hand-drawn ranch maps. Unusual documents include slave deeds, papers related to the treatment of Indians by white ranchers in the late 1870's, and deeds transferring Creek and Cherokee Indian lands to white settlers in Georgia, 1826-50.

SEE: NUCMC, 1980.

SEE: Hinding.

SEE ALSO: James M. Day, *Handbook of Texas Archival and Manuscript Depositories* (Texas Library and Historical Commission, 1966). Inventories of some collections are available at the institution.

AMARILLO

TX21-50
Amarillo Public Library
Local History Collection and
John L. McCarty Papers
413 East 4th Street
Amarillo TX

MAILING ADDRESS:
Box 2171
Amarillo TX 79189

(806) 378-3054

OPEN: M-Th 9-9, F, Sa 9-6, Su 2-6; closed holidays
COPYING FACILITIES: yes
MATERIALS SOLICITED: Materials dealing with the history, growth and development of the Texas Panhandle, especially Amarillo and Potter County; manuscripts of area authors.

HOLDINGS:
  Total volume: 18 c.f.
  Inclusive dates: 1840 - 1950
  Description: Materials relating to the history and growth of the Texas Panhandle, especially Amarillo. Included are genealogical materials, family records, letters, photographs, correspondence, diaries, music scores by Radie Brittain Moeller, manuscripts of books by area authors, architectural drawings by Guy Carlander, scrapbooks of community groups, minutes of organization meetings, materials relating to Maximilian, Emperor of Mexico, a physician's ledger, and other materials.

SEE ALSO: James M. Day, *Handbook of Texas Archival and Manuscript Depositories* (Texas Library and Historical Commission, 1966).

TX21-690
Roman Catholic Diocese of Amarillo
Diocesan Archives
1800 North Spring Street
Amarillo TX

MAILING ADDRESS:
P.O. Box 5644
Amarillo TX 79107

(806) 383-2243

OPEN: M-F 10-5; closed weekends, Christmas and Easter

ACCESS: serious students in church history
COPYING FACILITIES: yes
MATERIALS SOLICITED: Materials documenting history of the Roman Catholic church in western Texas.

HOLDINGS:
Total volume: 1,000 items
Inclusive dates: 1876 -
Description: Account books, letters, parish histories, parish records of baptisms, deaths and marriages, and other materials.

ANGLETON

TX35-90
Brazoria County Library System
401 East Cedar
Angleton TX 77515

(409) 849-5711, Ext. 1505

OPEN: M, Tu 9-8, W-Sa 9-6; closed Sundays and holidays
COPYING FACILITIES: yes
MATERIALS SOLICITED: Family histories relating to Brazoria County.

HOLDINGS:
Total volume: 24 l.f.
Inclusive dates: 19th century -
Description: Oral histories and correspondence relating to early settlers.

OPEN: by appointment

ARLINGTON

TX42-810
University of Texas at Arlington Library
Division of Special Collections
Arlington TX

MAILING ADDRESS:
P.O. Box 19497
Arlington TX 76019

(817) 273-3391

OPEN: M-F 8-5, Sa 10-2; closed Sundays and holidays
COPYING FACILITIES: yes
MATERIALS SOLICITED: Items relating to Texas and Southwestern history, Mexican War history; cartography; Texas writers; 20th century Texas politics and labor unions; oral history; university archives; genealogy; history of Yucatan and Honduras. Materials supporting research interests of the University accepted.

HOLDINGS:
Total volume: 4,000 l.f.; 2,500 reels; 24,000 items
Inclusive dates: 1500's -
Description: The Jenkins Garrett Library on the history of Texas, the Southwest and the Mexican War; the Cartographic History Library; the Robertson Colony Papers relating to the settlement of Texas from Colonization through the present State Constitution; the Texas Labor Archives; the Knoerzer Foundation Collection of Western Art; documents, microfilm and newspapers relating to of-

ficial state, notarial and ecclesiastical archives of the Mexican state of Yucatan.

SEE: NUCMC, 1972-74, 76-77, 79.

SEE: Hinding.

SEE ALSO: Alan M. Meckler and Ruth McMullin, comps., *Oral History Collections* (Bowker, 1975); Ann Novotny, ed., *Picture Sources 3* (Special Libraries Assn., 1975); Howard Lackman and George Green, 'Origin and Progress of the Texas Labor Archives,' *Labor History* 11 (Summer 1970); and the following publications of the University of Texas at Arlington Library: Jan Hart Cohen, comp., *Descriptive Guide to the Collections* (1974); and *Labor Archives in the University of Texas at Arlington Library* (n.d.).

AUSTIN

TX56-25
Archives of the Episcopal Church, USA
606 Rathervue Place
Austin TX 78705

MAILING ADDRESS:
P.O. Box 2247
Austin TX 78768

(512) 472-6816

OPEN: M-F 8:30-4:30; closed weekends and holidays
ACCESS: serious researchers only; two references requested
COPYING FACILITIES: yes
MATERIALS SOLICITED: Records of and pertaining to the Episcopal church.

HOLDINGS:
Total volume: 2,000 l.f.
Inclusive dates: 17th century -
Description: Archives of the Episcopal church, including records of the House of Bishops, the House of Deputies, the Executive Council, and agencies of the church. Also included are photographs, films, slides, and private papers and manuscripts of clergy and laypeople.

SEE: Hamer; NUCMC, 1965, 68 (as Church Historical Society).

SEE ALSO: James M. Day, *Handbook of Texas Archival and Manuscript Depositories* (Texas Library and Historical Commission, 1966); Robert O. Collins and Peter Duignan, *Americans in Africa* (Hoover Institution, 1963). Descriptions of the collections have been published in *The Historical Magazine*, the official publication of the Historical Society.

TX56-30
Austin Presbyterian Theological Seminary
Stitt Library
100 East 27th Street
Austin TX 78705

no telephone

SEE: NUCMC, 1965.

Questionnaire not returned.

TX56-50
Austin Public Library
Austin-Travis County Collection
810 Guadalupe
Austin TX 78705

MAILING ADDRESS:
Box 2287
Austin TX 78767

(512) 472-5433, Ext. 280

OPEN: Su 2-6, M-Th 9-9, F, Sa 9-6; closed holidays
COPYING FACILITIES: yes
MATERIALS SOLICITED: Material pertaining to Austin or Travis County.

HOLDINGS:
Total volume: 734 l.f.
Inclusive dates: 1685 -
Description: More than 200 collections pertaining to the history of the Austin-Travis County area and its settlers. Included are correspondence, diaries, and family account books; records of organizations, businesses, and early city departments; oral history recordings and transcripts; sound recordings of Austin musicians; and photographs.

SEE: Hamer; NUCMC, 1979.

SEE: Beers - Southwest; Hinding.

SEE ALSO: Ann Novotny, ed., *Picture Sources 3* (Special Libraries Assn., 1975); James M. Day, *Handbook of Texas Archival and Manuscript Depositories* (Texas Library and Historical Commission, 1966); Albert Krichmar, *The Women's Rights Movement in the United States, 1848-1970: A Bibliography and Sourcebook* (Scarecrow Press, 1972); Katherine Hart, 'Administering the Local History Collection,' *Texas Libraries* 29 (Fall 1967).

TX56-110
Catholic Archives of Texas
16th and Congress
Austin TX

MAILING ADDRESS:
P.O. Box 13327
Capital Station
Austin TX 78711

(512) 476-4888

OPEN: M-F 8:30-4:30; closed weekends and National and religious holidays
COPYING FACILITIES: yes
MATERIALS SOLICITED: Materials related to Catholic activities throughout Texas and the Southwest, especially histories of Catholic parishes in Texas. Will also accept other Texas historical materials.

HOLDINGS:
Total volume: 350 l.f.
Inclusive dates: 1690 -
Description: Materials on the history of the Catholic church in Texas and the Southwest. Included are copies of documents at other institutions. Materials consist of records of the Knights of Columbus Historical Commission and its successor organization; Spanish and Mexican government records; diocesan, mission, parish and church records; photographs; personal papers such as correspondence, financial records, diaries, reports, military

inspections, land grants and titles, proclamations, and inventories.

Also includes the Texas Catholic Conference Collection (1969-75), the George W. Strake collection, and records of Volunteers for Educational and Social Services Collection (1968-77).

GUIDES: Claude Lane, *Catholic Archives of Texas: History and Preliminary Inventory* (1961).

SEE: Hamer; NUCMC, 1978.

SEE: Beers - Southwest; Hinding.

SEE ALSO: James M. Day, *Handbook of Texas Archival and Manuscript Depositories* (Texas Library and Historical Commission, 1966).

TX56-160

Daughters of the Republic of Texas, Inc.
Museum
112 East 11th Street
Austin TX 78701

(512) 477-1822

OPEN: M-F 9-5; closed weekends and holidays
COPYING FACILITIES: no
MATERIALS SOLICITED: Will accept materials dealing with Texas history before 1849.

HOLDINGS:
Total volume: not specified
Inclusive dates: not specified
Description: A small collection of manuscripts and photographs pertaining to the history of Texas, particularly in the 19th century.

TX56-200

Elisabet Ney Museum
304 East 44th Street
Austin TX 78751

(512) 458-2255

OPEN: Tu-F 11-4:30, Sa, Su 2-4:30; closed Mondays and holidays
COPYING FACILITIES: no
MATERIALS SOLICITED: Manuscripts and photographs relating to Elisabet Ney. Will also accept materials relating to sculpture.

HOLDINGS:
Total volume: 6 file drawers; 20 l.f. books
Inclusive dates: 1850's -
Description: Seventy photographs relating to sculptor Elisabet Ney and three hundred copies of Ney's papers, including notebooks and letters to friends and business associates.

SEE: Hinding.

Most of the copies are from Ney manuscripts at the University of Texas at Austin, Humanities Research Center.

TX56-490

Lutheran Church in America
Texas-Louisiana Synod
408 West 45th Street
Austin TX

MAILING ADDRESS:
P.O. Box 4367
Austin TX 78765

(512) 459-0090, 1000

OPEN: M-F 8:30-5; closed weekends and holidays
ACCESS: advance arrangements required
COPYING FACILITIES: yes
MATERIALS SOLICITED: Biographical data of ordained ministers of the synod and historical information on organizations. Will also accept historical material relating to congregations of the synod and official records of disbanded congregations.

HOLDINGS:
Total volume: 15 l.f.
Inclusive dates: 1851
Description: Records of the Lutheran Church in America, Texas-Louisiana Synod, and its predecessor organizations, the Texas-Louisiana Synod of the United Lutheran Church and the Texas Conference of the Augustana Lutheran Church, including correspondence, minutes of conventions, directories of clergy, biographical information relating to clergy, some historical material on congregations of the synod, account books and membership records of disbanded congregations, synod newspapers, and historical records of synod organizations.

TX56-520

Lyndon Baines Johnson Library
2313 Red River
Austin TX 78705

(512) 482-5137

OPEN: M-F 9-5, Sa by appointment; closed Sundays and holidays
COPYING FACILITIES: yes
MATERIALS SOLICITED: Materials relating to the life and career of Lyndon Baines Johnson and his friends, family, and associates; American politics and major issues of the 1930's through the 1970's.

HOLDINGS:
Total volume: 34,000,000 pages
Inclusive dates: 1927 -
Description: Materials relating to the life and political career of Lyndon Baines Johnson. Included are his Congressional, Senatorial, Vice Presidential, and Presidential papers, papers of friends and associates, oral history interviews and records of committees and commissions appointed by Johnson as President. Also included are motion pictures, video tape recordings, sound recordings, and still pictures documenting Johnson's life, career, and administration.

GUIDES: *Historical Materials in the Lyndon B. Johnson Library* (1977).

SEE: NUCMC, 1974, 76.

SEE: Davis; Paszek.

SEE ALSO: Ann Novotny, ed., *Picture Sources 3* (Special Libraries Assn., 1975); Chester A. Newland, 'The Lyndon Baines Johnson Library: New Dimensions of the Presidency and Presidential Papers,' *The Library Chronicle of the University of Texas* 1 (March 1970).

TX56-720

St. Edward's University
Archives
3001 South Congress Avenue
Austin TX 78704

(512) 448-8400

OPEN: M-F 8-12, by appointment in afternoons; closed weekends and holidays
COPYING FACILITIES: yes
MATERIALS SOLICITED: Materials relating to St. Edward's University and High School. Will also accept records relating to the Order of Preachers, Dominicans; Sisters, Servants of the Immaculate Heart of Mary; Congregation of the Holy Cross; and the Roman Catholic church in the southwest United States.

HOLDINGS:
Total volume: 104 drawers, 187 boxes
Inclusive dates: not specified
Description: Records of St. Edward's University and St. Edward's High School; records on members of the Congregation of Holy Cross; the Order of Preachers; Sisters, Servants of the Immaculate Heart of Mary; and the Roman Catholic church in the southwestern United States.

TX56-780

Texas Parks and Wildlife Department
Records Section
4200 Smith School Road
Austin TX 78744

(512) 479-4800

OPEN: M-F 8-5; closed weekends and holidays
MATERIALS SOLICITED: Historically significant records, including correspondence, diaries, and photographs, relating to the history of the Department. Will also accept other material pertinent to the conservation of natural resources.

HOLDINGS:
Total volume: 150 c.f.
Inclusive dates: 1902 -
Description: Departmental financial records, mostly microfilmed (1932-74), and materials relating to game, fish, and park management, such as construction contracts, records of public meetings and grants-in-aid projects, statistical reports, annual reports, audits, and sand, shell, and gravel surveys. There also is a State parks collection consisting of letters, photographs, Civilian Conservation Corps drawings and plans, and other documentation (1932-62).

TX56-790

Texas State Historical Association
2.306 Sid Richardson Hall
University Station
Austin TX 78712

(512) 471-1525

OPEN: M-F 8-5; closed weekends and
holidays
COPYING FACILITIES: no
MATERIALS SOLICITED: Photographs of
Texas and the Southwest.

HOLDINGS:
Total volume: 7,000 items
Inclusive dates: 19th century -
Description: A collection of 4,000 nega-
tives and 3,000 photographic prints illus-
trating various aspects of the history of
Texas and the American Southwest.

TX56-800

Texas State Library
Archives Division
1201 Brazos Street
Austin TX

MAILING ADDRESS:
P.O. Box 12927
Capitol Station
Austin TX 78711

(512) 475-2166

OPEN: M-F 8-5; closed weekends and
holidays
COPYING FACILITIES: yes
MATERIALS SOLICITED: Texas history.

HOLDINGS:
Total volume: 20,000 c.f.
Inclusive dates: 1733 -
Description: Materials relating to the
history of Texas and its governments. Included are the Nacogdoches Archives
(1733-1836), documenting the Spanish
and Mexican regimes; records of the Republic period, such as those of the Adjutant General's Office, the offices and
departments of Indian Affairs, State, and
Treasury, the Customs House, and the
Texas Congress; and for the statehood
period, the records of most State agencies, some local government records, and
papers of governors and other political
leaders.

SEE: Hamer; NUCMC, 1959-62.

SEE ALSO: Walter Schatz, ed., Directory of
Afro-American Resources (Bowker,
1970); Ann Novotny, ed., Picture
Sources 3 (Special Libraries Assn.,
1975); James M. Day, Handbook of
Texas Archival and Manuscript Deposi-
tories (Texas Library and Historical
Commission, 1966); Irene Sanchez,
comp., 'Index to Census and Manu-
script Microfilm Materials in Texas
State Archives,' Texas Libraries 23
(May/June 1961); James M. Day,
comp., Maps of Texas, 1527-1900: The
Map Collection of the Texas State Ar-
chives (Pemberton Press, 1964);
Dorman H. Winfrey, 'The Texas State
Archives,' Texas Libraries 22
(Sept./Oct. 1960); and the following
publications of the Library: Louise

Horton, Samuel Bell Maxey Papers: An
Inventory (1969); and John M. Kinney,
comp., Index to Applications for Texas
Confederate Pensions (1975). Typed inventories to individual collections are
available at the Library.

TX56-850

University of Texas at Austin
E. C. Barker Texas History Center
Austin TX 78713-7330

(512) 471-5961

OPEN: M-Sa 8-5; closed Sundays and
holidays
ACCESS: photographic identification
required
COPYING FACILITIES: yes
MATERIALS SOLICITED: Materials relating
to the development of Texas, the
American South and Southwest, and
the University of Texas.

HOLDINGS:
Total volume: 41,000 l.f.
Inclusive dates: 16th century -
Description: Over 3,000 collections relating to the historical development of
Texas, the American South and Southwest, and the University of Texas. Included are papers, related printed and
nontextual material and tape recordings
of individuals and families, records of
business concerns, organizations, and institutions, and the University Archives.
Primary concentration is in the 19th and
20th centuries. Fields of activity documented include agriculture, commerce,
cultural affairs, education, genealogy, government, industry, military affairs, politics, religion, science, and social affairs.

GUIDES: The University of Texas Archives:
A Guide to the Historical Manuscripts
Collections in the University of Texas
Library (Univ. of Texas Press, 1968).

SEE: Hamer; NUCMC, 1959-64, 69-73.

SEE: Schatz; Hounshell; Meckler and
McMullin; Davis; Spalek; Beers -
Southwest; Beers - Confederate; Allard,
Crawley, and Edmison; Hinding.

TX56-860

University of Texas at Austin
General Libraries
Nettie Lee Benson Latin American
Collection
Austin TX 78713-7330

(512) 471-3818

OPEN: M-F 9-5, Sa 1-5; closed Sundays
and holidays
COPYING FACILITIES: yes
MATERIALS SOLICITED: Material relating
to Latin America, the Caribbean, the
Spanish-speaking in the United States,
and areas of the United States at the
time they were under the Spanish or
Mexican government.

HOLDINGS:
Total volume: 515 l.f.; 2,250
microfilm reels
Inclusive dates: 16th century -
Description: Manuscript collections
covering the history and culture of Latin
America, the Caribbean, the Spanish-
speaking in the United States, and areas

of the United States at the time they
were under the Spanish or Mexican government. Included are records of organizations, papers of individuals, manuscript
maps, photographs, motion pictures, oral
history tapes and transcripts, sound recordings, and microfilm from foreign repositories documenting explorations, religious affairs, economic conditions, family
history, military and diplomatic history,
revolutionary upheavals, activities of governments, and the language and
ethnology of Meso-American and South
American Indians.

SEE: Hamer.

SEE: Hinding; Robbins; Beers - Southwest.

SEE ALSO: Catalog of the Latin American
Collection of the University of Texas
Library (G. K. Hall, 1969), First Sup-
plement (1971), Second Supplement
(1973), Third Supplement (1975); Jack
Autrey Dabbs, The Mariano Riva
Palacio Archives: A Guide (Editorial
Jus, 1967); Pablo Max Ynsfran,
Catalogo de los manuscritos del archivo
de don Valentin Gomez Farias:
Obrantes en la Universidad de Texas,
Coleccion Latinoamericana (Editorial
Jus, 1968); and publications describing
individual collections available at the
institution.

TX56-890

University of Texas at Austin
Humanities Research Center Library
21st and Guadalupe
Austin TX

MAILING ADDRESS:
P.O. Box 7219
Austin TX 78712

(512) 471-9119

OPEN: M-F 9-5, Sa 9-noon; closed
Sundays and holidays
ACCESS: researchers must make written
application to the faculty Committee
on the Use of Historical and Literary
Manuscripts
COPYING FACILITIES: yes
MATERIALS SOLICITED: English, French,
and American literature, 18th-20th centuries; and history of science, photography, theater arts, book arts and publishing history.

HOLDINGS:
Total volume: 8,400 l.f.; 250,000
photographs
Inclusive dates: 14th century -
Description: More than 450 collections
of literary manuscripts and correspondence of English, French, and American
authors, primarily from the 20th century.
Also included are Italian manuscripts and
materials relating to the history of science, photography, bibliography and theater arts.

SEE: Hamer; NUCMC, 1971.

SEE: Spalek; Martin.

SEE ALSO: Ann Novotny, ed., Picture
Sources 3 (Special Libraries Assn.,
1975); Source Materials for the Recent
History of Astronomy and Astrophysics:
A Checklist of Manuscript Collections in
the United States (American Institute
of Physics, 1971); Warren Roberts,

'The Humanities Research Center at the University of Texas,' *Manuscripts* 27 (Fall 1975); Frederick J. Hunter, comp., *Catalog of the Norman Bel Geddes Theatre Collections, Humanities Research Center, University of Texas at Austin* (G. K. Hall, 1973); Warren Roberts, *Twentieth Century Research Materials: A Decade of Library Development and Utilization* (1972).

The Library has published guides to specific collections, including manuscripts of Maxwell Anderson, Elizabeth Barrett and Robert Browning, Lord Byron, Charles Dickens, T. S. Eliot, Lillian Hellman, Joseph Hergesheimer, Johanna Southcott, and Louis Zukofsky. Unpublished guides to various collections are also available at the Library.

BASTROP

TX63-80
Bastrop County Historical Society
Museum
702 Main Street
Bastrop TX

MAILING ADDRESS:
P.O. Box 279
Bastrop TX 78602

(512) 321-6177

OPEN: Sa, Su 1-5 and by appointment; closed weekdays, holidays, Jan. and Feb.
COPYING FACILITIES: no
MATERIALS SOLICITED: Materials of historical value, especially those pertaining to Bastrop County, and particularly relating to early settlers and area industries.

HOLDINGS:
Total volume: 200 file folders; 20 maps; 75 vols.
Inclusive dates: 1800's -
Description: Materials relating to the history of Bastrop County, including manuscript maps, scrapbooks, ledgers, proceedings of civic organizations, minutes of Ayuntamiento (1834) and Bastrop (1839-56), school records, church records, photographs, muster rolls, deeds, and other items.

SEE: NUCMC, 1975.

SEE: Hinding.

BEAUMONT

TX70-770
Tyrrell Historical Library
695 Pearl Street
Beaumont TX

MAILING ADDRESS:
P.O. Box 3827
Beaumont TX 77704

(409) 838-0780

OPEN: Tu-Th, Sa 9-6; closed other days and holidays
COPYING FACILITIES: yes
MATERIALS SOLICITED: Texas history and genealogy.

HOLDINGS:
Total volume: 8,358 vols.
Inclusive dates: 1850's -
Description: Photographs and essays concerning Texas subjects, and manuscript poetry and plays.

BIG BEND NATIONAL PARK

TX91-80
Big Bend National Park
Big Bend National Park TX 79834

(915) 477-2251

OPEN: daily 8-5
ACCESS: advance arrangements required
COPYING FACILITIES: no
MATERIALS SOLICITED: Materials relating to the Big Bend area, including photographs of ranching, mining and early exploration; oral history interviews with area pioneers; and scientific papers and documents concerning natural history, geology and other aspects of Big Bend National Park.

HOLDINGS:
Total volume: 2 c.f.; 20 file drawers
Inclusive dates: 1930's -
Description: Historic and scientific documents used for the management of and research on Big Bend National Park and its immediate vicinity. Included is a photograph collection dating primarily after 1940.
Collection includes oral histories and some 16mm motion picture films.

SEE: Hinding.

SEE ALSO: James M. Day, *Handbook of Texas Archival and Manuscript Depositories* (Texas Library and Historical Commission, 1966).

BONHAM

TX105-720
Sam Rayburn Library
Bonham TX 75418

no telephone

SEE: Hamer; NUCMC, 1966, 74.

Questionnaire not returned.

CANYON

TX128-640
Panhandle-Plains Historical Museum
Historic Research Center
2401 4th Avenue
Canyon TX

MAILING ADDRESS:
Box 967
W. T. Station
Canyon TX 79016

(806) 655-7191

OPEN: M-F 9-5; closed weekends, Thanksgiving, Dec. 24-26, and New Year's
COPYING FACILITIES: yes

MATERIALS SOLICITED: Material dealing with the economic, geographic, cultural, archaeological, legal, political and social development of the Texas Panhandle and the surrounding region.

HOLDINGS:
Total volume: 11,000 c.f.
Inclusive dates: 1868 -
Description: A collection of manuscripts relating to the settlement and development of the Texas Panhandle. Included are personal and family papers, records of ranches and other businesses, county records, interviews with and memoirs of pioneers, and papers of National and State political leaders. There is also a photograph collection relating to local history.

SEE: Hamer; NUCMC, 1965, 73, 76, 80.

SEE ALSO: James M. Day, *Handbook of Texas Archival and Manuscript Depositories* (Texas Library and Historical Commission, 1966).

COLLEGE STATION

TX181-780
Texas A & M University
Libraries
Special Collections
College Station TX 77843

(409) 845-1951

OPEN: M-F 8-5; closed weekends, Thanksgiving, Christmas and spring vacations
COPYING FACILITIES: yes
MATERIALS SOLICITED: Materials relating to range livestock, science fiction, the Ku Klux Klan, and Texas.

HOLDINGS:
Total volume: 350 items
Inclusive dates: 1900 -
Description: Materials relating to the 19th century range cattle industry west of the Mississippi, science fiction, the Ku Klux Klan, and the history and geography of Texas.

SEE: NUCMC, 1977.

SEE: Robbins; Hinding.

TX181-790
Texas A & M University
University Archives and Manuscripts
Collection
College Station TX 77843

(409) 845-1815

OPEN: M-F 8-5; closed weekends, holidays, and spring vacations
COPYING FACILITIES: yes
MATERIALS SOLICITED: Records dealing with agriculture in Texas, technology, modern politics of Texas, and Texas A & M University, its faculty, and alumni.

HOLDINGS:
Total volume: 3,300 l.f.
Inclusive dates: 1850 -
Description: Historical manuscripts relating to agriculture in Texas, technology in the Southwest, and modern politics of Texas. Included are records of organiza-

tions and individuals including State legislators, members of Congress, and University faculty members in several disciplines. There are also records of several administrative units of Texas A & M University, Texas Agricultural Experiment Station, Texas Agricultural Extension Service, and Texas Engineering Experiment Station.

GUIDES: Charles R. Schultz, *A Descriptive Guide to the Holdings of the University Archives and Manuscripts Collections, Texas A & M University* (Texas A & M Univ. Library, 1974).

SEE: Hinding.

COLORADO CITY

TX189-520

Mitchell County Public Library
340 Oak Street
Colorado City TX 79512

(915) 728-3968

OPEN: Tu 12-8, W-Sa 9-5:30; closed
    Sundays, Mondays, and holidays
COPYING FACILITIES: yes
MATERIALS SOLICITED: Materials relating
    to Mitchell County and Texas.

HOLDINGS:
    Total volume: not specified
    Inclusive dates: 19th century -
    Description: Manuscripts relating chiefly to Mitchell County. Included are biographies of early settlers, a photograph collection, oral history interviews relating to the County, reminiscences of pioneers, and research papers on early education in the County, the history of the Mitchell County Library, the pioneer era, and local black history.

COMMERCE

TX210-200

East Texas State University
James G. Gee Library
Oral History Program
Commerce TX

MAILING ADDRESS:
East Texas Station
Commerce TX 75428

(214) 886-5739

OPEN: M-F 8-5; closed weekends,
    Thanksgiving, Christmas, and spring
    break
ACCESS: serious researchers
COPYING FACILITIES: yes
MATERIALS SOLICITED: Materials relating
    to the history of railroads, blacks,
    cotton and medicine in East Texas; the
    diplomatic career of Fletcher Warren;
    and the political career of A. M. Aikin,
    Jr.

HOLDINGS:
    Total volume: 350 hours of tapes
    Inclusive dates: 1973 -
    Description: Oral history materials relating chiefly to the history of railroads, blacks, cotton and medicine in East Texas; the diplomatic career of Fletcher Warren; and the political career of A. M. Aikin, Jr.

TX210-230

East Texas State University
University Archives
Commerce TX

MAILING ADDRESS:
East Texas Station
Commerce TX 75428

(214) 886-5737

OPEN: M-F 8-5; closed weekends,
    Thanksgiving, Christmas, and spring
    break
COPYING FACILITIES: yes
MATERIALS SOLICITED: East Texas State
    University records. Will also accept local history materials.

HOLDINGS:
    Total volume: 650 l.f.
    Inclusive dates: 1840 -
    Description: Manuscripts relating mainly to the history of Hopkins County and East Texas. Included are letters from Civil War soldiers, politicians, and religious leaders. There are also records on the Indians of the area, various communities of the East Texas area, and East Texas State University.

SEE: Hinding.

SEE ALSO: unpublished finding aids available at the repository.

CORPUS CHRISTI

TX217-480

La Retama Public Library
Local History Collection
505 North Mesquite Street
Corpus Christi TX 78401

(512) 882-1937

OPEN: M-Th 9-9, F, Sa 9-6; closed
    Sundays and holidays
COPYING FACILITIES: yes
MATERIALS SOLICITED: Materials relating
    to Nueces County and Corpus Christi,
    Texas.

HOLDINGS:
    Total volume: 10,000 items
    Inclusive dates: 19th century -
    Description: Materials relating to the history of Nueces County and Corpus Christi, Texas, including family papers, biographies, municipal and county records, oral histories, diaries and photographs.

CROCKETT

TX228-320

Historical and Cultural Activities
    Center
of Houston County, TX, Inc.
629 North 4th
Crockett TX 75835

(409) 544-3269

OPEN: by appointment only
ACCESS: serious researchers only

COPYING FACILITIES: yes
MATERIALS SOLICITED: Materials relating
    to the volunteer Ranger Company,
    1838-40, and John Wortham, commanding officer; Trinity and Neches
    River Bluff shipping points for Houston County, 1837-40; east Texas area
    participation in the Civil War, the Reconstruction and the Ku Klux Klan;
    cotton farming, Trinity River plantations and the transition to mechanization, 1820-1930; medicines and apothecary advancement to pharmacies and
    drug stores, 1870-1940. Will also accept Houston County records, 1850-65.

HOLDINGS:
    Total volume: 7 c.f.
    Inclusive dates: 1838 -
    Description: Personal papers of Major John Wortham, 1838-60; documentation and correspondence pertaining to historical markers; materials relating to the Monroe-Crook and the Downes-Aldrich houses, listed in the National Register; photographs, 1870- ; and records of Houston County community groups and schools.

CROSBYTON

TX231-120

Crosby County Pioneer Memorial
101 Main Street
Crosbyton TX

MAILING ADDRESS:
P.O. Box 386
Crosbyton TX 79322

(806) 675-2331

OPEN: Tu-Sa 9-5; closed Sundays,
    Mondays, holidays, and Christmas
    vacation
COPYING FACILITIES: yes
MATERIALS SOLICITED: Materials relevant to the south plains area of Texas,
    1870-1950. Will also accept materials
    applicable to the development of western Texas.

HOLDINGS:
    Total volume: 12 l.f.
    Inclusive dates: 1862 -
    Description: Materials relating to settlement and agricultural development in Crosby County and western Texas. Notable collections include papers of Henry Clay Smith, an early settler; correspondence of the first large ranch in the region; and several thousand photographs of farming and ranching. There are also oral histories, pioneer daybooks, and land and military records.

SEE: Hinding.

CUERO

TX245-160

De Witt County Historical Museum, Inc.
312 East Broadway
Cuero TX

MAILING ADDRESS:
P.O. Box 745
Cuero TX 77954

(512) 275-6322

OPEN: Th, F 9-5; closed other days and holidays
COPYING FACILITIES: no
MATERIALS SOLICITED: Materials relating to De Witt County. Will also accept materials relating to Texas.

HOLDINGS:
Total volume: 2 file cabinets
Inclusive dates: 1890 -
Description: Material pertaining to De Witt County families and institutions in the 19th and 20th centuries; research notes taken from 1940 to the present; 200 photographs; and church records.

DALLAS

TX252-80

Bishop College
Library
Southwest Research Center and Museum of African American Life and Culture
3837 Simpson-Stuart Road
Dallas TX 75241

(214) 372-8734, 8000

OPEN: M-F 8-4; closed weekends, Easter, Christmas and New Year's
COPYING FACILITIES: yes
MATERIALS SOLICITED: Black Baptist church history archives, blacks in the Southwest, and archives and non-current records of the College. Will also accept materials related to the black experience and African materials.

HOLDINGS:
Total volume: not specified
Inclusive dates: 1929 -
Description: A collection of papers (1929-52) of Dr. J. J. Rhoads, first black president of the College. Included are records of the Texas Council of Negro Organizations, Texas State Colored Teachers Association and the NAACP. There are also four boxes of papers of a Texas State Representative (1973-75) dealing with revision of the State constitution.

TX252-120

Dallas City Secretary
200 City Hall
Dallas TX 75201

(214) 670-3738

OPEN: M-F 8:15-5:15; closed weekends and holidays
COPYING FACILITIES: yes
MATERIALS SOLICITED: City of Dallas government documents.

HOLDINGS:
Total volume: 200,000 items
Inclusive dates: 1888 -
Description: City government records pertaining to actions by Dallas City Council. Included are ordinances, resolutions of the Council, land instruments, zoning maps and files, reports from special committees, commissions, and consultants, and tape recordings of Council meetings since 1961.

TX252-150

Dallas Historical Society
Research Center Library and Archives
Hall of State
Fair Park
Dallas TX

MAILING ADDRESS:
Box 26038
Dallas TX 75226

(214) 421-5136

OPEN: M-F 9-5, Saturdays by appointment; closed Sundays and holidays
ACCESS: researchers must complete use form and obtain use card
COPYING FACILITIES: yes
MATERIALS SOLICITED: Photographs, maps, and other materials relating to Dallas history, north and central Texas history, especially social and urban, and the John F. Kennedy assassination. Will also accept other materials which might be useful to researchers in this area.

HOLDINGS:
Total volume: 1,600,000 items
Inclusive dates: 1590 -
Description: Archive collection of over 1,600,000 pieces covering the history of Texas from the period of Spanish control to the present, with emphasis on the history of the Dallas area. Included are papers of individuals, unpublished memoirs, diaries, histories, records of institutions, maps, photographs, autograph collections, and scrapbooks.

SEE: Hamer; NUCMC, 1962-64.

SEE: Beers - Southwest.

SEE ALSO: Albert Krichmar, *The Women's Rights Movement in the United States, 1848-1970: A Bibliography and Sourcebook* (Scarecrow Press, 1972). A brochure listing major collections is available from the Historical Society.

TX252-170

Dallas Public Library
Archives and Research Center for Texas and Dallas History
1515 Young Street
Dallas TX 75201

(214) 749-4151

OPEN: M-Th 9-9, F-Sa 9-5, Su 1-5; closed holidays
COPYING FACILITIES: yes
MATERIALS SOLICITED: Materials relating to the history of the city of Dallas and Dallas County. Will also accept materials relating to other areas in Texas.

HOLDINGS:
Total volume: 750 c.f.
Inclusive dates: 1809 -
Description: Materials relating to the Dallas area, primarily in the 20th century. Included are oral history tapes and transcripts, correspondence, business records, diaries, photographs, maps, and architectural drawings and blueprints.

SEE: Hamer; NUCMC, 1966, 76, 79.

SEE: Schatz; Novotny.

TX252-200

Diocese of Dallas of the Episcopal Church
1630 North Garrett
Dallas TX 75206

(214) 826-8310

OPEN: M-F 8:30-4:30; closed weekends and holidays
ACCESS: arrangements with Historiographer recommended
COPYING FACILITIES: yes
MATERIALS SOLICITED: Materials pertaining to bishops Alexander C. Garrett, Harry Tunis Moore, and C. Avery Mason, and other clergy of the diocese; Episcopal churches of the diocese; St. Mary's College; and St. Matthew's Home for Children.

HOLDINGS:
Total volume: 10 file drawers
Inclusive dates: 1874 -
Description: Diaries and letters of Bishop Moore and other bishops of the diocese; microfilmed and typescript copies of Bishop Garrett's diaries; histories about Bishop Garrett; records of defunct parishes; and news clippings, photographs, and other historical materials about diocesan churches and parishes.

TX252-320

Historic Preservation League, Inc.
2013 Kidwell Street
Dallas TX

MAILING ADDRESS:
P.O. Box 140460
Dallas TX 75214

(214) 827-5800

OPEN: M-F 1-5; closed weekends, Christmas, and New Year's
COPYING FACILITIES: no
MATERIALS SOLICITED: Visual documents of research or archival value, especially photographs, architectural drawings, and related materials. Will also accept manuscripts and archives relating to Dallas' past.

HOLDINGS:
Total volume: 3,000 items
Inclusive dates: 1900 -
Description: A collection of records, photographs, architectural line drawings, surveys, legal material, and other data relating to the architectural and physical history of the city of Dallas.

TX252-322

Society of Independent Professional
Earth Scientists
Archives Committee
1 Energy Square, Suite 170
4925 Greenville
Dallas TX 75206

(214) 363-1780

OPEN: by appointment only
ACCESS: members of the Society
COPYING FACILITIES: no

HOLDINGS:
Total volume: 1 file cabinet
Inclusive dates: 1962 -
Description: A collection of the Society's correspondence and other papers.

In 1984 the Society moved to its present quarters from 406 W. Wall Street, Midland, Texas.

TX252-730

Southern Methodist University
Fikes Hall of Special Collections and
DeGolyer Library
3rd Floor, Science Information
Library
Dallas TX 75275

(214) 692-3231

OPEN: M-F 8:30-5; closed weekends and
holidays
ACCESS: identification required; advance
arrangements suggested
COPYING FACILITIES: yes
MATERIALS SOLICITED: History of the
American West, especially that of
railroads, business, mining, land development, exploration, overland travel,
and agriculture and ranching. Special
interest in Spanish Borderlands. Will
also accept materials pertaining to the
oil industry and general transportation.

HOLDINGS:
Total volume: 1,500 l.f. manuscripts;
300,000 photographs
Inclusive dates: 1600 -
Description: Letters, drawings, and other materials on Texas and the American
West, mainly in the 19th century, concerning business, mining and geology,
land development, and transportation.
There is particular emphasis on locomotive manufacturing, railroad industries,
and the oil and gas industry. Also included are materials on Mexican and
Spanish-American history, and 300,000
photographs, largely concerning the
railroad industry.

SEE: NUCMC, 1959-64, 69 (as DeGolyer
Foundation Library).

SEE: Schatz; Novotny; Beers - Southwest;
Parkinson; Hinding.

TX252-760

Southern Methodist University
Perkins School of Theology
Methodist Historical Collections
Bridwell Library, SMU
Dallas TX 75275

(214) 692-2363

OPEN: M-F 9-5; closed weekends and
holidays; schedule varies with school
calendar
COPYING FACILITIES: yes
MATERIALS SOLICITED: Materials relating
to the development of the Methodist
church in England and North America;
of the Methodist Episcopal Church,
South; of Methodism in Texas and the
south central region of the US, and of
the Perkins School of Theology, SMU.
Will also accept materials relating to
theological or biblical studies and to
English or American history of the
Christian churches.

HOLDINGS:
Total volume: 420 c.f.
Inclusive dates: 1740 -
Description: Correspondence and other
papers of principal figures in the development of the Methodist church, especially
in Texas, and of Southern Methodist
University. Included are letters of John
Wesley and important American Methodist bishops, photographs, and church
records.

SEE: Hamer; NUCMC, 1959-61.

SEE: Robbins; Hinding.

TX252-770

Southern Methodist University
Science/Engineering Library
6425 Airline Road
Dallas TX 75275

(214) 692-2277

OPEN: M-Th 8-11, F 8-6, Sa 8:30-5, Su
2-11; closed holidays
COPYING FACILITIES: yes
MATERIALS SOLICITED: History of earth
sciences. Will also accept materials relating to the history of science and engineering.

HOLDINGS:
Total volume: 18 l.f.
Inclusive dates: 19th century -
Description: Primarily the papers of
Robert Thomas Hill, Texas geologist who
also contributed significantly to National
and international geologic studies. Included are field notebooks, personal correspondence, photographs, manuscript
maps and reports.

TX252-780

Southern Methodist University
Underwood Law Library
Dallas TX 75275

(214) 692-3258

OPEN: M-F 9-5; closed weekends and
holidays
COPYING FACILITIES: yes

HOLDINGS:
Total volume: 11 l.f.
Inclusive dates: 1955 -
Description: Papers compiled by
Charles O. Galvin while a member of the
National Commission on Marijuana and
Drug Abuse (1970-73); correspondence of
the Texas Legislative Council Statutory
Revision Study Committee concerning
the Texas Business and Commerce Code
(1966-67); correspondence and drafts of
the State Bar of Texas Committee on
Revision of the Texas Non-profit Corporation Act (1955-59); research and
drafting files of the State Bar of Texas
and the Texas Legislative Council concerning a proposed revision of the Texas
Penal Code (1966-70); and correspondence of the State Bar of Texas Committee on Revision of Corporation Laws
(1959-61).

TX252-790

Southern Methodist University
University Archives
302 Fondren Library West
Dallas TX

MAILING ADDRESS:
Box 313
Southern Methodist University
Dallas TX 75275

(214) 692-2261

OPEN: M-F 9-5; closed weekends and
holidays
COPYING FACILITIES: yes
MATERIALS SOLICITED: Records, correspondence, photographs, or other
memorabilia dealing with the history
and development of the University.

HOLDINGS:
Total volume: 438 l.f.
Inclusive dates: 1910 -
Description: Papers, records, photographs, documents, and letters relating to
the history of the University; an oral history collection relating to the history of
the University and the city of Dallas; and
papers and correspondence of Ellis
Shuler, Texas geologist.
Also includes papers of S.W. Geiser,
Texas biologist and historian; and Paul
van Katwijk, Texas musician and educator.

DECATUR

TX259-880

Wise County Heritage Museum
Wise County Historical Commission
Archive
1602 South Trinity
Decatur TX

MAILING ADDRESS:
P.O. Box 427
Decatur TX 76234

(817) 627-5586

OPEN: M-Sa 9:30-4:30, Su 1-4:30; closed
holidays
USER FEES: small charges for use of
microfilm readers
COPYING FACILITIES: no

MATERIALS SOLICITED: Family histories, county histories, cemetery records, muster roll lists, and other local history manuscripts, as well as materials concerned broadly with American and Texas history. Will also accept photographs and maps.

HOLDINGS:
Total volume: 500 vols.
Inclusive dates: 19th century -
Description: A local history collection of photographs, oral histories, and family histories, including a 19th century account of a girl captured by Indians.

DEER PARK

TX266-720
San Jacinto Museum of History
Association
San Jacinto Monument
Deer Park TX

MAILING ADDRESS:
P.O. Box 758
Deer Park TX 77536

no telephone

SEE: Hamer (listed under San Jacinto Monument, TX).

Questionnaire not returned.

DENISON

TX273-160
Denison Public Library
300 West Gandy
Denison TX 75020

(214) 465-1797

OPEN: M, Tu, F, Sa 9-6, W, Th 9-8, Su 1-5; closed holidays
COPYING FACILITIES: yes
MATERIALS SOLICITED: Materials relating to the Grayson County area.

HOLDINGS:
Total volume: 13 items
Inclusive dates: 1923 - 1944
Description: Papers of naval officer Adolphus Andrews, including scrapbooks, clippings, correspondence, speeches, and a diary kept while he was captain of the Presidential yacht in 1925.

SEE: Allard, Crawley, and Edmison.

DENTON

TX280-540
North Texas State University
University Archives
A.M. Willis, Jr. Library
Denton TX

MAILING ADDRESS:
Box 5188 NT Station
Denton TX 76203

(817) 565-2766

OPEN: M-F 8-5; closed weekends, holidays, and during spring break
COPYING FACILITIES: yes

MATERIALS SOLICITED: Business collections and regional material. Will also accept Texas and Southwest collections.

HOLDINGS:
Total volume: 1,359 l.f.
Inclusive dates: 1826 -
Description: Historical manuscript collections pertaining to the 19th century include the Mrs. Anson Jones Collection (letters of the family of the last president of the Republic of Texas) and letters and diaries concerning the Civil War, gold mining in Colorado, and social history in Texas, Indiana, Iowa, Minnesota, and Ohio.

Historical manuscript collections from the 20th century include the political, military, and diplomatic papers of Alvin Owsley covering North America and Europe; administrative records of the Oral History Association; the equal rights political papers of Hermine Tobolowsky of Texas; and other collections dealing with Texas political, social, and economic history.

Business collections from the 20th century include the Fort Worth Stockyard records and labor union records of the Screwmen's Benevolent Association of Galveston and the Brotherhood of Railroad Trainmen of Cleburne, TX. University records include presidential papers, retired faculty collections, and university photographs.

Oral history materials include 490 transcripts concerning Pearl Harbor, prisoners of war, the Texas legislature and ex-governors, the U.S. Congress, the New Deal, and Texas businessmen and women. The archives is also a depository for Montague County records.

SEE: Hamer; NUCMC, 1979.

SEE: Meckler and McMullin; Spalek; Hinding; Beers-Southwest.

SEE ALSO: *American Archivist*, vol. 42, no. 2, April 1979, pp. 249-250; *Journal of American History*, vol. 66, no. 2, September 1979; *Oral History Collection*, NTSU Bulletin, 1980.

EDINBURG

TX319-640
Pan American University
Library
Special Collections
Edinburg TX 78539

(512) 381-2799

OPEN: M-Th 7:45-10:30, F 7:45-5:30, Sa 8-5, Su 2-10; closed holidays and spring break
COPYING FACILITIES: yes
MATERIALS SOLICITED: Records of Pan American University; records of Cameron, Willacy, Hidalgo, Starr, Jim Hogg, Webb, and Zapata counties; and manuscripts, archives, and oral histories pertaining to the Rio Grande Valley and northeastern Mexico, especially the state of Tamaulipas. Will also accept materials of local historical significance, such as records of civic clubs.

HOLDINGS:
Total volume: 48 l.f.; 7 microfilm reels; 20 photographs; 2 oral histories
Inclusive dates: 1925 -
Description: Pan American University archives; minutes and other records of the Edinburg Study Club, a women's cultural organization; and photographs and oral histories relating to the Rio Grande Valley and northeastern Mexico.

SEE: Hinding.

EL PASO

TX326-160
Diocese of the Rio Grande, Protestant Episcopal Church
Archives
810 North Campbell
El Paso TX 79902

(915) 533-4915

OPEN: M-Th 8-4, F 8-3; closed weekends and holidays
COPYING FACILITIES: no
MATERIALS SOLICITED: Materials having to do with the diocese and its churches.

HOLDINGS:
Total volume: 41 file cabinets; 12 items
Inclusive dates: 1870 -
Description: Correspondence and papers concerning diocesan missions and parishes, including work with Indians, the girls' school in Santa Fe, the church tuberculosis sanitarium in Albuquerque, and the Mexican mission in El Paso. Other diocesan materials include registers of baptisms, confirmations, and deaths; journals; business records and financial ledgers; personal correspondence and sermons; and the manuscript of *Lighting the Candle*, by Bishop James M. Stoney.

TX326-210
El Paso Public Library
Southwest Collection
501 North Oregon
El Paso TX 79901

(915) 541-4869

OPEN: M-Th 9-9, F, Sa 9-5:30; closed Sundays and holidays
ACCESS: advance notice is necessary for use of certain archival materials
COPYING FACILITIES: yes
MATERIALS SOLICITED: Material pertaining to El Paso, trans-Pecos Texas, southern New Mexico, and the Mexican Revolution in northern Mexico. Will also accept material pertaining to any part of the American Southwest or northern Mexico.

HOLDINGS:
Total volume: 900 manuscript items; 10,000 photographs
Inclusive dates: 1813 -
Description: Materials pertaining to El Paso, trans-Pecos Texas, and the Mexican Revolution. Included are business records, court records, correspondence, legal papers, scrapbooks, photographs of El Paso and the Mexican Revolution, literary manuscripts by J. Frank Dobie, C.

L. Sonnichsen, and Tom Lea, and Carl Hertzog ephemera.

SEE: Robbins.

SEE ALSO: James M. Day, *Handbook of Texas Archival and Manuscript Depositories* (Texas Library and Historical Commission, 1966).

TX326-770

The University of Texas at El Paso
El Paso Centennial Museum
Manuscript Collection
El Paso TX 79968

(915) 747-5565

OPEN: by appointment only
COPYING FACILITIES: yes
MATERIALS SOLICITED: Materials pertaining to archaeological and historical sites, and to the human and natural history of the El Paso area. Will also accept materials relating to local history.

HOLDINGS:
   Total volume: 4 file cabinets
   Inclusive dates: 1940 -
   Description: Manuscripts relating to the archaeological and historical research of the Museum staff, including archaeological surveys and records, such as field notes and maps, of 8,200 sites. Also includes manuscripts by the staff on Spanish Colonial history.

TX326-780

University of Texas at El Paso
Institute of Oral History
Room 334, Liberal Arts Building
El Paso TX 79968

(915) 747-5508

OPEN: M-F 8-5; closed weekends and holidays
ACCESS: researchers are asked to sign agreement concerning restrictions on individual interviews, proper credit citation, and permission for extensive use of interviews
COPYING FACILITIES: yes
MATERIALS SOLICITED: Interviews concerning the history of El Paso and Ciudad Juarez and the surrounding area, especially Mexican-Americans, other ethnic groups, and issues of the United States-Mexico border. Will also accept diaries, family histories, pictures, tapes of speeches, and video tapes.

HOLDINGS:
   Total volume: 335 items
   Inclusive dates: 1966 -
   Description: Subject areas include the Mexican Revolution, World War I, prohibition, the Depression, immigration, World War II, recent social and economic issues of the US-Mexico border area, and labor history.

GUIDES: An unpublished catalogue of the collection (1977) is available from the institution.

SEE: Meckler and McMullin.

TX326-800

University of Texas at El Paso
Library
Department of Special Collections and Archives
El Paso TX 79968

(915) 747-5697

OPEN: M, W 8-9, Tu, Th, F 8-5; closed weekends, holidays and school vacations; shorter hours in summer
COPYING FACILITIES: yes
MATERIALS SOLICITED: Materials pertaining to the history of the City of El Paso, El Paso County, the State of Texas, the old Southwest and northern Mexico (with emphasis on the Mexican Revolution of 1910).

HOLDINGS:
   Total volume: 1,500 c.f.
   Inclusive dates: 1631 -
   Description: Records of the El Paso and Northeastern Railroad Co. (1897-1905), the El Paso and Southwestern Railroad Co. (1905-24), and the Rio Grande Division of the Southern Pacific Co. (1924-58); correspondence, clippings and interviews from the files of military historian S. L. A. Marshall; municipal, church and judicial archives on microfilm from Chihuahua, Durango, Janos, and Ciudad Juarez, Mexico (1745-1900; 1,600 reels); and personal papers, documents and photographs pertaining to individuals and institutions prominent in the history of the El Paso area. The Department also serves as a regional depository for selected city and county records.

GUIDES: R. P. Daguerre, ed., *List of Archival Accessions* (1975); Mildred Torok, comp., *The University of Texas at El Paso Archives* (1972).

SEE: Hamer (as El Paso Centennial Museum, Texas Western College); NUCMC, 1969-70.

SEE: Beers - Southwest.

SEE ALSO: Ann Novotny, ed., *Picture Sources 3* (Special Libraries Assn., 1975); James M. Day, *Handbook of Texas Archival and Manuscript Depositories* (Texas Library and Historical Commission, 1966).

FORT STOCKTON

TX367-40

Annie Riggs Memorial Museum
301 South Main Street
Fort Stockton TX 79735

(915) 336-2167

OPEN: M-Sa 10-5; closed Sundays and holidays
USER FEES: fifty cents for first visit
COPYING FACILITIES: no
MATERIALS SOLICITED: Will accept materials pertaining to Pecos County, TX, and the Southwest.

HOLDINGS:
   Total volume: 3 l.f.
   Inclusive dates: late 1800's -
   Description: Materials concerning the history of Pecos County, TX, including aerial photographs of the entire county,

pioneer memorabilia, unpublished dissertations, and photographs.

FORT WORTH

TX374-40

Amon Carter Museum
Department of Photographs
3501 Camp Bowie Blvd.
Fort Worth TX

MAILING ADDRESS:
P.O. Box 2365
Fort Worth TX 76101

(817) 738-1933

OPEN: Tu-F 10-5; closed weekends, Mondays, and holidays
ACCESS: advance arrangements required
COPYING FACILITIES: yes
MATERIALS SOLICITED: 19th and 20th century American photographs.

HOLDINGS:
   Total volume: 200,000 items
   Inclusive dates: 1840's -
   Description: A broad collection of American photography with a special emphasis on the American West. Highlights of the collection include: the Laura Gilpin photographic estate, the Mazzulla collection of historic western American photography, and holdings relating to western survey photography and 19th-century Plains Indians (including several hundred photographs by William Henry Jackson). Also included are significant groups of work by Ansel Adams, John K. Hillers, Lewis Hine, Dorothea Lange, Carleton Watkins, Todd Webb, and Edward Weston.

SEE: Novotny.

TX374-240

Fort Worth Museum of Science and History
Collections Library
1501 Montgomery
Fort Worth TX 76107

(817) 732-1631

OPEN: M-F 9-5; closed weekends and holidays
ACCESS: qualified scholars by arrangement with the Executive Director or Curator of Collections
COPYING FACILITIES: yes
MATERIALS SOLICITED: Materials relating to archaeology, ethnology, history, pre-Columbian art, biology, acarology, astronomy, paleontology, and geology.

HOLDINGS:
   Total volume: 130 items
   Inclusive dates: 1807 - 1935
   Description: Primarily sources of information related to identification of artifacts and specimens currently in the museum collection. Especially strong collection of Pre-Columbian archaeological information. Historical photographs of Fort Worth, published sources of Southwestern native American cultures, Texas and U.S. history, and scientific literature are also included. Library holdings are intended to serve research needs of museum staff.

TX374-250

Fort Worth Public Library
Southwest and Genealogy Department
300 Taylor
Fort Worth TX 76102

(817) 870-7740

OPEN: M-Th 9-9, F, Sa 10-6; closed
Sundays and holidays

SEE: Hamer.

Questionnaire not returned.

TX374-550

National Archives and Records
Service
Federal Archives and Records Center
Archives Branch
4900 Hemphill Street
Fort Worth TX

MAILING ADDRESS:
P.O. Box 6216
Fort Worth TX 76115

(817) 334-5515

OPEN: M-F 8-4:30; closed weekends and
holidays
ACCESS: Records are open, subject to
Federal agency restrictions and
restrictions based upon current
legislation relevant to confidentiality
and security classification. See General
Information Leaflet No. 27, 'General
Restrictions on Access to Records in
the National Archives of the United
States.'
COPYING FACILITIES: yes
MATERIALS SOLICITED: Non-current
records of agencies of the Federal government in Arkansas, Louisiana, Oklahoma, and Texas. Will also accept other materials subject to the appropriate
guidelines of the National Archives and
Records Service.

HOLDINGS:
Total volume: 24,161 c.f.
Inclusive dates: 1806 - 1952
Description: Federal records, primarily
for Arkansas, Louisiana, Oklahoma, and
Texas. Heaviest concentration is on the
records of District and Circuit Courts,
such as docket and minute books and
case files. There are significant holdings
for the Bureau of Indian Affairs in Texas
and Oklahoma, including correspondence,
tribal census and annuity rolls, allotment
and lease files, and trust accounts.

SEE: Hamer.

SEE: Davis; Hinding.

SEE ALSO: James M. Day, Handbook of
Texas Archival and Manuscript Deposi-
tories (Texas Library and Historical
Commission, 1966).

TX374-720

Southwestern Baptist Theological
Seminary
Webb Roberts Library
2001 West Seminary Drive
Fort Worth TX

MAILING ADDRESS:
Box 22000-2E
Fort Worth TX 76122

(817) 923-1921, Ext. 333

OPEN: M-F 8-5; closed weekends,
Thanksgiving, and Christmas week
COPYING FACILITIES: yes
MATERIALS SOLICITED: Texas Baptist
history. Will also accept Baptist materi-
als from outside of Texas.

HOLDINGS:
Total volume: 1,916 l.f.
Inclusive dates: 1870 -
Description: Papers of Texas and Louisiana Baptist clergy and professionals,
primarily presidents and faculty members
of Southwestern Baptist Theological
Seminary and other Baptist colleges.
There are also records of the Baptist General Convention of Texas and of miscellaneous Texas Baptist churches.

SEE: Hamer.

TX374-750

Texas Christian University
Library
Fort Worth TX 76129

no telephone

SEE: NUCMC, 1959-61.

Questionnaire not returned.

FREDERICKSBURG

TX381-280

Gillespie County Historical Society
and Commission
Vereins Kirche Archives and Local
History Collection
Pioneer Plaza
P.O. Box 765
Fredericksburg TX 78624

(512) 997-7832

OPEN: M-F 2-4:30; closed weekends and
holidays
COPYING FACILITIES: no
MATERIALS SOLICITED: Materials relative
to Gillespie County and German Settlement in that area.

HOLDINGS:
Total volume: not specified
Inclusive dates: 1847 -
Description: Materials documenting the
founding of the colony of Fredericksburg,
1846, of Gillespie County, 1848, and the
Vereins Kirche, 1847.

GAINESVILLE

TX390-140

Cooke County Heritage Society, Inc.
Morton Museum of Cooke County
210 S. Dixon
Gainesville TX

MAILING ADDRESS:
P.O. Box 150
Gainesville TX 76240

(817) 668-8900

OPEN: Tu-Sa 12-5, Su 2-5; closed
Mondays, Christmas and New Year's
ACCESS: advance arrangements
recommended
COPYING FACILITIES: no
MATERIALS SOLICITED: Records documenting Cooke County personalities
and life, including politics, technology,
agriculture, and social life.

HOLDINGS:
Total volume: not specified
Inclusive dates: 1850 -
Description: Collections pertaining to
the development of Cooke County, including correspondence, diaries,
reminiscences, photographs, and manuscripts.

GALVESTON

TX397-690

Rosenberg Library
Archives Department
2310 Sealy
Galveston TX 77550

(409) 763-8854, Ext. 27

OPEN: Tu-Sa 10-5; closed Sundays,
Mondays, and holidays
ACCESS: registration and identification
required
COPYING FACILITIES: yes
MATERIALS SOLICITED: Manuscript materials dealing with Texas as a colony
and a republic, especially Galveston
and the upper Texas Gulf coast area in
the 19th and 20th centuries.

HOLDINGS:
Total volume: 900 l.f.
Inclusive dates: 1655 -
Description: Materials relating chiefly
to the colonization of Texas, the Texas
revolution, the Texas Republic, immigration, and land and railroad speculation.
Manuscripts of Galveston interest relate
to the development of the port, the Civil
War and the Battle of Galveston, yellow
fever epidemics, hurricanes, seawall construction and grade raising, and Galveston's commission form of government.

GUIDES: Michael Wilson and Jane
Kenamore, A Guide to Manuscripts in
the Rosenberg Library (1981).

SEE: Hamer; NUCMC, 1967.

SEE: Beers - Southwest; Allard, Crawley,
and Edmison; Robbins; Hinding.

SEE ALSO: Walter Schatz, ed., *Directory of Afro-American Resources* (Bowker, 1970); James M. Day, *Handbook of Texas Archival and Manuscript Depositories* (Texas Library and Historical Commission, 1966); Ann Novotny, ed., *Picture Sources 3* (Special Libraries Assn., 1975).

TX397-790
University of Texas Medical Branch
Moody Medical Library
History of Medicine and Archives
  Department
Galveston TX 77550

(409) 761-2397

OPEN: M-F 8-5; closed weekends and
  holidays
COPYING FACILITIES: yes
MATERIALS SOLICITED: Materials concerning medicine and allied fields.

HOLDINGS:
  Total volume: 130 l.f.
  Inclusive dates: 1810 -
  Description: Papers of medical educators, biomedical scientists, practicing physicians, records of medical societies, and UTMD Archives. Materials concerning the development of medicine, the medical profession, and medical education in Texas. Also included are materials relating to medicine in other areas of the United States and Europe.

SEE: NUCMC, 1980.

SEE: Hinding.

GEORGETOWN

TX404-120
Southwestern University
Cody Memorial Library
Department of Special Collections
Georgetown TX 78626

(512) 863-1568

OPEN: M-F 8-5; closed weekends,
  Thanksgiving, Christmas and spring
  vacations
COPYING FACILITIES: yes
MATERIALS SOLICITED: Materials relating to the history of Southwestern University.

HOLDINGS:
  Total volume: 150 l.f.
  Inclusive dates: 1840 -
  Description: Materials relating to the history of Southwestern University including correspondence, photographs, scrapbooks and ephemera; and the Isabel Gaddis Collection of J. Frank Dobie letters and manuscripts.

SEE: Robbins.

GONZALES

TX425-280
Gonzales Historical Museum
East St. Lawrence Street
Gonzales TX 78629

(512) 672-6350

OPEN: M-Sa 10-5, Su 1-5
COPYING FACILITIES: no
MATERIALS SOLICITED: Materials pertaining to early Texas history or subjects of general historical interest.

HOLDINGS:
  Total volume: 46 items
  Inclusive dates: 1705 - 1866
  Description: Collection includes founding records of Gonzales, property deeds, land records, bills of sale of its citizens and several miscellaneous Spanish documents, 1705- .

SEE: Beers-Southwest.

GRAPEVINE

TX439-280
Grapevine Public Library
307 W. Dallas Road
Grapevine TX 76051

(817) 481-0336

OPEN: Tu, Th 10-8, W, F 10-6, Sa 10-3;
  closed Sundays, Mondays and holidays
COPYING FACILITIES: yes
MATERIALS SOLICITED: Materials related to the history of Grapevine. Will also accept family histories.

HOLDINGS:
  Total volume: 1 file drawer
  Inclusive dates: 19th century -
  Description: Materials relating to the history of Grapevine, including family histories, manuscript histories, photographs, deeds, and records of social clubs.

HARLINGEN

TX446-320
Harlingen Public Library
504 East Tyler Avenue
Harlingen TX 78550

no telephone

SEE: NUCMC, 1969.

Questionnaire not returned.

HILLSBORO

TX476-320
Hill Junior College
History Complex
Confederate Research Center
Hillsboro TX

MAILING ADDRESS:
P.O. Box 619
Hillsboro TX 76645

(817) 582-2555

OPEN: M-F 8-5; closed weekends and
  holidays
COPYING FACILITIES: yes
MATERIALS SOLICITED: Letters, diaries, and other manuscripts pertaining to Confederate Texas, particularly Hood's Texas Brigade. Will also accept materials relating to 19th century American military history.

HOLDINGS:
  Total volume: 25 l.f.
  Inclusive dates: 1850 - 1875
  Description: Letters, diaries, reminiscences, photographs, and other manuscripts relating to Texas units in the Confederate army. Most of the holdings focus on Hood's Texas Brigade.

HOUSTON

TX483-160
Diocese of Galveston-Houston
Chancery Archives and Research
1700 San Jacinto
Houston TX

MAILING ADDRESS:
P.O. Box 907
Houston TX 77001

(409) 659-5461, Ext. 250

OPEN: M-F 8:30-4:30; closed weekends,
  holidays, and holy days
ACCESS: permission must be obtained
  from the Bishop or Chancellor of the
  Diocese
COPYING FACILITIES: yes
MATERIALS SOLICITED: Correspondence between parish officials and bishops, correspondence and photographs of Diocesan priests, and photographs of churches. Will also accept other materials relating to the Diocese.

HOLDINGS:
  Total volume: not specified
  Inclusive dates: 1840 -
  Description: Records of the Diocese, including office files, former bishops' files, annual reports to the Vatican, annual parish reports, and correspondence with institutions affiliated with the Diocese. There are records of Diocesan convents, hospitals, orphanages, churches, secondary schools, and seminaries, including deeds and abstracts to property, blueprints, financial records, correspondence, and photographs. Also included are files of marriage dispensations and probate records.

TX483-280
Harris County Heritage Society
1100 Bagby
Houston TX 77002

(713) 223-8367

OPEN: M-F 9:30-4; closed weekends and
  holidays
ACCESS: by appointment
COPYING FACILITIES: yes
MATERIALS SOLICITED: Houston history and 19th century decorative arts. Will also accept materials relating to Texas history.

HOLDINGS:
Total volume: 3,000 photographs; other items
Inclusive dates: 1837 - 1940's
Description: The Litterst-Dixon photograph collection containing 3,000 scenes of Houston buildings and people (1890's-1940's). There are also holdings of diaries, letterbooks, and deeds from the Houston area, primarily from the 19th century.

TX483-320

Houston Public Library
Houston Metropolitan Research Center
500 McKinney
Houston TX 77002

(713) 236-1313

OPEN: M-Sa 9-6; closed Sundays and holidays
COPYING FACILITIES: yes
MATERIALS SOLICITED: Materials relating to the development of the Houston metropolitan area. Will also accept materials relating to Texas history.

HOLDINGS:
Total volume: 5,000 l.f.
Inclusive dates: 1830's -
Description: Collections primarily relating to the history of urban development in the Houston metropolitan area. Included are non-current records of organizations and local governments, papers of individuals, unpublished memoirs and histories, photographs, and oral history recordings.

SEE: Hamer; NUCMC, 1959-61, 70.

SEE: Beers - Southwest; Hinding.

SEE ALSO: Walter Schatz, ed., *Directory of Afro-American Resources* (Bowker, 1970); James M. Day, *Handbook of Texas Archival and Manuscript Depositories* (Texas Library and Historical Commission, 1966). A guide to collections is available from the Library.

TX483-322

Incarnate Word Convent
Archives
3400 Bradford Place
Houston TX 77025

(713) 668-0423

OPEN: M-F by appointment; closed weekends
COPYING FACILITIES: no
MATERIALS SOLICITED: Will accept materials pertaining to Houston, TX, that are of relevance to the Sisters of the Incarnate Word and Blessed Sacrament.

HOLDINGS:
Total volume: 100 l.f.
Inclusive dates: 1872 -
Description: Photographs, financial records, annals, and other materials pertaining to the history of the Sisters of the Incarnate Word and Blessed Sacrament in Houston, TX.

SEE: Hinding.

TX483-480

Lunar Science Institute
Photo/Map Library
3303 NASA Road 1
Houston TX 77058

(713) 486-2134

OPEN: M-F 8:30-5; closed weekends and holidays
ACCESS: by appointment only
COPYING FACILITIES: yes
MATERIALS SOLICITED: Lunar photographs. Will also accept photographic materials pertaining to the planets.

HOLDINGS:
Total volume: 800 l.f.
Inclusive dates: 1968 -
Description: A collection of lunar and planetary photographs, including photographs of lunar rocks.

SEE: Novotny.

TX483-560

National Aeronautics and Space Administration
Lyndon B. Johnson Space Center
History Office
Building 35A
Johnson Space Center
Houston TX

MAILING ADDRESS:
BE4
Johnson Space Center
Houston TX 77058

(713) 483-3544

OPEN: by appointment only
ACCESS: advance arrangements required
COPYING FACILITIES: yes
MATERIALS SOLICITED: Aeronautics and astronautics. Will also accept materials in related subjects.

HOLDINGS:
Total volume: 900 c.f.
Inclusive dates: 1958 -
Description: A collection of materials on aeronautics and astronautics, with greatest emphasis on recent American civilian activities, especially those connected with NASA or its predecessor agency, the National Advisory Committee for Aeronautics. Material in related fields, such as foreign and military aeronautics and astronautics, science, technology, and public policy, is also held. Greatest emphasis is on manned space flight.

SEE: Allard, Crawley, and Edmison.

TX483-690

Rice University
Fondren Library
Woodson Research Center
6100 South Main Street
Houston TX

MAILING ADDRESS:
P.O. Box 1892
Houston TX 77001

(713) 527-8101, Ext. 2586

OPEN: M-F 9-5; closed weekends and holidays
COPYING FACILITIES: yes

MATERIALS SOLICITED: Papers of individuals influential in history of Houston and Rice University; Houston and Texas business records; Civil War papers; and historical manuscripts relating to Austria. Will also accept other materials.

HOLDINGS:
Total volume: 2,200 l.f.; 15,000 vols.
Inclusive dates: 1600 -
Description: A collection relating chiefly to Texas history. Included are papers of individuals and families prominent in development of the State's Gulf coast region. Other fields of concentration are the Civil War, especially in Texas; French intervention in Mexico; 19th century Austria; the British Navy in the 18th and 19th centuries; modern literature; and the archives of Rice University.
Also included are the papers of Sir Julian Huxley.

SEE: Hamer.

SEE: Allard, Crawley, and Edmison; Robbins; Hinding.

TX483-810

Texas Gulf Coast Historical Association
University of Houston Library
Houston TX 77004

(713) 749-2727, 4680

OPEN: M-F 9-5; closed weekends and holidays
COPYING FACILITIES: yes
MATERIALS SOLICITED: Private manuscripts and business history records relating primarily to Texas social, political, and economic development since 1865.

HOLDINGS:
Total volume: 1,000 l.f.
Inclusive dates: 1800's -
Description: Personal and business papers of Texas oilmen J. S. Cullinan, George A. Hill, Charles A. Warner, and Robert A. Welch; records of Houston Oil Company; papers of lumberman John Henry Kirby; papers of women activists Minnie Fisher Cunningham and Ida Darden; and political correspondence of Palmer Bradley and Joe H. Eagle.

SEE ALSO: James M. Day, *Handbook of Texas Archival and Manuscript Depositories* (Texas Library and Historical Commission, 1966); Albert Krichmar, *The Women's Rights Movement in the United States, 1848-1970: A Bibliography and Sourcebook* (Scarecrow Press, 1972).

TX483-820

Texas Southern University
Library
Heartman Negro Collection
3201 Wheeler
Houston TX 77004

(713) 527-7149

OPEN: M-F 8-11, Sa 8-6:30, Su 2-8; closed academic holidays
COPYING FACILITIES: yes

MATERIALS SOLICITED: Material by or about black people, especially papers of prominent figures. Will also accept material produced by Texas Southern University.

HOLDINGS:
Total volume: 450 items; 4 file drawers; 2 shelves
Inclusive dates: 1830's -
Description: Texas slave papers, including records of court cases and transportation of slaves. Also included is the Texas Southern University archives (1947-).

SEE: Schatz.

KINGSVILLE

TX529-770
Texas A & I University
John E. Conner Museum
805 West Santa Gertrudis
Kingsville TX

MAILING ADDRESS:
Box 2172
Station 1
Kingsville TX 78363

(512) 595-2819

OPEN: M-F 10-5, Sa 9-noon, Su 2:30-5; closed Christmas and New Year's
ACCESS: upon request to Museum Director
COPYING FACILITIES: yes
MATERIALS SOLICITED: Materials, including photographs, related to the history of the area of Texas from San Antonio southward, especially materials on Spanish and Mexican heritage. Will also accept materials relating to other areas of Texas, but only if in sufficient quantity on one topic to provide primary source materials for University students' research papers.

HOLDINGS:
Total volume: 46 c.f.
Inclusive dates: 1820 - 1930
Description: Manuscripts related chiefly to southern Texas, including account books of ranches, diaries, records of local businesses, civic organizations, and Texas A & I University, architectural drawings, photographs of the area, and recordings of *corridas* (Mexican border ballads). Photographs deal with development of area towns and ranching, farming, and migrant workers.
The institution is also a regional county records depository.

SEE: Hinding.

LAREDO

TX543-560
Nuevo Santander Museum
West End Washington Street
Laredo TX 78040

(512) 722-8351, Ext. 321

OPEN: Su 1-5, M-F 8-5; closed Saturdays
COPYING FACILITIES: yes
MATERIALS SOLICITED: Materials relating to the Nuevo Santander region.

HOLDINGS:
Total volume: 36 l.f.
Inclusive dates: 1850's -
Description: Materials including the papers of author John Z. Leyendecker; papers of Antonio Armengol, including twelve general store ledgers and other business papers; and Laredo Air Force Base class books and scrapbooks.

LEVELLAND

TX555-720
South Plains Museum
608 Avenue H
Levelland TX

MAILING ADDRESS:
P.O. Box 1305
Levelland TX 79336

(806) 894-7547

OPEN: Tu-Sa 2-5; closed Sundays and Mondays
ACCESS: advance arrangements required
COPYING FACILITIES: no
MATERIALS SOLICITED: Materials pertaining to Hockley County, Texas.

HOLDINGS:
Total volume: not specified
Inclusive dates: 1920 -
Description: A small collection of local photographs.

LIBERTY

TX560-720
Sam Houston Regional Library and Research Center
Farm Road 1011
Liberty TX

MAILING ADDRESS:
P.O. Box 989
Liberty TX 77575

(409) 336-7097

OPEN: M-F 8-5, Sa 10-4; closed Sundays and holidays
COPYING FACILITIES: yes
MATERIALS SOLICITED: Manuscripts, diaries, journals, account books, non-current county records, and visual documents of research or archival value relative to the Southeast Texas-Atascosito District of 1826 and the counties which now comprise this area.

HOLDINGS:
Total volume: 8,760 c.f.
Inclusive dates: 1805 -
Description: A collection of letters, diaries, pioneer reminiscences, and other papers relating to the ten counties of southeastern Texas and the Atascosito District: Chambers, Hardin, Jasper, Jefferson, Liberty, Newton, Orange, Polk, San Jacinto, and Tyler counties.
Included are literary manuscripts; correspondence, land grant papers, maps, diaries, journals, surveyors field notes, notes on river navigation, photographs, non-current organizations, institutions, cities, counties, business, and financial records. Among the items are a Jean Laffite journal, the papers of Captain

William Logan, a card index pertaining to Sam Houston, and William B. Duncan's Confederate papers.

LUBBOCK

TX590-760
Texas Tech University
Southwest Collection
106 Mathematics Building
Lubbock TX

MAILING ADDRESS:
P.O. Box 4090
Lubbock TX 79409

(806) 742-3749

OPEN: M, W-F 8-5, Tu 8-7, Sa 8-noon; closed Sundays, holidays, and Christmas vacation
COPYING FACILITIES: yes
MATERIALS SOLICITED: Personal papers, business and organization records, photographs, and tape recordings relating to the American Southwest, especially western Texas. Subject focuses include Texas Tech University, ranching, oil, and cotton.

HOLDINGS:
Total volume: 15,000,000 items
Inclusive dates: 19th century -
Description: A collection relating to western Texas and the American Southwest, consisting of more than 10 million leaves and 150,000 feet of microfilm of personal papers and business and organization records; 100,000 photographs; and 2,000 oral histories. Emphasis is on local history and such topics as ranching, cotton, agriculture, pioneer life, and athletics. In addition, the Southwest Collection houses the archives of Texas Tech University.

SEE: Hamer; NUCMC, 1962, 69-70.

SEE: Davis; Paszek; Parkinson; Beers - Southwest.

SEE ALSO: Walter Schatz, ed., *Directory of Afro-American Resources* (Bowker, 1970); Alan M. Meckler and Ruth McMullin, comps., *Oral History Collections* (Bowker, 1975); James M. Day, *Handbook of Texas Archival and Manuscript Depositories* (Texas Library and Historical Commission, 1966); Roy Sylvan Dunn, 'The Southwest Collection at Texas Tech,' *American Archivist* 28 (July 1965). Descriptive lists of materials relating to western Texas, women, ethnic groups, irrigation, petroleum, cattle ranching, and medicine are available at the institution.

MARSHALL

TX604-220
East Texas Baptist College
Mamye Jarrett Learning Center
Special Collections
1209 North Grove
Marshall TX 75670

(214) 935-7963

OPEN: M-F 8-5; closed weekends,
Thanksgiving, Christmas and spring
vacation
ACCESS: advance appointment required
COPYING FACILITIES: no
MATERIALS SOLICITED: Historical materials pertaining to Marshall and Harrison counties and the East Texas Baptist Association. Will also accept any
materials pertaining to Texas history.

HOLDINGS:
    Total volume: 300 items
    Inclusive dates: 1836 -
    Description: Materials include minutes
of East Texas Baptist Associations; original manuscripts relating to the history of
Marshall and Harrison counties, including biographical data, reminiscences and
a diary of economic life at Mimosa Hall
Plantation.

MIDLAND

TX625-640
Permian Basin Petroleum Museum,
    Library and Hall of Fame
Archives Center
1500 Interstate 20 West
Midland TX 79701

(915) 683-4403

OPEN: M-F 9-5; closed weekends,
Thanksgiving and Christmas
ACCESS: advance arrangements requested
COPYING FACILITIES: yes
MATERIALS SOLICITED: Materials per-
taining to history of the oil industry in
west Texas and southeastern New
Mexico. Will also accept materials re-
lating to the general history of these
areas.

HOLDINGS:
    Total volume: 60,000 items
    Inclusive dates: 1880 -
    Description: Collection includes origi-
nal research materials for Myres' *The
Permian Basin*; 300 photos of oil industry
people and scenes; 200 voice tapes with
transcriptions of oil industry pioneers in
this region; aerial photos of the Permian
Basin, 1940's; and a limited collection of
geological maps and materials from the
Basin.

NACOGDOCHES

TX632-200
East Texas Historical Association
Rooms 316 & 318, Rusk Building
Stephen F. Austin State University
Nacogdoches TX

MAILING ADDRESS:
Box 6223 SFA Station
Nacogdoches TX 75962

(409) 569-2407

OPEN: M-F 8-5; closed weekends and
holidays
COPYING FACILITIES: yes
MATERIALS SOLICITED: Eastern Texas
history.

HOLDINGS:
    Total volume: several folders
    Inclusive dates: 20th century -
    Description: A collection of photo-
graphs, mostly of the eastern Texas oil
industry in the 1930's.

TX632-720
Stephen F. Austin State University
Ralph W. Steen Library
Special Collections Department
Nacogdoches TX

MAILING ADDRESS:
P.O. Box 13055, SFASU Station
Nacogdoches TX 75962

(409) 569-4100, 4101

OPEN: M-F 8-5, Sa 10-6; closed Sundays
and University holidays
COPYING FACILITIES: yes
MATERIALS SOLICITED: Materials relating
to the life, culture, economy and history of East Texas, with special emphasis on forestry. Will also accept materials produced by or about East Tex-
ans or East Texas.

HOLDINGS:
    Total volume: 1,590 l.f.
    Inclusive dates: 1812 -
    Description: A collection of manu-
scripts relating chiefly to East Texas or
which have been produced by East Tex-
ans. Included are literary manuscripts,
correspondence, land grant and title papers, business papers, miscellaneous personal papers, public documents, photographs, maps and Stephen F. Austin State
University archival records. There are
also extensive non-current business
records of several lumber companies, as
well as the non-current records of other
East Texas organizations and businesses.

GUIDES: *Special Collections Stephen F.
Austin State University Library: A
Guide* (1975).

SEE: Hamer; NUCMC, 1966, 74, 81.

SEE: Davis; Hinding.

SEE ALSO: James M. Day, *Handbook of
Texas Archival and Manuscript Depositories* (Texas Library and Historical
Commission, 1966); Robert S. Maxwell, 'Manuscript Collections at Stephen F. Austin State College,' *American Archivist* 28 (July 1965).
Unpublished calendars of some collections are available for use at the Library.

NEW BRAUNFELS

TX640-720
Sophienburg Memorial Association
Sophienburg Archives
401 West Coll Street
New Braunfels TX 78130

(512) 629-1572

OPEN: Tu, Th 10-2; closed other days
and holidays
COPYING FACILITIES: yes
MATERIALS SOLICITED: Historical materials, including photographs, oral history tapes, unpublished manuscripts
and institutional records, pertaining to
New Braunfels and Comal County and
early German migration to Texas. Will
also accept materials which relate to
the German settlements established in
Texas in the mid to late-nineteenth
century.

HOLDINGS:
    Total volume: 333 c.f.; 3 file cabinets;
60 boxes
    Inclusive dates: 1840's - 1970's
    Description: Materials relating to New
Braunfels and Comal County, Texas and
the German immigration movement of
the *Gesellschaft zum Schutze Deutscher
Auswanderer nach Texas* (German Immigration Society), 1845-47, including
documents, unpublished translations of
manuscripts, original manuscripts, diaries, correspondence, music, business
records, genealogical source material, literary manuscripts, school records, photographs, and a growing oral history collection.

ODESSA

TX654-640
Presidential Museum
Library of the Presidents
622 North Lee
Odessa TX 79761

(915) 332-7123

OPEN: M-F 10-5; closed weekends and
holidays
COPYING FACILITIES: yes
MATERIALS SOLICITED: Documents, messages, papers, letters and other written
material produced by any of the 37
Presidents. Will also accept material
used in Presidential campaigns or produced by Presidential candidates.

HOLDINGS:
    Total volume: 2,000 items
    Inclusive dates: 1793 -
    Description: Documents, messages, let-
ters and other papers relating to the
Presidents of the United States, as well as

Presidential candidates, political parties, elections, and related subjects.

PANHANDLE

TX691-130
Carson County Square House
  Museum
5th & Elsie Streets
Panhandle TX

MAILING ADDRESS:
P.O. Box 276
Panhandle TX 79068

(806) 537-3118

OPEN: M-Sa 9-5:30, Su 1-5:30; closed
  holidays
COPYING FACILITIES: yes
MATERIALS SOLICITED: Materials pertaining to the history of Carson County and surrounding areas including pioneer chronicals, military records, oral history tapes from World Wars I and II, personal papers and photographs.

HOLDINGS:
  Total volume: 4,650 items
  Inclusive dates: 1870's - 1940's
  Description: Collection of historical materials pertaining to Carson County and surrounding areas, including the business records of the British-owned Francklyn Land and Cattle Company; land grants; Civil War release papers; school records; diaries and photographs documenting the development of the area.

SEE: Hinding.

PARIS

TX695-640
Paris Junior College
Mike Rheudasil Learning Center
A. M. and Welma Aikin Regional
  Archives
2400 Clarksville Street
Paris TX 75460

(214) 785-7661

OPEN: M-F 8-5; closed weekends and
  state holidays
COPYING FACILITIES: yes
MATERIALS SOLICITED: Materials relating to the political career of A. M. Aikin, Jr., Dean Emeritus of the Texas Senate from the first Senatorial District; archival records of institutions and organizations; materials related to early settlers, political figures, and leaders in northeastern Texas, including manuscripts, correspondence, diaries, maps, charts, photographs; video and oral history tapes of research and archival value; materials relating to the junior college movement in Texas; and records and materials dealing with Paris Junior College, its faculty and alumni.

HOLDINGS:
  Total volume: 285 c.f.; 58 vols.
  Inclusive dates: 1841 -
  Description: Non-current records of local government; materials relating to the political career of Senator A. M. Aikin,

Jr.; administrative records and correspondence of Paris Junior College; records of organizations and individuals of local and state significance within the region; genealogical records from the four-county area; research papers on early history and education in Lamar County; research materials from the Joseph Ligon Chapter of the Daughters of the American Revolution; literary manuscripts; and private collections.

PLAINVIEW

TX712-880
Wayland Baptist College
Van Howeling Memorial Library
Caprock-Plains Historical Collection
1900 West 7th
Plainview TX 79072

(806) 296-5521, Ext. 29

OPEN: M-Th 8-10, F 8-5:30, Sa 10-5;
  closed Sundays and holidays
COPYING FACILITIES: yes
MATERIALS SOLICITED: Materials relating to the settlement of the South Plains of Texas and the Llano Estacado, including such topics as economics, social and cultural history, and agriculture. Will also accept machine readable records in special situations.

HOLDINGS:
  Total volume: 500 l.f.
  Inclusive dates: 1845 -
  Description: Economic, social, and religious materials relating to the development of the Llano Estacado region of Texas, with particular emphasis on railroad records. Records of churches, clubs, and other organizations are also represented.

SEE ALSO: unpublished guides to specific collections available at the Library.

PORT ARTHUR

TX719-640
Port Arthur Public Library
3601 Cultural Center Drive
Port Arthur TX 77640

(409) 985-8838

OPEN: M-F 9-9, Sa 9-5, Su 2-5; closed
  holidays and Sundays in summer
COPYING FACILITIES: yes
MATERIALS SOLICITED: Archives, manuscripts, and visual and audible documents relating to Port Arthur history.

HOLDINGS:
  Total volume: 30 items
  Inclusive dates: 1898 -
  Description: Oral history interviews and scrapbooks of the photographs and newspaper clippings, all related to the history of Port Arthur.

PORTLAND

TX726-80
Bell Public Library
8th and Austin Street
Portland TX 78374

(512) 643-6527

OPEN: M, Tu, Th 9-6, W 9-7, F 9-5, Sa
  10-2; closed Sundays and holidays
COPYING FACILITIES: yes
MATERIALS SOLICITED: Texas genealogy, items pertaining to the 1919 storm, Bayview College history.

HOLDINGS:
  Total volume: 1 l.f.
  Inclusive dates: 1921 -
  Description: An unpublished history of the Portland area, an unpublished biography of J. S. McKamey, and oral history tapes and transcripts of interviews with early settlers of the area.

SEE: Hinding.

PRAIRIE VIEW

TX733-640
Prairie View A & M University
W. R. Banks Library
Prairie View TX 77445

(409) 857-2012

OPEN: M-F 8-5; closed weekends and
  holidays
COPYING FACILITIES: yes
MATERIALS SOLICITED: Records concerning the education of blacks in Texas, the history of the Agricultural Extension Service, and the early history of Prairie View A & M University, its faculty and alumni. Will also accept materials relating to the history of community.

HOLDINGS:
  Total volume: 22,415 items
  Inclusive dates: 1899 -
  Description: Manuscripts relating to the following state-wide programs: Interscholastic League, Agricultural Extension Service, and Educational Conference, including papers and business correspondence of persons directing these programs. There are also records relating to units of the Prairie View A & M University and to the history of Waller County.

RICHARDSON

TX742-680
Richardson Public Library
900 Civic Center
Richardson TX 75080

(214) 238-8251

OPEN: M-Th 10-9, F, Sa 10-6; closed
  Sundays and holidays
COPYING FACILITIES: yes
MATERIALS SOLICITED: Materials relating to Richardson history.

HOLDINGS:
Total volume: 21 l.f.; 197 items
Inclusive dates: 1883 -
Description: Materials relating chiefly to the history of Richardson. Included are the archives of the Richardson Historical Society, records of the Richardson Jaycees, video tapes of Richardson centennial celebrations, and slides of Texas wildflowers, historic Richardson homes, and other aspects of Richardson's history.

TX742-690

Rockwell International
Collins Commercial
  Telecommunications Division
1200 North Alma Road
Richardson TX 75081

(214) 996-5000

OPEN: M-F 8-5; closed weekends and holidays
USER FEES: special permission necessary
COPYING FACILITIES: yes
MATERIALS SOLICITED: Business records, engineering designs and technical documents relating to Rockwell International, Collins Commercial Telecommunications Division.

HOLDINGS:
Total volume: 10,000 boxes
Inclusive dates: 1950 -
Description: Primarily engineering and business records of Rockwell International.

TX742-800

University of Texas at Dallas
Department of Special Collections
History of Aviation Collection
Richardson TX

MAILING ADDRESS:
P.O. Box 830643
Richardson TX 75083-0643

(214) 690-2570

OPEN: M-F 9-5; closed weekends and holidays
COPYING FACILITIES: yes
MATERIALS SOLICITED: Materials relating to the history of aviation, aviation pioneers, and dirigibles. Will also accept materials relating to the history of technology.

HOLDINGS:
Total volume: 1,500 l.f.
Inclusive dates: 1870 - 1978
Description: Scrapbooks, logbooks, personal papers, photographs, reports, and other materials of aviation pioneers and developers, covering heavier-than-air fixed winged craft, as well as lighter-than-air craft. Coverage extends to European and American aviation, helicopters, rockets, jet and propeller driven airplanes, airline development, and business use of airplanes. Included is the archives of *Flight* magazine, containing correspondence files and unpublished articles of the previous 48 years.

RICHMOND

TX749-246

Fort Bend County Museum
  Association
Museum
400 Houston Street
Richmond TX

MAILING ADDRESS:
P.O. Box 251
Richmond TX 77469

(713) 342-6478

OPEN: Tu-F 10-4, Sa, Su 1-5; closed Mondays, Christmas through New Year's, Easter, Thanksgiving
COPYING FACILITIES: yes
MATERIALS SOLICITED: Materials relating to the history of Fort Bend County and Texas.

HOLDINGS:
Total volume: 185 c.f.
Inclusive dates: 1822 - 1945
Description: Collection pertaining to the history of Fort Bend County including county and business records, papers and correspondence of local residents, oral histories and photographs.

ROUND TOP

TX754-880

The University of Texas
Winedale Historical Center
FM Road 2714
Round Top TX

MAILING ADDRESS:
P.O. Box 11
Round Top TX 78954

no telephone

OPEN: M-F 9-5, Sa 10-5, Su noon-5; closed holidays
ACCESS: advance appointment required
COPYING FACILITIES: yes
MATERIALS SOLICITED: Materials relating to German culture, the history of Fayette County, and Texas furniture makers of the 19th century.

HOLDINGS:
Total volume: not specified
Inclusive dates: 19th century
Description: Letters, diaries and other materials relating to German immigration to Texas, and materials on 19th century cabinetmakers.

SAN ANGELO

TX770-240

Fort Concho National Historic
  Landmark
Archives
213 East Avenue D
San Angelo TX 76903

(915) 655-9121, Ext. 441

OPEN: M-F 8-5; closed weekends and holidays
ACCESS: advance arrangements required
COPYING FACILITIES: yes

MATERIALS SOLICITED: History of Fort Concho, San Angelo and Tom Green County to 1900 with emphasis on Hispanics, Blacks, Native Americans. Will also accept local historical materials to 1920, and materials relating to Indians of the southern Plains, westward expansion, and the Plains Indian Wars.

HOLDINGS:
Total volume: 36,120 c.f.
Inclusive dates: 1850 - 1920
Description: Collection consists of materials on Fort Concho (1867-89) including the papers of Captain George Gibson Huntt, military telegrams and architectural drawings. Regional historical materials on San Angelo and Tom Green County, including photographs by pioneer photographer M. C. Ragsdale, the papers of architect Oscar Ruffini and records of several 19th century physicians.

GUIDES: *A Guide to Archival Collections at Fort Concho* (1980).

SEE ALSO: A finding aid is available at the institution.

SAN ANTONIO

TX777-30

Archdiocese of San Antonio
Catholic Archives at San Antonio
2718 W. Woodlawn
San Antonio TX

MAILING ADDRESS:
P.O. Box 28410
San Antonio TX 78284

(512) 734-2620

OPEN: M-F 8:30-4:30; closed weekends, holidays, and holy days
ACCESS: manuscript collections for serious researchers only
COPYING FACILITIES: yes
MATERIALS SOLICITED: Texas materials relating to the history of the Roman Catholic church, including historical and biographical source materials, ethnic history documents, and microform and other copies.

HOLDINGS:
Total volume: 280 l.f.; 357 microfilm rolls
Inclusive dates: 1485 -
Description: Civil, church-related, and biographical documents from the early Mission period to the present. Included are correspondence, diaries, journals, and such individual collections as the Galveston Archives, parts of the Texas-related New Orleans papers, and the Bejar Archives (civil). Microfilm holdings are primarily vital records of the parishes within the Archdiocese of San Antonio.

TX777-80

Bexar County Archives
Office of the County Clerk
San Antonio TX 78205

(512) 220-2587

OPEN: M-F 8-5; closed weekends and holidays

SEE: Hamer; NUCMC, 1975.

Questionnaire not returned.

TX777-160

The Daughters of the Republic of Texas
Library
The Alamo
San Antonio TX

MAILING ADDRESS:
P.O. Box 2599
San Antonio TX 78299

(512) 225-1071

OPEN: M-Sa 9-5; closed Sundays and holidays
COPYING FACILITIES: yes
MATERIALS SOLICITED: Texas history. Will also accept genealogical materials if the family has a Texas connection.

HOLDINGS:
    Total volume: 14,000 items
    Inclusive dates: 1600 -
    Description: A collection of regal and viceregal documents concerning Texas under Spanish rule; collections on Texas as a Mexican colony (in Spanish); materials on Texas as a Republic, in early statehood, and during the Civil War, including papers of Sam Houston, the Stephen F. Austin family, and other prominent figures. Collections contain diaries, land grant papers, unpublished memoirs, family histories, and photographs.

GUIDES: The Texas History Collection of the Daughters of the Republic of Texas Library (1977).

SEE: Hinding.

SEE ALSO: James M. Day, Handbook of Texas Archival and Manuscript Depositories (Texas Library and Historical Commission, 1966); Ann Novotny, ed., Picture Sources 3 (Special Libraries Assn., 1975).

TX777-620

Our Lady of the Lake University
Libraries
Texana Collection
411 Southwest 24th Street
San Antonio TX 78285

(512) 434-6711, Ext. 332

OPEN: M-F 8-6, Sa 10-5, Su 12-6; closed Christmas and Easter
COPYING FACILITIES: yes

HOLDINGS:
    Total volume: 6 microfilm reels
    Inclusive dates: 1688 - 1867
    Description: Archives of Saltillo, former capital of the State of Coahuila in Mexico.

SEE ALSO: an index to the archives available at the institution.

TX777-640

The Protestant Episcopal Church in the Diocese of West Texas
Cathedral House Archives
111 Torcido Drive
San Antonio TX

MAILING ADDRESS:
P.O. Box 6885
San Antonio TX 78209

(512) 824-5387

OPEN: M-F 9-5; closed weekends, holidays, and Holy Week
COPYING FACILITIES: yes
MATERIALS SOLICITED: Materials relating to the Episcopal church in southern and western Texas.

HOLDINGS:
    Total volume: 50 l.f.
    Inclusive dates: 1874 -
    Description: A collection of letters, minutes, diaries, records, scrapbooks, and other manuscripts relating to the history of the Episcopal church in the Diocese of West Texas; its institutions, including St. Philip's College, St. Mary's Hall and Texas Military Institute; parishes; and bishops, clergy and lay leaders.

TX777-670

St. Mary's University of San Antonio
Academic Library
Special Collections
One Camino Santa Maria
San Antonio TX 78284

(512) 436-3441

OPEN: M-F 8:30-5; closed weekends, holidays and semester breaks
COPYING FACILITIES: yes
MATERIALS SOLICITED: Collections pertaining to the historical development of the Spanish Southwest. Will also accept materials on Texas, especially the border lands, military science, and mathematics.

HOLDINGS:
    Total volume: 12 l.f.
    Inclusive dates: 1749 - 1930
    Description: Collection consists of official documentation of founding and development of Laredo, Texas (1749-1872) including land grants, records of schools, courts, churches and local government. Also included are materials on Henry Castro and his colonists in Medino County, Texas (1844-98) and the records of the Old Spanish Trail Association, 1915-30, which planned the preservation of historical sites along the southern highway system.

SEE: NUCMC, 1970.

SEE: Beers - Southwest.

TX777-700

San Antonio Conservation Society
Library
107 King William Street
San Antonio TX 78204

(512) 224-6163

OPEN: M, Tu 9-4; closed W-Su, holidays and week of April 21
ACCESS: advance appointment required
COPYING FACILITIES: yes
MATERIALS SOLICITED: Records relating to the history of San Antonio and Texas.

HOLDINGS:
    Total volume: 5,000 items
    Inclusive dates: not specified
    Description: Materials relating primarily to San Antonio, Bexar County, and San Antonio Conservation Society including manuscripts, photographs, slides and directories emphasizing history, preservation, conservation and restoration techniques, zoning, and historic district surveys.

TX777-710

San Antonio Museum Association
Research Library
3810 Broadway
San Antonio TX 78209

(512) 226-5544

OPEN: M-F 9-5; closed weekends and holidays
COPYING FACILITIES: yes
MATERIALS SOLICITED: San Antonio and Texas history.

HOLDINGS:
    Total volume: 1,000 items
    Inclusive dates: 1791 -
    Description: Manuscripts, institutional records, and photographs emphasizing Texas and San Antonio in the 19th century.

SEE ALSO: James M. Day, Handbook of Texas Archival and Manuscript Depositories (Texas Library and Historical Commission, 1966), as Witte Memorial Museum.

TX777-720

San Antonio Public Library
203 South St. Mary's Street
San Antonio TX 78205

(512) 299-7813

OPEN: M-F 9-9, Sa 9-6; closed Sundays and holidays
COPYING FACILITIES: yes
MATERIALS SOLICITED: Historical materials, especially relating to Texas. Will also accept circus materials.

HOLDINGS:
    Total volume: not specified
    Inclusive dates: 1850's -
    Description: Texas and San Antonio historical collections, composed of literary manuscripts and personal papers, genealogical source data, records of social organizations, early photographs of San Antonio, and other materials. There is also the Hertzberg Circus Collection, containing a 19th century manuscript circus

history and 1,000 photographs, many dating from the turn of the century.

SEE: Hinding; Robbins.

SEE ALSO: James M. Day, *Handbook of Texas Archival and Manuscript Depositories* (Texas Library and Historical Commission, 1966).

TX777-760

Trinity University
Library
Special Collections
715 Stadium Drive
San Antonio TX 78284

(512) 736-7355, 8127

OPEN: by appointment only
COPYING FACILITIES: yes

HOLDINGS:
    Total volume: 485 l.f.; 4,375 reels
    Inclusive dates: 1599 -
    Description: Primarily Trinity University archival material and microfilm copies of municipal and parochial archives of the state of Nuevo Leon, Mexico.

SEE: NUCMC, 1967.

SEE: Robbins.

SEE ALSO: James M. Day, comp., *Handbook: Texas Archival and Manuscript Depositories* (Texas Library and Historical Commission, 1966); Henry Putney Beers, *Spanish & Mexican Records of the American Southwest: A Bibliographical Guide to Archive and Manuscript Sources* (Univ. of Arizona Press, 1979); Robert Alvin Houze, 'The Texas Consortium for Microfilming the Mexican Archives,' *Library Journal* 45 (Fall 1969).

TX777-790

The University of Texas Health
    Science Center at San Antonio
Library
Special Collections
7703 Floyd Curl Drive
San Antonio TX 78284

(512) 691-6271

OPEN: M-F 8:30-5; closed weekends and holidays
COPYING FACILITIES: yes
MATERIALS SOLICITED: Materials relating to the health care history of Texas, particularly South Texas and Bexar County.

HOLDINGS:
    Total volume: 36 l.f.
    Inclusive dates: 1893 -
    Description: Journals, account books, photographs, and oral history tapes of San Antonio physicians, 1893- ; correspondence and other records of Bexar County Medical Society, 1898-1955; manuscripts of Dr. P. I. Nixon relating to medicine in San Antonio and Texas, 1920-65; archives of The University Texas Health Science Center at San Antonio, including correspondence and minutes, 1965- .

TX777-810

University of Texas at San Antonio
John Peace Library
Special Collections
San Antonio TX 78285

(512) 691-4570

OPEN: by appointment
COPYING FACILITIES: yes
MATERIALS SOLICITED: Materials emphasizing the Spanish and Mexican colonization of Texas, 1600-1800. Will also accept other materials.

HOLDINGS:
    Total volume: 34 l.f.
    Inclusive dates: 1514 - 1920
    Description: Manuscripts documenting the political, social, and military history of Texas and Mexico. Included are documents from Spanish and Mexican regimes, correspondence concerning Mexican revolutions, land grants, and Sam Houston, Antonio Lopez de Santa Anna, and other military leaders of the Texas-Mexican War of 1836.

SEE: Robbins.

SAN MARCOS

TX791-730

Southwest Texas State University
Library
Special Collections
San Marcos TX 78666

(512) 245-2313

OPEN: by appointment only
COPYING FACILITIES: yes
MATERIALS SOLICITED: Will accept materials relating to early Texas and the Southwest, Lyndon Baines Johnson, John Wesley Hardin, and T. E. Lawrence.

HOLDINGS:
    Total volume: 43 c.f.
    Inclusive dates: 1870's -
    Description: Primarily Southwest Texas State University archival materials and John Wesley Hardin papers.

SEE ALSO: Boyd H. Grimes, *Chronological Calendar of the Letters in the John Wesley Hardin Collection in the Southwest Texas State University Library* (Southwest Texas State Univ., 1971).

SEGUIN

TX797-760

Texas Lutheran College
Blumberg Memorial Library
Seguin TX 78155

(512) 379-4161, Ext. 230

OPEN: M-Th 8-11, F 8-5, Sa 9-5, Su 2-11 Sept.-May; closed holidays
COPYING FACILITIES: yes
MATERIALS SOLICITED: Materials pertaining to Texas Lutheran College and to the Southwestern District of the American Lutheran church.

HOLDINGS:
    Total volume: not specified
    Inclusive dates: 1891 -
    Description: Archives of the history of Texas Lutheran College and of materials relating to the history of the American Lutheran church in Texas, Oklahoma, Louisiana and Arkansas.

TEMPLE

TX851-690

Railroad and Pioneer Museum, Inc.
P.O. Box 5126
Temple TX

MAILING ADDRESS:
P.O. Box 5126
Temple TX 76501

(817) 778-6873

OPEN: Tu-Sa 1-4; closed Su, M, Thanksgiving, between Christmas and New Year's
USER FEES: fifty cents
COPYING FACILITIES: yes
MATERIALS SOLICITED: Materials relating to the railroad industry and to pioneers, settlement, and Indians within a 50 mile radius of Temple.

HOLDINGS:
    Total volume: not specified
    Inclusive dates: 1881 -
    Description: Manuscripts, diaries, journals, logbooks, account books, financial records, and literary manuscripts of railroad workers, city employees, researchers, and historians. There are also records of social and other organizations and institutions; maps, charts, and technical drawings of railroad and early town lots; photographs of pioneers and businesses; oral histories; and manuscripts in the Swedish language.

TEXARKANA

TX865-750

Texarkana Historical Society and Museum
219 State Line Avenue
Texarkana TX

MAILING ADDRESS:
P.O. Box 2343
Texarkana TX 75501

(214) 793-4831

OPEN: M-F 10-4, Sa, Su 12-3; closed holidays
COPYING FACILITIES: yes
MATERIALS SOLICITED: Materials relating to the history of the Texarkana area.

HOLDINGS:
    Total volume: 14,665 items
    Inclusive dates: 1873 -
    Description: Materials relating to the history of Texarkana, including photographs, land deeds, tax records, oral histories, post cards, personal correspondence, and genealogical materials.

TYLER

TX890-720
Smith County Historical Society
Archives
Room 216
409 West Erwin
Tyler TX

MAILING ADDRESS:
Goodman Museum
624 North Broadway
Tyler TX 75702

(214) 597-5304

OPEN: Tu 10-5, by appointment
COPYING FACILITIES: no
MATERIALS SOLICITED: Materials relating to eastern Texas.

HOLDINGS:
    Total volume: 9 file drawers
    Inclusive dates: 1850's -
    Description: A collection of diaries, letters, business correspondence, photographs, and other materials, covering the Civil War, Reconstruction, and the turn of the century era in eastern Texas.

SEE ALSO: James M. Day, *Handbook of Texas Archival and Manuscript Depositories* (Texas Library and Historical Commission, 1966).

VICTORIA

TX923-840
Victoria College
Library
Local History Collection
Victoria TX 77901

(512) 576-3157

OPEN: M-Sa 9-10, Su 1-5; closed holidays
COPYING FACILITIES: yes
MATERIALS SOLICITED: Primary source materials relating to Victoria and its surrounding counties. Will also accept materials relating to Texas.

HOLDINGS:
    Total volume: 50 l.f.
    Inclusive dates: early 1800's -
    Description: Correspondence, journals, store records, early photographs, and other materials. Included are papers of prominent pioneers, historical research notes on Victoria County, and papers of naturalists J. D. Mitchell and Gilbert Onderdonk.
    Collection also includes papers of Texas rancher George Tyng, tapes and written interviews of area residents, and retired records of six area counties.

WACO

TX933-65
Baylor University
Armstrong Browning Library
700 Speight
Waco TX

MAILING ADDRESS:
Box 6336
Waco TX 76706

(817) 755-3566

OPEN: M-F 9-4, Sa 9-12; closed Sundays, holidays and spring break
COPYING FACILITIES: yes
MATERIALS SOLICITED: Letters and manuscripts relating to or owned by Robert and Elizabeth Barrett Browning. Will also accept letters and manuscripts of the Browning family or their contemporaries.

HOLDINGS:
    Total volume: 20 file drawers
    Inclusive dates: 1816-1889
    Description: Collection of over 2,000 original letters and other manuscripts written by and to Robert Browning and Elizabeth Barrett Browning.

SEE: Robbins.

SEE ALSO: Philip Kelley and Ronald Hudson, comps., *The Brownings' Correspondence: A Checklist* (The Browning Institute and Wedgstone Press, 1978).

TX933-80
Baylor University
The Texas Collection
Waco TX 76798

MAILING ADDRESS:
P.O. Box 6396
Waco TX 76706

(817) 754-0189

OPEN: M-Th 9-5 (9-10 during fall and spring), F 9-5, Sa 9-12 during fall and spring; closed Sundays and holidays
COPYING FACILITIES: yes
MATERIALS SOLICITED: Manuscripts, photographs, maps and ephemeral materials providing substantive documentation of any aspect of past or present activity and experience in Texas. Prominent subject areas of interest include transportation, religion, education, ethnic groups and special-interest organizations. Also desired are unpublished or privately-published memoirs which recount personal experiences in Texas.

HOLDINGS:
    Total volume: 3,800 l.f.
    Inclusive dates: 1800 -
    Description: Personal manuscripts collections and institutional records, photographs and transcribed oral memoirs which document social and economic trends in Texas, and depict interests and activities of Texans. Particular emphasis upon period 1860-date. Archives of Baylor University, as well as personal papers of faculty, administrators and alumni, and historical materials pertaining to the University.

SEE: NUCMC, 1959-62.

SEE: Hinding; Robbins; Schatz; Beers - Southwest.

WASHINGTON

TX940-720
Star of the Republic Museum
Washington-on-the-Brazos State Historical Park
Washington TX

MAILING ADDRESS:
P.O. Box 317
Washington TX 77880

(713) 878-2461

OPEN: M-F 10-5; closed weekends and holidays
ACCESS: by appointment with Curator
COPYING FACILITIES: yes
MATERIALS SOLICITED: Materials relating to the economic, agricultural, military, political, and social history of the Republic of Texas, 1836-1846.

HOLDINGS:
    Total volume: 1,000 items
    Inclusive dates: 1775 - 1800's
    Description: Government documents and other papers relating to Texas, primarily for the period 1830-80.

WAXAHACHIE

TX947-720
Southwestern Assemblies of God College
Nelson Memorial Library
1200 Sycamore
Waxahachie TX 75165

(214) 937-4010, Ext. 59

OPEN: M-Th 8-10, Sa 10-5; closed F, Su, holidays
COPYING FACILITIES: yes
MATERIALS SOLICITED: Materials on the history of the Assemblies of God denomination in the southwestern and south central United States. Will also accept historical material related to the other pentecostal church groups.

HOLDINGS:
    Total volume: 97 c.f.
    Inclusive dates: 1900 -
    Description: Historical materials relating to the history of the Assemblies of God in the south central and southwestern United States, including oral history tapes of denomination leaders.

WICHITA FALLS

TX968-520
Midwestern State University
Moffett Library
3400 Taft Street
Wichita Falls TX 76308

(817) 692-6611, Ext. 204

OPEN: M-Th 7:45-11, F 7:45-5, Sa 9-5, Su 2-11; closed holidays

COPYING FACILITIES: yes
MATERIALS SOLICITED: Materials relating to the economic, social, and political history of the Wichita Falls area.

HOLDINGS:
Total volume: 12 boxes; 8 file drawers; 1,000 items
Inclusive dates: 1908 - 1970
Description: Papers of State Senator George Moffett, 1931-64, and land elevation maps of the Missouri-Kansas-Texas Railroad, Northwestern Division, between Forgan, OK, and Wichita Falls.

UTAH

The Utah State Archives and Records Service is responsible for local public records preservation, continuing a statewide program initiated in 1951. Counties and municipalities in Utah normally retain control of their permanently valuable records. The State Archives in Salt Lake City also houses many of these documents, in addition to more than 8,000 reels of microfilm of county government and district court records.

CEDAR CITY

UT152-720
Southern Utah State College
Library
Special Collections Department
351 W. Center Street
Cedar City UT 84720

(801) 586-7945, 7933

OPEN: M-F 9-4; closed weekends and holidays; shorter hours in June and July; closed in August
COPYING FACILITIES: yes
MATERIALS SOLICITED: Southern Utah history, including Mormon and Indian history. Will also accept materials relating to the American West, Utah, women in Utah, and Shakespeare or his plays.

HOLDINGS:
  Total volume: 500 l.f.
  Inclusive dates: 1847 -
  Description: A collection of manuscripts, pictures, and oral history tapes dealing with the history of southern Utah and its twin themes of Mormon and Indian history. Included are personal collections of between 25 and 50 individuals, in addition to diaries, minute books of organizations, letters, records of businesses and pioneer industries, and a few records of early county agencies.

SEE: Hinding.

SEE ALSO: Everett L. Cooley, 'Manuscript and Archival Holdings in Utah Universities and Colleges,' *Intermountain Archivist* (June 1976); Alan M. Meckler and Ruth McMullin, comps., *Oral History Collections* (Bowker, 1975).

LOGAN

UT380-810
Utah State University
Merrill Library
Special Collections and Archives
Logan UT 84322-3000

(801) 750-2663

OPEN: M, W, F 8-5, Tu, Th 8-8; closed weekends and holidays
COPYING FACILITIES: yes
MATERIALS SOLICITED: Materials relating to the history of Utah, Idaho, and Arizona; Mormon history; the western cattle and sheep industry; and archives of Utah State University. Will also accept personal papers.

HOLDINGS:
  Total volume: 4,000 l.f.
  Inclusive dates: 18th century -
  Description: Private and institutional papers emphasizing irrigation and agriculture in the intermountain region; literary manuscripts, including those of Jack London, Charmian London, and Bernard DeVoto; 2,000 reels of microfilm of manuscripts in private hands; and 10,000 photographs.

SEE: NUCMC, 1970, 72, 76.

SEE: Davis; Hinding; Robbins.

SEE ALSO: registers and calendars available for major collections.

OGDEN

UT456-900
Weber State College
Stewart Library
Special Collections and Howell
  Library
3750 Harrison Boulevard
Ogden UT 84408-2901

(801) 626-6416

OPEN: M-F 8-5; closed weekends and holidays
COPYING FACILITIES: yes
MATERIALS SOLICITED: Non-current records of Weber State College and historical and literary documents relating to Utah and the West. Will also accept materials about the College or College-related events.

HOLDINGS:
  Total volume: not specified
  Inclusive dates: 19th century -
  Description: Collections documenting the history of Utah and the West. Of special interest are the papers of Utah Congressman Lawrence Burton and a small collection of materials concerning writer Bernard DeVoto. There are also literary manuscripts, photographs of Weber County, blueprints of pioneer buildings in Ogden, and the archives of Weber State College, including 100 oral history recordings.

SEE ALSO: Everett L. Cooley, 'Manuscript and Archival Holdings in Utah Universities and Colleges,' *Intermountain Archivist* (June 1976).

PROVO

UT684-80
Brigham Young University
Harold B. Lee Library
Special Collections Division
Archives and Manuscripts
  Department
Provo UT 84602

(801) 378-3514, 2932

OPEN: M-F 8-5; closed weekends and holidays
COPYING FACILITIES: yes
MATERIALS SOLICITED: Materials relating to: Mormons and the Church of Jesus Christ of Latter-day Saints; Brigham Young University; Utah and the American West with emphasis on transportation, mining, culture, the native American, and politics; arts and communication in Utah and America with emphasis on motion pictures, journalism, television, theater and radio; women's history; Mesoamerican archives; and British and American literary manuscripts (1820 - present).

HOLDINGS:
  Total volume: 3,500,000 items
  Inclusive dates: 1500 -
  Description: Collections relating chiefly to the history of Utah and the intermountain West, the Church of Jesus Christ of Latter-day Saints, and Brigham Young University. 2,000 collections in the Mormon History Archives (1820-) include church records and papers of church leaders, Mormon pioneers, and Mormons prominent in business, politics, and law. U.S. Senator Reed Smoot is among those whose papers are held. Utah and the West Archives (1847-) consists of hundreds of collections relating to educators, scientists, businesspersons, politicians, farmers, artists, and writers.
  Other significant holdings include the University Archives and the Communications Archives, featuring papers concerning Cecil B. DeMille, Boris Karloff, Howard Hawks, and other representatives of the film industry. The Western Transportation Archives consists of 10 collections of western railroad materials, and

the Photograph Archives contains 25,000 glass plate negatives documenting the American West (1890-1920).

SEE: Hamer; NUCMC, 1959-64, 68, 75.

SEE: Davis; Paszek; Parkinson; Mehr; Allard, Crawley, and Edmison; Hines.

SEE ALSO: Alan M. Meckler and Ruth McMullin, comps., *Oral History Collections* (Bowker, 1975); Everett L. Cooley, 'Manuscript and Archival Holdings in Utah Universities and Colleges,' *Intermountain Archivist* (June 1976); Hyrum L. Andrus and Richard E. Bennett, comps., *Mormon Manuscripts to 1846* (Brigham Young Univ. Press, 1977). Published and unpublished guides to collections are available from the Library.

ST. GEORGE

UT836-880
Washington County Library
55 West Tabernacle
St. George UT 84770

(801) 628-3621

OPEN: M-F 10-8, Sa 10-6; closed Sundays and holidays
COPYING FACILITIES: yes
MATERIALS SOLICITED: Will accept materials relating to the history of the St. George area.

HOLDINGS:
    Total volume: 10 c.f.
    Inclusive dates: 1847 - 1939
    Description: Diaries and journals relating chiefly to southern Utah, reminiscences of pioneers in southern Utah, and papers on such subjects as missions, exploration, Mormon colonization, and experiences with Indians.

SEE: Hamer; NUCMC, 1968.

SALT LAKE CITY

UT912-110
Church of Jesus Christ of Latter-day Saints
Genealogical Society
50 East North Temple
Salt Lake City UT 84150

(801) 531-2331

OPEN: M 7:30-6, Tu-F 7:30-10, Sa 7:30-5; closed Sundays and holidays
COPYING FACILITIES: yes
MATERIALS SOLICITED: Genealogical records and similar materials.

HOLDINGS:
    Total volume: 1,000,000 microfilm reels; 170,000 vols.
    Inclusive dates: 13th century -
    Description: Family histories, vital statistics, and other material of a genealogical nature with large collections from the United States, Latin America, Great Britain, Europe, and the Orient.

SEE: Hamer; NUCMC, 1968.

SEE: Bean and Vane; Hines; Beers - Southwest.

SEE ALSO: Mary J. Brown, *Handy Index to the Holdings of the Genealogical Society of Utah* (Everton Publishing Co., 1971); D. Gail Saunders and E. A. Carson, *Guide to the Records of the Bahamas* (Commonwealth of the Bahamas, Government Printing Dept., 1973); Larry T. Wimmer and Clayne L. Pope, 'The Genealogical Society Library of Salt Lake City: A Source of Data for Economic and Social Historians,' *Historical Methods Newsletter* 8 (March 1975); Alan M. Meckler and Ruth McMullin, comps., *Oral History Collections* (Bowker, 1975).

Microfilms of many of the Genealogical Society's holdings are available at the Society's branch libraries throughout the United States.

UT912-120
The Church of Jesus Christ of Latter-day Saints
Historical Department
Church Library-Archives
50 East North Temple Street
Salt Lake City UT 84150

(801) 531-2786

OPEN: M-F 8-4:30; closed weekends and holidays
ACCESS: researchers required to demonstrate a legitimate need before receiving a search room pass
COPYING FACILITIES: yes
MATERIALS SOLICITED: Materials relating to Mormonism, documenting the official activities of The Church of Jesus Christ of Latter-day Saints at all levels, the activities and lives of its members, and activities of non-Mormon groups or individuals which have influenced the church or its members. Will also accept materials relating to groups or organizations which have a common origin with the church and materials relating to the areas in which the church flourished, especially Utah and surrounding western States, western New York, northern Ohio, western Illinois, and western Missouri.

HOLDINGS:
    Total volume: 19,880 l.f.
    Inclusive dates: 1800 -
    Description: Archives of the Mormon church, consisting of records of 150 general church departments, divisions, and offices, including records of the presidency, the presiding bishopric, the building department, and the missionary department. There are records of more than 15,000 local church units throughout the world, including minutes of public and executive meetings, historical and financial reports, and membership records. There are also more than 5,000 manuscript collections, consisting primarily of the papers of church members and leaders, including journals and diaries of 1,300 individuals, mostly 19th century; records of church related and sponsored institutions and organizations, such as schools, businesses, and cultural associations; 100,000 photographs in 800 collections, many from the 19th century, and including the work of early photographers of the West; oral histories; sound recordings; and video tapes and motion pictures.

SEE: Hamer; NUCMC, 1959-61, 72, 74-75.

SEE: Armstrong; Hinding.

SEE ALSO: Max J. Evans and Ronald G. Watt, 'Sources for Western History at the Church of Jesus Christ of Latter-day Saints,' *The Western Historical Quarterly* 8 (July 1977); and the following publications of the Historical Department: *Guide to James Moyle Oral History Program in the LDS Church Archives* (1977); *Guide to Sources for Studies of Mormon Women in the Church Archives* (1976); *Guide to the Oral History Program of the Historical Department* (1974, 1975); *Register of the James Henry Moyle Collection in the Church Archives* (1975); *Register of the Stephen Post Papers in the Church Archives* (1975); and *Register of the Joseph Smith Collection in the Church Archives* (1973).

Ronald G. Watt, 'LDS Church Records on Immigration,' *Genealogical Journal* 6 (March 1977); David M. Mayfield, 'LDS Genealogical Sources at the Church Historical Department,' *Genealogical Journal* 6 (June 1977).

UT912-200
Episcopal Diocese of Utah
Archives
231 East First South
Salt Lake City UT 84111

(801) 322-3400

OPEN: M-F 9-4; closed weekends and holidays
ACCESS: by prior arrangement
COPYING FACILITIES: no
MATERIALS SOLICITED: Materials related to the Episcopal church in Utah and its parishes and missions. Will also accept materials concerning religious life in the western United States.

HOLDINGS:
    Total volume: 65 c.f.
    Inclusive dates: 1867 -
    Description: Records of the Diocese, consisting of journals of annual conventions, confirmation records, financial records, parish statistical reports, and diaries and registers of clergy.

UT912-550
National Society, Daughters of Utah Pioneers
300 North Main Street
Salt Lake City UT 84103

(801) 533-5759

SEE: Hamer.

Questionnaire not returned.

UT912-820
University of Utah
Library
Special Collections Department
Salt Lake City UT 84112

(801) 581-8863

OPEN: M-F 8-5; closed weekends and holidays
ACCESS: oral interview with staff member required
COPYING FACILITIES: yes
MATERIALS SOLICITED: Materials relating to Utah, Mormonism, the American West (especially the intermountain States), and the Middle East (especially Arabic), and the University archives. Will also accept materials relating to authors such as Fawn Brodie, Bernard DeVoto, Dale Morgan, and Wallace Stegner.

HOLDINGS:
    Total volume: 7,072 l.f.; 3,658 reels; 45,000 photographs
    Inclusive dates: 1450 -
    Description: Over 500 collections dealing mostly with Utah and Mormonism. Included are diaries, memoirs, autobiographies, reminiscences, correspondence, photographs, minute books, account books, military records, labor union records, ethnic materials, 1,500 oral history interviews with western Indians, and records of Utah political leaders. There are also music scores, architectural drawings, literary manuscripts, manuscripts and papyri from the Middle East, and materials on Islamic history and literature, as well as the University's archives.

SEE: Hamer; NUCMC, 1959-61, 69-72, 76, 79.

SEE: Spalek; Martin; Parkinson; Hinding; Robbins.

SEE ALSO: G. Q. Flynn, 'The New Deal and Local Archives: the Pacific Northwest,' *American Archivist* 33 (Jan. 1970); Everett L. Cooley, 'Manuscript and Archival Holdings in Utah Universities and Colleges,' *Intermountain Archivist* (June 1976); Alan M. Meckler and Ruth McMullin, comps., *Oral History Collections* (Bowker, 1975); and published and unpublished registers and other finding aids available from the institution.

UT912-840
Utah State Archives and Records Service
2333 South 2300 West
Salt Lake City UT

MAILING ADDRESS:
Room 28, State Capitol
Salt Lake City UT 84114

(801) 533-5250

OPEN: M-F 8-5; closed weekends and holidays
COPYING FACILITIES: yes
MATERIALS SOLICITED: Public records of Utah.

HOLDINGS:
    Total volume: 19,000 c.f.; 29,000 microfiche; 47,900 microfilm reels
    Inclusive dates: 1847 -
    Description: Utah territorial, State, and county records.

GUIDES: *Guide to Utah State Archives* (1977).

SEE: Hamer.

SEE: Armstrong; Bean and Vane.

UT912-850
Utah State Historical Society
Library
300 Rio Grande
Salt Lake City UT 84101

(801) 533-5755

OPEN: M-F 8-5, Sa 10-2; closed Sundays, holidays and July 24
COPYING FACILITIES: yes
MATERIALS SOLICITED: Utah, Mormon, and western history. Will also accept materials relating to Indians, exploration, and similar subjects.

HOLDINGS:
    Total volume: 3,500 l.f.
    Inclusive dates: 1830 -
    Description: A collection of manuscripts relating to the Church of Jesus Christ of Latter-day Saints and the settlement of Utah, including diaries, journals, personal histories, photographs, and oral history tapes and transcripts.

GUIDES: *A Guide to the Unpublished Materials at the Utah State Historical Society* (1980).

SEE: Hamer; NUCMC, 1977.

SEE: Davis; Mehr; Bean and Vane; Armstrong; Parkinson; Hinding.

SEE ALSO: Alan M. Meckler and Ruth McMullin, comps., *Oral History Collections* (Bowker, 1975); Ann Hinckley, 'The Stanley Snow Ivins' Collection,' *Intermountain Archivist* (June 1976); Ann Novotny, ed., *Picture Sources 3* (Special Libraries Assn., 1975). Registers to individual collections are available at the institution.

VERNAL

UT988-40
Ashley National Forest
Forest Supervisor's Office
1680 W. Highway 40
Vernal UT 84078

(801) 789-1181

OPEN: M-F 8-5; closed weekends and holidays
ACCESS: advance arrangements required
COPYING FACILITIES: yes
MATERIALS SOLICITED: Materials related to the administration of the Uintah Forest Reserve, 1897-1908, and administration of Ashley National Forest, 1908- . Will also accept materials related to exploration, settlement, and development of northeastern Utah and southwestern Wyoming, including Ute Indian history.

HOLDINGS:
    Total volume: 20 c.f.
    Inclusive dates: 1900 -
    Description: A collection of manuscripts, official correspondence, reports, studies, statistical compilations, publications, and photographs related to the establishment and administration of Ashley National Forest.

VERMONT

Since 1955 the Public Records Division of the Vermont Agency of Administration has been responsible for a statewide program to preserve local public records. Local governments normally retain custody of their records, but the Public Records Division in Montpelier has more than 2.5 million file cards duplicating township and city vital records, alphabetized by name. Additionally, the Public Records Division makes available to researchers more than 3,000 microfilm reels of vital, land, probate, and other township records.

Most of the filmed records predate 1851 and were filmed by the Church of Jesus Christ of Latter-day Saints or by the Division. A card index to the microfilmed records has been compiled. The Division has begun a program to microfilm local government records from the period after 1850.

ARLINGTON

VT16-120
Canfield Memorial Library
Russell Vermontiana Collection
Arlington VT 05250

(802) 375-6153

OPEN: by appointment
COPYING FACILITIES: no
MATERIALS SOLICITED: Vermont local history and genealogy.

HOLDINGS:
    Total volume: 20,000 items
    Inclusive dates: 1750 - 1900
    Description: Letters, manuscript literary works, diaries, account books, justice of the peace records, manuscript maps, and photographs relating to Vermont local history.

BELLOWS FALLS

VT32-80
Bellows Falls Historical Society
Adams' Old Stone Grist Mill Museum
Mill Street
Bellows Falls VT

MAILING ADDRESS:
21 Center Street
Bellows Falls VT 05101

no telephone

OPEN: July - Aug., weekends 2-4 or by appointment; closed rest of year
COPYING FACILITIES: no
MATERIALS SOLICITED: Materials relating to Bellows Falls history. Will also accept family records and correspondence on conversion of the Mill from water power to electricity.

HOLDINGS:
    Total volume: 3 boxes; 40 items
    Inclusive dates: 1831 - 1960's
    Description: Records of the Mill; oral history tapes on logging, railroading, and the paper industry; and photographs of Mill owners and town events.

BENNINGTON

VT48-90
The Bennington Museum
Genealogical Library
Bennington VT 05201

(802) 447-1571

OPEN: M-F 9:30-4:30; closed weekends, holidays and Dec. - Feb.
USER FEES: $2; courtesy free readmission may be arranged
COPYING FACILITIES: limited
MATERIALS SOLICITED: Materials related to Vermont, chiefly the Bennington area; family genealogies and records.

HOLDINGS:
    Total volume: 4 file drawers
    Inclusive dates: 1800 - 1950's
    Description: Bennington area family letters and papers, primarily late 19th and early 20th century, including diaries (1806-23) kept by a local farmer.

SEE: Hamer.

SEE: Hinding.

BRATTLEBORO

VT128-80
Brooks Memorial Library
Local History and Genealogy
  Collection and
Brattleboro Photography Collection
224 Main Street
Brattleboro VT 05301

(802) 254-5290

OPEN: M-Th 9-9, F 9-6, Sa 9-12; closed Sundays and holidays
ACCESS: serious researchers by appointment; identification required
COPYING FACILITIES: yes

MATERIALS SOLICITED: Brattleboro history. Will also accept materials relating to Windham County and Vermont history.

HOLDINGS:
    Total volume: not specified
    Inclusive dates: 19th century -
    Description: Local history collection includes local directories, town reports, scrap books, maps, broadsides, advertising materials, and other 19th-century material. Photography collection pertains to the locality.

SEE: Hinding.

BROWNINGTON

VT160-600
Orleans County Historical Society, Inc.
Old Stone House Museum
Brownington VT

MAILING ADDRESS:
P.O. Box 27
Brownington VT 05860

(802) 754-2022

OPEN: by appointment only
ACCESS: advance arrangements required
COPYING FACILITIES: no
MATERIALS SOLICITED: Manuscripts by Orleans County authors and materials relating to people, places, and things in the County.

HOLDINGS:
    Total volume: 100 l.f.
    Inclusive dates: 1800 -
    Description: Materials relating to the history of the region, especially Orleans County, including manuscripts, archival materials, photographs, and cassette tapes.

BURLINGTON

VT176-690
Roman Catholic Diocese of
  Burlington
Diocesan Archives
Bishop Brady Center
351 North Avenue
Burlington VT 05401

(802) 658-6110

OPEN: M-F 9:30-5; closed weekends, holidays, and holy days
ACCESS: advance arrangements required
COPYING FACILITIES: yes

MATERIALS SOLICITED: Anything pertaining to the history of the Catholic church in Vermont. Will also accept other materials of interest pertaining to the history and traditions of the Catholic church.

HOLDINGS:
Total volume: 2,500 l.f.
Inclusive dates: 1815 -
Description: Materials relating to the Roman Catholic church in Vermont and elsewhere in the United States, including photographs, missionary papers, architectural drawings, parochial and diocesan records, papers of bishops, hospital and school records, reports of religious orders, and an oral history collection, consisting mostly of interviews with priests and laypeople connected with the Burlington Diocese.

SEE: NUCMC, 1968.

VT176-790
University of Vermont
Archives
Waterman Building
Burlington VT

MAILING ADDRESS:
Box 19
Burlington VT 05401

(802) 656-3235

OPEN: M-F 8:30-5; closed weekends and holidays
USER FEES: none for scholarly use; for commercial use, inquire at repository
COPYING FACILITIES: yes
MATERIALS SOLICITED: Materials concerned with the operation of the University of Vermont. Will also accept private papers, scrapbooks, photographs, and similar materials from alumni, fraternities, sororities, faculty, and staff.

HOLDINGS:
Total volume: 3,000 l.f.
Inclusive dates: 1791 -
Description: Archives of the University, including minutes and working papers of the trustees, 1791-1948; papers of presidents and deans of colleges; private papers of faculty and students; publications of faculty and student organizations; files and photographs relating to faculty, staff and students; tape recordings of public occasions; oral history interviews; and plans and pictures of buildings and grounds.

SEE: Hamer; NUCMC, 1963-64.

SEE: Hinding.

SEE ALSO: T. D. S. Bassett, 'Sources for the Study of Vermont at the University of Vermont,' Vermont Libraries 4 (Sept.-Oct. 1975); Alan M. Meckler and Ruth McMullin, comps., Oral History Collections (Bowker, 1975).

VT176-810
University of Vermont
Guy W. Bailey Library
Wilbur Special Collections
Burlington VT 05401

(802) 656-2138

OPEN: M-Th 8:30-9, F 8:30-5, Sa 9-12; closed Sundays, holidays, and Saturdays and evenings between sessions
ACCESS: advance appointments are recommended
COPYING FACILITIES: yes
MATERIALS SOLICITED: Materials dealing with Vermont, and areas adjacent to Vermont which relate to Vermont history; manuscripts of John Masefield. Will also accept materials of National or international significance, especially papers of literary figures, artists and craftspeople, politicians, extremist organizations, publishers, and businesses dealing with various aspects of book production and distribution.

HOLDINGS:
Total volume: 4,000 l.f.
Inclusive dates: 1700 -
Description: Archives, manuscripts, photographs, tape recordings, and other materials relating chiefly to Vermont. The Collection is strong in 19th and 20th century manuscripts, especially in art, literature, business, industry, education, farming and rural life, labor, land and natural resources, military activities, photography, politics and government, religion and social action, recreation and tourism, and transportation.

SEE: Hamer; NUCMC, 1962-66, 68-69, 71-72, 74, 78, 81.

SEE: Davis; Allard, Crawley, and Edmison; Hines; Robbins.

SEE ALSO: T. D. S. Bassett, 'Sources for the Study of Vermont at the University of Vermont,' Vermont Libraries 4 (Sept. - Oct. 1975).

CUTTINGSVILLE

VT215-720
Shrewsbury Historical Society, Inc.
Cuttingsville VT 05738

(802) 492-3378

OPEN: by appointment only
COPYING FACILITIES: no
MATERIALS SOLICITED: Records relating to Shrewsbury, VT.

HOLDINGS:
Total volume: not specified
Inclusive dates: 18th century -
Description: Diaries, correspondence, account books, and photographs relating to the Town of Shrewsbury and Rutland County, VT.

FERRISBURG

VT296-690
Rowland E. Robinson Memorial Association
Rokeby Museum
Archives
Route 7
Ferrisburg VT

MAILING ADDRESS:
RFD 1, Route 7
Ferrisburg VT 05456

(802) 877-3406

OPEN: M, W-Sa 9:30-5, Su 11-5; closed Tuesdays and holidays
USER FEES: membership fee of $2 for the Robinson Memorial Association is suggested
COPYING FACILITIES: no
MATERIALS SOLICITED: Will accept material pertaining to Robinson family members or specific organizations or topics related to them, such as the Vermont Anti-Slavery Society, Ferrisburg artists, reform movements, and the Society of Friends.

HOLDINGS:
Total volume: 26 l.f.; 4 c.f.
Inclusive dates: 1790's - 1940's
Description: Materials from the families of Rowland Thomas Robinson and Clark Stevens dealing with the political, economic and social history of Vermont, with particular emphasis on social reforms (antislavery and temperance) and religious movements (Quakerism and spiritualism) in the 18th and 19th centuries. Other topics covered include the Civil War, the western frontier, Vermont Indians, farms, sheep, artistic movements, women's rights and women as teachers. There are also the correspondence and literary manuscripts of Rowland Evans Robinson, naturalist and folkwriter.

GRAFTON

VT312-280
Grafton Historical Society, Inc.
Main Street opposite store
Grafton VT 05146

(802) 843-2388

OPEN: May 30 - Oct. 12, weekends 2:30-4:30; other hours by appoointment
COPYING FACILITIES: no
MATERIALS SOLICITED: Materials relating to Grafton history prior to 1900.

HOLDINGS:
Total volume: 1,000 items
Inclusive dates: not specified
Description: Materials relating to the history of Grafton, including photographs, diaries, manuscripts, genealogical records, account books, and public documents.

LUDLOW

VT374-80

Black River Academy Museum
Statesman's Archives
High Street
Ludlow VT

MAILING ADDRESS:
P.O. Box 73
Ludlow VT 05149

(802) 228-5050

OPEN: F-Tu 9:30-5:30; closed
Wednesdays, Thursdays, and Oct. 18 -
May 20 except by appointment
COPYING FACILITIES: yes

HOLDINGS:
Total volume: 12 items
Inclusive dates: 19th century - 20th
century
Description: Letters and photographs
of Calvin Coolidge and his associates.

MIDDLEBURY

VT432-520

Middlebury College
Starr Library
Flanders Ballad Collection
Middlebury VT 05753

(802) 388-3711, Ext. 5653

OPEN: by appointment only
ACCESS: advance appointment
recommended
COPYING FACILITIES: yes
MATERIALS SOLICITED: Ballads and folk-
lore.

HOLDINGS:
Total volume: 4,400 recordings
Inclusive dates: 1940 - 1950
Description: Original recordings of folk
songs of British and American origin,
made in New England. Also included are
typewritten sheets of the transcribed
lyrics of these songs.

VT432-530

Middlebury College
Starr Library
Special Collections
Middlebury VT 05753

(802) 388-3711, Ext. 5502

OPEN: M-F 8-5; closed weekends and
holidays
ACCESS: qualified researchers
COPYING FACILITIES: yes
MATERIALS SOLICITED: Middlebury Col-
lege archives and materials relating to
American literature and the history of
the town of Middlebury and Addison
County. Will also accept other materi-
als.

HOLDINGS:
Total volume: 35 l.f.
Inclusive dates: 1800 -
Description: Manuscript and archival
material relating to Middlebury College,
the town of Middlebury and its surrounding area, and American literature. There
are extensive manuscript holdings of the
work of William Carlos Williams, Julia
Dorr, Marguerite Wilkinson, Robert
Pack, and Henry David Thoreau.

SEE: Hamer; NUCMC, 1959-61.

SEE: Hinding; Robbins.

VT432-720

Sheldon Museum
Swift Research Center
1 Park Street
Middlebury VT 05753

(802) 388-2117

OPEN: M-F 1-5; morning and evening
hours vary with season; closed holidays
and Dec. 24 - Jan. 1
USER FEES: one dollar or Museum
membership
COPYING FACILITIES: yes
MATERIALS SOLICITED: Addison County
material, especially account books,
records of businesses and organizations,
letters, diaries, architectural drawings,
maps, and photographs, of any date.

HOLDINGS:
Total volume: 230 l.f.
Inclusive dates: 1764 -
Description: Included are letters, scrapbooks, photographs, account books, diaries, records of businesses and organizations, tax records, genealogical data, maps
and charts, court dockets, public proclamations, petitions, and court orders relating chiefly to Middlebury and Addison
County. Most of the papers are from the
19th century.

MIDDLETOWN SPRINGS

VT448-520

The Middletown Springs Historical
Society, Inc.
Middletown Springs VT 05757

(802) 235-2127

OPEN: by appointment only by
contacting the President at (802)
235-2302
COPYING FACILITIES: no

HOLDINGS:
Total volume: not specified
Inclusive dates: late 1700's -
Description: Photographs and memorabilia of Middletown Springs; photographs
and manuscripts of Dana S. Carpenter,
botanist; papers of Henry Gray, M. I. T.
professor; family records; records of St.
Margaret's Episcopal Church; photographs of early buildings and individuals;
correspondence and other records of
Montvert and Mineral Springs; records
and drawings of A. W. Gray, manufacturer; school records and photographs;
Congregational and other church records;
and birth, marriage, death, and land
records of Middletown Springs.

MONTPELIER

VT464-560

Norwich University
Vermont College Division
Gary Memorial Library
College Street
Montpelier VT 05602

(802) 229-0522, Ext. 253

OPEN: by appointment only
COPYING FACILITIES: yes
MATERIALS SOLICITED: Newbury Seminary, Montpelier Seminary and Vermont Junior College archives and materials. Will also accept other items.

HOLDINGS:
Total volume: 200 l.f.
Inclusive dates: 1834 -
Description: Archives and non-current
records of Vermont College. Included are
records of Newbury Seminary, Montpelier Seminary, and Vermont Junior College, as well as other materials.

VT464-800

Vermont Agency of Administration
Public Records Division
6 Baldwin Street
Montpelier VT

MAILING ADDRESS:
State Administration Building
Montpelier VT 05602

(802) 828-3288

OPEN: M-F 8-4; closed weekends and
holidays
COPYING FACILITIES: yes
MATERIALS SOLICITED: Records of Vermont State government agencies. Will
also accept microforms of local government records, including vital records,
deeds, grand lists, charters, and town
proceedings.

HOLDINGS:
Total volume: 900 c.f.; 14,200
microfilm reels; 843 c.f. of card files of
vital records
Inclusive dates: 1776 -
Description: Post-1900 State records
other than those deposited with the Secretary of State's office. Included are
records of executive agencies, and legislative manuscript bills and committee reports. Microfilm holdings include Vermont governors' correspondence; town
and county records, including deeds, proprietors' records, town proceedings, vital
statistics, church records, charters and
maps; highway deeds; and probate
records.

SEE: Hamer (as Public Records Commission).

VT464-820

Vermont Department of Libraries
Law and Documents Unit
Supreme Court Building
Montpelier VT 05602

(802) 828-3268

OPEN: M-F 8-4:30; closed weekends and
holidays

COPYING FACILITIES: yes

HOLDINGS:
> *Total volume:* 70 vols.; 19 l.f.
> *Inclusive dates:* 1790 - 1968
> *Description:* Manuscript censuses of Vermont, 1790-1880, and aerial photographs taken in Vermont in 1962 and 1968.

VT464-840
Vermont Historical Society
Library
Pavilion Building
109 State Street
Montpelier VT 05602

(802) 828-2291

OPEN: M-F 8-4:30; closed weekends and holidays
COPYING FACILITIES: yes
MATERIALS SOLICITED: Will accept materials relating to Vermont local history and genealogy, and the genealogy of other New England States, New York, and southern Canada.

HOLDINGS:
> *Total volume:* 493 c.f.; 70 l.f.; 81 file drawers
> *Inclusive dates:* 1740 -
> *Description:* Materials relating to Vermont, including personal correspondence, diaries, charters, account books, church records, and manuscript town histories. Topics covered include the French and Indian War, World War II, and other wars; perfectionism; antimasonry; and the antislavery movement. Also held are many manuscript letters from Vermonters living outside the state, describing local conditions in the South, Midwest, and West.

SEE: Hamer; NUCMC, 1962-65, 67, 69.

SEE: Davis; Hines; Robbins; Hinding.

SEE ALSO: Walter Schatz, ed., *Directory of Afro-American Resources* (Bowker, 1970); Ann Novotny, ed., *Picture Sources 3* (Special Libraries Assn., 1975); 'Personal Narratives of the Civil War in the Collection of the Vermont Historical Society,' *Vermont History* 31 (1963).

VT464-850
Vermont Secretary of State
State Papers Division
Redstone Building
Montpelier VT 05602

(802) 828-2369

OPEN: M-F 8-4:30; closed weekends and holidays
COPYING FACILITIES: yes
MATERIALS SOLICITED: State papers as mandated by Vermont statute. Will also accept occasional materials relating to the State Papers.

HOLDINGS:
> *Total volume:* 500 c.f.; 735 vols.
> *Inclusive dates:* 1774 -
> *Description:* The archives of the State of Vermont, chiefly prior to 1900, and predominantly 1774-1850. Certain record series continue to be deposited with the State Papers Division. These include legislative records such as the original acts of the legislature, committee records and constitutional amendment records; federal, state, county, and town election records; executive records and governors' correspondence; and deeds, leases, agreements and compacts in which the state is party.
>
> The records of the Vermont Bicentennial Commission are also held by the division.

SEE: Hamer.

SEE ALSO: Marlene Wallace, 'A Guide to the Vermont State Papers,' *Vermont Libraries* 4 (July - Aug. 1975); Marlene Wallace and John Williams, 'Vermont State Papers: Rich Sources for the Study of Vermont History,' *Vermont History* 38 (Summer 1970).

NORTH BENNINGTON

VT496-640
The Park-McCullough House
  Association, Inc.
Library
Manuscript Collection and Archive
Park and West Streets
North Bennington VT 05257

(802) 442-2747

OPEN: M-F 9-4; closed weekends and holidays
ACCESS: appointment required
COPYING FACILITIES: yes
MATERIALS SOLICITED: Materials relating to the Hall, Park, and McCullough families, and to Vermont, especially Bennington and North Bennington.

HOLDINGS:
> *Total volume:* 70 l.f.
> *Inclusive dates:* 1757 - 1967
> *Description:* Manuscripts, papers, and documents relating to Hiland Park, congressman and governor; Trenor Park; John G. McCullough, governor; Arthur L. Van Benthuysen; and other members of the Park-McCullough family. Papers relating to the family's involvement in the San Francisco Vigilance Movement, the Panama Canal and railroad, the Mariposa Gold Mine, Rutland Railroad, Erie Railroad, First National Bank of North Bennington, and Bennington College. Also includes manuscripts and poems of Esther Morgan McCullough.
>
> Papers relating to New York land grants disputed by Vermont and to California and Virginia land claims; papers of David Robinson and George J. Stannard, Civil War generals; photographs, oral history tapes, genealogical charts of family members; architectural plans and records of building costs of the Park-McCullough house, built by Diaper and Dudley; and papers of the Park-McCullough House Association, 1965- .

SEE: Hinding.

NORTHFIELD

VT528-560
Norwich University
Library
Special Collections
Northfield VT 05663

(802) 485-5011, Ext. 248

OPEN: M-F 9-4; closed weekends and holidays
COPYING FACILITIES: yes
MATERIALS SOLICITED: Materials relating to the history of Norwich University and to the achievements of its alumni and faculty. Will also accept local history materials.

HOLDINGS:
> *Total volume:* 125 l.f.
> *Inclusive dates:* late 18th century -
> *Description:* A collection of manuscripts, photographs, and motion pictures relating to Norwich University and its faculty and alumni. Of special interest are the papers of Alden Partridge, founder of the institution, which reflect his interest in education, mathematics, surveying, engineering, politics, and military affairs. Collections relating to alumni include materials on Truman B. Ransom, Grenville Dodge, Gideon Welles, Alonzo Jackman, E. N. Harmon, I. D. White, and Barksdale Hamlett.

SEE: Hamer.

PROCTOR

VT632-640
Proctor Free Library
Proctor VT 05765

(802) 459-3539

SEE: NUCMC, 1979.

Questionnaire not returned.

PUTNEY

VT640-640
Putney Historical Society
Town Hall
Putney VT 05346

(802) 387-5862

OPEN: W-Sa 2-4; closed other days
COPYING FACILITIES: yes
MATERIALS SOLICITED: Materials relating to Putney town history.

HOLDINGS:
> *Total volume:* not specified
> *Inclusive dates:* not specified
> *Description:* Documents related to Putney since its earliest settlement.

ROYALTON

VT688-690
Royalton Historical Society
South Royalton VT 05068

(802) 763-8830

OPEN: by appointment
COPYING FACILITIES: no
MATERIALS SOLICITED: Manuscripts relating to Royalton. Will also accept materials dealing with neighboring towns and the State of Vermont.

HOLDINGS:
  Total volume: 66.6 l.f.
  Inclusive dates: 1780 -
  Description: Manuscripts and photographs relating to Royalton. Included are diaries, reminiscences of early settlers and residents, account books, early business records, correspondence of Royalton residents, genealogical materials, and materials relating to the Bank of Royalton, cemeteries, architecture, schools, and the Royalton Academy.

RUTLAND

VT704-280
Green Mountain National Forest
Rutland VT

MAILING ADDRESS:
P.O. Box 519
Rutland VT 05701

(802) 775-2579

OPEN: M-F 8-4:30; closed weekends and holidays
USER FEES: standard fee for clerical search time
COPYING FACILITIES: yes
MATERIALS SOLICITED: Files and records of the Green Mountain National Forest, Vermont, and Hector Land Use Area, New York.

HOLDINGS:
  Total volume: 6 c.f.
  Inclusive dates: 1934 -
  Description: Material on the history of the Green Mountain National Forest and Civilian Conservation Corps camps of the 1930's.

VT704-690
Rutland Historical Society
101 Center Street
Rutland VT 05701

(802) 773-3417

OPEN: by appointment
ACCESS: mature, serious researchers
COPYING FACILITIES: no
MATERIALS SOLICITED: Material pertaining to the history of Rutland. Will also accept materials relating to Rutland County, with emphasis on Lemuel Haynes, Julia C. R. Dorr, John A. Graham, W. Y. Ripley, and William Henry Jackson.

HOLDINGS:
  Total volume: 2 l.f.
  Inclusive dates: 1830 - 1930
  Description: Minute books of early fire companies in Rutland and West Rutland; farmer's diaries of the mid-19th century; account books of merchants; letters and collections of letters (1870-1900); hotel registers; and lawyer's letter books (1834-50).

ST. ALBANS

VT720-710
St. Albans Free Library
Maiden Lane
St. Albans VT 05478

(802) 524-3804

OPEN: M, W, F, 10-9, Tu, Th 2-9, Sa 2-5; closed Sundays and holidays
USER FEES: $2, nonresidents; $3 per family per year
COPYING FACILITIES: yes

HOLDINGS:
  Total volume: 12 items; 1 vol.
  Inclusive dates: late 19th century
  Description: Photographs of St. Albans in the late 19th century.

VT720-720
St. Albans Historical Society, Inc.
Franklin County Museum
Corner Church & Bishop Streets
St. Albans VT 05478

MAILING ADDRESS:
P.O. Box 722
St. Albans VT 05478

(802) 527-7933 or 524-2865

OPEN: by appointment May, June, Tu-Sa afternoons July-Nov. and March, April; closed Dec.-March
COPYING FACILITIES: no
MATERIALS SOLICITED: Material on the St. Albans Raid of 1864, Confederate Raid on the banks; genealogical material; and information in general about Franklin County.

HOLDINGS:
  Total volume: 2 file cabinets
  Inclusive dates: 19th century -
  Description: Correspondence, photographs, and eye-witness accounts of St. Albans Confederate Raid; diary of Judge James C. Davis; records of local families, including Brainerd, Governor Smith, Dutcher, and Aldis; records relating to Revolutionary soldiers; material relating to railroads and fire department; press copies of correspondence of Warren R. Austin and Roswell C. Austin, attorneys; maps; prescription books and ledgers; and local cemetery records.

ST. JOHNSBURY

VT736-240
Fairbanks Museum and Planetarium
Main and Prospect Streets
St. Johnsbury VT 05819

(802) 748-2372

OPEN: by appointment only
ACCESS: advance arrangements advisable
COPYING FACILITIES: yes
MATERIALS SOLICITED: Materials relating to northeastern Vermont.

HOLDINGS:
  Total volume: 5,000 items
  Inclusive dates: 1800 -
  Description: Materials pertaining to the history of northeastern Vermont, and especially to the Fairbanks family.

SEE: Hamer.

SHELBURNE

VT784-720
Shelburne Museum
Library
Shelburne VT 05482

(802) 985-3346

OPEN: M-F 9-5; closed weekends
USER FEES: $15 yearly membership fee; no fee for students
COPYING FACILITIES: yes
MATERIALS SOLICITED: Materials relating to Vermont and the museum collections of decorative and folk arts, as well as papers of artists and museum patrons.

HOLDINGS:
  Total volume: 4 file drawers
  Inclusive dates: late 18th century -
  Description: Theses, artists' letters, and other materials relating to the decorative arts and folk art; papers of Thomas Macdonough, commander of U.S. naval forces at the Battle of Plattsburgh in the War of 1812; materials concerning Vermont since the late 18th century; and correspondence and documents relating to steamship transportation and life on Lake Champlain.

SEE: Novotny.

SPRINGFIELD

VT864-730
Springfield Town Library
43 Main Street
Springfield VT 05156

(802) 885-3108

OPEN: Tu-Th 9-8, F 9-5, Sa 9-1; closed Su, M and holidays
USER FEES: $5 a year for non-Vermont residents
COPYING FACILITIES: yes

HOLDINGS:
  Total volume: 25 l.f.
  Inclusive dates: late 1800's -
  Description: Photographs of Springfield and the surrounding area; town records; records of the Library; and oral history

tapes relating to the machine tool industry in Springfield.

SEE: Hinding.

STRAFFORD

VT880-720
Strafford Historical Society
Strafford VT 05072

no telephone

SEE: NUCMC, 1959-61, 70 (as Stafford Historical Society).

Questionnaire not returned.

WINOOSKI

VT964-720
St. Michael's College
Archives and Special Collections
Jeremiah K. Durick Library
St. Michael's College
Winooski VT 05404

(802) 655-2000, Ext. 2408

OPEN: M-F 8:30-4; closed weekends and holidays
ACCESS: advance arrangements required
COPYING FACILITIES: yes

MATERIALS SOLICITED: Will accept faculty papers and literary manuscripts of faculty and alumni authors.

HOLDINGS:
Total volume: 100 l.f.
Inclusive dates: 1900 -
Description: Manuscripts; music scores in manuscript; correspondence of faculty and alumni of St. Michael's College; audible documents of ecumenical symposia; and visual documents pertaining to the history of St. Michael's College, the Society of St. Edmund and the Diocese of Burlington, Vermont.

VIRGIN ISLANDS

Although there is no comprehensive program for preserving local public records of the Virgin Islands of the United States, small collections pertaining to St. Thomas, St. Croix, and St. John are available in the Islands' public and academic libraries. Materials include tax and court records and annual reports of government departments. A small body of local tax, police, court and other records, mostly pre-dating 1917, is located in the National Archives in Washington, DC.

ST. CROIX

VI300-240
Florence A. Williams Public Library
49-50 King Street
Christiansted
St. Croix VI 00820

(809) 773-5715

OPEN: M-F 8-5; closed weekends and holidays
COPYING FACILITIES: yes

HOLDINGS:
Total volume: 1,700 items
Inclusive dates: 1800 -
Description: A collection of manuscript ledgers, 1800-1930, from the government of the Danish West Indies and the early United States administration, and records of the territorial governments and legislatures, 1930 - .

ST. THOMAS

VI700-360
Island Resources Foundation
Harms Lagoon Marina
St. Thomas, U.S. Virgin Islands

MAILING ADDRESS:
Red Hook Center Box 33
St. Thomas, U.S. Virgin Islands 00801

(809) 775-3225

OPEN: M-F 7-7; closed weekends and holidays
ACCESS: advance notification required
COPYING FACILITIES: yes
MATERIALS SOLICITED: West Indian history.

HOLDINGS:
Total volume: 8 l.f.; 1,200 items
Inclusive dates: 1752 - 1790
Description: A collection of manuscript reproductions relating chiefly to the British West Indies in the era of the American Revolution. Included are official letters and reports from the Admiralty, War Office and Colonial Office papers at the London Public Record Office, as well as private correspondence from British, American, and West Indian repositories relating to West Indian Affairs generally and West Indian plantations and slavery specifically. Also included in the collection are documents concerning the Danish West Indies and complete reproductions of the 'Joseph Senhouse Memoirs' from the Cumberland Record Office and the 'Christopher Vail Manuscript' from the Library of Congress, accounts of the West Indian Islands during the American Revolution.

SEE ALSO: George F. Tyson, Jr., and Carolyn Tyson, *Preliminary Report on Manuscript Materials in British Archives Relating to the American Revolution in the West Indian Islands* (1974).

VI700-800
Virgin Islands Department of Conservation and Cultural Affairs
Bureau of Libraries and Museums
20 Dronningens Gade
Charlotte Amalie
St. Thomas VI

MAILING ADDRESS:
P.O. Box 390
Charlotte Amalie
St. Thomas VI 00801

(809) 774-0630

OPEN: M-F 8-5; closed weekends and holidays
COPYING FACILITIES: yes
MATERIALS SOLICITED: Records and papers of the government of the Virgin Islands of the United States and of prominent Virgin Islands residents. Will also accept records and papers pertaining to other Caribbean islands and their peoples.

HOLDINGS:
Total volume: 300 c.f.
Inclusive dates: 1672 -
Description: A collection relating to the Caribbean islands, with emphasis on Virgin Islands' materials, including the Governor's annual reports, and records of other executive departments. There are also microfilm copies of dispatches of U.S. consuls, archives of the Danish West Indies, and church records.

VIRGINIA

Since 1972 the Archives and Records Division of the Virginia State Library has administered a statewide program to preserve local public records through inventorying, scheduling, and microfilming, under the auspices of its Records Branch. Permanently valuable county and municipal records are scheduled for retention either in the locality or in the Archives Branch, State Library, in Richmond. More than 19,450 cubic feet, primarily county and circuit court records from the 18th and 19th centuries, have been transferred to the State Library.

The Archives Branch also provides researchers with more than 6,400 reels of pre-1865 vital, land, probate, and other microfilmed records for almost all counties and municipalities, filmed by the Church of Jesus Christ of Latter-day Saints and the State Library. A preliminary inventory to the microfilm is available.

ALEXANDRIA

VA20-40
Alexandria Library
Lloyd House Archives
220 North Washington Street
Alexandria VA 22314

(703) 838-4577

OPEN: M-F 9-5; closed Sundays and holidays; Sa 9-1, June-Aug., Sa 9-5 Sept.-May
COPYING FACILITIES: yes
MATERIALS SOLICITED: Materials relating to Alexandria and Virginia. Will also accept materials relating to the Civil War and early America.

HOLDINGS:
Total volume: 7,500 items
Inclusive dates: 1650 - 1937
Description: Materials pertaining primarily to Alexandria. Included are letters, merchants' ledgers, receipts, tax records, photographs, and other materials.

VA20-322
National Council of Negro Women
National Archives for Black Women's History
701 N. Fairfax Street, Suite 330
Alexandria VA 22314

(703) 684-5733

OPEN: M-F 9-5; closed weekends and holidays
ACCESS: advance arrangements required
COPYING FACILITIES: yes
MATERIALS SOLICITED: Personal papers of black women, records of black women's organizations, and other historical documentation about black women in the United States.

HOLDINGS:
Total volume: 200 l.f.
Inclusive dates: 1935 -
Description: Historical records of the National Council of Negro Women, including local Council sections and affiliated black women's organizations, and other manuscript collections. Included are organization records, personal papers, photographs, audio-visual materials, and ephemera. The materials relate to civil rights, women's issues, education, employment, health, housing, consumer issues, and international relations.

VA20-666
National Rural Letter Carriers' Association
1448 Duke Street
Alexandria VA 22314

(703) 684-5545

OPEN: M-F 7:30-5:30; closed weekends and holidays
COPYING FACILITIES: yes

HOLDINGS:
Total volume: not specified
Inclusive dates: 1903 -
Description: Records of the National Rural Letter Carriers' Association, including annual reports of the Association's National officers, photographs of employees and officials, and official correspondence.

SEE ALSO: Paul Lewinson and Morris Rieger, 'Labor Union Records in the United States,' *American Archivist* 25 (Jan. 1962).

ARLINGTON

VA50-30
American Gas Association
Library
1515 Wilson Boulevard
Arlington VA 22209

(703) 841-8415

OPEN: M-F 9-5; closed weekends and holidays
ACCESS: non-members by appointment only
COPYING FACILITIES: yes
MATERIALS SOLICITED: Materials relating to the natural gas industry in the US including manuscripts, diaries, journals, unpublished translations, records of non-current gas associations, photographs and drawings.

HOLDINGS:
Total volume: 5,000 items
Inclusive dates: 1816 -
Description: Records of companies and associations in the American gas industry, 1816- .

VA50-50
Arlington County Public Library
Virginiana Collection
1015 North Quincy Street
Arlington VA 22201

(703) 527-4777, Ext. 52

OPEN: Su 1-9, M-Th 9-10, F, Sa 9-5; closed holidays
ACCESS: an appointment is advisable
COPYING FACILITIES: yes
MATERIALS SOLICITED: Oral history of Arlington County, specifically personal recollections of inhabitants about their social, political, government, educational, and civic experiences, 1895- . Will also accept personal photographs, diaries, correspondence, and records relating to civic or political groups.

HOLDINGS:
Total volume: 24 boxes; 60 items; other materials
Inclusive dates: 1895 -
Description: Correspondence, notebooks, and records of individuals active in civic and political affairs in Arlington County; and oral history interviews with long-time Arlington residents and others prominent in Arlington affairs, covering such topics as rural life, urban development, business, civic activities, government, schools, social life, vanished landmarks, churches, and celebrations.

SEE: Hinding.

VA50-65

Arlington House, the Robert E. Lee
  Memorial
Arlington National Cemetery
Arlington VA

MAILING ADDRESS:
Arlington House
c/o George Washington Memorial
  Parkway
Turkey Run Park
McLean VA 22101

(703) 557-0613

OPEN: by appointment only
ACCESS: appointment requested
COPYING FACILITIES: no
MATERIALS SOLICITED: Manuscripts, correspondence, diaries, journals, genealogical material, sheet music, maps,
  photographs, scrapbooks, and oral history tapes relating to Arlington House
  and its residents.

HOLDINGS:
  Total volume: not specified
  Inclusive dates: 1780 -
  Description: Collection of correspondence, journals, maps, and photographs
  relating to: Robert E. Lee and his immediate family; George Washington Parke
  Custis and his immediate family; Arlington House and its construction, furnishings, grounds, farm operation, slaves and
  restoration; general American social, cultural, and political life, 1800-61, relating
  to the Arlington estate, northern Virginia,
  Washington, D.C. and environs.

VA50-240

Forest Service
Office of Information
Audio/Visual Group
Photo Library
1621 North Kent Street
Arlington VA

MAILING ADDRESS:
51 LL-RPE
Washington DC 20013

(703) 235-8215

OPEN: M-F 8-4:45; closed weekends and
  holidays
COPYING FACILITIES: yes
MATERIALS SOLICITED: Historical photographs relating to U.S. National Forests, the lumber industry, forest fire
  and brush fire fighting, and important
  figures in forestry. Will also accept recent photographs of people's activities
  on National Forest land.

HOLDINGS:
  Total volume: 600,000 items
  Inclusive dates: 1870 -
  Description: A collection of black-
  and-white and color negatives, prints, and
  slides relating to forestry, National Forests, scenic public lands, people's activities on National Forest land, and the harvesting of timber. Included is a comprehensive visual record of Smokey Bear
  and Woodsy Owl and photographs of
  many tree species.

SEE: Novotny.

VA50-530

Air Force Military Airlift Command
Aerospace Audiovisual Service
1361st Audiovisual Squadron
1221 South Fern Street
Arlington VA 22202

(202) 697-3810

OPEN: M-F 7:45-4:30; closed weekends
  and holidays
COPYING FACILITIES: no
MATERIALS SOLICITED: Photographs of
  Air Force activities of a historical or
  newsworthy nature.

HOLDINGS:
  Total volume: 300,000 items
  Inclusive dates: early 1900's -
  Description: Still photographs covering
  the history of aviation from the Wright
  brothers era to the present.

Pre-1954 photographs have been
transferred to: Smithsonian Institution, National Air and Space Museum, Records Management Division,
Washington, DC 20560. (202)
357-3133. Photographs, 1954-85, have
been transferred to Department of
Defense, Audio Visual Agency, DOD
Still Media Depository, Code LGP-R,
Washington, DC 20374-1681. (202)
433-2166

ASHLAND

VA60-690

Randolph-Macon College
Library
Ashland VA 23005

no telephone

SEE: Hamer; NUCMC, 1959-62, 76, 78.

Questionnaire not returned.

BLACKSBURG

VA90-840

Virginia Polytechnic Institute and
  State University
Carol M. Newman Library
Special Collections
Blacksburg VA 24061

(703) 961-6308

OPEN: Su 1-5, M, W, F 8-5, Tu, Th 8-8;
  closed Saturdays and holidays; reduced
  hours between sessions and in summer
COPYING FACILITIES: yes
MATERIALS SOLICITED: Materials relating
  to the history of VPI&SU, including
  faculty, student, and alumni papers.
  Materials relevant to the history of
  Southwest Virginia, including personal
  papers, business records, and photographs. Professional papers relating to
  twentieth-century developments in science and technology.

HOLDINGS:
  Total volume: 750 l.f.
  Inclusive dates: 1820 -
  Description: Materials related to Southwest Virginia include the papers of Governor J. Hoge Tyler; Martin P. and Andrew L. Farrier; John S. Apperson; Harvey Black; William Preston, 150 items;
  account books of general stores, hotels,
  and other businesses; and the records of
  the Blacksburg Methodist Church,
  Blacksburg Community Concert Association, Blacksburg Women's Club, and
  other local organizations.
    Materials dealing with twentieth-
  century developments in science and
  technology include the papers of John W.
  Landis, James R. Randolph, and Samuel
  Herrick. The University Archives contains not only non-current administrative
  records but also the papers of faculty and
  alumni, including those of Ralph M.
  Brown, Dayton M. Kohler, and J.
  Ambler Johnston.

SEE: NUCMC, 1980.

SEE: Robbins.

BRIDGEWATER

VA115-80

Bridgewater College
Alexander Mack Memorial Library
College Archives
Bridgewater VA 22812

(703) 828-2501, Ext. 510

OPEN: M-F 8-5; closed weekends and
  holidays
ACCESS: permission of Head Librarian
  required
COPYING FACILITIES: yes
MATERIALS SOLICITED: Diaries, manuscripts, church records, personal correspondence, Fraktur, oral history
  tapes, video tapes and motion pictures,
  sound recordings relating to the College. Will also accept pictures pertaining to the college and Church of the
  Brethren.

HOLDINGS:
  Total volume: 75 l.f.
  Inclusive dates: 18th century - 20th
  century
  Description: Materials include the John
  W. Wayland diaries; Nettie Sanger work
  books; several account books from the
  Timberville Orphan's Home (1800's); a
  16mm film about Bridgewater College;
  video tapes and cassette and reel tape
  recordings; miscellaneous Civil War letters; and a holograph book belonging to
  Joseph Funk, local printer and musician.

BRISTOL

VA120-80

Bristol Public Library
701 Goode Street
Bristol VA 24201

(703) 669-9444

OPEN: M-Th 9-9, F, Sa 9-5; closed
  Sundays and holidays
COPYING FACILITIES: yes

HOLDINGS:
   Total volume: 1,500 items
   Inclusive dates: 1800 -
   Description: Records relating to geneal-
   ogy and the local history of Bristol, VA,
   and Bristol, TN.

CHARLOTTESVILLE

VA145-40
Albemarle County Historical Society
220 Court Square
Charlottesville VA 22901

(804) 296-1492

OPEN: Tu 10-12, W 10-4:30, Th 1-4:30,
   F 12-4:30, Sa 10-12:30; closed Su, M
   and holidays

SEE: Hamer.

Questionnaire not returned.

VA145-780
University of Virginia
Library
Manuscripts Department and
   University Archives
Charlottesville VA 22901

(804) 924-3025

OPEN: M-F 9-5, Sa 9-1; closed Sundays,
   holidays, and Christmas vacation
ACCESS: identification required
COPYING FACILITIES: yes
MATERIALS SOLICITED: Materials relating
   to the history of Virginia and the
   southeastern United States; Virginia
   and American literary materials; and
   University of Virginia records, either of
   permanent value or required legally for
   retention.

HOLDINGS:
   Total volume: 10,000,000 items
   Inclusive dates: 1200 -
   Description: Over 12,000 collections
   relating to Virginia and the southeastern
   United States, including those of literary
   figures and other individuals, organizations, businesses, educational institutions,
   and professional associations. The collection consists of manuscripts, records, diaries, letters, photographs, audio and video
   tapes, oral history interviews, and other
   items.

SEE: Hamer; NUCMC, 1959-65, 67, 69,
   71-72, 74, 77, 81.

SEE: Allard, Crawley, and Edmison; Bean
   and Vane; Beers - Confederate;
   Hinding; Ingram; Leventhal and Mooney - III; Parkinson; Paszek; Robbins.

SEE ALSO: Peter Duignan, *Handbook of
   American Resources for African Studies*
   (Hoover Institution, 1967); Ann Novotny,
   ed., *Picture Sources 3* (Special Libraries
   Assn., 1975); Walter Schatz, ed., *Directory
   of Afro-American Resources* (Bowker,
   1970); David A. Hounshell, comp.,
   *Manuscripts in U.S. Depositories Relating
   to the History of Electrical Science and
   Technology* (Smithsonian Institution,
   n.d.); *Source Materials for the Recent History of Astronomy and Astrophysics: A*

*Checklist of Manuscript Collections in the
United States* (American Institute of
Physics, 1971); Joan N. Warnow, *A Selec-
tion of Manuscripts Collections at Ameri-
can Repositories* (American Institute of
Physics, 1969).

Albert Krichmar, *The Women's Rights
Movement in the United States,
1848-1970: A Bibliography and
Sourcebook* (Scarecrow Press, 1972);
Thomas H. English, *Roads to Research:
Distinguished Literary Collections of the
Southeast* (Univ. of Georgia Press, 1968);
Richard C. Davis, *North American Forest
History: A Guide to Archives and Manu-
scripts in the United States and Canada*
(Clio Books, 1977); Michael F. Plunkett,
*A Guide to Latin American Materials in
the Manuscripts Department, University of
Virginia Library* (Univ. of Virginia,
1972). There are also other finding aids
to literary collections and other materials
held by the University Library.

CHESAPEAKE

VA165-120
Chesapeake Public Library
Wallace Memorial Room of the
Norfolk County Historical Society of
   Chesapeake
300 Cedar Road
Chesapeake VA 23320

(804) 547-6591

OPEN: M-Th 9-9, F, Sa 9-5, Su 1-5;
   closed holidays
COPYING FACILITIES: yes
MATERIALS SOLICITED: Materials relating
   to Virginia, Norfolk County and the
   city of Chesapeake. Will also accept
   genealogical materials and family histories.

HOLDINGS:
   Total volume: not specified
   Inclusive dates: 1687 -
   Description: Maps concentrating on the
   early history (1687-1787) of Norfolk,
   Norfolk County, and Tidewater Virginia;
   including a good selection of maps de-
   picting the development of waterways
   (Albemarle & Chesapeake Canal, Dismal
   Swamp Canal) in Southeastern Virginia.
   Reports of the Albemarle & Chesapeake
   Canal Co., 1855, 1857-81, 1885. Other
   manuscripts relating chiefly to Norfolk
   County and its people.

DANVILLE

VA185-160
Danville Historical Society
116 South Ridge Street
Danville VA 24541

MAILING ADDRESS:
P.O. Box 2
Danville VA 24543

(804) 792-6762

OPEN: by appointment only
COPYING FACILITIES: yes
MATERIALS SOLICITED: Local and regional historical materials, including manuscripts, archives of institutions and or-

ganizations, visual and audible documents, scrapbooks, and photographs.

HOLDINGS:
   Total volume: 50 l.f.
   Inclusive dates: 1815 -
   Description: Collections relating to the
   history of Danville, Pittsylvania County
   and some parts of Virginia, including account books, correspondence, public documents, business records, memorabilia,
   non-current records of institutions, maps,
   photographs, and oral history tapes. The
   majority of the material dates from the
   period 1870-1930.

EMORY

VA195-200
Emory & Henry College
Library
Emory VA

MAILING ADDRESS:
P.O. Drawer G
Emory VA 24327

(703) 944-3121

OPEN: M-F 8-11:30, Sa 9-5, Su
   2:30-10:30; closed holidays
COPYING FACILITIES: yes
MATERIALS SOLICITED: Documents per-
   taining to the history of the Holston
   Annual Conference of the United
   Methodist church, and folklore and
   oral history of Washington County,
   VA, and southwestern Virginia.

HOLDINGS:
   Total volume: 120 l.f.; 350 hours of
   interviews
   Inclusive dates: 1800 -
   Description: A collection of manuscripts, diaries, reports, memoirs, and
   minutes, 1800-1900, relating to the
   Holston Annual Conference of the United Methodist church and its activities in
   southwestern Virginia and eastern Tennessee; Emory & Henry College archives,
   consisting of trustees' reports, minutes of
   trustees' meetings, journals and daybooks
   of the business office, and miscellaneous
   manuscripts, memoirs, and memorials of
   the faculty, alumni, and other persons
   connected with the College or the local
   area; and oral history interviews, primarily biographical, but containing information on mining, agriculture, business, education, community development, labor
   unions, and religion in southwestern Virginia.

SEE: Parkinson; Hinding.

SEE ALSO: Alan M. Meckler and Ruth
   McMullin, comps., *Oral History Collec-
   tions* (Bowker, 1975); *The Appalachian
   Oral History Project Union Catalog*
   (Appalachian Oral History Project,
   1977).

FAIRFAX

VA205-290
George Mason University
Research Center for the Federal
 Theater Project
4400 University Drive
Fairfax VA

MAILING ADDRESS:
English Department
George Mason University
Fairfax VA 22030

(703) 323-2251

OPEN: M-F 8:30-5; closed weekends and
 holidays
USER FEES: research requests by mail:
 first hour of research, no charge; $5 per
 hour each subsequent hour
ACCESS: permission of Curator required
COPYING FACILITIES: yes
MATERIALS SOLICITED: Materials from
 and related to the Federal Theater
 Project. Will also accept material relating to drama of the 1920's and 1930's.

HOLDINGS:
 Total volume: 2,156 c.f.
 Inclusive dates: 1935 - 1939
 Description: Play research papers; reports; photographs; play and radio scripts;
 music scores; and costume, set, and lighting diagrams from the Federal Theater
 Project and other productions around the
 country. Also included are administrative
 papers of the Federal Theater Project.

SEE: NUCMC, 1979.

SEE: Robbins.

SEE ALSO: a newsletter, *Federal One,*
 available on request.

FALLS CHURCH

VA215-40
American Automobile Association
Library
8111 Gatehouse Road
Falls Church VA 22042

(703) 222-6466

OPEN: M-F 8:30-5; closed weekends and
 holidays
ACCESS: advance permission required
COPYING FACILITIES: yes
MATERIALS SOLICITED: Materials related
 to automobile travel.

HOLDINGS:
 Total volume: 200 items
 Inclusive dates: 1910's -
 Description: Photographs, many of historical interest, of early cars, emergency
 road service vehicles, driver's education
 training programs, school safety patrols,
 and other automobile-related subjects.
 There are also several scrapbooks containing photographs of trips of A. L.
 Westgard, who scouted automobile routes
 for the American Automobile Association
 in the 1910's.

FERRUM

VA235-230
Ferrum College
Blue Ridge Institute
Stanley Library
Ferrum VA 24088

(703) 365-2121, Ext. 416

OPEN: by appointment only; closed
 weekends and holidays
COPYING FACILITIES: yes
MATERIALS SOLICITED: Materials pertaining to the folk culture of Virginia
 with special emphasis on folk music
 and the folk culture of the Blue Ridge
 Mountains and southwestern Virginia.
 Will also accept materials relating to
 folk music of the Blue Ridge Mountains in West Virginia, Tennessee, and
 Kentucky.

HOLDINGS:
 Total volume: 7,500 items
 Inclusive dates: 1780 -
 Description: Correspondence, video
 tapes, and audio tapes of oral history,
 folk legends, traditional crafts, music, and
 customs of Virginia, particularly the Blue
 Ridge Mountain area. Some transcripts
 are available, as well as written interviews. Included is a collection of audio
 tapes on traditional music.

VA235-250
Ferrum College
Stanley Library
Franklin County Historical Society
 Collection
Ferrum VA 24088

(703) 365-2121, Ext. 426

OPEN: F 10-4 March-Oct., other times
 by appointment
COPYING FACILITIES: yes
MATERIALS SOLICITED: Personal papers,
 genealogical source material, literary
 manuscripts, records of organizations,
 business records, photographs, oral history tapes, and sound recordings concerning Franklin County and its people.

HOLDINGS:
 Total volume: 872 items
 Inclusive dates: 1831 -
 Description: Reminiscences, mercantile
 records, records of organizations, recordings of folk songs, photographs, manuscripts for books, and other materials relating to Franklin County.

FORT BELVOIR

VA245-800
U.S. Army Engineer Museum
Building 1000
16th Street and Belvoir Road
Fort Belvoir VA 22060

(703) 664-3171

OPEN: M-F 8-4:30, Sa 1-4; closed
 Sundays and holidays
COPYING FACILITIES: no

MATERIALS SOLICITED: Manuscripts and
 visual and audible documents pertaining to the history of the Corps of Engineers, the Fort Belvoir military installation, and Belvoir Plantation.

HOLDINGS:
 Total volume: 10 l.f.
 Inclusive dates: 1694 -
 Description: Manuscripts and visual
 documents focusing primarily on Army
 Corps of Engineers history. Included are
 French maps and journals of the siege of
 Yorktown; correspondence and diaries of
 prominent military engineers; Presidential
 letters; photographs and slides of military
 engineer activities and personalities; and
 photographs and slides pertaining to the
 history of the Fort Belvoir military installation. There are also photographs and
 slides documenting the Belvoir Plantation
 archaeological excavations, 1931-32 and
 1972-76.

FORT EUSTIS

VA255-800
Army Transportation Museum
Fort Eustis VA

MAILING ADDRESS:
Building 300
Fort Eustis VA 23604-5260

(804) 878-3603, 3480

OPEN: Su 12-5, M-F 8-5, Sa 10-5; closed
 Christmas and New Year's
COPYING FACILITIES: yes
MATERIALS SOLICITED: Materials relating
 to the history of the Transportation
 Corps or to transportation in the U.S.
 Army. Will also accept materials relat-
 ing to American military history.

HOLDINGS:
 Total volume: 100 l.f.; 250 films;
 2,000 photographs
 Inclusive dates: 1914 -
 Description: A collection of films and
 photographs relating to the history of
 transportation in the U.S. Army and the
 history of the Transportation Corps.
 There are also non-current records of the
 U.S. Army Transportation Center and
 School, 1957- .

FORT MONROE

VA275-240
Fort Monroe
Casemate Museum
Reference Library
Fort Monroe VA

MAILING ADDRESS:
Box 341
Fort Monroe VA 23651

(804) 727-3391

OPEN: daily 10:30-5; closed
 Thanksgiving, Christmas and New
 Year's
ACCESS: 24-hours advance notice
 required
COPYING FACILITIES: yes

MATERIALS SOLICITED: Materials relating to the U.S. Army Coast Artillery, seacoast fortifications, Old Point Comfort, Fort Monroe, the Civil War in Virginia. Will also accept materials pertaining to the history of Hampton, Newport News, and Hampton Roads.

HOLDINGS:
> *Total volume:* 50 l.f.; 1,000 vols.
> *Inclusive dates:* 1820 -
> *Description:* Materials pertaining to the history of Old Point Comfort, especially those relating to the history of Fort Monroe and the Civil War.

FREDERICKSBURG

VA285-240

Fredericksburg and Spotsylvania
   National Military Park
Fredericksburg VA

MAILING ADDRESS:
P.O. Box 679
Fredericksburg VA 22404

(703) 373-4461

OPEN: daily 9-5; closed Christmas and New Year's
ACCESS: by arrangement with the Park Historian
COPYING FACILITIES: yes
MATERIALS SOLICITED: Civil War manuscripts.

HOLDINGS:
> *Total volume:* 1,000 items
> *Inclusive dates:* 1840 - 1930
> *Description:* A collection of manuscripts and archives dealing primarily with the Civil War campaigns in central Virginia, and secondarily with people and sites of Fredericksburg and its environs.

SEE: Hamer; NUCMC, 1965.

VA285-400

James Monroe Law Office Museum
   and Memorial Library
908 Charles Street
Fredericksburg VA 22401

(703) 373-8426

OPEN: by appointment only
COPYING FACILITIES: no
MATERIALS SOLICITED: Papers of James Monroe. Will also accept materials relating to Monroe, his family and descendants, his presidency, and the effects of his administration in the United States and abroad.

HOLDINGS:
> *Total volume:* 300 items
> *Inclusive dates:* 1780 - 1836
> *Description:* Materials on James Monroe and papers of other persons living during the period.

SEE: Hamer.

VA285-440

Kenmore Association, Inc.
1201 Washington Avenue
Fredericksburg VA 22401

(703) 373-3381

OPEN: April 1 - Oct. 31, daily 9-5; rest of year, daily 9-4; closed Thanksgiving, Christmas, and New Year's
USER FEES: $15 per day
ACCESS: researchers should write Director for permission to use archives
COPYING FACILITIES: no
MATERIALS SOLICITED: Materials pertaining to Fielding Lewis and his immediate family. Will also accept materials relating to 18th century Virginia and 19th century materials of Fielding Lewis's descendants.

HOLDINGS:
> *Total volume:* 515 items
> *Inclusive dates:* 1750 - 1824
> *Description:* Letters and bills of Fielding Lewis.

SEE: Hinding.

VA285-520

Mary Washington College
E. Lee Trinkle Library
Rare Books Room and College
   Archives
1301 College Avenue
Fredericksburg VA 22401-5358

(703) 899-4665

OPEN: M-F 8-5; closed weekends and holidays
ACCESS: advance appointment recommended
COPYING FACILITIES: yes
MATERIALS SOLICITED: Materials appropriate to the holdings of a college library.

HOLDINGS:
> *Total volume:* 250 items
> *Inclusive dates:* 1860's -
> *Description:* Approximately 250 file boxes, folders, and papers consisting chiefly of literary manuscripts by Virginia authors or relating to Virginia. Included are papers of Hamilton J. Eckenrode, Virginia State historian, among which are unpublished biographies of Confederate General Joseph Eggleston Johnston and Horace Greeley. In addition, there are the archives of the College and a collection of letters written from the Fredericksburg area by U.S. soldiers during the Civil War.

SEE: Hamer; NUCMC, 1980.
SEE: Robbins.

GALAX

VA290-760

City of Galax
Jeff Matthews Memorial Museum
606 West Stuart Drive
Galax VA 24333

no telephone

OPEN: W-F 1-5, Sa 11-4, Su 1-4; closed M, Tu

COPYING FACILITIES: no
HOLDINGS:
> *Total volume:* 16 items
> *Inclusive dates:* not specified
> *Description:* Photographs and land grants of Galax, including one signed by Daniel Boone.

HAMPDEN-SYDNEY

VA310-320

Hampden-Sydney College
Eggleston Library
Special Collections
Via Sacra
Hampden-Sydney VA

MAILING ADDRESS:
P.O. Box 7
Hampden-Sydney VA 23943

(804) 223-4381, Ext. 190

OPEN: M-Sa 8:30-4:30; closed Sundays and holidays
COPYING FACILITIES: yes
MATERIALS SOLICITED: Materials dealing with Hampden-Sydney College, its immediate surroundings, and the people associated with it.

HOLDINGS:
> *Total volume:* 30 l.f.
> *Inclusive dates:* 1778 - 1966
> *Description:* A collection relating to Hampden-Sydney College and the people associated with it.

SEE: Hamer; NUCMC, 1959-62, 71, 73.
SEE: Schatz; Robbins.

HAMPTON

VA315-310

Hampton Center for the Arts and
   Humanities
22 Wine Street
Hampton VA 23669

(804) 723-1776

OPEN: M-F 10-6; closed weekends and holidays
COPYING FACILITIES: yes
MATERIALS SOLICITED: Hampton city documents, including the former Elizabeth City County and Phoebus and Fox Hill townships, with emphasis on black cultural heritage. Will also accept materials on Virginia history.

HOLDINGS:
> *Total volume:* 4 file drawers
> *Inclusive dates:* 1607 -
> *Description:* Archaeological records and reports of property ownership and excavations of Hampton, and the papers of S. D. Banks of the Hampton Institute.

HANOVER

VA330-320

Hanover County Historical Society
Museum
Old Jail Box 91
Hanover VA 23069

MAILING ADDRESS:
Rt. 4 Box 182
Ashland VA 23005

(804) 537-5502

OPEN: by appointment only
ACCESS: written inquiries only
COPYING FACILITIES: no
MATERIALS SOLICITED: Records of Hanover County, before 1865, including plats, deeds, indentures, wills, letters, account books, genealogical data, maps, and photographs.

HOLDINGS:
Total volume: 5 l.f.
Inclusive dates: 1774 - 1865
Description: Maps, wills, plats, and photographs of Hanover County.

HARRISONBURG

VA350-200

Eastern Mennonite College
Menno Simons Historical
Library/Archives
Harrisonburg VA 22801

(703) 433-2771, Ext. 177, 178

OPEN: M-F 10-5, Sa 9-12; closed Sundays, holidays, college vacation, and Saturdays in summer
ACCESS: advance arrangements recommended
COPYING FACILITIES: yes
MATERIALS SOLICITED: Virginia Mennonite history. Will also accept local Shenandoah Valley historical materials.

HOLDINGS:
Total volume: 455 l.f.; 34 file cabinets
Inclusive dates: 1810 -
Description: A collection of archival and manuscript materials related to Mennonites, especially the Virginia Mennonite Conference and its subsidiary organizations, including records of the historical and current activities of congregations. The files of Eastern Mennonite College are a major part of the archives. There are also some Shenandoah Valley area collections.

SEE: NUCMC, 1959-61.

VA350-320

Harrisonburg-Rockingham Historical
Society
301 South Main Street
Harrisonburg VA 22801

(703) 434-4762

OPEN: M-F 10-4; closed weekends and holidays, and December 15-April 1
COPYING FACILITIES: yes
MATERIALS SOLICITED: Materials on Rockingham County and its citizens. Will also accept other materials.

HOLDINGS:
Total volume: 30 l.f.; 6 file cabinets
Inclusive dates: 1760 -
Description: Land grants, maps, deeds, and other papers, including military records dating from early wars with American Indians through World War II. Also included are copies of early church records.

HOLLINS COLLEGE

VA360-320

Hollins College
Fishburn Library
Hollins College VA 24020

(703) 362-6000

OPEN: M-F 9-4:30; closed weekends and College holidays
ACCESS: advance arrangements recommended
COPYING FACILITIES: yes
MATERIALS SOLICITED: Records of College board of trustees meetings, faculty correspondence, and manuscripts of English and American authors. Will also accept audio-visual materials, music scores by Hollins College faculty, and other materials.

HOLDINGS:
Total volume: 55 l.f.
Inclusive dates: 15th century -
Description: 15th and 16th century manuscript books and leaves; a Virginia Adjutant General's Office order book, 1814; letters and literary manuscripts by English and American authors; miscellaneous letters, including some written in Liberty, VA; materials relating to Hollins College and the Cocke family, consisting of minutes of the College board of trustees, letters, diaries, account books, unpublished memoirs, audio-visual materials, and ephemera; and music scores, chiefly by members of the Hollins faculty.

SEE: Hamer.

SEE: Robbins.

LANCASTER

VA400-520

Mary Ball Washington Museum and
Library
Route 3 at the Lancaster Courthouse
Lancaster VA

MAILING ADDRESS:
Box 97
Lancaster VA 22503

(804) 462-7280

OPEN: Tu-F 10-5, and by appointment; closed other days and holidays
COPYING FACILITIES: yes
MATERIALS SOLICITED: Letters, manuscripts, genealogical materials, photographs, and other materials pertaining to Lancaster County, the Northern Neck, Virginia, and the United States.

HOLDINGS:
Total volume: 81 l.f.
Inclusive dates: 1651 -
Description: Primarily sermon manuscripts and photographs from early camp meetings on the Northern Neck. Other holdings include oral history tapes, and manuscripts, letters, diaries, and account books of families from the Lancaster area.

LEXINGTON

VA430-280

George C. Marshall Research Library
Virginia Military Institute Parade
Ground
Lexington VA

MAILING ADDRESS:
P.O. Drawer 1600
Lexington VA 24450

(703) 463-7103

OPEN: M-F 8:30-4:30; closed weekends and holidays
COPYING FACILITIES: yes
MATERIALS SOLICITED: Materials relating to military history, diplomatic history, foreign affairs, and the Red Cross, 1900-60, with special concentration on World Wars I and II, post-war China, the Marshall Plan, the Cold War, and the Korean War.

HOLDINGS:
Total volume: 1,250 l.f.
Inclusive dates: 1820 -
Description: Materials documenting military and diplomatic history, 1900-60, with special emphasis on the career of George C. Marshall and his service as an Army officer and Chief of Staff, Special Ambassador to China, Secretary of State, president of the American Red Cross, and Secretary of Defense.
Other collections include the papers of William R. Arnold, Marshall S. Carter, William F. Friedman, Collas Harris, John Letcher, Cecilia Martin, Frank McCarthy, Francis Pickens Miller, Frank Price, Harry B. Price, Forrest C. Pogue, Lucian K. Truscott; 400 reels of microfilmed records from the National Archives; photographs, books, posters, and periodicals.

SEE: Hamer; NUCMC, 1973, 75, 80.

SEE: Paszek; Meckler and McMullin; Novotny; Hinding.

VA430-690

Rockbridge County Historical Society
Washington and Lee University
The University Library
Special Collections
Lexington VA

MAILING ADDRESS:
P.O. Box 878
Lexington VA 24450

(703) 463-8663, 8640

OPEN: M-F 9-5; closed weekends and holidays
COPYING FACILITIES: yes
MATERIALS SOLICITED: Rockbridge County history.

HOLDINGS:
> *Total volume:* 40 l. f.
> *Inclusive dates:* 1800 -
> *Description:* Rockbridge County family letters, scrapbooks, business journals, and oral history tapes, and records of the Society.

SEE: NUCMC, 1970.

SEE ALSO: unpublished guides available at the institution.

VA430-840
Virginia Military Institute
Preston Library
Archives/Special Collections
Virginia Military Institute Parade
  Ground
Lexington VA 24450

(703) 463-6228

OPEN: M-F 8-4:30; closed weekends and holidays
COPYING FACILITIES: yes
MATERIALS SOLICITED: Papers of VMI alumni; VMI-related photographs (particularly pre-1900 photographs); and all materials of archival value to the Institute.

HOLDINGS:
> *Total volume:* 1,200 l.f.
> *Inclusive dates:* 1839 - 1960
> *Description:* Official non-current records of the Virginia Military Institute (1839-1960), including Superintendents' correspondence and financial records. Manuscripts held are primarily correspondence, diaries, scrapbooks and other memorabilia of alumni. There is also a photograph collection of ca. 3,000 items, most documenting some aspect of VMI history.

SEE: Hamer; NUCMC, 1959-61, 74.

VA430-870
Washington and Lee University
The University Library
Special Collections
Lexington VA 24450

(703) 463-8663

OPEN: M-F 9-5; closed weekends, holidays, and University vacations; shorter hours in summer
ACCESS: scholarly researchers with proper identification
COPYING FACILITIES: yes
MATERIALS SOLICITED: Materials relating to Washington and Lee University, Lexington and Rockbridge County, and the Shenandoah Valley. Will also accept other materials.

HOLDINGS:
> *Total volume:* 165 l.f.
> *Inclusive dates:* 1750 - 1975
> *Description:* Manuscript collections relating primarily to Lexington and Rockbridge County families of the late 18th and 19th centuries, Washington and Lee University, and the Civil War. Included are logbooks of three 19th century literary-debating societies, and archives of Washington and Lee University, 1776-1930.

GUIDES: *Guide to the Manuscripts at Cyrus Hall McCormick Library, Washington and Lee University* (1976).

SEE: Hamer; NUCMC, 1963-64, 71, 74, 76, 78.

SEE: Robbins.

LYNCHBURG

VA470-470
Lynchburg College
Knight/Capron Library
Lynchburg VA 24501

(804) 522-8204

OPEN: M-F 9-5; closed weekends and Thanksgiving, Christmas and college vacations
COPYING FACILITIES: yes
MATERIALS SOLICITED: Materials relating to the history and growth of Lynchburg College, especially photographs. Will also accept historical data on the central Virginia area.

HOLDINGS:
> *Total volume:* not specified
> *Inclusive dates:* 19th century -
> *Description:* Manuscripts, photographs and oral history interviews relating to the history and growth of Lynchburg College.

VA470-690
Randolph-Macon Woman's College
Lipscomb Library
Rivermont Avenue
Lynchburg VA 24503

(804) 846-7392, Ext. 241, 242

OPEN: Su 10-11, M-F 7:30-11, Sa 10-11; closed College vacations, Christmas, spring break, and summer
COPYING FACILITIES: yes

HOLDINGS:
> *Total volume:* 75 l.f.
> *Inclusive dates:* 1795 -
> *Description:* Papers of John Randolph of Roanoke, 1795-1810, and some autograph letters and literary manuscripts of English and American authors.

SEE: Hamer; NUCMC, 1966.

SEE: Robbins.

MANASSAS

VA480-520
Manassas National Battlefield
Library
Research Collection
Manassas VA

MAILING ADDRESS:
P.O. Box 1830
Manassas VA 22110

(703) 754-7107

OPEN: daily 9-5; closed Christmas
ACCESS: advance arrangements required
COPYING FACILITIES: no
MATERIALS SOLICITED: Materials relating to the battles of Manassas during the Civil War. Will also accept materials

dealing with Manassas area history of the Civil War period.

HOLDINGS:
> *Total volume:* not specified
> *Inclusive dates:* 1860 - 1865
> *Description:* A collection of manuscripts relating chiefly to the two Civil War battles fought at Manassas. Included are diaries, personal accounts, Bibles, one original map, and enlistment records and discharge papers of several individuals.

SEE: Hamer; NUCMC, 1966.

SEE: Hinding.

MCLEAN

VA500-322
Glass Packaging Institute
6845 Elm Street, Suite 209
McLean VA 22101

(703) 790-0800

OPEN: by appointment only; closed holidays
COPYING FACILITIES: no
MATERIALS SOLICITED: Photographs of containers and their recycling and manufacturing.

HOLDINGS:
> *Total volume:* 4,000 items
> *Inclusive dates:* 20th century -
> *Description:* 1,000 black and white photographs of early bottles, some manufactured in the 18th century. Also included are 3,000 color slides of containers, and their manufacture and recycling.

SEE: Novotny.

MOUNT VERNON

VA540-520
Mount Vernon Ladies' Association of the Union
Library
Mount Vernon VA 22121

(703) 780-2000

OPEN: M-F 9-5; closed weekends and holidays except Washington's Birthday
ACCESS: advance appointment required
COPYING FACILITIES: yes
MATERIALS SOLICITED: Materials relating to George Washington and the Washington family, the Curtis and Lewis families, the Mount Vernon estate, the Mount Vernon Ladies Association, plantation life, colonial and 18th century Virginia, slavery, 18th century agriculture, domestic and decorative arts, historic preservation, early views and description of Mount Vernon, and Fairfax County local history.

HOLDINGS:
> *Total volume:* 10,000 vols.; 15,000 manuscripts; other materials
> *Inclusive dates:* 1601 -
> *Description:* Materials focusing on the domestic lives of George and Martha Washington and the history of the Mount Vernon estate. Manuscripts relate to the Washington family at Mount Vernon throughout their ownership, with concentration on George Washington's tenure,

and including correspondence, account books, receipts, journals, surveys, and inventories. The early records of the Mount Vernon Ladies' Association document the rescue, preservation, and restoration of Mount Vernon from the founding of the Association in 1853.

SEE: Hamer; NUCMC, 1966.

SEE: Novotny; Robbins.

NEW MARKET

VA550-520
New Market Battlefield Park
George Collins Parkway
New Market VA

MAILING ADDRESS:
P.O. Box 1864
New Market VA 22844

(703) 740-3101

OPEN: by appointment only
COPYING FACILITIES: yes
MATERIALS SOLICITED: Civil War documents, particularly those associated with the Battle of New Market, the Virginia Military Institute cadets who fought in the Battle, and the War in the Shenandoah Valley. Will also accept materials relating to the Virginia Military Institute during the Civil War.

HOLDINGS:
    Total volume: 48 items
    Inclusive dates: 1861 - 1923
    Description: Materials relating to the Civil War, including 114 letters, diaries, Virginia Military Institute diplomas, Confederate bonds, an oath of allegiance, a military pardon, and 21 photographs of persons and places.

NEWPORT NEWS

VA560-333
Chesapeake and Ohio Historical
    Society, Inc.
Christopher Newport College, Captain
    John Smith Library
50 Shoe Lane
Newport News VA 23606

no telephone

OPEN: by appointment only
ACCESS: advance arrangements required
COPYING FACILITIES: no
MATERIALS SOLICITED: Manuscripts and other items giving information about the Chesapeake and Ohio Railway, its subsidiaries, and its predecessor companies, including photographic prints, negatives and transparencies, engineering drawings, and other primary sources of written and visual data. Especially of interest are items relating to its locomotives, rolling stock, structures, and right of way.

HOLDINGS:
    Total volume: 5,000 items
    Inclusive dates: 1870's - 1970's
    Description: Materials concerning the Chesapeake and Ohio Railway in Virginia, West Virginia, Kentucky, Ohio, and Indiana; the Hocking Valley Railroad

in Ohio; the Pere Marquette Railroad in Michigan and Ontario; and predecessor companies of all these lines. The collection includes nearly 4,000 photographic negatives and prints and transparencies, mainly 1930's through 1950's; several hundred engineering drawings, track charts, and other maps and plans, as well as related printed materials, such as annual reports and company magazines.

VA560-520
The Mariners Museum
Library
Newport News VA 23606

(804) 595-0368

OPEN: M-Sa 9-5; closed Sundays and holidays
COPYING FACILITIES: yes
MATERIALS SOLICITED: Materials in maritime history.

HOLDINGS:
    Total volume: 243 logbooks; 150,000 photographs; other items
    Inclusive dates: not specified
    Description: Materials relating to maritime history, including maps, charts, logbooks, ships' papers, and photographs.

SEE: Hamer; NUCMC, 1959-61.

SEE: Allard, Crawley, and Edmison; Ingram.

SEE ALSO: Ann Novotny, ed., Picture Sources 3 (Special Libraries Assn., 1975); Catalog of Maps, Ships' Papers and Logbooks, The Mariners Museum Library (G. K. Hall, 1964); Catalog of Marine Photographs, The Mariners Museum Library (G. K. Hall, 1964).

VA560-880
War Memorial Museum of Virginia
Library
9285 Warwick Blvd.
Newport News VA 23607

(804) 247-8523

OPEN: M-F 9-5, Sa 1-5; closed Sundays and holidays
USER FEES: adults, 50 cents; children, 25 cents
ACCESS: access to rare books, photographs, films, and historical files is limited to W-F 12-5 or by appointment
COPYING FACILITIES: yes
MATERIALS SOLICITED: U.S. military history archival material from 1776 to the present, especially relating to World Wars I and II, including letters, documents, orders, newspapers, photographs, diaries and films. Foreign military archival materials dealing with World Wars I and II are also desired.

HOLDINGS:
    Total volume: 14,000 items
    Inclusive dates: 1776 -
    Description: Maps, photographs, films, tapes, and manuscripts relating to military history.

NORFOLK

VA580-520
MacArthur Memorial
Archives and Library
MacArthur Square
Norfolk VA 23510

(804) 441-2965

OPEN: M-F 8:30-5; closed weekends and holidays
COPYING FACILITIES: yes
MATERIALS SOLICITED: Correspondence of General Douglas MacArthur prior to 1941. Will also accept documents and correspondence concerning persons on General MacArthur's staffs, 1941-51, especially Courtney Whitney, Charles A. Willoughby, R. K. Sutherland, R. J. Marshall, and H. E. Eastwood.

HOLDINGS:
    Total volume: 696 l.f.; 4,000 vols.
    Inclusive dates: 1880 - 1964
    Description: Correspondence of Douglas MacArthur; staff files, 1941-51, of General MacArthur's various commands; the manuscript of Reminiscences; photographs covering MacArthur's career; and papers of generals Charles A. Willoughby, Courtney Whitney, and H. E. Eastwood.

SEE: Novotny; Paszek; Hinding.

SEE ALSO: Typed finding aids for each of the record groups are available upon request from the institution.

VA580-550
Naval Amphibious Base, Little Creek
Naval Amphibious Museum
Norfolk VA 23521

(804) 464-8130, 7563

OPEN: Sa, Su 1-5, M-F by appointment only; closed holidays
ACCESS: advance arrangements required
COPYING FACILITIES: no
MATERIALS SOLICITED: Records relating to amphibious warfare, especially during World War II and the Vietnam War.

HOLDINGS:
    Total volume: not specified
    Inclusive dates: World War II -
    Description: Correspondence, diaries, journals, logbooks, maps, aerial and ground photographs, audio-visual displays and scrapbooks all pertaining to amphibious warfare, pre- and post-World War II and Vietnam eras. The majority of the material is on loan to the Naval Amphibious Museum from the Curator for the Navy, Naval Historical Center.

VA580-570
Norfolk Public Library
Sargeant Memorial Room
301 East City Hall Avenue
Norfolk VA 23510

(804) 441-2503

OPEN: M, Tu, Th-Sa 9-5, W 9-9; closed Sundays and holidays
COPYING FACILITIES: yes

MATERIALS SOLICITED: History and genealogy of Norfolk and Virginia. Will also accept materials from North Carolina and other surrounding States.

HOLDINGS:
Total volume: 4,000 items
Inclusive dates: 17th century -
Description: Materials on Norfolk history; manuscripts and typescripts of local authors; diaries and letters from Civil War and Revolutionary War writers; records of businesses and organizations; Walter Herron Taylor papers; William C. Whittle papers; unpublished genealogies; photographs of Norfolk, 1860 to the present.

SEE: NUCMC, 1967.

SEE: Allard, Crawley, and Edmison.

VA580-600
Old Dominion University
University Library
Department of Archives and
  Manuscripts
Hampton Blvd.
Norfolk VA 23508

(804) 440-4483

OPEN: M-F 8-5, Sa 9-1; closed Sundays, holidays, and Dec. 24
COPYING FACILITIES: yes
MATERIALS SOLICITED: Non-current records of Old Dominion University; personal papers of emeritus faculty, retired administrators, and members of the Board of Visitors; and papers of citizens of the Tidewater area who have distinguished themselves in public service.

HOLDINGS:
Total volume: 1,598 l. f.
Inclusive dates: 1776 - 1980
Description: More than 48 manuscript collections concerned principally with the history of Tidewater, from the early national period to the present, including correspondence, diaries, legislative and mayoral files, family papers, scrapbooks, photographs, business papers, music scores in manuscript, political files, and legal files.
  Included are papers of Moses Myers, early 19th century Norfolk merchant; Lieutenant Governor Henry E. Howell, Jr.; lawyer and civic leader Robert M. Hughes; Lieutenant Governor A. E. S. Stephens; Norfolk Mayor Joseph D. Wood; and Norfolk Redevelopment and Housing Authority executive director Lawrence M. Cox.
  Also included are non-confidential records of the Florence Crittenton Services, Inc., of Norfolk, 1891-1977; non-current university records; and oral history and photographic materials pertaining to the university.

SEE: NUCMC, 1978, 80.

SEE: Allard, Crawley, and Edmison; Hinding.

PETERSBURG

VA630-640
Petersburg National Battlefield
Route 36
Petersburg VA

MAILING ADDRESS:
P.O. Box 549
Petersburg VA 23814

(804) 732-3531

OPEN: daily 8-5; closed Christmas and New Year's
ACCESS: scholars only; appointment required
COPYING FACILITIES: yes
MATERIALS SOLICITED: Letters and personal diaries related directly to Petersburg and the 1864 campaign.

HOLDINGS:
Total volume: 120 items
Inclusive dates: 1861 - 1865
Description: Letters, reports and personal diaries of northern and southern origin, dealing with Petersburg and the 1864 siege.

SEE: Hamer; NUCMC, 1967.

SEE: Schatz.

VA630-840
Virginia State University
Johnston Memorial Library
Special Collections
Petersburg VA 23803

(804) 520-6181

OPEN: M-Sa 8-5; closed Sundays and holidays
COPYING FACILITIES: yes
MATERIALS SOLICITED: Organization, business and family papers relating to blacks in Virginia. Will also accept other material having archival value.

HOLDINGS:
Total volume: 526 c.f.
Inclusive dates: 1880 -
Description: 11 manuscript groups which relate to the black experience in Virginia. Included are the papers of the Virginia Teachers Association, the Virginia Intercollegiate Athletic Association, the Prince Edward County (Virginia) Free School, 1963-64, Luther Porter Jackson, James Hugo Johnston, William Henry Johnson, John Manuel Gandy, Edna Meade Colson of the National Association of College Women, and Robert Prentiss Daniel, as well as Virginia State College memorabilia dating from 1888.

SEE: Hamer.

SEE: Schatz.

PORTSMOUTH

VA640-650
Portsmouth Public Library
Local History
601 Court Street
Portsmouth VA 23704

(804) 393-8501

OPEN: M-F 9-9, Sa 9-5; closed Sundays and holidays
ACCESS: special card required, available from Library Director weekdays 9-5, or by previous arrangement
COPYING FACILITIES: yes
MATERIALS SOLICITED: Photographs, manuscripts, letters, and diaries relating to Portsmouth, Norfolk County, the Norfolk Naval Shipyard, and the Portsmouth Naval Hospital; oral history interviews; and materials relating to lighthouses and lightships.

HOLDINGS:
Total volume: 2,035 items
Inclusive dates: 1636 - 1926
Description: Letters, deeds, warrants, court proceedings, wills, inventories, loading bills, receipts, and other materials from Norfolk County. There are unpublished manuscripts from the War of 1812 and Civil War, including applications of Confederate soldiers to the veterans association, minute books, a daybook from the period of Union occupation of Portsmouth, and John A. Foreman diaries, 1866-90. The collection also includes oral history tapes and photographs of the city dating from 1870.

QUANTICO

VA660-510
Marine Corps Development and
  Education Command
Education Center
James Carson Breckinridge Library
  and Amphibious Warfare Research
  Facility
Quantico VA 22134

(703) 640-2248

OPEN: M-F 8-4:30; closed weekends and holidays
COPYING FACILITIES: yes
MATERIALS SOLICITED: Amphibious operations. Will also accept materials relating to the Marine Corps.

HOLDINGS:
Total volume: 470 l. f.
Inclusive dates: 1925 -
Description: History of the doctrinal aspects of the evolution of amphibious warfare and defense of advanced naval bases. Included are materials relating to the history of the Marine Corps and of the Command. Oral history transcripts are provided by the History and Museums Division, Headquarters, U.S. Marine Corps for the collection.

SEE: Paszek.

RADFORD

VA670-690

Radford University
John Preston McConnell Library
Alumni-Special Collections
Radford VA 24142

(703) 731-5471

OPEN: M-F 8-5; closed weekends and
holidays
COPYING FACILITIES: yes
MATERIALS SOLICITED: Materials relating
to Virginia local and State history, the
Christiansburg Institute, and Radford
College.

HOLDINGS:
Total volume: 20,000 items
Inclusive dates: 1830 -
Description: Manuscript collections,
photographs, slides, tapes, and other materials relating to the institutions, people,
and culture of southwestern Virginia. Included are Civil War items, folklore,
unpublished literary manuscripts, and a
collection on the Christiansburg Institute,
originally a black Freedmen's Bureau
school.

RICHMOND

VA690-240

Federal Reserve Bank of Richmond
Archives
701 East Byrd Street
Richmond VA

MAILING ADDRESS:
P.O. Box 27622
Richmond VA 23261

(804) 643-1250

OPEN: M-F 8:30-4:30; closed weekends
and holidays
ACCESS: by appointment
COPYING FACILITIES: yes
MATERIALS SOLICITED: Materials relating
to the Federal Reserve Bank of Richmond.

HOLDINGS:
Total volume: not specified
Inclusive dates: 1913 -
Description: A historical collection relating to the Bank, including information
on its early history, early administrative
records, records of various statistical series published by the Bank and of Bank
departments, and material relating to
Bank Governor George J. Seay and Bank
President Hugh Leach, including correspondence, speeches, biographical data,
and other information.

GUIDES: Inventory of Historical Collection
(1976), available from the Bank.

VA690-400

John Marshall House
9th and Marshall Streets
Richmond VA 23219

no telephone

SEE: Hamer.

Questionnaire not returned.

VA690-530

The Museum of the Confederacy
1201 East Clay Street
Richmond VA 23219

(804) 649-1861

OPEN: M-F 10-4; closed weekends and
holidays
ACCESS: appointments preferred
COPYING FACILITIES: yes
MATERIALS SOLICITED: Materials relating
to the history of the South, 1850-77,
including manuscripts, visual documents, and scrapbooks. Will also accept
audible documents and microforms.

HOLDINGS:
Total volume: 155 l.f.
Inclusive dates: 1810 -
Description: Primary resource materials relating to the Confederacy, the decades leading to Civil War, and the
postwar years of reconstruction and after.
Items include diaries, letters, reports, logs,
and the official records of combat, hospital, navy, political, and social units.

SEE: Hamer; NUCMC, 1967 (as Confederate Museum).

SEE: Schatz, Allard, Crawley and Edmison;
Beers-Confederate.

VA690-690

Richmond Academy of Medicine
Library
1200 East Clay Street
Richmond VA 23219

no telephone

SEE: NUCMC, 1959-61.

Questionnaire not returned.

VA690-700

Richmond National Battlefield Park
3215 East Broad Street
Richmond VA 23223

(804) 226-1981

OPEN: M-F 9-5; closed weekends,
Christmas, and New Year's
ACCESS: by appointment only
COPYING FACILITIES: yes
MATERIALS SOLICITED: Materials relating
to the Civil War, 19th century Virginia
history, 19th century military history,
history of the Park, and the National
Park Service.

HOLDINGS:
Total volume: 400 items
Inclusive dates: 1825 -
Description: Diaries and letters relating
chiefly to the Civil War; non-current
records of the Battlefield Parks Corporation and the National Park Service; and
visual documents relating to the Civil
War and the history of the Park.

VA690-740

Richmond Newspapers, Inc.
Library
333 East Grace Street
Richmond VA

MAILING ADDRESS:
P.O. Box C-32333
Richmond VA 23293

(804) 649-6283

OPEN: M-Sa 9-5:30; closed Sundays and
holidays
COPYING FACILITIES: yes
MATERIALS SOLICITED: Will accept biographical and some historical materials.

HOLDINGS:
Total volume: not specified
Inclusive dates: 1852 -
Description: Primarily news clippings
and pictures from the Richmond Times-
Dispatch and the Richmond News Lead-
er.

VA690-750

Union Theological Seminary in
Virginia
The Library
3401 Brook Road
Richmond VA 23227

(804) 355-0671

OPEN: M-F 8:30-5, Sa by appointment;
closed Sundays and holidays
COPYING FACILITIES: yes
MATERIALS SOLICITED: Materials relating
to the Presbyterian Church in the United States, Synod of the Virginias, and
to faculty and alumni of Union Theological Seminary in Virginia. Will also
accept materials relating to southern
Presbyterians in general.

HOLDINGS:
Total volume: 750 vols.
Inclusive dates: 1750 -
Description: Materials relating to the
Presbyterian Church in the United States,
especially the Synod of the Virginias and
the Synod of North Carolina, consisting
of synod minutes and those of their component presbyteries, and session minutes,
marriage registers, and baptismal registers
of local churches. There are also a few
diaries, letters relating to colonial and
19th century church history, and papers
of William Henry Foote and Robert Lewis Dabney.

SEE: Hamer; NUCMC, 1971.

Microfilms of Presbyterian church
records are available for interlibrary
loan.

VA690-760

United Daughters of the Confederacy
Caroline Meriwether Goodlett Library
328 North Boulevard
Richmond VA 23220

(804) 355-1636

OPEN: by appointment to members and
historians
ACCESS: appointment required
COPYING FACILITIES: no

MATERIALS SOLICITED: Will accept Civil War letters and documents.

HOLDINGS:
> Total volume: not specified
> Inclusive dates: 1849 - 1877
> Description: Diaries, correspondence, passes, furloughs, paroles, and hospital records relating to the Confederate period.

VA690-770

University of Richmond
Library
Archives
Richmond VA 23173

(804) 289-8000

OPEN: M-F 8:30-4:30; closed weekends, Thanksgiving, Christmas, and New Year's
COPYING FACILITIES: yes
MATERIALS SOLICITED: Materials relating to the history of the University of Richmond.

HOLDINGS:
> Total volume: 180 l.f.; 44 file drawers
> Inclusive dates: 1830-
> Description: Materials relating to the history of the University of Richmond.

SEE: Robbins.

VA690-810

Valentine Museum of the Life and History of Richmond
Library and Research Center
1015 East Clay Street
Richmond VA 23219

(804) 649-0711

OPEN: Tu-F 10-5 by appointment; closed Sa-M and holidays
USER FEES: members free; adults, one dollar; students 50 cents
COPYING FACILITIES: yes
MATERIALS SOLICITED: Personal manuscripts, such as letters and diaries, dealing with Richmond history and social life, and photographic records. Will also accept material relating to government, history, local prehistory, prominent local individuals, business and crafts, and Richmond photographs and materials illustrating the development of photography.

HOLDINGS:
> Total volume: not specified
> Inclusive dates: 1607 -
> Description: Manuscript and graphic materials dealing with the history and life of Richmond. Included are correspondence of Edgar Allan Poe, Daniel Call, George S. Cook, James Chaffin, the Valentine family, the Wickham family, and others; transcripts of Virginia Quaker records, 1673-1844; 50,000 photographs with primary focus on the Victorian period; and materials relating to the tobacco industry.

SEE: Hamer; NUCMC, 1967.

SEE: Novotny; Schatz; Beers - Confederate; Robbins.

VA690-815

Virginia Baptist Historical Society
P.O. Box 34
University of Richmond
Richmond VA 23173

(804) 289-8434

OPEN: M-F 9-4:30 by appointment; closed weekends and holidays
ACCESS: advance appointments recommended
COPYING FACILITIES: yes
MATERIALS SOLICITED: Materials relating to the history of the Baptist church in Virginia. Will also accept materials relating to Christianity in general, Virginia, and genealogy.

HOLDINGS:
> Total volume: 1500 vols.; 14 file cabinets
> Inclusive dates: 1750 -
> Description: Records of the Baptist denomination in Virginia, including individual church minutes, associational minutes, correspondence, sermons, diaries, journals, genealogical source data, and biographical information relating to clergy and lay people.

SEE: Hamer.

VA690-830

Virginia Commonwealth University
James Branch Cabell Library
Special Collections Department
901 Park Avenue
Richmond VA

MAILING ADDRESS:
P.O. Box 2033
Richmond VA 23284-0001

(804) 257-1108

OPEN: M-F 8-5; closed weekends and holidays
COPYING FACILITIES: yes
MATERIALS SOLICITED: Materials relating to women's history of Virginia and the South, post-1970 American poets, James Branch Cabell, and 20th-century American comic art; Richmond Professional Institute (1917-1968) and Virginia Commonwealth University (1968-); Richmond-area urban studies emphasizing associations, businesses, and ethnic communities.

HOLDINGS:
> Total volume: 1,000 l.f.
> Inclusive dates: 1887 -
> Description: Material relating to Richmond business history, Richmond ethnic history, urban studies, women's history, Virginia authors, post-1970 American poets, James Branch Cabell, 20th-century American comic art, and archives of Richmond Professional Institute and the University.

SEE: Hinding; Robbins.

VA690-840

Virginia Commonwealth University
Medical College of Virginia
Tompkins-McCaw Library
Archives Department
509 N. 12th Street
Richmond VA

MAILING ADDRESS:
P.O. Box 582, M.C.V. Station
Richmond VA 23298

(804) 786-9898

OPEN: M-F 8-5; closed weekends and holidays
COPYING FACILITIES: yes
MATERIALS SOLICITED: Records of MCV administration and of affiliated or supportive organizations; papers of faculty and alumni; materials relating to the history of medicine in Virginia, particularly in the Richmond area.

HOLDINGS:
> Total volume: 250 l.f.
> Inclusive dates: 1802 -
> Description: Records of the Medical College of Virginia and the University College of Medicine (1893-1913); manuscript and photograph collections and other materials relating chiefly to the development of MCV and to the history of medical sciences in Richmond.

VA690-850

Virginia Genealogical Society
P.O. Box 7469
Richmond VA 23221

no telephone

OPEN: by appointment only
COPYING FACILITIES: no
MATERIALS SOLICITED: Materials pertaining to Virginia families.

HOLDINGS:
> Total volume: 400 items
> Inclusive dates: 1970 -
> Description: Genealogical charts pertaining to Virginia families.

VA690-860

Virginia Historic Landmarks Commission
221 Governor Street
Richmond VA 23219

(804) 786-3143

OPEN: M-F 8:15-5; closed weekends and holidays
COPYING FACILITIES: yes
MATERIALS SOLICITED: Architectural and historical information on buildings, structures, and sites in Virginia.

HOLDINGS:
> Total volume: 15,000 files; 142,000 photographs
> Inclusive dates: 1600's -
> Description: Information and photograph files concerning over 15,000 buildings, structures, and sites in Virginia.

SEE ALSO: Virginia Historic Landmarks Commission, Virginia Landmarks Register (Dietz Press, 1976). Other finding aids are available at the Commission.

VA690-870

Virginia Historical Society
428 North Blvd.
Richmond VA

MAILING ADDRESS:
P.O. Box 7311
Richmond VA 23221

(804) 358-4901

OPEN: M-Sa 9-5; closed Sundays and
holidays
ACCESS: two items of identification
required
COPYING FACILITIES: yes
MATERIALS SOLICITED: Materials on Virginia
history, colonial American history,
Confederate history, and English
history.

HOLDINGS:
Total volume: 2,800,000 items;
100,000 vols.
Inclusive dates: 1607 -
Description: Manuscript holdings include
papers of prominent leaders of the
colonial, Revolutionary, Federal, and
Confederate periods, along with family,
personal, corporate, and institutional papers
from 19th century Virginia.

SEE: Hamer; NUCMC, 1959-65, 67,
69-70, 72, 74, 76-78, 81.

SEE: Allard, Crawley, and Edmison; Beers
- Confederate; Davis; Duignan;
Hounshell; Ingram; Leventhal and
Mooney - III; Robbins; Schatz.

VA690-910

Virginia State Library
Archives and Records Division
Archives Branch
12th and Capitol Streets
Richmond VA 23219

(804) 786-2306

OPEN: M-Sa 8:15-5; closed Sundays and
holidays
COPYING FACILITIES: yes
MATERIALS SOLICITED: Noncurrent public
records received as the State's
archival agency. Will also accept other
papers relating to Virginia and the
South.

HOLDINGS:
Total volume: 18,378,080 items;
42,086 reels microfilm
Inclusive dates: 1607 -
Description: Public and private records
pertaining to Virginia. Public records include
surviving records of the colonial
government and records of the executive,
legislative, and judicial departments of
the state government. Also included in
this category are original and microfilmed
records of county and municipal governments
and microfilm copies of colonial
records in public and private repositories
in England, Scotland, Ireland, France,
and Belgium.
Private papers include collections of
personal papers, church records, Bible
records, genealogical notes and charts,
business records, and records of organizations.
There is also an extensive map
collection focusing on Virginia and the
southeastern United States.

SEE: Hamer; NUCMC, 1959-62, 65, 67,
69, 71, 74.

SEE: Allard, Crawley, and Edmison; Beers
- Confederate; Davis; Hinding;
Krichmar; Leventhal and Mooney - III;
Novotny; Parkinson; Robbins; Schatz.

SPRINGFIELD

VA700-322

Washington Gas Light Company
Corporate Library
6800 Industrial Road
Springfield VA 22151

(703) 750-7927

OPEN: M-F 8:30-5; closed weekends and
holidays
ACCESS: advance arrangements by
telephone or mail required
COPYING FACILITIES: yes

HOLDINGS:
Total volume: 3 file cabinets
Inclusive dates: 1848 -
Description: Records of the Washington
Gas Light Company, such as bills,
annual reports, publications, press
clippings, training brochures, correspondence,
and photographs of employees and
other subjects.

STAUNTON

VA750-880

Woodrow Wilson Birthplace
Foundation, Inc.
Research Library and Archives
20 North Coalter Street
Staunton VA

MAILING ADDRESS:
P.O. Box 24
Staunton VA 24401

(703) 885-0897

OPEN: M-F 9-5; closed weekends,
Thanksgiving, Christmas, and New
Year's
ACCESS: prior appointment preferred
COPYING FACILITIES: no
MATERIALS SOLICITED: Materials relating
to the life and times of Woodrow Wilson.

HOLDINGS:
Total volume: 3,000 items
Inclusive dates: 1840 - 1960
Description: A collection of manuscripts
and photographs relating to the
life and times of Woodrow Wilson, his
family, the Manse in which he was born,
and the Foundation which has maintained
his birthplace as a museum since
1938. Important personal papers include
those of Wilson and his second wife,
Edith Bolling Galt Wilson.

STRATFORD

VA760-690

Robert E. Lee Memorial Association,
Inc.
Stratford Hall Plantation
Archives & Manuscripts Collection
Stratford VA 22558

(804) 493-8038, 8039

OPEN: M-F 9-5; weekends and holidays
by appointment
ACCESS: advance arrangements required
COPYING FACILITIES: no
MATERIALS SOLICITED: Records and materials
dealing with the Robert E. Lee
Memorial Association, and the ancestry
of the Lees of Stratford.

HOLDINGS:
Total volume: not specified
Inclusive dates: 1929 -
Description: Records of the Robert E.
Lee Memorial Association including correspondence,
account books, business and
financial records, journals and log books;
and genealogical data on the Lees of
Stratford.

SWEET BRIAR

VA780-720

Sweet Briar College
Library
Sweet Briar VA 24595

(804) 381-6138

OPEN: M-F 9-5; closed weekends

SEE: NUCMC, 1963-64.

Questionnaire not returned.

TAZEWELL

VA800-320

Historic Crab Orchard Museum and
Pioneer Park, Inc.
Rt. 19/460
Tazewell VA

MAILING ADDRESS:
P.O. Box 12
Tazewell VA 24651

(703) 988-6755

OPEN: Tu-Sa 10-5, Su 2-5 Apr.-Oct.;
closed Mondays and holidays
COPYING FACILITIES: yes
MATERIALS SOLICITED: Genealogical and
historical materials relating to southwest
Virginia, especially Tazewell
County. Will also accept literary manuscripts
and college theses about the
area.

HOLDINGS:
Total volume: 350 items
Inclusive dates: Late 16th century -
20th century
Description: Predominantly personal
letters and records pertaining to the history
of Tazewell County and surrounding
counties.

VIRGINIA BEACH

VA810-40

Association for Research and Enlightenment
Edgar Cayce Foundation Archives
67th and Atlantic Avenue
Virginia Beach VA

MAILING ADDRESS:
P.O. Box 595
Virginia Beach VA 23451

(804) 428-3588, Ext. 131

OPEN: M-Sa 9-10, Su 1-10 June-Sept., Su 9-5 Oct.-May; closed Christmas and Thanksgiving
ACCESS: by prior arrangement with the Edgar Cayce Foundation
COPYING FACILITIES: yes
MATERIALS SOLICITED: Will accept materials relating to psychic readings and research, philosophy, world religions, metaphysics, and ancient history.

HOLDINGS:
 Total volume: 500 l.f.
 Inclusive dates: 1844 -
 Description: Over 14,000 psychic readings given by Edgar Cayce between 1903 and 1944, with supplementary data and reports documenting this psychic material; other materials relating to Edgar Cayce, including readings, correspondence, diaries, photographs, oral histories, and lectures; records of early organizations formed around the work of Cayce, as well as records of the Association for Research and Enlightenment; medical, archaeological, and parapsychological research of these organizations; and collections relating to other psychics.

SEE ALSO: an introductory brochure and inventory available from the Foundation.

WARM SPRINGS

VA820-80

Bath County Historical Society, Inc.
Warm Springs VA

MAILING ADDRESS:
Box 212
Warm Springs VA 24484

(703) 839-2543

OPEN: May 1 - Oct. 31, F, Sa 3-5; closed holidays and rest of year
COPYING FACILITIES: yes
MATERIALS SOLICITED: Materials relating to Bath County, including manuscripts, correspondence, journals, deeds, public documents, genealogical source data, and visual documents. Will also accept audible documents, microfilm, and photographs.

HOLDINGS:
 Total volume: several hundred items
 Inclusive dates: 1740 - 1900
 Description: Manuscripts and photographs of 18th and 19th century Bath County and western Virginia. Included are a few journals, deeds, and public documents relating to the springs of Virginia,

especially Hot and Warm Springs in Bath County.

WILLIAMSBURG

VA870-40

Abby Aldrich Rockefeller Folk Art Collection
307 S. England Street
Williamsburg VA

MAILING ADDRESS:
P.O. Drawer C
Williamsburg VA 23187

(804) 229-1000, Ext. 2424

OPEN: M-F 10-5; closed weekends and holidays
ACCESS: qualified researchers with advance appointments
COPYING FACILITIES: yes
MATERIALS SOLICITED: Documentation relating to works of art or to artists represented in the Folk Art Collection.

HOLDINGS:
 Total volume: 200 items
 Inclusive dates: 18th century -
 Description: A small collection of 19th century papers relating to American folk art. Included are several artists' letters and a collection of handwritten vital documents (Fraktur) in German script.

VA870-110

College of William and Mary
Earl Gregg Swem Library
Manuscripts and Rare Books Department/College Archives
Williamsburg VA 23185

(804) 253-4550, 4661

OPEN: M-F 10-4:45, Sa 9-12:45; closed Sundays and holidays
COPYING FACILITIES: yes
MATERIALS SOLICITED: Virginia family papers, papers of College of William and Mary alumni and faculty, papers of Virginia political figures, records of local organizations, manuscripts relating to King William and Queen Mary, literary manuscripts of local authors; materials relating to the College and the people associated with it.

HOLDINGS:
 Total volume: 700,000 manuscript items; 2,500 l.f. of archival materials
 Inclusive dates: 1650 -
 Description: Letters, documents, diaries, account books, and other materials on the social, economic, and political history of the colony and Commonwealth of Virginia, with particular strength in the period from the American Revolution to the Civil War, as well as several collections of the 20th century.
 Records of the College of William and Mary, including correspondence; financial records; reports; Board of Visitors and Faculty minutes and papers; photographs; tape recordings; Oral History Project transcripts and tape recordings; students' lecture notes; unofficial information such as news clippings; and materials, official and otherwise, relating to people associated with the College.

SEE: Hamer; NUCMC, 1966-67, 69, 73-74, 79.

SEE: Allard, Crawley, and Edmison; Beers - Confederate; Hinding; Ingram; Leventhal and Mooney - III; Robbins.

SEE ALSO: Walter Schatz, ed., *Directory of Afro-American Resources* (Bowker, 1970); Peter Duignan, *Handbook of American Resources for African Studies* (Hoover Institution, 1967); Morris Rieger, 'Africa-Related Papers of Persons and Organizations in the United States,' *African Studies Bulletin* 8 (Dec. 1965); Richard C. Davis, *North American Forest History: A Guide to Archives and Manuscripts in the United States and Canada* (Clio Books, 1977).

VA870-130

Colonial Williamsburg Foundation
Audiovisual Library
Goodwin Building
Prince George and South Henry Streets
Williamsburg VA

MAILING ADDRESS:
Drawer C
Williamsburg VA 23185

(804) 229-1000, Ext. 2119

OPEN: M-F 8:30-5; closed weekends and holidays
COPYING FACILITIES: yes
MATERIALS SOLICITED: Audio-visual materials relating to Colonial Williamsburg and its collections, activities, and history. Will also accept materials relating to other restorations and projects, graphic arts of Revolutionary War subjects, and the architecture of Tidewater Virginia.

HOLDINGS:
 Total volume: 210,000 items; 1,000,000 feet of film
 Inclusive dates: 1890's -
 Description: Photographs and other audio-visual materials relating to Williamsburg. Included are pre-restoration views of the town; progress shots of the restoration process; and views of restored rooms and their furnishings, restoration of gardens and grounds, and personalities and events of importance to Colonial Williamsburg, particularly the Rockefeller family in Williamsburg. Also included are materials concerning early interpretation of the restored town.

VA870-150

Colonial Williamsburg Foundation
Research Archives
Francis and South Henry Streets
Williamsburg VA

MAILING ADDRESS:
Drawer C
Williamsburg VA 23185

(804) 229-1000, Ext. 2572

OPEN: M-F 8:30-5, Sa 9-1; closed Sundays and holidays
COPYING FACILITIES: yes

MATERIALS SOLICITED: Virginia material through 1800 and Williamsburg material through 1900. Will also accept non-Virginia manuscripts which may relate to collections already in the repository.

HOLDINGS:

Total volume: 12,000 items; 110 vols.; 2,700 microfilm reels

Inclusive dates: 1600 - 1900

Description: Collections of manuscripts, mainly 1660-1860, relating chiefly to Virginia, but containing also a considerable quantity of papers of wider interest. Papers include account books; business, personal, and family papers; and materials relating to the British colonies in the West Indies and North America. There are microfilm copies of manuscripts located throughout the United States and Great Britain concerning colonial Virginia. Microfilms and translations of material in French repositories relate to French participation in the American Revolution, particularly the Battle of Yorktown.

GUIDES: Marylee G. McGregor, comp., *Guide to the Manuscript Collections of Colonial Williamsburg* (1969).

SEE: Hamer; NUCMC, 1959-62, 68, 77-78.

SEE: Hinding; Ingram; Leventhal and Mooney - III.

SEE ALSO: Walter Schatz, ed., *Directory of Afro-American Resources* (Bowker, 1970).

WINCHESTER

VA880-320

The Handley Library
100 West Piccadilly Street
Winchester VA 22601

MAILING ADDRESS:
P.O. Box 58
Winchester VA 22601

(703) 662-9041

OPEN: M-F 10-9, Sa 9-5; closed Sundays and holidays

COPYING FACILITIES: yes

MATERIALS SOLICITED: Material relating to the lower Shenandoah Valley including the city of Winchester and the counties of Frederick, Shenandoah, Clarke, and Warren in Virginia and Berkeley, Hardy, Hampshire, and Morgan in West Virginia. Will also accept material relating to the migration of settlers and their activities in the Shenandoah Valley.

HOLDINGS:

Total volume: 200 l.f.

Inclusive dates: 1744 -

Description: Collections dealing primarily with people, organizations, institutions, and events of the lower Shenandoah Valley region of Virginia.

SEE: NUCMC, 1977.

VA880-720

Shenandoah College and Conservatory of Music
Howe Library
Winchester VA 22601

(703) 665-4553

OPEN: M-Th 8-11, F 8-5, Sa 10-4:30, Su 1:30-11; closed holidays and semester breaks

COPYING FACILITIES: yes

MATERIALS SOLICITED: Materials relating to the formation, organization, and operation of the United Brethren and the Evangelical United Brethren churches of the Virginia Annual Conference to the time of merger with the Methodist church in 1970 and personal papers and photographs of leading ministerial and lay members of these churches.

HOLDINGS:

Total volume: not specified

Inclusive dates: 1800 - 1970

Description: A collection relating to the Virginia Conferences of the United Brethren and Evangelical United Brethren churches, including histories, diaries, biographies, autobiographies, theological studies, and General Conference minutes.

WISE

VA890-120

Clinch Valley College of the University of Virginia
John Cook Wyllie Library
Wise VA 24293

(703) 328-2431, Ext. 233

OPEN: M-F 8-4:30; closed weekends and holidays

COPYING FACILITIES: yes

MATERIALS SOLICITED: Will accept materials dealing with history of southwestern Virginia.

HOLDINGS:

Total volume: 94 l.f.

Inclusive dates: 1779 -

Description: Materials relating to southwestern Virginia's political, social and economic history. Included are records of businesses and newspaper publishers, papers of educators and individuals and unpublished diaries and histories.

SEE: NUCMC, 1969.

WYTHEVILLE

VA900-880

Wytheville Community College Library
Kegley Collection
1000 East Main Street
Wytheville VA 24382

(703) 228-5541

OPEN: M-F 8-5; closed weekends and holidays

COPYING FACILITIES: yes

MATERIALS SOLICITED: Materials relating to Wythe County and the history of southwest Virginia.

HOLDINGS:

Total volume: 600 items

Inclusive dates: 1900 -

Description: Materials relating to the history of southwest Virginia and particularly to Wythe County. Included are original maps, Works Progress Administration Historical Inventory papers, church records, genealogical records, and oral history interviews relating to the area.

WASHINGTON

The Washingon State Historical Records and Archives Survey, completed in 1980, showed the existence of more than 6,500 private records collections held by museums, libraries, and historical societies. A further 3,500 public record series, amounting to over 30,000 cubic feet of holdings, are held by the Washington State Archives and the State Archives Regional Depository System. Many more thousands of cubic feet of historical public records are still in the custody of local and state government agencies, slated for gradual accession into the Archives System.

ABERDEEN

WA2-680
Aberdeen Public Library
121 East Market
Aberdeen WA 98520

(206) 533-2360

OPEN: M-F 10-9, Sa 10-6; closed Sundays and holidays
ACCESS: limited access due to physical condition of materials
COPYING FACILITIES: yes

HOLDINGS:
    Total volume: 10 c.f.
    Inclusive dates: 1880's - 1940's
    Description: Photographs, draft histories, diaries, maps, and other materials, chiefly the collection of a disbanded local historical society.

SEE: *Washington Repository Guide.*

ANACORTES

WA25-40
Anacortes Museum of History and Art
1305 8th Street
Anacortes WA 98221

(206) 293-5198

OPEN: by permission of director or curator
COPYING FACILITIES: no
MATERIALS SOLICITED: Materials from Anacortes, Fidalgo Island, Whidbey Island, Guemes Island, and other islands along the ferry route.

HOLDINGS:
    Total volume: 11 c.f.
    Inclusive dates: 1860's -
    Description: Photographs, business records, miscellaneous personal papers, scrapbooks, and maps, all chiefly concerned with Anacortes, Washington, and vicinity.

SEE: *Washington Repository Guide;* Winroth.

WA25-60
Anacortes Public Library
1209 9th Street
Anacortes WA 98221

(206) 293-2700

OPEN: M-W 12:30-9, Th 10-9, F 12:30-5, Sa 10-4:30, Su 1-4:30
COPYING FACILITIES: yes

HOLDINGS:
    Total volume: 1 c.f.
    Inclusive dates: 1850's - 1940's
    Description: Library board records and a photograph collection assembled by the Skagit County Oral History Project.

SEE: *Washington Repository Guide.*

ANDERSON ISLAND

WA27-40
Anderson Island Historical Society
Anderson Island WA 98303

(206) 884-2135

OPEN: by appointment
COPYING FACILITIES: no
MATERIALS SOLICITED: Anderson Island history; will also accept materials concerning the Puget Sound area.

HOLDINGS:
    Total volume: 9.2 c.f.; 5 vols.
    Inclusive dates: 1855 -
    Description: Area voter registers, community organization records, a general photograph collection, and materials concerning the evacuation of adjacent McNeil Island for use as a Federal prison.

SEE: *Washington Repository Guide.*

ARLINGTON

WA34-40
Arlington Public Library
135 N. Washington Avenue
Arlington WA 98223

(206) 435-3033

OPEN: M-F 2-9, Sa 10-6; closed Sundays and legal holidays
COPYING FACILITIES: yes

HOLDINGS:
    Total volume: 2 c.f.
    Inclusive dates: 1914 - 1950
    Description: Records ofthe Stillaguamish Pioneer Association, along with local history reference materials.

SEE: *Washington Repository Guide.*

ASHFORD

WA35-520
Mount Rainier National Park Administration
Tahoma Woods
Star Route
Ashford WA 98304

(206) 569-2211

OPEN: M-F 8:30-4:30 by appointment; closed weekends and holidays
COPYING FACILITIES: no

HOLDINGS:
    Total volume: 110 c.f.
    Inclusive dates: 1897 -
    Description: Records of the park administration which have historical reference value, along with maps, photographs, diaries of park employees, collected draft writings about the park, and other similar materials, all concerning Mount Rainier National Park.

SEE: *Washington Repository Guide.*

ASOTIN

WA36-50
Asotin County Historical Society Museum
Third & Filmore
Asotin WA 99402

MAILING ADDRESS:
P.O. Box 367
Asotin WA 99402

(509) 243-4659

OPEN: W-F 1-5 May-Oct., other times by appointment

COPYING FACILITIES: no

HOLDINGS:
> *Total volume:* not specified
> *Inclusive dates:* 1880 -
> *Description:* Principally photographs and maps of Asotin County, Washington.

SEE: *Washington Repository Guide.*

AUBURN

WA37-540
Mukleshoot Tribal Council
Mukleshoot Tribal Center
Auburn WA 98002

(206) 939-3311

OPEN: by appointment
COPYING FACILITIES: no

HOLDINGS:
> *Total volume:* not specified
> *Inclusive dates:* 1850's -
> *Description:* Various historical materials, many in copy, pertaining to tribal people.

SEE: *Washington Repository Guide.*

WA37-880
White River Valley Historical Society Museum
918 H Street S.E.
Auburn WA 98002

(206) 939-2783

OPEN: S, Th 1-5
COPYING FACILITIES: no
MATERIALS SOLICITED: Materials pertaining to the White River Valley.

HOLDINGS:
> *Total volume:* 83 vols.; 12.5 c.f.
> *Inclusive dates:* 1847 - 1970's
> *Description:* Historical reference files; assembled collections of photographs, scrapbooks, family histories, business records, and public records; and records of three volunteer associations, all materials predominantly from the towns of Auburn and Kent.

SEE: *Washington Repository Guide;* Winroth.

BATTLE GROUND

WA44-240
Fort Vancouver Regional Library
Battle Ground Branch Library
Parkway and Main Streets
Battle Ground WA 98604

(206) 687-2322

OPEN: M-F 10-8, Sa 10-5; closed Sundays and holidays
COPYING FACILITIES: yes
MATERIALS SOLICITED: Materials pertaining to Battle Ground and Clark County.

HOLDINGS:
> *Total volume:* 0.5 c.f.
> *Inclusive dates:* 1950's -
> *Description:* Historical reference file of reports, clippings and ephemera pertaining to Battle Ground history.

SEE: *Washington Repository Guide.*

BELLEVUE

WA56-100
Bellevue Community College
Community Relations Office
3000 Landerholm Circle, S.E.
Bellevue WA

MAILING ADDRESS:
P.O. Box 92700
Bellevue WA 98009-2037

(206) 641-2281

OPEN: M-F 8-5; closed weekends and legal holidays
COPYING FACILITIES: yes

HOLDINGS:
> *Total volume:* 1 c.f.
> *Inclusive dates:* 1967 -
> *Description:* College maintains a scrapbook as a historical reference tool.

SEE: *Washington Repository Guide.*

BELLINGHAM

WA60-80
Bellingham Public Library
210 Central
Bellingham WA 98225

(206) 676-6860

OPEN: M-W 10-9, Th-Su 10-6
COPYING FACILITIES: yes

HOLDINGS:
> *Total volume:* 18 c.f.
> *Inclusive dates:* 1880 - 1974
> *Description:* Library records, area scrapbooks, records of a recreation organization, and papers of an author, Ella Higginson.

SEE: *Washington Repository Guide;* Hinding; Robbins.

WA60-160
Daughters of the Pioneers
Pickett House
7th and Dupont
Bellingham WA 98225

no telephone

OPEN: by appointment
COPYING FACILITIES: no
MATERIALS SOLICITED: Material relating to Bellingham pioneers.

HOLDINGS:
> *Total volume:* 10 vols.
> *Inclusive dates:* 1930 -
> *Description:* Scrapbooks concerning Bellingham-area pioneers and history, and chapter minutes.

SEE: *Washington Repository Guide.*

WA60-220
Eldridge Area Historical Center
1807 Eldridge Avenue
Bellingham WA 98225

(206) 734-8491

OPEN: by appointment only
COPYING FACILITIES: no
MATERIALS SOLICITED: Material pertaining to the Eldridge area of Bellingham.

HOLDINGS:
> *Total volume:* 1.5 c.f.
> *Inclusive dates:* 1881 -
> *Description:* Photographs and other background reference documents concerning the historic Eldridge District of Bellingham, Washington.

SEE: *Washington Repository Guide.*

WA60-510
Lummi Indian Tribal Center
2616 Kwina Road
Bellingham WA 98226

(206) 384-1489

OPEN: M-F 8-5; closed weekends and legal holidays
COPYING FACILITIES: yes
MATERIALS SOLICITED: Materials dealing with legal matters involving the Lummi Indian Tribe. Will also accept other Lummi-related materials.

HOLDINGS:
> *Total volume:* 88 c.f.
> *Inclusive dates:* 1854 - 1974
> *Description:* Photographs, maps, and oral histories of the Lummi people, and duplicated records of the Tulalip Indian Agency, assembled for historical and legal use.

SEE: *Washington Repository Guide.*

WA60-800
Washington Department of General Administration
Division of Archives and Records Management
Western Washington Regional State Archives
Western Washington University
Bellingham WA 98225

(206) 676-3125

OPEN: M-F 8-5; closed weekends and legal holidays
ACCESS: some records restricted by rights of privacy
COPYING FACILITIES: yes
MATERIALS SOLICITED: Materials related to local government from northwest Washington region. Will also accept public records from the state and local governmental agencies.

HOLDINGS:
> *Total volume:* 3,032 c.f. (includes 4,211 vols.)
> *Inclusive dates:* 1852 - 1977
> *Description:* The Washington State Archives' Western Regional Archives serves as a depository for county, city, and other public archival records generated by local government agencies. The seven counties in northwest Washington served by the depository include Whatcom, Snohomish,

Skagit, Island, San Juan, Clallam, and Jefferson.

GUIDES: *Historical Records of Washington State: Guide to Records in State Archives and its Regional Depositories* (Washington State Archives and Washington State Historical Records Advisory Board, 1981).

SEE ALSO: David W. Hastings, *A Guide to the Records of San Juan County* (1977).

WA60-860
Western Washington University
Center for Pacific Northwest Studies
High Street
Bellingham WA 98225

(206) 676-3278

OPEN: M-F 9-5 during academic sessions
ACCESS: some materials involve restrictions accepted by the repository
COPYING FACILITIES: yes
MATERIALS SOLICITED: Pacific Northwest materials, especially from northwest Washington, and covering all aspects of economic and cultural life. Will also accept Alaskan materials.

HOLDINGS:
> *Total volume:* 350 l.f.
> *Inclusive dates:* 1850's -
> *Description:* Materials relating to the Pacific Northwest, especially northwest Washington. Included are business records, especially of the railroad and transportation industries, papers of local organizations, including the YMCA; collections of photographs, manuscripts and other materials, all chiefly related to several local historians, and personal papers of a number of civic and political figures from northwest Washington.

SEE: *Washington Repository Guide;* Winroth.

SEE ALSO: James H. Hitchman, 'Primary Source Materials in Washington Maritime History,' *Pacific Northwest Quarterly* 65 (April 1974).

WA60-870
Western Washington University
Library
Bellingham WA 98225

(206) 676-3050

OPEN: M-F 8-5; closed weekends and legal holidays
COPYING FACILITIES: yes

HOLDINGS:
> *Total volume:* 8 c.f.
> *Inclusive dates:* 1949 -
> *Description:* A small quantity of university records are retained in conjunction with a collection of university publications and documents.

SEE: *Washington Repository Guide.*

WA60-885
Whatcom Museum of History and Art
121 Prospect Avenue
Bellingham WA 98225

(206) 676-6981

OPEN: Tu-Sa 8-5 by appointment; closed Su, M and holidays
COPYING FACILITIES: yes

HOLDINGS:
> *Total volume:* 100 c.f.
> *Inclusive dates:* 1850 -
> *Description:* The Darius Kinsey lumber industry photograph collection, a large general photograph collection, a historical reference file, scrapbooks, maps, and internal museum records.

SEE: *Washington Repository Guide;* Davis; Winroth.

WA60-895
Whatcom Genealogical Society

MAILING ADDRESS:
P.O. Box 1493
Bellingham WA 98225

no telephone

OPEN: by appointment
COPYING FACILITIES: no

HOLDINGS:
> *Total volume:* not specified
> *Inclusive dates:* 1850's -
> *Description:* Copies of cemetery and census records from Whatcom, Skagit, and San Juan counties.

SEE: *Washington Repository Guide.*

BLACK DIAMOND

WA70-80
Black Diamond Historical Society
32627 Baker Street
Black Diamond WA

MAILING ADDRESS:
P.O. Box 232
Black Diamond WA 98010

(206) 886-1168

OPEN: Sa, Su 12-3, Th 9-3, or by appointment
COPYING FACILITIES: no
MATERIALS SOLICITED: Black Diamond area historical materials.

HOLDINGS:
> *Total volume:* 2 c.f.; 12 reels of recording tape
> *Inclusive dates:* 1870's -
> *Description:* Photographs and oral history recordings related to the Black Diamond area.

SEE: *Washington Repository Guide.*

WA70-90
Black Diamond Library
4th and Lawson Streets
Black Diamond WA

MAILING ADDRESS:
P.O. Box 306
Black Diamond WA 98018

(206) 886-1105

OPEN: M, W 1:30-9, F 1:30-6
COPYING FACILITIES: no

HOLDINGS:
> *Total volume:* 0.6 c.f.
> *Inclusive dates:* 1949 -
> *Description:* The library maintains a historical reference file of clippings, photographs, and draft histories.

SEE: *Washington Repository Guide.*

BOTHELL

WA78-80
Bothell Historical Museum Society
9919 Northeast 180th
Bothell WA

MAILING ADDRESS:
P.O. Box 313
Bothell WA 98011

(206) 486-1889

OPEN: Su 1-4, and by appointment
COPYING FACILITIES: no
MATERIALS SOLICITED: Historical materials relative to Bothell and Woodinville.

HOLDINGS:
> *Total volume:* 5 c.f.
> *Inclusive dates:* 1871 -
> *Description:* Bothell-area records and papers from businesses, churches, and persons, along with photographs and legal documents from early Bothell.

SEE: *Washington Repository Guide;* Winroth.

WA78-90
Bothell Library
9654 N.E. 182nd
Bothell WA 98011

(206) 486-7811

OPEN: M-Th 11-9, F, Sa 10-5
Copyingfacilities:—yes
MATERIALS SOLICITED: Bothell history materials.

HOLDINGS:
> *Total volume:* 4 c.f.
> *Inclusive dates:* 1890's -
> *Description:* Scrapbooks, photographs, and draft writings, all concerning Bothell pioneers, history and genealogy, and financial records of the Bothell City Treasurer.

SEE: *Washington Repository Guide.*

BREMERTON

WA84-450
Kitsap Regional Library
Regional History Collection
1301 Sylvan Way
Bremerton WA 98310

(206) 377-7601

OPEN: M-Th 9:30-9, F, Sa 9:30-5:30, Su 1-5:30; closed holidays
COPYING FACILITIES: yes
MATERIALS SOLICITED: History of Kitsap County.

HOLDINGS:
> Total volume: 12 l.f.
> Inclusive dates: 1900 -
> Description: A collection of manuscripts and other materials relating chiefly to the early history of Kitsap County, including reminiscences of pioneers.

WA84-455
Olympic College
Library
16th and Chester
Bremerton WA 98310

(206) 478-4511

OPEN: M-F 8-10, Sa 10-10, Su 12-10
COPYING FACILITIES: yes

HOLDINGS:
> Total volume: 4 c.f.
> Inclusive dates: 1940 - 1966
> Description: Olympic College maintains a collection of mountaineering materials.

SEE: *Washington Repository Guide.*

WA84-720
Puget Sound Naval Shipyard Museum
Ferry Terminal Building
151 1st Street
Bremerton WA 98310

(206) 479-7447

OPEN: W-Su 12:30-4
COPYING FACILITIES: no

HOLDINGS:
> Total volume: 6.2 c.f.
> Inclusive dates: 1876 - 1970
> Description: Photographs and a shipyard log from the Bremerton Naval Shipyard, established in 1892.

SEE: *Washington Repository Guide.*

WA86-95
Bridgeport Public Library
1200 Columbia Street
Bridgeport WA 98813

(509) 686-7281

OPEN: Tu, Th 12:30-5:30, 7-9, Sa 12:30-5:30
COPYING FACILITIES: no

HOLDINGS:
> Total volume: 0.5 c.f.
> Inclusive dates: 1899 - 1916
> Description: The library maintains a photograph collection on local history.

SEE: *Washington Repository Guide.*

BUCODA

WA94-720
South Thurston County Historical Society
7th and Nenant
Bucoda WA 98530

no telephone

OPEN: by appointment
COPYING FACILITIES: no
MATERIALS SOLICITED: Thurston County history, especially pertaining to the territorial prison; will also accept other materials.

HOLDINGS:
> Total volume: 13 c.f.
> Inclusive dates: 1878 -
> Description: Records, documents, and photographs relating to the Washington territorial penitentiary at Seatco (now Bucoda), and to the towns of Tono, Tenino, and Bucoda.

SEE: *Washington Repository Guide.*

BURIEN

WA97-100
Burien Public Library
14700 6th Avenue S.W.
Burien WA 98166

(206) 243-3490

OPEN: M-Th 10-9, F, Sa 10-6
COPYING FACILITIES: yes

HOLDINGS:
> Total volume: 20 c.f.
> Inclusive dates: 1925 -
> Description: Holdings consist of a reference file of materials relative to Burien-area history, and several scrapbooks.

SEE: *Washington Repository Guide.*

WA97-320
Highline Historical Society
421 146th Street S.W.
Burien WA 98166

no telephone

OPEN: by appointment
COPYING FACILITIES: no
MATERIALS SOLICITED: Materials documenting the Burien-Des Moines-Highline area.

HOLDINGS:
> Total volume: 0.5 c.f.
> Inclusive dates: 1922 - 1933
> Description: Holdings consist of a variety of materials related to planting 'memorial trees' honoring World War I dead.

SEE: *Washington Repository Guide.*

BURLINGTON

WA98-100
Burlington Library
Fairhaven Avenue
Burlington WA 98233

(206) 755-0760

OPEN: M-F 9-5; closed weekends and legal holidays
COPYING FACILITIES: no

HOLDINGS:
> Total volume: 5 c.f.
> Inclusive dates: 1910 - 1970
> Description: The library maintains a collection of library association and women's social club records.

SEE: *Washington Repository Guide.*

CAMAS

WA102-105
Camas Public Library
421 N.E. Franklin
Camas WA 98607

(206) 834-4692

OPEN: M-Th 10-9, F, Sa 10-6; closed Sundays and holidays
COPYING FACILITIES: no
MATERIALS SOLICITED: Materials of interest to the general public.

HOLDINGS:
> Total volume: 1 c.f.
> Inclusive dates: 1890's - 1974
> Description: A historical reference file including a variety of materials illustrative of the history of Camas.

SEE: *Washington Repository Guide.*

CASHMERE

WA112-880
Willis Carey Historical Museum
Sunset Highway
Cashmere WA

MAILING ADDRESS:
P.O. Box 22
Cashmere WA 98815

(509) 782-3230

OPEN: May-Oct., daily 10-5
COPYING FACILITIES: no
MATERIALS SOLICITED: Materials from the area of Cashmere, Washington, are sought; will consider accepting other materials.

HOLDINGS:
> Total volume: not specified
> Inclusive dates: 1891 -
> Description: Principal documentary holdings are collected photographs.

SEE: *Washington Repository Guide;* Hines.

CATHLAMET

WA115-890
Wahkiakum County Historical Society
Museum
Route 1
Cathlamet WA 98612

(206) 795-3954

OPEN: Tu-Sa 1-4; closed Sundays,
Mondays and legal holidays
COPYING FACILITIES: no
MATERIALS SOLICITED: Materials per-
taining to Wahkiakum County.

HOLDINGS:
Total volume: 7.5 c.f.
Inclusive dates: 1867 -
Description: Photographs, miscella-
neous legal documents, deeds, maps, and
unidentified diaries, all pertaining to
Wahkiakum County, Washington.

SEE: Washington Repository Guide.

CENTRALIA

WA122-100
Centralia College
Library
West Locust and South Oak
Centralia WA 98531

(206) 736-9391

OPEN: M-F 8-9; closed legal holidays and
quarter breaks
COPYING FACILITIES: yes

HOLDINGS:
Total volume: 30 c.f.
Inclusive dates: 1940's -
Description: A pamphlet/reference file,
including some historical materials con-
cerning Centralia and Chehalis.

SEE:	Washington	Repository	Guide;
Winroth.

WA122-110
Centralia Public Library
110 S. Silver Street
Centralia WA 98531

(206) 736-0183

OPEN: M-F 10-9, Sa 10-6
COPYING FACILITIES: yes
MATERIALS SOLICITED: Centralia history,
Lewis County history.

HOLDINGS:
Total volume: 18 c.f.
Inclusive dates: 1841 -
Description: The Centralia Public Library contains a collection of materials
on the history, Indians, industry, agriculture, early settlers, places, and activities
of Centralia and Lewis County, Washington.

SEE: Washington Repository Guide.

CHATTAROY

WA123-333
Owen Pioneer Museum
Route 1
Chattaroy WA 99003

no telephone

OPEN: Th-Tu 10-6; closed Wednesdays
COPYING FACILITIES: no
MATERIALS SOLICITED: Materials per-
taining to Washington Territory and
State. Will also accept records docu-
menting the pioneer spirit of the West.

HOLDINGS:
Total volume: 18 l.f.
Inclusive dates: 1760 -
Description: Materials pertaining to the
history of Washington's northeastern
counties, including a special collection of
photographs of local buildings and the
lumber industry.

CHEHALIS

WA124-110
Chehalis Public Library
76 N.E. Park Street
Chehalis WA 98532

(206) 748-3301

OPEN: M-F 11-5
COPYING FACILITIES: yes

HOLDINGS:
Total volume: 43 c.f.
Inclusive dates: 1841 -
Description: Pamphlet and reference
file with historical material, a genealogy-
oriented index of Chehalis newspapers,
and library records.

SEE: Hamer.

SEE: Washington Repository Guide.

WA124-480
Lewis County Historical Society
Museum
599 Northwest Front Street
Chehalis WA 98532

(206) 748-0831

OPEN: by appointment only
COPYING FACILITIES: no
MATERIALS SOLICITED: Materials relating
to the history of Lewis County, including manuscripts, archives, and non-
current records of institutions and organizations, oral history tapes, and area
photographs. Will also accept other historical reference material.

HOLDINGS:
Total volume: 25 c.f.
Inclusive dates: 1854 -
Description: Materials relating to Lewis
County, Washington. Includes materials
related to the Chehalis Indians, papers of
Ernest Bechly, minutes and scrapbooks of
local civic organizations, business records,
photographs, oral history tapes, and other
historical reference material.

SEE:	Washington	Repository	Guide;
Hinding; Winroth.

CHELAN

WA125-100
North Central Regional Library
Chelan Branch Library
133 Johnson Street
Chelan WA 98816

(509) 682-5131

OPEN: M, Tu 12:30-5, Tu 7-9, W
10-2:30, Th 7-9, F 1-5
COPYING FACILITIES: no

HOLDINGS:
Total volume: 1 vol.; .5 c.f.
Inclusive dates: 1892 - 1941
Description: Small collection of local
photographs and a manuscript history of
the library.

SEE: Washington Repository Guide.

WA125-490
Lake Chelan Museum
204 East Woodin
Chelan WA

MAILING ADDRESS:
P.O. Box 697
Chelan WA 98816

no telephone

OPEN: June-Sept., daily 1-4
ACCESS: use subject to permission of the
Lake Chelan Historical Society
COPYING FACILITIES: no
MATERIALS SOLICITED: Materials per-
taining to the Lake Chelan area, and to
north central Washington.

HOLDINGS:
Total volume: 70 c.f.
Inclusive dates: 1869 -
Description: Several local photograph
collections along with area maps, business
records, civic association records and personal papers, most from Chelan County.

SEE: Washington repository Guide.

CHENEY

WA144-110
Cheney Historical Museum
Wren-Pierson Building
312 'C' Street
Cheney WA 99004

no telephone

OPEN: W noon to 4:30, and by
appointment
COPYING FACILITIES: no
MATERIALS SOLICITED: Local materials.

HOLDINGS:
Total volume: 14 c.f.
Inclusive dates: 1884 -
Description: Business, government, and
personal papers, along with photographs,
all relative to the Cheney region.

SEE: Washington Repository Guide.

WA144-190
Eastern Washington University
Department of Geography
Isle Hall
Cheney WA 99004

(509) 359-2433

OPEN: M-F 9-5; closed weekends and
legal holidays
ACCESS: appointment recommended
COPYING FACILITIES: yes

HOLDINGS:
Total volume: 22 c.f.
Inclusive dates: 1921 - 1964
Description: Material produced or collected by geographer Otis W. Freeman,
consisting of photographs, maps, charts,
field notes, motion pictures, glass lantern
slides, correspondence, and manuscript
books.

SEE: Washington Repository Guide.

WA144-210
Eastern Washington University
Library
Archives Section
Cheney WA 99004

(509) 359-2475

OPEN: M-F 8-5
COPYING FACILITIES: yes
MATERIALS SOLICITED: Business records
from eastern Washington and northern
Idaho, materials relating to Pacific
Northwest fisheries and angling, materials concerning recreation and tourism, and records of Eastern Washington University. Will also accept diaries,
manuscripts, oral history tapes, and
photographs of the inland Northwest.

HOLDINGS:
Total volume: 250 c.f.
Inclusive dates: 1853 -
Description: Materials relating to eastern Washington, northern Idaho, and
western Montana, emphasizing business
and public agencies. Principal subject focuses include Northwest folklife, hydroelectric power development, angling and
fisheries in the Columbia and Snake River drainages, the history and development
of social welfare and community action
programs in Spokane, Washington, the
history and development of teacher education in eastern Washington, rural banking in the 1920's and 1930's, and local
government in eastern Washington. Holdings also include a variety of transcribed
documents and draft writings concerning
the early history of the inland Pacific
Northwest, which are part of the C.S.
Kingston Collection of Northwest Americana.

SEE: Washington Repository Guide;
Hinding; Winroth.

SEE ALSO: Finding aids for individual collections are available at the repository.

WA144-840
Office of the Secretary of State
Division of Archives and Records
Management
Eastern Washington Regional State
Archives
Eastern Washington University
Cheney WA

MAILING ADDRESS:
Mail Stop 84
Eastern Washington University
Cheney WA 99004

(509) 359-2475

OPEN: M-F 8-5; closed weekends and
holidays
ACCESS: limited; some records restricted
by rights of privacy
COPYING FACILITIES: yes
MATERIALS SOLICITED: Local government records from the eastern Washington region. Will also accept other
state and local public records.

HOLDINGS:
Total volume: 1,850 c.f. (includes
1,219 vols.); 151 microfilm reels
Inclusive dates: 1860 - 1977
Description: Eastern Washington Regional State Archives serves local government agencies in eastern Washington by
providing records management assistance
and storing archival records. The area
served includes Ferry, Stevens, Pend
Oreille, Lincoln, Spokane, Adams, Whitman, Franklin, Walla Walla, Columbia,
Garfield, and Asotin counties.

GUIDES: Historical Records of Washington
State: Guide to Records in State Archives and its Regional Depositories
(Washington State Archives and Washington State Historical Records Advisory Board, 1981).

SEE: Washington Repository Guide;
Hinding.

CHEWELAH

WA145-105
Chewelah Historical Society
Museum
E. 3rd Street
Chewelah WA

MAILING ADDRESS:
Box 913
Chewelah WA 99109

no telephone

OPEN: W-Su 1-4 Memorial-Labor Day;
closed Mondays and Tuesdays
COPYING FACILITIES: no
MATERIALS SOLICITED: Chewelah area
materials.

HOLDINGS:
Total volume: 26 c.f.
Inclusive dates: 1846 -
Description: A photograph collection,
primarily of local pictures; miscellaneous
area business records; three collections of
personal papers and office records; and
some public records of local government
agencies. Subject focus is local history
and mining.

SEE: Washington Repository Guide.

WA145-110
Chewelah Public Library
Washington Avenue and 2nd Street
Chewelah WA 99109

(509) 935-6805

OPEN: M, W 2-8, Sa 1-5; closed legal
holidays
COPYING FACILITIES: no

HOLDINGS:
Total volume: 0.4 c.f.
Inclusive dates: 1964 - 1976
Description: Two mimeographed his-
tories of Chewelah and Stevens County,
Washington.

SEE: Washington Repository Guide.

CLARKSTON

WA151-40
Asotin County Library
6th and Chestnut Streets
Clarkston WA 99403

(509) 758-5454

OPEN: M-F 10-8:30, Sa 10-6
COPYING FACILITIES: yes

HOLDINGS:
Total volume: 4 vols.
Inclusive dates: 1910 -
Description: Principally transcriptions
of an oral history project and a historical
clippings collection.

SEE: Washington Repository Guide.

CLAYTON

WA152-125
Clayton Memorial Museum and
Vagabond House Studio
Clayton WA 99110

no telephone

OPEN: daily; appointment may be
advisable
USER FEES: one dollar donation is
requested
COPYING FACILITIES: no
MATERIALS SOLICITED: Materials related
to Clayton, especially the Washington
Brick, Lime, and Sewer Pipe Company,
and to the Prestini family, especially
photographs.

HOLDINGS:
Total volume: 10 c.f.
Inclusive dates: 1900 (approx.) -
Description: The central theme of the
Clayton Museum is the artistic work,
principally paintings, of Lino Prestini
(1906-63). Holdings include supporting
documentation related to the art work.
Museum also has photographs of the
Clayton area, of the Washington Brick,
Lime, and Sewer Pipe Company plant,
and certain records of that firm.

SEE: Washington Repository Guide; Hines.

CLE ELUM

WA153-125
Cle Elum Historical Telephone
   Museum
1st and Wright
Cle Elum WA 98922

(509) 674-5702

OPEN: summer months, Tu-Su 1:30-4:30
COPYING FACILITIES: no
MATERIALS SOLICITED: Cle Elum-area
   historical materials.

HOLDINGS:
> *Total volume:* 4 vols.; 1.1 c.f.
> *Inclusive dates:* 1890's - 1966
> *Description:* Although the principal
> theme of the museum concerns early tele-
> phones and switchboards, holdings in-
> clude clippings about the museum, Cle
> Elum area photographs, and ledgers from
> a local grocery.

SEE: *Washington Repository Guide.*

WA153-128
Carpenter Memorial Library
1301 Pennsylvania Avenue
Cle Elum WA 98922

(509) 674-2313

OPEN: M, Th 10-9, W 11-7
COPYING FACILITIES: no

HOLDINGS:
> *Total volume:* 1 vol.
> *Inclusive dates:* 1949
> *Description:* The library holds a vol-
> ume listing the accomplishments of Cle
> Elum-area men in World Wars I and II.

SEE: *Washington Repository Guide.*

WA153-130
Cle Elum-Roslyn School District
Rt. 4
Cle Elum WA 98922

(509) 649-2291

OPEN: by appointment
COPYING FACILITIES: no

HOLDINGS:
> *Total volume:* 0.5 c.f.
> *Inclusive dates:* 1970 -
> *Description:* The school serves as cus-
> todian for recordings of local
> reminiscences collected in a history class.

SEE: *Washington Repository Guide.*

COLFAX

WA164-890
Whitman County Historical Society
Perkins House Museum
623 N. Perkins
Colfax WA

MAILING ADDRESS:
P.O. Box 67
Colfax WA 99111

(509) 397-2555

OPEN: Th, Sa afternoon and by
   appointment
COPYING FACILITIES: no
MATERIALS SOLICITED: Manuscripts,
   photographs, and ephemera relative to
   Whitman County.

HOLDINGS:
> *Total volume:* 8 c.f.
> *Inclusive dates:* 1761 -
> *Description:* Business records, personal
> papers, photographs, justice court records,
> and a reference file of local histories.

SEE: *Washington Repository Guide.*

SEE ALSO: Margot H. Knight, ed., *Guide
to the Whitman County, Washington,
Oral History Collection* (1980).

WA164-895
Whitman County Library
Main Street
Colfax WA 99111

(509) 397-4366

OPEN: M-F 8-5, Sa 9-5
COPYING FACILITIES: no

HOLDINGS:
> *Total volume:* 2 c.f.
> *Inclusive dates:* 1900 (approx.) -
> *Description:* Vertical file including
> items relevant to the history of Whitman
> County and Washington.

SEE: *Washington Repository Guide.*

WA164-900
Whitman County Parks and
   Recreation Department
Room 3, ONB Building
Colfax WA 99111

(509) 397-4304

OPEN: M-F 8-4:30; closed weekends and
   legal holidays
COPYING FACILITIES: no

HOLDINGS:
> *Total volume:* 22 c.f.
> *Inclusive dates:* 1896 -
> *Description:* Oral history projects, city
> records, and business records from the
> abandoned town of Elberton, Washing-
> ton; also oral histories concerning Rock
> Lake, Washington.

SEE: *Washington Repository Guide.*

COLVILLE

WA168-130
Colville National Forest
695 S. Main
Colville WA 99114

(509) 684-3711

OPEN: M-F 8-5; closed legal holidays
COPYING FACILITIES: yes

HOLDINGS:
> *Total volume:* 5.5 c.f.
> *Inclusive dates:* 1820's -
> *Description:* Reminiscences, draft his-
> tories, oral history interviews, photo-
> graphs, and selected forest service docu-
> ments combined into a historical refer-
> ence file.

WA168-135
Colville Public Library
195 S. Oak
Colville WA 99114

(509) 684-6620

OPEN: Tu, Th-Sa 2-5, W 11-9; closed
   legal holidays
COPYING FACILITIES: no

HOLDINGS:
> *Total volume:* 2 c.f.
> *Inclusive dates:* 1859 - 1977
> *Description:* Material relative to the
> Colville Bicentennial Pageant, a copy of a
> drawing of Fort Colville, and notes of an
> amateur historian.

SEE: *Washington Repository Guide.*

WA168-750
Stevens County Historical Society
   Museum
137 N. Wynee
Colville WA

MAILING ADDRESS:
P.O. Box 25
Colville WA 99114

(509) 684-5968

OPEN: Tu-Su 10-5; closed Mondays
COPYING FACILITIES: no
MATERIALS SOLICITED: Materials related
   to Stevens County.

HOLDINGS:
> *Total volume:* 25 c.f.
> *Inclusive dates:* 1880's -
> *Description:* Area photographs, busi-
> ness records, civic group records, and pio-
> neer reminiscences.

SEE: *Washington Repository Guide;*
Winroth.

COUPEVILLE

WA181-360
Island County Historical Society
903 Alexander Street
Coupeville WA

MAILING ADDRESS:
P.O. Box 305
Coupeville WA 98239

(206) 678-4470, 4343

OPEN: April - May, Sa, Su 1-5; June -
   Sept. W-Su 1-5
COPYING FACILITIES: no
MATERIALS SOLICITED: Materials relating
   to historical development of central
   Whidby Island.

HOLDINGS:
> *Total volume:* 29 c.f.
> *Inclusive dates:* 1851 -
> *Description:* Principal holding is a his-
> torical reference collection of draft
> writings and assembled material; holdings
> also include scattered records from Island
> County civic organizations, women's
> clubs, businesses and agencies of local
> government.

SEE: *Washington Repository Guide;*
Winroth.

DARRINGTON

WA200-322
Sauk-Suiattle Indian Tribe
5318 Chief Brown Lane
Darrington WA 98241

(206) 435-8366, 436-0131

OPEN: by appointment
ACCESS: by permission
MATERIALS SOLICITED: Material containing information on the history of the Sauk-Suiattle.

HOLDINGS:
Total volume: 2 c.f.
Inclusive dates: 1850's -
Description: Assembled materials, many in copy, related to the Sauk-Suiattle Indian tribe.

SEE: *Washington Repository Guide.*

DAVENPORT

WA240-250
Fort Spokane Interpretive Center
State Highway 21
Davenport WA

MAILING ADDRESS:
HCR Box 51
Davenport WA 99122

(509) 725-2715, 633-1360, Ext. 441

OPEN: daily 9-6; shorter and intermittent hours in winter
COPYING FACILITIES: no
MATERIALS SOLICITED: Photographs, including copies, of the fort, the Indian agency, and the area. Will also accept reminiscences relative to the fort and the immediate region.

HOLDINGS:
Total volume: 5 c.f.
Inclusive dates: 1880 -
Description: Photographs, maps, and documents, principally copies, concerning Fort Spokane, a military post from 1880 to 1898, and an Indian agency school and hospital from about 1900 to 1940.

SEE: *Washington Repository Guide.*

WA240-480
Lincoln County Historical Society Museum
Davenport WA 99122

(509) 725-7021

OPEN: May-Sept., daily 10-4
COPYING FACILITIES: no
MATERIALS SOLICITED: Personal reminiscences, photographs, and display items relevant to Lincoln County, Washington.

HOLDINGS:
Total volume: 14 c.f.
Inclusive dates: 1877 -
Description: Materials on Lincoln County history, particularly in the frontier period, including photographs, land grant (homestead) papers, and family histories written by local residents.

SEE: *Washington Repository Guide.*

DAYTON

WA241-160
Dayton Memorial Library
Clay and 3rd Streets
Dayton WA

MAILING ADDRESS:
Box 74
Dayton WA 99328

(509) 382-4131

OPEN: M-Th 3-5, 7-9, Sa 10-12, 3-5; closed F, Su and holidays
COPYING FACILITIES: no
MATERIALS SOLICITED: Local history and genealogical materials.

HOLDINGS:
Total volume: 4 c.f.
Inclusive dates: 1870's -
Description: Principal holding is a genealogical and historical reference file which includes many local reminiscences and draft histories concerning a number of Columbia County topics.

SEE: *Washington Repository Guide.*

WA241-170
Dayton Historical Depot Society
Clay and 3rd Streets
Dayton WA 99328

(509) 382-2045

OPEN: by appointment
COPYING FACILITIES: no

HOLDINGS:
Total volume: 8 c.f.
Inclusive dates: 1872 - 1967
Description: Holdings stress the history of Columbia County, Washington, and include photographs, materials relating to the local volunteer military unit, maps, some local government records and miscellaneous legal documents, such as land patents.

SEE: *Washington Repository Guide; Hines.*

DES MOINES

WA246-170
Greater Des Moines-Zenith Historical Society
728 225th Street S.
Des Moines WA

MAILING ADDRESS:
P.O. Box 98055
Zenith WA 98188

(206) 878-7552

OPEN: by appointment
COPYING FACILITIES: no
MATERIALS SOLICITED: Materials related to the history of Des Moines and Zenith.

HOLDINGS:
Total volume: 14 c.f.
Inclusive dates: 1889 -
Description: Records of several civic organizations from Des Moines and Zenith; and an assembled historical reference file.

SEE: *Washington Repository Guide.*

DRYDEN

WA258-160
Dykes Dryden Museum
Main and Division Streets
Dryden WA

MAILING ADDRESS:
P.O. Box 321
Dryden WA 98821

(509) 782-2443

OPEN: summer months, M-F 1-5
COPYING FACILITIES: no

HOLDINGS:
Total volume: 3 c.f.
Inclusive dates: 1915 -
Description: Photographs from Chelan County, Washington, and a few documenting items, used for display purposes.

SEE: *Washington Repository Guide.*

DU PONT

WA259-160
Du Pont Historical Museum
207 Brandywine Avenue
Du Pont WA 98327

(206) 964-8895

OPEN: by appointment
COPYING FACILITIES: no
MATERIALS SOLICITED: Du Pont area history, Fort Nisqually, and E. I. Du Pont Company.

HOLDINGS:
Total volume: 15 c.f.
Inclusive dates: 1832 -
Description: Papers, publications, and memorabilia relating to the history of the Du Pont area, specifically Fort Nisqually and the E. I. Du Pont Company (explosives manufacturer), as well as materials about the town of Du Pont.

SEE: *Washington Repository Guide.*

DUVALL

WA263-160
Duvall Historical Society

MAILING ADDRESS:
P.O. Box 324
Duvall WA 98019

no telephone
MATERIALS SOLICITED: Materials related to the history of the Duvall area.
Description: The society (formed in 1977) holds no papers or records, but can provide researchers with names of local parties who hold such materials.

WA263-165
Duvall Library
Main Street
Duvall WA 98019

(206) 788-1173

OPEN: Tu 1-5, W 1-9, Sa 1-4
COPYING FACILITIES: no

HOLDINGS:
> Total volume: 1 c.f.
> Inclusive dates: 1970 -
> Description: The library has a local history collection of published and unpublished histories of Duvall and the Snoqualmie River Valley.

SEE: Washington Repository Guide.

EASTSOUND

WA265-600
Orcas Island Historical Society
North Beach Road
Eastsound WA

MAILING ADDRESS:
P.O. Box 134
Eastsound WA 98245

(206) 376-4849

OPEN: daily 1-4; closed fall and winter seasons
COPYING FACILITIES: no
MATERIALS SOLICITED: Any material pertaining to Orcas Island and the surrounding areas; will also accept other items of historical interest.

HOLDINGS:
> Total volume: 25 c.f.
> Inclusive dates: 1831 - 1916
> Description: A photograph collection, historical reference files, and miscellaneous school and business records from Orcas Island in the San Juan group. Holdings also include a few items from Ohio and Manitoba.

SEE: Washington Repository Guide.

EDMONDS

WA272-190
Edmonds Public Library
250 Fifth Avenue N.
Edmonds WA 98020

(206) 774-0900

OPEN: M-F 10-9, Sa 10-5; closed Sundays and legal holidays
COPYING FACILITIES: no

HOLDINGS:
> Total volume: 1 c.f.
> Inclusive dates: 1910 -
> Description: Records pertaining to library development and a newspaper clipping file on area history.

SEE: Washington Repository Guide.

WA272-210
Edmonds-South Snohomish County
  Historical Society
118 Fifth Avenne N.
Edmonds WA

MAILING ADDRESS:
P.O. Box 52
Edmonds WA 98020

(206) 774-0900

OPEN: Su, Tu, Th 1-4
COPYING FACILITIES: no
MATERIALS SOLICITED: Material relating to the history of south Snohomish County and Edmonds.

HOLDINGS:
> Total volume: 1 c.f.
> Inclusive dates: 1880's - 1940's
> Description: The museum maintains small photograph and document collections.

SEE: Washington Repository Guide.

ELLENSBURG

WA280-105
Central Washington University
Archives
c/o Earl Glauert
100-B Shaw-Smyser Hall
Central Washington University
Ellensburg WA 98926

(509) 963-1244

OPEN: by appointment
COPYING FACILITIES: yes
MATERIALS SOLICITED: Pacific Northwest history materials, especially from central Washington, and records of Central Washington University.

HOLDINGS:
> Total volume: 165 vols.; 55 c.f.
> Inclusive dates: 1891 -
> Description: Records of Central Washington University and affiliated staff and student organizations, along with several manuscript collections from the area of central Washington.

SEE: Washington Repository Guide; Meckler and McMullin; Winroth.

WA280-200
Ellensburg Public Library
3rd Avenue and Ruby Street
Ellensburg WA 98926

(509) 962-9863

OPEN: M-F 10-9, Sa, Su 1-5; closed holidays
COPYING FACILITIES: yes
MATERIALS SOLICITED: Seeks materials from the Kittitas Valley; will accept materials from throughout central Washington.

HOLDINGS:
> Total volume: 21 vols.; 25 c.f.; 90 microfilm reels
> Inclusive dates: 1854 -
> Description: Oral histories, maps, photographs, and personal papers, all generally illustrative of the history of Kittitas County, Washington, along with

microform copies of a broader range of Pacific Northwest documents.

SEE: Washington Repository Guide. Meckler and McMullin; Winroth.

WA280-440
Kittitas County Museum
114 E. 3rd
Ellensburg WA

MAILING ADDRESS:
P.O. Box 265
Ellensburg WA 98926

(509) 925-3778

OPEN: M-Sa 1-5
COPYING FACILITIES: no
MATERIALS SOLICITED: No active solicitation; will accept materials dealing with Kittitas County subjects.

HOLDINGS:
> Total volume: 55 vols.; 7.5 c.f.
> Inclusive dates: 1872 -
> Description: Holdings consist of records of businesses and civic associations from Ellensburg and Kittitas County, oral reminiscences, collected amateur historical writings on local topics and a photograph collection.

SEE: Washingon Repository Guide.

WA280-885
Office of the Secretary of State
Division of Archives and Records
  Management
Central Washington Regional State
  Archives
3rd Avenue and Poplar Street
Ellensburg WA

MAILING ADDRESS:
Central Washington University
Ellensburg WA 98926

(509) 963-2136

OPEN: by appointment; closed weekends and legal holidays
ACCESS: some records restricted by rights of privacy
COPYING FACILITIES: yes
MATERIALS SOLICITED: Materials related to local government from the central Washington region. Will also accept public records at the state and local levels.

HOLDINGS:
> Total volume: 2,854 c.f. (includes 3,056 vols.)
> Inclusive dates: 1874 - 1979
> Description: The Central Washington Regional State Archives depository serves as one of four branches in a statewide system which holds state, county, city and other local government records. The eight county area served by the Central depository includes Benton, Chelan, Douglas, Grant, Kittitas, Klickitat, Okanogan, and Yakima counties.
> In addition to records from all eight county governments, the Central depository holds records from the cities of Bingen, Ellensburg, Richland, White Salmon, Kennewick and Yakima, the Washington State Potato Commission, Educational Service District Number 171, Klickitat County Port District Number 1,

and the Washington State Historical Records and Archives Project.

GUIDES: *Historical Records of Washington State: Guide to Records in State Archives and its Regional Depositories* (Washington State Archives and Washington State Historical Records Advisory Board, 1981).

ENTIAT

WA288-200
Entiat Community Museum
Lake Shore Drive
Entiat WA

MAILING ADDRESS:
10750 Entiat River Road
Entiat WA 98822

no telephone

OPEN: Sa, Su by appointment June-Sept.
COPYING FACILITIES: no

HOLDINGS:
Total volume: 5 c.f.
Inclusive dates: 1905 -
Description: Collection of photographs from area, along with some maps and clippings.

SEE: *Washington Repository Guide.*

ENUMCLAW

WA289-200
Enumclaw Public Library
Pioneer Room
1309 Myrtle Avenue
Enumclaw WA 98022

(206) 825-2938

OPEN: M-F 9-5
COPYING FACILITIES: yes
MATERIALS SOLICITED: Enumclaw-area historical materials. Will also accept materials from King and Pierce counties.

HOLDINGS:
Total volume: 14 c.f.
Inclusive dates: 1883 -
Description: Photographs, oral-history recordings, a historical reference file, family papers, and records of local businesses, a women's rights group, and school district records.

SEE: *Washington Repository Guide.*

EPHRATA

WA290-200
Ephrata Public Library
339 First Street S.W.
Ephrata WA 98823

(509) 754-3971

OPEN: M-Th 10-9, F, Sa 12-5; closed Sundays and holidays
COPYING FACILITIES: yes

HOLDINGS:
Total volume: 1.2 c.f.
Inclusive dates: 1870 -
Description: A genealogical/historical reference file which includes draft histories, photographs, and records pertaining to Grant County history.

SEE: *Washington Repository Guide.*

WA290-285
Grant County Historical Museum
742 Basin Street N.W.
Ephrata WA

MAILING ADDRESS:
P.O. Box 1141
Ephrata WA 98823

(509) 754-3334

OPEN: May-Oct., daily 10-5
COPYING FACILITIES: no
MATERIALS SOLICITED: Will accept materials concerning the history of Grant County.

HOLDINGS:
Total volume: 3 vols.; 2 c.f.
Inclusive dates: 1906 -
Description: Photographs, oral histories, and some records of local government agencies, all pertaining to county history.

SEE: *Washington Repository Guide.*

EVERETT

WA300-80
Bureau of Indian Affairs
Western Washington Office
3006 Colby Avenue
Everett WA 98201

(206) 258-2651

OPEN: by appointment
ACCESS: apply to the Superintendent of the Bureau for western Washington
COPYING FACILITIES: no

HOLDINGS:
Total volume: 166 c.f.
Inclusive dates: 1875 -
Description: This office, which serves 23 Indian tribes and groups in western Washington, has assembled various documents concerning these tribes. Included are census rolls, birth records, claim award files, and other materials. Many records pertain to legal claims of membership in tribal groups.

SEE: *Washington Repository Guide.*

WA300-172
Everett Community College
Library
801 Wetmore
Everett WA 98201

(206) 259-7151

OPEN: M-F 8-5
COPYING FACILITIES: yes

HOLDINGS:
Total volume: 0.6 c.f.
Inclusive dates: 1899 - 1905 (approx.)
Description: Photographs and newspapers from a socialist utopian colony and a small photograph collection concerning Everett.

SEE: *Washington Repository Guide.*

WA300-175
Everett Fire Department
Museum
2801 Oakes
Everett WA 98201

(206) 259-8892

OPEN: M-F 8-5
COPYING FACILITIES: no

HOLDINGS:
Total volume: 7.5 c.f.
Inclusive dates: 1898 -
Description: Fire department records from Everett and a photograph collection stressing the Everett Fire Department.

SEE: *Washington Repository Guide.*

WA300-200
Everett Public Library
2702 Hoyt
Everett WA 98201

(206) 259-8851, Ext. 20

OPEN: M, Tu, Th-Sa 9-4:30; closed Su, W and holidays
COPYING FACILITIES: yes
MATERIALS SOLICITED: Everett area history; will also accept material concerning Snohomish County.

HOLDINGS:
Total volume: 30 c.f.; 522 reels of microfilm
Inclusive dates: 1882 -
Description: Photographs by several Everett photographers, materials concerning Everett police, and oral history materials.

SEE: *Washington Repository Guide;* Winroth.

WA300-730
Snohomish County Historical Society
Museum
Legion Park
Everett WA

MAILING ADDRESS:
2602 Rainier Avenue
Everett WA 98201

(206) 252-7974

OPEN: Su 2-5
COPYING FACILITIES: no
MATERIALS SOLICITED: Snohomish County material.

HOLDINGS:
Total volume: 18 c.f.
Inclusive dates: 1874 -
Description: The museum maintains a collection of photographs, local public records, records of businesses and social clubs, and a diary.

SEE: *Washington Repository Guide.*

FAIRFIELD

WA304-720
Southeast Spokane County Historical
  Society
c/o Donna deFord
Route 1
Fairfield WA 99012

no telephone

OPEN: by appointment
COPYING FACILITIES: no
MATERIALS SOLICITED: Will accept materials from southern Spokane County,
  pending available storage.

HOLDINGS:
  Total volume: 1 vol.
  Inclusive dates: 1912 - 1959
  Description: Treasurer's records from
  Waverly Township, Spokane County,
  Washington.

SEE: *Washington Repository Guide.*

FEDERAL WAY

WA310-240
Federal Way Public Library
848 S. 320th
Federal Way WA 98104

(206) 839-0257

OPEN: M-Th 10-9, F, Sa 10-6
COPYING FACILITIES: yes

HOLDINGS:
  Total volume: 2.7 c.f.
  Inclusive dates: 1952 -
  Description: The library's holdings in-
  clude a local activities file which contains
  some historical material.

SEE: *Washington Repository Guide.*

WA310-880
Weyerhaeuser Company
Historical Archives
32820 32nd Avenue South
Federal Way WA

MAILING ADDRESS:
Tacoma WA 98477

(206) 924-5053

OPEN: M-F 8-4:30; closed weekends
ACCESS: open to approved scholars
  working on a specific project and
  sponsored by a reputable organization
COPYING FACILITIES: yes
MATERIALS SOLICITED: Company
  records, photographs, films, slides, and
  paintings, supplemented by an oral interview program and contributions of
  materials from outside the company.
  Will also accept materials concerning
  the history of the forest products industry.

HOLDINGS:
  Total volume: 1,000 c.f.
  Inclusive dates: 1875 -
  Description: Weyerhaeuser's archives
  collection includes correspondence, financial records, minute books, ledgers, journals, statements, speeches, photographs,
  films, maps, drawings, oral interviews, genealogies, scrapbooks, and other business
  records of Weyerhaeuser Company, its
  subsidiaries, and acquired companies.

SEE: *Washington Repository Guide;* Davis.

FORKS

WA319-260
Forks Memorial Library
B Street S.E. and 1st Avenue
Forks WA

MAILING ADDRESS:
P.O. Box 1817
Forks WA 98331

(206) 374-6402

OPEN: Tu-Sa 1-8
COPYING FACILITIES: no

HOLDINGS:
  Total volume: 2 c.f.
  Inclusive dates: 1890 -
  Description: Area photographs and
  scrapbooks, along with the Library's ad-
  ministrative records.

SEE: *Washington Repository Guide.*

FORT LEWIS

WA320-230
Fort Lewis Military Museum
Bldg. 4320
Fort Lewis WA 98433

(206) 967-7206

OPEN: Tu-F 12-4 by appointment; closed
  Sa-M and holidays
COPYING FACILITIES: no
MATERIALS SOLICITED: Military history,
  especially about Fort Lewis. Will also
  accept Pierce and Thurston County
  materials.

HOLDINGS:
  Total volume: 45 c.f.
  Inclusive dates: 1840's -
  Description: Photographs, personal nar-
  ratives, scrapbooks, draft essays, and
  maps concerning military history, espe-
  cially of the United States Army and Fort
  Lewis, Washington.

SEE: *Washington Repository Guide;*
Winroth.

FOX ISLAND

WA322-240
Fox Island Historical Society
Fox Island Museum
Fox Island WA 98335

(206) 549-2461

OPEN: Sa 2-4, and by appointment
COPYING FACILITIES: no
MATERIALS SOLICITED: Fox Island his-
  tory.

HOLDINGS:
  Total volume: 25 c.f.
  Inclusive dates: 1840's -
  Description: Area historical reference
  materials such as clippings, photographs,
  and essays, along with a collection of legal documents and records of a cemetery
  association.

SEE: *Washington Repository Guide.*

FRIDAY HARBOR

WA327-735
San Juan Historical Society
405 Price Street
Friday Harbor WA

MAILING ADDRESS:
P.O. Box 441
Friday Harbor WA 98250

no telephone

OPEN: W, Sa 2-4, and by appointment;
  closed fall and winter seasons
ACCESS: prior arrangement with
  historical society officers is advisable
COPYING FACILITIES: no
MATERIALS SOLICITED: Photographs and
  histories associated with the San Juan
  Islands; will also accept other historial
  material.

HOLDINGS:
  Total volume: 8.4 c.f.
  Inclusive dates: 1867 - 1974
  Description: The society holds photo-
  graphs, area business records, local court
  dockets, and a historical reference file.

SEE: *Washington Repository Guide;*
Winroth.

WA327-740
San Juan Island National Histórical
  Park
Friday Harbor WA 98250

(206) 378-2240

OPEN: by appointment
ACCESS: with superintendent's
  permission
COPYING FACILITIES: no

HOLDINGS:
  Total volume: 6 c.f.
  Inclusive dates: 1859 -
  Description: Photographs and research
  files concerning the San Juan Islands
  boundary dispute, the history and description of San Juan Island, and the development of a National Historical Park
  on the island.

SEE: *Washington Repository Guide.*

GIG HARBOR

WA350-650
Peninsula Historical Society
3510 Rosedale Street
Gig Harbor WA

MAILING ADDRESS:
P.O. Box 774
Gig Harbor WA 98335

(206) 858-6722

OPEN: W 12-4, other times by appointment
MATERIALS SOLICITED: Materials concerning Gig Harbor and Pierce County.

HOLDINGS:
Total volume: 12 c.f.
Inclusive dates: 1833 -
Description: Family histories, draft writings, photographs, and similar historical-reference materials relative to the Gig Harbor area, along with government records from the same area.

SEE: *Washington Repository Guide;* Winroth.

GOLDENDALE

WA360-440
Klickitat County Historical Society Museum
427 W. Broadway
Goldendale WA 98620

(509) 773-4303

OPEN: Tu-Su 10-5 June-Sept.; closed Mondays
COPYING FACILITIES: no

HOLDINGS:
Total volume: 11 vols.; 25 c.f.
Inclusive dates: 1865 -
Description: General collection of materials, including records of a few Klickitat County businesses, social organizations and civic groups, along with local government items, and assembled collections of photographs, certificates, correspondence and scrapbooks.

SEE: NUCMC, 1959-61.

SEE: *Washington Repository Guide;* Winroth.

WA360-520
Maryhill Museum of Art
Highway 14
Goldendale WA

MAILING ADDRESS:
Star Route 677, Box 23
Goldendale WA 98620

(509) 773-4792

OPEN: daily 9-5; closed Nov. 16-March 14
USER FEES: adults $1.50, students 50 cents
ACCESS: apply to museum director for access
COPYING FACILITIES: no
MATERIALS SOLICITED: Biographical materials relating to Samuel Hill, Alma de Bretteville Spreckles, Marie, Queen of Romania, and artists featured at the museum.

HOLDINGS:
Total volume: 33 c.f.
Inclusive dates: 1881 -
Description: Administrative files of the museum, photographs, and personal papers, including those of the museum's founder, Samuel Hill (1857-1931), and of Alma de Bretteville Spreckles, principal member of the museum board.

SEE: *Washington Repository Guide.*

GRANDVIEW

WA366-90
Bleyhl Community Library
311 Division Street
Grandview WA

MAILING ADDRESS:
207 W. 2nd Street
Grandview WA 98930

(509) 882-2807

OPEN: M-W 1-8, Th 10-8, F 1-6, Sa 1-5; closed Sundays
COPYING FACILITIES: no

HOLDINGS:
Total volume: 3 c.f.
Inclusive dates: 1894 -
Description: Holdings include records of a few local civic associations, a local history file, and the library's records.

SEE: *Washington Repository Guide.*

WA366-640
R. E. Powell Museum
313 Division Street
Grandview WA 98930

(509) 882-2070

OPEN: Tu-Su 2-4; closed Mondays and legal holidays
COPYING FACILITIES: no
MATERIALS SOLICITED: Records and papers from the Grandview area.

HOLDINGS:
Total volume: 74 vols.
Inclusive dates: 1896 -
Description: Materials primarily relating to the history of the Grandview-Toppenish area of Yakima County, Washington, including photographs and maps, along with records of several local business and civic organizations, and of the City of Grandview; the museum also holds the Earl Reisner photograph collection.

SEE: *Washington Repository Guide.*

GRANGER

WA367-280
Granger Library
109 W. A Street
Granger WA 98932

(509) 854-1446

OPEN: M, W 2-5, Tu, Th 2-8

HOLDINGS:
Total volume: 2 vols.; 2 c.f.
Inclusive dates: 1910 -
Description: Library records, local clippings, and draft of a community history of Granger, Washington.

SEE: *Washington Repository Guide.*

GRANITE FALLS

WA368-280
Granite Falls Historical Society
Corner of Wabash and Indiana
Granite Falls WA

MAILING ADDRESS:
P.O. Box 135
Granite Falls WA 98252

(206) 691-7640

OPEN: by appointment only
COPYING FACILITIES: no
MATERIALS SOLICITED: Materials relating to the history of the Granite Falls/Monte Cristo area.

HOLDINGS:
Total volume: 9 vols.; 9.3 c.f.
Inclusive dates: 1890's -
Description: Photographs, oral history tapes, scrapbooks, and city government records, all concerning Granite Falls, Monte Cristo, and Silverdale.

SEE: *Washington Repository Guide.*

HARRAH

WA380-320
Harrah Public Library
1 E. Pioneer
Harrah WA 98933

(509) 848-2432

OPEN: Tu 2-4, F 2-8
COPYING FACILITIES: no

HOLDINGS:
Total volume: 1 vol.
Inclusive dates: 1911
Description: Library holds one volume of business records of the town's founder.

SEE: *Washington Repository Guide.*

HARRINGTON

WA381-330
Harrington Public Library
11 South Third Street
Harrington WA 99134

(509) 253-4345

OPEN: Tu, Sa 2-5
COPYING FACILITIES: no
MATERIALS SOLICITED: Will accept local materials of limited quantity.

HOLDINGS:
Total volume: 3 vols.
Inclusive dates: 1870 - 1912
Description: Three display items, consisting of Harrington Volunteer Fire Department records, an account book of a pioneer merchant, and a personal scrapbook.

SEE: *Washington Repository Guide.*

HOQUIAM

WA395-320
Hoquiam Public Library
621 K Street
Hoquiam WA 98550

(206) 532-1710

OPEN: M-F 10-9, Sa 10-6
COPYING FACILITIES: yes
MATERIALS SOLICITED: Materials relative to Hoquiam-area history.

HOLDINGS:
    Total volume: 30 c.f.
    Inclusive dates: 1890's -
    Description: Draft histories of local focus, a historical reference file, a photograph collection, pioneer reminiscences, and the records of the library.

SEE: *Washington Repository Guide.*

WA395-640
Polson Park and Museum Historical Society
1611 Riverside Avenue
Hoquiam WA

MAILING ADDRESS:
P.O. Box 432
Hoquiam WA 98550

(206) 533-5862

OPEN: W-Su 12-4 summers; Sa, Su 12-4 winters; closed M, Tu and holidays
COPYING FACILITIES: no
MATERIALS SOLICITED: Materials relevant to the history of Grays Harbor County.

HOLDINGS:
    Total volume: 6.5 c.f.
    Inclusive dates: 1880's -
    Description: Area photographs, maps, and draft histories, along with records on two lumbering firms and several community organizations.

SEE: *Washington Repository Guide.*

IONE

WA407-760
Ione Club Library
Town Hall
Ione WA 99139

(509) 442-3611

OPEN: irregular hours
COPYING FACILITIES: no

HOLDINGS:
    Total volume: 1 c.f.
    Inclusive dates: 1950's -
    Description: Policy and administrative records of this volunteer library, serving as a public library in Ione.

SEE: *Washington Repository Guide.*

ISSAQUAH

WA408-360
Issaquah Historical Society
165 S.E. Andrews Street
Issaquah WA

MAILING ADDRESS:
P.O. Box 695
Issaquah WA 98027

(206) 392-3500

OPEN: second and fourth Sundays of each month 1-5
COPYING FACILITIES: no
MATERIALS SOLICITED: Issaquah history.

HOLDINGS:
    Total volume: 6 c.f.
    Inclusive dates: 1870's
    Description: General reference file of photographs and personal accounts, mining maps, city records, school records, post office records, and business records.

SEE: *Washington Repository Guide.*

WA408-370
Issaquah Library
130 East Sunset Way
Issaquah WA

MAILING ADDRESS:
P.O. Box 1048
Issaquah WA 98027

(206) 392-5430

OPEN: M-W 1-8:30, F, Sa 11-5
COPYING FACILITIES: yes

HOLDINGS:
    Total volume: 0.1 c.f.
    Inclusive dates: 1975 - 1976
    Description: Draft history of Issaquah and a tape recording relative to a mural painting in the library.

SEE: *Washington Repository Guide.*

KALAMA

WA413-440
Kalama Public Library
First Street
Kalama WA

MAILING ADDRESS:
P.O. Box 576
Kalama WA 98625

(206) 673-3060

OPEN: Tu, Th, F 1-6, W 1-8; closed Sa, Su, M
COPYING FACILITIES: no

HOLDINGS:
    Total volume: 0.2 c.f.
    Inclusive dates: 1960 -
    Description: File of press clippings concerning local news.

SEE: *Washington Repository Guide.*

KELSO

WA417-140
Cowlitz County Historical Society Museum
405 Allen Street
Kelso WA 98626

(206) 577-3119

OPEN: Tu-Su 1-5, mornings by appointment; closed Mondays and holidays
COPYING FACILITIES: no
MATERIALS SOLICITED: Materials concerning Cowlitz County.

HOLDINGS:
    Total volume: 27 c.f.
    Inclusive dates: 1850 - 1945
    Description: Holdings stress Cowlitz County history and include photographs, diaries and the records of a 19th century logging company.

SEE: *Washington Repository Guide;* Winroth.

KENNEWICK

WA420-520
Mid-Columbia Regional Library
405 S. Dayton
Kennewick WA 99336

(509) 586-3156

OPEN: M-F 10-9, Sa 10-5
COPYING FACILITIES: yes

HOLDINGS:
    Total volume: 11 vols.
    Inclusive dates: 1948 -
    Description: Archival holdings consist of the library's records.

SEE: *Washington Repository Guide.*

KENT

WA421-440
Kent Library
232 S. 4th
Kent WA 98031

(206) 872-3330

OPEN: M-Th 9:30-8:30, F, Sa 9:30-5:30, Su 1-5 except summer; closed holidays
COPYING FACILITIES: yes

HOLDINGS:
    Total volume: 1 c.f.
    Inclusive dates: 1885 -
    Description: The library's vertical file collection includes some miscellaneous documents from the local area.

SEE: *Washington Repository Guide.*

KIRKLAND

WA427-440
Kirkland Historical Commission
Kirkland WA 98033

no telephone

OPEN: by appointment
COPYING FACILITIES: no
MATERIALS SOLICITED: Materials dealing
with history of Kirkland.

HOLDINGS:
Total volume: 1 c.f.
Inclusive dates: 1880's - 1920's
Description: Photographs of local subjects.

SEE: *Washington Repository Guide.*

WA427-450
Kirkland Public Library
406 Kirkland Avenue
Kirkland WA 98033

(206) 822-2459

OPEN: M-Th 10-9, F, Sa 10-6
COPYING FACILITIES: yes

HOLDINGS:
Total volume: 7 c.f.
Inclusive dates: 1892 -
Description: Local history reference file
and records of the Kirkland Parent-
Teacher Association.

SEE: *Washington Repository Guide.*

WA427-550
Northwest College of the Assemblies
of God
Library
11102 N.E. 53rd Avenue
Kirkland WA

MAILING ADDRESS:
P.O. Box 579
Kirkland WA 98033

(206) 822-8266

OPEN: M-Th 7:30-10, F 7:30-5, Sa
9-4:30; closed Sundays and holidays
ACCESS: limited; by permission
COPYING FACILITIES: yes

HOLDINGS:
Total volume: 1 c.f.
Inclusive dates: 1949 -
Description: The Northwest College of
the Assemblies of God is a private religious college which has a two year liberal
arts program and a four year Bible program. It trains ministers amd missionaries. The Library maintains a small historical file.

SEE: *Washington Repository Guide.*

WA427-560
Northwest Seaport, Inc.
218-B Kirkland Ave.
Kirkland WA

MAILING ADDRESS:
P.O. Box 395
Kirkland WA 98033

(206) 447-9800

OPEN: by appointment
ACCESS: permission of the executive
director required
COPYING FACILITIES: no
MATERIALS SOLICITED: Maritime history
materials.

HOLDINGS:
Total volume: 8 c.f.
Inclusive dates: 1863 -
Description: Photographs of ships, fishing, and harbors, diaries and journals
from ships, lighthouses and seamen.

SEE: *Washington Repository Guide;*
Winroth.

LA CONNER

WA468-720
Skagit County Historical Society
501 S. 4th Street
La Conner WA

MAILING ADDRESS:
P.O. Box 818
La Conner WA 98257

(206) 466-3365

OPEN: M-Th 10-4; closed F, Sa, Su and
holidays
ACCESS: permission required
COPYING FACILITIES: yes
MATERIALS SOLICITED: Materials pertaining to Skagit County, Washington,
and the Pacific Northwest.

HOLDINGS:
Total volume: 70 c.f.
Inclusive dates: 1800 -
Description: A large photographic collection, along with Skagit County business records, school records, civic group
records, and personal papers. Holdings
also include oral history recordings.

SEE: *Washington Repository Guide;*
Hinding; Winroth.

LACEY

WA472-720
Saint Martin's Abbey
Archives
College Way
Lacey WA 98503

(206) 491-4700

OPEN: by appointment
ACCESS: permission required
COPYING FACILITIES: no

HOLDINGS:
Total volume: 48 vols.; 130 c.f.
Inclusive dates: 1895 -
Description: Saint Martin's Abbey is
the only abbey in the state and is the
governing body of Saint Martin's College.
The records document the functions of
the Benedictine Abbey and the college.
Included are administrative files, minutes, correspondence, monks' papers, religious relics, photographs and maps of the
area, and other materials of importance
to the history of Saint Martin's Abbey.

SEE: *Washington Repository Guide.*

LANGLEY

WA478-480
Langley Library
105 Cascade Avenue
Langley WA 98260

(206) 321-4383

OPEN: M 2-9, W 2-5, Sa 10-3
COPYING FACILITIES: no

HOLDINGS:
Total volume: 1.5 c.f.
Inclusive dates: 1880's -
Description: Holdings consist of various local materials grouped as a historical reference file.

SEE: *Washington Repository Guide.*

LEAVENWORTH

WA483-560
North Central Regional Library
Leavenworth Branch Library
819 Front Street
Leavenworth WA

MAILING ADDRESS:
P.O. Box 208
Leavenworth WA 98826

(509) 548-7923

OPEN: M, W 12:30-8:30, Tu, Th 12:30-5,
F 10:30-3:30; closed weekends and
holidays
COPYING FACILITIES: no

HOLDINGS:
Total volume: 7 vols.; 2 c.f.
Inclusive dates: 1929 - 1965
Description: Photographs, local scrapbooks, and draft reports.

SEE: *Washington Repository Guide.*

LIND

WA489-40
Adams County Historical Society
Museum
Phillips Building
Lind WA

MAILING ADDRESS:
c/o Georgia Hays
103 5th Street
Lind WA 99341

(509) 677-3219

OPEN: by appointment
COPYING FACILITIES: no

HOLDINGS:
Total volume: 32 vols.; 9.7 c.f.
Inclusive dates: 1850 -
Description: Papers and records, mostly from Lind and Adams County, relating
to banking, retail businesses, wheat warehouses, fraternal organizations, and
individuals. There is also a reference file
of draft histories, along with a photograph collection.

SEE: *Washington Repository Guide.*

LONGVIEW

WA495-500
Longview Public Library
Longview Room
1600 Louisiana Street
Longview WA 98632

(206) 577-3380

OPEN: M-Th 10-9, F, Sa 10-5
COPYING FACILITIES: yes
MATERIALS SOLICITED: Materials relating to cities of Longview and Kelso, to Cowlitz County, and to the Pacific Northwest.

HOLDINGS:
Total volume: 87 l.f.
Inclusive dates: 1921 -
Description: Holdings stress the history of Longview and include some correspondence and business records of the Long-Bell Lumber Company, developer of the planned city of Longview, along with other records, papers and photographs relating to the Longview area.

SEE: NUCMC, 1980.

SEE: *Washington Repository Guide;* Winroth.

LOPEZ VILLAGE

WA498-480
Lopez Island Historical Society
Lopez Island Museum
Weeks Road and Washburn Place
Lopez Village WA

MAILING ADDRESS:
P.O. Box 163
Lopez Island WA 98261

(206) 468-2049

OPEN: Sa, Su 11-4 and by appointment; closed July 4, Dec. 25, Jan. 1
COPYING FACILITIES: yes
MATERIALS SOLICITED: Materials concerning Lopez Island. Will also accept materials relating to the San Juan Islands.

HOLDINGS:
Total volume: 15 boxes
Inclusive dates: 1860 -
Description: Family papers, business records, school records, manuscript histories, and photographs dealing with Lopez Island history.

SEE: *Washington Repository Guide.*

LYNDEN

WA505-480
Lynden Pioneer Museum
Third and Front Streets
Lynden WA

MAILING ADDRESS:
P.O. Box 371
Lynden WA 98264

(206) 354-3675

OPEN: M-Sa 10-4 summer; W-Sa 10-4 winter; closed Sundays and holidays
COPYING FACILITIES: no
MATERIALS SOLICITED: Materials relating to the Lynden area.

HOLDINGS:
Total volume: 1 c.f.
Inclusive dates: 1880 -
Description: A small body of photographs and scrapbooks.

SEE: *Washington Repository Guide.*

LYNNWOOD

WA506-480
Lynnwood Public Library
19100 44th Avenue
Lynnwood WA 98043

no telephone

OPEN: M-Sa 10-5; closed Sundays and legal holidays
COPYING FACILITIES: yes

HOLDINGS:
Total volume: 1 c.f.
Inclusive dates: 1908 - 1934
Description: Miscellaneous manuscripts dealing with Fort Casey and Mt. Rainier National Park.

SEE: *Washington Repository Guide.*

MABTON

WA508-520
Mabton Public Library
B Street
Mabton WA 98935

(509) 894-4128

OPEN: M, W 1-9, Tu, Th-Sa 1-5

HOLDINGS:
Total volume: 5 vols.; 1.75 c.f.
Inclusive dates: 1906 -
Description: Area photographs, scattered school and post office records, files of the Friends of the Library, and a scrapbook collection.

SEE: *Washington Repository Guide.*

MANSON

WA517-560
North Central Regional Library
Manson Branch Library
Manson WA

MAILING ADDRESS:
Box A
Manson WA 98831

no telephone

OPEN: Tu, Sa 12:30-5:30, F 7-9

HOLDINGS:
Total volume: 7 vols.
Inclusive dates: 1969 - 1976
Description: The library holds a photograph collection related to a Chelan County civic celebration, the Apple Blossom Festival.

SEE: *Washington Repository Guide.*

MAPLE VALLEY

WA520-280
Greater Maple Valley Historical Society
Maple Valley Library
22424 Maple Valley Road
Maple Valley WA

MAILING ADDRESS:
P.O. Box 123
Maple Valley WA 98038

(206) 255-7588

OPEN: by appointment only
COPYING FACILITIES: yes
MATERIALS SOLICITED: History of the greater Maple Valley area.

HOLDINGS:
Total volume: 1 c.f.
Inclusive dates: 1894 - 1975
Description: Reminiscences, oral history interviews, photographs, and miscellaneous documents relative to the greater Maple Valley area.

SEE: *Washington Repository Guide.*

MARYSVILLE

WA528-520
Marysville Historical Society
Pioneer Association
c/o Valda Bloom
Bloom's Store
3rd and State Streets
Marysville WA 98270

(206) 659-2511

OPEN: by appointment
COPYING FACILITIES: no

HOLDINGS:
Total volume: 1 vol.; .5 c.f.
Inclusive dates: 1921 -
Description: The society maintains Marysville area pioneer biographies.

SEE: *Washington Repository Guide.*

WA528-530
Marysville Library
4820 72nd Street N.E.
Marysville WA 98270

(206) 659-2364

OPEN: M-F 12-9, Sa 10-5; closed Sundays and legal holidays
COPYING FACILITIES: yes

HOLDINGS:
Total volume: 33 vols.
Inclusive dates: 1905 -
Description: The library maintains a collection of Marysville High School yearbooks.

WA528-780
Tulalip Tribal Reservation
6700 Totem Beach Road
Marysville WA 98270

(206) 653-4585

OPEN: by appointment
COPYING FACILITIES: no

HOLDINGS:
Total volume: 2 vols.; .5 c.f.
Inclusive dates: 1850 -
Description: Oral histories, a photograph catalog, and certain tribal records.

SEE: *Washington Repository Guide.*

MCCLEARY

WA535-200
Eastern Grays Harbor County
Historical Society
McCleary WA

MAILING ADDRESS:
P.O. Box 554
McCleary WA 98557

no telephone

OPEN: by appointment
COPYING FACILITIES: no
MATERIALS SOLICITED: Eastern Grays
Harbor County materials.

HOLDINGS:
Total volume: 4 c.f.
Inclusive dates: 1902 -
Description: A reference file of draft histories, clippings, and oral histories, a photograph collection, and one volume of accounting records from a lumber company, all materials from the vicinity of McCleary.

SEE: *Washington Repository Guide.*

MERCER ISLAND

WA542-520
Mercer Island Historical Society
9111 Fortuna Drive
Mercer Island WA 98040

(206) 232-0745

OPEN: by appointment
COPYING FACILITIES: no

HOLDINGS:
Total volume: 2 c.f.
Inclusive dates: 1890's - 1960's
Description: Mercer Island photographs, historical reference materials consisting of draft essays and similar items, and civic organization records.

SEE: *Washington Repository Guide.*

WA542-530
Mercer Island Library
4400 80th Avenue S.E.
Mercer Island WA 98040

(206) 233-3537

OPEN: M-Th 11-9, Sa 10-5; closed
Sunday, Friday and legal holidays
COPYING FACILITIES: yes

HOLDINGS:
Total volume: 2 vols.
Inclusive dates: 1959 - 1979
Description: A small quantity of draft reminiscences and local histories.

SEE: *Washington Repository Guide.*

METALINE FALLS

WA545-760
Metalines Recreation Club Public
Library
Town Hall
Metaline Falls WA 99153

no telephone

OPEN: Th 11-7

HOLDINGS:
Total volume: .1 c.f.
Inclusive dates: 1965 (approx.)
Description: The library holds a short draft history of the town of Metaline Falls.

SEE: *Washington Repository Guide.*

MONROE

WA560-520
Monroe Historical Society
Monroe WA

no telephone

OPEN: by appointment
COPYING FACILITIES: no
MATERIALS SOLICITED: Material relating
to the history and development of
Monroe.

HOLDINGS:
Total volume: 1 c.f.
Inclusive dates: 1880 - 1930
Description: Photographs of Monroe and vicinity.

SEE: *Washington Repository Guide.*

MORTON

WA564-200
Eastern Lewis County Historical
Society
Old Settlers Memorial Museum
567 Darid Lake Road
Morton WA

MAILING ADDRESS:
P.O. Box 777
Morton WA 98356

(606) 496-5602

OPEN: by appointment
COPYING FACILITIES: no
MATERIALS SOLICITED: Eastern Lewis
County history; will also accept other
Lewis County materials.

HOLDINGS:
Total volume: 2 c.f.
Inclusive dates: 1887 - 1970's
Description: Photographs, family histories, histories of local communities, oral history tapes, and newspaper clippings.

SEE: *Washington Repository Guide.*

MOSES LAKE

WA565-40
Adam East Museum
5th and Balsam Streets
Moses Lake WA

MAILING ADDRESS:
P.O. Box 940
Moses Lake WA 98837

no telephone

OPEN: March-Oct., daily 1-5, also
mornings during summer months
COPYING FACILITIES: no

HOLDINGS:
Total volume: 6 vols.; .2 c.f.
Inclusive dates: 1905 -
Description: Scrapbooks of local focus, correspondence of East, founder of the museum, and a small photograph collection which stresses Indians.

SEE: *Washington Repository Guide;* Hines.

WA565-520
Moses Lake Public Library
418 E. 5th
Moses Lake WA 98837

(509) 765-3489

OPEN: M-Th 10-9, F, Sa 9-5
COPYING FACILITIES: no

HOLDINGS:
Total volume: 0.5 c.f.
Inclusive dates: 1910 -
Description: Collected photographs pertaining to Moses Lake area.

SEE: *Washington Repository Guide.*

MOUNT VERNON

WA570-540
Mount Vernon Public Library
315 Snoqualmie Street
Mount Vernon WA 98273

(206) 336-6209

OPEN: M-Th 11-8, F, Sa 11-5, Su 1-5;
closed holidays
COPYING FACILITIES: yes

HOLDINGS:
Total volume: 3 vols.; 5.1 c.f.
Inclusive dates: 1910 -
Description: Library records and a 1920 Mount Vernon city budget.

SEE: *Washington Repository Guide.*

MOUNTLAKE TERRACE

WA571-520
Mountlake Terrace Library
5102 236th S.W.
Mountlake Terrace WA 98043

(206) 776-8722

OPEN: M-F 1-9, Sa 10-5; closed Sundays
and legal holidays

HOLDINGS:
Total volume: 4 vols.
Inclusive dates: 1948 -
Description: The library maintains a
scrapbook collection concerning
Mountlake Terrace history and a master's
thesis in geography relating to the area.

SEE: *Washington Repository Guide.*

MUKILTEO

WA573-520
Mukilteo Historical Society
c/o Opel McConnel
718 Front Street
Mukilteo WA

MAILING ADDRESS:
c/o Opel McConnel
Box 675
Mukilteo WA 98265

(206) 355-3411

OPEN: by appointment
COPYING FACILITIES: no
MATERIALS SOLICITED: Material pertaining to Mukilteo and environment, as
specified in the society's charter.

HOLDINGS:
Total volume: 4 c.f.
Inclusive dates: 1870 -
Description: Mukilteo area photographs, lighthouse records, civic club
records, and records of the historical society.

SEE: *Washington Repository Guide.*

NEAH BAY

WA578-520
Makah Museum
Neah Bay WA

MAILING ADDRESS:
P.O. Box 95
Neah Bay WA 98357

(206) 645-2711

OPEN: W-F mornings and afternoon;
closed other times
COPYING FACILITIES: no

HOLDINGS:
Total volume: 6 c.f.; 75 reels of
recording tape
Inclusive dates: 1840 -
Description: Oral histories of the
Makah tribe, archaeological records related to excavations at Ozette, Washington, and a historical reference file composed of documents copied from the National Archives and other sources.

SEE: *Washington Repository Guide.*

NEWPORT

WA584-645
Pend Oreille County Historical
Society
Museum
Washington Street and Highway 2
Newport WA

MAILING ADDRESS:
Box 457
Newport WA 99156

(509) 447-5388

OPEN: May 31-Labor Day, M-F 9-4;
closed rest of year
COPYING FACILITIES: no
MATERIALS SOLICITED: Historical materials from northeastern Washington,
particularly Pend Oreille County.

HOLDINGS:
Total volume: 20 c.f.
Inclusive dates: 1890's -
Description: The museum maintains a
collection of oral history tapes, photographs, scrapbooks, maps, genealogical
materials, and public records dealing with
Pend Oreille County history, especially
steamboating on the Pend Oreille River.

SEE: *Washington Repository Guide;*
Meckler and McMullin; Winroth.

NORTH BEND

WA592-560
North Bend Library
4th Street
North Bend WA

MAILING ADDRESS:
P.O. Box 312
North Bend WA 98045

(206) 888-0554

OPEN: Tu, W 1-9, F 1-5, Sa 1-4
COPYING FACILITIES: no

HOLDINGS:
Total volume: 12 vols.
Inclusive dates: 1956 - 1976
Description: Holdings consist of several
draft histories of state and local focus.

SEE: *Washington Repository Guide.*

WA592-720
Snoqualmie Valley Historical Society
320 N. Bend Boulevard S.
North Bend WA

MAILING ADDRESS:
P.O. Box 179
NorthBend WA 98045

(206) 888-0062, 3200

OPEN: Sa, Su 1-5
ACCESS: permission of curator required
COPYING FACILITIES: no
MATERIALS SOLICITED: History of the
Snoqualmie valley.

HOLDINGS:
Total volume: 5.5 c.f.
Inclusive dates: 1858 - 1974
Description: Tape-recorded interviews,
family papers, scrapbooks, records of
businesses and organizations, all relative
to the Snoqualmie valley, especially the
towns of North Bend and Snoqualmie.

SEE: *Washington Repository Guide;*
Hinding.

OAK HARBOR

WA596-600
Oak Harbor Historical Society
Oak Harbor WA 98277

no telephone

OPEN: by appointment
COPYING FACILITIES: no
MATERIALS SOLICITED: Oak Harbor his-
torical materials.

HOLDINGS:
Total volume: not specified
Inclusive dates: 1854 -
Description: Principal holding is a col-
lection of photographs from the Oak Har-
bor vicinity.

SEE: *Washington Repository Guide.*

OAKESDALE

WA597-600
Oakesdale Public Library
Town Hall
Oakesdale WA 99158

no telephone

OPEN: Tu, Sa 1-4

HOLDINGS:
Total volume: 1 item
Inclusive dates: 1887
Description: Display item - agreement
for a subscription school.

SEE: *Washington Repository Guide.*

OCEAN SHORES

WA601-680
Ocean Shores Public Library
Point Brown Avenue
Ocean Shores WA

MAILING ADDRESS:
P.O. Box 668
Ocean Shores WA 98569

(206) 289-3919

OPEN: M-F 9-4
COPYING FACILITIES: yes
MATERIALS SOLICITED: Ocean Shores
history.

HOLDINGS:
Total volume: 3 c.f.
Inclusive dates: 1850 -
Description: Photographs, maps, and
local histories documenting the history of
the local area.

SEE: *Washington Repository Guide;*
Winroth.

ODESSA

WA602-600
Odessa Historical Society
Odessa Historische Museum
Fourth and Elm Streets
Odessa WA 99159

(509) 982-2539

OPEN: Su 2-5, and by appointment
COPYING FACILITIES: no
MATERIALS SOLICITED: Local materials.

HOLDINGS:
Total volume: 11 c.f.
Inclusive dates: 1880's -
Description: Odessa area photographs, miscellaneous documents, business records, and scrapbooks. Material tends to emphasize dry-farming agriculture and the Russian-German origin of a large segment of the local population.

SEE: *Washington Repository Guide;* Hines.

WA602-610
Odessa Public Library
21 E. 1st Avenue
Odessa WA 99159

(509) 982-2654

OPEN: W, Sa 2-5

HOLDINGS:
Total volume: 1.5 c.f.
Inclusive dates: 1975 - 1976
Description: Principal manuscript holding is a sequence of family histories, mostly compiled on forms.

SEE: *Washington Repository Guide.*

OKANOGAN

WA604-590
Okanogan County Historical Museum
1410 2nd Avenue N.
Okanogan WA

MAILING ADDRESS:
P.O. Box 1129
Okanogan WA 98840

(509) 422-4272

OPEN: daily 11-5; closed Oct. through April
COPYING FACILITIES: yes
MATERIALS SOLICITED: Any materials related to Okanogan County history.

HOLDINGS:
Total volume: 40 c.f.
Inclusive dates: 1867 -
Description: Photographs, scrapbooks, financial records, diaries, local government records, school records, and draft writings, all focusing on Okanogan County history.

SEE: *Washington Repository Guide;* Winroth.

OLYMPIA

WA616-240
The Evergreen State College
Daniel Evans Library
Olympia WA 98505

(206) 866-6000

OPEN: M-F 8-5; closed weekends and legal holidays
COPYING FACILITIES: yes
MATERIALS SOLICITED: Records of the Evergreen State College.

HOLDINGS:
Total volume: 127 c.f.
Inclusive dates: 1965 -
Description: Records of the College president, accounting files, and public relations office files, dating from the inception of the school.

SEE: *Washington Repository Guide.*

WA616-400
Judge Daniel R. Bigelow House
918 Glass Avenue
Olympia WA 98506

(206) 357-6198

OPEN: by appointment
COPYING FACILITIES: no
MATERIALS SOLICITED: Bigelow family materials.

HOLDINGS:
Total volume: 5 vols.; 5 c.f.
Inclusive dates: 1828 - 1899
Description: Diary (1848-54) kept by Bigelow at Harvard Law School, on the journey overland to Washington, and during the early years of Washington Territory. Also correspondence and other materials of Bigelow.

SEE: *Washington Repository Guide.*

WA616-444
Office of the Secretary of State
Division of Archives and Records Management
King County Regional State Archives
12th and Washington Streets
Olympia WA 98504

(206) 754-1492

OPEN: M-F by appointment only; closed weekends and legal holidays
ACCESS: some records restricted by rights of privacy
COPYING FACILITIES: yes
MATERIALS SOLICITED: Materials related to local governments in King County, Washington. Will also accept public records from state and local government agencies.

HOLDINGS:
Total volume: 3,487 c.f. (includes 969 vols.); 20 microfilm reels
Inclusive dates: 1850 - 1970
Description: The Washington State Archives' King County Archives serves as a depository for county, city, and other public archival records from King County, Washington.

GUIDES: *Historical Records of Washington State: Guide to Records in State Archives and its Regional Repositories* (Washington State Archives and Washington State Historical Records Advisory Board, 1981).

SEE ALSO: David W. Hastings, *A Guide to the Judicial Records of King County* (1977).

WA616-610
Olympia Public Library
8th and Franklin
Olympia WA 98501

(206) 352-0595

OPEN: M-Th 10-9, F, Sa 10-6
COPYING FACILITIES: yes
MATERIALS SOLICITED: Genealogy; will also accept materials concerning Olympia and Thurston County history.

HOLDINGS:
Total volume: 26 c.f.
Inclusive dates: 1849 -
Description: The library maintains a historical reference file, genealogical information, and scrapbooks on Olympia Public Library history.

SEE: *Washington Repository Guide.*

WA616-620
Olympic National Forest
Federal Building
Capitol Way
Olympia WA 98501

(206) 753-9544

OPEN: M-F 8-5; closed weekends and legal holidays
ACCESS: permission required
COPYING FACILITIES: yes
MATERIALS SOLICITED: Olympic National Forest history.

HOLDINGS:
Total volume: 17 c.f.
Inclusive dates: 1900 (approx.) -
Description: The Olympic National Forest maintains a collection of maps, photographs, correspondence, business records, and reminiscences of forest service employees.

SEE: *Washington Repository Guide;* Davis; Winroth.

WA616-870
Office of the Secretary of State
Division of Archives and Records Management
Washington State Archives
P.O. Box 9000
Olympia WA 98504

(206) 753-5485

OPEN: M-F 8-5; closed weekends and holidays
ACCESS: Compliance with the Public Disclosure Act requires a written request or a letter from the appropriate office of record to gain access to specified records. All records are open to the public unless specifically exempted under the terms of the Public Disclosure Act.
COPYING FACILITIES: yes

MATERIALS SOLICITED: State and local government records of Washington.

HOLDINGS:
> *Total volume:* 30,886 c.f.
> *Inclusive dates:* 1854 -
> *Description:* Records of the state and territorial governments of Washington, including those of the Governor's Office, the Legislature, the Supreme Court, and territorial and state agencies and programs. Also included are oral history collections, and special collections documenting specific events such as the Indian Wars, the Seattle World's Fair, and the Centralia Massacre.
>
> In addition to territorial and state records, the State Archives holds extensive collections of county and city government records at its five regional depositories located in Bellingham, Burien, Cheney, Ellensburg, and Olympia.

GUIDES: *Historical Records of Washington State: Guide to Records in State Archives and its Regional Depositories* (1981).

SEE: Hamer.

SEE: Davis; Hinding; Winroth.

SEE ALSO: John Burns, et al., *Washington State Archives Guide to the Governor's Papers* (1977); G. Q. Flynn, 'The New Deal and Local Archives: The Pacific Northwest,' *American Archivist* 33 (Jan. 1970); James H. Hitchman, 'Primary Source Materials in Washington Maritime History,' *Pacific Northwest Quarterly* 65 (April 1974); Raymond G. McInnis, 'Opportunities for Historical Research in Washington State,' *Studies in History and Society* 1 (April 1969).

Ann Rune, comp., *Oral History Index: Washington State Oral/Aural History Program, 1974-1977* (1977).

Guides to individual collections are available at the institution.

WA616-895
Office of the Secretary of State
Division of Archives and Records Management
Southwest Washington Regional State Archives
12th and Washington Streets
Olympia WA

MAILING ADDRESS:
218 General Administration Building
Olympia WA 98504

(206) 753-5467

OPEN: M-F 8-5; closed weekends and legal holidays
ACCESS: some records restricted by rights of privacy
MATERIALS SOLICITED: Materials related to southwest Washington local government records. Will also accept public records from state and local governments.

HOLDINGS:
> *Total volume:* 1,661 c.f. (includes 5,445 vols.)
> *Inclusive dates:* 1847 - 1976
> *Description:* The Southwest Washington Regional State Archives provides records management and archival storage

services for local governments in southwest Washington. The area served includes Grays Harbor, Mason, Pierce, Thurston, Lewis, Pacific, Cowlitz, Skamania, Wahkiakum, Kitsap, and Clark Counties. The records made available for archival research at the Regional State Archives originate from county, city, port, and special district governments.

GUIDES: *Historical Records of Washington State: Guide to Records in State Archives and its Regional Depositories* (Washington State Archives and Washington State Historical Records Advisory Board, 1981).

WA616-915
Washington State Capital Museum
211 W. 21st Street
Olympia WA 98504

(206) 753-2580

OPEN: Tu-F 10-4; closed weekends and Mondays
COPYING FACILITIES: no
MATERIALS SOLICITED: Historical papers of local interest; will also accept materials related to Washington and Oregon history.

HOLDINGS:
> *Total volume:* 150 c.f.
> *Inclusive dates:* 1790's -
> *Description:* Olympia-area records of businesses, civic organizations, and women's clubs; scrapbooks; a general photograph collection featuring Olympia subjects; and various recollections, personal narratives, and family histories.

SEE: Hamer.

SEE: *Washington Repository Guide;* Winroth.

WA616-950
Washington State Library
Washington Northwest Room
Olympia WA 98504

(206) 753-4024

OPEN: M-F 8-5; closed weekends and legal holidays
COPYING FACILITIES: yes
MATERIALS SOLICITED: Material related to Washington state government; will also accept materials relative to the general history of Washington, and manuscripts of writings by Washington authors.

HOLDINGS:
> *Total volume:* 420 c.f.
> *Inclusive dates:* 1830's -
> *Description:* Primary components within the holdings are personal papers of territorial and state officials of Washington; diaries and personal accounts of overland journeys and frontier experiences from throughout the state; interviews and other materials related to a state-wide 'pioneer project;' a Northwest photograph collection of general scope; literary materials of Washington authors; and area-history materials, chiefly from Olympia, Thurston County, and Lewis County.

SEE: Hamer; NUCMC, 1959-62, 70, 74.

SEE: *Washington Repository Guide;* Hinding; Novotny; Robbins; Winroth.

SEE ALSO: James H. Hitchman 'Primary Source Materials in Washington Maritime History,' *Pacific Northwest Quarterly* 65 (April 1974); Raymond G. McInnis, 'Opportunities for Historical Research in Washington State,' *Studies in History and Society* 1 (April 1969); Joan Hoff Wilson and Lynn B. Donovan, 'Women's History: A Listing of West Coast Archival and Manuscript Sources, Part II,' *California Historical Quarterly* 55 (Summer 1976).

Raymond G. McInnis, 'Thar's Gold in Them Stacks: Rich Resources for Historical Research in State Libraries,' *Library News Bulletin* 38 (Jan.-March 1971); Hazel E. Mills, 'New Manuscript Collection in the Washington State Library: The Alanson Wesley Smith Papers,' *Library News Bulletin* 38 (Jan.-March 1971); *Washington Newspapers and Historical Materials on Microfilm in the Washington State Library* (1966).

OMAK

WA617-90
North Central Regional Library
Omak Branch Library
30 S. Ash
Omak WA 98841

(509) 826-1820

OPEN: M-Th 11-8, F-Sa 11-5

HOLDINGS:
> *Total volume:* 1 c.f.
> *Inclusive dates:* 1860 - 1963
> *Description:* The library has a collection of local pioneer biographies, and other local history reference materials.

SEE: *Washington Repository Guide.*

ORTING

WA626-600
Orting Town Museum
202 S. Washington
Orting WA 98360

(206) 893-2219

OPEN: irregular summer hours and by appointment
COPYING FACILITIES: no
MATERIALS SOLICITED: Orting-area history; will also accept other materials of historical interest.

HOLDINGS:
> *Total volume:* not specified
> *Inclusive dates:* 1889 - 1947
> *Description:* Orting-area photographs, and miscellaneous personal papers of two Orting residents.

SEE: *Washington Repository Guide.*

OTHELLO

WA629-655

Othello Community Museum
3rd and Lurch Streets
Othello WA

MAILING ADDRESS:
P.O. Box 121
Othello WA 99344

(509) 488-2268

OPEN: Sa, Su 1-5
COPYING FACILITIES: no
MATERIALS SOLICITED: Materials from Othello and western Adams County.

HOLDINGS:
   Total volume: 6 c.f.
   Inclusive dates: 1880's -
   Description: Photographs, especially a collection which relates to railroading, other railroad materials, public school records, city water department records, and miscellaneous deeds, certificates and so forth, with most materials from the vicinity of Othello.

SEE: *Washington Repository Guide;* Hines.

PASCO

WA647-135

Columbia Basin College
Library
c/o Franklin County Public Utility District
1411 West Clark
Pasco WA 99301

(509) 547-0511

OPEN: M-Th 7:30-9:30, F 7:30-4:30
COPYING FACILITIES: yes
MATERIALS SOLICITED: Will accept materials dealing with the college.

HOLDINGS:
   Total volume: 8 c.f.
   Inclusive dates: 1955 -
   Description: Irregularly deposited College records and ephemera and printed matter issued by the College.

SEE: *Washington Repository Guide.*

WA647-270

Franklin County Historical Society
305 North 4th Street
Pasco WA 99301

(509) 547-3714

OPEN: W-Su 1-5; closed Mondays and Tuesdays

HOLDINGS:
   Total volume: 2 c.f.
   Inclusive dates: 1912 - 1914
   Description: Photographs of schools in Franklin County, guest register from a hotel at Pasco, and correspondence of the Pasco Chamber of Commerce.

SEE: *Washington Repository Guide;* Hines; Winroth.

WA647-640

Pasco Public Library
1320 W. Hopkins
Pasco WA 99301

(509) 545-3451

OPEN: M-Sa 10-5
COPYING FACILITIES: yes

HOLDINGS:
   Total volume: 58 vols.; 8 c.f.
   Inclusive dates: 1912 -
   Description: Library records, a draft history of Pasco, and a Northwest reference file of various materials, with emphasis on the Tri-Cities area (Pasco-Kennewick-Richland).

SEE: *Washington Repository Guide.*

POMEROY

WA672-160

Denny Ashby Memorial Library
856 Arlington Street
Pomeroy WA 99347

MAILING ADDRESS:
P.O. Box 670
Pomeroy WA 99347

(509) 843-3710

OPEN: Tu, Th 2-5:30, 7-9, W 2-5:30; closed F-M and holidays
COPYING FACILITIES: no

HOLDINGS:
   Total volume: 4 c.f.
   Inclusive dates: 1880's - 1950's
   Description: Family papers of the John J. Ashby family, benefactors of the Library, along with draft writings on local history and a few photographs.

SEE: *Washington Repository Guide.*

WA672-290

Garfield County Historical Association
Museum
7th and Columbia Streets
Pomeroy WA 99347

(509) 843-1316

OPEN: F 1-4
COPYING FACILITIES: no

HOLDINGS:
   Total volume: 6 c.f.
   Inclusive dates: 1860's - 1977
   Description: Photographs and business records from Garfield County, along with draft writings of A. G. Farley, 'Poet Laureate of Washington State.'

SEE: *Washington Repository Guide.*

PORT ANGELES

WA676-135

Clallam County Historical Society
Clallam County Museum
223 East Fourth
Port Angeles WA

MAILING ADDRESS:
P.O. Box 1024
Port Angeles WA 98362

(206) 452-7831, Ext. 364

OPEN: M-F 10-4; closed weekends and holidays
COPYING FACILITIES: yes
MATERIALS SOLICITED: Materials relating to Clallam County, Washington.

HOLDINGS:
   Total volume: 10 c.f.
   Inclusive dates: 1860 -
   Description: Local photograph and oral history collections, along with a few records of the Clallam County Engineer's Office, and the working papers for a recent county history.

SEE: *Washington Repository Guide;* Winroth.

WA676-560

Port Angeles Library
Campbell Northwest Room
207 S. Lincoln
Port Angeles WA 98362

(206) 452-9253

OPEN: M-Th 9-8, F, Sa 9-6
COPYING FACILITIES: yes
MATERIALS SOLICITED: Material relating to the history of Port Angeles, Clallam County and the Olympic Peninsula.

HOLDINGS:
   Total volume: 22 c.f.
   Inclusive dates: 1880 (approx.) -
   Description: Draft histories, photographs, oral histories, maps, and other materials integrated into a reference file, all stressing Port Angeles, Clallam County, and the Olympic Peninsula.

SEE: *Washington Repository Guide.*

WA676-610

Olympic National Park
Pioneer Memorial Visitor Center
2800 Hurricane Ridge Road
Port Angeles WA 98362

(206) 452-4501, Ext. 230

OPEN: daily 8-4; closed Christmas
ACCESS: appointment required
COPYING FACILITIES: no

HOLDINGS:
   Total volume: 23 items
   Inclusive dates: 1895 - 1962
   Description: Manuscripts relating to books published on Olympic National Park; trout records from Lake Crescent, 1913-33; Lake Crescent area hotel registers, 1905-44; and photographs of Olympic National Park backcountry.

SEE: *Washington Repository Guide;* Davis; Winroth.

PORT GAMBLE

WA678-650
Port Gamble Historic Museum
Port Gamble WA

MAILING ADDRESS:
P.O. Box 217
Port Gamble WA 98364

(206) 297-3341

OPEN: M-F 8-5 by appointment; closed
  weekends and holidays
COPYING FACILITIES: no
MATERIALS SOLICITED: History of Port
  Gamble.

HOLDINGS:
  Total volume: 2.5 c.f.
  Inclusive dates: 1853 -
  Description: The museum, located in
  Port Gamble, an unincorporated company town founded by the Pope and Talbot Lumber Company, maintains a collection of photographs, maps, and a
  ship's log, all detailing both company and
  town history.

SEE: *Washington Repository Guide.*

PORT ORCHARD

WA680-480
Log Cabin Museum
Sidney Road
Port Orchard WA 98366

(206) 876-3693

OPEN: M 10-noon, Su 1-4
COPYING FACILITIES: no

HOLDINGS:
  Total volume: 1 c.f.
  Inclusive dates: 1860's - 1960
  Description: A small body of miscella-
  neous personal papers and business
  records, chiefly from Port Orchard.

SEE: *Washington Repository Guide;*
Winroth.

PORT TOWNSEND

WA681-250
Coast Artillery Museum at Fort
  Worden
Administration Building
Fort Worden State Park
Port Townsend WA

MAILING ADDRESS:
433 Ranger Drive, S.E.
Olympia WA 98503

(206) 491-2906

OPEN: by appointment
COPYING FACILITIES: no
MATERIALS SOLICITED: Military history
  relating to the 248th Coast Artillery.

HOLDINGS:
  Total volume: 1.5 c.f.
  Inclusive dates: 1914 - 1945
  Description: Correspondence, photo-
  graphs, and a newspaper of the Coastal
  Artillery unit station at the Fort Worden
  Coastal Defense station.

SEE: *Washington Repository Guide.*

WA681-400
Jefferson County Historical Society
City Hall
Port Townsend WA 98368

(206) 385-1003

OPEN: Th-M 10-4; closed Tu, W and
  holidays
COPYING FACILITIES: no
MATERIALS SOLICITED: Seeks materials
  documenting Jefferson County history.
  Will also accept materials relative to
  history of the Olympic Peninsula.

HOLDINGS:
  Total volume: 90 c.f.
  Inclusive dates: 1850's -
  Description: Family papers, business
  records, city and county government
  records, photographs, records of civic and
  social organizations, reference files and
  other components of a general collection
  of materials relative to Port Townsend,
  Jefferson County, and the Olympic Peninsula.

SEE: NUCMC, 1962-64, 73, 75.

SEE: *Washington Repository Guide;* Bean
and Vane; Hinding; Winroth.

WA681-670
Port Townsend Library
1200 Lawrence
Port Townsend WA 98368

(206) 385-3181

OPEN: Tu-Th, Sa 1-8, F 1-5
COPYING FACILITIES: no

HOLDINGS:
  Total volume: 8.5 c.f.
  Inclusive dates: 1898 -
  Description: Holdings consist of the
  records of the library and of a local wom-
  en's club.

SEE: *Washington Repository Guide.*

POULSBO

WA685-640
Poulsbo Marine Science Center
17771 Fjord Drive, N.E.
Poulsbo WA 98370

(206) 779-5549

OPEN: M-F 1-4; closed weekends
COPYING FACILITIES: no
MATERIALS SOLICITED: Pacific marine
  life.

HOLDINGS:
  Total volume: 40 c.f.
  Inclusive dates: 1960's -
  Description: Photographs, maps, re-
  ports, papers, charts, and scientific stud-
  ies of a center for the study of Pacific
  Northwest marine life, operated by the
  public school districts of the area.

SEE: *Washington Repository Guide.*

WA685-650
Poulsbo Public Library
700 Lincoln Street
Poulsbo WA 98370

(206) 779-2915

OPEN: M, W 1-8:30, F, Sa 10-5:30
COPYING FACILITIES: no
MATERIALS SOLICITED: History of north
  Kitsap County.

HOLDINGS:
  Total volume: 0.7 c.f.
  Inclusive dates: 1870's -
  Description: The library's collection in-
  cludes a local history file, photographs,
  and newspaper and magazine articles on
  Poulsbo history.

SEE: *Washington Repository Guide.*

PROSSER

WA687-90
Benton County Historical Museum
City Park
Prosser WA

MAILING ADDRESS:
P.O. Box 591
Prosser WA 99350

(509) 786-3842

OPEN: M-Sa 10-4, Su 1-5
USER FEES: fifty cents
COPYING FACILITIES: no

HOLDINGS:
  Total volume: 10 vols.; 8 c.f.
  Inclusive dates: 1895 - 1965
  Description: Holdings include area
  photographs, draft histories and a collec-
  tion of publicity brochures.

SEE: *Washington Repository Guide;* Hines.

PULLMAN

WA724-490
Neill Public Library
N. 210 Grand
Pullman WA 99163

(509) 334-4555

OPEN: M-Sa 9-9
COPYING FACILITIES: no

HOLDINGS:
  Total volume: 1 c.f.
  Inclusive dates: 1880's -
  Description: Pullman-area photographs.

SEE: *Washington Repository Guide;*
Winroth.

WA724-890
Washington State University
Libraries
Manuscripts, Archives, and Special
  Collections Division
Pullman WA 99164

(509) 335-6691

OPEN: M-F 8-5:30; other hours by
  appointment
COPYING FACILITIES: yes
MATERIALS SOLICITED: Pacific Northwest materials, chiefly eastern Washington. Will also accept other materials
  complementary to existing holdings, including photographs and oral histories.

HOLDINGS:
  Total volume: 2,300 l.f.
  Inclusive dates: 1500 -
  Description: Materials relating to the
  Pacific Northwest, chiefly eastern Washington, with some holdings from throughout the world. Included are personal papers and records of political figures, businesses, professional people, authors, scientists, and others, including a certain number of 'common people.' Subject focuses
  include agriculture, aviation, banking,
  botany, mining, naval history, the Columbia River basin, the Klondike, and
  Northwest Plateau Indians.

GUIDES: *Selected Manuscript Resources in
  the Washington State University Library* (1974).

SEE: Hamer; NUCMC, 1962-64, 66,
  69-72, 74, 76-77, 79.

SEE: *Washington Repository Guide;* Allard,
  Crawley, and Edmison; Davis;
  Hinding; Hines; Hounshell; Novotny;
  Paszek; Robbins; Winroth.

SEE ALSO: Joan Hoff Wilson and Lynn B.
  Donovan, 'Women's History: A Listing
  of West Coast Archival and Manuscript
  Sources, Part II,' *California Historical
  Quarterly* 55 (Summer 1976); James H.
  Hitchman, 'Primary Source Materials
  in Washington Maritime History,' *Pacific Northwest Quarterly* 65 (April
  1974); Terry Abraham, comp., *Union
  List of the Papers of Members of Congress from the Pacific Northwest* (1976).

Finding aids to individual collections are
  available at the library; eighteen have
  been published.

WA724-895
Washington State University
Libraries
University Archives
MASC Division
Washington State University Library
Pullman WA 99164

(509) 335-6691

OPEN: M-F 8-5:30, and by appointment
COPYING FACILITIES: yes
MATERIALS SOLICITED: Inactive records
  of the university and related campus
  organizations.

HOLDINGS:
  Total volume: 650 c.f.
  Inclusive dates: 1891 -
  Description: Inactive materials released
  to the archives by University offices, departments, research stations, and campus
  organizations. The institution has been
  successively known as Washington Agricultural College, Washington State College, and Washington State University.

SEE: Hamer; NUCMC, 1972.

SEE: *Washington Repository Guide.*

PUYALLUP

WA726-200
Ezra Meeker Historical Society
321 E. Pioneer
Puyallup WA

MAILING ADDRESS:
P.O. Box 103
Puyallup WA 98371

(206) 848-1770

OPEN: W-Su 1-5; closed M, Tu,
  Christmas-New Year's
USER FEES: one dollar donation
  requested
COPYING FACILITIES: no
MATERIALS SOLICITED: Early photo-
  graphs of the Meeker family, material
  relative to the Meeker family and
  Meeker Mansion, and items pertaining
  to Puyallup Valley history.

HOLDINGS:
  Total volume: 18 c.f.
  Inclusive dates: 1790's -
  Description: Chiefly materials pertaining to Ezra Meeker, a Puyallup settler
  who long personified the Northwest pioneer, along with various Puyallup-area
  business records, and collected documents concerning area history, including
  Hudson's Bay Company subjects.

SEE: *Washington Repository Guide.*

WA726-440
Paul H. Karshner Memorial Museum
426 Fourth Street N.E.
Puyallup WA 98371

(206) 841-8748

OPEN: M-F 9-3
ACCESS: available for special projects
  only
  Inclusive dates: 1872 - 1970's
  Description: An area photographs collection, miscellaneous personal papers of
  a resident, and town council minute
  books from the 1880's.

SEE: *Washington Repository Guide.*

WA726-640
Puyallup Public Library
Beta Women's Club Collection
324 Meridian S.
Puyallup WA 98371

(206) 841-5454

OPEN: M-Th 9-9, F, Sa 9-5; closed
  Sundays and holidays

MATERIALS SOLICITED: Puyallup Valley
  pioneer residents' papers.

HOLDINGS:
  Total volume: 15 c.f.
  Inclusive dates: 1834 - 1976
  Description: Records of Puyallup civic
  and women's organizations, a family-
  history reference collection, and records
  of a Puyallup fruit canner.

SEE: *Washington Repository Guide.*

QUINAULT

WA729-820
Olympic National Forest
Quinault Ranger Station
Quinault WA 98575

(206) 288-2525

OPEN: M-F 7:45-4:30; closed weekends
  and holidays
COPYING FACILITIES: no
MATERIALS SOLICITED: History of Lake
  Quinault area.

HOLDINGS:
  Total volume: 10.3 c.f.
  Inclusive dates: 1894 -
  Description: Photographs, maps, plans,
  and memorabilia concerning the history
  of the district of the Olympic National
  Forest administered by the Quinault
  Ranger Station.

SEE: *Washington Repository Guide.*

QUINCY

WA730-880
William Conlon Memorial Library
108 B Street S.E.
Quincy WA 98848

(509) 787-2359

OPEN: M 12:30-5:30, Tu, Th 12:30-8, F
  10-5:30, Sa 12-5; closed Su, W and
  holidays
COPYING FACILITIES: yes

HOLDINGS:
  Total volume: 8 vols.
  Inclusive dates: 1950 - 1965
  Description: Scrapbook concerning the
  library.

SEE: *Washington Repository Guide.*

RAYMOND

WA734-680
Raymond Public Library
507 Duryea
Raymond WA 98577

(206) 942-2408

OPEN: M-F 10-4; closed legal holidays
COPYING FACILITIES: yes

HOLDINGS:
  Total volume: 10 c.f.
  Inclusive dates: 1849 -
  Description: The library maintains a
  collection of local history manuscripts
  and historical reference clippings scrapbooks.

SEE: *Washington Repository Guide.*

REARDAN

WA735-680
Reardan Public Library
Town Hall/Library
Reardan WA 99029

(509) 796-3921

OPEN: W, Sa 2-5; closed legal holidays
COPYING FACILITIES: no

HOLDINGS:
Total volume: 3 vols.
Inclusive dates: 1954 - 1973
Description: Library holds Reardan Parent-Teacher Association scrapbooks.

SEE: *Washington Repository Guide.*

REDMOND

WA736-440
King County Historical Association
Marymoor Museum
Marymoor Park
Redmond WA

Mailing address:
P.O. Box 162
Redmond WA 98052

(206) 885-3684

OPEN: by appointment
COPYING FACILITIES: no
MATERIALS SOLICITED: Will accept local history materials.

HOLDINGS:
Total volume: 8.5 c.f.
Inclusive dates: 1869 - 1977
Description: Area photographs, records of civic associations, family papers, and personal papers and photographs of Edwin C. Chalcraft, 19th century Indian agent at Puyallup, Washington.

SEE: *Washington Repository Guide.*

WA736-680
Redmond Library
15810 N.E. 85th
Redmond WA 98052

(206) 885-1861

OPEN: M, Tu 11-9, W, Th 1-9, Sa 10-5
COPYING FACILITIES: yes

HOLDINGS:
Total volume: 8 vols.; 1 c.f.
Inclusive dates: 1909 -
Description: Records of the Nokomis Club of Redmond, historical reference materials, and tape recordings of the Redmond City Council.

SEE: *Washington Repository Guide.*

RENTON

WA738-670
Renton Historical Museum
235 Mill Avenue S.
Renton WA 98055

(206) 255-3624

OPEN: Su 2-5, and by appointment
COPYING FACILITIES: no
MATERIALS SOLICITED: Materials pertaining to the Pacific Northwest; will accept other materials of historical interest.

HOLDINGS:
Total volume: 45 vols.; 6 c.f.
Inclusive dates: 1889 -
Description: Family papers, records of Renton civic groups, draft histories and biographies, and collections of photographs and scrapbooks; all materials generally focusing on the Renton area.

SEE: *Washington Repository Guide;* Winroth.

WA738-690
Renton Public Library
100 Mill Avenue S.
Renton WA 98055

(206) 235-2610

OPEN: M-W 9-9, F, Sa 9-6, Su 1-5
COPYING FACILITIES: yes

HOLDINGS:
Total volume: 6 c.f.
Inclusive dates: 1913 -
Description: Scrapbooks kept by the library, maps, and a historical reference file, all pertaining to Renton and vicinity.

SEE: *Washington Repository Guide.*

REPUBLIC

WA739-240
Ferry County Historical Society Museum
N. Adams Street
Republic WA

Mailing address:
Box 356
Republic WA 99166

(509) 775-3351

OPEN: daily 1-4 Memorial-Labor Days
COPYING FACILITIES: no
MATERIALS SOLICITED: Materials relative to the history of Ferry County.

HOLDINGS:
Total volume: 3 c.f.
Inclusive dates: 1897 - 1960's
Description: Holdings include a photograph collection, a dental register, draft histories, and a soldier's diary from World War I, with all materials related to the history of Ferry County, Washington.

SEE: *Washington Repository Guide;* Winroth.

RICHLAND

WA742-690
Richland Public Library
Swift and Northgate Streets
Richland WA 99352

(509) 943-9117

OPEN: M-Th 10:30-9, F 5-9, Sa 10:30-5:30
COPYING FACILITIES: yes

HOLDINGS:
Total volume: 60 vols.; 110 c.f.
Inclusive dates: 1949 -
Description: Reference file which includes historical materials, and a body of documentation consisting of draft reports, statements and studies related to the nuclear energy industry.

SEE: *Washington Repository Guide.*

RITZVILLE

WA747-680
Ritzville Public Library
302 W. Main Street
Ritzville WA 99169

(509) 659-1222

OPEN: M, W 2-9, Tu, Th 11-9, F 2-5; closed weekends and holidays
COPYING FACILITIES: no

HOLDINGS:
Total volume: 0.1 c.f.
Inclusive dates: 1902
Description: Display items relative to library, principally Daniel Buchanan's Act of Donation, which established the library.

SEE: *Washington Repository Guide.*

ROSALIA

WA759-680
Rosalia Battle Days Museum
W. 106 5th Street
Rosalia WA

Mailing address:
P.O. Box 277
Rosalia WA 99170

(509) 523-5991

OPEN: Tu 7-9, Th, Sa 10-1; closed other times
COPYING FACILITIES: no
MATERIALS SOLICITED: Local materials.

HOLDINGS:
Total volume: 6 c.f.
Inclusive dates: 1883 - 1927
Description: Local items, mostly business records and personal miscellany, relating to small businesses, agriculture, public education, and social conditions ca. 1880-1920.

SEE: *Washington Repository Guide.*

ROSLYN

WA761-680

Roslyn Historical Museum
28 Pennsylvania Avenue
Roslyn WA 98941

no telephone

OPEN: variable hours, depending on season
USER FEES: one dollar
COPYING FACILITIES: no
MATERIALS SOLICITED: Seeks materials from Roslyn, Washington, and upper Kittitas County.

HOLDINGS:
    Total volume: 44 vols.; 10 c.f.
    Inclusive dates: 1884 - 1940
    Description: Maps, photographs, scrapbooks and records of local businesses and associations, with the focus on the mining industry. Materials are not arranged, but are grouped in a few broad catagories.

SEE: *Washington Repository Guide.* Hines.

SEATTLE

WA820-92

The Boeing Company
Historical Services
7755 E. Marginal Way, S.
Seattle WA

Mailing address:
P.O. Box 3707
Mail Stop 1R-24
Seattle WA 98124

(206) 655-4586

OPEN: M-Th 8-2, F 2-4 by appointment; closed weekends and holidays
ACCESS: appointment required
COPYING FACILITIES: yes
MATERIALS SOLICITED: Non-current materials about the Boeing Company, its employees, and its products. Will also accept selected non-Company material.

HOLDINGS:
    Total volume: 150 c.m.; 100,000 items
    Inclusive dates: 1915 -
    Description: Business and technological records, including 100,000 photographs, of the Boeing Company, its predecessors, and subsidiary businesses.

SEE: Hinding.

WA820-147

Coast Guard Museum/Northwest
1519 Alaskan Way S. (Pier 36)
Seattle WA 98134

(206) 442-5019

OPEN: M, Tu, F 9:30-3:30; closed W, Th, Sa, Su, Christmas and New Year's Day
COPYING FACILITIES: no
MATERIALS SOLICITED: Materials related to the United States Coast Guard in the Pacific Northwest and Alaska.

HOLDINGS:
    Total volume: 16 c.f.
    Inclusive dates: 1868 -
    Description: Manuscripts, charts, photographs, and scrapbooks relating to the United States Coast Guard and its predecessor services in the Pacific Northwest and Alaska. Materials concern lighthouses, Coast Guard cutters, icebreakers, the Bering Sea Patrol, the Lifesaving Service, and the Revenue Service.

SEE: *Washington Repository Guide;* Allard, Crawley, and Edmison; Winroth.

WA820-200

Episcopal Diocese of Olympia
1551 Tenth Avenue E.
Seattle WA

Mailing address:
P.O. Box 12126
Seattle WA 98102

(206) 325-4200

OPEN: M-F 9-5
COPYING FACILITIES: yes
MATERIALS SOLICITED: Papers of prominent church-related persons.

HOLDINGS:
    Total volume: not specified
    Inclusive dates: 1879 -
    Description: Diocesan registers of ministerial acts, such as baptisms and confirmations; correspondence of John Adams Paddock, first Bishop of Washington; and records of conventions and assemblies. The repository also holds a variety of newsletters and other printed materials related to the Diocese.

SEE: *Washington Repository Guide.*

WA820-261

Foster Public Library
4205 S. 142nd
Seattle WA

Mailing address:
Box 68697
Seattle WA 98188

(206) 242-1640

OPEN: Tu, Th 12:30-8:30, F 1-5
COPYING FACILITIES: no

HOLDINGS:
    Total volume: 0.5 c.f.
    Inclusive dates: 1954 -
    Description: A small reference file contains a few items pertaining to the history of the Foster area.

SEE: *Washington Repository Guide.*

WA820-325

Historic Seattle: Preservation and Development Authority
207 1/2 1st Avenue S.
Seattle WA 98104

(206) 622-6952

OPEN: M-F 8-5; closed weekends and legal holidays

HOLDINGS:
    Total volume: 4.2 c.f.
    Inclusive dates: 1899 -
    Description: Reference files on historic buildings and properties in Seattle, and papers associated with Joshua Green and the Green House, a local landmark.

SEE: *Washington Repository Guide.*

WA820-465

Lake Forest Park Public Library
11171 Bothell Way N.E.
Seattle WA 98155

(206) 362-8860

OPEN: M, W 1-9, Tu, F 1-5, Sa 11-5
COPYING FACILITIES: no

HOLDINGS:
    Total volume: 0.5 c.f.
    Inclusive dates: 1910 (approx.) - 1972
    Description: Photographs and materials used in a master's thesis relative to the Lyon Creek (Lake Forest Park-Mountlake Terrace) area.

SEE: *Washington Repository Guide.*

WA820-550

National Archives and Records Administration
Federal Archives and Records Center
Archives Branch
6125 Sand Point Way N.E.
Seattle WA 98115

(206) 526-6507

OPEN: M-F 8-4:30; closed weekends and legal holidays
ACCESS: Records are open, subject to Federal agency restrictions and restrictions based upon current legislation relevant to confidentiality and security classification. See General Information Leaflet No. 27, 'General Restrictions on Access to Records in the National Archives of the United States.'
COPYING FACILITIES: yes
MATERIALS SOLICITED: Records of regional offices of Federal agencies in the States of Alaska, Idaho, Oregon, and Washington. Will also accept public and private records closely related to Federal records in the legal custody of the Branch.

HOLDINGS:
    Total volume: 13,966 c.f.; 26,872 microfilm reels
    Inclusive dates: 1639 -
    Description: Records of Federal agencies in the Pacific Northwest, including the Bureau of Indian Affairs, the U.S. District Courts, the 13th and 17th Naval Districts, the Bureau of Land Management, the Army Corps of Engineers, the Bureau of Customs, and the Bureau of the Mint. Additionally, the facility holds a large volume of microfilmed materials, principally from the National Archives in Washington, DC. This material reflects broad themes of American history, and the involvement of Federal agencies in the Pacific Northwest during the 19th century.

GUIDES: Richard Hobbs, comp., *Guide to the Seattle Archives Branch* (1977).

SEE: Hamer.

SEE: *Washington Repository Guide;* Allard, Crawley, and Edmison; Davis; Hinding.

SEE ALSO: Elmer W. Lindgard, 'Records of the Office of the Governor of Alaska (Territory),' *Pacific Northwest Quarterly* 53 (April 1962); G. Q. Flynn, 'The New Deal and Local Archives: The Pacific Northwest,' *American Archivist* 33 (Jan. 1970); Raymond G. McInnis, 'Opportunities for Historical Research in Washington State,' *Studies in History and Society* 1 (April 1969); James H. Hitchman, 'Primary Source Materials in Washington Maritime History,' *Pacific Northwest Quarterly* 65 (April 1974).

Preliminary inventories are available from the institution.

WA820-613

Pacific Northwest Aviation Historical Foundation
2325 Financial Center
1215 Fourth Avenue
Seattle WA 98161

no telephone

OPEN: by appointment
COPYING FACILITIES: no
MATERIALS SOLICITED: Materials related to Pacific Northwest aviation history. Will also accept materials on aviation history in general.

HOLDINGS:
　　Total volume: 440 c.f.
　　Inclusive dates: 1851 - 1970's
　　Description: Personal papers of parties related to the aviation industry in the Pacific Northwest; and photographs and technical documents concerning aircraft.

SEE: *Washington Repository Guide.*

WA820-619

Pioneer Association of Washington
1642 43rd E.
Seattle WA 98105

(206) 325-0888

OPEN: by appointment
ACCESS: permission of directors required
MATERIALS SOLICITED: Letters, papers and photographs.

HOLDINGS:
　　Total volume: 6 c.f.
　　Inclusive dates: 1868 -
　　Description: Genealogical materials, photographs, family histories, and oral reminiscences related to early settlers in Washington, especially the Seattle area.

SEE: *Washington Repository Guide.*

WA820-635

Puget Sound Maritime Historical Society
2700 24th E.
Seattle WA 98112

(206) 324-1125

OPEN: Tu-F 11-5, Sa 10-3; closed Sundays and Mondays
ACCESS: permission required

COPYING FACILITIES: yes
MATERIALS SOLICITED: Puget Sound maritime history.

HOLDINGS:
　　Total volume: 100 c.f.
　　Inclusive dates: 1885 -
　　Description: Photographs, reference files, logbooks, ledgers, and similar materials concerning maritime history of Puget Sound, the coastal Pacific Northwest, and Alaska.

SEE: *Washington Repository Guide.*

SEE ALSO: James H. Hitchman, 'Primary Source Materials in Washington Maritime History,' *Pacific Northwest Quarterly* 65 (April 1974).

WA820-653

Richmond Beach Public Library
2402 N.W. 195th Place
Seattle WA 98177

(206) 546-3522

OPEN: M, Tu 1-9, Th 1-6, Sa 12:30-5; closed other days
COPYING FACILITIES: no

HOLDINGS:
　　Total volume: 4 vols.; .7 c.f.
　　Inclusive dates: 1910 -
　　Description: A historical reference file, which includes records of the library board, along with scrapbooks and similar materials from local voluntary associations.

SEE: *Washington Repository Guide.*

WA820-715

Seattle Central Community College Library
1701 Broadway
Seattle WA 98122

(206) 587-4050

OPEN: M-Th 7:30-9, F 7:30-4:30, Sa 8-2
COPYING FACILITIES: yes

HOLDINGS:
　　Total volume: 0.5 c.f.
　　Inclusive dates: 1965 -
　　Description: The library of this two-year college maintains a historical file relative to college affairs.

SEE: *Washington Repository Guide.*

WA820-770

Seattle Historical Society
Museum of History and Industry
Sophie Frye Bass Memorial Library
2700 24th Avenue E.
Seattle WA 98112

(206) 324-1125

OPEN: Tu-F 11-5, Sa 10-5
ACCESS: an appointment is advised
COPYING FACILITIES: yes
MATERIALS SOLICITED: Materials on Seattle and King County history, Alaska, western Washington, British Columbia, maritime subjects, northern Pacific exploration, and other western topics.

HOLDINGS:
　　Total volume: 120 c.f.
　　Inclusive dates: 1850 -
　　Description: Materials relating primarily to Seattle and King County, and to a lesser extent to Alaska, western Washington, British Columbia, maritime history, exploration in the Northern Pacific, and other topics in western history. Included is a photograph collection relating to Puget Sound and Alaska, ledgers, ships' logbooks, and materials on Seattle pioneers. A large number of Seattle-area scrapbooks are also included in the holdings.

SEE: *Washington Repository Guide;* Hinding; Novotny; Winroth.

SEE ALSO: James H. Hitchman, 'Primary Source Materials in Washington Maritime History,' *Pacific Northwest Quarterly* 65 (April 1974); *Bicentennial Photo Reproduction Project Index* (1976).

WA820-772

Seattle Pacific University
Weter Memorial Library
Omar Allen Burns Room
3307 Third Avenue W.
Seattle WA 98119

(206) 281-2228

OPEN: M-F 9-5; closed weekends and legal holidays
COPYING FACILITIES: yes
MATERIALS SOLICITED: Will accept materials related to the University, and to Free Methodist church history.

HOLDINGS:
　　Total volume: 32 c.f.
　　Inclusive dates: 1853 -
　　Description: Principal holdings are historical reference materials of Seattle Pacific University, founded in 1892 as Seattle Seminary, a Free Methodist affiliated college. Holdings also include papers of persons affiliated with the school and with Northwest methodism.

SEE: *Washington Repository Guide.*

WA820-774

Seattle Public Library
1000 Fourth Avenue
Seattle WA 98104

(206) 625-2665

OPEN: M-Th 9-9, F, Sa 9-6; closed Sundays and holidays
COPYING FACILITIES: yes
MATERIALS SOLICITED: Will accept materials compatible with existing holdings.

HOLDINGS:
　　Total volume: 150 c.f.
　　Inclusive dates: 1800 -
　　Description: Holdings include scrapbooks concerned with Seattle-related topics, records of civic associations, such as the Seattle Chamber of Commerce, personal papers of literary figures, musical and theatrical materials, the Lenggenhager photographs of historic structures, and a variety of pioneer accounts and genealogical materials.

SEE: Hamer; NUCMC, 1959-61.

SEE: *Washington Repository Guide;* Hinding; Novotny; Winroth.

Materials are located in the following Library departments: Literature, History, Technology, Art, Map, and Music.

WA820-775
Seattle Public Library
Municipal Reference Library
600 Fourth Avenue
Seattle WA 98104

(206) 625-2853

OPEN: by appointment
COPYING FACILITIES: yes

HOLDINGS:
> *Total volume:* 135 c.f.
> *Inclusive dates:* 1884 -
> *Description:* Minutes, reports, budgets, planning papers, maps, and similar documents concerning municipal government in the greater Seattle area, including materials from voluntary associations closely affiliated with the city government.

SEE: *Washington Repository Guide.*

WA820-780
Seattle University
Jesuit Residence Archives
Loyola Building
Seattle WA 98122

(206) 626-6485

OPEN: M-F 8-5; closed weekends and legal holidays
ACCESS: use restricted to applicants approved by representatives of the Society of Jesus
COPYING FACILITIES: yes

HOLDINGS:
> *Total volume:* 50 c.f.
> *Inclusive dates:* 1880 - 1970
> *Description:* Records of the Society of Jesus at Seattle, and personal papers of individual members of the Society, along with a theatrical collection and Seattle fire insurance maps.

SEE: *Washington Repository Guide.*

WA820-810
Shoreline Historical Museum
  Association
N. 175th and Linden
Seattle WA

Mailing address:
P.O. Box 7171
Seattle WA 98133

(206) 542-7111

OPEN: Th, F 10-4, Sa, Su 1-4; closed M, Tu, W and holidays
COPYING FACILITIES: no
MATERIALS SOLICITED: Materials relevant to the history of the Shoreline area.

HOLDINGS:
> *Total volume:* 10 c.f.
> *Inclusive dates:* 1895 - 1977
> *Description:* Photographs, historical reference materials, records of a civic group, of a parent-teacher association and

of public schools, all relative to the Shoreline region, which consists of the communities of Richmond Beach, Lago Vista, Lake Forest Park, Ronald, Happy Valley, Echo Lake, and Innis Arden.

SEE: *Washington Repository Guide.*

WA820-815
Shoreline Public Library
345 N.E. 175th Street
Seattle WA 98133

(206) 362-7550

OPEN: M-Th 10-9, F, Sa 10-6
COPYING FACILITIES: yes

HOLDINGS:
> *Total volume:* 1 c.f.
> *Inclusive dates:* 1957 -
> *Description:* The library maintains a historical reference file of pamphlets, draft writings and other materials relative to the Shoreline region.

SEE: *Washington Repository Guide.*

WA820-820
Sisters of Providence
Sacred Heart Province Archives
4800 37th Avenue S.W.
Seattle WA 98126

no telephone

OPEN: by appointment
COPYING FACILITIES: yes
MATERIALS SOLICITED: Materials concerning inactive missions, hospitals, and schools operated by the community, and the lives of individual sisters.

HOLDINGS:
> *Total volume:* 312 c.f.
> *Inclusive dates:* 1856 -
> *Description:* Records of this religious community in Washington, Alaska, Oregon, and California, and of hospitals, schools, and social welfare institutions operated by the community, personal papers of individual sisters, principally Mother Joseph, leader of the community in the 19th Century.

SEE: *Washington Repository Guide;* Hinding.

SEE ALSO: Unpublished finding aids available at the institution.

WA820-824
Snoqualmie and Mount
  BakerNational Forest
Recreation Cultural Visual Resources
  Division
1022 First Avenue
Seattle WA 98104

(206) 442-5400

OPEN: M-F 8-4:30

HOLDINGS:
> *Total volume:* 12 c.f.
> *Inclusive dates:* 1900 -
> *Description:* Reference materials concerning historic and archaeological features of the Snoqualmie and Mount Baker National Forests, including photographs, oral history recordings, Forest Service diaries, and other materials.

SEE: *Washington Repository Guide.*

WA820-828
Steamer Virginia V Foundation, Inc.
4250 21st Avenue W.
Seattle WA 98199

no telephone

OPEN: by appointment
MATERIALS SOLICITED: Materials dealing with the *Virginia V.*

HOLDINGS:
> *Total volume:* 3 c.f.
> *Inclusive dates:* 1911 -
> *Description:* Operating records, builder's drawings, and photographs of the *Virginia V,* a vessel of the Puget Sound 'mosquito fleet,' which is being restored by the foundation.

SEE: *Washington Repository Guide.*

WA820-840
The Thomas Burke Memorial
  Washington State Museum
DB-10
University of Washington
Seattle WA 98195

(206) 543-5590

OPEN: Su, Tu-F 10-4:30, Sa noon-4:30; closed Mondays and holidays
MATERIALS SOLICITED: Seeks archaeological and ethnological materials. Will also accept materials of prominent Pacific Northwest families.

HOLDINGS:
> *Total volume:* 156 c.f.
> *Inclusive dates:* 1830 -
> *Description:* Holdings consist of a variety of research materials, including photographs, related to anthropological and ethnological investigations among native peoples of North America and the Pacific.

SEE: *Washington Repository Guide;* Winroth.

SEE ALSO: Richard I. Ford, *Systematic Research Collections in Anthropology: An Irreplaceable Resource* (Peabody Museum, 1977).

WA820-880
University of Washington
Libraries
Manuscripts and University Archives
  Division
Seattle WA 98195

(206) 543-1879

OPEN: M-F 8-5; closed weekends and holidays
COPYING FACILITIES: yes
MATERIALS SOLICITED: Urban history and problems; specific communities and geographic areas, primarily in the Pacific Northwest; ethnic history, particularly of Afro-Americans, Chinese-Americans, Filipino-Americans, American Indians, Japanese-Americans, Mexican-Americans, Scandinavian-Americans, and other Asian and European groups of importance in Washington; organized labor; business; literature; art; public administration; poli-

tics; education; and religion. Will also accept oral histories and copied material; photographic materials are referred to the Library's Special Collections Division.

HOLDINGS:
> *Total volume:* 13,000 l.f.
> *Inclusive dates:* 1450 -
> *Description:* Over 2,600 collections, chiefly relating to the Pacific Northwest, especially western Washington. Materials focus on the following subjects: politics, public administration, urbanization, electric power development, mining, railroads, forest industries, international fisheries, environmental issues, labor movements, ethnic minorities, and the arts.

GUIDES: Marilyn Priestley, comp., *Comprehensive Guide to the Manuscripts Collection and to the Personal Papers in the University Archives* (1980).

SEE: Hamer; NUCMC, 1959-67, 69, 71, 76.

SEE: *Washington Repository Guide;* Allard, Crawley, and Edmison; Bean and Vane; Davis; Hinding; Hounshell; Meckler and McMullin; Robbins; Schatz.

SEE ALSO: James H. Hitchman, 'Primary Source Materials in Washington Maritime History,' *Pacific Northwest Quarterly* 65 (April 1974); 'The Manuscript Collection of the University of Washington Libraries,' *University of Washington Libraries Library Leaflet,* No. 1 (Nov. 1967); Joan Hoff Wilson and Lynn B. Donovan, 'Women's History: A Listing of West Coast Archival and Manuscript Sources, Part II,' *California Historical Quarterly* 55 (Summer 1976).

Terry Abraham, comp., *Union List of the Papers of Members of Congress from the Pacific Northwest* (Washington State Univ. Library, 1976); Richard C. Berner, 'Sources for Research in Forest History: The University of Washington Manuscripts Collection,' *Business History Review* 35 (Autumn 1961); G. Q. Flynn, 'The New Deal and Local Archives: The Pacific Northwest,' *American Archivist* 33 (Jan. 1970); James R. McLeod, *Theodore Roethke, A Manuscript Checklist* (Kent State Univ. Press, 1971).

Finding aids to individual collections are available at the library. Finding aids for six collections have been published.

WA820-883
University of Washington
Libraries
Manuscripts and University Archives
Division
University Archives
3902 Cowlitz Road, N.E.
Seattle WA 98195

(206) 543-6509

OPEN: M-F 8-5; closed weekends and legal holidays
ACCESS: access is open according to the guidelines of public records laws and privacy legislation
COPYING FACILITIES: yes

MATERIALS SOLICITED: Records of the University of Washington and affiliated organizations.

HOLDINGS:
> *Total volume:* 800 c.f.
> *Inclusive dates:* 1860 -
> *Description:* Inactive university records, along with records of some affiliated campus organizations. The personal papers of many university employees are also maintained within this section.

SEE: *Washington Repository Guide.*

SEE ALSO: Marilyn Priestley, comp., *Comprehensive Guide to the Manuscripts Collection and to the Personal Papers in the University Archives* (1980).

Finding aids for individual record groups are available at the archives.

WA820-886
University of Washington
Libraries
East Asia Library
Gowen Hall DO-27
Seattle WA 98195

(206) 543-4490

OPEN: Su-F 8-10, Sa 12-4; closed on legal holidays
COPYING FACILITIES: yes
MATERIALS SOLICITED: Will accept materials pertaining to East Asia.

HOLDINGS:
> *Total volume:* 3.1 c.f.
> *Inclusive dates:* early twentieth century
> *Description:* Holdings consist of materials of the Chinese Empire Reform Association, a Chinese-American organization with chapters throughout the western United States.

SEE: *Washington Repository Guide.*

WA820-889
University of Washington
Law School Library
Condon Hall JB-20
Seattle WA 98195

(206) 543-4089

OPEN: M-F 8-5; closed weekends and legal holidays
COPYING FACILITIES: yes
MATERIALS SOLICITED: Biographical material concerning Washington lawyers and judges.

HOLDINGS:
> *Total volume:* 25 c.f.
> *Inclusive dates:* 1850's -
> *Description:* An unpublished history of the Washington bar by Arthur Beardsley and a biographical reference file on lawyers and judges of Washington.

SEE: Hamer; NUCMC, 1962.

SEE: *Washington Repository Guide;* Novotny.

WA820-892
University of Washington
Libraries
Special Collections Division
Suzzallo Library
University of Washington
Seattle WA 98195

(206) 543-1929

OPEN: M-F 10-5, Sa 1-5; closed Sundays and holidays
COPYING FACILITIES: yes
MATERIALS SOLICITED: History of photography in the American West, particularly in the Pacific Northwest, including original prints and negatives, as well as documentation of the introduction and development of photography, photographic equipment, and techniques, and also of individual photographers. Will also accept manuscript monographs on historical photography and the work of photographers of the 19th century and the American West, and other materials complementing existing holdings.

HOLDINGS:
> *Total volume:* 350 c.f.
> *Inclusive dates:* 1860 -
> *Description:* Primary components within the Division's holdings include the Historical Photography Collection, emphasizing the Pacific Northwest and Alaska; a scrapbook collection of similar scope; the Architectural Plans and Drawings Collection, chiefly concerning Seattle and the Puget Sound area; and other historical reference materials such as clippings files and quasi-published materials held within the Pacific Northwest Collection.

SEE: *Washington Repository Guide;* Novotny; Winroth; Mehr.

SEE ALSO: Ann Novotny, ed., *Picture Sources 3* (Special Libraries Assn., 1975).

WA820-893
University of Washington
Instructional Media Services (DG-10)
23 Kane Hall
Seattle WA 98195

(206) 543-9906

The University of Washington no longer maintains the Phonoarchives. The original discs have been deposited at the National Archives and Records Service, entry DC14-250, and duplicates deposited at the Federal Archives and Records Center, **WA820-550.**

WA820-895
University of Washington
School of Medicine
Department of Biomedical History
SB-20
Seattle WA 98105

(206) 543-5447

OPEN: M-F 8-5; closed weekends and legal holidays

MATERIALS SOLICITED: Materials pertaining to biomedical history.

HOLDINGS:
Total volume: 4 c.f.
Inclusive dates: 1920's -
Description: The department offers classes in biomedical history, and maintains historical reference materials as part of its program.

SEE: *Washington Repository Guide.*

WA820-966
Wing Luke Memorial Museum
414 Eighth Avenue South
Seattle WA 98104

(206) 623-5124

OPEN: Tu-F 11-4:30
ACCESS: permission of director required
COPYING FACILITIES: no
MATERIALS SOLICITED: Materials relating to the history of the Chinese in the Pacific Northwest.

HOLDINGS:
Total volume: 5 c.f.
Inclusive dates: 1895 -
Description: Family photographs, Boy Scout scrapbooks, immigration documents, and miscellaneous materials, relating to Chinese in the Pacific Northwest, principally Seattle.

SEE: *Washington Repository Guide.*

SEDRO WOOLLEY

WA832-560
North Cascades National Park
800 State Street
Sedro Woolley WA 98284

(206) 855-1331

OPEN: M-F 8:30-4:30
MATERIALS SOLICITED: Anything on the early history of the area administered by the National Park Service.

HOLDINGS:
Total volume: 2 c.f.
Inclusive dates: 1859 - 1972
Description: The National Park maintains scientific and historical records, including oral histories, personal papers, photographs, and government records.

SEE: *Washington Repository Guide.*

SEE ALSO: Karyl Winn, ed., *North Cascades Archival Resources in Washington State Repositories* (University of Washington, 1974).

SEQUIM

WA836-740
Sequim-Dungeness Museum
175 W. Cedar
Sequim WA

Mailing address:
P.O. Box 1002
Sequim WA 98382

(206) 682-8110

OPEN: by appointment

COPYING FACILITIES: no
HOLDINGS:
Total volume: 5 c.f.
Inclusive dates: 1859 -
Description: Area photographs and maps, inactive voters' registers, scrapbooks, and an autograph book from Iowa.

SEE: *Washington Repository Guide.*

SHAW ISLAND

WA844-720
Shaw Island Library and Historical Society
Shaw Island WA 98296

no telephone

OPEN: M, W, Sa 2-4; closed other days
USER FEES: one dollar (annual membership fee)
ACCESS: members of the Society
COPYING FACILITIES: no
MATERIALS SOLICITED: Materials pertinent to the history of Shaw Island. Will also accept manuscripts dealing with the history of the San Juan Islands.

HOLDINGS:
Total volume: 6 l.f.
Inclusive dates: 1870 -
Description: Grange records, ferry schedules, school records, pioneer letters, and a collection of photographs, all relating to the history of Shaw Island.

SHELTON

WA845-720
Shelton Public Library
Shelton WA 98584

(206) 426-3512

OPEN: M, W, F 10-5, Tu, Th, Sa 10-7
COPYING FACILITIES: yes
MATERIALS SOLICITED: Mason County history and activities.

HOLDINGS:
Total volume: 3.2 c.f.
Inclusive dates: 1890's -
Description: Holdings consists of a local history file, writings, newspaper clippings, and maps.

SEE: *Washington Repository Guide.*

SILVERDALE

WA848-440
Kitsap County Historical Society
3343 N.W. Byron Street
Silverdale WA 98383

(206) 692-1949

OPEN: daily 1-4
COPYING FACILITIES: no
MATERIALS SOLICITED: Kitsap County history; will also accept other historical items.

HOLDINGS:
Total volume: 65 c.f.
Inclusive dates: 1855 -
Description: Photographs, scrapbooks, county government records, personal papers, business records, community organization records, and a large reference file, all chiefly from Kitsap County and the Kitsap Peninsula.

SEE: *Washington Repository Guide;* Winroth.

WA848-720
Silverdale Public Library
Carlton Street
Silverdale WA

Mailing address:
P.O. Box 1068
Silverdale WA 98383

(206) 692-2779

OPEN: M, W 1-9, F 9-5, Sa 1-5
COPYING FACILITIES: no

HOLDINGS:
Total volume: 2 vols.
Inclusive dates: 1920's -
Description: Library scrapbooks and a commemorative scrapbook for a Silverdale school teacher.

SEE: *Washington Repository Guide.*

SNOHOMISH

WA855-80
Snohomish Historical Society
Blackman Museum
118 Avenue B
Snohomish WA

Mailing address:
P.O. Box 174
Snohomish WA 98290

(206) 568-5400

OPEN: Sa, Su 12-4; closed Easter and Christmas
COPYING FACILITIES: no
MATERIALS SOLICITED: All material relating to the history of Snohomish.

HOLDINGS:
Total volume: 12 vols.; 5.6 c.f.
Inclusive dates: 1853 -
Description: The museum maintains a collection including Snohomish, Washington, oral histories, club records, scrapbooks, photographs, and also a study of the Snohomish Indians.

SEE: *Washington Repository Guide;* Winroth.

WA855-735
Snohomish Public Library
1st and Cedar
Snohomish WA 98290

(206) 568-2898

OPEN: M-F 2-9, Sa 10-5; closed Sundays and legal holidays
COPYING FACILITIES: no

HOLDINGS:
> *Total volume:* 21.6 c.f.; 3 vols.
> *Inclusive dates:* 1885 -
> *Description:* Library records and a 19th century diary from Illinois.

SEE: *Washington Repository Guide.*

SNOQUALMIE

WA856-100
Puget Sound Railroad Historical
  Association
109 King Street
P.O. Box 459
Snoqualmie WA 98065

Mailing address:
1709 204th Place S.E.
Maple Valley WA 98038

(206) 746-4025
ACCESS: permission of curator required
COPYING FACILITIES: no

HOLDINGS:
> *Total volume:* 4 cartons
> *Inclusive dates:* 1940's - 1950's
> *Description:* Records of a local Brotherhood of Firemen and Engineers.

SEE: *Washington Repository Guide.*

SOAP LAKE

WA857-720
Soap Lake Public Library
32 Main Street E.
Soap Lake WA

Mailing address:
P.O. Box 86
Soap Lake WA 98851

(509) 246-1313

OPEN: Tu, W 12:30-9, Th 12:30-5, F, Sa 1-5; closed Su, M and holidays
COPYING FACILITIES: no

HOLDINGS:
> *Total volume:* 7 vols.; .2 c.f.
> *Inclusive dates:* 1956 -
> *Description:* Draft history of the community and scrapbooks reflecting the town's public issues.

SEE: *Washington Repository Guide.*

SOUTH BEND

WA859-650
Pacific County Historical Society
Pacific County Museum
1008 W. Robert Bush Drive
South Bend WA

Mailing address:
P.O. Box P
South Bend WA 98586

(206) 875-5224

OPEN: daily 12-4 by appointment; closed Christmas and Thanksgiving
ACCESS: advance arrangement necessary
COPYING FACILITIES: no

MATERIALS SOLICITED: Pacific County history; will also accept materials relative to the history of southwestern Washington in general.

HOLDINGS:
> *Total volume:* 55 c.f.
> *Inclusive dates:* 1849 -
> *Description:* Pacific County business records, community organization records, maps, personal papers, photographs, public records, and scrapbooks.

SEE: *Washington Repository Guide.*

SPOKANE

WA880-120
Catholic Diocese of Spokane
Chancery Archives
West 1023 Riverside Avenue
Spokane WA

Mailing address:
P.O. Box 1453
Spokane WA 99210

(509) 456-7100

OPEN: by appointment
USER FEES: $5 per hour for genealogical records; no charge for other materials
ACCESS: permission required
COPYING FACILITIES: yes
MATERIALS SOLICITED: Materials relating to church history in the Pacific Northwest. Will also accept manuscript journals and diaries of Oregon Trail and other early pioneer settlers.

HOLDINGS:
> *Total volume:* 500 vols.; 5,000 microfilm reels
> *Inclusive dates:* 1847 - 1956
> *Description:* Materials dealing with the history of the Catholic church in the Pacific Northwest since 1837, specifically with the Catholic Diocese of Spokane since 1914. The records include materials relating to the State of Washington east of the Columbia River from the Canadian to the Oregon borders.

WA880-190
Eastern Washington State Historical
  Society
Library
W. 2316 First Avenue
Spokane WA 99204

(509) 456-3931

OPEN: Tu-Sa 10-5; closed Sundays, Mondays, and legal holidays
COPYING FACILITIES: yes
MATERIALS SOLICITED: The Society's charter directs it to collect and purchase materials illustrative of the history of Washington, especially concerning the area from the Idaho border to the ridge of the Cascade Mountains.

HOLDINGS:
> *Total volume:* 800 c.f.
> *Inclusive dates:* 1700's -
> *Description:* Manuscript and photographic material relative to Northwest history, especially of eastern Washington. Includes correspondence, diaries, reminiscences, and photographs of early settlers, authors, political figures, and

prominent persons, as well as business records, many relating to the founding and development of Spokane and other inland Northwest cities, and to mining and hydrology. Portions of the holdings are organized into a biographic reference file, arranged in a sequence separate from that of the manuscript collections. The library also holds materials related to Northwest Indians.

SEE: Hamer; NUCMC, 1959-64, 66, 71, 77.

SEE: *Washington Repository Guide;* Davis; Hinding; Hines; Winroth.

SEE ALSO: Raymond G. McInnis, 'Opportunities for Historical Research in Washington State,' *Studies in History and Society* 1 (April 1969).

Inventories of individual collections are available at the library.

WA880-260
Fort Wright College
Historical Museum
W. 4000 Randolph Road
Spokane WA

Mailing address:
P.O. Box 7496
Spokane WA 99207

(509) 328-2970, Ext. 38

OPEN: Sa, Su 1-5, and by appointment
COPYING FACILITIES: no
MATERIALS SOLICITED: Spokane social and military history; will also accept other offerings.

HOLDINGS:
> *Total volume:* 19 c.f.
> *Inclusive dates:* 1800 - 1976
> *Description:* Photographs and architectural drawings of Fort George Wright, personal papers of Spokane residents, Civil War and ante-bellum South papers, and Spokane local government records.

SEE: *Washington Repository Guide;* Winroth.

WA880-280
Gonzaga University
Crosby Library
Oregon Province Archives of the
  Society of Jesus
E. 502 Boone Avenue
Spokane WA 99258

(509) 328-4220

OPEN: M-Th 8:30-5, F 8:30-2; closed weekends and legal holidays
ACCESS: advance arrangements required
COPYING FACILITIES: yes
MATERIALS SOLICITED: Material concerning Catholic missions and the Society of Jesus in the Oregon and Alaska provinces; will also accept Northwest history materials.

HOLDINGS:
> *Total volume:* 350 c.f.
> *Inclusive dates:* 1843 -
> *Description:* Materials relating chiefly to Jesuit missionary activities in Alaska, Idaho, Montana, Oregon, Washington, and Wyoming. Included are correspondence between missionaries and Roman

Catholic church and U.S. government officials, diaries and reports of missions, personal diaries and notes, 20,000 photographs, 50 reels of motion picture film (primarily of Alaska), and papers of laypeople, including Spokane pioneers.

SEE: Hamer.

SEE: *Washington Repository Guide;* Hines; Winroth.

SEE ALSO: Thomas T. McAvoy, 'Catholic Archives and Manuscript Collections,' (materials transferred from Mount St. Michael's to Oregon Province Archives) *American Archivist* 24 (Oct. 1961).

WA880-290

Gonzaga University
Crosby Library
Rare Book and Manuscript Collection
E. 502 Boone Avenue
Spokane WA 99258

(509) 328-4220, Ext. 343

OPEN: M-F 8-5; closed weekends and legal holidays
ACCESS: permission of library director required
COPYING FACILITIES: yes
MATERIALS SOLICITED: Materials complementing existing holdings.

HOLDINGS:
Total volume: 27 l.f.
Inclusive dates: 1876 -
Description: Papers of James Edward O'Sullivan relating to irrigation in eastern Washington, papers of Hector Chevigny concerning the history of Russian America, and memorabilia of Harry Lillis (Bing) Crosby.

SEE: NUCMC, 1959-61.

SEE: *Washington Repository Guide.*

WA880-370

Inland Empire Railway Historical
Society
Columbia Cycle Shop
N. 1818 Monroe
Spokane WA

Mailing address:
P.O. Box 4537
Spokane WA 99202

(509) 327-1465

OPEN: by appointment
COPYING FACILITIES: no
MATERIALS SOLICITED: Railway related material.

HOLDINGS:
Total volume: 32.5 c.f.
Inclusive dates: 1890's -
Description: Materials relating to railroads, principally in the inland northwest.

SEE: *Washington Repository Guide.*

WA880-495

Lincoln Mutual Savings Bank
Washington Mutual Lincoln Division
Lincoln Plaza
W. 818 Riverside
Spokane WA 99201

(509) 838-3101

OPEN: M-Th 9-4, F 9-6; closed weekends and holidays
COPYING FACILITIES: no

HOLDINGS:
Total volume: 2 c.f.
Inclusive dates: 1839 - 1906
Description: Photographs, letters, legal documents, and printed materials related to the life of Abraham Lincoln.

SEE: *Washington Repository Guide.*

WA880-550

Museum of Native American Cultures
E. 200 Cataldo
Spokane WA 99202

(509) 326-4550

OPEN: M-Sa 9-5:30, Su noon-5:30; closed holidays
ACCESS: qualified researchers only; prior arrangements recommended
COPYING FACILITIES: yes
MATERIALS SOLICITED: Materials relating to Northwest Indians.

HOLDINGS:
Total volume: 4 c.f.
Inclusive dates: 1830's - 1900 (approx.)
Description: Indian language materials, associated primarily with Catholic missions in the Pacific Northwest and northern Rocky Mountains.

SEE: *Washington Repository Guide;* Hines.

WA880-590

Northwest Regional Foundation
E. 525 Mission Avenue
Spokane WA 99202-1824

(509) 484-6733

OPEN: M-F 9-5; closed weekends and legal holidays
COPYING FACILITIES: yes
MATERIALS SOLICITED: Ephemera and drafts of writings/speeches relative to futurism, alternative lifestyles and technology, citizen involvement, networks, energy and natural resources, and environmental concerns.

HOLDINGS:
Total volume: 37 c.f.
Inclusive dates: 1950's -
Description: Reference file of ephemera, drafts, and some manuscript material concerning futurism and related matters, as well as some records related to the Spokane International Exposition (EXPO '74).

SEE: *Washington Repository Guide.*

WA880-710

Sisters of Providence
St. Ignatius Province
Archives
West 12 Ninth Avenue
Spokane WA 99204

(509) 838-2594, Ext. 21

OPEN: M-F 8-4; closed weekends
COPYING FACILITIES: yes
MATERIALS SOLICITED: Diaries, biographical data, school records, histories of institutions, and photographs relating to the history of the Sisters of Providence in eastern Washington, Idaho, and Montana.

HOLDINGS:
Total volume: 500 items
Inclusive dates: 1843 -
Description: A collection relating to the Sisters of Providence in eastern Washington, Idaho, and Montana, covering religious, political, social and economic subjects. Included are records of institutions maintained by the Sisters, unpublished theses, and audio-visual materials.

WA880-753

Sisters of the Holy Names of Jesus
and Mary Convent
Archives
W. 2911 Fort Wright Drive
Spokane WA 99204

(509) 328-4310

OPEN: M-F 9-4:30; other times by appointment
ACCESS: permission required
COPYING FACILITIES: no

HOLDINGS:
Total volume: 68 vols.; 37 c.f.
Inclusive dates: 1880's -
Description: Chronicles, clippings, photographs, and miscellaneous business records of the Community of the Sisters of the Holy Names at Spokane, Pomeroy, and Uniontown, relating to their work as teachers and to their other activities.

SEE: *Washington Repository Guide.*

Some records are transferred to the order's Oregon Province Archives, Marylhurst, Oregon.

WA880-775

Spokane Public Library
W. 906 Main
Spokane WA 99201

(509) 838-3361

OPEN: M, Tu, Th 9-9, W 1-6, F, Sa 9-6; closed Sa June-Sept., Su all year
ACCESS: use of most material is contingent on library permission, which is routinely granted
COPYING FACILITIES: yes
MATERIALS SOLICITED: Genealogical materials in concert with Eastern Washington Genealogical Society; Northwest history materials, including oral history tapes, and manuscript collections of manageable quantity.

HOLDINGS:
> *Total volume:* 38 c.f.
> *Inclusive dates:* 1834 - 1975
> *Description:* Miscellaneous Northwest public and private records, mostly single-item or fragmentary collections or groups. Many items are relative to Northwest Indian missions and Indian wars. The library also works in concert with the Eastern Washington Genealogical Society and its efforts to amass holdings of the Genealogical Room.

SEE: Hamer.

SEE: *Washington Repository Guide;* Hinding; Meckler and McMullin; Winroth.

WA880-790

Spokane Valley Historical Society
Spokane WA

Mailing address:
c/o Virginia Straughn
Greenacres WA 99016

(509) 926-3581

OPEN: by appointment

HOLDINGS:
> *Total volume:* 2.5 c.f.
> *Inclusive dates:* 1861 -
> *Description:* Chiefly reminiscences and scrapbooks from the Spokane Valley. There is also an 1861 diary of an overland journey to California.

SEE: *Washington Repository Guide.*

SPRAGUE

WA881-740

Sprague Public Library
2nd & C Streets
Sprague WA

Mailing address:
P.O. Box 264
Sprague WA 99032

(509) 257-2662

OPEN: M-F 9-5
COPYING FACILITIES: no

HOLDINGS:
> *Total volume:* 0.3 c.f.
> *Inclusive dates:* 1889 - 1940
> *Description:* One pioneer letter and one statement of reminiscences.

SEE: *Washington Repository Guide.*

STANWOOD

WA885-720

Stanwood Historical Society
Pearson House
Stanwood WA

Mailing address:
P.O. Box 69
Stanwood WA 98292

no telephone

OPEN: Su 2-4
COPYING FACILITIES: no

MATERIALS SOLICITED: Material relating to the history and development of Stanwood.

HOLDINGS:
> *Total volume:* 50 vols.; .5 c.f.
> *Inclusive dates:* 1884 - 1930's
> *Description:* Photographs of local origin, general store records, and a local voter register.

SEE: *Washington Repository Guide.*

STEILACOOM

WA889-560

Nathaniel Orr House
1811 Rainier Street
Steilacoom WA

MAILING ADDRESS:
P.O. Box 16
Steilacoom WA 98388

(206) 588-8115

OPEN: by appointment
ACCESS: at the discretion of the Steilacoom Historical Museum Association
MATERIALS SOLICITED: Materials relating to the Orr family.

HOLDINGS:
> *Total volume:* 6 c.f.
> *Inclusive dates:* 1879 - 1974
> *Description:* Letters, clippings, blueprints, construction plans, photos, postcards, bank books, and pamphlets of the Orr family, Steilacoom pioneers and owners of this historic building.

SEE: *Washington Repository Guide.*

WA889-720

Steilacoom Historical Museum
  Association
Main Street
Steilacoom WA

MAILING ADDRESS:
P.O. Box 16
Steilacoom WA 98388

(206) 588-8115

OPEN: by appointment only
COPYING FACILITIES: no
MATERIALS SOLICITED: Steilacoom area history.

HOLDINGS:
> *Total volume:* 40 c.f.
> *Inclusive dates:* 1835 -
> *Description:* Photographs, maps, correspondence, writings on Steilacoom history, club scrapbooks and minutes of clubs, Indian language vocabularies and writings, an original letter by Narcissa Whitman, records of Steilacoom businesses and local public agencies, and family papers of Steilacoom pioneers.

SEE: *Washington Repository Guide.*

WA889-880

Western State Hospital
Library
Interpretive Center
Steilacoom Boulevard
Steilacoom WA 98388

(206) 756-2518

OPEN: by appointment
MATERIALS SOLICITED: Western State Hospital; early treatment of the mentally ill.

HOLDINGS:
> *Total volume:* 34 c.f.
> *Inclusive dates:* 1803 -
> *Description:* Photographs, reports, newspaper clippings, publications, maps, correspondence, and other materials documenting the history of the hospital and the care of the mentally ill.

SEE: *Washington Repository Guide.*

STEVENSON

WA892-725

Skamania County Historical Society
Skamania County Historical Museum
Courthouse Annex
Vancouver Avenue
Stevenson WA

MAILING ADDRESS:
P.O. Box 396
Stevenson WA 98648

(509) 427-5141, Ext. 218

OPEN: Th, F 12-5 by appointment; closed holidays
COPYING FACILITIES: yes
MATERIALS SOLICITED: Skamania County and Columbia River history.

HOLDINGS:
> *Total volume:* 30 c.f.
> *Inclusive dates:* 1804 -
> *Description:* Public records, oral history tapes, photographs, government studies, and maps pertaining to Stevenson, Skamania County, the Columbia River, and its tributaries.

SEE: *Washington Repository Guide;* Winroth.

SUMAS

WA896-720

Sumas Public Library
Sumas WA 98295

(206) 988-2501

OPEN: M-W, Sa 1-5; closed legal holidays
COPYING FACILITIES: no

HOLDINGS:
> *Total volume:* 3 vols.
> *Inclusive dates:* 1891 - 1976
> *Description:* Library records and manuscript histories of Sumas, Washington.

SEE: *Washington Repository Guide.*

SUMNER

WA898-740

Sumner Historical Society
1228 Main Street
Sumner WA

MAILING ADDRESS:
P.O. Box 517
Sumner WA 98390

(206) 863-8936, 5567

OPEN: Sa, Su 1-4; closed Nov.-March
MATERIALS SOLICITED: Sumner pioneer
family materials; will also accept other
historical items.

HOLDINGS:
   Total volume: 3 vols.
   Inclusive dates: 1855 - 1960's
   Description: Scrapbooks of Sumner
area historical reference materials.

SEE: *Washington Repository Guide.*

WA898-820

Sumner Public Library
1228 Main
Sumner WA 98390

(206) 863-0441

OPEN: M, Th-Sa 12-5, Tu 12-8
COPYING FACILITIES: yes
MATERIALS SOLICITED: Local historical
material referred to the Sumner Historical Society.

HOLDINGS:
   Total volume: 3 c.f.
   Inclusive dates: 1889 -
   Description: Reference file for local
history, several genealogies, and records
of the library, which is now part of the
Pierce County Library System.

SUNNYSIDE

WA900-730

Sunnyside Museum
704 S. 4th
Sunnyside WA

MAILING ADDRESS:
P.O. Box 782
Sunnyside WA 98944

(509) 837-6010

OPEN: Su, Tu, Th 1:30-4:30
COPYING FACILITIES: no

HOLDINGS:
   Total volume: 3.5 c.f.
   Inclusive dates: 1898 -
   Description: Various local materials,
assembled into three collections: photo-
graphs, scrapbooks, and correspondence.

SEE: *Washington Repository Guide; Hines.*

TACOMA

WA904-50

Archives of Pacific Northwest Annual
   Conference
United Methodist Church
University of Puget Sound
1500 N. Warner
Tacoma WA 98416

(206) 627-0700

OPEN: by appointment
ACCESS: apply to the archivist
MATERIALS SOLICITED: Methodist
church records.

HOLDINGS:
   Total volume: 275 c.f.
   Inclusive dates: 1830 -
   Description: Records of the conferences
and annual sessions of the Methodist
church, the Methodist Episcopal church,
and the United Methodist church in the
Pacific Northwest; also records of district
parishes principally in the metropolitan
regions of Washington, materials related
to early Methodist missions in the Pacific
Northwest, and records of auxiliary organizations of the church.

GUIDES: Published inventory available
from the repository.

SEE: *Washington Repository Guide.*

WA904-100

Camp Six Logging Museum
Point Defiance Park
Tacoma WA 98407

(206) 752-0047

OPEN: daily 10-3; closed in winter
COPYING FACILITIES: no
MATERIALS SOLICITED: Logging history.

HOLDINGS:
   Total volume: 4 c.f.
   Inclusive dates: 1880's - 1940's
   Description: Photographs of logging op-
erations, chiefly in Washington.

SEE: *Washington Repository Guide.*

WA904-260

Fort Nisqually Museum
Point Defiance Park
Tacoma WA 98407

(206) 591-5339

OPEN: by appointment only

HOLDINGS:
   Total volume: 4 c.f.
   Inclusive dates: 1837 - 1890
   Description: Letters, deeds, legal documents, photographs, and copies of a
logbook of the original Fort Nisqually
used in museum displays at this reconstruction of a Hudson's Bay Company
fort and fur trade station.

SEE: *Washington Repository Guide.*

WA904-635

Pacific Lutheran University
Archives
Park Avenue and S. 121 Street
Tacoma WA 98447

(206) 535-7587

OPEN: M-F 8-5; closed weekends and
holidays
COPYING FACILITIES: yes

HOLDINGS:
   Total volume: 115 c.f.
   Inclusive dates: 1861 -
   Description: Records of the University,
of Columbia College at Everett, and of
Spokane College at Spokane; records of
campus organizations; and some materi-
als concerning the Lutheran church in
Washington.

SEE: *Washington Repository Guide;*
Hinding.

WA904-640

Pacific Lutheran University
Library
Nisqually Plains Room
Park Avenue S. and S. 121st Street
Tacoma WA 98447

(206) 535-7500

OPEN: M-Sa 10-4; closed Sundays and
legal holidays
MATERIALS SOLICITED: South Puget
Sound history; will also accept materials on western Washington history.

HOLDINGS:
   Total volume: 28 c.f.
   Inclusive dates: 1882 -
   Description: Photographs, oral history
materials, and reference files of research
papers concerning the history of western
Washington.

SEE: *Washington Repository Guide.*

WA904-665

Pierce County Library System
Headquarters
2356 Tacoma Avenue S.
Tacoma WA 98402

(206) 572-6760

OPEN: M-F 8-5; closed weekends and
legal holidays
COPYING FACILITIES: yes

HOLDINGS:
   Total volume: 13 c.f.
   Inclusive dates: 1898 -
   Description: Library records, including
those of a 'friends of the library' organi-
zation, and records of a Pierce County,
Washington, good-roads association.

SEE: *Washington Repository Guide.*

WA904-760

Tacoma General Hospital
School of Nursing
School Historical Collection
314 South K Street
Tacoma WA 98405

(206) 594-1000

OPEN: M-F 8-4; closed weekends and
holidays
ACCESS: advance permission of director
of the school is required
COPYING FACILITIES: yes
MATERIALS SOLICITED: Manuscripts and
photographs pertaining to the School of
Nursing. Will also accept related oral
history recordings.

HOLDINGS:
Total volume: 2.5 l.f.
Inclusive dates: 1895 -
Description: Records and manuscripts
relating to the Tacoma General Hospital
School of Nursing, including memoirs,
photographs of graduating classes, infor-
mation on prominent graduates, and ma-
terials relating to Bishop John Adams
Paddock, founder of the Hospital, and
Dr. Charles McCutcheon, founder of the
School of Nursing.

SEE: Hinding.

WA904-770

Tacoma Public Library
1102 Tacoma Avenue S.
Tacoma WA 98402

(206) 591-5600

OPEN: M-F 9-9, Sa 9-6; closed Sundays
and legal holidays
COPYING FACILITIES: yes
MATERIALS SOLICITED: Materials relating
to the Pacific Northwest, especially
concerning railroads, the forest industry, exploration, and settlement; and
papers and photographic materials pertaining to individuals, organizations,
and units of government.

HOLDINGS:
Total volume: 630 l.f.
Inclusive dates: 1828 -
Description: Railroad and transportation company papers, including the local
division of the Northern Pacific Railroad,
and traction companies; records of
Tacoma-area businesses, architectural
firms, professional, social, and cultural associations, and churches; papers of local
business people, professional, and literary
figures; records of the Tacoma city government and other regional local governments; and a photograph collection of
123,000 items, 1854- , covering Tacoma,
Fort Lewis, Washington, and the Cascade
Mountains.
There are also oral history materials
relating to local history, especially to European immigrants.

SEE: NUCMC, 1970-72, 74, 80.

SEE: Washington Repository Guide; Davis;
Hinding; Meckler and McMullin;
Schatz; Winroth.

SEE ALSO: Joan Hoff Wilson and Lynn B.
Donovan, 'Women's History: A Listing
of West Coast Archival and Manuscript
Sources, Part II,' California Historical
Quarterly 55 (Summer 1976).

WA904-780

Tenzler Branch Library
6300 Wildare Road
Tacoma WA 98499

(206) 582-6040

OPEN: M-W 11-9; Th-Sa 11-6
COPYING FACILITIES: yes

HOLDINGS:
Total volume: 3 c.f.
Inclusive dates: 1886 -
Description: A historical reference file
of clippings, chiefly about the southern
part of Tacoma, and records of a local
literary club of the 1880's.

SEE: Washington Repository Guide.

WA904-790

University of Puget Sound
Geology Library
Thompson Hall
Tacoma WA 98416

(206) 756-3129

OPEN: by appointment

HOLDINGS:
Total volume: 3 c.f.
Inclusive dates: 1920's - 1940's
Description: Mining and geological re-
ports on the Skykomish area.

SEE: Washington Repository Guide.

WA904-800

University of Puget Sound
Manuscript Collection
1500 N. Warner
Tacoma WA 98416

(206) 756-3258

OPEN: M-F 9-4 by appointment; closed
weekends and holidays
COPYING FACILITIES: yes
MATERIALS SOLICITED: Materials relating
to the University of Puget Sound, Tacoma, Puget Sound, the Methodist
church, and the Pacific Northwest.

HOLDINGS:
Total volume: not specified
Inclusive dates: not specified
Description: Records and documents,
primarily acquired from faculty members
and others connected with the University,
relating to the University, Puget Sound,
the Methodist church, Tacoma, and Albert Schweitzer.

SEE: Washington Repository Guide.

WA904-810

University of Puget Sound
University Archives
1500 N. Warner
Tacoma WA 98416

(206) 756-3257

OPEN: M-F 8-5; closed weekends and
legal holidays

MATERIALS SOLICITED: University of
Puget Sound.

HOLDINGS:
Total volume: 150 c.f.
Inclusive dates: 1890 -
Description: Records of governing and
administrative bodies and associated or-
ganizations at the University of Puget
Sound, a Methodist church educational
institution founded in 1888.

SEE: Washington Repository Guide.

WA904-870

Washington State Historical Society
Library
315 N. Stadium Way
Tacoma WA 98403

(206) 593-2830

OPEN: Tu-Sa 9:30-5
COPYING FACILITIES: yes
MATERIALS SOLICITED: Materials, includ-
ing manuscripts and manuscript collec-
tions, for research, education, and pub-
lic information regarding Pacific
Northwest history, particularly that of
Washington.

HOLDINGS:
Total volume: 450 c.f.
Inclusive dates: 1308 -
Description: A general collection of his-
torical materials from throughout Wash-
ington, emphasizing pioneer papers, the
Tacoma area, Northwest labor move-
ments, Indian relations, and Pacific
Northwest political history.

SEE: Hamer; NUCMC, 1970.

SEE: Washington Repository Guide; Davis;
Hinding; Hines; Novotny; Robbins;
Winroth.

SEE ALSO: James H. Hitchman, 'Primary
Source Materials in Washington Mari-
time History,' Pacific Northwest Quar-
terly 65 (April 1974); Raymond C.
McInnis, 'Opportunities for Historical
Research in Washington State,' Studies
in History and Society 1 (April 1969);
Joan Hoff Wilson and Lynn B. Dono-
van, 'Women's History: A Listing of
West Coast Archival and Manuscript
Sources, Part II,' California Historical
Quarterly 55 (Summer 1976).

Karyl Winn, ed., North Cascades Archival
Resources in Washington State Repositories (Univ. of Washington, 1974).

Finding aids for four collections have been
published; unpublished finding aids for
other holdings are available at the repository.

WA904-890

Western Wright Marine, Inc.
Museum
1525 Commerce Street
Tacoma WA 98402

(206) 272-5065

OPEN: M-F 8-5; closed weekends and
legal holidays
ACCESS: appointment advised
COPYING FACILITIES: no
MATERIALS SOLICITED: Tacoma water-
front and maritime history.

HOLDINGS:
> *Total volume:* 1.7 c.f.
> *Inclusive dates:* 1900 -
> *Description:* Engineering drawings and instruction manuals, along with photographs, in support of the museum collection of engines for small boats and ships.

SEE: *Washington Repository Guide.*

TEKOA

WA909-760
Tekoa Historical Museum
City Hall
Tekoa WA 99033

no telephone

OPEN: currently open on July 4th only
MATERIALS SOLICITED: Tekoa-area items, especially those with display value.

HOLDINGS:
> *Total volume:* 12 c.f.
> *Inclusive dates:* 1880's -
> *Description:* Local photographs, business materials, farm records, scrapbooks, and a few personal papers.

SEE: *Washington Repository Guide;* Hines.

TONASKET

WA919-560
North Central Regional Library
Tonasket Branch Library
City Hall
Whitcomb Avenue
Tonasket WA

MAILING ADDRESS:
P.O. Box 629
Tonasket WA 98855

(509) 486-2366

OPEN: Tu, Th 12:30-9, W 12:30-5:30, F 1-5, Sa 10-2; closed Su, M and holidays
COPYING FACILITIES: no

HOLDINGS:
> *Total volume:* 8 vols.
> *Inclusive dates:* 1912 - 1948
> *Description:* The library maintains a collection of social club meeting minutes.

SEE: *Washington Repository Guide.*

TOPPENISH

WA921-950
Yakima Indian Nation
Archives
Toppenish WA

MAILING ADDRESS:
P.O. Box 151
Toppenish WA 98948

(509) 865-2800, Ext. 445

OPEN: M-F 8:30-8, Sa, Su 12-6; closed Thanksgiving, Christmas, and New Year's
COPYING FACILITIES: yes

MATERIALS SOLICITED: Yakima Indian Nation; will also accept materials on Pacific Northwest Indians.

HOLDINGS:
> *Total volume:* 42 vols.; 42 c.f.
> *Inclusive dates:* 1775 - 1970's
> *Description:* Photographs and recordings from tribal people, along with a body of reproduced documentation, which has been assembled from a number of archival and manuscript repositories and which constitutes comprehensive historical documentation of the Yakima Indian Nation.

SEE: *Washington Repository Guide;* Winroth.

TUKWILA

WA927-780
Tukwila Historical Society
5827 S. 144th Street
Tukwila WA 98168

(206) 244-7857

OPEN: by appointment
COPYING FACILITIES: no
MATERIALS SOLICITED: History of Tukwila and vicinity.

HOLDINGS:
> *Total volume:* 0.8 c.f.
> *Inclusive dates:* 1910 - 1977
> *Description:* Photographs, oral interviews and draft writings on the Tukwila area.

SEE: *Washington Repository Guide.*

UNIONTOWN

WA935-770
Twin Willows Museum
Uniontown WA

MAILING ADDRESS:
P.O. Box 125
Uniontown WA 99179

(509) 229-3396

OPEN: March 1-Nov. 1, Su noon-5, M 9-5; closed rest of year
USER FEES: one dollar
ACCESS: approval of owner of museum required

HOLDINGS:
> *Total volume:* 10 c.f.
> *Inclusive dates:* 1875 - 1940's
> *Description:* Business records from Uniontown, a general photograph collection, and a copy of an overland journey diary of a Uniontown pioneer.

SEE: *Washington Repository Guide.*

VANCOUVER

WA943-125
Clark College
Library
800 E. McLaughlin Blvd.
Vancouver WA 98663

(206) 699-0152

OPEN: M-Th 8-10, F 8-4:30
COPYING FACILITIES: yes

HOLDINGS:
> *Total volume:* 1 c.f.
> *Inclusive dates:* 1940's - 1960's
> *Description:* The Hermine Decker drama collection, which relates to the College's theater.

SEE: *Washington Repository Guide.*

WA943-240
Fort Vancouver Historical Society
Clark County Historical Museum
1511 Main Street
Vancouver WA

MAILING ADDRESS:
P.O. Box 1834
Vancouver WA 98668

(206) 695-4681

OPEN: Tu-Su 1-5; closed Mondays and legal holidays
COPYING FACILITIES: yes
MATERIALS SOLICITED: Clark County and the Pacific Northwest.

HOLDINGS:
> *Total volume:* 125 c.f.
> *Inclusive dates:* 1820 -
> *Description:* Personal papers, Civil War diaries, county government records, Vancouver area business records, civic association records, scrapbooks, oral history materials, and local history reference items.

SEE: *Washington Repository Guide;* Hinding.

WA943-245
Fort Vancouver National Historic Site
E. Evergreen Blvd.
Vancouver WA 98661

(206) 696-7655

OPEN: daily 9-4; closed holidays
COPYING FACILITIES: no

HOLDINGS:
> *Total volume:* 12 c.f.
> *Inclusive dates:* 1778 -
> *Description:* Photographs, field notes, reports and reproductions of source documents relating to the National Park Service's interpretive programs and archaeological investigations concerning the Hudson's Bay Company and the United States Army at Vancouver during the 19th century.

SEE: *Washington Repository Guide.*

WA943-250
Fort Vancouver Regional Library
System
Vancouver Community Library
1007 E. Mill Plain Boulevard
Vancouver WA 98660

(206) 695-1566

OPEN: M-Th 10-8, F, Sa 10-5
COPYING FACILITIES: no

HOLDINGS:
>*Total volume:* 11 c.f.
>*Inclusive dates:* 1844 -
>*Description:* Materials assembled by
>Carl Landerholm, a local historian, and
>Charles A. Gauld, author of several arti-
>cles concerning the United States Army
>and Fort Vancouver.

SEE: *Washington Repository Guide.*

WA943-280
Gifford Pinchot National Forest
500 W. 12th Street
Vancouver WA 98660

(206) 696-7500

OPEN: M-F 7:45-4:30
COPYING FACILITIES: yes

HOLDINGS:
>*Total volume:* 52 c.f.
>*Inclusive dates:* 1905 -
>*Description:* Historical reference files,
>photographs, scrapbooks, maps, and
>drawings pertaining to the area admin-
>istered by the Pinchot National Forest.

SEE: *Washington Repository Guide.*

WA943-333
Grant House Museum
1106 E. Evergreen Boulevard
Vancouver WA 98661

(206) 694-4002

OPEN: Tu-F 1-4, Sa, Su 1-5; closed
Mondays and holidays
COPYING FACILITIES: no
MATERIALS SOLICITED: Materials related
to Ulysses S. Grant; 19th century
Americana.

HOLDINGS:
>*Total volume:* 4 c.f.
>*Inclusive dates:* 1824 - 1900
>*Description:* Photographs and a few
>other documents, relating chiefly to 19th
>century Vancouver and to Ulysses S.
>Grant, in whose house the museum is
>located.

SEE: *Washington Repository Guide.*

WA943-725
Washington State School for the Blind
Library
2214 E. 13th Street
Vancouver WA 98661

(206) 696-6228

OPEN: M-F 7:20-4:15; closed weekends
and legal holidays
COPYING FACILITIES: yes

HOLDINGS:
>*Total volume:* 2 vols.
>*Inclusive dates:* 1918 - 1974
>*Description:* Scrapbook concerning the
>school.

SEE: *Washington Repository Guide.*

WA943-730
Washington State School for the Deaf
Learning Resource Center
611 Grand
Vancouver WA 98661

(206) 696-6223, 6113

OPEN: M-F 7:30-4; closed weekends,
holidays, and summer vacation
COPYING FACILITIES: yes

HOLDINGS:
>*Total volume:* 1 c.f.
>*Inclusive dates:* 1900 -
>*Description:* A small number of
>brochures, pamphlets, scrapbooks, and
>slides depicting the history and develop-
>ment of the school.

SEE: *Washington Repository Guide.*

VAUGHN

WA948-440
Key Peninsula Historical Society
Vaughn WA

MAILING ADDRESS:
P.O. Drawer F
Vaughn WA 98394

no telephone

OPEN: by appointment
COPYING FACILITIES: no
MATERIALS SOLICITED: Key Peninsula
area materials; will also accept other
historical material.

HOLDINGS:
>*Total volume:* 3 c.f.
>*Inclusive dates:* 1887 -
>*Description:* Newspapers, photographs,
>and manuscript histories relating to the
>history of the Key Peninsula area.

SEE: *Washington Repository Guide.*

VERLOT

WA950-840
Snoqualmie and Mount Baker
National Forest
Verlot Ranger Station
Verlot WA

MAILING ADDRESS:
c/o Snoqualmie-Mt. Baker National
Forest
1022 First Avenue
Seattle WA 98104

(206) 691-7791

OPEN: daily 9-6

HOLDINGS:
>*Total volume:* 5.5 c.f.
>*Inclusive dates:* 1908 -
>*Description:* Reference materials, in-
>cluding some records of the Verlot Rang-
>er Station and its predecessor at
>Silverton, and collected photographs, all
>related to activities of the Monte Cristo
>Ranger District of the Mount Baker Na-
>tional Forest.

SEE: *Washington Repository Guide.*

WAITSBURG

WA952-80
Bruce Memorial Museum
Main Street
Waitsburg WA 99361

(509) 337-6688

OPEN: by appointment
COPYING FACILITIES: no

HOLDINGS:
>*Total volume:* 2 c.f.
>*Inclusive dates:* 1880's - 1920's
>*Description:* Photographs from
>Waitsburg and vicinity.

SEE: *Washington Repository Guide;*
Winroth.

WA952-880
Weller Public Library
Main Street
Waitsburg WA 99361

(509) 337-6371

OPEN: M 2-4, W 10-11, Sa 1-5
COPYING FACILITIES: no

HOLDINGS:
>*Total volume:* 10 vols.; .5 c.f.
>*Inclusive dates:* 1870's - 1960's
>*Description:* Papers and notebooks of
>John R. White, a historian of southeast-
>ern Washington, and local photographs.

SEE: *Washington Repository Guide.*

WALLA WALLA

WA954-40
American Political Items Collectors
Education Division
1008 Bonsella
Walla Walla WA 99362

no telephone

OPEN: by appointment
ACCESS: materials are available for use
to subscribers of APIC
COPYING FACILITIES: no
MATERIALS SOLICITED: American political and social movements, and American presidents and presidential candidates.

HOLDINGS:
>*Total volume:* not specified
>*Inclusive dates:* 1790's -
>*Description:* Materials related to
>American political campaigns, chiefly
>presidential elections, and to political and
>social movements and presidents. They

include audio cassettes and photographic slides.

GUIDES: *American Political Audio-Visual Library, Catalog Number 1* (Feb. 1976).

SEE: *Washington Repository Guide;* Hinding.

WA954-240

Fort Walla Walla Museum Complex
Myra Road
Walla Walla WA

MAILING ADDRESS:
P.O. Box 1616
Walla Walla WA 99362

(509) 525-7703

OPEN: July and August, Tu-Su 1-5, May, June, and Sept., Sa, Su, and holidays 1-5; closed other times
COPYING FACILITIES: no

HOLDINGS:
　Total volume: not specified
　Inclusive dates: 19th century -
　Description: Photographs of historical subjects in the Walla Walla Valley and the Pacific Northwest.

WA954-845

Walla Walla Community College
Library
500 Tausick Way
Walla Walla WA 99362

(509) 527-4293

OPEN: M-F 8-5; closed weekends and legal holidays
COPYING FACILITIES: no

HOLDINGS:
　Total volume: 1 c.f.
　Inclusive dates: 1973 - 1976
　Description: Approximately 60 audio recordings of interviews and historical talks, all relative to Walla Walla area history.

SEE: *Washington Repository Guide.*

WA954-880

Whitman College
Penrose Memorial Library
Eells Northwest Room
345 Boyer Street
Walla Walla WA 99362

(509) 527-5191

OPEN: M-F 9-4
COPYING FACILITIES: yes
MATERIALS SOLICITED: Materials relating to Walla Walla and to Whitman College. Will also accept Pacific Northwest materials, especially from the inland region.

HOLDINGS:
　Total volume: 600 c.f.
　Inclusive dates: 1804 -
　Description: A general collection relating to the inland Northwest, with emphasis on missionaries affiliated with the American Board of Commissioners for Foreign Missions. Also included are materials concerning missionary activities and ethnological observation on the Skokomish Indian Reservation,

1874-1907, business and civic association records from Walla Walla, and the archives of Whitman College.

SEE: Hamer.

SEE: *Washington Repository Guide;* Hinding; Hines; Robbins; Winroth.

WA954-885

Whitman Mission National Historic Site
Highway 12 W.
Walla Walla WA

MAILING ADDRESS:
Route 2
Walla Walla WA 99362

(509) 522-6360

OPEN: M-F 8-4:30; closed weekends and holidays
COPYING FACILITIES: yes

HOLDINGS:
　Total volume: 6 l.f.
　Inclusive dates: 1834 -
　Description: Source documents concerning the Whitman (Wailatpu) Mission, chiefly copied material assembled by National Park Service historians, along with correspondence and reminiscences of mission personnel.

SEE: NUCMC, 1959-61.

SEE: *Washington Repository Guide.*

WAPATO

WA956-880

Wapato Public Library
100 East 5th Street
Wapato WA 98951

(509) 877-2882

OPEN: M, Tu, Th-Sa 9-5, W 9-8; closed Sundays and holidays

HOLDINGS:
　Total volume: 3 c.f.
　Inclusive dates: 1935 -
　Description: Holdings include scrapbooks of local associations.

SEE: *Washington Repository Guide.*

WASHOUGAL

WA958-240

Fort Vancouver Regional Library System
Washougal Branch Library
1661 C Street
Washougal WA 98671

(206) 835-5393

OPEN: M, W, F, Sa 10-6, Tu, Th 10-8
COPYING FACILITIES: yes

HOLDINGS:
　Total volume: 0.5 c.f.
　Inclusive dates: 1900 (approx.) -
　Description: Historical reference file of photographs, clippings and draft histories, all pertaining to Washougal.

SEE: *Washington Repository Guide.*

WATERVILLE

WA960-170

Douglas County Historical Museum
Central and Walnut Streets
Waterville WA

MAILING ADDRESS:
P.O. Box 573
Waterville WA 98858

no telephone

OPEN: daily 11-5; closed Oct. 1 - May 30
COPYING FACILITIES: no
MATERIALS SOLICITED: Douglas County historical materials; will also accept American Indian photographs and U.S. history ephemera.

HOLDINGS:
　Total volume: 22 c.f.
　Inclusive dates: 1888 -
　Description: Local school, business and government records, along with some materials from local associations and a photograph collection.

SEE: *Washington Repository Guide;* Hines.

WA960-880

Waterville Public Library
Waterville WA

MAILING ADDRESS:
Box 508
Waterville WA 98858

(509) 745-8354

OPEN: Tu, F 1-5, W 10-12:30
COPYING FACILITIES: yes

HOLDINGS:
　Total volume: 3 vols.
　Inclusive dates: 1919 - 1961
　Description: Holdings consist of the minutes of the Library Board.

SEE: *Washington Repository Guide.*

WENATCHEE

WA966-115

Church of the Brethren
Washington District Archives
535 Okanogan Street
Wenatchee WA 98801

(509) 662-3681

OPEN: M, Tu, Th, F 8-4, W 8-12:30; closed weekends and holidays
ACCESS: use subject to approval of District Historical Committee and the District Archives
COPYING FACILITIES: no
MATERIALS SOLICITED: Materials of individual Brethren churches.

HOLDINGS:
　Total volume: 65 vols.; 10.5 c.f.
　Inclusive dates: 1895 -
　Description: Administrative records of the District, a historical collection, and records of individual churches within the District's jurisdiction.

SEE: *Washington Repository Guide.*

WA966-320
Heritage Society of the Mid-Columbia
1101 Wedgewood
Wenatchee WA 98801

(509) 663-6473

OPEN: by appointment
COPYING FACILITIES: no

HOLDINGS:
Total volume: 25 c.f.
Inclusive dates: 1919 -
Description: Recordings, drafts, and transcriptions of presentations at society meetings, mostly relating to local history. There are also a few items from Chelan and Okanogan counties.

SEE: *Washington Repository Guide.*

WA966-550
North Central Regional Library
Wenatchee Branch Library
310 Douglas Street
Wenatchee WA 98801

(509) 662-5021

OPEN: M-Sa 9-5
COPYING FACILITIES: yes

HOLDINGS:
Total volume: 2 c.f.
Inclusive dates: 1915 (approx.) -
Description: The library's vertical file holdings include a few draft histories and some copies of local reminiscences.

SEE: *Washington Repository Guide.*

WA966-560
North Central Washington Museum
127 S. Mission
Wenatchee WA 98801

(509) 662-4728

OPEN: M-F 10-4, Sa, Su 1-4; closed holidays
COPYING FACILITIES: no
MATERIALS SOLICITED: Materials relating to the north central Washington fruit industry, the Cascade Division of the Great Northern Railway, Clyde E. Pangborn's trans-Pacific flight, and central Washington.

HOLDINGS:
Total volume: 22 c.f.
Inclusive dates: 1872 -
Description: Local photographs and films; records of businesses, civic groups, and local government agencies; and some unidentified diaries and collections of personal papers.

SEE: *Washington Repository Guide.*

WA966-905
Wenatchee Valley College
Library
1300 Fifth Street
Wenatchee WA 98801

(509) 664-2520

OPEN: M-F 7:30-5:30

HOLDINGS:
Total volume: 2 c.f.
Inclusive dates: 1864 -
Description: Principally copied and transcribed materials, mostly local diaries, and some draft writings.

SEE: *Washington Repository Guide.*

WHITE SWAN

WA972-240
Fort Simcoe State Park
White Swan WA 98952

(509) 874-2372

OPEN: M-F 8-5; closed winters

HOLDINGS:
Total volume: 1 vol.
Inclusive dates: 1858 - 1861
Description: Small quantity of records relative to the active military period of Fort Simcoe's history.

SEE: *Washington Repository Guide.*

WILBUR

WA975-80
Big Bend Historical Society
Museum
Wilbur WA 99185

no telephone

OPEN: Sa 2-5 May 21-Sept.; other times by appointment
COPYING FACILITIES: no
MATERIALS SOLICITED: Will accept local materials.

HOLDINGS:
Total volume: 17 c.f.
Inclusive dates: 1817 -
Description: A general collection of a variety of organization, business, and personal papers, including photographs, principally from the vicinity of Wilbur. Some items involve Samuel Wilbur (Wild Goose Bill) Condit, founder of the town, and Marion E. Hay, Governor of Washington, 1909-13, known as the 'Merchant Prince of Wilbur.'

SEE: *Washington Repository Guide;* Hines.

WINLOCK

WA982-880
Winlock Public Library
322 N.E. 1st Street
Winlock WA 98596

(206) 785-3461

OPEN: M, Tu, Th, F 1-5, W 1-6
COPYING FACILITIES: no
MATERIALS SOLICITED: Winlock history.

HOLDINGS:
Total volume: 1.2 c.f.
Inclusive dates: 1873 - 1970's
Description: The library's historical records include photographs, newspaper clippings, an 1873 letter, and a history of Winlock.

SEE: *Washington Repository Guide.*

WINSLOW

WA984-80
Bainbridge Island Historical Society
High School Road
Winslow WA 98110

(206) 842-3433

OPEN: Sa 11-3
COPYING FACILITIES: no
MATERIALS SOLICITED: Bainbridge Island and Kitsap County history.

HOLDINGS:
Total volume: 17 c.f.
Inclusive dates: 1860's -
Description: The historical society maintains a collection of old photographs, club minutes, school and county records, hotel registers, and a plat book, all pertaining to Bainbridge Island history.

SEE: *Washington Repository Guide.*

WA984-90
Bainbridge Island Library
1270 Madison Avenue N.
Winslow WA 98110

(206) 842-4162

OPEN: M-Sa 10-5
MATERIALS SOLICITED: Bainbridge Island history; will also accept other historical materials.

HOLDINGS:
Total volume: 3.8 c.f.
Inclusive dates: 1874 -
Description: Short histories, photographs, and other materials relating to Bainbridge Island and Kitsap County history.

SEE: *Washington Repository Guide.*

WINTHROP

WA985-720

Okanogan County Historical Society
Shaffer Museum
Winthrop WA

MAILING ADDRESS:
Box 15
Winthrop WA 98862

no telephone

OPEN: daily 10-5 summer; closed Oct. -
April
COPYING FACILITIES: no

HOLDINGS:
Total volume: 6 c.f.
Inclusive dates: 1899 -
Description: Photographs, business
records, and public records.

SEE: *Washington Repository Guide.*

SEE ALSO: Karyl Winn, ed., *North Cascades Archival Resources in Washington
State Repositories* (University of Washington, 1974).

WOODINVILLE

WA990-280

Greater Woodinville Historical
Museum Foundation
Woodinville WA

MAILING ADDRESS:
P.O. Box 216
Woodinville WA 98072

(206) 483-2811

OPEN: by appointment only
ACCESS: permission of foundation
officers required
COPYING FACILITIES: no
MATERIALS SOLICITED: History of the
greater Woodinville area.

HOLDINGS:
Total volume: 1 c.f.
Inclusive dates: 1976 -
Description: Oral history interviews re-
lating to the Woodinville area.

SEE: *Washington Repository Guide.*

YAKIMA

WA994-690

Catholic Diocese of Yakima
Room 222, Washington Mutual
Building
32 N. 3rd Street
Yakima WA

MAILING ADDRESS:
P.O. Box 505
Yakima WA 98907

(509) 248-6857

OPEN: M-F 8-5; closed weekends and
legal holidays
ACCESS: with permission of the bishop

HOLDINGS:
Total volume: 23 vols.
Inclusive dates: 1951 - 1970
Description: Principally scrapbooks of
press releases, memoranda and correspon-
dence.

SEE: *Washington Repository Guide;*
Hinding.

WA994-925

Yakima Valley Genealogical Society
Yakima Valley Museum and
Historical Association
2105 Tieton Drive
Yakima WA 98902

(509) 248-0747

OPEN: Tu-F 10-5, Sa, Su noon-5

HOLDINGS:
Total volume: 10 c.f.
Inclusive dates: 1889 -
Description: Information for indexes of
genealogical sources in the Yakima Valley
and central Washington.

SEE: *Washington Repository Guide.*

WA994-935

Yakima Valley Museum and
Historical Association
210 W. Tieton
Yakima WA 98902

(509) 248-0747

OPEN: W-Sa 9-5, Su 10-6; closed other
days
COPYING FACILITIES: yes
MATERIALS SOLICITED: Materials from
the Yakima Valley.

HOLDINGS:
Total volume: 45 vols.; 30 c.f.
Inclusive dates: 1853 -
Description: Personal papers; business,
local government, and civic organization
records; photographs; and reminiscences.
Most materials are from Yakima County,
with some from outside Washington and
the United States.

SEE: *Washington Repository Guide;*
Hinding; Hines; Winroth.

WA994-940

Yakima Valley Regional Library
102 N. 3rd Street
Yakima WA 98901

(509) 452-8541

OPEN: M-Sa 8-10, Su 10-10; closed legal
holidays
COPYING FACILITIES: yes

HOLDINGS:
Total volume: 80 c.f.
Inclusive dates: 1826 - 1929
Description: Papers of Clifford Curtis
(Click) Relander, consisting of his per-
sonal papers and a large number of col-
lected and transcribed documents pertain-
ing to the history of central Washington,
especially to the Yakima and Wanapum
Indian tribes.

SEE: *Washington Repository Guide;*
Winroth.

SEE ALSO: Published guide to Relander
collections.

WEST VIRGINIA

West Virginia does not have a statewide program for preserving local public records. Local officials normally retain custody of permanently valuable records, but the West Virginia Collection at the West Virginia University Library includes extensive county court records for eight counties and partial holdings for seven other counties. The Department of Culture and History in Charleston makes available to researchers over 5,000 reels of microfilm of vital, probate, land, and other records which were filmed by the Church of Jesus Christ of Latter-day Saints.

BETHANY

WV100-80
Bethany College
T. W. Phillips Library
Alexander Campbell Archives
Bethany WV 26032

(304) 829-4258, 7321

OPEN: M-F 7:45-11, Sa 9-5, Su 1-11; closed holidays
ACCESS: approval of College Archivist required
COPYING FACILITIES: yes
MATERIALS SOLICITED: Diaries, letters, other manuscripts, and photographs relating to Alexander Campbell, Thomas Campbell, their Bethany colleagues, and family.

HOLDINGS:
  Total volume: 2,000 l.f.
  Inclusive dates: 1800 -
  Description: Material related to Bethany College's founder and first president Alexander Campbell, his father Thomas Campbell, their Bethany associates, and family. Subjects covered include the history of the College and the religious movement, Disciples of Christ, that Campbell founded, and West Virginia and western Pennsylvania regional and intellectual history of the 19th century.

WV100-90
Bethany College
T. W. Phillips Library
College Archives
Bethany WV 26032

(304) 829-7321

OPEN: M-Th 8-11, F 8-10, Sa 10-5, Su 1-11; summer hours M-F 8-4:30; closed weekends and holidays

ACCESS: approval of College Archivist required
COPYING FACILITIES: yes
MATERIALS SOLICITED: Records of the College, including manuscripts, printed and published documents, sound recordings, and microforms.

HOLDINGS:
  Total volume: 500 l.f.
  Inclusive dates: 1840 -
  Description: Archives of Bethany College, including publications, minutes of governing bodies, faculty and student diaries, office records, and oral history recordings.

BUCKHANNON

WV200-880
West Virginia Wesleyan College
Annie Merner Pfeiffer Library
Buckhannon WV 26201

(304) 473-8000

OPEN: M-F 8-10:30, Sa 8-5, Su 2-10:30; closed variable times; variable summer hours
ACCESS: with permission of Librarian
COPYING FACILITIES: yes
MATERIALS SOLICITED: Materials relating to Pearl S. Buck and the United Methodist church in West Virginia. Will also accept other materials on a limited basis.

HOLDINGS:
  Total volume: 46 l.f.; 137 vols.
  Inclusive dates: 1848 -
  Description: Conference journals, local West Virginia church histories, diaries, and other materials created and collected by the West Virginia Annual Conference of the United Methodist church; and literary manuscripts by Pearl S. Buck, including those of 34 novels, as well as short stories, plays, and speeches.

CHARLESTON

WV225-860
West Virginia Department of Culture and History
Archives and History Division
The Cultural Center
Capitol Complex
Charleston WV 25305

(304) 348-0230

OPEN: M-F 9-5, Sa 1-5; closed Sundays and holidays
COPYING FACILITIES: yes

MATERIALS SOLICITED: Family histories and correspondence, Civil War materials, West Virginia State government records, and other materials of importance to the history of West Virginia and Virginia. Will also accept materials on coal mining and other industries in West Virginia.

HOLDINGS:
  Total volume: 3,500 l.f.
  Inclusive dates: 1729 -
  Description: West Virginia State and local history collection, including some Virginia materials. There are strong holdings of early West Virginia governors' papers, records of Virginia and West Virginia State agencies, family letters and papers, account books and ledgers of early businesses, and Civil War record books. The repository also houses a large collection of West Virginia county courthouse records reproduced on microfilm.

SEE: Hamer; NUCMC, 1959-62, 70, 73-74.

SEE: Parkinson.

CLARKSBURG

WV250-320
Harrison County Historical Society
123 West Main Street
Clarksburg WV

MAILING ADDRESS:
P.O. Box 2074
Clarksburg WV 26301

(304) 842-3073

OPEN: M, F 2-4, and by appointment Tu-Th, Sa; closed Sundays and holidays
USER FEES: 25 cents
COPYING FACILITIES: no
MATERIALS SOLICITED: Materials concerning local history and genealogy.

HOLDINGS:
  Total volume: 1.5 l.f.
  Inclusive dates: 1900 - 1930
  Description: Papers of Melville Davisson Post, author, including correspondence with his publishers and with John W. Davis.

HARPERS FERRY

WV350-560
National Park Service
Archives
Harpers Ferry Center
Harpers Ferry WV 25425

(304) 535-6371, Ext. 6493

OPEN: M-Th 8-5, F 8-4:30; closed
weekends and holidays
ACCESS: with approval of archivist
COPYING FACILITIES: yes
MATERIALS SOLICITED: Materials related
to National Park Service history and
activities, and to past NPS employees;
materials on tourism as it pertains to
national parks, monuments and historic
sites; and materials on the Civilian
Conservation Corps. Will also accept
materials concerned with the history of
museums, historic preservation, environmental and historical interpretation,
and the conservation movement in general.

HOLDINGS:
Total volume: 600 c.f.
Inclusive dates: 1860 -
Description: Papers of Ronald Lee,
Harold Peterson, and other officials associated with the National Park Service;
photographs of National Park system
areas, Civilian Conservation Corps operations, museums, etc.; oral history interviews, including 450 with long-time employees of NPS and 130 dealing with the
history of women in the NPS; and supporting research materials.

SEE: NUCMC, 1972.

SEE: Meckler and McMullin.

HILLSBORO

WV375-640
Pearl S. Buck Birthplace Foundation
Box 126
Hillsboro WV 24946

(304) 653-4430

OPEN: by appointment only
COPYING FACILITIES: no
MATERIALS SOLICITED: Works of Pearl
S. Buck and materials concerning her
family.

HOLDINGS:
Total volume: 200 items
Inclusive dates: 1850's -
Description: Materials concerning author Pearl S. Buck, including photographs, unpublished family histories, the
manuscript of her father's autobiography,
and family correspondence.

HUNTINGTON

WV435-520
Marshall University
James E. Morrow Library
Special Collections Department
Huntington WV 25705

(304) 696-2320

OPEN: M-Th 8-10, F 8-4:30, Sa 9-5, Su
1-10; closed holidays; shorter hours
between sessions
COPYING FACILITIES: yes
MATERIALS SOLICITED: Materials relating
to the tri-State area of West Virginia,
Ohio, and Kentucky, to Appalachia,
and to the Civil War. Will also accept
materials documenting southern history.

HOLDINGS:
Total volume: 450 l.f.
Inclusive dates: late 1700's -
Description: Manuscript collections relating chiefly to the history of the tri-State
region of West Virginia, Ohio, and Kentucky. Included are diaries, letters, business records, photographic negatives,
Marshall University archives, and a substantial number of oral history recordings
and transcriptions consisting of interviews with coal miners, school teachers,
government officials, and others.

KEYSER

WV500-640
Potomac State College
Mary F. Shipper Library
Mineral County Collection
Keyser WV 26726

(304) 788-3011, Ext. 250

OPEN: M-Th 8-10, F 8-5, Su 7-10;
summer, M-F 8-5; closed other days
COPYING FACILITIES: yes

HOLDINGS:
Total volume: 44 folders; 2 l.f.
Inclusive dates: 1700 - 1910
Description: Typescripts dealing with
the history of Mineral County, WV. Included are copies of land grants, deeds,
property titles, wills, and genealogical material on 15 early settlers in the area. 9
folders contain a WPA history of Mineral
County from 1700 to 1850. Supporting
research data is also available.

LEWISBURG

WV550-280
Greenbrier Historical Society
100 Church Street
Lewisburg WV

MAILING ADDRESS:
309 S. Court Street
Lewisburg WV 24901

(304) 645-3398

OPEN: April-Oct. Th 1-4:30; or by
appointment
USER FEES: members free; others one
dollar

COPYING FACILITIES: no
MATERIALS SOLICITED: Materials concerning the Greenbrier Valley of West
Virginia and its residents. Will also accept materials about West Virginia,
and Virginia prior to 1863, with emphasis on western Virginia.

HOLDINGS:
Total volume: not specified
Inclusive dates: not specified
Description: Manuscripts relating chiefly to the Greenbrier Valley of West Virginia, including some correspondence,
diaries, account books, minutes of a local
United Daughters of the Confederacy organization and a garden club, and photographs.

MARLINTON

WV575-640
Pocahontas County Historical Society
810 2nd Avenue
Marlinton WV 24954

(304) 799-4973

OPEN: June - Aug., M-Sa 11-5, Su 1-5;
Sept. - Oct., Sa 11-5, Su 1-5; closed
other days and rest of year
COPYING FACILITIES: no
MATERIALS SOLICITED: Items relating to
the history of Pocahontas County.

HOLDINGS:
Total volume: 20 l.f.
Inclusive dates: 1880's - 1960's
Description: A collection of 2,000 photographs, primarily of Pocahontas County
subjects, 1890-1960, and manuscript materials, including correspondence and
writings of clergyman William T. Price
and several of his children.

MARTINSBURG

WV600-280
General Adam Stephen Memorial
Association, Inc.
309 East John Street
Martinsburg WV

MAILING ADDRESS:
P.O. Box 862
Martinsburg WV 25401

(304) 267-4434

OPEN: Sa, Su 1-5, May - Oct.; other
times by appointment
ACCESS: advance arrangements necessary
COPYING FACILITIES: no
MATERIALS SOLICITED: Materials relating
to General Adam Stephen.

HOLDINGS:
Total volume: 4 notebooks
Inclusive dates: 1700's -
Description: Correspondence of Gen-
eral Adam Stephen.

MORGANTOWN

WV650-520
Morgantown Public Library
West Virginia Collection and Archives
373 Spruce Street
Morgantown WV 26505

(304) 291-7425

OPEN: M 10-8, Tu-Th 10-6, F, Sa 10-5;
closed Sundays and holidays
COPYING FACILITIES: yes
MATERIALS SOLICITED: West Virginia
material, particularly for Monongalia
County, and materials concerning
southwestern Pennsylvania, western
Maryland, and eastern Ohio. Will also
accept all historical materials.

HOLDINGS:
  Total volume: not specified
  Inclusive dates: 1820's -
  Description: Materials documenting
  Morgantown history, including photo-
  graphs, genealogical notes, and the
  Moreland family collection of diaries, let-
  ters, and other manuscripts, primarily
  post-Civil War.

WV650-890
West Virginia University
Library
West Virginia and Regional History
Colson Hall
Morgantown WV 26506

(304) 293-3536, 3537

OPEN: M-F 8-5, Sa 9-5; closed Sundays
and holidays
COPYING FACILITIES: yes
MATERIALS SOLICITED: Materials relating
to West Virginia history; the history of
Appalachia and the upper Ohio Valley;
the coal industry; labor history; and
genealogy, including personal papers;
business records; State, county, and local government records; photographs;
maps; recordings; tapes; and films.

HOLDINGS:
  Total volume: 20,000 l.f.
  Inclusive dates: 1690 -
  Description: A collection of personal
  papers, business records, State and local
  government and court records, oral history recordings, photographs, maps,
  unpublished genealogies, and other materials relating to the history of the State
  of West Virginia, West Virginia University, the upper Ohio Valley, Appalachia,
  the coal industry, and organized labor.

GUIDES: James W. Hess, *A Guide to
Manuscripts and Archives in the West
Virginia Collection* (1974).

SEE: Hamer; NUCMC, 1959-62, 66, 69,
77.

SEE: Meckler and McMullin; Schatz;
Hounshell; Krichmar; Davis; Parkin-
son; Paszek; Allard, Crawley, and
Edmison; Hines; Hinding; Robbins.

PHILIPPI

WV775-40
Alderson Broaddus College
Pickett Library Media Center
Philippi WV 26416

(304) 457-1700, Ext. 258

OPEN: M-Th 8-10, F 8-4:30, Sa 1-5, Su
1:30-10; closed Christmas, New Year's
and Easter
COPYING FACILITIES: yes

MATERIALS SOLICITED: College reports
and photographs. Will also accept other
materials relevant to College and Baptist history.

HOLDINGS:
  Total volume: not specified
  Inclusive dates: 1870 -
  Description: Baptist materials, including minutes of National and local Baptist
  associations and local church records.
  There are also College archives consisting
  of annual reports, trustee minutes, College bulletins, and 4,000 photographs and
  slides.

WELLSBURG

WV900-80
Brooke County Historical Society
10th and Main Streets
Wellsburg WV

MAILING ADDRESS:
1200 Pleasant Avenue
Wellsburg WV 26070

no telephone

OPEN: M-F 1-9, Sa 9-5; closed Sundays
and holidays
ACCESS: scholars only
COPYING FACILITIES: yes

HOLDINGS:
  Total volume: not specified
  Inclusive dates: 1798 -
  Description: Business ledgers, court
  records, diaries, genealogies, oral histor-
  ies, and photographs pertaining to the
  Wellsburg area and to navigation on the
  Ohio River.

WISCONSIN

Since 1949 the Wisconsin State Historical Society has administered a statewide program for preserving local records. Most permanently valuable local records still remain in the custody of local officials, but more than 8,000 cubic feet of county, town and municipal records have been transferred to the Historical Society in Madison and to Area Research Centers located on 12 four-year University of Wisconsin campuses and at Northland College. Materials may be loaned from any of the 14 institutions to another at the request of researchers.

The Society maintains a central descriptive system for local government records.

ANTIGO

WI38-480
Langlade County Historical Museum
404 Superior Street
Antigo WI 54409

(715) 627-4464

OPEN: Tu, Th-Su 2-5, May 1 - Oct. 1; closed Mondays and Wednesdays
COPYING FACILITIES: yes

HOLDINGS:
Total volume: not specified
Inclusive dates: 1876 -
Description: A collection dealing with many facets of Langlade County history, including papers on the German, Austrian, Polish, Scandinavian, Czechoslovakian, and Yankee populations, the logging industry, and the founder of the city of Antigo, Francis A. Deleglise.

SEE: Hamer.

SEE ALSO: a list of holdings available from the institution.

APPLETON

WI46-360
The Institute of Paper Chemistry
The Dard Hunter Paper Museum
1043 East South River Street
Appleton WI

MAILING ADDRESS:
Box 1039
Appleton WI 54912

(414) 734-9251

OPEN: M-F 7:30-4; closed weekends and holidays
COPYING FACILITIES: yes
MATERIALS SOLICITED: Will accept manuscripts, works of art on paper, photographs, and other materials pertaining to the history and technology of papermaking.

HOLDINGS:
Total volume: not specified
Inclusive dates: 1754 -
Description: Materials pertaining to the history and technology of papermaking.

SEE: NUCMC, 1966.

WI46-480
Lawrence University
Library
Appleton WI 54912

MAILING ADDRESS:
Box 599
Appleton WI 54912

(414) 735-6750

OPEN: by appointment only
COPYING FACILITIES: yes

HOLDINGS:
Total volume: not specified
Inclusive dates: 1847 -
Description: Materials pertinent to the histories of Lawrence University and Milwaukee Downer College.

SEE: Hamer.
SEE: Robbins.

WI46-600
Outagamie County Historical Society, Inc.
320 North Durkee Street
Appleton WI 54911

(414) 733-8445

OPEN: M-Sa 1-5, other times by appointment; closed Sundays and holidays
ACCESS: advance arangements requested
COPYING FACILITIES: yes
MATERIALS SOLICITED: Materials relating to the history of the city of Appleton and Outagamie County.

HOLDINGS:
Total volume: 3,000 items
Inclusive dates: 1823 - 1978
Description: Manuscripts relating to the City of Appleton, and Outagamie County, Wisconsin. Included are records from the city and county clerk's offices, 1867-1969; biographies and reminiscences of early pioneers; church histories; local business records; photographs; oral interviews; papers and pho-

tographs from the DeLanglade-Grignon family, 1823-1948; and papers and photographs from journalist and historian Lillian Mackesy, 1929-1978.

ASHLAND

WI54-560
Northland College
Dexter Library
1411 Ellis Avenue
Ashland WI 54806

(715) 682-4531, Ext. 279

OPEN: Su 1-11, M-Th 8-11, F 8-5, Sa 12-5; closed holidays
COPYING FACILITIES: yes
MATERIALS SOLICITED: Will accept institutional records and publications.

HOLDINGS:
Total volume: 50 l.f.
Inclusive dates: 1908 -
Description: Materials pertinent to College history, and publications of the College and College organizations.

SEE: NUCMC, 1978.

BARABOO

WI70-120
Circus World Museum
Library and Research Center
415 Lynn Street
Baraboo WI

MAILING ADDRESS:
425 Water Street
Baraboo WI 53913

(608) 356-8341

OPEN: May-Aug. M-F 8-5; other months by appointment; closed weekends and holidays
COPYING FACILITIES: yes
MATERIALS SOLICITED: Circus and wild West show materials.

HOLDINGS:
Total volume: 400 l.f.
Inclusive dates: 1840 -
Description: Materials relating to circuses and wild West shows, mainly in America. Included are several thousand photographs and negatives; several hundred movies; business archives and records; correspondence, notes, and manuscripts of notable showpeople and circus historians; and biographical records, logbooks, and diaries of circus personnel.

SEE: NUCMC, 1979.

SEE: Robbins; Hinding.

The Museum is administered by The State Historical Society of Wisconsin.

WI70-720
Sauk County Historical Society
531 4th Avenue
Baraboo WI

MAILING ADDRESS:
Box H
Baraboo WI 53913

(608) 356-4484

OPEN: mid-May - mid-Sept. Tu-Su 2-5; closed Mondays and rest of year.
ACCESS: advance arrangements recommended
COPYING FACILITIES: no
MATERIALS SOLICITED: Materials, including photographs, relating to the Sauk County area.

HOLDINGS:
    Total volume: 5.5 c.f.
    Inclusive dates: 1871 -
    Description: Materials relating to Sauk County. Included are account books, journals, literary manuscripts, photographs, scrapbooks, records of community groups, and county records.

SEE: Hamer.

BEAVER DAM

WI77-160
Dodge County Historical Society, Inc.
Museum
127 South Spring Street
Beaver Dam WI 53916

(414) 887-1266

OPEN: Tu 11-1, W-Sa 1-5; closed Sundays and Mondays
COPYING FACILITIES: no
MATERIALS SOLICITED: Diaries and records relating to early citizens of the area and industrial and cultural growth; architectural plans for significant buildings and homes; and photographs.

HOLDINGS:
    Total volume: not specified
    Inclusive dates: early 1800's -
    Description: Photographs of the area's first settlers, city plat books, and other materials.

SEE: Hinding.

BELOIT

WI82-90
Beloit Historical Society
Lincoln Center
845 Hackett Street
Beloit WI 53511

(608) 365-7835

SEE: NUCMC, 1970 (as Bartlett Memorial Historical Museum).

Questionnaire not returned.

BLACK RIVER FALLS

WI98-390
Jackson County Historical Society
Gallery
South First Street
Black River Falls WI

MAILING ADDRESS:
223 North 4th Street
Black River Falls WI 54615

no telephone

OPEN: by appointment, and Tu 1-4 during warm weather; closed winter months
COPYING FACILITIES: yes
MATERIALS SOLICITED: Photographic materials concerning Jackson County history from 1870 to the present.

HOLDINGS:
    Total volume: 15,500 items
    Inclusive dates: 1870 - 1920
    Description: Photographs, slides, and glass negatives of Jackson County. The Van Schaick collection includes 3,100 pictures of the Winnebago Indians.

WI98-400
Jackson County Historical Society
Library
Black River Falls Public Library
321 Main Street
Black River Falls WI 54615

(715) 284-4112

OPEN: M-F 1:30-9, Sa 1:30-5:30; closed Sundays and holidays
COPYING FACILITIES: yes
MATERIALS SOLICITED: History of Jackson County, contiguous counties, and the Black River logging industry.

HOLDINGS:
    Total volume: 3 file cabinets
    Inclusive dates: 1850 -
    Description: Organization and business records, correspondence, diaries, and genealogical data relating to the history of Jackson County, including the Black River logging industry, cranberry production, iron mining, archaeology and dairying.

BURLINGTON

WI114-80
Burlington Historical Society
Burlington WI 53105

no telephone

SEE: Hamer.

Questionnaire not returned.

CEDARBURG

WI118-600
Ozaukee County Historical Society
W61 N619 Mequon Avenue
Cedarburg WI

MAILING ADDRESS:
P.O. Box 307
Port Washington WI 53074

(414) 377-4510, 242-6788

OPEN: by appointment only
COPYING FACILITIES: no
MATERIALS SOLICITED: Materials relating to Ozaukee County.

HOLDINGS:
    Total volume: 50 items
    Inclusive dates: 1900's -
    Description: Photographs, newspaper clippings, and manuscripts relating to Ozaukee County.

DE PERE

WI130-720
St. Norbert Abbey
Archives
1016 North Broadway
De Pere WI 54115

(414) 336-1321

OPEN: by appointment only
COPYING FACILITIES: yes
MATERIALS SOLICITED: History of the Premonstratensian Order. Will also accept materials relating to the history of the Catholic church in northeastern Wisconsin.

HOLDINGS:
    Total volume: 120 l.f.
    Inclusive dates: 1893 -
    Description: Manuscripts, noncurrent records, visual and audible documents pertaining to the activities of the Premonstratensian Order in the United States.

WI130-730
St. Norbert College
Todd Wehr Library
Special Collections
Grant Street
De Pere WI 54115

(414) 337-3280

OPEN: M-F 8-4; closed weekends, Memorial Day, July 4, and Christmas
ACCESS: advance arrangements with special collections librarian
COPYING FACILITIES: yes
MATERIALS SOLICITED: Archives and noncurrent records of St. Norbert College and its students, faculty, and administration. Will also accept materials on Wisconsin Indians.

HOLDINGS:
    Total volume: 150 l.f.
    Inclusive dates: 1898 -
    Description: St. Norbert College archives are arranged under ten headings: history, administration, correspondence, faculty, students, alumni, biography, par-

ents' association, committees, and miscellaneous. There is also a collection of Menominee Indian materials consisting of correspondence, tribal council reports, photographs, documents, and clippings relating to the termination and restoration proceedings of the tribe.

SEE ALSO: a typed paper listing, *The Menominee Indian Archives*, available upon request.

DELAFIELD

WI134-320
Hawks Inn Historical Society
428 Wells Street
Delafield WI

MAILING ADDRESS:
P.O. Box 105
Delafield WI 53018

(414) 646-2140

OPEN: by appointment only
COPYING FACILITIES: no
MATERIALS SOLICITED: The history of the Delafield area and the history and genealogy of the Hawks family.

HOLDINGS:
Total volume: 30 c.f.
Inclusive dates: 1800 - 1920's
Description: Collections dealing with local history, including photographs, oral histories, documents, ledgers and other materials. Also included are the family records and genealogy of the Hawks family.

EAU CLAIRE

WI142-120
Chippewa Valley Museum
Eau Claire WI

MAILING ADDRESS:
Box 1204
Eau Claire WI 54701

(715) 834-7871

OPEN: Tu-Su 1-5; closed Mondays, Thanksgiving, Christmas, and New Year's
COPYING FACILITIES: no
MATERIALS SOLICITED: Manuscripts, documents, diaries, scrapbooks, and photographs pertaining to people and events of the Chippewa Valley area. Will also accept oral history tapes.

HOLDINGS:
Total volume: 90 l.f.
Inclusive dates: early 1800's -
Description: Materials relating to the Chippewa Valley area of northern Wisconsin, with particular focus on the lumber industry. Included are journals, diaries, and scrapbooks of lumbermen, typed biographies of local residents, cemetery records, business ledgers, Civil War letters, and oral histories on the lumber industry and life in Wisconsin.

GUIDES: State Historical Society of Wisconsin, *Guide to Archives and Manuscripts in the Chippewa Valley Museum, Eau Claire Public Library, and Univer-*

sity of Wisconsin - Eau Claire Area Research Center & Archives (1977).

SEE: Hinding.

WI142-800
University of Wisconsin at Eau Claire
William D. McIntyre Library
University Archives and Area
    Research Center
Eau Claire WI 54701

(715) 836-2739

OPEN: M-F 8-5, additional hours by appointment
COPYING FACILITIES: yes
MATERIALS SOLICITED: Wisconsin local history materials relating to the geographical area of interest of this Area Research Center, including coverage of such topics as business, women's history, professional activities, mass communications, and ethnic groups; county, town, and city records; records and other materials relating to the University of Wisconsin at Eau Claire. Will also accept other personal papers, and records of labor unions, social and fraternal organizations, churches, and political groups.

HOLDINGS:
Total volume: 1,500 l.f.
Inclusive dates: 1837 -
Description: Archives and manuscripts documenting local history in the geographical area of interest of this Area Research Center. Included are local government records; business records, especially those pertaining to banking and lumbering; records of labor unions and social organizations; photographs; and other materials. There are also archives and manuscripts relating to the history of the University of Wisconsin at Eau Claire, including records of faculty and student organizations, oral history interviews, photographs, and recordings of campus events.

GUIDES: State Historical Society of Wisconsin, *Guide to Archives and Manuscripts in the Chippewa Valley Museum, Eau Claire Public Library, and University of Wisconsin - Eau Claire Area Research Center & Archives* (1977).

SEE: NUCMC, 1963-64, 68 (as State Historical Society of Wisconsin, Area Research Center, Eau Claire), 81.

SEE: Davis; Hinding.

SEE ALSO: Richard A. Erney and F. Gerald Ham, 'Wisconsin's Area Research Centers,' *American Libraries* (Feb. 1972); Richard A. Erney, 'Wisconsin's Area Research Centers,' *American Archivist* 29 (Jan. 1966); Josephine L. Harper, ed., *Guide to the Manuscripts of the State Historical Society of Wisconsin: Supplement Number Two* (State Historical Society of Wisconsin, 1966).

FOND DU LAC

WI170-230
Fond Du Lac County Historical
    Society
Historic Galloway House and Village
336 Old Pioneer Road
Fond Du Lac WI

MAILING ADDRESS:
33 3rd Street
Fond Du Lac WI 54935

(414) 921-4543

OPEN: Memorial Day-Labor Day, daily 1-4; weekends only in Sept.; closed rest of year
ACCESS: members only or by special permission
COPYING FACILITIES: no
MATERIALS SOLICITED: Materials pertaining to Fond Du Lac. Will also accept materials relating to eastern Wisconsin.

HOLDINGS:
Total volume: not specified
Inclusive dates: 1830 -
Description: Materials relating to State and local history, diaries, correspondence, photographs, and genealogical records.

FORT ATKINSON

WI178-240
Fort Atkinson Historical Society
Hoard Historical Museum
407 Merchants Avenue
Fort Atkinson WI 53538

(414) 563-4521

OPEN: first Sunday of the month 1-5, Tu-Sa 9:30-3:30; closed other Sundays, Mondays and holidays
COPYING FACILITIES: yes
MATERIALS SOLICITED: Materials relating to Jefferson County and Ft. Atkinson. Materials relating to Wisconsin Indians, particularly the Winnebago, and the Black Hawk War of 1832. Will also accept materials relating to dairying, for inclusion in the National Dairy Shrine.

HOLDINGS:
Total volume: 7,995 artifacts; 5,254 books, manuscripts, etc.; 4,823 pictures
Inclusive dates: 1832 -
Description: Manuscripts relating chiefly to Jefferson County. Included are copies of the majority of the Black Hawk War letters of General Henry Atkinson and Albert Sidney Johnston; original Mary Atkinson letters; Civil War diaries, letters, records, and rolls; and other material on American wars, such as the Spanish-American War and the Vietnam War. Also included are family genealogies and records of local pioneers.

SEE ALSO: William J. Schereck and Jane A. Smith, eds., *A Bibliography of the History of Jefferson County* (State Historical Society of Wisconsin, 1975).

GREEN BAY

WI202-120

Catholic Diocese of Green Bay
Diocesan Pastoral Office
Chancery
1910 South Webster Avenue
Green Bay WI

MAILING ADDRESS:
P.O. Box 66
Green Bay WI 54305

(414) 435-4406

OPEN: M-F 9-5; closed weekends and
holidays
ACCESS: by appointment only
COPYING FACILITIES: yes
MATERIALS SOLICITED: Histories of the
parishes of Green Bay Diocese. Will
also accept other documents of the
Catholic church in northeastern Wisconsin.

HOLDINGS:
  Total volume: 250 l.f.; 900 microfilm
reels
  Inclusive dates: 1832 -
  Description: Diocesan archives, includ-
ing Chancery correspondence, deeds,
records of ordinations and consecration
of sacred places, and parish histories.
  Also included are collections of Msgr.
Joseph Marx, P.A. (diocesan historian),
Rev. Nicholas Diedrich (local historian),
Msgr. John Gehl (local historian), Rev.
Nicholas Gross (diocesan historian), and
Msgr. Chester Ropella, S.T.D., J.C.D.,
P.A. (canon lawyer).

SEE: Hinding.

WI202-560

Neville Public Museum
210 Museum Place
Green Bay WI 54303

(414) 497-3767

OPEN: M, Tu, F, Sa 9-5, W, Th 9-9, Su
12-5; closed holidays
ACCESS: appointment and identification
required
COPYING FACILITIES: yes
MATERIALS SOLICITED: Materials relating to northeastern Wisconsin.

HOLDINGS:
  Total volume: 26,600 items
  Inclusive dates: 1645 -
  Description: Materials relating chiefly
to the Green Bay area. Included are papers of and concerning James Duane
Doty, Morgan L. Martin, Melancton
Smith, Eleazer Williams, and John Williams of Deerfield, MA. There are also
papers and correspondence of two local
law firms, records of the Cigarmakers'
Union local in Green Bay from 1893 to
1933, land grant documents and deeds,
Indian treaties, World War I draft
records, 8,000 photographs and slides,
10,000 negatives of photographs from a
local newspaper, and 600 newsreels from
a local television station.

SEE: Hamer.

WI202-790

University of Wisconsin at Green Bay
Library Learning Center
Area Research Center
Green Bay WI 54301

(414) 465-2539

OPEN: M, Tu, Th, F, 8:30-5, W 12:30-9;
W hours in summer 8:30-5; closed
weekends and holidays
COPYING FACILITIES: yes
MATERIALS SOLICITED: Papers and
records of persons, institutions, businesses, organizations, and local governments of Brown, Calumet, Door, Florence, Kewaunee, Manitowoc,
Marinette, Menominee, Oconto,
Outagamie, and Shawano counties.
Will also accept materials from other
areas.

HOLDINGS:
  Total volume: 1,115 l.f.
  Inclusive dates: 1830 -
  Description: Manuscripts and government records relating to northeastern
Wisconsin. Included are diaries; personal
papers; business, organization, and labor
union records; and local government
records, chiefly from Brown County.

SEE: NUCMC, 1981.

SEE: Davis.

WI202-810

University of Wisconsin at Green Bay
Library Learning Center
Special Collections
Green Bay WI 54302

(414) 465-2539

OPEN: M, Tu, Th, F 8:30-5, W 8:30-9;
closed weekends and holidays
COPYING FACILITIES: yes
MATERIALS SOLICITED: Materials on
Belgian-Americans in Door, Brown,
and Kewaunee counties. Will also ac-
cept other materials on northeastern
Wisconsin, in particular those dealing
with Brown, Calumet, Door, Florence,
Kewaunee, Manitowoc, Marinette,
Menominee, Oconto, Outagamie, and
Shawano counties.

HOLDINGS:
  Total volume: 349 items
  Inclusive dates: late 1800's -
  Description: Oral history tapes, architectural surveys, and photographs dealing
with the settlement of Walloon Belgians
in Door, Brown, and Kewaunee counties
from 1853 to the present.

SEE ALSO: *Belgian-American Research
Materials: A Selected Bibliography*
(Univ. of Wisconsin at Green Bay, Li-
brary, Special Collections, 1976).

HALES CORNERS

WI214-700

Sacred Heart Fathers and Brothers
North American Province
Provincialate Archives
Hales Corners WI 53130

(414) 425-5575

OPEN: M-F 9-4:30; closed weekends,
holidays, and holy days
ACCESS: serious researchers only: prior
approval of Archivist required
COPYING FACILITIES: yes
MATERIALS SOLICITED: Materials relating to the work of the Sacred Heart Fathers and Brothers in their North
American Province, including records
of Provincial Administration, major
and minor seminaries, colleges and
high schools, domestic and foreign missions, as well as the papers of deceased
members of the community. Will also
accept other materials which are in
some way related to the history of the
Order.

HOLDINGS:
  Total volume: 500 l.f.
  Inclusive dates: 1878 -
  Description: Historical manuscripts relating to the North American Province of
the Sacred Heart Order. Included are
records of minutes and reports, Provincial Offices and Administrations, correspondence, diaries and house journals,
unpublished translations of the writings
of Fr. Leo John Dehon, the Founder of
the Order, oral history interviews, a photograph and slide collecton, motion pictures, videotapes, seminary and college
records, mission materials, and the personal papers of deceased brothers and
priests.

SEE: Meckler and McMullin.

HUDSON

WI230-720

St. Croix County Historical Society
The Octagon House
1004 Third Street
Hudson WI 54016

(715) 386-2654

OPEN: Tu-Sa 10-5, Su 2-5; closed
Mondays and holidays
ACCESS: appointment required
COPYING FACILITIES: no
MATERIALS SOLICITED: Oral history
tapes, photographs, and genealogical information. Will also accept county-
wide records of clubs and schools, historical manuscripts pertaining to county residents, and county plat maps.

HOLDINGS:
  Total volume: not specified
  Inclusive dates: 1840 -
  Description: Photographs, oral history
tapes, and genealogical information relat-
ing to the history of St. Croix County.

JANESVILLE

WI250-690

Rock County Historical Society
10 South High Street
Janesville WI

MAILING ADDRESS:
P.O. Box 896
Janesville WI 53545

(608) 752-4519

OPEN: M-F 9-4:30, Sa by appointment;
closed Sundays and holidays
ACCESS: advance arrangements advisable
COPYING FACILITIES: yes
MATERIALS SOLICITED: Historical materials relating to Rock County.

HOLDINGS:
Total volume: 3,000 items
Inclusive dates: 1840's -
Description: Materials describing the geographic, political, institutional, and religious history of Rock County. Included are diaries, letters, ledgers, 2,000 photographs, 15 oral history recordings on the black labor movement, and 10 transcripts of oral history interviews with descendants of early settlers.

SEE: Schatz.

WI250-800

University of Wisconsin Center -
Rock County
Library
2909 Kellogg Avenue
Janesville WI 53545

(608) 755-2831

OPEN: M-Th 8-9, F 8-5, Su 2-8; closed
Saturdays and holidays
COPYING FACILITIES: yes
MATERIALS SOLICITED: Archival materials relating to the Center.

HOLDINGS:
Total volume: 6 file drawers
Inclusive dates: 1966 -
Description: Archives of the Center, including memoranda, reports, news releases, publications, and constitutions of student organizations.

KENOSHA

WI266-430

Kenosha County Historical Museum
Library
6300 Third Avenue
Kenosha WI 53140

(414) 654-5770

OPEN: Tu, Th 2-4:30, first Sunday of
month 2-4:30, M, W, F by
appointment; closed weekends and
holidays
COPYING FACILITIES: yes

HOLDINGS:
Total volume: 2,500 items; 60 c.f.
Inclusive dates: 1836 -
Description: Photographs and slides of pioneers, industrialists, buildings and homes, and other local history subjects. Manuscripts relating to Kenosha history

include correspondence and reminiscences of settlers, diaries, shipping manifests, and records of Kemper Hall, a women's college, (1870's-1970's).

SEE: Hamer.

SEE: Novotny.

WI266-820

University of Wisconsin at Parkside
University Archives and Area
Research Center
Kenosha WI 53140

MAILING ADDRESS:
Box 2000
Kenosha WI 53141

(414) 553-2411

OPEN: M-F 8-4:30; closed weekends and
holidays
COPYING FACILITIES: yes
MATERIALS SOLICITED: Local history materials, including University of Wisconsin at Parkside, records of governments and private institutions, and personal papers. Will also accept other materials relating to Wisconsin history.

HOLDINGS:
Total volume: 1,700 l.f.
Inclusive dates: 1836 -
Description: The Area Research Center consists of local government records as well as business, labor, education, religious, ethnic, political, and private collections from Racine and Kenosha counties. The University Archives contains administrative files, reports, faculty and student publications, photographs, and recording tapes, dating from 1946, but with emphasis on the period after 1967.

GUIDES: State Historical Society of Wisconsin, Checklist of Archives and Manuscripts in the University of Wisconsin - Parkside Area Research Center (1977).

SEE: NUCMC, 1978, 1981.

SEE: Davis; Hinding.

LA CROSSE

WI298-120

Catholic Diocese of La Crosse
4238 Mormon Coulee Road
La Crosse WI

MAILING ADDRESS:
Box 69
La Crosse WI 54601

(608) 788-7700, Ext. 220

OPEN: M-F 9-4; closed weekends, holy
days, and the day after Christmas and
Easter
COPYING FACILITIES: yes

HOLDINGS:
Total volume: 45 l.f.
Inclusive dates: 1868 -
Description: A collection of ecclesiastical documents and letters dealing with the history of the Catholic church in the Diocese of La Crosse.

WI298-250

Franciscan Sisters of Perpetual
Adoration
St. Rose Convent
912 Market Street
La Crosse WI 54601

(608) 782-5610

OPEN: M-F 9-5; closed weekends and
holidays
COPYING FACILITIES: yes
MATERIALS SOLICITED: Materials relating to the Franciscan Sisters of Perpetual Adoration community.

HOLDINGS:
Total volume: not specified
Inclusive dates: 1858 -
Description: The Archives include personal histories and papers of each member of the order; oral history tapes; constitutions, articles, and bylaws; scrapbooks and jubilee celebrations; official correspondence; financial records and deeds; photographs; material dealing with the Franciscan Sisters of the Eucharist; newsletters; annals of missions; historical maps; and correspondence of Archbishop Michael Heiss who figured prominently in the founding of the Community.

SEE: Hinding.

WI298-470

La Crosse County Historical Society
112 South 9th Street
La Crosse WI

(608) 782-1980

SEE: Hamer.

Questionnaire not returned.

WI298-480

La Crosse County Library
Courthouse
400 North 4th Street
La Crosse WI 54601

(608) 786-2111

OPEN: M-F 8-5, Sa 8:30-12:30; closed
Sundays and holidays
COPYING FACILITIES: yes
MATERIALS SOLICITED: Local history.

HOLDINGS:
Total volume: 2 l.f.
Inclusive dates: 1860 -
Description: Manuscripts of local author Alvin Peterson, and a few business ledgers and journals from La Crosse County.

WI298-490

La Crosse Public Library
Department of Local History and
Archives
800 Main Street
La Crosse WI 54601

(608) 784-8623, Ext. 36

OPEN: Su 1-5, M-Th 12-9, F, Sa 10-5;
closed holidays and Sundays in August
COPYING FACILITIES: yes
MATERIALS SOLICITED: Manuscripts and private records relating to the history of La Crosse, the Mississippi River in

the La Crosse area, and La Crosse County. Will also accept manuscripts and records relating to the history of the Iowa-Minnesota-Wisconsin tri-state area, and to counties in Wisconsin adjacent to La Crosse County.

HOLDINGS:
   Total volume: 25 l.f.; 40 items
   Inclusive dates: 1857 - 1976
   Description: Materials relating to the history of La Crosse and the surrounding area.

WI298-810
University of Wisconsin at La Crosse
Murphy Library
Special Collections and Area Research
   Center
1631 Pine Street
La Crosse WI 54601

(608) 785-8511

OPEN: M-F 9-5, Sa 1-4, reduced hours when University not in session; closed Sundays and holidays
COPYING FACILITIES: yes
MATERIALS SOLICITED: Materials relating to Wisconsin and upper Mississippi River regional history, as well as life and lore of the Mississippi River, particularly steamboating. Will also accept rare and unusual books and documents and materials on U.S. history.

HOLDINGS:
   Total volume: 300 l.f.
   Inclusive dates: 1700 -
   Description: Manuscripts, books, maps, photographs, tapes, relating to Wisconsin and upper Mississippi River region, with particular emphasis on southwestern Wisconsin and La Crosse County area. Substantial holdings in public records, photographs, and steamboating data from mid-19th century to present, and in family and small business records for southwest Wisconsin.
      Also included are 600 reels of oral history, with emphasis on social life, customs, and domestic-professional aspects of area history; 30,000 photos relating to steamboating, river history, and local history.

SEE: Hamer (as Wisconsin State College Library); NUCMC, 1968 (as State Historical Society of Wisconsin, Area Research Center, La Crosse) 78, 81.

SEE: Meckler and McMullin; Davis; Hinding; Robbins.

LAONA

WI326-120
Camp Five Foundation Museum
Laona WI 54541

(715) 674-3414

OPEN: Memorial Day - Labor Day, M-Sa 10-4; closed Sundays and rest of year
COPYING FACILITIES: yes
MATERIALS SOLICITED: Photographs and maps relating to the lumber industry.

HOLDINGS:
   Total volume: 200 items
   Inclusive dates: 1872 -
   Description: Photographs of the lumber industry, railroads, and the ecology of the North Woods.

MADISON

WI346-240
Forest Service
Forest Products Laboratory
North Walnut Street
Madison WI

MAILING ADDRESS:
P.O. Box 5130
Madison WI 53705

(608) 264-6500

OPEN: M-F 8-4; closed weekends and holidays
COPYING FACILITIES: yes
MATERIALS SOLICITED: Clippings, memorabilia, and other materials relating to laboratory history, activities, and personnel.

HOLDINGS:
   Total volume: 40 l.f.
   Inclusive dates: 1909 -
   Description: History of the establishment of the Forest Products Laboratory; correspondence regarding development and accomplishment of its research programs; clippings; 30 oral history tapes; biographies of prominent staff members; photographs, glass slides, and scrapbooks.

WI346-280
Grand Army of the Republic
   Memorial Hall Museum
Capitol 419 North
Madison WI 53702

(608) 266-1680

OPEN: M-F 9-4:30; open summer weekends 9-4:30; closed other weekends and holidays
ACCESS: advance arrangements advised
COPYING FACILITIES: yes
MATERIALS SOLICITED: Wisconsin Civil War and Civil War veterans' organizations materials. Will also accept Wisconsin-related and foreign military materials on the Spanish-American War, World Wars I and II, Korean War, and Vietnam War.

HOLDINGS:
   Total volume: 85 l.f.
   Inclusive dates: 1860 - 1973
   Description: A collection of records of Grand Army of the Republic posts in Wisconsin, 1883-1930; similar scattered records for the Womans Relief Corps, United Spanish War Veterans, and Sons of Veterans, 1910-45; and a few records of Wisconsin Civil War regiments, including ledgers, muster rolls, diaries, and post-War accounts.

SEE: Hinding.

WI346-720
The State Historical Society of
   Wisconsin
Archives Division
816 State Street
Madison WI 53706

(608) 262-3338

OPEN: M-Sa 8-5; closed Sundays and holidays
ACCESS: advance arrangements advised
COPYING FACILITIES: yes
MATERIALS SOLICITED: Wisconsin history and government; and National materials relating to labor, industry, agriculture, socialism, civil rights, student activism, contemporary social, economic, and political movements, and mass communications. Will also accept manuscripts, maps, sound recordings, and visual documents which relate to other areas in American history, with emphasis on the upper Midwest and the Great Lakes region.

HOLDINGS:
   Total volume: 68,000 c.f.
   Inclusive dates: 1660 -
   Description: Public records of Wisconsin, 26,000 c.f., from 1799 to date, including papers of governors, the State legislature, courts, State agencies, and county and local governments; and manuscripts, 28,000 c.f., including the Draper Collection on the trans-Allegheny frontier, the McCormick Collection on the personal interests and business activities of Cyrus H. McCormick and his family, and collections on the history of Wisconsin and such National areas of interest as the labor movement, socialism, civil rights, mass communications, and contemporary social action movements.
      There are also more than 25,000 maps, with emphasis on Wisconsin and the Great Lakes region; audible and visual documents emphasizing rural and small town life in the upper Midwest, 1880-1920's, as well as contemporary Wisconsin; and materials deposited by organizations, including papers of the Wisconsin Conference of the United Church of Christ and its predecessors, 1839-1968, the American Council for Judaism papers, and pharmaco-historical manuscripts of the American Institute of the History of Pharmacy.

SEE: Hamer; NUCMC, 1959-65, 68, 73, 78, 81.

SEE: Meckler and McMullin; Schatz; Duignan; Novotny; Hounshell; Krichmar; Davis; Robbins; Hinding; Allard, Crawley, and Edmison; Bean and Vane; Spalek; Beers - Southwest; White.

SEE ALSO: The following publications of the Society: David J. Delgado, comp., *Guide to the Wisconsin State Archives* (1966); William G. Paul, comp., *Wisconsin's Civil War Archives* (1965); Margaret R. Hafstad, ed., *Guide to the McCormick Collection of The State Historical Society of Wisconsin* (1967); F. Gerald Ham, comp., *Labor Manuscripts in The State Historical Society of Wisconsin* (1967); Josephine L. Harper, ed., *Guide to the Manuscripts of The State Historical Society of Wisconsin, Supplement 2* (1966); James P. Danky and Eleanor McKay, *Women's History: Resources at The State Historical Society of Wisconsin* (1975); Janice O'Connell, comp., *The Collections of the Mass Communications History Center of The State Historical Society of Wisconsin and The Collections of the Wisconsin Center for Theatre Research of the University of Wisconsin and The State Historical Society of Wisconsin* (1974).

Additional guides to individual collections are available at the Archives Division.

WI346-840

University of Wisconsin at Madison
Library
Rare Books Department
728 State Street
Madison WI 53706

(608) 262-3243

OPEN: M-F 8-5; closed weekends and holidays

SEE: Hamer (as University of Wisconsin, Memorial Library); NUCMC, 1970-71.

Questionnaire not returned.

WI346-850

University of Wisconsin at Madison
Map and Air Photo Library
384 Science Hall
550 North Park Street
Madison WI 53706

(608) 262-1471

OPEN: M-F 8-5; closed weekends and holidays; shorter hours during University vacations
COPYING FACILITIES: yes
MATERIALS SOLICITED: Aerial photographs of Wisconsin. Will also accept maps of Wisconsin and other areas of the world.

HOLDINGS:
Total volume: 28 file drawers
Inclusive dates: 1930's -
Description: A collection of approximately 80,000 aerial photographs and 1,200 mosaic indexes of the State of Wisconsin. About 25,000 photographs covering other parts of the United States and the world are also in the collection.

SEE ALSO: a list of air photo mosaic indexes, available upon request.

WI346-870

University of Wisconsin at Madison
School of Pharmacy
F. B. Power Pharmaceutical Library
Kremers Reference Files
425 North Charter Street
Madison WI 53706

(608) 262-2894

OPEN: by appointment only; closed weekends and holidays
COPYING FACILITIES: yes
MATERIALS SOLICITED: All areas of pharmacy, pharmacology, toxicology and related health sciences.

HOLDINGS:
Total volume: 360 file drawers
Inclusive dates: 1850's -
Description: Letters, laboratory records, minute books of organizations, biographical sketches, prescriptions, pictures, and other matter mainly relating to pharmaceutical subjects. Housed with these files are the Kremers manuscript encyclopedia of historical pharmacy; pharmaceutical corporation reports; and representative prescription books of pharmacies.

SEE: Hamer (as American Institute of the History of Pharmacy); NUCMC, 1959-61.

WI346-890

University of Wisconsin at Madison
System Archives
B134 Memorial Library
Madison WI 53706

(608) 262-3290

OPEN: M-F 8-5; closed weekends and holidays
COPYING FACILITIES: yes
MATERIALS SOLICITED: Materials on University development and operations. Will also accept manuscripts and personal papers of faculty and administrators.

HOLDINGS:
Total volume: 16,000 c.f.
Inclusive dates: 1848 -
Description: University records, including those of the central administration, the Madison campus, University extensions, and the Center System, most dating after 1886. Included are papers of administrators, faculty, staff, students, and other individuals associated with the University; official records of departments and agencies of the University; oral history interviews of administrators and emeriti faculty; and 35,000 photographs and negatives of University academic and social life.

SEE: Davis; Robbins.

WI346-900

Wisconsin Center for Film and
  Theater Research
816 State Street
Madison WI

MAILING ADDRESS:
6039 Vilas Communication Hall
University of Wisconsin
Madison WI 53706

(608) 262-9706, 0585

OPEN: M-F 8-5, Sa 8-4; closed Sundays, holidays, and Saturday afternoons during University vacations
ACCESS: restricted to persons with legitimate specified research purpose; advance arrangements advised
COPYING FACILITIES: yes
MATERIALS SOLICITED: Film, television, and theater materials. Will also accept materials in music and dance.

HOLDINGS:
Total volume: 6,000 c.f.
Inclusive dates: 1900 -
Description: Primary source material relating to the performing arts in 20th century America and their role in social and cultural history. Over 150 collections document the development of theater, motion pictures, radio, and television.

GUIDES: Janice O'Connell, comp., *The Collections of the Mass Communications History Center of The State Historical Society of Wisconsin and The Collections of the Wisconsin Center for Theatre Research of the University of Wisconsin and The State Historical Society of Wisconsin* (1974).

SEE ALSO: Barbara J. Kaiser, 'Resources in the Wisconsin Center for Theatre Research,' *American Archivist* 30 (July 1967); Ted Perry, ed., *Performing Arts Resources* (Drama Book Specialists, 1975); Ann Novotny, ed., *Picture Sources 3* (Special Libraries Assn., 1975); Josephine L. Harper, *Guide to the Manuscripts of The State Historical Society of Wisconsin, Supplement 2* (State Historical Society of Wisconsin, 1966).

The Center is administered jointly by The State Historical Society of Wisconsin and the University of Wisconsin.

MANITOWOC

WI354-520

Manitowoc Maritime Museum
809 South 8th Street
Manitowoc WI 54220

(414) 684-0218

OPEN: M-F 9-5; closed weekends and holidays
COPYING FACILITIES: yes
MATERIALS SOLICITED: Materials relating to the maritime history of the Great Lakes. Will also accept materials relating to maritime history of other areas.

HOLDINGS:
Total volume: 12,000 items
Inclusive dates: 1870 -
Description: Records relating to the maritime history of the Great Lakes, including photographs, manuscripts, and scrapbooks.

MARINETTE

WI362-520

Marinette County Historical Society
Stephenson Island
Marinette WI

MAILING ADDRESS:
P.O. Box 262
Marinette WI 54143

(715) 732-0831 (summer only)

OPEN: M-Sa 10-4, Su noon-4; closed July 4th
USER FEES: adults one dollar; senior citizens 75 cents; students 50 cents, except when studying records

COPYING FACILITIES: no
MATERIALS SOLICITED: Materials pertaining to all aspects of Marinette County history, including the history of the logging and commercial fishing industries.

HOLDINGS:
Total volume: 5,000 items
Inclusive dates: 1850 -
Description: A collection of manuscripts and photographs relating to logging in Marinette County; materials relating to Marinette County communities; and oral history tapes of reminiscences on commercial fishing, logging, agriculture, and medical practice in the area.

MAYVILLE

WI378-520
Mayville Historical Society, Inc.
Museum Complex
11 North German Street
Mayville WI 53050

(414)387-5530, 4295

OPEN: May - Oct., second and fourth Sundays, 1:30-4:30 or by appointment; closed Nov. - April
COPYING FACILITIES: yes
MATERIALS SOLICITED: Company records of early Mayville. Will also accept any records relating to Mayville.

HOLDINGS:
Total volume: not specified
Inclusive dates: not specified
Description: Photographs and records relating to Mayville and its iron ore industry.

MAZOMANIE

WI382-520
Mazomanie Historical Society
Research Center
51 Crescent Street
Mazomanie WI 53560

(608) 795-2216

OPEN: by appointment
COPYING FACILITIES: no
MATERIALS SOLICITED: Will accept materials relating to State and local history, such as family records, municipal and town records, records of churches and schools, photographs, tax and voting records, and miscellaneous manuscripts.

HOLDINGS:
Total volume: not specified
Inclusive dates: 1843 -
Description: Records relating to the village of Mazomanie and Mazomanie Township, including cemetery records, census reports, election registers, Grand Army of the Republic and Civil War records, plat maps, school attendance records, and tax records.

MCFARLAND

WI390-520
McFarland Historical Society
Museum
5814 Main Street
McFarland WI

MAILING ADDRESS:
Box 62
McFarland WI 53558

(608) 838-4185

OPEN: Memorial Day-Sept. 30, Su 1-5
COPYING FACILITIES: no

HOLDINGS:
Total volume: not specified
Inclusive dates: 19th century -
Description: Logbooks of the local post office and railway depot, photographs of the McFarland area, and manuscript local histories.

MENOMONIE

WI418-520
Mabel Tainter Memorial Library
205 Main Street
Menomonie WI 54751

(715) 235-5558

SEE: Hamer.

Questionnaire not returned.

WI418-800
University of Wisconsin at Stout
Library Learning Center
Area Research Center
Menomonie WI 54751

(715) 232-2300

OPEN: M-Th 8-9, F 8-5, Sa 11-4, Su 7-9; hours vary during University recesses
ACCESS: appointment requested
COPYING FACILITIES: yes
MATERIALS SOLICITED: Materials relating to Barron and Dunn counties, WI; records of the University of Wisconsin at Stout; and papers and other materials of its faculty, staff, and alumni. Will also accept manuscripts relating to home economics, industrial education, vocational rehabilitation, industry, and technology, as well as genealogies of families of northwestern Wisconsin.

HOLDINGS:
Total volume: 450 l.f.
Inclusive dates: 1858 -
Description: Materials relating to Barron and Dunn counties, WI, consisting of business records, genealogies, church histories, cemetery records, community organization records, personal papers, reminiscences, photographs, recordings, and local government records. Also included are records, photographs, manuscripts, and recordings relating to the University of Wisconsin at Stout and its faculty and alumni.

SEE: NUCMC, 1981.

SEE: Davis.

MEQUON

WI426-111
Concordia College
College Archives and Archives of the South Wisconsin District of the Lutheran Church-Missouri Synod
12800 N. Lake Shore Drive
Mequon WI 53092

(414) 243-5700, Ext. 527

OPEN: M-F 8:30-4; closed weekends, holidays, and school vacations
COPYING FACILITIES: yes
MATERIALS SOLICITED: Records of or relating to Concordia College and the South Wisconsin District, local congregations, and affiliated auxiliary agencies. Will also accept records relating to Lutheranism in southern Wisconsin and the life, work, and activities of Lutherans, especially the Lutheran Church-Missouri Synod.

HOLDINGS:
Total volume: 256 l.f.
Inclusive dates: 1896 -
Description: Manuscripts and documents of or relating to Concordia College and the South Wisconsin District, Wisconsin District, and Northern District of the Lutheran Church-Missouri Synod.

WI426-120
Crafts Museum
11458 North Laguna Drive 21W
Mequon WI 53092

(414) 242-1571

OPEN: by appointment only
ACCESS: written permission required
COPYING FACILITIES: yes
MATERIALS SOLICITED: Materials relating to natural ice harvesting, storage, and delivery, and to wooden shoe making.

HOLDINGS:
Total volume: 325 items
Inclusive dates: 1900 -
Description: Home-made movies, photographs, logbooks, and letters relating to ice harvesting, storage, and delivery. There is also material relating to wooden shoe making and other woodworking.

MIDDLETON

WI442-530
Middleton Public Library
7426 Hubbard Avenue
Middleton WI 53562

(608) 831-5564

OPEN: M-Th 10-9, F, Sa 10-5; closed Sundays and holidays
COPYING FACILITIES: yes
MATERIALS SOLICITED: Materials relating to Middleton.

HOLDINGS:
Total volume: 45 items
Inclusive dates: 1972 -
Description: Oral history tapes relating to Middleton.

MILTON

WI450-530

Milton Historical Society
Library
744 East Madison Avenue
Milton WI

MAILING ADDRESS:
P.O. Box 245
Milton WI 53563

(608) 868-7772

OPEN: by appointment
COPYING FACILITIES: no
MATERIALS SOLICITED: Materials relating
to local history. Will also accept business records.

HOLDINGS:
   Total volume: not specified
   Inclusive dates: 1836 -
   Description: Materials relating chiefly
   to Milton, including diaries, letters, land
   grant documents, maps, account books,
   photographs, genealogical records of local
   interest, and oral history tapes.

MILWAUKEE

WI456-490

Legislative Reference Bureau
Room 404, City Hall
200 East Wells Street
Milwaukee WI 53202

(414) 278-2295

OPEN: M-F 8-4:45; closed weekends and
   holidays
COPYING FACILITIES: yes
MATERIALS SOLICITED: Milwaukee city
   government documents, and records relating broadly to city planning, public
   finance, public administration, housing,
   urban affairs, and employment.

HOLDINGS:
   Total volume: 225 l.f.
   Inclusive dates: 1846 -
   Description: Official documents, such
   as annual reports, special reports, and
   minutes, of Milwaukee city government
   since its incorporation in 1846. Also held
   are some records of the Milwaukee school
   board, Milwaukee County, and the State
   of Wisconsin.

SEE ALSO: Harry H. Anderson, 'Historical
   Research Resources and Opportunities
   in Metropolitan Milwaukee,' *Historical
   Messenger of the Milwaukee County
   Historical Society* 30 (Spring 1974);
   John A. Fleckner and Stanley Mallach,
   eds., *Guide to Historical Resources in
   Milwaukee Area Archives* (Milwaukee
   Area Archives Group, 1976).

WI456-495

Marquette University
Memorial Library
Department of Special Collections and
University Archives
1415 West Wisconsin Avenue
Milwaukee WI 53233

(414) 224-7256

OPEN: M-F 8-5; closed weekends and
   holidays
COPYING FACILITIES: yes
MATERIALS SOLICITED: Written and audible documents pertaining to social
   change, particularly Catholic social action in 20th century America; materials
   concerning the sociology of religion;
   Catholic Indian mission records of
   North America; and archives of Marquette University. Will also accept papers of Marquette alumni, particularly
   in the fields of broadcasting, entertainment, and State and National politics;
   literary manuscripts; and personal papers and organization records from the
   Milwaukee area.

HOLDINGS:
   Total volume: 4,200 c.f.
   Inclusive dates: 1850 -
   Description: 60 archival and manuscript collections, 1,300 c.f., relating primarily to American social change and the
   contributions of Catholic church organizations and individuals to interracial justice; economic reform; fair employment;
   women's, minority and welfare rights;
   agrarian reform; and international peace.
   Post-war anti-Communist activity, broadcasting, social criticism and literature also
   are represented. There are also the University Archives, 1,500 c.f., and records
   of the Bureau of Catholic Indian Missions, 400 c.f.

SEE: NUCMC, 1959-61.

SEE: Robbins; Meckler and McMullin.

WI456-500

Medical College of Wisconsin
Todd Wehr Library
8701 Watertown Plank Road
Milwaukee WI

MAILING ADDRESS:
P.O. Box 26509
Milwaukee WI 53226

(414) 257-8302

OPEN: M-F 8:30-4; closed weekends and
   holidays
ACCESS: by prior arrangement only,
   seven day advance notice minimum
COPYING FACILITIES: yes
MATERIALS SOLICITED: History of medicine materials.

HOLDINGS:
   Total volume: 8 file drawers; 1 l.f.
   Inclusive dates: 1880's -
   Description: Records and correspondence of the Milwaukee Academy of
   Medicine, founded in 1886, and other
   manuscripts and notebooks relating to the
   history of medicine.

SEE: Hamer (as Milwaukee Academy of
   Medicine).

WI456-530

Milwaukee Art Center
Prairie Archives
750 North Lincoln Memorial Drive
Milwaukee WI 53202

(414) 271-9508, Ext. 209

OPEN: by appointment M-F 9-4; closed
   weekends and holidays

COPYING FACILITIES: yes
MATERIALS SOLICITED: Manuscripts, visual documents and scrapbooks documenting the early modern history of
   Midwestern, especially Milwaukee area,
   architectural interiors. Will also accept
   Midwestern architectural materials.

HOLDINGS:
   Total volume: 400 c.f.
   Inclusive dates: 1897 - 1975
   Description: Records relating to interior design and related architecture of
   Wisconsin and the Midwest including
   drawings and office records of
   Niedecken-Walbridge Company and
   George Niedecken, designer.

WI456-540

Milwaukee County Historical Society
910 North 3rd Street
Milwaukee WI 53203

(414) 273-8288

OPEN: M-F 9-5; closed weekends and
   holidays
COPYING FACILITIES: yes
MATERIALS SOLICITED: Materials relating
   to socialism, Milwaukee, ethnic groups,
   Charles King, Douglas MacArthur, and
   William Mitchell. Will also accept materials relating to Wisconsin, the Great
   Lakes, and labor history, as well as papers of hereditary and patriotic societies.

HOLDINGS:
   Total volume: 5,000 c.f.
   Inclusive dates: 1820 -
   Description: Over 5,000 collections relating to individuals and private and public institutions in Milwaukee County. Included are correspondence, business
   records, photographs, maps, and 500 cubic feet of local court records, 1837-1928.

GUIDES: *A Preliminary Survey of Manuscript and Archival Collections of the
   Milwaukee County Historical Society*
   (1967).

SEE: Hamer; NUCMC, 1967, 69, 80.

SEE: Allard, Crawley, and Edmison; Robbins; Hinding.

SEE ALSO: John A. Fleckner and Stanley
   Mallach, eds., *Guide to Historical Resources in Milwaukee Area Archives*
   (Milwaukee Area Archives Group,
   1976); Walter Schatz, ed., *Directory of
   Afro-American Resources* (Bowker,
   1970).

WI456-550

Milwaukee Public Library
Local History and Marine Room
814 West Wisconsin Avenue
Milwaukee WI 53233

(414) 278-3074

OPEN: M 12:30-9, Tu-Sa 12:30-5:15;
   Tuesday following Monday holiday
   12:30-9; closed Sundays and holidays
COPYING FACILITIES: yes
MATERIALS SOLICITED: Materials relating
   to Milwaukee and vicinity, the Great
   Lakes, Wisconsin, and American socialism.

HOLDINGS:
Total volume: 4,335 c.f.
Inclusive dates: 1800 -
Description: Manuscripts relating to the history of Milwaukee, the State of Wisconsin and surrounding States, and the Great Lakes. Included are photographs, papers of literary and political figures, and records of local businesses, shipping interests, and the Socialist Party. The Library is the city archives repository, housing extensive financial records and departmental correspondence, as well as records of miscellaneous Milwaukee agencies.

SEE: Hamer; NUCMC, 1959-64.

SEE: Robbins.

SEE ALSO: Harry H. Anderson, 'Historical Research Resources and Opportunities in Metropolitan Milwaukee,' *Historical Messenger of the Milwaukee County Historical Society* 30 (Spring 1974); John A. Fleckner and Stanley Mallach, eds., *Guide to Historical Resources in Milwaukee Area Archives* (Milwaukee Area Archives Group, 1976); Gerald Friedberg, 'Sources for the Study of Socialism in America, 1901-1919,' *Labor History* 6 (Spring 1965). The Library has published a guide to its Socialist Party holdings.

WI456-560

Milwaukee Public Museum
History Division
800 West Wells Street
Milwaukee WI 53233

(414) 278-2744

OPEN: M-F 9-4:30; closed weekends and holidays
USER FEES: for non-scholarly research only: one dollar for Milwaukee County residents, $2 for non-residents
COPYING FACILITIES: yes
MATERIALS SOLICITED: Business records and other materials relating to watches and clocks, typewriters, office machines, bicycles, firearms, tools, and machinery.

HOLDINGS:
Total volume: 12,200 items; 6 file drawers
Inclusive dates: 1860's - 1960's
Description: Correspondence between the inventor of the typewriter C. L. Sholes and the Densmore brothers, promoters of the machine, especially James Densmore. Materials relate to Merritt, Densmore, and Remington typewriters and to typewriters in general. There is also a patent file and index from the Elgin National Watch Company, and materials relating to Milwaukee history.

SEE: Hamer.

WI456-720

St. Francis Seminary
Salzmann Library
3257 South Lake Drive
Milwaukee WI 53207

(414) 483-1979

OPEN: M-F 8-4:30; closed weekends and holidays
ACCESS: advance arrangements advised

COPYING FACILITIES: yes

HOLDINGS:
Total volume: not specified
Inclusive dates: 1856 -
Description: Archives of St. Francis Seminary, including papers of Seminary faculty and rectors and papers and records of Seminary students.

SEE: NUCMC, 1966.

WI456-730

School Sisters of St. Francis
Archives
1501 South Layton Blvd.
Milwaukee WI 53215

(414) 384-4105, Ext. 394

OPEN: M-F 9-4; closed weekends and holidays
COPYING FACILITIES: yes
MATERIALS SOLICITED: Materials pertaining to School Sisters of St. Francis.

HOLDINGS:
Total volume: 600 c.f.
Inclusive dates: 1866 -
Description: Manuscripts, records, diaries, photographs, motion pictures, sound recordings, and other materials documenting the founding and growth of the SSSF and their works, including rural and urban mission schools for Native Americans, immigrants, blacks and other Americans; the SSSF hospitals; the Congregation's life and work in India, China and Latin America in the 20th century; and the SSSF contribution to American music education and liturgical music.

SEE: Hinding.

WI456-734

Sisters of St. Francis of Assisi
Archives
3221 South Lake Drive
Milwaukee WI 53207

(414) 744-1160

OPEN: M-F 9-5; weekends by appointment
COPYING FACILITIES: no
MATERIALS SOLICITED: Materials relating to the Sisters of St. Francis of Assisi and churches and organizations in which members have been active.

HOLDINGS:
Total volume: 60 c.f.
Description: Materials relating to the Sisters of St. Francis of Assisi including manuscripts, institutional records, photographs and recordings.

WI456-735

Sisters of the Divine Savior
North American Province
Archives
Sisters of the Divine Savior
Community House
4311 North 100th Street
Milwaukee WI 53222

(414) 466-0810

OPEN: M-F 8:30-4:30; closed weekends, holidays and holy days
COPYING FACILITIES: yes

MATERIALS SOLICITED: All administrative, historical, and other pertinent records and papers of the Provincial Administration, convents, institutions, schools and various apostolates and ministries in which the Sisters of the Divine Savior are engaged. Will also accept records related to our Congregation, and our Sisters working in various areas.

HOLDINGS:
Total volume: 136 volumes; 65 boxes
Inclusive dates: 1895 -
Description: Records of the Sisters of the Divine Savior, particularly of the North American Province in Alabama, Illinois, Minnesota, South Dakota, Washington and Wisconsin. Included are the papers of the Founder and Foundress, and of the Major Supervisors; the papers and records of deceased or former Sisters; financial, administrative, retirement, foreign mission and Roman records; Roman manuscripts; chronicles and annals; oral history tapes; other recordings; photographs and scrapbooks relating to the Sisters of the Divine Savior.

WI456-740

Socialist Party
Library and Archives
Suite 325
135 West Wells Street
Milwaukee WI 53203

(414) 276-0773

OPEN: by appointment only
COPYING FACILITIES: yes

HOLDINGS:
Total volume: 50 l.f.
Inclusive dates: 1920 -
Description: Correspondence, financial records, public documents, archives and non-current records of the Socialist Party of Milwaukee County, as well as photographs, audio tapes, membership records, minutes of the Wisconsin State Socialist Party Executive Committee, 1906- , convention transcripts, policy statements, and other materials.

WI456-810

University of Wisconsin at Milwaukee
Library
Archives and Special Collections
Milwaukee WI 53201

(414) 963-5402

OPEN: M-F 8-4:30; closed weekends and holidays
COPYING FACILITIES: yes
MATERIALS SOLICITED: Local history and University history.

HOLDINGS:
Total volume: 1,304 c.f.
Inclusive dates: 1792 -
Description: As an Area Research Center of the State Historical Society of Wisconsin, the Library is a depository for personal papers, business records, and government documents from Milwaukee County and four surrounding counties. The University archives contains 300 cubic feet of catalogs, publications, and correspondence. There are also two collections of correspondence, one of the *Are-*

na, a literary magazine published in Ireland from 1963 to 1965, and the other of the *Little Review,* including letters of Edith Sitwell, James Joyce, Ezra Pound, Ernest Hemingway, T. S. Eliot, Ben Hecht, Margaret Anderson, and Jane Heap.

SEE: NUCMC, 1968, 78, 81.

SEE: Robbins; Hinding.

SEE ALSO: John A. Fleckner and Stanley Mallach, eds., *Guide to Historical Resources in Milwaukee Area Archives* (Milwaukee Area Archives Group, 1976); Richard C. Davis, *North American Forest History: A Guide to Archives and Manuscripts in the United States and Canada* (Clio Books, 1977).

MINERAL POINT

WI462-520
Mineral Point Historical Society
Gundry House
234 Madison Street
Mineral Point WI

MAILING ADDRESS:
515 Maiden Street
Mineral Point WI 53565

no telephone

OPEN: May-Sept. daily 10-4; Oct.-April by appointment
ACCESS: by permission of Board of Directors
COPYING FACILITIES: no
MATERIALS SOLICITED: Genealogical materials and other items relating to Iowa County. Will also accept other materials relating to Wisconsin.

HOLDINGS:
Total volume: 700 items
Inclusive dates: 1827 - 1927
Description: Materials relating to early Iowa County. Included are legal documents, papers of pioneers, account books and records of firms, Civil War diaries, and 350 glass plate negatives showing activities, homes, and businesses in Mineral Point in the 1860's and 1870's.

MONONA

WI474-520
Monona Public Library
1000 Nichols Road
Monona WI 53716

(608) 222-6127

OPEN: M-Th 10-9, F 10-6, Sa 9-5; closed Sundays and holidays
COPYING FACILITIES: yes
MATERIALS SOLICITED: Materials on the greater Madison area, with special emphasis on the area which is now the city of Monona and the rural and urban areas of the original Blooming Grove Township, as well as materials from other Wisconsin communities. Will also accept photographs, newspaper clippings, church and other organization records, films, manuscript maps, and tape recordings.

HOLDINGS:
Total volume: 2 file drawers; 18 oral history tapes
Inclusive dates: 1850 -
Description: Genealogical materials, oral history recordings, and municipal records concerning the history of the village of Blooming Grove, the city of Monona, and vicinity, with emphasis on early settlers. The collection includes the holdings of the Historic Blooming Grove Historical Society.

NASHOTAH

WI498-560
Nashotah House
Library
Nashotah WI 53058

(414) 646-3371

OPEN: M-F 8:30-4:30; closed weekends and holidays
COPYING FACILITIES: yes
MATERIALS SOLICITED: Materials pertaining to Nashotah House and its history. Will also accept materials pertaining to its alumni and such faculty members as James Lloyd Breck, James Dekoven, Jackson Kemper, and William Adams, as well as the Episcopal church in Wisconsin and local history.

HOLDINGS:
Total volume: 25 l.f.
Inclusive dates: 1842 -
Description: Materials pertaining to Nashotah House since its establishment, with emphasis on 19th century materials. Included are official records, personal papers of those associated with the institution, lecture notes, diaries, photographs, and letters, in addition to personal papers, letters, and diaries of Bishop W. W. Webb of Milwaukee.

NEENAH

WI502-440
Kimberly-Clark Corporation
North Lake Street
Neenah WI 54956

(414) 721-2000

OPEN: M-F 8-4; closed weekends and holidays
ACCESS: scholars on request and with approval
COPYING FACILITIES: yes

HOLDINGS:
Total volume: 50 file drawers
Inclusive dates: 1872 -
Description: Photographs, annual reports, financial records, house organs, press clippings, training brochures, pamphlets, minutes, articles of incorporation, and correspondence of the Kimberly-Clark Corporation.

SEE: Davis.

NORTH FREEDOM

WI530-520
Mid-Continent Railway Historical Society, Inc.
Mid-Continent Railway Museum
Foot of Walnut Street
North Freedom WI

(608) 522-4261

OPEN: by appointment only M-F 9-4; closed weekends and holidays
ACCESS: advance arrangements required
COPYING FACILITIES: no
MATERIALS SOLICITED: Material relating to railroads of the upper Midwest, with special emphasis on Wisconsin. Will also accept other material relating to railroads, and railroad industries and associations within the United States.

HOLDINGS:
Total volume: 30 l.f.
Inclusive dates: 1880 - 1950
Description: Over 5,000 technical drawings of railroad structures, steam locomotive assemblies, and rolling stock, the majority relating to the Chicago and North Western Railroad; several hundred photographs of midwestern railroads taken in the early 1900's; depot freight logs; personal pay records; and Interstate Commerce Commission reports.

OSHKOSH

WI554-480
University of Wisconsin-Oshkosh
Libraries and Learning Resources
University Archives/Area Research Center
800 Algoma Blvd.
Oshkosh WI 54901

(414) 424-3347

OPEN: M-F 7:45-4:30; closed weekends and holidays
ACCESS: appointment required
COPYING FACILITIES: yes
MATERIALS SOLICITED: Materials relating to northeastern Wisconsin, including photographs, maps, and clippings relating to the University of Wisconsin at Oshkosh or its faculty and students.

HOLDINGS:
Total volume: 1,035 l.f.
Inclusive dates: 1838 -
Description: Records of the University of Wisconsin-Oshkosh, including faculty and student organizations, and campus events; papers of John Strange, politician and business leader, 1902-35; records of the Menasha Wooden Ware Corporation, 1857-1946; microfilmed records of the Ladies Benevolent Society of Oshkosh, 1890-1963; and reminiscences of Albert Cook, a Ripon carriage maker.

SEE: NUCMC, 1968, 78, 81.

SEE: Davis.

WI554-600
Oshkosh Public Museum
1331 Algoma Blvd.
Oshkosh WI 54901

(414) 236-5150

OPEN: M-F 1-5; closed weekends and
holidays
COPYING FACILITIES: yes
MATERIALS SOLICITED: Materials relating
to local history and biography, including local industries, such as logging and
lumbering, steamboats, logging marks,
and clubs and social organizations,
such as the Inland Lakes Yachting Association and the Arts Association.

HOLDINGS:
  Total volume: 120 l.f.
  Inclusive dates: 1800 -
  Description: Documents, photographs,
  letters, diaries, and other manuscripts re-
  lating to Oshkosh and the Fox River Val-
  ley, with special emphasis on lumbering,
  logging, and steamboating on Lake
  Winnebago and the Fox and Wolf rivers.
  There are also materials relating to such
  local figures as the Sawyer family, Jessie
  Jack Hooper, and Mary Mears.

SEE: Hamer; NUCMC, 1966.

SEE: Davis.

PRAIRIE DU CHIEN

WI594-110
Campion Jesuit Community
South Minnesota Street
Prairie du Chien WI 53821

no telephone

OPEN: by appointment
USER FEES: at the discretion of the
institution
COPYING FACILITIES: yes

HOLDINGS:
  Total volume: not specified
  Inclusive dates: 1829 -
  Description: Papers, correspondence,
  and photographs of poet Joyce Kilmer,
  materials pertaining to the history of
  Prairie du Chien, manuscripts relating to
  area residents, 1857- , and materials per-
  taining to Campion High School and the
  Jesuit community.

RACINE

WI606-680
Racine County Courthouse
County Clerk's Office
Wisconsin and Seventh Streets
Racine WI 53403

(414) 636-3121

SEE: Hamer.

Questionnaire not returned.

WI606-710
Racine Public Library
75 Seventh Street
Racine WI 53403

(414) 636-9241

OPEN: M-F 9-9, Sa 9-5:30; closed
Sundays and holidays
COPYING FACILITIES: yes

HOLDINGS:
  Total volume: 2 vols.; 135
  photographs; other items
  Inclusive dates: 1880 -
  Description: Correspondence, photographs, and other items concerning the
  use of Horlick's malted products on various polar expeditions (1900-35); photographs of the Racine area (1880-1900);
  and materials relating to the Racine black
  community (1960-).

RIPON

WI646-670
Ripon College
Library
Ripon WI 54971

(414) 748-8328

OPEN: M-Sa 8-5, Su 2-10, shorter
summer hours
COPYING FACILITIES: yes
MATERIALS SOLICITED: Materials relating
to Ripon College and local history.

HOLDINGS:
  Total volume: 25 file drawers; 50 l.f.
  Inclusive dates: 1843 -
  Description: Archives of Ripon Col-
  lege, including photographs, official Col-
  lege publications, and other materials.

RIVER FALLS

WI654-790
University of Wisconsin at River Falls
Chalmer Davee Library
St. Croix Valley Historical Research
Center
River Falls WI 54022

(715) 425-3567

OPEN: M-Th 8-10, F 8-4, Sa 2-5, Su
7-10; summer, M-F 8-5; hours vary
with University vacations
COPYING FACILITIES: yes
MATERIALS SOLICITED: History of western Wisconsin and the St. Croix River
Valley; Wisconsin history; American
history; genealogy; and University history.

HOLDINGS:
  Total volume: 600 l.f.; 1,500 vols.;
  9,000 photographs; 580 reels oral history
  tapes
  Inclusive dates: 1750 -
  Description: Manuscripts, photographs,
  oral histories, maps, and other materials
  with the history of western Wisconsin
  and the University of Wisconsin at River
  Falls as a central focus, but including
  materials on the history of the Old
  Northwest, of the United States and of a
  number of foreign countries.

Also included is the Wisconsin census,
1840-1905.

GUIDES: State Historical Society of Wisconsin, *Guide to Archives and Manuscripts in the University of Wisconsin -
River Falls Area Research Center*
(1975).

SEE: NUCMC, 1963-64, 68 (as State Historical Society of Wisconsin, Area Research Center, River Falls) 78, 81.

SEE: Hines; Hinding.

SEE ALSO: Alan M. Meckler and Ruth
McMullin, comps., *Oral History Collec-
tions* (Bowker, 1975); Richard A. Erney
and F. Gerald Ham, 'Wisconsin's Area
Research Centers,' *American Libraries*
(Feb. 1972); Richard A. Erney,
'Wisconsin's Area Research Centers,'
American Archivist 29 (Jan. 1966); Jo-
sephine L. Harper, ed., *Guide to the
Manuscripts of the State Historical So-
ciety of Wisconsin, Supplement Two*
(State Historical Society of Wisconsin,
1966).

SHEBOYGAN

WI670-720
Sheboygan County Historical Museum
3110 Erie Avenue
Sheboygan WI

MAILING ADDRESS:
P.O. Box 754
Sheboygan WI 53081

(414) 458-1103

OPEN: April - Sept., Tu-Sa 10-5, Su 1-5;
closed Mondays, Easter, Good Friday,
Independence Day, and Oct. - March
USER FEES: adults 50 cents; children 25
cents
ACCESS: advance arrangements required
COPYING FACILITIES: no

HOLDINGS:
  Total volume: not specified
  Inclusive dates: 1750 -
  Description: Materials relating to
  Sheboygan County history, including
  County government records, business
  records, and photographs.

SEE: Hamer.

SINSINAWA

WI698-730
Sinsinawa Dominican Sisters
Dominican Archives
Sinsinawa WI 53824

(608) 748-4411

OPEN: M-Sa 9-5, Su 1-4; closed Easter,
Christmas, and New Year's
COPYING FACILITIES: yes
MATERIALS SOLICITED: Records, including visual documents, relating to local
and state history of Wisconsin, eastern
Iowa, and northwestern Illinois; church
history of the nineteenth century, including missionaries, educational institutions and studies, and women. Will
also accept family records and diaries

of early settlers and Irish and German ethnic studies, 1830-65.

HOLDINGS:
Total volume: 1,070 l.f.; 35 microfilms; 240 taped interviews
Inclusive dates: 1800 -
Description: Records and papers of the missionary, Rev. Samuel Mazzuchelli, O.P., including diary, daybooks, and writings; congregation records including charters, constitutions, papers of major superiors, minutes of chapter assemblies, correspondence with ecclesiastical and civic officials, financial books, legal papers and documents; records of members, photographs, limited genealogical data, scrapbooks, published articles, and theses; oral histories documenting work and history of the congregation; and early educational materials.

SEE: NUCMC, 1980.

SEE: Hinding.

SOUTH MILWAUKEE

WI706-720
South Milwaukee Historical Society
717 Milwaukee Avenue
South Milwaukee WI

MAILING ADDRESS:
104 Brookdale Drive
South Milwaukee WI 53172

no telephone

OPEN: June - Aug., Su 2-4, and by appointment
ACCESS: appointment required
COPYING FACILITIES: yes
MATERIALS SOLICITED: Materials relating to the history of South Milwaukee and Oak Creek.

HOLDINGS:
Total volume: not specified
Inclusive dates: 1836 -
Description: Materials dealing primarily with the South Milwaukee and Oak Creek area, including business records, Civil War letters, genealogical records, oral history tapes and photographs.

SPARTA

WI714-520
Monroe County Historical Society
Monroe County Local History Room
Community Services Bldg.
Route 1
Sparta WI

MAILING ADDRESS:
P.O. Box 422
Sparta WI 54656

(608) 269-8680, 372-8680

OPEN: M-F 8-4; closed weekends and holidays
USER FEES: adults 50 cents; children 10 cents
COPYING FACILITIES: yes
MATERIALS SOLICITED: Materials related to the history of Monroe County and adjacent areas of Wisconsin, including genealogy, photographs, biographies,

business records, cemetery records, oral history, county government records, school histories and records, and area maps.

HOLDINGS:
Total volume: 12 file drawers; 80 l.f.
Inclusive dates: 1842 - 1920
Description: Correspondence, diaries, journals, photographs, genealogical records, cemetery records, marriage documents, oral history recordings, school records, maps, military and Post Office history, records of social organizations, and microfilm copies of newspapers and census records of Monroe County.

WI714-525
Monroe County Local History Room
and Library
Rt. 2, Box 21
Community Services Building
Sparta WI 54656

(608) 269-8680, 372-8680

OPEN: M-F 8-4:30; closed weekends and holidays
COPYING FACILITIES: yes
MATERIALS SOLICITED: Materials relating to Monroe County, including family Bibles, biographical family group sheets, photographs, maps and church histories. Will also accept materials pertaining to Wisconsin.

HOLDINGS:
Total volume: 3,000 photographs; 120 l.f. books; 5 file cabinets
Inclusive dates: 1848 -
Description: Materials relating to Monroe County, including cemetery records, church records, records of Grand Army of the Republic posts, biographical histories, church histories, school census records and school histories, business ledgers, photographs, family Bibles, family genealogical group charts, and oral history interviews of pioneer families.

WI714-880
Wisconsin Map Society
418 East Main Street
Sparta WI 54656

no telephone

OPEN: by appointment
COPYING FACILITIES: no
MATERIALS SOLICITED: Manuscript maps, correspondence, journals, and other papers dealing with surveying and exploration of the Monroe County area.

HOLDINGS:
Total volume: 8 items
Inclusive dates: 1838 - 1854
Description: Correspondence and travel journals concerning early exploration and settlement of the Monroe County area.

STEVENS POINT

WI722-770
University of Wisconsin at Stevens Point
Area Research Center
Stevens Point WI 54481

(715) 346-2586

OPEN: M-F 8-4:30; closed weekends and holidays
COPYING FACILITIES: yes
MATERIALS SOLICITED: Materials relating to local history, including photographs and local government records. Will also accept ethnic, North American Indian, and genealogical materials.

HOLDINGS:
Total volume: 850 l.f.
Inclusive dates: 1840 -
Description: Records and papers of individuals, businesses, churches, institutions, and local governments in the Wisconsin counties of Adams, Forest, Langlade, Lincoln, Marathon, Oneida, Portage, Vilas, Waupaca, Waushara, and Wood.

GUIDES: *Checklist of Archives and Manuscript Holdings in the Wisconsin State University-Stevens Point Area Research Center* (n.d.).

SEE: NUCMC, 1968 (as State Historical Society of Wisconsin, Area Research Center in Wisconsin State University), 81.

SEE: Davis.

SEE ALSO: Richard C. Davis, *North American Forest History: A Guide to Archives and Manuscripts in the United States and Canada* (Clio Books, 1977).

WI722-830
University of Wisconsin at Stevens Point
University Archives and
Portage County Historical Society Collection
Room 012, Old Main
Stevens Point WI 54481

(715) 346-2586

OPEN: M-F 9-4; closed weekends and holidays
COPYING FACILITIES: yes
MATERIALS SOLICITED: Manuscripts, photographs, audio and video tapes, and other materials relating to the history, development and traditions of the University of Wisconsin at Stevens Point.

HOLDINGS:
Total volume: 1,500 l.f.
Inclusive dates: 1840's
Description: Archives and manuscript collections documenting the history and development of the University of Wisconsin at Stevens Point since its establishment in 1894. Included are manuscripts, photographs, tapes, faculty committee minutes, yearbooks, administrative correspondence and reports, catalogs, bulletins, tapes of events and activities, and personnel records. Holdings in the Portage County Historical Society Collection

include records, papers, and photographs, of individuals and institutions of Stevens Point and central Wisconsin.

SEE: Hinding.

SUN PRAIRIE

WI733-333
United Methodist Church
Wisconsin Conference
Archives
P.O. Box 220
Sun Prairie WI 53590

(608) 837-7320

OPEN: by appointment only
COPYING FACILITIES: no
MATERIALS SOLICITED: Materials relating to the United Methodist church in Wisconsin and its predecessor denominations, including biographical data on both clergy and lay persons.

HOLDINGS:
Total volume: 25 l.f.
Inclusive dates: 1848 -
Description: Church related records and other materials relating to the United Methodist church in Wisconsin. Included are records of such predecessor denominations as the Evangelische Gemeinschaft, the Evangelical Association, the Evangelical church, the United Brethren in Christ, the Evangelical United Brethren church, Bible Christians, the Methodist Episcopal church, and the Methodist church. Some of the materials are in the German language.

SUPERIOR

WI754-170
Douglas County Historical Museum
906 East 2nd Street
Superior WI 54880

(715) 394-5712

OPEN: Tu-F 9-5, Sa 1-5, Su 2-5; closed Mondays, holidays, and Jan. - Feb.
USER FEES: identification required; advance arrangements required
COPYING FACILITIES: no
MATERIALS SOLICITED: Manuscript material pertaining to the Douglas County area, its history, and its arts.

HOLDINGS:
Total volume: 70 vols.
Inclusive dates: 1830 - 1940
Description: A collection of manuscripts, including WPA histories of Douglas County and the surrounding area, diaries of Douglas County residents dating from 1830, voting records of Superior, 1890-1935, police records, and papers of author Zoa Grace, including contracts, correspondence, and original manuscripts.

SEE: Hamer; NUCMC, 1962.

SEE: Novotny; Davis.

WI754-720
Superior Public Library
1204 Hammond Avenue
Superior WI 54880

(715) 394-0252

OPEN: M-Th 9-9, F 9-6, Sa 9-5, Su 2-5; closed holidays and weekends during the summer
COPYING FACILITIES: yes
MATERIALS SOLICITED: Materials relating to genealogy, ethnic history, primarily Scandinavian, and to Douglas County, northern Wisconsin, and northeastern Minnesota.

HOLDINGS:
Total volume: not specified
Inclusive dates: mid 19th century - early 20th century
Description: 19th and early 20th century manuscripts relating to Douglas County and surrounding area including biographies of early settlers, diaries, and records of local institutions and industries.

VIROQUA

WI774-840
Vernon County Historical Museum
606 W. Broadway
Viroqua WI

MAILING ADDRESS:
c/o C. Stephen - Curator
619 East Linton
Viroqua WI 54665

(608) 637-7396

OPEN: T-Su 1-5; closed Mondays
COPYING FACILITIES: no
MATERIALS SOLICITED: Materials and artifacts relating to the history of Vernon County, including genealogical, church, school, and cemetery records.

HOLDINGS:
Total volume: not specified
Inclusive dates: late 1800's -
Description: Genealogical data, diaries, photographs, and oral histories pertaining to Vernon County history.

WATERTOWN

WI786-880
Watertown Historical Society
919 Charles Street
Watertown WI 53094

(414) 261-2796

OPEN: by appointment only, daily 10-5; historic buildings closed Nov. 1-April 30

SEE: Hamer.

Questionnaire not returned.

WAUKESHA

WI794-120
Carroll College
Library
100 North East Avenue
Waukesha WI 53186

(414) 547-1211, Ext. 175

OPEN: by appointment only
COPYING FACILITIES: yes
MATERIALS SOLICITED: Materials relating to Carroll College.

HOLDINGS:
Total volume: 10 c.f.
Inclusive dates: 1822 -
Description: Manuscripts and archival records relating chiefly to Carroll College (1846-) and its predecessor, Prairieville Academy (1840-46). Included are the minutes of the Board of Trustees, papers of several presidents and a faculty member, letters of an early student, tapes of oral history interviews with several alumni, and photographs.

SEE: NUCMC, 1976.

SEE: Hinding.

WI794-880
Waukesha County Historical Museum
Research Center
101 West Main Street
Waukesha WI 53186

(414) 548-7186

OPEN: M-F 9-4:30; closed weekends and holidays
ACCESS: adults unrestricted; high school students with teacher approval
COPYING FACILITIES: yes
MATERIALS SOLICITED: Manuscript, archival, and visual material relating to Waukesha County.

HOLDINGS:
Total volume: 662 c.f.
Inclusive dates: 1834 -
Description: Materials relating chiefly to Waukesha County. Included are diaries, marriage records, naturalization records, census records, records of the civil court from 1846 to 1930, manuscript maps, tax records, genealogical materials, photographs, post cards, Civil War journals, notebooks of data on County pioneers, cemetery records, and a compilation of medical biographical records.

SEE: Hamer (as Waukesha County Historical Society, Museum).

SEE: Allard, Crawley, and Edmison; Hinding.

SEE ALSO: the following publications of the Museum by Pamela D. Berger: *Guide to Genealogical Research in Waukesha County* (1973); *Pioneer Schools of Waukesha County* (1975); *Waukesha County Churches: The First Hundred Years* (1976).

WAUSAU

WI814-480
Lutheran Church-Missouri Synod
North Wisconsin District
Archives
3103 Seymour Lane
Wausau WI 54401

(715) 845-8241

OPEN: M-F 8-4:30; closed weekends and
holidays
COPYING FACILITIES: yes
MATERIALS SOLICITED: Congregational
histories and documents, and documents and records of the District.

HOLDINGS:
Total volume: 62 l.f.; 9 file cabinets
Inclusive dates: 1916 -
Description: Manuscripts and histories
relating chiefly to the North Wisconsin
District of the Lutheran Church-Missouri
Synod. The collection includes materials
pertaining to the history of the Lutheran
church in Wisconsin, and Wisconsin
itself. A collection of biographical sketches of prominent Wisconsin Lutherans is
also included.

WI814-510
Marathon County Historical Museum
403 McIndoe
Wausau WI 54401

(715) 848-6143

OPEN: M-F 9-5, Su 2-5; closed Saturdays
and holidays
COPYING FACILITIES: no
MATERIALS SOLICITED: Will accept Marathon County and Wisconsin materials.

HOLDINGS:
Total volume: 22 l.f.; 15 c.f.
Inclusive dates: 1839 -
Description: Materials focusing on
Wausau and Marathon County. Included
are diaries, journals, letters, scrapbooks,
3,000 photographs, post cards, account
books and logbooks for over 100 busi-
nesses, and the logbook of the frigate
Brandywine, 1834-37.

SEE: Hamer.

SEE: Hinding.

WEST ALLIS

WI834-40
Allis-Chalmers Corporation
Communication Services
1126 South 70th Street
West Allis WI

MAILING ADDRESS:
P.O. Box 512
Milwaukee WI 53201

(414) 475-2000

OPEN: M-F 8:30-5; closed weekends and
holidays
COPYING FACILITIES: yes
MATERIALS SOLICITED: Material relating
to the history of Allis-Chalmers.

HOLDINGS:
Total volume: 2,000,000 pages; other
items
Inclusive dates: 1860 -
Description: Material relating to the
history of Allis-Chalmers and its many
plants, including photographs and films
of plants and products.

Most material has been microfilmed; microfilm indexes are available at the repository.

WEST BEND

WI836-322
Washington County Historical Society
Museum
340 5th Avenue
West Bend WI

MAILING ADDRESS:
506 3rd Avenue
West Bend WI 53095

(414) 338-8287

OPEN: Tu 2-4, Th 1-4, second Sunday of
month 2-4; closed other days, holidays,
and December-April 1
ACCESS: users of materials must be
supervised by a society member
COPYING FACILITIES: yes
MATERIALS SOLICITED: Materials relating
to Washington County.

HOLDINGS:
Total volume: 2,000 documents;
2,000 pictures
Inclusive dates: 1830's -
Description: Materials relating to the
history of Washington and Ogaukee
Counties, including genealogies, tax
records, marriage records, maps, court
records, church records, cemetery records,
photographs, and slides.

WEST SALEM

WI853-880
West Salem Historical Society, Inc.
Hamlin Garland Homestead
357 West Garland Street
West Salem WI 54669

(608) 786-1399

OPEN: daily 10-5 Memorial Day - Labor
Day; by appointment Labor Day -
Memorial Day
ACCESS: appointment required
COPYING FACILITIES: no
MATERIALS SOLICITED: Records relating
to Hamlin Garland and his family,
West Salem, and the surrounding area.
Will also accept records relating to La
Crosse County and Wisconsin, and to
Wisconsin authors.

HOLDINGS:
Total volume: 300 items
Inclusive dates: 1850 -
Description: Letters, poems, photographs, and scrapbooks of Hamlin Garland; and records, photographs, and oral
history tapes relating to West Salem.

WESTFIELD

WI855-520
Marquette County Historical Society
Cochrane - Nelson House
213 Lawrence Street
Westfield WI 53964

no telephone

OPEN: W 1-3 in summer; closed other
times
COPYING FACILITIES: no
MATERIALS SOLICITED: Items pertaining
to the history of Marquette County.

HOLDINGS:
Total volume: 7 file drawers
Inclusive dates: 1865 -
Description: A collection of photo-
graphs and documents relating to the his-
tory of Marquette County.

WHITEWATER

WI858-810
University of Wisconsin at
Whitewater
Harold Andersen Library
Whitewater WI 53190

(414) 472-1017, 4671

SEE: NUCMC, 1968, 78, 81.

Questionnaire not returned.

WILLIAMS BAY

WI874-940
University of Chicago
Yerkes Observatory
Williams Bay WI 53191

(414) 245-5555

OPEN: by appointment only
ACCESS: permission to use materials
must be requested of Observatory
Director
COPYING FACILITIES: yes

HOLDINGS:
Total volume: 73 file drawers; 6,000
pages
Inclusive dates: 1891 -
Description: Correspondence of astronomers at Yerkes Observatory
(1895-1930's), business papers of the Observatory and its directors, logbooks of
observations at the Observatory, photographs, and blueprints.

SEE ALSO: Ann Novotny, ed., *Picture
Sources 3* (Special Libraries Assn.,
1975); *Source Materials for the Recent
History of Astronomy and Astrophysics:
A Checklist of Manuscript Collections in
the United States* (American Institute
of Physics, 1971).

WISCONSIN DELLS

WI890-320
H. H. Bennett Studio
215 Broadway
Wisconsin Dells WI

MAILING ADDRESS:
P.O. Box 145
Wisconsin Dells WI 53965

(608) 253-2261

OPEN: by appointment
COPYING FACILITIES: no
HOLDINGS:
  Total volume: 5,000 items; other materials
  Inclusive dates: 1848 -
  Description: Primarily glass plate negatives taken by H. H. Bennett from 1865 to 1908, including photographs of Wisconsin Dells, Devil's Lake, rock formations, Milwaukee in the 1880's, railroads, steamboats, raftsmen on the Wisconsin River, Winnebago Indians, and the St. Paul, MN, ice carnival. There are also business records and letters of the Bennett family.

SEE: Novotny.

WYOMING

The Archives and Records Management Division of the Wyoming State Archives administers a statewide program for preserving local public records, acting under the authority of legislation passed in 1953.

Permanently valuable local public records normally remain in the custody of local officials, but some county and municipal records have been transferred to the State Archives in Cheyenne. The State Archives also makes available to researchers some 10,000 reels of microfilmed records, predominantly county land records.

BUFFALO

WY90-410

Johnson County Library Annex
90 North Main
Buffalo WY 82834

(307) 684-9007

OPEN: M-F 10:30-4; closed weekends and holidays
COPYING FACILITIES: yes
MATERIALS SOLICITED: Oral history recordings and transcripts on the history of Johnson County.

HOLDINGS:
  Total volume: 75 items
  Inclusive dates: 1971 -
  Description: Recordings and transcripts of narratives by people of Johnson County.

SEE ALSO: Alan M. Meckler and Ruth McMullin, comps., *Oral History Collections* (Bowker, 1975).

CHEYENNE

WY135-860

Wyoming Archives, Museums and Historical Department
Archives and Records Management Division
Barrett Building
Cheyenne WY 82002

(307) 777-7826

OPEN: M-F 8-5; closed weekends and holidays
COPYING FACILITIES: yes
MATERIALS SOLICITED: Public records of Wyoming's state and local governments.

HOLDINGS:
  Total volume: 15,000 c.f.; 42,000 microfilm reels
  Inclusive dates: 1868 -
  Description: Public records from most state agencies, including the Governor's Office, and all counties, some municipalities, nearly all school districts, and other political subdivisions from the creation of Wyoming Territory in 1868 to the present. The records are from all areas of the state and include information on land, water rights, marriages, corporations, taxes, state institutions, legislation, elections, courts, law enforcement, territorial and state governors, schools, and other topics.

SEE: Hamer.

WY135-865

Wyoming Archives, Museums and Historical Department
Historical Research and Publications Division
Barrett Building
Cheyenne WY 82002

(307) 777-7518

OPEN: M-F 8-5; closed weekends and holidays
COPYING FACILITIES: yes
MATERIALS SOLICITED: Materials relating to Wyoming history from pre-territorial days to the present. Will also accept materials relating to Western history pertinent to Wyoming.

HOLDINGS:
  Total volume: 544.5 c.f.
  Inclusive dates: 1850 -
  Description: Materials related to Wyoming history, including economic, social, political, military, geographical, and cultural history. Included are manuscripts, diaries, correspondence, financial records, public records such as the Wyoming Works Progress Administration collection, genealogical source data, community group records, business records, maps, architectural plans and blueprints, photograph collections such as the Stimson collection of 8,000 negatives, oral history tapes and transcripts, and microfilm copies of documents, journals, and other materials.

SEE: Hamer; NUCMC, 1973, 76.

SEE: Meckler and McMullin; Novotny; Davis; Parkinson; Hinding.

WY135-880

Wyoming Archives and Museums
Historical Division
Cheyenne WY 82002

(307) 777-7697

OPEN: M-F 8-5; closed weekends and holidays
COPYING FACILITIES: no
MATERIALS SOLICITED: Materials relative to Wyoming history, particularly historic sites.

HOLDINGS:
  Total volume: 3 l.f.
  Inclusive dates: 1867 -
  Description: Collections generated by historic preservation activities in Wyoming. Included are correspondence concerning historic sites; nominations to the National Register of Historic Places; drawings of historic places and structures; and photographs.

CODY

WY155-80

Buffalo Bill Historical Center
Cody WY

MAILING ADDRESS:
Box 1000
Cody WY 82414

(307) 587-4771

SEE: Hamer.

Questionnaire not returned.

ENCAMPMENT

WY245-280

Grand Encampment Museum, Inc.
Encampment WY

MAILING ADDRESS:
Box 395
Encampment WY 82325

no telephone

OPEN: June - Aug., daily 1-5; Sept. - Oct., weekends 1-5; closed rest of year
COPYING FACILITIES: no
MATERIALS SOLICITED: Materials relating to the history of the Encampment area.

HOLDINGS:
  Total volume: 6 l.f.
  Inclusive dates: 1845 -
  Description: Materials relating to the history of mining in the Encampment area, including manuscripts, diaries, letters, photographs, city records, and hotel registers.

SEE: Svoboda and Dunning.

FORT LARAMIE

WY305-240
Fort Laramie National Historic Site
Fort Laramie WY 82212

(307) 837-2221

OPEN: daily 8-4:30; summer, daily 8-8;
   closed Christmas and New Year's
COPYING FACILITIES: yes
MATERIALS SOLICITED: Records concerning officers, soldiers or civilians who
   served or lived at Fort Laramie,
   1849-90, and documents about emi-
   grants who passed through Fort
   Laramie on the overland trails before
   1890. Will also accept manuscripts of
   individuals relating to the Rocky
   Mountain fur trade during the first half
   of the 19th century, and records about
   the northern Plains Indians concerning
   Fort Laramie, 1834-90.

HOLDINGS:
   Total volume: 17 boxes; 4 vols.
   Inclusive dates: 1840 - 1900
   Description: Manuscripts relating chiefly to historic Fort Laramie. Included are
   correspondence, diaries, reports, and photographs of soldiers and civilians who
   lived at or visited the Fort or were concerned in some way with its history.

SEE: Hamer.

GREEN RIVER

WY365-710
Sweetwater County Historical
   Museum
County Courthouse
50 West Flaming Gorge Way
Green River WY

MAILING ADDRESS:
Box 25
Green River WY 82935

(307) 875-2611, Ext. 263

OPEN: M-F 10-4:30; closed weekends
   and holidays
COPYING FACILITIES: yes
MATERIALS SOLICITED: Manuscripts and
   photographs relating to Wyoming local
   history, especially for Sweetwater
   County and southwestern Wyoming.

HOLDINGS:
   Total volume: 15 c.f.
   Inclusive dates: 1870 -
   Description: Records of the Union Pacific Coal Company, including ledgers,
   account books, photographs, maps, and
   publications; local school records and annuals; lodge account books; records of
   local organizations, including the Woman's Club and Boy Scouts; and records of
   Sweetwater County and the town of
   Green River.

SEE: Hinding.

LARAMIE

WY500-480
Laramie Plains Museum
603 Ivinson Avenue
Laramie WY 82070

(307) 742-4448

OPEN: June 15 - Aug. 31, M-F 9-4; rest
   of year, M-F 2-4; closed weekends,
   holidays, and month of Dec.
USER FEES: arranged with individual
   user
COPYING FACILITIES: yes
MATERIALS SOLICITED: Materials pertaining to the Laramie Plains. Will accept some material on famous Wyoming residents or historical incidents.

HOLDINGS:
   Total volume: 1 file cabinet
   Inclusive dates: 1870 - 1940
   Description: Photographs of early busi-
   nesses, buildings, and families in the
   Laramie area, as well as a few family
   reminiscences and diaries.

SEE: Svoboda and Dunning.

WY500-800
University of Wyoming
Library
Division of Rare Books and Special
   Collections
Laramie WY

MAILING ADDRESS:
Box 3334, University Station
Laramie WY 82071

(307) 766-4114

OPEN: M-F 8-5; closed weekends and
   holidays
COPYING FACILITIES: yes
MATERIALS SOLICITED: Materials relating
   to petroleum; military history of the
   West; western ranching; business in the
   West; contemporary politics and business; literature; film; television; Hollywood, CA; conservation; reclamation;
   journalists; mining; women; revisionist
   historians; scientists; psychologists;
   mathematics and statistics; soil and
   range sciences; and architecture.

HOLDINGS:
   Total volume: 7,000 l.f.
   Inclusive dates: 1762 -
   Description: Materials, including
   10,000 photographs and other visual
   items, concentrating on ranching, petroleum, business, military history, mining,
   conservation, reclamation, and political
   history of the American West. There are
   also materials relating to revisionist historians, individuals involved in the Pearl
   Harbor culpability debate, and early aviation pioneers; corporate records of Trans
   World Airways and Standard Oil of New
   Jersey; genealogical materials relating to
   the Cranch family of Massachusetts, including John Adams and Adams family
   correspondence; manuscript music for the
   'big bands,' as well as that written by
   motion picture composers and arrangers;
   manuscripts of television and motion picture writers; and materials relating to
   women's history.

SEE: Hamer; NUCMC, 1966, 74-75, 77,
   80.

SEE: Spalek; Parkinson; Allard, Crawley,
   and Edmison; Svoboda and Dunning.

SEE ALSO: Ann Novotny, ed., *Picture
   Sources 3* (Special Libraries Assn.,
   1975); Gene M. Gressley, 'Oil and History Do Mix: The Petroleum History
   and Research Center of the University
   of Wyoming,' *Special Libraries* 61 (Oct.
   1970); Richard C. Davis, *North American Forest History: A Guide to Archives
   and Manuscripts in the United States
   and Canada* (Clio Books, 1977); Alan
   M. Meckler and Ruth McMullin,
   comps., *Oral History Collections*
   (Bowker, 1975); Lawrence J. Paszek,
   comp., *United States Air Force History:
   A Guide to Documentary Sources*
   (Office of Air Force History, 1973).

MOOSE

WY560-280
Grand Teton National Park
Moose WY

MAILING ADDRESS:
P.O. Box 170
Moose WY 83012

(307) 543-2851

OPEN: by appointment only
ACCESS: by appointment with librarian
   in charge of archives
COPYING FACILITIES: no
MATERIALS SOLICITED: Materials relating
   to the natural history of Grand Teton
   National Park and to persons associ-
   ated with the Park. Will also accept
   materials concerning the National Park
   Service.

HOLDINGS:
   Total volume: 15 items
   Inclusive dates: 1879 -
   Description: Fragment of a diary by
   Thomas Moran, 1879, detailing his travels in the American West; an interview
   with Horace Albright, Director of the National Park Service from 1929 to 1933;
   and original and copy information on the
   establishment of Grand Teton National
   Park and Jackson Hole National Monument.

SEE ALSO: Richard C. Davis, *North
   American Forest History: A Guide to
   Archives and Manuscripts in the United
   States and Canada* (Clio Books, 1977).

THERMOPOLIS

WY800-320
Hot Springs County Museum
Museum and Cultural Center
7th and Broadway
Thermopolis WY

MAILING ADDRESS:
P.O. Box 1311
Thermopolis WY 82443

(307) 864-5183

OPEN: M-F 9-5; closed weekends and
   holidays

COPYING FACILITIES: no
MATERIALS SOLICITED: Historical materials on Hot Springs County and the Big Horn Basin. Will also accept materials pertaining to the American West, especially emigration.

HOLDINGS:
> *Total volume:* not specified
> *Inclusive dates:* 1900 -
> *Description:* Diaries, records of voluntary organizations, photographs, and other materials on the history of Hot Springs County.

YELLOWSTONE NATIONAL PARK

WY950-940
Yellowstone National Park
Research Library
Horace M. Albright Visitor Center

MAILING ADDRESS:
P.O. Box 117
Yellowstone National Park WY 82190

(307) 344-7381, Ext. 2352

OPEN: by appointment only
COPYING FACILITIES: yes
MATERIALS SOLICITED: Materials regarding Yellowstone National Park. Will also accept related materials.

HOLDINGS:
> *Total volume:* not specified
> *Inclusive dates:* 1824 -
> *Description:* Private papers relating to the Park and surrounding areas, covering scientific and historical topics. Included are research papers, diaries, and correspondence.

SEE: Hamer.

SEE: Davis.

WY950-945
Yellowstone National Park
Still Photographic Section
Park Photographer
Yellowstone National Park WY

MAILING ADDRESS:
P.O. Box 168
Yellowstone National Park WY 82190

(307) 344-7381, Ext. 350

OPEN: M-F 8-4:30; closed weekends and holidays
COPYING FACILITIES: no
MATERIALS SOLICITED: Clear black and white photographs of early Yellowstone National Park.

HOLDINGS:
> *Total volume:* 106,000 items
> *Inclusive dates:* 1871 -
> *Description:* A collection of photographs of Yellowstone National Park, depicting Park features, early explorers and visitors, Park personnel and animals.

SEE: Novotny.

WY950-950
Yellowstone National Park
Yellowstone Archives
Horace M. Albright Visitor Center
Yellowstone National Park WY 82190

(307) 344-7381, Ext. 2267

OPEN: M-F 8-5; closed weekends and holidays
COPYING FACILITIES: yes
MATERIALS SOLICITED: Records generated by administrative functions of the National Park Service in Yellowstone.

HOLDINGS:
> *Total volume:* 207 l.f.
> *Inclusive dates:* 1872 -
> *Description:* Administrative records of Yellowstone Park, including over 77,000 pages for the period before 1916. Included are correspondence, reports, station logs, and scout diaries.

SEE: Hinding.

SEE ALSO: Aubrey Haines, 'The Yellowstone Archives: A Unique Source of History,' *Proceedings of the Montana Academy of Sciences* 22 (1963). Guides to portions of the Archives are available from the repository.

REPOSITORY INDEX

A

A. A. BEDIKIAN LIBRARY, *NJ630-40*

A. C. BUEHLER LIBRARY, *IL246-190*

A. K. SMILEY PUBLIC LIBRARY, SPECIAL COLLECTIONS AND LINCOLN MEMORIAL SHRINE, *CA628-40*

A. M. AND WELMA AIKIN REGIONAL ARCHIVES, *TX695-640*

A. R. BOWMAN HISTORICAL MUSEUM, *OR736-40*

AARON BURR ASSOCIATION, *NJ339-40*

ABBOTT LABORATORIES, ARCHIVES, *IL629-40*

ABBOTT-NORTHWESTERN HOSPITAL, SISTER KENNY INSTITUTE, *MN541-16*

ABBY ALDRICH ROCKEFELLER FOLK ART COLLECTION, *VA870-40*

ABDEL ROSS WENTZ LIBRARY, *PA325-490*

ABERDEEN PUBLIC LIBRARY, *WA2-680*

ABIGAIL E. WEEKS MEMORIAL LIBRARY, *KY24-800*

ABRAHAM A. BRILL LIBRARY, *NY592-640*

ABRAHAM LINCOLN BIRTHPLACE NATIONAL HISTORIC SITE, *KY358-40*

ACADEMY OF AMERICAN FRANCISCAN HISTORY, LIBRARY, *MD703-40*

ACADEMY OF CALIFORNIA CHURCH HISTORY, *CA274-40*

ACADEMY OF CALIFORNIA CHURCH HISTORY AND MONTEREY-FRESNO DIOCESAN CHANCERY, *CA274-40*

ACADEMY OF MEDICINE OF BROOKLYN, LIBRARY, *NY591-240*

ACADEMY OF MOTION PICTURE ARTS & SCIENCES, MARGARET HERRICK LIBRARY, *CA90-30*

ACADEMY OF NATURAL SCIENCES OF PHILADELPHIA, *PA725-15*

ACADEMY OF THE NEW CHURCH, ARCHIVES, *PA130-30*

ACADEMY OF THE NEW CHURCH, SWEDENBORGIANA LIBRARY, *PA130-50*

ACADIA NATIONAL PARK, ISLESFORD HISTORICAL MUSEUM, *ME453-40*

ACTION (THE AGENCY FOR VOLUNTEER SERVICE), PHOTO LIBRARY, *DC1-40*

ADAM EAST MUSEUM, *WA565-40*

ADAMS CENTER FOR ECOLOGICAL STUDIES, *MI518-860*

ADAMS COUNTY (PA) HISTORICAL SOCIETY, *PA325-40*

ADAMS COUNTY HISTORICAL SOCIETY, ARCHIVES, *NE496-40*

ADAMS COUNTY HISTORICAL SOCIETY, MUSEUM, *WA489-40*

ADAMS, JAMES P., LIBRARY, ARCHIVES, *RI700-660*

ADAMS' OLD STONE GRIST MILL MUSEUM, *VT32-80*

ADDISON PUBLIC LIBRARY, *NY5-40*

ADELPHI UNIVERSITY, LIBRARIES, SPECIAL COLLECTIONS, *NY315-30*

ADENA STATE MEMORIAL, *OH166-590*

ADIRONDACK HISTORICAL ASSOCIATION, *NY104-40*

ADIRONDACK MUSEUM, *NY104-40*

ADJUTANT GENERAL OF MISSOURI, RECORDS AND ARCHIVES, *MO410-40*

ADORERS OF THE BLOOD OF CHRIST, PROVINCE OF RUMA, *IL770-40*

ADRIAN COLLEGE, SHIPMAN LIBRARY, *MI8-20*

ADRIAN PUBLIC LIBRARY, *MI8-30*

ADRIANCE MEMORIAL LIBRARY, LOCAL HISTORY COLLECTION, *NY726-40*

AEROSPACE AUDIOVISUAL SERVICE, 1361ST AUDIOVISUAL SQUADRON, *VA50-530*

AFRICAN METHODIST EPISCOPAL CHURCH, FINANCIAL DEPARTMENT, *DC1-160*

AFRICAN-AMERICAN HISTORICAL AND CULTURAL SOCIETY, SAN FRANCISCO, *CA720-10*

AFTON FREE LIBRARY, *NY6-40*

AGENCY FOR INTERNATIONAL DEVELOPMENT (AID), BUREAU FOR EXTERNAL AFFAIRS, *DC1-180*

AGRICULTURAL AND TECHNICAL COLLEGE, STATE UNIVERSITY OF NEW YORK AT ALFRED, WALTER HINKLE LIBRARY, *NY18-720*

AGRICULTURE, DEPARTMENT OF, NATIONAL AGRICULTURAL LIBRARY, *MD133-160*

AIKIN, A. M. AND WELMA, REGIONAL ARCHIVES, *TX695-640*

AIR FORCE ACADEMY, U.S., LIBRARY, SPECIAL COLLECTIONS BRANCH, *CO180-750*

AIR FORCE MILITARY AIRLIFT COMMAND, AEROSPACE AUDIOVISUAL SERVICE, 1361ST AUDIOVISUAL SQUADRON, *VA50-530*

AIR FORCE, OFFICE OF AIR FORCE HISTORY, *DC1-200*

AKRON CARNEGIE PUBLIC LIBRARY, *IN5-40*

ALABAMA A & M UNIVERSITY, J. F. DRAKE MEMORIAL LEARNING RESOURCES CENTER, *AL640-40*

ALABAMA DEPARTMENT OF ARCHIVES AND HISTORY, *AL620-20*

ALABAMA STATE ARCHIVES, *AL620-20*

ALABAMA STATE UNIVERSITY, LEVI WATKINS LEARNING CENTER, UNIV. LIBRARY, UNIV. ARCH. & SPEC. COLL., *AL620-60*

ALAN MASON CHESNEY MEDICAL ARCHIVES, *MD76-315*

ALASKA DIVISION OF STATE LIBRARIES AND MUSEUMS, ALASKA HISTORICAL LIBRARY, *AK500-20*

ALASKA HISTORICAL LIBRARY, *AK500-20*

ALASKA NATIVE LANGUAGE CENTER, *AK350-815*

ALASKA NATIVE LANGUAGE CENTER, UNIVERSITY OF ALASKA, *AK350-815*

ALASKA PICTORIAL SERVICE, *AK50-25*

ALASKA STATE ARCHIVES, *AK500-40*

ALASKA, OFFICE OF THE SECRETARY OF, *AK500-40*

ALASKAN AIR COMMAND, OFFICE OF HISTORY, *AK320-40*

ALBANY CITY ARCHIVES, *NY10-60*

ALBANY DEPARTMENT OF HUMAN RESOURCES, BUREAU FOR HISTORICAL SERVICES, CITY RECORDS LIBRARY, *NY10-60*

ALBANY INSTITUTE OF HISTORY AND ART, MCKINNEY LIBRARY, *NY10-80*

ALBANY MEDICAL COLLEGE, SCHAFFER LIBRARY OF HEALTH SCIENCES, *NY10-800*

ALBANY PUBLIC LIBRARY, *NY10-100, OR16-40*

ALBEMARLE COUNTY HISTORICAL SOCIETY, *VA145-40*

ALBEN W. BARKLEY MUSEUM, *KY604-40*

ALBERT F. SIMPSON HISTORICAL RESEARCH CENTER, *AL560-720*

ALBERT SCHWEITZER FRIENDSHIP HOUSE, *MA349-30*

ALBION COLLEGE, STOCKWELL MEMORIAL LIBRARY, *MI12-10*

ALBRIGHT COLLEGE, LIBRARY, *PA755-40*

ALBUQUERQUE MUSEUM OF ART, HISTORY AND SCIENCE, *NM114-35*

ALCO HISTORIC PHOTOS, *NY804-560*

ALCORN STATE UNIVERSITY, LIBRARY, *MS570-40*

ALCOTT, LOUISA MAY, MEMORIAL ASSOCIATION, ORCHARD HOUSE, *MA217-480*

ALDERSON BROADDUS COLLEGE, PICKETT LIBRARY MEDIA CENTER, *WV775-40*

ALEXANDER CAMPBELL ARCHIVES, *WV100-80*

ALEXANDER GRAHAM BELL ASSOCIATION FOR THE DEAF, LIBRARY, *DC22-500*

ALEXANDER MACK MEMORIAL LIBRARY, BRIDGEWATER COLLEGE ARCHIVES, *VA115-80*

ALEXANDER MITCHELL PUBLIC LIBRARY, SOUTH DAKOTA COLLECTION, *SD18-40*

ALEXANDER, WILL W., LIBRARY, *LA600-160*

ALEXANDRIA LIBRARY, LLOYD HOUSE ARCHIVES, *VA20-40*

ALEXIAN BROTHERS, CONGREGATION OF, PROVINCIAL ARCHIVES, *IL245-322*

ALEXIS CARREL COLLECTION, *DC7-660*

ALFRED M. HESTON COLLECTION, *NJ20-40*

ALFRED P. SLOAN, JR., MUSEUM, *MI314-60*

ALFRED UNIVERSITY, HERRICK LIBRARY, *NY18-40*

ALGER COUNTY HISTORICAL SOCIETY, *MI670-40*

ALICE LLOYD COLLEGE, APPALACHIAN ORAL HISTORY PROJECT, *KY630-40*

ALLAIRE VILLAGE AUXILIARY LIBRARY, *NJ8-160*

ALLEGAN PUBLIC LIBRARY, *MI120-50*

ALLEGANY COUNTY DEPARTMENT OF HISTORY, ALLEGANY COUNTY MUSEUM, *NY87-40*

ALLEGANY COUNTY HISTORICAL SOCIETY, *NY87-50*

ALLEGANY COUNTY HISTORICAL SOCIETY, HISTORY HOUSE, *MD304-80*

ALLEGANY COUNTY MUSEUM, *NY87-40*

ALLEGHENY COLLEGE, PELLETIER LIBRARY, *PA555-40*
ALLEN COUNTY HISTORICAL SOCIETY, ALLEN COUNTY MUSEUM, *OH451-40*
ALLEN COUNTY MUSEUM, *OH451-40*
ALLEN COUNTY-FORT WAYNE HISTORICAL SOCIETY, *IN231-40*
ALLEN J. ELLENDER ARCHIVES, *LA920-560*
ALLEN KNIGHT MARITIME MUSEUM, *CA480-500*
ALLEN MEMORIAL LIBRARY, *ND876-830*
ALLEN, GEORGE E., LIBRARY, *MS140-560*
ALLIANCE HISTORICAL SOCIETY, *OH16-30*
ALLIANCE KNIGHT MUSEUM, *NE32-40*
ALLIED ORDERS OF THE GRAND ARMY OF THE REPUBLIC, MEMORIAL SHRINE TO THE GRAND ARMY OF THE REPUBLIC, *MA108-10*
ALLIS-CHALMERS CORPORATION, COMMUNICATION SERVICES, *WI834-40*
ALMA COLLEGE, MONTEITH LIBRARY, ARCHIVES, *MI32-40*
ALMOND HISTORICAL SOCIETY, *NY20-40*
ALTOONA AREA PUBLIC LIBRARY, PENNSYLVANIA ROOM, *PA35-40*
AMALGAMATED TRANSIT UNION, *DC1-280*
AMANA HERITAGE SOCIETY, *IA22-40*
AMARILLO PUBLIC LIBRARY, LOCAL HISTORY COLLECTION AND JOHN L. MCCARTY PAPERS, *TX21-50*
AMBROSE SWASEY LIBRARY, *NY752-110*
AMERICAN ACADEMY AND INSTITUTE OF ARTS AND LETTERS, LIBRARY AND ARCHIVES, *NY586-180*
AMERICAN ACADEMY OF ARTS AND SCIENCES, *MA169-30*
AMERICAN ALLIANCE FOR HEALTH, PHYSICAL EDUCATION AND RECREATION, ARCHIVES, *DC1-295*
AMERICAN ALPINE CLUB, AMERICAN ALPINE LIBRARY, *NY586-220*
AMERICAN ALPINE LIBRARY, *NY586-220*
AMERICAN ANTIQUARIAN SOCIETY, *MA985-70*
AMERICAN ARCHIVES OF THE FACTUAL FILM, *IA33-364*
AMERICAN ASSOCIATION FOR THE ADVANCEMENT OF SCIENCE, *DC1-300*
AMERICAN ASSOCIATION OF UNIVERSITY WOMEN, ARCHIVES, *DC1-340*
AMERICAN AUTOMOBILE ASSOCIATION, LIBRARY, *VA215-40*
AMERICAN AVIATION HISTORICAL SOCIETY, *CA770-40*
AMERICAN BAPTIST CHURCHES IN THE U.S.A., INTERNATIONAL MINISTRIES LIBRARY AND CENTRAL FILES, *PA905-60*
AMERICAN BAPTIST-SAMUEL B. COLGATE HISTORICAL LIBRARY, *NY752-40*
AMERICAN BAR FOUNDATION, PROGRAM ON ORAL HISTORY, *IL169-52*
AMERICAN BIBLE SOCIETY, LIBRARY, *NY586-280*
AMERICAN CATHOLIC HISTORICAL SOCIETY OF PHILADELPHIA, HISTORICAL COLLECTIONS, *PA725-45*
AMERICAN CETACEAN SOCIETY, *CA762-40*
AMERICAN CLOCK AND WATCH MUSEUM, EDWARD INGRAHAM LIBRARY, *CT48-40*
AMERICAN COLLEGE OF LIFE UNDERWRITERS, ORAL HISTORY CENTER, *PA135-40*
AMERICAN COLLEGE TESTING PROGRAM, LIBRARY, *IA466-40*
AMERICAN COUNCIL FOR THE ARTS, LIBRARY, *NY586-330*
AMERICAN CRAFT COUNCIL, LIBRARY, *NY586-360*
AMERICAN DENTAL ASSOCIATION, BUREAU OF LIBRARY SERVICES, *IL169-78*
AMERICAN FEDERATION OF LABOR AND CONGRESS OF INDUSTRIAL ORGANIZATIONS, LIBRARY, *DC1-400*
AMERICAN FILM INSTITUTE, LOUIS B. MAYER LIBRARY, *CA421-015*
AMERICAN FORESTRY ASSOCIATION, *DC1-460*
AMERICAN FOUNDATION FOR THE BLIND, HELEN KELLER ARCHIVES, *NY586-440*
AMERICAN FOUNDATION FOR THE BLIND, RECORDS CENTER/ARCHIVES, *NY586-443*
AMERICAN FRIENDS SERVICE COMMITTEE, ARCHIVES, *PA725-60*
AMERICAN GAS ASSOCIATION, LIBRARY, *VA50-30*
AMERICAN HISTORICAL ASSOCIATION, PACIFIC COAST BRANCH, *CA421-20*
AMERICAN HISTORICAL SOCIETY OF GERMANS FROM RUSSIA, ARCHIVES AND HISTORICAL LIBRARY, *CO498-40*
AMERICAN HISTORY RESEARCH CENTER, *OH399-420*
AMERICAN HUMANE ASSOCIATION, ROBERTA WRIGHT REEVES MEMORIAL LIBRARY, *CO252-30*
AMERICAN INDIAN RESEARCH PROJECT, *SD792-800*
AMERICAN INSTITUTE FOR EXPLORATION, MAIN ADMINISTRATIVE OFFICE AND LIBRARY, *MI518-50*
AMERICAN INSTITUTE FOR MARXIST STUDIES, *NY586-520*
AMERICAN INSTITUTE OF ARCHITECTS, LIBRARY, *DC1-480*
AMERICAN INSTITUTE OF PHYSICS, CENTER FOR HISTORY OF PHYSICS, NIELS BOHR LIBRARY, *NY586-580*
AMERICAN INSTITUTE OF THE HISTORY OF PHARMACY, *WI346-870*

AMERICAN INTERNATIONAL COLLEGE, ORAL HISTORY CENTER, *MA804-50*
AMERICAN IRISH HISTORICAL SOCIETY, *NY586-600*
AMERICAN IRON AND STEEL INSTITUTE, PHOTO LIBRARY, *DC1-500*
AMERICAN JEWISH ARCHIVES, *OH171-20*
AMERICAN JEWISH COMMITTEE, BLAUSTEIN LIBRARY, *NY586-640*
AMERICAN JEWISH COMMITTEE, WILLIAM E. WIENER ORAL HISTORY LIBRARY, *NY586-650*
AMERICAN JEWISH HISTORICAL SOCIETY, LIBRARY, *MA871-40*
AMERICAN LAWN BOWLS ASSOCIATION, *FL560-40*
AMERICAN LEGION NATIONAL HEADQUARTERS, LIBRARY, *IN363-40*
AMERICAN LEPROSY MISSIONS, *NJ222-333*
AMERICAN LIBRARY ASSOCIATION, ARCHIVES, *IL916-40*
AMERICAN LISZT SOCIETY COLLECTION, *KY496-725*
AMERICAN LUTHERAN CHURCH, ARCHIVES (IA), *IA244-30*
AMERICAN LUTHERAN CHURCH, ARCHIVES (MN), *MN763-50*
AMERICAN MATHEMATICAL SOCIETY, *PA90-30*
AMERICAN MEDICAL COLLEGES, ASSOCIATION OF, ARCHIVES, *DC1-890*
AMERICAN MUSEUM OF IMMIGRATION, LIBRARY, *NY594-390*
AMERICAN MUSEUM OF NATURAL HISTORY, LIBRARY SERVICES DEPARTMENT, ARCHIVES AND PHOTOGRAPHIC COLL., *NY586-720*
AMERICAN NATIONAL RED CROSS, ARCHIVES, *DC1-560*
AMERICAN NUMISMATIC SOCIETY, LIBRARY, *NY586-770*
AMERICAN OLD TIME FIDDLERS ASSOCIATION, FIDDLING ARCHIVE, *NE560-50*
AMERICAN PATRIOT ARCHIVES SOCIETY, *MS80-40*
AMERICAN PETROLEUM INSTITUTE, PUBLIC RELATIONS, PHOTOGRAPHIC AND FILM SERVICES, *DC1-580*
AMERICAN PHARMACEUTICAL ASSOCIATION FOUNDATION, *DC1-600*
AMERICAN PHILOSOPHICAL SOCIETY, LIBRARY, *PA725-75*
AMERICAN POETRY ARCHIVES, *CA720-548*
AMERICAN POLITICAL ITEMS COLLECTORS, EDUCATION DIVISION, *WA954-40*
AMERICAN PSYCHIATRIC ASSOCIATION, LIBRARY AND ARCHIVES, *DC1-640*
AMERICAN SADDLE HORSE MUSEUM, *KY464-50*
AMERICAN SEPHARDI FEDERATION, RESEARCH DEPARTMENT, *NY586-880*
AMERICAN SOCIETY FOR PSYCHICAL RESEARCH, *NY586-910*
AMERICAN SOCIETY OF AGRICULTURAL ENGINEERS, *MI845-40*
AMERICAN SOCIETY OF ANESTHESIOLOGISTS, WOOD LIBRARY-MUSEUM OF ANESTHESIOLOGY, *IL708-40*
AMERICAN SWEDISH HISTORICAL MUSEUM, JOHN ERICSSON COLLECTION, *PA725-120*
AMERICAN SWEDISH INSTITUTE, *MN541-64*
AMERICAN TRUCKING ASSOCIATIONS, *DC1-680*
AMERICAN UNIVERSITY, BATTELLE MEMORIAL LIBRARY, UNIVERSITY ARCHIVES, *DC1-700*
AMERICAN UNIVERSITY, MUSIC LIBRARY, *DC1-705*
AMERICAN-CANADIAN GENEALOGICAL SOCIETY, *NH600-30*
AMERIND FOUNDATION, *AZ225-40*
AMES LIBRARY OF SOUTH ASIA, *MN541-822*
AMESBURY PUBLIC LIBRARY, *MA17-40*
AMHERST COLLEGE, ROBERT FROST LIBRARY, ARCHIVES AND SPECIAL COLLECTIONS, *MA21-40*
AMISTAD RESEARCH CENTER, *LA600-20*
AMITYVILLE HISTORICAL SOCIETY, MUSEUM, RESEARCH LIBRARY, *NY26-40*
AMON CARTER MUSEUM, DEPARTMENT OF PHOTOGRAPHS, *TX374-40*
AMOS JUDSON LIBRARY, *PA930-240*
AMOS MEMORIAL PUBLIC LIBRARY, *OH778-40*
ANACORTES MUSEUM OF HISTORY AND ART, *WA25-40*
ANACORTES PUBLIC LIBRARY, *WA25-60*
ANCHORAGE HISTORICAL AND FINE ARTS MUSEUM, *AK50-66*
ANCIENT AND HONORABLE ARTILLERY COMPANY OF MASSACHUSETTS, *MA108-80*
ANCIENT FREE AND ACCEPTED MASONS OF MARYLAND, GRAND LODGE, MUSEUM, *MD76-20*
ANCIENT FREE AND ACCEPTED MASONS, GRAND LODGE OF IOWA, IOWA MASONIC LIBRARY, *IA99-40*
ANDERSEN, HAROLD, LIBRARY, *WI858-810*
ANDERSON COLLEGE, SCHOOL OF THEOLOGY, LIBRARY, *IN22-50*
ANDERSON COUNTY PUBLIC LIBRARY, *KY410-40*
ANDERSON ISLAND HISTORICAL SOCIETY, *WA27-40*
ANDERSON LEARNING CENTER-LIBRARY, *ME837-560*
ANDOVER FREE LIBRARY, *NY29-40*
ANDOVER HISTORICAL SOCIETY, *MA25-40*
ANDOVER NEWTON THEOLOGICAL SCHOOL, LIBRARY, *MA593-40*
ANDOVER-HARVARD THEOLOGICAL LIBRARY, MANUSCRIPT DEPARTMENT, *MA169-230*

ANDREW CARNEGIE LIBRARY, AFRO-AMERICAN STUDIES, *NC730-480*
ANDREWS UNIVERSITY, JAMES WHITE LIBRARY, HERITAGE ROOM, *MI90-30*
ANDROSCOGGIN HISTORICAL SOCIETY, *ME25-30*
ANGELICA FREE LIBRARY, *NY32-50*
ANNAWAN HISTORICAL SOCIETY OF REHOBOTH, *MA708-40*
ANNE RAND RESEARCH LIBRARY, *CA720-356*
ANNIE MERNER PFEIFFER LIBRARY, *WV200-880*
ANNIE RIGGS MEMORIAL MUSEUM, *TX367-40*
ANNIE S. KEMERER MUSEUM, *PA90-40*
ANNISQUAM HISTORICAL SOCIETY, *MA338-840*
ANNMARY BROWN MEMORIAL, *RI700-45*
ANOKA COUNTY HISTORICAL/GENEALOGICAL SOCIETY, *MN42-40*
ANONYMOUS ARTS RECOVERY SOCIETY, *NY587-80*
ANTHONY, SUSAN B., MEMORIAL, *NY752-790*
ANTHROPOLOGY FILM CENTER, VISUAL ANTHROPOLOGY RESOURCE COLLECTION, *NM722-30*
ANTIETAM NATIONAL BATTLEFIELD SITE, LIBRARY, *MD798-40*
ANTIOCH COLLEGE, ANTIOCHIANA, *OH986-40*
ANTIQUARIAN AND LANDMARKS SOCIETY OF CONNECTICUT, *CT316-40*
ANTIQUE WIRELESS ASSOCIATION, ELECTRONIC COMMUNICATION MUSEUM, *NY396-40*
APACHE-SITGREAVES NATIONAL FOREST, *AZ700-40*
APPALACHIAN MUSEUM, *KY80-70*
APPALACHIAN ORAL HISTORY PROJECT, *KY630-40*
APPALOOSA HORSE CLUB, MUSEUM, *ID480-40*
ARCADIA PUBLIC LIBRARY, *CA40-60*
ARCHAEOLOGICAL INSTITUTE OF AMERICA, *NY587-180*
ARCHBISHOP CORRIGAN MEMORIAL LIBRARY, *NY984-710*
ARCHDIOCESE OF BALTIMORE, ARCHIVES, *MD76-30*
ARCHDIOCESE OF CINCINNATI, ARCHDIOCESAN ARCHIVES, *OH171-50*
ARCHDIOCESE OF DETROIT, ARCHIVES, *MI230-50*
ARCHDIOCESE OF LOS ANGELES, CHANCERY ARCHIVES, *CA421-30*
ARCHDIOCESE OF NEW ORLEANS, ROMAN CATHOLIC ARCHIVES, *LA600-40*
ARCHDIOCESE OF PORTLAND IN OREGON, HISTORY AND ARCHIVES DEPARTMENT, *OR720-40*
ARCHDIOCESE OF SANTA FE, ARCHIVES, *NM114-50*
ARCHDIOCESE OF WASHINGTON, CHANCERY OFFICE, *DC1-740*
ARCHIBALD MACLEISH COLLECTION, *MA352-270*
ARCHITECTURAL LEAGUE OF NEW YORK, ARCHIVE OF WOMEN IN ARCHITECTURE, *NY587-190*
ARCHIVE FOR HISTORY OF QUANTUM PHYSICS, *CA86-895*
ARCHIVE FOR RESEARCH IN ARCHETYPAL SYMBOLISM, *NY590-740*
ARCHIVE OF WOMEN IN ARCHITECTURE, *NY587-190*
ARCHIVES OF AMERICAN ART, *DC19-320*
ARCHIVES OF APPALACHIA, *TN435-220*
ARCHIVES OF COOPERATIVE LUTHERANISM, *NY591-40*
ARCHIVES OF DEPAUW UNIVERSITY AND INDIANA UNITED METHODISM, *IN275-150*
ARCHIVES OF INDUSTRIAL SOCIETY, *PA735-790*
ARCHIVES OF LABOR HISTORY AND URBAN AFFAIRS, *MI230-880*
ARCHIVES OF LEHIGH COUNTY, *PA25-60*
ARCHIVES OF PACIFIC NORTHWEST ANNUAL CONFERENCE, UNITED METHODIST CHURCH, *WA904-50*
ARCHIVES OF THE BRETHREN IN CHRIST CHURCH AND MESSIAH COLLEGE, *PA340-520*
ARCHIVES OF THE EPISCOPAL CHURCH, USA, *TX56-25*
ARCHIVES OF THE FIRST CHURCH IN CAMBRIDGE, CONGREGATIONAL, *MA169-40*
ARCHIVES OF THE HISTORY OF AMERICAN PSYCHOLOGY, *OH11-800*
ARCHIVES OF THE MENNONITE CHURCH, *IN264-40*
ARCHIVES OF THE MORAVIAN CHURCH, *PA90-500*
ARCHIVES OF THE SOUTH WISCONSIN DISTRICT OF THE LUTHERAN CHURCH-MISSOURI SYNOD, *WI426-111*
ARCHIVO GENERAL DE PUERTO RICO, *PR720-360*
ARENTS COLLECTIONS, *NY592-680*
ARENTS, GEORGE, RESEARCH LIBRARY, MANUSCRIPT COLLECTIONS, *NY872-800*
ARENTS, GEORGE, RESEARCH LIBRARY, SYRACUSE UNIVERSITY ARCHIVES, *NY872-810*
ARGONNE NATIONAL LABORATORY, TECHNICAL INFORMATION SERVICES DEPARTMENT, *IL35-40*
ARIZONA DEPARTMENT OF LIBRARY, ARCHIVES AND PUBLIC RECORDS, ARCHIVES DIVISION, *AZ550-040*
ARIZONA HISTORICAL FOUNDATION, *AZ750-10*
ARIZONA HISTORICAL SOCIETY, MANUSCRIPTS DIVISION, *AZ800-30*
ARIZONA HISTORICAL SOCIETY, PHOENIX CHAPTER, *AZ550-45*
ARIZONA HISTORICAL SOCIETY, YUMA COUNTY HISTORICAL SOCIETY COLLECTIONS, *AZ950-40*
ARIZONA PIONEERS' HISTORICAL SOCIETY, *AZ800-30*

ARIZONA STATE ARCHIVES, *AZ550-040*
ARIZONA STATE MUSEUM, DOCUMENTARY RELATIONS OF THE SOUTHWEST, *AZ800-790*
ARIZONA STATE MUSEUM, LIBRARY, *AZ800-800*
ARIZONA STATE MUSEUM, PHOTOGRAPHIC COLLECTIONS, *AZ800-803*
ARIZONA STATE PARKS, *AZ75-240, AZ950-950*
ARIZONA STATE UNIVERSITY, DEPARTMENT OF MUSIC, SOUTHWEST TAPE ARCHIVE, *AZ750-32*
ARIZONA STATE UNIVERSITY, LIBRARY, *AZ750-45*
ARKANSAS DEPARTMENT OF NATURAL AND CULTURAL HERITAGE, ARKANSAS TERRITORIAL RESTORATION, *AR510-13*
ARKANSAS HISTORY COMMISSION, *AR510-25*
ARKANSAS LIBRARY COMMISSION, *AR510-30*
ARKANSAS POST COUNTY MUSEUM, *AR360-40*
ARKANSAS STATE ARCHIVES, *AR510-25*
ARKANSAS STATE UNIVERSITY, DEAN B. ELLIS LIBRARY, ARKANSAS ROOM, *AR890-20*
ARKANSAS STATE UNIVERSITY, MUSEUM LIBRARY, *AR890-30*
ARKANSAS TERRITORIAL RESTORATION, *AR510-13*
ARLINGTON COUNTY PUBLIC LIBRARY, VIRGINIANA COLLECTION, *VA50-50*
ARLINGTON HISTORICAL SOCIETY, *MA29-40*
ARLINGTON HOUSE, ROBERT E. LEE MEMORIAL, *VA50-65*
ARLINGTON PUBLIC LIBRARY, *WA34-40*
ARMED FORCES INSTITUTE OF PATHOLOGY, ARMED FORCES MEDICAL MUSEUM, OTIS HISTORICAL ARCHIVES, *DC1-760*
ARMED FORCES MEDICAL MUSEUM, OTIS HISTORICAL ARCHIVES, *DC1-760*
ARMENIAN ASSEMBLY OF AMERICA, ORAL HISTORY PROJECT, *DC1-775*
ARMENIAN LIBRARY AND MUSEUM OF AMERICA, ARCHIVES AND MANUSCRIPTS DEPT. AND ORAL HISTORY COLLECTION, *MA84-50*
ARMENIAN MISSIONARY ASSOCIATION OF AMERICA, A. A. BEDIKIAN LIBRARY, *NJ630-40*
ARMS MUSEUM, *OH990-510*
ARMSTRONG BROWNING LIBRARY, *TX933-65*
ARMSTRONG COLLEGE, LIBRARY, *CA86-50*
ARMSTRONG WORLD INDUSTRIES, MANAGEMENT REFERENCE SERVICES, *PA470-40*
ARMSTRONG, JUDGE GEORGE W., LIBRARY, *MS640-400*
ARMY AVIATION MUSEUM, *AL380-800*
ARMY CENTER OF MILITARY HISTORY, *DC3-320*
ARMY COMMUNICATIONS-ELECTRONICS MUSEUM, *NJ270-800*
ARMY CORPS OF ENGINEERS, CANAL PARK MARINE MUSEUM, *MN261-40*
ARMY CORPS OF ENGINEERS, OFFICE OF THE CHIEF OF ENGINEERS, LIBRARY, *DC1-805*
ARMY CORPS OF ENGINEERS, OFFICE OF THE CHIEF OF ENGINEERS, PUBLIC AFFAIRS, AUDIO VISUAL DIVISION, *DC1-810*
ARMY SIGNAL CORPS MUSEUM, *NJ270-800*
ARMY TRANSPORTATION MUSEUM, *VA255-800*
ARMY 101ST AIRBORNE DIVISION AND FORT CAMPBELL, DON F. PRATT MUSEUM, *KY250-160*
ARMY, ARMOR SCHOOL, LIBRARY, *KY272-45*
ARNETT LIBRARY, *GA90-60*
ARNOLD ARBORETUM, *MA169-190*
ARNOLD B. TOFIAS INDUSTRIAL ARCHIVES, *MA615-710*
ARNOLD H. CRANE LIBRARY OF PHOTOGRAPHY, *IL169-127*
ARNOLD SCHOENBERG INSTITUTE, ARCHIVES, *CA421-40*
ARNOT ART MUSEUM, *NY272-40*
ARROTT COLLECTION AND SPANISH AND MEXICAN ARCHIVES, *NM513-560*
ARROW ROCK STATE HISTORICAL SITE, *MO30-80*
ART INSTITUTE OF CHICAGO, RYERSON AND BURNHAM LIBRARIES, *IL169-130*
ARTHUR A. HOUGHTON, JR., LIBRARY, *NY214-100*
ARTHUR AND ELIZABETH SCHLESINGER LIBRARY ON THE HISTORY OF WOMEN IN AMERICA, *MA169-860*
ARTHUR LAKES LIBRARY, *CO458-130*
ARTZ, C. BURR, LIBRARY, *MD399-240*
ARVADA CENTER FOR THE ARTS AND HUMANITIES, MUSEUM, *CO36-40*
ASBURY COLLEGE, MORRISON-KENYON LIBRARY, *KY886-30*
ASBURY FIRST METHODIST CHURCH, LIBRARY, *NY752-60*
ASBURY THEOLOGICAL SEMINARY, B. L. FISHER LIBRARY, *KY886-50*
ASHBY, DENNY, MEMORIAL LIBRARY, *WA672-160*
ASHER LIBRARY, CHICAGO JEWISH ARCHIVES, *IL170-780*
ASHLAND COLLEGE, LIBRARY, JOHN W. BROWN CENTER FOR CURRENT GOVERNMENT STUDIES, *OH26-40*
ASHLAND HISTORICAL SOCIETY, *MA41-40*
ASHLEY NATIONAL FOREST, FOREST SUPERVISOR'S OFFICE, *UT988-40*
ASOTIN COUNTY HISTORICAL SOCIETY, MUSEUM, *WA36-50*

ASOTIN COUNTY LIBRARY, *WA151-40*
ASPEN HISTORICAL SOCIETY, *CO54-40*
ASSOCIATION FOR CHILDHOOD EDUCATION INTERNATIONAL, ARCHIVES, *DC1-860*
ASSOCIATION FOR NORTHERN CALIFORNIA RECORDS AND RESEARCH, *CA136-40*
ASSOCIATION FOR RESEARCH AND ENLIGHTENMENT, EDGAR CAYCE FOUNDATION ARCHIVES, *VA810-40*
ASSOCIATION OF AMERICAN MEDICAL COLLEGES, ARCHIVES, *DC1-890*
ASSOCIATION OF AMERICAN RAILROADS, OFFICE OF INFORMATION AND PUBLIC AFFAIRS, *DC1-920*
ASSOCIATION OF CHILD PSYCHOANALYSIS, *NY587-300*
ASSOCIATION OF ROMANIAN CATHOLICS OF AMERICA, ARCHIVES SECTION, *IN187-40*
ASSOCIATION OF THE BAR OF THE CITY OF NEW YORK, LIBRARY, *NY587-340*
ASSUMPTION ABBEY, ARCHIVES, *ND824-40*
ASTOR FUR POST, STUART HOUSE MUSEUM OF, *MI590-720*
ASTORIA PUBLIC LIBRARY, *OR48-40*
ATASCADERO HISTORICAL SOCIETY, MUSEUM, *CA48-40*
ATCHISON PUBLIC LIBRARY, *KS80-40*
ATHENAEUM OF PHILADELPHIA, *PA725-150*
ATHENS COUNTY MUSEUM, *OH35-40*
ATKINS LIBRARY, *NC160-800*
ATLANTA HISTORICAL SOCIETY, ARCHIVES, *GA90-30*
ATLANTA UNIVERSITY CENTER, ARNETT LIBRARY, *GA90-60*
ATLANTIC CITY FREE PUBLIC LIBRARY, ALFRED M. HESTON COLLECTION, *NJ20-40*
ATLANTIC COUNTY HISTORICAL SOCIETY, *NJ786-40*
ATONEMENT, FRANCISCAN SISTERS OF THE, *NY318-240*
ATONEMENT, FRIARS OF THE, *NY318-260*
ATTICA HISTORICAL SOCIETY, *NY50-40*
ATTLEBORO AREA INDUSTRIAL MUSEUM, *MA48-20*
ATTLEBORO PUBLIC LIBRARY, JOSEPH L. SWEET MEMORIAL, *MA48-40*
AUBURN (MA) PUBLIC LIBRARY, *MA52-50*
AUBURN (ME) PUBLIC LIBRARY, *ME25-50*
AUBURN AUTOMOTIVE HERITAGE, AUBURN-CORD-DUESENBERG MUSEUM, *IN33-40*
AUBURN UNIVERSITY, ARCHIVES, *AL80-40*
AUBURN-CORD-DUESENBERG MUSEUM, *IN33-40*
AUGSBURG COLLEGE, GEORGE SVERDRUP LIBRARY, ARCHIVES, *MN541-80*
AUGUSTANA COLLEGE, LIBRARY, SPECIAL COLLECTIONS, *IL801-20*
AURARIA HIGHER EDUCATION CENTER, LIBRARY, UNIVERSITY ARCHIVES AND SPECIAL COLLECTIONS, *CO252-42*
AURORA COLLEGE, LIBRARY, *IL45-30*
AURORA COLONY HISTORICAL SOCIETY, OX BARN MUSEUM, *OR56-40*
AURORA HISTORICAL MUSEUM, *IL45-45*
AURORA HISTORICAL SOCIETY AND AURORA TOWN HISTORIAN, *NY250-50*
AURORA TOWN HISTORIAN AND AURORA HISTORICAL SOCIETY, *NY250-50*
AUSTIN PEAY STATE UNIVERSITY, FELIX G. WOODWARD LIBRARY, *TN75-50*
AUSTIN PRESBYTERIAN THEOLOGICAL SEMINARY, STITT LIBRARY, *TX56-30*
AUSTIN PUBLIC LIBRARY, AUSTIN-TRAVIS COUNTY COLLECTION, *TX56-50*
AUSTIN-TRAVIS COUNTY COLLECTION, *TX56-50*
AUSTIN, STEPHEN F., STATE UNIVERSITY, RALPH W. STEEN LIBRARY, SPECIAL COLLECTIONS DEPARTMENT, *TX632-720*
AUSTRO-AMERICAN ASSOCIATION OF BOSTON, *MA108-110*
AVERY ARCHITECTURAL AND FINE ARTS LIBRARY, *NY588-820*
AVOCA FREE LIBRARY, *NY54-40*

B

B. L. FISHER LIBRARY, *KY886-50*
B'NAI B'RITH MUSEUM, ARCHIVAL COLLECTION, *DC2-200*
BABSON COLLEGE, HORN LIBRARY, SPECIAL COLLECTIONS, *MA891-80*
BABSON LIBRARY, DR. ERNEST M. BEST ARCHIVES ROOM, *MA804-710*
BABYLON PUBLIC LIBRARY, *NY56-80*
BACON MEMORIAL PUBLIC LIBRARY, LOCAL HISTORY COLLECTION, *MI982-80*
BACON, FRANCIS, FOUNDATION, FRANCIS BACON LIBRARY, *CA143-240*
BACON, FRANCIS, LIBRARY, *CA143-240*
BAECK, LEO, INSTITUTE, *NY590-840*
BAHA'I, NATIONAL, ARCHIVES, *IL981-560*

BAILEY, GUY W., LIBRARY, WILBUR SPECIAL COLLECTIONS, *VT176-810*
BAILEY, OLIN C., LIBRARY, *AR240-320*
BAINBRIDGE FREE LIBRARY, *NY59-80*
BAINBRIDGE ISLAND HISTORICAL SOCIETY, *WA984-80*
BAINBRIDGE ISLAND LIBRARY, *WA984-90*
BAKER COUNTY PUBLIC LIBRARY, OREGON ROOM COLLECTION, *OR64-80*
BAKER HISTORICAL COLLECTION, *MA943-880*
BAKER LIBRARY, MANUSCRIPTS AND ARCHIVES DEPARTMENT, *MA108-750*
BAKER MEMORIAL LIBRARY, *CA421-520*
BAKER UNIVERSITY, ARCHIVES AND HISTORICAL LIBRARY, SPECIAL COLLECTIONS, *KS108-70*
BAKER-VANGUARD LIBRARY, BENTLEY COLLEGE ARCHIVES, *MA871-60*
BAKERY AND CONFECTIONERY WORKERS INTERNATIONAL UNION, PUBLIC RELATIONS, *MD575-333*
BAKHMETEFF ARCHIVE OF RUSSIAN AND EAST EUROPEAN HISTORY AND CULTURE, *NY588-825*
BALCH INSTITUTE FOR ETHNIC STUDIES, *PA725-165*
BALDWIN-WALLACE COLLEGE, LIBRARY, *OH82-50*
BALL STATE UNIVERSITY, BRACKEN LIBRARY, ALTHEA L. STOECKEL DELAWARE CTY. ARCH. & LOC. HIS., *IN539-80*
BALL STATE UNIVERSITY, BRACKEN LIBRARY, CENTER FOR MIDDLETOWN STUDIES, *IN539-83*
BALL STATE UNIVERSITY, BRACKEN LIBRARY, MUSIC ARCHIVES, *IN539-86*
BALL STATE UNIVERSITY, BRACKEN LIBRARY, SPECIAL COLLECTIONS, *IN539-90*
BALL STATE UNIVERSITY, COLLEGE OF ARCHITECTURE AND PLANNING, ARCHIVE OF DRAWINGS AND DOCUMENTS, *IN539-100*
BALTIMORE COUNTY HISTORICAL SOCIETY, *MD266-80*
BALTIMORE COUNTY PUBLIC LIBRARY, CATONSVILLE BRANCH, *MD209-80*
BALTIMORE COUNTY PUBLIC LIBRARY, REISTERSTOWN BRANCH, *MD745-690*
BALTIMORE DEPARTMENT OF LEGISLATIVE REFERENCE, DIVISION OF CITY ARCHIVES AND RECORDS MANAGEMENT, *MD76-60*
BALTIMORE HEBREW COLLEGE, JOSEPH MEYERHOFF LIBRARY, *MD76-70*
BALTIMORE MUSEUM OF ART, CONE COLLECTION, ARCHIVES, *MD76-80*
BALZEKAS MUSEUM OF LITHUANIAN CULTURE, *IL169-169*
BANCROFT LIBRARY, MANUSCRIPTS DIVISION, *CA86-780*
BANCROFT LIBRARY, MARK TWAIN PROJECT, *CA86-790*
BANCROFT LIBRARY, REGIONAL ORAL HISTORY OFFICE, *CA86-810*
BANCROFT LIBRARY, UNIVERSITY ARCHIVES, *CA86-815*
BANCROFT MEMORIAL LIBRARY, *MA411-80*
BANDELIER NATIONAL MONUMENT, LIBRARY AND PHOTO FILE, *NM570-80*
BANDON HISTORICAL SOCIETY, *OR72-80*
BANGOR HISTORICAL SOCIETY, *ME50-70*
BANGOR PUBLIC LIBRARY, *ME50-80*
BANK OF AMERICA ARCHIVES 3218, *CA720-104*
BANK OF AMERICA NT&SA, BANK OF AMERICA ARCHIVES 3218, *CA720-104*
BANK OF NEW YORK, ARCHIVES, *NY587-460*
BANKS, W. R., LIBRARY, *TX733-640*
BANKS, WILLIAM AND EVELYN, LIBRARY, *GA660-480*
BANNING PUBLIC LIBRARY, *CA66-80*
BAPTIST GENERAL CONFERENCE, ARCHIVES, *MN763-80*
BAR HARBOR HISTORICAL SOCIETY, *ME62-80*
BARAGA, BISHOP, ASSOCIATION, *MI605-80*
BARBERTON PUBLIC LIBRARY, *OH54-80*
BARBOUR, CLIFFORD E., LIBRARY, *PA735-630*
BARCO PHOTO AGENCY, *NY587-500*
BARD COLLEGE, LIBRARY, *NY35-80*
BARKER, DARWIN R., LIBRARY, HISTORICAL MUSEUM, *NY310-160*
BARKER, E. C., TEXAS HISTORY CENTER, *TX56-850*
BARKLEY, ALBEN W., MUSEUM, *KY604-40*
BARLOW SOCIETY FOR THE HISTORY OF MEDICINE, *CA421-385*
BARMES, FLOSSIE WILLS, MUSEUM, *AZ100-120*
BARNARD COLLEGE, ARCHIVES, *NY587-510*
BARNES COUNTY HISTORICAL SOCIETY, *ND876-80*
BARRE HISTORICAL SOCIETY, *MA70-70*
BARRINGTON AREA HISTORICAL SOCIETY MUSEUM, *IL55-80*
BARRY COUNTY HISTORICAL SOCIETY, *MO160-80*
BARTHOLOMEW COUNTY HISTORICAL SOCIETY, *IN121-80*
BARTLE, GLENN G., LIBRARY, SPECIAL COLLECTIONS, *NY101-720*
BARTLESVILLE PUBLIC LIBRARY, HISTORY ROOM, *OK118-70*
BARTLETT MEMORIAL HISTORICAL MUSEUM, *WI82-90*
BASQUE STUDIES PROGRAM, *NV940-800*
BASS, SOPHIE FRYE, MEMORIAL LIBRARY, *WA820-770*

BASTROP COUNTY HISTORICAL SOCIETY, MUSEUM, *TX63-80*
BATES COLLEGE, LIBRARY, *ME487-90*
BATH COUNTY HISTORICAL SOCIETY, *VA820-80*
BATH COUNTY LIBRARY, *KY602-80*
BATTELLE MEMORIAL LIBRARY, AMERICAN UNIVERSITY ARCHIVES, *DC1-700*
BATTLE GROUND BRANCH LIBRARY, *WA44-240*
BATTLEGROUND HISTORICAL SOCIETY, *NJ822-80*
BAY AREA ELECTRIC RAILROAD ASSOCIATION, WESTERN RAILWAY MUSEUM, *CA650-322*
BAY COUNTY HISTORICAL SOCIETY, HISTORICAL MUSEUM OF BAY COUNTY, *MI64-70*
BAYARD TAYLOR MEMORIAL LIBRARY, *PA440-80*
BAYLISS PUBLIC LIBRARY, JUDGE JOSEPH R. STEERE ROOM, *MI865-80*
BAYLOR UNIVERSITY, ARMSTRONG BROWNING LIBRARY, *TX933-65*
BAYLOR UNIVERSITY, TEXAS COLLECTION, *TX933-80*
BEAMAN MEMORIAL PUBLIC LIBRARY, WEST BOYLSTON COLLECTION, *MA904-80*
BEATRICE S. SWEENEY LIBRARY, *NY795-320*
BEAUFORT COUNTY LIBRARY, *SC54-80*
BEDFORD HISTORICAL SOCIETY, *MA77-80*
BEDFORD PUBLIC LIBRARY, INDIANA ROOM, OLD LAWRENCE COLLECTION, *IN55-80*
BEDIKIAN, A. A., LIBRARY, *NJ630-40*
BEINECKE RARE BOOK AND MANUSCRIPT LIBRARY, *CT505-890*
BELCHERTOWN HISTORICAL ASSOCIATION, STONE HOUSE, *MA81-80*
BELFAST MUSEUM, *ME87-80*
BELFAST PUBLIC LIBRARY, *NY82-80*
BELFER AUDIO LABORATORY AND ARCHIVES, *NY872-760*
BELL PUBLIC LIBRARY, *TX726-80*
BELL, ALEXANDER GRAHAM, ASSOCIATION FOR THE DEAF, LIBRARY, *DC22-500*
BELL, JAMES FORD, LIBRARY, *MN541-854*
BELLARMINE COLLEGE, LIBRARY, *KY496-70*
BELLARMINE COLLEGE, THOMAS MERTON COLLECTION, *KY496-90*
BELLEVUE COMMUNITY COLLEGE, COMMUNITY RELATIONS OFFICE, *WA56-100*
BELLINGHAM PUBLIC LIBRARY, *WA60-80*
BELLOWS FALLS HISTORICAL SOCIETY, ADAMS' OLD STONE GRIST MILL MUSEUM, *VT32-80*
BELMONT (MARY HELP OF CHRISTIANS) ABBEY, BELMONT ABBEY COLLEGE, *NC090-080*
BELMONT ABBEY COLLEGE, *NC090-080*
BELMONT LITERARY AND HISTORICAL SOCIETY FREE LIBRARY, *NY87-80*
BELOIT HISTORICAL SOCIETY, *WI82-90*
BEMIDJI STATE UNIVERSITY, LIBRARY, UNIVERSITY ARCHIVES, *MN63-70*
BEMIDJI STATE UNIVERSITY, NORTH CENTRAL MINNESOTA HISTORICAL CENTER, *MN63-75*
BEN FERREL-PLATTE COUNTY MUSEUM, *MO675-640*
BENBOW, LILLIAN PIERCE, ROOM OF SPECIAL COLLECTIONS, *MS870-760*
BENEDICTINE SISTERS OF COVINGTON, KENTUCKY, ST. WALBURG CONVENT, COMMUNITY ARCHIVES, *KY176-720*
BENNETT COLLEGE, THOMAS F. HOLGATE LIBRARY, *NC380-80*
BENNETT, H. H., STUDIO, *WI890-320*
BENNINGTON MUSEUM, GENEALOGICAL LIBRARY, *VT48-90*
BENSON, NETTIE LEE, LATIN AMERICAN COLLECTION, *TX56-860*
BENTLEY COLLEGE, BAKER-VANGUARD LIBRARY, COLLEGE ARCHIVES, *MA871-60*
BENTLEY HISTORICAL LIBRARY, MICHIGAN HISTORICAL COLLECTIONS, *MI40-784*
BENTON COUNTY (AR) HISTORICAL SOCIETY, *AR200-322*
BENTON COUNTY (MN) HISTORICAL SOCIETY, *MN794-80*
BENTON COUNTY HISTORICAL MUSEUM, *OR704-80, WA687-90*
BENTON COUNTY HISTORICAL SOCIETY, BENTON COUNTY HISTORICAL MUSEUM, *OR704-80*
BENTON HARBOR PUBLIC LIBRARY, *MI80-80*
BEREA COLLEGE, APPALACHIAN MUSEUM, *KY80-70*
BEREA COLLEGE, LIBRARY, SPECIAL COLLECTIONS, *KY80-90*
BERGEN COUNTY HISTORICAL SOCIETY, *NJ304-80*
BERKELEY, LAWRENCE, LABORATORY, ARCHIVES AND RECORDS, *CA86-882*
BERKSHIRE ATHENAEUM, LOCAL HISTORY AND LITERATURE SERVICES, *MA677-70*
BERKSHIRE FREE LIBRARY, *NY91-80*
BERNARDSVILLE PUBLIC LIBRARY, SPINNING ROOM, *NJ66-80*
BERNICE P. BISHOP MUSEUM, LIBRARY AND SOUND ARCHIVES, *HI350-73*
BERNICE P. BISHOP MUSEUM, PACIFIC SCIENTIFIC INFORMATION CENTER, *HI350-80*
BERRY SCHOOLS, ARCHIVES, *GA810-80*

BERRY, E. Y., LIBRARY/LEARNING CENTER, CASE LIBRARY AND BERRY MANUSCRIPT COLLECTION, *SD720-80*
BERRY, E. Y., MANUSCRIPT COLLECTION, *SD720-80*
BERTRAND, ELLEN CLARKE, LIBRARY, *PA500-80*
BEST, DR. ERNEST M., ARCHIVES ROOM, *MA804-710*
BETHANY COLLEGE, T. W. PHILLIPS LIBRARY, ALEXANDER CAMPBELL ARCHIVES, *WV100-80*
BETHANY COLLEGE, T. W. PHILLIPS LIBRARY, COLLEGE ARCHIVES, *WV100-90*
BETHANY COLLEGE, WALLERSTEDT LEARNING CENTER, *KS555-80*
BETHANY THEOLOGICAL SEMINARY AND NORTHERN BAPTIST THEOLOGICAL SEMINARY, LIBRARY, SP. COLL. & ARCH., *IL644-80*
BETHEL COLLEGE, HISTORICAL LIBRARY, *KS676-520*
BETHEL HISTORICAL SOCIETY, MOSES MASON MUSEUM, *ME95-80*
BETHEL UNITED METHODIST CHURCH, *SC144-70*
BETHLEHEM HISTORICAL ASSOCIATION, *NY818-760*
BETHLEHEM PUBLIC LIBRARY, *PA90-80*
BETTENDORF PUBLIC LIBRARY, *IA43-80*
BETTY CRONK MEMORIAL LIBRARY, *NY752-665*
BEVERLY HISTORICAL SOCIETY AND MUSEUM, CABOT HOUSE, *MA92-70*
BEVERLY PUBLIC LIBRARY, *MA92-90*
BEXAR COUNTY ARCHIVES, *TX777-80*
BEXLEY HALL, *NY752-110*
BIBLIOTHEQUE MALLET, *RI945-800*
BIDDLE LAW LIBRARY, *PA726-750*
BIDWELL MANSION STATE HISTORIC PARK, *CA136-90*
BIEL, JOHN G., LIBRARY, *IN825-830*
BIERCE LIBRARY, ARCHIVAL SERVICES, *OH11-810*
BIG BEND ARCHIVES, *TX14-720*
BIG BEND HISTORICAL SOCIETY, MUSEUM, *WA975-80*
BIG BEND NATIONAL PARK, *TX91-80*
BIG FLATS HISTORICAL SOCIETY, *NY98-80*
BIG SPRINGS HISTORICAL SOCIETY, *NY139-80*
BIG STONE COUNTY HISTORICAL SOCIETY, *MN632-80*
BIGELOW, JUDGE DANIEL R., HOUSE, *WA616-400*
BILLY GRAHAM CENTER, ARCHIVES, *IL976-850*
BILLY ROSE THEATRE COLLECTION, *NY592-880*
BILOXI CHAMBER OF COMMERCE, *MS80-80*
BINGHAMTON PUBLIC LIBRARY, *NY101-70*
BIRMINGHAM PUBLIC LIBRARY, DEPARTMENT OF ARCHIVES AND MANUSCRIPTS, *AL120-100*
BIRMINGHAM PUBLIC LIBRARY, SOUTHERN WOMEN'S ARCHIVES, *AL120-104*
BIRMINGHAM-SOUTHERN COLLEGE, CHARLES ANDREW RUSH LEARNING CENTER, SPECIAL COLLECTIONS, *AL120-110*
BISHOP BARAGA ASSOCIATION, *MI605-80*
BISHOP COLLEGE, LIBRARY, SOUTHWEST RESEARCH CENTER AND MUSEUM OF AFRICAN AMERICAN LIFE AND CULTURE, *TX252-80*
BISHOP PLANETARIUM AND SOUTH FLORIDA MUSEUM, *FL60-720*
BISHOP SKILLMAN LIBRARY, *PA270-470*
BISHOP, BERNICE P., MUSEUM, LIBRARY AND SOUND ARCHIVES, *HI350-73*
BISHOP, BERNICE P., MUSEUM, PACIFIC SCIENTIFIC INFORMATION CENTER, *HI350-80*
BLACK ARCHIVES, RESEARCH CENTER, AND MUSEUM, *FL800-200*
BLACK DIAMOND HISTORICAL SOCIETY, *WA70-80*
BLACK DIAMOND LIBRARY, *WA70-90*
BLACK HERITAGE RESEARCH CENTER, *SC860-600*
BLACK HILLS STATE COLLEGE, BERRY LIBRARY/LEARNING CENTER, CASE LIBRARY AND BERRY COLLECTION, *SD720-80*
BLACK RIVER ACADEMY MUSEUM, STATESMAN'S ARCHIVES, *VT374-80*
BLACK, COLONEL, HOUSE, *ME337-120*
BLACKMAN MUSEUM, *WA855-80*
BLAIR COUNTY HISTORICAL SOCIETY, *PA35-80*
BLAISDELL INSTITUTE FOR ADVANCED STUDY IN WORLD CULTURES AND RELIGIONS, *CA143-80*
BLAUSTEIN LIBRARY, *NY586-640*
BLAZER LIBRARY, *KY288-460*
BLESSED SACRAMENT SEMINARY, LIBRARY, *OH181-80*
BLEYHL COMMUNITY LIBRARY, *WA366-90*
BLOOMFIELD COLLEGE,LIBRARY, *NJ76-70*
BLOOMFIELD PUBLIC LIBRARY, *NY251-80*
BLOOMSBURG STATE COLLEGE, H. A. ANDRUSS LIBRARY, COLLGE ARCHIVES, *PA100-80*
BLOUGH, ROGER M., LEARNING CENTER, *PA800-720*
BLUE CROSS OF CALIFORNIA, FRANCES B. LINKE LIBRARY, *CA421-100*
BLUE EARTH COUNTY HISTORICAL SOCIETY, *MN506-80*
BLUE FOUR GALKA SCHEYER ARCHIVE, *CA578-630*
BLUE HILL PUBLIC LIBRARY, *ME112-80*
BLUE RIDGE INSTITUTE, *VA235-230*
BLUMBERG MEMORIAL LIBRARY, *TX797-760*

BOB WHEELER MUSEUM, *KY514-120*
BOEING COMPANY, HISTORICAL SERVICES, *WA820-92*
BOHR, NIELS, LIBRARY, *NY586-580*
BOISE STATE UNIVERSITY, LIBRARY, SPECIAL COLLECTIONS DEPARTMENT, *ID80-90*
BOLIVAR FREE LIBRARY, *NY106-80*
BOLTON HISTORICAL SOCIETY, *MA104-80*
BOLTON, JAMES C., LIBRARY, *LA26-480*
BOND COUNTY HISTORICAL SOCIETY, HISTORICAL SOCIETY MUSEUM, *IL354-80*
BONNER COUNTY HISTORICAL SOCIETY, BONNER COUNTY MUSEUM, *ID880-80*
BONNER COUNTY MUSEUM, *ID880-80*
BOONE COUNTY PUBLIC LIBRARY, *KY240-80*
BOONTON TOWNSHIP HISTORICAL SOCIETY, *NJ84-320*
BOOTH, CYRENIUS H., LIBRARY, *CT533-120*
BORDERLAND STATE PARK, *MA615-80*
BOSTON ATHENAEUM, *MA108-140*
BOSTON COLLEGE, LIBRARIES, SPECIAL COLLECTIONS, *MA199-90*
BOSTON COLLEGE, UNIVERSITY ARCHIVES, *MA199-100*
BOSTON MEDICAL LIBRARY, *MA108-770*
BOSTON PUBLIC LIBRARY, *MA108-200*
BOSTON SOCIETY OF NATURAL HISTORY, *MA109-380*
BOSTON UNIVERSITY, MUGAR LIBRARY, DEPARTMENT OF SPECIAL COLLECTIONS, *MA108-240*
BOSTONIAN SOCIETY, LIBRARY, *MA108-320*
BOSWELL, JAMES, YALE EDITIONS OF THE PRIVATE PAPERS OF, *CT505-977*
BOTHELL HISTORICAL MUSEUM SOCIETY, *WA78-80*
BOTHELL LIBRARY, *WA78-90*
BOULDER PUBLIC LIBRARY, CARNEGIE BRANCH LIBRARY, *CO108-85*
BOUND BROOK MEMORIAL LIBRARY, *NJ92-80*
BOURBON COUNTY-PARIS LIBRARY, *KY61A-640*
BOVINA HISTORICAL SOCIETY, MUSEUM, *NY111-60*
BOVINA PUBLIC LIBRARY, *NY111-80*
BOWDOIN COLLEGE, LIBRARY, SPECIAL COLLECTIONS, *ME162-120*
BOWDOIN COLLEGE, PEARY-MACMILLAN ARCTIC MUSEUM, *ME162-100*
BOWERS MUSEUM, *CA770-120*
BOWLBY, EVA K., PUBLIC LIBRARY, ORAL HISTORY COLLECTION, *PA940-300*
BOWLING GREEN STATE UNIVERSITY, NORTHWEST OHIO-GREAT LAKES RESEARCH CENTER, *OH97-80*
BOWLING LIBRARY, *AL540-400*
BOWMAN, A. R., HISTORICAL MUSEUM, *OR736-40*
BOXFORD HISTORIC DOCUMENTS CENTER, *MA903-80*
BOYCE, WILLIAM T., LIBRARY, *CA278-240*
BOYD COUNTY HISTORICAL SOCIETY, *KY2A-80*
BOYLSTON PUBLIC LIBRARY, *MA123-80*
BRACKEN LIBRARY, CENTER FOR MIDDLETOWN STUDIES, *IN539-83*
BRACKEN LIBRARY, MUSIC ARCHIVES, *IN539-86*
BRADFORD COUNTY HISTORICAL SOCIETY, *PA875-80*
BRADLEY COUNTY HISTORICAL SOCIETY, *TN90-80*
BRADLEY UNIVERSITY, CULLOM-DAVIS LIBRARY, VIRGINIUS H. CHASE SPEC. COLL. CENTER, *IL723-80*
BRANCHPORT FREE LIBRARY, *NY112-80*
BRANDEIS UNIVERSITY, DRETZIN LIVING BIOGRAPHIES PROGRAM, *MA871-85*
BRANDEIS UNIVERSITY, GOLDFARB LIBRARY, SPECIAL COLLECTIONS, *MA871-90*
BRANDYWINE CONSERVANCY, BRANDYWINE RIVER MUSEUM, LIBRARY, *PA175-80*
BRANFORD ELECTRIC RAILWAY ASSOCIATION, BRANFORD TROLLEY MUSEUM, KUHN MEMORIAL LIBRARY, *CT198-80*
BRANFORD TROLLEY MUSEUM, KUHN MEMORIAL LIBRARY, *CT198-80*
BRATTLEBORO PHOTOGRAPHY COLLECTION, *VT128-80*
BRAZORIA COUNTY LIBRARY SYSTEM, *TX35-90*
BREATHITT COUNTY PUBLIC LIBRARY, *KY38U-80*
BRECKINRIDGE, JAMES CARSON, LIBRARY, *VA660-510*
BRETHREN HISTORICAL LIBRARY AND ARCHIVES, *IL241-120*
BRETHREN, CHURCH OF THE, WASHINGTON DISTRICT ARCHIVES, *WA966-115*
BREWSTER LADIES' LIBRARY, *MA134-80*
BRICK STORE MUSEUM, *ME460-80*
BRIDGEPORT PUBLIC LIBRARY, *WA86-95*
BRIDGEPORT PUBLIC LIBRARY, HISTORICAL COLLECTIONS, *CT36-80*
BRIDGEWATER COLLEGE, ALEXANDER MACK MEMORIAL LIBRARY, COLLEGE ARCHIVES, *VA115-80*
BRIDGEWATER PUBLIC LIBRARY, HISTORICAL ROOM, *MA139-90*
BRIGGS, HILTON M., LIBRARY, ARCHIVES, *SD54-715*
BRIGHAM YOUNG UNIVERSITY - HAWAII CAMPUS, *HI450-80*
BRIGHAM YOUNG UNIVERSITY - HAWAII CAMPUS, ARCHIVES AND MANUSCRIPTS, *HI450-75*

BRIGHAM YOUNG UNIVERSITY, HAROLD B. LEE LIBRARY, ARCHIVES AND MANUSCRIPTS, *UT684-80*
BRILL, ABRAHAM A., LIBRARY, *NY592-640*
BRISTOL HISTORICAL SOCIETY, *NY124-60*
BRISTOL PUBLIC LIBRARY, *CT48-80, VA120-80*
BROADCAST PIONEERS LIBRARY, *DC2-600*
BROADCASTING, MUSEUM OF, *NY591-690*
BRONSON, SILAS, LIBRARY, *CT870-730*
BRONX COUNTY HISTORICAL SOCIETY, RESEARCH LIBRARY, *NY587-720*
BROOKE COUNTY HISTORICAL SOCIETY, *WV900-80*
BROOKLINE HISTORICAL SOCIETY, *MA154-640*
BROOKLINE PUBLIC LIBRARY, *MA154-640*
BROOKLYN BOTANIC GARDEN, LIBRARY, *NY587-740*
BROOKLYN COLLEGE, LIBRARY, SPECIAL COLLECTIONS DIVISION, *NY588-300*
BROOKLYN MUSEUM, LIBRARIES, *NY587-780*
BROOKLYN PUBLIC LIBRARY, HISTORY DIVISION, BROOKLYN COLLECTION, *NY587-800*
BROOKS MEMORIAL LIBRARY, LOCAL HISTORY AND GENEALOGY COLLECTION AND BRATTLEBORO PHOTOGRAPH COLL., *VT128-80*
BROOME COMMUNITY COLLEGE, CECIL B. TYRRELL LIBRARY, *NY101-80*
BROOME COUNTY HISTORICAL SOCIETY, *NY101-90*
BROWN COUNTY HISTORICAL SOCIETY, *MN618-80*
BROWN COUNTY HISTORICAL SOCIETY, ARCHIVES, ORAL HISTORY, GENEALOGY, *IN550-80*
BROWN UNIVERSITY, ANNMARY BROWN MEMORIAL, *RI700-45*
BROWN UNIVERSITY, ARCHIVES, *RI700-50*
BROWN UNIVERSITY, HAFFENREFFER MUSEUM OF ANTHROPOLOGY, *RI105-320*
BROWN UNIVERSITY, JOHN CARTER BROWN LIBRARY, *RI700-70*
BROWN UNIVERSITY, JOHN HAY LIBRARY, *RI700-100*
BROWN, ANNMARY, MEMORIAL, *RI700-45*
BROWN, GEORGE H. AND LAURA E., LIBRARY, *NC850-120*
BROWN, JAMES V., LIBRARY, *PA965-400*
BROWN, JOHN CARTER, LIBRARY, *RI700-70*
BROWN, JOHN W., CENTER FOR CURRENT GOVERNMENT STUDIES, *OH26-40*
BROWNELL, LOIS, RESEARCH LIBRARY, *MO700-720*
BROWNING, ARMSTRONG, LIBRARY, *TX933-65*
BROWNSTOWN PUBLIC LIBRARY, *IN92-80*
BRUCE MEMORIAL MUSEUM, *WA952-80*
BRUTE LIBRARY, *IN902-80*
BRYAN WILDENTHAL MEMORIAL LIBRARY, ARCHIVES OF THE BIG BEND, *TX14-720*
BRYANT LIBRARY, LOCAL HISTORY COLLECTION, *NY760-90*
BRYN MAWR COLLEGE, ARCHIVES, *PA135-80*
BUCK, PEARL S., BIRTHPLACE FOUNDATION, *WV375-640*
BUCKNELL UNIVERSITY, ELLEN CLARKE BERTRAND LIBRARY, *PA500-80*
BUCKNELL UNIVERSITY, LIBRARY, ARCHIVES, *PA500-70*
BUCKS COUNTY HISTORICAL SOCIETY, *PA260-80*
BUCKSPORT HISTORICAL SOCIETY, *ME175-80*
BUD WERNER MEMORIAL LIBRARY, ROUTT COUNTY COLLECTION, *CO856-80*
BUEHLER, A. C., LIBRARY, *IL246-190*
BUFFALO AND ERIE COUNTY HISTORICAL SOCIETY, ICONOGRAPHY DEPARTMENT, *NY134-50*
BUFFALO AND ERIE COUNTY HISTORICAL SOCIETY, MANUSCRIPTS DEPARTMENT, *NY134-60*
BUFFALO AND ERIE COUNTY PUBLIC LIBRARY, NORTH JEFFERSON BRANCH, CENTER FOR AFRO-AMERICAN HISTORY, *NY134-85*
BUFFALO AND ERIE COUNTY PUBLIC LIBRARY, RARE BOOK ROOM, *NY134-90*
BUFFALO BILL HISTORICAL CENTER, *WY155-80*
BUFFALO BILL MEMORIAL MUSEUM, *CO458-80*
BUND ARCHIVES FOR THE JEWISH LABOR MOVEMENT, *NY587-820*
BURCHFIELD CENTER, *NY134-710*
BUREAU COUNTY HISTORICAL SOCIETY, *IL762-80*
BUREAU OF AMERICAN ETHNOLOGY, ARCHIVES, *DC19-520*
BUREAU OF INDIAN AFFAIRS, WESTERN WASHINGTON OFFICE, *WA300-80*
BURIEN PUBLIC LIBRARY, *WA97-100*
BURKE LIBRARY, *NY197-310*
BURKE, THOMAS, MEMORIAL WASHINGTON STATE MUSEUM, *WA820-840*
BURLING LIBRARY, *IA377-280*
BURLINGTON COUNTY HISTORICAL SOCIETY, *NJ100-80*
BURLINGTON COUNTY LIBRARY, *NJ552-70*
BURLINGTON COUNTY LYCEUM OF HISTORY AND NATURAL SCIENCES (MOUNT HOLLY LIBRARY), *NJ552-80*
BURLINGTON HISTORICAL SOCIETY, *WI114-80*
BURLINGTON LIBRARY, *WA98-100*
BURLINGTON PUBLIC LIBRARY, *IA66-80*

BURNDY CORPORATION, LIBRARY, *CT582-80*
BURNHAM TAVERN MUSEUM, *ME512-80*
BURNHAM, GUY H., MAP AND AERIAL PHOTOGRAPH LIBRARY, *MA985-120*
BURNHAM, RYERSON AND, LIBRARIES, *IL169-130*
BURR, AARON, ASSOCIATION, *NJ339-40*
BURRITT, ELIHU, LIBRARY, *CT477-130*
BURROW LIBRARY, *TN630-740*
BURTON HISTORICAL COLLECTION, *MI230-165*
BURTON PUBLIC LIBRARY, *OH112-80*
BURWELL SCHOOL, COLLECTIONS ON WOMEN'S EDUCATION IN EARLY NORTH CAROLINA, *NC430-340*
BUSCH-REISINGER MUSEUM, GROPIUS ARCHIVES AND FEININGER ARCHIVES, *MA169-200*
BUSH CENTER, HILL MONASTIC MANUSCRIPT LIBRARY, *MN226-720*
BUSH MEMORIAL LIBRARY, ARCHIVES, *MN763-310*
BUSHWHACKER MUSEUM, ARCHIVES, *MO620-80*
BUSINESS AND PROFESSIONAL WOMEN'S CLUBS, NATIONAL FEDERATION OF, ARCHIVES DEPARTMENT, *DC14-420*
BUSINESS AND PROFESSIONAL WOMEN'S FOUNDATION, LIBRARY, *DC2-850*
BUTEN MUSEUM OF WEDGWOOD, *PA575-80*
BUTLER COUNTY (KS) HISTORICAL SOCIETY, MUSEUM, *KS269-80*
BUTLER COUNTY (OH) HISTORICAL SOCIETY, MUSEUM, *OH360-80*
BUTLER UNIVERSITY, IRWIN LIBRARY, *IN363-90*
BUTLER, E. H., LIBRARY, ARCHIVES/SPECIAL COLLECTIONS, *NY134-730*
BUTTERICK ARCHIVES/LIBRARY, *NY587-840*
BYRON R. LEWIS HISTORICAL COLLECTIONS LIBRARY, *IN902-840*

C

C. A. DANA - LIFE LIBRARY, *NE144-160*
C. BURR ARTZ LIBRARY, *MD399-240*
C. W. POST CENTER, LIBRARY, SPECIAL COLLECTIONS, *NY355-480*
CABELL, JAMES BRANCH, LIBRARY, SPECIAL COLLECTIONS DEPARTMENT, *VA690-830*
CABOT HOUSE (BEVERLY MA), *MA92-70*
CADY, GEORGE P. AND SUSAN PLATT, LIBRARY, *NY605-280*
CAIRO PUBLIC LIBRARY, *IL109-130*
CALAIS FREE LIBRARY, *ME200-120*
CALAVERAS COUNTY MUSEUM AND ARCHIVES, *CA692-130*
CALDWELL PARSONAGE MUSEUM, *NJ844-800*
CALEDONIA LIBRARY ASSOCIATION, *NY139-120*
CALHOUN COUNTY HISTORICAL SOCIETY, *IA833-120*
CALHOUN COUNTY MUSEUM, ARCHIVES AND RESEARCH, *SC792-120*
CALIFON HISTORICAL SOCIETY, *NJ108-120*
CALIFORNIA ACADEMY OF SCIENCES, LIBRARY, *CA720-148*
CALIFORNIA DEPARTMENT OF CONSERVATION, DIVISION OF MINES AND GEOLOGY, LIBRARY, *CA720-161*
CALIFORNIA DEPARTMENT OF PARKS AND RECREATION, *CA410-120*
CALIFORNIA DEPARTMENT OF PARKS AND RECREATION, BIDWELL MANSION STATE HISTORIC PARK, *CA136-90*
CALIFORNIA DEPARTMENT OF PARKS AND RECREATION, SHASTA STATE HISTORIC PARK, *CA814-120*
CALIFORNIA HISTORICAL SOCIETY, LIBRARY, *CA720-180*
CALIFORNIA HISTORICAL SOCIETY, SOUTHERN CALIFORNIA BRANCH, *CA421-115*
CALIFORNIA INSTITUTE OF TECHNOLOGY, *CA578-560*
CALIFORNIA INSTITUTE OF TECHNOLOGY, ARCHIVES, *CA578-130*
CALIFORNIA MUSEUM OF PHOTOGRAPHY, *CA652-795*
CALIFORNIA OFFICE OF THE SECRETARY OF STATE, CALIFORNIA STATE ARCHIVES, *CA676-110*
CALIFORNIA PETROLEUM INDUSTRY COLLECTION, *CA414-470*
CALIFORNIA POLYTECHNIC STATE UNIVERSITY, LIBRARY, SPECIAL COLLECTIONS SECTION, *CA744-120*
CALIFORNIA STATE AND LOCAL HISTORY, SOURISSEAU ACADEMY FOR, *CA728-850*
CALIFORNIA STATE ARCHIVES, *CA676-110*
CALIFORNIA STATE COLLEGE, LOUIS L. MANDERINO LIBRARY, ARCHIVES, *PA145-120*
CALIFORNIA STATE COLLEGE, STANISLAUS, LIBRARY, *CA906-120*
CALIFORNIA STATE LIBRARY, CALIFORNIA SECTION, *CA676-130*
CALIFORNIA STATE LIBRARY, SUTRO BRANCH, *CA720-203*
CALIFORNIA STATE POLYTECHNIC UNIVERSITY, LIBRARY, *CA601-120*
CALIFORNIA STATE UNIVERSITY, CHICO, LIBRARY, SPEC. COLLECT. & ASSOC. FOR N. CAL. RECS. & RESEARCH, *CA136-120*
CALIFORNIA STATE UNIVERSITY, EDUCATIONAL RESOURCES CENTER, *CA222-120*
CALIFORNIA STATE UNIVERSITY, FRESNO, HENRY MADDEN LIBRARY, *CA274-120*

CALIFORNIA STATE UNIVERSITY, FULLERTON, GEOGRAPHY DEPARTMENT, MAP LIBRARY, *CA278-120*
CALIFORNIA STATE UNIVERSITY, FULLERTON, LIBRARY, UNIVERSITY ARCHIVES AND SPECIAL COLLECTIONS, *CA278-130*
CALIFORNIA STATE UNIVERSITY, HAYWARD, LIBRARY, SPECIAL COLLECTIONS, *CA314-120*
CALIFORNIA STATE UNIVERSITY, LONG BEACH, LIBRARY, SPECIAL COLLECTIONS, *CA414-150*
CALIFORNIA STATE UNIVERSITY, NORTHRIDGE, MAP LIBRARY, *CA524-140*
CALIFORNIA STATE UNIVERSITY, NORTHRIDGE, URBAN ARCHIVES PROJECT, *CA524-160*
CALIFORNIA STATE UNIVERSITY, SACRAMENTO, LIBRARY, UNIVERSITY ARCHIVES, *CA676-140*
CALUMET REGIONAL ARCHIVES, *IN253-360*
CALVERT MARINE MUSEUM, *MD836-120*
CALVIN COLLEGE AND SEMINARY, HERITAGE HALL-LIBRARY, COLONIAL ORIGINS COLLECTION, *MI355-110*
CAMAS PUBLIC LIBRARY, *WA102-105*
CAMBRIA COUNTY HISTORICAL SOCIETY, MUSEUM AND LIBRARY, *PA275-120*
CAMBRIDGE HISTORICAL COMMISSION, *MA169-50*
CAMDEN ARCHIVES, *SC108-100*
CAMDEN COUNTY HISTORICAL SOCIETY, *NJ112-120*
CAMDEN-ROCKPORT HISTORICAL SOCIETY, OLD CONWAY HOMESTEAD, CRAMER MUSEUM, *ME212-120*
CAMDEN, JOHNSON, LIBRARY, SPECIAL COLLECTIONS, *KY558-520*
CAMERON COUNTY PUBLIC LIBRARY, *PA295-130*
CAMP FIVE FOUNDATION MUSEUM, *WI326-120*
CAMP SIX LOGGING MUSEUM, *WA904-100*
CAMPBELL UNIVERSITY, CARRIE RICH MEMORIAL LIBRARY, *NC130-120*
CAMPBELL, ALEXANDER, ARCHIVES, *WV100-80*
CAMPBELLSVILLE COLLEGE, LIBRARY, *KY126-120*
CAMPION JESUIT COMMUNITY, *WI594-110*
CAMPUS MARTIUS MUSEUM, *OH486-660*
CANADIAN COUNTY HISTORICAL MUSEUM, *OK338-120*
CANAL MUSEUM, RESEARCH LIBRARY, *PA270-320*
CANAL PARK MARINE MUSEUM, *MN261-40*
CANAL SOCIETY OF NEW JERSEY, MUSEUM, *NJ804-120*
CANDOR FREE LIBRARY, *NY148A-12*
CANFIELD MEMORIAL LIBRARY, RUSSELL VERMONTIANA COLLECTION, *VT16-120*
CANISIUS COLLEGE, ARCHIVES, *NY134-120*
CANNON, CHARLES A., MEMORIAL LIBRARY, *NC200-120*
CANTON HISTORICAL MUSEUM, LIBRARY, *CT108-120*
CANTON HISTORICAL SOCIETY, CANTON HISTORICAL MUSEUM, LIBRARY, *CT108-120*
CAPE COD COMMUNITY COLLEGE, LIBRARY-LEARNING RESOURCE CENTER, *MA901-120*
CAPE FEAR TECHNICAL INSTITUTE, LIBRARY LEARNING RESOURCE CENTER, *NC900-120*
CAPE MAY COUNTY HISTORICAL AND GENEALOGICAL SOCIETY, *NJ120-120*
CAPITAL UNIVERSITY, ARCHIVES, *OH203-100*
CAPROCK-PLAINS HISTORICAL COLLECTION, *TX712-880*
CAPRON/KNIGHT LIBRARY, *VA470-470*
CAPTAIN CHARLES H. HURLEY LIBRARY, *MA165-520*
CARDINAL HAYES LIBRARY, *NY591-100*
CAREY, WILLIS, HISTORICAL MUSEUM, *WA112-880*
CARL AND LILY PFORZHEIMER FOUNDATION, CARL H. PFORZHEIMER LIBRARY, *NY587-880*
CARL H. PFORZHEIMER LIBRARY, *NY587-880*
CARL S. SWISHER LIBRARY, *FL280-420*
CARLETON COLLEGE, LIBRARY, *MN625-120*
CARLTON COUNTY HISTORICAL SOCIETY, *MN185-120*
CARMELITE MONASTERY OF BALTIMORE, ARCHIVES, *MD76-100*
CARMELITE ORDER, PROVINCE OF THE MOST PURE HEART OF MARY, ARCHIVE, *IL55-120*
CARMICHAEL LIBRARY, ARCHIVES, *AL600-800*
CARNEGIE LIBRARY OF PITTSBURGH, PENNSYLVANIA DIVISION, *PA735-110*
CARNEGIE PUBLIC LIBRARY (CLARKSDALE MS), *MS200-120*
CARNEGIE PUBLIC LIBRARY (SAULT STE. MARIE MI), *MI865-80*
CARNEGIE PUBLIC LIBRARY (TRINIDAD CO), *CO910-120*
CARNEGIE-MELLON UNIVERSITY, HUNT INSTITUTE FOR BOTANICAL DOCUMENTATION, *PA735-140*
CARNEGIE-MELLON UNIVERSITY, HUNT LIBRARY, FINE AND RARE BOOK ROOMS, *PA735-150*
CARNEGIE, ANDREW, LIBRARY, AFRO-AMERICAN STUDIES, *NC730-480*
CAROL M. NEWMAN LIBRARY, SPECIAL COLLECTIONS, *VA90-840*
CAROLINA ART ASSOCIATION, GIBBES ART GALLERY, *SC144-90*
CAROLINE MARTIN-MITCHELL MUSEUM, *IL609-120*
CAROLINE MERIWETHER GOODLETT LIBRARY, *VA690-760*
CARPENTER CENTER FOR THE VISUAL ARTS, *MA169-210*
CARPENTER MEMORIAL LIBRARY, *WA153-128*

CARREL, ALEXIS, COLLECTION, *DC7-660*
CARRIE MCLAIN MEMORIAL MUSEUM, *AK700-120*
CARRIE RICH MEMORIAL LIBRARY, *NC130-120*
CARROLL COLLEGE, LIBRARY, *WI794-120*
CARROLL COUNTY HISTORICAL SOCIETY, *MD978-320*
CARSON COUNTY SQUARE HOUSE MUSEUM, *TX691-130*
CARTER, AMON, MUSEUM, DEPARTMENT OF PHOTOGRAPHS, *TX374-40*
CARVER, GEORGE WASHINGTON, NATIONAL MONUMENT, *MO240-280*
CARY LIBRARY, *ME437-120*
CASA GRANDE RUINS NATIONAL MONUMENT, *AZ175-120*
CASA GRANDE VALLEY HISTORICAL SOCIETY, FLOSSIE WILLS BARMES MUSEUM, *AZ100-120*
CASE MEMORIAL LIBRARY, ARCHIVES, *CT316-330*
CASE WESTERN RESERVE UNIVERSITY, ARCHIVES, *OH181-110*
CASE WESTERN RESERVE UNIVERSITY, LIBRARIES, SPECIAL COLLECTIONS, *OH181-130*
CASE WESTERN RESERVE UNIVERSITY, SEARS LIBRARY, ARCHIVE OF SCIENCE AND TECHNOLOGY, *OH181-130*
CASE, LELAND D., LIBRARY FOR WESTERN HISTORICAL STUDIES, *SD720-80*
CASEY COUNTY PUBLIC LIBRARY, *KY467-120*
CASS COUNTY HISTORICAL SOCIETY, MUSEUM, *NE720-120*
CASTILE HISTORICAL SOCIETY, *NY156-120*
CASTILLO DE SAN MARCOS NATIONAL MONUMENT AND FORT MATANZAS NATIONAL MONUMENT, *FL660-120*
CASTINE SCIENTIFIC SOCIETY, ARCHIVES DEPARTMENT, *ME231-120*
CATAWBA COLLEGE, LIBRARY, *NC730-120*
CATAWBA COUNTY HISTORICAL MUSEUM, *NC650-120*
CATHEDRAL HOUSE ARCHIVES, *TX777-640*
CATHER, WILLA, HISTORICAL CENTER, *NE736-560*
CATHERWOOD, M. P., LIBRARY, LABOR-MANAGEMENT DOCUMENTATION CENTER, *NY439-150*
CATHOLIC ARCHIVES AT SAN ANTONIO, *TX777-30*
CATHOLIC ARCHIVES OF TEXAS, *TX56-110*
CATHOLIC CENTER, ARCHIVES, *IN363-50*
CATHOLIC CHANCERY OFFICE (DUBUQUE IA), *IA244-120*
CATHOLIC DIOCESE OF BAKER, CHANCERY OFFICE, *OR64-120*
CATHOLIC DIOCESE OF FAIRBANKS, *AK350-120*
CATHOLIC DIOCESE OF GREEN BAY, DIOCESAN PASTORAL OFFICE, CHANCERY, *WI202-120*
CATHOLIC DIOCESE OF GREENSBURG, DIOCESAN ARCHIVES, *PA350-160*
CATHOLIC DIOCESE OF JACKSON, *MS550-120*
CATHOLIC DIOCESE OF LA CROSSE, *WI298-120*
CATHOLIC DIOCESE OF PITTSBURGH, DIOCESAN HISTORICAL ARCHIVES, *PA735-160*
CATHOLIC DIOCESE OF SPOKANE, CHANCERY ARCHIVES, *WA880-120*
CATHOLIC DIOCESE OF YAKIMA, *WA994-690*
CATHOLIC HISTORICAL SOCIETY OF SAINT PAUL, *MN763-100*
CATHOLIC UNIVERSITY OF AMERICA, DEPARTMENT OF ARCHIVES, MANUSCRIPTS, AND MUSEUM COLLECTIONS, *DC3-210*
CATHOLIC UNIVERSITY OF AMERICA, THE OLIVEIRA LIMA LIBRARY, *DC3-226*
CATLIN HISTORICAL SOCIETY, *NY159-120*
CATO FREE LIBRARY, *NY160-120*
CATSKILL MOUNTAIN AND HUDSON RIVER STUDIES, CENTER FOR, *NY574-710*
CATTARAUGUS AREA HISTORICAL SOCIETY, CATTARAUGUS HISTORICAL CENTER, *NY163-120*
CATTARAUGUS COUNTY HISTORIAN, *NY496-120*
CATTARAUGUS HISTORICAL CENTER, *NY163-120*
CAYCE, EDGAR, FOUNDATION ARCHIVES, *VA810-40*
CAYUGA COUNTY COMMUNITY COLLEGE, LIBRARY, *NY51-90*
CAYUGA COUNTY HISTORIAN, *NY51-100*
CAYUGA MUSEUM OF HISTORY AND ART, *NY51-140*
CAYUGA OWASCO LAKES HISTORICAL SOCIETY, HISTORY HOUSE, *NY563-120*
CBS-KIRO MILO RYAN PHONOARCHIVES, *WA820-893*
CEC-SEABEE MUSEUM, *CA605-510*
CECIL B. TYRRELL LIBRARY, *NY101-80*
CEDAR FALLS HISTORICAL SOCIETY, *IA88-120*
CEDAR GROVE HISTORICAL SOCIETY, *NJ128-120*
CENTENARY COLLEGE OF LOUISIANA, MAGALE LIBRARY, CLINE ROOM, *LA885-120*
CENTENARY COLLEGE, TAYLOR MEMORIAL LIBRARY LEARNING RESOURCE CENTER, CENTENARIAN COLLECTION, *NJ308-120*
CENTER FOR CATSKILL MOUNTAIN AND HUDSON RIVER STUDIES, *NY574-710*
CENTER FOR CREATIVE PHOTOGRAPHY, *AZ800-820*
CENTER FOR ERIE STUDIES, *PA305-510*
CENTER FOR HISTORY OF PHYSICS, NIELS BOHR LIBRARY, *NY586-580*

CENTER FOR LOCAL AFRO-AMERICAN HISTORY & RESEARCH, *NY134-85*
CENTER FOR MENNONITE BRETHREN STUDIES, HIEBERT LIBRARY, *CA274-130*
CENTER FOR MIDDLETOWN STUDIES, *IN539-83*
CENTER FOR MIGRATION STUDIES, ARCHIVES, *NY587-940*
CENTER FOR PACIFIC NORTHWEST STUDIES, *WA60-860*
CENTER FOR REFORMATION RESEARCH, *MO810-190*
CENTER FOR RESEARCH LIBRARIES, *IL169-247*
CENTER FOR THE STUDY OF THE CONSUMER MOVEMENT, *NY569-120*
CENTER MORICHES FREE PUBLIC LIBRARY, *NY169-120*
CENTER OF MILITARY HISTORY, *DC3-320*
CENTER OF SOUTHWEST STUDIES, *CO270-240*
CENTERVILLE HISTORICAL SOCIETY, *OH152-120*
CENTERVILLE HISTORICAL SOCIETY AND MUSEUM, *MA180-120*
CENTRAL COLLEGE, LEARNING RESOURCE CENTER, DEPARTMENT OF ARCHIVES, *IA811-110*
CENTRAL CONNECTICUT STATE UNIVERSITY, ELIHU BURRITT LIBRARY, *CT477-130*
CENTRAL COUNCIL OF POLISH ORGANIZATIONS OF PITTSBURGH, POLISH HISTORICAL COMMISSION, *PA735-170*
CENTRAL METHODIST COLLEGE, GEORGE M. SMILEY MEMORIAL LIBRARY, METHODIST COLLECTION, *MO290-120*
CENTRAL MICHIGAN UNIVERSITY, CLARKE HISTORICAL LIBRARY, *MI665-120*
CENTRAL MINNESOTA HISTORICAL CENTER, *MN742-700*
CENTRAL MISSOURI UNIVERSITY, WARD EDWARDS LIBRARY, SPECIAL COLLECTIONS, *MO920-120*
CENTRAL OREGON COMMUNITY COLLEGE, LIBRARY, *OR96-120*
CENTRAL WASHINGTON REGIONAL STATE ARCHIVES, *WA280-885*
CENTRAL WASHINGTON UNIVERSITY, ARCHIVES, *WA280-105*
CENTRALIA COLLEGE, LIBRARY, *WA122-100*
CENTRALIA PUBLIC LIBRARY, *WA122-110*
CENTRE COUNTY LIBRARY AND HISTORICAL MUSEUM, *PA80-110*
CHADWICK, J. RAYMOND, LIBRARY, ARCHIVES, *IA688-360*
CHAGRIN FALLS HISTORICAL SOCIETY, *OH157-120*
CHALMER DAVEE LIBRARY, ST. CROIX VALLEY HISTORICAL RESEARCH CENTER, *WI654-790*
CHAMINADE EDUCATION CENTER, MARIANIST ARCHIVES, *HI350-720*
CHAMPAIGN COUNTY LIBRARY, *OH853-130*
CHAPEL, JOHN MARK, MUSEUM, *NY273-800*
CHAPIN LIBRARY OF RARE BOOKS, *MA961-870*
CHAPIN MEMORIAL LIBRARY, *KY62G-120*
CHAPMAN HISTORICAL MUSEUM, *NY331-280*
CHARITON COUNTY HISTORICAL SOCIETY, *MO830-120*
CHARITY, SISTERS OF, OF CINCINNATI, OHIO, MT. ST. JOSEPH MOTHERHOUSE, *OH593-720*
CHARLES A. CANNON MEMORIAL LIBRARY, *NC200-120*
CHARLES A. MOCK LIBRARY, *IA544-880*
CHARLES A. WEYERHAEUSER MEMORIAL MUSEUM, *MN466-520*
CHARLES ANDREW RUSH LEARNING CENTER, SPECIAL COLLECTIONS, *AL120-110*
CHARLES COUNTY COMMUNITY COLLEGE, LEARNING RESOURCE CENTER, SOUTHERN MARYLAND ROOM, *MD580-120*
CHARLES H. STEWART & CO., *MA772-120*
CHARLES WILLARD COE MEMORIAL LIBRARY, *CA421-470*
CHARLESTON COUNTY LIBRARY, SOUTH CAROLINA ROOM, *SC144-100*
CHARLESTON DIVISION OF ARCHIVES AND RECORDS, *SC144-105*
CHARLESTON LIBRARY SOCIETY, *SC144-130*
CHARLESTON MUSEUM, *SC144-140*
CHARLOTTE AND MECKLENBURG COUNTY LIBRARY, SPECIAL COLLECTIONS, *NC160-120*
CHARLTON W. TEBEAU LIBRARY OF FLORIDA HISTORY, *FL440-320*
CHASE MANHATTAN BANK, ARCHIVES, *NY588-60*
CHASE, VIRGINIUS H., SPECIAL COLLECTIONS CENTER, *IL723-80*
CHATHAM PUBLIC LIBRARY, *NY178-120*
CHATHAM-EFFINGHAM-LIBERTY REGIONAL LIBRARY, REFERENCE DEPARTMENT, GEORGIA HISTORY COLLECTION, *GA895-120*
CHATSWORTH HISTORICAL SOCIETY, HISTORICAL COLLECTION, *CA132-120*
CHATTANOOGA-HAMILTON COUNTY BICENTENNIAL LIBRARY, *TN60-120*
CHAUTAUQUA INSTITUTION, SMITH MEMORIAL LIBRARY, CHAUTAUQUA COLLECTION, *NY179-120*
CHAVEZ COUNTY HISTORICAL MUSEUM, PECOS VALLEY COLLECTION, *NM684-120*
CHAVEZ COUNTY HISTORICAL SOCIETY, CHAVEZ COUNTY HISTORICAL MUSEUM, PECOS VALLEY COLLECTION, *NM684-120*
CHEHALIS PUBLIC LIBRARY, *WA124-110*
CHELAN BRANCH LIBRARY, *WA125-100*

CHELMSFORD HISTORICAL SOCIETY, *MA190-120*
CHEMUNG COUNTY HISTORICAL SOCIETY, *NY272-120*
CHENANGO COUNTY HISTORIAN'S OFFICE, *NY618-115*
CHENANGO COUNTY HISTORICAL SOCIETY, *NY618-120*
CHENEY HISTORICAL MUSEUM, *WA144-110*
CHEROKEE COUNTY HISTORICAL SOCIETY, *IA122-120*
CHEROKEE COUNTY PUBLIC LIBRARY, *SC414-110*
CHEROKEE NATIONAL HISTORICAL MUSEUM, *OK778-120*
CHEROKEE NATIONAL HISTORICAL SOCIETY, CHEROKEE
    NATIONAL HISTORICAL MUSEUM, *OK778-120*
CHEROKEE STRIP LANDRUSH MUSEUM, *KS52-120*
CHERRY HILL FREE PUBLIC LIBRARY, *NJ138-120*
CHERRY VALLEY HISTORICAL SOCIETY, *NY187-120*
CHESANING PUBLIC LIBRARY, *MI164-120*
CHESAPEAKE AND OHIO HISTORICAL SOCIETY, *VA560-333*
CHESAPEAKE BAY MARITIME MUSEUM, LIBRARY, *MD770-120*
CHESAPEAKE PUBLIC LIBRARY, WALLACE MEMORIAL ROOM,
    NORFOLK COUNTY HISTORICAL SOCIETY OF CHESAPEAKE,
    VA165-120
CHESNEY, ALAN MASON, MEDICAL ARCHIVES, *MD76-315*
CHESTER COUNTY HISTORICAL SOCIETY, LIBRARY, *PA945-120*
CHESTER FRITZ LIBRARY, DEPARTMENT OF SPECIAL
    COLLECTIONS (FORMERLY ORIN G. LIBBY MSS. COLL.),
    ND486-800
CHESTERFIELD HISTORICAL SOCIETY, EDWARDS MEMORIAL
    MUSEUM, *MA196-120*
CHESTERWOOD LIBRARY, *MA334-120*
CHESTNUT HILL COLLEGE, LOGUE LIBRARY, *PA725-195*
CHEWELAH HISTORICAL SOCIETY, MUSEUM, *WA145-105*
CHEWELAH PUBLIC LIBRARY, *WA145-110*
CHICAGO ACADEMY OF SCIENCES, *IL169-286*
CHICAGO HISTORICAL SOCIETY, *IL169-325*
CHICAGO JEWISH ARCHIVES, *IL170-780*
CHICAGO NATURAL HISTORY MUSEUM, *IL169-729*
CHICAGO PUBLIC LIBRARY, CONRAD SULZER REGIONAL
    LIBRARY, *IL169-396*
CHICAGO PUBLIC LIBRARY, PULLMAN BRANCH, *IL169-403*
CHICAGO PUBLIC LIBRARY, SPECIAL COLLECTIONS DIVISION,
    IL169-416
CHICAGO STATE UNIVERSITY, DOUGLAS LIBRARY, *IL169-468*
CHICAGO THEOLOGICAL SEMINARY, HAMMOND LIBRARY,
    IL169-507
CHILD DEVELOPMENT FILM ARCHIVES, *OH11-840*
CHILDREN'S LITERATURE RESEARCH COLLECTIONS, *MN541-838*
CHILDREN'S MUSEUM, *IN363-110*
CHILI TOWN HISTORIAN, *NY752-100*
CHILKAT VALLEY HISTORICAL SOCIETY, SHELDON MUSEUM,
    AK400-720
CHINESE HISTORICAL SOCIETY OF AMERICA, *CA720-220*
CHIPPEWA COUNTY HISTORICAL SOCIETY, *MN555-120*
CHIPPEWA NATIONAL FOREST, *MN198-120*
CHIPPEWA VALLEY MUSEUM, *WI142-120*
CHIRICAHUA NATIONAL MONUMENT, *AZ850-120*
CHISHOLM TRAIL MUSEUM, *KS934-120*
CHISHOLM TRAIL MUSEUM AND GOVERNOR A. J. SEAY
    MANSION, *OK456-120*
CHRIST CHURCH, LIBRARY, *PA726-37*
CHRISTIAN BROTHERS COLLEGE, ARCHIVES, *TN630-120*
CHRISTIAN CHURCH HISTORY COLLECTION, *NC310-200*
CHRISTIAN SCIENCE CHURCH, ARCHIVES, *MA108-600*
CHRISTIAN THEOLOGICAL SEMINARY, MANUSCRIPT
    COLLECTION, *IN363-125*
CHURCH HISTORICAL SOCIETY, *TX56-25*
CHURCH OF JESUS CHRIST OF LATTER-DAY SAINTS,
    GENEALOGICAL SOCIETY, *UT912-110*
CHURCH OF JESUS CHRIST OF LATTER-DAY SAINTS,
    GENEALOGICAL SOCIETY, LOS ANGELES BRANCH LIBRARY,
    CA421-180
CHURCH OF JESUS CHRIST OF LATTER-DAY SAINTS, HISTORICAL
    DEPARTMENT, CHURCH LIBRARY-ARCHIVES, *UT912-120*
CHURCH OF THE BRETHREN, GENERAL BOARD, BRETHREN
    HISTORICAL LIBRARY AND ARCHIVES, *IL241-120*
CHURCH OF THE BRETHREN, WASHINGTON DISTRICT
    ARCHIVES, *WA966-115*
CHURCH OF THE NAZARENE, INTERNATIONAL HEADQUARTERS,
    ARCHIVES, *MO430-120*
CHURCH OF THE NEW JERUSALEM, NEW CHURCH LIBRARY,
    OH171-95
CHURCHILL COUNTY MUSEUM AND ARCHIVES, *NV450-120*
CINCINNATI AND HAMILTON COUNTY, PUBLIC LIBRARY OF,
    DEPT. OF RARE BOOKS AND SPECIAL COLLECTIONS, *OH171-650*
CINCINNATI ART MUSEUM-ART ACADEMY OF CINCINNATI,
    ARCHIVES, *OH171-100*
CINCINNATI HISTORICAL SOCIETY, *OH171-110*
CINCINNATI OBSERVATORY, *OH171-130*
CIRCUS WORLD MUSEUM, LIBRARY AND RESEARCH CENTER,
    WI70-120

CITADEL, ARCHIVES-MUSEUM, *SC144-150*
CITIZENS FOR FARM LABOR, *CA86-120*
CITIZENS UNITED FOR RACIAL EQUALITY, *CA712-120*
CITY ARCHIVES OF PHILADELPHIA, *PA725-240*
CITY COLLEGE, LIBRARY, ARCHIVES/SPECIAL COLLECTIONS,
    NY588-340
CITY OF CORAL GABLES HISTORICAL ARCHIVES, *FL80-120*
CITY OF GALAX, JEFF MATTHEWS MEMORIAL MUSEUM,
    VA290-760
CITY OF GREELEY MUSEUMS, *CO498-270*
CITY OF SARATOGA SPRINGS, ARCHIVES, *NY795-120*
CITY UNIVERSITY OF NEW YORK, BROOKLYN COLLEGE,
    LIBRARY, SPECIAL COLLECTIONS DIVISION, *NY588-300*
CITY UNIVERSITY OF NEW YORK, CITY COLLEGE, LIBRARY,
    ARCHIVES/SPECIAL COLLECTIONS, *NY588-340*
CITY UNIVERSITY OF NEW YORK, GRADUATE SCHOOL AND
    UNIVERSITY CENTER, LIBRARY, *NY588-380*
CITY UNIVERSITY OF NEW YORK, HUNTER COLLEGE, LIBRARY,
    COLLEGE ARCHIVES, *NY588-420*
CITY UNIVERSITY OF NEW YORK, JOHN JAY COLLEGE OF
    CRIMINAL JUSTICE, LIBRARY, *NY588-440*
CITY UNIVERSITY OF NEW YORK, QUEENS COLLEGE,
    HISTORICAL DOCUMENTS COLLECTION, *NY588-520*
CITY UNIVERSITY OF NEW YORK, QUEENSBOROUGH
    COMMUNITY COLLEGE, *NY588-560*
CLAFLIN COLLEGE, H. V. MANNING LIBRARY, *SC720-120*
CLALLAM COUNTY HISTORICAL SOCIETY, CLALLAM COUNTY
    MUSEUM, *WA676-135*
CLALLAM COUNTY MUSEUM, *WA676-135*
CLARA WALDRON HISTORICAL ROOM, *MI910-770*
CLAREMONT COLLEGES, GALLERIES, CLAREMONT UNIVERSITY
    CENTER, COLLECTIONS (PHOTOGRAPHY), *CA143-280*
CLAREMONT COLLEGES, LIBRARIES, HONNOLD LIBRARY,
    SPECIAL COLLECTIONS DEPARTMENT, *CA143-470*
CLAREMONT COLLEGES, LIBRARIES, NORMAN F. SPRAGUE
    MEMORIAL LIBRARY, *CA143-480*
CLAREMONT COLLEGES, LIBRARIES, POMONA COLLEGE,
    GEOLOGY LIBRARY, *CA143-490*
CLAREMONT SCHOOL OF THEOLOGY, *CA143-720*
CLAREMONT UNIVERSITY CENTER, COLLECTIONS
    (PHOTOGRAPHY), *CA143-280*
CLARENCE METCALF RESEARCH LIBRARY, *OH863-280*
CLARION COUNTY HISTORICAL SOCIETY, *PA200-110*
CLARK COLLEGE, LIBRARY, *WA943-125*
CLARK COUNTY HISTORICAL ASSOCIATION ARCHIVES, *AR60-600*
CLARK COUNTY HISTORICAL MUSEUM, *WA943-240*
CLARK COUNTY HISTORICAL SOCIETY, *OH788-120*
CLARK COUNTY LIBRARY, *AR60-120*
CLARK UNIVERSITY, ARCHIVES, *MA985-100*
CLARK UNIVERSITY, GODDARD LIBRARY, DEPARTMENT OF
    RARE BOOKS AND SPECIAL COLLECTIONS, *MA985-110*
CLARK UNIVERSITY, GRADUATE SCHOOL OF GEOGRAPHY, GUY
    H. BURNHAM MAP AND AERIAL PHOTOGRAPH LIBRARY,
    MA985-120
CLARK, EMMA S., MEMORIAL LIBRARY, THREE VILLAGE LOCAL
    HISTORY COLLECTION, *NY824-200*
CLARK, HAROLD TERRY, LIBRARY, *OH181-240*
CLARK, WILLIAM ANDREWS, MEMORIAL LIBRARY, *CA421-774*
CLARK, WILLIAM, MARKET HOUSE MUSEUM, *KY604-890*
CLARKE HISTORICAL LIBRARY*MI665-120*
CLARKE MEMORIAL MUSEUM, *CA250-120*
CLAUSEN MEMORIAL MUSEUM, *AK750-120*
CLAWSON HISTORICAL COMMISSION, CLAWSON HISTORICAL
    MUSEUM, *MI172-120*
CLAWSON HISTORICAL MUSEUM, *MI172-120*
CLAWSON, DR. CHARLES DELAND, MEDICAL COLLECTION,
    NY562-720
CLAY COUNTY ARCHIVES, *MO530-110*
CLAY COUNTY HISTORICAL SOCIETY, *MN562-110*
CLAY COUNTY HISTORICAL SOCIETY, CLAY COUNTY ARCHIVES,
    MO530-110
CLAY COUNTY MUSEUM ASSOCIATION, LIBRARY AND
    ARCHIVES, *MO530-120*
CLAYTON MEMORIAL MUSEUM AND VAGABOND HOUSE
    STUDIO, *WA152-125*
CLE ELUM HISTORICAL TELEPHONE MUSEUM, *WA153-125*
CLE ELUM-ROSLYN SCHOOL DISTRICT, *WA153-130*
CLEARWATER NATIONAL FOREST, *ID600-130*
CLEMENTS, WILLIAM L., LIBRARY, *MI40-820*
CLEMSON AGRICULTURAL COLLEGE, *SC185-120*
CLEMSON UNIVERSITY, ROBERT MULDROW COOPER LIBRARY,
    SPECIAL COLLECTIONS, *SC185-120*
CLENDENING HISTORY OF MEDICINE LIBRARY, *KS475-800*
CLERMONT COUNTY HISTORICAL SOCIETY, *OH63-110*
CLERMONT COUNTY PUBLIC LIBRARY, *OH63-130*
CLEVELAND HEALTH SCIENCES LIBRARY, HISTORICAL DIVISION,
    OH181-180

CLEVELAND MUSEUM OF NATURAL HISTORY, HAROLD TERRY CLARK LIBRARY, *OH181-240*
CLEVELAND PUBLIC LIBRARY, *OH181-270*
CLEVELAND STATE COMMUNITY COLLEGE, LIBRARY, *TN90-130*
CLEVELAND STATE UNIVERSITY, ARCHIVES, *OH181-290*
CLEVELAND STATE UNIVERSITY, LIBRARIES, AUDIO/MUSIC SERVICES, *OH181-310*
CLIFFORD E. BARBOUR LIBRARY, *PA735-630*
CLIFFORD MEMORIAL LIBRARY, ARCHIVES, *IN209-800*
CLIFTON M. MILLER LIBRARY, *MD228-870*
CLIFTON SPRINGS LIBRARY, *NY195-120*
CLINCH VALLEY COLLEGE OF THE UNIVERSITY OF VIRGINIA, JOHN COOK WYLLIE LIBRARY, *VA890-120*
CLINE ROOM, *LA885-120*
CLINTON COUNTY HISTORICAL ASSOCIATION, MUSEUM, *NY708-120*
CLINTON COUNTY HISTORICAL SOCIETY, *OH953-120*
CLINTON HISTORICAL SOCIETY, *NY197-120*
CLINTON HISTORICAL SOCIETY, HOLDER MEMORIAL, *MA207-120*
CLINTON, GENERAL JAMES, FREE LIBRARY, *NY262-280*
CLOUD COUNTY HISTORICAL MUSEUM, *KS213-120*
CLOVIS-CARVER PUBLIC LIBRARY, *NM304-320*
CLYDE PUBLIC LIBRARY, *OH194-120*
COAST ARTILLERY MUSEUM AT FORT WORDEN, *WA681-250*
COAST GUARD MUSEUM/NORTHWEST, *WA820-147*
COASTAL GEORGIA HISTORICAL SOCIETY, MUSEUM OF COASTAL HISTORY, *GA885-120*
COBLESKILL PUBLIC LIBRARY, *NY200-120*
COCA-COLA COMPANY, ARCHIVES, *GA90-130*
COCHRANE-NELSON HOUSE, *WI855-520*
CODY MEMORIAL LIBRARY, DEPARTMENT OF SPECIAL COLLECTIONS, *TX404-120*
COE, CHARLES WILLARD, MEMORIAL LIBRARY, *CA421-470*
COHOCTON HISTORICAL SOCIETY, *NY201-120*
COLBY COLLEGE, LIBRARY, SPECIAL COLLECTIONS, *ME925-130*
COLD SPRING HARBOR LABORATORY, LIBRARY, *NY205-120*
COLE COUNTY HISTORICAL SOCIETY, *MO410-120*
COLE, RUSSELL D., LIBRARY, *IA699-120*
COLEBROOK HISTORICAL SOCIETY, *CT102-120*
COLEMAN LIBRARY, LILLIAN PIERCE BENBOW ROOM OF SPECIAL COLLECTIONS, *MS870-760*
COLES COUNTY HISTORICAL SOCIETY, *IL154-130*
COLGATE ROCHESTER DIVINITY SCHOOL, LIBRARY, *NY752-110*
COLGATE ROCHESTER/BEXLEY HALL/CROZER THEOLOGICAL SEMINARIES, AMBROSE SWASEY LIBRARY, *NY752-110*
COLLEGE OF CHARLESTON, LIBRARY, DEPARTMENT OF ARCHIVES AND MANUSCRIPTS, *SC144-170*
COLLEGE OF IDAHO, REGIONAL STUDIES CENTER, FOLKLORE ARCHIVES, *ID160-130*
COLLEGE OF MEDICAL EVANGELISTS, *CA406-480*
COLLEGE OF NOTRE DAME OF MARYLAND, ARCHIVES, *MD76-118*
COLLEGE OF PHYSICIANS OF PHILADELPHIA, LIBRARY, HISTORICAL COLLECTIONS, *PA725-285*
COLLEGE OF SAINT BENEDICT, LIBRARY, *MN749-120*
COLLEGE OF SAINT ELIZABETH, ARCHIVES, *NJ178-110*
COLLEGE OF SAINT ELIZABETH, MAHONEY LIBRARY, PHILLIPS RARE BOOKS AND MANUSCRIPTS LIBRARY, *NJ178-115*
COLLEGE OF ST. CATHERINE, LIBRARY, ARCHIVES, *MN763-110*
COLLEGE OF ST. ROSE, LIBRARY, ARCHIVES, *NY10-150*
COLLEGE OF ST. TERESA, ARCHIVES, *MN975-120*
COLLEGE OF ST. THOMAS, ARCHIVES, *MN763-120*
COLLEGE OF THE BIBLE, *KY464-490*
COLLEGE OF THE HOLY CROSS, ARCHIVES, *MA985-130*
COLLEGE OF THE HOLY CROSS, LIBRARY, *MA985-140*
COLLEGE OF WILLIAM AND MARY, EARL GREGG SWEM LIBRARY, MSS. AND RARE BOOKS DEPT./COLLEGE ARCHIVES, *VA870-110*
COLLEGE OF WOOSTER, LIBRARY, *OH968-120*
COLLEGIATE REFORMED DUTCH CHURCH, *NY588-700*
COLLINGSWOOD FREE PUBLIC LIBRARY, NEW JERSEY ROOM, COLLINGSWOOD COLLECTION, *NJ162-110*
COLLINS COMMERCIAL TELECOMMUNICATIONS DIVISION, *TX742-690*
COLMAN, HOWARD, LIBRARY, ARCHIVES, *IL806-695*
COLONEL BLACK HOUSE, *ME337-120*
COLONIAL ORIGINS COLLECTION, *MI355-110*
COLONIAL WILLIAMSBURG FOUNDATION, AUDIOVISUAL LIBRARY, *VA870-130*
COLONIAL WILLIAMSBURG FOUNDATION, RESEARCH ARCHIVES, *VA870-150*
COLORADO COLLEGE, LIBRARY, SPECIAL COLLECTIONS, *CO180-120*
COLORADO DEPARTMENT OF ADMINISTRATION, DIVISION OF STATE ARCHIVES AND PUBLIC RECORDS, *CO252-70*
COLORADO DEPARTMENT OF NATURAL RESOURCES, DIVISION OF MINES, *CO252-80*

COLORADO DEPARTMENT OF NATURAL RESOURCES, DIVISION OF PARKS AND OUTDOOR RECREATION, *CO252-90*
COLORADO HISTORICAL SOCIETY, STEPHEN H. HART LIBRARY, *CO252-100*
COLORADO METHODIST HISTORICAL SOCIETY, *CO252-360*
COLORADO MOUNTAIN CLUB, *CO252-120*
COLORADO MOUNTAIN HISTORICAL COLLECTION, *CO640-480*
COLORADO RAILROAD HISTORICAL FOUNDATION, COLORADO RAILROAD MUSEUM, *CO458-110*
COLORADO RAILROAD MUSEUM, *CO458-110*
COLORADO SCHOOL OF MINES, ARTHUR LAKES LIBRARY, *CO458-130*
COLORADO STATE ARCHIVES, *CO252-70*
COLORADO STATE UNIVERSITY, GERMANS FROM RUSSIA IN COLORADO STUDY PROJECT, *CO378-110*
COLORADO STATE UNIVERSITY, LIBRARIES, SPECIAL COLLECTIONS, UNIVERSITY ARCHIVES, *CO378-120*
COLTON HALL MUSEUM, *CA480-120*
COLTON, HAROLD S., MEMORIAL LIBRARY, MUSEUM ARCHIVES AND MANUSCRIPTS COLLECTION, *AZ250-520*
COLUMBIA BASIN COLLEGE, LIBRARY, *WA647-135*
COLUMBIA BIBLE COLLEGE, *SC216-110*
COLUMBIA COLLEGE, LIBRARY, *CA159-120*
COLUMBIA COUNTY (PA) HISTORICAL SOCIETY, *PA100-320*
COLUMBIA COUNTY HISTORICAL SOCIETY, *NY466-120*
COLUMBIA HISTORICAL SOCIETY, LIBRARY, *DC3-550*
COLUMBIA STATE COMMUNITY COLLEGE, JOHN W. FINNEY MEMORIAL LIBRARY, *TN120-120*
COLUMBIA UNIVERSITY, DEPARTMENT OF ART HISTORY AND ARCHAEOLOGY, PHOTOGRAPH COLLECTION, *NY588-780*
COLUMBIA UNIVERSITY, LIBRARIES, AVERY ARCHITECTURAL AND FINE ARTS LIBRARY, *NY588-820*
COLUMBIA UNIVERSITY, LIBRARIES, BAKHMETEFF ARCHIVE OF RUSSIAN AND EAST EUROPEAN HISTORY & CULTURE, *NY588-825*
COLUMBIA UNIVERSITY, LIBRARIES, COLUMBIANA COLLECTION, *NY588-830*
COLUMBIA UNIVERSITY, LIBRARIES, HERBERT H. LEHMAN PAPERS, *NY588-850*
COLUMBIA UNIVERSITY, LIBRARIES, LAW LIBRARY, *NY588-860*
COLUMBIA UNIVERSITY, LIBRARIES, RARE BOOK AND MANUSCRIPT LIBRARY, *NY588-900*
COLUMBIA UNIVERSITY, ORAL HISTORY COLLECTION, *NY588-940*
COLUMBIA UNIVERSITY, TEACHERS COLLEGE, MILBANK MEMORIAL LIBRARY, SPECIAL COLLECTIONS, *NY588-970*
COLUMBIANA AND FAIRFIELD TOWNSHIP, HISTORICAL SOCIETY OF, *OH199-320*
COLUMBIANA COLLECTION, *NY588-830*
COLUMBUS COLLEGE, ARCHIVES, *GA245-110*
COLVILLE NATIONAL FOREST, *WA168-130*
COLVILLE PUBLIC LIBRARY, *WA168-135*
COMMUNITY OF ST. MARY, *NY687-120*
CON FOSTER MUSEUM, *MI925-120*
CONCEPTION ABBEY, ARCHIVES, *MO220-120*
CONCORD FREE PUBLIC LIBRARY, *MA217-130*
CONCORD HISTORICAL SOCIETY, *NY855-120*
CONCORDIA COLLEGE (IL), ARCHIVES, *IL772-120*
CONCORDIA COLLEGE, COLLEGE ARCHIVES AND ARCHIVES OF S. WI DIST. OF LUTHERAN CHURCH-MO SYNOD, *WI426-111*
CONCORDIA HISTORICAL INSTITUTE, *MO810-200*
CONCORDIA TEACHERS COLLEGE (NE), ARCHIVES, *NE800-110*
CONCORDIA THEOLOGICAL SEMINARY, ARCHIVES, *IN231-130*
CONE COLLECTION, ARCHIVES, *MD76-80*
CONE LIBRARY, ARCHIVES, *IA188-520*
CONFEDERATE RESEARCH CENTER, *TX476-320*
CONGREGATION MIKVEH ISRAEL, ARCHIVES, *PA725-330*
CONGREGATION OF ALEXIAN BROTHERS, PROVINCIAL ARCHIVES, *IL245-322*
CONGREGATION OF OUR LADY OF THE CENACLE, CENTRAL ARCHIVES, *IL169-565*
CONGREGATION OF THE HOLY UNION OF THE SACRED HEARTS, SACRED HEART PROVINCE, *MA356-120*
CONGREGATION OF THE SISTERS, SERVANTS OF THE IMMACULATE HEART OF MARY, *PA795-120*
CONGREGATIONAL LIBRARY, *MA108-480*
CONGRESSIONAL LEADERSHIP RESEARCH CENTER, *IL718-200*
CONLON, WILLIAM, MEMORIAL LIBRARY, *WA730-880*
CONNECTICUT AERONAUTICAL HISTORICAL ASSOCIATION, NEW ENGLAND AIR MUSEUM, *CT963-120*
CONNECTICUT AGRICULTURAL EXPERIMENT STATION, *CT505-120*
CONNECTICUT COLLEGE, LIBRARY, DEPARTMENT OF SPECIAL COLLECTIONS, *CT512-120*
CONNECTICUT HISTORICAL SOCIETY, *CT316-110*
CONNECTICUT STATE ARCHIVES, *CT316-120*
CONNECTICUT STATE LIBRARY, ARCHIVES, HISTORY AND GENEALOGY UNIT, *CT316-120*

CONNECTICUT VALLEY HISTORICAL MUSEUM, *MA804-130*
CONNER PRAIRIE PIONEER SETTLEMENT, CONNER PRAIRIE RESEARCH LIBRARY, *IN594-120*
CONNER PRAIRIE RESEARCH LIBRARY, *IN594-120*
CONNER, JOHN E., MUSEUM, *TX529-770*
CONOCOCHEAGUE DISTRICT LIBRARY, FRANKLIN COUNTY LIBRARY, *PA180-120*
CONRAD SULZER REGIONAL LIBRARY, *IL169-396*
CONSTABLE HALL ASSOCIATION, *NY208-120*
CONSTITUTION ISLAND ASSOCIATION, *NY949-120*
CONSUMERS UNION FOUNDATION, CENTER FOR THE STUDY OF THE CONSUMER MOVEMENT, *NY569-120*
CONTRA COSTA COUNTY LIBRARY, CENTRAL LIBRARY AT PLEASANT HILL, *CA594-120*
CONWAY HOMESTEAD, OLD, CRAMER MUSEUM, *ME212-120*
CONWELLANA-TEMPLANA COLLECTION, *PA726-600*
COOK COUNTY HISTORICAL SOCIETY, *MN356-120*
COOK COUNTY HOSPITAL, LIBRARIES AND ARCHIVES, *IL169-580*
COOKE COUNTY HERITAGE SOCIETY, MORTON MUSEUM OF COOKE COUNTY, *TX390-140*
COOKE MEMORIAL LIBRARY, SPECIAL COLLECTIONS, *KY304-280*
COOPER UNION FOR THE ADVANCEMENT OF SCIENCE AND ART, LIBRARY, COOPER-HEWITT COLLECTION, *NY589-100*
COOPER-HEWITT COLLECTION, *NY589-100*
COOPER, ROBERT MULDROW, LIBRARY, SPECIAL COLLECTIONS, *SC185-120*
COPLEY PRESS, JAMES S. COPLEY LIBRARY, *CA368-120*
COPLEY, JAMES S., LIBRARY, *CA712-810*
COPLEY, JAMES S., LIBRARY (COPLEY PRESS), *CA368-120*
CORCORAN GALLERY OF ART, ARCHIVES, CURATORIAL LIBRARY, *DC3-750*
CORCORAN GALLERY OF ART, PERMANENT COLLECTION, *DC3-760*
CORDELIA A. GREENE LIBRARY, *NY156-140*
CORDOVA HISTORICAL SOCIETY, *AK250-110*
CORGAN, D. LEONARD, LIBRARY, SPECIAL COLLECTIONS, *PA960-440*
CORNELL COLLEGE, RUSSELL D. COLE LIBRARY, *IA699-120*
CORNELL MEDICAL CENTER, MEDICAL ARCHIVES, *NY592-480*
CORNELL UNIVERSITY, LIBRARIES, DEPARTMENT OF MANUSCRIPTS AND UNIVERSITY ARCHIVES, *NY439-120*
CORNELL UNIVERSITY, LIBRARIES, DEPARTMENT OF RARE BOOKS, *NY439-140*
CORNELL UNIVERSITY, LIBRARIES, HISTORY OF SCIENCE COLLECTIONS, *NY439-145*
CORNELL UNIVERSITY, LIBRARIES, M. P. CATHERWOOD LIBRARY, LABOR-MANAGEMENT DOCUMENTATION CENTER, *NY439-150*
CORNELL UNIVERSITY, LIBRARIES, WASON COLLECTION, *NY439-156*
CORNERSTONE GENEALOGICAL SOCIETY, *PA940-120*
CORNING COMMUNITY COLLEGE, ARTHUR A. HOUGHTON, JR., LIBRARY, *NY214-100*
CORNING GLASS WORKS, THE ARCHIVES, *NY214-120*
CORNING MUSEUM OF GLASS, *NY214-140*
CORNING PUBLIC LIBRARY, *NY214-150*
CORNING-PAINTED POST HISTORICAL SOCIETY, *NY214-160*
CORNWALL FREE LIBRARY, *CT120-120*
CORNWALL HISTORICAL SOCIETY, *CT120-120*
CORONADO HISTORICAL ASSOCIATION, INC., *CA168-120*
CORONADO NATIONAL MEMORIAL, *AZ375-120*
CORONADO-QUIVERA HISTORICAL MUSEUM, *KS579-690*
CORRIGAN, ARCHBISHOP, MEMORIAL LIBRARY, *NY984-710*
CORTLAND COUNTY HISTORICAL SOCIETY, LIBRARY, *NY216-120*
CORTLAND FREE LIBRARY, *NY216-130*
COSMETIC, TOILETRY & FRAGRANCE ASSOCIATION, *DC3-800*
COTTON COUNCIL OF AMERICA, NATIONAL, *TN630-590*
COTTONWOOD COUNTY HISTORICAL SOCIETY, *MN968-120*
COUNCIL ON FOREIGN RELATIONS, ARCHIVES, *NY589-160*
COUNTRY MUSIC FOUNDATION, LIBRARY AND MEDIA CENTER, *TN690-110*
COUNTWAY, FRANCIS A., LIBRARY OF MEDICINE, *MA108-770*
COUNTY CENTER HISTORICAL SOCIETY, *MN884-880*
COVINGTON PUBLIC LIBRARY, FOUNTAIN COUNTY HISTORICAL SOCIETY COLLECTION, *IN143-120*
COWEETA HYDROLOGIC LABORATORY, *NC656-720*
COWLES LIBRARY, SPECIAL COLLECTIONS, *IA233-160*
COWLEY COUNTY HISTORICAL SOCIETY, MUSEUM AND LIBRARY, *KS962-120*
COWLITZ COUNTY HISTORICAL SOCIETY, MUSEUM, *WA417-140*
CRAB ORCHARD MUSEUM AND PIONEER PARK, *VA800-320*
CRABBE LIBRARY, TOWNSEND ROOM, *KY680-190*
CRAFTS MUSEUM, *WI426-120*
CRAMER MUSEUM, *ME212-120*
CRANBROOK EDUCATIONAL COMMUNITY, ARCHIVES, *MI110-120*
CRANBURY HISTORICAL AND PRESERVATION SOCIETY, MUSEUM RESEARCH CENTER, *NJ182-110*

CRANDALL LIBRARY, LOCAL HISTORY COLLECTION, *NY331-120*
CRANE & COMPANY, MUSEUM, *MA227-120*
CRANE SCHOOL OF MUSIC, LIBRARY, *NY723-715*
CRANE, ARNOLD H., LIBRARY OF PHOTOGRAPHY, *IL169-127*
CRANFORD HISTORICAL SOCIETY, MUSEUM, *NJ186-110*
CRATER LAKE LIBRARY, *OR176-120*
CRATER LAKE NATIONAL PARK, CRATER LAKE LIBRARY, *OR176-120*
CRAWFORD COUNTY (KS) HISTORICAL SOCIETY, *KS746-120*
CRAWFORD COUNTY (PA) HISTORICAL SOCIETY, *PA555-120*
CREEK COUNCIL HOUSE MUSEUM, ARCHIVES, *OK609-120*
CREIGHTON UNIVERSITY, ALUMNI MEMORIAL LIBRARY, *NE624-130*
CRERAR, JOHN, LIBRARY, *IL170-39*
CRITTENDEN COUNTY HISTORICAL SOCIETY, BOB WHEELER MUSEUM, *KY514-120*
CRITTENDEN COUNTY PUBLIC LIBRARY, *KY514-130*
CROMAINE LIBRARY, *MI414-120*
CRONK, BETTY, MEMORIAL LIBRARY, *NY752-665*
CROSBY COUNTY PIONEER MEMORIAL, *TX231-120*
CROSBY LIBRARY, RARE BOOK AND MANUSCRIPT COLLECTION, *WA880-290*
CROTON FREE LIBRARY, HISTORICAL REFERENCE ROOM, *NY222-110*
CROWLEY RIDGE REGIONAL LIBRARY, *AR480-130*
CROZER THEOLOGICAL SEMINARY, *NY752-110*
CRUMB, FREDERICK W., MEMORIAL LIBRARY, *NY723-720*
CUBA CIRCULATING LIBRARY ASSOCIATION, *NY228-110*
CUDAHY, E. M., MEMORIAL LIBRARY, *IL170-78*
CULLMAN, HOWARD S., LIBRARY, *NY594-680*
CULLOM-DAVIS LIBRARY, VIRGINIUS H. CHASE SPECIAL COLLECTIONS CENTER, *IL723-80*
CULVER PICTURES, *NY589-200*
CULVER-STOCKTON COLLEGE, LIBRARY, *MO120-120*
CUMBERLAND COLLEGE, HAGAN MEMORIAL LIBRARY, *KY876-120*
CUMBERLAND COLLEGE, MITCHELL LIBRARY, ARCHIVES, *TN495-120*
CUMBERLAND COUNTY HISTORICAL SOCIETY AND HAMILTON LIBRARY ASSOCIATION, *PA160-120*
CUNNINGHAM MEMORIAL LIBRARY, DEPARTMENT OF RARE BOOKS AND SPECIAL COLLECTIONS, *IN825-350*
CUPOLA HOUSE ASSOCIATION, *NC290-120*
CURTIS INSTITUTE OF MUSIC, LIBRARY, *PA725-345*
CURTISS, GLENN H., MUSEUM OF LOCAL HISTORY, *NY367-270*
CUSHING-MARTIN LIBRARY, JOSEPH W. MARTIN COLLECTION, *MA615-720*
CUSTER BATTLEFIELD NATIONAL MONUMENT, *MT270-130*
CUYAHOGA COUNTY ARCHIVES, *OH181-325*
CYNTHIANA PUBLIC LIBRARY, *KY189-320*
CYRENIUS H. BOOTH LIBRARY, *CT533-120*
CZECHOSLOVAK SOCIETY OF AMERICA FRATERNAL LIFE, ARCHIVES, *IL84-120*

D

D. LEONARD CORGAN LIBRARY, SPECIAL COLLECTIONS, *PA960-440*
D'YOUVILLE COLLEGE, ARCHIVES, *NY134-170*
DACOTAH PRAIRIE MUSEUM, *SD18-160*
DACUS LIBRARY, ARCHIVES AND SPECIAL COLLECTIONS DEPARTMENT, *SC774-880*
DADE COUNTY PUBLIC SCHOOLS, SOCIAL STUDIES OFFICE, BLACK ARCHIVES AND ORAL HISTORY COLLECTION, *FL440-150*
DAG HAMMARSKJOLD LIBRARY, MAP COLLECTION, *NY595-40*
DAHLGREN, JOHN VINTON, MEMORIAL LIBRARY, ALEXIS CARREL COLLECTION, *DC7-660*
DAKOTA STATE COLLEGE, KARL E. MUNDT LIBRARY, KARL E. MUNDT ARCHIVES, *SD450-150*
DAKOTA TERRITORIAL MUSEUM, YANKTON COUNTY HISTORICAL SOCIETY, *SD936-950*
DAKOTA WESLEYAN UNIVERSITY, LAYNE LIBRARY, *SD522-160*
DALLAS CITY SECRETARY, *TX252-120*
DALLAS HISTORICAL SOCIETY, RESEARCH CENTER LIBRARY AND ARCHIVES, *TX252-150*
DALLAS PUBLIC LIBRARY, ARCHIVES AND RESEARCH CENTER FOR TEXAS AND DALLAS HISTORY, *TX252-170*
DALLES-WASCO COUNTY PUBLIC LIBRARY, *OR848-160*
DANA COLLEGE, C. A. DANA - LIFE LIBRARY, *NE144-160*
DANA, C. A. - LIFE LIBRARY, *NE144-160*
DANBURY SCOTT-FENTON MUSEUM AND HISTORICAL SOCIETY, *CT144-150*
DANFORTH LIBRARY, *NH396-560*
DANIEL EVANS LIBRARY, *WA616-240*
DANISH BROTHERHOOD IN AMERICA, *NE624-150*
DANSVILLE PUBLIC LIBRARY, *NY234-165*

DANVERS ARCHIVAL CENTER, *MA231-640*
DANVILLE HISTORICAL SOCIETY, *VA185-160*
DANVILLE PUBLIC LIBRARY, *IL186-170*
DARD HUNTER PAPER MUSEUM, *WI46-360*
DARLINGTON COUNTY HISTORICAL COMMISSION, *SC270-160*
DARLINGTON MEMORIAL LIBRARY, *PA735-800*
DARMS, REV. ANTON, LIBRARY, *IL996-980*
DARTMOUTH COLLEGE, LIBRARY, *NH372-160*
DARWIN R. BARKER LIBRARY, HISTORICAL MUSEUM, *NY310-160*
DATAPRODUCTS CORPORATION, *CA132-160*
DAUGAVAS VANAGI OF BOSTON, MASSACHUSETTS, LIBRARY OF
    LATVIAN PLAYS AND THEATER, *MA172-160*
DAUGHTERS OF CHARITY OF ST. VINCENT DE PAUL, MATER DEI
    PROVINCIALATE, ARCHIVES, *IN209-140*
DAUGHTERS OF CHARITY OF ST. VINCENT DE PAUL, ST.
    JOSEPH'S PROVINCIAL HOUSE, *MD380-160*
DAUGHTERS OF CHARITY, NORTHEAST PROVINCE, ARCHIVES,
    NY10-160
DAUGHTERS OF HAWAII, QUEEN EMMA SUMMER PALACE,
    HI350-150
DAUGHTERS OF THE AMERICAN REVOLUTION (LEROY NY),
    NY484-160
DAUGHTERS OF THE AMERICAN REVOLUTION, COLONEL
    WILLIAM PRESCOTT CHAPTER, *NY597-130*
DAUGHTERS OF THE AMERICAN REVOLUTION, NATIONAL
    SOCIETY OF, AMERICANA COLLECTION, *DC14-590*
DAUGHTERS OF THE AMERICAN REVOLUTION, NATIONAL
    SOCIETY OF, GENEALOGICAL LIBRARY, *DC14-600*
DAUGHTERS OF THE PIONEERS (BELLINGHAM WA CHAPTER),
    WA60-160
DAUGHTERS OF THE REPUBLIC OF TEXAS, LIBRARY, *TX777-160*
DAUGHTERS OF THE REPUBLIC OF TEXAS, MUSEUM, *TX56-160*
DAUGHTERS OF UTAH PIONEERS, NATIONAL SOCIETY, *UT912-550*
DAUPHIN COUNTY HISTORICAL SOCIETY, *PA380-320*
DAVEE, CHALMER, LIBRARY, ST. CROIX VALLEY HISTORICAL
    RESEARCH CENTER, *WI654-790*
DAVENPORT HISTORICAL SOCIETY, *NY235-160*
DAVENPORT MUSEUM, *IA188-650*
DAVENPORT PUBLIC LIBRARY, *IA188-160*
DAVID A. HOWE PUBLIC LIBRARY, *NY942-160*
DAVID LIBRARY OF THE AMERICAN REVOLUTION, *PA925-160*
DAVID O. MCKAY LEARNING RESOURCES CENTER, ARCHIVES
    AND SPECIAL COLLECTIONS, *ID680-690*
DAVIDSON COLLEGE, LIBRARY, ARCHIVES DEPARTMENT,
    NC240-160
DAVIS MEMORIAL LIBRARY, LAFAYETTE ROOM, *NC330-520*
DAVIS, HARWELL G., LIBRARY, *AL120-720*
DAWES MEMORIAL LIBRARY, *OH486-510*
DAYTON AND MONTGOMERY COUNTY PUBLIC LIBRARY,
    DAYTON COLLECTION, *OH223-160*
DAYTON HISTORICAL DEPOT SOCIETY, *WA241-170*
DAYTON MEMORIAL LIBRARY, *WA241-160*
DE FOREST MEMORIAL LIBRARY, *CA418-200*
DE WITT COUNTY HISTORICAL MUSEUM, *TX245-160*
DEACONESS COMMUNITY OF THE LUTHERAN CHURCH IN
    AMERICA, ARCHIVES, *PA330-160*
DEADWOOD PUBLIC LIBRARY, CENTENNIAL ARCHIVES,
    SD144-160
DEAN B. ELLIS LIBRARY, ARKANSAS ROOM, *AR890-20*
DEARBORN DEPARTMENT OF LIBRARIES, HENRY FORD
    CENTENNIAL LIBRARY, AUDIO-VISUAL DIVISION, *MI214-140*
DEARBORN HISTORICAL MUSEUM, *MI214-150*
DEATH VALLEY NATIONAL MONUMENT, *CA210-160*
DEBS, EUGENE V., MUSEUM AND LIBRARY, *IN825-200*
DECATUR COUNTY HISTORICAL SOCIETY, LAST INDIAN RAID IN
    KANSAS MUSEUM, *KS690-160*
DEDHAM HISTORICAL SOCIETY, *MA235-150*
DEER ISLE-STONINGTON HISTORICAL SOCIETY, *ME275-160*
DEERE & COMPANY, CORPORATE ARCHIVES, *IL548-150*
DEGOLYER LIBRARY, *TX252-730*
DEL NORTE COUNTY HISTORICAL SOCIETY, MAIN MUSEUM,
    CA180-160
DELAWARE ART MUSEUM, LIBRARY, *DE810-150*
DELAWARE COUNTY ARCHIVES, *IN539-80*
DELAWARE COUNTY HISTORICAL ASSOCIATION, *NY240-160*
DELAWARE COUNTY HISTORICAL SOCIETY, *PA185-160*
DELAWARE COUNTY INSTITUTE OF SCIENCE, *PA565-160*
DELAWARE DIVISION OF HISTORICAL AND CULTURAL AFFAIRS,
    BUREAU OF ARCHIVES AND RECORDS, *DE90-140*
DELAWARE HISTORICAL SOCIETY, LIBRARY, *DE810-330*
DELAWARE PUBLIC ARCHIVES COMMISSION, *DE90-140*
DELAWARE STATE ARCHIVES, *DE90-140*
DELAWARE TOWNSHIP COMMITTEE, *NJ766-160*
DELIUS COLLECTION, *FL280-390*
DELTA STATE UNIVERSITY, W. B. ROBERTS LIBRARY, *MS230-160*
DENISON PUBLIC LIBRARY, *TX273-160*
DENISON UNIVERSITY, W. H. DOANE LIBRARY, *OH350-170*

DENNIS HISTORICAL SOCIETY, JOSIAH DENNIS MANSE LIBRARY,
    MA242-160
DENNIS, JOSIAH, MANSE LIBRARY, *MA242-160*
DENNY ASHBY MEMORIAL LIBRARY, *WA672-160*
DENVER MUSEUM OF NATURAL HISTORY, ARCHIVES
    DEPARTMENT, *CO252-152*
DENVER PUBLIC LIBRARY, COLLECTION DEVELOPMENT,
    CO252-159
DENVER PUBLIC LIBRARY, CONSERVATION LIBRARY, *CO252-163*
DENVER PUBLIC LIBRARY, GENEALOGY DIVISION, *CO252-172*
DENVER PUBLIC LIBRARY, WESTERN HISTORY DEPARTMENT,
    CO252-181
DEPARTMENT OF AGRICULTURE, NATIONAL AGRICULTURAL
    LIBRARY, *MD133-160*
DEPARTMENT OF AGRICULTURE, OFFICE OF GOVERNMENTAL
    AFFAIRS, PHOTOGRAPHIC DIVISION, *DC4-260*
DEPARTMENT OF ARCHIVES, NEW ORLEANS PUBLIC LIBRARY,
    LA600-555
DEPARTMENT OF ENERGY, HISTORY DIVISION, *DC4-322*
DEPARTMENT OF HOUSING AND URBAN DEVELOPMENT,
    PRINTING AND VISUAL ARTS DIVISION, *DC4-450*
DEPARTMENT OF THE NAVY, HEADQUARTERS, U.S. MARINE
    CORPS, HISTORY AND MUSEUMS DIVISION, *DC13-210*
DEPAUL UNIVERSITY, LIBRARIES, LINCOLN PARK CAMPUS
    LIBRARY, DEPARTMENT OF SPECIAL COLLECTIONS, *IL169-599*
DEPAUW UNIVERSITY, ARCHIVES OF DEPAUW UNIVERSITY AND
    INDIANA UNITED METHODISM, *IN275-150*
DEPAUW UNIVERSITY, ROY O. WEST LIBRARY, *IN275-170*
DEPOSIT FREE LIBRARY, *NY241-160*
DEPOT PARK MUSEUM, *CA838-720*
DERBY HISTORICAL SOCIETY, GEN. DAVID HUMPHREYS HOUSE,
    CT4-160
DERMATOLOGY FOUNDATION OF MIAMI, TAPE STUDIO AND
    LIBRARY, *FL80-160*
DERMODY, WILLIAM E., FREE PUBLIC LIBRARY, *NJ124-240*
DES MOINES PUBLIC LIBRARY, FRANKLIN AVENUE LIBRARY,
    IA233-640
DES PLAINES HISTORICAL SOCIETY, MUSEUM, *IL207-160*
DESCHUTES COUNTY LIBRARY, *OR96-150*
DESERTED VILLAGE AT ALLAIRE, ALLAIRE VILLAGE AUXILIARY
    LIBRARY, *NJ8-160*
DESOTO NATIONAL WILDLIFE REFUGE, *IA661-160*
DETROIT INSTITUTE OF ARTS, MUSEUM ARCHIVES AND
    RECORDS CENTER, *MI230-148*
DETROIT INSTITUTE OF ARTS, REGISTRAR'S OFFICE, *MI230-153*
DETROIT INSTITUTE OF ARTS, RESEARCH LIBRARY, *MI230-155*
DETROIT PUBLIC LIBRARY, BURTON HISTORICAL COLLECTION,
    MI230-165
DEUEL COUNTY HISTORICAL MUSEUM, *SD41-160*
DEVEREAUX LIBRARY, *SD648-710*
DEWITT HISTORICAL SOCIETY OF TOMPKINS COUNTY, *NY439-180*
DEXTER AREA MUSEUM, *MI235-160*
DEXTER HISTORICAL SOCIETY, *ME287-160*
DEXTER LIBRARY, *WI54-560*
DIBNER LIBRARY, *DC19-641*
DICKINSON COLLEGE, LIBRARY, SPECIAL COLLECTIONS,
    PA160-160
DICKINSON COUNTY HISTORICAL SOCIETY, *KS10-150*
DICKINSON, JAMES, LIBRARY, SPECIAL COLLECTIONS
    DEPARTMENT, *NV630-800*
DIGHTON HISTORICAL SOCIETY, *MA246-160*
DILLARD UNIVERSITY, WILL W. ALEXANDER LIBRARY, *LA600-160*
DIMOCK GALLERY, *DC7-510*
DIMOND LIBRARY, SPECIAL COLLECTIONS, *NH206-800*
DIOCESE OF BETHLEHEM OF THE EPISCOPAL CHURCH, *PA90-160*
DIOCESE OF CENTRAL NEW YORK, *NY872-150*
DIOCESE OF CHARLESTON, CHARLESTON DIOCESAN ARCHIVES,
    SC144-190
DIOCESE OF COLUMBUS, ARCHIVES, *OH203-170*
DIOCESE OF COVINGTON, ARCHIVES, *KY176-160*
DIOCESE OF CROOKSTON, CHANCERY OFFICE, *MN233-160*
DIOCESE OF DALLAS OF THE EPISCOPAL CHURCH, *TX252-200*
DIOCESE OF DELAWARE, *DE810-170*
DIOCESE OF GALVESTON-HOUSTON, CHANCERY ARCHIVES AND
    RESEARCH, *TX483-160*
DIOCESE OF GRAND RAPIDS, DIOCESAN ARCHIVES, *MI355-160*
DIOCESE OF HELENA, *MT530-690*
DIOCESE OF LAFAYETTE IN INDIANA, CHANCERY ARCHIVES,
    IN440-160
DIOCESE OF LAFAYETTE, ARCHIVES, *LA358-160*
DIOCESE OF LAKE CHARLES, ARCHIVES, *LA358-165*
DIOCESE OF LITTLE ROCK, ARCHIVES, *AR510-145*
DIOCESE OF NORTHERN CALIFORNIA, *CA676-170*
DIOCESE OF OGDENSBURG, ARCHIVES, *NY634-160*
DIOCESE OF PROVIDENCE, ARCHIVES, *RI700-160*
DIOCESE OF SAVANNAH, CHANCERY ARCHIVES AND DIOCESAN
    ARCHIVES, *GA895-160*

DIOCESE OF SIOUX CITY, *IA866-160*
DIOCESE OF SOUTHERN OHIO, *OH171-165*
DIOCESE OF THE RIO GRANDE, PROTESTANT EPISCOPAL CHURCH, ARCHIVES, *TX326-160*
DIOCESE OF WINONA, *MN975-160*
DIRKSEN, EVERETT MCKINLEY, CONGRESSIONAL LEADERSHIP RESEARCH CENTER, *IL718-200*
DISCIPLES OF CHRIST HISTORICAL SOCIETY, LIBRARY AND ARCHIVES, *TN690-170*
DISCOVERY HALL MUSEUM, RESEARCH LIBRARY, *IN792-160*
DISNEY, WALT, ARCHIVES, *CA114-880*
DISNEY, WALT, PRODUCTIONS, WALT DISNEY ARCHIVES, *CA114-880*
DIVINE PROVIDENCE, SISTERS OF, PROVIDENCE HEIGHTS ARCHIVES, *PA30-720*
DIVISION OF LAND RECORDS (PA), *PA380-665*
DIXON, JOHN, LIBRARY, ARCHIVES COLLECTION, *NJ420-490*
DOANE COLLEGE, PERKINS LIBRARY, COLLEGE ARCHIVES, *NE288-160*
DOANE, W. H., LIBRARY, *OH350-170*
DOCUMENTARY RELATIONS OF THE SOUTHWEST, *AZ800-790*
DODGE COUNTY HISTORICAL SOCIETY, LOUIS E. MAY MUSEUM, LIBRARY, *NE368-160*
DODGE COUNTY HISTORICAL SOCIETY, MUSEUM, *WI77-160*
DODGE, HISTORIC GENERAL, HOUSE, *IA177-320*
DOHENY, EDWARD LAURENCE, MEMORIAL LIBRARY, ESTELLE DOHENY COLLECTION, *CA118-720*
DOHENY, ESTELLE, COLLECTION, *CA118-720*
DOMINICAN COLLEGE, *DC15-50*
DOMINICAN COLLEGE, LIBRARY, *CA764-160*
DOMINICAN CONVENT OF SAN RAFAEL, *CA764-165*
DOMINICAN FATHERS, PROVINCE OF ST. JOSEPH, ARCHIVES, *DC15-50*
DOMINICAN SISTERS OF ST. CATHARINE OF SIENA, ARCHIVES, *KY710-160*
DOMINICAN, SINSINAWA, SISTERS, DOMINICAN ARCHIVES, *WI698-730*
DON F. PRATT MUSEUM, *KY250-160*
DONALDSON, LUFKIN & JENRETTE SECURITIES CORPORATION, *NY589-340*
DONNELLEY LIBRARY, LAKE FOREST COLLEGE ARCHIVES, *IL434-490*
DORCHESTER HISTORICAL SOCIETY, *MA250-160*
DORDT COLLEGE, ARCHIVES AND DUTCH MEMORIAL COLLECTION, *IA855-150*
DOSSIN GREAT LAKES MUSEUM, SHIP DATA REGISTRY, *MI230-180*
DOUGLAS COUNTY HISTORICAL MUSEUM, *WA960-170, WI754-170*
DOUGLAS COUNTY HISTORICAL SOCIETY, ELIZABETH M. WATKINS COMMUNITY MUSEUM, LIBRARY, *KS527-160*
DOUGLAS COUNTY MUSEUM OF HISTORY AND NATURAL HISTORY, HISTORY CENTER LIBRARY, *OR768-170*
DOUGLAS LIBRARY, *IL169-468*
DOUGLASS COLLEGE, AMERICAN STUDIES DEPARTMENT, NEW JERSEY FOLKLORE ARCHIVE, *NJ568-625*
DOUGLASS, FREDERICK, INSTITUTE, ARCHIVES, *DC19-440*
DOUGLASS, FREDERICK, INSTITUTE, ELIOT ELISOFON ARCHIVES, *DC19-450*
DOVER HISTORICAL SOCIETY, J. E. REEVES HOME AND MUSEUM, *OH237-160*
DOVER LIBRARY, SPECIAL COLLECTIONS, *NC100-280*
DOVER PUBLIC LIBRARY, *NH194-160*
DOWNEY HISTORICAL SOCIETY, *CA226-170*
DOWNS, JOSEPH, MANUSCRIPT AND MICROFILM COLLECTION, *DE900-320*
DR. CHARLES DELAND CLAWSON MEDICAL COLLECTION, *NY562-720*
DR. ERNEST M. BEST ARCHIVES ROOM, *MA804-710*
DRAKE MEMORIAL LIBRARY, *NY125-720*
DRAKE UNIVERSITY, COWLES LIBRARY, SPECIAL COLLECTIONS, *IA233-160*
DRAKE UNIVERSITY, DIVINITY SCHOOL LIBRARY, *IA233-160*
DRAKE WELL MUSEUM, *PA870-160*
DRAKE, J. F., MEMORIAL LEARNING RESOURCES CENTER, *AL640-40*
DRETZIN LIVING BIOGRAPHIES PROGRAM, *MA871-85*
DREW COUNTY HISTORICAL MUSEUM, SOUTHEAST RESEARCH AND ARCHIVES CENTER, *AR600-160*
DREW UNIVERSITY, LIBRARY, *NJ464-150*
DREXEL COLLECTION, *PA725-375*
DREXEL UNIVERSITY, LIBRARIES, DREXEL COLLECTION, *PA725-375*
DROPSIE UNIVERSITY, LIBRARY, *PA725-405*
DU PONT HISTORICAL MUSEUM, *WA259-160*
DU PONT, HENRY FRANCIS, WINTERTHUR MUSEUM, JOSEPH DOWNS MANUSCRIPT AND MICROFILM COLLECTION, *DE900-320*

DU PONT, HENRY FRANCIS, WINTERTHUR MUSEUM, WINTERTHUR ARCHIVES, *DE900-330*
DUBUQUE COUNTY HISTORICAL SOCIETY, *IA244-160*
DUCKWORTH LIBRARIES, *GA990-940*
DUERSON-OLDHAM COUNTY PUBLIC LIBRARY, *KY41E-160*
DUGGAN LIBRARY, *IN319-330*
DUKE UNIVERSITY, ARCHIVES, *NC260-150*
DUKE UNIVERSITY, MEDICAL LIBRARY, TRENT COLLECTION, *NC260-160*
DUKE UNIVERSITY, WILLIAM R. PERKINS LIBRARY, MANUSCRIPT DEPARTMENT, *NC260-170*
DUKES COUNTY HISTORICAL SOCIETY, *MA285-160*
DULUTH PUBLIC LIBRARY, *MN261-170*
DUMBARTON OAKS RESEARCH LIBRARY, DUMBARTON OAKS GARDEN LIBRARY, *DC4-940*
DUNDEE AREA HISTORICAL SOCIETY, *NY247-160*
DUNN LIBRARY, *IA455-720*
DUPONT, JESSIE BALL, LIBRARY, *TN840-800*
DUPRE LIBRARY, SOUTHWESTERN ARCHIVES AND MANUSCRIPTS COLLECTION, *LA358-800*
DUQUESNE UNIVERSITY, LIBRARY, *PA735-200*
DURHAM CENTER MUSEUM, *NY254-160*
DUTCH HERITAGE COLLECTION, *IA755-560*
DUTCH MEMORIAL COLLECTION, *IA855-150*
DUVALL HISTORICAL SOCIETY, *WA263-160*
DUVALL LIBRARY, *WA263-165*
DUXBURY RURAL AND HISTORICAL SOCIETY, *MA265-160*
DWIGHT D. EISENHOWER LIBRARY, *KS10-170*
DYER MEMORIAL LIBRARY, *MA5-160*
DYER-YORK LIBRARY AND MUSEUM, *ME750-160*
DYKE COLLEGE, LIBRARY RESOURCE CENTER, ARCHIVAL COLLECTION, *OH181-400*
DYKES DRYDEN MUSEUM, *WA258-160*

E

E. C. BARKER TEXAS HISTORY CENTER, *TX56-850*
E. E. RASMUSON LIBRARY, ARCHIVES AND MANUSCRIPT COLLECTIONS, *AK350-800*
E. H. BUTLER LIBRARY, ARCHIVES/SPECIAL COLLECTIONS, *NY134-730*
E. J. MEYER MEMORIAL HOSPITAL, CENTRAL PHOTO LAB, *NY134-510*
E. LEE TRINKLE LIBRARY, RARE BOOKS ROOM AND MARY WASHINGTON COLLEGE ARCHIVES, *VA285-520*
E. M. CUDAHY MEMORIAL LIBRARY, *IL170-78*
E. R. SQUIBB & SONS, *NJ692-190*
E. Y. BERRY LIBRARY/LEARNING CENTER, CASE LIBRARY AND BERRY MANUSCRIPT COLLECTION, *SD720-80*
E. Y. BERRY MANUSCRIPT COLLECTION, *SD720-80*
EARL GREGG SWEM LIBRARY, *VA870-110*
EARL K. LONG LIBRARY, ARCHIVES AND MANUSCRIPTS/SPECIAL COLLECTIONS DEPARTMENT, *LA600-775*
EARLHAM COLLEGE, LILLY LIBRARY, *IN704-200*
EARTH RESOURCES OBSERVATION SYSTEMS DATA CENTER, *SD684-280*
EARTH SCIENTISTS, SOCIETY OF INDEPENDENT, ARCHIVES COMMITTEE, *TX252-322*
EAST CAROLINA UNIVERSITY, EAST CAROLINA MANUSCRIPT COLLECTION, *NC390-200*
EAST CHICAGO HISTORICAL SOCIETY, *IN187-200*
EAST CLEVELAND PUBLIC LIBRARY, MAIN BRANCH, *OH246-200*
EAST HADDAM HISTORICAL SOCIETY, *CT174-200*
EAST HAMPTON FREE LIBRARY, LONG ISLAND COLLECTION, *NY257-190*
EAST ORANGE PUBLIC LIBRARY, REFERENCE DEPARTMENT, *NJ212-200*
EAST ROCHESTER VILLAGE HISTORIAN, *NY262-200*
EAST TENNESSEE STATE UNIVERSITY, SHERROD LIBRARY, ARCHIVES OF APPALACHIA, *TN435-220*
EAST TEXAS BAPTIST COLLEGE, MAMYE JARRETT LEARNING CENTER, SPECIAL COLLECTIONS, *TX604-220*
EAST TEXAS HISTORICAL ASSOCIATION, *TX632-200*
EAST TEXAS STATE UNIVERSITY, JAMES G. GEE LIBRARY, ORAL HISTORY PROGRAM, *TX210-200*
EAST TEXAS STATE UNIVERSITY, UNIVERSITY ARCHIVES, *TX210-230*
EAST, ADAM, MUSEUM, *WA565-40*
EASTERN ARIZONA MUSEUM AND HISTORICAL SOCIETY OF GRAHAM COUNTY, *AZ600-200*
EASTERN GRAYS HARBOR COUNTY HISTORICAL SOCIETY, *WA535-200*
EASTERN KENTUCKY UNIVERSITY, ARCHIVES DIVISION, *KY680-180*
EASTERN KENTUCKY UNIVERSITY, CRABBE LIBRARY, TOWNSEND ROOM, *KY680-190*

EASTERN LEWIS COUNTY HISTORICAL SOCIETY, OLD SETTLERS MEMORIAL MUSEUM, *WA564-200*
EASTERN MENNONITE COLLEGE, MENNO SIMONS HISTORICAL LIBRARY/ARCHIVES, *VA350-200*
EASTERN MICHIGAN UNIVERSITY, CENTER OF EDUCATIONAL RESOURCES, UNIV. ARCHIVES AND SPEC. COLLECTIONS, *MI990-180*
EASTERN MONTANA COLLEGE, LIBRARY, SPECIAL COLLECTIONS, *MT100-200*
EASTERN NAZARENE COLLEGE, ARCHIVES, *MA978-200*
EASTERN NEW MEXICO UNIVERSITY, GOLDEN LIBRARY, SPECIAL COLLECTIONS AND ARCHIVES, *NM668-210*
EASTERN OREGON STATE COLLEGE, WALTER M. PIERCE LIBRARY, *OR464-200*
EASTERN WASHINGTON REGIONAL STATE ARCHIVES, *WA144-840*
EASTERN WASHINGTON STATE HISTORICAL SOCIETY, LIBRARY, *WA880-190*
EASTERN WASHINGTON UNIVERSITY, DEPARTMENT OF GEOGRAPHY, *WA144-190*
EASTERN WASHINGTON UNIVERSITY, LIBRARY, ARCHIVES SECTION, *WA144-210*
EASTHAM HISTORICAL SOCIETY, 1869 SCHOOLHOUSE MUSEUM, *MA278-200*
EASTMAN KODAK COMPANY, ARCHIVES, *NY752-200*
EASTMAN SCHOOL OF MUSIC, SIBLEY MUSIC LIBRARY, *NY752-840*
EASTON AREA PUBLIC LIBRARY, *PA270-200*
EBENEZER MEMORIAL AND HISTORICAL ASSOCIATION, *SC540-200*
EDDY FAMILY ASSOCIATION, *MA542-200*
EDDY HISTORICAL & GENEALOGICAL COLLECTION, *MI824-320*
EDDY, MARY BAKER, MUSEUM, *MA154-480*
EDEN HISTORICAL SOCIETY, TOWN HISTORIAN'S OFFICE, *NY263-210*
EDGAR CAYCE FOUNDATION ARCHIVES, *VA810-40*
EDGAR FAHS SMITH COLLECTION IN THE HISTORY OF CHEMISTRY, *PA726-765*
EDGEWATER FREE PUBLIC LIBRARY, *NJ220-200*
EDINA HISTORICAL SOCIETY, *MN275-200*
EDISON BIRTHPLACE MUSEUM, *OH550-200*
EDISON NATIONAL HISTORIC SITE, *NJ910-200*
EDISON WINTER HOME AND MUSEUM, *FL180-210*
EDITH B. FORD MEMORIAL LIBRARY, *NY664-200*
EDMESTON FREE LIBRARY AND MUSEUM, *NY264-200*
EDMONDS PUBLIC LIBRARY, *WA272-190*
EDMONDS-SOUTH SNOHOMISH COUNTY HISTORICAL SOCIETY, *WA272-210*
EDUCATIONAL TESTING SERVICE, ARCHIVES, *NJ692-210*
EDWARD G. MINER LIBRARY, *NY752-885*
EDWARD INGRAHAM LIBRARY, *CT48-40*
EDWARD LAURENCE DOHENY MEMORIAL LIBRARY, ESTELLE DOHENY COLLECTION, *CA118-720*
EDWARD MINER GALLAUDET MEMORIAL LIBRARY, ARCHIVES, *DC7-100*
EDWARD R. MURROW CENTER FOR PUBLIC DIPLOMACY, *MA528-740*
EDWARD RHODES STITT LIBRARY, *MD152-560*
EDWARDS MEMORIAL MUSEUM, *MA196-120*
EDWARDS, JACOB, LIBRARY, *MA797-400*
EDWARDS, WARD, LIBRARY, SPECIAL COLLECTIONS, *MO920-120*
EFFIGY MOUNDS NATIONAL MONUMENT, *IA622-200*
EGGLESTON LIBRARY, SPECIAL COLLECTIONS, *VA310-320*
EHRHART, OTTO E. - PAULDING COUNTY HISTORICAL SOCIETY, *OH21-600*
EIGHTEEN HUNDRED SIXTY NINE (1869) SCHOOLHOUSE MUSEUM, *MA278-200*
EISENHOWER, DWIGHT D., LIBRARY, *KS10-170*
EISENHOWER, MAMIE DOUD, BIRTHPLACE, MUSEUM AND LIBRARY, *IA58-540*
EISENHOWER, MILTON S., LIBRARY, *MD76-360*
EL PASO CENTENNIAL MUSEUM, *TX326-800*
EL PASO CENTENNIAL MUSEUM, MANUSCRIPT COLLECTION, *TX326-770*
EL PASO PUBLIC LIBRARY, SOUTHWEST COLLECTION, *TX326-210*
EL PUEBLO DE LOS ANGELES STATE HISTORIC PARK, HISTORY AND PUBLIC AFFAIRS, *CA421-218*
EL RENO CARNEGIE LIBRARY, *OK338-200*
ELBERT HUBBARD LIBRARY-MUSEUM, *NY250-212*
ELBERT IVEY MEMORIAL LIBRARY, *NC410-200*
ELDRIDGE AREA HISTORICAL CENTER, *WA60-220*
ELECTRONIC COMMUNICATION MUSEUM, *NY396-40*
ELEUTHERIAN MILLS-HAGLEY FOUNDATION, *DE270-200*
ELEVENTH BOMBARDMENT GROUP (H) ASSOCIATION, HISTORICAL ARCHIVES, *FL750-200*
ELIHU BURRITT LIBRARY, *CT477-130*
ELIJAH P. LOVEJOY LIBRARY, MAP SECTION, *IL236-730*
ELIJAH P. LOVEJOY LIBRARY, RESEARCH COLLECTIONS, *IL236-760*
ELIOT ELISOFON ARCHIVES, *DC19-450*
ELISABET NEY MUSEUM, *TX56-200*

ELISOFON, ELIOT, ARCHIVES, *DC19-450*
ELIZABETH M. WATKINS COMMUNITY MUSEUM, LIBRARY, *KS527-160*
ELIZABETH SETON COLLEGE, LIBRARY, *NY984-200*
ELIZABETHTOWN COLLEGE, ZUG MEMORIAL LIBRARY, *PA285-200*
ELKHART COUNTY HISTORICAL SOCIETY, *IN77-200*
ELLA SHARP MUSEUM, *MI510-200*
ELLEN CLARKE BERTRAND LIBRARY, *PA500-80*
ELLENDER MEMORIAL LIBRARY, ALLEN J. ELLENDER ARCHIVES, *LA920-560*
ELLENDER, ALLEN J., ARCHIVES, *LA920-560*
ELLENSBURG PUBLIC LIBRARY, *WA280-200*
ELLENVILLEPUBLIC LIBRARY AND MUSEUM, *NY269-200*
ELLIS COUNTY HISTORICAL SOCIETY, *KS377-200*
ELLIS, DEAN B., LIBRARY, ARKANSAS ROOM, *AR890-20*
ELLISON LIBRARY, ST. ALBANS ARCHIVES, *DC19-40*
ELMHURST COLLEGE, A. C. BUEHLER LIBRARY, *IL246-190*
ELMHURST HISTORICAL MUSEUM, *IL246-200*
ELMIRA COLLEGE, ARCHIVES, *NY272-200*
ELON COLLEGE, LIBRARY, CHRISTIAN CHURCH HISTORY COLLECTION, *NC310-200*
ELYRIA PUBLIC LIBRARY, *OH266-200*
EMERSON COLLEGE, LIBRARY, *MA108-520*
EMERSON, RALPH WALDO, ROOM, *MN541-600*
EMHART INDUSTRIES, HARTFORD DIVISION LIBRARY, *CT961-210*
EMIL LORIKS HERITAGE HOUSE, *SD550-600*
EMMA B. KING LIBRARY, *NY637-720*
EMMA S. CLARK MEMORIAL LIBRARY, THREE VILLAGE LOCAL HISTORY COLLECTION, *NY824-200*
EMMA WILLARD SCHOOL, *NY890-200*
EMORY & HENRY COLLEGE, LIBRARY, *VA195-200*
EMORY UNIVERSITY, OXFORD COLLEGE, LIBRARY, *GA825-200*
EMORY UNIVERSITY, PITTS THEOLOGY LIBRARY, *GA90-190*
EMORY UNIVERSITY, ROBERT W. WOODRUFF LIBRARY, SPECIAL COLLECTIONS DEPARTMENT, *GA90-200*
EMORY UNIVERSITY, SCHOOL OF DENTISTRY, SHEPPARD W. FOSTER LIBRARY, *GA90-210*
EMPIRE TOWNSHIP HISTORICAL MUSEUM, *MI268-200*
EMPORIA STATE UNIVERSITY, WILLIAM ALLEN WHITE LIBRARY, SPECIAL COLLECTIONS DIVISION, *KS283-200*
ENCINO HISTORICAL SOCIETY, LIBRARY, *CA246-480*
ENGEL, LEHMAN, COLLECTION, *MS550-460*
ENGELBRECHT LIBRARY, WARTBURG COLLEGE ARCHIVES, *IA944-880*
ENGINEERING SOCIETIES LIBRARY, *NY589-460*
ENGLEWOOD PUBLIC LIBRARY, *CO306-200*
ENOCH PRATT FREE LIBRARY, *MD76-190*
ENTIAT COMMUNITY MUSEUM, *WA288-200*
ENTOMOLOGICAL SOCIETY OF AMERICA, *MD285-200*
ENUMCLAW PUBLIC LIBRARY, *WA289-200*
ENVIRONMENTAL PROTECTION AGENCY, PROJECT DOCUMERICA, *DC5-600*
EPHRATA PUBLIC LIBRARY, *WA290-200*
EPISCOPAL CHURCH, USA, ARCHIVES OF, *TX56-25*
EPISCOPAL DIOCESE OF ALABAMA, *AL120-200*
EPISCOPAL DIOCESE OF BETHLEHEM, *PA90-160*
EPISCOPAL DIOCESE OF CENTRAL NEW YORK, *NY872-150*
EPISCOPAL DIOCESE OF CHICAGO, ARCHIVES AND HISTORICAL COLLECTIONS, *IL169-651*
EPISCOPAL DIOCESE OF CONNECTICUT, ARCHIVES, *CT316-210*
EPISCOPAL DIOCESE OF DALLAS, *TX252-200*
EPISCOPAL DIOCESE OF DELAWARE, *DE810-170*
EPISCOPAL DIOCESE OF EASTERN OREGON, OFFICE OF THE HISTORIOGRAPHER, *OR464-322*
EPISCOPAL DIOCESE OF KANSAS, DIOCESAN OFFICE, *KS878-200*
EPISCOPAL DIOCESE OF KENTUCKY, *KY496-200*
EPISCOPAL DIOCESE OF LONG ISLAND, *NY315-200*
EPISCOPAL DIOCESE OF MASSACHUSETTS, DIOCESAN LIBRARY AND ARCHIVES, *MA108-580*
EPISCOPAL DIOCESE OF MINNESOTA, *MN541-216*
EPISCOPAL DIOCESE OF MISSOURI, ARCHIVES, *MO810-590*
EPISCOPAL DIOCESE OF NEW YORK, ARCHIVES, *NY593-590*
EPISCOPAL DIOCESE OF NORTH CAROLINA, *NC680-200*
EPISCOPAL DIOCESE OF NORTHERN CALIFORNIA, *CA676-170*
EPISCOPAL DIOCESE OF OHIO, ARCHIVES, *OH181-430*
EPISCOPAL DIOCESE OF OLYMPIA, *WA820-200*
EPISCOPAL DIOCESE OF OREGON, *OR720-200*
EPISCOPAL DIOCESE OF ROCHESTER, NEW YORK, ARCHIVES, *NY752-220*
EPISCOPAL DIOCESE OF SOUTH DAKOTA, *SD684-200*
EPISCOPAL DIOCESE OF SOUTHERN OHIO, *OH171-165*
EPISCOPAL DIOCESE OF SPRINGFIELD, *IL866-200*
EPISCOPAL DIOCESE OF TENNESSEE, *TN630-200*
EPISCOPAL DIOCESE OF THE CENTRAL GULF COAST, OFFICE OF THE BISHOP, *AL580-650*
EPISCOPAL DIOCESE OF THE RIO GRANDE, ARCHIVES, *TX326-160*
EPISCOPAL DIOCESE OF UTAH, ARCHIVES, *UT912-200*

EPISCOPAL DIOCESE OF WASHINGTON, ARCHIVES, *DC5-800*
EPISCOPAL DIOCESE OF WEST TEXAS, CATHEDRAL HOUSE ARCHIVES, *TX777-640*
EPISCOPAL DIOCESE OF WESTERN NEW YORK, *NY134-660*
EPISCOPAL THEOLOGICAL SCHOOL, LIBRARY, *MA169-110*
ERICSSON, JOHN, COLLECTION, *PA725-120*
ERIE CANAL MUSEUM, *NY872-120*
ERIE COUNTY HISTORICAL SOCIETY, *PA305-190*
ERIE HISTORICAL MUSEUM AND PLANETARIUM, *PA305-210*
ERIE STUDIES, CENTER FOR, *PA305-510*
ERIN HISTORICAL SOCIETY, *NY274-200*
ERNIE SIMON COLLECTION, *NY717-640*
EROS DATA CENTER, *SD684-280*
ERSKINE COLLEGE, MCCAIN LIBRARY, *SC306-200*
ERWIN LIBRARY AND INSTITUTE, *NY107-200*
ESCONDIDO HISTORICAL SOCIETY, *CA248-200*
ESPERANCE HISTORICAL SOCIETY, *NY277-200*
ESSENTIAL CLUB FREE LIBRARY, *NY148-200*
ESSEX HISTORICAL SOCIETY, ESSEX SHIPBUILDING MUSEUM, *MA293-200*
ESSEX INSTITUTE, JAMES DUNCAN PHILLIPS LIBRARY, *MA733-210*
ESSEX SHIPBUILDING MUSEUM, *MA293-200*
ESTELLE DOHENY COLLECTION, *CA118-720*
ESTHER RAUSHENBUSH LIBRARY, *NY128-720*
ESTO PHOTOGRAPHICS, *NY519-200*
EUGENE FIELD HOUSE AND TOY MUSEUM, *MO810-260*
EUGENE SHEDDEN FARLEY LIBRARY, *PA960-870*
EUGENE V. DEBS MUSEUM AND LIBRARY, *IN825-200*
EUREKA COLLEGE, MELICK LIBRARY, *IL256-200*
EUREKA PIONEER MUSEUM OF MCPHERSON COUNTY, *SD153-200*
EVA K. BOWLBY PUBLIC LIBRARY, ORAL HISTORY COLLECTION, *PA940-300*
EVANGELICAL AND REFORMED CHURCH AND UNITED CHURCH OF CHRIST, *MO810-270*
EVANGELICAL COVENANT CHURCH OF AMERICA, COVENANT ARCHIVES/HISTORICAL LIBRARY, *IL169-677*
EVANGELICAL LUTHERAN CHURCH, ARCHIVES, *MN763-50*
EVANGELICAL THEOLOGICAL SEMINARY, *IL261-280*
EVANS MEMORIAL LIBRARY, HISTORICAL DIVISION, *MS20-200*
EVANS, DANIEL, LIBRARY, *WA616-240*
EVANSTON HISTORICAL SOCIETY, *IL261-200*
EVANSVILLE MUSEUM OF ARTS AND SCIENCE, ARCHIVES OFFICE, *IN209-200*
EVERETT COMMUNITY COLLEGE, LIBRARY, *WA300-172*
EVERETT FIRE DEPARTMENT, MUSEUM, *WA300-175*
EVERETT MCKINLEY DIRKSEN CONGRESSIONAL LEADERSHIP RESEARCH CENTER, *IL718-200*
EVERETT PUBLIC LIBRARY, *WA300-200*
EVERGREEN STATE COLLEGE, DANIEL EVANS LIBRARY, *WA616-240*
EXCELSIOR LAKE MINNETONKA HISTORICAL SOCIETY, *MN307-200*
EXETER HISTORICAL SOCIETY, *NY811-200*
EXETER PUBLIC LIBRARY, *NH254-210*
EXPLORATION, AMERICAN INSTITUTE FOR, MAIN ADMINISTRATIVE OFFICE AND LIBRARY, *MI518-50*
EXPLORERS CLUB, *NY589-500*
EZRA MEEKER HISTORICAL SOCIETY, *WA726-200*

F

F. B. POWER PHARMACEUTICAL LIBRARY, KREMERS REFERENCE FILES, *WI346-870*
FAIRBANKS MUSEUM AND PLANETARIUM, *VT736-240*
FAIRCHILD AERIAL PHOTOGRAPHY COLLECTION AT WHITTIER COLLEGE, *CA966-860*
FAIRFIELD HISTORICAL SOCIETY, *CT234-230*
FAIRFIELD PUBLIC LIBRARY, *CT234-250*
FAIRFIELD UNIVERSITY, NYSELIUS LIBRARY, UNIVERSITY ARCHIVES, *CT234-260*
FAIRLEIGH DICKINSON UNIVERSITY, FRIENDSHIP LIBRARY, *NJ464-240*
FAIRLEIGH DICKINSON UNIVERSITY, MESSLER LIBRARY, NEW JERSEY ROOM, *NJ756-240*
FAKE, WARREN H., LIBRARY, *PA725-690*
FALES LIBRARY, *NY593-90*
FALL RIVER HISTORICAL SOCIETY, *MA304-230*
FALMOUTH HISTORICAL SOCIETY, *MA307-230*
FALVEY MEMORIAL LIBRARY, *PA910-840*
FANT, J. C., MEMORIAL LIBRARY, *MS300-520*
FARLEY MEMORIAL LIBRARY, *NJ408-280*
FARLEY, EUGENE SHEDDEN, LIBRARY, *PA960-870*
FARLOW REFERENCE LIBRARY, *MA169-270*
FARM AND INDUSTRIAL EQUIPMENT INSTITUTE, *IL169-703*
FARMINGTON MUSEUM, *CT247-240*

FARMINGTON VILLAGE GREEN AND LIBRARY ASSOCIATION, FARMINGTON MUSEUM, *CT247-240*
FARNSWORTH, WILLIAM A., LIBRARY AND ART MUSEUM, *ME725-880*
FAYETTE COUNTY HELPERS CLUB AND HISTORICAL SOCIETY, *IA972-240*
FAYETTE COUNTY-LEXINGTON HISTORIC COMMISSION, *KY464-495*
FAYETTE HISTORIC STATE PARK, *MI343-280*
FAYETTEVILLE FREE LIBRARY, *NY286-240*
FEDERAL ARCHIVES AND RECORDS CENTER, *CA386-560, CA704-560, CO252-550, IL170-280, MO430-540, NJ46-560, TX374-550*
FEDERAL ARCHIVES AND RECORDS CENTER, ARCHIVES BRANCH, *GA405-560, MA871-540, PA726-7, WA820-550*
FEDERAL RESERVE BANK OF RICHMOND, ARCHIVES, *VA690-240*
FEDERAL WAY PUBLIC LIBRARY, *WA310-240*
FEINBERG LIBRARY, SPECIAL COLLECTIONS DEPARTMENT, NORTH COUNTRY HISTORY CENTER, *NY708-720*
FEININGER ARCHIVES AND GROPIUS ARCHIVES, *MA169-200*
FELIX G. WOODWARD LIBRARY, *TN75-50*
FEMINIST HISTORY RESEARCH PROJECT, *CA886-240*
FENTON HISTORICAL SOCIETY, LIBRARY, *NY442-230*
FERDINAND HAMBURGER, JR., ARCHIVES, *MD76-325*
FERREL, BEN, PLATTE COUNTY MUSEUM, *MO675-640*
FERRIS STATE COLLEGE, LIBRARY, COLLEGE ARCHIVES, *MI100-240*
FERRUM COLLEGE, BLUE RIDGE INSTITUTE, *VA235-230*
FERRUM COLLEGE, STANLEY LIBRARY, FRANKLIN COUNTY HISTORICAL SOCIETY COLLECTION, *VA235-250*
FERRY COUNTY HISTORICAL SOCIETY, MUSEUM, *WA739-240*
FIDDLING ARCHIVE, *NE560-50*
FIELD ARTILLERY AND FORT SILL MUSEUM, MUSEUM ARCHIVAL LIBRARY, *OK372-240*
FIELD MUSEUM OF NATURAL HISTORY, LIBRARY, *IL169-729*
FIELD, EUGENE, HOUSE AND TOY MUSEUM, *MO810-260*
FIKES HALL OF SPECIAL COLLECTIONS AND DEGOLYER LIBRARY, *TX252-730*
FINDLAY COLLEGE, LIBRARY, *OH281-240*
FINNEY COUNTY HISTORICAL SOCIETY, *KS335-240*
FINNEY, JOHN W., MEMORIAL LIBRARY, *TN120-120*
FINNISH-AMERICAN HISTORICAL ARCHIVES, *MI390-720*
FIRE LANDS HISTORICAL SOCIETY, *OH660-240*
FIRE MUSEUM OF TRENTON, *NJ838-530*
FIRESTONE TIRE AND RUBBER COMPANY, ARCHIVES DEPARTMENT, *OH11-240*
FIRST BAPTIST CHURCH IN AMERICA, *RI700-240*
FIRST CENTRAL CONGREGATIONAL CHURCH (UNITED CHURCH OF CHRIST), CHURCH HISTORY COLLECTION, *NE624-240*
FIRST CHURCH IN CAMBRIDGE, CONGREGATIONAL, ARCHIVES, *MA169-40*
FIRST CHURCH OF CHRIST, SCIENTIST, ARCHIVES AND LIBRARY OF THE MOTHER CHURCH, *MA108-600*
FIRST NATIONAL BANK OF ATLANTA, CORPORATE SECRETARY'S DEPARTMENT, *GA90-230*
FIRST NATIONAL BANK OF CHICAGO, LIBRARY, *IL169-753*
FIRST SETTLERS MUSEUM, *MN391-310*
FISH AND WILDLIFE SERVICE, OFFICE OF AUDIO VISUAL, *DC6-500*
FISHBURN LIBRARY, *VA360-320*
FISHER, B. L., LIBRARY, *KY886-50*
FISHER, JONATHAN, MEMORIAL, *ME112-400*
FISHKILL HISTORICAL SOCIETY, VAN WYCK HOMESTEAD MUSEUM, *NY289-240*
FISK UNIVERSITY, LIBRARY AND MEDIA CENTER, SPECIAL COLLECTIONS, *TN690-220*
FITCHBURG HISTORICAL SOCIETY, *MA311-240*
FITZGERALD LIBRARY, *MN975-720*
FIVE CIVILIZED TRIBES MUSEUM, *OK541-240*
FLAGLER, HENRY MORRISON, MUSEUM, *FL580-320*
FLANDERS BALLAD COLLECTION, *VT432-520*
FLANNERY O'CONNOR COLLECTION, *GA780-270*
FLEMING LIBRARY, *TX374-720*
FLESH PUBLIC LIBRARY, *OH709-240*
FLETCHER SCHOOL OF LAW AND DIPLOMACY, EDWARD R. MURROW CENTER FOR PUBLIC DIPLOMACY, *MA528-740*
FLETCHER, J. V., LIBRARY, HISTORICAL COLLECTIONS, *MA931-400*
FLINT PUBLIC LIBRARY, MICHIGAN ROOM, *MI314-250*
FLORENCE A. WILLIAMS PUBLIC LIBRARY, *VI300-240*
FLORIDA A & M UNIVERSITY, BLACK ARCHIVES, RESEARCH CENTER, AND MUSEUM, *FL800-200*
FLORIDA ATLANTIC UNIVERSITY, LIBRARY, *FL40-250*
FLORIDA BAPTIST HISTORICAL SOCIETY, *FL140-240*
FLORIDA BUREAU OF STATE LANDS, *FL800-235*
FLORIDA DEPARTMENT OF NATURAL RESOURCES, DIVISION OF RESOURCE MANAGEMENT, BUREAU OF STATE LANDS, *FL800-235*
FLORIDA DIVISION OF ARCHIVES, HISTORY AND RECORDS MANAGEMENT, FLORIDA STATE ARCHIVES, *FL800-245*

FLORIDA FOLKLIFE ARCHIVE, *FL940-240*
FLORIDA FOLKLIFE PROGRAM, FLORIDA FOLKLIFE ARCHIVE,
  FL940-240
FLORIDA HISTORICAL SOCIETY, LIBRARY, *FL820-240*
FLORIDA INSTITUTE OF TECHNOLOGY, LIBRARY, *FL420-240*
FLORIDA STATE ARCHIVES, *FL800-245*
FLORIDA STATE LIBRARY, *FL800-245*
FLORIDA STATE MUSEUM, *FL220-792*
FLORIDA STATE PHOTOGRAPHIC ARCHIVES, *FL800-266*
FLORIDA STATE UNIVERSITY, ROBERT MANNING STROZIER
  LIBRARY, SPECIAL COLLECTIONS, *FL800-262*
FLORIDA STATE UNIVERSITY, STATE PHOTOGRAPHIC ARCHIVES,
  FL800-266
FLORIDA, NATIONAL FORESTS IN, *FL800-575*
FLOSSIE WILLS BARMES MUSEUM, *AZ100-120*
FLUVANNA FREE LIBRARY, *NY442-250*
FLYNT, HENRY N., LIBRARY OF HISTORIC DEERFIELD, *MA238-520*
FOGG ART MUSEUM, ARCHIVES DEPARTMENT, *MA169-300*
FOGLER, RAYMOND H., LIBRARY, SPECIAL COLLECTIONS
  DEPARTMENT, *ME650-810*
FOLGER SHAKESPEARE LIBRARY, *DC6-600*
FOLKLORE ARCHIVES, *IN66-340*
FOLKLORE INSTITUTE, FOLKLORE ARCHIVES, *IN66-340*
FOND DU LAC COUNTY HISTORICAL SOCIETY, HISTORIC
  GALLOWAY HOUSE AND VILLAGE, *WI170-230*
FONDREN LIBRARY, WOODSON RESEARCH CENTER, *TX483-690*
FONDULAC DISTRICT LIBRARY, LOCAL HISTORY COLLECTION,
  IL231-240
FOOTHILL ELECTRONICS MUSEUM, *CA418-200*
FOOTHILL ELECTRONICS MUSEUM, DE FOREST MEMORIAL
  LIBRARY, *CA418-200*
FORBES LIBRARY, *MA624-240*
FORD ARCHIVES, *MI214-260*
FORD FOUNDATION, ARCHIVES, *NY589-560*
FORD, EDITH B., MEMORIAL LIBRARY, *NY664-200*
FORD, GERALD R., LIBRARY, *MI40-300*
FORD, HENRY, CENTENNIAL LIBRARY, AUDIO-VISUAL DIVISION,
  MI214-140
FORD, HENRY, MUSEUM AND GREENFIELD VILLAGE, FORD
  ARCHIVES, *MI214-260*
FORD, HENRY, MUSEUM AND GREENFIELD VILLAGE, ROBERT
  HUDSON TANNAHILL RESEARCH LIBRARY, *MI214-280*
FORD'S THEATRE NATIONAL HISTORIC SITE, LINCOLN LIBRARY,
  DC6-650
FORDHAM UNIVERSITY, LIBRARY, *NY589-580*
FOREST HISTORY SOCIETY, *CA782-240*
FOREST LAWN MEMORIAL PARKS, FOREST LAWN MUSEUM,
  CA290-240
FOREST LAWN MUSEUM, *CA290-240*
FOREST PRODUCTS LABORATORY, *WI346-240*
FOREST SERVICE *See also*individual National forests, and other
  facilities*AZ700-40, CA94-360, CA274-720, CA624-740, CA978-520,
  CA998-440, ID600-130, MN198-120, MN261-730, NC60-240, NC656-720,
  NE240-560, NM760-280, OR224-880, OR464-490, OR688-820, UT988-40,
  VT704-280, WA616-620*
FOREST SERVICE, FOREST PRODUCTS LABORATORY, *WI346-240*
FOREST SERVICE, NATIONAL FORESTS IN FLORIDA, *FL800-575*
FOREST SERVICE, OFFICE OF INFORMATION, AUDIO/VISUAL
  GROUP, PHOTO LIBRARY, *VA50-240*
FOREST SERVICE, RECREATION MANAGEMENT STAFF,
  CULTURAL RESOURCE MANAGEMENT, RESEARCH AND
  ARCHIVES, *CA720-307*
FORESTRY AND ENVIRONMENTAL STUDIES LIBRARY, YALE
  UNIVERSITY, *CT505-905*
FORESTRY AND RANGE SCIENCES LABORATORY, *OR464-490*
FORKS MEMORIAL LIBRARY, *WA319-260*
FORSYTH LIBRARY, ARCHIVES COLLECTION, *KS377-250*
FORT ATKINSON HISTORICAL SOCIETY, HOARD HISTORICAL
  MUSEUM, *WI178-240*
FORT BEND COUNTY MUSEUM ASSOCIATION, MUSEUM,
  TX749-246
FORT CAMPBELL, DON F. PRATT MUSEUM, *KY250-160*
FORT COLLINS MUSEUM, *CO378-250*
FORT COLLINS PUBLIC LIBRARY, LOCAL HISTORY, *CO378-260*
FORT CONCHO NATIONAL HISTORIC LANDMARK, ARCHIVES,
  TX770-240
FORT CROOK HISTORICAL SOCIETY, FORT CROOK MUSEUM,
  CA258-240
FORT CROOK MUSEUM, *CA258-240*
FORT DELAWARE MUSEUM, *DE60-240*
FORT FREDERICA NATIONAL MONUMENT, PARK LIBRARY,
  GA885-240
FORT HAYS KANSAS STATE UNIVERSITY, FORSYTH LIBRARY,
  ARCHIVES COLLECTION, *KS377-250*
FORT JOHNSON MANSION, *NY297-520*
FORT LARAMIE NATIONAL HISTORIC SITE, *WY305-240*
FORT LARNED NATIONAL HISTORIC SITE, *KS513-250*

FORT LAUDERDALE HISTORICAL SOCIETY, *FL160-240*
FORT LEBOEUF MUSEUM, AMOS JUDSON LIBRARY, *PA930-240*
FORT LEE FREE PUBLIC LIBRARY, SILENT FILM PHOTO
  COLLECTION, *NJ266-240*
FORT LEWIS COLLEGE, LIBRARY, CENTER OF SOUTHWEST
  STUDIES, *CO270-240*
FORT LEWIS MILITARY MUSEUM, *WA320-230*
FORT MATANZAS NATIONAL MONUMENT, *FL660-120*
FORT MCHENRY NATIONAL MONUMENT AND HISTORIC
  SHRINE, LIBRARY, *MD76-240*
FORT MONROE CASEMATE MUSEUM, *VA275-240*
FORT NISQUALLY MUSEUM, *WA904-260*
FORT ROBINSON MUSEUM, *NE284-560*
FORT SILL AND FIELD ARTILLERY MUSEUM, MUSEUM
  ARCHIVAL LIBRARY, *OK372-240*
FORT SIMCOE STATE PARK, *WA972-240*
FORT SPOKANE INTERPRETIVE CENTER, *WA240-250*
FORT ST. JOSEPH MUSEUM, *MI700-240*
FORT TICONDEROGA MUSEUM, *NY881-260*
FORT VANCOUVER HISTORICAL SOCIETY, CLARK COUNTY
  HISTORICAL MUSEUM, *WA943-240*
FORT VANCOUVER NATIONAL HISTORIC SITE, *WA943-245*
FORT VANCOUVER REGIONAL LIBRARY SYSTEM, VANCOUVER
  COMMUNITY LIBRARY, *WA943-250*
FORT VANCOUVER REGIONAL LIBRARY SYSTEM, WASHOUGAL
  BRANCH LIBRARY, *WA958-240*
FORT VANCOUVER REGIONAL LIBRARY, BATTLE GROUND
  BRANCH LIBRARY, *WA44-240*
FORT VERDE STATE HISTORIC PARK, *AZ75-240*
FORT WALLA WALLA MUSEUM COMPLEX, *WA954-240*
FORT WASHINGTON HISTORICAL SOCIETY, *PA315-320*
FORT WAYNE PUBLIC LIBRARY, INDIANA COLLECTION, *IN231-240*
FORT WILKINS STATE PARK, *MI200-240*
FORT WORDEN, COAST ARTILLERY MUSEUM AT, *WA681-250*
FORT WORTH MUSEUM OF SCIENCE AND HISTORY, *TX374-240*
FORT WORTH PUBLIC LIBRARY, SOUTHWEST AND GENEALOGY
  DEPARTMENT, *TX374-250*
FORT WRIGHT COLLEGE HISTORICAL MUSEUM, *WA880-260*
FOSSIL STATION MUSEUM, *KS774-690*
FOSTER COUNTY HISTORICAL SOCIETY, *ND117-240*
FOSTER PUBLIC LIBRARY, *WA820-261*
FOSTER, CON, MUSEUM, *MI925-120*
FOSTER, RALPH, MUSEUM, LOIS BROWNELL RESEARCH
  LIBRARY, *MO700-720*
FOSTER, SHEPPARD W., LIBRARY, *GA90-210*
FOSTER, STEPHEN, MEMORIAL, *PA735-760*
FOULGER, PETER, MUSEUM, LIBRARY, *MA572-560*
FOUNDATION FOR SAN FRANCISCO'S ARCHITECTURAL
  HERITAGE, *CA720-316*
FOUNDATION HISTORICAL ASSOCIATION, *NY51-240*
FOUNTAIN COUNTY HISTORICAL SOCIETY COLLECTION,
  IN143-120
FOX ISLAND HISTORICAL SOCIETY, FOX ISLAND MUSEUM,
  WA322-240
FOX ISLAND MUSEUM, *WA322-240*
FOXBOROUGH HISTORICAL COMMISSION, *MA319-240*
FOXFIRE FUND, *GA840-240*
FRAMINGHAM HISTORICAL AND NATURAL HISTORY SOCIETY,
  MA323-250
FRAMINGHAM NATURAL HISTORY AND HISTORICAL SOCIETY,
  MA323-250
FRAMINGHAM PUBLIC LIBRARY, FRAMINGHAM ROOM,
  MA323-230
FRANCES CARRICK THOMAS LIBRARY, SPECIAL COLLECTIONS
  DEPARTMENT, *KY464-760*
FRANCES E. WILLARD MEMORIAL LIBRARY, *IL261-545*
FRANCES LOEB LIBRARY, *MA169-305*
FRANCIS A. COUNTWAY LIBRARY OF MEDICINE, *MA108-770*
FRANCIS BACON FOUNDATION, FRANCIS BACON LIBRARY,
  CA143-240
FRANCIS BACON LIBRARY, *CA143-240*
FRANCIS HARVEY GREEN LIBRARY, *PA945-880*
FRANCIS MARION COLLEGE, ROGERS LIBRARY, ARCHIVES,
  SC378-250
FRANCIS RUSSELL HART NAUTICAL COLLECTIONS, *MA169-610*
FRANCISCAN FRIARS, PROVINCE OF THE IMMACULATE
  CONCEPTION, ARCHIVES, *NY589-620*
FRANCISCAN MONASTERY, LIBRARY, *DC6-800*
FRANCISCAN SISTERS OF PERPETUAL ADORATION, ST. ROSE
  CONVENT, *WI298-250*
FRANCISCAN SISTERS OF THE ATONEMENT, *NY318-240*
FRANCISCAN SISTERS OF THE EUCHARIST, *WI298-250*
FRANKENMUTH HISTORICAL ASSOCIATION, FRANKENMUTH
  HISTORICAL MUSEUM, *MI322-240*
FRANKENMUTH HISTORICAL MUSEUM, *MI322-240*
FRANKFORD HISTORICAL SOCIETY, *PA725-710*
FRANKFORT COMMUNITY PUBLIC LIBRARY, *IN237-240*

FRANKLIN AND MARSHALL COLLEGE, LIBRARY, *PA470-240*
FRANKLIN COLLECTION, *CT505-945*
FRANKLIN COLLEGE, LIBRARY, SPECIAL COLLECTIONS, *IN242-230*
FRANKLIN COUNTY (VA) HISTORICAL SOCIETY COLLECTION, *VA235-250*
FRANKLIN COUNTY HISTORICAL SOCIETY, *WA647-270*
FRANKLIN COUNTY LIBRARY, *PA180-120*
FRANKLIN COUNTY MUSEUM, *VT720-720*
FRANKLIN D. ROOSEVELT LIBRARY, *NY427-240*
FRANKLIN INSTITUTE, HISTORICAL COLLECTIONS, *PA725-495*
FRANKLIN PUBLIC LIBRARY, *NH312-240*
FRANKLIN-JOHNSON COUNTY PUBLIC LIBRARY, *IN242-250*
FRAUNCES TAVERN MUSEUM, *NY594-220*
FRAZAR MEMORIAL LIBRARY, ARCHIVES AND SPECIAL COLLECTIONS, *LA395-520*
FREDERIC LEWIS (PHOTOGRAPH REPOSITORY), *NY589-640*
FREDERICK COUNTY PUBLIC LIBRARIES, C. BURR ARTZ LIBRARY, *MD399-240*
FREDERICK DOUGLASS INSTITUTE, ARCHIVES, *DC19-440*
FREDERICK DOUGLASS INSTITUTE, ELIOT ELISOFON ARCHIVES, *DC19-450*
FREDERICK MADISON SMITH LIBRARY, RESTORATION HISTORY MANUSCRIPT COLLECTION, *IA533-280*
FREDERICK W. CRUMB MEMORIAL LIBRARY, *NY723-720*
FREDERICKSBURG AND SPOTSYLVANIA NATIONAL MILITARY PARK, *VA285-240*
FREE LIBRARY OF PHILADELPHIA, RARE BOOK DEPARTMENT, *PA725-510*
FREE METHODIST CHURCH OF NORTH AMERICA, MARSTON MEMORIAL HISTORICAL CENTER, *IN990-240*
FREE PUBLIC LIBRARY (COUNCIL BLUFFS IA), *IA177-240*
FREE PUBLIC LIBRARY (TRENTON NJ), *NJ838-240*
FREE PUBLIC LIBRARY OF LIVINGSTON, *NJ444-240*
FREE WILL BAPTIST BIBLE COLLEGE, FREE WILL BAPTIST HISTORICAL COLLECTION, *TN690-240*
FREE WILL BAPTIST HISTORICAL COLLECTION, *NC610-520, TN690-240*
FREEBORN COUNTY HISTORICAL SOCIETY, MUSEUM AND RESEARCH LIBRARY, *MN28-240*
FREEMAN JUNIOR COLLEGE, LIBRARY, HISTORICAL LIBRARY, *SD234-250*
FREER GALLERY OF ART, DEPARTMENT OF NEAR EASTERN ART, *DC19-327*
FREER GALLERY OF ART, LIBRARY, *DC19-330*
FRESNO COUNTY FREE LIBRARY, LOCAL HISTORY COLLECTION, *CA274-240*
FRESNO COUNTY HISTORICAL SOCIETY, *CA274-250*
FRESNO STATE COLLEGE, *CA274-120*
FRIARS OF THE ATONEMENT, *NY318-260*
FRICK ART REFERENCE LIBRARY, *NY589-680*
FRIENDS FREE LIBRARY OF GERMANTOWN, *PA725-540*
FRIENDS HISTORICAL LIBRARY, *PA860-710, PA860-730*
FRIENDS HOSPITAL, WEINER PROFESSIONAL LIBRARY, ARCHIVES, *PA725-525*
FRIENDS UNITED MEETING, WIDER MINISTRIES COMMISSION ARCHIVES, *IN704-240*
FRIENDS UNIVERSITY, LIBRARY, QUAKER COLLECTION, *KS948-240*
FRIENDSHIP FREE LIBRARY, *NY313-240*
FRIENDSHIP LIBRARY, *NJ464-240*
FRISELL, HOLLIS BURKE, LIBRARY, *AL820-765*
FRITZ, CHESTER, LIBRARY, DEPARTMENT OF SPECIAL COLLECTIONS (FORMERLY ORIN G. LIBBY MSS. COLL.), *ND486-800*
FRONTENAC HISTORICAL SOCIETY, *NY895-240*
FROST, ROBERT, LIBRARY, ARCHIVES AND SPECIAL COLLECTIONS, *MA21-40*
FRUITLANDS MUSEUMS, *MA383-240*
FULLERTON COLLEGE, WILLIAM T. BOYCE LIBRARY, *CA278-240*
FULTON COUNTY (IN) HISTORICAL SOCIETY, *IN726-240*
FULTON COUNTY HISTORICAL AND GENEALOGICAL SOCIETY, *IL119-240*
FULTON COUNTY HISTORICAL SOCIETY, *PA540-240*
FULTON COUNTY MUSEUM, *NY334-240*
FURMAN UNIVERSITY, LIBRARY, SPECIAL COLLECTIONS, *SC450-240*

G

G. W. BLUNT WHITE LIBRARY, *CT463-520*
GAAR, JULIA MEEK, WAYNE COUNTY HISTORICAL MUSEUM, *IN704-880*
GABRIEL D. HACKETT, PHOTOGRAPHY AND PICTURE ARCHIVES, *NY589-690*
GAINESVILLE PUBLIC LIBRARY, REFERENCE DEPARTMENT, *FL220-280*

GALEN FREE LIBRARY, *NY198-280*
GALENA HISTORICAL MUSEUM, *IL301-280*
GALESBURG PUBLIC LIBRARY, SPECIAL COLLECTIONS, *IL305-280*
GALLATIN COUNTY PUBLIC LIBRARY, *KY85G-290*
GALLAUDET COLLEGE, EDWARD MINER GALLAUDET MEMORIAL LIBRARY, ARCHIVES, *DC7-100*
GALLAUDET, EDWARD MINER, MEMORIAL LIBRARY, ARCHIVES, *DC7-100*
GALLERIES OF THE CLAREMONT COLLEGES, CLAREMONT UNIVERSITY CENTER COLLECTIONS (PHOTOGRAPHY), *CA143-280*
GANSER LIBRARY, ARCHIVES AND SPECIAL COLLECTIONS, *PA595-530*
GAR MEMORIAL HALL, LIBRARY, *PA726-508*
GARDEN GROVE HISTORICAL SOCIETY, STANLEY HOUSE MUSEUM, *CA282-280*
GARDNER RARE BOOK ROOM, *MO810-690*
GARDNER-WEBB COLLEGE, DOVER LIBRARY, SPECIAL COLLECTIONS, *NC100-280*
GARDNER, ISABELLA STEWART, MUSEUM, *MA108-940*
GARFIELD COUNTY HISTORICAL ASSOCIATION, MUSEUM, *WA672-290*
GARFIELD COUNTY PUBLIC LIBRARY, *CO730-280*
GARLAND COUNTY HISTORICAL SOCIETY, *AR390-280*
GARLAND, HAMLIN, HOMESTEAD, *WI853-880*
GARRARD COUNTY PUBLIC LIBRARY, *KY41M-280*
GARRETT BIBLICAL INSTITUTE, *IL261-280*
GARRETT-EVANGELICAL THEOLOGICAL SEMINARY, LIBRARY, *IL261-280*
GARRETT, JOHN WORK, LIBRARY, *MD76-340*
GARY MEMORIAL LIBRARY, *VT464-560*
GEAUGA COUNTY HISTORICAL SOCIETY, *OH112-280*
GEAUGA COUNTY PUBLIC LIBRARY, *OH161-240*
GEE, JAMES G., ORAL HISTORY PROGRAM, *TX210-200*
GEM VILLAGE MUSEUM, *CO90-280*
GENEALOGICAL SOCIETY, CHURCH OF JESUS CHRIST OF LATTER-DAY SAINTS, *UT912-110*
GENERAL ADAM STEPHEN MEMORIAL ASSOCIATION, *WV600-280*
GENERAL ELECTRIC COMPANY, MAIN LIBRARY, *NY804-280*
GENERAL FEDERATION OF WOMEN'S CLUBS, ARCHIVES, *DC7-300*
GENERAL JAMES CLINTON FREE LIBRARY, *NY262-280*
GENERAL MOTORS INSTITUTE, ALUMNI FOUNDATION'S COLLECTION OF INDUSTRIAL HISTORY, *MI314-265*
GENERAL THEOLOGICAL SEMINARY, ST. MARK'S LIBRARY, *NY589-710*
GENESEE COUNTY DEPARTMENT OF HISTORY, LIBRARY, *NY69-280*
GENESEE PUBLIC LIBRARY, *NY494-280*
GENEVA HISTORICAL SOCIETY, ARCHIVES, *NY323-280*
GEOLOGICAL SURVEY OF ALABAMA, LIBRARY, *AL840-280*
GEOLOGICAL SURVEY, EARTH RESOURCES OBSERVATION SYSTEMS DATA CENTER, *SD684-280*
GEOLOGICAL SURVEY, ILLINOIS STATE, *IL916-360*
GEORGE ARENTS RESEARCH LIBRARY, MANUSCRIPT COLLECTIONS, *NY872-800*
GEORGE ARENTS RESEARCH LIBRARY, SYRACUSE UNIVERSITY ARCHIVES, *NY872-810*
GEORGE C. MARSHALL RESEARCH LIBRARY, *VA430-280*
GEORGE C. RUHLE LIBRARY, *MT870-280*
GEORGE E. ALLEN LIBRARY, *MS140-560*
GEORGE F. JOHNSON MEMORIAL LIBRARY, *NY273-280*
GEORGE H. AND LAURA E. BROWN LIBRARY, *NC850-120*
GEORGE M. SMILEY MEMORIAL LIBRARY, METHODIST COLLECTION, *MO290-120*
GEORGE MASON UNIVERSITY, RESEARCH CENTER FOR THE FEDERAL THEATER PROJECT, *VA205-290*
GEORGE P. AND SUSAN PLATT CADY LIBRARY, *NY605-280*
GEORGE PEABODY LIBRARY, *MD76-333*
GEORGE SVERDRUP LIBRARY, ARCHIVES, *MN541-80*
GEORGE W. STEVENS COLLECTION, *OH823-770*
GEORGE WASHINGTON CARVER NATIONAL MONUMENT, *MO240-280*
GEORGE WASHINGTON UNIVERSITY, DIMOCK GALLERY, *DC7-510*
GEORGE WASHINGTON UNIVERSITY, LIBRARY, SPECIAL COLLECTIONS DIVISION, *DC7-540*
GEORGE WILLIAMS COLLEGE, LIBRARY, *IL212-280*
GEORGETOWN COLLEGE, COOKE MEMORIAL LIBRARY, SPECIAL COLLECTIONS, *KY304-280*
GEORGETOWN SOCIETY, *CO414-280*
GEORGETOWN UNIVERSITY, ARCHIVES, *DC7-650*
GEORGETOWN UNIVERSITY, LIBRARY, SPECIAL COLLECTIONS DIVISION, *DC7-650*
GEORGETOWN UNIVERSITY, MEDICAL CENTER, JOHN VINTON DAHLGREN LIBRARY, ALEXIS CARREL COLLECTION, *DC7-660*
GEORGIA AGRIRAMA DEVELOPMENT AUTHORITY, STATE MUSEUM OF AGRICULTURE, *GA940-280*
GEORGIA BAPTIST HISTORICAL COLLECTION, *GA735-520*

GEORGIA COLLEGE, LIBRARY, FLANNERY O'CONNOR COLLECTION, *GA780-270*

GEORGIA COLLEGE, LIBRARY, SPECIAL COLLECTIONS, *GA780-290*

GEORGIA COLLEGE, MUSEUM AND ARCHIVES OF GEORGIA EDUCATION, *GA780-310*

GEORGIA DEPARTMENT OF ARCHIVES AND HISTORY, *GA90-260*

GEORGIA DEPARTMENT OF NATURAL RESOURCES, PARKS, RECREATION, AND HIST. SITES DIV., HIST. PRES. SEC., *GA90-265*

GEORGIA DEPARTMENT OF STATE, SURVEYOR GENERAL DEPARTMENT, *GA90-270*

GEORGIA HISTORICAL SOCIETY, *GA895-280*

GEORGIA INSTITUTE OF TECHNOLOGY, LIBRARY, *GA90-280*

GEORGIA SALZBURGER SOCIETY MUSEUM, *GA860-280*

GEORGIA SOUTHERN COLLEGE, LIBRARY, *GA915-280*

GEORGIA STATE ARCHIVES, *GA90-260*

GEORGIA STATE UNIVERSITY, SOUTHERN LABOR ARCHIVES, *GA90-300*

GEORGIAN COURT COLLEGE, FARLEY MEMORIAL LIBRARY, *NJ408-280*

GERALD R. FORD LIBRARY, *MI40-300*

GERMAN SOCIETY OF PENNSYLVANIA, JOSEPH HORNER LIBRARY, *PA725-585*

GERMANS FROM RUSSIA IN COLORADO STUDY PROJECT, *CO378-110*

GERMANTOWN HISTORICAL SOCIETY, LIBRARY, *PA725-600*

GERMANTOWN MENNONITE CHURCH CORPORATION, ARCHIVES, *PA725-608*

GERONIMO SPRINGS MUSEUM, *NM912-280*

GETTYSBURG COLLEGE, MUSSELMAN LIBRARY/LEARNING RESOURCES CENTER, *PA325-280*

GIBBES ART GALLERY, *SC144-90*

GIFFORD PINCHOT NATIONAL FOREST, *WA943-280*

GILA NATIONAL FOREST, *NM760-280*

GILBERTSVILLE FREE LIBRARY, HISTORICAL SECTION, *NY326-280*

GILES COUNTY HISTORICAL SOCIETY, *TN765-280*

GILLESPIE COUNTY HISTORICAL SOCIETY AND COMMISSION, VEREINS KIRCHE ARCHIVES AND LOCAL HISTORY COLL.*TX381-280*

GIRARD COLLEGE, STEPHEN GIRARD PAPERS, *PA725-615*

GIRARD, STEPHEN, COLLECTION, *PA725-615*

GIRL SCOUTS OF THE U.S.A., *NY589-720*

GIRL SCOUTS OF THE U.S.A., JULIETTE GORDON LOW GIRL SCOUT NATIONAL CENTER, *GA895-290*

GLACIER NATIONAL PARK, GEORGE C. RUHLE LIBRARY, *MT870-280*

GLASS PACKAGING INSTITUTE, *VA500-322*

GLASSBORO STATE COLLEGE, SAVITZ LIBRARY, STEWART ROOM, *NJ280-270*

GLEBE HOUSE, *CT982-280*

GLEESON, RICHARD A., LIBRARY, SPECIAL COLLECTIONS DEPARTMENT, *CA720-910*

GLENDALE PUBLIC LIBRARIES, SPECIAL COLLECTIONS, *CA290-280*

GLENN G. BARTLE LIBRARY, SPECIAL COLLECTIONS, *NY101-720*

GLENN H. CURTISS MUSEUM OF LOCAL HISTORY, *NY367-270*

GLENS FALLS-QUEENSBURY HISTORICAL ASSOCIATION, CHAPMAN HISTORICAL MUSEUM, *NY331-280*

GLENVIEW AREA HISTORICAL SOCIETY, *IL325-270*

GLENVIEW PUBLIC LIBRARY, *IL325-290*

GLOUCESTER COUNTY HISTORICAL SOCIETY, LIBRARY, *NJ982-280*

GLOUCESTER LYCEUM & SAWYER FREE LIBRARY, AUDIO-VISUAL DEPARTMENT, *MA338-280*

GLOVER LIBRARY, MISSIONARY BAPTIST ARCHIVES, *AR510-520*

GLOVERSVILLE FREE LIBRARY, *NY334-280*

GODDARD LIBRARY, DEPARTMENT OF RARE BOOKS AND SPECIAL COLLECTIONS, *MA985-110*

GOLDEN BALL TAVERN TRUST, *MA937-280*

GOLDEN LIBRARY, SPECIAL COLLECTIONS AND ARCHIVES, *NM668-210*

GOLDFARB LIBRARY, SPECIAL COLLECTIONS, *MA871-90*

GOLDSTEIN LIBRARY, *CA86-385*

GONZAGA UNIVERSITY, CROSBY LIBRARY, OREGON PROVINCE ARCHIVES OF THE SOCIETY OF JESUS, *WA880-280*

GONZAGA UNIVERSITY, CROSBY LIBRARY, RARE BOOK AND MANUSCRIPT COLLECTION, *WA880-290*

GONZALES HISTORICAL MUSEUM, *TX425-280*

GOOD, LEROY V., LIBRARY, *NY752-525*

GOODLETT, CAROLINE MERIWETHER, LIBRARY, *VA690-760*

GOODNOW PUBLIC LIBRARY, *MA788-280*

GOODSPEED MEMORIAL LIBRARY, *ME937-870*

GOODWIN LIBRARY, *NH266-280*

GOODYEAR TIRE AND RUBBER COMPANY, *OH11-290*

GORDON COUNTY HISTORICAL SOCIETY, *GA180-280*

GORDON-NASH LIBRARY, *NH688-280*

GORE PLACE SOCIETY, *MA871-280*

GOSCHENHOPPEN HISTORIANS, INC., FOLK LIFE LIBRARY AND MUSEUM, *PA345-280*

GOSHEN HISTORICAL SOCIETY, *CT261-280*

GOSHEN LIBRARY AND HISTORICAL SOCIETY, *NY340-280*

GOVERNOR A. J. SEAY MANSION, *OK456-120*

GOVERNORS STATE UNIVERSITY, LIBRARY, *IL703-300*

GRACE THEOLOGICAL SEMINARY, LIBRARY, *IN990-280*

GRACELAND COLLEGE, FREDERICK MADISON SMITH LIBRARY, RESTORATION HISTORY MANUSCRIPT COLLECTION, *IA533-280*

GRADUATE THEOLOGICAL UNION, LIBRARY, *CA86-280*

GRAFTON HISTORICAL SOCIETY, *VT312-280*

GRAHAM COUNTY HISTORICAL SOCIETY, *KS385-280*

GRAHAM HISTORICAL SOCIETY, *MO350-280*

GRAHAM, BILLY, CENTER, ARCHIVES, *IL976-850*

GRAN QUIVIRA NATIONAL MONUMENT, LIBRARY, *NM646-280*

GRAND ARMY MEMORIAL, *MA108-10*

GRAND ARMY OF THE REPUBLIC MEMORIAL HALL MUSEUM, *WI346-280*

GRAND CANYON NATIONAL PARK, STUDY COLLECTION, *AZ350-290*

GRAND ENCAMPMENT MUSEUM, *WY245-280*

GRAND RAPIDS PUBLIC LIBRARY, MICHIGAN ROOM, *MI355-270*

GRAND RAPIDS PUBLIC MUSEUM, PICTORIAL MATERIALS COLLECTION, *MI355-290*

GRAND TETON NATIONAL PARK, *WY560-280*

GRAND VALLEY STATE COLLEGE, ZUMBERGE LIBRARY, ARCHIVES, *MI28-280*

GRAND VIEW COLLEGE, LIBRARY, ARCHIVES COLLECTION, *IA233-280*

GRAND, R. W., LODGE (PENNSYLVANIA FREE AND ACCEPTED MASONS), *PA726-057*

GRANDVILLE HISTORICAL ASSOCIATION AND MUSEUM, *MI360-280*

GRANGER COLLECTION, *NY589-800*

GRANGER HOMESTEAD SOCIETY, *NY147-280*

GRANGER LIBRARY, *WA367-280*

GRANITE CITY PUBLIC LIBRARY, *IL340-280*

GRANITE FALLS HISTORICAL SOCIETY, *WA368-280*

GRANT COUNTY HISTORICAL MUSEUM, *WA290-285*

GRANT COUNTY HISTORICAL SOCIETY, GRANT COUNTY MUSEUM, *KS892-280, OK524-280*

GRANT COUNTY MUSEUM, *KS892-280, OK524-280*

GRANT HOUSE MUSEUM, *WA943-333*

GRAPEVINE PUBLIC LIBRARY, *TX439-280*

GRAPHIC SKETCH CLUB, *PA725-660*

GRASSELLI LIBRARY, *OH843-400*

GRAVES COUNTY PUBLIC LIBRARY, *KY520-280*

GRAY HERBARIUM, *MA169-310*

GRAYSON COUNTY PUBLIC LIBRARY, *KY430-280*

GREAT LAKES HISTORICAL SOCIETY, CLARENCE METCALF RESEARCH LIBRARY, *OH863-280*

GREAT PLAINS, MUSEUM OF THE, LIBRARY AND ARCHIVES, *OK490-520*

GREAT SMOKY MOUNTAINS NATIONAL PARK, *TN285-280*

GREATER DES MOINES-ZENITH HISTORICAL SOCIETY, *WA246-170*

GREATER MAPLE VALLEY HISTORICAL SOCIETY, *WA520-280*

GREATER MIAMI VALLEY RESEARCH CENTER, *OH223-880*

GREATER PORTLAND LANDMARKS, RESOURCE LIBRARY, *ME712-280*

GREATER WOODINVILLE HISTORICAL MUSEUM FOUNDATION, *WA990-280*

GREECE TOWN HISTORIAN, *NY752-250*

GREEN COUNTY PUBLIC LIBRARY, *KY316-280*

GREEN MOUNTAIN NATIONAL FOREST, *VT704-280*

GREEN TREE (MUTUAL ASSURANCE COMPANY), *PA725-990*

GREEN, FRANCIS HARVEY, LIBRARY, *PA945-880*

GREENBELT BRANCH LIBRARY, REXFORD G. TUGWELL ROOM, *MD513-640*

GREENBRIER HISTORICAL SOCIETY, *WV550-280*

GREENE COUNTY DISTRICT LIBRARY, GREENE COUNTY ROOM, LOCAL HISTORY DEPARTMENT, *OH982-280*

GREENE COUNTY HISTORICAL SOCIETY, *PA940-280*

GREENE COUNTY HISTORICAL SOCIETY, VEDDER MEMORIAL LIBRARY, *NY219-290*

GREENE COUNTY LIBRARY SYSTEM, EVA K. BOWLBY PUBLIC LIBRARY, ORAL HISTORY COLLECTION, *PA940-300*

GREENE, CORDELIA A., LIBRARY, *NY156-140*

GREENFIELD COMMUNITY COLLEGE, ARCHIBALD MACLEISH COLLECTION, *MA352-270*

GREENFIELD PUBLIC LIBRARY, *IN286-280*

GREENFIELD VILLAGE AND HENRY FORD MUSEUM, FORD ARCHIVES, *MI214-260*

GREENFIELD VILLAGE AND HENRY FORD MUSEUM, ROBERT HUDSON TANNAHILL RESEARCH LIBRARY, *MI214-280*

GREENSBORO PUBLIC LIBRARY, CALDWELL-JONES COLLECTION, *NC380-280*

GREENWICH LIBRARY, ORAL HISTORY COLLECTION, *CT275-280*

GREYTON H. TAYLOR WINE MUSEUM, *NY367-290*

GRINNELL COLLEGE, BURLING LIBRARY, *IA377-280*

GROLIER CLUB, LIBRARY, *NY589-840*
GROPIUS ARCHIVES AND FEININGER ARCHIVES, *MA169-200*
GROSSMAN, JACOB AND ROSE, LIBRARY, *MA154-310*
GROTON HISTORICAL ASSOCIATION, *NY358-760*
GROTON PUBLIC LIBRARY, *NY358-280*
GROUT MUSEUM OF HISTORY AND SCIENCE, *IA922-280*
GRUMMAN CORPORATION, HISTORY CENTER, *NY95-280*
GUERNSEY MEMORIAL LIBRARY, *NY618-280*
GUILFORD COLLEGE, LIBRARY, QUAKER COLLECTION, *NC380-290*
GUILFORD FREE LIBRARY, *CT288-280*
GUILFORD KEEPING SOCIETY, *CT288-280*
GUILFORD TOWNSHIP HISTORICAL COLLECTION, *IN660-640*
GUNDRY HOUSE, *WI462-520*
GUNLOCKE MEMORIAL LIBRARY, *NY936-280*
GUNN MEMORIAL LIBRARY, HISTORICAL MUSEUM, *CT863-280*
GUNPOWDER FALLS STATE PARK, *MD475-280*
GUSTAVUS ADOLPHUS COLLEGE, COLLEGE AND MINNESOTA
  SYNOD OF LUTHERAN CHURCH IN AMERICA ARCHIVES,
  MN769-280
GUY H. BURNHAM MAP AND AERIAL PHOTOGRAPH LIBRARY,
  MA985-120
GUY W. BAILEY LIBRARY, WILBUR SPECIAL COLLECTIONS,
  VT176-810

H

H. A. ANDRUSS LIBRARY, COLLEGE ARCHIVES, *PA100-80*
H. H. BENNETT STUDIO, *WI890-320*
H. V. MANNING LIBRARY, *SC720-120*
HAAS LIBRARY, *PA25-520*
HAAS, RUTH A., LIBRARY, ARCHIVES, *CT144-880*
HACKETT, GABRIEL D., PHOTOGRAPHY AND PICTURE
  ARCHIVES, *NY589-690*
HACKETTSTOWN HISTORICAL SOCIETY, MUSEUM, *NJ308-320*
HACKLEY PUBLIC LIBRARY, *MI675-320*
HADASSAH MEDICAL RELIEF ASSOCIATION, HADASSAH
  WOMEN'S ZIONIST ORGANIZATION OF AMERICA AND,
  NY589-900
HADASSAH WOMEN'S ZIONIST ORGANIZATION OF AMERICA
  AND HADASSAH MEDICAL RELIEF ASSOCIATION, *NY589-900*
HADDON HEIGHTS PUBLIC LIBRARY, *NJ312-320*
HADDONFIELD HISTORICAL SOCIETY, *NJ316-330*
HADDONFIELD PUBLIC LIBRARY, *NJ316-310*
HAFFENREFFER MUSEUM OF ANTHROPOLOGY, *RI105-320*
HAGAN MEMORIAL LIBRARY, *KY876-320*
HAGAN, HELEN, RARE BOOK ROOM, *NC900-810*
HAGLEY MUSEUM AND LIBRARY, *DE270-200*
HAHNEMANN UNIVERSITY, ARCHIVES AND HISTORY OF
  MEDICINE COLLECTIONS (FORMERLY WARREN H. FAKE LIB.),
  PA725-690
HALIFAX HISTORICAL SOCIETY, *FL120-330*
HALL COUNTY HISTORICAL SOCIETY, *NE416-320*
HALL OF FAME OF THE TROTTER, *NY340-320*
HAMBURGER, FERDINAND, JR., ARCHIVES, *MD76-325*
HAMILTON COLLEGE, BURKE LIBRARY, *NY197-310*
HAMILTON LIBRARY ASSOCIATION, *PA160-120*
HAMLIN GARLAND HOMESTEAD, *WI853-880*
HAMLIN TOWN HISTORIAN'S OFFICE, *NY365-340*
HAMLINE UNIVERSITY, BUSH MEMORIAL LIBRARY, ARCHIVES,
  MN763-310
HAMMARSKJOLD, DAG, LIBRARY, MAP COLLECTION, *NY595-40*
HAMMERSTEIN, ROGERS AND, ARCHIVES OF RECORDED SOUND,
  NY592-878
HAMMOND LIBRARY, *IL169-507*
HAMMOND PUBLIC LIBRARY, CALUMET ROOM COLLECTION,
  IN308-330
HAMMONDSPORT PUBLIC LIBRARY, *NY367-320*
HAMPDEN-BOOTH THEATRE LIBRARY, *NY593-485*
HAMPDEN-SYDNEY COLLEGE, EGGLESTON LIBRARY, SPECIAL
  COLLECTIONS, *VA310-320*
HAMPDEN, WALTER-EDWIN BOOTH THEATRE COLLECTION AND
  LIBRARY, *NY593-485*
HAMPTON CENTER FOR THE ARTS AND HUMANITIES, *VA315-310*
HAMPTON HISTORICAL SOCIETY, MEETING HOUSE GREEN
  MEMORIAL AND HISTORICAL ASSN., TUCK MEMORIAL MUS.,
  NH368-320
HANCOCK COUNTY HISTORICAL SOCIETY, *IL139-320*
HANCOCK SHAKER VILLAGE, *MA677-720*
HANDLEY LIBRARY, *VA880-320*
HANFORD MILLS MUSEUM, *NY261-320*
HANOVER AREA HISTORICAL SOCIETY, *PA370-310*
HANOVER COLLEGE, DUGGAN LIBRARY, *IN319-330*
HANOVER COUNTY HISTORICAL SOCIETY MUSEUM, *VA330-320*
HANOVER PUBLIC LIBRARY, *PA370-330*
HARDIN SIMMONS UNIVERSITY, RICHARDSON LIBRARY,
  RICHARDSON RESEARCH CENTER, *TX7-320*

HARDYSTON HERITAGE SOCIETY, OLD MONROE SCHOOLHOUSE
  MUSEUM, *NJ318-320*
HARFORD COMMUNITY COLLEGE, LEARNING RESOURCES
  CENTER, LIBRARY SERVICES DIVISION, *MD114-310*
HARFORD COUNTY HISTORICAL SOCIETY, *MD114-330*
HARLINGEN PUBLIC LIBRARY, *TX446-320*
HARNEY COUNTY LIBRARY, *OR112-335*
HAROLD ANDERSEN LIBRARY, *WI858-810*
HAROLD B. LEE LIBRARY, ARCHIVES AND MANUSCRIPTS,
  UT684-80
HAROLD D. STRUNK LEARNING RESOURCE CENTER, *KY78J-760*
HAROLD S. COLTON MEMORIAL LIBRARY, MUSEUM ARCHIVES
  AND MANUSCRIPTS COLLECTION, *AZ250-520*
HAROLD TERRY CLARK LIBRARY, *OH181-240*
HARRAH PUBLIC LIBRARY, *WA380-320*
HARRINGTON PUBLIC LIBRARY, *WA381-330*
HARRIS COUNTY HERITAGE SOCIETY, *TX483-280*
HARRIS TEACHERS COLLEGE/STOWE TEACHERS COLLEGE
  ARCHIVES, *MO810-330*
HARRIS-STOWE STATE COLLEGE, LIBRARY, HARRIS TEACHERS
  COLLEGE/STOWE TEACHERS COLLEGE ARCHIVES, *MO810-330*
HARRISON COUNTY HISTORICAL SOCIETY, *WV250-320*
HARRISON COUNTY HISTORICAL VILLAGE, *IA600-322*
HARRISON MEMORIAL PUBLIC LIBRARY, *CA122-320*
HARRISON, PRESIDENT BENJAMIN, MEMORIAL HOME, *IN363-660*
HARRISONBURG-ROCKINGHAM HISTORICAL SOCIETY, *VA350-320*
HARRODSBURG HISTORICAL SOCIETY, LIBRARY, *KY352-320*
HARRY M. TROWBRIDGE RESEARCH LIBRARY, *KS136-880*
HARRY S. TRUMAN LIBRARY, *MO400-320*
HART, FRANCIS RUSSELL, NAUTICAL COLLECTIONS, *MA169-610*
HART, STEPHEN H., LIBRARY, *CO252-100*
HARTFORD MEDICAL SOCIETY, LIBRARY, *CT316-310*
HARTFORD PUBLIC LIBRARY, HARTFORD COLLECTION,
  CT316-320
HARTFORD SEMINARY FOUNDATION, CASE MEMORIAL
  LIBRARY, ARCHIVES, *CT316-330*
HARTT COLLEGE OF MUSIC, LIBRARY, *CT891-820*
HARTWICK COLLEGE, ARCHIVES, *NY648-310*
HARTWICK HISTORICAL SOCIETY, *NY373-320*
HARTWICK PINES STATE PARK, INTERPRETIVE CENTER AND
  LOGGING CAMP MUSEUM, *MI368-320*
HARVARD COLLEGE LIBRARY, FINE ARTS LIBRARY, *MA169-340*
HARVARD COLLEGE LIBRARY, HOUGHTON LIBRARY,
  MANUSCRIPT DEPARTMENT, *MA169-370*
HARVARD UNIVERSITY, ARCHIVES, *MA169-170*
HARVARD UNIVERSITY, ARNOLD ARBORETUM, *MA169-190*
HARVARD UNIVERSITY, BUSCH-REISINGER MUSEUM, GROPIUS
  ARCHIVES AND FEININGER ARCHIVES, *MA169-200*
HARVARD UNIVERSITY, CARPENTER CENTER FOR THE VISUAL
  ARTS, *MA169-210*
HARVARD UNIVERSITY, DIVINITY SCHOOL,
  ANDOVER-HARVARD THEOLOGICAL LIBRARY, MANUSCRIPT
  DEPARTMENT, *MA169-230*
HARVARD UNIVERSITY, FARLOW REFERENCE LIBRARY,
  MA169-270
HARVARD UNIVERSITY, FOGG ART MUSEUM, ARCHIVES
  DEPARTMENT, *MA169-300*
HARVARD UNIVERSITY, FRANCIS A. COUNTWAY LIBRARY OF
  MEDICINE, *MA108-770*
HARVARD UNIVERSITY, GRADUATE SCHOOL OF BUS. ADMIN.,
  BAKER LIBRARY, MSS. AND ARCHIVES DEPT., *MA108-750*
HARVARD UNIVERSITY, GRADUATE SCHOOL OF DESIGN,
  FRANCES LOEB LIBRARY, *MA169-305*
HARVARD UNIVERSITY, GRAY HERBARIUM, *MA169-310*
HARVARD UNIVERSITY, HARVARD COLLEGE LIBRARY, FINE
  ARTS LIBRARY, *MA169-340*
HARVARD UNIVERSITY, HARVARD COLLEGE LIBRARY,
  HOUGHTON LIBRARY, MANUSCRIPT DEPARTMENT, *MA169-370*
HARVARD UNIVERSITY, HARVARD-YENCHING LIBRARY,
  MA169-400
HARVARD UNIVERSITY, INDUSTRIAL RELATIONS LIBRARY,
  MA169-460
HARVARD UNIVERSITY, LAW SCHOOL, MANUSCRIPT DIVISION,
  MA169-440
HARVARD UNIVERSITY, LITTAUER CENTER OF PUBLIC
  ADMINISTRATION, LIBRARY, *MA169-460*
HARVARD UNIVERSITY, LITTAUER CENTER, MANPOWER AND
  INDUSTRIAL RELATIONS LIBRARY, *MA169-460*
HARVARD UNIVERSITY, MUSEUM OF COMPARATIVE ZOOLOGY,
  MA169-500
HARVARD UNIVERSITY, PEABODY MUSEUM, TOZZER LIBRARY,
  MA169-530
HARVARD-YENCHING LIBRARY, *MA169-400*
HARVEY HELM MEMORIAL HISTORICAL LIBRARY AND
  MUSEUM, *KY79F-320*
HARWELL G. DAVIS LIBRARY, *AL120-720*
HASBROUCK, JEAN, MEMORIAL HOUSE, *NY574-320*

HASTINGS HISTORICAL SOCIETY, *NY376-320*
HASTINGS MUSEUM, *NE496-330*
HAVERFORD COLLEGE, JAMES P. MAGILL LIBRARY, TREASURE ROOM, *PA395-320*
HAVERHILL HISTORICAL SOCIETY, *MA394-330*
HAVERHILL PUBLIC LIBRARY, *MA394-330*
HAVILAND RECORDS ROOM, *NY593-710*
HAWAII CHINESE HISTORY CENTER, *HI350-295*
HAWAII DEPARTMENT OF ACCOUNTING AND GENERAL SERVICES, ARCHIVES DIVISION, *HI350-300*
HAWAII STATE ARCHIVES, *HI350-300*
HAWAII STATE LIBRARY, HAWAII AND PACIFIC SECTION, HAWAII DOCUMENTS CENTER, *HI350-311*
HAWAIIAN HISTORICAL SOCIETY, LIBRARY, *HI350-315*
HAWAIIAN MISSION CHILDREN'S SOCIETY LIBRARY, *HI350-320*
HAWKS INN HISTORICAL SOCIETY, *WI134-320*
HAWLEY, ROSE, MUSEUM-ARCHIVES, *MI585-520*
HAY, JOHN, LIBRARY, *RI700-100*
HAYES, CARDINAL, LIBRARY, *NY591-100*
HAYES, RUTHERFORD B., LIBRARY, *OH301-690*
HAYWARD AREA HISTORICAL SOCIETY, *CA314-320*
HAYWOOD COUNTY PUBLIC LIBRARY, *NC860-320*
HAZEN MEMORIAL LIBRARY, *MA761-320*
HEARST, PHOEBE APPERSON, FREE LIBRARY, *SD414-640*
HEARTMAN NEGRO COLLECTION, *TX483-820*
HEBREW COLLEGE, JACOB AND ROSE GROSSMAN LIBRARY, *MA154-310*
HEBREW UNION COLLEGE-JEWISH INSTITUTE OF RELIGION, KLAU LIBRARY, *OH171-320*
HEBREW UNION COLLEGE, SKIRBALL MUSEUM, *CA421-250*
HEDRICH-BLESSING (PHOTOGRAPH REPOSITORY), *IL169-826*
HEIDELBERG COLLEGE, ARCHIVES, *OH813-310*
HEIDRICH, HERMAN J., LIBRARY AND ST. BERNARD ABBEY, *AL130-333*
HELEN CROCKER RUSSELL LIBRARY, *CA720-798*
HELEN HAGAN RARE BOOK ROOM, *NC900-810*
HELEN KELLER ARCHIVES, *NY586-440*
HELM, HARVEY, MEMORIAL HISTORICAL LIBRARY AND MUSEUM, *KY79F-320*
HEMPSTEAD PUBLIC LIBRARY, *NY382-310*
HENDERSON MEMORIAL PUBLIC LIBRARY, *OH394-320*
HENDRICK HUDSON CHAPTER HOUSE, *NY416-320*
HENDRIX COLLEGE, OLIN C. BAILEY LIBRARY, *AR240-320*
HENNEPIN COUNTY HISTORICAL SOCIETY, *MN541-320*
HENRY A. MURRAY RESEARCH CENTER, *MA169-885*
HENRY CHARLES LEA LIBRARY OF MEDIEVAL HISTORY, *PA726-770*
HENRY COUNTY HISTORICAL MUSEUM, *IN572-320*
HENRY COUNTY HISTORICAL SOCIETY, *KY230-320*
HENRY COUNTY LIBRARY AND HENRY COUNTY HISTORICAL SOCIETY, *KY230-320*
HENRY F. MOELLERING MEMORIAL LIBRARY, *IN858-850*
HENRY FORD CENTENNIAL LIBRARY, AUDIO-VISUAL DIVISION, *MI214-140*
HENRY FORD MUSEUM AND GREENFIELD VILLAGE, FORD ARCHIVES, *MI214-260*
HENRY FORD MUSEUM AND GREENFIELD VILLAGE, ROBERT HUDSON TANNAHILL RESEARCH LIBRARY, *MI214-280*
HENRY FRANCIS DU PONT WINTERTHUR MUSEUM, JOSEPH DOWNS MANUSCRIPT AND MICROFILM COLLECTION, *DE900-320*
HENRY FRANCIS DU PONT WINTERTHUR MUSEUM, WINTERTHUR ARCHIVES, *DE900-330*
HENRY MADDEN LIBRARY, DEPARTMENT OF SPECIAL COLLECTIONS, *CA274-120*
HENRY MORRISON FLAGLER MUSEUM, *FL580-320*
HENRY N. FLYNT LIBRARY OF HISTORIC DEERFIELD, *MA238-520*
HENRY PFEIFFER LIBRARY, *IL394-500*
HENRY T. SAMPSON LIBRARY, SPECIAL COLLECTIONS, *MS550-410*
HERBERT H. LAMSON LIBRARY, *NH772-640*
HERBERT H. LEHMAN PAPERS, *NY588-850*
HERBERT HOOVER LIBRARY, *IA966-320*
HERITAGE SOCIETY OF OIL CITY, *PA705-320*
HERITAGE SOCIETY OF THE MID-COLUMBIA, *WA966-320*
HERKIMER COUNTY HISTORICAL SOCIETY, *NY385-320*
HERKIMER HOME STATE HISTORIC SITE, *NY493-320*
HERMAN J. HEIDRICH LIBRARY AND ST. BERNARD ABBEY, *AL130-333*
HERMITAGE, THE, *TN345-480*
HERRICK LIBRARY, *NY18-40*
HERRICK MEMORIAL PUBLIC LIBRARY, *OH906-320*
HERRICK PUBLIC LIBRARY, *MI445-310*
HERRICK, MARGARET, LIBRARY, *CA90-30*
HERSKOVITS, MELVILLE J., LIBRARY OF AFRICAN STUDIES, *IL261-566*
HESTON, ALFRED M., COLLECTION, *NJ20-40*

HEYE FOUNDATION, HUNTINGTON FREE LIBRARY AND READING ROOM, *NY591-820*
HIBBING HISTORICAL SOCIETY, FIRST SETTLERS ASSOCIATION, FIRST SETTLERS MUSEUM, *MN391-310*
HICKMAN COUNTY PUBLIC LIBRARY, *KY17S-320*
HIEBERT LIBRARY, *CA274-130*
HIGH PLAINS HISTORICAL FOUNDATION, *NM304-320*
HIGH POINT COLLEGE, LIBRARY, *NC420-310*
HIGHLAND PARK HISTORICAL SOCIETY, *IL374-310*
HIGHLINE HISTORICAL SOCIETY, *WA97-320*
HILL JUNIOR COLLEGE, HISTORY COMPLEX, CONFEDERATE RESEARCH CENTER, *TX476-320*
HILL MEMORIAL LIBRARY, *LA62-500*
HILL MONASTIC MANUSCRIPT LIBRARY, *MN226-720*
HILL, JAMES JEROME, REFERENCE LIBRARY, *MN763-400*
HILL, LISTER, LIBRARY OF THE HEALTH SCIENCES, ALABAMA HEALTH SCIENCES COLLECTION, *AL120-810*
HILL, LISTER, LIBRARY OF THE HEALTH SCIENCES, REYNOLDS HISTORICAL LIBRARY, *AL120-815*
HILLSDALE COLLEGE, MOSSEY LEARNING RESOURCES CENTER, *MI440-320*
HILTON M. BRIGGS LIBRARY, ARCHIVES, *SD54-715*
HILTON VILLAGE HISTORIAN, *NY393-320*
HINGHAM BICENTENNIAL COLLECTION, *MA398-330*
HINGHAM PUBLIC LIBRARY, HINGHAM BICENTENNIAL COLLECTION, *MA398-330*
HINKLE, WALTER C., MEMORIAL LIBRARY, COLLEGE ARCHIVES AND WESTERN NEW YORK HISTORICAL COLLECTIONS, *NY18-720*
HINKLEY FOUNDATION MUSEUM, *NY439-310*
HINSDALE PUBLIC LIBRARY, *IL384-320*
HIRAM COLLEGE, LIBRARY, COLLEGE ARCHIVES, *OH370-310*
HIRAM TOWNSHIP HISTORICAL SOCIETY, *OH370-330*
HIRSHHORN MUSEUM AND SCULPTURE GARDEN, *DC19-340*
HISPANIC SOCIETY OF AMERICA, MANUSCRIPTS AND RARE BOOKS, *NY590-40*
HISTORIC AUTOMOTIVE DATA COLLECTION, *IN132-310*
HISTORIC BETHLEHEM, *PA90-320*
HISTORIC CHERRY HILL, *NY10-320*
HISTORIC CRAB ORCHARD MUSEUM AND PIONEER PARK, *VA800-320*
HISTORIC FALLSINGTON, *PA308-320*
HISTORIC GALLOWAY HOUSE AND VILLAGE, *WI170-230*
HISTORIC GENERAL DODGE HOUSE, *IA177-320*
HISTORIC HILLSBOROUGH COMMISSION, BURWELL SCHOOL, COLLECTIONS ON WOMEN'S EDUCATION IN EARLY NC, *NC430-340*
HISTORIC HOPE FOUNDATION, HOPE PLANTATION, *NC915-320*
HISTORIC LANDMARK SOCIETY OF MONTANA, *MT430-320*
HISTORIC LYME VILLAGE, LIBRARY, *OH77-330*
HISTORIC NEW ORLEANS COLLECTION, ARCHIVES-MANUSCRIPTS DIVISION, *LA600-310*
HISTORIC PRESERVATION LEAGUE, *TX252-320*
HISTORIC SEATTLE: PRESERVATION AND DEVELOPMENT AUTHORITY, *WA820-325*
HISTORIC SPEEDWELL, *NJ548-720*
HISTORIC ST. GEORGE'S UNITED METHODIST CHURCH, MUSEUM AND LIBRARY COMPLEX, *PA725-700*
HISTORICAL AND CULTURAL ACTIVITIES CENTER OF HOUSTON COUNTY, TX, *TX228-320*
HISTORICAL AND GENEALOGICAL SOCIETY OF INDIANA COUNTY, *PA425-320*
HISTORICAL AND PHILOSOPHICAL SOCIETY OF OHIO, *OH171-110*
HISTORICAL ASSOCIATION OF SOUTHERN FLORIDA, CHARLTON W. TEBEAU LIBRARY OF FLORIDA HISTORY, *FL440-320*
HISTORICAL FOUNDATION OF THE PRESBYTERIAN AND REFORMED CHURCHES, *NC590-320*
HISTORICAL RUGBY, *TN825-690*
HISTORICAL SOCIETY OF BERKS COUNTY, *PA755-320*
HISTORICAL SOCIETY OF BOONTON TOWNSHIP, *NJ84-320*
HISTORICAL SOCIETY OF CARROLL COUNTY, *MD978-320*
HISTORICAL SOCIETY OF COLUMBIANA AND FAIRFIELD TOWNSHIP, *OH199-320*
HISTORICAL SOCIETY OF DAUPHIN COUNTY, *PA380-320*
HISTORICAL SOCIETY OF DELAWARE, LIBRARY, *DE810-330*
HISTORICAL SOCIETY OF FORT WASHINGTON, *PA315-320*
HISTORICAL SOCIETY OF FRANKFORD, *PA725-710*
HISTORICAL SOCIETY OF GLASTONBURY, *CT254-320*
HISTORICAL SOCIETY OF GRAHAM COUNTY, *AZ600-200*
HISTORICAL SOCIETY OF HADDONFIELD, *NJ316-330*
HISTORICAL SOCIETY OF HARFORD COUNTY, *MD114-330*
HISTORICAL SOCIETY OF HOPKINS COUNTY, *KY504-310*
HISTORICAL SOCIETY OF LONG BEACH, *CA414-320*
HISTORICAL SOCIETY OF MIDDLETOWN AND THE WALLKILL PRECINCT, *NY542-320*
HISTORICAL SOCIETY OF MONTGOMERY COUNTY, *PA690-320*

HISTORICAL SOCIETY OF NEWBURGH BAY AND THE HIGHLANDS, LIBRARY, *NY599-320*
HISTORICAL SOCIETY OF OKALOOSA AND WALTON COUNTIES, MUSEUM, *FL860-320*
HISTORICAL SOCIETY OF PENNSYLVANIA, MANUSCRIPTS DEPARTMENT, *PA725-720*
HISTORICAL SOCIETY OF POTTAWATTAMIE COUNTY, *IA177-340*
HISTORICAL SOCIETY OF PRINCETON, LIBRARY, *NJ692-320*
HISTORICAL SOCIETY OF QUAKER HILL, *NY681-320*
HISTORICAL SOCIETY OF QUINCY AND ADAMS COUNTY, *IL767-320*
HISTORICAL SOCIETY OF SARATOGA SPRINGS, MUSEUM, BEATRICE S. SWEENEY LIBRARY, *NY795-320*
HISTORICAL SOCIETY OF SCHUYLKILL COUNTY, *PA740-320*
HISTORICAL SOCIETY OF THE CENTRAL KANSAS CONFERENCE, *KS962-800*
HISTORICAL SOCIETY OF THE MERRICKS, *NY537-320*
HISTORICAL SOCIETY OF THE PHILADELPHIA ANNUAL CONFERENCE OF THE METHODIST EPISCOPAL CHURCH, *PA725-700*
HISTORICAL SOCIETY OF THE ROCKAWAYS, *NJ330-320*
HISTORICAL SOCIETY OF THE TARRYTOWNS, *NY878-320*
HISTORICAL SOCIETY OF THE TOWN OF EAST BLOOMFIELD, *NY251-320*
HISTORICAL SOCIETY OF TRAPPE, LIBRARY, *PA880-320*
HISTORICAL SOCIETY OF WESTERN PENNSYLVANIA, *PA735-320*
HISTORICAL SOCIETY OF YORK COUNTY, LIBRARY AND ARCHIVES, *PA975-320*
HOARD HISTORICAL MUSEUM, *WI178-240*
HOBART AND WILLIAM SMITH COLLEGES, WARREN HUNTING SMITH LIBRARY, *NY323-320*
HOBART HISTORICAL SOCIETY, PLEAK MEMORIAL LIBRARY, *IN341-320*
HOBSON-HUNTSINGER UNIVERSITY ARCHIVES, *NM494-570*
HOGAN, WILLIAM RANSOM, JAZZ ARCHIVE, *LA600-764*
HOLDER MEMORIAL, *MA207-120*
HOLGATE, THOMAS F., LIBRARY, *NC380-80*
HOLLAND PATENT FREE LIBRARY, *NY398-320*
HOLLAND PURCHASE HISTORICAL SOCIETY, *NY69-280*
HOLLAND SOCIETY OF NEW YORK, *NY590-80*
HOLLINS COLLEGE, FISHBURN LIBRARY, *VA360-320*
HOLLIS BURKE FRISELL LIBRARY, *AL820-765*
HOLLIS HISTORICAL SOCIETY, *NH430-320*
HOLLISTON HISTORICAL SOCIETY, *MA407-320*
HOLLYWOOD MUSEUM COLLECTION, *CA421-360*
HOLMAN LIBRARY, *IL444-720*
HOLMES, OLIVER WENDELL, LIBRARY, *MA25-650*
HOLY ANGELS CONVENT, *AR480-320*
HOLY CROSS, COLLEGE OF THE, ARCHIVES, *MA985-130*
HOLY CROSS, COLLEGE OF THE, LIBRARY, *MA985-140*
HOLY FAMILY COLLEGE, ARCHIVES, *PA725-765*
HOLY FAMILY OF NAZARETH, SISTERS OF, IMMACULATE CONCEPTION PROVINCE, ARCHIVES, *PA726-495*
HOLY NAME COLLEGE, LIBRARY, *DC8-500*
HOLY NAMES OF JESUS AND MARY, SISTERS OF, OREGON PROVINCE, ARCHIVES, *OR528-718*
HOMER SOCIETY OF NATURAL HISTORY, PRATT MUSEUM, *AK450-320*
HOMOSEXUAL INFORMATION CENTER, LIBRARY, *CA318-320*
HONEOYE FALLS VILLAGE HISTORIAN, *NY407-320*
HONEOYE PUBLIC LIBRARY, *NY406-320*
HONNOLD LIBRARY, SPECIAL COLLECTIONS DEPARTMENT, *CA143-470*
HONOLULU MUNICIPAL REFERENCE & RECORDS CENTER, *HI350-340*
HOOVER INSTITUTION ON WAR, REVOLUTION AND PEACE, ARCHIVES, *CA858-320*
HOOVER, HERBERT, LIBRARY, *IA966-320*
HOPE COLLEGE, ARCHIVES, *MI445-320*
HOPE PLANTATION, *NC915-320*
HOPEWELL MUSEUM, *NJ358-320*
HOPKINS COUNTY HISTORICAL SOCIETY, *KY504-310*
HOPKINS HISTORICAL SOCIETY, *MN405-320*
HOQUIAM PUBLIC LIBRARY, *WA395-320*
HORN LIBRARY, SPECIAL COLLECTIONS, *MA891-80*
HORNBY HISTORICAL SOCIETY, *NY78-320*
HORNE, MARILYN, ARCHIVES, *CA414-490*
HORNELL PUBLIC LIBRARY, *NY410-320*
HORNER MUSEUM, *OR144-610*
HORNER, JOSEPH, LIBRARY, *PA725-585*
HORRMANN LIBRARY, *NY595-360*
HORSEHEADS CULTURAL CENTER AND HISTORICAL SOCIETY, *NY411-320*
HOSPITAL SISTERS OF THIRD ORDER OF ST. FRANCIS, ST. FRANCIS CONVENT, *IL866-320*
HOT SPRINGS COUNTY MUSEUM, MUSEUM AND CULTURAL CENTER, *WY800-320*

HOTEL DIEU HOSPITAL, LIBRARY, *LA600-320*
HOUGHTON COLLEGE, WILLARD J. HOUGHTON LIBRARY, *NY413-320*
HOUGHTON COUNTY HISTORICAL MUSEUM, *MI530-320*
HOUGHTON LIBRARY, MANUSCRIPT DEPARTMENT, *MA169-370*
HOUGHTON MEMORIAL LIBRARY, *AL620-320*
HOUGHTON, ARTHUR A., JR., LIBRARY, *NY214-100*
HOUGHTON, WILLARD J., LIBRARY, *NY413-320*
HOUSING AND URBAN DEVELOPMENT, DEPARTMENT OF, PRINTING AND VISUAL ARTS DIVISION, *DC4-450*
HOUSTON METROPOLITAN RESEARCH CENTER, *TX483-320*
HOUSTON PUBLIC LIBRARY, HOUSTON METROPOLITAN RESEARCH CENTER, *TX483-320*
HOUSTON, SAM, REGIONAL LIBRARY AND RESEARCH CENTER, *TX560-720*
HOVERTER, TERENCE J., MEMORIAL ARCHIVES, *NY872-720*
HOWARD COLMAN LIBRARY, ARCHIVES, *IL806-695*
HOWARD COUNTY HISTORICAL MUSEUM, *IN407-320*
HOWARD COUNTY HISTORICAL SOCIETY, LIBRARY, *MD361-320*
HOWARD PUBLIC LIBRARY, *NY414-320*
HOWARD S. CULLMAN LIBRARY, *NY594-680*
HOWARD UNIVERSITY, MOORLAND-SPINGARN RESEARCH CENTER, MANUSCRIPT DIVISION, *DC8-850*
HOWARD-TILTON MEMORIAL LIBRARY, SPECIAL COLLECTIONS DIVISION, *LA600-755*
HOWARD-TILTON MEMORIAL LIBRARY, SPECIAL COLLECTIONS DIVISION, SOUTHEASTERN ARCHITECTURAL ARCHIVE, *LA600-761*
HOWARD-TILTON MEMORIAL LIBRARY, SPECIAL COLLECTIONS DIVISION, WILLIAM RANSOM HOGAN JAZZ ARCHIVE, *LA600-764*
HOWE LIBRARY, *VA880-720*
HOWE, DAVID A., PUBLIC LIBRARY, *NY942-160*
HOWELL LIBRARY, *UT456-900*
HOWLAND, PILGRIM JOHN, SOCIETY, *RI945-760*
HOYT PUBLIC LIBRARY, EDDY HISTORICAL & GENEALOGICAL COLLECTION, *MI824-320*
HUBBARD FREE LIBRARY, *ME425-320*
HUBBARD, ELBERT, LIBRARY-MUSEUM, *NY250-212*
HUDSON PUBLIC LIBRARY, *MI476-320*
HUDSON RIVER MUSEUM, *NY984-320*
HUDSON, HENDRICK, CHAPTER HOUSE, *NY416-320*
HUFELAND MEMORIAL LIBRARY, *NY577-330*
HUGH J. PHILLIPS LIBRARY, *MD380-520*
HUGH MOORE PARK, CANAL MUSEUM, RESEARCH LIBRARY, *PA270-320*
HUGHES, LANGSTON, MEMORIAL LIBRARY, *CA421-322*
HUGUENOT HISTORICAL SOCIETY, *NY574-320*
HUGUENOT-THOMAS PAINE HISTORICAL ASSOCIATION, HUFELAND MEMORIAL LIBRARY, *NY577-330*
HUMILITY OF MARY, SISTERS OF THE, VILLA MARIA COMMUNITY CENTER, ARCHIVES OFFICE, *PA908-720*
HUMPHREYS, GEN. DAVID, HOUSE, *CT4-160*
HUNGERFORD, T. A., MEMORIAL LIBRARY, *CT323-320*
HUNT INSTITUTE FOR BOTANICAL DOCUMENTATION, *PA735-140*
HUNT LIBRARY, FINE AND RARE BOOK ROOMS, *PA735-150*
HUNTER COLLEGE, LIBRARY, COLLEGE ARCHIVES, *NY588-420*
HUNTER LIBRARY, SPECIAL COLLECTIONS, *NC210-870*
HUNTER, DARD, PAPER MUSEUM, *WI46-360*
HUNTINGDON COLLEGE, HOUGHTON MEMORIAL LIBRARY, *AL620-320*
HUNTINGDON COUNTY HISTORICAL SOCIETY, *PA415-320*
HUNTINGTON COLLEGE, LOEW-ALUMNI LIBRARY, HUNTINGTON COLLEGE ARCHIVES, *IN352-320*
HUNTINGTON FREE LIBRARY AND READING ROOM, *NY591-820*
HUNTINGTON HISTORICAL SOCIETY, LIBRARY, *NY419-310*
HUNTINGTON LIBRARY, *CA756-320*
HUNTINGTON MEMORIAL LIBRARY, *NY648-330*
HUNTINGTON PUBLIC LIBRARY, *NY419-330*
HUNTINGTON, OFFICE OF THE HISTORIAN, *NY419-350*
HURLEY, CAPTAIN CHARLES H., LIBRARY, *MA165-520*
HYATTSVILLE BRANCH LIBRARY, MARYLAND ROOM, *MD551-640*
HYDE PARK HISTORICAL SOCIETY, *MA432-320*

I

I. D. WEEKS LIBRARY, RICHARDSON ARCHIVES, *SD792-820*
IBM CORPORATION, ARCHIVES, *NY40-360*
IDA PUBLIC LIBRARY, *IL74-360*
IDAHO MUSEUM OF NATURAL HISTORY, *ID640-360*
IDAHO ORAL HISTORY CENTER, *ID80-375*
IDAHO STATE ARCHIVES, *ID80-365*
IDAHO STATE HISTORICAL SOCIETY, DIVISION OF MANUSCRIPTS AND IDAHO STATE ARCHIVES, *ID80-365*
IDAHO STATE HISTORICAL SOCIETY, IDAHO ORAL HISTORY CENTER, *ID80-375*

IDAHO STATE UNIVERSITY, ARCHIVES, *ID640-345*
IDAHO STATE UNIVERSITY, IDAHO MUSEUM OF NATURAL HISTORY, *ID640-360*
ILIFF SCHOOL OF THEOLOGY, IRA J. TAYLOR LIBRARY, *CO252-360*
ILLINOIS BENEDICTINE COLLEGE, THEODORE LOWNIK LIBRARY, *IL459-360*
ILLINOIS COLLEGE, SCHEWE LIBRARY, *IL394-360*
ILLINOIS DEPARTMENT OF ENERGY AND NATURAL RESOURCES, ILLINOIS STATE GEOLOGICAL SURVEY DIVISION, *IL140-322*
ILLINOIS HISTORICAL SURVEY, LIBRARY, *IL916-795*
ILLINOIS OFFICE OF THE SECRETARY OF STATE, ARCHIVES DIVISION, *IL866-355*
ILLINOIS PRAIRIE DISTRICT PUBLIC LIBRARY, *IL542-360*
ILLINOIS STATE ARCHIVES, *IL866-355*
ILLINOIS STATE GEOLOGICAL SURVEY, *IL140-322*
ILLINOIS STATE HISTORICAL LIBRARY, *IL866-365*
ILLINOIS STATE UNIVERSITY, MILNER LIBRARY, MAP ROOM, *IL624-370*
ILLINOIS STATE UNIVERSITY, MILNER LIBRARY, SPECIAL COLLECTIONS/UNIVERSITY ARCHIVES, *IL624-380*
ILLINOIS WESLEYAN UNIVERSITY, SHEEN LIBRARY, *IL94-360*
IMMACULATE HEART OF MARY, SERVANTS OF THE, *PA420-720*
IMMIGRANT CITY ARCHIVES, *MA451-360*
IMMIGRATION HISTORY RESEARCH CENTER, *MN763-790*
INA CORPORATION, ARCHIVES, *PA725-780*
INCARNATE WORD CONVENT, ARCHIVES, *TX483-322*
INDEPENDENCE NATIONAL HISTORICAL PARK, *PA725-795*
INDIAN AND COLONIAL RESEARCH CENTER, *CT603-360*
INDIANA COMMISSION ON PUBLIC RECORDS, ARCHIVES DIVISION, *IN363-342*
INDIANA COUNTY HISTORICAL AND GENEALOGICAL SOCIETY, *PA425-320*
INDIANA HISTORICAL SOCIETY, LIBRARY, *IN363-350*
INDIANA JEWISH HISTORICAL SOCIETY, *IN231-370*
INDIANA STATE ARCHIVES, *IN363-342*
INDIANA STATE LIBRARY, ARCHIVES DIVISION, *IN363-342*
INDIANA STATE LIBRARY, INDIANA DIVISION, *IN363-360*
INDIANA STATE UNIVERSITY AT EVANSVILLE, SPECIAL COLLECTIONS AND UNIVERSITY ARCHIVES, *IN209-360*
INDIANA STATE UNIVERSITY, CUNNINGHAM MEMORIAL LIBRARY, DEPT. OF RARE BOOKS & SPEC. COLL., *IN825-350*
INDIANA UNITED METHODISM, ARCHIVES OF, AND DEPAUW UNIVERSITY, *IN275-150*
INDIANA UNIVERSITY NORTHWEST, CALUMET REGIONAL ARCHIVES, *IN253-360*
INDIANA UNIVERSITY OF PENNSYLVANIA, LIBRARY, SPECIAL COLLECTIONS, *PA425-360*
INDIANA UNIVERSITY-PURDUE UNIVERSITY AT INDIANAPOLIS, ARCHIVES, *IN363-385*
INDIANA UNIVERSITY, FOLKLORE INSTITUTE, FOLKLORE ARCHIVES, *IN66-340*
INDIANA UNIVERSITY, LIBRARIES, LILLY LIBRARY, MANUSCRIPTS DEPARTMENT, *IN66-380*
INDIANA UNIVERSITY, MUSEUM, *IN66-385*
INDIANA UNIVERSITY, ORAL HISTORY RESEARCH PROJECT, *IN66-390*
INDIANA UNIVERSITY, SCHOOL OF MUSIC, LIBRARY, *IN66-395*
INDIANA YEARLY MEETING OF FRIENDS, CUSTODIAN OF RECORDS, *IN704-360*
INDIANAPOLIS MOTOR SPEEDWAY HALL OF FAME, *IN803-360*
INDIANAPOLIS-MARION COUNTY PUBLIC LIBRARY, *IN363-400*
INFORMATION CENTER ON CHILDREN'S CULTURES, *NY595-180*
INGALLS MEMORIAL LIBRARY ASSOCIATION, BOXFORD HISTORIC DOCUMENTS CENTER, *MA903-80*
INGRAHAM MEMORIAL RESEARCH LIBRARY, *CT393-480*
INGRAHAM, EDWARD, LIBRARY, *CT48-40*
INLAND EMPIRE RAILWAY HISTORICAL SOCIETY, *WA880-370*
INLAND RIVERS LIBRARY, *OH171-650*
INLOW FOUNDATION, LIBRARY, *IN781-360*
INSTITUTE FOR SEX RESEARCH, *IN66-350*
INSTITUTE FOR THE STUDY OF RELIGIOUS DIMENSIONS IN UKRAINIAN CULTURE, *PA725-430*
INSTITUTE OF AMERICAN INDIAN ARTS, MUSEUM, *NM722-360*
INSTITUTE OF BEHAVIORAL SCIENCE, *CO108-740*
INSTITUTE OF CONTEMPORARY ART, *MA108-900*
INSTITUTE OF OUTDOOR DRAMA, *NC150-790*
INSTITUTE OF PAPER CHEMISTRY, DARD HUNTER PAPER MUSEUM, *WI46-360*
INSTITUTE OF SOCIAL ETHICS, NATIONAL GAY LIBERATION ARCHIVES, *CT316-360*
INSTITUTO DE CULTURA PUERTORRIQUENA, ARCHIVO GENERAL DE PUERTO RICO, *PR720-360*
INSURANCE LIBRARY ASSOCIATION OF BOSTON, *MA108-920*
INTER-CHURCH CHILD CARE SOCIETY, *PA725-810*
INTERDENOMINATIONAL THEOLOGICAL CENTER, ARCHIVES AND SPECIAL COLLECTIONS, *GA90-360*

INTERLAKEN HISTORICAL SOCIETY, *NY433-350*
INTERLAKEN PUBLIC LIBRARY, *NY433-370*
INTERNATIONAL ART REGISTRY, *NY590-360*
INTERNATIONAL BANK FOR RECONSTRUCTION AND DEVELOPMENT (WORLD BANK), PHOTO LIBRARY, *DC9-450*
INTERNATIONAL BUSINESS MACHINES CORPORATION, ARCHIVES, *NY40-360*
INTERNATIONAL FEDERATION OF PROFESSIONAL AND TECHNICAL ENGINEERS, *MD800-322*
INTERNATIONAL FORTEAN ORGANIZATION (INFO), *MD285-360*
INTERNATIONAL LADIES' GARMENT WORKERS' UNION, ARCHIVES, *NY590-430*
INTERNATIONAL LONGSHOREMEN'S AND WAREHOUSEMEN'S UNION, ANNE RAND RESEARCH LIBRARY, *CA720-356*
INTERNATIONAL MUSEUM OF PHOTOGRAPHY AT GEORGE EASTMAN HOUSE, *NY752-330*
INTERNATIONAL TENNIS HALL OF FAME AND TENNIS MUSEUM, *RI560-360*
INTERSTUDY, LIBRARY - INFORMATION CENTER, *MN307-360*
INYO NATIONAL FOREST, *CA94-360*
IONE CLUB LIBRARY, *WA407-760*
IOWA DEPARTMENT OF TRANSPORTATION, LIBRARY, *IA33-350*
IOWA MASONIC LIBRARY, *IA99-40*
IOWA STATE ARCHIVES, *IA233-360*
IOWA STATE HISTORICAL DEPARTMENT, DIVISION OF HISTORICAL MUSEUM AND ARCHIVES, *IA233-360*
IOWA STATE HISTORICAL DEPARTMENT, STATE HISTORICAL SOCIETY DIVISION, MANUSCRIPT COLL., *IA466-360*
IOWA STATE HISTORICAL SOCIETY, MANUSCRIPT COLLECTION, *IA466-360*
IOWA STATE MEDICAL LIBRARY, *IA233-450*
IOWA STATE UNIVERSITY, LIBRARY, AMERICAN ARCHIVES OF THE FACTUAL FILM, *IA33-364*
IOWA STATE UNIVERSITY, LIBRARY, DEPARTMENT OF SPECIAL COLLECTIONS, *IA33-370*
IOWA WESLEYAN COLLEGE, J. RAYMOND CHADWICK LIBRARY, ARCHIVES, *IA688-360*
IOWA-ILLINOIS GAS & ELECTRIC COMPANY, *IA188-360*
IPSWICH HISTORICAL SOCIETY, *MA436-350*
IPSWICH PUBLIC LIBRARY, *MA436-360*
IPSWICH TOWN HALL, *MA436-370*
IRA J. TAYLOR LIBRARY, *CO252-360*
IRON COUNTY MUSEUM, *MI130-360*
IRON RANGE HISTORICAL SOCIETY, DIVISION OF HISTORICAL SERVICES, RESEARCH LIBRARY AND ARCHIVES, *MN338-360*
IRONDEQUOIT, TOWN OF, HISTORIAN, *NY752-820*
IROQUOIS COUNTY GENEALOGY SOCIETY, GENEALOGY LIBRARY, *IL946-360*
IRVINGTON PUBLIC LIBRARY, *NJ376-360*
IRWIN LIBRARY, *IN363-90*
ISABELLA STEWART GARDNER MUSEUM, *MA108-940*
ISLAND COUNTY HISTORICAL SOCIETY, *WA181-360*
ISLAND RESOURCES FOUNDATION, *VI700-360*
ISLESFORD HISTORICAL MUSEUM, *ME453-40*
ISSAQUAH HISTORICAL SOCIETY, *WA408-360*
ISSAQUAH LIBRARY, *WA408-370*
ITASCA COUNTY HISTORICAL SOCIETY, MUSEUM, *MN363-360*
ITHACA COLLEGE, LIBRARY, *NY439-360*
IVEY, ELBERT, MEMORIAL LIBRARY, *NC410-200*
IZARD COUNTY HISTORICAL SOCIETY, *AR270-360*

J

J. C. FANT MEMORIAL LIBRARY, *MS300-520*
J. E. REEVES, HOME AND MUSEUM, *OH237-160*
J. F. DRAKE MEMORIAL LEARNING RESOURCES CENTER, *AL640-40*
J. PORTER SHAW LIBRARY, *CA720-485*
J. RAYMOND CHADWICK LIBRARY, ARCHIVES, *IA688-360*
J. V. FLETCHER LIBRARY, HISTORICAL COLLECTIONS, *MA931-400*
J. WALTER THOMPSON COMPANY, ARCHIVES, *NY590-535*
J-B PUBLISHING COMPANY, *NE288-400*
JACK LONDON STATE HISTORIC PARK, *CA288-400*
JACKSON - MADISON COUNTY LIBRARY, *TN390-390*
JACKSON CITY PUBLIC LIBRARY, *MI510-390*
JACKSON COUNTY HISTORICAL SOCIETY, GALLERY, *WI98-390*
JACKSON COUNTY HISTORICAL SOCIETY, LIBRARY, *WI98-400*
JACKSON COUNTY HISTORICAL SOCIETY, RESEARCH LIBRARY AND ARCHIVES, *MO400-400*
JACKSON COUNTY PUBLIC LIBRARY, *KY53N-400*
JACKSON HOMESTEAD, HISTORICAL CENTER AND COMMUNITY MUSEUM, *MA590-400*
JACKSON STATE UNIVERSITY, HENRY T. SAMPSON LIBRARY, SPECIAL COLLECTIONS, *MS550-410*
JACKSON, JOHN HERRICK, MUSIC LIBRARY, *CT505-910*

JACKSON, LEVI, WILDERNESS ROAD STATE PARK, MOUNTAIN LIFE MUSEUM, *KY48V-495*

JACKSON, WALTER CLINTON, LIBRARY, SPECIAL COLLECTIONS, *NC380-800*

JACKSONVILLE HISTORICAL SOCIETY, *FL280-380*

JACKSONVILLE MUSEUM, ARCHIVES AND LIBRARY, *OR400-720*

JACKSONVILLE PUBLIC LIBRARY, *IL394-400*

JACKSONVILLE PUBLIC LIBRARY, DELIUS COLLECTION, *FL280-390*

JACKSONVILLE PUBLIC LIBRARY, FLORIDA COLLECTION, *FL280-400*

JACKSONVILLE UNIVERSITY, CARL S. SWISHER LIBRARY, *FL280-420*

JACOB AND ROSE GROSSMAN LIBRARY, *MA154-310*

JACOB EDWARDS LIBRARY, *MA797-400*

JAMES A. KELLY LOCAL HISTORICAL STUDIES INSTITUTE, *NY593-900*

JAMES BRANCH CABELL LIBRARY, SPECIAL COLLECTIONS DEPARTMENT, *VA690-830*

JAMES C. BOLTON LIBRARY, *LA26-480*

JAMES CARSON BRECKINRIDGE LIBRARY, *VA660-510*

JAMES DICKINSON LIBRARY, SPECIAL COLLECTIONS DEPARTMENT, *NV630-800*

JAMES DUNCAN PHILLIPS LIBRARY, *MA733-210*

JAMES E. MORROW LIBRARY, SPECIAL COLLECTIONS DEPARTMENT, *WV435-520*

JAMES FORD BELL LIBRARY, *MN541-854*

JAMES G. GEE LIBRARY, ORAL HISTORY PROGRAM, *TX210-200*

JAMES JEROME HILL REFERENCE LIBRARY, *MN763-400*

JAMES M. MILNE LIBRARY, SPECIAL COLLECTIONS CENTER, *NY648-720*

JAMES MONROE LAW OFFICE MUSEUM AND MEMORIAL LIBRARY, *VA285-400*

JAMES P. ADAMS LIBRARY, ARCHIVES, *RI700-660*

JAMES P. MAGILL LIBRARY, TREASURE ROOM, *PA395-320*

JAMES S. COPLEY LIBRARY *CA712-810*

JAMES S. COPLEY LIBRARY (COPLEY PRESS), *CA368-120*

JAMES V. BROWN LIBRARY, *PA965-400*

JAMES WHITE LIBRARY, HERITAGE ROOM, *MI90-30*

JAMIESON, SIMMS A., MEMORIAL LIBRARY, *MD532-880*

JAPANESE AMERICAN CITIZENS LEAGUE, NATIONAL HEADQUARTERS, *CA720-365*

JARRETT, MAMYE, LEARNING CENTER, SPECIAL COLLECTIONS, *TX604-220*

JASPER FREE LIBRARY, *NY443-400*

JAY, JOHN, COLLEGE OF CRIMINAL JUSTICE, LIBRARY, *NY588-440*

JEAN HASBROUCK MEMORIAL HOUSE, *NY574-320*

JEFF MATTHEWS MEMORIAL MUSEUM, *VA290-760*

JEFFERSON COUNTY ARCHIVES AND RECORDS SERVICE, *KY496-400*

JEFFERSON COUNTY HISTORICAL SOCIETY, *NY930-410, WA681-400*

JEFFERSON NATIONAL EXPANSION MEMORIAL NATIONAL HISTORICAL SITE, *MO810-390*

JENKS, W. L., HISTORICAL COLLECTION, *MI775-710*

JERICHO HISTORICAL SOCIETY, *NY6-400*

JERSEY CITY PUBLIC LIBRARY, NEW JERSEY ROOM, *NJ386-380*

JERVIS PUBLIC LIBRARY, *NY757-400*

JESSE BESSER MUSEUM, *MI36-400*

JESSIE BALL DUPONT LIBRARY, *TN840-800*

JET PROPULSION LABORATORY OF THE CALIFORNIA INSTITUTE OF TECHNOLOGY, *CA578-560*

JEWISH FEDERATION OF NASHVILLE AND MIDDLE TENNESSEE, *TN690-360*

JEWISH HISTORICAL SOCIETY OF GREATER HARTFORD, *CT891-400*

JEWISH HISTORICAL SOCIETY OF GREATER WASHINGTON, LILIAN AND ALBERT SMALL JEWISH MUSEUM, *DC10-500*

JEWISH HISTORICAL SOCIETY OF MARYLAND, *MD76-300*

JEWISH HISTORICAL SOCIETY OF OREGON, INC., *OR720-400*

JEWISH INSTITUTE OF RELIGION, KLAU LIBRARY, *OH171-320*

JEWISH THEOLOGICAL SEMINARY OF AMERICA, LIBRARY, *NY590-680*

JOHN C. PACE LIBRARY, *FL600-800*

JOHN CARROLL UNIVERSITY, GRASSELLI LIBRARY, *OH843-400*

JOHN CARTER BROWN LIBRARY, *RI700-70*

JOHN COOK WYLLIE LIBRARY, *VA890-120*

JOHN CRERAR LIBRARY, *IL170-39*

JOHN DIXON LIBRARY, ARCHIVES COLLECTION, *NJ420-490*

JOHN E. CONNER MUSEUM, *TX529-770*

JOHN G. BIEL LIBRARY, *IN825-830*

JOHN F. KENNEDY LIBRARY, *MA108-965*

JOHN GREENLEAF WHITTIER HOME, *MA17-400*

JOHN HAY LIBRARY, *RI700-100*

JOHN HERRICK JACKSON MUSIC LIBRARY, *CT505-910*

JOHN J. TYLER ARBORETUM, PAINTER LIBRARY, *PA512-400*

JOHN JAY COLLEGE OF CRIMINAL JUSTICE, LIBRARY, *NY588-440*

JOHN L. MCCARTY PAPERS, *TX21-50*

JOHN MARK CHAPEL MUSEUM, *NY273-800*

JOHN MARSHALL HOUSE, *VA690-400*

JOHN PACKARD LIBRARY OF YUBA COUNTY, *CA452-400*

JOHN PEACE LIBRARY, SPECIAL COLLECTIONS, *TX777-810*

JOHN PRESTON MCCONNELL LIBRARY, ALUMNI-SPECIAL COLLECTIONS, *VA670-690*

JOHN VINTON DAHLGREN MEMORIAL LIBRARY, ALEXIS CARREL COLLECTION, *DC7-660*

JOHN W. BROWN CENTER FOR CURRENT GOVERNMENT STUDIES, *OH26-40*

JOHN W. FINNEY MEMORIAL LIBRARY, *TN120-120*

JOHN WESLEY POWELL MEMORIAL MUSEUM, *AZ500-400*

JOHN WORK GARRETT LIBRARY, *MD76-340*

JOHN XXIII LIBRARY, *LA600-710*

JOHNS HOPKINS MEDICAL INSTITUTIONS, ALAN MASON CHESNEY MEDICAL ARCHIVES, *MD76-315*

JOHNS HOPKINS UNIVERSITY, FERDINAND HAMBURGER, JR., ARCHIVES, *MD76-325*

JOHNS HOPKINS UNIVERSITY, GEORGE PEABODY LIBRARY, *MD76-333*

JOHNS HOPKINS UNIVERSITY, JOHN WORK GARRETT LIBRARY, *MD76-340*

JOHNS HOPKINS UNIVERSITY, MILTON S. EISENHOWER LIBRARY, *MD76-360*

JOHNSON CAMDEN LIBRARY, SPECIAL COLLECTIONS, *KY558-520*

JOHNSON COUNTY LIBRARY ANNEX, *WY90-410*

JOHNSON SAFARI MUSEUM, *KS164-520*

JOHNSON, GEORGE F., MEMORIAL LIBRARY, *NY273-280*

JOHNSON, LYNDON B., SPACE CENTER, HISTORY OFFICE, *TX483-560*

JOHNSON, LYNDON BAINES, LIBRARY, *TX56-520*

JOHNSTON MEMORIAL LIBRARY, SPECIAL COLLECTIONS, *VA630-840*

JOHNSTOWN FLOOD MUSEUM ASSOCIATION, JOHNSTOWN FLOOD MUSEUM, *PA435-400*

JOHNSTOWN HISTORICAL SOCIETY, *NY447-400*

JOINT COLLECTION, UNIV. OF MISSOURI WEST. HIST. MSS. COLLECTION & STATE HIST. SOC. OF MISSOURI MSS.*MO210-815, MO430-800, MO760-800, MO810-800*

JOINT FREE PUBLIC LIBRARY OF MORRISTOWN AND MORRIS TOWNSHIP, *NJ548-400*

JOLIET PUBLIC LIBRARY, *IL404-410*

JONATHAN FISHER MEMORIAL, *ME112-400*

JONES COUNTY IOWA HISTORICAL SOCIETY, *IA840-400*

JONES LIBRARY, SPECIAL COLLECTIONS, *MA21-400*

JONES, PERRIE, MEMORIAL ROOM, *MN763-710*

JONSON GALLERY, *NM114-870*

JOSEPH DOWNS MANUSCRIPT AND MICROFILM COLLECTION, *DE900-320*

JOSEPH HORNER LIBRARY, *PA725-585*

JOSEPH L. SWEET MEMORIAL, *MA48-40*

JOSEPH MEYERHOFF LIBRARY, *MD76-70*

JOSEPH PILSUDSKI INSTITUTE OF AMERICA FOR RESEARCH IN MODERN HISTORY OF POLAND, *NY590-700*

JOSEPH W. MARTIN COLLECTION, *MA615-720*

JOSEPHINE COUNTY HISTORICAL SOCIETY, *OR288-400*

JOSLYN ART MUSEUM, *NE624-400*

JUDAH L. MAGNES MEMORIAL MUSEUM, GOLDSTEIN LIBRARY, *CA86-385*

JUDAH L. MAGNES MEMORIAL MUSEUM, WESTERN JEWISH HISTORY CENTER, *CA86-400*

JUDGE DANIEL R. BIGELOW HOUSE, *WA616-400*

JUDGE GEORGE W. ARMSTRONG LIBRARY, *MS640-400*

JUDGE JOSEPH R. STEERE ROOM, *MI865-80*

JUDSON COLLEGE, BOWLING LIBRARY, *AL540-400*

JUDSON, AMOS, LIBRARY, *PA930-240*

JUILLIARD SCHOOL, LILA ACHESON WALLACE LIBRARY, *NY590-720*

JULIA MEEK GAAR WAYNE COUNTY HISTORICAL MUSEUM, *IN704-880*

JULIETTE GORDON LOW GIRL SCOUT NATIONAL CENTER, *GA895-290*

JUNIATA COLLEGE, LIBRARY, *PA415-400*

JUNIPERO SERRA MUSEUM, *CA712-708*

K

KALAMA PUBLIC LIBRARY, *WA413-440*

KALAMAZOO COLLEGE, LIBRARY, COLLEGE AND BAPTIST ROOM, *MI518-425*

KALAMAZOO PUBLIC LIBRARY, REFERENCE DIVISION, *MI518-445*

KALAMAZOO PUBLIC MUSEUM, *MI518-455*

KANDIYOHI COUNTY HISTORICAL SOCIETY, *MN961-440*

KANKAKEE COUNTY HISTORICAL SOCIETY, LIBRARY, KANKAKEE COUNTY COLLECTION, *IL409-440*

KANSAS CITY MUSEUM OF HISTORY AND SCIENCE, ARCHIVES, *MO430-420*
KANSAS CITY PUBLIC LIBRARY, *KS475-440*
KANSAS CITY RAILROAD MUSEUM, *KS850-720*
KANSAS STATE ARCHIVES, *KS878-430*
KANSAS STATE HISTORICAL SOCIETY, *KS878-430*
KANSAS STATE UNIVERSITY, LIBRARY, SPECIAL COLLECTIONS AND UNIVERSITY ARCHIVES, *KS607-450*
KANSAS WESLEYAN UNIVERSITY, MEMORIAL LIBRARY, WESLEYAN ARCHIVES, *KS833-440*
KANSAS WEST CONFERENCE, UNITED METHODIST CHURCH, COMMISSION ON ARCHIVES AND HISTORY, *KS962-800*
KARL E. MUNDT ARCHIVES, *SD450-150*
KARL E. MUNDT LIBRARY, KARL E. MUNDT ARCHIVES, *SD450-150*
KARSHNER, PAUL H., MEMORIAL MUSEUM, *WA726-440*
KEARNEY COUNTY HISTORICAL SOCIETY, *NE592-440*
KEENE STATE COLLEGE, MASON LIBRARY, PRESTON COLLECTION, *NH468-800*
KEENE VALLEY PUBLIC LIBRARY, *NY456-440*
KEENELAND ASSOCIATION, LIBRARY, *KY464-440*
KEGLEY COLLECTION, *VA900-880*
KELCE, MERL, LIBRARY, *FL820-810*
KELLER, HELEN, ARCHIVES, *NY586-440*
KELLY, JAMES A., LOCAL HISTORICAL STUDIES INSTITUTE, *NY593-900*
KEMERER, ANNIE S., MUSEUM, *PA90-40*
KENDALL WHALING MUSEUM, *MA748-440*
KENDALL YOUNG LIBRARY, *IA955-440*
KENILWORTH HISTORICAL SOCIETY, *IL414-440*
KENMORE ASSOCIATION, *VA285-440*
KENNEBEC HISTORICAL SOCIETY, *ME37-440*
KENNEBUNK FREE LIBRARY, *ME460-440*
KENNEBUNKPORT HISTORICAL SOCIETY, *ME462-440*
KENNEDY, JOHN F., LIBRARY, *MA108-965*
KENNESAW MOUNTAIN NATIONAL BATTLEFIELD PARK, *GA765-440*
KENNETH SPENCER RESEARCH LIBRARY, DEPARTMENT OF SPECIAL COLLECTIONS, MSS. SECT., *KS527-790*
KENNETH SPENCER RESEARCH LIBRARY, KANSAS COLLECTION, *KS527-795*
KENNETH SPENCER RESEARCH LIBRARY, UNIVERSITY OF KANSAS ARCHIVES, *KS527-805*
KENNY, SISTER, INSTITUTE, *MN541-16*
KENOSHA COUNTY HISTORICAL MUSEUM, LIBRARY, *WI266-430*
KENT COLLEGE, LIBRARY, *TN90-440*
KENT LIBRARY, *WA421-440*
KENT MEMORIAL LIBRARY, HISTORICAL ROOM, *CT793-440*
KENT STATE UNIVERSITY, LIBRARIES, AMERICAN HISTORY RESEARCH CENTER, *OH399-420*
KENT STATE UNIVERSITY, LIBRARIES, DEPARTMENT OF SPECIAL COLLECTIONS, *OH399-440*
KENT STATE UNIVERSITY, LIBRARIES, UNIVERSITY ARCHIVES, *OH399-450*
KENT-DELORD MUSEUM, *NY708-440*
KENTON COUNTY PUBLIC LIBRARY, *KY188-440*
KENTUCKIANA REGIONAL LIBRARY, *KY230-440*
KENTUCKY ARTS COUNCIL, *KY288-395*
KENTUCKY CHRISTIAN COLLEGE, LUSBY MEMORIAL LIBRARY, *KY310-440*
KENTUCKY DEPARTMENT OF LIBRARY AND ARCHIVES, DIVISION OF ARCHIVES AND RECORDS MANAGEMENT, *KY288-425*
KENTUCKY HISTORICAL SOCIETY, *KY288-440*
KENTUCKY LIBRARY, WESTERN KENTUCKY UNIVERSITY, *KY96-870*
KENTUCKY MEDICAL ASSOCIATION, MCDOWELL HOUSE AND APOTHECARY SHOP, *KY192-200*
KENTUCKY RIVERS COALITION, *KY464-460*
KENTUCKY STATE ARCHIVES, *KY288-425*
KENTUCKY STATE UNIVERSITY, BLAZER LIBRARY, *KY288-460*
KENYON COLLEGE, ARCHIVES, *OH320-430*
KEOKUK PUBLIC LIBRARY, *IA511-450*
KERR, WILLIAM JASPER, LIBRARY, *OR144-620*
KEUKA COLLEGE, LIGHTNER LIBRARY, *NY462-440*
KEWANEE HISTORICAL SOCIETY, *IL417-440*
KEWEENAW HISTORICAL SOCIETY, *MI530-320*
KEY PENINSULA HISTORICAL SOCIETY, *WA948-440*
KEYPORT HISTORICAL SOCIETY, *NJ398-440*
KIMBALL HOUSE HISTORICAL SOCIETY OF BATTLE CREEK, *MI60-420*
KIMBERLY-CLARK CORPORATION, *WI502-440*
KING COUNTY HISTORICAL ASSOCIATION, MARYMOOR MUSEUM, *WA736-440*
KING COUNTY REGIONAL STATE ARCHIVES, *WA616-444*
KING LIBRARY AND ARCHIVES, *GA90-490*
KING LIBRARY, DEPARTMENT OF SPECIAL COLLECTIONS, *KY464-800*

KING, EMMA B., LIBRARY, *NY637-720*
KING, MARTIN LUTHER, JR., CENTER FOR SOCIAL CHANGE, KING LIBRARY AND ARCHIVES, *GA90-490*
KING'S COLLEGE, D. LEONARD CORGAN LIBRARY, SPECIAL COLLECTIONS, *PA960-440*
KING'S DAUGHTERS FREE LIBRARY, *NY672-440*
KINGMAN MUSEUM OF NATURAL HISTORY, *MI60-440*
KINGSBOROUGH HISTORICAL SOCIETY, *NY590-760*
KINGSTON FREE LIBRARY, LITTLE REST ARCHIVES, *RI420-440*
KINNEY MEMORIAL LIBRARY, *NY373-440*
KIRBY POLITICAL SCIENCE MUSEUM, *PA270-480*
KIRKLAND HISTORICAL COMMISSION, *WA427-440*
KIRKLAND PUBLIC LIBRARY, *WA427-450*
KIT CARSON MEMORIAL FOUNDATION, HISTORICAL RESEARCH LIBRARY AND ARCHIVES, *NM874-440*
KITSAP COUNTY HISTORICAL SOCIETY, *WA848-440*
KITSAP REGIONAL LIBRARY, REGIONAL HISTORY COLLECTION, *WA84-450*
KITTITAS COUNTY MUSEUM, *WA280-440*
KITTSON COUNTY HISTORICAL SOCIETY, *MN433-440*
KLAMATH COUNTY MUSEUM, *OR448-450*
KLAMATH NATIONAL FOREST, *CA998-440*
KLAU LIBRARY, *OH171-320*
KLICKITAT COUNTY HISTORICAL SOCIETY MUSEUM, *WA360-440*
KNIGHT/CAPRON LIBRARY, *VA470-470*
KNIGHT, ALLEN, MARITIME MUSEUM, *CA480-500*
KNOX COLLEGE, SEYMOUR LIBRARY, COLLEGE ARCHIVES, *IL305-430*
KNOXVILLE-KNOX COUNTY PUBLIC LIBRARY, MCCLUNG HISTORICAL COLLECTION, *TN465-440*
KOOCHICHING COUNTY HISTORICAL SOCIETY, *MN419-440*
KORNHAUSER HEALTH SCIENCES LIBRARY, *KY496-795*
KRANNERT GRADUATE SCHOOL OF MANAGEMENT, KRANNERT LIBRARY, *IN935-640*
KRANNERT LIBRARY, *IN935-640*
KREMERS REFERENCE FILES, *WI346-870*
KRESGE LEARNING RESOURCES CENTER, MEHARRY MEDICAL COLLEGE ARCHIVES, *TN690-510*
KRITZECK COLLECTION, *MN226-700*
KUHN MEMORIAL LIBRARY, *CT198-80*

L

LA CROSSE COUNTY HISTORICAL SOCIETY, *WI298-470*
LA CROSSE COUNTY LIBRARY, *WI298-480*
LA CROSSE PUBLIC LIBRARY, DEPARTMENT OF LOCAL HISTORY AND ARCHIVES, *WI298-490*
LA GRANDE PUBLIC LIBRARY, *OR464-470*
LA GRANGE AREA HISTORICAL SOCIETY, *IL424-480*
LA GRANGE COLLEGE, WILLIAM AND EVELYN BANKS LIBRARY, *GA660-480*
LA PUENTE VALLEY HISTORICAL SOCIETY, *CA376-480*
LA PURISIMA MISSION STATE HISTORICAL PARK, *CA410-120*
LA RETAMA PUBLIC LIBRARY, LOCAL HISTORY COLLECTION, *TX217-480*
LA RUE COUNTY PUBLIC LIBRARY, *KY358-480*
LABOR HISTORY AND URBAN AFFAIRS, ARCHIVES OF, *MI230-880*
LABOR RELATIONS AND RESEARCH CENTER, *MA21-800*
LABOR-MANAGEMENT DOCUMENTATION CENTER, *NY439-150*
LAC QUI PARLE COUNTY HISTORICAL SOCIETY, HISTORIC CENTER, *MN499-480*
LACKAWANNA HISTORICAL SOCIETY, *PA795-480*
LACKAWANNA PUBLIC LIBRARY, *NY472-480*
LADIES' HERMITAGE ASSOCIATION, *TN345-480*
LADIES' SOCIAL LIBRARY, *ME112-80*
LAFAYETTE COLLEGE, DAVID BISHOP SKILLMAN LIBRARY, *PA270-470*
LAFAYETTE COLLEGE, KIRBY POLITICAL SCIENCE MUSEUM, *PA270-480*
LAFAYETTE HISTORICAL SOCIETY, *CA382-480*
LAFAYETTE ROOM, *NC330-520*
LAHAINA RESTORATION FOUNDATION, *HI400-480*
LAIRD LUCAS MEMORIAL LIBRARY, *MN975-860*
LAKE CHELAN MUSEUM, *WA125-490*
LAKE COUNTY (CA) HISTORICAL SOCIETY, *CA390-480*
LAKE COUNTY (FL) HISTORICAL SOCIETY, *FL840-480*
LAKE COUNTY (MN) HISTORICAL SOCIETY, *MN863-480*
LAKE COUNTY FOREST PRESERVE HEADQUARTERS, LAKE COUNTY MUSEUM, *IL951-480*
LAKE COUNTY LIBRARY, *OR512-480*
LAKE COUNTY MUSEUM, *IL951-480*
LAKE COUNTY PUBLIC LIBRARY, COLORADO MOUNTAIN HISTORICAL COLLECTION, *CO640-480*
LAKE FOREST COLLEGE, DONNELLEY LIBRARY, COLLEGE ARCHIVES, *IL434-490*
LAKE FOREST PARK PUBLIC LIBRARY, *WA820-465*

LAKE SUPERIOR STATE COLLEGE, LIBRARY, *MI865-480*
LAKE TAHOE HISTORICAL SOCIETY, *CA846-480*
LAKES, ARTHUR, LIBRARY, *CO458-130*
LAKEWOOD HISTORICAL SOCIETY, OLD STONE HOUSE MUSEUM, *OH426-470*
LAKEWOOD PUBLIC LIBRARY, *OH426-490*
LAMBERTVILLE HISTORICAL SOCIETY, MARSHALL HOUSE MUSEUM, *NJ412-480*
LAMONT MEMORIAL FREE LIBRARY, *NY537E-60*
LAMSON, HERBERT H., LIBRARY, *NH772-640*
LANCASTER COUNTY HISTORICAL SOCIETY, *PA470-460*
LANCASTER COUNTY LIBRARY, *PA470-470*
LANCASTER HISTORICAL COMMISSION, *MA448-470*
LANCASTER MENNONITE CONFERENCE, HISTORICAL SOCIETY, *PA470-480*
LANCASTER TOWN LIBRARY, *MA448-490*
LAND RECORDS, DIVISION OF (PA), *PA380-665*
LANDMARK SOCIETY OF WESTERN NEW YORK, WENRICH MEMORIAL LIBRARY, *NY752-480*
LANE COUNTY HISTORICAL MUSEUM, *OR224-480*
LANE COUNTY HISTORICAL SOCIETY, MUSEUM, *KS241-480*
LANE MEDICAL LIBRARY, *CA858-895*
LANE PUBLIC LIBRARY, REFERENCE DEPARTMENT, *OH360-480*
LANGLADE COUNTY HISTORICAL MUSEUM, *WI38-480*
LANGLEY LIBRARY, *WA478-480*
LANGLEY-ADAMS LIBRARY, *MA359-480*
LANGSTON HUGHES MEMORIAL LIBRARY, *CA421-322*
LARAMIE PLAINS MUSEUM, *WY500-480*
LAST INDIAN RAID IN KANSAS MUSEUM, *KS690-160*
LATAH COUNTY HISTORICAL SOCIETY, *ID480-480*
LATIN AMERICAN LIBRARY, *LA600-760*
LAURA G. WILLGOOSE ARCHIVES ROOM, *MA580-550*
LAURA INGALLS WILDER MEMORIAL SOCIETY, *SD126-480*
LAURA INGALLS WILDER PARK & MUSEUM, *IA74-480*
LAURA PARSON PRATT ARCHIVES AND RESEARCH CENTER, *NY595-740*
LAUREL COUNTY PUBLIC LIBRARY, *KY48V-480*
LAVA HOT SPRINGS MUSEUM, *ID400-720*
LAVERY LIBRARY, *NY752-780*
LAWRENCE BERKELEY LABORATORY,ARCHIVES AND RECORDS, *CA86-882*
LAWRENCE UNIVERSITY, LIBRARY, *WI46-480*
LAWRENCEVILLE SCHOOL, JOHN DIXON LIBRARY, ARCHIVES COLLECTION, *NJ420-490*
LAWS RAILROAD MUSEUM AND HISTORICAL SITE, *CA94-480*
LAYNE LIBRARY, *SD522-160*
LE SUEUR COUNTY HISTORICAL SOCIETY, *MN300-480*
LEA, HENRY CHARLES, LIBRARY OF MEDIEVAL HISTORY, *PA726-770*
LEAVENWORTH BRANCH LIBRARY, *WA483-560*
LEAVENWORTH COUNTY HISTORICAL SOCIETY, *KS541-470*
LEAVENWORTH PUBLIC LIBRARY, *KS541-490*
LEBANON COUNTY HISTORICAL SOCIETY, LIBRARY, *PA490-480*
LEBANON VALLEY COLLEGE, LIBRARY, *PA45-480*
LEE COUNTY PUBLIC LIBRARY, *KY3S-480*
LEE, HAROLD B., LIBRARY, ARCHIVES AND MANUSCRIPTS, *UT684-80*
LEE, ROBERT E., MEMORIAL, *VA50-65*
LEE, ROBERT E., MEMORIAL ASSOCIATION, STRATFORD HALL PLANTATION, ARCHIVES AND MANUSCRIPTS COLL., *VA760-690*
LEES JUNIOR COLLEGE, LIBRARY-ORAL HISTORY CENTER, *KY38U-470*
LEETONIA PUBLIC LIBRARY, *OH441-480*
LEGISLATIVE REFERENCE BUREAU (MILWAUKEE WI), *WI456-490*
LEHIGH COUNTY ARCHIVES, *PA25-60*
LEHIGH COUNTY HISTORICAL SOCIETY, SCOTT ANDREW TREXLER II LIBRARY, *PA25-480*
LEHIGH UNIVERSITY, LIBRARIES, *PA90-480*
LEHMAN ENGEL COLLECTION, *MS550-460*
LEHMAN, HERBERT H., PAPERS, *NY588-850*
LELAND D. CASE LIBRARY FOR WESTERN HISTORICAL STUDIES, *SD720-80*
LENAWEE COUNTY HISTORICAL MUSEUM, *MI8-480*
LEO BAECK INSTITUTE, ARCHIVES DIVISION, *NY590-840*
LEO J. WARD MEMORIAL LIBRARY, RARE BOOK COLLECTION AND ARCHIVES, *MI230-720*
LEROY HISTORICAL SOCIETY, *NY484-480*
LEROY V. GOOD LIBRARY, *NY752-525*
LESLIE COUNTY LIBRARY, *KY37S-480*
LETCHWORTH STATE PARK MUSEUM, *NY156-480*
LEVI JACKSON WILDERNESS ROAD STATE PARK, MOUNTAIN LIFE MUSEUM, *KY48V-495*
LEVI WATKINS LEARNING CENTER, UNIVERSITY LIBRARY, UNIVERSITY ARCHIVES AND SPECIAL COLLECTIONS, *AL620-60*
LEWIS AND CLARK COLLEGE, WATZEK LIBRARY, COLLEGE ARCHIVES, *OR720-440*
LEWIS COUNTY HISTORICAL SOCIETY, *NY511-480*

LEWIS COUNTY HISTORICAL SOCIETY, MUSEUM, *WA124-480*
LEWIS, BYRON R., HISTORICAL COLLECTIONS LIBRARY, *IN902-840*
LEWIS, FREDERIC (PHOTOGRAPH REPOSITORY), *NY589-640*
LEWIS, SINCLAIR, FOUNDATION, *MN790-720*
LEWIS, TED, MUSEUM, HISTORICAL AND GENEALOGICAL LIBRARY, *OH176-650*
LEXINGTON COUNTY MUSEUM, *SC576-480*
LEXINGTON HISTORICAL SOCIETY, *MA462-480*
LEXINGTON LIBRARY AND HISTORICAL ASSOCIATION, LEXINGTON HISTORICAL MUSEUM, *MO520-440*
LEXINGTON THEOLOGICAL SEMINARY, LIBRARY, *KY464-490*
LEXINGTON-FAYETTE COUNTY HISTORIC COMMISSION, *KY464-495*
LIBBY, ORIN G., MANUSCRIPT COLLECTION, *ND486-800*
LIBERTYVILLE-MUNDELEIN HISTORICAL SOCIETY, *IL449-480*
LIBRARIES OF THE CLAREMONT COLLEGES, HONNOLD LIBRARY, SPECIAL COLLECTIONS DEPARTMENT, *CA143-470*
LIBRARIES OF THE CLAREMONT COLLEGES, NORMAN F. SPRAGUE MEMORIAL LIBRARY, *CA143-480*
LIBRARIES OF THE CLAREMONT COLLEGES, POMONA COLLEGE, GEOLOGY LIBRARY, *CA143-490*
LIBRARY ASSOCIATION OF PORTLAND, *OR720-450*
LIBRARY COMPANY OF PHILADELPHIA, *PA725-870*
LIBRARY OF CONGRESS, AFRICAN AND MIDDLE EASTERN DIVISION, HEBRAIC SECTION, *DC12-100*
LIBRARY OF CONGRESS, AFRICAN AND MIDDLE EASTERN DIVISION, NEAR EAST SECTION, *DC12-105*
LIBRARY OF CONGRESS, ASIAN DIVISION, *DC12-150*
LIBRARY OF CONGRESS, GEOGRAPHY AND MAP DIVISION, *DC12-190*
LIBRARY OF CONGRESS, HISPANIC DIVISION, *DC12-200*
LIBRARY OF CONGRESS, MANUSCRIPT DIVISION, *DC12-300*
LIBRARY OF CONGRESS, MICROFORM READING ROOM SECTION, *DC12-400*
LIBRARY OF CONGRESS, MOTION PICTURE, BROADCASTING AND RECORDED SOUND DIVISION, *DC12-450*
LIBRARY OF CONGRESS, MUSIC DIVISION, REFERENCE SECTION, *DC12-510*
LIBRARY OF CONGRESS, ORIENTALIA DIVISION, *DC12-100, DC12-105, DC12-150*
LIBRARY OF CONGRESS, PRINTS AND PHOTOGRAPHS DIVISION, *DC12-600*
LIBRARY OF CONGRESS, RARE BOOK AND SPECIAL COLLECTIONS DIVISION, *DC12-650*
LIBRARY OF LATVIAN PLAYS AND THEATER, *MA172-160*
LIBRARY OF MICHIGAN, INFORMATION SERVICES UNIT, *MI550-505*
LIBRARY OF THE PRESIDENTS, *TX654-640*
LIFE UNDERWRITERS, AMERICAN COLLEGE OF, ORAL HISTORY CENTER, *PA135-40*
LIFWYNN FOUNDATION, *CT926-480*
LIGHTFOOT COLLECTION, *NY354-480*
LIGHTNER LIBRARY, *NY462-440*
LILA ACHESON WALLACE LIBRARY, *NY590-720*
LILIAN AND ALBERT SMALL JEWISH MUSEUM, *DC10-500*
LILLIAN PIERCE BENBOW ROOM OF SPECIAL COLLECTIONS, *MS870-760*
LILLY LIBRARY (EARLHAM COLLEGE), *IN704-200*
LILLY LIBRARY (INDIANA UNIVERSITY), MANUSCRIPTS DEPARTMENT, *IN66-380*
LILLY LIBRARY (WABASH COLLEGE), *IN154-880*
LIMA PUBLIC LIBRARY, *NY488-480*
LIMA, OLIVEIRA, LIBRARY, *DC3-226*
LINCOLN COLLEGE, LIBRARY, *IL454-470*
LINCOLN COUNTY CULTURAL AND HISTORICAL ASSOCIATION, LINCOLN COUNTY MUSEUM, ARCHIVES, *ME950-480*
LINCOLN COUNTY HISTORICAL MUSEUMS, *OR624-480*
LINCOLN COUNTY HISTORICAL SOCIETY, MUSEUM, *WA240-480*
LINCOLN COUNTY MUSEUM, ARCHIVES, *ME950-480*
LINCOLN HISTORICAL SOCIETY, *ME500-480*
LINCOLN LIBRARY, SANGAMON VALLEY COLLECTION, *IL866-480*
LINCOLN MEMORIAL SHRINE, *CA628-40*
LINCOLN MEMORIAL UNIVERSITY, *TN315-480*
LINCOLN MUTUAL SAVINGS BANK, WASHINGTON MUTUAL LINCOLN DIVISION, *WA880-495*
LINCOLN NATIONAL LIFE FOUNDATION, *IN231-470*
LINCOLN PUBLIC LIBRARY, *MA466-480*
LINCOLN STATE MONUMENT, *NM532-520*
LINCOLN UNIVERSITY, LIBRARY, *PA516-480*
LINCOLN, ABRAHAM, BIRTHPLACE NATIONAL HISTORIC SITE, *KY358-40*
LINDENHURST HISTORICAL SOCIETY, OLD VILLAGE HALL MUSEUM, *NY490-480*
LINDENWOOD COLLEGES, LINDENWOOD COLLEGE ARCHIVES, *MO770-480*
LINDSAY, VACHEL, ASSOCIATION, *IL866-840*
LINN COUNTY ARCHIVES, *KS760-480*

LINN COUNTY HISTORICAL SOCIETY, LINN COUNTY ARCHIVES, *KS760-480*
LIPSCOMB LIBRARY, *VA470-690*
LISLE FREE LIBRARY, *NY491-480*
LISTER HILL LIBRARY OF THE HEALTH SCIENCES, ALABAMA HEALTH SCIENCES COLLECTION, *AL120-810*
LISTER HILL LIBRARY OF THE HEALTH SCIENCES, REYNOLDS HISTORICAL LIBRARY, *AL120-815*
LITCHFIELD HISTORICAL SOCIETY, INGRAHAM MEMORIAL RESEARCH LIBRARY, *CT393-480*
LITHUANIAN AMERICAN COUNCIL, *IL170-53*
LITHUANIAN PHOTO LIBRARY, *IL170-61*
LITTAUER CENTER, MANPOWER AND INDUSTRIAL RELATIONS LIBRARY, *MA169-460*
LITTLE FALLS TOWNSHIP HISTORICAL SOCIETY, *NJ440-490*
LITTLE NINE PARTNERS HISTORICAL SOCIETY, *NY699-480*
LITTLE REST ARCHIVES, *RI420-440*
LIVINGSTON COUNTY HISTORIAN'S OFFICE, *NY321-480*
LIVINGSTON LIBRARY, *NY327-880*
LIVINGSTONE COLLEGE, ANDREW CARNEGIE LIBRARY, AFRO-AMERICAN STUDIES, *NC730-480*
LIVONIA PUBLIC LIBRARY, *NY500-480*
LLOYD HOUSE, *VA20-40*
LLOYD LIBRARY AND MUSEUM, *OH171-470*
LLOYD, ALICE, COLLEGE, APPALACHIAN ORAL HISTORY PROJECT, *KY630-40*
LOCK HAVEN UNIVERSITY, ARCHIVES AND RECORDS CENTRE, *PA520-470*
LOCK MUSEUM OF AMERICA, *CT797-480*
LOCKWOOD LIBRARY, POLISH COLLECTION, *NY24-725*
LOEB, FRANCES, LIBRARY, *MA169-305*
LOEW-ALUMNI LIBRARY, HUNTINGTON COLLEGE ARCHIVES, *IN352-320*
LOG CABIN MUSEUM, *WA680-480*
LOGAN HELM-WOODFORD COUNTY PUBLIC LIBRARY, *KY834-480*
LOGUE LIBRARY, *PA725-195*
LOIS BROWNELL RESEARCH LIBRARY, *MO700-720*
LOMA LINDA UNIVERSITY, LIBRARY, *CA406-480*
LOMBARD COLLEGE, MEADVILLE THEOLOGICAL SCHOOL OF, *IL170-195*
LOMBARD HISTORICAL SOCIETY, MUSEUM, *IL469-480*
LONDON, JACK, STATE HISTORIC PARK, *CA288-400*
LONG BEACH COLLECTION, *CA414-480*
LONG BEACH HISTORICAL SOCIETY, *CA414-320*
LONG BEACH PUBLIC LIBRARY, CALIFORNIA PETROLEUM INDUSTRY COLLECTION, *CA414-470*
LONG BEACH PUBLIC LIBRARY, LONG BEACH COLLECTION, *CA414-480*
LONG BEACH PUBLIC LIBRARY, MARILYN HORNE ARCHIVES, *CA414-490*
LONG BEACH PUBLIC LIBRARY, RANCHO LOS CERRITOS, HISTORICAL COLLECTION, *CA414-500*
LONG ISLAND COLLECTION, *NY257-190*
LONG ISLAND HISTORICAL SOCIETY, *NY590-940*
LONG ISLAND UNIVERSITY, BROOKLYN CENTER, LIBRARY, ARCHIVES DEPARTMENT, *NY590-960*
LONG ISLAND UNIVERSITY, C. W. POST CENTER, LIBRARY, SPECIAL COLLECTIONS, *NY355-480*
LONG, EARL K., LIBRARY, ARCHIVES AND MANUSCRIPTS/SPECIAL COLLECTIONS DEPARTMENT, *LA600-775*
LONG, LOUIS JEFFERSON, LIBRARY, *NY53-880*
LONGFELLOW NATIONAL HISTORIC SITE, *MA169-590*
LONGMONT PIONEER MUSEUM, ARCHIVES, *CO676-480*
LONGVIEW PUBLIC LIBRARY, LONGVIEW ROOM, *WA495-500*
LONGWOOD LIBRARY, *DE270-200*
LONGYEAR HISTORICAL SOCIETY, MARY BAKER EDDY MUSEUM, *MA154-480*
LOPEZ ISLAND HISTORICAL SOCIETY, *WA498-480*
LORAIN COUNTY HISTORICAL SOCIETY, *OH266-480*
LORAIN COUNTY METROPOLITAN PARK DISTRICT, *OH266-490*
LORAIN PUBLIC LIBRARY, *OH471-480*
LORAS COLLEGE, WAHLERT MEMORIAL LIBRARY, *IA244-480*
LORD, STEWART M., MEMORIAL HISTORICAL MUSEUM, *ME187-730*
LORENZO STATE HISTORIC SITE, *NY164-570*
LORETTE WILMOT LIBRARY, *NY752-560*
LORIKS, EMIL, HERITAGE HOUSE, *SD550-600*
LOS ALAMOS COUNTY HISTORICAL MUSEUM AND SOCIETY, *NM570-480*
LOS ANGELES (INNER CITY) CULTURAL CENTER, LIBRARIES, LANGSTON HUGHES MEMORIAL LIBRARY, *CA421-322*
LOS ANGELES CITY ARCHIVES, *CA421-330*
LOS ANGELES CITY CLERK'S OFFICE, LOS ANGELES CITY ARCHIVES, *CA421-330*
LOS ANGELES CITY COLLEGE, EARTH SCIENCE DEPARTMENT, *CA421-340*

LOS ANGELES CITY RECREATION AND PARKS DEPARTMENT, HOLLYWOOD MUSEUM COLLECTION, *CA421-360*
LOS ANGELES COUNTY MUSEUM OF NATURAL HISTORY, HISTORY DIVISION HISTORIC RECORDS CENTER, *CA421-390*
LOS ANGELES HARBOR COLLEGE, LIBRARY, *CA982-480*
LOS ANGELES PUBLIC LIBRARY, CENTRAL LIBRARY, *CA421-400*
LOS ANGELES STATE AND COUNTY ARBORETUM, HISTORICAL SECTION, *CA40-480*
LOS ENCINOS STATE HISTORIC PARK, ARCHIVES AND ENCINO HISTORICAL SOCIETY, LIBRARY, *CA246-480*
LOST CITY MUSEUM OF ARCHAEOLOGY, *NV870-480*
LOUIS B. MAYER LIBRARY, *CA421-015*
LOUIS E. MAY MUSEUM, LIBRARY, *NE368-160*
LOUIS JEFFERSON LONG LIBRARY, *NY53-880*
LOUIS L. MANDERINO LIBRARY, ARCHIVES, *PA145-120*
LOUISA MAY ALCOTT MEMORIAL ASSOCIATION, ORCHARD HOUSE, *MA217-480*
LOUISIANA ARMY AND AIR NATIONAL GUARD, OFFICE OF THE ADJUTANT GENERAL, MILITARY LIBRARY, *LA600-455*
LOUISIANA COLLEGE, NORTON MEMORIAL LIBRARY, *LA670-480*
LOUISIANA DEPARTMENT OF CULTURE, RECREATION, AND TOURISM, LA STATE MUS., LA HIST. CENTER, *LA600-465*
LOUISIANA DIVISION OF HISTORIC PRESERVATION, *LA62-430*
LOUISIANA HISTORICAL CENTER, *LA600-465*
LOUISIANA SECRETARY OF STATE, ARCHIVES AND RECORDS DIVISION, *LA62-470*
LOUISIANA STATE ARCHIVES, *LA62-470*
LOUISIANA STATE LIBRARY, LOUISIANA DIVISION, *LA62-490*
LOUISIANA STATE MUSEUM, LOUISIANA HISTORICAL CENTER, *LA600-465*
LOUISIANA STATE PARKS AND RECREATION COMMISSION, *LA465-480*
LOUISIANA STATE UNIVERSITY AT ALEXANDRIA, JAMES C. BOLTON LIBRARY, *LA26-480*
LOUISIANA STATE UNIVERSITY, HILL MEMORIAL LIBRARY, SPECIAL COLLECTIONS, *LA62-500*
LOUISIANA STATE UNIVERSITY, MEDICAL CENTER, DIVISION OF LIBRARIES, *LA600-490*
LOUISIANA STATE UNIVERSITY, SHREVEPORT, LIBRARY, ARCHIVES DEPARTMENT, *LA885-480*
LOUISIANA TECH UNIVERSITY, PRESCOTT MEMORIAL LIBRARY, UNIVERSITY ARCHIVES, *LA780-490*
LOUISVILLE FREE PUBLIC LIBRARY, IROQUOIS BRANCH LIBRARY, *KY496-498*
LOUISVILLE FREE PUBLIC LIBRARY, SOUTHWEST BRANCH LIBRARY, *KY496-518*
LOUISVILLE FREE PUBLIC LIBRARY, WESTERN BRANCH LIBRARY, *KY496-520*
LOUISVILLE PRESBYTERIAN THEOLOGICAL SEMINARY, LIBRARY, *KY496-530*
LOUISVILLE ZOOLOGICAL GARDEN AND LOUISVILLE ZOOLOGICAL SOCIETY, *KY496-540*
LOUISVILLE ZOOLOGICAL SOCIETY AND LOUISVILLE ZOOLOGICAL GARDEN, *KY496-540*
LOVEJOY, ELIJAH P., LIBRARY, MAP SECTION, *IL236-730*
LOVEJOY, ELIJAH P., LIBRARY, RESEARCH COLLECTIONS, *IL236-760*
LOVELAND PUBLIC LIBRARY, *CO685-480*
LOVELY LANE MUSEUM, *MD76-790*
LOW, JULIETTE GORDON, GIRL SCOUT NATIONAL CENTER, *GA895-290*
LOWELL OBSERVATORY, ARCHIVES, *AZ250-480*
LOWNDES COUNTY HISTORICAL SOCIETY, *GA950-480*
LOWNIK, THEODORE, LIBRARY, *IL459-360*
LOYOLA COLLEGE, ARCHIVES, *MD76-478*
LOYOLA UNIVERSITY OF CHICAGO, ARCHIVES, E. M. CUDAHY MEMORIAL LIBRARY, *IL170-78*
LOYOLA UNIVERSITY OF NEW ORLEANS, LIBRARY, SPANISH DOCUMENTS PROJECT, *LA600-505*
LUCAS, LAIRD, MEMORIAL LIBRARY, *MN975-860*
LUCE, STEPHEN B., LIBRARY, ARCHIVES, *NY594-340*
LUMBERMAN'S MUSEUM, *ME667-480*
LUMMI INDIAN TRIBAL CENTER, *WA60-510*
LUNAR SCIENCE INSTITUTE, PHOTO/MAP LIBRARY, *TX483-480*
LUSBY MEMORIAL LIBRARY, *KY310-440*
LUTHER COLLEGE, LIBRARY, *IA211-480*
LUTHERAN ARCHIVES CENTER AT PHILADELPHIA, *PA725-885*
LUTHERAN CHURCH IN AMERICA, ARCHIVES, *IL170-91*
LUTHERAN CHURCH IN AMERICA, FLORIDA SYNOD, *FL820-480*
LUTHERAN CHURCH IN AMERICA, INDIANA-KENTUCKY SYNOD, *IN363-480*
LUTHERAN CHURCH IN AMERICA, MARYLAND SYNOD, *MD76-490*
LUTHERAN CHURCH IN AMERICA, METROPOLITAN NEW YORK SYNOD, ARCHIVES, *NY591-35*
LUTHERAN CHURCH IN AMERICA, MINNESOTA SYNOD ARCHIVES, *MN769-280*

LUTHERAN CHURCH IN AMERICA, NORTH CAROLINA SYNOD, ARCHIVES, *NC730-500*
LUTHERAN CHURCH IN AMERICA, OHIO SYNOD, ARCHIVES, *OH788-600*
LUTHERAN CHURCH IN AMERICA, TEXAS-LOUISIANA SYNOD, *TX56-490*
LUTHERAN CHURCH OF AMERICA, WESTERN PENNSYLVANIA-WEST VIRGINIA SYNOD, ARCHIVES, *PA355-760*
LUTHERAN CHURCH-MISSOURI SYNOD, ATLANTIC DISTRICT, ARCHIVES, *NY128-480*
LUTHERAN CHURCH-MISSOURI SYNOD, CALIFORNIA AND NEVADA DISTRICT ARCHIVES, *CA720-405*
LUTHERAN CHURCH-MISSOURI SYNOD, INDIANA DISTRICT ARCHIVES, *IN231-490*
LUTHERAN CHURCH-MISSOURI SYNOD, NEBRASKA DISTRICT, ARCHIVES, *NE800-480*
LUTHERAN CHURCH-MISSOURI SYNOD, NORTH WISCONSIN DISTRICT, ARCHIVES, *WI814-480*
LUTHERAN CHURCH-MISSOURI SYNOD, NORTHWEST DISTRICT, *OR720-470*
LUTHERAN CHURCH-MISSOURI SYNOD, SOUTH DAKOTA DISTRICT ARCHIVES, *SD684-480*
LUTHERAN CHURCH-MISSOURI SYNOD, SOUTHEASTERN DISTRICT, *DC12-900*
LUTHERAN COUNCIL IN THE USA, ARCHIVES OF COOPERATIVE LUTHERANISM, *NY591-40*
LUTHERAN HISTORICAL SOCIETY, LIBRARY, *PA325-470*
LUTHERAN THEOLOGICAL SEMINARY, ABDEL ROSS WENTZ LIBRARY, *PA325-490*
LYCOMING COLLEGE, LIBRARY, *PA965-470*
LYCOMING COUNTY HISTORICAL MUSEUM, *PA965-490*
LYCOMING COUNTY HISTORICAL SOCIETY, LYCOMING COUNTY HISTORICAL MUSEUM, *PA965-490*
LYMAN HOUSE MEMORIAL MUSEUM, *HI250-480*
LYME HISTORICAL SOCIETY, ARCHIVES, *CT596-480*
LYNCHBURG COLLEGE, KNIGHT/CAPRON LIBRARY, *VA470-470*
LYNDEN PIONEER MUSEUM, *WA505-480*
LYNDON B. JOHNSON SPACE CENTER, HISTORY OFFICE, *TX483-560*
LYNDON BAINES JOHNSON LIBRARY, *TX56-520*
LYNN HISTORICAL SOCIETY, MANUSCRIPT COLLECTION, *MA486-470*
LYNNWOOD PUBLIC LIBRARY, *WA506-480*
LYONS SCHOOL DISTRICT PUBLIC LIBRARY, *NY510-480*

M

M. P. CATHERWOOD LIBRARY, LABOR-MANAGEMENT DOCUMENTATION CENTER, *NY439-150*
MABEE LIBRARY, CONGREGATIONAL COLLECTION AND WASHBURN ARCHIVES, *KS878-880*
MABEL TAINTER MEMORIAL LIBRARY, *WI418-520*
MABTON PUBLIC LIBRARY, *WA508-520*
MACALESTER COLLEGE, LIBRARY, *MN763-500*
MACARTHUR MEMORIAL, ARCHIVES AND LIBRARY, *VA580-520*
MACCRACKEN, WILLIAM P., JR., MEMORIAL LIBRARY, *TN630-730*
MACK, ALEXANDER, MEMORIAL LIBRARY, BRIDGEWATER COLLEGE ARCHIVES, *VA115-80*
MACKINAC ISLAND STATE PARK COMMISSION, *MI590-520*
MACLEISH, ARCHIBALD, COLLECTION, *MA352-270*
MACMURRAY COLLEGE, HENRY PFEIFFER LIBRARY, *IL394-500*
MACON COUNTY HISTORICAL SOCIETY, MACON COUNTY MUSEUM COMPLEX, STATE AND LOCAL HISTORY ROOM, *IL192-510*
MADERA COUNTY MUSEUM, *CA432-520*
MADISON (CT) HISTORICAL SOCIETY, *CT400-520*
MADISON (NH) HISTORICAL SOCIETY, *NH588-520*
MADISON (NJ) HISTORICAL SOCIETY, *NJ464-510*
MADISON COUNTY (IL) HISTORICAL SOCIETY, *IL236-520*
MADISON COUNTY (IN) HISTORICAL SOCIETY, *IN22-510*
MADISON COUNTY (NY) HISTORICAL SOCIETY, *NY646-520*
MADISON TOWNSHIP HISTORICAL SOCIETY, THOMAS WARNE HISTORICAL MUSEUM AND LIBRARY, *NJ622-690*
MADISONVILLE COMMUNITY COLLEGE, LEARNING RESOURCE CENTER, *KY504-510*
MADONNA CEMETERY AND MAUSOLEUM, *NJ266-520*
MAGALE LIBRARY, CLINE ROOM, *LA885-120*
MAGILL, JAMES P., LIBRARY, TREASURE ROOM, *PA395-320*
MAGNES, JUDAH L., MEMORIAL MUSEUM, GOLDSTEIN LIBRARY, *CA86-385*
MAGNES, JUDAH L., MEMORIAL MUSEUM, WESTERN JEWISH HISTORY CENTER, *CA86-400*
MAHONEY LIBRARY, PHILLIPS RARE BOOKS AND MANUSCRIPTS LIBRARY, *NJ178-115*
MAHONING VALLEY HISTORICAL SOCIETY, ARMS MUSEUM, *OH990-510*

MAINE HISTORICAL SOCIETY, *ME712-530*
MAINE MARITIME MUSEUM, LIBRARY/ARCHIVES, *ME75-520*
MAINE STATE ARCHIVES, *ME37-525*
MAINE STATE LIBRARY, *ME37-535*
MAINE STATE MUSEUM, *ME37-540*
MAINE WOMEN WRITERS COLLECTION, *ME712-880*
MAKAH MUSEUM, *WA578-520*
MALKI MUSEUM, *CA66-520*
MALLET LIBRARY, *RI945-800*
MALLOCH RARE BOOK AND HISTORY OF MEDICINE ROOM, *NY592-260*
MALONE COLLEGE, LIBRARY, *OH137-520*
MAMIE DOUD EISENHOWER BIRTHPLACE, MUSEUM AND LIBRARY, *IA58-540*
MAMYE JARRETT LEARNING CENTER, SPECIAL COLLECTIONS, *TX604-220*
MANASSAS NATIONAL BATTLEFIELD, LIBRARY, RESEARCH COLLECTION, *VA480-520*
MANCHESTER CITY LIBRARY, NEW HAMPSHIRE ROOM, *NH600-510*
MANCHESTER HISTORIC ASSOCIATION, *NH600-530*
MANCHESTER HISTORICAL SOCIETY, *MA499-520*
MANHATTAN COLLEGE, CARDINAL HAYES LIBRARY, *NY591-100*
MANHATTANVILLE COLLEGE, LIBRARY, RARE BOOKS (SPECIAL COLLECTIONS) AND ARCHIVES, *NY732-520*
MANITOWOC MARITIME MUSEUM, *WI354-520*
MANKATO STATE UNIVERSITY, SOUTHERN MINNESOTA HISTORICAL CENTER, *MN506-530*
MANNES COLLEGE OF MUSIC, LIBRARY, *NY591-140*
MANNING, H. V., LIBRARY, *SC720-120*
MANOR OF ST. GEORGE MUSEUM, *NY536-520*
MANPOWER AND INDUSTRIAL RELATIONS LIBRARY, HARVARD UNIVERSITY, *MA169-460*
MANSFIELD HISTORICAL SOCIETY, *CT779-520*
MANSFIELD STATE COMMEMORATIVE AREA, *LA465-480*
MANSFIELD-RICHLAND COUNTY PUBLIC LIBRARY, *OH481-530*
MANSON BRANCH LIBRARY, *WA517-560*
MANTOR LIBRARY, *ME350-800*
MAPLEWOOD MEMORIAL LIBRARY, *NJ482-520*
MARATHON COUNTY HISTORICAL MUSEUM, *WI814-510*
MARBLEHEAD HISTORICAL SOCIETY, *MA506-520*
MARCELLUS HISTORICAL SOCIETY, MUSEUM, *NY525-520*
MARGARET HERRICK LIBRARY, *CA90-30*
MARIA MITCHELL ASSOCIATION, NANTUCKET, *MA572-540*
MARIANIST ARCHIVES, *HI350-720*
MARIETTA COLLEGE, DAWES MEMORIAL LIBRARY, *OH486-510*
MARILYN HORNE ARCHIVES, *CA414-490*
MARIN COUNTY FREE LIBRARY, CALIFORNIA HISTORY COLLECTION, *CA764-510*
MARINE CORPS DEVELOPMENT AND EDUCATION COMMAND, EDUCATION CENTER, JAMES CARSON BRECKINRIDGE LIBRARY *VA660-510*
MARINE CORPS, HISTORY AND MUSEUMS DIVISION, *DC13-210*
MARINE HISTORICAL ASSOCIATION, *CT463-520*
MARINELAND, *FL660-510*
MARINERS MUSEUM, LIBRARY, *VA560-520*
MARINETTE COUNTY HISTORICAL SOCIETY, *WI362-520*
MARION COUNTY PUBLIC LIBRARY, *KY418-520*
MARION E. WADE COLLECTION, *IL976-900*
MARITIME COLLEGE, STATE UNIVERSITY OF NEW YORK, STEPHEN B. LUCE LIBRARY, ARCHIVES, *NY594-340*
MARK OSTERLIN LIBRARY, *MI925-560*
MARK TWAIN BIRTHPLACE STATE HISTORIC SITE, *MO870-520*
MARK TWAIN HOME BOARD, MARK TWAIN MUSEUM, *MO370-520*
MARK TWAIN MEMORIAL, *CT316-520*
MARK TWAIN PROJECT, *CA86-790*
MARLBOROUGH COUNTY LIBRARY, *SC72-510*
MARLBOROUGH PUBLIC LIBRARY, *MA513-530*
MARQUETTE COUNTY (MI) HISTORICAL SOCIETY, *MI605-520*
MARQUETTE COUNTY HISTORICAL SOCIETY, COCHRANE-NELSON HOUSE, *WI855-520*
MARQUETTE UNIVERSITY, MEMORIAL LIBRARY, DEPARTMENT OF SPECIAL COLLECTIONS AND UNIVERSITY ARCHIVES, *WI456-495*
MARRS LIBRARY, *KY54G-520*
MARS HILL COLLEGE, MEMORIAL LIBRARY, APPALACHIAN ROOM, *NC570-530*
MARSHALL COUNTY HISTORICAL MUSEUM, *MS520-520*
MARSHALL COUNTY HISTORICAL SOCIETY, *IL429-520*
MARSHALL COUNTY HISTORICAL SOCIETY, MARSHALL COUNTY HISTORICAL MUSEUM, *MS520-520*
MARSHALL COUNTY HISTORICAL SOCIETY, MUSEUM, *IN671-520*
MARSHALL COUNTY PUBLIC LIBRARY, *KY5M-520*
MARSHALL HISTORICAL SOCIETY, MUSEUM, ARCHIVES, *MI609-520*
MARSHALL HOUSE MUSEUM, *NJ412-480*

MARSHALL UNIVERSITY, JAMES E. MORROW LIBRARY, SPECIAL
    COLLECTIONS DEPARTMENT, *WV435-520*
MARSHALL, GEORGE C., RESEARCH LIBRARY, *VA430-280*
MARSHALL, JOHN, HOUSE, *VA690-400*
MARSTON MEMORIAL HISTORICAL CENTER OF THE FREE
    METHODIST CHURCH, *IN990-240*
MARTIN AND OSA JOHNSON SAFARI MUSEUM, *KS164-520*
MARTIN COUNTY HISTORICAL SOCIETY, PIONEER MUSEUM,
    MN314-520
MARTIN LUTHER KING, JR., CENTER FOR SOCIAL CHANGE,
    KING LIBRARY AND ARCHIVES, *GA90-490*
MARTIN LUTHER KING, JR., MEMORIAL LIBRARY,
    WASHINGTONIANA DIVISION, *DC13-300*
MARTIN VAN BUREN PAPERS, *PA565-640*
MARTIN-MITCHELL, CAROLINE, MUSEUM, *IL609-120*
MARTIN, JOSEPH W., COLLECTION, *MA615-720*
MARTINS FERRY AREA HISTORICAL SOCIETY, SEDGWICK
    MUSEUM, *OH495-510*
MARY BAKER EDDY MUSEUM, *MA154-480*
MARY BALL WASHINGTON MUSEUM AND LIBRARY, *VA400-520*
MARY F. SHIPPER LIBRARY, MINERAL COUNTY COLLECTION,
    WV500-640
MARY HOLMES COLLEGE, LIBRARY, ORAL HISTORY PROGRAM,
    MS970-520
MARY SURRATT HOUSE, SURRATT SOCIETY LIBRARY, *MD255-720*
MARY WASHINGTON COLLEGE, E. LEE TRINKLE LIBRARY, RARE
    BOOKS ROOM AND COLLEGE ARCHIVES, *VA285-520*
MARY WILCOX MEMORIAL LIBRARY, *NY968-520*
MARY, SOCIETY OF, PROVINCE OF CINCINNATI, ARCHIVES,
    OH223-720
MARYCREST COLLEGE, CONE LIBRARY, ARCHIVES, *IA188-520*
MARYGROVE COLLEGE, LIBRARY, *MI230-500*
MARYHILL MUSEUM OF ART, *WA360-520*
MARYKNOLL SISTERS OF ST. DOMINIC, ARCHIVES, *NY529-530*
MARYLAND DEPARTMENT OF GENERAL SERVICES, MARYLAND
    HALL OF RECORDS, *MD57-500*
MARYLAND HALL OF RECORDS, *MD57-500*
MARYLAND HISTORICAL SOCIETY, MANUSCRIPTS DIVISION,
    MD76-515
MARYLAND HISTORICAL SOCIETY, ORAL HISTORY OFFICE,
    MD76-525
MARYLAND HISTORICAL SOCIETY, PRINTS AND PHOTOGRAPHS
    DIVISION, *MD76-526*
MARYLAND HOUSE AND GARDEN PILGRIMAGE, *MD950-520*
MARYLAND PARK SERVICE, *MD475-280*
MARYLAND STATE ARCHIVES, *MD57-500*
MARYMOOR MUSEUM, *WA736-440*
MARYMOUNT COLLEGE, ARCHIVES, *NY878-510*
MARYSVILLE HISTORICAL SOCIETY, PIONEER ASSOCIATION,
    WA528-520
MARYSVILLE LIBRARY, *WA528-530*
MASON COUNTY HISTORICAL SOCIETY, ROSE HAWLEY
    MUSEUM-ARCHIVES, *MI585-520*
MASON COUNTY MUSEUM, *KY526-520*
MASON LIBRARY, PRESTON COLLECTION, *NH468-800*
MASON, MOSES, MUSEUM, *ME95-80*
MASSACHUSETTS DEPARTMENT OF ENVIRONMENTAL
    MANAGEMENT, DIVISION OF FORESTS AND PARKS, *MA615-80*
MASSACHUSETTS HISTORICAL SOCIETY, *MA109-120*
MASSACHUSETTS HORTICULTURAL SOCIETY, LIBRARY,
    MA109-140
MASSACHUSETTS INSTITUTE OF TECHNOLOGY, INSTITUTE
    ARCHIVES AND SPECIAL COLLECTIONS, *MA169-650*
MASSACHUSETTS INSTITUTE OF TECHNOLOGY, MUSEUM,
    MA169-625
MASSACHUSETTS INSTITUTE OF TECHNOLOGY, MUSEUM,
    FRANCIS RUSSELL HART NAUTICAL COLLECTIONS, *MA169-610*
MASSACHUSETTS MARITIME ACADEMY, CAPTAIN CHARLES H.
    HURLEY LIBRARY, *MA165-520*
MASSACHUSETTS METROPOLITAN DISTRICT COMMISSION,
    MA109-180
MASSACHUSETTS NEW-CHURCH UNION, SWEDENBORG
    LIBRARY, *MA109-200*
MASSACHUSETTS SECRETARY OF STATE, ARCHIVES DIVISION,
    MA109-220
MASSACHUSETTS SOCIETY OF MAYFLOWER DESCENDANTS,
    MA109-230
MASSACHUSETTS STATE ARCHIVES, *MA109-220*
MASSACHUSETTS STATE LIBRARY, *MA109-240*
MASSACOH PLANTATION, *CT718-720*
MASSENGILL MUSEUM OF OVERMOUNTAIN HISTORY, *TN750-690*
MASSILLON MUSEUM, *OH505-510*
MASSILLON PUBLIC LIBRARY, *OH505-520*
MASTERSON HOUSE, PORT WILLIAM HISTORICAL SOCIETY,
    KY13Y-120
MATAS, RUDOLPH, MEDICAL LIBRARY, *LA600-765*

MATTATUCK HISTORICAL SOCIETY, MATTATUCK MUSEUM,
    CT870-520
MATTATUCK MUSEUM, *CT870-520*
MATTHEWS, JEFF, MEMORIAL MUSEUM, *VA290-760*
MAXWELL MUSEUM OF ANTHROPOLOGY, *NM114-880*
MAY DEPARTMENT STORES COMPANY, CORPORATE
    INFORMATION CENTER, *MO810-470*
MAY, LOUIS E., MUSEUM, LIBRARY, *NE368-160*
MAYER, LOUIS B., LIBRARY, *CA421-015*
MAYFLOWER DESCENDANTS, MASSACHUSETTS SOCIETY OF,
    MA109-230
MAYFLOWER SOCIETY HOUSE, *MA685-520*
MAYO FOUNDATION, ARCHIVES, *MN721-520*
MAYO HAYES O'DONNELL LIBRARY, *CA480-510*
MAYVILLE HISTORICAL MUSEUM, *MI615-520*
MAYVILLE HISTORICAL SOCIETY, MUSEUM COMPLEX, *WI378-520*
MAZOMANIE HISTORICAL SOCIETY, RESEARCH CENTER,
    WI382-520
MCCAIN LIBRARY, *SC306-200*
MCCAIN, WILLIAM DAVID, LIBRARY AND ARCHIVES, *MS490-810*
MCCARTY, JOHN L., PAPERS, *TX21-50*
MCCLUNG HISTORICAL COLLECTION, *TN465-440*
MCCONNELL, JOHN PRESTON, LIBRARY, ALUMNI-SPECIAL
    COLLECTIONS, *VA670-690*
MCCORMICK THEOLOGICAL SEMINARY, MCGAW LIBRARY,
    IL170-182
MCCREARY COUNTY PUBLIC LIBRARY, *KY87S-520*
MCCULLOUGH-PARK HOUSE ASSOCIATION, INC., LIBRARY,
    MANUSCRIPT COLLECTION AND ARCHIVE, *VT496-640*
MCDONALD MEMORIAL LIBRARY, *OH171-920*
MCDOWELL HOUSE AND APOTHECARY SHOP, *KY192-200*
MCFARLAND HISTORICAL SOCIETY, MUSEUM, *WI390-520*
MCFARLAND STATE HISTORICAL PARK, *AZ275-520*
MCGAW LIBRARY, *IL170-182*
MCHENRY MUSEUM OF ART AND HISTORY, *CA476-520*
MCINTYRE, WILLIAM D., LIBRARY, UNIVERSITY ARCHIVES AND
    AREA RESEARCH CENTER, *WI142-800*
MCKAY LIBRARY, *MI44-520*
MCKAY, DAVID O., LEARNING RESOURCES CENTER, ARCHIVES
    AND SPECIAL COLLECTIONS, *ID680-690*
MCKEAN COUNTY HISTORICAL SOCIETY, *PA820-520*
MCKELDIN LIBRARY, ARCHIVES AND MANUSCRIPTS
    DEPARTMENT, *MD285-805*
MCKENDREE COLLEGE, HOLMAN LIBRARY, *IL444-720*
MCKINLEY MUSEUM OF HISTORY, SCIENCE, AND INDUSTRY,
    RAMSAYER LIBRARY, *OH137-730*
MCKINNEY LIBRARY, *NY10-80*
MCKUNE MEMORIAL LIBRARY, *MI160-520*
MCLAIN, CARRIE, MEMORIAL MUSEUM, *AK700-120*
MCLAUGHLIN LIBRARY, ARCHIVES & SPECIAL COLLECTIONS,
    NJ798-720
MCLEAN COUNTY HISTORICAL SOCIETY, *IL94-510*
MCLEOD COUNTY HISTORICAL SOCIETY, *MN412-520*
MCNEESE STATE UNIVERSITY, FRAZAR MEMORIAL LIBRARY,
    ARCHIVES AND SPECIAL COLLECTIONS, *LA395-520*
MCPHERSON COLLEGE, MILLER LIBRARY, BRETHREN
    COLLECTION, *KS593-510*
MEADE COUNTY PUBLIC LIBRARY, *KY98-520*
MEADVILLE THEOLOGICAL SCHOOL OF LOMBARD COLLEGE,
    IL170-195
MEANS LIBRARY, *MA425-520*
MEDFORD HISTORICAL SOCIETY, *MA528-510*
MEDICAL AND CHIRURGICAL FACULTY OF THE STATE OF
    MARYLAND, LIBRARY, *MD76-527*
MEDICAL COLLEGE OF PENNSYLVANIA, ARCHIVES AND SPECIAL
    COLLECTIONS ON WOMEN IN MEDICINE, *PA725-900*
MEDICAL COLLEGE OF VIRGINIA, TOMPKINS-MCCAW LIBRARY,
    ARCHIVES DEPARTMENT, *VA690-840*
MEDICAL COLLEGE OF WISCONSIN, TODD WEHR LIBRARY,
    WI456-500
MEDICAL MISSION SISTERS (SOCIETY OF CATHOLIC MEDICAL
    MISSIONARIES), *PA725-908*
MEDICAL RESEARCH LIBRARY OF BROOKLYN, *NY591-240*
MEDICAL UNIVERSITY OF SOUTH CAROLINA, HEALTH AFFAIRS
    LIBRARY, WARING HISTORICAL LIBRARY, *SC144-520*
MEDIEVAL INSTITUTE, UNIVERSITY OF NOTRE DAME, *IN627-810*
MEDINA DISTRICT PUBLIC LIBRARY, *OH530-240*
MEEKER COUNTY HISTORICAL SOCIETY, *MN459-520*
MEEKER, EZRA, HISTORICAL SOCIETY, *WA726-200*
MEETING HOUSE GREEN MEMORIAL AND HISTORIAL
    ASSOCIATION, TUCK MEMORIAL MUSEUM, *NH368-320*
MEHARRY MEDICAL COLLEGE, LIBRARY, KRESGE LEARNING
    RESOURCES CENTER, COLLEGE ARCHIVES, *TN690-510*
MEIGS COUNTY MUSEUM, *OH714-510*
MEIGS COUNTY PIONEER AND HISTORICAL SOCIETY, MEIGS
    COUNTY MUSEUM, *OH714-510*
MEIKLEJOHN CIVIL LIBERTIES INSTITUTE, *CA86-520*

MELICK LIBRARY, *IL256-200*

MELVILLE J. HERSKOVITS LIBRARY OF AFRICAN STUDIES, *IL261-566*

MELVILLE WHALING ROOM COLLECTION, *MA584-550*

MEMORIAL HALL LIBRARY, *MA25-520*

MEMORIAL LIBRARIES, HENRY N. FLYNT LIBRARY AND POCUMTUCK VALLEY MEMORIAL ASSOCIATION LIBRARY, *MA238-520*

MEMORIAL PIONEER LOG CABIN AND MUSEUM, *NY71-715*

MEMORIAL SHRINE TO THE GRAND ARMY OF THE REPUBLIC, *MA108-10*

MEMPHIS PINK PALACE MUSEUM, *TN630-510*

MEMPHIS STATE UNIVERSITY, LIBRARIES, MISSISSIPPI VALLEY COLLECTION/SPECIAL COLLECTIONS DEPT., *TN630-530*

MEMPHIS/SHELBY COUNTY PUBLIC LIBRARY AND INFORMATION CENTER, MEMPHIS ROOM, *TN630-570*

MENAUL SCHOOL, MENAUL HISTORICAL LIBRARY, *NM114-525*

MENDHAM FREE PUBLIC LIBRARY, *NJ502-520*

MENDOCINO HISTORICAL RESEARCH, *CA454-520*

MENDOCINO NATIONAL FOREST, RECREATION AND CULTURAL RESOURCES BRANCH, *CA978-520*

MENDON HISTORICAL MUSEUM, *MA538-520*

MENDON HISTORICAL SOCIETY, MENDON HISTORICAL MUSEUM, *MA538-520*

MENDON TOWN HISTORIAN, *NY407-520*

MENLO PARK HISTORICAL ASSOCIATION, HISTORY ROOM, *CA456-530*

MENLO PARK PUBLIC LIBRARY, LOCAL HISTORY COLLECTION AND MENLO PARK HISTORICAL ASSN., HISTORY ROOM, *CA456-530*

MENNINGER FOUNDATION, DIVISION OF MUSEUMS AND ARCHIVES, *KS878-520*

MENNO SIMONS HISTORICAL LIBRARY/ARCHIVES, *VA350-200*

MENNONITE ARCHIVES, *IA499-520*

MENNONITE BRETHREN STUDIES, CENTER FOR, HIEBERT LIBRARY, *CA274-130*

MENNONITE CHURCH, ARCHIVES, *IN264-40*

MENNONITE HISTORIANS OF EASTERN PENNSYLVANIA, MENNONITE HISTORICAL LIBRARY & ARCH. OF EAST. PENNA., *PA478-530*

MENNONITE HISTORICAL LIBRARY, *OH92-520*

MENNONITE HISTORICAL LIBRARY AND ARCHIVES OF EASTERN PENNSYLVANIA, *PA478-530*

MENNONITE HISTORICAL SOCIETY OF IOWA, MENNONITE ARCHIVES, *IA499-520*

MENNONITE LIBRARY AND ARCHIVES, *KS676-520*

MENOMINEE COUNTY HISTORICAL SOCIETY, MENOMINEE COUNTY MUSEUM, *MI620-520*

MENOMINEE COUNTY MUSEUM, *MI620-520*

MERCER COUNTY HISTORICAL MUSEUM, RILEY HOME, ARCHIVES, *OH147-520*

MERCER COUNTY HISTORICAL SOCIETY, *PA570-520*

MERCER ISLAND HISTORICAL SOCIETY, *WA542-520*

MERCER ISLAND LIBRARY, *WA542-530*

MERCER UNIVERSITY, STETSON MEMORIAL LIBRARY, GEORGIA BAPTIST HISTORICAL COLLECTION, *GA735-520*

MERCY HOSPITAL OF PITTSBURGH, ARCHIVES, *PA735-515*

MERCYHURST COLLEGE, ARCHIVES, CENTER FOR ERIE STUDIES, *PA305-510*

MEREDITH HAVENS FIRE MUSEUM OF TRENTON, *NJ838-530*

MERGENTHALER LINOTYPE COMPANY, *NY705-560*

MERL KELCE LIBRARY, *FL820-810*

MERNER-PFEIFFER LIBRARY, *TN15-760*

MERRICK COUNTY HISTORICAL MUSEUM, *NE224-520*

MERRILL LIBRARY, SPECIAL COLLECTIONS AND ARCHIVES, *UT380-810*

MERRILL MEMORIAL LIBRARY, *ME965-520*

MERRITT-WRIGHT ROOM, *NY150-760*

MERTON, THOMAS, COLLECTION, *KY496-90*

MESA COUNTY PUBLIC LIBRARY, *CO476-520*

MESA MUSEUM, *AZ435-520*

MESSIAH COLLEGE, ARCHIVES OF THE BRETHREN IN CHRIST CHURCH AND MESSIAH COLLEGE, *PA340-520*

MESSLER LIBRARY, NEW JERSEY ROOM, *NJ756-240*

METALINES RECREATION CLUB PUBLIC LIBRARY, *WA545-760*

METCALF-FRITZ PHOTOGRAPH COLLECTION, *CA86-850*

METCALF, CLARENCE, RESEARCH LIBRARY, *OH863-280*

METHODIST COLLEGE, DAVIS MEMORIAL LIBRARY, LAFAYETTE ROOM, *NC330-520*

METHODIST HISTORICAL COLLECTIONS, *TX252-760*

METHODIST HISTORICAL SOCIETY, *NE560-810*

METHODIST HISTORICAL SOCIETY OF THE BALTIMORE CONFERENCE, *MD76-790*

METHODIST MUSEUM, *GA885-520*

METHODIST PUBLISHING HOUSE, *TN690-890*

METROPOLITAN DISTRICT COMMISSION, *MA109-180*

METROPOLITAN MUSEUM OF ART, DEPARTMENT OF PRINTS AND PHOTOGRAPHS, *NY591-350*

METROPOLITAN MUSEUM OF ART, THOMAS J. WATSON LIBRARY, *NY591-380*

METROPOLITAN OPERA ARCHIVES, *NY591-420*

METROPOLITAN OPERA ASSOCIATION, METROPOLITAN OPERA ARCHIVES, *NY591-420*

MEYER, E. J., MEMORIAL HOSPITAL, CENTRAL PHOTO LAB, *NY134-510*

MEYERHOFF, JOSEPH, LIBRARY, *MD76-70*

MIAMI COUNTY HISTORICAL MUSEUM, *IN649-520*

MIAMI COUNTY HISTORICAL SOCIETY, MIAMI COUNTY HISTORICAL MUSEUM, *IN649-520*

MIAMI COUNTY HISTORICAL SOCIETY, PUTERBAUGH MUSEUM, *IN649-650*

MIAMI PURCHASE ASSOCIATION FOR HISTORIC PRESERVATION, *OH171-530*

MIAMI UNIVERSITY, KING LIBRARY, WALTER HAVIGHURST SPECIAL COLLECTIONS, *OH680-540*

MIAMI-DADE PUBLIC LIBRARY, FLORIDA COLLECTION, *FL440-530*

MICHAEL NOVAK PAPERS, *MA615-730*

MICHEL ORRADRE LIBRARY, *CA778-800*

MICHIGAN CITY HISTORICAL SOCIETY, OLD LIGHTHOUSE MUSEUM, *IN517-520*

MICHIGAN DEPARTMENT OF NATURAL RESOURCES, *MI200-240, MI343-280, MI368-320, MI590-520*

MICHIGAN DEPARTMENT OF STATE, MICHIGAN HISTORY DIVISION, STATE ARCHIVES UNIT, *MI550-530*

MICHIGAN HISTORICAL COLLECTIONS, *MI40-784*

MICHIGAN HISTORICAL COMMISSION, ARCHIVES, *MI550-530*

MICHIGAN HISTORY DIVISION, STATE ARCHIVES UNIT, *MI550-530*

MICHIGAN STATE ARCHIVES, *MI550-530*

MICHIGAN STATE UNIVERSITY, LIBRARIES, SPECIAL COLLECTIONS DIVISION, *MI255-530*

MICHIGAN STATE UNIVERSITY, UNIVERSITY ARCHIVES AND HISTORICAL COLLECTIONS, *MI255-545*

MICHIGAN TECHNOLOGICAL UNIVERSITY, LIBRARY, ARCHIVES, *MI464-530*

MICHIGAN, LIBRARY OF, INFORMATION SERVICES UNIT, *MI550-505*

MID-COLUMBIA REGIONAL LIBRARY, *WA420-520*

MID-CONTINENT BAPTIST BIBLE COLLEGE, *KY520-530*

MID-CONTINENT RAILWAY HISTORICAL SOCIETY, MID-CONTINENT RAILWAY MUSEUM, *WI530-520*

MID-CONTINENT RAILWAY MUSEUM, *WI530-520*

MIDDLE AMERICAN RESEARCH INSTITUTE LIBRARY, *LA600-760*

MIDDLE GEORGIA HISTORICAL SOCIETY, ARCHIVES AND SPECIAL COLLECTIONS, *GA735-540*

MIDDLEBOROUGH HISTORICAL ASSOCIATION, *MA542-520*

MIDDLEBURY COLLEGE, STARR LIBRARY, FLANDERS BALLAD COLLECTION, *VT432-520*

MIDDLEBURY COLLEGE, STARR LIBRARY, SPECIAL COLLECTIONS, *VT432-530*

MIDDLESEX COUNTY HISTORICAL SOCIETY, *CT428-520*

MIDDLETON PUBLIC LIBRARY, *WI442-530*

MIDDLETOWN PUBLIC LIBRARY, OHIO SECTION, GENEALOGY ROOM, *OH545-530*

MIDDLETOWN SPRINGS HISTORICAL SOCIETY, *VT448-520*

MIDWAY COLLEGE, MARRS LIBRARY, *KY54G-520*

MIDWAY VILLAGE - ROCKFORD MUSEUM, *IL806-705*

MIDWEST CHINA CENTER, *MN763-510*

MIDWEST INTER-LIBRARY CENTER, *IL169-247*

MIDWEST OLD SETTLERS AND THRESHERS ASSOCIATION, MUSEUM OF REPERTOIRE AMERICA, *IA688-520*

MIDWESTERN STATE UNIVERSITY, MOFFETT LIBRARY, *TX968-520*

MIGRATION STUDIES, CENTER FOR, ARCHIVES, *NY587-940*

MIKE RHEUDASIL LEARNING CENTER, A. M. AND WELMA AIKIN REGIONAL ARCHIVES, *TX695-640*

MILFORD HISTORICAL SOCIETY, *CT435-520*

MILITARY AIRLIFT COMMAND, AEROSPACE AUDIOVISUAL SERVICE, 1361ST AUDIOVISUAL SQUADRON, *VA50-530*

MILITARY ORDER OF THE LOYAL LEGION OF THE UNITED STATES, WAR LIBRARY AND MUSEUM, *PA725-930*

MILL VALLEY HISTORICAL SOCIETY, *CA460-520*

MILLER F. WHITTAKER LIBRARY, SOUTH CAROLINA STATE COLLEGE HISTORICAL COLLECTION, *SC720-710*

MILLER LIBRARY, BRETHREN COLLECTION, *KS593-510*

MILLER, CLIFTON M., LIBRARY, *MD228-870*

MILLER, W. EVERETT, LIBRARY OF VEHICLES, *CA282-480*

MILLERSBURG MILITARY INSTITUTE, ALUMNI OFFICE, *KY54Q-520*

MILLERSVILLE UNIVERSITY OF PENNSYLVANIA, GANSER LIBRARY, ARCHIVES AND SPECIAL COLLECTIONS, *PA595-530*

MILLS COLLEGE, LIBRARY, *CA540-520*

MILLS MEMORIAL LIBRARY, *FL960-690*

MILLSAPS COLLEGE, MILLSAPS-WILSON LIBRARY, LEHMAN ENGEL COLLECTION, *MS550-460*

MILLSAPS-WILSON LIBRARY, LEHMAN ENGEL COLLECTION, *MS550-460*

MILNE LIBRARY, *NY321-720*

MILNE, JAMES M., LIBRARY, SPECIAL COLLECTIONS CENTER, *NY648-720*

MILNER LIBRARY, MAP ROOM, *IL624-370*

MILNER LIBRARY, SPECIAL COLLECTIONS/ILLINOIS STATE UNIVERSITY ARCHIVES, *IL624-380*

MILTON HISTORICAL SOCIETY, LIBRARY, *WI450-530*

MILTON S. EISENHOWER LIBRARY, *MD76-360*

MILWAUKEE ART CENTER, PRAIRIE ARCHIVES, *WI456-530*

MILWAUKEE COUNTY HISTORICAL SOCIETY, *WI456-540*

MILWAUKEE PUBLIC LIBRARY, LOCAL HISTORY AND MARINE ROOM, *WI456-550*

MILWAUKEE PUBLIC MUSEUM, HISTORY DIVISION, *WI456-560*

MINER, EDWARD G., LIBRARY, *NY752-885*

MINERAL COUNTY COLLECTION, *WV500-640*

MINERAL POINT HISTORICAL SOCIETY, GUNDRY HOUSE, *WI462-520*

MINERVA FREE LIBRARY, *NY830-520*

MINERVA HISTORICAL SOCIETY, TOWN HISTORIAN, *NY550-520*

MINISINK VALLEY HISTORICAL SOCIETY, *NY714-560*

MINNEAPOLIS HISTORY COLLECTION, *MN541-592*

MINNEAPOLIS INSTITUTE OF ARTS, *MN541-496*

MINNEAPOLIS PUBLIC LIBRARY AND INFORMATION CENTER, ART/MUSIC DEPARTMENT AND ATHENAEUM, *MN541-512*

MINNEAPOLIS PUBLIC LIBRARY AND INFORMATION CENTER, MINNEAPOLIS HISTORY COLLECTION, *MN541-592*

MINNEAPOLIS PUBLIC LIBRARY AND INFORMATION CENTER, NORTH REGIONAL LIBRARY, RALPH WALDO EMERSON ROOM*MN541-600*

MINNESOTA HISTORICAL SOCIETY, AUDIO-VISUAL LIBRARY, *MN763-530*

MINNESOTA HISTORICAL SOCIETY, DIVISION OF ARCHIVES AND MANUSCRIPTS, *MN763-540*

MINNESOTA HISTORICAL SOCIETY, REGIONAL RESEARCH CENTERS, *MN63-75, MN261-810, MN506-530, MN520-700, MN562-520, MN583-920, MN742-700, MN975-730*

MINNESOTA PIONEER PARK, *MN38-520*

MINNESOTA STATE AGRICULTURAL SOCIETY, MINNESOTA STATE FAIR HISTORY MUSEUM, *MN763-573*

MINNESOTA STATE ARCHIVES, *MN763-540*

MINNESOTA STATE FAIR HISTORY MUSEUM, *MN763-573*

MINNESOTA STATE LAW LIBRARY, *MN763-580*

MINOT STATE COLLEGE, MEMORIAL LIBRARY, *ND652-520*

MINT MUSEUM, *NC160-520*

MINUTE MAN NATIONAL HISTORICAL PARK, *MA217-520*

MISS PORTER'S SCHOOL, ARCHIVES, *CT247-640*

MISSION MILL MUSEUM ASSOCIATION, *OR816-530*

MISSION SAN ANTONIO, *CA352-520*

MISSION SAN JOSE, ARCHIVES, *CA270-520*

MISSIONARY BAPTIST SEMINARY, GLOVER LIBRARY, MISSIONARY BAPTIST ARCHIVES, *AR510-520*

MISSIONARY RESEARCH LIBRARY, *NY591-500*

MISSISSIPPI COLLEGE, LIBRARY, *MS260-500*

MISSISSIPPI COUNTY HISTORICAL SOCIETY, MUSEUM, *MO170-520*

MISSISSIPPI DEPARTMENT OF ARCHIVES AND HISTORY, ARCHIVES AND LIBRARY DIVISION, *MS550-500*

MISSISSIPPI METHODIST ARCHIVES, *MS550-540*

MISSISSIPPI STATE ARCHIVES, *MS550-500*

MISSISSIPPI STATE UNIVERSITY, MITCHELL MEMORIAL LIBRARY, SPECIAL COLLECTIONS, *MS610-520*

MISSISSIPPI UNIVERSITY FOR WOMEN, J. C. FANT MEMORIAL LIBRARY, *MS300-520*

MISSISSIPPI UNIVERSITY FOR WOMEN, M.U.W. ARCHIVES AND MUSEUM, *MS300-550*

MISSISSIPPI VALLEY COLLECTION/SPECIAL COLLECTIONS DEPARTMENT, *TN630-530*

MISSOURI BOTANICAL GARDEN, ARCHIVES, *MO810-490*

MISSOURI DEPARTMENT OF NATURAL RESOURCES, DIVISION OF GEOLOGY AND LAND SURVEY, *MO760-530*

MISSOURI DEPARTMENT OF NATURAL RESOURCES, DIVISION OF PARKS AND RECREATION, *MO490-880, MO870-520*

MISSOURI HISTORICAL SOCIETY, ARCHIVES, *MO810-510*

MISSOURI OFFICE OF SECRETARY OF STATE, RECORDS MANAGEMENT AND ARCHIVES SERVICE, *MO410-545*

MISSOURI STATE ARCHIVES, *MO410-545*

MITCHELL COUNTY HISTORICAL SOCIETY, MUSEUM, *IA766-520*

MITCHELL COUNTY PUBLIC LIBRARY, *TX189-520*

MITCHELL LIBRARY, ARCHIVES, *TN495-120*

MITCHELL MEMORIAL LIBRARY, SPECIAL COLLECTIONS, *MS610-520*

MITCHELL, ALEXANDER, PUBLIC LIBRARY, SOUTH DAKOTA COLLECTION, *SD18-40*

MITCHELL, MARIA, ASSOCIATION, NANTUCKET, *MA572-540*

MITRE CORPORATION, *MA77-520*

MOBERLY HISTORICAL AND RAILROAD MUSEUM, *MO607-520*

MOBILE PUBLIC LIBRARY, SPECIAL COLLECTIONS DIVISION, *AL580-510*

MOBILE, MUSEUM OF THE CITY OF, *AL580-530*

MOCK, CHARLES A., LIBRARY, *IA544-880*

MODERN GREEK STUDIES ASSOCIATION, *MA169-800*

MOELLERING, HENRY F., MEMORIAL LIBRARY, *IN858-850*

MOFFETT LIBRARY, *TX968-520*

MONMOUTH COLLEGE (IL), LIBRARY, *IL553-520*

MONMOUTH COUNTY HISTORICAL ASSOCIATION, LIBRARY, *NJ276-510*

MONONA PUBLIC LIBRARY, *WI474-520*

MONROE COMMUNITY COLLEGE, LEROY V. GOOD LIBRARY, *NY752-525*

MONROE COUNTY HISTORIAN'S OFFICE, *NY752-530*

MONROE COUNTY HISTORICAL COMMISSION, ARCHIVES, *MI650-510*

MONROE COUNTY HISTORICAL SOCIETY, LIBRARY, *PA850-520*

MONROE COUNTY HISTORICAL SOCIETY, MONROE COUNTY LOCAL HISTORY ROOM, *WI714-520*

MONROE COUNTY LIBRARY SYSTEM, *MI650-530*

MONROE COUNTY LOCAL HISTORY ROOM, *WI714-520*

MONROE COUNTY LOCAL HISTORY ROOM AND LIBRARY, *WI714-525*

MONROE COUNTY PUBLIC LIBRARY, INDIANA ROOM, *IN66-520*

MONROE HISTORICAL SOCIETY, *WA560-520*

MONROE, JAMES, LAW OFFICE MUSEUM AND MEMORIAL LIBRARY, *VA285-400*

MONTANA HISTORICAL SOCIETY, DIVISION OF ARCHIVES AND MANUSCRIPTS, *MT530-500*

MONTANA STATE ARCHIVES, *MT530-500*

MONTANA STATE UNIVERSITY, LIBRARY, SPECIAL COLLECTIONS, *MT130-540*

MONTANA STATE UNIVERSITY, ROLAND R. RENNE LIBRARY, ARCHIVES, *MT130-535*

MONTAUK, *IA133-520*

MONTCLAIR PUBLIC LIBRARY, *NJ532-515*

MONTEITH LIBRARY, ARCHIVES, *MI32-40*

MONTEREY HISTORY AND ART ASSOCIATION, ALLEN KNIGHT MARITIME MUSEUM, *CA480-500*

MONTEREY HISTORY AND ART ASSOCIATION, MAYO HAYES O'DONNELL LIBRARY, *CA480-510*

MONTEREY PUBLIC LIBRARY, *CA480-530*

MONTGOMERY COUNTY (MD) HISTORICAL SOCIETY, *MD760-530*

MONTGOMERY COUNTY (NY) HISTORICAL SOCIETY, FORT JOHNSON MANSION, *NY297-520*

MONTGOMERY COUNTY (OH) HISTORICAL SOCIETY, *OH223-520*

MONTGOMERY COUNTY (PA) HISTORICAL SOCIETY, *PA690-320*

MONTGOMERY COUNTY COMMUNITY COLLEGE, LEARNING RESOURCE CENTER, *PA105-520*

MONTGOMERY COUNTY DEPARTMENT OF HISTORY AND ARCHIVES, *NY292-520*

MONTGOMERY COUNTY PUBLIC LIBRARY, *KY56N-520*

MONTGOMERY COUNTY-NORRISTOWN PUBLIC LIBRARY, STEINBRIGHT LOCAL HISTORY COLLECTION, *PA690-520*

MONTOUR FALLS MEMORIAL LIBRARY, *NY562-510*

MOODY BIBLE INSTITUTE, LIBRARY, HISTORICAL COLLECTION, *IL170-234*

MOODY MEDICAL LIBRARY, HISTORY OF MEDICINE AND ARCHIVES DEPT., *TX397-790*

MOON, F. FRANKLIN, LIBRARY, *NY872-720*

MOORE COUNTY HISTORICAL ASSOCIATION, *NC760-520*

MOORE MEMORIAL LIBRARY, *NY353-520*

MOORE, HUGH, PARK, CANAL MUSEUM, RESEARCH LIBRARY, *PA270-320*

MOORHEAD STATE UNIVERSITY, NORTHWEST MINNESOTA HISTORICAL CENTER, *MN562-520*

MOORLAND-SPINGARN RESEARCH CENTER, MANUSCRIPT DIVISION, *DC8-850*

MORAGA HISTORICAL SOCIETY, ARCHIVE, *CA488-520*

MORAVIAN ARCHIVES (NC), *NC930-510*

MORAVIAN ARCHIVES (PA), *PA90-500*

MORAVIAN CHURCH IN AMERICA, SOUTHERN PROVINCE, MORAVIAN ARCHIVES, *NC930-510*

MORAVIAN MUSIC FOUNDATION, *NC930-530*

MORE, THOMAS, COLLEGE, ARCHIVES, *KY280-760*

MOREELL COLLECTION, *CA605-520*

MOREELL LIBRARY, MOREELL COLLECTION, *CA605-530*

MOREHEAD STATE UNIVERSITY, JOHNSON CAMDEN LIBRARY, SPECIAL COLLECTIONS, *KY558-520*

MORGAN COUNTY (IL) HISTORICAL SOCIETY, *IL394-400*

MORGAN COUNTY (MO) HISTORICAL SOCIETY, *MO902-520*

MORGAN STATE UNIVERSITY, SOPER LIBRARY, *MD76-540*

MORGAN, PIERPONT, LIBRARY, *NY593-460*

MORGANTOWN PUBLIC LIBRARY, WEST VIRGINIA COLLECTION AND ARCHIVES, *WV650-520*

MORISON, SAMUEL ELIOT, LIBRARY, *MA109-850*

MORLEY LIBRARY, GENEALOGICAL COLLECTION, *OH684-520*

MORRIS COUNTY FREE LIBRARY, NEW JERSEY ROOM, *NJ950-520*
MORRIS COUNTY HISTORICAL SOCIETY, *NJ548-520*
MORRIS LIBRARY, SPECIAL COLLECTIONS, *IL124-725*
MORRISON COUNTY HISTORICAL SOCIETY, CHARLES A.
  WEYERHAEUSER MEMORIAL MUSEUM, *MN466-520*
MORRISON HISTORICAL SOCIETY, *IL567-520*
MORRISON-KENYON LIBRARY, *KY886-30*
MORRISSON-REEVES LIBRARY, *IN704-520*
MORRISTOWN AND MORRIS TOWNSHIP, JOINT FREE PUBLIC
  LIBRARY OF, *NJ548-400*
MORRISTOWN LIBRARY, *NJ548-400*
MORRISTOWN NATIONAL HISTORICAL PARK, *NJ548-530*
MORROW, JAMES E., LIBRARY, SPECIAL COLLECTIONS
  DEPARTMENT, *WV435-520*
MORSE INSTITUTE, LIBRARY, *MA576-520*
MORTON ARBORETUM, STERLING MORTON LIBRARY, *IL459-520*
MORTON MUSEUM OF COOKE COUNTY, *TX390-140*
MORTON, STERLING, LIBRARY, *IL459-520*
MOSES LAKE PUBLIC LIBRARY, *WA565-520*
MOSES MASON MUSEUM, *ME95-80*
MOSS ARCHIVES, *NJ751-520*
MOSSEY LEARNING RESOURCES CENTER, *MI440-320*
MOTOR BUS SOCIETY, *NJ918-520*
MOTOROLA, ARCHIVES, *IL841-520*
MOULTRIE COUNTY HISTORICAL AND GENEALOGICAL SOCIETY,
  IL886-520
MOUNT BAKER NATIONAL FOREST, *See* Snoqualmie and Mount Baker
  National Forest
MOUNT HERMON LIBRARIES, *MA568-560*
MOUNT HOLLY LIBRARY, *NJ552-80*
MOUNT HOLYOKE COLLEGE, SKINNER MUSEUM, *MA776-515*
MOUNT HOLYOKE COLLEGE, WILLISTON MEMORIAL LIBRARY,
  MA776-530
MOUNT MICHAEL BENEDICTINE ABBEY AND HIGH SCHOOL,
  NE320-520
MOUNT MORRIS LIBRARY, *NY566-540*
MOUNT OLIVE COLLEGE, MOYE LIBRARY, FREE WILL BAPTIST
  HISTORICAL COLLECTION, *NC610-520*
MOUNT PLEASANT HISTORICAL CENTER, *OH588-520*
MOUNT RAINIER NATIONAL PARK, ADMINISTRATION, *WA35-520*
MOUNT SAINT MARY'S COLLEGE, CHARLES WILLARD COE
  MEMORIAL LIBRARY, *CA421-470*
MOUNT SAINT MARY'S COLLEGE, HUGH J. PHILLIPS LIBRARY,
  MD380-520
MOUNT SINAI SCHOOL OF MEDICINE, ARCHIVE, *NY591-600*
MOUNT ST. JOSEPH MOTHERHOUSE, *OH593-720*
MOUNT UNION COLLEGE, LIBRARY, *OH16-520*
MOUNT VERNON LADIES' ASSOCIATION OF THE UNION,
  LIBRARY, *VA540-520*
MOUNT VERNON PUBLIC LIBRARY, *IL599-520, WA570-540*
MOUNTAIN LIFE MUSEUM, *KY48V-495*
MOUNTAIN VIEW PIONEER AND HISTORICAL ASSOCIATION,
  PIONEER ROOM, *CA496-520*
MOUNTLAKE TERRACE LIBRARY, *WA571-520*
MOWER COUNTY HISTORICAL SOCIETY, *MN49-520*
MOYE LIBRARY, FREE WILL BAPTIST HISTORICAL COLLECTION,
  NC610-520
MUGAR LIBRARY, DEPARTMENT OF SPECIAL COLLECTIONS,
  MA108-240
MUHLENBERG COLLEGE, HAAS LIBRARY, *PA25-520*
MUKILTEO HISTORICAL SOCIETY, *WA573-520*
MUKLESHOOT TRIBAL COUNCIL, *WA37-540*
MUNCIE PUBLIC LIBRARY, *IN539-545*
MUNCY HISTORICAL SOCIETY, *PA625-520*
MUNDELEIN COLLEGE, LEARNING RESOURCE CENTER, *IL170-250*
MUNDT, KARL E., ARCHIVES, *SD450-150*
MUNDT, KARL E., LIBRARY, KARL E. MUNDT ARCHIVES,
  SD450-150
MUNICIPAL REFERENCE LIBRARY (SEATTLE WA), *WA820-775*
MUNSON-WILLIAMS-PROCTOR INSTITUTE, AUTOGRAPH
  COLLECTION, *NY899-520*
MURFREESBORO HISTORICAL ASSOCIATION, *NC620-520*
MURPHY LIBRARY, SPECIAL COLLECTIONS AND AREA
  RESEARCH CENTER, *WI298-810*
MURRAY STATE UNIVERSITY, POGUE SPECIAL COLLECTIONS
  LIBRARY, *KY564-520*
MURRAY, HENRY A., RESEARCH CENTER, *MA169-885*
MURROW, EDWARD R., CENTER FOR PUBLIC DIPLOMACY,
  MA528-740
MUSEUM AND ARCHIVES OF GEORGIA EDUCATION, *GA780-310*
MUSEUM OF AFRICAN AMERICAN LIFE AND CULTURE, *TX252-80*
MUSEUM OF AFRICAN ART AND FREDERICK DOUGLASS
  INSTITUTE, ARCHIVES, *DC19-440*
MUSEUM OF AFRICAN ART AND FREDERICK DOUGLASS
  INSTITUTE, ELIOT ELISOFON ARCHIVES, *DC19-450*
MUSEUM OF AMERICAN JEWISH HISTORY, *PA725-980*
MUSEUM OF AMERICAN TEXTILE HISTORY, *MA606-530*

MUSEUM OF ANESTHESIOLOGY-WOOD LIBRARY, *IL708-40*
MUSEUM OF BROADCASTING, *NY591-690*
MUSEUM OF COASTAL HISTORY, *GA885-120*
MUSEUM OF COMPARATIVE ZOOLOGY, HARVARD UNIVERSITY,
  MA169-500
MUSEUM OF FINE ARTS, LIBRARY, *MA109-360*
MUSEUM OF HISTORY AND INDUSTRY, SOPHIE FRYE BASS
  MEMORIAL LIBRARY, *WA820-770*
MUSEUM OF INDEPENDENT TELEPHONY, *KS10-520*
MUSEUM OF MODERN ART, FILM STUDY CENTER, *NY591-760*
MUSEUM OF MODERN ART, LIBRARY, *NY591-780*
MUSEUM OF MODERN ART, PHOTOGRAPHIC ARCHIVES,
  NY591-700
MUSEUM OF NATIVE AMERICAN CULTURES, *WA880-550*
MUSEUM OF NAVAHO CEREMONIAL ART, *NM722-510*
MUSEUM OF NEW MEXICO, HISTORY BUREAU, HISTORY
  LIBRARY, *NM722-530*
MUSEUM OF NEW MEXICO, LABORATORY OF ANTHROPOLOGY,
  NM722-535
MUSEUM OF NEW MEXICO, MONUMENT DIVISION, LINCOLN
  STATE MONUMENT, *NM532-520*
MUSEUM OF NORTH IDAHO, *ID240-520*
MUSEUM OF NORTHERN ARIZONA, HAROLD S. COLTON
  MEMORIAL LIBRARY, MUSEUM ARCHIVES AND MSS.
  COLLECT., *AZ250-520*
MUSEUM OF REPERTOIRE AMERICA, *IA688-520*
MUSEUM OF SCIENCE, *MA109-380*
MUSEUM OF SCIENCE AND INDUSTRY, LIBRARY, *IL170-273*
MUSEUM OF SOUTHWESTERN BIOLOGY, HERBARIUM AND
  MUSEUM OF BOTANY, *NM114-825*
MUSEUM OF THE AMERICAN INDIAN, HEYE FOUNDATION,
  HUNTINGTON FREE LIBRARY AND READING ROOM,
  NY591-820
MUSEUM OF THE CITY OF MOBILE, *AL580-530*
MUSEUM OF THE CITY OF NEW YORK, LIBRARY, *NY591-840*
MUSEUM OF THE CITY OF NEW YORK, THEATRE AND MUSIC
  COLLECTION, *NY591-850*
MUSEUM OF THE CONFEDERACY, *VA690-530*
MUSEUM OF THE GREAT PLAINS, LIBRARY AND ARCHIVES,
  OK490-520
MUSEUM OF WESTERN COLORADO, ARCHIVES, *CO476-540*
MUSEUM VILLAGE IN ORANGE COUNTY, *NY558-520*
MUSEUMS OF STONY BROOK, ARCHIVES, *NY866-520*
MUSKEGON COUNTY MUSEUM, *MI675-510*
MUSKINGUM COUNTY PIONEER AND HISTORICAL SOCIETY, DR.
  INCREASE MATHEWS HOUSE, *OH996-520*
MUSSELMAN LIBRARY/LEARNING RESOURCES CENTER,
  PA325-280
MUTUAL ASSURANCE COMPANY, *PA725-990*
MUTUAL OF OMAHA INSURANCE COMPANY, *NE624-520*
MYERS LIBRARY, *KS718-600*
MYNDERSE PUBLIC LIBRARY, *NY821-520*
MYRTLE BANK GALLERIES, *MS640-520*
MYSTIC SEAPORT MUSEUM, G. W. BLUNT WHITE LIBRARY,
  CT463-520

N

N.O.A.A., ENVIRONMENTAL DATA INFORMATION SERVICE,
  NATIONAL CLIMATIC DATA CENTER, *NC60-160*
NANTUCKET HISTORICAL ASSOCIATION, PETER FOULGER
  MUSEUM, LIBRARY, *MA572-560*
NANTUCKET MARIA MITCHELL ASSOCIATION, SCIENCE
  LIBRARY, MARIA MITCHELL MEMORABILIA, *MA572-540*
NAPA COUNTY HISTORICAL SOCIETY, *CA500-560*
NAPERVILLE HERITAGE SOCIETY, NAPER SETTLEMENT,
  CAROLINE MARTIN-MITCHELL MUSEUM, *IL609-120*
NAPLES LIBRARY, *NY569A-56*
NARRAGANSETT HISTORICAL SOCIETY, *MA845-560*
NASH COUNTY HISTORICAL ASSOCIATION, *NC710-540*
NASH LIBRARY, *OK228-610*
NASHOTAH HOUSE, LIBRARY, *WI498-560*
NASHUA PUBLIC LIBRARY, *NH672-570*
NASHVILLE AND DAVIDSON COUNTY PUBLIC LIBRARY,
  NASHVILLE ROOM, *TN690-600*
NASSAU COUNTY HISTORICAL MUSEUM AND LIBRARY,
  NY260-560
NASSAU COUNTY MUSEUM, REFERENCE LIBRARY, *NY260-560*
NASSON COLLEGE, ANDERSON LEARNING CENTER-LIBRARY,
  ME837-560
NATAS-UCLA TELEVISION LIBRARY, *CA421-760*
NATCHEZ TRACE PARKWAY, LIBRARY, *MS880-560*
NATHAN TAYLOR YORKERS MUSEUM, *NY847-560*
NATHANIEL ORR HOUSE, *WA889-560*
NATIONAL ACADEMY OF DESIGN, *NY591-920*
NATIONAL ACADEMY OF SCIENCES, *DC14-100*

NATIONAL AERONAUTICS AND SPACE ADMINISTRATION, AUDIO-VISUAL BRANCH, *DC14-120*

NATIONAL AERONAUTICS AND SPACE ADMINISTRATION, HEADQUARTERS HISTORY OFFICE, *DC14-140*

NATIONAL AERONAUTICS AND SPACE ADMINISTRATION, JET PROPULSION LABORATORY, CALTECH, *CA578-560*

NATIONAL AERONAUTICS AND SPACE ADMINISTRATION, LYNDON B. JOHNSON SPACE CENTER, HISTORY OFFICE, *TX483-560*

NATIONAL AGRICULTURAL LIBRARY, *MD133-160*

NATIONAL AIR AND SPACE MUSEUM, LIBRARY, *DC19-500*

NATIONAL ANTHROPOLOGICAL ARCHIVES, *DC19-520*

NATIONAL ARBORETUM, *DC14-180*

NATIONAL ARCHIVES AND RECORDS ADMINISTRATION, DWIGHT D. EISENHOWER LIBRARY, *KS10-170*

NATIONAL ARCHIVES AND RECORDS ADMINISTRATION, FEDERAL ARCHIVES AND RECORDS CENTER, *CA386-560, CA704-560, CO252-550, IL170-280, MO430-540, NJ46-560, TX374-550*

NATIONAL ARCHIVES AND RECORDS ADMINISTRATION, FEDERAL ARCHIVES AND RECORDS CENTER, ARCHIVES BRANCH, *GA405-560, MA871-540, PA726-7, WA820-550*

NATIONAL ARCHIVES AND RECORDS ADMINISTRATION, FRANKLIN D. ROOSEVELT LIBRARY, *NY427-240*

NATIONAL ARCHIVES AND RECORDS ADMINISTRATION, GERALD R. FORD LIBRARY, *MI40-300*

NATIONAL ARCHIVES AND RECORDS ADMINISTRATION, HARRY S. TRUMAN LIBRARY, *MO400-320*

NATIONAL ARCHIVES AND RECORDS ADMINISTRATION, HERBERT HOOVER LIBRARY, *IA966-320*

NATIONAL ARCHIVES AND RECORDS ADMINISTRATION, JOHN F. KENNEDY LIBRARY, *MA108-965*

NATIONAL ARCHIVES AND RECORDS ADMINISTRATION, LYNDON BAINES JOHNSON LIBRARY, *TX56-520*

NATIONAL ARCHIVES AND RECORDS ADMINISTRATION, OFFICE OF THE NATIONAL ARCHIVES, *DC14-250, NY949-780*

NATIONAL ARCHIVES FOR BLACK WOMEN'S HISTORY, *VA20-322*

NATIONAL ASSOCIATION OF WATCH AND CLOCK COLLECTORS MUSEUM, INC., LIBRARY, *PA215-560*

NATIONAL AUDUBON SOCIETY, LIBRARY, *NY592-20*

NATIONAL BAHA'I ARCHIVES, *IL981-560*

NATIONAL BASEBALL HALL OF FAME AND MUSEUM, NATIONAL BASEBALL LIBRARY, *NY211-540*

NATIONAL BOARD OF THE YOUNG WOMEN'S CHRISTIAN ASSOCIATION OF THE UNITED STATES OF AMERICA, ARCHIVES*NY592-30*

NATIONAL BOARD OF YOUNG MEN'S CHRISTIAN ASSOCIATIONS OF THE UNITED STATES, *IL170-283*

NATIONAL BUSINESS LEAGUE, *DC14-350*

NATIONAL CAPITAL HISTORICAL MUSEUM OF TRANSPORTATION, NATIONAL CAPITAL TROLLEY MUSEUM, *MD985-560*

NATIONAL CAPITAL PLANNING COMMISSION, *DC14-370*

NATIONAL CAPITAL TROLLEY MUSEUM, *MD985-560*

NATIONAL CATHOLIC NEWS SERVICE, *DC14-380*

NATIONAL CITY PUBLIC LIBRARY, ARCHIVES ROOM, *CA504-560*

NATIONAL CLIMATIC CENTER, *NC60-160*

NATIONAL COLLECTION OF FINE ARTS, *DC19-536*

NATIONAL COTTON COUNCIL OF AMERICA, *TN630-590*

NATIONAL COUNCIL OF NEGRO WOMEN, NATIONAL ARCHIVES FOR BLACK WOMEN'S HISTORY, *VA20-322*

NATIONALDEFENSE UNIVERSITY, LIBRARY, *DC14-410*

NATIONAL FEDERATION OF BUSINESS AND PROFESSIONAL WOMEN'S CLUBS, ARCHIVES DEPARTMENT, *DC14-420*

NATIONAL FORESTS IN FLORIDA, *FL800-575*

NATIONAL FORESTS IN NORTH CAROLINA, *NC60-240*

NATIONAL GALLERY OF ART, LIBRARY, *DC14-450*

NATIONAL GALLERY OF ART, PHOTOGRAPHIC ARCHIVES, *DC14-460*

NATIONAL GAY LIBERATION ARCHIVES, *CT316-360*

NATIONAL GENEALOGICAL SOCIETY, *DC14-470*

NATIONAL GEOPHYSICAL DATA CENTER, *CO108-560*

NATIONAL GRANGE, MEMORIAL LIBRARY, *DC14-490*

NATIONAL GUARD ASSOCIATION OF THE UNITED STATES, *DC14-500*

NATIONAL INSURANCE ASSOCIATION, *IL170-312*

NATIONAL LIBRARY OF MEDICINE, HISTORY OF MEDICINE DIVISION, *MD152-550*

NATIONAL MARITIME MUSEUM, J. PORTER SHAW LIBRARY, *CA720-485*

NATIONAL MUSEUM OF AMERICAN ART, ARCHIVES, *DC19-536*

NATIONAL MUSEUM OF AMERICAN ART, SLIDE AND PHOTOGRAPH ARCHIVE, *DC19-539*

NATIONAL MUSEUM OF AMERICAN HISTORY, ARCHIVES CENTER, *DC19-542*

NATIONAL MUSEUM OF AMERICAN HISTORY, DEPT. OF HIST. OF SCI. & TECH., DIV. OF ARMED FORCES HIST., *DC19-621*

NATIONAL MUSEUM OF AMERICAN HISTORY, DEPT. OF HIST. OF SCI. & TECH., DIV. OF ELECTR. & PHYSICS, *DC19-586*

NATIONAL MUSEUM OF AMERICAN HISTORY, DEPT. OF HIST. OF SCI. & TECH., DIV. OF EXTRACT. INDUS., *DC19-591*

NATIONAL MUSEUM OF AMERICAN HISTORY, DEPT. OF HIST. OF SCI. & TECH., DIV. OF MATHEMATICS, *DC19-596*

NATIONAL MUSEUM OF AMERICAN HISTORY, DEPT. OF HIST. OF SCI. & TECH., DIV. OF MECH. & CIV. ENG., *DC19-601*

NATIONAL MUSEUM OF AMERICAN HIST., DEPT. OF HIST. OF SCI. & TECH., DIV. OF MECHANISMS, *DC19-606*

NATIONAL MUSEUM OF AMERICAN HISTORY, DEPT. OF HIST. OF SCI. & TECH., DIV. OF MEDICAL SCIENCES, *DC19-611*

NATIONAL MUSEUM OF AMERICAN HISTORY, DEPT. OF HIST. OF SCI. & TECH., DIV. OF MILITARY HIST., *DC19-616*

NATIONAL MUSEUM OF AMERICAN HISTORY, DEPT. OF HIST. OF SCI. & TECH., DIV. OF PHOTOGR. HIST., *DC19-626*

NATIONAL MUSEUM OF AMERICAN HISTORY, DEPT. OF HIST. OF SCI. & TECH., DIV. OF PHYSICAL SCIENCES, *DC19-631*

NATIONAL MUSEUM OF AMERICAN HISTORY, DEPT. OF HIST. OF SCI. & TECH., DIV. OF TRANSPORTATION, *DC19-636*

NATIONAL MUSEUM OF AMERICAN HISTORY, DEPT. OF SOC. & CULT. HIST., DIV. OF CERAMICS AND GLASS, *DC19-545*

NATIONAL MUSEUM OF AMERICAN HISTORY, DEPT. OF SOC. & CULT. HIST., DIV. OF COMMUNITY LIFE, *DC19-550*

NATIONAL MUSEUM OF AMERICAN HISTORY, DEPT. OF SOC. & CULT. HIST., DIV. OF COSTUMES, *DC19-555*

NATIONAL MUSEUM OF AMERICAN HISTORY, DEPT. OF SOC. & CULT. HIST., DIV. OF DOMESTIC LIFE, *DC19-560*

NATIONAL MUSEUM OF AMERICAN HISTORY, DEPT. OF SOC. & CULT. HIST., DIV. OF GRAPHIC ARTS, *DC19-565*

NATIONAL MUSEUM OF AMERICAN HISTORY, DEPT. OF SOC. & CULT. HIST., DIV. OF MUSICAL INSTRUMENTS, *DC19-570*

NATIONAL MUSEUM OF AMERICAN HISTORY, DEPT. OF SOC. & CULT. HIST., DIV. OF POLITICAL HISTORY, *DC19-576*

NATIONAL MUSEUM OF AMERICAN HISTORY, DEPT. OF SOC. & CULT. HIST., DIV. OF TEXTILES, *DC19-581*

NATIONAL MUSEUM OF AMERICAN HISTORY, DIBNER LIBRARY, *DC19-641*

NATIONAL MUSEUM OF AMERICAN HISTORY, NATIONAL NUMISMATICS COLLECTIONS, *DC19-646*

NATIONAL MUSEUM OF AMERICAN HISTORY, NATIONAL PHILATELIC COLLECTIONS, *DC19-651*

NATIONAL NAVAL MEDICAL CENTER, NAVAL MEDICAL SCHOOL, EDWARD RHODES STITT LIBRARY, *MD152-560*

NATIONAL OCEAN SERVICE, CHARTING AND GEODETIC SERVICES, DATA CONTROL SECTION, *MD755-560*

NATIONAL OCEANIC AND ATMOSPHERIC ADMIN., NATIONAL OCEAN SERVICE, CHARTING AND GEODETIC SERVICES, *MD755-560*

NATIONAL OCEANIC AND ATMOSPHERIC ADMINISTRATION, ENVIRONMENTAL DATA INFORMATION SERVICE, *NC60-160*

NATIONAL OCEANIC AND ATMOSPHERIC ADMINISTRATION, NATIONAL GEOPHYSICAL DATA CENTER, *CO108-560*

NATIONAL OPINION RESEARCH CENTER, LIBRARY AND DATA ARCHIVES, *IL170-891*

NATIONAL ORGANIZATION FOR WOMEN, *DC14-520*

NATIONAL PARK SERVICE *See also* individual National parks, monuments, and other sites; and Parks, National, in subject index *AZ175-120, AZ350-290, AZ375-120, AZ450-640, AZ850-120, CA210-160, CA882-720, CA994-940, DC6-650, FL660-120, GA765-440, GA885-240, IA622-200, KS513-250, KY358-40, MA169-590, MA217-520, MD76-240, MD798-40, ME453-40, MN674-650, MO240-280, MO730-800, MO810-390, MS880-560, MT270-130, MT870-280, NJ548-530, NJ910-200, NM570-80, NM646-280, NY861-720, OR176-120, PA725-795, TN675-720, TN870-720, TX91-80, VA50-65, VA285-240, VA480-520, VA630-640, VA690-700, WY305-240, WY560-280, WY950-940, WY950-945, WY950-950*

NATIONAL PARK SERVICE, ARCHIVES, *WV350-560*

NATIONAL PARK SERVICE, DIVISION OF CULTURAL RESOURCES MANAGEMENT, *DC14-530*

NATIONAL PARK SERVICE, FORT SPOKANE INTERPRETIVE CENTER, *WA240-250*

NATIONAL PARK SERVICE, PHOTO LIBRARY, *DC14-540*

NATIONAL PRESS CLUB, ARCHIVES, *DC14-552*

NATIONAL RAILWAY HISTORICAL SOCIETY, MOHAWK AND HUDSON CHAPTER, ALCO HISTORIC PHOTOS, *NY804-560*

NATIONAL RAILWAY HISTORICAL SOCIETY, PACIFIC NORTHWEST CHAPTER, *OR720-560*

NATIONAL RURAL LETTER CARRIERS' ASSOCIATION, *VA20-666*

NATIONAL SHRINE OF THE IMMACULATE CONCEPTION, *DC14-580*

NATIONAL SOCIETY OF THE DAUGHTERS OF THE AMERICAN REVOLUTION, AMERICANA COLLECTION, *DC14-590*

NATIONAL SOCIETY OF THE DAUGHTERS OF THE AMERICAN REVOLUTION, GENEALOGICAL LIBRARY, *DC14-600*

NATIONAL SOCIETY, DAUGHTERS OF UTAH PIONEERS, *UT912-550*

NATIONAL SPELEOLOGICAL SOCIETY, ARCHIVES, *AL440-560*

NATIONAL SPIRITUAL ASSEMBLY OF THE BAHA'IS IN THE UNITED STATES, NATIONAL BAHA'I ARCHIVES, *IL981-560*
NATIONAL TEMPLE HILL ASSOCIATION, *NY902-560*
NATIONAL THEATRE, LIBRARY, *DC14-850*
NATIONAL TRUST FOR HISTORIC PRESERVATION, AUDIOVISUAL COLLECTIONS, *DC14-640*
NATIONAL TRUST FOR HISTORIC PRESERVATION, LIBRARY, *DC14-650*
NATIONAL WEATHER RECORDS CENTER, *NC60-160*
NATIONAL WOMAN'S CHRISTIAN TEMPERANCE UNION, FRANCES E. WILLARD MEMORIAL LIBRARY, *IL261-545*
NATIONALITY ROOM ARCHIVES, *PA735-825*
NATIONALITY ROOMS AND INTERCULTURAL EXCHANGE PROGRAMS, NATIONALITY ROOM ARCHIVES, *PA735-825*
NATURAL HISTORY AND LIBRARY SOCIETY OF SOUTH NATICK, *MA785-720*
NAVAJO TRIBAL MUSEUM, RESEARCH SECTION, *AZ900-560*
NAVAL AMPHIBIOUS BASE, LITTLE CREEK, NAVAL AMPHIBIOUS MUSEUM, *VA580-550*
NAVAL AMPHIBIOUS MUSEUM, *VA580-550*
NAVAL AVIATION HISTORY OFFICE, *DC14-715*
NAVAL HISTORICAL CENTER, NAVAL HISTORY DIVISION, CURATOR BRANCH, PHOTOGRAPHIC SECTION, *DC14-720*
NAVAL HISTORICAL CENTER, NAVAL HISTORY DIVISION, NAVY DEPARTMENT LIBRARY, *DC14-725*
NAVAL HISTORICAL FOUNDATION, *DC14-740*
NAVAL HISTORY DIVISION, CURATOR BRANCH, PHOTOGRAPHIC SECTION, *DC14-720*
NAVAL HISTORY DIVISION, NAVY DEPARTMENT LIBRARY, *DC14-725*
NAVAL IMAGING COMMAND, FILM DEPOSITORY DIVISION, *DC14-770*
NAVAL IMAGING COMMAND, STILL PICTURE DEPOSITORY, *DC14-780*
NAVAL MEDICAL SCHOOL, EDWARD RHODES STITT LIBRARY, *MD152-560*
NAVAL OBSERVATORY, LIBRARY, *DC14-750*
NAVAL OCEANOGRAPHIC OFFICE, TECHNICAL PUBLICATIONS GROUP, *MS50-560*
NAVAL SCHOOL, CIVIL ENGINEER CORPS OFFICERS, MOREELL LIBRARY, MOREELL COLLECTION, *CA605-530*
NAVAL TRAINING CENTER, HISTORICAL MUSEUM, *CA712-570*
NAVAL WAR COLLEGE, NAVAL HISTORICAL COLLECTION, *RI560-510*
NAVARRE-BETHLEHEM TOWNSHIP HISTORICAL SOCIETY, ARCHIVES, *OH603-560*
NAVY, CEC-SEABEE MUSEUM, *CA605-510*
NAZARETH COLLEGE, LORETTE WILMOT LIBRARY, *NY752-560*
NAZARETH CONVENT AND ACADEMY, NAZARETH MOTHERHOUSE ARCHIVES, *KS213-560*
NAZARETH MORAVIAN HISTORICAL SOCIETY, *PA640-570*
NEBRASKA NATIONAL FOREST, *NE240-560*
NEBRASKA STATE ARCHIVES, *NE560-550*
NEBRASKA STATE HISTORICAL SOCIETY, FORT ROBINSON MUSEUM, *NE284-560*
NEBRASKA STATE HISTORICAL SOCIETY, STATE ARCHIVES DIVISION, *NE560-550*
NEBRASKA STATE HISTORICAL SOCIETY, WILLA CATHER HISTORICAL CENTER, *NE736-560*
NEEDHAM FREE PUBLIC LIBRARY, LAURA G. WILLGOOSE ARCHIVES ROOM, *MA580-550*
NEEDHAM HISTORICAL SOCIETY, *MA580-570*
NEILL PUBLIC LIBRARY, *WA724-490*
NEILSON, WILLIAM ALLAN, LIBRARY, RARE BOOK ROOM, *MA624-750*
NELSON MEMORIAL LIBRARY, *CA32-640, TX947-720*
NEPTUNE HISTORICAL MUSEUM, *NJ564-560*
NETHERLANDS MUSEUM, *MI445-560*
NETTIE LEE BENSON LATIN AMERICAN COLLECTION, *TX56-860*
NEVADA COUNTY HISTORICAL SOCIETY, SEARLS HISTORICAL LIBRARY, *CA508-560*
NEVADA HISTORICAL SOCIETY, *NV940-560*
NEVADA STATE ARCHIVES, *NV90-530*
NEVADA STATE LIBRARY, DIVISION OF STATE, COUNTY, AND MUNICIPAL ARCHIVES, *NV90-530*
NEVERSINK VALLEY AREA MUSEUM, *NY229-560*
NEVILLE PUBLIC MUSEUM, *WI202-560*
NEW ALBANY-FLOYD COUNTY PUBLIC LIBRARY, INDIANA HISTORY ROOM, *IN561-560*
NEW BALTIMORE PUBLIC LIBRARY, *MI690-560*
NEW BEDFORD FREE PUBLIC LIBRARY, MELVILLE WHALING ROOM COLLECTION, *MA584-550*
NEW BERLIN LIBRARY, *NY570-560*
NEW BRITAIN PUBLIC LIBRARY, LOCAL HISTORY ROOM, *CT477-570*
NEW BRUNSWICK HISTORICAL CLUB, *NJ568-540*
NEW BRUNSWICK THEOLOGICAL SEMINARY, LIBRARY, *NJ568-570*

NEW CANAAN HISTORICAL SOCIETY, *CT484-550*
NEW CANAAN LIBRARY, *CT484-570*
NEW CASTLE ARCHIVES AND RECORDS COMMITTEE, *NH680-760*
NEW CASTLE FREE PUBLIC LIBRARY, *PA645-560*
NEW CASTLE HISTORICAL SOCIETY, *NY172-120*
NEW CHURCH LIBRARY, *OH171-95*
NEW ENGLAND AIR MUSEUM, *CT963-120*
NEW ENGLAND COLLEGE, DANFORTH LIBRARY, *NH396-560*
NEW ENGLAND CONSERVATORY OF MUSIC, LIBRARIES AND AUDIO DEPARTMENT, *MA109-440*
NEW ENGLAND FIRE AND HISTORY MUSEUM, *MA134-560*
NEW ENGLAND HISTORIC GENEALOGICAL SOCIETY, *MA109-460*
NEW ENGLAND METHODIST HISTORICAL SOCIETY, LIBRARY, *MA109-480*
NEW ENGLAND QUAKER RESEARCH LIBRARY, *MA603-560*
NEW GLOUCESTER HISTORICAL SOCIETY, *ME575-560*
NEW HAMPSHIRE ANTIQUARIAN SOCIETY, *NH444-560*
NEW HAMPSHIRE DEPARTMENT OF STATE, DIVISION OF RECORDS MANAGEMENT AND ARCHIVES, *NH134-530*
NEW HAMPSHIRE HISTORICAL SOCIETY, *NH134-540*
NEW HAMPSHIRE STATE ARCHIVES, *NH134-530*
NEW HAMPSHIRE STATE LIBRARY, *NH134-560*
NEW HARMONY WORKINGMEN'S INSTITUTE, *IN583-560*
NEW HAVEN COLONY HISTORICAL SOCIETY, LIBRARY, *CT505-560*
NEW IPSWICH HISTORICAL SOCIETY, *NH696-560*
NEW JERSEY DEPARTMENT OF CONSERVATION AND ECONOMIC DEVELOPMENT, *NJ838-550*
NEW JERSEY DEPARTMENT OF STATE, BUREAU OF ARCHIVES & RECS. PRES., DIV. OF ARCH. & RECS. MGMT., *NJ838-580*
NEW JERSEY FOLKLORE ARCHIVE, *NJ568-625*
NEW JERSEY HISTORICAL SOCIETY, LIBRARY, *NJ578-510*
NEW JERSEY INSTITUTE OF TECHNOLOGY, ARCHIVES, *NJ578-515*
NEW JERSEY STATE ARCHIVES, *NJ838-580*
NEW JERSEY STATE MUSEUM, BUREAU OF ARCHAEOLOGY AND ETHNOLOGY, *NJ838-600*
NEW JERSEY STATE MUSEUM, BUREAU OF CULTURAL HISTORY, *NJ838-610*
NEW LONDON COUNTY HISTORICAL SOCIETY, SHAW MANSION, *CT512-550*
NEW MARKET BATTLEFIELD PARK, *VA550-520*
NEW MARKET HISTORICAL SOCIETY, STONE SCHOOL MUSEUM, *NH720-560*
NEW MEXICO ANNUAL CONFERENCE ARCHIVES, *NM200-800*
NEW MEXICO HIGHLANDS UNIVERSITY, LIBRARY, ARROTT COLLECTION AND SPAN. & MEX. ARCHIVES, *NM513-560*
NEW MEXICO STATE ARCHIVES, *NM722-570*
NEW MEXICO STATE RECORDS CENTER AND ARCHIVES, HISTORICAL SERVICES DIVISION, *NM722-570*
NEW MEXICO STATE UNIVERSITY, LIBRARY, RIO GRANDE HIST. COLLS./HOBSON-HUNTSINGER UNIV. ARCHS., *NM494-570*
NEW MILFORD HISTORICAL SOCIETY, *CT519-560*
NEW NATIONAL THEATRE CORPORATION, NATIONAL THEATRE, LIBRARY, *DC14-850*
NEW ORLEANS BAPTIST THEOLOGICAL SEMINARY, LIBRARY, *LA600-540*
NEW ORLEANS PUBLIC LIBRARY, LOUISIANA DIVISION, *LA600-555*
NEW PROVIDENCE HISTORICAL SOCIETY, MUSEUM AND LIBRARY, *NJ574-560*
NEW YORK ACADEMY OF MEDICINE, LIBRARY, MALLOCH RARE BOOK AND HISTORY OF MEDICINE ROOM, *NY592-260*
NEW YORK ACADEMY OF SCIENCES, *NY592-280*
NEW YORK BARTOK ARCHIVE, *NY166-80*
NEW YORK BOTANICAL GARDEN, LIBRARY, MANUSCRIPTS AND ARCHIVES, *NY592-320*
NEW YORK CITY DEPARTMENT OF RECORDS AND INFORMATION SERVICES, DIVISION OF MUNICIPAL ARCHIVES, *NY592-350*
NEW YORK COUNTY, COUNTY CLERK AND CLERK OF THE SUPREME COURT, DIVISION OF OLD RECORDS, *NY592-420*
NEW YORK GENEALOGICAL AND BIOGRAPHICAL SOCIETY, *NY592-440*
NEW YORK HISTORICAL SOCIETY, MANUSCRIPT DEPARTMENT, *NY592-460*
NEW YORK HOSPITAL-CORNELL MEDICAL CENTER, MEDICAL ARCHIVES, *NY592-480*
NEW YORK LAW INSTITUTE, LIBRARY, *NY592-540*
NEW YORK LIFE INSURANCE COMPANY, ARCHIVES, *NY592-580*
NEW YORK MUSEUM OF TRANSPORTATION, *NY383-560*
NEW YORK PSYCHOANALYTIC INSTITUTE, ABRAHAM A. BRILL LIBRARY, *NY592-640*
NEW YORK PUBLIC LIBRARY, ARENTS COLLECTIONS, *NY592-680*
NEW YORK PUBLIC LIBRARY, JEWISH DIVISION, *NY592-760*
NEW YORK PUBLIC LIBRARY, MANUSCRIPTS AND ARCHIVES DIVISION, *NY592-800*
NEW YORK PUBLIC LIBRARY, ORIENTAL DIVISION, *NY592-860*
NEW YORK PUBLIC LIBRARY, PERFORMING ARTS RESEARCH CENTER, ARCHIVES OF RECORDED SOUND, *NY592-878*

NEW YORK PUBLIC LIBRARY, PERFORMING ARTS RESEARCH CENTER, DANCE COLLECTION, *NY592-870*
NEW YORK PUBLIC LIBRARY, PERFORMING ARTS RESEARCH CENTER, MUSIC DIVISION, *NY592-875*
NEW YORK PUBLIC LIBRARY, PERFORMING ARTS RESEARCH CENTER, THE BILLY ROSE THEATRE COLLECTION, *NY592-880*
NEW YORK PUBLIC LIBRARY, SCHOMBURG CENTER FOR RESEARCH IN BLACK CULTURE, *NY592-930*
NEW YORK PUBLIC LIBRARY, SPENCER COLLECTION, *NY592-970*
NEW YORK SOCIETY, LIBRARY, *NY593-10*
NEW YORK STATE DEPARTMENT OF STATE, COMMUNITY AFFAIRS LIBRARY, *NY10-570*
NEW YORK STATE DEPARTMENT OF TRANSPORTATION, MAP INFORMATION UNIT, *NY10-580*
NEW YORK STATE HISTORICAL ASSOCIATION, SPECIAL COLLECTIONS, *NY211-580*
NEW YORK STATE LIBRARY, MANUSCRIPTS AND SPECIAL COLLECTIONS, *NY10-640*
NEW YORK STATE PARKS AND RECREATION, LORENZO STATE HISTORICAL SITE, *NY164-570*
NEW YORK STOCK EXCHANGE, OFFICE OF THE SECRETARY, ARCHIVES, *NY593-040*
NEW YORK TIMES, NYT PICTURES-THE NEW YORK TIMES PHOTO SYNDICATE, *NY593-60*
NEW YORK UNIVERSITY, FALES LIBRARY, *NY593-90*
NEW YORK UNIVERSITY, INSTITUTE OF FINE ARTS, PHOTOGRAPHIC ARCHIVES, *NY593-100*
NEW YORK UNIVERSITY, LIBRARIES, TAMIMENT LIBRARY, *NY593-120*
NEW YORK YEARLY MEETING, HAVILAND RECORDS ROOM, RELIGIOUS SOCIETY OF FRIENDS, *NY593-710*
NEW YORK ZOOLOGICAL SOCIETY, ARCHIVES, *NY593-130*
NEW YORK, MUSEUM OF THE CITY OF, LIBRARY, *NY591-840*
NEW YORK, MUSEUM OF THE CITY OF, THEATRE AND MUSIC COLLECTION, *NY591-850*
NEWARK MUSEUM, *NJ578-530*
NEWARK PUBLIC LIBRARY, *NY597-520*
NEWARK PUBLIC LIBRARY, ART AND MUSIC DEPARTMENT, *NJ578-540*
NEWARK VALLEY HISTORICAL SOCIETY, *NY598-560*
NEWBERRY COLLEGE, WESSELS LIBRARY, SPECIAL COLLECTION, *SC684-550*
NEWBERRY LIBRARY, *IL170-351*
NEWBURGH BAY AND THE HIGHLANDS, HISTORICAL SOCIETY OF, LIBRARY, *NY599-320*
NEWBURGH FREE LIBRARY, *NY599-560*
NEWMAN, CAROL M., LIBRARY, SPECIAL COLLECTIONS, *VA90-840*
NEWPORT HISTORICAL SOCIETY, *RI560-570*
NEWSPAPER GUILD, *DC14-870*
NEWTON FREE LIBRARY, *MA590-570*
NEWTON, PHINEHAS S., LIBRARY, *MA725-640*
NEY, ELISABET, MUSEUM, *TX56-200*
NIAGARA FALLS PUBLIC LIBRARY, LOCAL HISTORY DEPARTMENT, *NY602-570*
NIAGARA UNIVERSITY, ARCHIVES, *NY604-560*
NICHOLAS COUNTY MEMORIAL LIBRARY, *KY13U-560*
NICHOLLS STATE UNIVERSITY, ELLENDER MEMORIAL LIBRARY, ALLEN J. ELLENDER ARCHIVES, *LA920-560*
NICOLLET COUNTY HISTORICAL MUSEUM, *MN769-560*
NICOLLET COUNTY HISTORICAL SOCIETY, *MN769-560*
NIELS BOHR LIBRARY, *NY586-580*
NILES COMMUNITY LIBRARY, *MI700-560*
NIMITZ LIBRARY, SPECIAL COLLECTIONS DIVISION, *MD57-810*
NINETY-NINES, INC., LIBRARY AND ARCHIVES, *OK592-570*
NINETY-SECOND STREET YOUNG MEN'S AND YOUNG WOMEN'S HEBREW ASSOCIATION, ARCHIVES, *NY593-132*
NO MAN'S LAND HISTORICAL MUSEUM, *OK389-560*
NOAH WEBSTER FOUNDATION AND HISTORICAL SOCIETY OF WEST HARTFORD, *CT891-550*
NOBLESVILLE PUBLIC LIBRARY, *IN594-560*
NODAWAY COUNTY HISTORICAL SOCIETY, MUSEUM, *MO570-560*
NOOK FARM RESEARCH LIBRARY, STOWE-DAY MEMORIAL LIBRARY, *CT316-560*
NORDICA MEMORIAL ASSOCIATION, *ME350-560*
NORFOLK COUNTY HISTORICAL SOCIETY OF CHESAPEAKE, *VA165-120*
NORFOLK PUBLIC LIBRARY, SARGEANT MEMORIAL ROOM, *VA580-570*
NORMAN COUNTY HISTORICAL SOCIETY, MUSEUM, *MN14-560*
NORMAN F. SPRAGUE MEMORIAL LIBRARY, *CA143-480*
NORRIS CITY ARCHIVES, *TN705-560*
NORTH ANDOVER HISTORICAL SOCIETY, *MA606-560*
NORTH BALTIMORE PUBLIC LIBRARY, *OH646-560*
NORTH BEND LIBRARY, *WA592-560*
NORTH CAROLINA BAPTIST HISTORICAL COLLECTION AND WAKE FOREST UNIVERSITY ARCHIVES, *NC930-840*
NORTH CAROLINA COLLECTION, *NC150-810*

NORTH CAROLINA DEPARTMENT OF CULTURAL RESOURCES, NORTH CAROLINA STATE ARCHIVES, *NC680-460*
NORTH CAROLINA STATE ARCHIVES, *NC680-460*
NORTH CAROLINA STATE UNIVERSITY, ARCHIVES, *NC680-550*
NORTH CASCADES NATIONAL PARK, *WA832-560*
NORTH CENTRAL MINNESOTA HISTORICAL CENTER, *MN63-75*
NORTH CENTRAL REGIONAL LIBRARY, CHELAN BRANCH LIBRARY, *WA125-100*
NORTH CENTRAL REGIONAL LIBRARY, LEAVENWORTH BRANCH LIBRARY, *WA483-560*
NORTH CENTRAL REGIONAL LIBRARY, MANSON BRANCH LIBRARY, *WA517-560*
NORTH CENTRAL REGIONAL LIBRARY, OMAK BRANCH LIBRARY, *WA617-90*
NORTH CENTRAL REGIONAL LIBRARY, TONASKET BRANCH LIBRARY, *WA919-560*
NORTH CENTRAL REGIONAL LIBRARY, WENATCHEE BRANCH LIBRARY, *WA966-550*
NORTH CENTRAL WASHINGTON MUSEUM, *WA966-560*
NORTH COUNTRY HISTORY CENTER, *NY708-720*
NORTH DAKOTA INSTITUTE FOR REGIONAL STUDIES, *ND375-570*
NORTH DAKOTA SCHOOL OF FORESTRY, *ND80-560*
NORTH DAKOTA STATE ARCHIVES, *ND43-730*
NORTH DAKOTA STATE HISTORICAL SOCIETY, *ND43-730*
NORTH DAKOTA STATE UNIVERSITY AT BOTTINEAU, LIBRARY, *ND80-560*
NORTH DAKOTA STATE UNIVERSITY, NORTH DAKOTA INSTITUTE FOR REGIONAL STUDIES, *ND375-570*
NORTH IDAHO COLLEGE, LIBRARY, *ID240-560*
NORTH PARK COLLEGE, LIBRARY, *IL170-403*
NORTH PLATTE VALLEY HISTORICAL ASSOCIATION, NORTH PLATTE VALLEY MUSEUM, *NE384-560*
NORTH PLATTE VALLEY MUSEUM, *NE384-560*
NORTH TEXAS STATE UNIVERSITY, UNIVERSITY ARCHIVES, *TX280-540*
NORTHAM COLONISTS HISTORICAL SOCIETY, *NH194-560*
NORTHAMPTON COUNTY HISTORICAL AND GENEALOGICAL SOCIETY, *PA270-560*
NORTHAMPTON HISTORICAL SOCIETY, *MA624-560*
NORTHBOROUGH HISTORICAL SOCIETY, *MA627-560*
NORTHEAST ARCHIVES OF FOLKLORE AND ORAL HISTORY, *ME650-780*
NORTHEAST LOUISIANA UNIVERSITY, SANDEL LIBRARY, SPECIAL COLLECTIONS, *LA535-560*
NORTHEAST MINNESOTA HISTORICAL CENTER, *MN261-810*
NORTHEAST MISSOURI STATE UNIVERSITY, PICKLER MEMORIAL LIBRARY, *MO460-560*
NORTHEAST REGIONAL LIBRARY, GEORGE E. ALLEN LIBRARY, *MS140-560*
NORTHEASTERN NEVADA MUSEUM, *NV270-560*
NORTHEASTERN OKLAHOMA STATE UNIVERSITY, LIBRARY/LEARNING RESOURCES CENTER, *OK778-560*
NORTHEASTERN STATE COLLEGE, LIBRARY, *OK778-560*
NORTHEASTERN UNIVERSITY, LIBRARIES, UNIVERSITY ARCHIVES, *MA109-530*
NORTHERN ARIZONA UNIVERSITY, LIBRARY, SPECIAL COLLECTIONS DIVISION, *AZ250-575*
NORTHERN BAPTIST THEOLOGICAL SEMINARY AND BETHANY THEOLOGICAL SEMINARY, LIBRARY, SP. COLL. & ARCH., *IL644-80*
NORTHERN ILLINOIS UNIVERSITY, REGIONAL HISTORY CENTER, *IL202-550*
NORTHERN INDIANA HISTORICAL SOCIETY, *IN792-560*
NORTHERN OKLAHOMA COLLEGE, LIBRARY, *OK812-560*
NORTHFIELD MOUNT HERMON SCHOOL, MOUNT HERMON LIBRARIES, *MA568-560*
NORTHFIELD PUBLIC LIBRARY, LOCAL HISTORY COLLECTION, *MN625-550*
NORTHLAND COLLEGE, DEXTER LIBRARY, *WI54-560*
NORTHPORT PUBLIC LIBRARY, REFERENCE DEPARTMENT, *NY615-560*
NORTHUMBERLAND COUNTY HISTORICAL SOCIETY, *PA855-560*
NORTHVILLE HISTORICAL SOCIETY, *MI705-560*
NORTHWEST ARCHITECTURAL ARCHIVES, *MN763-800*
NORTHWEST COLLEGE OF THE ASSEMBLIES OF GOD, LIBRARY, *WA427-550*
NORTHWEST MINNESOTA HISTORICAL CENTER, *MN562-520*
NORTHWEST NAZARENE COLLEGE, ARCHIVES, *ID560-560*
NORTHWEST OAKLAND COUNTY HISTORICAL SOCIETY, *MI450-560*
NORTHWEST REGIONAL FOUNDATION, *WA880-590*
NORTHWEST SEAPORT, *WA427-560*
NORTHWESTERN COLLEGE, RAMAKER LIBRARY, DUTCH HERITAGE COLLECTION, *IA755-560*
NORTHWESTERN MEMORIAL HOSPITAL, ARCHIVES, *IL170-416*
NORTHWESTERN MICHIGAN COLLEGE, MARK OSTERLIN LIBRARY, *MI925-560*

NORTHWESTERN OKLAHOMA STATE UNIVERSITY, LIBRARY, *OK42-560*
NORTHWESTERN STATE UNIVERSITY OF LOUISIANA, WATSON LIBRARY, ARCHIVES DIVISION, *LA570-540*
NORTHWESTERN UNIVERSITY, DENTAL SCHOOL LIBRARY, *IL170-429*
NORTHWESTERN UNIVERSITY, LAW LIBRARY, *IL170-442*
NORTHWESTERN UNIVERSITY, LIBRARY, MAP COLLECTION, *IL261-565*
NORTHWESTERN UNIVERSITY, LIBRARY, MELVILLE J. HERSKOVITS LIBRARY OF AFRICAN STUDIES, *IL261-566*
NORTHWESTERN UNIVERSITY, LIBRARY, MUSIC LIBRARY, *IL261-568*
NORTHWESTERN UNIVERSITY, LIBRARY, SPECIAL COLLECTIONS, *IL261-570*
NORTHWESTERN UNIVERSITY, LIBRARY, UNIVERSITY ARCHIVES, *IL261-585*
NORTHWESTERN UNIVERSITY, MEDICAL SCHOOL, LIBRARY, *IL170-455*
NORTON MEMORIAL LIBRARY, *LA670-480*
NORTON SIMON MUSEUM OF ART AT PASADENA, BLUE FOUR GALKA SCHEYER ARCHIVE, *CA578-630*
NORTON, R. W., ART GALLERY, REFERENCE LIBRARY, *LA885-690*
NORWALK HISTORICAL COMMISSION, NORWALK HISTORICAL REFERENCE LIBRARY, *CT582-550*
NORWALK HISTORICAL REFERENCE LIBRARY, *CT582-550*
NORWALK PUBLIC LIBRARY, *OH660-560*
NORWEGIAN-AMERICAN HISTORICAL ASSOCIATION, *MN625-570*
NORWICH UNIVERSITY, LIBRARY, SPECIAL COLLECTIONS, *VT528-560*
NORWICH UNIVERSITY, VERMONT COLLEGE DIVISION, GARY MEMORIAL LIBRARY, *VT464-560*
NORWOOD HISTORICAL SOCIETY, *MA642-560*
NOTRE DAME DE NAMUR, SISTERS OF, CALIFORNIA PROVINCE, *CA78-740*
NOTRE DAME DE NAMUR, SISTERS OF, OHIO PROVINCE, ARCHIVES, *OH171-730*
NOTTINGHAM HISTORICAL SOCIETY, *NH732-560*
NOVAK, MICHAEL, PAPERS, *MA615-730*
NUEVO SANTANDER MUSEUM, *TX543-560*
NYSELIUS LIBRARY, FAIRFIELD UNIVERSITY ARCHIVES, *CT234-260*

O

O'BRIEN COUNTY HISTORICAL SOCIETY, *IA822-600*
O'CONNOR, FLANNERY, COLLECTION, *GA780-270*
O'DONNELL, MAYO HAYES, LIBRARY, *CA480-510*
OAK HARBOR HISTORICAL SOCIETY, *WA596-600*
OAK PARK PUBLIC LIBRARY, LOCAL HISTORY AND LOCAL AUTHORS COLLECTION, *IL649-600*
OAKESDALE PUBLIC LIBRARY, *WA597-600*
OAKLAND COUNTY PIONEER AND HISTORICAL SOCIETY, *MI770-600*
OAKLAND MUSEUM, HISTORY DEPARTMENT, *CA540-590*
OAKLAND PUBLIC LIBRARY, OAKLAND HISTORY ROOM, *CA540-610*
OAKLAND UNIVERSITY LIBRARY, *MI795-600*
OBERLIN COLLEGE, ARCHIVES, *OH665-580*
OBERLIN COLLEGE, LIBRARY, *OH665-580, OH665-590*
OCCIDENTAL COLLEGE, LIBRARY, SPECIAL COLLECTIONS DEPARTMENT, *CA421-510*
OCEAN SHORES PUBLIC LIBRARY, *WA601-680*
OCTAGON HOUSE, *WI230-720*
ODELL PUBLIC LIBRARY, *IL567-600*
ODESSA HISTORICAL SOCIETY, ODESSA HISTORISCHE MUSEUM, *WA602-600*
ODESSA HISTORISCHE MUSEUM, *WA602-600*
ODESSA PUBLIC LIBRARY, *WA602-610*
OFFICE OF THE SECRETARY OF ALASKA, *AK500-40*
OFFICE OF THE SECRETARY OF STATE, DIV. OF ARCH. & RECS. MGMT., CENTRAL WA REG. STATE ARCHIVES, *WA280-885*
OFFICE OF THE SECRETARY OF STATE, DIV. OF ARCH. & RECS. MGMT., E. WASHINGTON REG. STATE ARCHIVES, *WA144-840*
OFFICE OF THE SECRETARY OF STATE, DIV. OF ARCH. & RECS. MGMT., KING COUNTY REG. STATE ARCHIVES, *WA616-444*
OFFICE OF THE SECRETARY OF STATE, DIV. OF ARCH. & RECS. MGMT., SOUTHWEST WA REG. STATE ARCHIVES, *WA616-895*
OFFICE OF THE SECRETARY OF STATE, DIV. OF ARCH. & RECS. MGMT., WASHINGTON STATE ARCHIVES, *WA616-870*
OGDEN, WILLIAM B., FREE LIBRARY, *NY915-880*
OGDENSBURG PUBLIC LIBRARY, *NY634-600*
OGLETHORPE UNIVERSITY, LIBRARY, *GA90-600*
OGUNQUIT FREE LIBRARY, *ME625-600*
OHIO AGRICULTURAL RESEARCH AND DEVELOPMENT CENTER, *OH968-600*

OHIO GENEALOGICAL SOCIETY, LIBRARY, *OH481-610*
OHIO HISTORICAL SOCIETY, ADENA STATE MEMORIAL, *OH166-590*
OHIO HISTORICAL SOCIETY, ARCHIVES-MANUSCRIPTS DIVISION, *OH203-600*
OHIO HISTORICAL SOCIETY, CAMPUS MARTIUS MUSEUM, *OH486-660*
OHIO STATE ARCHIVES, *OH203-600*
OHIO STATE UNIVERSITY, DEPARTMENT OF PHOTOGRAPHY AND CINEMA, *OH203-630*
OHIO STATE UNIVERSITY, LIBRARIES, DIVISION OF SPECIAL COLLECTIONS, *OH203-650*
OHIO STATE UNIVERSITY, THEATRE RESEARCH INSTITUTE, *OH203-670*
OHIO STATE UNIVERSITY, UNIVERSITY ARCHIVES, *OH203-680*
OHIO UNIVERSITY, LIBRARY, SPECIAL COLLECTIONS AND UNIVERSITY ARCHIVES, *OH35-610*
OHIO WESLEYAN UNIVERSITY, LIBRARY, *OH232-600*
OKALOOSA AND WALTON COUNTIES, HISTORICAL SOCIETY OF, MUSEUM, *FL860-320*
OKANOGAN COUNTY HISTORICAL MUSEUM, *WA604-590*
OKANOGAN COUNTY HISTORICAL SOCIETY, SHAFFER MUSEUM, *WA985-720*
OKLAHOMA BAPTIST UNIVERSITY, *OK736-600*
OKLAHOMA CHRISTIAN COLLEGE, OKLAHOMA LIVING LEGENDS, *OK592-580*
OKLAHOMA DEPARTMENT OF LIBRARIES, ARCHIVES AND RECORDS DIVISION, *OK592-620*
OKLAHOMA HERITAGE ASSOCIATION, ARCHIVES, *OK592-630*
OKLAHOMA HISTORICAL SOCIETY, INDIAN ARCHIVES DIVISION, *OK592-640*
OKLAHOMA HISTORICAL SOCIETY, LIBRARY, *OK592-650*
OKLAHOMA HISTORICAL SOCIETY, OKLAHOMA TERRITORIAL MUSEUM, *OK406-600*
OKLAHOMA LIVING LEGENDS, *OK592-580*
OKLAHOMA STATE ARCHIVES, *OK592-620*
OKLAHOMA STATE UNIVERSITY, LIBRARY, SPECIAL COLLECTIONS AND MAP ROOM, *OK753-600*
OKLAHOMA TERRITORIAL MUSEUM, *OK406-600*
OLANA STATE HISTORIC SITE, *NY416-600*
OLD ACADEMY MUSEUM LIBRARY, *CT933-890*
OLD BARRACKS ASSOCIATION, OLD BARRACKS, *NJ838-630*
OLD BRUTUS HISTORICAL SOCIETY, *NY941-600*
OLD CATHEDRAL LIBRARY, *IN902-80*
OLD CHRIST CHURCH IN PHILADELPHIA, ARCHIVES, *PA726-37*
OLD COLONY HISTORICAL SOCIETY, *MA841-600*
OLD CONWAY HOMESTEAD, CRAMER MUSEUM, *ME212-120*
OLD COURT HOUSE MUSEUM, *MS950-830*
OLD DARTMOUTH HISTORICAL SOCIETY, *MA584-600*
OLD DOMINION UNIVERSITY, UNIVERSITY LIBRARY, DEPARTMENT OF ARCHIVES AND MANUSCRIPTS, *VA580-600*
OLD ECONOMY VILLAGE, *PA40-600*
OLD FORT NIAGARA ASSOCIATION, *NY990-600*
OLD FORT NUMBER 4, *NH118-600*
OLD LIGHTHOUSE MUSEUM, *IN517-520*
OLD MONROE SCHOOLHOUSE MUSEUM, *NJ318-320*
OLD ONAQUAGA HISTORICAL SOCIETY, ST. LUKE'S MUSEUM, *NY368-600*
OLD SLAVE MART MUSEUM, BLACK HERITAGE RESEARCH CENTER, *SC860-600*
OLD SOUTH MEETING HOUSE, *MA109-560*
OLD STONE HOUSE MUSEUM, *OH426-470, VT160-600*
OLD STONE MUSEUM, *NY973-600*
OLD STURBRIDGE VILLAGE, RESEARCH LIBRARY, *MA823-610*
OLD VILLAGE HALL MUSEUM, *NY490-480*
OLD WASHINGTON HISTORIC STATE PARK, *AR950-600*
OLD WOODBURY HISTORICAL SOCIETY, *CT982-600*
OLD YORK HISTORICAL SOCIETY, *ME980-600*
OLD YORK ROAD HISTORICAL SOCIETY, *PA430-600*
OLDHAM COUNTY-DUERSON PUBLIC LIBRARY, *KY41E-160*
OLDHAM LIBRARY AND HISTORICAL ASSOCIATION, EMIL LORIKS HERITAGE HOUSE, *SD550-600*
OLIN C. BAILEY LIBRARY, *AR240-320*
OLIVEIRA LIMA LIBRARY, *DC3-226*
OLIVER WENDELL HOLMES LIBRARY, *MA25-650*
OLIVET COLLEGE, LIBRARIES, COLLEGE ARCHIVES, *MI720-600*
OLMSTED COUNTY HISTORICAL SOCIETY, RESEARCH CENTER, *MN721-600*
OLYMPIA PUBLIC LIBRARY, *WA616-610*
OLYMPIC COLLEGE LIBRARY, *WA84-455*
OLYMPIC NATIONAL FOREST, *WA616-620*
OLYMPIC NATIONAL FOREST, QUINAULT RANGER STATION, *WA729-820*
OLYMPIC NATIONAL PARK, PIONEER MEMORIAL VISITOR CENTER, *WA676-610*
OMAHA PUBLIC LIBRARY, *NE624-620*
OMAK BRANCH LIBRARY, *WA617-90*
OMS INTERNATIONAL, *IN297-600*

ONE, BAKER MEMORIAL LIBRARY, *CA421-520*
ONEIDA HISTORICAL SOCIETY, *NY899-600*
ONONDAGA COUNTY PUBLIC LIBRARY, LOCAL HISTORY AND
 GENEALOGY DEPARTMENT, *NY872-590*
ONONDAGA HISTORICAL ASSOCIATION, *NY872-610*
ONTARIO COUNTY HISTORIAN'S OFFICE, *NY147-595*
ONTARIO COUNTY HISTORICAL SOCIETY, *NY147-600*
ONTONAGON COUNTY HISTORICAL SOCIETY, MUSEUM,
 MI725-600
ORANGE COUNTY HISTORICAL COMMISSION, *FL560-590*
ORANGE EMPIRE RAILWAY MUSEUM, *CA582-600*
ORCAS ISLAND HISTORICAL SOCIETY, *WA265-600*
ORCHARD HOUSE, *MA217-480*
ORDER OF PREACHERS, PROVINCE OF ST. JOSEPH, ARCHIVES,
 DC15-50
ORDER OF SERVANTS OF MARY, EASTERN PROVINCE,
 PROVINCIAL ARCHIVES, *IL84-600*
ORDER OF SERVANTS OF MARY, WESTERN PROVINCE,
 SOMERSET ARCHIVES, *CA110-600*
OREGON ART INSTITUTE, PORTLAND ART MUSEUM, *OR720-660*
OREGON COLLEGE OF EDUCATION, LIBRARY, *OR576-600*
OREGON DEPARTMENT OF GEOLOGY AND MINERAL
 INDUSTRIES, LIBRARY, *OR720-580*
OREGON ELECTRIC RAILWAY HISTORICAL SOCIETY, *OR424-322*
OREGON HISTORICAL SOCIETY, LIBRARY, *OR720-590*
OREGON PROVINCE ARCHIVES OF THE SOCIETY OF JESUS,
 WA880-280
OREGON SECRETARY OF STATE, ARCHIVES DIVISION, OREGON
 STATE ARCHIVES AND RECORDS CENTER, *OR816-590*
OREGON STATE ARCHIVES AND RECORDS CENTER, *OR816-590*
OREGON STATE UNIVERSITY, ARCHIVES, *OR144-600*
OREGON STATE UNIVERSITY, HORNER MUSEUM, *OR144-610*
OREGON STATE UNIVERSITY, WILLIAM JASPER KERR LIBRARY,
 OR144-620
ORGANIZATION OF AMERICAN STATES, RECORDS
 MANAGEMENT CENTER, *DC15-500*
ORIENTAL INSTITUTE MUSEUM, ARCHAEOLOGICAL ARCHIVES,
 IL170-897
ORIN G. LIBBY MANUSCRIPT COLLECTION, *ND486-800*
ORLEANS COUNTY HISTORICAL SOCIETY, OLD STONE HOUSE
 MUSEUM, *VT160-600*
ORR, NATHANIEL, HOUSE, *WA889-560*
ORRADRE, MICHEL, LIBRARY, *CA778-800*
ORTHODOX CHURCH IN AMERICA, DEPARTMENT OF HISTORY
 AND ARCHIVES, *NY870-600*
ORTING TOWN MUSEUM, *WA626-600*
OSAGE COUNTY HISTORICAL SOCIETY, OSAGE COUNTY
 MUSEUM, *KS569-600*
OSAGE COUNTY MUSEUM, *KS569-600*
OSHKOSH PUBLIC MUSEUM, *WI554-600*
OSSINING HISTORICAL SOCIETY, MUSEUM, *NY657-600*
OSTERLIN, MARK, LIBRARY, *MI925-560*
OSWEGO COUNTY HISTORICAL SOCIETY, *NY660-600*
OTEGO HISTORICAL SOCIETY, *NY661-620*
OTHELLO COMMUNITY MUSEUM, *WA629-655*
OTIS HISTORICAL ARCHIVES, *DC1-760*
OTTAWA COUNTY HISTORICAL MUSEUM, *KS635-600*
OTTAWA UNIVERSITY, MYERS LIBRARY, *KS718-600*
OTTER TAIL COUNTY HISTORICAL SOCIETY, *MN328-600*
OTTERBEIN COLLEGE, COURTRIGHT MEMORIAL LIBRARY,
 OH925-600
OTTO E. EHRHART - PAULDING COUNTY HISTORICAL SOCIETY,
 OH21-600
OUACHITA BAPTIST UNIVERSITY, RILEY LIBRARY, CLARK
 COUNTY HISTORICAL ASSOCIATION ARCHIVES, *AR60-600*
OUACHITA PARISH PUBLIC LIBRARY, SPECIAL COLLECTIONS,
 LA535-600
OULEHOUDT VALLEY HISTORICAL SOCIETY, *NY303-600*
OUR LADY OF SORROWS BASILICA, ARCHIVES, *IL170-475*
OUR LADY OF THE LAKE UNIVERSITY, LIBRARIES, TEXANA
 COLLECTION, *TX777-620*
OUTAGAMIE COUNTY HISTORICAL SOCIETY, *WI46-600*
OUTDOOR DRAMA, INSTITUTE OF, *NC150-790*
OVER, W. H., MUSEUM, *SD792-880*
OWEN COUNTY HISTORICAL SOCIETY, *KY600-600*
OWEN COUNTY PUBLIC LIBRARY AND OWEN COUNTY
 HISTORICAL SOCIETY, *KY600-600*
OWEN PIONEER MUSEUM, *WA123-333*
OWENSBORO-DAVIESS COUNTY PUBLIC LIBRARY, KENTUCKY
 ROOM, *KY598-600*
OWSLEY COUNTY PUBLIC LIBRARY, *KY9U-600*
OWYHEE COUNTY HISTORICAL MUSEUM, *ID520-600*
OX BARN MUSEUM, *OR56-40*
OXFORD COLLEGE, LIBRARY, *GA825-200*
OXFORD FREE PUBLIC LIBRARY, OXFORD MUSEUM, *MA654-590*
OXFORD HISTORICAL SOCIETY, *NY667-580*
OXFORD MEMORIAL LIBRARY, *NY667-600*

OXFORD MUSEUM, *MA654-590*
OYSTERPONDS HISTORICAL SOCIETY, *NY654-600*
OZAUKEE COUNTY HISTORICAL SOCIETY, *WI118-600*

P

P. K. YONGE LIBRARY OF FLORIDA HISTORY, *FL220-795*
PACE, JOHN C., LIBRARY, *FL600-800*
PACIFIC CENTER FOR WESTERN HISTORICAL STUDIES, *CA862-810*
PACIFIC COUNTY HISTORICAL SOCIETY, *WA859-650*
PACIFIC GROVE PUBLIC LIBRARY, *CA566-640*
PACIFIC LUTHERAN UNIVERSITY, ARCHIVES, *WA904-635*
PACIFIC LUTHERAN UNIVERSITY, LIBRARY, NISQUALLY PLAINS
 ROOM, *WA904-640*
PACIFIC NORTHWEST ARCHAEOLOGY, ARCHIVE OF, *ID480-770*
PACIFIC NORTHWEST AVIATION HISTORICAL FOUNDATION,
 WA820-613
PACIFIC NORTHWEST FOREST AND RANGE EXPERIMENT
 STATION, FORESTRY AND RANGE SCIENCES LABORATORY,
 OR464-490
PACIFIC PIONEER BROADCASTERS, *CA318-640*
PACIFIC REGIONAL ORAL HISTORY PROGRAM, *HI350-790*
PACIFIC SCHOOL OF RELIGION, ARCHIVES, *CA86-630*
PACIFIC SCIENTIFIC INFORMATION CENTER, *HI350-80*
PACIFIC TELEPHONE AND TELEGRAPH COMPANY, LIBRARY,
 CA720-546
PACIFIC UNION COLLEGE, NELSON MEMORIAL LIBRARY,
 CA32-640
PACIFIC UNIVERSITY, LIBRARY, *OR256-650*
PACIFIC UNIVERSITY, MUSEUM, *OR256-650*
PACK MEMORIAL PUBLIC LIBRARY, NORTH CAROLINA
 COLLECTION AND THOMAS WOLFE COLLECTION, *NC60-640*
PACKWOOD HOUSE MUSEUM, *PA500-640*
PADUCAH COMMUNITY COLLEGE, LIBRARY, *KY604-630*
PADUCAH PUBLIC LIBRARY, *KY604-640*
PAINE, THOMAS, MEMORIAL HOUSE, *NY577-330*
PAINTER LIBRARY, *PA512-400*
PAJARO VALLEY HISTORICAL ASSOCIATION, WILLIAM H. VOLCK
 MUSEUM, *CA958-640*
PALEONTOLOGICAL RESEARCH INSTITUTION, *NY439-640*
PALOS PARK HISTORICAL SOCIETY, *IL693-640*
PALOS VERDES LIBRARY DISTRICT, *CA574-640*
PAN AMERICAN UNION, *DC15-500*
PAN AMERICAN UNIVERSITY, LIBRARY, SPECIAL COLLECTIONS,
 TX319-640
PANHANDLE-PLAINS HISTORICAL MUSEUM, HISTORIC
 RESEARCH CENTER, *TX128-640*
PARAMOUNT NORTH ISLAND CENTRE, ARCHIVES, *IL45-640*
PARIS JUNIOR COLLEGE, MIKE RHEUDASIL LEARNING CENTER,
 A. M. AND WELMA AIKIN REGIONAL ARCHIVES, *TX695-640*
PARIS-BOURBON COUNTY LIBRARY, *KY61A-640*
PARISH OF TRINITY CHURCH, OFFICE OF PARISH ARCHIVES,
 NY593-290
PARK CONGREGATIONAL CHURCH, ARCHIVES, *NY272-640*
PARK-MCCULLOUGH HOUSE ASSOCIATION, INC., LIBRARY,
 MANUSCRIPT COLLECTION AND ARCHIVE, *VT496-640*
PARMA TOWN HISTORIAN, *NY393-640*
PARSONS MEMORIAL LIBRARY, *ME12-640*
PASADENA ART MUSEUM, *CA578-630*
PASADENA HISTORICAL SOCIETY AND MUSEUM, *CA578-640*
PASADENA URBAN CONSERVATION DEPARTMENT, *CA578-675*
PASCO PUBLIC LIBRARY, *WA647-640*
PASSAIC COUNTY HISTORICAL SOCIETY, *NJ646-630*
PATERSON PUBLIC LIBRARY, *NJ646-660*
PATTERSON LIBRARY, *NY958-640*
PATTERSON, RAYMOND, ALUMNI ARCHIVE, *MA928-730*
PATTON MUSEUM OF CAVALRY AND ARMOR, *KY272-635*
PAUL H. KARSHNER MEMORIAL MUSEUM, *WA726-440*
PAUL SMITH'S COLLEGE, LIBRARY, *NY675-640*
PAULDING COUNTY - OTTO E. EHRHART HISTORICAL SOCIETY,
 OH21-600
PAYSON LIBRARY, *CA436-640*
PEABODY CONSERVATORY OF MUSIC, LIBRARY, *MD76-640*
PEABODY HISTORICAL SOCIETY, *MA662-640*
PEABODY INSTITUTE LIBRARY, DANVERS ARCHIVAL CENTER,
 MA231-640
PEABODY MUSEUM OF NATURAL HISTORY, *CT505-980*
PEABODY MUSEUM OF SALEM, PHILLIPS LIBRARY, *MA733-660*
PEABODY MUSEUM, TOZZER LIBRARY, *MA169-530*
PEABODY, GEORGE, LIBRARY, *MD76-333*
PEACE, JOHN, LIBRARY, SPECIAL COLLECTIONS, *TX777-810*
PEALE MUSEUM, *MD76-650*
PEARL HARBOR SURVIVORS ASSOCIATION, GRANITE STATE
 CHAPTER NO. 1 N.H., *NH784-620*
PEARL S. BUCK BIRTHPLACE FOUNDATION, *WV375-640*
PEARY-MACMILLAN ARCTIC MUSEUM, *ME162-100*

PECK MEMORIAL LIBRARY, *CT351-640, NY524-640*
PEJEPSCOT HISTORICAL SOCIETY, ARCHIVES ROOM, *ME162-640*
PELLETIER LIBRARY, *PA555-40*
PEMBER LIBRARY AND MUSEUM, *NY347-640*
PEND OREILLE COUNTY HISTORICAL SOCIETY MUSEUM, *WA584-645*
PENDLETON DISTRICT HISTORICAL AND RECREATIONAL COMMISSION, RESEARCH DIVISION, *SC738-640*
PENFIELD LIBRARY, SUCO SPECIAL COLLECTIONS, *NY660-720*
PENINSULA HISTORICAL SOCIETY, *WA350-650*
PENN YAN PUBLIC LIBRARY, *NY693-640*
PENNSYLVANIA ACADEMY OF THE FINE ARTS, *PA726-43*
PENNSYLVANIA DUTCH FOLK CULTURE SOCIETY, *PA495-640*
PENNSYLVANIA FARM MUSEUM OF LANDIS VALLEY, *PA470-640*
PENNSYLVANIA FREE AND ACCEPTED MASONS, R. W. GRAND LODGE, *PA726-057*
PENNSYLVANIA HISTORICAL AND MUSEUM COMMISSION, *PA40-600, PA840-690, PA870-160*
PENNSYLVANIA HISTORICAL AND MUSEUM COMMISSION, DIVISION OF ARCHIVES AND MANUSCRIPTS, *PA380-650*
PENNSYLVANIA HISTORICAL AND MUSEUM COMMISSION, DIVISION OF LAND RECORDS, *PA380-665*
PENNSYLVANIA HISTORICAL AND MUSEUM COMMISSION, SOMERSET HISTORICAL CENTER, *PA825-720*
PENNSYLVANIA HOSPITAL, MEDICAL LIBRARY, *PA726-60*
PENNSYLVANIA STATE ARCHIVES, *PA380-650*
PENNSYLVANIA STATE UNIVERSITY, AGRICULTURAL EXTENSION SERVICE, *PA895-680*
PENNSYLVANIA STATE UNIVERSITY, DELAWARE COUNTY CAMPUS, PAPERS OF MARTIN VAN BUREN, *PA565-640*
PENNSYLVANIA STATE UNIVERSITY, LIBRARIES, SPECIAL COLLECTIONS DIVISION, *PA895-710*
PENOBSCOT MARINE MUSEUM, *ME762-640*
PENROSE LIBRARY, *CO252-820*
PENROSE MEMORIAL LIBRARY, EELLS NORTHWEST ROOM, *WA954-880*
PENSACOLA HISTORICAL MUSEUM, *FL600-640*
PEORIA PUBLIC LIBRARY, *IL723-650*
PEPPERDINE UNIVERSITY, PAYSON LIBRARY, *CA436-640*
PEQUOT LIBRARY, *CT751-640*
PERFORMING ARTS RESEARCH CENTER, DANCE COLLECTION, NEW YORK PUBLIC LIBRARY, *NY592-870*
PERFORMING ARTS RESEARCH CENTER, MUSIC DIVISION, NEW YORK PUBLIC LIBRARY, *NY592-875*
PERFORMING ARTS RESEARCH CENTER, RODGERS AND HAMMERSTEIN ARCHIVES OF RECORDED SOUND, *NY592-878*
PERFORMING ARTS RESEARCH CENTER, THE BILLY ROSE THEATRE COLLECTION, NEW YORK PUBLIC LIBRARY, *NY592-880*
PERINTON HISTORICAL SOCIETY, *NY281-640*
PERKINS HOUSE MUSEUM, *WA164-890*
PERKINS LIBRARY, DOANE COLLEGE ARCHIVES, *NE288-160*
PERKINS SCHOOL OF THEOLOGY, METHODIST HISTORICAL COLLECTIONS, *TX252-760*
PERKINS, WILLIAM R., LIBRARY, MANUSCRIPT DEPARTMENT, *NC260-170*
PERMIAN BASIN PETROLEUM MUSEUM, LIBRARY AND HALL OF FAME, ARCHIVES CENTER, *TX625-640*
PERQUIMANS COUNTY HISTORICAL SOCIETY, *NC405-640*
PERRIE JONES MEMORIAL ROOM, *MN763-710*
PERRY PUBLIC LIBRARY, *NY694-640*
PETER FOULGER MUSEUM, LIBRARY, *MA572-560*
PETERBOROUGH HISTORICAL SOCIETY, *NH748-630*
PETERBOROUGH TOWN LIBRARY, *NH748-650*
PETERSBURG NATIONAL BATTLEFIELD, *VA630-640*
PETERSHAM HISTORICAL SOCIETY, *MA673-640*
PETTIGREW MUSEUM OF NATURAL ARTS AND HISTORY, *SD684-640*
PETZINGER MEMORIAL LIBRARY, *CA862-630*
PFEIFFER, ANNIE MERNER, LIBRARY, *WV200-880*
PFEIFFER, HENRY, LIBRARY, *IL394-500*
PFORZHEIMER, CARL AND LILY, FOUNDATION, *NY587-880*
PFORZHEIMER, CARL H., LIBRARY, *NY587-880*
PHELPS COMMUNITY MEMORIAL LIBRARY, *NY695-640*
PHELPS HISTORICAL SOCIETY, *NY695-650*
PHELPS-STOKES FUND, ARCHIVES, *NY593-380*
PHILADELPHIA ARCHDIOCESAN ARCHIVES, *PA726-105*
PHILADELPHIA CAMP 200, SONS OF UNION VETERANS OF THE CIVIL WAR, GAR MEMORIAL HALL, LIBRARY, *PA726-508*
PHILADELPHIA CITY ARCHIVES, *PA725-240*
PHILADELPHIA COLLEGE OF ART, LIBRARY, *PA726-135*
PHILADELPHIA CONTRIBUTIONSHIP, *PA725-208*
PHILADELPHIA JEWISH ARCHIVES CENTER, *PA726-225*
PHILADELPHIA MARITIME MUSEUM, LIBRARY, *PA726-240*
PHILADELPHIA MUSEUM OF ART, ARCHIVES, *PA726-255*
PHILADELPHIA MUSEUM OF ART, DEPARTMENT OF PRINTS, DRAWINGS, AND PHOTOGRAPHS, *PA726-270*

PHILLIPS ACADEMY, OLIVER WENDELL HOLMES LIBRARY, *MA25-650*
PHILLIPS COLLECTION, *DC16-300*
PHILLIPS EXETER ACADEMY, LIBRARY, *NH254-640*
PHILLIPS FREE LIBRARY, *NY404-640*
PHILLIPS LIBRARY, *MA733-660*
PHILLIPS MEMORIAL LIBRARY, PROVIDENCE COLLEGE ARCHIVES, *RI700-640*
PHILLIPS RARE BOOKS AND MANUSCRIPTS LIBRARY, *NJ178-115*
PHILLIPS UNIVERSITY, GRADUATE SEMINARY LIBRARY, *OK355-640*
PHILLIPS, HUGH J., LIBRARY, *MD380-520*
PHILLIPS, JAMES DUNCAN, LIBRARY, *MA733-210*
PHILLIPS, T. W., LIBRARY, ALEXANDER CAMPBELL ARCHIVES, *WV100-80*
PHILLIPS, T. W., LIBRARY, BETHANY COLLEGE ARCHIVES, *WV100-90*
PHINEHAS S. NEWTON LIBRARY, *MA725-640*
PHOEBE APPERSON HEARST FREE LIBRARY, *SD414-640*
PHOENIX PUBLIC LIBRARY, ARIZONA ROOM, *AZ550-640*
PHOENIXVILLE PUBLIC LIBRARY, *PA730-640*
PHOTO TRENDS (PHOTOGRAPH REPOSITORY), *NY593-420*
PHOTOPHILE (PHOTOGRAPH REPOSITORY), *CA712-630*
PICKAWAY COUNTY HISTORICAL SOCIETY, TED LEWIS MUSEUM, HISTORICAL AND GENEALOGICAL LIBRARY, *OH176-650*
PICKERING-BEACH HISTORICAL MUSEUM, *NY769-640*
PICKERING, TIMOTHY, LIBRARY, *MA897-880*
PICKETT LIBRARY MEDIA CENTER, *WV775-40*
PICKLER MEMORIAL LIBRARY, *MO460-560*
PIERCE COUNTY LIBRARY SYSTEM, HEADQUARTERS, *WA904-665*
PIERCE, WALTER M., LIBRARY, *OR464-200*
PIERPONT MORGAN LIBRARY, *NY593-460*
PIKE COUNTY HISTORICAL SOCIETY, *PA590-640*
PIKE LIBRARY, *NY698-650*
PIKES PEAK REGIONAL LIBRARY DISTRICT, LOCAL HISTORY COLLECTION, *CO180-640*
PILGRIM JOHN HOWLAND SOCIETY, *RI945-760*
PILGRIM SOCIETY, *MA685-630*
PILSUDSKI, JOSEPH, INSTITUTE OF AMERICA FOR RESEARCH IN MODERN HISTORY OF POLAND, *NY590-700*
PIMERIA ALTA HISTORICAL SOCIETY MUSUEM, LIBRARY AND ARCHIVES, *AZ475-640*
PINCHOT NATIONAL FOREST, *WA943-280*
PIONEER ASSOCIATION OF WASHINGTON, *WA820-619*
PIONEER MEMORIAL VISITOR CENTER, *WA676-610*
PIONEER MUSEUM, *MN314-520*
PIONEER MUSEUM AND ART CENTER, *OK956-640*
PIONEER MUSEUM AND HAGGIN GALLERIES, PETZINGER MEMORIAL LIBRARY, *CA862-630*
PIONEER OIL MUSEUM OF NEW YORK, *NY106-640*
PIONEER PARK, *VA800-320*
PIONEER PICTURE GALLERY, *OR104-640*
PIONEER STUDY CENTER, *MI925-640*
PIONEERS' MUSEUM, LIBRARY AND ARCHIVES, *CO180-650*
PIPE SPRING NATIONAL MONUMENT, MONUMENT LIBRARY, *AZ450-640*
PIPESTONE COUNTY HISTORICAL SOCIETY, *MN674-630*
PIPESTONE NATIONAL MONUMENT, *MN674-650*
PITTS THEOLOGY LIBRARY, *GA90-190*
PITTSBURG STATE UNIVERSITY, LIBRARY, *KS746-640*
PITTSBURGH THEOLOGICAL SEMINARY, CLIFFORD E. BARBOUR LIBRARY, *PA735-630*
PITTSFORD TOWN HISTORIAN, *NY702-660*
PIUS XII MEMORIAL LIBRARY, VATICAN FILM LIBRARY, *MO810-730*
PLAIN DEALER, LIBRARY, *OH181-630*
PLAINFIELD FRIENDS MEETING, WESTERN YEARLY MEETING OF FRIENDS, *IN660-620*
PLAINFIELD PUBLIC LIBRARY, GUILFORD TOWNSHIP HISTORICAL COLLECTION, *IN660-640*
PLAINS INDIANS AND PIONEER HISTORICAL FOUNDATION, PIONEER MUSEUM AND ART CENTER, *OK956-640*
PLATTE COUNTY HISTORICAL SOCIETY, BEN FERREL-PLATTE COUNTY MUSEUM, *MO675-640*
PLATTSBURGH PUBLIC LIBRARY, LOCAL COLLECTION, *NY708-640*
PLAYERS, THE, THE HAMPDEN-BOOTH THEATRE LIBRARY, *NY593-485*
PLEAK MEMORIAL LIBRARY, *IN341-320*
PLEASANT VALLEY PRESERVATION SOCIETY, *NJ175-333*
PLIMOTH PLANTATION, RESEARCH DEPARTMENT, *MA685-640*
PLUMAS COUNTY MUSEUM, *CA613-640*
PLYMOUTH HISTORICAL SOCIETY, ARCHIVES, *MI765-640*
PLYMOUTH STATE COLLEGE, HERBERT H. LAMSON LIBRARY, *NH772-640*
POCAHONTAS COUNTY HISTORICAL SOCIETY, *WV575-640*
POCUMTUCK VALLEY MEMORIAL ASSOCIATION LIBRARY, *MA238-520*

POETRY CENTER, AMERICAN POETRY ARCHIVES, *CA720-548*
POGUE SPECIAL COLLECTIONS LIBRARY, *KY564-520*
POLISH INSTITUTE OF ARTS AND SCIENCES OF AMERICA, *NY593-500*
POLISH MUSEUM OF AMERICA, LIBRARY, *IL170-520*
POLSON PARK AND MUSEUM HISTORICAL SOCIETY, *WA395-640*
POMONA COLLEGE, GEOLOGY LIBRARY, *CA143-490*
POMONA PUBLIC LIBRARY, SPECIAL COLLECTIONS DEPARTMENT, *CA601-640*
PONCA CITY CULTURAL CENTER MUSEUM, *OK634-640*
PONTIAC CITY LIBRARY, *MI770-640*
PONY EXPRESS STABLES MUSEUM, *MO800-730*
PORT ANGELES LIBRARY, CAMPBELL NORTHWEST ROOM, *WA676-560*
PORT ARTHUR PUBLIC LIBRARY, *TX719-640*
PORT CHESTER PUBLIC LIBRARY, *NY71S-720*
PORT GAMBLE HISTORIC MUSEUM, *WA678-650*
PORT HURON MUSEUM OF ARTS AND HISTORY, *MI775-520*
PORT TOWNSEND LIBRARY, *WA681-670*
PORT WASHINGTON PUBLIC LIBRARY, ERNIE SIMON COLLECTION, *NY717-640*
PORT WILLIAM HISTORICAL SOCIETY, MASTERSON HOUSE, *KY13Y-120*
PORTAGE COUNTY HISTORICAL SOCIETY COLLECTION, *WI722-830*
PORTER PHELPS HUNTINGTON FOUNDATION, PORTER PHELPS HUNTINGTON HOUSE MUSEUM, *MA363-640*
PORTER PHELPS HUNTINGTON HOUSE MUSEUM, *MA363-640*
PORTLAND ART MUSEUM, *OR720-660*
PORTLAND STATE UNIVERSITY, DEPARTMENT OF GEOGRAPHY, MAP ROOM, *OR720-670*
PORTSMOUTH ATHENAEUM, LIBRARY, *NH784-630*
PORTSMOUTH PUBLIC LIBRARY, *OH724-630*
PORTSMOUTH PUBLIC LIBRARY, LOCAL HISTORY, *VA640-650*
PORTVILLE FREE LIBRARY, *NY720-640*
POSEY COUNTY HISTORICAL SOCIETY, *IN533-640*
POST, C. W., CENTER, LIBRARY, SPECIAL COLLECTIONS, *NY355-480*
POTOMAC STATE COLLEGE, MARY F. SHIPPER LIBRARY, MINERAL COUNTY COLLECTION, *WV500-640*
POTSDAM PUBLIC MUSEUM, *NY723-640*
POTTAWATOMIE COUNTY HISTORICAL SOCIETY, SANTA FE DEPOT MUSEUM, *OK736-640*
POTTER COUNTY HISTORICAL SOCIETY, *PA235-640*
POULSBO MARINE SCIENCE CENTER, *WA685-640*
POULSBO PUBLIC LIBRARY, *WA685-650*
POWELL, JOHN WESLEY, MEMORIAL MUSEUM, *AZ500-400*
POWELL, R. E., MUSEUM, *WA366-640*
POWER, F. B., PHARMACEUTICAL LIBRARY, KREMERS REFERENCE FILES, *WI346-870*
POWERS LIBRARY ASSOCIATION, *NY563-322*
PRAIRIE ARCHIVES, *WI456-530*
PRAIRIE HISTORIANS, *IL936-640*
PRAIRIE VIEW A & M UNIVERSITY, W. R. BANKS LIBRARY, *TX733-640*
PRATT INSTITUTE, LIBRARY, *NY593-560*
PRATT MUSEUM, *AK450-320*
PRATT, DON F., MUSEUM, *KY250-160*
PRATT, ENOCH, FREE LIBRARY, *MD76-190*
PRATT, LAURA PARSONS, ARCHIVES AND RESEARCH CENTER, *NY595-740*
PREACHERS, ORDER OF, PROVINCE OF ST. JOSEPH, ARCHIVES, *DC15-50*
PRESBYTERIAN AND REFORMED CHURCHES, HISTORICAL FOUNDATION OF, *NC590-320*
PRESBYTERIAN CHURCH (U.S.A.), PRESBYTERIAN HISTORICAL SOCIETY, *PA726-713*
PRESBYTERIAN HISTORICAL SOCIETY, *PA726-713*
PRESCOTT HISTORICAL SOCIETY, SHARLOT HALL MUSEUM, *AZ625-630*
PRESCOTT MEMORIAL LIBRARY, LOUISIANA TECH UNIVERSITY ARCHIVES, *LA780-490*
PRESIDENT BENJAMIN HARRISON MEMORIAL HOME, *IN363-660*
PRESIDENTIAL MUSEUM, LIBRARY OF THE PRESIDENTS, *TX654-640*
PRESIDIO ARMY MUSEUM, *CA720-550*
PRESIDIO OF MONTEREY, *CA480-800*
PRESTON COLLECTION, *NH468-800*
PRESTON LIBRARY, ARCHIVES/SPECIAL COLLECTIONS, *VA430-840*
PRESTONSBURG COMMUNITY COLLEGE, LIBRARY, *KY64C-640*
PRIESTS OF HOLY CROSS, INDIANA PROVINCE, PROVINCE ARCHIVES CENTER, *IN627-640*
PRIMITIVE BAPTIST LIBRARY AND ARCHIVES, *NC310-640*
PRINCE GEORGE'S COUNTY MEMORIAL LIBRARY, GREENBELT BRANCH LIBRARY, REXFORD G. TUGWELL ROOM, *MD513-640*
PRINCE GEORGE'S COUNTY MEMORIAL LIBRARY, HYATTSVILLE BRANCH LIBRARY, MARYLAND ROOM, *MD551-640*
PRINCETON HISTORICAL SOCIETY, *NJ692-320*

PRINCETON THEOLOGICAL SEMINARY, SPEER LIBRARY, *NJ692-610*
PRINCETON UNIVERSITY, ART MUSEUM, *NJ692-620*
PRINCETON UNIVERSITY, LIBRARY, DEPARTMENT OF RARE BOOKS AND SPECIAL COLLECTIONS, MANUSCRIPT DIV., *NJ692-660*
PRINCIPIA COLLEGE, ARCHIVES, *IL251-630*
PROCESS EQUIPMENT CORPORATION, *MI68-640*
PROCTOR FREE LIBRARY, *VT632-640*
PROJECT DOCUMERICA, *DC5-600*
PROPRIETARY HOUSE ASSOCIATION, *NJ666-650*
PROTESTANT EPISCOPAL CHURCH IN THE DIOCESE OF THE CENTRAL GULF COAST, OFFICE OF THE BISHOP, *AL580-650*
PROTESTANT EPISCOPAL CHURCH IN THE DIOCESE OF WEST TEXAS, CATHEDRAL HOUSE ARCHIVES, *TX777-640*
PROTESTANT EPISCOPAL CHURCH, DIOCESE OF CHICAGO, ARCHIVES AND HISTORICAL COLLECTIONS, *IL169-651*
PROTESTANT EPISCOPAL CHURCH, DIOCESE OF MISSOURI, DIOCESAN ARCHIVES, *MO810-590*
PROTESTANT EPISCOPAL CHURCH, DIOCESE OF NEW YORK, ARCHIVES, *NY593-590*
PROTESTANT EPISCOPAL DIOCESE OF WESTERN NEW YORK, *NY134-660*
PROVIDENCE ATHENAEUM, *RI700-620*
PROVIDENCE COLLEGE, PHILLIPS MEMORIAL LIBRARY, COLLEGE ARCHIVES, *RI700-630*
PROVIDENCE HEIGHTS ARCHIVES, SISTERS OF DIVINE PROVIDENCE, *PA30-720*
PROVIDENCE PUBLIC LIBRARY, SPECIAL COLLECTIONS, *RI700-640*
PROVIDENCE, SISTERS OF, ST. IGNATIUS PROVINCE, ARCHIVES, *WA880-710*
PROVINCE OF THE MOST PURE HEART OF MARY, CARMELITE ORDER, ARCHIVE, *IL55-120*
PSYCHOLOGY, AMERICAN, ARCHIVES OF THE HISTORY OF, *OH11-800*
PUBLIC BROADCASTING SERVICE, PROGRAM DATA AND ANALYSIS, *DC16-680*
PUBLIC LIBRARY OF BROOKLINE, *MA154-640*
PUBLIC LIBRARY OF CINCINNATI AND HAMILTON COUNTY, DEPARTMENT OF RARE BOOKS AND SPECIAL COLLECTIONS, *OH171-650*
PUBLIC LIBRARY OF DES MOINES, FRANKLIN AVENUE LIBRARY, *IA233-640*
PUBLIC LIBRARY OF NASHVILLE AND DAVIDSON COUNTY, NASHVILLE ROOM, *TN690-600*
PUBLIC LIBRARY OF YOUNGSTOWN AND MAHONING COUNTY, *OH990-640*
PUBLIC RECORDS COMMISSION (VT), *VT464-800*
PUEBLO LIBRARY DISTRICT, WESTERN RESEARCH ROOM, *CO768-640*
PUGET SOUND MARITIME HISTORICAL SOCIETY, *WA820-635*
PUGET SOUND NAVAL SHIPYARD MUSEUM, *WA84-720*
PUGET SOUND RAILROAD HISTORICAL ASSOCIATION, *WA856-100*
PULASKI COUNTY HISTORICAL SOCIETY, *KY78J-650*
PULASKI COUNTY PUBLIC LIBRARY AND PULASKI COUNTY HISTORICAL SOCIETY, *KY78J-650*
PULTENEY FREE LIBRARY, *NY728-640*
PURDUE UNIVERSITY AT INDIANAPOLIS-INDIANA UNIVERSITY, ARCHIVES, *IN363-385*
PURDUE UNIVERSITY CALUMET LIBRARY, ARCHIVES AND SPECIAL COLLECTIONS, *IN308-640*
PURDUE UNIVERSITY, KRANNERT GRADUATE SCHOOL OF MANAGEMENT, KRANNERT LIBRARY, *IN935-640*
PURDUE UNIVERSIY, LIBRARIES, SPECIAL COLLECTIONS, *IN935-650*
PUTERBAUGH MUSEUM, *IN649-650*
PUTNAM COUNTY DISTRICT LIBRARY, *OH675-640*
PUTNAM COUNTY HISTORICAL SOCIETY, *IN275-640*
PUTNAM COUNTY HISTORICAL SOCIETY, MUSEUM, *OH397-640*
PUTNAM MUSEUM, *IA188-650*
PUTNEY HISTORICAL SOCIETY, *VT640-640*
PUYALLUP PUBLIC LIBRARY, *WA726-640*

Q

QUABEAG HISTORICAL SOCIETY, *MA910-680*
QUAKER COLLECTION, FRIENDS UNIVERSITY, *KS948-240*
QUAKER COLLECTION, GUILFORD COLLEGE, *NC380-290*
QUAKER HILL, HISTORICAL SOCIETY OF, *NY681-320*
QUAPAW QUARTER ASSOCIATION, *AR510-680*
QUEEN EMMA SUMMER PALACE, *HI350-150*
QUEENS BOROUGH PUBLIC LIBRARY, LONG ISLAND DIVISION, *NY593-600*
QUEENS COLLEGE, HISTORICAL DOCUMENTS COLLECTION, *NY588-520*
QUEENSBOROUGH COMMUNITY COLLEGE, *NY588-560*

QUINAULT RANGER STATION, *WA729-820*
QUINCY AND ADAMS COUNTY, HISTORICAL SOCIETY OF, *IL767-320*
QUINCY COLLEGE, LIBRARY, *IL767-680*
QUINCY HISTORICAL SOCIETY, LIBRARY AND MUSEUM, *MA697-680*

R

R. E. POWELL MUSEUM, *WA366-640*
R. P. STRATHEARN HISTORICAL PARK, *CA830-720*
R. W. GRAND LODGE (PENNSYLVANIA FREE AND ACCEPTED MASONS), *PA726-057*
R. W. NORTON ART GALLERY, REFERENCE LIBRARY, *LA885-690*
RACINE COUNTY COURTHOUSE, COUNTY CLERK'S OFFICE, *WI606-680*
RACINE PUBLIC LIBRARY, *WI606-710*
RADCLIFFE COLLEGE, ARCHIVES, *MA169-855*
RADCLIFFE COLLEGE, ARTHUR AND ELIZABETH SCHLESINGER LIBRARY ON THE HISTORY OF WOMEN IN AMERICA, *MA169-860*
RADCLIFFE COLLEGE, HENRY A. MURRAY RESEARCH CENTER, *MA169-885*
RADCLIFFE WOMEN'S ARCHIVES, *MA169-860*
RADFORD UNIVERSITY, JOHN PRESTON MCCONNELL LIBRARY, ALUMNI-SPECIAL COLLECTIONS, *VA670-690*
RADNOR HISTORICAL SOCIETY, *PA935-690*
RAILROAD AND PIONEER MUSEUM, *TX851-690*
RAILROAD HOUSE HISTORICAL ASSOCIATION, *NC740-690*
RAILROAD MUSEUM OF PENNSYLVANIA, *PA840-690*
RALPH FOSTER MUSEUM, LOIS BROWNELL RESEARCH LIBRARY, *MO700-720*
RALPH W. STEEN LIBRARY, SPECIAL COLLECTIONS DEPARTMENT, *TX632-720*
RALPH WALDO EMERSON ROOM, *MN541-600*
RALSTON HISTORICAL ASSOCIATION, *NJ502-690*
RAMAKER LIBRARY, DUTCH HERITAGE COLLECTION, *IA755-560*
RAMONA PIONEER HISTORICAL SOCIETY AND MUSEUM, *CA616-690*
RAMSAYER LIBRARY, *OH137-730*
RANCHO LOS CERRITOS, HISTORICAL COLLECTION, *CA414-500*
RANCHO SANTA ANA BOTANIC GARDEN, *CA143-690*
RAND, ANNE, RESEARCH LIBRARY, *CA720-356*
RANDALL, WILLIAM MADISON, LIBRARY, HELEN HAGAN RARE BOOK ROOM, *NC900-810*
RANDOLPH TOWNSHIP PUBLIC LIBRARY, HISTORICAL ROOM, *NJ708-690*
RANDOLPH-MACON COLLEGE, LIBRARY, *VA60-690*
RANDOLPH-MACON WOMAN'S COLLEGE, LIPSCOMB LIBRARY, *VA470-690*
RAPID CITY PUBLIC LIBRARY, *SD648-690*
RASMUSON, E. E., LIBRARY, ARCHIVES AND MANUSCRIPT COLLECTIONS, *AK350-800*
RAUSHENBUSH, ESTHER, LIBRARY, *NY128-720*
RAWLINS COUNTY HISTORICAL MUSEUM, *KS94-690*
RAYBURN, SAM, LIBRARY, *TX105-720*
RAYMOND H. FOGLER LIBRARY, SPECIAL COLLECTIONS DEPARTMENT, *ME650-810*
RAYMOND HISTORICAL SOCIETY, *NH796-690*
RAYMOND PATTERSON ALUMNI ARCHIVE, *MA928-730*
RAYMOND PUBLIC LIBRARY, *WA734-680*
READING ANTIQUARIAN SOCIETY, *MA705-680*
REARDAN PUBLIC LIBRARY, *WA735-680*
RED CROSS, AMERICAN NATIONAL, ARCHIVES, *DC1-560*
REDINGTON MUSEUM, *ME925-870*
REDMOND LIBRARY, *WA736-680*
REDWOOD CITY PUBLIC LIBRARY, *CA636-690*
REED COLLEGE, LIBRARY, *OR720-700*
REED LIBRARY, *NY310-720*
REED MEMORIAL LIBRARY, *OH733-690*
REEVES LIBRARY, SETON HILL COLLEGE ARCHIVES, *PA350-720*
REEVES, J. E., HOME AND MUSEUM, *OH237-160*
REEVES, ROBERTA WRIGHT, MEMORIAL LIBRARY, *CO252-30*
REFORMED CHURCH IN AMERICA, ARCHIVES, *NJ568-570*
REFORMED PROTESTANT DUTCH CHURCH OF KINGSTON, NY, HERITAGE COMMITTEE, MUSEUM SUBCOMMITTEE, *NY469-600*
REGIS COLLEGE, LIBRARY, *CO252-680*
RELIGIOUS SISTERS OF MERCY, ARCHIVES, LOUISIANA AREA, *LA600-690*
RELIGIOUS SOCIETY OF FRIENDS, NEW YORK YEARLY MEETING, HAVILAND RECORDS ROOM, *NY593-710*
REMINGTON-CARPENTER TOWNSHIP PUBLIC LIBRARY, *IN687-690*
RENNE, ROLAND R., LIBRARY, ARCHIVES, *MT130-535*
RENSSELAER COUNTY HISTORICAL SOCIETY, LIBRARY, *NY890-680*
RENSSELAER POLYTECHNIC INSTITUTE, ARCHIVES, *NY890-700*
RENSSELAERVILLE HISTORICAL SOCIETY, *NY742-690*

RENTON HISTORICAL MUSEUM, *WA738-670*
RENTON PUBLIC LIBRARY, *WA738-690*
REORGANIZED CHURCH OF JESUS CHRIST OF LATTER DAY SAINTS, HISTORY COMMISSION, CHURCH ARCHIVES, *MO400-690*
RESEARCH AND ENLIGHTENMENT, ASSOCIATION FOR, EDGAR CAYCE FOUNDATION ARCHIVES, *VA810-40*
RESEARCH CENTER FOR THE FEDERAL THEATER PROJECT, *VA205-290*
RESEARCH FOUNDATION FOR JEWISH IMMIGRATION, *NY593-720*
RESTORATION HISTORY MANUSCRIPT COLLECTION, *IA533-280*
REV. ANTON DARMS LIBRARY, *IL996-980*
REVERE PUBLIC LIBRARY, *MA711-690*
REXFORD G. TUGWELL ROOM, *MD513-640*
REYNOLDS HISTORICAL LIBRARY, *AL120-815*
RHEES, RUSH, LIBRARY, DEPARTMENT OF RARE BOOKS, MANUSCRIPTS AND ARCHIVES, *NY752-880*
RHEUDASIL, MIKE, LEARNING CENTER, A. M. AND WELMA AIKIN REGIONAL ARCHIVES, *TX695-640*
RHODE ISLAND COLLEGE, JAMES P. ADAMS LIBRARY, ARCHIVES, *RI700-660*
RHODE ISLAND HISTORICAL SOCIETY, LIBRARY, *RI700-680*
RHODE ISLAND JEWISH HISTORICAL ASSOCIATION, *RI700-690*
RHODE ISLAND MEDICAL SOCIETY, LIBRARY, *RI700-710*
RHODE ISLAND SECRETARY OF STATE, ARCHIVES DIVISION, *RI700-740*
RHODE ISLAND STATE ARCHIVES, *RI700-740*
RHODES COLLEGE, BURROW LIBRARY, *TN630-740*
RIALTO HISTORICAL SOCIETY, *CA640-640*
RICE COUNTY HISTORICAL SOCIETY, *MN321-690*
RICE UNIVERSITY, FONDREN LIBRARY, WOODSON RESEARCH CENTER, *TX483-690*
RICH, CARRIE, MEMORIAL LIBRARY, *NC130-120*
RICHARD A. GLEESON LIBRARY, SPECIAL COLLECTIONS DEPARTMENT, *CA720-910*
RICHARD B. RUSSELL MEMORIAL LIBRARY, *GA75-790*
RICHARD SALTER STORRS LIBRARY, *MA474-690*
RICHARDSON ARCHIVES, *SD792-820*
RICHARDSON LIBRARY, RICHARDSON RESEARCH CENTER, *TX7-320*
RICHARDSON MEMORIAL LIBRARY, *MO810-600*
RICHARDSON PUBLIC LIBRARY, *TX742-680*
RICHARDSON RESEARCH CENTER, *TX7-320*
RICHBURG COLONIAL LIBRARY, *NY744-680*
RICHEY HISTORICAL SOCIETY, RICHEY MUSEUM, *MT750-690*
RICHFIELD SPRINGS PUBLIC LIBRARY, *NY745-690*
RICHLAND COUNTY GENEALOGICAL SOCIETY, RICHLAND COUNTY MUSEUM, *OH446-690*
RICHLAND COUNTY MUSEUM, *OH446-690*
RICHLAND PUBLIC LIBRARY, *WA742-690*
RICHMOND ACADEMY OF MEDICINE, LIBRARY, *VA690-690*
RICHMOND BEACH PUBLIC LIBRARY, *WA820-653*
RICHMOND COLLECTION, *CA644-690*
RICHMOND COUNTY HISTORICAL SOCIETY, *GA105-690*
RICHMOND NATIONAL BATTLEFIELD PARK, *VA690-700*
RICHMOND NEWSPAPERS, LIBRARY, *VA690-740*
RICHMOND PUBLIC LIBRARY, RICHMOND COLLECTION, *CA644-690*
RICHTER LIBRARY, ARCHIVES DIVISION, *FL80-820*
RICKS COLLEGE, DAVID O. MCKAY LEARNING RESOURCES CENTER, ARCHIVES AND SPECIAL COLLECTIONS, *ID680-690*
RIDGWAY MEMORIAL LIBRARY, *KY760-720*
RIGGS, ANNIE, MEMORIAL MUSEUM, *TX367-40*
RILEY COUNTY HISTORICAL MUSEUM, *KS607-690*
RILEY LIBRARY, CLARK COUNTY HISTORICAL ASSOCIATION ARCHIVES, *AR60-600*
RIO GRANDE HISTORICAL COLLECTIONS/HOBSON-HUNTSINGER UNIVERSITY ARCHIVES, *NM494-570*
RIORDAN STATE HISTORIC PARK, *AZ250-690*
RIPON COLLEGE, LIBRARY, *WI646-670*
RITZVILLE PUBLIC LIBRARY, *WA747-680*
RIVERTON FREE LIBRARY, *NJ736-690*
ROBERSON CENTER FOR THE ARTS AND SCIENCES, *NY101-690*
ROBERT BENNETT FORBES HOUSE, ARCHIVES, *MA554-530*
ROBERT E. LEE MEMORIAL, *VA50-65*
ROBERT E. LEE MEMORIAL ASSOCIATION, STRATFORD HALL PLANTATION, ARCHIVES AND MANUSCRIPTS COLLECTION, *VA760-690*
ROBERT FROST LIBRARY, ARCHIVES AND SPECIAL COLLECTIONS, *MA21-40*
ROBERT HUDSON TANNAHILL RESEARCH LIBRARY, *MI214-280*
ROBERT MANNING STROZIER LIBRARY, SPECIAL COLLECTIONS, *FL800-262*
ROBERT MULDROW COOPER LIBRARY, SPECIAL COLLECTIONS, *SC185-120*
ROBERT W. WOODRUFF LIBRARY, SPECIAL COLLECTIONS DEPARTMENT, *GA90-200*

ROBERTA WRIGHT REEVES MEMORIAL LIBRARY, CO252-30, CO306-40
ROBERTS COUNTY HISTORICAL SOCIETY, SD702-690
ROBERTS WESLEYAN COLLEGE, ARCHIVES, NY752-660
ROBERTS, W. B., LIBRARY, MS230-160
ROBERTS, WEBB, LIBRARY, TX374-720
ROBESON COUNTY PUBLIC LIBRARY, NC540-690
ROBINSON HOUSE MUSEUM, PA943-760
ROBINSON, ROWLAND E., MEMORIAL ASSOCIATION, ROKEBY MUSEUM, ARCHIVES, VT296-690
ROCHESTER BUSINESS INSTITUTE, BETTY CRONK MEMORIAL LIBRARY, NY752-665
ROCHESTER INSTITUTE OF TECHNOLOGY, WALLACE MEMORIAL LIBRARY, ARCHIVES AND SPECIAL COLLECTIONS, NY752-700
ROCHESTER MUSEUM AND SCIENCE CENTER, LIBRARY, NY752-720
ROCHESTER PUBLIC LIBRARY, NH820-690
ROCHESTER PUBLIC LIBRARY, LOCAL HISTORY DIVISION, NY752-740
ROCK COUNTY HISTORICAL SOCIETY, WI250-690
ROCKBRIDGE COUNTY HISTORICAL SOCIETY, VA430-690
ROCKEFELLER ARCHIVE CENTER, NY612-690
ROCKEFELLER UNIVERSITY, ARCHIVES, NY593-840
ROCKEFELLER UNIVERSITY, ROCKEFELLER ARCHIVE CENTER, NY612-690
ROCKEFELLER, ABBY ALDRICH, FOLK ART COLLECTION, VA870-40
ROCKFORD COLLEGE, HOWARD COLMAN LIBRARY, ARCHIVES, IL806-695
ROCKFORD MUSEUM - MIDWAY VILLAGE, IL806-705
ROCKFORD PUBLIC LIBRARY, LOCAL HISTORY AND GENEALOGY DIVISION, IL806-710
ROCKINGHAM COMMUNITY COLLEGE, LEARNING RESOURCES CENTER, NC870-690
ROCKINGHAM-HARRISONBURG HISTORICAL SOCIETY, VA350-320
ROCKTON TOWNSHIP HISTORICAL SOCIETY, IL811-690
ROCKWELL INTERNATIONAL, COLLINS COMMERCIAL TELECOMMUNICATIONS DIVISION, TX742-690
ROCKWOOD MUSEUM, RESEARCH ARCHIVES, DE810-690
ROCKY HILL HISTORICAL SOCIETY, ACADEMY HALL MUSEUM-LIBRARY, CT673-690
ROCKY MOUNT HISTORICAL ASSOCIATION, MASSENGILL MUSEUM OF OVERMOUNTAIN HISTORY, TN750-690
RODGERS AND HAMMERSTEIN ARCHIVES OF RECORDED SOUND, NY592-878
RODMAN PUBLIC LIBRARY, ORAL HISTORY DIVISION, OH16-690
ROGER M. BLOUGH LEARNING CENTER, PA800-720
ROGERS LIBRARY, ARCHIVES, SC378-250
ROGERS, THELMA, GENEALOGICAL AND HISTORICAL SOCIETY, NY945-760
ROGERS, WILL, MEMORIAL, WILL ROGERS MEMORIAL LIBRARY, OFFICE OF THE CURATOR, OK245-880
ROGUE RIVER NATIONAL FOREST, OR560-690
ROKEBY MUSEUM, ARCHIVES, VT296-690
ROLAND R. RENNE LIBRARY, ARCHIVES, MT130-535
ROLLINS COLLEGE, ARCHIVES, FL960-680
ROLLINS COLLEGE, MILLS MEMORIAL LIBRARY, FL960-690
ROLLS ROYCE OWNERS' CLUB FOUNDATION, LIBRARY, PA560-690
ROMAN CATHOLIC ARCHDIOCESE OF BALTIMORE, ARCHIVES, MD76-30
ROMAN CATHOLIC ARCHDIOCESE OF BOSTON, ARCHIVES, MA109-595
ROMAN CATHOLIC ARCHDIOCESE OF CINCINNATI, ARCHDIOCESAN ARCHIVES, OH171-40
ROMAN CATHOLIC ARCHDIOCESE OF DETROIT, ARCHIVES, MI230-50
ROMAN CATHOLIC ARCHDIOCESE OF LOS ANGELES, CHANCERY ARCHIVES, CA421-30
ROMAN CATHOLIC ARCHDIOCESE OF NEW ORLEANS, ARCHIVES OF THE, LA600-40
ROMAN CATHOLIC ARCHDIOCESE OF PHILADELPHIA, ARCHIVES, PA726-105
ROMAN CATHOLIC ARCHDIOCESE OF PORTLAND IN OREGON, HISTORY AND ARCHIVES DEPARTMENT, OR720-40
ROMAN CATHOLIC ARCHDIOCESE OF SAN ANTONIO, CATHOLIC ARCHIVES AT SAN ANTONIO, TX777-30
ROMAN CATHOLIC ARCHDIOCESE OF SAN FRANCISCO, CA720-579
ROMAN CATHOLIC ARCHDIOCESE OF SANTA FE, ARCHIVES, NM114-50
ROMAN CATHOLIC ARCHDIOCESE OF WASHINGTON, CHANCERY OFFICE, DC1-740
ROMAN CATHOLIC CHANCERY OFFICE (DUBUQUE IA), IA244-120
ROMAN CATHOLIC DIOCESE OF ALBANY, ARCHIVES, NY10-675
ROMAN CATHOLIC DIOCESE OF AMARILLO, DIOCESAN ARCHIVES, TX21-690
ROMAN CATHOLIC DIOCESE OF BAKER, CHANCERY OFFICE, OR64-120

ROMAN CATHOLIC DIOCESE OF BROOKLYN, CHANCERY, NY587-930
ROMAN CATHOLIC DIOCESE OF BURLINGTON, DIOCESAN ARCHIVES, VT176-690
ROMAN CATHOLIC DIOCESE OF CHARLESTON, CHARLESTON DIOCESAN ARCHIVES, SC144-190
ROMAN CATHOLIC DIOCESE OF COVINGTON, ARCHIVES, KY176-160
ROMAN CATHOLIC DIOCESE OF CROOKSTON, CHANCERY OFFICE, MN233-160
ROMAN CATHOLIC DIOCESEOF FAIRBANKS, AK350-120
ROMAN CATHOLIC DIOCESE OF GALVESTON-HOUSTON, CHANCERY ARCHIVES AND RESEARCH, TX483-160
ROMAN CATHOLIC DIOCESE OF GRAND RAPIDS, DIOCESAN ARCHIVES, MI355-160
ROMAN CATHOLIC DIOCESE OF GREEN BAY, DIOCESAN PASTORAL OFFICE, CHANCERY, WI202-120
ROMAN CATHOLIC DIOCESE OF GREENSBURG, DIOCESAN ARCHIVES, PA350-160
ROMAN CATHOLIC DIOCESE OF HARRISBURG, BUREAU OF HISTORY AND ARCHIVES, PA380-700
ROMAN CATHOLIC DIOCESE OF HELENA, MT530-690
ROMAN CATHOLIC DIOCESE OF JACKSON, MS550-120
ROMAN CATHOLIC DIOCESE OF LA CROSSE, WI298-120
ROMAN CATHOLIC DIOCESE OF LAFAYETTE IN INDIANA, CHANCERY ARCHIVES, IN440-160
ROMAN CATHOLIC DIOCESE OF LAFAYETTE, ARCHIVES, LA358-160
ROMAN CATHOLIC DIOCESE OF LAKE CHARLES, ARCHIVES, LA358-165
ROMAN CATHOLIC DIOCESE OF LITTLE ROCK, ARCHIVES, AR510-145
ROMAN CATHOLIC DIOCESE OF MONTEREY-FRESNO, CHANCERY AND ACADEMY OF CALIFORNIA CHURCH HISTORY, CA274-40
ROMAN CATHOLIC DIOCESE OF NASHVILLE, TN690-690
ROMAN CATHOLIC DIOCESE OF OGDENSBURG, ARCHIVES, NY634-160
ROMAN CATHOLIC DIOCESE OF PATERSON, ARCHIVES, NJ154-690
ROMAN CATHOLIC DIOCESE OF PITTSBURGH, DIOCESAN HISTORICAL ARCHIVES, PA735-160
ROMAN CATHOLIC DIOCESE OF PROVIDENCE, ARCHIVES, RI700-160
ROMAN CATHOLIC DIOCESE OF SAVANNAH, CHANCERY ARCHIVES AND DIOCESAN ARCHIVES, GA895-160
ROMAN CATHOLIC DIOCESE OF SIOUX CITY, IA866-160
ROMAN CATHOLIC DIOCESE OF SPOKANE, CHANCERY ARCHIVES, WA880-120
ROMAN CATHOLIC DIOCESE OF WINONA, MN975-160
ROMANIAN CATHOLICS OF AMERICA, ASSOCIATION OF, ARCHIVES SECTION, IN187-40
ROMEO HISTORICAL SOCIETY, MI812-690
ROOSEVELT UNIVERSITY, ARCHIVES, IL170-637
ROOSEVELT UNIVERSITY, ORAL HISTORY PROJECT, IL170-650
ROOSEVELT, FRANKLIN D., LIBRARY, NY427-240
ROPER PUBLIC OPINION RESEARCH CENTER, CT779-812
ROSALIA BATTLE DAYS MUSEUM, WA759-680
ROSE HAWLEY MUSEUM-ARCHIVES, MI585-520
ROSE, BILLY, THEATRE COLLECTION, NY592-880
ROSEAU COUNTY HISTORICAL SOCIETY, MN728-690
ROSEAU COUNTY MUSEUM, MN728-690
ROSENBACH MUSEUM AND LIBRARY, PA726-412
ROSENBERG LIBRARY, ARCHIVES DEPARTMENT, TX397-690
ROSLYN HISTORICAL MUSEUM, WA761-680
ROSLYN LANDMARK SOCIETY, NY760-690
ROSS COUNTY HISTORICAL SOCIETY, OH166-690
ROSWELL MUSEUM AND ART CENTER, NM684-690
ROUTT COUNTY COLLECTION, CO856-80
ROWAN PUBLIC LIBRARY, HISTORY ROOM, NC730-710
ROWLAND E. ROBINSON MEMORIAL ASSOCIATION, ROKEBY MUSEUM, ARCHIVES, VT296-690
ROXBURY PUBLIC LIBRARY, NY763-680
ROY O. WEST LIBRARY, IN275-170
ROYALSTON VILLAGE IMPROVEMENT AND HISTORICAL SOCIETY, MA725-320
ROYALTON HISTORICAL SOCIETY, VT688-690
ROYALTON HISTORICAL SOCIETY, LIBRARY AND MUSEUM, MN735-690
RUDOLPH MATAS MEDICAL LIBRARY, LA600-765
RUHLE, GEORGE C., LIBRARY, MT870-280
RUSH RHEES LIBRARY, DEPARTMENT OF RARE BOOKS, MANUSCRIPTS AND ARCHIVES, NY752-880
RUSH TOWN HISTORIAN, NY763-690
RUSH, CHARLES ANDREW, LEARNING CENTER, SPECIAL COLLECTIONS, AL120-110
RUSHFORD HISTORICAL SOCIETY, NY764-690
RUSSELL COUNTY HISTORICAL SOCIETY, FOSSIL STATION MUSEUM, KS774-690

RUSSELL COUNTY PUBLIC LIBRARY, *KY380-720*
RUSSELL D. COLE LIBRARY, *IA699-120*
RUSSELL SAGE COLLEGE, LIBRARY, *NY890-740*
RUSSELL VERMONTIANA COLLECTION, *VT16-120*
RUSSELL, HELEN CROCKER, LIBRARY, *CA720-798*
RUSSELL, RICHARD B., MEMORIAL LIBRARY, *GA75-790*
RUTGERS UNIVERSITY, DOUGLASS COLLEGE, AMERICAN STUDIES DEPARTMENT, NEW JERSEY FOLKLORE ARCHIVE, *NJ568-625*
RUTGERS UNIVERSITY, UNIVERSITY LIBRARIES, SPECIAL COLLECTIONS DEPARTMENT, *NJ568-670*
RUTGERS UNIVERSITY, UNIVERSITY LIBRARIES, UNIVERSITY ARCHIVES, *NJ568-680*
RUTH A. HAAS LIBRARY, ARCHIVES, *CT144-880*
RUTHERFORD B. HAYES LIBRARY, *OH301-690*
RUTLAND HISTORICAL SOCIETY, *VT704-690*
RYE HISTORICAL SOCIETY, *NY766-690*
RYERSON AND BURNHAM LIBRARIES, *IL169-130*

S

S. ARTHUR WATSON LIBRARY, QUAKER COLLECTION/WILMINGTON COLLEGE ARCHIVES, *OH953-870*
SACRAMENTO HISTORY CENTER, SACRAMENTO MUSEUM AND HISTORY DIVISION, *CA676-740*
SACRAMENTO MUSEUM AND HISTORY DIVISION, *CA676-740*
SACRAMENTO PIONEER ASSOCIATION, *CA676-750*
SACRED HEART FATHERS AND BROTHERS, NORTH AMERICAN PROVINCE, PROVINCIALATE ARCHIVES, *WI214-700*
SACRED HEART SEMINARY, LEO J. WARD MEMORIAL LIBRARY, RARE BOOK COLLECTION AND ARCHIVES, *MI230-720*
SACRED HEARTS, CONGREGATION OF THE HOLY UNION OF THE, SACRED HEART PROVINCE, *MA356-120*
SAINT . . . *See also* St.
SAINT ANNE CONVENT, *KY532-720*
SAINT JOSEPH'S COLLEGE, ARCHIVES, *IN693-710*
SAINT MARTIN'S ABBEY, ARCHIVES, *WA472-720*
SAINT MARY COLLEGE, DEPAUL LIBRARY, SPECIAL COLLECTIONS DEPARTMENT, *KS541-720*
SAINT MARY'S COLLEGE, ARCHIVES, *IN627-720*
SAINT MEINRAD ARCHABBEY, LIBRARY, *IN759-710*
SAINTS MARY AND ELIZABETH HOSPITAL, *KY496-687*
SALEM COUNTY HISTORICAL SOCIETY, *NJ760-720*
SALEM HEIGHTS ARCHIVES, *OH223-710*
SALEM HISTORICAL SOCIETY, *NH832-720*
SALEM PUBLIC LIBRARY, *OH753-720*
SALINAS PUBLIC LIBRARY, JOHN STEINBECK COLLECTION, *CA688-720*
SALISBURY ASSOCIATION, *CT687-710*
SALISBURY HISTORICAL SOCIETY, *NY245-720*
SALMON BROOK HISTORICAL SOCIETY, REFERENCE AND EDUCATIONAL CENTER, *CT268-720*
SALT MUSEUM, *NY499-720*
SALVATION ARMY, ARCHIVES BUREAU, *NY594-20*
SALZMANN LIBRARY, *WI456-720*
SAM HOUSTON REGIONAL LIBRARY AND RESEARCH CENTER, *TX560-720*
SAM RAYBURN LIBRARY, *TX105-720*
SAMFORD UNIVERSITY, HARWELL G. DAVIS LIBRARY, *AL120-720*
SAMPSON, HENRY T., LIBRARY, SPECIAL COLLECTIONS, *MS550-410*
SAMUEL ELIOT MORISON LIBRARY, *MA109-850*
SAN ANTONIO CONSERVATION SOCIETY LIBRARY, *TX777-700*
SAN ANTONIO MISSION, *CA352-520*
SAN ANTONIO MUSEUM ASSOCIATION, RESEARCH LIBRARY, *TX777-710*
SAN ANTONIO PUBLIC LIBRARY, *TX777-720*
SAN ANTONIO VALLEY HISTORICAL ASSOCIATION, *CA360-720*
SAN BERNARDINO COUNTY LIBRARY, *CA700-720*
SAN BERNARDINO COUNTY MUSEUM, *CA628-720*
SAN BERNARDINO PUBLIC LIBRARY, *CA700-760*
SAN BUENAVENTURA MISSION, *CA934-720*
SAN DIEGO COUNTY LAW LIBRARY, *CA712-700*
SAN DIEGO HISTORICAL SOCIETY, RESEARCH ARCHIVES, *CA712-708*
SAN DIEGO MUSEUM OF MAN, PHOTO ARCHIVES AND ARCHAEOLOGICAL ARCHIVES, *CA712-713*
SAN DIEGO PUBLIC LIBRARY, CALIFORNIA ROOM, *CA712-720*
SAN DIEGO SOCIETY OF NATURAL HISTORY, NATURAL HISTORY MUSEUM, LIBRARY, *CA712-726*
SAN DIEGO STATE UNIVERSITY, LIBRARY, CENTER FOR REGIONAL HISTORY, *CA712-750*
SAN DIEGO STATE UNIVERSITY, MAP COLLECTION, *CA712-743*
SAN FRANCISCO CONSERVATORY OF MUSIC, LIBRARY, *CA720-623*
SAN FRANCISCO PUBLIC LIBRARY, SAN FRANCISCO ROOM, *CA720-675*

SAN FRANCISCO THEOLOGICAL SEMINARY, LIBRARY, *CA696-720*
SAN GABRIEL MISSION CHURCH, ARCHIVES, *CA724-730*
SAN JACINTO MUSEUM OF HISTORY ASSOCIATION, *TX266-720*
SAN JOAQUIN COUNTY ARCHIVES, *CA402-720*
SAN JOAQUIN COUNTY HISTORICAL MUSEUM, SAN JOAQUIN COUNTY ARCHIVES, *CA402-720*
SAN JOSE HISTORICAL MUSEUM, *CA728-730*
SAN JUAN COUNTY ARCHAEOLOGICAL RESEARCH CENTER AND LIBRARY AT SALMON RUIN, *NM398-720*
SAN JUAN COUNTY MUSEUM ASSOCIATION, *NM398-720*
SAN JUAN HISTORICAL SOCIETY, *WA327-735*
SAN JUAN ISLAND NATIONAL HISTORICAL PARK, *WA327-740*
SAN LEANDRO COMMUNITY LIBRARY CENTER, *CA740-710*
SAN MATEO COUNTY HISTORICAL ASSOCIATION AND MUSEUM, *CA760-710*
SANDEL LIBRARY, SPECIAL COLLECTIONS, *LA535-560*
SANDOR TESZLER LIBRARY, ARCHIVES DEPARTMENT, *SC846-890*
SANDWICH ARCHIVES & HISTORICAL CENTER, *MA738-700*
SANDWICH GLASS MUSEUM, *MA738-720*
SANDWICH HISTORICAL SOCIETY, MUSEUM, *NH108-720*
SANDWICH HISTORICAL SOCIETY, SANDWICH GLASS MUSEUM, *MA738-720*
SANFORD MEMORIAL LIBRARY, *FL740-720*
SANFORD MUSEUM AND PLANETARIUM, *IA122-720*
SANGAMON STATE UNIVERSITY, LIBRARY, UNIVERSITY ARCHIVES AND SPECIAL COLLECTIONS, *IL866-715*
SANGAMON STATE UNIVERSITY, ORAL HISTORY OFFICE, *IL866-720*
SANGAMON VALLEY COLLECTION, *IL866-480*
SANTA BARBARA COLLEGE LIBRARY, UNIVERSITY OF CALIFORNIA, GOLETA, *CA774-800*
SANTA BARBARA HISTORICAL SOCIETY, LIBRARY, *CA774-710*
SANTA BARBARA MISSION, ARCHIVE-LIBRARY, *CA774-720*
SANTA CLARA COUNTY HISTORICAL AND GENEALOGICAL SOCIETY, *CA778-710*
SANTA CRUZ COUNTY HISTORICAL MUSEUM, *CA782-720*
SANTA CRUZ HISTORICAL SOCIETY, *CA782-730*
SANTA FE DEPOT MUSEUM, *OK736-640*
SANTA FE TRAIL CENTER, RESEARCH LIBRARY, *KS513-720*
SANTA MONICA PUBLIC LIBRARY, CALIFORNIA SPECIAL COLLECTION, *CA790-720*
SAPULPA HISTORICAL MUSEUM, *OK685-710*
SAPULPA HISTORICAL SOCIETY, SAPULPA HISTORICAL MUSEUM, *OK685-710*
SAPULPA PUBLIC LIBRARY, *OK685-720*
SARAH LAWRENCE COLLEGE, ESTHER RAUSHENBUSH LIBRARY, *NY128-720*
SARATOGA COUNTY HISTORIAN'S OFFICE, *NY795-710*
SARATOGA COUNTY HISTORICAL SOCIETY, *NY66-720*
SARATOGA NATIONAL HISTORICAL PARK, LIBRARY, *NY861-720*
SARATOGA SPRINGS PUBLIC LIBRARY, *NY792-720*
SARATOGA SPRINGS, HISTORICAL SOCIETY OF, *NY795-320*
SARGEANT MEMORIAL ROOM, *VA580-570*
SAUK COUNTY HISTORICAL SOCIETY, *WI70-720*
SAUK-SUIATTLE INDIAN TRIBE, *WA200-322*
SAUSALITO HISTORICAL SOCIETY, MUSEUM, *CA810-700*
SAVITZ LIBRARY, STEWART ROOM, *NJ280-270*
SAVONA FREE LIBRARY, *NY797-720*
SAWYER FREE LIBRARY & GLOUCESTER LYCEUM, AUDIO-VISUAL DEPARTMENT, *MA338-280*
SCHAFFER LIBRARY OF HEALTH SCIENCES, *NY10-800*
SCHAFFER LIBRARY, SPECIAL COLLECTIONS, *NY804-800*
SCHENECTADY CITY HISTORY CENTER, *NY804-700*
SCHENECTADY COUNTY HISTORICAL SOCIETY, *NY804-720*
SCHENECTADY COUNTY PUBLIC LIBRARY, *NY804-740*
SCHEVCHENKO SCIENTIFIC SOCIETY, *NY594-080*
SCHEWE LIBRARY, *IL394-360*
SCHLESINGER LIBRARY, *MA169-860*
SCHLOW MEMORIAL LIBRARY, *PA837-720*
SCHMINCK MEMORIAL MUSEUM, *OR512-720*
SCHOENBERG, ARNOLD, INSTITUTE, ARCHIVES, *CA421-40*
SCHOHARIE COUNTY HISTORICAL SOCIETY, REFERENCE LIBRARY, *NY807-730*
SCHOMBURG CENTER FOR RESEARCH IN BLACK CULTURE, *NY592-930*
SCHOOL OF THE OZARKS, RALPH FOSTER MUSEUM, LOIS BROWNELL RESEARCH LIBRARY, *MO700-720*
SCHOOL OF THEOLOGY AT CLAREMONT, *CA143-720*
SCHOOL SISTERS OF ST. FRANCIS, ARCHIVES, *WI456-730*
SCHUYLER COUNTY HISTORICAL SOCIETY, DR. CHARLES DELAND CLAWSON MEDICAL COLLECTION, *NY562-720*
SCHWENKFELDER LIBRARY, *PA715-720*
SCIENCE AND HISTORY, FORT WORTH MUSEUM OF, *TX374-240*
SCIENCE FICTION MUSEUM, *CA318-700*
SCIENCES, NATIONAL ACADEMY OF, *DC14-100*
SCIO FREE LIBRARY, *NY813-720*
SCOTIA HISTORY CENTER, *NY814-720*

SCOTLAND COUNTY HISTORICAL SOCIETY, *MO590-720*
SCOTT ANDREW TREXLER II, *PA25-480*
SCOTT MEMORIAL LIBRARY, *PA726-690*
SCOTTISH RITE OF FREEMASONRY, SUPREME COUNCIL, ARCHIVES, *DC19-130*
SCOVILLE MEMORIAL LIBRARY, *CT687-730*
SCRANTON PUBLIC LIBRARY, *PA795-710*
SCRIPPS INSTITUTION OF OCEANOGRAPHY, HISTORICAL ARCHIVES SECTION, *CA368-820*
SEAMEN'S CHURCH INSTITUTE OF NEW YORK, *NY594-060*
SEARLS HISTORICAL LIBRARY, *CA508-560*
SEATTLE CENTRAL COMMUNITY COLLEGE, LIBRARY, *WA820-715*
SEATTLE HISTORICAL SOCIETY, MUSEUM OF HISTORY AND INDUSTRY, SOPHIE FRYE BASS MEMORIAL LIBRARY, *WA820-770*
SEATTLE PACIFIC UNIVERSITY, WETER MEMORIAL LIBRARY, OMAR ALLEN BURNS ROOM, *WA820-772*
SEATTLE PUBLIC LIBRARY, *WA820-774*
SEATTLE PUBLIC LIBRARY, MUNICIPAL REFERENCE LIBRARY, *WA820-775*
SEATTLE UNIVERSITY, JESUIT RESIDENCE ARCHIVES, *WA820-780*
SEAY, GOVERNOR A. J., MANSION, *OK456-120*
SEDGWICK MUSEUM, *OH495-510*
SEDGWICK-BROOKLIN HISTORICAL SOCIETY, *ME775-720*
SEMINOLE NATION MUSEUM, *OK922-720*
SENATE HOUSE STATE HISTORIC SITE, *NY469-720*
SENATE, HISTORICAL OFFICE, *DC19-160*
SENECA FALLS HISTORICAL SOCIETY, MUSEUM, *NY821-720*
SEQUIM-DUNGENESS MUSEUM, *WA836-740*
SEQUOIA NATIONAL PARK, DIVISION OF INTERPRETATION, *CA882-720*
SERVANTS OF MARY, ORDER OF, WESTERN PROVINCE, SOMERSET ARCHIVES, *CA110-600*
SERVANTS OF THE IMMACULATE HEART OF MARY, *PA420-720, PA795-120*
SETON HALL UNIVERSITY, MCLAUGHLIN LIBRARY, ARCHIVES & SPECIAL COLLECTIONS, *NJ798-720*
SETON HILL COLLEGE, REEVES LIBRARY, COLLEGE ARCHIVES, *PA350-720*
SETON MEMORIAL LIBRARY AND MUSEUM, *NM266-720*
SEVENTH DAY BAPTIST HISTORICAL SOCIETY, *NJ674-720*
SEVENTH DAY BAPTIST MISSIONARY SOCIETY, *RI910-730*
SEVENTH-DAY ADVENTIST THEOLOGICAL SEMINARY, LIBRARY, *MI90-30*
SEVENTH-DAY ADVENTISTS, GENERAL CONFERENCE, ARCHIVES, *DC19-220*
SEYMOUR LIBRARY, *NY51-730, NY125-700*
SEYMOUR LIBRARY, KNOX COLLEGE ARCHIVES, *IL305-430*
SHADELANDS RANCH HISTORICAL MUSEUM, *CA954-720*
SHAFFER MUSEUM, *WA985-720*
SHAKER MUSEUM, EMMA B. KING LIBRARY, *NY637-720*
SHARLOT HALL MUSEUM, *AZ625-630*
SHARP, ELLA, MUSEUM, *MI510-200*
SHASTA COLLEGE, MUSEUM AND RESEARCH CENTER, *CA624-710*
SHASTA HISTORICAL SOCIETY, *CA624-730*
SHASTA STATE HISTORIC PARK, *CA814-120*
SHASTA-TRINITY NATIONAL FOREST, *CA624-740*
SHAW ISLAND LIBRARY AND HISTORICAL SOCIETY, *WA844-720*
SHAW MANSION, *CT512-550*
SHAW, J. PORTER, LIBRARY, *CA720-485*
SHEBOYGAN COUNTY HISTORICAL SOCIETY, *WI670-720*
SHEEN LIBRARY, *IL94-360*
SHELBURNE MUSEUM, LIBRARY, *VT784-720*
SHELBY COUNTY HISTORICAL AND GENEALOGICAL LIBRARY, *IL851-720*
SHELBY COUNTY LIBRARY, *KY76Y-760*
SHELBY COUNTY/MEMPHIS PUBLIC LIBRARY AND INFORMATION CENTER, MEMPHIS ROOM, *TN630-570*
SHELDON MUSEUM, *AK400-720*
SHELDON MUSEUM, SWIFT RESEARCH CENTER, *VT432-720*
SHELTER ISLAND HISTORICAL SOCIETY, DOCUMENTS COMMITTEE, *NY827-720*
SHELTON PUBLIC LIBRARY, *WA845-720*
SHENANDOAH COLLEGE AND CONSERVATORY OF MUSIC, HOWE LIBRARY, *VA880-720*
SHEPPARD W. FOSTER LIBRARY, *GA90-210*
SHERBURNE PUBLIC LIBRARY, *NY829-720*
SHERROD LIBRARY, ARCHIVES OF APPALACHIA, *TN435-220*
SHERWIN-WILLIAMS COMPANY, *OH181-660*
SHIAWASSEE COUNTY HISTORICAL SOCIETY, *MI735-720*
SHILOH HOUSE, *IL996-980*
SHILOH NATIONAL MILITARY PARK, *TN870-720*
SHIMER COLLEGE, LIBRARY, *IL585-720*
SHIP DATA REGISTRY, *MI230-180*
SHIPBUILDERS COUNCIL OF AMERICA, *DC19-250*
SHIPMAN LIBRARY, *MI8-20*
SHIPPENSBURG HISTORICAL SOCIETY, *PA810-700*

SHIPPER, MARY F., LIBRARY, MINERAL COUNTY COLLECTION, *WV500-640*
SHIRLEY HISTORICAL SOCIETY, *MA761-720*
SHORELINE HISTORICAL MUSEUM ASSOCIATION, *WA820-810*
SHORELINE PUBLIC LIBRARY, *WA820-815*
SHORTER COLLEGE, MEMORABILIA ROOM, *GA870-730*
SHREWSBURY HISTORICAL SOCIETY, *MA765-730, VT215-720*
SIBLEY MUSIC LIBRARY, *NY752-840*
SIDNEY HISTORICAL SOCIETY, *NY839-720*
SIENA HEIGHTS COLLEGE, LIBRARY, *MI8-720*
SIERRA COUNTY HISTORICAL SOCIETY, GERONIMO SPRINGS MUSEUM, *NM912-280*
SIERRA NATIONAL FOREST, INFORMATION OFFICE, *CA274-720*
SILAS BRONSON LIBRARY, *CT870-730*
SILENT FILM PHOTO COLLECTION, *NJ266-240*
SILVER CITY MUSEUM, *NM760-720*
SILVERADO MUSEUM, *CA680-720*
SILVERDALE PUBLIC LIBRARY, *WA848-720*
SIMI VALLEY HISTORICAL SOCIETY, R. P. STRATHEARN HISTORICAL PARK, *CA830-720*
SIMMONS COLLEGE, ARCHIVES, *MA109-630*
SIMMS A. JAMIESON MEMORIAL LIBRARY, *MD532-880*
SIMON, ERNIE, COLLECTION, *NY717-640*
SIMONS, MENNO, HISTORICAL LIBRARY/ARCHIVES, *VA350-200*
SIMPSON COLLEGE, DUNN LIBRARY, *IA455-720*
SIMPSON, ALBERT F., HISTORICAL RESEARCH CENTER, *AL560-720*
SIMSBURY HISTORICAL SOCIETY, MASSACOH PLANTATION, *CT718-720*
SINCLAIR LEWIS FOUNDATION, *MN790-720*
SINSINAWA DOMINICAN SISTERS, *WI698-730*
SINSINAWA DOMINICAN SISTERS, DOMINICAN ARCHIVES, *WI698-730*
SIOUX CITY PUBLIC MUSEUM, *IA866-730*
SISKIYOU COUNTY MUSEUM, *CA998-720*
SISTER KENNY INSTITUTE, *MN541-16*
SISTERS OF CHARITY OF CINCINNATI, OHIO, MT. ST. JOSEPH MOTHERHOUSE, *OH593-720*
SISTERS OF CHARITY OF NAZARETH, ARCHIVAL CENTER, *KY569-720*
SISTERS OF DIVINE PROVIDENCE OF KENTUCKY, SAINT ANNE CONVENT, *KY532-720*
SISTERS OF DIVINE PROVIDENCE, PROVIDENCE HEIGHTS ARCHIVES, *PA30-720*
SISTERS OF LORETTO, ARCHIVES, *KY57W-720*
SISTERS OF MERCY OF ERIE COUNTY, ARCHIVES, *PA305-720*
SISTERS OF MERCY OF THE UNION, GENERALATE ARCHIVES, *MD152-720*
SISTERS OF MERCY, ARCHIVES, *NY10-710*
SISTERS OF MERCY, PROVINCE OF PROVIDENCE, PROVINCIAL ARCHIVES, *RI210-720*
SISTERS OF MERCY, PROVINCE OF SCRANTON, PROVINCE ARCHIVES, *PA240-720*
SISTERS OF NOTRE DAME DE NAMUR, CALIFORNIA PROVINCE, ARCHIVES, *CA78-740*
SISTERS OF NOTRE DAME DE NAMUR, OHIO PROVINCE, ARCHIVES, *OH171-730*
SISTERS OF PROVIDENCE, SACRED HEART PROVINCE ARCHIVES, *WA820-820*
SISTERS OF PROVIDENCE, ST. IGNATIUS PROVINCE, ARCHIVES, *WA880-710*
SISTERS OF SOCIAL SERVICE, ARCHIVES, *CA421-565*
SISTERS OF ST. FRANCIS OF ASSISI, ARCHIVES, *WI456-734*
SISTERS OF ST. FRANCIS OF MILLVALE, *PA735-720*
SISTERS OF ST. FRANCIS OF PENANCE AND CHRISTIAN CHARITY, HOLY NAME PROVINCE, ARCHIVES, *NY859-720*
SISTERS OF ST. FRANCIS OF PHILADELPHIA, *PA50-720*
SISTERS OF ST. JOSEPH OF CARONDELET, ALBANY NY PROVINCE, ARCHIVES, *NY481-720*
SISTERS OF ST. JOSEPH OF CARONDELET, ST. LOUIS PROVINCE, ARCHIVES DEPARTMENT, *MO810-750*
SISTERS OF ST. JOSEPH OF CARONDELET, ST. PAUL PROVINCE, *MN763-720*
SISTERS OF ST. JOSEPH OF PHILADELPHIA, ARCHIVES, *PA726-480*
SISTERS OF ST. JOSEPH, ARCHIVES DEPARTMENT, *NY115-720*
SISTERS OF ST. MARY OF NAMUR, ARCHIVES, *NY459-520*
SISTERS OF ST. MARY OF THE THIRD ORDER OF ST. FRANCIS, *MO810-760*
SISTERS OF THE BLESSED SACRAMENT, ARCHIVES, *PA85-730*
SISTERS OF THE DIVINE SAVIOR, NORTH AMERICAN PROVINCE, ARCHIVES, *WI456-735*
SISTERS OF THE HOLY FAMILY OF NAZARETH, IMMACULATE CONCEPTION PROVINCE, ARCHIVES, *PA726-495*
SISTERS OF THE HOLY NAMES OF JESUS AND MARY CONVENT, ARCHIVES, *WA880-753*
SISTERS OF THE HOLY NAMES OF JESUS AND MARY, OREGON PROVINCE, ARCHIVES, *OR528-718*
SISTERS OF THE HUMILITY OF MARY, *IA188-777*

SISTERS OF THE HUMILITY OF MARY, VILLA MARIA COMMUNITY CENTER, ARCHIVES OFFICE, *PA908-720*
SISTERS OF THE PRECIOUS BLOOD, SALEM HEIGHTS ARCHIVES, *OH223-710*
SISTERS OF THE PRESENTATION OF THE BLESSED VIRGIN MARY, PRESENTATION ARCHIVES, *CA720-739*
SISTERS, SERVANTS OF THE IMMACULATE HEART OF MARY, *PA420-720*
SISTERS, SERVANTS OF THE IMMACULATE HEART OF MARY, ARCHIVES, *MI650-720*
SIUSLAW PUBLIC LIBRARY, *OR240-240*
SKAGIT COUNTY HISTORICAL SOCIETY, *WA468-720*
SKAMANIA COUNTY HISTORICAL SOCIETY, *WA892-725*
SKINNER MUSEUM, *MA776-515*
SKIRBALL MUSEUM, *CA421-250*
SLEEPY HOLLOW RESTORATIONS, LIBRARY, *NY878-720*
SLIPPERY ROCK STATE COLLEGE, LIBRARY, COLLEGE ARCHIVES, *PA815-710*
SLOAN, ALFRED P., JR., MUSEUM, *MI314-60*
SMALL, LILIAN AND ALBERT, JEWISH MUSEUM, *DC10-500*
SMILEY, A. K., PUBLIC LIBRARY, SPECIAL COLLECTIONS AND LINCOLN MEMORIAL SHRINE, *CA628-40*
SMILEY, GEORGE M., MEMORIAL LIBRARY, METHODIST COLLECTION, *MO290-120*
SMITH COLLEGE, ARCHIVES, *MA624-700*
SMITH COLLEGE, SOPHIA SMITH COLLECTION, *MA624-740*
SMITH COLLEGE, WILLIAM ALLAN NEILSON LIBRARY, RARE BOOK ROOM, *MA624-750*
SMITH COUNTY HISTORICAL SOCIETY, ARCHIVES, *TX890-720*
SMITH MEMORIAL LIBRARY, CHAUTAUQUA COLLECTION, *NY179-120*
SMITH, EDGAR FAHS, COLLECTION IN THE HISTORY OF CHEMISTRY, *PA726-765*
SMITH, FREDERICK MADISON, LIBRARY, RESTORATION HISTORY MANUSCRIPT COLLECTION, *IA533-280*
SMITH, SOPHIA, COLLECTION, *MA624-740*
SMITH, STANLEY W., COLLECTION, *MA67-720*
SMITH, WARREN HUNTING, LIBRARY, *NY323-320*
SMITHSONIAN INSTITUTION, ARCHIVES, *DC19-310*
SMITHSONIAN INSTITUTION, ARCHIVES OF AMERICAN ART, *DC19-320*
SMITHSONIAN INSTITUTION, FREER GALLERY OF ART, DEPARTMENT OF NEAR EASTERN ART, *DC19-327*
SMITHSONIAN INSTITUTION, FREER GALLERY OF ART, LIBRARY, *DC19-330*
SMITHSONIAN INSTITUTION, HIRSHHORN MUSEUM AND SCULPTURE GARDEN, *DC19-340*
SMITHSONIAN INSTITUTION, MUSEUM OF AFRICAN ART AND FREDERICK DOUGLASS INSTITUTE, ARCHIVES, *DC19-440*
SMITHSONIAN INSTITUTION, MUSEUM OF AFRICAN ART AND FREDERICK DOUGLASS INSTITUTE, ELISOFON ARCH., *DC19-450*
SMITHSONIAN INSTITUTION, MUSEUM OF AMER. HIST., ARCHIVES CENTER, *DC19-542*
SMITHSONIAN INSTITUTION, MUSEUM OF AMER. HIST., DEPT. HIST. OF SCI. & TECH., DIV. OF ARM. FORCES, *DC19-621*
SMITHSONIAN INSTITUTION, MUSEUM OF AMER. HIST., DEPT. HIST. OF SCI. & TECH., DIV. OF ELECTR., *DC19-586*
SMITHSONIAN INSTITUTION, MUSEUM OF AMER. HIST., DEPT. HIST. OF SCI. & TECH., DIV. OF ENGINEER., *DC19-601*
SMITHSONIAN INSTITUTION, MUSEUM OF AMER. HIST., DEPT. HIST. OF SCI. & TECH., DIV. OF EXTR. IN., *DC19-591*
SMITHSONIAN INSTITUTION, MUSEUM OF AMER. HIST., DEPT. HIST. OF SCI. & TECH., DIV. OF MATH., *DC19-596*
SMITHSONIAN INSTITUTION, MUSEUM OF AMER. HIST., DEPT. HIST. OF SCI. & TECH., DIV. OF MECH., *DC19-606*
SMITHSONIAN INSTITUTION, MUSEUM OF AMER. HIST., DEPT. HIST. OF SCI. & TECH., DIV. OF MED. SC., *DC19-611*
SMITHSONIAN INSTITUTION, MUSEUM OF AMER. HIST., DEPT. HIST. OF SCI. & TECH., DIV. OF MIL. HIST., *DC19-616*
SMITHSONIAN INSTITUTION, MUSEUM OF AMER. HIST., DEPT. HIST. OF SCI. & TECH., DIV. OF PHOTOGR., *DC19-626*
SMITHSONIAN INSTITUTION, MUSEUM OF AMER. HIST., DEPT. HIST. OF SCI. & TECH., DIV. OF PHYS. SC., *DC19-631*
SMITHSONIAN INSTITUTION, MUSEUM OF AMER. HIST., DEPT. HIST. OF SCI. & TECH., DIV. OF TRANSPOR., *DC19-636*
SMITHSONIAN INSTITUTION, MUSEUM OF AMER. HIST., DEPT. OF SOC. & CULT. HIST., DIV. OF CER. & GLASS, *DC19-545*
SMITHSONIAN INSTITUTION, MUSEUM OF AMER. HIST., DEPT. OF SOC. & CULT. HIST., DIV. OF COMMUNITY LIFE*DC19-550*
SMITHSONIAN INSTITUTION, MUSEUM OF AMER. HIST., DEPT. OF SOC. & CULT. HIST., DIV. OF COSTUMES, *DC19-555*
SMITHSONIAN INSTITUTION, MUSEUM OF AMER. HIST., DEPT. OF SOC. & CULT. HIST., DIV. OF DOMESTIC LIFE, *DC19-560*
SMITHSONIAN INSTITUTION, MUSEUM OF AMER. HIST., DEPT. OF SOC. & CULT. HIST., DIV. OF GRAPHIC ARTS, *DC19-565*
SMITHSONIAN INSTITUTION, MUSEUM OF AMER. HIST., DEPT. OF SOC. & CULT. HIST., DIV. OF MUSICAL INST., *DC19-570*

SMITHSONIAN INSTITUTION, MUSEUM OF AMER. HIST., DEPT. OF SOC. & CULT. HIST., DIV. OF POLIT. HIST., *DC19-576*
SMITHSONIAN INSTITUTION, MUSEUM OF AMER. HIST., DEPT. OF SOC. & CULT. HIST., DIV. OF TEXTILES, *DC19-581*
SMITHSONIAN INSTITUTION, MUSEUM OF AMER. HIST., DIBNER LIBRARY, *DC19-641*
SMITHSONIAN INSTITUTION, MUSEUM OF AMER. HIST., NATIONAL NUMISMATICS COLLECTIONS, *DC19-646*
SMITHSONIAN INSTITUTION, MUSEUM OF AMER. HIST., NATIONAL PHILATELIC COLLECTIONS, *DC19-651*
SMITHSONIAN INSTITUTION, NATIONAL AIR AND SPACE MUSEUM, LIBRARY, *DC19-500*
SMITHSONIAN INSTITUTION, NATIONAL ANTHROPOLOGICAL ARCHIVES, *DC19-520*
SMITHSONIAN INSTITUTION, NATIONAL MUSEUM OF AMERICAN ART, ARCHIVES, *DC19-536*
SMITHSONIAN INSTITUTION, NATIONAL MUSEUM OF AMERICAN ART, SLIDE AND PHOTOGRAPH ARCHIVE, *DC19-539*
SMITHTOWN HISTORICAL SOCIETY, *NY842-720*
SMITHTOWN LIBRARY, LONG ISLAND ROOM, *NY842-730*
SMOKY HILL RAILWAY MUSEUM AND HISTORICAL SOCIETY, KANSAS CITY RAILROAD MUSEUM, *KS850-720*
SMYTH PUBLIC LIBRARY, *NH600-740*
SNOHOMISH COUNTY HISTORICAL SOCIETY, MUSEUM, *WA300-730*
SNOHOMISH HISTORICAL SOCIETY, BLACKMAN MUSEUM, *WA855-80*
SNOHOMISH PUBLIC LIBRARY, *WA855-735*
SNOQUALMIE AND MOUNT BAKER NATIONAL FOREST, RECREATION CULTURAL VISUAL RESOURCES DIVISION, *WA820-824*
SNOQUALMIE AND MOUNT BAKER NATIONAL FOREST, VERLOT RANGER STATION, *WA950-840*
SNOQUALMIE VALLEY HISTORICAL SOCIETY, *WA592-720*
SOAP LAKE PUBLIC LIBRARY, *WA857-720*
SOCIAL LAW LIBRARY, *MA109-660*
SOCIAL SERVICE, SISTERS OF, ARCHIVES, *CA421-565*
SOCIAL WELFARE HISTORY ARCHIVES, *MN541-902*
SOCIALIST PARTY OF MILWAUKEE COUNTY, LIBRARY AND ARCHIVES, *WI456-740*
SOCIETY FOR THE PRESERVATION OF COLONIAL CULTURE, *MA478-730*
SOCIETY FOR THE PRESERVATION OF LONG ISLAND ANTIQUITIES, *NY824-720*
SOCIETY FOR THE PRESERVATION OF NEW ENGLAND ANTIQUITIES, LIBRARY, *MA109-680*
SOCIETY OF CALIFORNIA PIONEERS, LIBRARY, *CA720-746*
SOCIETY OF FRIENDS, BALTIMORE YEARLY MEETING, *MD76-720*
SOCIETY OF FRIENDS, WESTERN YEARLY MEETING, *IN660-620*
SOCIETY OF INDEPENDENT EARTH SCIENTISTS, ARCHIVES COMMITTEE, *TX252-322*
SOCIETY OF JESUS, OREGON PROVINCE ARCHIVES, *WA880-280*
SOCIETY OF MARY, PROVINCE OF CINCINNATI, ARCHIVES, *OH223-720*
SOCIETY OF THE CINCINNATI, *DC19-700*
SOCIETY OF WIRELESS PIONEERS, *CA798-720*
SOCIETY OF WOMAN GEOGRAPHERS, *DC19-750*
SODUS FREE LIBRARY, *NY844-720*
SOIL CONSERVATION SERVICE, INFORMATION DIVISION, AUDIO-VISUAL BRANCH, *DC19-800*
SOJOURNER TRUTH LIBRARY, *NY574-730*
SOLDIERS AND SAILORS MEMORIAL HALL, COUNTY OF ALLEGHENY, *PA735-730*
SOMERS (CT) HISTORICAL SOCIETY, *CT723-720*
SOMERS (NY) HISTORICAL SOCIETY, *NY845-720*
SOMERSET ARCHIVES, *CA110-600*
SOMERSET COMMUNITY COLLEGE, HAROLD D. STRUNK LEARNING RESOURCE CENTER, *KY78J-760*
SOMERSET COUNTY HISTORICAL SOCIETY, *NJ792-720*
SOMERSET HISTORICAL CENTER, *PA825-720*
SONNENBERG GARDENS, *NY147-720*
SONNICHSEN COLLECTION, *CA456-730*
SONOMA VALLEY HISTORICAL SOCIETY, DEPOT PARK MUSEUM, *CA838-720*
SONS OF THE REVOLUTION IN THE STATE OF NEW YORK, FRAUNCES TAVERN MUSEUM, *NY594-220*
SONS OF THE REVOLUTION LIBRARY, *CA290-720*
SONS OF UNION VETERANS OF THE CIVIL WAR, PHILADELPHIA CAMP 200, GAR MEMORIAL HALL, LIBRARY, *PA726-508*
SOPER LIBRARY, *MD76-540*
SOPHIA SMITH COLLECTION, *MA624-740*
SOPHIE FRYE BASS MEMORIAL LIBRARY, *WA820-770*
SOPHIENBURG ARCHIVES, *TX640-720*
SOPHIENBURG MEMORIAL ASSOCIATION, SOPHIENBURG ARCHIVES, *TX640-720*
SOURISSEAU ACADEMY FOR CALIFORNIA STATE AND LOCAL HISTORY, *CA728-850*

SOUTH BANNOCK COUNTY HISTORICAL CENTER, LAVA HOT SPRINGS MUSEUM, *ID400-720*

SOUTH BEND PUBLIC LIBRARY, LOCAL HISTORY DEPARTMENT, *IN792-720*

SOUTH CAROLINA DEPARTMENT OF ARCHIVES AND HISTORY, *SC216-720*

SOUTH CAROLINA HISTORICAL SOCIETY, *SC144-730*

SOUTH CAROLINA STATE ARCHIVES, *SC216-720*

SOUTH CAROLINA STATE COLLEGE, MILLER F. WHITTAKER LIBRARY, COLLEGE HISTORICAL COLLECTION, *SC720-710*

SOUTH CAROLINIANA LIBRARY, MANUSCRIPTS DIVISION, *SC216-820*

SOUTH DAKOTA OFFICE OF HISTORY, HISTORICAL RESOURCE CENTER, *SD558-720*

SOUTH DAKOTA ORAL HISTORY PROJECT, *SD792-850*

SOUTH DAKOTA SCHOOL OF MINES AND TECHNOLOGY, DEVEREAUX LIBRARY, *SD648-710*

SOUTH DAKOTA STATE ARCHIVES, *SD558-710*

SOUTH DAKOTA STATE HISTORICAL SOCIETY, *SD558-720*

SOUTH DAKOTA STATE LIBRARY & ARCHIVES, STATE ARCHIVES, *SD558-710*

SOUTH DAKOTA STATE UNIVERSITY, HILTON M. BRIGGS LIBRARY, ARCHIVES, *SD54-715*

SOUTH END HISTORICAL SOCIETY, *MA109-720*

SOUTH FLORIDA MUSEUM AND BISHOP PLANETARIUM, *FL60-720*

SOUTH GEORGIA REGIONAL LIBRARY, *GA950-720*

SOUTH MILWAUKEE HISTORICAL SOCIETY, *WI706-720*

SOUTH NEW BERLIN FREE LIBRARY, *NY847-720*

SOUTH PASADENA PUBLIC LIBRARY, *CA850-720*

SOUTH PLAINS MUSEUM, *TX555-720*

SOUTH PORTLAND PUBLIC LIBRARY, *ME825-730*

SOUTH STREET SEAPORT MUSEUM, LIBRARY, *NY594-240*

SOUTH SUBURBAN GENEALOGICAL AND HISTORICAL SOCIETY, *IL856-730*

SOUTH THURSTON COUNTY HISTORICAL SOCIETY, *WA94-720*

SOUTHEAST MICHIGAN COUNCIL OF GOVERNMENTS, *MI230-730*

SOUTHEAST MINNESOTA HISTORICAL CENTER, *MN975-730*

SOUTHEAST RESEARCH AND ARCHIVES CENTER, *AR600-160*

SOUTHEAST SPOKANE COUNTY HISTORICAL SOCIETY, *WA304-720*

SOUTHEASTERN ARCHITECTURAL ARCHIVE, *LA600-761*

SOUTHEASTERN BAPTIST THEOLOGICAL SEMINARY, LIBRARY, *NC840-720*

SOUTHEASTERN COMMUNITY COLLEGE, LIBRARY, *NC880-720*

SOUTHEASTERN FOREST EXPERIMENT STATION, *NC60-720*

SOUTHEASTERN FOREST EXPERIMENT STATION, COWEETA HYDROLOGIC LABORATORY, *NC656-720*

SOUTHEASTERN LOUISIANA UNIVERSITY, LIBRARY, ARCHIVES DEPARTMENT, *LA286-720*

SOUTHEASTERN MASSACHUSETTS UNIVERSITY, LIBRARY COMMUNICATION CENTER, ARCHIVES & SPEC. COLLS., *MA612-720*

SOUTHERN BAPTIST CONVENTION, HISTORICAL COMMISSION, *TN690-740*

SOUTHERN BAPTIST CONVENTION, SUNDAY SCHOOL BOARD, *TN690-750*

SOUTHERN BAPTIST THEOLOGICAL SEMINARY, LIBRARY, *KY496-720*

SOUTHERN BAPTIST THEOLOGICAL SEMINARY, SCHOOL OF CHURCH MUSIC, AMERICAN LISZT SOC. COLL., *KY496-725*

SOUTHERN COLLEGE OF OPTOMETRY, WILLIAM P. MACCRACKEN, JR., MEMORIAL LIBRARY, *TN630-730*

SOUTHERN EDUCATION FOUNDATION, *GA90-700*

SOUTHERN HIGHLANDS RESEARCH CENTER, *NC60-810*

SOUTHERN HISTORICAL COLLECTION, *NC150-800*

SOUTHERN ILLINOIS UNIVERSITY AT CARBONDALE, MORRIS LIBRARY, SPECIAL COLLECTIONS, *IL124-725*

SOUTHERN ILLINOIS UNIVERSITY, ELIJAH P. LOVEJOY LIBRARY, MAP SECTION, *IL236-730*

SOUTHERN ILLINOIS UNIVERSITY, ELIJAH P. LOVEJOY LIBRARY, RESEARCH COLLECTIONS, *IL236-760*

SOUTHERN LABOR ARCHIVES, *GA90-300*

SOUTHERN METHODIST UNIVERSITY, FIKES HALL OF SPECIAL COLLECTIONS AND DEGOLYER LIBRARY, *TX252-730*

SOUTHERN METHODIST UNIVERSITY, PERKINS SCHOOL OF THEOLOGY, METHODIST HISTORICAL COLLECTIONS, *TX252-760*

SOUTHERN METHODIST UNIVERSITY, SCIENCE/ENGINEERING LIBRARY, *TX252-770*

SOUTHERN METHODIST UNIVERSITY, UNDERWOOD LAW LIBRARY, *TX252-780*

SOUTHERN METHODIST UNIVERSITY, UNIVERSITY ARCHIVES, *TX252-790*

SOUTHERN MINNESOTA HISTORICAL CENTER, *MN506-530*

SOUTHERN OREGON HISTORICAL SOCIETY, JACKSONVILLE MUSEUM, RESEARCH LIBRARY, *OR400-720*

SOUTHERN OREGON STATE COLLEGE, LIBRARY, *OR32-720*

SOUTHERN UNIVERSITY, LIBRARY, BLACK HERITAGE COLLECTION, *LA62-710*

SOUTHERN UTAH STATE COLLEGE, LIBRARY, SPECIAL COLLECTIONS DEPARTMENT, *UT152-720*

SOUTHERN WOMEN'S ARCHIVES, *AL120-104*

SOUTHPORT HISTORICAL SOCIETY, *NY851-720*

SOUTHWEST AUDIO-VISUAL COLLECTION, *NM722-730*

SOUTHWEST COLLECTION, EL PASO PUBLIC LIBRARY, *TX326-210*

SOUTHWEST COLLECTION, TEXAS TECH UNIVERSITY, *TX590-760*

SOUTHWEST FOUNDATION FOR AUDIO-VISUAL RESOURCES, SOUTHWEST AUDIO-VISUAL COLLECTION, *NM722-730*

SOUTHWEST MINNESOTA HISTORICAL CENTER, *MN520-700*

SOUTHWEST MUSEUM, LIBRARY, *CA421-610*

SOUTHWEST RESEARCH CENTER, BISHOP COLLEGE, *TX252-80*

SOUTHWEST STATE UNIVERSITY, SOUTHWEST MINNESOTA HISTORICAL CENTER, *MN520-700*

SOUTHWEST TAPE ARCHIVE, *AZ750-32*

SOUTHWEST TEXAS STATE UNIVERSITY, LIBRARY, SPECIAL COLLECTIONS, *TX791-730*

SOUTHWEST WASHINGTON REGIONAL STATE ARCHIVES, *WA616-895*

SOUTHWESTERN ARCHIVES AND MANUSCRIPTS COLLECTION, *LA358-800*

SOUTHWESTERN ASSEMBLIES OF GOD COLLEGE, NELSON MEMORIAL LIBRARY, *TX947-720*

SOUTHWESTERN BAPTIST THEOLOGICAL SEMINARY, WEBB ROBERTS LIBRARY (FORMERLY FLEMING LIBRARY), *TX374-720*

SOUTHWESTERN COLLEGE, MEMORIAL LIBRARY, *KS962-730*

SOUTHWESTERN OREGON COMMUNITY COLLEGE, LEARNING RESOURCE CENTER, *OR128-720*

SOUTHWESTERN UNIVERSITY, CODY MEMORIAL LIBRARY, DEPARTMENT OF SPECIAL COLLECTIONS, *TX404-120*

SOUTHWORTH LIBRARY ASSOCIATION, *NY246-720*

SOUTHWORTH LIBRARY, MERRITT-WRIGHT ROOM, *NY150-760*

SPALDING COLLEGE, ARCHIVES, *KY496-730*

SPANISH DOCUMENTS PROJECT (LOYOLA UNIVERSITY OF NEW ORLEANS), *LA600-505*

SPARTANBURG COUNTY PUBLIC LIBRARY, *SC846-730*

SPEEDWELL VILLAGE, *NJ548-720*

SPEER LIBRARY, *NJ692-610*

SPENCER HISTORICAL SOCIETY, MUSEUM, *NY852-720*

SPENCER LIBRARY, *NY852-730*

SPENCER, KENNETH, RESEARCH LIBRARY, DEPARTMENT OF SPECIAL COLLECTIONS, MSS. SECT., *KS527-790*

SPENCER, KENNETH, RESEARCH LIBRARY, KANSAS COLLECTION, *KS527-795*

SPENCER, KENNETH, RESEARCH LIBRARY, UNIVERSITY OF KANSAS ARCHIVES, *KS527-805*

SPERTUS COLLEGE OF JUDAICA, ASHER LIBRARY, CHICAGO JEWISH ARCHIVES, *IL170-780*

SPOKANE PUBLIC LIBRARY, *WA880-775*

SPOKANE VALLEY HISTORICAL SOCIETY, *WA880-790*

SPORT BALLOON SOCIETY OF THE UNITED STATES OF AMERICA, SONNICHSEN COLLECTION, *CA456-730*

SPRAGUE PUBLIC LIBRARY, *WA881-740*

SPRAGUE, NORMAN F., MEMORIAL LIBRARY, *CA143-480*

SPRING VALLEY COMMUNITY HISTORICAL SOCIETY, *MN821-720*

SPRINGFIELD COLLEGE, BABSON LIBRARY, DR. ERNEST M. BEST ARCHIVES ROOM, *MA804-710*

SPRINGFIELD HISTORICAL SOCIETY, *NJ800-720*

SPRINGFIELD TOWN LIBRARY, *VT864-730*

SQUIBB, E. R., & SONS, *NJ692-190*

ST. . . . *See also* Saint

ST. ALBANS ARCHIVES, *DC19-40*

ST. ALBANS FREE LIBRARY, *VT720-710*

ST. ALBANS HISTORICAL SOCIETY, FRANKLIN COUNTY MUSEUM, *VT720-720*

ST. ALBANS SCHOOL FOR BOYS, ELLISON LIBRARY, ST. ALBANS ARCHIVES, *DC19-40*

ST. ANTHONY-ON-HUDSON LIBRARY, *NY741-720*

ST. AUGUSTINE HISTORICAL SOCIETY, *FL660-720*

ST. BENEDICT'S ABBEY, ARCHIVES, *KS80-720*

ST. BENEDICT'S CONVENT, ARCHIVES, *MN749-720*

ST. BERNARD ABBEY, *AL130-333*

ST. BERNARD'S INSTITUTE, LIBRARY, *NY752-760*

ST. BONAVENTURE UNIVERSITY, LIBRARY, ARCHIVE COLLECTION, *NY775-720*

ST. CATHARINE OF SIENA, DOMINICAN SISTERS OF, ARCHIVES, *KY710-160*

ST. CHARLES COUNTY HISTORICAL SOCIETY, ARCHIVES AND LIBRARY, *MO770-710*

ST. CHARLES PUBLIC LIBRARY DISTRICT, *IL826-730*

ST. CLAIR COUNTY LIBRARY, W. L. JENKS HISTORICAL COLLECTION, *MI775-710*

ST. CLAIR SHORES HISTORICAL COMMISSION'S ARCHIVAL COLLECTIONS, *MI828-720*

ST. CLAIR SHORES PUBLIC LIBRARY, ST. CLAIR SHORES
HISTORICAL COMMISSION'S ARCHIVAL COLLECTIONS,
MI828-720

ST. CLEMENT UKRAINIAN CATHOLIC UNIVERSITY IN ROME,
PHILADELPHIA CENTER, INST. FOR UKRAINIAN CULT.,
PA725-430

ST. CLOUD STATE UNIVERSITY, CENTRAL MINNESOTA
HISTORICAL CENTER, *MN742-700*

ST. CLOUD STATE UNIVERSITY, LEARNING RESOURCES
SERVICES, UNIV. ARCHIVES & RARE BOOKS & MSS., *MN742-720*

ST. CROIX COUNTY HISTORICAL SOCIETY, OCTAGON HOUSE,
WI230-720

ST. DOMINIC, MARYKNOLL SISTERS OF, ARCHIVES, *NY529-530*

ST. EDWARD'S UNIVERSITY, ARCHIVES, *TX56-720*

ST. FRANCIS COLLEGE, JAMES A. KELLY LOCAL HISTORICAL
STUDIES INSTITUTE, *NY593-900*

ST. FRANCIS CONVENT, *IL866-320*

ST. FRANCIS MONASTERY, PAPERS, *KS819-720*

ST. FRANCIS OF PENANCE AND CHRISTIAN CHARITY, SISTERS
OF, HOLY NAME PROVINCE, ARCHIVES, *NY859-720*

ST. FRANCIS OF PHILADELPHIA, SISTERS OF, *PA50-720*

ST. FRANCIS SEMINARY, SALZMANN LIBRARY, *WI456-720*

ST. FRANCIS, HOSPITAL SISTERS OF THIRD ORDER OF, ST.
FRANCIS CONVENT, *IL866-320*

ST. JOHN FISHER COLLEGE, LAVERY LIBRARY, *NY752-780*

ST. JOHN'S ABBEY, ARCHIVES, *MN226-705*

ST. JOHN'S ABBEY, KRITZECK COLLECTION, *MN226-700*

ST. JOHN'S CHURCH, *NH784-700*

ST. JOHN'S SEMINARY, EDWARD LAURENCE DOHENY
MEMORIAL LIBRARY, ESTELLE DOHENY COLLECTION,
CA118-720

ST. JOHN'S UNIVERSITY (MN), BUSH CENTER, HILL MONASTIC
MANUSCRIPT LIBRARY, *MN226-720*

ST. JOHN'S UNIVERSITY (MN), UNIVERSITY ARCHIVES, *MN226-725*

ST. JOHN'S UNIVERSITY (NY), LIBRARY, *NY593-940*

ST. JOSEPH MUSEUM AND PONY EXPRESS STABLES MUSEUM,
MO800-730

ST. JOSEPH OF CARONDELET, SISTERS OF, ALBANY NY
PROVINCE, *NY481-720*

ST. JOSEPH OF CARONDELET, SISTERS OF, ST. LOUIS PROVINCE,
ARCHIVES DEPARTMENT, *MO810-750*

ST. JOSEPH OF CARONDELET, SISTERS OF, ST. PAUL PROVINCE,
MN763-720

ST. JOSEPH OF PHILADELPHIA, SISTERS OF, ARCHIVES, *PA726-480*

ST. JOSEPH, SISTERS OF, ARCHIVES DEPARTMENT, *NY115-720*

ST. JOSEPH'S PROVINCIAL HOUSE, DAUGHTERS OF CHARITY OF
ST. VINCENT DE PAUL, *MD380-160*

ST. JOSEPH'S SEMINARY, ARCHBISHOP CORRIGAN MEMORIAL
LIBRARY, *NY984-710*

ST. LAWRENCE COUNTY HISTORICAL ASSOCIATION, *NY150-700*

ST. LAWRENCE UNIVERSITY, ARCHIVES, *NY150-740*

ST. LAWRENCE UNIVERSITY, MUSEUM, *NY150-740*

ST. LEO ABBEY, LIBRARY, *FL680-720*

ST. LOUIS ART MUSEUM, RICHARDSON MEMORIAL LIBRARY,
ARCHIVES DIVISION, *MO810-600*

ST. LOUIS COUNTY DEPARTMENT OF PARKS AND RECREATION,
MO200-720

ST. LOUIS COUNTY HISTORICAL SOCIETY, *MN261-810*

ST. LOUIS MEDICAL MUSEUM, *MO810-650*

ST. LOUIS MERCANTILE LIBRARY ASSOCIATION, *MO810-630*

ST. LOUIS METROPOLITAN MEDICAL SOCIETY, ST. LOUIS SOC.
FOR MED. AND SCI. EDUC., ST. LOUIS MED. MUS.*MO810-650*

ST. LOUIS POST-DISPATCH, REFERENCE DEPARTMENT, *MO810-670*

ST. LOUIS PUBLIC LIBRARY, GARDNER RARE BOOK ROOM,
MO810-690

ST. LOUIS SCIENCE CENTER, *MO810-700*

ST. LOUIS SOCIETY FOR MEDICAL AND SCIENTIFIC EDUCATION,
ST. LOUIS MEDICAL MUSEUM, *MO810-650*

ST. LOUIS UNIVERSITY, PIUS XII MEMORIAL LIBRARY, VATICAN
FILM LIBRARY, *MO810-730*

ST. LOUIS-CHAMINADE EDUCATION CENTER, MARIANIST
ARCHIVES, *HI350-720*

ST. LUKE'S HOSPITAL OF KANSAS CITY, ARCHIVES, *MO430-700*

ST. LUKE'S MUSEUM, *NY368-600*

ST. MARK'S CHURCH IN-THE-BOWERY, ARCHIVES, *NY593-970*

ST. MARK'S LIBRARY, *NY589-710*

ST. MARY OF NAMUR, SISTERS OF, ARCHIVES, *NY459-520*

ST. MARY OF THE PLAINS COLLEGE, ARCHIVES, *KS255-720*

ST. MARY OF THE THIRD ORDER OF ST. FRANCIS, SISTERS OF,
MO810-760

ST. MARY, COMMUNITY OF, *NY687-120*

ST. MARY'S COLLEGE OF CALIFORNIA, *CA488-720*

ST. MARY'S COLLEGE, FITZGERALD LIBRARY, *MN975-720*

ST. MARY'S COLLEGE, LIBRARY, *NC680-720*

ST. MARY'S COLLEGE, SOUTHEAST MINNESOTA HISTORICAL
CENTER, *MN975-730*

ST. MARY'S COUNTY HISTORICAL SOCIETY, *MD608-710*

ST. MARY'S DOMINICAN COLLEGE, JOHN XXIII LIBRARY,
LA600-710

ST. MARY'S UNIVERSITY OF SAN ANTONIO, ACADEMIC LIBRARY,
SPECIAL COLLECTIONS, *TX777-670*

ST. MICHAEL'S COLLEGE, ARCHIVES AND SPECIAL COLLECTIONS,
VT964-720

ST. MICHAEL'S EPISCOPAL CHURCH, *SC144-710*

ST. NORBERT ABBEY, ARCHIVES, *WI130-720*

ST. NORBERT COLLEGE, ARCHIVES, *WI130-730*

ST. OLAF COLLEGE, ARCHIVES, *MN625-710*

ST. PAUL COMPANIES, LIBRARY, *MN763-690*

ST. PAUL PUBLIC LIBRARY, HIGHLAND PARK BRANCH, PERRIE
JONES MEMORIAL ROOM, *MN763-710*

ST. PAUL'S CHURCH, *GA105-720*

ST. PETERSBURG HISTORICAL SOCIETY, WATERFRONT MUSEUM,
FL720-720

ST. ROSE CONVENT, *WI298-250*

ST. VINCENT ARCHABBEY AND COLLEGE, *PA485-720*

ST. VINCENT DE PAUL, DAUGHTERS OF CHARITY OF, MATER
DEI PROVINCIALATE, ARCHIVES, *IN209-140*

ST. VINCENT DE PAUL, DAUGHTERS OF CHARITY OF, ST.
JOSEPH'S PROVINCIAL HOUSE, *MD380-160*

ST. WALBURG CONVENT, COMMUNITY ARCHIVES, *KY176-720*

STAMFORD GENEALOGICAL SOCIETY, LIBRARY, *CT765-710*

STAMFORD VILLAGE LIBRARY, *NY858-720*

STANFORD COLLECTION, *CA858-820*

STANFORD UNIVERSITY, LIBRARIES, ARCHIVE OF RECORDED
SOUND, *CA858-790*

STANFORD UNIVERSITY, LIBRARIES, DEPARTMENT OF SPECIAL
COLLECTIONS, MANUSCRIPTS DIVISION, *CA858-810*

STANFORD UNIVERSITY, LIBRARIES, UNIVERSITY ARCHIVES,
CA858-820

STANFORD UNIVERSITY, SCHOOL OF MEDICINE, LANE MEDICAL
LIBRARY, *CA858-895*

STANLEY HOUSE MUSEUM, *CA282-280*

STANLEY LIBRARY, FRANKLIN COUNTY HISTORICAL SOCIETY
COLLECTION, *VA235-250*

STANLEY W. SMITH COLLECTION, *MA67-720*

STANLEY-WHITMAN HOUSE, *CT247-240*

STANLY COUNTY HISTORIC PROPERTIES COMMISSION, *NC30-715*

STANTON COUNTY HISTORICAL SOCIETY, *KS461-720*

STANTON COUNTY MUSEUM, *NE712-760*

STANWOOD HISTORICAL SOCIETY, *WA885-720*

STAR OF THE REPUBLIC MUSEUM, *TX940-720*

STARK COUNTY HISTORICAL SOCIETY, MCKINLEY MUSEUM OF
HISTORY, SCIENCE, & INDUSTRY, RAMSAYER LIBRARY,
OH137-730

STARR LIBRARY, FLANDERS BALLAD COLLECTION, *VT432-520*

STARR LIBRARY, SPECIAL COLLECTIONS, *VT432-530*

STATE HISTORICAL SOCIETY OF NORTH DAKOTA, *ND43-730*

STATE HISTORICAL SOCIETY OF WISCONSIN, ARCHIVES
DIVISION, *WI346-720*

STATE HISTORICAL SOCIETY OF WISCONSIN, AREA RESEARCH
CENTER, LA CROSSE, *WI298-810*

STATE HISTORICAL SOCIETY OF WISCONSIN, AREA RESEARCH
CENTER, MILWAUKEE, *WI456-810*

STATE HISTORICAL SOCIETY OF WISCONSIN, AREA RESEARCH
CENTER, WHITEWATER, *WI858-810*

STATE HISTORICAL SOCIETY OF WISCONSIN, AREA RESEARCH
CENTERS, *WI142-800, WI202-790, WI266-820, WI418-800, WI554-480,
WI654-790, WI722-770*

STATE LIBRARY OF MASSACHUSETTS, *MA109-240*

STATE UNIVERSITY OF NEW YORK AT ALBANY, UNIVERSITY
LIBRARIES, SPECIAL COLLECTIONS, *NY10-770*

STATE UNIVERSITY OF NEW YORK AT ALFRED, AGRICULTURAL
AND TECHNICAL COLLEGE, WALTER HINKLE LIBRARY,
NY18-720

STATE UNIVERSITY OF NEW YORK AT BINGHAMTON, GLENN G.
BARTLE LIBRARY, SPECIAL COLLECTIONS, *NY101-720*

STATE UNIVERSITY OF NEW YORK AT BUFFALO, LIBRARIES,
POETRY/RARE BOOKS, *NY24-735*

STATE UNIVERSITY OF NEW YORK AT BUFFALO, LIBRARIES,
UNIVERSITY ARCHIVES, *NY24-720*

STATE UNIVERSITY OF NEW YORK AT BUFFALO, LOCKWOOD
LIBRARY, POLISH COLLECTION, *NY24-725*

STATE UNIVERSITY OF NEW YORK AT COBLESKILL,
AGRICULTURE AND TECHNICAL COLLEGE, LEARNING RES.
CTR., *NY200-720*

STATE UNIVERSITY OF NEW YORK AT STONY BROOK, LIBRARY,
DEPARTMENT OF SPECIAL COLLECTIONS, *NY866-710*

STATE UNIVERSITY OF NEW YORK AT STONY BROOK, WILLIAM
BUTLER YEATS ARCHIVES, *NY866-730*

STATE UNIVERSITY OF NEW YORK, AGRICULTURAL AND
TECHNICAL COLL., SOUTHWORTH LIB., MERRITT-WRIGHT
RM.*NY150-760*

STATE UNIVERSITY OF NEW YORK, AGRICULTURAL AND
TECHNICAL COLLEGE AT DELHI, LIBRARY, *NY240-720*

STATE UNIVERSITY OF NEW YORK, COLLEGE AT BROCKPORT, DRAKE MEMORIAL LIBRARY, *NY125-720*
STATE UNIVERSITY OF NEW YORK, COLLEGE AT BROCKPORT, EDUCATIONAL CUMMUNICATIONS CENTER, *NY125-740*
STATE UNIVERSITY OF NEW YORK, COLLEGE AT BUFFALO, BURCHFIELD CTR., WEST. NY FORUM FOR AMERICAN ART, *NY134-710*
STATE UNIVERSITY OF NEW YORK, COLLEGE AT BUFFALO, BUTLER LIBRARY, ARCHIVES/SPECIAL COLLECTIONS, *NY134-730*
STATE UNIVERSITY OF NEW YORK, COLLEGE AT CORTLAND, MEMORIAL LIBRARY, *NY216-720*
STATE UNIVERSITY OF NEW YORK, COLLEGE AT FREDONIA, REED LIBRARY, *NY310-720*
STATE UNIVERSITY OF NEW YORK, COLLEGE AT GENESEO, MILNE LIBRARY, *NY321-720*
STATE UNIVERSITY OF NEW YORK, COLLEGE AT NEW PALTZ, CTR. FOR CATSKILL MTN. AND HUDSON RIVER STUDIES*NY574-710*
STATE UNIVERSITY OF NEW YORK, COLLEGE AT NEW PALTZ, SOJOURNER TRUTH LIBRARY, *NY574-730*
STATE UNIVERSITY OF NEW YORK, COLLEGE AT ONEONTA, JAMES M. MILNE LIBRARY, SPECIAL COLLECTIONS CTR., *NY648-720*
STATE UNIVERSITY OF NEW YORK, COLLEGE AT OSWEGO, PENFIELD LIBRARY, SUCO SPECIAL COLLECTIONS, *NY660-720*
STATE UNIVERSITY OF NEW YORK, COLLEGE AT PLATTSBURGH, FEINBERG LIBRARY, NORTH COUNTRY HISTORY CTR., *NY708-720*
STATE UNIVERSITY OF NEW YORK, COLLEGE AT POTSDAM, CRANE SCHOOL OF MUSIC, LIBRARY, *NY723-715*
STATE UNIVERSITY OF NEW YORK, COLLEGE AT POTSDAM, FREDERICK W. CRUMB MEMORIAL LIBRARY, *NY723-720*
STATE UNIVERSITY OF NEW YORK, COLLEGE AT PURCHASE, LIBRARY, *NY732-730*
STATE UNIVERSITY OF NEW YORK, COLLEGE OF ENVIRONMENTAL SCIENCE AND FORESTRY, MOON LIBRARY, *NY872-720*
STATE UNIVERSITY OF NEW YORK, MARITIME COLLEGE, STEPHEN B. LUCE LIBRARY, ARCHIVES, *NY594-340*
STATEN ISLAND HISTORICAL SOCIETY, *NY594-360*
STATEN ISLAND INSTITUTE OF ARTS AND SCIENCES, ARCHIVES AND LIBRARY, *NY594-380*
STATUE OF LIBERTY NATIONAL MONUMENT, AMERICAN MUSEUM OF IMMIGRATION, LIBRARY, *NY594-390*
STEAMER VIRGINIA V FOUNDATION, INC., *WA820-828*
STEAMSHIP HISTORICAL SOCIETY COLLECTION, *MD76-810*
STEARNS COUNTY HISTORICAL SOCIETY, *MN742-750*
STEELE COUNTY HISTORICAL SOCIETY, *MN646-720*
STEELE COUNTY HISTORICAL SOCIETY, LIBRARY, *ND523-720*
STEELE MEMORIAL LIBRARY, *NY272-720*
STEEN, RALPH W., LIBRARY, SPECIAL COLLECTIONS DEPARTMENT, *TX632-720*
STEERE, JUDGE JOSEPH R., ROOM, *MI865-80*
STEILACOOM HISTORICAL MUSEUM ASSOCIATION, *WA889-720*
STEINBRIGHT LOCAL HISTORY COLLECTION, *PA690-520*
STEPHEN B. LUCE LIBRARY, ARCHIVES, *NY594-340*
STEPHEN F. AUSTIN STATE UNIVERSITY, RALPH W. STEEN LIBRARY, SPECIAL COLLECTIONS DEPARTMENT, *TX632-720*
STEPHEN FOSTER MEMORIAL, *PA735-760*
STEPHEN GIRARD COLLECTION, *PA725-615*
STEPHEN H. HART LIBRARY, *CO252-100*
STEPHEN, GENERAL ADAM, MEMORIAL ASSOCIATION, *WV600-280*
STEPHENSON COUNTY HISTORICAL MUSEUM, *IL296-720*
STERLING MEMORIAL LIBRARY, FRANKLIN COLLECTION, *CT505-945*
STERLING MEMORIAL LIBRARY, HISTORICAL SOUND RECORDINGS, *CT505-976*
STERLING MEMORIAL LIBRARY, MANUSCRIPTS AND ARCHIVES, *CT505-960*
STERLING MEMORIAL LIBRARY, MAP COLLECTION, *CT505-970*
STERLING MEMORIAL LIBRARY, VERTICAL FILES COLLECTION, *CT505-975*
STERLING MORTON LIBRARY, *IL459-520*
STETSON MEMORIAL LIBRARY, GEORGIA BAPTIST HISTORICAL COLLECTION, *GA735-520*
STETSON UNIVERSITY, ARCHIVES, *FL140-710*
STEUBEN COUNTY AGRICULTURAL SOCIETY, MEMORIAL PIONEER LOG CABIN AND MUSEUM, *NY71-715*
STEUBEN COUNTY HISTORICAL SOCIETY, *NY71-720*
STEVENS COUNTY HISTORICAL SOCIETY, MUSEUM, *WA168-750*
STEVENS INSTITUTE OF TECHNOLOGY, LIBRARY, *NJ346-720*
STEVENS MEMORIAL LIBRARY, *MA606-720*
STEVENS, GEORGE W., COLLECTION, *OH823-770*
STEVENSON HOUSE STATE HISTORICAL MONUMENT, *CA480-720*
STEWART LIBRARY, SPECIAL COLLECTIONS AND HOWELL LIBRARY, *UT456-900*

STEWART M. LORD MEMORIAL HISTORICAL MUSEUM, *ME187-730*
STEWART ROOM, *NJ280-270*
STILLWATER PUBLIC LIBRARY, MINNESOTA ROOM, *MN835-720*
STILLWATER TOWN HISTORIAN, *NY861-740*
STITT LIBRARY, *TX56-30*
STITT, EDWARD RHODES, LIBRARY, *MD152-560*
STOCKBRIDGE LIBRARY ASSOCIATION, HISTORICAL ROOM, *MA811-720*
STOCKTON-SAN JOAQUIN COUNTY PUBLIC LIBRARY, CALIFORNIA ROOM, *CA862-730*
STOCKWELL MEMORIAL LIBRARY, *MI12-10*
STONE HOUSE (BELCHERTOWN MA), *MA81-80*
STONE SCHOOL MUSEUM, *NH720-560*
STONEHILL COLLEGE, ARNOLD B. TOFIAS INDUSTRIAL ARCHIVES, *MA615-710*
STONEHILL COLLEGE, CUSHING-MARTIN LIBRARY, JOSEPH W. MARTIN COLLECTION, *MA615-720*
STONEHILL COLLEGE, MICHAEL NOVAK PAPERS, *MA615-730*
STONES RIVER NATIONAL BATTLEFIELD, *TN675-720*
STONINGTON HISTORICAL SOCIETY, LIBRARY, *CT772-720*
STORRS, RICHARD SALTER, LIBRARY, *MA474-690*
STOUGHTON HISTORICAL SOCIETY, *MA817-720*
STOWE-DAY MEMORIAL LIBRARY, *CT316-560*
STRAFFORD HISTORICAL SOCIETY, *VT880-720*
STRATFORD HALL PLANTATION, ARCHIVES AND MANUSCRIPT COLLECTIONS, *VA760-690*
STRATFORD HISTORICAL SOCIETY, *CT786-720*
STRATHEARN, R. P., HISTORICAL PARK, *CA830-720*
STRAWBERY BANKE, *NH784-720*
STROH BREWERY COMPANY, *MI230-740*
STROZIER, ROBERT MANNING, LIBRARY, SPECIAL COLLECTIONS, *FL800-262*
STRUNK, HAROLD D., LEARNING RESOURCE CENTER, *KY78J-760*
STRYBING ARBORETUM SOCIETY, HELEN CROCKER RUSSELL LIBRARY, *CA720-798*
STUART HOUSE MUSEUM OF ASTOR FUR POST, *MI590-720*
STUHR MUSEUM OF THE PRAIRIE PIONEER, STUHR RESEARCH LIBRARY, *NE416-720*
STUHR RESEARCH LIBRARY, *NE416-720*
STURGIS LIBRARY, STANLEY W. SMITH COLLECTION, *MA67-720*
STURGIS PUBLIC LIBRARY, *KY800-760, MI890-720, SD756-720*
SUBMARINE FORCE LIBRARY AND MUSEUM, *CT282-720*
SUCO SPECIAL COLLECTIONS, *NY660-720*
SUE BENNETT COLLEGE, LIBRARY, *KY48V-720*
SUFFOLK COUNTY HISTORICAL SOCIETY, *NY749-720*
SUFFOLK COUNTY WHALING MUSEUM OF SAG HARBOR, LONG ISLAND, *NY772-720*
SUFFOLK MARINE MUSEUM, *NY952-720*
SUL ROSS STATE UNIVERSITY, BRYAN WILDENTHAL MEMORIAL LIBRARY, ARCHIVES OF THE BIG BEND, *TX14-720*
SULLIVAN COUNTY HISTORICAL SOCIETY, *NY424-720*
SULPICIAN ARCHIVES BALTIMORE, *MD76-748*
SULZER, CONRAD, REGIONAL LIBRARY, *IL169-396*
SUMAS PUBLIC LIBRARY, *WA896-720*
SUMMIT FREE PUBLIC LIBRARY, *NJ812-710*
SUMNER HISTORICAL SOCIETY, *WA898-740*
SUMNER PUBLIC LIBRARY, *WA898-820*
SUNNYSIDE MUSEUM, *WA900-730*
SUNNYVALE HISTORICAL MUSEUM, *CA870-710*
SUNNYVALE HISTORICAL SOCIETY AND MUSEUM ASSOCIATION, SUNNYVALE HISTORICAL MUSEUM, *CA870-710*
SUOMI COLLEGE, FINNISH-AMERICAN HISTORICAL ARCHIVES, *MI390-720*
SUPERIOR NATIONAL FOREST, *MN261-730*
SUPERIOR PUBLIC LIBRARY, *WI754-720*
SUPREME COURT OF THE UNITED STATES, CURATOR'S OFFICE, *DC19-900*
SURRATT SOCIETY LIBRARY, MARY SURRATT HOUSE, *MD255-720*
SURRY COMMUNITY COLLEGE, LEARNING RESOURCES CENTER, SURRY COUNTY LOCAL HISTORY COLLECTION, *NC250-720*
SURVEYOR GENERAL DEPARTMENT (GA), *GA90-270*
SUSAN B. ANTHONY MEMORIAL, *NY752-790*
SUSQUEHANNA COUNTY HISTORICAL SOCIETY AND FREE LIBRARY ASSOCIATION, *PA615-720*
SUSQUEHANNA UNIVERSITY, ROGER M. BLOUGH LEARNING CENTER, *PA800-720*
SUSSEX COUNTY HISTORICAL SOCIETY, MANUSCRIPTS COLLECTION, *NJ586-720*
SUSSEX COUNTY LIBRARY, SUSSEX COUNTY HISTORY ROOM, *NJ273-740*
SUTLIFF MUSEUM, *OH878-720*
SUTTER'S FORT STATE HISTORICAL MONUMENT, *CA676-770*
SVERDRUP, GEORGE, LIBRARY, ARCHIVES, *MN541-80*
SWAN LIBRARY, *NY12-720*
SWANSEA HISTORICAL SOCIETY, *MA837-720*
SWANTON PUBLIC LIBRARY, *OH803-720*

SWARTHMORE COLLEGE, FRIENDS HISTORICAL LIBRARY, *PA860-710*
SWARTHMORE COLLEGE, PEACE COLLECTION, *PA860-730*
SWASEY, AMBROSE, LIBRARY, *NY752-110*
SWEDENBORG LIBRARY, *MA109-200*
SWEDENBORG MEMORIAL LIBRARY, *OH853-800*
SWEDENBORG SCHOOL OF RELIGION, LIBRARY, *MA590-720*
SWEDENBORGIANA LIBRARY, *PA130-50*
SWEENEY, BEATRICE S., LIBRARY, *NY795-320*
SWEET BRIAR COLLEGE, LIBRARY, *VA780-720*
SWEET, JOSEPH L., MEMORIAL, *MA48-40*
SWEETWATER COUNTY HISTORICAL MUSEUM, *WY365-710*
SWEM, EARL GREGG, LIBRARY, *VA870-110*
SWIFT RESEARCH CENTER, *VT432-720*
SWIGART MUSEUM, LIBRARY, *PA415-720*
SWISHER, CARL S., LIBRARY, *FL280-420*
SYRACUSE PUBLIC LIBRARY, *NY872-590*
SYRACUSE UNIVERSITY, LIBRARIES, BELFER AUDIO LABORATORY AND ARCHIVES, *NY872-760*
SYRACUSE UNIVERSITY, LIBRARIES, GEORGE ARENTS RESEARCH LIBRARY, MANUSCRIPT COLLECTIONS, *NY872-800*
SYRACUSE UNIVERSITY, LIBRARIES, GEORGE ARENTS RESEARCH LIBRARY, UNIVERSITY ARCHIVES, *NY872-810*

T

T. W. PHILLIPS LIBRARY, ALEXANDER CAMPBELL ARCHIVES, *WV100-80*
T. W. PHILLIPS LIBRARY, BETHANY COLLEGE ARCHIVES, *WV100-90*
T.A. HUNGERFORD MEMORIAL LIBRARY, *CT323-320*
TACOMA GENERAL HOSPITAL, SCHOOL OF NURSING, SCHOOL HISTORICAL COLLECTION, *WA904-760*
TACOMA PUBLIC LIBRARY, *WA904-770*
TAINTER, MABEL, MEMORIAL LIBRARY, *WI418-520*
TALBOT COUNTY FREE LIBRARY, MARYLAND ROOM, *MD323-520*
TALBOTT LIBRARY, WESTMINSTER CHOIR COLLEGE ARCHIVES, *NJ692-880*
TALCOTT FREE LIBRARY, *IL811-760*
TALLADEGA COLLEGE HISTORICAL COLLECTIONS, *AL760-760*
TALLADEGA COLLEGE, TALLADEGA COLLEGE HISTORICAL COLLECTIONS, *AL760-760*
TALLMADGE HISTORICAL SOCIETY, *OH808-760*
TAMIMENT LIBRARY, *NY593-120*
TANNAHILL, ROBERT HUDSON, RESEARCH LIBRARY, *MI214-280*
TARRYTOWNS, HISTORICAL SOCIETY OF THE, *NY878-320*
TAYLOR COUNTY HISTORICAL SOCIETY, *KY126-760*
TAYLOR COUNTY PUBLIC LIBRARY, *KY126-770*
TAYLOR MEMORIAL LIBRARY, LEARNING RESOURCE CENTER, CENTENARIANA COLLECTION, *NJ308-120*
TAYLOR, BAYARD, MEMORIAL LIBRARY, *PA440-80*
TAYLOR, GREYTON H., WINE MUSEUM, *NY367-290*
TAYLOR, IRA J., LIBRARY, *CO252-360*
TAYLOR, NATHAN, YORKERS MUSEUM, *NY847-560*
TEANECK PUBLIC LIBRARY, ORAL HISTORY PROJECT AND LOCAL HISTORY PROJECT, *NJ816-760*
TEBEAU, CHARLTON W., LIBRARY OF FLORIDA HISTORY, *FL440-320*
TECUMSEH PUBLIC LIBRARY, CLARA WALDRON HISTORICAL ROOM, *MI910-770*
TED LEWIS MUSEUM, HISTORICAL AND GENEALOGICAL LIBRARY, *OH176-650*
TEHAMA COUNTY LIBRARY, CALIFORNIANA SECTION, *CA620-760*
TEKOA HISTORICAL MUSEUM, *WA909-760*
TELEPHONE PIONEER MUSEUM, *NM114-760*
TELEPHONE PIONEERS OF AMERICA, ZIA COUNCIL, TELEPHONE PIONEER MUSEUM, *NM114-760*
TEMPE HISTORICAL MUSEUM, *AZ750-760*
TEMPE HISTORICAL SOCIETY, TEMPE HISTORICAL MUSEUM, *AZ750-760*
TEMPLE B'RITH KODESH, MUSEUM, *NY752-800*
TEMPLE UNIVERSITY, LIBRARIES, CONWELLANA-TEMPLANA COLLECTION, *PA726-600*
TEMPLE UNIVERSITY, LIBRARIES, RARE BOOK AND MANUSCRIPT COLLECTION, *PA726-615*
TEMPLE UNIVERSITY, LIBRARIES, URBAN ARCHIVES CENTER, *PA726-630*
TENNESSEE STATE ARCHIVES, *TN690-780*
TENNESSEE STATE LIBRARY AND ARCHIVES, ARCHIVES AND MANUSCRIPTS SECTION, *TN690-780*
TENNESSEE STATE MUSEUM, *TN690-770*
TENNESSEE VALLEY AUTHORITY, TECHNICAL LIBRARY, *TN465-760*
TENNESSEE WESLEYAN COLLEGE, MERNER-PFEIFFER LIBRARY, *TN15-760*
TENNIS MUSEUM, *RI560-360*

TENZLER BRANCH LIBRARY, *WA904-780*
TERENCE J. HOVERTER MEMORIAL ARCHIVES, *NY872-720*
TESZLER, SANDOR, LIBRARY, ARCHIVES DEPARTMENT, *SC846-890*
TEXACO, ARCHIVES, *NY964-322*
TEXARKANA HISTORICAL SOCIETY AND MUSEUM, *TX865-750*
TEXAS A & I UNIVERSITY, JOHN E. CONNER MUSEUM, *TX529-770*
TEXAS A & M UNIVERSITY, LIBRARIES, SPECIAL COLLECTIONS, *TX181-780*
TEXAS A & M UNIVERSITY, UNIVERSITY ARCHIVES AND MANUSCRIPTS COLLECTION, *TX181-790*
TEXAS CHRISTIAN UNIVERSITY, LIBRARY, *TX374-750*
TEXAS COLLECTION, *TX933-80*
TEXAS GULF COAST HISTORICAL ASSOCIATION, *TX483-810*
TEXAS LUTHERAN COLLEGE, BLUMBERG MEMORIAL LIBRARY, *TX797-760*
TEXAS PARKS AND WILDLIFE DEPARTMENT, RECORDS SECTION, *TX56-780*
TEXAS SOUTHERN UNIVERSITY, LIBRARY, HEARTMAN NEGRO COLLECTION, *TX483-820*
TEXAS STATE ARCHIVES, *TX56-800*
TEXAS STATE HISTORICAL ASSOCIATION, *TX56-790*
TEXAS STATE LIBRARY, ARCHIVES DIVISION, *TX56-800*
TEXAS TECH UNIVERSITY, SOUTHWEST COLLECTION, *TX590-760*
TEXAS WESTERN COLLEGE, EL PASO CENTENNIAL MUSEUM, *TX326-800*
THAYER COUNTY HISTORICAL MUSEUM, *NE112-760*
THE FILSON CLUB, MANUSCRIPT DEPARTMENT, *KY496-765*
THE TEMPLE, LIBRARY, *OH181-730*
THEATRE AND FILM ARTS, *CA421-620*
THEATRE HISTORICAL SOCIETY, *IN627-760*
THELMA ROGERS GENEALOGICAL AND HISTORICAL SOCIETY, *NY945-760*
THEODORE LOWNIK LIBRARY, *IL459-360*
THIEL COLLEGE, COLLEGE ARCHIVES AND ARCHIVES OF LUTHERAN CHURCH OF AMERICA, WESTERN PA-WV SYNOD, *PA355-760*
THOMAS BURKE MEMORIAL WASHINGTON STATE MUSEUM, *WA820-840*
THOMAS COUNTY HISTORICAL SOCIETY, *KS192-760*
THOMAS F. HOLGATE LIBRARY, *NC380-80*
THOMAS GILCREASE INSTITUTE OF AMERICAN HISTORY AND ART, *OK829-520*
THOMAS J. WATSON LIBRARY, *NY591-380*
THOMAS JEFFERSON UNIVERSITY, SCOTT MEMORIAL LIBRARY, *PA726-690*
THOMAS MERTON COLLECTION, *KY496-90*
THOMAS MORE COLLEGE, ARCHIVES, *KY280-760*
THOMAS PAINE MEMORIAL HOUSE, *NY577-330*
THOMAS WARNE HISTORICAL MUSEUM AND LIBRARY, *NJ622-690*
THOMAS, FRANCES CARRICK, LIBRARY, SPECIAL COLLECTIONS DEPARTMENT, *KY464-760*
THOMPSON FREE LIBRARY, *ME300-760*
THOMPSON HOME LIBRARY, MICHIGAN COLLECTION, *MI505-760*
THOMPSON, J. WALTER, COMPANY, ARCHIVES, *NY590-535*
THOUSAND ISLANDS SHIPYARD MUSEUM, *NY194-760*
THREE RIVERS PUBLIC LIBRARY, *MI920-760*
THREE VILLAGE LOCAL HISTORY COLLECTION, *NY824-200*
TICONDEROGA HISTORICAL SOCIETY, *NY881-750*
TILLAMOOK COUNTY PIONEER MUSEUM, *OR880-760*
TILTON SCHOOL, *NH904-760*
TIME, ARCHIVES, *NY594-640*
TIMOTHY PICKERING LIBRARY, *MA897-880*
TIOGA COUNTY HISTORICAL SOCIETY, MUSEUM, *NY665-760*
TIOGA COUNTY HISTORICAL SOCIETY, ROBINSON HOUSE MUSEUM, *PA943-760*
TIOGA POINT MUSEUM, *PA55-760*
TIPPECANOE COUNTY HISTORICAL ASSOCIATION, *IN440-760*
TOBACCO MERCHANTS ASSOCIATION OF THE UNITED STATES, HOWARD S. CULLMAN LIBRARY, *NY594-680*
TODD WEHR LIBRARY, *WI456-500*
TOFIAS, ARNOLD B., INDUSTRIAL ARCHIVES, *MA615-710*
TOLEDO MUSEUM OF ART, GEORGE W. STEVENS COLLECTION, *OH823-770*
TOLEDO-LUCAS COUNTY PUBLIC LIBRARY, LOCAL HISTORY DEPARTMENT, *OH823-750*
TOMBSTONE COURTHOUSE STATE HISTORICAL PARK, *AZ760-760*
TOMPKINS CORTLAND COMMUNITY COLLEGE, DIVISION OF INSTRUCTIONAL AND LEARNING RESOURCES, *NY246-760*
TOMPKINS COUNTY PUBLIC LIBRARY, *NY439-760*
TOMPKINS-McCAW LIBRARY, ARCHIVES DEPARTMENT, *VA690-840*
TONASKET BRANCH LIBRARY, *WA919-560*
TOPSFIELD HISTORICAL SOCIETY, *MA849-750*
TORREYSON LIBRARY, *AR240-810*
TORRINGTON HISTORICAL SOCIETY, *CT821-760*
TOUGALOO COLLEGE, COLEMAN LIBRARY, LILLIAN PIERCE BENBOW ROOM OF SPECIAL COLLECTIONS, *MS870-760*

TOWN OF BETHLEHEM HISTORICAL ASSOCIATION, *NY818-760*
TOWN OF ERWIN MUSEUM, *NY670-760*
TOWN OF GROTON HISTORICAL ASSOCIATION, *NY358-760*
TOWN OF HUNTINGTON, OFFICE OF THE HISTORIAN, *NY419-350*
TOWN OF IRONDEQUOIT HISTORIAN, *NY752-820*
TOWN OF MIDDLEFIELD HISTORICAL ASSOCIATION, *NY540-760*
TOWN OF WARREN HISTORICAL ASSOCIATION, *NY450-760*
TOWSON STATE UNIVERSITY, ARCHIVES, *MD950-760*
TOZZER LIBRARY, *MA169-530*
TRANS UNION CORPORATION, *IL170-832*
TRANSYLVANIA UNIVERISTY, FRANCES CARRICK THOMAS
    LIBRARY, SPECIAL COLLECTIONS DEPARTMENT, *KY464-760*
TRAVELERS INSURANCE COMPANIES, CORPORATE LIBRARY,
    CT316-750
TRENT COLLECTION, *NC260-160*
TRENTON HISTORICAL MUSEUM, *MI930-760*
TRENTON PSYCHIATRIC HOSPITAL, *NJ838-730*
TRENTON STATE COLLEGE, DEPARTMENT OF GEOGRAPHY,
    NJ838-740
TRENTON STATE COLLEGE, LIBRARY, SPECIAL COLLECTIONS,
    NJ838-750
TREVECCA NAZARENE COLLEGE, LIBRARY, TREVECCA
    ARCHIVES, *TN690-850*
TREXLER, SCOTT ANDREW, II, LIBRARY, *PA25-480*
TRI-CITIES HISTORICAL SOCIETY, MUSEUM, *MI350-760*
TRI-LAKES REGIONAL LIBRAY, *AR390-760*
TRIMBLE COUNTY LIBRARY, *KY42-800*
TRINITY CHURCH PARISH, OFFICE OF PARISH ARCHIVES,
    NY593-290
TRINITY COLLEGE, ARCHIVES, *DC20-600*
TRINITY COLLEGE, LIBRARY, ARCHIVES, *CT316-763*
TRINITY COLLEGE, WATKINSON LIBRARY, *CT316-770*
TRINITY UNIVERSITY, LIBRARY, SPECIAL COLLECTIONS,
    TX777-760
TRINKLE, E. LEE, LIBRARY, RARE BOOKS ROOM AND MARY
    WASHINGTON COLLEGE ARCHIVES, *VA285-520*
TROTTER, HALL OF FAME OF THE, *NY340-320*
TROUTDALE HISTORICAL SOCIETY, *OR901-760*
TROWBRIDGE, HARRY M., RESEARCH LIBRARY, *KS136-880*
TROY CONFERENCE HISTORICAL SOCIETY, *NY881-770*
TROY MUSEUM, *MI935-770*
TROY STATE UNIVERSITY, LIBRARY, *AL780-760*
TRUMAN, HARRY S., LIBRARY, *MO400-320*
TRUTH, SOJOURNER, LIBRARY, *NY574-730*
TUBAC PRESIDIO STATE HISTORIC PARK, *AZ775-790*
TUCK MEMORIAL MUSEUM, *NH368-320*
TUCUMCARI HISTORICAL RESEARCH INSTITUTE, MUSEUM,
    NM950-270
TUFTS LIBRARY, *MA947-880*
TUFTS UNIVERSITY, FLETCHER SCHOOL OF LAW AND
    DIPLOMACY, MURROW CENTER FOR PUBLIC DIPLOMACY,
    MA528-740
TUFTS UNIVERSITY, LIBRARY, ARCHIVES AND SPECIAL
    COLLECTIONS, *MA528-780*
TUGWELL, REXFORD G., ROOM, *MD513-640*
TUKWILA HISTORICAL SOCIETY, *WA927-780*
TULALIP TRIBAL RESERVATION, *WA528-780*
TULANE UNIVERSITY, HOWARD-TILTON MEMORIAL LIBRARY,
    SPECIAL COLL. DIV., MSS. COLL., *LA600-755*
TULANE UNIVERSITY, HOWARD-TILTON MEMORIAL LIBRARY,
    SPECIAL COLLECTIONS, SOUTHEAST ARCHIT. ARCHIVE,
    LA600-761
TULANE UNIVERSITY, HOWARD-TILTON MEMORIAL LIBRARY,
    SPECIAL COLLECTIONS, W. R. HOGAN JAZZ ARCHIVE,
    LA600-764
TULANE UNIVERSITY, LATIN AMERICAN LIBRARY, *LA600-760*
TULANE UNIVERSITY, MIDDLE AMERICAN RESEARCH
    INSTITUTE LIBRARY, *LA600-760*
TULANE UNIVERSITY, RUDOLPH MATAS MEDICAL LIBRARY,
    LA600-765
TULARE COUNTY FREE LIBRARY, HISTORICAL RESEARCH
    COLLECTION, *CA942-940*
TULSA COUNTY HISTORICAL SOCIETY, *OK829-770*
TUOLUMNE COUNTY HISTORICAL SOCIETY, *CA842-760*
TUSCULUM COLLEGE, ARCHIVES, *TN300-760*
TUSKEGEE INSTITUTE, HOLLIS BURKE FRISELL LIBRARY,
    AL820-765
TWAIN, MARK, BIRTHPLACE STATE HISTORIC SITE, *MO870-520*
TWAIN, MARK, MEMORIAL, *CT316-520*
TWAIN, MARK, MUSEUM, *MO370-520*
TWAIN, MARK, PROJECT, *CA486-790*
TWENTIETH CENTURY CLUB LIBRARY, *NY20-760*
TWIN WILLOWS MUSEUM, *WA935-770*
TYLER, JOHN J., ARBORETUM, PAINTER LIBRARY, *PA512-400*
TYRRELL HISTORICAL LIBRARY, *TX70-770*
TYRRELL, CECIL B., LIBRARY, *NY101-80*

U

U.S. . . . *See also* United States. . .
U.S. AIR FORCE MUSEUM, RESEARCH DIVISION, *OH978-120*
U.S. ARMY ENGINEER MUSEUM, *VA245-800*
U.S. ARMY MILITARY HISTORY INSTITUTE, *PA165-790*
U.S. ARMY MUSEUM, PRESIDIO OF MONTEREY, *CA480-800*
U.S. INFORMATION AGENCY, ASSOCIATE DIRECTORATE FOR
    PROGRAMS, AGENCY LIB., AGENCY ARCHIVES, *DC9-580*
UCLA FILM ARCHIVES, *CA421-763*
UCLA RADIO ARCHIVES, *CA421-766*
UKRAINIAN MUSEUM, ARCHIVES, *OH181-780*
UKRAINIAN-AMERICAN ARCHIVES AND MUSEUM, *MI230-780*
ULYSSES PHILOMATHIC LIBRARY, *NY891-800*
UMATILLA COUNTY LIBRARY, *OR688-810*
UMATILLA NATIONAL FOREST, *OR688-820*
UNADILLA PUBLIC LIBRARY, *NY894-800*
UNDERWOOD LAW LIBRARY, *TX252-780*
UNION COLLEGE, ABIGAIL E. WEEKS MEMORIAL LIBRARY,
    KY24-800
UNION COLLEGE, SCHAFFER LIBRARY, SPECIAL COLLECTIONS,
    NY804-800
UNION COUNTY (OH) HISTORICAL SOCIETY, *OH500-800*
UNION COUNTY (OR) MUSEUM, *OR907-800*
UNION COUNTY CULTURAL AND HERITAGE PROGRAMS
    ADVISORY BOARD, *NJ926-840*
UNION LEAGUE OF PHILADELPHIA, *PA726-705*
UNION MUTUAL LIFE INSURANCE COMPANY, *ME712-790*
UNION PACIFIC HISTORICAL MUSEUM, *NE624-800*
UNION PRESBYTERIAN CHURCH OF ENDICOTT, JOHN MARK
    CHAPEL MUSEUM, *NY273-800*
UNION SAINT-JEAN-BAPTISTE, BIBLIOTHEQUE MALLET, *RI945-800*
UNION THEOLOGICAL SEMINARY IN VIRGINIA, LIBRARY,
    VA690-750
UNION THEOLOGICAL SEMINARY, LIBRARY, *NY594-860*
UNION TOWNSHIP HISTORICAL SOCIETY, CALDWELL
    PARSONAGE MUSEUM, *NJ844-800*
UNION UNIVERSITY, ALBANY MEDICAL COLLEGE, SCHAFFER
    LIBRARY OF HEALTH SCIENCES, *NY10-800*
UNIONTOWN PUBLIC LIBRARY, *PA890-800*
UNITARIAN AND UNIVERSALIST GENEALOGICAL SOCIETY,
    MD266-800
UNITARIAN UNIVERSALIST ASSOCIATION, *MA109-750*
UNITED BANK OF DENVER, ARCHIVES CENTER, *CO252-780*
UNITED BOARD FOR CHRISTIAN HIGHER EDUCATION IN ASIA,
    NY594-880
UNITED BRETHREN IN CHRIST, ARCHIVES, *IN352-800*
UNITED CHURCH OF CHRIST, CONNECTICUT CONFERENCE,
    CT316-105
UNITED CHURCH OF CHRIST, HISTORICAL COUNCIL,
    LANCASTER ARCHIVES, *PA470-800*
UNITED CHURCH OF CHRIST, NEBRASKA CONFERENCE,
    HISTORY AND ARCHIVES ROOM, *NE560-790*
UNITED DAUGHTERS OF THE CONFEDERACY, CAROLINE
    MERIWETHER GOODLETT LIBRARY, *VA690-760*
UNITED METHODIST CHURCH, BOARD OF HIGHER EDUCATION
    AND MINISTRY, *TN690-880*
UNITED METHODIST CHURCH, CENTRAL ILLINOIS
    CONFERENCE, CONFERENCE HISTORICAL SOCIETY, *IL94-800*
UNITED METHODIST CHURCH, DETROIT CONFERENCE,
    ARCHIVES AND HISTORY, *MI8-800*
UNITED METHODIST CHURCH, GENERAL BOARD OF
    DISCIPLESHIP, UPPER ROOM DEVOTIONAL LIBRARY,
    TN690-885
UNITED METHODIST CHURCH, GENERAL COMMISSION ON
    ARCHIVES AND HISTORY, *NJ464-666*
UNITED METHODIST CHURCH, KANSAS WEST CONFERENCE,
    COMMISSION ON ARCHIVES AND HISTORY, *KS962-800*
UNITED METHODIST CHURCH, KENTUCKY CONFERENCE,
    COMMISSION ON ARCHIVES AND HISTORY, *KY464-780*
UNITED METHODIST CHURCH, MINNESOTA ANNUAL
    CONFERENCE, COMMISSION ON ARCHIVES AND HISTORY,
    MN541-777
UNITED METHODIST CHURCH, NEBRASKA CONFERENCE,
    HISTORICAL CENTER, *NE560-810*
UNITED METHODIST CHURCH, NEW HAMPSHIRE CONFERENCE,
    HISTORICAL SOCIETY, *MA540-800*
UNITED METHODIST CHURCH, NEW MEXICO ANNUAL
    CONFERENCE ARCHIVES, HISTORICAL LIBRARY, *NM200-800*
UNITED METHODIST CHURCH, NORTH DAKOTA CONFERENCE,
    ND486-770
UNITED METHODIST CHURCH, NORTHWEST TEXAS ANNUAL
    CONFERENCE, ARCHIVES DEPOSITORY, *TX7-800*
UNITED METHODIST CHURCH, OKLAHOMA ANNUAL
    CONFERENCE, COMMISSION ON ARCHIVES AND HISTORY,
    ARCHIVES, *OK592-780*

UNITED METHODIST CHURCH, SOUTH DAKOTA CONFERENCE, COMMISSION ON ARCHIVES AND HISTORY, *SD522-800*

UNITED METHODIST CHURCH, SOUTHERN NEW JERSEY CONFERENCE, HISTORICAL SOCIETY, *NJ658-840*

UNITED METHODIST CHURCH, TENNESSEE CONFERENCE, COMMISSION ON ARCHIVES AND HISTORY, *TN765-800*

UNITED METHODIST CHURCH, WEST MICHIGAN CONFERENCE, COMMISSION ON ARCHIVES AND HISTORY, *MI12-10*

UNITED METHODIST CHURCH, WESTERN NEW YORK UNITED METHODIST CONFERENCE, ARCHIVES CENTER, *NY970-840*

UNITED METHODIST CHURCH, WISCONSIN CONFERENCE, ARCHIVES, *WI733-333*

UNITED METHODIST HISTORICAL SOCIETY, LOVELY LANE MUSEUM, *MD76-790*

UNITED METHODIST PUBLISHING HOUSE, LIBRARY, *TN690-890*

UNITED NATIONS, ARCHIVES, *NY595-20*

UNITED NATIONS, DAG HAMMARSKJOLD LIBRARY, MAP COLLECTION, *NY595-40*

UNITED NEGRO COLLEGE FUND, ARCHIVES, *NY595-130*

UNITED STATES . . . *See also* U.S. . . .

UNITED STATES AIR FORCE ACADEMY, LIBRARY, SPECIAL COLLECTIONS BRANCH, *CO180-750*

UNITED STATES ARMY AVIATION MUSEUM, *AL380-800*

UNITED STATES ARMY COMMUNICATIONS-ELECTRONICS MUSEUM, *NJ270-800*

UNITED STATES ARMY MILITARY HISTORY INSTITUTE, *PA165-790*

UNITED STATES ARMY MUSEUM, HAWAII, *HI350-770*

UNITED STATES COAST GUARD ACADEMY, LIBRARY, *CT512-800*

UNITED STATES COMMITTEE FOR UNICEF, INFORMATION CENTER ON CHILDREN'S CULTURES, *NY595-180*

UNITED STATES MILITARY ACADEMY, ARCHIVES, *NY949-780*

UNITED STATES MILITARY ACADEMY, LIBRARY, SPECIAL COLLECTIONS DIVISION, *NY949-830*

UNITED STATES NAVAL ACADEMY, MUSEUM, *MD57-800*

UNITED STATES NAVAL ACADEMY, NIMITZ LIBRARY, SPECIAL COLLECTIONS DIVISION, *MD57-810*

UNITED STATES NAVAL HISTORY DIVISION, OPERATIONAL ARCHIVES, *DC14-730*

UNITED STATES NAVAL INSTITUTE, ORAL HISTORY OFFICE, *MD57-820*

UNITED STATES NAVAL INSTITUTE, PHOTOGRAPHIC LIBRARY, *MD57-830*

UNITED STATES TOBACCO MUSEUM, *CT275-800*

UNITED TECHNOLOGIES CORPORATION, ARCHIVES, *CT186-800*

UNITED THEOLOGICAL SEMINARY, LIBRARY, *OH223-790*

UNITY SCHOOL OF CHRISTIANITY, LIBRARY, *MO894-800*

UNIVERSALIST HISTORICAL SOCIETY, LIBRARY, *MA528-800*

UNIVERSITY HOSPITALS OF CLEVELAND, HOSPITAL ARCHIVES, *OH181-790*

UNIVERSITY OF AKRON, ARCHIVES OF THE HISTORY OF AMERICAN PSYCHOLOGY, *OH11-800*

UNIVERSITY OF AKRON, BIERCE LIBRARY, ARCHIVAL SERVICES, *OH11-810*

UNIVERSITY OF AKRON, CHILD DEVELOPMENT FILM ARCHIVES, *OH11-840*

UNIVERSITY OF ALABAMA AT BIRMINGHAM, HILL LIBRARY OF HEALTH SCIENCES, ALA. HEALTH SCIENCES COLL., *AL120-810*

UNIVERSITY OF ALABAMA AT BIRMINGHAM, HILL LIBRARY OF HEALTH SCIENCES, REYNOLDS HISTORICAL LIBRARY, *AL120-815*

UNIVERSITY OF ALABAMA AT HUNTSVILLE, LIBRARY, ARCHIVES AND SPECIAL COLLECTIONS, *AL440-800*

UNIVERSITY OF ALABAMA, LIBRARY, SPECIAL COLLECTIONS, *AL840-820*

UNIVERSITY OF ALASKA, *AK350-815*

UNIVERSITY OF ALASKA, ANCHORAGE, LIBRARY SYSTEM, ARCHIVES AND MANUSCRIPTS DEPARTMENT, *AK50-800*

UNIVERSITY OF ALASKA, E. E. RASMUSON LIBRARY, ARCHIVES AND MANUSCRIPT COLLECTIONS, *AK350-800*

UNIVERSITY OF ALBUQUERQUE, CENTER FOR LEARNING AND INFORMATION RESOURCES, *NM114-800*

UNIVERSITY OF ARIZONA, ARIZONA STATE MUSEUM, DOCUMENTARY RELATIONS OF THE SOUTHWEST, *AZ800-790*

UNIVERSITY OF ARIZONA, ARIZONA STATE MUSEUM, LIBRARY, *AZ800-800*

UNIVERSITY OF ARIZONA, ARIZONA STATE MUSEUM, PHOTOGRAPHIC COLLECTIONS, *AZ800-803*

UNIVERSITY OF ARIZONA, LIBRARY, CENTER FOR CREATIVE PHOTOGRAPHY, *AZ800-820*

UNIVERSITY OF ARIZONA, LIBRARY, SPECIAL COLLECTIONS, *AZ800-830*

UNIVERSITY OF ARKANSAS AT LITTLE ROCK, LIBRARY, ARCHIVES AND SPECIAL COLLECTIONS, *AR510-810*

UNIVERSITY OF ARKANSAS FOR MEDICAL SCIENCES, LIBRARY, HISTORY OF MEDICINE/ARCHIVES DIVISION, *AR510-825*

UNIVERSITY OF ARKANSAS, LIBRARIES, SPECIAL COLLECTIONS, *AR330-830*

UNIVERSITY OF BALTIMORE, BALTIMORE REGION INSTITUTIONAL STUDIES CENTER, *MD76-800*

UNIVERSITY OF BALTIMORE, LIBRARY, STEAMSHIP HISTORICAL SOCIETY COLLECTION, *MD76-810*

UNIVERSITY OF CALIFORNIA, BERKELEY, BANCROFT LIBRARY, MANUSCRIPTS, *CA86-780*

UNIVERSITY OF CALIFORNIA, BERKELEY, BANCROFT LIBRARY, MARK TWAIN PROJECT, *CA86-790*

UNIVERSITY OF CALIFORNIA, BERKELEY, BANCROFT LIBRARY, REGIONAL ORAL HISTORY OFFICE, *CA86-810*

UNIVERSITY OF CALIFORNIA, BERKELEY, BANCROFT LIBRARY, UNIVERSITY ARCHIVES, *CA86-815*

UNIVERSITY OF CALIFORNIA, BERKELEY, DEPARTMENT OF ARCHITECTURE, DOCUMENTS COLLECTION, *CA86-820*

UNIVERSITY OF CALIFORNIA, BERKELEY, FORESTRY LIBRARY, METCALF-FRITZ PHOTOGRAPH COLLECTION, *CA86-850*

UNIVERSITY OF CALIFORNIA, BERKELEY, LAWRENCE BERKELEY LABORATORY, ARCHIVES AND RECORDS, *CA86-882*

UNIVERSITY OF CALIFORNIA, BERKELEY, MUSIC LIBRARY, *CA86-890*

UNIVERSITY OF CALIFORNIA, BERKELEY, OFF. FOR HIST. & TECH., ARCH. FOR HIST. OF QUANT. PHYS., *CA86-895*

UNIVERSITY OF CALIFORNIA, BERKELEY, UNIVERSITY HERBARIUM, *CA86-910*

UNIVERSITY OF CALIFORNIA, BERKELEY, WATER RESOURCES CENTER, ARCHIVES, *CA86-920*

UNIVERSITY OF CALIFORNIA, DAVIS, LIBRARY, DEPARTMENT OF SPECIAL COLLECTIONS, *CA206-790*

UNIVERSITY OF CALIFORNIA, LOS ANGELES, BIOMEDICAL LIBRARY, HISTORY & SPECIAL COLLECTIONS DIV., *CA421-660*

UNIVERSITY OF CALIFORNIA, LOS ANGELES, BUREAU OF GOVERNMENTAL RESEARCH, LIBRARY, *CA421-665*

UNIVERSITY OF CALIFORNIA, LOS ANGELES, LAW LIBRARY, *CA421-710*

UNIVERSITY OF CALIFORNIA, LOS ANGELES, MUSIC LIBRARY, *CA421-750*

UNIVERSITY OF CALIFORNIA, LOS ANGELES, THEATER ARTS DEPARTMENT, NATAS-UCLA TELEVISION LIBRARY, *CA421-760*

UNIVERSITY OF CALIFORNIA, LOS ANGELES, THEATER ARTS DEPARTMENT, UCLA FILM ARCHIVES, *CA421-763*

UNIVERSITY OF CALIFORNIA, LOS ANGELES, THEATER ARTS DEPARTMENT, UCLA RADIO ARCHIVES, *CA421-766*

UNIVERSITY OF CALIFORNIA, LOS ANGELES, UNIVERSITY RESEARCH LIBRARY, SPECIAL COLLECTIONS, *CA421-770*

UNIVERSITY OF CALIFORNIA, LOS ANGELES, WILLIAM ANDREWS CLARK MEMORIAL LIBRARY, *CA421-774*

UNIVERSITY OF CALIFORNIA, MEDICAL CENTER, LIBRARY, *CA720-890, CA720-894*

UNIVERSITY OF CALIFORNIA, RIVERSIDE, CALIFORNIA MUSEUM OF PHOTOGRAPHY, *CA652-795*

UNIVERSITY OF CALIFORNIA, RIVERSIDE, LIBRARY, *CA652-800*

UNIVERSITY OF CALIFORNIA, SAN DIEGO, LIBRARY, *CA368-800*

UNIVERSITY OF CALIFORNIA, SAN DIEGO, SCRIPPS INSTITUTION OF OCEANOGRAPHY, HIST. ARCHIVES SECTION, *CA368-820*

UNIVERSITY OF CALIFORNIA, SAN FRANCISCO, LIBRARY, ORIENTAL MEDICINE DIVISION, *CA720-886*

UNIVERSITY OF CALIFORNIA, SAN FRANCISCO, LIBRARY, SPECIAL COLLECTIONS: ARCHIVES, *CA720-890*

UNIVERSITY OF CALIFORNIA, SAN FRANCISCO, LIBRARY, SPECIAL COLLECTIONS: HISTORY, *CA720-894*

UNIVERSITY OF CALIFORNIA, SANTA BARBARA, LIBRARY, DEPARTMENT OF SPECIAL COLLECTIONS, *CA774-800*

UNIVERSITY OF CALIFORNIA, SANTA CRUZ, LIBRARY, *CA782-800*

UNIVERSITY OF CENTRAL ARKANSAS, TORREYSON LIBRARY, *AR240-810*

UNIVERSITY OF CHICAGO, LIBRARY, DEPARTMENT OF SPECIAL COLLECTIONS, *IL170-884*

UNIVERSITY OF CHICAGO, NATIONAL OPINION RESEARCH CENTER, LIBRARY AND DATA ARCHIVES, *IL170-891*

UNIVERSITY OF CHICAGO, ORIENTAL INSTITUTE MUSEUM, ARCHAEOLOGICAL ARCHIVES, *IL170-897*

UNIVERSITY OF CHICAGO, YERKES OBSERVATORY, *WI874-940*

UNIVERSITY OF CINCINNATI, LIBRARIES, ARCHIVES AND RARE BOOKS DEPARTMENT, *OH171-800*

UNIVERSITY OF COLORADO, INSTITUTE OF BEHAVIORAL SCIENCE, *CO108-740*

UNIVERSITY OF COLORADO, LIBRARIES, WESTERN HISTORICAL COLLECTIONS, *CO108-810*

UNIVERSITY OF CONNECTICUT, CENTER FOR ORAL HISTORY, *CT779-800*

UNIVERSITY OF CONNECTICUT, LIBRARIES, HISTORICAL MANUSCRIPTS AND ARCHIVES, *CT779-785*

UNIVERSITY OF CONNECTICUT, LIBRARIES, MUSIC LIBRARY, *CT779-790*

UNIVERSITY OF CONNECTICUT, ROPER PUBLIC OPINION RESEARCH CENTER, *CT779-812*

UNIVERSITY OF DAYTON, LIBRARY, UNIVERSITY ARCHIVES, *OH223-800*

UNIVERSITY OF DAYTON, LIBRARY, WRIGHT BROTHERS-CHARLES F. KETTERING ORAL HISTORY PROJECT, *OH223-810*

UNIVERSITY OF DELAWARE, ARCHIVES, *DE540-780*

UNIVERSITY OF DELAWARE, LIBRARIES, DEPARTMENT OF SPECIAL COLLECTIONS, *DE540-790*

UNIVERSITY OF DENVER, PENROSE LIBRARY, *CO252-820*

UNIVERSITY OF DETROIT, MAIN LIBRARY, RARE BOOK ROOM AND ARCHIVES, *MI230-800*

UNIVERSITY OF EVANSVILLE, CLIFFORD MEMORIAL LIBRARY, ARCHIVES, *IN209-800*

UNIVERSITY OF FLORIDA, FLORIDA STATE MUSEUM, *FL220-792*

UNIVERSITY OF FLORIDA, LIBRARIES, P. K. YONGE LIBRARY OF FLORIDA HISTORY, *FL220-795*

UNIVERSITY OF FLORIDA, LIBRARIES, RARE BOOKS AND MANUSCRIPTS DEPARTMENT, *FL220-800*

UNIVERSITY OF FLORIDA, LIBRARIES, UNIVERSITY ARCHIVES, *FL220-805*

UNIVERSITY OF GEORGIA, LIBRARIES, RICHARD B. RUSSELL MEMORIAL LIBRARY, *GA75-790*

UNIVERSITY OF GEORGIA, LIBRARIES, SCIENCE LIBRARY, MAP COLLECTION, *GA75-800*

UNIVERSITY OF GEORGIA, LIBRARIES, SPECIAL COLLECTIONS, MANUSCRIPT DEPARTMENT, *GA75-810*

UNIVERSITY OF HARTFORD, HARTT COLLEGE OF MUSIC, LIBRARY, *CT891-820*

UNIVERSITY OF HAWAII AT MANOA, DEPARTMENT OF HISTORY, PACIFIC REGIONAL ORAL HISTORY PROGRAM, *HI350-790*

UNIVERSITY OF HAWAII AT MANOA, LIBRARY, ARCHIVES AND MANUSCRIPTS, *HI350-808*

UNIVERSITY OF IDAHO, ARCHIVE OF PACIFIC NORTHWEST ARCHAEOLOGY, *ID480-770*

UNIVERSITY OF IDAHO, LIBRARY, SPECIAL COLLECTIONS AND ARCHIVES, *ID480-810*

UNIVERSITY OF ILLINOIS AT CHICAGO CIRCLE, LIBRARY, MANUSCRIPT DEPARTMENT, *IL170-910*

UNIVERSITY OF ILLINOIS AT THE MEDICAL CENTER, LIBRARY OF THE HEALTH SCIENCES, ARCH. & SPEC. COLL., *IL170-936*

UNIVERSITY OF ILLINOIS, ILLINOIS HISTORICAL SURVEY, LIBRARY, *IL916-795*

UNIVERSITY OF ILLINOIS, UNIVERSITY ARCHIVES, *IL916-810*

UNIVERSITY OF ILLINOIS, UNIVERSITY LIBRARIES, MUSIC LIBRARY, *IL916-820*

UNIVERSITY OF IOWA, LIBRARIES, SPECIAL COLLECTIONS DEPARTMENT, *IA466-800*

UNIVERSITY OF KANSAS, LIBRARIES, KENNETH SPENCER RESEARCH LIBRARY, DEPARTMENT OF SPECIAL COLLECTION*KS527-790*

UNIVERSITY OF KANSAS, LIBRARIES, KENNETH SPENCER RESEARCH LIBRARY, KANSAS COLLECTION, *KS527-795*

UNIVERSITY OF KANSAS, LIBRARIES, KENNETH SPENCER RESEARCH LIBRARY, UNIVERSITY ARCHIVES, *KS527-805*

UNIVERSITY OF KANSAS, MEDICAL CENTER, COLLEGE OF HEALTH SCIENCES AND HOSPITAL, CLENDENING LIBRARY, *KS475-800*

UNIVERSITY OF KENTUCKY, KING LIBRARY, DEPARTMENT OF SPECIAL COLLECTIONS, *KY464-800*

UNIVERSITY OF LOUISVILLE, ARCHIVES AND RECORDS CENTER, *KY496-785*

UNIVERSITY OF LOUISVILLE, KORNHAUSER HEALTH SCIENCES LIBRARY, *KY496-795*

UNIVERSITY OF LOUISVILLE, LAW LIBRARY, *KY496-800*

UNIVERSITY OF LOUISVILLE, MEDICAL SCHOOL LIBRARY, *KY496-795*

UNIVERSITY OF LOUISVILLE, MUSIC LIBRARY, *KY496-808*

UNIVERSITY OF LOUISVILLE, ORAL HISTORY CENTER, *KY496-812*

UNIVERSITY OF LOUISVILLE, UNIVERSITY LIBRARY, PHOTOGRAPHIC ARCHIVES, *KY496-823*

UNIVERSITY OF LOUISVILLE, UNIVERSITY LIBRARY, RARE BOOKS AND SPECIAL COLLECTIONS, *KY496-825*

UNIVERSITY OF LOWELL, LIBRARIES, SPECIAL COLLECTIONS, *MA478-800*

UNIVERSITY OF MAINE AT FARMINGTON, MANTOR LIBRARY, *ME350-800*

UNIVERSITY OF MAINE AT ORONO, DEPARTMENT OF ANTHROPOLOGY, ARCHIVES OF FOLKLORE AND ORAL HISTORY, *ME650-780*

UNIVERSITY OF MAINE AT ORONO, RAYMOND H. FOGLER LIBRARY, SPECIAL COLLECTIONS DEPARTMENT, *ME650-810*

UNIVERSITY OF MARYLAND, MCKELDIN LIBRARY, ARCHIVES AND MANUSCRIPTS DEPARTMENT, *MD285-805*

UNIVERSITY OF MASSACHUSETTS AT AMHERST, ARCHIVES AND MANUSCRIPTS DEPARTMENT, *MA21-770*

UNIVERSITY OF MASSACHUSETTS AT AMHERST, LABOR RELATIONS AND RESEARCH CENTER, *MA21-800*

UNIVERSITY OF MASSACHUSETTS AT BOSTON, LIBRARY, MANUSCRIPTS AND ARCHIVAL COLLECTIONS DEPARTMENT, *MA109-830*

UNIVERSITY OF MIAMI, RICHTER LIBRARY, ARCHIVES DIVISION, *FL80-820*

UNIVERSITY OF MICHIGAN AT FLINT, LIBRARY, *MI314-840*

UNIVERSITY OF MICHIGAN, BENTLEY HISTORICAL LIBRARY, MICHIGAN HISTORICAL COLLECTIONS, *MI40-784*

UNIVERSITY OF MICHIGAN, ENGINEERING-TRANSPORTATION LIBRARY, *MI40-796*

UNIVERSITY OF MICHIGAN, HISTORY OF ART DEPARTMENT, ASIAN ART ARCHIVES, *MI40-800*

UNIVERSITY OF MICHIGAN, LIBRARY, DEPARTMENT OF RARE BOOKS AND SPECIAL COLLECTIONS, *MI40-808*

UNIVERSITY OF MICHIGAN, MUSEUM OF ANTHROPOLOGY, *MI40-814*

UNIVERSITY OF MICHIGAN, WILLIAM L. CLEMENTS LIBRARY, *MI40-820*

UNIVERSITY OF MINNESOTA AT DULUTH, LIBRARY, UNIVERSITY ARCHIVES, *MN261-830*

UNIVERSITY OF MINNESOTA AT DULUTH, NORTHEAST MINNESOTA HISTORICAL CENTER, *MN261-810*

UNIVERSITY OF MINNESOTA AT MORRIS, MORRIS CAMPUS ARCHIVES, *MN583-890*

UNIVERSITY OF MINNESOTA AT MORRIS, WEST CENTRAL MINNESOTA HISTORICAL CENTER, *MN583-920*

UNIVERSITY OF MINNESOTA, IMMIGRATION HISTORY RESEARCH CENTER, *MN763-790*

UNIVERSITY OF MINNESOTA, LIBRARIES, AMES LIBRARY OF SOUTH ASIA, *MN541-822*

UNIVERSITY OF MINNESOTA, LIBRARIES, CHILDREN'S LITERATURE RESEARCH COLLECTIONS, *MN541-838*

UNIVERSITY OF MINNESOTA, LIBRARIES, JAMES FORD BELL LIBRARY, *MN541-854*

UNIVERSITY OF MINNESOTA, LIBRARIES, MANUSCRIPTS DIVISION, *MN763-800*

UNIVERSITY OF MINNESOTA, LIBRARIES, MAP DIVISION, *MN541-934*

UNIVERSITY OF MINNESOTA, LIBRARIES, SOCIAL WELFARE HISTORY ARCHIVES, *MN541-902*

UNIVERSITY OF MINNESOTA, LIBRARIES, SPECIAL COLLECTIONS DEPARTMENT, *MN541-918*

UNIVERSITY OF MINNESOTA, LIBRARIES, UNIVERSITY ARCHIVES, *MN541-925*

UNIVERSITY OF MISSISSIPPI, JOHN DAVIS WILLIAMS LIBRARY, DEPARTMENT OF ARCHIVES AND SPECIAL COLLEC.*MS900-870*

UNIVERSITY OF MISSOURI AT COLUMBIA, CENTRAL ADMINISTRATION, UNIVERSITY ARCHIVES, *MO210-780*

UNIVERSITY OF MISSOURI AT COLUMBIA, JOINT COLLECTION, WEST. HIST. MSS. & HIST. SOC. OF MO MSS., *MO210-815*

UNIVERSITY OF MISSOURI AT COLUMBIA, MUSEUM OF ANTHROPOLOGY, ARCHIVES, *MO210-840*

UNIVERSITY OF MISSOURI AT KANSAS CITY, ARCHIVES, *MO430-775*

UNIVERSITY OF MISSOURI AT KANSAS CITY, CONSERVATORY LIBRARY, *MO430-790*

UNIVERSITY OF MISSOURI AT KANSAS CITY, JOINT COLLECTION, WEST. HIST. MSS. & HIST. SOC. OF MO MSS., *MO430-800*

UNIVERSITY OF MISSOURI AT ROLLA, ARCHIVES, *MO760-760*

UNIVERSITY OF MISSOURI AT ROLLA, DEPARTMENT OF GEOLOGY AND GEOPHYSICS, *MO760-780*

UNIVERSITY OF MISSOURI AT ROLLA, JOINT COLLECTION, WEST. HIST. MSS. & HIST. SOC. OF MISSOURI MSS., *MO760-800*

UNIVERSITY OF MISSOURI AT ST. LOUIS, ARCHIVES, *MO810-780*

UNIVERSITY OF MISSOURI AT ST. LOUIS, JOINT COLLECTION, WEST. HIST. MSS. & HIST. SOC. OF MO. MSS., *MO810-800*

UNIVERSITY OF MISSOURI WESTERN HIST. MSS. COLLECTION AND STATE HIST. SOCIETY OF MISSOURI MSS., *MO210-815, MO430-800, MO760-800, MO810-800*

UNIVERSITY OF MONTANA, LIBRARY, *MT700-800*

UNIVERSITY OF MONTEVALLO, CARMICHAEL LIBRARY, ARCHIVES, *AL600-800*

UNIVERSITY OF NEBRASKA AT LINCOLN, LIBRARY, SPECIAL COLLECTIONS DIVISION, *NE560-860*

UNIVERSITY OF NEBRASKA AT LINCOLN, LIBRARY, UNIVERSITY ARCHIVES, *NE560-870*

UNIVERSITY OF NEBRASKA, MEDICAL CENTER, LIBRARY OF MEDICINE, *NE624-830*

UNIVERSITY OF NEVADA AT LAS VEGAS, JAMES DICKINSON LIBRARY, SPECIAL COLLECTIONS DEPARTMENT, *NV630-800*

UNIVERSITY OF NEVADA AT RENO, LIBRARY, BASQUE STUDIES PROGRAM, *NV940-800*

UNIVERSITY OF NEVADA AT RENO, LIBRARY, SPECIAL COLLECTIONS DEPARTMENT, *NV940-810*

UNIVERSITY OF NEW HAMPSHIRE, DIMOND LIBRARY, SPECIAL COLLECTIONS, *NH206-800*

UNIVERSITY OF NEW HAMPSHIRE, KEENE STATE COLLEGE, MASON LIBRARY, PRESTON COLLECTION, *NH468-800*

UNIVERSITY OF NEW MEXICO, DEPT. OF BIOLOGY, MUSEUM OF S.W. BIOLOGY, HERBARIUM & MUS. OF BOTANY, *NM114-825*

UNIVERSITY OF NEW MEXICO, JONSONGALLERY, *NM114-870*

UNIVERSITY OF NEW MEXICO, MAXWELL MUSEUM OF ANTHROPOLOGY, *NM114-880*

UNIVERSITY OF NEW MEXICO, ZIMMERMAN LIBRARY, SPECIAL COLLECTIONS DEPARTMENT, *NM114-900*

UNIVERSITY OF NEW ORLEANS, EARL K. LONG LIBRARY, ARCHIVES AND MSS./SPEC. COLL. DEPARTMENT, *LA600-775*

UNIVERSITY OF NORTH CAROLINA AT ASHEVILLE, SOUTHERN HIGHLANDS RESEARCH CENTER, *NC60-810*

UNIVERSITY OF NORTH CAROLINA AT CHAPEL HILL, GEOLOGY LIBRARY, *NC150-780*

UNIVERSITY OF NORTH CAROLINA AT CHAPEL HILL, INSTITUTE OF OUTDOOR DRAMA, *NC150-790*

UNIVERSITY OF NORTH CAROLINA AT CHAPEL HILL, LIBRARY, MSS. DEPT. AND SOUTHERN HISTORICAL COLL., *NC150-800*

UNIVERSITY OF NORTH CAROLINA AT CHAPEL HILL, LIBRARY, NORTH CAROLINA COLLECTION, *NC150-810*

UNIVERSITY OF NORTH CAROLINA AT CHAPEL HILL, LIBRARY, RARE BOOK COLLECTION, *NC150-860*

UNIVERSITY OF NORTH CAROLINA AT CHARLOTTE, ATKINS LIBRARY, *NC160-800*

UNIVERSITY OF NORTH CAROLINA AT GREENSBORO, WALTER CLINTON JACKSON LIBRARY, SPECIAL COLLECTIONS, *NC380-800*

UNIVERSITY OF NORTH CAROLINA AT WILMINGTON, RANDALL LIBRARY, HELEN HAGAN RARE BOOK ROOM, *NC900-810*

UNIVERSITY OF NORTH DAKOTA, CHESTER FRITZ LIBRARY, DEPARTMENT OF SPECIAL COLLECTIONS, *ND486-800*

UNIVERSITY OF NORTH DAKOTA, GEOGRAPHY DEPARTMENT, *ND486-810*

UNIVERSITY OF NORTHERN IOWA, LIBRARY, SPECIAL COLLECTIONS, *IA88-800*

UNIVERSITY OF NOTRE DAME, ARCHIVES, *IN627-780*

UNIVERSITY OF NOTRE DAME, LIBRARIES, DEPARTMENT OF RARE BOOKS AND SPECIAL COLLECTIONS, *IN627-800*

UNIVERSITY OF NOTRE DAME, MEDIEVAL INSTITUTE, *IN627-810*

UNIVERSITY OF OKLAHOMA, LIBRARIES, WESTERN HISTORY COLLECTIONS, DIVISION OF MANUSCRIPTS, *OK558-790*

UNIVERSITY OF OREGON, LIBRARY, *OR224-800*

UNIVERSITY OF OREGON, MAP LIBRARY, *OR224-810*

UNIVERSITY OF PENNSYLVANIA, ARCHIVES, *PA726-725*

UNIVERSITY OF PENNSYLVANIA, LAW SCHOOL, BIDDLE LAW LIBRARY, *PA726-750*

UNIVERSITY OF PENNSYLVANIA, MUSEUM, *PA726-795*

UNIVERSITY OF PENNSYLVANIA, SCHOOL OF DENTAL MEDICINE, LIBRARY, *PA726-810*

UNIVERSITY OF PENNSYLVANIA, VAN PELT LIBRARY, EDGAR FAHS SMITH COLLEC. IN HIST. OF CHEMISTRY, *PA726-765*

UNIVERSITY OF PENNSYLVANIA, VAN PELT LIBRARY, HENRY CHARLES LEA LIBRARY OF MEDIEVAL HISTORY, *PA726-770*

UNIVERSITY OF PENNSYLVANIA, VAN PELT LIBRARY, SPECIAL COLLECTIONS, *PA726-775*

UNIVERSITY OF PITTSBURGH, LIBRARIES, ARCHIVES OF INDUSTRIAL SOCIETY, *PA735-790*

UNIVERSITY OF PITTSBURGH, LIBRARIES, DARLINGTON MEMORIAL LIBRARY, *PA735-800*

UNIVERSITY OF PITTSBURGH, NATIONALITY ROOMS AND INTERCULTURAL EXCHANGE PROGRAMS, NAT. ROOM ARCHIVES*PA735-825*

UNIVERSITY OF PITTSBURGH, STEPHEN FOSTER MEMORIAL, *PA735-760*

UNIVERSITY OF PITTSBURGH, UNIVERSITY LIBRARIES, UNIVERSITY ARCHIVES, *PA735-780*

UNIVERSITY OF PORTLAND, ARCHIVES, *OR720-740*

UNIVERSITY OF PUERTO RICO AT RIO PIEDRAS, HISTORICAL RESEARCH CENTER, *PR600-800*

UNIVERSITY OF PUGET SOUND, GEOLOGY LIBRARY, *WA904-790*

UNIVERSITY OF PUGET SOUND, MANUSCRIPT COLLECTION, *WA904-800*

UNIVERSITY OF PUGET SOUND, UNIVERSITY ARCHIVES, *WA904-810*

UNIVERSITY OF RHODE ISLAND, LIBRARY, *RI420-800*

UNIVERSITY OF RICHMOND, LIBRARY, ARCHIVES, *VA690-770*

UNIVERSITY OF ROCHESTER, EASTMAN SCHOOL OF MUSIC, SIBLEY MUSIC LIBRARY, *NY752-840*

UNIVERSITY OF ROCHESTER, RUSH RHEES LIBRARY, DEPARTMENT OF RARE BOOKS, MANUSCRIPTS AND ARCHIVES, *NY752-880*

UNIVERSITY OF ROCHESTER, SCHOOL OF MEDICINE AND DENTISTRY, EDWARD G. MINER LIBRARY, *NY752-885*

UNIVERSITY OF SAN DIEGO, JAMES S. COPLEY LIBRARY, *CA712-810*

UNIVERSITY OF SAN FRANCISCO, RICHARD A. GLEESON LIBRARY, SPECIAL COLLECTIONS DEPARTMENT, *CA720-910*

UNIVERSITY OF SANTA CLARA, ARCHIVES, *CA778-780*

UNIVERSITY OF SANTA CLARA, MICHEL ORRADRE LIBRARY, *CA778-800*

UNIVERSITY OF SCIENCE AND ARTS OF OKLAHOMA, NASH LIBRARY, *OK228-610*

UNIVERSITY OF SCRANTON, ALUMNI MEMORIAL LIBRARY, SPECIAL COLLECTIONS, *PA795-800*

UNIVERSITY OF SOUTH ALABAMA, LIBRARY, SPECIAL COLLECTIONS DEPARTMENT, *AL580-800*

UNIVERSITY OF SOUTH CAROLINA, MUSEUM AND ARCHIVES, DEPARTMENT OF ARCHIVES AND RECORDS MANAGEMENT, *SC216-800*

UNIVERSITY OF SOUTH CAROLINA, SOUTH CAROLINIANA LIBRARY, MANUSCRIPTS DIVISION, *SC216-820*

UNIVERSITY OF SOUTH DAKOTA, AMERICAN INDIAN RESEARCH PROJECT, *SD792-800*

UNIVERSITY OF SOUTH DAKOTA, I. D. WEEKS LIBRARY, RICHARDSON ARCHIVES, *SD792-820*

UNIVERSITY OF SOUTH DAKOTA, SCHOOL OF MEDICINE, HEALTH SCIENCE LIBRARY, *SD792-830*

UNIVERSITY OF SOUTH DAKOTA, SOUTH DAKOTA ORAL HISTORY PROJECT, *SD792-850*

UNIVERSITY OF SOUTH FLORIDA, LIBRARY, SPECIAL COLLECTIONS DEPARTMENT, *FL820-780*

UNIVERSITY OF SOUTHERN CALIFORNIA, LIBRARY, SPECIAL COLLECTIONS DEPARTMENT, *CA421-830*

UNIVERSITY OF SOUTHERN CALIFORNIA, LIBRARY, UNIVERSITY ARCHIVES, *CA421-825*

UNIVERSITY OF SOUTHERN MISSISSIPPI, WILLIAM DAVID MCCAIN LIBRARY AND ARCHIVES, *MS490-810*

UNIVERSITY OF SOUTHWESTERN LOUISIANA, DUPRE LIBRARY, SOUTHWESTERN ARCHIVES AND MANUSCRIPTS COLL., *LA358-800*

UNIVERSITY OF TAMPA, MERL KELCE LIBRARY, *FL820-810*

UNIVERSITY OF TENNESSEE AT KNOXVILLE, LIBRARY, SPECIAL COLLECTIONS, *TN465-800*

UNIVERSITY OF TEXAS AT ARLINGTON, LIBRARY, DIVISION OF SPECIAL COLLECTIONS, *TX42-810*

UNIVERSITY OF TEXAS AT AUSTIN, E. C. BARKER TEXAS HISTORY CENTER, *TX56-850*

UNIVERSITY OF TEXAS AT AUSTIN, GENERAL LIBRARIES, NETTIE LEE BENSON LATIN AMERICAN COLLECTION, *TX56-860*

UNIVERSITY OF TEXAS AT AUSTIN, HUMANITIES RESEARCH CENTER LIBRARY, *TX56-890*

UNIVERSITY OF TEXAS AT DALLAS, DEPARTMENT OF SPECIAL COLLECTIONS, HISTORY OF AVIATION COLLECTION, *TX742-800*

UNIVERSITY OF TEXAS AT EL PASO, EL PASO CENTENNIAL MUSEUM, MANUSCRIPT COLLECTION, *TX326-770*

UNIVERSITY OF TEXAS AT EL PASO, INSTITUTE OF ORAL HISTORY, *TX326-780*

UNIVERSITY OF TEXAS AT EL PASO, LIBRARY, DEPARTMENT OF SPECIAL COLLECTIONS AND ARCHIVES, *TX326-800*

UNIVERSITY OF TEXAS AT SAN ANTONIO, JOHN PEACE LIBRARY, SPECIAL COLLECTIONS, *TX777-810*

UNIVERSITY OF TEXAS MEDICAL BRANCH, MOODY MEDICAL LIBRARY, HISTORY OF MEDICINE AND ARCHIVES DEPT., *TX397-790*

UNIVERSITY OF TEXAS, HEALTH SCIENCE CENTER AT SAN ANTONIO, LIBRARY, SPECIAL COLLECTIONS, *TX777-790*

UNIVERSITY OF TEXAS, WINEDALE HISTORICAL CENTER, *TX754-880*

UNIVERSITY OF THE DISTRICT OF COLUMBIA, LEARNING RESOURCES DIVISION, ARCHIVES AND SPECIAL COLLECT., *DC21-510*

UNIVERSITY OF THE PACIFIC, PACIFIC CENTER FOR WESTERN HISTORICAL STUDIES, *CA862-810*

UNIVERSITY OF THE SOUTH, JESSIE BALL DUPONT LIBRARY, *TN840-800*

UNIVERSITY OF TOLEDO, WILLIAM S. CARSON LIBRARY, WARD M. CANADAY CENTER & UNIV. OF TOLEDO ARCHIVES, *OH823-800*

UNIVERSITY OF TULSA, LIBRARY, *OK829-790*

UNIVERSITY OF UTAH, LIBRARY, SPECIAL COLLECTIONS DEPARTMENT, *UT912-820*

UNIVERSITY OF VERMONT, ARCHIVES, *VT176-790*

UNIVERSITY OF VERMONT, GUY W. BAILEY LIBRARY, WILBUR SPECIAL COLLECTIONS, *VT176-810*

UNIVERSITY OF VIRGINIA, LIBRARY, MANUSCRIPTS DEPARTMENT AND UNIVERSITY ARCHIVES, *VA145-780*

UNIVERSITY OF WASHINGTON, INSTRUCTIONAL MEDIA SERVICES, *WA820-893*

UNIVERSITY OF WASHINGTON, LAW SCHOOL LIBRARY, *WA820-889*

UNIVERSITY OF WASHINGTON, LIBRARIES, EAST ASIA LIBRARY, *WA820-886*

UNIVERSITY OF WASHINGTON, LIBRARIES, MANUSCRIPTS AND
UNIVERSITY ARCHIVES DIVISION, *WA820-880, WA820-883*
UNIVERSITY OF WASHINGTON, LIBRARIES, SPECIAL
COLLECTIONS DIVISION, *WA820-892*
UNIVERSITY OF WASHINGTON, SCHOOL OF MEDICINE,
DEPARTMENT OF BIOMEDICAL HISTORY, *WA820-895*
UNIVERSITY OF WEST FLORIDA, JOHN C. PACE LIBRARY,
FL600-800
UNIVERSITY OF WISCONSIN AT EAU CLAIRE, LIBRARY,
UNIVERSITY ARCHIVES AND AREA RESEARCH CENTER,
WI142-800
UNIVERSITY OF WISCONSIN AT GREEN BAY, LIBRARY
LEARNING CENTER, AREA RESEARCH CENTER, *WI202-790*
UNIVERSITY OF WISCONSIN AT GREEN BAY, LIBRARY
LEARNING CENTER, SPECIAL COLLECTIONS, *WI202-810*
UNIVERSITY OF WISCONSIN AT LA CROSSE, MURPHY LIBRARY,
SPECIAL COLLECTIONS AND AREA RESEARCH CENTER,
WI298-810
UNIVERSITY OF WISCONSIN AT MADISON, LIBRARY, RARE
BOOKS DEPARTMENT, *WI346-840*
UNIVERSITY OF WISCONSIN AT MADISON, MAP AND AIR PHOTO
LIBRARY, *WI346-850*
UNIVERSITY OF WISCONSIN AT MADISON, SCHOOL OF
PHARMACY, POWER LIBRARY, KREMERS REFERENCE FILES,
WI346-870
UNIVERSITY OF WISCONSIN AT MADISON, SYSTEM ARCHIVES,
WI346-890
UNIVERSITY OF WISCONSIN AT OSHKOSH, LIBRARY,
UNIVERSITY ARCHIVES/AREA RESEARCH CENTER, *WI554-480*
UNIVERSITY OF WISCONSIN AT PARKSIDE, UNIVERSITY
ARCHIVES AND AREA RESEARCH CENTER, *WI266-820*
UNIVERSITY OF WISCONSIN AT RIVER FALLS, CHALMER DAVEE
LIBRARY, ST. CROIX VALLEY HIST. RES. CTR., *WI654-790*
UNIVERSITY OF WISCONSIN AT STEVENS POINT, AREA
RESEARCH CENTER, *WI722-770*
UNIVERSITY OF WISCONSIN AT STEVENS POINT, UNIVERSITY
ARCHIVES AND PORTAGE COUNTY COLLECTION, *WI722-830*
UNIVERSITY OF WISCONSIN AT STOUT, LIBRARY LEARNING
CENTER, AREA RESEARCH CENTER, *WI418-800*
UNIVERSITY OF WISCONSIN AT WHITEWATER, HAROLD
ANDERSEN LIBRARY, *WI858-810*
UNIVERSITY OF WISCONSIN CENTER - ROCK COUNTY, LIBRARY,
WI250-800
UNIVERSITY OF WISCONSIN, MEMORIAL LIBRARY, *WI346-840*
UNIVERSITY OF WYOMING, LIBRARY, DIVISION OF RARE BOOKS
AND SPECIAL COLLECTIONS, *WY500-800*
UNIVERSITY OF WISCONSIN AT MILWAUKEE, LIBRARY,
ARCHIVES AND SPECIAL COLLECTIONS, *WI456-810*
UPPER ROOM DEVOTIONAL LIBRARY, *TN690-885*
UPPER SUSQUEHANNA HISTORICAL SOCIETY, HISTORICAL
MUSEUM, *NY648-800*
URBAN ARCHIVES PROJECT, *CA524-160*
URBANA COLLEGE, SWEDENBORG MEMORIAL LIBRARY,
OH853-800
URBANA FREE LIBRARY, ARCHIVES, *IL916-840*
URSINUS COLLEGE, LIBRARY, *PA210-800*
URSULINE SISTERS OF THE IMMACULATE CONCEPTION OF
LOUISVILLE, KENTUCKY, ARCHIVES, *KY496-850*
USS CONSTITUTION MUSEUM, SAMUEL ELIOT MORISON
LIBRARY, *MA109-850*
UTAH INTERNATIONAL, ARCHIVES, *CA720-955*
UTAH STATE ARCHIVES AND RECORDS SERVICE, *UT912-840*
UTAH STATE HISTORICAL SOCIETY, *UT912-850*
UTAH STATE UNIVERSITY, MERRILL LIBRARY, SPECIAL
COLLECTIONS AND ARCHIVES, *UT380-810*
UTE PASS HISTORICAL SOCIETY, *CO150-840*
UTICA PUBLIC LIBRARY, *NY899-800*

V

VACHEL LINDSAY ASSOCIATION, *IL866-840*
VALDEZ HISTORICAL SOCIETY, *AK900-840*
VALDRES SAMBAND, *MN370-920*
VALENTINE MUSEUM OF THE LIFE AND HISTORY OF
RICHMOND, LIBRARY AND RESEARCH CENTER, *VA690-810*
VALENTOWN MUSEUM, *NY288-840*
VALLEJO NAVAL AND HISTORIC MUSEUM, RESEARCH AND
ACCESSIONS DIVISION, *CA922-840*
VALLEY CITY STATE COLLEGE, ALLEN MEMORIAL LIBRARY,
ND876-830
VALLEY FORGE HISTORICAL SOCIETY, *PA905-840*
VALPARAISO UNIVERSITY, ARCHIVES, *IN858-835*
VALPARAISO UNIVERSITY, HENRY F. MOELLERING MEMORIAL
LIBRARY, *IN858-850*
VAN BUREN, MARTIN, PAPERS, *PA565-640*
VAN HORNESVILLE COMMUNITY CORPORATION, *NY905-840*

VAN HOWELING MEMORIAL LIBRARY, CAPROCK-PLAINS
HISTORICAL COLLECTION, *TX712-880*
VAN WYCK HOMESTEAD MUSEUM, *NY289-240*
VANCOUVER COMMUNITY LIBRARY, *WA943-250*
VANDALIA HISTORICAL SOCIETY, JAMES HALL LIBRARY,
IL921-840
VANDERBILT TELEVISION NEWS ARCHIVE, *TN690-980*
VANDERBILT UNIVERSITY ARCHIVES, *TN690-975*
VANDERBILT UNIVERSITY, EDUCATION LIBRARY, *TN690-950*
VANDERBILT UNIVERSITY, LIBRARY, SPECIAL COLLECTIONS
AND VANDERBILT UNIVERSITY ARCHIVES, *TN690-975*
VANDERBILT UNIVERSITY, LIBRARY, VANDERBILT TELEVISION
NEWS ARCHIVE, *TN690-980*
VANDERBILT UNIVERSITY, MEDICAL CENTER LIBRARY, SPECIAL
COLLECTIONS, *TN690-960*
VASSAR COLLEGE, LIBRARY, *NY726-850*
VATICAN FILM LIBRARY, *MO810-730*
VEDDER MEMORIAL LIBRARY, *NY219-290*
VENTURA COUNTY AND CITY FREE LIBRARY, *CA934-835*
VENTURA COUNTY FREE LIBRARY, *CA934-835*
VENTURA COUNTY HISTORICAL MUSEUM, HISTORICAL
LIBRARY, *CA934-835*
VEREINS KIRCHE ARCHIVES AND LOCAL HISTORY COLLECTION,
TX381-280
VERLOT RANGER STATION, *WA950-840*
VERMONT AGENCY OF ADMINISTRATION, PUBLIC RECORDS
DIVISION, *VT464-800*
VERMONT COLLEGE, GARY MEMORIAL LIBRARY, *VT464-560*
VERMONT DEPARTMENT OF LIBRARIES, LAW AND DOCUMENTS
UNIT, *VT464-820*
VERMONT HISTORICAL SOCIETY, LIBRARY, *VT464-840*
VERMONT SECRETARY OF STATE, STATE PAPERS DIVISION,
VT464-850
VERMONT STATE ARCHIVES, *VT464-800, VT464-850*
VERNON COUNTY HISTORICAL MUSEUM, *WI774-840*
VESTAL HISTORICAL SOCIETY, MUSEUM, *NY909-840*
VESTAL PUBLIC LIBRARY, *NY909-850*
VICKSBURG AND WARREN COUNTY HISTORICAL SOCIETY, OLD
COURT HOUSE MUSEUM, *MS950-830*
VICTOR FREE LIBRARY, *NY910-840*
VICTOR HISTORICAL SOCIETY, VALENTOWN MUSEUM, *NY288-840*
VICTOR TOWN HISTORIAN, *NY910-860*
VICTORIA COLLEGE, LIBRARY, LOCAL HISTORY COLLECTION,
TX923-840
VIGO COUNTY HISTORICAL SOCIETY, JOHN G. BIEL LIBRARY,
IN825-830
VIGO COUNTY PUBLIC LIBRARY, SPECIAL COLLECTIONS,
IN825-850
VILLA BELVIDERE, *NY87-900*
VILLAGE HALL ASSOCIATION, ANNISQUAM HISTORICAL
SOCIETY, *MA338-840*
VILLAGE LIBRARY OF MORRIS, *NY564-840*
VILLANOVA UNIVERSITY, FALVEY MEMORIAL LIBRARY,
PA910-840
VINCENNES UNIVERSITY, BYRON R. LEWIS HISTORICAL
COLLECTIONS LIBRARY, *IN902-840*
VINELAND HISTORICAL AND ANTIQUARIAN SOCIETY, *NJ874-840*
VINITA PUBLIC LIBRARY, ARCHIVES DIVISION, *OK854-840*
VIRGIN ISLANDS DEPARTMENT OF CONSERVATION AND
CULTURAL AFFAIRS, BUREAU OF LIBRARIES AND MUSEUMS,
VI700-800
VIRGINIA BAPTIST HISTORICAL SOCIETY, *VA690-815*
VIRGINIA COMMONWEALTH UNIVERSITY, JAMES BRANCH
CABELL LIBRARY, SPECIAL COLLECTIONS DEPARTMENT,
VA690-830
VIRGINIA COMMONWEALTH UNIVERSITY, MEDICAL COLLEGE
OF VIRGINIA, LIBRARY, ARCHIVES DEPARTMENT, *VA690-840*
VIRGINIA GENEALOGICAL SOCIETY, *VA690-850*
VIRGINIA HISTORIC LANDMARKS COMMISSION, *VA690-860*
VIRGINIA HISTORICAL SOCIETY, *VA690-870*
VIRGINIA MILITARY INSTITUTE, PRESTON LIBRARY,
ARCHIVES/SPECIAL COLLECTIONS, *VA430-840*
VIRGINIA POLYTECHNIC INSTITUTE AND STATE UNIVERSITY,
CAROL M. NEWMAN LIBRARY, SPECIAL COLLECTIONS,
VA90-840
VIRGINIA STATE ARCHIVES, *VA690-910*
VIRGINIA STATE LIBRARY, ARCHIVES AND RECORDS DIVISION,
ARCHIVES BRANCH, *VA690-910*
VIRGINIA STATE UNIVERSITY, JOHNSTON MEMORIAL LIBRARY,
SPECIAL COLLECTIONS, *VA630-840*
VIRGINIUS H. CHASE SPECIAL COLLECTIONS CENTER, *IL723-80*
VISUAL STUDIES WORKSHOP, *NY752-890*
VOLCK, WILLIAM H., MUSEUM, *CA958-640*

W

W. B. ROBERTS LIBRARY, *MS230-160*
W. EVERETT MILLER LIBRARY OF VEHICLES, *CA282-480*
W. H. DOANE LIBRARY, *OH350-170*
W. H. OVER MUSEUM, *SD792-880*
W. L. JENKS HISTORICAL COLLECTION, *MI775-710*
W. R. BANKS LIBRARY, *TX733-640*
WABASH CARNEGIE PUBLIC LIBRARY, *IN913-880*
WABASH COLLEGE, LILLY LIBRARY, *IN154-880*
WABASH COUNTY HISTORICAL MUSEUM, *IN913-900*
WABASHA COUNTY HISTORICAL SOCIETY, *MN438-880*
WADE, MARION E., COLLECTION, *IL976-900*
WADING RIVER HISTORICAL SOCIETY, *NY911-880*
WADLEIGH MEMORIAL LIBRARY, *NH660-880*
WADSWORTH ATHENEUM, *CT316-880*
WAGNER COLLEGE, HORRMANN LIBRARY, *NY595-360*
WAGNER FREE INSTITUTE OF SCIENCE, *PA726-855*
WAHKIAKUM COUNTY HISTORICAL SOCIETY, MUSEUM, *WA115-890*
WAHLERT MEMORIAL LIBRARY, *IA244-480*
WAKARUSA PUBLIC LIBRARY, *IN917-880*
WAKE FOREST COLLEGE BIRTHPLACE SOCIETY, *NC840-880*
WAKE FOREST UNIVERSITY, NORTH CAROLINA BAPTIST HISTORICAL COLLECTION AND UNIVERSITY ARCHIVES, *NC930-840*
WAKEFIELD HISTORICAL SOCIETY, MUSEUM, *MA865-880*
WALDRON, CLARA, HISTORICAL ROOM, *MI910-770*
WALLA WALLA COMMUNITY COLLEGE, LIBRARY, *WA954-845*
WALLACE MEMORIAL LIBRARY, ARCHIVES AND SPECIAL COLLECTIONS, *NY752-700*
WALLACE MEMORIAL ROOM, NORFOLK COUNTY HISTORICAL SOCIETY OF CHESAPEAKE, *VA165-120*
WALLACE, LILA ACHESON, LIBRARY, *NY590-720*
WALLERSTEDT LEARNING CENTER, *KS555-80*
WALLINGFORD HISTORICAL SOCIETY, *CT849-880*
WALLOWA COUNTY MUSEUM, *OR424-880*
WALT DISNEY ARCHIVES, *CA114-880*
WALT DISNEY PRODUCTIONS, WALT DISNEY ARCHIVES, *CA114-880*
WALT WHITMAN ASSOCIATION, *NJ112-880*
WALT WHITMAN BIRTHPLACE ASSOCIATION, *NY421-880*
WALTER C. HINKLE MEMORIAL LIBRARY, COLLEGE ARCHIVES AND WESTERN NEW YORK HISTORICAL COLLECTIONS, *NY18-720*
WALTER CLINTON JACKSON LIBRARY, SPECIAL COLLECTIONS, *NC380-800*
WALTER M. PIERCE LIBRARY, *OR464-200*
WALTER REED ARMY MEDICAL CENTER, LIBRARIES, *DC23-70*
WALTERS ART GALLERY, DEPARTMENT OF MANUSCRIPTS AND RARE BOOKS, *MD76-880*
WALTHAM HISTORICAL SOCIETY, *MA871-860*
WALTHAM MUSEUM, *MA871-870*
WALTHAM PUBLIC LIBRARY, GENEALOGY AND LOCAL HISTORY ROOM, *MA871-890*
WALTON HISTORICAL SOCIETY, *NY915-870*
WAPATO PUBLIC LIBRARY, *WA956-880*
WAR MEMORIAL MUSEUM OF VIRGINIA, *VA560-880*
WARD EDWARDS LIBRARY, SPECIAL COLLECTIONS, *MO920-120*
WARD, LEO J., MEMORIAL LIBRARY, RARE BOOK COLLECTION AND ARCHIVES, *MI230-720*
WARDER PUBLIC LIBRARY, *OH788-870*
WARDMAN LIBRARY, *CA966-880*
WARING HISTORICAL LIBRARY, *SC144-520*
WARNE, THOMAS, HISTORICAL MUSEUM AND LIBRARY, *NJ622-690*
WARREN COUNTY HISTORICAL SOCIETY, ARCHIVES, *PA915-870*
WARREN COUNTY HISTORICAL SOCIETY, MUSEUM, HISTORICAL AND GENEALOGICAL LIBRARY, *OH436-880*
WARREN H. FAKE LIBRARY, *PA725-690*
WARREN HUNTING SMITH LIBRARY, *NY323-320*
WARREN PUBLIC LIBRARY, *OH878-880*
WARSAW HISTORICAL SOCIETY, *NY923-880*
WARSAW PUBLIC LIBRARY, *NY923-890*
WARTBURG COLLEGE, ENGELBRECHT LIBRARY, COLLEGE ARCHIVES, *IA944-880*
WARWICK HISTORICAL SOCIETY, *RI875-880*
WASCO COUNTY LIBRARY, *OR848-160*
WASHBURN UNIVERSITY OF TOKEKA, MABEE LIBRARY, CONGREGATIONAL COLLECTION AND WASHBURN ARCHIVES, *KS878-880*
WASHINGTON AND JEFFERSON COLLEGE, LIBRARY, HISTORICAL COLLECTION, *PA920-890*
WASHINGTON AND LEE UNIVERSITY, UNIVERSITY LIBRARY, SPECIAL COLLECTIONS, *VA430-870*
WASHINGTON CARNEGIE PUBLIC LIBRARY, *OH883-880*

WASHINGTON CATHEDRAL, CENTRAL FILES, *DC23-100*
WASHINGTON CATHEDRAL, LIBRARY, *DC5-800*
WASHINGTON COLLEGE, CLIFTON M. MILLER LIBRARY, ARCHIVES, *MD228-870*
WASHINGTON COUNTY (AR) HISTORICAL SOCIETY, *AR330-880*
WASHINGTON COUNTY (IN) HISTORICAL SOCIETY, *IN770-880*
WASHINGTON COUNTY (MD) HISTORICAL SOCIETY, SIMMS A. JAMIESON MEMORIAL LIBRARY, *MD532-880*
WASHINGTON COUNTY (MN) HISTORICAL MUSEUM, *MN835-880*
WASHINGTON COUNTY (NE) HISTORICAL ASSOCIATION, WASHINGTON COUNTY HISTORICAL MUSEUM, *NE352-880*
WASHINGTON COUNTY (NE) HISTORICAL MUSEUM, *NE352-880*
WASHINGTON COUNTY (OH) PUBLIC LIBRARY, *OH486-890*
WASHINGTON COUNTY (OR) MUSEUM, *OR352-900*
WASHINGTON COUNTY (PA) HISTORICAL SOCIETY, *PA920-870*
WASHINGTON COUNTY (UT) LIBRARY, *UT836-880*
WASHINGTON COUNTY (WI) HISTORICAL SOCIETY, MUSEUM, *WI836-322*
WASHINGTON DEPARTMENT OF GENERAL ADMINISTRATION, DIVISION OF ARCHIVES AND RECORDS MANAGEMENT, *WA60-800*
WASHINGTON GAS LIGHT COMPANY, CORPORATE LIBRARY, *VA700-322*
WASHINGTON HOSPITAL CENTER, MEDICAL LIBRARY, *DC23-250*
WASHINGTON STATE ARCHIVES, *WA616-870*
WASHINGTON STATE CAPITAL MUSEUM, *WA616-915*
WASHINGTON STATE HISTORICAL SOCIETY, LIBRARY, *WA904-870*
WASHINGTON STATE LIBRARY, WASHINGTON NORTHWEST ROOM, *WA616-950*
WASHINGTON STATE SCHOOL FOR THE BLIND, LIBRARY, *WA943-725*
WASHINGTON STATE SCHOOL FOR THE DEAF, LEARNING RESOURCE CENTER, *WA943-730*
WASHINGTON STATE UNIVERSITY, LIBRARIES, MANUSCRIPTS, ARCHIVES, AND SPECIAL COLLECTIONS DIVISION, *WA724-890*
WASHINGTON STATE UNIVERSITY, LIBRARIES, UNIVERSITY ARCHIVES, *WA724-895*
WASHINGTON UNIVERSITY, GALLERY OF ART, *MO810-880*
WASHINGTON UNIVERSITY, LIBRARIES, DEPARTMENT OF RARE BOOKS AND SPECIAL COLLECTIONS, *MO810-920*
WASHINGTON UNIVERSITY, LIBRARIES, UNIVERSITY ARCHIVES AND RESEARCH COLLECTION, *MO810-940*
WASHINGTON UNIVERSITY, SCHOOL OF MEDICINE, LIBRARY, ARCHIVES, *MO810-960*
WASHINGTON, MARY BALL, MUSEUM AND LIBRARY, *VA400-520*
WASHINGTON'S HEADQUARTERS STATE HISTORIC SITE, *NY599-880*
WASHOUGAL BRANCH LIBRARY, *WA958-240*
WASHTENAW HISTORICAL SOCIETY, *MI40-880*
WASON COLLECTION, *NY439-156*
WATER RESOURCES CENTER, ARCHIVES, *CA86-920*
WATERFRONT MUSEUM, *FL720-720*
WATERLOO LIBRARY AND HISTORICAL SOCIETY, *NY928-880*
WATERTOWN (CT) HISTORICAL SOCIETY, *CT884-870*
WATERTOWN (WI) HISTORICAL SOCIETY, *WI786-880*
WATERTOWN LIBRARY, *CT884-890*
WATERVILLE HISTORICAL SOCIETY, *NY932-880*
WATERVILLE HISTORICAL SOCIETY, REDINGTON MUSEUM, *ME925-870*
WATERVILLE PUBLIC LIBRARY, *WA960-880*
WATKINS WOOLEN MILL STATE HISTORIC SITE, *MO490-880*
WATKINS, ELIZABETH M., COMMUNITY MUSEUM, LIBRARY, *KS527-160*
WATKINS, LEVI, LEARNING CENTER, UNIVERSITY LIBRARY, UNIVERSITY ARCHIVES AND SPECIAL COLLECTIONS, *AL620-60*
WATKINSON LIBRARY, *CT316-770*
WATONWAN COUNTY HISTORICAL SOCIETY, *MN492-880*
WATROUSVILLE-CARO AREA HISTORICAL SOCIETY, *MI126-880*
WATSON LIBRARY, ARCHIVES DIVISION, *LA570-540*
WATSON, S. ARTHUR, LIBRARY, QUAKER COLLECTION/WILMINGTON COLLEGE ARCHIVES, *OH953-870*
WATSON, THOMAS J., LIBRARY, *NY591-380*
WATZEK LIBRARY, LEWIS AND CLARK COLLEGE ARCHIVES, *OR720-440*
WAUKEGAN HISTORICAL SOCIETY, LIBRARY, *IL956-870*
WAUKESHA COUNTY HISTORICAL MUSEUM, RESEARCH CENTER, *WI794-880*
WAVELAND STATE SHRINE, *KY464-880*
WAYLAND BAPTIST COLLEGE, VAN HOWELING MEMORIAL LIBRARY, CAPROCK-PLAINS HISTORICAL COLLECTION, *TX712-880*
WAYLAND FREE PUBLIC LIBRARY, *MA883-870*
WAYNE COUNTY (KY) HISTORICAL SOCIETY, *KY55L-920*
WAYNE COUNTY (OH) HISTORICAL SOCIETY, *OH968-880*
WAYNE COUNTY (PA) HISTORICAL SOCIETY, *PA410-880*
WAYNE COUNTY HISTORIAN'S OFFICE, *NY510-880*
WAYNE COUNTY HISTORICAL MUSEUM, *IN704-880*

WAYNE COUNTY PUBLIC LIBRARY AND WAYNE COUNTY HISTORICAL SOCIETY, *KY55L-920*

WAYNE STATE UNIVERSITY, ARCHIVES OF LABOR HISTORY AND URBAN AFFAIRS, *MI230-880*

WAYNE STATE UNIVERSITY, DEPARTMENT OF ANTHROPOLOGY, MUSEUM OF ANTHROPOLOGY, *MI230-890*

WAYNE STATE UNIVERSITY, UNIVERSITY ARCHIVES, *MI230-905*

WEBB DEANE STEVENS MUSEUM, *CT933-870*

WEBB HOUSE, *CT933-870*

WEBB INSTITUTE OF NAVAL ARCHITECTURE, LIVINGSTON LIBRARY, *NY327-880*

WEBB ROBERTS LIBRARY, *TX374-720*

WEBER STATE COLLEGE, STEWART LIBRARY, SPECIAL COLLECTIONS AND HOWELL LIBRARY, *UT456-900*

WEBSTER COUNTY PUBLIC LIBRARY, *KY22W-920*

WEBSTER TOWN HISTORIAN, *NY938-890*

WEBSTER VILLAGE HISTORIAN, *NY938-900*

WEBSTER, NOAH, FOUNDATION AND HISTORICAL SOCIETY OF WEST HARTFORD, *CT891-550*

WEDSWORTH MEMORIAL LIBRARY, *MT180-880*

WEEKS, ABIGAIL E., MEMORIAL LIBRARY, *KY24-800*

WEEKS, I. D., LIBRARY, RICHARDSON ARCHIVES, *SD792-820*

WEHR, TODD, LIBRARY, *WI456-500*

WEINER PROFESSIONAL LIBRARY, ARCHIVES, *PA725-525*

WELLER LIBRARY, *NY553-880*

WELLER PUBLIC LIBRARY, *WA952-880*

WELLESLEY COLLEGE, ARCHIVES, *MA891-860*

WELLESLEY COLLEGE, LIBRARY, SPECIAL COLLECTIONS, *MA891-880*

WELLFLEET HISTORY SOCIETY, *MA894-880*

WELLS COLLEGE, LOUIS JEFFERSON LONG LIBRARY, *NY53-880*

WELLS FARGO BANK, ARCHIVES, *CA720-960*

WENATCHEE BRANCH LIBRARY, *WA966-550*

WENATCHEE VALLEY COLLEGE LIBRARY, *WA966-905*

WENHAM HISTORICAL ASSOCIATION AND MUSEUM, TIMOTHY PICKERING LIBRARY, *MA897-880*

WENRICH MEMORIAL LIBRARY, *NY752-480*

WENTZ, ABDEL ROSS, LIBRARY, *PA325-490*

WERNER, BUD, MEMORIAL LIBRARY, ROUTT COUNTY COLLECTION, *CO856-80*

WESLEY THEOLOGICAL SEMINARY, LIBRARY, *DC23-500*

WESLEYAN ARCHIVES, *KS833-440*

WESLEYAN CHURCH, ARCHIVES AND HISTORICAL LIBRARY, *IN506-870*

WESLEYAN UNIVERSITY, ARCHIVES, *CT428-865*

WESSELS LIBRARY, SPECIAL COLLECTION, *SC684-550*

WEST BOYLSTON COLLECTION, *MA904-80*

WEST CENTRAL MINNESOTA HISTORICAL CENTER, *MN583-920*

WEST CHESTER STATE COLLEGE, FRANCIS HARVEY GREEN LIBRARY, *PA945-880*

WEST FLORIDA REGIONAL LIBRARY, LOCAL HISTORY COLLECTION, *FL600-880*

WEST GEORGIA COLLEGE, LIBRARY, SPECIAL COLLECTIONS, *GA210-880*

WEST GEORGIA REGIONAL LIBRARY, SPECIAL COLLECTIONS, *GA210-900*

WEST HENNEPIN PIONEERS ASSOCIATION, *MN473-880*

WEST SALEM HISTORICAL SOCIETY, HAMLIN GARLAND HOMESTEAD, *WI853-880*

WEST VIRGINIA AND REGIONAL HISTORY, *WV650-890*

WEST VIRGINIA COLLECTION AND ARCHIVES, *WV650-520*

WEST VIRGINIA DEPARTMENT OF CULTURE AND HISTORY, *WV225-860*

WEST VIRGINIA STATE ARCHIVES, *WV225-860*

WEST VIRGINIA UNIVERSITY, LIBRARY, WEST VIRGINIA AND REGIONAL HISTORY, *WV650-890*

WEST VIRGINIA WESLEYAN COLLEGE, ANNIE MERNER PFEIFFER LIBRARY, *WV200-880*

WEST, ROY O., LIBRARY, *IN275-170*

WESTBOROUGH HISTORICAL SOCIETY, *MA925-880*

WESTBROOK COLLEGE, MAINE WOMEN WRITERS COLLECTION, *ME712-880*

WESTCHESTER COUNTY HISTORICAL SOCIETY, *NY893-890*

WESTERLY PUBLIC LIBRARY, *RI910-880*

WESTERN AMERICA INSTITUTE FOR EXPLORATION, *OR848-40*

WESTERN CAROLINA UNIVERSITY, HUNTER LIBRARY, SPECIAL COLLECTIONS, *NC210-870*

WESTERN CONNECTICUT STATE COLLEGE, RUTH A. HAAS LIBRARY, ARCHIVES, *CT144-880*

WESTERN HISTORICAL COLLECTIONS, UNIVERSITY OF COLORADO, *CO108-810*

WESTERN HISTORY COLLECTIONS, DIVISION OF MANUSCRIPTS, UNIVERSITY OF OKLAHOMA, *OK558-790*

WESTERN ILLINOIS UNIVERSITY, LIBRARY, ARCHIVES AND SPECIAL COLLECTIONS DEPARTMENT, *IL489-890*

WESTERN JEWISH HISTORY CENTER, *CA86-400*

WESTERN KENTUCKY UNIVERSITY, ARCHIVES, *KY94-845*

WESTERN KENTUCKY UNIVERSITY, FOLK-LORE, FOLK-LIFE AND ORAL HISTORY ARCHIVES, *KY96-850*

WESTERN KENTUCKY UNIVERSITY, KENTUCKY LIBRARY, *KY96-870*

WESTERN MARYLAND COLLEGE, ARCHIVES, *MD978-880*

WESTERN MICHIGAN UNIVERSITY, ADAMS CENTER FOR ECOLOGICAL STUDIES, *MI518-860*

WESTERN MICHIGAN UNIVERSITY, ARCHIVES AND REGIONAL HISTORY COLLECTIONS, *MI518-870*

WESTERN MICHIGAN UNIVERSITY, LIBRARY, *MI518-870*

WESTERN MONROE HISTORICAL SOCIETY, *NY125-880*

WESTERN NEW MEXICO UNIVERSITY, MUSEUM, *NM760-900*

WESTERN NEW YORK FORUM FOR AMERICAN ART, *NY134-710*

WESTERN NEW YORK UNITED METHODIST CONFERENCE, ARCHIVES CENTER, *NY970-840*

WESTERN NORTH CAROLINA HISTORICAL ASSOCIATION, *NC60-880*

WESTERN PENNSYLVANIA, HISTORICAL SOCIETY OF, *PA735-320*

WESTERN RAILWAY MUSEUM, *CA650-322*

WESTERN RESERVE HISTORICAL SOCIETY, HISTORY LIBRARY, *OH181-880*

WESTERN RESERVE UNIVERSITY, LIBRARY, *OH181-110, OH181-130*

WESTERN STATE HOSPITAL, LIBRARY, INTERPRETIVE CENTER, *WA889-880*

WESTERN THEOLOGICAL SEMINARY, *MI445-880*

WESTERN TOWNSHIP PUBLIC LIBRARY, *IL674-880*

WESTERN WASHINGTON REGIONAL STATE ARCHIVES, *WA60-800*

WESTERN WASHINGTON UNIVERSITY, CENTER FOR PACIFIC NORTHWEST STUDIES, *WA60-860*

WESTERN WASHINGTON UNIVERSITY, LIBRARY, *WA60-870*

WESTERN WRIGHT MARINE, MUSEUM, *WA904-890*

WESTERN YEARLY MEETING OF FRIENDS, *IN660-620*

WESTFIELD STATE COLLEGE, RAYMOND PATTERSON ALUMNI ARCHIVE, *MA928-730*

WESTMAR COLLEGE, CHARLES A. MOCK LIBRARY, *IA544-880*

WESTMINSTER CHOIR COLLEGE, TALBOTT LIBRARY, COLLEGE ARCHIVES, *NJ692-880*

WESTMINSTER THEOLOGICAL SEMINARY, LIBRARY, *PA726-870*

WESTMORELAND COUNTY HISTORICAL SOCIETY, *PA350-880*

WESTON HISTORICAL SOCIETY, *CT919-880*

WESTTOWN SCHOOL, HISTORICAL LIBRARY, *PA950-880*

WESTWOOD PUBLIC LIBRARY, BAKER HISTORICAL COLLECTION, *MA943-880*

WETER MEMORIAL LIBRARY, OMAR ALLEN BURNS ROOM, *WA820-772*

WETHERSFIELD HISTORICAL SOCIETY, OLD ACADEMY MUSEUM LIBRARY, *CT933-890*

WEXFORD COUNTY HISTORICAL SOCIETY-MUSEUM, *MI122-880*

WEYERHAEUSER COMPANY, HISTORICAL ARCHIVES, *WA310-880*

WEYERHAEUSER, CHARLES A., MEMORIAL MUSEUM, *MN466-520*

WEYMOUTH PUBLIC LIBRARIES, TUFTS LIBRARY, *MA947-880*

WHALING MUSEUM SOCIETY, *NY205-880*

WHATCOM GENEALOGICAL SOCIETY, *WA60-895*

WHATCOM MUSEUM OF HISTORY AND ART, *WA60-885*

WHEATON COLLEGE, BUSWELL MEMORIAL LIBRARY, ARCHIVES AND SPECIAL COLLECTIONS, *IL976-890*

WHEATON COLLEGE, BUSWELL MEMORIAL LIBRARY, BILLY GRAHAM CENTER, ARCHIVES, *IL976-850*

WHEATON COLLEGE, BUSWELL MEMORIAL LIBRARY, MARION E. WADE COLLECTION, *IL976-900*

WHEATON COLLEGE, LIBRARY, COLLEGE ARCHIVES, *MA636-880*

WHEELER, BOB, MUSEUM, *KY514-120*

WHITE PINE COUNTY HISTORICAL SOCIETY, *NV200-920*

WHITE RIVER VALLEY HISTORICAL SOCIETY, MUSEUM, *WA37-880*

WHITE, G. W. BLUNT, LIBRARY, *CT463-520*

WHITE, JAMES, LIBRARY, HERITAGE ROOM, *MI90-30*

WHITE, WILLIAM ALANSON, PSYCHIATRIC FOUNDATION, ARCHIVES, *DC23-800*

WHITE, WILLIAM ALLEN, LIBRARY, SPECIAL COLLECTIONS DIVISION, *KS283-200*

WHITEFRIARS HALL, LIBRARY, *DC23-700*

WHITESVILLE PUBLIC LIBRARY, *NY967-880*

WHITMAN COLLEGE, PENROSE MEMORIAL LIBRARY, EELLS NORTHWEST ROOM, *WA954-880*

WHITMAN COUNTY HISTORICAL SOCIETY, PERKINS HOUSE MUSEUM, *WA164-890*

WHITMAN COUNTY LIBRARY, *WA164-895*

WHITMAN COUNTY PARKS AND RECREATION DEPARTMENT, *WA164-900*

WHITMAN MISSION NATIONAL HISTORIC SITE, *WA954-885*

WHITMAN, WALT, ASSOCIATION, *NJ112-880*

WHITMAN, WALT, BIRTHPLACE ASSOCIATION, *NY421-880*

WHITTAKER, MILLER F., LIBRARY, SOUTH CAROLINA STATE COLLEGE HISTORICAL COLLECTION, *SC720-710*

WHITTIER COLLEGE, DEPARTMENT OF GEOLOGY, FAIRCHILD AERIAL PHOTOGRAPHY COLLECTION, *CA966-860*

WHITTIER COLLEGE, WARDMAN LIBRARY, *CA966-880*

WHITTIER, JOHN GREENLEAF, HOME, *MA17-400*
WICHITA CITY LIBRARY, *KS948-880*
WICHITA HISTORICAL MUSEUM, *KS948-870*
WICHITA PUBLIC LIBRARY, REFERENCE DEPARTMENT, *KS948-880*
WICHITA STATE UNIVERSITY, LIBRARY, SPECIAL COLLECTIONS,
    KS948-890
WIDE AWAKE CLUB LIBRARY, *NY287-880*
WIDE WORLD PHOTOS, INC., *NY595-480*
WIDER MINISTRIES COMMISSION ARCHIVES, *IN704-240*
WIENER, WILLIAM E., ORAL HISTORY LIBRARY, *NY586-650*
WILBERFORCE UNIVERSITY, ARCHIVES AND SPECIAL
    COLLECTIONS, *OH939-860*
WILBUR SPECIAL COLLECTIONS, *VT176-810*
WILCOX, MARY, MEMORIAL LIBRARY, *NY968-520*
WILDENTHAL, BRYAN, MEMORIAL LIBRARY, ARCHIVES OF THE
    BIG BEND, *TX14-720*
WILDER, LAURA INGALLS, PARK & MUSEUM, *IA74-480*
WILKES COLLEGE, EUGENE SHEDDEN FARLEY LIBRARY,
    PA960-870
WILKES COMMUNITY COLLEGE, LEARNING RESOURCES
    CENTER, *NC890-880*
WILKIN COUNTY HISTORICAL SOCIETY, *MN126-880*
WILL COUNTY HISTORICAL SOCIETY, *IL464-880*
WILL ROGERS MEMORIAL, WILL ROGERS MEMORIAL LIBRARY,
    OFFICE OF THE CURATOR, *OK245-880*
WILL W. ALEXANDER LIBRARY, *LA600-160*
WILLA CATHER HISTORICAL CENTER, *NE736-560*
WILLAMETTE NATIONAL FOREST, HISTORICAL COLLECTION,
    OR224-880
WILLAMETTE UNIVERSITY, LIBRARY, *OR816-890*
WILLARD J. HOUGHTON LIBRARY, *NY413-320*
WILLARD LIBRARY OF EVANSVILLE, REGIONAL AND FAMILY
    HISTORY CENTER, *IN209-880*
WILLARD LIBRARY, LOCAL HISTORY COLLECTION, *MI60-880*
WILLARD, FRANCES E., MEMORIAL LIBRARY, *IL261-545*
WILLET STAINED GLASS STUDIOS, *PA726-895*
WILLGOOSE, LAURA G., ARCHIVES ROOM, *MA580-550*
WILLIAM A. FARNSWORTH LIBRARY AND ART MUSEUM,
    ME725-880
WILLIAM ALANSON WHITE PSYCHIATRIC FOUNDATION,
    ARCHIVES, *DC23-800*
WILLIAM ALLAN NEILSON LIBRARY, RARE BOOK ROOM,
    MA624-750
WILLIAM ALLEN WHITE LIBRARY, SPECIAL COLLECTIONS
    DIVISION, *KS283-200*
WILLIAM AND EVELYN BANKS LIBRARY, *GA660-480*
WILLIAM ANDREWS CLARK MEMORIAL LIBRARY, *CA421-774*
WILLIAM B. OGDEN FREE LIBRARY, *NY915-880*
WILLIAM BUTLER YEATS ARCHIVES, *NY866-730*
WILLIAM CLARK MARKET HOUSE MUSEUM, *KY604-890*
WILLIAM CONLON MEMORIAL LIBRARY, *WA730-880*
WILLIAM D. MCINTYRE LIBRARY, UNIVERSITY ARCHIVES AND
    AREA RESEARCH CENTER, *WI142-800*
WILLIAM DAVID MCCAIN LIBRARY AND ARCHIVES, *MS490-810*
WILLIAM E. DERMODY FREE PUBLIC LIBRARY, *NJ124-240*
WILLIAM E. WIENER ORAL HISTORY LIBRARY, *NY586-650*
WILLIAM H. VOLCK MUSEUM, *CA958-640*
WILLIAM JASPER KERR LIBRARY, *OR144-620*
WILLIAM L. CLEMENTS LIBRARY, *MI40-820*
WILLIAM MADISON RANDALL LIBRARY, HELEN HAGAN RARE
    BOOK ROOM, *NC900-810*
WILLIAM P. MACCRACKEN, JR., MEMORIAL LIBRARY, *TN630-730*
WILLIAM R. PERKINS LIBRARY, MANUSCRIPT DEPARTMENT,
    NC260-170
WILLIAM RANSOM HOGAN JAZZ ARCHIVE, *LA600-764*
WILLIAM SMITH, HOBART AND, COLLEGES, WARREN HUNTING
    SMITH LIBRARY, *NY323-320*
WILLIAM T. BOYCE LIBRARY, *CA278-240*
WILLIAMS COLLEGE, CHAPIN LIBRARY OF RARE BOOKS,
    MA961-870
WILLIAMS COLLEGE, LIBRARY, *MA961-890*
WILLIAMS, FLORENCE A., PUBLIC LIBRARY, *VI300-240*
WILLINGTON HISTORICAL SOCIETY, *CT905-880*
WILLIS CAREY HISTORICAL MUSEUM, *WA112-880*
WILLISTON MEMORIAL LIBRARY, *MA776-530*
WILMINGTON COLLEGE, S. ARTHUR WATSON LIBRARY, QUAKER
    COLLECTION/COLLEGE ARCHIVES, *OH953-870*
WILMINGTON SOCIETY OF THE FINE ARTS, *DE810-150*
WILMOT, LORETTE, LIBRARY, *NY752-560*
WILSON, WOODROW, BIRTHPLACE FOUNDATION, RESEARCH
    LIBRARY AND ARCHIVES, *VA750-880*
WILSON'S CREEK NATIONAL BATTLEFIELD, *MO730-800*
WILTON FREE PUBLIC LIBRARY (GOODSPEED MEMORIAL),
    ME937-870
WILTON HERITAGE MUSEUM, *CT947-880*
WILTON HISTORICAL SOCIETY, WILTON HERITAGE MUSEUM,
    CT947-880

WIMODAUGHSIAN FREE LIBRARY, *NY148B-88*
WINCHENDON HISTORICAL SOCIETY, *MA964-880*
WINCHESTER ARCHIVAL CENTER, *MA967-880*
WINDSOR HISTORICAL SOCIETY, *CT961-880*
WINE INSTITUTE, *CA720-980*
WINEDALE HISTORICAL CENTER, *TX754-880*
WING LUKE MEMORIAL MUSEUM, *WA820-966*
WINLOCK PUBLIC LIBRARY, *WA982-880*
WINONA COUNTY HISTORICAL SOCIETY, LAIRD LUCAS
    MEMORIAL LIBRARY, *MN975-860*
WINTERTHUR ARCHIVES, *DE900-330*
WINTHROP COLLEGE, DACUS LIBRARY, ARCHIVES AND SPECIAL
    COLLECTIONS DEPARTMENT, *SC774-880*
WINTHROP PUBLIC LIBRARY, *MA970-890*
WISCONSIN CENTER FOR FILM AND THEATER RESEARCH,
    WI346-900
WISCONSIN DEPARTMENT OF VETERANS AFFAIRS, WISCONSIN
    VETERANS MUSEUMS, *WI346-280*
WISCONSIN MAP SOCIETY, *WI714-880*
WISCONSIN STATE ARCHIVES, *WI346-720*
WISCONSIN STATE COLLEGE, LIBRARY, *WI298-810*
WISCONSIN STATE HISTORICAL SOCIETY, ARCHIVES DIVISION,
    WI346-720
WISCONSIN VETERANS MUSEUMS, *WI346-280*
WISE COUNTY HERITAGE MUSEUM, WISE COUNTY HISTORICAL
    COMMISSION ARCHIVE, *TX259-880*
WISE COUNTY HISTORICAL COMMISSION ARCHIVE, *TX259-880*
WITCO CHEMICAL CORPORATION, *NJ990-322*
WITTE MEMORIAL MUSEUM, *TX777-710*
WITTENBERG UNIVERSITY, ARCHIVES, *OH788-880*
WOBURN PUBLIC LIBRARY, *MA975-890*
WOFFORD COLLEGE, SANDOR TESZLER LIBRARY, ARCHIVES
    DEPARTMENT, *SC846-890*
WOLCOTT TOWN HISTORIAN, *NY974-890*
WOMAN GEOGRAPHERS, SOCIETY OF, *DC19-750*
WOMAN'S COLLEGE LIBRARY, UNIVERSITY OF NORTH
    CAROLINA, *NC380-800*
WOMEN'S CLUBS, GENERAL FEDERATION OF, ARCHIVES, *DC7-300*
WOMEN'S EDUCATIONAL CENTER, WOMEN'S MOVEMENT
    ARCHIVES, *MA169-970*
WOMEN'S MOVEMENT ARCHIVES, *MA169-970*
WOMEN'S STUDY CLUB AND LIBRARY, *NY247-880*
WOOD COUNTY HISTORICAL SOCIETY, *OH97-890*
WOOD LIBRARY, *NY147-880*
WOOD LIBRARY-MUSEUM OF ANESTHESIOLOGY, *IL708-40*
WOODFORD COUNTY-LOGAN HELM PUBLIC LIBRARY, *KY834-480*
WOODROW WILSON BIRTHPLACE FOUNDATION, RESEARCH
    LIBRARY AND ARCHIVES, *VA750-880*
WOODRUFF, ROBERT W., LIBRARY, SPECIAL COLLECTIONS
    DEPARTMENT, *GA90-200*
WOODS HOLE OCEANOGRAPHIC INSTITUTION, DATA
    LIBRARY/ARCHIVE, *MA981-890*
WOODSON RESEARCH CENTER, *TX483-690*
WOODSTOCK LIBRARY, *NY975-890*
WOODWARD, FELIX G., LIBRARY, *TN75-50*
WORCESTER FREE LIBRARY, *NY978-870*
WORCESTER HISTORICAL MUSEUM, *MA985-860*
WORCESTER HISTORICAL SOCIETY, *NY978-880*
WORCESTER POLYTECHNIC INSTITUTE, ARCHIVES, *MA985-870*
WORCESTER PUBLIC LIBRARY, *MA985-890*
WORLD BANK, PHOTO LIBRARY, *DC9-450*
WRIGHT BROTHERS-CHARLES F. KETTERING ORAL HISTORY
    PROJECT, *OH223-810*
WRIGHT STATE UNIVERSITY, LIBRARY, ARCHIVES/SPECIAL
    COLLS., GREATER MIAMI VALLEY RESEARCH CENTER,
    OH223-880
WYANDOTTE COUNTY MUSEUM, HARRY M. TROWBRIDGE
    RESEARCH LIBRARY, *KS136-880*
WYANDOTTE MUSEUMS, *MI982-880*
WYLLIE, JOHN COOK, LIBRARY, *VA890-120*
WYOMING ARCHIVES AND MUSEUMS, HISTORICAL DIVISION,
    WY135-880
WYOMING ARCHIVES, MUSEUMS AND HISTORICAL
    DEPARTMENT, ARCHIVES AND RECORDS MANAGEMENT
    DIVISION, *WY135-860*
WYOMING ARCHIVES, MUSEUMS AND HISTORICAL
    DEPARTMENT, HISTORICAL RESEARCH AND PUBLICATIONS
    DIVISION, *WY135-865*
WYOMING COUNTY HISTORICAL CENTER, *NY923-910*
WYOMING HISTORICAL AND GEOLOGICAL SOCIETY, *PA960-910*
WYOMING STATE ARCHIVES, *WY135-860*
WYTHEVILLE COMMUNITY COLLEGE, LIBRARY, KEGLEY
    COLLECTION, *VA900-880*

X

XAVIER UNIVERSITY OF LOUISIANA, LIBRARY, BLACK
COLLECTION, *LA600-920*
XAVIER UNIVERSITY, MCDONALD MEMORIAL LIBRARY,
OH171-920

Y

YADKIN COUNTY PUBLIC LIBRARY AND YADKIN COUNTY
HISTORICAL SOCIETY, HISTORY ROOM, *NC950-940*
YAKIMA INDIAN NATION, ARCHIVES, *WA921-950*
YAKIMA VALLEY GENEALOGICAL SOCIETY, *WA994-925*
YAKIMA VALLEY MUSEUM AND HISTORICAL ASSOCIATION,
WA994-935
YAKIMA VALLEY REGIONAL LIBRARY, *WA994-940*
YALE DIVINITY SCHOOL, LIBRARY, *CT505-900*
YALE EDITIONS OF THE PRIVATE PAPERS OF JAMES BOSWELL,
CT505-977
YALE LAW SCHOOL, LIBRARY, *CT505-960*
YALE UNIVERSITY, LIBRARIES, BEINECKE RARE BOOK AND
MANUSCRIPT LIBRARY, *CT505-890*
YALE UNIVERSITY, LIBRARIES, DIVINITY SCHOOL LIBRARY,
CT505-900
YALE UNIVERSITY, LIBRARIES, FORESTRY AND
ENVIRONMENTAL STUDIES LIBRARY, *CT505-905*
YALE UNIVERSITY, LIBRARIES, JOHN HERRICK JACKSON MUSIC
LIBRARY, *CT505-910*
YALE UNIVERSITY, LIBRARIES, MEDICAL LIBRARY, HISTORICAL
LIBRARY, *CT505-930*
YALE UNIVERSITY, LIBRARIES, STERLING MEMORIAL LIBRARY,
FRANKLIN COLLECTION, *CT505-945*
YALE UNIVERSITY, LIBRARIES, STERLING MEMORIAL LIBRARY,
MANUSCRIPTS AND ARCHIVES, *CT505-960*
YALE UNIVERSITY, LIBRARIES, STERLING MEMORIAL LIBRARY,
MAP COLLECTION, *CT505-970*
YALE UNIVERSITY, LIBRARIES, STERLING MEMORIAL LIBRARY,
VERTICAL FILES COLLECTION, *CT505-975*
YALE UNIVERSITY, LIBRARIES, STERLING MEMORIAL LIBRARY,
YALE COLLECTION OF RECORDINGS, *CT505-976*
YALE UNIVERSITY, LIBRARIES, YALE EDITIONS OF THE PRIVATE
PAPERS OF JAMES BOSWELL, *CT505-977*
YALE UNIVERSITY, LIBRARY OF THE SCHOOL OF MUSIC,
CT505-910
YALE UNIVERSITY, LIBRARY, HISTORICAL MANUSCRIPTS
COLLECTION, *CT505-960*
YALE UNIVERSITY, LIBRARY, WESTERN AMERICANA
COLLECTION, *CT505-890*
YALE UNIVERSITY, LIBRARY, YALE COLLECTION OF AMERICAN
LITERATURE, *CT505-890*
YALE UNIVERSITY, LIBRARY, YALE COLLECTION OF GERMAN
LITERATURE, *CT505-890*
YALE UNIVERSITY, LIBRARY, YALE UNIVERSITY ARCHIVES,
CT505-960

YALE UNIVERSITY, PEABODY MUSEUM OF NATURAL HISTORY,
CT505-980
YAMHILL COUNTY HISTORICAL MUSEUM, *OR480-940*
YANKTON COLLEGE, LIBRARY, ARCHIVE COLLECTION, *SD936-930*
YANKTON COUNTY HISTORICAL SOCIETY, *SD936-950*
YATES COUNTY GENEALOGICAL AND HISTORICAL SOCIETY,
NY693-920
YEATS, WILLIAM BUTLER, ARCHIVES, *NY866-730*
YELLOWSTONE ARCHIVES, *WY950-950*
YELLOWSTONE NATIONAL PARK, RESEARCH LIBRARY,
WY950-940
YELLOWSTONE NATIONAL PARK, STILL PHOTOGRAPHIC
SECTION, *WY950-945*
YELLOWSTONE NATIONAL PARK, YELLOWSTONE ARCHIVES,
WY950-950
YERKES OBSERVATORY, *WI874-940*
YESHIVA UNIVERSITY, DIVISION OF ARCHIVES AND
MANUSCRIPT COLLECTIONS, *NY595-660*
YESHIVA UNIVERSITY, MUSEUM, *NY595-670*
YIVO INSTITUTE FOR JEWISH RESEARCH, ARCHIVES, *NY595-700*
YOLO COUNTY LIBRARY, DAVIS BRANCH, *CA206-940*
YONGE, P. K., LIBRARY OF FLORIDA HISTORY, *FL220-795*
YORK COUNTY HISTORICAL SOCIETY, LIBRARY AND ARCHIVES,
PA975-320
YORK INSTITUTE, *ME750-160*
YOSEMITE NATIONAL PARK, RESEARCH LIBRARY AND RECORDS
CENTER, *CA994-940*
YOUNG HARRIS COLLEGE, DUCKWORTH LIBRARIES, *GA990-940*
YOUNG MEN'S AND YOUNG WOMEN'S HEBREW ASSOCIATION,
NINETY-SECOND STREET, ARCHIVES, *NY593-132*
YOUNG MEN'S CHRISTIAN ASSOCIATIONS OF THE UNITED
STATES, NATIONAL BOARD OF, *IL170-283*
YOUNG WOMEN'S CHRISTIAN ASSOCIATION OF THE UNITED
STATES OF AMERICA, ARCHIVES, *NY592-30*
YOUNG WOMEN'S CHRISTIAN ASSOCIATION, CITY OF NEW
YORK, LAURA PARSON PRATT ARCHIVES, *NY595-740*
YOUNG, KENDALL, LIBRARY, *IA955-440*
YOUNGSTOWN AND MAHONING COUNTY, PUBLIC LIBRARY OF,
OH990-640
YOUR HOME PUBLIC LIBRARY, *NY446-920*
YPSILANTI HISTORICAL MUSEUM, *MI990-940*
YUMA COUNTY HISTORICAL SOCIETY COLLECTIONS, *AZ950-40*
YUMA TERRITORIAL PRISON STATE HISTORIC PARK, *AZ950-950*

Z

ZELIENOPLE HISTORICAL SOCIETY, *PA986-960*
ZIMMERMAN LIBRARY, SPECIAL COLLECTIONS DEPARTMENT,
NM114-900
ZION HISTORICAL SOCIETY, SHILOH HOUSE, REV. ANTON
DARMS LIBRARY, *IL996-980*
ZIONIST LIBRARY AND ARCHIVES, *NY595-760*
ZUG MEMORIAL LIBRARY, *PA285-200*
ZUMBERGE LIBRARY, ARCHIVES, *MI128-280*

SUBJECT INDEX

A

A. W. GRAY (MANUFACTURER)
VT448-520
AASGAARD, JOHAN ARNDT
MN763-50
ABBEYS
WA472-720
ABBOT-DOWNING COMPANY
NH134-540
ABBOT, ABIEL
NH748-650
ABBOT, CHARLES G.
DC19-310
ABBOTT, WALLACE CALVIN
IL629-40
ABDURAHMAN, A.
IL261-566
ABEL, JOHN JACOB
MD76-315
ABOLITIONISM
See Antislavery movement
ABOUREZK, JAMES
SD792-820
ABRAHAM LINCOLN BIRTHPLACE NATIONAL HISTORIC SITE
KY358-480
ACADEMIC LIBRARY ASSOCIATION OF OHIO
OH223-800
ACADEMY OF NEWARK (DE)
DE540-780
ACCIDENTS
DC1-680
ACCOUNTING
MA871-60
EDUCATION
MA871-60
ACTIVE CORPS OF EXECUTIVES (ACTION)
DC1-40
ACTIVISTS
IL170-910, NY134-85, PA735-790
ACTORS
IA688-520, IN726-240, NY593-485
ACTRESSES
IA688-520, NY593-485
ACUPUNCTURE
CA720-886
ADAIR, ISAAC
MO920-120
ADAMS FAMILY
MA109-120, WY500 -800
ADAMS, ANSEL
AZ800-820, DC3-760, TX374-40
ADAMS, CLARK K.
NY240-160
ADAMS, JOHN
MA109-660, NY594-220, WY500-800
ADAMS, JOHN, FAMILY
DC19-576
ADAMS, THEODORE FLOYD
NC840-720
ADANSON, MICHEL
PA735-140
ADDAMS, JANE
IL170-910, IL296-720, IL806-695

ADE, GEORGE
IN275-170, IN935-650, MA961-870
ADIRONDACK MOUNTAINS
NY150-700, NY331-120, NY447-400, NY708-720, NY872-720
ADLER AND SULLIVAN (ARCHITECTURAL FIRM)
IL169-130
ADMINISTRATION
OR816-590
HISTORICAL AGENCIES
DC14-650
ADOPTION
MN541-902
ADVENT CHRISTIAN CHURCH
IL45-30
ADVENT MOVEMENT
MI90-30
ADVENTURE TOMORROW (TELEVISION PROGRAM)
CA278-130
ADVENTURES OF TOM SAWYER, BY MARK TWAIN
MO870-520
ADVERTISING
CT316-750, DC19-542, GA90-130, IN533-640, IN792-160, MI214-260, MT430-320, NJ464-240, NY587-840, NY590-535
RADIO
GA90-130
TELEVISION
GA90-130
AERIAL PHOTOGRAPHY
See Topography
AERONAUTICS
See also Aviation , CA421-830, CA578-130, CA578-560, CO180-750, DC14-140, DC19-500, IA33-350, MO810-510, NY95-280, OH223-810, OH223-880, TX483-560*
AERONAUTICS, NATIONAL ADVISORY COMMITTEE FOR
TX483-560
AERONAUTS
CA456-730
AEROSPACE INDUSTRY
NY95-280, WA820-92
AEROSTATS
CA456-730, OH11-810
AESTHETICS
LITERATURE
NY125-740
AFFLICTIONS
See Deformities
AFRICA
See also individual countries and regions, *AL620-20, AL840-820, AZ800-30, AZ800-803, AZ800-830, ,A86-630, ,A86-780, CA421-770, CA756-320, CA858-320, CA858-810, CT316-330, CT463-520, CT505-960, DC3-226, DC7-650, DC8-850, DC12-300, DC12-400, DC12-450, DC12-600, DC12-650, DC14-250, DC19-440, DC19-450, DE540-790, GA90-200, GA90-360, IA233-360, IL169-247, IL169-325, IL170-884, IL261-566, IN297-600, KY288-460, KY464-490, KY464-800, LA62-500, LA600-20, LA600-920, MA92-70, MA108-240, MA108-750, MA109-120, MA169-370, MA572-560, MA584-600, MA733-210,*

MA733-660, MA776-530, MA871-40, MA985-70, MA985-130, MD76-515, MI40-820, MI255-530, MI255-545, MO810-200, NC260-170, NC730-480, NH134-540, NJ568-670, NJ578-530, NJ692-660, NY134-60, NY260-560, NY439-120, NY536-520, NY587-780, NY588-900, NY592-30, NY592-460, NY592-800, NY592-860, NY592-930, NY752-880, NY872-800, OH939-860, OR224-800, PA160-160, PA325-490, PA340-520, PA395-320, PA725-75, PA725-720, PA726-713, PA860-710, RI560-570, SC860-600, TN690-170, TN690-220, TN690-740, TN690-890, TX56-25, VA145-780, VA690-870, VA870-110, WI346-720
ART
DC19-440, DC19-450
BAHA'I
IL981-560
ECONOMIC AID TO
NY589-560
EDUCATION
NY593-380
EXPLORATION
KS164-520
EXPLORERS
MI255-530
FOREIGN AID
DC1-180
HOSPITALS
PA725-908
MEDICINE
MA108-770
MISSIONARIES
AL760-760, LA600-505, NC390-200, NC590-320, NJ222-333, NY529-530, OH223-720, PA725-908, RI910-730
MUSIC
AZ750-32
ORGANIZATIONS
IL261-566
TRADE WITH UNITED STATES
MA733-660
AFRICA, WESTERN
NY593-380
TRADE WITH UNITED STATES
MA733-210
AFRICAN METHODIST EPISCOPAL CHURCH
NY134-85, OH939-860
CLERGY
OH939-860
AFRICAN METHODIST EPISCOPAL ZION CHURCH
NC730-480
AFRICAN STUDIES ASSOCIATION
IL261-566
AFRO-AMERICAN STUDIES
See Blacks
AGAOGLU, MEHMET
DC19-327
AGASSIZ, ALEXANDER
MA169-500
AGASSIZ, LOUIS
MA169-500
AGED AND AGING
MN541-902, OH203-630
AGRARIAN REFORM
WI456-495
AGRICULTURAL EXTENSION SERVICE
TX733-640

AGRICULTURAL IMPLEMENTS
See Farm equipment

AGRICULTURAL SOCIETY (BURTON OH)
OH112-280

AGRICULTURAL STABILIZATION AND CONSERVATION SERVICE
GA75-800, IL624-370

AGRICULTURAL WORKERS ASSOCIATION
CA86-120

AGRICULTURAL WORKERS ORGANIZING COMMITTEE
CA86-120

AGRICULTURE
See also Farming; Farms; Plantations; and
related terms, *AR510-25, CA86-810,
CA143-470, CA206-790, CA432-520,
CA540-590, CA676-740, CA712-630,
CA862-810, CA998-720, CT234-230,
CT275-800, DC1-180, DC4-260,
DC9-450, DC14-490, DC19-591,
DC19-800, DE900-330, IA33-370,
IL202-550, IL866-355, IL866-720,
IN143-120, IN363-342, MA871-280,
MD285-805, ME437-120, MI40-784,
MI255-530, MI255-545, MI845-40,
MN562-520, MN763-530, MO210-815,
MS610-520, MT130-535, MT130-540,
MT530-500, NC200-120, NC260-170,
ND375-570, NJ756-240, NM494-570,
NV450-120, NY150-760, NY200-720,
NY211-580, NY540-760, NY612-690,
OH203-650, OH968-600, PA725-615,
PA895-680, SC738-640, TN465-760,
TX56-850, TX181-790, TX231-120,
TX590-760, TX733-640, VA195-200,
VT296-690, WA122-110, WA724-890,
WA759-680, WI362-520*

CHEMISTRY
CT428-865

DRY-FARMING
WA602-600

EDUCATION
HI450-80

EXPERIMENTATION
CT505-120

GOVERNMENT AGENCIES
OR816-590

INDIANS
GA90-270

LABOR
*CA86-120, CA778-800, CA858-810,
HI350-790, MI230-880, NY439-150,
TX529-770*

MACHINERY
CA132-120, CA206-790

MOVEMENTS
DC2-200

ORGANIZATIONS
*CA226-170, CT477-570, CT673-690,
DC4-260, KY600-600, MA897-880,
ME437-120, MI518-445, MN275-200,
MN520-700, MN728-690, ND486-800,
NY71-715, NY251-320, OH112-280,
OH223-880, OH906-320, PA965-490,
SC185-120, SD550-600, TN435-220,
TX733-640, WA280-885, WA844-720*

RICE
LA358-800

ROCKY MOUNTAIN REGION
UT380-810

SCOTLAND
CT505-977

TECHNOLOGY
CA862-630, NV450-120

TOBACCO
NC390-200

AGRICULTURE, MASSACHUSETTS SOCIETY FOR PROMOTING
MA897-880

AIKEN, CONRAD
NH206-800

AIKIN, A. M., JR.
TX210-200

POLITICAL CAREER
TX695-640

AIR COMBAT
CO180-750

WORLD WAR II
FL750-200

AIR FORCE
*AK320-40, AL560-720, AZ800-830,
CA421-770, CA578-130, CA858-320,
CO108-810, CO180-750, CO252-550,
CT505-890, DC12-300, DC12-600,
DC13-210, DC14-250, DC14-410,
DC14-725, DC14-725, DC14-730,
DC14-770, DC14-780, DC19-500,
DE90-140, DE270-200, GA405-560,
IA377-280, IA966-320, IL169-325,
IL170-884, IL866-365, IL916-810,
KS10-170, KS878-430, KY96-870,
MA108-240, MA108-750, MA108-965,
MA109-120, MA169-170, MD152-550,
MI40-784, MI214-260, MN763-540,
MO210-815, MO400-320, MS900-870,
NC390-200, NE560-550, NJ270-800,
NJ692-660, NM114-35, NY427-240,
NY439-120, NY872-800, OH978-120,
OK558-790, OR768-170, PA165-790,
PA725-495, SC144-150, TX56-520,
TX543-560, TX590-760, UT684-80,
VA145-780, VA430-280, VA580-520,
VA660-510, WA724-890, WV650-890,
WY500-800*

AIR CORPS TACTICAL SCHOOL
AL560-720

GERMANY
AL560-720, DC1-200

GREAT BRITAIN
AL560-720

AIR LINE PILOTS ASSOCIATION
MI230-880

AIR TRANSPORTATION
See Aviation

AIRCRAFT
*AL560-720, CA770-40, CT186-800,
DC14-715, DC14-770, DC14-780,
KS948-890, MA981-890, MD57-830,
NY367-270, OH968-600, OH978-120,
TX742-800, WA820-613*

PILOTS
MI230-880

AIRGLOW
CO108-560

AIRPORTS
NJ178-110

AIRSHIPS
AL560-720, DC19-500, TX742-800

AKRON METHODIST CHURCH (AKRON IN)
IN5-40

AKRON PA
MENNONITE CENTRAL COMMITTEE
IN264-40

ALABAMA
DC14-600, WI456-735

ALASKA
*CA778-780, MI518-50, OR848-40,
WA820-770, WA820-892, WA880-280*

ARCHAEOLOGY
ID480-770

COAST GUARD
WA820-147

ESKIMOS
MO210-840

GOVERNORS
WA820-550

JEWS
CA86-400

LANGUAGES, NATIVE
NY870-600

MARITIME HISTORY
WA820-635

MISSIONARIES
IL169-677, OH953-870, WA880-280

MORAVIAN CHURCH
PA90-500

ORTHODOX CHURCH
NY870-600

SISTERS OF PROVIDENCE
WA820-820

ALBANY COLLEGE
OR720-440

ALBEMARLE & CHESAPEAKE CANAL CO.
VA165-120

ALBERT B. LEWIS LUMBER COMPANY
PA960-910

ALBERT, CARL
OK558-790

ALBERTA, CANADA
ARCHAEOLOGY
ID480-770

ALBRIGHT, HORACE
WY560-280

ALBUQUERQUE NM
TX326-160

ALCATRAZ ISLAND, INDIAN OCCUPATION OF
CA720-675

ALCHEMY
CT505-890, PA726-765

ALCO (LOCOMOTIVE MANUFACTURER)
NY804-560

ALCOA TELEVISION PROGRAMS
CA421-760

ALCOHOLICS
NY594-20

ALCOTT FAMILY
MA217-480

ALCOTT, AMOS BRONSON
MA217-130

ALCOTT, LOUISA MAY
MA217-130

ALDEN, JAMES
ID880-80

ALDINGTON, RICHARD
PA726-615

ALDIS FAMILY
VT720-720

ALDRICH-DOWNES HOUSE
TX228-320

ALEUTIAN ISLANDS
MI518-50, OR848-40

ALEUTS
MI518-50, NY591-820

ALEXANDER FAMILY (MECKLENBURG COUNTY NC)
NC160-520

ALEXANDER, ARCHIBALD
NJ692-610

ALEXANDER, MARGARET WALKER
MS550-410

ALEXANDER, WILLIAM DEWITT
HI350-315

ALEXANDERSON, ERNST F. W.
NY804-800

ALEXANDRIA VA
DC14-370, DC19-560

ALFRED, WILLIAM
NY588-300

ALGER HOUSE
MI230-148

ALIENS
ILLEGAL
TX326-780

ALLAIRE FAMILY
NJ8-160

ALLAIRE, JAMES P.
NJ8-160

ALLEN & KELLY (ARCHITECTURAL FIRM)
IN539-100

ALLEN UNIVERSITY
DC1-160

ALLEN, NATHAN H.
CT316-770

ALLIANCE OF CATHOLIC LAITY
IL170-78

ALMANACS
CT512-120

ALMIRA COLLEGE
IL354-80

ALSTON, THEODOSIA BURR
NJ339-40

ALTIERI, ALICE LAFOND
RI700-630

ALUMNI ASSOCIATION OF HUNTER COLLEGE
NY588-420

AMBROSIANA LIBRARY (MILAN, ITALY)
IN627-810

AMERICA'S CUP RACES
NY952-720
AMERICAN ACADEMY OF ARTS AND
  LETTERS
NY586-180
AMERICAN ACADEMY OF RELIGION
  SOUTHEASTERN SECTION
GA90-190
AMERICAN ANTI-SLAVERY SOCIETY
OH878-720
AMERICAN ASSOCIATION OF
  UNIVERSITY WOMEN
IN704-520
  ST. CLOUD (MN) BRANCH
MN742-700
AMERICAN AUTOMOBILE ASSOCIATION,
  CONTEST BOARD
IN803-360
AMERICAN BALLET THEATRE
NY592-870
AMERICAN BAPTIST CHURCH
MA593-40,   NY752-40
  MISSIONARIES
NY752-40,   PA905-60
  ORGANIZATIONS
NY752-40
AMERICAN BAPTIST FOREIGN MISSION
  SOCIETY
NY752-40
AMERICAN BAPTIST HOME MISSION
  SOCIETY
NY752-40
AMERICAN BAR ASSOCIATION
IL169-52
AMERICAN BAR ENDOWMENT
IL169-52
AMERICAN BISON SOCIETY
NY593-300
AMERICAN BOARD OF COMMISSIONERS
  FOR FOREIGN MISSIONS
HI350-320,   IL169-507,   WA954-880
AMERICAN CASSINESE FEDERATION OF
  THE ORDER OF SAINT BENEDICT
PA485-720
AMERICAN CHEMICAL SOCIETY
  DIVISION OF CHEMICAL EDUCATION
PA726-765
AMERICAN CIVIL LIBERTIES UNION
NY866-710
AMERICAN COMMITTEE FOR
  INTERNATIONAL PROTECTION OF
  WILD LIFE
NY593-130
AMERICAN COMMITTEE TO KEEP BIAFRA
  ALIVE
IL261-566
AMERICAN COUNCIL ON EDUCATION
NJ692-210
AMERICAN DANCE FESTIVAL
CT512-120
AMERICAN ECONOMIC ASSOCIATION
IL261-570
AMERICAN ECONOMIC REVIEW
IL261-570
AMERICAN ENGINEERING COUNCIL
NY589-460
AMERICAN ENTOMOLOGICAL SOCIETY
PA725-15
AMERICAN EVANGELICAL LUTHERAN
  CHURCH
IL170-91
AMERICAN EXPEDITIONARY FORCES
  RUSSIA
MI445-320
AMERICAN FEDERATION OF JEWS FROM
  CENTRAL EUROPE
NY593-720
AMERICAN FEDERATION OF LABOR
DC1-400,   DC3-210
AMERICAN FEDERATION OF LABOR AND
  CONGRESS OF INDUSTRIAL
  ORGANIZATIONS
MA21-800,   PA895-710
AMERICAN FEDERATION OF STATE,
  COUNTY AND MUNICIPAL
  EMPLOYEES
MI230-880

AMERICAN FEDERATION OF TEACHERS
MI230-880
AMERICAN FIELD SERVICE
NJ178-115
AMERICAN FOREST INSTITUTE
CA782-240
AMERICAN FORESTRY ASSOCIATION
CA782-240
AMERICAN FUR COMPANY
MI865-80
AMERICAN INDUSTRIAL ARTS
  ASSOCIATION
PA595-530
AMERICAN INSTITUTE OF ARCHITECTS
  NEW ORLEANS CHAPTER
LA600-761
AMERICAN INSTITUTE OF THE HISTORY
  OF PHARMACY
WI346-720
AMERICAN LEGION AUXILIARY
ND876-80
AMERICAN LOCOMOTIVE COMPANY
NY804-800
AMERICAN LUTHERAN CHURCH
TX797-760
AMERICAN OPTOMETRIC ASSOCIATION
TN630-730
AMERICAN PSYCHOANALYTIC
  ASSOCIATION
CT926-480
AMERICAN RELIEF SERVICE
NJ178-115
AMERICAN REVOLUTION
  See also Daughters of the American
  Revolution,   *CA368-120,   CA756-320,*
  CT36-80,   CT120-120,   CT316-770,
  CT519-560,   DC1-810,   DC12-190,
  DC14-590,   DC14-600,   DC19-700,
  DE90-140,   IL169-325,   KS541-720,
  MA48-20,   MA81-80,   MA109-220,
  MA231-640,   MA250-160,   MA462-480,
  MA478-730,   MA506-520,   MA624-560,
  MA677-70,   MA931-400,   MA985-110,
  MD57-500,   ME750-160,   MI40-820,
  NC680-460,   NH134-530,   NH772-640,
  NJ66-80,   NJ92-80,   NJ175-333,
  NJ182-110,   NJ276-510,   NJ548-530,
  NJ578-510,   NJ622-690,   NJ692-610,
  NJ692-660,   NJ838-630,   NJ838-750,
  NJ982-280,   NY10-640,   NY51-100,
  NY51-140,   NY292-520,   NY493-320,
  NY577-330,   NY587-720,   NY589-580,
  NY592-800,   NY594-220,   NY595-360,
  NY599-560,   NY599-880,   NY757-400,
  NY878-320,   NY899-600,   NY923-880,
  NY949-830,   OH181-880,   OH823-800,
  PA25-480,   PA55-760,   PA160-120,
  PA380-650,   PA380-665,   PA395-320,
  PA726-765,   PA735-800,   PA905-840,
  PA920-890,   PA925-160,   PA960-870,
  RI700-45,   RI700-680,   VA580-570,
  VA690-870,   VI700-360,   VT720-720
  BICENTENNIALS
MS80-40
  FINANCE
NY589-340
  FRANCE
VA870-150
  LOYALISTS
  CT316-110,   CT316-120,   CT316-770,
  CT393-480,   CT505-960,   DC12-300,
  DC14-250,   DE90-140,   DE810-330,
  FL220-800,   FL280-400,   FL660-120,
  FL660-720,   GA75-810,   GA405-560,
  GA895-280,   MA108-140,   MA108-240,
  MA108-320,   MA108-580,   MA109-120,
  MA109-460,   MA169-170,   MA169-370,
  MA235-150,   MA285-160,   MA506-520,
  MA528-780,   MA554-530,   MA624-240,
  MA677-70,   MA733-210,   MA804-130,
  MA811-720,   MA841-600,   MA985-70,
  MD76-515,   ME712-530,   NC260-170,
  NC390-200,   NH134-530,   NH134-540,
  NH206-800,   NH784-630,   NH784-700,
  NJ548-530,   NJ578-510,   NJ838-580,
  NY10-80,   NY10-640,   NY211-580,
  NY257-190,   NY260-560,   NY292-520,

  NY297-520,   NY419-350,   NY587-780,
  NY587-800,   NY588-520,   NY588-900,
  NY589-710,   NY590-940,   NY591-840,
  NY592-260,   NY592-440,   NY592-460,
  NY593-600,   NY593-900,   NY594-360,
  NY749-720,   NY804-720,   NY842-730,
  NY878-720,   PA725-75,   PA725-240,
  PA725-285,   PA725-600,   PA726-37,
  PA860-710,   PA945-120,   RI700-740,
  SC216-720,   SC216-820,   VA145-780,
  VA690-870,   VA690-910,   VA870-110,
  VA870-150
  NAVY
CT512-550
  NEW JERSEY
PA925-160
  SULLIVAN-CLINTON CAMPAIGN
NY566-540
  VETERANS
NH588-520,   OH486-890
AMERICAN SAMOA
  GOVERNMENT AGENCIES,
  TERRITORIAL
CA704-560
AMERICAN SHIPBUILDING COMPANY
OH863-280
AMERICAN SOCIETY OF ANESTHETISTS
IL708-40
AMERICAN SOCIETY OF CIVIL
  ENGINEERS
NY589-460
AMERICAN SOCIETY OF MECHANICAL
  ENGINEERS
NY589-460
AMERICAN SOCIETY OF PLANT
  TAXONOMISTS
NY592-320
AMERICAN SUNDAY SCHOOL UNION
PA726-713
AMERICAN UNITARIAN ASSOCIATION
MA169-230
AMES FAMILY
MA615-80,   MA624-740
AMES MANUFACTURING COMPANY
MA804-130
AMES SHOVEL COMPANY
MA615-710
AMES, BLANCHE AMES
MA615-80
AMES, FISHER
MA235-150
AMES, NATHANIEL
MA235-150
AMES, OAKES
MA615-80
AMHERST, JEFFREY (1ST BARON
  AMHERST)
MA21-40
AMHERST, LORD JEFFREY (JEFFREY
  AMHERST, 1ST BARON AMHERST)
MA21-40
AMINO ACIDS
CT505-120
AMISH CHURCH
IA499-520
AMISH MENNONITES
  See also Mennonites,   *IA499-520,*
IN264-40
AMOS 'N' ANDY (RADIO PROGRAM)
NY591-690
AMOSKEAG CORPORATION
NH600-510
AMOSKEAG MANUFACTURING COMPANY
NH600-530
AMUSEMENT PARKS
CA114-880,   DC19-560,   NY590-760
  PARAGON PARK
MA425-520
AN ACCOUNT OF CORSICA, BY JAMES
  BOSWELL
CT505-977
ANABAPTISTS
OH92-520
  CANADA
OH92-520
  FRANCE
OH92-520

GERMANY
OH92-520
SWITZERLAND
OH92-520
ANATOMY
CA720-886
ANDERSON, LARZ, FAMILY
DC19-700
ANDERSON, MARGARET
WI456-810
ANDERSON, MAXWELL
TX56-890
ANDERSON, SHERWOOD
IN275-170, MI720-600
ANDERSON, VERNON
IL261-566
ANDERSONVILLE GA
NY101-70
ANDOVER THEOLOGICAL SEMINARY
MA593-40
ANDRADE, CARRERA
NY866-710
ANDRE, JOHN
NY878-320
ANDREWS, ADOLPHUS
TX273-160
ANDREWS, ALFRED
CT477-570
ANESTHESIA
CA720-894
ANESTHESIOLOGY
IL708-40
ANGELL, NORMAN
IN539-90
ANGLING
See Fishing
ANGLO-ROMAN UNION
NY318-260
ANGOLA
MISSIONARIES
CA143-280
ANIMALS
AZ250-520, CA712-630, FL220-792,
KY496-540
DISEASES
OH588-520
EQUALITY
NY125-740
HEALTH
KY496-540
WELFARE
CO252-30
ANKENBRAND, FRANK
PA726-600
ANTHONY WAYNE, BY HARRY EMERSON
WILDER
IN363-400
ANTHONY, SUSAN B.
NY752-720
ANTHROPOLOGY
AZ225-40, CA66-520, CA421-610,
CO252-152, CT505-980, CT603-360,
DC3-210, DC19-520, HI350-73,
ID640-360, MI40-814, MI518-50,
MT100-200, NJ464-240, NM722-30,
NY586-720, NY591-820, NY752-880,
OR848-40, PA90-500, WA820-840,
WI456-560
MOTION PICTURES
NM722-30
ORGANIZATIONS
DC19-520
PACIFIC OCEAN
WA820-840
ANTHROPOLOGY OF VISUAL
COMMUNICATIONS, SOCIETY FOR
THE
NM722-30
ANTI-COMMUNISM
SD450-150, WI456-495
ANTI-MASONRY
VT464-840
ANTI-SALOON LEAGUE OF AMERICA
OH203-600
ANTI-SEMITISM
OH171-20

ANTI-SHAKESPEAREANS
CA143-240
ANTI-WAR PROTEST
MO810-940
ANTIOCH COLLEGE
OH982-290
ANTIQUARIANS
MA849-750
ANTIQUES
NY590-360
ANTISLAVERY MOVEMENT
CT316-560, DE810-330, KY80-90,
LA600-160, MA17-400, MA231-640,
MA486-470, MA947-880, ME200-120,
MI40-820, NC260-170, NJ100-80,
NY51-730, OH181-880, OH505-520,
OH665-580, OH878-720, PA860-710,
VT296-690, VT464-840
APICULTURE
See Bees
APPALACHIA
GA840-240, KY80-70, KY80-90,
KY38U-470, KY464-800, KY630-40,
NC210-870, NC570-530, TN435-220,
VA195-200, WV650-890
FOLK MUSIC
NC570-530
APPALACHIAN MOUNTAINS
WILDERNESS
NC210-870
APPERSON, JOHN S.
VA90-840
APPLES
CA206-790, DC14-180
APPLETON ACADEMY
NH696-560
APPLETON FAMILY
MA169-590, MA606-720
APPLIANCES, ELECTRIC
See Electric appliances
APPRENTICES
NY757-400
AQUARIUMS
NY593-130
ARABIA
FOLK MUSIC
NY166-80
ARBITRATION
NY439-150
ARBORETUMS
PA512-400
ARBUCKLE, DANIEL
NY240-160
ARCHAEOLOGISTS
MI40-814
ARCHAEOLOGY
AZ175-120, AZ250-520, AZ800-800,
AZ900-560, CA410-120, CA421-610,
CA712-713, CO90-280, DC14-530,
DC14-540, DC14-640, HI350-73,
IA122-720, IA622-200, ID480-770,
ID640-360, KY496-518, MA169-305,
MI230-890, MI355-270, MI518-50,
MO800-730, MT100-200, NJ8-160,
NJ838-600, NM114-880, NM570-80,
NM646-280, NV870-480, NY591-820,
NY752-780, OR848-40, VA245-800,
VA315-310, VA810-40, WI98-400
ALASKA
ID480-770
ALBERTA, CANADA
ID480-770
BRITISH COLUMBIA
ID480-770
CALIFORNIA
ID480-770
CENTRAL AMERICA
RI105-320
CHANNEL ISLANDS
CA712-713
CLASSICAL
NY587-180
INDIANS
AZ800-803, WA578-520
MEXICO
AZ800-803, NY587-180

MIDDLE AMERICA
NM722-535
MIDDLE EAST
IL170-897
MONTANA
ID480-770
NORTH AMERICA
RI105-320, WA820-840
OREGON
ID480-770
PACIFIC NORTHWEST
ID480-770, WA943-245
PALESTINE
OH171-320
SOUTH AMERICA
CA421-610, RI105-320
SOUTHWESTERN US
AZ800-803, CA712-713, NM722-535,
NM874-440, NY587-180, TX326-770
UNDERWATER
NY101-720
WASHINGTON
ID480-770
ARCHDIOCESE OF LOUISVILLE
KY496-70
ARCHITECTS
CA86-820, CA480-530, CA578-675,
IN539-100, MA169-50, MN763-800,
NY588-900, NY591-380, OH181-325,
PA725-150
MARINE
DC19-636
WOMEN
CA86-820, NY587-190
ARCHITECTURAL DRAWINGS
CA410-120
ARCHITECTURAL HISTORIANS, SOCIETY
OF, MISSOURI VALLEY CHAPTER
MO430-800
ARCHITECTURE
See also Buildings, *AR510-680,*
AZ850-120, CA40-60, CA48-40,
CA86-820, CA136-90, CA410-120,
CA414-150, CA414-500, CA421-218,
CA421-250, CA480-510, CA488-720,
CA504-560, CA692-130, CA712-700,
CA712-708, CA712-720, CA720-316,
CA720-675, CA740-710, CA760-710,
CA782-720, CA958-640, CO108-85,
CO180-640, CO414-280, CT36-80,
CT316-520, CT316-560, CT316-750,
CT316-763, CT428-865, CT435-520,
CT505-960, DC1-480, DC4-450,
DC6-600, DC12-600, DC14-460,
DC14-530, DC14-540, DC14-640,
DC15-50, DC19-536, DC19-560,
DE810-690, FL80-120, FL580-320,
GA90-30, GA90-210, GA90-600,
GA810-80, IA88-120, ID160-130,
ID560-560, IL74-360, IL169-130,
IL169-325, IL169-416, IL170-273,
IL261-585, IL414-440, IL424-480,
IL649-600, IL866-355, IL866-480,
IN209-200, IN231-40, IN231-130,
IN539-100, KY94-845, LA62-430,
LA600-40, LA600-760, MA108-140,
MA108-940, MA109-680, MA109-720,
MA169-50, MA169-200, MA169-305,
MA169-340, MA169-625, MA334-120,
MA466-480, MA478-800, MA590-400,
MA590-720, MA606-530, MA606-560,
MA624-560, MA673-640, MA849-750,
MA964-880, MA970-890, MD76-30,
MD76-118, MD76-315, MD76-340,
MD76-650, MD114-330, MD266-80,
MD950-520, MD950-760, ME37-535,
ME62-80, ME712-280, ME725-880,
ME750-160, MI122-880, MI214-150,
MI230-148, MI235-160, MI605-520,
MI650-510, MN391-310, MN541-496,
MN541-925, MN625-550, MN763-800,
MN975-160, MO430-800, MO770-710,
MO810-600, MO810-940, MS300-550,
NC200-120, NC380-280, NC405-640,
NC620-520, NE284-560, NH772-640,
NJ8-160, NJ154-690, NJ266-520,
NJ804-120, NJ822-80, NJ926-840,

NM114-900, NM570-480, NV270-560, NY10-150, NY10-320, NY10-675, NY10-710, NY24-720, NY87-50, NY134-50, NY134-170, NY169-120, NY216-120, NY235-160, NY246-720, NY331-120, NY355-480, NY385-320, NY416-600, NY419-310, NY439-120, NY450-760, NY510-480, NY519-200, NY542-320, NY574-710, NY587-720, NY588-780, NY588-820, NY590-840, NY590-940, NY590-960, NY591-350, NY591-420, NY592-350, NY592-460, NY592-480, NY592-880, NY593-290, NY594-20, NY693-920, NY702-660, NY708-440, NY708-720, NY752-480, NY752-525, NY760-690, NY824-720, NY859-720, NY878-320, NY878-720, NY990-600, OH152-120, OH171-530, OH181-110, OH181-325, OH181-430, OH203-170, OH203-680, OK389-560, OR64-120, OR720-40, OR720-560, OR720-660, PA90-320, PA90-500, PA305-720, PA370-330, PA420-720, PA725-150, PA725-208, PA725-510, PA725-765, PA726-725, PA950-880, PR720-360, RI560-570, RI700-680, SC72-510, SC144-170, SC144-730, SC860-600, TX21-50, TX252-170, TX252-320, TX374-40, TX483-160, TX483-280, TX529-770, TX742-680, TX770-240, UT456-900, UT912-820, VA690-860, VA870-130, VT176-690, VT176-790, VT496-640, VT688-690, WA820-325, WA820-774, WA820-892, WA904-770, WI202-810, WI266-430, WI456-530, WI462-520, WY135-865, WY135-880, WY500-480

BOGGS AND BUHL (DEPARTMENT STORE)
PA986-960
CHURCHES
PA726-37, PA726-895, SC144-710
CONNECTICUT
DC19-560
EDUCATION
CA86-820
EUROPE
DC1-480, NY591-350
FRANCE
NY588-820
GREAT BRITAIN
NY588-820
HOSPITALS
PA735-515
ITALY
NY588-820
MARINE
WA820-828
MIDWESTERN US
IL169-826
ORNAMENTATION
NY587-80
PERU
LA600-760
SOUTHEASTERN US
LA600-761
THEATER
IL45-640, IN627-760
ARCHIVES
WA280-885
ARCTIC
AK350-800, ME175-80, MI518-50
CANADA
MI518-50
ARCTIC COAL COMPANY
MI464-530
ARCTIC REGION
EXPEDITIONS
ME175-80
EXPLORATION
ME162-100, ME162-120
ARENA (LITERARY MAGAZINE)
WI456-810
ARENDS, LESLIE C.
IL94-360
ARENSBERG, LOUISE STEVENS
MA606-720

ARENSBERG, WALTER CONRAD
CA143-240, MA606-720
ARGENTINA
NY588-940
BAPTIST CHURCH
TN690-740
MISSIONARIES
OH223-720
ARISTOTLE
DC19-641
ARIZONA
CA421-610, CA712-743, TX7-320
CHRISTIAN CHURCH
CA143-720
DISCIPLES OF CHRIST
CA143-720
GOVERNMENT AGENCIES, NATIONAL
CA386-560
PROTESTANT EPISCOPAL CHURCH
CA143-720
UNITED METHODIST CHURCH
CA143-720
ARKANSAS
GOVERNMENT AGENCIES, NATIONAL
TX374-550
ARLINGTON COUNTY VA
DC14-370
ARMBRUSTER SCENIC STUDIO
OH203-670
ARMED FORCES
See also Military history; and related terms. *NY594-20*
MEDICINE
DC1-760
WOMEN
AL560-720, DC1-200, DC1-340, MD57-820
ARMENGOL, ANTONIO
TX543-560
ARMENIA
CT316-330, DC1-775, MA84-50
IMMIGRATION AND EMIGRATION
DC1-775, MA84-50
ARMENIAN-AMERICANS
DC1-775, MA84-50
ARMENIANS
MASSACRES
DC1-775, MA84-50
ARMERDING, HUDSON T.
IL976-890
ARMISTEAD, GEORGE, FAMILY
MD76-240
ARMORY SHOW
DC19-340
ARMSTRONG, THOMAS J.
NC900-810
ARMY
AL560-720, CA720-550, DC3-320, HI350-770, IL94-510, KS513-250, NM513-560, NV90-530, PA165-790, VA430-280, VA580-520, WA320-230
AIRBORNE DIVISION 101
KY250-160
AIRBORNE DIVISION 11
KY250-160
ARMY AIR FORCE
FL750-200
AVIATION
AL380-800
CAMP FREMONT
CA456-530
CAVALRY
NY125-720
COAST ARTILLERY 248
WA681-250
COMMUNICATIONS EQUIPMENT
NJ270-800
CORPS OF ENGINEERS
DC1-805, DC1-810, DC19-636, MA871-540, MS300-550, PA726-7, VA245-800, WA820-550
ELECTRONICS EQUIPMENT
NJ270-800
FORT SPOKANE
WA240-250
FORT VANCOUVER
WA943-245, WA943-250

GREAT BRITAIN, 10TH FOOT REGIMENT
MA478-730
HOSPITALS
MD76-240
MCCARTHY HEARINGS
SD450-150
MEDICAL MUSEUM
DC1-760
MUSICIANS
SD936-950
QUARTERMASTER GENERAL
PA726-7
SEVENTH CAVALRY
MT100-200, MT270-130
TELEGRAPH BATTALION
NJ270-800
TRANSPORTATION
VA255-800
TRANSPORTATION CENTER AND SCHOOL
VA255-800
TRANSPORTATION CORPS
VA255-800
YOSEMITE NATIONAL PARK
CA994-940
ARMY BALLOON SCHOOL, WORLD WAR I
CA40-60
ARMY WAR COLLEGE
PA165-790
ARNOLD, BENEDICT
NY878-320
ARNOLD, WILLIAM R.
VA430-280
ARNOT, MATTHIAS H.
NY272-40
ARSENAL-COMMANDANT'S QUARTERS (DEARBORN MI)
MI214-150
ART
CA86-810, CA421-250, CA644-690, CA814-120, CA862-810, CT234-230, CT316-880, DC1-480, DC7-300, DC14-460, DC19-539, IL169-127, IL169-416, IN66-380, IN363-400, LA600-20, LA600-760, MA108-900, MA108-940, MA169-300, MA169-340, MA338-280, MD76-80, MD76-880, MI230-153, MI230-165, MN541-496, MO810-600, NM114-870, NM722-730, NY257-190, NY588-780, NY589-680, NY590-360, NY591-700, NY591-920, NY592-460, NY592-800, NY593-100, NY595-700, NY872-800, OH171-100, OH171-650, PA175-80, PA470-240, PA726-43, PA726-255, PA960-440, SC144-90, TN690-780, TX252-170, VT176-810, VT296-690, WA152-125, WA820-880
AFRICA
DC19-440, DC19-450
ARCHETYPAL IMAGERY
NY590-740
ARMORY SHOW
DC19-340
ASIA
MA169-400
ASIA, EASTERN
MI40-800
ASIA, SOUTHEASTERN
MI40-800
ASIA, SOUTHERN
MI40-800
BELGIUM
NY593-100
BLACKS
DC19-450
BRAZIL
DC3-226
COLLECTORS
DC3-750, MD76-80, NY587-780, OR720-660
COLONIES
CT596-480
COMIC
NJ464-240, VA690-830

CRITICS
IL806-695
DEALERS
DC3-750, MD76-880, MI230-153
EDUCATION
DC19-320, IN363-385, KY288-395, MI110-120, PA726-43, PA726-135
ETHNIC GROUPS
CA143-280
EUROPE
DC1-480, NY589-680, NY593-100
FOLK
VA870-40, VT784-720
GALLERIES
DC19-340
INDIANS
CA421-322, NM722-360, OR720-660
ISLAM
MI40-800
ITALY
NY593-100
JAPAN
DC12-150
LUXEMBOURG
NY593-100
MANUSCRIPTS
MA169-340
MEDICINE
MD76-880
MODERN
DC16-300, NY591-780
MUSEUMS
DC19-320, DC19-340, MO810-600, NY272-40, WA360-520
NETHERLANDS
NY593-100
ORGANIZATIONS
DC19-320, IL169-130, NY591-920
PERU
LA600-760
PHOTOGRAPHIC
DC19-626
PORTUGAL
DC3-226
SPORTS
KS746-640
THEFT
NY590-360
ART INSTITUTE OF CHICAGO
IL169-416
ARTHRITIS
OH181-180
ARTHURS, STANLEY MASSEY
DE810-150, PA175-80
ARTILLERY
OK372-240
ARTISANS
MA823-610, ME925-870, NY665-760
ARTISTS
AZ250-520, CA578-630, CA728-850, CA764-510, CA810-700, CA814-120, CT316-880, DC3-750, DC14-450, DC19-320, DC19-340, DE810-150, IA955-440, IL169-130, IL169-416, IN209-200, KY288-395, MA169-200, MA169-300, MD76-340, MD76-525, MD76-880, MI230-155, MS520-520, NJ578-530, NM266-720, NM722-730, NY51-730, NY134-710, NY416-600, NY586-180, NY589-680, NY591-380, NY591-700, NY591-920, NY844-720, NY866-520, NY899-520, OH823-770, OH906-320, OK829-520, OR224-800, PA726-270, SC144-90, SC144-730, TX374-40, UT684-80, VA870-40
BLACKS
NY588-340
BOTANICAL
PA735-140
EUROPE
OH823-770
FOLK
FL940-240
GREAT BRITAIN
DE810-150
WOMEN
NY591-920

ARTS
See also Performing arts, *DC16-680, MA624-740, NY586-330, NY593-970, NY612-690*
ASIAN-AMERICANS
CA421-322
BLACKS
CA421-322
DECORATIVE
DE900-320, NY824-720, PA90-40, PA725-150, VT784-720
VISUAL
DC19-320, MA169-860
WOMEN
CA414-490, DC14-450, DE810-150, IL169-130, MS520-520, TX56-200
ARTS AND LETTERS, AMERICAN ACADEMY OF
NY586-180
ARTS AND LETTERS, NATIONAL INSTITUTE OF
NY586-180
ASA MAHAN SOCIETY
KY886-50
ASBURY METHODIST CHURCH (ROCHESTER NY)
NY752-60
ASBURY, FRANCIS
DC23-500, MD76-790, TN690-885
ASCHER, LEO
PA595-530
ASHBY, JOHN J., FAMILY
WA672-160
ASIA
See also individual countries and regions, *CA858-320, HI350-73, OH171-650, PA725-510*
ART
MA169-400
ART COLLECTORS
NY587-780
BAHA'I
IL981-560
EASTERN
MA169-400
ECONOMIC AID TO
NY589-560
FOREIGN AID
DC1-180
HOSPITALS
PA725-908
MISSIONARIES
NJ222-333, NY529-530, PA725-908
RELIGION
MA169-400, NJ578-530
TRADE WITH UNITED STATES
MA338-840
ASIA, CENTRAL
GREAT BRITAIN, RELATIONS WITH
OH181-270
ASIA, EASTERN
CA143-80, DC1-480, DC1-560, DC3-210, DC7-650, DC12-150, DC12-450, DC13-210, DC14-250, DC14-730, DC14-770, DC14-780, DC19-310, DC19-327, DC19-500, DC19-520, DE540-790, HI350-770, MD285-805, MN541-854, NY439-156, UT912-110
ART
MI40-800
LITERATURE
CT505-890
MEDICINE
CA858-895
MISSIONARIES
IN297-600
TRADE WITH UNITED STATES
MA733-660
ASIA, SOUTHEASTERN
AL560-720, IL170-884, IN66-380, MI518-50, NJ578-530, NY439-156
ART
MI40-800
ASIA, SOUTHERN
DC12-150, MN541-822
ART
MI40-800

POLITICS
MN541-822
ASIAN-AMERICAN STUDIES
CA421-770
ASIAN-AMERICANS
ARTS
CA421-322
ASPEN INSTITUTE OF HUMANISTIC STUDIES
CO54-40
ASPEN MUSIC FESTIVAL
CO54-40
ASSASSINATIONS
DC6-650, DC14-410, FL820-810, MD255-720, NY775-720, TN630-530
ASSEMBLIES OF GOD
TX947-720
ASSOCIATE PRESBYTERIAN CHURCH
NC590-320
ASSOCIATED COLLEGES OF UPPER NEW YORK
NY101-720
ASSOCIATED EXECUTIVE COMMITTEE OF FRIENDS ON INDIAN AFFAIRS
IN704-200
ASSOCIATED REFORMED PRESBYTERIAN CHURCH
SC306-200
ASSOCIATION FOR CREATIVE CHANGE
OH223-800
ASSOCIATION OF COLLEGE AND RESEARCH LIBRARIES
DELAWARE VALLEY CHAPTER
PA725-375
ASSOCIATION OF COLLEGIATE ALUMNAE
DC1-340
ASSOCIATION OF GRADUATES, UNITED STATES MILITARY ACADEMY
NY949-780
ASSOCIATION OF LIVING HISTORICAL FARMS AND AGRICULTURAL MUSEUMS
DC19-591
ASTRONAUTICS
CA578-560, DC14-140, DC19-500, MA985-110, NM684-690, NY95-280, TX483-560
ASTRONAUTS
DC19-500
ASTRONOMERS
TN690-975
ASTRONOMY
AZ250-480, AZ250-575, CA86-780, CA756-320, CA782-800, CT505-960, DC7-650, DC12-300, DC14-120, DC14-750, DC19-500, DC19-641, IL170-884, MA169-170, MA169-650, MA572-540, MI40-784, MO210-815, NJ692-660, NY586-580, NY586-720, NY588-900, NY726-850, OH181-110, PA395-320, PA725-75, PA735-790, TN690-975, TX56-890, TX483-480, VA145-780, WI874-940
ASTROPHYSICS
AZ250-480, CA86-780, CA756-320, CA782-800, DC12-300, MA169-170, MA169-650, MI40-784, MO210-815, NJ692-660, NY586-580, NY588-900, NY726-850, OH181-110, PA395-320, PA725-75, PA735-790, TN690-975, TX56-890, VA145-780, WI874-940
ASYLUM COMPANY
PA55-760
ATCHISON, TOPEKA AND SANTA FE RAILWAY
KS878-430
ATHENS ACADEMY
PA55-760
ATHLETES
DC19-550, RI560-360
BASEBALL
IN990-280
ATHLETICS
See also Sports, *MA21-770, MD76-478, MS550-410, NY134-120, NY211-540, OK753-600, TX590-760, VA630-840*

ORGANIZATIONS
CA278-130, CA456-730
ATKINSON, HENRY
WI178-240
ATKINSON, MARY
WI178-240
ATL, DR. (PSEUDONYM OF GERARDO MURILLO)
CA274-120
ATLANTA DENTAL COLLEGE
GA90-210
ATLANTA SOUTHERN DENTAL COLLEGE
GA90-210
ATLANTIC & ST. LAWRENCE RAILROAD
ME162-120
ATLANTIC AND GREAT WESTERN RAILWAY
PA555-40
ATOMIC BOMB
MANHATTAN PROJECT
NM570-480
ATOMIC ENERGY COMMISSION
DC4-322, IL35-40, NM570-480
ATONEMENT, SOCIETY OF THE
NY318-260
ATTORNEYS
See also Legal profession, *CA712-700, CT505-977, ID80-365, IL169-52, IL170-280, KY96-870, KY496-800, MA169-440, MA797-400, ME925-870, MS20-120, NC850-120, NJ358-320, NM950-270, NY240-160, NY842-730, PA520-470, PA740-320, SC576-480, TN630-730, TX7-320, VA90-840, VT704-690, VT720-720, WA820-889, WI202-560*
ORGANIZATIONS
GA90-490
ATWATER, RICHARD M.
NY214-140
ATWATER, WILBUR OLIN
CT428-865
ATWOOD, WALLACE W.
MA985-100
AUBURN (AUTOMOBILE MODEL)
IN33-40
AUCHINLECK, SCOTLAND
CT505-977
AUCTIONS
PRICES
NY586-770
AUDIO-VISUAL COMMUNICATIONS ASSOCIATION OF MINNESOTA
MN742-720
AUGSBURG COLLEGE AND THEOLOGICAL SEMINARY
MN541-80
AUGUSTANA LUTHERAN CHURCH
IL170-91
MINNESOTA CONFERENCE
MN769-280
TEXAS CONFERENCE
TX56-490
AURORA COLONY
OR56-40
AURORA ELECTRIC LIGHT COMPANY
NY53-880
AURORAS
CO108-560
AUSTERLITZ CEMETERY ASSOCIATION
NY178-120
AUSTIN, ROSWELL
VT720-720
AUSTIN, STEPHEN F., FAMILY
TX777-160
AUSTIN, WARREN R.
VT720-720
AUSTRALASIA
BAHA'I
IL981-560
AUSTRALIA
MISSIONARIES
OH223-720
MORMONS
MO400-690

AUSTRIA
MA108-110, MN226-720, TX483-690
IMMIGRATION AND EMIGRATION
GA860-280
MISSIONARIES
OH223-720
AUSTRIAN-AMERICANS
MA108-110, WI38-480
AUTHORS
See also Literary figures; Literary manuscripts; Literature; Writers, *CA86-790, CA118-720, CA764-510, CO252-42, CT477-570, FL40-250, FL220-800, FL440-530, FL820-810, GA660-480, GA825-200, HI350-808, IA233-160, IA955-440, IL459-360, IL649-600, IL866-480, IL921-840, IN209-880, IN242-230, IN275-170, IN627-800, KS283-200, KY96-870, KY22W-920, KY304-280, KY496-825, KY564-520, KY604-640, MA21-400, MA123-80, MA217-520, MA615-730, MA636-880, MI925-560, MN763-800, NC100-280, NH206-800, NH600-510, NJ568-670, NJ692-660, NY51-90, NY134-730, NY169-120, NY272-120, NY272-200, NY588-900, NY592-680, PA395-320, PA725-195, PA725-510, PA726-412, SD126-480, TN690-600, TX404-120, TX625-640, VA285-520, VA360-320, VA470-690, VA690-830, WA724-890, WA880-190, WI298-480, WV375-640*
CHILDREN'S
ME825-730
EUROPE
DC19-641
GREAT BRITAIN
NY588-900, PA726-412, VA360-320
NEW ENGLAND
MN541-600
ROMAN CATHOLIC CHURCH
IN627-800
SOVIET UNION
MA21-770
WOMEN
FL220-800, IA74-480, IL261-570, IL459-520, IL976-890, IN704-520, KS283-200, KY496-825, KY61A-640, MA92-90, MA108-940, ME712-880, WA60-80
AUTOMATION
CT505-975
AUTOMOBILE INDUSTRY
DC19-601, IN33-40, IN132-310, IN539-83, IN792-160, MA871-870, MI214-260, MI230-880, MI255-545, MI314-60
AUTOMOBILE, AEROSPACE AND AGRICULTURAL IMPLEMENT WORKERS OF AMERICA, UNITED
MI230-880
AUTOMOBILES
CA282-480, IN33-40, IN132-310, MA871-870, MI230-165, PA415-720, PA560-690, VA215-40
DESIGN
NH600-530, PA560-690
GREAT BRITAIN
PA560-690
HORNS
PA415-720
MANUFACTURING
PA560-690
RACING
IN803-360
TRAFFIC
NC160-520
AVE MARIA (RADIO PROGRAM)
NY318-260
AVERY, DAVID
NJ692-610
AVIATION
See also Aeronautics, *CA143-480, CA421-390, CA770-40, CA778-780, CT186-800, CT505-960, CT963-120, DC19-500, IN935-650, MI230-800,*

MO430-420, NM114-35, NY101-720, NY367-270, NY367-320, NY588-940, OH223-810, TN630-730, TX56-890, TX742-800, VA50-530, WA724-890, WA820-613, WY500-800,
ARMY
AL380-800
EUROPE
TX742-800
MARINE CORPS
DC14-715
MILITARY
AL560-720, DC1-200, MD57-820
NAVY
DC14-715
WOMEN
OK592-570
AVIATORS
DC19-500, IN935-650, NY367-270, TX742-800
AYER, ALFRED J.
NY125-740
AYUNTAMIENTOS (SPANISH COLONIAL GOVERNMENT)
TX63-80
AZILUM
PA55-760

B

B.U.I.L.D.
NY134-85
B'NAI BRITH BUILDING ASSOCIATION
OR720-400
BABCOCK, W. WAYNE
PA726-600
BABSON, ROGER W.
MA891-80
BACH, JOHANN SEBASTIAN
CT505-976
BACHE, ALEXANDER DALLAS
PA725-495
BACHELLER, IRVING
NY899-520
BACON, A. O.
GA735-520
BACON, ALBION FELLOWS
IN209-880
BACON, FRANCIS
CA143-240
BACON, HENRY
CT428-865
BADIN, STEPHEN T.
KY569-720
BAHA'I
IL981-560
AFRICA
IL981-560
ASIA
IL981-560
AUSTRALASIA
IL981-560
CENTRAL AMERICA
IL981-560
EUROPE
IL981-560
SOUTH AMERICA
IL981-560
BAHAMAS
FL440-320, MN226-705, UT912-110
MISSIONARIES
MN749-720
BAIER, KURT
NY125-740
BAILEY FAMILY
MA606-720
BAIN, WINIFRED E.
DC1-860
BAIRD, SPENCER F.
DC19-310
BAJA CALIFORNIA
CA720-579
BAJA CALIFORNIA, MEXICO
CA712-726, CA720-910
BAKER FAMILY
MA154-480

BAKER, BRYANT
    OK634-640
BAKER, CHARLES F.
    PA185-160
BAKER, RAY JEROME
    HI350-315
BAKERIES
    LABOR
        MD575-333
BALDWIN RANCH
    CA40-480
BALDWIN SOUTHWARK CORPORATION
    DC19-601
BALDWIN, ANITA
    CA40-60
BALDWIN, E. J. (LUCKY)
    CA40-60
BALDWIN, JAMES H.
    NJ358-320
BALDWIN, JOHN F.
    CA594-120
BALL, JOHN
    MI355-270
BALL, LUCILLE
    NY591-690
BALLET
    OH203-670,   OH223-880
BALLOONS
    AL560-720,   CA40-60,   CA456-730,
    DC19-500,   IL806-705,   TX742-800
BALLOU, ADIN
    MA411-80
BALLOU, HOSEA, II
    MA528-780
BALTIMORE AND OHIO RAILROAD
    MD76-525,   MD304-80
BALTIMORE CATHEDRAL
    MD76-30
BALTIMORE CITY PLANNING
    DEPARTMENT
    MD76-800
BALTIMORE COUNTY ALMS HOUSE
    MD266-80
BALTIMORE MD
    LUTHERAN CHURCH IN AMERICA
        PA330-160
BANCROFT, MARY R.
    DE810-150
BANCROFT, SAMUEL, JR.
    DE810-150
BAND MUSIC
    See also Music
BANDON FIRES
    OR72-80
BANDS (MUSIC)
    CA782-730
BANK OF ROYALTON
    VT688-690
BANK OF THE MANHATTAN COMPANY
    NY588-60
BANK OF WESTERN PENNSYLVANIA
    PA555-120
BANKERS
    NC850-120,   NY978-880
BANKHEAD, TALLULAH
    NY593-485
BANKING
    CA676-130,   CA720-104,   CO252-780,
    DC9-450,   GA90-230,   IA33-370,
    ID80-365,   IL866-355,   IN363-342,
    KY496-800,   ME925-870,   MN728-690,
    MT430-320,   MT530-500,   NC850-120,
    NM950-270,   NY10-770,   NY358-760,
    NY537-320,   NY588-60,   NY588-940,
    NY592-460,   OH481-530,   PA555-120,
    PA725-615,   VA690-240,   VT688-690,
    WA489-40,   WA724-890,   WI142-800
    RURAL
        WA144-210
    WESTERN US
        CA720-960
BANKRUPTCY
    NY592-420
BANKS, S. D.
    VA315-310
BAPTIST ASSOCIATION
    IL644-80

BAPTIST ASSOCIATION, TAYLOR COUNTY
    KY126-120
BAPTIST CHURCH
    See also American Baptist church,
    AL120-720,   AR510-520,   FL140-240,
    GA180-280,   GA735-520,   IN242-230,
    KS718-600,   KY126-120,   KY520-530,
    LA600-540,   MI518-425,   MS260-500,
    NC100-280,   NC310-640,   NC570-530,
    NC930-840,   NY263-210,   NY484-480,
    NY752-110,   OK736-600,   RI700-240,
    SC450-240,   TN690-240,   TN690-740,
    TN690-750,   TX374-720,   VA690-815,
    WV775-40
    ARGENTINA
        TN690-740
    BLACKS
        NC930-840
    BRAZIL
        TN690-740,   TN690-750
    CLERGY
        IN242-230,   MA593-40,   MN763-80,
        NC840-720,   PA726-600,   TX374-720,
        VA690-815
    EDUCATION
        LA600-540
    GERMANY
        TN690-750
    GREAT BRITAIN
        TN690-750
    ISRAEL
        TN690-750
    MEXICO
        TN690-740
    MISSIONARIES
        MN763-80,   NC840-720,   NY752-110
    NEW ENGLAND
        MA593-40
    ORGANIZATIONS
        KY520-530,   NY895-240,   OK736-600,
        TN690-740,   TX604-220,   WV775-40
    SOUTHERN US
        TN690-740
BAPTIST GENERAL CONVENTION OF
    OKLAHOMA
    OK736-600
BAPTIST GENERAL CONVENTION OF
    TEXAS
    TX374-720
BAPTIST MISSIONARY TRAINING
    SCHOOL
    NY752-110
BAPTISTS, RUSSELL CREEK ASSOCIATION
    OF
    KY126-120
BAR ASSOCIATIONS
    IL169-52,   WA820-889
BARBADOS
    DC12-300,   MA109-120,   MA199-90,
    MA733-210,   MA871-40,   PA725-720,
    RI700-70
BARBER, SAMUEL
    PA725-345
BARBOUR, PHILIP L.
    KY496-825
BARFIELD, OWEN
    IL976-900
BARGES
    NY818-760
BARING, WALTER S.
    NV90-530
BARKLEY, ALBEN W.
    KY604-40,   KY604-640,   KY604-890
BARLOW, CLAUDE W.
    NY612-690
BARNARD, EDWARD E.
    TN690-975
BARNARD, GEORGE GREY
    PA726-255
BARNARD, HENRY
    CT316-770,   NY593-90
BARNES, EDWARD
    MA513-530
BARNES, JULIUS
    MN261-810
BARNES, SILAS
    MA513-530

BARNUM AND BAILEY CIRCUS
    IL624-380
BARNUM, PHINEAS TAYLOR
    CT36-80,   MA528-780
BARNUM, PHINEAS TAYLOR, FAMILY
    CT435-520
BARRIE, JAMES MATTHEW
    CT505-890
BARROW, JOSEPH LOUIS (JOE LOUIS)
    DC19-550
BARRY, DAVID F.
    MT100-200
BARRY, JOHN
    PA726-240
BARTEL, S. G.
    IN539-100
BARTLETT, ROBERT A.
    ME162-120
BARTOK, BELA
    NY166-80
BARTON, CLARA
    MA654-590
BARUS, CARL
    RI700-50
BASEBALL
    NY160-120,   NY211-540
    ATHLETES
        IN990-280
BASKETBALL
    FL80-820,   NY978-880
BASKETMAKERS
    CA143-280
BASKETS
    CA143-280
BASQUES
    EXHIBITIONS AND FAIRS
        NV940-800
    FRANCE
        NV940-800
    IMMIGRATION AND EMIGRATION
        NV940-800
    SHEEPHERDING
        NV940-800
    SPAIN
        NV940-800
    WESTERN US
        NV940-800
BASSE FAMILY
    PA986-960
BASSETT, WHEELER A.
    NY433-370
BATCHELLER, GEORGE SHERMAN,
    FAMILY
    NY795-320
BATH HOUSES
    AR390-760
BATTLEFIELD PARKS CORPORATION
    VA690-700
BATTLES
    DC14-715,   MD57-800,   MD57-830
    CONCORD
        MA478-730
    GALVESTON
        TX397-690
    LEXINGTON
        MA478-730
    LITTLE BIG HORN
        MT270-130,   SD414-640
    MANASSAS
        VA480-520
    MONMOUTH
        NJ276-510
    NEW ORLEANS
        LA600-310
    PLATTSBURGH
        VT784-720
    STONES RIVER
        TN675-720
    TIPPECANOE
        IN440-760
    WILSON'S CREEK MO
        MO730-800
    YORKTOWN
        VA870-150
BAUER, HAROLD
    CA720-623

BAUER, WALTER F.
CA132-160
BAUHAUS
MA169-200
BAY CITY TIMES
MI64-70
BEACH FAMILY
NY769-640
BEACH, AMY
NH206-800
BEACHES
MA425-520, NY590-760
BEACON HILL FREE SCHOOL
MA109-830
BEAL, ROBERT
IL429-520
BEAN FAMILY
TN750-690
BEAR CREEK ICE COMPANY
PA960-910
BEAR, SMOKEY
VA50-240
BEAUFORT COLLEGE AND FEMALE
SEMINARY
SC54-80
BEAUMONT, WILLIAM
MO810-960
BEAUTIFICATION
CIVIC
NY160-120
BEAVEN, ALBERT W.
NY752-40
BECHLY, ERNEST
WA124-480
BEDFORD FLAG
MA77-80
BEEBE, C. WILLIAM
NY593-130
BEECHER, HENRY WARD
NY310-160
BEECHER, LYMAN
CT316-560
BEECHMONT CIVIC CLUB
KY496-498
BEEKMAN FAMILY
NY878-720
BEERS, CLIFFORD
KS878-520
BEES
CA206-790
BEGALA, JOHN
OH399-420
BEGEL, J. J.
IA188-777
BEGEL, JOHN JOSEPH
PA908-720
BEISSEL, JOHANN CONRAD
PA415-400
BELCHERTOWN STATE SCHOOL,
FRIENDS OF THE
MA21-770
BELEN NM
RELIGIOUS COMMUNITIES
CA110-600
BELGIAN-AMERICANS
WI202-810
BELGIUM
ART
NY593-100
MISSIONARIES
NY459-520
BELIZE
RELIGIOUS COMMUNITIES
RI210-720
BELL TELEPHONE HOUR (RADIO AND
TELEVISION PROGRAM)
NY439-360
BELL, ALEXANDER GRAHAM
DC22-500
BELL, ALEXANDER MELVILLE
DC22-500
BELLAMY FAMILY
NY566-540
BELLAMY, JOHN HALEY
ME725-880 BELLAMY, PAUL E.
SD792-820

BELLOWS, GEORGE
ME725-880
BELVEDERE HOTEL CORPORATION
MD76-800
BELVOIR PLANTATION
VA245-800
BEN-GURION, DAVID
MA871-85
BENDER, ALBERT M.
CA540-520
BENDER, LAURETTA
NY588-300
BENEDICTINES
MO220-120, NC090-080, PA485-720
BENJAMIN PATTERSON INN
NY214-160
BENJAMIN, ASHER
MA109-680
BENNETT FAMILY
WI890-320
BENNETT, EDWARD H.
IL169-130
BENNETT, H. H.
WI890-320
BENNETT, JOHN GEORGE
IN440-160
BENNETT, WILLIAM
OH603-560
BENNINGTON COLLEGE
VT496-640
BENNY, JACK
CA421-760, CA421-766, NY591-690
BENTEEN-GOLDIN FAMILY
OK829-520
BENTLEY AUTOMOBILES
PA560-690
BENTLEY SCHOOL OF ACCOUNTING AND
FINANCE
MA871-60
BENTLEY, HARRY CLARK
MA871-60
BENTLEY, WILLIAM
MA528-780
BENTON, THOMAS HART
OH171-920
BERENSON, BERNHARD
DC14-450
BERING SEA PATROL (COAST GUARD)
WA820-147
BERKELEY FOLK FESTIVAL
IL261-570
BERLE, ADOLF A.
NY427-240
BERNDTSON, PETER
PA735-150
BERNHEIM FOREST
KY760-720
BERNSTEIN, DAVID
NY101-720
BERRY, DON
IA455-720
BERRY, E. Y.
SD720-80
BERRY, MARTHA
GA810-80
BERRYMAN, JOHN
NY125-740, OH181-130
BERTIE COUNTY HISTORICAL SOCIETY
NC915-320
BERTRAND (STEAMBOAT)
IA661-160
BESSEY NURSERY
NE240-560
BEST, ERNEST M.
MA804-710
BETHANY BIBLICAL SEMINARY
IL644-80
BETHEL A.M.E. CHURCH
NY134-85
BETHEL ACADEMY
KY886-30
BETHEL COLLEGE
KS676-520
BETHEL COLLEGE AND SEMINARY
MN763-80
BETHEL COLONY
OR56-40

BETHLEHEM PA
MUSIC
NC930-530
BETHLEHEM PROTECTIVE ASSOCIATION
NY818-760
BETTMAN, ALFRED
OH171-800
BETTMAN, GILBERT
OH171-800
BEXAR COUNTY MEDICAL SOCIETY
TX777-790
BEXLEY HALL
OH320-430
BIBLE
KS541-720, MA108-600, MA154-310,
MI255-545, NY586-280, PA130-50
WASHBURN
KS878-880
BIBLE CHRISTIANS
WI733-333
BIBLIOGRAPHY
OH203-650, TX56-890
BIBLIOPHILES
MI40-820
BIBRING, GRETE
MA871-85
BICENTENNIAL CELEBRATION
(PHILADELPHIA, 1976)
PA725-240
BICENTENNIALS
AMERICAN REVOLUTION
CA601-640, KY189-320, MS80-40,
NJ440-490, NY240-160, PA726-37,
WA168-135
BIDWELL FAMILY
CA136-90
BIDWELL, ANNIE
CA136-90
BIDWELL, JOHN
CA136-90
BIG BASIN STATE PARK
CA728-850
BIG BEND
TX14-720, TX374-40
BIG EIGHT CONFERENCE
MS550-410
BIG SANDY RIVER
KY2A-80
BIGELOW CARPET COMPANY
MA207-120
BIGELOW, DANIEL R.
WA616-400
BIGGS, E. POWER
DC19-570
BILBO, THEODORE GILMORE
MS490-810
BILLBOARDS
NJ464-240 BILLINGS BRIDGE
COMPANY
MT100-200
BILTMORE FOREST SCHOOL
NC60-240, NC680-550
BINGHAM, WILLIAM
NY101-90
BIO-MEDICINE
RESEARCH
NY593-840
BIOCHEMISTRY
MA169-650, PA725-75
BIOECOLOGY
MI518-50
BIOGEOGRAPHY
HI350-80
BIOGRAPHY
CT234-230, CT505-977, OK592-630,
PA726-725
BIOLOGY
DC14-100, IL409-440
MARINE
MI518-50
MOLECULAR
CA578-130
BIRDS
See also Ornithology, AZ250-520,
CA850-720
BIRDSELL MANUFACTURING COMPANY
IN792-160

BIRDSEYE, CLARENCE
MA338-280
BIRMINGHAM COLLEGE
AL120-110
BIRTH CONTROL
CA774-800, DC9-450, MA169-860,
MA624-740, MD76-800, MN541-902,
NY586-440
BISHOP FAMILY
IL856-730
BISHOP, JIM
NY775-720
BISHOP, R.
IN539-100
BISHOP, ROBERT H.
OH680-540
BISHOP, SERENO
HI350-315
BISON SOCIETY, AMERICAN
NY593-130
BIXBY FAMILY
CA414-500
BLACK HAWK WAR
IL866-355, IL866-365, WI178-240
BLACK HILLS
SD144-160, SD648-710, SD720-80
BLACK HILLS REGION
CO36-40
BLACK MOUNTAIN COLLEGE
LITERARY FIGURES
NY866-710
BLACK SASH
IL261-566
BLACK, FREDERICK
MI795-600
BLACK, GREENE YARDEMAN
IL170-429
BLACK, HARVEY
VA90-840
BLACK, JULIAN
DC19-550
BLACKS
AL120-100, AL580-510, AL620-20,
AL620-60, AL640-40, AL760-760,
AL840-820, AR330-830, AR510-25,
AZ800-30, AZ800-830, CA86-520,
CA86-630, CA118-720, CA143-470,
CA386-560, CA421-390, CA421-770,
CA540-590, CA644-690, CA676-110,
CA712-720, CA720-180, CA720-675,
CA756-320, CA774-800, CA858-320,
CA858-810, CO252-100, CT316-110,
CT316-120, CT316-560, CT316-770,
CT463-520, CT505-890, CT505-960,
CT512-120, CT772-720, CT779-785,
CT786-720, DC3-210, DC8-850,
DC12-300, DC14-250, DC19-320,
DC19-450, DC19-550, DE90-140,
DE810-330, FL440-150, FL800-200,
FL800-262, GA75-810, GA90-200,
GA90-360, GA90-490, GA90-700,
GA405-560, GA895-280, IA33-370,
IA233-360, IA455-720, IA466-800,
IA688-360, IL45-30, IL124-725,
IL169-325, IL169-416, IL170-283,
IL170-884, IL170-891, IL170-910,
IL261-566, IL394-500, IL866-355,
IL866-365, IL866-720, IL916-810,
IL976-890, IN209-880, IN231-470,
IN363-350, IN363-360, IN704-200,
IN792-720, KS527-790, KS527-795,
KS541-720, KS746-640, KS878-430,
KS948-890, KY80-90, KY288-440,
KY288-460, KY464-800, KY496-520,
KY496-765, KY496-800, KY496-812,
LA62-500, LA358-800, LA570-540,
LA600-20, LA600-160, LA600-310,
LA600-755, LA600-920, MA21-400,
MA21-770, MA92-70, MA108-140,
MA108-240, MA108-480, MA108-750,
MA108-965, MA109-120, MA169-370,
MA169-860, MA217-130, MA584-550,
MA590-720, MA624-240, MA624-740,
MA627-560, MA636-880, MA733-210,
MA733-660, MA776-530, MA871-40,
MA891-880, MA985-70, MA985-860,
MD57-500, MD76-360, MD76-515,
MD76-790, MD285-805, ME162-120,
MI40-784, MI40-808, MI40-820,
MI230-165, MI230-800, MI230-880,
MI550-505, MI550-530, MI665-120,
MN541-902, MN625-570, MN763-530,
MN763-540, MO210-815, MO240-280,
MO400-320, MO810-200, MO810-510,
MO810-690, MO810-920, MO810-940,
MS550-500, MS610-520, MS870-760,
MS970-520, NC100-280, NC150-800,
NC260-170, NC380-80, NC590-320,
NC680-460, NC730-480, NE560-550,
NH134-540, NH194-160, NJ280-270,
NJ568-670, NJ568-680, NJ578-510,
NJ692-660, NJ982-280, NV940-810,
NY10-80, NY10-640, NY51-90,
NY134-60, NY134-85, NY134-90,
NY211-580, NY427-240, NY439-120,
NY466-120, NY577-330, NY586-180,
NY588-900, NY588-940, NY592-460,
NY592-800, NY592-930, NY592-930,
NY593-120, NY593-380, NY593-710,
NY594-380, NY595-700, NY646-520,
NY752-740, NY752-880, NY804-720,
NY872-800, NY878-320, NY949-830,
OH147-520, OH171-20, OH171-110,
OH181-270, OH181-880, OH203-630,
OH223-790, OH223-880, OH301-690,
OH399-420, OH665-580, OH823-750,
OH878-720, OH939-860, OH953-870,
OH990-640, OK558-790, OK829-520,
OK922-720, OR224-800, PA85-730,
PA160-160, PA380-320, PA380-650,
PA395-320, PA470-460, PA555-40,
PA725-75, PA725-720, PA725-870,
PA726-630, PA726-713, PA726-775,
PA735-790, PA735-800, PA860-710,
PA895-710, PA945-120, RI560-570,
RI700-100, RI700-660, RI700-680,
SC144-170, SC144-730, SC216-720,
SC216-820, SC450-240, SC720-710,
SC860-600, TN465-800, TN630-530,
TN630-740, TN690-170, TN690-220,
TN690-510, TN690-740, TN690-780,
TN690-880, TN690-975, TN765-280,
TN840-800, TX56-800, TX56-850,
TX189-520, TX210-200, TX252-80,
TX252-170, TX252-730, TX397-690,
TX483-320, TX483-820, TX590-760,
VA145-780, VA310-320, VA630-640,
VA630-840, VA690-530, VA690-810,
VA690-870, VA690-910, VA870-110,
VA870-150, VI700-360, VT464-840,
WA820-880, WA904-770, WI250-690,
WI346-720, WI456-540, WI606-710,
WV650-890
ART
DC19-450
ARTISTS
NY588-340
ARTS
CA421-322
BAPTIST CHURCH
NC930-840
BUSINESS
DC14-350
COLLEGES
NY595-130
EDUCATION
AL760-760, DC1-160, GA90-700,
MS550-410, NY593-380, NY595-130,
VA670-900, WI456-730
EDUCATORS
GA780-310
LABOR
WI250-690
LITERATURE
NY592-930
MUSIC
AZ750-32, IN66-395, MI230-165,
NY592-930
ORGANIZATIONS
DC14-350, FL800-200, GA90-360,
GA90-490, IL170-312, IL261-566,
NY134-85, NY592-930, TX252-80,
VA20-322
ORPHANAGES
MD76-315
POETS
OH823-800
PUBLISHING
IN66-390
RELIGION
AL760-760, GA90-360
SOCIAL WELFARE
MA931-400
THEATER
GA735-540
WESTERN US
CA720-10
WITH JEWS IN CIVIL RIGHTS
MOVEMENT
NY586-650
WOMEN
MS550-410, NY51-730, VA20-322
BLACKSBURG COMMUNITY CONCERT
ASSOCIATION
VA90-840
BLACKSBURG METHODIST CHURCH
VA90-840
BLACKSBURG WOMAN'S CLUB
VA90-840
BLACKSMITHING
MA134-560, MA673-640, MA883-870
BLACKWELL, ALICE STONE
MA891-880
BLAIR, W. REID
NY593-130
BLAISDELL FAMILY
CA143-80
BLAISDELL, JAMES A.
CA143-80
BLAKE, EUGENE C.
PA726-713
BLAKELY, HAROLD
KY272-635
BLANCHARD, CHARLES
IL976-890
BLANCHARD, JONATHAN
IL976-890
BLANDSHARD, BRAND
NY125-740
BLAUSTEIN, JACOB
NY586-650
BLENNERHASSETT ISLAND
OH486-660
BLIND PERSONS
NY586-440, NY586-443
EDUCATION
WA943-725
BLINDNESS
NY586-443
BLISS, PORTER CORNELIUS
LA600-760
BLOCH, ALBERT
NY899-520
BLOCH, ERNST
CA86-890, CA720-623
BLOOD VESSELS
DC7-660
BLOOMER, AMELIA
IA177-240
BLOW, SUSAN ELIZABETH
DC1-860, MO810-690
BLUE FOUR (ARTISTS' GROUP)
CA578-630
BLUE RIDGE INSTITUTE FOR SOUTHERN
COMMUNITY SERVICE EXECUTIVES
FL800-262
BLUE RIDGE MOUNTAINS
FOLKLORE
VA235-230
BLUE RIDGE PARKWAY
NC60-810
BLUE, THOMAS F.
KY496-520
BLUFFTON COLLEGE
OH92-520
BOARD OF AID TO LANDOWNERSHIP
TN825-690
BOARD OF COMMISSIONERS OF STATE
INSTITUTIONS (FL)
FL800-245

BOARD OF CONTROL (OR)
OR816-590

BOARD OF EDUCATION (NEW YORK CITY NY)
NY588-970

BOARD OF EDUCATION (SARATOGA SPRINGS NY)
NY795-120

BOARD OF EDUCATION (WARREN OH)
OH878-880

BOARD OF FIRE COMMISSIONERS (TRENTON NJ)
NJ838-530

BOARD OF FOREIGN MISSIONS
IL261-566

BOARD OF HIGHER EDUCATION (NEW YORK CITY NY)
NY588-340

BOARDMAN, DANIEL
CT519-560

BOARDMAN, DOUGLAS
NY439-180

BOATS
AK400-720, MA293-200, NJ804-120, OH171-650, PA145-120
CHESAPEAKE BAY
MD770-120
ENGINES
WA904-890

BOE, LARS W.
MN625-710

BOETHIUS, ANICIUS MANLIUS SEVERINUS
DC19-641

BOGAN, LOUISE
MA21-40

BOGART, DANIEL, FAMILY
NY760-90

BOGGS AND BUHL (DEPARTMENT STORE)
PA986-960

BOGGS, MAE HELENE BACON
CA814-120

BOHEMIA
IRON INDUSTRY
MA108-750

BOHEMIAN-AMERICANS
MN405-320

BOLITHO, HECTOR
OH399-440

BOLIVAR, SIMON
PA725-615

BOLMAN, SILAS
MA513-530

BONAPARTE FAMILY
PA725-615

BONAPARTE, NAPOLEON
See Napoleon I (Emperor of France)

BOND, HORACE MANN
MA21-770

BONHAM, JERIAH
IL429-520

BOOK TRADE
CA143-480, MA985-70, PA415-400, PA726-615

BOOK-OF-THE-MONTH CLUB
NY588-940

BOOKS
CA143-480, DC12-650, MN226-720, MO810-920, NY592-680, NY905-840
ILLUSTRATION
NY592-970

BOONE, ALBERT G.
CA421-774

BOONE, DANIEL
CA778-800, VA290-760

BOOTH FAMILY
FL820-810

BOOTH, EDWIN
NY593-485

BOOTH, EVANGELINE
NY594-20

BOOTH, GEORGE C.
MI110-120

BOOTH, JOHN WILKES
DC6-650, FL820-810, MD255-720, MI795-600

BOOTT, FRANCIS
PA735-140

BORDEN'S DREAM (HISTORY OF WALTER REED ARMY MEDICAL CENTER)
DC23-70

BORNEO
EXPLORATION
KS164-520

BORNSTEIN, BERTA
NY592-640

BOSTON & SANDWICH GLASS COMPANY
MA738-720, MI214-280

BOSTON MANUFACTURING CO.
MA871-870

BOSTON SCHOOL (COMPOSERS)
MA109-440

BOSTON SYMPHONY ORCHESTRA
MA108-240

BOSWELL, JAMES
CT505-890, CT505-977

BOSWELL, JAMES, FAMILY
CT505-977

BOTANISTS
MA169-310, PA735-140

BOTANY
See also Plants, *AL840-280, CA86-910, CA143-690, CA278-130, CT505-980, DC14-180, FL960-690, GA90-270, IL74-360, LA570-540, MA169-190, MA169-270, MI518-50, MI650-530, MO810-490, NM114-825, NY592-320, OH203-650, OR464-490, PA725-75, VT448-520, WA724-890*
CHINA
DC14-180, MA169-190
CRYPTOGAMIC
MA169-270
INDIA
CA720-798, MA169-190
JAPAN
MA169-190
RUSSIA
DC14-180

BOTKIN, BENJAMIN
NE560-860

BOTTLING INDUSTRY
GA90-130

BOUDINOT, ELIAS
NJ280-270, NJ692-620, OK541-240

BOUGHTON FAMILY
NY910-840

BOUNDARIES
ME37-535, PA920-890
CANADA AND THE UNITED STATES
WA327-740
DISPUTES
NY588-860, WA327-740
MEXICO AND UNITED STATES
CA712-750, TX326-780
SURVEYS
GA90-270

BOUNDARY WATERS CANOE AREA
MN261-730

BOVA, BEN
PA726-615

BOWERS, CLAUDE G.
IN237-240

BOWERS, CLEMENT
NY101-90

BOWERS, LAMONT MONTGOMERY
NY101-720

BOWLING
FL560-40

BOWSER PUMP COMPANY
IN231-40

BOWSHER, N. P., MANUFACTURING COMPANY
IN792-160

BOXERS (ATHLETES)
DC19-550

BOY SCOUTS
WA820-966

BOY SCOUTS (GREEN RIVER WY)
WY365-710

BOYNTON, CHARLES
CO676-480

BOYS TOWN NE
IL245-322

BRACEROS (DAY LABORERS)
CA728-850

BRACKENRIDGE, HENRY MARIE
PA735-800

BRACKENRIDGE, HUGH HENRY
PA735-800

BRADFORD DURFEE TEXTILE INSTITUTE
MA612-720

BRADLEY, DAN BEACH
OH665-590

BRADLEY, OMAR M.
MO607-520

BRADLEY, PALMER
TX483-810

BRADSTREET FAMILY
MA606-720

BRADSTREET, ANNE
MA606-720

BRADY, MATHEW B.
CT477-130, DC12-600

BRAGDON, CLAUDE
NY752-480

BRAHMS, JOHANNES
DC12-510, PA725-345

BRAIN, ALFRED
IN539-86

BRAINERD FAMILY
VT720-720

BRAND, OSCAR
NY588-300

BRANDEIS, LOUIS DEMBITZ
KY496-800

BRANDT SCHOOL
SD41-160

BRANDYWINE (SHIP)
WI814-510

BRANNING, HENRY
IN231-40

BRATTER, HERBERT H.
DC19-646

BRAVO, MANUEL
DC3-760

BRAZIL
DC3-226, NC590-320
ART
DC3-226
BAPTIST CHURCH
TN690-740, TN690-750
FRANCISCANS
MD703-40
MISSIONARIES
KS213-560

BREMERTON NAVAL SHIPYARD
WA84-720

BRETHREN IN CHRIST CHURCH
PA340-520

BRETON, JULES
MO810-880

BREVOORT, HENRY
NY878-720

BREWERIES
DC19-601, MI230-740

BREWSTER, WILLIAM
MA169-500

BRICKS
MANUFACTURING
NY818-760, WA152-125

BRIDGES
DC1-680, ME925-870, MT100-200, NE288-400, NY272-720, NY890-700
CONSTRUCTION
DC19-601

BRIDGES, HARRY R.
CA720-356

BRIDGES, STYLES
NH396-560

BRIGGS AND NELSON (ARCHITECTURAL FIRM)
OH181-325

BRIGGS, LUTHER
MA109-680

BRIGHAM FAMILY
MA513-530

BRINGHURST FAMILY
DE810-690

BRISTOL TN
VA120-80
BRITISH ACTORS ORPHANAGE FUND
NY593-485
BRITISH COLUMBIA
WA820-770
ARCHAEOLOGY
ID480-770
BROADCASTING
NY588-940, WI456-495
BROOK FARM
MA109-120
BROOKHOUSER, FRANK
PA726-600
BROOKLYN BRIDGE
NY890-700
BROOKLYN MUSIC SCHOOL
NY587-500
BROOKS, PHILLIPS
MA606-720
BROOKSIDE SCHOOL
MI110-120
BROOMALL, ANNA
PA185-160
BROOME COUNTY MEDICAL SOCIETY
NY101-720
BROTHERHOOD OF FIREMEN AND
ENGINEERS
WA856-100
BROTHERHOOD OF LOCOMOTIVE
ENGINEERS
IA244-480
BROTHERHOOD OF LOCOMOTIVE
FIREMEN
IN825-200
BROTHERHOOD OF RAILROAD
TRAINMEN
TX280-540
BROWN, EDGAR A.
SC185-120
BROWN, EDMUND GERALD (PAT)
CA86-810
BROWN, ELAM
CA54-120
BROWN, FRANK CHOUTEAU
MA109-680
BROWN, FRED R.
NY10-770
BROWN, GEORGE
CA132-160, NH600-510
BROWN, JOHN
MO620-80
BROWN, JOHN W.
OH26-40
BROWN, MARGARET WISE
RI910-880
BROWN, OLYMPIA
OH986-40
BROWN, RALPH M.
VA90-840
BROWN, THOMAS A.
CA594-120
BROWN'S SCHOOLHOUSE
NC260-150
BROWNE, GEORGE H.
NH772-640
BROWNING FAMILY
NJ280-270
BROWNING, ELIZABETH BARRETT
MA891-880, TX56-890, TX933-65
BROWNING, ROBERT
MA891-880, TX56-890, TX933-65
BRUMBAUGH, MARTIN GROVE
PA415-400
BRUNSWICK-ALTAMAHA CANAL
GA885-120
BRUTUS, DENNIS
IL261-566
BRYAN, WILLIAM JENNINGS
CA421-510
BRYANT FAMILY
IL762-80
BRYANT, BILLY
OH181-270
BRYANT, WILLIAM CULLEN
MA961-870, NY760-90

BRYOPHYTES
CA278-130
BUCHANAN, JAMES
PA160-160, PA470-240, PA725-720
BUCHANAN, JOSEPH
KY464-760
BUCHTEL COLLEGE
OH11-810
BUCK, JONATHAN
ME175-80
BUCK, PEARL S.
WV200-880, WV375-640
BUCK, PEARL S., FAMILY
WV375-640
BUCKLEY FAMILY
MO920-120
BUDDHISM
*CA720-886, DC12-150, DC19-327,
MA169-400*
BUDENZ, LOUIS F.
RI700-630
BUFFALO BILL
See William F. Cody
BUFFALO COOPERATIVE ECONOMIC
SOCIETY
NY134-85
BUFFALO SOCIETY OF ARTISTS
NY134-710
BUFORD, S. R., COMPANY
MT430-320
BUHL FAMILY
PA986-960
BUILDING SUPPLIES
NY851-720
BUILDING TRADES
MA169-50
BUILDINGS
See also Architecture; Historic
preservation, *CA578-675, CA764-510,
CA838-720, CO768-640, CT254-320,
CT316-750, CT512-120, CT793-440,
CT863-280, DC3-550, DE900-320,
GA895-290, HI400-480, ID80-375,
ID400-720, IL169-729, IL354-80,
IL384-320, IL414-440, IN77-200,
IN363-342, KS80-40, KS527-160,
KY76Y-760, KY834-480, MA278-200,
MA624-700, MD76-478, MD266-80,
MD580-120, MI828-720, MO350-280,
MT180-880, NE288-400, NJ822-80,
NY24-720, NY197-120, PA415-320,
PA740-320, PR720-360, WA123-333*
CONSTRUCTION
DC14-552
BUKOFZER, MANFRED
CA86-890
BULFINCH, CHARLES
ME37-535
BULKELEY, GERSHOM
CT316-310
BULKLEY, CHARLES
OR720-450
BULL, EPHRAIM WALES
MA217-130
BULLIET, CLARENCE
IL806-695
BULLOCK, WYNN
AZ320-820
BUNDY, OMAR
IN572-320
BUNN, BENNETT
NC710-540
BURCHFIELD, CHARLES EPHRAIM
NY134-710
BUREAU OF CATHOLIC INDIAN MISSIONS
WI456-495
BUREAU OF CUSTOMS
*CA386-560, CA704-560, MA285-160,
MA584-550, MA733-210, MA871-540,
ME275-160, ME462-440, ME762-640,
MI775-520, NJ46-560, NY772-720,
PA726-7, RI560-570, WA820-550*
BUREAU OF EDUCATION AND CULTURAL
AFFAIRS
DC9-580

BUREAU OF INDIAN AFFAIRS
*CA386-560, CO252-550, IL170-280,
TX374-550, WA820-550*
ST. LOUIS SUPERINTENDENCY
KS878-430
BUREAU OF INDIAN AFFAIRS, CROW
AGENCY
MT100-200
BUREAU OF LAND MANAGEMENT
CA386-560, CO252-550, WA820-550
BUREAU OF RECLAMATION
CO252-550
BUREAU OF THE MINT
WA820-550
BURGES, WILLIAM
CT316-763
BURGTHEATER (VIENNA, AUSTRIA)
OH203-670
BURK, J. H.
RI910-880
BURKE, EDMUND
CT505-977
BURKE, KENNETH
PA895-710
BURKE, THOMAS M. A.
NY10-675
BURLESQUE
NY593-485
BURLINGTON COUNTY ABOLITION
SOCIETY
NJ100-80
BURMA
MN541-822
BURNELLI AIRCRAFT COMPANY
CT963-120
BURNHAM AND ROOT (ARCHITECTURAL
FIRM)
IL169-130
BURNHAM, D. H., AND COMPANY
(ARCHITECTURAL FIRM)
IL169-130
BURNHAM, DANIEL H.
IL169-130
BURNTVEDT, T. O.
MN763-50
BURR FAMILY
NJ339-40
BURR, AARON
MA961-870, NJ339-40
BURRITT, ELIHU
CT477-130, CT477-570
BURROW, TRIGANT
CT926-480
BURTON CONGREGATIONAL CHURCH
OH112-80
BURTON, LAWRENCE
UT456-900
BURWELL SCHOOL
NC430-340
BUSES
NJ918-520
TERMINALS
NJ918-520
BUSH, C. J.
NY303-600
BUSINESS
General references to Business *have been
deleted due to frequency of terms.*
ADMINISTRATION
CA86-50
BLACKS
DC14-350
EDUCATION
NY752-665, OH181-400
INCORPORATION
NY592-420
LEGISLATION
TX252-780
ORGANIZATIONS
*CA524-160, DC14-350, KY380-720,
KY598-600, NC200-120, NV940-560,
NY59-80, NY433-350, TN435-220,
WA366-640*
BUSINESS AND PROFESSIONAL WOMEN'S
CLUB (JAMESTOWN KY)
KY380-720

BUSINESS AND PROFESSIONAL WOMEN'S CLUBS, INTERNATIONAL FEDERATION OF
DC14-420

BUSINESS AND PROFESSIONAL WOMEN'S CLUBS, NATIONAL FEDERATION OF
DC2-850

BUSINESS RECORDS
General references to Business records have been deleted due to frequency.

BUSINESSPERSONS
CA132-160, CA720-180, DC2-850, DC14-420, GA245-110, MA776-515, MD76-525, MI230-165, MI314-265, MN763-510, OR352-900, OR720-590, PA425-360, PA735-790, SC144-730, TN465-800

BUTLER FAMILY
CT891-550, MA615-80

BUTLER, BENJAMIN FRANKLIN
MA615-80

BUTLER, E. G. W., FAMILY
LA600-310

BUTLER, EVA L.
CT603-360

BUTLER, WILLIAM
NY241-160

BUTLER, ZEBULON
PA960-910

BUTTONS
MANUFACTURING
CT870-520

BUTTRICK, WALLACE
NY612-690

BUTZ, EARL L.
IN935-650

BYINGTON, JOHN
MI90-30

BYNNER, WITTER
NH206-800

BYRNES, JAMES FRANCIS
SC185-120

BYRON, GEORGE GORDON (6TH BARON BYRON)
IN825-850, TX56-890

BYRON, LORD (GEORGE GORDON BYRON, 6TH BARON BYRON)
IN825-850, TX56-890

C

CABELL, JAMES BRANCH
VA690-830

CABILDOS (SPANISH COLONIAL GOVERNMENT)
LA600-465

CABLE, GEORGE WASHINGTON
LA600-755

CADY FAMILY
NY605-280

CADY, ISAAC
NY563-322

CAFETERIAS
See Restaurants

CAHILL SCHOOL
MN275-200

CAIRO, EGYPT
KARAITES
CA86-385

CALDWELL, CHARLES
KY464-760

CALDWELL, JANET TAYLOR
NY134-90

CALHOUN, JOHN CALDWELL
SC144-130, SC185-120

CALIFORNIA
NE624-400
ARCHAEOLOGY
ID480-770
CHRISTIAN REFORMED CHURCH
MI355-110
FRANCISCANS
MD703-40
GOLD RUSHES
NY288-840, NY990-600

INDIANS
AK500-20, AZ800-30, AZ800-800, AZ800-830, DC12-300, DC19-520, IL169-729, IL170-351, IL170-884, IN66-385, KY496-765, MA169-170, MA733-210, MA985-70, MI40-784, MI40-814, MI230-165, MI665-120, MN763-540, MO400-320, MO810-200, MO810-510, NV940-810, NY427-240, NY439-120, NY586-720, NY587-780, NY591-820, NY592-460, NY592-800, OH301-690, OK558-790, OK592-640, OK829-520, OR448-450, PA395-320, PA725-720, UT912-110, UT912-840, UT912-850, VA145-780, VA145-780, WA681-400, WA820-880, WI346-720

SISTERS OF PROVIDENCE
WA820-820

TRAVEL
WA880-790

WRITERS
PA726-600

CALIFORNIA FEDERATION OF TEACHERS
CA524-160

CALIFORNIA SOUTHERN RAILROAD
CA582-600

CALIFORNIA SPEECH AND HEARING ASSOCIATION
CA278-130

CALIFORNIA STATE UNIVERSITY AND COLLEGES
CA744-120

CALIFORNIA, NORTHERN
INDIANS
OR96-120

CALIFORNIA, SOUTHERN
INDIANS
MO210-840

CALL, DANIEL
VA690-810

CALLAHAN, HARRY
AZ800-820

CALLERY, IDA HAYMAN
KS746-640

CALLERY, PHIL
KS746-640

CALLIOPES
NY563-322

CALVERT FAMILY
MD76-515

CAMBODIA
REFUGEES
NY10-160

CAME, CHARLES
NY288-840

CAMELLIAS
SC144-170

CAMERON, DUGALD
NY87-900

CAMERON, SIMON
PA380-320

CAMEROON
MISSIONARIES
NY459-520

CAMP CRESCENDO
KY760-720

CAMP FIRE CLUB
NY593-130

CAMP FREMONT (ARMY)
CA456-530

CAMP GRANT
WORLD WAR II
IL806-710

CAMP MEETINGS
VA400-520

CAMP SHANTITUCK
KY760-720

CAMPBELL, ALEXANDER
WV100-80

CAMPBELL, PERSIA
NY569-120

CAMPBELL, THOMAS
WV100-80

CAMPBELL, WILLIAM (BOOKSTORE)
PA726-615

CAMPION, S. B.
NY858-720

CAMPS
NY593-132

CANADA
See also individual provinces, *IA74-480, IN627-780, NC590-320, NH600-30*
ANABAPTISTS
OH92-520
ARCTIC
MI518-50
CARMELITE ORDER
IL55-120
CHRISTIAN REFORMED CHURCH
MI355-110
DUTCH-AMERICANS
IA855-150
EDUCATION, MEDICAL
DC1-890
FRIARS MINOR CONVENTUAL
NY741-720
GAY RIGHTS MOVEMENT
CT316-360
HOSPITALS
DC1-890
IMMIGRATION AND EMIGRATION, FROM NETHERLANDS
MI355-110
IMMIGRATION AND EMIGRATION, FROM UKRAINE
MI230-780
INDIANS
SD792-800
LUTHERAN CHURCH IN AMERICA
IL170-91
MENNONITE BRETHREN
CA274-130
MENNONITE CHURCH
IN264-40
MENNONITES
OH92-520
MISSIONARIES
NY459-520, OH223-720
ORTHODOX CHURCH
NY870-600

CANADA, MARITIME PROVINCES
FOLKLIFE
ME650-780
FOLKLORE
ME650-780

CANADA, WESTERN
JEWS
CA86-400

CANADIAN-AMERICANS
NH600-30

CANAL ZONE
MD755-560

CANAL ZONE BIOLOGICAL STATION
DC14-100

CANALS
See also individual canals, *AZ435-520, AZ600-200, CT268-720, CT505-560, DC1-805, DC7-650, DC19-130, DC19-591, GA885-120, IL464-880, IL866-355, IN143-120, IN363-342, IN913-900, MA70-70, MA478-800, MD304-80, NJ804-120, NY229-560, NY269-200, NY714-560, NY752-530, NY752-720, NY757-400, NY821-520, NY872-120, NY941-600, NY949-830, OH545-530, OH990-640, PA55-760, PA90-480, PA270-320, PA410-880, PA740-320, PA960-910, PA965-490, VA165-120, VT496-640*
CENTRAL AMERICA
DC1-805
CONSTRUCTION
DC19-591, FL60-720, PA875-80
TRAVEL
NY10-160

CANBY, EDWARD RICHARD SPRIGG
AL580-530

CANDLER SCHOOL OF THEOLOGY
GA90-190

CANNING
DE270-200
FRUIT
WA726-640

CANOEING
MN261-730
CAPE CANAVERAL
FL420-240
CAPE COD
MA242-160
CAPE COD, BY HENRY DAVID THOREAU
MA894-880
CAPE KENNEDY
FL420-240
CAPE VERDE CLUB
CA720-10
CAPEN, PARSON, HOUSE
M.4849-750
CAPITAL PUNISHMENT
AZ550-040
CAPITAL TRANSIT COMPANY
DC3-550
CAPITOL RECONSTRUCTION
COMMISSION (OR)
OR816-590
CAPITOL, U.S.
DC1-480, DC1-810
CARBERRY, JOHN JOSEPH
IN440-160
CARELTON, WILL
MI440-320
CARIBBEAN
See also Danish West Indies; West Indies;
and individual islands, CA86-780,
CA756-320, CT316-110, CT316-120,
CT772-720, DC1-40, DC1-180,
DC1-560, DC3-210, DC3-226, DC7-650,
DC8-850, DC12-600, DC12-650,
DC13-210, DC14-250, DC14-720,
DC14-730, DC14-780, DC15-500,
DC19-310, DC19-520, DE90-140,
DE810-330, DE900-330, FL220-800,
GA895-280, IL169-325, IL170-351,
IL170-884, IN66-380, KS527-790,
LA600-755, MA108-140, MA108-240,
MA108-750, MA109-120, MA169-170,
MA169-370, MA199-90, MA733-210,
MA733-660, MA871-40, MA985-70,
MD76-515, MI40-784, MI40-820,
MI1230-165, MS550-500, NC150-800,
NC680-460, NH784-630, NY10-640,
NY427-240, NY439-120, NY588-900,
NY590-680, NY591-820, NY592-460,
NY592-800, NY592-930, NY872-800,
OH171-20, PA90-500, PA725-75,
PA725-285, PA725-405, PA725-885,
PA860-710, RI700-70, RI700-680,
RI700-740, SC144-730, SC216-720,
TX56-860, VA145-780, VA560-520,
VA690-870, VA870-110, VA870-150
ETHNOGRAPHY
FL220-792
LITERATURE
DC12-200
MORAVIAN CHURCH
PA90-500
NATURAL HISTORY
FL220-792
CARLANDER, GUY
TX21-50
CARLISLE INDIAN SCHOOL
PA160-120
CARLSON FAMILY
IA58-540
CARLYLE, THOMAS
CA782-800
CARMELITE ORDER
DC23-700
CARNATION COMPANY
CA421-766
CARNEGIE CORPORATION
NY588-940
CARNEGIE FOUNDATION FOR THE
ADVANCEMENT OF TEACHING
NJ692-210
CARNEGIE FREE PUBLIC LIBRARY (KY)
KY598-600
CAROUSELS
DC19-560
CARPENTER, DANA S.
VT448-520

CARPENTER, EDMUND N.
PA960-910
CARPETS
MANUFACTURING
MA207-120
CARR, JAMES
CA778-800
CARR, JUNE H.
SC414-110
CARRANZA, VENUSTIANO
CA274-120
CARREL, ALEXIS
DC7-660
CARRIAGE INDUSTRY
CA282-480, NH134-540, WI554-480
CARROLL, AUSTIN
LA600-690
CARROLL, CHARLES
CA720-910
CARROLL, LEWIS
See Charles Lutwidge Dodgson
CARTER, GEORGE C.
NH600-510
CARTER, JIMMY
INAUGURATION
NY591-690
CARTER, MARSHALL S.
VA430-280
CARTER, MYRA INMAN
TN90-130
CARTOGRAPHY
See also Maps, AR510-25, CT505-970,
DC12-190, DC14-370, GA90-270,
IL624-370, KS878-430, MS50-560
EUROPE
PA325-280
GREAT BRITAIN
CT505-970
CARTOONS
DC14-552, NY411-320
ANIMATED
CA114-880, CA421-763
EDITORIAL
CA862-630
POLITICAL
IL169-416
CARUSO, ENRICO
MD76-640
CARVER, GEORGE WASHINGTON
IA455-720, MO240-280
CARVER, JOHN
PA725-150
CASCADE MOUNTAINS
WA832-560, WA904-770
CASE INSTITUTE OF TECHNOLOGY
OH181-110
CASE SCHOOL OF APPLIED SCIENCE
OH181-110
CASE, CLIFFORD P.
NJ568-670
CASE, FRANCIS
SD522-160
CASEMENT, DANIEL D.
KS607-450
CASEMENT, STEVEN J.
KS607-450
CASEY, ROSEMARY
PA735-150
CASSATT, MARY
DC14-450, IL169-130
CASSEBEER, WALTER
NY752-480
CASSEL, ABRAHAM HARLEY
PA415-400
CASTRO, HENRY
TX777-670
CATHEDRAL CHAPTER LIBRARY (MONZA,
ITALY)
IN627-810
CATHER, WILLA SIBERT
NE736-560
CATHERINE II (EMPRESS OF RUSSIA)
MD76-880
CATHERINE THE GREAT
See Catherine II (Empress of Russia)
CATHOLIC CHURCH
See Roman Catholic church

CATHOLIC CHURCH EXTENSION SOCIETY
IL170-78
CATHOLIC INDIAN MISSIONS, BUREAU
OF
WI456-495
CATHOLIC MEDICAL BOARD
NY318-260
CATHOLIC NEAR EAST WELFARE
ASSOCIATION
NY318-260
CATHOLIC RELIGIOUS ORDER OF OUR
LADY OF MOUNT CARMEL
See Carmelite Order
CATS
CA290-280
CATSKILL MOUNTAINS
NY219-290, NY574-710, NY574-730
CATSKILL-CANAJOHARIE RAILROAD
NY254-160
CATT, CARRIE CHAPMAN
MA624-740
CATTLE
AZ750-10, CA274-120, DC19-591,
DE900-330, NY263-210, NY763-680,
NY905-840, TX181-780
BRANDS
AZ435-520
RANCHING
AZ435-520
SOUTH DAKOTA
CO36-40
CATTLEMEN
MO810-390
CATTON, BRUCE
SC144-150
CAVALRY ASSOCIATION, SECOND NEW
JERSEY
NJ838-530
CAVES
AL440-560, NY200-720
CAVING
AL440-560
CAWSTON'S OSTRICH FARM
CA850-720
CAYCE, EDGAR
VA810-40
CAYUGA AND SENECA CANAL
NY821-520
CAYUGA LAKE ACADEMY
NY53-880
CELEBRATIONS
IN92-80, IN143-120, KY496-725,
VA50-50, WA517-560, WI890-320
CEMETERY COMPANIES
CA640-640, NJ266-520, NY178-120,
PA185-160, WA322-240
CENSUS
AR360-40, CA180-160, DC3-550,
IL866-355, IN363-342, KY526-520,
MA109-220, MI775-710, MO210-840,
NC680-460, NY71-720, NY87-50,
NY292-520, NY321-480, NY323-280,
NY550-520, NY648-330, NY752-530,
NY858-720, NY909-850, OH778-40,
PA915-870, RI700-740, TX56-800,
VT464-820, WI382-520, WI794-880
CENSUS OF THE CITY AND TOWN OF
WATERBURY, CONNECTICUT, 1876,
BY STURGES M. JUDD
CT870-730
CENTENNIAL EXHIBITION
(PHILADELPHIA 1876)
PA725-240
CENTERVILLE PUBLIC LYCEUM
MA180-120
CENTRAL AMERICA
See also Latin America; South America;
and individual countries and regions,
AZ800-803, CA86-780, CA712-570,
LA600-760, NY592-30
ARCHAEOLOGY
RI105-320
BAHA'I
IL981-560
CANALS
DC1-805

ETHNOLOGY
RI105-320
POLITICIANS
LA600-760
CENTRAL CONFERENCE OF AMERICAN
RABBIS
OH181-730
CENTRAL DISPENSARY AND EMERGENCY
HOSPITAL
DC23-250
CENTRAL WESLEYAN COLLEGE
MO460-560
CENTURY OF PROGRESS EXPOSITION
(CHICAGO)
IL170-273
CERAMICS
DC19-545, MI40-800, PA575-80
MANUFACTURING
DC19-545
CERLETTI, UGO
KS878-520
CHADDOCK COLLEGE
IL94-360
CHADEAYNE FAMILY
NY878-720
CHAFFIN, JAMES
VA690-810
CHAIKEN, JOSEPH
OH399-440
CHALCRAFT, EDWIN C.
WA736-440
CHAMBER OF COMMERCE
NEW ORLEANS
LA600-775
CHAMBER OF COMMERCE (BOULDER CO)
CO108-85
CHAMBER OF COMMERCE (MANHATTAN
KS)
KS607-690
CHAMBER OF COMMERCE (PASCO WA)
WA647-270
CHAMBER OF COMMERCE (SAN
FRANCISCO CA)
CA720-180
CHAMBER OF COMMERCE (SEATTLE WA)
WA820-774
CHAMBERLIN, WILLIAM H.
RI700-630
CHAMBREAU, EDOUARD
OR720-700
CHAMIER, DANIEL
CA368-120
CHAMINADE, WILLIAM
OH223-720
CHANNEL ISLANDS
ARCHAEOLOGY
CA712-713
CHANNING, WILLIAM ELLERY
IL170-195
CHANTS
HI350-73
CHAPIN, E. Y.
KY62G-120
CHAPMAN, DAVID
TN285-280
CHAPMAN, ISAAC A.
PA960-910
CHAPPAQUA MOUNTAIN INSTITUTE
NY172-120
CHARCOAL IRON INDUSTRY
MI343-280
CHARITIES
IL169-651, IN363-342
ORGANIZATIONS
MA894-880, ME437-120, OH97-80,
TN690-880
CHARLES COUNTY MD
DC14-370
CHASE NATIONAL BANK
NY588-60
CHASE, PHILANDER
IL723-80, OH320-430
CHASE, SALMON P.
PA725-720
CHASE, STEPHEN
NH784-720

CHATHAM TURNPIKE
NY178-120
CHATHAM VILLAGE LITERARY SOCIETY
NY178-120
CHATHAM, EARL OF (WILLIAM PITT)
CT505-977, PA735-800
CHAUTAUQUA MOVEMENT
PA726-600
CHAVEZ, DENNIS E.
NM114-800
CHEMICAL INDUSTRY
DE270-200, NJ990-322
CHEMISTRY
DC19-631, DC19-641, NY890-700,
PA726-765
AGRICULTURE
CT428-865
EUROPE
PA726-765
NORTH AMERICA
PA726-765
CHEMISTS
MA606-530
CHEROKEE STRIP
KS52-120
CHERRY TREES
DC14-180
JAPAN
DC14-180
CHERRY, FRANCIS
AR890-20
CHESAPEAKE AND OHIO CANAL
MD304-80
CHESAPEAKE AND OHIO RAILWAY
VA560-333
CHESAPEAKE BAY
MD836-120
BOATS
MD770-120
LIGHTHOUSES
MD770-120
CHESAPEAKE, BY JAMES A. MICHENER
MD323-520
CHESEBROUGH FAMILY
CT772-720
CHESLER, HARRY
NJ464-240
CHESLOCK, LOUIS
MD76-640
CHESNUTT, CHARLES WADDELL
OH181-270
CHESS
OH181-270
CHESTER RURAL CEMETERY
PA185-160
CHESTER UNITED METHODIST CHURCH
PA185-160
CHESTERTON, GILBERT KEITH
IL976-900, OH843-400
CHEVIGNY, HECTOR
WA880-290
CHIAPAS, MEXICO
MO210-840
CHICAGO AND NORTH WESTERN
RAILROAD
WI530-520
CHICAGO AUDITORIUM ASSOCIATION
IL170-637
CHICAGO COMMUNITY RENEWAL
SOCIETY
IL169-507
CHICAGO INTER-STUDENT CATHOLIC
ACTION
IL170-78
CHICAGO RAILROAD FAIR (1950)
IL170-273
CHICAGO WHITE STOCKINGS (BASEBALL
TEAM)
IN990-280
CHICAGO, BURLINGTON AND QUINCY
RAILROAD
IL170-351
CHIEF OF NAVAL OPERATIONS, OFFICE
OF
DC14-730
CHIHUAHUA, MEXICO
AZ225-40, TX326-800

CHILD DEVELOPMENT
OH11-840
CHILD WELFARE LEAGUE (KALAMAZOO
MI
MI518-445
CHILDREN
MO810-590, NY595-180, OH11-840
ABUSE
NY594-20
COPY BOOKS
NJ838-630
FACTORY WORKERS
NY586-440
GREECE
OH11-840
HOSPITALS
NY687-120
INDIAN CAPTIVES
TX259-880
LABOR
NY586-440
LITERATURE
AR890-20, DE900-320, KS283-200,
ME825-730, MN541-838, MS490-810,
OH788-870, OK42-560, RI910-880
NIGERIA
OH11-840
NORTH AMERICA
OH11-840
ORGANIZATIONS
DC1-860, GA895-290, IN704-200,
NY589-720, WY365-710
PROTECTION
CO252-30
PSYCHOANALYSIS
NY587-300
SOCIAL WELFARE
MA109-830, NJ568-670
WELFARE
IL170-910, MI518-445, MN541-902,
NY594-20
CHILDS, GEORGE W.
PA725-375
CHILE
PA420-720
MISSIONARIES
DC15-50, IL55-120, OH223-720
CHINA
See also Taiwan, CT505-960, DC12-190,
MA169-400, MA169-590, MA891-880,
MN763-510, NJ578-530, NJ692-660,
NY439-156, NY592-30, NY612-690,
NY949-830, PA735-825, VA430-280,
WI456-730
BOTANY
DC14-180, MA169-190
BOXER REBELLION
CA712-713
CHURCH OF THE BRETHREN
IL241-120
DIPLOMACY
NY439-156
IMMIGRATION AND EMIGRATION
WA820-966
MEDICINE
CA720-886
MING DYNASTY
MA169-400
MISSIONARIES
CT505-900, DC15-50, IL45-30,
KY464-490, KY57W-720, MA81-80,
MI445-880, MN749-720, MN763-50,
MN763-510, NC390-200, NC590-320,
NJ568-570, NY439-156
ORGANIZATIONS
HI350-295
RELIGIOUS COMMUNITIES
IL866-320
TRADE WITH UNITED STATES
CT772-720, MA554-530, MA733-210
WORLD WAR II
IN297-600
CHINA RELIEF EXPEDITION
NY949-830
CHINA TRADE WITH UNITED STATES
PA725-615

CHINATOWN FACTFINDING COMMITTEE
CA720-220

CHINESE
IN HAWAII
HI350-295

CHINESE CONSTITUTIONALIST PARTY
CA720-220

CHINESE EMPIRE REFORM ASSOCIATION
WA820-886

CHINESE-AMERICANS
CA86-630, CA274-250, CA720-220,
DC1-920, HI350-295, LA600-20
ORGANIZATIONS
WA820-886
PACIFIC NORTHWEST
WA820-966

CHIVERS, THOMAS H.
KY464-760

A CHOICE OF BOOKS, BY ISABELLA
  STEWART GARDNER
MA108-940

CHRIST CHURCH CRANBROOK
MI110-120

CHRIST CHURCH HOSPITAL
PA726-37

CHRIST EPISCOPAL CHURCH
GA735-540

CHRIST REFORMED CHURCH
  (BEARYTOWN NY)
NY928-880

CHRIST'S CHURCH (RYE NY)
NY766-690

CHRISTENBERRY, WILLIAM
DC3-760

CHRISTIAN BROTHERS
TN630-120

CHRISTIAN CHURCH
See also Disciples of Christ, *CA86-630,*
CA86-780, CA143-720, IN363-125,
KY54G-520, NC310-200, TN690-170
ARIZONA
CA143-720
CLERGY
KY464-490
GREAT BRITAIN
IN363-125
VIRGINIA
NC310-200

CHRISTIAN FAMILY MOVEMENT
IN627-780

CHRISTIAN HOLINESS ASSOCIATION
KY886-50

CHRISTIAN REFORMED CHURCH
IA855-150, MI355-110
CALIFORNIA
MI355-110
CANADA
MI355-110
COLORADO
MI355-110
MIDWESTERN US
MI355-110
NEW JERSEY
MI355-110
NEW YORK
MI355-110
WASHINGTON
MI355-110

CHRISTIAN SCIENCE CHURCH
MA108-600

CHRISTIANITY
DC19-327, IN902-80, KY464-780,
MO894-800, PA725-700
REFORMATION
MO810-190

CHRISTIANSBURG INSTITUTE
VA670-690

CHRISTIANSEN, F. MELIUS
MN625-710

CHRISTMAS
OH788-870

CHRISTY, ARTHUR
IL976-890

CHURCH HISTORY
See also Religion; and individual
denominations and faiths, *CA862-810,*
DC6-800, FL660-120, GA180-280,
KY126-120, MA108-580, MI40-784,
MI214-150, MI390-720, NM722-570

MIDWESTERN US
KS878-880
NETHERLANDS
IA811-110

CHURCH MISSIONARY SOCIETY
IL261-566

CHURCH OF CHRIST
CA436-640, KY22W-920

CHURCH OF GOD
IN22-50

CHURCH OF JESUS CHRIST OF
  LATTER-DAY SAINTS
See Mormons

CHURCH OF THE BRETHREN
KS593-510, PA285-200, PA415-400,
VA115-80
CHINA
IL241-120
CLERGY
PA285-200
ECUADOR
IL241-120
INDIA
IL241-120
NIGERIA
IL241-120
ORGANIZATIONS
IL241-120

CHURCH OF THE NAZARENE
TN690-850
HOLINESS ASSOCIATIONS
MO430-120
IOWA
MO430-120
MISSIONARIES
MO430-120
NORTH DAKOTA
MO430-120
NORTHEASTERN US
MO430-120
SOUTHEASTERN US
TN690-850
TENNESSEE
MO430-120
TEXAS
MO430-120
WESTERN US
MO430-120

CHURCH OF THE NEW JERUSALEM
MA590-720, PA130-30

CHURCH OF THE UNITED BRETHREN IN
  CHRIST
MN541-777, NJ464-666

CHURCH RECORDS
See Church history; Religion; and
individual denominations and faiths

CHURCH UNITY OCTAVE
NY318-260

CHURCH-STATE RELATIONS
KY496-850

CHURCH, FREDERIC EDWIN
NY416-600

CHURCH, JOHN BARKER
NY32-50, NY87-900

CHURCH, PHILIP
NY32-50, NY87-40, NY87-900,
NY228-110

CIGAR STORE FIGURES
DC19-560

CIGARMAKERS' UNION, GREEN BAY (WI)
  LOCAL
WI202-560

CINCINNATI ADVERTISER (NEWSPAPER)
OH171-920

CIRCUSES
CT36-80, DC1-680, IL624-380,
MI255-530, NY101-690, NY845-720,
TX777-720, WI70-120
HISTORIANS
WI70-120

CIST, JACOB
PA960-910

CITIES
CT779-785, DC1-680, MI518-455,
TX374-40, WA880-190
EDUCATION
NY588-970

CITIZENS UNITED FOR RACIAL EQUALITY
CA712-750

CITIZENSHIP
NY592-420, WI794-880

CITRICULTURE
CA601-640, CA770-120

CITRUS FRUIT
CA278-130

CITY FEDERATION OF WOMEN'S CLUBS
  (WARREN OH)
OH878-880

CITY PLANNING
See also Regional planning, *DC7-540,*
IL414-440, IN539-100, MA169-305,
MD76-650, MD76-800, NJ138-120,
NJ950-520, NY590-960, OH54-80,
PA90-500, PA726-630, WA495-500

CIUDAD JUAREZ, MEXICO
TX326-780, TX326-800

CIVIL DEFENSE
WORLD WAR I
NY899-600
WORLD WAR II
CT870-730

CIVIL ENGINEERING
See Engineering, civil

CIVIL ENGINEERS, AMERICAN SOCIETY
  OF
NY589-460

CIVIL LIBERTIES
CA86-520, MA21-770, NY586-640,
NY866-710

CIVIL LIBERTIES UNION OF
  MASSACHUSETTS,
  HAMPSHIRE-FRANKLIN COUNTY
  CHAPTER
MA21-770

CIVIL RIGHTS
See also Race relations, *AL120-100,*
AL580-800, AL760-760, AR510-810,
CA86-520, CA712-120, CA720-10,
DC2-200, DC8-850, GA90-200,
IN363-342, LA600-555, MD76-525,
MO810-800, MO810-940, MS870-760,
NY586-640, NY586-650, NY588-850,
NY588-940, OH171-20, VA20-322,
WI346-720
LAW
MS870-760
ORGANIZATIONS
GA90-360, GA90-490, MI40-808,
MS870-760
SOUTHERN US
CA858-790

CIVIL RIGHTS MOVEMENT
GA90-490
BLACKS AND JEWS
NY586-650

CIVIL RIGHTS, U.S. COMMISSION ON
MS870-760

CIVIL SERVICE
OH301-690

CIVIL WAR
See also Confederate States of America;
Grand Army of the Republic, *AL580-530,*
AL840-820, AR60-120, AR360-40,
AR890-30, CA274-120, CA436-640,
CA628-40, CA756-320, CA774-800,
CA858-810, CA862-810, CT36-80,
CT120-120, CT144-150, CT144-880,
CT268-720, CT316-330, CT316-770,
CT323-320, CT477-570, CT519-560,
DC1-760, DC6-650, DC12-600,
DC19-621, DE60-240, GA90-200,
GA765-440, GA895-160, GA915-280,
IA188-650, IA211-480, IA466-360,
IA511-450, IA600-322, IA922-280,
IL74-360, IL94-510, IL109-130,
IL169-325, IL169-416, IL170-884,
IL212-280, IL296-720, IL301-280,
IL609-120, IL674-880, IL762-80,
IL767-320, IL866-355, IL866-365,
IN77-200, IN154-880, IN242-250,
IN363-360, IN649-520, IN649-650,
IN913-900, KS513-250, KS513-720,
KS541-720, KS878-430, KY5M-520,
KY96-870, KY464-880, KY496-765,

LA62-500, LA465-480, LA570-540,
LA600-310, LA600-465, LA600-755,
LA885-690, MA25-520, MA108-10,
MA109-220, MA109-460, MA207-120,
MA246-160, MA250-160, MA506-520,
MA624-560, MA761-320, MA904-80,
MA964-880, MA970-890, MD76-60,
MD152-720, MD380-160, MD798-40,
ME37-535, ME162-120, ME750-160,
ME825-730, MI40-784, MI40-820,
MI64-70, MI255-545, MI505-760,
MI518-455, MI675-510, MI765-640,
MN14-560, MN835-720, MO730-800,
MO920-120, MS20-200, MS550-500,
NC30-715, NC260-170, NC680-460,
NC850-120, NC900-810, NE624-400,
NH134-530, NH600-510, NH832-720,
NJ276-510, NJ838-530, NJ982-280,
NM912-280, NY51-240, NY101-70,
NY107-200, NY125-720, NY147-600,
NY150-700, NY214-160, NY228-110,
NY247-160, NY272-120, NY288-840,
NY292-520, NY439-180, NY566-540,
NY569A-56, NY599-560, NY618-120,
NY618-280, NY660-600, NY672-440,
NY699-480, NY732-520, NY752-720,
NY830-520, NY915-870, NY923-880,
NY973-600, OH181-880, OH199-320,
OH301-690, OH370-310, OH788-120,
OH823-750, OH982-290, OK778-560,
PA25-480, PA55-760, PA160-120,
PA270-200, PA275-120, PA325-280,
PA500-70, PA555-40, PA645-560,
PA725-930, PA726-508, PA726-600,
PA740-320, PA920-870, PA920-890,
RI700-45, RI700-100, RI700-640,
RI700-680, SC144-150, TN630-740,
TN675-720, TN690-975, TN765-280,
TX7-320, TX56-800, T TX210-230,
TX280-540, TX397-690, TX476-320,
TX483-690, TX691-130, TX777-160,
TX890-720, VA275-240, VA285-240,
VA285-520, VA430-870, VA480-520,
VA550-520, VA580-570, VA630-640,
VA640-650, VA670-690, VA690-530,
VA690-760, VA690-870, VT296-690,
VT464-840, VT496-640, WA880-260,
WA943-240, WI142-120, WI178-240,
WI346-280, WI346-720, WI382-520,
WI462-520, WI706-720, WI794-880,
WV225-860

DRAFT (MILITARY)
  NY106-80
MILITARY PERSONNEL
  ME460-440
NURSING
  NY115-720
PRISONERS OF WAR
  DE60-240
VETERANS
  NH588-520, NH672-570, NY672-440
CIVIL WAR VETERANS (NEW BRITAIN CT)
  CT477-570
CIVILIAN CONSERVATION CORPS
  CO252-550, NC60-240, NM570-80,
  OR560-690, TX56-780, VT704-280,
  WV350-560
CLARA DE HIRSCH HOME FOR WORKING
  GIRLS
  NY593-132
CLARK COUNTY NV
  GOVERNMENT AGENCIES, NATIONAL
  CA386-560
CLARK, BADGER
  SD522-160
CLARK, JOHN S.
  NY51-140
CLARK, KATE FREEMAN
  MS520-520
CLARK, MARK W.
  SC144-150
CLARK, STEPHEN W.
  NY251-320
CLARK, WILLIAM
  KY604-890, OR720-450
CLARKSON FAMILY
  NY466-120

CLAWSON FAMILY
  NY562-510
CLAWSON, CHARLES DELAND
  NY562-720
CLAY, HENRY
  KY464-760
CLEMENS, SAMUEL LANGHORNE
  See also Mark Twain, *CA86-790,*
  CT316-560, MO370-520, MO870-520,
  NY134-90, NY272-120, NY272-200,
  NY310-160
CLEMENS, SAMUEL LANGHORNE,
  FAMILY
  CT316-520, MO370-520
CLEMENT MANUFACTURING COMPANY
  MA804-130
CLEMENT, ADA
  CA720-623
CLEMMER, J. D.
  TN90-130
CLERGY
  CT4-160, CT505-900, KS108-70,
  KY96-870, KY514-120, LA600-20,
  MA108-140, MA169-230, MA528-780,
  MA823-610, ME112-400, MN321-690,
  MN763-790, MO810-270, NH194-160,
  NH820-690, NJ266-520, NJ692-610,
  NY187-120, PA90-80, PA986-960,
  RI910-880, SC72-510, WV575-640
  AFRICAN METHODIST EPISCOPAL
    CHURCH
    OH939-860
  BAPTIST CHURCH
    IN242-230, MA593-40, MN763-80,
    NC840-720, PA726-600, TX374-720,
    VA690-815
  CHRISTIAN CHURCH
    KY464-490
  CHURCH OF THE BRETHREN
    PA285-200
  CONGREGATIONAL CHURCH
    IL169-507, MA593-40, NY272-640,
    NY334-280
  EPISCOPAL CHURCH
    AL120-200, AL580-650, CT316-210,
    DC5-800, DE810-170, IL169-651,
    IL866-200, KS878-200, KY496-200,
    MA108-580, MO810-590, NC680-200,
    NH784-700, NY134-660, NY589-710,
    NY593-290, NY752-220, NY872-150,
    OH171-165, OH181-430, OR464-322,
    OR720-200, PA726-37, SC144-710,
    SD684-200, TN630-200, TX56-25,
    TX252-200, TX326-160, TX777-640,
    UT912-200, WA820-200, WI498-560
  EVANGELICAL COVENANT CHURCH
    IL169-677
  EVANGELICAL UNITED BRETHREN
    CHURCH
    OH223-790
  JUDAISM
    OH181-730
  LUTHERAN CHURCH
    LA600-775, MD76-490, NY591-35,
    PA25-520, PA325-490, TX56-490
  LUTHERAN CHURCH IN AMERICA
    PA725-885
  LUTHERAN CHURCH-MISSOURI SYNOD
    SD684-480
  METHODIST CHURCH
    GA885-520, IL261-280, MD76-790,
    MS550-540, NE560-810, NM200-800,
    PA555-40, TN690-885, TN690-890,
    TX7-800, TX252-760
  MORAVIAN CHURCH
    PA90-320
  NORWEGIAN LUTHERAN CHURCH
    IA211-480
  ORTHODOX CHURCH
    NY870-600
  PRESBYTERIAN CHURCH
    NY569A-56
  REFORMED CHURCH IN AMERICA
    MI445-880

  ROMAN CATHOLIC CHURCH
    AR480-320, AR510-145, DC1-740,
    DC3-210, DC14-380, DC14-580,
    IA188-777, IL55-120, IL866-320,
    IN363-50, IN440-160, IN627-720,
    IN627-780, IN627-800, KY57W-720,
    LA358-160, LA358-165, LA600-40,
    MD76-30, MD380-160, MI230-50,
    MN763-100, MO220-120, MT530-690,
    NJ798-720, NY10-675, NY587-930,
    NY752-560, NY752-760, OH171-50,
    OH171-730, OH203-170, OR720-40,
    PA380-700, PA485-720, PA725-45,
    PA726-105, RI210-720, SC144-190,
    TN690-690, VT176-690, WI698-730
  SWEDISH-AMERICANS
    IL801-20
  UNITARIAN CHURCH
    IL170-195
  UNITARIAN UNIVERSALISTS
    MA109-750
  UNITED BRETHREN IN CHRIST
    IN352-800
  UNITED CHURCH OF CHRIST
    PA470-800
  UNITED METHODIST CHURCH
    AL620-320, IA688-360, IL94-800,
    IN275-150, KS962-800, MN541-777,
    NJ464-666, NJ658-840
  UNIVERSALIST CHURCH
    IL170-195
CLEVELAND CITY CLUB
  WEEKLY FORUMS
    OH181-310
CLEVELAND CLINIC
  OH181-180
CLEVELAND CLINICAL CLUB
  OH181-180
CLEVELAND LAW SCHOOL
  OH181-290
CLEVELAND MEDICAL LIBRARY
  ASSOCIATION
  OH181-180
CLEVELAND-MARSHALL COLLEGE OF
  LAW
  OH181-290
CLEVELAND-MARSHALL LAW SCHOOL
  OH181-290
CLIMATE
  NC60-160, NC656-720
CLINTON WIRE CLOTH COMPANY
  MA207-120
CLINTON, DEWITT
  NY310-160, NY599-880
CLINTON, GEORGE
  NY599-880
CLOCK MAKERS
  CT48-40, MA837-720
CLOCKS
  DC19-606
  MANUFACTURING
    CT48-40
CLOSE BROTHERS COMPANY
  MN674-630
CLOTHING
  DC19-555, MI122-880, NY587-840,
  NY866-520
  PATTERNS
    NY587-840
  WOMEN
    IL192-510
CLOUDS
  ND486-810
CLOUGH, GEORGE LAFAYETTE
  NY51-730
CLUNY, FRANCE
  MA169-305
CLYDE PROGRESS CLUB
  OH194-120
COAL
  DE270-200, PA726-855, PA740-320,
  PA960-910, WY365-710
COAL MINING
  AK500-20, AL120-100, AR330-830,
  CA86-780, CA421-770, CA756-320,
  CO108-740, CO108-810, CO252-80,
  CO252-100, CO252-181, CO768-640,

DC1-500, DC3-210, DC12-300,
DC14-250, DC19-591, DE270-200,
DE540-790, IA33-370, IA233-360,
IA466-360, IA466-800, IA966-320,
IL124-725, IL169-325, IL170-351,
IL170-637, IL170-884, IL170-910,
IL866-365, IL866-715, IL866-720,
IL916-810, IN66-380, IN363-350,
IN363-360, IN627-780, IN704-200,
IN825-200, IN902-840, KS10-170,
KS878-430, KY2A-80, KY96-870,
KY288-425, KY38U-470, KY464-800,
KY496-765, KY496-785, KY504-310,
KY569-720, KY630-40, MA108-750,
MD57-500, MD76-515, MI214-260,
MI230-165, MI230-880, MI255-530,
MI464-530, MI550-505, MI824-320,
MN763-540, MN763-790, MO210-815,
MO400-320, MT130-540, MT530-500,
NC150-800, NM114-900, NM722-570,
NY427-240, NY439-150, NY588-900,
NY588-940, NY592-460, NY592-800,
NY612-690, NY752-880, NY872-800,
OH35-40, OH181-880, OH203-600,
OH301-690, OH399-420, OH588-520,
OK558-790, OK592-620, OR224-800,
OR720-580, PA160-160, PA380-650,
PA725-15, PA725-60, PA725-75,
PA735-790, PA920-890, TN60-120,
TN465-800, TN690-780, TX252-730,
TX590-760, UT684-80, UT912-820,
UT912-850, VA145-780, VA195-200,
VA690-910, WV225-860, WV435-520,
WV650-890, WY135-865, WY500-800

MACHINERY
DC19-591
COAST GUARD
CT512-800, DC19-621, MA871-540,
MD57-820, MD57-830
ALASKA
WA820-147
PACIFIC NORTHWEST
WA820-147
COASTAL AREAS
MD755-560
COBB FAMILY
TN750-690
COBB, IRVIN S.
KY604-640, KY680-190
COBBETT, WILLIAM
NY315-30
COBURN AND BARNUM (ARCHITECTURAL FIRM)
OH181-325
COCKE FAMILY
VA360-320
CODMAN FAMILY
MA109-680
CODMAN, OGDEN, JR.
MA109-680
CODY, WILLIAM F.
CO458-80
COFFIN FAMILY (NEWBURY, MA)
MA109-680
COFFINBERRY, WRIGHT L.
MI355-270
COGGIN, WALTER
NC090-080
COGHILL, GEORGE ELLETT
KS527-790, KS527-790
COLD SPRING WHALING COMPANY
NY205-880
COLD WAR
KS10-170
COLE, THOMAS
MI230-155
COLGATE THEOLOGICAL SEMINARY
NY752-110
COLLEGE ENTRANCE EXAMINATION BOARD
NJ692-210
COLLEGE OF CALIFORNIA
CA86-815
COLLEGES
See also Education; Universities; and
names of specific institutions in repository
index, IL94-800, IL354-80

BLACKS
NY595-130
COLLEGE IN THE COUNTRY CONCEPT
GA210-880
COLLINS AND AUTENRIETH
PA725-150
COLLINS COMPANY
CT108-120
COLLINS, W. J.
CO36-40
COLLINS, ZACCHEUS
PA725-15
COLMER, WILLIAM M.
MS490-810
COLOMBIA
MISSIONARIES
IL169-677, OH223-720
COLOMBUS, DIEGO
OK829-520
COLONIAL PERIOD (AMERICAN)
DC12-190, IN902-840, MA108-240,
MA776-515, MI40-820, PA735-825
COLONIAL POLICY
GREAT LAKES
IL916-795
COLONIES
DENMARK
VI300-240, VI700-360
FRANCE
AL580-510, GA895-160, IN902-840,
LA358-800, LA600-465, LA600-505,
LA600-555, MO810-510, MS550-500,
NY634-160, PA55-760
GREAT BRITAIN
FL220-795, FL660-120, IN902-840,
LA358-800, MS550-500, NC150-790,
VA870-150, VI700-360
MEXICO
CA782-800, NM722-570, TX56-800,
TX56-860, TX777-160, TX777-810
NETHERLANDS
CA756-320, CT316-120, DC12-300,
DE810-330, MA109-120, MA109-220,
NJ548-530, NJ568-570, NJ578-510,
NY10-80, NY10-640, NY427-240,
NY469-720, NY588-700, NY590-940,
NY591-840, NY592-460, NY593-600,
NY593-900, NY804-800, PA725-720
PORTUGAL
DC3-226
SPAIN
AL580-510, AZ225-40, AZ550-040,
AZ775-790, AZ800-30, AZ800-830,
CA86-630, CA86-780, CA118-720,
CA352-520, CA386-560, CA421-30,
CA421-390, CA421-610, CA421-774,
CA676-110, CA676-130, CA704-560,
CA712-708, CA720-180, CA720-746,
CA720-910, CA724-730, CA728-730,
CA756-320, CA770-120, CA774-720,
CA778-800, CA782-800, CA858-810,
CA934-720, CO252-70, CO252-100,
CO252-550, CO270-240, CT505-960,
DC14-250, FL220-795, FL660-120,
GA895-160, IL170-884, LA62-500,
LA358-800, LA600-465, LA600-505,
LA600-555, LA600-760, MA169-310,
MD76-515, MD703-40, MI40-820,
MI230-165, MO810-510, MO810-730,
MS550-500, NM114-50, NM114-900,
NM722-530, NM722-570, NY592-460,
NY592-800, OK829-520, PR600-800,
PR720-360, RI700-70, TX56-50,
TX56-110, TX56-800, TX56-850,
TX56-860, TX252-150, TX252-730,
TX280-540, TX326-770, TX326-800,
TX397-690, TX425-280, TX483-320,
TX590-760, TX777-160, TX777-670,
TX777-760, TX777-810, TX933-80,
UT912-110, WI346-720
UNITED STATES
PR720-360
COLONIZATION
RI700-70
EUROPE
MN541-854

MORMONS
AZ250-575, UT836-880
RUSSIA IN AMERICA
WA880-290
COLORADO
CA712-743, TX374-40
CHRISTIAN REFORMED CHURCH
MI355-110
MINING
TX280-540
RELIGIOUS COMMUNITIES
OH593-720
COLORADO FORESTRY ASSOCIATION
CO378-120
COLORADO RIVER
AZ350-290, AZ500-400, AZ550-040,
AZ950-40
COLORADO SEMINARY
CO252-820
COLORADO STATE UNIVERSITY
CO378-260
COLORADO WOMEN'S CONFERENCE
CO252-42
COLORED MUSICIANS OF BUFFALO
NY134-85
COLORED ORPHAN'S ASYLUM
MD76-315
COLSON, EDNA MEADE
VA630-840
COLT, SAMUEL
CT316-880, MO810-690
COLTON HALL SCHOOL
CA480-120
COLUM, MARY M.
NY101-720
COLUM, PADRAIC
NY101-720
COLUMBIA COLLEGE (EVERETT WA)
WA904-635
COLUMBIA INSTITUTION FOR THE DEAF
DC7-100
COLUMBIA RIVER
OR901-760, WA892-725
BASIN
WA724-890
FISHING
WA144-210
FISHING INDUSTRY
OR48-40, WA144-210
PLATEAU AREA
ID480-40
COLUMBIA RIVER PACKERS ASSOCIATION
OR48-40
COLUMBIA WORKSHOP (RADIO PROGRAM)
NY591-690
COLUMBIAN FEDERATION
CO768-640
COMANCHE AND KIOWA CAPTIVES IN OKLAHOMA, BY HUGH D. CORWIN
OK228-610
COMEDIANS
NY591-690
COMEDIE-FRANCAISE (THEATER)
OH203-670
COMEDY
CA421-763
COMIC ART
VA690-830
COMMERCE
See also Trade, CA676-740, MA109-680,
MN42-40, MN763-530, NM494-570,
NY208-120, PA875-80, TX56-850
EUROPE
MN541-854, NY208-120
LEGISLATION
TX252-780
SANTA FE TRAIL
KS513-720
COMMISSION ON CIVIL RIGHTS
MS870-760
COMMISSIONER OF EDUCATION (FL)
FL800-245
COMMITTEE FOR MARITIME UNITY
CA720-356

COMMITTEE ON EMIGRES
OR720-400
COMMUNES
JEWS
NY590-840, NY595-660
COMMUNICATIONS
*AK500-20, DC9-580, IL841-520,
MN742-720, MO800-730, NM114-760,
NY396-40, NY594-640, TX742-690,
UT684-80*
CORPORATE
CT234-260
ELECTRONICS
DC19-542
EQUIPMENT, ARMY
NJ270-800
POLITICAL
CT234-260
COMMUNISM
SD450-150
COMMUNISM, OPPOSITION TO
See Anti-Communism
COMMUNIST PARTY (US)
GA90-200, MI255-530
COMMUNITARIANISM
*IL916-795, IN583-560, MA109-120,
MA411-80, MA677-720, NJ276-510,
NY590-680, NY637-720, OH505-520,
OR56-40, PA40-600, TN825-690,
WA300-172*
ORGANIZATIONS
MA109-120
COMMUNITY COLLEGE OF DENVER
CO252-42
COMMUNITY COLLEGES
IL866-715
COMMUNITY DEVELOPMENT
CA774-800, VA195-200
COMMUNITY RESEARCH ASSOCIATES
NY10-770
COMPOSERS
*CA86-890, CA421-40, CA421-750,
CA421-774, CT505-910, DC12-510,
FL280-390, KY496-725, LA670-480,
MA109-440, MN541-512, MO430-790,
MS900-870, NH600-510, NY166-80,
NY272-200, NY586-180, NY592-875,
PA725-345*
GERMANY
IL170-637
WOMEN
CA421-750
COMPUTER INDUSTRY
CA132-160
COMPUTERS
DC1-680, DC19-596
CONANT, KENNETH J.
MA169-305
CONCESSIONS (BUSINESS)
CA994-940
CONCORD COACH
NH134-540
CONCORDIA TEACHERS COLLEGE
NE800-480
**CONDIT, SAMUEL WILBUR (WILD GOOSE
BILL)**
WA975-80
CONDUCTORS (MUSIC)
CA86-890
CONE FAMILY
IL856-730
CONE, CLARIBEL
MD76-80
CONE, ETTA
MD76-80
CONFEDERATE STATES OF AMERICA
*AL620-20, AR510-25, AZ750-45,
FL220-795, GA75-810, GA405-560,
GA895-280, LA62-500, LA600-465,
LA600-755, MA528-780, MS610-520,
NC150-800, NC260-170, NC680-460,
NY588-900, NY592-800, RI700-45,
SC108-100, SC216-720, SC216-820,
TX56-800, TX56-850, VA145-780,
VA690-530, VA690-810, VA690-870,
VA690-910, VA870-110, WV550-280*

ARMY
KY5M-520, TX476-320
MILITARY RECORDS
LA600-455
POSTAL SERVICE
AL120-100
RAIDS
VT720-720
CONFEDERATION CONGRESS
DC14-250
CONGO
MI255-530
MISSIONARIES
IL45-30, KY464-490, NY459-520
UNITED NATIONS
NY595-20
CONGREGATION OF HOLY CROSS
IN627-640
CONGREGATION OF THE HOLY CROSS
TX56-720
CONGREGATIONAL CHRISTIAN CHURCH
CT316-105, NC310-200
MISSIONARIES
CT316-105
VIRGINIA
NC310-200
CONGREGATIONAL CHURCH
See also United Church of Christ,
*CA86-630, CT484-550, CT505-900,
CT905-880, IA377-280, IL169-507,
IL567-600, MA108-480, MA169-40,
MA761-720, MA811-720, MA894-880,
NE288-160, NY263-210, OH112-80,
OH665-590, OK854-840, SD936-930,
VT448-520*
CLERGY
*IL169-507, MA593-40, NY272-640,
NY334-280*
GREAT BRITAIN
IL169-507
NEW ENGLAND
MA108-480, MA593-40
CONGRESS
*CT477-130, DC14-490, DC14-725,
DC16-680, HI350-300, MI255-545,
TX280-540, WA820-880*
HOUSE COMMITTEE ON UN-AMERICAN
ACTIVITIES
CA86-520
REPRESENTATIVES
*AL440-800, AR510-810, AR890-20,
CA594-120, CA676-140, DC12-450,
DC19-130, FL820-810, GA75-790,
IA466-360, IL489-890, IL718-200,
IL866-365, IN231-40, KS377-200,
KS948-890, LA286-720, MA615-720,
MI20-50, MI40-300, MS80-40,
MS490-810, MT130-540, MT530-500,
MT700-800, NC60-810, NC900-810,
ND486-800, NH206-800, NY723-720,
OH399-420, OH878-720, OK558-790,
OR224-800, OR720-590, PA25-520,
PA90-480, PA425-360, PA500-80,
PA645-560, PA960-440, SD720-80,
TX56-520, TX181-790, UT456-900,
VT496-640, WA724-890*
SENATORS
*AZ275-520, AZ750-10, AZ750-45,
AZ750-760, CA620-760, DC19-160,
GA75-790, GA735-520, ID640-345,
IL718-200, IL866-365, KS948-890,
KY514-120, LA62-500, LA920-560,
MI20-50, MI1100-240, MI1440-320,
MS80-40, MS490-810, MS520-520,
MS610-520, MT130-540, MT530-500,
MT700-800, ND486-800, NH396-560,
NJ568-670, NM114-800, NY150-700,
NY323-320, OK558-790, OR224-800,
OR720-590, PA380-320, SD450-150,
SD522-160, TN630-570, TX56-520,
UT684-80, WA724-890*
CONGRESS (TX)
TX56-800

**CONGRESS OF INDUSTRIAL
ORGANIZATIONS**
See also American Federation of Labor and
Congress of Industrial Organizations,
DC1-400, DC3-210
CONGRESS OF RACIAL EQUALITY
GA90-490
CONKLIN FAMILY
NY878-720
CONKLING, ROSCOE
NY899-520
CONNECTICUT
MA804-50, OH878-720, PA55-760
ARCHITECTURE
DC19-560
COLONIAL PERIOD
RI700-45
SOCIETY OF FRIENDS
NY593-710
CONNECTICUT HOME GUARD
CT268-720
CONNECTICUT LAND COMPANY
OH112-280
CONNECTICUT RIVER VALLEY
MA804-50, NH468-800
CONNER, JOHN COGGSWELL, FAMILY
IN594-120
CONNER, WILLIAM, FAMILY
IN594-120
CONNOLLY, MAURICE
IA244-480
CONRAD, EARL
NY51-90
CONRAD, JOSEPH
CT505-890
CONRADT, HENRY, FAMILY
IN649-650
CONRAIL
See Consolidated Rail Corporation
CONROY, JOHN JOSEPH
NY10-675
CONSCIENTIOUS OBJECTORS
KS676-520, MI40-784, PA725-60
CONSERVATION
*CA86-810, CA360-720, CA774-800,
CA782-240, CO252-163, DC4-260,
MI40-784, NE624-520, TX56-780,
WY500-800*
LATIN AMERICA
CO252-163
SOIL
DC19-800
WILDLIFE
NY593-130
CONSERVATION FOUNDATION
NY593-130
CONSERVATIONISTS
CA728-850
CONSERVATISM (POLITICS)
OR224-800
**CONSOLIDATED RAIL CORPORATION
(CONRAIL)**
*CT463-520, CT779-785, DE270-200,
MA108-750, NJ838-580*
CONSTABLE & COMPANY (PUBLISHER)
PA726-615
CONSTABLE FAMILY
NY208-120
CONSTABLE, WILLIAM C.
NY208-120
CONSTELLATION (SHIP)
MD532-880
CONSTITUTION (SHIP)
MA109-850
CONSTITUTIONS
CONVENTION OF 1787 (UNITED
STATES)
DC14-590
CONVENTION OF 1849 (CALIFORNIA)
CA480-120
CONVENTION OF 1967 (MARYLAND)
MD114-310
STATE
IL866-355, ME37-535, TX252-80
UNITED STATES
CA118-720

CONSTRUCTION
AZ175-120, CA605-510, CA720-955,
CT512-120, DC1-810, DC23-100,
FL220-805, FL660-120, IL374-310,
IL866-355, KY496-498, MA109-180,
MA883-870, PA735-790, TX56-780
BRIDGES
DC19-601
BUILDINGS
DC14-552
CANALS
DC19-591, FL60-720, PA875-80
CHURCHES
DC14-580
DAMS
CA720-955, DC19-601, IA511-450,
NY222-110
EQUIPMENT
MA109-180
LIGHTHOUSES
GA885-120
LOCKS (WATERWAYS)
IA511-450
RAILROADS
CA720-955, DC1-920, DC19-591,
DC19-601
ROADS
IA33-350
SEAWALLS
TX397-690
SUBMARINES
CT282-720
TUNNELS
DC19-601
CONSULAR RELATIONS
GREAT BRITAIN AND HAWAII
HI350-311
INDIA AND UNITED STATES
MA92-70, MA108-750, MA109-120,
MA733-210, MA733-660, PA725-75,
PA725-720, RI700-70
CONSUMER MOVEMENT
NY569-120
**CONSUMER-FARMER MILK
COOPERATIVE**
NY569-120
CONSUMER'S LEAGUE OF NEW JERSEY
NJ568-670
CONSUMERS
MO810-800, VA20-322
AGENCIES
MD513-640, NJ568-670
COOPERATIVES
MN541-902, NY134-85
CONSUMERS UNION OF UNITED STATES
NY569-120
CONTAINERS
GLASS
CT961-210, VA500-322
CONTINENTAL CONGRESS
DC14-250
CONTRACTORS
MN763-800
CONTROL, BOARD OF (OR)
OR816-590
CONWAY, MONCURE
PA160-160
CONWELL, RUSSELL HERMAN
PA726-600
COOK ACADEMY
NY562-510
COOK COUNTY SCHOOL OF NURSING
IL169-580
COOK, ALBERT
WI554-480
COOK, GEORGE S.
VA690-810
COOK, MARIMON
OH112-80
COOKE, JAY
PA725-720
COOKE, SAMUEL
MA29-40
COOKING
See also Food, CT961-880
COOKSON, JOSEPH
NY598-560

COOLIDGE, CALVIN
MA624-240, VT374-80
COOLIDGE, JOHN
MA169-300
COOPER MEDICAL COLLEGE
CA858-895
COOPER, JAMES FENIMORE
CT505-890
COOPER, PETER
NY589-100
COOPERATIVES
FARMING
SD550-600, TN435-220
COPPER
MINING
CA624-710, MI464-530
COPPER RIVER
AK250-110
COPYRIGHT
DC12-650
CORBETT, JOHN T.
IA244-480
CORBIT-SHARPE HOUSE
DE900-320
CORD (AUTOMOBILE MODEL)
IN33-40
CORELLI, MARIE
MI230-800
CORK
MANUFACTURING
PA470-40
CORMIER, RAYMOND J.
PA726-600
CORN
MI255-530
HUSKING
IL417-440
CORNELL UNIVERSITY
MEDICAL COLLEGE
NY592-480
**CORNELL UNIVERSITY-NEW YORK
HOSPITAL SCHOOL OF NURSING**
NY592-480
CORNELL, DOROTHY
NY439-180
CORNELL, KATHERINE
MA285-160
CORNPLANTER
PA915-870
CORONERS
CA624-710, NY752-720
**CORPORATION FOR THE PROPAGATION
OF THE GOSPEL IN NEW ENGLAND**
MA109-460
CORRECTIONAL SERVICES
NY594-20
CORRIDAS (MEXICAN BORDER BALLADS)
TX529-770
CORSICA
CT505-977
CORWIN, HUGH D.
OK228-610
COSMETICS INDUSTRY
DC3-800
COSMIC RAYS
CO108-560
COSTUMES
See also Clothing; Fashions, NY591-350,
NY866-520, PA415-720, VA205-290
EUROPE
NY591-350
COTTER, JOSEPH
KY496-520
COTTON
MA837-720, TN630-590, TN630-740,
TX210-200, TX590-760
COTTON, NORRIS
NH206-800
**COUNCIL FOR CHRISTIAN SOCIAL
ACTION**
CT505-900
**COUNCIL OF DEFENSE, UNITED WAR
WORK CAMPAIGN (WORLD WAR I)**
CA942-940

**COUNCIL OF NATIONAL DEFENSE,
ADVISORY COMMITTEE OF (WORLD
WAR I)**
DC1-400
COUNTY FAIR BOARD (BURTON OH)
OH112-280
**COURSE OF OUR TIMES (RADIO
PROGRAM)**
MA871-85
COURTS
CA712-700, OH778-40
OPINIONS
MA108-920
RECORDS
AR360-40, AZ550-040, CA274-250,
CA488-520, CT603-360, DE900-320,
FL120-330, HI400-480, IA177-340,
IA811-110, IL301-280, KY126-760,
KY48V-495, KY496-400, KY514-130,
LA600-465, MA108-140, MA109-180,
MA109-660, MA231-640, MA624-560,
MD57-500, MD361-320, MN314-520,
MN433-440, MN728-690, MN975-730,
MS550-500, NC730-710, NJ304-80,
NJ578-515, NY66-720, NY219-290,
NY373-320, NY588-440, NY592-350,
PA920-890, PR720-360, RI560-570,
SC576-480, TX326-210, TX483-820,
WV650-890, WV900-80, WY135-860
RECORDS, COUNTY
AR890-30, CA676-110, IA922-280,
IL866-715, IN275-640, KS335-240,
KS385-280, KS774-690, KY98-520,
KY55L-920, KY78J-650, NJ982-280,
NM760-720, NY592-420, NY618-120,
OH394-320, OH878-880, OR288-400,
PA80-110, PA325-40, PA380-320,
TN90-80, TN435-220, VA690-870,
VT432-720, WV225-860
RECORDS, INDIANS
OK609-120
RECORDS, LOCAL
CA476-520, CT144-880, CT174-200,
IL856-730, IL946-360, IN539-80,
IN660-640, KY526-520, MA928-730,
MI350-760, MO530-120, NH680-760,
NY235-160, NY592-420, NY978-880,
OH436-880, OH481-530, OH481-610,
OH803-720, OH968-880, PA25-60,
PA470-460, PA725-240, VA640-650,
WA164-890, WA327-735, WI456-540,
WI794-880
RECORDS, MEXICO
TX326-800
RECORDS, NATIONAL
CA704-560, GA405-560
RECORDS, STATE
FL800-245, IA233-360, IN363-342,
KS878-430, LA600-775, MA817-720,
ME37-525, MN763-580, NH134-530,
NY588-520, OR816-590, PA920-870,
RI700-740, TN690-780, WI346-720
SCOPES TRIAL
KY604-640
U.S. APPEALS
NJ46-560, PA726-7
U.S. CIRCUIT
IL170-280, MA871-540, TX374-550
U.S. DISTRICT
AR890-20, CA386-560, CO252-550,
DC14-250, IL170-280, MA871-540,
NJ46-560, OK592-650, PA726-7,
TX374-550, WA820-550
U.S. SUPREME
DC14-250, DC19-900, KY496-800
U.S. TERRITORIAL
CA386-560
COUSINS, NORMAN
NY588-300
COVINGTON, SAMUEL F.
OH680-540
COWBOYS
ID480-40
COWLES, BETSY MIX
OH399-420
COWLES, GILES HOOKER
OH399-420

COX, ABRAHAM B.
NY187-120
COX, JAMES M.
OH223-880
COX, LAWRENCE M.
VA580-600
COXEY, JACOB
OH505-510
CRAB APPLES
DC14-180
CRACIUN, JOSEPH J.
OH399-420
CRAFT, GEORGE A.
IA833-120
CRAFTS
DC9-450, DC19-560, KY604-640,
NM722-730, NY592-460, NY637-720,
NY646-520, VA235-230
INDIANS
NM722-360
ORGANIZATIONS
TN435-220
CRAFTSPEOPLE
CT234-230, DC19-320, DE900-320,
FL940-240, IN66-520, MD76-525,
NJ838-630, NM722-730, NY586-360
GREAT BRITAIN
DE900-320
CRAIG, GORDON
NY592-870
CRAMER, WILLIAM C.
FL820-810
CRAMP SHIPBUILDING COMPANY
PA726-240
CRANBERRIES
WI98-400
CRANBROOK ACADEMY OF ART
MI110-120
CRANBROOK EDUCATIONAL
COMMUNITY
MI110-120
CRANBROOK FOUNDATION
MI110-120
CRANBROOK INSTITUTE OF SCIENCE
MI110-120
CRANBROOK SCHOOL
MI110-120
CRANCH FAMILY (MA)
WY500-800
CRANDALL, LEE S.
NY593-130
CRANE FAMILY
MA227-120, NJ548-520
CRANE, HART
OH399-440
CRANE, JOSHUA
MA139-90
CRANE, R. C.
TX7-320
CRANE, STEPHEN
MA961-870
CRAWFORD, MERRITT
NY591-760
CREDIT FONCIER OF SINALOA COMPANY
CA274-120
CREIGHTON, EDWARD
NE624-130
CREIGHTON, JOHN ANDREW
NE624-130
CREMATORY
PA920-870
CRESSON, MARGARET FRENCH
MA334-120
CRESSON, WILLIAM PENN
MA334-120
CRET, PAUL
PA725-150
CRETIN, JOSEPH
MN763-100
CRIME
CA862-810, IN242-250, IN539-83,
NY590-360
CRIMEAN WAR
MD152-720

CRIMINAL JUSTICE
NY588-440, NY978-880, PA726-630
WORLD WAR II
CA32-640
CRIMINAL LAW
TX252-780
CRIMINALS
CA862-810, KY288-440, NY588-440
WOMEN
DC14-410
CRIMINOLOGISTS
PA726-600
CROOK-MONROE HOUSE
TX228-320
CROSBY, HARRY LILLIS (BING)
CA421-766, WA880-290
CROSS-CULTURAL STUDIES, INSTITUTE
FOR
DC19-440
CROSS, FRED WILDER
MA725-640
CROW AGENCY, BUREAU OF INDIAN
AFFAIRS
MT100-200
CROW MEADOW HORSE THIEF
ASSOCIATION
IL429-520
CROWE, JOHN FINLEY
IN319-330
CRYPT OF CIVILIZATION (PERIODICAL)
GA90-600
CRYPTOGAMIC BOTANY
MA169-270
CRYPTOGRAPHY
OH399-440
CUBA
FL440-320, NC590-320
MISSIONARIES
IN704-240
REFUGEES
NY10-160
SPANISH-AMERICAN WAR
FL60-720
CUBAN-AMERICANS
FL940-240
CUKOR, GEORGE
CA90-30
CULIN, STEWART
NY587-780
CULLEN, THOMAS
MD76-315
CULLIGAN WATER COMPANY
CA712-810
CULLIGAN, EMMETT
CA712-810
CULLINAN, J. S.
TX483-810
CULLUM, GEORGE W.
PA555-40
CULTURAL ACTIVITIES
CT36-80, DC19-550, IL169-325,
IL170-910, NM494-570
CULTURAL ANTHROPOLOGY
PA90-500
CUMBERLAND PRESBYTERIAN CHURCH
NC590-320
CUNNINGHAM, MINNIE FISHER
TX483-810
CURRAN, JOHN R.
NJ838-610
CURRENCY
OH301-690, TX326-780
CURTIS, VIVIAN
NY564-840
CURTIS, WILLIAM E., FAMILY
CT316-763
CURTISS, GLENN HAMMOND
NY367-270, NY367-320
CURWEN FAMILY
PA725-150
CUSHING, FRANK HAMILTON
CA421-610
CUSICK, WILLIAM CONKLIN
OR464-490
CUSTER, GEORGE ARMSTRONG
MI650-510, MI650-530, MT100-200,
MT270-130, SD414-640, SD936-950

CUSTER, MILO
IL94-510
CUSTIS, GEORGE WASHINGTON PARKE
VA50-65
CUSTOMS, BUREAU OF
CA386-560, CA704-560, MA285-160,
MA584-550, MA733-210, MA871-540,
ME275-160, ME462-440, ME762-640,
MI775-520, NJ46-560, NY772-720,
PA726-7, RI560-570, WA820-550
CUTLER, EPHRAIM
OH486-510
CUTLER, WILLIAM PARKER
OH486-510
CYBERNETICS
MA169-650
CYPRUS
NY595-40
CYPRUS WAR OF INDEPENDENCE
MA169-800
CZECHOSLOVAKIA
NE560-860, NY588-825, PA735-825
IMMIGRATION AND EMIGRATION
IL459-360
CZECHOSLOVAKIAN-AMERICANS
FL940-240, IL84-120, IL459-360,
MN405-320, NE560-860, WI38-480
NEBRASKA
IL459-360

D

D. H. BURNHAM AND COMPANY
(ARCHITECTURAL FIRM)
IL169-130
D. S. MORGAN COMPANY
NY125-720
D'ASCENZO STAINED GLASS STUDIO
PA725-150
D'AUTREMONT, MARIE D'OHENT
NY32-50
D'HAPPART, JOSEPH LEGER
PA735-800
DABNEY, ROBERT LEWIS
VA690-750
DAGGETT, R. F., JR.
IN539-100
DAGGETT, R. F., SR.
IN539-100
DAGGETT, R. P.
IN539-100
DAGUERREOTYPISTS
OH203-630
DAIRY PRODUCTS
WI98-400, WI606-710
DAIRYING
COOPERATIVES
NY569-120
DAKOTA WESLEYAN UNIVERSITY
SD522-800
DALLAPICCOLA, LUIGI
CA86-890
DALLAS, GEORGE MIFFLIN
PA725-720
DALTON, JOHN
DC19-641
DALY, AUGUSTIN
DC6-600
DAMS
DC19-800, ID680-690
CONSTRUCTION
CA720-955, DC19-601, IA511-450,
NY222-110
DANA FAMILY
MA169-590
DANA, EDMUND L.
PA960-910
DANCE
CT512-120, MN763-800, NY587-800,
NY591-420, NY592-870, NY593-970,
OH203-670
DANE, NATHAN
MA891-880
DANIEL BOONE (TELEVISION SERIES)
CA778-800

DANIEL PAYNE COLLEGE
  DC1-160
DANIEL, PERCY
  KS746-640
DANIEL, ROBERT PRENTISS
  VA630-840
DANISH BAPTIST CHURCH (US)
  NY752-40
DANISH BAPTIST THEOLOGICAL
  SEMINARY
  IL644-80
DANISH EVANGELICAL LUTHERAN
  CHURCH
  IA233-280
DANISH WEST INDIES
  See also Caribbean; West Indies; and
  individual islands, *VI300-240, VI700-360,
  VI700-800*
DANISH-AMERICANS
  NE624-150
  LUTHERAN CHURCH
  IA244-30
DANNETT, SYLVIA P. L.
  NC730-480
DANSPACE
  NY593-970
DANSVILLE SHAKESPEARE CLUB
  NY234-165
DARDEN, IDA
  TX483-810
DARLINGTON, WILLIAM
  PA945-880
DARMS, ANTON
  IL996-980
DARWIN D. MARTIN HOUSE
  NY24-720
DARWIN, CHARLES ROBERT
  NY592-320, OH181-180
DAUGHTERS OF THE AMERICAN
  REVOLUTION
  *IN704-520, MI80-80, MI824-320,
  MI890-720, ND876-80, NY839-720,
  PA500-70, PA615-720*
  BLAND BALLARD CHAPTER
  KY230-440
  HANNAH WESTON CHAPTER
  ME512-80
  JOSEPH LIGON CHAPTER
  TX695-640
  MARY WEED MARTIN CHAPTER
  NY915-870
  SOMERSET CHAPTER
  KY78J-650
DAUGHTERS OF THE AMERICAN
  REVOLUTION (EAST SPRINGFIELD
  NY)
  NY262-280
DAUGHTERS OF THE AMERICAN
  REVOLUTION (EMINENCE KY)
  KY230-320
DAUGHTERS OF 1812
  NEW YORK STATE SOCIETY
  NY292-520
DAVID, JOHN BAPTIST MARY
  KY569-720
DAVIES, A. POWELL
  IL170-195
DAVIESS COUNTY HISTORICAL SOCIETY
  KY598-600
DAVIS FAMILY
  IA511-450
DAVIS, DAVID
  IL866-365
DAVIS, DOROTHY SALISBURY
  NY588-300
DAVIS, JAMES C.
  VT720-720
DAVIS, JEFFERSON
  KY464-760, LA885-690, OH680-540
DAVIS, JOHN W.
  NY288-840, WV250-320
DAVIS, VARINA
  NC330-520
DAVISVILLE, BY JOAN LEACH LARKEY
  CA206-940
DAWES COMMISSION (1896-1906)
  OK541-240

DAWES, CHARLES G.
  IL261-200, IL261-570
DAWSON, MOSES
  OH171-920
DAY CARE CENTERS
  NY594-20
DAY, ALBERT
  KY886-50
DAY, JOSEPH, FAMILY
  KY430-280
DAY, KATHARINE SEYMOUR
  CT316-560
DAYTON BALLET COMPANY
  OH223-880
DAYTON MALLEABLE INC.
  OH223-880
DAYTON MANUFACTURING COMPANY
  OH223-520
DE FOREST, LEE
  CA418-200, PA725-495
DE HIRSCH, CLARA, HOME FOR
  WORKING GIRLS
  NY593-132
DE HUECK, CATHERINE
  NY318-260
DE LA MARE, WALTER
  PA726-615
DE LAUSSAT, PIERRE CLEMENT
  LA600-310
DE MALESHERBES, CHRETIEN
  LAMOIGNON
  PA735-140
DE MENDONCA CORTE-REAL, DIOGO
  DC3-226
DE MILLE, AGNES
  NY592-870
DE OLIVEIRA LIMA, MANOEL, FAMILY
  DC3-226
DE SOTO, HERNANDO
  OK829-520
DE VIMEUR, JEAN BAPTISTE DONATIEN
  (COMTE DE ROCHAMBEAU)
  FL220-800, NJ692-660
DE WITT, WILLIAM R.
  PA380-320
DEADWOOD SD
  CO36-40
DEAF PERSONS
  DC7-100, DC22-500, NY586-440
  EDUCATION
  DC7-100, DC22-500, WA943-730
  ORGANIZATIONS
  DC7-100
DEANE, STEPHEN R.
  ME725-880
DEARBORN, HENRY
  MI214-150
DEATH OF A SALESMAN, BY ARTHUR
  MILLER
  NY315-200
DEBATING
  VA430-870
DEBS, EUGENE V.
  IN825-200, IN825-350
DEBS, THEODORE
  IN825-350
DECLARATION OF INDEPENDENCE
  *CA118-720, CT751-640, DC14-590,
  IL170-250, MA685-520, OH823-800,
  PA726-725, PA945-880*
DECLERQUE, GILBERT
  NY101-90
DECORATIVE ARTS
  See Arts, decorative
DECOYS (WILDFOWL)
  NY866-520
DEERE, JOHN
  IL548-150
DEERFIELD MA
  WI202-560
DEFENSE
  See Armed forces; Military history
DEFENSE AUDIO-VISUAL AGENCY
  DC13-210
DEFENSE COUNCIL (OR)
  OR816-590

DEFOE, DANIEL
  KS948-240
DEFORD, MIRIAM ALLEN
  PA726-600
DEFORMITIES
  OH203-630
DEHON, LEO JOHN
  WI214-700
DELANGLADE FAMILY
  WI46-600
DELANO FAMILY
  NY427-240
DELANO, JANE A.
  NY562-510
DELAWARE
  PA725-720
  DUTCH-AMERICANS
  NY590-80
  GOVERNMENT AGENCIES, NATIONAL
  PA726-7
  SOCIETY OF FRIENDS
  PA860-710
DELAWARE AND HUDSON CANAL
  *NY229-560, NY269-200, NY714-560,
  PA410-880*
DELAWARE PLANK ROAD COMPANY
  NY915-870
DELAWARE RIVER
  PA726-240
DELEGLISE, FRANCIS A.
  WI38-480
DELHI TOURIST CLUB
  NY240-160
DELIUS, FREDERICK
  FL280-390, FL280-420
DELORD FAMILY
  NY708-440
DELPHI (FRATERNITY)
  NY216-720
DELTA MINISTRY
  GA90-490, MS870-760
DEMILLE, CECIL B.
  CA90-30, UT684-80
DEMOCRATIC PARTY
  NY842-730
  POLITICIANS
  IN231-40
DEMOGRAPHY
  CA712-750, HI350-320, PA725-330
DEN BOER, ARIE F.
  DC14-180
DENISON, FREDERICK
  RI910-880
DENMARK
  IL261-566
  COLONIES
  VI300-240, VI700-360
  IMMIGRATION AND EMIGRATION
  IA233-280, NE144-160
DENNIS, JOSIAH
  MA242-160
DENSMORE BROTHERS
  WI456-560
DENSMORE, JAMES
  WI456-560
DENTISTRY
  *AL120-810, AL120-815, CA720-894,
  GA90-210, IL169-78, IL170-429,
  NY752-885, PA726-810, TN690-780,
  WA739-240*
  EDUCATION
  CA720-890, NY752-885
  ORGANIZATIONS
  GA90-210
DENTISTS
  DC19-611, KS213-120, PA726-810
DENVER CO
  RELIGIOUS COMMUNITIES
  CA110-600
DENVER MINT
  CO252-550
DEPARTMENT OF DEFENSE
  DC3-320
DEPARTMENT OF STATE
  BUREAU OF EDUCATION AND
  CULTURAL AFFAIRS
  DC9-580

DEPARTMENT OF STATE (TX)
TX56-800
DEPARTMENT OF THE INTERIOR
DC4-322,   RI945-800
DEPARTMENT OF TREASURY (TX)
TX56-800
DEPASQUALI, BERNICE
MA425-520
DEPRESSION (1930'S)
*MN562-520,   NY594-20,   PA726-37,
SD792-850,   TX326-780*
DERMATOLOGISTS
FL80-160
DERRICK PUBLISHING COMPANY
PA705-320
DESAUSSURE, J. M.
SC108-100
DESEGREGATION
See Civil rights; Race relations
DESIGN
MA169-300
  AUTOMOBILES
    NH600-530,   PA560-690
  INDUSTRIAL
    NY591-350
  INTERIOR
    NY591-350
  SUBMARINES
    CT282-720
  THEATER
    NY591-850,   OH203-670,   VA205-290
  TIRES
    NH600-530
DESMOND, THOMAS C.
NY10-770
DESOTO (AUTOMOBILE MODEL)
IN33-40
DETECTIVES
IN242-250
DETROIT MEDICAL COLLEGE
MI230-905
DETROIT PUBLISHING COMPANY
MI214-280
DETROIT UNITED RAILWAY LINES
MI40-796
DEUTSCH, BABETTE
MO810-690
DEVAULT FAMILY
TN750-690
DEVEREUX FAMILY
NY775-720
DEVOTO, BERNARD
UT456-900
  LITERARY MANUSCRIPTS
    UT380-810
DEWAR, CHARLES A.
MT100-200
DEWING, THOMAS W.
DC19-330
DEWITT, SIMEON
NY439-180
DEWOLF, JAMES M.
MT100-200
DIABETES
OH181-180
DIAGHILEV, SERGEI PAVLOVICH
NY592-870
DIAPER AND DUDLEY (ARCHITECTS)
VT496-640
DICK, DAVID
PA555-120
DICKENS, CHARLES
PA725-510,   TX56-890
DICKEY, JAMES
NY125-740
DICKINSON, DANIEL S.
NY101-90
DICKINSON, EMILY
MA21-40,   MA21-400,   MN541-600
DICKINSON, FAIRLEIGH S., JR.
NJ756-240
DICKINSON, JOHN
PA725-720
DIEDRICH, NICHOLAS
WI202-120
DIESELDORFF, ERWIN PAUL
LA600-760

DIETEL, WILLIAM M.
NY890-200
DILLON, ASA
KS948-240
DIOCESE OF BURLINGTON, VT
VT964-720
DIPLOMACY
*CA858-320,   DC7-650,   DC15-500,
DE540-790,   KS10-170,   KS527-790,
MA108-750,   MD57-800,   MD76-340,
NY247-160,   NY588-940,   NY590-700,
PA210-800,   PA725-45,   RI560-510,
TX56-860,   TX210-200,   VA430-280*
  CHINA
    NY439-156
  PORTUGAL
    DC3-226
DIPLOMATS
LA600-760,   OH906-320,   PA725-615
DIRIGIBLES
OH11-810,   TX742-800
DIRKSEN, EVERETT MCKINLEY
IL718-200
DISASTERS
See also Fires; Floods; Tornados; and
similar events,   *CA798-720,   OH863-280,
OH982-290,   PA435-400,   SD648-690,
SD792-850,   SD792-880*
  RELIEF
    *DC1-180,   DC1-560,   DC14-500,
    NY594-20*
DISCIPLES OF CHRIST
See also Christian church,   *CA86-630,
CA143-720,   KY464-490,   WV100-80*
  ARIZONA
    CA143-720
DISEASES
NY752-885
  ANIMALS
    OH588-520
DISINGER, FOSTER
NY101-90
DISMAL SWAMP CANAL
VA165-120
DISNEY, WALT
CA114-880
DISTRICT OF COLUMBIA
MD985-560,   NY574-320,   NY593-420
DITMARS, RAYMOND L.
NY593-130
**DIVINE PROVIDENCE, SISTERS OF, OF ST.
JEAN DE BASSEL, FRANCE**
KY532-720
DIVORCE
MA169-885,   PR720-360
DIX, DOROTHEA LYNDE
KS878-520,   NJ838-610,   NJ838-730
**DIX, DOROTHY (ELIZABETH
MERIWETHER GILMER)**
TN75-50
DIXON, JOSEPH
IN66-385
DIXON, THOMAS
NC100-280
DOANE, THOMAS
NE288-160
DOBIE, JAMES FRANK
TX326-210,   TX404-120
DOBRITCH INTERNATIONAL CIRCUS
IL624-380
DOCK STREET THEATER
SC144-90
DOCTORS
See Physicians
DOD, THADDEUS
PA920-890
DODGE FAMILY
IA177-320
DODGE MEIGS (LUMBER MILL)
GA885-520
DODGE, GRENVILLE MELLEN
IA177-240,   IA177-320,   VT528-560
DODGSON, CHARLES LUTWIDGE
NY593-90
DOGGETT, LAWRENCE L.
MA804-710

DOLAN, BROOKE
PA725-15
DOLBEAR, AMOS EMERSON
MA528-780,   MA528-780
DOLLEY, SARAH ADAMSON
NY752-885
DOMINICANS
  ORDER OF PREACHERS
    TX56-720
DONAHUE, MAURICE A.
MA21-770
DONOVAN, RICHARD
CT505-910
DOOLITTLE, JAMES ROOD
NY323-320
DOORLEY, JOSEPH A., JR.
RI700-630
DORR, JULIA
VT432-530
DORSCH, EDUARD
MI650-530
DOTY, JAMES DUANE
WI202-560
DOUBLE EAGLE II (BALLOON)
IL806-705
DOUD FAMILY
IA58-540
DOUGLAS, EMILY
IL169-468
DOUGLAS, PAUL
IL169-468
DOUGLAS, STEPHEN A.
IL866-365
DOW, GEORGE FRANCIS
MA849-750
DOWIE, JOHN ALEXANDER
IL996-980
DOWNES-ALDRICH HOUSE
TX228-320
DOYLE, ARTHUR CONAN
IL459-360
DRAFT (MILITARY)
MO810-940
  BOARDS
    OH968-880
  CIVIL WAR
    NY106-80
  WORLD WAR I
    WI202-560
DRAKE, EDWIN L.
PA870-160
DRAKE, MARGARET T.
NY214-160
DRAMA
See also Theater,   *AR60-600,   CA318-700,
CA421-322,   CA778-800,   DC6-600,
FL820-780,   IA688-520,   KY496-520,
MI650-530,   NY234-165,   PA440-80,
RI700-100,   VA205-290,   WA168-135,
WA943-125*
  LATVIA
    MA172-160
  LATVIAN-AMERICANS
    MA172-160
  OUTDOOR
    NC150-790
  TELEVISION
    DC16-680
  YIDDISH CULTURE
    OH171-20
DRAPER FAMILY
MA411-80
DRAPER, EDWARD B.
ME37-535
DRAPER, JOHN WILLIAM, FAMILY
DC19-631
DREISER, THEODORE
CA421-400
DREXEL FAMILY
PA85-730,   PA725-375
DREXEL, ANTHONY JOSEPH
PA725-375
DREYFUS, ALFRED
MA871-90
DRINKWATER, JOHN
PA160-160

DRISCOLL, ALFRED E.
NJ316-310
DRISCOLL, CHARLES BENEDICT
KS948-880
DRIVER'S EDUCATION
VA215-40
DROWNE, SOLOMON
RI700-50
DRUG ADDICTS
NY594-20
DRUGS
See also Pharmacy, *CA720-886,*
OH495-510, TX252-780, WI346-870
  MANUFACTURING
  IL629-40
DRURY LANE THEATRE
DC6-600
DRYDEN, HUGH LATIMER
MD76-360
**DU BOIS, WILLIAM EDWARD
  BURGHARDT**
MA21-770
**DU MOTIER, MARIE JOSEPH PAUL YVES
  ROCH GILBERT (MARQUIS DE
  LAFAYETTE)**
CT505-945, GA660-480, NC330-520,
NY439-140
DU PONT FAMILY
DE270-200, DE900-330
DU PONT, E. I., COMPANY
WA259-160
DU PONT, HENRY ALGERNON
DE900-330
DU PONT, HENRY FRANCIS
DE900-330
DUBLIN GATE THEATRE
IL261-570
DUBOIS, CONSTANCE GODDARD
CA712-713
DUBOIS, FRED THOMAS
ID640-345
DUCASSE, C. J.
RI700-50
DUCK, DONALD
CA114-880
DUELL, PRENTICE
MA169-340
DUESENBERG (AUTOMOBILE MODEL)
IN33-40
DULLES, JOHN FOSTER
NJ692-660
DULUTH-SUPERIOR HARBOR
MN261-40
DULUTH-SUPERIOR TRANSIT COMPANY
MN261-810
DUMONT, GABRIEL
RI945-800
DUNBAR, PAUL LAURENCE
OH203-600
DUNCAN GLASS
PA920-870
DUNCAN, ISADORA
NY592-870
DUNCAN, ROBERT
OH399-440
DUNCAN, WILLIAM B.
TX560-720
DUNDAS FAMILY (VISCOUNTS MELVILLE)
MI40-820
DUNHAM, BARROWS
PA726-600
DUNHAM, LAWRENCE B.
NY612-690
DUNLAP, WILLIAM
NY589-680
**DUNSANY, LADY (MRS. EDWARD JOHN
  MORETON DRAX PLUNKETT, 18TH
  BARONESS DUNSANY)**
NY101-720
**DUNSANY, LORD (EDWARD JOHN
  MORETON DRAX PLUNKETT, 18TH
  BARON DUNSANY)**
NY101-720
DURANGO, MEXICO
TX326-800
DURANT, WILLIAM C.
MI1314-265

DURANZO MINE
AZ475-640
DURYEA, J. FRANK
CA282-480
DUSENBURY, J. E.
NY720-640
DUSTIN, FRED
MT100-200
DUTCH CHURCH, REFORMED
NY588-700
DUTCH-AMERICANS
IA855-150, MI355-110, MI445-310,
MI445-320, MI445-880, NY590-80
  CANADA
  IA855-150
  DELAWARE
  NY590-80
  MINNESOTA
  IA855-150
  NEW JERSEY
  NY590-80
  NORTH DAKOTA
  IA855-150
  PENNSYLVANIA
  NY590-80
  SOUTH DAKOTA
  IA855-150
DUTCHER FAMILY
VT720-720
DYERS
MA606-530

E

EAGLE LOCK COMPANY
CT797-480
EAGLE, JOE H.
TX483-810
EAKINS, THOMAS
DC19-340, PA135-80
EARHART, AMELIA
IN935-650
EARLY, ELEANOR
MA199-90
EARTH SCIENCE
DC19-500, TX252-322
EARTHQUAKES
CO108-560, SC144-105
  TOKYO, JAPAN
  IN297-600
**EAST METHODIST SOCIETY (ROCHESTER
NY)**
NY752-60
EAST ORANGE HISTORICAL SOCIETY
NJ212-200
EAST SUDBURY MINISTERIAL FUND
MA883-870
EAST SUDBURY SOCIAL LIBRARY
MA883-870
EAST TEXAS BAPTIST ASSOCIATION
TX604-220
EAST, ADAM
WA565-40
EASTERN US
CA524-140, NC60-640, PA420-720
  EDUCATION
  KY496-850
  LANDSCAPE ARCHITECTURE
  CA86-820
  LUTHERAN CHURCH
  PA325-490
  MENNONITES
  PA470-480
EASTON, MARY
MO770-480
EASTWOOD, H. E.
VA580-520
EATON, D. M.
NC650-120
EBREO, GIORGIA
NY592-870
ECKENRODE, HAMILTON J.
VA285-520
ECKHART (AUTOMOBILE MODEL)
IN33-40

ECKHERD, JACOB
SC144-710
ECOLOGY
GA90-270, OR848-40, WI326-120
ECONOMIC DEVELOPMENT
CA421-390, CA712-750, DC9-450,
KY41E-160
ECONOMIC HISTORY
IN363-360, ME37-540, NC260-170,
UT912-110, WY135-865
  SOUTHERN US
  LA62-500
ECONOMICS
AL840-280, DC3-210, FL820-780,
GA810-80, IA966-320, IL170-910,
IN77-200, KS10-170, KY288-425,
MD114-330, MI40-808, NY211-580,
OR224-800, PA90-500, PA725-870,
PA895-710, PA965-490, TX56-860,
TX712-880
  INDIANS
  NM722-360
  LATIN AMERICA
  PA325-280
  ORGANIZATIONS
  IL261-570
ECONOMISTS
NY569-120
ECUADOR
  CHURCH OF THE BRETHREN
  IL241-120
  MISSIONARIES
  IL169-677
ECUMENICAL METHODIST CONFERENCE
NC730-480
EDDY FAMILY
IL856-730, MA542-200
EDDY, MARY BAKER
MA108-600, MA154-480
EDEL, LEON
IN275-170
EDELMANN, JOHN H.
OH181-325
EDEN SEMINARY
MO810-270
EDINA MILLS
MN275-200
EDINBURG STUDY CLUB
TX319-640
EDISON, THOMAS ALVA
FL180-210, MI214-280, NJ910-200,
NY872-760
EDITORS
DC13-300, KY96-870, TN690-890
EDMAN, V. RAYMOND
IL976-890
EDUCATION
See also Schools; Teachers; and specific
institutions in repository index,
AK350-120, AL120-100, CA421-322,
CA720-739, CA764-165, CA862-810,
CO54-40, CT36-80, CT505-560,
CT926-480, DC1-180, DC7-300,
DC9-450, DC19-550, DE540-790,
GA75-810, GA780-310, IA33-364,
IA88-800, ID80-90, IL169-325, IL170-91,
IL866-355, IL866-365, IN363-342,
IN583-560, KY496-518, KY760-720,
LA885-480, MA169-860, MI214-150,
MI518-445, MN42-40, MN562-520,
MN763-720, NC260-170, NJ444-240,
NY10-160, NY53-880, NY115-720,
NY128-720, NY179-120, NY272-720,
NY540-760, NY587-940, NY588-940,
NY588-970, NY592-460, NY595-700,
NY612-690, NY795-120, NY872-800,
OH203-170, OH203-650, OH301-690,
OH593-720, OH878-880, OR528-718,
PA55-760, PA725-540, PA726-630,
PA860-710, SD792-820, TN435-220,
TN690-780, TN690-880, TX56-850,
TX189-520, TX695-640, TX733-640,
VA20-322, VA145-780, VA195-200,
VA630-840, VT176-810, VT528-560,
WA280-885, WI266-820, WI698-730
  ACCOUNTING
  MA871-60

AFRICA
  NY593-380
AGRICULTURE
  HI450-80
ARCHITECTURE
  CA86-820
ART
  DC19-320, IN363-385, KY288-395,
  MI110-120, PA726-43, PA726-135
BAPTIST CHURCH
  LA600-540
BILINGUAL
  AK350-815
BLACKS
  AL760-760, DC1-160, GA90-700,
  MS550-410, NY593-380, NY595-130,
  VA670-690, WI456-730
BLIND PERSONS
  WA943-725
BUSINESS
  NY752-665, OH181-400
CITIES
  NY588-970
CONTINUING
  GA210-880, NY128-720
DEAF PERSONS
  DC7-100, DC22-500, WA943-730
DENTISTRY
  CA720-890, NY752-885
EARLY CHILDHOOD
  DC1-860
EASTERN US
  KY496-850
ELEMENTARY
  DC1-340
ENGINEERING
  MA985-870
ENVIRONMENT
  KY464-460, NY593-130
EUROPE
  MD76-527
HIGHER
  CO108-810, DC1-340, DC7-540,
  IN154-880, IN627-720, MD76-118,
  MD114-310, MO220-120, MO810-940,
  NC150-800, OH953-870, RI700-660,
  SC774-880, TN690-880
HIGHER, BLACKS
  NY595-130
INDIANS
  NM722-360, PA160-120, SD936-930,
  WA240-250, WI456-730
INSURANCE
  PA135-40
INTERNATIONAL
  MI255-545
JAPAN
  NJ568-670
JEWS
  NY595-660, TN690-360
LABOR
  AR890-30, NY439-150
LAW
  CA421-710, MA169-440, NC950-940,
  PA726-750
LIBRARIANS
  IL916-40
LITCHFIELD CT
  NY297-520
LOS ALAMOS RANCH SCHOOL
  NM570-480
MARITIME
  MA165-520, NY594-340
MEDICINE
  CA720-886, CA720-890, CA720-894,
  DC1-890, MD76-315, MD76-527,
  MI230-905, MO810-650, NE624-830,
  NY591-600, NY592-480, NY593-840,
  NY752-885, OH203-680, PA725-690,
  PA725-900, PA726-690, PA726-725,
  SD792-830, TN690-510, TX397-790,
  VA690-840, WA904-760
MIDWESTERN US
  KY496-850
MORMONS
  HI450-80

MUSIC
  MN541-902, NY587-500, NY590-720,
  WI456-730
NURSING
  IL169-580, IL245-322, NY588-970
ORGANIZATIONS
  CA524-160, DC1-860, DC15-500,
  MO520-440, NJ138-120, NJ692-210,
  NV940-560, NY334-240, PA726-225,
  TN690-880, TX733-640, WA427-450,
  WA735-680
PERU
  KY496-850
PHARMACY
  CA720-890, DC1-600
PHILOSOPHY OF
  MA804-710
PHYSICS
  NY586-580
POLAND
  NY593-500
POLISH-AMERICANS
  PA725-765
PROGRESSIVE
  NY128-720
PUBLIC
  WA759-680
PUERTO RICO
  NY115-720
RELIGION
  DC1-160, GA90-360, IA377-280,
  IL261-280, IN264-40, NY247-160,
  NY752-40, OH171-730, PA145-120,
  PA726-37, PA726-713, TN690-880,
  TX483-160, WA427-550, WI498-560
ROMAN CATHOLIC CHURCH
  LA600-40, MO220-120, NY481-720,
  PA726-495
RURAL
  NY310-720
SCIENCE
  MI110-120, PA726-765, PA726-855
SECONDARY
  DC1-340, DC19-40, NY197-120,
  TX483-160, WI594-110
SOCIAL WORK
  MN541-902
SOUTHERN US
  GA90-700, KY496-850
SOUTHWESTERN US
  NM114-525
TEACHERS
  WA144-210
TESTING
  IA466-40, NJ692-210
URBAN
  NY588-970
WOMEN
  DC1-340, IL806-695, KY54Q-520,
  MA109-630, MA572-540, MA776-530,
  MA891-860, NC430-340, NC680-720,
  NJ276-510, NY10-150, NY297-520,
  NY588-420, NY595-130, PA725-900,
  SC54-80, SC774-880, TX326-160,
  WI266-430
WRITING (CREATIVE)
  NY125-740
EDUCATION, BOARD OF (NEW YORK CITY
  NY)
  NY588-970
EDUCATION, BOARD OF HIGHER (NEW
  YORK CITY NY)
  NY588-340
EDUCATION, COMMISSIONER OF (FL)
  FL800-245
EDUCATIONAL ALLIANCE
  SURPRISE LAKE CAMP
  NY593-132
EDUCATIONAL CONFERENCE
  TX733-640
EDUCATIONAL SERVICE DISTRICT
  NUMBER 171
  WA280-885
EDUCATORS
  CT316-330, CT316-770, GA735-520,
  HI350-808, KY496-785, KY514-120,
  MN763-510, NH904-760, NM760-900,

  OH223-790, OH986-40, OR720-590,
  PA726-600, TN465-800, UT684-80,
  VA890-120
  BLACKS
    GA780-310
  MEDICINE
    TX397-790
  WOMEN
    DC1-860
EDWARD WATERS COLLEGE
  DC1-160
EDWARD WINSLOW HOUSE
  MA685-520
EDWARDS FAMILY
  MA811-720
EDWARDS, HARRY STILLWELL
  GA735-540
EDWARDS, R. M.
  TN90-130
EGBERT, JAMES DEWEY
  NY288-840
EGGERS, GEORGE WILLIAM
  NY134-710
EGGLESTON, WILLIAM
  DC3-760
EGGS
  CA830-720
EHRHART, OTTO E.
  OH21-600
EHRMANN, MAX
  IN275-170
EIDSON, JOHN O.
  GA915-280
EILSHEMIUS, LOUIS
  DC19-340
EINSTEIN, ALBERT
  DC19-641
EINSTEIN, ALFRED
  CA86-890
EISENHOWER FAMILY
  IA58-540
EISENHOWER, DWIGHT DAVID
  IA58-540, KS10-170, MS140-560,
  NY588-940
EISENHOWER, MAMIE DOUD
  IA58-540
EISENHOWER, MAMIE DOUD,
  BIRTHPLACE FOUNDATION
  IA58-540
EISENMANN, JOHN
  OH181-325
EISENSCHIML, OTTO
  IL169-416
EL PASO AND NORTHEASTERN
  RAILROAD COMPANY
  TX326-800
EL PASO AND SOUTHWESTERN
  RAILROAD COMPANY
  TX326-800
EL SALVADOR
  MO210-840
ELECTIONS
  See also Voting, IN363-342, KY288-440,
  NY263-210, NY967-880, OH481-530,
  SD450-150, TX654-640, VT464-850
ELECTRIC APPLIANCES
  IN231-40
  MANUFACTURING
    OH223-520
ELECTRIC POWER
  CO270-240, NY602-570, NY804-280,
  TN465-760, WA144-210, WA820-880
  COMPANIES
    IA188-360, NY53-880
ELECTRICAL SCIENCE
  See also Electronics, AK350-800,
  AR330-830, AZ800-30, CA86-780,
  CA86-920, CA756-320, CA858-810,
  CA858-820, CO252-181, CT316-110,
  CT505-960, DC12-300, DC14-250,
  DC19-310, DC19-542, DC19-586,
  DC19-641, DE270-200, GA75-810,
  IA466-800, IL124-725, IL169-325,
  IL916-810, IN363-360, KS10-170,
  MA108-750, MA169-170, ME712-530,
  MI40-784, MI214-260, MI230-165,
  MI665-120, MN763-540, NC150-800,

NC260-170, NC680-460, ND486-800,
NE560-550, NJ568-670, NJ578-510,
NJ910-200, NY427-240, NY439-120,
NY586-580, NY588-900, NY592-460,
NY592-800, NY752-740, NY866-710,
NY872-800, OH181-130, OH181-880,
OH203-600, OR224-800, PA380-650,
PA500-70, PA725-495, PA725-720,
PA735-790, SC185-120, TX56-850,
VA145-780, VA690-870, WA724-890,
WA820-880, WI346-720, WV650-890

ELECTRICAL, RADIO AND MACHINE WORKERS, INTERNATIONAL UNION OF
NJ568-680

ELECTRICITY
NY804-280, PA725-75

ELECTRONICS
See also Electrical science, CA418-200
COMMUNICATIONS
DC19-542
EQUIPMENT, ARMY
NJ270-800
MANUFACTURING
PA295-130

ELEVATED RAILROADS
NY587-500

ELGIN NATIONAL WATCH COMPANY
WI456-560

ELIOT, CHARLES
MA169-305

ELIOT, THOMAS STEARNS
TX56-890, WI456-810

ELISOFON, ELIOT
DC19-450

ELIZABETH NJ
IL245-322

ELIZABETH SETON SCHOOL AND JUNIOR COLLEGE
NY984-200

ELLENDER, ALLEN J.
LA920-560

ELLET, CHARLES, JR.
MI40-796

ELLICOTT, ANDREW
DC19-631

ELLING BANK
MT430-320

ELLIOT, THOMAS LAMB
OR720-700

ELLIOT, ZO
NH600-510

ELLIOTT, ELIZABETH SHIPPEN GREEN
DE810-150

ELLIOTT, HARRIET WISEMAN
NC380-800

ELLIS ISLAND NY
NY594-390

ELLSWORTH, JAMES W.
IL169-416

ELSTON, ISAAC COMPTON
IN154-880

ELWELL, HERBERT
OH181-310

ELY, EDMUND F.
MN261-810

ELY, HERMAN
OH266-200

EMERGENCY PREPAREDNESS, OFFICE OF (DC)
DC13-300

EMERSON, CHARLES WESLEY
MA108-520

EMERSON, RALPH WALDO
MA217-130, MA961-870, MN541-600, NY134-90

EMERSONIAN READING CLUB
NY698-650

EMIGRATION
See Immigration and emigration; Migration

EMIGRES
See Exiles

EMPIRE STATE FOREST PRODUCTS ASSOCIATION
NY872-720

EMPLOYMENT
See also Labor, DC1-340, VA20-322
PUBLIC
NY439-150
WOMEN
NY592-30

ENDANGERED SPECIES
DC6-500
PLANTS
NM114-825

ENDICOTT-JOHNSON CORPORATION
NY273-280, NY446-920

ENERGY
DC4-322, DC14-540, NM684-690, VA50-30
DEVELOPMENT
ND486-800, VA50-30
NUCLEAR
WA742-690
PHOTOGRAPHY
DC4-322
SOLAR
PA725-120

ENERGY RESEARCH AND DEVELOPMENT ADMINISTRATION
DC4-322

ENGINEERING
CA136-120, CA159-120, CA488-720,
CA624-710, CA692-130, CO108-85,
DC1-810, DC14-100, DC19-601,
HI350-340, IL169-580, IN539-100,
MA478-800, MA871-540, MA970-890,
MI605-520, MI725-600, MN391-310,
MO810-940, NJ646-660, NY10-675,
NY134-50, NY589-460, NY593-290,
NY890-700, PA725-495, PA725-765,
SC144-105, TX181-790, TX742-690,
VT528-560, WA676-135
CHEMICAL
TN465-760
CIVIL
CA605-510, CA605-530, MA169-650
EDUCATION
MA985-870
MARINE
MA169-610
MILITARY
VA245-800
POWER
MA606-530
TEXTILE INDUSTRY
MA606-530
TRAFFIC
NC160-520
WATER
CA86-920

ENGINEERING COUNCIL, AMERICAN
NY589-460

ENGINEERS
DC19-601, DC19-621, MN763-800,
NY804-800, PA725-120
CIVIL
MI40-796, MT100-200, OH54-80

ENGINES
BOATS
WA904-890
SHIPS
WA904-890

ENGLAND
See Great Britain

ENGLE, CLAIR
CA620-760

ENGRAVING
DC19-565

ENOLOGY
CA206-790

ENTERTAINERS
OK245-880

ENTERTAINMENT
CO458-80, DC12-450, DC19-550,
NY592-460, NY592-880, OH481-530,
TX374-40, WI70-120

ENTOMOLOGY
MA169-500, MD285-200, MI255-530,
PA725-15, PA725-75

ENTREPRENEURS
NJ548-720

ENVIRONMENT
CA862-810, CO252-163, DC5-600,
DC19-800, IL459-520, KY464-460,
MO810-800, MT130-540, NM722-730,
WA820-880
EDUCATION
KY464-460, NY593-130
ORGANIZATIONS
IN66-390, NY866-710

EPIDEMICS
NY10-160, NY752-885, PA725-615,
TN630-570, TX397-690

EPISCOPAL CHURCH
See also Protestant Episcopal church,
CT484-550, DC23-100, GA105-720,
KY496-200, LA600-755, NH784-700,
NV940-560, NY589-710, NY593-290,
OH181-430, OH320-430, PA726-37,
SC144-710, VT448-520, WA820-200,
WI498-560
CLERGY
AL120-200, AL580-650, CT316-210,
DC5-800, DE810-170, IL169-651,
IL866-200, KS878-200, KY496-200,
MA108-580, MO810-590, NC680-200,
NH784-700, NY134-660, NY589-710,
NY593-290, NY752-220, NY872-150,
OH171-165, OH181-430, OR464-322,
OR720-200, PA726-37, SC144-710,
SD684-200, TN630-200, TX56-25,
TX252-200, TX326-160, TX777-640,
UT912-200, WA820-200, WI498-560
FLORIDA
AL580-650
IDAHO
MO810-590
MISSIONARIES
IL169-651, IL866-200, SD684-200
MONTANA
MO810-590
NEW ENGLAND
CT316-210
ORGANIZATIONS
DE810-170, GA90-490, IL169-651,
MA108-580
RELIGIOUS COMMUNITIES
NY687-120
UTAH
MO810-590

EPISCOPAL CHURCH WOMEN
DE810-170

EPISCOPAL DIOCESE OF LEXINGTON KY
KY464-800

EPISCOPAL DIOCESE OF NEVADA
NV940-560

EPISCOPAL DIOCESE OF NEW YORK
NY752-220

EPISCOPAL DIOCESE OF SOUTH CAROLINA
SC144-130

EPISCOPAL DIOCESE OF WESTERN MICHIGAN
MI40-784

EPISCOPAL DIOCESE OF WESTERN NEW YORK
NY752-220

EPISCOPAL EYE, EAR AND THROAT HOSPITAL
DC23-250

EPISCOPAL SOCIETY FOR CULTURAL AND RACIAL UNITY
GA90-490

EPITAPHS
SC216-820

EQUIPMENT
CONSTRUCTION
MA109-180

EQUITABLE TRUST COMPANY
NY588-60

ERA CLUB
LA600-555

ERDMAN, LOULA GRACE
MO920-120

ERICSSON, JOHN
PA725-120

ERIE CANAL
  NY752-720, NY757-400, NY872-120,
  NY941-600
ERIE RAILROAD
  VT496-640
EROSION
  SOIL
    DC19-800, TN465-760
ERTMAN, IRENE P.
  KS746-640
ESKIMOS
  AK50-800, AK700-120, CA712-713,
  DC19-520, MI518-50, NY591-820
  ALASKA
    MO210-840
ESTHER (BOOK)
  DC2-200
ESTUARIES
  OR128-720
ETHICS
  MA154-310, TN690-780
  SOCIAL
    MA169-210
  TECHNOLOGY
    NY125-740
ETHIOPIA
  MN226-720
  MISSIONARIES
    IA244-30
ETHNIC GROUPS
  See also individual nationalities and
    countries, *AL840-820, AR510-25,*
    AZ800-800, CA40-60, CA720-675,
    CA862-810, CO108-810, CO180-120,
    CO180-650, CO252-70, CO252-100,
    CO768-640, CT779-785, DC19-550,
    HI250-480, IL170-280, IL170-910,
    IL202-550, IL245-322, IL866-720,
    IN253-360, KS10-170, KS94-690,
    KS377-250, KS607-690, KS676-520,
    KS878-430, KS962-800, LA600-20,
    LA600-760, LA600-775, MA108-750,
    MN338-360, MN562-520, MN763-790,
    MT130-540, MT530-500, MT700-800,
    ND486-800, NE496-40, NE560-550,
    NE560-860, NE736-560, NH600-30,
    NM722-360, NY587-940, NY870-600,
    NY870-600, OH35-40, OH181-880,
    OH823-750, OK558-790, OK753-600,
    PA725-165, PA735-780, PA735-790,
    PA735-825, PA960-440, RI700-630,
    RI700-660, SD558-710, TX590-760,
    UT912-820, VA690-830, WA820-880,
    WI266-820, WY245-280, WY500-480,
    WY500-800
  ART
    CA143-280
  MIDWESTERN US
    DC14-250
  ORGANIZATIONS
    MI824-320, NE624-150, OH181-780,
    PA305-510
ETHNOBOTANY
  MI40-814, MI518-50, OR848-40
ETHNOGRAPHY
  AK50-66, CA540-590, CA712-713,
  FL220-792, LA600-760, NM722-30,
  NY592-878
  CARIBBEAN
    FL220-792
ETHNOHISTORY
  AZ800-790, CO252-550
ETHNOLOGY
  AZ800-800, DC19-520, MI518-50,
  NM114-880, NY591-820, TX56-860
  CENTRAL AMERICA
    RI105-320
  INDIANS
    AZ800-803, TX56-860, TX56-860,
    WA954-880
  MEXICO
    AZ800-803
  MIDDLE AMERICA
    NM722-535
  NORTH AMERICA
    RI105-320, WA820-840

PACIFIC OCEAN
    WA820-840
  SOUTH AMERICA
    RI105-320
  SOUTHWESTERN US
    AZ800-803
ETHNOMUSICOLOGY
  MEXICO, NORTHWESTERN
    AZ750-32
  SOUTHWESTERN US
    AZ750-32
EUROPE
  See also individual countries and regions,
    AZ800-803, CA858-320, CA858-810,
    CT505-960, DC3-226, DC7-540,
    DC7-650, DC12-400, DC12-450,
    DC12-600, DC14-250, DC14-730,
    DC19-310, DC19-320, DC19-500,
    IL170-351, IL170-884, IN627-780,
    IN627-800, KY496-823, MN541-854,
    NC150-800, NC150-860, NJ578-530,
    NY589-690, NY595-670, OH171-320,
    PA725-720, TN630-510, UT912-110
  ARCHITECTURE
    DC1-480, NY591-350
  ART
    DC1-480, NY589-680, NY593-100
  ART COLLECTORS
    NY587-780
  ARTISTS
    OH823-770
  AUTHORS
    DC19-641
  AVIATION
    TX742-800
  BAHA'I
    IL981-560
  CARTOGRAPHY
    PA325-280
  CHEMISTRY
    PA726-765
  COLONIZATION
    MN541-854
  COMMERCE
    MN541-854, NY208-120
  COSTUMES
    NY591-350
  ECONOMIC AID TO
    NY589-560
  EDUCATION
    MD76-527
  FURNITURE
    NY591-350
  GAY RIGHTS MOVEMENT
    CT316-360
  GLASS
    NY214-140
  IMMIGRATION AND EMIGRATION
    MN763-790, WA904-770
  INDUSTRIAL DESIGN
    NY591-350
  INTERIOR DESIGN
    NY591-350
  JEWS
    NY590-680
  LAW
    MO430-420
  LITERARY MANUSCRIPTS
    MD285-805
  LITERATURE
    CT505-977
  LOGGING
    CA86-850
  LUTHERAN CHURCH
    MN625-710
  MEDICINE
    MD76-527, NY592-260
  MEDIEVAL
    CA143-240, CA756-320, DC12-650,
    IL170-351, IN627-810, IN825-850,
    KS527-790, MA891-880, MN226-720,
    MO810-190, NE624-400, NJ692-660,
    NY214-100, NY592-800, NY775-720,
    OH171-650, OR720-450, PA725-510,
    PA726-770, PA795-800, PA910-840

MILITARY GOVERNMENT AFTER
    WORLD WAR II
    MA21-770
  MILITARY HISTORY
    NY949-830
  MORAVIAN CHURCH
    PA90-500
  MUSIC
    IL916-820, NC930-530, NY588-380,
    NY872-760
  MUSICIANS
    NY590-720
  NEUROSCIENCES
    CA421-660
  POLITICIANS
    DC14-590
  POLITICS
    CT505-977
  PRE-WORLD WAR II
    CA578-130
  RELIGIOUS COMMUNITIES
    DC23-700
  RENAISSANCE
    CA143-240, CA143-240, CA756-320,
    DC6-800, DC12-650, IN627-810,
    MA891-880, MD76-880, MO810-190,
    NE624-400, NJ692-660, NY592-800,
    NY593-100, NY775-720, OH171-650,
    OR720-450, PA726-770, PA795-800,
    PA910-840
  SCIENTISTS
    MA169-310
  THEATER
    OH203-670
  TRADE WITH UNITED STATES
    MA338-840
  TRANSPORTATION
    NY591-350
  TRAVEL
    IL296-720, IN583-560
  UNIVERSITIES
    IN627-810
EUROPE, CENTRAL
  JEWS
    NY590-840, NY595-660
  REFUGEES
    NY593-720
EUROPE, EASTERN
    NY590-700
  JEWS
    NY586-650, NY587-820, NY595-660
  LABOR MOVEMENT
    NY587-820
  ORTHODOX CHURCH
    NY870-600
  WORLD WAR I
    MI230-780
  WORLD WAR II
    MI230-780
EUROPE, SOUTHERN
  MUSIC
    OH181-310
EUROPE, WESTERN
    DE540-790
EUTHANASIA
  MORALITY
    NY125-740
EVANGELICAL AND REFORMED CHURCH
  See also United Church of Christ,
    IL169-507, NY263-210, PA470-800
EVANGELICAL ASSOCIATION
    IA688-360, MN541-777, NJ464-666,
    WI733-333
EVANGELICAL CHURCH
    MN541-777, NJ464-666, OH813-310,
    WI733-333
EVANGELICAL COVENANT CHURCH
  CLERGY
    IL169-677
  MISSIONARIES
    IL169-677
  ORGANIZATIONS
    IL169-677
EVANGELICAL SYNOD OF NORTH
    AMERICA
    MO810-270

EVANGELICAL UNITED BRETHREN CHURCH
See also United Methodist church,
CO252-360, IA688-360, KS108-70,
MN541-777, NJ464-666, NJ464-666,
NM200-800, OH223-790, PA160-160,
WI733-333
CLERGY
OH223-790
VIRGINIA CONFERENCE
VA880-720
EVANGELISCHE GEMEINSCHAFT
WI733-333
EVANGELISM
IL976-850, PA645-560
EVANGELISTS
IN990-280, KY310-440
EVANS, MAURICE
NY593-485
EVANS, THOMAS W.
PA726-810
EVANS, WALKER
DC3-760
EVANSVILLE COLLEGE
IN209-800
EVANSVILLE, SUBURBAN AND NEWBURGH RAILWAY COMPANY
IN209-200
EVOLUTION
PA725-75
EWING PRESBYTERIAN CHURCH
NJ838-750
EXCELSIOR SOCIETY
NY303-600
EXHIBITIONS AND FAIRS
CA143-280, IL169-130, IL169-416,
IL170-273, MN763-573, MO810-600,
NY240-160, NY246-720, NY288-840,
OH112-280, OR720-450, PA725-240,
WA616-870, WA880-590
BASQUES
NV940-800
FOLKLORE
IL261-570
HORSES
MO400-400
INDIANS
NM722-360
LIVESTOCK
MO400-400
EXILES
See also Immigration and emigration;
Refugees, NY588-900
FRANCE
NY32-50
GERMANY
NH206-800
LITHUANIA
IL170-53
EXIT LAUGHING, BY IRVIN S. COBB
KY604-640
EXPEDITIONS
AZ500-400, MA169-190, MA169-500,
MI518-50, NY586-720
ARCTIC REGION
ME175-80
JAPAN
NY288-840
POLAR REGIONS
WI606-710
SCIENCE
DC14-180, HI350-73, PA725-15
EXPLORATION
AZ250-520, CO476-540, CT772-720,
DC1-805, DC1-810, DC12-190,
ME175-80, ME837-560, MI518-50,
MO810-510, NY589-500, OR624-480,
OR720-450, OR848-40, PA726-412,
TX56-860, UT836-880, WI714-880
AFRICA
KS164-520
ARCTIC REGION
ME162-100, ME162-120
BORNEO
KS164-520
BY GREAT BRITAIN
OR720-590

BY RUSSIA
OR720-590
BY SPAIN
CA756-320, CO270-240, OR720-590
MOUNTAINS
NY586-220
OLYMPIC MOUNTAINS
WA676-610
PACIFIC OCEAN, NORTHERN
WA820-770
PACIFIC OCEAN, SOUTHERN
KS164-520
SPACE
CA578-560, DC14-120, DC14-715,
SD684-280
TROPIC REGIONS
MO810-490
WESTERN US
CO252-181, MO810-490, OK558-790
EXPLORERS
CA778-780, MO810-390, OR464-490,
WY950-945
AFRICA
MI255-530
RUSSIA
MI518-50
EXPLOSIVES
MANUFACTURING
DE270-200, WA259-160
EXPO '74
See Spokane International Exposition
(1974)

F

FACTORIES
See Industry; Manufacturing; Mills
FACTORS WHICH MAKE JOLIET A GOOD CONVENTION CITY, BY JOLIET ASSOCIATION OF COMMERCE
IL404-410
FAIRBANK FAMILY
MA242-160
FAIRBANKS, THADDEUS
VT736-240
FAIRCHILD AERIAL SURVEYS
CA966-860
FAIRCHILD, CHARLES S.
NY164-570
FAIRFAX COUNTY VA
DC14-370
FAIRFIELD COLLEGE PREPARATORY SCHOOL
CT234-260
FAIRLESS HILLS PA
NJ838-750
FAIRS
See Exhibitions and fairs
FALKE, UMAR
IL261-566
FAMILY PLANNING
DC1-180, MD76-800
FAMILY RELATIONS
NY592-30
FANTASY
CA318-700
FAR EAST
See Asia, eastern
FAR WEST MO
IA533-280
FARGO COLLEGE
SD936-930
FARIAS, VALENTIN GOMEZ
TX56-860
FARLEY, A. G.
WA672-290
FARLOW HERBARIUM
MA169-270
FARLOW, WILLIAM G.
MA169-270

FARM EQUIPMENT
CA132-120, DC1-680, IN242-250,
NY125-700, NY261-320, WI834-40
MANUFACTURING
IL169-703, IL548-150, IN792-160,
NY125-720, OH223-880, OH223-880,
WI834-40
FARM SECURITY ADMINSTRATION
MD513-640
FARMER'S UNION
ND486-800
FARMERS
CT582-550, MA823-610, MA837-720,
NY254-160, PA965-490, SC306-200,
UT684-80, VT48-90, VT704-690
FARMERS' WIVES SOCIETY
IA600-322
FARMING
See also Agriculture; Farms; Plantations;
and related terms, CA624-710,
CA850-720, IL916-795, MA108-750,
MN363-360, ND375-570, NM494-570,
NY654-600, OH878-720, PA595-530,
PA965-490, SC270-160, TX231-120,
TX529-770, VA50-65, VT176-810,
VT296-690
COOPERATIVES
SD550-600, TN435-220
FARMINGTON CANAL
CT268-720
FARMINGTON CANAL COMPANY
CT505-560
FARMS
See also Agriculture; Farming; Plantations;
and related terms, CA620-760,
CT144-150, DE900-330, FL580-320,
IL567-520, KY358-40, ME287-160,
MI510-200, MI518-455, NJ358-320,
NY111-80, NY910-840, PA512-400,
PA935-690, WA909-760
COLONIES
NY594-20
FARNHAM, LYNNWOOD
PA725-345
FARNSWORTH, WILLIAM A.
ME725-880
FARR ALPACA
MA804-130
FARRAGUT, DAVID G.
AL580-530, MD57-800
FARRAND, BEATRIX
CA86-820
FARRELL, JAMES T.
NY125-740
FARRIER, ANDREW L.
VA90-840
FARRIER, MARTIN P.
VA90-840
FASHION INDUSTRY
WOMEN
DC19-555
FASHIONS
See also Clothing; Costumes, DC19-555,
NY587-840
FAULKNER, WILLIAM
LA600-755, MA961-870
FAUNCE, WILLIAM HERBERT PERRY
RI700-50
FAW FAMILY
GA765-440
FAWCETT, JOHN J.
RI700-630
FEDERAL AGENCIES
See Government agencies, National
FEDERAL ENERGY ADMINISTRATION
DC4-322
FEDERAL PERIOD
NY589-580
FEDERAL THEATER PROJECT
See Work Projects Administration
FEDERAL WRITERS' PROJECT
See Work Projects Administration
FEININGER, LYONEL
CA578-630, MA169-200, NY899-520
FELLAND, O. G.
MN625-710

FELLOWS, HENRY COFFIN
    KS948-240
FELLOWS, JOSEPH
    NY288-840
FELTON, CYRUS
    MA513-530
FEMINISM
    MA169-860
FEMINISTS
    NY286-240, NY587-880
FENCES
    ID160-130
FENN COLLEGE
    OH181-290
FENOLLOSA, MARY MCNEIL
    AL580-530
FERGUSON-JAYNE FAMILY
    NY235-160
FERGUSON, FERN
    NY978-880
FERNS
    MA169-270
FERRELL, JOHN A.
    NY612-690
FERRIES
    CA700-720, WA844-720
FERRIS, SCOTT
    OK490-520
FERRIS, WOODBRIDGE NATHAN
    MI100-240
FERTILIZER
    TN465-760
FESTIVALS
    See Celebrations
FETHERSTON, JOHN T.
    PA500-640
FICTION
    See Literature
FIDDLERS
    NE560-50
FIDDLES
    NE560-50
FIDLER, NOAH
    TN690-885
FIELD ARTILLERY
    OK372-240
FIELD FAMILY
    MA811-720
FIELD, CHARLES KELLOGG
    MA21-400
FIELD, EUGENE
    CO252-159, MO810-260, PA725-195
FIELD, ISOBEL
    CA680-720
FIFIELD FAMILY
    MA947-880
FIFTY YEARS IN THE ONION BUSINESS,
    BY RUSSELL RICE
    IA43-80
FIJI
    CA782-800
FILLMORE, MILLARD
    NY660-720
FILM
    See Motion pictures
FILSINGER, SARA TEASDALE
    IN275-170
FINANCE
    DC19-646, IA33-370, IL866-355,
    IN363-342, LA395-520, MI214-260,
    NY593-040
    AMERICAN REVOLUTION
        NY589-340
    WESTERN US
        CA720-960
FINANCE AND ADMINISTRATION
    DEPARTMENT (OR)
    OR816-590
FINE ARTS
    DC19-565, MO810-600
FINLAND
    MI390-720
FINN, FRANCIS J., JR.
    OH171-920
FINNEGANS WAKE, BY JAMES JOYCE
    NY323-320

FINNISH (SUOMI) EVANGELICAL
    LUTHERAN CHURCH
    IL170-91
FINNISH-AMERICANS
    MI390-720
    FOLKLORE
        OR48-40
FIRE COMMISSIONERS, BOARD OF
    (TRENTON NJ)
    NJ838-530
FIRE FIGHTING
    AL580-530, CA810-700, DC19-636,
    MA108-920, MA134-560, MA943-880,
    ME175-80, MI360-280, NC60-240,
    NC160-520, NH194-560, NJ124-240,
    NJ386-380, NJ574-560, NJ578-530,
    NJ838-530, NY353-520, NY433-350,
    NY587-720, NY858-720, OH968-880,
    PA725-240, PA725-780, SC54-80,
    VT704-690, VT720-720, WA300-175,
    WA381-330
FIRE INSURANCE
    DE900-320, PA725-780
FIRE PROTECTION
    OIL INDUSTRY
        DC1-580
FIREMEN AND ENGINEERS,
    BROTHERHOOD OF
    WA856-100
FIRES
    See also Disasters, ID600-130,
    MA108-920, NJ838-530, NY331-120,
    OR560-690
FIRESTONE FAMILY
    OH11-240
FIRESTONE, HARVEY S.
    OH11-240
FIRESTONE, HARVEY S., JR.
    OH11-240
FIRST CHRISTIAN CHURCH (FRANKFORT
    IN)
    IN237-240
FIRST CHRISTIAN CHURCH (RIALTO CA)
    CA640-640
FIRST CHURCH (NEW BRITAIN CT)
    CT477-130
FIRST CONGREGATIONAL CHURCH
    NE624-240
FIRST CORPS OF CADETS
    (MASSACHUSETTS)
    MA108-240
FIRST METHODIST CHURCH (MT.
    VERNON IA)
    IA699-120
FIRST METHODIST CHURCH (ROCHESTER
    NY)
    NY752-60
FIRST NATIONAL BANK OF NORTH
    BENNINGTON (VT)
    VT496-640
FISH
    OR901-760, TX56-780
FISHER, CHARLES
    NY288-840
FISHER, JONATHAN
    ME112-400, ME725-880
FISHERIES
    MI36-400, NY139-80, TN465-760
FISHING
    CA278-130, DC9-450, MA338-280,
    NY675-640, WA427-560, WA616-620
    COLUMBIA RIVER
        WA144-210
    SNAKE RIVER
        WA144-210
FISHING INDUSTRY
    AK750-120, DC19-591, NY590-760,
    OR720-590, WA820-880, WI362-520
    COLUMBIA RIVER
        OR48-40, WA144-210
    SNAKE RIVER
        WA144-210
FISKE, JENNIE MCGRAW
    NY439-180
FISKE, THADDEUS
    MA29-40

FITCH, GEORGE
    MA169-400
FITCH, GERALDINE
    MA169-400
FITZPATRICK, T. J.
    KS527-790
FLAGET, BENEDICT JOSEPH
    KY569-720
FLAGLER SYSTEM
    FL580-320
FLAGLER, HENRY MORRISON
    FL580-320
FLAGS
    DC14-720, DC19-616
FLAGSTAD, KIRSTEN
    CA720-180
FLAHERTY, ROBERT
    CA143-720
FLEISHER ART MEMORIAL
    PA726-255
FLEMING, GEORGE
    NY51-140
FLETCHER, JOHN GOULD, JR.
    AR510-810
FLETCHER, THOMAS
    PA725-150
FLIGHT (MAGAZINE)
    TX742-800
FLINT FAMILY
    CA414-500
FLOOD, DANIEL J.
    PA960-440
FLOODS
    See also Disasters, KY2A-80, KY42-800,
    NJ574-560, NY272-720, OH545-530,
    PA435-400, SD648-690, SD792-850,
    SD792-880
    CONTROL
        AZ550-040, DC1-810, DC9-450,
        DC19-800, NH784-720, OH223-880,
        OH990-640, PA520-470
    TETON DAM
        ID680-690
FLOOR COVERING INDUSTRY
    PA470-40
FLORENCE CRITTENTON SERVICES, INC.
    VA580-600
FLORIDA
    EPISCOPAL CHURCH
        AL580-650
    ROMAN CATHOLIC CHURCH
        PA726-495
FLORIDA FOLK FESTIVAL
    FL940-240
FLOWERS
    SC144-170, TX742-680
    ARRANGEMENT
        MA109-140
FLYING CLOUD (SHIP)
    CA480-500
FOCHT, BENJAMIN K.
    PA500-80
FOGARTY, JOHN E.
    RI700-630
FOHR, GERMANY
    CA314-120
FOLGER, EMILY JORDAN
    DC6-600
FOLGER, HENRY CLAY
    DC6-600
FOLK ART
    PA90-40, VA870-40, VT784-720
FOLK ARTISTS
    FL940-240
FOLK MEDICINE
    OH788-120
FOLK MUSIC
    CO180-120, KY96-850, NY166-80,
    NY872-760, VA235-230, VA235-250,
    VT432-520
    APPALACHIA
        NC570-530
    ARABIA
        NY166-80
    GREAT BRITAIN
        VT432-520

HUNGARY
NY166-80
ROMANIA
NY166-80
RUTHENIA
NY166-80
SLOVAKIA
NY166-80
TURKEY
NY166-80
YUGOSLAVIA
NY166-80
FOLKLIFE
CANADA, MARITIME PROVINCES
ME650-780
FOLKLORE
AL840-820, AL840-820, AR330-830,
AR330-830, CA136-120, CA143-470,
CA159-120, CA862-810, CO108-810,
CO180-120, CO252-100, DC7-650,
DC12-300, DE270-200, DE540-790,
FL940-240, GA840-240, GA895-280,
HI350-73, ID80-365, ID240-520,
ID480-480, ID480-810, ID880-80,
IL169-325, IN66-340, IN66-350,
IN363-350, IN627-780, KS377-250,
KY96-850, KY96-870, KY22W-920,
KY630-40, MA169-860, ME162-120,
ME650-780, MI230-165, MN763-540,
MO210-815, MS900-870, NJ568-625,
NJ568-670, NJ786-40, NY10-640,
NY200-720, NY574-710, NY595-700,
NY708-720, NY949-830, OH181-270,
OH181-880, OH301-690, OK592-580,
OR96-120, PA735-110, PA960-440,
TN690-780, UT684-80, UT912-110,
VA235-230, VA670-690, VT176-810,
VT296-690, VT464-840, WA112-880,
WA144-210, WA152-125, WA241-170,
WA565-40, WA602-600, WA629-655,
WA647-270, WA687-90, WA724-890,
WA761-680, WA880-190, WA880-280,
WA880-550, WA900-730, WA904-870,
WA909-760, WA954-880, WA960-170,
WA975-80, WA994-935, WI654-790,
WV650-890
BLUE RIDGE MOUNTAINS
VA235-230
CANADA, MARITIME PROVINCES
ME650-780
EXHIBITIONS AND FAIRS
IL261-570
FINNISH-AMERICANS
OR48-40
KENTUCKY
IN66-340
MICHIGAN
IN66-340
OHIO
IN66-340
FONDA FAMILY
NY297-520
FOOD
See also Cooking; Recipes
DISTRIBUTION
NY594-20
PACKING HOUSES
CA770-120
PROCESSING
DC19-591
FOOT, PHILLIPA
NY125-740
FOOTE, WILLIAM HENRY
VA690-750
FORAND, AIME J.
RI700-630
FORBES, EDWARD W.
MA169-300
FORBES, ESTHER
MA985-110
FORD FAMILY
MI214-140
FORD MOTOR COMPANY
MI214-260
FORD, FORD MADDOX
MI720-600

FORD, GERALD R.
MI40-300, MS80-40
FORD, HENRY
MI214-140, MI214-260
FORD, LUCINDA E.
NY82-80
FORD, WILLIAM L.
NY101-90
FOREIGN AID
DC9-450
AFRICA
DC1-180
ASIA
DC1-180
LATIN AMERICA
DC1-180
FOREIGN RELATIONS
NY589-160, SD450-150
GREAT BRITAIN
IN66-390, MA169-370
GREECE
MA169-800
FOREMAN, JOHN A.
VA640-650
FORENSIC MEDICINE
OH181-180
FOREST PRODUCTS INDUSTRY
WA310-880
FOREST SERVICE
See also under repository index,
CO252-550, OR560-690, WA168-130,
WA729-820, WA820-824, WA943-280,
WA950-840
FORESTRY
AZ700-40, CA86-850, CA720-307,
CA782-240, CO252-163, DC1-460,
DC4-260, NC680-550, OR144-610,
TN465-760, VA50-240
OREGON
CA86-850
ORGANIZATIONS
CA782-240
RANGERS
NE240-560
WASHINGTON
CA86-850
FORESTS
AK350-800, AL80-40, AL620-20,
AL840-820, AR330-830, AZ250-575,
AZ350-290, AZ700-40, AZ750-45,
AZ800-30, AZ800-830, CA86-780,
CA86-810, CA86-850, CA86-920,
CA94-360, CA136-120, CA206-790,
CA274-120, CA274-250, CA274-720,
CA386-560, CA421-770, CA421-774,
CA624-740, CA676-110, CA676-130,
CA700-720, CA704-560, CA720-180,
CA756-320, CA760-710, CA774-800,
CA782-240, CA782-800, CA858-320,
CA858-810, CA862-810, CA882-720,
CA994-940, CO108-810, CO252-70,
CO252-100, CO252-163, CO252-181,
CO252-550, CO378-120, CT505-890,
CT505-960, DC7-650, DC12-300,
DC14-250, DC19-310, DE90-140,
DE270-200, DE540-790, DE810-330,
FL220-795, FL600-640, FL600-800,
FL800-245, FL800-262, FL800-575,
GA90-200, GA90-270, GA90-300,
GA405-560, HI350-300, IA33-370,
IA233-360, IA466-360, IA466-800,
IA966-320, ID80-365, ID240-520,
ID480-810, ID600-130, IL124-725,
IL169-325, IL170-280, IL170-351,
IL170-884, IL170-910, IL866-355,
IL866-365, IL916-795, IL916-810,
IN66-380, IN275-150, IN363-350,
IN363-360, IN935-650, KS10-170,
KS527-795, KS878-430, KY96-870,
KY288-425, KY496-765, KY760-720,
LA62-500, LA570-540, LA600-755,
LA780-490, MA70-70, MA108-750,
MA108-965, MA109-120, MA169-270,
MA627-560, MA673-640, MA733-210,
MA733-660, MA871-540, MA985-70,
MA985-860, MD76-515, ME37-525,
ME37-535, ME37-540, ME162-640,

ME200-120, ME650-780, ME650-810,
ME712-530, ME750-160, ME925-870,
MI40-784, MI40-796, MI40-820,
MI64-70, MI214-260, MI214-280,
MI230-165, MI230-880, MI255-545,
MI355-290, MI445-560, MI464-530,
MI550-530, MI605-520, MI665-120,
MI675-320, MI824-320, MN198-120,
MN321-690, MN541-925, MN625-570,
MN763-400, MN763-540, MO210-815,
MO400-320, MO430-540, MO810-490,
MS610-520, MS900-870, MT130-540,
MT530-500, MT700-800, MT870-280,
NC60-640, NC60-720, NC150-800,
NC210-870, NC260-150, NC260-170,
NC680-460, NC680-550, NC930-840,
NE284-560, NE560-550, NE560-870,
NH134-540, NJ46-560, NJ112-120,
NJ548-400, NJ548-530, NJ568-670,
NJ578-510, NJ838-580, NM114-900,
NV940-560, NV940-810, NY10-640,
NY139-120, NY211-580, NY419-310,
NY427-240, NY439-120, NY439-150,
NY439-180, NY586-180, NY588-940,
NY592-320, NY592-460, NY592-800,
NY594-380, NY720-640, NY752-880,
NY872-720, NY872-800, OH35-610,
OH97-80, OH171-110, OH181-880,
OH203-600, OH203-680, OK558-790,
OK592-620, OK592-640, OR144-600,
OR176-120, OR224-800, OR224-880,
OR400-720, OR464-490, OR688-820,
OR720-590, OR720-700, OR816-590,
PA40-600, PA90-500, PA160-160,
PA380-650, PA470-40, PA725-75,
PA725-240, PA725-720, PA726-7,
PA726-240, PA726-615, PA726-855,
PA735-140, PA740-320, PA755-320,
PA860-710, PA895-710, PA915-870,
PA945-120, PA960-910, SC216-720,
SC216-820, SD450-150, SD558-720,
SD792-820, TN285-280, TN630-530,
TN690-780, TN840-800, TX56-520,
TX56-850, TX374-550, TX590-760,
TX632-720, UT380-810, UT684-80,
UT912-850, UT988-40, VA50-240,
VA145-780, VA690-870, VA690-910,
VA870-110, VT176-810, VT464-840,
VT704-280, WA616-870, WA676-610,
WA724-890, WA820-550, WA820-880,
WA880-190, WA904-770, WA904-870,
WI142-800, WI202-790, WI266-820,
WI298-810, WI346-720, WI346-890,
WI418-800, WI456-810, WI502-440,
WI554-480, WI554-600, WI722-770,
WI754-170, WV650-890, WY135-865,
WY500-800, WY560-280, WY950-940
FIRES
ID600-130, NC60-240
PRODUCTS
NY594-640, WI346-240
FORESTS, NATIONAL
See Forest Service; and individual National
Forests in repository index
FORMAN, SAMUEL
NY164-570
FORMOSA
MI518-50
FORT ATKINSON
IA211-480, NE352-880
FORT BELVOIR
VA245-800
FORT BOWIE NATIONAL HISTORIC SITE
AZ850-120
FORT BOWYER
AL580-530
FORT CAMPBELL
KY250-160
FORT CASEY
WA506-480
FORT COLVILLE
WA168-135
FORT CONCHO
TX770-240
FORT CONSTITUTION
NH680-760

FORT DELAWARE
DE60-240
FORT FREDERICA
GA885-240
FORT GEORGE WRIGHT
WA880-260
FORT GRATIOT
MI775-520
FORT KNOX
KY272-635
FORT LA PRESENTATION
NY634-160
FORT LARAMIE
WY305-240
FORT LARNED
KS513-250, KS513-720
FORT LEWIS
WA320-230, WA904-770
FORT MACKINAC
MI590-520
FORT MCHENRY
MD76-240
FORT MCNAIR
DC14-410
FORT MERVINE
CA480-800
FORT MONROE
VA275-240
FORT NISQUALLY
WA259-160, WA904-260
FORT RENO
OK338-200
FORT ROBINSON PRISON CAMP
NE284-560
FORT SCHUYLER
NY594-340
FORT SILL
OK372-240
FORT SPOKANE
WA240-250
FORT ST. JOSEPH
MI700-560
FORT UNION
NM513-560
FORT VANCOUVER
WA943-250
FORT WILLIAM AND MARY
NH680-760
FORT WORDEN COASTAL DEFENSE
STATION
WA681-250
FORT WORTH STOCKYARD
TX280-540
FORT YATES ND
MO220-120
FORTIFICATIONS
NY949-830
FORTS
See also Frontier defences; and individual
forts, *AR60-120, DC19-616, FL660-120,
MI1200-240, NH118-600, NM513-560,
NY990-600, SD792-880, TX374-40,
TX770-240*
FOSTER GRANDPARENT PROGRAM
(ACTION)
DC1-40
FOSTER, JOHN G.
NH672-570
FOSTER, STEPHEN
NH748-650
FOUNDATIONS (PHILANTHROPIC)
DC2-850, GA90-700
FOURTH DISTRICT AGRICULTURAL AND
MECHANICAL SCHOOL
GA210-880
FOUST, JULIUS I.
NC380-800
FOWLER, LAURENCE HALL
MD76-340
FOX RIVER
WI554-600
FOX, JOHN
SC576-480
FOX, NELSON L.
NY915-870
FOXCROFT FAMILY
MA108-240

FRAKTUR
PA725-510
FRAKTUR (PENNSYLVANIA GERMAN
FOLK ART)
PA90-40, VA870-40
FRANCE
*DC6-600, DC12-300, DC19-700,
NC590-320, PA735-825, PA986-960*
AMERICAN REVOLUTION
VA870-150
ANABAPTISTS
OH92-520
ARCHITECTURE
NY588-820
BASQUES
NV940-800
COLONIES
*AL580-510, GA895-160, IN902-840,
LA358-800, LA600-465, LA600-505,
LA600-555, MO810-510, MS550-500,
NY634-160, PA55-760*
EXILES
NY32-50
IMMIGRATION AND EMIGRATION
IL866-355
INTERVENTION IN MEXICO
TX483-690
LITERATURE
CT505-890, MO810-690, TX56-890
MADAGASCAR WAR
MI255-530
MENNONITES
OH92-520
MILITARY OFFICERS
DC14-590
MISSIONARIES
OH223-720
PAINTERS
CA143-240
POETS
PA726-615
RELIGIOUS COMMUNITIES
*IA188-777, IL169-565, KY496-850,
KY532-720, MA169-305, PA726-480*
ROYALTY
MN226-700, PA960-870
SIEGE, YORKTOWN VA
VA245-800
SUPERIOR COUNCIL (LA)
LA600-465
THEATER
OH203-670
WORLD WAR I
FL60-720
FRANCIS, ROBERT
MA21-770
FRANCISCANS
MD703-40, NM114-50
BRAZIL
MD703-40
CALIFORNIA
MD703-40
LATIN AMERICA
MD703-40
NEW MEXICO
MD703-40
FRANCK, JAMES
IL170-884
FRANCKLYN LAND AND CATTLE
COMPANY
TX691-130
FRANCONIA MENNONITE CONFERENCE
PA478-530
FRANK STREET METHODIST CHURCH
(ROCHESTER NY)
NY752-60
FRANK, GLENN
MO460-560
FRANK, LEO
MA871-90
FRANK, WERNER
CA132-160
FRANKLIN, BENJAMIN
CT505-945, MA961-870, PA820-520
FRANKLIN, BENJAMIN, FAMILY
CT505-945

FRANKLIN, WILLIAM
NJ666-650
FRASER, CHARLES
SC144-90
FRASER, WILLARD E.
MT100-200
FRATERNITIES
IL723-80, NY216-720, OH853-800
FRECHETTE-HOWELLS FAMILY
NY18-40
FREDERIC, HAROLD
MI255-530
FREDONIA ACADEMY
NY310-160
FREE BAPTIST CHURCH
NY752-40
FREE BED ASSOCIATION OF THE
AROOSTOOK HOSPITAL
ME437-120
FREE METHODIST CHURCH
NY752-660, WA820-772
MISSIONARIES
IN990-240
FREE WILL BAPTIST CHURCH
NC610-520
ORGANIZATIONS
TN690-240
FREEDMAN'S AID AND SOUTHERN
EDUCATION SOCIETY
TN690-880
FREEDMEN'S AID SOCIETY (METHODIST
EPISCOPAL CHURCH)
GA90-360
FREEDMEN'S BUREAU
ME162-120, OH953-870, VA670-690
FREEMAN, CHARLES W.
IL170-429
FREEMAN, JAMES EDWARD
DC5-800
FREEMAN, OTIS W.
WA144-190
FREER, CHARLES L.
DC19-330
FREIGHTING
MT530-500
FRENCH AND INDIAN WAR
*CT316-330, MA81-80, NH118-600,
NH134-530, NY923-880, VT464-840*
FRENCH MADAGASCAR WAR
MI255-530
FRENCH REVOLUTION
CA206-790, PA725-615
FRENCH-AMERICANS
LA358-800, ME437-120, RI945-800
HUGUENOTS
NY574-320
FRENCH-CANADIANS
NH600-30, RI945-800
FRENCH, BURTON L.
OH680-540
FRENCH, DANIEL CHESTER
MA334-120
FRENCH, HENRY FLAGG
MA334-120
FRENCH, MARY
MA334-120
FREUD, ANNA
KS878-520, NY587-300, NY592-640
FREUD, SIGMUND
NY592-640
FRIARIES
IL55-120
FRIARS MINOR CONVENTUAL
NY741-720
CANADA
NY741-720
FRIEDENWALD, HARRY
MD76-70, MD76-300
FRIEDMAN, WILLIAM F.
VA430-280
FRIENDS ASYLUM
PA725-525
FRIENDS OF THE BELCHERTOWN STATE
SCHOOL
MA21-770
FRIGIDAIRE COMPANY
OH223-520

FRIGIDAIRE CORPORATION
MI314-265
FROEBEL, FRIEDRICH
DC1-860
FRONCZAK, FRANCIS E.
NY134-730
FRONTIER
DC3-210, VT296-690, WI346-720
DEFENCES
GA90-270
GUIDES
CA954-720
FROST, ELINOR
CT512-120, IN275-170
FROST, LESLEY
CT512-120
FROST, ROBERT
CT316-770, CT512-120, MA21-40,
MA108-240, NH206-800, NH772-640,
OH320-430
FRUIT
CA206-790, CA770-120, DC14-180
CANNING
WA726-640
FUGITIVE/AGRARIAN MOVEMENT
(LITERATURE)
TN690-975
FULLER FAMILY (OHIO)
OH399-420
FULLER, MARGARET
CT512-120
FULLER, MURIEL
PA726-600
FULTON, ROBERT
MD57-800
FUNERALS
See also Undertakers, *LA535-600,*
NH194-160
FUNGI
MA169-270
FUNK, JOSEPH
VA115-80
FUNSTON, FREDERICK
KS878-430
FUR TRADE
CA862-810, MI865-80, MN261-810,
MO810-510, MT130-540, MT530-500,
OR720-590, SD558-720, WA904-260
MINNESOTA
CA86-780, CT505-960, DC12-300,
DC14-250, MI1230-165, MI865-80,
NY592-460, WI346-720
FURLONG, CHARLES WELLINGTON
OR688-810
FURNITURE
DC14-640, DC19-560, NY574-320,
NY590-360, NY591-350, TX754-880,
VA870-130
EUROPE
NY591-350
GREAT BRITAIN
DE900-320
NEW ENGLAND
DE900-320
FUTURISM
WA880-590

G

GAG, WANDA HAZEL
MN541-838
GAGE, MATILDA JOSLYN
NY286-240
GALLAGHER, RAYMOND JOSEPH
IN440-160
GALLIMORE, ARTHUR RAYMOND
NC840-720
GALLOWAY, WILLIAM A.
OH982-290
GALLUP FAMILY
CT512-120
GALVIN, CHARLES O.
TX252-780
GAMBLE, ANNA DILL
PA380-700

GAMBLE, THOMAS
GA895-120
GAMBLING
LA600-555, NV630-800, NY795-320
GAMES
See also names of specific games,
OH181-270
GANDHI, MOHANDAS KARAMCHAND
(MAHATMA GANDHI)
DC12-150
GANDY, JOHN MANUEL
VA630-840
GANTT, HORSLEY
MD76-315
GARDENING
MA109-140 GARDENS
DC14-640, DE900-330, NY147-720,
NY147-880, VA870-130, WV550-280
GARDNER, OLIVER MAX
NC100-280
GARFIELD MEMORIAL HOSPITAL
DC23-250
GARFIELD, JAMES ABRAM
OH481-530
GARLAND JUNIOR COLLEGE
MA109-630
GARLAND, HAMLIN
IN275-170, WI853-880
GARMENT INDUSTRY
DC19-555, NY439-150, NY590-430
GARRETT, ALEXANDER C.
TX252-200
GARRETT, JOHN WORK
MD76-340
GARRICK, DAVID
CT505-977, DC6-600
GARRISON FAMILY
MA624-740
GARRISON, WILLIAM LLOYD
KS948-890
GARVIN, ROBERT
NY101-90
GAS COMPANIES
IA188-360, VA50-30, VA700-322
GAS INDUSTRY
LA885-480, TX252-730, VA50-30
TECHNOLOGY
VA50-30
GASOLINE PUMPS
MANUFACTURING
IN231-40
GASOLINE STATIONS
DC1-580
GATES COLLEGE
NE288-160
GATES FAMILY
MA513-530
GATES, FREDERICK T.
NY612-690
GATHINGS, E. C.
AR890-20
GAUNTLETT, JOHN C.
NY439-180
GAUSS, THAYER
NY251-320
GAY RIGHTS MOVEMENT
CA421-520, CT316-360
CANADA
CT316-360
EUROPE
CT316-360
GAYARRE, CHARLES
LA600-755
GEHL, JOHN
WI202-120
GEISER, S. W.
TX252-790
GELLETT, EDWIN C.
PA725-600
GENERAL LAND OFFICE
CO252-550
GENERAL MISSIONARY SOCIETY OF
WESTERN NEW YORK
NY928-880
GENERAL MOTORS CORPORATION
MI314-60

GENERAL STORES
See also Mercantile activities, *CA814-120,*
GA940-280, KY604-640, MA837-720,
NY111-60, NY240-160, NY720-640,
OR424-880, WA885-720
GENESEE COUNTRY (NY)
NY752-720
GENESEE RIVER VALLEY
NY321-720
GENESEE VALLEY CANAL
NY752-720
GENETICS
CT505-120, PA725-75
GENSMAN, L. M.
OK490-520
GEOGRAPHERS
WOMEN
DC19-750
GEOGRAPHY
AL840-280, CA432-520, CT234-230,
DC19-750, GA90-270, HI350-80,
IL261-565, IN55-80, IN902-80,
MA985-120, MO760-530, NJ838-740,
NY593-420, PA915-870, SD684-280,
WA144-190
SOUTHWESTERN US
NM874-440
GEOLOGISTS
OR720-580
GEOLOGY
AL840-280, AZ250-520, CA143-490,
CA421-340, CA720-161, DC14-540,
GA90-270, IL140-322, IL801-20,
KS635-600, MI518-50, MO760-530,
MO760-780, NC150-780, NJ464-240,
NJ838-740, NY10-570, NY586-720,
OH203-650, OH370-310, OR720-580,
OR848-40, PA725-75, TX252-730,
TX252-770, TX252-790, WA904-790,
WI890-320
MARINE
CO108-560
GEOMAGNETISM
CO108-560
GEOPHYSICS
CA720-161, MD755-560
MARINE
CO108-560
GEORGE II (KING OF ENGLAND)
NC900-810
GEORGE III (KING OF ENGLAND)
NJ552-80
GEORGE JUNIOR REPUBLIC
NY439-120
GEORGE PEABODY COLLEGE FOR
TEACHERS
TN690-975
GEORGE, HARRY L.
MO800-730
GEORGE, WILLIAM REUBEN
NY439-120
GEORGIA
AL80-40, NC150-800
LAND, RECORDS
TX14-720
GEORGIA HISTORICAL COMMISSION
GA90-265
GEORGIA STATE DENTAL SOCIETY
GA90-210
GERMAN FREE BED SOCIETY
MA451-360
GERMAN IMMIGRATION SOCIETY
TX640-720
GERMAN METHODIST COLLEGE
IA688-360
GERMAN REFORMED CHURCH
MO810-270, OH813-310, PA210-800,
PA470-800
GERMAN SCHOOL
MA451-360
GERMAN SOUTHWEST AFRICA
RAILROADS
MI255-530
GERMAN-AMERICANS
IL246-190, IL770-40, MI322-240,
OH147-520, PA210-800, TX381-280,
TX640-720, WI138-480

LUTHERAN CHURCH
IA244-30
MUSICIANS
NY590-720
ORGANIZATIONS
MA451-360
SCHOOLS
MA451-360
GERMAN, GEORGE B.
SD936-950
GERMANS, FROM RUSSIA (IMMIGRANTS)
CO378-110, CO498-40, WA602-600
GERMANTOWN FRIENDS SCHOOL
PA725-540
GERMANY
CA314-120, CA858-320, PA735-825,
PA986-960
AIR FORCE
AL560-720, DC1-200
ANABAPTISTS
OH92-520
BAPTIST CHURCH
TN690-750
COMPOSERS
IL170-637
EXILES
NH206-800
GOVERNMENT AGENCIES
IL169-247
IMMIGRATION AND EMIGRATION
CA86-780, CA86-890, CA90-30,
CA314-120, CA421-40, CA421-750,
CA421-830, CA540-520, CA578-130,
CA774-800, CA858-320, CA858-820,
CT428-865, CT505-890, CT505-910,
CT505-960, DC1-640, DC12-300,
DC14-250, DC19-310, DC19-320,
DC19-327, DC19-641, GA75-810,
IA466-800, IL124-725, IL169-729,
IL170-78, IL170-637, IL170-884,
IL170-897, IL170-910, IL770-40,
IL916-810, IL916-820, IN66-380,
IN66-395, IN627-780, KS527-790,
LA600-760, MA108-240, MA108-750,
MA169-170, MA169-200, MA169-230,
MA169-370, MA871-90, MD76-360,
ME925-130, MI230-165, MI440-320,
MN541-902, MN763-540, MN763-790,
MO210-815, NJ578-530, NY134-90,
NY310-720, NY427-240, NY439-120,
NY493-320, NY586-580, NY588-900,
NY590-840, NY590-940, NY591-420,
NY591-780, NY591-840, NY592-800,
NY593-120, NY593-840, NY595-700,
NY899-600, OH147-520, OH171-800,
OH665-590, PA25-520, PA725-75,
PA725-495, PA860-710, TX56-850,
TX56-890, TX280-540, UT912-820,
WI346-720, WY500-800
JEWS
MD76-70, NY590-680, NY590-840
LABOR MOVEMENTS
NY590-840
LITERARY FIGURES
MD76-360
LITERATURE
CA206-790, CT505-890
MENNONITES
OH92-520
METHODISM
IA688-360
MILITARY HISTORY
SC144-150
MORAVIANS
PA90-320
MOTION PICTURES
DC12-450
MUSICIANS
NY590-720
NAVY
DC14-730
OCCUPATION BY UNITED STATES
NY18-40
RELIGIOUS COMMUNITIES
IL866-320, KY496-850, PA30-720
THEOLOGY
IA244-30

WAR CRIMES
NY588-860
WRITERS
IL170-637
GERMANY (HESSE)
MILITARY PERSONNEL
NJ548-530, NY594-360, NY595-360
GERONIMO
AZ475-640
GERRARD, C. W.
IN539-100
GESELL, ARNOLD
OH11-840
GHANA
MISSIONARIES
MO810-750
GIBBONS, EDMUND F.
NY10-675
GIBSON, FRANCIS MARION
MT100-200
GIDDINGS, JOSHUA REED
OH878-720
GIFFORD, WILLIAM
NY51-140
GILBRETH, FRANK BUNKER
IN935-650
GILBRETH, LILLIAN MOLLER
IN935-650
GILL, ERIC
CA421-774, CA720-910
GILL, EVERETT
NC840-720
GILL, H. S.
CT435-520
GILLETTE, WILLIAM H.
CT316-560
GILLIE, GEORGE
IN231-40
GILMAN, DANIEL COIT
MD76-360
GILMAN, GORHAM
HI350-315
**GILMER, ELIZABETH MERIWETHER
(DOROTHY DIX)**
TN75-50
GILMORE, MELVIN R.
MI40-814
GILPIN, LAURA
CO180-640, TX374-40
GIRARD, STEPHEN
PA725-615
GIRL SCOUTS
GA895-290
GIROD ASYLUM
LA600-555
GISSING, GEORGE ROBERT
NY587-880
GLACIERS
NY10-570
NORTH AMERICA
NY586-220
GLASHEEN, ADALINE
NY323-320
GLASS
DC19-545, NY214-140, PA726-895
CONTAINERS
CT961-210, VA500-322
EUROPE
NY214-140
MANUFACTURING
CT961-210, MA738-720, MI214-280,
NY214-120, NY214-140, NY269-200,
VA500-322
MIDDLE EAST
NY214-140
RECYCLING
VA500-322
GLEN FAMILY
NY804-720
GLENS FALLS INSURANCE COMPANY
NY331-280
GOBATTI MANUFACTURING COMPANY
CO768-640
GODDARD FAMILY
MA985-110
GODDARD, ROBERT HUTCHINGS
MA985-110, NM684-690

GODDELL, WILLIAM
PA945-880
GODFREY, EDWARD SETTLE
MT100-200
GOETHE, CHARLES M.
CA676-140
GOFF, IVAN
CA436-640
GOGARTY, OLIVER ST. JOHN
PA500-80
GOIRAN, HENRI
MA528-780
GOITER
OH181-180
GOLD
MINING
CA624-710, CA676-130, DC1-810,
NV200-920, TX280-540
GOLD RUSHES
AK700-120, CA720-180, CA782-730,
CA814-120, CO252-181, MA70-70
CALIFORNIA
NY288-840, NY990-600
GOLDSMITH, OLIVER
CT505-977, PA725-510
GOLDWATER, BARRY M.
AZ750-10, MI440-320
GOMPERS, SAMUEL
DC1-400
GOOD COMRADES, BY FELIX SALTEN
IN363-400
GOOD NEWS (PUBLISHER)
KY886-30
GOOD-ROADS MOVEMENT
ORGANIZATIONS
WA904-665
GOODMAN THEATRE
IL169-416
GOODWIN, SAMUEL
ME950-480
GOODWIN, SAMUEL, FAMILY
ME950-480
GOODYEAR, CHARLES
OH11-290
GOOL, Z.
IL261-566
GORDOA FAMILY
LA600-760
GORDON FAMILY
GA895-290, NJ175-33
GORDON, MAX
NY593-485
GORDON, MYRON
NY593-130
GORDON, THOMAS, FAMILY
NY240-160
GORE FAMILY
MA871-280
GORE, CHRISTOPHER
MA871-280
GORE, T. P.
OK490-520
GORHAM, NATHANIEL
NY288-840
GOSCHENHOPPEN AREA
PA345-280
GOSPEL DOLLAR LEAGUE
KY310-440
GOSPEL TRUMPET (PUBLISHER)
IN22-50
GOSSAGE, JOHN
DC3-760
GOTHIC REVIVAL (ARCHITECTURE)
DC19-560
GOUCHER, JOHN FRANKLIN
MD76-790
GOVERNMENT
CA862-730, DE810-330, GA75-790,
IN792-560, KY496-800, KY760-720,
MA108-965, MA169-860, MI40-784,
MI214-150, MT530-500, NM494-570,
NY872-800, PA100-320, TX56-850,
TX56-860, VA50-50, VT176-810
COMMISSION FORM OF
TX397-690
EMPLOYEES
MI230-880

LEADERS
CA421-774, MA108-240, NJ692-660

OFFICIALS
CA778-800, DC14-725, HI350-300,
HI350-808, IN242-230, IN902-840,
NV90-530, SC144-730, SC185-120,
SC576-480, VA430-280, WV435-520

OFFICIALS, LOCAL
AK250-110, IN572-320, IN649-520,
TN630-570, TX851-690

OFFICIALS, NATIONAL
MA797-400, MS80-80, NY164-570,
WA880-280

OFFICIALS, STATE
AK250-110, MS80-80

GOVERNMENT AGENCIES
See also Public documents; listings
beginning Department of. . ., CA86-882,
CA480-510, CA712-708, CA764-510,
CA922-840, CO252-163, DC19-320,
DE540-790, IN209-140, KY78J-650,
MN419-440, MN742-750, MO810-940,
NY590-700, TN60-120, TX940-720

AGRICULTURE
OR816-590

COUNTY
MO410-545

GERMANY
IL169-247

GREAT BRITAIN
IL169-247, OR720-590

JAPAN
DC12-150, DC12-400, IL169-247

LOCAL
AK350-120, AK500-20, AK900-840,
AL120-100, AL580-530, AL620-20,
AZ475-640, AZ550-040, AZ600-200,
CA136-40, CA168-120, CA314-320,
CA382-480, CA421-330, CA500-560,
CA504-560, CA578-675, CA624-710,
CA676-140, CA676-740, CA692-130,
CA700-720, CA720-675, CA728-730,
CA760-710, CA770-120, CA810-700,
CA870-710, CA934-835, CA942-940,
CO54-40, CO252-70, CO306-200,
CT36-80, CT120-120, CT144-880,
CT484-550, CT505-560, CT596-480,
CT603-360, CT718-720, CT870-520,
DC3-550, DC13-300, DC14-370,
DC14-600, DE90-140, FL440-150,
FL590-550, FL660-720, FL800-245,
GA90-30, GA105-720, GA950-480,
HI350-340, IA122-120, IA122-120,
IA244-480, IA600-322, ID400-720,
IL55-80, IL124-725, IL186-170,
IL202-550, IL236-520, IL246-200,
IL261-200, IL305-430, IL325-290,
IL424-480, IL469-480, IL542-360,
IL567-600, IL599-520, IL624-380,
IL866-480, IL866-715, IL916-840,
IN22-510, IN77-200, IN121-80,
IN187-200, IN209-360, IN209-880,
IN231-40, IN253-360, IN275-640,
IN440-760, IN539-80, IN594-560,
KS10-150, KS136-880, KS335-240,
KS385-280, KS513-720, KS593-510,
KS607-690, KS760-480, KS774-690,
KS878-430, KS934-120, KY188-440,
KY288-425, KY464-800, KY496-400,
KY496-785, KY598-600, LA62-470,
LA600-555, LA600-920, LA885-480,
MA29-40, MA154-640, MA196-120,
MA217-130, MA231-640, MA238-520,
MA242-160, MA246-160, MA293-200,
MA323-230, MA398-330, MA432-320,
MA466-480, MA478-800, MA580-550,
MA580-570, MA590-570, MA624-240,
MA654-590, MA673-640, MA708-40,
MA725-320, MA738-700, MA761-720,
MA817-720, MA823-610, MA837-720,
MA871-860, MA947-880, MA970-890,
MD57-500, MD76-60, MD76-515,
MD76-800, MD513-640, MD760-530,
ME37-525, ME112-80, ME187-730,
ME453-40, ME460-440, ME950-480,
MI8-480, MI20-50, MI60-880,
MI126-880, MI230-165, MI355-270,

MI360-280, MI445-560, MI550-530,
MI620-520, MI650-510, MI675-510,
MI700-560, MI705-560, MI775-520,
MI795-600, MI828-720, MI925-560,
MI935-770, MI982-80, MN38-520,
MN185-120, MN261-170, MN261-810,
MN307-200, MN314-520, MN363-360,
MN506-80, MN562-520, MN618-80,
MN674-630, MN728-690, MN763-540,
MN975-730, MO400-400, MO770-710,
MO810-510, MS550-500, NC30-715,
NC160-520, NC680-460, ND117-240,
ND523-720, NE368-160, NE560-550,
NE720-120, NH108-720, NH134-540,
NH206-800, NH600-510, NH680-760,
NH688-280, NH696-560, NH732-560,
NH796-690, NH832-720, NJ92-80,
NJ100-80, NJ138-120, NJ304-80,
NJ358-320, NJ386-380, NJ444-240,
NJ574-560, NJ708-690, NJ766-160,
NJ838-580, NJ950-520, NJ982-280,
NM570-480, NM722-570, NM760-720,
NV90-530, NV450-120, NY10-60,
NY10-570, NY18-720, NY20-40,
NY29-40, NY69-280, NY82-80,
NY101-90, NY111-60, NY124-60,
NY148A-12, NY150-700, NY172-120,
NY187-120, NY216-120, NY219-290,
NY222-110, NY235-160, NY240-160,
NY246-720, NY250-50, NY264-200,
NY274-200, NY292-520, NY331-280,
NY382-310, NY385-320, NY393-320,
NY393-640, NY404-640, NY407-320,
NY411-320, NY419-350, NY439-180,
NY443-400, NY490-480, NY510-880,
NY542-320, NY550-520, NY562-510,
NY563-120, NY563-322, NY587-720,
NY592-350, NY593-900, NY594-360,
NY599-560, NY602-570, NY618-115,
NY648-800, NY667-600, NY693-920,
NY702-660, NY726-40, NY752-250,
NY752-720, NY795-120, NY795-710,
NY827-720, NY893-890, NY902-560,
NY923-880, NY932-880, NY958-640,
NY978-880, OH11-810, OH35-610,
OH97-80, OH112-280, OH157-120,
OH171-800, OH181-325, OH203-600,
OH223-160, OH223-880, OH399-420,
OH505-510, OH665-580, OH684-520,
OH714-510, OH968-880, OK524-280,
OK592-650, OK854-840, OR400-720,
OR816-590, OR880-760, PA25-60,
PA130-30, PA160-120, PA325-40,
PA370-330, PA470-460, PA640-570,
PA705-320, PA725-240, PA735-790,
PA755-320, PA880-320, PA890-800,
PA935-690, PA960-910, PA975-320,
PR720-360, RI560-570, RI700-680,
SC54-80, SC108-100, SC144-105,
SC144-730, SC216-720, SD558-710,
TN435-220, TN630-570, TN690-780,
TN705-560, TN840-800, TX56-50,
TX56-800, TX63-80, TX128-640,
TX252-120, TX280-540, TX326-800,
TX483-320, TX695-640, TX749-246,
TX777-670, UT912-840, VA690-870,
VA690-910, VT448-520, VT464-800,
VT864-730, WA60-800, WA78-90,
WA144-110, WA144-210, WA144-840,
WA145-105, WA164-900, WA181-360,
WA241-170, WA280-885, WA290-285,
WA300-730, WA304-720, WA350-650,
WA360-440, WA368-280, WA408-360,
WA570-540, WA604-590, WA616-444,
WA616-870, WA616-895, WA629-655,
WA676-135, WA681-400, WA726-440,
WA736-680, WA820-775, WA848-440,
WA859-650, WA880-260, WA889-720,
WA892-725, WA904-770, WA943-240,
WA960-170, WA966-560, WA984-80,
WA994-935, WI70-720, WI142-800,
WI202-790, WI266-820, WI298-810,
WI346-720, WI418-800, WI456-490,
WI456-550, WI456-810, WI474-520,
WI670-720, WI722-770, WI754-170,
WV225-860, WV650-890, WY135-860,
WY245-280, WY365-710

MAINE
MA109-220

MEXICO
TX56-110, TX326-800, TX777-620

NATIONAL
AK350-120, AK500-20, CA386-560,
CA704-560, CO252-550, CO378-120,
DC1-40, DC1-805, DC4-322, DC9-580,
DC14-250, FL800-235, GA405-560,
IL170-53, IL170-280, MA871-540,
ME460-440, MI40-300, MI775-520,
MN763-540, MO400-320, MS300-550,
NJ46-560, NY427-240, NY589-160,
NY589-900, NY593-380, NY593-420,
NY594-390, NY870-600, OK592-620,
OK592-640, PA470-460, PA726-7,
TX56-520, TX374-550, WA820-550,
WA832-560, WI346-240, WV350-560,
WY950-950

SPAIN
TX56-110

STATE
AK350-120, AK500-40, AL620-20,
CO252-70, DC12-400, DE90-140,
FL800-235, FL800-245, GA895-280,
HI350-300, IA233-360, IL866-355,
IN363-342, KS527-795, KS878-430,
KY288-425, KY288-440, LA62-470,
LA600-465, LA600-775, MA21-770,
MA109-180, MA109-220, MA109-240,
MD57-500, MD76-515, ME37-525,
MI550-530, MN763-540, MO410-545,
MS550-500, MT530-500, NC680-460,
NE560-550, NH134-530, NJ666-650,
NJ804-120, NJ838-580, NM722-570,
NV90-530, NY588-850, OH26-40,
OH203-600, OK592-620, OR720-590,
OR816-590, PA380-650, PA380-665,
PR720-360, RI700-680, RI700-740,
SC216-720, SD558-710, SD558-720,
SD648-710, TN285-280, TN690-780,
TX56-800, UT912-840, VA360-320,
VA690-910, VT464-800, VT464-850,
WA60-800, WA144-840, WA280-885,
WA616-444, WA616-870, WA616-950,
WI346-720, WI456-490, WV225-860,
WV650-890, WY135-860

TERRITORIES
VI300-240, VI700-800

GOVERNORS
AR890-20, AZ275-520, AZ550-040,
CA86-810, CO252-70, FL800-245,
FL820-240, IA133-520, IA233-360,
IA866-730, IL866-355, IL866-365,
IN363-342, KS527-795, KS878-430,
KY288-440, KY604-890, KY680-180,
LA62-500, MA871-280, MS490-810,
NC100-280, ND486-800, NH134-530,
NH396-560, NH468-800, NJ316-310,
NY150-700, OH26-40, OH823-800,
OK592-650, OK753-600, OR816-590,
PA415-400, TN690-780, TX56-800,
TX280-540, VA90-840, VT464-800,
VT464-850, VT496-640, VT720-720,
WA616-870, WA975-80, WI346-720,
WV225-860, WY135-860

ALASKA
WA820-550

GRAAS, JOHN
IN539-86

GRABOWSKY, ADOLF
MI255-530

GRACE, ZOA
WI754-170

**GRADUATE SCHOOL OF SACRED
THEOLOGY**
IN627-720

GRAF, OSCAR MARIA
NH206-800

GRAHAM, BILLY
IL976-850

GRAIN

MILLS
IL170-273, MA823-610, MI28-280,
MN541-320, NY289-240, PA90-320,
VT32-80

WAREHOUSES
WA489-40
GRAND ARMY OF THE REPUBLIC
*IL169-416, MA108-10, MA904-80,
MA947-880, MA964-880, MI824-320,
MI890-720, MN14-560, NJ838-530,
NY672-440, OH223-880, PA726-508,
PA735-730, WI346-280, WI382-520,
WI714-525*
**GRAND ARMY OF THE REPUBLIC (BEN
MARVIN POST 209)**
NY240-160
GRAND CANYON
AZ350-290
GRAND RIVER
MI360-280
GRAND TRAVERSE REGION
MI925-640
GRANGE
*DC14-490, ME437-120, MI505-760,
MN275-200, NY124-60, NY251-320,
WA844-720*
GRANGER, GIDEON
NY147-280
GRANITE INDUSTRY
ME112-80
GRANT, MADISON
NY593-130
GRANT, ULYSSES SIMPSON
*DC7-510, IL296-720, IL301-280,
MO810-690, NY899-520, PA920-870,
WA943-333*
GRAPES
CA206-790, CA700-720
GRAPHIC ARTS
DC19-565, KS878-880
GRAPHIC ARTS INTERNATIONAL UNION
PA895-710
GRAVEL
TX56-780
GRAVES, ROBERT RANKE
CA720-910, IL124-725, NY24-735
GRAY, ASA
MA92-90, MA169-310
GRAY, ELISHA
DC19-586
GRAY, HENRY
VT448-520
GRAY, JAMES M.
IL170-234
GRAZING
CA720-307, CO252-163
GREAT BRITAIN
See also Scotland, *CA143-240,
CA421-770, CA480-530, IL170-884,
CA756-320, DC6-600, IL170-884,
MA108-240, MA624-750, MI40-820,
NC260-170, NC590-320, NY593-420,
PA735-825, UT912-110*
ADMIRALTY
VI700-360
AIR FORCE
AL560-720
AIR MINISTRY
AL560-720
AND AMERICAN REVOLUTION
NJ548-530
ARCHITECTURE
NY588-820
ARMY
MA478-730
ARTISTS
DE810-150
ASIA, CENTRAL, RELATIONS WITH
OH181-270
AUTHORS
NY588-900, PA726-412, VA360-320
AUTOMOBILES
PA560-690
BAPTIST CHURCH
TN690-750
CARTOGRAPHY
CT505-970
CHRISTIAN CHURCH
IN363-125
COLONIAL OFFICE
IL261-566, VI700-360

COLONIES
*FL220-795, FL660-120, IN902-840,
LA358-800, MS550-500, NC150-790,
VA870-150, VI700-360*
CONGREGATIONAL CHURCH
IL169-507
CONSULAR RELATIONS WITH HAWAII
HI350-311
CRAFTSPEOPLE
DE900-320
EMPIRE
NC260-170
EXPLORATION BY
OR720-590
FOLK MUSIC
VT432-520
FOREIGN RELATIONS
IN66-390, MA169-370
FURNITURE
DE900-320
GOVERNMENT AGENCIES
IL169-247, OR720-590
IMMIGRATION AND EMIGRATION
IL866-355, TN825-690
INDENTURES
MO810-690
INDIA, RELATIONS WITH
OH181-270
LAND GRANTS
NC900-810
LANDSCAPE ARCHITECTURE
CA86-820
LAW
PA726-750
LITERARY MANUSCRIPTS
GA90-200
LITERATURE
*CA206-790, CA421-770, CA421-774,
CA540-520, CA680-720, CA756-320,
CA858-810, CO180-120, CT505-890,
DC7-650, IA466-800, IL624-380,
IL976-900, IN66-380, IN627-800,
IN627-800, KS527-790, KS948-240,
MA21-40, MA169-370, ME925-130,
MI230-800, MO810-920, NJ692-660,
NY134-90, NY592-680, NY593-90,
NY752-880, OH399-440, PA895-710,
TX56-890, TX933-65, VA470-690*
MANUFACTURING
PA560-690
MASONS (ORGANIZATION)
MD76-20
METHODIST CHURCH
CT428-865
MISSIONARIES
NY459-520
MORMONS
MO400-690
NAVY
DC14-730, TX483-690, VI700-360
PAINTERS
MI230-800
PALESTINE MANDATE
NY589-900
PARLIAMENT
DC6-600, NJ838-750
POETS
*CO180-120, DE810-150, NY24-735,
TX933-65*
POLITICS
KS527-790
POTTERY
PA575-80
PRIVY COUNCIL
CA143-240
PUBLISHING
PA726-615
RAILROADS
NE288-400
ROYALTY
MN226-700, PA960-870
THEATER
*CT505-975, DC6-600, NY593-485,
OH203-670*
TRADE
RI700-630

TRADE WITH UNITED STATES
MA931-400
TREASURY
IL261-566
WAR OFFICE
VI700-360
WORLD WAR II
IN66-390
WRITERS
*CA782-800, MI230-800, OH843-400,
PA135-80*
GREAT BROOK RESERVOIR ASSOCIATION
CT870-520
GREAT LAKES
*MD755-560, MI64-70, MI230-180,
MI665-120, MI865-80, MI865-480,
NY134-60, OH97-80, OH863-280,
WI346-720, WI456-550*
COLONIAL POLICY
IL916-795
MARITIME HISTORY
WI354-520
SHIPPING
MI230-180
SHIPS
MI230-180, MN261-40
**GREAT LAKES-ST. LAWRENCE
TIDEWATER ASSOCIATION**
MN261-810
**GREAT NORTHERN IRON ORE
PROPERTIES TRUST CASE**
MN763-400
GREAT NORTHERN RAILROAD
MN763-400
GREAT PLAINS, NORTHERN
MT530-500
INDIANS
SD792-820
GREAT SMOKY MOUNTAINS
NC860-320, TN285-280
**GREAT SMOKY MOUNTAINS NATIONAL
PARK**
NC860-320
GREATER BALTIMORE COMMITTEE
MD76-800
GREECE
NC590-320, PA735-825
CHILDREN
OH11-840
FOREIGN RELATIONS
MA169-800
MARSHALL PLAN
MA169-800
WORLD WAR II
MA169-800
GREEK-AMERICANS
FL940-240
GREELEY, HORACE
NY172-120, NY310-160, VA285-520
GREEN FAMILY
MA985-890
GREEN HOUSE
WA820-325
GREEN RIVER
AZ500-400
GREEN, CHARLES SUMNER
CA86-820
GREEN, JOHN, II
MA985-890
GREEN, JOSHUA
WA820-325
GREEN, MELVILLE S.
PA726-600
GREEN, PAUL ELIOT
NC150-790
GREEN, WILLIAM
DC1-400
GREENAWAY, KATE
PA725-510, PA735-140
GREENBELT CONSUMER SERVICES
MD513-640
GREENE, CLAY MEREDITH
CA778-800
GREENE, CORDELIA A.
NY156-140
GREENE, NATHANAEL
CT512-120

GREENWOOD, JOHN
IL170-429

GREGG, JOSIAH
OK829-520

GREGORIAN CHANT
MN541-512

GRESHAM WI
IL245-322

GREYSTONE NIGHT CLUB
OH481-530

GRIFFES, CHARLES T.
NY272-200

GRIFFIN, MATTHEW
NY240-160

GRIFFIS, WILLIAM ELIOT
NJ568-670

GRIFFITH, DAVID WARK
NY591-760

GRIGNON FAMILY
WI46-600

GRIMES, JONATHAN, HOUSE
MN275-200

GRINNELL, GEORGE BIRD
CA421-610

GROCERY STORES
See also Mercantile activities, *IL231-240,*
WA153-125

GROOVER, JAN
DC3-760

GROPIUS, WALTER
MA169-200

GROSS, NICHOLAS
WI202-120

GROSSHUT, FRIEDRICH
NH206-800

GROTON MONUMENT
CT512-120

GROTTOS
AL440-560

GROUP ANALYSIS
CT926-480

GROUP FOR THE ADVANCEMENT OF
PSYCHIATRY
KS878-520

GUATEMALA
LA600-760,   MO210-840
IXIL MAYA INDIANS
NM722-30
RELIGIOUS COMMUNITIES
CA720-739

GUFFEY, JOSEPH F.
PA920-890

GUIDES
FRONTIER
CA954-720
MOUNTAIN
NY675-640

GULF COAST
AL580-510,   TX483-690

GULF COAST, CIVIL RIGHTS MOVEMENT
AL580-800

GULICK, LUTHER H.
MA804-710

GUNS
CONTROL
IL489-890

GURNEY, HENRY
MS640-520

GUTHE, CARL E.
MI40-814

GUTHRIE, SAMUEL
DC19-611

GUYANA
MISSIONARIES
RI910-730

H

H. P. BUILDING COMPANY
IL374-310

HADASSAH ISRAEL EDUCATION
SERVICES
NY589-900

HADDON, ELIZABETH
NJ280-270

HADDONFIELD CIVIC ASSOCIATION
NJ316-310

HAENSCHEN, GUSTAVE
NY439-360

HAGGERTY, WILLIAM J.
NY574-730

HAID, LEO
NC090-080

HAIGIS, JOHN W.
MA21-770

HAINES FAMILY
NJ280-270

HAITI
FL220-800,   NY247-160,   NY592-930

HALDEMAN-JULIUS, E.
KS746-640

HALE FAMILY
MA624-740

HALE, BENJAMIN
NY323-320

HALE, EDWARD EVERETT
MO810-690

HALL FAMILY
NY427-240

HALL, DONALD
NH206-800

HALL, G. STANLEY
MA985-100

HALL, JAMES
IL921-840

HALL, JAMES NORMAN
IA377-280

HALL, WILLIAM HAMMOND
CA720-798

HALLAM, GLEN
MT100-200

HALLIBURTON, RICHARD
IN275-170

HALLMARK CARDS
CA421-766

HALLMARK HALL OF FAME
CA421-760

HALSELL, WILLIE, COLLEGE
OK854-840

HAMERIK, ASGER
MD76-640

HAMILL, WILLIAM A.
CO414-280

HAMILTON FAMILY
NY878-720

HAMILTON STANDARD
CT186-800

HAMILTON WATCH COMPANY
PA215-560

HAMILTON, ALEXANDER
CT512-800

HAMILTON, ALICE
CT512-120

HAMILTON, ALLEN
IN231-40

HAMILTON, JAMES
PA160-120

HAMLETT, BARKSDALE
VT528-560

HAMMER, WILLIAM JOSEPH
DC19-586

HAMMOND, JOHN W.
NY804-280

HAMPDEN, WALTER
NY593-485

HAMPTON INSTITUTE
VA315-310

HAMPTON, WADE, III
SC144-130

HAN-MIN, HU
MA169-400

HANCOCK, JOHN
MA109-460,   MA109-660,   PA55-760

HANCOCK, JOHN, FAMILY
DC19-576

HANCOCK, NATHANIEL
MA285-160

HANCOCK, THOMAS
MA109-460

HAND, JAMES, JR.
MS230-160

HANDICAPPED PERSONS
NY594-20

HANDLIN, OSCAR
NY588-300

HANFORD BROTHERS (BUSINESS FIRM)
NY261-320

HANKE, LEWIS
LA600-760

HANKS, NANCY, FAMILY
IN231-470

HANNA, RICHARD
CA414-150

HANNA, SAMUEL
IN231-40

HANNAFORD, MARK
CA414-150

HANSELL, CLARENCE WESTON
NY866-710

HAPPY LAND, BY MACKINLAY KANTOR
IA955-440

HARBESON, JOHN
PA725-150

HARBORS
DC1-805,   MD76-810,   NH680-760,
OH863-280,   WA427-560,   WA616-620

HARDENBURGH, JOHN L.
NY51-140

HARDEST WIFE TO BE, BY BOOTH
TARKINGTON
IN363-400

HARDIN, JOHN WESLEY
TX791-730

HARDING, ALFRED
DC5-800

HARDING, WARREN GAMALIEL
OH203-600

HARDING, WILLIAM L.
IA866-730

HARDWARE
NM760-720,   PA380-320

HARDY, THOMAS
ME925-130

HARE, HOBART
SD684-200

HARE, R. M.
NY125-740

HARGRAVES FAMILY
DE810-690

HARKER, JOSEPH R.
IL394-500

HARKNESS, WILLIAM
DC14-750

HARLAN, JOHN MARSHALL (1833-1911)
KY496-800

HARLEM RENAISSANCE
NY592-930

HARMON, E. N.
VT528-560

HARMONY SOCIAL CLUB
NV450-120

HARMONY SOCIETY
PA40-600
INDIANA
PA40-600

HARMOUNT'S UNCLE TOM'S CABIN
COMPANY
OH203-670

HARN, W. S.
OK592-650

HARRIET LANE HOME
MD76-315

HARRIMAN, AVERELL
MA871-85

HARRINGTON, JOHN PEABODY
CA66-520

HARRIS, COLLAS
VA430-280

HARRIS, FRED
OK490-520

HARRIS, GILBERT D.
NY439-640

HARRIS, HUGH P.
SC144-150

HARRIS, THOMAS LAKE
NY595-360

HARRIS, TOWNSEND
NY588-340

HARRISON FAMILY (PALMYRA NY)
  NY672-440
HARRISON, BENJAMIN
  IN363-660
HARRISON, WILLIAM HENRY
  OH171-920
HARTFORD CT
  OH505-520
HARTLEY, HOWSON H.
  NY978-870
HARTMAN THEATRE
  OH203-670
HARTSVILLE COLLEGE
  IN352-320
HARTWICK SEMINARY
  NY648-310
HARTWICK, EDWARD E.
  MI368-320
HARTWICK, JOHN C.
  NY648-310
HARVARD UNIVERSITY
  LAW SCHOOL
    NJ316-310
HARVEY, MARTHA HALE
  MA338-840
HASBROUCK, JOSIAH
  NY574-320
HASBROUCK, LEVI
  NY574-320
HASIDISM
  MA154-310
HASSAN, IHAB
  NY125-740
HATCH, ALDEN
  FL220-800
HATHAWAY FAMILY
  CA414-500
HATHEWAY INSTITUTE
  MI690-560
HATS
  MA673-640
  MANUFACTURING
    CT144-150
HAUPTMANN, GERHART
  NY315-30
HAVEN SEED COMPANY
  CA278-130
HAVEN, JOSEPH
  NH820-690
HAVENS, B. F.
  NC850-120
HAVENS, JONATHAN
  NC850-120
HAVILAND, JOHN
  PA725-150
HAWAII
  GOVERNMENT AGENCIES, NATIONAL
    CA704-560
  JEWS
    CA86-400
  MISSIONARIES
    NY481-720
  SISTERS OF NOTRE DAME DE NAMUR
    CA78-740
HAWKES, THOMAS G., & COMPANY
  NY214-140
HAWKINS, MICAH
  NY866-520
HAWKINS, RUSH C.
  RI700-45
HAWKS FAMILY
  WI134-320
HAWKS, HOWARD
  UT684-80
HAY, JOHN
  RI700-100
HAY, MARION E.
  WA975-80
HAY, SARAH HENDERSON
  PA735-150
HAYDEN, CARL T.
  AZ750-45,   AZ750-760
HAYDEN, CHARLES TRUMBULL
  AZ750-760
HAYDEN, RICHARD V.
  ME200-120

HAYES, PATRICK
  PA726-240
HAYES, RUTHERFORD BIRCHARD
  OH301-690
HAYNES FAMILY
  KY430-280
HAZARDS
  GEOLOGIC
    CA720-161
HAZLEHURST AND HUCKLE
  PA725-150
HEALTH
    CT36-80,   DC1-295,   DC1-340,
    MA169-860,   NY156-120,   NY592-30,
    PA725-240,   TN465-760,   VA20-322
  ANIMALS
    KY496-540
  INSURANCE
    MN307-360
  MENTAL
    DC1-640,   MN226-725,   NJ838-730,
    PA860-710
  PERIODICALS
    MI60-880
  PUBLIC
    MN541-902
HEALTH AND HOSPITALS GOVERNING
    COMMISSION OF COOK COUNTY
    IL169-580
HEALTH CARE
    AL120-810,   CA421-100,   CT505-960,
    KY37S-480,   MN307-360,   MN541-902,
    NY10-160,   NY481-720,   OH593-720,
    TX326-160
  WOMEN
    IL192-510
HEALTH PROFESSIONS
  MD152-550
HEALTH SCIENCES
    See also Medicine; Physicians,   *CA720-894,*
    IL170-936,   PA725-525,   PA726-600,
    PA726-713,   PA726-725,   PA726-765,
    PA726-810
HEALY, GEORGE PETER ALEXANDER
  NY589-680
HEAP, JANE
  WI456-810
HEARING
  ORGANIZATIONS
    CA278-130
HEARST, WILLIAM RANDOLPH
  CA744-120
HEAVILON FAMILY
  IN237-240
HEBREW BENEVOLENT ASSOCIATION OF
    CAMDEN (SC)
    SC108-100
HEBRIDES, SCOTLAND
  CT505-977
HECHT, BEN
  WI456-810
HEDDING COLLEGE
  IL94-360
HEIMENDAHL, W. EDWARD
  MD76-640
HEINRICHS, ALBEN
  NJ646-660
HEINRICHS, CHARLES, SR.
  NJ646-660
HEINRICHS, DOROTHY
  NJ646-660
HEISS, MICHAEL
  WI298-250
HELICOPTERS
  TX742-800
HELLER, FRANKLIN
  NY593-485
HELLMAN, LILLIAN
  TX56-890
HEMBERGER, THEODORE
  MD76-640
HEMINGWAY, ERNEST
  IL649-600,   WI456-810
HEMMING, FRANCIS
  MI255-530
HENDERSON STOCK COMPANY
  MI255-530

HENDRICK, THOMAS A.
  NY752-560
HENREY, MADELEINE
  MA891-880
HENRY, E. L.
  NY447-400
HENRY, JOSEPH
  DC19-310
HENRY, MILTON
  TN75-50
HENRY, WILLIAM MELLORS
  CA421-510
HEPPLE, ALEX
  IL261-566
HERALDRY
  CA143-240
HERBS
  CA720-886,   MA134-560
HERFORD, OLIVER
  MA961-870
HERGESHEIMER, JOSEPH
  TX56-890
HERKIMER FAMILY
  NY493-320
HERMAN, JAN
  IL261-570
HERRESHOFF MANUFACTURING
    COMPANY
    MA169-610
HERRICK, C. JUDSON
  KS527-790,   KS527-790
HERRICK, MYRON TIMOTHY
  OH906-320
HERRICK, SAMUEL
  VA90-840
HERRMAN, AUGUST
  NY211-540
HERRON, JOHN, SCHOOL OF ART
  IN363-385
HERSETH, RALPH
  SD792-820
HERSHEY, LEWIS B.
  PA165-790
HERSHOLT, JEAN
  CA90-30
HERSKOVITS, MELVILLE J.
  IL261-566
HERTZ, ALFRED
  CA86-890
HERTZOG, CARL
  TX326-210
HERZFELD, ERNST EMIL
  DC19-327
HESSE (GERMANY)
  MILITARY PERSONNEL
    NJ548-530,   NY594-360,   NY595-360
HESSIANS (REVOLUTIONARY WAR
    SOLDIERS)
    See Hesse (Germany), military personnel
HEWITT, ABRAM S.
  NY589-100
HEWITT, FRANK L.
  NY214-160
HIDALGO, MEXICO
  MO210-840
HIGGINSON, ELLA
  WA60-80
HIGGINSON, THOMAS WENTWORTH
  CT316-560,   MA961-870
HIGHWAY DIVISION (OR)
  OR816-590
HIGHWAYS
    See Roads
HILDRETH, SAMUEL PRESCOTT
  OH486-510
HILL, ANDREW P.
  CA728-850
HILL, GEORGE A.
  TX483-810
HILL, GRACE LIVINGSTON
  NY447-400
HILL, PATTY SMITH
  DC1-860
HILL, ROBERT THOMAS
  TX252-770
HILL, SAMUEL (1857-1931)
  WA360-520

HILLERS, JOHN K.
  TX374-40
HILLMAN LAND & IRON COMPANY
  TN75-50
HINDERER, J. G.
  MN541-512
HINDUISM
  DC19-327
HINE, LEWIS
  DC3-760,   TX374-40
HIPPS, JOHN BURDER
  NC840-720
HISPANIC AMERICAN HISTORICAL
  REVIEW
  NC260-150
HISPANIC-AMERICANS
  LA600-20,   TX56-860,   TX252-730
  MUSIC
  AZ750-32
HISTORIANS
  CT316-330,   DC3-210,   LA600-760,
  MT100-200,   NY587-800,   NY588-940,
  PA380-700,   PA425-360,   TN465-800,
  VA285-520,   WA60-860,   WI46-600
  CIRCUSES
  WI70-120
  LOCAL
  CT477-570,   NY147-600
  REVISIONIST
  WY500-800
  WOMEN
  ID640-345,   PA380-700
HISTORIC AMERICAN BUILDINGS
  SURVEY
  IN539-100,   ME37-535,   NJ926-840,
  NY752-480
HISTORIC AMERICAN MERCHANT
  MARINE SURVEY
  See Work Projects Administration
HISTORIC BLOOMING GROVE
  HISTORICAL SOCIETY
  WI474-520
HISTORIC DISTRICTS
  WA60-220
HISTORIC PRESERVATION
  CA410-120,   CO108-85,   DC14-640,
  DC14-650,   GA90-265,   HI350-150,
  IA58-540,   IL45-640,   KY358-40,
  KY418-520,   LA62-430,   MA109-680,
  MA837-720,   MA849-750,   ME712-280,
  MS640-400,   NM570-80,   NY10-570,
  NY824-720,   NY878-720,   NY990-600,
  OH171-530,   TN825-690,   TX252-320,
  TX777-670,   VA540-520,   VA690-860,
  VA870-130,   WA820-325,   WY135-880
  LEGISLATION
  DC14-650
  WOMEN AND
  NY587-190
HISTORIC SITES
  GA90-265,   KY358-40,   KY358-480,
  KY464-495,   MD580-120
HISTORICAL AGENCIES
  ADMINISTRATION
  DC14-650
HISTORICAL MARKERS
  TX228-320
HISTORICAL RECORDS SURVEY
  See Work Projects Administration
HISTORICAL SOCIETY OF THE SOUTH
  CAROLINA CONFERENCE OF THE
  UNITED METHODIST CHURCH
  SC846-890
HISTORY
  CA862-810,   MI40-808,   NY726-850
HITZ, JOHN
  DC22-500
HOBART, GARRET A.
  NJ756-240
HOBBIES
  OH203-630
HOCKING VALLEY RAILROAD
  VA560-333
HODGE, CHARLES
  NJ692-610
HODGE, FREDERICK WEBB
  CA421-610

HODGES, J. E.
  NC650-120
HODGHEAD, LILLIAN
  CA720-623
HOGAN, J. J.
  IA188-777
HOGARTH, WILLIAM
  NY589-680
HOGE, JOHN
  PA920-890
HOHOKAM-PIMA NATIONAL MONUMENT
  AZ175-120
HOLDEN, PERRY G.
  MI255-530
HOLIDAY IN DIXIE
  COTILLION BOARD
  LA885-690
HOLLAND
  See Netherlands
HOLLAND AMERICA LINE (STEAMSHIPS)
  NY594-390
HOLLAND LAND COMPANY
  NY164-570,   PA555-120
HOLLAND LAND COMPANY
  (CHAUTAUQUA COUNTY)
  NY958-640
HOLLAND, CECILIA
  CT512-120
HOLLAND, JOHN PHILIP
  CT282-720,   NJ646-660
HOLLAND, LOU E.
  MO430-800
HOLLENBACK, GEORGE
  PA960-910
HOLLENBACK, MATTHIAS
  PA960-910
HOLLEY, MARY AUSTIN
  KY496-825
HOLLOWAY, EPHRAIM S.
  OH199-320
HOLLOWAY, REUBEN ROSS, MRS.
  MD76-240
HOLLOWELL, FRED S.
  NY693-920
HOLLYWOOD CA
  NY593-420
HOLM, MIKE
  MN728-690
HOLME, CONSTANCE
  OH399-440
HOLMES, DANIEL
  NY125-700
HOLMES, JOHN
  MA528-780
HOLMES, MARY JANE
  NY125-700
HOLMES, NATHANIEL
  NH748-650
HOLMES, OLIVER WENDELL (1809-1894)
  MN541-600
HOLMES, SHERLOCK
  IL459-360
HOLOCAUST (WORLD WAR II)
  CA86-385,   NY586-650,   NY587-820,
  NY595-660,   NY595-700
HOLT, HAMILTON
  FL960-690
HOLY ROMAN EMPIRE
  ROYALTY
  MN226-700
HOME DEMONSTRATION UNIT (EAST
  SPRINGFIELD NY)
  NY262-280
HOME ECONOMICS
  PA895-680
  ORGANIZATIONS
  KY230-320
HOMEMAKERS CLUB
  KY230-320
HOMEMAKING
  See Home economics
HOMEOPATHY
  CA720-894,   PA725-690
HOMER, WINSLOW
  ME162-100
HOMESTEAD GRANTS
  AR360-40,   CO768-640,   WA240-480

HOMESTEADING
  SD792-850
HOMOSEXUALITY
  CA318-320,   CA421-520,   CT316-360
HONDURAS
  MISSIONARIES
  MO810-270
  RELIGIOUS COMMUNITIES
  RI210-720
HONEYWELL, INC.
  IN913-880
HONEYWELL, MARK C.
  IN913-880
HONG KONG
  MISSIONARIES
  MN763-50
HOOD, JOHN BELL
  TX476-320
HOOD'S TEXAS BRIGADE
  TX476-320
HOOKER, ISABELLA BEECHER
  CT316-560
HOOKWORM
  NY612-690
HOOPER, JESSIE JACK
  WI554-600
HOOVER, HERBERT CLARK
  CA143-480,   IA966-320,   IN539-90,
  MN261-810
HOOVER, JOHN EDGAR
  MS140-560
HOPEDALE COMMUNITY
  MA411-80
HOPKINS WOMEN'S CLUB
  MN405-320
HOPKINS, HARRY L.
  NY427-240
HOPPER, HEDDA
  CA90-30
HOPPING, FORREST
  CA942-940
HORIZON, JOHNNY, PROGRAM
  IL489-890
HORLICK'S MALTED PRODUCTS
  WI606-710
HORNADAY, WILLIAM T.
  NY593-130
HORNE, MARILYN
  CA414-490
HORNELL FAMILY
  NY410-320
HORNS
  AUTOMOBILES
  PA415-720
HORNS (MUSICAL INSTRUMENTS)
  IN539-86
HORSES
  CA601-120,   CA720-886,   KY464-50
  KY464-440,   NY818-760
  APPALOOSA
  ID480-40
  EXHIBITIONS AND FAIRS
  MO400-400
  RACING
  KY464-440,   NY795-320
  STANDARDBRED
  NY340-320
  THEFT
  IL429-520,   IN154-880,   IN242-250
HORTICULTURE
  CA206-790,   DE900-330,   FL960-690,
  IL459-520,   MA109-140,   MO810-490,
  PA725-615,   PA950-880,   SC144-170
HORTICULTURISTS
  PA725-600,   PA735-140
HOSKINS, GAYLE PORTER
  DE810-150
HOSMER, HARRIET
  MO810-880
HOSPITAL OBSTETRICAL SOCIETY OF
  OHIO
  OH181-180
HOSPITALS
  AZ900-560,   CA858-895,   CO768-640,
  CT505-930,   DC1-890,   DC19-611,
  DC23-250,   IL94-800,   IL109-130,
  IL169-580,   IL170-416,   IL245-322,

IL866-320, IN209-140, KY496-687,
LA600-320, LA600-690, MA478-800,
MA970-890, MD76-240, MD76-315,
ME437-120, MN749-720, MN763-720,
MO430-700, MO810-760, NJ838-730,
NY10-160, NY592-260, NY592-480,
NY594-20, OH97-890, OH181-180,
OH181-790, OH223-790, PA30-720,
PA380-700, PA725-525, PA725-690,
PA725-900, PA725-908, PA726-37,
PA726-495, PA726-690, PA735-515,
PA908-720, SC144-520, TX483-160,
VT176-690, WA904-760
AFRICA
PA725-908
ASIA
PA725-908
CHILDREN
NY687-120
INDIANS
WA240-250
MARYLAND
MD76-527
MENTAL HOSPITALS
DC1-640
RENO NV
CA764-165
SCHOOL SISTERS OF ST. FRANCIS
WI456-730
SISTERS OF PROVIDENCE
WA820-820
SOUTH AMERICA
PA725-908
HOT SPRINGS SD
CO36-40
HOTELS
See also Taverns, CA692-130,
CO180-650, CO640-480, FL120-330,
FL560-590, FL580-320, FL860-320,
IA922-280, IL567-600, KY604-640,
MA425-520, MD76-800, ME62-80,
MN38-520, MO902-520, NE368-160,
NJ20-40, NM760-720, NM912-280,
NM950-270, NY594-20, NY654-600,
NY675-640, NY795-320, NY807-730,
NY932-880, OH394-320, OK389-560,
OR624-480, PA235-640, VA90-840,
VT704-690, WA647-270, WA676-610,
WA984-80, WY245-280
HOULTON PLANTATION
ME437-120
HOULTON WOMAN'S CLUB
ME437-120
HOUSEHOLD SCIENCE CLUB
IL567-520
HOUSING
DC1-340, DC4-450, IL170-910,
MA606-530, NY10-570, NY592-30,
NY593-380, PA726-630, VA20-322
HOUSING ASSOCIATION OF DELAWARE
VALLEY
PA726-630
HOUSTON OIL COMPANY
TX483-810
HOUSTON, SAMUEL
LA885-690, TX777-160, TX777-810
HOVEY, EDMUND OTIS
IN154-880
HOVEY, RICHARD
MA606-720
HOWARD UNIVERSITY
ME162-120
HOWARD, JOHN GALEN
CA86-820
HOWARD, MINNIE FRANCIS
ID640-345
HOWARD, OLIVER OTIS
ME162-120
HOWE, CHAUNCEY J.
MI100-240
HOWE, JULIA WARD
MA961-870
HOWE, SAMUEL GRIDLEY
MA961-870
HOWELL FAMILY
NJ280-270

HOWELL WORKS (FACTORY)
NJ8-160
HOWELL, HENRY W., JR.
VA580-600
HOWELLS-FRECHETTE FAMILY
NY18-40
HOWELLS, WILLIAM DEAN
NJ568-670, NY18-40, OH680-540
HOWLAND FAMILY
RI945-760
HOWLAND, JOHN
RI945-760
HOWORTH, LUCY S.
MS230-160
HOYT NURSERY
CT484-550
HOYT, C. H.
KS513-250
HOYT, HENRY M.
PA960-910
HUBBARD, BERNARD
CA778-780
HUBBARD, ELBERT
NY134-90, NY250-212
HUBBARD, GARDINER GREENE
DC22-500
HUBBELL AND BENES (ARCHITECTURAL
FIRM)
OH181-325
HUBBELL TRADING POST
AZ800-830
HUBBS, CARL P.
CA368-820
HUBER, WALTER LEROY
CA86-920
HUCKLEBERRY FINN, BY MARK TWAIN
NY134-90
HUDSON RIVER
NY219-290, NY466-120, NY574-730,
NY818-760
HUDSON RIVER DAY LINE
MD76-810
HUDSON RIVER VALLEY
NY574-710
HUDSON RIVER VALLEY, MID-HUDSON
REGION
NY469-720
HUDSON RIVER, NEW YORK
CONVENTION OF THE
REPRESENTATIVES, COMMITTEE
FOR OBSTRUCTING THE (1776)
NY599-880
HUDSON'S BAY COMPANY
OR720-590, WA726-200, WA904-260,
WA943-245
HUEGELY MILL (GRAIN)
IL170-273
HUFF, W.A.
GA735-540
HUGHES, LANGSTON
CT505-890
HUGHES, ROBERT M.
VA580-600
HUGHES, TED
OH181-130
HUGHES, THOMAS
TN825-690
HUGUENOTS
NY574-320, SC144-130
HUIDEKOPER FAMILY
PA555-120
HULCE, MARTIAL
NY241-160
HULIHEE PALACE
HI350-150
HULL-HOUSE
IL296-720, IL806-695
HULL, ISAAC
CT4-160
HUMAN RELATIONS
NY592-30
HUMANE MOVEMENT
CO252-30
HUMANISM
ITALY
IN627-810

HUMANISTS
NY594-080
HUMANITIES
NY612-690
HUMORISTS
KY496-520, KY604-640, NY795-320
HUMPHREY, DORIS
NY592-870
HUMPHREYS, DAVID
CT4-160
HUNEKER, JAMES GIBBONS
PA725-195
HUNGARIAN-AMERICANS
CT234-250
HUNGARY
NY588-825, PA735-825
FOLK MUSIC
NY166-80
RELIGIOUS COMMUNITIES
CA421-565
HUNLEY (SUBMARINE)
AL580-510
HUNT AND HUNT (ARCHITECTURAL
FIRM)
DC1-480
HUNT, GEORGE W. P.
AZ550-040
HUNT, LEIGH
IA466-800
HUNT, MABEL LEIGH
IN275-170
HUNT, RICHARD MORRIS
DC1-480
HUNTER, EUGENIA
DC1-860
HUNTER, WILLIAM
MA891-880
HUNTING
NY675-640
DECOYS
NY866-520
HUNTINGTON, DAN
MA363-640
HUNTINGTON, ELIZABETH WHITING
PHELPS
MA363-640
HUNTINGTON, FREDERICK DAN
MA363-640
HUNTINGTON, JAMES LINCOLN
MA363-640
HUNTINGTON, JAMES OTIS SARGENT
MA363-640
HUNTT, GEORGE GIBSON
TX770-240
HUNTTING, ISAAC
NY699-480
HURD-MEAD, KATE
PA725-900
HURLBUT, STEPHEN AUGUSTUS
IL296-720
HURRICANES
See also Disasters, TX397-690
HURST, FANNIE
MO810-690
HURSTON, ZORA NEALE
FL220-800
HUTCHINSON FAMILY
MA486-470
HUTCHINSON FAMILY SINGERS
MA486-470
HUTTERIAN BRETHREN
SD234-250
HUXLEY, ALDOUS
KS878-520
HUXLEY, SIR JULIAN
TX483-690
HYATT, JAMES
MD76-790
HYDE PARK WATER COMPANY
MA432-320
HYDRAULICS
MI725-600
HYDROELECTRIC POWER
DC1-810
PEE DEE RIVER
NC30-715

YADKIN RIVER
  NC30-715
HYDROGRAPHY
  MA981-890,   MD755-560,   MS50-560
HYDROLOGY
  NC656-720,   WA880-190
HYMNS
  KY464-490,   PA415-400,   TN690-885

I

ICE
  PA960-910,   WI426-120
ICE CARNIVALS
  ST. PAUL MN
    WI890-320
ICE CREAM
  MI230-740
ICEBREAKERS
  WA820-147
ICELAND
  MD76-360
ICONOGRAPHY
  NY593-100
IDAHO
  EPISCOPAL CHURCH
    MO810-590
  INDIANS
    SD792-800
  MISSIONARIES
    WA880-280
  NORTHERN
    WA144-210
  SISTERS OF PROVIDENCE
    WA880-710
IL'IN, ALEXANDER
  MI255-530
ILLINOIS
  IA188-650,   IN308-330,   WA855-735,
  WI456-735
  MORMONS
    MO400-690
  SOCIETY OF FRIENDS
    PA860-710
  SONS OF TEMPERANCE
    IN209-200
  VOLUNTEER REGIMENT 33 (CIVIL WAR)
    IL94-510
  VOLUNTEER REGIMENT 94 (CIVIL WAR)
    IL94-510
ILLINOIS AND MICHIGAN CANAL
  IL464-880,   IL866-355
ILLINOIS CENTRAL RAILROAD
  IL170-351
**ILLINOIS TRAINING SCHOOL FOR
  NURSES**
  IL169-580
ILLINOIS, SOUTHERN
  IN209-880
ILLUSTRATION
  PA175-80
  BOOKS
    NY592-970
ILLUSTRATORS
  KS283-200,   MS490-810,   NY592-680,
  OR224-800,   PA725-510
IMMIGRANTS
  GERMAN-MENNONITES, FROM RUSSIA
    KS676-520
IMMIGRATION AND EMIGRATION
  See also Exiles; Migration; Refugees,
  CT779-785,   DC19-550,   IA22-40,
  IL170-650,   IL245-322,   IL599-520,
  IL856-730,   LA600-465,   MA338-280,
  MA451-360,   MD57-500,   MI40-784,
  NY588-850,   NY592-30,   NY594-20,
  NY594-390,   OH171-20,   OH778-40,
  PA726-225,   PA735-790,   PA908-720,
  TX397-690,   UT912-120
  ARMENIA
    DC1-775,   MA84-50
  AUSTRIA
    GA860-280
  BASQUES
    NV940-800

CHINA
  WA820-966
CZECHOSLOVAKIA
  IL459-360
DENMARK
  IA233-280,   NE144-160
EUROPE
  MN763-790,   WA904-770
FRANCE
  IL866-355
GERMAN-SPEAKING
  NY586-180,   NY872-800
GERMAN, FROM RUSSIA
  CO378-110,   CO498-40
GERMAN, TO TEXAS
  TX640-720,   TX754-880
GERMANY
  CA86-780,   CA86-890,   CA90-30,
  CA314-120,   CA421-40,   CA421-750,
  CA421-830,   CA540-520,   CA578-130,
  CA774-800,   CA858-320,   CA858-820,
  CT428-865,   CT505-890,   CT505-910,
  CT505-960,   DC1-640,   DC12-300,
  DC14-250,   DC19-310,   DC19-320,
  DC19-327,   DC19-641,   GA75-810,
  IA466-800,   IL124-725,   IL169-729,
  IL170-78,   IL170-637,   IL170-884,
  IL170-897,   IL170-910,   IL770-40,
  IL916-810,   IL916-820,   IN66-380,
  IN66-395,   IN627-780,   KS527-790,
  LA600-760,   MA108-240,   MA108-750,
  MA169-170,   MA169-200,   MA169-230,
  MA169-370,   MA871-90,   MD76-360,
  ME925-130,   MI230-165,   MI440-320,
  MN541-902,   MN763-540,   MN763-790,
  MO210-815,   NJ578-530,   NY134-90,
  NY310-720,   NY427-240,   NY439-120,
  NY493-320,   NY586-580,   NY588-900,
  NY590-840,   NY590-940,   NY591-420,
  NY591-780,   NY591-840,   NY592-800,
  NY593-120,   NY593-840,   NY595-700,
  NY899-600,   OH147-520,   OH171-800,
  OH665-590,   PA25-520,   PA725-75,
  PA725-495,   PA860-710,   TX56-850,
  TX56-890,   TX280-540,   UT912-820,
  WI346-720,   WY500-800
GREAT BRITAIN
  IL866-355,   TN825-690
IRELAND
  MA109-595
ITALY
  NY587-940
JAPAN
  CA720-365
JEWS
  DC2-200,   NY593-720,   NY595-660,
  NY595-700
MENNONITES
  KS676-520
MEXICO
  TX326-780
MIDDLE EAST
  MN763-790
NETHERLANDS
  IA855-150,   MI355-110,   MI445-560,
  NY289-240
NETHERLANDS, TO CANADA
  MI355-110
NORWAY
  MN625-570
RUSSIA
  CA86-810,   NY586-650
SALZBURG, AUSTRIA
  GA860-280
SCOTLAND
  FL860-320
SWEDEN
  IL801-20,   MN541-64
UKRAINE
  MI230-780
UKRAINE, TO CANADA
  MI230-780
**IMMIGRATION AND NATURALIZATION
  SERVICE**
  IL170-280,   NJ46-560
IMP (AUTOMOBILE MODEL)
  IN33-40

IMPERSONATIONS
  MO370-520
INDENTURES
  CT905-880,   TX7-320
  GREAT BRITAIN
    MO810-690
INDEPENDENCE SANITARIUM
  IA533-280
INDEPENDENT ORDER OF ODD FELLOWS
  MD76-800
INDIA
  AL580-530,   DC3-226,   IL170-884,
  NC260-170,   NJ578-530,   WI456-730
  BOTANY
    CA720-798,   MA169-190
  CHURCH OF THE BRETHREN
    IL241-120
  CONSULAR RELATIONS WITH UNITED
    STATES
    MA92-70,   MA108-750,   MA109-120,
    MA733-210,   MA733-660,   PA725-75,
    PA725-720,   RI700-70
  GREAT BRITAIN, RELATIONS WITH
    OH181-270
  MISSIONARIES
    IA244-30,   IL45-30,   IN297-600,
    MI445-880,   MO810-270,   NJ568-570
  TRADE WITH UNITED STATES
    MA92-70,   MA108-750,   MA109-120,
    MA733-210,   MA733-660,   PA725-75,
    PA725-720,   RI700-70
**INDIAN AFFAIRS, ASSOCIATED
  EXECUTIVE COMMITTEE OF
  FRIENDS ON**
  IN704-200
INDIAN AFFAIRS, BUREAU OF
  CA386-560,   CO252-550,   IL170-280,
  TX374-550,   WA820-550
INDIAN AFFAIRS, OFFICE OF (TX)
  TX56-800
INDIAN AGENTS
  OK338-200,   WA736-440
INDIAN CAPTIVES
  CHILDREN
    TX259-880
INDIAN RIGHTS ASSOCIATION
  PA725-720
INDIAN SCOUTS
  AZ900-560,   OK956-640,   OR720-700
INDIAN TERRITORY
  OK592-640,   OK592-650
  SCHOOLS
    OH953-870
INDIAN TRADERS
  CA421-774
INDIANA
  TX280-540
  GOVERNMENT AGENCIES, NATIONAL
    IL170-280
  HARMONY SOCIETY
    PA40-600
  QUAKERS
    OH953-870
INDIANA LAND COMPANY
  PA920-890
INDIANS
  See also Native peoples; individual tribes
  and nations, *AZ100-120,   AZ175-120,*
  AZ475-640,   AZ550-040,   AZ800-800,
  CA66-80,   CA206-790,   CA250-120,
  CA258-240,   CA421-610,   CA432-520,
  CT505-960,   CT603-360,   DC3-210,
  DC14-250,   DC19-520,   GA895-160,
  IA622-200,   ID400-720,   ID640-345,
  IL170-351,   IL801-20,   IL811-690,
  IN66-385,   IN649-650,   IN704-200,
  IN902-80,   KS690-160,   KS878-430,
  KS948-240,   LA570-540,   LA600-20,
  MA383-240,   MA733-660,   MA811-720,
  MA894-880,   MD475-280,   MI60-440,
  MI64-70,   MI230-890,   MI322-240,
  MI735-720,   MI865-80,   MN42-40,
  MN541-838,   MN749-720,   MN763-530,
  MO210-840,   MO220-120,   MO800-730,
  MO810-390,   MT130-540,   MT270-130,
  MT530-500,   ND824-40,   NE624-400,
  NJ622-690,   NM114-35,   NM722-360,

NM722-730, NV940-810, NY156-480,
NY272-120, NY591-820, NY592-460,
NY593-380, NY634-160, NY766-690,
OH203-630, OH301-690, OK228-610,
OK338-200, OK372-240, OK558-790,
OK592-640, OK592-780, OK634-640,
OK812-560, OK829-520, OK854-840,
OR72-80, OR624-480, OR688-810,
PA85-730, PA90-500, PA350-880,
PA395-320, PA725-75, PA860-710,
PA945-120, RI700-45, RI875-880,
RI945-800, SD792-800, SD792-820,
SD792-880, TN690-780, TX14-720,
TX210-230, TX326-160, TX374-40,
TX374-550, UT152-720, UT836-880,
UT912-820, VA350-320, VT296-690,
WA122-110, WA300-80, WA565-40,
WA724-890, WA736-440, WA904-870,
WI202-560, WI456-495

AGRICULTURE
GA90-270
ARCHAEOLOGY
AZ800-803, WA578-520
ART
CA421-322, NM722-360, OR720-660
CALIFORNIA
AK500-20, AZ800-30, AZ800-800,
AZ800-830, CA66-520, CA86-520,
CA86-630, CA86-780, CA118-720,
CA136-90, CA143-280, CA143-470,
CA159-120, CA180-160, CA206-790,
CA386-560, CA390-480, CA402-720,
CA410-120, CA414-500, CA421-390,
CA421-400, CA421-610, CA421-710,
CA480-510, CA500-560, CA504-560,
CA578-640, CA613-640, CA624-710,
CA628-40, CA676-110, CA676-130,
CA700-720, CA700-760, CA704-560,
CA712-708, CA712-720, CA712-810,
CA720-180, CA720-675, CA720-910,
CA724-730, CA756-320, CA760-710,
CA770-120, CA774-720, CA782-800,
CA858-810, CA858-820, CA862-810,
CA934-720, DC12-300, DC19-520,
IL169-729, IL170-351, IL170-884,
IN66-385, KY496-765, MA169-170,
MA733-210, MA985-70, MI40-784,
MI40-814, MI230-165, MI665-120,
MN763-540, MO400-320, MO810-200,
MO810-510, NV940-810, NY427-240,
NY439-120, NY586-720, NY587-780,
NY591-820, NY592-460, NY592-800,
OH301-690, OK558-790, OK592-640,
OK829-520, OR448-450, PA395-320,
PA725-720, UT912-110, UT912-840,
UT912-850, VA145-780, VA145-780,
WA681-400, WA820-880, WI346-720
CALIFORNIA, NORTHERN
OR96-120
CALIFORNIA, SOUTHERN
MO210-840
CANADA
SD792-800
CAPTIVES
TX259-880
CHEHALIS
WA124-480
CHEROKEE
GA90-270, NC210-870, OK541-240,
OK592-640, OK778-120, OK778-560,
OK854-840, TN90-80, TX14-720
CHICKASAW
OK541-240, OK592-640
CHIPPEWA
MI865-480, MN763-540
CHOCTAW
OK541-240, OK592-640
COURT RECORDS
OK609-120
CRAFTS
NM722-360
CREEK
GA90-270, OK541-240, OK592-640,
OK609-120, TX14-720
DAKOTA
MN541-838, MN763-540, SD792-880

DELAWARE
OK118-70, PA90-500
ECONOMICS
NM722-360
EDUCATION
NM722-360, PA160-120, SD936-930,
WA240-250, WI456-730
ETHNOLOGY
AZ800-803, TX56-860, TX56-860,
WA954-880
EXHIBITIONS AND FAIRS
NM722-360
FIVE CIVILIZED TRIBES
OK829-520
FOX
IL801-20
GREAT PLAINS, NORTHERN
SD792-820
HAVASUPAI
AZ250-520
HOHOKAM
AZ435-520
HOPI
AZ250-520
HOSPITALS
WA240-250
IDAHO
SD792-800
IXIL MAYA
NM722-30
KAW
OK634-640
KICKAPOO
IL94-510
KIOWA
OK228-610
LAND
OR880-760
LAND OWNERSHIP
MS20-200
LANGUAGES
AK350-815, MD703-40, RI700-70,
TX56-860, WA880-550, WA889-720
LATIN AMERICA
DC12-300, MI40-820, NJ692-660,
NY592-800, TX56-860
LINGUISTICS
DC7-650, PA725-75, RI700-70
LUMMI
WA60-510
MAKAH
WA578-520
MARICOPA
AZ250-520
MAYA
NM722-30, OH181-270
MENOMINEE
WI130-730
MEXICO
AZ800-803, CA712-713, LA600-760,
MI60-440, NM114-880
MIAMI
IN649-650
MICMAC
MA891-880
MINNESOTA
SD792-800
MISSIONS
WA880-775
MIWOK
CA159-120
MODOC
OR448-450
MOHAWK
NY150-700
MONTANA
SD792-800
MOUNDS
GA90-270
MUKLESHOOT
WA37-540
MUSIC
SD792-800
NAVAJO
AZ250-520, AZ900-560
NEZ PERCE
ID480-40, OK812-560

OJIBWAY
MI865-480, MN541-838
ORGANIZATIONS
DC19-520
OSAGE
OK634-640, OK812-560
OTOE
OK634-640
OTOE AND MISSOURIA
OK812-560
OTTAWA
KS718-600
PACIFIC NORTHWEST
WA880-550
PAWNEE
OK812-560
PLAINS
OK490-520
POLITICS
NM722-360
POMO
CA390-480
PONCA
OK634-640, OK812-560
POWWOWS
NM722-360
PUEBLO
CA421-610
QUAPAW
OK812-560
RELIGION
SD792-800
REMOVAL FROM GEORGIA
GA90-270
RESERVATIONS
GA90-270
ROCKY MOUNTAIN REGION
WA880-550
RODEOS
NM722-360
SANTEE NE
SD936-930
SAUK
IL801-20
SAUK-SUIATTLE
WA200-322
SEMINOLE
FL60-720, FL940-240, OK541-240,
OK592-640, OK922-720
SHAWNEE
OH982-290
SIOUX
MN618-80, NE284-560, SD558-720,
SD792-880
SKOKOMISH
WA954-880
SNOHOMISH
WA855-80
SOUTH AMERICA
CA712-713
SOUTHEASTERN US
NC60-640, OK541-240
SOUTHWESTERN US
AZ800-803, CA421-115, CA421-610
TONKAWA
OK634-640, OK812-560
TRADE
IN363-360
TULALIP
WA528-780
UTE
CO252-550, CO270-240, CO476-540
WALAPAI
AZ250-520
WANAPUM
WA994-940
WAR
IL866-365, KS513-720, NY272-120,
OR448-450, WA616-870, WA880-775,
WI178-240
WASHINGTON
SD792-800
WESTERN US
CA712-713
WINNEBAGO
IA211-480, WI98-390, WI890-320

WISCONSIN
SD792-800
YAKIMA
WA921-950, WA921-950, WA994-940
INDONESIA
NY595-40
INDUSTRIAL ARTS
PA595-530
INDUSTRIAL ASSOCIATION OF SAN
FERNANDO VALLEY
CA524-160
INDUSTRIAL DESIGN
NY591-350
EUROPE
NY591-350
INDUSTRIAL HOMES
NY594-20
INDUSTRIAL MUTUAL ASSOCIATION OF
FLINT MICHIGAN
MI314-265
INDUSTRIAL RELATIONS
NY439-150, NY592-30
INDUSTRIAL STANDARDS
PA725-495
INDUSTRIAL TECHNOLOGY
PA90-320
INDUSTRIAL WORKERS OF THE WORLD
MI230-880
INDUSTRIALISTS
NY821-720, PA725-495
INDUSTRY
See also Manufacturing; Mills, AR510-25,
CA540-590, CA676-740, CA712-630,
CT234-230, CT316-560, CT477-570,
CT582-550, CT905-880, DC9-450,
IL169-826, IL767-320, IL806-705,
IN66-390, IN121-80, IN187-200,
KS541-470, KY504-310, MA307-230,
MA677-70, MA823-610, MD114-330,
ME175-80, MI36-400, MI314-265,
MI314-840, MN419-440, MN721-600,
MN763-530, NC200-120, NY10-570,
NY358-760, NY594-360, NY637-720,
NY804-280, NY821-720, OH21-600,
OH588-520, OH823-750, OK118-70,
OR128-720, PA520-470, PA810-700,
PA895-710, TX56-850, VA90-840,
VT176-810, WA122-110, WI266-430,
WI754-720
PENNSYLVANIA
DE270-200
INFORMATICS (BUSINESS FIRM)
CA132-160
INFORMATION SCIENCE ABSTRACTS
PA725-375
INLAND WATERWAYS
CA922-840
INNSKEEP FAMILY
NJ280-270
INQUISITOR'S CLUB
KY189-320
INSECTS
See Entomology
INSTITUTE FOR CROSS-CULTURAL
STUDIES
DC19-440
INSTITUTE FOR SOCIAL ANTHROPOLOGY
DC19-520
INSTITUTE FOR STUDIES IN AMERICAN
MUSIC
MO430-790
INSTITUTE OF MEDICINE
DC14-100
INSTITUTE OF MUSICAL ART
NY590-720
INSURANCE
CA226-170, CA870-710, CT316-750,
CT505-560, CT512-550, IL84-120,
IL170-312, KS878-430, KY496-800,
MA108-920, ME712-790, NY10-770,
NY331-280, NY592-580, PA135-40,
PA725-208, PA725-780, PA725-990
EDUCATION
PA135-40
FIRE
DE900-320, MN763-690, NH784-630,
PA725-780, WA820-780

HEALTH
CA421-100, MN307-360
LAW
NY588-860
MARINE
CT463-520, MN763-690, NH784-630,
PA725-780
INSURANCE COMPANY OF NORTH
AMERICA
PA725-780
INTELLECTUAL HISTORY
CA578-130, CA858-320
SOUTHERN US
LA62-500
INTER-AMERICAN COUNCIL FOR
EDUCATION, SCIENCE AND
CULTURE
DC15-500
INTER-AMERICAN ECONOMIC AND
SOCIAL COUNCIL
DC15-500
INTER-AMERICAN JURIDICAL
COMMITTEE
DC15-500
INTERIOR DESIGN
DE900-320, NY591-350, WI456-530
EUROPE
NY591-350
INTERLAKEN BUSINESS MEN'S
ASSOCIATION
NY433-350
INTERLAKEN FIRE DEPARTMENT
NY433-350
INTERNAL REVENUE SERVICE
DC19-651, NJ46-560
INTERNATIONAL ASSOCIATION OF
MACHINISTS
GA90-300
INTERNATIONAL BIOGRAPHICAL
ARCHIVES OF CENTRAL EUROPEAN
EMIGRES
NY593-720
INTERNATIONAL BRIGADE
SPANISH CIVIL WAR
NY315-30
INTERNATIONAL BROTHERHOOD OF
POTTERY AND ALLIED WORKERS
OH399-420
INTERNATIONAL COMMITTEE OF YOUNG
MEN'S CHRISTIAN ASSOCIATIONS
IL170-283
INTERNATIONAL FEDERATION OF
BUSINESS AND PROFESSIONAL
WOMEN'S CLUBS
DC14-420
INTERNATIONAL FEDERATION OF
UNIVERSITY WOMEN
DC1-340
INTERNATIONAL HORN SOCIETY
IN539-86
INTERNATIONAL INFORMATION
ADMINISTRATION
DC9-580
INTERNATIONAL INSTITUTE (LAWRENCE
MA)
MA451-360
INTERNATIONAL KINDERGARTEN UNION
DC1-860
INTERNATIONAL MARINE ARCHIVES,
INC.
MA584-600
INTERNATIONAL NEW THOUGHT
ALLIANCE
MO894-800
INTERNATIONAL ORGANIZATIONS
CA858-320, DC15-500, NY595-20
INTERNATIONAL PENAL AND
PENITENTIARY COMMISSION
NY595-20
INTERNATIONAL REFUGEE
ORGANIZATION
NY595-20
INTERNATIONAL RELATIONS
CA858-320, DC7-540, DC9-580,
NY588-900, NY588-940, NY590-700,
VA20-322

LABOR
NY590-430
ORGANIZATIONS
NY588-900
INTERNATIONAL UNION OF ELECTRICAL,
RADIO AND MACHINE WORKERS
NJ568-680
INTERNATIONAL WOODWORKERS OF
AMERICA
GA90-300
INTERSCHOLASTIC LEAGUE
TX733-640
INTERSEMINARY COMMISSION
CT505-900
INTERSTATE COMMERCE COMMISSION
WI530-520
INVENTIONS
NJ910-200
INVENTORS
DC19-606, DC19-621, DC19-631,
FL180-210, GA245-110, MA606-530,
MI214-280, NJ578-515, NJ646-660,
NY101-720, PA725-120
INVESTIGATORS CLUB
KY598-600
IONOSPHERE
CO108-560
IOWA
NE624-400, TX280-540
CHURCH OF THE NAZARENE
MO430-120
LUTHERAN CHURCH IN AMERICA
IL170-91
MORMONS
MO400-690
IOWA STATE HIGHWAY COMMISSION
IA33-350
IOWA STATE TEACHERS COLLEGE
IA88-800
IRAQ
MISSIONARIES
MO810-270
IRELAND
AL120-720, IL170-884, MA199-90,
PA735-825
IMMIGRATION AND EMIGRATION
MA109-595
LITERARY MANUSCRIPTS
GA90-200
LITERATURE
ME925-130, NY101-720, NY866-730,
PA500-80, WI456-810
MUSIC
NY984-200
RELIGIOUS COMMUNITIES
IL84-600, MD152-720
IRELAND, JOHN
MN763-100
IRELAND, JOSEPH
OH181-325
IRELAND, MARK
MI164-120
IRELAND, NORTHERN
NC590-320
IRENE (COSTUME DESIGNER)
CA90-30
IRISH-AMERICANS
NY586-600
LITERATURE
NY101-720
PREJUDICE AGAINST
NY10-160
IRON
MINING
DC1-500, DC19-591, MN261-810,
NJ330-320, NJ756-240, NY708-720,
WI98-400
IRON INDUSTRY
AL120-100, DC1-500, DC19-601,
DE270-200, KY2A-80, MI343-280,
MN763-400, NJ8-160, NJ276-510,
NJ330-320, NJ548-530, NJ548-720,
NY708-720, PA270-200, PA735-150,
PA890-800, WI378-520
BOHEMIA
MA108-750

IRRIGATION
  CA274-250, DC4-260, DC19-800,
  TX590-760, WA880-290
  ROCKY MOUNTAIN REGION
  UT380-810
IRVING FAMILY
  NY878-720
IRVING, WASHINGTON
  NY310-160, NY447-400, NY878-720
ISABELLA I (QUEEN OF CASTILE)
  IL170-250
ISLAM
  CA86-780, CA756-320, CA858-895,
  CT316-330, CT316-770, CT316-880,
  CT505-930, DC7-650, DC12-105,
  DC19-327, GA90-200, IA466-800,
  IL170-351, IL170-884, IL170-897,
  IL261-570, IN66-380, IN627-810,
  KS475-800, KS527-790, KY464-760,
  LA600-755, MA21-40, MA108-140,
  MA108-770, MA169-300, MA169-370,
  MA733-660, MA871-90, MD76-360,
  MD76-880, MD152-550, MI140-808,
  MI230-155, MN226-720, MN541-496,
  MN541-822, NE560-860, NE624-130,
  NJ568-570, NJ578-530, NJ692-660,
  NY101-720, NY134-60, NY134-90,
  NY439-140, NY588-900, NY590-680,
  NY592-860, NY726-850, OH171-100,
  OH171-800, OH181-270, OH823-770,
  OR224-800, PA90-480, PA270-470,
  PA395-320, PA725-405, PA725-510,
  PA725-540, PA725-870, RI700-50,
  SC144-130, TX56-890, UT912-820
  ART
  MI40-800
  LITERATURE
  UT912-820
  METALWORK
  DC19-327
  SCIENCE
  DC12-105
ISLE ROYALE
  MI464-530
ISRAEL
  NY589-900, NY595-660, NY595-670,
  NY595-760
  BAPTIST CHURCH
  TN690-750
  SEPHARDIM
  NY586-880
ITALIAN VINEYARD COMPANY
  CA700-720
ITALIAN-AMERICANS
  NY587-940
  ORGANIZATIONS
  CO768-640
ITALY
  DC6-600, IA244-480, KS527-790,
  NC150-860
  ARCHITECTURE
  NY588-820
  ART
  NY593-100
  HUMANISM
  IN627-810
  IMMIGRATION AND EMIGRATION
  NY587-940
  JEWS
  NY592-760
  MATHEMATICS
  CA578-130
  MEDIEVAL
  DC12-400, PA726-615
  MISSIONARIES
  OH223-720
  MOTION PICTURES
  DC12-450
  MUSIC
  CA86-890
  RELIGIOUS COMMUNITIES
  KY496-850
  ROMAN CATHOLIC CHURCH
  DC15-50
  THEATER
  OH203-670

**ITHACA CONSERVATORY OF MUSIC AND
  AFFILIATED SCHOOLS**
  NY439-360
ITHACA GRANGE
  MI505-760
ITZEL, JOHN
  MD76-640
IVES, BURL
  IL489-890
IVES, CHARLES E.
  CT144-150, CT505-910, MS900-870
IVINS, STANLEY SNOW
  UT912-850

J

JACKMAN, ALONZO
  VT528-560
JACKSON HOLE NATIONAL MONUMENT
  WY560-280
JACKSON IRON COMPANY
  MI343-280
JACKSON, ANDREW
  OH171-920, OK829-520
JACKSON, CHEVALIER
  PA726-600
JACKSON, HUGH
  NY588-850
JACKSON, LUTHER PORTER
  VA630-840
JACKSON, MARY ANN MORRISON
  NC330-520
JACKSON, OSCAR L.
  PA645-560
JACKSON, ROBERT G. A.
  NY588-850
JACKSON, SHELDON
  NJ692-610, PA726-713
JACKSON, STUART
  CT505-945
JACKSON, WILLIAM HENRY
  CO180-640, TX374-40
JAGGAR, T. J.
  CA782-800
JAMAICA
  MA199-90
  MISSIONARIES
  IN704-240, RI910-730
  NATURAL HISTORY
  MA199-90
JAMES FAMILY (HULL MA)
  MA425-520
JAMES LEFFEL & CO.
  OH223-880
JAMES, GEORGE WHARTON
  CA421-115
JAMES, JESSE
  MN625-550
JAMES, JOHN H.
  OH680-540
JAMES, JOSHUA
  MA425-520
JAMES, OLLIE M.
  KY514-120
JAMES, WILLIAM
  IN275-170
JAMESON, STORM
  MA891-880
JANOS, MEXICO
  TX326-800
JAPAN
  AL580-530, CT505-960, DC12-150,
  DC12-190, MA169-400, MA169-590,
  MA554-530, MN226-705, NJ578-530,
  NY588-340, NY592-30
  ART
  DC12-150
  BOTANY
  MA169-190
  CHERRY TREES
  DC14-180
  EDUCATION
  NJ568-670
  EXPEDITIONS
  NY288-840

  GOVERNMENT AGENCIES
  DC12-150, DC12-400, IL169-247
  IMMIGRATION AND EMIGRATION
  CA720-365
  MATTHEW C. PERRY MISSION TO
  (1852-54)
  DC19-621
  MEDICINE
  CA720-886
  MISSIONARIES
  IL45-30, IL169-677, MI445-880,
  MN749-720, MO810-270, MO810-750,
  NC390-200, NC590-320, NJ568-570,
  NY481-720, OH223-720
  MOTION PICTURES
  DC12-450
  NAVY
  DC14-730
  OCCUPATION BY UNITED STATES
  MD285-805, NY588-940
  PEARL HARBOR ATTACK
  NH784-620
  RELIGIOUS COMMUNITIES
  IL866-320
  WAR CRIMES
  NY588-860
  WORLD WAR II
  CA32-640
JAPAN, NORTHERN
  MI518-50
JAPANESE-AMERICANS
  CA40-60, CA86-630, CA720-365
  RESETTLEMENT
  CA720-365
  WORLD WAR II
  CA720-365, TN690-880
JARDINE, J. T.
  OR464-490
JARRELL, RANDALL
  NC380-800
JARVES, DEMING
  MA738-720
JAWLENSKY, ALEXIS
  CA578-630
JAY, JOHN
  NY588-440
JAYCEES (RICHARDSON TX)
  TX742-680
JAYNE-FERGUSON FAMILY
  NY235-160
JAZZ
  LA600-764, NY592-878
  RECORDINGS
  CT505-976
JEANES FUND
  GA90-700
**JEANNERET, CHARLES EDOUARD (LE
  CORBUSIER)**
  MA169-305
JEFFERS, ROBINSON
  CA421-510
JEFFERSON BARRACKS
  MO200-720
JEFFERSON MEDICAL COLLEGE
  PA726-690
JEFFERSON, THOMAS
  MD76-30, NY594-220
JEKYLL, GERTRUDE
  CA86-820
JELLIFFE, SMITH ELY
  NY592-640
JEMISON, MARY
  NY566-540
JENNINGS FAMILY
  PA986-960
JENSEN FAMILY
  CA314-120
JENSEN, ERICH RICKERT
  CA314-120
JENSEN, JENS
  IL459-520
JENSEN, JENS CHRISTIAN
  CA314-120
JERICHO PLANK ROAD COMPANY
  NY382-310
JEROME ROBBINS' BALLETS: U.S.A.
  NY592-870

JERSEY CITY FIRE DEPARTMENT
NJ386-380
JERUSALEM
DC6-800
JERUSALEM LUTHERAN CHURCH
GA860-280
JERVIS, JOHN BLOOMFIELD
NY757-400
JESSOP, CHARLES
MD266-80
JESSYE, EVA
KS746-640
JESUITS
    See also Society of Jesus, *DC7-650,*
    WA820-780, WI594-110
  MISSIONARIES
    AZ800-790
JEWETT, GEORGE FREDERICK
ID480-810
JEWETT, SARAH ORNE
MA109-680, ME925-130, NY899-520
JEWISH COMMUNITY CENTER
(NASHVILLE TN)
TN690-360
JEWISH EDUCATION ASSOCIATION
OR720-400
JEWISH FAMILY SERVICES (NASHVILLE
TN)
TN690-360
JEWISH NATIONAL FUND
NY589-900
JEWISH WORLD RELIEF ORGANIZATION
CA86-385
JEWS
    CA86-400, CA86-810, CA421-250,
    CT891-400, DC2-200, DC10-500,
    DC12-100, IN231-370, KY496-812,
    MA154-310, MA169-370, MA871-40,
    MD76-70, MD76-300, NJ816-760,
    NY586-650, NY590-680, NY590-840,
    NY592-760, NY593-720, NY595-660,
    NY595-670, NY595-700, NY595-760,
    NY752-800, OH171-20, OH171-320,
    OH181-730, OH181-880, OR720-400,
    PA725-330, PA725-405, PA725-980,
    PA726-225, RI560-570, RI700-680,
    RI700-690, TN90-440, TN690-360,
    TN765-280
  ALASKA
    CA86-400
  CANADA, WESTERN
    CA86-400
  COMMUNES
    NY590-840, NY595-660
  EDUCATION
    NY595-660, TN690-360
  EUROPE
    NY590-680
  EUROPE, CENTRAL
    NY590-840, NY595-660
  EUROPE, EASTERN
    NY586-650, NY587-820, NY595-660
  GERMAN-SPEAKING
    NY590-840
  GERMANY
    MD76-70, NY590-680, NY590-840
  HAWAII
    CA86-400
  IMMIGRATION AND EMIGRATION
    DC2-200, NY593-720, NY595-660,
    NY595-700
  ITALY
    NY592-760
  LABOR MOVEMENTS
    NY587-820
  LITERATURE
    NY590-840, NY595-700
  MEXICO
    CA86-400
  MIDDLE EAST
    NY590-680
  MUSIC
    NY590-840
  ORGANIZATIONS
    CA86-385, DC10-500, IL170-780,
    IN231-370, MA871-40, NY593-132,
    NY595-660, NY595-700, PA726-225

  POLAND
    NY595-660
  POLITICAL BEHAVIOR
    NY586-650
  RABBIS
    OH181-730
  REFUGEES
    NY593-720
  RHODE ISLAND
    MA871-40
  SEPHARDIM
    NY586-880
  SOCIAL WELFARE
    CA86-385
  WOMEN
    NY595-760
JILLSON, WILLARD R.
KY680-190
JIMENEZ, JUAN RAMON
PR600-800
JOHN HERRON SCHOOL OF ART
IN363-385
JOHN MARSHALL LAW SCHOOL
OH181-290
JOHNNY HORIZON PROGRAM
IL489-890
JOHNS HOPKINS HOSPITAL
MD76-315
JOHNS HOPKINS UNIVERSITY
  SCHOOL OF ART AS APPLIED TO
  MEDICINE
    MD76-880
  SCHOOL OF HEALTH SERVICES
    MD76-315
  SCHOOL OF HYGIENE AND PUBLIC
  HEALTH
    MD76-315
  SCHOOL OF NURSING
    MD76-315
  WELCH MEDICAL LIBRARY
    MD76-315
JOHNSON FAMILY
MA606-720
JOHNSON, ANDREW
OH481-530
JOHNSON, FREEMAN
NY752-720
JOHNSON, GEORGE
SC144-90
JOHNSON, GEORGE F.
NY273-280
JOHNSON, HAROLD K.
PA165-790
JOHNSON, HARRY
KY272-635
JOHNSON, JAMES WELDON
CT505-890
JOHNSON, KEEN
KY680-180
JOHNSON, LUCINDA
NY564-840
JOHNSON, LYNDON BAINES
TX56-520
JOHNSON, MARTIN
KS164-520
JOHNSON, OAKLEY C.
NY866-710
JOHNSON, OSA
KS164-520
JOHNSON, SAMUEL
CT505-977
JOHNSON, SAMUEL W.
CT505-120
JOHNSON, SIR WILLIAM
NY447-400
JOHNSON, THOMAS
MD399-240
JOHNSON, WALTER NATHAN
NC840-720
JOHNSON, WILLIAM HENRY
VA630-840
JOHNSTON, ALBERT SIDNEY
WI178-240
JOHNSTON, ANNIE FELLOWS
IN209-880
JOHNSTON, J. AMBLER
VA90-840

JOHNSTON, JAMES HUGO
VA630-840
JOHNSTON, JOSEPH EGGLESTON
VA285-520
JOHNSTON, LUCY B.
KS878-430
JOHNSTON, WILLIAM ALEXANDER
OH54-80
JOLIET ASSOCIATION OF COMMERCE
IL404-410
JONA, ABRAHAM
NY592-760
JONATHAN GRIMES HOUSE
MN275-200
JONES FAMILY
CT484-550
JONES FAMILY (MASSACHUSETTS)
MA513-530
JONES, ANSON, FAMILY
TX280-540
JONES, DONALD F.
CT505-120
JONES, ERNEST LARUE
MI230-800
JONES, HORATIO, JR.
NY752-40
JONES, HORATIO, SR.
NY752-40
JONES, HOWARD PALFREY
NY10-770
JONES, ISAAC
MA937-280
JONES, JENKIN LLOYD
IL170-195
JONES, JOHN PAUL
MD57-800, SC144-130
JONES, MARCUS
CA143-690
JONES, NARD
OR848-160
JONES, ROBERT E.
AL440-800
JONES, SAMUEL (GOLDEN RULE)
OH823-750
JONSON, RAYMOND
NM114-870
JOSEFFY, RAFAEL
IL916-820
JOSEPH, MOTHER
WA820-820
JOSLIN, ELLIOTT P.
MA654-590
JOURNAL ET CORRESPONDENCE
ARTISTIQUE, BY CHARLES MERYON
OH823-770
JOURNALISM
    See also Newspapers, *CA86-780,*
    CT505-960, DC7-540, DC14-870,
    LA570-540, MA108-240, MI40-784,
    MI230-880, MI390-720, MI675-510,
    MN541-902, NY717-640, OH320-430,
    RI700-680, TN690-980, WI202-560
JOURNALISTS
    DC14-552, FL960-690, GA90-200,
    IA455-720, IL429-520, KS283-200,
    KY680-180, MA528-740, MN763-790,
    NY101-720, NY187-120, NY594-080,
    NY717-640, PA425-360, PA870-160,
    WI46-600
  WOMEN
    GA245-110, PA870-160
JOY, KENNETH
ME460-440
JOYCE, JAMES
    NY24-735, NY323-320, NY439-140,
    WI456-810
JUBB FAMILY
MA931-400
JUBILEE COLLEGE
IL723-80
JUDAISM
  CLERGY
    OH181-730
  HASIDISM
    MA154-310
  YEMEN
    NY592-760

JUDAISM, AMERICAN COUNCIL FOR
WI346-720
JUDD, STURGES M.
CT870-730
JUDD, SYLVESTER
MA624-240
JUDGES
CA594-120, CA712-700, KY496-400,
KY496-800, KY680-180, MA169-440,
NY842-730, PA740-320, VT720-720,
WA820-889
SUPREME COURT
AZ275-520
JUDSON FAMILY
PA905-60
JUDSON FAMILY (OR)
OR816-530
JUDSON, ADONIRAM
PA905-60
JUMEL, ELIZA BOWEB
NJ339-40
JUNG, C. G.
NY590-740
JUNIOR LEAGUE
MN541-902
JUSTICE
CRIMINAL
NY588-440
JUSTICE COURTS
WA164-890
JUSTICE DEPARTMENT (OR)
OR816-590
JUSTICE, DONALD
NY125-740
JUSTICES OF THE PEACE
See also Courts - Records, local,
IN704-880, KS377-200, NY419-350,
NY720-640, PA875-80, VT16-120
JUVENILE DELINQUENTS
IL489-890, MA169-440, NY588-440,
NY594-20

K

KABBALA
MA154-310, NY592-760
KAHN, ALBERT
MI230-155
KALAMAZOO COUNTY AGRICULTURAL
SOCIETY
MI518-445
KALER, JAMES OTIS
ME825-730
KANDINSKY, WASSILY
CA578-630
KANNER, LEO J.
MD76-70
KANSAS
AR890-30
KANSAS YEARLY MEETING OF FRIENDS
KS948-240
KANTOR, MACKINLAY
IA955-440, IN275-170
KARAITES
CAIRO, EGYPT
CA86-385
KARLOFF, BORIS
UT684-80
KARPOVICH, PETER V.
MA804-710
KASHMIR
NY595-40
KATE FENNIGATE, BY BOOTH
TARKINGTON
IN363-400
KATWIJK, PAUL VAN
TX252-790
KAWEAH CO-OPERATIVE
COMMONWEALTH COMPANY
CA882-720
KAY, ROBIN
HI350-315
KAZAN, ELIA
CT428-865
KEAN, CHARLES
DC6-600

KEATING, MOTHER DE CHANTAL
NY115-720
KEELER, W. W.
OK778-120
KEEN, WILLIAM WILLIAMS
RI700-50
KELKER, FREDERICK
PA380-320
KELLAS, ELIZA
NY890-200
KELLER, HELEN ADAMS
DC22-500, NY586-440
KELLNER, ESTHER
IN704-520
KELLOGG ARABIAN HORSE RANCH
CA601-120
KELLOGG, JOHN HARVEY
MI60-880
KELLY, HOWARD
MD76-315
KELSEY, THEODORE
HI350-315
KEMPER HALL
WI266-430
KENDAL SOCIETY
OH505-520
KENNEBEC PURCHASE COMPANY
ME950-480
KENNEBUNK SOLDIERS' RELIEF SOCIETY
ME460-440
KENNEDY INSURANCE AGENCY
SC108-100
KENNEDY, CLARENCE
MA169-340
KENNEDY, JOHN FITZGERALD
CA421-760, MA108-965, MS140-560,
NY775-720
KENNEDY, JOHN PENDLETON
MD76-333
KENNICOTT GROVE
IL325-290
KENNY, ELIZABETH
MN541-16
KENRICK, FRANCIS PATRICK
PA726-105
KENSETT, JOHN FREDERICK
NY589-680
KENT FAMILY
IN237-240
KENTUCKY
IL170-884, WV435-520
COURTS, RECORDS
IN231-470
FOLKLORE
IN66-340
LUTHERAN CHURCH IN AMERICA
IN363-480
LUTHERAN CHURCH-MISSOURI SYNOD
IN231-490
ROMAN CATHOLIC CHURCH
DC15-50
KENTUCKY ACADEMY OF SCIENCE
KY680-180
KENTUCKY FEMALE ORPHAN SCHOOL
KY54G-520
KENTUCKY HERITAGE COMMISSION
KY464-495
KENTUCKY, WESTERN
IN209-880
KENYA
MISSIONARIES
DC15-50, IN704-240, OH223-720
KENYON REVIEW
OH320-430
KEOKUK RIFLES (MILITIA)
IA511-450
KERN, RICHARD
PA725-15
KERSHAW COUNTY MEDICAL SOCIETY
SC108-100
KERSHAW, JOSEPH
SC108-100
KERSHAW, JOSEPH BREVARD
SC108-100
KERSTEN COMMITTEE
IL170-53

KETCHUM FAMILY
NY708-440
KETTERING, CHARLES FRANKLIN
MI314-265, OH223-810
KEY, FRANCIS SCOTT, FAMILY
MD76-240
KEY, JOSEPH STAUNTON
GA90-190
KIBELE, C.
IN539-100
KIBLINGER (AUTOMOBILE MODEL)
IN33-40
KIESTER FAMILY
PA815-710
KILMER, JOYCE
WI594-110
KILPATRICK, W. H.
GA735-520
KIMBALL, FISKE
MA169-340, PA726-255
KIMBALL, FRANCIS H.
CT316-763
KIMMEL, STANLEY P.
FL820-810
KINDERGARTENS
DC1-860, GA245-110
KING FAMILY
IL866-365
KING, HORTENSE FLEXNER
KY496-825
KING, MACKENZIE
IN275-170
KING, MARTIN LUTHER, JR.
GA90-490, MA108-240, TN630-530
KING, WILLIAM
NC915-320
KING'S COLLEGE (NY)
NY588-830
KING'S MOUNTAIN BAPTIST
ASSOCIATION
NC100-280
KINGFISHER COLLEGE
OK456-120
KINGS CANYON NATIONAL PARK
CA882-720
KINGSWOOD SCHOOL
MI110-120
KINNELL, GALWAY
OH181-130
KINSEY, DARIUS
WA60-885
KIRBY, JOHN HENRY
TX483-810
KIRKLAND, MURIEL
NY593-485
KIRKLAND, SAMUEL
NY197-310
KIRTLAND OH
IA533-280
KITTRELL JOB CORPS CENTER
DC1-160
KLEE, PAUL
CA578-630
KLICKITAT COUNTY PORT DISTRICT
NUMBER 1
WA280-885
KLIPPLE, MAY AUGUSTA
OH181-270
KLONDIKE
WA724-890
KNEIP, RICHARD F.
SD792-820
KNIGHT, GOODWIN
CA86-810
KNIGHTS OF COLUMBUS (TX)
HISTORICAL COMMISSION
TX56-110
KNIGHTS OF LABOR
AR510-810, DC3-210
KNIGHTS OF PYTHIAS
IL567-520
KNOWLES, DANIEL
NH904-760
KNOX, ROSE
NY447-400
KOANGA, BY FREDERICK DELIUS
FL280-420

KOBLER, JOHN
 MD76-790
KOHLER, DAYTON M.
 VA90-840
KOLB, EMERY
 AZ250-575
KOONTZ, ELIZABETH D.
 NC730-480
KOREA
 DC12-190, NC590-320, NY595-20
 MISSIONARIES
 OH223-720
KOREAN WAR
 AL380-800, CO180-750, CT36-80,
 HI350-770, IL866-355, KY272-45,
 MN14-560, PA325-280
KOVACS, ERNIE
 NY591-690
KU KLUX KLAN
 IN539-83, IN539-90, IN913-880,
 TN765-280, TX181-780
KUDZU (UNDERGROUND NEWSPAPER)
 MS870-760
KUHNLE, WESLEY
 CA414-150
KUMIN, MAXINE
 NY125-740
KUPER, LEO
 IL261-566

L

L'ENGLE, MADELINE
 IL976-890
L'OUVERTURE, TOUSSAINT
 PA725-615
LA MAMA EXPERIMENTAL THEATRE
 CLUB
 NY593-485
LABOR
 AZ550-040, CA728-850, CO108-810,
 CT779-785, DC3-210, DC7-540,
 DC14-250, IL170-637, IL170-650,
 IL866-365, LA600-775, MA169-860,
 MI230-880, MI255-530, MN338-360,
 MN763-530, MN975-730, MO210-815,
 MO810-800, NY439-150, NY592-30,
 NY804-280, OR816-590, PA726-630,
 PA895-710, TN630-530, VT176-810,
 WA820-880, WI266-820
 AGRICULTURE
 CA86-120, CA778-800, CA858-810,
 HI350-790, MI230-880, NY439-150,
 TX529-770
 BAKERIES
 MD575-333
 BLACKS
 WI250-690
 BUREAUS
 NY594-20
 CHILDREN
 NY586-440
 EDUCATION
 AR890-30, NY439-150
 INTERNATIONAL RELATIONS
 NY590-430
 LEADERS
 DC1-400, MD800-322, MN763-790,
 MT100-200
 LEGISLATION
 NY439-150, NY590-430
 MARITIME
 NY594-060
 MOVEMENTS
 DC19-550, MI314-840, NY586-440,
 WA904-870
 MOVEMENTS, GERMANY
 NY590-840
 MOVEMENTS, JEWS
 NY587-820
 NURSERIES (TREE)
 NE240-560
 ORGANIZATIONS
 CA524-160, CA712-750, DC1-280,
 DC14-870, GA90-300, ID80-365,
 IL866-365, MD575-333, MD800-322,

 MI230-880, NY439-150, NY588-940,
 NY593-120, NY595-700, OH223-880,
 PA920-890, TX42-810, VA20-666,
 WI346-720, WV650-890
 POLITICS
 NY590-430
 RAILROADS
 DC1-920, OH451-40, OK389-560,
 TX280-540
 TEXTILE INDUSTRY
 MA606-530
 UNIONS
 AR510-810, CA86-120, CA720-356,
 DC1-400, DC3-210, GA90-300,
 IA244-480, IN253-360, IN825-200,
 KY564-520, MA21-800, MI230-880,
 NC260-170, NJ568-680, NY439-150,
 NY587-940, NY590-430, NY593-120,
 OH11-810, OH399-420, PA520-470,
 PA726-225, PA726-630, PA735-790,
 PA895-710, TN435-220, TX42-810,
 TX280-540, UT912-820, VA195-200,
 WA856-100, WI142-800, WI202-560,
 WI202-790
 WOMEN
 NY586-440
 WORLD WAR II
 DC1-400
LABOR BUREAU (OR)
 OR816-590
LABOR RELATIONS
 IL866-720
LABORATORIES
 SCIENCE
 PA725-495
LABRADOR, CANADA
 MORAVIAN CHURCH
 PA90-500
LACROSSE
 MA21-770
LADD FAMILY
 NJ280-270
LADIES AID SOCIETY (DAVENPORT NY)
 NY235-160
LADIES BENEVOLENT SOCIETY OF
 OSHKOSH
 WI554-480
LADIES LIBRARY ASSOCIATION
 MI775-520
LADIES READING CLUB (NILES MI)
 MI700-560
LADIES TEMPERANCE SOCIETY
 NY178-120
LAFAYETTE, MARQUIS DE (MARIE
 JOSEPH PAUL YVES ROCH GILBERT
 DU MOTIER)
 CT505-945, GA660-480, NC330-520,
 NY439-140
LAFFITE, JEAN
 TX560-720
LAHR, BERT
 NY591-690
LAKE CHAMPLAIN
 STEAMBOATS AND STEAMSHIPS
 VT784-720
LAKE CHAMPLAIN VALLEY
 NY708-440, NY708-720
LAKE ERIE
 PA305-210
LAKE ERIE-OHIO RIVER CANAL
 OH990-640
LAKE GEORGE
 NY331-120
LAKE HURON
 MI64-70
LAKE MICHIGAN
 LIGHTHOUSES
 IN517-520
 SHIPPING
 IN517-520
LAKE SUPERIOR
 MI865-480
 PORTS
 MN261-40
LAKE TAHOE
 CA846-480

LAKE WINNEBAGO
 WI554-600
LAKE, SIMON
 CT282-720
LAKEY FAMILY (PALMYRA NY)
 NY672-440
LAMAR, LUCIUS QUINTUS CINCINNATUS
 MS520-520
LAMB, FRED
 NH600-510
LAMBER, JOHN S.
 NY310-720
LAMONT, THOMAS W.
 MA108-750
LAMPTON FAMILY
 MO370-520
LAMY, J. B.
 RI945-800
LANCASTER GINGHAM MILLS
 MA207-120
LANCASTER LIBRARY COMPANY
 KY41M-280
LAND
 ACQUISITION
 CA456-530, CA640-640, CA942-940,
 IL856-730, MA109-180, MI355-270,
 MI865-80, NJ444-240, NY288-840,
 TN285-280, TX397-690
 AGENTS
 PA820-520
 CLAIMS
 PA55-760
 DEVELOPMENT
 FL580-320, GA90-270, NY842-730,
 TN285-280, TX252-730
 FEDERAL
 CO252-163
 INDIANS
 OR880-760
 RAILROADS
 TX968-520
 RECLAMATION
 AZ550-040, CA402-720, CA676-740,
 WY500-800
 RECORDS
 AR890-30, CA601-640, CA770-120,
 CA942-940, CT174-200, CT435-520,
 FL800-235, FL800-245, FL800-575,
 IA499-520, IA811-110, IL236-520,
 IL693-640, IL866-355, IL866-715,
 IL916-795, IL946-360, IN363-342,
 KS241-480, KY42-800, KY288-440,
 LA62-430, LA62-470, MA606-560,
 MA738-700, MA797-400, MA894-880,
 MD361-320, MD608-710, ME37-525,
 MN618-80, MN674-630, MO350-280,
 MO530-110, NC30-715, NC60-240,
 ND117-240, NH468-800, NH600-510,
 NJ280-270, NJ736-690, NJ822-80,
 NJ838-610, NY32-50, NY69-280,
 NY87-40, NY87-900, NY147-600,
 NY228-110, NY240-160, NY297-520,
 NY327-880, NY407-320, NY511-480,
 NY577-330, NY708-120, NY752-525,
 NY807-730, OH176-650, OH588-520,
 OK592-650, OR224-480, OR816-590,
 PA25-480, PA185-160, PA305-210,
 PA325-40, PA380-665, PA430-600,
 PA555-120, PA740-320, PA920-890,
 PA945-120, PA960-910, RI945-760,
 SC144-730, TN690-780, TX14-720,
 TX231-120, TX425-280, TX632-720,
 TX691-130, TX777-160, TX865-750,
 VT176-810, VT496-640, WY135-860
 SETTLEMENT
 OK558-790, PA726-412, WI714-880
 SPAIN
 FL800-235
 SURVEYS
 NJ756-240, NJ838-610
 USE
 CA86-810, CA578-675, CA966-860,
 DC14-370, GA90-270, MI230-890,
 NY10-570, NY878-320, OR720-670

LAND GRANTS
  CA700-720, GA780-290, IL866-355,
  KY96-870, KY464-880, KY526-520,
  KY604-890, MI450-560, NC950-940,
  NE720-120, NM114-900, NY648-800,
  OH112-280, OH788-120, PA380-665,
  TN390-390, TX56-110, TX777-670,
  TX777-810, VA290-760, VA350-320,
  VT496-640, WA241-170, WI202-560,
  WI450-530, WV500-640
  GREAT BRITAIN
    NC900-810
  MEXICO
    CA676-110
  SPAIN
    CA676-110, CO252-181, OK829-520
LAND MANAGEMENT, BUREAU OF
  CA386-560, CO252-550, WA820-550
LAND OFFICE
  CO252-550, FL800-235
LAND OWNERSHIP
  CA456-530, LA26-480, LA600-920,
  ME925-870
  INDIANS
    MS20-200
LAND, H. JACK
  OH181-130
LANDMARKS
  VA50-50
LANDON, ALF M.
  KS878-430
LANDS DIVISION (OR)
  OR816-590
LANDSCAPE
  NM722-730
LANDSCAPE ARCHITECTS
  CA578-675
LANDSCAPE ARCHITECTURE
  CA86-820, CO252-42, DC14-640,
  IA58-540, IL459-520, IN539-100,
  MA169-305, MO810-490, NY416-600
  EASTERN US
    CA86-820
  GREAT BRITAIN
    CA86-820
LANE, G. T.
  CA720-798
LANE, HENRY SMITH
  IN154-880
LANGE, DOROTHEA
  TX374-40
LANGLEY, JAMES W.
  GA765-440
LANGLEY, SAMUEL P.
  DC19-310
LANGUAGES
  See also Linguistics, PA595-530
  AMERINDIAN
    LA600-760
  INDIANS
    MD703-40, RI700-70, TX56-860,
    WA880-550, WA889-720
  INDIANS, LATIN AMERICA
    TX56-860
  NATIVE
    AK350-815, NY870-600
LANIER, SIDNEY
  GA735-540, MD76-340
LANMAN, CHARLES
  CT477-130
LANSING, JOHN
  CA368-120
LAPHAM, ROGER D.
  CA720-910
LARCOM, LUCY
  MA92-90, MA636-880
LAREDO AIR FORCE BASE
  TX543-560
LARKEY, JOAN LEACH
  CA206-940
LARKIN, THOMAS
  NH784-630
LARRABEE, WILLIAM, FAMILY
  IA133-520
LARSEN, NILS PAUL
  HI350-311

LASKY, JESSE L.
  CA90-30
LATHROP, JULIA
  IL806-695
LATIN AMERICA
  See also Central America; South America;
  and individual countries and regions,
  CA774-720, CA858-320, CA862-810,
  CT505-960, DC1-40, DC1-560,
  DC3-210, DC3-226, DC7-650, DC8-850,
  DC12-600, DC12-650, DC13-210,
  DC14-250, DC14-720, DC14-730,
  DC14-780, DC15-500, DC19-310,
  DC19-520, DE540-790, IN66-380,
  LA600-760, MI40-820, NC150-800,
  NY592-800, TX56-860, UT912-110,
  VA145-780, WI456-730
  CONSERVATION
    CO252-163
  ECONOMIC AID TO
    NY589-560
  ECONOMICS
    PA325-280
  FOREIGN AID
    DC1-180
  FRANCISCANS
    MD703-40
  INDIANS
    DC12-300, MI40-820, NJ692-660,
    NY592-800, TX56-860
  LITERATURE
    DC12-200
  MISSIONARIES
    NC390-200, NY529-530
  MUSIC
    AZ750-32, IN66-395
  TRAVEL
    LA600-760
LATIN PATRIARCH OF JERUSALEM
  DC6-800
LATROBE, HENRY
  MD76-30
LATVIA
  DRAMA
    MA172-160
LATVIAN-AMERICANS
  DRAMA
    MA172-160
LAUGHLIN, HARRY
  MO460-560
LAUGHLIN, LEDLIE I.
  DE900-320
LAURA SPELMAN ROCKEFELLER
  MEMORIAL
  NY612-690
LAURENS FAMILY
  NY594-220
LAUSSAT, PIERRE CLEMENT DE
  LA600-310
LAVIN, MARY
  NY101-720
LAW
  CA86-780, CA421-710, CA508-560,
  CA782-800, DE540-790, GA75-810,
  IN363-342, KY96-870, KY496-800,
  MA109-220, MA109-660, MA871-90,
  MA871-890, MI214-260, MN961-440,
  MO210-815, NJ386-380, NJ756-240,
  NY51-140, NY586-440, NY588-520,
  NY588-940, NY592-460, NY594-20,
  NY667-580, NY895-240, OH171-320,
  OH360-480, OH878-720, OH982-290,
  OK736-640, PA725-510, PA725-615,
  PA726-750, RI700-45, RI700-100,
  SC576-480, SD792-820, TX252-320,
  UT684-80, VA580-600, WI462-520
  CIVIL RIGHTS
    MS870-760
  CRIMINAL
    MA169-440, TX252-780
  EDUCATION
    CA421-710, MA169-440, NC950-940,
    PA726-750
  EUROPE
    MO430-420
  GREAT BRITAIN
    PA726-750

  INSURANCE
    NY588-860
  INTERNATIONAL
    DC15-500, MA169-440
  MAYA INDIANS
    OH181-270
  MEXICO
    OH181-270
  ORGANIZATIONS
    CA712-700
  REFORM
    TX252-780
  WATER
    CA86-920
LAW ENFORCEMENT
  OK338-120, WY135-860
LAWES, LEWIS E.
  NY588-440
LAWN BOWLS
  FL560-40
LAWYERS
  See Attorneys
LAWYERS CONSTITUTIONAL DEFENSE
  COMMITTEE
  MS870-760
LE CORBUSIER (CHARLES EDOUARD
  JEANNERET)
  MA169-305
LE GALLIENNE, RICHARD
  CA720-910
LEA, ALBERT MILLER
  MN28-240
LEA, HENRY CHARLES
  PA726-770
LEA, TOM
  TX326-210
LEACH, HUGH
  VA690-240
LEAD
  MINING
    IL301-280
LEAGUE OF NATIONS
  NY588-940
LEAGUE OF WOMEN VOTERS
  CA720-180, MI355-270, NJ568-670
LEAGUE OF WOMEN VOTERS
  (ZELIENOPLE PA)
  PA986-960
LEAGUE OF WOMEN VOTERS OF
  GREATER LOS ANGELES
  CA524-160
LEAMING FAMILY
  NJ280-270
LEARNED, HENRY DEXTER
  PA726-600
LEARY & COMPANY (BOOKSTORE)
  PA726-615
LEATHER
  IN242-250
  MANUFACTURING
    DE270-200, NY447-400
LEBAMOFF, IVAN
  IN231-40
LEBANON
  PA735-825
LEBANON (OHIO) NATIONAL NORMAL
  UNIVERSITY
  OH953-870
LEDYARD DYKE
  NY286-240
LEDYARD, JONATHAN D.
  NY164-570
LEE FAMILY (STRATFORD VA)
  VA760-690
LEE, D. BOARDMAN
  NY439-180
LEE, G. W. CUSTIS
  NC330-520
LEE, ROBERT E.
  VA50-65
LEE, RONALD
  WV350-560
LEEPER, MARY
  DC1-860
LEESON, CECIL
  IN539-86

LEGAL PROFESSION
  See also Attorneys, *IL169-52, IN66-390*
LEGAL RECORDS
  See Law
LEGISLATION
  CA594-120, NJ838-750, TN630-590,
  TN690-780, VA580-600, WY135-860
  BUSINESS
    TX252-780
  COMMERCE
    TX252-780
  HISTORIC PRESERVATION
    DC14-650
  LABOR
    NY439-150, NY590-430
  STATE
    IL866-355
LEGISLATIVE ASSEMBLY (OR)
  OR816-590
LEGISLATURES
  STATE
    IA233-360, IN363-342, KS527-795,
    MN583-920, TX280-540
LEHIGH AND WILKES-BARRE COAL
  COMPANY
  PA960-910
LEHIGH CANAL
  PA90-480
LEHIGH COAL AND NAVIGATION
  COMPANY
  PA90-480
LEHMAN, HERBERT H.
  NY588-850
LEIDSEN, ERIK
  NY594-20
LEIDY, JOSEPH
  PA725-15
LEMHI INDIAN AGENCY
  ID640-345
LEMOYNE FAMILY
  PA920-870
LENGGENHAGER
  WA820-774
LENNON, ALTON
  NC900-810
LENSKI, LOIS
  AR890-20, KS283-200, NY134-730,
  OH788-870
LEONARD, A. W.
  MD76-790
LEONARD, ELMORE
  MI1230-800
LEONARD, ROBERT Z.
  CA90-30
LEOPOLD, NATHAN
  IL169-416
LEPROSY
  NJ222-333
LESUEUR, C. A.
  PA725-15
LET'ER BUCK, BY CHARLES WELLINGTON
  FURLONG
  OR688-810
LETCHER, JOHN
  VA430-280
LETCHWORTH STATE PARK
  NY566-540
LETCHWORTH, WILLIAM P.
  NY156-480
LETCHWORTH, WILLIAM PRYOR
  NY321-720
LETTS, JAMES M.
  NY247-160
LEVENSON, SAM
  NY588-300
LEVERTOV, DENISE
  NY125-740
LEVY, NEWMAN
  NY593-485
LEWIS FAMILY
  NY288-840
LEWIS, ALBERT B., LUMBER COMPANY
  PA960-910
LEWIS, CLIVE STAPLES
  IL976-900
LEWIS, E. G.
  CA48-40

LEWIS, FIELDING
  VA285-440
LEWIS, MERIWETHER
  OR720-450
LEWIS, PERCY WYNDHAM
  NY24-735, NY439-140
LEWISLATTES, FRED
  IN275-170
LEXICOGRAPHY
  DC7-650
LEY, WILLY
  AL440-800
LEYENDECKER, JOHN Z.
  TX543-560
LHEVINNE, JOSEF
  CA720-623
LIBERIA
  NY593-380
LIBRARIANS
  IL916-40, MN742-720, MS550-410
  EDUCATION
    IL916-40
LIBRARIES
  CA40-60, CA850-720, CA862-730,
  IL916-40, MA883-870, OH813-310,
  PA690-520, PA725-375
  MEDICINE
    OH181-180
  ORGANIZATIONS
    IL916-40, NY698-650, OH486-890
LICENSE PLATES
  PA415-720
LICK OBSERVATORY
  CA782-800
LIFE AND ADVENT UNION
  IL45-30
LIFE OF JOHNSON, BY JAMES BOSWELL
  CT505-977
LIFESAVING
  MA425-520, OH863-280
LIFESAVING SERVICE (COAST GUARD)
  WA820-147
LIGHTHOUSES
  CT512-800, DC19-621, DC19-636,
  MI36-400, MI1200-240, MI925-560,
  NY818-760, NY952-720, OH863-280,
  WA427-560, WA573-520, WA616-620,
  WA820-147
  CHESAPEAKE BAY
    MD770-120
  CONSTRUCTION
    GA885-120
  LAKE MICHIGAN
    IN517-520
LIGHTING
  THEATER
    VA205-290
LIGHTING THE CANDLE, BY JAMES M.
  STONEY
  TX326-160
LILIETHAL, MAX
  CA86-385
LILLIE, BEATRICE (LADY PEEL)
  NY591-690
LIMA LOCOMOTIVE WORKS
  OH451-40
LIME
  MANUFACTURING
    WA152-125
LIMESTONE
  MINING
    DC1-500
LIMON, JOSE ARCADIO
  NY592-870
LINCKLEAN, JOHN
  NY164-570
LINCOLN FARM ASSOCIATION
  KY358-40
LINCOLN REPUBLICAN CLUB (OAKLAND
  COUNTY MI)
  MI1770-600
LINCOLN, ABRAHAM
  CA628-40, DC6-650, DC14-410,
  FL820-810, IL429-520, IL459-520,
  IL767-320, IL866-365, IL921-840,
  IN231-470, KS213-120, KY24-800,

  KY358-40, MD255-720, MN835-720,
  NE624-800, NY942-160, RI700-100,
  WA880-495
LINCOLN, ABRAHAM, BIRTHPLACE
  NATIONAL HISTORIC SITE
  KY358-480
LINCOLN, ABRAHAM, FAMILY
  KY358-480
LINCOLN, ELMO
  IN726-240
LINCOLN, MARY TODD
  DC6-650
LINDBERGH, CHARLES AUGUSTUS
  NY591-690
LINDSAY, ALBERT MUMFORD
  DE810-150
LINDSAY, NICHOLAS VACHEL
  IL866-480, IL866-840, IN275-170
LINGNAM UNIVERSITY (CANTON, CHINA)
  MA169-400
LINGUISTIC ATLAS OF NEW ENGLAND
  MA21-770
LINGUISTICS
  See also Languages, *AK350-815,*
  AZ800-800, HI350-73, MA21-770,
  MI518-50, OR848-40
  INDIANS
    DC7-650, PA725-75, RI700-70
LINK, EDWIN ALBERT, JR.
  NY101-720
LINOTYPE MACHINES
  NY705-560
LIPPINCOTT FAMILY
  NJ280-270
LIPPINCOTT, J. B.
  CA86-920
LISZT, FRANZ
  KY496-725, MA108-240, PA725-345
LITCHFIELD CT
  EDUCATION
    NY297-520
  WOMEN
    NY297-520
LITERACY
  NY594-390
LITERARY AGENTS
  NY588-900
LITERARY CRITICS
  CO252-42
LITERARY FIGURES
  See also Authors; Literary manuscripts;
  Literature; Writers, *CA720-180, DC4-940,*
  GA90-200, IA955-440, IL305-430,
  MA108-140, MD76-340, PA726-725,
  PA726-775, SC144-730, TN465-800,
  TN630-570, TN840-800, WA820-774,
  WA904-770, WI456-550
  BLACK MOUNTAIN COLLEGE
    NY866-710
  GERMANY
    MD76-360
LITERARY MANUSCRIPTS
  See also Authors; Literary figures;
  Literature; Writers, *AK500-20, AL620-20,*
  AR330-830, AR890-20, AR890-30,
  AZ750-45, AZ800-30, AZ800-830,
  CA86-780, CA86-790, CA118-720,
  CA122-320, CA143-240, CA143-470,
  CA288-400, CA290-240, CA421-40,
  CA421-400, CA421-510, CA421-610,
  CA421-770, CA421-774, CA421-830,
  CA480-510, CA480-530, CA540-520,
  CA540-610, CA601-640, CA628-40,
  CA676-130, CA680-720, CA688-720,
  CA712-810, CA720-180, CA720-675,
  CA720-910, CA756-320, CA760-710,
  CA774-800, CA778-800, CA858-320,
  CA858-810, CA862-810, CA958-640,
  CA966-880, CO180-120, CO180-640,
  CO180-650, CO252-100, CO252-820,
  CO378-120, CT36-80, CT316-110,
  CT316-120, CT316-320, CT316-330,
  CT316-520, CT316-560, CT393-480,
  CT428-865, CT463-520, CT477-130,
  CT477-570, CT505-560, CT512-120,
  CT779-785, DC4-940, DC6-600,
  DC7-540, DC7-650, DC8-850,

DC12-650, DC19-536, DC20-600,
DE270-200, DE540-790, FL40-250,
FL80-820, FL220-800, FL440-320,
FL440-530, FL800-262, FL960-690,
GA75-810, GA90-30, GA90-200,
GA90-600, GA735-540, GA780-270,
GA895-280, HI350-73, HI350-808,
IA33-370, IA233-160, IA233-360,
IA377-280, IA466-360, IA466-800,
IA955-440, ID480-810, IL55-80,
IL124-725, IL169-325, IL169-416,
IL169-599, IL170-351, IL170-884,
IL170-910, IL202-550, IL261-570,
IL305-430, IL394-360, IL394-500,
IL444-720, IL624-380, IL762-80,
IL866-365, IL866-480, IL866-840,
IL916-795, IL916-810, IL921-840,
IN66-380, IN154-880, IN209-360,
IN231-470, IN275-150, IN275-170,
IN363-90, IN363-360, IN363-360,
IN363-400, IN539-90, IN583-560,
IN627-780, IN627-800, IN704-200,
IN825-200, IN825-350, IN825-830,
IN902-840, IN935-650, KS283-200,
KS475-800, KS527-790, KS527-795,
KS541-720, KS746-640, KS878-430,
KS948-880, KS948-890, KY80-90,
KY96-870, KY288-440, KY352-320,
KY464-800, KY496-90, KY496-765,
KY496-825, KY496-850, KY564-520,
KY680-190, LA62-500, LA570-540,
LA600-555, LA600-755, LA600-775,
MA17-40, MA17-400, MA21-770,
MA25-650, MA108-140, MA108-580,
MA108-770, MA108-940, MA108-965,
MA109-120, MA109-220, MA109-460,
MA154-480, MA154-640, MA219-310,
MA169-400, MA169-440, MA169-590,
MA169-860, MA199-90, MA217-520,
MA235-150, MA334-120, MA352-270,
MA478-800, MA513-530, MA528-780,
MA538-520, MA584-550, MA593-40,
MA624-240, MA624-740, MA624-750,
MA677-70, MA733-210, MA811-720,
MA871-40, MA871-90, MA891-880,
MA961-870, MA985-70, MA985-110,
MA985-860, MD76-360, MD76-515,
MD228-870, MD285-805, MD323-520,
MD950-760, ME162-120, ME162-120,
ME650-810, ME825-730, ME925-130,
MI132-40, MI40-784, MI40-808,
MI40-820, MI255-530, MI650-530,
MI775-710, MN226-720, MN419-440,
MN541-600, MN541-902, MN541-925,
MN763-120, MN763-500, MN763-540,
MN763-800, MO210-815, MO370-520,
MO810-690, MO810-730, MO870-520,
MO920-120, MS230-160, MS490-810,
MS550-410, MS550-500, MS900-870,
MT530-500, MT700-800, NC60-640,
NC150-800, NC150-810, NC240-160,
NC380-280, NC380-800, NC390-200,
NC680-460, ND486-800, ND876-830,
NE560-550, NE560-860, NH134-540,
NH206-800, NH254-640, NH772-640,
NJ112-120, NJ178-115, NJ280-270,
NJ444-240, NJ548-400, NJ548-530,
NJ568-670, NJ756-240, NJ982-280,
NM114-900, NM722-530, NV940-810,
NY10-80, NY10-640, NY24-735,
NY51-90, NY51-240, NY134-60,
NY134-730, NY147-600, NY150-740,
NY169-120, NY197-310, NY211-580,
NY250-212, NY257-190, NY260-560,
NY272-200, NY310-720, NY315-200,
NY421-880, NY427-240, NY439-140,
NY529-530, NY586-180, NY586-440,
NY587-510, NY587-800, NY587-880,
NY588-300, NY588-340, NY588-420,
NY588-520, NY589-460, NY589-560,
NY589-580, NY590-720, NY590-940,
NY591-840, NY592-640, NY593-90,
NY593-485, NY593-560, NY593-600,
NY594-380, NY595-700, NY599-560,
NY615-560, NY637-720, NY654-600,
NY708-720, NY726-850, NY752-40,
NY752-110, NY752-330, NY752-700,

NY752-720, NY752-740, NY757-400,
NY760-90, NY766-690, NY775-720,
NY804-800, NY845-720, NY866-710,
NY872-800, NY878-320, NY878-720,
NY949-830, NY967-880, OH35-610,
OH97-80, OH171-20, OH171-320,
OH171-650, OH171-800, OH171-920,
OH181-130, OH181-270, OH181-880,
OH203-600, OH203-680, OH223-800,
OH301-690, OH320-430, OH370-310,
OH399-420, OH665-590, OH680-540,
OH788-870, OH823-750, OH823-800,
OH853-800, OH986-40, OK245-880,
OK558-790, OK753-600, OK829-520,
OR224-800, OR720-590, OR848-160,
PA90-480, PA135-80, PA160-160,
PA270-470, PA325-280, PA370-330,
PA380-650, PA395-320, PA425-360,
PA440-80, PA470-240, PA500-70,
PA555-40, PA595-530, PA725-45,
PA725-75, PA725-195, PA725-285,
PA725-510, PA725-540, PA725-720,
PA725-765, PA726-412, PA726-412,
PA726-600, PA726-775, PA735-110,
PA735-150, PA860-710, PA895-710,
PA910-840, PA945-880, PA986-960,
RI700-50, RI700-620, RI700-660,
RI700-680, RI700-740, SC144-130,
SC144-170, SC144-730, SC185-120,
SC216-820, SC846-890, SC860-600,
SD126-480, TN465-800, TN630-530,
TN690-220, TN690-600, TN690-780,
TN690-975, TX21-50, TX56-860,
TX56-890, TX56-890, TX70-770,
TX181-780, TX252-760, TX326-160,
TX326-210, TX326-210, TX3 97-690,
TX404-120, TX483-690, TX632-720,
TX695-640, TX777-720, TX777-720,
TX777-760, TX777-810, TX851-690,
TX933-65, TX933-80, UT380-810,
UT456-900, UT912-820, UT912-820,
VA90-840, VA145-780, VA205-290,
VA285-520, VA285-520, VA310-320,
VA360-320, VA360-320, VA430-870,
VA470-690, VA470-690, VA540-520,
VA580-570, VA670-690, VA690-770,
VA690-810, VA690-830, VA690-870,
VA690-910, VA870-110, VT16-120,
VT176-810, VT432-530, VT464-840,
WA60-80, WA616-950, WA672-290,
WA724-890, WA904-870, WA954-880,
WI46-480, WI70-120, WI70-720,
WI298-810, WI346-720, WI346-890,
WI456-495, WI456-540, WI456-550,
WI456-810, WI754-170, WV200-880,
WV650-890

EUROPE
MD285-805
GREAT BRITAIN
GA90-200
IRELAND
GA90-200
LITERARY PERIODICALS
DE540-790, NY51-90, NY240-720,
WI456-810
LITERATURE
See also Authors; Literary figures; Literary
manuscripts; Writers, AR510-810,
CA86-780, CA86-790, CA206-790,
CA290-240, CA540-520, CA756-320,
CA858-810, CT316-770, CT505-890,
CT505-945, CT926-480, DC12-300,
DC12-400, DE540-790, FL220-800,
FL820-780, GA75-810, IA99-40,
IA466-800, ID80-90, IL169-416,
IL170-351, IL170-884, IL624-380,
IN66-380, IN363-400, IN627-720,
IN627-800, KY496-520, KY564-520,
MA17-400, MA21-40, MA108-240,
MA108-940, MA169-860, MA217-130,
MA338-280, MA383-240, ME925-130,
MI40-808, MI230-165, MI230-800,
MI665-120, MI720-600, MN625-570,
MN763-800, MO810-260, MO810-510,
MO810-920, NE560-860, NJ464-240,
NJ578-540, NY125-740, NY134-90,
NY323-320, NY592-460, NY592-680,

NY592-800, NY593-90, NY726-850,
NY752-880, NY866-710, NY872-800,
OH203-650, OH399-440, OR224-800,
PA895-710, RI700-100, TN630-510,
TN630-530, TN630-740, TN690-975,
TX56-890, VA145-780, VT17 6-810,
VT432-530, WI456-495
AESTHETICS
NY125-740
ASIA, EASTERN
CT505-890
AVANT GARDE
CA774-800
BERKSHIRE REGION
MA677-70
BLACKS
NY592-930
CARIBBEAN
DC12-200
CHILDREN
AR890-20, DE900-320, KS283-200,
ME825-730, MN541-838, MS490-810,
OH788-870, OK42-560, RI910-880
EUROPE
CT505-977
FRANCE
CT505-890, MO810-690, TX56-890
GERMANY
CA206-790, CT505-890
GREAT BRITAIN
CA206-790, CA421-770, CA421-774,
CA540-520, CA680-720, CA756-320,
CA858-810, CO180-120, CT505-890,
DC7-650, IA466-800, IL624-380,
IL976-900, IN66-380, IN627-800,
IN627-800, KS527-790, KS948-240,
MA21-40, MA169-370, ME925-130,
MI230-800, MO810-920, NJ692-660,
NY134-90, NY592-680, NY593-90,
NY752-880, OH399-440, PA895-710,
TX56-890, TX933-65, VA470-690
IRELAND
ME925-130, NY101-720, NY866-730,
PA500-80, WI456-810
IRISH-AMERICANS
NY101-720
ISLAM
UT912-820
JEWS
NY590-840, NY595-700
LATIN AMERICA
DC12-200
MODERN
TX483-690
MYSTERY
CA421-510
NEW ENGLAND
MA169-370
ORGANIZATIONS
IA699-120, IL444-720, IL567-520,
IL624-380, IL976-990, IN319-330,
IN352-320, KY598-600, MI40-808,
MI700-560, MO810-920, NC240-160,
NY241-160, OH194-120, PA755-40,
SC144-150, SC846-890, VA430-870
PACIFIC AREA
HI350-73
POLAND
NY593-500
PORTUGAL
DC12-200
RECORDINGS
CT505-976
RUSSIA
CT505-890, MA169-370
SOUTHERN US
NC260-170
SPAIN
DC12-200, PR600-800
WESTERN US
CA862-810
WOMEN
NE736-560, NY564-840

LITHUANIA
IL169-169, IL170-53, IL170-61,
PA735-825
EXILES
IL170-53
**LITHUANIAN NATIONAL CATHOLIC
CHURCH**
MA451-360
**LITHUANIAN SOCIAL CAMP
ASSOCIATION**
MA451-360
LITHUANIAN-AMERICANS
IL170-53, IL170-61
ORGANIZATIONS
MA451-360
LITITZ PA
MUSIC
NC930-530
LITSCH GENERAL STORE
CA814-120
LITSEY, EDWIN CARLILE
KY418-520
LITTLE REVIEW (LITERARY MAGAZINE)
WI456-810
LITTLE TENNESSEE RIVER
NC656-720
LITTLE THEATER OF SHREVEPORT
LA885-690
LITTLE, CYRUS
NH600-510
LITTLE, MOSES
NY563-120
LITURGY
IN627-810, MA154-310, MI255-545,
PA725-885
LIVESTOCK
EXHIBITIONS AND FAIRS
MO400-400
LIVESTOCK INDUSTRY
MT130-540, MT530-500
STOCKYARDS
TX280-540
LIVINGSTON FAMILY
NY427-240
LIVINGSTON FAMILY (NY)
NY726-40
LLANO ESTACADO (SOUTHWESTERN US)
TX712-880
**LOCAL COUNCIL OF WOMEN OF NEW
ORLEANS**
LA600-555
LOCKS (HARDWARE)
MANUFACTURING
CT797-480
LOCKS (WATERWAYS)
IL429-520, MI865-480, OH171-650
CONSTRUCTION
IA511-450
**LOCOMOTIVE FIREMEN, BROTHERHOOD
OF**
IN825-200
LOCOMOTIVES
See also Railroads, IL170-273,
NY804-560, NY804-800, TX252-730
MANUFACTURING
DC19-636, OH451-40
LODER, LEWIS A.
KY62G-120
LOESER, CHRISTOPHER
PA740-320
LOEW'S (THEATER CHAIN)
IN627-760
LOGAN, JAMES
PA725-720
LOGAN, WILLIAM
TX560-720
LOGGING
See also Lumbering, CA250-120,
CA620-760, CA720-307, CA782-240,
CA998-720, ME437-120, ME667-480,
MI122-880, MI368-320, MI620-520,
MI925-640, MN185-120, MN198-120,
MN363-360, MN735-690, NY675-640,
NY708-720, NY872-720, OR96-120,
VT32-80, WA417-140, WA904-100,
WI38-480, WI198-400, WI1362-520,
WI554-600

EUROPE
CA86-850
RAILROADS
CA720-307
LOMBARD COLLEGE
IL305-430
LOMBARD, LOUIS
MD76-640
LONDON, CHARMIAN
LITERARY MANUSCRIPTS
UT380-810
LONDON, JACK
CA288-400, CA540-610
LITERARY MANUSCRIPTS
UT380-810
LONG ISLAND RAILROAD
NY866-710
**LONG ISLAND SOCIETY OF
ANESTHETISTS**
IL708-40
**LONG-BELL LUMBER COMPANY
(LONGVIEW, WASHINGTON)**
WA495-500
LONG, HANIEL
PA735-150
LONG, HUEY PIERCE
LA62-500
LONGFELLOW FAMILY
MA169-590
LONGFELLOW, HENRY WADSWORTH
MA169-590, MN541-600
LOOKABOUT CLUB
NY563-322
**LORAIN COUNTY AGRICULTURAL
SOCIETY**
OH906-320
LORD AND BURHAM CORPORATION
NY592-320
LORENZ, KONRAD
KS878-520
LORIKS, EMIL
SD550-600
LOS ALAMOS RANCH SCHOOL
NM570-480, NM722-730
LOS ANGELES CA
SISTERS OF ST. JOSEPH OF
CARONDELET
NY481-720
**LOS ANGELES COUNTY FEDERATION OF
LABOR**
CA524-160
**LOS NIETOS AND RANCHITO WALNUT
GROWERS ASSOCIATION**
CA226-170
LOSSING, BENSON J.
NY726-40
LOUDOUN COUNTY VA
DC14-370
LOUGHBOROUGH, JOHN N.
MI90-30
**LOUIS H. SULLIVAN (ARCHITECTURAL
FIRM)**
IL169-130
LOUIS XIV (KING OF FRANCE)
NY592-870
LOUIS, AH, FAMILY
CA720-220
LOUIS, JOE (JOSEPH LOUIS BARROW)
DC19-550
LOUISIANA
NY439-640
GOVERNMENT AGENCIES, NATIONAL
TX374-550
LOUISIANA HISTORICAL ASSOCIATION
LA600-755
LOUISIANA LANDMARKS SOCIETY
LA600-761
**LOUISIANA PURCHASE EXPOSITION
(1904)**
MO810-600
LOUISIANA RELIEF COMMITTEE
LA600-310
LOUISIANA SUPREME COURT
LA600-775
LOUISVILLE & NASHVILLE RAILROAD
FL860-320, KY496-812

LOUISVILLE HISTORICAL LEAGUE
KY496-70
LOUISVILLE ZOOLOGICAL COMMISSION
KY496-540
LOVEJOY FAMILY
IL762-80
LOW, JULIETTE GORDON
GA895-290, NY589-720
LOWELL OBSERVATORY
AZ250-575
LOWELL, JAMES RUSSELL
MA961-870, MN541-600
LOWELL, ROBERT
OH320-430
LUCAS, GEORGE A.
MD76-880
LUCE, STEPHEN B.
RI560-510
LUCIHE FAMILY
MA425-520
LUHRS, DOROTHY
NM114-880
LUMBERING
See also Logging, AZ250-575, CA86-850,
CA180-160, CA274-120, CA432-520,
CA454-520, CA624-710, DC1-680,
GA885-120, GA885-520, IA211-480,
ID80-365, ID600-130, ID880-80,
KY2A-80, MA823-610, ME37-535,
ME200-120, ME650-780, MI40-784,
MI64-70, MI255-545, MI585-520,
MI675-510, MI824-320, MN763-530,
MN835-720, MO210-815, MS900-870,
NY274-200, OR128-720, OR144-610,
OR720-590, PA520-470, PA726-855,
PA740-320, PA960-910, PA965-490,
TN285-280, TX483-810, TX632-720,
WA60-885, WA123-333, WA395-640,
WA535-200, WA678-650, WI142-120,
WI142-800, WI298-810, WI326-120,
WI554-600
NORTH CAROLINA
PA726-855
PACIFIC NORTHWEST
MI824-320
SOUTH DAKOTA
CO36-40
LUMMIS, CHARLES FLETCHER
CA421-510, CA421-610
LUTHER SEMINARY
IA211-480
LUTHER, BERTHA
NY563-120
LUTHER, LESTER
NY563-120
LUTHERAN CHURCH
GA860-280, IA211-480, IA233-280,
IA244-30, LA600-775, MN625-710,
MN763-50, NY591-40, PA325-280,
PA325-490, PA705-320, PA986-960,
TX797-760, WA904-635
CLERGY
LA600-775, MD76-490, NY591-35,
PA25-520, PA325-490, TX56-490
DANISH-AMERICANS
IA244-30
EASTERN US
PA325-490
EUROPE
MN625-710
GERMAN-AMERICANS
IA244-30
MISSIONARIES
IA244-30, IL170-91, MI322-240,
MN763-50, MO810-200
NEW ENGLAND
NY591-35
NEW JERSEY
NY591-35
NORWEGIAN-AMERICANS
IA211-480, MN763-50
ORGANIZATIONS
MN625-710
SYNOD OF THE NORTWEST
MN769-280
THEOLOGIANS
MO810-190

LUTHERAN CHURCH IN AMERICA
FL820-480, MO810-200, PA725-885
CANADA
IL170-91
CLERGY
PA725-885
IOWA
IL170-91
KENTUCKY
IN363-480
MISSIONARIES
PA725-885
RELIGIOUS COMMUNITIES
PA330-160
TENNESSEE SYNOD
NC730-500
LUTHERAN CHURCH-MISSOURI SYNOD
IN231-130, IN231-490, MI322-240,
MO810-200, WI426-111
CENTRAL DISTRICT
IN231-490
CLERGY
SD684-480
KENTUCKY
IN231-490
MISSIONARIES
OR720-470
NEVADA
CA720-405
NEW ENGLAND
NY128-480
NEW JERSEY
NY128-480
NORTHERN DISTRICT
WI426-111
OHIO
IN231-490
ORGANIZATIONS
OR720-470
SOUTH WISCONSIN DISTRICT
WI426-111
SOUTHERN DISTRICT
LA600-775
WEST VIRGINIA
IN231-490
WISCONSIN DISTRICT
WI426-111
LUTHERAN LAYMEN'S LEAGUE
MO810-200, NE800-480, OR720-470
LUTHERAN WOMEN'S MISSIONARY
LEAGUE
MO810-200, NE800-480, OR720-470
LUTHERAN WORLD FEDERATION
MN625-710
LUXEMBOURG
ART
NY593-100
LYCEUMS
IL674-880
LYING-IN HOSPITAL OF NEW YORK
NY592-480
LYON, IRVING PHILLIPS
DE900-320
LYON, IRVING W.
DE900-320
LYON, ISRAEL WHITNEY
CA480-500
LYON, LUCIUS
MI20-50
LYON, MARY
MA776-530

M

MACARTHUR, DOUGLAS
MI440-320, PA325-280, VA580-520
MACCRACKEN, WILLIAM P., JR.
TN630-730
MACDONALD, GEORGE
IL976-900
MACDOWELL, EDWARD
NH748-650
MACDUFFIE, MARSHALL
NY588-850
MACFADDEN, FAY
CA278-130

MACGIMSEY, ROBERT HUNTER
LA670-480
MACHINE TOOL INDUSTRY
DC19-601, VT864-730
MACHINERY
DC19-606, DE270-200, MI122-880
AGRICULTURE
CA132-120, CA206-790
COAL MINING
DC19-591
MANUFACTURING
DC19-601
TEXTILES
MA606-530
MACHINISTS, INTERNATIONAL
ASSOCIATION OF
GA90-300
MACK, STEPHEN, FAMILY
IL811-690
MACKAY, CLARENCE H.
NY760-90
MACKAYE, BENTON
MA761-720
MACKAYE, HAZEL
MA761-720
MACKAYE, PERCEY
MA761-720
MACKAYE, STEELE
MA761-720
MACKENZIE, JAMES C.
NJ420-490
MACKENZIE, RODERICK D.
AL580-530
MACKESY, LILLIAN
WI46-600
MACKINAC, STRAITS OF
MI590-520
MACLEISH, ARCHIBALD
NY125-740
MACMILLAN, DONALD B.
ME162-100
MACRAE, ELMER
DC19-340
MADAGASCAR
MISSIONARIES
MN763-50
WAR WITH FRANCE
MI255-530
MADDUX FAMILY
TN15-760
MAGAZINER, LOUIS
PA725-150
MAGIC
NY593-485
MAGNETISM
DC19-641
MAHAN, ALFRED THAYER
RI560-510
MAHAN, ASA
MI8-20
MAHLER, MARGARET
OH11-840
MAHURIN, S. F.
IN231-40
MAINE
GOVERNMENT AGENCIES
MA109-220
MAINE, SOUTHWESTERN
NH784-700
MAJOR, CHARLES
IN935-650
MAKAH INDIANS
WA578-520
MALACOLOGY
PA725-15
MALAWI
MISSIONARIES
RI910-730
MALCOLM, NORMAN
NY125-740
MALLET, EDMOND
RI945-800
MALONE, EDMUND
CT505-977
MALTA
MN226-720

MALTED MILK PRODUCTS
WI606-710
MAMIE DOUD EISENHOWER
BIRTHPLACE FOUNDATION
IA58-540
MANHATTAN COMPANY, BANK OF THE
NY588-60
MANHATTAN MATERNITY AND
DISPENSARY
NY592-480
MANHATTAN PROJECT
ATOMIC BOMB
NM570-480
MANHATTANVILLE ACADEMY
NY732-520
MANION FORUM (RADIO PROGRAM)
MI440-320
MANION, CLARENCE E.
MI440-320
MANITOBA, CANADA
WA265-600
MANN FAMILY
OH986-40
MANN, ARTHUR
NY588-300
MANN, HORACE
MA235-150, OH986-40
MANNES, DAVID
NY591-140
MANNING, JAMES
RI700-50
MANNING, SARA MORGAN
NY125-720, NY125-880
MANNING, WARREN, FAMILY
MA478-800
MANSFIELD, RICHARD
CT4-160
MANSON, GRANT
IL649-600
MANTELL, ROBERT B.
NY593-485
MANTON, ROBERT
NH206-800
MANUFACTURERS PERFUMERS
ASSOCIATION
DC3-800
MANUFACTURING
See also Industry; Mills, *CA862-630,*
CO768-640, CT36-80, IL192-510,
IL866-355, IN363-342, IN539-83,
MA823-610, MI1230-890, NH600-510,
RI875-880, TX252-730
AUTOMOBILES
PA560-690
BRICKS
NY818-760, WA152-125
BUTTONS
CT870-520
CARPETS
MA207-120
CERAMICS
DC19-545
CLOCKS
CT48-40
CORK
PA470-40
DRUGS
IL629-40
ELECTRIC APPLIANCES
OH223-520
ELECTRONICS
PA295-130
EXPLOSIVES
DE270-200, WA259-160
FARM EQUIPMENT
IL169-703, IL548-150, IN792-160,
NY125-720, OH223-880, OH223-880,
WI834-40
GASOLINE PUMPS
IN231-40
GLASS
CT961-210, MA738-720, MI214-280,
NY214-120, NY214-140, NY269-200,
VA500-322
GREAT BRITAIN
PA560-690

HATS
CT144-150
LEATHER
DE270-200, NY447-400
LIME
WA152-125
LOCKS (HARDWARE)
CT797-480
LOCOMOTIVES
DC19-636, OH451-40
MACHINERY
DC19-601
MEXICO
TX326-780
OHIO
DC19-601
PAPER
DC19-601, DE270-200, MA227-120,
MA823-610, VT32-80, WI46-360
SEWER PIPE
WA152-125
SHOES
MA486-470, NH720-560
SHOVELS
MA615-710
STOVES
OH495-510
TILE
IN242-250
TOBACCO
NC390-200
WAGONS
IN792-160
WATCHES
CT48-40, MA871-870, PA215-560
WOOL
MO490-880, NY240-160, OH505-520
WORLD WAR II
CT870-730
MANUSCRIPTS
ART
MA169-340
MAORI AGRICULTURAL COLLEGE
HI450-80
MAPS
See also Cartography, IL236-730,
NJ692-660, TN465-760
MARANDA, ELLI KONGAS
OR48-40
MARBLEHEAD ACADEMY
MA506-520
MARCH OF TIME (RADIO PROGRAM)
NY594-640
MARCH, ALDEN
NY10-800
MARCONI, GUGLIELMO
DC19-641
MARCY FAMILY
MA797-400
MARCY, WILLIAM
MA797-400
MARE ISLAND NAVAL SHIPYARD
CA922-840
MARIANISTS
See Society of Mary, in repository index
MARIE (QUEEN OF ROMANIA)
OH399-440
MARIETTA LIBRARY ASSOCIATION
OH486-890
MARIJUANA
TX252-780
MARIJUANA AND DRUG ABUSE,
NATIONAL COMMISSION ON
TX252-780
MARINE BIOLOGY
MI518-50
MARINE CORPS
DC13-210, DC19-621, MD57-830
AVIATION
DC14-715
MARINE GEOLOGY
CO108-560
MARINE GEOPHYSICS
CO108-560
MARINE INSURANCE
CT463-520, PA725-780

MARINE LIFE
PACIFIC NORTHWEST
WA685-640
MARINE SCIENCE
NY586-720
MARINE SOCIETY OF THE CITY OF NEW
YORK
NY594-340
MARIPOSA GOLD MINE
VT496-640
MARITIME EDUCATION
MA165-520, NY594-340
MARITIME FEDERATION OF THE PACIFIC
CA720-356
MARITIME HISTORY
CA250-120, CA480-500, CA676-130,
CA720-485, CA982-480, CT463-520,
CT505-560, CT512-550, CT751-640,
DC14-740, KY96-870, MA307-230,
MA572-560, MA733-210, MA837-720,
MD836-120, ME75-520, ME275-160,
ME762-640, MI620-520, NY427-240,
NY594-060, NY594-340, NY952-720,
PA726-240, VA560-520, WA427-560,
WA616-620, WA616-870, WA616-950,
WA724-890, WA820-550, WA820-770,
WA820-880
ALASKA
WA820-635
GREAT LAKES
WI354-520
NEW ENGLAND
CT463-520
NORTHEASTERN US
CT463-520
PACIFIC NORTHWEST
WA820-635
PUGET SOUND
WA820-635
MARITIME PRESERVATION
DC14-640
MARKETING
MA606-530, NC390-200, NY587-840
MARKHAM, EDWIN
IN275-170, NY595-360
MARKS, JEANNETTE
MA891-880
MARLAND, E. W.
OK634-640
MARRIAGE
FL800-245, IL261-280, MA169-885,
TX483-160
MARRIED LADIES READING CLUB
KY598-600
MARSHALL FAMILY
NY660-720
MARSHALL PLAN
GREECE
MA169-800
MARSHALL, ALEXANDER
PA725-15
MARSHALL, GEORGE C.
VA430-280
MARSHALL, S. L. A.
TX326-800
MARTIN, CECILIA
VA430-280
MARTIN, DARWIN D., HOUSE
NY24-720
MARTIN, GEORGE, FAMILY
IL609-120
MARTIN, JOSEPH W.
MA615-720
MARTIN, MORGAN L.
WI202-560
MARVIN FAMILY
OH878-720
MARX, JOSEPH
WI202-120
MARYKNOLL TEACHERS COLLEGE
NY529-530
MARYLAND
DC14-600, DE810-330
HOSPITALS
MD76-527
PHYSICIANS
MD76-527

RELIGIOUS COMMUNITIES
DC7-650
ROMAN CATHOLIC CHURCH
PA726-495
SOCIETY OF FRIENDS
PA860-710
UNITED CHURCH OF CHRIST
PA470-800
MARYLAND CONFERENCE FOR SOCIAL
CONCERN
MD76-800
MARYLAND COUNCIL OF CHURCHES
MD76-800
MARYLAND STATE NORMAL SCHOOL
MD950-760
MASEFIELD, JOHN
OH181-130
MASON, GEORGE
MA961-870
MASON, GREGORY
MA961-870
MASONS (ORGANIZATION)
DC19-130, IA99-40, MD76-20,
NH468-800, VT464-840
GREAT BRITAIN
MD76-20
MASS COMMUNICATIONS
MI40-784, WI346-720
MASS TRANSIT
DC1-680
MASSACHUSETTS
CRANCH FAMILY
WY500-800
MASSACHUSETTS BAY COLONY
MA841-600
MASSACHUSETTS SOCIETY FOR
PROMOTING AGRICULTURE
MA897-880
MASSACHUSETTS SUPREME JUDICIAL
COURT
MA109-660
MASSACHUSETTS, WESTERN
NY178-120
MASSACRES
ARMENIANS
DC1-775, MA84-50
MASSEE, MAY
KS283-200
MASSENGILL FAMILY
TN750-690
MASTERS, EDGAR LEE
IL489-890, MA961-870
MATHEMATICIANS
NY216-720
MATHEMATICS
DC19-596, NC240-160, NY125-740,
OH481-530, PA90-30, VT528-560
ITALY
CA578-130
MATHER, COTTON
MA513-530
MATHER, INCREASE
MA513-530
MATHEWS, MITFORD MCLEOD
IN825-350
MATTOX FAMILY
TN15-760
MAUJEAN, CATHERINE (MOTHER MARY
OF THE ANGELS)
IA188-777
MAUVE, ANTON
NY589-680
MAUZEY, MERRITT
MS490-810
MAXEY, SAMUEL BELL
TX56-800
MAXIMILIAN (EMPEROR OF MEXICO)
TX21-50
MAXWELL, GEORGE HEBARD
AZ550-040, LA600-465
MAXWELL, VOLNEY
PA960-910
MAYBECK, BERNARD
CA86-820
MAYER, ALBERT
IL170-884

MAYFLOWER (SHIP)
MA685-520
MAYHEW FAMILY
MA108-240
MAYORS
AR390-760, CA720-910, GA735-540, GA895-120, IN231-40, MD76-60, MT100-200, VA580-600
MAYTORENA, JOSE MARIA
CA143-470
MAZZUCHELLI, SAMUEL
WI698-730
MCAULEY, CATHERINE
LA600-690, MD152-720
MCCALLEY, HENRY
AL840-280
MCCARRAN, PATRICK
NV90-530
MCCARTHY, FRANK
VA430-280
MCCARTHY, JOSEPH RAYMOND
SD450-150
MCCARTHY, KATHERYN O'LOUGHLIN
KS377-200
MCCARTHYISM
NY588-850
MCCLELLAN, WALTER S.
NY792-720
MCCLINTOCK, JAMES HARVEY
AZ550-640
MCCLOSKEY, JOHN
NY10-675
MCCOMB, JOHN, JR.
NY101-70
MCCONNELL, DANIEL
PA540-240
MCCORMACK, JOHN W.
MA108-240
MCCORMICK, CYRUS HALL (1809-1884)
WI346-720
MCCOY, ISAAC
KS878-430
MCCOY, LEO
CA620-760
MCCULLOUGH, ESTHER MORGAN
VT496-640
MCCULLOUGH, JOHN G.
VT496-640
MCCULLY, F. D.
OR424-880
MCCUTCHEON, CHARLES
WA904-760
MCCUTCHEON, GEORGE BARR
MA961-870
MCCUTCHEON, JOHN TINNEY
IL169-416, IN935-650
MCDEVITT, PHILIP R.
PA380-700
MCDONALD, GERALD DOAN
OH953-870
MCDONALD, JAMES GROVER
NY588-850
MCDONALD, JOHN D.
FL220-800
MCDONOGH, JOHN
LA600-465
MCDONOUGH, THOMAS
VT784-720
MCDOWELL, EDWARD ALLISON, JR.
NC840-720
MCDOWELL, EPHRAIM
KY192-200
MCELHANY, JAMES L.
MI90-30
MCFADDEN-ROSS HOUSE (DEARBORN MI)
MI214-150
MCFARLAND, E.W.
AZ275-520
MCGLYNN, THOMAS M.
RI700-630
MCGRATH, J. HOWARD
RI700-630
MCGUFFEY, WILLIAM H.
OH680-540
MCILVAINE, CHARLES PETTIT
OH320-430

MCINERNEY, FRANCIS J.
NY10-675
MCINTOSH, DONALD
MT100-200
MCINTYRE (AUTOMOBILE MODEL)
IN33-40
MCINTYRE, THOMAS
NH206-800
MCIVER, CHARLES DUNCAN
NC380-800
MCKAMEY, J. S.
TX726-80
MCKAY, VERNON
IL261-566
MCKAY, WILLIAM
OR688-810
MCKELLAR, KENNETH D.
TN630-570
MCKIM, MEAD, AND WHITE (ARCHITECTURAL FIRM)
IL169-130
MCKINLEY, WILLIAM
OH481-530
MCKINSTRY FAMILY
NY466-120
MCKNIGHT, ROBERT
PA735-800
MCLAUGHLIN, JAMES
ND824-40
MCLAUGHLIN, LEO P.
AR390-760
MCLEAN COUNTY HOME BUREAU
IL94-510
MCMURTRIE, DOUGLAS C.
MI255-530
MCNAMARA, ROBERT F.
NY214-160
MCNAMARA, THOMAS R.
VA580-600
MCNEESE, JOHN
LA395-520
MCPHERSON FREEDOM MEMORIAL COLLECTION
LA600-160
MCQUAID, BERNARD J.
NY752-760
MCVICCAR, JOHN
NY286-240
MCVICKER, GEORGE
NE368-160
MEAD, ELWOOD
CO378-120
MEAD, MARGARET
KS878-520
MEAD, MRS.
NY915-880
MEARS, MARY
WI554-600
MEASON, ISAAC
PA735-150
MECHANICAL ENGINEERS, AMERICAN SOCIETY OF
NY589-460
MECHANICS
PA725-495
ORGANIZATIONS
KY600-600
MECHANICS INSTITUTE
NY752-700
MEDARIS, JOHN B.
FL420-240
MEDICAL PROFESSION
WOMEN
CA720-890, PA725-900
MEDICI FAMILY
MA108-750
MEDICINE
See also Health sciences; Physicians, AL120-810, AL120-815, AR510-825, CA421-660, CA720-894, CA858-895, CA862-810, CT316-310, CT505-930, CT673-690, DC1-760, DC3-320, DC7-660, DC14-100, DC19-611, FL80-160, IN902-80, KS475-800, KY192-200, KY604-890, LA600-755, MA108-770, MA169-860, MD76-360, MD152-550, MI40-784, MI518-50,

MI824-320, MN541-16, MO430-700, MO810-510, MO810-650, MO810-960, NE624-830, NJ108-120, NJ222-333, NJ756-240, NY10-800, NY101-720, NY134-510, NY562-720, NY588-940, NY591-600, NY592-260, NY592-480, NY593-840, NY612-690, NY752-885, OH171-800, OH181-180, OH181-790, OH588-520, OK338-120, PA725-75, PA725-285, PA725-690, PA725-720, PA725-870, RI700-710, SC144-105, SC144-520, TN690-510, TN690-780, TN690-960, TX210-200, TX397-790, TX590-760, VA810-40, WI362-520, WI456-500, WI794-880
AFRICA
MA108-770
ART
MD76-880
ASIA, EASTERN
CA858-895
BIOMEDICINE
WA820-895
CHINA
CA720-886
EDUCATION
CA720-886, CA720-890, CA720-894, DC1-890, MD76-315, MD76-527, MI1230-905, MO810-650, NE624-830, NY591-600, NY592-480, NY593-840, NY752-885, OH203-680, PA725-690, PA725-900, PA726-690, PA726-725, SD792-830, TN690-510, TX397-790, VA690-840, WA904-760
EDUCATORS
TX397-790
EUROPE
MD76-527, NY592-260
FOLK
OH788-120
HERBAL
MA134-560
JAPAN
CA720-886
LIBRARIES
OH181-180
MEXICO
CA720-894
MILITARY
DC1-760, NM513-560, VA690-530
NEW ENGLAND
MA108-770
ORGANIZATIONS
CA720-894, IL708-40, IN792-720, MI1230-905, MO810-650, NH600-510, NY101-720, NY318-260, NY589-900, NY592-260, OH181-180, PA725-285, TX397-790, WI456-500
PHILOSOPHY
NY125-740
SOUTHWESTERN US
NM114-525
SPANISH-AMERICAN WAR
OH181-180
WOMEN
OH181-180, PA725-900
WORLD WAR I
OH181-180
MEDITERRANEAN
TRAVEL
CT512-120
MEEHAN, THOMAS
PA725-600
MEISSNER, BENJAMIN F.
IN935-650
MELANESIA
FL60-720, HI350-73
MELLOR, MEIGS AND HOWE
PA725-150
MELLOR, WILLIAM J.
OK42-560
MELVILLE, HERMAN
MA677-70
MELVILLE, VISCOUNTS (DUNDAS FAMILY)
MI40-820

MEMMINGER, CHRISTOPHER GUSTAVUS
  NC150-800
MEN AND VOLTS, BY JOHN W. HAMMOND
  NY804-280
MENASHA WOODEN WARE CORPORATION
  WI554-480
MENCKEN, HENRY LOUIS
  KY496-825, MD323-520, PA325-280
MENDELSSOHN, FELIX
  DC12-510
MENNINGER FAMILY
  KS878-520
MENNINGER, KARL
  KS878-520
MENNINGER, WILLIAM CLAIRE
  KS878-520
MENNONITE BRETHREN
  CA274-130
  CANADA
    CA274-130
  MISSIONARIES
    CA274-130
  SOUTH AMERICA
    CA274-130
MENNONITE CENTRAL COMMITTEE
  AKRON PA
    IN264-40
MENNONITE CENTRAL COMMITTEE (AKRON PA)
  IN264-40
MENNONITE CHURCH
  IA499-520, PA470-480, PA478-530, SD234-250, VA350-200
  CANADA
    IN264-40
  GENERAL CONFERENCE
    KS676-520
  MISSIONARIES
    IN264-40
  NEBRASKA
    IA499-520
  ORGANIZATIONS
    IN264-40
MENNONITES
  IA499-520, IN264-40, OH92-520, PA470-480, PA478-530, PA715-720, PA725-608, SD234-250, VA350-200
  CANADA
    OH92-520
  EASTERN US
    PA470-480
  FRANCE
    OH92-520
  GERMANY
    OH92-520
  IMMIGRATION AND EMIGRATION
    KS676-520
  ONTARIO, CANADA
    PA470-480
  SWITZERLAND
    OH92-520
MENOTTI, GIAN-CARLO
  PA725-345
MENTAL HEALTH
  See also Psychiatry, *IL866-355, IL866-720, KS878-520, NJ838-730, PA860-710, WA889-880*
MENTALLY ILL PERSONS
  NY594-20
MENTALLY RETARDED PERSONS
  MA21-770
MERCANTILE ACTIVITIES
  See also General stores; Grocery stores, *AZ250-575, AZ750-10, AZ800-830, CA180-160, CT36-80, CT582-550, CT947-880, IL192-510, KY126-760, KY600-600, MA108-750, MA338-840, MA673-640, MA837-720, ME667-480, MI126-880, NC405-640, NC710-540, NC950-940, NH588-520, NH600-530, NJ108-120, NJ358-320, NJ502-690, NJ574-560, NY10-770, NY150-700, NY261-320, NY274-200, NY550-520, NY577-330, NY598-560, NY654-600, NY760-690, NY839-720, NY851-720,*

NY861-740, NY915-870, OH996-520, OK685-710, PA55-760, PA180-120, TX923-840, VA20-40, VA90-840, VA235-250, VT704-690, WA489-40
MERCER, GEORGE J.
  CA282-480
MERCHANDISING
  DE270-200, MA109-120, MI214-260, MT430-320, MT530-500
MERCHANT MARINE
  DC19-636, MD57-830, NY594-060
  SHIPS
    MD57-810
MERCHANTS
  CT234-230, CT772-720, DE900-320, ID80-365, IN917-880, MA108-140, MA823-610, ME925-870, NJ838-630, NY665-760, OH112-280, PA380-320, VT704-690, WA381-330
  TOBACCO
    NY594-680
MERCURY (SHIP) CASE
  CA421-400
MEREDITH, GEORGE
  CT505-890
MEREDITH, SAMUEL
  PA960-910
MERRILL, ELMER D.
  MA169-190
MERRIMAN FAMILY
  MI510-200
MERRITT FAMILY
  MN261-810
MERTENS, FRANZ CARL
  PA735-140
MERTON, THOMAS
  KY496-90, MA199-90, NY775-720
MERWIN FAMILY
  NY466-120
MERWIN, W. S.
  OH181-130
MERYON, CHARLES
  OH823-770
MES OBSERVATIONS, BY CHARLES MERYON
  OH823-770
A MESSAGE TO GARCIA, BY ELBERT HUBBARD
  NY134-90
MESSENGER, GEORGE
  MS230-160
MESSMER, JOSEPH
  DC6-650
METALLURGICAL LABORATORY
  IL35-40
METALLURGY
  CA143-480
METALWORK
  ISLAM
    DC19-327
METCALF, GEORGE
  NY51-90
METEOROLGY
  CA778-780
METEOROLOGY
  See also Weather, *CA206-790, CT512-120, DC14-770, DC19-631, MA572-540, NC60-160, ND486-810, OR720-450, SC108-100, SC144-170*
METHODISM
  IA688-360
  GERMANY
    IA688-360
  MISSOURI
    IA688-360
METHODIST CHURCH
  See also United Methodist church, Free Methodist church and other Methodist churches, *AL120-110, CA86-630, CO252-360, CT428-865, CT484-550, DC23-500, GA825-200, IA699-120, IL394-500, IN5-40, KY464-780, KY48V-720, MI8-800, MI126-880, MN541-777, MO290-120, NC260-150, NJ464-666, NM950-270, NY235-160, NY263-210, NY752-60, NY872-800, NY945-760, OH223-790, OR816-530, PA160-160, PA295-130, PA725-700, TN690-890, TN765-800, TX252-760, WA904-800, WI733-333*

  CLERGY
    GA885-520, IL261-280, MD76-790, MS550-540, NE560-810, NM200-800, PA555-40, TN690-885, TN690-890, TX7-800, TX252-760
  GREAT BRITAIN
    CT428-865
  HOLSTON CONFERENCE
    TN15-760
  MIDWESTERN US
    IL261-280
  MISSIONARIES
    GA885-520, KY886-30, NY752-60, WA904-50
  NEW ENGLAND
    MA109-480
  NORTH GEORGIA CONFERENCE
    GA90-190
  ORGANIZATIONS
    GA90-190, NY752-60, NY895-240, TX7-800
  PUBLISHING
    KY886-30, TN690-890
  SOUTH GEORGIA CONFERENCE
    GA885-520
  SOUTHERN US
    GA90-200, MS550-540
  WOMEN
    GA885-520
METHODIST EPISCOPAL CHURCH
  DC23-500, IA455-720, IA688-360, KS108-70, LA885-120, MN541-777, NJ464-666, NM200-800, TN765-800, WA904-50, WI733-333
  FREEDMEN'S AID SOCIETY
    GA90-360
  ORGANIZATIONS
    GA90-360
METHODIST EPISCOPAL CHURCH, SOUTH
  AR240-320, NJ464-666, NM200-800, TN765-800
METHODIST PROTESTANT CHURCH
  AR240-320, DC23-500, IA688-360, KS108-70, LA885-120, NJ464-666
METROPOLITAN CHURCH FEDERATION OF GREATER ST. LOUIS
  MO810-590
METROPOLITAN STATE COLLEGE
  CO252-42
METZ AUTOMOBILE CO.
  MA871-870
MEXICAN WAR
  CA720-180, DC1-810, IL866-355, IN363-360, PA920-890, TX42-810, TX777-810
MEXICAN-AMERICANS
  CA143-470, CA778-800, MN763-530, MN763-540
MEXICO
  AZ225-40, AZ550-040, AZ800-30, AZ800-803, AZ800-830, CA66-80, CA86-630, CA86-780, CA118-720, CA274-120, CA352-520, CA386-560, CA421-30, CA421-390, CA421-510, CA421-610, CA676-130, CA704-560, CA712-708, CA720-180, CA720-579, CA720-746, CA720-910, CA724-730, CA728-730, CA756-320, CA770-120, CA774-720, CA778-800, CA858-810, CA934-720, CO252-70, CO252-100, CO252-550, CO270-240, CT505-960, DC7-650, DC14-250, LA600-760, MA169-310, MD76-515, MD703-40, MI40-820, MI230-165, MN226-705, MO200-720, MO210-840, MO810-730, NM114-50, NM722-530, NM722-570, NY592-460, NY592-800, OK829-520, PA726-412, RI700-70, TX21-50, TX56-50, TX56-850, TX56-860, TX252-150, TX252-730, TX326-800, TX397-690, TX425-280, TX483-320, TX590-760, TX777-760, TX777-810, UT912-110, WI346-720
  ARCHAEOLOGY
    AZ800-803, NY587-180

BAPTIST CHURCH
TN690-740
COLONIES
CA782-800, NM722-570, TX56-800, TX56-860, TX777-160, TX777-810
ETHNOLOGY
AZ800-803
FRENCH INTERVENTION IN
TX483-690
GOVERNMENT AGENCIES
TX56-110, TX326-800, TX777-620
IMMIGRATION AND EMIGRATION
TX326-780
INDIANS
AZ800-803, CA712-713, LA600-760, MI60-440, NM114-880
JEWS
CA86-400
LAND GRANTS
CA676-110
LAW
OH181-270
MANUFACTURING
TX326-780
MEDICINE
CA720-894
MISSIONARIES
IL169-677, IN704-240, NC590-320, TX326-160
MUSIC
DC19-570, TX529-770
ORTHODOX CHURCH
NY870-600
RELATIONS WITH UNITED STATES
CA712-750, MA108-750
RELIGIOUS COMMUNITIES
CA720-739
REVOLUTION
TX326-210, TX326-780
MEXICO, NORTHEASTERN
TX319-640
MEXICO, NORTHERN
AZ800-790
MEXICO, NORTHWESTERN
AZ800-800
ETHNOMUSICOLOGY
AZ750-32
MEYER, ADOLF
MD76-315
MEYEROWITZ, EVA L.R.
IL261-566
MEYNELL, ALICE
MA199-90
MEYNELL, WILFRID
MA199-90
MIAMI-ERIE CANAL
OH147-520, OH545-530
MICHALSKY, DONAL
CA278-130
MICHENER, JAMES A.
MD323-520
MICHIGAN
MN541-934
FOLKLORE
IN66-340
GOVERNMENT AGENCIES, NATIONAL
IL170-280
MINING
MN338-360
RELIGIOUS COMMUNITIES
OH593-720
MICHIGAN BAPTIST STATE CONVENTION
MI518-425
MICHIGAN ROAD
IN363-342
MICHLS CIGAR STORE
IL192-510
MICRONESIA
HI350-73, HI350-80
MIDDLE AMERICA
ARCHAEOLOGY
NM722-535
ETHNOLOGY
NM722-535

MIDDLE ATLANTIC US
ETHNIC GROUPS
PA725-165
RELIGIOUS COMMUNITIES
NY10-160
MIDDLE EAST
CA858-320, CT316-330, CT505-890, DC6-800, DC12-100, DC12-105, DC12-400, DC19-327, NC590-320, NJ692-660, NY592-30, NY592-860, NY595-760, OH171-320, UT912-820
ARAB-JEWISH RELATIONS
NY589-900
ARCHAEOLOGY
IL170-897
ECONOMIC AID TO
NY589-560
GLASS
NY214-140
IMMIGRATION AND EMIGRATION
MN763-790
JEWISH-ARAB RELATIONS
NY589-900
JEWS
NY590-680
MEDIEVAL
PA725-405
ORTHODOX CHURCH
NY870-600
PHILOLOGY
IL170-897
SOCIAL WELFARE
NY318-260
MIDDLESEX CANAL COMPANY
MA478-800
MIDDLETOWN AND BERLIN TURNPIKE
CT477-130
MIDVALE, FRANK
AZ435-520
MIDWEST PROGRAM ON AIRBORNE
TELEVISION INSTRUCTION
IN935-650
MIDWESTERN US
IA33-370, IA466-800, IL916-795, IN66-385, MN763-510, MO220-120, OH223-710, VT464-840, WI346-720, WI456-550
ARCHITECTURE
IL169-826
CHRISTIAN REFORMED CHURCH
MI355-110
CHURCH HISTORY
KS878-880
EDUCATION
KY496-850
ETHNIC GROUPS
DC14-250
METHODIST CHURCH
IL261-280
MISSIONARIES
MD76-30
RAILROADS
WI530-520
ROMAN CATHOLIC CHURCH
MN763-100, OH171-50
UNITARIAN CHURCH
IL170-195
UNIVERSALIST CHURCH
IL170-195
MIDWIFERY
PA725-908
MIGRANT LABOR
TX529-770
MIGRATION
See also Immigration and emigration, *GA90-270, MT530-500, OH878-720*
WESTERN US
IL170-351
MIGRATION PATTERNS
CA274-130, CA712-750, CA858-320, HI350-320, NY590-700
MILES, MILTON
RI560-510
MILES, NELSON A.
OH481-530
MILHAUD, DARIUS
CA86-890

MILITARY DEPARTMENT (OR)
OR816-590
MILITARY HISTORICAL SOCIETY OF
MASSACHUSETTS
MA108-240
MILITARY HISTORY
See also Armed forces, *AL620-20, AZ75-240, AZ550-040, CA290-240, CA605-510, CA712-750, CA720-550, CA858-320, CO180-750, CO270-240, CT36-80, CT505-960, DC12-300, DC13-210, DC14-140, DC14-500, DC19-616, DE810-330, FL660-120, GA75-810, GA885-240, IL866-365, IN363-40, KS10-170, KY272-635, LA570-540, MA48-40, MA108-10, MA109-220, MA154-640, MA293-200, MA398-330, MA615-80, MA624-560, MA673-640, MA871-540, MA985-70, MI620-520, MI665-120, MN14-560, MN618-80, MO200-720, MO810-510, MO810-940, MS20-200, MT530-500, NC390-200, NC680-460, NH108-720, NH784-620, NH784-630, NJ182-110, NJ376-360, NJ548-530, NJ838-630, NM513-560, NM570-480, NM722-570, NY134-60, NY289-240, NY590-700, NY592-460, NY599-880, NY648-800, NY654-600, NY708-440, NY708-720, NY915-870, NY949-830, NY973-600, OH199-320, OH778-40, OH878-720, OH978-120, OK372-240, OR816-590, PA165-790, PA380-650, PA380-665, PA735-110, PA975-320, RI560-510, RI700-100, SC144-150, TN675-720, TN690-780, TX56-110, TX56-850, TX56-860, TX63-80, TX231-120, TX280-540, TX326-800, TX777-640, UT912-820, VA245-800, VA350-320, VA430-280, VA550-520, VA560-880, VA580-520, VA660-510, VA690-530, VT176-810, VT528-560, WA320-230, WA972-240, WY135-865, WY305-240, WY500-800*
EUROPE
NY949-830
GERMANY
SC144-150
WESTERN US
OK558-790
MILITARY INSTALLATIONS
NY590-760
MILITARY MEDICINE
OH181-180
MILITARY OFFICERS
CT4-160, CT120-120, DC1-810, DC14-410, DC14-725, IA177-320, IA188-777, IA955-440, IL296-720, IL301-280, KY272-635, MI440-320, MO607-520, MT100-200, NH672-570, NY844-720, OH823-800, PA740-320, SD414-640, SD936-950, VT496-640, WV600-280
FRANCE
DC14-590
MILITARY PERSONNEL
AL620-20, DC1-340, DC14-720, DC14-780, DC19-616, FL820-810, IN231-370, IN363-40, IN363-342, MN763-510, MO700-720, MO810-390, NE284-560, NY107-200, NY160-120, PA25-480, PA165-790, PA725-930, PA726-508, RI910-880, TN390-390, VA285-520, VA480-520, VA640-650
CIVIL WAR
ME460-440
GERMANY (HESSE)
NJ548-530, NY594-360, NY595-360
HESSE (GERMANY)
NJ548-530, NY594-360, NY595-360
SOCIAL WELFARE
MA931-400
SPANISH-AMERICAN WAR
FL60-720
WORLD WAR I
KY514-130, WA153-128

WORLD WAR II
CT870-730, IN237-240, KY558-520, WA153-128
MILITARY RECORDS
AR330-880, CT144-880, DC3-320, DC19-616, HI350-770, IL866-355, IN770-880, KS513-250, KY288-440, LA62-500, LA600-455, MA513-530, MA738-700, ME37-525, MI200-240, MI355-270, MN499-480, MN721-600, MO410-40, NV90-530, NY6-400, NY18-40, NY101-90, NY187-120, NY240-160, NY562-510, NY667-600
CONFEDERATE STATES OF AMERICA
LA600-455
MILITARY STRATEGY
RI560-510
MILITIA
CT268-720, IA511-450, NY254-160
LOCAL
GA735-540, NJ182-110, WA241-170
STATE
NH134-540, NH600-510
MILLER FAMILY
TN750-690
MILLER, ARTHUR
NY315-200
MILLER, EMMA GUFFEY
PA815-710
MILLER, FRANCIS PICKENS
VA430-280
MILLER, HERBERT A.
PA726-600
MILLER, SAMUEL
NJ692-610
MILLER, WILLIAM
HI350-311, IL45-30
MILLERSBURG FEMALE COLLEGE
KY54Q-520
MILLIKAN, ROBERT ANDREWS
CA578-130
MILLS
See also Industry; Manufacturing,
IA58-540, MN275-200, MO400-400, NC430-340, NJ358-320, NJ502-690, NY261-320, PA935-690
FEED
IN792-160
GRAIN
IL170-273, MA823-610, MI28-280, MN541-320, NY289-240, PA90-320, VT32-80
PAPER
MA823-610
SAW
MA823-610, NY274-200
STARCH
MA823-610
TEXTILES
MA606-530, MA823-610, ME112-80, MO490-880
WATER
PA370-330
MILLS, ABRAHAM G.
NY211-540
MILLS, ROBERT
SC144-710
MILLWORK COMPANIES
IA466-360
MILWAUKEE ACADEMY OF MEDICINE
WI456-500
MILWAUKEE DOWNER COLLEGE
WI46-480
MIMOSA HALL PLANTATION
TX604-220
MINER FAMILY
CT772-720
MINER, CHARLES
PA960-910
MINERAL SPRINGS
ID400-720, NY792-720, NY795-320, VA820-80
MINERALS
IL140-322
PERU
CA274-120

MINERS
CA159-120, MO810-390, WV435-520
MINING
See also Coal mining, *AK50-66, AK400-720, AL600-800, AZ250-520, AZ350-290, AZ475-640, AZ750-10, AZ800-830, CA143-480, CA159-120, CA432-520, CA508-560, CA692-130, CA720-180, CA720-307, CA720-746, CA720-955, CA728-850, CA862-810, CA998-720, CO54-40, CO108-85, CO108-810, CO252-80, CO270-240, CO414-280, CO458-130, CO640-480, ID80-365, ID480-810, ID520-600, IL140-322, MI130-360, MI200-240, MI464-530, MI725-600, MN338-360, MN363-360, MN763-530, MT130-540, MT530-500, NM494-570, NM760-720, NM912-280, NV270-560, NV450-120, NV940-560, NV940-810, OR64-80, OR560-690, OR720-580, PA740-320, PA960-870, SD648-710, TN690-780, TX14-720, TX252-730, VA195-200, WA145-105, WA408-360, WA724-890, WA761-680, WA820-880, WA880-190, WA904-790, WY245-280, WY500-800*
COLORADO
TX280-540
COPPER
CA624-710, MI464-530
GOLD
CA624-710, CA676-130, DC1-810, NV200-920, TX280-540
IRON
DC1-500, DC19-591, MN261-810, NJ330-320, NJ756-240, NY708-720, WI98-400
LEAD
IL301-280
LIMESTONE
DC1-500
MICHIGAN
MN338-360
SILVER
CA676-130, CO54-40, NV200-920
SOUTH DAKOTA
CO36-40
TECHNOLOGY
PA960-870
WISCONSIN
MN338-360
ZACATECAS, MEXICO
LA600-760
MINISTERS
See Clergy
MINISTRY OF FOREIGN AFFAIRS (JAPAN)
DC12-400
MINNEAPOLIS AQUATENNIAL
MN541-592
MINNEAPOLIS TIMES
PHOTOGRAPHS
MN541-592
MINNEHAHA GRANGE
MN275-200
MINNESOTA
TX280-540, WI456-735
DUTCH-AMERICANS
IA855-150
FUR TRADE
CA86-780, CT505-960, DC12-300, DC14-250, MI230-165, MI865-80, NY592-460, WI346-720
GOVERNMENT AGENCIES, NATIONAL
IL170-28 0
INDIANS
SD792-800
MINNESOTA ACADEMY OF SCIENCE
MN541-592
MINNESOTA ASSOCIATION OF SCHOOL LIBRARIANS
MN742-720
MINNESOTA COLLEGE
MN769-280
MINNESOTA, WESTERN
ND375-570
MINOR, CLARK H.
NY241-160

MINORITY GROUPS
AL840-820, CA858-810, NY586-640, TN690-880, WI456-495
MINT
RUSH-BOUDINOT U.S. MINT CONTROVERSY
NJ280-270
MINT, BUREAU OF THE
WA820-550
MINT, DENVER
CO252-550
MISSILES
MILITARY
CA578-560
MISSING PERSONS
NY594-20
MISSIONARIES
CA86-630, CA720-579, CT316-330, CT505-900, CT505-960, HI350-320, IL169-507, IL976-850, IN297-600, IN440-160, IN704-240, KS108-70, KS878-880, LA600-20, LA600-160, MA776-530, MI90-30, MI445-880, MI518-425, MN261-810, MN541-80, MN541-854, MN749-720, NC590-320, NJ692-610, NY928-880, OH223-790, OH665-580, OH813-310, OK592-640, OR224-800, OR720-590, PA725-700, PA725-908, SD18-160, TN690-170, TX326-160, UT836-880, VT176-690, WA954-885
AFRICA
AL760-760, LA600-505, NC390-200, NC590-320, NJ222-333, NY529-530, OH223-720, PA725-908, RI910-730
ALASKA
IL169-677, OH953-870, WA880-280
AMERICAN BAPTIST CHURCH
NY752-40, PA905-60
ANGOLA
CA143-280
ARGENTINA
OH223-720
ASIA
NJ222-333, NY529-530, PA725-908
ASIA, EASTERN
IN297-600
AUSTRALIA
OH223-720
AUSTRIA
OH223-720
BAHAMAS
MN749-720
BAPTIST CHURCH
MN763-80, NC840-720, NY752-110
BELGIUM
NY459-520
BRAZIL
KS213-560
CAMEROON
NY459-520
CANADA
NY459-520, OH223-720
CHILE
DC15-50, IL55-120, OH223-720
CHINA
CT505-900, DC15-50, IL45-30, KY464-490, KY57W-720, MA81-80, MI445-880, MN749-720, MN763-50, MN763-510, NC390-200, NC590-320, NJ568-570, NY439-156
CHURCH OF THE NAZARENE
MO430-120
COLOMBIA
IL169-677, OH223-720
CONGO
IL45-30, KY464-490, NY459-520
CONGREGATIONAL CHRISTIAN CHURCH
CT316-105
CUBA
IN704-240
ECUADOR
IL169-677
EPISCOPAL CHURCH
IL169-651, IL866-200, SD684-200

ETHIOPIA
IA244-30
EVANGELICAL COVENANT CHURCH
IL169-677
FRANCE
OH223-720
FREE METHODIST CHURCH
IN990-240
GHANA
MO810-750
GREAT BRITAIN
NY459-520
GUYANA
RI910-730
HAWAII
NY481-720
HONDURAS
MO810-270
HONG KONG
MN763-50
IDAHO
WA880-280
INDIA
IA244-30, IL45-30, IN297-600,
MI445-880, MO810-270, NJ568-570
IRAQ
MO810-270
ITALY
OH223-720
JAMAICA
IN704-240, RI910-730
JAPAN
IL45-30, IL169-677, MI445-880,
MN749-720, MO810-270, MO810-750,
NC390-200, NC590-320, NJ568-570,
NY481-720, OH223-720
JESUITS
AZ800-790
KENYA
DC15-50, IN704-240, OH223-720
KOREA
OH223-720
LATIN AMERICA
NC390-200, NY529-530
LUTHERAN CHURCH
IA244-30, IL170-91, MI322-240,
MN763-50, MO810-200
LUTHERAN CHURCH IN AMERICA
PA725-885
LUTHERAN CHURCH-MISSOURI SYNOD
OR720-470
MADAGASCAR
MN763-50
MALAWI
RI910-730
MENNONITE BRETHREN
CA274-130
MENNONITE CHURCH
IN264-40
METHODIST CHURCH
GA885-520, KY886-30, NY752-60,
WA904-50
MEXICO
IL169-677, IN704-240, NC590-320,
TX326-160
MIDWESTERN US
MD76-30
MONTANA
WA880-280
MORMONS
IA533-280, MO400-690, UT912-120
NEW ENGLAND
MA109-460, MD76-30
NEW GUINEA
IA244-30
NIGERIA
TN690-740
OREGON
WA880-280
ORGANIZATIONS
IA699-120, IL261-566, IN22-50
PACIFIC ISLANDS
NY529-530
PACIFIC NORTHWEST
RI945-800, WA954-880
PAKISTAN
DC15-50

PALESTINE
IL55-120, IN704-240
PERSIA
NY672-440
PERSIAN GULF
NJ568-570
PERU
DC15-50, IL55-120, NY481-720,
OH223-720
PITCAIRN ISLAND
MI90-30
PRESBYTERIAN CHURCH
NM114-525, PA726-713
PUERTO RICO
MN749-720
QUAKERS
KS948-240, OH953-870
ROMAN CATHOLIC CHURCH
DC3-210, GA895-160, IN209-140,
KS213-560, KY57W-720, LA600-505,
MD76-30, MD380-160, MD703-40,
MO220-120, NM114-50, NY318-240,
NY459-520, NY481-720, NY529-530,
OH223-720, OR720-590, PA50-720,
PA485-720, PA908-720, RI945-800,
SC144-190, WI456-495, WI698-730
RWANDA
NY459-520
SEVENTH DAY BAPTIST CHURCH
RI910-730
SEVENTH-DAY ADVENTIST CHURCH
DC19-220
SIAM
OH665-590
SOCIETY OF JESUS
WA880-280
SO UTH AFRICA
MN763-50
SOUTH AMERICA
IN297-600, KY57W-720, MO810-750,
NJ222-333, PA725-908
SOUTHWESTERN US
NM114-525
SPAIN
AZ800-830, OH223-720
SWITZERLAND
OH223-720
TAIWAN
IL169-677, MN763-50
THAILAND
IL169-677
UNITED BRETHREN IN CHRIST
IN352-800
UNITED CHURCH OF CHRIST
CT316-105
UNITED METHODIST CHURCH
KS962-800, OK592-780
WESTERN US
NJ568-570
WYOMING
WA880-280
ZAIRE
IL169-677
MISSIONARY SOCIETY OF CONNECTICUT
CT316-105
MISSIONS
INDIANS
WA880-775
MISSIONS (BUILDINGS)
CA352-520, CA410-120, CA724-730,
CA774-720, CA778-780, CA934-720
MISSISSIPPI BAPTIST CONVENTION
MS260-500
MISSISSIPPI BAPTIST HISTORICAL
COMMISSION
MS260-500
MISSISSIPPI FREEDOM DEMOCRATIC
COMMITTEE
GA90-490
MISSISSIPPI MISSION CONFERENCE
LA600-160
MISSISSIPPI NEGRO ACCREDITING
COMMISSION
MS550-410

MISSISSIPPI RIVER
LA885-480, WI298-810
STEAMBOATS AND STEAMSHIPS
KY96-870, MN975-860
MISSISSIPPI RIVER VALLEY
IL916-795, LA62-500, TN630-530
ROMAN CATHOLIC CHURCH
DC15-50
MISSOURI
METHODISM
IA688-360
MISSOURI RIVER
IA661-160, NE624-400
MISSOURI-KANSAS-TEXAS RAILROAD,
NORTHWESTERN DIVISION
TX968-520
MITCHELL COLLEGE
NC430-340
MITCHELL, EDWARD GRANT, FAMILY
IL609-120
MITCHELL, ELISHA
NC150-780
MITCHELL, J. D.
TX923-840
MITCHELL, MARGARET
GA915-280
MITCHELL, MARIA
MA572-540
MIYUKI, MOKUSEN
CA143-80
MOBERLY (U.S. COAST GUARD FRIGATE)
MO607-520
MODDOX FAMILY
TN15-760
MODEL BALLOON LEAGUE
CA456-730
MODEL CITIES (HUD PROGRAM)
DC4-450
MODEL SECONDARY SCHOOL FOR THE
DEAF
DC7-100
MODOC INDIAN WAR
OR448-450
MODOC INDIANS
OR448-450
MOELLER, RADIE BRITTAIN
TX21-50
MOFFETT, GEORGE
TX968-520
MOHAWK RIVER
NY447-400
MOHR, CHARLES
AL840-280
MOLECULAR BIOLOGY
CA578-130
MOLLY MAGUIRES
PA920-890
MONASTERIES
AL130-333, IL170-475
MONDAY NIGHT CLUB
NY240-160
MONETARY POLICY
DC19-646
MONETARY REFORM
OH301-690
MONEY
PESO DEVALUATION
TX326-780
MONGAN, AGNES
MA169-300
MONITOR (SHIP)
PA725-120
MONONGAHELA RIVER
PA145-120
MONROE COUNTY HISTORICAL SOCIETY
IN66-520
MONROE MI
PA420-720
MONROE-CROOK HOUSE
TX228-320
MONROE, GORDON
MA169-610
MONROE, HARRIET
IN275-170
MONROE, JAMES
VA285-400

MONROE, JOHN D.
NY240-160
MONROE, VAUGHN
MA109-440
MONT AMEONA SEMINARY
NC730-500
MONTANA
CA421-774, MN541-934, SD792-880
ARCHAEOLOGY
I D480-770
EPISCOPAL CHURCH
MO810-590
INDIANS
SD792-800
MISSIONARIES
WA880-280
ROMAN CATHOLIC CHURCH
MN749-720
SISTERS OF PROVIDENCE
WA880-710
MONTANA EXPERIMENT STATION
MT130-535
MONTANA EXTENSION SERVICE
MT130-535
MONTANA, WESTERN
WA144-210
MONTGOMERY COUNTY MD
DC14-370
MONTGOMERY, CHARLES F.
DE900-320
MONTGOMERY, JOHN J.
CA778-780
MONTOUR FALLS HISTORICAL SOCIETY
NY562-510
MONTPELIER SEMINARY
VT464-560
MONUMENTS
CT512-120, DC14-540
MOODY, DWIGHT LYMAN
IL170-234, MA568-560, PA645-560
MOOERS FAMILY
NY708-440
MOON
TX483-480
MOORE, CHARLES H.
MA169-300
MOORE, CORNELIUS
RI700-630
MOORE, GEORGE
KS527-790
MOORE, HARRY TUNIS
TX252-200
MOORE, J. LYONS
RI700-630
MOORE, JOHN BASSETT
NY588-860
MOORE, MARIANNE
PA726-412
MOORE, ORLANDO
MI518-455
MOOREHOUSE, LEE
OR688-810
MOORES HILL COLLEGE
IN209-800
MORAL AND POLITICAL SURVEY..., BY NATHAN DANE
MA891-880
MORALITY
EUTHANASIA
NY125-740
MORAN FAMILY
NY257-190
MORAN, THOMAS
NY257-190, OK829-520, WY560-280
MORAVIA CALLIOPEAN SOCIETY
NY563-322
MORAVIA WATER WORKS COMPANY
NY563-120
MORAVIAN CHURCH
PA90-320, PA90-500, PA640-570
ALASKA
PA90-500
CARIBBEAN
PA90-500
CLERGY
PA90-320

EUROPE
PA90-500
LABRADOR, CANADA
PA90-500
MORAVIANS
PA640-570
GERMANY
PA90-320
MUSIC
NC930-530
MORAZAN, FRANCISCO
LA600-760
MOREELL, BEN
CA605-530
MOREHOUSE AND WELLS (HARDGOODS STORE)
IL192-510
MORELAND FAMILY
WV650-520
MORGAN FAMILY
NY53-880, NY125-880
MORGAN, D. S., COMPANY
NY125-720
MORGAN, JULIA
CA86-820, CA744-120
MORGAN, SUSAN JOSLYN
NY125-720
MORGAN, WILLIAM E.
CO378-120
MORGENTHAU, HENRY M., JR.
NY427-240
MORICE, CHARLES
PA726-615
MORLEY, CHRISTOPHER
NY760-90
MORMONS
See also Reorganized Church of Jesus
Christ of Latter Day Saints, *AZ450-640,*
IA177-240, IA533-280, ID680-690,
IL124-725, IL261-280, MO400-690,
UT152-720, UT684-80, UT912-120,
UT912-820, UT912-850
AUSTRALIA
MO400-690
COLONIZATION
AZ250-575, UT836-880
EDUCATION
HI450-80
GREAT BRITAIN
MO400-690
ILLINOIS
MO400-690
IOWA
MO400-690
MISSIONARIES
IA533-280, MO400-690, UT912-120
NEW YORK
MO400-690
OHIO
MO400-690
ORGANIZATIONS
UT912-120
POLYNESIA
MO400-690
MORRIS BROWN COLLEGE
DC1-160
MORRIS FAMILY (NJ)
NJ568-670
MORRIS, GOUVERNEUR
NY208-120
MORRIS, ROBERT
PA726-240
MORRIS, THERON A.
NY851-720
MORRISON, JAMES H.
LA286-720
MORROW, DWIGHT WHITNEY
MA21-40
MORSE, CARLTON E.
PA726-615
MORSE, LEMUEL
MA708-40
MORSE, SAMUEL F. B.
NJ548-720
MORTON, JOY
IL459-520

MORTON, STERLING
IL459-520
MORTON, WILLIAM THOMAS GREEN
DC19-611
MOSHER, CHARLES A.
OH399-420
MOSKOWITZ, BELLE
CT512-120
MOSS, JOHN E.
CA676-140
MOTE, D. W.
OR424-880
MOTHER JOSEPH
WA820-820
MOTHER LODE REGION CA
CA159-120
MOTHERS
SINGLE
MN541-902, NY594-20
MOTION PICTURES
CA421-763, CA421-830, CA676-740,
DC12-450, DC14-250, DC14-770,
DC16-680, IA33-364, MI214-140,
NM722-570, NY591-760, WA820-892,
WI346-900
ANTHROPOLOGY
NM722-30
GERMANY
DC12-450
HISTORY
AZ750-45, AZ800-30, CA90-30,
CA114-880, CA143-470, CA143-720,
CA206-790, CA318-700, CA414-150,
CA414-320, CA421-015, CA421-360,
CA421-390, CA421-400, CA421-470,
CA421-510, CA421-770, CA676-130,
CA712-708, CA712-720, CA756-320,
CA774-800, CA778-800, CA782-800,
CA858-810, CO252-100, GA735-540,
ID480-810, IN231-240, IN627-760,
MA108-240, NJ266-240, NJ910-200,
OH181-270, OR224-800, UT684-80,
UT912-850
ITALY
DC12-450
JAPAN
DC12-450
MUSIC
CA421-750, NY592-878, WY500-800
SCRIPTS
CA436-640, WY500-800
TARZAN
IN726-240
MOTT, CHARLES STEWART
MI314-265
MOUNT FAMILY
NY866-520
MOUNT HERMON SCHOOL
MA568-560
MOUNT LASSEN
CA620-760, CA624-710
MOUNT MITCHELL
NATIONAL PARK (PROPOSED)
NC60-810
MOUNT PLEASANT INSTITUTE
NC730-500
MOUNT RAINIER NATIONAL PARK
WA506-480
MOUNT SINAI HOSPITAL
NY591-600
MOUNT ST. MARY'S SEMINARY
OH171-50
MOUNT VERNON
VA540-520
MOUNT VERNON FURNACE COMPANY
PA735-150
MOUNT, SHEPARD ALONZO
NY866-520
MOUNT, WILLIAM SIDNEY
NY866-520
MOUNTAIN MEN
ID480-40, MO810-390
MOUNTAINEERING
CO252-120, WA84-455
MOUNTAINS
EXPLORATION
NY586-220

MOUSE, MICKEY
  CA114-880
MOXIBUSTION
  CA720-886
MOYLE, JAMES HENRY
  UT912-120
MOZART, WOLFGANG AMADEUS
  PA725-345
MUDGE, LEWIS S.
  PA726-713
MUHLENBERG FAMILY
  PA25-520
MUHLENBERG, FREDERICK AUGUSTUS
  CONRAD
  PA25-520
MUHLENBERG, HENRY AUGUSTUS
  PHILIP
  PA25-520
MUHLENBERG, HENRY MELCHIOR
  PA725-885
MULCAHY, GEORGE D.
  PA380-700
MUNDT, KARL E.
  SD450-150
MUNJOR TOWN AND GRAZING
  COMPANY
  KS377-200
MUNSON FAMILY
  NY899-600
MUNSON, GORHAM
  CT428-865
MUNZ, PHILIP
  CA143-690
MURICATA CLUB
  CA566-640
MURILLO, GERARDO (DR. ATL)
  CA274-120
MURILLO, LUIS
  CA274-120
MURPHY, MARTIN, JR., FAMILY
  CA870-710
MURRAY, SAMUEL
  DC19-340
MURROW, EDWARD ROSCOE
  MA528-740
MUSEUM OF CONTEMPORARY CRAFTS
  NY586-360
MUSEUM OF WESTWARD EXPANSION
  MO810-390
MUSEUMS
  DC19-591, MI40-800 , PA726-255,
  WV350-560
  ADMINISTRATION
  MA108-940, NY586-720 , WA360-520
  ART
  DC19-320, DC19-340, MO810-600,
  NY272-40, WA360-520
  COLLECTIONS
  MO210-840
  EXHIBITIONS
  MA169-300, NY591-700
  PATRONS
  MA169-300
  SCIENCE
  IL170-273, PA725-495
  MUSIC
  CA86-890, CA136-120, CA278-130 ,
  CA318-640 , CA414-150, CA421-40,
  CA421-322 , CA421-620, CA421-750,
  CA421-763 , CA778-800, CO54-40,
  CO378-250, CT316-320, CT316-770,
  CT505-910, CT723-720, CT961-880,
  DC4-940 , DC12-450, DC12-510,
  DC14-850, FL280-390, FL280-420,
  GA75-810, HI350-73, IA533-280,
  IA688-520, IA833-120 , IL170-351 ,
  IL246-200, IL261-568 , IL916-820,
  IN66-340, IN66-395, IN693-710,
  KY96-850, KY496-520 , KY496-725 ,
  LA600-310, LA600-764 , LA920-560,
  MA108-240, MA108-940, MA109-440,
  MA169-860, MA338-280 , MA841-600,
  MD76-340, MD76-640, MD285-805,
  ME50-70, ME87-80, MI40-808,
  MI1390-720, MI1824-320 , MN541-512,
  MN625-710, MN763-800, MO430-790,
  MS550-460, MS900-870, NC380-800,

  NC570-530, NC930-530, NE560-50,
  NH206-800, NH600-530 , NH748-650,
  NJ578-540, NJ692-880 , NY166-80,
  NY439-360, NY586-180 , NY587-500,
  NY588-380, NY590-720, NY591-140,
  NY591-420, NY591-850, NY592-875,
  NY593-132 , NY660-600, NY708-720,
  NY866-520 , NY872-760, OH171-320,
  OH181-270, OH223-880, PA90-500,
  PA90-500, PA440-80, PA725-45 ,
  PA725-345, RI210-720, RI700-640,
  SC860-600, TN 690-780, TX21-50,
  TX56-50, TX640-720, UT912-820,
  VA205-290, VA360-320, VT432-520,
  VT964-720, WA820-774
  AFRICA
  AZ750-32
  BAND
  AL780-760, CA782-730, WY500-800
  BETHLEHEM PA
  NC930-530
  BLACKS
  AZ750-32, IN66-395, MI230-165,
  NY592-930
  CLASSICAL
  NY592-878
  COUNTRY AND WESTERN
  TN690-110
  CRITICS
  IL806-695
  EDUCATION
  MN541-902, NY587-500, NY590-720,
  WI456-730
  EUROPE
  IL916-820, NC930-530, NY588-380,
  NY872-760
  EUROPE, SOUTHERN
  OH181-310
  FOLK
  AZ750-32, CO180-120, KY96-850,
  NC570-530, NY166-80, NY872-760,
  VA235-230, VA235-250, VT432-520
  GREGORIAN CHANT
  MN541-512
  HISPANIC-AMERICANS
  AZ750-32
  INDIANS
  SD792-800
  IRELAND
  NY984-200
  ITALY
  CA86-890
  JAZZ
  NY592-878
  JEWS
  NY590-840
  LATIN AMERICA
  AZ750-32, IN66-395
  LITITZ PA
  NC930-530
  MEDIEVAL
  IL916-820
  MEXICO
  DC19-570, TX529-770
  MILITARY
  DC13-210
  MORAVIANS
  NC930-530
  MOTION PICTURES
  CA421-750, NY592-878, WY500-800
  NAZARETH PA
  NC930-530
  NORTH CAROLINA
  DC19-570
  ORGANIZATIONS
  IN539-86, MO430-790, NY563-322
  POPULAR
  CA421-750, NY592-878, WY500-800
  RECORDINGS
  CT505-976
  RELIGIOUS
  IL170-91, LA670-480, SC144-710,
  WI456-730
  RENAISSANCE
  IL916-820
  SOUTH AMERICA
  NY872-760

  TELEVISION
  CA421-750, DC16-680
  TRADITIONAL
  DC19-570
  VERMONT
  DC19-570
  VIETNAM
  AZ750-32
  VIRGINIA
  DC19-570
  WOMEN
  MA109-440
MUSICAL INSTRUMENTS
  DC19-570, IN539-86, NE560-50
MUSICAL THEATER
  RECORDINGS
  CT505-976
MUSICIANS
  CA414-490, CA421-774, DC12-510,
  MA486-470, MD76-640, MO430-790,
  NE560-50, NY134-85, NY590-720,
  NY592-875, SC144-170, TN690-110
  ARMY
  SD936-950
  EUROPE
  NY590-720
  GERMAN-AMERICANS
  NY590-720
  GERMANY
  NY590-720
MUSICOLOGY
  CA86-890
MUTUAL LAND & WATER COMPANY
  CA640-640
MYERS, JEROME
  DE810-150
MYERS, MOSES
  VA580-600
MYNDERSE, ROBERT
  NY439-180
MYRES (SURNAME)
  TX625-640

N

N. P. BOWSHER MANUFACTURING
  COMPANY
  IN792-160
NANTASKET BEACH (MA)
  MA425-520
NANTUCKET MA
  OH505-520
NAPOLEON I (EMPEROR OF FRANCE)
  IL169-599
NASH AND ROLLOCK SCHOOL
  NC430-340
NASSAU, ROBERT HAMILL
  NJ692-610
NATCHEZ PILGRIMAGE
  MS640-400
NATCHEZ TRACE PARKWAY
  MS880-560
NATIONAL ACADEMY OF ENGINEERING
  DC14-100
NATIONAL ADVISORY COMMITTEE FOR
  AERONAUTICS
  CA578-560, DC14-140, TX483-560
NATIONAL AGRICULTURAL WORKERS
  UNION
  CA86-120
NATIONAL APPLIANCE RETAIL
  DEALERS ASSOCIATION
  IN231-40
NATIONAL ASSOCIATION FOR THE
  ADVANCEMENT OF COLORED
  PEOPLE
  AL580-800, TX252-80
  EDUCATIONAL COMMITTEE
  CA720-10
  LEGAL DEFENSE FUND
  MS870-760
NATIONAL ASSOCIATION OF COLLEGE
  WOMEN
  VA630-840

NATIONAL ASSOCIATION OF DENTAL FACULTIES
  GA90-210
NATIONAL ASSOCIATION OF GEOLOGY TEACHERS
  IL801-20
NATIONAL BUSINESSWOMEN'S WEEK
  DC14-420
NATIONAL CATHEDRAL FOUNDATION, CATHEDRAL CHAPTER
  DC19-40
NATIONAL CATHOLIC RURAL LIFE CONFERENCE
  CA778-800
NATIONAL COMMISSION ON MARIJUANA AND DRUG ABUSE
  TX252-780
NATIONAL COUNCIL OF CHURCHES
  PA726-713
NATIONAL COUNCIL OF PRIMARY EDUCATION
  DC1-860
NATIONAL COUNCIL OF STATE SOCIOLOGICAL ASSOCIATIONS
  PA595-530
NATIONAL FEDERATION OF BUSINESS AND PROFESSIONAL WOMEN'S CLUBS
  DC2-850
NATIONAL FEDERATION OF TEMPLE SISTERHOODS
  RICHMOND SISTERHOOD
    IN704-520
NATIONAL FOREST PRODUCTS ASSOCIATION
  CA782-240
NATIONAL FORESTS
  See Forest Service and individual National Forests in repository index
NATIONAL GUARD
  CA942-940
NATIONAL HISTORIC LANDMARKS
  IL325-290, MA849-750
NATIONAL HORSE THEFT DETECTIVE ASSOCIATION
  IN154-880
NATIONAL INSTITUTE OF ARTS AND LETTERS
  NY586-180
NATIONAL LABOR RELATIONS BOARD
  NY439-150
NATIONAL LAWYERS GUILD
  CA86-520, GA90-490
NATIONAL LUTHERAN COUNCIL
  MN625-710, NY591-40
NATIONAL NEGRO BUSINESS LEAGUE
  DC14-350
NATIONAL NEGRO INSURANCE ASSOCIATION
  IL170-312
NATIONAL PALACE MUSEUM (TAIWAN)
  MI40-800
NATIONAL PARK SERVICE
  See also under repository index, *PA726-7*
NATIONAL PIKE
  PA920-870
NATIONAL PRESS BUILDING (WASHINGTON DC)
  DC14-552
NATIONAL RECOVERY ADMINISTRATION
  AZ550-040
NATIONAL REGISTER OF HISTORIC PLACES
  LA62-430, WY135-880
NATIONAL RESEARCH COUNCIL
  DC14-100, MI40-814
NATIONAL SOCIALIST (NAZI) PARTY
  NY18-40
NATIONAL TRANSIT COMPANY
  PA705-320
NATIONAL WEATHER SERVICE
  DC19-631
NATIONAL WILDLIFE REFUGES
  DC6-500
NATIVE PEOPLES
  AK50-800, AK500-20

NATURAL HISTORY
  CA712-726, CA774-800, CO90-280, CO252-152, CT505-980, FL220-792, HI350-73, IL169-286, KS527-790, MA109-380, ME837-560, MT870-280, NC60-640, NM266-720, NY586-720, NY592-320, NY594-380, NY749-720, PA725-15
  CARIBBEAN
    FL220-792
  JAMAICA
    MA199-90
  ORGANIZATIONS
    OH181-240
  WEST INDIES
    MA199-90
NATURAL RESOURCES
  CO252-90, DC4-260, DC14-540, IN363-342, MI40-784, MT530-500, NM494-570, NY10-570, VT176-810
NATURAL RESOURCES COUNCIL OF AMERICA
  CA782-240
NATURAL RESOURCES COUNCIL OF ONONDAGA COUNTY
  NY872-720
NATURAL WONDERS
  KS635-600
NATURALISTS
  MA109-380, OH181-240, PA725-15, TX923-840, VT296-690
NATURALIZATION
  IL856-730, IL946-360
NATURE
  NY593-420, OH203-630, PA965-490
NAVAL ARCHITECTURE
  MA169-610
NAVAL HISTORY
  AL80-40, AL580-510, AL620-20, CA86-780, CA386-560, CA421-770, CA421-830, CA605-530, CA704-560, CA720-180, CA756-320, CA858-320, CA858-810, CA922-840, CO252-100, CT282-720, CT316-110, CT316-120, CT316-770, CT393-480, CT463-520, CT505-560, CT505-960, CT512-800, DC1-560, DC3-210, DC7-650, DC12-300, DC12-600, DC13-210, DC14-120, DC14-140, DC14-250, DC14-590, DC14-720, DC14-725, DC14-740, DC14-750, DC19-310, DC19-320, DC19-500, DC19-576, DC19-621, DC19-636, DC19-700, DE270-200, DE810-330, DE900-320, FL220-795, FL600-800, FL800-245, GA75-810, GA405-560, GA895-280, HI350-73, HI350-300, HI350-808, IA466-360, IA966-320, IL169-325, IL170-280, IL170-884, IL866-365, IL916-810, IN66-380, IN363-40, IN363-350, IN627-780, KS10-170, KS878-430, KS948-890, LA62-500, MA108-140, MA108-240, MA108-750, MA108-965, MA109-120, MA109-220, MA109-460, MA169-170, MA169-370, MA169-860, MA217-130, MA584-600, MA733-210, MA733-660, MA871-40, MA871-540, MA985-70, MD76-240, MD76-340, MD76-515, MD76-810, MD152-550, ME650-810, ME712-530, MI40-820, MI1230-165, MN763-540, MO210-815, MO400-320, MO430-540, MO810-510, MS550-500, NC260-170, NC680-460, NE560-550, NH134-540, NH784-720, NJ568-670, NJ578-510, NJ692-660, NY134-60, NY211-580, NY272-120, NY439-120, NY586-720, NY588-900, NY592-800, NY599-880, NY872-800, NY890-700, NY949-780, OH97-80, OH171-20, OH171-110, OH171-650, OH181-880, OH203-600, OH301-690, OK558-790, OR224-800, PA160-160, PA380-650, PA395-320, PA470-240, PA725-15, PA725-75, PA725-495, PA725-720, PA726-240, PA735-110, PA735-790, RI700-50, RI700-70, RI700-680, RI700-740,

  SC144-150, SC144-730, SC185-120, SC216-720, SC216-820, TN690-780, TN840-800, TX56-850, TX273-160, TX397-690, TX483-560, TX483-690, UT684-80, VA145-780, VA560-520, VA580-570, VA580-600, VA690-530, VA690-870, VA690-910, VA870-110, VT176-810, WI346-720, WI456-540, WI794-880, WV650-890, WY500-800
NAVAL STORES
  GA885-120
NAVAL WARFARE
  RI560-510
NAVIGATION
  DC1-810, IL841-520, OH171-650, PA725-615, TN465-760, WV900-80
NAVY
  CA712-570, CA922-840, CT282-720, DC12-300, DC13-210, DC14-250, DC14-720, DC14-725, DC14-730, DC14-770, DC14-780, DC19-621, MA92-70, MD57-500, MD57-800, MD57-810, MD57-820, MD57-830, MI214-280, MS50-560, NC150-800, NH784-720, NY240-720, NY427-240, RI560-510, TX273-160, WA724-890, WA820-880
  AMERICAN REVOLUTION
    CT512-550
  AVIATION
    DC14-715
  BASES
    CA605-510
  BUREAU OF YARDS AND DOCKS
    CA605-510
  CEC-SEABEE MUSEUM
    CA605-510
  CIVIL ENGINEER CORPS
    CA605-510
  GERMANY
    DC14-730
  GREAT BRITAIN
    DC14-730, TX483-690, VI700-360
  JAPAN
    DC14-730
  NAVAL CONSTRUCTION FORCE (SEABEES)
    CA605-510, CA605-530
  NAVY DISTRICT 13
    WA820-550
  NAVY DISTRICT 17
    WA820-550
  OFFICERS
    DC19-621, HI350-311, IL296-720, MA109-850, ME162-100, PA725-615, VT784-720
  PERSONNEL
    DC19-621
  SECRETARY OF
    MA109-850, MD76-333
  SHIPS
    MA169-610, MD57-800, MD57-810, MD57-830
  YARDS AND DOCKS, BUREAU OF
    CA605-510
NAZARETH ACADEMY
  KY569-720
NAZARETH COLLEGE
  KY496-730
NAZARETH PA
  MUSIC
    NC930-530
NEAL, R. B.
  KY310-440
NEAR EAST
  See Middle East
NEBRASKA
  CZECHOSLOVAKIAN-AMERICANS
    IL459-360
  MENNONITE CHURCH
    IA499-520
NECROLOGY
  OH181-630
NEEDLEWORK
  MA238-520
NEGROES
  See Blacks

NEILSON, JOHN, FAMILY
  NY861-720
NELSON, HORATIO
  MD57-800
NERINCKX, CHARLES
  KY57W-720
NETHERLANDS
  IL261-566, MI445-310, NC590-320,
  NJ568-570
 ART
  NY593-100
 CHURCH HISTORY
  IA811-110
 COLONIES
  CA756-320, CT316-120, DC12-300,
  DE810-330, MA109-120, MA109-220,
  NJ548-530, NJ568-570, NJ578-510,
  NY10-80, NY10-640, NY427-240,
  NY469-720, NY588-700, NY590-940,
  NY591-840, NY592-460, NY593-600,
  NY593-900, NY804-800, PA725-720
 IMMIGRATION AND EMIGRATION
  IA855-150, MI355-110, MI445-560,
  NY289-240
NETTL, BRUNO
  IN66-395
NEUBERGER MUSEUM
  NY732-730
NEUMANN, JOHN NEPOMUCENE
  PA726-105
NEUROLOGISTS
  KS527-790
NEUROSCIENCES
 EUROPE
  CA421-660
 NORTH AMERICA
  CA421-660
NEUVA VIZCAYA (SPANISH COLONIAL
  PERIOD)
  AZ225-40
NEVADA
  CA94-360, CA676-110, CA676-130,
  CA720-180, CA756-320, CA764-165,
  DC14-250, NY726-850, UT912-120,
  UT912-840, UT912-850
 GOVERNMENT AGENCIES, NATIONAL
  CA704-560
 LUTHERAN CHURCH-MISSOURI SYNOD
  CA720-405
 UNITED METHODIST CHURCH
  CA86-630
NEVADA FEDERATION OF WOMEN'S
  CLUBS
  NV940-560
NEVELSON, LOUISE
  ME725-880
NEW ALMADEN MINE
  CA728-850
NEW BEDFORD MA
  OH505-520
NEW BEDFORD TEXTILE INSTITUTE
  MA612-720
NEW BRITAIN INSTITUTE
  CT477-570
NEW BRITAIN TRACT SOCIETY
  CT477-570
NEW BRUNSWICK, CANADA
  ME200-120
NEW CANAAN CONGREGATIONAL
  CHURCH
  CT484-550
NEW DEAL
  AK350-800, CA700-720, CT144-880,
  ID80-365, LA62-490, MA871-890,
  MD513-640, MO210-815, NC60-240,
  NM570-80, NY427-240, NY588-940,
  NY714-560, OK490-520, OK592-620,
  OK592-640, OR224-800, OR816-590,
  SD792-820, TX56-780, TX280-540,
  UT912-820, VA205-290, VT704-280,
  WA616-870, WA820-550, WA820-880,
  WI754-170, WV500-640
NEW ENGLAND
  AR890-30, CA454-520, CT234-230,
  CT316-120, CT316-880, CT603-360,
  MA21-40, MA108-750, MA109-120,

  MA109-460, MA109-680, MA169-370,
  MA823-610, ME162-120, ME925-130,
  NY10-770, NY419-310, OH778-40
 AUTHORS
  MN541-600
 BAPTIST CHURCH
  MA593-40
 CONGREGATIONAL CHURCH
  MA108-480, MA593-40
 EPISCOPAL CHURCH
  CT316-210
 FURNITURE
  DE900-320
 LITERATURE
  MA169-370
 LUTHERAN CHURCH
  NY591-35
 LUTHERAN CHURCH-MISSOURI SYNOD
  NY128-480
 MARITIME HISTORY
  CT463-520
 MEDICINE
  MA108-770
 METHODIST CHURCH
  MA109-480
 MISSIONARIES
  MA109-460, MD76-30
 QUAKERS
  RI560-570
 RELIGIOUS COMMUNITIES
  NY10-160
 SERMONS
  CT316-330
 TOMBSTONES
  DC19-560
 WOMEN
  MA169-860
NEW ENGLAND ALMANAC AND
  FARMER'S FRIEND (PUBLICATION)
  CT512-120
NEW ENGLAND EMIGRANT AID
  COMPANY
  KS878-430
NEW ENGLAND FREEDMEN'S AID
  SOCIETY
  MA931-400
NEW ENGLAND INTERCOLLEGIATE
  LACROSSE LEAGUE
  MA21-770
NEW ENGLAND WOMEN'S AUXILIARY
  ASSOCIATION
  MA931-400
NEW GARDEN BOARDING SCHOOL
  NC380-290
NEW GUINEA
 MISSIONARIES
  IA244-30
NEW HAMPSHIRE
  DC14-600, MA154-480
NEW HAMPSHIRE FIRE AND MARINE
  INSURANCE COMPANY
  NH784-630
NEW HAMPSHIRE MEDICAL SOCIETY
  NH600-510
NEW HAMPSHIRE MILITIA
  NH600-510
NEW HAMPTON SCHOOL
  NH688-280
NEW HARMONY COMMUNITY OF
  EQUALITY
  IN583-560
NEW HAVEN WATER COMPANY
  CT505-560
NEW JERSEY
  OH778-40, PA725-720
 AMERICAN REVOLUTION
  PA925-160
 CHRISTIAN REFORMED CHURCH
  MI355-110
 DUTCH-AMERICANS
  NY590-80
 LUTHERAN CHURCH
  NY591-35
 LUTHERAN CHURCH-MISSOURI SYNOD
  NY128-480
 RELIGIOUS COMMUNITIES
  NY859-720

 ROMAN CATHOLIC CHURCH
  PA726-495
 SOCIETY OF FRIENDS
  NY593-710, PA860-710
NEW JERSEY ABOLITION SOCIETY
  NJ100-80
NEW JERSEY ASSEMBLY
  NJ666-650
NEW JERSEY LEAGUE OF WOMEN
  VOTERS
  NJ568-670
NEW JERUSALEM, CHURCH OF THE
  MA590-720, PA130-30
NEW LEBANON NY
 SHAKERS
  MA677-720
NEW MEXICO
  AZ550-040, CA421-610
 FRANCISCANS
  MD703-40
 MIDWIFERY
  PA725-908
 PUEBLOS
  RI945-800
 RELIGIOUS COMMUNITIES
  CA720-739, OH593-720
NEW ORLEANS LA
  TX777-30
NEW SALEM MA
  ME437-120
NEW SPAIN
  AZ225-40
NEW THOUGHT ALLIANCE,
  INTERNATIONAL
  MO894-800
NEW YORK
  CT603-360, DC14-600, MN226-705,
  PA725-720
 CHRISTIAN REFORMED CHURCH
  MI355-110
 GOVERNMENT AGENCIES, NATIONAL
  NJ46-560
 MORMONS
  MO400-690
 PUBLIC SCHOOL CONTROVERSY
  NY752-760
 SHIPS
  MD76-810
NEW YORK AQUARIUM
  NY593-130
NEW YORK ASYLUM FOR LYING-IN
  WOMEN
  NY592-480
NEW YORK CENTRAL RAILROAD
  COMPANY, ROCHESTER DIVISION
  NY383-560
NEW YORK CLOAK JOINT BOARD
  NY590-430
NEW YORK CONVENTION OF THE
  REPRESENTATIVES, COMMITTEE
  FOR OBSTRUCTING THE HUDSON
  RIVER (1776)
  NY599-880
NEW YORK DRESS JOINT BOARD
  NY590-430
NEW YORK FOREST OWNERS
  ASSOCIATION
  NY872-720
NEW YORK HOSPITAL
  NY592-480
NEW YORK INFANT ASYLUM
  NY592-480
NEW YORK MILLS
  NY899-600
NEW YORK NURSERY AND CHILD'S
  HOSPITAL
  NY592-480
NEW YORK NY
  NJ548-520
NEW YORK PSYCHOANALYTIC SOCIETY
  NY592-640
NEW YORK SHIPBUILDING COMPANY
  PA726-240
NEW YORK SOCIETY OF ANESTHETISTS
  IL708-40
NEW YORK STATE BARGE CANAL
  NY872-120

NEW YORK STATE COLONIZATION SOCIETY
NY593-380

NEW YORK STATE FEDERATION OF WOMEN'S CLUBS
NY272-200

NEW YORK STATE FORESTRY AND PARK ASSOCIATION
NY872-720

NEW YORK ZOOLOGICAL PARK
NY593-130

NEW ZEALAND
HI450-80

NEWBURY SEMINARY
VT464-560

NEWCOMB, FRANCES
NM114-880

NEWGATE PRISON
CT268-720

NEWLANDS RECLAMATION PROJECT
NV450-120

NEWMAN, LIONEL
CA778-800

NEWMAN, RALPH G.
IL169-416

NEWMARKET MANUFACTURING COMPANY
NH720-560

NEWORLD (PERIODICAL)
CA421-322

NEWPORT CASINO
RI560-360

NEWS
NY595-480,   RI700-680,   WI202-560
    TELEVISION
    DC16-680,   NY134-50,   TN690-980

NEWS JOURNAL (KY NEWSPAPER)
KY126-120

NEWSOM, EMMA DAY
IA688-360

NEWSOM, HUGH
MD76-640

NEWSOM, JOHN EDWARD
IA688-360

NEWSPAPER GUILD
MI230-880

NEWSPAPERS
See also Journalism, *AZ550-640,*
DC13-300, ID80-365, MI64-70,
NY595-700, NY717-640, OH171-920
    PHOTOGRAPHS
    MN541-592, MO810-670
    PUBLISHING
    VA890-120
    UNDERGROUND
    MS870-760

NEWTON FAMILY
MA513-530

NEWTON THEOLOGICAL INSTITUTION
MA593-40

NEWTON, A. EDWARD
PA725-510

NEWTON, ISAAC
DC19-641, MA891-80

NEY, ELISABET
TX56-200

NEY, PETER S.
NC240-160

NIAGARA FRONTIER
NY134-50, NY134-60

NICKEL PLATE RAILROAD
IN231-40

NIEBUHR, REINHOLD
MO810-270

NIEBUHR, RICHARD
MO810-270

NIEDECKEN-WALBRIDGE COMPANY
WI456-530

NIEDECKEN, GEORGE M.
WI456-530

NIGERIA
    CHILDREN
    OH11-840
    CHURCH OF THE BRETHREN
    IL241-120
    MISSIONARIES
    TN690-740

NIGERIA, NORTHERN
IL261-566

NIGHTINGALE, FLORENCE
AL120-815,   CA421-660,   IL169-580,
MA108-240

NIJINSKY, VASLAV
NY592-870

NIMITZ, CHESTER
MD57-820

NIN, ANAIS
IL261-570

NISBET, CHARLES
PA735-800

NIXON, JUSTIN WROE
NY752-40

NIXON, P. I.
TX777-790

NIXON, RICHARD MILHOUS
CA966-880, MS140-560

NOBEL PRIZE
DC19-641

NOBILI, JOHN
CA778-780

NOKOMIS CLUB
WA736-680

NOLAN, S.
IN539-100

NOLAND, TURLEY
KY680-190

NOLL, JOHN FRANCIS
IN440-160

NON-ELITES
MA804-50

NONPARTISAN LEAGUE
ND486-800

NONVIOLENCE
PA860-730

NORBECK, PETER
SD792-820

NORDICA, LILLIAN
ME350-560

NORFOLK AND WESTERN RAILROAD
MO607-520

NORMAL COLLEGE
NC260-150

NORMAL COLLEGE OF THE AMERICAN GYMNASTIC UNION
IN363-385

NORMAN, EARL
MS640-520

NORMAN, HENRY
MS640-520

NORRISTOWN LIBRARY COMPANY
PA690-520

NORTH AMERICA
See also individual countries and regions,
AZ800-803, CA712-570, TN630-510,
VA870-150
    ARCHAEOLOGY
    RI105-320, WA820-840
    CHEMISTRY
    PA726-765
    CHILDREN
    OH11-840
    ETHNOLOGY
    RI105-320, WA820-840
    EXPLORATION, MOUNTAINS
    NY586-220
    GLACIERS
    NY586-220
    LINGUISTICS, INDIANS
    DC7-650
    MOUNTAINS, EXPLORATION
    NY586-220
    NEUROSCIENCES
    CA421-660
    RAILROADS
    NE288-400

NORTH AMERICAN LAND COMPANY
PA920-890

NORTH AMERICAN PHALANX
NJ276-510

NORTH CAROLINA
    APPALACHIA
    GA840-240
    LUMBERING
    PA726-855

MUSIC
    DC19-570
PRESBYTERIAN CHURCH
    VA690-700, VA690-750
UNITED CHURCH OF CHRIST
    PA470-800

NORTH CAROLINA COUNCIL OF WOMEN'S ORGANIZATIONS
NC380-800

NORTH DAKOTA
CA712-743, MN226-705, MN541-934,
MN763-720
    CHURCH OF THE NAZARENE
    MO430-120
    DUTCH-AMERICANS
    IA855-150
    ROMAN CATHOLIC CHURCH
    MN749-720

NORTH DAKOTA AGRICULTURAL COLLEGE
ND375-570

NORTH LOUISIANA HISTORICAL ASSOCIATION
LA885-120

NORTH PLATTE RIVER VALLEY
NE384-560

NORTHEASTERN US
PA90-480
    CHURCH OF THE NAZARENE
    MO430-120
    MARITIME HISTORY
    CT463-520

NORTHERN ARIZONA PIONEERS' HISTORICAL SOCIETY
AZ250-575

NORTHERN IRELAND
NC590-320

NORTHERN PACIFIC RAILROAD
MN763-400, WA904-770

NORTHWEST RAILROAD
AK250-110

NORTHWEST TERRITORY
See also Old Northwest, *IN363-350,*
IN902-80, MI665-120, OH486-510

NORTHWESTERN CLASSICAL ACADEMY
IA755-560

NORTHWESTERN JUNIOR COLLEGE AND ACADEMY
IA755-560

NORTHWESTERN US
MN763-540

NORWAY
MN625-570, PA735-825
    IMMIGRATION AND EMIGRATION
    MN625-570

NORWEGIAN BAPTIST THEOLOGICAL SEMINARY
IL644-80

NORWEGIAN LUTHERAN CHURCH
    CLERGY
    IA211-480

NORWEGIAN LUTHERAN CHURCH OF AMERICA
IA211-480

NORWEGIAN-AMERICANS
IA211-480, MN370-920
    LUTHERAN CHURCH
    IA211-480, MN763-50

NOTMAN, JOHN
PA725-150

NOVAK, MICHAEL
MA615-730

NOWELL, F. H.
CA712-713

NOYES FAMILY
CT484-550, RI910-880

NOYES, THEODORE
DC13-300

NUCLEAR ENERGY INDUSTRY
WA742-690

NUEVO LEON, MEXICO
TX777-760

NUMISMATICS
DC19-646, NY586-770

NURSERIES (CHILDREN)
NY594-20

NURSERIES (TREE)
NE240-560
  LABOR
  NE240-560
NURSES
CA421-660, WA904-760
NURSING
AL120-810, CA720-894, MA108-240, MD76-315, MD152-720, MO430-700, NY592-480, WA904-760
  CIVIL WAR
  NY115-720
  EDUCATION
  IL169-580, IL245-322, NY588-970
NURSING HOMES
IL245-322
NUTRITION
TN690-960
NUTTER, MCCLENNEN, AND FISH (LAW FIRM)
KY496-800

O

O. S. KELLY COMPANY
OH223-880
O'CONNOR, FLANNERY
GA780-270
O'HARA, JOHN
PA895-710
O'KEEFFE, GEORGIA
IL169-130
O'NEILL, EUGENE
CT505-890, CT512-120
O'SHAUGHNESSY, A. E. W.
KS527-790
O'SULLIVAN, JAMES EDWARD
WA880-290
OAK SWAMP BAPTIST CHURCH
MA708-40
OAKLEY, THORNTON
PA175-80
OAKLEY, VIOLET
DE810-150
OAKMONT CLUB
NY895-240
OAKS, MAEBEL E.
NY695-640
OATES, JOYCE CAROL
NY125-740
OBERHOFFER, EMIL
MN541-512
OBERHOLZER, EMIL
KS878-520
OBRESKY, JOSEPH
MA21-770
OBRESKY, TAMARA
MA21-770
OBSERVATORIES
AZ250-480, AZ250-575, CA782-800
OBSTETRICS
OH181-180
OCCULTISTS
NY866-730
OCCUPATIONS
CA712-630, OH203-630
OCEANOGRAPHY
CA368-820, MA169-500, MA981-890, MS50-560
OCEANS
CA86-920, FL660-510
ODD FELLOWS, INTERNATIONAL ORDER OF, SENECA LODGE NO. 694
NY433-350
ODENBACH, FREDERICK LOUIS
OH843-400
OFFICE OF CHIEF OF NAVAL OPERATIONS
DC14-730
OFFICE OF EMERGENCY PREPAREDNESS (DC)
DC13-300
OFFICE OF INDIAN AFFAIRS (TX)
TX56-800
OFFICE OF THE SURGEON GENERAL
DC3-320

OFFICE OF WAR INFORMATION
DC9-580
OGDEN, WILLIAM B.
NY915-880
OHIO
TX280-540, WA265-600, WV435-520
  FOLKLORE
  IN66-340
  GOVERNMENT AGENCIES, NATIONAL
  IL170-280
  LUTHERAN CHURCH-MISSOURI SYNOD
  IN231-490
  MANUFACTURING
  DC19-601
  MORMONS
  MO400-690
  RELIGIOUS COMMUNITIES
  NY859-720, OH593-720
  ROMAN CATHOLIC CHURCH
  DC15-50
  SOCIETY OF FRIENDS
  PA860-710
OHIO AGRICULTURAL EXPERIMENT STATION
OH968-600
OHIO COMPANY OF ASSOCIATES
OH486-510
OHIO MEDICAL UNIVERSITY
OH203-680
OHIO RIVER
IN209-200, KY2A-80, OH714-510, WV900-80
  STEAMBOATS AND STEAMSHIPS
  KY96-870
OHIO RIVER VALLEY
IL170-884, KY464-800
  ROMAN CATHOLIC CHURCH
  DC15-50
OHIO RIVER VALLEY, UPPER
WV650-890
OHIO VALLEY ATHLETIC CONFERENCE
KY680-180
OIL
CA414-470, DE270-200, NY594-520, NY964-322, OH646-560 , TX56-850, TX252-730, TX483-810, TX590-760, TX625-640, TX632-200, WY500-800
OIL INDUSTRY
DC1-580, KY496-823, LA885-480, NY106-640, PA705-320, PA870-160, TX625-640
  FIRE PROTECTION
  DC1-580
  PENNSYLVANIA
  DC1-580
  TECHNOLOGY
  DC1-580
  TEXAS
  DC1-580
OIL SHALE
CO476-540
OKLAHOMA
MN226-705
  GOVERNMENT AGENCIES, NATIONAL
  TX374-550
  TOPOGRAPHY
  TX968-520
  UNITED CHURCH OF CHRIST
  KS878-880
OKLAHOMA HALL OF FAME
OK592-630
OLD BURNSIDE
KY78J-760
OLD EBENEZER CHURCH
SC540-200
OLD LYME ART COLONY
CT596-480
OLD NATCHEZ TRACE
MS880-560
OLD NORTHWEST
See also Northwest Territory, *IL916-795, MI230-165, OH181-880, WI654-790*
OLD SETTLERS (ORGANIZATION)
KS760-480
OLD SETTLERS MEMORIAL MUSEUM
WA564-200

OLD SPANISH TRAIL ASSOCIATION
TX777-670
OLDPORT ASSOCIATION, INC.
RI560-570
OLIVER CHILLED PLOW COMPANY
IN792-160
OLIVETAN BENEDICTINE SISTERS
AR480-320
OLMSTED, FREDERICK LAW
MA169-305
OLMSTED, JOHN CHARLES
MA169-305
OLSON, CHARLES
MA338-280
OLYMPIC MOUNTAINS
  EXPLORATION
  WA676-610
OMAHA MEDICAL COLLEGE
NE624-830
OMAHA NE
  LUTHERAN CHURCH IN AMERICA
  PA330-160
OMNIBUS (TELEVISION PROGRAM)
CT428-865, NY591-690
OMS (PERIODICAL)
IN297-600
ONDERDONK, GILBERT
TX923-840
ONE HUNDRED AND ONE RANCH (101 RANCH)
OK634-640
ONE WORLD FLIGHT (RADIO PROGRAM)
NY591-690
ONEIDA COUNTY HOME DEFENSE
NY899-600
ONEONTA CLUB
CA850-720
ONIONS
IA43-80
ONTARIO, CANADA
  MENNONITES
  PA470-480
ONTON SCHOOL
KY22W-920
OOLOGY
CA830-720
OPEN THEATER
OH399-440
OPERA
CA720-180, CA774-800, ME350-560, NY439-360, NY591-420, NY872-760
  WOMEN
  MA425-520
OPERATION BREAKTHROUGH (HUD PROGRAM)
DC4-450
OPERETTA
PA595-530
OPTICAL EQUIPMENT
DC19-626
OPTOMETRISTS
MI100-240
OPTOMETRY
AL120-810, TN630-730
ORAL HISTORY ASSOCIATION
TX280-540
ORANGEBURGH DISTRICT SC
SC792-120
ORDER OF PREACHERS
  DOMINICANS
  TX56-720
ORDER OF SERVANTS OF MARY
See Servites
ORDNANCE
DC19-616
OREGON
CA712-743, CA862-810, NE624-400, PA726-412
  ARCHAEOLOGY
  ID480-770
  FORESTRY
  CA86-850
  MISSIONARIES
  WA880-280
  SISTERS OF NOTRE DAME DE NAMUR
  CA78-740

SISTERS OF PROVIDENCE
WA820-820
WHITMAN MASSACRE
RI945-800
ORGAN TRANSPLANTATION
DC7-660
ORGANISTS
DC19-570
ORGANIZATIONS
ACTIVIST
PA726-630
AFRICA
IL261-566
AGRICULTURE
CA226-170, CT477-570, CT673-690,
DC4-260, KY600-600, MA897-880,
ME437-120, MI518-445, MN275-200,
MN520-700, MN728-690, ND486-800,
NY71-715, NY251-320, OH112-280,
OH223-880, OH906-320, PA965-490,
SC185-120, SD550-600, TN435-220,
TX733-640, WA280-885, WA844-720
AMERICAN BAPTIST CHURCH
NY752-40
ANTHROPOLOGY
DC19-520
ART
DC19-320, IL169-130, NY591-920
ATHLETICS
CA278-130, CA456-730
ATTORNEYS
GA90-490
BAPTIST CHURCH
KY520-530, NY895-240, OK736-600,
TN690-740, TX604-220, WV775-40
BLACKS
DC14-350, FL800-200, GA90-360,
GA90-490, IL170-312, IL261-566,
NY134-85, NY592-930, TX252-80,
VA20-322
BUSINESS
CA524-160, DC14-350, KY380-720,
KY598-600, NC200-120, NV940-560,
NY59-80, NY433-350, TN435-220,
WA366-640
CHARITIES
MA894-880, ME437-120, OH97-80,
TN690-880
CHILDREN
DC1-860, GA895-290, IN704-200,
NY589-720, WY365-710
CHINA
HI350-295
CHINESE-AMERICANS
WA820-886
CHURCH OF THE BRETHREN
IL241-120
CIVIC
AL120-100, CA676-140, IL246-200,
IN55-80, KY496-498, KY564-520,
MN307-200, NY866-710, NY915-870,
OH11-810, PA520-470, TX529-770,
WA27-40, WA124-480, WA125-490,
WA168-750, WA181-360, WA246-170,
WA280-440, WA360-440, WA366-90,
WA366-640, WA468-720, WA542-520,
WA573-520, WA616-915, WA681-400,
WA726-640, WA736-440, WA738-670,
WA820-774, WA820-810, WA943-240,
WA954-880, WA960-170, WA966-560,
WA994-935
CIVIL RIGHTS
GA90-360, GA90-490, MI40-808,
MS870-760
COMMUNAL
NY590-680
COMMUNITARIANISM
MA109-120
COMMUNITY
WA395-640, WA848-440, WA859-650
CRAFTS
TN435-220
CULTURAL
AZ600-200, DC15-500, MO430-420,
MO520-440, NY234-165, SC144-90,
WA904-770

DEAF PERSONS
DC7-100
DENTISTRY
GA90-210
DEVELOPMENT
TN435-220
ECONOMICS
IL261-570
EDUCATION
CA524-160, DC1-860, DC15-500,
MO520-440, NJ138-120, NJ692-210,
NV940-560, NY334-240, PA726-225,
TN690-880, TX733-640, WA427-450,
WA735-680
ENVIRONMENT
IN66-390, NY866-710
EPISCOPAL CHURCH
DE810-170, GA90-490, IL169-651,
MA108-580
ETHNIC GROUPS
MI824-320, NE624-150, OH181-780,
PA305-510
EVANGELICAL COVENANT CHURCH
IL169-677
FORESTRY
CA782-240
FRATERNAL
CO768-640, DC19-130, IA99-40,
IL84-120, IL723-80, IN5-40, IN539-80,
MD76-20, MI824-320, MN763-790,
NV940-560, NY433-350, PA308-320,
PA380-665, PA520-470, PA726-225,
SC270-160, WA34-40, WA489-40,
WY365-710
FREE WILL BAPTIST CHURCH
TN690-240
GERMAN-AMERICANS
MA451-360
GOOD-ROADS MOVEMENT
WA904-665
GOVERNMENT-RELATED
WA820-775
HEARING
CA278-130
HISTORICAL
NJ212-200
HOME ECONOMICS
KY230-320
HUMANITARIAN
NY899-600, PA725-60, PA726-630,
TX42-810
INDIANS
DC19-520
INTERNATIONAL
CA858-320, DC15-500, NY595-20
INTERNATIONAL RELATIONS
NY588-900
ITALIAN-AMERICANS
CO768-640
JEWS
CA86-385, DC10-500, IL170-780,
IN231-370, MA871-40, NY593-132,
NY595-660, NY595-700, PA726-225
LABOR
CA524-160, CA712-750, DC1-280,
DC14-870, GA90-300, ID80-365,
IL866-365, MD575-333, MD800-322,
MI230-880, NY439-150, NY588-940,
NY593-120, NY595-700, OH223-880,
PA920-890, TX42-810, VA20-666,
WI346-720, WV650-890
LAW
CA712-700
LIBRARIES
IL916-40, NY698-650, OH486-890
LITERARY
NY178-120, NY698-650, PA920-890,
PA950-880, WA904-780
LITERATURE
IA699-120, IL444-720, IL567-520,
IL624-380, IL976-890, IN319-330,
IN352-320, KY598-600, MI40-808,
MI700-560, MO810-920, NC240-160,
NY241-160, OH194-120, PA755-40,
SC144-150, SC846-890, VA430-870
LITHUANIAN-AMERICANS
MA451-360

LOCAL
WA60-860, WI142-800
LUTHERAN CHURCH
MN625-710
LUTHERAN CHURCH-MISSOURI SYNOD
OR720-470
MECHANICS
KY600-600
MEDICINE
CA720-894, IL708-40, IN792-720,
MI230-905, MO810-650, NH600-510,
NY101-720, NY318-260, NY589-900,
NY592-260, OH181-180, PA725-285,
TX397-790, WI456-500
MENNONITE CHURCH
IN264-40
METHODIST CHURCH
GA90-190, NY752-60, NY895-240,
TX7-800
METHODIST EPISCOPAL CHURCH
GA90-360
MISSIONARIES
IA699-120, IL261-566, IN22-50
MORMONS
UT912-120
MUSIC
IN539-86, MO430-790, NY563-322
NATURAL HISTORY
OH181-240
PARENT-TEACHER
WA820-810
PATRIOTISM
IN363-40, KY230-320, KY230-440,
MA108-10, MA108-80, MA109-120,
MA904-80, MA964-880, MA970-890,
ME512-80, MI824-320, MI890-720,
ND876-80, NJ838-530, PA500-70,
WI346-280
PHARMACY
DC1-600
PHILANTHROPY
IL170-780, LA600-755, NY589-560
POLITICS
MA154-640, MI770-600
PRESBYTERIAN CHURCH
NC590-320
PROFESSIONAL
CT926-480, DC1-480, DC2-850,
DC14-420, DC19-220, KY380-720,
KY598-600, MI845-40, MN742-720,
NC200-120, NY59-460, NY589-460,
PA595-530, PA725-375, TX252-322,
VA145-780, WA904-770
PSYCHICS
VA810-40
RADICALS
NY593-120
RECREATION
WA60-80
REFORM
PA726-630, TX42-810
RELIGION
LA600-40, TN435-220
RELIGIOUS
CT505-900, DC19-40, IA699-120,
ID80-365, IL170-780, IL976-850,
IN187-40, IN627-720, KY3S-480,
KY886-50, LA600-20, MA837-720,
MO810-590, NJ222-333, PA500-70,
PA726-225, TN690-170, WI456-735
ROMAN CATHOLIC CHURCH
DC14-380, IL170-78, OH203-170,
WI456-495
SCIENCE
DC15-500, IA99-40, IL567-520,
KY680-180, MA169-30, NY586-580,
PA725-15, PA725-75, PA726-765,
PA735-140
SOCIAL
AL120-100, IN275-640, MI770-600,
MN307-200, OH157-120, PA305-510,
PA935-690, RI700-680, SC144-730,
TX439-280, WA300-730, WA681-400,
WA889-720, WA904-770, WA919-560

SOCIAL WELFARE
   DC3-210, KY886-50, MA931-400,
   MA947-880, ME460-440, MI824-320,
   MN391-310, ND876-80, NE800-480,
   NY895-240
SOCIETY OF FRIENDS
   IN704-200
SPEECH
   CA278-130
STUDENTS
   GA90-490
TEMPERANCE
   CT477-570, IL261-545, IN209-200,
   MI518-445, MN14-560, NE112-760,
   NY148B-88, NY178-120, NY598-560,
   NY720-640, NY928-880, OH203-600,
   OH733-690
TEXTILE INDUSTRY
   MA606-530
UNITED METHODIST CHURCH
   IL94-800, OK592-780
VETERANS
   CT477-570, NV450-120, NY563-120,
   WI346-280
VOLUNTARY
   CA524-160, IN154-880, MA169-860,
   OH97-80, WY800-320
WELFARE
   MN541-902
WOMEN
   CA524-160, CA566-640, CO252-42,
   CT477-570, DC1-340, DC2-850,
   DC7-300, DC14-420, DC14-520,
   DC19-750, DE810-170, HI350-150,
   IA600-322, IA955-440, IN22-50,
   IN539-80, IN704-520, KY230-320,
   KY230-440, KY380-720, KY558-520,
   KY598-600, LA600-555, MA169-970,
   MA931-400, MA947-880, ME437-120,
   ME512-80, MI355-270, MI700-560,
   MI824-320, MI890-720, MN14-560,
   MN185-120, MN391-310, MN405-320,
   MN541-592, MN742-700, MO810-200,
   NC380-800, ND486-770, ND876-80,
   NE112-760, NE352-880, NJ20-40,
   NV940-560, NY148B-88, NY235-160,
   NY262-280, NY272-200, NY593-132,
   NY595-740, NY598-560, NY720-640,
   NY839-720, NY858-720, NY866-710,
   NY915-870, OH878-880, OR720-470,
   PA500-70, TX7-800, TX319-640,
   VA20-322, WA98-100, WA181-360,
   WA616-915, WA681-670, WA726-640,
   WV550-280, WY365-710
YOUTH
   IL170-283, NY589-900, OH181-780,
   OR720-470, TX7-800
ZIONISM
   OH181-730
ORGANS (MUSICAL INSTRUMENTS)
   DC19-570
ORIENT
   See Asia, eastern
ORIENTAL MISSIONARY SOCIETY
   IN297-600
ORNAMENTATION
   ARCHITECTURE
      NY587-80
ORNITHOLOGY
   See also Birds, MA169-500, PA725-15
ORNSTEIN, LEO
   CT505-910
ORPHANAGES
   GA245-110, IN440-160, LA600-555,
   MN749-720, NY10-160, NY481-720,
   PA380-700, PA986-960, SC144-105,
   TX483-160
   BLACKS
      MD76-315
ORPHANS
   NY593-485
   WOMEN
      KY54G-520
ORR FAMILY
   WA889-560
ORR, ELLISON
   IA622-200

ORR, JAMES L.
   IN209-200
ORTHODOX CHURCH
   ALASKA
      NY870-600
   CANADA
      NY870-600
   CLERGY
      NY870-600
   EUROPE, EASTERN
      NY870-600
   MEXICO
      NY870-600
   MIDDLE EAST
      NY870-600
   SOUTH AMERICA
      NY870-600
OSBORN LABORATORIES OF MARINE
   SCIENCES
   NY593-130
OSBORN, ARTHUR
   IN572-320
OSBORN, FAIRFIELD
   NY593-130
OSBORN, HENRY FAIRFIELD
   NY593-130
OSBORNE FAMILY (MECKLENBURG
   COUNTY NC)
   NC160-520
OSBORNE, THOMAS B.
   CT505-120
OSHKOSH WI
   IL245-322
OSLER, WILLIAM
   AL120-815, CA720-894, CT316-310
OSTEOMETRY
   ID480-770
OSTRICHES
   CA850-720
OTIS, HARRISON GRAY
   MA109-680
OTIS, JAMES, JR.
   MA109-660
OUACHITA JUNIOR COLLEGE
   LA535-560
OUR LADY OF MOUNT CARMEL,
   CATHOLIC RELIGIOUS ORDER OF
   See Carmelite Order
OUR LADY OF SORROWS PARISH
   IL170-475
OUSA MEQUIN CLUB
   MA139-90
OUTDOOR ADVERTISING
   NJ464-240
OVERSEAS FRIENDSHIP CENTER
   NY899-600
OWEN COUNTY UNION AGRICULTURAL
   AND MECHANICAL ASSOCIATION
   KY600-600
OWEN, RICHARD
   IN935-650
OWEN, ROBERT
   OH505-520
OWENITES
   OH505-520
OWL, WOODSY
   VA50-240
OWSLEY, ALVIN
   TX280-540
OXFORD UNIVERSITY
   CA143-470
OYSTER HOUSES (SEAFOOD BUSINESSES)
   MD836-120
OZARK MOUNTAINS
   AR270-360, AR330-830, MO700-720

P

PACIFIC AREA
   DE540-790
   GOVERNMENT AGENCIES, NATIONAL
      CA704-560
   LITERATURE
      HI350-73
   WORLD WAR II
      FL750-200

PACIFIC COAST
   CA143-470
PACIFIC COAST MARITIME INDUSTRY
   BOARD
   CA720-356
PACIFIC ISLANDS
   HI350-73, HI350-80, HI350-770
   MISSIONARIES
      NY529-530
   TRADE WITH UNITED STATES
      MA733-660
PACIFIC NORTHWEST
   CA862-810, ID80-365, MT130-540,
   MT530-500, OR224-810, OR576-600,
   OR720-590, WA60-860, WA280-200,
   WA616-950, WA647-640, WA724-890,
   WA820-550, WA820-892, WA880-775,
   WA954-240
   ARCHAEOLOGY
      ID480-770, WA943-245
   CHINESE-AMERICANS
      WA820-966
   COAST GUARD
      WA820-147
   INDIANS
      WA880-550
   INLAND AREA
      WA144-210, WA880-190
   LABOR MOVEMENTS
      WA904-870
   LUMBERING
      MI824-320
   MARINE LIFE
      WA685-640
   MARITIME HISTORY
      WA820-635
   METHODIST CHURCH
      WA904-50
   MISSIONARIES
      RI945-800, WA954-880
   POLITICS
      OR224-800, WA904-870
   RAILROADS
      OR720-560, OR901-760, WA880-370
   ROMAN CATHOLIC CHURCH
      WA880-120
PACIFIC OCEAN
   HI450-75, OR720-590
   ANTHROPOLOGY
      WA820-840
   ETHNOLOGY
      WA820-840
PACIFIC OCEAN, NORTHERN
   EXPLORATION
      WA820-770
PACIFIC OCEAN, SOUTHERN
   CA782-800
   EXPLORATION
      KS164-520
PACIFISM
   MI40-784
PACK, ROBERT
   VT432-530
PACKARD, VANCE
   PA895-710
PACKING HOUSES
   FOOD
      CA770-120
PADDOCK, JOHN ADAMS
   WA820-200, WA904-760
PADUCAH JUNIOR COLLEGE
   KY604-630
PAGE, RUTH
   NY592-870
PAHLMANN, WILLIAM G.
   DE900-320
PAINE, THOMAS
   NY577-330
PAINT INDUSTRY
   OH181-660
PAINTERS
   FRANCE
      CA143-240
   GREAT BRITAIN
      MI230-800

PAINTING
See also Art, *DC14-460, DC19-320, DC19-340, MA169-340, MA383-240, MD76-80, MO810-880, NY574-710, NY590-360, WA408-370*

PAIRPOINT MANUFACTURING COMPANY
NY214-140

PAKISTAN
MISSIONARIES
DC15-50

PALACES
HI350-150

PALEONTOLOGISTS
NY439-640
WOMEN
NY439-640

PALEONTOLOGY
AZ250-520, CT505-980, MA169-500, NY439-640, NY586-720

PALESTINE
CA421-250, NY589-900, NY595-40, NY595-660, NY595-760
ARCHAEOLOGY
OH171-320
MISSIONARIES
IL55-120, IN704-240

PALMER FAMILY
CT772-720

PALMER, E. D.
NY53-880

PAMOND GRANGE
ME437-120

PANAMA
VT496-640

PANAMA CANAL
DC1-805, DC7-650, DC19-130, FL60-720, NY949-830

PANAMA CANAL EXPOSITION
LA600-465

PANAMA-CALIFORNIA INTERNATIONAL EXPOSITION (1916)
CA143-280

PAPER
MANUFACTURING
DC19-601, DE270-200, MA227-120, MA823-610, VT32-80, WI46-360
MILLS
MA823-610

PARADES
MA943-880, NJ440-490

PARAGON PARK
MA425-520

PARAMOUNT STUDIOS
CA90-30, CA421-763

PARAMOUNT THEATER
IL45-640

PARAPSYCHOLOGY
NY586-910, VA810-40

PARDEE, HENRY
NY288-840

PARENT-TEACHER ASSOCIATION (CHERRY HILL NJ)
NJ138-120

PARENT-TEACHER ASSOCIATION (REARDAN WA)
WA735-680

PARIS PEACE CONFERENCE (1918)
DC1-400

PARK HOUSES
PA726-255

PARK, HILAND
VT496-640

PARK, TRENOR
VT496-640

PARKER, HORATIO
CT505-910

PARKER, J. C.
AR890-20

PARKER, LINUS
GA90-190

PARKS
CA578-675, CA728-850, DC4-450, DC14-540, IL459-520, KY760-720, MA109-180, MD475-280, NC60-810, OH266-490
MANAGEMENT
MT870-280, TX56-780, TX91-80

NATIONAL
See also National Park Service and National parks in repository index, *CA86-810, CA942-940, DC14-530, MI60-440, NC860-320, WA35-520, WA506-480, WA676-610, WA832-560, WA943-245*
STATE
CA86-810

PARRIS, ALEXANDER
MA109-680

PARRISH, WILLIAM
NJ838-610

PARRY, EDWIN OWEN
PA740-320

PARSON CAPEN HOUSE
MA849-750

PARSONS FAMILY
NY566-540

PARSONS LUMBER COMPANY
OH399-420

PARSONS, LOUELLA
CA90-30

PARTCH, HARRY
IL916-820

PARTRIDGE, ALDEN
VT528-560

PARVIN, T. S.
IA99-40

PASQUALI, BERNICE DE
MA425-520

PASSAVANT FAMILY
PA986-960

PASSMAN, OTTO E.
LA535-560

PASTEUR CLUB
OH181-180

PASTEUR, LOUIS
AL120-815

PASTORE, JOHN O.
RI700-630

PATENTS
DC19-581, DC19-586, MA738-720, NJ910-200, NY292-520, PA726-810, WI346-240
WATCHES
WI456-560

PATHOLOGY
DC1-760, OH181-180

PATMORE, COVENTRY
MA199-90

PATRIARCHAL SOCIETY
PA725-430

PATRIOTISM
ORGANIZATIONS
IN363-40, KY230-320, KY230-440, MA108-10, MA108-80, MA109-120, MA904-80, MA964-880, MA970-890, ME512-80, MI824-320, MI890-720, ND876-80, NJ838-530, PA500-70, WI346-280

PATRONS OF HUSBANDRY
See Grange

PATTERAN SOCIETY
NY134-710

PATTERNS
CLOTHING
NY587-840

PATTERSON FAMILY
OH223-520

PATTON FAMILY
TN750-690

PATTON, GEORGE S.
KY272-635

PATTON, WILLARD
MN541-512

PATUXENT RIVER
MD836-120

PAUL QUINN COLLEGE
DC1-160

PAUL, JOHN
KY886-50

PAULDING, JOHN
NY878-320

PAYNE THEOLOGICAL SEMINARY
DC1-160

PAYNE, DAVID L.
OK592-650

PEABODY EDUCATION FUND
TN690-975

PEABODY FAMILY
OH986-40

PEABODY FUND
GA90-700

PEABODY INSTITUTE
MD76-640

PEACE
CA676-140, CO378-120, MA21-770, MA624-740, NY586-440, PA325-280, PA725-60, PA860-710, PA860-730, WI456-495
TREATIES
DC3-226

PEACE COLLEGE
NC430-340

PEACE CORPS
CO378-120

PEACE CORPS (ACTION)
DC1-40

PEACE OF UTRECHT
DC3-226

PEARL HARBOR
NH784-620

PEARL HARBOR CULPABILITY DEBATE
WY500-800

PEARY, ROBERT EDWIN
ME162-100, ME175-80

PECHAN, ALBERT R.
PA425-360

PECK, G. W.
NY563-120

PECK, RICHARD E.
PA726-600

PECOS RIVER VALLEY
NM684-120

PEE DEE RIVER
HYDROELECTRIC POWER
NC30-715

PEIRCE, CHARLES SANDERS
MA169-370

PEIRCE, DANIEL
NH784-630

PEIRCE, JOHN
NH784-630

PELOT FAMILY
MO920-120

PENMANSHIP
CT961-880
SPENCERIAN
OH181-400

PENN, WILLIAM
PA380-665, PA725-720

PENNOYER FAMILY
CT484-550

PENNSYLVANIA
DE810-330, IL624-370, OH778-40
DUTCH-AMERICANS
NY590-80
INDUSTRY
DE270-200
OIL INDUSTRY
DC1-580

PENNSYLVANIA ABOLITION SOCIETY
PA725-720

PENNSYLVANIA COLLEGE OF DENTAL SURGERY
PA726-810

PENNSYLVANIA GERMANS
PA210-800

PENNSYLVANIA LIBRARY CLUB
PA725-375

PENNSYLVANIA MUSEUM AND SCHOOL OF INDUSTRIAL ART
PA726-135, PA726-255

PENNSYLVANIA POPULATION COMPANY
PA305-210

PENNSYLVANIA RAILROAD
PA35-40

PENNSYLVANIA SOCIOLOGICAL ASSOCIATION
PA595-530

PENNSYLVANIA STATE MODERN LANGUAGE ASSOCIATION
PA595-530
PENNSYLVANIA, WESTERN
OH990-640, WV100-80
PENSACOLA DAM
OK854-840
PENSACOLA FL
AL580-510
PENSIONS, STATE BOARD OF (FL)
FL800-245
PENTECOSTALISM
TN90-440
PEOPLE'S INSTITUTE (NEW YORK CITY NY)
NY589-100
PERE MARQUETTE RAILROAD
VA560-333
PERFECTIONISM
VT464-840
PERFORMING ARTS
CA421-400, CA421-830, MN763-800, MS550-460, NY586-330, NY592-460, NY592-878, TN690-110, WA820-880, WI346-900
  WOMEN
    MA108-520, NY592-870
PERIODICALS
IL261-570
  HEALTH
    MI60-880
  LITERARY
    DE540-790, NY51-90, NY240-720, WI456-810
PERISHABLE PRESS
NY866-710
PERKINS REALTY COMPANY
OH878-880
PERKINS, FRANCES
CT512-120
PERKINS, HAYES
CA566-640
PERKINS, JUSTIN
NY672-440
PERMANENT WILD LIFE PROTECTION FUND
NY593-130
PERRY, BLISS
IN275-170
PERRY, MATTHEW CALBRAITH
DC19-621, NY288-840
PERSIA
DC19-327
  MISSIONARIES
    NY672-440
PERSIAN GULF
  MISSIONARIES
    NJ568-570
PERU
LA600-760, NY439-120, PA420-720, PA726-412
  ARCHITECTURE
    LA600-760
  ART
    LA600-760
  EDUCATION
    KY496-850
  MINERALS
    CA274-120
  MISSIONARIES
    DC15-50, IL55-120, NY481-720, OH223-720
PESO DEVALUATION
TX326-780
PESTICIDES
OH968-600
PETER A. JULEY AND SON (PHOTOGRAPHIC FIRM)
DC19-539
PETER, ROBERT
KY464-760
PETERKIN, JULIA
SC846-890
PETERS, ROBERTA
NY439-360
PETERSON, ALVIN
WI298-480

PETERSON, HAROLD
WV350-560
PETROGLYPHS
AZ435-520
PETROLEUM
See Oil
PETTIT, JAMES M.
NY588-300
PEWTER IN AMERICA, BY LEDLIE I. LAUGHLIN
DE900-320
PHARMACOLOGY
WI346-870
PHARMACY
See also Drugs, CA720-894, DC19-542, DC19-611, NJ692-190, OH495-510, PA725-285, WI346-720, WI346-870
  EDUCATION
    CA720-890, DC1-600
  ORGANIZATIONS
    DC1-600
PHELON, JOSEPH
NY187-120
PHELPS, ELIZABETH PORTER
MA363-640
PHELPS, WILLIAM LYON
IN275-170
PHENIX CITY AL
GA245-110
PHENOMENA
MD285-360
PHILADELPHIA MUSEUM AND SCHOOL OF INDUSTRIAL ART
PA726-135
PHILADELPHIA MUSEUM COLLEGE OF ART
PA726-135
PHILADELPHIA MUSEUM SCHOOL OF ART
PA726-135
PHILANTHROPISTS
CA720-180
PHILANTHROPY
GA90-700, IL170-884, IL170-910, MA109-595, MA871-60, NY589-560, NY612-690
  ORGANIZATIONS
    IL170-780, LA600-755, NY589-560
PHILATELY
AK900-840, DC19-651
PHILIPPINE WAR
NY949-830
PHILIPPINES
IL170-351, IN66-380, MI40-784, MI40-814, MN226-705
  ROMAN CATHOLIC CHURCH
    NY752-560
  SPANISH-AMERICAN WAR
    FL60-720
PHILIPSE FAMILY
NY878-720
PHILLEO, PRUDENCE CRANDALL
CT512-120
PHILLIPS FAMILY
MA25-650
PHILOLOGY
CT316-770
  MIDDLE EAST
    IL170-897
PHILOSOPHY
DC3-210, IN627-800, NY637-720, OH171-320
  MEDICINE
    NY125-740
PHOTOGRAPHERS
AZ800-820, DC19-626, MS20-200, MT100-200, OH203-630
PHOTOGRAPHS
AK50-25, AK50-66, AK50-800, AZ250-575, AZ750-10, AZ800-820, CA676-740, CA712-630, CO36-40, CO180-640, CO252-163, CO252-181, CO252-550, CO378-260, CT282-720, DC1-40, DC1-180, DC1-460, DC1-500, DC1-580, DC1-680, DC1-810, DC1-920, DC3-550, DC3-760, DC4-260, DC4-450, DC5-600, DC6-500, DC9-450,

DC12-600, DC13-300, DC14-120, DC14-380, DC14-460, DC14-540, DC14-640, DC14-720, DC14-780, DC15-500, DC19-160, DC19-450, DC19-500, DC19-539, DC19-542, DC19-636, DC19-800, FL160-240, FL440-320, FL440-530, FL600-640, FL800-266, GA90-30, GA840-240, HI350-80, IL169-127, IL169-826, IL202-550, IL459-360, IL624-370, IL866-365, IN66-350, IN66-385, IN231-240, IN627-810, KS527-795, KS878-430, KY496-823, MA109-680, MA169-50, MA169-210, MA169-625, MA981-890, MD57-810, MD57-830, MD76-526, MD76-650, MD76-810, MD152-550, MI40-796, MI40-800, MI214-260, MI230-800, MI230-880, MI230-905, MI355-290, MN541-592, MN541-925, MN541-934, MN763-530, MO400-320, MO810-670, MS640-520, MT530-500, MT700-800, NC620-5 20, NE624-800, NH134-540, NJ568-670, NJ646-660, NJ918-520, NM114-35, NY331-280, NY354-480, NY586-720, NY587-800, NY589-200, NY589-640, NY589-690, NY589-900, NY591-700, NY591-850, NY593-60, NY593-100, NY595-480, NY708-120, NY752-890, NY804-560, OH181-630, OH203-680, OH301-690, OH486-510, OR720-670, PA35-40, PA895-680, RI105-320, SD558-720, SD684-280, TN285-280, TN465-760, TN690-110, TX56-890, TX326-210, TX374-40, TX590-760, UT380-810, UT684-80, UT912-120, UT912-820, VA50-240, VA50-530, VA560-520, VA690-810, WA820-92, WA820-774, WA880-280, WA904-770, WI70-120, WI98-390, WI202-560, WI298-810, WI346-850, WI346-890, WY950-945
PHOTOGRAPHY
CA652-795, DC19-626, MA642-560, NY752-200, NY752-330, TX56-890, VT176-810, WA820-892
  ENERGY
    DC4-322
  EQUIPMENT, MANUFACTURERS
    OH203-630
PHOTOMICROSCOPY
DC1-760
PHYLOBIOLOGY
CT926-480
PHYSICAL EDUCATION
DC1-295, IN363-385, NC380-800
PHYSICAL SCIENCES
CA578-130
PHYSICIANS
See also Health sciences; Medicine, CA720-894, CT316-310, CT505-930, DC6-650, DC19-611, DC23-250, IA511-450, IL139-320, IL429-520, IN917-880, KS475-800, KY192-200, KY514-120, MD76-70, ME925-870, MN763-510, NC710-540, NE112-760, NJ358-320, NY111-60, NY134-730, NY288-840, NY303-600, NY382-310, NY592-480, NY752-885, NY923-880, OH112-280, OH181-180, PA725-285, PA920-870, RI700-710, SC144-520, TX21-50, TX397-790, TX770-240, TX777-790
  HOMEOPATHIC
    PA725-690
  MARYLAND
    MD76-527
  WOMEN
    NY752-885, PA725-900
PHYSICISTS
CA86-895, NY586-580
PHYSICS
CA578-130, DC12-300, DC19-586, DC19-641, IL170-884, MO810-940, NC260-150, NJ692-660, NY439-120, NY586-580, VA145-780

EDUCATION
NY586-580
QUANTUM
CA86-895, MA169-650, NC260-150,
NY586-580, PA725-75
PIANOS
RECORDINGS
CT505-976
PICKERING FAMILY
NY769-640
PICKERING, TIMOTHY
NY599-880, PA960-910
PIEDMONT AREA SC
NC160-800
PIERCE, C. C.
CA421-115
PIERCE, FRANKLIN
NH134-540
PIERRE & WRIGHT (ARCHITECTURAL FIRM)
IN539-100
PIKE READING ROOM AND LIBRARY ASSOCIATES
NY698-650
PIKE, ALBERT
DC19-130
PIKE, JAMES SHEPHERD
ME200-120
PIKES PEAK
CO180-650
PILGRIMS
MA242-160, MA265-160, MA685-630,
MA685-640
PILOTS
AIRCRAFT
MI230-880
PINCHOT, GIFFORD
OR464-490
PINCKNEY, THOMAS
NJ812-710
PINE RIVER
CO90-280
PINEAPPLES
PLANTATIONS
HI350-790
PINKERTON, ALLAN
PA920-890
PIOLETT, VICTOR E.
PA960-910
PIONEER DAUGHTERS
ND876-80
PIONEER WOMAN STATUE
OK634-640
PIOUS FUND
CA720-579
PIRATES
KS948-880
SPAIN
KS948-880
PITCAIRN ISLAND
MISSIONARIES
MI90-30
PITT FAMILY
PA735-800
PITT, WILLIAM (1ST EARL OF CHATHAM)
CT505-977, PA735-800
PITT, WILLIAM (1759-1806)
PA735-800
PIZZA BROTHERS (BUSINESS FIRM)
NY261-320
PLACE OF THE BIG ROCK, BY MARK IRELAND
MI164-120
PLACE, ENOCH
NH194-160
PLACE, WILLIAM
MA109-680
PLANCK, MAX KARL ERNST LUDWIG
DC19-641
PLANETS
DC14-120, DC19-500, TX483-480
PLANNED COMMUNITIES
IL414-440
PLANNED PARENTHOOD
MD76-800, NY586-440

PLANNING
LOCAL GOVERNMENT
NY10-570
REGIONAL
DC14-370, MI230-730, MO810-940,
NJ444-240
PLANNING BOARD (OR)
OR816-590
PLANT CULTURE
MA109-140
PLANT HUNTERS
OR464-490
PLANT SCIENCE
PA735-140
PLANTATIONS
See also Agriculture; Farming; Farms; and
related terms, *AL840-820, GA780-290,*
GA895-280, LA62-500, LA570-540,
LA600-755, LA885-480, SC144-730,
SC216-820, SC576-480, TX604-220,
VA50-65, VA245-800, VA540-520,
VI700-360
PINEAPPLES
HI350-790
SUGAR
HI350-790, LA920-560
PLANTERS
SC144-730, SC576-480
SUGAR
HI350-808
PLANTS
See also Botany, *AZ250-520, CA601-640,*
DC6-500, DC14-540, MA169-190,
NC656-720, OR464-490, TN285-280
ENDANGERED SPECIES
NM114-825
SOUTHWESTERN US
NM114-825
PLAST (UKRAINIAN-AMERICAN YOUTH ORGANIZATION)
OH181-780
PLATH, SYLVIA
OH181-130
PLATT FAMILY
NY605-280, NY708-440
PLATTE RIVER
NE384-560
PLAYHOUSE IN THE PARK (CINCINNATI OH)
OH399-440
PLAYWRIGHTS
NC150-790, NY187-120
PLUMB FAMILY
OH878-720
PLUME & ATWOOD COMPANY
CT870-520
PLUMMER, FREDERICK B.
NY439-640
PLUMMER, HELEN JEANNE
NY439-640
PLUNKETT, EDWARD JOHN MORETON DRAX (18TH BARON DUNSANY)
NY101-720
PLUNKETT, EDWARD JOHN MORETON DRAX, MRS. (18TH BARONESS DUNSANY)
NY101-720
PLYMOUTH COLONY
MA109-220, MA242-160, MA685-640,
MA841-600
POE, EDGAR ALLAN
PA725-510, VA690-810
POETRY
CA720-548, CA858-790, ID80-90,
IL94-510, IL404-410, IL866-840,
KS948-240, KY496-520, MA17-400,
MA154-310, MA352-270, MA891-880,
MI650-530, MO810-920, NC240-160,
NY125-740, NY564-840, NY592-460,
NY593-132, NY593-970, NY967-880,
RI700-100
RECORDINGS
CT505-976
POETRY PROJECT
NY593-970

POETS
AR330-830, AR510-810, GA990-940,
IL866-480, IL866-840, IN825-850,
MA352-270, MA606-720, MI440-320,
MN763-790, NJ568-670, NY24-735,
NY421-880, NY588-340, OH203-600,
OH320-430, OR720-700, PA725-150,
PA735-150, SD522-160, VA690-830,
WA672-290, WI594-110
BLACKS
OH823-800
FRANCE
PA726-615
GREAT BRITAIN
CO180-120, DE810-150, NY24-735,
TX933-65
QUAKERS
KS948-240
POGUE, FORREST C.
VA430-280
POINSETT, JOEL R.
PA725-720
POLAND
NY24-725, NY588-825, NY590-700,
NY593-500, PA735-825
EDUCATION
NY593-500
JEWS
NY595-660
LITERATURE
NY593-500
POLITICAL SCIENCE
NY593-500
RELIGIOUS COMMUNITIES
IL866-320
SOCIOLOGY
NY593-500
WORLD WAR II
NY587-820
POLAR REGIONS
EXPEDITIONS
WI606-710
POLETTI, CHARLES
NY588-850
POLEY, HORACE S.
CO180-640
POLICE
NJ444-240, NJ574-560, NY587-720,
NY752-720, OK338-200, PA725-240,
SC144-130, WA300-200, WI754-170
POLING, JAMES
NY169-120
POLIOMYELITIS
MN541-16
POLISH FALCONS
MI824-320
POLISH-AMERICANS
NY134-730, NY590-700, PA725-765,
WI38-480
EDUCATION
PA725-765
POLITICS
PA725-765
SCIENCE
PA725-765
POLITICAL BEHAVIOR
JEWS
NY586-650
POLITICAL CAMPAIGNS
WA954-40
POLITICAL COMMUNICATION
CT234-260
POLITICAL IDEOLOGY
CA858-320, NY590-700
POLITICAL SCIENCE
DC7-650, MD76-360
POLAND
NY593-500
POLITICIANS
CA118-720, CA414-150, CA720-180,
FL220-795, GA75-790, GA245-110,
GA810-80, IA177-320, I A955-440,
IL305-430, IL718-200, IL866-365,
IL916-795, IN649-520, KY96-870,
KY496-785, KY514-120, KY564-520,
KY680-180, LA600-755, MD76-340,
MI230-165, MN763-790, MO430-420,

MS20-200, MS900-870, ND486-800,
NJ548-530, NV940-560, NY588-900,
NY866-730, OK490-520, OR352-900,
OR720-590, PA90-480, PA380-320,
TN60-120, TN465-800, TX210-230,
UT912-820, VA580-600, WA60-860,
WA724-890, WA880-190, WI456-550,
WI554-480

CENTRAL AMERICA
LA600-760
DEMOCRATIC PARTY
IN231-40
EUROPE
DC14-590
LOCAL
NY866-710
NATIONAL
AL840-820, AZ750-10, AZ750-45,
MS140-560, MS490-810, NH396-560,
OK558-790, TX128-640
STATE
AL840-820, AZ750-45, MN520-700,
MN742-700, MS490-810, NH134-540,
NH396-560, OH26-40, OK558-790,
TX42-810, TX128-640, TX181-790,
TX252-80
WOMEN
CA86-810
POLITICS
AK350-800, AR510-810, AZ250-690,
AZ625-630, CA86-780, CA290-240,
CA432-520, CA540-590, CA578-130,
CA720-220, CA858-790, CA862-810,
CO108-810, CT505-945, CT779-785,
DC2-200, DC7-540, DC12-300,
DC16-680, DC19-576, DE540-790,
DE810-330, GA75-810, IA99-40,
IA966-320, ID80-90, IL169-325,
IN66-380, IN363-360, IN363-400,
IN583-560, KS10-170, KY288-425,
KY760-720, LA395-520, LA885-480,
MA108-965, MA109-660, MA169-590,
MA169-860, MA615-80, MA615-720,
MA615-730, MA871-280, MA985-70,
MD76-515, MD285-805, MI665-120,
MO210-815, MT530-500, MT700-800,
ND486-800, NH784-630, NJ578-510,
NJ756-240, NJ838-630, NM494-570,
NV940-810, NY272-720, NY592-460,
NY592-800, NY592-878, NY593-900,
NY842-730, OH171-650, OH181-310,
OH481-530, OK778-560, OR224-800,
PA380-650, PA470-240, PA725-870,
PA726-630, PA735-790, PA895-710,
PA960-440, RI700-620, RI700-740,
SD450-150, SD558-720, SD792-820,
SD792-850, TN435-220, TN630-530,
TN630-570, TN840-800, TX56-800,
TX56-850, TX210-200, TX483-810,
TX654-640, TX777-810, UT684-80,
VA50-50, VA90-840, VT176-810,
VT528-560, WA820-880, WA954-40,
WI266-820, WY135-865
ASIA, SOUTHERN
MN541-822
EUROPE
CT505-977
GREAT BRITAIN
KS527-790
INDIANS
NM722-360
JACKSONIAN PERIOD
OH171-920, PA25-520
LABOR
NY590-430
ORGANIZATIONS
MA154-640, MI770-600
PACIFIC NORTHWEST
OR224-800, WA904-870
POLISH-AMERICANS
PA725-765
RELIGION
KY464-780
SOUTHERN US
GA90-200, LA62-500

STATE
AZ550-040, IL866-720, IN66-390,
MN583-920, MO810-510, MS230-160,
MS610-520, NY588-850, RI700-630,
RI700-640, TX181-790
POLK, JAMES K.
OH171-920
POLK, WILLIS
CA86-820
POLLUTION
DC1-680, DC4-260, DC19-800
POLYGAMY
IL261-280
POLYNESIA
HI350-73, HI350-80
MORMONS
MO400-690
POLYPHONY
IL916-820
POMEROY, JULIUS
MA109-680
POMEROY, R. (MRS.)
MA970-890
POMOLOGY
See also Apples, CA206-790
PONCE DE LEON, JUAN
OK829-520
PONY EXPRESS
MO800-730
POOLE CHURCH OF CHRIST
KY22W-920
POPE AND TALBOT LUMBER COMPANY
WA678-650
POPE, ARTHUR
MA169-300
POPE, EDITH
FL220-800
POPENOE, FREDERICK WILSON
PA735-140
POPOWSKI, BERT
SD54-715
POPULIST PARTY
AR510-810
PORCELAIN
NY590-360
PORCUPINE MINING CO.
AK400-720
PORGY, BY DUBOSE HEYWARD
SC144-130
PORNOGRAPHY
IN66-350
PORTER FAMILY
KS527-790, NY602-570
PORTER, COLE
CT505-976
PORTER, DAVID DIXON
IL296-720
PORTER, KATHERINE ANNE
MI720-600
PORTER, QUINCY
CT505-910
PORTLAND ME
MA169-590
PORTLAND OR
RELIGIOUS COMMUNITIES
CA110-600
PORTLAND TRACTION COMPANY
OR424-322
PORTS
CA712-570, NY594-060, OH97-80,
TX397-690, WA280-885
LAKE SUPERIOR
MN261-40
PORTSMOUTH NAVAL SHIPYARD
NH784-720
PORTUGAL
DC3-226, IL170-351, KS527-790
ART
DC3-226
COLONIES
DC3-226
DIPLOMACY
DC3-226
LITERATURE
DC12-200
POST OFFICE DEPARTMENT
DC19-651

POST OFFICES
WA408-360, WA508-520
POST, MELVILLE DAVISSON
WV250-320
POST, STEPHEN
UT912-120
POSTAGE STAMPS
AK900-840, DC19-651
POSTAL SERVICE
AL120-100, AR890-30, CA180-160,
DC19-651, IL236-520, KS569-600,
MI350-760, MO902-520, NE288-400,
NY720-640, OR736-40, VA20-666,
WI390-520
CONFEDERATE STATES OF AMERICA
AL120-100
RECORDS
DC19-651, MI925-560
POSTELTHWAITE, SAMUEL
PA160-120
POSTMASTERS
NY851-720
POTATOES
WA280-885
POTOMAC PARK (WASHINGTON DC)
JAPANESE FLOWERING CHERRY TREES
DC14-180
POTTAG, MAX
IN539-86
POTTER, BEATRIX
PA725-510
POTTERY
DC19-560, OH399-420, PA575-80
GREAT BRITAIN
PA575-80
POTTERY AND ALLIED WORKERS,
INTERNATIONAL BROTHERHOOD
OF
OH399-420
POUND, EZRA
CT505-890, MI720-600, WI456-810
POUND, ROSCOE
CA421-710
POVERTY
NY419-350, PA725-240, PA935-690
POWELL, JOHN WESLEY
AZ500-400
POWELL, MAUD
IL916-820
POWER ENGINEERING
MA606-530
POWER, ELECTRIC
See Electric power
POWWOWS
INDIANS
NM722-360
POYNTER, LIDA
PA725-900
PRAIRIEVILLE ACADEMY
WI794-120
PRATT & WHITNEY AIRCRAFT
CT186-800
PRATT, CHARLES
NY593-560
PRATT, FREDERIC BAYLEY
NY593-560
PRATT, JOHN
SC306-200
PRATT, JOHN LEE
MI314-265
PRATT, JULIUS W.
NY134-90
PRATT, THEODORE
FL40-250
PRATT, WILLIAM VEAZIE
RI560-510
PRE-RAPHAELITES
DE810-150
PREJUDICE
NY10-160, NY586-640
PREMONSTRATENSIAN ORDER
WI130-720
PRESBYTERIAN (OLD STONE) CHURCH
NY277-200

PRESBYTERIAN CHURCH
IL261-566, KY37S-480, KY496-530, NC590-320, NJ76-70, NJ692-610, NJ838-750, PA160-160, PA726-713, PA986-960, TN300-760, VA690-750
CLERGY
NY569A-56
MISSIONARIES
NM114-525, PA726-713
NORTH CAROLINA
VA690-700, VA690-750
ORGANIZATIONS
NC590-320
SOUTHWESTERN US
NM114-525
PRESBYTERIAN CHURCH IN THE U.S.A., BOARD OF FOREIGN MISSIONS
NJ692-610
PRESCOTT, WILLIAM HICKLING
CA756-320, CT505-960, IN66-380, MA109-120, MA169-370, NY592-460
PRESIDENTS
See also individual Presidents, CA628-40, CT316-880, CT435-520, DC3-550, DC6-650, DC7-510, DC14-590, DC14-725, FL820-810, IA58-540, IA966-320, IL429-520, IL459-360, IL609-120, IL767-320, IL866-365, IL921-840, IN231-470, IN363-660, IN539-90, KS10-170, KY24-800, KY358-40, KY358-480, LA885-690, MA108-240, MA108-965, MA871-85, MA961-870, MD76-30, MD3 99-240, MI40-300, MN226-700, MN835-720, MO400-320, MS80-40, MS140-560, NC240-160, NE624-800, NH134-540, NJ548-530, NJ692-620, NJ812-710, NY222-110, NY427-240, NY592-800, NY660-720, NY942-160, OH171-920, OH203-600, OH481-530, OH823-770, OH823-800, PA55-760, PA90-480, PA160-160, PA305-210, PA325-280, PA470-240, PA565-640, PA725-510, PA725-615, PA905-840, PA925-160, PA960-870, RI700-100, TX56-520, TX273-160, TX654-640, VA245-800, VA750-880, VT374-80, WA954-40
CAMPAIGNS
NY586-650
SPOUSES
DC14-590, IA58-540
PRESTINI, LINO
WA152-125
PRESTON, WILLIAM
VA90-840
PREVOST, THEODOSIA BARTOW
NJ339-40
PRICE, FRANK
VA430-280
PRICE, GEORGE MCCREADY
MI90-30
PRICE, HARRY B.
VA430-280
PRICE, WILLIAM T.
WV575-640
PRIESTLEY, JOSEPH
PA160-160
PRIMITIVE BAPTIST CHURCH
NC930-840
PRIMITIVE METHODIST CHURCH OF AMERICA
NJ464-666
PRINCE EDWARD COUNTY FREE SCHOOL
VA630-840
PRINCE EDWARD ISLAND, CANADA
CA454-520
PRINCE GEORGES COUNTY MD
DC14-370
PRINCE WILLIAM COUNTY VA
DC14-370
PRINT CLUB OF PHILADELPHIA
PA725-720
PRINTING
CA86-810, CA180-160, CA421-774, DC19-565, IL170-351, MA961-870, MI255-530, NY592-800, NY705-560

WESTERN US
CA720-180
PRIOR, MATTHEW
OH680-540
PRISON
REFORM
OH301-690
PRISONERS OF WAR
MD57-820, TX280-540
CIVIL WAR
DE60-240
WORLD WAR II
NE284-560
PRISONS
AZ550-040, AZ950-950, CA480-530, CT268-720, IL866-355, IN77-200, IN363-342, KS569-600, KY464-760, MA169-860, NY51-730, NY101-70, NY588-440, PA25-60, PA725-240, WA27-40, WA94-720
REFORM
AZ550-040, PA860-710
PRIVATEERING
NY599-880
PROCTOR FAMILY
NY899-600
PROFESSIONS
CT870-520, DC1-340, GA940-280, IL916-795, MO210-815, NY254-160, PA325-40, WA724-890
WOMEN
DC2-850, DC14-420, MA169-885, NY588-940
PROGRAMS IN ETHNOGRAPHIC FILM
NM722-30
PROGRESSIVE READING CIRCLE
IL567-520
PROGRESSIVISM
IL170-910, OH823-750
PROHIBITION
MI40-784, TX326-780
PROPAGANDA
NY586-640
WORLD WAR II
NY591-690
PROPAGANDA FIDE
IL261-566
PROPAGANDA FIDE (ROMAN CATHOLIC CHURCH)
LA600-505, MD76-30
PROTEST
See also Protest movements; Radicals
ANTI-WAR
MO810-940
DEMONSTRATIONS
DC13-300
STUDENTS
CA858-790, MO810-940, OH399-450
PROTEST MOVEMENTS
See also Protest; Radicals, MI40-808
PROTESTANT EPISCOPAL CHURCH
CA143-720
ARIZONA
CA143-720
PROUTY, OLIVE HIGGINS
MA985-110
PSYCHIATRISTS
DC1-640, DC23-800
PSYCHIATRY
See also Mental health, CT926-480, DC1-640, KS878-520, NY592-640
PSYCHIATRY, GROUP FOR THE ADVANCEMENT OF
KS878-520
PSYCHIC RESEARCH
NY586-910, VA810-40
PSYCHICS
VA810-40
ORGANIZATIONS
VA810-40
PSYCHOANALYSIS
CT926-480, NY592-640
CHILDREN
NY587-300

PSYCHOANALYSTS
NY592-640
WOMEN
NY592-640
PSYCHOLOGISTS
OH11-800
PSYCHOLOGY
CA421-322, DC19-596, OH11-800
COLLECTIVE UNCONSCIOUS
NY590-740
PSYCHOTHERAPY
NJ464-240
PUBLIC ADMINISTRATION
NY612-690, NY872-800, WA820-880
PUBLIC AFFAIRS
CT779-785, MN763-540, NC260-170, NY592-30
PUBLIC DOCUMENTS
See also Government agencies, CA862-730, HI250-480, LA62-500, MA811-720, ME750-160, MN794-80, NJ756-240, NY752-740, OK829-770, SC216-720, TN630-510, VT312-280
PUBLIC DOMAIN
FL800-235
PUBLIC FIGURES
IN66-390
PUBLIC HEALTH
DC1-180, IN363-342, MD76-315, MN541-902, NY593-840, NY612-690
PUBLIC OPINION SURVEYS
IL170-891
PUBLIC POLICY
CA578-560, DC14-140, NJ692-660, TX483-560
PUBLIC RELATIONS
MI214-260
PUBLIC UTILITIES
See also Electric power; Gas companies; Water companies, CT144-880, CT505-560, IA188-360, IN363-342, MA425-520, NY978-880, PR720-360, VA90-840, WA629-655
PUBLIC WORKS
See also specific types of public works, DC1-805, DC4-450, HI350-340, IL866-355, IN77-200, IN363-342, MA425-520, MI214-150, PR720-360
SEWAGE
MA109-180
PUBLICATIONS
HISTORY
NC260-150
PUBLISHING
IA211-480, IN22-50, IN66-380, MI214-280, MN763-790, MO810-920, NY588-900, NY592-800, NY594-640, NY866-710, PA175-80, PA705-320, WV250-320
BLACKS
IN66-390
GREAT BRITAIN
PA726-615
METHODIST CHURCH
KY886-30, TN690-890
NEWSPAPERS
VA890-120
RELIGION
IN264-40, NY752-40
WESTERN US
CA720-180
PUCKETT, NEWBELL N.
OH181-270
PUEBLO GRANDE DE NEVADA (LOST CITY)
NV870-480
PUEBLOS
NM722-730
NEW MEXICO
RI945-800
PUERTO RICO
MD755-560, MN226-705
EDUCATION
NY115-720
GOVERNMENT AGENCIES, NATIONAL
NJ46-560

MISSIONARIES
MN749-720
ROMAN CATHOLIC CHURCH
PA726-495
PUGET SOUND
WA820-770, WA904-800
MARITIME HISTORY
WA820-635
PULLMAN CARS (RAILROADS)
DC19-636
PULLMAN COMPANY
IL170-351
PULTENEY, SIR WILLIAM
NY752-720
PULVER, E. C.
NY563-120
PUPPETRY
MI230-148
PURDUE, JOHN
IN935-650
PUTNAM, RUFUS
OH486-510
PYLE, HOWARD
DE810-150, PA175-80

Q

QUABBIN RESERVOIR
MA109-180
QUAKERS
See also Society of Friends, *CA966-880,*
DE810-690 , IN649-650, KS948-240,
MA486-470, MA603-560, MD57-500,
NC380-290, NC430-340 , NJ280-270,
NY172-120, OH505-520, OH953-870 ,
PA395-320, PA725-540, PA860-710,
PA945-120 , VA690-810, VT296-690
INDIANA
OH953-870
MISSIONARIES
KS948-240, OH953-870
NEW ENGLAND
RI560-570
POETS
KS948-240
QUARRIES
MA338-280
**QUARTERMASTER GENERAL, OFFICE OF
THE**
PA726-7
QUEEN'S CHAPEL
NH784-700
QUEENS COLLEGE (NORTH CAROLINA)
NC430-340
QUINCY FAMILY
MA109-120
QUINN, ROBERT E.
RI700-630
QUISLING, VIDKUN
PA800-720

R

R.K.O. RADIO PICTURES
CA90-30
**RABBIS, AMERICAN, CENTRAL
CONFERENCE OF**
OH181-730
RACE RELATIONS
See also Civil rights, *KY80-90, LA600-20,*
PA860-710
SCHOOLS
KY496-812
RACHMANINOFF, SERGEI
DC12-510
RACIAL DISCRIMINATION
FL440-150
RACIAL JUSTICE
NY592-30
RACING
AUTOMOBILES
IN803-360
HORSES
KY464-440 , NY795-320

RACKHAM, ARTHUR
PA725-510
**RADCLIFFE COLLEGE BLACK WOMEN
ORAL HISTORY PROJECT**
MS550-410
RADICALISM
NY593-120
RADICALS
See also Protest; Protest movements,
NY439-150
ORGANIZATIONS
NY593-120
RADIO
CA114-880, CA143-720, CA206-790,
CA418-200, CA421-015 , CA421-360,
CA421-400, CA421-470, CA421-510,
CA421-750, CA421-763 , CA421-770,
CA421-830, CA712-708, CA756-320,
CA774-800, CA858-790 , CA858-810,
CO252-100 , DC2-600, GA245-110 ,
IN539-545 , IN792-720, MA108-240,
MN226-725 , MN625-710, NJ270-800,
NY396-40 , NY439-360, NY588-940,
NY594-640, NY872-760, PA726-615,
VA205-290, WI346-900
ADVERTISING
GA90-130
NEWSCASTS
IN209-880
PROGRAMS
CA318-640, CA318-700, CA421-766,
MA871-85, MI440-320, NY318-260,
NY591-690, NY752-760, PA690-520,
PA725-430
RADIO CORPORATION OF AMERICA
NY905-840
RADIOLOGY
IA99-40
RAFINESQUE, C. S.
KY464-760
RAFTS
WI890-320
RAGSDALE, M. C.
TX770-240
RAIGUEL, WILLIAM O.
CA480-530
**RAILROAD TRAINMEN, BROTHERHOOD
OF**
TX280-540
RAILROADS
See also Locomotives and names of
individual lines, *AK50-66, AK250-110,*
CA250-120, CA421-510, CA582-600,
CA650-322, CA676-740, CA810-700,
CO270-240, CO458-110, CT36-80,
CT505-560, CT505-960, CT779-785,
CT870-520, DC1-680, DC1-810,
DC1-920, DC19-591, DC19-636,
DC19-651, DE270-200, FL580-320,
FL860-320, IA33-350, IA177-240,
IA177-320, IA188-650, ID880-80,
IL170-273, IL170-351, IL936-640,
IN77-200, IN209-200, IN231-40,
IN825-350, KS850-720, KY496-785,
KY496-812, MA108-750, MA615-710,
MA964-880, MD76-525, MD304-80,
ME162-120, MI40-796, MI360-280,
MI824-320, MN763-400, MN763-540,
MO160-80, MO607-520, MS20-200,
NC740-690, NE560-860, NE624-800,
NH134-530, NJ386-380, NJ838-580,
NM950-270, NV270-560, NY10-770,
NY254-160, NY288-840, NY383-560,
NY439-150, NY574-710, NY590-960,
NY618-120, NY757-400, NY804-560,
NY866-710, NY890-700, OH97-80,
OH451-40, OH680-540, OK338-120,
PA35-40, PA55-760, PA410-880,
PA555-40, PA740-320, PA960-910,
PA965-490, PR720-360, SD144-160,
SD792-880, TN285-280, TX210-200,
TX252-730, TX326-800, TX374-40,
TX712-880, TX851-690, TX968-520,
UT684-80, VA560-333, VT32-80,
VT496-640, VT720-720, WA60-860,

WA629-655, WA820-880, WA904-770,
WI326-120, WI390-520, WI530-520,
WI890-320
CONSTRUCTION
CA720-955, DC1-920, DC19-591,
DC19-601
ELECTRIC
CT198-80, MD985-560, NY804-280
ELEVATED
NY587-500
EQUIPMENT
DC1-920, NY804-800, WI530-520
GERMAN SOUTHWEST AFRICA
MI255-530
GREAT BRITAIN
NE288-400
LABOR
DC1-920, OH451-40, OK389-560,
TX280-540
LABOR UNIONS
IN825-200, WA856-100
LAND
TX968-520
LOGGING
CA720-307
NORTH AMERICA
NE288-400
PACIFIC NORTHWEST
OR720-560, OR901-760, WA880-370
ROCKY MOUNTAIN REGION
CO252-820
SPECULATION
TX397-690
STATIONS
NE288-400, NY240-160, NY818-760
RAILSBACK, THOMAS
IL489-890
RAILWAY MAIL SERVICE
DC19-651
RAINFALL
NC656-720
RALEIGH NEWS AND OBSERVER
NC680-460
RALEIGH, WALTER
NC150-810
RALSTON, JOHN
NJ502-690
RAMSAY, WILLIAM
DC19-560
RANCHERS
OK389-560, OR464-490
RANCHING
AZ475-640, CA40-60, CA40-480,
CA601-120, CA720-746, CA830-720,
ID80-365, NM494-570, NV270-560,
SD792-850, TX7-320, TX14-720,
TX128-640, TX231-120, TX529-770,
TX590-760, WY500-800
CATTLE
AZ435-520
SOUTH DAKOTA
CO36-40
ZACATECAS, MEXICO
LA600-760
RANCHO SANTA ANITA
CA40-60
RAND SCHOOL OF SOCIAL SCIENCES
NY593-120
RANDOLPH, JAMES R.
VA90-840
RANDOLPH, JOHN
OH147-520, VA470-690
RANGE LAND
AZ700-40, OR464-490
RANGERS
NE240-560
RANKIN AND KELLOGG
PA725-150
RANKIN FAMILY (ALBANY NY)
NY10-320
RANKIN, JOHN C.
NY101-90
RANSOHOFF, MARTHA
OH171-800
RANSOM, JAY ELLIS
OR848-40

RANSOM, JOHN CROWE
OH320-430
RANSOM, TRUMAN B.
VT528-560
RANSOME, REVERDY CASSIUS
OH939-860
RAPID CITY SD
CO36-40
RAPID TRANSIT
See Transportation
RAPP, GEORGE
PA40-600
RASKOB, JOHN J.
DE270-200
RASMUSSEN, AXEL
OR720-660
RAUSCHENBUSCH, WALTER
NY752-40
RAVENNA TEMPERANCE SOCIETY
OH733-690
RAVINIA FESTIVAL
IL374-310
RAVOUX, AUGUSTIN
MN763-100
RAWLINGS, M. K.
FL220-800
REACTIONARIES
NY439-150
**READING THE LANDSCAPE OF AMERICA,
BY MAY THEILGAARD WATTS**
IL459-520
**READING THE LANDSCAPE OF EUROPE,
BY MAY THEILGAARD WATTS**
IL459-520
REAL ESTATE
AL120-100, CA48-40, IA188-777,
IL84-120, MA738-700, ME453-40,
ME460-440, NY915-880, OH878-880,
OR624-480, PA725-615, TN465-760,
VA315-310
REARDON, JAMES
MN763-100
REAVIS, JAMES ADDISON
MO620-80
RECIPES
See also Food, CT961-880
RECLAMATION
CA402-720, WY500-800
LAND
AZ550-040, CA402-720, CA676-740,
WY500-800
RECLAMATION, BUREAU OF
CO252-550
RECONCILIATION
PA725-60
RECONSTRUCTION
LA600-310, LA600-465, NC30-715,
NC260-170, NC740-690, OH203-600,
OH301-690, TN690-780, TX890-720,
VA690-530
RECREATION
AZ700-40, CA720-307, DC1-295,
DC14-540, MA425-520, ME287-160,
MN541-902, NY10-570, OR560-690,
VT176-810
ORGANIZATIONS
WA60-80
RECYCLING
GLASS
VA500-322
RED CROSS
DC1-560, MN391-310, NY563-120,
VA430-280
RED CROSS (DAYTON OH)
OH223-880
RED CROSS (UNION SPRINGS NY)
NY895-240
RED RIVER
LA885-480
RED RIVER CAMPAIGN (CIVIL WAR)
LA465-480
RED RIVER VALLEY
ND375-570
REDDING, THOMAS B.
IN572-320
REDDIX, JACOB L.
MS550-410

REDFIELD COLLEGE
SD936-930
REDMOND, GEORGE H.
NY240-160
REDOUTE, PIERRE-JOSEPH
PA735-140
REDWOODS
CA454-520
REECE, BYRON HERBERT
GA990-940
REED, DANIEL
NY310-720
REED, NELSON
MD76-790
REED, SIMEON GANNETT
OR720-700
REESE, LIZETTE WOODWORTH
MD266-80
REEVE, CHARLES MCCORMICK
NY234-165
REEVE, JULIET
KS948-240
REEVES, DAVID WALLACE
RI700-640
REFORM
MOVEMENTS
CT505-960
SOCIAL
MA169-210
REFORMED CHURCH
NC590-320, OH813-310
REFORMED CHURCH IN AMERICA
IA755-560, MI445-880
CLERGY
MI445-880
REFORMED CHURCH IN THE U.S.
PA470-800
REFORMED DUTCH CHURCH
NY588-700
REFORMED EPISCOPAL CHURCH
IL169-651
REFUGEES
See also Exiles; Immigration and
emigration, DC1-340, MI230-780,
NY588-850
CAMBODIA
NY10-160
CUBA
NY10-160
EUROPE, CENTRAL
NY593-720
JEWS
NY593-720
VIETNAM
NY10-160
REGIONAL PLANNING
See also City planning, DC14-370,
MI230-730, MO810-940, NJ444-240
REHDER, ALFRED
MA169-190
REID, ALEX J.
KY886-30
REID, BERNARD J.
CA778-780
REIDSVILLE SEMINARY
NC430-340
REIK, THEODOR
NY592-640
REISCHAUER, EDWIN
MA871-85
RELANDER, CLIFFORD CURTIS (CLICK)
WA994-940
RELIEF
See Social welfare
RELIGION
See also Church history; and individual
denominations and faiths, AK900-840,
AR510-25, CA143-80, CA712-750,
DC12-150, DC12-300, DE810-330,
GA810-80, IL169-325, IL170-884,
IL866-365, IN902-80, LA62-500,
LA395-520, MA109-460, MA154-310,
MA624-740, MA985-70, MD114-330,
MD266-800, MI665-210, MN226-700,
MO210-815, NC260-170, NJ578-510,
NY187-120, NY588-940, NY592-460,
NY637-720, NY732-520, NY872-800,

OH171-320, OR720-700, PA40-600,
PA470-470, PA715-720, PA725-700,
PA735-630, PA795-800, PA960-440,
SD558-720, TN435-220, TN690-780,
TN690-885, TX56-720, TX56-850,
TX56-860, TX210-230, TX712-880,
VA195-200, VA400-520, VT176-810,
VT296-690, VT964-720, WI266-820
ASIA
MA169-400, NJ578-530
BLACKS
AL760-760, GA90-360
ECUMENICAL MOVEMENT
NY318-260
EDUCATION
DC1-160, GA90-360, IA377-280,
IL261-280, IN264-40, NY247-160,
NY752-40, OH171-730, PA145-120,
PA726-37, PA726-713, TN690-880,
TX483-160, WA427-550, WI498-560
INDIANS
SD792-800
ORGANIZATIONS
LA600-40, TN435-220
PENTECOSTAL
TN90-440, TX947-720
POLITICS
KY464-780
PUBLISHING
IN264-40, NY752-40
**RELIGION, AMERICAN ACADEMY OF
SOUTHEASTERN SECTION**
GA90-190
RELIGIOUS COMMUNITIES
NY587-940, NY741-720, WA820-820
BELEN NM
CA110-600
BELIZE
RI210-720
CHINA
IL866-320
COLORADO
OH593-720
DENVER CO
CA110-600
EPISCOPAL CHURCH
NY687-120
EUROPE
DC23-700
FRANCE
IA188-777, IL169-565, KY496-850,
KY532-720, MA169-305, PA726-480
GERMANY
IL866-320, KY496-850, PA30-720
GUATEMALA
CA720-739
HONDURAS
RI210-720
HUNGARY
CA421-565
IRELAND
IL84-600, MD152-720
ITALY
KY496-850
JAPAN
IL866-320
LUTHERAN CHURCH IN AMERICA
PA330-160
MARYLAND
DC7-650
MEXICO
CA720-739
MICHIGAN
OH593-720
MIDDLE ATLANTIC US
NY10-160
NEW ENGLAND
NY10-160
NEW JERSEY
NY859-720
NEW MEXICO
CA720-739, OH593-720
OHIO
NY859-720, OH593-720
POLAND
IL866-320

PORTLAND OR
  CA110-600
ROMAN CATHOLIC CHURCH
  AR480-320, CA78-740, CA110-600,
  CA421-565, CA720-739, CA764-165,
  DC7-650, DC23-700, IA188-777,
  IL55-120, IL84-600, IL169-565,
  IL170-475, IL245-322, IL770-40,
  IL866-320, IN209-140, IN627-640,
  KS213-560, KY176-720, KY496-850,
  KY532-720, KY569-720, KY57W-720,
  KY710-160, LA600-690, MA356-120,
  MD76-100, MD152-720, MD380-160,
  MD703-40, MI650-720, MN226-705,
  MN749-720, MN763-720, MO810-750,
  MO810-760, ND824-40, NE320-520,
  NY10-160, NY10-710, NY115-720,
  NY318-240, NY318-260, NY459-520,
  NY481-720, NY529-530, NY604-560,
  NY859-720, OH171-730, OH223-710,
  OH593-720, OR528-718, PA30-720,
  PA50-720, PA240-710, PA305-720,
  PA420-720, PA485-720, PA725-908,
  PA726-480, PA726-495, PA735-720,
  PA795-120, PA908-720, RI210-720,
  TN630-120, TX483-160, TX483-322,
  VT176-690, VT964-720, WA472-720,
  WA820-820, WA880-710, WA880-753,
  WI130-720, WI214-700, WI298-250,
  WI594-110
  SOUTH AFRICA
    IL84-600
  SOUTH CAROLINA
    NY859-720
  TAIWAN
    IL866-320
  WASHINGTON
    CA720-739
  WEST VIRGINIA
    NY859-720
  WOMEN
    AR480-320, CA78-740, CA110-600,
    CA421-565, CA720-739, CA764-165,
    IA188-777, IL109-130, IL169-565,
    IL770-40, IL866-320, IN209-140,
    KS213-560, KY176-720, KY496-850,
    KY532-720, KY569-720, KY57W-720,
    KY710-160, LA600-690, MD76-100,
    MD152-720, MD380-160, MI650-720,
    MN763-720, MO810-750, MO810-760,
    NY10-160, NY10-710, NY115-720,
    NY318-240, NY459-520, NY481-720,
    NY529-530, NY687-120, NY859-720,
    OH171-730, OH223-710, OH593-720,
    PA30-720, PA50-720, PA85-730,
    PA305-720, PA330-160, PA420-720,
    PA725-908, PA726-480, PA726-495,
    PA735-720, PA795-120, PA908-720,
    RI210-720, TX483-322, WA820-820,
    WA880-710, WA880-753, WI298-250
RELIGIOUS ORDERS
  See Religious communities
REMEY, GEORGE COLLIER
  MN763-710
REMINGTON, FREDERIC
  DC14-450, LA885-690
REMINISCENCES, BY DOUGLAS
    MACARTHUR
  VA580-520
RENAISSANCE
  See Europe, Renaissance
RENO NV
  HOSPITALS
    CA764-165
RENO, JOHN
  IN92-80
RENSSELAERSWYCK MANOR
  NY10-80
REORGANIZED CHURCH OF JESUS
    CHRIST OF LATTER DAY SAINTS
  IA533-280
REPARATIONS
  NY905-840
REPERTOIRE COMPANIES (THEATER)
  IA688-520

REPRESENTATIVE MEN, BY RALPH
    WALDO EMERSON
  NY134-90
REPRESENTATIVES
  CONGRESS
    AL440-800, AR510-810, AR890-20,
    CA594-120, CA676-140, DC12-450,
    DC19-130, FL820-810, GA75-790,
    IA466-360, IL489-890, IL718-200,
    IL866-365, IN231-40, KS377-200,
    KS948-890, LA286-720, MA615-720,
    MI20-50, MI40-300, MS80-40,
    MS490-810, MT130-540, MT530-500,
    MT700-800, NC60-810, NC900-810,
    ND486-800, NH206-800, NY723-720,
    OH399-420, OH878-720, OK558-790,
    OR224-800, OR720-590, PA25-520,
    PA90-480, PA425-360, PA500-80,
    PA645-560, PA960-440, SD720-80,
    TX56-520, TX181-790, UT456-900,
    VT496-640, WA724-890
  STATE
    GA75-790, IL866-365, MA725-640,
    MN562-520, NM760-900
REPUBLIC OF SOUTH AFRICA
  See South Africa
REPUBLIC PICTURES
  CA421-763
REPUBLICAN PARTY
  AR510-810, GA735-540, NH194-560
RESEARCH
  BIO-MEDICINE
    NY593-840
RESERVOIRS
  CT870-520, DC19-800, MA123-80,
  NY334-240, OH990-640, TN465-760
RESETTLEMENT
  JAPANESE-AMERICANS
    CA720-365
RESISTANCE MOVEMENTS
  CA858-320, NY590-700
RESORTS
  GA885-120, ID400-720, MA425-520,
  NJ66-80, NY590-760, OR624-480,
  RI560-360
RESTAURANTS
  CAFETERIAS
    NY594-20
  TRUCK STOPS
    DC1-680
RETAILING
  See Mercantile activities
RETIRED SENIOR VOLUNTEER PROGRAM
    (ACTION)
  DC1-40
RETIREMENT
  MA169-885
REVENUE-CUTTER SERVICE (COAST
    GUARD)
  WA820-147
REVERE, PAUL
  MA109-660
REVOLUTIONARY WAR
  See American Revolution
REVOLUTIONS
  CA206-790, CA858-320, NY590-700,
  TX56-860, TX326-210, TX326-780,
  TX777-810
REW, HENRY C.
  NY597-520
REYNOLDS WOMENS RELIEF CORPS
  MA947-880
REYNOLDS, HELEN WILKINSON
  NY726-40
REYNOLDS, JOHN E.
  PA555-120
REYNOLDS, JOSHUA
  CT505-977
RHOADS, J. J.
  TX252-80
RHODE ISLAND
  JEWS
    MA871-40
RIALTO CEMETERY ASSOCIATION
  CA640-640

RICE
  AGRICULTURE
    LA358-800
RICE FAMILY
  MA513-530
RICE PADDY WAR
  RI560-510
RICE, EMILY
  MA513-530
RICE, LABAN LACY
  KY22W-920
RICE, RUSSELL
  IA43-80
RICE, WILLIAM H.
  PA90-320
RICHARD, GABRIEL
  MD76-30, MI230-720
RICHARDSON HISTORICAL SOCIETY
  TX742-680
RICHARDSON JAYCEES
  TX742-680
RICHARDSON, H. H.
  MA169-305
RICHARDSON, ROY D.
  NY588-300
RICHMOND ART CENTER
  CA644-690
RICHMOND HILL LAW SCHOOL
  NC950-940
RICHMOND SISTERHOOD (VA)
  IN704-520
RICHMOND, GRACE
  NY310-720
RICKENBACKER, EDDIE
  MI440-320
RICOEUR, PAUL
  NY125-740
RIDGELY FAMILY
  DE90-140
RIDGWAY, MATTHEW B.
  PA165-790
RIEL, LOUIS
  RI945-800
RIGGS FAMILY
  SD936-930
RIIS, JACOB
  NY899-520
RILEY, JAMES
  OH147-520
RILEY, JAMES WATSON
  OH147-520
RILEY, JAMES WHITCOMB
  IN363-400, PA725-195
RILKE, RAINER MARIA
  MA169-370
RINGLING BROTHERS CIRCUS
  IL624-380
RIO GRANDE SOUTHERN RAILROAD
  CO270-240
RIO GRANDE VALLEY
  TX319-640
RIORDAN FAMILY
  AZ250-690
RIOTS
  DC4-450, DC14-500
RIPPLE (YACHT)
  FL60-720
RITTER, WILLIAM EMERSON
  CA368-820
RIVER BASIN SURVEYS
  DC19-520
RIVERS
  CA402-720, CA922-840, DC1-805,
  IA33-350, KY464-460, OH171-650
  ESTUARIES
    OR128-720
  TRANSPORTATION
    CA676-740, KY2A-80, WI298-810
RIVERS, L. MENDEL
  SC144-150
RIVERTON IMPROVEMENT COMPANY
  NJ736-690
RIVERTON YACHT CLUB
  NJ736-690

ROADS
AK500-20, CA624-710, DC1-680,
DC1-805, GA90-270, IA33-350,
IL936-640, IN363-342, MA235-150,
MA738-700, MD76-525, NE368-160,
NJ464-240, NY178-120, NY251-320,
NY254-160, NY263-210, NY382-310,
NY419-350, NY915-870, OR816-590,
PA890-800, PR720-360, VT464-800
CONSTRUCTION
IA33-350
GOOD-ROADS MOVEMENT
WA904-665
TURNPIKES
CT268-720, PA960-910, TN690-780
ROBBINS, JEROME
NY592-870
ROBERTO, MARCUS A.
OH399-420
ROBERTS, BENJAMIN TITUS
NY752-660
ROBERTS, DENNIS J.
RI700-630
ROBERTS, NORMAN
IL956-870
ROBERTSON COLONY
TX42-810
ROBESON, PAUL
NJ568-680
ROBIDOUX, JOSEPH, FAMILY
MO800-730
ROBIDOUX, JULIUS
MO800-730
ROBINS, MARGARET DREIER
FL220-800
ROBINSON, CHARLES MULFORD
MA169-305
ROBINSON, DAVID
VT496-640
ROBINSON, EDWIN ARLINGTON
CT316-770, ME925-130, NH206-800
ROBINSON, ROWLAND EVANS
VT296-690
ROBINSON, ROWLAND THOMAS
VT296-690
ROBINSON, THEODORE
NY589-680
ROBITSCHEK, ROBERT
MN763-710
**ROCHAMBEAU, COMTE DE (JEAN
BAPTISTE DONATIEN DE VIMEUR)**
FL220-800, NJ692-660
ROCHESTER ACADEMY OF MEDICINE
NY752-885
**ROCHESTER ATHENAEUM AND
MECHANICS INSTITUTE**
NY752-700
ROCHESTER THEOLOGICAL SEMINARY
NY752-110
ROCK ISLAND RAILROAD
OK338-120
ROCK ISLAND SASH AND DOOR WORKS
IL801-20
ROCK, JOSEPH
PA735-140
ROCKEFELLER FAMILY
VA870-130
ROCKEFELLER FOUNDATION
NY612-690
**ROCKEFELLER INSTITUTE FOR MEDICAL
RESEARCH**
NY593-840
**ROCKEFELLER SANITARY COMMISSION
FOR THE ERADICATION OF
HOOKWORM DISEASE**
NY612-690
ROCKEFELLER, JOHN D.
NY612-690
**ROCKEFELLER, LAURA SPELMAN,
MEMORIAL**
NY612-690
ROCKEFELLER, NELSON ALDRICH
MS80-40
ROCKETRY
DC14-120, DC19-500, MA985-110,
NM684-690, TX742-800

ROCKFORD FEMALE SEMINARY
IL806-695
ROCKWELL, NORMAN
NY844-720
ROCKY MOUNTAIN REGION
CO108-810, CO252-120, CO252-181,
CO252-550, UT684-80
AGRICULTURE
UT380-810
INDIANS
WA880-550
IRRIGATION
UT380-810
RAILROADS
CO252-820
**ROCKY MOUNTAIN UNITED METHODIST
CONFERENCE**
CO252-360
ROCKY MOUNTAINS
DC1-810, MT530-500
RODBAURN STORE AND SAWMILL
NY274-200
RODEOS
INDIANS
NM722-360
RODIN MUSEUM
PA726-255
ROETHKE, THEODORE
PA895-710, WA820-880
ROGERS COLLEGE
NY529-530
ROGERS, BRUCE
IN935-650
ROGERS, JACOB
NJ646-660
ROGERS, MALCOLM J.
CA712-713
ROGERS, WILLIAM PENN ADAIR (WILL)
OK245-880, OK753-600
ROLLS-ROYCE AUTOMOBILES
PA560-690
ROMAN CATHOLIC CHURCH
AL130-333, CA270-520, CA720-579,
CA720-910, CA724-730, CA778-800,
DC3-210, DC7-650, DC14-380,
DC14-580, DC15-50, HI350-720,
IA244-480, IA866-160, IL245-322,
IN627-780, IN627-800, KS527-790,
KY418-520, KY532-720, LA358-160,
MA451-360, MD76-748, MD380-520,
MN226-700, MN763-110, MO810-730,
MO810-750, NC090-080, ND824-40,
NY10-675, NY10-710, NY587-930,
NY587-940, NY775-720, OH171-730,
OH203-170, PA726-495, RI700-160,
TX56-110, WA880-280, WA994-690,
WI130-720, WI456-720
ARCHDIOCESE OF LOUISVILLE
KY496-70
ARCHDIOCESE OF NEW ORLEANS
LA358-160, LA358-165
ARCHDIOCESE OF NEWARK
NJ798-720
AUTHORS
IN627-800
CLERGY
AR480-320, AR510-145, DC1-740,
DC3-210, DC14-380, DC14-580,
IA188-777, IL55-120, IL866-320,
IN363-50, IN440-160, IN627-720,
IN627-780, IN627-800, KY57W-720,
LA358-160, LA358-165, LA600-40,
MD76-30, MD380-160, MI230-50,
MN763-100, MO220-120, MT530-690,
NJ798-720, NY10-675, NY587-930,
NY752-560, NY752-760, OH171-50,
OH171-730, OH203-170, OR720-40,
PA380-700, PA485-720, PA725-45,
PA726-105, RI210-720, SC144-190,
TN690-690, VT176-690, WI698-730
DIOCESE OF LAFAYETTE
LA358-165
DIOCESE OF ROCHESTER
NY752-760
DIOCESE OF ROCKVILLE CENTRE
NY587-930

DIOCESE OF ST. JOSEPH, MO
IA188-777
DIOCESE OF VINCENNES
IN363-50
DIOCESE OF YOUNGSTOWN
OH399-420
EDUCATION
LA600-40, MO220-120, NY481-720,
PA726-495
FLORIDA
PA726-495
ITALY
DC15-50
KENTUCKY
DC15-50
MARYLAND
PA726-495
MIDWESTERN US
MN763-100, OH171-50
MISSIONARIES
DC3-210, GA895-160, IN209-140,
KS213-560, KY57W-720, LA600-505,
MD76-30, MD380-160, MD703-40,
MO220-120, NM114-50, NY318-240,
NY459-520, NY481-720, NY529-530,
OH223-720, OR720-590, PA50-720,
PA485-720, PA908-720, RI945-800,
SC144-190, WI456-495, WI698-730
MISSIONS (BUILDINGS)
CA352-520, CA724-730, CA774-720,
CA778-780, CA934-720
MISSISSIPPI RIVER VALLEY
DC15-50
MONTANA
MN749-720
NEW JERSEY
PA726-495
NORTH DAKOTA
MN749-720
OHIO
DC15-50
OHIO RIVER VALLEY
DC15-50
ORGANIZATIONS
DC14-380, IL170-78, OH203-170,
WI456-495
PACIFIC NORTHWEST
WA880-120
PHILIPPINES
NY752-560
POPES
IN627-800, MN226-700
PREJUDICE AGAINST
NY10-160
PUERTO RICO
PA726-495
RELIGIOUS COMMUNITIES
AR480-320, CA78-740, CA110-600,
CA421-565, CA720-739, CA764-165,
DC7-650, DC23-700, IA188-777,
IL55-120, IL84-600, IL169-565,
IL170-475, IL245-322, IL770-40,
IL866-320, IN209-140, IN627-640,
KS213-560, KY176-720, KY496-850,
KY532-720, KY569-720, KY57W-720,
KY710-160, LA600-690, MA356-120,
MD76-100, MD152-720, MD380-160,
MD703-40, MI650-720, MN226-705,
MN749-720, MN763-720, MO810-750,
MO810-760, ND824-40, NE320-520,
NY10-160, NY10-710, NY115-720,
NY318-240, NY318-260, NY459-520,
NY481-720, NY529-530, NY604-560,
NY859-720, OH171-730, OH223-710,
OH593-720, OR528-718, PA30-720,
PA50-720, PA240-710, PA305-720,
PA420-720, PA485-720, PA725-908,
PA726-480, PA726-495, PA735-720,
PA795-120, PA908-720, RI210-720,
TN630-120, TX483-160, TX483-322,
VT176-690, VT964-720, WA472-720,
WA820-820, WA880-710, WA880-753,
WI130-720, WI214-700, WI298-250,
WI594-110
SAINTS
MN226-700

SCHOOLS
 NE320-520, NY459-520, PA380-700,
 WI456-730
SOCIAL WELFARE
 NJ798-720
SOUTHWESTERN US
 TX56-720
UTAH
 MN749-720
VATICAN I
 NY752-760
WASHINGTON
 MN749-720
WESTERN US
 CA421-30
WISCONSIN
 MN749-720
ROMANIA
 IN187-40, OH399-440, PA735-825
 FOLK MUSIC
 NY166-80
ROMANIAN-AMERICANS
 IN187-40
ROMBERG, SIGMUND
 CA86-890
ROMMEL, ERWIN
 SC144-150
ROMULO, CARLOS
 MA871-85
ROONEY, FRED C.
 PA90-480
ROOSEVELT (SHIP)
 ME175-80
ROOSEVELT FAMILY
 NY427-240, PA795-800
ROOSEVELT, ANNA ELEANOR
 MA636-880, NY427-240, OK42-560
ROOSEVELT, FRANKLIN DELANO
 MS140-560, NY588-940, NY726-40,
 PA325-280, PA795-800
ROOSEVELT, THEODORE
 MA108-240, MD76-30, NY222-110
ROOT, CHESTER
 AL580-530
ROPELLA, CHESTER
 WI202-120
ROSE, WICKLIFFE
 NY612-690
ROSECRANS FAMILY
 CA421-770
ROSECRANS, WILLIAM STARKE
 CA421-770
ROSEDALE MILLS
 NJ358-320
ROSEN, ISRAEL
 MD76-640
ROSENBERG REPORT ON HIGHER
 EDUCATION IN MARYLAND
 MD114-310
ROSS, JOHN
 OK778-120
ROSS, WILLIAM P.
 OK778-120
ROSSETTI FAMILY
 KS527-790
ROSSETTI, DANTE GABRIEL
 DE810-150
ROTARY CLUB
 KY598-600, NC200-120, NY59-80
ROTCH, THOMAS
 OH505-520
ROUNDUPS
 OR688-810
ROUSSEAU, JEAN JACQUES
 CT505-977
ROYAL ACADEMY OF DANCE (LONDON)
 NY592-870
ROYALTON ACADEMY
 VT688-690
ROYALTY
 CA118-720, HI350-300, NJ552-80,
 PA395-320
 FRANCE
 MN226-700, PA960-870
 GREAT BRITAIN
 MN226-700, PA960-870

HAWAII
 HI350-73
HOLY ROMAN EMPIRE
 MN226-700
RUSSIA
 MD76-880, MN226-700
SPAIN
 MN226-700
ROYCROFTERS
 NY250-212
RUBAIYAT OF DOC SIFERS, BY JAMES
 WHITCOMB RILEY
 PA725-195
RUBBER
 OH11-240, OH11-290, OH11-810
RUFFINI, OSCAR
 TX770-240
RUGE, FRIEDRICH
 SC144-150
RUGGLES, CARL
 CT505-910
RUNDLET-MAY COLLECTION
 MA109-680
RURAL LIFE
 MA823-610, MO830-120, SC414-110,
 SD792-850, VA50-50, VT176-810
 SOUTHERN US
 GA810-80
RUSH-BOUDINOT U.S. MINT
 CONTROVERSY
 NJ280-270
RUSH, BENJAMIN
 NJ280-270, PA160-160
RUSK, HOWARD
 MA871-85
RUSKIN, JOHN
 MA891-880
RUSSELL CREEK ASSOCIATION OF
 BAPTISTS
 KY126-120
RUSSELL FAMILY
 NJ756-240
RUSSELL, CHARLES M.
 LA885-690
RUSSELL, RICHARD B.
 GA75-790
RUSSIA
 See also Soviet Union; and individual
 republics, CA578-130, CA858-320,
 CT505-960, NY587-820, NY588-825,
 PA735-825
 AMERICAN EXPEDITIONARY FORCES
 MI445-320
 BOTANY
 DC14-180
 COLONIES IN AMERICA
 WA880-290
 EXPLORATION BY
 OR720-590
 EXPLORERS
 MI518-50
 GERMANS FROM (IMMIGRANTS)
 CO378-110, CO498-40
 IMMIGRATION AND EMIGRATION
 CA86-810, NY586-650
 LITERATURE
 CT505-890, MA169-370
 ROYALTY
 MD76-880, MN226-700
 RUSSO-AMERICAN TELEGRAPH
 EXPEDITION
 OR720-450
 SOCIAL WELFARE
 CA86-385
RUSSIAN ORTHODOX CHURCH
 AK500-20
RUTHENIA
 FOLK MUSIC
 NY166-80
RUTHERFORD-RUSSELL-WATTS FAMILY
 NJ756-240
RUTHERFORD, ERNEST (1ST BARON
 RUTHERFORD OF NELSON)
 NY586-580
RUTLAND RAILROAD
 VT496-640

RUTLEDGE, JOHN
 SC144-130
RWANDA
 MISSIONARIES
 NY459-520
RYCHLIE, CHARLES V.
 OH181-270

S

S. R. BUFORD COMPANY
 MT430-320
S.S. CORDOVA (SHIP)
 AK450-320
SABBATARIANISM
 TN90-440
SABIN, ALBERT
 OH171-800
SACANDAGA RESERVOIR
 NY334-240
SACCO-VANZETTI CASE
 MA871-90
SACCO, NICOLA
 MA871-90
SACHAR, ABRAM L.
 MA871-85
SACHS, PAUL J.
 MA169-300
SACRA CONGREGATIO DE PROPAGANDA
 FIDE (ROMAN CATHOLIC CHURCH)
 LA600-505
SACRAMENTO CITIZENS COMMITTEE ON
 LOCAL GOVERNMENTAL
 REORGANIZATION
 CA676-140
SACRAMENTO PEACE CENTER
 CA676-140
SACRAMENTO RIVER
 CA402-720, CA676-740
SACROBOSCO, JOHANNES DE
 DC19-641
SADLER'S WELLS BALLET
 OH203-670
SAFETY
 TN465-760
SAFETY PATROLS (SCHOOLS)
 VA215-40
SAFRAN PRINTING COMPANY
 MI255-530
SAGE, MARGARET OLIVIA SLOCUM
 NY890-200
SAGINAW GENEALOGICAL SOCIETY
 MI824-320
SAGINAW SYMPHONY
 MI824-320
SAIA, D. J.
 KS746-640
SAIL MAKING
 ME462-440
SAILLY FAMILY
 NY708-440
SALT INDUSTRY
 KY760-720, MI824-320, NY499-720
SALT LAKE CITY UT
 CA628-720, IA533-280
SALT RIVER VALLEY
 AZ550-45
SALTEN, FELIX
 IN363-400
SALTILLO, COAHUILA, MEXICO
 TX777-620
SALTONSTALL FAMILY
 MA109-120
SALZBURG, AUSTRIA
 IMMIGRATION AND EMIGRATION
 GA860-280
SALZEDO, CARLOS
 PA725-345
SAM SMITH SHOE COMPANY
 NH720-560
SAMOA
 HI450-80
SAMPSON, ARTHUR W.
 OR464-490
SAN DIEGO ELECTRIC RAILWAY
 CA582-600

SAN FRANCISCO BAY
CA922-840
SAN FRANCISCO EARTHQUAKE (PERIODICAL)
IL261-570
SAN FRANCISCO VIGILANCE MOVEMENT
VT496-640
SAN JOAQUIN RIVER
CA402-720
SAN JOAQUIN VALLEY
CA274-240
SAN JOSE CA
IL245-322
SANBORN, FRANKLIN BENJAMIN
MA217-130
SAND
TX56-780
SANDBURG, CARL
IL169-416, PA160-160
SANDER, AUGUST
DC3-760
SANDERSON, GEORGE L.
PA425-360
SANDOZ, MARI
NE560-860
SANDWICH ISLANDS
HI350-311
SANDY HOOK PILOTS' ASSOCIATION
NY594-340
SANGER, MARGARET HIGGINS
MA624-740
SANGER, NETTIE
VA115-80
SANITARIUMS
MI60-880, NY156-120
SANKEY, IRA D.
PA645-560
SANTA ANITA ASSEMBLY CENTER FOR JAPANESE-AMERICANS, WORLD WAR II
CA40-60
SANTA ANNA, ANTONIO LOPEZ DE
TX777-810
SANTA CLARA MISSION
CA778-780
SANTA FE NM
TX326-160
SANTA FE TRAIL
KS569-600
  COMMERCE
KS513-720
SANTEE NE
  INDIANS
SD936-930
SANTO DOMINGO, AUDENCIA DE (SPANISH COLONIAL GOVERNMENT)
LA600-505
SARATOGA SPRINGS RESERVATION
NY792-720
SARGENT, CHARLES SPRAGUE
MA169-190
SARGENT, JOHN SINGER
IL169-130
SASKATCHEWAN, CANADA
MN226-705
SATTERLEE HOSPITAL (PHILADELPHIA PA)
NY10-160
SATTERLEE, HENRY YATES
DC5-800
SAUNDERS FAMILY
RI910-880
SAWYER FAMILY
WI554-600
SAXON, LYLE
LA600-755
SAXOPHONES
IN539-86
  MUSIC FOR
MA109-440
SAXTON, CARLON
NY563-120
SAY, THOMAS
MA169-500, PA725-15
SAYERS, DOROTHY L.
IL976-900

SAYLES, HENRY
TX7-320
SAYLOR, JOHN P.
PA425-360
SCANDINAVIA
MN433-440, MN562-520
  CHILDREN'S LITERATURE
MN541-838
SCANDINAVIAN-AMERICANS
MN433-440, MN562-520, WI38-480
SCANDRETT, RICHARD B., JR.
NY588-850
SCARBROUGH, W. S.
OH939-860
SCARLET SISTER MARY, BY JULIA PETERKIN
SC846-890
SCHELLENBERG, THEODORE
KS878-430
SCHENCK, CARL ALWYN
NC60-240, NC680-550
SCHENCK, ROBERT C.
OH680-540
SCHEYER, GALKA
CA578-630
SCHILDER, PAUL F.
NY588-300
SCHMIDT, CARL
NY321-720
SCHMITT, GLADYS
PA735-150
SCHOENBERG, ARNOLD
CA421-40
SCHOLARS
NY594-080
SCHOLARSHIPS
  AFRICAN STUDENTS
NY593-380
SCHOLL, L. W.
IN539-100
SCHOLTE, HENDRIK PETER
IA811-110
SCHOOL OF ART AS APPLIED TO MEDICINE, JOHNS HOPKINS UNIVERSITY
MD76-880
SCHOOL SISTERS OF ST. FRANCIS
  HOSPITALS
WI456-730
SCHOOLS
  See also Education, *CT102-120, CT120-120, IL169-651, IL296-720, IL946-360, IN77-200, KS241-480, KS579-690, KY22W-920, KY37S-480, KY41E-160, KY760-720, LA600-690, MA109-595, MA823-610, MI122-880, MN275-200, MN419-440, MN749-720, NE352-880, NJ318-320, NJ358-320, NJ548-520, NJ622-690, NM912-280, NY10-160, NY87-50, NY112-80, NY178-120, NY241-160, NY331-280, NY510-880, NY550-520, NY562-510, NY587-800, NY654-600, NY720-640, NY763-690, NY807-730, NY858-720, NY861-740, NY895-240, NY910-860, NY915-870, NY967-880, NY968-520, NY978-880, OH223-520, OR128-720, OR720-40, PA30-720, PA90-500, PA908-720, VA50-50, VT176-690, VT688-690, WA265-600, WA289-200, WA408-360, WA468-720, WA498-480, WA508-520, WA597-600, WA604-590, WA629-655, WA647-270, WA820-810, WA984-80, WI456-490, WY135-860*
  GERMAN-AMERICANS
MA451-360
  INDIAN TERRITORY
OH953-870
  ONE-ROOM
IN726-240, KY514-120, MO830-120
  PUBLIC
CA676-110, CT144-880, MI518-445, MO810-330, NY752-760
  RACE RELATIONS
KY496-812
  RANCH
NM722-730

RECORDS
CA168-120, CA180-160, CO180-640, CO768-640, CT234-230, CT254-320, CT505-560, CT512-550, CT673-690, CT786-720, GA105-690, IA244-160, IA600-322, IA822-260, IA855-150, IL139-320, IL424-480, IN66-520, IN92-80, IN209-140, IN649-520, IN770-880, IN917-880, KS10-150, KS385-280, KS513-720, KS527-160, KY57W-720, KY886-30, MA109-830, MA761-720, MD304-80, MI126-880, MI585-520, MI675-510, MN307-200, MN506-80, MN674-630, MN742-750, MT750-690, NE32-40, NY20-40, NY54-40, NY78-320, NY82-80, NY148-200, NY148A-12, NY228-110, NY240-160, NY246-720, NY247-160, NY251-320, NY264-200, NY373-320, NY404-640, NY411-320, NY439-180, NY491-480, NY537E-60, NY563-120, NY563-322, NY587-720, NY618-115, NY618-120, NY661-620, NY667-580, NY667-600, NY764-690, NY847-560, NY847-720, NY852-720, OK854-840, OR480-940, OR704-80, PA80-110, PA235-640, PA880-320, PA920-870, PA920-890, SD153-200, TX640-720, TX777-670, VT448-520, WI714-525
ROMAN CATHOLIC CHURCH
NE320-520, NY459-520, PA380-700, WI456-730
SAFETY PATROLS
VA215-40
SCHOOL BOARDS
OH397-640
SISTERS OF PROVIDENCE
WA820-820
SCHOONERS
  See also Boats, *MA293-200, ME453-40*
SCHOONOVER, FRANK E.
DE810-150, PA175-80
SCHUBERT, FRANZ
PA725-345
SCHULTZ, EDWARD A.
OH399-420
SCHULTZE, JOHN S.
NJ756-240
SCHUMANN, ROBERT
PA725-345
SCHUYLER FAMILY
NY254-160, NY878-720
SCHUYLER, JAMES DIX
CA86-920
SCHWEINFURTH, CHARLES
OH181-325
SCHWEINITZ, L. D. VON
PA725-15
SCHWEITZER, ALBERT
WA904-800
SCHWENKFELDERS
PA715-720
SCIENCE
AL120-815, AL440-560, CA86-780, CA86-882, CA86-920, CA143-80, CA421-770, CA578-130, CA578-560, CT36-80, CT505-945, CT926-480, DC1-300, DC12-300, DC14-100, DC14-140, DC16-680, DC19-310, DC19-542, DC19-641, FL180-210, IA33-370, IA99-40, IL170-273, IN363-360, IN583-560, IN627-810, IN935-650, KS527-790, KY288-425, MA109-380, MA169-170, MA169-500, MA169-650, MA615-80, MD76-360, MD152-550, MI40-796, MI40-808, MI40-820, MI214-260, MI230-165, MI230-740, MI255-530, MI355-270, MI550-530, MI605-520, MI665-120, MO810-700, MO810-940, NY205-120, NY592-280, NY592-800, NY592-860, NY593-420, NY593-840, NY594-380, OH171-110, OH171-650, OH181-110, OH181-130, OH181-790, OH181-880, OH203-600, OH203-650, OH301-690, OH436-880, OH505-520, OH588-520, OH925-600, OH968-600, OH990-510,

PA470-240, PA725-15, PA725-75,
PA725-495, PA725-870, TX56-850,
TX56-890, TX483-560, WA832-560,
WY950-940
APPLIED
NY890-700
EDUCATION
MI110-120, PA726-765, PA726-855
EXPEDITIONS
DC14-180, HI350-73, PA725-15
ISLAM
DC12-105
LABORATORIES
PA725-495
MUSEUMS
IL170-273, PA725-495
ORGANIZATIONS
DC15-500, IA99-40, IL567-520,
KY680-180, MA169-30, NY586-580,
PA725-15, PA725-75, PA726-765,
PA735-140
POLISH-AMERICANS
PA725-765
SPACE
AL440-800, CO108-560, SD684-280
SCIENCE (MAGAZINE)
DC1-300
SCIENCE ADVISORY BOARD
DC14-100
SCIENCE FICTION
CA278-130, CA318-700, CO252-42,
KS746-640, NM668-210, NY872-800,
PA726-615, TX181-780
SCIENTIFIC INSTRUMENTS
CT505-980, DC19-586, DC19-631
SCIENTISTS
AL440-800, AZ250-520, CA578-130,
CA720-894, DC19-631, DC19-641,
HI350-808, IL305-430, KY496-785,
MA169-310, NY592-320, NY593-840,
NY804-800, OH181-240, OH823-800,
PA90-480, PA395-320, PA725-495,
SC144-730, TN465-800, TX397-790,
UT684-80, WA724-890
EUROPE
MA169-310
SCIO COLLEGE
OH16-520
SCOFIELD, LEVI
OH181-325
SCOPES TRIAL
KY604-640
SCOPES, JOHN
KY604-640
SCOPES, LELA
KY604-640
SCOTLAND
IL609-120, NC590-320, PA735-825
AGRICULTURE
CT505-977
IMMIGRATION AND EMIGRATION
FL860-320
WRITERS
CT505-977
SCOTLAND TRINITY CHURCH
(BRIDGEWATER MA)
MA139-90
SCOTT, LAVINIA
IL261-566
SCOTT, ROBERT K.
OH203-600
SCOUTS
See also Indian scouts, WY950-950
SCREWMEN'S BENEVOLENT
ASSOCIATION
TX280-540
SCRIBNER'S (PUBLISHER)
PA175-80
SCRIPPS FAMILY (CA)
CA368-820
SCULL & CO.
AR360-40
SCULPTORS
MA334-120, ME725-880, TX56-200

SCULPTURE
See also Art, DC14-460, DC19-320,
DC19-340, MA169-300, MA169-340,
MD76-80, MI40-800, NY590-360,
NY594-390
SEABEES
See Navy, Naval Construction Force
(Seabees)
SEAFOOD INDUSTRY
MD770-120, MD836-120
SEALING (HUNTING)
CT772-720
SEALS (ANIMALS)
DC14-770
SEATTLE WORLD'S FAIR
WA616-870
SEAWALLS
CONSTRUCTION
TX397-690
SEAY, GEORGE J.
VA690-240
SECOND CONGREGATIONAL CHURCH
(WELLFLEET MA)
MA894-880
SECOND NEW JERSEY CAVALRY
ASSOCIATION
NJ838-530
SECRETARIES
CA712-700
SECRETARY OF STATE (AZ)
AZ550-040
SECRETARY OF STATE (FL)
FL800-245
SECRETARY OF STATE (OR)
OR816-590
SECURITY SAVINGS AND LOAN
COMPANY
OH481-530
SEDGWICK FAMILY
MA811-720
SEEDS
CA278-130
SEEGAL, DAVID
MA871-85
SEELEY FAMILY
CT484-550
SEIDEL, HERMAN
MD76-70, MD76-300
SEISMOLOGY
CA778-780, CO108-560
SELIG, WILLIAM N.
CA90-30
SELLERS, WILLIAM
PA725-495
SEMI-TROPIC LAND & WATER COMPANY
CA640-640
SEMINOLE WAR
CA274-120
SEMMES, RAPHAEL
AL580-530
SEMPLE, LETITIA TYLER
NC330-520
SENATORS
CONGRESS
AZ275-520, AZ750-10, AZ750-45,
AZ750-760, CA620-760, DC19-160,
GA75-790, GA735-520, ID640-345,
IL718-200, IL866-365, KS948-890,
KY514-120, LA62-500, LA920-560,
MI20-50, MI100-240, MI440-320,
MS80-40, MS490-810, MS520-520,
MS610-520, MT130-540, MT530-500,
MT700-800, ND486-800, NH396-560,
NJ568-670, NM114-800, NY150-700,
NY323-320, OK558-790, OR224-800,
OR720-590, PA380-320, SD450-150,
SD522-160, TN630-570, TX56-520,
UT684-80, WA724-890
STATE
IL866-365, PA425-360, TX695-640,
TX968-520
SENECA LODGE NO. 694, INTERNATIONAL
ORDER OF ODD FELLOWS
NY433-350
SENHOUSE, JOSEPH
VI700-360

SENNETT, MACK
CA90-30
SEPARATE STAR, BY LOULA GRACE
ERDMAN
MO920-120
SEQUOIA NATIONAL PARK
CA942-940
SEQUOYAH CHILDREN'S BOOK AWARD
OK42-560
SERGEANT FAMILY
MA811-720
SERMONS
CT247-240, CT254-320, CT316-330,
CT477-130, CT519-560, CT723-720,
DC23-100, DC23-500, DE810-170,
GA90-190, IL170-195, IL261-280,
IN22-50, IN990-240, IN990-280,
KY464-490, LA600-540, MA29-40,
MA108-140, MA725-320, MA871-890,
ME750-160, MI32-40, NH820-690,
PA470-800, PA735-630, SC306-200,
TX326-160, VA400-520
SERVICE CORPS OF RETIRED
EXECUTIVES (ACTION)
DC1-40
SERVICE EMPLOYEES INTERNATIONAL
UNION
GA90-300
SERVITES
IL170-475
NOVENA OF OUR SORROWFUL
MOTHER
IL84-600
OUR LADY OF SORROWS PROVINCE
IL84-600
SESQUICENTENNIAL EXHIBITION
(PHILADELPHIA, 1926)
PA725-240
SESQUICENTENNIALS
KY17S-320
SESSIONS, RUTH HUNTINGTON
MA363-640
SETON, ELIZABETH ANN BAYLEY
MD380-160
SETON, ERNEST THOMPSON
NM266-720
SETON, JULIA M. BUTREE
NM266-720
SETTLEMENT
See Land, settlement
SETTLEMENT HOUSES
GA245-110, IL170-910, IN253-360,
KY496-785, MA169-860, MN541-902,
NY594-20, PA726-630
SEVEN DECADES THAT CHANGED
AMERICA, BY THE AMERICAN
SOCIETY OF AGRICULTURAL
ENGINEERS
MI845-40
SEVENTH CAVALRY
SD936-950
SEVENTH DAY BAPTIST CHURCH
MISSIONARIES
RI910-730
SEVENTH-DAY ADVENTIST CHURCH
CA406-480, IL45-30, MI60-880,
MI90-30
MISSIONARIES
DC19-220
SEVERN, ARTHUR
MI230-800
SEWAGE
NY10-570
PUBLIC WORKS
MA109-180
SEWALL & CO. (SHIPBUILDERS)
ME75-520
SEWARD FAMILY
NY51-240
SEWARD, WILLIAM HENRY
NY51-240
SEWER PIPE
MANUFACTURING
WA152-125
SEWERS
See Public works

SEWING
  DC19-581, NY587-840
SEXUAL BEHAVIOR
  IN66-350
SEYFFARTH, GUSTAVUS
  NY587-780
SHAKERS
  *DE900-320, KY96-870, KY352-320,
  MA383-240, MA677-70, MA677-720,
  NY566-540, NY637-720, OH181-880*
  NEW LEBANON NY
  MA677-720
**SHAKESPEARE WAR (RADIO
  CONTROVERSY)**
  NY591-690
SHAKESPEARE, WILLIAM
  CA143-240, DC6-600
SHANE, JOHN D.
  PA726-713
SHANE, NORMAN A., SR.
  IN209-880
SHARKS
  DC14-770
SHARP FAMILY
  MI510-200
SHARPE, WEISS COAL COMPANY
  PA960-910
SHAVER, DOROTHY
  DC19-555
SHAW, GEORGE BERNARD
  ME925-130, PA500-80, PA725-195
SHAW, HENRY
  MO810-490
SHAW, HOWARD VAN DOREN
  IL169-130
SHAW, LEMUEL
  MA109-660
SHAW, NATHANIEL, JR.
  CT512-550
SHAWN, EDWIN M. (TED)
  MA961-870, NY592-870
SHAY ENGINE
  MI122-880
SHAY'S REBELLION
  MA250-160, MA673-640
SHEEN, FULTON JOHN
  NY752-760
SHEEP
  NY763-680, OH505-520, VT296-690
SHEEPHERDING
  BASQUES
  NV940-800
SHEIP, MARIE LEYETTE
  AL580-530
SHELDEN FAMILY
  CT891-550
SHELDON, HENRY L.
  HI350-311
**SHELL FAMILY (MECKLENBURG COUNTY
  NC)**
  NC160-520
SHELLEY, PERCY BYSSHE
  NY587-880
SHELLS
  TX56-780
**SHELTERING ARMS CHILDREN'S
  SERVICES**
  NJ568-670
SHEPTYTZKY, ANDREW
  PA725-430
SHERMAN, AUGUSTUS F.
  NY594-390
SHERMAN, JOHN
  OH481-530
SHERMAN, PHILIP H.
  MS230-160
SHERMAN, WILLIAM
  NY958-640
SHERMAN, WILLIAM TECUMSEH
  IL296-720, OH481-530
SHERWOOD FAMILY
  NY240-160
SHERWOOD, CARRIE MINER
  NE736-560
SHIELDS, DAN A.
  IA188-777

SHIELDS, FREDERICK
  KS527-790
SHIELDS, JAMES
  IA188-777
SHINN, EVERETT
  DE810-150
SHINTO
  DC12-150
SHIP CAPTAINS
  CA480-500, MA134-80, MA307-230
SHIPBUILDING
  *DC19-601, DC19-636, DE270-200,
  MA169-610, MA265-160, MA293-200,
  MA338-280, MA733-660, ME75-520,
  ME175-80, ME21 2-120, ME460-80,
  ME462-440, ME762-640, ME965-520,
  NY327-880, OH97-80, OH863-280,
  OR72-80, PA726-240, WA84-720*
  WORLD WAR I
  GA885-120
  WORLD WAR II
  GA885-120
SHIPLEY FAMILY
  DE810-690
SHIPPING
  *CA720-485, CA720-675, CA720-960,
  CA798-720, CT36-80, CT512-550,
  CT751-640, CT772-720, DE270-200,
  HI400-480, LA600-465, MA108-750,
  MA109-120, MA338-280, MA338-840,
  MA733-210, MA837-720, MA937-280,
  MD76-810, ME75-520, ME200-120,
  ME453-40, ME462-440, ME950-480,
  MI36-400, MI200-240, MI865-80,
  MN261-810, NH134-540, NH784-630,
  NJ786-40, NY592-460, NY594-060,
  NY594-240, OH171-650, OH505-520,
  OH863-280, PA305-210, PA725-615,
  RI875-880, WI266-430, WI456-550,
  WI530-520*
  GREAT LAKES
  MI230-180
  LAKE MICHIGAN
  IN517-520
SHIPS
  See also Boats; Schooners; Steamboats and
  steamships, *AK450-320, CA368-820,
  CA454-520, CA480-500, CA798-720,
  CT463-520, CT512-120, CT512-800,
  CT772-720, DC1-680, DC6-800,
  DC14-720, DC14-770, DC14-780,
  DC19-621, DC19-636, DE540-790,
  KS948-880, LA600-505, MA109-120,
  MA109-850, MA165-520, MA169-610,
  MA180-120, MA285-160, MA307-230,
  MA338-840, MA584-550, MA584-600,
  MA733-660, MA981-890, MD57-830,
  MD76-810, MD532-880, MD836-120,
  ME162-120, ME175-80, ME212-120,
  ME231-120, ME453-40, ME762-640,
  MI518-50, MN541-822, MO607-520,
  NH254-640, NH784-720, NJ786-40,
  NY327-880, NY594-240, NY654-600,
  NY772-720, OH97-80, OH863-280,
  OR880-760, PA725-120, PA725-615,
  PA726-240, RI560-570, RI700-70,
  WA427-560, WA678-650, WA820-770,
  WA820-828, WI814-510*
  ENGINES
  WA904-890
  GREAT LAKES
  MI230-180, MN261-40
  MERCHANT MARINE
  MD57-810
  NAVY
  *MA169-610, MD57-800, MD57-810,
  MD57-830*
  NEW YORK
  MD76-810
  PASSENGERS
  MD76-60, NY594-390
  SAILING
  DC19-636
SHIPS' LOGS
  PA725-615

SHIPWRECKS
  *MA278-200, MA425-520, NJ276-510,
  NY952-720*
SHOEMAKERS
  MA837-720
SHOES
  MANUFACTURING
  MA486-470, NH720-560
  WOODEN
  WI426-120
SHOLES, CRISTOPHER LATHAM
  WI456-560
SHORTER JUNIOR COLLEGE
  DC1-160
SHORTHAND
  PA725-45
SHOVELS
  MANUFACTURING
  MA615-710
SHRINES
  KY760-720
SHULER, ELLIS
  TX252-790
SIAM
  MISSIONARIES
  OH665-590
SIBLEY, GEORGE CHAMPLAIN
  MO770-480
SIDNEY, MARGARET
  MA217-520
SIERRA FOREST RESERVE
  CA274-720
SIGMA PHI (FRATERNITY)
  IL723-80
**SIGNAL CORPS ASSOCIATION, U.S.
  VETERANS**
  NJ270-800
SIGNAL MOUNTAIN TN
  IL245-322
SIGOURNEY, LYDIA HUNTLEY
  CT316-560, CT512-120
SIKORSKY AIRCRAFT
  CT186-800
SILETZ INDIAN RESERVATION
  OR624-480
SILLERS FAMILY
  MS230-160
SILLERS, FLORENCE WARFIELD
  MS230-160
SILLERS, WALTER, SR.
  MS230-160
SILLIMAN FAMILY
  CT484-550
SILLIMAN, BENJAMIN
  DC19-641
SILVER
  MINING
  CA676-130, CO54-40, NV200-920
SILVER, ABBA HILLEL
  OH181-730
SILVERSMITHS
  PA725-150
SIMMONS SCHOOL OF SOCIAL WORK
  MA109-630
SIMON, ERNEST
  NY717-640
SIMPSON, EDWARD
  CA712-570
SIMPSON, JOHN, FAMILY
  NC900-120
SIMS, CHARLES CARROLL
  SC216-820
SING SING PRISON
  NY588-440
SINGERS
  TN690-110
SINGING
  STYLES OF
  CT505-976
SINGLE MOTHERS
  See Mothers, single
SIPES, FLOYD
  PA540-240
SISKIND, AARON
  AZ800-820
SISTERS OF CHARITY OF ST. JOSEPH
  MD380-160

SISTERS OF DIVINE PROVIDENCE OF ST.
JEAN DE BASSEL, FRANCE
KY532-720
SISTERS OF PROVIDENCE
HOSPITALS
WA820-820
SISTERS OF ST. JOSEPH OF CARONDELET
LOS ANGELES CA
NY481-720
ST. LOUIS
NY481-720
ST. PAUL MN
NY481-720
SISTERS OF THE DIVINE SAVIOR
WI456-735
SISTERS OF THE HOLY CROSS
IL109-130
SISTERS, SERVANTS OF THE
IMMACULATE HEART OF MARY
TX56-720
SITWELL, EDITH
WI456-810
SKIING
CO54-40
SKINNER, JOSEPH ALLEN
MA776-515
SKUBITZ, JOSEPH
KS746-640
SLADE, WILLIAM
NY563-120
SLATER FUND
GA90-700
SLAVE TRADE
NY592-930
SLAVERY
See also Blacks, AL580-530, AR360-40,
GA245-110, KY288-440, LA26-480,
LA62-490, LA62-500, LA600-310,
LA600-755, LA600-920, NJ280-270,
NJ982-280, NY577-330, NY592-460,
NY592-930, NY757-400, OH147-520,
OH481-530, PA725-45, PA860-710,
SC860-600, TX14-720, TX483-820,
VA50-65, VI700-360
SLICER, HENRY
MD76-790
SLOVAKIA
FOLK MUSIC
NY166-80
SLUMS
NY594-20
SMITH COLLEGE
COUNCIL OF INDUSTRIAL STUDIES
MA804-130
SMITH FAMILY
NY536-520, NY842-730, VT720-720
SMITH, ALANSON WESLEY
WA616-950
SMITH, ALICE RAVENEL HUGER
SC144-90
SMITH, DAVID EUGENE
NY216-720
SMITH, DON
CA620-760
SMITH, EUGENE ALLEN
AL840-280
SMITH, H. H.
AL840-280
SMITH, HELEN FAIRCHILD
NY53-880
SMITH, HENRY CLAY
TX231-120
SMITH, J. LAWRENCE
NY842-730
SMITH, JESSIE WILLCOX
DE810-150
SMITH, JOSEPH
UT912-120
SMITH, LILLIAN
FL220-800
SMITH, LOGAN PEARSALL
OH399-440
SMITH, MELANCTON
WI202-560
SMITH, MYRON BEMENT
DC19-327

SMITH, PERSIFER F.
PA945-880
SMITH, ROY L.
KS962-800
SMITH, SAM, SHOE COMPANY
NH720-560
SMITH, THADDEUS
MI518-455
SMITH, W. GENE
AZ800-820
SMITH, WILLIAM (TANGIER)
NY536-520
SMITHSONIAN INSTITUTION
IL169-286
SMOKEY BEAR
VA50-240
SMOKING
NY594-680
SMOOT, REED
UT684-80
SMUGGLING
CA421-400
SNAKE RIVER
FISHING
WA144-210
FISHING INDUSTRY
WA144-210
SNELL, BERTRAND H.
NY723-720
SNETHEN, NICHOLAS
DC23-500
SNOHOMISH INDIANS
WA855-80
SNYDER, AGNES
DC1-860
SNYDER, GARY
OH399-440
SNYDER, SIMON
MT100-200
SNYDER, WILLIAM G.
NY851-720
SOCIAL ACTION
VT176-810
SOCIAL ANTHROPOLOGY, INSTITUTE
FOR
DC19-520
SOCIAL CONDITIONS
IL169-325, MA169-210
SOCIAL CREDIT
CT428-865
SOCIAL ETHICS
MA169-210
SOCIAL ISSUES
OH181-310
SOCIAL LIFE
IN56-350, IN77-200, IN363-360,
NC260-170, NM494-570
SOCIAL REFORM
CA886-240, IL170-910, IN209-880,
IN583-560, MA169-210, MN541-902,
NY589-720, VT296-690, WI456-495
SOCIAL REFORMERS
KY496-785
SOCIAL SCIENCE
NY612-690, NY726-850
SOCIAL SECURITY
NY588-940
SOCIAL STUDIES
IN209-360, KY288-425
SOCIAL WELFARE
See also Welfare, DC3-210, GA245-110,
IL94-800, IL170-910, IL296-720,
IL806-695, IN77-200, IN363-342,
MA169-860, MA196-120, MD76-800,
MD266-80, NY10-160, NY587-940,
NY591-40, NY594-20, NY602-570,
NY612-690, OH171-20, OH203-170,
PA725-60, PA726-225, SC144-105,
WA144-210, WA954-40
AGENCIES
DC1-560, DC2-200, DC9-450,
IL170-780, IN209-140, MA109-595,
MA109-830, MN541-902, NY593-132,
PA726-37, PA726-630, VA430-280
BLACKS
MA931-400

CHILDREN
MA109-830, NJ568-670
JEWS
CA86-385
MIDDLE EAST
NY318-260
MILITARY PERSONNEL
MA931-400
ORGANIZATIONS
DC3-210, KY886-50, MA931-400,
MA947-880, ME460-440, MI824-320,
MN391-310, ND876-80, NE800-480,
NY895-240
ROMAN CATHOLIC CHURCH
NJ798-720
RUSSIA
CA86-385
SISTERS OF PROVIDENCE
WA820-820
UKRAINE
CA86-385
WORLD WAR I
NJ178-115, NY595-660
WORLD WAR II
NY595-660
SOCIAL WORK
MA109-630, MN541-902, NY592-30
EDUCATION
MN541-902
SOCIAL WORKERS
NY134-85
SOCIALISM
CT505-960, DC12-300, IL170-884,
IN363-360, IN825-200, MA871-90,
MO810-800, NC260-170, NY587-820,
NY592-800, NY593-120, NY595-700,
PA860-710, WA300-172, WI346-720,
WI456-550, WI456-740
SOCIALIST PARTY
NC260-170, WI456-550
SOCIETY FOR ECONOMIC BOTANY
NY592-320
SOCIETY FOR ESTABLISHING USEFUL
MANUFACTURES
NJ646-660
SOCIETY FOR THE ADVANCEMENT OF
TRUTH IN ART
IL169-130
SOCIETY FOR THE ANTHROPOLOGY OF
VISUAL COMMUNICATIONS
NM722-30
SOCIETY OF AMERICAN FORESTERS
CA782-240
SOCIETY OF AMERICAN FORESTERS-NEW
YORK SECTION
NY872-720
SOCIETY OF ARCHITECTURAL
HISTORIANS, MISSOURI VALLEY
CHAPTER
MO430-800
SOCIETY OF BRETHREN
MA593-40
SOCIETY OF FRIENDS
See also Quakers, CA966-880, IN572-320,
IN704-200, IN704-240, IN704-360,
NC380-290, NY593-710, PA395-320,
PA860-710
BALTIMORE YEARLY MEETING
PA395-320
CONNECTICUT
NY593-710
DELAWARE
PA860-710
HADDONFIELD WOMEN'S MEETING
NJ280-270
ILLINOIS
PA860-710
MARYLAND
PA860-710
NEW JERSEY
NY593-710, PA860-710
OHIO
PA860-710
ORGANIZATIONS
IN704-200
PHILADELPHIA YEARLY MEETING
PA395-320

PHILADELPHIA YEARLY MEETING,
SCHOOL COMMITTEE
PA950-880
VERMONT
NY593-710
SOCIETY OF INQUIRY
MA593-40
SOCIETY OF JESUS
See also Jesuits
MARYLAND PROVINCE
DC7-650
MISSIONARIES
WA880-280
MISSOURI PROVINCE
DC7-650
SOCIETY OF ST. EDMUND
VT964-720
SOCIETY OF THE ATONEMENT
NY318-260
SOCIETY OF THE CINCINNATI
MA109-120
SOCIO-ECONOMIC DEVELOPMENT
CA421-390
SOCIOLOGISTS
PA726-600
SOCIOLOGY
IL170-884, PA90-500
POLAND
NY593-500
SOD HOUSES
ND375-570
SODBUSTERS
MO810-390
SOIL
AZ700-40, IL45-640, NC656-720
CONSERVATION
DC19-800
EROSION
DC19-800, TN465-760
SURVEYS
NY10-570
SOIL CONSERVATION SERVICE
CA360-720, GA75-800
SOLAR ACTIVITY
CO108-560
SOLAR SYSTEM
AZ250-480
SOLDIER'S AID SOCIETY (WESTFORD MA)
MA931-400
SOLDIERS
See Military personnel
SOLERI, PAOLO
AZ750-45
SOMERS, FREDERICK
AZ800-820
SOMERVILLE, LUCY NUGENT
MS230-160
SONNICHSEN, C. L.
TX326-210
SONORA, MEXICO
AZ475-640
**SONS AND DAUGHTERS OF PIMA
PIONEERS**
AZ600-200
SONS OF TEMPERANCE
IN209-200
SONS OF THE AMERICAN REVOLUTION
OLD SUFFOLK CHAPTER
MA970-890
**SONS OF UNION VETERANS OF THE
CIVIL WAR**
NJ838-530
SONS OF VETERANS
WI346-280
SORORITIES
OH853-800
SOSSNITZ, JOSEPH JUDAH LOB
NY592-760
SOUSA CORREIA, ARTUR DE
DC3-226
SOUTH AFRICA
IL261-566
MISSIONARIES
MN763-50
RELIGIOUS COMMUNITIES
IL84-600

SOUTH AMERICA
See also Central America; Latin America;
and individual countries and regions,
AZ800-803, CA712-570, NY592-30
ARCHAEOLOGY
CA421-610, RI105-320
BAHA'I
IL981-560
ETHNOLOGY
RI105-320
HOSPITALS
PA725-908
INDIANS
CA712-713
MENNONITE BRETHREN
CA274-130
MISSIONARIES
*IN297-600, KY57W-720, MO810-750,
NJ222-333, PA725-908*
MUSIC
NY872-760
ORTHODOX CHURCH
NY870-600
TRADE WITH UNITED STATES
MA338-840
SOUTH CAROLINA
GA105-690
RELIGIOUS COMMUNITIES
NY859-720
SOUTH CAROLINA BAPTIST CONVENTION
SC450-240
SOUTH CAROLINA POETRY SOCIETY
SC144-150
SOUTH CAROLINA, PIEDMONT AREA
NC160-800
SOUTH DAKOTA
MN226-705, MN541-934, WI456-735
CATTLE
CO36-40
DUTCH-AMERICANS
IA855-150
LUMBERING
CO36-40
MINING
CO36-40
RANCHING
CO36-40
SOUTH PACIFIC
See Pacific Ocean, southern
SOUTH PACIFIC COMMISSION
CA782-800
SOUTH PASADENA LIBRARY BOARD
CA850-720
SOUTH UNION SOCIETY OF BELIEVERS
KY96-870
SOUTHCOTT, JOHANNA
TX56-890
**SOUTHEASTERN MASSACHUSETTS
TECHNOLOGICAL INSTITUTE**
MA612-720
SOUTHEASTERN THEATRE CONFERENCE
NC380-800
SOUTHEASTERN US
*AL80-40, GA75-810, GA90-280,
GA405-560, TN465-800, VA145-780,
VA690-910*
ARCHITECTURE
LA600-761
CHURCH OF THE NAZARENE
TN690-850
INDIANS
NC60-640, OK541-240
**SOUTHERN ASSOCIATION OF COLLEGE
WOMEN**
DC1-340
**SOUTHERN ASSOCIATION OF PHYSICAL
EDUCATION FOR WOMEN**
NC380-800
SOUTHERN BAPTIST CHURCH
NC930-840
SOUTHERN CHRISTIAN INSTITUTION
TN690-170
**SOUTHERN CHRISTIAN LEADERSHIP
CONFERENCE**
GA90-490

SOUTHERN PACIFIC COMPANY
RIO GRANDE DIVISION
TX326-800
SOUTHERN UNIVERSITY
AL120-110
SOUTHERN US
*AL840-820, FL820-780, GA90-200,
GA90-360, KY569-720, LA62-500,
MS20-200, NC150-800, NC260-170,
NC590-320, NC610-520, NC680-460,
TN630-510, TN690-780, TN690-880,
TN690-975, TX56-850, VA690-870,
VT464-840, WA880-260*
BAPTIST CHURCH
TN690-740
CIVIL RIGHTS
CA858-790
ECONOMIC HISTORY
LA62-500
EDUCATION
GA90-700, KY496-850
INTELLECTUAL HISTORY
LA62-500
LABOR, UNIONS
GA90-300
LITERATURE
NC260-170
METHODIST CHURCH
GA90-200, MS550-540
POLITICS
GA90-200, LA62-500
RURAL LIFE
GA810-80
WRITERS
TN630-740
SOUTHERN UTE AGENCY
CO252-550
**SOUTHWEST INDIANA HISTORICAL
SOCIETY**
IN209-880
SOUTHWESTERN COLLEGE
KS962-800
SOUTHWESTERN US
*AR950-600, AZ625-630, AZ750-45,
AZ800-30, AZ800-790, AZ800-800,
AZ800-803, AZ800-830, CA601-640,
CA712-726, CA966-860, CO180-120,
CO270-240, NM114-880, NM114-900,
NM668-210, NM684-120, NM722-530,
NM722-730, NM760-900, NM874-440,
OK558-790, TX56-790, TX56-850,
TX590-760*
ARCHAEOLOGY
*AZ800-803, CA712-713, NM722-535,
NM874-440, NY587-180, TX326-770*
ART COLLECTORS
NY587-780
EDUCATION
NM114-525
ETHNOLOGY
AZ800-803
ETHNOMUSICOLOGY
AZ750-32
FOUR CORNERS AREA
NM398-720
INDIANS
AZ800-803, CA421-115, CA421-610
LLANO ESTACADO
TX712-880
MEDICINE
NM114-525
MEXICAN PERIOD
TX280-540, TX777-670, TX777-760
MISSIONARIES
NM114-525
PLANTS
NM114-825
PRESBYTERIAN CHURCH
NM114-525
ROMAN CATHOLIC CHURCH
TX56-720
TECHNOLOGY
TX181-790
SOVIET UNION
See also Russia; and individual republics,
*CA858-320, DC1-560, DC7-540,
DC13-210, DC14-250, DC14-780,*

DC19-310, DC19-320, DC19-327,
DC19-500, MA169-500, MD152-550,
MN541-902, NY588-825, PA725-430
AUTHORS
MA21-770
PERSECUTION OF LITHUANIANS
IL170-53
SPACE
EXPLORATION
CA578-560, DC14-120, DC14-715,
SD684-280
SCIENCE
AL440-800, CO108-560, SD684-280
SPAIN
CA774-720, IL170-351, LA600-760,
MN226-720, TX425-280
BASQUES
NV940-800
CABILDO (LA)
LA600-465
CIVIL WAR
MA871-90
COLONIES
AL580-510, AZ225-40, AZ550-040,
AZ775-790, AZ800-30, AZ800-830,
CA86-630, CA86-780, CA118-720,
CA352-520, CA386-560, CA421-30,
CA421-390, CA421-610, CA421-774,
CA676-110, CA676-130, CA704-560,
CA712-708, CA720-180, CA720-746,
CA720-910, CA724-730, CA728-730,
CA756-320, CA770-120, CA774-720,
CA778-800, CA782-800, CA858-810,
CA934-720, CO252-70, CO252-100,
CO252-550, CO270-240, CT505-960,
DC14-250, FL220-795, FL660-120,
GA895-160, IL170-884, LA62-500,
LA358-800, LA600-465, LA600-505,
LA600-555, LA600-760, MA169-310,
MD76-515, MD703-40, MI40-820,
MI230-165, MO810-510, MO810-730,
MS550-500, NM114-50, NM114-900,
NM722-530, NM722-570, NY592-460,
NY592-800, OK829-520, PR600-800,
PR720-360, RI700-70, TX56-50,
TX56-110, TX56-800, TX56-850,
TX56-860, TX252-150, TX252-730,
TX280-540, TX326-770, TX326-800,
TX397-690, TX425-280, TX483-320,
TX590-760, TX777-160, TX777-670,
TX777-760, TX777-810, TX933-80,
UT912-110, WI346-720
EXPLORATION BY
CA756-320, CO270-240, OR720-590
GOVERNMENT AGENCIES
TX56-110
LAND
FL800-235
LAND GRANTS
CA676-110, CO252-181, OK829-520
LITERATURE
DC12-200, PR600-800
MISSIONARIES
AZ800-830, OH223-720
PIRATES
KS948-880
ROYALTY
MN226-700
SPALDING, CATHERINE
KY569-720
SPALDING, MARTIN JOHN
KY569-720
SPANISH AMERICAN WAR
IL866-355
SPANISH CIVIL WAR
INTERNATIONAL BRIGADE
NY315-30
SPANISH-AMERICAN WAR
IN913-880, KY96-870, MD152-720,
MD380-160, MD532-880, MO200-720,
NY10-160, NY967-880, OH301-690,
OR880-760, WI178-240, WI346-280
CUBA
FL60-720
MEDICINE
OH181-180

MILITARY PERSONNEL
FL60-720
PHILIPPINES
FL60-720
SPANISH-AMERICANS
CA862-810, CO270-240
SPAS
See also Resorts, NY795-320, VA820-80
SPEARS, GEORGE M.
KY304-280
SPEECH
ORGANIZATIONS
CA278-130
SPEED, G. H.
NY439-180
SPEER, ROBERT E.
NJ692-610
SPELEOLOGY
AL440-560
SPELMAN FUND OF NEW YORK
NY612-690
SPENCER, PLATT ROGERS
OH181-400
SPENDER, STEPHEN
NY125-740
SPINDEN, HERBERT J.
RI105-320
SPIRITUALISM
VT296-690
SPITZBERGEN ISLAND
MI464-530
SPLIT ROCK SPRING
NY197-120
SPOKANE COLLEGE
WA904-635
SPOKANE INTERNATIONAL EXPOSITION
(1974)
WA880-590
SPOKANE, PORTLAND AND SEATTLE
RAILWAY
OR720-560
SPORTS
See also Athletics, CA712-630, FL560-40,
IN627-800, MA985-130, MI824-320,
MN541-592, NY595-480, TX590-760
ART
KS746-640
SPRECKLES, ALMA DE BRETTEVILLE
WA360-520
SPRINGFIELD IL
DC6-650
SPRINGS, GEOLOGICAL
See Mineral springs
SPROSS, CHARLES GILBERT
NY726-40
SPRUANCE, RAYMOND AMES
RI560-510
SQUIBB, EDWARD ROBINSON
NJ692-190
SQUIER, EPHRAIM GEORGE
LA600-760
ST. CROIX VALLEY
ME200-120
ST. DENIS, RUTH
NY592-870
ST. EDWARD'S HIGH SCHOOL
TX56-720
ST. IGNATIUS COLLEGE
IL170-78
ST. JAMES CHURCH
PA726-37
ST. JOSEPH MO
IA188-777
ST. JOSEPH ORPHANAGE
IN440-160
ST. JOSEPH, SISTERS OF CHARITY OF
MD380-160
ST. LAWRENCE RIVER
MI230-180, NY150-700
ST. LAWRENCE SEAWAY
NY634-600, OH990-640
ST. LOUIS
SISTERS OF ST. JOSEPH OF
CARONDELET
NY481-720
ST. LOUIS ACADEMY OF SCIENCE
MO810-700

ST. LOUIS COLLEGE
HI350-720
ST. LOUIS MO
IL245-322
ST. LOUIS SCHOOL AND MUSEUM OF
FINE ARTS
MO810-600
ST. LOUIS WORLD'S FAIR (1904)
MO810-600
ST. MARGARET'S EPISCOPAL CHURCH
VT448-520
ST. MARK'S ART PROJECTS
NY593-970
ST. MARK'S EPISCOPAL CHURCH
CT484-550
ST. MARY'S FREE HOSPITAL FOR
CHILDREN
NY687-120
ST. MARY'S HALL
TX777-640
ST. MARY'S PARISH (ALBANY NY)
NY741-720
ST. MARY'S SEMINARY
MD76-748
ST. MARY'S UNIVERSITY
MD76-748
ST. OLAF CHOIR
MN625-710
ST. PAUL FIRE AND MARINE INSURANCE
COMPANY
MN763-690
ST. PAUL MN
ICE CARNIVALS
WI890-320
SISTERS OF ST. JOSEPH OF
CARONDELET
NY481-720
ST. PETERS CHURCH
PA726-37
ST. PHILIP'S COLLEGE
TX777-640
ST. PROCOPIUS ABBEY
IL459-360
ST. PROCOPIUS COLLEGE
IL459-360
ST. SOPHIA RELIGIOUS ASSOCIATION OF
UKRAINIAN CATHOLICS
PA725-430
STAGECOACHES
TRAVEL
NY10-160
STAINED GLASS
See also Glass, DC19-545, PA726-895
STAMFORD (NY) FIRE DEPARTMENT
NY858-720
STAMFORD (NY) SEMINARY AND UNION
FREE SCHOOL
NY858-720
STAMFORD (NY) WOMEN'S CLUB
NY858-720
STANDARD OIL COMPANY
PA705-320
STANDARD OIL OF NEW JERSEY
WY500-800
STANDARD OIL OF NEW JERSEY
COMPANY
KY496-823
STANDING ROCK INDIAN RESERVATION
MO220-120
STANLEY, MARIE
AL580-530
STANNARD, GEORGE J.
VT496-640
STANTON FAMILY
CT772-720
STANTON, ELIZABETH CADY
NY447-400
STAPLETON, JOHN
IN66-520
STAR-SPANGLED BANNER, BY FRANCIS
SCOTT KEY
MD76-240
STARCH
MILLS
MA823-610
STARKEY SEMINARY
NY247-160

STARLING MEDICAL COLLEGE
OH203-680
STARR, ELLEN GATES
MA624-740
STATE BAR OF TEXAS
TX252-780
  COMMITTEE ON REVISION OF
    CORPORATION LAWS
    TX252-780
  COMMITTEE ON REVISION OF THE
    TEXAS NON-PROFIT CORPORATION
    ACT
    TX252-780
STATE BOARD OF PENSIONS (FL)
FL800-245
STATE NORMAL SCHOOL
MA901-120
STATE TEACHERS COLLEGE AT TOWSON
MD950-760
STATE UNIVERSITY OF NEW YORK
NY101-80
STATE UNIVERSITY OF NEW YORK,
  COLLEGE AT PURCHASE,
  PERFORMING ARTS CENTER
  NY732-730
STATE, COUNTY AND MUNICIPAL
  EMPLOYEES, AMERICAN
  FEDERATION OF
  MI230-880
STATE, DEPARTMENT OF (TX)
TX56-800
STATE, SECRETARY OF (FL)
FL800-245
STATESMEN
PA395-320, PA725-615
STATISTICS
CA508-560
STATUE OF LIBERTY
NY594-390
STEADMAN FAMILY
RI910-880
STEAMBOATS AND STEAMSHIPS
  CA720-485, IA188-650, IA661-160,
  IL109-130, IL429-520, IN561-560,
  KY96-870, LA600-755, MD76-810,
  MO210-815, MS20-200, ND375-570,
  NJ276-510, OH171-650, OH486-510,
  PA145-120, SD792-880, WA584-645,
  WI298-810, WI554-600, WI890-320
  LAKE CHAMPLAIN
    VT784-720
  MISSISSIPPI RIVER
    KY96-870, MN975-860
  OHIO RIVER
    KY96-870
STEEL INDUSTRY
  AL120-100, DC1-500, DE270-200,
  KY2A-80, NJ838-750
STEELE, FLETCHER
NY872-720
STEENHUYSEN, E.
NJ838-610
STEICHEN, EDWARD J.
MD57-810
STEIN, GERTRUDE
CT505-890, MD76-80
STEIN, LEO
MD76-80
STEINBECK, JOHN
CA688-720, IN539-90
STEINMETZ, CHARLES PROTEUS
NY804-800
STENNIS, JOHN C.
MS610-520
STEPHEN, ADAM
WV600-280
STEPHENS, A. E. S.
VA580-600
STEPHENS, JAMES
OH399-440
STERILIZATION (HUMAN
  REPRODUCTION)
  MN541-902
STERLING, GEORGE
MO810-690

STEUBEN COUNTY AGRICULTURAL
  SOCIETY
  NY71-715
STEVENS FAMILY (MASSACHUSETTS)
MA513-530
STEVENS, CLARK
VT296-690
STEVENS, GEORGE
CA90-30
STEVENS, NETTIE MARIA
MA931-400
STEVENS, WILMOT E.
OH112-80
STEVENSON, GEORGE
PA160-120
STEVENSON, ROBERT LOUIS
CA680-720, CT505-890
STEWART, GEORGE W.
CA942-940
STEWART, THOMAS S.
PA725-150
STILLAGUAMISH PIONEER ASSOCIATION
WA34-40
STOCKS
  TRADING
    NY593-040
STOCKTON, RICHARD, FAMILY
NJ692-320
STOCKWELL FAMILY
NY59-80
STODDARD, SENECA RAY
NY331-280
STOKES, JOHN
HI350-315
STOKOWSKI, LEOPOLD
PA725-345
STOLLER, EZRA
NY519-200
STONE, DAVID
NC915-320
STONE, L. JOSEPH
OH11-840
STONE, WITMER
PA725-15
STONEY, JAMES M.
TX326-160
STONG, PHILIP DUFFIELD
IA233-160
STORES
  See Mercantile activities
STORK, CHARLES WHARTON
PA725-150
STORMS
  See Meteorology; Weather
STORY OF A LIFE, BY JAMES A.
  BLAISDELL
  CA143-80
STORY OF THE RENO GANG, BY JOHN
  RENO
  IN92-80
STORY, GEORGE
NY928-880
STOVES
  MANUFACTURING
    OH495-510
STOWE TEACHERS COLLEGE
MO810-330
STOWE, HARRIET BEECHER
CT316-560
STRAITS OF MACKINAC
MI590-520
STRAKE, GEORGE W.
TX56-110
STRANGE, JOHN
WI554-480
STRANGEWAY, ANDREW T.
NY111-60
STRASSER, WILLIAM
PA725-345
STRATEGY, MILITARY
  See Military strategy
STRATON, JOHN ROACH
NY752-40
STRAUS AND ASSOCIATES
  (ARCHITECTURAL FIRM)
  IN231-40

STREET RAILWAYS
  See also Transportation, *CA250-120,*
  CA582-600, CT198-80, DC19-636,
  OR424-322, PA960-870
STRICKLAND, WILLIAM
PA725-495
STRIKES
  See also Labor and related terms,
  DC1-400, DC14-870, MO810-800,
  TN630-530
  FLINT SIT-DOWN STRIKE OF 1935
    MI314-840
STRUBE, GUSTAV
MD76-640
STRYKER, ROY
KY496-823
STUART, JESSE
IN825-350
STUB, JACOB AALL OTTESEN
MN763-50
STUDEBAKER BROTHERS
  MANUFACTURING COMPANY
  IN792-160
STUDENT NONVIOLENT COORDINATING
  COMMITTEE
  GA90-490
STUDENT VOLUNTEER MOVEMENT FOR
  FOREIGN MISSIONS
  CT505-900
STUDENTS
  ORGANIZATIONS
    GA90-490
  PROTEST
    CA858-790, MO810-940, OH399-450
STUDENTS FOR A DEMOCRATIC SOCIETY
MI255-530
STUDIO ONE (TELEVISION PROGRAM)
NY591-690
STUKAS, JACK
OH399-420
STURGES ACADEMY
CA700-720
STUYVESANT, PETER
NJ838-610
SUBMARINES
  AL580-510, CT282-720, MA981-890,
  MD57-820, NJ646-660
  CONSTRUCTION
    CT282-720
  DESIGN
    CT282-720
SUDSWORTH, GEORGE B.
OR464-490
SUFFOLK INFERIOR COURT OF COMMON
  PLEAS
  MA109-660
SUFFRAGE
  AL580-530, DE810-330
  WOMEN
    AZ550-040, CA720-910, CT316-560,
    DC1-340, IN363-400, MA169-860,
    MA624-740, MO810-510, MO810-940,
    NY586-440
SUFFRAGISTS
OR720-590
SUGAR
  PLANTATIONS
    HI350-790, LA920-560
  PLANTERS
    HI350-808
SULLIVAN, ANNIE
DC22-500
SULLIVAN, FRANCIS JOHN (FRANK)
NY795-320
SULLIVAN, HARRY STACK
DC23-800
SULLIVAN, JOHN
NY272-120
SULLIVAN, LOUIS H. (ARCHITECTURAL
  FIRM)
  IL169-130
SULLIVAN, LOUIS HENRI
IL169-130
SULPICIAN SEMINARIES
MD76-748
SUMMERALL, CHARLES P.
SC144-150

SUMMIT ATHENEUM (NJ)
NJ812-710
SUMNER, CHARLES
MA891-880
SUNDAY SCHOOL TEACHERS UNION
NY178-120
SUNDAY, HELEN (MRS. WILLIAM A.)
IN990-280
SUNDAY, WILLIAM A. (BILLY)
IN990-280
**SUPREME COMMITTEE FOR THE
    LIBERATION OF LITHUANIA**
IL170-53
SUPREME COURT
   JUDGES
AZ275-520
SUPREME COURT (AZ)
AZ550-040
SUPREME COURT (FL)
FL800-245
SUPREME COURT (IL)
IL866-355
SUPREME COURT (OR)
OR816-590
SUPREME COURT OF LOUISIANA
LA600-775
SURGEON GENERAL, OFFICE OF THE
DC3-320
SURGEONS
   See also Physicians, *PA726-600*
SURGERY
   See also Medicine, *DC1-760, KY496-687,
    OH181-180*
SURRATT, MARY E.
DC14-410, MD255-720
SURVEILLANCE
CA418-200
SURVEYING
*GA90-270, ID880-80, IN66-520,
    KY464-880, LA62-470, MA81-80,
    MA624-560, ME175-80, ME187-730,
    ME200-120, MT100-200, NJ838-610,
    NY87-40, NY269-200, PA325-40,
    PA380-665, VT528-560*
SURVEYOR-GENERAL OF FLORIDA (US)
FL800-235
SURVEYORS
DC19-631
SUSQUEHANNA RIVER VALLEY, CENTRAL
PA500-640
SUSQUEHANNA TURNPIKE
NY254-160
SUTHERLAND, DONALD
CO252-42
SUTLIFF FAMILY
OH878-720
SUTLIFF, PHEBE LORD MARVIN
OH878-720
SUTRO, ADOLPH
CA720-910
SWADOS, HARVEY
MA21-770
SWAMPS
NJ178-110
SWANN, WILLIAM F. G.
PA725-495
SWEDEN
PA735-825
   IMMIGRATION AND EMIGRATION
IL801-20, MN541-64
SWEDENBORG, EMANUEL
PA130-50
SWEDENBORGIAN CHURCH
   See New Jerusalem, Church of the
**SWEDISH BAPTIST GENERAL
    CONFERENCE OF AMERICA**
MN763-80
SWEDISH-AMERICANS
IL801-20, ME437-120, MN541-64
   CLERGY
IL801-20
SWEENEY, JOHN D.
CA620-760
SWENSSON, CARL AARON
KS555-80
SWETLAND FAMILY
NY708-440

SWETNAM, GEORGE A.
PA425-360
**SWIFT FLOWS THE RIVER, BY NARD
    JONES**
OR848-160
SWINNERTON, HENRY ULYATE
NY187-120
SWITZERLAND
OH223-710
   ANABAPTISTS
OH92-520
   MENNONITES
OH92-520
   MISSIONARIES
OH223-720
**SWORDS AND PLOWSHARES, BY
    MAXWELL DAVENPORT TAYLOR**
DC14-410
SYKES, COLUMBUS
GA765-440
SYLVAN HEIGHTS HOME FOR GIRLS
PA380-700
SYLVANIA ELECTRONIC PRODUCTS
PA295-130
SYMONDS, ROBERT WEMYSS
DE900-320
SYNAGOGUE AHAVAI SHOLOM
OR720-400
SYNAGOGUES
   See also Jews, *CA421-250, DC10-500,
    LA600-755, NY595-670*
SYRIA
MA169-370, PA735-825
**SYSTEM OF ORNAMENT, BY LOUIS
    HENRI SULLIVAN**
IL169-130
SZIGETI, JOSEPH
IL916-820
SZOLD, BENJAMIN
MD76-300
SZOLD, HENRIETTA
MD76-300, NY589-900
SZOLD, MACHON
NY589-900

T

TABOR COLLEGE
NE288-160
TABOR GRAND HOTEL
CO640-480
TAFT, WILLIAM HOWARD
MD76-30
TAINTER, CHARLES SUMNER
DC19-606
TAIWAN
   See also China
   MISSIONARIES
IL169-677, MN763-50
   RELIGIOUS COMMUNITIES
IL866-320
TALBOT, EMILY F.
MA961-870
TALBOT, ISRAEL T.
MA961-870
**TALLMADGE AND WATSON
    (ARCHITECTURAL FIRM)**
IL169-130
TALLY, MARY QUINN
IA188-777
TALMUD
   See also Jews, *MA154-310, NY592-760*
TAMIRIS, HELEN
NY592-870
TANDLER, RICHARD
NY978-880
TANEY, ROGER BROOKE
PA160-160
TANKS (MILITARY)
KY272-635
TANNAHILL, ROBERT H.
MI230-148
TARBELL, IDA M.
PA555-40, PA870-160

TARIFFS
   TEXTILE INDUSTRY
MA606-530
TARKINGTON, BOOTH
IN363-400
TAU ALPHA KAPPA SOCIETY
NY178-120
TAVERNS
   See also Hotels, *CT863-280, MA937-280,
    NJ982-280, NY214-160, NY263-210,
    PA935-690*
TAXONOMISTS
OR464-490
TAYLOR COUNTY BAPTIST ASSOCIATION
KY126-120
TAYLOR, BAYARD
PA440-80
TAYLOR, FRANCIS HENRY
PA726-255
TAYLOR, KENNETH
IL976-890
TAYLOR, MAXWELL DAVENPORT
DC14-410
TAYLOR, NATHANIEL WILLIAM
CT519-560
TAYLOR, ROY ARTHUR
NC60-810
TAYLOR, THOS
DC3-760
TAYLOR, VINCENT
NC090-080
TAYLOR, WALTER HERRON
VA580-570
TEACHERS
*AR890-30, IN917-880, KY514-120,
    LA600-20, MA823-610, MI230-880,
    MO810-800, MO902-520, PA965-490,
    SD684-480, WA880-753, WV435-520*
   EDUCATION
WA144-210
   WOMEN
MA92-90, VT296-690
TEACHERS, AMERICAN FEDERATION OF
MI230-880
TEACHING
   See Education
TECHNOLOGY
*CA421-770, CA578-130, CA578-560,
    CT505-975, DC14-140, DC19-542,
    DC19-641, DE540-790, IA33-370,
    IL841-520, IN363-360, IN583-560,
    IN935-650, MA169-650, MI40-784,
    MI40-796, MI40-820, MI214-260,
    MI230-165, MI230-740, MI255-530,
    MI355-270, MI550-530, MI605-520,
    MI665-120, MO760-800, OH171-110,
    OH171-650, OH181-110, OH181-130,
    OH181-180, OH181-880, OH203-600,
    OH301-690, OH436-880, OH505-520,
    OH588-520, OH925-600, OH968-600,
    OH990-510, PA90-320, PA725-495,
    SD648-710, TX483-560*
   AGRICULTURE
CA862-630, NV450-120
   ETHICS
NY125-740
   GAS INDUSTRY
VA50-30
   MINING
PA960-870
   NAVAL
MD57-800, RI560-510
   OIL INDUSTRY
DC1-580
   SOUTHWESTERN US
TX181-790
   TEXTILE INDUSTRY
MA606-530
TECUMSEH
OH982-290
TECUMSEH (SHIP)
DC19-621
TEE-VAN, JOHN
NY593-130
TEETERS, NEGLEY
PA726-600

TELECOMMUNICATIONS
 TX742-690
TELEGRAPHY
 CA418-200, CA798-720, DC19-586,
 NJ270-800, NJ548-720, OR720-450
TELEKI, SAMUEL
 MI255-530
TELEPHONE
 KS10-520, NM114-760, NY178-120,
 NY967-880, WA153-125
TELEPHONE CO-OPERATIVE
 NY178-120
TELESCOPES
 DC14-750
TELEVISION
 CA114-880, CA414-490, CA418-200,
 CA421-015, CA421-360, CA421-400,
 CA421-510, CA421-770, CA421-830,
 CA676-740, CA712-708, CA756-320,
 CA774-800, CA778-800, CA858-810,
 CO252-100, DC2-600, ID480-810,
 MA108-240, NY439-360, PA726-615,
 RI700-680, WI346-900
 ADVERTISING
  GA90-130
 DRAMA
  DC16-680
 MUSIC
  CA421-750, DC16-680
 NEWS
  DC16-680, NY134-50, TN690-980
 PROGRAMS
  CA278-130, CA318-640, CA318-700,
  CA421-760, CT428-865, DC12-450,
  DC16-680, MA109-440, ME50-70,
  NY591-690, NY752-760, WI202-560
 PUBLIC
  DC16-680
 SCRIPTS
  CA436-640, WY500-800
TEMPERANCE
 DE810-330, IL261-545, IN77-200,
 MI40-784, MI390-720, OH665-580,
 PA725-45, PA860-710, VT296-690
 ORGANIZATIONS
  CT477-570, IL261-545, IN209-200,
  MI518-445, MN14-560, NE112-760,
  NY148B-88, NY178-120, NY598-560,
  NY720-640, NY928-880, OH203-600,
  OH733-690
TEMPLE FAMILY
 CA414-500
TEMPLE, HENRY WILLSON
 PA920-890
TENNESSEE
 LA600-20, NC680-460
 CHURCH OF THE NAZARENE
  MO430-120
 GOVERNMENT AGENCIES, LOCAL
  DC14-600
TENNESSEE RIVER VALLEY
 TN465-760
TENNESSEE-TOMBIGBEE WATERWAY
 DEVELOPMENT AUTHORITY
 MS300-550
TENNESSEE, EASTERN
 UNITED METHODIST CHURCH
  VA195-200
TENNESSEE, WESTERN
 KY564-520
TENNIS
 RI560-360
TENNYSON, ALFRED
 KS527-790
TERRY, DAVID D., JR.
 AR510-810
TESTING
 EDUCATION
  IA466-40, NJ692-210
TETON DAM
 FLOODS
  ID680-690
TEUSCHER, GEORGE W.
 IL170-429

TEXAS
 CA712-743, NY288-840
 CHURCH OF THE NAZARENE
  MO430-120
 OIL INDUSTRY
  DC1-580
TEXAS (OUTDOOR DRAMA)
 NC150-790
TEXAS AGRICULTURAL EXPERIMENT
 STATION
 TX181-790
TEXAS AGRICULTURAL EXTENSION
 SERVICE
 TX181-790
TEXAS COMPANY
 NY964-322
TEXAS COUNCIL OF NEGRO
 ORGANIZATIONS
 TX252-80
TEXAS ENGINEERING EXPERIMENT
 STATION
 TX181-790
TEXAS LEGISLATIVE COUNCIL
 TX252-780
 STATUTORY REVISION STUDY
  COMMITTEE
  TX252-780
TEXAS MILITARY INSTITUTE
 TX777-640
TEXAS STATE BAR
 TX252-780
TEXAS STATE COLORED TEACHERS
 ASSOCIATION
 TX252-80
TEXAS-MEXICAN WAR OF 1836
 TX777-810
TEXTILE INDUSTRY
 AL120-100, DC19-555, DC19-581,
 DC19-591, DE270-200, MA108-750,
 MA207-120, MA478-800, MA606-530,
 MA776-515, MA823-610, MA837-720,
 MO490-880, NH600-530, NH720-560,
 NY899-600, OH505-520
 ENGINEERING
  MA606-530
 LABOR
  MA606-530
 LABOR UNIONS
  MA21-800
 ORGANIZATIONS
  MA606-530
 TARIFFS
  MA606-530
 TECHNOLOGY
  MA606-530
TEXTILE WORKERS OF AMERICA, UNITED
 GA90-300
TEXTILES
 DC19-581, NY595-670
 MACHINERY
  MA606-530
 MILLS
  MA606-530, MA823-610, ME112-80,
  MO490-880
 TRADE
  MA606-530
THAILAND
 MISSIONARIES
  IL169-677
THATCHER, GEORGE
 ME750-160
THATCHER, HOWARD
 MD76-640
THATCHER, MAURICE H.
 DC19-130
THAYER, ABBOTT H.
 DC19-330
THE JOURNAL OF A TOUR TO THE
 HEBRIDES, BY JAMES BOSWELL
 CT505-977
THE MAD BOOTHS OF MARYLAND, BY
 STANLEY P. KIMMEL
 FL820-810
THE OUTSIDER (PERIODICAL)
 IL261-570
THE PERMIAN BASIN, BY MYRES
 TX625-640

THEATER
 See also Drama, *CA278-130, CA421-620,*
 CA862-730, CA862-810, CT316-560,
 CT505-975, DC6-600, DC14-850,
 GA75-810, IL45-640, IL261-570,
 IN66-390, IN363-400, KS527-790,
 KY496-823, LA62-500, LA885-690,
 MA108-240, MA108-940, MA169-860,
 MI40-808, MN763-800, MS550-460,
 NC380-800, NY591-850, NY592-880,
 NY593-485, NY593-970, NY595-700,
 OH181-270, OH203-670, OH399-440,
 PA725-540, PA726-600, SC144-90,
 TX56-890, VA205-290, WA820-774,
 WA820-780, WI346-900
 ARCHITECTURE
  IL45-640, IN627-760
 BLACKS
  GA735-540
 DESIGN
  NY591-850, OH203-670, VA205-290
 EUROPE
  OH203-670
 FRANCE
  OH203-670
 GREAT BRITAIN
  CT505-975, DC6-600, NY593-485,
  OH203-670
 ITALY
  OH203-670
 LIGHTING
  VA205-290
 MUSICAL
  NY592-878
 RECORDINGS
  CT505-976
 REPERTOIRE COMPANIES
  IA688-520
 VAUDEVILLE
  GA735-540
 YIDDISH CULTURE
  NY591-850, NY592-760
THEATER FOR THE FORGOTTEN
 NY588-440
THEATERS
 MA772-120
THEATRE GENESIS
 NY593-970
THEFT
 ART
  NY590-360
 HORSES
  IL429-520, IN154-880, IN242-250
THEOLOGIANS
 CT316-330, KY886-50
 LUTHERAN CHURCH
  MO810-190
THEOLOGY
 DC3-210, IN627-720, IN627-800,
 MA109-595, MI230-800, NC150-860,
 NY637-720, PA470-480
 GERMANY
  IA244-30
THIRD GREAT WESTERN TURNPIKE
 NY164-570
THOBURN, JAMES MATTHEW
 PA555-40
THOMAS G. HAWKES & COMPANY
 NY214-140
THOMAS, CAROLYN B. MCCLESTER
 NY134-85
THOMAS, DYLAN
 NY24-735
THOMAS, JOHN CHARLES
 MD76-640
THOMAS, RICHARD
 HI350-311
THOMAS, VINCENT
 CA414-150
THOMASON, CAROLINE WASSON
 OR424-880
THOMPSON, BRADBURY
 KS878-880
THOMPSON, FRANCIS
 MA199-90
THOMPSON, RICHARD WIGGINTON
 IN231-470

THOMSON, ELIHU
DC19-586, PA725-495
THOMSON, FRANK
PA725-375
THOMSON, JAMES H.
NY111-80
THOMSON, VIRGIL
CT505-910
THOREAU, HENRY DAVID
MA217-130, MA894-880, MN541-600,
OH181-130, VT432-530
THORNTON, WILLIAM
DC1-480
THOUSAND ISLANDS
NY194-760
THREATENED AND ENDANGERED
  SPECIES SURVEY OF NEW MEXICO
  AND ARIZONA
NM114-825
THURMOND, STROM
SC185-120
THYROID GLANDS
OH181-180
TIBET
DC12-150, NJ578-530
TILE
  MANUFACTURING
IN242-250
TILLMAN, BENJAMIN RYAN
SC185-120
TIMBERVILLE ORPHAN'S HOME
VA115-80
TIPTON, FRENCH
KY680-190
TIRES
  See also Rubber, *OH11-240, OH11-290*
  DESIGN
NH600-530
TISSUE CULTIVATION
DC7-660
TOAST OF THE TOWN (TELEVISION
  PROGRAM)
NY591-690
TOBACCO
CT275-800, NC390-200, NY592-680,
NY594-680, VA690-810
  AGRICULTURE
NC390-200
  MANUFACTURING
NC390-200
  MERCHANTS
NY594-680
TOBOLOWSKY, HERMINE
TX280-540
TOBY TYLER, BY JAMES OTIS KALER
ME825-730
TOCH, ERNST
CA421-750
TOKLAS, ALICE B.
CT512-120
TOKYO, JAPAN
  EARTHQUAKES
IN297-600
TOLAN, BRENTWOOD J.
IN231-40
TOLKIEN, JOHN RONALD REUEL
IL976-900
TOMASH, ERWIN
CA132-160
TOMBSTONES
NJ92-80, PA270-200, PA370-310
  CARVING
DC19-560
  NEW ENGLAND
DC19-560
TONGA ISLANDS
HI450-80
TOPOGRAPHY
CA278-120, CA488-720, CA504-560,
CA524-140, CA578-675, CA692-130,
CA712-743, CA966-860, CT505-970,
GA75-800, IL261-565, IL424-480,
IL624-370, KY496-518, MD755-560,
MN541-934, NY101-90, OR224-810,
SD684-280, TX968-520, WI346-850
  OKLAHOMA
TX968-520

WORLD WAR I
MN321-690
TOPOLOBAMPO, MEXICO
CA274-120
TOPP, ROBERTSON
TN630-740
TORELLO, ANTON
PA725-345
TORNADOS
  See also Meteorology; Weather,
OH982-290
TORREY BOTANICAL CLUB
NY592-320
TORREY, JOHN
NY592-320
TORREY, REUBEN ARCHER
IL170-234
TORRY, JASON
PA960-910
TOURISM
AK500-20, AZ350-290, DC9-450,
MA338-280, VT176-810
TOURISTS
OR624-480
TOWNSEND, CHARLES H.
NY593-130
TOWNSEND, JAMES H.
PA870-160
TOWNSEND, JOHN WILSON
KY680-190
TOWSON STATE COLLEGE
MD950-760
TOYS
DE900-320
TRACTION COMPANIES
  See also Transportation, *WA904-770*
TRADE
  See also Commerce, *NJ756-240,*
NY592-460, RI700-630, TN630-740
  AFRICA AND UNITED STATES
MA733-660
  AFRICA, WESTERN, AND UNITED
  STATES
MA733-210
  ASIA AND UNITED STATES
MA338-840
  ASIA, EASTERN, AND UNITED STATES
MA733-660
  CHINA AND UNITED STATES
CT772-720, MA554-530, MA733-210,
PA725-615
  EUROPE AND UNITED STATES
MA338-840
  FOREIGN
MA108-750, MN541-854
  GREAT BRITAIN
RI700-630
  GREAT BRITAIN AND UNITED STATES
DE810-690, MA931-400
  INDIA AND UNITED STATES
MA92-70, MA108-750, MA109-120,
MA733-210, MA733-660, PA725-75,
PA725-720, RI700-70
  INDIANS
IN363-360
  PACIFIC ISLANDS AND UNITED STATES
MA733-660
  SOUTH AMERICA AND UNITED STATES
MA338-840
  TEXTILES
MA606-530
  WEST INDIES AND UNITED STATES
MA733-210
TRADERS
IN792-560, MI230-165, MO810-390
TRAILS
IA33-350, KS569-600
TRANS WORLD AIRWAYS
WY500-800
TRANSFORMERS (ELECTRICAL)
DC19-586
TRANSPORTATION
  See also specific forms of transportation,
CA582-600, CA676-130, CA858-810,
CA862-810, CO476-540, CT234-250,
DC1-280, DC1-500, DC3-550, DC9-450,
DC14-370, DC14-640, DC19-636,

DE270-200, IA188-360, IA188-650,
IL202-550, IN363-342, MA425-520,
MD114-330, MD304-80, MI40-796,
MI214-150, MI314-265, MO810-940,
NH134-540, NJ444-240, NJ918-520,
NM494-570, NY10-570, NY289-240,
NY331-120, NY383-560, NY590-960,
NY591-350, NY593-900, PA920-870,
PA960-870, TX252-730, UT684-80,
VT176-810, WA60-860, WA904-770
  AIR
NM114-35
  ARMY
VA255-800
  EUROPE
NY591-350
  PUBLIC
CA582-600
  RIVERS
CA676-740, KY2A-80, WI298-810
TRAPIER, PAUL
SC144-710
TRAPPERS
CA954-720, ID400-720, MO810-390
TRAVEL
CA676-130, CA712-630, GA870-730,
IN583-560, IN825-850, MA108-940,
MA169-590, MA624-560, MI518-455,
MT530-500, NH832-720, NY586-720,
NY597-520, PA90-500, PA325-280,
PA986-960, SC144-730, TN75-50,
WI714-880, WY560-280
  CALIFORNIA
WA880-790
  CANALS
NY10-160
  EUROPE
IL296-720
  LATIN AMERICA
LA600-760
  MEDITERRANEAN
CT512-120
  STAGECOACHES
NY10-160
  WESTERN US
CA86-780, WA880-790
TRAVELER'S AID
MN541-902
TRAVELERS
CA210-160
TREASURER (OR)
OR816-590
TREASURY (PR)
PR720-360
TREASURY, DEPARTMENT OF (TX)
TX56-800
TREATIES
  PEACE
DC3-226
TREES
CA86-850, DC1-460, DC14-180,
DE900-330, VA50-240
  AS MEMORIALS
WA97-320
  NURSERIES
NE240-560
TRIANGLE UNIVERSITIES COMPUTATION
  CENTER
NC260-150
TRINITY CHURCH IN THE CITY OF
  BOSTON
MA109-460
TRINITY COLLEGE
NC260-150
TRIPARTITE COMMITTEE
NY589-460
TROLLEYS
NY383-560
TROPIC REGIONS
  EXPLORATION
MO810-490
TROUP, ROBERT
NY87-900
TRUAX, RHODA
PA725-900
TRUCKS
DC1-680

TRUMAN, HARRY S.
MA871-85, MO400-320, MS140-560
TRUMAN, JAMES C.
CA601-640
TRUMBAUER, HORACE
PA725-150
TRUMBULL FAMILY
CT772-720
TRUMBULL, JAMES HAMMOND
CT316-770
TRUMBULL, JOHN
CT316-880
TRUSCOTT, LUCIAN K.
VA430-280
TRUTH, SOJOURNER
NY574-730
TRYON, DWIGHT W.
DC19-330
TUBERCULOSIS
IN792-720
TUBMAN, HARRIET
NY51-730
TUCKER FAMILY
MA606-720
TUESDAY CLUB
ND876-80
TUFTS, COTTON
MA947-880
TULALIP INDIAN AGENCY
WA60-510
TULANE SCHOOL OF ARCHITECTURE
LA600-761
TUNNELS
CONSTRUCTION
DC19-601
TURKEY
FOLK MUSIC
NY166-80
MASSACRE OF ARMENIANS
DC1-775, MA84-50
TURNER THEOLOGICAL SEMINARY
DC1-160
TURNER, JOHN CLYDE
NC840-720
TURNER, SCOTT
MI464-530
TURNPIKES
CT268-720, PA960-910
TURPENTINE
GA940-280
TURRILL, JOEL
HI350-315
TUTTLE, DANIEL SYLVESTER
MO810-590
TUTTLE, JOSEPH FARRAND
IN154-880
TWAIN, MARK
See Samuel Langhorne Clemens
**TWENTIETH CENTURY-FOX FILM
CORPORATION**
CA421-763
TYLER, ERNEST
OK42-560
TYLER, J. HOGE
VA90-840
TYNG, GEORGE
TX923-840
TYPEFACES
NY705-560
TYPEWRITERS
NY705-560, WI456-560
TYPOGRAPHICAL UNION
GA90-300
TYPOGRAPHY
DC19-565

U

U.S. FOREST SERVICE
NC60-810
U.S.S. OMAHA (SHIP)
CA712-570
U.S.S.R.
See Russia; Soviet Union; and individual
republics

UKRAINE
NY588-825, PA725-430
IMMIGRATION AND EMIGRATION
MI230-780
SOCIAL WELFARE
CA86-385
UKRAINIAN-AMERICANS
MI230-780, OH181-780, PA725-430
UMATILLA INDIAN AGENCY
OR688-810
UNDERTAKERS
NM760-720, NY923-880
UNICEF
See United Nations Children's Fund
UNION COLONY
CO498-270
UNION INSTITUTE
NC260-150
UNION PACIFIC COAL COMPANY
WY365-710
UNION PACIFIC RAILROAD
MA615-710, NE624-800
UNION SQUARE THEATRE
NY593-485
UNIONS
See Labor, unions; Labor, organizations
UNITARIAN CHURCH
IL170-195, MA169-230
CLERGY
IL170-195
MIDWESTERN US
IL170-195
**UNITARIAN UNIVERSALIST SERVICE
COMMITTEE**
MA169-230
UNITARIAN UNIVERSALISTS
CLERGY
MA109-750
UNITED AUTO WORKERS
See United Automobile, Aerospace and
Agricultural Implement Workers of
America
**UNITED AUTOMOBILE, AEROSPACE AND
AGRICULTURAL IMPLEMENT
WORKERS OF AMERICA**
MI230-880
UNITED BRETHREN CHURCH
IA688-360, IN352-320
VIRGINIA CONFERENCE
VA880-720
UNITED BRETHREN IN CHRIST
WI733-333
CLERGY
IN352-800
MISSIONARIES
IN352-800
**UNITED CHRISTIAN MISSIONARY
SOCIETY**
TN690-170
UNITED CHURCH OF CHRIST
See also Congregational church; Evangelical
and Reformed church, CA86-630,
CT316-105, MO810-270, NC310-200,
NE288-160, NE624-240, PA470-800
CLERGY
PA470-800
KANSAS-OKLAHOMA CONFERENCE
KS878-880
MARYLAND
PA470-800
MISSIONARIES
CT316-105
NORTH CAROLINA
PA470-800
NORTHERN CALIFORNIA CONFERENCE
CA86-630
OKLAHOMA
KS878-880
VIRGINIA
NC310-200, PA470-800
WISCONSIN CONFERENCE
WI346-720
**UNITED DAUGHTERS OF THE
CONFEDERACY**
WV550-280
UNITED EVANGELICAL CHURCH
NJ464-666

UNITED FARM WORKERS
MI230-880
**UNITED FARM WORKERS ORGANIZING
COMMITTEE**
CA86-120
UNITED FUND (MANCHESTER NH)
NH600-530
UNITED KINGDOM
See Great Britain; Ireland, Northern
**UNITED LUTHERAN CHURCH IN
AMERICA**
IL170-91
**UNITED LUTHERAN CHURCH,
TEXAS-LOUISIANA SYNOD**
TX56-490
UNITED METHODIST CHURCH
See also Methodist church and related
denominations, CA86-630, CA143-720,
CO252-360, IN275-150, LA885-120,
PA185-160, SC144-70, SC846-890,
SD522-160, WV200-880
(SOUTH) ALABAMA-WEST FLORIDA
CONFERENCE
AL620-320
ARIZONA
CA143-720
BALTIMORE CONFERENCE
MD76-790
BOARD OF EVANGELISM
TN690-885
CALIFORNIA-NEVADA CONFERENCE
CA86-630
CENTRAL KANSAS CONFERENCE,
BOARD OF MISSIONS
KS962-800
CLERGY
AL620-320, IA688-360, IL94-800,
IN275-150, KS962-800, MN541-777,
NJ464-666, NJ658-840
HOLSTON ANNUAL CONFERENCE
VA195-200
LOUISIANA CONFERENCE
LA885-120
MISSIONARIES
KS962-800, OK592-780
NEVADA
CA86-630
ORGANIZATIONS
IL94-800, OK592-780
SOUTHERN ILLINOIS CONFERENCE
IL444-720
TENNESSEE, EASTERN
VA195-200
WASHINGTON CONFERENCE
MD76-790
WEST VIRGINIA ANNUAL CONFERENCE
WV200-880
UNITED METHODIST CHURCH OF IOWA
IA688-360
UNITED MINE WORKERS
DC3-210
UNITED NATIONS
SD450-150
CONGO
NY595-20
UNITED NATIONS CHILDREN'S FUND
NY595-20, NY595-180
**UNITED NATIONS DEVELOPMENT
PROGRAM**
NY595-20
UNITED NATIONS EMERGENCY FORCE
NY595-20
**UNITED NATIONS PREPARATORY
COMMISSION**
NY595-20
**UNITED NATIONS RELIEF AND
REHABILITATION ADMINISTRATION**
NY588-850, NY595-20
**UNITED PRESBYTERIAN CHURCH IN THE
UNITED STATES OF AMERICA**
INDIANA SYNOD
IN319-330
UNITED SERVICE ORGANIZATION
NY592-30
UNITED SOCIETY OF BELIEVERS
See Shakers

UNITED SPANISH WAR VETERANS
WI346-280
UNITED STATES
See specific regions
UNITED STATES (FRIGATE)
CT512-120
UNITED STATES GOVERNMENT
See Government agencies, National; and
individual Federal agencies in repository
index
UNITED STATES INFORMATION AGENCY
DC9-580
UNITED STATES MILITARY ACADEMY
ME162-120
ASSOCIATION OF GRADUATES
NY949-780
UNITED STATES STEEL CORP.
NJ838-750
UNITED STATES VETERANS SIGNAL
CORPS ASSOCIATION
NJ270-800
UNITED STATES VOLLEYBALL
ASSOCIATION
CA278-130
UNITED STEELWORKERS OF AMERICA
PA895-710
UNITED TEXTILE WORKERS OF AMERICA
GA90-300
UNIVERSALIST CHURCH
IL170-195, PA715-720
CLERGY
IL170-195
MIDWESTERN US
IL170-195
UNIVERSALIST CHURCH OF AMERICA
MA169-230
UNIVERSITIES
EUROPE
IN627-810
UNIVERSITY CITY MO
CA48-40
UNIVERSITY COLLEGE OF MEDICINE
VA690-840
UNIVERSITY OF BUFFALO
NY24-720
UNIVERSITY OF COLORADO AT DENVER
CO252-42
UNIVERSITY OF DAYTON
OH223-720
UNIVERSITY OF KENTUCKY
BOARD OF TRUSTEES
KY504-510
SENATE RULES COMMITTEE
KY504-510
UNIVERSITY OF MARYLAND
MEDICAL AND CHIRURGICAL
FACULTY
DC19-611
UNIVERSITY OF MICHIGAN
MI518-445
UNIVERSITY OF NASHVILLE
TN690-975
UNTO THESE HILLS (OUTDOOR DRAMA)
NC150-790
UNWED MOTHERS
See Mothers, single
UPDIKE, DANIEL BERKELEY
RI700-640
UPLAND COLLEGE
PA340-520
UPPER PENINSULA (MI)
MI865-480
URBAN DESIGN
MA169-305
URBAN DEVELOPMENT
CA48-40, CA624-710, CA712-750,
CA966-860, DC2-200, GA90-270,
IL202-550, LA600-775, NC160-520,
OH823-750, TX483-320, VA50-50,
WA820-880
URBAN LEAGUE (DETROIT)
MI40-784
URBAN LEAGUE (SPRINGFIELD OH)
OH223-880
URBAN LEAGUE OF RHODE ISLAND
RI700-630

URBAN PLANNING
See City planning; Regional planning
URBAN RENEWAL
DC4-450, MN541-902
URBAN STUDIES
IN253-360, OH171-800, OH181-880,
OH203-600, VA690-830
UTAH
AZ500-400, CA712-743
EPISCOPAL CHURCH
MO810-590
ROMAN CATHOLIC CHURCH
MN749-720
UTILITIES
See Public utilities

V

VACCINES
POLIOMYELITIS
MN541-16
VAIL, ALFRED
NJ548-720
VAIL, CHRISTOPHER
VI700-360
VAIL, STEPHEN
NJ548-720
VALENTINE FAMILY
VA690-810
VALLEY PEACE CENTER OF AMHERST
MA21-770
VALLEY STATION CHRISTIAN CHURCH
KY496-518
VAN ALLEN, JOHN
IL169-130
VAN ALSTYNE FAMILY
NY466-120
VAN BENTHUYSEN, ARTHUR L.
VT496-640
VAN BUREN FAMILY
NY466-120, PA565-640
VAN BUREN, JOHN
PA565-640
VAN BUREN, MARTIN
CT435-520, OH171-920, PA565-640
VAN CAMPEN
NY87-40
VAN CLEEF, CHARLES E.
NY439-180
VAN CORTLANDT FAMILY
NY878-720
VAN DYKE, J. N.
NY187-120
VAN GAASBEEK, PETER
NY469-720
VAN ITALLIE, JEAN CLAUDE
OH399-440
VAN KIRK, BENJAMIN
NJ358-520
VAN KLEECK, EDWIN ROBERT
NY10-770
VAN KLEECK, MARY
MA624-740
VAN RENSSELAER FAMILY
NY254-160
VAN RENSSELAER FAMILY (ALBANY NY)
NY10-320
VAN SANTVOORD FAMILY
NY466-120
VAN VOORHEES, KOERT S.
KS513-250
VAN WART, ISAAC
NY878-320
VAN WYCK FAMILY
NY878-720
VANDERBURGH HISTORICAL AND
BIOGRAPHICAL SOCIETY
IN209-880
VANDERCOOK, JOHN
NY240-160
VANDERLYN, JOHN
NY469-720
VANDERPOEL FAMILY
NY466-120
VANZETTI, BARTOLOMEO
MA871-90

VARIAN, RUSSELL HARRISON
DC19-586
VASSAR, MATTHEW, JR.
NY726-40
VATICAN (PAPAL GOVERNMENT)
DC1-740, DC3-226, DC14-380
VAUGHAN, THOMAS WAYLAND
CA368-820
VAUSE, GEORGE
OR848-160
VEGETATION
See Plants
VEHICLES
CA282-480
ELECTRIC
NY804-280
HORSE-DRAWN
NY866-520
VENDOME HOTEL
CO640-480
VENDORS
MA109-180
VERMONT
NH468-800
MUSIC
DC19-570
SOCIETY OF FRIENDS
NY593-710
VERMONT JUNIOR COLLEGE
VT464-560
VERPLANCK, ROBERT NEWLIN
NY726-40
VESTAL, OPHELIA
OK490-520
VETERANS
NY148-200, NY321-480, NY510-880,
NY752-530, OR816-590, PA726-508
AMERICAN REVOLUTION
NH588-520, OH486-890
CIVIL WAR
NH588-520, NH672-570, NY672-440
ORGANIZATIONS
CT477-570, NV450-120, NY563-120,
WI346-280
WORLD WAR I
NY672-440
WORLD WAR II
NY672-440
VETERANS OF FOREIGN WARS
NV450-120
VETERANS OF FOREIGN WARS, JUNIOR
UNIT (MORAVIA NY)
NY563-120
VETERINARIANS
NE112-760
VETERINARY MEDICINE
CA720-886, OH588-520
VICE PRESIDENTS
IL261-570, KY604-40, KY604-640,
KY604-890, MI40-300, MS80-40,
NJ339-40, SC185-120, TX56-520
VICTORIA MINING COMPANY
MI725-600
VIETNAM
MUSIC
AZ750-32
REFUGEES
NY10-160
VIETNAM WAR
AL380-800, AL560-720, CO180-750,
CT36-80, DC14-770, HI350-770,
MN14-560, PA325-280, WI178-240
VILLA, PANCHO
MO200-720
VILLARREAL, JOSE
CA778-800
VINATIERI, FELIX VILLIET
SD936-950
VINCENT FAMILY
PA815-710
VINCENT, ARTHUR P.
PA815-710
VINCENTIAN FATHERS
NY604-560
VIOLINS
NE560-50

VIRGIN ISLANDS
MD755-560
VIRGINIA
NY288-840,   OH778-40,   OH853-130,
WV225-860
  BOUNDARY DISPUTE WITH PA
  PA920-890
  CHRISTIAN CHURCH
  NC310-200
  CONGREGATIONAL CHRISTIAN
    CHURCH
  NC310-200
  COURT RECORDS
  PA920-870,   PA920-890
  MUSIC
  DC19-570
  UNITED CHURCH OF CHRIST
  NC310-200,   PA470-800
VIRGINIA INTERCOLLEGIATE ATHLETIC
ASSOCIATION
VA630-840
VIRGINIA MENNONITE CONFERENCE
VA350-200
VIRGINIA MILITARY INSTITUTE
VA550-520
VIRGINIA TEACHERS ASSOCIATION
VA630-840
VIRGINIA V (SHIP)
WA820-828
VIRUSES
MN541-16
VISUAL ANTHROPOLOGY
NM722-30
VISUAL ARTS
See Arts, visual
VITAMINS
CT505-120
VITICULTURE
See Grapes
VIZZARD, JAMES L.
CA778-800
VOCATIONAL GUIDANCE
NY592-30
VOICE OF AMERICA
DC9-580
VOICE OF FIRESTONE (TELEVISION
PROGRAM)
MA109-440
VOICE OF THE UKRAINIAN COMMUNITY
(RADIO PROGRAM)
PA725-430
VOIGT COMPANY
MI28-280
VOLCANOES
CA620-760,   CA624-710
VOLLEYBALL
CA278-130
VOLTAIRE (FRANCOIS MARIE AROUET)
CT505-977
VOLUNTEER FIRE DEPARTMENT OF
CARLSTADT (NJ)
NJ124-240
VOLUNTEERS
DC1-40,   IL231-240,   NY592-30
VOLUNTEERS IN SERVICE TO AMERICA
(ACTION)
DC1-40
VON KETTELER, WILLIAM E.
PA30-720
VONNEGUT, KURT, JR.
MA636-880
VOORHEES, DONALD
NY439-360
VOORHIS, H. JERRY
CA143-470
VOTER REGISTRATION
CA86-520,   WA885-720
VOTING
See also Elections,   CA700-720,
CT102-120,   CT144-880,   CT533-120,
IL354-80,   NJ568-670,   NJ574-560,
NM912-280,   NY261-320,   OH603-560,
PA735-790,   WI382-520,   WI754-170

W

W. J. COLLINS
CO36-40
WABASH AND ERIE CANAL
IN143-120,   IN363-342,   IN913-900
WABASH RAILROAD
MO607-520
WADSWORTH FAMILY
MA169-590,   NY321-720
WADSWORTH, JEREMIAH, FAMILY
CT316-880
WAGES
  EQUAL PAY
  DC1-340
WAGGENER, HEWITT A.
IN539-86
WAGNER, FRANK
CA132-160
WAGNER, RICHARD
PA725-345
WAGNER, WILLIAM
PA726-855
WAGONS
  MANUFACTURING
  IN792-160
WAKE FOREST COLLEGE
NC840-880
WALCOTT, CHARLES D.
DC19-310
WALD, LILLIAN
CT512-120
WALES, ARVINE
OH505-520
WALES, ARVINE C.
OH505-520
WALKER AND WEEKS (ARCHITECTURAL
FIRM)
OH181-325
WALKER, ANDREW
ME460-440
WALKER, JOSEPH REDDEFORD
CA954-720
WALLACE, MARY
PA726-600
WALLACE, WILLIAM L.
KY680-180
WALLIN, THEODORE B.
IL976-890
WALNUTS
CA226-170
WALPOLE, HUGH
IN275-170
WALRUS MANUFACTURING COMPANY
IL192-510
WALTER, FRANCIS E.
PA90-480
WALTER, H. E.
RI700-50
WALTER, THOMAS USTICK
PA725-150
WALTERS, HENRY
MD76-880
WALTERS, WILLIAM
MD76-880
WALTHALL, EDWARD CARY
MS520-520
WALTHAM WATCH COMPANY
MA871-870
WALTHER LEAGUE
NE800-480,   OR720-470
WALTON CIVIC CLUB
NY915-870
WALTON, DOROTHY
AL580-530
WALTON, GEORGE
AL580-530
WALWORTH FAMILY
NY708-440
WALWORTH, REUBEN HYDE, FAMILY
NY795-320
WANTLING, WILLIAM
IL94-510
WAPPENBUCHER (MEDIEVAL BOOKS)
MN226-720

WAR
See also names of individual wars,
CA605-510,   GA180-280,   IA972-240,
IL762-80,   IL866-355,   IN297-600,
KS676-520,   NC680-460,   NY949-830,
PA860-730,   VT464-840,   WI178-240
  AMPHIBIOUS
  VA580-550,   VA660-510
  ARMISTICES
  NY595-40
  INDIANS
  IL866-365,   KS513-720,   NY272-120,
  OR448-450,   WA616-870,   WA880-775,
  WI178-240
  LIBRARIANS
  IL916-40
  NAVAL
  DC14-720,   RI560-510
  PRISONERS
  DE60-240,   MD57-820
  RELIEF
  CA858-320,   DC1-560,   DC3-210,
  MI390-720,   NY590-700,   NY595-660,
  PA725-765
WAR ASSETS ADMINISTRATION
CO252-550
WAR CRIMES
  GERMANY
  NY588-860
  JAPAN
  NY588-860
  WORLD WAR II
  NY588-860
WAR OF INDEPENDENCE, HAITI
FL220-800
WAR OF 1812
CT36-80,   CT435-520,   GA915-280,
IN363-360,   MA506-520,   MD76-60,
MD76-240,   MI40-820,   NY708-440,
OH823-750,   PA920-870,   PA920-890,
VA640-650,   VT784-720
WAR PRODUCTION BOARD (US)
DC19-606
WAR? OR GOOD? IT'S OUR CHOICE, BY
JOSIAH S. WATSON
IL404-410
WARD, ARTEMAS
MA513-530
WARE, EUGENE F.
KS878-430
WAREHOUSES
  GRAIN
  WA489-40
WARFIELD & BOONE
CA421-774
WARFIELD, ALEXANDER
CA421-774
WARFIELD, BENJAMIN B.
NJ692-610
WARNE, COLSTON E.
NY569-120
WARNER BROTHERS
CA421-763
WARNER FAMILY
NY949-120
WARNER INN
OH394-320
WARNER PRESS
IN22-50
WARNER, ANNA BARTLETT
NY949-120
WARNER, CHARLES A.
TX483-810
WARNER, CHARLES DUDLEY
CT316-560,   CT316-770
WARNER, DAVID SIDNEY
IN22-50
WARNER, SUSAN BOGERT
NY949-120
WARREN, CHARLES F.
NC850-120
WARREN, E. J.
NC850-120
WARREN, EARL
CA86-810,   MA871-85
WARREN, FLETCHER
TX210-200

WASHINGTON
CA712-743, MN226-705, OR224-800, WI456-735
ARCHAEOLOGY
ID480-770
CHRISTIAN REFORMED CHURCH
MI355-110
FORESTRY
CA86-850
INDIANS
SD792-800
RELIGIOUS COMMUNITIES
CA720-739
ROMAN CATHOLIC CHURCH
MN749-720
SISTERS OF NOTRE DAME DE NAMUR
CA78-740
WASHINGTON AGRICULTURAL COLLEGE
WA724-895
WASHINGTON BRICK, LIME, AND SEWER PIPE COMPANY
WA152-125
WASHINGTON DAILY NEWS (NEWSPAPER)
DC13-300
WASHINGTON DC
See District of Columbia
WASHINGTON FAMILY
VA540-520
WASHINGTON GALLERY OF MODERN ART
DC3-750
WASHINGTON STAR (NEWSPAPER)
DC13-300
WASHINGTON STATE COLLEGE
WA724-895
WASHINGTON STATE HISTORICAL RECORDS AND ARCHIVES PROJECT
WA280-885
WASHINGTON STATE POTATO COMMISSION
WA280-885
WASHINGTON UNIVERSITY MEDICAL CENTER
MO810-960
WASHINGTON, BOOKER TALIAFERRO
DC14-350, GA90-700, NY310-160
WASHINGTON, GEORGE
CT512-120, DC7-510, DC14-590, IL170-429, MD76-30, MD399-240, MO810-690, NJ548-530, NJ692-620, NJ812-710, NY594-220, NY599-880, OH823-770, PA55-760, PA905-840, PA925-160, SC144-130, VA540-520
WASHINGTON, MARTHA
KS213-120, VA540-520
WASHINGTON, SOUTHEASTERN
OR688-820
WATCHES
MANUFACTURING
CT48-40, MA871-870, PA215-560
PATENTS
WI456-560
WATCHES (TIMEPIECES)
DC19-606
WATER
LAW
CA86-920
WATER COMPANIES
See also Public utilities, *CA601-640, CA640-640, CA712-810, CT505-560, MA109-180, MA432-320, MA883-870, NY563-120, NY923-880*
WATER POWER
MA478-800, MA606-530
WATER RESOURCES
AZ700-40, CA86-810, CA86-920, CA143-470, CA770-120, CA782-720, CO252-163, CO270-240, CO768-640, NC656-720, NM494-570, NV940-810, NY10-570, NY588-60, OH990-640, OR560-690, WA629-655, WY135-860
WATER SPORTS
MN541-592
WATER WORKS
See Water companies

WATERBURY BUTTON COMPANY
CT870-520
WATERGATE SCANDAL
IL489-890
WATERLOO FEMALE TEMPERANCE SOCIETY
NY928-880
WATERMELONS
IN92-80
WATERWAYS
DC19-636, MS300-550, PR720-360, VA165-120
WATERWHEELS
PA90-320, PA370-330
WATKINS, CARLETON
TX374-40
WATKINS, W. L., FAMILY
MO490-880
WATSON, JOHN MICHENER
OH953-870
WATSON, JOSIAH
IL404-410
WATTS FAMILY
NJ756-240
WATTS, MAY THEILGAARD
IL459-520
WATTS, TED
KS746-640
WATTSON, PAUL JAMES FRANCIS (LEWIS WATTSON)
NY318-260
WAVES (NAVY)
MD57-820
WAYLAND, FRANCIS
RI700-50
WAYLAND, J. A.
KS746-640
WAYLAND, JOHN W.
VA115-80
WAYNE-GORDON HOUSE (SAVANNAH GA)
GA895-290
WAYNE, ANTHONY
NY844-720, PA945-880
WCAL (RADIO STATION)
MN625-710
WEATHER
See also Meteorology, *CA180-160, CT512-120, FL660-510, KS461-720, MA278-200, NC60-160, ND486-810, NY18-720, NY766-690, OH863-280, SC144-170*
WEATHER SERVICE (EVANSVILLE IN, STATION)
IN209-880
WEAVERS
DC19-581, MA606-530, NY222-110
WEBB FAMILY
NY708-440
WEBB SHIPYARDS
NY327-880
WEBB, FAY
NC100-280
WEBB, TODD
TX374-40
WEBB, W. W.
WI498-560
WEBB, WILLIAM H.
NY327-880
WEBBER, W. T.
OR464-490
WEBSTER, DANIEL
MA871-90
WEBSTER, W. A.
NH600-510
WEDGWOOD COMPANY
PA575-80
WEDGWOOD, JOSIAH
PA575-80
WEEDON, GEORGE
RI700-45
WEEK OF PRAYER FOR CHRISTIAN UNITY
NY318-260
WEIDENSALL, ROBERT
IL212-280
WEINBERG, ROBERT CHARLES
NY590-960

WELCH, ROBERT A.
TX483-810
WELCH, WILLIAM HENRY
MD76-315
WELFARE
See also Social welfare, *CT36-80 , CT144-880, MN541-902 , WI456-495*
ANIMALS
CO252-30, CO306-40
CHILDREN
IL170-910, MI518-445, MN541-902, NY594-20
ORGANIZATIONS
MN541-902
WELLES, GIDEON
VT528-560
WELLFLEET MARINE BENEVOLENT SOCIETY
MA894-880
WELLMAN, PAUL ISELIN
KS948-880
WELLS, HENRY
NY53-880
WELLS, J. STUART
NY101-90
WENTWORTH, BENNING
NH468-800
WESLEY, JOHN
DC23-500, TN690-885, TX252-760
WESLEYAN CHURCH
IN506-870
WESLEYAN METHODIST CHURCH
RECORDS
NY413-320
WESSELMANN, THOMAS
MO810-880
WEST INDIES
See also Caribbean; Danish West Indies; and individual islands, *MA199-90, VA870-150, VI300-240, VI700-360, VI700-800*
NATURAL HISTORY
MA199-90
TRADE WITH UNITED STATES
MA733-210
TRAVEL
IN583-560
WEST VIRGINIA
GOVERNMENT AGENCIES, LOCAL
DC14-600
LUTHERAN CHURCH-MISSOURI SYNOD
IN231-490
RELIGIOUS COMMUNITIES
NY859-720
WEST, JESSAMYN
CA966-880, MA636-880
WEST, JOSEPH
CT863-280
WESTERLY RIFLE COMPANY
RI910-880
WESTERN ASSOCIATION OF COLLEGIATE ALUMNAE
DC1-340
WESTERN CHAPTER OF THE NORTHLAND CHAPTER, RED CROSS
MN391-310
WESTERN COLLEGE ASSOCIATION
CA143-470
WESTERN COLORADO POWER COMPANY
CO270-240
WESTERN RESERVE COLLEGE
OH181-110
WESTERN RESERVE UNIVERSITY
OH181-110
WESTERN UNION COLLEGE
IA544-880
WESTERN US
CA66-80, CA86-780, CA86-810, CA540-590, CA636-690, CA858-810, CO180-120, CO252-181, CT505-890, DC3-210, IL170-351, NM722-530, OK558-790, OR848-40, TX252-730, TX374-40, UT380-810, UT456-900, UT684-80, UT912-120, VT464-840, WY500-800, WY560-280
BANKING
CA720-960

BASQUES
  NV940-800
BLACKS
  CA720-10
CHURCH OF THE NAZARENE
  MO430-120
EXPLORATION
  CO252-181, MO810-490, OK558-790
FINANCE
  CA720-960
INDIANS
  CA712-713
LITERATURE
  CA862-810
MIGRATION
  IL170-351
MILITARY HISTORY
  OK558-790
MISSIONARIES
  NJ568-570
PRINTING
  CA720-180
PUBLISHING
  CA720-180
ROMAN CATHOLIC CHURCH
  CA421-30
TRAVEL
  CA86-780, WA880-790
WESTGARD, A.L.
  VA215-40
WESTMINSTER CATHEDRAL
  MO810-190
WESTMORELAND, WILLIAM C.
  SC144-150
WESTON, EDWARD
  NJ578-515, TX374-40
WESWIG, CARL M.
  MN763-50
WETMORE, ALEXANDER
  DC19-310
WGN (RADIO STATION)
  IL916-820
WHALEN, PHILIP
  OR720-700
WHALING (HUNTING)
  CA762-40, CT268-720, CT512-550,
  CT772-720, HI400-480, MA285-160,
  MA307-230, MA572-560, MA584-550,
  MA584-600, MA748-440, NY205-880,
  NY257-190, NY593-600, NY772-720,
  OH505-520, RI700-640
WHARFS
  OH171-650
WHEAT
  IL170-273
WHEATON FAMILY
  MA636-880
WHEELER, CHARLES B.
  MO430-800
WHIPPLE, AMIEL WEEKS
  OK592-650
WHIPPLE, GEORGE HOYT
  NY752-885
WHIPPLE, HENRY B.
  MN321-690
WHISKEY HILL, ATHERTON AND MENLO
  OAKS BALLOONING AND SPORTING
  SOCIETY
  CA456-730
WHISKEY REBELLION
  PA735-110, PA890-800, PA920-890
WHISTLER, JAMES ABBOTT MCNEILL
  DC19-330
WHISTLERS
  LA670-480
WHITAKER, CHARLES H.
  IL169-130
WHITE HOUSE CONFERENCE ON
  CHILDREN AND YOUTH
  DC1-340
WHITE, ALVAN
  NM760-900
WHITE, DAVID
  KS513-250
WHITE, FRANCIS
  MD76-340

WHITE, I. D.
  KY272-635, VT528-560
WHITE, JULES
  CA90-30
WHITE, MABEL
  CA601-640
WHITE, MARY
  CA601-640, KS283-200
WHITE, WILLIAM
  PA726-37
WHITE, WILLIAM ALLEN
  KS283-200
WHITE, WILLIAM ALLEN, FAMILY
  KS283-200
WHITEHILL, ROBERT
  PA160-120
WHITELY, JOHN, FAMILY
  KY430-280
WHITESVILLE AND BEECH HILL
  TELEPHONE COMPANY
  NY967-880
WHITESVILLE UNION SCHOOL AND
  ACADEMY
  NY967-880
WHITLEY, EDNA TALBOTT
  KY61A-640
WHITLOCK, BRAND
  IL866-480
WHITMAN MASSACRE
  OREGON
  RI945-800
WHITMAN, MARCUS
  NY693-920
WHITMAN, NARCISSA
  WA889-720
WHITMAN, WALT
  CT505-890, MA961-870, NJ568-670,
  NY421-880
WHITNEY FAMILY
  NY602-570
WHITNEY, COURTNEY
  VA580-520
WHITNEY, JOSHUA
  NY101-90
WHITTIER, JOHN GREENLEAF
  CA966-880, MA17-400, MN541-600
WHITTLE, WILLIAM C.
  VA580-570
WHORF, HARRY
  MA970-890
WIANT, JOHN, FAMILY
  OH853-130
WICKHAM FAMILY
  VA690-810
WIDNEY, LYMAN S.
  GA765-440
WIESELMAN, IRVING L.
  CA132-160
WILBERFORCE UNIVERSITY
  DC1-160, OH982-290
WILBOUR, CHARLES EDWIN
  NY587-780
WILBUR, RICHARD
  NY125-740
WILBURN, HIRAM C.
  NC860-320
WILD KINGDOM (TELEVISION PROGRAM)
  NE624-520
WILD LIFE PROTECTION FUND,
  PERMANENT
  NY593-130
WILD LIFE, AMERICAN COMMITTEE FOR
  INTERNATIONAL PROTECTION OF
  NY593-130
WILD WEST SHOWS
  CO458-80, TX374-40, WI70-120
WILDE, OSCAR
  CA421-774
WILDER IN THE WEST, BY LAURA
  INGALLS WILDER
  SD126-480
WILDER, HARRY EMERSON
  IN363-400
WILDER, LAURA INGALLS
  IA74-480, SD126-480
WILDER, THORNTON NIVEN
  NY323-320

WILDERNESS
  APPALACHIAN MOUNTAINS
  NC210-870
WILDLIFE
  CO252-163, DC4-260, DC6-500,
  DC14-540, MI60-440, OR560-690 ,
  TN465-760, TX56-780, WY950-945
CONSERVATION
  NY593-130
HABITAT PRESERVATION
  NY593-130
MANAGEMENT
  NY593-130
PROPAGATION
  NY593-130
WILKES, JOHN
  CT505-977
WILKIN, ALEXANDER
  MN763-690
WILKINSON, JAMES
  LA600-465
WILKINSON, JEMIMA
  NY693-920
WILKINSON, MARGUERITE
  VT432-530
WILLAMETTE MISSION
  OR816-530
WILLARD, ARCHIBALD M.
  OH906-320
WILLARD, EMMA HART
  NY890-200
WILLARD, FRANCES E.
  IL261-545
WILLET FAMILY
  PA726-895
WILLHAM, OLIVER
  OK753-600
WILLIAM ALLEN WHITE CHILDREN'S
  BOOK AWARD
  KS283-200
WILLIAM CAMPBELL (BOOKSTORE)
  PA726-615
WILLIAM REITH STAINED GLASS STUDIO
  PA725-150
WILLIAMS FAMILY
  CT772-720, NY899-600
WILLIAMS, CHARLES
  IL976-900
WILLIAMS, DAVID
  NY878-320
WILLIAMS, ELEAZER
  WI202-560
WILLIAMS, FRANKLIN DELANO
  MA943-880
WILLIAMS, JAMES WATSON
  NY899-520
WILLIAMS, JOAN
  TN630-740
WILLIAMS, JOHN
  WI202-560
WILLIAMS, JOSIAH B.
  NY439-180
WILLIAMS, MAYNARD OWEN
  MI518-425
WILLIAMS, MILO
  OH853-800
WILLIAMS, ROBERT L.
  OK592-650
WILLIAMS, TENNESSEE
  LA600-755
WILLIAMS, WILLIAM CARLOS
  CT505-890, NY24-735, OH399-440,
  VT432-530
WILLIAMSBURG SEMINAR FOR
  HISTORICAL ADMINISTRATORS
  DC14-650
WILLIE HALSELL COLLEGE
  OK854-840
WILLING, SIMS AND TALBUTT
  PA725-150
WILLIS, CHARLES
  MD114-310
WILLOUGHBY, CHARLES A.
  VA580-520
WILSON-WARNER HOUSE
  DE900-320

WILSON, ALEXANDER FORD
IL996-980
WILSON, ANGUS
IA466-800
WILSON, E. H.
MA169-190
WILSON, EDITH BOLLING GALT
VA750-880
WILSON, EDWIN BIDWELL
DC14-100
WILSON, FRANCIS MAIRS HUNTINGTON
PA210-800
WILSON, SLOAN
NY134-90
WILSON, WOODROW
NC240-160, VA750-880
WIMMER, BONIFACE
PA485-720
WINANS, F. N.
NY303-600
WINDOWS
STAINED GLASS
PA726-895
WINE
CA86-810, CA206-790, CA720-980,
NY367-290
WING, JOHN
IN231-40
WINSLOW, EDWARD, HOUSE
MA685-520
WINSTON, CLARA
NY588-300
WINSTON, ELLEN
NC380-800
WINSTON, RICHARD
NY588-300
WINTER WAR (FINLAND)
MI390-720
WINTER, WILLIAM
DC6-600
WINTHROP COMMUNITY HOSPITAL
MA970-890
WINTHROP, GRENVILLE L.
MA169-300
WIRELESS TELEGRAPHY
CA798-720
WISCONSIN
MN541-934
GOVERNMENT AGENCIES, NATIONAL
IL170-280
INDIANS
SD792-800
MINING
MN338-360
ROMAN CATHOLIC CHURCH
MN749-720
WISCONSIN STATE SOCIALIST PARTY
EXECUTIVE COMMITTEE
WI456-740
WISSENSCHAFT (19TH CENTURY GERMAN-JEWISH MOVEMENT)
NY590-680
WITCHCRAFT
MA231-640, RI700-45
WITHERBEE FAMILY
MA513-530
WITTELS, FRITZ
NY592-640
WOIWODE, AUDREY
ND876-830
WOIWODE, E. C.
ND876-830
WOIWODE, LARRY
ND876-830
WOLF RIVER
WI554-600
WOLFE, HENRY CUTLER
NJ178-115
WOLFE, THOMAS
NC60-640, NC150-810
WOLFF, M. MADELEVA
IN627-720
WOMAN'S CHRISTIAN TEMPERANCE UNION
MN14-560, NY148B-88

WOMAN'S CHRISTIAN TEMPERANCE UNION (KALAMAZOO MI)
MI518-445
WOMAN'S CHRISTIAN TEMPERANCE UNION (NEW BRITAIN CT)
CT477-570
WOMAN'S CHRISTIAN TEMPERANCE UNION (NEWARK VALLEY NY)
NY598-560
WOMAN'S CHRISTIAN TEMPERANCE UNION (PORTVILLE NY)
NY720-640
WOMAN'S CHRISTIAN TEMPERANCE UNION (POUGHKEEPSIE NY)
NY726-40
WOMAN'S CHRISTIAN TEMPERANCE UNION (THAYER COUNTY NE)
NE112-760
WOMAN'S CLUB (GREEN RIVER WY)
WY365-710
WOMAN'S GENERAL HOSPITAL
OH181-180
WOMAN'S MEDICAL COLLEGE OF PENNSYLVANIA
PA725-900
WOMAN'S MISSIONARY SOCIETY
IN22-50
WOMAN'S RESEARCH CLUB (ATLANTIC CITY NJ)
NJ20-40
WOMANS RELIEF CORPS
See also Women's Relief Corps,
WI346-280
WOMEN
AK50-66, AK400-720, AK500-20,
AL80-40, AL120-104, AL120-815,
AL380-800, AL540-400, AL560-720,
AL580-530, AL620-20, AL620-60,
AL760-760, AR240-810, AR330-830,
AR510-13, AR510-25, AZ250-575,
AZ550-040, AZ625-630, AZ750-45,
AZ800-30, AZ800-800, AZ800-830,
AZ950-950, CA86-400, CA86-520,
CA86-780, CA90-30, CA118-720,
CA136-120, CA143-470, CA206-790,
CA206-940, CA226-170, CA274-250,
CA314-120, CA314-320, CA386-560,
CA410-120, CA414-480, CA421-015,
CA421-390, CA421-610, CA421-660,
CA421-760, CA421-763, CA421-766,
CA421-770, CA421-830, CA454-520,
CA508-560, CA540-520, CA540-610,
CA578-630, CA578-640, CA601-640,
CA628-720, CA636-690, CA676-110,
CA676-130, CA676-130, CA676-140,
CA680-720, CA704-560, CA712-700,
CA712-708, CA712-713, CA712-720,
CA720-180, CA720-675, CA720-910,
CA724-730, CA740-710, CA756-320,
CA760-710, CA770-120, CA774-800,
CA782-800, CA814-120, CA858-320,
CA858-810, CA858-820, CA858-895,
CA862-730, CA862-810, CA870-710,
CA886-240, CO108-85, CO108-810,
CO180-120, CO180-640, CO252-70,
CO252-100, CO252-181, CO252-550,
CO378-120, CO768-640, CT36-80,
CT120-120, CT275-280, CT316-105,
CT316-120, CT316-210, CT316-330,
CT316-560, CT316-763, CT316-770,
CT428-865, CT463-520, CT505-560,
CT505-900, CT505-910, CT505-960,
CT512-120, CT519-560, CT603-360,
CT673-690, DC1-340, DC1-560,
DC1-640, DC1-760, DC2-600, DC2-850,
DC3-210, DC7-100, DC7-650, DC8-850,
DC12-300, DC13-210, DC14-100,
DC14-250, DC14-420, DC14-730,
DC19-220, DC19-310, DC19-520,
DC19-536, DC19-576, DC19-640,
DC20-600, DC22-500, DE270-200,
DE810-330, FL220-795, FL600-640,
FL600-800, FL720-720, FL800-245,
FL800-262, FL800-266, FL820-240,
FL820-780, GA75-810, GA90-30,
GA90-190, GA90-200, GA90-300,
GA780-310, GA885-120, GA895-280,

GA895-290, GA950-720, HI350-300,
HI350-320, HI350-808, IA22-40,
IA33-370, IA66-80, IA99-40, IA122-720,
IA177-240, IA188-520, IA211-480,
IA233-360, IA244-30, IA377-280,
IA466-360, IA466-800, IA499-520,
IA688-360, IA699-120, IA755-560,
IA833-120, IA866-730, IA955-440,
IA966-320, ID80-90, ID80-365,
ID480-810, ID680-690, IL45-30,
IL94-360, IL94-510, IL124-725,
IL169-325, IL169-396, IL169-580,
IL169-677, IL169-729, IL170-78,
IL170-91, IL170-234, IL170-250,
IL170-280, IL170-351, IL170-416,
IL170-637, IL170-650, IL170-780,
IL170-891, IL170-897, IL170-910,
IL202-550, IL207-160, IL245-322,
IL246-200, IL251-630, IL261-200,
IL261-280, IL261-545, IL261-568,
IL261-570, IL261-585, IL296-720,
IL305-430, IL374-310, IL384-320,
IL394-500, IL444-720, IL449-480,
IL459-520, IL469-480, IL489-890,
IL609-120, IL624-380, IL767-320,
IL770-40, IL801-20, IL806-695,
IL806-695, IL806-710, IL851-720,
IL866-365, IL866-720, IL916-810,
IL921-840, IL946-360, IL951-480,
IL956-870, IL996-980, IN66-380,
IN66-390, IN154-880, IN209-360,
IN209-800, IN209-880, IN231-370,
IN231-470, IN242-230, IN264-40,
IN275-150, IN275-640, IN341-320,
IN352-320, IN352-800, IN363-125,
IN363-350, IN363-360, IN363-400,
IN363-660, IN440-760, IN539-90,
IN583-560, IN627-720, IN627-780,
IN660-640, IN704-200, IN726-240,
IN792-560, IN825-200, IN825-850,
IN902-840, IN935-650, KS10-150,
KS10-170, KS108-70, KS136-880,
KS164-520, KS335-240, KS377-250,
KS593-510, KS607-450, KS607-690,
KS676-520, KS746-640, KS833-440,
KS878-200, KS878-430, KS878-520,
KS878-880, KS948-870, KS948-880,
KS948-890, KS962-800, KY80-90,
KY96-870, KY288-425, KY288-440,
KY352-320, KY464-490, KY464-800,
KY496-530, KY496-730, KY496-765,
KY496-812, KY564-520, KY630-40,
KY680-190, LA62-470, LA62-490,
LA62-500, LA358-800, LA570-540,
LA600-20, LA600-310, LA600-320,
LA600-465, LA600-555, LA600-755,
LA600-764, LA600-775, LA885-120,
MA21-40, MA21-770, MA25-520,
MA25-650, MA70-70, MA92-70,
MA108-140, MA108-240, MA108-580,
MA108-600, MA108-750, MA108-770,
MA109-460, MA134-80, MA154-480,
MA154-640, MA169-170, MA169-230,
MA169-270, MA169-300, MA169-310,
MA169-370, MA169-440, MA169-500,
MA169-590, MA169-625, MA169-650,
MA169-855, MA169-860, MA169-885,
MA231-640, MA238-520, MA246-160,
MA250-160, MA278-200, MA285-160,
MA323-230, MA334-120, MA338-840,
MA356-120, MA363-640, MA383-240,
MA432-320, MA448-470, MA478-800,
MA486-470, MA499-520, MA506-520,
MA513-530, MA572-540, MA590-570,
MA593-40, MA606-530, MA606-720,
MA615-80, MA624-240, MA624-560,
MA624-700, MA624-740, MA624-750,
MA636-880, MA654-590, MA677-720,
MA733-210, MA733-660, MA738-700,
MA748-440, MA797-400, MA811-720,
MA823-610, MA871-40, MA891-860,
MA891-880, MA897-880, MA931-400,
MA943-880, MA964-880, MA970-890,
MA985-70, MA985-100, MA985-110,
MA985-860, MD57-800, MD76-70,
MD76-80, MD76-315, MD76-333,
MD76-515, MD76-525, MD76-800,

MD76-880, MD152-550, MD266-80,
MD285-805, MD950-760, MD978-320,
MD978-880, ME37-525, ME37-535,
ME37-540, ME95-80, ME112-80,
ME162-120, ME275-160, ME460-440,
ME512-80, ME650-780, ME650-810,
ME712-530, ME837-560, ME925-130,
ME925-870, MI8-480, MI40-784,
MI40-808, MI40-820, MI160-880,
MI214-150, MI230-165, MI230-880,
MI230-905, MI255-545, MI314-60,
MI445-310, MI445-320, MI445-560,
MI445-880, MI450-560, MI510-200,
MI518-50, MI518-445, MI550-505,
MI550-530, MI665-120, MI675-320,
MI720-600, MI865-80, MN42-40,
MN63-70, MN261-810, MN275-200,
MN300-480, MN328-600, MN419-440,
MN520-700, MN541-16, MN541-777,
MN541-902, MN541-925, MN562-520,
MN583-920, MN625-550, MN625-570,
MN625-710, MN721-600, MN742-720,
MN749-720, MN763-50, MN763-80,
MN763-110, MN763-510, MN763-530,
MN763-540, MN763-790, MN884-880,
MN968-120, MN975-120, MN975-730,
MN975-860, MO210-780, MO210-815,
MO290-120, MO350-280, MO400-320,
MO400-400, MO400-690, MO410-545,
MO430-420, MO430-540, MO430-790,
MO490-880, MO700-720, MO770-480,
MO770-710, MO810-200, MO810-260,
MO810-330, MO810-490, MO810-510,
MO810-590, MO810-760, MO810-780,
MO810-800, MO810-960, MS20-200,
MS230-160, MS260-500, MS300-520,
MS490-810, MS550-500, MS610-520,
MS900-870, MT100-200, MT130-535,
MT130-540, MT530-500, MT700-800,
NC150-800, NC260-150, NC260-170,
NC330-520, NC380-80, NC380-280,
NC380-800, NC390-200, NC570-530,
NC650-120, NC680-460, ND486-800,
NE112-760, NE416-720, NE496-40,
NE560-50, NE560-550, NE560-810,
NE560-860, NE560-870, NE624-130,
NE624-830, NH134-540, NH194-160,
NH206-800, NH820-690, NJ112-120,
NJ178-110, NJ276-510, NJ280-270,
NJ330-320, NJ339-40, NJ444-240,
NJ464-510, NJ464-666, NJ532-515,
NJ548-720, NJ564-560, NJ568-570,
NJ568-670, NJ568-680, NJ574-560,
NJ578-510, NJ578-540, NJ622-690,
NJ646-660, NJ692-210, NJ692-660,
NJ786-40, NJ838-580, NJ982-280,
NM114-35, NM114-870, NM114-880,
NM114-900, NM722-530, NM722-570,
NV90-530, NV270-560, NV940-810,
NY10-80, NY10-150, NY10-640,
NY10-770, NY12-720, NY18-40,
NY24-720, NY32-50, NY51-100,
NY53-880, NY82-80, NY101-720,
NY125-700, NY125-720, NY125-880,
NY128-720, NY134-60, NY134-90,
NY150-740, NY156-140, NY214-100,
NY214-120, NY216-120, NY219-290,
NY250-50, NY250-212, NY254-160,
NY263-210, NY272-120, NY286-240,
NY323-320, NY326-280, NY427-240,
NY439-120, NY439-140, NY439-360,
NY563-120, NY564-840, NY566-540,
NY569-120, NY586-180, NY586-443,
NY586-580, NY586-650, NY587-300,
NY587-510, NY587-720, NY587-800,
NY587-840, NY587-940, NY588-300,
NY588-520, NY588-820, NY588-830,
NY588-900, NY588-940, NY588-970,
NY589-710, NY589-720, NY589-900,
NY590-720, NY590-940, NY590-960,
NY591-420, NY591-840, NY592-260,
NY592-320, NY592-460, NY592-480,
NY592-800, NY592-880, NY592-930,
NY593-90, NY593-120, NY593-560,
NY593-590, NY593-600, NY594-20,
NY594-380, NY595-20, NY602-570,
NY612-690, NY646-520, NY648-310,

NY657-600, NY660-600, NY660-720,
NY693-920, NY708-720, NY723-720,
NY726-850, NY749-720, NY752-40,
NY752-330, NY752-530, NY752-720,
NY752-720, NY752-740, NY752-880,
NY752-890, NY760-90, NY792-720,
NY795-320, NY795-710, NY821-720,
NY861-740, NY866-710, NY872-800,
NY872-810, NY878-510, NY890-200,
NY915-880, NY928-880, OH11-810,
OH11-840, OH35-610, OH92-520,
OH171-20, OH171-100, OH171-110,
OH171-800, OH181-110, OH181-270,
OH181-630, OH181-880, OH181-880,
OH203-600, OH203-600, OH203-680,
OH223-520, OH399-420, OH399-450,
OH505-510, OH665-580, OH823-750,
OH878-720, OH925-600, OH978-120,
OH982-290, OH986-40, OH986-40,
OK42-560, OK118-70, OK228-610,
OK389-560, OK490-520, OK490-520,
OK524-280, OK592-580, OK592-620,
OK592-630, OK753-600, OK829-770,
OR56-40, OR128-720, OR144-600,
OR224-480, OR224-800, OR224-800,
OR400-720, OR424-880, OR528-718,
OR720-590, OR768-170, PA130-30,
PA135-80, PA160-120, PA160-760,
PA305-510, PA325-490, PA380-320,
PA380-650, PA395-320, PA435-400,
PA470-240, PA470-460, PA470-480,
PA555-40, PA725-15, PA725-75,
PA725-120, PA725-165, PA725-240,
PA725-285, PA725-375, PA725-495,
PA725-600, PA726-105, PA726-240,
PA726-412, PA726-630, PA735-780,
PA735-790, PA860-730, PA895-710,
PA945-120, PR720-360, RI560-360,
RI700-630, RI700-660, RI700-680,
RI700-740, SC144-90, SC144-105,
SC144-130, SC144-520, SC144-730,
SC216-720, SC216-820, SC270-160,
SC738-640, SC774-880, SC792-120,
SD18-160, SD558-720, SD558-720,
SD792-820, SD792-820, SD936-930,
TN75-50, TN300-760, TN465-800,
TN630-530, TN690-170, TN690-220,
TN750-690, TN840-800, TX14-720,
TX42-810, TX56-110, TX56-850,
TX56-860, TX63-80, TX91-80,
TX181-780, TX181-790, TX210-230,
TX231-120, TX252-730, TX252-760,
TX280-540, TX374-550, TX397-690,
TX397-790, TX483-320, TX483-322,
TX483-690, TX529-770, TX590-760,
TX590-760, TX632-720, TX691-130,
TX726-80, TX777-160, TX777-720,
TX933-80, UT152-720, UT380-810,
UT912-120, UT912-120, UT912-820,
UT912-850, VA50-50, VA145-780,
VA195-200, VA285-440, VA430-280,
VA480-520, VA580-520, VA580-600,
VA630-840, VA690-830, VA690-910,
VA870-110, VA870-150, VT48-90,
VT128-80, VT176-790, VT296-690,
VT464-840, VT496-640, VT864-730,
WA124-480, WA144-210, WA144-840,
WA468-720, WA592-720, WA616-870,
WA616-950, WA681-400, WA724-890,
WA820-92, WA820-550, WA820-770,
WA820-774, WA820-880, WA880-190,
WA880-775, WA904-635, WA904-760,
WA904-770, WA904-870, WA943-240,
WA954-40, WA954-880, WA994-690,
WA994-935, WI70-120, WI77-160,
WI142-120, WI202-120, WI266-820,
WI298-250, WI298-810, WI346-280,
WI346-720, WI456-540, WI456-730,
WI456-810, WI554-600, WI654-790,
WI698-730, WI722-830, WI794-120,
WI794-880, WI814-510, WV650-890,
WY135-865, WY500-800, WY950-950

ARCHITECTS
   CA86-820, NY587-190
ARMED FORCES
   AL560-720, DC1-200, DC1-340,
   MD57-820

ARTISTS
   NY591-920
ARTS
   CA414-490, DC14-450, DE810-150,
   IL169-130, MS520-520, TX56-200
AUTHORS
   FL220-800, IA74-480, IL261-570,
   IL459-520, IL976-890, IN704-520,
   KS283-200, KY496-825, KY61A-640,
   MA92-90, MA108-940, ME712-880,
   WA60-80
AVIATION
   OK592-570
BLACKS
   MS550-410, NY51-730, VA20-322
CLOTHING
   IL192-510
COMPOSERS
   CA421-750
CRIMINALS
   DC14-410
DISTINGUISHED SERVICE AWARD
   AL120-104
EDUCATION
   DC1-340, IL806-695, KY54Q-520,
   MA109-630, MA572-540, MA776-530,
   MA891-860, NC430-340, NC680-720,
   NJ276-510, NY10-150, NY297-520,
   NY588-420, NY595-130 , PA725-900,
   SC54-80, SC774-880, TX326-160 ,
   WI266-430
EDUCATORS
   DC1-860
EMPLOYMENT
   NY592-30
FACTORY WORKERS
   NY586-440
FASHION INDUSTRY
   DC19-555
GEOGRAPHERS
   DC19-750
HEALTH CARE
   IL192-510
HISTORIANS
   ID640-345, PA380-700
IN HISTORIC PRESERVATION
   NY587-190
INSURANCE INDUSTRY
   PA135-40
JEWS
   NY595-760
JOURNALISTS
   GA245-110, PA870-160
LABOR
   NY586-440
LITCHFIELD CT
   NY297-520
LITERATURE
   NE736-560, NY564-840
MEDICAL PROFESSION
   CA720-890, PA725-900
MEDICINE
   OH181-180
METHODIST CHURCH
   GA885-520
MUSIC
   MA109-440
NATIONAL PARK SERVICE
   WV350-560
NEW ENGLAND
   MA169-860
OPERA
   MA425-520
ORGANIZATIONS
   CA524-160, CA566-640, CO252-42,
   CT477-570, DC1-340, DC2-850,
   DC7-300, DC14-420, DC14-520,
   DC19-750, DE810-170, HI350-150,
   IA600-322, IA955-440, IN22-50,
   IN539-80, IN704-520, KY230-320,
   KY230-440, KY380-720, KY558-520,
   KY598-600, LA600-555, MA169-970,
   MA931-400, MA947-880, ME437-120,
   ME512-80, MI355-270, MI700-560,
   MI824-320, MI890-720, MN14-560,
   MN185-120, MN391-310, MN405-320,
   MN541-592, MN742-700, MO810-200,

NC380-800, ND486-770, ND876-80,
NE112-760, NE352-880, NJ20-40,
NV940-560, NY148B-88, NY235-160,
NY262-280, NY272-200, NY593-132,
NY595-740, NY598-560, NY720-640,
NY839-720, NY858-720, NY866-710,
NY915-870, OH878-880, OR720-470,
PA500-70, TX7-800, TX319-640,
VA20-322, WA98-100, WA181-360,
WA616-915, WA681-670, WA726-640,
WV550-280, WY365-710

ORPHANS
KY54G-520

PALEONTOLOGISTS
NY439-640

PERFORMING ARTS
MA108-520, NY592-870

PHYSICIANS
NY752-885, PA725-900

POLITICIANS
CA86-810

PRESIDENTS' (US) WIVES
DC6-650

PROFESSIONS
DC2-850, DC14-420, MA169-885,
NY588-940

PSYCHOANALYSTS
NY592-640

PUBLIC OFFICE
DC1-340

RELIGIOUS COMMUNITIES
AR480-320, CA78-740, CA110-600,
CA421-565, CA720-739, CA764-165,
IA188-777, IL109-130, IL169-565,
IL770-40, IL866-320, IN209-140,
KS213-560, KY176-720, KY496-850,
KY532-720, KY569-720, KY57W-720,
KY710-160, LA600-690, MD76-100,
MD152-720, MD380-160, MI650-720,
MN763-720, MO810-750, MO810-760,
NY10-160, NY10-710, NY115-720,
NY318-240, NY459-520, NY481-720,
NY529-530, NY687-120, NY859-720,
OH171-730, OH223-710, OH593-720,
PA30-720, PA50-720, PA85-730,
PA305-720, PA330-160, PA420-720,
PA725-908, PA726-480, PA726-495,
PA735-720, PA795-120, PA908-720,
RI210-720, TX483-322, WA820-820,
WA880-710, WA880-753, WI298-250

SUFFRAGE
AZ550-040, CA720-910, CT316-560,
DC1-340, IN363-400, MA169-860,
MA624-740, MO810-510, MO810-940,
NY586-440

TEACHERS
MA92-90, VT296-690

WORK FORCE
NY439-150

WORLD WAR I
IL231-240, NY592-30

WORLD WAR II
NY592-30

WRITERS
AR890-20, GA780-270, GA915-280,
IN275-170, MD76-80, MN541-600,
MN541-838, MO810-690, NE736-560,
NY125-740, NY134-730, NY297-520,
NY949-120, OH788-870, PA555-40,
PA726-600, PA735-150, RI910-880,
SC846-890, TN630-740, VT432-530,
WI456-810, WV200-880

WOMEN'S ANTI-LOTTERY LEAGUE
LA600-555

WOMEN'S ARCHIVES, WORLD CENTER FOR
DC14-420

WOMEN'S BOARD OF MISSIONS FOR THE PACIFIC
CA86-630

WOMEN'S CLUBS, NEW YORK STATE FEDERATION OF
NY272-200

WOMEN'S EDUCATIONAL AND INDUSTRIAL UNION
MA109-630

WOMEN'S RELIEF CORPS
See also Womans Relief Corps,
MI824-320, ND876-80

WOMEN'S RIGHTS MOVEMENT
AZ550-040, CA86-780, CA86-810,
CA601-640, CA720-180, CA756-320,
CA858-810, CO108-810, CO252-100,
CT316-120, DC8-850, DC12-300,
GA75-810, GA90-30, IA33-370,
IA177-240, IA233-360, IL124-725,
IL169-325, IL170-884, IL261-545,
IN363-360, KS527-805, KS878-430,
KY464-800, KY496-765, LA62-500,
LA600-555, LA600-755, MA109-120,
MA169-860, MA169-970, MA624-740,
MA871-40, MI230-165, MI518-445,
MI550-505, MN763-540, MO810-510,
MO810-940, MS550-500, MS610-520,
MS900-870, NC260-170, NC590-320,
NE560-550, NJ578-510, NY10-770,
NY427-240, NY588-900, NY821-720,
NY872-800 , OH181-270, OH203-600,
OH823-800, PA395-320, PA735-790,
PA860-710, PA895-710, TN690-975 ,
TX56-50, TX252-150, TX483-810,
VA145-780, VA690-910 , WA289-200,
WI456-495, WV650-890

WOOD CARVING
ME725-880

WOOD, JOSEPH D.
VA580-600, VA580-600

WOOD, MYRON
CO180-640

WOODBURY, LEVI
OH171-920

WOODCROFT HOSPITAL
CO768-640

WOODEN SHOES
WI426-120

WOODS, EMMA K.
MD266-80

WOODSMALL, RUTH FRANCES
MA624-740

WOODSTOCK COLLEGE
DC7-650

WOODSY OWL
VA50-240

WOODWAY HOMES
MD513-640

WOODWORKERS OF AMERICA, INTERNATIONAL
GA90-300

WOODWORKING
WI426-120

WOOL
MANUFACTURING
MO490-880, NY240-160, OH505-520

WOOLLETT, WILLIAM L., JR.
NY899-520

WOOTEN FAMILY
TN90-130

WORCESTER ACADEMY
OK854-840

WORCHESTER, DEAN C.
MI40-814

WORDSWORTH, WILLIAM
MA21-40, MA891-880

WORK PROJECTS ADMINISTRATION
CA421-390, CT144-880, DC14-600,
IL340-280, KS774-690, NY714-560,
OH246-200, OK490-520, OK592-640,
WI754-170, WV500-640, WY135-865

FEDERAL THEATER PROJECT
VA205-290

FEDERAL WRITERS' PROJECT
CA700-720, IN825-350, LA62-490,
LA535-600, SD792-820

HISTORIC AMERICAN BUILDING SURVEY
ME712-280, ME725-880

HISTORIC AMERICAN MERCHANT MARINE SURVEY
DC19-636

HISTORICAL RECORDS SURVEY
FL800-235, IL866-355, MA871-890,
OK592-620, SD792-820, VA900-880

WORKMAN, ROWLAND
CA376-480

WORKS PROGRESS ADMINISTRATION
See Work Projects Administration

WORLD ALLIANCE OF YOUNG MEN'S CHRISTIAN ASSOCIATIONS
IL170-283

WORLD BANK
NY588-940

WORLD CENTER FOR WOMEN'S ARCHIVES
DC14-420

WORLD STUDENT CHRISTIAN FEDERATION
CT505-900

WORLD WAR I
CA40-60, CA456-530, CA942-940,
CO180-750, CT36-80, DC1-400,
IA211-480, IL246-190, IL567-600,
IN66-390, KY96-870, KY464-880,
KY496-800, MA246-160, MA624-560,
MI445-320, MN14-560, MO20-720,
MO902-520, MS20-200, NC850-120,
NH134-530, OK592-650, OR816-590,
SD550-600 , TX326-780, WA739-240

ARMY TELEGRAPH BATTALION
NJ270-800

CIVIL DEFENSE
NY899-600

DRAFT (MILITARY)
WI202-560

EUROPE, EASTERN
MI230-780

FRANCE
FL60-720

MEDICINE
OH181-180

MEMORIAL ACTIVITIES
WA97-320

MILITARY PERSONNEL
KY514-130, WA153-128

REPARATIONS
NY905-840

SHIPBUILDING
GA885-120

SOCIAL WELFARE
NJ178-115, NY595-660

TOPOGRAPHY
MN321-690

VETERANS
NY672-440

VETERANS STATE AID COMMISSION (OR)
OR816-590

WOMEN
IL231-240, NY592-30

WORLD WAR II
AK320-40, AL380-800, AL560-720,
CA40-60, CA278-130, CO180-750,
CT36-80, CT870-730, DC1-810,
DC14-250, DC14-725, DC14-730,
DC19-606, HI350-808, IA966-320,
KS10-170, KY96-870, KY250-160,
KY272-45, MA108-965, MD57-810,
MI390-720, MN14-560, MN562-520,
MO400-320, MS20-200, NC850-120,
NJ376-360, NY101-90, NY160-120,
NY247-160, NY427-240, NY590-840,
NY915-870, OK592-650, PA325-280,
RI910-880, TX326-780, VA350-320,
VT464-840

AIR COMBAT
FL750-200

CAMP GRANT
IL806-710

CHINA
IN297-600

CIVIL DEFENSE
CT870-730

CRIMINAL JUSTICE
CA32-640

EUROPE, EASTERN
MI230-780

EUROPEAN MILITARY GOVERNMENT
MA21-770

GREAT BRITAIN
IN66-390

GREECE
MA169-800
HOLOCAUST
CA86-385, NY586-650, NY587-820, NY595-660, NY595-700
JAPAN
CA32-640
JAPANESE-AMERICANS
CA720-365, TN690-880
LABOR
DC1-400
MANUFACTURING
CT870-730
MILITARY PERSONNEL
CT870-730, IN237-240, KY558-520, WA153-128
PACIFIC AREA
FL750-200
PEARL HARBOR
NH784-620, TX280-540
PEARL HARBOR CULPABILITY DEBATE
WY500-800
POLAND
NY587-820
PRISONERS OF WAR
NE284-560
PROPAGANDA
NY591-690
SHIPBUILDING
GA885-120
SOCIAL WELFARE
NY595-660
V-J DAY
NY591-690
VETERANS
NY672-440
WAR CRIMES
NY588-860
WOMEN
NY592-30
WORLD'S COLUMBIAN EXPOSITION (1893)
IL169-130, IL169-416
WORTHAM, JOHN
TX228-320
WORTHINGTON, THOMAS, FAMILY
OH166-590
WRECKS
OH863-280
WRIGHT, FRANK LLOYD
IL169-130, IL649-600, NY24-720
WRIGHT, HENDRIK B.
PA960-910
WRIGHT, HERBERT PERRY
MO430-800
WRIGHT, JOHN S.
IL169-416
WRIGHT, MILTON S. J.
OH939-860
WRIGHT, ORVILLE
OH223-810, OH223-880
WRIGHT, RICHARD
CT505-890
WRIGHT, SILAS
NY150-700
WRIGHT, WILBUR
OH223-810, OH223-880
WRITERS
See also Authors; Literary figures; Literary manuscripts; Literature, *CO252-159, IL429-520, LA62-490, MD76-80, MD76-525, MI720-600, MN763-790, NC60-640, NM266-720, NY125-740, NY240-160, NY586-180, NY594-080, NY866-730, OH823-800, OR720-590, PA90-480, PA500-80, PA735-150, PA895-710, PA960-870, RI700-620, SD792-820, UT456-900, UT684-80, WI456-810, WI754-170, WV200-880, WV250-320*
CALIFORNIA
PA726-600
GERMANY
IL170-637
GREAT BRITAIN
CA782-800, MI230-800, OH843-400, PA135-80

SCOTLAND
CT505-977
SOUTHERN US
TN630-740
WOMEN
AR890-20, GA780-270, GA915-280, IN275-170, MD76-80, MN541-600, MN541-838, MO810-690, NE736-560, NY125-740, NY134-730, NY297-520, NY949-120, OH788-870, PA555-40, PA726-600, PA735-150, RI910-880, SC846-890, TN630-740, VT432-530, WI456-810, WV200-880
WRITING
CA86-810
WRITING (CREATIVE)
EDUCATION
NY125-740
WUERTEMBERG, GERMANY, HARMONY SOCIETY
PA40-600
WURSTER, WILLIAM
CA86-820
WYER, ROBERT
NY240-160
WYETH, N. C.
PA175-80
WYLES, WILLIAM
CA774-800
WYLLYS, SAMUEL
RI700-45
WYNKOOP, GEORGE C.
PA740-320
WYNN, ED
CA421-766
WYOMING
MISSIONARIES
WA880-280

Y

YACHTING
NY952-720, OH863-280
YACHTS
FL60-720, MA169-610, NJ736-690, TX273-160
YADKIN RIVER
HYDROELECTRIC POWER
NC30-715
YALE MEDICAL SCHOOL
CT505-930
YALE NEW HAVEN MEDICAL CENTER
CT505-930
YALE TECHNOLOGY PROJECT
CT505-975
YALE, ELISHA
NY334-280
YATES, ANDREW
NY804-800
YATES, ELIZABETH
KS283-200
YEATS FAMILY
KS527-790, NY866-730
YEATS, WILLIAM BUTLER
NY866-730
YEGEN, LAURA BELL CLARK
MT100-200
YELLOW FEVER
PA725-615, TN630-570, TX397-690
YELLOWSTONE NATIONAL PARK
MT130-540
YEMEN
JUDAISM
NY592-760
YIDDISH CULTURE
NY587-820, NY595-700
DRAMA
OH171-20
THEATER
NY591-850, NY592-760
YORK COLLEGE
IA544-880
YOSEMITE NATIONAL PARK
CA728-850
YOST, DANIEL
PA740-320

YOUNG FRIENDS
IN704-200
YOUNG MEN'S AND YOUNG WOMEN'S HEBREW ASSOCIATION
NY593-132
YOUNG MEN'S CHRISTIAN ASSOCIATION
IL170-283, IL212-280
STUDENT DIVISION
CT505-900
YOUNG MEN'S CHRISTIAN ASSOCIATION (BELLINGHAM WA)
WA60-860
YOUNG MEN'S CHRISTIAN ASSOCIATION (GLENS FALLS NY)
NY331-280
YOUNG MEN'S CHRISTIAN ASSOCIATION (SAN FRANCISCO CA)
CA720-180
YOUNG MEN'S CHRISTIAN ASSOCIATION SCHOOL OF TECHNOLOGY, SCHOOL OF COMMERCE, AND PREP. SCHOOL
OH181-290
YOUNG MEN'S CHRISTIAN ASSOCIATIONS, INTERNATIONAL COMMITTEE OF
IL170-283
YOUNG MEN'S CHRISTIAN ASSOCIATIONS, WORLD ALLIANCE OF
IL170-283
YOUNG MEN'S HEBREW ASSOCIATION
NY593-132
YOUNG MEN'S HEBREW ASSOCIATION SURPRISE LAKE CAMP
NY593-132
YOUNG WOMEN'S CHRISTIAN ASSOCIATION (LAWRENCE MA)
MA451-360
YOUNG WOMEN'S CHRISTIAN ASSOCIATION (NEW YORK NY)
NY595-740
YOUNG WOMEN'S HEBREW ASSOCIATION
NY593-132
YOUNG, AMMI BURNHAM
DC1-480
YOUNG, CALE
KY22W-920
YOUNG, OWEN D.
NY905-840
YOUNG, THOMAS
SC144-710
YOUR SHOW OF SHOWS (TELEVISION PROGRAM)
NY591-690
YOUTH
ORGANIZATIONS
IL170-283, NY589-900, OH181-780, OR720-470, TX7-800
YUCATAN, MEXICO
TX42-810
YUGOSLAVIA
NY588-825, PA735-825
FOLK MUSIC
NY166-80
YUKON TERRITORY, CANADA
AK500-20

Z

ZABRISKIE, A.
NJ386-380
ZACATECAS, MEXICO
MINING
LA600-760
RANCHING
LA600-760
ZAIRE
NC590-320
MISSIONARIES
IL169-677
ZAMBIA
IL261-566
ZANTZINGER, BORIE AND MEDARY
PA725-150

ZEIS, HAROLD
IN231-40
ZEISL, ERIC
CA421-750
ZILBOORG, GREGORY
KS878-520
ZIMBALIST, MARY LOUISE CURTIS BOK
PA725-345
ZIMMERLY, R. K.
IN539-100
ZIMMERMAN (AUTOMOBILE MODEL)
IN33-40
ZIMMERMAN, EUGENE (ZIM)
NY411-320
ZIMRING, FRED
PA726-600
ZIONISM
KY496-800, NY589-900, NY595-760
ORGANIZATIONS
OH181-730
ZONING
NJ138-120, NJ574-560, NY10-570,
TX252-120
ZOOLOGY
CT505-980, MA169-500, NY586-720
ZOOS
KY496-540, NY593-130
ZUKOFSKY, LOUIS
TX56-890
ZWEIG, STEFAN
NY310-720
ZWIERLEIN, FREDERICK
NY752-760